# AMERICAN CAESARS

Nigel Hamilton is one of Britain's most distinguished biographers. He began his career with *The Brothers Mann*, a life of two of Germany's greatest twentieth-century authors. He then won the Whitbread Prize and Templer Medal for *Monty*, his definitive, three-volume official life of Field Marshal Bernard Montgomery, following which his *JFK: Reckless Youth* proved an international bestseller and was filmed as an ABC mini-series. His subsequent two-volume biography of Bill Clinton was published to great critical acclaim. He became the first Professor of Biography in Britain, at De Montfort University, and currently lives in Boston, Massachusetts.

NIGEL HAMILTON

# American Caesars

Lives of the US Presidents
from Franklin D. Roosevelt to
George W. Bush

**VINTAGE BOOKS**
London

Published by Vintage 2011

10 9

Copyright © Nigel Hamilton 2010

Nigel Hamilton has asserted his right under the
Copyright, Designs and Patents Act 1988
to be identified as the author of this work

First published in Great Britain in 2010
by The Bodley Head

Vintage
Random House, 20 Vauxhall Bridge Road,
London SW1V 2SA

www.vintage-books.co.uk

Addresses for companies within The Random House Group Limited
can be found at: www.randomhouse.co.uk/offices.htm

The Random House Group Limited Reg. No. 954009

A CIP catalogue record for this book
is available from the British Library

ISBN 9780099520412

Typeset in Dante MT by Palimpsest Book Production Limited,
Falkirk, Stirlingshire

Penguin Random House is committed to a sustainable future for
our business, our readers and our planet. This book is made from
Forest Stewardship Council® certified paper.

Printed and bound in Great Britain by Clays Ltd, St Ives plc

# Contents

# Preface

Gaius Suetonius Tranquillus – known as Suetonius – had written a whole series of biographies of Roman poets, orators and historians (*The Lives of Illustrious Men*) when the idea came to him, early in the second century AD, to address the first twelve Caesars of Rome. Beginning with the dictator Julius Caesar, he recounted the lives of emperors Augustus, Tiberius, Caligula, Claudius, Nero, Galba, Otho, Vitellius, Vespasian, Titus and Domitian.

The result was *The Twelve Caesars*, which became a classic of classical times: a virtuoso imperial portrait gallery by a distinguished author, remarkable not only for its frank, often salacious accounts (in contrast to contemporary commemorations) of Rome's emperors, but also because the twelve men whose lives he chronicled were the embodiment – both good and awful – of Rome's greatest century and a half, between 49 BC and AD 96.

As Roman hegemony became more contested in the second century AD, and ultimately fractured into the decline and fall that Gibbon later chronicled, Suetonius' extraordinary work only increased in interest. Some of his chosen Caesars had been deified, but Suetonius showed little reverence for the divine, preferring to chronicle their lives as human beings, each with his own story from birth to supreme power. His emperors were thus portrayed not as sanctified icons, but as distinctive individuals, often effective but also perverse – ruthless characters whom Suetonius treated fairly, without needing to curtsey. Here was the prototype of Lytton Strachey's later masterpiece, *Eminent Victorians*, published in 1918, but without the need for irony, and unforgettable not only as portraits, but because the selected group personified the 'beautiful and the base' that Dr Johnson later saw as essential facets of 'useful' biography rather than hagiography. Bucking the contemporary approach taken by Greek and Roman biographers, moreover, Suetonius divided each portrait into three parts: first an account of how the Caesar rose to power; then his public life as emperor; and finally, an account of the emperor's private life.

Fast-forward to today. Though few US citizens care for the word 'empire' to describe their own country, American historians have reluctantly begun to accept the designation, since by most indices – military, economic and cultural – the United States has incontrovertibly been the world's dominant hegemony since its entry into World War II in 1941. With its massive rearmament programme, its struggle to defeat Hitler's Third Reich and fascism, and its use of the atom bomb to defeat the Japanese Empire, it stepped up to the plate in defence of democracy. Then, after the war's end, it did not turn away from international leadership as it had done after World War I, but undertook a role as ongoing guardian of its allies and those countries which espoused democratic values – and also some that didn't, as long as it was in America's interest to do so. Isolationism thus died, and the United States attempted, as best it could, to maintain a Pax Americana, or liberal peace, across much of the post-war world, using its economic, military, diplomatic and even subversive power. At times the Pax turned distinctly belligerent, as it did under presidents Truman, Johnson, Nixon, Bush Sr and Bush Jr – indeed, by the beginning of the twenty-first century, a presidential adviser at the imperial court could shamelessly tell reporters: 'We're an empire now, and when we act, we create our own reality.'[1] Overseas US military bases increased from fourteen in 1938 to more than a thousand in the new millennium.[2]

In writing this account of the last twelve American presidents and using, somewhat loosely, the words 'Caesars', 'imperial' and 'empire', my object is not to scorn the difficulties which the United States has faced and still faces today. Rather, my purpose is to look back over the past six decades since the United States became the world's foremost military and economic power, and to shine a spotlight on the men who have led their often unruly nation on its post-World War II 'imperial' journey. Although there have been empires and emperors aplenty in the world since Roman times, I doubt there has been a succession of such remarkable individuals who have launched and led a hegemony as potent as that of the United States, paralleling the might of the Roman Empire.

Who were they, then, these American 'Caesars'? How did they get
to be president? How did they confront the challenges of empire once
they got there? How effectively did they assert their growing power
in the Oval Office, in the role that came to be called the 'imperial
presidency'? How authoritatively did they assert Pax Americana
through the long years of Cold War, and thereafter? And what, for
good or ill, was the course of their private lives? These are the questions I have sought to answer, as a biographer, within the context of
recent American and global history. Of the twelve men who held the
office of US president from the onset of World War II, four showed
undoubted (to me) greatness. As in ancient Rome some American
Caesars started wars; others ended them. Some authorized assassination attempts on foreign leaders threatening American hegemony;
almost all became victims of assassination attempts; one was actually
murdered in office. But from the time of America's entry into World
War II, each president was required, on a world stage, to show leadership – and it is the quality of each one's imperial leadership that I have
tried to judge in *American Caesars*.

Each chapter tells the story of a human journey, as its protagonist
makes his way to the heart of American power, and there confronts
the salient challenges of his time. The book begins with the greatest
of American emperors, the Caesar Augustus of his time: President
Franklin D. Roosevelt. It continues with the lives of his great successors, Harry S. Truman, Dwight D. Eisenhower and John F. Kennedy;
then examines the lives of Lyndon Johnson, Richard Nixon, Gerald
Ford, Jimmy Carter, Ronald Reagan, George H. W. Bush and Bill
Clinton; and ends with arguably the worst of all the American Caesars,
George W. Bush, and his deputy Dick Cheney, who wilfully and recklessly destroyed so much of the moral basis of American leadership
in the modern world.

Where the American Empire will go from here – how long it will
last, as it competes with other, rising empires, and how it will manage
its epic struggle to embrace the values enshrined in its great
Constitution – is not for me to predict. In the meantime there are too
many lessons to be learned from the lives of these twelve men to
neglect or forget them. The reader will not necessarily agree with my
judgements, embedded in these life stories. The reader will also have
his or her own views on which of the twelve American Caesars (and

deputy Caesars) most resemble Suetonius' heroes – or his tyrants such as Tiberius, Caligula and Nero. Whether we like it or not, however, these were the men chosen, one after another, to lead the United States in what will be regarded as its greatest days in the role of dominant world superpower. They surely deserve to be seen, as Suetonius saw their Roman forebears, unflinchingly and yet with charity, together with their private lives that remind us, in their affections, how intensely human and individual they were, despite the great burdens they undertook on behalf of the empire.

That said, let us begin with the greatest Caesar of all.

# CHAPTER ONE

# FRANKLIN D. ROOSEVELT

Later Deified

Democrat
32nd President
(March 4, 1933–April 12, 1945)

## Part One: The Road to the White House

Franklin Delano Roosevelt was born on January 30, 1882, at Springwood, Hyde Park, a grand estate overlooking the Hudson River, seventy-five miles above New York City. The birth of the ten-pound baby, which lasted twenty-six hours, almost killed his mother, Sara Delano Roosevelt. Because of the difficult parturition she was advised not to have more children.

FDR was suckled at his mother's breast – unusual at the time – and was kept in dresses and long curls until the age of five, schooled at home, wore kilts, and then pants for the first time at age seven. He had his first bath alone at age nine. In Washington DC, President Cleveland patted FDR's curly head and, reflecting on the burdens of the Oval Office, pronounced 'a strange wish for you. It is that you may never be president of the United States.'[1]

The wish would not be granted.

Mr and Mrs James Roosevelt doted on FDR – so much so, they made do with private tutors and took him with them to Europe, visiting it no less than eight times in FDR's first fourteen years. It was only then, reluctantly, they let him go to his first full-time school, Groton, three years later than his contemporaries. They had forbidden him to try for entry to naval college at Annapolis, saying they would miss him too much if he went to sea.

The sea, nevertheless, became part of FDR's lifeblood. Mr James, as his father was known to all, had built a summer home in 1883 off the coast of Maine on the island of Campobello, and there FDR learned to sail, being given his first yacht, the *New Moon*, at age sixteen, as well as Alfred Thayer Mahan's works on the influence of sea power in history. He began a collection of stamps, stuffed birds, naval prints and books, all of which he catalogued meticulously.

At Harvard FDR finished his four-year degree course in three, and became a much admired editor-in-chief of the university newspaper, the *Crimson*. He had a fine singing voice, learned nothing by rote, but instead developed from an early age a surprisingly independent mind, confident in his own opinions, and positive in his outlook on life. Standing 6' 2" tall, he towered over most of his contemporaries; handsome, energetic, blessed with a genial sense of humour, yet as happy alone as with companions.

The secret of FDR's early success was his mother, Sara. On Mr James' death in 1900 FDR inherited half his father's financial estate, from which he drew an annuity of $12,000, but Sara retained ownership of the Springwood mansion; moreover she controlled the principal of FDR's inheritance. The following year, on the death of her own father she inherited a fortune of $1.2 million ($28 million in today's money). A very rich widow, she avoided fortune hunters and rented an apartment in Boston, Massachusetts, to be close to her son across the Charles River, at Harvard. After graduating, he married in 1905 and Sara built him a house (which she continued to own) close to hers in Manhattan.

'Nothing like keeping the name in the family' remarked Republican President Theodore Roosevelt when he insisted on being allowed to give away his orphaned but wealthy niece, Eleanor Roosevelt, to her fifth cousin, FDR.[2] It was Sara Delano, however, not Eleanor, who continued to be the linchpin of FDR's rising career, socially, professionally and emotionally. Sara encouraged FDR not to overestimate his talents, but to use his abundant skills – his intelligence, charm, humour, education and connections – to make his way in the world beyond the inbred Roosevelts, just as her father had done when facing bankruptcy after the 1857 financial meltdown. She was, and remained all her life, FDR's litmus test in considering his options. When he began to support the local Democratic Party, she supported his decision, recalling later that 'I was one of the few sympathizers Franklin had among his own people. Many of our friends said it was a shame for so fine a young man to associate with "dirty" politicians.'[3]

So close was FDR to his mother, in fact, that he was almost rejected by the local Democratic Party as a mama's boy. Asked by a state committeeman if he would like to run for the New York State legislature as an assemblyman in 1910, he responded he would first have to ask his mother. 'Frank,' the committeeman responded, as he looked up at the building where they'd parked, 'the men that are looking out that window are waiting for an answer. They won't like to hear that you had to ask your *mother*.'[4]

FDR never concealed his political ambition. A fellow law clerk at Carter, Ledyard and Milburn, who had also been at Harvard with FDR, recalled how, in 1907, FDR confided to his young colleagues he was determined to become president of the United States, like his uncle-in-law, and outlined the exact steps by which he would do so: a seat in the New York State Assembly, Assistant Secretary of the Navy, governor of New York, the White House. None mocked him; it seemed, as his colleague recalled, 'entirely reasonable'.[5]

In fact Roosevelt stood for the New York State Senate rather than the Assembly – and won. His resounding victory made him, at age twenty-eight, a force to be reckoned with in the New York Democratic Party in 1911. However, in the same way that the Republican Party split between progressives and conservatives, so did the Democrats. FDR found himself a progressive, fighting the forces of corruption in his own party, known in New York as Tammany Hall.

Beaten in every fight for legislation and party appointments, it was only when FDR threw his support to the Democratic outsider, Governor Woodrow Wilson of New Jersey, in the 1912 presidential election that he was given his chance to leapfrog the closed ranks of Tammany Hall Democrats into the corridors of Washington power. Wilson won. As a reward for his help FDR was offered the posts of Assistant Secretary of the Treasury or the Navy. He chose the Navy.

FDR was the youngest man (at thirty) ever to hold the office. Like Winston Churchill – First Lord of the Admiralty in Britain at the time – FDR was energetic, impetuous, arrogant. His boss, Josephus Daniels, was a short, rumpled newspaper owner from Raleigh, North Carolina, who knew nothing of the sea or the navy, in fact was a pacifist and teetotaller who ordered naval officers' messes to stop serving alcohol. Daniels did, though, know a lot about America and its people. While the European nations allowed power to devolve on to the military once war began, leaving their politicians powerless either to overrule the generals or to make peace, Daniels taught FDR the greatest lesson of the twentieth century: 'the politicians' must retain control of the generals, and must use that power wisely.

Under Daniels' tutelage, FDR learned the exercise of political command. In peacetime the US Navy absorbed 20 per cent of America's annual federal budget, employed 63,000 servicemen in all ranks, and provided employment for hundreds of thousands more in shipyards across the nation, with 197 ships on active service.[6] When President Wilson reluctantly asked Congress to authorize national rearmament involving the building of 176 new ships – the biggest peacetime construction project in the nation's history (ten battleships, a hundred submarines, six battle cruisers, fifty destroyers and ten light cruisers) – FDR applied his formidable energies to the task. Not only did he propose a Council of National Defense to oversee war production, but while Daniels was out of Washington he created, in September 1916, a 50,000-strong Naval Reserve. Thus, by the time President Wilson declared war on April 4, 1917, in response to the kaiser's authorization of unrestricted submarine warfare against neutral countries, FDR was considered indispensable, and the president – narrowly re-elected in November 1916 – refused to hear of FDR's request to join up as a naval officer. 'Tell the young man to stay where he is' Wilson instructed Daniels.[7]

In the 1880s the US economy had become the biggest in the world. With the surrender of the German armed forces at Compiègne on November 11, 1918, the United States finally established its claim to be a world empire in all but name, boasting an army of five million men and a navy of half a million, second only to that of the British Empire, once the German fleet was scuttled at Scapa Flow. America's moral power, however, was founded in a revered Constitution, idealistic principles of justice and, in Wilson's view, the ideal of self-determination by all nations. On his way to the Versailles Peace Conference, Wilson – welcomed by his Assistant Secretary of the Navy – was celebrated at Brest with banners reading 'Hail the Champion of the Rights of Man', and in Paris by two million people as 'Wilson the Just'.

War-weariness in America, however, quickly set in, leading to renewed isolationism. On his return, President Wilson barnstormed across America to sell his League of Nations accord – the core of the Versailles Treaty – in the fall of 1919, but suffered first a minor and then a massive stroke. 'He looked as if he were dead' a White House usher recalled candidly, and although, over time, the president regained some speech and movement in his right arm, his new wife, Edith, kept him out of sight even of his secretaries.[8]

It was in these circumstances that, with the president clearly unable to run for a third term in the summer of 1920, the Assistant Secretary of the Navy put himself forward as a candidate for the number two place on the Democratic Party's presidential ticket, next to the Ohio governor James M. Cox, and was nominated. He was only thirty-eight.

To launch their campaign, Cox and FDR went to the White House to meet President Wilson and get his blessing, Cox having agreed that the League of Nations would be, as FDR recalled, 'the paramount issue' of their platform, in deference to Wilson. 'It was one of the most impressive scenes', the Democratic vice-presidential nominee afterwards described, 'I have ever witnessed.'[9]

The truth was rather different. Roosevelt had greeted the president in full health in France only a year before. Now, 'as we came in sight of the portico, we saw the president in a wheelchair', FDR later confided.[10] A shawl covered President Wilson's left arm, his head hung down, the left side of his face was paralyzed, and his words were barely audible. Without realizing it, FDR was staring at his own destiny.

Amazingly, the press declined to publish the truth of the president's condition. Wilson was awarded that year's Nobel Peace Prize (which he was too ill to collect). But the further west that FDR travelled as vice-presidential candidate, the more he recognized that the United States, a nation of immigrants, was not yet ready to assume the mantle and responsibilities of world leadership.

President Wilson's aide, Joseph M. Tumulty, recalled the White House as the 'loneliest place on election night' in 1920. Not only were Cox and Roosevelt soundly defeated by the Republican senator, Warren G. Harding of Ohio – 404 to 127 in the Electoral College, and by almost two to one in the popular vote – but the vote was seen as a total 'defeat of the solemn referendum on the League of Nations'. It was also the Democratic Party's worst showing since the Civil War.

Roosevelt soon had his own medical disaster to face. Travelling to Campobello for his summer vacation in July 1921, he made good a promise he'd made to attend, as chairman of the New York Boy Scouts, a youth camp by the Hudson River. His enthusiasm and energy were infectious, but so was something else. In Maine, sailing and playing with his children, his legs gave way beneath him. The local doctor diagnosed a summer cold, while a nearby specialist, when summoned, a spinal clot. But with the lower half of FDR's body paralyzed, his trusted aide, Louis Howe, wrote urgently to FDR's uncle Fred in New York, telling him the symptoms. A diagnosis of polio was confirmed by the national authority on the disease the moment he reached the island of Campobello.

Polio changed FDR's life. He had already begun planning a run for the US Senate in 1922. Unkind people now called him a cripple. Even his mother Sara thought he should retire to Springwood, Hyde Park, and become a country squire, though this seemed premature when he was only thirty-nine. There was no way, however, in which the illness could be kept from the public. On its front page the *New York Times* announced 'F. D. ROOSEVELT ILL OF POLIOMYELITIS.'[11]

Since the majority of polio patients recovered at least partial use of their limbs, FDR's team stressed to the media that the former vice-presidential candidate was heading towards recovery, not disability. This was untrue, but not wholly dishonest. Roosevelt's willpower in learning to walk with two fourteen-pound steel braces holding him upright from his heels to his hips, mesmerized those who met him. When he swung himself forward on crutches to the podium at Madison Square Garden in New York to give the nominating speech for Governor Al Smith as candidate for the Democratic presidential nomination on June 26, 1924, no one dared breathe, as Frances Perkins – later Secretary of Labor – recalled. 'Eight thousand delegates, alternates, and spectators watched spellbound while FDR fought his way across the stage, the personification of courage' one biographer recounted.[12] 'When he finally reached the podium, unable to wave for fear of falling but flashing that famous smile, head thrown back, shoulders high, the Garden erupted with a thunderous ovation.'[13]

Four years later, in Houston, FDR again gave the nominating speech for Governor Smith – without crutches this time, and with 15,000 people in the audience, as well as radio microphones transmitting his speech. By using the arm of his son for support on one side, and a cane in his other hand, FDR gave the impression of mild, residual stiffness, but otherwise rude good health. A president, he declared in his lilting tenor voice, needed a 'quality of soul' that 'makes him a strong help to those in sorrow or trouble, that quality which makes him not merely admired but loved by all of the people – the quality of sympathetic understanding of the human heart, or real interest in one's fellow man.'[14] He was extolling Smith, but the words applied much more to himself.

Asked to stand for the governorship of New York, FDR decided to take his chances, despite the fact that Wall Street was experiencing an unregulated, feverish speculation bonanza and he had no real hope of winning. 'Mess is no name for it' Louis Howe wired him.[15] Speaking as many as fourteen times a day, Roosevelt criss-crossed the state, and finally went home to bed in Manhattan on election night, assuming he had lost the battle. He awoke to hear his mother shouting from the front door (she still lived in the next house) that he was governor-elect.

Inaugurated on January 1, 1929, Governor Roosevelt predicted neither the Great Crash that year, nor the Great Depression that followed. However, thanks to his farm and rehabilitation centre in Warm Springs, Georgia, FDR's finger was on the pulse of American life in an unusual way. In the state capitol in Albany, the new governor responded to the economic collapse that took place as he had in his Navy Department days, using government purchasing power to modernize not a fleet but a state. He set up the first state commission in the nation to stabilize employment, and became the first governor in America to endorse unemployment insurance. He pushed for a massive electrification programme, stressed farm relief and employment projects. In 1930, running for re-election as governor, more than 90 per cent of registered voters went to the polls in New York City, giving FDR the largest win in New York history, as well as returning Democratic majorities in both houses of the state legislature. The way was clear to presidential nomination in 1932.

As national unemployment doubled to eight million, the bread and soup lines grew longer. FDR called the New York Assembly into special session, asking for an immediate $20 million to provide work, and where work was not feasible, 'food against starvation'. President Hoover had claimed that 'mutual self-help' was the answer – principles which, if departed from, would strike at the very 'roots of self-government'. By contrast, FDR claimed it was the duty of 'modern society, acting through its government' to prevent starvation as 'a matter of social duty'. In August 1931, he set up a Temporary Emergency Relief Administration (TERA) to distribute state funding, and raised state income taxes. TERA would, over the following five years, assist 40 per cent of New York State residents, five million people – with 70 per cent returning to employment.[16]

FDR's activist success was not appreciated by his rival, former New York Governor Al Smith. But with Democratic leaders across the country despairing of their losing streak in presidential elections since 1920, they wanted a winner, and early polls showed FDR as the only front-runner who could beat President Hoover in 1932. A scurrilous campaign to damn FDR's chances on the grounds that he was physically unfit for the rigours of the presidency was scotched by a panel of distinguished doctors, given free access to Governor Roosevelt during his workday. They reported him 'able to take more punishment than many men ten years younger'. When asked her own opinion, FDR's wife, Eleanor, remarked sourly: 'If the infantile paralysis didn't kill him, the presidency won't.'[17]

At Oglethorpe University in Georgia on May 22, 1932, FDR gave one of his most famous speeches. 'Must the country remain hungry and jobless while raw materials stand unused and factories idle?' he asked, and gave his famous answer: 'The country needs, the country demands, bold, persistent experimentation. Take a method and try it. If it fails admit it frankly and try another. But above all, try something.'[18]

Imaginative, pragmatic, non-partisan and activist in his response to a growing national emergency: this was Roosevelt's contribution to the history of democracy, at a time when more draconian solutions were being aired in Europe and the Far East.

For President Herbert Hoover, the 1932 election campaign proved a fiasco. The self-made millionaire and former mining engineer lost to FDR by almost seven million votes out of a record forty million cast. Huge new Democratic majorities in both houses of Congress, moreover, meant that no Republican filibuster would suffice to stop the president-elect's New Deal programme, once his official inauguration took place in March 1933. A bullet, however, could – and nearly did, when an unemployed Italian bricklayer in Miami, having bought a handgun at a local pawnshop, took aim at the president-elect, sitting in his open, parked car as he talked to the Chicago mayor, Anton Cermak. A spectator swung her purse and deflected his shot. Cermak was mortally wounded: FDR was unscathed.

## Part Two: The Presidency

'This great Nation will endure as it has endured,' declared the 32nd president in his historic inaugural speech on March 4, 1933, 'will revive and will prosper. So first of all, let me assert my firm belief that the only thing we have to fear is fear itself – nameless, unreasoning, unjustified terror which paralyzes needed efforts to convert retreat into advance.'

Those who scorned FDR's words as empty rhetoric received a rude awakening. Summoning Congress back into emergency session, the new president made good on his promise: using the federal government to put capitalism back on its feet. Issuing a proclamation closing the nation's banks, he sought the means to keep them solvent. Within days he had it; the government would issue the money, backed not by gold but by its own security. The ruse worked. A week later – after federal scrutiny – banks reopened, with federal insurance backing them, and they stayed open. The dollar soared. 'Capitalism', as Raymond Moley, one of FDR's 'brain trust', remarked, 'was saved in eight days.'[19]

In a series of initiatives he pushed through with the cooperation of Republicans and Democrats, as well as the support of the nation's state governors and the press, FDR then kept Congress in session – repealing Prohibition, increasing farm incomes by tackling surpluses (paying for the reduction by special taxes), refinancing farm mortgages threatened by foreclosure, and creating a Civilian Conservation Corps that would offer employment to three million young people. 'It smacks of fascism, of Hitlerism, of a form of sovietism' the president of the American Federation of Labor complained, afraid the measure would depress ordinary workers' wages. But the Boy Scout in Franklin Roosevelt would not back down. Some 2,500 camps across the nation were set up, FDR taking the president of the AFL to see the first of them, that summer, in Shenandoah National Park.

The creation of the CCC presaged the creation of the Federal Emergency Relief Agency, assisting seventeen million people that year, with a staff of only 121. A public works bill was also put before Congress, with $3.3 billion of federal stimulus funding approved by June 16, 1933, less than a hundred days since FDR entered the White House.

Regulation of Wall Street, the revival of the Tennessee Valley hydroelectric programme stalled since its opening in World War I, in deference to the objection that it offered unfair federal competition with private energy companies – and the creation of a Homeowners' Loan Corporation to rescue the collapsing housing market; these and other measures added to the president's remarkable domestic achievement. A week after the inauguration, the president had also begun broadcasting 'fireside chats' in which, via radio, he explained to listeners across America in articulate yet homey language what he was seeking to do, and why. Instantly, a new bond was established between the president and the public. What surprised listeners most was Roosevelt's sheer energy, confidence, humour and faith, a testament both to his indomitable courage as a paraplegic, and his positive temperament. As his mother Sara put it, his 'disposition is such that he can accept responsibilities and not let them wear him out'.[20]

In contrast to Adolf Hitler – who was granted full emergency powers by the German Reichstag on March 23, 1933, and who in *his* first days as dictator announced he would rule Germany with an iron, anti-Semitic fist ('Treason towards the nation and the people shall in future be stamped out with ruthless barbarity' Hitler declared, as he ordered the rounding up of his political opponents, to be held in concentration camps) – FDR's first Hundred Days showed America and the world that democracy could be saved, without barbarism.

Try as the Republican right did, it was difficult to portray as a mad fascist, or as a Nazi or Soviet dictator, a patrician president working so closely with the nation's Congress and governors. Four of Roosevelt's senior cabinet members were Republicans, and the president went out of his way to show he was not *parti pris*, but party-free. He took the United States off the gold standard, insisted on balancing the national budget, cut the pay of government officials – including himself – and radiated courage, optimism and confidence. Marxist historians who interpreted history as the implacable movement of economic and social forces would never be able to explain the impact made by a single such individual, drawn from the 'landed gentry', who marshalled the positive energies of his nation, rather than the punitive.

The November 1934 midterm elections returned even larger Democratic majorities in both House and Senate. With that fair wind FDR announced the Securities and Exchange Commission, the new regulatory agency for Wall Street, and a revolutionary federal programme to provide unemployment pay, sick pay and old-age pensions. 'Keep it simple', FDR ordered his Secretary of Labor. 'So simple that everybody will understand it.'[21] To fend off opposition and make sure the programme could never be derailed by later congressional budget manoeuvres, he made it self-financing through contributions by employers and employees rather than the government. Signed by the president on August 14, 1935, the Social Security Act became FDR's signature domestic achievement as president of the United States, and a demonstration to both fascists and Communists across the world that there was a middle way.[22]

Social-security legislation was followed by the Works Progress Administration, whereby Congress gave FDR power to disburse $4.8 billion to employ 'the maximum number of persons in the shortest time possible'. Using the Army Corps of Engineers, his chief overseer, Harry Hopkins, set to work, employing 8.5 million people over the following eight years and injecting $11 billion into the working economy. Without being aware of it, FDR was in fact rehearsing the nation for the moment when the US government would have to administer an even bigger programme: the manning of a military empire.

Unemployment was cut by two thirds, national income rose 50 per cent, industrial production doubled, stock prices went up, as did corporate profits and farm income. The Rural Electrification Administration Act of 1935 appealed to those outside the cities, while the Wagner Act, recognizing (in the wake of growing violence in San Francisco, Minneapolis and Toledo) workers' rights to unionize, appealed to urban industrial voters. Criticized by economists for his employment initiatives, rather than the provision of a dole, FDR was unrepentant. 'That is true' he allowed, with regard to his rejection of a weekly handout rather than federally funded employment. 'But the men who tell me that', he pointed out, 'have, unfortunately, too little contact with the true America to realize most Americans want to give something for what they get. That something, which in this case is honest work, is the saving barrier between them and moral degradation.'[23]

FDR's empathy with the lot of ordinary Americans was the quality that raised him head and shoulders above his contemporaries. At the Democratic National Convention in Philadelphia in June 1936, a crowd of 100,000, as well as half the population of America who owned radios, listened as the president – who fell on the way to the podium when one of his leg braces failed to lock tight – was lifted back on to his feet and

gave thanks to those who had helped defeat the Depression. Candidly
and with humility he acknowledged the mistakes made along the way.
'Governments can err. Presidents do make mistakes' he acknowledged.
But there was, he said, echoing Dante, a difference between 'the sins of
the cold-blooded and the sins of the warm-hearted'. As he put it – thinking
of former president Herbert Hoover, who was currently stomping across
the country in an attempt to recast his own bruised legend – 'Better the
occasional faults of a government that lives in a spirit of charity than the
consistent omissions of a government frozen in the ice of its own indifference.' Then, lowering his voice a register, FDR came to the words
that would define his presidency: 'To some generations much is given.
Of other generations much is asked. This generation of Americans has
a rendezvous with destiny.'

For ten long minutes the cheering overwhelmed the rhetoric in the
formal start to an election that again made history when, on November
3, 1936, FDR won by the largest margin in electoral annals to that date:
carrying 523 electoral votes to Governor Alf Landon's eight, and
trouncing his opponent by a margin of more than eleven million votes
in the popular vote.

Father Coughlin, who had helped launch a new party to split
Roosevelt's support, had boasted he would 'teach' the public 'how to
hate'. 'Religion and patriotism,' Coughlin urged Congressman Lemke
and the new Union Party, 'keep going on that. It's the only way you
can get them really "het up"' – a view that so alarmed Pope Pius XI
that he dispatched Cardinal Pacelli to America to calm concerns over
Coughlin's increasingly anti-Semitic invective.[24] Fortunately for
Roosevelt, however, the Union Party's showing proved even worse on
election night than that of the Republican Party.

Roosevelt's second term, ironically, proved as disappointing as his
first had been inspiring. Not only did his Supreme Court-packing
agenda fail miserably (as well as proving unnecessary, once vacancies
on the court allowed FDR to nominate his own replacements), but
he backed off his great economic stimulus package at the point of
its maximum success, fearing inflation and loss of control over the
national deficit. The result was a balanced budget, but a new recession.
Unionization in big industrial plants such as the Republic steelworks
in South Chicago led to brutality and mass murder by the police,
with FDR caught in the metaphorical middle. Similarly, an anti-

lynching bill split the Democratic Party in the South, and the president, for all his sympathy for the black cause, was loath to intervene lest he lose his traditional Dixiecrat base, should southern Democrats turn to the Republicans. The stock market crashed, unemployment rose by two million in two months, and the president suddenly seemed mortal again – unsure whether to restimulate the economy or sit tight.

By the spring of 1938, as the 'Roosevelt recession' worsened, FDR was finally persuaded to abandon his balanced budget demands, and instead revive the Public Works Administration, as well as the Works Progress Administration, with billions of dollars in new federal spending. This duly did the Keynesian trick – though not swiftly enough to avoid a midterm election reverse for Democrats in Congress, the party losing eighty-one seats in the House, eight in the Senate, and thirteen governorships across the country. The outlook for FDR, if he wished to run again for the presidency in 1940, looked unpromising.

It was at this juncture, however, that foreign affairs began to play a major part in the role of the American president, for the first time since Republicans refused to ratify the League of Nations and the United States opted out of a global role in the post-World War I universe.

Roosevelt had recognized the USSR in 1933, and withdrawn American troops from Haiti as part of his 'Good Neighbor' policy, but American appeasement seemed only to encourage war elsewhere, not halt it. When Japanese troops invaded China and their warplanes deliberately attacked and sank the USS *Panay* at anchor in the Yangtse River in December 1937, neither Congress nor the American navy seemed anxious to retaliate. Instead, the State Department sent the Japanese government a bill! This the Japanese happily paid.

In Europe, the same was the case. Neutrality Acts forbade the trading of American war materials with belligerents, let alone American military intervention, unless with congressional approval. Annual immigration quotas had been set by Congress in 1924, with no caveats for refugees, and remained unaltered despite the worsening situation in Europe. No effort was made by the US to make an issue of General Franco's insurgency, backed militarily by Italian and German forces, against the elected Spanish Republican government. American impotence to intervene abroad was illustrated yet again when Hitler annexed Austria with impunity on March 11, 1938, then went on to challenge the major European powers by threatening war if western Czechoslovakia (which included the Sudetenland) was not also ceded to the Nazi Third Reich.

The fact was, with only 185,000 men in its army, the United States of America now ranked a lowly eighteenth on the scale of military forces in the world. It could do nothing to help Britain, France and Russia in protesting Hitler's opportunism, even had Congress wished. 'We in the United States do not seek to impose on any other people either our way of life or our internal government' FDR assured the international community. 'But we are determined', he warned, 'to maintain and protect that way of life and form of government for ourselves.' Beyond offering help to Canada if it was attacked, however, the truth was that the president of the United States was, thanks to public sentiment and congressional pusillanimity, powerless: an extraordinary reversal of its situation at the end of World War I.

'It's a terrible thing to look over your shoulder when you are trying to lead', FDR told one of his speechwriters, who was Jewish, '– and to find no one there.'[25] News of Kristallnacht in November 1938 shocked Americans. 'I myself could scarcely believe such things could occur in a twentieth-century civilization' FDR commented, but outrage led neither to higher immigration quotas for Jewish refugees, nor to a change in American isolationist sentiment.[26] Protected by the Atlantic, the New World seemed to be severing its links with the Old.

With Hitler's march into the rest of Czechoslovakia and seizure of Prague in March 1939, the situation resembled, as Winston Churchill memorably commented, 'feeding the crocodiles'. German troops duly drove into Poland on September 1, 1939, from the west, followed two weeks later by Russian troops advancing from the east as part of a Nazi–Soviet Pact. To Hitler's surprise, however, Britain declared war in order to honour its agreement to aid Poland, followed by France. World war was now unleashed – with the United States, as in 1914, on the sidelines.

FDR's experience in the Navy Department under Josephus Daniels in World War I now became invaluable. By remaining neutral in Europe's struggle, rather than rushing in, the United States had been able to intercede in 1917 with decisive effect. FDR's approach therefore mirrored that of President Wilson twenty-five years before: declaring a steadfast faith in democracy, but avoiding any commitment abroad, while quietly increasing American preparedness, should war be forced upon the United States.

For FDR, this 'phony war' period became perhaps the greatest trial of his political life. France, Britain and Russia had all held firm in the face of German military attack in 1914, but would they do so now, in the face of modern air warfare and German troops, sent into battle by a ruthless Nazi dictator? American aviator Charles Lindbergh thought not, as did Roosevelt's ambassador to London, Joseph P. Kennedy. Their defeatist views were amply confirmed when Hitler overran Denmark and Norway in April 1940, then invaded Holland, Belgium and France on May 10. No Battle of the Marne came to save the Allies. Instead, surrounded on three sides, the British Army was authorized by the new prime minister, Winston Churchill, to evacuate at Dunkirk, and several weeks later Marshal Pétain surrendered on behalf of a provisional French government in Vichy. This left Hitler master of western and central Europe by sheer force of arms, only six years since becoming chancellor of a bankrupt Weimar Republic, facing massive unemployment.

'I suppose Churchill was the best man in England' FDR said, reluctantly acknowledging King George VI's wisdom in choosing Winston Churchill rather than Lord Halifax to be prime minister, 'even if he was drunk half of his time.'[27] The president found it difficult to forget Churchill's snooty attitude when FDR had tried to visit British Admiralty units on behalf of the US Navy Department in 1916, and then in person in London at a banquet in 1918. Now, however, their roles were reversed: Churchill (who had conveniently forgotten his faux pas) begged for material US assistance in pleading telegrams each day.

President Hoover would have scoffed, but Roosevelt was torn. It was an election year, and although the public remained predominantly isolationist, the president found it hard to take pride in one form of democratic life in North America, yet turn his back on it in Europe. Churchill might be an alcoholic, but Hitler was far worse: a 'madman', as FDR had called him already in 1933, drunk with power.[28] The president made up his mind to assist Churchill, as far as he could, overruling his ambassador in London, and treating Britain as an outpost of the US.

This was the turning point in the history of American Empire and the modern world, as the president chose to align the United States with the one major surviving, embattled democracy left in combat in Europe in the summer of 1940. The president had made General George C. Marshall, who had served on the staff of General Pershing in World War I, head of the US Army. Within weeks of the fall of France, under a 'cash and carry' bill he had pushed Congress to pass the previous autumn, FDR and Marshall more than made up for the weapons British troops had left at Dunkirk. From London, Ambassador Kennedy continued to predict defeat for England, but the aerial Battle of Britain – equivalent to the Battle of the Marne in 1914 – ended Hitler's hopes of a swift German invasion that summer. With the Luftwaffe's failure in the air, the course of the war became a matter not of blitzkrieg but of attrition; a war Hitler knew from his economic and military advisors he could not win, yet would not as Führer relinquish.

Whether FDR could win re-election for a third term in November 1940, meanwhile, was far from a foregone conclusion. The president was still only fifty-eight, but his long struggle with polio and his eight taxing years in the presidency, leading his country out of the Depression, had worn him out. In February he had suffered what his doctor called 'a very slight heart attack', falling unconscious across the table. He'd already signed a contract to be contributing editor of *Collier's* magazine after he left the White House (at $75,000 per year), and had confided to the Teamsters union president 'I am tired. I really am. I can't be president again.' He wanted to 'have a rest' and to 'write history', not have to make it. 'No, I just can't do it.'[29] But with the war in Europe heating up, and calls from Chicago that there were 'nine hundred leaderless delegates milling about like worried sheep waiting for the inspiration of leadership that only you can give them', he had to accede.[30] FDR thus became the first elected president in American history to be nominated as his party's candidate for a third consecutive term in office.

The autumn of 1940, FDR knew, would determine America's survival, as he struggled to stop isolationist sentiment across America from preventing his re-election. In August he announced he favoured a selective military service bill or draft, to increase the nation's defence forces – the first ever in peacetime. If Wendell Willkie, chairman of the largest utility holding company and the Republican presidential nominee, had chosen to denounce the president's proposal at that point, he might well have carried the election, such was the nervousness in the country about being dragged into a war that seemed unwinnable for the democracies in Europe. 'I would rather not win the election than do that' Willkie nobly declared, however.[31] Congress passed the Selective Service Bill in September, and by October, 1940, some sixteen million Americans between the ages of twenty-one and thirty-five were registered for a year's military training.

From a mere 189,000 men America's tiny army would grow by the following summer to 1.4 million. Willkie, seeing his polls slide, was urged by his Republican advisers to try a dirty tricks strategy accusing the president of 'secret agreements' to take America into war if he were re-elected. This time Willkie cooperated, and immediately the polls swung in his favour as the 'peace candidate'. Stung, the president travelled to Philadelphia. There, in the cradle of American constitutional democracy, he gave a ringing, categorical denial of the charges. 'There is no secret treaty, no secret obligation, no secret commitment, no secret understanding in any shape or form, direct or indirect, with any other government, to involve this nation in any war or for any other purpose' the president declared.[32] And to nail down the lid on Willkie's coffin, he proclaimed in Boston, where the American Revolution had begun: 'I have said before, but I shall say it again and again and again. Your boys are not going to be sent into any foreign wars.'[33]

'That hypocritical son of a bitch. This is going to beat me' Willkie sighed as he listened to his opponent on the radio.[34] It did. On November 5, 1940, FDR won his third presidential election with fifty million people voting, the largest number in American history. The president received 449 electoral votes to Willkie's meagre eighty-two, and in the popular vote FDR won five million more ballots than Willike. It was not quite the landslide of 1936, but given the isolationist temper of the times in America, it was a magnificent achievement. With selective military service launched and Congress authorizing massive supplementary funding for military production, the US would be in a position not only to defend itself if it was attacked, but to intervene where and when the president and Congress decided.

In 1936, in addressing domestic policy, Roosevelt had spoken of America's 'rendezvous with destiny'. Now, abjuring as an 'obvious delusion' the isolationist notion of America as 'a lone island in a world dominated by the philosophy of force', as he put it in the summer of 1940, he saw a second destiny: that America should rise not only to the challenge of modern social equality and dignity in a free capitalist society, but gird itself to become the world's leading power in international affairs, once its defence forces were rebuilt.[35] For that to happen, he needed Britain to hold out against the Nazi offensive. At Churchill's request he therefore not only pushed through a naval-destroyers-for-bases deal, by which fifty mothballed American World War I destroyers could be traded with Britain for strategically import-ant military garrison rights in the western hemisphere, but pressed Congress to ignore Britain's impending bankruptcy and continue to supply it on unspecified credit, or 'Lend-Lease'.

Roosevelt's Lend-Lease proposal was bitterly opposed by many Republicans, even by Democrats like Joseph P. Kennedy, the US ambas-sador to Britain. But by flattering Kennedy – who left his post in London to exert pressure on FDR and sink Lend-Lease as wasted money ('Democracy is finished in England') – the president was able to pressure Congress into passing the bill, while keeping America out of the war.

Speaking to the nation, the president's fireside chat of December 29, 1940, provided a vivid example of the difference between the everyday democratic values expressed by the elected leader of America in the White House and the venomous, mesmerizing rhetoric of Adolf Hitler. 'The experience of the past two years has proven beyond doubt that no nation can appease the Nazis' FDR explained – and poured cold water on the notion of an American 'negotiated peace' with Hitler, such as Ambassador Kennedy was proposing.[36] 'Nonsense! Is it a nego-tiated peace if a gang of outlaws surrounds your community and on threat of extermination makes you pay tribute to save your skins?' he asked listeners. Hitler was not only clinically insane, but implacable. 'No man can tame a tiger into a kitten by stroking it. There can be no appeasement with ruthlessness' the president declared. 'If Britain goes down, the Axis powers will control the continents of Europe, Asia, Africa, Australasia, and the high seas – and they will be in a position to bring enormous military and naval resources against this hemisphere.' In that case, 'Crawling into bed and pulling the cover over our heads' was no answer. 'The people of Europe who are defending themselves do not ask us to do their fighting. They ask us for the implements of war,' he spelled out, 'the planes, the tanks, the guns that will enable them to fight for their liberty and for our security.' And with that the president used the phrase that would redefine the status of the United States in 1941: 'the arsenal of democracy'.[37]

Several days later, in his State of the Union address, the president raised the stakes still further, urging Americans to lift their sights from mercantilism to a restatement of fundamental democratic principles, setting out what became known as 'the essential Four Freedoms' of modern democratic life: the freedoms of speech and of worship, from want and from fear.[38]

Lend-Lease, endorsed by Wendell Willkie, was signed by Roosevelt into law on March 11, 1941 – not only the largest congressional appropriation in American history but, as FDR put it, 'the end of any attempts at appeasement'.[39]

Appeasement might be over as a policy for the United States, but entering the war was a different issue. Eighty-one per cent of Americans still opposed American involvement. As German troops went on to invade Greece, the cradle of western civilization, after overrunning Bulgaria and Yugoslavia, Churchill again appealed to Roosevelt to join Britain as an ally and declare war on Nazi Germany, to no avail. Using paratroopers, Hitler's Wehrmacht even seized Crete, birthplace of Zeus and considered an impregnable island, dominating the Mediterranean. With General Rommel racing his Panzerarmee across North Africa towards Tobruk, and the Mediterranean controlled by Axis air power, the future for democracy looked bleak, even if the US were to declare war.

In view of Hitler's blitzkrieg success, then, the question arose: were isolationists such as Ambassador Kennedy, Colonel Lindbergh, Senator Burton K. Wheeler and Herbert Hoover right? Was Britain doomed? Between them, Hitler's Third Reich, Mussolini's Italian Empire, and Stalin's Soviet Union would in that case become the ultimate masters of a modern industrial, militarized, totalitarian Europe.

As if to prove the wisdom of Roosevelt's warning about stroking tigers, however, Hitler now shocked the world – though not intelligence services – by attacking his own ally, Russia. Beginning before dawn on the same day of the same month in which Napoleon had once attacked Russia, June 22, almost four million German troops, marshalled in 180 infantry and Panzer divisions, crossed the German–Soviet border in 1941, and made for Leningrad, Moscow, Minsk and the Crimea, executing Russian political commissars and Jews as they went, and herding hundreds of thousands of bewildered Soviet soldiers into captivity.

For FDR, Hitler's apparent success, though welcomed by many in America as a blow against Bolshevism, only increased the threat of

Nazism – the more so if, as Hitler was requesting, Japan were also to declare and wage war on Russia in the Far East, forcing the Soviets to fight on two fronts. The Japanese would thereby increase their growing hegemony in the Far East, following their invasions of China and Indochina, while Hitler would become the undisputed master of all Europe and Russia. The United States of America would then be forced into yet further isolation, indeed be pressed to start appeasement negotiations with the Third Reich and the Empire of Japan, in a new Munich.

The fate of the democratic world now rested, to an extraordinary extent, in one man's hands. Mulling over the situation, President Roosevelt sent word via his emissary Harry Hopkins to Prime Minister Churchill that he'd like to meet him – in secret. Their 'summit' aboard the battleships *Augusta* and *Prince of Wales* in Placentia Bay, off the coast of Newfoundland, early in August 1941, infuriated Hitler, who felt upstaged; but it disappointed Churchill too.

Churchill had assumed Roosevelt would not have suggested such a meeting – fraught with danger for the prime minister in avoiding German U-boats as he sailed across the Atlantic with his senior staff – unless the president 'contemplated some further forward step': namely an announcement of America's entry into the war, on the British Empire's side, and that of the Soviet Union, too, in resisting fascism.[40] However, though the two leaders clasped hands and began their summit by calling each other 'Winston' and 'Franklin', and though they lunched, dined and sang rousing English hymns together, and though they reviewed the global scenario in considerable detail, and though FDR made sympathetic noises, no formal commitment was given by the president beyond further Lend-Lease aid and a decision, in the light of the recent dispatch of US Marines to help defend Iceland, that the Atlantic Ocean between the United States and Iceland would be declared an American maritime security zone, patrolled by US warships. Beyond that, FDR would not go. Instead, the president proposed, they should jointly issue a declaration of principles.

Principles? Churchill was driven almost apopletic with rage. Buoyed by a report from an emissary to Moscow whom he trusted, however, the president was certain that both Russian and British forces would hold out. He was therefore determined to step into the shoes of President Wilson, whose 'Fourteen Points' had been the only explicit statement of war aims presented by any side in World War I. Where

Wilson had produced his document in January 1918, ten months *after* America's declaration of war, however, FDR wanted his charter to *precede* America's entry into the world conflict, and thus inspire not only those peoples still holding out against the tide of Nazi aggression, but the American public. To Churchill's chagrin, therefore, Roosevelt insisted in the joint declaration that there be no post-war territorial gains coveted by, or given to, the US or Britain; that any alteration in national boundaries should only take place by consent of the peoples concerned; and that all peoples – including those in the colonies – had the right to self-determination. This sent ice running through Churchill's veins.

Churchill's dream of the continuation of the British Empire, with the ongoing subjection of India, Burma, Singapore, Malaya and other colonies in Africa, the Middle East and the Far East, was thus shaken. FDR himself stood behind the American version of the declaration, however, and Churchill, desperate for America to become a participating ally (Field Marshal Smuts, his strategic adviser, had reported that the war against Germany could never be won without American intervention), was forced to present the document to his cabinet in London as a fait accompli.[41] The joint declaration henceforth became known as the Atlantic Charter, without even a commitment that the US would fight. It was on Roosevelt's part a masterstroke, though a bitter pill for the beleaguered British prime minister to swallow, as he read newspaper reports of what the president had told reporters on his return to Washington: the US was no closer to 'entering the war' as a result of the summit.[42]

The Atlantic Charter, though never formally signed, spelled the end of British colonial imperialism – indeed the imminent end of Britain as a world power. As Roosevelt congratulated himself when telling his wife about his trip, Churchill had been 'the orator', but he had been the realist.[43]

Because Roosevelt did not survive World War II, he was unable to write his memoirs; whereas Churchill, purloining most of Downing Street's secret documents, was able later to portray himself, in his multi-volume history of the war, as the master strategist of ultimate Allied victory. Despite Churchill's undoubted moral and physical courage, this was to say the least debatable.

In truth, FDR exhibited a far better feel for the likely course the war would follow than Churchill, indeed than any senior politician in the world. With his now legendary powers of persuasion he had gone before Congress to get the Selective Service Act renewed and extended to eighteen months. Congress responded by passing the measure by only a single vote on August 12, against growing resistance from isolationists. Meanwhile the president accelerated war production of planes, tanks, guns, ships and munitions to the point where, unhampered by bombs or invading armies, US output of material in 1942, as a still neutral country, promised to dwarf that of all belligerents combined. If Russia and Britain could survive until the winter, the US would thus be in a position, FDR calculated, to intervene decisively, and thereby emerge as the master of the post-war universe; an economic and military mastery that would, thanks to the Atlantic Charter, be predicated on *moral* principles.

Roosevelt's political, strategic, industrial and diplomatic skill in guiding the US not only on the sidelines of a world war, but with a clearly articulated moral framework for the world that would come thereafter, was – and remains – perhaps the greatest example of presidential leadership in American history. To the relief of those like Frances Perkins who feared the clash of prima donnas in Placentia Bay, the president had afterwards remarked that he'd liked Churchill, indeed had found him much improved since 1918. 'I'm sure that he's got a greater mind than he had twenty years ago' he remarked of the prime minister. 'He's got a more developed mind.'[44] If this was true of Churchill, it was doubly so of Roosevelt. By extending his American security zone as far as Iceland in the summer of 1941, and by then placing an embargo on oil exports to Japan, the president now turned the screw on the Axis alliance, challenging both the Third Reich and the Empire of the Rising Sun to respond in the only way they knew how: by force of arms, thus giving the United States a *casus belli* that would turn the isolationist tide at home.

Bogged down in his titanic struggle to crush the Soviet Union's armies before winter, Hitler was forced to cede control of the western Atlantic to the US Navy, and he gave U-boat captains direct orders to avoid any incident that might provoke an American declaration of war. Japan was equally loath to incite war with the US. Without essential raw materials such as oil from America, however, it was stymied in its plans to expand its Greater East Asia Co-prosperity Sphere. Aware from decrypts of Japanese secret signals how hysterical the Japanese leaders were becoming, FDR ratcheted up his diplomatic pressure, not only refusing to lift his embargo on the export of oil and other materials to Japan, but demanding that the Japanese withdraw from conquered territories in China.

Convinced that the United States would declare war on Japan if they invaded the Dutch East Indies and Malaya, the new hard-line Japanese government headed by Hideki Tojo therefore proposed in November 1941 a pre-emptive attack on American forces in the Pacific before US units could be reinforced. The war was becoming a game of cat and mouse; but America, thanks to Roosevelt's massive rearmament programme and military draft, was the cat.

Aware of Japanese intentions from intercepts, Roosevelt ordered all American commanders in the Pacific to be on the highest alert, and sent a squadron of new B-17s to Hawaii. Not even FDR, however, could credit the utter ineptitude of the peacetime US garrison at Pearl Harbor, when now attacked in broad daylight on December 7, 1941: the 'day of infamy', as the president called it in his speech to Congress. In two hours Admiral Yamamoto's attack on Pearl Harbor managed to sink eighteen American warships, including no less than eight battleships, smash or cripple 283 aircraft, and kill 2,403 servicemen, with almost total impunity.

Hitler, with his armies beleaguered in snow outside Moscow and lacking winter clothing, was ecstatic when he heard the news (he had not been informed by the Japanese in advance), but completely misread the fact that the US had, in the aftermath, declared war only on Japan. Four days after Pearl Harbor the Führer made a long, impassioned speech to deputies in the Reichstag in Berlin. In it he announced something that would cost him the war – and his life.

President Roosevelt, Hitler explained to Reichstag deputies, 'comes from a family rolling in money', with social advantages that 'pave the way and secure success in life in the democracies'. By contrast, Hitler himself had returned from World War I 'just as poor as I had left for it in the autumn of 1914'. While Roosevelt the millionaire had then pursued the 'career of a normal politician, who is experienced in business, has economic backing, and is protected by his birth, I fought as a nameless and unknown man for the resurrection of my *Volk*, a people which had just suffered the greatest injustice in its history. The course

of the two lives!' the Führer reflected, amazed to think how different
they were, as men and leaders. 'When Franklin Roosevelt became the
head of the United States, he was the candidate of a thoroughly capitalist party, which used him. When I became the chancellor of the
German Reich, I was the Führer of a popular movement which I
myself had created.' Where Roosevelt was guided by a 'brain trust'
of Jews – people 'we once fought in Germany as a parasitic phenomenon of mankind, and which we had begun to remove from public
life' – he, Adolf Hitler, had fought against such people on behalf of
'the fate of my *Volk* and my sacred inner beliefs'.[45] Roosevelt's and
Churchill's Atlantic Charter was 'tantamount to a bald hairdresser
recommending his unfailing hair restorer. These gentlemen, who live
in socially retarded states, should have taken care of their unemployed
instead of agitating for war' the Führer commented. Germany, whose
*Volk* had 'a history of nearly two thousand years', had 'never been as
united and unified as it is today and as it will be in the future', nor
'so aware of its honour'. As Führer, he announced, he had therefore
given the American chargé d'affaires his passport and had told him to
leave Berlin. He was declaring war on the United States.

The challenge that now faced the Third Reich would not only be
one of arms, but of will and ruthlessness. 'Just as we were mercilessly
harsh in our struggle for power,' the Führer warned, 'we will be merciless and harsh in our struggle for the preservation of our *Volk*.' Any
German who questioned, criticized, mocked or sabotaged 'the efforts
of the homeland' would be executed.[46] Six days later, on December
17, 1941, having arrived back at his Rastenburg headquarters in East
Prussia, Hitler then relieved Field Marshal von Brauchitsch of his post
as commander-in-chief of the army, and made himself supreme
commander or generalissimo of the Wehrmacht and Waffen SS.
'Anyone can do that little bit of operational planning' he sneered.

For his part, FDR also took on the role of generalissimo, yet took
care while exercising his constitutional authority as commander-in-
chief to direct the strategy of the war but not to interfere with its
implementation, as Hitler now did, to the cost of his armies' chances
of battlefield success. In casting Roosevelt as a mere functionary and
'profiteer' in the 'shadow' of President Wilson in World War I, Hitler
– who had never visited America – had made a big mistake. FDR's
eight years in the US Navy Department, from 1913 to 1920, had given

him the very training Hitler lacked – indeed it is impossible for an historian to imagine how otherwise a huge but militarily impotent democracy, which had refused to militarize in the inter-war years, could have transformed itself into the Rome of the twentieth century as, under Roosevelt's presidency, the United States now did.

From that earlier administrative experience in Washington, working with Josephus Daniels, FDR had learned the fundamental lesson of war, as set out by Clausewitz and other military thinkers: the organization of a nation's resources is crucial to achieving success – the means that enable the end. The fact that Yamamoto's daring sneak attack had proven so damaging to America's naval and military standing in the Far East was shameful (FDR could not understand why, despite his warnings sent to Hawaii, the battleships were 'tied up in rows', and the airplanes parked by their runways as at a polo meet), but the president was not downcast.[47] His 500-word speech to Congress on December 8, 1941 on the infamy of Pearl Harbor would go down in history alongside Lincoln's Gettysburg Address, but it was his State of the Union address four weeks later that actually *made* history.

On January 6, 1942, outlining American production targets for the coming year, President Roosevelt announced numbers that took Congress' and the world's breath away: six million tons of new ships; 45,000 tanks; 60,000 airplanes – in 1942 alone! On this basis, there could be no doubt who would win the war, only how long it would take.

Churchill, hearing these figures from Roosevelt himself while staying in the White House for three weeks, was reborn. In a fireside chat two days after Pearl Harbor FDR had told listeners that there would be 'bad news and good news', 'defeats and victories', but that these were the 'fortunes of war' – and would be shared by the nation. The fundamental fact was that 'we are all in it – all the way. Every single man, woman and child is a partner in the most tremendous undertaking in American history.'[48]

The first eight months of 1942 bore out the president's warning about bad news. Hong Kong, Guam, Wake Island, New Britain, the Gilbert Islands and most of the Solomon Islands had fallen to the Japanese. On January 2, the capital of the Philippines, Manila, fell too, forcing the Americans to fall back into the Bataan Peninsula, while another Japanese army captured Kuala Lumpur in Malaya, advanced through Borneo and invaded New Guinea, to the north of Australia.

General Rommel raced to Benghazi, routing the British
Commonwealth army in North Africa, while Hitler, authorizing the
annihilation of all German and captured Jews, told his propaganda
minister Dr Goebbels not to 'get sentimental' about the Hebrews, but
to 'speed up the process with cold brutality', whatever the 'resistance
in some circles'. (As Goebbels coyly noted in his diary several weeks
later, in relation to the mass deportation of Jews to extermination
camps in the east: 'Here will be used a fairly barbarous method which
one can't come close to describing; not much will remain of the Jews
themselves. On the whole, it can be determined that 60 per cent of
them will have to be liquidated, only 40 per cent being usable for the
purposes of labour.')[49]

German barbarity was matched by Japanese atrocities committed
against captured enemy troops in Asia, South East Asia and the
Pacific. In February, the Japanese invaded Burma, and after landing
in Malaya, took Singapore, together with 85,000 troops defending it.
In the Battle of the Java Sea, all five Allied cruisers were sunk, and
five of the nine accompanying destroyers. The Dutch East Indies
also fell to Japanese invaders, and Japanese warplanes began bombing
Darwin on the northern Australian peninsula. And worse was to
come.

As the spring of 1942 turned to summer, German forces launched
another spectacular armoured offensive in the Crimea. The Japanese
took the surrender of General King's 76,000-strong army in the Bataan
Peninsula of the Philippines – the largest surrender in American history,
and precursor to the infamous Bataan Death March. With the Russian
armies defeated in the Crimea, opening the gateway to the rich oilfields
of the Caucasus, Stalin sent his foreign minister Vyacheslav Molotov
to Washington to plead for more American munitions and an urgent
invasion of France to create a second front and relieve the pressure
on Russia.

Roosevelt's and Churchill's responses to the pleas of the Soviet
Union differed markedly. To Molotov's appeal for a second front,
Roosevelt replied yes: the Allies would launch an invasion of France
in 1942, to draw off German air squadrons and divisions, and drive
straight for Berlin. Churchill, when he heard what Roosevelt had
verbally promised Molotov, was appalled. The Allies would never be
able to launch such an amphibious attack across the often stormy seas

of the English Channel; no one had done so successfully since 1066. As the Spanish Armada had come to grief in 1588, so too had Hitler's mighty Luftwaffe in the Battle of Britain; it was an impossible task. In June 1942, therefore, Churchill made haste to Washington to attempt to dissuade FDR against mounting a second front – at least, across the Channel. It was in the White House, in fact, that Churchill's defeatism in terms of head-to-head battle with the German armies was seemingly justified, when Roosevelt relayed to him the bad news. Tobruk in North Africa, with its entire British garrison of 33,000 soldiers, had surrendered to Rommel's German-Italian Panzerarmee without serious fighting. 'Defeat is one thing,' Churchill commented, in shame at British cowardice, 'disgrace is another.'[50]

Roosevelt was remarkably unfazed. For him, it was another indication of Britain's need for more and better equipment – which America could provide. He thus magnanimously offered a convoy of the latest American Sherman tanks and 105 mm self-propelled artillery guns to be re-routed to Suez, to ensure that Egypt, too, was not lost.[51]

By the summer of 1942, then, it was clear that Washington DC – not London or Moscow – was the epicentre of the Allies' war on Germany and Japan. To prosecute the war, Roosevelt had established a Joint Chiefs of Staff Committee, with its offices forming the Anglo-American High Command headquarters, and the new Pentagon – the world's largest office building – to house it. Meanwhile FDR also set up a series of War Boards to maximize US industrial output, and gave the green light to the development of a highly secret weapon of mass destruction: the Manhattan Project.

With Congress' backing, FDR was, in short, not only the US president but now the generalissimo of the Allied cause, weighing carefully the political, economic and military priorities in winning the war. Aged sixty that year, and despite the military reverses overseas, he radiated confidence and vitality, sure that he could manage the leaders of the various supplicant nations and emissaries seeking his aid. He was, in this sense, the pharaoh not only of peacetime, but of war. America, he was certain, would win in the end, with its subordinate partners. He had only to communicate positive energy and compassion, and exercise good judgement, and the United States would emerge as leader of a democratic New World it could oversee economically and, if necessary, by superior force.

Roosevelt's patience was the quality that perhaps raised him above all his peers. To the apoplexy of his generals he not only accepted Churchill's argument that Germany should be defeated first, then Japan (since the fall of Germany would inevitably lead to the fall of Japan, whereas the reverse was not true), but deferred to Churchill's qualms about a cross-Channel attack on France in 1942. He therefore delayed the undertaking for two years, until American forces were seasoned enough by battles in North Africa and Italy, to launch what would be the decisive battle of World War II: D-Day, on June 6, 1944. 'If anything happens to that man, I couldn't stand it' Churchill said with tears in his eyes as Roosevelt's plane took off from Casablanca, where they concerted plans in January 1943. 'He is the truest friend; he has the furthest vision; he is the greatest man I have ever known.'[52]

Meeting President Roosevelt in Casablanca on behalf of the Free French, quartered in London, General de Gaulle did not agree. De Gaulle was incensed by the president's presumptuousness regarding the future. 'Roosevelt meant the peace to be an American peace, convinced that he must be the one to dictate its structure,' de Gaulle later chronicled, 'and that France in particular should recognize him as its saviour and its arbiter.' Given the tens of thousands of Americans, Britons and Canadians who would still have to give their lives to liberate France, this seemed a fair presumption to most combatants, but not to de Gaulle. The Frenchman was furious that 'beneath his mask of courtesy, Roosevelt regarded me without benevolence'.[53]

Malevolence might have been more accurate. Roosevelt remarked to Supreme Court Justice Felix Frankfurter that de Gaulle was 'a bit touched' in the head, and later 'a nut'.[54] At any event, with allies such as these, the president would have been forgiven for wishing, like his military staff, to return his forces to the US and concentrate on the defeat of Japan – where, in crucial naval battles in the Coral Sea and Midway, US naval superiority had been reasserted in the summer of 1942, and the campaign to retake the Solomon Islands had begun in earnest at Guadalcanal. Yet to his lasting credit Roosevelt resisted, aware that this time, unlike 1918, the United States must take a more effective leadership role in the post-war world, not back away.

Upon his success in first setting the United States back on the path to economic prosperity in the 1930s, then commanding America's war effort, and finally in positioning the United States to guide the post-war world, Franklin Delano Roosevelt must ultimately be judged. None were easy tasks – in fact it is hard to imagine any other American figure who could have managed what FDR achieved. Compromise in keeping the Grand Alliance unified was in this respect Roosevelt's greatest contribution to grand strategy, and though mocked by those who counselled a more rational, clear-cut American military approach, time would prove him right. Roosevelt, as generalissimo-in-chief, was vindicated, able to take heed of Churchill's warnings, overrule his military advisers, use his understanding of the Vichy French, and prosecute a patient strategy that allowed the Allies to employ their combination of forces – naval, air and ground troops, as well as military intelligence – that promised to defeat even the most fanatical German armies. Moreover he ensured that Stalin would refuse possible German offers of an armistice, knowing that the Americans were, eventually, coming, and would not accept anything but the 'unconditional surrender' of the Nazis, as FDR announced at Casablanca.

By the fall of 1943, with the Soviets pushing back Hitler's armies towards Prussia, Anglo-American forces in control of the Mediterranean, and General MacArthur making headway in the Solomon Islands, the war certainly seemed to have reversed itself since the dark days of 1941. Even the U-boat menace in the Atlantic – where, in the spring of 1943, more than 200 German submarines had caused havoc in intercepting Allied convoys – was lifted when Roosevelt ordered back sixty long-range Liberator airplanes from the Pacific, which led to the sinking of eighty German submarines, and Hitler's order to withdraw the remainder.

American war production hit new records that year, with the US producing a new B-24 bomber every sixty-three minutes, tens of thousands of tanks, thousands of ships, and hundreds of thousands of vehicles of all kinds; more than the output of all other combatants combined. It was small wonder that, at a summit in Tehran in November 1943, Stalin raised his glass to acknowledge what 'the president and the United States have done to win this war. The most important thing in this war are machines. The United States has proven it can turn out 10,000 planes a month. Russia can turn out, at most, 3,000 airplanes a month. The United States is a country with machines' the Russian dictator remarked with awe. 'Without the use of those machines, through Lend-Lease, we would lose this war.'

This was, in the end, Roosevelt's greatest single achievement. Fearing an English Channel running with English blood, Churchill had frankly never believed in an Allied invasion of France. The Germans themselves had baulked at a cross-channel assault in 1940. The one-day assault on Dieppe in 1942 (in which more than 1,000 Canadian soldiers had been mown down in a few hours, and 2,000 captured) had proven an unmitigated catastrophe, completely defeating its strategic aim of proving to the Russians that the Allies were serious in preparing for a cross-Channel invasion of France. Moreover Churchill's pet project, his personally promoted amphibious landing near Rome at Anzio, in January 1944, was an even greater disaster, incurring a horrific 29,000 American and British casualties to little, if any, purpose. In overruling Churchill, therefore, and insisting the Allies must and *would* carry out Operation Overlord, Roosevelt showed supreme patience and, at the appropriate moment, decisive judgement. Moreover, in deciding that General Eisenhower, not General Marshall, should command the Allied D-Day invasion, Roosevelt once again demonstrated his talent for choosing effective subordinates.

D-Day, June 6, 1944, was thus the triumph of President Roosevelt's role as generalissimo-in-chief. It would become the greatest successful military operation of the twentieth century, mounted under the supreme command of an American general, and combining the arms not only of all the services, but all the western Allies. When Churchill telegraphed Stalin to say the D-Day landings would commence the next day, the marshal – who had waited two long years for the moment – sneered: 'if there is no fog. Until now there was always something that interfered. I suspect tomorrow it will be something else. Maybe they'll meet up with some Germans! What if they meet up with some Germans! Maybe there won't be a landing then, but just promises as usual.'[55]

The Russian dictator, however, was stunned and surprised by the ferocity of the Allied onslaught. Landing almost 200,000 troops in Normandy in a single day, in overwhelming force, across a storm-blown sea, and reinforcing them with two million troops in the weeks thereafter, the western Allies finally proved they could not only supply the means to fight the Nazis, but the will, determination and professionalism to do so – and to win. It was a lesson that not only the Germans, but also the Soviets, took to heart.

Summoning James Byrnes back from the Supreme Court to act as his domestic affairs deputy, Roosevelt increasingly concentrated his unique political skills on the business of working with America's allies, and plans for a post-war world. Inevitably, the latter impinged on the former; Churchill recalled how, at the Tehran summit, 'I sat with the Russian bear on the one side of me, with paws outstretched, and on the other side the great American buffalo, and between the two sat the poor little English donkey who was the only one', he claimed, 'who knew the right way home.'[56]

But did he? Churchill had proven an historic figure when England stood alone against the Nazis after the fall of France, Russia complacent in its Nazi–Soviet Pact, the United States still in isolation mode. But as World War II wound to its climax, Churchill's vision of a Britain restored to colonial greatness, at the heart of a global empire, rang hollow to Roosevelt's ears, for all Churchill's eloquence. When Stalin jokingly suggested, at Tehran, shooting 50,000 German officers at the conclusion of the war, and Roosevelt demurred, suggesting 49,000 as a better number, Churchill walked out of the room, chased by Stalin and Molotov, who insisted it was a jest.[57] 'I would rather be taken out into the garden here and now and be shot myself than sully my own country's honour by such infamy' Churchill had protested: the voice of a great humanitarian, but one who looked to revive an imperial past, not embrace a post-colonial future.

President Roosevelt, though later criticized for his naivety in dealing with his Russian counterpart, was far more prescient than Churchill about the future of the democratic rather than the Communist world. Churchill evinced little interest in the concept of a United Nations organization, or UN trusteeships that would, against strict timetables, immediately prepare former colonized countries for swift independence. The colonial system, Roosevelt had told his son Elliott at Casablanca, was not merely unjust, but inevitably it led to protest, terrorism and war. 'Exploit the resources of an India, a Burma, a Java; take all the wealth out of those countries but never put anything back into them, things like education, decent standards of living, minimum health requirements – all you're doing is storing up the kind of trouble that leads to war.'[58] Churchill was still so opposed to Indian self-rule that Roosevelt had told Stalin, at Tehran, 'it would be better not to discuss the question of that country's independence with Churchill', given the prime minister's Tory views.[59] Roosevelt felt similarly about

French colonialism – indeed with regard to Indochina, FDR had also agreed '100%' with Stalin in wishing to stop France from taking it back as a colony, stating bluntly that 'after 100 years of French rule in Indochina, the inhabitants were worse off than they had been'.[60]

One British historian of the Tehran conference wondered, forty years later, if it had 'crossed Stalin's mind that Roosevelt was, wittingly or unwittingly, pointing towards a world of Soviet/American dictatorship' – later to be called 'hegemonism'.[61] Whether or not it did, the prospect certainly crossed many a British (and French) mind, with concerns as to whether such a dual dictatorship of the world could possibly work without eventual war between the two, given their contrary systems of government.

Roosevelt had no illusions either about Soviet Communism or Stalin. To his lasting credit, however, FDR felt impelled at least to try to co-opt Russian involvement in shaping a free and democratic post-war world. Certainly no other American figure could have attempted to reach an accommodation with Stalin, nor with such legendary charm, humour and goodwill. If Soviet–American relations were destined to go down the drain after the war, given a Bolshevist system based upon fear, intimidation and indifference to human life, Roosevelt was determined that, on his watch, he would first do everything in his power to make the dual hegemony work. And this, by standing for election for an unprecedented fourth term as president of the United States, despite failing health, he was determined to achieve.

His hand shook when he poured tea, he had long since stopped using the White House swimming pool, and he rarely stood, finding his leg braces too heavy and the effort too tiring. Deep circles below his eyes began to make his huge, once handsome face, with his trademark small pince-nez, seem haggard – yet still the president insisted, in the summer of 1944, he was fit to run. Eventually, at the insistence of his daughter Anna, he went for a check-up at the Bethesda Naval Hospital, where he was found to be suffering congestive heart failure, causing his face, lips and nail beds to discolour. If not treated, he was given a year to live.

Aged sixty-two, the president suddenly looked seventy-two, and should never have placed his name in contention, given his prognosis. Instead, the press was told he was in fine health and, after being nominated on the first ballot at the Democratic Party Convention in July

1944, he set off for Hawaii to mediate between General MacArthur and Admiral Nimitz over strategy in the Pacific – having dropped the unpopular vice president, Henry Wallace, from the ticket, and having taken Senator Harry S. Truman of Missouri as his running mate.

Few who met the president in person were confident he would stand up to the rigours of an election campaign. After conferring with FDR aboard the USS *Baltimore*, MacArthur told his wife on July 26, 1944, 'In six months he will be in his grave.' The president was, MacArthur felt, 'just a shell of the man I knew'.[62] Roosevelt had lost nineteen pounds, and when he spoke to dock workers in Washington State, after donning his leg braces for the first time in a year, he rambled and was almost incoherent. 'It's going to look mighty sad when he begins to trade punches with young Dewey' the *Washington Post* predicted, referring to the Republican candidate, Governor Thomas E. Dewey of New York.[63]

In fact the campaign that autumn turned out to be the reverse, as Roosevelt twitted the young governor for 'attacking my little dog, Fala'. Addressing an audience in Washington, FDR added: 'Well, of course, I don't resent attacks, and my family doesn't resent attacks, but Fala does resent them.'[64] Campaigning in New York the president appeared before three million people in October 1944, riding in an open White House car, even in pouring rain, and speaking before 125,000 people in Chicago's Soldier Field (with 150,000 outside), ending with an appearance in Boston, where Frank Sinatra warmed up the crowd. There, in the city's Fenway Park, the president reminded his audience that America was a nation of immigrants, and it was 'our duty to make sure that, big as our country is, there is no room in it for racial or religious intolerance' – nor for 'snobbery'.[65]

Six months later, Roosevelt's partner in the Grand Alliance, Winston Churchill, would be ejected from the prime ministership by British voters, but for his part FDR seemed in November 1944 just as popular as when first elected, winning the presidential election by three million more votes than in 1932, and receiving 432 electoral votes to Dewey's ninety-nine.

The president was over the moon; but under the weather. He had lost more weight, had no appetite, and his blood pressure was higher than ever. 'He looked like an invalid who had been allowed to see guests for the first time and the guests had stayed too long' Frances

Perkins recalled, after congratulating him on his win.[66] The president
gave his fourth inaugural speech under the South Portico of the White
House on January 20, 1945, before 7,000 people gathered in the snow
– his last ever while standing. Peace was now close, 'a just and honorable peace, a durable peace' that America would work for, 'as today
we work and fight for total victory in war'. In working for peace, moreover, 'We shall strive for perfection' he declared; a goal that would not
be achieved 'immediately – but we shall still strive. We may make
mistakes – but they must never be mistakes which result from faint-
ness of heart or abandonment of moral principle.' He reminded his
audience that the US Constitution was not a perfect instrument, but a
'firm base upon which all manner of men, of all races and colors and
creeds, could build our solid structure of democracy', a democracy he
had sought, as president, to protect. 'We have learned', he stated, 'that
we cannot live alone, at peace; that our well-being is dependent on the
well-being of other nations far away . . . We have learned to be citizens of the world.' Isolationism, in other words, was dead.

Two days later the ailing president sailed to Malta, then flew to
Yalta on the Black Sea, where the sequel to the Tehran summit was
to be held, beginning on February 4, 1945.

No conference in World War II would later give rise to more partisan
argument than Yalta. Reversing their role as the party of isolationism
up to World War II, Republicans would assert the summit was a sell-out
by a sick president to Stalin. Yalta was, they claimed, a veritable invitation to diehard Soviet Communists to do what Hitler had failed to do:
control Europe and infect the globe with their ideological doctrines.[67]

The president was certainly unwell – indeed was dying, whether
of heart disease or cancer, or both. Edith Wilson, the widow of
President Wilson, had commented at the inauguration that Roosevelt
looked 'exactly as my husband did when he went into his decline'.[68]
But with the war not yet over in either Europe or the Far East – and
anywhere between half a million and a million American casualties
estimated as necessary to force the Japanese to accept unconditional
surrender – the president was determined to get Stalin's formal agreement to join the US in defeating Japan, once Berlin fell. Moreover,
he wanted the mechanism of the United Nations – successor to the
League of Nations – locked down, while Stalin still supported the
notion. The rest, he recognized, would be a matter of barter.

Barter there certainly was at Yalta. The Soviets were already occupying much of Poland, having refused to support the Warsaw uprising, clearly determined to use the country as a permanent buffer against any future Barbarossa-like attack from the West. Poland would thus be part of a Soviet cordon sanitaire against Germany and any other western power seeking to invade Russia – a form of paranoid Soviet isolationism that would, behind a veil of mischief-making in foreign parts, characterize Russian relations with the West for the next half-century.

Roosevelt, fully aware of this, did his best at Yalta to charm and encourage Stalin in a less negative approach to the future world. It was, sadly, a losing battle. Moreover, the president was still adamant that the British should honour the Atlantic Charter and abandon their dreams of post-war colonial paradise, putting him on a confrontational course with Winston Churchill.

Roosevelt did his dying best at the eight-day Yalta conference. He fudged a compromise over Poland, knowing he was clothing rape; he agreed to Far Eastern bases for the Soviet military, in order not only to get Russian entry into the war against Japan, but to build a co-bulwark against renascent Japanese military adventurism in post-war years. He settled for a four-power occupation of Germany in distinct zones, including Berlin. He engineered a joint declaration on Liberated Europe, pledging free elections that would be 'broadly representative of all democratic elements', knowing that Russia, in those countries it overran on its own, would stretch the word 'democratic' to breaking point. Above all, he got agreement on the set-up for the United Nations, with a preparatory conference to assemble in San Francisco that April.

Sailing back to America aboard the USS *Quincy*, the president was depressed. Meeting King Ibn Saud of Saudi Arabia on Great Bitter Lake in the Suez Canal on February 12, 1945, Roosevelt attempted to get the king's agreement to 10,000 more Jewish refugees being allowed to settle in Palestine. Ibn Saud refused, saying the refugees should be sent back to the countries from which they came, compelling the president to promise that whatever Congress or the American media might say, he himself 'would do nothing to assist the Jews against the Arabs and would make no move hostile to the Arab people', while confiding to his new Secretary of State, Edward Stettinius, that Jews and Arabs, sadly, were on a collision course, but that he would do his best to find a way of avoiding war between them.[69] 'I didn't say the result was good,' FDR said to an aide on his return to Washington, 'I said it was the best I could do.'[70]

On March 1, 1945, the president made his last speech to a joint session of Congress, asking the senators and congressmen to forgive him if he remained seated, given the weight of his steel leg braces – the first time he had ever mentioned his disability. As one historian noted, 'His voice faltered, he was hoarse, he hesitated or lost his place fourteen times' and kept departing from the text.[71] He joked that he wanted to do in one hour 'what Winston did in two', and made reference to the Roosevelts' reputation for travel.[72] 'No plan is perfect' he said of his efforts at Yalta to assure the democratic freedom of Poland and other countries in Europe, but he hoped that overall the summit marked 'the end of the system of unilateral action', or heedless war by militarist states, and even – if the United Nations worked as was hoped – the end of imperial 'balances of power, and all other expedients that have been tried for centuries – and have always failed'. He denied he was unwell – unfounded 'rumors' that had circulated in his absence, but which could be seen, he claimed, to be untrue.

It was a bravura performance. Six weeks later, having travelled to Warm Springs to recover his failing energy, he was signing papers when he felt a terrible headache, slumped forward, and died.

## Part Three: Private Life

Pampered by a rich, devoted, somewhat imperious mother, FDR grew up in very privileged circumstances, as Hitler noted, but as an only, often lonely child. Wanting to please his mother, yet also wanting to escape her control over his financial and social life, were the twin leitmotifs of his early manhood as he courted a number of eligible girls while at Harvard. He seemed, in fact, almost feminine in his desperation to get married before he graduated, proposing to at least three teenagers.

The most beautiful and serious of these student infatuations was tiny Alice Sohier, daughter of a wealthy businessman, who bewitched him.[73] Her doctor claimed her womb was too small to bear children, so Franklin's declaration that he wanted to have six fell on unfavourable Sohier ears ('I did not wish to be a cow' she told a friend afterwards).[74]

Whether from pique or *noblesse oblige*, FDR then courted another teenager, a girl he had known all his life: the orphaned daughter of his godfather, Elliott Roosevelt. She was the legendary ugly duckling of the family, unnaturally tall for those days (5' 10"), with big feet, big protruding teeth, and a receding chin. Plain was a euphemism. Moreover, she had no sense of humour and was – after several years in a finishing school in Paris, run by a left-wing lesbian martinet, Mlle Souvestre – dedicated to helping the poor and disadvantaged, which would free her from the trite and unattainable expectations of her class.

However, thanks to her deceased parents Eleanor Roosevelt was set to inherit a lot of money. To cap this, her uncle (the brother of her deceased father) was none other than the president of the United States. Franklin – who never kissed her before they were engaged, and certainly never went further than kissing before they were married – called her an 'angel' in his diary, and 'Babs' in conversation. Looks aside, he was proud of his 'catch'. He had grown tall and hugely handsome by the time he left Harvard, and was politically ambitious. Eleanor, who was well read, compassionate and obedient to the point of subservience in her adoration of him, would do fine. He wanted to be admired and loved, but by someone other than just his mother. And by Eleanor he was, once they married in 1905. They would have six children (one died), and houses full of servants. What more could he want?

Yachting, hiking, golf. Parties too, at which he was not only the tallest at 6' 2" but also the most handsome, intelligent, witty and charming. Eleanor herself predicted she would 'never be able to hold him', telling her cousin Ethel 'He's too attractive.'[75] Exhausted after child number six, Eleanor did not refuse to have further sex, but she did ask for, and get, her own bedroom and a good night's sleep in 1916.[76] In terms of marital stitching, however, it was a mistake, as she eventually discovered.

In 1918 Roosevelt sailed to England and France in order to inspect the US Navy's installations there, and to see the US Marine Corps in combat in the final year of World War I. On the way home he caught flu, in the global pandemic, and arrived aboard the *Leviathan* having barely survived a high fever and difficulty in breathing. Eleanor, alerted by telegram, met the ship at New York and arranged his conveyance by ambulance to his mother Sara's house on East 65th Street. As she unpacked his things, she came to his leather valise, and opened it.

Inside were beribboned love letters addressed to him from Eleanor's former secretary, Lucy Mercer.

Eleanor had already fired the twenty-six-year-old Ms Mercer in 1917 for being too intimate with Franklin, only for Lucy to join the navy as a yeoman, and Franklin to hire her in the Assistant Secretary of the Navy's office. There too Lucy had been fired, by Franklin's boss, Josephus Daniels, who knew that in Washington tongues wagged harder than in any other city. FDR still saw the stunningly beautiful Miss Lucy, however, and supported her financially when she lost her job. The discovery of the cache of her love letters – which she had continued to send while Franklin was in Europe – was an affront Eleanor could not endure.

'The bottom dropped out of my world' Eleanor later wrote. To her daughter Anna she later confided that she 'questioned' her husband about his intentions, if he was so in love with the woman, and 'offered him a divorce and asked that he think things over before giving her a definite answer'.[77]

No one in the Roosevelt family had ever been divorced, however, and though Eleanor herself had told a friend in a similar predicament 'not to accept ½ loaf of love', this was what, in the event, she was forced to take. For when FDR's mother, Sara, heard of Franklin's plans to divorce, she put her foot down, telling FDR he would not get another penny from her, nor would he inherit Springwood. FDR's amanuensis, Louis Howe, said the same thing, only more bluntly. FDR would be dismissed as Assistant Secretary of the Navy by Josephus, and his career would be ruined.

Thanks to Sara and to Howe, the crisis was averted. FDR lied to Lucy, telling her Eleanor would not agree to a divorce. But knowing FDR so well – they had conducted the affair for two years – Lucy also knew FDR was slated for greatness. Divorce, even if Eleanor did agree to one, would end all talk of his reaching the presidency one day. Lucy thus released him from any obligation, he 'returned' to his wife, and by the summer of 1920 FDR was campaigning as the Democratic candidate for the vice presidency of the United States, posing as a happily married man with five children.

To her credit, Lucy Mercer faded completely into the background – indeed emulated Franklin's mother, by marrying a fabulously wealthy widower twice her age, Winty Rutherfurd, by whom she also had a child. She continued to correspond with FDR, as a 'friend', but allowed no hint of their relationship to surface in her lifetime.

Eleanor, by contrast, was neither convinced that, as a result of his treachery, FDR still had the makings of greatness in him, nor could she exonerate him for loving Lucy, whose beauty made her feel exactly as she'd felt (and suffered) throughout her childhood: ugly and unwanted. 'I have the memory of an elephant. I can forgive, but never forget' she later confessed.[78] She took to visiting Rock Creek Cemetery and sitting before Saint-Gaudens' memorial statue to Clover Adams, who had killed herself in grief over her husband's love affair.[79] She lost weight and threw up so much the acid caused her teeth to separate and appear even more prominent.[80] She had once declared her belief in his future; now she appeared indifferent. When New York governor Al Smith ran for the presidency in 1928, and Franklin ran for the governor's mansion that Smith would vacate, she worked for Smith, not for FDR. 'Governor Smith's election means something,' she told a friend, 'but whether Franklin spends two years in Albany or not matters comparatively very little.' And when Smith lost, and FDR won, she was sour. 'I don't care' she snorted to a journalist. 'What difference does it make to me?'[81]

Eleanor's humourless, punitive response to FDR's betrayal changed their marriage into one of lingering convenience. She nursed him almost single-handedly when he was struck by polio, out of charity and duty, but at a deeper level considered it his just reward. When he began going down to Warm Springs to build his polio centre, to which polio sufferers of all backgrounds could come for treatment, she did not accompany him. She even ignored rumours that he had 'girlfriends' there, among them, Marguerite (Missy) LeHand, a former campaign worker who became his secretary and girl Friday. Young, lively, but neither beautiful nor from a classy background, Missy was accepted by Eleanor as a substitute wife for her husband. Sex, Eleanor told her daughter, 'is an ordeal to be borne'; she was perfectly happy for Franklin to have it, à la française, in his post-polio state (his potency not being affected by the paralysis in his lower limbs), if that was what he wanted, since she did not.[82] What she insisted upon was discretion ('I haven't told Mama that Missy is back' Eleanor wrote FDR in the spring of 1924, because Sara would have 'more peace of mind when she doesn't know such things'), while she carved a career for herself as an activist for social causes.[83]

Though he had promised Eleanor he would never see Lucy again, it was a promise Franklin and Lucy found difficult to keep. Lucy Mercer's husband proved more jealous of FDR than Eleanor of Lucy. Franklin and Lucy therefore maintained a clandestine correspondence throughout the 1920s and 1930s, and it was only when her husband's health failed in his mid-seventies, and he required full-time nursing that, in 1937, the relationship was revived in person. In 1935 FDR had suggested to author Fulton Oursler a magazine series by different detective novelists, devoted to the theme of how a rich man, 'married for twenty years' but with a wife who 'bores him' and tired of the 'hollowness of all the superficial friendship surrounding him', could engineer a getaway in order 'to begin a secret life in some small town where he can escape his past' – the series to be called 'The President's Mystery Story'. Oursler complied, earning $9,000 for the president (who gave it to his polio foundation).

The president had found his own secret solution: being driven to Q Street in Georgetown, picking Lucy up ('Go look out the window,' Lucy's niece would shout, 'President Roosevelt is coming to pick up Aunt Lucy!') and taking a ride with her in his car through Rock Creek Park.[84] In 1940, Lucy attended FDR's third inauguration as his guest, and when her husband suffered a stroke in 1941, the president took to meeting her in small lanes in the Virginia countryside. ('There seems to be a lady waiting on the road. Let us ask her if she needs a ride' he'd tell his driver.)[85]

On June 5, 1941, under the alias Mrs Paul Johnson in the White House log, Lucy visited the president in the Oval Office for the first time, while Eleanor was away at Hyde Park where she had her own house, Stone Cottage, or Val-Kill.[86]

FDR had always enjoyed the thrill of subterfuge, which appealed to his adventurous nature. Some have speculated that the knowledge of Lucy's impending visit to the White House caused Missy LeHand to have the first stroke that disabled her, on June 4, 1941, so possessive had she become as FDR's 'office wife' and gatekeeper. If so, FDR showed no guilt. Not only did he see Lucy for an hour and a half on June 6, but kept seeing her thereafter, either at the White House, Hyde Park, her estate at Allamuchy, or at Warm Springs. At the White House, one biographer noted, Eleanor's departure and Lucy's arrival 'suggested the banging doors in a French bedroom farce'.[87]

Lucy – whose husband died in 1944 – had worried lest she be

burdening the president by such clandestine trysts. 'This kind of letter is best unwritten and unmailed, and poor darling, to give you one more thing to read or think about is practically criminal'[88] she acknowledged in one missive – yet she still mailed it, knowing how lonely he was in the 'white sepulcher' of the White House, and how their romance allowed him, however nostalgically, to fantasize about a 'small house' that would be 'a joy', where 'one could grow vegetables as well as flowers'. 'I know one should be proud, very proud of your greatness,' she mused, 'instead of wishing for the soft life, of joy – and the world shut out.'[89]

By initiating his daughter Anna in the subterfuge, FDR was able to see Lucy time and time again – even at Bernard Baruch's estate at Hobcaw, in South Carolina, in April 1944, before D-Day – and taking her to Shangri-La, a Maryland summer camp in the Catoctin Mountains, seventy-five miles from Washington (later called Camp David) in July. In November 1944, he had her to stay at Warm Springs again, in the Little White House, like husband and wife. On a drive to Dowdell's Knob nearby, he told her in confidence of 'the real problems facing the world now', and his plan to meet Stalin and Churchill in the hope of committing Russia to the war against Japan – matters he simply couldn't share with Eleanor who, instead of hearing him out, would have pressed her own views, as FDR's daughter said. 'Mother was not capable of giving him this – just listening' Anna reflected.[90]

Another house guest, Daisy Suckley, a neighbour from Hyde Park, noted in her diary how concerned Lucy was about the president's health. 'She has worried & does worry terribly, about him, & has felt for years that he has been terribly lonely ... We got to the point of literally weeping on each other's shoulders & we kissed each other, I think because we each feel thankful that the other understood & wants to help Franklin.'[91]

This was, sadly, no longer the case with Eleanor, who spent only a few days with FDR in his last two years. The affection he inspired in those around him, from world leaders to his black maid at Warm Springs, was remarkable. Born an American aristocrat, he had become a man of the people. Lizzie McDuffie 'told funny stories, laughed unrestrainedly, & gestured most amusingly & even poked him on the shoulder on one occasion to press home her point. She then resumed her position as maid', Daisy noted.[92]

As his health failed, FDR almost gave up the subterfuge, having Lucy travel with him on his special train back to Washington in December, and taking her with him to Hyde Park in January before his fourth inauguration. After Yalta, they were almost never apart. Recognizing how close to the end her father might be, Anna saw nothing morally wrong in the relationship; 'they were occasions', she later confided, 'which I welcomed for my father because they were light-hearted and gay, affording a few hours of much needed relaxation for a loved father and world leader in a time of crisis'.[93]

In Warm Springs, the president became so excited by Lucy's imminent arrival, on April 9, 1945, that he told his chauffeur to drive him eighty miles to Macon, Georgia, to intercept her as she came from her estate at Ridgely Hall in Aiken, South Carolina. Finally, at Manchester, they met up, and shooing away Ms Shoumatoff – who was to paint his portrait at Lucy's suggestion – to finish the journey on her own, FDR had Lucy sit beside him in the back of his automobile, enchanted. The following evening he insisted on driving Lucy himself in his hand-controlled car, with Fala, up to Dowdell's Knob to see the sun go down. Again, the next day, he drove Lucy, with Daisy Suckley and the dog in the back, for a two-hour drive. 'Lucy is so sweet with F—' Daisy noted in her diary that night. 'No wonder he loves having her around – Toward the end of the drive, it began to be chilly and she put her sweater over his knees.'[94]

It was the president's last drive. The next morning he worked on his government papers, then telephoned Washington to ensure he would get the first stamp commemorating the United Nations Conference he was to address on April 25, and began sitting for Ms Shoumatoff at midday. Lucy, next to him, was talking to Daisy about the barbecue planned for the evening when he collapsed.[95] He'd been haggard, but happy, a last idyll that came to an end several hours later at 3.35 p.m., when the enlightened pharaoh of the twentieth century was pronounced dead. By then Lucy, ever discreet, had slipped away into an obscurity that would last for decades thereafter.

# CHAPTER TWO

# HARRY S. TRUMAN

Later deified

Democrat
33rd President
(April 12, 1945–January 20, 1953)

## Part One: The Road to the White House

Harry S. Truman was born on May 8, 1884, in Lamar, Missouri, the eldest son of a Baptist farmer and cattle futures trader. (The S in his name was left unpunctuated on Truman's birth certificate. It is said to have referred to his grandfather, Sol Young, a Confederate sympathizer in the Civil War.)

Truman suffered from deformed eyeballs. Without thick glasses he was, he admitted later, 'blind as a mole'.[1] Adored by his mother, he was only sent to school at age eight; at age ten his right side was paralyzed by diphtheria, and for a time he was unable to walk. His mother, who came from a well-off landowning family, was convinced he was a prodigy he read so much (history, biography and poetry). She insisted the family move from Lamar to Independence, where there were better schools. She paid for piano lessons through high school, encouraging Truman to believe he could make a career in music. Once his father lost everything in 1902 and went effectively bankrupt, there was insufficient money, and Truman never attended college. (He later took night-school courses in law, but never graduated.) 'My choice early in life was either to be a piano player in a whorehouse, or a politician' he later joked – adding there was little difference.

In actuality Truman's early reading of the Roman historians, from Julius Caesar to Plutarch and Tacitus, caused him to set his sights on a career in the military. His application to West Point in 1902 was rejected, however, owing to his optical 'deformity'.

To help support his family, Truman studied basic bookkeeping and worked for the local railroad, where he learned 'all the cuss words in the English language, not by ear, but by note'.[2] Switching to clerking in a bank, he finally joined his father and brother in 1906, working on his uncle's farm close to Grandview, Jackson County, without plumbing or electricity. His brother left to start a family of his own; Truman stayed on for a decade with his taciturn, implacable father, who would shout from the bottom of the stairs at 5 a.m. every day to rouse him to the fields.

For those early adult years Truman ploughed, fed pigs and cattle, cut wheat, shucked corn and kept the farm's books. 'We always owed the bank something – sometimes more, sometimes less – but we always owed the bank.'[3]

Meanwhile, to fulfil his childhood dream, and despite his eyesight, Truman applied to join the Missouri National Guard in 1905 as a junior lieutenant in the field artillery. His grandmother, whose property had been razed by Union troops for siding with the Confederacy in Kentucky, was appalled. Eyeing him standing proudly in his blue dress uniform, she thundered: 'Harry, this is the first time since 1863 that a blue uniform has been in this house. Don't bring it here again!'[4] (He didn't.)

Farming taught Truman how to get along with a demanding father, in an occupation to which he was entirely unsuited. He was at least spared the temptations of the big city in his twenties, learned the value of relentlessly hard work, and appreciated the joviality, tensions and loyalty of a close family. Most of all, he trained himself to get along with rural people of lesser intelligence and ambition, but no less wisdom. His vision of democracy – American democracy – was thus forged on farmland, a very different outlook from that of his patrician predecessor as president, FDR. Truman regretted that the US had not stopped immigration to America in the 1880s; then 'we'd have been an agricultural country forever', he said. 'When it is made up of factories and large cities it soon becomes depressed and makes classes among people.'[5] Yet it would be these growing American cities, ironically, that would later ensure his election when all opinion polls showed him going down to defeat.

A four-year lawsuit over his grandmother's will (which brought the still almost bankrupt Trumans 518 acres of her high-value land, but also heartbreaking family strife) altered Truman's nostalgia – especially the sight of a white-haired aunt 'tearing up truth just for a few dollars'. The suit only ended after the death of the aunt, when a settlement, or family peace treaty, was concluded. This, and a lawsuit over a few hundred barren acres in another state that went before the Supreme Court, caused Truman to temper his idealization of the land. 'No man that's any good would be a farmhand', he reflected in 1914, and by 1917, although well past draft age, he was ready to re-enlist in the National Guard and, if possible, serve overseas.[6]

Cheating on the eye test Truman joined the 2nd Missouri Field Artillery Regiment, where troopers elected their officers. The unit was soon federalized as the 129th. During training he befriended a fellow volunteer, James Pendergast, whose uncle, Tom Pendergast, was the political 'boss' of Kansas City. Truman also ran a successful unit canteen to make extra money with the help of a Jewish subordinate, Eddie Jacobson, who would have a profound influence on Truman's future.

Truman was soon promoted to artillery captain. His battery, shipped to Europe, took part in a series of actions in support of infantry in north-east France against German forces in the autumn of 1918. Truman's steadfastness under fire earned him a high reputation and official commendation that would help him greatly when later seeking political office. His moral fury over French extortionism – 'These people love francs better than their country and they are extracting just as many of them from us as they possibly can' – also gave him an increasing scepticism about human greed.[7]

Following the November 1918 Armistice Truman was recommended for a major's appointment in the regular US Army, which would have enabled him to serve with all the significant generals whom he would later direct as commander-in-chief of the US armed services, from Eisenhower to MacArthur, Bradley, Patton, Marshall and Ridgway. Instead, he turned down the opportunity and set up a haberdashery with Eddie Jacobson in Kansas City, Missouri.

'Truman & Jacobson' failed. The experience taught Truman many lessons, however, from tact with difficult customers to stoicism in the face of insolvency. Saddled with debts that would take a decade to pay off (he declined to declare bankruptcy), Truman was forced to face up to reality: he was too small a figure to be playing alone in the big leagues. If he was ever to win elected office – as, increasingly, the ex-artillery captain wished to do – he would need not only support from fellow veterans (he became a reserve officer, rising to colonel commanding the 381st Field Artillery Regiment in 1932), but financial and political 'sponsors'.

It was young Jim Pendergast's father, Mike Pendergast, who first suggested Truman run for eastern county judge, Jackson County, Missouri, in 1922. ('Judge' was the name given for what was, effectively, a county governor, responsible for appointing most public officials and overseeing the financial running of the community through its tax revenues.) With the 'help' of Tom Pendergast, the 'boss' of Kansas City, Truman – though an execrable speaker – duly 'won' the Democratic Party nomination and the post.

'Machine' politics and the 'boss' system were a political equivalent of the mafia in major US cities. Providing a guarantee of victory for their candidates through intimidation, multiple voting and ballot theft, the system was a Faustian bargain for someone with higher than local aspirations. By accepting such help, Truman the would-be politician was tainted from the start, though there was no other way in which, lacking money, charisma or rhetorical ability, the thick-bespectacled former haberdasher from Independence could make his way up the electoral ladder. Without Pendergast's support Truman lost re-election for eastern country judge in 1924, took up Masonry in a big way, became membership secretary of the Auto Club of Kansas City in 1925, lost yet more money when taking over a Citizens Community Bank in 1926 (it failed), and was fortunate to be sponsored again by Tom Pendergast (who had become the 'boss of bosses' in Kansas City politics) for presiding judge for the entire region in the autumn of 1926.

Truman seems to have been personally incorruptible, pocketing none of the rake-offs that Pendergast notoriously took from major public contracts. 'Am I a fool or an ethical giant?' he asked himself in his diary, hurt by press excoriation of his fealty to a corrupt political puppeteer.[8] Concerned lest newspaper readers send his family poisoned gifts he forbade them to eat anything delivered to the door. Without Pendergast, however, he was, in terms of election, a Missouri nobody; indeed, he only visited the nation's capital for the first time at age forty-four. He had joined a slew of associations in a bid to gain wider recognition, but without financial and organizational backing in the nuts and bolts of running an election campaign he remained, in the end, beholden to Pendergast.

Missouri had straddled both sides in the American Civil War, but had formally sided with the Union. Its population of Scots, Irish, Germans, Jews and blacks was tough, socially conservative, segregated, and in the 1920s equally divided between rural and urban Americans. The Ku Klux Klan was active, as were gangsters and loan sharks in Kansas City and St Louis. Truman stood out among political leaders in the state because, as Judge Truman, he held greedy contractors to a strict budget, while his literary and cultural interests caused him to want his community to boast better services, from roads and schools to libraries and concert halls. When the Great Depression hit Missouri, therefore, he did not hesitate in promoting a massive public works program: major public investments that were brought in on time, under budget, with full employment. He was twice re-elected presiding judge, despite worsening gangsterism and political corruption in Kansas City itself.

In 1934 Truman's Faustian bargain reached a crossroads. He had been made director of the Federal Re-employment Service in Missouri, answering to Harry Hopkins in Washington DC, and had found work for some 100,000 Missourians. He had thought about running either for tax collector, with Pendergast's backing – which would have given him a safe salary of $10,000 per annum – or for Congress. He was fifty years old, unknown outside his home state and unable to make up his mind. Pendergast made it up for him. He was told to run for the US Senate.

Despite Mussolini's dictatorship in Italy, the clampdown by Stalin in the Soviet Union, and the rise of Hitler in Germany, as well as worsening problems in Asia, there was zero interest among new or old immigrant Missourians in foreign affairs. Interest in how their next senator would work in tandem with the Roosevelt administration in handling jobs, welfare and mortgage relief was, however, high, and though some saw Truman as a mere pawn in Tom Pendergast's corrupt political machine, others were impressed by the honesty, candour, simplicity, courage and dependability of the candidate. 'You folks won't get a chance very often to vote for a farmer for United States senator' one Democrat introduced Truman at a picnic gathering. 'He's our kind of people. Why, his hands fit cultivator handles just like owls' claws fit a limb.'[9]

Not even a car crash which broke two of his ribs stopped Truman from barnstorming for the Democratic nomination under the Rooseveltian banner of 'A New Deal for Missouri'. To a large extent, however, this remained show. In truth, Truman relied heavily on Pendergast, who controlled the Kansas City vote, in a fight against the boss of St Louis, who controlled the Democratic primary vote there. Election records reflected the corruption: Kansas City recorded a staggering 137,529 votes for Truman, but only 1,525 for his opponent, John Cochran; in St Louis, by contrast, Cochran polled 121,048 votes, against Truman's meagre 4,614. At any event, Truman won the Democratic senatorial nomination in November 1934 almost entirely thanks to Pendergast.

Once installed in Washington DC, Senator Truman found himself the poorest member of the legislature. His wife and family stayed in Independence, where there was insufficient money to pay off the loans on the family farm, which was repossessed by the banks. In itself this was the ultimate demonstration that Truman himself was incorruptible, however much he relied on Pendergast for electoral support in the jungle of urban interwar politics. 'My connection with Pendergast was, of course, purely political' the senator explained to a journalist when Pendergast was eventually indicted and imprisoned for election fraud, at the prompting of Roosevelt's Justice Department. 'He has been a friend to me when I needed it. I am not one to desert a ship when it starts to go down.'[10] But down it went.

In the Senate Truman focused on interstate commerce and transportation – rail and air – as the most practical means to combat the Depression and revive America's economic prosperity. With Pendergast imprisoned, his mother's farm foreclosed and no capital, Truman faced an uphill re-election battle for the Senate in 1940, when his six-year term ended. 'He is a dead cock in the pit' as the St Louis *Post-Dispatch* commented.[11] Unsure whether or not to resign, Truman filed for re-nomination and had the fight of his life with a rival, popular Democratic governor, Lloyd Stark. Tall, handsome and a charismatic speaker, Governor Stark looked unbeatable: a distinguished World War I veteran who had inherited the world's largest apple-growing farm, had supported all Roosevelt's New Deal programmes, and had done his best to clean up election fraud in Missouri – especially Pendergast's. Stark was even bruited as a possible vice president if Roosevelt ran a third time.

Roosevelt ran, but didn't choose Stark. Down 11,000 votes, Truman went to bed on primary polling day, August 6, 1940, thinking he'd lost; 'I guess this is one time I'm beaten' he sighed, but was woken early the next morning to hear he was re-elected, thanks to the state's two great urban populations: Kansas City, where Truman's loyalty to the convicted Pendergast was admired, and St Louis, where the machine boss now also plumped for him.[12] It was a victory he then repeated against his Republican opponent in the November 1940 contest.

Roosevelt had been re-elected on the promise that he would keep America's sons out of foreign wars. There was no guarantee, though, that foreign wars would keep out America's sons. Appointed to the Senate Military Affairs Committee, Truman asked to head a special subcommittee to investigate the national defence programme, known thereafter as the Truman Committee.

Truman's job thus became central to America's reluctant preparation for its new 'manifest destiny'. By getting to know and assess every major (and many a minor) military installation and supplier in the United States, and as the boss finally of his own organization (albeit tiny in staff and funding), the senator grew twelve inches – until the Japanese attack on Pearl Harbor on December 7, 1941. Assuming his investigatory subcommittee would be unnecessary in actual war – indeed might embarrass the president (and the country's enemies) by exposing gaps and failures in the country's war machinery – Truman volunteered for the military again. He was turned down in person by General Marshall with the immortal words: 'We don't need old stiffs like you – this will be a young man's war.'[13]

Returning to his Senate subcommittee work, Truman realized that, as the president reassured him, it would probably be more important than ever. 'The chairman is a fine fellow, presiding like some trim, efficient, keen-minded businessman,' a journalist described, 'which is just what he looks like, with his neat appearance, heavy-lensed glasses and quick, good-natured smile.'[14] Truman boasted he saved the country billions of dollars, ensured the manufacture of vital synthetic rubber, facilitated the employment of an army of factory women, and stopped Standard Oil from choking 'the country to death' – for his suspicion of the greed of American big business corporations, as well as union labour racketeers, was sincere, if tinged with envy.[15] 'I'm glad I can sleep well' he solaced himself, despite his relative impecuniousness – still unable to buy back the family farm, and without real hope of advancement.[16]

Then, on Thursday July 20, 1944, Roosevelt finally made up his mind whom he wanted as his new vice-presidential nominee, having dropped Henry Wallace. A colleague from St Louis took the call from the president at the Blackstone Hotel.

'Bob, have you got that fellow lined up?' the president demanded.

'No, he is the contrariest Missouri mule I've ever dealt with.'[17]

'Well, tell the senator that if he wants to break up the Democratic party by staying out', Roosevelt shouted, it 'is his responsibility.'

The colleague looked at Truman.

'Jesus Christ!' Truman exploded, after saying yes (despite his wife's objections; she feared his assassination if he succeeded to the presidency). 'But why the hell didn't he tell me [he wanted me] in the first place?'[18]

Truman criss-crossed America on behalf of the Roosevelt-Truman ticket in the 1944 autumn election campaign, aware that, though the president's mind still seemed alert, 'physically he's just going to pieces'.[19] The result, nevertheless, on November 8, 1944, was FDR's triumphant re-election to a fourth term. Thereafter, Truman did not travel to Yalta, saw the president only twice following the inauguration, and was totally unprepared for the moment when, out of the blue on April 12, 1945, came the shattering news from Warm Springs, Georgia, that President Roosevelt was dead.

## Part Two: The Presidency

Even in the Soviet Union black-bordered flags flew on government buildings, while in Washington DC the Stars and Stripes above the White House were lowered to half-mast for the first time since the death of President Harding in office in 1923. In the Cabinet Room at the White House, President Truman was sworn in by Chief Justice Harlan Fiske at 6 p.m.

The cabinet was then summoned. 'He looked to me like a very little man as he sat waiting in a huge leather chair' FDR's press secretary later recalled.[20] It seemed an impossible seat to fill, in a nation inheriting the mantle of empire – but a nation which, since throwing off the yoke of England's monarchical empire in 1777, professed an aversion to thinking of itself in imperial terms. After all, in 1919 the Senate had forced the country to reject its own president's founding role in setting up and joining the League of Nations. Twenty-five years later, with a new president who had only once been to Europe and lacked even a college degree, how would the nation rise to the looming challenges? Would there be a retreat into isolationism, as in the 1920s – after ensuring German industry was first razed, as Treasury Secretary Morgenthau recommended, so that there could never be a Fourth Reich (or commercial competitor)?

Truman claimed his predecessor's death struck him like a 'bolt of lightning'.[21] If so, it seemed to others not to paralyze so much as galvanize him. Lunching with the main congressional leaders, the former senator assured them that Congress would be an equal partner in fashioning post-war America and America's place in the post-war world. Congressmen and senators were pleased, unaware how quickly the two competing secular ideologies of the 1920s and 1930s, Communism and capitalism, would rise up in revived mutual confrontation, once the war against Hitler and Hirohito was won.

World events moved swiftly after FDR's sad demise. Only two weeks later, Italian dictator Benito Mussolini and his mistress were executed by his fellow countrymen; then, on April 30, news came that Adolf Hitler had shot himself and his mistress, lest execution be his fate too. By May 7, Hitler's successor, Grand Admiral Dönitz, agreed unconditional German surrender to the Allied supreme commander, General Dwight D. Eisenhower.

The American divisions (sixty in Europe by May 1945), backed by a vast air force of bomber and fighter aircraft, had ended the German threat to western civilization. On May 8, 1945 the war in Europe ended, though the war against Japan had still to be won. Roosevelt's widow, Eleanor, finally moved out of the White House (requiring two months and twenty army trucks), so that the Trumans (requiring one) could move in.

The global balance of power was now set to shift completely. The Dutch and French empires were bankrupt after their defeat in 1940 and appeared doomed, even as Allied troops reasserted control of German- and Japanese-occupied territories across the world. The British Empire, which had prevailed in its long struggle against Hitler's

Third Reich, was – at least in terms of its mother country – effectively penniless. Whatever the fantasies of its redoubtable prime minister, Winston Churchill, the United Kingdom seemed ill-placed to police a global network of colonies, at a time when its indigenous population was exhausted by six years of war. This left only China, the Soviet Union and the United States of America to take up the batons of supranational rule. Since China no longer had an emperor and was embroiled in a civil war between Communists, led by Mao Zedong, and Nationalists, led by Chiang Kai-shek, it would be several years before its destiny would become manifest. Thus the rest of the world looked to Stalin and to America's new generalissimo, President Truman, to see not only how the world war would end, but how the post-war world would be shaped. They did not have long to wait.

Thanks to his four years inspecting American war production (and from 1943 helping prepare for reconversion to a post-war economy) Truman was initially, if naively, confident in his ability to take over the reins of the Roosevelt administration. For the most part, he re-employed Roosevelt's cabinet and senior appointees. 'It won't be long until I can sit back and study the picture and tell 'em what is to be done in each department' he wrote in a letter to his wife. 'When things come to that stage there'll be no more to running this job than there was to running Jackson County and not any more worry.'[22]

These were famous last words, reflecting the innocence of a rising empire. The notion that the United States, let alone large parts of the economically dependent world, could be run by a board of American directors and a happy-go-lucky chairman was quickly challenged when Prime Minister Churchill warned on May 12, 1945, that, with regard to Soviet behaviour and intentions in central and eastern Europe, 'an iron curtain' had been 'drawn down'.[23]

Ignoring Churchill, Truman instructed Harry Hopkins, on a mission to Moscow in May 1945, not only to try and get a fig leaf to cover Soviet tyranny in Soviet-occupied Poland but also to tell Stalin – who outraged the diplomatic community by arresting the members of Poland's government-in-exile when they flew to Moscow – that Romania, Bulgaria, Czechoslovakia, Austria, Yugoslavia and the Baltic states were not important to US 'interests'. 'The smart boys in the State Department, as usual, are against the best interests of the US' he noted naively in his diary, 'if they can circumvent a straightforward hard hitting trader for the home front.' That trader, of course, was Truman himself. 'I shall expect our interests to come first' he emphasized as he made his way to the Big Three summit in Potsdam, close to Sanssouci, the mini Versailles on the outskirts of Berlin established by Frederick the Great of Prussia. 'I'm not working for any interest but the Republic of the United States. I [am] giving nothing away except to save starving people and even then I hope we can only help them to help themselves.'[24]

Potsdam, however, would change Truman's life, and the course of American history, as the president awoke not only to global reality, but to America's destiny.

Truman was driven from his villa – aptly called Number 2 Kaiserstrasse, or Caesar Street – on July 16, 1945, in an open car, along an avenue lined with US soldiers and tanks, into the ruined capital of the Third Reich. Coming from Washington, he found the utter devastation surreal. The ruined Reich Chancellery, in the basement of which Hitler had recently committed suicide, Truman dubbed 'Hitler's Folly'. As he noted in his diary, Hitler 'overreached himself by trying to take in too much territory. He had no morals and the people backed him up. Never did I see a more sorrowful sight.'[25]

The bookworm child was taken back to his early reading. As he recorded that night: 'I thought of Carthage, Baalbeck, Jerusalem, Rome, Atlantis, Peking, Babylon, Nineveh; Scipio, Rameses II, Titus, Herman, Sherman, Jenghis Khan, Alexander, Darius the Great.'[26] Though he shrank from adding his name or Washington DC to that imperial pantheon, and reflected humbly how humans were but 'termites on a planet', he was acutely aware from latest communications with the White House that the United States was about to become more powerful than any nation in history, having successfully developed an atomic bomb. The question now arose whether to use it to destroy the empire of Japan. And how to handle America's partner on the world-historical stage, the USSR.

Truman's first meeting with Churchill did not impress him. Churchill's golden-tongued unctuousness contrasted poorly with the no-nonsense demeanour of Joseph Stalin, who raised a host of questions about the post-imperial world – from getting rid of the fascist dictator Franco in Spain to the future of territories once mandated by the League of Nations in the Middle East, even in Africa.

Compared to Churchill, Stalin was of a different, more bracing (and less alcoholic) calibre. Stalin's list was 'dynamite – but I have some dynamite too which I'm not exploding now' Truman noted cryptically in his diary.[27] The two emperors of the world now measured each other over the fate of Poland, in an effort to see how powerful the other truly was.

For Truman the realist, Poland's doom was a fait accompli, already occupied by hundreds of thousands of Soviet troops. Meanwhile Truman needed the USSR to participate actively in the newly created United Nations, whose founding he had just attended, if it was ever to succeed as an international body. He also needed Russia to follow through and enter, as promised, the fight against Japan, if conventional war was to be pursued to the bitter end. Truman therefore accepted the saddest, yet unavoidable compromise: recognizing a Polish puppet government that did not look like espousing democracy – and wouldn't be permitted to for the next fifty years. This was deplorable, but inexorable. As Churchill feared, Communists throughout Europe would feel emboldened by the Polish example to seize power in their own countries, and win protection from the USSR and fellow Communist regimes, if they could – indeed it was already happening in Bulgaria, Albania and Greece. There, following the exit of Nazi occupiers, Communist insurgents, supported by arms furnished by the Yugoslav Communist dictator Tito, were causing British liberation forces grave concern. If most of the nations of Europe merely exchanged the swastika for the hammer and sickle, Truman began to wonder, what purpose would the removal of Adolf Hitler have served, in terms of American interests?

Despite his reservations about the 'striped pants' diplomats of the US State Department, therefore, Truman was forced at Potsdam to recognize that the looming confrontation between the USSR and the USA was less about Marxist ideologies and democratic ideals – Communism and capitalism – than between two systems of *power*: dictatorship and electoral-based democracy.

Having learned how to handle 'Boss' Pendergast in Missouri, Truman remained amazingly, if innocently, confident he could, within limits, handle both Stalin and Soviet opportunism. Don't contest what you cannot control; be firm as a rock over those things you can; give financial help to rebuild industry and commerce among your allies;

trust in God. 'I can deal with Stalin. He is honest – but smart as hell' Truman recorded in his diary after their first meeting. The next day he invited him to visit the US.

Like FDR, Truman laboured under no illusions about the Russian quest for 'security'. Soviet troops occupied all of central Europe to the Elbe and the Danube. What Truman could and did do was hold Stalin to the Yalta agreement on the four occupation zones of Germany. 'If Russia chooses to allow Poland to occupy a part of her [German occupation] zone I am agreeable but title to territory cannot and will not be settled here' Truman made clear as chairman of the super-power summit, and began to listen more attentively to America's 'striped pants' brigade, especially those who were stationed in Communist countries, or where Communists were seeking power.[28] The 'Russian variety' of Communism 'isn't Communism at all but just police government pure and simple' the president noted. 'A few top hands just take clubs, pistols and concentration camps and rule the people on lower levels. The Communist Party in Moscow is no different in its methods and actions toward the common man than were the czar and the Russian Nobleman (so-called: they were anything but noble). Nazis and Fascists were worse.'[29]

With the news on July 26 that Churchill had been defeated in the British general election, and Stalin's 'indisposition' on July 30, however, Truman began to reflect on the prospects for post-war peace if Stalin were to die. 'If some demagogue on horseback gained control of the efficient Russian military machine he could play havoc with European peace for a while. I also wonder if there is a man with the necessary strength and following to step into Stalin's place and maintain peace and solidarity at home . . . Our only hope for good from the European War is restored prosperity to Europe and future trade with them. It is', he reflected, 'a sick situation.'[30]

Years later, Truman considered he had been 'an innocent idealist' at Potsdam. Stalin showed no interest in Truman's proposals to inter-nationalize the main arterial waterways of Europe or to restore European prosperity, and broke most of the Potsdam agreements as soon as he returned to the Soviet Union.[31] 'And I like the little son of a bitch' Truman afterwards lamented. 'He was a good six inches shorter than I am and even Churchill was only three inches taller than Joe! Yet I was the little man in stature and intellect! So the Press said.'[32]

Was the press right? Had Truman been too compliant? Russian-occupied eastern Europe was certainly confirmed as lost to democracy at Potsdam; but without the US declaring war on the Soviet Union (which Congress would not have supported), it is difficult to see how Truman could have saved the defenceless, 'Soviet-liberated' nations. He proved correct in seeing Stalin as the linchpin of Russian Communism – a barbaric dictator, but one who was at least forthright and consistent, especially in comparison with his successor, Nikita Khrushchev.

However naive Truman was, then, it was he who stepped up to the plate at Potsdam, and on behalf of the western world. It was in Potsdam that he recognized the bankruptcy and impotence of the once awe-inspiring British Empire as it attempted to hang on to 'control [of] the Eastern Mediterranean', and to 'keep India, oil in Persia, the Suez Canal and whatever else was floating loose' – imperial interests that would all too soon be shorn away.[33] This left the United States a simple choice: either return to its pre-war isolationism, keeping its distance, or take up the fallen baton and lead the free world by imposing a new Pax Americana on the territories that Stalin's troops had not already overrun.

On July 24 in Potsdam, Truman had given his approval for the new weapon to be used on Japan as soon as possible, after due warning – 'asking the Japs to surrender and save lives'. 'I'm sure they will not do that,' he noted laconically in his diary, 'but we will have given them the chance.'[34] Since Roosevelt's death, 50,000 American servicemen had died in the Pacific and another quarter of a million would be killed, he was told by the chief of staff of the army, General Marshall, if Japan refused to surrender and the US had to invade with conventional forces.[35] In his diary the president had written that the weapon was 'to be used against Japan between now and August 10th. I have told the Sec of War, Mr Stimson, to use it so that military objectives and soldiers and sailors are the target and not women and children. Even if the Japs are savages, ruthless, merciless and fanatic, we as the leader of the world for the common welfare cannot drop this terrible bomb on the old capital or the new. He & I are in accord . . . It is certainly a good thing for the world that Hitler's crowd or Stalin's did not discover the bomb.'[36]

Reviewing the situation with the US ambassador to Moscow, Averell

Harriman, and the other 'Wise Men' of the State Department on his return from Potsdam, Truman expressed satisfaction that, although it took two atomic bombs, dropped on Hiroshima on August 6 and Nagasaki on August 9, to achieve, the Japanese government finally surrendered unconditionally to the Allies on August 10, saving countless American (and Japanese) lives and ending World War II without the need for Russian intervention. But Potsdam, he also made clear to Harriman, had clarified his own new view: that the United States must embrace a global post-war leadership role and, in effect, become a counter-empire to the Communist USSR.

Thus, before either the famous Kennan policy of containment or the Marshall Plan were mooted, Truman not only made a momentous decision regarding the use of the world's first atomic weapon, but also grasped at Potsdam in essence how and why he would direct American quasi-imperial power in the post-war world. It was a guns-and-butter vision that lacked Roosevelt's noble rhetoric, and it would expose him to attacks from both right and left in America. It would also lead the United States, under the leadership of subsequent imperial presidents, into countless strategic difficulties and questionable actions, including major wars. It is difficult to imagine, however, that Roosevelt would not have done the same had he lived.

In due course Truman would have to contend with schisms in his own Democratic Party, caused in part by liberals, and also by union greed. He would suffer nefarious attacks from rabid anti-Communist Republicans such as the young Richard Nixon (who would call him a traitor – an insult Truman never forgave). Nevertheless Truman's epiphany at Potsdam gave rise to the essential architecture of American empire, for good and bad, for the next half-century and more.

Leftist historians would argue that a more Russia-friendly policy by the United States might have encouraged a less repressive, less paranoid Soviet system over time. It is more likely, however, that the opposite would have been the case. The USSR's boasts of higher agricultural, industrial and commercial output in the ensuing decades were almost all fabrications which, behind its 'iron curtain', could only escape exposure by denying access to independent reporters, and by absolute control of the media. Only by ruling its constituent and satellite peoples with 'clubs, pistols and concentration camps' (exemplified in Soviet military clampdowns in Hungary and later Czechoslovakia) and cheap bread, was the Soviet Union able to stave off the collapse of an inherently unworkable system for so many decades. In short, the USSR *had* to continue to tyrannize its Communist empire merely in order to survive, forcing the United States to find a counterweight if its democratic vision was to prevail in the West.

Given the weak state of Europe's liberated western countries, Truman's historic role, he recognized, was to reverse the conduct of post-World War I America in foreign affairs. This he decided to do by maintaining a major American military presence in Europe (later establishing, equipping and leading the forces of NATO), while pumping money into the rebuilding of European nations with whom the United States could trade – and profit. It was enlightened capitalistic imperialism such as had characterized relations between the United Kingdom and its dominions; but like the British Empire (which had traded slaves for cotton, opium for tea, and upheld many a corrupt ruler in order to maintain its overall hegemony) its record would be less than honourable in the more contested reaches of its influence.

As Britain divested itself of its imperial obligations under its new prime minister, Clement Attlee, the US was faced with grave decisions. If Britain had 'stumbled into empire' as one historian put it, it was now stumbling out of it, leaving its former American colony, under President Truman, to pick up the pieces – and the tab.[37] On February 21, 1947, Attlee announced the end of British rule in India – the 'jewel' in the British crown that had made Queen Victoria an empress – no later than June the following year. The next day Attlee told Truman's new Secretary of State, General Marshall, that Britain was effectively bankrupt, and could no longer afford the cost and troops (which would be withdrawn before April 1) to guarantee either security in Greece – where Communist insurgents were inciting civil war – or aid to Turkey, which was being subjected to Soviet pressure over the Dardanelles Straits.

Truman's advisers begged him to be less diffident in public and to galvanize post-war America as he had the nation when ending World War II: to be an American warrior, with a vision for the country. Addressing Congress on Wednesday March 12, 1947, Truman finally did so. 'It had to be clear and free of hesitation or double talk' Truman later recalled instructing his speech writers, and wisely invited the leading lawmakers of Congress to the White House to hear him explain his policy two days before he gave the speech, and to ask questions.[38]

Whether or not the president was exaggerating the threat posed by the USSR or was wise to exhort America to challenge Communism 'on every front', his speech made history. As he recorded in his memoirs, 'I could never quite forget the strong hold which isolationism had gained over our country after World War I. Throughout my years in the Senate I listened each year as one of the senators would read Washington's farewell address. It served little purpose to point out to the isolationists that Washington had advised a method suitable under conditions of *his* day to achieve the great end of preserving the nation . . . For the isolationists this address was like a biblical text.'[39] His own speech to Congress became, by contrast, as he put it, 'the turning point in America's foreign policy, which now declared that wherever aggression, direct or indirect, threatened the peace, the security of the United States was involved' – the Truman Doctrine, as it became known.[40] American Empire, under the rubric of Pax Americana, was thus born, and the bill sanctioning aid to Greece and Turkey was passed by 287 to 107 on May 9, 1947 by the new Republican-dominated House of Representatives.

Backing Truman's bill with finance and implied military assistance, Congress thus ensured that Greece avoided a Communist coup and Turkey maintained its army and complete independence, in spite of Soviet threats and pressure. Both nations would join NATO in 1952, with their forces serving under an American supreme commander.

American isolationism, or non-imperialism, was dead; the burdens of empire were lifted from the shoulders of the floundering British, and assumed now by the United States. 'At the present moment in world history nearly every nation must choose between alternative ways of life' Truman explained. 'The choice is too often not a free one. One way of life is based upon the will of the majority, and is distinguished by free institutions, representative government, free elections, guarantees of individual liberty, freedom of speech and religion and freedom from political oppression. The second way of life is based upon the will of a minority forcibly imposed upon the majority. It relies upon terror and oppression, a controlled press and radio, fixed elections, and the suppression of personal freedoms.'[41]

In the years that followed, as in ancient Rome, many aspects of

democracy, both within the United States and in the actions of its official and unofficial personnel abroad, would be compromised. Yet
almost no historian has doubted Truman's integrity or honesty in
switching America's course from isolationism to world dominance.
'The world looks to us for leadership' Truman stated at the Jefferson
Day dinner on April 5, 1947. 'The force of events makes it necessary
that we assume that role.'[42]

The president was not exaggerating. Marshal Voroshilov, the Soviet
commander in Hungary, had ignored the results of the 1945 election in
which the Independent Smallholders' Party won 57 per cent of the votes.
Voroshilov insisted that the Hungarian Communist Party be invited to
participate in a coalition government, followed by executions, purges,
show trials, political imprisonment, exile to Siberia and savage repression of criticism or uprising. Czechoslovakia suffered a similar fate, as
did Romania and Albania; only Tito in Yugoslavia dared claim a certain
murderous independence (all Yugoslav monarchists were executed).

Truman's espousal of the Marshall Plan, which he persuaded
Congress to take up in 1947 following his 'Doctrine' speech, demonstrated the man from Independence at his best. Truman wanted to
aid *all* the shattered economies of post-war Europe, not simply Greece
and the strategically critical Turkey. On the urging of his Secretary of
State, George Marshall, he therefore offered massive American financial aid to free as well as to Communist countries, including the USSR.

Stalin, who had gratefully accepted grain and convoys of materiel
from the US during World War II, had already made a speech
denouncing capitalism and the US in February 1946. Now, a year later,
he forbade all Soviet satellite countries in eastern and central Europe,
as well as the USSR, to accept American aid. His Foreign Secretary
denounced the US plan as 'dollar imperialism'. Czechoslovakia and
Poland had agreed to send representatives to the Paris conference on
the Marshall Plan, but they were summoned to Moscow and warned
not to think of attending. Even the nominally independent Finland
declined Marshall Plan aid in order not to antagonize Stalin. Isolationist
Republicans in Congress also protested against the plan, as did Henry
Wallace, the former Democratic vice president. Once news came in
of the elected government of Czechoslovakia being overthrown by
Stalinists, however, Congress relented, and after six months' wran-
gling, passed a $12.4 billion aid package.

Economic historians later claimed that the Marshall Plan was a wolf in sheep's clothing that helped US trade and industry more than the western European beneficiaries (for example, half of all purchases had to be transported in US vessels). Nevertheless, the plan proved to be the touchstone of renewed European economic confidence among the democracies; indeed in many ways it became the building block for the creation of the European Economic Community (today the EU). Moreover Truman, selflessly, was quite content to have the plan named after the man he called 'the greatest living American' – the 'organizer of victory' in World War II, General George C. Marshall – rather than himself. (Marshall won the Nobel Peace Prize in 1953 for the plan). 'The assistance we gave, which averted stark tragedy and started progress towards recovery in many areas of the world, was in keeping both with the American character and with America's new historic responsibility' Truman later wrote.[43] (He also confided how he had to order Marshall to accept authorship of the plan: 'He blushed . . . He was just about the most modest man I ever did know, and he said, "I can't allow a thing like that to happen, Mr President."'[44]) It also helped guarantee America's security, for by 'rebuilding Europe and Asia, we would help to establish that healthy economic balance which is essential to the peace of the world' – even if Third World economists later questioned how healthy such a balance really was, for them.[45]

As the effects of the Marshall Plan began to be felt, the British, French and American governments authorized not only a commercial merging of the three western occupation sectors of Germany, but also a common West German currency (the Deutschmark, replacing the Reichsmark or Imperial Mark) to hasten economic recovery. This signalled the first major, inexorable step towards a West German constitution and republic, rather than the gutted, compliant and, above all, demilitarized or neutered state that the Soviets (and Allies, originally) had in mind.

Germany – at least that part occupied by American, British and French forces – would thus be rebuilt. Given that Germany had twice invaded Russia in the past thirty-three years, Stalin was furious, and decided to twist off the growing serpent's head. Relying on a legal loophole, since there was no formal, signed document permitting road and rail access from West German occupation zones to the capital,

Berlin, Stalin ordered a blockade. The Allied occupation zones of the city, merged as West Berlin, would starve.

If Stalin thought blockading West Berlin would force the western Allies to back down over German economic revival in the summer of 1948, he was misguided. It had the opposite effect. The western Allies could do nothing to rescue Poland, Hungary or Czechoslovakia (which was taken over completely by Quisling-style Communists the following year). American troops, however, were still stationed, fully armed, in Berlin. On June 28, 1948, Truman made the decision that 'we would stay, period', and reaffirmed it in the days afterwards. The Secretary of State, Jim Byrnes, 'wants to hedge', Truman snorted in his diary on July 19; 'he always does'. The president had made his decision and stuck with it. 'I don't pass the buck, nor do I alibi out of any decision I make.'[46]

Overriding his US Air Force chief of staff, General Vandenberg, Truman authorized a massive airlift until a diplomatic solution was found. The airlift was expected to take three weeks; brilliantly marshalled by General William Turner – who had organized from Burma the famous 'Hump' air supply of General Stilwell's forces fighting the Japanese in China in World War II – it lasted, in the event, almost a year. French engineers built the new Tegel airfield, while pilots from Britain, Australia, Canada and South Africa flew 50,000 of the staggering 277,000 unarmed American and RAF flights required, bringing more than 2.3 million tons of food and supplies into the beleaguered city, at the cost of sixty-five Allied lives. At one point, an Allied supply aircraft was landing every minute in West Berlin.

Stalin – who did not dare permit an unarmed Allied transport plane to be shot down, lest he thereby provoke a third world war – eventually brought the Russian fiasco to an end in the spring of 1948. He had played poker, even risking atomic war, and had lost.

The net result of the Berlin airlift was that, as Truman later wrote, 'we demonstrated to the people of Europe that with their cooperation we would act, and act resolutely, when their freedom was threatened. Politically it brought the peoples of western Europe more closely to us.'[47] This was not an exaggeration. Five of the west European nations formed a new military alliance, Western Union, in March 1948, which was the basis for the twelve-nation North Atlantic Treaty Organization, or NATO, set up in April 1949 under American supreme command. The Federal Republic of West Germany was then established on May 23, 1949.

Instead of offering the downtrodden nations of central Europe an example of socialism at its best, Russia had thus shown itself at its worst. Though they would maintain a vice-like military grip upon its 'liberated' nations for another four decades, Soviets became as hated as the Nazis had been – with, sadly, no single political, cultural, economic or social benefit to show their puppet states, in retrospect, for all the years of occupation, save for ballet, good (if heavily censored) public education, and vodka. By contrast, Harry Truman, the haberdasher from Kansas City, emerged from the Berlin airlift as one of the greatest of modern emperors in the eyes of most people in the free world: a simple man, but, for all that, a well-intentioned, brave internationalist, generous with American aid, firm in conflict, and cautious in taking advice from wilder-minded military advisers and subordinates.

Not all Truman's decisions as American emperor worked as successfully as the Marshall Plan, the Berlin airlift and NATO. Two, in particular, would adversely affect the peace and stability of the world, though each was pursued with the best of intentions: Palestine and Korea.

If Truman's performance over the Berlin airlift was exemplary, his performance over the crisis in Palestine in 1948 was the opposite. War upon war, hatred piled upon hatred was the result of what writer Robert Fisk would call 'an epic tragedy whose effects have spread around the world and continue to poison the lives not only of the participants but of our entire western political and military policies towards the Middle East and the Muslim lands'.[48]

What Truman faced in 1945 was, however, a veritable debacle not of his own or American making: namely an ongoing contractual obligation by Britain, signed and sealed under international law more than twenty years before in 1923, to 'reconstitute' a homeland for Jews in Palestine, 2,000 years after their expulsion by the Romans. That obligation, incurred in 1917 (the Balfour Declaration) in an effort to secure Jewish support for the Allies in World War I, directly contradicted promises made to the Arab tribes and kingdoms of the Middle East when securing their help in overthrowing the Ottoman Turkish Empire.

Protests – and ultimately revolts by Palestinian Arabs in the 1930s – had caused the British (who had been awarded a League of Nations Mandate to govern the country while establishing the Jewish homeland) to limit annual Jewish immigration lest it create, overnight, civil war in an Arab territory considered strategically vital to Britain's commercial and military empire. By the end of World War II, however, the situation was reaching crisis levels once again. Some five to six million European Jews, it was realized, had been murdered in the coldest blood by the Nazis. Their survivors were in refugee camps for 'displaced persons'. A safe homeland in Palestine seemed the obvious, least expensive and most compassionate solution for them. Truman, who had never visited the Middle East, felt so, at any rate; indeed he pressured the British government to grant 100,000 immigration visas into Palestine immediately, and offered to pay all transport and feeding costs. Such people would, the legendary president of the Jewish World Zionist Organization, Chaim Weizmann, assured Truman, 'make the desert bloom'.

Truman, brought up on the stories of the Bible, was entranced by Chaim Weizmann, and moved by the tears of his haberdashery partner Eddie Jacobson, who had persuaded Truman to meet the Zionist leader. He was also deluged by letters and telephone calls from Jewish voters across America who wanted the US to ease the plight of the refugees. Between 1945 and 1948 he attempted vainly to steer a neutral course. 'I am not a New Yorker' Truman told one pleader of the Jewish cause. 'All these people are pleading for a special cause. I am an American.'[49] He received delegations from neighbouring Arab states who warned of the consequences of 'giving away' Arab land to European Jews; he was warned by his own State Department officials not to destabilize Britain's unenviable task in keeping order in Palestine – where Jewish terrorists of the Haganah, Irgun and Stern Gang groups were taking British soldiers hostage, executing them, and exploding bombs in British buildings, such as the King David Hotel. ('They seem to have the same attitude toward the "underdog" [i.e. Arabs] when they are on top as they have [suffered] as "underdogs" themselves' Truman fumed.)[50] 'Jesus Christ couldn't please them when he was here on earth,' Truman said in exasperation over Zionist lobbyists, 'so how could anyone expect that I would have any luck?'[51] Their number reflected, however, a political reality in America. 'I am sorry, gentlemen,' he told a group of US diplomats working on the Middle East, 'but I have to answer to hundreds of thousands who are anxious for the success of Zionism; I do not have hundreds of thousands of Arabs among my constituents.'[52]

Truman's heart, in the end, was with the European refugees – and, by extension, the minority of Jews in Palestine (625,000 out of a population of almost two million) who would look after them. His advisers (the 'Wise Men' George Marshall, Dean Acheson, Averell Harriman, Charles Bohlen, James Forrestal) explained the long-term consequences of instability in the Middle East, especially in regard to the supply of oil to the West, and the possibility that Arab nations might turn towards the USSR, thus giving the Soviets new influence in the region, even a base in the Mediterranean. However, other political and electoral advisers warned the president that if he did not support the Jewish refugee exodus to Palestine, then Republicans would, with politically fatal consequences for Democrats, first in the 1946 midterm elections, then in the 1948 presidential election.

Truman was thus caught between two stools. Had he employed the same robust, far-sighted determination that he'd evinced in promulgating the Truman Doctrine, the Marshall Plan and the Berlin airlift, he could have accepted American responsibility to ensure a just, internationally negotiated settlement in Palestine. Instead, with the US refusing to grant extra immigrant visas to Jewish refugees and Holocaust survivors, he meddled from afar, to the point where the British Foreign Secretary, Ernest Bevin, washed his hands of Palestine's fate in September 1947, announcing that Britain, in one of the worst examples of spinelessness in its history, would withdraw all forces in May the following year, and surrender its Mandate back to the UN – which had *no* forces to keep order.

Fairly or unfairly, the UN eventually recommended partition of Palestine, by a two-thirds majority, in November 1947. When neither the Palestinian leaders nor the surrounding Arab neighbours accepted the terms of the UN partition (which awarded 53 per cent of the country, including the Negev Desert, the home of Bedouin Arabs for 4,000 years, to the Jews), Truman then recognized the new State of Israel only eleven minutes after the official departure of the last British troops, on May 14, 1948. This did nothing to assuage Arab despair or acceptance of the UN partition plan, or to advance UN calls for a temporary trusteeship while further negotiations took place, or to head off plans for military attack by neighbouring Arab countries.

Throughout the sad saga Truman, urged on by his former naval aide and subsequently White House adviser, Captain Clark Clifford, had acted against the warnings of his own State Department. As Under Secretary Acheson put it to Truman, by surrendering the Mandate in the face of mounting American calls for more Jewish immigration, the British prime minister had by 1947 'deftly exchanged the United States for Britain as the most disliked power in the Middle East'.[53] It is a title the US still holds.

Secretary of State General Marshall was driven to the point of unique insubordination (for a trained soldier), telling the commander-in-chief and chief executive of the United States to his face that if the US election was taking place that day, he would 'vote against the president'.[54] It was a savage indictment of Truman's conflicted conduct. Thinking to do right by his former partner Eddie Jacobson, Dr Weizmann and Clark Clifford (who warned Truman even before the British departure he would lose the 1948 election unless he recognized the establishment of Israel), and the many Jewish Americans agitating for a Jewish homeland rather than for issuing more visas into the US, Truman had ensured an accelerated homeland for Holocaust survivors and Jews – but at a terrible cost. 'There'd never been anything like it before,' Truman later recalled the pressure he was under, 'and there wasn't after. Not even when I fired MacArthur.'[55] In the second half of 1947 alone, 135,000 letters, telegrams and petitions bombarded him.

Though recognized by Truman's fiat in a matter of minutes, Israel would never survive, isolated in the heartland of Islam, without American financial and military aid, or achieve peace in the long run without negotiated treaties with the former Palestinian majority and its Arab neighbours, thus dragging the United States into a responsibility it had never sought, or wanted, and which continues to this day.

Truman's opponent in the 1948 presidential election turned out to be the silk-spoken Republican governor of New York State, Thomas Dewey, whose polls suggested such an inevitable victory that on an election platform in Idlewild, Truman was reported to have muttered, 'Tom, when you get to the White House, for God's sake do something about the plumbing.'[56] (Not only the plumbing but the entire interior of the White House was due to be gutted and rebuilt.)

Aware he was behind both in public opinion in media support, Truman became as energized as he'd been in 1940 when running against another governor, Lloyd Stark, telling an aide that he knew 'he was catching up and he was confident that on election day he would be out front'.[57] He even predicted the states he would win to the last handful. While Dewey stayed home, Truman grounded his presidential airplane, the *Independence*, and took out the 'Presidential Special' train with its bombproof Pullman car: the 'Ferdinand Magellan', equipped with microphone and loudspeakers. In cities like Detroit he spoke to crowds of industrial workers as many as 100,000 strong. He gave up reading speeches in his hopeless monotone and spoke extempore, as he had in his earlier days, lambasting Dewey, the Republican 'do nothing' Congress, and Republican 'red-baiters' and 'red-herring' chasers, earning the sobriquet 'Give 'em hell Harry'. With former vice president Henry Wallace running as an independent, as well as the southern Democrat Strom Thurmond standing in opposition to Truman's civil rights bill, which Dixiecrats had killed, Truman felt licensed to let rip – and did, coming across as the people's underdog president, while Dewey (like Stark before him) looked aristocratic and out of touch with ordinary Americans.

It was a masterly self-reinvention on Truman's part, combative and firm in standing up to Communism abroad, without risking accidental or thoughtless war. He secretly took a room in a hotel in Missouri on election night. NBC television called the race for Dewey, and Truman went to bed. He was woken at 4 a.m. by aides telling him that Illinois, the tell-tale state, had plumped for Truman. 'That's it!' Truman responded. 'Now let's go back to sleep, and we'll go down tomorrow and wait for the telegram from the other fellow.' It was hard for aides not to feel admiration for such a boss – especially when the president eyed the bottle of bourbon on his dresser and added: 'Well, boys, we'll have one and then we'll all go to sleep. I'll pour the first one.'[58]

Reversing Gallup poll predictions, Truman won the election on November 2, 1948, by 49.5 per cent to Dewey's 45.1 per cent, which translated into 303 electoral delegates to Dewey's 189, and segregationist Thurmond's thirty-nine. (Wallace won nil.)

Truman's unexpected second (though first elected) presidential term turned out to be far less fulfilling than his first three years in the White House – or 'Great White Jail' as he and his wife called it. With the

Truman Doctrine helping to stabilize a Cold War (a term invented in 1947) in Europe, but unable to stop an Arab–Israeli war in the Middle East from breaking out in 1948, Truman was unwilling to commit troops or ask Congress for vast monies to prop up the Nationalist regime of Chiang Kai-shek in China – where General Marshall had attempted fruitlessly to sponsor a coalition between Chiang and the Communist leader, Mao Zedong. As Marshall predicted, the Nationalists were too corrupt and badly led to be worth supporting militarily. By late 1949 Mao's forces seized Beijing, and together with two million refugees, the Nationalist forces finally retreated to Taiwan. Mao proclaimed a Communist People's Republic of China on the mainland, comprising 550 million people. Britain and other countries immediately recognized Mao's regime de facto, just as the US had instantly recognized Israel. Truman, in deference to Congress, declined to do so, however – putting US–Chinese relations into deep sleep for a generation – with right-wing American imperialists berating Truman for having 'lost' China to Mao.

The US had never had China to 'lose', but this did not stop Republicans turning from isolationists into warmongers. Though lucky to avoid a war in Asia that would have dwarfed in casualties even the magnitude of the war against Japan, Truman would not be so fortunate in Korea.

Under Japanese imperial rule since 1910, Korea had been divided at the end of World War II into two territories, North and South, under Russian and American UN trusteeship. On June 24, 1950, a North Korean Communist army under Kim Il-sung ('Our Great Leader') swept south across the 38th Parallel into the American zone. This put Truman in a fix he could not easily escape.

Attacking at dawn on a Sunday when most South Korean soldiers were off duty, Kim Il-sung's invasion, employing 135,000 troops, 242 Soviet-made tanks, and 180 Soviet-made aircraft, was a military master-stroke, but a political disaster. Stalin had stopped him the year before, and more recently had warned him not to invade the southern zone unless he was satisfied he could swiftly win. Everything thus depended on speed.

Receiving reports of the North Korean attack, President Truman flew straight back to Washington from Independence, Missouri, where he was staying the weekend. In order to save time he immediately placed the matter before the UN's Security Council, without waiting for a formal resolution in Congress. Since the USSR had temporarily walked out of the Council – reflecting Stalin's ambivalence over the issue – Truman was able to avoid a Soviet veto; he asked for, and got, a clear resolution (later three), condemning the attack and calling upon the North Koreans to withdraw or face economic and military sanctions.

Thus far, Truman had taken the lead international role, and elicited the applause of the entire free world. Events thereafter spiralled out of political control, thanks to General Douglas MacArthur.

MacArthur was now seventy years old. Tall, egocentric to the point of paranoia, he had remained the commander-in-chief of US forces in East Asia and Allied supreme commander, stationed in Japan. When South Korean troops abandoned the capital, Seoul, and continued to fall back south, MacArthur, appointed generalissimo of UN forces, dispatched American troops from Japan. These men could only slow the North Korean advance, not stop it. But by landing a fresh contingent behind the North Korean lines, on the midwest coast of the peninsula at Inchon on September 15, 1950, MacArthur then brilliantly routed Kim Il-sung's invading army, and was soon back in possession of the 38th Parallel, gung-ho to pursue the enemy northwards and unify Korea not as a Communist but as as a democratic nation, under American protection.

On September 28, 1950, the Cold War became red hot. The history of the American Empire may be said to have hinged on two men: MacArthur and Truman. Certainly, in the flush of a great victory at Inchon (an operation he had ordered despite a thousand voices counselling him against such a precarious landing), MacArthur was certain he had routed the enemy, and could destroy the remnants of the fleeing North Korean army in a matter of weeks, if not days – if permitted to cross the 38th Parallel. From there he would strike north to the frontiers of China and the Soviet Union. MacArthur thus cabled Washington, demanding consent.

The UN resolution, however, had not authorized a crossing of the 38th Parallel. The Pentagon was also concerned lest Soviet and Chinese forces become involved by an American-led advance, Chinese foreign minister Chou En-lai having warned of military action if the Parallel was crossed. All too easily the war might escalate into a third world war.

In a miscalculation that proved to be one of the colossal errors in military history, MacArthur dismissed such fears, assuring Washington that there were negligible Sino-Soviet forces in North Korea, and no signs of outside forces being readied to enter the country.

Had Truman overruled MacArthur and stopped all US–UN forces on the 38th Parallel, and then threatened atomic warfare if the North Koreans dared repeat their incursion, historians could not have faulted him – indeed he might have gone down as one of the greatest of American presidents, in the same league as Franklin Roosevelt. He might even have been asked to stand again for a second elected term in the White House as the quiet but firm guardian of international peace and security. Neither the Soviets nor the Chinese Communists had yet committed troops to the front line – and would have been unlikely to do so, merely to aid a second, doomed North Korean attack on the forces of the UN. Historians, however, only write history – they do not make it.

Later, Truman cursed himself for not having dismissed MacArthur. 'I've given it a lot of thought, and I have finally concluded', he told an interviewer, 'that there were times when he [MacArthur] . . . well, I'm afraid, when he wasn't right in the head . . . He just wouldn't let anybody near him who wouldn't kiss his ass . . . I should have fired him.'[59] Firing such a legendary figure – who had masterminded World War II in the Pacific and taken the Japanese surrender – was, however, something no one in the Truman administration was anxious to do, lest it stir further accusations of being 'soft' on Communism. At a meeting of the inner cabinet and Joint Chiefs of Staff, Truman 'told them I wanted to fire him, and I wanted to send over General Bradley to take his place. But they talked me out of it. They said it would cause too much uproar, so I didn't do it, and I was wrong.'[60]

Truman's advisers were right about Republican uproar; when Truman fired his Secretary of Defense, Louis Johnson, a few days later and appointed General Marshall in his stead, Marshall was denounced by Republicans at his confirmation hearing in the Senate as 'a frontman for traitors'.[61]

With MacArthur promising total victory (and thus the reunification of Korea by force as a democratic state), Truman and his advisers, including Marshall, gambled on MacArthur's battlefield prowess.

As Kim Il-sung had hoped to present the UN with a fait accompli, so did MacArthur. General Marshall radioed MacArthur on September 29, 1950 to keep quiet about crossing the 38th Parallel, while he wrapped up his campaign.

Betting on a headstrong, seventy-year-old general worried President Truman, however. He ordered the CIA (an organization he had set up after World War II to take over the role of the fabled OSS) to check out MacArthur's assertion that no Chinese armies would, or could, intervene. The CIA confirmed MacArthur's view; nevertheless, Truman remained sceptical.

In the midst of patriotic jubilation over MacArthur's victory at Inchon, Truman dared not face accusations of halting his country's star general on the cusp of sudden, 'definitive' American victory. However, every fibre of his humble Missouri background cautioned him against hubris. Truman flew 14,000 miles to meet MacArthur in person, for the first and only time in his life, on the island of Wake in the mid-Pacific, on 15 September, 1950. There, like Julius Caesar first attempting collegial relations with Pompey, the president tried to be civil and get to know, face to face, the notoriously vain, self-seeking general – who once again, both privately and in front of witnesses (including the Joint Chiefs of Staff and the Secretary of the Army) assured Truman that 'organized resistance throughout Korea will be ended by Thanksgiving' (November 23, 1950); that he would have the troops of the US Eighth Army back in Japan 'by Christmas'; and that neither the Soviets nor the Chinese would 'throw good money after bad' by entering the conflict.[62]

The result was disaster. The Chinese *did* commit troops to battle, and in vast numbers (260,000), since they could not sit idly by and watch their Communist next-door neighbour be destroyed, even though Kim Il-sung had brought the business on himself. 'The Chinese have come in with both feet' Truman memorably remarked, but resisted calls from colleagues that he should fire MacArthur, feeling that national unity was more important than scapegoating.[63]

Truman's magnanimity towards MacArthur was not reciprocated. The campaign in Korea became a bloodbath – with Seoul changing hands four times, and atrocities committed on both sides. What had been a brilliant demonstration of UN-supported firmness in the face of Communist military invasion turned into a moral as well as physical quagmire. By the beginning of December 1950, most US military and diplomatic officials favoured evacuation of Korea entirely. The head of the US Army, General 'Lightnin' Joe' Collins, felt Korea was 'not worth a nickel',[64] while the head of the CIA felt it important to 'get out of Korea'.[65] MacArthur, by contrast, condemned such 'Munich defeatism'; he favoured, instead, taking the war into China, blockading its seaports, attacking its cities from the air, using atomic weapons, bringing Nationalist Chinese forces from Taiwan to fight in Korea, launching an attack on the mainland of China from Taiwan . . .

Truman's gamble had needlessly turned a potential silk purse into a sow's ear in two fatal months. The leadership of the United States, so brilliantly asserted in a 'UN policing' role in September 1950 (as Stalin had warned Kim Il-sung in 1949), had led to a major war: the wrong war, as the chairman of the Joint Chiefs of Staff, General Bradley, had warned, at the wrong time, in the wrong place. Moreover, it was now a war to salvage America's military pride and honour (General Walker had been forced to make the longest retreat of an American army since the Civil War, chased by the Chinese), supporting a right-wing Korean nationalist, Syngman Rhee, about whom no American knew anything. UN cohesion, fused in facing the North Korean invasion, had also been exploded – McArthur's atomic-bomb sabre-rattling giving understandable rise to grave strains among European allies of the United States, whose NATO solidarity, in 1950, was of far greater import to the future of democratic freedoms in the world than the fortunes of a former Japanese colony.

In every respect, MacArthur's misjudgement, and Truman's acquiescence in it, had altered America's destiny – for the worse. When in the spring of 1951 MacArthur proceeded to publicly blame Truman and his administration (in an open letter to the Republican Minority Leader in Congress), rather than himself, Truman finally relieved him of his post. On Monday April 9, 1951, Truman told General Bradley: 'The son of a bitch isn't going to resign on me' and go into politics. 'I want him fired.'[66]

It was too late. MacArthur's 'martyrdom' (he was feted with ticker-tape parades attended by millions on his return to the US) only inflamed the rhetorical fantasies of 'the China lobby' in America, as well as those who advocated atomic measures to assert American hegemony abroad. Meanwhile at home, the monster of McCarthyism – Senator Joe McCarthy's crusade to root out secret Communists he saw in every area of government, industry and entertainment in America – was treated to a luscious bone.

Declaring a national emergency on December 15, 1950, Truman was forced to pay for MacArthur's mistake by the ruin of his own legacy, and terrible slaughter. The two years that followed were marked by stoic heroism on the battlefront – to little purpose, other than to restore what the US had achieved by September 1950: restitution of the 38th Parallel as the border between North and South Korea. The US armed services suffered almost 137,000 casualties: 33,686 dead in combat and 103,284 wounded. Other UN forces sustained 16,000 dead, while the South Koreans suffered a staggering 415,000 mortalities, military and civilian. North Korean dead were estimated at an even more staggering 520,000 – with an estimated 900,000 Chinese military casualties.

On November 1, 1950, two assassins from New York, having travelled by train and taken rooms in Washington DC's Harris Hotel, walked to Blair House, the temporary residence of the president, and opened fire on the security detail outside the building, intending to rush in and kill Truman.

It being a hot day, Truman was resting on his bed in his underwear, after a worrying morning meeting across the road, in the West Wing of the White House, at which the CIA director had announced the CIA had made a mistake, and that some 15,000–20,000 Chinese troops were in combat in northern Korea.

Had the Puerto Rican nationalists carried more powerful weapons than two pistols (a Luger and a P-38, with sixty-nine rounds of ammunition) they might well have been successful. Within two minutes twenty-seven shots were fired; one assassin was dead, and one White House policeman; the other assassin and two White House policemen were badly wounded. When the president ran and looked out of the open window to see for himself the source of the commotion, a voice from the sidewalk barked 'Get back! Get back!'[67] Undaunted, Truman dressed, went downstairs and attended an unveiling ceremony for a statue of Churchill's military representative during World War II, Field Marshal Sir John Dill, in Arlington Cemetery.

Convicted and sentenced to death, the surviving assassin was surprised, afterwards, to have his sentence commuted to life imprisonment – by the president. 'My opinion has always been that if you're in an office like that and someone wants to shoot you, they'll probably do it, and there's nothing much can help you out. It just goes with the job, and I don't think there's any way to prevent it' Truman mused later.[68] The secret service disagreed. He was provided with an armoured limousine with a landmine-proof floor and grenade-secure roof simply to cross Pennsylvania Avenue, and forbidden to walk. He had, he reflected, become a prisoner of the presidency.[69]

Assassination attempts by Puerto Ricans were one thing, but why, historians later asked, when the United States emerged as the most powerful economic and military nation on earth after World War II, did it become so infected by the bug that was eventually called McCarthyism? Moreover, why did Truman not do more to nip the disease in the bud before it became a pandemic, reducing the US for years to the status, in some respects, of a near police state with the FBI acting as a sort of western STASI rather than a criminal investigation bureau, with 'political' files on almost every actual and potential political leadership figure in the country, and many thousands of ordinary citizens?

The answer is that Truman did attempt to head off the looming scourge. By executive order on March 21, 1947, he set up a Loyalty Review Board in the Civil Service Commission tasked with investigating any and every government employee against whom a rumour or allegation of 'disloyalty' to the United States was made. The board, using FBI investigators, examined tens of thousands of people. Between 400 and 1,200 were fired during Truman's presidency. Between 1,000 and 6,000 resigned, many in disgust and protest.[70] This seemed a small, indeed pathetic, number in such a huge empire, with more than 2.5 million government employees, but rather than demonstrating the patriotism and reliability of the vast majority of Americans, the results only seemed to feed fear and loathing among anxious citizens seeking scapegoats in a difficult post-war reconstruction environment, as prices rose and news broke that atomic secrets had been stolen and given to the Russians. Inevitably, a politician stepped forward to ride the wave of apprehension, even panic: Senator Joe McCarthy.

At Wheeling, West Virginia, on February 9, 1950, Senator McCarthy, an alcoholic loudmouth who had switched from the Democratic to the Republican Party, achieved grotesque notoriety by holding up a phony piece of paper, claiming it contained the names of more than 200 Communist 'spies' currently working in the American government.[71] The list was fictitious, the assertion a lie, and the senator a corrupt charlatan; almost everything in his curriculum vitae was, in fact, a fabrication, from heroism as 'Tail-Gunner Joe' to war wounds. Nevertheless, with the help of Senator Robert Taft, who hated Truman and was eyeing the next presidential election, and J. Edgar Hoover, the director of the FBI who also despised the president, McCarthy's position as chair of the Senate Subcommittee on Investigations gave him carte blanche to paint the inner workings of American government as red.

Perhaps all empires are prone to internal pogroms in the pursuit or maintenance of power. Joseph McCarthy's hate-ridden sallies against the great and the good in America's government smacked of the social misfit, poisoned by envy rather than any observable ideology. In the context of bitter war against Communists in Korea, and concerns over the leaking of America's atom bomb secrets, however, his talk of spies and accusations of treachery in the highest places began to gain political and social traction.

Alarmed lest the unity of the nation, in a grave national emergency, be subverted by the Wisconsin demagogue, President Truman summoned a meeting of advisers on February 28, 1951. Congressional privilege had allowed McCarthy to speak without fear of slander, encouraging 'hectoring and innuendo', 'dirty tricks' and a 'bully's delight in the ruin of innocent'.[72] Where would it end, the president asked, and what would they suggest he do?

The Attorney General had come prepared for just such a question, and to the assembled group he confided he had a 'thick and devastating dossier'[73] on McCarthy and his corrupt financial and private life, including details of his bedmates over recent years – 'enough to blow Senator McCarthy's show sky high'.[74]

The president banged the table with the flat of his hand but, fatefully, it was not to announce they now had the means to expose the Wisconsin phony. The writer John Hersey, who was present, later recalled Truman's reasons for not leaking the dossier. 'You must not ask the president of the United States to get down in the gutter with a guttersnipe. Nobody, not even the president, can approach too close to a skunk, in skunk territory, and expect to get anything out of it except a bad smell. If you think someone is telling a lie about you, the only way to answer is with the whole truth.'[75]

This was Trumanian naivety of a tragic kind. The result was worse than anyone imagined. As one cultural chronicler of the period, Joseph Goulden, noted, fear, apathy and ignorance meant that 'for a full decade, that of the 1950s, America went into a holding period – intellectually, morally, politically'.[76] Dean Acheson, Truman's valiant Secretary of State, wrote of the '1950s' shameful and nihilistic orgy' of 'irresponsible character assassination'[77] which had a dire effect on the US government, as well as universities, and the Civil Services (whose members had to submit to loyalty oaths and FBI investigation) – requiring 'a decade to recover from this sadistic pogrom'.[78] Clark Clifford, who was also present at the McCarthy-dossier meeting, later wrote: 'It is easy to make light of McCarthy today, when even conservatives use the word "McCarthyism" to mean unfair political smear tactics – but the harsh fact, which must never be forgotten, is that until he destroyed himself . . . Joe McCarthy literally terrorized Washington and much of the nation', giving free ammunition to Communists abroad who could legitimately describe America as a quasi-police state, not a genuine democracy.[79] Too honourable to sink to McCarthy's level, Truman thereby permitted him to pursue his 'tricks' for a further three years, and his influence lasted for even longer.

Truman was in his fifth year as Caesar when he decided, in the spring of 1950, before the Korean War even began, that he would not stand again. 'Cincinnatus and Washington pointed the way. When Rome forgot Cincinnatus its downfall began' he noted tersely in his diary on April 16, 1950, reflecting on the way that, after their public duties were over, President Washington and Cincinnatus had both returned to their farms, the latter after his time as temporary dictator of Rome ended in 439 BC. By the end of his elected term Truman had served as president for seven years and nine months. 'I am not a candidate,' he wrote (but did not announce publicly, lest it cause him to be seen as a lame-duck president), 'and will not accept the nomination for another term.'[80]

As it happened, Truman would not be offered the nomination. The continuing stalemate in the Korean War, and the defection of more and more southern Democratic segregationists to the Republican Party, meant there was little or no support left for the beleaguered president among congressmen and senators anxious about their own re-election chances. Wherever his name was entered by others on primary presidential nomination ballot lists, Truman was roundly beaten. Moreover, when General Eisenhower, as the hugely popular supreme commander of NATO in Europe, indicated that he would resign his command and stand for the presidency as a Republican if drafted by the Republican Party at its summer 1952 political convention, Truman – who had hoped the general might stand as a Democrat – was mortified.

Eisenhower's victory in the presidential election in November 1952, as well as the clean sweep by the Republicans in the Senate and House of Representatives, reflected a nation tired of war. General Eisenhower had promised that the first thing he would do would be to 'go to Korea', and end the stalemate: either fighting the war to a definitive conclusion, or bringing the troops home. Biting his tongue, Truman offered the president-elect his plane, transition briefings with his staff, and a personal meeting in the newly refurbished White House.

There, in the Oval Office, Harry Truman gave back the globe which Eisenhower had given him some years before, in recognition of Truman's imperial responsibilities. In private, Truman was disconsolate. 'He'll sit right here,' Truman's daughter Margaret recalled her father's prediction, 'and he'll say do this, do that!! And nothing will happen. Poor Ike – it won't be a bit like the army. He'll find it very frustrating.'[81]

And with that, the Cincinnatus of modern America – former farmer and haberdasher – left the White House, without even a bodyguard, let alone a pension.

## Part Three: Private Life

Harry S. Truman differed both in background and character from his predecessor, FDR. Where Franklin Roosevelt was expansive – overwhelming people with his presence and the toss of his great lion-like head when he laughed or dismissed his opponents – Truman was compact in build with alert, penetrating eyes behind his thick glasses.

He was the only president in the twentieth century, in fact, to wear spectacles permanently – which he kept on, even when swimming in the White House pool.

Truman stood 5' 10", and weighed a steady 185 lb as president. He liked to wear a double-breasted, light-coloured suit, with immaculately laundered shirts, a five-pointed handkerchief in the breast pocket, and a World War I veteran's pin in his lapel. He had no disarming warmth, only an air of no-nonsense honesty and firmness. It was said that on charisma alone, Dwight Eisenhower, had he run for president in 1948 rather than 1952, would have beaten Truman easily.

Recognizing his lack of photogenic or charismatic appeal, Truman adopted early on in life a self-deprecating, humorous way of talking in company, while constantly clarifying his own thoughts and feelings in his diary and in letters, many hundreds of them not sent.

Truman adored his wife, Bess. When she greeted him coldly in Independence, after he had flown from Washington in a snowstorm to be with her for Christmas, he was hurt almost beyond words. 'You can never appreciate', he wrote in a letter, 'what it means to me to come home as I did the other evening after doing at least 100 things I didn't want to do [as president in 1945] and have the only person in the world whose approval and good opinion I value look at me like I'm something the cat dragged in and tell me I've come in at last because I couldn't find any reason to stay away . . .'[82] He did not send it.

The truth was that for all his high sense of responsibility and goodwill, Truman was by temperament short in patience and irascible. Very rarely, however, did he ever allow himself to lose his cool in public, although there were occasions when his mask would slip: when the *Washington Post*'s music correspondent dared criticize his daughter Margaret's first singing concert, for example, the president's rage knew no bounds. The vitriolic letter he penned he actually stamped and posted himself. 'Some day I hope to meet you' he wrote the hapless journalist. 'When that happens you'll need a new nose, a lot of beefsteak for black eyes, and perhaps a supporter below!'[83]

Truman's lack of observable ego caused others with greater egos to imagine they could best him, from Lloyd Stark to James Byrnes and Douglas MacArthur. None did. Truman's mother-in-law, wealthy Madge Wallace, was a great trial, however. For years she would not give her blessing to her daughter Bess' marriage to Truman, whom she considered a mere 'dirt farmer'. It took many years of courtship before Truman could persuade Bess, the object of his childhood adoration (he first met her in Bible class at age six) to finally persuade her mother to accept him as her son-in-law. True to form, at the wedding she criticized him for wearing a light woollen suit with waistcoat, instead of linen.

Madge Wallace's own husband had been a no-good, loudmouth alcoholic who shot himself in his bath, causing Mrs Wallace to cling to her daughter and pursue respectability at all costs. The price she exacted for her eventual agreement to the wedding was that she should be permitted to live with her daughter and her daughter's husband in every one of their residences – which she did. She died in the White House the month before Truman left office.

One of the president's English biographers called Truman 'about the most devoted husband in American presidential history'.[84] He was certainly one of the most faithful letter-writers to his spouse, which pleased historians, about whom Bess was sceptical. Dubbed 'dull, dumpy and distant' as First Lady, she espoused no grand (or minor) causes; her hands perspired if she had to speak in public (which she attempted always to avoid); she did not believe in advancing women's rights; she was attacked by the black congressman Adam Clayton Powell for once attending a reception of the segregated Daughters of the American Revolution; was excoriated for crossing a picket line to see Ingrid Bergman act in a still racially segregated theatre. Nevertheless Bess was and remained throughout Truman's life his one and only love, along with their daughter, Margaret ('Margie').

Bess Wallace never went out to work after completing finishing school. Content with being a homemaker, she helped Truman keep his books as a haberdasher, and with his paperwork when a senator. He rarely wrote a speech or letter that she did not vet before he gave or sent it, knowing that her intensely private, cautious, principled character was the necessary counterpoise to his feistier, fiery-tempered, often impetuous nature. 'How does it feel being engaged to a clodhopper who has ambitions to be governor of Missouri and chief executive of the US?' Truman asked his new fiancée in a letter in 1913. 'He'll do well if he gets to be a retired farmer' he added; 'I intend to keep peggin' away and I suppose I'll arrive at something. You'll never be sorry if you take me for better or for worse because I'll always try to make it better.'[85]

Truman's loyalty to his wife knew no bounds. If anyone spoke or wrote ill of her, he or she was forever banished. As Bess aged, Truman's devotion only grew more pronounced. Seeing an advertisement for Marilyn Monroe in *Gentlemen Prefer Blondes*, he memorably commented: 'real gentlemen prefer gray'. His letters to Bess numbered in the thousands, written every day they were apart. When later he found Bess burning some of their correspondence, he asked what on earth she was doing. 'I'm burning your letters to me.' 'Bess!' he objected, 'You oughtn't to do that.' 'Why not? I've read them several times.' 'But think of history!' 'I *have*' Bess remarked.[86]

How many of Truman's letters Bess destroyed, we do not know. More than 1,000 survive, however, providing a fascinatingly intimate insight into Truman's witty, observant, ambitious, entertaining, loyal and sharing heart.

Once, at Potsdam, Truman gave a ride back to his villa to a young American officer who offered to do anything for the president, even 'you know, like women'. Truman cut him short. 'Listen, son, I married my sweetheart' he said. 'She doesn't run around on me, and I don't run around on her. I want that understood. Don't ever mention that kind of stuff to me again.'[87]

If Truman was a marital paragon in comparison to his predecessor FDR (and his successors Eisenhower, Kennedy and Johnson), he was by no means a prude, or averse to boisterous company, especially if it involved music. At a stage show for servicemen shortly after his 1945 inauguration as vice president, he astonished the world by playing an upright piano in front of 800 people with Lauren Bacall perched, long-legged, on the piano. (The photo elicited sacks of mail from 'old ladies' who felt it unbecoming for a vice president.) He even astonished Prime Minister Churchill, according to Lord Moran, Churchill's doctor. 'When he was on his way out, passing a piano in one of the rooms,' Moran noted in his diary at Potsdam, 'he stopped and, pulling up a chair, played for a while.'[88] At Number 2 Kaiserstrasse in Potsdam, the president gave a party for both Stalin and Churchill at which the he played Paderewski's Minuet in G, which Paderewski himself had helped Truman master as a child after a concert in Kansas City, when Truman was twelve. Then, when Clement Attlee, a former infantry major, replaced Churchill as British prime minister, the two World War I veterans sang bawdy soldiers' songs they'd learned at the front. During the live televised reopening of the White House in May 1952 Truman suddenly sat down at the Steinway grand – 'the most wonderful tones of any piano I have ever heard' – and played part of Mozart's Ninth Sonata. His favourite was Chopin's A flat Waltz, Opus 42.[89] When he left the White House he claimed his record collection took up more space on the moving truck than his files. Music, clearly, was in Truman's bones.

Best of all, however, Truman loved to drink bourbon on the rocks and play poker with colleagues and cronies, who were obliged to tell tales along with him, tall as well as true. He insisted on a loss-limit for individuals, with a common bank, made up from a portion of winner's chips for losers to draw on. He played poker, it was said, recklessly and with gusto. 'He drank bourbon continuously but never got tight' an aide recalled. 'He just got exhilarated and told terrible stories.'[90]

Truman was a modest man who lived modestly. In contrast to Churchill, who rose late and stayed up late, Truman rose early and retired early, save when partying, when he rose early and retired late. Even as vice president of the United States he continued to live in a rented five-room apartment on Connecticut Avenue. Once he, his wife, their daughter and Mrs Madge Wallace, moved into the White House, they treated the White House staff as equals, to the astonishment – and delight – of the personnel. 'He could talk to anyone! He could talk to the lowly peasant. He could talk to the king of England' one of his secret service agents recalled. 'He never got swellheaded – never got, you know, swagly.'[91] 'They treated the staff with respect' the assistant to the chief usher reflected. 'When a butler or doorman or usher would enter the room, the Trumans would introduce him to whoever happened to be sitting in the room, even if it were a king or a prime minister. They introduced all the staff to their visitors – something I've never seen the Roosevelts do.'[92]

Truman's personal honesty was, in the context of American politics, power and temptation, remarkable. From 1935 Truman had no income other than his salary as senator, vice president and finally president, which reached $100,000 by 1952, but was insufficient to cover the costs of his thirteen staff, let alone formal White House hospitality expenses. (He had to be voted a further $50,000 by Congress to help run the White House.[93]) When he left the Oval Office at age sixty-nine, he had nothing bar his savings and his military pension, amounting to $112.56 per month. He moved back to his wife's family home at 219 North Delaware Street in Independence, Missouri. Five years later in 1958, Congress voted him (and subsequent ex-presidents) a pension and office expenses – and, after the Kennedy assassination, a bodyguard.

In the corrupt world of American politics, Harry S. Truman had been personally incorruptible. On December 26, 1972, he died in a Kansas City hospital, aged eighty-eight. He was buried in the court-yard of the Presidential Library bearing his name – 'the captain with the mighty heart', as Dean Acheson once called him.[94]

# CHAPTER THREE

# DWIGHT D. EISENHOWER

### Later Deified

Republican
34th President
(January 20, 1953–January 20, 1961)

## Part One: The Road to the White House

Dwight David Eisenhower (named Dwight after a popular evangelist preacher of the time) was born on October 14, 1890 in the small town of Denison, Texas. His father, David Eisenhower, had moved there to find work as a railway-engine wiper, earning $10 per week (his general store in Abilene, Kansas, had failed and he had consumed his promised inheritance).

Engine-wiping offered little future, however, and after several years in Texas David Eisenhower and his Jehovah's Witness wife, Ida, returned to Abilene with $24, three small children, and a fourth on the way. The third of David's and Ida's six boys (one of whom died), Dwight Eisenhower grew up from age two in the once lawless Wild West town and railroad cattle centre, pacified and made famous by Wild Bill Hickok. All his life Eisenhower would be addicted to Westerns.

The Eisenhowers' small house in Abilene had no indoor plumbing, and the boys had to help their mother keep chickens, two cows, poultry and rabbits to supplement their father's meagre income as a maintenance man at the local dairy. (He never earned more than $150 per month in his life.) Like his brothers – 'those little roughnecks from the wrong side of the tracks' people said of them – Eisenhower (nicknamed 'The Swede', and later 'Ike') wished to get out of Abilene as fast as possible.[1] At school he was good at maths, and athletic. Tall for the time (5' 10"), with unusually large hands, bright blue eyes and a smooth, handsome head, 'The Swede' made an agreement with his brother: one would work for several years to pay for the other to go to college, then reverse the arrangement. His older brother Edgar duly went to the University of Michigan – but never returned the favour.

It did not matter. After working eighty-six hours per week for two years at the local creamery following high-school graduation, Eisenhower won through competitive exams and high recommendations a place at West Point, which he entered as a cadet in 1911. He was a born leader, had a good memory, and inherited from his father an explosive temper which he spent his life controlling. 'He who conquers his temper is greater than he who taketh the city' his mother instilled in him.[2] It helped Eisenhower, too, to conceal his real views. As he later confided, 'I got where I did by knowing how to hide my ego and my intelligence.'[3]

Commissioned a second lieutenant in 1915, the West Point graduate was impecunious but popular, capable but unpretentious, and a magnet to both men and women, despite his shyness with the latter. In 1916 at Fort Sam Houston he married the daughter of a millionaire meatpacking businessman, who forbade the lieutenant go into the army's nascent aviation wing lest his daughter become a young widow. Instead, after US entry into World War I, Eisenhower was asked to organize the training of some 10,000 tank personnel for combat in France. To his chagrin he proved so effective as an administrator that he was retained in America, as the army mushroomed from a mere 106,000 men in 1916 to 2.4 million three years later. He was awarded the Distinguished Service Medal for his work.

Reduced from temporary lieutenant colonel to captain, then rising again to major and lieutenant colonel over the next twenty years in the military, Eisenhower never did hold combat field command. He was, however, highly regarded for his skills as a football coach, as a superlative staff officer – and chain-smoking poker player.

Interested in modernization and mechanization, despite the contraction of the post-war army to 300,000 men, in 1919 Eisenhower participated as an observer in the army's first transcontinental road crossing by a motorized army formation – the genesis of his US highway system, commissioned during his presidency. He served in Panama, then in Europe (on General Pershing's American Battlefields Commission), and Washington DC. There, as a staff officer serving as assistant to the then chief of staff of the US Army, General Douglas MacArthur, he witnessed MacArthur refuse to take direct orders from the Secretary of the Army. In an act of deliberate defiance of political authority, MacArthur instructed US Army units (led by tanker

George S. Patton) to cross the Anacostia Bridge and destroy the shanty town ('Hooverville') of World War I army veterans pleading for early payment of their promised bonuses, on July 28, 1932, at the height of the Depression. It was 'one of the most disgraceful incidents in American history' Eisenhower's military biographer later considered.[4]

'I just can't understand how such a damn fool could ever have gotten to be a general' Eisenhower said later of MacArthur.[5] But at the time, as a mere major, he was unwilling to confront his aristocratic boss, who considered the Bonus Marchers to be Communists and malingerers. Though he considered himself to have been 'a slave in the War Department' under MacArthur, Eisenhower's five years in the capital nevertheless enabled him to meet, break bread with, and work with cabinet ministers, senators and congressmen – a political experience invaluable as preparation for later elective office, and a merciful counter to his years in 'exile' in the Pacific.[6]

Posted to the Philippines (a US colony slated for independence in 1945) by FDR in 1934 as head of the US Military Mission, General MacArthur took the absurd rank of field marshal of the skeletal Philippine Army – and insisted Eisenhower accompany him, in the rank of a Philippine general. Eisenhower agreed to go but refused the rank, earning MacArthur's enduring spite. 'He was the best clerk who ever served under me' MacArthur later derided the tireless staff officer.[7]

Had he remained in the Philippines, Eisenhower might well have ended the war in Japanese captivity – if he had survived the Bataan Death March and horrific POW conditions. Instead, the lieutenant colonel – who had spent much of his time at the presidential palace in Manila playing bridge with the Philippine president, Manuel Quezon, and had been deprived of further contact with his army contemporaries – was posted back to the United States late in 1939. He commanded briefly a battalion on manoeuvres, then served as chief of staff of a corps, first as a full colonel, then brigadier general. His clear mind and capacity for hard work eventually paid off when, following Pearl Harbor in December 1941, he became part of General George Marshall's War Department operations planning team. In that capacity he was sent to England by Marshall the following spring to assess the feasibility of an Allied cross-Channel invasion in 1942.

Well liked by the British, Eisenhower was soon appointed US

commander for the European theatre. As he wrote home to his wife, he had to be 'a bit of a diplomat – lawyer – promoter – salesman – social hound – *liar* (at least to get out of social affairs) – mountebank – actor – Simon Legree – humanitarian – orator and incidentally (sometimes I think most damnably incidentally) a soldier!'[8]

Eisenhower fulfilled most of these conditions brilliantly. His strategic and tactical ideas were questionable, as were his assessments of effective commanders. (He was impressed by a young British admiral, Lord Louis Mountbatten, for example, and argued strongly for D-Day to be launched in 1942 with a single division; when Mountbatten did mount such a one-division attack across the English Channel at Dieppe that August, more than 3,500 Canadian and Allied troops were killed, wounded or captured in a single day, discouraging any further notions of cross-Channel invasion for two years.) Yet Eisenhower's absolute sincerity and his supranational dedication made up for his failings in a war the Allies could not lose – so long as the Russians kept fighting in the east, and the American war machine kept making planes, ships, tanks and artillery.

In deference to the US decision to follow a 'Germany First' strategy, Eisenhower – having been made Allied commander-in-chief of the air, naval and ground forces for Operation Torch, the Allied invasion of north-west Africa in November 1942 – made his name and reputation as a supreme commander who could weld a truly international team, despite his unease in such a rear-headquarters role. 'I used to read about commanders of armies and envied them what I supposed to be great freedom in action and decision' he wrote his wife from Algiers, many hundreds of miles from the battlefield. 'What a notion! My life is a mixture of politics and war. The latter is bad enough – but I've been trained for it!' Politics, by contrast, was 'straight and unadulterated venom' – demanding not only his valuable time, but 'my good disposition' in order to marshal the Allied cause.[9]

The surrender of all German and Axis troops in North Africa on May 12, 1942 at Tunis made the politics and the venom worthwhile, however, and the subsequent Allied invasions of Sicily in July 1943, and finally the mainland of Italy in September 1943, added lustre to Eisenhower's growing reputation. On December 7, the second anniversary of Pearl Harbor, the president visited Eisenhower in Tunis on his way back from his summit with Churchill and Stalin in Tehran.

'Well, Ike,' FDR announced, 'you are going to command Overlord' – the D-Day invasion, set for the spring of 1944.[10]

Asked afterwards by his son James why he had chosen Eisenhower rather than General Marshall, FDR explained: 'Eisenhower is the best politician among the military men. He is a natural leader who can convince other men to follow him, and this is what we need in his position more than any other quality.'[11] Projecting transparent openness of mind and firm purpose, Eisenhower transcended the internecine squabbling that bedevils coalition warfare. Even Stalin was impressed by his character, remarking 'General Ike is a very great man, not only because of his military accomplishments but because of his human, friendly, kind and frank nature. He is not a "grubyi" [coarse] man like most military.'[12]

Eisenhower's ability to lead the senior combat team of the western Allies paid off. As supreme commander he backed General Montgomery's plans for the D-Day landings, then General Bradley's plans for the breakout in Normandy (using heavy bombers to blast a way out of the Normandy *bocage*), then Patton's race to the Loire – and Germany. He would be criticized by military historians for taking personal field command in September 1944, leading to the dispersion of his forces ('broad front'), failure at Arnhem (the 'Bridge Too Far') and worst of all, the German counteroffensive in the Ardennes (the 'Battle of the Bulge'), in which the US armies suffered 80,000 casualties. Montgomery and Patton closed down this German counter-attack, and two months later had forces across the Rhine racing for Berlin and Vienna.

Eisenhower was criticized for not ordering the seizure of Berlin from the west after American troops had already crossed the Elbe, and for failing to secure written terms from the Russians for Allied access to the city. However, his absolute sincerity of Allied purpose outshone his naivety and tactical shortcomings. After German unconditional surrender on May 7, 1945, he became the hero of liberated Europe, and the most honoured American on the continent – indeed he emerged from the Allied 'Crusade In Europe' (as he titled his subsequent account) so popular in the United States that there were growing calls for him to stand, like victorious General Ulysses S. Grant after the Civil War, for the presidency.

So great was Eisenhower's popularity back home that the new president, Harry Truman – only three months in office and on his way to the summit at Potsdam – generously assured Eisenhower that if he stood for election as a Democrat, Truman would be happy to stand down and serve again as vice president.[13] The general assured the president, however, that he had no political ambitions, having never voted in a presidential election in his life.

On General Marshall's retirement following the Japanese surrender, Eisenhower took Marshall's place as chief of staff of the army, having been made a five-star general – a heady achievement for an engine-wiper's son. (His father died in 1942, before Eisenhower's meteoric rise, but his mother lived to see him return triumphantly from Europe.) On a tour of American forces serving abroad (including China, where he was briefed by the president's emissary, General Marshall, on the inevitability of Chiang Kai-shek's defeat), Eisenhower visited Japan. It was there that he met with his former commanding officer, and fellow five-star general: the commander of US forces in the Far East, Douglas MacArthur.

In the library of the general's residence next to the US embassy in Tokyo, the two American supreme commanders of World War II faced each other after dinner on May 10, 1946, Eisenhower now technically MacArthur's boss. The unspoken matter of the 1948 presidential election, still two years away, hung over them. Both men were considered prime candidates to be nominated by acclamation. When Eisenhower finally raised the subject, MacArthur claimed that, at age sixty-six and by ten years the older man, he was too old to stand a chance, but was certain Ike would be asked. Eisenhower resisted. 'That's right,' MacArthur said, with a twisted smile. 'You go on like that and you'll get it for sure!'[14]

As Eisenhower's official biographer noted, 'Neither man convinced the other.'[15] Upon his retirement as head of the US Army Eisenhower did become president, but of New York's Columbia University, not the United States. In the fall of 1950, with deepening strategic anxiety over Russian intentions in the wake of the bitter war in Korea, President Truman asked Eisenhower to return to military duty as the first supreme commander of NATO in Europe. Dutifully accepting the appointment, General Eisenhower took up his post in Paris in January 1951. As he sought to weld the nations of western Europe into a cohesive military defence force, American politics were never far away, especially when the prospective Republican contender for the 1952 election, Senator Robert Taft (son of President Taft), protested against American involvement in NATO, and said he wished to bring home all American forces still in Europe.[16]

Concerned lest the United States slide back into isolationism under a Taft-led Republican administration, as it had after World War I, Eisenhower tore up a note he'd penned, to the effect that he would remain at NATO as a soldier and would 'repudiate' any efforts to draft him for the Republican nomination the following year.[17] Instead, he indicated, he was open to the notion of running for president – and stamping out Taft's isolationist movement in America.

After being shown, in Paris, a hand-delivered film of a tumultuous two-hour Madison Square Garden rally in New York in February 1952, with huge crowds sporting 'I Like Ike' buttons and chanting 'We want Ike!' (the film had been flown over by the aviator Jacqueline Cochran, who tellingly addressed him as 'Mr President'), Eisenhower then made his historic decision to resign from the army, if nominated, and stand.[18] As a Republican.

At the White House, Truman – who had hoped Eisenhower would run in order to 'keep the isolationists out of the White House' – was gutted, noting sardonically that Republicans were showing the general 'gates of gold and silver', which the president was quite certain 'will turn out but copper and tin'.[19]

There were, Eisenhower quickly recognized, Faustian-like bargains he would have to make in joining the ranks of politicians, a breed for which he had professed contempt all his life.[20]

Fortunately Eisenhower had become a master at swallowing his pride and seeking compromise, as well as taming his temper, throughout his career. Years later, when an interviewer implied that he was not cut out to be a politician, he retorted: 'What the hell are you talking about? I have been in politics, the most active sort of politics, most of my adult life. There's no more active political organization in the world than the armed services of the US.'[21]

In the event, thanks to the hard work of Senator Lodge and his team, General Dwight D. Eisenhower pipped Senator Taft to the post on the first ballot at the Chicago Republican Convention on July 11, 1952 and became the first US general in the twentieth century to be nominated by a political party as its presidential candidate. Eisenhower's triumph, however, raised the question of running mate.

To unify Republicans, Eisenhower was advised, a candidate was required who would be acceptable to those who had supported his isolationist opponent – the 'reactionaries', as Eisenhower called them, or 'Old Guard'. There was such a man, who nursed – as his biographer wrote – a 'Cassius-like appetite for power': Senator Richard M. Nixon of California.[22]

Eisenhower had met with Nixon for an hour in Paris while still supreme commander of NATO in 1951, and had found the Californian unctuous but clever. Nixon had gained a national reputation for Communist-bashing, but he promised to bring geographical balance to the ticket by representing the West Coast. Thus, immediately after Eisenhower's nomination, the general summoned Nixon to his suite in the Blackstone Hotel and asked if Nixon would join his 'crusade of ideals'.[23] Nixon said yes. It was an offer Ike would deeply regret.

## Part Two: The Presidency

On November 4, 1952, having covered 21,000 miles by whistle-stop campaign train and 30,000 miles by air, and having reluctantly kept Nixon on as his vice-presidential running mate despite allegations of a 'Secret Nixon Fund', Eisenhower won the presidency easily – 55 per cent to 45 per cent in the popular vote, and 442 to eighty-nine in the Electoral College.

Chagrined – especially over Eisenhower's failure to rein in Republican denunciations of General Marshall for having 'lost' China – Truman magnanimously invited the president-elect, who seemed uncommonly grumpy, to the White House. There, the president offered the first genuine transition assistance in history by instructing his staff to brief the president-elect's team; Eisenhower was even offered Truman's plane, the *Independence*, to take him to Korea on the fact-finding mission he had promised the public.

From afar, Eisenhower had considered MacArthur's 1950 landings at Inchon and his bold campaign across the 38th Parallel to be militarily 'perfect' – even favouring McArthur's controversial willingness to use atomic weapons. But his visit to Korea as president-elect (though in an ordinary military plane) brought him up against reality. General Mark Clark, the UN commander, favoured another MacArthur-style attack against the North Korean and Chinese forces. Seeing for himself the 300-mile-wide front and rugged terrain, the veteran commander-in-chief of campaigns in Morocco, Tunisia, Sicily, Italy, France and Germany estimated it would require at least 300,000 American troops. 'I know how you feel, militarily,' he told Clark, 'but I feel I have a mandate from the people to stop this fighting. That's my decision.'[24] There would be no UN attack.

MacArthur, meanwhile, announced he had his own 'secret plan' to end the Korean War – one that he would only reveal in person to the president-elect. In New York on December 14, 1952, the would-be Caesar explained to the about-to-be Caesar his solution – threatening Mao Zedong, the ruler of Communist China, he would mercilessly bomb China's main cities with atomic weapons and destroy the Chinese industrial base. If this failed, MacArthur proposed dropping a radioactive belt across the Chinese–North Korean border, to stop Chinese troops crossing into North Korea, while the US–UN forces were to cross the 38th Parallel and mount new amphibious and land offensives.

Eisenhower, knowing that the sixteen UN participant nations would not, as America's allies in Korea, consent to such World War III measures, realized he was talking to a madman. His own historic responsibility, he recognized, was not to pursue fantasies, but to keep the world safe and if possible at peace.

The president-elect's response to MacArthur's plan was admirably cool. However, his behaviour towards President Truman, still his commander-in-chief, was less worthy. Asked to step into the White House for traditional coffee before the inauguration of 20 January, 1953, Eisenhower declined. The car ride to the reviewing stand at the Capitol was equally frosty. When Eisenhower found his son John on the stand, brought back from military duty in Korea for the occasion, he was furious and demanded to know who had ordered him home. Truman stared in disbelief at Ike. 'The president of the United States ordered your son to attend your inauguration' Truman responded.[25]

Three days later, Eisenhower thanked Truman for his thoughtfulness, in a letter, but the damage was done; for the next eight years the two greatest living American emperors did not speak or communicate with each other.

The strain of the election campaign, and the problem of how to end the war in Korea, were clearly weighing on the new president, as his contempt for the command set-up in the White House showed, once he took office. 'If I'd had a staff like this during the war, we'd have lost it' Eisenhower fumed.[26] He soon instituted a more imperial staff structure at the White House, appointing for the first time in presidential history a no-nonsense chief of staff, Sherman Adams, a first-class secretariat, weekly National Security Council meetings, regular press conferences, and weekly cabinet meetings – which did not vote, but advised the president. This was the start of modern White House headquarters-style administration: the imperial presidency, as it would later be termed. 'Organization cannot make a genius out of a dunce' he would say. 'But it can provide its head with the facts he needs, and help him avoid misinformed mistakes.'[27] The president started early, disliked the telephone, encouraged one-page summaries of documents from his staff, listened patiently, asked penetrating questions and took time to mull over his decisions, even at the risk of appearing indecisive.

By the spring of 1953, with the death of Stalin and the failure of another massive Chinese ground attack in Korea, prospects for a ceasefire in Korea grew. The seventy-nine-year-old South Korean president, Syngman Rhee, refused to accept a divided nation, but Eisenhower bluntly told him he must accept such a compromise or the United States would pull out its forces altogether. Meanwhile Eisenhower prepared nuclear-tipped artillery and fighter-borne weapons for potential combat, and sent a message via the Indian prime minister that they would be used if China launched another invasion of the South (a threat Truman should have used, had he resolutely forbidden MacArthur to cross the 38th Parallel two years earlier). On July 26, 1953, an armistice was signed. As Eisenhower went to the White House Broadcast Room to announce the end of hostilities, he told a photographer: 'The war is over – I hope my son is coming home soon.'[28]

Eisenhower's judgement, whether about people or issues, was certainly not infallible, but he had the crucial blessing Napoleon had looked for in a general: luck. Moreover he was not an ideologue, or self-serving. Given Senator Taft's death from cancer in 1954 and the resultant elevation of MacArthur to the presidency that would have occurred had the two men been the successful Republican candidates in the 1952 election, historians could only marvel in retrospect at America's good fortune in having had Eisenhower at the imperial helm. With his high intelligence, noble ideals and ability to weld people – from prima donnas to effective public servants – into a team, Eisenhower proved more successful in his first year in office than his detractors ever thought possible. His popularity regularly reached 70 per cent, and 80 per cent of his legislation was passed by the Republican-controlled Congress (Eisenhower had wisely taken to golfing with the Senate Majority Leader). He had promised a reduction of taxes, but refused to fulfil that promise until the budget was balanced. He issued a new National Security Council directive outlining American strategy in supporting and protecting western Europe and Japan, with defence of Taiwan, South Korea and Israel as the perhaps unfortunate 'extra' legacies of the Truman era, yet an inheritance America could not, morally, abandon. It was an overall strategy that would make certain America stayed out of foreign wars for the rest of Eisenhower's presidency, indeed a strategy that would last for fifty years, ensuring the United States' continuing wealth as the world's largest economy. Yet at every step he was crossed, not by the Democrats, but the right-wing extremists in his own party – beginning with Senator McCarthy.

Later, after McCarthy self-destructed, people found it difficult to understand the fear and trembling he had aroused by his Senate investigations, so similar to the dreaded Inquisition during the Spanish Empire, or the Soviet Union's worst show trials; but this was to treat McCarthy as an aberration in an otherwise civilized American society – which was unfair to aberrants. The truth was, McCarthy represented not only himself but the dark side of political extremism in America, expressed in both the Republican Party and the Democratic Party. Like many a turncoat, the former Democrat became more aggressive and fanatical once a Republican than most Republicans – and when a Republican president and Congress assumed power in 1953, McCarthy's power to create headlines and headaches increased exponentially. At the start of the 81st Congress, with a Republican majority in both houses (albeit by only one vote in the Senate), McCarthy was appointed chairman of the Senate Committee on Government Operations – and made himself chair of its Permanent Subcommittee on Investigations, normally a backwater, without objection.

No sooner was Eisenhower's 1953 inauguration over than, to his amazement, McCarthy dared contest the nomination of General Walter Bedell Smith, Eisenhower's famous wartime chief of staff and subsequent US ambassador to Russia and first director of the CIA, to be Under Secretary of State. When Eisenhower, furious, managed to warn off McCarthy via the Senate Majority Leader, McCarthy switched to the nomination of Dr James B. Conant, the president of Harvard, as US high commissioner to Germany. Though Eisenhower again got McCarthy to withdraw his opposition – this time via McCarthy's former Senate colleague, the vice president – he then found McCarthy contesting the nomination as US ambassador to Russia of Charles E. Bohlen, a career officer who had been present at Yalta and whom McCarthy targeted for not repudiating the Yalta agreement.

Bohlen's Senate hearing lasted four entire days, by which time Eisenhower had a clearer picture of the Republican Party in action. McCarthy's subcommittee then began hearings on supposed subversives in the new administration. No lie became too gross, no accusation too outrageous, no libel too exaggerated, no demonization too grotesque for McCarthy, aided by his legal counsel Roy Cohn, to pass up in his self-appointed pogrom to expose the Communist enemy within America – an ideology supposedly responsible for all the ills without. A paranoid culture of fear and suspicion was deliberately inculcated in the manner – ironically – of Stalin's and Hitler's purges. He coerced John Foster Dulles, Eisenhower's new Secretary of State, to demand 'loyalty statements' from all 16,500 State Department employees and to purge the State Department of 'Communists, left-wingers, New Dealers, radicals and pinkos' – reducing the Voice of America to rank propaganda, and eliminating all liberal or leftist literature from American embassy libraries worldwide.

A poor and rambling speaker, McCarthy was a strangely repellent demagogue, the last of a breed of politicians who for centuries had grabbed headlines in print, and by their congressional immunity were able to lie and slander with impunity. Like his predecessor in the Oval Office, Eisenhower refused to speak to or deal directly with McCarthy, declaring privately, 'I will not get into a pissing contest with that skunk.'[29] The president tellingly blamed 'the people who have built him up, namely writers, editors, publishers. I really believe', Eisenhower noted in his diary, 'that nothing will be so effective in combating his particular kind of troublemaking as to ignore him. This he cannot stand.'[30]

Eisenhower was right about McCarthy's reaction, but wrong about the senator's troublemaking, never dreaming that he might go for the very organization the president most revered: the US Army.

The army had dared draft G. David Schine, who was the favourite aide of McCarthy's chief counsel, Roy Cohn. Furious, McCarthy turned his spotlight on the Pentagon, and the army's top personnel soon found themselves subpoenaed by McCarthy's Senate committee. The army responded by claiming that McCarthy and Cohn (a homosexual who later died of AIDS) had improperly used their power to get special treatment for Schine. The hearings, chaired by Senator Karl Mundt once McCarthy was forced to step down, became a national spectacle and were the first congressional inquiry to be fully televised, gavel to gavel, with an audience of twenty million.

Live coverage of McCarthy berating one of the army's senior officers, Brigadier General Ralph Zwicker (who had landed on D-Day, was wounded and decorated), as 'not fit to wear' his uniform, and lacking even the 'brains of a five-year-old child', proved scandalous. The TV hearings became a uniquely American disgrace. With McCarthy demanding access to Pentagon documents and subpoenaing White House officials on Eisenhower's staff, however, it was not only the Senate that was open to world ridicule. McCarthy and McCarthyism had got out of hand, the president belatedly recognized, causing him to feel shame for the Republican Party as well as the Senate.[31] While watching McCarthy's antics on his television set at the White House, he was heard to remark 'It saddens me that I must feel ashamed for the United States Senate.'[32]

Eisenhower, whose friends were all millionaires and who was an anti-Communist to his fingertips, could no longer stand by and watch McCarthy transform America into a version of the USSR through accusation, intimidation, fear and show trials aired on national TV. There was even talk of McCarthy running for the presidency in 1956, a prospect that prompted Eisenhower, who had only intended to serve a single term, to say the 'only reason I would consider running again would be to run against him'.[33] 'He's ambitious', Eisenhower judged McCarthy's supposed presidential aspirations, but 'he's the last guy in the whole world who'll ever get there, if I have anything to say.'[34]

Having hitherto downplayed the McCarthy threat, the president became so deeply concerned that he confided to aides he might leave the Republican Party, with its clique of right-wing desperadoes

including Senator Barry Goldwater, and 'set quietly about the formation of a new party'. He considered making a personal appeal to every
member of Congress and every governor 'whose general political
philosophy [is] the middle way'. In the meantime, however, he became
determined to beat McCarthy over the army hearings.

Instead of denouncing McCarthy directly, as president, the former
supreme commander decided on a different strategy. Summoning his
Attorney General, Herbert Brownell, Eisenhower invented a new judicial rule: 'executive privilege', a rule that would bar Congress from
subpoenaing any serving employee on the president's team, or his or
her documents, lest they thereby inhibit the president of the United
States in the execution of his constitutional duties as chief executive
of the country. Not one member of his staff would therefore go before
McCarthy's kangaroo court.

'Executive privilege' undoubtedly changed the nature of the presidential power in America, cementing for good or ill what had already
become, thanks to American military and economic power across the
globe, an increasingly imperial presidency. It certainly stymied
McCarthy's witch-hunt. Denied victims or their documents, McCarthy
was helpless. The president had then only to wait for McCarthy himself
to be investigated over his alleged improprieties in the Schine case.
On the afternoon of June 9, 1954, the subcommittee hearings finally
reached their climax. In a pre-hearing contractual arrangement,
McCarthy had agreed not to make personal accusations of
Communism against any member of the army counsel's legal team.
Now, under cross-examination himself, McCarthy gave way to a malevolence he could no longer control. On camera, he suddenly announced
a new charge: accusing the army chief counsel's law office of
harbouring a lawyer with Communist sympathies.

Before twenty million viewers the army's chief lawyer, Joseph
Welch, paused, and after a deep breath addressed the Republican
senator. 'Until this moment, Senator, I think I never really gauged
your cruelty or your recklessness . . . Have you no sense of decency,
sir, at long last? Have you left no sense of decency?' As McCarthy
attempted to respond, Welch cut him off, asking the chairman, Senator
Mundt, to 'call the next witness'.[35] Spectators in the gallery erupted
with applause. McCarthy, slain on live TV, turned to Cohn and in a
stunned voice, croaked: 'What happened?' The president, watching

in the White House, was ecstatic, and invited Welch to the Oval Office in order to congratulate him in person. 'You handled a tough job like a champion' Eisenhower beamed.[36]

Eisenhower's close encounter with McCarthy's evil altered his view of his own role as US president or Caesar. Senator McCarthy was declared *persona non grata* at the White House, indeed all government receptions, on the express orders of the president. In retaliation McCarthy announced he was 'breaking' with the Republican leader and accused the president publicly of 'weakness and supineness' in ferreting out Communists, indeed claimed he himself had made a terrible mistake – namely to have voted for Eisenhower in 1952 as a staunch anti-Communist.[37]

The president was undaunted. He seemed, in fact, energized by the fight with McCarthy, telling his press secretary, Jim Hagerty, he was 'glad the break has come'. 'I have just one purpose, outside of keeping this world at peace,' Eisenhower explained, 'and that is to build up a strong progressive Republican Party in this country. If the right wing wants a fight, they're going to get it. If they want to leave the Republican Party and form a third party, that's their business, but before I end up, either this Republican Party will reflect progressivism or I won't be with them anymore.'[38] And if the fanatics thought they could nominate a right-wing ideologue like McCarthy for the presidency, he declared, 'they've got another thought coming. I'll go up and down this country, campaigning against them. I'll fight them right down the line.'[39]

The American Empire was, in effect, at the crossroads. 'There is so much resentment,' Eisenhower reflected upon the very Republicans who had helped make him president, 'and those people will never give up.' The dieharders wanted to ban all trade with Communist countries, refusing to accept Eisenhower's view that once those countries were lifted out of poverty, the appeal of Communism would wither. 'Trade is the strongest weapon of the diplomat and it should be used more', not less, the president declared. 'Anyone who says that to trade with a Red country is in effect advocating a traitorous act just doesn't know what he is talking about' he snorted.[40] When the vice president began using the same hard-line language as McCarthy, Eisenhower called him to the White House and told him to 'back off'. When Nixon gave the excuse that he had meant to attack only Acheson and

Truman, not the entire Democratic Party, Eisenhower cut him short. Use of the word treason was 'indefensible', he told Nixon, and ordered him to stop it, immediately.[41]

Scapegoating and an almost fascistic patriotism had produced a potent right-wing Republican brew – moreover a uniquely dangerous one, given the power of America's growing atomic arsenal. The US was producing a new atomic bomb *every day*, in addition to the 1,600 bombs it had when Eisenhower became president. By contrast the Soviet Union had no nuclear weapons deployed operationally. As a result McCarthy called for General MacArthur to replace John Foster Dulles, in order to exert a more muscular American foreign policy. Again, Eisenhower ignored him, knowing that had 'the Old Guard', as Eisenhower termed them, been privy to the USSR's weakness in operational nuclear weapons, McCarthy's bellicosity would have been even harder to control.

Vietnam became a test case. The newly fortified French position at Dien Bien Phu supposedly guarded the Laotian border, across which Vietnam's nationalist-Communist insurgent leader Ho Chi Minh got the supplies he needed to evict the French colonists. The French had claimed their garrison was impregnable, but once in danger of being surrounded and overrun by Ho Chi Minh's troops, they asked for American help.

Eisenhower had already sent Under Secretary of State General Bedell Smith to study the French situation. Worried about the expansion of Communism in South East Asia, Bedell Smith recommended using Chiang Kai-shek's Nationalist Chinese Army, while Admiral Radford, the chairman of the Joint Chiefs of Staff, recommended the use of atomic weapons. 'You boys must be crazy' Eisenhower said. 'We can't use those awful things against Asians for the second time in less than ten years. My God!'[42] A Franco-American war in the jungles of Vietnam made no military sense to Eisenhower, nor did there seem any chance that members of Congress would condone a US-led war in Vietnam, when no American to date had been attacked and no American commercial trade route, major market or mineral source was affected.

Having rehearsed all the options (and changed his mind a dozen times), Eisenhower wisely overruled his advisers. He let the French be defeated at Dien Bien Phu. In June 1954, an armistice was signed in Geneva, similar to the one Eisenhower had obtained in Korea. This ended hostilities in Indochina, partitioning Vietnam temporarily on the 17th Parallel, its sovereign independence formally granted by the evacuating French, and national reunification elections slated for 1956.

In September 1955 Eisenhower suffered a heart attack, the severity of which was hushed up. Recovering, the president attempted to dump Nixon, suggesting on December 26 that, since Nixon's popularity was still low, he would benefit from more experience, in a cabinet position to which Eisenhower could appoint him, and then easily dismiss him. Eisenhower even spoke of running for re-election as a Democrat, perhaps with the Democratic governor of Ohio, Frank Lausche, or the progressive chief justice, Earl Warren, or the navy secretary, Robert Anderson, even his brother Milton, as his vice president. Anyone rather than with Nixon. 'He never liked me . . . he's always been against me' Nixon complained.[43] Backed by his wife, Pat, Nixon declined to quit, however, lining up as many pledges of support for the summer Republican National Convention as possible by having his name specially written in on tens of thousands of New Hampshire presidential primary ballots as vice-presidential nominee, and getting former colleagues in Congress to give written support for his continued place as a good anti-Communist and anti-tax Republican on the ticket.

It was clear that Richard Milhous Nixon, unlike FDR's vice president Henry Wallace in 1944, would not surrender his claim to the vice-throne. Belatedly, Eisenhower realized the time to dump Nixon had been in 1952, at the time of Nixon's financial scandal. Now, however, it was too late. Eisenhower had to grit his teeth and renew his offer of the vice-presidential ticket, hoping that his frail health (he suffered an attack of ileitis, requiring an emergency bypass operation on his small intestine, performed on June 8, 1956) would see him through the inevitable crises of a second term, if re-elected – for the nation's sake.

The next major crisis came, in fact, before the election could even take place. On June 29, 1956, the president had finally been able to sign the Federal Aid Highway Act he'd been urging on Congress for over a year, to create a national system of intercity highways comparable to the great Roman roads of classical times.[44] On August 22 the president was re-nominated by acclamation at the Republican National Convention in San Francisco. Soon after, a major international crisis arose in the Middle East over ownership of the Suez Canal.

At first Eisenhower, recovering from his surgery, could not believe Britain and France would take unilateral military action without UN support, or act secretly in concert with Israel, a country which above all other states in the Middle East needed the goodwill of its Arab neighbours. Eisenhower at first assumed such reported plans to be the brainchild of Winston Churchill, whose notions and misadventures from Gallipoli in World War I to the Dodecan Islands in World War II had taxed the patience of all who had to work with, and under, him. In fact, however, the Suez invasion was the idea of Churchill's successor, Sir Anthony Eden, who insisted that Abdel Gamal Nasser, the president of Egypt, was a second Hitler in the making.

Eisenhower did not share Eden's view. Nasser's decision in July 1956 to nationalize the Suez Canal had certainly reignited the dying embers of British and French imperialism ('The fat was now really in the fire' Eisenhower wrote in his memoirs[45]) but the president felt Nasser was 'in his rights' to take over the canal, under eminent domain, and ridiculed the British assertion that Egyptian pilots would be unable to guide vessels through it without British supervision.[46] (Within the first week Egyptian pilots had shepherded 254 ships without help, a canal record.) Moreover, while 'initial military successes might be easy', Eisenhower warned Prime Minister Eden, 'the eventual price might become too heavy'.[47]

Once again Eisenhower's savvy was pitted against members of his own party. The Senate Majority Leader, Democrat Lyndon B. Johnson, counselled Eisenhower to 'tell them [the British and the French] they have our moral support and go on in'.[48] John Foster Dulles, as Secretary of State, also favoured American strong-arm tactics. Again, Eisenhower demurred. He would only risk embroilment in war if the nation was threatened or attacked. To his great credit, he urged Eden 'not [to] make Nasser an Arab hero', given that Nasser loved drama; as in Truman's magnificent Berlin airlift approach to such a challenge, Eden should, he advised, quietly work on supertankers, new oil pipelines and oil supply from the US, while the United States built upon its special relationship with Saudi Arabia.[49]

Neither Eden nor the Israelis complied. Flying over the Middle East, Ike's new spy plane, the U-2, discovered that Israel had obtained sixty French Mystère fighter planes, not the twenty-four it had owned up to under the 1950 Tripartite Declaration, which maintained the military status quo in the region. Reports indicated, moreover, that the British and French were preparing an invasion force on the island of Cyprus, while the Israelis were doing likewise – ready, it was believed, to invade Jordan. Urged by the CIA to approve the assassination of Nasser, Eisenhower refused permission, point blank. It would inflame 'the Arab world' even if it succeeded, and besides, Nasser might be followed by a far worse leader. Eisenhower instructed Dulles to tell the Israelis to drop any idea of attacking Jordan, since that would only force other Arabs to turn to the Soviet Union for weapons with which to defend themselves, and 'the ultimate effect would be to sovietize the whole region'.[50]

To Eisenhower's chagrin, the British, French and Israelis persisted. The Israeli prime minister, David Ben-Gurion, seemed determined to take the West Bank, gambling on American distraction over the presidential election, the support of Jews in America, and Egyptian preoccupation with defending its newly nationalized canal against the French and British. Such an Israeli offensive, Eisenhower warned bluntly, 'cannot fail to bring catastrophe'.[51] In fact Eisenhower began to wonder whether he would 'have to use force' to stop the Israelis, even if this lost him the election. 'There would go New York, New Jersey, and Connecticut at least' he mused. But, as he told Dulles, he was not going to allow that fear 'to influence my judgement'.[52] 'I just can't figure out what the Israelis think they're up to. Maybe they're thinking they just *can't* survive without more land' Eisenhower confided to an aide. But how would expansionist Israeli tactics make more sense than Hitler's had, in the long run? 'I don't see how they can survive without coming to some honorable and peaceful terms with the whole Arab world that surrounds them.'[53]

On October 28, 1956, the Israelis attacked – not Jordan, as the CIA had predicted, but across the Egyptian-held Sinai Desert towards the Suez Canal, which they hoped the Egyptians would then close, giving the British and French a *casus belli* to invade also. The 'catastrophe' Eisenhower predicted had begun.

The London Tripartite Declaration, which Britain, France and the US had signed on May 25, 1950, had warned that, in the interests of peace and stability in the Middle East, the signatories would take military action if Israel or any of the Arab states violated 'frontiers or armistice lines'. With absolute indifference to their own Declaration,

France and Britain now worked not to stop the Israelis from violating borders, but to assist them, threatening to invade Egypt unless it withdrew its canal staff and military forces ten miles from the canal. Appalled, President Eisenhower issued a White House statement deploring such perfidy; 'he did not care in the slightest whether he is re-elected or not' his staff secretary noted; if the voting public threw him out the following week, at the November election, 'so be it'.[54] The president felt he had been double-crossed, and sided with Egypt. 'I've never seen great powers make such a complete mess and botch of things' Eisenhower lamented.[55] It was 'the biggest error of our time' he declared, and he called not only for a ceasefire, but also a military and trade embargo against Israel until it withdrew its forces.[56]

The smaller nations at the UN were overwhelmed with admiration for Eisenhower, as were American voters. Yet Eden simply ignored the president, went ahead with the Anglo-French part of the plot and on October 31, 1954 authorized the bombing of Cairo. Nasser retaliated by ordering the sinking of block-ships in the canal. In the last speech of his re-election campaign, Eisenhower said of the Middle East imbroglio and arrant colonialism on the part of his allies, 'We cannot subscribe to one law for the weak, another for the strong; one law for those opposing us, another for those allied with us. There can be only one law – or there shall be no peace.'[57]

Saddest of all to Eisenhower was that Britain's and France's myopia gave Russia a perfect opportunity to bring a popular anti-Soviet uprising in Hungary, which had begun on October 23, to heel with impunity. The USSR had promised to withdraw its troops; instead, it dispatched some 200,000 soldiers and 4,000 tanks to Budapest, where they murdered 40,000 Hungarian protesters. The CIA recommended airdropping supplies to the dissidents, while others urged Eisenhower to invade Hungary with US troops from bases in Germany, but he shook his weary head. Hungary, behind the Iron Curtain, was as 'inaccessible to us as Tibet'.[58] Ignoring world outrage over the crackdown (the Hungarian prime minister was forced to seek diplomatic asylum, but was intercepted by the Russians and executed), the Soviet prime minister, Nikolai Bulganin, suggested in a letter to Eisenhower that Russia and the US should join forces and together send troops into Egypt. 'If this war is not stopped', the Russian emperor warned his American counterpart, it could 'grow into a Third World War'.[59]

Eisenhower ignored Bulganin's suggestion, instead insisting that the UN police a ceasefire, with no troops permitted in the area from the Big Five powers: a ceasefire that, on November 6, 1956 – American election day – Prime Minister Eden reluctantly accepted, though Ben-Gurion did not.

In a major international crisis, the president had acted calmly, and had refused to go along with recidivist Anglo-French colonial imperialism, or Israeli adventurism. Although Democrats made further gains in the Senate and House of Representatives in the election, Eisenhower's personal popularity swept him back into the Oval Office, trouncing his presidential election opponent, Adlai Stevenson, for a second time. It was a landslide victory, Eisenhower defeating the Democrat by 457 to seventy-three in the Electoral College, and by almost ten million votes in ballots cast.

With Eisenhower commanding such manifest popular support, Republican and Democratic warmongers in Congress were silenced. The president was allowed to impose sanctions on Ben-Gurion – cutting off $40 million in private American tax gifts made to Israel and $60 million raised in bonds – in order to force him to submit to the UN resolution and withdraw Israeli forces from Gaza.

Ben-Gurion resisted, demanding the right to administer and police the 'strip' and to get international guarantees so that Israel could use the Gulf of Aqaba. But if Ben-Gurion hoped the Jewish lobby in America would compel Congress to force Eisenhower to follow such an agenda, as had been the case in Truman's presidency, he had mistaken Eisenhower's firmness. Congressional leaders left the matter up to the president, and on March 1, 1957, a chastened Golda Meir, on behalf of Ben-Gurion, announced Israel's 'full and complete withdrawal' from the territory it had overrun in the Suez war. Nasser thereupon ordered the Suez Canal – which would now be an Egyptian waterway – to be cleared. The war was over.

In retrospect Eisenhower's calmness throughout the Suez crisis bespoke his long military training and experience of war. By staying out of hostilities in the Middle East, and compelling the participants to withdraw – while ensuring the Soviets were denied a new presence in the region, or a reward for their mass butchery in Hungary – Eisenhower had shown great leadership.

Crises abroad were not the only ones Eisenhower sought to defuse.

In his handling of America's foreign policy the president enjoyed the support of the vast majority of Americans, as well as most members of Congress, and he was loath to endanger that buttress by espousing domestic causes that were divisive, such as civil rights. Events, however, now forced his hand.

The Supreme Court's *Brown* vs *Board of Education* ruling in 1954 'gave some time' to begin integrating segregated public schools in America, from kindergarten to twelfth grade, he had reminded his cabinet before the 1956 election. 'Our complaint is, that time is not being used' he warned. 'Instead states have merely sat down to say "We Defy."'[60] Even the right to vote was not being accorded to blacks. Out of almost a million African Americans living in Mississippi, for instance, only 7,000 were permitted to vote![61] Despite defeat in a monumental Civil War over slavery and states rights, southern Democrats had successfully resisted civil rights legislation since Reconstruction, and were clearly not going to give up on segregation without a fight. The FBI reported that membership of the Ku Klux Klan was soaring, as were sales of handguns in the South. As racial tensions escalated, and more blacks were murdered without law enforcement or judicial response (since white juries refused to find white defendants guilty), the danger of civil insurrection arose.

Eisenhower's natural instinct was to wait out the venom, but since it showed no sign of abating, he reluctantly – and to the fury of southern political leaders – submitted to Congress a modest civil rights bill in 1957, involving federal rather than state judicial process. The House of Representatives passed the bill on June 18, but southern senators baulked, and with a filibuster, which lasted a record twenty-four hours, mounted by Strom Thurmond (despite the senator having secretly fathered a child by a black woman) and other bigots, Lyndon Johnson as Majority Leader was forced to limit the legislation to an emasculated voting and housing rights bill which Eisenhower felt would require a decade to revisit. One northern senator called the bill 'a soup made from the shadow of a crow which had starved to death'.[62] Eisenhower signed the bill into law on September 9, 1957. Far from calming tempers in the South, however, it seemed only to inflame them, on both sides.

Even more threatening to whites in the South than voting rights was the impending desegregation of public schools, on which southern racists were prepared to take matters into their own hands. When schools reopened after the summer and education boards attempted to introduce black children into hitherto white-only schools, mob violence ensued – but with state governors backing the white mobs, not the black children. Governor Orval Faubus of Arkansas became an international celebrity by ordering the state's National Guard to stop nine black children from attending Little Rock's Central High School. It was not a message the president wanted to be broadcast to the world, and fearing further insurrection, Eisenhower – who was vacationing in Newport – summoned Governor Faubus to Rhode Island to explain himself.

On September 14, 1957, Faubus faced the president. The governor had been an infantry major in Europe in World War II, serving under General Eisenhower, who as president now had the power to federalize the National Guard unless Faubus followed the law. A trial of strength between the president and a state governor could have only one outcome, Eisenhower warned: 'the state will lose'.[63] He recommended the governor return to Arkansas and ensure the black children be permitted to enter the school in safety. Faubus promised Eisenhower he would do so but, once back in Arkansas, reneged on his word, resulting in mayhem as hordes of white racists, summoned by telephone and radio, poured into Little Rock with guns and steel bars to bar the black children from entering.

By September 23, 1957, the situation had become both a national and an international disaster. Shortly after midday Eisenhower called the head of the US Army, General Maxwell Taylor – a paratroop commander who had dropped on D-Day, under Eisenhower's supreme command – and by nightfall some 500 paratroopers of the 101st Airborne Division had assumed positions in the centre of the city, with bayonets fixed. Governor Faubus went on national television to decry the 'warm red blood of patriotic citizens staining the cold, naked, unsheathed knives' of the airborne division's soldiers holding back the white mob, while Senator Richard Russell charged the president with using Hitler-like storm-trooper tactics on ordinary Americans.[64]

For Eisenhower, these charges took a great deal of swallowing. The fact that the US Army had to be called out to protect less than a dozen students seeking to go to school was a terrible indictment of white bigotry. The Soviets, Eisenhower said, were 'gloating over this incident and using it everywhere to misrepresent our whole nation'.[65] Did Faubus and his ilk have no shame? 'Failure to act', he replied in a letter to Senator Russell, 'would be tantamount to acquiescence in anarchy and the dissolution of the union.'[66]

A Gallup poll three weeks later showed 58 per cent of respondents supported Eisenhower's 'handling of the situation at Little Rock'. Over 30 per cent disapproved, however, and in Arkansas Faubus became a folk hero, especially when, as Eisenhower feared, Faubus closed the school altogether once the National Guard was defederalized at the end of the school year. No high-school education, in the governor's view, was better than integration.

Eisenhower's decision to send the 101st Airborne Division into Little Rock marked the pinnacle of his presidency, as an upholder of the Constitution: a signal to the world that, in the struggle of free peoples against the tyranny of Communism, he would not accept the tyranny of white bigots and lynch mobs in his own country. As he clarified in his letter to Senator Russell, 'I completely fail to comprehend your comparison of our troops to Hitler's storm troopers. In one case military power was used to further the ambitions and purposes of a ruthless dictator; in the other to preserve the institutions of free government.'[67]

Eisenhower was ill-rewarded for his reluctant firmness, however. Though liberals congratulated him, he knew from his dealings with Faubus – a Democratic governor – that anti-black racism could not be cauterized permanently by force, any more than it had been by Union troops in and after the Civil War. It was a peculiarly American disease that had infected successive waves of white European immigrants to the South for 300 years, and in the months following the Central High School crisis, Eisenhower's popularity, once so unassailable, began to dip – especially after news was broadcast on October 4, 1957 that Russia had successfully fired into orbit a satellite they called the 'travelling companion': Sputnik 1.

Americans were stunned by First Secretary Khrushchev's statement in Moscow that the USSR had 'won' the space race – and, by extension, the arms race. With no bombers able to strike the United States, the USSR seemed to have performed an end run: capable now, by implication, of launching not only a satellite but nuclear-armed intercontinental ballistic missiles, reminiscent of V-2 bombs in World War II.

Such missiles would be capable of striking every American city with impunity, since interception would be impossible. Even subsequent retaliation was questionable, given that three quarters of the American B-52 fleet would be destroyed on the ground in the initial Russian onslaught. Some US advisers even counselled Eisenhower to launch an immediate pre-emptive atomic holocaust on the Soviet Union, before its missile launchers were operational.

The president demurred, though he did give the go-ahead for more hydrogen-bomb testing, more B-52s to be churned out, and accelerated competition between the navy and army in developing America's own sputnik.

Making haste, unfortunately, only produced less speed. On December 6, 1957, America's first attempted satellite launch ended ignominiously – the rocket exploded only a few seconds after blast-off. The sequel, on February 5, 1958, fared no better, exploding within the first minute. Moreover it carried only a 4 lb payload, as compared with *Sputnik 3*'s successful 3,000 lb payload, launched into orbit in May 1958.

By then Eisenhower's once magisterial presidency was reeling, the president having suffered a stroke on November 25, 1957, aged sixty-seven.

Though in due course he recovered all his faculties, Eisenhower fell into depression. In January 1958, he told his Secretary of State, John Foster Dulles, that given his heart attack, his ileitis and then the stroke, he should, if he was unable to attend a planned meeting of NATO, perhaps 'abdicate'.[68]

Fearful of Richard Nixon, the vice president, commanding the US nuclear arsenal, Dulles dissuaded the president. Nevertheless the writing appeared to be on the wall. Eisenhower had never liked or trusted Nixon, nor did he feel confident about Nixon holding the reins of America's imperial power. More important, Eisenhower was losing confidence in himself. A number of the president's most senior cabinet officials had already abandoned ship, America was in the grip of an economic recession, unemployment was approaching 8 per cent, and there was pressure to offer federal funding for people to build their own nuclear shelters. Though Eisenhower tried to pour oil on troubled waters in his press conferences, speeches and addresses to the nation, he had never been an articulate speaker (as opposed to writer), and his paternalistic phrasing made him appear increasingly out of touch and unreasonably complacent, thus providing ammunition to ambitious Democrats like Lyndon Johnson to begin eyeing the throne.

At the nadir of his depression in February 1958, Eisenhower drew up a secret personal agreement with the vice president, allowing Nixon to decide whether to assume presidential power if Eisenhower was too incapacitated to hand over authority. Dulles was himself terminally ill; the mood was bleak. Then on March 27, 1958, Bulganin resigned. Nikita Sergeyevich Khrushchev became both Soviet premier and party leader, and thus the effective leader of the USSR. It was possible, Eisenhower reckoned, that by personal diplomacy the relationship between the two world superpowers could be transformed – for the better.

Given the attention paid to the later legendary nuclear confrontation between Kennedy and Khrushchev, which brought the world to the very brink of World War III, its prequel should not be forgotten.

As president, Dwight Eisenhower saw his role as that of a conservative brake on younger imperialistic hotheads, far preferring to use what historians called 'hidden hand' strategy: using the CIA to police compliant regimes across the world, such as Iran (where the CIA overthrew the prime minister and put the Shah back on his Peacock Throne) and South America (where the president of Guatemala was overthrown). Dealing with Khrushchev, however, was of a different order, and Eisenhower's failure would, sadly, tarnish his legacy after six extraordinary years of world leadership.

It was not for want of trying. Deploring the arms race, and saddened by the death on May 24, 1958 of his Secretary of State, John Foster Dulles, Eisenhower decided to try personal peacemaking with the USSR. On July 10, 1958, the president therefore issued an invitation to Khrushchev to visit the US and twelve days later Khrushchev accepted, the visit scheduled for the summer of 1959. It would be the first time a leader of the Soviet Union had ever visited the United States, its former ally – but since World War II's aftermath, its sworn 'imperialist enemy'.

Khrushchev's tape-recorded memoirs later revealed the profound suspicion he had to overcome before leaving the USSR in September 1959. 'I'll admit I was worried' he recalled. He'd already travelled to India and to England, 'But this was different – this was America.' He didn't think the US was necessarily superior to Britain in culture, 'but American power was of decisive significance'.[69] Power *mattered*.

Khrushchev had in fact met General Eisenhower twice before, in Moscow in 1945 and Geneva in 1955. He'd sparred with Vice President Nixon at the opening of the American National Exhibition in Moscow in late July 1959, in the show kitchen of a labour-saving modern American home (the so-called 'Kitchen Debate'). That, however, had been on Russian soil, where Khrushchev could mercilessly mock idle American consumerism before compliant Soviet reporters. Now, however, he would be on American soil, with only his foreign minister, Andrei Gromyko, and their wives. Even the planned visit to the president's hideaway home in Maryland, renamed Camp David for Eisenhower's grandson, aroused paranoid fears (calmed when informed it was simply a dacha, and thus a special honour). 'You shouldn't forget that all during Stalin's life, right up to the day he died', Khrushchev noted in his memoirs, the Russian dictator 'kept telling us we'd never be able to stand up to the forces of imperialism, that the first time we came into contact with the outside world our enemies would smash us to pieces; we would get confused and be unable to defend our land. In his words, we would become "agents" of some kind.'[70]

Khrushchev admitted to having butterflies, his nerves 'strained with excitement' that he 'was about to meet with the leader of the country which represented the biggest military threat in the world and to discuss with him the major issues of the times: peaceful coexistence, an agreement on the ban of nuclear weapons, the reduction of armed forces, the withdrawal of troops, and the liquidation of bases on foreign territories. I was also looking forward to establishing contacts with the American business world.'[71]

Eisenhower was also nervous with anticipation. He and Khrushchev shared many common experiences. Khrushchev, three years younger than Eisenhower and even balder, had been born the son of an illiterate peasant and raised in rural poverty. 'Our countries have different social systems' Khrushchev acknowledged at the state dinner held in his honour at the White House. 'We believe our system to be better – and you believe yours to be better. But surely we should not bring quarrels out on to the arena of open struggle. Let history judge which of us is right. If we agree this principle, then we can build our relations on the basis of peace and friendship.'[72]

If only! Eisenhower took the Russian premier in his presidential helicopter to Camp David, where Khrushchev regaled the president with stories of Comrade Stalin and the war in Russia. Known as 'The Butcher of the Ukraine', Khrushchev had, as political commissar, been responsible for ensuring Stalin's orders were carried out on the battlefields of Kiev, Kharkov, Stalingrad and Kursk – with monumental, often criminal casualties (such as Stalin's refusal to evacuate the city of Stalingrad and to fight on the more defensible high ground to the east), as Khrushchev told Eisenhower.

The president admitted to finding Khrushchev's war stories 'fascinating'. But in the context of the post-war world, the question was how could the two empires coexist more peacefully in the present, and future. Eisenhower even took Khrushchev to see his farm at Gettysburg and promised to send one of his prime Angus cattle to Russia. The two men confided in each other that they were constantly being badgered and cajoled by their military advisers to spend more money on weapons and defence, thus constantly ratcheting up the arms race, as before World War I. ('How many times can you kill the same man?' Eisenhower had asked one of his Republican gadflies from Congress, in exasperation.[73]) But when the two imperial leaders discussed practical measures to further 'peace and friendship', it became clear there was little either emperor could do without impeachment, removal or assassination. Congress, dominated since the 1958 midterm elections by right-leaning Democrats on defence, would never agree to arms control that would inhibit American nuclear superiority; the Soviets would never allow weapons inspections in their closed society. Beyond the military stand-off, moreover, there was the political system divide. Khrushchev was used to banging the table in order to get things done, indeed prided himself on his power as a virtual dictator, imagining that, though 'you [Americans] are richer than we are at present . . . tomorrow', by the ability of the Politburo to direct the Soviet economy, 'we will be as rich as you are, and the day after tomorrow we will be even richer'.[74]

Eisenhower could only shake his head. He had sent Khrushchev across America to visit American people and factories for ten days, and to see at first hand state and city – as opposed to federal – government. He had arranged for him to visit Hollywood and privately owned farms, hoping the premier might see the cumulative, peaceful energy of individualism, once unleashed and encouraged in an educated, democratic society observing a written constitution and federal, state and local laws.

The effort, however, seemed to have the opposite effect to the one Eisenhower had intended. Though impressing Khrushchev with capitalism's undeniable virtues, the trip seemed actually to raise Khrushchev's anxiety level rather than diminish it, increasing his sense of Soviet inferiority in everything save repressive militarism and secret police. Moreover Eisenhower was polite but implacable over West Berlin, and the need for access routes from the West to remain under western Allied military aegis; was unwilling to countenance the disbandment of NATO merely on the promise of Russian military withdrawal from the occupied countries of eastern Europe; was unable to promise an end to Congress' trade embargo, or forgiveness of debt, since he did not have that power.

The talks between the two emperors – both born into the 'working class' – thus 'failed', as Khrushchev put it. The arms race – or rather, the Russian race to try and catch up with America's technological advances – would go on. The 'Americans had us surrounded on all sides with their military bases' Khrushchev noted. Russia 'lagged significantly behind the US in both warheads and missiles, and the US was out of range of our bombers. We could blast into dust America's allies in Europe and Asia, but America itself – with its huge economic and military potential – was beyond our reach . . . I was convinced that as long as the US held a big advantage over us, we couldn't submit to international disarmament'[75] or to having 'inspectors criss-crossing around the Soviet Union' who 'would have discovered that we were in a relatively weak position', leading them 'to attack us'.[76]

'I could tell Eisenhower was deflated' Khrushchev recalled. 'He looked like a man who had fallen through a hole in the ice and been dragged from the river with freezing water still dripping off of him. Lunchtime came. It was more like a funeral than a wedding feast. Well, maybe that's going too far: it wasn't so much like a funeral as it was like a meal served at the bedside of a critically ill patient.' The two men then travelled from Camp David to Washington by car. 'I could see how depressed and worried Eisenhower was; and I knew how he felt, but there wasn't anything I could do to help him.'[77]

Khrushchev's visit convinced him the United States was outstripping the USSR in every area of production, both civilian and military. Like a chess player who knows he will lose if a game is continued methodically, on his return to Moscow Khrushchev sought every opportunity to turn the tables by provoking dramas that would put the United States (and its allies) on the defensive. The first was sabre-rattling over Berlin. When Eisenhower refused to be disconcerted by Khrushchev's threatened deadline for the western Allies to vacate West Berlin (a deadline Khrushchev had to keep postponing), thus leading the Russian premier to lose face at home, Khrushchev grew even more denunciatory of American 'imperialism' in his speeches. Nothing seemed to go his way, however, until, to his surprise and delight, he was presented on May 1, 1960 with the perfect opportunity to trick the man who, by virtue of his patience, goodwill and firmness, had become his nemesis.

A disarmament and détente summit meeting had been planned to take place in Paris in mid-May, and in order to have a better idea of current Russian operational missile capability, President Eisenhower had authorized the use of the high-flying American spy planes, the U-2s. Aware that, if shot down by a new Russian SAM missile, this might jeopardize the Paris summit, as well as his own visit to the USSR planned thereafter (in return for Khrushchev's to the US the previous September), Eisenhower only permitted a single final flight which confirmed that there was no missile 'gap', as both Democrat and Republican loudmouths were proclaiming. The US still had overwhelming nuclear superiority.

Had Eisenhower accepted the CIA report, and had he refused to sanction another, he might well have saved his presidency from the abyss into which it now fell – much as Truman's opportunity to stop General MacArthur's forces from crossing the 38th Parallel in 1950 might have saved his. But the deputy director of the CIA begged for one more U-2 flight to confirm the lack of Russian ICBMs, and Eisenhower reluctantly gave his authorization.

The U-2, unreachable by Soviet fighter planes, was, however, hit by lucky Russian anti-aircraft fire, and brought down on May 1, 1960, hundreds of miles inside Russian territory, exactly as Eisenhower had feared. CIA officials hoped against hope that its pilot, Captain Gary Powers, had been killed, and could tell no tales.

Unfortunately for them, Powers parachuted to safety, thereby giving Khrushchev a wholly unexpected way to trap Eisenhower and administer a humiliating snub to the Americans. It was childlike, yet would have dire consequences.

For days Khrushchev deliberately kept the survival of the American pilot quiet, as well as the tell-tale remnants of his plane. As news of a missing plane got out, Eisenhower and the US government were compelled to issue a series of ever more embarrassing lies, beginning with outright denial of any mishap, followed by an assertion that the flight had only been a weather-reporting plane over Turkey that had strayed. Finally, like a magician, Khrushchev brought the drama to a climax by exhibiting on Soviet state television the captive pilot, Gary Powers, his incriminating spy film and bits of the U-2.

Premier Khrushchev's performance, as public theatre, was masterly, even claiming the flight had been a deliberate affront to the Soviet Union's May Day festival. In a country relying on patriotism rather than home appliances, it earned the delight of the Politburo and the outrage of the Russian people: a propaganda victory of the first magnitude in an otherwise losing imperial game. However, in then demanding that President Eisenhower – whom Khrushchev portrayed as having been probably unaware of what his intelligence services were doing – issue a humiliating rebuke to his subordinate military advisers in America, and fire someone senior in order to complete the Russian global propaganda coup, 'The Butcher of the Ukraine' made an unfortunate miscalculation.

Eisenhower was a man of his word, and of great natural dignity. He was also a soldier by training as well as having a long, distinguished career in the military. His high sense of honour – rather than his political common sense – refused to let him either scapegoat anyone else, or deny his own decision as commander-in-chief. He thus took personal and public responsibility for the mission, explaining in a statement that intelligence-gathering was often regrettable, but part of national security in the real world. Yet for the very reason of national security – i.e. secrecy – he could not explain publicly the most vital aspect of the affair: that the previous spy flight had proved there was no disadvantageous missile 'gap' between the United States and the USSR, as Democratic hopefuls such as senators John F. Kennedy and Lyndon B. Johnson were claiming in the presidential primaries.

Keeping silent over the U-2's revelation, Eisenhower was thus forced to fall on his sword, not only causing him to look ineffective at home, but giving Khrushchev another huge propaganda opportunity. A veritable battle between the two empires began to rage in their countries' press, radio and television, with neither side backing down. The issue grew bigger by the day, and threatened to overwhelm what should have been a constructive Paris summit conference, in the interests of détente, only two weeks after the downed flight.

Instead of Gary Powers' flight thus providing Eisenhower with the quiet confidence to be magnanimous at the Paris conference table, safe in the knowledge that America enjoyed nuclear operational superiority, his May Day mission had turned into a Mayday call.

Eisenhower flew to Paris intending to confess to Khrushchev that as he had indeed authorized the U-2 mission, but had now ordered that no more spy flights would ever be flown over Russia – in part because orbiting American satellite rockets would soon be able to do the job. He left it too late, however. According to his diplomatic aide Oleg Troyanovsky, Khrushchev decided on a whim to sabotage the summit, and use American embarrassment as the launch pad for a new propaganda campaign that would mask Russian military inferiority – indeed give the Soviet Union time to catch up militarily with the United States. He would therefore stage a new opera, demanding at the conference that Eisenhower openly apologize for the violation of Russian airspace 'and punish those responsible. He went on to say that it seemed next to impossible that Eisenhower could accept those terms. Consequently the summit would almost certainly collapse before really starting.' Those Russians who were present felt sick: 'most, if not all, were upset at the realization that we were sliding back to the worst times of the Cold War and would have to start from Square One again.' The deputy Russian foreign minister went around the embassy in Paris repeating 'What a situation! What a situation!'[78]

The charade duly took place on May 16, 1960, when Khrushchev asked his host, President de Gaulle, for the right to speak first. Then, to the consternation of the assembled world leaders and their staffs, the Soviet premier began his promised tirade against President Eisenhower and the American government, and their perfidy over the U-2 incident. De Gaulle asked Khrushchev to lower his voice as 'the acoustics in this room are excellent. We can all hear the chairman.'[79] Even the Russian delegation became concerned how to 'keep him from overplaying the part of a person outraged at the insult suffered'.[80] When Khrushchev raised his arm, pointing at the ceiling, and complained he had been 'overflown', de Gaulle pointed out that France, too, had already been overflown eighteen times by *Sputnik 4*, launched the previous day, 'without my permission. How do I know you do not have cameras aboard which are taking pictures of my country?'

At this, Khrushchev became even angrier, denying the possibility in strangely religious terms for a Communist atheist: 'As God is my witness, my hands are clean. You don't think I would do a thing like that?'[81] Eisenhower then attempted to cool the temperature. He said he was sad, but not upset that Khrushchev had seen fit to withdraw his invitation to visit the USSR, but he hoped they could move on to the more substantive matters of disarmament.

It was no good, however; attitudes had been struck, pride ruffled, dignity compromised.[82] Khrushchev recalled how, when he was done ranting, he 'sat down. Frankly, I was all worked up, feeling combative and exhilarated. As my kind of simple folk would say, I was spoiling for a fight. I had caused quite a commotion.' He claimed that when Eisenhower and his delegation stood up, the summit came to an end. 'Then we all left. We had set off an explosion that scattered the four delegations into their separate chambers. The conference table, which was to have united us, had crumbled into dust.'[83] Metaphorically this was true; the chance for meaningful détente between the competing empires was set back by decades.

With his failure to force the West to surrender West Berlin or its access routes to the city, then his amateur dramatics in Paris, Khrushchev had turned himself into a world heavyweight shadow-boxer instead of wise peacemaker. 'We had shown that anyone who slapped us on our cheek would get his head kicked off' said the former commissar, recalling his pride over the Paris summit. 'The Americans had been taught a lesson. They had learned the limit of our toler-ance. They now knew that American imperialism would not go unpunished if it overstepped this limit. We showed the whole world that while all other western powers might crawl on their bellies in front of America's mighty financial and industrial capital, we wouldn't bow down – not for one second.' Under no circumstances would he or his fellow Soviets 'let ourselves be abused and degraded'.[84] Instead, he would – as at Stalingrad and Kursk – switch to counter-attack. In America.

Travelling to New York and denouncing the 'mighty' American 'imperialists' at the United Nations General Assembly in the autumn of 1960, castigating the old colonial nations for their slowness in granting independence to their colonies, and publicly befriending the new Cuban dictator Fidel Castro at his downtrodden hotel in Harlem, Khrushchev now posed and strutted as a Communist hero to the Third World. Wherever there were cameras, he felt obliged to make a scene. In the Big Apple on September 29, 1960, for example, he famously banged the United Nations podium with his fists, then, on October 11, his desk with his shoe. As Oleg Troyanovsky (who accompanied Khrushchev) euphemistically recalled, there had always been something 'puckish' in Khrushchev's nature, but now it was exhibited in 'an irresistible urge to humiliate the prince of Darkness, as he had begun to regard Eisenhower'.

For Eisenhower, the sight of Premier Khrushchev, emperor of the Soviet Union, turning into a dangerous and unpredictable clown, was disheartening. Eisenhower had had to deal with other bombastic leaders in his lifetime – MacArthur, Montgomery and Patton in particular – and he did not allow Khrushchev's antics to spoil his day. Nevertheless the picture of Khrushchev acting out in the final weeks before the 1960 election (which would mark the end of Eisenhower's distinguished eight-year presidency) was depressing. The two nominated American presidential candidates of the major parties – Vice President Nixon and Senator John F. Kennedy – seemed now to be competing not to pursue peace, but to be seen as toughest on defence and military spending, with ridiculous allegations of a missile 'gap' between the US and Russia, and nonsensical rhetoric over Cuba. The chance to make quiet progress with Russia over nuclear disarmament (especially in the knowledge that Communist China was building an atomic bomb) had gone up in U-2's smoke, ruining Eisenhower's imperial legacy.

In a televised farewell address from the Oval Office, Eisenhower memorably warned against the country's own 'military industrial complex' becoming too potent. An 'immense military establishment' and a 'large arms industry', acting in concert, were seeking 'unwarranted influence' in 'every city, every statehouse, every office of the federal government,' thus posing the risk of a 'disastrous rise of misplaced power'.[85] Then, on January 20, 1961, Eisenhower handed over the burdens of office to his successor, the young Democratic senator and president-elect John F. Kennedy, who had beaten Nixon by the narrowest of margins in the November 1960 election. 'I had longed to give the world a lasting peace' Eisenhower would write in retirement. 'I was only able to contribute', he lamented, 'a stalemate.'[86]

## Part Three: Private Life

From the time he was a child the people around Dwight Eisenhower wanted to win his affection, and his approval. This was the secret of his leadership in war, but also in peace, as a politician. Highly intelligent, with a great gift of empathy, Eisenhower was astute enough to recognize the power of benevolent charisma in modern communications, as FDR had shown. And with the era of television, after World War II, he found himself in a position to apply his famous smile to the living-room screen. Eisenhower became the first president to give televised press conferences. Taking instruction and advice from American television's star anchor, Edward R. Murrow, and from Hollywood actor Robert Montgomery, he learned how to put himself across not as an actor but as himself: a man with natural dignity, modesty and genuineness – a man you would be proud to have living next door. Thenceforth 'likeability' would become a crucial ingredient in the public's expectations of a presidential candidate – to the detriment of Eisenhower's heir apparent, 'Tricky Dick' Nixon, who sounded wise on radio, but looked like a crook on television.

The ability to inspire affection raised, of course, the question of fidelity. Few charismatic male leaders exude magnetism without being tempted by the rewards. Like Franklin D. Roosevelt, Eisenhower was no exception. His strict upbringing by his Jehovah's Witness mother was a lifelong moral compass, but not enough to fight all temptation. From schooldays onwards Eisenhower chain-smoked as many as four packs a day. He adored football, and was gutted when a knee injury at West Point precluded further play. He also hunted and loved to fish. Once rain and darkness fell, however, poker and bridge, with bourbon, were Eisenhower's favourite pastime, as they were for Truman. Eisenhower's prowess at the poker table helped fund his cadetship at West Point, to the point where he was sometimes barred from groups.

Eisenhower's love life followed an equally conventional course. Like Truman, he had first set his marital sights on a fellow high-school student: a blue-eyed blonde beauty named Gladys Harding. On August

5, 1915, on his graduation from West Point, Eisenhower asked Gladys
to marry him. As in Truman's case the romance was sabotaged by the
young lady's parent – in Gladys Harding's case her father, who predicted
that 'That Eisenhower kid will never amount to anything.'[87]

Fearful of her father's reaction, Gladys – who was set on making
a career as a pianist – temporized, leading Eisenhower to pour his
heart out in a series of lovelorn letters that demonstrated how romantic
he was, behind his disciplined, ambitious facade. 'More than ever, now,
I want to hear you say the three words [I love you] with "Better than
I ever have anyone in the world"' he implored Gladys. 'If you can say
that to me . . . then I'll know that I've won. From that time – if it
ever comes – I'll know you're mine – no matter where you go – or
what you do . . . For girl I do love you and want you to KNOW it –
to be as certain of it as I am – and to believe in me and trust me as
you would your dad.'[88]

Gladys Harding wouldn't, however, citing her own musical ambition. Thus, when the handsome young second lieutenant on the
rebound was posted to Fort Sam Houston in San Antonio, Texas, he
turned his attention to a new campaign: this time to win the heart of
a flighty eighteen-year-old, Mamie Doud: the short, pretty, spoiled
daughter of a rich dad who would deny his daughter nothing, and
who condoned the romance. The pair made an unlikely couple – 'a
classic romantic mismatch' in the words of one biographer, between
a twenty-five-year-old penniless infantry officer (known as a 'woman-
hater' after the collapse of his relationship with Gladys Harding) and
an 'outrageous flirt', a vivacious teenage air-head, fresh out of
'finishing' school.[89]

'The girl I'm running around with now is named Miss Doud, from
Denver' Eisenhower wrote to another high-school friend. '[She] winters
here. Pretty nice – but awful strong for society – which often bores
me. But we get along well together – and I'm at her house whenever
I'm off duty.'[90] Perhaps hoping his letter would be passed on to Gladys
Harding, the unrequited love of his life, he repeated he would write
more fully 'about the girl I run around with *since* I learned that
G[ladys]. H[arding]. cared so terribly for her *work*'.[91]

The wedding of Dwight D. Eisenhower and Miss Mamie Doud
took place on July 1, 1916, in the Doud family home in Denver. For a
man of such high intelligence and ambition, however, marriage to

Mamie – an inveterate socialite – became a trial, as did the profession of soldiering after World War I. Their first son, Little Ike or 'Ikky', died of scarlet fever and meningitis in 1921, and something of the light went out of Eisenhower's genial personality, causing people to find him difficult to fathom. 'Ike has the most engaging grin of anybody I ever met' his wife would later say of him. 'Though when he turns it off,' she added, 'his face is as bleak as the plains of Kansas.'[92]

The death of their first son steeled both Ike and Mamie for the difficult years that followed in different postings, from Panama to the Philippines. It was neither a passionate nor a spiritual union, neither calming nor mentally stimulating. Instead it became yet another test of Eisenhower's loyalty and patience – as was his career, serving under men like Douglas MacArthur – and in curbing his own explosive temper.

For Mamie Doud it was also a long trial. Eisenhower preferred to stay at home and read, or spend time with close friends, rather than party or 'socialize'. 'Ike is the kind', she would say ruefully, 'who would rather give you a fried egg in his own home than take you to the finest nightclub in the world.'[93] He was obstinate, too. 'No woman can run him' she confided to a girlfriend. And later to her grand-daughter-in-law: 'There can be only one star in the heaven, Sugar, and there is only one way to live with an Eisenhower. Let him have his own way.'[94] Divorce was mooted in 1922 and again in 1936, in view of Mamie's flirtations, but neither she nor Eisenhower wanted the stigma or the adverse effect it might have on their surviving second son, David. They loyally soldiered on, so to speak, until in 1942 Eisenhower's female driver, resurrecting shades of Gladys Harding, turned the general's head.

A former model for Worth, Kay Summersby was a stunningly attractive, tall, slender, Irish redhead, daughter of a British cavalry officer, married to a British officer in India and being sued for divorce for carrying on an affair with an American officer in England when Eisenhower became her boss. Thereafter she devoted herself to Eisenhower's welfare and comfort. Inevitably tongues wagged – including Kay's. She later wrote two books, *Eisenhower Was My Boss* and *Past Forgetting*, the latter claiming that she'd had a wartime love affair with Eisenhower, with much fun, tenderness and kissing but no sexual consummation, after a trial-and-error performance had ended in impotence on the general's return to London, prior to D-Day. This may indeed have been the simple truth; Eisenhower's deep loyalty to Mamie, after almost thirty years of marriage and the death of their first child, may well have made the sexual act of infidelity, or gratification, simply too frightening, given also the enormous responsibilities he carried as supreme commander in Europe and the hopes and fears of so many millions of soldiers and citizens of the free world vested in him.

If Eisenhower could not consummate his love affair with Kay, however, did he propose marriage to Mrs Summersby, which might allow him to become potent again? No less a person than President Truman later believed so, recalling a letter which Eisenhower purportedly sent General Marshall at the end of World War II, 'saying that he wanted to come back to the United States and divorce Mrs Eisenhower so that he could marry this Englishwoman'. It was, Truman remembered, 'a very, very shocking thing to have done, for a man who was a general in the army of the United States' – a five-star general, no less. 'Well,' Truman went on, 'Marshall wrote him back a letter the like of which I never did see. He said that if . . . Eisenhower even came close to doing such a thing, he'd not only bust him out of the army, he'd see to it that never for the rest of his life would he be able to draw a peaceful breath . . . a living hell. General Marshall didn't often lose his temper, but when he did, it was a corker.' And, Truman claimed, 'one of the last things I did as president, I got those letters from his file in the Pentagon, and I destroyed them'.[95]

Published in 1973 by a journalist and interviewer, Truman's allegation could never be verified – indeed the journalist's recording of the conversation was never found.[96] Most historians discounted it as the rambling of an old man, the summer before his own death, and four years after Eisenhower's. Could such a story have been invented out of thin air? Even Mamie suspected (and accused) Eisenhower of having an affair with Kay, and Eisenhower did admit to Mamie that he had briefly been infatuated. Enough to countenance retirement from the army and a post-war life with Kay, though? If so, he would not have been the first American to dread return to a sterile marriage at home, after the extraordinary experience of struggle and military conquest in Europe; moreover the days he'd spent with Mamie at her apartment in New York, before flying to England to undertake command of the D-Day invasion, had been miserable and had held out little prospect of post-war happiness.

Whatever the truth, reality set in once he was home. 'Kay, it's impossible. There's nothing I can do' Eisenhower had said when accidentally meeting Kay in New York in 1948 (he had arranged for her to become an American citizen).[97] The great general, vanquisher of the German armies in the West, thus opted for the nobler, more loyal outcome – and became, as a result, the hugely popular president of the United States, with Mamie an all-American, beloved and devoted First Lady, who said she liked to reach over in the double bed she'd ordered for Ike's return from the war 'and pat Ike on his old bald head anytime I want to'.[98] The bed, in a refurbished pink and green room, became Mamie's command post, from which she rarely rose before midday, relishing the White House personal staff and the social distinction that came with the title after so many years of isolation, while 'the general' was away fighting.

Something of his long-suffering stoicism, along with his genial nature, was thus the mark of Eisenhower's character, and gave confidence to Americans that the empire was in safe hands. Even his passion for golf, though mocked by comedians, symbolized a president who knew the importance of relaxation as a counterpart to his high sense of duty (and his constantly controlled temper). He read Westerns in the same way – as escapism from the problems he faced by day. In 1950 he had purchased a farmhouse at Gettysburg as a country retreat (the first house he ever owned). There, inspired by Winston Churchill, he began to paint, avidly and therapeutically. He accepted gifts, just as he took for granted the valet who dressed him each day, the drivers and pilots who transported him, the staff who worked for him, as well as the millionaire companions who vacationed and visited with him. Yet woe betide any who expected special favours as a result! He prided himself on his absolute impartiality, which made him the greatest internationalist American since FDR, perhaps even greater. 'Without allies or associates the leader is just an adventurer like Genghis Khan' he liked to say.[99]

Legions of subordinates, from MacArthur to Patton and Bradley, decried this impartiality, accusing Eisenhower of being insufficiently nationalistic; yet it was this very quality that made him stand head and shoulders above any other American of his time. He was slow to advance the cause of racial integration at home (and wholly ignorant of the merits of feminism), but in accepting the Supreme Court decision on public education, and in ordering the 101st Airborne Division to Little Rock, he had shown he would not shirk his ultimate duty. Though disparaged by racists, moreover, he never questioned the rightness of his action. He had become, he recognized, the embodiment of the noble American in an age of empire, with a duty to represent all Americans, not simply a party.

As President Theodore Roosevelt had famously recommended, Eisenhower talked softly abroad, but wielded a big, indeed atomic, stick – which, unlike his predecessor, he never had occasion to use. Under his presidency America flourished economically, without bankrupting itself through military expenditure and overreach. 'Rarely in American history has the craving for tranquility and moderation commanded more general support' wrote the pioneer political pollster Samuel Lubell, who did door-to-door research.[100] Though mocked by historians after his departure from the White House for his lack of flamboyance in the new 1960s decade – he was ranked twenty-second of thirty-one presidents, just above Andrew Johnson, who was impeached – Eisenhower had fulfilled his generation's trust.[101] He died on March 28, 1969, at Walter Reed Army Hospital in Washington DC, and was buried in the grounds of the Presidential Library established in his name. He was, after Theodore Roosevelt, Woodrow Wilson and FDR, probably the greatest American president of the twentieth century – and, in the years after his departure from the White House, his calm, worldly experience and safe hands would be sorely missed.

# CHAPTER FOUR

# JOHN F. KENNEDY

Later deified

Democrat
35th President
(January 20, 1961–November 22, 1963)

## Part One: The Road to the White House

John Fitzgerald Kennedy was born in Brookline, a suburb of Boston, Massachusetts on May 29, 1917. He was named after his maternal grandfather, John 'HoneyFitz' Fitzgerald, who made history as a congressman and then as the first Irish-American Catholic mayor of Boston, a New England port-city in which WASP (White Anglo-Saxon Protestant) elitism had secured virtually all senior political posts since the Pilgrims landed in 1620. 'No Irish Need Apply' had still been a common sign on hiring boards when HoneyFitz grew up. Hugely popular, funny and hardworking, Fitzgerald *had* applied, however – and had won. Thereafter he humorously referred to the difference between himself and the Cabots and the Lodges, whose families had arrived early in the seventeenth century, as the difference of 'only a few ships'.

John F. Kennedy's father, by contrast, was a man of little humour, save that of cynicism. Son of an East Boston bar owner, Joseph P. Kennedy was clever, ruthlessly ambitious, and made history in America in a different way: first as its youngest bank president, then wartime shipyard manager, stock-market swindler, millionaire movie production company owner, and first chairman of the Securities Exchange Commission (SEC) in New York (appointed by FDR as 'a thief to catch a thief'). As reward for his support for FDR, Kennedy asked to be made US ambassador to London in 1938. A passionate isolationist (he had avoided military service in World War I), Kennedy opposed involvement in Europe's troubles, and by 1940, as Britain faced Hitler's Third Reich alone, Ambassador Kennedy became Churchill's bitterest foe in London.

Joseph P. Kennedy Jr, Joseph P. Kennedy's eldest son, was a chip off the block – a devoted but shallow-minded mouthpiece for his father's sympathies with the Nazis and American isolationism in 1940 and 1941. Ambassador Kennedy's second son, John F. Kennedy, however, was made of different stuff. Suffering recurrent illnesses, he spent much of his childhood in either a hospital, sick room or sanatorium. He disliked the Catholic boarding school to which his devout but distant mother sent him, so was switched at age fourteen to his brother's Episcopalian boarding school, Choate, in Connecticut. There he scored at the top of intelligence tests, read voraciously, yet did little class work and was finally threatened with expulsion for irreverence and subversion. When asked by a school-affiliated psychologist why he so misbehaved, the seventeen-year-old replied: 'If my brother were not so efficient, it would be easier for me to be efficient. He does it so much better than I do.'[1]

While no other member of the Kennedy family had ever willingly picked up a book, 'Jack' Kennedy was never without one. Endowed with a near-photographic memory and self-deprecating humour he was, like Dwight Eisenhower, blessed with a magnetic charm. Even his Choate school headmaster, who was tormented for four years by Kennedy's anti-Establishment, schoolboy subversion, later recalled how winning Jack could be, with his tousled hair, wide cheeks, perfect teeth and mischievous blue eyes. 'His smile was, as a young boy, when he first came to school – well, in any school he would have got away with some things just on his smile.'[2]

To the smile was added a quick, sharp mind, and a fascination with world politics. As a Harvard University student he interned at the US embassies in London and Paris, then travelled through Russia and Germany in the weeks before the Nazi invasion of Poland in September 1939. He took charge of American survivors of the first passenger vessel to be sunk by a German submarine in World War II (the SS *Athenia*) on behalf of his father, and chose as the subject of his senior thesis at Harvard Britain's failure to rearm in time to meet Hitler's aggression, a subject so topical it was issued as a book, *Why England Slept*, in the summer of 1940, as France fell and the people of Britain prepared for Nazi invasion. Thereafter, in California, deeply involved in a peace conference, the young author took issue with his father, who had disobeyed Roosevelt and blackmailed the president to be able to return to America from the London embassy prior to the November 1940 presidential election.

'If England is defeated America is going to be alone in a strained and hostile world' the twenty-three-year-old warned his father in a letter – indeed, Britain might be 'on the verge of defeat or defeated – by a combination of totalitarian powers. Then there will be a general turning of the people's opinions. They will say "Why were we so stupid not to have given Britain all possible aid."'[3]

The letter was brilliantly effective. Ambassador Kennedy withdrew his planned opposition to the Lend-Lease Bill. Britain did survive, and was able to join the United States in declaring war on the Japanese Empire after Pearl Harbor.

By then JFK had wangled a doctor's pass to serve in the US Navy, first in naval intelligence in Washington before transferring to high-speed wooden torpedo boats. Posted to the Solomon Islands in 1943 he took command of the ill-fated PT-109, which was rammed and sunk by a steel-hulled Japanese destroyer at night, when the lead US boat, equipped with radar, quit the patrol and returned to base. Two crew members were killed, but Kennedy brought the remaining nine back to safety after four days and five nights behind Japanese lines.

Written up by novelist John Hersey in the New Yorker in 1944, the PT-109 story made Kennedy a minor national hero, but the episode was disastrous for Kennedy's physical health, eventually causing him to be medically discharged. The death of his healthy older brother, who had joined the navy as a pilot, upset him so deeply that he wrote a collection of essay tributes to Joe Jr, who had been expected to go into politics after the war.

The privately published volume was a mark of fierce family loyalty, and perfectly sincere, yet avoided the bitter truth – that Joe Jr lacked an independent mind and good political judgement (he was an early admirer of Hitler, and had opposed FDR's re-nomination at the Democratic National Convention in 1940). By contrast JFK seemed not only to have inherited his grandfather's legendary charm and compassion, but also evinced precociously mature political judgement. Encouraged by his college and navy friends, with his father's backing and at the urging of his adoring grandfather, JFK thus ran for a vacant congressional seat in Massachusetts in 1946. To Ambassador Kennedy's amazement – in view of his son's appalling health – JFK proved a born campaigner, exuding a kind of natural grace both on the platform and in person, and concealing his exceptional intelligence behind his quick humour. He was well informed, well travelled, inquisitive, competitive, ruggedly handsome, tough, and happy-go-lucky. Women adored him; men were less easily seduced, but his mix of insouciance and thoughtfulness, for a decorated young veteran, eventually won their votes too. He was elected three times as a congressman for Massachusetts between 1946 and 1950, then ran for the Senate in 1952 against the distinguished incumbent, Republican Henry Cabot Lodge, who had moved mountains to draft Eisenhower for the presidency.

In a memorable campaign, despite a national landslide for Republicans, JFK triumphed and took Lodge's Senate seat. The difference of a few ships had worked in JFK's favour, putting him ahead of his WASP rival as the young representative of an old state in which veterans, immigrants, community groups and college faculty now warmed to his liberal, Truman-style notion of government: firm on defence and international alliances, and compassionate on domestic issues from veteran's housing to education, the minimum wage and social security.

Marrying Jacqueline Bouvier, a New England WAFC (White Anglo-French Catholic), added to the allure of the freshman senator, who defied his father's wishes, and ran for vice president at the 1956 Democratic Convention – the same summer that Vice President Richard Nixon stood for re-nomination as the Republican vice-presidential candidate.

Nixon was successful in his bid; Kennedy was not. The Democratic vice-presidential nomination went to Senator Estes Kefauver by a handful of votes. The convention was televised, however, and Kennedy's performance (which included his narration of the official thirty-minute documentary film on the history of the Democratic Party, as well as his beguiling concession remarks) garnered Kennedy national face-and-voice recognition as a young candidate, barely thirty-nine, to be reckoned with.

Determined to show he was on a rising tide, JFK stood again for election to the US Senate in 1958, and won by the largest majority in Massachusetts history, as well the largest in that year's elections to the Senate. With Adlai Stevenson withdrawing from the presidential fray after two defeats, unless drafted, the time seemed propitious for JFK to make his expected bid for the Democratic presidential nomination in 1960. His work in the Senate was undistinguished but, once promoted to a place on the Senate Foreign Relations Committee, he spoke widely on foreign policy. His youthfulness, his idealism, his intelligence, his photogenic (and expensively dressed) new wife, and his own good looks augured well in the television age. His third book, *Profiles in Courage*, though largely researched and first-drafted by others (like Winston Churchill's books) had won a Pulitzer Prize for biography in 1957, which gave him an unusual literary pedigree. Moreover his heroic war record mitigated his youth and executive inexperience, making Governor Stevenson look fusty even to many liberals.

The national press, like the public, thus found much to laud in Kennedy's candidature, though many remained disturbed not only by JFK's faith (no Catholic had ever been elected to the presidency), but by his sinister father, Joseph P. Kennedy, in the background, bankrolling his candidature.

To run successfully against powerful Democratic rivals such as the supremely effective Senate Majority Leader, Lyndon B. Johnson, JFK thus needed to campaign vigorously, widely and combatively, in order that his distinctive personality emerge and win over sceptics. To this end his father furnished him with his own plane, *The Caroline* (named after his daughter, born in 1957). Despite recurrent (and sedulously concealed) ill health, JFK duly won the party nomination in Los Angeles in August 1960, offering his beaten rival, Lyndon Johnson, the vice presidency as a gesture of magnanimity and respect, though never dreaming Johnson would surrender his powerful legislative position in the Senate to accept it.

To Kennedy's surprise Johnson did, and in a thrilling campaign that autumn, the race for the presidency looked too close to call.

Two confrontations helped tip the national scales towards Kennedy: a brave appearance in Houston, Texas, before a meeting of 300 Protestant ministers, where he defended his right as a Catholic to run for the nation's highest office; and the first ever televised presidential debates, to which his opponent, Republican Richard Nixon, an excellent debater with a deep baritone voice, agreed. On radio, where Nixon's voice conveyed his vice-presidential stature, he seemed to win the three debates, but on television the reverse seemed to be the case (according to Gallup polls), the vice president sweating profusely under the klieg lamps, and looking untrustworthy beside the confident, smiling, handsome Democrat.

The presidential election on November 8, 1960, proved one of the closest in American history, indeed closer than that of Truman against Dewey in 1948. The difference between winning and losing appeared to boil down to a number of disputed counties in Illinois, where Chicago Mayor Daley's machine was operating, and where large amounts of cash (organized by Joe Kennedy) changed hands and fraudulent voting was suspected. ('Mr President, with a little bit of luck and the help of a few close friends, you are going to carry Illinois' Daley had confidently promised earlier that evening.[4])

Kennedy, when asked how he would take the news if he were to lose the election, admitted: 'Badly. But I won't take it as hard as Nixon will.'[5] He was right.

Nixon was urged to contest the result. Such an investigation might, however, have encountered electoral fraud on Nixon's own behalf. At 9 a.m. Nixon's press secretary conceded. Nixon did not, and in fact only officially conceded on January 6, 1961, in Congress, after Kennedy had visited him by helicopter in Florida and offered him a senior position in the new administration (which Nixon declined).

## Part Two: The Presidency

On January 20, 1961, John Fitzgerald Kennedy, aged forty-three, took the oath of office as thirty-fifth president of the United States, with Lyndon Baines Johnson sworn in as the new vice president, standing beside the outgoing thirty-fourth president, Dwight D. Eisenhower, and outgoing vice president, Richard Nixon. Together they comprised four consecutive presidents of the United States, none of whom had ever served as a state governor, the traditional means of ascent.

Kennedy's inaugural speech, written by the even younger Ted Sorensen, was widely considered the best of its kind in American annals. 'Let the word go forth from this time and place,' Kennedy declared in his confident tenor voice, with its distinctive Boston intonation, 'to friend and foe alike, that the torch has been passed to a new generation of Americans – born in this century, tempered by war, disciplined by a hard and bitter peace, proud of our ancient heritage – and unwilling to witness or permit the slow undoing of those human rights to which this nation has always been committed, and to which we are committed today at home and around the world. Let every nation know, whether it wishes us well or ill, that we shall pay any price, bear any burden, meet any hardship, support any friend, oppose any foe, in order to assure the survival and the success of liberty.' Televised across the world, it signalled a new captain at America's imperial helm.

With Kennedy's younger brother Robert F. Kennedy nominated as Attorney General, and JFK's Senate seat 'kept warm' for when his youngest brother Ted would be old enough to serve, as well as Joseph Kennedy operating in the background as a grey eminence, the British prime minister Harold Macmillan likened the Kennedy clan to a medieval Italian family taking over the capital. The Kennedys were, of course, Irish-American, but there was undeniably something of a Medici feel to the takeover, following the staid, solid and respectable Eisenhowers, who suddenly looked like yesterday's pudding, despite the international crises Eisenhower had so maturely met, and the domestic wonders he had performed as president.

Living standards had risen more than 30 per cent during Eisenhower's two terms; almost every American home had television; grand highways were being constructed to connect the main cities of the continent from coast to coast and north to south; no wars had been declared; no riots had marred the rising national prosperity after Little Rock; and there was little if any inflation. President Eisenhower was understandably miffed. 'This is the biggest defeat of my life' he had remarked the morning after the election, sensing that, with a new era beginning, his legacy would quickly be forgotten, even trampled.[6] In particular he deplored 'naive' reporters who welcomed JFK as 'a new genius in our midst who is incapable of making any mistakes, and therefore deserving no criticism whatever'.[7]

Certainly, having raised public – indeed world – expectations on behalf of a new generation, Kennedy had to work hard to meet them. The first great achievement of his new administration took place some weeks later, in March 1961: the establishment of the Peace Corps, a volunteer programme to send young Americans abroad to help especially in Third World countries, and which tapped into the native idealism of a younger American generation.

The Peace Corps would exemplify the best and most inspiring element of the new broom in Washington, where the White House was swiftly transformed by the 'best and brightest' new incumbents, such as Defense Secretary Robert McNamara, former head of Ford Motor Company, and National Security Adviser McGeorge Bundy, the former (and youngest ever) Dean of the Faculty at Harvard. The First Lady had just given birth to a boy, in addition to their daughter Caroline, so the private quarters were quickly transformed into a charming nursery. The press was captivated by the picture, later memorialized as a modern Camelot.

Peace Corps volunteers fanned across the Second and Third Worlds, without weapons. Fidel Castro, by contrast, favoured the export both of Marxist ideas *and* weapons, thus posing a potent threat in the poorer countries of Latin America. President Eisenhower had already warned 'we could lose all of South America' unless the US took action, yet felt the United States must 'conduct itself in precisely the right way' lest it merely fan the flames of anti-Americanism.[8] A straightforward imperialist invasion of Cuba was off the table, in Eisenhower's view, since it would only confirm Castro's depiction of the US as a military empire out of control; he had therefore favoured the same hidden-hand tactic he'd used in Iran and Guatemala: a coup, backed by Cuban exiles, covertly sponsored by the CIA, with a $13 million budget. Eisenhower directed that no US military personnel be sanctioned for the mission, however, at least in combat status; nor was Vice President Nixon allowed to be part of the planned operation. Finally, Eisenhower insisted, there had to be a credible alternative leader to put in Castro's place.

Operation Zapata had thus hardly promised to be a great success before President Kennedy took office, and it certainly did not promise to become better in the weeks after his inauguration, for all the talk of paying any price and bearing any burden. The truth was, it was already ridiculed by diplomats: the plan 'known all over Latin America' and even 'discussed in UN circles', as Eisenhower's Under Secretary of State, Douglas Dillon (whom Kennedy had made Treasury Secretary), protested.[9] Kennedy's new Secretary of State, Dean Rusk, felt similarly unenthusiastic, as was the chairman of the Senate Foreign Relations Committee, William Fulbright. Castro could not but be aware of the impending operation, and threw out most of the American embassy personnel in Havana, calling it, correctly, 'a nest of spies'.

Swollen to 1,500 men and targeted on to another Cuban beachhead, the CIA-supported Cuban exiles, still lacking a leader, were authorized by President Kennedy to invade Cuba on April 17, 1961, at the so-called

Bay of Pigs. Within hours the landing threatened to become a catastrophe.

Certainly the Kremlin expected US forces to invade. But Kennedy
did not take either course. As the entire rebel force was reported as
having been killed or taken captive, the First Lady and White House
staff found JFK weeping at the needless loss of life and liberty. 'A great
nation must be willing to use its strength' Senator Goldwater told the
president, urging him to snatch victory from the jaws of defeat. 'Power
belongs to those who use it [and] I would do whatever is necessary to
assure the invasion is a success.'[10] Richard Nixon said the same, while
Richard Bissell, on behalf of the CIA, begged for at least two US jets
to 'shoot down enemy aircraft'. 'No,' Kennedy responded, 'I've told
you over and over again, our forces won't engage in combat.'[11] When
the chief of the US Navy Staff, Admiral Burke (Kennedy's former naval
commander in the Solomon Islands) asked permission to send a US
destroyer into action to knock out Castro's advancing tanks, the president again refused: 'Burke, I don't want the United States involved in
this' – and in the ensuing days, as calamity became a rout, he held by
that decision.[12]

Instead, the president did the unthinkable. He accepted failure – and
turned down Nixon's offer, on behalf of the Republican Party, to publicly
support him if he now launched a formal US invasion of Cuba (using,
if necessary, a phony threat to the naval base at Guantanamo as a
pretext). At the president's live press conference on April 21, 1961, a
reporter defied the injunction (in the interests of national security)
against questions over Cuba; the president paused, then looked the
journalist in the eye without irritation. 'There's an old saying that victory
has a hundred fathers,' he stated, 'and defeat is an orphan. I am the
responsible officer of this government.'[13]

Defeat, then, it was. Viewers – like the reporters present – were
stunned. And impressed. Even Kennedy was amazed at the public's
response to his admission of responsibility for the blunder. In a Gallup
survey his popularity rating jumped *ten* points, hitting 83 per cent
approval. 'Jesus, it's just like Ike' he mocked the results of the poll
with typically self-deprecating wit. 'The worse you do, the better they
like you.'[14]

As became clear to the president, a commander-in-chief must in the
end live with his own conscience and ignore the gung-ho chiding of

subordinates eager for imperial glory, usually at the cost of other men's lives. In his heart of hearts, tempered by savage war in the Solomon Islands, JFK had not really believed in Operation Zapata, either as an operation of war or as a political objective, given that no replacement for Castro was at hand. He himself had visited Cuba (and its massage parlours) numerous times in its pre-Castro, Batista era. Was Batista's corrupt political, social and economic system what the United States should be seeking to restore, along with the United Fruit Company's property? What credible leader or government were the Cuban rebels offering the poor in Cuba?

The 1960s were not the 1890s, the president recognized from the young people he was meeting in launching his Peace Corps. The idealistic rhetoric that had brought him the presidency (but only just) was based on an inspirational, *moral* quality he exuded in spades, not cynicism, or the methods the Soviets had used in Hungary. Chastened by the disaster, he assured Eisenhower that the next time he would not mess up; he would choose his battlefields more carefully.

Cuba was not the only point of maximum impact between capitalism and Communism. Alongside the drama of the Bay of Pigs, the world was treated in the spring of 1961 to a race between the two nuclear superpowers to see which of them could, following the success of the sputnik programme, be the first to put a human being into orbit around the earth. The race was won by the Soviet Union when Lieutenant Yuri Gagarin was rocketed into space on April 12, 1961, beating US astronaut Alan Shepard – who only reached a height of 115 miles, and did not orbit the earth – by three weeks. It secured another great propaganda victory for the Soviets, fostering the illusion not only of technological superiority over the capitalist world, but also of the USSR's peaceful intentions.

Eisenhower's response as president would have been to ignore the propaganda, and proceed patiently with the science. President Kennedy, however, was nothing if not sensitive to the battle of modern ideas between the US and USSR. In the wake of Lieutenant Gagarin's triumph he therefore ordered a crash programme to put the first man on the moon – though it would not happen in his lifetime.

No sooner had the waves of Cuba and Lieutenant Gagarin subsided, than Kennedy emplaned to meet his fellow emperor in Vienna.

The summit meeting, on June 3, 1961, was a second disaster for

Kennedy in as many months. Kennedy's charm and good manners had entranced America, and the majority of people had forgiven his freshman faux pas over Cuba; but his charm now acted as a disadvantage in confronting 'The Butcher of the Ukraine'.

Kennedy admitted afterwards to James Reston, a *New York Times* journalist, that the confrontation was the 'roughest thing in my life'.[15] Dean Rusk, Kennedy's Secretary of State, recalled that the president was 'very upset. He wasn't prepared for the brutality of Khrushchev's presentation' – a *nyet*-studded performance during which Khrushchev rejected any nuclear disarmament that entailed military inspection; proposed again to recognize East Germany and thereby abandon four-power control and access to Berlin; and insisted Russia would continue to back Communist movements worldwide, whatever the danger of miscalculation leading to inadvertent nuclear war.[16]

Drugged with cortisone for his Addison's disease – an invariably fatal, progressive deterioration of the adrenal glands – novocaine for his back pain, and a concoction devised by Dr Max Jacobson for celebrities to combat his low energy level, Kennedy seemed to Khrushchev 'very inexperienced, even immature. Compared to him, Eisenhower was a man of intelligence and vision.'[17]

Back in Moscow Khrushchev spoke of Kennedy as 'the boy': a president who 'doesn't have any backbone' or, worse still, 'the courage to stand up to a serious challenge'.[18] A KGB operative in America confided to Robert Kennedy that Khrushchev's bombast in Vienna seemed to have downright 'scared' the president. 'When you have your hand up a girl's dress,' the operative sneered, 'you expect her to scream, but you don't expect her to be scared.'[19] Better in fact that war 'begin now', over Berlin, the Russian premier had told Kennedy, than later, when even more destructive weaponry would be developed by the two empires. 'If that's true,' Kennedy had sighed, 'it's going to be a cold winter.'[20]

To America's allies, the president was disturbingly pessimistic in the aftermath of Vienna. Prime Minister Macmillan, whom Kennedy visited in London on his way back to America, noted in his diary that the president was still in shock and that for Kennedy the Vienna summit had been 'rather like somebody meeting Napoleon (at the height of his power) for the first time'.[21] 'Talking to *Time*'s correspondent Hugh Sidey, Kennedy said 'I talked about how a nuclear exchange would kill seventy million people in ten minutes and he just looked at me as if to say, "So what?"'[22] Vice President Johnson said 'Khrushchev scared the poor little fellow dead' and later imitated JFK falling to his knees in abject supplication to the Russian premier.[23]

Those seeking to understand the Russian premier's Napoleonic posturing did not have far too look. The fact was, Khrushchev – a man with a tough, peasant approach to negotiating – had been amazed by apparent American pusillanimity over Cuba, and had fully expected Castro to be overwhelmed by a full-scale American invasion force in a matter of days. When no American troops landed, however, he'd been puzzled. 'I don't understand Kennedy,' he had told his son Sergei one evening. 'What's wrong with him? Can he really be that indecisive? Perhaps he lacks determination.'[24]

The results of JFK's failed charm offensive in Vienna, on top of his Bay of Pigs 'weakness', thus tipped the scales in the now icy Cold War. The Russian premier had never underestimated President Eisenhower's imperial resolve, especially after seeing for himself the magnitude of America's industrial might and energy; but Eisenhower was like an older brother, four years older than Khrushchev, whereas 'the boy' Kennedy was twenty-three years younger – younger even than Khrushchev's son. In Moscow Khrushchev was soon heard discussing with aides 'what we can do in our [Soviet] interest and at the same time subject Kennedy to a test of strength'.[25]

If Khrushchev was an opportunist, JFK was a pragmatist. Growing up with a ruthless businessman for a father, JFK was no stranger to tough goliaths driven by their own manic agendas. What Kennedy misunderstood – as Eisenhower had – was the extent to which Khrushchev was out of his intellectual depth, and at war with the world, both at home and abroad; a denouncer of Stalin who was himself a tyrant; a man who thrived on hand-to-hand combat in the pursuit of power, like a Roman gladiator. Thus, to test Kennedy's mettle, Khrushchev had announced at Vienna that he was going to separate West Berlin from the West, a threat that had caused even Khrushchev's own fellow Presidium members to wince. Seeking to wield the initiative in inter-empire relations was one thing; but testing American resolve by risking nuclear war over *Berlin*? Should tens of millions of Russian lives be put in jeopardy, Presidium members asked, over western access to a fragment of a bombed-out German city, a place forever linked with Adolf Hitler and the Nazis, which they would

then have to hand over to the very people Khrushchev and his generation had fought to the death to defeat in World War II? Even
Khrushchev, pondering his own gambler's impetuousness, recognized
why his colleagues were baulking at that. Thus when Kennedy belatedly made clear at Vienna, as Eisenhower had done at Camp David,
that the US would never surrender West Berlin, but implied that the
US would not go to war over East Berlin, Khrushchev had seen his
chance: namely the opportunity to partition the still-open city permanently and physically, with a wall. At a stroke he could thereby halt
the tide of East German nationals currently fleeing the so-called
German Democratic Republic in their tens of thousands. He made a
personal, secret tour of Berlin in an unmarked limousine. Then, in
an inspired example of 'imperial' Soviet leadership, Khrushchev ramped
up his public rhetoric about the many hundreds of millions who would
die in a nuclear holocaust if the US became belligerent over Berlin,
while secretly giving orders for barbed wire to be rolled out on August
13, 1961, followed by demolitions and the erection of the wall. He then
waited for western reaction.

Had the western Allies or West Berliners begun immediately tearing
down the wire, Khrushchev had in reality no idea what he would do,
believing in Napoleon's dictum, *on s'engage, et puis on voit*: you throw
yourself into the fray, then see what happens.

'Father was delighted' Sergei Khrushchev remembered, however, for
the building of the Berlin Wall went entirely unopposed. Once again
Khrushchev emerged the propaganda victor; Kennedy implicitly
accepted the Soviet challenge by doing nothing beyond sending 1,500
Marines to guarantee military access to East Berlin, under the old four-
power World War II agreement.

The fact was, the Berlin Wall, however unfortunate for East Germans,
was a blessed relief to President Kennedy, since it finally removed Berlin
as a potential *casus belli* after months of dire Soviet threats and warnings – a draconian yet peaceful resolution, at a moment when the US
was facing up to its own barrier, between whites and blacks. Attacks
on Freedom Riders in the South had become murderous, and then, in
September 1962, the first major race riot of Kennedy's presidency took
place as a crowd of 2,000 white students and troublemakers gathered
on the campus of the University of Mississippi, in Oxford, to stop the
first ever black student from registering. Wielding lead pipes and guns,

and throwing rocks and Molotov cocktails, they met the federal marshals whom the Attorney General Robert Kennedy had sent in, with bullets – inviting bloodshed. 'Go to hell, JFK!' was one epithet they screamed; 'Go to Cuba, nigger lovers, go to Cuba!' another.[26]

President Kennedy held his fire, finally appearing on national television at 10 p.m. on Sunday September 30, 1962, in the Oval Office. Taking his cue from his predecessor during the Little Rock crisis, he appealed to the honour and dignity of Mississippians in accepting the ruling of the Fifth Circuit southern judges who had voted to send the black student, James Meredith, to Old Miss. The law was the law – even if the governor, Ross Barnett, was afraid to uphold it, as Governor Faubus had defied President Eisenhower in 1957. 'Our nation is founded on the principle that observance of the law is the eternal safeguard of liberty,' the president reminded viewers, 'and defiance of the law is the surest road to tyranny. The law which we obey includes the final rulings of the courts, as well as the enactments of our legislative bodies. Even among law-abiding men few laws are universally loved, but they are uniformly respected and not resisted . . . The eyes of the nation and all the world are upon you and upon all of us' the president ended. 'I am certain the great majority of the students will uphold that honor.'[27]

The majority did – but a vocal, armed minority, however, held out for drama and the sight of blood. Tear gas had to be fired to prevent hysterical rioters from becoming a lynch mob; photographs of US marshals wearing gas masks were flashed across the world. An Agence France Press journalist was killed by the rioters, as well as a bystander. Twenty-eight marshals were shot, and several hundred sustained other injuries from bricks and projectiles. 'People are dying in Oxford. This is the worst thing I've seen in forty-five years' Kennedy yelled at the Defense Secretary and chief of the US Army, telling them to transmit his orders to General Billingslea, a distinguished paratroop leader who'd fought in North Africa, Sicily, Italy and the Netherlands, but who, as designated area commander, had not gotten the military police in to protect Meredith, an American in his own country.[28] Finally, reluctantly, the president ordered regular army units to be flown from Tennessee to Oxford, just as Eisenhower had been compelled to do at Little Rock five years before.

No sooner had President Kennedy dealt with the crisis in Mississippi – the 'most interesting time' he'd had 'since the Bay of Pigs' he remarked in mocking understatement, as he sent 23,000 soldiers to protect Meredith – than he was compelled to meet an even greater challenge: nuclear weapons being secretly shipped by the Soviet Union to Cuba.[29]

Neither Kennedy nor his cabinet had believed the CIA warnings that Soviet vessels might be shipping nuclear missiles to Castro. Had not Khrushchev, in an exchange of letters (dubbed the 'pen pal letters'), personally denied that Russia had any intention of introducing offensive missiles into the hemisphere? Had not Khrushchev's unofficial emissaries vowed the same, in confidential meetings with Robert Kennedy and others? Above all, why would Khrushchev take such a premeditated risk, requiring not only absolute secrecy until the weapons were fully installed and operational – when they could be announced as a fait accompli – but a progression of lies that would poison hopes of better relations between East and West for another generation? It didn't make sense, prompting the president to ridicule the CIA director's dire predictions.

Kennedy did worry, however, about the political ramifications at home of a Russian military build-up in Cuba. Right-wing post-McCarthyites (McCarthy had died in 1957) had been calling Kennedy a pushover ever since the Bays of Pigs disaster, and had bayed for renewed invasion of Cuba, this time with overwhelming American force. To placate them and show that his administration would not bow to Soviet warmongering, Kennedy had approved Operation Mongoose, a CIA plan to destabilize Cuba by any means possible. He also called up another 150,000 reservists, while at the same time authorizing an official speech, by the Deputy Secretary of Defense, that would reveal for the first time, publicly and officially, that he had been mistaken when campaigning against Vice President Nixon over a perceived missile gap in favour of the Soviets. Not only was there no such gap, but the truth was – as President Eisenhower's U-2 flights had shown – the US had a huge superiority in nuclear weapons and delivery systems from the ground, sea and air. Even if the USSR did launch a first atomic strike, the US would be able to retaliate with such force it would eradicate the entire Soviet Union in a matter of hours.

The official speech mollified American hawks, but proved, in the event, a terrible miscalculation, egging the Soviet leader even further in his search for an opportunity to 'stick it' to the United States. 'Rodion Yakovlevich,' Khrushchev had said to Malinovsky, his defence minister, in April that year, 'what if we throw a hedgehog down Uncle Sam's pants?'[30] With the Berlin crisis effectively defused by the new wall, there were still many other opportunities to humiliate the American government, such as in Laos or the Congo, but these were far, far from the American continent. Using Cuba, only ninety miles from the Florida Keys, as the platform for weapons aimed at the mainland, offered Khrushchev the chance to make Americans understand how Russians felt, surrounded by American nuclear missiles from Norway to Turkey.

When Kennedy first learned of the successful transfer of nuclear weapons to Cuba, after breakfast at the White House on October 16, 1962, he was stunned by the sheer audacity of Khrushchev's new gamble. For months Khrushchev and his underlings must have deliberately lied, the president recognized, while Russian vessels quietly shipped the nuclear arsenal across the Atlantic. The new US photos – ironically taken by a U-2 spy plane, as well as by satellite – provided unmistakeable evidence. Castro's Cuba was to be transformed into a Russian nuclear missile base.

In the years that followed, commentators and historians would rake over the ashes, origins, context, steps and missteps that constituted the Cuban Missile Crisis. Kennedy's initial misreading of the situation certainly put the US government on the spot. Both Truman and Eisenhower would doubtlessly have sent in the air force to obliterate the missile sites, followed by naval and ground forces – as Castro predicted when being told of Khrushchev's plan. But Khrushchev, a wily veteran of World War II, had first checked with his marshals. As he reassured Castro, it would take a full week for the US to mount an amphibious invasion after an air strike. During that interval Khrushchev would announce he was standing behind Cuba, and warn that any US invasion would trigger World War III. A rock-solid, nuclear-tipped mutual-support pact between Cuba and the USSR would then be signed in public in November, Khrushchev promised, insisting that, in the meantime, secrecy was essential so that the Americans would be faced with a fait accompli. Once the Soviet intercontinental and medium-range ballistic missiles were *in situ* (with 50,000 accompanying troops) on November 6, it would be too late for the US to risk attacking them, Khrushchev was certain.[31] Kennedy, soft and indecisive, would have to climb down. 'The missiles will already be in place,' Khrushchev explained his reasoning later, 'ready to fire. Before taking the decision to eliminate them by military means, the United States would have to think twice. America could knock out some of those installations, but not all. What if a quarter, or one-tenth survived . . .'

Khrushchev's reasoning was correct. 'We are probably going to have to bomb them' were the president's first words, which he quickly withdrew, however, when he examined the timetable.[32] Nuclear missiles or bombs were probably already on the island, complicating any notion of instant reprisal such as US bombing, which could not be guaranteed to be 100 per cent effective. (Four decades later, historians confirmed the appraisal: a slew of medium-range Soviet missiles had arrived in mid-September, followed by their nuclear warheads on October 4, and by October 16, the nuclear warheads for the intercontinental ballistic missiles had also reached Cuba, although they remained in port on a Russian ship, waiting to be unloaded.[33] By the time Kennedy saw the U-2 photographs there were thus already 'eighty cruise missile warheads, six atomic bombs for Il-28 bombers and twelve Luna warheads' in Cuba, as Khrushchev's biographer summarized.[34])

Beyond the uncertainty about whether nuclear weapons had already arrived and were operational, there was the looming political fallout for Kennedy in having failed to credit his own CIA director's warnings. 'He thought', one biographer later wrote, 'he was going to go down as the commander-in-chief who looked the other way while the Soviets put nuclear missiles ninety miles from the United States.'[35] As he set down the photos, Kennedy realized he had been snookered.

Perhaps no plan since the blitzkrieg campaigns of Adolf Hitler – often against the advice of his generals – so demonstrated the role of individuals in history as Khrushchev's fantastical plot. 'It was his brainchild,' his aide Troyanovsky recalled, 'and he clung to it in spite of all the dangers and warnings.'[36]

To his great credit, the president finally recognized what the former Secretary of State, Dean Acheson, had said of Khrushchev: they were 'dealing with a madman'.[37] Even Khrushchev's own generals thought he had taken leave of his senses and, as Admiral Amelko remarked, that the Cuban venture was 'a crackpot scheme'.[38] The 'crackpot' Soviet premier, however, had made it impossible for Kennedy to take military action without risking a nuclear disaster, either by accident or chain of events. The question was, how would Kennedy react.

Over six fateful days in October, the president reviewed his options.

The Russians had kept silent about what they were doing. Very well, then, Kennedy determined, so would we. He deliberately said nothing to the Soviet foreign minister, Gromyko, who visited him at the White House on October 18. 'It was incredible to sit there and watch the lies coming out of his mouth' the president afterwards told an aide – but still said nothing.[39] Finally, having obtained further incontrovertible evidence of the Soviet missile bases, and having lined up his ducks, Kennedy said he was going to make an important announcement on national television.

At 9.30 p.m. on October 22, 1962, having sent copies of his text by special delivery to Moscow and the capitals of the globe, President Kennedy addressed the world. Composed in part by Ted Sorensen (who was summoned from hospital, where he was being treated for ulcers), the broadcast set out in harrowing detail the new threat ninety miles off the coast of Florida, with Soviet nuclear missiles being transferred to Cuban launch sites at that very moment 'under a cloack of secrecy and deception'. The president called upon Khrushchev to 'halt and eliminate this clandestine, reckless and provocative threat to world peace and to stable relations between our two nations' by withdrawing them from the western hemisphere, or face the consequences. In the meantime, the president announced, he had ordered the establishment of a naval blockade or 'quarantine' around Cuba, so that no more nuclear weapons could be shipped to the island. Addressing his countrymen, the president ended his speech with an appeal for calm and unity of American purpose:

> The path we have chosen for the present is full of hazards, as all paths are; but it is the one most consistent with our character and courage as a nation and our commitments around the world. The cost of freedom is always high, but Americans have always paid it. And one path we shall never choose, and that is the path of surrender or submission.
>
> Our goal is not the victory of might, but the vindication of right; not peace at the expense of freedom, but both peace and freedom, here in this hemisphere, and, we hope, around the world. God willing, that goal will be achieved.
>
> Thank you and good night.

Khrushchev, reading the advance text at the Kremlin, was shocked. Having brimmed with pride at sending to Cuba, without detection, a vast shipment of nuclear weapons that would alter the entire balance of power between the two empires at a stroke, he was now beside himself with anger, fear and frustration. He called for a crisis meeting of the Presidium. 'The missiles aren't operational yet. They're defenceless; they can be wiped out from the air in one swipe' he confessed in panic to his son.[40] To his colleagues in the Kremlin he now backpedalled, explaining he'd never wanted to provoke the threat of nuclear war, he 'just wanted to intimidate' the Americans in order to deter 'the anti-Cuban [i.e. exile] forces'.[41]

For hours the meeting became surreal, as different options were debated, from a 'big war' between Russia and the US, to a small one between Cuba and the US, with the Soviets washing their hands and handing over 'tactical' (i.e. battlefield) nuclear weapons to the Cubans. Eventually the meeting broke up in dissension. As Khrushchev's biographer noted, the premier, not the president, had screwed up. 'Instead of preventing war, his masterstroke might trigger one' – and all for an island more inconsequential than Berlin, which no Berlin-type airlift from the Soviet Union could now save, nor Soviet ships even reach, since they could not breach the imminent US blockade without inciting war.[42]

Intense and secret negotiations went on between Washington and the Kremlin, while across the world people protested, blamed, excused, and vented their anxiety. Finally Khrushchev backed down. On October 24, six Russian vessels laden with military material approached the 500-mile exclusion perimeter – then stopped dead in the water. Dean Rusk, the Secretary of State, turned to McGeorge Bundy, the national security adviser, and made the remark for which he would become famous: 'We're eyeball to eyeball, and I think the other fellow just blinked.'[43]

Khrushchev had. He had gambled, and only two weeks away from triumph, had to admit defeat. In the following days, in return for Russian withdrawal, he obtained a non-binding promise from a magnanimous Kennedy that the United States would never invade Communist Cuba, and also that, some time later and without public admission of the arrangement, redundant American nuclear missiles would be removed from Turkey, on the Soviet Union's border. This was, in actuality, a not inconsiderable outcome, though bringing the world to the very brink of nuclear war to achieve it was not considered a victory by anybody in the Kremlin, or in Havana.

To his own surprise, President John F. Kennedy emerged a global hero. All twenty members of the Organization of American States had voted to support Kennedy's quarantine, and thereafter continued to impose it as a commercial quarantine. Instead of becoming the Lenin of Latin America, Fidel Castro became a pariah; his Communist revolution, for all its supposedly idealistic socialist aims and objectives, was stillborn. Furious, Castro bad-mouthed Khrushchev ('Son of a bitch . . . bastard . . . asshole . . . No *cojones. Maricón*'), and excoriated the 44,000 departing Russian troops and their precious hardware, claiming later that he could never find out who had dreamed up such a crazy scheme in the first place.

In the greatest international crisis since World War II, Kennedy had shown firmness and great statesmanship, overruling the hawks in his own country and ensuring the peaceful resolution of an extraordinary adventure. Without bluff and bluster, Khrushchev 'was lost' and would soon be deposed.[44] To his chagrin, moreover, it was Mao Zedong who took over the propaganda role of godfather to the Marxist-Leninist revolutionary world, accusing Khrushchev's Cuban policy of being nothing but 'adventurism' followed by 'capitulationism'.[45]

As 1962 came to a close, with the Cuban Missile Crisis thankfully over, President Kennedy's approval rating rose to the upper seventies.

While the Soviet Union retreated into an ageing imperial shell, its agriculture still failing to feed its people and its industry incapable of furnishing the things people really wanted, from refrigerators to cars, the United States seemed to have overcome its shame over the sputnik programme, and to be exploding with young, creative energy in manufacturing, commerce, science, pop music, pop art, literature, and access to college education. In a special one-hour ABC television interview on December 16, 1962, the president was asked about his two years in office to date. Had they matched his expectations?

Kennedy shook his head. The problems he'd encountered were, he said, 'more difficult than I had imagined they were. The responsibilities placed on the United States are greater than I imagined them to be, and there are greater limitations upon our ability to bring about a favorable result than I imagined them to be. And I think that is probably true of anyone who becomes the president, because there is such a difference between those who advise or speak or legislate, and between the man who must select from the various alternatives proposed and say that this shall be the policy of the United States.' Wistfully he pointed out that 'If you take the wrong course, and on occasion I have, the president bears the burden of the responsibility quite rightly. The advisers', he added tartly, 'may move on to new advice.'[46]

This was John F. Kennedy at his most reflective – and realistic. Nevertheless he did allow himself and his American viewers a brief moment of pride in the accomplishments of the United States as a great power since World War II – 'One hundred and eighty million people' who, 'for almost twenty years, have been the great means of defending the world against the Nazi threat, and since then against the Communist threat, and if it were not for us, the Communists would be dominant in the world today . . . I think that is a pretty good record with 6 per cent of the world's population. I think we ought to be rather pleased with ourselves this Christmas.'[47]

In the glow of prosperity (the US had emerged from a minor recession in 1960–1, and was beginning to boom), as well as peaceful resolution of the Cuban Missile Crisis, the president enumerated to his secretary the twenty-seven probable troubles requiring solution in 1963.[48] Neither civil rights nor Vietnam were on the list.

Like Eisenhower at the time of the *Brown* vs *Board of Education* case, Kennedy hoped against hope he could defer the matter of civil rights to his second term, after the 1964 election, walking in the meantime on eggshells in order to placate both whites and blacks. Yet the very energy that was impelling the 1960s – with gross national product (GNP) rising by 4 per cent per capita in 1962 made black leaders less rather than more patient. The very aspirations aroused by Kennedy's 1960 rhetoric could not now be stopped, or shelved, merely because the president feared he might then lose the 1964 election. A civil rights voting bill the president introduced to Congress in February 1963 was mocked by blacks as whitewashing. In April, the city of Birmingham, Alabama, saw protest marches, and the arrest of Dr King for leading them. By May, when, released from jail, Dr King turned to children for his marches, the temperature rose higher still. Thousands were arrested. Alarming photos were transmitted across the world of Eugene 'Bull' Connor, the Commissioner of Public Safety, turning fire hoses on 1,000 black children as they came out of a Baptist church, and German shepherd dogs being used against them. After the humiliation of the Cuban Missile Crisis, Radio Moscow now had ample opportunity to hit back, in the court of world opinion.

Kennedy was called upon to get off the fence and to use his presidential bully pulpit, whether or not it sundered his own or the Democratic Party's re-election chances. He resisted, but as a summer of increasing civil rights demonstrations in the face of southern intransigence promised to grow hotter and hotter, the day of reckoning came. George Wallace, the governor of Alabama, arrived on the campus of the state university on June 11, 1963, vowing he would personally halt court-ordered desegregation by stopping the university's first two black students from registering.

Many had mocked Kennedy's book, *Profiles in Courage*, as the work of Ted Sorensen, Kennedy's talented young speechwriter from Nebraska. Yet the notion of political courage as the willingness to challenge conventional power structures had been Kennedy's own, and he had been sincere in his admiration of those figures in political history who had shown it. Now, at last, his own turn had come. Hitherto he had, like Eisenhower, sheltered behind his legal and constitutional responsibility to carry out the laws of the land, as chief executive of the nation. Now, in an eighteen-minute television address at 8 p.m. on June 11, having federalized the Alabama National Guard under his own ultimate command, the president set out the inequities of education, society, business, finance, employment and health care as they affected black people of America. 'This is not even a legal or legislative issue alone,' he declared in the 'deeper', stronger voice Eleanor Roosevelt had recommended he adopt, shortly before she died. 'We are confronted primarily with a moral issue. It is as old as the Scriptures,' he added for the benefit of segregationists in the Bible Belt, 'and is as clear as the American Constitution.' Who 'among us' would change 'his skin' if faced by unending segregation and humiliation in public places, in restaurants, public schools, and in the denial of the right to vote; 'Who among us would then be content with the counsels of patience and delay?' he asked. 'We face, therefore, a moral crisis as a country and as a people. It cannot be met with repressive police action. It cannot be left to increased demonstrations in the streets ... It is time to act in the Congress, in your state and local legislative body, and above all in our daily lives. A great change is at hand, and our task, our obligation, is to make that revolution, that change, peaceful and constructive for all.'

With those words, the president announced he would be introducing a new comprehensive civil rights bill into Congress. Aware that this might mean the loss of the southern Democrats, he'd told his legislative counsellor he was well aware that 'I can kiss the South goodbye.' But he had, at last, chosen sides.[49]

Led by Martin Luther King Jr, a march on Washington took place at the end of August 1963. 'The Vandals are coming to sack Rome' one Washington newspaper warned, but the march proved peaceful, and the voices of Mahalia Jackson and Dr King made history. Kennedy was moved. 'He's damned good. Damned good!' he remarked with genuine admiration as he watched and listened to King's passionate 'I have a dream' speech on television.[50] After the march was over, he invited Dr King to a private meeting in the Cabinet Room of the White House, and there congratulated the preacher – who was twelve years younger than himself – in person. Together, the two most inspirational figures of their generation began detailed discussions on how enough votes could be secured in Congress for a civil rights bill. 'It's going to be a crusade, then' said seventy-four-year-old Philip Randolph, founder of the Brotherhood of Sleeping Car Porters. 'And I think that nobody can lead this crusade but you, Mr President.'[51] Taking a deep breath, Kennedy vowed he would.

Even as civil rights marches and protests dominated the agenda at home, meanwhile, the difficulty of leading and cheerleading the democratic nations of the world proved just as challenging, especially in a prosperous empire bristling with hawks. In June, the president gave a deeply idealistic speech on world peace at the American University in Washington to reinforce his view of the impending negotiations in Moscow over a limited nuclear test-ban treaty which, to the disgust of the Chinese Communists, the Russians agreed to sign on July 25. 'What kind of peace do we speak?' Kennedy asked rhetorically. 'Not a Pax Americana, enforced on the world by American weapons of war' but one in which inevitable tensions were eased by 'mutual tolerance' and respect.

In the light of the US–Soviet brokered settlement reached in Laos, long considered the 'hot spot' of South East Asia, as well as the ultimately peaceful resolution of the Cuban Missile Crisis, this sounded noble and realistic – but as Khrushchev pointed out to Averell Harriman (the chief US negotiator of the test-ban treaty), such words, though broadcast uncut on Soviet radio and television, did not make Americans any the less 'imperialist'. There were, Khrushchev explained, 'many capitalists who only deal with matters in their own country, whereas an imperialist is a capitalist who interferes in other people's affairs, as you are in South Vietnam.'[52]

Coming from Khrushchev, after his imperialist fiasco in Cuba, this was rich – but not unmerited. Two years before, President de Gaulle had warned Kennedy that intervention in Vietnam 'will be an endless entanglement', as the French had cause to know. 'You will sink into a bottomless military and political quagmire, however much you spend in men and money.'[53] He was right, but had little idea how loud the drums of war echoed in the citadel of American democracy. Twenty years before, Republican isolationists had stopped the president from committing troops to defend democracy in Europe; now, Kennedy had spent the first two years of his presidency attempting to shoot down hawks he had himself appointed to his administration, in an effort to show bipartisanship over American security: Dean Rusk, Robert MacNamara, Walt Rostow and the brothers William and McGeorge Bundy. The president 'expressed his strong feeling' against committing US troops to Vietnam, since America's primary allies, France and Britain, were against such a move, as the minutes of the National Security Meeting on November 14, 1961 had recorded. Going to war in Vietnam without the support of allies would invoke 'sharp domestic criticism' as well as 'strong objections from other nations in the world' the president warned, pointing out that he could make 'a rather strong case against intervening in an area 10,000 miles away against 16,000 [Vietcong] guerrillas,' backed by 200,000 nationalist Communist troops in North Vietnam – a region where 'millions have been spent for years and with no success'.

Instead of simply silencing the hawks, however, the president had sought to placate them by agreeing to what turned out to be a disastrous compromise – sending, between 1961 and 1963, some 16,000 US military 'advisers', tasked with propping up the thoroughly corrupt and ineffective, undemocratic government of the self-appointed South Vietnamese ruler, Ngo Dinh Diem.

Kennedy had no illusions. After all, he had fought in bitter combat against the Japanese in the Solomon Islands in 1943, and knew the level of air, navy and infantry required to dislodge entrenched enemy troops, particularly guerrillas, in tropical conditions. He had been to Vietnam (North and South) in 1951, where he had concluded that the French were not only wrong to remain in colonial occupation of the country, but also deluded in thinking they could ever subdue Ho Chi Minh's essentially nationalist uprising. He acknowledged in a press conference in December 1962 the 'great difficulty' in 'fighting a guerrilla war', especially, he emphasized, 'in terrain as difficult as South Vietnam'.[54] He told his navy chief, Arleigh Burke, that the distinguished fighting admiral was 'wrong' when he said the United States *had* to fight in Laos, and had declined to give further CIA support to anti-Communist General Phoumi Nosavan, who failed miserably in fighting the Communist Pathet Lao. 'General Phoumi is a total shit' Kennedy told a journalist friend, and he rejected Admiral Burke's insistence that, if not in Laos, at least in South Vietnam the US must stand and fight.[55] 'And if it's not South Vietnam, is it going to be Thailand?' Burke had sneered – to the president's discomfort.[56]

Kennedy appreciated that great empires could only prosper when able to establish and protect their sources of wealth and sustenance; in doing so, they had to focus on vital spheres of influence, not be sidetracked into expensive and distracting conflict that only added to their headaches. President Eisenhower had overruled his advisers and had declined to help the French maintain Vietnam as a non-Communist colony. Having hopefully mollified the hawks of his administration and the Pentagon, JFK desperately tried to keep Vietnam off the administration's agenda, out of its press conferences, and away from the front pages of American newspapers, in the forlorn hope he could erase it as a political issue in America and in due course either negotiate a settlement, or abandon President Diem and his associates to their own national destiny. But patience was required, he felt. Divided Berlin – where on July 26, 1963 Kennedy had given the massively popular '*Ich bin ein Berliner*' speech before a million cheering West Berliners – was still the most potent symbol of the Cold War and western democratic resolve. But South Vietnam, where Buddhist monks were incinerating themselves in protest against Diem's corrupt regime? Senator Mike Mansfield, the Senate Majority Leader, advised the president not to listen to the CIA and the military, who were gung-ho to exploit the opportunity for bloodshed far away from Washington control, and stressed the 'the relatively limited importance of the area in terms of specific US interests'. In words that would ring through subsequent American history, the senator urged the president to ask himself whether 'South Viet Nam' was truly as 'important to us' as the supposed advocates for fighting there claimed.[57] Kennedy nodded, as he calculated how a withdrawal could be effected.[58] 'If I tried to pull out completely now from Vietnam,' he explained to an aide after talking with Mansfield, 'we would have another Joe McCarthy scare on our hands, but I can do it after I'm re-elected' in 1964.

Beset by other troubles and issues, from civil rights to re-election concerns, and finding his group of advisers on the subject of Vietnam equally divided between hawks and doves, Kennedy now made the same intrinsic mistake he'd made over the Bay of Pigs and Operation Mongoose. To appease the right he appointed a fiercely anti-Communist Republican, the former senator Cabot Lodge, as the new American ambassador to Saigon, and in a cable he would regret to the day he died, gave Lodge the green light to support a coup against Diem that would supposedly usher in a military junta, with whom the CIA and the military could better work in fighting the Vietcong insurgency.

How this American-sponsored junta in South Vietnam could be seen as an outpost of 'democracy', and whether it would prove any less corrupt or more effective in administering the Asian country, were questions Kennedy failed to ask in the autumn of 1963, let alone demand an answer to. He did not have Eisenhower's experience and prestige as a general in high command, dealing with the military; moreover he lacked Eisenhower's 'hidden hand' intimacy with the CIA. Most of all, he lacked Eisenhower's luck.

Belatedly, in the days after cabling Lodge, he realized he'd made a poor, indeed potentially awful decision, and tried to recall or reverse the cable. He was, he realized, trapped; if the coup failed, the US would look exactly like the nefarious, imperial, meddling Uncle Sam it had been portrayed as over the Bay of Pigs. 'If we miscalculate, we could lose our entire position in South East Asia overnight' he signalled to Lodge.[59] Were it to succeed, though, it would still look the same, with no guarantee the new junta, even with American help, would be any more successful in fighting the Communist insurgency than Diem.

The Vietnam coup thus went ahead, with secret American backing, at 1.45 p.m. on November 1, 1963. President Diem and his brother were taken prisoner on the orders of the South Vietnamese generals, and despite Kennedy's attempts to arrange for the brothers to be flown out of the country, they were swiftly assassinated in the personnel carrier in which they were travelling, along with the $1 million in cash the CIA was supplying to ease their exile. The chairman of the Joint Chiefs of Staff, General Maxwell Taylor (who did not favour the plan for a coup), recalled how, when the news was passed to Kennedy, he 'leaped to his feet and rushed from the room with a look of shock and dismay on his face'.[60] Upstairs, he burst into tears, as Jackie recalled.[61] Like Julius Caesar, he saw it not only as a mistake, but as an omen.

Kennedy blamed himself. He went into depression, knowing he had been party not only to a *coup d'état*, in a faraway, difficult country whose fortunes should not have skewed American strategy, but also to the killing in cold blood of Diem, a man he'd met and admired. Was this the act of a great democracy, that had overthrown the British yoke in 1776 and set down the world's most precious political document, the Constitution of the United States? 'I should never have given my consent to it without a round-table conference,' he said in a statement taped for the record three days later. 'I was shocked by the death of Diem and Nhu. I'd met Diem with Justice Douglas many years ago. He was an extraordinary character. While he became increasingly difficult in the last months, nevertheless over a ten-year period, he'd held his country together, maintained its independence under very adverse conditions. The way he was killed made it particularly abhorrent.'[62]

A fortnight later Kennedy was himself assassinated, seemingly by a lone gunman, Lee Harvey Oswald, who was in turn murdered while in police custody two days later.[63]

## Part Three: Private Life

JFK's father suffered lifelong stomach problems, and was rendered mute and unable to walk by a massive stroke in 1961; his sister Eunice also suffered from mild Addison's disease, but JFK's ill health was of a completely different order, resulting in disabilities almost as severe as FDR's polio and heart disease, and requiring the same magnitude of courage. Scarlet fever, chicken pox, bronchitis, German measles, mumps, whooping cough, ear infections; these were easily diagnosable, if almost incessant, illnesses during JFK's childhood. During adolescence and early manhood, however, his afflictions became more serious and less easy to identify, beyond 'colitis', suspected leukaemia and gastritis. He neither smoked nor drank, and only ate bland food such as soup. Doctors had no idea what caused his frequent physical collapses.

At college, and with the help of his best friend from school (who was homosexual and adored him slavishly), JFK began a checkered romantic career as 'Don Juan' or 'Don John Kennedy', as he described himself.[64] Mozart's Don Giovanni, had, according to his servant Leporello, racked up some 2,085 conquests. It was a catalogue raisonné that JFK was resolved to match in his own lifetime. Handsome, witty, educated, well travelled and exciting to be with, against all the medical odds he seemed to be succeeding when, at twenty-four, Ensign John F. Kennedy fell in love in late 1941 with a beautiful, exotic – and married – siren.

Six years older than JFK, Inga Arvad was the only woman who came near to stealing his almost proverbially stone heart; indeed, Inga might well have become Mrs John F. Kennedy had war and J. Edgar Hoover not intervened. Radiantly attractive, sensitive and intelligent, Inga exuded more charm even than her young Massachusetts beau. A former Miss Denmark, then successful journalist, she had followed her second husband, Hungarian anthropologist and film-maker Paul Fejos, to New York. After retraining at the Columbia School of Journalism, she was writing an interview column for the *Washington Herald* when introduced to Kennedy.

For the first and only time in his life, JFK became utterly infatuated and they quickly became a Washington item, causing Inga's jealous husband to pay for a private detective to trail her, and her female colleagues to denounce her to the FBI as a possible enemy spy. (While in Denmark in the 1930s Inga had got exclusive interviews with Hitler and a number of senior Nazis in neighbouring Germany.)

The denunciations were groundless, but once the FBI began a surveillance operation on Mrs Fejos, alarm bells sounded when the man staying overnight at her apartment was identified as the son of the US ambassador to Great Britain. More worrying still, in the case of a woman being investigated as a possible German spy, the junior officer was found to be working in the office of the chief of naval intelligence, raising the possibility of a scandal neither the navy nor the ambassador to Great Britain were keen, in the wake of Pearl Harbor, to see explode. JFK was therefore swiftly removed from his intelligence post in Washington and sent to Charleston, South Carolina, where he was assigned to training and security duties.

Warned not to continue the affair, JFK simply refused to comply – indeed begged Inga to marry him. Head over heels in love, he wanted to have a baby with her. 'Dammit, Jack, she's already married!' his father protested, but Jack 'said he didn't care', Inga's newspaper editor recalled.[65]

To the end of his days, JFK kept Inga's love letters, as she kept his. But the love affair, ignited just as the US Navy suffered the worst defeat in its history, was itself doomed to defeat, Inga realized – especially when told so by none other than Ambassador Kennedy. To Inga, JFK's ambition seemed both real and achievable, despite his youth, given his personality, intelligence and talents. Transcripts of their lovemaking, taped by the FBI as part of their ongoing investigation, revealed not only repeated carnal relations but JFK's relentless dissections of world affairs, the probable future course of the war, and his ambition to become president of the United States.

'We are so well matched' Inga reflected, knowing marriage was impossible yet certain JFK would one day get to the very pinnacle of politics. 'Should I die before you reach to the top of the golden ladder, then Jack, dear – if there is a life after death, as you believe in – be I in heaven or hell, that is the moment when I shall stretch a hand out and try to keep you balancing on that – the most precarious of all steps.'[66]

Even had JFK followed his smitten heart rather than his head and married Inga, pursuing thereafter a career as a writer and political journalist (as he did briefly, after the war), could Inga have altered his Don Juan behaviour? The serious biographer must doubt it. Nevertheless Inga was, without doubt, the only woman in JFK's life who bewitched him 'von Kopf bis Fuss' ('from head to toe', as Marlene Dietrich had mesmerizingly sung in The Blue Angel), and of whom he was sexually jealous: a true femme fatale. Blonde, quick-witted, instinctively empathetic, gifted in languages, well travelled, experienced in life, not afraid of sex, profoundly feminine and so beautiful men old and young melted before her, 'Inga Binga' (as JFK dubbed her) tormented the young ensign – indeed his decision to leave his 'safe' shore-based post in Charleston, South Carolina, and volunteer for active duty at sea, despite his chronic ill health, can be seen as a crazed reaction to the battle for Inga – a battle he could only have won by getting himself dishonourably discharged from the navy, in wartime, and ignoring his father's warnings. Given his patriotism and vaulting ambition, that was something he would not do.

In the Solomon Islands, where he played Sinatra love ballads incessantly on a portable Victrola between night sorties behind the Japanese lines, JFK dreamed of Inga. He seemed unfazed by the prospect of death, impelled by love and his old standby, his self-deprecating sense of humour. When he crashed his PT boat against the dock, racing back to base after one mission, and faced court martial for recklessly endangering government property, he was unapologetic and is reported to have said, 'Well, you can't stop that PT-109!'[67]

Certainly JFK could not be stopped after his affair with Inga; indeed there was something almost suicidal in his behaviour. Telling Inga in a letter how much he longed to see her again, he wrote 'If anything happens to me I have this knowledge that if I had lived to be a hundred, I could only have improved the quantity of my life, not the quality. This sounds gloomy as hell . . . I'll cut it . . . You are the only person I'd say it to anyway. As a matter of fact knowing you has been the brightest point in an extremely bright twenty-six years'.[68]

How had a privileged, repeatedly sick, gangly youth got himself into combat anyway, his colleagues wondered? Wherever he went, men were magnetized. His courage in saving his surviving crew after the sinking of his PT boat would become legendary, but when captaining a subsequent vessel, PT-59, he demonstrated even more determination under fire, as well as being promoted executive officer of his squadron with a perfect 4.0 rating for overall performance and leadership. Though JFK had written lovelorn letters to Inga from the tropics, he weighed only 140 lb, was yellow, barely able to walk for back pain, and 'just looked like hell' Inga later told her son.[69] It was over.

Along with broken health and the disillusioning, death-filled experience of war, the end of the affair with Inga marked the end of innocence in the life of JFK. His brother Joe Jr was killed while courageously piloting a navy bomber packed with explosives on a secret mission over England in August 1944.[70] Then in September, his sister Kathleen's young husband, Captain Lord Hartington, was killed in Belgium during the Allied breakout from Normandy.

With Inga elsewhere, his brother dead and his sister widowed, JFK alternated between depression and a sort of manic determination to make every second count in terms of his two obsessions: politics and women. On a whim, shortly after his election to Congress, he is believed to have secretly married a pretty, petite, blonde, twice-divorced Inga lookalike, Durie Malcolm, an Episcopalian socialite in Palm Beach.

If true, and if JFK thought this act of insouciant defiance of his fate would go down well in the Kennedy compound, he was much mistaken. His father 'went ballistic' recalled his friend Chuck Spalding, who was ordered by Joe Kennedy to get the marriage 'eradicated' at the County Court, which (in days of handwritten paper records) was swiftly done.[71]

The problem of an unwise first marriage was less fatal to JFK's political aspirations, however, than the revelation, in 1947, that his recurrent illnesses were due to the fact that he was slowly dying of a fatal disease – Addison's. On a trip to Ireland and England as a young congressman, JFK was given this shocking diagnosis by the king's doctor, Sir Daniel Davis. Seeing JFK's suspiciously bronzed flesh, he diagnosed advanced Addison's disease – and gave Kennedy perhaps a year to live. Aboard the *Queen Elizabeth* on the way home, JFK again fell ill and it seemed even that prognosis was optimistic; a Catholic priest administered the last rites. Fortunately for Kennedy, an American doctor Dr George Thorn, had pioneered the use of synthetic cortisone to treat Addisonian patients. In great secrecy the congressman began taking Thorn's medication, and the terminal disease was arrested – for how long no doctor could say. In 1951, on a visit to Japan, JFK suffered a repeat Addisonian crisis, and was again given the last rites – but survived.

Life, which had always been a game that JFK played competitively and for maximum amusement, now became a serious challenge: how, like FDR after polio, to become a real politician with a clear vision, and cheat death, to fulfil not only his own long-standing ambition, but the dreams of his family, the good wishes of his friends, the expectations of colleagues, and the hopes of his growing number of supporters who believed in his sad-looking, disabled yet magnetic leadership ability.

As in Shakespeare's portrait of young Prince Hal, JFK now threw himself into his political career in Washington while ensuring his Massachusetts base was covered. Politics – in terms of issues and personalities – proved to be a new battlefield. Political calculation marked every decision, even that of marriage. Interviewed in the late 1940s, Congressman Kennedy claimed he'd like to marry a 'homebody type of girl. One who is quiet and would make a nice, understanding wife and mother for [my] children. The color of her hair or her height wouldn't make much difference. Just as long as she's a homebody is all that counts. When I find her, even politics will take a back seat then.'[72]

This was garbage. JFK neither looked for such a consort seriously, nor would he ever allow politics to take a back seat; indeed after the affair with Inga and the putative marriage to Durie Malcolm, he showed no inclination to marry at all. So little did he date 'homebody' types, or even eligible women, in fact, that his father, as his chief funder, launderer and political rooter, grew anxious over his son's playboy reputation, as did others on JFK's staff. Marrying Inga, a divorced woman, would have spelled the end of any presidential aspirations (as would his secretly expunged nuptials with Durie) – but remaining unmarried made Kennedy an equally vulnerable candidate.

It was in this way that Senator John Fitzgerald Kennedy, the most eligible bachelor in Congress following his victory over Senator Lodge in 1952, surrendered to his father's importunings and the following year took Jackie Bouvier, daughter of divorced parents but a Roman Catholic, as his bride.

Jackie Bouvier was well mannered (she had been named Debutante of the Year in the 1947–8 Newport, Rhode Island, season) and well educated, having attended Vassar, the Sorbonne and George Washington University. Significantly, she was working as the Inquiring Photographer on the *Washington Times-Herald* – the same position that Inga Arvad had held – when JFK met her. There the similarity ended, however. Jackie was twelve years younger than the senator, and not considered conventionally beautiful, with wide shoulders, no figure, size-ten shoes, an accomplished equestrienne and a budding cultural snob par excellence. As an impecunious stepdaughter of the very wealthy Standard Oil heir, Hugh D. Auchincloss of Hammersmith Farm in Connecticut, she was also obsessed with what she termed 'real money'.[73]

There was tantalizingly little initial interest or affection on JFK's part. A sullen, desultory romance ensued with but a single postcard sent by JFK to his fiancée when out of town. When one of JFK's ushers danced with her at the big wedding on September 12, 1953, and asked when had she first fallen in love with JFK, Jackie stopped dancing and demanded: 'Who says I am in love with him?'[74] Yet when a photographer took JFK's picture as he danced with another attractive woman

– rumoured to be one of his paramours – she smashed the photographer's camera.[75]

Jackie's efforts at self-protection were futile, however. Like most women who fell under his spell, she adored him, in her case as helplessly as she'd loved her own errant father, 'Black Jack' Bouvier, who had proven too drunk to give her away on her wedding day. Thus began the tragic marriage of Mr and Mrs John F. Kennedy.

In *The Twelve Caesars*, Suetonius described the private life of the emperor Caligula with undisguised disgust. 'It would be hard to say whether the way he got married, the way he dissolved his marriages, or the way he behaved as a husband was the more disgraceful.' Certainly there were many sad similarities between Caligula's and JFK's marital and extramarital conduct. According to his friends, JFK dated more women during his *fiançailles* than ever, as if determined to prove he would not be tamed. Certainly he refused to give up the chase afterwards, as if punishing Jackie for imagining they could be a real couple.

JFK's travels in pre-war Europe had given him an understanding of the European class system, a set-up whereby the privileged upper classes could, behind a mask of 'polite behaviour', do exactly as they pleased in whatever beds they pleased, protected by a hierarchical social structure and strict libel laws. This amorality was much to JFK's liking, as the privileged son of an American multimillionaire; its ethos would always define his reckless private life. However, in contrast to his wife's sincere and gushing admiration for all things European – clothes, cuisine, history – JFK was, and remained, all-American in his tastes, interests and, above all, in his aggressive approach to living. He loved competitive sports – football, touch-football, sailing, golf. He loved dancing, show business, Broadway and Hollywood, priding himself on bedding more stars of the silver screen in his career than almost any actor, from Gene Tierney and Grace Kelly to Jayne Mansfield and Marilyn Monroe. Uncertain how long he had to live, he demanded – and got – the maximum out of life, whether in politics or in pleasure. As a journalist friend, Gloria Emerson, later recalled, at weekend parties he walked around 'half naked, with just a towel wrapped around him – all bone, all rib, all shank. You have to have tremendous self-assurance to do that. I've never met anyone like that again. It was the audaciousness, the intensity, the impatience, the brusqueness. Here was a man who wasn't going to wait; he was going to get what he wanted. He was going to go from the House to the Senate to the White House. And it was quite thrilling.'[76]

In 1954 JFK's sister Pat married the British actor Peter Lawford, who then facilitated JFK's intimacy with Sinatra's jet-setting entertainment mafia, the so-called 'Rat Pack'. Though as president he would eventually be forced to spurn Sinatra and his naked poolside orgies for fear of stories leaking in the press, JFK's recklessness did not diminish. He despised Jackie's pretentious social and artistic snobbery (she was nicknamed 'the Deb' in the Kennedy family), and found her whims and moodiness unbearable when he was in almost constant pain. His life by 1953 had reduced to two demands: sexual distraction or serious, challenging political engagement, neither of which, given the differences of their personalities, Jackie supplied. ('Oh, Jack, I'm so sorry for you that I'm such a dud' she apologized.[77]) He had always been cruelly indifferent to women, at heart – save for Inga, who had broken his. Now he took it out on Jackie that, for purely political and dynastic reasons, he had felt obliged to take her as his wife: their wedding, their honeymoon and their marriage, in his eyes, as much a sham as his first – merely more pretentious.

For Jackie, this was far more than she had bargained for. By 1959, it was later reported, her feelings had turned from love to despair – as was all too understandable, given JFK's behaviour. She had nursed him through his back surgeries but had got little in return since, like JFK's parents, siblings, friends and colleagues she was sworn to secrecy about the severity of his ailments and the extent of his womanizing. Concerned lest his sexually transmitted diseases might have made him impotent, JFK had had himself tested for fertility, the results of which were positive. Nevertheless Jackie had miscarried once, and was understandably careful when she became pregnant again in 1956, at the time of the Chicago Democratic Convention. Once the politicking was over, JFK simply flew to Europe without her, disappearing on a privately rented yacht in the Mediterranean with his younger brother and a fellow philanderer, wealthy William Thomson, to 'relax' with young women. When Jackie haemorrhaged and the baby died in America, JFK simply sailed on, only returning home when a friend in the Senate, George Smathers, called from Washington and read him the riot act. It was small wonder Jackie eventually wanted out, demanding, it was said, a huge money-guarantee from the 'paymaster', Joseph P. Kennedy, for her to drop her divorce application and continue as the senator's spouse for the duration of the 1960 presidential election campaign. Convinced that he could ensure his son's election, but that Jackie's defection could damn it, Joseph Kennedy willingly agreed.

When JFK won the election – just – Jackie played fair to the agreement. JFK, however, had not made any agreement regarding his conduct. When asked by his deputy speechwriter, Dick Goodwin, whether being president in the White House cramped his philandering, given the intense media scrutiny, he grinned and shook his head. 'Dick,' he responded, 'it's never been easier!'[78]

Jackie had loyally borne JFK two healthy children – a girl in 1957 and a boy in 1960. In the White House, to her great credit, she made a new role for herself as First Lady. She would not be a toiling feminist and defender of the rights of the poor, like Eleanor Roosevelt, nor would she stay out of the limelight under her mother's watchful eye, like shy Beth Truman. Nor did she aspire to quiet TV dinners with her husband once he returned from the Oval Office to the family quarters, as Mamie Eisenhower had done. Instead Jackie set herself the task of becoming not only the mother of young children in the White House, complete with nursery and crèche, but also the photogenic young doyenne of modern taste, fashionable clothes and appreciation of cultural history, casting a spell on invited foreign dignitaries, artists and diplomats in the manner of a twentieth-century Cleopatra, while decorating with flair a hideaway country estate, Glen Ora, that she rented in Virginia's horse country, where she was able to indulge her love of fox-hunting.

Warming to his role of father, JFK's attitude towards Jackie softened, even if his extramarital behaviour didn't change. As Jackie became a world celebrity in her own right as First Lady, he also began to appreciate her style, famously remarking in Paris, on his way to Vienna, that he was but the 'man who accompanied Jacqueline Kennedy to Paris'.[79] His wit, self-deprecating and worldly-wise, together with Jackie's trendsetting fashion sense and dignity, made the Kennedys an entrancing couple, especially when photographed or filmed with their children (which Jackie only permitted by tasteful photographers such as Richard Avedon).

Behind the super-elegant facade, however, JFK found himself more challenged by the job of president than he'd expected, and more and more in need of medication, both pharmaceutical and extramarital. The tougher the responsibilities of presidency became, the fiercer grew his addiction, and the more his staff worried – especially once his father was out of the picture, following his stroke. It was as if Jackie's immaculately dressed, beautifully manicured posing (she adopted a husky whisper when talking to people she wished to beguile), though graceful and fashionable, only reinforced JFK's desire to 'stick it' to those who bowed to such elitism and snobbery. His mother Rose's cold, dry insistence on aping the manners of the upper classes, as well as her obsession with top dressmakers, had infuriated him as a child, and was now replicated as Jackie and Rose fought for the title of 'best-dressed woman in America'. For all his legendary compassion, JFK seemed unable to see that such pretensions were their answer to otherwise crushing marital infidelity.

The more Jackie dressed, the more, it seemed, JFK undressed, even receiving visitors in the nude, such as his paralyzed father's nurse, after his father's stroke. 'All I could really think of was what in heaven's name does one say to a naked president?' Rita Dallas later recalled – and how she had thrown a washcloth into the bath with the words 'For heaven's sake, cover up.'[80] Such playfulness masked, however, a much deeper, almost pathological subversion by which, in his private life, JFK deliberately cocked a snook at decorum. In public, he was famed for his quick, intelligent articulateness, which his speechwriter Ted Sorensen further refined, adding noble cadences; but in private, impatient with those who bored, crossed or disappointed him, JFK cussed and swore like a proverbial trooper, his speech peppered with 'prick' and 'shit' and 'fuck' and 'nuts' and 'bastard' and 'son of a bitch'.[81] A speed-reader with a photographic memory, he was famously able to absorb information and distil its essence. But working at high velocity, at once inspirational and realistic, intelligent and compassionate, his private life, he felt, was his own, to do as he pleased. And what pleased him was casting off the uniform of the presidency, almost literally, as he sought nudity and 'fun' in the White House swimming pool, or the family compound at Palm Beach.

Because he was president, the secret services were able (and obliged) to protect such privacy, even as, amazed, they witnessed the leader of the free world casting caution to the four winds and behaving, when Jackie was not present, like a teenager whose parents were on vacation. His White House staff became his pimps, escorting 'Jane Does' into the residence whenever Jackie was away, without logging their names or bothering with security at the gates. The White House pool often resembled a Roman bathhouse, the scene of orgy after orgy, which the secret services were compelled to protect both from assassins and from public view.

'Was he really that bad?' an Argentine girlfriend, who had known JFK from the age of nineteen, later asked, distressed at revelations concerning Kennedy's many hundreds of extramarital 'conquests', ranging from mafia trollops like Judith Campbell, to well brought up daughters of the upper class. 'How could he have had the *time*?'[82]

The answer was perhaps that the president spent so little time with each of his belles. Even Jackie, according to her psychotherapist (who spoke after her death), complained that JFK had no idea of foreplay. The president seemed not to be interested in loving intimacy – something which remained a distant and somewhat forbidding city. In matters of public policy such as poverty or mental retardation or racial oppression, JFK felt and could uninhibitedly show curiosity, compassion and a determination to effect change through political courage; but in matters of after-hours distraction he became, as his life went on and he continued to cheat death, simply too addicted to stop. It was, moreover, an area where not even his closest male friends, marvelling at the polarities of his character, could restrain him. Thus in his public life he could be the most disciplined and rational of men, yet in his private life could simply ignore danger or even – perhaps especially – decency. At the end of a private lunch with his friend Chuck Spalding in JFK's suite in the Carlyle in New York, JFK asked Spalding's new young girlfriend if she'd like to go into the bedroom with him for 'dessert' – which she did. Recalling the episode almost thirty years later, Spalding could not explain why he had neither stopped JFK, nor called him on his *droit de seigneur* behaviour, then or afterwards. 'I didn't . . . I just didn't' Spalding shrugged. 'That's how he was.'[83] And that was the man Spalding loved, as a friend.

This was, perhaps, the crux of the matter. While JFK seemed unable, after Inga, to show love in a reciprocal, caring relationship, this did not stop people – of both sexes – loving *him*. Jackie's response was exactly the same as that of Spalding. She called JFK 'Bunny' for his insatiable need for sex, and would at times introduce visitors to her twenty-three-year-old secretary with the words 'This is Miss Turnure – with whom my husband is sleeping.'[84] Two young campaign assistants, twenty-year-old Priscilla Wear and Jill Cowan, were put on the White House payroll as secretaries, yet were known to all as 'Fiddle' and 'Faddle' with instructions to service the president whenever summoned. They, too, would be introduced to certain visitors by Jackie as 'my husband's tarts'. 'Why? Are you starting to get ambitious?' the president asked when Priscilla announced she'd like to take a typing course.[85]

Air hostesses, women journalists, artists, mothers and wives (like Marella Agnelli, the wife of the boss of Fiat) all succumbed, often unaware, like Helen Chavchavadze, a classmate of Jackie's sister Lee, that JFK was simultaneously carrying on similar affairs with other women. 'It was a compulsion, a quirk in his personality' Helen would later reflect, having had a breakdown. 'He was out of control.'[86] 'He's like a god, fucking anybody he wants to,' remarked political aide Fred Dutton, 'anytime he feels like it.'[87] Even Jackie was reduced to finding attractive young women, such as Mary Meyer, Robyn Butler, Fifi Fell and Mary Gimbel, to amuse her husband at table – and beneath. As Helen Chavchavadze put it, 'Jackie was in charge' of the harem – indeed Jackie later commissioned and edited, at Doubleday, a book on eastern harems: 'choosing his playmates. It was very French.'[88] Less French and more Roman was the president's penchant for group sex, perhaps ensuring his partners understood the terms of trade as much as for enhanced excitement; sex as distraction, in other words, not love, which was something else, long buried in the past.

Though the JFK's private shenanigans astonished newcomer aides and secret servicemen, none 'ratted', in large part because such private misbehaviour could not be seen as adversely affecting the president's professional performance in the White House. Indeed the opposite might be said. From initial naivety in handling the presidency, JFK had grown more and more confident in his unique role as youthful leader or steward of the free world, as his handling of the Cuban Missile Crisis showed.

Was it, then, as Jackie believed, an abiding fear of boredom, of wasting precious off-duty hours in a life he was certain from the start would be short, that explained JFK's recklessness as president? Was the chase, the planning, the constant challenge of promiscuity with pretty – and young – women an escape, however temporary, from often crippling pain, age and depression? Was it, in the White House, a tried and tested means to slough off the relentless expectations and heavy burdens of head of state?

Whatever it was that impelled JFK to take such risks it went back too far, too deep, and was too insistent in its urgency for him to countenance reform. Moreover the women he bedded were the last to complain, raised in an era when 'it was assumed that women compete with each other for the best men' as one young mistress recalled.[89] 'Somehow it didn't register with me at any deep level that what I was doing was absolutely immoral, absolutely atrocious behavior' – a twenty-year-old reflected, describing 'having dinner in the White House' with sex to follow in 'the Abraham Lincoln bedroom'.[90]

How long such behaviour could have continued without becoming public knowledge is a question that vexed many writers in subsequent years. Certainly it made the president vulnerable to blackmail; indeed by the autumn of 1963 he was being warned by well-meaning friends about serious financial corruption on the part of his personal staff in the White House, corruption he chose not to investigate or rein in lest, in return, the accused accuse him of other, scandalous improprieties.[91]

In any event, JFK himself never abandoned his primary love: politics. He was determined to stand for re-election in 1964, and to win with a significant majority. With this in mind he persuaded Jackie to accompany him on November 21, 1963 to Fort Worth, Texas, to rally support for the Democratic Party. He'd once told Clare Booth Luce 'I can't go to sleep without a lay.'[92] He'd wanted Jackie to come, yet whenever Jackie was with him, one of his secret service agents recalled, his private life 'was no fun. He just had headaches. You really saw him droop because he wasn't getting laid. He was like a rooster getting hit with a water hose.'[93] Nevertheless he was grateful she'd agreed to accompany him into what he called 'nut country', knowing how she hated campaigning and having to meet 'common' people who called her 'Jackie' instead of her preferred 'Jacqueline'.[94]

The next day, 22 November, 1963, the president and First Lady flew to Love Field outside Dallas, where they got into their open limousine and made their way downtown where there was to be a $100-a-plate fundraising luncheon at the Trade Mart. Amazingly, it was the first time since the inauguration in 1961 that she had ever been west of her house at Glen Ora, Virginia – despite a number of trips abroad, including a recent month-long stay in Europe as house guest of Aristotle Onassis.

While JFK beamed his warm, grateful smile at the crowds, hoping the estimated 200,000 would all vote Democrat in the next year's election, Jackie seemed unable or unwilling to fake delight, insisting on wearing dark sunglasses, as if married to a South American dictator. JFK asked her to take them off, so that well-wishers lining the route could see her better.

Jackie took them off, but the bright sunlight hurt her eyes. 'Jackie: *take your glasses off!*' the president repeated, when she put them back on. They were his last words to her. Just as the open Lincoln Continental (he had rejected the covered limousine that had been offered as an alternative) picked up gentle speed after slowing down to walking pace around the right-angle bend on Dealey Plaza, a shot rang out. 'If someone wants to shoot me from a window with a rifle, nobody can stop it', the president had remarked earlier.[95] He was right. The bullet, aimed from above, went through his neck. Two more shots made it murder most foul, ending the life of the last of the Great Caesars.

# CHAPTER FIVE

# LYNDON B. JOHNSON

Later reviled

Democrat
36th President
(November 22, 1963–January 20, 1969)

## Part One: The Road to the White House

Lyndon Baines Johnson was born on August 27, 1908 in a two-room shack by the Pedernales, a small, muddy tributary of the Colorado River, in the Hill Country, sixty-five miles from Austin, Texas.[1]

A speculator on cotton futures, Lyndon's father Sam Ealy Johnson Jr had lost all but the clothes on his back. Rebekah Baines Johnson, Lyndon's mother, was a devout, college-educated journalist, big on literacy, poetry and dreams. The Baines family had a rich tradition of producing Baptist preachers and politicians – her father, a lawyer, became a Secretary of State for Texas – but had then gone bankrupt.

For the first five years of his life Lyndon was brought up in rural poverty until the family finally moved to a rented house in the small town of Johnson City. Becoming a real-estate broker, Lyndon's father – who had once before been elected to the Texas state legislature in Austin – was re-elected three times following the end of World War I. However the Johnsons remained short of money, and their house remained without indoor plumbing.

When her husband was away, Rebekah, a strong-willed woman, kept Lyndon, her firstborn, in her bed. Though she gave birth to four more children, Lyndon – smart, gangly and wild – would always be her favourite.

At age fifteen Lyndon ran away from home with a group of friends to work in California for a year. Further months labouring on highway construction in rural Texas convinced him that without an education he was never going to achieve much in life. On a working scholarship he therefore attended San Marcos College in south-west Texas, studying first for a two-year teaching certificate then a full four-year BS degree in education and history. To earn his tuition money he worked as an aide to the college principal, and for a year took a job as a principal himself in a small rural Mexican American school – an experience that made him a lifelong warrior for the poor, the wronged and the racially oppressed. He became a high-school teacher in Houston in 1930.

Johnson had been called 'incorrigibly delinquent' as a teenager, but his phenomenal energy on behalf of his Mexican American students, then his Houston High students, bespoke responsibility and ambitions that would not be contained in a classroom. As a youth he had acted as a messenger for his father in the state legislature in Austin, where he had fallen in love with democracy – expressed in a marbled atmosphere of ritual, oratory, legal niceties, constantly quoted history and political barter behind closed doors. When approached for help in running a local politician's campaign for the state legislature, he offered his services to be his campaign manager. He was then asked to go to Washington DC in 1931, as legislative secretary to his local congressman, Richard Kleberg.

No man in the history of Congress embraced the everyday business of Capitol Hill as did Lyndon Baines Johnson upon his arrival in Washington. Alternately obsequious in his willingness to be of service to superiors, and tyrannically domineering towards those over whom he had power, LBJ was from the start a phenomenon. He revived a discussion group, Little Congress, and became its Speaker at age twenty-three. On March 4, 1933 he attended Roosevelt's inauguration, dreaming of one day standing there as president himself, instead of as a mere legislative secretary. In a delusion of Napoleonic grandeur the junior congressional aide, who slept only four to five hours per night, even put himself forward to be president of Texas College of Arts and Industries in Kingsville, South Texas. Turned down for presumptuousness he was, however, offered a $10,000 per year job as lobbyist for General Electric, and was on the point of accepting when Roosevelt announced on June 26, 1935 the formation by executive order of a new National Youth Administration. There would be, it was also announced, a director for each of the forty-eight states, and a $27 million budget.

Johnson pounced, and with the help of his mentor, Texas congressman Sam Rayburn, he got FDR to revoke the appointment of an experienced union boss as the Texas director, and instead assign twenty-six-year-old Lyndon Johnson to the post in Austin.

The youngest director of any New Deal programme in America, Johnson – who had married in 1934 – saw a chance, with twenty million people nationwide on relief, not only to help find employment (and, thereby, college funding) for the 125,000 young Texans who needed work and direction, but to prove his ability as a leader. He did. By the following year Eleanor Roosevelt, on a visit to Texas – which comprises a ninth of the area of the continental United States – asked to meet the young director who was 'doing such an effective job.'[2]

By then, in fact, Johnson had already begun plotting his electoral ascent. A seat in the Texas State Senate initially looked appealing, but he had reservations. He had promised his colleagues at the Capitol in Washington he would return one day as an elected congressman, and in February 1937 he made a successful bid for the House of Representatives for the Tenth District of Texas, in a special election. Johnson thereby not only became the youngest member of Congress, but got to meet the president, who was visiting Galveston on a trip aboard the presidential yacht in the Gulf of Mexico that spring, and who asked to meet the young Democratic prodigy. Greeting FDR as he came ashore, the newly elected congressman 'came on like a freight train', Roosevelt later commented. Johnson accompanied the president the next day on his way to Kingsville, and from there to Fort Worth. 'I've just met a remarkable young man. Now I like this boy, and you're going to help him with anything you can' the president told his key strategist Tommy Corcoran, once back in Washington.[3] 'That was all it took' remarked Corcoran years later, 'one train ride.'[4]

So successful was Congressman Johnson in getting Works Progress Administration (WPA) projects, housing and rural electrification to his area of Texas that Roosevelt asked him to become head of the Rural Electrification Administration (REA) itself. Johnson declined. His relationship with the president continued to prosper in the years that followed, however, to mutual benefit: Roosevelt steered huge military contracts Johnson's way in Texas, and in turn Johnson steered them to Brown & Root, Inc., which financed Texas-for-Roosevelt campaigns, as well as Brown-for-Lyndon support. So certain did Johnson become that he could vault into the US Senate, that when Texas senator Morris Sheppard died of a brain haemorrhage in April 1941, shortly after Roosevelt's third inauguration, the thirty-two-year-old congressman threw his ten-gallon hat into the ring and fought a tough race against his fellow Democrat, Texas governor 'Pappy' O'Daniel.

All his adult life Johnson had done everything possible to ensure that, when he went out to attain something, no stone was left unturned. On election night, however, having unwisely made public the tiny margin of his victory, Johnson went exhausted to his hotel room in Johnson City to sleep, his door guarded by Rebekah, his proud mother, against all intrusion. When he awoke it was to find his opponent had raided the ballot boxes kept in various judges' homes. Johnson eventually lost by 1,311 'late' votes. 'Lyndon,' the president said, tipping back his head in laughter when the distraught congressman came back to see him at the White House on July 30, 1941, 'apparently you Texans haven't learned one of the first things we learned up in New York State, and that is that when the election is over, you have to sit on the ballot boxes.'[5]

With the Japanese attack on Pearl Harbor in December 1941, Johnson's failed Senate campaign receded into the background. He had already unsuccessfully volunteered for service in the US Navy in 1940, when Roosevelt revived the draft; moreover, he had helped save the year-old Selective Service Act, or draft, from defeat by isolationists the following year, by a single vote. In recognition the navy now ignored his poor medical report and commissioned him as a lieutenant commander. The navy drew the line at active service at sea, however, since Johnson did not know one end of a vessel from the other. Granted leave of absence by the House, the young congressman commander was instead charged with gingering naval war production in Texas and the Southwest, under the auspices of the Secretary of the Navy's office.

Frustrated that he was not the boss, Lieutenant Commander Johnson pressed the president first to make him an admiral in charge of all wartime navy production, then, following a harrowing mission to Australia and the Solomon Islands on behalf of the president, Secretary of the Navy.[6]

Roosevelt, a lifelong sailor, had been Assistant Secretary of the Navy for eight years, but had never made Secretary, and was not going to appoint to that position a junior congressman aged thirty-four. With Roosevelt blocking naval promotion, and his chairmanship of a House subcommittee on problems in wartime production overshadowed by

Senator Truman's powerful, high-profile Senate subcommittee, Johnson languished. By April 1945, when Roosevelt died and Truman became president, Johnson feared the worst. Roosevelt had, at least, been impressed by the young congressman's superhuman energy and drive. Truman, aware of murky financial dealings in Texas, refused to have anything to do with him.

With no hope of attaining a full committee chairmanship for a further twenty years owing to House seniority rules, Johnson thus decided to make another bid for the Senate in 1948, at age thirty-nine.

Johnson's 1948 Senate campaign was as brutal as Congressman Nixon's simultaneous contest in California – only in Texas, Johnson was crusading against 'Coke' Stevenson, a fellow Democrat who was the state's most popular former Speaker of the House of Representatives, former lieutenant governor, and former governor, from 1941 to 1947. Twenty years older than Johnson, Stevenson opposed the Marshall Plan, axed funding for the needy, and had, as governor of the state, ignored a lynching in Texarkana with the words 'certain members of the Negro race' deserved to be lynched.[7]

The run-off campaign for the Democratic nomination proved to be the fight of Johnson's life. Stevenson – a quiet, simple man, known as 'our cowboy governor' – was backed by Texas oil interests and conservative, largely racist sentiment; Johnson by a mix of political and financial supporters. With both sides spending almost $1 million the campaign was so surreal it could have been a rehearsal for George Orwell's novel *Nineteen Eighty-Four* (published the following year): Johnson pioneered the use of a campaign helicopter, a sixty-foot-long Sikorsky S-51 with three rotor blades (quickly christened the 'Flying Windmill')[8] that hovered over Texas farms and constituents. 'Hello down there!' Johnson would blare through a loudspeaker attached to the wheel struts, 'This is your friend, Lyndon Johnson, your candidate for United States Senate. I hope you'll vote for me on Primary Day. And bring along your relatives to vote, too!'[9]

This was not *deus ex machina*, but Lyndon Johnson's version of it. Advance men paved his way in the cities and radio advertising blasted night and day, as the young congressman battled the ageing former governor. Taking Roosevelt's words to heart, Johnson not only sat on the ballot boxes, but concealed the interim tallies from his opponent, the better to amend them when, as feared, Stevenson outpolled him.

In the days following the election Johnson thus whittled Stevenson's lead down to zero, and then overtook him. At eighty-seven votes' majority for Johnson, it was the tightest result in Texas history.

The vicious 1948 Texas campaign was the making of Lyndon B. Johnson. Like Richard M. Nixon, who became senator in 1950, Johnson had supped with the devil to get there, and like Nixon he instantly used his formidable energies to aim higher. Within two years he was appointed Democratic Party whip, and within four he became the Democratic Minority Party Leader in the Senate.

Where Nixon had used his political acumen to boost Joe McCarthy, however, Johnson used it to destroy his fellow senator. In the spring of 1954 Johnson authorized and arranged for McCarthy's army hearings to be televised so that the American people could see, as Johnson put it, 'what the bastard is up to'.[10] In the autumn he then orchestrated Senate hearings that, by sixty-seven votes to twenty-two, recommended Senator McCarthy be 'condemned' for having abused Senate rules and pilloried an innocent American general.[11] By 1955, when a Republican senator changed his party affiliation, Johnson became, at age forty-six, Senate Majority Leader – the swiftest ascent in the history of an institution known for its white hair.

Inevitably, 'The Tornado' was spoken of as a future president. But in the fickle way that American populist politics ran – and would continue to run – an alternative Democratic contender came forward in 1956 who seemed at first glance too young, too charming, too spoiled, too handsome, too father-dominated, and too lightweight to win the deputy Democratic crown as vice-presidential candidate: Senator John F. Kennedy.

Kennedy failed in his bid for the vice-presidential nomination in 1956, but when he won the nomination for the number one spot at the Democratic National Convention four years later in Los Angeles and as a courtesy asked Johnson to be his running mate, Johnson surprised even his closest aides by taking the offer seriously. John Adams had called the post 'the most insignificant office that ever the invention of man contrived', but Johnson did the maths. Unknown to the general public Kennedy was suffering from Addison's disease, an often terminal illness. Kennedy's offer would give Johnson a better than one-in-four chance of reaching the Oval Office by reason of the incumbent's death – a goal he might otherwise never achieve on his own, he calculated. To Kennedy's surprise, Johnson therefore accepted. In a presidential election that also made history for its ballot stuffing and bloc-voting, the Kennedy–Johnson ticket then squeezed past the winning post in November 1960. Johnson thus became, in January 1961, vice president of the United States, taking the place of his nemesis, outgoing vice president Richard Nixon.

Nixon had made the same calculation when surrendering his Senate seat to run for the vice presidency in 1952, next to General Eisenhower, but in his case the gamble had not paid off. Once elected, Nixon had been almost wholly sidelined by the president save at campaign times – and in much the same way, from January 1961 to the fall of 1963, Vice President Lyndon B. Johnson found himself largely ignored by Kennedy, spending less than two hours in one-on-one discussion with him in the whole of 1963.[12] Worse still, without Johnson's masterly influence in the Senate as Majority Leader, President Kennedy had a tough time pushing his liberal legislative agenda through Congress. Then, on November 22, 1963 – a day that, like Pearl Harbor, would live in infamy – disaster struck.

## Part Two: The Presidency

To the end of his life Johnson suspected a more nefarious plot behind the Kennedy assassination than the lone-gunman conclusion arrived at by the Warren Commission, which the new president straightaway established. No serious evidence emerged, however, of such a conspiracy, notwithstanding suspicions of mafia involvement and/or Cuban exiles, still smarting over the Bay of Pigs.

Johnson had been a human tornado in the years of his ascent. As the 36th president of the US he now became a hurricane. Within two days of the assassination he was masterminding successful passage through Congress of Kennedy's imperilled civil rights bill and $11 billion of tax cuts. As Truman had begun his surprise presidency, in a moment of national mourning, with an address to Congress, so President Johnson prepared a special speech three days after Kennedy's death, dictating for his speechwriters 'a whole page' of notes on hate: 'hate internationally – hate domestically – and just to say this hate that produces inequality, this hate that produces poverty, that's why we've got to have a tax bill

– the hate that produces injustice – that's why we've got to have a civil rights bill. It's a cancer that just eats out our national existence.'[13]

Johnson was as good as his word. Whatever Johnson wanted badly enough, he got, as when he overcame the resistance of his mentor and all-powerful southern senator, Richard Russell of Georgia, against serving on the Warren Commission, one week after the assassination. 'You've never turned your country down' Johnson barked on the telephone, working on Russell's patriotism. 'This is not me. This is your country . . . You're my man on that *commission*, and you're going to *do* it! And don't tell me what you can do and what you *can't* because I can't *arrest* you and I'm not going to put the *FBI* on you. But you're *goddammed* sure going to *serve* – I tell you *that!*'[14]

Russell served. Then, to the slain president's interrupted legislative agenda, Johnson added a third rail: a war on poverty. 'This administration,' he memorably declared in his famous State of the Union address to Congress on January 8, 1964, 'today, here and now, declares unconditional war on poverty in America . . . Our aim is not only to relieve the symptom of poverty, but to cure it and, above all, to prevent it.'[15]

Backed by liberal Democrats wanting to turn the tragedy into an opportunity for real change in America, Johnson was unstoppable. The 'smear and fear' tactics of Republicans and conservative Dixiecrats would unfortunately continue, Senator Hubert Humphrey of Minnesota stated, but 'while they are digging there, we will just be building a better America': rebuilding the republic on the basis of 'war on poverty, economic growth, world peace, security and medicare, human dignity, human rights, education, opportunity for the young.' To which Johnson responded 'Goddamn, that couldn't be better; that's as fine a statement as I ever saw of that view in a few words', and eight months later chose him as his election running mate.[16]

In due course Johnson's and Humphrey's visionary dreams would turn sour. But for the moment, at the opening stage in Johnson's crusade as a liberal, he swept aside all obstacles in the greatest demonstration of domestic presidential leadership since FDR's first term. As vice president, Johnson had been shunned by his former colleagues in the Senate, to the point where, as Senate president, he had stopped stepping down on to the Senate floor, or even going into the Democratic cloakroom where for twelve years he had held court, so unwelcome did the bullying former 'Master of the Senate' feel. Now, however, he had a mission, blazing a trail on behalf of his country, and was determined to use the assassination of his predecessor as his launch pad to greatness. 'I had to take the dead man's program and turn it into a martyr's cause' he later explained, his goal being to clarify the cause, in terms of legislation, and to turn it into reality. 'That way,' as he put it, 'Kennedy would live on forever and so would I.'[17]

Kennedy aficionados were not necessarily grateful, however. The Widow Jacqueline – a Paris-educated lover of style over substance par excellence – innocently fashioned, in her grief, a romantic legend of a lost Camelot, while former Kennedy operatives connived and calculated the chances of putting another Kennedy sibling on the imperial throne. Faint whiffs of treason thus emanated from Massachusetts and certain suburbs of the capital, reminding historians of Shakespeare's history plays, with their tart insights into the machinations of a perpetually jockeying Renaissance court.

Johnson's political courage made such murmurings of discontent in his own Democratic Party especially unworthy. 'I'm going to be the president who finishes what Lincoln began' Johnson insisted. When Senator Russell warned the president not to steamroller Kennedy's stalled civil rights bill through Congress, Johnson responded, 'Dick, you've got to get out of my way. I'm going to run over you. I don't intend to cavil or compromise.' And when Russell warned that 'it's going to cost you the South and cost the election', the president tilted his powerful head lower still. 'If that's the price I've got to pay,' he thundered, 'I'll pay it gladly.'[18]

Russell was unmoved. 'We will resist to the bitter end any measure or movement which would have a tendency to bring about social equality' the senator declared openly. At the end of March 30, 1964, however, following fifty-four days of Republican-Dixiecrat filibuster in the Senate, Johnson's civil rights bill was judged to have enough votes (two thirds of the Senate) to merit cloture, which concluded legislative opposition to racial integration in America, a century after the Civil War.

Signing the Civil Rights Act on July 2, 1964 in front of a hundred witnesses in the East Room of the White House, Johnson could take pride in an extraordinary accomplishment. It was, literally and metaphorically, his signature achievement as president of the United States, rectifying an injustice that had plagued America since colonial times. Yet although the president had used every tactic in his huge arsenal of persuasion, both public and private, to get the bill passed as a bipartisan measure, he was nervous about marking the ceremony with television cameras, knowing it would accelerate the ending of Dixiecrat support for the Democratic Party.

As Senator Russell had warned, the Civil Rights Act would have profound consequences for the Democrats. Johnson's aide, Bill Moyers, found the president far from elated in his bedroom that night. Asked why he looked so depressed, Johnson sighed: 'Because, Bill, I think we just delivered the South to the Republican Party for a long time to come.'[19]

If so, it would not happen overnight. In the meantime Johnson obtained a huge, Keynesian tax cut for the American middle class, lowering taxes an average of 19 per cent for eighty million individuals, with low-income earners paying little or none at all, and corporations also benefiting from a 2 per cent reduction in company tax rates. This was a stimulus bill that would, it was claimed, lead to increased consumer spending, higher industrial investment, reduced unemployment, and a higher gross national product. Reaction to the tax cuts was immediate. The stock market broke its 800-point ceiling for the first time, causing Democrats to anticipate a landslide in the November election, despite the contentious civil rights legislation.

Would Johnson stand, however? It was a quirk in his tornado-like character that, at certain times, he would lose faith in himself and, recalling his hardscrabble childhood, would suddenly feel too wounded, too unlovable, too sinful, too humble in terms of his background to go on. Compared with most northern liberals he was a southern progressive who had actually known poverty, yet he still felt inferior, at times, to those who talked poverty so eloquently. To them, he claimed, 'my name is shit and always has been and always will be. I got their goddamn legislation passed for them, but they gave me no credit.'[20] In particular, a spat he had with privileged Robert F. Kennedy, whom he had kept on as his Attorney General but whom he had decided not to take as his running mate if he ran, rankled. 'I don't want to have to go down in history', Johnson – a worrier to his toenails – explained, 'as the guy to have the dog wagged by the tail and have the vice president elect me.'[21]

The feeling was mutual. For his part, Robert Kennedy described the president as 'mean, bitter, vicious – an animal in many ways', a carnivore 'able to eat people up, and even people who are considered rather strong figures – I mean Mac Bundy or Bob McNamara. There's nothing left of them. *Our* president [Kennedy] was a gentleman and a human being. This man is not.'[22]

Johnson may have been an animal, but whatever was said of him, he was the leader who had brought the country together after his predecessor's shocking assassination, and who had used the tragedy to push a liberal agenda through Congress in posthumous homage to JFK. What concerned Johnson at a much deeper level were the antics at the Republican National Convention in New Jersey, especially those of Senator Barry Goldwater.

Like many Democrats, Johnson did not initially believe Senator Goldwater's *Conscience of a Conservative* political philosophy (against big government at home, yet for big American government action abroad) could win Goldwater the Republican nomination. Domestically, the Republicans 'don't stand for anything' the president mocked. 'And if they don't stand for something – hell if they just come out here and talk revival of the corn tassel or . . . Tom Watson's[23] watermelons, it would be something, but they're just, by God, *against* things – against everything,' he commented, 'and trying to smear and fear.'[24]

The smearing worked, however, not only against Democrats but against opponents in Goldwater's own party. Thus moderate Republican governor Nelson Rockefeller of New York, who had bucked Goldwater's call for 'values' by daring to get divorced in 1961 and remarrying in 1963, was trounced by Goldwater in the California Republican primary, and neither Nixon nor Senator Lodge found it possible to halt the wave of support that Goldwater's jingoism was creating. There was 'a bunch of screwballs in California', as Johnson put it, with money to burn – and a potential nominee 'as nutty as a fruitcake',[25] calling to send the Marines in Vietnam and to 'bomb' the North Vietnamese[26] – yet Goldwater was winning enough delegates to become the official presidential candidate of the Republican Party. 'He wants to drop atomic bombs on everybody' the president sighed. 'I don't believe the people will stand for that' – but even he acknowledged that, in a country as ornery as America, they 'may do it'.[27]

Republicans *did* – many of them, like Clare Boothe Luce, the wife of *Time* magazine founder Henry Luce, delighted that Goldwater had voted against the civil rights bill on June 18. At the Republican National Convention in San Francisco the next month Goldwater duly seized the Republican Party crown – ironically, the party of emancipator Abraham Lincoln – and in his nomination acceptance speech on July 16, 1964, Goldwater proceeded to excoriate America's decades-old containment policy.

Goldwater's rhetoric was chilling in its fanaticism: 'It's been during Democratic years that our strength to deter war has stood still, and even gone into a planned decline. It has been during Democratic years that we have weakly stumbled into conflict, timidly refusing to draw our own lines against aggression, deceitfully refusing to tell even our people of our full participation, and tragically, letting our finest men die on battlefields unmarked by purpose, unmarked by pride or the prospect of victory.'

To those who'd wondered what on earth he meant, Goldwater was all too clear. 'The administration which we shall replace', he sneered, 'has talked and talked and talked and talked the words of freedom' but had done no actual face-to-face fighting on its behalf. American policy since JFK's election, he claimed, had been nothing but a wilful belief in 'the illusion that a world of conflict will somehow mysteriously resolve itself into a world of harmony, if we just don't rock the boat or irritate the forces of aggression' – a continuing containment policy that he called 'hogwash'. Failures in the fight against Communism, he maintained, 'cement the wall of shame in Berlin. Failures blot the sands of shame at the Bay of Pigs. Failures mark the slow death of freedom in Laos. Failures infest the jungles of Vietnam . . . Failures proclaim lost leadership, obscure purpose, weakening wills, and the risk of inciting our sworn enemies to new aggressions and to new excesses.'

What all this was leading to, Goldwater revealed, was a new showdown in South East Asia. 'Yesterday it was Korea. Tonight it is Vietnam. Make no bones of this. Don't try to sweep this under the rug. We are at war in Vietnam. And yet the president, who is commander-in-chief of our forces, refuses to say – *refuses* to say, mind you – whether or not the objective over there is victory. And his Secretary of Defense continues to mislead and misinform the American people, and enough of it has gone by.' The would-be

Republican president wanted to 'set the tides running again in the cause of freedom'; indeed to hysterical cheering he reminded his audience 'that extremism in the defense of liberty is no vice'.[28] The former ferry-pilot from World War II gave notice he would, if elected, give up the timid policy of American 'advisers' helping the South Vietnamese junta in its attempts to deal with the Vietcong insurgency. He wanted war.

As publication of Johnson's secret White House tapes revealed three decades later, the president and the senior members of his administration and the Democratic Congress were all intimately aware of the disastrous French experience in the 1950s and were not anxious to repeat it. Time and again through the spring and early summer of 1964 Johnson had discussed the nightmare scenario of direct American intervention in a war in the jungles of the Vietnamese peninsula with his colleagues, opponents, members of the press and academics, as the primaries took place and the Democratic National Convention in Atlantic City drew closer.[29] 'It's a tragic situation. It's one of those places where you can't win', Senator Russell warned the president on May 27, 1964 as the two men talked through the worsening conditions in South Vietnam, where national elections – mandated by the Geneva Peace Accords – had been turned down by the United States government lest the Communists win. The latest 'democratic' government in Saigon was no more than a right-wing military junta, capitalizing on its *coup d'état* against President Diem nine months before. 'Anything that you do is wrong' commented Senator Russell, chairman of the Senate Armed Services Committee. As he memorably put it, the US was 'like the damn cow over a fence out there in Vietnam'.[30] 'The French report that they lost 250,000 men and spent a couple billion of their money and two billion of ours down there and just got the hell whipped out of them' he reminded the president.[31] At which point Johnson posed the $64,000 question: 'How important is it to us?' Russell shook his head. 'It isn't important a damned bit, with all these new missile systems' with which the United States could deter possible Soviet aggression.[32]

South Vietnam, however, *was* important to Goldwater, a symbol of his mission to export American 'spiritual values' and 'to bomb' those who disagreed, as Johnson noted in frustration. Behind Goldwater, moreover, stood Nixon, Ronald Reagan and the ageing

Republican conservatives who had savaged Truman over the 'loss' of China in 1948.[33]

Like Senator Russell, the president thus felt sandwiched between his predecessor's fateful decision to station 16,000 American military 'advisers' in South Vietnam, on the one hand, and Goldwater's gung-ho war rhetoric – with its shades of MacArthur's willingness to use nuclear weapons in Korea – on the other. Truman had eventually fired MacArthur; but did Johnson have the same strength of will to over-rule his own military advisers by withdrawing those in Vietnam? Would he not be called defeatist, chicken, and worse?

Johnson, in terms of foreign policy, was no Truman. At heart he felt fatally torn: doomed if he allowed the US to become directly engaged in a Vietnamese civil war it could no more win than the French had been able to in the early 1950s, but damned by Goldwater's Republican tribe – indeed fearful of 'impeachment' – if he pulled Kennedy's 16,000 American 'advisers' out of Vietnam.[34] Afraid that Goldwater would turn the American tide against Democrats in November, Johnson attempted to toe a line of cautious indecision, refusing to allow himself to be stampeded by Goldwater Republicans as the Democratic National Convention in Atlantic City approached.

On August 4, 1964, an alarming report reached the White House that the USS *Maddox*, a World War II specialist communications destroyer operating off the coast of North Vietnam in the Gulf of Tonkin, was under attack by North Vietnamese PT boats. Johnson was urged by his advisers to bomb North Vietnamese installations in reprisal.

'It looks to me like the weakness of our position is that we respond only to an action and we don't have any [strategy] of our own' the president wisely reflected.[35] By taking punitive retaliatory action, America would get lured into war without a real plan, and with the initiative held by the enemy. What if American bombing didn't scare the North Vietnamese, but on the contrary encouraged them to goad the US into outright war? President Eisenhower's emissary to South East Asia, General Matt Ridgway, had famously told Eisenhower that taking up the falling French colonial baton in Vietnam would require eight US divisions and eight years. Senator Russell had told Eisenhower it would take fifty years.[36] Was America up for such a struggle, in support of a corrupt, unpopular and completely undemocratic mili-tocracy in South Vietnam?

The president therefore demanded proof that North Vietnamese vessels had attacked US ships. He was right to question the evidence: Admiral Sharp's initial reports from his headquarters in Honolulu – 6,000 miles from the Gulf of Tonkin, where the incident was said to have taken place – turned out to be less than firm, once challenged. 'Freak weather' conditions had apparently affected the US destroyer's radar, its captain reported, and the ship's sonar operator might, he warned, have been seeing things that weren't there. No North Vietnamese vessels had actually been identified, he admitted. He therefore recommended no further action be taken until a 'complete evaluation' had been undertaken.

It was too late, however. The die was cast at the height of a presidential election-year battle, Johnson ultimately deciding that the minor incident would give him his chance to defang Goldwater warmongers without having to go to war, so long as he, as commander-in-chief, exercised a restraining hand on those in the US military and among his national security staff who were spoiling for bigger blood. On August 7 and 8, 1964, after McNamara had issued a series of outright lies to conceal US direction of, and participation in, the CIA's operations, Johnson got Congress to grant him retaliatory war powers, yet insisted in a national television broadcast that he was only authorizing an American airstrike on North Vietnam in response to 'open aggression on the high seas', and was *not* thereby escalating the US advisory mission in Vietnam into outright war.

Only two senators dared oppose the Tonkin Gulf Resolution, and no congressmen. With wisdom and guile Johnson seemed thereby to have cauterized the growing threat from Senator Goldwater by demonstrating his own firmness of purpose as president.

Just over a hundred American 'advisers' had been killed in support of South Vietnamese forces between 1961 and 1964. The Tonkin Gulf Resolution, however, would change that picture: a veritable death sentence, as Senator Russell had feared, for more than 59,000 American sons in the coming years. It would also spell wounds and disability, drug addiction and trauma for hundreds of thousands of American servicemen, who survived service in Vietnam. Instead of teaching the North Vietnamese a lesson in the Gulf of Tonkin – namely to desist from attacking American military personnel – the American 'retaliatory' bombing and naval-shelling raid on the North Vietnam PT boat base achieved the opposite; indeed evoked the great lesson of war in history: it is far easier to get into hostilities than out of them.

Since the Geneva conference of 1954, North Vietnam had thus far committed no regular forces south of the Demilitarized Zone, or 17th Parallel. Under American protection the South had then teetered in a long, festering civil strife, not only between South Vietnamese non-Communists and Communists (the Vietcong), but between Buddhists and Catholics. The Gulf of Tonkin Resolution, however, changed the dynamic, licensing the militaries of both North Vietnam and the United States to prepare for outright war, with only Lyndon B. Johnson able to halt the slide.

Johnson's genius as a politician had always been to watch for bad omens, an example of which was his refusal ever to let his wife send his 'lucky' shoes away to be resoled, lest they not be available in a crisis. Now, in the summer of 1964, Johnson hesitated. In a declaration to be read to the Democratic National Convention, he claimed he was not 'physically and mentally' equipped to carry the burden of the presidency – the 'responsibilities of the bomb and the world and the Negroes and the South'. The dangers America faced were such that he rightly doubted he could be his country's leader. There were, he told his aide Walter Jenkins, 'younger men and better-prepared men and better-trained men and Harvard-educated men. I know my limitations.'[37] He would not therefore stand for the nomination. 'My God, he's going up there tomorrow [to] resign; the convention will be thrown into chaos', said a long-time assistant, recalling the panic that gripped him and others.[38]

Johnson's withdrawal statement was serious; indeed it presaged his actual withdrawal from the presidency four years later. But in the summer of 1964, with his war on poverty proposals having been officially submitted to Congress in March and his civil rights bill just signed, the still-unelected president knew, in his heart of hearts, he couldn't simply back out of the White House and leave Senator Goldwater to take the reins of American Empire. Robert Kennedy, Johnson's only real rival in the Democratic Party, would never hold the South in a presidential election, and would never beat Goldwater in November that year. Besides, Kennedy held the same views as Johnson domestically and in foreign policy, including (at this time) Vietnam. Withdrawing from the presidential race would make Johnson a lame-duck president for his remaining five months, with waning power to hold back the forces of patriotic gore in the wake of Tonkin.

In the end, what the president had wanted was loving reassurance and, once his wife gave it (telling him he was 'as brave a man as Harry Truman – or FDR – or Lincoln' and 'to step out now would be wrong for your country', leaving his 'enemies jeering' and nothing but a 'lonely wasteland for your future'), Johnson rescinded his resignation statement.[39] He thus accepted his party's unanimous nomination on August 29, and went all out to defeat Goldwater in the fall election on November 3.

Using the 'Daisy' (nuclear mushroom cloud) television ad, Johnson's election team cast his maverick Arizona opponent as unstable and liable to cause an atomic war, leading to a landslide victory for the president (forty-three million votes to twenty-seven million, the highest popular vote percentage – 61 per cent – in US history), as well as winning the largest Democratic majorities in both chambers of Congress since FDR in 1936. Lyndon Baines Johnson had been elected president of the United States in his own right.

With the country enjoying a forty-two-month economic boom, and every prospect of the war on poverty rivalling FDR's New Deal, Democrats were delighted. Johnson's victory at the polls, however, did not mean the problem of Vietnam went away. It got worse.

On the campaign trail in New Hampshire the president had insisted he was not going to allow 'American boys to do the fighting for Asian boys'. But if Asian boys would not fight, he had little option, unless he ordered the national elections, mandated by the Geneva Accords, or got the South Vietnamese junta to fight better. Choosing the latter course, Johnson was infuriated by the farce taking place in Saigon. Following the CIA-assisted assassination of President Diem, a second coup had ousted General Minh in January 1964, and resulted in yet another general, Nguyen Khanh, taking power. In August, 1964, Khanh – who recommended that South Vietnamese forces attack North Vietnam – himself faced an attempted coup. Acting Prime Minister Oanh, a Harvard-educated economist, lasted three days; the former mayor of Saigon became titular 'president' while General Khanh held military power. Then, on September 13, 1964, Khanh faced yet another military coup attempt. President Johnson's aide, Jack Valenti, searched later for an apt metaphor for the exasperation felt by the White House:

'I guess you might call [it] . . . a *turnstile*, for God's sake. You know, coups were like fleas on a dog, and Johnson said, "I don't want to hear any more about this coup shit. I've had enough of it, and we've got to find a way to stabilize those people out there."'[40] In the absence of a competent national authority in South Vietnam, Johnson's military advisers and the chiefs of staff pressed him to let American forces take over the job, as they had in Korea.

The Under Secretary of State, George Ball, reminded his colleagues Korea had been different: that in 1950 the American government had been responding to a massive land invasion by regular North Korean forces, and moreover had acted under the aegis and banner of the United Nations. Ball, however, was speaking into the wind – the wind of war.

The sheer imperial hubris of Johnson's military planners and advisers takes the historian's breath away half a century later, ranging from their pre-emptive plans to bomb China's nuclear weapons production plants to plans for mass bombing of North Vietnam, with utter disregard for the need for allies, or even for the danger of losing respect across the world if the plans failed.

As John F. Kennedy had allowed himself to be browbeaten into greenlighting the disastrous Bay of Pigs operation in 1961 and the subsequent dispatch of 16,000 'advisers' to South Vietnam, so Johnson now, in his turn, hesitantly but inexorably allowed himself to be infected by the Goldwater-led vision of 'kicking ass' in the winter of 1964–5 following his election: the notion of teaching the world a lesson about modern American military firepower in confronting 'Communism'. It would serve, Johnson was assured, as a potent warning to both Russia and China, and to any smaller countries that accepted help from them.

In vain the State Department warned that neither Japan nor Thailand – Vietnam's neighbour, beyond Laos – wanted a US air or ground war, and that not even the countries in the region believed the 'domino' theory: that 'losing' South Vietnam would entail the 'loss' of all South East Asia to Communism. Moreover, a turn to war – especially a mass-bombing war – would, the State Department cautioned, not impress Russia and China. Nor would it impress America's NATO allies, who felt it misguided and unlikely to produce a political solution – indeed it would probably *rule out* a political solution.

The superlative judgement that had enabled Lyndon Johnson to get his domestic agenda enacted over the past year, even without having been elected president, now failed him completely. Instead of taking charge of the issue and pressing for an internationally mediated settlement, or national Vietnamese elections as mandated by the Geneva Accords, Johnson handed the matter over to 'the experts', his military advisers, allowing them to set and define his choices, whereupon he would, he promised, select what he thought was the best option. This was not only government by committee, but also unilateral imperialism, in that it was prosecuted 'regardless of opinion in other [foreign] quarters' as the US chief planner put it.

The concept of unilateral American Empire pursuing its destiny regardless of allies now swept aside the patient work of presidents Roosevelt, Truman and Kennedy. Two weeks after Johnson's inauguration, a mortar attack on an American airfield at Pleiku on February 7, 1965, killed eight Americans. Like the Tonkin incident, this was the *casus belli* the US military had been praying for.

Having summoned the Senate Majority Leader and House Speaker to the Oval Office, the president explained how he and his cabinet had 'kept our gun over the mantle and our shells in the basement for a long time now. And what was the result? They are killing our men while they sleep in the night. I can't ask our American soldiers out there to continue to fight with one hand tied behind their backs.'[41] Claiming that 'cowardice has gotten us into more wars than response has', Johnson told them he had, finally, authorized massive US bombing raids over North Vietnam.[42] The Vietnam War now formally began.

In vain George Ball warned that 'Once on the tiger's back we cannot be sure of picking the place to dismount.'[43] Instead of searching for ways to defuse the growing crisis by diplomacy, in conjunction with America's allies, the president now hunkered down with his generals and national security advisers, hoping to find, or invent, an all-American military solution. Even if it meant ultimate withdrawal from Vietnam, Johnson wanted first to make a grand show of American military might, lest anyone question imperial American power and superiority. Thus, instead of educating the public on the need for an internationally negotiated resolution to preserve the peace, Johnson greenlighted immediate – and secret – preparations for modern war that would use America's unrivalled arsenal of latest weaponry: still unsure, however, as commander-in-chief, whether the new jungle war should be conducted from the air, on the ground or at sea – and how to avoid it spilling over into war with China and the Soviet Union.

By opting for graduated bombing raids, codenamed Rolling Thunder, beginning March 2, 1965, Johnson certainly succeeded in avoiding Goldwater's preference for nuclear warefare, in direct confrontation with the Chinese or Russians. By the same token, though, he thereby invoked a bloodbath of holocaust proportions over the next several years: between 52,000[44] and 182,000[45] North Vietnamese civilians were slaughtered in American air attacks that dropped some 864,000 tons of high-explosive bombs.

The president had been warned – as had Kennedy before him – that air power alone would be ineffective in bombing the North Vietnamese to America's negotiating table, indeed would only redouble North Vietnamese determination, just as the Nazi bombing blitz over England had done in 1940 and 1941. Bombing, in other words, would only encourage the North Vietnamese to send more, not fewer troops to help the Vietcong in South Vietnam. This, in turn, would make it harder, not easier, to 'win the war' in South Vietnam, since ground combat in the forbidding jungle terrain was fraught with problems for the US military. And so it transpired; instead of forcing the North Vietnamese to back off, Operation Rolling Thunder merely incited them to commit to a war unto the death.

The story of Johnson's direction of US forces over the subsequent four years, as *de jure* generalissimo, turned out to be a nightmare of argument, disagreement, disappointment, anger, recrimination – and bloodshed on an ever increasing scale, perhaps as many as a million civilian deaths by the end. 'Bomb, bomb, bomb. That's all you know. Well, I want to know why there's nothing else' the president berated his chief airman. 'You generals have all been educated at taxpayer's expense, and you're not giving me any ideas and any solutions for this damn little piss-ant country.'[46] Yet if Johnson thought there was a solution other than negotiating peace via the South Vietnamese government, not simply the North Vietnamese, he was to be terribly mistaken.

Despairing of North Vietnamese willingness to negotiate in response to US carpet-bombing from the air (with relatively few American casualties), the president was inevitably compelled to order a ground war in South Vietnam, using US forces operating on their own, without even a semblance of South Vietnamese involvement: mercenaries by any other name. By June 1965, some 75,000 US troops were in the country; by July, another 100,000 were authorized, with a further 100,000 to be sent over in 1966.

Though well armed and well led, they offered easy targets to Vietcong guerrilla units, backed by weapons and personnel from North Vietnam via the Ho Chi Minh Trail, which the US Air Force was unable to interdict even for a single day, just as Senator Russell had warned, from bitter experience in Korea. American casualties mounted. A third of the US Army had already comprised conscripts; all too soon huge numbers of new draftees between the ages of eighteen and twenty-seven were being sent out from the United States, fuelling an anti-war movement that took fire in what was already being termed a generational cultural revolution in America and the West.

Within months, Johnson's war in Vietnam thus produced the very opposite results to those he had intended. His wife, Lady Bird, later claimed he 'had no stomach for it, no heart for it; it wasn't the war he wanted', but that whenever he went before a crowd to talk about civil rights and poverty and combating disease, the 'audience would begin to shift their feet and be restive and silent and maybe hostile. But then the moment you said something about defending liberty around the world – bear any burden – everybody would go cheering.'[47] Polls showed Mrs Johnson partially right: three quarters of Americans favoured negotiations to resolve the Vietnamese imbroglio, but even more, 83 per cent, supported the bombing of North Vietnam, and 79 per cent still credited the 'domino theory' of Communism.

Clearly, the war in Vietnam, embarked upon with patriotic fervour, was not unifying America but dividing it, threatening to ruin the very causes Johnson had made his own: racial justice and the war on poverty.

Five days after the Rolling Thunder bombing sorties over North Vietnam began, racial unrest in the US showed the world the most alarming face of an America in violent social transition. At Selma, Alabama, the Reverend Martin Luther King Jr led a peaceful 'Black Sunday' civil rights march across the Edmund Pettus Bridge in support of voting rights, only to be attacked by state and local police brandishing clubs and tear gas. Only a third of the marchers reached Montgomery, with three killed. Though Johnson was able to push through his Voting Rights Act, which he signed into law on August 6, 1965, outlawing racial discrimination at the polling station, this proved a pyrrhic victory when, five days later, one of the worst urban riots in American history broke out in a section of Los Angeles known as Watts. Most of the area was razed, thirty-five people were killed, and 4,000 arrested. The mayor blamed 'Communists', while the predominantly black population, enduring 30 per cent unemployment in an otherwise booming Californian economy, blamed the 5,000 strong white police force, whom they saw as armed 'pigs'.

A just war, such as World War II, might have unified the country, and helped Johnson's domestic agenda. But in choosing to send hundreds of thousands of young Americans to fight for a military junta halfway across the world, Johnson soon found himself attacked on all fronts. Far from galvanizing NATO and his allies, Johnson's decision to go to war in Vietnam exasperated the French president Charles de Gaulle, who in 1966 withdrew France from NATO's command structure and expelled NATO's headquarters in France. With no NATO country willing to support American combat in Vietnam, the Atlantic Alliance fell into disarray, while the North Vietnamese took heart from American protest demonstrations and refusals by draftees to serve.

Like many political leaders of empire before him, Johnson had initially calculated it would be a short war, fought by regulars. Once Hanoi saw that the US was serious in shoring up South Vietnam's coup-riddled, chaotic regime and was going to apply its vast military forces to stamp out the Vietcong insurgency and stop any talk of Communists sharing power, the North Vietnamese would negotiate a peace treaty. The terms would then be the same as in Korea: a commitment by the Vietnamese in the North to leave an American-protected, non-Communist South Vietnamese authority in power, thus allowing the US to withdraw its forces in 'six months', as Johnson declared – indeed, in a desperate televised plea, the president even offered billions of dollars in funding to Communist North Vietnam, if it would only leave South Vietnam to follow its junta-led destiny. Since this destiny was conceived only as a sort of Americanized puppet nation under the eagle-like wing of the US president as a global imperial patriarch, with no Communist participation in government permitted, the North Vietnamese refused to countenance such terms. Johnson had gambled on the use of force, in what his national security adviser called 'all-out limited war' to keep the country partitioned. It was not working.

Johnson's political skill had always been his ability to put himself in the shoes of an opponent, and calculate what was needed to get his way. In the case of South Vietnam, however, the giant Texan found that by embracing rather than rejecting war, he had committed himself to a mistake. 'If I were Ho Chi Minh, I would never negotiate' he admitted, forcing the US into a 'long war' for which the American people would have little stomach.[48]

From being a 'trouble spot' few Americans were even aware of, Vietnam now became the overarching issue dominating America's airwaves and political debate, as the war's financial costs, the military draft, and growing public opposition escalated. Congress had passed Johnson's request for a special supplemental appropriation to fund expansion of the war effort by 408 votes to seven in May 1965, but only out of patriotism and in the hope of a quick fix. Where would such an open-ended commitment end, more and more people began to ask. With the tap turned on, who could turn it off? At a White House meeting that Johnson convened, his Defense Secretary Robert McNamara urged expanding the army by another 200,000 men and an even larger call-up of 225,000 reserves, while George Ball, Under Secretary of Defense, countered 'We can't win': that the war would be a 'long protracted' campaign with a 'messy conclusion' – namely defeat and withdrawal, as the French had learned. A 'great power cannot beat guerrillas' he cautioned; this, not respect for American resolve, would be the lesson others would take from the war, if it was pursued. For Johnson it was a bitter pill, and as president of the United States, he simply refused to swallow it.

Though the war had initially provided a stimulus to the buoyant American economy, its escalation was another matter. Inexorably interest rates began to rise, and the budget deficit started to explode. To continue the war in Vietnam would, Johnson recognized, drain the treasury and signal the end of his war on poverty in America; in fact the Voting Rights Act of 1965 turned out to be the last major civil rights legislation enacted in America. A tax increase was necessary to pay for the war, but since the Tonkin Resolution gave Johnson only a congressional mandate to prosecute retaliatory military action and he lacked a popular mandate for a longer war, the tax was considered too politically dangerous to impose. By the spring of 1966 Johnson had to ask Congress for yet another $4.8 billion supplemental appropriation, and by the summer of 1966 was having to propose massive cuts in federal expenditures, at the very moment when his ambitious social legislation needed financial reinforcement if it was to succeed without more violence.

Violence came, irrespective of finance. The summer of 1966 saw urban riots in some thirty-eight American cities, from Chicago to Philadelphia, as newly empowered blacks vented their frustration over the disparity between white and black incomes, education and urban blight, symbolized in destructive young black rioters screaming 'Burn, baby, burn.'

Thus arose the ultimate contradiction of the 1960s: the American government marshalling its financial, military and political forces to impose a fantasy notion of American 'democracy' abroad, on a fractured and fractious people – Buddhists, Catholics and others – almost 10,000 miles away, while in America itself the ideal of a Great Society, unified and strong, disintegrated into urban mayhem, characterized by student protests and rising social tensions ranging from black militancy to gay rights and feminism.

Punctuating the era of violence were repeated assassinations. On February 21, 1965, Malcolm X – an African American minister who had dared join the Nation of Islam, then had left it to become a Sunni Muslim – was murdered by black Muslims in Manhattan. More and more Johnson feared for his own life when travelling outside the White House – and not without reason.

Vietnam gradually infected every part of American life, most especially since the war could not be fought without calling up reserves and untrained conscripts. Unwilling students sought to avoid the draft by deferments or exile – eventually more than 100,000 fled abroad to escape serving – which further contributed to the increasing generational divide. Paying for the war also became an ever worsening problem; by 1967, some 400,000 US troops had been committed and a two-year surcharge on individual taxpayer's income became inevitable, as well as complete cessation of new Great Society spending programmes and cutbacks in recently instituted ones.

Detroit led the urban riots and burn-downs that summer, breaking Johnson's heart after all the effort and determination he had invested in civil rights legislation and his war on poverty. Yet inasmuch as he had chosen, as president and commander-in-chief, to go to war in

Vietnam, he had only himself to blame. With American casualties mounting week by week, gradually reaching into the tens of thousands, Johnson's approval rating sank to 34 per cent. Even his loyal aide Jack Valenti resigned from the White House, begging Johnson to 'find some way out of Vietnam. All that you strive for and believe in, and are accomplishing is in danger, as long as this war goes on'.[49]

Surrounded by loyal national security advisers and generals promising eventual victory if he but stayed the course, Johnson shook his lined, tormented head. As the 'told-you-sos' berated him in the media, he burned with shame and frustration. 'Don't give me another goddamn history lesson' he roared at Senator McGovern. 'I don't need a lecture on where we went wrong. I've got to deal with where we are now.' But since he refused either to withdraw, or to offer meaningful terms of negotiation, or to force the South Vietnamese to go along with whatever he decided, he was effectively a prisoner of his own mistake. 'I can't get out' he lamented. 'So what the hell can I do?'[50]

Another casualty of Johnson's war in Vietnam, meanwhile, was peace in the Middle East. For three years Johnson had known of Israel's race to build an atomic bomb at Dimona, in the Negev desert. By 1966 evidence showed that Israel was putting nuclear warheads into missiles, but Johnson was so committed to his unilateral full-scale war in Vietnam that he found himself unable to object. Matters could only get worse. When, early in June, 1967, a special adviser asked Johnson if he was going to ask Israel to be patient in waiting for an international initiative to open the Strait of Tiran, which President Nasser of Egypt had closed to shipping the week before (thus depriving Israel of access to the Red Sea and Indian Ocean), Johnson shook his head. The Israelis wouldn't wait, he told John Roche – and America was impotent to intercede. 'They're going to hit' Johnson confided, having received secret intelligence reports of massive Israeli mobilization. 'There's nothing we can do about it.'[51] Israel was going to war.

Perhaps no other catastrophe so demonstrated the price of American imperial overreach in Vietnam as the Six Day War, launched by Israel on June 5, 1967. In less than a week Israel managed to secure all its planned military conquests without the use of its nuclear weaponry, defeating the Egyptian and Syrian armies, seizing the Egyptian Sinai desert, occupying the entire West Bank, capturing East Jerusalem, and taking the Golan Heights.

Johnson, who saw Israel's victory as a disaster for the Middle East and the security of the western world, was now, thanks to his imbroglio in Vietnam, as helpless in restraining Israeli ambitions as he had been in restraining Nasser from closing the Tiran Straits.[52] Jews in America berated the president for insisting on American neutrality during Israel's war, while Arabs across the Middle East damned him for covertly equipping, aiding and resupplying Israel's blitzkrieg. 'You Zionist dupe!' Johnson shouted at his aide Larry Levinson when Levinson begged him to address a pro-Israel rally in Washington's Lafayette Park and thus garner more Jewish support – especially from Jewish anti-Vietnam voters – by backing Israel. 'Why can't you see I'm doing all I can for Israel? That's what you should be telling people', the president cried, knowing he was as powerless to break up the brawl as he had been to stop it from starting.[53]

Several days later US impotence was stunningly illustrated when in broad daylight, Israeli bombers and three Israeli PT boats attacked the USS *Liberty*, an American naval intelligence vessel similar in purpose to the *Maddox* but operating in international waters off Port Said. After strafing the American warship with cannon and napalm, the PT boats launched five torpedoes which further crippled the smoking vessel. Thirty-four American crew were killed, and another 171 were wounded. Though Israel afterwards excused the attack as one of mistaken identity, no one was taken in. As historian Robert Dallek noted, 'The Israelis were determined to avoid a repeat of 1956, when US, Soviet, and UN pressure forced them to give up the fruits of their victory against Egypt.'[54] The US Navy would not be permitted to monitor Israeli progress, let alone pass on information about it to their enemies.

Chastened, Johnson could do nothing. Once Israel had achieved its objectives – tripling the size of Israel from 8,000 to 26,000 square miles, forcing a third of a million Arabs to flee from the West Bank, which Israel then annexed, conquering the whole city of Jerusalem, securing the 'Kashmir of the Middle East', the Golan Heights, and racing its armoured forces right up to the banks of the Suez Canal, as well as the Gulf of Suez and the Gulf of Tiran coastlines – a UN ceasefire was arranged.

Although the ceasefire mandated eventual Israeli withdrawal from the territories it had conquered, the document was worthless, save as a testament to Israeli's astonishing military success. Holding on to most of its military conquests for another forty years, it not only permitted Israelis to establish settlements in what became 'the occupied territories', but also allowed it to refuse for the next half-century to withdraw from any land seized unless an agreement was signed by its former owner accepting Israel's 'right to exist' and other terms, such as no right of return by Palestinian refugees to their former homes. Thus, while defeat in Vietnam would go down as the greatest military reverse in America's history, for Israel the Six Day War would represent the greatest triumph in its military annals.

To add to Johnson's woes, the American debacle in Vietnam meant that the US was unable to take advantage of what otherwise would have been a signal opportunity to improve East–West relations. The Soviet Union had become deeply concerned about the hostile attitude of its former ally and Communist partner, the People's Republic of China, to which it had once given technical assistance in developing an atomic bomb. Now the Chinese had developed a hydrogen bomb, and felt not only the equal of Russia, but a rival for North Vietnamese affections. Instead of being able to exploit this inter-Communist rivalry to America's advantage, Johnson's war in Vietnam achieved the very opposite.

In challenging Ho Chi Minh to armed combat, Johnson found himself grappling with an opponent increasingly able to get both Moscow and Peking to compete with each other to offer assistance. Observers and chroniclers of the region could thus only watch in bemused disbelief as France, having extricated its defeated army from Vietnam in 1954, recognized the People's Republic of China in 1964 and began trading profitably with Beijing, a move that prompted Washington to send a diplomatic note deploring President de Gaulle's decision as 'unwise and untimely'.[55] By contrast President Johnson found himself not only stuck with France's abandoned war in Vietnam, but also without access to China's trade market. Moreover, thanks to Israel's triumphant victory in the Middle East, America's access to oil was severly curtailed at the very moment when American oil production was falling, in relation to its industrial, commercial and domestic needs.

With China and Israel developing their own nuclear weapons, the Soviet premier, Aleksei Kosygin, reckoned it was time for a summit with his fellow emperor, President Johnson. Two weeks after the Israeli ceasefire he proposed that they meet in New York, on the occasion of his visit to the UN. But in a vivid illustration of the negative repercussions of the Vietnam War, Johnson was forced to turn down the Russian proposal – for fear of anti-war demonstrations by his own people.

Johnson was now at the nadir of his presidential fortunes. Eventually it was decided to hold the summit at a small state college in New Jersey, Glassboro State College (later renamed Rowan University) on June 23, 1967, out of sight and reach of protesters and assassins.

Glassboro demonstrated what no one was willing to admit: both the Soviet and the American empires had reached the limits of their imperial hegemony. The states to which Russia had sent arms – Egypt and Syria – had been trounced in combat, while the crippling of the USS *Liberty* and America's inability to influence its own client state in the Six Day War had demonstrated US impotence, despite its vast wealth and power. In the interests of stability in the region, Kosygin asked Johnson to join with Russia in pressuring Israel to withdraw from the territories it had just conquered in order to start permanent peace talks, but Johnson knew it would be political suicide in terms of the following year's presidential election, and warned Kosygin to back off. When Kosygin asked Johnson to withdraw American forces from Vietnam, the dialogue chilled even more.

What might have been a decade of détente after the Cuban Missile Crisis – thus disproving Goldwater's belligerent 1964 rhetoric – had frozen into mutual finger-wagging. No nuclear arms reduction was agreed; indeed the arms race would continue full tilt, as the Russians attempted to deploy as many ABMs as possible to counter American offensive capability, and the two most inflammable conflicts in the world went unresolved.

As if to prove the impotence of the summit leaders, Ho Chi Minh – who was now dying – directed a mass uprising against military and civilian control centres across South Vietnam to break the military deadlock. Beginning on January 31, 1968, the day of Tet Nguyen Dan (the Vietnamese festival celebrating the lunar start of the New Year), the offensive stunned American commanders as well as South Vietnamese officers by its ferocity and breadth. A 'Battle of the Bulge' attack had been expected by Johnson and the generals, targeted on the US Marine base of Khe Sanh. Instead, the Communists simultaneously besieged some thirty-six provincial capitals, five of the half-dozen largest cities, and 30 per cent of South Vietnam's district centres.

At first, President Johnson's polls went up, as Americans rallied around the flag. But as the weeks and months went by, Johnson could not prevent the casualty figures from being broadcast and public opposition to the war resumed. Though the battlefields were far away from ordinary American life, television brought the pity of war finally home, especially after reports of an American massacre at My Lai (codenamed 'Pinkville') of South Vietnamese civilians, many hundreds of them women and children. The victims had been beaten, tortured, raped, and their bodies mutilated. Though the three US servicemen who tried to stop the massacre were vilified on their return home, the majority of the American public was now wearied of the war and ashamed of its excesses. The Defense Secretary, Robert McNamara, had admitted to the president and his colleagues the previous autumn that 'everything I and Dean Rusk have tried to do since 1961 has been a failure', and he warned that to continue the war 'would be dangerous, costly in lives, and unsatisfactory'.[56]

At a State Department meeting on February 27, 1968, McNamara's 'controlled exterior cracked', his successor Clark Clifford recalled later. 'Speaking between suppressed sobs', he burst out with the words: 'The goddamned air force, they're dropping more on North Vietnam than we dropped on Germany in the last year of World War II, and it's not doing anything! We simply have to end this thing . . . It is out of control.'[57]

Johnson described McNamara as mentally unbalanced, disoriented by stress, even suicidal, and accepted his resignation; but Johnson's own health, mental and physical, almost four years since Tonkin, was taking a tremendous beating. His war had split the nation, the administration, and Johnson himself. He'd flown to Vietnam on the eve of Christmas 1967, when he temporarily halted the bombing of Hanoi, and had encouraged US troops to 'nail that coonskin to the wall' in the pursuit of 'victory' on the ground, but in private he'd begun to do what he had refused to allow for four years: pressure the corrupt South Vietnamese president to open talks with the Communist National Liberation Front, even flying to Rome and begging the Pope to see if he could persuade Lieutenant Colonel Thieu, a Roman Catholic, to agree to negotiate with the NLF in South Vietnam.

Thieu refused, thus forcing Johnson back into fighting for American 'honor', in support of an odious regime. 'I'm not going to be the first American president to lose a war' Johnson said, continuing to defend his own obstinacy, and hoped against hope that in beating back the Tet Offensive, he might yet compel the North Vietnamese to negotiate.[58] But with 525,000 US troops in the field in Vietnam – the largest army fielded by the United States since World War II – and the Joint Chiefs of Staff asking for another 205,000 reserves to be called up, as well as Congress baulking at having to pass an unpopular tax to pay the ever escalating cost, General Westmoreland's gung-ho optimism was not shared by Clark Clifford, the new Secretary of Defense.

On March 4, 1968, Clifford gave the president his task force's assessment of the situation. Keeping his voice deliberately low and dispassionate, using 'the dry-as-dust language of a Dickensian lawyer', he quietly laid out the sheer impossibility of winning a misbegotten war in support of a corrupt regime in a distant country, at punitive cost to America's spiralling deficit, its young men, its gold reserves, its responsibilities in the rest of the world, its standing with its allies, and its fracturing national morale. 'We are not sure that a conventional military victory, as commonly defined, can be achieved.' The prospects were dim. 'We seem to have gotten caught in a sinkhole' he said bluntly. Reversing the view he'd expressed only a few months before, he made clear he now saw 'no end in sight'. Sending another 205,000 men to the meat grinder would only prolong the agony.[59]

At a moment when the president was being fed positive reports of US combat units in countering the Tet Offensive, Clifford's assessment forced Johnson to stop focusing on tactical operations and to see the utter vacuousness of his grand strategy. 'Clifford changed the course of US policy' Johnson's press secretary, George Reedy, considered. Westmoreland's intelligence chief later claimed that Johnson had 'fired a doubting Thomas [i.e. McNamara] only to replace him with a Judas', but similar accusations had been made against those of Hitler's advisers like Rommel who had counselled the Führer to make peace in 1944 after the Allied invasion of Normandy.[60] Even Dean Acheson, who had been the toughest of hawks over Vietnam, now described the war as 'unwinnable'.

Reluctantly Johnson recognized, even if he capped the number of

US troops in South Vietnam and stopped the bombing of North Vietnam, he would not necessarily be able to persuade the South Vietnamese junta to accept a power-sharing peace deal, let alone sit down with the North Vietnamese. As more advisers pressed for Johnson to hold firm, indeed to escalate the war still further, others now joined Clifford's camp, forcing Johnson to face up to the impasse to which he had led his beloved country.

The president's brother Sam Houston Johnson recalled a domino game they played one night in the White House: 'He just sat there, staring way off yonder.' 'It's your move Lyndon' he reminded the president. 'That's just the trouble,' LBJ finally spoke, 'it's always my move.' With 'his big tough fingers', he played with the blank domino in his hand. 'Sam Houston,' he finally said. 'I've just got to choose between my opposing experts. No way of avoiding it. But I sure as hell wish I could *really* know what's right.'[61]

In the end, and despite the defections of McNamara, Acheson and Clifford, Johnson opted to continue the war. 'He had never, in his entire life, learned to confess error,' Reedy reflected later, 'and this quality – amusing or exasperating in a private person – resulted in cosmic tragedy for a president. He had to prove he was right all along.'[62]

Clifford, as a consummate Washington insider, had never known such a crisis in American government. The war was threatening to tear the nation apart at every level: in families (President Johnson's own daughter hysterically opposed the war, as her husband was shipped out to Vietnam), in anti-war demonstrations, in the media, in Congress, in the administration. Johnson had promised to make a national broadcast at the end of the month to address the issue, but what would he decide to do, and what would he say?

Once again he summoned his advisers, the majority of whom now recommended he 'stop the bombing and negotiate' with the North Vietnamese. Johnson was stunned. 'Who poisoned the well with these guys?' he demanded afterwards, like an angry headmaster whose staff had crossed his plans. 'The Establishment bastards have bailed out' he sneered.[63] Yet he knew in his heart of hearts that the Wise Men were right and that only he, as American Caesar, could manage the next step: negotiating a peace agreement while his troops held the fort. Having swallowed that bitter pill, however, Johnson then made the biggest error since Tonkin in trying to put his decision into effect.

On March 31, 1968, he went before the cameras in the Oval Office and made his historic statement. He would stop bombing North Vietnam and seek a peace agreement with the North Vietnamese. But there was a further announcement he wished to make. 'With America's sons in the fields far away, with America's future under challenge right here at home, with our hopes and the world's hopes for peace in the balance every day, I do not believe that I should devote an hour or a day of my time to any personal partisan causes or to any duties other than the awesome duties of this – the presidency of your country. Accordingly, I shall not seek, and I will not accept, the nomination of my party for another term as your president.' His political career was over.

No one, including his own wife, could ever quite explain this. Though the announcement seemed to bring him a brief moment of comfort as the burden of the imperial crown finally lifted from his shoulders, the notion that the leader of the free world could simply and suddenly terminate his duties, in the midst of a war, without diminishing his authority as president and mortally wounding his own political party, was an illusion. Shock and disbelief greeted the news among his cabinet, staff and citizens, especially Democrats. Whatever his failings, Lyndon Johnson had been, by force of personality, a far bigger, more dominating figure in the firmament of American politics than his detractors – from East Coast Kennedy-liberals to southern Dixiecrats – had ever allowed.

Nineteen sixty-eight, the year of Tet, now turned into one of the worst years in American history. Four days after the president's announcement, on April 4, 1968, Dr Martin Luther King Jr was assassinated in Memphis, Tennessee. America descended into a nationwide orgy of urban rioting. City by city, including Washington, America went up in flames.

'By the dawn of April 6, a pall of black smoke hung over the national monuments' one observer wrote. 'The capital of the United States was under military occupation', some 75,000 soldiers having been deployed lest the country disintegrate into anarchy.[64] Then on June 4, Senator Robert F. Kennedy was assassinated in Los Angeles, having just won the California Democratic presidential primary, leaving only Eugene McCarthy and the vice president, Hubert Humphrey, to fight it out for the Democratic nomination in Chicago in July.

For a moment Johnson, regretting his decision not to stand, explored whether the convention might draft him, but, given the fury of anti-war protests outside and the president's ever deepening unpopularity, it was a mirage. His ratings had remained stuck in the mid-thirties, and negotiations in Paris were deadlocked thanks to the continued American bombing that Johnson would not halt. His 'fantasy that the convention would be such a mess that he would go in on a flying carpet and be acclaimed as the nominee' was derided even by his own press secretary.[65] In any event, Mayor Daley's police brutality at Chicago in dealing with anti-war protesters put the final kibosh on the idea, making it unsafe for the embattled president even to go near the city, or face crowds chanting 'Hey, hey, LBJ, how many kids did you kill today?' On August 28, 1968, Johnson sent word to the party chairman that his name 'not be considered by the convention', and Vice President Hubert Humphrey was duly nominated.[66]

Instead of backing him, however, Johnson now did the unthinkable: he deliberately destroyed Humphrey's candidacy.

After visiting Saigon, Secretary of Defense Clark Clifford had reported to the President that he was 'absolutely certain' the South Vietnamese government did not want an end to the war while they were protected by over 500,000 American troops and a 'golden flow of money'. In other words, the South Vietnamese were the problem, not the Communists. But when Hubert Humphrey recommended forcing the South Vietnamese to compromise, in order to get peace, Johnson labelled him a turncoat and gave orders that Humphrey's telephone was to be tapped. Thus when Humphrey – still vice president of the United States – came to see Johnson at the White House after campaigning in Maryland in September 1968, Johnson refused to meet with him. 'You tell the president he can cram it up his ass!' the distraught vice president expostulated as he left the White House.[67] Johnson thereafter refused to campaign for Humphrey in Texas and key border states on the grounds that Richard Nixon, the nominated Republican candidate for the presidency in the November election, 'is following my policies more closely than Humphrey'.[68]

Johnson's misreading of Richard Nixon – who had promised never to speak ill of the president if he continued bombing North Vietnam – would now doom the American Empire to yet more years of bloodshed. On October 2, 1968, word came that the North Vietnamese, nervous lest Nixon become president, were prepared to negotiate

seriously with the representatives of the South Vietnamese government present at the table in Paris, in return for a cessation of American
bombing. Johnson immediately made preparations for the bombing
to stop. 'Nixon will be disappointed' he acknowledged, but decided
at long last that peace in Vietnam was more important than helping
Nixon defeat Humphrey.[69]

It was too late. 'He promised me he would not [end the bombing]'
Nixon screamed, unwilling at first to credit the report from his double
agent, working under Johnson at the White House; 'He has sworn
he would not.'[70] Told 'It's going to happen', however, Nixon searched
for ways to sabotage Johnson's peace negotiations, lest his fight for
the presidency be lost at the eleventh hour, with Vice President
Humphrey garnering the fruits of an October surprise: peace. When
Johnson called Nixon to confirm the breakthrough, and that he was
going to halt the bombings now that North Vietnam had agreed to
his conditions, Nixon 'reaffirmed his support for a deal on that
basis'[71] but in reality went ahead with a plan he'd secretly drawn up
to derail the peace talks: persuading the South Vietnamese *not* to
participate.[72]

Illegally tapping Nixon's phones, Johnson quickly became aware of
Nixon's skullduggery: Nixon and his chief of staff, John Mitchell, had
used Anna Chennault – the co-chair of 'Republican Women for Nixon'
– to persuade President Thieu in Saigon not to participate in the talks,
on the promise of better terms for the South Vietnamese if he held
out and Nixon were elected. 'I was constantly in touch with Mitchell
and Nixon' boasted Mrs Chennault decades later, but at the time there
was nothing the president could do, lest his wiretapping became
known.[73] Like Eisenhower before him, he had become trapped by his
own clandestine operations.

Johnson yelled at his aides that it was 'treason' on Nixon's part,
'American boys dying in the service of Nixon's political ambitions'.[74]
He even telephoned Nixon to complain, but Nixon swore 'There was
absolutely no truth in it, as far as he knew.' Nixon and his staff then
'collapsed with laughter' after he put the phone down.[75]

'We must tell them [the South Vietnamese] we won't stand for
them vetoing this' Johnson railed. 'We have attained what we worked
for. We must not let this get away from us.'[76] But with President
Thieu stonewalling, the peace negotiations failed. Nixon, not Vice

President Humphrey, won the election on November 5 to become the thirty-seventh president of the United States – by 0.7 per cent in the popular vote.

## Part Three: Private Life

Explosive forces seemed to drive Lyndon Johnson's larger-than-life nature. Everything about him, from his ears to his nose to his height and his feet, was outsize – and his personality was the same. From the start of his career, colleagues, relatives and chroniclers noted that whatever Lyndon undertook, he took over, not so much because he was a control freak (though he was) as because his tremendous energy, intelligence and drive made such an outcome inevitable. Moreover, in relentless hard work he discovered a talent that would have ensured he reach the top in any profession he chose: namely the ability to read with relentless cynicism other people's motives, their characters and their weaknesses. He was not always right, but his often sneering 'fix' on others enabled him either to bend them to his will or, if they did not bend, to thwart their attempts to best him. The most sensible, the most sensitive, and the best walked away from him; but those who remained were broken, and enchained.

Where Johnson's cynicism came from is hard to know. Certainly his humble circumstances as a child in Texas, his restless adolescence, his familiarity with the soil, farms and their folk, domestic animals, wild animals, hunting, the Texas range, meant that although he'd never gone without food or needed to do manual work, he had no illusions or compunctions about human nature as animal nature: including his own. Inasmuch as he despised himself for not having a purer, more noble character, he sought to compensate by working harder, aiming higher, doing more for the less privileged or empowered – not mechanically but manically. There was no spiritual or religious component to this ceaseless drive; indeed he was never religious from childhood on, and until he reached the White House, his brother said, he never attended a church. What propelled him was nothing biblical or even political in any ideological or carefully thought-out sense. But like those men who go into the armed services and rise to the highest rank, he was by nature – that is, by temperament and inclination – a *warrior*: a political warrior. He was born to fight, not with his fists (a fellow student would recall his utter cowardice if there was any danger of physical violence) but with intensity and relentless determination to get his own way, whether by guile or by exerting himself harder than anyone else.

Succeeding, almost from the word go, he recognized what many a leader of men before him had discovered: strength of will trumped all. Human beings were like pack wolves, with himself as the alpha wolf. Fighting for 'the poor' or weak or disadvantaged actually increased his dominance. Moreover, to maintain that dominance, especially with rivals, he instinctively applied his X-ray ability, measuring their boundaries in morality and endurance, exploiting their gratitude, their fear, their greed or their innocence.

At every step in his ascent to supreme power Johnson first attached himself to mentors – older men to whom by industry and servility he could be useful – until he himself inherited their power.

Love was an early casualty in this grand quest. At eighteen, while he was at San Marcos College, Johnson met Carol Davis, an unusually tall (6'), stunningly attractive fellow student. However much he boasted ('Well, I've got to take ol' Jumbo here and give him some exercise' he would declare, sporting himself naked after a shower at his shared apartment), and however much he groomed his wavy, slicked locks and clothes for a night out, he was disliked by the majority of girls he dated, who found his braggadocio and exaggerations almost pathological.[77] Carol, however, was two years older than Johnson, clever and shy. She was also rich. 'I fell in love with her the first moment we met' Johnson claimed. She 'played the violin and wrote poetry', he recalled, but also had a big white convertible her father – owner of a major wholesale grocery business in San Marcos – had bought her. The romance lasted two years. 'Lying next to the river in a waste-high mass of weeds,' Johnson related, 'we began to talk about marriage', but the relationship, though it promised him access to money and power (her father had been mayor of San Marcos) was doomed. Not only was Carol not interested in politics ('Miss Sarah,' Johnson complained to his landlady, 'this girl loves opera. But I'd rather sit down on an old log with a farmer and talk'[78]), but her father wasn't interested in Lyndon as a suitor, having already moved his wife and four daughters from Dripping Springs to San Marcos lest they be inclined to 'marry those goatherders up there' in the Hill Country, where Johnson came from.[79] 'I won't let you, I won't have my daughter marrying into that no-account Johnson family' Carol's father told her. 'I've known that bunch all my life, one generation after another of shiftless dirt farmers and grubby politicians . . . None of them will ever amount to a damn.'[80]

If Johnson was hurt by Carol's rejection after two years' courting, he did not show it; indeed the episode merely reinforced his view that romantic love was a waste of energy. Sex could be had with whores or women of easy virtue.[81] What he wanted in a wife was a woman of means, who would devote herself to his career, night and day – but keep out of his way when not required. When he met petite Claudia Alta in 1934, he was certain he'd found the right partner. On their first date – morning coffee at a store in Austin – he could sense he was making a big impression and wasted no time. He told her about his job (secretary to Congressman Kleberg), his salary, his insurance policies, his family – then asked her to marry him.

Claudia, nicknamed Lady Bird since infancy, lived alone with her widower father, a millionaire businessman and landowner with tens of thousands of acres to his name. Still only twenty-one, she already had two degrees from the University of Texas, and though working as a journalist, was almost pathologically shy. 'I thought it was some kind of joke' she said later of Johnson's proposal.[82]

It wasn't. The next day Johnson whisked Lady Bird off to meet his parents in Johnson City. 'The house was extremely modest' she recalled. 'Lyndon knew it, and I knew it, and he was kind of watching me look at it.'[83] No beauty – indeed considered by her peers and even her friends to be plain and dowdy – Claudia thought Lyndon strikingly handsome: 'excessively thin, but very, very good-looking, with lots of black wavy hair, and the most outspoken, straightforward, determined manner I had ever encountered'.[84]

Lady Bird asked him to wait twelve months while they got to know each other better, but Lyndon refused. He pressed for an immediate engagement, and a wedding. 'I see something I know I want – I immediately exert efforts to get it' he said of his character and modus operandi in the frankest of love letters to her, sent from his congressman's office in Washington. 'You see something you might want . . . You tear it to pieces in an effort to determine if you should want it . . . Then you . . . conclude that maybe the desire isn't an "ever-lasting" one and the "sane" thing to do is to wait a year or so'.[85] Less courting than pressuring, this was a manner of business he was making his own: working on people's weaknesses, hesitations, uncertainty, while contrasting these with his own tough-love energy, focus and determination.

Ten weeks later the twenty-six-year-old congressman's secretary drove the car he'd borrowed from his boss the 1,300 miles from Washington to Texas and gave Claudia an ultimatum. 'We either get married now or we never will. And if you say goodbye to me, it just proves to me that you just don't love me enough to dare to. And I can't bear to go on and keep wondering if it will ever happen.'[86]

Lady Bird caved in. They were married forthwith without any member of either of their families present, using a $2.50 ring purchased from a Sears, Roebuck store across the street for the hastily arranged civil ceremony in St Mark's Episcopal Church, San Antonio. 'Lyndon and I committed matrimony last night' Lady Bird telephoned the stunned friend who'd first introduced her to Johnson.[87]

From insistent, adoring suitor, Lyndon Baines Johnson, alias Dr Jekyll, instantly turned into a Mr Hyde, trampling over Lady Bird as though she were a servant, not his wife. 'He'd embarrass her in public. Just yell at her across the room, tell her to do something' one person recalled. 'All the people from Texas felt very sorry for Lady Bird. I don't know how she stands for it.'[88] 'Put your lipstick on' he'd snarl when they went out. 'You don't sell for what you're worth.'[89]

Lady Bird did as ordered – as others did, too – because Lyndon was Lyndon: a human tsunami, sweeping all in his path, men as well as women. Her father was similarly tall (6' 2"), dictatorial, obsessively neat and at the same time foul-mouthed. Lyndon was no different. He seemed to enjoy defying convention or good manners: 'a very intense crudity,' George Reedy reflected, 'an obviously deliberate effort to be disgusting' in the sight of snobs or sophisticates.[90] He was rude, boorish, taunting, humiliating, thinking nothing of urinating into the sink in his office while still interviewing someone,[91] standing naked in company,[92] or later, when he had his own bathroom, leaving the door open and defecating while dictating, or speaking with an aide or visitor. 'Have you ever seen anything as big as this?' he asked a friend visiting from Texas, unzipping his pants.[93]

Behind Johnson's outrageously boorish behavior was an unspoken challenge: accept me as I am, or get out. He rendered Lady Bird unhappy by his more or less constant fornication, practised in Washington on a truly pasha-like scale using every space, from his office desk to his car and closet. Unlike JFK, who charmed ladies to surrender their virtue in the hope of love, he never allowed any of his conquests to even dream of usurping his wife's place. He believed – or made himself believe – he was unique in his drive and ambition; his attention was thus a gift a man or a woman rejected at his or her cost or peril. His Washington harem was compared by one observer to *The King and I*. 'It worked that way; you know, the scene where she sits at the table and all the babes – Lady Bird was the head wife.'[94]

Lyndon's behaviour, in Lady Bird's eyes, simply reflected the biological dynamism of an oversexed man – *her* man. 'You have to understand,' she later explained to a journalist, 'my husband loved people. All people. And half the people in the world were women. You don't think I could have kept my husband away from half the people?'[95] Lyndon's womanizing did upset her, however, when he went overboard, and sex became affection that took him away from her emotionally, rather than being the expression of mere exuberance. His seven-year affair with Alice Marsh, the mistress and later wife of his Texas patron Charles Marsh, was a case in point. Likened to a 'Viking princess', the tall, red-haired beauty fell deeply in love with Lyndon who, together with Charles Marsh, agreed to a *ménage à trois*. Lyndon needed Marsh's money for his campaigns; she (twenty-four years younger than her husband) needed Johnson's youthful ardour; while Marsh – who felt he owned Lyndon – was content to let her amuse herself. Only Lady Bird lost out, suffering miscarriage after miscarriage, and only finally giving birth to two daughters in her thirties.

Apart from Alice Marsh, however, Lady Bird was in no danger from Lyndon's myriad conquests. 'Yes, but that's just one side of him,' she excused him to a friend who seemed outraged by Lyndon's philandering.[96] Johnson made no secret of it, either. As a newly minted senator he met a beautiful twenty-three-year-old radio ad executive at a party in Dallas, and had her flown to Austin. 'I threw away all my morals for him' she sighed later, knowing she was not alone.[97] Helen Gahagan Douglas, wife of actor Melvyn Douglas, was a congresswoman whom Richard Nixon later defeated in their fight for the Senate;

she too discarded her morals when Congressman Johnson hit on her in 1944, continuing to have an 'on-call' sexual relationship with him for the following twenty years. 'Bird knows everything about me, and all my lady friends are hers, too' Lyndon assured Speaker Sam Rayburn when Rayburn warned him not to endanger his marriage.[98] And it was true, as Lady Bird's confidences, interviews and her diary attest.[99]

'Sex to Johnson was one of the spoils of victory' George Reedy would later say.[100] It was also a means to evade the shadow of the Grim Reaper. When his mother died of cancer in September 1958, just after he had turned fifty, Lyndon began to behave more like a high-school dropout than the Senate Majority Leader. 'He intermingled, almost daily, childish tantrums; threats of resignation; wild drinking bouts; a remarkably non-paternal yen for young girls; and an almost frantic desire to be in the company of young people' said Reedy.[101] Five years later, the corrupting influence – or mystique – of the White House only fanned the excesses to which Johnson was prone. Flirtation with 'a very pretty young woman' led to casual sex on an office desk, as one of his many willing 'victims' recalled.[102] In fact there were so many that, in a moment of boastfulness and sneering, Johnson claimed he'd 'had more women by accident than Kennedy had on purpose'.[103]

Working eighteen hours a day in the Oval Office Johnson came to feel he *deserved* the brief spoils of imperial victory, unworried by the parallels with Caligula and Nero. As Jackie Kennedy had become her husband's enabler, so too did Lady Bird, soothing his brow, maintaining her composure, and continuing to adore her husband as Vietnam and riots incinerated the dreams they had once shared.

Another White House aide, the Princeton historian Eric Goldman, blamed Texas – not so much for its border traditions of wild Scots-Irish behaviour as for the lack of an early education to match the sheer natural intellect of the man. 'After years of meeting first-rate minds in and out of universities, I am sure I have never met a more intelligent person than Lyndon Johnson' he wrote, correcting those who saw only the loudmouth, the exaggerator, the liar. By intelligence the professor meant 'in terms of sheer IQ, a clear swift, penetrating mind, with an abundance of its own type of imagination and subtleties'. Yet for all his gifts, Johnson was a 'great sonofabitch', a throwback to the Huey Longs of the 1930s, a man who, despite his elevation to the highest office in the land – indeed the world – 'could not command that respect, affection and rapport which alone permit an American president genuinely to lead' in a modern democratic world.[104]

'If he did not exist, we'd have to invent him' Charles de Gaulle had said, *pace* Voltaire, of the new 'Texas cowboy' president of the United States he had met at the funeral of President Kennedy in 1963. A whole era of American imperial grandeur – its conduct of power across the world tempered by presidents of global vision and wisdom – was coming to an end, de Gaulle recognized, with Johnson's accession. 'Roosevelt and Kennedy were masks over the real face' of the United States, de Gaulle felt. By contrast 'Johnson is the very portrait of America. He reveals the country to us as it really is, rough and raw' – and the world would have to live with the consequences.[105]

Convinced that her husband's health would not permit him to serve out a second elected term, Lady Bird had also been a proponent of his decision not to run again for the presidency in 1968. But retirement to the Texas ranch was, if anything, worse for Johnson's health. He had stopped chain-smoking after a heart attack in 1955, and had followed a strict diet throughout his years in the White House, exercising regularly. All this he abandoned once 'home' in Texas. On January 22, 1973, Lyndon Baines Johnson suffered another heart attack, aged sixty-four. This time it was fatal.

Lady Bird was distraught (Lyndon had died in his study alone, his biggest dread). Though African Americans felt gratitude, the majority of the nation, sickened by Johnson's mad war in Vietnam, was unforgiving, and hardly mourned his passing. After a state memorial service in Washington the great champion of civil rights and equality was buried in the Johnson family plot by the Pedernales River, whence he had come.

# CHAPTER SIX

# RICHARD NIXON

Later reviled

Republican
37th President
(January 20, 1969–August 9, 1974)

## Part One: The Road to the White House

Richard Milhous Nixon was born in Yorba Linda, in southern California, on January 9, 1913. He was the second son of a devout Quaker, Hannah Milhous, and her uneducated but hard-working, irascible Irish-American husband, Frank Nixon.

Frank Nixon made his living as a repairman, carpenter, streetcar driver, citrus picker and finally orange and lemon grove farmer on the ten acres his wife's family gave him. The simple Sears, Roebuck house Frank built was tiny, with a diminutive, five-foot high attic room for their five boys, two of whom died of tuberculosis in childhood; but it did have an indoor bathroom and plumbing. Unable to afford fertilizer, and not making enough to survive, Frank gave up his failed lemon grove in 1919, worked for Union Oil while his wife worked as a lemon packer, and in 1922 started a gas station and grocery store in nearby Whittier.

Working in the summers as a picker in the bean fields for twelve hours a day, at age seven and eight, Richard – named after King Richard the Lionheart – grew up a somewhat morose, introspective child, walking to school barefoot, carrying his shoes and socks in a paper bag.

Though he never learned to read music, Nixon was blessed with near total recall, and learned to play the piano in the family's small sitting room; indeed for a while he seemed destined, like Harry Truman, for a musical career. At age eleven he applied, unsuccessfully, for a job at the *Los Angeles Times*. He did brilliantly at school and was pressed to apply to Harvard University, but for financial reasons was unable to do so. Instead, because his grandfather had left a $250 bequest for members of the family to study locally, he attended tiny Whittier College (its student body totalling only 300) nearby, where he achieved prominence as an organizer, debater, student president and amateur actor.

Just under six feet tall, with wavy hair, an extruded nose and deep baritone voice, Nixon was thought by his drama teacher to be talented enough to become a professional actor – which in certain ways is what he did become. He was not unattractive, but was too self-absorbed, emotionally brittle and self-seeking to attract women. His mother hoped he might become a clergyman. Instead he devoted himself to getting ahead in the temporal world, beginning with law, which he studied on a scholarship at Duke Law School in North Carolina. In 1940 he voted against Franklin Roosevelt in the presidential election.

When the United States was attacked at Pearl Harbor, Nixon – who had been turned down for a job in the FBI and had become a small-town lawyer and assistant city attorney in Whittier – served in Washington as a government price control official, then in the navy as a logistics officer. He saw brief service in the Pacific, in administrative work behind the front lines, before returning to the States as a base administrator in California.

Posted to Washington DC in the autumn of 1945 as a navy contract lawyer, Lieutenant Commander Nixon was approached by the Committee of One Hundred, mostly arch right-wingers of the Twelfth Congressional District of California. 'Are you serious?' Nixon responded to the phone call, and promised to give the post-war battle his all. He'd married a local secondary school teacher; with her earnings and his own (including poker winnings) he had $5,000 to contribute to his campaign. The rest came from a cabal of local Republicans, including the owner of the *Los Angeles Times*.

The Committee of One Hundred judged their man correctly. 'I always felt, because he was poor,' reflected California governor Pat Brown later, 'he got in with those rich Republicans, who changed him.'[1]

Since he had not stood for office before, Nixon could not be attacked on his record; by contrast he attacked his opponent's record with everything he was able, as a trained lawyer, to research and misrepresent. Using identical tactics to Joe McCarthy in Wisconsin, Nixon was thus able to smear the five-term Democratic incumbent, Congressman

Jerry Voorhis, as pro-Communist. The climax came in the first of five debates to which Voorhis unwisely challenged the challenger. Held on September 13, 1946, in South Pasadena High School, the debate treated its audience to Richard Nixon's first political drama, starring himself: a performance in which, like Iago using Desdemona's stolen handkerchief, he suddenly waved a phony document, which he claimed as 'proof' that his opponent was a near-Communist.[2]

That Congressman Voorhis, son of a millionaire and a dedicated liberal, could be smeared as a pro-Communist was a testament to Richard Nixon's success as a campaigner. 'I like to win and I play hard to win' he would later admit. 'You have to fight all the way; you never get on the defensive. Nice guys and sissies don't win many elections.'[3] 'Of course, I knew that Jerry Voorhis wasn't a Communist' he confessed after the election, which he won by 64,784 votes to 49,431.[4] He was, also, a 'marked man', as a member of the Committee of One Hundred warned him in a congratulatory phone call.[5]

Licensed – and paid – to become his party's attack dog against powerful unions ('I was elected to smash the labor bosses' he confided) and to target influential 'pinkos' during the two years when Republicans held majorities in both chambers of Congress, from 1947 to 1949, Nixon was determined to seize his opportunity.[6] He had no distinguished record of combat experience like his fellow congressman John F. Kennedy, but he did have a credential that could catapult him into the headlines. 'I was the only lawyer on the committee, so that's why I played such a major role' he later explained his high profile on the House Un-American Activities Committee (HUAC).[7] Though nothing of substance was ever unearthed by the committee, in a climate where the director of the FBI was publicly claiming there were 'at least 100,000 Communists at large in the country', HUAC would set the course of virulent McCarthyism for the following seven years, specializing in guilt and personal ruin via calculated leaks and innuendo.[8] Nixon himself was responsible for the Mundt-Nixon bill, requiring registration of American Communist Party members, denial of passports, and barring of non-elective federal jobs, which even the FBI objected to, since it would only drive Communists underground. For Nixon, however, it provided the necessary kudos he needed for his next political step: the congressional investigation of a specific, high-profile government 'pinko', Alger Hiss.

Using his amateur theatrical experience as well as his training as a lawyer, Nixon deliberately portrayed Hiss – a distinguished senior State Department official who had advised President Roosevelt at Yalta and was founding secretary of the United Nations – as the quintessential, pinstriped New Dealer, while casting himself as the patriotic all-American commoner. Since Hiss was a self-made man whose father had been a bankrupt who committed suicide, the polarity was entirely manufactured, but it more than achieved the national attention the young congressman desired. Nixon deliberately leaked confidential information he'd been given, spread unsubstantiated rumours, and promised his main witness freedom from perjury for having lied about his own treason in the 1930s, while working night and day to 'get' Hiss. He did. Indicted for perjury in January 1950, Alger Hiss was found guilty and imprisoned for four years in a federal penitentiary. Nixon, meanwhile, emerged a national figure, re-elected to Congress, and his name a byword as a dedicated, no-holds-barred Republican anti-Communist prosecutor. Inevitably, he raised his sights to the Senate.

In private, Nixon was – to Democrats – a surprisingly liberal figure: a strong proponent of health care, public education and civil rights, 'a liberal', as he himself put it, 'but not a flaming liberal', representing 'Main Street rather than Wall Street', a believer in bipartisanship and 'practical liberalism' or 'progressive liberalism'. As a prosecutor and campaigner, by contrast, he was ruthless, vindictive, amoral, and wholly devoted to his own cause: namely self-advancement. The Speaker of Congress, Sam Rayburn, declared Nixon, even after a single term, to be 'the most devious face of all those who have served in the Congress in all the years I've been here', but Nixon was unbowed.[9] He began plotting his campaign for the Senate in 1949, eighteen months before the election. Tarring Democrats as the party of 'state socialism', he declared 'They can call it a planned economy, the Fair Deal, or social welfare. It's still the same old socialist baloney any way you slice it.'[10] Thanks to the Hiss case, he boasted, he had won publicity 'on a scale that most congressmen only dream of achieving'.[11]

Nixon's 1950 Senate campaign against Helen Gahagan Douglas, a fellow member of Congress, would become infamous. He proceeded to tar and feather Douglas – with whom he had hitherto been on collegial, first-name terms – as a Communist fellow traveller, 'pink down to her underwear'.[12]

Nixon vowed to 'put on a fighting, rocking, socking campaign'.[13] With anonymous phone calls, half a million libellous copies of 'The Pink Sheet' and the support of Republican financiers and oil men, he proceeded to do so. No claim or accusation was too outrageous as Nixon called for American forces to cross the 38th Parallel in Korea following the invasion of the South by North Korea, and damned Congresswoman Douglas for advocating Chiang Kai-shek's seat on the UN Security Council should be given to the Communist Chinese government – the very policy he would himself espouse two decades later, to Douglas' incredulity.

As best she could, Douglas attempted to warn voters of Nixon's willingness to lie and cheat, coining the epithet 'Tricky Dick', but to no effect. Wherever he campaigned, Nixon claimed 'personal know-ledge' of HUAC files containing frightening information on Communist fifth-columnist intentions in America, including the poisoning of the nation's water and food supplies, attacking public facilities, derailing trains, seizing armouries and the like.[14] With J. Edgar Hoover declaring that there were now over half a million subversives at large in the country, and Joe McCarthy having waved before reporters a phony list of 205 active Communists in the higher echelons of the US government, this was rank demagoguery on Nixon's part. It won him the Senate seat, however, by a near-landslide (2.1 million votes to Douglas' 1.5 million), on November 7, 1950.

Nixon was only thirty-seven, the second youngest member of the upper chamber, representing the second most populous state in America. There, as Senator Nixon, he could have remained for the rest of his life, had he so chosen – a politician able and willing to back enough social causes in Washington, from civil rights to health care, to be amenable to Democrats, while posing as a diehard right-wing anti-Communist and anti-New Dealer in election campaigns. Nixon almost immediately evinced, however, higher aspirations. Travelling to Europe in the early summer of 1951, he visited the supreme commander of NATO, General Eisenhower. Thereafter he let it be known to Eisenhower's main promoter, Senator Henry Cabot Lodge of Massachusetts, that he would be able to help in getting California delegates at the 1952 Republican National Convention to back the general – and did, earning himself the offer of the vice-presidential ticket.

Matters did not then go according to Nixon's plan. On September 18, 1952, under the headline 'Secret Rich Men's Trust Fund Keeps Nixon in Style Far Beyond His Salary', an article in the *New York Post* claimed Nixon was a kept man, funded by Republican backers in California. A scandal erupted.

Eisenhower, running on a campaign slogan of absolute probity in government (following scandals dogging several outgoing Truman administration officials), was distraught at the notion of losing the presidential election because of an ambitious but corrupt young running mate, about whom he had always had qualms. For his 'crusade' to be successful, Eisenhower insisted his team be 'as clean as a hound's tooth'. In at least two cases, Nixon had interceded with the Justice Department on behalf of rich contributors, despite his demand that key Democrats resign from Congress for similar favours. Eisenhower therefore favoured dumping Nixon immediately. Nixon, however, refused.

Aboard his campaign train, Nixon declared at whistle-stops he was the victim of a 'filthy left-wing smear' – an irony, given his own past election tactics. A first-class lawyer, he recognized that his accusers had exaggerated some of their claims to include his home furnishings and his wife's fur coat – an article of clothing she did not possess. Nixon therefore pleaded with Eisenhower for the chance, at least, to clear his name in a television broadcast. Uncertain whether to give him that leeway lest it only attract more public attention to the business, Eisenhower procrastinated, prompting Nixon to exclaim: 'General, a time comes in politics when you have to shit or get off the pot!'[15]

It is impossible to overstate the critical importance of the 'Checkers speech' (as it became known) to the survival of Richard Nixon as a politician. Even Eisenhower, used to the histrionics of generals like George Patton, Bernard Montgomery and Charles de Gaulle, was awed by Nixon's performance in a national broadcast before sixty million viewers – the largest television audience ever for a political speech.

Ironically, Nixon's wife had earlier begged him not to take Eisenhower's offer of the vice-presidential ticket, and thereby have to surrender his safe Senate seat. The fur-coat scandal now threatened to ruin Nixon's career, however, even if his resignation saved Eisenhower and the Republican Party. Were he to 'crawl away', she

warned him, 'you will destroy yourself. Your life will be marred
forever and the same will be true of your family and, particularly,
your daughters.'[16] 'Just tell them that I haven't the slightest idea [what
I'll say],' Nixon snapped back at Eisenhower's emissary, Governor
Dewey, 'and if they want to find out they'd better listen to the broadcast. And tell them', he added, ominously, 'I know something about
politics too!'[17]

Nixon did. He later confided he 'staged' the entire show, from the
desk in front of which he stood, to his wife in a chair by his side in
a home-made woollen dress, and the absence of a script, using only
notes that he held. 'He oscillated between the slick southern California
salesman and Uriah Heep', one biographer described, but the performance was magnetically effective, as Nixon first refuted the allegations
made against him, then turned the tables.[18]

Listing his assets and his liabilities, the embattled senator declared:
'Well, that's about it. That's what we have and that's what we owe.
It isn't very much, but Pat and I have the satisfaction that every dime
we have is honestly ours. I should say this, that Pat doesn't have a
mink coat. But she does have a respectable Republican cloth coat and
I always tell her that she would look good in anything.' He then
corrected himself, saying they *had* accepted one gift, after the last election. 'A man in Texas heard Pat on the radio mention the fact that
our two young daughters would like to have a dog. And, believe it or
not, the day before we left on this campaign trip we got a message
from Union Station in Baltimore saying they had a package for us . . .
It was a little cocker spaniel dog in a crate that he sent all the way
from Texas. Black and white and spotted, and our little girl, Tricia,
the six-year-old, named it Checkers. And you know, the kids love the
dog and I just want to say this right now, that regardless of what they
say about it, we're going to keep it.'

Many viewers wept at this. But it was not all. The senator then
made a plea for 'the little man' in American politics, saying Eisenhower's
Democratic opponent, Governor Adlai Stevenson, was a wealthy man
who inherited a fortune from his father, which was fine, but men 'of
modest means' deserved a chance too, he said, quoting Republican
president Abraham Lincoln, who had remarked, 'God must have loved
the common people – he made so many of them.' Thereupon Nixon
called upon Governor Stevenson and other candidates to 'come

before the American people as I have and make a complete statement as to their financial history. And if they don't it will be an admission that they have something to hide.'[19]

The Checkers speech made political and television history. Though Eisenhower waited another day before making up his mind – in order to show who was boss – the vast positive public response made it impossible for him to dump Nixon. Eisenhower would have to put up with him – as would America.

Nixon had read the public mind and its need to identify with the candidate as an ordinary, not extraordinary American: a man with a spouse, children, a house, a mortgage, debts and a dog. With his own heavy-jowled, morose, underdog face he shamelessly played upon the ordinary viewer's sympathy – and got it. No subsequent American Caesar would be able to campaign successfully without making that familial, human connection, presented on television.

'You're my boy!' General Eisenhower declared when summoning Nixon to a meeting in Virginia and let him rip on the campaign trail (though even he blanched when Nixon referred to President Truman as a 'traitor').

Once he had won the 1952 election and was installed as president, however, Eisenhower barely allowed Nixon entry to the White House. He would not tolerate the vice president's participation in cabinet and senior government meetings, save as an observer, and censored Nixon's speeches. Moreover, he tried to remove him from the re-election ticket in 1956 by offering him a senior cabinet post, which Nixon understandably declined lest he thereby miss the opportunity to inherit the crown if the president died in office. Four years later, Eisenhower's tepid imprimatur ensured that Nixon did not succeed him when the vice president was beaten in the 1960 election by Senator John F. Kennedy.

Nixon was gutted by the president's ill will, especially given the fact that Eisenhower's grandson, David, had wedded Nixon's attractive daughter Julie. In any event, Nixon's years in the wilderness now began. He declined offers to join a New York law firm and returned to California as an attorney. On President Kennedy's advice he wrote a book, Six Crises, which became a bestseller and enabled him to buy a nice house in Bel Air next to Groucho Marx. 'Let's not run, let's stay at home. Let's be a private family' his wife begged, hoping she could persuade him to abandon his political dream.[20] Despite his promises, however, Nixon was far from being done with politics. Against his wife's advice, and that of many advisers, in autumn 1961 he threw his hat into the ring for the governorship of California, a stepping stone to the presidency.

Times had changed, however. 'That's what you have to expect from these fucking local yokels' Nixon complained when attendance at his campaign meetings was thin. 'I wouldn't give them the sweat off my balls.'[21] Nixon's concession speech made history for its mournful bitterness, following a night of drinking and, according to some sources, spousal abuse so severe his wife could not go out in public. 'One last thing,' Nixon told reporters, 'as I leave you I want you to know – just think how much you're going to be missing. You won't have Nixon to kick around any more because, gentlemen, this is my last press conference.'[22] He was, he claimed, leaving political life for good; it had been his 'last play'. 'Barring a miracle,' *Time* magazine declared, 'Richard Nixon can never hope to be elected to any political office again.'[23]

With President Kennedy's approval polls rising to record levels after the safe conclusion to the Cuban Missile Crisis that autumn, Nixon concentrated on making money ($250,000 per annum) and cultivating wealthy connections, from Walter Annenberg to Elmer Bobst, Bebe Rebozo and Don Kendall. He moved to a twelve-room apartment on Fifth Avenue, New York City, and began to travel the world as a youthful elder statesman of the Republican Party, gaining audiences with the world's leaders from General Franco to Willy Brandt, de Gaulle to Gamal Nasser. He also visited Vietnam.

With Rockefeller and Goldwater first tearing each other apart for the 1964 presidential nomination, then Goldwater being trounced by President Johnson, Nixon's gubernatorial misstep in California was gradually forgotten. Despite the new statesmanlike role he had adopted, however, even people who worked with him remained worried by his weird psyche. 'He is', Tom Wicker warned in the *New York Times*, 'as difficult as ever to know, driven still by deep inner compulsion toward power and personal vindication, painfully conscious of slights and failures, a man who has imposed upon himself a self-control so rigid as to be all but invisible' to all but his wife – and his psychiatrist.

Though sworn to secrecy, Dr Arnold Hutschnecker was especially concerned. When looking in a mirror, Nixon confided to him, 'it was as if there were nobody there'. Nixon continued to suffer from insomnia and depression, and seemed to have difficulty in living up to the exalted, saintly figure of his Quaker mother. At the same time, he seemed oddly at home with his own duplicity, in a political world largely based upon dissembling and 'dirty tricks'. 'John,' Nixon said to an aide after telling 'some pretty awful lies' to an audience, 'I can say things that when other people say them, they are lies, but when I say them people don't believe them anyway!' From then on, the aide recalled, 'I realized I was dealing with a very complicated person.'[24]

Journalists might write Nixon off as a has-been, a self-pitying failure, sour and out of sync with flower power and the 1960s, but his influence in Republican circles remained strong. As President Johnson's Great Society began to crumble in the face of mounting casualties in an unpopular war in Vietnam and race riots at home, Nixon's hour again approached. He assembled the largest Republican financial backing in history, and won the early primaries for the 1968 Republican presidential nomination against governors Romney, Rockefeller and Reagan (nicknamed the Three Rs). At the national convention in Miami in August 1968, he won an overwhelming first-ballot victory, but to general consternation then chose an unknown (and uninvestigated) governor of Maryland, Spiro T. Agnew, as his vice presidential running mate, instead of the more distinguished Senator George Romney – an ominous, if little noticed, indication of Nixon's distrust of others and inability to share the limelight, in an otherwise extraordinary act of self-reinvention.

Measured, statesmanlike rhetoric characterized Nixon's second bid for the White House, with new speechwriters Pat Buchanan and William Safire reaching for a Republican high road. 'As we look at America, we see cities enveloped in smoke and flame. We hear sirens in the night. We see Americans dying on distant battlefields abroad' Nixon had said in his acceptance speech in Miami. 'We see Americans hating each other; killing each other at home. And as we see and hear these things, millions of Americans cry out in anguish: Did we come all this way for this? Did American boys die in Normandy and Korea and Valley Forge for this?' Pausing first, he heard an 'answer to these questions': another, quieter voice 'in the tumult of the shouting. It is the voice of the great majority of Americans, the forgotten Americans, the non-shouters, the non-demonstrators. They're good people. They're decent people. They work and they save and they pay taxes and they care. They work in American factories, they run American businesses, they serve in government. They provide most of the soldiers who die to keep it free. They give drive to the spirit of America. They give life to the American dream.'[25]

This was a vastly different approach from the anti-Communist, anti-tax, anti-government 'values' Republicanism that Governor Ronald Reagan was trumpeting. Moreover it represented the better, compassionate, responsible voice of Richard Nixon himself: the 'good' son of Quaker Hannah Milhous: a dutiful, hard-working son who had helped his father buy, stock and sell, even deliver, vegetables for his small grocery store in Yorba Linda, long before Nixon turned to rich backers and gave in to the demons in his soul. Sadly, it was a side of Nixon that was completely contradicted by what he next did – namely, in an act of rank treason, sabotage President Johnson's last-minute breakthrough in peace negotiations with North Vietnam to end the Vietnam War.

By dissuading President Thieu from attending the Paris peace talks, Nixon brilliantly scotched the president's triumph, and destroyed Vice President Hubert Humphrey's challenge for the 1968 presidential crown. At midnight on November 5, 1968, Humphrey seemed to be leading by almost 1 per cent, but in the Electoral College the picture was less rosy. At 3 a.m. Nixon, calculating his Electoral College numbers on his familiar yellow legal pad, claimed success. He had won victory by a sliver – a margin of less than 1 per cent of votes cast – snatching it from the jaws of defeat and avenging his loss to John F. Kennedy in 1960.

## Part Two: The Presidency

Immediately after his inauguration on January 20, 1969, Nixon shunned the Oval Office. Instead, he selected a secret suite or hideaway: Room EOB 175, in the Old Executive Office Building next door along Pennsylvania Avenue, amid a rabbit warren of offices. He had assembled a cabinet of mediocrities, including a Secretary of State, William

Rogers, who would be a cipher, so that he could himself direct and manage American foreign policy – with political scientist Dr Henry Kissinger, from Harvard University, as his national security adviser.

From Room 175, using his coterie of protective loyalists and henchmen, the new president now issued edicts and instructions without having to meet people face to face. 'I have never met such a gang of self-seeking bastards in my life' Kissinger remarked of Nixon's clique, reminiscent of a medieval monarch's courtiers – worse even than Kissinger's colleagues at Harvard.[26] William Rogers, however, saw Kissinger as the problem: 'Machiavellian, deceitful, egotistical, arrogant, and insulting.'[27]

Voters had been made to believe Nixon had a better chance of immediately ending the war than his opponent by virtue of a 'secret plan',[28] but as historian Robert Dallek noted, this had been 'nothing more than an election ploy'[29] that turned into national disaster when Nixon now found it impossible to shift President Thieu's opposition to a peace settlement with North Vietnam. Nixon and Kissinger were thus stymied; they 'had no good alternative for ending the war except the application of more force' against North Vietnam.[30]

Protected by his chief of staff Bob Haldeman, and his domestic affairs czar John Ehrlichman, Nixon ate lunch alone in Room 175, and kept late hours there, brooding, plotting, spinning, dictating, as he set out to recast American foreign policy while dismissing domestic concerns as 'building outhouses in Peoria'.[31] He thus declined to give a State of the Union address, refused to give press conferences on a regular basis, and decided to rely on occasional, very carefully controlled appearances. As far as possible he even shut down direct contact with the State Department and foreign diplomats. Instead, he began to fly from one hideaway to another with a retinue of staffers, while Dr Kissinger, Haldeman and Ehrlichman were under orders to translate his decisions into direct action, without reference to the cabinet or Congress or even the Pentagon. He also relied on loyalist John Mitchell, whom he made Attorney General, to police any leaks to the Fourth Estate. Anyone publishing details or revelations of the president's intentions or decisions was immediately subjected to wiretapping – including Kissinger himself. The first victim of this new secretive approach to the presidency was to be Cambodia.

How, historians later asked, was a democratically elected leader of the United States able to recast the constitutional role of the presidency, and bypass the famed checks and balances, namely Congress, the Supreme Court, and a free press?

The answer – as it would be three decades later – was the veil of war. President Johnson had launched the war in Vietnam to satisfy jingoists and armchair strategists preoccupied by domino theories of Soviet expansionism. He had then acted as the chairman of successive committees of advisers. Nixon had no such interest. As Kennedy had 'hit the Republicans from the right', in the parlance of historians, Nixon's intention was equally radical: namely to hit Democrats from the left, hoping to reverse his old anti-Communist agenda and seek a new world order based on rapprochement and equivalence between the US, the Soviet Union and Communist China as the world's three superpowers, each with their own spheres of influence. To achieve this, however, he needed to close down the Vietnam War as swiftly as possible. With President Thieu resisting all blandishments, Nixon decided he would have to escalate the war, on a scale not seen since World War II.

Using his commander-in-chief's prerogative, Nixon thus drew up, in his second month in office, a secret new bombing plan to interdict the Ho Chi Minh Trail, the gateway for the North Vietnamese army's supplies and troops to operations in the South.

The US Air Force bombed Cambodia and southern Laos (Operation MENU) from March 18 to May 26, 1969, without the Secretary of the Air Force or the outside world knowing – using phony coordinates, in literal double-entry bookkeeping.

Had the secret escalation worked, Nixon and his national security adviser might have been able to excuse such deliberate mass murder as a necessity in achieving peace. But to Dr Kissinger's disappointment, the bombing evinced no change in Hanoi's position, indeed produced nothing save the tipping of Cambodia into a catastrophic spiral of civil war, the creation of 600,000 refugees in Laos (20 per cent of its population), and the start of yet more illegal wiretapping in America when the *New York Times* finally revealed the bomber raids on Cambodia.

By the summer of 1969 Nixon was privately admitting that there was no possibility of 'victory', or even an armistice, along the lines of Korea, with the country remaining divided into two. The question was simply one of American imperial pride: how the commander-in-chief could get the US Army out of Vietnam without America's standing as the most powerful nation in the free world suffering too severely.

President de Gaulle had recommended swallowing national pride and making a simple decision to leave the country, as the French had left Algeria. However, France had been a waning empire, with withdrawal a mark of painful adjustment to a post-colonial, European reality. Though some commentators predicted the imminent collapse of the American Empire as evidenced by its anarchic, draft-burning, drug-taking, campus-occupying and anti-war-protesting students, Nixon was sure they were wrong; in this, at least, he was right. The American economy, despite inflation and unemployment, was more productive than ever, busting to expand on a global scale, if only the troops could be brought home.

Finding an 'honourable' Vietnam exit strategy thus posed the same problem that it had for President Johnson. Still beholden to President Thieu for his role in getting him elected, Nixon kept Operation MENU secret for another four years, during which some half a million tons of bombs were dropped. In the meantime he and his national security adviser lurched from one alternative exit to the next, unwilling to accept the 'first defeat in the nation's history', as Nixon put it.[32]

Not to be able to smash up 'a fourth-rate power like North Vietnam' without resorting to nuclear weapons tormented Nixon. He refused to believe Ho Chi Minh 'doesn't have a breaking point'. He even explored the possibility of applying his 'Madman Theory', namely feigning crazy and unpredictable behaviour. Like Nikita Khrushchev before him, he would, he told Kissinger, thus be seen by North Vietnam and their 'sponsors' as a wild card, dangerous and nuclear-tipped, so that North Vietnam would *have* to negotiate a settlement in Paris, if only for safety's sake. 'We'll just slip the word to them' the President explained to his chief of staff. The enemy would be compelled to cower, saying: 'We can't restrain him when he is angry – and he has his hand on the nuclear button.' 'Ho Chi Minh himself will be in Paris in two days,' the president fantasized, 'begging for peace.'[33]

Not even Nixon, a consummate actor, believed he would get away with this on its own, however. He therefore ordered plans to be drawn up for a monster-offensive to be called Operation Duck Hook, which would apply 'maximum political, military, and psychological shock' on the enemy – indeed the president regretted he hadn't kicked off with such clout on winning the White House. 'We should have bombed the hell out of them the minute we took office' he told his speech-writer, Bill Safire. Simultaneously he also continued to pursue his 'Madman' idea. Word thus went round the White House that 'the Old Man is going to have to drop the bomb before the year is out and that will be the end of the war'.[34] To further the 'madman-as-president' notion, Nixon even ordered the dispatch of 'nuclear capable forces to their operating bases' in an effort to intimidate the Russians into pressuring the North Vietnamese to relent.

Nothing worked, however; indeed protests in America grew ever more vocal. Finally, in response to the Moratorium, a huge national anti-war protest held on October 15, 1969, Nixon finally bowed to the un-silent majority in America, just as President Johnson had before him. He wished to win the midterm congressional elections in 1970, and if possible be re-elected as president in 1972. He therefore rejected Kissinger's proposals to increase the bombing or send over more American troops. Instead he proposed the opposite: namely to force Thieu to accept 'de-Americanization' of the conflict: a policy that was quickly retitled 'Vietnamization'.

'Vietnamization' sounded a lot better than defeat, but was based on the same premise: that South Vietnam was doomed, since the South Vietnamese could no more defend themselves effectively, without American help, than the South Koreans.

In a speech on November 3, 1969, Nixon attempted to put a brave face on his failure to resolve the conflict in Vietnam, blaming the North Vietnamese for refusing to cave in. Meanwhile, pretending the war was going well, he announced he would begin withdrawing tens of thousands of troops as part of his successful 'Vietnamization' policy. He also announced the termination of the draft, once the war – for America – ended, addressing the young people of America with the words 'I want peace as much as you do.'[35]

Behind a veil of pretence – that the South Vietnamese were suddenly and miraculously able to shoulder the burden of fighting the Vietcong and North Vietnamese – the Great Retreat was beginning. By the end of the year, Nixon had ordered the repatriation of more than 115,000 American troops, with huge numbers slated to follow them home the following year.

Nixon the politician had gauged correctly, if belatedly. His public approval rating leaped to an all-time high (68 per cent). By continuing a punitive B-52 bombing policy, meantime, he hoped he could at least play to the patriotic American gallery. 'If, when the chips are down, the world's most powerful nation, the United States of America, acts like a pitiful, helpless giant,' he claimed, 'the forces of totalitarianism and anarchy will threaten free nations and free institutions throughout the world.' As a rationale for continuing mass slaughter from the air, especially in laying waste a poor and neutral country such as Cambodia by massive carpet-bombing, it proved unconvincing to protesters, and filled later historians with indignation – poor Cambodia becoming 'the most heavily bombed country in history'.[36] Transcripts of Nixon's deliberations with Henry Kissinger, released decades later, certainly make sickening reading. 'They [the USAF] have got to go in there and I mean really go in,' Nixon emphasized to Kissinger in 1970. 'I want everything that can fly to go in there and crack the hell out of them. There is no limitation on mileage and there is no limitation on budget. Is that clear?' Lest there be any doubt (since Kissinger had warned that the US Air Force was trained to attack Soviet air forces and conventional armies, not guerrillas embedded in civilian communities[37]), Nixon reiterated: 'I want a plan where every goddamn thing that can fly goes into Cambodia and hits every target that is open . . . everything. I want them to use the big planes, the small planes, everything they can.'[38]

The Cambodian 'Sideshow', as William Shawcross sarcastically called it – a campaign in which 15,000 American troops invaded the country, without congressional approval, while 2.75 million tons of bombs were dropped by the US Air Force – was a veritable holocaust from a humanitarian point of view. Upwards of 10 per cent of the bombing was indiscriminate, resulting not only in some 600,000 Cambodian deaths, it was later estimated in a Finnish government report, but also the death of a further million Cambodian civilians by starvation, and the rise of Pol Pot's Khmer Rouge.

Meanwhile huge advances in western technology and the manufacture of consumer appliances in the 1960s had proved Nixon, in his Kitchen Debate with Nikita Khrushchev in 1959, correct: consumer capitalism *was* fulfilling ordinary people's desires for a better life more effectively than ideological Marxism was doing. Thanks to President

Kennedy's decision to fund a race to the moon, moreover, even the Soviet Union's one scientific and engineering triumph, sputnik, was relegated to a footnote when, on Sunday July 20, 1969, nearly a billion people around the world – the largest television audience ever – watched as the *Eagle* (the lunar module of *Apollo 11*) landed, and two American astronauts set foot on the moon's powdery surface.

'This certainly has to be the most historic telephone call ever made from the White House' Nixon declared excitedly as he spoke to the men, Neil Armstrong and Buzz Aldrin. It was the 'beginning of a new age' he claimed. 'For one priceless moment in the whole history of man all the people on this earth are truly one.' Welcoming the men three days later aboard an American aircraft carrier in the Pacific Ocean, Nixon then congratulated them in person, saying (to the consternation of evangelical Christians) that it was 'the greatest week in the history of the world since the Creation'.[39]

As five further manned moon landings then built upon the American achievement over the following three years, the question arose: might the 1970s usher in that 'new age', an age of peaceful coexistence, leading to an end to the Cold War? If so, how far could the United States push that process, while turning it to its own economic and security advantage? Did the answer lie in what, after the first moon landing, Nixon called his new 'Doctrine'?

Speaking to journalists in Guam, Nixon had described his view of US policy across the world, in particular the face-saving 'Vietnamization'. Reading reporters' articles afterwards, he decided to give it the title 'Nixon Doctrine', in contrast to the Truman Doctrine, and Cambodia, he declared, 'is the Nixon doctrine in its purest form'.[40]

Pure was a relative term. In his new approach to foreign affairs there would be 'no more Vietnams'. Although the US would do its best to help meet Communist insurgencies when they arose, it 'would not fight the war' for other people's democracies.[41] Instead, America would pursue a radically new approach to empire: seeking an accommodation with the Soviets, a freeze on the arms race, and reversal of his own long-held attitude towards Communist China by embracing it now as a 'neighbour' in the Pacific, with the prospect of real trade between the continents – once a major facet of the United States economy. The Cold War would thus no longer be fought as a struggle to be won, but would be recast as the interplay of great powers, as in the nineteenth century, with 'spheres' of influence but no direct colonization.

Reporters who had covered Nixon since the 1940s rubbed their eyes in disbelief. Was such a volte-face real? And could Nixon put it into effect?

In seeking psychiatric help in the 1950s, Nixon had attempted to alter his political persona into one he could accept in the mirror and with which he could be more comfortable. The result had been, for the most part, a more dignified, statesmanlike Richard Nixon, willing to see the world more realistically than many of his Republican, even Democratic colleagues: the foundation for his new Nixon Doctrine. But, as his deliberate stymieing of President Johnson's peace negotiations had demonstrated, the old Richard Nixon – ambitious, resentful, tormented – had not gone away, and in the bunker-style life he then led as president, protected by amoral courtiers, it was bound eventually to resurface. 'Isolation', Kissinger said of him later, 'had become almost a spiritual necessity' – a 'tormented man who insisted on his loneliness'.[42]

Unable to share the limelight or give credit to others, the president was, Kissinger described, 'a very odd man, an unpleasant man. He didn't enjoy people.'[43] Nixon himself was aware of this. Of President Eisenhower he said in amazement, 'Everybody loved Ike. But the reverse of that was that Ike loved everybody . . . Ike didn't hate anybody. Ike was puzzled by that sort of thing. He didn't think of people who disagreed with him as being the "enemy". He just thought: "They don't agree with me."'[44] This was not how Richard Nixon felt or worked, with the consequence that the bunker mentality that pervaded his presidency poisoned even the most progressive of his initiatives.

The Strategic Arms Limitation Treaty (SALT) between the United States and the Soviet Union was an example of Nixon at his best – and worst. Halting the arms race had been a goal of presidents since Dwight Eisenhower. It had been pursued by Kennedy, who got a treaty ban against testing nuclear weapons, and again by President Johnson, who got the Soviets to agree a common approach to the spread of nuclear weapons. Yet it was President Nixon who got Congress to ratify Johnson's nuclear non-proliferation treaty and, in a tied vote in the Senate (broken by the vice president) to back a failing US anti-ballistic-missile (ABM) programme, as a bargaining tool in getting a strategic missile limitation. Instead of proceeding methodically through his SALT team and Secretary of State, however, Nixon pursued a tortuous up-and-down, back-room, ad hoc series of 'negotiations' as Byzantine as they were protracted, all conducted with, or through, his National Security Adviser, Kissinger, lest the State Department or defence experts garner any credit or acclaim.

This was the 'Madman Theory' written into the script of the increasingly imperial White House itself: an American Empire propelled by capitalist wealth, investment, trade and hard work, but led by a whim-driven president who seemed able only to operate in secret, hoping that his eccentric, maverick style would keep everybody guessing and thereby preserve the initiative in his own hands. Thus, instead of getting a considered arms treaty with the Soviets in reasonable time, Nixon attempted endless manoeuvres as part of his negotiating tactics to try and trick-or-treat them into pressuring the North Vietnamese to make peace – a linkage that failed completely, and left Nixon, facing growing unpopularity over continuation of the Vietnam War in May 1972, having to agree to a five-year arms moratorium that was largely specious.

Characteristically the president announced SALT to the world as if it were the beginning of the end of the Cold War. Moreover, having used Dr Kissinger rather than his formal team to get the agreement, he became paranoid lest Kissinger take credit for it. 'It won't mean a damn thing' he privately acknowledged of the SALT agreement, but agreed with Kissinger it might well produce a worthwhile outcome by stealing the peacenik thunder from under Democrats' noses, and thus 'break the back of this generation of Democratic leaders'.[45] More so, in fact, if he and Kissinger pursued their dual-Machiavellian approach to government. 'We've got to break – we've got to destroy the confidence of the people in the American Establishment' the president confided to Kissinger, so that 'the people' of America would turn to Richard M. Nixon as their true leader.[46]

This was no longer a matter of an imperial presidency, centred on the White House, in other words, but of a maverick president operating from a hidden office, on the sly, *away* from the White House; unpredictable, isolated, often out of control. Certainly, it was becoming clear to many observers abroad that America was being ruled by a new kind of leader, an untrustworthy chief executive playing poker on a world stage while exploiting the docility and support of a 'silent majority' at home.

For all Nixon's mistakes and self-isolation, however, such observers had to admit he was amazingly clever at keeping the initiative; indeed he *was* representing the centrist majority of voters, both Republican and Democratic. The majority of Americans wanted the US military to leave Vietnam, as did Nixon. The majority favoured détente with the Russians – as did Nixon, however irrationally he conducted negotiations and however specious the first SALT agreement. The majority wished for a rapprochement with Communist China – as did Nixon. The very man who had fanned the flames of fear and even hysteria against the Communists of the USSR and China for two long decades, trampling every liberal in his path, became the first president to obtain a signed agreement that codified nuclear parity and coexistence with the Soviets. And then, to the disbelief of diehard Republican anti-Communists but to the applause of the 'silent majority', Nixon reversed his attitude towards Communist China too, going all out to woo Chairman Mao. Observers could only scratch their heads in astonishment. Had the politician who had, at the start of his career, called himself a 'progressive liberal' actually become a liberal?

On Sunday August 15, 1971, after a secret economic summit at Camp David involving thirteen helicoptered assistants and advisers, including the chairman of the Federal Reserve Board, Arthur Burns, Nixon had gone on national television to make an important announcement. With inflation continually rising, along with unemployment, foreign speculators were demanding gold for their dollars. The United States, then, would simply abandon the gold standard and allow the dollar to float, effectively devaluing it at a stroke.

Foreign governments, oil producers and currency speculators were stunned by such a unilateral, surprise decision, which Nixon managed to keep from leaking until the moment he went on air. Moreover he announced a temporary freeze on prices and wages, as well as a raft of economic measures that scandalized right-wing Republican backers and reduced George McGovern, his probable opponent in the 1972 presidential election, to apoplexy. McGovern called the speech 'sheer bunk, irrelevancy and mystery' – especially the abandonment of the gold standard as 'a disgrace that amounts to a backdoor devaluation'.[47]

It did – but a highly effective one. As a result, the Dow Jones recorded the biggest one-day rise in its history. Nixon's address, moreover, was masterly. American troops were coming home faster than anyone had believed possible the year before; South Vietnam would soon be left on its own, leaving the United States to do what it did best: create wealth. 'America has its best opportunity today to achieve two of its greatest ideals,' Nixon began: 'to bring about a full generation of peace and to create a new era of prosperity.' The American dollar was never again to be 'a hostage in the hands of international speculators.' A 10 per cent tax on all imports would be levied, with price controls to ensure American speculators did not get in on the act. Federal spending would be cut, while investment credits would be given to businesses and a fifty-dollar bonus to every taxpayer. Foreign aid would be cut by 10 per cent. Lest this sound like Father Christmas in America and Scrooge abroad, Nixon ended with a call to economic arms. 'Every action I have taken tonight is designed to nurture and stimulate that competitive spirit to help us snap out of self-doubt, the self-disparagement that saps our energy and erodes our confidence in ourselves . . . Whether the nation stays number one depends on your competitive spirit, your sense of personal destiny, your pride in your country and yourself.'[48]

As a lawyer and as a campaign pugilist Nixon had always looked for weaknesses in an opponent's defences. Recognizing that the tensions between the USSR and China could be exploited to American advantage, Nixon the global strategist attempted to offer himself as an ally to the Soviets in their gathering dispute with Mao, while doing the same with the Chinese in their growing hostility towards the Soviet Union. He thus discussed (but did not agree to) a Soviet pre-emptive strike against Chinese nuclear weapon-producing sites; simultaneously he pressed for a personal meeting with Mao, and eventually got it. 'They're scared of the Russians. That's got to be it', Nixon remarked to Kissinger, on hearing Chou En-lai's invitation that he visit Peking.[49]

Nixon was right – and rightly seized the opportunity. His epithet 'Tricky Dick' was now earned in spades as he cast aside his long-held loyalty to Chinese Nationalist leader Chiang Kai-shek, buttered up Mao Zedong ('The Chairman's writings moved a nation and have changed the world' he said unctuously, when Mao deprecated his own books), expressed awe at the Great Wall of China, accepted two pandas for the Washington National Zoo, and agreed a communiqué which not only obligated the United States to oppose with China any move by the USSR to achieve 'hegemony in the Asia Pacific region', but also recognized Communist China's claim that Taiwan was 'a part of China'. Recommending that there be a 'peaceful settlement of the Taiwan question by the Chinese themselves', the president committed the US to an 'ultimate objective of the withdrawal of all US forces and military installations from Taiwan'.[50] Such a statement, had it been issued by a politician when Nixon was in Congress, would have had him on the floor denouncing the speaker as a traitor. Now it was wisdom – Nixon's wisdom.

Back home, where the president's extraordinary week-long trip in February 1972 had been broadcast on evening network television (thanks to the time difference), he immediately declared 'This was the week that changed the world' – a play on John Reed's famous account of the Russian Revolution. Inasmuch as he had spent half a lifetime opposing the change, it was patently disingenuous. Nixon the maverick had every reason to crow, however, since only a maverick could have changed his spots so swiftly, utterly and shamelessly. The leader of the free world, after decades of 'pinko-trashing', had entered the lion's den, and stretched out a hand of potential friendship between the world's foremost capitalist superpower and the world's most populous Communist nation (871 million people, having added 200 million, the size of the US population, in a single decade). This was an extraordinary achievement, however much of a turncoat Nixon might be as a Republican. 'Tricky Dick' had, in effect, tricked his own right-wing anti-Communist funders and supporters, confounding them by his use of the 'silent majority', which by an overwhelming margin supported his initiative.

Later that year Nixon won re-nomination as the Republican presidential candidate, despite outrage among Republican hardliners, diehards and extremists over his liberal actions. Then, with a peace agreement being tortuously negotiated with North Vietnam, he won one of the biggest electoral landslide victories in presidential history, trouncing George McGovern on November 5, 1972, by forty-seven million votes to twenty-nine million. For a politician who had committed genocide in South East Asia and provoked virtual civil war at home in his first two years in office, this was a truly extraordinary resurrection.

In his second term, Richard Nixon seemed determined to continue to recast America's power abroad. Moreover he would exercise it no longer as the leader of the western allies, but in the pursuit of raw American self-interest, as the world's strongest economic and military power. 'Here's those little cocksuckers right in there' Nixon had sneered when pointing to Vietnam on a map of the world in May 1972 shortly before his re-election, thumping the table as he spoke. 'Here's the United States (thump). Here's western (thump) Europe, that *cocky* little place that's caused so much devastation – Here's the Soviet Union (thump), here's the (thump) mid-East . . . Here's the (thump) silly Africans . . . And (thump) the not-quite-so-silly Latin Americans. Here *we* are. They're taking on the United States. Now, goddamit we're gonna *do* it. We're going to *cream* them [bomb the North Vietnamese]. This is not in anger or anything. This old business, that I'm "petulant", that's bullshit. I should have done it long ago,' he'd rasped in an almost Hitlerian monologue, 'I just didn't follow my instincts.'[51]

This maverick, individual, cynical, dangerous but also game-changing approach to global issues was Nixon's contribution to what became known the next year as the 'Imperial Presidency'.[52] Instead of working in conjunction with Congress, Nixon directed his US bombing operations and simultaneous negotiating efforts with Hanoi almost entirely without reference to Capitol Hill – just as he made each of his about-turns *ex cathedra*, from his visit to China to his abandonment of the gold standard. But such benevolent-dictator behaviour could only work successfully if there were no leaks; and leaks came to obsess him to the point of paranoia.

Nixon had always hated the press for criticizing him; now he hated it for daring to publish the truth – truths which people on his own team must be leaking, he suspected. In this respect, Nixon was not Richard the Lionheart but Richard III: an inveterate schemer, suspicious even of his colleagues, and constantly issuing vindictive, retaliatory orders, which his loyal chief of staff, Bob Haldeman, for the most part took upon himself to execute – and often quietly ditched. Among the orders that Haldeman didn't ditch was one that would have disastrous results for the president and his trusted servants: Watergate.

Had Nixon been psychologically better balanced, or had he had a sense of humour, the break-in that became known as Watergate might never have happened.

Watergate would be the iceberg that sank his presidency, but it was only the tip. Blaming 'fucking Jews' and using a Special Investigations Unit, familiarly known as 'the Plumbers', Nixon had already personally ordered the burglary of the office and files of a psychiatrist believed to be treating an opponent of the Vietnam War, Daniel Ellsberg. The president had also demanded IRS investigations of all who had contributed to his Democratic opponent Hubert Humphrey, and Senator Muskie: 'the Jews, you know, that are stealing—'. When his White House aide John Ehrlichman suggested the Plumbers break into the National Archives – the very repository of the US Constitution – Nixon concurred. 'You can do that,' the president said, his voice captured for posterity on his own self-taping system.

Even before his re-election, Nixon had prompted growing concern for the way he shut out members of his own administration, of Congress and even senior military leaders who threatened to steal his limelight. He had his own national security adviser, Dr Kissinger, wiretapped, and accused him of entertaining 'delusions of grandeur' when Kissinger offered to fly personally to Hanoi to negotiate with the North Vietnamese.[53] In a bizarre twist, Nixon insisted Kissinger see a psychiatrist, so paranoid did he feel Kissinger was becoming about leaks and 'internal weakness'.[54] (Kissinger even began taping his own telephone conversations to protect himself.)

It was small wonder, then, that in a White House morass of mutual suspicion, wiretapping, burglary, leak and planted denunciatory rumour, one of the Plumbers' illegal 'investigations' would eventually backfire. On May 28, 1972, a year after the Ellsberg affair began, with Nixon still in Leningrad after signing the SALT I treaty with Leonid Brezhnev, First Secretary of the Communist Party, the Plumbers managed to pick the locks of a new target: the headquarters of the National Democratic Committee, on the sixth floor of the Watergate office and apartment complex in Foggy Bottom, Washington DC.

The first break-in went without a hitch. Three weeks later, however, hubris overtook caution. On June 13, 1972, Nixon ordered his special counsel, Charles Colson, to carry out round-the-clock secret surveillance of his Democratic opponent, Senator McGovern, up to the November election. The next night, dissatisfied with the results from the bugs they'd earlier planted in the Democratic National Committee headquarters, Nixon's aides Gordon Liddy and Howard Hunt ordered the burglars back into the Watergate building. This time the President's men were caught *in flagrante*: three Cuban Americans and two former CIA agents, one of whom worked for the Committee to Re-elect the President (the CRP or, later, CREEP).

'Well, it sounds like a comic opera' Nixon chuckled as he listened to initial stories circulating about the burglary, mocking the accents of the Cubans and shaking his head over the $100 bills found in their pockets.[55] He felt secure: Gordon Liddy, his strong-arm lieutenant, was willing to be put 'in front of a firing squad' rather than betray his president, he was assured. The Democratic National Committee duly sued the CRP for $1 million for invasion of privacy, while Nixon – who had ordered the burglary, and had paid the Plumbers – attempted to remain above the fray, issuing a statement from the White House that 'this kind of activity has no place whatever in our electoral process, or in our governmental process'. This was followed by the categorical declaration that 'the White House has had no involvement whatever in this particular incident'.[56]

For a while it seemed as if the murky scandal would blow over, despite the detective work of two *Washington Post* reporters, Bob Woodward and Carl Bernstein. Nixon thus rejoiced in his massive victory at the November 1972 polls – validation, as he saw it, of all his efforts as president during his first term. Having withdrawn virtually all ground forces from Vietnam, he was relying on the might of the US Air Force, once again, to obtain a formal end to the war – or rather, America's part in it. This, he decided, would be achieved by massive new bombing of military targets in Hanoi and Haiphong, code-named Linebacker II. Over twelve days at Christmas 1972 (while Congress was in recess for the holiday break and could not object) vast aerial armadas of B-52 bombers were ordered to drop more tons of high explosive on North Vietnam than in World War II – 'the most savage and senseless act of war ever visited, over a scant ten days, by one sovereign people over another' as the *Washington Post* protested – a 'stone-age tactic' that might cause the president to be impeached, once congressmen returned to Washington.[57]

Since North Vietnam persisted in its refusal to sign a peace treaty guaranteeing South Vietnamese independence, Dr Kissinger's deputy, General Alexander Haig, favoured even more aggressive bombing to compel the North Vietnamese to withdraw their forces from the South.

Kissinger, in Paris, also wanted to end the fruitless negotiations, blaming the Vietnamese, whom he called 'Tawdry, filthy shits. They make the Russians look good.' But the South Vietnamese junta leader, President Thieu, was no better – an 'insane son-of-a-bitch', in Kissinger's parlance, since Thieu obstinately, but understandably, still refused the settlement Nixon had got him to reject four years before.

Times had changed, however. Almost 70 per cent of Americans now felt the war to have been a mistake, from the start. The ceaseless American bombing was becoming an international disgrace, with calls for Nuremberg war trials, given the untold civilian casualties; and all because, from Kissinger's viewpoint, President Thieu would not agree to South Vietnam's suicide. A 'bilateral arrangement' between the US and North Vietnam – one that would simply ignore the South Vietnamese – thus became the American position. The North Vietnamese, who had exhausted their last anti-aircraft missiles around Hanoi, had had enough too. A ceasefire was therefore announced in Paris on January 23, 1973, with President Thieu bowing to the inevitable.

All parties, including the Vietcong who signed up to the agreement, knew the Paris Peace Accords were a charade. Kissinger confided to a journalist that the North Vietnamese would 'probably start the war again on the first of February' 1973 – i.e. after Nixon's re-inauguration – and President Thieu's deputy denounced it as 'a sell-out'. Nevertheless American honour, if it could be called that, had been satisfied, and the US could finally and legally abandon South Vietnam to its fate. Kissinger predicted that, if lucky, South Vietnam could last a year before being overrun by the North Vietnamese, while he sought to get back some 600 American POWs.[58] It was a sad conclusion to a war that could have been terminated in the same way some four years before, had Nixon not sabotaged President Johnson's negotiations. A further 20,000 US servicemen had been killed, but at least it was now over for America.

Behind the general rejoicing, however, all was not well as the president's role in the Watergate burglary became the subject of a media manhunt.

Why Nixon's aides and subordinates should have been willing to go to the wall for him would never be clear, beyond promises of cash; but by continuing to operate his secret taping system, and keeping his incriminating tapes rather than destroying them, the president – who was pathologically anxious lest Kissinger upstage him and write memoirs that would steal the credit for Nixon's triumphs over China, SALT I and the ending of the war in Vietnam – sealed his own ultimate demise. On February 7, 1973, a Senate Watergate Committee was established. By April 30, the first resignations of White House staff began with those of Haldeman and Ehrlichman (both of whom would go to prison, as well as White House counsel John Dean). On May 18, Archibald Cox was then appointed Special Prosecutor by the Attorney General.

Cox's hearings were televised, just as the McCarthy hearings had been. Some 85 per cent of Americans watched at least some of the process. The first crack came in late June, when the 'master manipulator of the cover-up', John Dean, became a witness for the prosecution in return for a reduced jail sentence. Nixon asked Haig, who had become the White House chief of staff in May, if he thought he should resign as president, the first such resignation in US history.

Haig recommended against, as did Kissinger, who blamed 'bastard traitors', namely the press and members of Congress who 'are now trying to deprive you of any success'. By hanging tough, 'You can go down in history', he promised the president as his would-be Bismarck ('My idol', Kissinger boasted), 'as the man who brought about the greatest revolution in foreign policy ever'.[59]

Kissinger, born in Germany, had never truly understood the system of checks and balances that made the US Constitution such a unique document in world history, or the anti-monarchical sentiment that had fuelled the American Revolution. As the rats began to leave the sinking ship, however, Nixon's downfall became inevitable. On July 13, 1973, the deputy White House chief of staff, Alexander Butterfield, a decorated air force pilot, revealed under questioning the existence of White House audio surveillance tapes, a secret originally known only to three people. Immediately the tapes were subpoenaed both by Cox and by Congress. Nixon resisted, citing – like Eisenhower during the McCarthy hearings – 'executive privilege'.

Eisenhower had had, at least, the backing of his Attorney General in asserting such a privilege. Nixon did not; indeed he now fired his newly minted Attorney General, Elliot Richardson, and the Deputy Attorney General, for refusing to fire Cox. Fighting the Congress and his own Justice Department was, however, a poker-driven strategy that could only end badly. Although the Solicitor General, Robert Bork, agreed to do the president's bidding by firing Cox, a move to impeach Nixon in Congress began to gather momentum.

The president now knew what it was like to be Alger Hiss. Weighing his options, Nixon nevertheless decided he would hang on to the presidency, come what may. At a meeting of 400 Associated Press editors in Orlando, Florida, he admitted mistakes but said he had not obstructed justice, would not resign, and, while he acknowledged that 'people have got to know whether or not their president is a crook', he wanted them to know, via the editors, he wasn't.[60]

Adopting a stonewalling strategy, Nixon lurched between self-pity and bravado. His whole life, since childhood, had been a struggle to offset his disadvantages – his humble background, his morose character – by exercising his tough, relentless, competitive and wily intellect. At times he seemed actually to relish the cat-and-mouse struggle to deflect the long arm of the law, in a constitutional system he considered weighted towards dunces and second-raters. 'How much money do you need?' he asked John Dean, on March 21, 1973 – their conversation captured on tape. 'If you need the money, you could get the money . . . You could get it in cash. I know where it could be gotten . . . I mean it's not easy but it could be done,' he confided, assuring Haldeman he could raise a million dollars.[61] 'There is no problem in that.'[62] He could not, however, promise his Plumbers would avoid prison. 'We can't provide the clemency', he made clear; the money would have to compensate for that, he explained – and thereupon arranged for $75,000 to be taken from his secret safe and delivered to Hunt's home that night.[63]

More and more, the president's machinations resembled those of Caligula. Alternating daily between illegal and drastic options – the provision of illegal hush-money; efforts to get Mitchell, Dean and others to take sole blame for Watergate; instructions to the prosecutor not to offer immunity (which would encourage whistle-blowers); pretending meanwhile to his Plumbers that they could rely on him to grant them a presidential pardon so they would not go to jail – Nixon seemed to relish the adrenalin rush of playing, as always, such a high-stakes game. 'For a guy who you say is sometimes a little loose upstairs, he looks pretty clever to me', Dean's attorney was moved to remark.[64]

American affairs of state, meanwhile, went to pot as the president became more and more embattled, leaving Kissinger to conduct US foreign policy. Kissinger's indifference to civilian suffering in Cambodia and Laos – where another 350,000 civilians lost their lives – caused observers, historians and, later, genocide lawyers, to question his role as national security adviser in the Nixon administration, even to call for his indictment. Cambodia and Laos, moreover, were not the only areas where Kissinger indulged, it would be claimed, in mass murder and even individual murder – as when, on September 11, 1973, a second CIA-sponsored coup against the democratically elected president of Chile, Dr Salvador Allende, led to him being surrounded in his presidential palace and forced to commit suicide. 'I mean,' Kissinger congratulated the president five days later, 'we helped them – created the conditions as great as possible' for the coup to succeed. To which Nixon added, thinking of Watergate, he was grateful that 'our hand doesn't show on this one' – yet.[65] Nor did it the following month, when war broke out in the Middle East.

The first news of war in the Middle East came early on October 6, 1973. More than any other ill tidings, its reception in Washington DC bespoke the state of Nixon's crippled presidency, sixteen days before impeachment proceedings were opened by the House Judiciary Committee. 'For two and a half hours after he heard about war dangers from the Israelis at 6 a.m. on October 6,' one historian later wrote, the newly promoted Secretary of State, Kissinger, 'did not consult Nixon, who was in Key Biscayne, Florida, where he had taken shelter from mounting judicial and congressional pressures.'[66]

The president was, in fact, seldom in Washington. Records indicate that, in the seven months between April and the end of November 1973, Nixon only spent a total of thirty-two days in the capital, 'ten of them as a patient, with pneumonia, at Walter Reed Army Hospital'.[67]

Nixon's absenteeism, after sidelining the State Department throughout his presidency in order to concentrate power in his own and Kissinger's hands, now proved fatal to peace in the Middle East. The fact was, 'in October 1973, Nixon was in no condition to execute US policy in the Middle East' wrote another historian.[68] Depressed, he reverted to drinking; his new national security adviser, Brent Scowcroft, was told to refuse a call from the British prime minister Edward Heath, during the crisis, because the president of the United States was 'loaded'.[69]

Egypt's and Syria's attack, launched to retrieve the Sinai and the Golan Heights that Israel had refused to vacate after the 1967 war, made far more headway than Kissinger's analysts had forecast. Besieged by Israeli pleas for urgent military help, however, Kissinger presented the crisis to President Nixon not as a war between Jews and Arabs over the Occupied Territories, but as a war between America and the Soviet Union for domination of the Middle East and its oil for the next generation.

Sobering up, Nixon allowed himself to be persuaded, despite his concern over the consequences. He therefore approved Kissinger's rescue plan: a larger airlift of military supplies to Israel in a few days than the entire humanitarian Berlin airlift against Soviet pressure in 1948–9. The twenty-day Yom Kippur War thus ended on October 26 in a triumph not for the Egyptians and Syrians in liberating the Occupied Territories, but for the intransigent Israelis. Kissinger would claim it was his greatest achievement, a great coup against the Soviets – the very empire with which the president was seeking détente – but in terms of peace in the Middle East, it would prove to be a disaster.

To add to Nixon's misfortunes, a new scandal took place in Washington as the Yom Kippur War raged. On October 10, 1973, Nixon's vice president, Spiro T. Agnew, was forced to resign and face charges over earlier financial improprieties while governor of Maryland.

Characteristically, Nixon refused to grant Agnew a pardon, and looked for a replacement vice president who would help him fight Congress' ongoing Watergate investigation. Eventually he settled on a member of Congress itself: Minority House Leader Gerald R. Ford of Michigan.

If the president hoped thereby to mollify the Congress, however, he was to be bitterly disappointed. The Watergate hearings continued apace, taking a terrible toll on Nixon's mental health. As 1973 came to an end, his sanity seemed, to those who were allowed to meet him in person, to be deteriorating alarmingly. At Christmas, Senator Goldwater found him talking 'gibberish' and 'making no sense'.[70] 'I asked myself whether I was witnessing a slow-motion collapse of Nixon's mental balance', Goldwater noted, but declined to raise the issue of the president's competence in the Senate.[71] Fearful for the implications for the Republican lock on the presidency after the recent resignation of the vice president, Goldwater merely put his notes in his safe.

From landslide popular re-election in 1972, a bare year before, President Nixon's second term in office had turned into a travesty, his family, doctor and remaining intimates aware that he was no longer rational. The chief of naval operations, Admiral Zumwalt, considered that Nixon, Kissinger and General Haig were now clinically 'paranoid', raising grave concerns for the safety of the world. 'It was clear he saw the attacks on him', Zumwalt afterwards described, 'as part of a vast plot by intellectual snobs to destroy a president who was representative of the man in the street.'[72]

Had Nixon been a man in the street, he might well have been locked up, but with Kissinger feeding Nixon's paranoia ('They are out to get you . . . We will show them') the tragedy for America would drag on for many more months, with the danger that the very office of president of the United States would lose its dignity and authority unless the President, whose polls had dipped to the twenties, resigned.[73]

Behind Nixon's back, Kissinger promised Vice President Ford he would stay on as Secretary of State in a Ford administration, if the president was persuaded to step down; but Kissinger continued to toady and fawn to Nixon, as he had since Nixon's campaign of 1968. Emboldened, and despite rumours of resignation swirling throughout January 1974, Nixon warned Congress he would not resign 'under any circumstances'. The alternative was for Congress to impeach him, but if it did, he warned in what was in effect blackmail, it would bring upon the nation an even greater humiliation, for he would 'fight like hell, even if only one senator stands with him'.[74]

In truth there existed one other alternative: a Caine Mutiny. Under the Twenty-fifth Amendment, Section 3, passed by Congress in 1965 and ratified by the states in 1967, a president could stand down or be removed by virtue of his inability to 'discharge the powers and duties of his office'. But with no one yet willing to officially challenge the president's sanity, the future of America thus rested on judicial process: namely whether Congress dared proceed with the first impeachment of an incumbent president in the twentieth century, based on subpoenaing Nixon's tapes as material evidence.

Vainly, Nixon hoped he could rescue his fortunes, as he had so often managed before, by another Checkers-style speech. He therefore made plans to announce with great fanfare in his State of the Union address in January 1974 that he had personally persuaded Middle East oil producers to drop their oil embargo, currently crippling the American economy. The Arab oil-producing states, however, declined to oblige until they saw real progress in getting a withdrawal by Israel from the Occupied Territories. Israel simply refused to pull back from the captured Golan Heights; the Arabs would not lift their oil embargo; and nothing Nixon could say or threaten would move either side. The lines he'd planned for his State of the Union address were dropped, while the lines at American gas stations grew longer and longer throughout the spring of 1974.

For the president the punitive Arab oil embargo was a catastrophe. Inflation rose to 15 per cent, affecting everyone, while thanks to the Watergate revelations, distrust of the government rose to a near 70 per cent level. Once again Nixon attempted a Checkers-like broadcast on April 29, 1974, after issuing a sanitized version of transcripts of some of the tapes he was withholding.

Nixon's 1952 Checkers speech had saved his vice-presidential candidacy. Twenty-two years later, with the indictment of no less than seven White House officials by a federal grand jury announced in Washington in March 1974, and the Supreme Court rejecting Nixon's appeal to withhold subpoenaed tapes from the Public Prosecutor on the grounds of 'executive privilege', it didn't work. Despite acute phlebitis, the president then insisted on travelling to Europe and the Middle East in June, in an effort to show that, for the time being at least, he was too critical to world peace for Congress to start the impeachment process. That effort, too, led nowhere. Kissinger merely raised the question whether, by deliberately flying against his doctor's advice, Nixon had a death wish. (General Haig thought he had.) In Moscow, Nixon's attempt to get a SALT II agreement proved abortive and he was unfocused, purportedly 'listening to White House tapes' in his room rather than preparing for the next day's talks.

In public (or semi-public) Nixon claimed 'the Office of the presidency must never be weakened, because a strong America and a strong American president is something which is absolutely indispensable' – but this begged the question of whether by hanging on, Nixon was deliberately weakening the office.[75] In any event, his protracted manoeuvrings proved to no avail. On July 27, 1974, the House Judiciary Committee passed its historic vote to recommend impeachment of the president for only the second time in the nation's history. The specified articles of suggested impeachment extended in succeeding days to a total of three: first, obstruction of justice; second, the illegal use of executive agencies; and third, defying committee subpoenas.

All attention now narrowed to the tapes themselves, which were combed for incriminating material before being released. When the president's aides listened to the 'smoking gun' tape of June 23, 1972, however, with its record of Nixon's role in ordering the CIA to deliberately prevent the FBI from investigating the Watergate break-in, the die was cast. A brief segment, short enough to appear accidental, had been erased; nevertheless it was reported to the president that, in view of what remained, he now had no chance of fighting off a successful impeachment in the House, let alone winning the subsequent trial in the Senate. Nixon himself described the tape as resembling 'slow-fused dynamite waiting to explode,' and he rued the day when, suffering pneumonia in July 1973, he had resisted the temptation (and others' recommendations) to destroy it.[76]

The final farce now began. On August 1, 1974, Nixon told his chief of staff, General Haig, he would resign – but wanted Vice President Ford to promise he would pardon him, once Ford succeeded to the presidency. Ford baulked, unsure of the implications and consequences. At Camp David that weekend Nixon, now in limbo, was persuaded to fight on and face impeachment by his distraught family, who had no idea of the true contents of the tapes, or his involvement in the Watergate and other burglaries. (Later, Nixon's wife suffered a stroke when reading transcripts of the tapes.)

On August 7, the White House issued a statement saying the president 'had no intention of resigning'. But the truth was he had made the decision to resign, as he confided to Kissinger that evening, after hearing his support in the Senate was down to six or seven votes, meaning certain defeat. Nixon vividly foresaw not only the end of all his political dreams, but prosecution for his High Crimes and Misdemeanors – and burst into tears.

Kissinger sobbed as well, saying he too would resign, prompting Nixon to beg him not to. As Kissinger, relieved, made his way to the elevator, Nixon asked him to stop, and to kneel with him and pray. Afterwards the president called Kissinger and begged him never to reveal what had happened. Kissinger promised, but once Nixon was gone, reneged.

The next day, August 8, 1974, at 9.01 p.m., Nixon finally ended the excruciating saga of Watergate, broadcasting live from the Oval Office to some 160 million people. 'In all the decisions I have made in my public life, I have always tried to do what was best for the nation', he claimed – parsing the 'wrong' decisions he'd made not as criminal or vengeful, but as mere 'judgements' in what he believed 'at the time to be the best interests of the country'. It was vintage RN, as he liked to refer to himself, as 'duplicitous as the man himself', Senator Goldwater sneered, standing on the Stage of History, with one of the largest audiences in the annals of television and radio for a presidential broadcast.[77]

At moments the voice of another Richard could be discerned by viewers and listeners: Shakespeare's Richard II, which Nixon had devoured at school. Schlock and bathos were larded for maximum effect, echoing his Checkers speech two decades before. 'I have never been a quitter' he claimed in one final attempt to paint himself as victim rather than as responsible for his own misfortune. 'To leave office before my term is completed is abhorrent to every instinct in my body' he explained truthfully. 'But as president, I must put the interest of America first. America needs a full-time president and a full-time Congress, particularly at this time with problems we face at home and abroad.' After more than a year of covering up, of lies to Congress, of indictments of his closest aides – a whole year after the Watergate conspiracy began to consume his attention – he would now therefore set aside the selfish temptation to 'continue to fight through the months ahead for my personal vindication' and would ask Vice President Ford to take over the presidency at noon the following day.

On August 9, as Nixon boarded his helicopter to be whisked to Andrews Air Force Base and then by jet to exile in California, demonstrators waved placards reading 'Jail to the Chief'. It was a sorry end to a genocidal presidency.


## Part Three: Private Life


Of all American Caesars, Richard Milhous Nixon's personality was the most conflicted. Fear of his irascible, Irish-American father was balanced by adoration of his Quaker, saintly mother. Neither parent, however, believed in showing physical affection. 'No one projected warmth and affection more than my mother did', Nixon later explained. 'But she never indulged in the present-day custom, which I find nauseating, of hugging and kissing her children or others for whom she had great affection.'78

Nauseated or not, with two of his brothers dying of tuberculosis, Nixon seems to have felt guilty at surviving, tormented especially by the memory of his youngest brother, Arthur, who, when Nixon returned home from nearly a year away at a grammar school, asked if he could buck the Milhous-Nixon family rule, and kiss his older brother. 'He put his arms around me and kissed me on the cheek', Nixon later remembered – recalling, too, the weeks during which he wept in secret when little Arthur, whom the whole family loved, died at age six. The next year his older brother Harold also came down with tuberculosis, which took five heartbreaking years before it killed him.

Snubbed at school for his brains and for being teacher's pet, Nixon was nicknamed 'Gloomy Gus' by girls (for whom the shy, studious and intensely private student, lonely and lacking a sister, showed zero interest). Later, he would analyze his own competitive streak and relentless ambition, in the face of constant taunts and snubs as a child. 'If you are reasonably intelligent and if your anger is deep enough and strong enough,' he reflected, 'you learn that you can change those attitudes by excellence, personal gut performance, while those who have everything are sitting on their fat butts.'79

Nixon had many significant relationships with men in his life, from his father and brothers to men like Haldeman, Ehrlichman, Dean, Mitchell, Rebozo and Kissinger. He had only three significant relationships with women, however, in his whole life.

The first was Hannah Milhous, Nixon's mother. Hannah had trained as a schoolteacher before her wedding, and was proficient in Latin and Greek; she was considered to have 'married beneath her'. Nixon became her star pupil, able to translate Latin without difficulty, and well versed in Roman history. Her moral rectitude hung over him all his life; in fact part of Nixon's later objection to publication of transcripts of his tapes was his horror lest the 'damns and 'goddamns' be made public, which would make his mother 'turn in her grave'.

While his brothers faced down his cantankerous father (there were times when 'shouting could be heard all through the neighborhood', a contemporary recalled), Nixon was too afraid of his father's notorious Irish temper to risk his ire – or a belting.[80] 'Perhaps my own aversion to personal confrontations dates back to these', he later reflected, having watched his mother's quiet, tenacious way of defeating his father, who had left school with only a third-grade education.[81] Hannah's incisive tongue was, to the children, more stinging than their father's strap. 'Tell her to give me a spanking', Nixon's younger brother is said to have cried when caught smoking. 'I just can't stand it to have her talk to me.'[82]

His first girlfriend was initially out of his romantic league. Ola Welch was the stunningly beautiful daughter of the local police chief, a Democrat who revered Franklin Roosevelt and espoused opposing views to those of Nixon's father, a stalwart Republican. 'Oh, how I hate Richard Nixon' Ola wrote in her diary at Whittier High School.[83] But when they acted together in a (Latin) school play, in which the school 'nerd' had to kiss her, she softened her stance, and became intrigued by the talented but psychologically contorted valedictorian, a young man she thought amazingly gifted in his stage presence and 'rapport with an audience', and the speed with which he learned his lines and stage directions.[84] She thus allowed Nixon to date her, platonically, for the following five years, during which they became engaged and saved for a wedding ring. 'He was a real enigma' she said of him later.[85] 'Most of the time I just couldn't figure him out.'[86]

Moody, hard-working, riven between morality and ambition, Nixon worried people early on by his brilliant potential, which might be put to ill use. Ola's sister Dorothy read Nixon's palm at age nineteen, when he was in college. 'I got quite a shock' she remembered later. 'What I saw in his palm was a path of incredibly brilliant success and then the most terrible black cloud like a disaster or something.'[87]

Returning for the vacation from Duke Graduate Law School in the summer of 1935, Nixon asked to come over to Ola's home in Whittier. Pressed to give a reason why she said no, Ola explained that she had another boyfriend there, talking to her parents.

Nixon was beside himself. 'He was really furious. He shouted, "If I ever see you again it will be too soon."'[88] Though Ola returned the money he had contributed towards the purchase of a wedding ring, he kept writing to her, calling himself 'a bad penny' yet unable to relent.[89] Finally, in February 1936, after nine months he gave up, writing that he 'realized more than ever the perfection, the splendor, the grandeur of my mother's character. Incapable of selfishness she is to me a supreme ideal. And you', he explained to Ola, 'have taken her place in my heart – as an example for which all men should strive.'[90]

Nixon's stilted, idealizing prose masked a black hole in his psyche. Between his 'superdrive' on the one hand, and his 'inhibitions' on the other, even his psychiatrist later found him 'an enigma, not only to me but to himself'.[91] Though Ola Welch's termination of their engagement hurt him deeply, Nixon was fortunate enough, two years later, to meet – again through amateur dramatics – another beautiful woman. This time it was a twenty-six-year-old schoolteacher, blessed with golden-red hair and film-star looks, Thelma Ryan, who'd changed her name to Patricia. Nixon asked her for a date on January 16, 1938, the evening he first met her (acting in the ominously named play *The Dark Tower*). When she turned him down, he announced: 'You may not believe this but I am going to marry you some day.'[92]

Pat Ryan rebuffed Nixon's notions of courtship throughout the spring of 1938, but found it impossible to shake him off. They shared similar family stories, as well as common feelings of resentment towards those who came from more privileged backgrounds. Her father had also been a virtually uneducated, poverty-stricken Irish-American, a goldminer-trucker-farmer with a foul temper who died of silicosis when Pat was sixteen. Her mother had been a German immigrant, who bore her husband's violent outbursts with stoicism until she died in 1924, when Pat was twelve. Pat had worked her way all through college (in part as a movie extra in Hollywood), was a non-believer, and though, like Ola, she definitively terminated the relationship with Gloomy Gus, no better or more tenacious candidate came forward during the ensuing two years; Nixon even ferried her to and from her dates with other men to show the depth of his attachment. Pat finally agreed to marry him in the summer of 1940, when she was twenty-eight. She refused, however, to go through the hypocrisy of a church wedding, and the ceremony took place at an inn in Riverside, California, attended by only a handful of relatives. Pat and Dick would remain married for over fifty years until her death, in 1993, at eighty-one; but it was often a triumph of willpower more than affection.

Like many a young bride, Pat attempted to reinforce the better side of her husband's nature. She was, however, unable to thwart its darker, more satanic elements. As Stephen Ambrose, Nixon's biographer, later wrote, 'she hated politics' and there was no joy in the marriage beyond their two daughters.[93] Though they separated for a time in 1956, and he promised time and again thereafter to give up politics, he could not do so, addicted as he was to the excitement and dismissive of the 'boredom' that life as a lawyer would entail, indeed claiming it would 'kill him in four years'.

Nixon's mother had wanted him to become a preacher, but he had had insufficient faith; for politics, however, he possessed many of the most important credentials, beginning with deceit. 'You're never going to make it in politics', he told a fellow law student. 'You just don't know how to lie.'[94] In Nixon's mind, lies – especially political lies – were white, as long as they led to power, the greatest aphrodisiac. 'Nixon depended on Pat because he trusted her, and she stayed with him', Nixon's psychiatrist remarked after Nixon's death and his oath of confidentiality was at an end. 'But that was for politics. The truth is, his only passion was politics.'[95]

Between deceit and power there was the field of political battle, which energized and obsessed the grocer's son. Politics – especially taking on 'the Establishment' – challenged his theatrical, debating, analytical, predictive and conspiratorial abilities as nothing else. Weaving a personal myth of noble quest in pursuit of high ideals, moreover, permitted him to play upon public gullibility, excusing his less attractive traits. For this outwardly noble quest he needed Pat as a public symbol of his purity, even as he overruled her objections. 'His destiny', she recognized, 'was her fate.'[96]

Henry Kissinger later wondered how much more Nixon might have accomplished, had the president been 'loved' – failing to recognize that Nixon had been loved by his family, despite (perhaps because of) his awkward personality.[97] Amazingly, he drew copious examples of love, of admiration, and, above all, of extraordinary loyalty from his family, from certain companions, and from his intimate staff, even when they should have known better. The problem was not, then, in the lack of available love and devotion, but that it was never enough to satisfy Nixon's tormented psyche, which expressed itself in a constant mix of high rhetoric and black vindictiveness. Together they formed a relentless, insatiable ambition to vault the necessary steps leading to the highest political office in the empire, and then to retain it at any cost, however duplicitous, immoral, illegal, illicit or criminal his conduct became, as his tapes would ultimately reveal.

For his wife Pat, as for those innocents who had supported the rise of a hugely gifted American lawyer from a humble background, this was the deepest disappointment. For those who knew the demon in Richard Nixon, either in private or as evidenced early in his public career during the Hiss case and rampant McCarthyism, there was, by contrast, only a sense of déjà vu – as well as fear as to where a man of such profound narcissism, hate, depression and bouts of paranoia might, together with his many talents, lead (or mislead) America.

Behind Nixon's devotion to mythic political ideals such as anti-Communism and his low-life, vindictive pursuit of power at any cost, his psychiatrist saw a never-ending struggle between idealization of his saintly, puritanical mother and anger over the fear inspired in him as a child by his tyrannical, brutal and loud-mouthed father. It was not a struggle that Nixon succeeded in overcoming, the doctor lamented, especially when dishonesty and vindictiveness actually *rewarded* Nixon, emotionally, financially and politically.[98] As a candle draws moths to the flame, Nixon drew men of dubious, dishonest nature to him, attracting them not only to indulge their greed and eye for opportunity, but also appealing beyond them to a 'silent majority': the great white jury of American, mostly male, voters who did not know his underlying character, and who, once won over by his bathos-ridden theatrics, unwittingly licensed his secretive criminal behaviour and megalomaniacal conduct of America's vast military power.

In this latter-day role of Iago, Nixon demonstrated unmatched talents. Of all post-war US presidents, he was by far and away the most skilful in his use of courtroom techniques. His childhood love of Latin and his reading of Roman history gave him a powerful command of outward 'order and logic' in forming his appeal; to this he added telling infusions of sentimentality, schlock, entertaining invective and well-chosen lies, making him a compelling orator as well as formidable opponent whom even Ronald Reagan, in his prime, could not match.

Nixon always kept by him a lined yellow legal pad on which he would draft his thoughts, his speeches, his ambitions. He was forever *calculating*, and forever manipulating others for his own purposes. He worked at times as if demented, requiring at one point nine secretaries. His wife recalled that when he was a senator, he would often spend the whole night on the Hill. 'He'll work over there until the small hours of the morning . . . He'll curl up on the couch and get a few hours' sleep. Then he'll get a little breakfast and shave, and go right down to the Senate chambers to work.'[99] Posing as a man with a noble mission – beginning with anti-Communism, then switching to the accommodation of Communism – each time he was defeated he was able to solicit personal pity and compassion; so much so, in fact, that his own wife, and later his daughters, would refuse each time to believe the bad things said or documented about him. 'Richard Nixon is a man who has never lied, not even a white lie, to his family or to the American people', his daughter Tricia would say,[100] despite the testimony of Nixon's own Watergate attorney, Fred Buzhardt, who considered Nixon 'the most transparent liar he had ever met'.[101]

It was a masterly real-life performance in which the actor never actually paid for any of his sins, but was always rewarded or pardoned, forgiven and rehabilitated to the very end of his life, despite the swathe of destruction he left around and behind him. Thus the one-time pauper, who rented a hut without plumbing as a law student at Duke to save money, became, despite his defeats and criminal conduct, rich beyond his early dreams, able to dispose of huge amounts of cash from dubious sources to further his nefarious plots, like a medieval caliph.

Herein, sadly, lay the deeper tragedy for America, since not only was Richard Nixon irremediably corrupt, but in his manic determination to gain and to wield absolute power as president or Caesar of the United States, he succeeded in overturning a two-centuries-old American system of governance, claiming he was doing the best thing for his country of 'silent' Americans, but setting an example of quasi-dictatorship in which his contempt for the Senate and House of Representatives, two chambers in which he himself had briefly served, was absolute.

By a brilliant, Ciceronian ability to spin his own presidential story, Nixon had continually gilded a public self-portrait in which he, in search of greatness, was the noble victim of spite and snobbery, rather than an increasingly unstable, even mad quasi-dictator. 'The only place

where you and I disagree,' Nixon had told Kissinger in the spring of
1972, 'is with regard to the bombing' of North Vietnam, Cambodia
and Laos. 'You're so goddamned concerned about civilians,' Nixon
remarked, 'and I don't give a damn. I don't care.'[102] Contemptuous of
humanitarian-minded critics, Nixon insisted 'we ought to take the
North Vietnamese dikes out now. Will that drown people?' he asked
his national security adviser, who responded that it would kill 'About
200,000.' 'No, no, no' protested Nixon, not from compassion but from
the very insufficiency of such measures. 'I'd rather use the nuclear
bomb', he told the open-mouthed Kissinger. 'Have you got that,
Henry?'

Kissinger, though tantamount to a fellow mass-murderer by this
point, thought it 'would just be too much'. Nixon sneered. 'The nuclear
bomb, does that bother you?' he said. 'I just want you to think big,
Henry, for Christsakes.'[103]

'Hare-brained scheming, half-baked conclusions and hasty decisions
and actions divorced from reality, bragging and bluster, attraction to
rule by fiat' – these and other accusations had been made by *Pravda*
against another emperor, Premier Nikita Khrushchev, who had had
to be removed by his political colleagues before he endangered the
planet, in 1964.[104] Nixon and Khrushchev were thus both considered
by their peers to be dangerously loose cannons: clever but unstable,
relentless in the pursuit of power, and propelled by deep resentments
and feelings of personal insecurity. Both were responsible for the deaths
of tens of thousands of people. To Nixon it was immaterial whether
or not Thieu's South Vietnam, or its people, survived; what was important was 'the United States *cannot* lose. Which means, basically, I have
made the decision. Whatever happens to South Vietnam, we are going
to *cream* North Vietnam', irrespective of congressional approval. 'For
once, we've got to use the maximum power of this country . . . against
this *shit-ass* little country: to win the war.' Surgical strikes against
Haiphong were not what Nixon had in mind. 'I want that place bombed
to *smithereens*. If we draw the sword, we're gonna bomb those bastards
all over the place. Let it fly, *let it fly*.'[105]

It was small wonder Pat Nixon was stricken by thrombosis, reading
transcripts such as these. Nixon had, as his psychiatrist later confided,
always been on the margin of sanity; by the end, even Kissinger called
him 'a basket case'.[106] Whether he was truly mad is impossible to

know, but the 'Madman Theory' (or practice) certainly came in handy – invoking compassion and, astonishingly, even forgiveness, once he left office.

Spinning tales of innocence in the pursuit of greatness for his country, he would decline ever to admit to deliberate wrongdoing; obtained a controversial presidential pardon; fought tooth and nail to keep his tapes from being made available to the general public; and lived out his remaining twenty years in considerable wealth, dying in New York on April 22, 1994. His funeral in Yorba Linda, California was attended by five US presidents.

# CHAPTER SEVEN

# GERALD FORD

Respected

Republican
38th President
(August 9, 1974–January 20, 1977)

## Part One: The Road to the White House

Baptized as Leslie Lynch King Jr, Ford was born in Omaha, Nebraska, on July 14, 1913. Two weeks later his mother took him to her family's home in Grand Rapids, Michigan, refusing to tolerate the violent, abusive behaviour of her husband, wool-merchant-heir Leslie Lynch King Sr.

Four years after her return to Grand Rapids, the divorcee remarried, this time choosing a humble local housepainter, Gerald Rudolf Ford, whose name was informally taken by her little son, once he went to school in Grand Rapids. Only in his twenties in 1934 did 'Jerry', as he was known to all, then legally change his name to Gerald Rudolph Ford Jr.

'I am a Ford, not a Lincoln' was the self-deprecating line Gerald Ford would later use. No great intellect but sensible, focused, tenacious and a fiercely loyal youth, Ford grew up to be six feet tall, broad-shouldered, fair-haired, blue-eyed, good-looking, and a fine football player – which counted for more in conservative Michigan than brains.[1] Gaining a football scholarship to Michigan State University, he played in the famous match against Georgia Tech, who refused to compete if Michigan's only coloured player, Willis Ward (who roomed with Ford on away-game trips), were allowed on to the field. Ward insisted Ford should play – and win. The Michigan Wolverines trounced the racists 9–2, to Ward's delight.

On graduation Ford, who had waited tables and washed dishes to survive, took a position as an athletics coach at Yale, where he was eventually accepted into the university's famed law school. Genial and respected, he was a young man 'who has an attractive personality, and is a gentleman of considerable bearing and poise', but was 'not conceited in the slightest, and is very handsome', as the athletics director reported.[2] Ford then returned to his home state to practise law.

As for many of Ford's contemporaries – men such as McCarthy, Kennedy, Lyndon Johnson and George H. W. Bush – World War II proved for him the stepping stone to political success. His application to serve in naval intelligence (as John F. Kennedy did) was not accepted, but despite bad knees he was accepted into the seagoing US Navy in April 1942, serving with courage and distinction as an anti-aircraft gun director and assistant navigator aboard the converted aircraft carrier, USS *Monterey*, in the South Pacific. He left the service, like Nixon, as a lieutenant commander, in 1946 – but, unlike Nixon, having earned some sixteen battle stars in 1943 and 1944.

From Midwest American isolationism (Ford had worked for Wendell Willkie's presidential campaign in 1940, and attended the Republican National Convention in Philadelphia), Ford became an ardent internationalist once the United States was attacked, and then defeated the Japanese and German empires. Thereafter he favoured America accepting the leadership of the free world in confronting Soviet postwar domination. Keen on carving out a political career in Grand Rapids, however, he found his path stymied by a Michigan political machine boss, Frank D. McKay.

Ignoring McKay, Ford filed at the last minute in the local Michigan Republican primary for Congress. To the surprise of all (including himself and his fiancée) he beat the incumbent congressman for the Fifth District, isolationist Bartel Jonkman, 23,632 votes to 14,341, on his first attempt – thereby assuring himself, in a safe Republican district, election to the House of Representatives in November 1948. It was a seat he never lost, in thirteen consecutive elections.

Given his popularity and principled, hard-working conduct, Ford would be repeatedly asked to stand for the Senate, but his seat on the Appropriations Committee in the House of Representatives guaranteed him growing importance and fulfilment. Unlike 'Tricky Dick' Nixon, who had immediately befriended him as a fellow congressman in 1949, Ford thus rested content with his political lot, becoming in due course Republican Minority Leader and nursing the hope that, if the Republicans ever won back their majority in the House after the 1950 debacle, he would one day become Speaker of the House.

In the event, the Republicans not only failed to gain a majority in Congress, but suffered a 'negative landslide' when Senator Goldwater contested the presidential election, resulting in the loss of some thirty-six Republican seats in the House in 1964. Ford declared his own agenda as pursuing 'the high middle road of moderation'. He was, he made clear, committed to 'firmly resist[ing] the takeover of our party by any elements that are not interested in building a party, but only in advancing their own narrow interests'.[3]

As a moderate Republican and stalwart, anti-Communist patriot Ford supported President Johnson's commitment of American troops to combat in Vietnam, as well as the president's subsequent escalation of the war, having rejected the Senate Republican Policy Committee's 1967 report that recommended peace and withdrawal. Ford was not a gifted speaker, but his position in Congress, his Eisenhowerian integrity and his moderate views on domestic issues made him a welcome mid-American middle-of-the-road speaker across the country with Republican audiences, so much so that he was tipped to be chosen as Nixon's running mate in the summer of 1968.

Former Vice President Richard Nixon had other ideas, however, preferring an unknown, inexperienced and therefore uncompeting understudy: the former governor of Maryland, Spiro T. Agnew. 'I shook my head in disbelief', Ford later recalled.[4]

Returning to the Capitol following Nixon's narrow victory in November 1968, Ford loyally backed Nixon's re-escalation of the Vietnam War, but was otherwise ignored by the president. To Ford's face, Nixon was unctuously grateful for the 'little errands' he did for him, such as denouncing Teddy Kennedy 'on the House floor', as Ford's chief of staff complained. But behind his back, Nixon did not even bother to disguise his contempt for Congress or its Republican Minority Leader, John Ehrlichman sneering that 'Jerry might have become a pretty good Grand Rapids insurance salesman' if he had not chosen politics; 'he played a good game of golf, but he wasn't excessively bright'.[5]

Ford had promised his wife he would step down from his congressional seat at the 1976 election, given the Republican Party's disappointing showing in the 1972 congressional elections and the unlikelihood that he would ever reach his cherished goal of Speaker of the House. But Nixon's trust in Ford's loyalty was well placed. When Agnew was compelled to resign for financial impropriety in October 1973, Nixon made his historic choice, which was approved by the House without serious objection. In accordance with the Twenty-fifth Amendment to the US Constitution, the former Leslie Lynch King Jr thus became, on December 6, 1973, the first appointed vice president of the United States of America – under a president increasingly besieged by Watergate investigators.

Had Nelson Rockefeller, Ronald Reagan or John Connally – the three alternatives recommended by senior members of the Republican Party – been appointed vice president, they would have had few qualms in condemning Nixon's abuse of presidential authority, and – as experienced governors of major states – in subsequently wielding their own new brooms once he was forced to resign. Jerry Ford, by contrast, was made of different stuff – a prisoner, in many ways, of his own high sense of loyalty. As vice president he now remained stubbornly and personally beholden to President Nixon for having chosen him, rather than to Congress for having favoured him in representations to the president, as mandated under the Twenty-fifth Amendment; moreover he continued to defer to Nixon as a leader who he thought, correctly, was significantly smarter than himself. In the following months he flew more than 100,000 miles across America as vice president to reassure Republicans and voters of Nixon's innocence – a noble, if obtuse, effort, given mounting suspicions, evidence and White House obstructionism. To the last moments, Ford refused to read or listen to evidence of Nixon's transgressions, enabling him to claim he was sincere in considering the president to be the victim of a vast left-wing conspiracy.

Ford, an Episcopalian, was a devout Christian, and prayed a lot for strength and guidance. He worked hard, meant well, and took people at their word. His radiant honesty and defence of the President, however, could not keep the chief executive afloat forever. Once the Supreme Court ruled that the 'smoking gun' tape be handed over to Judge Sirica, Nixon was cornered. On Thursday August 1, 1974, with Nixon confiding to Al Haig, his chief of staff, that he would resign if he could be spared prison, Haig embarked on a unique form of extortion. He asked to meet secretly, one on one, with the vice president, and made clear that Nixon would resign only if promised an a priori pardon.

Haig explained he had consulted a lawyer who claimed that the Founding Fathers had specifically mentioned the preservation of the 'tranquility of the Commonwealth', in the words of Alexander Hamilton, as the exceptional circumstance giving a president the right to grant such clemency.

Though trained at Yale Law School, Ford had never studied Hamilton's argument, which warned against taking any step that might, in the offering of a pardon, 'hold out the prospect of impunity' to rebels or miscreants in obstructing justice, and thereby set a poor example.[6] Instead the vice president fatefully took it for granted Haig and his lawyer were correct.

Ford's staff was aghast at the implications, which would destroy Ford's one great virtue, his integrity, if the claim was made he had exchanged a pardon in order to attain the presidency. Even his wife told him 'You can't do that, Jerry.'[7]

Reluctantly Ford, whose commendable and natural instinct was to spare the country the shame and humiliation of impeachment if the president hung on to power, called Haig the next day to tell him he had misspoken, and that there was 'No deal'. He even destroyed Haig's colleague's notes, lest they implicate him later.[8]

Nixon was stunned by Ford's reversal, and told his chief of staff that in that case he had changed his mind about resigning. 'Let them impeach me' Nixon told Haig. 'We'll fight it out to the end.'[9] The *opéra bouffe* of Nixon's last days in office now approached its climax.

Loyal as ever, Ford continued to claim in public that the president was innocent of any wrongdoing. 'I believe the president is innocent of any impeachable offense and I haven't changed my mind,' he stated on August 3, 1974.[10] But with the revelations of the 'smoking gun' tape on August 4, which proved Nixon had had full knowledge of the Watergate burglary from the very beginning, Ford could no longer pretend they would ride out the storm. Even Al Haig admitted to Republican leaders 'I don't see how we can survive this one.'[11]

With impeachment in the House now inevitable – and the prospect of losing his pension if convicted in a consequent Senate trial – Nixon was skewered. Publication of the transcript of the 'smoking gun' tape made even his own family recognize the game might be up. Yet *still* the president held on to his crown, issuing a crazed, thousand-word statement denying culpability, and asking his cabinet to meet on August 6, 1974.

For the first time Nixon was not applauded as he entered. Clearing his throat he began the meeting with the words 'I would like to discuss the most important issue confronting the nation, inflation.'[12]

'My God!' Ford later recalled thinking, it was surreal.[13] It became more so when the president, once they got round to the constitutional crisis, insisted that his decision to order the CIA to stop the FBI investigation of Watergate had been made solely for reasons of national security. He was, therefore, determined to go ahead and face impeachment and trial by Congress. With an air of injured nobility, Nixon added, 'I will accept whatever verdict the Senate hands down.'

Was Nixon acting? It seemed 'ludicrous' to Ford, especially when the president explained he had made the tapes available to prove his innocence, not because the Supreme Court had compelled him to. Yet so amazing was Nixon's performance in its pathos – like a wounded fox, before the kill – that he elicited personal compassion rather than concern for the interests of the nation. Finally, the vice president spoke.

Instead of explaining that the president must, in all conscience, stand down to save the nation, Ford looked ahead to impeachment proceedings in the House, following by a trial in the Senate, whose outcome 'I can't predict.' As vice president, Ford would of course have to recuse himself in public, during the trial, as he was 'a party of interest' – meaning he stood to gain if the president was forced to resign. Nevertheless he wanted Nixon to know he had 'given us the finest foreign policy this country has ever had', and that, if the president was convicted and Ford succeeded him, he would 'expect to support the administration's foreign policy and the fight against inflation'.[14]

There was stunned silence. The declaration, as Ford's aide afterwards recalled, fell far short of the 'Declaration of Independence' they had hoped for; indeed it seemed positively mealy-mouthed.[15] The other cabinet officers were as bad; in the worst domestic crisis of modern American government, no one dared ask the president to step down.

Could this really be the epicentre of the world's most powerful empire? Had Richard Nixon reduced his administration to a handful of gibbering idiots? Ford's chief of staff Robert Hartmann found himself in shock. After the meeting, when Republican members of Congress begged the vice president again to speak up, in order to end what was now a constitutional crisis of the first magnitude, Ford demurred, citing his conflict of interest – though he assured his aides it was only a matter of days before Nixon surrendered to the inevitable. It was important, Ford declared, to avoid rocking the sinking ship; rumours were circulating in the White House that the president might commit suicide if pressed further.[16] In the circumstances, Ford made clear, no one should push the president of the United States, with his finger on the nuclear trigger, into doing something crazy. Patiently allowing Nixon the time to accept his fate gracefully seemed the wisest policy.

Graceful would never be an appropriate epithet for Nixon, but finally, on August 7, 1974, three long days after the 'smoking gun' evidence pulled the rug from beneath him, he capitulated. He would, he decided, resign – after another two days. He did not even summon Ford to tell him the decision, but relied on his chief of staff to relay his decision – and to describe his state of mind. The next day the president agreed to see Ford. 'I have made my decision to resign', he told the vice president in the Oval Office, as if for the first time. 'It's in the best interests of the country.'[17] Watergate was never mentioned. Nixon then put his feet on the desk, and proceeded to give his successor an hour-long tutorial on American foreign and domestic policy – something he had failed to do for the past ten months.

Nixon's behaviour defied comprehension, at one moment in another world, the next, earnest and engaged with the real world. Ford, rendered almost speechless by Nixon's latest performance, told him he felt he was 'ready to do the job and I think I am fully qualified to do it'.[18] But was he?

When he read the draft of the speech the new president would give after taking the oath of office, written by his chief of staff Bob Hartmann, Ford said he wanted to remove the phrase 'Our long national nightmare is over.' 'Isn't that a little hard on Dick?' the vice president asked Hartmann. 'Could we soften that?'

'No, no, no!' Hartmann protested. 'Don't you see, that's your whole speech. That's what you have to proclaim to the whole country – to the whole world. That's what everybody needs to hear, wants to hear, has got to hear you say . . . You have to turn the country around.'[19]

'Okay, Bob' Ford responded. 'I guess you're right. I hadn't thought about it that way.'[20]

What, then, *had* the former Michigan football star been thinking? The phrase stayed in, to Hartmann's relief, but Ford's anxiety not to be seen by the outgoing President as hard-hearted raised serious concerns about the new President's backbone, as well as connection with his fellow Americans.

President Nixon left the White House on the morning of August 9, 1976. Gerald Ford's inauguration followed at 12.03 in the East Room.

## Part Two: The Presidency

'I think he'll make a good president', Ford's new deputy press secretary, Bill Roberts – a former *Time* correspondent – noted on the eve of the handover. The nation's new chief executive 'had some dark circles under his eyes and it looked as though he hadn't slept very much. But he also was very calm and very serious and very intent on what he was doing. Whatever happens to me, I have great confidence in him. I think he'll make a good president simply because he does have confidence in himself, which is one of the things Richard Nixon lacked, and which I think a president needs.' Roberts also thought 'Harry Truman and Gerald R. Ford have a great deal in common in their approach to life and to the presidency.'[21]

Rarely can a former Washington bureau chief of *Time* magazine have been so mistaken. Ford was no Truman. His 'simplicity', however, certainly came as a relief after the tortured character of 'Tricky Dick'. Nixon had even insisted the press be locked inside the press room lest they see him emerge for a final time from his secret hideaway in the Eisenhower Executive Office Building. 'What a sad commentary on the Nixon administration', Roberts reflected, delighting in the fact that, by contrast, after dancing with Queen Alia of Jordan at a White House reception, the new president came back inside and had a long dance with his press secretary's wife, 'who is a very attractive Asiatic gal, dancing to the tune of "Big Bad LeRoy Brown" with a whole crowd attending and clapping hands. Mrs Nessen was doing a sort of modified rock and roll . . . The girls all say the president's a very good dancer. But the whole point was that people kept saying, "What a change. What a change. What a wonderful place this White House can be, people are having fun.'"[22]

The days of fun, however, would be short-lived – something the president-to-be had been warned about the night before. 'Christ, Jerry, isn't this a wonderful country?' the Democratic House Majority Leader Tip O'Neill had remarked when Ford had called him. 'Here we can talk like this and you and I can be friends, and eighteen months from now I'll be going around the country kicking your ass in.' Ford had been taken aback. 'That's a hell of a way to speak to the next President of the United States' he'd responded, and they'd both erupted in laughter.

Ford's unique ascent to the office of president and his lack of personal preparation would hold many lessons for future rulers of the empire. He had read little or no history, had limited vision, and no foresight. What he did have was a very attractive, dependable, loyal yet obstinate personality – which now worked to his own impediment.

Instead of asserting his new authority, Ford made the inexplicable decision to keep General Haig on, for the time being, as his own White House chief of staff.

Ford's staff, accompanying him from the vice president's office, were disbelieving. Haig had made no secret of the fact that he would not leave Washington until he had got Nixon a pardon, and had deliberately shipped Nixon's subpoenaed tapes to Nixon's home in San Clemente, California, even as 'staff members were stuffing an inordinately high amount of papers in their "burn bags". These bags later were macerated chemically', Ford's legal adviser, Benton Becker, recalled with shock.[23]

Haig's hubris was, in fact, stunning. He considered he had been 'acting president' in Nixon's last months, and seemed intent on continuing that role for as long as possible thereafter. Thus on Ford's first day as president, August 9, 1974, Haig asked him if he would address Nixon's old staff, both to thank them and to ask them to stay on for the moment, to facilitate an orderly transition. He even asked Ford to especially emphasize in his address, as Haig put it in a briefing memo, 'Point 3': namely the 'special and heroic role of Al Haig'.

Haig's self-aggrandizing memorandum was just one indication of the 'arrogance of the people who worked for the Nixon administration', Roberts noted several days later. Another was the attitude of

Nixon's other henchman, Henry Kissinger, who had, in a supreme historical irony, been awarded the 1973 Nobel Peace Prize.

Instead of considering an alternative Secretary of State, Ford had immediately given in to Kissinger's pressure not only to be left in control of the State Department, but to be the sole conduit of foreign affairs information, cutting out Ford's own team of advisers. Ford's vice-presidential staff begged him not to listen so cravenly to Haig or to Kissinger, especially in their recommendations of a pardon for the disgraced Nixon. By a substantial margin public opinion polls showed voters were opposed to an immediate pardon, at least until the truth be divulged, now that Nixon could no longer stonewall the Justice Department, the Special Prosecutor or Congress.

Having watched the tragicomedy of Nixon's last year in office, Ford's staff were now treated to a fresh episode of Nixonian man-oeuvring as Ford listened to Haig's recommendations. The new president 'does like and respect Al Haig and thinks he's a great guy', Bill Roberts noted. 'I'm not so sure of that.'[24]

Nor were others, especially when Haig kept urging that Ford re-employ Nixon's White House staff. As Ford's speechwriter Milton Friedman confided to Bill Roberts on August 18, 'there is a very serious and intense battle going on between General Haig and Bob Hartmann . . . General Haig simply wants to take over the whole operation and is arguing with the president that he should not throw away this great structure of administration which has been built up over so many years, and Hartmann is going completely the other way, arguing that the structure is what brought about the Nixon downfall.'[25]

As Ford's chief aide, Hartmann had good cause to be worried. Haig, who had never commanded a unit higher than a battalion in combat but had got himself promoted to general, remained in intimate, secret communication with Nixon. Throughout the rest of August 1974, they were in daily, sometimes hourly contact while Haig was running the transition.

Finally, on August 28, Ford gave in to Haig's importunings on Nixon's behalf. In a secret meeting to prepare his staff for his decision, he explained he was going to trust not the polls, or congressional advice, but his 'conscience'. Rather than placing a terrible burden on the official Watergate prosecutor, Leon Jaworski, he would therefore, as president, take sole responsibility for the pardon-in-advance. 'My conscience tells me I must do this' he repeated. 'I have followed my conscience before – and look where it has brought me. I like where I am. I would like to stay. If what I am doing is judged wrong, I am willing to accept the consequences.'[26]

There was quiet consternation in the Oval Office at these words. The antique clock in the room shattered 'the silence like a burst of machine-gun fire', one adviser recalled.[27]

Why did Ford do it, and why had he moved towards his ultimate decision so privately, withholding his 'intention' from his own White House staff, save Haig and Hartmann? Was he really not aware of Haig's disloyalty? Or was it the performance of a lifetime by the disgraced former president himself?

Between them, General Haig and Richard Nixon certainly fooled Ford. Alarmed by Haig's reports that Nixon was sinking into suicidal despair in San Clemente, Ford sent a personal emissary, Benton Becker, to California, hoping Nixon would agree to an admission of guilt that would make a pardon palatable to the nation.

Nixon, however, was in no mood to admit guilt. Haig had secretly called him in advance to tell him the pardon would not be predicated on the admission of guilt. 'You don't have to give up anything, you don't have to apologize, you're gonna get the pardon', Haig assured him before Becker's plane even reached California.[28] Thus, to Becker's astonishment on arrival, no admission of guilt was forthcoming. As Nixon's lawyer announced to Becker, Nixon would 'make no statement of admission of complicity in return for a pardon from Jerry Ford'.[29]

Becker was furious. In that case, he made clear, he would return to the White House immediately. Persuaded to stay the night, however, the next day he was shown a draft statement. It 'reeked', Becker later recalled, with 'protestations of innocence'. When finally Becker got Nixon's lawyers to agree at least a vague statement acknowledging there had been an 'obstruction of justice', he was at last allowed to meet Nixon, who now played the part of mad King Richard II. 'He rose upon my entrance,' Becker noted several days afterwards in a memorandum, 'and appeared to demonstrate a sense of nervousness or almost fright at meeting me in person.'[30] Becker's 'first impression' of the former president in his new role was of 'freakish grotesqueness . . . [his] arms and body were so thin and frail as to project an

image of a head size disproportionate to a body . . . a man whom I
might more reasonably expect to meet at an octogenarian nursing
home. He was old. Had I never known of the man before and met
him for the first time, I would have estimated his age to be eighty-
five.'[31] Tears mingled with ramblings, musings, self-pity, football allu-
sions, small gifts and defiance, in no apparent order, as Nixon played
his part to perfection. 'If it was an act, it was a convincing one', his
admiring Conservative biographer, Jonathan Aitken, later acknowledged.[32] With his 'hair disheveled', Nixon appeared 'in the most
pathetic, sad frame of mind that I believe I have ever seen anyone in
my life', Becker noted, Whittier's star college drama student having
put on a mesmerizing show.[33]

Returning to the White House the next day, Ford's emissary, full
of compassion, thus gave a deeply sympathetic yet erroneous view of
Nixon's state of mind and health, unaware that Nixon was playacting,
and would live another twenty years. An incomparable poker player
since college, Nixon had played for the very highest stakes, and was
way above Ford's league in manipulation. Bound by his old-fashioned
sense of honour, and urged on by Haig (who was delighted by his
latest achievement and, deceitful to the very end of his life, claimed
in his memoirs that 'where Nixon's pardon was concerned, I played
no role at all'), Ford had allowed himself to be played for a sucker.[34]

In retirement, Ford would admit he'd been outfoxed by the wily
Nixon. 'I had thought he would be very receptive to the idea of clearing
the decks', he confided to a friend, but Nixon had 'not been as forthcoming as I had hoped. He didn't admit guilt . . . I was taking one
hell of a risk [in granting a pre-indictment pardon], and he didn't seem
to be responsive at all.'[35] Instead of calling Nixon's bluff, however, Ford
had nobly allowed his sympathy to overcome his scepticism, and on
the morning of Sunday September 8, he began to telephone the leaders
of Congress to inform them of his decision, beginning with the House
Majority Leader, Tip O'Neill.

'Tip,' he explained, 'I've made up my mind to pardon Nixon. I'm
doing it because I think it's right for the country, and because it feels
right in my heart. The man is so depressed, and I don't want to see
a former president go to jail.'

O'Neill was amazed. 'You're crazy' he responded. 'I'm telling you
right now, this will cost you the [next] election.' O'Neill added that

he hoped it was 'not part of any deal'. Ford denied that it was. 'Then why the hell are you doing it?' O'Neill asked, pertinently.[36]

Ford could only sigh: 'Tip, Nixon is a sick man.' Nixon's daughter Julie had, he added, kept 'calling me because her father is so depressed'.[37]

Ford's compassion for Nixon's 'suffering' did him proud as a human being, but his openness to manipulation was ominous for the world's most powerful new head of state. Nixon had aroused deep concern abroad by his maverick 'imperial presidency', so that the prospect of a new president with long experience in the House of Representatives, and seven months of on-the-job training as vice president, had calmed diplomats and financial markets across the globe. At home, however, the public was sure to be outraged by the 'deal', his staff warned, a prospect that became daily more worrying as Nixon kept altering the wording of the pardon document, demanding that his White House tapes be maintained under his complete control (with the Archivist of the United States acting merely as a temporary trustee).

The pardon – a 'Get Out of Jail Free' pass, as Senator Goldwater aptly called it – was finally announced publicly on September 8, 1974.[38] Ford's new press secretary, Jerald terHorst, immediately resigned in protest, saying he had been kept in the dark. Bill Roberts, Ford's loyal deputy press secretary, noted that night in his diary that 'I feel there must be some compelling reason that caused him to make the decision to grant the Pardon now, either health or mental problems with Nixon or something else. The Nixon people deny this, but it just seems to me there must be something that changed the president's mind', for 'at his first news conference in August, he'd stated he'd let the legal action take its course before he made his decision. Now he's moving to subvert the whole legal action which of course irritates a lot of people.' The press were disbelieving; Thomas DeFrank, *Newsweek*'s White House correspondent and Ford's friend, told Roberts: 'Oh he's blown it. The election is down the drain in 1976.'[39]

Ford's poll ratings immediately slumped more than 20 per cent – the largest and most precipitous drop since presidential polling began. Even his former law partner, Phil Buchen, whom Ford had promoted to White House Counsel, threatened to resign (though was talked out of it). Buchen's wife would note, several weeks later, that Buchen 'is constantly discouraged by Jerry's decisions, boners in making statements, and wavering (changing) positions. He doesn't trust Jerry's "instincts".'[40]

Far from unifying the country by his pardon, Ford found to his chagrin that the majority of American citizens were appalled, making his task as a national caretaker/healer president harder, not easier. 'Overnight the healing stopped', Tom DeFrank would later write. 'Ford had sought to cauterize the wound of Watergate; instead he'd ripped off the scab.'[41]

Tip O'Neill had been right. Instead of putting the Nixon 'nightmare' to rest, Ford had permitted Nixon to evade justice and avoid admitting anything other than a few 'mistakes', even allowing him to keep legal (though not physical) possession of the taped proof of his own criminal behaviour. Meanwhile the innocent Ford found himself being accused across the nation of everything from egregious conspiracy to wilful ignorance. The pardon was 'nothing less than the continuation of a cover-up', the *Washington Post* declared.[42] 'In granting President Nixon an inappropriate and premature grant of clemency,' the *New York Times* commented, 'President Ford has affronted the Constitution and the American system of justice. This blundering intervention is a body blow to the president's own credibility and to the public's reviving sense of confidence in the integrity of its government.'[43]

Belatedly, Ford recognized he'd misunderstood the temper of American voters, just as he had done when rooting for Nixon against what he'd labelled 'a relatively small group of activists'. The small group had become the majority of Americans.

Ford vainly attempted to make good on his mistake. His honour impugned, he cast aside all precedent and agreed, for the first time in the history of the American presidency, to testify in person and on oath before the House Judiciary Subcommittee, which had convened to ask for an explanation of the premature pardon. This prompted Congresswoman Elizabeth Holzman to pose the $64,000 question 'whether or not in fact there was a deal'.[44] The president hotly denied it ('no deal, period, under no circumstances'), but the precipitate, blanket, pardon-in-advance left a sour, suspicious taste across the nation.

It was clear that Gerald Ford's honeymoon was over. Henceforth he would have to prove himself, in his own right, if he was to have any chance of being elected in 1976. The first issue would be pardons for Vietnam draft dodgers.

Objection to Vietnam as an unjust war had caused huge numbers of young Americans to burn their draft cards, refuse to register, flee abroad, go underground, or go AWOL when inducted. As a former World War II naval combatant Ford had little sympathy for such lack of patriotism, and had always objected to amnesty for Vietnam draft dodgers and deserters. Nevertheless he now hoped that by a demonstration of compassion ('I am throwing the weight of the presidency on the side of leniency'), he might show himself to be a conciliatory commander-in-chief.[45] He thus proposed, in August 1974, 'earned reentry' into American society for the 115,000 or more offenders. Their cases, he proposed, would be reviewed by a specially created Presidential Clemency Board, with a requirement that offenders perform alternative service to the state.

As a compromise solution to an awkward issue for diehard patriotic Republicans, the proposal was perfectly sensible, but it immediately fell victim to Ford's controversial simultaneous announcement of the blanket pardon for the very man who had, for four years, prolonged the Vietnam War at the cost of more than 20,000 American soldiers' lives – the majority of them draftees. When the establishment of the new board was made public in mid-September 1974, its potential for healing the wounds of Vietnam was thus completely drowned out. Once convened, moreover, the board proved a bureaucratic nightmare. It only processed a handful of cases (less than twenty) before the November election meltdown, and over subsequent years processed but a tiny minority of eligible cases.

Congress' fury over the Nixon pardon would meanwhile be manifested in multiple ways. One of these was the treatment of Ford's nominee for appointment as vice president. Taking a secret straw poll, Ford was minded to recommend to Congress former congressman George Bush of Texas, currently chairman of the Republican National Party after serving as ambassador to the United Nations. However, Newsweek published a report that Bush had been given no less than $100,000 from Nixon's secret White House slush fund for his unsuccessful bid for a Senate seat in 1970. On August 17, 1974, Ford had therefore turned to Governor Nelson Rockefeller, the millionaire former governor of New York who had retired the previous December in order to prepare for his own renewed presidential run in 1976. (He had already run in three Republican primary campaigns in 1960, 1964 and 1968.)

Though by most people's standards a conservative who was tough on crime and favoured capital punishment, Rockefeller was considered a liberal by Republican diehards such as Senator Goldwater and Governor Reagan. A notable womanizer in the same mould as John F. Kennedy, Rockefeller rattled 'the cages of the [Republican] Right', as Nixon's speechwriter Pat Buchanan put it, while on the left, outraged Democrats, furious over the Nixon pardon, sharpened their sabres to punish Ford by delaying a confirmation vote. Governor Rockefeller was required to testify before Congress on seventeen separate days before he was finally confirmed by Congress on December 5, 1974, leaving Ford and the nation without a vice president for almost four months.

Meanwhile, matters were no easier in the White House itself. General Haig still attempted to run the Ford White House as his own fiefdom, but this time under a weak, instead of mad, president.

Ford's supine response in dealing with General Haig was galling to the president's staff, especially when Haig told him to fire his long-time chief assistant, Bob Hartmann. The problem, however, was not simply Haig's megalomania. Ford had clearly not prepared himself in any way for the presidency. He had no personnel plan lined up, either for a White House staff or a new cabinet, no clear idea how to manage a big organization, in fact no notion of how to choose or discipline subordinates. Haig – who aspired to be the next chairman of the Joint Chiefs of Staff, despite his nominal experience as a general – was for months allowed to run amok at the White House until Ford finally plucked up enough courage to get rid of him, by promoting him to supreme command of NATO in Europe (a move which, although deeply unpopular in Europe, did not require Senate confirmation).

Ford had said, both in fear of Haig and in ignorance of how a huge organization needs to be run, that he would dispense with a chief of staff altogether on Haig's eventual departure. Once again, this was a well-meant notion that sought to make him accessible to as many as possible, in contrast to his bunker-protected predecessor. In the modern, accelerated world of communications and decision-making, however, it was yet another major mistake.

Nature abhors a vacuum; so does empire. Ford's notion of six or seven co-equal assistants meeting him every day had worked well for him as a mere legislative congressman, but he was now president of the United States. The entire world was watching how he commanded his White House team, as well as how he directed American imperial policy across the globe. As Ford himself acknowledged later, 'I started out in effect not having a chief of staff and it didn't work . . . You need a filter, a person that you have total confidence in, who works so closely with you that in effect his is almost an alter ego. I just can't imagine a president not having an effective chief of staff.'[46] This was said, however, almost three decades later.

The challenge Ford faced in 1974 was to restore the American public's trust in government. On paper, he was the very best possible appointee. But, with the best of intentions, he blundered at every step.

Nixon, when president, had been almost invisible to the general public, concealing himself in his various hideaways, yet managing White House operations on the phone and through dedicated, ultra-loyal, combative henchmen; Ford was now not only visible, but visibly inept, along with an incompetent White House staff. In the months after the transition the White House turned into a managerial and public relations mess, with the right hand seeming not to know what the left hand was doing, and top meetings with Ford either ill-attended or him rambling without purpose or order: 'a White House staff completely incapable of structuring a workable White House–Cabinet relationship', as one political scientist put it, let alone a successful White House–Congress one.[47]

Aware that his new administration was tanking and his own polls sinking, Ford eventually recognized he must take restorative action. Instead of bringing in an experienced bipartisan manager who would reflect his own centrist approach, however, Ford chose yet another Nixon holdover to head up White House operations: former congressman Donald Rumsfeld.

Rumsfeld had loyally served in Nixon's White House, then been sent as US ambassador to NATO in August 1974, only to be brought back from his brief job to help Al Haig manage the initial transition, and had thereafter departed. Now Rumsfeld was brought in yet again, as chief of staff to the president. In this role he was eventually able to carry out Haig's plan to destroy Hartmann, as well as other Ford loyalists. In their place, Rumsfeld brought in yet another of Nixon's 'praetorian' guards, as his deputy: former congressman Dick Cheney. Managerial order was thereby restored to the chaotic White House, but at a high ethical and political cost. Both Rumsfeld and Cheney were highly competent managers who proved effective administrators, but they were conservative Republicans harbouring a Nixonian view of imperial White House power wholly at odds with a charming, well-intentioned non-imperialist on the throne. Thus arose the basic problem of the Ford presidency: a Caesar with no clear vision of what he wished to achieve, other than continuing Nixon's policies abroad and at home, and so incompetent in command of his White House team that he had found himself forced to use Nixon's most detestable but effective civil servants, who were constantly at loggerheads with Ford's diminishing number of loyalists. The result was a White House split into feuding camps, lacking presidential direction; a poor prescription, when added to his disastrous Nixon pardon, for Ford's chances of election in 1976, if he chose to run.

The US inflation rate had reached 12.8 per cent that summer, in large part due to the Arab oil embargo. Economists across the western world were divided about how best to tackle rocketing prices, higher wages *and* rising unemployment – a vicious circle they termed stagflation. With signs of a major recession, Ford – who refused to re-impose a cap on wages and prices – felt compelled to act, but found himself none the wiser after convening a high-level economic summit in August 1974. His decision to declare a national voluntary campaign to reduce demand (and thus prices) by cutting consumption, waste and unnecessary travel, entitled 'Whip Inflation Now' (WIN), became an object of national ridicule. The Secretary of the Treasury called the campaign – complete with WIN lapel-buttons – 'ludicrous', while Ford's own Economic Policy Board hid their 'heads in embarrassment'.[48] One corporation president wrote to the White House: 'Your appeal to the American public with the juvenile "WIN" promotion was more fitting for a high school pep club than a leader of one of the world's great countries.'[49] WIN became, in short, lose.

Ford's more important proposal, namely to impose a surtax on high-income earners, corporations and especially oil companies, fared no better. Congress forced him to rescind the measure and propose instead a tax cut, in order to stimulate the economy and bring down unemployment, which had already reached 7.1 per cent.[50] This only resulted in claims of 'flip-flopping', yet few would have traded shoes with Ford as he attempted to curb inflation on the one hand, and avoid a looming recession on the other. Both William Simon, the Treasury Secretary, and Alan Greenspan, the chair of the Council of Economic Advisers, counselled ignoring unemployment – a policy of 'let 'em eat cake' as Ford's adviser Robert Hartmann – worried about a midterm meltdown for Republicans in congressional elections – sneered.[51]

America's dilemma was little different from that of most European economies, and Ford's response – taking considered advice from a plethora of economists and business leaders – well motivated. But, thanks to the Nixon pardon, his relations with Congress had soured, dooming his attempts to restore unity and common purpose in leading the nation. The result was a near-catastrophic midterm election defeat in November 1974, when Democrats took a further forty-nine seats from the Republicans in the House. In the Senate the Republican Party lost a further four members, giving Democrats a 61–38 majority. The Democrats thereby achieved a veto-proof majority – marking the end of the 'imperial presidency'.

The disastrous midterm election now gave the whip hand to a Democratic-controlled Congress, not the Oval Office. The very advantage Ford had held over rivals Rockefeller, Reagan and Connally the previous year as a vice-presidential appointee – namely his fine, bipartisan record in Congress – had evaporated. When Ford vetoed Congress' bill to embargo any aid to America's ally, Turkey, after its invasion of Cyprus in response to a Greek military coup there, the House simply overrode the veto, and although he was allowed to delay implementation, the embargo was duly instituted by Congress, causing Turkey, a crucial member of NATO, to close all US intelligence and military installations save a single NATO base. 'The enormous reservoir of goodwill Ford had enjoyed, especially with his Democratic cronies on Capitol Hill, swiftly dissipated. His popularity plummeted', DeFrank recalled, making it impossible for Ford to 'craft a bipartisan agenda' and even 'harder for Ford to rally support for dealing with runaway inflation or the Vietnam War'.[52]

If few political leaders would have traded places with Ford in dealing with stagflation, even fewer would have done so with respect to Vietnam, where on December 13, 1974, the North Vietnamese launched their long-awaited offensive to unify the two halves of the country by force. Their military campaign was planned to take two years, but in the event it took only a few months. By January 6, 1975, the Communists had captured the provincial capital Phuoc Binh. Ford begged Congress to authorize emergency funds to at least aid the South Vietnamese military, but as one group of congressmen explained to him, 'We face our own war here at home against crippling economic developments, the crisis in energy and other public resources and other serious problems . . . We cannot confront and resolve these crises while the United States continues involvement in South East Asia.'[53]

Ford seemed genuinely distraught. 'It cannot be in our interest to cause our friends all over the world to wonder whether we will support them' he countered, but the die was cast.[54] His pardon to Nixon had made him a pariah to many Democrats in Congress, and the policy of 'Vietnamization' Nixon had used to cover the American retreat from Vietnam was a sham that had convinced no one. Financial aid and military supplies would not affect the course of the campaign. Even the South Vietnamese dictator, Thieu, was under no illusions now. He had long labelled the Paris Peace Accords 'tantamount to surrender' by leaving 150,000 North Vietnamese troops in South Vietnam, and had known it was only a matter of time before his own right-wing junta fell. Nevertheless, as the North Vietnamese forces advanced, he begged Ford for a B-52 bombing campaign and the 'necessary means' to repel the offensive. He was supported not only by Kissinger but also by General Weyand, the chief of staff of the army, who had flown to Saigon. 'We must not abandon our goal of a free and independent South Vietnam', Weyand reported to Ford.[55]

The young White House photographer who had accompanied Weyand to Asia, however, was blunt when Ford asked his opinion. 'Mr President, Vietnam has no more than a month left,' David Kennerly warned, 'and anyone who tells you different is bullshitting.'[56]

Kennerly was right. Amid rumours he was about to be deposed in yet another coup, Thieu resigned, but the fantasy that South Vietnam could become a South Korea, protected by huge numbers of US troops, was over. Ford stopped showing the drafts of his speeches to Kissinger, his Secretary of State, and at Tulane University, New Orleans, the president unequivocally announced (to tumultuous applause) that America would not be 'refighting a war that is finished as far as America is concerned'.[57] A coded message was broadcast on Saigon radio announcing a temperature of '105 degrees and rising', as thirty-four helicopters from aircraft carriers in the South China Sea swooped down to the American embassy which was besieged by Vietnamese civilians seeking flight to safety.

As evening fell on April 29, 1975, the last helicopter lifted above the building, having evacuated 1,400 Americans and 5,600 South Vietnamese. The next day, and only fifty-five days since the North Vietnamese offensive began, Saigon fell. It was then renamed Ho Chi Minh City. Meanwhile, as North Vietnamese forces overwhelmed Saigon, a simultaneous assault took place on the capital of Cambodia, Phnom Penh. The American-funded dictator, Lon Nol, stepped down on April 1, 1975, and a week later, Ford authorized commencement of the US evacuation plan for Cambodia, code-named Eagle Pull, which 'saved' 276 people in helicopter rescues.

The Nixon Doctrine 'in its purest form' had come to final grief, having served only to ruin two small countries, far from Washington, in a misbegotten effort to demonstrate American imperial determination.

With unemployment and inflation rising, growing dependency on foreign oil and a new president who had inexplicably made Congress his enemy, as well as polls showing increasing isolationism on the part of voters, America's leadership role in the free world looked greatly diminished. 'America – A Helpless Giant', the German *Frankfurter Allgemeine Zeitung* headed an editorial that spring, while *The Economist* used the headline: 'The Fading of America'.

Ford later acknowledged the necessity to listen less to the rhetoric of Nixon's former apparatchiks and be more realistic. 'Maybe we weren't a giant power, throwing our [weight] around, trying to tell everybody to do what we wanted', he reflected on the change. The American Empire was no longer quite the giant that it had been; but it was not, as Ford added, 'without power'.[58]

In which direction would the president now steer the American ship of state, diplomats across the world wondered. With America's allies questioning US resolve in the aftermath of the fall of South Vietnam and Cambodia, as well as its economic problems at home, Ford was given an opportunity to show where he stood – and what advice, as Caesar, he would and wouldn't take.

Less than a month after the fall of Saigon and Phnom Penh an American merchant ship, carrying military spare parts, was seized by Khmer Rouge sailors in the Gulf of Siam on its way to Thailand. As

Ford was informed on May 12, 1975, the captors declared the unarmed vessel, the SS *Mayaguez*, to have deliberately entered newly expanded Cambodian territorial waters. Summoning his national security staff and alerting US naval and military staffs in South East Asia, Ford decided to make the incident a test of his presidential resolve. The Secretary of Defense, James R. Schlesinger, favoured downplaying the incident, but Kissinger (who had joked he was 'the only Secretary of State who has lost two countries in three weeks'[59]) was loath to see America lose further face, and recommended 'ferocious' air bombing countermeasures on the Cambodian mainland.[60]

Ford listened patiently to Kissinger, and realized belatedly that his Secretary of State was, in some respects, as reckless, even as feral as Nixon. Yet a response of some sort was required. Dismissing Kissinger's notion of a massive aerial attack on the mainland, the former naval lieutenant commander now ordered US forces to instantly retake the ship, which had been anchored fifty miles off the coast of Cambodia, by the island of Koh Tang, before its crew could be taken to a mainland port.

Luck favoured the president. In the first ship-to-ship boarding by an American naval vessel since 1826, the US destroyer *Holt* secured the *Mayaguez* on May 15, 1975, using air-dropped tear-gas bombs. The next morning, responding to pressure from the Communist Chinese government, the captive sailors were ordered to be released from a fishing vessel where they'd been secreted by the Khmer Rouge, and transferred to the USS *Holt* unharmed.

Ford's approval rating leaped eleven points at home. He had weathered the first international crisis not attributable to his predecessor, and had drawn a line in the proverbial sand, refusing to escalate the incident, as Kissinger wished, but avoiding accusations of pusillanimity that had attached to North Korea's seizure of the USS *Pueblo* six years before.[61] It was, despite its relatively trivial nature, 'the biggest political victory of the Ford presidency', as one Ford biographer called it.[62]

With his polls rising, Ford now decided to assert his own post-Nixonite Ford Doctrine on a much larger stage. He not only announced he would be a candidate for the 1976 presidential nomination, but also that he would personally attend the Helsinki Conference on Security and Cooperation.

For the American right, still vexed over Nixon's accommodation with Mao Zedong and then the 'loss' of South Vietnam and Cambodia to Communist regimes, Ford's willingness to go to Europe and sign off on what conservative Republicans continued to consider the 'Yalta betrayal' aroused a firestorm of protest. In thunderous indignation from his exile in Vermont, the Nobel-prizewinning novelist Aleksandr Solzhenitsyn denounced the president's July trip as appeasement, the aim of the conference being to settle the ongoing dispute over post-war borders of eastern European nations, including the legitimization of Soviet control of Poland and 'bloc' countries, in the interests of détente.

Once again, Ford demonstrated his growing stature. An inter-nationalist since his distinguished naval service in World War II, and a centrist in the manner of President Eisenhower, who had tried desper-ately hard to find common ground with the Soviets, Ford had never espoused Nixon's earlier rabid anti-Communism, and had welcomed Nixon's volte-face and efforts at détente. He thus had no trouble in now openly pursuing his own sincere détente agenda, without need of Nixon's magic tricks. Bravely ignoring the right wing of his own party, Ford proposed the opposite of the 'Madman Theory': an open, common-sense policy of global security through good relations between governments, shared agreements, and transparency.

'Jerry, Don't Go' the *Wall Street Journal* implored. The president did go, however, meeting the Soviet leader Leonid Brezhnev for a second time, and seating himself among the leaders of thirty-five non-Communist and Communist nations, including a representative from the Vatican. The four categories of agreements, from human rights to trade and travel and future monitoring, represented a willingness by western countries not to threaten the ever touchy Soviet Union, in return for liberalizing contact, commerce, information and human rights in Europe – part of a common will 'to broaden, deepen and make continuing and lasting the process of détente', as the signatories accepted.[63]

Travelling to the conference in Finland, Ford was the first US presi-dent to visit eastern Europe since World War II – a trip that, along with the Helsinki Accords, had profound consequences in the years that followed.

'The fact is,' General Wesley Clark, the supreme commander of NATO, later pointed out when running himself for presidential

nomination, 'that the Soviet Union did not fall the way the neoconservatives say it did. The 1975 Helsinki Accords proved to be the crucial
step in opening the way for the subsequent peaceful democratization
of the Soviet bloc. The accords, signed by the Communist governments of the East, guaranteed individual human and political rights
to all peoples and limited the authority of governments to act against
their own citizens. However flimsy the human rights provisions seemed
at the time, they provided a crucial platform for dissidents such as
Russian physicist Andrei Sakharov. These dissidents, though often jailed
and exiled, built organizations that publicized their governments' many
violations of the accords, garnering western attention and support
and inspiring their countrymen with the knowledge that it was possible
to stand up to the political powers that be.'[64]

John Lewis Gaddis, historian of the Cold War, seconded General
Clark's view the following year, writing that the Helsinki commitment
to 'human rights and fundamental freedoms' became a trap for the
Soviet Union, as it faced ever bolder condemnations by dissidents.
'Thousands of people who lacked the prominence of Solzhenitsyn
and Sakharov', Gaddis reflected, 'began to stand with them in holding
the USSR and its satellites accountable for human rights.' In other
words, the 1975 Helsinki Accords became, as he put it, 'the basis for
legitimizing opposition to Soviet rule'.[65]

If Ford hoped his successful statesmanship in Finland and eastern
Europe would improve his approval polls at home, however, he was
to be disappointed. In conforming to his new Ford Doctrine in
American foreign policy, based on patience, stability and goodwill,
he relied like Eisenhower on his own reputation for honesty and
integrity. But the America of the 1970s was not that of the 1950s. To
redirect American foreign policy towards détente and accommodation with both China and the USSR, Nixon had relied on his genius
for self-contradiction and counter-attack to confuse his opponents.
Ford, however, was honest to a fault, lacked courtroom skills, and
had no knack for manipulating public opinion. The result was that,
instead of being hailed at home as the Peace President, he was treated
to a chorus of right-wing Republican disapproval – with ominous
repercussions.

Long frustrated by Richard Nixon's ability to outwit, outtalk and
outmanoeuvre their star mouthpieces from Barry Goldwater to Ronald

Reagan, the right wing of the Republican Party now charged that their new president was 'selling out' their platform, and was guilty of a 'betrayal of eastern Europe', as Solzhenitsyn called it.[66] Still rabidly anti-Communist, vexed over American defeat in Vietnam, and virulently anti-government in domestic matters, Republican ideologues derided Ford for his participation in the Helsinki Accords, and began to promote an alternative, right-wing candidate as the Republican presidential nominee for the 1976 election. This was ominous.

Ford himself acknowledged he had not done enough to communicate the rationale and importance of the Helsinki Accords ('a failure in public relations' for which 'I will have to accept a large share of the blame', he admitted later), or to proselytize his moderate, long-sighted gospel of détente after Helsinki, allowing right-wing Republicans and even his eventual Democratic opponent to scorn his statesmanlike efforts on behalf of America.[67] Over domestic issues, meanwhile, he was faced by the same problem: how to explain to an American public the difficulty of dealing with runaway inflation at the same time as rising unemployment – stagflation.

As over the Helsinki Accords, Ford found himself unable to garner due credit for what, in historical terms, would prove the second major achievement of his presidency: his efforts to goad Congress into passing an emergency tax-rebate bill in the spring of 1975 in order to stimulate the economy, while at the same time cutting government expenditure and closing tax loopholes in order to maintain government programmes without increasing the national deficit.

These efforts were, in retrospect, heroic. Ford's $23 billion tax rebate – largely confined to lower-income families, who would spend the money and thus hopefully cure the Great Recession – worked. Passed by Congress in May 1975, the consequences proved remarkable: unemployment fell, the stock market rose, and GNP increased by a staggering 11.2 per cent by the third quarter – the highest in two decades. But the public gave Ford little immediate credit; indeed in September, 1975, he would experience no less than two assassination attempts.

On September 5, 1975, Ford was in Sacramento, the state capital of California, to give a speech to its legislature and hold a private meeting with its Democratic governor, Jerry Brown, who had succeeded Ronald Reagan. Ironically, the subject of Ford's speech was crime.

'The weather that morning was clear; the sun was shining brightly'

Ford recalled, so he decided to walk from the Senator Hotel.[68] There were 'several rows of people standing behind a rope that lined the sidewalk to my left. They were applauding and saying nice things' Ford remembered; 'I was in a good mood, so I started shaking hands.'[69]

'That's when I spotted a woman, wearing a bright red dress. She was in the second or third row, moving right along with me as if she wanted to shake my hand. When I slowed down, I noticed immediately that she thrust her hand under the arms of the other spectators, I reached down to shake it – and looked into the barrel of a .45 caliber pistol pointed directly at me.'[70]

'I ducked' he said – but even so, he was extraordinarily lucky.[71] The twenty-six-year-old lover of mass-murderer Charles Manson was heard by a bystander to complain 'It didn't go off. Can you believe it?', astonished at her ill-luck as a secret service agent wrestled the gun from her hand.

Lynette 'Squeaky' Fromme was sentenced to jail for life, after warning the judge that 'If Nixon's reality-wearing-a-Ford-Face continues to run this country, your homes will be bloodier than the Tate-LaBianca houses and My Lai put together.' Her fellow concubine, Sandra Good, also warned that 'many people all over the world are due to be assassinated. This is just the beginning. Just the beginning of the many, many assassinations . . . People will be killed.'[72]

Good was right. Two weeks later, Ford was leaving the St Francis Hotel in San Francisco, following a television interview, when Sara Jane Moore, a bookkeeper for People in Need, drew a .38 calibre revolver and fired. This time the gun went off. The bullet missed the president, ricocheting off the hotel entrance fascia and hitting a taxi driver in the groin, at which point a fellow bystander grabbed Moore's arm and pulled her to the ground before she could fire a second time. 'I do regret I didn't succeed and allow the winds of change to start', the assassin – an admirer of Patty Hearst, the heiress who was abducted by terrorists and had joined the Symbionese Liberation Army – said afterwards. 'I wish I had killed him. I did it to create chaos.'[73]

In both assassination attempts President Ford showed the same physical courage he'd demonstrated aboard the USS *Monterey* as kamikaze pilots zeroed in on his vessel, and continued his schedule for the day without even mentioning the 'incident'. But if Ford joked to his scheduling staff that 'we're not going to schedule any more trips like that'[74] and refused to 'capitulate to those who want to undercut all that's good in America', the writing was on the wall.[75] 'You wouldn't be standing before me if we had an effective capital punishment law', the sentencing judge complained to Ms Moore, denouncing her as 'a product of our permissive society'.[76] Whether capital punishment could rectify the problems of the permissive society was debatable, but with the spectre of anarchy facing the country there would be a price to be paid for the excesses of the counter-culture 1960s radicals – a price that would now be paid in political currency, as right-wing Republicans began to gain greater traction within their own party. For Gerald Ford, as a centrist, progressive Republican, this would be bad news.

Détente with the USSR was hard enough, but 'No foreign policy challenges occupied more of my time in the early months of 1975', Ford later recalled, than Israel's refusal to withdraw from the territories it had occupied.[77] Thanks to American support, the Israelis 'were stronger militarily than all their Arab neighbors combined, yet peace was no closer than it had ever been. So I began to question the rationale for our policy. I wanted the Israelis to recognize that there had to be some quid pro quo. If we were going to build up their military capabilities, we in turn had to see some flexibility to achieve a fair, secure and permanent peace.'[78] Though the president attempted to bully the Israelis into withdrawal and negotiation by threatening, on NBC television, to turn resolution of the conflict and the future of Palestine over to a Geneva peace conference, and thus abandon Israel to its fate, it was to no avail. By providing Israel with the arms to win the October War, then arranging a ceasefire that left Israel in control of all its war spoils, Kissinger had turned Israel into an American puppet-state – but with the Israelis refusing to be a puppet. 'The Israelis kept stalling', Ford recalled his own exasperation. However, as one historian chronicled, Ford's threat to abandon Israel 'backfired. Instead of caving in to Ford's threat, the Israelis stiffened their resolve' – and with Kissinger cautioning against iron insistence, the president was stymied.[79] 'Their antics frustrated the Egyptians and made me mad as hell', Ford later said of the Israeli prime minister, Yitzhak Rabin (a former terrorist during the British Mandate in Palestine), and his colleagues.[80] 'Rabin fought over every kilometer', Ford lamented, but 'he didn't understand that only by giving do you get something in return'.[81]

In the end the United States, not the UN, became committed to providing a permanent monitoring force (the Sinai Field Mission) on a new border that was established between Egypt and Israel. In a series of secret side agreements or Memorandums of Understanding, later known as Sinai II, the US also committed to providing support 'on an ongoing and long-term basis' for 'Israel's military equipment and other defense requirements, and to its economic needs' at a cost of $4 billion annually, as well as making available F-16 fighter planes for its air force (already the third largest in the world) and Pershing missiles, guaranteeing Israel's oil requirements, and preparing plans for any future airlifts of military weapons during a crisis.[82] In addition, the US secretly promised (without informing the Egyptians) not to negotiate with the Palestine Liberation Organization (PLO) until it recognized Israel's right to exist, nor to negotiate with anyone in the Middle East before first consulting with Israel, or to follow any course of negotiation other than following existing UN resolutions. Rabin was justly delighted.

Pleased at least to have got back the Sinai and his surrounded Egyptian Army, as well as the Israeli-occupied Egyptian oilfields and the crucial Suez Canal (which Israelis would henceforth be permitted to use for non-military cargo vessels), in September 1975 Egypt's President Sadat reluctantly signed the Israel–Egypt Peace Treaty – and his own death warrant. He was assassinated six years later. (Rabin, too, would be assassinated twenty years later, after seeking too late in the day a compromise Israeli route to permanent peace, via the Oslo Accords.)

From the Middle East, President Ford then turned his attention back to a more peaceful approach to America's problems at home. In his State of the Union speech in January he had stated frankly that 'the state of the union is not good. Millions of Americans are out of work. Recession and inflation are eroding the money of millions more.' He accepted there were no simple solutions, and vowed now to continue to steer a centrist-Republican middle course. 'I believe that being in the middle of the road, as far as the Republicans are concerned, on a nationwide basis, is the right policy.'

Former governor of California Ronald Reagan disagreed, as did the Republican right. The right-wing *Manchester Union-Leader* began referring to the president as 'Jerry the Jerk', and deplored his vision of the

Republican Party as an 'umbrella of many colors' that could, and would, welcome independents and moderate Democrats. Reagan indicated he might well challenge for the party's presidential nomination, by coming forward as the standard-bearer of the right, which coerced Ford to move to the right himself, in order to deprive Reagan of a clear wind.

Ford now committed 'one of the few cowardly things I did in my life', as he later termed it.[83] At the urging of his chief of staff Donald Rumsfeld, who hoped he himself would then be picked, Ford decided to turn his back on his loyal, centrist vice president.[84] On October 28, 1975, after discussing 'the growing strength of the [Republican] right wing' with Vice President Nelson Rockefeller, the president asked him not to stand for election in 1976 as his prospective running mate.[85] Rockefeller agreed to stand down. It was, Ford acknowledged afterwards, not only the most egregious, but 'the biggest political mistake of my life'.[86]

The removal of Rockefeller from the prospective presidential ticket, while keeping Kissinger as Secretary of State, in no way appeased the right wing of the Republican Party, which was spoiling for a fight. On November 19, 1975, Ford took a phone call from Reagan, who had refused a cabinet post in the Ford administration. 'I am going to run for president' Reagan announced. 'I trust we can have a good contest, and I hope it won't be too divisive.'[87]

'How can you challenge an incumbent president of your own party and *not* be divisive?' Ford asked later.[88] Reagan's challenge hurt him deeply, yet in it he recognized much more than a personal duel. It would be, he saw, a struggle to define the very conception of Republicanism in modern America, as a centrist approach to government, governing, and imperial leadership across the globe.

The omens were not promising. By December 1975 a Gallup poll was already showing Ronald Reagan leading Ford by 40 per cent to 32 per cent among Republican voters.

For Ford's campaign team this was, belatedly, a wake-up call. Thereafter the campaign became the most memorable example of an incumbent having to fight off a fellow Republican rival since that of William Howard Taft in 1912, a titanic struggle that had split the Republican Party, alienated voters by its venom, and had resulted in a Democrat (Woodrow Wilson) regaining the White House. Would that be the case in 1976, pundits wondered?

The president certainly had his work cut out. Not only did he not possess Reagan's silver-tongued, screen actor's performance skills on the campaign trail, but he lacked Nixon's flair for theatrics. Nixon, moreover, refused to help the man who had pardoned him; indeed, far from being grateful for his liberty, Nixon now astonished Ford by appearing in rude good health, and reneging on his promise not to visit China before the election. Disregarding Ford's pleas, Nixon flew to Beijing on February 21, 1976, a bare three days before the crucial, traditionally first-held presidential primary, in New Hampshire. 'Nixon's a shit!' Ford's national security adviser, Brent Scowcroft – a man who never cursed – was heard to exclaim on hearing the news.[89]

The president did manage, in the event, to beat Reagan in the New Hampshire primary, but it was only by a sliver: 1,000 votes out of 100,000 cast. This presaged an even more divisive battle in the subsequent primaries.

Buoyed by his near-win, Reagan stepped up his attacks on the president and his Republican administration, with so many false accusations that neither Ford nor observers could keep up with them. Reagan accused Ford – a stalwart maintainer of American military supremacy, who got Congress to authorize the largest budget for the Pentagon since World War II – of allowing the US to become number two militarily among world empires. The accusation was knowingly and completely false, but it allowed Reagan to campaign on a platform to 'Make America No. 1 Again'.

Ford had tackled the American inflation-recession crisis with considerable managerial skill, utilizing the best economic advisers in the nation and working hand in hand with the Democratic-controlled Congress. The result had been that unemployment rolls had begun to tumble, productivity rose and inflation fell. Yet day after day Reagan battered the president for poor economic growth, proposed shifting most taxation to the states rather than federal IRS authority, criticized government as a useless bureaucracy, and vilified Ford for his foreign policy, to the point where, after losing the Nebraska primary to Reagan, Ford had to postpone announcement of an agreement with the Russians on the peaceful use of nuclear explosions, lest it add fuel to Reagan's denunciatory rhetoric. The president was even forced to back off a new SALT arms reduction agreement, and found himself assailed by Reagan over his Panama Canal talks. ('When it comes to the canal,'

Reagan declared in one-liner speeches across the country, 'we built it, we paid for it, it's ours, and . . . we're going to keep it.'[90])

If President Ford, the most honest and moderate chief executive since World War II, was often outmanoeuvred by Reagan in media coverage, he was equally schemed against by his own White House staff. In the so-called 'Sunday Morning Massacre' of November 2, 1975, the 'Vulcans' – a cabal of former Nixon adherents, marshalled by Donald Rumsfeld – had shown their teeth. William Colby, the CIA chief who had testified honestly before the Church and Rockefeller committees, was fired, and Ambassador George Bush, Nixon's protégé, was brought back from China to take his place at CIA headquarters, lest he become Ford's choice as vice-presidential nominee. Simultaneously Rumsfeld engineered the removal of the Secretary of Defense, James Schlesinger, for not having carried out the bombing of the Cambodian mainland during the *Mayaguez* incident, and succeeded in making himself Defense Secretary. Dick Cheney – a man who had avoided the Vietnam draft – then took over Rumsfeld's job as chief of staff. Cheney was a Thomas Cromwell-type figure of ice-cold ambition, whose penchant for secrecy, illegality and Nixon-like targeting of individuals worried colleagues.[91]

Ford ultimately had no one to blame but himself. He was, in effect, 'too much Mr Nice Guy', as the White House press secretary put it, which meant his only hope of surviving as president was either to steal Reagan's right-wing thunder, or to govern more imperially from the White House, as Nixon had done.[92] By dropping his loyal, centrist vice president and massacring moderate members of his administration on the one hand, and promoting Nixon's least ethical henchmen on the other, Ford had made a last-ditch effort to do both; whether this would win the party nomination, let alone save his presidency in November 1976, was an open question.

Amazingly, Ford had been elected thirteen times to Congress, yet had never fought an election for anything larger than his own congressional district of Grand Rapids. 'All of a sudden I found myself in a different ballpark', he later conceded. 'I didn't comprehend the vast difference between running in my district and running for president.'[93] It was an extraordinary admission.

Faced with relentless attack from the right, he proved all too vulnerable, especially in combating Reagan's memorable but outrageous anecdotal claims. The president's first campaign manager resigned, and his replacement inspired little confidence when declaring that his job was to continue his predecessor's work rather than 'rearrange the furniture on the deck of the *Titanic*'.[94]

Reagan's relentless criticism of his presidency, Ford later confided, was 'a demagogic attack. And I resented it.'[95] With the contestants barely a hundred delegates apart at the Republican National Convention, it was clear that, win or lose, Reagan was leading a massive conservative revolt against Ford's centrist policies. As the convention chairman John J. Rhodes recalled, 'The Reagan people were intent on doing everything they could to embarrass President Ford', especially in pressing the president to alter his foreign policy by voting a new platform, 'Morality in Foreign Policy'. Instead of steady détente and gradualism in encouraging Communist regimes to liberalize, Reagan insisted upon a new, anti-Communist crusade, with himself as chief crusader.

In the end Ford, honourable and admired by all for his integrity, scraped by, winning the nomination on the convention floor by a bare 117 votes on August 19, 1976. 'Thus ended one of the most tense and unpleasant chapters of my political life', the convention chairman later wrote. The next chapter, however, proved if anything worse.

With Reagan and his disappointed supporters refusing thereafter to come out and campaign for Ford (or even, in many cases, to vote for the man they mocked as 'Bozo the president'), the president led a fatally divided party. He could – and did – boast that, like President Eisenhower, he had ended a foreign war and that the nation was now at peace; détente was producing remarkable stability in the once threatening Cold War; stagflation was being beaten (inflation cut by half, unemployment way down), and economic indicators were positive. Yet the president's near-defeat for the Republican nomination at the hands of a sixty-five-year-old right-wing ideologue betokened more than political schism in the Republican Party. In a celebrity-led society in which modern media and advertising played a burgeoning role, it spotlighted the ever increasing importance of public relations in modern politics. And in this respect, the president was at a grave disadvantage, blessed with neither acting ability nor televisual presence. Without them, however hard they tried, his team was unable to present the public with a winning presence. Ford's second campaign manager, Rogers Morton, was soon fired. A third then took on the role as Ford, severely wounded by Reagan's earlier attacks, now faced former governor Jimmy Carter of Georgia, the charismatic nominee of the Democratic Party.

With two months to go before the November election, Ford pinned his hopes on three prime-time television debates, the first such debates since those between Kennedy and Nixon sixteen years before. Although he won the first debate on domestic policy, he made a bad stumble in the second. In defending the Helsinki Accords, he took issue with Carter's criticism of détente as appeasement. 'There is no Soviet domination of eastern Europe,' the President defended his policy, adding 'and there never will be under a Ford administration.'

No Soviet domination of eastern Europe? Seventy-five million viewers rubbed their eyes in disbelief as Ford added insult to injury, claiming that not only Yugoslavs but Romanians and Poles did not 'consider themselves dominated by the Soviet Union'. Seeking to explain what he meant, Ford claimed that 'each of those countries is independent, autonomous; it has its own territorial integrity. And the United States does not concede that those countries are under the domination of the Soviet Union.'

Carter, handed such a gaffe, responded that he'd like to see 'Mr Ford convince the Polish-Americans and the Czech-Americans and the Hungarian-Americans in this country' that their countries were 'not under the domination and supervision of the Soviet Union behind the Iron Curtain'.

Though the president attempted to fudge the issue afterwards, he failed, unwilling to correct his mistake. His assertion, in such a tight election race, proved disastrous, especially when his running mate, Senator Robert Dole, committed an additional faux pas. In his one vice-presidential debate, he excoriated Democrats as collectively responsible for all American wars in the twentieth century, resulting in the death of 1.6 million Americans - 'enough to fill the city of Detroit' as Dole, who was known for his snarling tongue, sneered. The deliberate smear struck a very poor chord among patriotic citizens of both parties; it was an outrageous remark that Vice President Rockefeller, had Ford kept him on, would never have delivered. Not only did Dole thereby lose the debate to Walter Mondale, but centrist public confidence in the Republican ticket plummeted, following an already divisive nomination campaign.

'Mister President,' even Ford's own chief strategist said to him in the Oval Office, 'as a campaigner, you're no fucking good.'[96] Still, compared with polls taken in the summer at the time of the party conventions, Ford did remarkably well in improving his opinion poll numbers by late October, erasing the inexperienced Carter's twenty-point lead in eight weeks to a statistical tie, convincing Ford he might just breast the tape ahead of his rival.

The president's comeback, however, was a mirage. A low turnout – a mere 54 per cent of eligible voters, the lowest in twenty-eight years – cast their ballots on November 2, 1976. Counting went on into the early hours of the next morning. Even at 1 a.m. Ford's chief of staff, Dick Cheney, was calculating that with Hawaii, California, Illinois, Michigan and Ohio, the president might just reach the fabled 270 electoral votes. 'Hawaii?' reporters muttered, looking at each other.

At 9 a.m. on November 3, 1976, Cheney finally conveyed the bitter news. Carter had won 297 electoral votes against Ford's 240: a comfortable win for the former peanut farmer from Plains, Georgia.[97] The president was gutted.

President Ford remained in the Oval Office a further two and a half months until his term ended, but he seemed inconsolable, leading to newspaper reports of 'Jerry Ford's Blues'. On January 20, 1977, the only US president never to have been elected flew off aboard Air Force 2600[98] to Rancho Mirage, the retirement home he had bought in the California desert near Palm Springs.[99] He had served only 816 days in the White House, the shortest tenure of the US presidency in the twentieth century.[100]

## Part Three: Private Life

Gerald Ford grew up in a strait-laced home, in the strait-laced community of Grand Rapids, his mother his sternest critic if he failed her expectations as a devout Episcopalian, his hard-working but financially strapped stepfather equally devout and principled. Watching over his three younger half-brothers, Ford knew he would have to work for everything he might covet.

For a time Ford struggled with a stutter. At age fifteen he was working in a local Grand Rapids restaurant, dishwashing and flipping hamburgers, when a man came in and, after twenty minutes staring at him, introduced himself: 'I'm Leslie King, your father. Can I take you to lunch?'[101]

King – who had never once paid the $50–75 per month he was supposed to contribute in child support – gave the boy $25 in cash, and lunch at another establishment. He also introduced his second wife. Then, in a brand new Lincoln – not a Ford – which he'd purchased in Detroit, he drove off home to Wyoming. That night, after telling his parents, Ford wept. He never saw his biological father again.

Ford had a fiery temper, which his mother taught him to control by dispatching him to his room, only allowing him to come down when ready to 'discuss rationally whatever I'd done wrong'.[102] Both parents drilled into him 'the importance of honesty'.[103] He was unusual in being left-handed when sitting down, but became right-handed when standing up. Ford thus wrote with his left hand, but threw a football with his right. His handsome features, his star athletic perform-ance at college, his willingness to work hard both on the field and in his studies, finally got him into Yale Law School in New Haven, along-side Cyrus Vance and Sargent Shriver. They also got him into the arms of eighteen-year-old Phyllis Brown who was slim, equally blonde, and stunningly beautiful, and who was attending nearby Connecticut College for Women.

Ford fell 'deeply in love for the first time in my life', as he later recorded, and the two quickly became an item.[104] Bewitchingly attrac-tive, Phyllis soon gave up her junior degree course and moved to New York as a Powers model, appearing frequently on the covers of *Cosmopolitan* and *Look* magazines. Her beau, the handsome law student and college football coach, even featured alongside her in a major five-page pictorial in *Look* in 1940, entitled: 'A New York girl and her Yale boy friend spend a hilarious holiday on skis' in Stowe, Vermont. One caption read: 'After a hot dinner at the Inn, they loaf, sing, drink beer, dance, talk skiing – and so to bed.'

Using his Yale coaching salary, Ford invested $1,000 in Phyllis' modelling agency. The 'torrid four-year love affair', as he termed it, transformed the retiring Midwesterner into a New York would-be playboy, as the couple wined and dined, played bridge and tennis, and embraced the theatre as well as skiing.[105] Ford was more in love than Phyllis, however; though they 'talked of getting married as soon as I earned my law degree and found a decent job', there was no marriage.[106] Ford was offered a job with a New York law firm, but felt out of his league and hankered to return to Grand Rapids. 'Phyllis' modeling career was blossoming in New York and she didn't think she could afford to leave', he recalled – as well as the 'anguish' their break-up caused.[107] She was 'very smart, very beautiful, very great', he reflected in the evening of life, 'really a great gal'. 'I talk to her on the phone about once every five years, or if I'm in Reno, I call up', he confided to a friend. 'But I don't have her come to my hotel room', he giggled, like 'the lovelorn young buck he once was'.[108]

It was not until after World War II, still living with his mother and stepfather – despite his three younger half-brothers having all married and moved out – that Ford was encouraged by his parents to date a pretty local divorcée, Betty Anne Bloomer Warren, a former dancer and model, who was working as a fashion coordinator for a department store in Grand Rapids. 'At first,' Ford candidly confessed, 'neither of us had thought the relationship was serious' but over time they recognized their compatibility. They became engaged, though Ford explained he had a secret he could not vouchsafe to her for another six months.

The Duke of Wellington, who became not only a great military field commander but a distinguished British prime minister, once said that the Battle of Waterloo was won on the playing fields of his old school, Eton. So, too, Gerald Ford believed competitive sport had prepared him not only for combat, but also, thanks to its fierce aficionados, for politics. 'As a football player,' he later reflected, 'you have critics in the stands and critics in the press', opinionated individuals who 'assume they know all the answers. Their comments helped me to develop a thick hide, and in later years whenever critics assailed me, I just let their jibes roll off my back.'[109]

Ford's secret was that he was going to run as a Republican for Congress and 'wasn't sure how voters might feel about his marrying a divorced ex-dancer'.[110] Betty did not take umbrage or demur (though the marriage was to cost her her health and, to some degree, her happiness). Ford still had campaigning mud on his shoes when he arrived at the altar for his wedding on October 15, 1948 – and the mud stuck. Handsome, honourable and dependable, he made it a rule to be home every Sunday, but was always 'on call' to his constituents, who came to revere him. (One local farmer was astonished when Ford, who had promised he'd milk the farmer's cows for two weeks if he won the election, arrived at 4.30 a.m. to do exactly that, following his victory.) But for Betty, the one-day-a-week marriage, while she raised their four children, was tough, and in part explained her addiction to painkillers, after a pinched nerve in the neck led to continuous suffering.

Ford, in his genial, dedicated way, found himself more fulfilled than he had ever dreamed possible, but Betty was not. By the mid-1960s Betty was mixing painkillers with alcohol and suffered a 'crack-up' as she put it, when she simply walked out on her home, unsure whether she would go back – one of a silent army of dissatisfied wives and mothers who 'have no selves, no sense of self'.¹¹¹ As she later wrote, 'Jerry, who has always been supportive, blamed himself for a good deal of my misery. He once admitted to a reporter that, because of his schedule, I'd had to be both mother and father to the children.'¹¹² She suffered pancreatitis, but once Ford became president, she 'flowered. Jerry was no longer away so much. And I was somebody, the First Lady.'¹¹³

Unfortunately, it was as First Lady that Betty was found, on routine examination, to have breast cancer – an upset that explained, in part, Ford's distracted mind at the time of his disastrous pardon of Nixon. Like the cancer, Ford wanted the Nixon problem to go away, as fast as possible. Betty recovered well from surgery, but alcohol certainly loosened her tongue when she gave what would become a famed interview with Morley Safer, for CBS' programme *Sixty Minutes*, broadcast on August 10, 1975. In this she described the Supreme Court's 1973 decision to legalize abortion, *Roe* vs *Wade*, as 'the best thing in the world . . . a great, great decision' and admitted that, as a girl, she 'probably' would have tried marijuana had it been widely used. She also said she assumed her children had 'all probably tried marijuana' since there was 'complete freedom among young people now'. The First Lady's most scandalous admission, however, was the one with which the next day's *New York Times* led its shocked report, under the headline 'Betty Ford Would Accept "An Affair" by Daughter'. Asked what her reaction would be if her eighteen-year-old daughter, Susan, confided that she was having an affair, the First Lady countered: 'Well, I wouldn't be surprised. She's a perfectly normal human being like all young girls.'

Stunned, the (male) interviewer had responded: 'She's pretty young to start affairs.' The First Lady had not batted an eyelid. 'Oh, yes,' Betty responded with pride, 'she's a big girl', and even 'suggested that in general, premarital relations with the right partner might lower the divorce rate'. Asked about the 'pressures on a woman living in Washington', the First Lady had then confessed there were many, 'And it depends on the family, the type of husband you have, whether he's a wanderer or whether he's a homebody.'[114]

No First Lady had ever spoken so candidly on national television, sending moralists of both parties into a tailspin. In Dallas, the pastor of the world's largest southern Baptist congregation declared at a news conference that he was 'aghast'. 'I cannot think', he fulminated, 'that the First Lady of this land would descend to such a gutter type of mentality. For her to offer her own daughter in this kind of illicit sexual relationship with a man is unthinkable. Her own daughter!'[115] CBS was inundated with the most mail it had ever received for a broadcast. Demonstrations took place outside the White House. After watching the programme, the President sighed as he puffed on his trademark pipe. 'Well, honey, there goes about twenty million votes,' he commented, 'but we'll make it.'[116]

'He didn't kick me out of the house,' the First Lady observed laughingly on holiday in Vail, Colorado, a week later, 'but he did throw a pillow at me.'[117]

William Loeb, publisher of the militant right-wing *Manchester Union-Leader*, called Betty 'stupid' and 'immoral'. As the days went by, however, pollsters found that although her pro-choice stance over abortion, premarital sex and mild drugs caused apoplexy among Christian fundamentalists and diehard Republican conservatives, the vast majority of respondents, some 75 per cent, supported the First Lady's right to speak her mind, and hold her own independent views. So did the chief executive of the country. 'The president', announced the White House press secretary in the aftermath, 'has long since ceased to be perturbed or surprised by his wife's remarks.'[118]

Voters were reminded of Eleanor Roosevelt. Though not a feminist, Betty became, overnight, a feminist icon – 'the very best kind of liberated woman', even Betty Friedan commented approvingly.[119]

Others, however, could not bring themselves to approve, nor were they amused. In his memoirs, Ford acknowledged that Reagan's challenge in the Republican primaries was, in part, triggered by the CBS interview, and certainly drew support from the outraged moralists it had provoked across middle and southern states.

In tolerating Betty's candour in such a public way, President Ford was, of course, demonstrating his love, loyalty and genuine respect for his wife. Unfortunately, he was also enabling her in other ways, too – such as her drinking. Ford's defeat in the 1976 presidential election, and their move to California, led to an alcoholic spiral that only ended when the whole family confronted Betty in 1978. To her great credit, she then faced up to the truth, admitting she now accepted she had become an alcoholic, even in the White House, 'because I was preoccupied whether alcohol was going to be served or not'. She went into rehab, and became the most eminent spokesperson for the treatment of alcoholism and medicinal drug addiction in the United States in the twentieth century, as president of the Betty Ford Center.

The two presidents – honest, courageous and devoted to each other – lived together in retirement in Rancho Mirage, in the Coachella Valley, ten miles from Palm Springs, California. One day Phyllis Brown appeared, asking if she could 'drop by for a quick hello with her old flame. Much to her chagrin,' Ford's friend recorded, 'the answer was no. They never spoke, but no doubt he was torn; his days with Phyllis Brown were among his happiest memories. But Betty Ford, understandably, had never been high on the brassy babe' who was married 'at least three times, maybe four', Ford recalled. There was simply 'no way the straightest of arrows would have seen her without telling Betty,' Thomas DeFrank considered, 'and after nearly sixty years of marital bliss, he wasn't about to risk hurting the uncontested love of his life, the woman he described a few weeks before his death as "the greatest of all my blessings".'[120]

Ford, the former isolationist, had become the humblest, least ambitious, most moderate and most tolerant of all American Caesars. He had stabilized the conduct of American power in the world, reassuring its allies and finding common ground with its adversaries – no small achievement in the history of empire. On December 26, 2006, the decorated World War II veteran suffered a fatal coronary thrombosis. He was ninety-three – the oldest man ever to have held the office of president of the United States – and was buried in the grounds of his museum in Grand Rapids.

# CHAPTER EIGHT

# JIMMY CARTER

Mocked, but later respected

Democrat
39th President
(January 20, 1977–January 20, 1981)

## Part One: The Road to the White House

James Earl Carter Jr – named after his father, James Earl Carter Sr – was born on October 1, 1924, in the hamlet of Plains, 120 miles south of Savannah, Georgia. 'Jesus and even Moses would have felt at home on a farm in the deep South during the first third of the century' Carter later wrote, for without mechanization life in rural Georgia was primitive.[1] As Richard Nixon's parents had built a family house in Yorba Linda, California, from a Sears, Roebuck catalogue, so Carter's parents had traded their first home for a similar dwelling, made from a Sears, Roebuck catalogue in Archery, next door to Plains.

James Earl Carter Sr was not tall (5' 8") but was powerfully built, and had been a lieutenant in the Quartermaster Corps in World War I. He had what neighbours enviously called 'the Midas touch': everything he touched seemed to turn to gold, from businesses to agriculture and property. Mixing strictness – especially with regard to punctuality – with after-hours pleasure, he liked to play poker away from home on Friday nights, as Carter's mother recalled, and 'raise hell' at the Elks Club on Saturday, where 'he would dance with most of the pretty women in our crowd'.[2]

Jimmy Carter, the eldest of James Earl Carter Sr's four children, idealized his father. Though he loved his son, Jimmy's father did not idealize Jimmy, however – indeed he mockingly gave him the ambiguous nickname 'Hot'. This was short for 'Hotshot', which aptly captured the boy's diminutive size and precociously righteous ego. It was a nickname that would stick to Carter all the way to college and beyond.

'Hot' was still only 5' 3" tall when he left high school, and weighed only 121 lb. He was determined, nevertheless, to leave Georgia and enter the US Navy, despite never having seen the sea, much less spent time afloat. His father spent two years working on the local congressman to support Jimmy's application to go to the naval academy at Annapolis. Eventually, having cooled his heels for a year at junior college in Archery, then another year at the Georgia Institute of Technology studying engineering and other subjects he would need, Carter was admitted to Annapolis. By then, the summer of 1943, America had been at war for almost two years and 'Hot' had grown to his full height – 5' 9" – with unusually thick lips and wide mouth, a permanent toothy smile, thick cornfield-blond hair, and still weighing less than 130 lb.

'Hot' Carter's self-confidence, for an eighteen-year-old peanut farmer's son, none of whose male family had ever finished high school, let alone college, and who himself had never before been East, was astonishing. It certainly irritated his seniors, resulting in hazing that bordered on savagery as they attempted to put him 'in his place' and wipe the smile off his face.

The hazing did not succeed. Carter had encountered similar confrontations for several years already, some of them potentially lethal. As a sixteen-year-old, for example, he had been physically assaulted for insisting that a certain farmer not be awarded the federal soil-conservation payment he expected. 'I was meticulous in my work' (as a part-time crop-planting surveyor on behalf of the government's Agricultural Adjustment Administration) Carter later maintained, proud that the area supervisor had upheld his calculations. Given that his own grandfather had been murdered as a result of just such a local 'disagreement' (over ownership of an office desk), however, it had been foolhardy for Carter to insist. He was 'relieved', he later admitted, when the next planting season came and he departed to college, thus avoiding a second murder in the family.[3]

Carter's moral rectitude was impressive, the sign of a fierce and unyielding determination, despite his small size. Having been whipped many times by his father as a child he did not object to the tradition of hazing at Annapolis, which he did not take personally; yet his failure to recognize or seek to alter the effect of his priggish, righteous attitudes upon others would become an Achilles heel in someone so otherwise gifted.

The Annapolis Class of '47 graduated in 1946, with Carter having already served aboard the battleship USS *New York* on coastal escort duty in 1944, then aboard the battleship USS *Wyoming*, and finally being allotted, on graduation, a berth on the bruised battleship USS *Mississippi*, veteran of the war in the Pacific. With President Truman's decision to drop the atom bomb and the ending of the war in the Pacific, however, a large part of the rest of the American fleet was mothballed, and Carter became, as he put it, 'most disillusioned with the navy and the military in general'.[4]

According to one classmate who later became a doctor, Francis Hertzog, Carter was 'a loner' unable or unwilling to form 'close intimate friendships'. In retrospect Hertzog saw this as a sign of strength, not weakness. Though genial in his general outlook and behaviour, Carter 'didn't need' people to support 'his own ego and personality – he had a very strong character'; indeed Carter already demonstrated at Annapolis outstanding leadership ability and a rare, analytical mind that he remained bent on putting to practical use, like his father. But was the contracting post-war US Navy the appropriate place, or was there another, more challenging platform? 'Maybe once in a thousand years,' Dr Hertzog mused later, 'a person comes along who will have the control of their mind and utilize it to the extent he can his.'[5]

Carter seriously considered resigning from the navy. His application for a Rhodes scholarship to Oxford was, however, rejected by a committee of former Rhodes scholars at the final screening interview. It was, Carter later maintained, the first of only two great 'failures' he was willing to acknowledge in his life before he became president. Typically, Carter blamed the committee; after all, he complained, he had answered correctly and fully 'every question they could think of', from current events to nuclear physics. Never having been to Oxford, Carter could not understand how the successful student, who declared he had zero interest in anything after the death of Elizabeth I in 1603, would be more at home amidst Oxford's ancient spires than himself. On the rebound, though, he applied to join the US Navy's submarine service.

This time, Carter's application – in both senses – succeeded. Following a simple wedding to a local Georgia girl in Plains, Georgia, and then submarine training in New London, Connecticut, the young lieutenant served long tours of duty aboard the USS *Pomfret*, a three-year-old 1,500-ton Baloa-class diesel-electric submarine. In one storm he was swept thirty feet off the conning tower, but miraculously landed on the deck, adding to his sense that Providence was on his side. He claimed to enjoy the claustrophobic isolation of life below sea level, where his leadership skills – a powerful intelligence, absolute confidence in his ability, and ease in getting along with a small team of colleagues and subordinates while maintaining a consistent personal reserve – were honed. Like his father he looked after his men – 'Watch it, these are my engineers' was the tag line given to him – and like his father (who had several hundred tenant farmers working on his various lands) he asked that they trust in his professionalism, in return for his own trust in them. He was subsequently assigned as engineering officer to a brand-new diesel-electric submarine USS *K-1*, later named the *Barracuda*, launched and commissioned in 1951, becoming over time its executive officer and 'Qualified for Command of Submarine'. When no command ensued, the following year, however, he applied for service in the US Navy's futuristic nuclear-powered submarine project, requiring special interview by legendary Captain Hyman Rickover, generally considered the most abusive commander in the navy. Rickover accepted him in October 1952.

Again, Lieutenant Carter made no friends, but was respected for his professionalism in carrying out his duties in a perfectionist environment (Rickover's famous 'Why not the best?'), as the US Navy set about modernizing its submarine fleet in the frigid waters of a Cold War growing ever colder.

Rickover proved a stern taskmaster, but prized his elite team. Carter was posted to the US Atomic Energy Commission in New York, then Washington DC, to help develop the navy's first two nuclear-powered submarines, following the laying down of the USS *Nautilus* (whose keel had been laid by President Truman in June 1952) and the USS *Seawolf*, a 337-foot vessel with thirteen officers and ninety-two enlisted men, whose engineering officer Senior Lieutenant Carter was slated to become.

When commissioned, the *Seawolf* would break the world record for continuous submersion, as well as achieving speeds of more than twenty knots under water – but Lieutenant Carter would not be aboard. In July 1953, he was summoned to Plains, Georgia, where his father, who had been appointed to the seat of a retired Democratic

Georgia state legislator, was unexpectedly diagnosed with terminal pancreatic cancer. He was fifty-eight.

Jimmy Carter was present in the room in Plains when on July 23, 1953, his father exhaled his 'last terrible breath'.[6]

'I was at the pinnacle of success for a young officer of my rank', Carter later recalled, certain that he could 'attain the navy's highest rank'.[7] The brief compassionate leave he spent at his father's deathbed in rural Georgia raised, however, the uncomfortable question whether God had in store for him a different challenge: namely that he should resign his commission and save the family agribusiness, comprising over 5,000 acres of land, stores, houses, warehouses and other buildings, which in his will his father had instructed should be divided up, so that they could more easily be sold off.

Jimmy Carter's wife, Rosalynn, had been proud to become the wife of a deep-diving, ambitious submarine officer; indeed they had barely revisited Plains in the past seven and a half years. She was understandably 'shocked and furious a few days later' when Lieutenant Carter, returning to Washington, told her he was set upon resigning from the US Navy and returning 'home'.[8] 'She almost quit me' Carter confided forty years later.[9] As in a biblical saga, Jimmy Carter's brother, aged sixteen, was also distraught at his older brother's decision to return. 'I was mad as hell' Billy admitted later.[10] Captain Rickover – embroiled at that time in a bitter struggle to be made an admiral – was also angry at losing one of his chosen disciples, and damned Carter's resignation of his commission as 'a breach of loyalty'.[11] The move to Plains thus proved traumatic. 'I became more and more dejected', Rosalynn recalled. 'I didn't want to live in Plains. I had left there, moved on, and changed . . . I thought the best part of my life had ended.'[12]

In fact the best part was beginning. 'Miss' Lillian, Carter's mother, was delighted. 'He had to come back', she later made clear. 'Everything we had was on the line.'[13]

Back in Plains, aged only twenty-nine, Carter turned out to have inherited his father's Midas touch, collecting over time the sums owed to his father, rationalizing the family's land holdings and properties, and above all investing in mechanization of the peanut business. He encouraged his mother to leave Plains, and forced his wife to overcome her shyness. Finally, in 1962, while serving as chairman of the

Sumter County school board, Carter was asked to run for Congress for the district.

He said no, having calculated he had no chance of winning; moreover, if he did win, a seat in Congress would take him away from his business. Soon afterwards, however, having been halted in his attempts to modernize the local educational system, he decided to swallow his dislike of most politicians and to stand as prospective Georgia state senator, under new rules of direct election.

In rural Georgia, which lagged almost a century behind the rest of the country, electoral felony was still endemic. Ballot boxes were routinely stuffed, non-compliant white voters were intimidated, while black voters were simply excluded, on pain of death. Though popular in his county, and though he won in lawful votes cast, the former nuclear submarine engineer lost the special primary.

With his wife's backing, Carter – who had witnessed in person the fraud being openly and unapologetically perpetrated at several voting stations – contested the outcome. More than 10 per cent of registered voters in the worst-affected county signed his petition declaring the state Senate race, like its predecessors, to have been cooked. To everyone's astonishment, after initially being rebuffed, and despite ongoing threats against his life and property, Carter succeeded – the *Atlanta Journal*, and then local radio and television news, reporting that 'every election law in the book' had been violated.[14] Having won his lawsuit, Jimmy Carter thus claimed his rightful place in the Georgia state Senate at the eleventh hour. He later said 'If I have one political attribute as the cause of my success, it would be tenacity.'[15]

Tenacity was certainly needed. Not only was southern politics a 'dirty business', as Carter's wife – fearful of threats to burn down their peanut warehouse – described it, but the issue of desegregation in schools and colleges was reaching its climax. President Kennedy had been reviled for his civil rights speech when enforcing the admission of black students to the University of Alabama. Lyndon Johnson's successful 'Great Society' Civil Rights Bill had been followed by a backlash: the rise of the white Republican right under Senator Barry Goldwater (using 'states' rights' as a code word for anti-integration). Even Carter's own father opposed integration (though dying in the arms of his loyal black nurse). Democratic state senator Jimmy Carter nevertheless plunged into the vortex of the defining issue of his age, and announced he would run for governor on a platform of civil rights.

It proved a mistake. Though Carter campaigned tirelessly as a fiscal conservative and moderate, he lost to the openly racist Lester Maddox. Denied a bed in the governor's mansion, Carter gave way to despair ('acute reactive depression' in the words of his friend, aide and biographer, psychiatrist Dr Peter Bourne). He was rescued by his sister Ruth, a fervent Baptist. Though dismissed from her job as an English teacher for talking exclusively about God, her impact on her older brother, at a moment of profound personal crisis, was seminal. Carter 'reassessed' his relationship with God and became a born-again Christian. It was the turning point in his life.

Accepting defeat and proselytizing for the Baptist missionary movement in Pennsylvania and Massachusetts as a 'witness' for Christ, Carter not only discovered the joy of helping make other people's lives 'more enjoyable' through direct Christian teaching in 1968, but was gradually able to integrate his evangelical dedication into renewed political ambition – namely to stand again for the Democratic nomination for governor of Georgia in 1970.

This time the tide began to run with Carter. On television and on radio the fair-haired, blue-eyed candidate with big lips came across well. In person, his charisma was mesmerizing as he radiated integrity, high intelligence and complete conviction. Even his most hostile political critic in Georgia considered Carter 'as good a campaigner as anybody you've seen in the last twenty-five or thirty years in American politics. One-on-one, he's probably as convincing as anybody I've ever seen.'[16] With opinion polls showing him ahead of his rivals – including the former governor, Carl Sanders, who was standing again – money flowed in from the very 'special interests' that Carter condemned as a populist.

Carter duly won the Democratic Party's gubernatorial nomination. On a platform of government reorganization, tax reform, open government, racial harmony and protection of the environment, the peanut farmer went on to win handily against his Republican rival in November 1970.

Reorganizing Georgia's staggeringly diffuse government bureaucracy, increasing its revenues, reforming its crony-run judicial system, and leaving a healthy surplus at the end of his four years in office,

Jimmy Carter proved a model governor of his state. In his inaugural address he had unabashedly announced 'The time for racial discrimination is past', and since Georgia then practised what its governor preached, Jimmy Carter was widely applauded as the embodiment of the 'New South'.[17]

Carter's eyes, however, were on a higher prize. In 1972, halfway through his gubernatorial term, he made a quiet bid for the vice-presidential post, correctly seeing himself as a politician who could deliver a healing New South to the Democratic Party's presidential ticket. He was thus mortified when George McGovern, the victorious Democratic anti-Vietnam War nominee, failed to choose him as his vice-presidential running mate at the party's National Convention that summer. Instead, McGovern chose Senator Thomas Eagleton, without doing a careful background check. When Eagleton was found to have a medical history of depression, requiring hospitalization, and had to drop his candidacy, McGovern still did not take Carter but chose Ted Kennedy's brother-in-law Sargent Shriver, who had directed the Peace Corps but had never been elected to anything. McGovern and Shriver were then trounced by President Nixon, 521 to seventeen in the Electoral College, and 46.6 million to 28.4 million in votes cast.

Disappointed by McGovern's snub, Carter vowed never again to try for second spot. 'You have to sidle up to people,' he explained, 'and I don't like that.'[18] Emboldened by a loyal coterie of enthusiasts who saw him as a new JFK, he began preparations for a personal march on Washington and the White House. He could be unabashedly acerbic, alongside his positive personality. Richard Nixon, especially, aroused his scorn. 'In 200 years of history,' he remarked following revelations about the Watergate break-in but before the 'smoking gun' tapes were made public, 'he's the most dishonest president we've ever had. I think he's disgraced the presidency. I'm a long-time Nixon hater from way back', he confessed. 'I lived in California when he ran against Helen Gahagan Douglas. It's not in the nature of that man [to resign]' he judged – rightly. But hanging on to the Oval Office would do Nixon no good; Nixon would be 'impeached', he was certain. 'I think the evidence is there ... the accumulated impact of a dozen culpable acts.'[19] When asked by the New York Times reporter Scotty Reston what he himself planned to do when his gubernatorial term ended

1. President-elect.
Franklin Delano Roosevelt, Democratic governor of New York, November 1932.

2. On the battlefield. President Roosevelt visits US troops in North Africa, 1943 – the first president to appear on the battlefield since Lincoln.

3. At the summit.
FDR confers with fellow Allied war leaders Churchill and Stalin, Yalta, January 1945.

4. Victory in Europe. President Harry Truman arrives in Berlin after the German surrender, 15 July 1945.

5. Potsdam. Truman studies his Soviet counterpart.

6. Dividing the spoils. Truman presides over the Potsdam conference.

7. Ike and Mamie.
Lieutenant Dwight D. Eisenhower and Miss Doud on their wedding day,
Denver, Colorado, 1 July 1916.

9. Korea.
President-elect Dwight Eisenhower
inspects UN troops, November 1952.

8. D–Day.
Supreme Commander
General Eisenhower
briefs US troops before
the invasion,
5 June 1944.

10. Sputnik.
President Eisenhower
and Vice President
Nixon humour
Premier Khrushchev
on his visit to the
Oval Office, 1958.

11. War in the Pacific.
Lieutenant John F. Kennedy skippers PT 109, Tulagi, Solomon Islands, 1943.

12. PT 109.
Skipper John F. Kennedy and his crew, shortly before their ship was sunk in the Blackett Strait.

13. The torch is passed. President Kennedy's inauguration on 20 January 1961 excited worldwide attention.

14. 'Ask not what your country …' Flanked by a former and two future incumbents, the 35th president holds forth.

15. Missile Crisis. President Kennedy works in the Oval Office, 1962.

16. Assassination.
The body of the murdered 35th president lies in state in the Capitol Rotunda, November 1963.

17. Vietnam.
As commander-in-chief,
President Johnson makes a
surprise visit to the battlefield, October 1966.

18. Debacle.
The 36th president listens to
a tape sent by his son-in-law,
a marine serving in the quagmire
of Vietnam, 1968.

19. Treason.
The would-be 37th president promises to support President Johnson in peace
negotiations over Vietnam, 1968.

20. Disgrace.
Flanked by the First Lady and his daughter Tricia, President Nixon announces
his historic resignation, 9 August 1974.

21. Pardon.
Dooming his chances
of election, President Ford
pardons his predecessor,
Oval Office,
8 September 1974.

22. Exit Vietnam.
A US Navy helicopter
evacuates the last personnel
from the American Embassy
in Saigon, 29 April 1975.

23. A winning smile.
Lieutenant Jimmy
Carter, US Navy,
on his wedding day,
7 July 1946.

24. Camp David Accord.
President Carter takes President Sadat and Prime Minister Begin to Gettysburg, 10 September 1978.

25. Hollywood actor. Ronald Reagan's movie career earned him the title 'the Errol Flynn of the B's' – *Santa Fe Trail*, 1940.

26. Activist. Reagan's anti-Communist career began early. Here he testifies before HUAC, Washington, 1947.

27. 'Mr Gorbachev, tear down this wall!' President Reagan in Berlin, 12 June 1987.

28. Navy combat pilot. Nineteen-year-old Lieutenant George H.W. Bush, in his TBM Avenger, South Pacific, 1944.

29. Desert Storm. President George H.W. Bush spends Thanksgiving with his troops in Iraq, 1990.

30. End of an empire. Congratulating President Gorbachev on the end of Soviet occupation of Europe, 1991.

31. The man from Hope.
The youngest-ever ex-governor of Arkansas,
Bill Clinton, with his wife Hillary, 1982.

32. Peace in Bosnia.
After a difficult start, President
Clinton proved an able peacemaker,
ending the war in Bosnia, 1995.

33. Democracy on trial.
In January 1999 William
Jefferson Clinton became
the first president to be
impeached since 1868.

34. Mission accomplished. President George W. Bush announces victory in Iraq, aboard USS *Abraham Lincoln*, 2003.

35. End of an era. The 44th president bids farewell to George W. Bush outside the US Capitol, 2009

(Georgia governors could not run for office in consecutive elections), he stunned the *Times'* editorial board by declaring 'I plan to run for president.'[20]

No sooner had he left the Georgia governor's mansion in January 1975 than Carter did just that, hoping as he did so that Senator Ted Kennedy of Massachusetts, the best-known Democrat in the country, would continue to sit out the quadrennial contest.

Carter's prayers were answered and Ted Kennedy did not enter the 1976 race. In a field of mediocrities Carter was initially unknown; in fact, at the National Press Club in Washington in December 1975, one editor was quoted saying 'Carter? Running for president? Nobody's ever heard of him. It's a joke.'[21] Carter soon made up for this on the campaign trail, however. Short in physical stature he might have been, but he towered above his rivals, Birch Bayh, George Wallace, Fred Harris, Morris Udall, Lloyd Bentsen, Henry Jackson and other presidential wannabees. Sharp in intellect, politically focused, and driven by determination and strong religious faith, he proved a formidable opponent. Boasting a commendable earlier career in uniform, a highly successful career in business and stellar current performance in state lawmaking and governance in the New South, he possessed outstanding credentials as a presidential candidate.

Wisely, Carter chose not to run against the interim president, Gerald Ford, but against the image of Ford's disgraced predecessor, Richard Nixon. Carter's election mantra became: 'I will never lie to you.' Time and again he reinforced his oath. 'If I ever tell a lie, if I ever mislead you, if I ever betray a trust or a confidence,' he would state, 'I want you to come and take me out of the White House.'[22]

Ford's Republican image of honesty and healing took some of the wind from Carter's planned sails, since both men were at heart conservative moderates, but here the former governor of Georgia was rescued by none other than the former governor of California: Republican Ronald Reagan, who month after month, from one state primary election and caucus to the next, hammered his party colleague from the right – and right on to the floor of the Republican convention. Thus, although President Ford emerged the ultimate Republican nominee, he was left with only a few post-convention weeks to repair the damage and fend off the challenge posed by Carter and his running mate, Senator Walter Mondale of Minnesota.

Ford managed to cut Carter's lead in the polls from twenty points to a dead heat, but there was insufficient time to reverse it. When, in the second presidential debate, Ford made a serious error in discussing Soviet domination of eastern Europe, Carter was able to exploit the gaffe and keep Ford in his sights as they approached the winning post. This, despite Carter's own gaffe when giving an interview to *Playboy* magazine.

Carter's inner strength was his born-again Christian religion. In a secular country founded upon a constitutional division between church and state, however, Carter's Baptist zeal had become the source of considerable anxiety among Catholic voters and non-Baptists. At the end of an unwise *Playboy* interview designed to prove he was not a religious fanatic, Carter went too far. Just as he was leaving the journalist's office, he attempted to show his independence of mind by taking direct issue with the teachings of Jesus. 'Christ said, "I tell you that anyone who looks on a woman with lust has already committed adultery."' As the former Governor pointed out, this was ridiculous, in fact, since taken literally it set 'impossible standards for us'. Like the majority of heterosexual men Carter himself had 'looked on a lot of women with lust; I've committed adultery, in my heart many times'.[23]

Carter's point went grievously awry; indeed it caused a sensation in cold print. As an evangelical Christian he was already unpopular amongst Jews. They liked his references to the Old Testament well enough, but not to the New. After the *Playboy* interview – gleefully distorted by a post-Watergate national press, dizzy with its new power to ridicule, even bring down a politician – Carter found himself being denounced by others, too – even fellow Baptists. Although most voters, in the end, chose to overlook the gaffe, it did raise the question of whether the nuclear submarine officer, peanut farmer and Georgia legislator was really up to the searing business of national politics, in a 'take no prisoners' age of journalistic muckraking and political smearing.

Exhausted, but still wearing his red 'good luck' tie, he watched television in Atlanta, Georgia, on election night, November 2, 1976, as Massachusetts, which had eluded him in the Democratic primary, fell into the Carter column. At 3.30 a.m. the next morning the state of Mississippi was conceded by Republicans, giving Carter the necessary

Electoral College numbers he needed to take the White House. He had won – just.[24]

## Part Two: The Presidency

True to his populist mantra, Carter insisted on becoming, after a brief inaugural speech and lunch in the Capitol, the first president in modern times to get out of his armoured limousine and walk on foot to the White House, accompanied by his wife. In addition he decided to send their youngest child – nine-year-old daughter Amy – to a local public school, Stevens Elementary.

These symbolic gestures were carried out with absolute sincerity on his part, determined as he was not to allow pride to turn his head. He banished the playing of 'Hail to the Chief' at official appearances, insisted on being driven in a sedan rather than an armoured limousine, and even invited his wife to become the first ever First Lady to sit in on the president's meetings, even cabinet meetings, as an adviser. At special 'town meetings' with ordinary citizens he tried to make every American feel he or she also had equal access to his decision-making.

An outsider from the South he might be, but Carter was equally courageous in the issues he proposed to tackle. Though he had long since left the US Navy, he was now commander-in-chief. 'I don't care if all one hundred of them are against me,' he snapped, when told that the majority of senators opposed a pardon for Vietnam War draft evaders. 'It's the right thing to do.'[25] And the day after the inauguration, January 21, 1977, he simply did it, signing an executive order to that effect. He also began the arduous process of preparing new legislation on a whole raft of issues, from health and welfare reform to energy conservation. The political missionary was up and running.

Initially the public responded well to Carter's new democratic approach. By March 1977, his public approval rating was the highest any president had enjoyed in the aftermath of inauguration since World War II. No empire, however, operates successfully without a measure of arrogance and pride; indeed these had been considered virtues at the height of the Roman Empire, replete as it was with monuments, arches, games, a Coliseum and Triumphs honouring victors of foreign wars (who were required to have killed at least 5,000 enemy soldiers in battle). Now, by contrast, the American Empire had as president a former navy lieutenant who immediately *pardoned* those who had refused to fight in such wars! Worse still, in the eyes of Washington insiders, he showed scant respect for senators, congressmen and even the number three in line to the presidency: the Speaker of the House of Representatives, and fellow member of the Democratic Party, Tip O'Neill.

O'Neill, in confidence, had warned the president-elect during the transition not to treat Congress as he had the Georgia legislature, namely going over the heads of elected representatives to the people. Carter said that was exactly what he was proposing to do. 'Hell, Mr President, you're making a big mistake' O'Neill had responded.[26] When Carter assigned O'Neill 'the worst seats in the room' for the pre-inaugural gala at the Kennedy Center, O'Neill was outraged – but the insults continued. 'Hell,' the corpulent Speaker complained when only coffee and a roll were served for the first congressional breakfast at the White House, instead of a full English meal, '*Nixon* treated us better than this!'[27]

The main course was the same. Crucial to the relationship between president and Congress was the liaison official whom the president selected to act as go-between. Carter's insistence, against all protestations, on appointing a Georgia friend, Frank Moore – a dud who was deeply unpopular on the Hill – was seen as a shot in the foot. 'I knew the Carter administration was finished the day I heard Moore was to be in charge' said the very man Carter had asked to head up his transition planning team, Jack Watson.[28] 'It immediately signaled the Congress that this was a bunch of amateurs,' commented another, an experienced Georgia congressman.[29] Tip O'Neill confided later that relations between the two supposedly allied strongholds were, as he put it, 'like a bad dream'.[30]

Had Carter been able to appoint and lead a tough and capable imperial team at the White House, he might just have got away with his treatment of Congress, especially by spinning the media to maintain the public support he was counting upon. But to the dismay of veteran politicians, he refused to appoint a chief of staff at all. 'I never wanted to have a major chief of staff between me and the people who worked for me', he later explained. 'I have always wanted to have a multiple, perhaps as many as ten people who had direct access to me all of the time without having to go through an interim boss . . . I don't even mind if those ten or twelve people are incompatible with each other.'³¹

This 'spokes of a wheel' approach to command (as Carter called it), with himself at the hub of a diffused (and often confused) White House administrative command structure, ensured that everyone competed for his attention and imprimatur. Ford at least later saw the error of having begun his presidency that way, but Jimmy Carter was constitutionally unable ever to admit error, then or later. After all, his reasoning went, had not President John F. Kennedy operated without a chief of staff, and made himself the most visible and accessible president since World War II, alongside his young wife? Had not President Lincoln encouraged a 'team of rivals' in his administration, with himself as the arbiter and visionary?

Unfortunately, Jimmy Carter was no Lincoln, nor Jack Kennedy, who had first spent fourteen years as a politician in Washington and had employed a de facto enforcer in his brother Bobby.

Carter's visionary agenda and accessibility did him proud, but his failure to recognize the limits of his own leadership ability in the White House was alarming to his staff. Flooding the Capitol with new proposals, they watched as almost all of them foundered. 'Look, we're trying to do too much' one of Carter's assistants from Georgia, Jody Powell, acknowledged in April 1977, only weeks after the inauguration.³² The president, like Captain Queeg, refused to listen to his crew, however, and the chaos in the White House grew only worse.

The issue Carter most wanted to resolve was America's energy crisis. In 1910 the United States had produced almost 70 per cent of the world's oil. By the time of his inauguration, it was importing 50 per cent. The empire had become an oil addict, which would inevitably affect its global hegemony unless it moved to rectify the situation. 'There was no doubt in my mind that our national security was at stake' Carter would later write, calling the energy challenge 'the moral equivalent of war'.³³

The solution to that war, he maintained, was to cut American dependency, thereby helping also to save the environment. By an open fire in the White House library, wearing a cardigan sweater to emphasize his point, Carter gave his first fireside chat, in the manner of Franklin D. Roosevelt, asking the American people on a freezing day in early February 1977 to turn down their thermostats (after the most severe winter in living memory) to sixty-five degrees Fahrenheit by day; at night, fifty-five degrees would be acceptable. In return he promised a new national energy plan within ninety days.

The president was buoyed by the immediate positive public response. Unfortunately it proved premature, and his plan too green – in the half-baked sense, not the environmental. Linking the main cities, commercial hubs and manufacturing centres of America, US highways were the modern equivalent of Roman roads. Though willing perhaps to wear an occasional cardigan or pullover, few American automobile or truck drivers were eager to trade down for more fuel-efficient vehicles. 'It was like pulling teeth' Carter later described the difficulty in getting Americans to accept that, as privileged citizens of the world's dominant empire, 'they should be ready to make some sacrifices or change their habits' without a Pearl Harbor or similar crisis to shock them into reality.[34] Despite heroic efforts by the House Speaker, Tip O'Neill, Congress failed to rise to Carter's challenge. All too soon the president's bill was stymied by seventeen different committees in the House of Representatives, and five in the Senate. It became clear that, as commander-in-chief, Carter could seek to protect the American Empire and its oil sources, but as president he was almost powerless to alter citizens' behaviour, especially in the buying and use of automobiles.

Carter's appreciation of both the short-term and long-term energy crisis for America was a credit to his intellect, but it spoke little of his realism. Thirty years later the situation would be little different, but in the meantime Carter lamented in his diary on June 9, 1977, how the 'influence of the special interest lobbies is almost unbelievable' as summer came and the Senate crushed the House's energy bill into a proliferation of committees working on the issue, while Republican intransigence was fuelled by the automobile and oil companies urging senators to threaten a filibuster. The acronym for the Moral Equivalent of War was 'MEOW', critics mocked. Carter's ninety-day wonder hadn't worked.

Observers noted Carter was not whim-driven so much as hyperactive, and in a strangely obstinate, wilful way, absorbing huge amounts of written and verbal information via his 'spokes of a wheel' staffing system, but a stranger to the business of commanding a unified political team. In a man who had trained to be a submarine commander this seemed difficult to understand, until analysts asked navy personnel and learned of the special conditions in which underwater vessels operate: comprising small, elite crews, whose few officers worked together without needing a strict hierarchical system to put orders into effect. Moreover, under the moniker 'the silent service', their job was to remain invisible, not only to the enemy but to the rest of the navy and shore.

The White House, however, was not a submarine. Far from working together in a collegial fashion, the president's staff fought like dogs, using deliberate leaks to an all too grateful press for extra leverage when internal methods failed. Moreover, to cap the litany of White House errors and disputes, there was another difficulty: unlike President Kennedy, who had captained a PT boat in combat against the Japanese, Lieutenant Carter had never actually commanded his submarine, and this lack of experience now showed as he gave orders then countermanded them. His promised support to American farmers was quickly dumped, once the fiscally conservative president weighed the costs, which would militate against his efforts to achieve a balanced budget. His promised $50 per person tax giveaway was withdrawn, he abandoned his welfare spending reform as too expensive, and his big, much-heralded tax reform bill, designed to be simpler and fairer to the less wealthy, also stalled in Congress, its provisions contested in every which way.

From 75 per cent initial approval, Carter's rating dipped to below 50 per cent by summer's end in 1977. The public deplored the dissension, bickering and mish-mash legislation coming out of Congress, which retaliated by blaming the White House and demanded if not the head of the emperor, then one of his henchmen. The director of the White House's Office of Management and Budget (OMB), Carter's close friend Bert Lance, was thus targeted by the Democrat-led Congress. On September 21, 1977, the president fed the innocent Lance to the lions – 'Probably one of the worst days I've ever spent', Carter noted in his diary.[35] But the sacrifice led to no amelioration, and by the end of the year, noting the rise in unfavourable impressions of the president from 6 per cent to more than 30 per cent of poll respondents, *Time* magazine described the two most common explanations: 'that Carter had not lived up to his promises and seems unable to get things done'.[36]

The political commentator Victor Lasky was far more trenchant: 'Rarely in the history of the Republic has there been an occupant of the Oval Office', he wrote unkindly, paraphrasing Winston Churchill, 'who demonstrated so quickly an inability to conduct even the simplest affairs of state.'[37]

What had gone wrong? James Schlesinger, the man Carter appointed to head up his new Energy Department, probably summed up the problem best. Jimmy Carter was, Schlesinger later noted, 'an instinctive reformer, not a calculating one'; he had 'blundered' into Washington on a magic carpet, feeling 'he had this relationship with the American public that would transcend the need to get along with the traditional power centers'. In addition, there seemed to be something about the president that the press did not *like* – though Schlesinger was unable to explain why, in a leader so patently sincere, and thus the opposite of the arch-villain Richard Nixon. Even more worrying, that hostility became mutual. Carter called the journalists who had helped bring down his friend Bert Lance 'vultures'. In the media, Schlesinger noted, the president became stereotyped as 'cold and mean' – which was just 'plain wrong' since, from his perspective, Jimmy Carter was a 'kind, considerate warm attractive man'. However, in his missionary zeal the president did take 'on too many things and scattered his efforts', with impossible deadlines. He had 'regarded himself as a man of destiny, in that he had been chosen by destiny – or the Almighty – to be president of the United States. But by the fall of 1977, he was in serious trouble, barely able to keep his nose above water.'[38]

Carter was working eighty hours a week instead of the fifty he had promised, was still without a chief of staff, and continued to rely on a 'spokes of a wheel' White House staff structure in which none of the nine or ten spokes ever met in the same room, let alone agreed on a combined strategy. 'The imperial presidency of Franklin Delano Roosevelt and his successors was no more' commented Victor Lasky, distraught at the sight of the White House deliberately transformed into a cacophonous town hall.[39]

Worse, Carter remained as anxious to avoid the accusation (or sin) of running an 'imperial presidency' abroad as well as at home. To Schlesinger the president had confided his hope that 'in my administration I will be able to put our relations with the Soviet Union on the same basis as they are with England'.[40]

The Soviet Union the same as the UK, America's main NATO ally? What could the president possibly mean by such a remark? That he would hold the USSR to the same standards as any western democracy? Or that, thanks to détente, the Cold War was over, in his mind? Bill Moyers, in a television interview with Carter long before the election, had observed that people 'have more doubts about your perception of reality than they do about your integrity'.[41] It was a profound insight.

The SALT I arms control agreement with the Russians was set to expire in October 1977; a SALT II was urgently needed, and was more or less ready to be signed when Carter took over the presidency. To assist him in dealing with foreign affairs, he appointed two highly competent but competing individuals, Cyrus Vance, a 'dove', as Secretary of State, and Zbigniew Brzezinski, a 'hawk,' as his national security adviser. But if Carter hoped he could thereby be both liberal and conservative on the world stage, he was to be cruelly educated. All too soon his plan unravelled, as Carter publicly lambasted Moscow for the trials of human rights activists such as Anatoly Sharansky, while at the same time encouraging Communist China's rivalry with the Soviet Union and refusing to compromise over SALT II treaty provisions enshrining America's nuclear advantage. By the summer of 1977 Leonid Brezhnev, the Soviet premier, was refusing Carter's offer of a summit meeting, raising the spectre of détente evaporating, and producing fury in Europe, where Chancellor Helmut Schmidt of West Germany was driven to exasperation by Carter's approach to imperial diplomacy.

Once again, Carter had allowed himself to speak from moral conviction, incensed at the Soviet arrest of Alexander Ginsburg, Yuri Orlov and Sharansky. By deliberately making himself the spokesman of the American in the street, however, he lost presidential authority, with the Kremlin confused as to the true intentions of the American Empire. It took a further two years to get SALT II signed, by which time it was too late to count upon Senate ratification. (It was never formally ratified.)

Chaired by Carter's vice president, Walter Mondale, the first meeting of the National Security Council had set Panama as one of the two top priorities for the incoming Carter administration, along with the Middle East. Disputed ownership of the Suez Canal had nearly led to world war in 1956 when Egypt's President Nasser seized it from its French and British owner-operators; Carter wished to avoid the same from happening over the Panama Canal, especially since Ronald Reagan had used the issue as his biggest stick in beating – but not defeating – President Ford for the Republican presidential nomination in 1976.

Reagan was intent on keeping America's vital waterway between the Pacific and Atlantic – a 553 square mile strip that had been signed over to the US in a dubious land deal in 1903 – in American hands. By contrast President Carter, as an anti-imperialist, felt that not only should the canal revert to Panamanian ownership in due course, but restitution should be effected in good time. Serious rioting in the 1960s had raised the spectre of armed conflict over ownership, with a Pentagon report indicating it would require 100,000 troops to re-secure the canal in the event of a Panamanian insurgency and seizure. If a renegotiated treaty safeguarded neutrality, security and the passage of vessels from all nations, the president argued, all sides would be satisfied. To his lasting credit, the Carter–Torrijos treaties were not only signed in September 1977, but ratified by the Senate the following year, after a titanic struggle on Capitol Hill and the final ratification vote a cliffhanger. 'I think', Carter admitted in a press conference, 'I would almost equate it with the difficulty of being elected president.'⁴²

If securing agreement over a Panama Canal treaty was tough, securing peace in the Middle East was even more difficult.

The irony of US 'interference' (as Brezhnev called it) in the internal affairs of another nation was that while Carter was willing to pressure the USSR about its treatment of its own and its neighbours' citizens, he found himself unable to criticize Israel's actions without accusations of anti-Semitism within America. Carter had a special interest in Palestine from his long devotion to the Bible, and had visited Israel at Prime Minister Golda Meir's invitation in 1973, while governor of Georgia. His support for the security of Israel had rested on a distant concern to preserve the antiquities of the biblical land, considered as sacred to Christians as to Jews. 'I had no strong feelings about the Arab countries' he explained later. 'I had never visited one and knew no Arab leaders.'⁴³ All this changed once he became president.

Since Israel, having fought four wars of self-creation and survival, seemed adamant it would neither return the territories it had won nor accept a Palestinian state (which the 1947 UN Commission had mandated), the prospect for American mediation – especially in view of the power of the Jewish vote and lobby in US elections – was slight. Nevertheless Carter decided to tackle the issue, which even his staff and advisers considered a 'losing proposition'.[44] He wanted to help Israel achieve lasting security, but he could not see this happening as long as Israel remained wedded to the lands it had conquered in the Sinai, Gaza, the West Bank and Golan Heights – territories it not only occupied by military force, but where it was encouraging Zionists to create expanding Jewish settlements. These would require road corridors from Israel for access, and military protection for each settlement, thus making eventual Jewish withdrawal – as called for in UN Resolution 242 – difficult, if not impossible.

To absorb Palestinians in a Greater Israel, given the fact that Palestinian Arabs outnumbered Jews, would be hard for Israeli politicians to accept; but to withdraw Israeli troops from the occupied territories and agree to a Palestinian nation alongside Israel would be a leap of faith beyond the will of most Israelis, given the vehemence of most Arabs to 'wipe Israel off the map'. Better to keep the upper hand militarily over the neighbouring states of Lebanon, Syria, Jordan and Egypt, Israeli right-wingers like Ariel Sharon and Yitzhak Rabin argued, while expanding Jewish settlements and keeping the dispossessed Palestinians destitute, impotent and as divided as possible.

To President Carter's credit, he foresaw no good coming of Israeli intransigence. Given the US need for oil from the Middle East, it was neither in America's strategic interest nor that of Israel, ultimately, if Israel wished to continue to be supported politically, militarily and economically by the western powers. Palestinians, Carter therefore declared, *must* have a homeland.

Seen in retrospect, Palestinian leaders had made a huge mistake in not accepting the British Peel Commission Partition Plan of 1937, which would have given Jewish settlers 15 per cent of Palestine, with 85 per cent for the Palestinians; they had then made another mistake in rejecting (along with Arab neighbours) the UN Partition Plan of 1947, at the end of the British Mandate, when 56 per cent of the Mandate territory of Palestine was still slated for them.[45] But should those past errors of judgement – the second made at a time when Palestinian Arabs outnumbered Jews by two to one, thus making the division seem unfair – necessitate their permanent enslavement under

Jewish military occupation as the result of war, or as hand-to-mouth refugees in other countries? President Carter wanted for the Palestinians 'the right to vote, the right to assemble and to debate issues that affected their lives, the right to own property without fear of its being confiscated, and the right to be free of military rule', leading to Palestinian statehood – albeit with 77 per cent of the former Arab country permanently ceded to the Israelis, once the Israelis withdrew from the occupied Arab territories.

Prospects for a positive solution in the Middle East did not look good when Carter became president. Nor did they improve when Prime Minister Yitzhak Rabin overreacted to the killing of thirty-five Israelis aboard a bus by a rogue element of the PLO, which sought to represent Palestinian Arabs. Invading South Lebanon, Rabin's forces killed many thousands of innocent civilians – raising comparisons, critics claimed, with Nazi brutality, even concern whether Israel might be seeking more *Lebensraum*, this time in Lebanon. Yet beyond banning the sale of more cluster bombs to Israel, there was little Carter was able to do, given the power of the Israeli lobby in America.

Almost in desperation, once Rabin was succeeded as prime minister by Menachem Begin, another right-wing Israeli, Carter called a summit at Camp David to see if he could at least get a resolution of the ongoing state of war between Israel and Egypt, whose president was Anwar Sadat. Reading the biographies of the two leaders, Carter learned that Begin had been born in Brest Litovsk, Belarus, and had been wanted by the British for mass murder as an Irgun terrorist in Palestine in 1946–7 (responsible for killing 91 people). As leader of the Herut Party in Israel, and advised by his Irgun associate Shmuel Katz, Begin had then become committed to the expansion of the Jewish settlements, especially in Judea and Samaria, rather than a permanent peace treaty (considered illusory) that would secure peace guarantees for the fragile state of Israel.

For his part, President Sadat had *also* opposed British rule, indeed had been imprisoned by the British in Egypt in World War II for helping Hitler's and Mussolini's 'liberating' efforts in North Africa. He too had become a revolutionary, and had later taken part in the Egyptian officers' coup that ousted King Farouk, becoming thereafter vice president to Colonel Nasser. Sadat's decision to attack the Sinai

Peninsula in the 1973 'October War', though it ultimately failed, had made Sadat the 'hero of the Crossing' in the Arab world – a status which, Carter astutely realized, might actually make Sadat strong enough to be able to reverse engines and sign a peace treaty with Israel, if Carter could wring concessions from Begin.

The three days assigned for the Camp David meeting with Sadat and Begin, beginning on September 5, 1978, became thirteen. Only the United States, as Israel's chief supplier of arms and funding, could pressure Israel into concessions that might lead to peace; but given the perceived power of Jewish opinion makers, lobbyists and voters in the US, no American president had ever dared risk the furore (and electoral backlash) that such a Palestinian-oriented approach would entail. Failure of the 'summit' would, Carter's aides warned, feed a growing impression that the president was well meaning but inept.

At Camp David, Begin proved more intransigent than Sadat. In the West Bank – the almost exclusively Muslim and Christian area which Jordan had administered after 1948 but which Jewish Israeli forces had occupied since the 1967 Suez war – the Palestinian Arab population had grown from 600,000 to 700,000, with fewer than 1 per cent Jews. Begin remained fiercely determined to change this. His aim was to increase the Jewish West Bank population from its 1977 level by a hundred times – a demographic strategy that would inevitably inflame Palestinian inhabitants, but if successful would present the world with a fait accompli, thus making a complete Israeli withdrawal politically impossible in the face of Zionist demands that the settlements be made permanent.[46]

The Camp David Accords that President Carter successfully nego-tiated in September 1978 were to bring lasting peace between Egypt and Israel, and rightly won the Nobel Peace Prize for President Sadat and Prime Minister Begin. Americans were awed by Carter's seem-ingly magic peace wand, and his polls rose fifteen points in four weeks; even the *Wall Street Journal* complimented him on his 'inspired leadership'.[47]

Behind the scenes, however, Camp David proved an unmitigated disaster, for although Begin agreed to pull Israeli troops and would-be settlers out of the Sinai, and thus release the still-surrounded Egyptian Army, for the Palestinians there was no improvement. Begin simply reneged on his commitment to stop Jewish settlement and withdraw Israeli military forces from the West Bank and Gaza. As Carter wrote in sadness thirty years later, 'The Israelis have never granted any appreciable autonomy to the Palestinians and instead of withdrawing their military and political forces, Israeli leaders have tightened their hold on the occupied territories.'[48] Belatedly, the president realized he had been 'had'.

As Carter's White House aide and biographer Peter Bourne wrote, Begin had fooled Carter into believing the Israelis had agreed to end all construction of Jewish settlements in the Palestinian West Bank. 'Although the record is clear', Bourne chronicled, Begin had simply twisted the truth to suit his Zionist agenda. 'Begin would later claim, after violating the agreement, that he had meant the building of settlements would be suspended for only three months' – indeed Begin and succeeding prime ministers authorized the settling of more than a quarter of a million Israelis in the West Bank in the thirty years after the accords, despite the express provisions agreed at Camp David for complete withdrawal.[49]

Carter was understandably disappointed as the full import of his failure became clear in subsequent decades. 'With the bilateral treaty, Israel removed Egypt's considerable strength from the military equation of the Middle East', allowing Israel 'renewed freedom to pursue the goals of a fervent and dedicated minority of its citizens to confiscate, settle, and fortify the occupied territories'.[50] For fanatical Zionists this was divine delivery, but for the United States it would prove ruinous, leading to anti-American protests across the Arab world, attacks on American installations and personnel, and mounting threats to America's homeland security. It was, in hindsight, a disaster.

Leadership of a mighty empire rather than a nation, historians noted, requires more than peaceful sincerity. Carter had attempted to act merely as an honest broker between two warring adversaries, not as an American emperor who, by virtue of Israel's dependence on the US for military and economic support, could compel Israel not only to withdraw from the Sinai, but halt its illegal settlement activity in Gaza and the West Bank, and ensure at least a moderate Palestinian homeland in the region. The threat of Soviet expansion in the region had evaporated as Egypt sent home its Russian advisers; indeed there was no Arab state in the Middle East that showed any significant interest in Communism. In the absence of a Soviet presence in the

Middle East, the United States could have acted as the region's impartial guarantor of peace – and oil. Instead, thanks to Camp David, Israel was seen to have formed 'an alliance with America in all but name'.

The consequences were not slow in coming. Other Arab nations, including Jordan and Saudi Arabia, were appalled and refused to cooperate in efforts at a wider, regional peace agreement, which had been Carter's real aim. At the Tokyo G7 economic summit in 1979, Carter was condemned by Chancellor Schmidt and other NATO nations for his 'meddling' in the Middle East that had infuriated Arab oil producers, who lifted oil prices for a fourth time in five months. Oil prices in America rose higher and higher, presaging serious domestic problems for a president who had relied upon popular rather than congressional or party support. With 90 per cent of gas stations in the New York area being closed over the July 4 weekend, people began to wonder 'What in hell is Carter doing in Japan and Korea when all the problems are here at home?' as his senior aide, Hamilton Jordan, told him.[51]

Deemed too soft by conservatives, and too conservative (and confusing) by liberals, Carter's presidency seemed not so much centrist as lacking in cohesion, judgement and direction. Walter Mondale, the vice president, confided he would like to resign since the president did not seem to be representing the Democratic Party any more, sharing 'the view of much of Washington that Carter and his staff were politically inept, incapable of understanding the inner workings of Congress, and unable to project a clear and compelling vision to the public', as Peter Bourne put it.[52] Eventually Mondale told Carter to his face that his approach to the presidency was all wrong.

To his credit, Carter made history by inviting 150 people to Camp David, over eight days, while he listened carefully to their criticisms and complaints. On July 15, 1979, he gave a thoughtful, well-received televised address to the nation, cognizant of the frustration felt by ordinary Americans waiting in gas lines, and focusing on energy as the great test of the nation's will. He then asked his entire cabinet and White House staff to resign.

The White House Massacre, as it was quickly termed, created the opposite impression from the house cleaning which Carter had intended. An air of national crisis now pervaded Washington. The president made Hamilton Jordan his chief of staff, but Zbigniew Brzezinski, the national security adviser, simply refused to take orders from him, and was not alone. As the weeks went by, the president's admired address of July 15 was conflated with the 'massacre' and the sense of crisis; it thereafter became known as 'the malaise' speech.

Malaise, indeed, seemed to afflict the president himself – literally. On September 15, 1979, having overruled the warnings of his entire staff, he ran in a sponsored ten-kilometre race near Camp David, collapsed before the cameras and had to be carried off – inviting every cartoonist in the world to use the incident as a symbol of the president's demise. This despite inflation held down to 6 per cent, while the economy grew at a similar pace and unemployment also stabilized at 6 per cent, as well as a raft of legislation that was finally passing through Congress: bills that dealt with energy conservation, created a Department of Education, accepted a major welfare reform package, provided financial assistance to middle-income students, ensured better funding for schools, and deregulated trucking, railways, banking and communications.

It was too little, too late, and too diffuse. At a lunch at the White House on September 20, 1979, Senator Ted Kennedy delivered his own bad news. Carter's chances of re-election were slight (70 per cent of people polled disbelieved he could win re-election), and Kennedy had therefore decided to run against him for their party's nomination.

Early in November, Kennedy duly prepared the formal announcement of his candidacy. Before he could do so, however, disaster of another kind struck.

The Shah of Persia had chosen temporary exile in January 1979, for 'rest and recuperation'. From exile in Paris the seventy-eight-year-old Ayatollah Khomeini had then flown into Tehran in February. Millions had paraded on the streets. The military had held back, waiting to see what would happen. A group of Marxist guerrillas had besieged the American embassy, only to be chased away by Khomeini supporters. Soon armed revolutionaries loyal to Khomeini were arresting and executing people across the country. Over the ensuing months Mehdi Bazargan's civil government and Khomeini's de facto religious authority had worked in an uneasy tandem, the Iranian government declaring its commitment to the Palestinian cause, reversing the Shah's pro-Israel policy, and yet declaring an equal commitment to good relations with the US. In the streets, however, mobs still rampaged shouting anti-US slogans, in view of its military and economic support for Israel, and demanding the return of the Shah to face trial.

How, in these circumstances, Carter allowed the fabulously wealthy Shah – who had moved his place of exile to the Bahamas, then to Mexico – to visit America for medical treatment is difficult in retrospect to understand. Carter was certainly warned by the remaining staff of the US embassy in Tehran not to do so, but Henry Kissinger and Zbigniew Brzezinski lobbied on the Shah's behalf, and thus contributed to one of the most disastrous decisions of the era (though characteristically neither would ever accept responsibility for it). The Bazargan government gave an assurance there would be no reprisals, but given the state of turmoil in the country, it was an empty promise. The Shah was duly admitted to the Sloan-Kettering Memorial Hospital, New York, in October 1979. Once word of this reached Iran, an armed mob of revolutionaries attacked the US embassy on November 4, this time without interference or objection by government or Khomeini forces. The insurgents took all sixty-three members of the embassy staff hostage, as well as three US diplomats visiting the Iranian foreign ministry that day.[33] They did so, moreover, in the name of Khomeini, demanding that the Shah be returned to Iran to face 'revolutionary justice'.

'Does somebody have the answer to what we do if the diplomats in our embassy are taken hostage?' Carter had asked his staff, presciently, some months earlier. Silence, even on the part of the vice president, had greeted the question. 'I gather not', the president had commented, and delivered his own prophecy. 'On that day,' he'd mused, 'we will all sit here with long drawn, white faces and realize we've been had.'[54]

The day had now come, and Brzezinski had no contingency plan. Carter ordered the US Sixth Fleet, with two aircraft carriers, closer to the Persian coast; but with Ayatollah Khomeini threatening to put the American hostages on trial and destroy the embassy if the US attempted to rescue them, Carter had to admit that, beyond terminating oil purchases from Iran and the freezing of all Iranian assets in the US, he was powerless unless he wished to go to war over the matter. He broke off diplomatic relations with Iran on April 7, 1980, then, on April 11, he told his national security staff he wanted a rescue mission, which the Pentagon had now planned, to go ahead.

Launched as Operation Eagle Claw on April 24, the mission used helicopters from the aircraft carrier USS *Nimitz* to rendezvous in the Iranian desert with the rescue force, ferried there aboard six C130s. Transferring to the *Nimitz*'s helicopters, the rescue force was then intended to land secretly outside Tehran in darkness, and snatch the hostages from their captors the following day.

That the president, a trained naval officer, could have approved such a cockamamie plan said little for his youthful ambition to become chief of naval operations. 'I'll guarantee you something will go wrong' the Secretary of State, Cyrus Vance, warned the vice president and tendered his resignation, to be effective as soon as the operation had taken place. 'It never works out the way they say it's going to work', Vance sighed.[55]

Amid dust storms, the unexpected presence of Iranian military personnel and a catastrophic fatal accident, Carter ordered the mission to be aborted, leaving not only eight American servicemen dead but six abandoned helicopters in the desert, a burned-out C130, and secret documents with the names of all CIA agents in Tehran. As Peter Bourne chronicled, the botched rescue attempt 'compounded the impression of a president impotent in defending the nation's honor against a Third World power'.[56]

The seizure of the American embassy in Tehran was not the only nightmare that afflicted Carter's presidency at this time. Instead of following his cautious prescription for détente with the USSR, he made another disastrous mistake, this time in relation to Afghanistan. The Soviet Union had supplied military advisers and weaponry to the Afghan monarch since 1933, and its Marxist dictator since 1973. In the summer of 1979, Carter allowed Zbigniew Brzezinski to try a new version of the 'Great Game', the age-old imperial contest for supremacy in Central Asia.

Brzezinski's plan was stunning in its stupidity, especially in a period of détente: to secretly provoke the Soviet Union into invading Afghanistan, where their armies would get bogged down in a Vietnam-style quagmire. The US would then be doing 'something', Brzezinski later boasted, 'that had never been done in the entire history of the Cold War . . . actively and directly supporting the resistance movement in Afghanistan, the purpose of which was to fight the Soviet army'.[57] According to the official version, 'CIA aid didn't start until after the

Russian invasion of Afghanistan,' Brzezinski later explained with pride, 'But the reality, which has been kept secret to this day [1998], was different: that in fact President Carter signed the first directive six months earlier, on July 3, 1979, instructing the CIA to give assistance to the opponents of the pro-Soviet Afghan regime. And on that day I wrote a note to the president in which I explained my view that this aid would lure the Soviets into an invasion.'[58]

Operation Cyclone, which President Carter authorized that day, began a major effort to secretly arm and fund the mujahidin insurrection in order to destabilize the Afghan regime and force the Soviets to intervene with more than advisers – just as the US had done in Vietnam in 1964. The killing of a hundred Russian advisers provided the *casus belli*. Wearing Afghan uniforms, the Russians seized Kabul by *coup de main* on December 27, 1979, murdered the Communist president, Hafizullah Amin, and installed a new, more compliant Communist puppet dictator. Under command of Marshal Sokolov, Soviet ground forces simultaneously invaded Afghanistan from the north. Brzezinski was over the moon.

Given that the Russians, however brutally, were intent on modernizing a fractious, feudal Islamic society in Afghanistan through the Kabul government, the United States would have been well advised to stay clear of the imbroglio, having no apparent dog in the fight. Thanks to Brzezinski, however, they did not.

Keeping silent over the CIA's deliberate enticement to invade, President Carter pretended to be shocked and disgusted by the Russian incursion. To the American public and to the world, he announced on January 4, 1980, that he was imposing a punitive grain embargo on the USSR, thus hurting his own highly productive American farmers as well as the Russians. He also decided that the US would boycott the 1980 Olympic Games in Moscow.

'You don't regret it today?' Brzezinski was asked in 1998. 'Regret what?' he retorted. 'The CIA operation was a *wonderful* idea . . . It succeeded in luring the Soviets into the Afghan trap and you want me to regret *that*? The day the Russians officially crossed the Afghan border I wrote President Carter, saying, in effect, "We've now our chance of giving the Russians their own Vietnam."'

In this, at least, he was right. The ten-year Russian war, fought in Afghanistan's mountainous, often impassable terrain, required more than 620,000 Soviet troops, almost 15,000 of whom would be killed, 54,000 wounded, and more than 415,000 fall sick before the Kremlin withdrew. It was, Brzezinski boasted, a decade-long millstone which 'in the end put paid to the Soviet empire'. 'What is more important in terms of world history?' he asked. 'The fall of the Soviet empire – or the Taliban? A handful of hysterical Islamists, or the liberation of central Europe and the end of the Cold War?' When reminded that Islamic fundamentalism was, by 1998, posing a 'global threat', Brzezinski cut the interviewer short with the immortal words: 'Don't be daft! . . . There is no global Islamic threat from the Orient. The notion of global Islamism is utterly stupid!'[59]

Born in Poland and stranded in Canada as a youngster during World War II, when Poland was invaded by the Nazis and then turned into a Soviet Communist puppet state, Zbigniew Brzezinski was a Cold War fanatic. Détente made no sense to him. Instead of seeing a faltering Communist empire that would gradually disintegrate through its own inherent disabilities, he subscribed to the Republican fear that the Soviets were once again on the march and would soon be at the gates of Washington DC and other capitals of the free world. 'The Soviets at that time were proclaiming over and over again', he claimed, 'that the scales of history were tipping in the favor of the Soviet Union: that the Soviet Union would outstrip us in economic performance, the Soviet Union was getting a strategic edge, the Soviet Union was riding the crest of the so-called national liberation struggles. The Soviet Union was moving into Africa, it had a foothold in Latin America.' To him this fully warranted the ditching of détente in favour of a more aggressive American policy, such as support for the Taliban insurgency in Afghanistan and – in 1980 – warnings to the Russians not to send more troops into Poland to crush Lech Walesa's Solidarity movement. '[W]e'll not have détente: we'll have competition across the board', Brzezinski characterized the new Carter Doctrine – a revived Cold War strategy that missed completely the growth of Islamism, and how this, rather than supposed Soviet expansionism, would affect the problem of America's huge dependence on oil.[60]

With détente out the window, unrestrained Israeli settlement activity in the occupied territories, continuing oil shortages and soaring gas prices at home, inflation rising again, the SALT II treaty unratified and the Iran hostage crisis unresolved, President Carter's appeal for each individual American to 'look and say what can we do to make our country great' looked moribund. Carter was now asking Congress for 5 per cent annual increases in defence spending – raised from 3 per cent – while in April 1980 inflation ballooned to 20 per cent, and the Federal Reserve's prime interest rate rose to 18 per cent. Unemployment in some urban areas like Chicago reached 25 per cent.[61] Despite Carter's rightward turn in confronting the Soviet Union, the economic outlook for ordinary Americans looked far bleaker than when Carter took office – playing into the hands of his opponents.

Whether the Carter administration's lurch to the right reflected an inevitable trend in American culture and politics, Brzezinski's obsession with Russian Communism opened the floodgates to Republicans such as Barry Goldwater and Ronald Reagan, especially when the Iran hostage crisis was not quickly resolved.

Brzezinski acknowledged the Iran hostage crisis was 'politically devastating' for his boss, but not for America. For Brzezinski it was of no significance beside America's larger imperial strategy – which he did not see as concerning itself with the rise of militant Islam.[62] If the Soviets could send an army into Afghanistan, might they not also send troops into Iran, he argued. 'Iran would be even more vulnerable to the Soviet Union,' he claimed, 'and in any case, the Persian Gulf would be accessible even to Soviet tactical air force from bases in Afghanistan. Therefore, the Soviet intervention in Afghanistan was viewed by us as of serious strategic consequence, irrespective of whatever may have been the Soviet motives for it.'[63]

Brzezinski's obsession with the Soviet Communist threat thus not only hijacked Carter's peace agenda, but left the president squarely between a rock and a hard place, since Carter believed passionately in human rights, but, compared with diehard right-wingers, was unconvincing in his Cold War rhetoric. His record in foreign affairs had become as convoluted as his domestic efforts, and he could easily be dislodged from his eyrie by a sufficiently right-wing opponent, Republican strategists calculated. Equally, his conservative domestic policies, ditching of détente and increase in military spending made him vulnerable to a liberal Democratic challenger such as Senator Ted Kennedy, Democratic strategists argued in the spring of 1980.

The majority of Americans had rallied patriotically behind their president in the first weeks of the Iran hostage crisis, but the 'long wait' thereafter (including ever higher gas prices) had become a ball and chain Carter could not escape. Jewish voters abandoned him in droves when he instructed his administration to support the UN resolution to dismantle the illegal settlements in the West Bank. 'Either the vote is reversed or you can kiss New York goodbye', Carter's campaign manager warned – and he was right: the president lost the New York Democratic primary (and neighbouring Connecticut) to Senator Kennedy by 16 per cent.[64] With Carter running two White Houses – 'one working on the hostages, the other working on everything else' – and his polls dropping ever lower, it looked increasingly as if the ultimate presidential election contest would be a knockabout between Kennedy and Reagan.[65]

In primary after primary in the spring of 1980, Kennedy excoriated his fellow Democrat from the left, while Reagan hammered him from the right. Carter refused to give in, though, counting on his religious faith as well as his faith in ordinary voters to see him through. Eventually, on the floor of the National Democratic Convention on August 12, 1980, President Carter clinched his re-nomination, but it was a near-run thing. According to most opinion polls he was estimated to be running a staggering 30 per cent behind Reagan with barely two months to close the gap.[66] Carter could only hope that, in an October surprise, he could negotiate the release of the remaining American hostages in Iran, and be seen to have triumphed through Christian patience and dedication rather than loudmouth bravado.

Jimmy Carter's stoicism did him great credit, but his time was up. Reagan had campaigned across the South proclaiming 'states rights' – a code for anti-integration, or racism – and despite the fact that he never attended church himself, he had mobilized widespread support among Christian evangelicals, who now abandoned their devout Baptist president in surprising numbers. In a period of economic distress and international confusion, Reagan's no-nonsense anti-Communist rhetoric – ridiculed for years by East Coast liberals – sounded a clearer note than the president's speeches. Carter's pardon of Vietnam draft evaders still irked right-wing patriots, while Reagan's simplistic calls for tax cuts and further deregulation of trade and industry found receptive ears among lobbyists, funders and voters.

Though a Democrat, Carter had never truly had a Democratic Party base, whether among party organizers, trade unions, congressmen or senators. He had always relied on the nebulous public, who in 1976 had responded to his idealistic promise of honesty after the years of Nixonian deceit, as well as his declared willingness to tackle the problem of energy and oil. But he hadn't tackled them, at least, not effectively – unless gas lines at the pump were considered an effective way of reducing consumption. Even his efforts at governmental reform – streamlining departments, vetoing pork-barrel spending, urging welfare reform – had failed to stop Reagan from urging his supporters to see government as the problem, not the solution, to America's problems.

In previous campaigns, Carter had always been the challenger, not the incumbent. Instead of presenting himself as the confident occupant of the Oval Office in difficult times, calmly setting out a vision of what a second Carter term would bring, he scrapped with Reagan's image as if in a dogfight, attacking him as a semi-psychopath who would 'launch an all-out nuclear arms race' while dismantling Johnson's Great Society; he was a hollow man, a B-movie actor, with stock lines but no substance: a public danger in a hostile world.[67] Against the advice of his staff, but to show the public what he meant, Carter agreed to a televised debate with Reagan. This proved a terrible mistake.

'When it came to understanding the issues of the day, Jimmy Carter was the smartest public official I've ever known', Tip O'Neill reflected later. 'The range and extent of his knowledge were outstanding: he could speak with authority about energy, the nuclear issue, space travel, the Middle East, Latin America, human rights, American history, and just about any other topic that came up.'[68] Intelligence, however, was not the issue: effective leadership and character were. Reagan had spent a lifetime portraying himself on the screen; now, in a single prime-time television duel, he had the chance to disprove Carter's characterization of him – and even Carter's aides trembled at the prospect.

By dint of energetic campaigning the president had by October 19, 1980 effaced Reagan's lead in opinion polls. In fact he was supposedly two points ahead as the debate in Cleveland, Ohio, approached on October 28, 1980. As virtually the entire television audience of the country got to listen to Reagan's slightly gravelly voice and humour, and compare his tall, ageing Hollywood good looks with the diminutive, smiling, smart, self-righteous but tense and sometimes irritable president, the maverick right-wing screen actor was elevated in the public mind to Oval Office status.

Despite everything Carter threw at him, Reagan was composed and difficult to rattle – and for a good reason. Incredibly, the president's secret briefing book on foreign policy had come into Reagan's hands, allowing him to meet every Carter argument or thrust. Carter's attempts to paint his opponent as a loose cannon now failed miserably. 'There you go again' Reagan would sigh, unperturbed, humorous and supremely confident.

'We rushed downstairs and greeted the president and Rosalynn as they came offstage' recalled Hamilton Jordan, Carter's chief of staff. 'How did I do?' Carter asked in trepidation. 'Grasping his hand,' Jordan recounted, 'I exclaimed, "You won, Mr President! You did it!"'[69]

He hadn't, however, as polls soon showed. Even Jordan's own brother admitted in a telephone call that it had been a failure. 'My boy, the Gipper did well' he told Jordan. 'He did better than Carter.'[70] Reagan's summing up had proved especially devastating. 'Looking straight into the television camera with an almost pained look, he asked, "Are you better off than you were four years ago? Is it easier for you to go and buy things in the store than it was four years ago? Is there less unemployment than there was four years ago? Is America as respected throughout the world as it was? Do you feel that our security is as safe, that we're as strong as we were four years ago?"' Jordan afterwards related that he had got Carter to use the same tactic – the so-called 'Misery Index' – against President Ford in 1976. Now it had come back to haunt them, and Carter looked as wooden in the limelight as Ford had done.

As if Reagan's possession of Carter's briefing book and his victory in the single presidential debate were not enough, there was – as in the case of Richard Nixon's sabotage of President Johnson's peace negotiations in October, 1968 – another, even more egregious reason for his success. Frightened of the president producing an 'October Surprise' by obtaining the release of the American embassy hostages in Iran, Reagan had for months used his campaign manager, William Casey, to pursue a secret 'arms for hostages' deal with Iran (which desperately needed weapons, once the Iran–Iraq War had broken out in September 1980). Carter had ruled out a deal on moral grounds, but Reagan had not. Release of the hostages, therefore, would be deliberately held back, Ayatollah Khomeini assured Casey, until after the US election, thus dooming Carter's last hope of beating Reagan.

In the history of US electoral politics there were few examples of such treasonable, yet effective, misconduct in gaining supreme power. Unaware of Reagan's malfeasance, Carter kept pursuing the release of the hostages along conventional diplomatic lines. No deals were made, and the administration waited for the Iranian government to decide. Thus, with the contenders 'neck and neck', as Hamilton Jordan remembered, the result of the election 'was now in the hands of unpredictable fanatics halfway around the world, revolutionaries who hated the United States and its chief executive. If something dramatic happened Monday [November 2] – like the release of the hostages – it would probably allow us to nose Reagan out; a bad signal from the Iranian Parliament Sunday would probably mean Reagan's election.'[71]

The news from Tehran when the president flew back to the White House from Chicago, where he was campaigning, was bad: the Majlis were setting *new* conditions. Casey's secret machinations (he would be rewarded by being made director of the CIA) had worked. On board Air Force One, Jordan recalled, Carter confessed it was 'a hell of a note' on which to end a presidential election, knowing the outcome would not be decided 'in Michigan or Pennsylvania or New York – but in Iran'.[72]

In truth the outcome had already been decided in America – by William Casey. On November 4, 1980, Carter duly lost the low-turnout election, buried by a landslide in the winner-takes-all Electoral College, where Carter managed only forty-nine votes to Reagan's 489.

Carter was gutted. Still unaware of Reagan's treason, the White House continued its efforts to obtain the release of the hostages in Tehran, buoyed by Ayatollah Khomeini's promise they would soon be freed. Even that post-election achievement would be denied Carter, however; he planned, if all went well, to fly to Germany to greet the hostages and be able to get back for the inauguration ceremony, but Reagan's team had promised yet more illegal arms to the Iranians if only they delayed signing off on the deal. Only at 6 o'clock on inauguration morning, January 20, 1981, was the deal finally signed by Iranian negotiators (in Algiers, as the US had broken off diplomatic relations with Iran). When Carter called Reagan to tell him the glad tidings, he was informed that Mr Reagan was still asleep and could not be disturbed. It was a humiliating end to a deeply disappointing, luckless presidency.

## Part Three: Private Life

Only a psychologist could divine the glue that bonded James Earl Carter Jr to Rosalynn Smith, a woman who, as Carter said in 1976 when running for the presidency, became an 'equal extension of myself'.[73] At eighteen Rosalynn was profoundly shy, even antisocial, having no close friends except perhaps Ruth Carter, Jimmy's sister. After one movie date, however, Ensign Carter announced to his mother he'd found the person he would marry: a consort to his own loner personality who would not only keep house for him and bear his children, but be his 'other half' – the only person in the world to whom he would be willing to unburden himself wholeheartedly, completely.

This Rosalynn became. She had been her 'Daddy's girl' until the age of thirteen when her father died, and like Jimmy, she became the older responsible sibling to the three other children in the Smith family. Trim, pretty, smart and neat – and having studied decorating and secretarial duties at Georgia Southwestern – she became a model officer's wife and then a model agribusinessman's wife (she acted as bookkeeper for the growing Carter peanut company). They did everything together, as one. Jimmy's adored mother Lillian had caused him to surrender his naval career to save the family business, against Rosalynn's wishes, but once Rosalynn accepted the career change, the competition between the two women was quickly over. Lillian moved out of the family home, even travelling to India to serve in the Peace Corps, while Rosalynn helped Jimmy run the agribusiness – and run for elective office.

Rosalynn saw her husband's political destiny as others often, in her view, did not. After all, she reasoned, one only had to look at Jimmy's brother, 'Buckshot' Billy Carter, to see how differently 'Hotshot' Jimmy's life could have wandered off course. Raised in the same family, in identical circumstances, Billy became Jimmy's polar opposite: a Republican segregationist who, after leaving the Marines and selling his share of the Carter inheritance, drove a manure spreader for the agribusiness, wasted much of his life as an alcoholic, was twice jailed, scorned the Baptist church (calling it 'a bunch of hypocrites'), used his older brother's name to enrich himself, gave rise to a Senate investigation (Billygate), failed to get elected mayor of Plains, sired six children, and died of cancer at age fifty-one – but was nevertheless known in Georgia as a 'good ol' boy'.[74]

As a faithful Christian, Jimmy Carter never criticized or turned against his brother, however much trouble and embarrassment he caused. Billy Carter represented lack of willpower – and willpower was the defining element of Jimmy Carter's character, the factor that caused others, over time, to follow him in his quest for political stardom. 'All the Carters submerge their needs to his', Carter's psychiatrist friend Dr Peter Bourne noted before the presidential election, starting with Rosalynn, who became Jimmy's backbone when matters looked bleak or they spun out of control, his companion by day and by night, able to read his thoughts, finish his sentences, pray with him, even, at times, bend him to her will (as when insisting he put her in charge of a Mental Health Commission, and allow her to sit in on cabinet meetings).

Whether such a close modern marital bond, in the case of a politician who needed to communicate to *others* his strength of will and authority, was a blessing or proved an impediment is a moot point. In that Rosalynn became Jimmy's rock, she certainly contributed more than any other human being to his rise to power and to his many achievements. But this tightest of bonds also walled him off from the the most important requirement of the US presidency at a time of empire – the leadership of others. For all his ambition, intelligence (Katharine Graham, publisher of the *Washington Post*, considered Carter 'by far the most intelligent president of my lifetime') self-training and moral determination, and for all that he had spent ten years of his adult life in the US Navy, Carter failed to apply the two most fundamental elements of command, at least at a higher national and international level of politics: the need to impose a clear vision that others can subscribe to, and the ability to delegate to others if that vision is to be carried out successfully.[75]

Jimmy Carter was hobbled by the fact that, from childhood on, he was a 'control freak': a term that was launched in the general vocabulary shortly after his inauguration in 1977.[76] It was said that when his son received poor grades in school, he spent a week learning the lessons himself, in order to instruct the child privately and improve his grade – which to Jimmy, not his son, was all-important. (*Why Not the Best?* was the title of Carter's campaign book in 1976.) It was also said that at the White House he not only read mountains of paperwork that an assistant or chief of staff should have first winnowed, but even drew up the precise daily schedule for use of the White House tennis court.

While exemplary in his commitment to his son's education, and to an orderly use of the White House tennis court, these instances spotlight the unfortunate, micromanaging flaw at the heart of Jimmy Carter's gem-like character: a flaw which his devoted, loyal, committed, sincere and caring wife Rosalynn kept from him, as did his uncritical staff.

Flanked by his wife and surrounding himself with his 'Georgia Mafia' on whose loyalty he could depend, the Prince of Plains betrayed, at times, a surprising insecurity, which perhaps reflected his backwoods roots. For all his high intellect, he seemed stilted and uncomfortable with people of equal or greater talent, expertise or facility. In turn this reflected a further, perhaps more significant facet: his failure to mature in the office of president. Almost all his predecessors had, in the course of their tenure in the White House, grown more, not less presidential, from FDR to Gerald Ford. But as his problems mounted, Jimmy Carter seemed to turn more inward than outward, increasingly relying on prayer and Rosalynn's encouragement. He also retreated more regularly to Camp David in his own version of Nixon's bunker mentality – but without Nixon's ability to manipulate, deceive, and magically produce his own swamp rabbit in virtuoso television performances that would reconnect him to the 'silent majority'. Carter's 'malaise' speech became an unfortunate illustration of his misreading of the public's expectations of their president. Instead, many felt his most compelling compact was with Rosalynn, proving to her and to God, not the public, his nobility of heart, his sincerity, integrity and stoic determination. 'There was no way I could understand our defeat' Rosalynn said after it, tellingly using the word 'our'. 'It didn't seem fair that everything we had hoped for, all our plans and dreams for the country, could have gone when the votes were counted on election day.'[77]

Abjuring until it was too late a tough chief of staff and a hierarchical system of command, Jimmy Carter had posed as a democrat, a common man, while acting often as a control-freak – moreover a weak and sometimes misguided one. Seldom if ever did he transmit to his staff genuine confidence in *their* abilities, which could be passed on and down to others in the pyramid of imperial power. Too often he conveyed, in fact, the very opposite: the feeling that, had he but the time, he would do their jobs so much better than they. Incensed at the many mistakes made by the Carter administration and the president's know-all airs, his holier-than-thou hardworking piety and his self-righteousness, the press turned against him. Eventually, so did the voters, his only real constituency.

That a former B-movie actor, with right-wing, often wacky ideas and misconceptions, would be able not only to defeat Carter in 1980, but also to demonstrate thereafter how a president *should* act, in terms of White House leadership, would provide the ultimate demonstration of Jimmy Carter's failure as an emperor.

Spurned by the new president, by the press and even by those subordinates whom he had mistakenly thought of as friends, Carter bought a twenty-acre lot in the mountains of Ellijay, Georgia, building with his own hands a cabin (and its furniture) for himself and Rosalynn. Such humility on the part of an ex-president found few admirers. There were difficulties over his Presidential Library (the mandatory repository for ex-emperors' papers) in Atlanta, and accusations that behind the facade of humility and ordinariness, he was too full of 'self-importance', that the people of Georgia were tired of his 'acting like a stuffed shirt' and 'puffing up like a blowfish'. 'We've always felt a little guilty about palming Carter off on the other forty-nine states,' the political editor of the *Atlanta Journal* sneered in 1983, 'and we don't appreciate having him around as a constant reminder.'[78]

Deeply distressed by his sister's and his mother's deaths in September and October 1983, Jimmy Carter never understood the hostility he provoked in certain people, just as he never understood his own role in the failure of his presidency. Nor, crucially, did Rosalynn, who effaced her humble origins with an unfortunate air of entitlement. Nevertheless, after their two-year self-exile in Ellijay they eventually picked themselves up, dusted themselves off, and thereupon, with Rosalynn at his side, Carter began a new life: devoting himself over the next three decades to peace, reconciliation and volunteer projects that addressed poverty, diplomacy and self-sustaining agriculture.

Carter's work for Habitat for Humanity would show his idealism at its most practical, yet it was his faith and sheer personal courage – physical and intellectual – in the pursuit of peace that would take him to every corner of the globe, from Port au Prince to Pyongyang, Darfur to the West Bank, Eritrea to Cuba, and which would be finally recognized in the United Nations Human Rights Award in 1998, and the Nobel Peace Prize in 2002.

James Earl Carter Jr might have lacked the priceless asset of good luck, and been a failure as an American emperor, but he was far from a failure after he left the White House, transforming the lives of countless people in need across the globe. Rather than be buried at his Presidential Library in Atlanta, or the National Cemetery at Arlington, Virginia, he characteristically asked that when he die, he be laid to rest in Plains, the little hamlet in Georgia he came from. As the eminent Indian scientist Dr Swaminathan remarked reflecting on Carter's relentless post-presidential work for humanity in retirement, Carter is 'the American Gandhi'.[79]

# CHAPTER NINE

# RONALD REAGAN

Later deified – by conservatives

Republican
40th President
(January 20, 1981–January 20, 1989)

## Part One: The Road to the White House

Ronald Wilson Reagan was born on February 6, 1911, in a rented apartment above a bank in the small town of Tampico, Illinois, where his father Jack was an itinerant shoe salesman. Wilson was his mother Nelle's maiden name, and Ronald was chosen as a last-minute substitute for Donald, which a sister of Nelle had used for her own child. Reagan hated it, and asked to be called 'Dutch' after the family anecdote in which his father, looking at the newborn, had said 'He looks like a fat little Dutchman. But who knows, he might grow up to be president one day.'[1]

Jack Reagan was of Irish-American stock, a lapsed Roman Catholic with dark good looks, and a born storyteller who, as Reagan later described him, was 'endowed with the gift of blarney and the charm of a leprechaun'.[2] Neither Jack nor Nelle – a devout, churchgoing Protestant, daughter of American Scots-English parents – had more than a few years' grade school education, and they assumed their children would follow their father (who hoped one day to own a shoe store) as shoe salesmen.

Deeply shy, small as a boy, the last of the Reagans' four children and for many years unaware he was short-sighted, Reagan grew to be tall (6' 1") and an athlete at the high school in nearby Dixon, where the family had moved when he was nine. Helped by his mother, who both acted in plays and recited dramatic passages at her church, he was also a thespian who relished acclaim. 'I don't remember what I said,' he later recalled – or couldn't recall – of his first performance, 'but I'll never forget the response: *People laughed and applauded.*'[3]

The shy Illinois shoe salesman's son who suffered from insecurity and claustrophobia (which later gave him a fear of flying) found himself liberated by applause. Almost everything he would undertake in life, from football to lifesaving to politics, stemmed from an unrelenting determination to earn the music of acclamation.

In 1928, Reagan won a Needy Student scholarship at the tiny Eureka College, Illinois. Washing dishes and waiting tables during term time, and working as a lifeguard in his vacations (he claimed to have rescued seventy-seven people from drowning), he graduated in economics with a C. He was hardly an intellectual, but, like Richard Nixon at Whittier, he was a talented amateur actor, bursting with ambition to play upon a larger stage. His father lost his job in the Depression – rescued only by President Roosevelt's Works Program – while Reagan coveted a career in radio as an announcer. He duly got it, at WOC in Davenport, Illinois. As 'Dutch' Reagan he performed so well he was made sports announcer at a 50,000-watt station, WHO in Des Moines, earning $75 a week. His father gave up work altogether, suffering the ravages of an alcoholism he couldn't beat.

Reagan's skill as a radio announcer, especially his ability to drama-tize in listeners' minds a vivid ball-game from the ticker-tape he was handed, made him an Illinois legend. After paying a visit to a Gene Autry film being shot at Republic Pictures in Hollywood, however, he was smitten by the movie bug. Following a screen test, Reagan received a telegram in April 1937 informing him Warner Brothers were willing to offer a seven-year contract at $200 per week. 'SIGN,' Reagan wisely wired his agent from Des Moines, 'BEFORE THEY CHANGE THEIR MINDS.'

Reagan's mother Nelle, as a stalwart member of the Dixon Disciples of Christ congregation, worried about 'Dutch' going 'to such a wicked place as Hollywood'.[4] By 1941 Reagan was already earning $52,000 per film, and his fan mail was second only to that of Errol Flynn – in fact Reagan began to call himself 'the Errol Flynn of Bs'.[5] He was drafted in August 1941, some months before Pearl Harbor, but obtained defer-ments. Only after the Japanese attack, and finishing a new film with Errol Flynn (*Desperate Journey*), did Reagan report for duty in the Army Cavalry – where, to his chagrin, his poor eyesight caused him to be disqualified for combat duty.

Seconded to Lieutenant Colonel Jack Warner's new First Motion Picture Unit of the Army Air Corps, Reagan rose to the rank of captain, introducing training films and acting as personnel director for the FMP unit.

Joining the Hollywood Democratic Committee, Reagan – an admirer of President Roosevelt throughout the Depression – remained a loyal party member. Putting the skills he'd developed in introducing air force training films to good use, Reagan volunteered as a speech-maker on behalf of Democratic organizations such as the American Veterans Committee, and the 3,000-strong Hollywood Independent Citizens Committee of the Arts, Sciences and Professions, which espoused an anti-nuclear war agenda. Asked in 1946 to stand for Congress as a Democrat, though, Reagan demurred. Not only could he not bring himself to abandon his movie ambitions, but, as East Coast Democrats tore themselves apart in left-wing power struggles and fears of Communist infiltration, he witnessed first-hand mob violence – in Hollywood.

Reagan had never seen combat, but at the Warner Brothers main gate he now did, beginning on October 5, 1945, in what would be called the Battle of Burbank. Striking carpenters fought with competing union workers, with the fate of 30,000 workers and film production in Hollywood held to ransom. Tear gas, chains, pipes and hammers were used, as well as fire-brigade hoses to cool tempers and the violence. So disenchanted did Reagan's boss Jack Warner become by the inter-union saga, he vowed never to vote Democrat again. Once Regan received an anonymous death threat, requiring the studio to issue him with a .32 Smith & Wesson pistol and shoulder holster, he found himself in the same position. As Robert Mitchum remarked, when being threat-ened in a similar fashion by union thugs, 'as an American you can ask me what to do, but damn it, don't *tell* me what to do'.[6]

The threats to his own life by left-wing unionists soured Reagan against liberals for the rest of his life. The Warner Brothers bus, on which he usually commuted to the Warners lot, was firebombed in front of him. As a member of the board of the Screen Actors Union he had become their chief negotiator, and in the fall of 1946, suspecting a Communist conspiracy to destroy Hollywood, he began to inform on his left-wing colleagues, taking the codename T-10, as one of eighteen FBI 'informants' in Hollywood.[7]

Without Screen Actors Guild support, the carpenters' fight even-tually collapsed, and in March 1947 Reagan was voted president of the

SAG, beating Gene Kelly. In 1948 Reagan voted Republican in a presidential election for the first time, casting his ballot for Thomas Dewey. Though Reagan would not formally change his registered Democratic Party membership for several years, he confided to a friend 'I've switched.'[8]

Reagan had sworn he would never 'sink' to television. When his Hollywood acting career tanked, however, General Electric offered Reagan a contract to introduce their weekly CBS television drama broadcast, at a princely salary of $125,000, which he accepted. At his own request, moreover, the handsome new TV host was permitted to tour America giving live speeches in GE's many factories, as part of their Employee and Community Relations Program. The television contract thus gave Reagan two new career boosts: national television name recognition, plus live audiences as a political preacher. Within four years he had spoken, it was claimed, to some 200,000 GE workers, with as many as fifteen speeches a day in company cafeterias, plants and auditoria. One GE executive told him he was 'more in demand as a public speaker than anyone in the country except President Eisenhower'.[9]

Anti-Communist to his bootstraps after the Battle of Burbank, Reagan relished the Cold War; indeed he stood considerably to the right of the Republican in the White House, refusing, for example, to attend the gala which President Eisenhower arranged for Nikita Khrushchev on his visit to Hollywood.

Though Reagan's views delighted his rich friends in California, men like millionaire Walter Annenberg, they drove his first wife to distraction and divorce, and disappointed his liberal acquaintances – especially when Reagan supported the John Birch Society and its political candidates, who were dedicated to getting rid of graduated income tax, social security, and opposed school buses. Reagan voted for Republican Richard Nixon in the 1960 presidential election, and again for Nixon in the California gubernatorial race in 1962. Finally, and irrevocably, Reagan then changed his political registration, later excusing his desertion with the claim that 'I didn't leave the Democrats, they left me.'[10] General Electric, however, also left him, after he refused to tone down the right-wing rhetoric in his speeches to employees. 'Ronnie was devastated', his second wife, Nancy, acknowledged.[11] 'What can I do, Charley,' Reagan begged the chairman of the agency handling the GE contract, 'I can't act anymore, I can't do anything else. How can I support my family?'[12]

The answer, as Senator Barry Goldwater – the most conservative ideologue in the Senate – and others told Reagan, was obvious: seek political office. In an age of increasing celebrity worship, the former movie actor – fondly known as 'the Gipper' for his role in *Knute Rockne: All American* – should set about translating his television name recognition into Republican electoral votes.

Reagan remained reluctant, not only embarrassed by his divorce, which might lead to nastiness in an election battle, but also sensing it was not the right moment, with Nixon trounced in his gubernatorial bid and President Kennedy's popularity growing, not declining. In 1963 Reagan thus made one last, desperate attempt to be a movie actor, in a made-for-TV film called *The Killers*. The film flopped, however, leaving him with only one avenue to money and acclamation: politics.

Communications, especially television, were everything in the modern world, Reagan recognized – as did his financial backers. Reagan's televised half-hour speech in support of Goldwater's 1964 campaign at the Republican National Convention became its high-light, with quotations from Lincoln (Republican) and FDR (Democrat). His ability to mask his right-wing views with folksy humour and deference to Democratic gods such as FDR made him far more acceptable to centrist voters than Goldwater himself. Money poured into the Republican Party coffers.

Finally, in February 1965, Reagan agreed to enter the 1966 California gubernatorial race as a Republican. California had now overtaken New York as the most populous state in the US, boasting nineteen million residents, and an economy estimated to be the sixth largest in the world. For Reagan it would mean overcoming his fear of flying, which he had refused to undertake since 1939 after a traumatic snowbound landing in Chicago, but with medication and therapeutic advice he was prepared to face the challenge. Nancy became his campaign personnel director, while his friends and movie colleagues became his financial backers and fund-raisers.

Reagan was already fifty-four, and had never previously stood for public office. He had no knowledge or understanding of how the California state government worked, or what its obligations were. Though he had backed Democratic and Republican candidates with speeches in the past, his rhetoric had been anti-Communist and anti-federal, with little indication of what he was *for*, beyond patriotism, individual liberty, lower taxes and opposition to government – especially government 'in a distant capital'. To his foes he was nothing but a divorced actor who had been born and raised in another state, and an anti-intellectual who had never been seen with a book (though he read voraciously the funny pages, the newspapers and *Reader's Digest*). Political observers noted, however, that the actor possessed credentials that opponents, in a televisual age, were unwise to ignore.

Like Richard Nixon, Ronald Reagan had an excellent memory for the things he wished to recall, and moreover was able to recall them when speaking extempore. Also like Nixon, Reagan came from a humble background, with an Irish-American father and a tough, devout mother whom he revered, thus upsetting any notion in the voter's mind that Republicans were de facto all snobs. Furthermore, as Richard Nixon parlayed his humble origins into a special relationship with the 'silent majority', so too did Ronald Reagan. Having erected such a broad tent and easily won the Republican nomination, on polling day in the autumn of 1966 Reagan attracted not only a record number of independents but almost half a million renegade Democrats, who liked what they saw as he travelled the state, as well as what he said. Above all they liked *how* he said it; speeches that he scripted himself were peppered with homey remarks that put people at ease, and which harped on basic American values that were for the most part not, per se, Republican or Democratic. Most of all, his old-time values were welcomed by voters appalled by the 1965 summer race riots in Watts, as well as the anarchy at UC Berkeley, the state's largest campus, where the university president seemed incapable of asserting authority.

Reagan beat the incumbent Democratic governor of California, Pat Brown, by almost a million votes in November 1966. Journalists tittered when he insisted on taking his inaugural oath at two minutes past midnight on January 2, 1967, because his wife's pet astrologer, Jeanne Dixon, deemed the timing more propitious. Their mockery gave way to reluctant admiration, however, as reporters watched the former movie actor in his new role. In a nation increasingly partisan – whether supporting sports teams or political parties – Governor Reagan was maddeningly, disarmingly polite. Moreover he was humorous and confident. He was obstinately attached to his core principles, which he drew from his reading of the Constitution (which he liked for its brevity), but was otherwise pragmatic. His ignorance of California politics or state administration did not embarrass him in any way; indeed he had a way of deflecting criticism that would one day merit the name 'the Teflon president'. 'I don't know – I've never played governor before', he would answer a difficult question. Asked aboard a plane how he had overcome his fear of flying, he retorted: 'Overcome it, hell. I'm holding this plane up in the air by sheer willpower.'[13]

Truman had had a sign on his desk: 'The buck stops here.' Reagan had a sign placed over his door that read 'Observe the rules or get out.'[14] He chose key or signature issues to tackle which would set the tone of his governorship and which would be remembered, come the next election. He got the president of UC Berkeley dismissed within days of his own inauguration. He authorized the execution of Aaron Mitchell, a black who had killed a policeman. (Outside Reagan's rented house in Sacramento a candlelight vigil was held, prompting Reagan to say only that he wondered why no bells rang 'every time there is a murder'.[15]) But, ever the lifeguard, he saved the life of a little black girl he saw drowning in his pool during a staff party (his seventy-eighth rescue), and signed into law an abortion bill he did not personally favour. As Martin Luther King was assassinated in Tennessee, then Senator Robert Kennedy in California, and the capital of France erupted in what looked like urban politico-civil war, Reagan remained calm, firm and amazingly upbeat. His ability to pick effective subordinates harked back to his time as personnel officer in the Army Air Corps' film unit, but most of all it was his cool demeanour that inspired his staff – responsible for directing 115,000 state employees – to serve him loyally and leak-free. As his official biographer would write, his governing style as chief executive was, for a man who said very little in meetings and worked short hours in the Capitol, stunningly effective: 'I can compare it only to the phenomenon of the conductor who beats time imperceptibly, often with eyes closed, before a band of players, few of whom even look up from their decks. Somehow, a concerted sound emerges.'[16]

Sending in the National Guard to Berkeley, which had descended into People's Park anarchy, Governor Reagan became a scourge of 1960s' hippies, and increasingly a hero to the right. Yet he was able to get the Speaker of the California Assembly, macho Democrat Bob

Moretti, to work with him on welfare reform. ('Governor, I don't like you. And I know you don't like me,' Moretti declared, 'but we don't have to be in love to work together.'[17])

Step by step, by charm and focus, Reagan appeared to be preparing himself for national, indeed international stewardship. It was noted, for example, how he seemed to fix on even the most elderly statesmen he met, studying them for their comportment, dignity, resolution and distinctive traits. After all, Churchill had made his bowler hat, cigar and romper suit trademark fixtures; why should Reagan not also stamp his personal image on his era? Tall, lanky, with broad shoulders and a short neck requiring specially tailored shirts, he decided he would avoid hats and make do with what his official biographer called his 'pompadour': his immaculate, signature, slicked-back hairstyle.

Democratic politicians, who had done little to keep Reagan in their ranks, excoriated the apostate. 'As a human being and an American,' former governor Pat Brown wrote in 1970, 'I am chilled to the bone at the thought of Ronald Reagan one day becoming president of the United States.'[18] But Brown's political days were over (he never won another electoral office), while Reagan's ascent seemed inexorable – stalled only by his fellow Republicans.

Reagan's contest with President Ford for the Republican Party nomination in 1976, two years after Reagan left Sacramento at the end of his second gubernatorial term (the state limit), came agonizingly close to victory. Reagan's 'Kitchen Cabinet' (as it was later called) told him not to worry, however: Ford's defeat in the November 1976 election, against Jimmy Carter, would leave Reagan as the heir presumptive four years on. And so it proved.

No other Republican candidate possessed Reagan's speaking skills, both live and on television, or his unique temperament as a leader. To the fury of his opponents he seemed unruffled by criticism, patient in adversity, dogged in stating his convictions, and supremely confident he could run America, Inc., if given the electoral support to win the White House as a 'responsible conservative'.

Martin Anderson, who advised Nixon and then Reagan on domestic policy, later characterized Reagan's leadership style as totally different from 'the model of the classic executive who exercised leadership by planning and scheming, and barking out orders to his subordinates'. He was like 'an ancient king or a Turkish pasha', Anderson described, 'passively letting his subjects serve him, selecting only those morsels of public policy that were especially tasty . . . He just sat back in a supremely calm, relaxed manner and waited until important things were brought to him. And then he would act, quickly, decisively.'[19]

Nowhere was Reagan's decisiveness better demonstrated than at the Republican National Convention in Detroit in the summer of 1980. As the Republican presidential candidate, Reagan offered the vice-presidential place on his ticket to the former president, Gerald Ford, never dreaming that Ford would accept. He was thus taken aback when Ford agreed to 'consider' it with his wife Betty.

Watching Ford being interviewed on television the next night, and hearing the interviewer use the term 'co-presidency', Reagan was appalled. He had heard rumours that Henry Kissinger, Alan Greenspan and Dick Cheney – all of them former Nixon men – had set up a triumvirate, as in ancient Rome, and were busy presenting a 'power-sharing' proposal to Reagan's aides whereby they, behind Ford as a vice-presidential figurehead, would become Reagan's chief-of-staff council and decide who would be appointed Secretary of State and Secretary of Defense. It was, as another of Reagan's biographers put it, 'one of the most bizarre episodes in modern political history'.[20] Infuriated, Reagan told his senior aide to get Kissinger on the phone immediately, and told him to back off. At 11 p.m. on July 15, 1980, Ford was pressed to withdraw his candidacy for the vice presidency. Then Reagan picked up the phone, explaining to his staff his purpose: 'I'm calling George Bush. I want this settled. Anyone have any objections?'[21]

No one did. George Herbert Walker Bush became the official Republican vice-presidential candidate, and twelve weeks later, at 8.15 p.m. on November 4, 1980, NBC News called the election for Ronald Wilson Reagan: 'a sports announcer, a film actor, a governor of California',[22] Reagan had beaten President Carter by forty-three million votes to thirty-five million. He would be the fortieth president of the United States.


## Part Two: The Presidency


In his inaugural address on January 20, 1981, Reagan cleared his throat and declared that 'in this present crisis government is not the solution to our problem, government *is* the problem'.

The speech, given for the first time from the West Front of the Capitol, was considered to be the most inspiring since that of John F. Kennedy twenty years before; this time, however, it was not a call to do what one could for one's country, but for oneself. Taxes – at least for the wealthy – would be reduced, not increased, stimulating economic growth and generating more government revenue – an erroneous idea espoused by Arthur Laffer, and thereafter known as the Laffer Curve. 'If we look at the answer as to why, for so many years, we achieved so much, prospered as no other people on earth,' Reagan nonetheless declared, 'it was because here, in this land, we unleashed the energy and individual genius of man to a greater extent than has ever been done before.'

Reagan was determined to be the herald of a new era for the individual, beginning unashamedly with himself and the First Lady. Whereas the Carters had shown a cheese-paring presidential style, with reduced hospitality, smaller cars and carry-one's-own-luggage humility, Reagan deliberately espoused the opposite. Frank Sinatra – a Democrat – performed at the gala ball. The new First Lady wore a $10,000 gown. Hollywood glamour now replaced Plains-style in Washington DC. 'Hail to the Chief' was reintroduced. Limousines came back with a vengeance.

The son of the Irish-American shoe salesman from Dixon, Illinois understood the nature of symbolism and imperial leadership in a way that his predecessor, for all his intelligence and sincerity, had not. 'Can we solve the problems confronting us?' he asked in his inaugural address. 'Well, the answer is yes. To paraphrase Winston Churchill, I did not take the oath I have just taken with the intention of presiding over the dissolution of the world's strongest economy.'

Reagan's faith in himself was stunning. Whereas Carter had seemed to know very few people in Washington, and to trust even fewer, causing him to rely on an amateur 'Georgia Mafia' to help run the White House, Reagan brought in his own experienced people from California and augmented them with Washington and other insiders. He made Bush's campaign manager, James Baker, his chief of staff, working alongside Ed Meese and Mike Deaver – 'the troika', as they would be called, Baker overseeing politics and Congress, Deaver his deputy in charge of scheduling and packaging the president's image, while Meese watched over policy and the National Security Council.

The troika met at 7.30 every morning, and one of them was with Reagan every hour of the day, filtering out inessential items before they reached his desk. Reagan was thereby allowed to do what he did best: decide among options, then communicate his decisions. With 1,700 employees in the Executive Office of the President, 350 White House staffers and almost two million federal government workers, it was seen initially as a model White House command structure, one that put his predecessor's to shame.

A Hollywood film, ironically, lay the behind the assassination attempt on the life of the former Hollywood movie actor on March 30, 1981, only two months after his new and greatest role had begun: Martin Scorcese's *Taxi Driver*. Spurred by an obsession with its star, Jodie Foster, a paranoid twenty-three-year-old Texas college student, John Hinckley Jr, came to Washington by Greyhound bus, determined to prove the depth of his love for Ms Foster by killing the US president. He very nearly succeeded, catching Reagan leaving the Washington Hilton where he had been giving a speech.

Reagan had been arguing the case for his forthcoming federal government cost-cutting programme, in order to reduce the 'wild and irresponsible spending' that was ballooning the national deficit, conveniently ignoring his Defense Secretary's push to increase defence funding by a mammoth 10 per cent. Cleverly reminding the union audience that he had been a lifetime card-carrying member of the AFL-CIO, Reagan presented his one-sided appeal as if it were the gospel word, and shortly after 2 p.m. left by a side entrance to get into his armoured limousine.

Hinckley's .22 'Devastator' bullet was designed to explode on impact. Mercifully it missed the president, hitting the bodywork of the limousine, which then squashed the projectile into a careening disc that bounced through the narrow gap between the open door and the car, where it carved its way under Reagan's arm, hit a rib, was deflected into his lung and stopped only a few millimetres from his heart. Ordering the secret service agent who had been shielding him to get off, Reagan accused the agent of having broken one of his ribs. Then, as blood began to pour from his lips, he commented. 'I think I've cut my mouth.'[23] At that point the agent ordered the driver to race to the nearest hospital, not the White House.

Although Reagan insisted on walking from the limousine to the

George Washington University hospital entrance, which the limo reached in three and a half minutes, he collapsed inside. 'I think we've lost him' the secret service agent muttered when the emergency nurse in Trauma Bay 5 was unable to register a pulse.

At the White House, an even more surreal drama was played out as the Nixon henchman whom Reagan had appointed Secretary of State, Al Haig, declared himself to be the acting president – and put the military on high alert. To the disbelief of those present who knew the presidential succession procedures as set out in the Twenty-fifth Amendment, Haig announced: 'Constitutionally, gentlemen, you have the president, the vice president, and the Secretary of State in that order.' Since the vice president was away in Texas, 'I am in control here, in the White House', he claimed.

'He's wrong,' the Secretary of Defense, Caspar Weinberger, commented. 'He doesn't have any such authority.' Donald Regan, the Treasury Secretary – responsible for the secret service – was even more aghast, asking: 'Is he mad?'[24]

White House aides, watching the unholy struggle for power, worried lest Haig was, as one reporter put it to Reagan's communications director, plotting 'a *coup d'état*'.[25] Even if the seventy-year-old president survived the assassination attempt, would he be weakened, either physically or mentally – or both? Would the rump-administration of Haig and his warring colleagues then be able to direct government operations? Would a debilitated Reagan – who had always been thought of by many as a mere movie actor, an empty shell, even 'an amiable dunce' in the parlance of Clark Clifford, the former Secretary of Defense (and adviser to four presidents) – be able to guide, let alone rule, the American Empire?

It is impossible to overstate the effect of Reagan's recovery on America's recovery, as significant in its own way as Franklin Delano Roosevelt's courage in triumphing over his paralysis when stricken by polio. Reagan's five hours of surgery, with copious amounts of morphine still required after the operation (during which he lost over half his blood), certainly tested his resilience.[26] His courage, insisting on walking to the hospital entrance despite a bullet lodged next to his heart, then his jokes to the doctors, nurses and his wife, became legendary. Was the doctor a Republican, he asked jokingly, before undergoing surgery. ('We're all Republicans now', the surgeon, a

Democrat, responded.) 'Who's holding my hand? Who's holding my hand?' he enquired of the nurse who was checking his pulse, 'Does Nancy know about us?'[27] And when Nancy got there, only ten minutes later, he was quick to explain: 'Honey, I forgot to duck.'[28] Unable to speak after regaining consciousness, he scribbled: 'I'd like to do this scene again – starting at the hotel.'[29]

Treating the murder attempt as a joke, indeed as a Hollywood film comedy, Reagan transformed a terrible moment – certainly the worst moment since the assassinations of JFK, Bobby Kennedy and Martin Luther King – into a moment of national deliverance, not mourning. His approval polls shot up – by more than ten points, to 73 per cent – as did the stock exchange. Presidential weakness was buried, not Reagan. After his emergence from hospital, Reagan was never again traduced as a mere Hollywood movie actor. 'As long as people remember the hospitalized president joshing his doctors and nurses' wrote David Broder in the *Washington Post*, '– and they will remember – no critic will be able to portray Reagan as a cruel or callow or heartless man.'[30]

As he worked his phone to get congressional backing for his cost-cutting, tax-cutting, increased military-spending budget – a plan that might otherwise have been trashed by the Democrat-led House of Representatives – the president breathed new life into his ambitious agenda, launching the 'Reagan Revolution': a new era of unfettered, low-tax entrepreneurial capitalism in which the rich would be encouraged to get richer, while the middle class would be palliated with a diet of revived nationalism and a steadying drumbeat of conservative 'American values'.

The Democratic Majority Leader in the House, Jim Wright, noted in his diary that the president's 'philosophical approach is superficial, overly simplistic and one-dimensional. What he preaches is pure economic pap, glossed over with uplifting homilies and inspirational chatter. Yet so far the guy is making it work', Wright admitted. By unrelenting behind-the-scenes phone calls and meetings, the recuperating chief executive overcame Democratic resistance to his budget bill, which passed 232 to 192 in the House, and eighty to fifteen in the Senate. 'Appalled by what seems to me a lack of depth,' Wright wrote, 'I stand in awe nevertheless of his political skill. I am not sure that I have seen its equal.'[31]

From a seasoned political opponent, a liberal Democrat from Texas, this was praise indeed. Reagan had personally met or talked with some 479 members of Congress – 'about 400 more than Jimmy Carter had spoken to in four years', as one biographer chronicled.[32] A political scientist put the transformation into a nutshell: 'Reagan has demonstrated, in a way that Jimmy Carter never did, that he understands how to be president' – not least in 'developing a working relationship with Congress'.[33]

By appointing the first woman ever to sit on the Supreme Court, Sandra Day O'Connor, Reagan bit back at right-wing conservatives demanding not only an anti-Communist crusader but an anti-abortionist whom religious fundamentalists could applaud. The president had interviewed O'Connor at the White House, and liked the fact that she loved horses, having grown up on a ranch, the Lazy-B. Reagan phoned Jerry Falwell, the leader of the Moral Majority movement, who opposed the choice of O'Connor. 'Jerry, I'm going to put forth a lady on the Supreme Court. You don't know anything about her. Nobody does, but I want you to trust me on this one.' 'I'll do that, sir' Falwell responded.[34]

The day the president returned to his desk in the Oval Office in May 1981, he was confronted by an air traffic controllers' strike. By law, air controllers could not walk off their jobs, but 'the only illegal strike is an unsuccessful one', their union leader, Robert Poli, sneered, and declared the strike would go ahead, however illegally. 'They cannot fly this country's planes without us' he taunted, and 'they can't get us to do our jobs if we are in jail, or facing excessive fines'.[35]

Clearly Poli had not read the president's bio. Reagan labelled the illegal walkout 'Desertion in the face of duty', and at 11 a.m. on August 3, 1981, in the White House Rose Garden, he gave the strikers exactly forty-eight hours to return to their posts or their positions would be 'terminated' – forever.

Thirteen thousand strikers ignored him. This proved a gross miscalculation on their part. On orders of the president in his role as commander-in-chief, military air controllers now took over from those men who did not return to their posts. New controllers were then taken on, breaking the strike. The strikers were never re-employed. Even the Soviets took note – 'a man who, when aroused, will go to the limit to back up his principles', a Kremlin watcher noted.[36]

The Russians were right to be concerned. On July 1, 1981, America had gone officially into recession, with the worst unemployment since 1941, and was facing ballooning national deficits for the foreseeable future. Reagan refused to give up the 'no new taxes' mantra of his Republican crusade, and he would not countenance the only possible alternative to cuts in federal welfare, education and health costs: a cut in military spending, which would adversely affect his key goal, the destruction of the Soviet Empire.

Reagan had never been to the USSR, nor had he ever met a Communist outside Beverly Hills. Nevertheless he was certain that behind its Cold War curtain the Soviet Union was faring even less well than the United States economically, and that the way to cause it to collapse was to compete more aggressively in military spending.[37]

This was a risky strategy in that it would intensify, not reduce, the risk of misunderstanding or accidental nuclear war. Moreover it left the Soviet Union no room to reduce military spending and reform its economy (as Communist China would be encouraged to do in subsequent years). Simplistic, deliberately confrontational and draconian, it was Reagan's personal plan: a proposal to ignore America's current economic woes, accept the biggest deficit in American history and go all out for broke, breaking the will of the Soviet Empire as it struggled in Afghanistan and in Europe, where the Polish Solidarity movement was again protesting the USSR's iron occupation, prompting the Polish puppet leader, Jaruzelski, to declare martial law to crush opposition more effectively on the Kremlin's behalf.

All American presidents since Harry Truman – who established the doctrine of 'containment' – had believed the Soviet Union would topple on its own, eventually. Reagan, however, was the first to be convinced that it could be 'encouraged' to fall. He was increasingly driven by a growing conviction he could topple the USSR not only by fending off its expansionist efforts worldwide, but by deliberately inciting a new arms race that, if successful, would bankrupt a bloated military empire that was already overstretched, especially in eastern Europe.

Thus, where Brzezinski had persuaded President Carter to end détente and react defensively to presumed Soviet intentions in the Near East and Middle East, Reagan used his degree in economics to back his intuition, as well as 'raw intelligence on the Soviet economy' from his national security adviser and the CIA, not to worry about the Soviet Union's strengths, but rather, to identify its weaknesses.[38] The Russians 'are in very bad shape', he wrote in his diary, 'and if we can cut off their credit they'll have to yell "Uncle" or starve'.[39] In a secret Decision Directive, he laid down America's express strategy against the Soviet Empire as a policy 'to weaken the Soviet alliance system by forcing the USSR to bear the brunt of its economic shortcomings'.[40]

Trident submarine missiles, a B-1 stealth bomber, navy F-14 fighters, the M-1 tank and an MX programme of new ICBMs were amongst the programmes that indicated the seriousness of Reagan's gamble. He would, at the very least, 'force them to the bargaining table', but his goal was even more ambitious. American policy would now be not only to 'contain' the Soviet Union, but to 'reverse' its postwar expansion.[41]

Although three quarters of British members of Parliament boycotted President Reagan's address to the British legislature on his official visit to London and Europe – with millions of people across the western world demonstrating in favour of a 'nuclear freeze', not a new American nuclear arms race – he seemed undeterred. No one, he was determined, would now stop him from explaining in his own words his 'plan'. In the cradle of parliamentary democracy Reagan thus reversed Marx's claim that it was the capitalist world that was in crisis and could only be rescued by Communism. Instead, he described a Soviet Union 'in deep economic difficulty', unable to 'feed its own people' and in 'decay', while it was the democratic societies that were 'prosperous'. 'I don't want to sound overly optimistic,' he stated in his address, but Marxism-Leninism would soon be left 'on the ash heap of history'.[42]

At a time when the United States was officially in recession and heading for its largest ever deficit, Reagan's boast sounded impossibly blinkered. Marvin Kalb, the dean of Washington correspondents, nevertheless saw it as a milestone that 'after sixty years in power' the Soviet leadership was, in Reagan's eyes, not only illegitimate, protected by guns, gulags and secret police, but doomed to *economic* defeat – with the seventy-year-old president mounted on his steed and ready to 'take on the entire Communist world'.[43] Even Reagan's colleagues were stunned by his confidence in this respect. 'We must keep the heat on these people', Reagan had told Senator Howard Baker, the Republican Majority Leader, in March. 'What I want is to bring them to their knees so that they will disarm and let us disarm; but we have got to do it by keeping the heat on. We can do it. We have them on the ropes economically', he emphasized.[44] And to prove his thesis, he added his trademark coda: a little detail, often erroneous, but which brought his point right home, into the family parlour: 'They are selling rat meat in the markets in Russia today.'[45]

Could the Soviet system of police and military oppression that had enforced the slavery of the peoples of eastern Europe since World War II have been challenged in a less dangerous American manner, via continued containment and détente? Historians were tempted to think so. Certainly it was the view held by most European liberals at the time, and by many in the US. Yet the history of dictatorship in the twentieth century did not proffer many examples of happy endings. Karl Marx's supposed 'withering away of the state' once true Communism was achieved, never happened anywhere – in fact the reverse was the case. By challenging the Soviet Union to an arms race it could not win, the former Eureka C-student and B-movie actor was determined, as an alpha president, to end Marx's nonsense. Moreover he had another arrow in his quiver: Star Wars.

Following his insistence on the largest increase in American military spending in the country's entire peacetime history, in 1981, the ageing president began to rethink the whole concept of nuclear deterrence. He had made a visit to the North American Aerospace Defense Command in Colorado, on Cheyenne Mountain, in 1979, and had talked there with the inventor of the hydrogen bomb, Professor Edward Teller, who suggested that modern technology might eventually make it possible to create a defensive shield against missile attack, much as the British had set up radar stations before World War II to help counter German bomber fleets in the event of hostilities. The discussion was filed away in Reagan's highly selective memory, and when, early in March 1983, he attended a five-day, top-level computerized war game code-named Ivy League, the die was cast.

Reagan, who had made his reputation simulating baseball play from ticker tapes, was enthralled by the game – and alarmed, especially by its culmination, namely the death of the president. The entire notion of MAD – mutually assured destruction – appeared more pointless to him than ever, since American retaliation for the loss of the president and his command staff would be punitive, but pyrrhic: the world irradiated, and literally in flames.

With the Russians having installed more than 500 SS-20 missiles with multiple independent re-entry nuclear warheads, and given the vulnerability of American land-based missiles to Soviet targeting, there were only two 'good' options: either nuclear disarmament or the development of defensive weapons to disable Russian long-range missiles in flight. Knowing that the former had been proposed, but would never be accepted either by the American or Russian militaries, Reagan now chose the latter. Several weeks after Ivy League, with only a handful of people informed in advance, Reagan announced in a televised speech from the Oval Office at 8 p.m. on March 23, 1983, that he was launching a new military programme 'with the promise of changing the course of human history': a Strategic Defensive Initiative, SDI, or, as it was instantly dubbed, 'Star Wars'.

Almost the entire White House staff and Reagan administration, including the Joint Chiefs, were against the idea. Even the speechwriter helping prepare the television address did so under duress and in disbelief. Vice President Bush was aghast, his chief of staff bursting into his office, waving the speech and shouting: 'We've got to take this out! If we go off half-cocked on this idea, we're going to bring on the biggest arms race in history!' George Shultz, the new Secretary of State (following the much-welcomed resignation of Al Haig), declared 'This is lunacy.'[46] Within hours it was being denounced on Soviet radio and television, as well as the capitals of Europe. It appeared to defy the ABM Treaty which President Nixon had signed, as well as committing the US to vast expenditure on research and development that would make the Manhattan Project look like child's play.

It was a measure of Reagan's utter self-confidence that, in his diary that night and in subsequent days, he stuck to his belief that his initiative 'would render nuclear missiles obsolete', even though this might 'take 20 yrs. or more but we had to do it. I felt good.'[47]

Few others did; indeed the storm that Reagan's announcement triggered damaged his standing in Europe and elsewhere for decades after. The world's press had a field day, trashing the notion of such a deterrent and accusing Reagan of ratcheting up the Cold War, with NATO's European citadels targeted as the first victims of a nuclear holocaust, instead of becoming, as was hoped, a nuclear-free zone by patient accommodation with the Soviets.

Reagan ignored his critics, even those on his own staff. 'I didn't expect them to cheer' he remarked.[48] A week later he explained to sceptical reporters that, once developed, the SDI shield could be offered to the Soviets in a real disarmament negotiation, 'to prove that there was no longer any need for keeping those [nuclear] missiles'.[49]

Few journalists, if any, believed Reagan, or even the feasibility of a missile shield. But public reaction in America warmed to the president's rhetoric of a 'shield', even if it was mythological. Was not Reagan a favourite son of Hollywood, the dream factory that had just produced the third film of the Star Wars series, *Return of the Jedi*, replete with Red Guards, an implacable emperor aboard a Death Star, defensive shields, a renewed arms race, space stations, dark sides and fighter planes in the form of cannon-armoured space craft? Reagan's conduct, rhetoric and vision thus seemed unexceptional to most moviegoing Americans. Indeed his earlier assertion of American power in the Mediterranean, off the coast of Libya, had appeared scripted for a Lucas movie: American F-14 fighters were ordered to shoot down (and did) any Libyan jets that attempted to overfly US naval man-oeuvres in the Gulf of Sidra, which Libyan dictator Muammar Qaddafi had declared Libyan territory.

Despite protests across the world, Reagan was implacable. The Soviets offered to dismantle half their SS-20s if the president would cancel the deployment of the Tomahawks and Pershings. Reagan rejected the offer. The two-year-long efforts at nuclear arms reduction agreements in Geneva were then abandoned. The crunch, officials on both sides agreed, was now coming – the 'countdown to nuclear war', as Soviet officers put it, when Able Archer 83, a secret ten-day NATO war game in November 1983, caused Russian and Warsaw Pact forces to go on high alert.[50]

Having waved his big stick, Reagan then stunned the Soviets by a new announcement on national television in January 1984. The United States was back in a position of global nuclear superiority. He therefore wanted to revert to 'peaceful competition' – i.e. economic war – and embrace 'constructive cooperation' with the Soviets.[51] Was he serious, the Russians wondered, and what did he mean?

Gromyko, the Russian foreign minister, had denounced Reagan in Stockholm as the author of 'maniacal plans', and of using 'criminal and dishonest methods' in pursuit of a 'pathological obsession' over SDI – a sign that Reagan's tough stance was unnerving the Kremlin.

However, the SDI research programme, his defiant deployment of new missiles in Europe and then appeal for cooperation or even a return to détente, not only caught the Russians off guard, but leaderless – for on February 9, 1984, the Russian premier, Yuri Andropov, a former KGB chief who was four years younger than Reagan, passed away. Asked if he would attend the Andropov funeral, Reagan snapped: 'I don't want to honor that prick.'[52]

Andropov's successor, Konstantin Chernenko, was a master of wiretapping and Politburo bureaucracy, but he too was a sick man, hardly seen in public. In an attempt to match Reagan's stepped-up Cold War symbolism, he ordered a Russian boycott of the 1984 summer Olympics in Los Angeles; refused to allow the East German ruler, Erich Honecker, to visit West Germany; and attempted to dampen talk of liberalization in eastern Europe. He also pointed to the economic difficulties being suffered by western capitalist economies.

It was too late, however, for such counter-rhetoric to sound plausible. The American economy had picked up dramatically, and Reagan was on a roll. He had stalwartly backed the tough anti-inflationary measures of the chairman of the Federal Reserve Bank, via high interest rates, and Americans were now seeing positive results. Inflation and unemployment were down, while the Soviet Union's prospects – weighed down by its own Vietnam-like struggle in Afghanistan – looked dimmer than for decades. To Reagan it seemed clear that the Russian straitjacket, which had kept eastern Europe colonized and enslaved for almost forty years, was nearing its demise, or 'assisted suicide'.

That summer, on the fortieth anniversary of D-Day, Reagan gave perhaps the most celebrated speech of his life, at the top of a near-vertical cliff in Normandy that US Rangers, despite great losses, had stormed on June 6, 1944, during the invasion of France: 'The boys of Pointe du Hoc'. 'These are the men', the president said, pointing to the sixty-two survivors present, 'who took the cliffs. These are the champions who helped free a continent.'

In the context of the Cold War, Reagan's words possessed an added piquancy. The sheer courage of young US servicemen in liberating an occupied continent was Reagan's deliberate theme. The days of ironfisted Soviet military repression in the cause of a faded and failing ideology were numbered – the Soviet Empire, as successor to Hitler's

Third Reich, was on the defensive as Soviet occupation troops guarded a new form of the Atlantic Wall, stretching from the Baltic Sea almost to the Adriatic and into Asia. Reagan's certainty that the US would win was remarkable – worryingly so. 'My fellow Americans,' he announced on his return when testing a microphone at his ranch, which he thought was not recording, 'I am pleased to tell you I just signed legislation which outlaws Russia forever. The bombing will begin in five minutes.'[53]

The joke caused many to be concerned that Reagan was losing his marbles. He made further slips that year, his mental agility showing signs of deterioration at age seventy-three, having survived a near-fatal assassination attempt. But with the United States winning the majority of the Olympic medals in Los Angeles to patriotic glee, and the economy beginning to boom, it was a very different America from four years previously. The prospect of electoral victory for Democratic nominee Walter Mondale, Carter's former vice president, looked steeper than the Pointe du Hoc. Democrats who had predicted disaster for global stability and for the American economy found themselves embarrassingly wrong-footed.

Increasingly, voters gave Reagan credit for the eventual upturn in their personal lives since the Carter era – which seemed all the more dreary in retrospect. There were now no gasoline lines. Inflation was a thing of the past. Taxes had been reduced by a whopping 25 per cent. Real incomes were rising. A new era in America seemed afoot, encapsulated in Reagan's re-election advertising campaign mantra, 'It's morning in America.'

Many critics, though, felt the chill, pointing out that by encouraging people to see taxes as a form of government theft, Reagan was deliberately appealing to ordinary citizens' self-centredness – thereby destroying a collective moral responsibility that had existed since FDR's New Deal, and had been continued under presidents Truman, Kennedy and Johnson: the notion that, as Supreme Court Justice Oliver Wendell Holmes Jr had once put it, 'taxes are what we pay for civilized society'. Vilifying federal government as an obstacle to economic and social progress; seeking to shift the burden of welfare from the federal government to the (often poor) states; seeking to 'liberate' entrepreneurship by deregulating business, but at the risk of unfettered freedom, corruption and unchecked market manipulation – these and other aspects of the Reagan domestic agenda threatened not only to alter the social fabric of American society, but also its communal wealth, in rapidly deteriorating transportation infrastructure and environmental damage. Supply-side, Laffer-curved, 'trickle-down' (from tax cuts for the rich) 'Reaganomics' became, such critics argued, a recipe for simple American materialism, greed, consumerism and collective myopia. Reagan's own response to a CBS news reporter's question seemed to epitomize a new indifference at the very top. Under his new tax-cut programme, the president stood to save, the reporter noted, some $28,000 on his joint tax return, if his proposal to reduce taxes for the rich went through. 'I think that just points out for everyone how advantageous the new tax system is', Reagan had remarked – oblivious to the meaning of the word 'everyone'.[54]

Critics might blame Reagan for inspiring rampant greed, in contrast to FDR's vision of collective security or Carter's appeals for collective Christian charity. Reagan, however, had demographics on his side in the 1980s: a two-to-one majority of voters under twenty-five years of age, casting their ballots for a seventy-three-year-old presidential nominee when he stood for re-election.

Reagan's war on Communism, meanwhile, was obsessive, consuming the majority of his waking hours and diary entries. He could not, and would not, let up. Blaming Congress for not supporting him over what amounted to serial right-wing dictatorship across Central America, he resorted to whatever illegal measures he deemed 'necessary'. In a special address to Congress on April 27, 1983, he had even dared, as a Republican, quote the Truman Doctrine, in order to picture El Salvador, Honduras, Guatemala, Costa Rica and Nicaragua as a sort of collective Korea far closer to the American heartland than the Asian peninsula. El Salvador 'is nearer to Texas than Texas is to Massachusetts', he pointed out. 'The national security of all the Americas is at stake in Central America . . . If we cannot defend ourselves there we cannot be expected to prevail elsewhere' – despite the absence of any Americans to *be* defended there. 'Our credibility would collapse, our alliances would crumble, and the safety of our homeland would be put in jeopardy.'

For all the president's magical communication skills, this peroration, for once, was received in stony silence – save when he promised, at least, not to send American troops to the 'new Korea'. American intervention would thus have to remain, he reluctantly accepted, illegal – while keeping voters' attention focused on the Soviet Union. The fate of twenty-five million mostly poor inhabitants of Central America, with an average income of only $500 per year, was thus ignored by most Americans in the US, who thought their elderly president misguided, even a bit wacky, on the issue, and simply looked the other way. As the Secretary of State, George Shultz, put it when silencing a senior State Department official who was fulminating against Reagan for his continuing support for Ferdinand Marcos, the corrupt former president of the Philippines, in the face of incontrovertible evidence that Marcos had attempted to rig the election: 'The president is the president. He has strong views; that is how he got to be president.'[55]

Seen historically, however, it was in the Middle East that Reagan's obsession with Communism most clearly mortgaged the future for Americans. By refusing to negotiate with any Palestinian group that did not first acknowledge Israel's right to exist, Israel's prime minister Menachim Begin made certain there would be no obstacles to his settler policies, and proceeded to order accelerated expansion of illegal Jewish settlements in the West Bank, ignoring Palestinian objections, as well as UN and world protests. Nor did he stop at that, once he made General Ariel Sharon his defence minister. In June 1981 Begin had ordered an air attack on Saddam Hussein's French-built nuclear power station outside Baghdad, using American F-4 and F-16 fighters in violation of US agreements barring their use in offensive actions, rather than working with allies to stop shipment from France of enriched uranium. 'I swear I believe Armageddon is near' Reagan had noted anxiously in his diary on June 7, 1981, but beyond suspending delivery of more F-16 fighters to Israel in the aftermath, Reagan had done nothing to halt the approach of war.[56] 'That fellow Begin makes it very hard for us to support Israel' the president confided to staffers.[57] But in his diary he noted that even if Congress decided to punish Israel for violating its agreement, he would 'grant a presidential waiver', given his own belief that Saddam Hussein, as well as Israel, was building an atomic bomb.[58]

Licensing Israel to become America's uncontrolled proxy in the Middle East, however, was a policy fraught with consequences. Seeing so much American ambivalence, Begin unilaterally moved ahead with his West Bank settlement policy and his plans to destroy the PLO. By the following summer Reagan had 'known for at least a year' that Begin – 'the waspishly aggressive little prime minister of Israel', as Reagan's official biographer wrote – 'was spoiling for war in the Middle East', which had come appreciably closer once Begin's government officially annexed the Golan Heights.[59] Though the Israeli ambassador was 'called in' to the State Department in Washington in protest, little beyond an American vote in the UN condemning the action had been done; indeed in Tel Aviv the protesting American ambassador to Israel was handed Prime Minister Begin's response: 'What kind of talk is this "punishing Israel"? Are we a vassal state of yours? Are we a banana republic? You will not frighten us with punishments.'[60] On June 6, 1982, Begin ordered the launching of his ill-fated re-invasion of the Lebanon, backed by his defence minister Ariel Sharon, but in open defiance of the majority of Israelis.

Attempting not only to clear southern Lebanon of PLO insurgents, but also to cleanse it of Palestinian refugees and punish the city of Beirut, the Israeli assault resulted in massive civilian casualties. Such calculated bloodshed aroused condemnation across the world, not least for the deployment of American-supplied cluster bombs, which Israel was forbidden to employ except in self-defence. 'The world is waiting for us to use our muscle and order Israel out', Reagan acknowledged in his diary on June 16, 1982. He declined to do so, however, believing that, even if guilty of literal overkill, Israel's proxy-intervention might provide 'the best opportunity we've had to reconcile the warring factors in Lebanon and bring about peace after seven years'.[61]

Such a fantasy proved short-lived. A new frenzy descended as the Israeli Air Force – the third largest in the world and almost entirely dependent on US aircraft and spare parts – got busy. 'Watching the Israeli Air Force smashing Beirut to pieces was like having to stand and watch a man slowly beating a sick dog to death' Newsweek reported, as the eighth week of Israeli bombing ended, and a ninth began.[62] Secretary of State George Shultz pleaded with the president to do something to stop the killing, lest American influence and standing in the Arab world be permanently destroyed. Reagan's loyal deputy chief of staff Mike Deaver then offered his resignation, saying to Reagan 'I can't be part of this anymore, the bombings, the killing of children. It's wrong. And you're the one person on the face of the earth who can stop it.'[63]

For a man so unshakeable in his simplistic beliefs and attitudes, whether about Communism or taxes, Reagan was surprisingly unwilling to face unpleasantness among his own staff. 'All you have to do is tell Begin you want it stopped', Deaver pleaded. This time the president listened and phoned Begin, shaming him by calling the Israeli assault by its proper name. 'I used the word holocaust deliberately' Reagan noted that night in his diary, having angrily told Begin that 'our entire future relationship was endangered'.[64] Twenty minutes later Begin called back to say the aerial massacre had been halted, 'and pled for our continued friendship' as well as blaming Sharon for ordering it.[65] 'I didn't know I had that power' Reagan confessed, amazed.[66]

Why, Reagan's aide wondered, had it taken two *months* of Israeli blitzkrieg in Lebanon and the relentless bombing of the city of Beirut – with its overtones of Guernica in 1937 – before Reagan would lift the phone? Above all, why did Reagan not recognize that Begin's and Sharon's oppression of the Palestinian Arabs (a policy opposed by Shimon Peres, the leader of the opposition party in Israel) would inevitably cause the United States to carry the can in the Islamic world for Israel's misdeeds? As Reagan sought to defuse the Lebanese time-bomb by sending in American peacekeepers, after the fact, the following months gave him ample demonstration of the anti-US sentiment which his sponsorship of Israeli aggression and expansion had inspired.

From his California ranch, on holiday on August 8, 1982, Reagan ordered some 800 American Marines to land in Beirut and take part in an ad hoc peacekeeping mission with French and Italian troops – the Multinational Force, or MNF. From an NBC studio in Hollywood he then declared in a prime-time address to the nation and to the world that the Palestinian problem *had* to be addressed, not simply crushed, as Hitler had crushed the Warsaw uprising.

Although he appreciated Israeli fury at being shelled 'by hostile Arabs' from across its borders and explained that he was not 'about to ask Israel to live that way again', he declared he was not impressed by Israel's response. 'The war in Lebanon has demonstrated another reality in the region . . . The departure of the Palestinians from Beirut dramatizes more than ever the homelessness of the Palestinian people. Palestinians feel strongly that their cause is more than a question of refugees. I agree.'[67] On September 1, 1982, he proposed a Reagan Plan, granting full autonomy to Palestinians in the West Bank and Gaza, in a federation supervised by Jordan, and the freezing of Israeli settlements installed and defended by Israeli forces in the years since their victory in 1967.

Reagan's speech fell on deaf ears. 'ISRAEL REJECTS REAGAN PLAN FOR PALESTINIAN SELF-RULE' was the *New York Times* headline on September 3. Two days later Begin announced he was giving $18.5 million for another ten settlements in the West Bank, and indeed hoped to increase the number of Jewish settlers by more than 300 per cent.

Saddened, Reagan washed his hands of the problem and pulled out the 800 Marines on September 10. On humanitarian grounds, however, he felt compelled to send them back in again on September 29, for by then the situation had spiralled into a mad bloodbath. Far from reconciling 'the warring factors' and enforcing peace after seven years of quasi-tribal violence, the Israeli invasion had produced unadulterated turmoil, with the entire world sickened over what were seen as Israel's crimes against humanity and the aftermath, in which Christian Lebanese militias were abetted by a secret pact with Israeli forces.

The president's second humanitarian intervention was no better than the first, and merely demonstrated the weakness of the belated American hand. Instead of destroying the PLO, Israel's invasion had turned its members into martyrs, had helped spawn Hezbollah, had sucked Syria into deeper involvement, and had intensified lingering civil strife in the country. As Israel finally abandoned its failed blitzkrieg and left Beirut, American peacekeepers were forced to call for American battleship firepower to defend themselves. By so doing, however, the peacekeepers became combatants – surrogates for the departed Israelis. The result was inevitable.

On October 22, 1983, an Islamic suicide bomber drove a truck carrying six tons of high explosive into the US Marine peacekeeping barracks at Beirut airport, setting off an explosion that lifted the entire building into the air and slaughtered at one stroke some 241 Americans. It was a harbinger of a new kind of kamikaze-style suicidal guerrilla warfare, against which simple roadblocks and security checks were ineffective.

The slaughter of hundreds of young Americans sickened the

American public, who urged the president to pull out the Marines altogether. Reagan, having refused to rein in Begin until it was too late, now refused to pull out American peacekeepers lest in doing so it broadcast the same signal that had come out of Carter's administration: the US was weak and would back down if challenged.[68] However, he did nothing to pressure the Israelis into backing the Reagan Plan. Instead, he gave the go-ahead for an American invasion of an island ninety miles off Venezuela.

With a population of 11,000, Grenada was the smallest independent nation in the western hemisphere, a former British colony ruled by a Marxist dictator, Maurice Bishop. When a second Marxist coup took place there on October 20, 1983, supported by Cuban troops and Russian trainers, some 250 American medical students were placed in possible peril, it was alleged. Questioning the chairman of the Joint Chiefs, John Vessey, as to how many men he had committed to a possible US invasion, if it was supported by neighbouring Caribbean nations and went ahead, Reagan listened to the general's response – then stunned him by ordering that Vessey double the number. Asked why, the president responded 'Because if Jimmy Carter had used eighteen helicopters for Desert One instead of nine, you'd be briefing him now instead of me.'[69]

Mocked by cartoonists and columnists in Europe, where millions had been protesting against the placement of new American intermediate nuclear missiles, Reagan showed remarkable self-assurance for a man who had, all his early life, yearned for applause, not derision. 'You are informing us, not asking us?' Speaker Tip O'Neill reacted, stunned, when Reagan summoned congressional leaders to the White House. 'Yes', the president coolly replied.

Despite his fury at Reagan's high-handedness, Tip O'Neill cautioned his colleagues and the press not to fault the president while American lives were at risk in Grenada, where Cuban mercenaries put up stiff resistance. Finally, as American forces mopped up, Reagan went on television on October 27 to explain the tragic loss of American life in Beirut in a peacekeeping role, and the reasons for invading Grenada. 'Grenada, we were told, was a friendly island paradise for tourism. Well, it wasn't. It was a Soviet-Cuba colony readied as a major bastion to export Communism and undermine democracy. We got there just in time.'[70] As the Defense Department paraded evidence at Andrews

Air Force base outside Washington – from armoured personnel carriers to anti-aircraft guns, and almost six million rounds of ammunition for rifles and machine guns, as well as records of almost 700 Cuban soldiers (almost as many as there were Grenadian soldiers) – Reagan's approval polls rose twenty points to 84 per cent. Days later, triggering yet more protests, the first shipment to American air bases in Europe of nuclear-tipped Tomahawk and Pershing II missiles duly arrived at Greenham Common in England. The message for those who confronted the American Empire was: beware.

Reagan's magic, like Roosevelt's, was his sheer optimism: a quality considered deeply American, however naive, and which, together with a sense of humour, had been in short supply since JFK's presidency. In speechmaking Reagan had a brilliant eye for the telling detail, whether sentimental or inspiring, and a fantastically deflating sense of humour. 'I've come to the conclusion that there is a worldwide plot to make my job more difficult on almost any day that I go to the office' was one typical aphorism that delighted his admirers, and in turn made the job of any contender for the office of president a tougher sell. Tall, always immaculately groomed and attired, even in cowboy gear, with a studied air of confident distinction (standing before the mirror, shaving in the morning, he would recite his mantra: 'I am the president'), he was hard to humble – as President Carter had relentlessly been humbled – by the press, by opponents, or even angry voters. 'I want you all to know,' Reagan jested in the second of the presidential debates against the former vice president Walter Mondale, the Democratic nominee, in October 1984, 'that I also will not make age an issue in this campaign. I am not going to exploit, for political purposes,' he added with a smile, 'my opponent's youth and inexperience.'[71]

Despite Mondale's criticisms of Reagan's leadership and of his command of the military, Reagan remained polite, reasonable, principled – and above all, firm. 'I know it will come as a surprise to Mr Mondale, but I *am* in charge', he retorted in the debate, not only confident in his vision of America's future prosperity and security, but pleasantly surprised to know, according to a new poll, he was leading the much younger Mondale (aged fifty-six) two to one among voters aged between eighteen and twenty-four – voters who were the future of America.

On November 6, 1984, Reagan won re-election for four more years, carrying forty-eight states to two: a landslide vindication of a presidency that would now witness an even more dramatic term.

A routine medical examination in 1985 found Reagan to be suffering from cancer of the skin and of the colon, requiring a three-hour operation to remove two feet of his intestine around the malignant polyp.

With a new, arrogant chief of staff, Donald Regan, running the White House, some pundits wondered – and worried – who was really running the country. If anything, however, Reagan seemed even more presidential than before, narrowing the focus of his leadership skills still further to concentrate on those issues central to his imperial vision of America: defeating the 'spread' of Communism, achieving military superiority over the Soviet Union, cutting taxes for the rich, and reviving American confidence and pride.

Abroad, this gave rise to greater protest and unpopularity, especially his continued funding of right-wing rebels in Nicaragua and his Star Wars programme, but at home his Teflon coating became increasingly impermeable as the economy continued to flourish, despite a $2 trillion national debt, with a $125 billion annual trade deficit. Moreover the ageing president remained endlessly patient, consistent, and humorous. Informed he would have to have the three-hour abdominal operation to remove his cancerous lesions he quipped 'You mean, the bad news is that I don't get to eat supper tonight?'[72] Like Margaret Thatcher, the British prime minister who was his most constant ally and cheerleader, he kept to his simple script, ignoring and deflecting the views of others – and since he was infinitely more likeable and self-deprecating than Mrs Thatcher, he won most of his battles at home without arousing the sort of personal vilification that greeted him (and her) abroad.

For a president who had attempted to savage social security in order to increase national security – failing in the first, but succeeding in the second – Reagan's continuing domestic popularity was no mean achievement. Certainly no one would ever forget his national television address on the day the US space shuttle *Challenger* blew up, killing all on board, including Christa McAuliffe, a thirty-six-year-old social sciences teacher from Concord, New Hampshire. Many of the nation's children had been watching on television screens at school as *Challenger* lifted off from Cape Canaveral on January 28, 1986, and then

exploded a bare ten miles above the launch pad. Stricken, the president cancelled his scheduled State of the Union address in Congress
and instead addressed a nation in shock. The 'Challenger crew were
pulling us into the future,' he declared, 'and we'll continue to follow
them. We will never forget them, nor the last time we saw them, this
morning as they prepared for their journey and waved goodbye – and
"slipped the surly bonds of Earth" to "touch the face of God".'[73]

In the majority of American voters' eyes the president had reasserted
American military and economic superpower. In terms of imperial
politics, Reagan was certainly playing a brilliant hand – indeed a far
more ruthless one than most observers knew at the time. Not only
did he persuade the Saudis to increase oil output from two million
barrels a year to nine million, thus flooding the world market, in return
for military supplies, but via the CIA he also stepped up Brzezinski's
surreptitious programme of support to the Taliban and mujahidin in
Afghanistan. In a still-secret presidential directive, NSDD-166, Reagan
ordered the CIA not simply to help the Muslim rebels in 'harassing'
Russian forces in Afghanistan – as President Carter had done – but to
start 'driving them out'. In 1985 the CIA proceeded to deliver 10,000
rocket-propelled grenades and 200,000 rockets – more than five times
the total for the previous five years (and fifteen times more in dollar
terms). The operation became the 'largest US covert action program
in the history of the CIA', as Reagan-apologist Paul Kengor later
crowed.[74] Reagan's CIA director, William Casey, was reputed to have
ordered one of his subordinates to 'go out and kill me 10,000 Soviets
until they give up'.[75] Sixteen thousand Soviet troops were, in fact, killed
in Afghanistan, and an incredible 269 Russian helicopters downed by
340 American-furnished Stinger anti-aircraft missiles.

On March 10, 1985, however, an event of far greater global consequence than the Russian quagmire in Afghanistan took place:
Konstantin Chernenko, the Soviet premier, died in Moscow. Reagan
had assumed it would be another decade before the colossus of Soviet
Communism could be brought down, but the advent of a new Soviet
leader, fifty-four-year-old Mikhail Gorbachev, altered Reagan's time
frame and his strategy.

Star Wars held out no prospect of being realized in the short term,
but such was America's lead in technology that the Russians could
not make this assumption; they were thus cornered, desperately hoping

they could trade an American decision not to proceed with the programme in return for nuclear arms reduction. Gorbachev was quick to respond to Reagan's invitation to visit Washington or, if not there, an alternative venue. In due course it was in Geneva, where Calvin had launched his Reformation four centuries earlier, that the two men met in November 1985.

Month after month in his diary, during preparations for the summit meeting, the president had set down his absolute determination in relation to Star Wars. 'I stand firm we cannot retreat on that,' he had already noted in December 1984, 'no matter what they offer.'[76] Nine months later, on September 10, 1985, he remained just as determined. 'Gorbachev is adamant we must cave in our SDI – well this will be a case of an irresistible force meeting an unmovable object.'[77] On November 19 the two emperors met, 'the "No. 1 Communist" and the "No. 1 Imperialist"' as Gorbachev later wrote.[78]

'[W]e did about 2 hours on SDI,' Reagan noted that evening in his rented house in Geneva. 'He's adamant but so am I.'[79] The next day 'the stuff really hit the fan' as Gorbachev 'fired back about SDI creating an arms race in space . . . He was really belligerent,' the son of the Irish-American alcoholic shoe salesman described, '& d—n it I stood firm.'[80]

Reagan was sure Gorbachev – hugely intelligent and representing a generation that had participated neither in the Russian Revolution nor World War II – was blustering, and would fold his cards if Reagan remained cool but implacable. Like the British government after World War II, the Politburo was having to face up to the fact that the Soviet Union could no longer afford the huge costs of empire, with restive colonies or puppet states agitating behind the Iron Curtain, and in competition with a far more economically productive western world; moreover, it was becoming prohibitively expensive for the USSR to maintain direct military rivalry with the United States on one flank and the Communist Chinese, boasting almost limitless manpower and soldiers, on the other.

Knowing Gorbachev's travails, the question for historians would thus arise, in the aftermath: could another, less ideologically driven American president have helped Gorbachev and the Soviet Union to retreat from its own empire and to modernize – as the Chinese Communist empire was encouraged to do – without deliberately

seeking to bankrupt it? A second question became: would an alternative American Caesar – a President Mondale, for example, had he
won the 1984 election – have thought through the consequences of
destroying the Soviet Union? While the world would be – and eventually became – undoubtedly a safer place without a nuclear arms
race, was it necessarily likely to be a safer place with the United States
exercising sole global hegemony? Would such monolithic power not
permit, even encourage, the US, under a future Caesar, to wield its
superpower unilaterally and irresponsibly?

At Geneva in November 1985, Gorbachev decided to come clean.
He astonished Reagan by describing openly how US policy was hurting
the Soviet Union, with an arms race it could not afford.[81] Gorbachev's
frankness, however, did not alter Reagan's agenda. Reagan had been
informed by his diplomatic and intelligence sources that the Soviet
Union was near-moribund; he now had it from the mouth of its
emperor, who begged Reagan to ditch SDI and improve US–Soviet
relations by agreeing arms limitation.[82] Moreover he pleaded with
Reagan to discard the American obsession with Soviet 'expansionism',
which he felt 'either a delusion or deliberate distortion', since such
post-McCarthyites, he assured Reagan, 'overemphasize the power of
the Soviet Union. We have no secret plans for world domination . . .
We support a settlement in Afghanistan, a political settlement under
the United Nations, if you help us. You accuse us of deploying troops,
but you work against us. You want our troops there, the longer the
better.'[83]

American commanders struggling in Afghanistan, twenty years later,
would have cause to remember such plaintive truth-telling. Reagan,
though, simply smiled at his adversary on December 21, 1985, and
refused to back down. Reagan 'appeared to me not simply a conservative, but a political "dinosaur",' the young Russian leader reported
sadly to his colleagues when he returned to Moscow, recognizing he
would have to launch perestroika without American help or support.
As his memoirs attest, it was a thankless, excruciating exercise,
mounted against entrenched bureaucracies and personalities. A catastrophic accident at Chernobyl in April 1986 was the worst nuclear
accident in history, a symbol of all that was wrong in Marxist-Leninist
Utopia. At a meeting of the Politburo two months after the disaster,
Gorbachev openly called Chernobyl a 'fiasco' that reflected bleakly

on state-run Communism. 'Throughout the entire system there has reigned a spirit of servility, fawning, clannishness and persecution of independent thinkers, window dressing, and personal and clan ties between leaders.'[84]

Had he seen the transcript of Gorbachev's peroration, Reagan would have chuckled. But he did not need to. Following his experience of inter-union venom in Hollywood, Reagan had seen the light. Reagan had never thereafter been seduced or intimidated by Communist or Russian posturing, and though he felt he could work with Gorbachev ('You're right,' he told one of his negotiating team, 'I did like him'), he was not about to agree to a draw in a global Cold War chess game that had gone on for four decades.[85] He did agree, however, to a second summit at Reykjavik the next year.

On October 10, 1986, Gorbachev again went all out to persuade Reagan to scrap SDI. When Reagan baulked, but promised to 'share' the fruits of SDI as a defensive shield rather than to protect aggression, Gorbachev burst out laughing – and asked the president not to talk in such 'banalities'. 'Excuse me, Mr President, but I cannot take your idea of sharing SDI seriously. You are not willing to share with us well equipment, digitally guided machine tools, or even milking machines. Sharing SDI would provoke a second American revolution! Let's be realistic.'[86]

Reagan held firm, however, and though the two leaders agreed to massive mutual reductions in their deployed nuclear arsenals under a new treaty – thus effectively freezing the nuclear arms race – there would be no rest for the Soviet Empire in military research spending requirements. Nor would American help be offered in resolving Russia's quagmire in Afghanistan.

A year later, on December 7, 1987, Gorbachev came to Washington for a third summit, where he asked Reagan even more plaintively, 'Why can't we be allies? We were allies at one time, why can't we be allies now?'[87] Beyond the smiles, however, Reagan remained – as always – implacable; indeed some months earlier he had gone on the offensive, at least rhetorically.

On June 12, 1987, before a huge crowd in West Berlin celebrating the city's 750th anniversary at the Brandenburg Gate, Reagan had delivered his *coup de grâce*. Against the advice of his staff, he decided to make a Kennedyesque declaration that would go down in history. He had already forced the Soviets – who had finally prepared plans to pull out their vanquished army from Afghanistan in January – on the defensive. 'We hear much from Moscow about a new policy of reform and openness. Are these the beginnings of profound changes in the Soviet state? Or, are they token gestures?'

The former radio announcer from Dixon, Illinois paused, having come to the high point of his speech. 'There is one sign the Soviets can make that would be unmistakable, that would advance dramatically the cause of freedom and peace', he declared, then lifted his voice almost into a shout as he addressed himself directly to the emperor of the Soviet Union: 'General Secretary Gorbachev, if you seek peace, if you seek prosperity for the Soviet Union and eastern Europe, if you seek liberalization: come here to this gate! Mr Gorbachev, open this gate! Mr Gorbachev, tear down this wall!'[88]

Poor Gorbachev, already dicing with death in challenging the ossified Communist military-political power structure in the Soviet Union, felt stabbed in the back and embarrassed. He could only hope that in a fourth summit, he could convince President Reagan to back off, and give Russia real assistance.

Reagan happily accepted the invitation to Moscow on May 29, 1988, where he made it his business to talk openly to young people and raise the question of freedom of speech and religion in the Russian heartland.

If anything Reagan's 'ideological luggage' (as Gorbachev called it when talking to George Shultz)[89] was getting heavier as his second and final term of office neared its end. His agenda remained implacably the same: continuation of SDI research, arms reductions only according to an American agenda, zero trade improvements, zero financial help. Even the piece of paper Gorbachev proffered containing the draft of a joint statement declaring that neither country would infringe on the independence or sovereignty of the other, was rejected after Reagan promised to think about it. 'I don't want to do it,' the president announced his decision, as eastern European countries rattled their chains.[90]

It was their last session together, June 2, 1988. Disappointed that Reagan would not sign the 'peaceful coexistence' protocol he'd drafted, Gorbachev seemed momentarily at a loss. Recovering, however, he stood up and took the seventy-seven-year-old president's hand. 'Mr President,' he smiled as he put his arm around Reagan's shoulder, 'we had a great time.'[91] Reagan, by contrast, seemed unaffected by the get-together. 'I think it's clear that Gorbachev wants to restore the Soviet economy' he told congressional leaders on his return. 'It's a terrific job and it will take him a long time if he succeeds at all, because he's got opposition there, very obviously so.' In sum, he concluded, 'we have to consider them an adversary, because of their foreign policy and controlled society at home'.[92]

Reagan's role in crippling the Soviet Union and causing its imminent demise would be the signature achievement of his presidency in most Americans' eyes. Certainly he was later proud of his part in the ending of the 'evil empire' (though in Moscow he had claimed that he no longer believed it was evil). In other respects, however, his second term as president proved less fortunate than his first.

Reagan's wife had opposed his decision to stand for re-election in 1984, fearing his health would not stand the strain, especially in the wake of near-assassination. The First Lady had been right, for his health declined visibly and audibly as he went into his seventies. Prostate surgery followed his colon cancer operation. His hearing became progressively more impaired. His memory – once so strong – began to fail, and he often appeared muddled, dropping his cue cards when negotiating with Gorbachev, for example, and seemingly at a loss as the young Russian leader bent to help him pick them up.

Inevitably Reagan's cabinet colleagues and staff acted according to what they thought the president had in mind, or wanted, rather than what he actually instructed. For the most part his legendary Lady Luck held, and he was able to maintain his presidential dignity in a manner that had eluded his predecessor. The raging increase in the national deficit he managed to sweep under the rug, given the prolonged economic boom the country was experiencing, with GNP doubling since the recession of 1981–2. Other things were not so easy to bat away with silver words.

As a conservative Republican, Reagan necessarily drew to himself the biggest anti-Communist loudmouths in America, including his Defense Secretary Caspar Weinberger, his ambassador to the UN Jeanne Kirkpatrick and his CIA chief William Casey. Their misreading of a Soviet 'threat' in the Middle East – particularly their concern about a Soviet influence in Iran – would skew the history of the western world, as they worked on their 'boss' to approve illegal sales of American arms, and even more illegal use of the money they thereby pocketed. In return for supposed Iranian 'influence' in getting the release of Americans who had been taken hostage in Lebanon, the plotters would not only sell clandestine arms to Tehran, but then use proceeds from those sales to fund illegal weapons and support for Nicaraguan right-wing insurgents fighting against the democratically elected government of Daniel Ortega in Nicaragua.

Secretary of State George Shultz had, from the beginning, warned the president that 'if we go out and try to get money' for the Contra insurgents 'from third countries, it is an impeachable offense'.[93] But, as Reagan's national security adviser 'Bud' McFarlane later explained when hauled before Congress, he had failed to stop his colleagues. 'To tell you the truth, probably the reason I didn't is because if I had done that, Bill Casey, Jeanne Kirkpatrick and Cap Weinberger would have said I was some kind of commie.'[94] It was a telling admission.

Reagan's anti-Soviet stance could, at least, be understood and vindicated in terms of the forty years of totalitarian repression of the nations of eastern Europe. But Iran and Nicaragua? It was a measure of Reagan's limited interest in any subject outside the crushing of the Soviet Empire, and his failure ever to think through the consequences of his policies, that he not only tolerated an arms-for-hostages imbroglio, organized illicitly by his national security adviser, but happily acted as the undoubted godfather to the scheme, which had gone underground in June 1984 when Speaker Tip O'Neill turned down a supplemental appropriation bill to fund pro-Contra support. 'Thursday, December 5, 1985: NSC briefing' Reagan had written in his diary, noting the 'complex undertaking with only a few of us in on it. I won't even write in the diary what we're up to.'[95]

An inner sanctum of Reagan operatives, nicknamed 'The Establishment', had been created in the White House, on much the same lines as Richard Nixon's Plumbers: men who were united in their contempt for Congress and love of clandestine operations. Reagan's pet henchman in carrying out the secret deal was the heavily decorated Vietnam veteran, Lieutenant Colonel Oliver North, who claimed 'The old man loves my ass.'[96] North was exaggerating – but not by much, since the president saw in the young colonel's brash adventurism a sort of active alter ego, as well as a quasi-son,

whose patriotism and devotion to the military bespoke Reagan's sentimental nature. Though Reagan had signed Boland II in 1984 – a bill
expressly forbidding the CIA from giving non-military support to the
Contras, in conjunction with Boland I of 1982, which forbade the Reagan
administration from giving any funds to overthrow the Sandinista
government – the President had then authorized Robert MacFarlane,
the national security adviser, to do just that.

The deal stank from start to finish, especially since it could only
encourage Hezbollah to seize more hostages. First, an American pilot
who was shot down in October 1986 confessed that the CIA were clan-
destinely directing the Contra insurgency using their own ships, planes,
pilots, arms, airfields and radio equipment. Several weeks later on
November 3, 1986, the Iranian arms-for-hostages deal hit the headlines
when the *Washington Post* reported stories in Beirut that, in connection with the release of an American hostage there, 'the United States
had sent spare parts and ammunition for American-built fighter planes
and tanks' to Iran. 'We will never pay off terrorists,' President Reagan
said, 'because that only encourages more of it' – yet this was precisely,
it became clear, what he *had* done, with even more clandestine machinations still to be uncovered: namely, that the proceeds from the arms
sales to Iran would be used to illegally fund the Contras in Nicaragua,
in defiance of Congress.

By March 4, 1987, Reagan was having to apologize to the whole
nation. On prime-time television he took 'full responsibility for my
own actions and for those of my administration' and expressed disappointment 'in some who served me'.[97] He then admitted that, only
a 'few months ago [November 13, 1986] I told the American people I
did not trade arms for hostages. My heart and my best intentions still
tell me that's true, but the facts and evidence tell me it is not' – words
that did not make sense but, rather, implied that the ageing president
was losing his mind.

The inference, however, was clear: he was a patriotic American who
had desperately wanted to rescue the five American hostages held by
Hezbollah in Lebanon. It was a brilliant stratagem, and to the consternation of most critics he was forgiven on grounds of old age for one
of the shoddiest contraventions of congressional and constitutional
injunctions.

Reagan's elliptical confession masked a sad truth. His actions had merely encouraged Hezbollah – supported by the Iranians – to take more American hostages. By the time Congress put a stop to it, six further hostages had been seized in place of the five traded, while 1,508 TOW missiles, eight Hawk missiles and top secret intelligence information had been given to the Iranians. Reagan's national security adviser, Robert McFarlane, resigned and attempted suicide, the CIA director William Casey developed a brain tumour and also resigned, and Reagan's approval ratings plummeted from 67 per cent to a meagre 36. Meanwhile for six months, while awaiting the report of the Tower investigative panel that Reagan himself appointed to get to the heart of the matter, the White House came to a near standstill. Oliver North shredded as much evidence of the matter as possible, and the president's staff and senior members of the administration, from the White House to the Secretary of Defense, laboured to protect the president while trying to avoid prison themselves for malfeasance and perjury.

The revelations of deliberate deceit, lying, secret fund-solicitations both in the United States and abroad, use of foreign countries to facilitate illegal transactions, criminal acts and, above all, the mix of presidential whim and vacuity, were devastating, barely a decade since Watergate – and for what? Disgusted by a saga so reminiscent of Richard Nixon's imperial presidency and contempt for Congress, the House of Representatives rejected Reagan's appeal for another $36.25 million to aid the Contras in February 1988, and under the Sapoa Accord ceasefire, the Contras were completely disbanded. More than 40,000 Nicaraguan people had by then become casualties, with an estimated 29,000 dead on both sides, more than 3,000 of whom were civilians.[98] Reagan's efforts had been for nought, and his good name, some claimed, ruined forever.

'Reagan Now Viewed as an Irrelevant President' ran one newspaper headline in the aftermath of Iran-Contra.[99] Most of his right-wing staff were indicted by the federal prosecutor. His nomination of the conservative ideologue Judge Robert Bork to the Supreme Court was rejected by the Senate. In acknowledging the AIDS epidemic Reagan had been forced to acknowledge the need for the use of condoms – the bête noire of conservatives. Memory lapses and moments of confusion suggested an elderly man, almost eighty, facing the onslaught of dementia. Though he anointed his vice president, George Bush, as his preferred successor – 'win one for the Gipper' as he exhorted at the finale of the Republican National Convention in New Orleans on August 15, 1988 – he seemed either too tired or too indifferent to campaign heartily for Bush as the Republican nominee. Parallels with Eisenhower's last year in office were abundant, with many Republicans fearing the same outcome: a Democratic administration.

As pundits pondered his eight years as emperor, Reagan's legacy seemed strangely contradictory. He had doubled the national debt in six years. Behind a smokescreen of 'no new taxes' they had increased by more than $80 billion per year. Unemployment – though down in his last year – had averaged 7.7 per cent, compared with 6.4 under Carter. US output had averaged only 2.6 per cent growth under Reagan, compared with 3 under Carter (though the figure was 4.2 if reckoned from the time the Reagan recession ended). Meanwhile federal government spending, far from being slashed as Reagan had promised his conservative base, had risen to its highest level in relation to national output in American history. Reagan's efforts to deregulate the economy, moreover, resulted in a Savings and Loan scandal that exploded in his second term, resulting in taxpayers being asked to cover probable losses of $64 billion by the time of his final budget – a sum that would in due course require $200 billion in taxpayers' bailout funding, to compensate customers of failed and often fraudulent, unregulated American companies. The income of the poorest 20 per cent of the population fell by more than a tenth during his presidency, while the income of the top 20 per cent increased by a fifth, hugely enlarging the gap between them. He deliberately reversed Carter's efforts on environmental protection and energy conservation, while refusing to take seriously Gorbachev's warning about the threat of fundamentalist Islamic terror in Afghanistan and in the Middle East. Revelations of Reagan administration malfeasance in the Iran-Contra scandal continued to remind citizens of the excesses of Richard Nixon's White House – Oliver North's secretary (who had dated the son of a Nicaraguan Contra leader[100]) claimed that 'There are times when you have to go above the written law',[101] and North himself defended his decision to shred incriminating documents with the words 'That's why the government of the United States gave me a shredder.'[102] This was hardly a presidential scoreboard of which to be proud.

Was it smoke and mirrors, then, that explained the American public's continuing love affair with Reagan as his second term of office came to an end? Aware that the Soviet Union's Communist empire was fraying – its troops withdrawing from Afghanistan, its occupied countries in eastern Europe showing signs of revolt – American voters for the most part sensed an uncertain new era approaching, at once positive in signs of change in Russia, yet aware that traditional American manufacturing industry jobs were diminishing and being assigned overseas, in what came to be called 'globalization' and 'outsourcing'.

For this reason, perhaps, voters seemed reluctant to see the ageing but unwavering 'Gipper' go, indulging, as Richard Reeves later put it, in 'premature nostalgia'.[103] The president's sins of omission, his forgetfulness, even manipulation of the facts, were forgivable, it was felt, in a man who had restored the prestige of America across the world, after Jimmy Carter's brief but haunted occupation of the Oval Office. Whether or not Reagan had twisted the truth, indulged in false statistics, quoted phony economic indicators, misconstrued strategic threats, or engaged in occasional deliberate deceit, the Soviet Union was now on the defensive, while the president of the United States 'stood tall'. 'We meant to change a nation,' he declared in his farewell address from the Oval Office on January 11, 1989, in words crafted by his favourite speechwriter, Peggy Noonan, 'and, instead, we changed a world.'[104]

Leaving the White House and Washington on January 20, 1989 the fortieth president retired to Bel Air, California, keeping his 688-acre property in the hills north-west of Santa Barbara as his vacation home, where the seventy-seven-year-old, who had so wanted to be a cowboy actor, could ride to his heart's content.

## Part Three: Private Life

Reagan's 'inner life remained a mystery,' admitted Lou Cannon, the California journalist who knew and reported on Reagan for a quarter-century, 'even to his friends'.[105]

It remained a mystery, too, to Reagan's wives, and his children. The wall that Reagan had begged Gorbachev to tear down seems never to have come down in his own private life. Most biographers, in explanation, pointed their psychological fingers at Reagan's childhood. The

Reagan family, it was noted, moved some ten times while Reagan was growing up. Even when settled, briefly, in one place, Reagan's father Jack would suffer 'week-long benders' unable to control 'the Irish disease' as his son called it. At one point, living away from the family, Jack took up with another woman and divorce was threatened, though eventually he returned to Nelle. She, meanwhile, did her best to keep the shame from the rest of the world, but it was impossible to conceal it at home. At age eleven, for example, Reagan found his father spread-eagled on the front porch and had to drag him by his overcoat into the house.

Though Nelle Reagan tried to help her boys see their father's downfall as a disease, not a choice, Ronald, as the youngest child, grew an outer shell that became impervious to insult or condescension, while his older brother Neil tackled such abuse with his fists, to the point of getting a police record.

The Reagan boys went their separate ways as adults, Ronald following his own star: half in the real world, half in his own. Like Richard Nixon he worshipped his devout Christian mother to the day she died. Like Nixon he worked menial jobs throughout his youth, uncomplainingly. Like Nixon he even paid for his parents to retire early to a house he bought for them, in California. But unlike Nixon, Reagan exuded goodwill and gratitude for the better things in life, especially the simple ones. Clean living and clean speaking, he got the reputation of a Mr Goody-two-shoes, was the idol of his Disciple of Christ mother, and the diametric opposite of his wastrel father, who died of drink and heart disease at age fifty-seven.

As with Richard Nixon, theatre allowed Reagan to express himself in a new dimension. Again like Nixon he fell in love with a fellow thespian, Margaret Cleaver, daughter of his local Christian Church pastor. Fiercely intelligent, Margaret at first rejected him because of his alcoholic father, but eventually consented to his courtship. She acted with him first in high school, then in college. It was she who encouraged him to study at tiny Eureka College – itself half the size of Nixon's college, Whittier. 'I loved three things: drama, politics, and sports' Reagan later said of his time in Eureka, omitting his love affair with Margaret, his constant companion, who even returned to Eureka from the University of Missouri to spend her senior year with him.[106] ('Oh, you found out about her, huh?' he sighed when his official biographer, Edmund Morris, tracked her down and told Reagan he had done so.[107])

Ms Cleaver was the smartest and sharpest-tongued student in her class – so sharp Reagan's brother Neil said she 'spat tacks'.[108]) Reagan and Margaret became engaged on graduation, Reagan forcing himself to live up to Margaret's high moral expectations of him. Seven years into their relationship, however, Margaret went with her sister to stay in Paris and fell in love with a young American diplomat. She returned Reagan's ring, married the diplomat, and shattered Reagan's romantic dreams. He wasn't, it was clear, good enough for her.

Reagan's career in the less serious realm of entertainment fared better, however, leading him from radio to the dream factory itself: Hollywood. His swift ascent there, at the seeming brink of movie fame, earned the 6' 1" hunk easy dates and unusual bedding rights in a prudish era, yet his partners all later described him as impossible to fathom behind his facade of good and gentle manners. He seemed happiest on the beach or riding on the ranch he soon bought, when not required on the film set; he remained devoted to his parents, whom he took care to see every week; and allowed no one to get too close, save for one individual: 'Little Button Nose', as he affectionately called the twenty-year-old he acted alongside in the film *Brother Rat* in 1938: Jane Wyman.

Née Sarah Jane Mayfield, Jane Wyman had first met Reagan at the Warner Brothers studio in 1937, where they were both under contract. She had also had a difficult domestic upbringing, fostered out when her father died, and 'raised with such strict discipline', she later said, 'that it was years before I could reason myself out of the bitterness I brought from my childhood'.[109] Blessed with a good singing voice, she had pursued a part-time career in radio, then, having faked her birth certificate, left high school in Missouri at age fifteen to get into movies in Hollywood. With her petite figure, snub nose, her sunny smile and her big dark brown eyes, the diminutive, twice-married (in fact still married) blonde captivated Reagan.

After Jane obtained her second divorce she and Ronald became, under the aegis of Hollywood gossip columnist Louella Parsons, *the* model married couple of the movie industry, once they were wedded in January 1940: Reagan turning twenty-nine, Jane turning twenty-three. They soon had a daughter, they adopted a son, had another baby (a daughter who died), but in 1948, after eight years of marriage, they divorced – an experience from which Reagan never quite recovered.

Tiny Ms Wyman was both girlish and all-woman – 'hard-boiled, intense and passionate' as a friend described. She loved gaiety, singing and nightclubs. Reagan, by contrast, was tall, handsome – 'a very sexy-looking man, of course – looked wonderful in swimming trunks' – but 'rather square'.[110] In a movie world of self-preening and insecure artists he exuded unusual steadiness, wholesomeness and a persistent, unshakeable optimism, as if he would allow nothing bad ever to get to him, and would always think the best of people. He was loyal to Wyman, even to the point of accompanying her to her sessions with her psychiatrist and encouraging her to have 'a fling' with her co-star Lew Ayres during the filming of *Johnny Belinda*.[111] 'I know Jane and I know she loves me' he insisted to Hedda Hopper when there were rumours of impending separation. 'I don't know what this is all about, and I don't know why Jane has done it. For my part, I hope to live with her for the rest of my life.'[112]

Wyman's defection – she was the cause of the divorce, he insisted – crippled him. She ejected him from their house, then gave him a turquoise Cadillac convertible for his thirty-seventh birthday on February 6, 1948. She took him back into their house, then threw him out again and filed for divorce for his unceasing, boorish talk of politics. 'The plain truth was that such a thing was so far from ever being imagined by me that I had no resources to call on' Reagan acknowledged later. He had been 'a prince' of Hollywood, the perfect gentleman of the Sunset Strip.

For months Reagan went into denial, certain his wife would take him back. Hope faded as the lawyers sharpened their quills and in June 1948 a divorce decree was granted, which became absolute in July 1949. By then Reagan was a wreck. 'He was heartbroken. He really was' recalled Patricia Neal, who'd replaced Wyman in Reagan's next movie, *John Loves Mary* (which flopped). At midnight on New Year's Eve 1948, Reagan had 'wept and wept on an older woman's arm'.[113]

Though he met Nancy Robbins Davis, a young aspiring actress, in the autumn of 1949, Reagan was simply unable to get over his divorce, simultaneously dating a seemingly unending series of 'Hollywood starlets, singers, models, and beauticians' as one biographer of Nancy Davis put it, from Doris Day and Rhonda Fleming to Adele Jergens, Kay Stewart, Ruth Roman, Monica Lewis, Penny Edwards, Ann Sothern . . . 'I hate to say he was weak,' recalled Doris Lilly, one of his many 'conquests', 'maybe a nicer word would be passive.' This was understandable because, as another of his companions recalled, Jane Wyman haunted him to the point of impotence. 'He was so in love with that woman that she had become an obsession with him. When she walked out on him, he couldn't function – couldn't go out of the house, couldn't work, couldn't cook, couldn't perform sexually', Jacqueline Park recalled – as well as the time he dropped his glass and, pointing to the shards, told her: 'That is what is going to happen to your heart if you stay in this town. One way or the other – if you make it or if you don't make it – this town will break your heart. That's how your heart will look if you decide to stay here.'[114] He got Jacqueline pregnant, but then refused to have anything to do with her, or the abortion she ended up having.[115] 'I woke up one morning,' he confessed later, 'and I couldn't remember the name of the girl I was in bed with. I said, "Hey, I gotta get a grip here."'[116] When Nancy Robbins Davis became pregnant by him at the end of 1949, he finally agreed to marry her, and reform his broken life.

Reagan's private reformation was not easy. It would be claimed he was seeing at least six other women at the time he agreed to marry Nancy; embarrassed and ashamed, he would only agree to a small wedding. Two witnesses were invited, and only afterwards did Reagan dare tell his mother what he had done. He even went on seeing one of his mistresses, red-headed actress Christine Larson, in the months afterwards – and was with her in bed, she claimed, when Nancy gave birth to their first child, Patti. He told Christine his life was ruined, and that he had been 'tricked' into marriage.[117] But it was too late. He had made his marital bed and must lie in it, he recognized, though he would, in consequence, grow a secret layer around his heart that no one would ever be able to pierce. 'You can get just so far with Ronnie, and then something happens' Nancy later confessed.[118] And she added, thoughtfully: 'Although he loves people, he often seems remote, and he doesn't let anybody get too close. There's a wall around him. He lets me come closer than anyone else, but there are times when even I feel that barrier.'[119] This view was seconded by

Reagan's son Ron who, like his mother, later puzzled over the fact that there was 'something that he holds back. You get just so far, and then the curtain drops.'[120] Ron described his relationship with his father as 'friendly and loving', but 'he gets a little bit antsy if you try and get too close and personal and too father-and-sonny'.[121] Reagan's daughter Patti was more forthright, however. 'I never knew who he was,' she described her disappointment, 'I could never get through to him.'[122]

Without Nancy Davis – stepdaughter of a Republican doctor – Reagan would probably not have managed to overcome his hurt at all. Nancy's tough, no-nonsense, businesslike approach to marriage and to the world transformed Reagan's life in Hollywood. Petite, prim, pointy-nosed and with a pronounced chin, at thirty years old she became, in effect, his business manager. She had pressed him to get her a seat on the Screen Actors Guild, she applauded rather than deplored his political views, pushed him in new directions – and erected a fence around his daily life as his moral guardian, effacing any mention of his former wife. Within the safety zone created around him by 'Mrs Nancy Reagan' – as she recast herself in Tinseltown, having given up acting – Reagan gradually blossomed: his faltering career was rescued by television work and increasing political engagements that eventually led him towards elected office. By learning to operate his memory selectively, he was able not only to erase Jane Wyman from his conscious life (he only gave Jane and his first marriage twenty-nine words in his 748-page autobiography, *An American Life*), but also to blot out what he did not wish to see, or recall, in politics. Instead he focused relentlessly on the reality show he was scripting for California and then America, in which he would take the leading role, and which in time he would direct.

What Jane Wyman had considered boring, Nancy Davis recognized as American genius as she set about creating a home environment that would glue Reagan's broken doll together and make him whole, the better to fulfil his unique talent as a political communicator: at once folksy and inspiring, passionately sincere and disarmingly humorous. Since he was gentle, almost passive, she would play bad cop to his good cop. In doing so she offended people who either didn't share her reverence for his leadership or who resented her KGB style of policing behind the scenes. ('There was no ambiguity ever with regard to her power' a long-time colleague noted. 'If she thought someone was disloyal to her Ronnie, that was a nuclear holocaust!' Any 'dealings with her were difficult at best'.)[123] Others mocked her abject reliance on soothsayers and astrologers, as in ancient Rome, considering her a witch. But by her absolute devotion to his welfare, contentment and success, she earned his admiration and loyalty, not least when he recognized that his once photographic memory was fading into dementia, and finally Alzheimer's, which was diagnosed in 1994.

Ronald Reagan died at his home in Bel Air on June 5, 2004, not having opened his eyes for four years.[124] He was buried on the hill below his Presidential Library in Simi Valley, California, six days later.

# CHAPTER TEN

# GEORGE H. W. BUSH

Republican
41st President
(January 20, 1989–January 20, 1993)

## Part One: The Road to the White House

Born in a suburb of Boston, Massachusetts on June 12, 1924, George Herbert Walker Bush was considered a quintessential American WASP, following a long line of American worthies: his great-grandfather was an Episcopalian minister on Staten Island, New York, his grandfather a fabulously wealthy industrialist in Ohio. His father, Prescott Bush, became a senator, having served in combat in France in World War I as a field artillery captain, like Harry Truman.

Prescott Bush had married a wealthy woman, Dorothy Walker, and worked in her father's big investment firm in New York. There, he became both rich and a pillar of the establishment. Commuting each day to Manhattan, but living in Greenwich, Connecticut, Prescott Bush employed a cook, a maid and a chauffeur; he also served as moderator of the 148-strong Greenwich Representative Town Meeting as 'an active practising Republican', and was founder of the Greenwich Taxpayers Association.

Gloomy and uncommunicative, the giant (6' 4") Prescott Bush left the upbringing of his five children largely to his wife Dorothy, a no-nonsense martinet who shared his conservative views. When the master of Saybrook College told an off-colour joke, Prescott turned to his wife and said: 'Dorothy, we're leaving.' And they left.[1] When his brother abandoned his wife and children to marry a Philadelphia socialite, Prescott severed all connection with his sibling.[2] There was right and there was wrong – and Dorothy, schooled at Miss Porter's, was equally firm in her judgement.

On his eighteenth birthday in June 1942, straight out of Phillips Andover school, George – who was expected to attend Yale, like his

elder brother – registered instead at the navy recruiting station in New
York. By the following summer he was the youngest trained pilot in
the US Navy, and by January 1944, at age nineteen, he was flying off
the aircraft carrier USS *San Jacito* in the Pacific, first in bombing runs
against Wake Island, then on Chichi Jima, where on September 2 his
plane – a TBF Avenger – was hit but managed to drop four 500 lb
bombs on its target. Baling out at 2,000 feet with another of his three-
man crew, whose parachute did not open, he was the only one to
survive, rescued by a US submarine, the *Finback*, while fellow pilots
strafed approaching Japanese vessels.[3] Like Lieutenant John F. Kennedy,
he refused to be repatriated to the United States, but flew a further
eight combat missions over the Japanese-occupied Philippines before
going home aged twenty-one, with the Distinguished Flying Cross,
fifty-eight missions and 126 carrier landings to his credit.

After marrying the daughter of the company director of a big
women's magazine, Bush duly attended Yale, where he was accepted
into the exclusive Skull and Bones society, captained the university
baseball team, concentrated on business and finance, and graduated
in 1948 after only two and a half years. Anxious to escape his mother
and mother-in-law's critical gaze, he declined to join his father's investment company in New York, and instead obeyed the American injunction 'Go West, young man, and grow up with the country.' Working
for a Yale classmate, Neil Mallon, and his company the International
Derrick & Equipment Company, he moved to West Texas as an
oilman. Settling down with his growing family among cattle ranchers
and 'black gold' riggers and prospectors, the 'Ivy League' salesman
learned to mask his preppy background and barbecue with people
of all stripes.

From supplying equipment to the Texas oil industry, George Bush
moved into lease prospecting for mineral rights, starting his own
company, Bush-Overby, with $350,000 loaned from his father, his uncle
and his family's friends, including one of his father's clients, the owner
of the *Washington Post*, Eugene Meyer. Switching then from leases to
oil drilling, Bush formed a new company, Zapata Oil, in 1953. Striking
rich in Coke County, he became a prospective millionaire in Midland,
Texas, moving to a house with a swimming pool, while his father
Prescott went to Washington as senator for Connecticut.

Though two inches shorter than his father, George Bush was still tall at 6' 2", a certified World War II hero, handsome and personable, a born conciliator-adventurer with few fixed views on anything. Wherever he was, he blended in: popular, well connected, modest, and open to suggestion. Soon he was building special rigs and drilling offshore, on contract to major distributors in the Gulf of Mexico, and going international in the Persian Gulf, in the South China Sea off Brunei, and in the Caribbean off Trinidad. As the first self-made millionaire among his transplanted Yale cohort, he was the envy of his colleagues. What they could not understand was why Bush – who seemed apolitical except where offshore drilling legislation was concerned – then decided to go into politics.

In part Bush was floating on the tide of oil, which made Houston, Texas – where Bush moved in 1960 – the 'oil and chemical capital' of America. In part, though, he was borne by the same political tide on which his father, as an Eisenhower Republican, had risen to prominence. Prescott Bush suffered ill health and had decided not to run again for the Senate, after two terms, in 1962. Though George gave no thought to succeeding him in Connecticut, which would have meant carpet-bagging, he decided to make a run for political office in his new home state of Texas which, in the wake of the Civil Rights tsunami, was turning increasingly Republican.

In the long run, Bush's political prescience was as marked as his oil prospecting instinct. However, it involved moral compromises that caused his 'leviathan of a father' deep concern.[4] In February 1963 Bush was elected chairman of the Republican Party of Harris County, embracing two congressional districts. He'd affected a slight Texas drawl, but still found it hard to evade his 'preppy Yale' persona among ten-gallon hats, Bible-thumpers, diehard anti-Communist nationalists and John Birch Society stalwarts. 'It was his nature to try to get along with everybody', a campaign colleague recalled, appalled that, in his naivety, Bush would even think of bringing Birchers into the Republican hierarchy.[5] 'He didn't understand', the campaigner remarked, not recognizing Bush's instinctive appreciation that, in order to offset his educated East Coast carpetbagger image, he needed to get the backing of good, Goldwater, values-obsessed, Texas extremists. In 1964, approaching his fortieth birthday, George Bush made his first run for the Senate, easily winning the Republican Party primary as a 'Goldwater Republican'.

Like Goldwater, Bush opposed Johnson's civil rights bill, declaring it a 'new civil rights bill to protect fourteen per cent of the people', and excoriated his anti-poverty measures. He also opposed admission of Red China to the United Nations, and even the Nuclear Test Ban Treaty, which he called 'foolishness'. 'The sun's going to shine in the Senate some day / George Bush is going to chase them liberals away' his Bush Bonnett Belles chanted in 200 Texas town squares, while Bush recklessly defamed his opponent and other Democrats, using guilt by association.[6] Anyone who had given money to Martin Luther King's movement, for example, he tarred as a near-terrorist, while the right-wing fanatical Birchers who were supporting him were lauded as sanctified patriots. On election day, however, he failed to dislodge Senator Ralph Yarborough, the popular sitting Democratic senator, for whom President Johnson campaigned, losing by a massive 300,000 votes. 'I just don't know how it happened', Bush confessed in shock to reporters. 'I guess I have a lot to learn about.'[7]

He had a lot to be ashamed of, also, his opponents felt.

Afterwards, Bush was contrite. So concerned were his parents by the extreme positions he'd taken that neither of them had come out to Texas to help campaign for him. To his Episcopalian minister, Bush confessed: 'You know, John, I took some of the far right positions to get elected. I hope I never do it again. I regret it.'[8] He even admitted in a speech the next year he was 'ashamed' not to have spoken out against the 'pandemonium' of right-wing hate groups and racists.[9] Shame could not obscure the fact, however, that oceans of oil money had 'talked' in the election, more than a million formerly Democratic votes in Texas helping to produce the biggest Republican turnout in Texan history.

If Senator Yarborough, once elected, expected the young war hero to go back to his oil wells, he was much mistaken. Political ambition now became an addiction for Bush, and with President Johnson starting the Vietnam War, then escalating it, Bush (who supported it) felt confident in standing for election as a congressman for the predominantly (90 per cent) white Seventh District of Texas in 1966, comprising Houston's north-west city and suburban wards.

To show his absolute determination, moreover, Bush resigned his CEO and chairman's position with Zapata, sold his stock and this time ran to the *left* of his Dixiecrat opponent, an old-fashioned district attorney, racist Frank Briscoe. Completely reversing his anti-civil rights platform of only two years before, Bush sponsored a black girls' softball team, the George Bush All-Stars, who went on to challenge and beat all five white teams in the Houston league. He deliberately had himself photographed presenting the trophies to winners and losers, yet the volte-face did him no harm, especially in the context of young students representing a new generation. From a six-to-one majority for the Democratic candidate in the previous election, voters not only turned out in record numbers, but gave Bush, as a Republican, a 57.6 per cent majority.

One of forty-seven freshman Republican representatives in January 1967, Congressman Bush was, a colleague recalled, 'pretty innocent of political ideas generally': a politician still in the making, and bereft of political vision other than to serve in the nation's Capitol. In some ways, this helped him stand out against the more partisan members of the House. He was strangely inarticulate on the stump or in front of large gatherings, yet movie-star handsome, alert, ambitious, but modest in person. With his father's help, he got a seat on the Ways and Means Committee and soon set his sights on higher things, namely the vice presidency, if the Democratic administration was brought down thanks to the very Vietnam War that Republicans, ironically, had pressed Johnson to declare.

Aware how strong LBJ's influence still was in Texas, Bush went out to Vietnam, where he was encouraged by what he saw of American soldiers fighting on the ground, as well as navy fliers setting off to bomb Hanoi. With General Westmoreland demanding another 200,000 troops, and the Tet Offensive demonstrating the weakness of the South Vietnamese junta, however, he had to acknowledge it was the 'wrong war' to have started. He felt certain the 'next struggle will be in the Middle East', not South East Asia. Yet how withdraw, without dishonouring the flag? He did not oppose Johnson or the war – but he did oppose an aspect of it that surprised his Texas constituents.

Seeing the disproportionate number of African Americans fighting in Vietnam, Bush found himself ashamed over housing discrimination at home. Bush therefore voted in the House for President Johnson's bill to outlaw discrimination in housing, knowing it could end his political career in Texas. 'I voted for the bill,' he wrote a Yale friend, 'and the roof is falling in – boy does the hatred surface. I have had

more mail on this subject than on Vietnam and taxes and sex all put
together.'¹⁰ He even received death threats but persevered, announcing
to voters of the Seventh District that he would be betraying his sacred
duty to follow his own moral judgement as their elected representative if he did not stand up for basic American decency. As someone
who had himself served his country in combat, he declared that no
one 'should have the door slammed in his face because he is a Negro
or speaks with a Latin-American accent. Open housing offers a ray of
hope for blacks and other minorities locked out by habit and discrimination.'¹¹ With those words Congressman Bush demonstrated, finally,
a moral backbone missing in action since he went into politics – and
to his astonishment no one dared oppose his 1968 re-election candidacy from either party.

Bush's moral courage, however, had been spurred by the fact that
he was not overly concerned about re-election. The truth was, he had
hoped the Republican nominee for president, Nixon, might select him
as his running mate that year, since no lesser person than President
Eisenhower – who had admired Senator Prescott Bush – had recommended young Bush as a candidate for the post, just as young Nixon
had been recommended to Eisenhower in 1952. Nixon, however, chose
an unknown former Democrat and former governor of Maryland,
Spiro T. Agnew.

Spurned by the president, Bush now set his sights for a second time
on a seat in the Senate, not only toadying up to Johnson in the hope
of getting his imprimatur (he attended Johnson's farewell to
Washington at Andrews Air Force Base instead of Nixon's post-
inaugural ceremonies), but also visiting the former president at his
Texas ranch later, asking Johnson if he should run. 'Son, the difference between being a member of the Senate and a member of the
House is the difference between chicken salad and chicken shit',
Johnson memorably advised. 'Do I make my point?'¹²

Bush took the advice, even where it meant transgressing campaign
ethics – approaching President Nixon for financial backing in 1970,
and happily taking $106,000 from Nixon's illegal 'Townhouse Fund',
in violation of campaign finance law.¹³

Bush's behaviour reflected the two sides of his political personality:
the fawning young man, willing to compromise his integrity and self-
respect in order to get ahead, and the *noblesse oblige*, an honourable

and courageous individual whom his high-minded aides – particularly his Texas lawyer friend and campaign manager, James Baker III – admired and respected.

Neither Bush's toadying nor his financial impropriety worked, however. Democratic Congressman Lloyd Bentsen, a self-made Texas millionaire in insurance and an even greater war hero than Bush (having been awarded the Distinguished Flying Cross, the Air Medal and three Oak Leaf Clusters as a bomber pilot in World War II in Europe) won.

'Like Custer, who said there were just too many Indians,' Bush said in an attempt to make light of his second defeat running for the Senate, 'I guess there were too many Democrats.' In truth, he was 'shattered by the loss', a close friend recalled, 'he said it was just the end of everything'.[14]

In his campaign Bush had, to his credit, refused to use the odious 'attack ads' that Nixon's 'evil genius', Charles Colson, had suggested to him as Special White House Counsel; in fact Bush had called the White House in a fury to say: 'Don't ever send anything of that nature up here again. Tell Mr Colson I called and be sure he understands.'[15] Such moral revulsion bespoke Bush's better nature: Colson would be indicted as one of the Watergate Seven, and later went to jail for organizing the burglary of whistle-blower Daniel Ellsberg's psychiatrist's office. The lesson of Bush's defeat was that, without using such 'derogatory' attack ads, as a Republican politician with poor speaking ability he simply could not get elected. As another friend noted, Bush was too inarticulate: 'his sentences were ragged, ran into each other, and tended to leave thoughts hanging and ideas incomplete' – much like 'General Eisenhower whom I had observed in 1952'.[16]

It was an apt comparison, save that Bush was not a world-famous American general. Distraught and determined not to be left out in the cold two years into a Republican administration, Bush appealed directly to President Nixon for the job of Treasury Secretary, which was becoming vacant. Nixon said no. Disappointed, Bush begged Nixon to appoint him, instead, to the post of US ambassador to the UN. Nixon expressed surprise. Even Bush's associates were nonplussed. 'George,' Bush's old Skull and Bones friend, Lud Ashley, exclaimed when he heard of the plan, 'what the fuck do you know about foreign affairs?'[17]

The answer was very little – but a willingness to learn, and a place in the Nixon cabinet. Duly appointed to the post at age forty-seven, Ambassador Bush underwent a crash course in world politics in New York. As important as it was as an introduction to world affairs, the position also offered a ringside cabinet seat in the secretive, manipulative world of Nixon's imperial White House, since Nixon and Kissinger, he soon found, were double-crossing him, especially over Taiwan and Communist China. Bush belatedly favoured American recognition of Red China, which he saw as a 'brilliant move', but resented being used as a fall guy at the United Nations, where on October 24, 1971, Taiwan was duly expelled by a 59–55 vote in the General Assembly.

'A total Nixon man. Doubt if you can do better than Bush', Nixon commented with smug gratitude at Camp David when Bush's name came up for the post of Deputy Treasury Secretary, following Nixon's re-election in 1972.[18] Bush was not impressed. He had brought rich gifts to the president's secret campaign table, including $100,000 from Bush's old partner in Texas, William Liedke; he therefore felt he was 'owed', and baulked at the notion of being appointed a mere 'super-secretary' troubleshooter at the Treasury. There was an alternative sinecure Nixon could bestow, Bush knew – and desired. However, it was one that would mean firing the current chairman of the Republican National Committee, Senator Bob Dole, whom Nixon in any case considered insufficiently obsequious. Stirred by the financial and electoral implications, Nixon warmed to the idea. Dole duly stood down, remarking later that he had been 'Bushwhacked'.

Bush's wife Barbara, who'd enjoyed living in New York, hated the idea of the RNC post in Washington – 'the last thing in the world' she thought her husband should do.[19] Her instinct was right. But from his illegal cash transactions, Bush knew exactly what he was getting into by entering the lion's den; indeed his eye for the main chance within government and politics was unerring. Dissembling, he told his wife he couldn't 'turn a president down', whereas in truth the idea had been his own.[20] The Republican chairmanship would allow him access to the Nixon administration at all levels, and to meet all the top people in Republican politics, sitting with the cabinet and networking with the richest funders across the country. At the very least this would guarantee a soft landing if his political career came to an early end.

No soft landing, however, was to be had. No sooner had Bush moved to Washington and taken over the Republican Party's national office than Nixon's house of cards began to shake, thanks to Watergate. Bush admitted privately he was 'sickened' by the growing revelations, yet he continued to tour the country as chairman of the RNC, defending the president and denying anything illegal had been done: a *tour d'excuse* in which he gave some 101 speeches, held seventy-eight news conferences, made eleven appearances on television and travelled almost 100,000 miles visiting thirty-three states.[21]

Bush's desperate cover-up of malfeasance did no good. In October 1973, Vice President Agnew was forced to resign on corruption charges. Once again Bush's name was touted as a possible appointee for the post, which would put him in the White House if Nixon was successfully impeached. Despite his stalwart, transnational defence of the president, however, Bush was turned down yet again by Nixon. Instead, the president selected the Minority Leader in the House, Congressman Gerald R. Ford.

Disappointed, Bush continued to support the president, though even his wife noted in her diary she was 'worried about George as he does not love his work. How could he? All this scandal.'[22] Nor was Nixon even grateful, calling Bush a 'worrywart' for his anxieties over Watergate. Nixon's daughter Julie was more direct: she telephoned Bush directly, 'and asked him why', as Barbara Bush later recalled, 'he wasn't defending her dad more'.[23]

Such loyal stonewalling by Bush merely helped buy Nixon time to explore further ways of evading justice. The president was able to erase the most criminal eight minutes from his White House tapes, but the many hundreds of undeleted hours were subpoenaed. Still George Bush defended his chief, however, for whom he felt genuine compassion. 'He has a different sense than the rest of people', Bush noted in his diary on August 5, 1974 as Nixon vowed to fight impeachment in Congress to the bitter end. 'He came up the hard way. He hung tough. He hunkered down. He stonewalled. He became president of the United States and a damn good one in many ways, but now it had all caught up with him. All the people he hated – Ivy League, press, Establishment, Democrats, privileged – all of this ended up biting him and bringing him down.'[24]

Bush's sensitivity to the president's inferiority complex did credit to the Ivy Leaguer's social antennae, but not to his moral compass. 'My temptation was to blast the president,' he noted in his diary, 'blast the lie, and then I thought, why add to the personal tragedy and the personal grief? Events were moving so fast that it just didn't seem right to kind of "pile it on".'[25]

At a cabinet meeting on August 6, 1974, Bush was, like Vice President Ford, less than courageous in declining to raise the issue of resignation, and contenting himself with remarks about the effect of Watergate on Republican chances at the forthcoming midterm election. 'Am I failing to lead?' Bush asked in his diary. On August 7, he plucked up courage to at least send a letter to the president, advising him to resign. With Senator Goldwater and others telling Nixon in person that he would not survive impeachment, the president caved in and agreed to stand down. Ford's succession then raised the question of who would fill the vice-presidential vacancy.

Once again, Bush's name was shortlisted for the post. His supporters, led by James Baker III, hounded the White House and engineered calls from across the nation on his behalf. It did no good. 'I let my hopes zoom unrealistically' Bush confided to a friend, gutted to learn he had been turned down in favour of the four-times governor of New York, moderate Republican Nelson Rockefeller.[26] Deeply disappointed, Bush went to China as head of the US Mission in Beijing, wondering as he flew there with his wife, 'Am I running away from something?'[27]

Unknown to him, he was – from a White House disaster. His year and a half in Beijing, meanwhile, allowed him to grow up politically, convincing him that the United States had nothing 'to fear' from China. 'The talk about how we lost China infuriates the Chinese and *now* it infuriates me. I can see where it is very clearly wrong. China was not ours to lose,' Bush candidly acknowledged in his diary, 'and that has been part of the problem.'[28] He determined, if he could get back on to the political ladder, that he would do his best to make Republican foreign policy more realistic and less ideological.

President Ford felt the same, but was a poor picker of men to serve him. Instead of distancing himself from the disgraced president, Ford pardoned Nixon and kept on Henry Kissinger as combined national security adviser and Secretary of State despite his involvement in Watergate. ('Bullshit', Nixon told his lawyer. '[Kissinger] knew what was going on in the Plumbers' activities . . . Don't let him give you that crap. He was – he was clear up to his ankles himself'.[29]) Ford then found himself so out of his depth he had to summon Donald Rumsfeld, Nixon's *éminence grise*, to restore order as his chief of staff. And to George Bush's chagrin, Rumsfeld hated George Bush.

After Saigon was overrun by the North Vietnamese, Rumsfeld got himself promoted to Secretary of Defense. Dick Cheney, Rumsfeld's right-hand man, then became chief of staff and together the two urged Ford to axe the centrist, progressive Republican, Vice President Rockefeller, from the forthcoming 1976 presidential ticket. Lest George Bush again became contender for the vice-presidential post, which Rumsfeld coveted for himself, they also arranged for Ford to recall Bush from Beijing and park him at the CIA, with a promise to Congress not to run for electoral office in 1976.

Bush's old partner, Hugh Liedke, warned Bush the appointment was political homicide. Even Bush himself saw it as a move to 'Bury Bush at the CIA', which he called 'a graveyard for politics', prompting his wife to invite more guests to Beijing to drive away her husband's blues.[30] For his part Rumsfeld was heard to say the appointment would 'sink the sonofabitch for good'.[31] His and Cheney's Machiavellian manipulations had succeeded, it appeared, in ending Bush's political career.

Directing 15,000 spooks and their handlers on a 'black budget' traditionally kept secret from the public and Congress, Bush now received a new crash course in imperial strategy and tactics – this time not in diplomacy, but below the radar. Given the corrupt way in which Nixon had sought to use the CIA, the spy agency was up against the ropes. Not only was Bush summoned fifty-one times to go before Congress – where the Church Committee held its celebrated hearings into government-sanctioned assassination and illegal wiretapping – but he also inherited the problem that his predecessor William Colby had postponed, but which was rearing its ugly head once more: pressure from right-wing extremists to bust détente.

Later known as the Rise of the Vulcans, this was Goldwater II: a clique of American diehards, indifferent to Chinese Communism but virulently anti-Soviet, and driven to despair over military defeat in Vietnam, as symbolized in the last American helicopters lifting people away from the abandoned US embassy in Saigon.[32] Their venom was now directed at the empire that had got away scot-free from the imbroglios in South East Asia: the Russians, whom they now accused of an accelerated military build-up, and of planning a pre-emptive nuclear strike against the US, concealed behind détente.

Should George Bush, as CIA director, have permitted what became known as the 'Team B Panel Report on Strategic Objectives', an in-famous minority report which damned current CIA estimates of Russian capabilities and argued for a tough termination of détente? Disciples of right-wing professors Leo Strauss (who had died in 1973) and Albert Wohlstetter of the University of Chicago, the self-styled 'neocons' included Norman Podhoretz, Irving Kristol, Richard Pipes, Harry Jaffa, Paul Wolfowitz and Abram Shulsky. Under Professor Pipes' Team B – which boasted Paul Nitze and Paul Wolfowitz – the team objected to the CIA's view of Russia as a crumbling economic edifice, best cauterized by containment. Instead, Pipes' radical right-wing team not only invented fantasy Russian military programmes, from nuclear-powered beam weapons to non-acoustic submarines, but refused to accept the role of the CIA as an objective intelligence-gathering body. Pipes thus damned existing CIA estimates, to which he became privy, as a gross underestimation of the Soviet Union's 'intensity, scope and implicit threat', arguing that, even if correct, the CIA had hitherto only assessed 'the adversary's *capabilities*', not 'his ideas, motives and aspirations'.[33]

Almost every claim in the Team B Report – in particular the asser-tion that the Soviet Union had a 'large and expanding Gross National Product' and was working towards a 'first strike' capability – was right-wing moonshine. 'I would say that all of it was fantasy' commented Dr Anne Cahn of the Arms Control and Disarmament Agency later. 'If you go through most of Team B's specific allegations about weapons systems, and you just examine them one by one, they were all wrong. *All* of them.'[34] Even Bush's CIA deputy director, Admiral Daniel Murphy, derided Team B's 'reality check' as a brash challenge that 'did not amount to a hill of beans'.[35] Giving them access to 'data' that was denied to any other group outside the CIA, Bush had, however, taken a tremendous risk, the more so once Team B leaked 'a tough estimate of the USSR's military build-up in order to stop [president-elect] Carter from cutting the defense budget' – a charge that 'couldn't be further from the truth', Bush protested on television.[36]

Was it, though? Right-wing extremism was certainly mounting in America. Carter won the 1976 presidential election, but his victory, though sufficient in Electoral College votes, was garnered by a mere percentage point in the popular vote. The entire western half of America, from the Pacific Ocean eastwards to a line running from Minnesota to Texas, had swung to the Republicans. Despite his failure to beat President Ford for the Republican nomination, Reagan vowed to continue his crusade for the presidency. Caught between two stools – a defeated but resurgent Republican right and an incoming Democratic president with a liberal agenda – Bush was playing safe: not siding with the neocons, but not opposing them either. Moreover, in a telling illustration of his essentially apolitical character he actually offered to serve a further year as CIA director under Carter.

Fortunately for Bush's political career, the president – a deeply religious man and genuine southerner, who had a visceral antipathy to the East Coast Establishment – took an instant dislike to Bush as a dissembler without convictions, and fired him. On January 20, 1977, Bush thus found himself without a job, an oil company, or – when leaving Washington – a home.

In Texas no Republican electoral office looked winnable to Bush, and he was proven right when his lawyer-aide James Baker III failed to win the Texas governorship in 1978, and Bush's eldest son George Jr, who ran for Congress in the Nineteenth District, was defeated. For a while, as Rumsfeld had intended, George H. W. Bush, the chameleon of the Republican Party, with ties to all but no fixed convictions, was all washed up.

Many men might have given up further political ambitions at this point. The Republican Party which his father had served as a senator, with its old-fashioned fiscal conservatism, libertarian creed and paternalistic sense of social responsibility, was dying. In its place a new confluence of evangelical Christians, moneybags and virulent ideological anti-Communists were moulding a potent greed-machine, peculiarly suited to a nation of immigrants imbued with the American dream of becoming individually rich, or at least richer. Led by Ronald Reagan, the 'father' of the American revolt against taxes (he had supported a ballot referendum that capped property taxes, Proposition 1, as governor of California in 1973), the simplistic prosperity gospel movement cast off old-fashioned European values of compassion and social responsibility. In their place the movement espoused a muscular, born-again Christianity based on personal faith, a community of fellow Born-Agains, and vilification of government, whether good or bad, for daring to redistribute personal wealth. Since George Bush had not been born again as a Christian, but remained the same Christian he had always been, this posed a challenge.

In the event Bush refused to advocate the teaching of creationism in science classes. He also refused to oppose abortion even in cases of rape or incest, or to demand the overthrow of the Equal Rights Amendment – the campaign planks of Ronald Reagan. Instead, drawing comfort from polls showing that Gerald Ford, a moderate, was still the most popular Republican in the nation, and on the assumption that Ford would not run a second time, George Bush announced his candidacy for his party's nomination for president of the United States on May 1, 1979.

Why, Bush's friends asked, did he do so when he had little or no chance of defeating Reagan? Bush was unfazed. If Reagan, aged sixty-eight, were to falter, Bush countered, he would be left in pole position. Against a weak field of competitors (the former vice-presidential candidate Senator Dole, Senator Howard Baker and Congressman John Anderson), he felt himself to be the strongest contender behind Reagan. Besides, Reagan might overreach himself in demonizing the Russians, leading the majority of registered Republicans to plump for Bush as a moderate. And finally, there was, once again, the matter of the second spot, the vice presidency. Although it had never happened in practice, in theory the successful candidate might select the runner-up at the Republican National Convention in a bid for swift party unity following the gruelling campaign for the nomination.

Given that George Bush was still virtually unknown to the general population, he performed remarkably well, beating Reagan in the first caucus of the campaign in Ohio in January 1980. With James Baker III as his campaign manager, Bush went on to win a number of important states thereafter. But in calling Reagan's economics 'voodoo' it was he, not Reagan, who overreached. If he attacked or ridiculed Reagan, his chief strategist warned, 'they'll hate you. You can't do that', Reagan being simply too popular among his Republican fans. What he had to do, Bush was advised, was to attack the *other* candidates, 'and you're there. And if [Reagan] fails, then you can get it.'[37]

Though Bush eventually dropped his strategist, he did as advised, prudently withdrawing from the contest well before the National Convention lest he become a spoiler in Reagan's quest to unseat President Carter. Reagan duly won the Republican nomination, and telephoned Bush personally to offer him the second slot – if Bush was willing to subscribe to Reagan's right-wing platform. He was.

Cresting a patriotic, evangelical tide of greed and indifference to the poor, the Reagan-Bush ticket duly won both the 1980 and 1984 elections, the latter by the largest landslide in electoral history, when Reagan took forty-nine states to Mondale's one. Before the embers had died down, however, the race to become Reagan's successor began. As Barbara Bush noted, on January 21, 1985, 'the 1988 campaign started'.[38]

By the spring of that year Vice President Bush was already holding his first formal campaign strategy meeting for the 1988 election, with a ruthless young advertising genius named Lee Atwater as his political director, and Bush's eldest son George Jr working as his enforcer. At their urging, Bush also began to court the nation's top televangelists – Jerry Falwell, Jim and Tammy Faye Baker, Jimmy Swaggart and Pat Robertson – while positioning himself to meet or roll with any challenge from the right of his own party. He got rid of all his old staff 'because he knew the mission he needed was different', explained a new Bush operative, Ron Kaufman. 'George Bush is much smarter, much tougher than people give him credit for, much more Machiavellian.'[39]

Ruthless ambition allied to opportunism was now propelling Bush closer and closer to the extremist fire, at whatever cost. 'I've got to fulfill this mission' he wrote in his diary as the election grew closer, aware that he had broken the law over Iran-Contra to keep both Reagan and himself from possible impeachment.[40] He thus continued to serve the faltering president in the waning months of the Reagan presidency loyally and uncritically. Then on October 13, 1987, he finally declared his official candidacy for the Republican Party's presidential nomination.

With President Reagan's tepid yet crucial imprimatur, and the backing of Falwell's Moral Majority, Bush was able to win the Republican primary campaign in the spring of 1988. However, Iran-Contra hearings in Congress and an economic recession made his aim to win the election seem dubious; indeed the Democrats were reported to be some seventeen points ahead, a lead they kept into the summer of 1988 when the party conventions were held.

Governor Mike Dukakis, the Democratic nominee and son of Greek immigrants, had a two-term reputation for sober governance of a large, modern state, Massachusetts, but had no idea what he would be up against. The chameleon vice president proclaimed his new, right-wing credentials – anti-abortion, anti-regulatory agencies, denial of the spiralling deficit, anti-taxes ('The Congress will push me to raise taxes, and I'll say no . . . And I'll say to them, Read my lips: no new taxes') as well as a mandatory Pledge of Allegiance in schools. Meanwhile Bush's hit squad, under Lee Atwater, went for Dukakis as a wild, out of control 'Liberal,' sneering at his environmental record in failing to clean up Boston Harbor, and putting out their infamous 'Willie Horton' racist ads: using the photo of a black Massachusetts murderer who had committed armed robbery and rape while on furlough, fourteen years after he was imprisoned.[41]

This was a new Bush, licensing Atwater and his accomplices to aim directly at Dukakis' supposed strength, namely his record as an effective modernizing governor of Massachusetts. Having 'test-marketed' the Willie Horton ads, Atwater later boasted to reporters: 'I realized right then that the sky was the limit on Dukakis' negatives.'[42] It was a tactic to 'strip the bark off the little bastard' and 'make Willie Horton his running mate'.[43]

American politics had always had a Wild West frontier quality, expressed in elections that were rife with real or supposed skullduggery. But Atwater's evil genius was to see, like the Nazis in the 1920s and 1930s, how modern media could be cynically manipulated to vilify opponents. As Bush's media consultant Roger Ailes confided to a journalist, Bush 'hates it, but he knows we'd be getting killed if we didn't go negative'.[44] Saturating television with the Willie Horton ads some 600 times, it was estimated eighty million Americans saw them at least once.

This was Bush's personal pact with the devil, which his honourable, loyal campaign manager and friend James Baker III abhorred.[45] In a moment of unusual misjudgement Bush had overruled Baker and chosen as his running mate a young, unknown, semi-literate but photogenic conservative senator from Indiana, Dan Quayle, who would appeal to evangelicals and the party's anti-abortionist, supply-sider base, yet was entirely unqualified to be 'a heartbeat away from the presidency', as the vice presidency was termed.

With the press revealing Quayle's draft-dodging and lack of credentials, Bush confessed in his diary that 'it was my decision, and I blew it, but I'm not about to say that I blew it'.[46] Instead, he licensed Atwater and Republican national campaign operatives and their funders to work even harder to destroy Dukakis. The *New York Times* observed that Ronald Reagan had at least run his campaigns on the basis of gaining the confidence of the American people, whereas Bush was aiming to destroy it, at least in relation to his presidential opponent.[47] Reeling, Dukakis found himself unable to beat off Atwater's personal attacks on his character, his liberalism, his environmental record, his patriotism, and, above all, his 'guilt' over Willie Horton, even though Dukakis had not been responsible for the Massachusetts rehabilitation-furlough programme, which his predecessor had introduced, and which Dukakis had terminated in the spring of 1988 as a failure. 'The only question is whether we depict Willie Horton with a knife in his hand or without it', Atwater admitted.[48] As Dukakis belatedly did his best to fight back, Atwater worried lest he might have overdone his tactic: 'If this sucker lasted forty-eight hours longer, I'm not sure we would make it.'[49] In the event, however, the 'sucker' failed to beat off Atwater's evisceration. Vice President George H. W. Bush won the White House on November 8, 1988, by a comfortable margin: 426 electoral votes to 112, and thereby became the forty-first President, at age sixty-four.

## Part Two: The Presidency

Aware that his father Senator Prescott Bush would turn in his grave had he known of his son's (and grandson's) use of Lee Atwater, the new president began his inaugural speech on January 20, 1989, with a plea to God. 'For we are given power not to advance our own purposes' his prayer for atonement ran, but to 'serve people. Help us to remember it, Lord. Amen.' Bush then declared he would do his best to celebrate the 'quieter successes that are made not of gold and silk, but of better hearts and finer souls'. His purpose was 'to make kinder the face of the nation and gentler the face of the world. My friends, we have work to do', from helping the homeless to assisting pregnant teenagers and the recovering junkies, in a 'thousand points of light'. 'And so,' he ended, 'today a chapter begins, a small and stately story of unity, diversity, and generosity – shared, and written, together.'

Clearly, the speech had not been written by Atwater, who was made chairman of the Republican National Committee. There, with the help of the young right-wing firebrand, Congressman Newt Gingrich, Atwater began another campaign of character assassination, targeting the new Democratic Speaker of Congress, Tom Foley, whom they insinuated was gay. Bush found Atwater's latest attack so 'disgusting' that although he allowed Atwater to keep his job, in deference to his role in his presidential victory, the president made Atwater fire his odious RNC communications director, Mark Goodin. When Gingrich then became Republican Minority Whip in the House of Representatives, however, there was nothing President Bush could do; the political stage was now set for bloodletting on a deeply divisive, partisan scale. It was as if Atwater's newly diagnosed brain cancer was metastasizing in the polity of America, dooming Bush's inaugural vision of America as a 'proud, free nation, decent and civil'.[50]

Bush had pleaded for more civility in politics, but to get elected he had adopted platforms he did not believe in, and made promises he could not keep. Anti-abortionists were outraged he would not appoint a diehard conservative to the Supreme Court to overthrow *Roe* vs *Wade*, while rabid conservatives became apoplectic when, to balance the budget and begin paying down the spiralling national deficit, he agreed to Congress' demand that he abandon his 'no new taxes' pledge. To the chagrin of New Right conservatives, Bush was proving no different from the very man he had destroyed, Governor Dukakis: a centrist. Unlike Dukakis, however, Bush had no vision of what he wanted to achieve in the White House.

Not having won electoral office on his own account in more than twenty years, Bush found himself at sea – a 'free-form presidency' as one political scientist called it, that had little sway over the Democratic-controlled chambers of Congress and even less over the Republican right. The only terrain where the president could make his mark was foreign affairs, and in 1989 and early 1990 the charismatically challenged

American emperor duly applied himself alongside the wildly popular young leader of the Soviet Union, Mikhail Gorbachev.

Gorbachev had wowed the young not only of Europe but also of the Far East. As China emerged from the long nightmare of Mao's Cultural Revolution, Gorbachev travelled to Beijing in May 1989 to celebrate the 'normalization' of relations between the two tottering empires, some ten days after students occupied Tiananmen Square. As he was driven to meet the eighty-four-year-old Chinese leader Deng Xiaoping, past students screaming his name and the word 'perestroika', Gorbachev wondered 'Who the hell is in charge here?'[51] Only when he returned to Moscow did he get his answer. In a ruthless massacre to re-establish Communist 'order' in the capital, 3,000 students were slaughtered and 10,000 wounded.

Observing the massacre from afar, Bush said nothing, wondering whether Tiananmen Square would preface similar crackdowns in the Communist countries of eastern Europe, where Gorbachev's rhetoric had aroused identical student expectations and unrest. It was becoming clear that, although the Cold War was thawing with glasnost, the *Götterdämmerung* would inevitably be contested by reactionaries – and could be bloody.

Lacking Gorbachev's rhetorical ability, President Bush, as leader of the most powerful empire in the world, nevertheless seemed born to the role of elder statesman. His often apolitical past proved now an asset, insulating him from Republican fealty and allowing him, as former US representative to the UN and Communist China, to see America's best interests in global, rather than local, terms. Given his CIA directorship, successive political appointments and lack of elective credentials, he was, ironically, more akin to a typical Russian leader than Mikhail Gorbachev himself. Guardedly, the two men – who had met at the United Nations General Assembly in New York in November 1988 – thus cosied up to one another in the aftermath of Tiananmen Square, with the fate of the world in their hands.

Anxious not to provoke a military coup in Russia that might lead to a new freeze or Cold War, Bush overruled his new Secretary of Defense, Dick Cheney, who counselled a policy of taking advantage of Soviet weakness to assert US global hegemony, and letting Gorbachev fail.[52] Equally, he ignored the 'hotheads', impatient human rights activists calling for more robust American support for pro-democracy movements not only in China but in the East European bloc – which could only give ammunition to Russia's hardliners. In defiance of Margaret Thatcher's howls of protest, he therefore talked openly of armed force reductions in western Europe, and of acceptance of eventual German reunification. In this quest Bush travelled to Amsterdam, Bonn, Paris, London, and then, in July 1989, to Warsaw and Budapest behind the once seemingly impenetrable Iron Curtain. There, he saw for himself the pent-up public aspiration for freedom from the shackles of Communism in everyday life, as half a million people turned out in Kossuth Square to greet him – much like Americans had been fêted at the end of World War II. Joyfully, Bush threw away his speech and basked in the glow of being an American who simply stood for good things, not guided missiles.

The times, Bush now recognized, were changing faster than American militarists, in their bunkers, had anticipated or thought possible. General Colin Powell, Bush's new chairman of the Joint Chiefs of Staff, had been told by Kremlinologists at the CIA in 1988 that Gorbachev could not last and would be rubbed out; instead, Gorbachev had 'fired a dozen or so generals and hardliners' and had defied the odds. As Powell noted later, 'With all their expertise' the Kremlinologists 'could no longer anticipate events much better than a layman watching television.'[53]

Whatever hawks or 'Vulcans' in America warned, President Bush decided to do his best to keep Gorbachev in power by offering serious reductions and compromises in American military strength, both in men and weapons. Second, he would not tempt fate by threatening American intervention in eastern Europe, as the countdown to Russian relaxation of its control over the bloc countries began. And third, by a personal, one-on-one relationship with Gorbachev, he would attempt to talk down the ailing but heavily armed Soviet nuclear airship, pilot to pilot. Grabbing a sheet of White House notepaper on Air Force One while travelling back to the United States, Bush secretly proposed a meeting with Gorbachev, to take place on battleships anchored by the island of Malta, much like Roosevelt and Churchill when drawing up the Atlantic Charter in August 1941, off Newfoundland – 'without thousands of assistants hovering over our shoulders'.

Gorbachev immediately agreed to the summit, which was duly scheduled to take place at the beginning of December 1989. Even that early date was outpaced by events, however. On October 16, 100,000 anti-government protesters marched through Leipzig, but Gorbachev issued an order that not a single one of the 380,000 Russian troops occupying East Germany would be allowed out of their barracks to support a government crackdown. Two days later, with a nod from Gorbachev, the East German dictator Erich Honecker was deposed. On October 23, Hungary – which had got Gorbachev to promise Soviet troops would not invade or intervene in the country's democratiza-tion, and had begun permitting East German holidaymakers to cross freely into Austria – declared itself an independent republic with free elections set for the spring of 1990. Two days later, as the *New York Times* reported on October 26, President Mikhail S. Gorbachev 'declared today that the Soviet Union has no moral or political right to interfere in the affairs of its East European neighbors'.[54]

This was, for a Soviet emperor, a most extraordinary public state-ment. Though he would exclude his remark from his memoirs, Gorbachev had, in truth, given protesters across the Soviet-occupied nations of eastern Europe the green light. In the most sensational month in post-war European history, the unimaginable happened: on November 9, 1989 the Berlin Wall, erected in 1962 to stem the flood of East German refugees to West Berlin and thence to West Germany, was stormed by a crowd of Germans who, hearing from the post-Honecker government that East Germans were free to visit the West, dared the guards to shoot them as they took sledgehammers to the iconic concrete Mauer.[55]

At the White House President Bush found himself agog at the tele-vised coverage – the fruit of his 'hands-off' policy, trusting that Gorbachev would succeed. The Brezhnev Doctrine (namely the Soviet Right to Intervene) was unmistakably over. The next day the Bulgarian leader, Todor Zhivkov, was dismissed by his own Politburo, and on November 24 the entire Politburo of Czechoslovakia resigned. It was clear that no one save elderly, privileged or self-serving functionaries believed in the old Communist system any more, at least in central and eastern Europe.

Like a snowball, Gorbachev's words and, most of all, his refusal to take or support punitive action by the Communist authorities, now accelerated across Europe. Those who mocked Bush for not showing more emotion at the fall of the Berlin Wall were mistaken. In truth he could hardly believe his eyes, and was minded to jump for joy. He was determined, however, not to do, say, or give anything away, even by gesture, that might make Gorbachev's position in the Kremlin less secure – encapsulated in his quiet dictum 'I'm not going to dance on the wall.'[56] He wrote to Gorbachev to assure him the US, under his leadership, wanted a 'calm and peaceful' transition to full democracy in Europe.[57]

Meeting aboard their battleships anchored in Valetta Harbour on December 2, 1989, the two emperors were lashed by sixteen-foot waves in a freak Mediterranean storm. Both men emerged from the Malta summit satisfied, however. Not only did they establish the basis for a real strategic arms reduction agreement the next year (START), but President Bush obtained a Russian promise not to intervene in the Baltic States as the tiny, defenceless countries declared their independence; meanwhile Gorbachev got verbal assurances Russia would obtain a free trade agreement with America and observer status at the next GATT tariff talks, as well as promises of American help in creating a stock market and establishing private investment and property laws.

Most important of all, perhaps, given Russia's history of being invaded first by Napoleon's imperial armies, then by Kaiser Wilhelm's Second Reich, then by Hitler's Third Reich forces, Malta ended forever the understandable Russian fear that it would be attacked again from the west – either by the forces of the United States or by European nations, including Germany. After forty years of Cold War, Gorbachev recognized that as the Soviet Union adjusted to a different ideological model for economic and political life, the presence of US forces as peacekeepers would actually be essential to the Soviet Union for stability in Europe – especially if Russian troops were withdrawn from the bloc countries. In other words, the American Empire, not the Russian Empire, would henceforth be the responsible guarantor of peace in liberated Europe, ensuring that a reunified Germany, in particular, would never threaten Russia again.

'The summit suggested to Gorbachev', wrote Kremlin watchers, 'that Bush was at last emerging from his fear of the American Right.'[58] Whether Gorbachev was entirely correct was, however, debatable. Even as they met in Valetta Harbour, Bush ordered jets to streak over the Philippines and indicate American willingness to intervene if the coup against President Cori Aquino's elected government succeeded, prompting one of Gorbachev's staff to quip that while the Soviets had abandoned the Brezhnev Doctrine, the US had adopted it. More dramatically, three weeks later, US troops invaded Panama in response to an unwise declaration of war by the Panamanian legislature.

Operation Just Cause was the biggest US military assault conducted since World War II. Moreover, it made US history since there was no rationale of anti-Communism or even anti-socialism, the invasion this time being classically imperial: to remove from power a leader in a foreign country deemed inimical to American interests. Gambling on his decades of paid service to the CIA and US Defense Department, Noriega – the self-styled 'chief executive officer' of the Panamanian Republic – had considered himself immune to American intervention as he ordered the murder of any who confronted or competed with him, assassinated one of the main opposition leaders, voided the spring 1989 elections, foiled two coup attempts and controlled the drug trade as an agent of the Medellin cartel. When the Panamanian legislature, under pressure from Noriega, objected to US military exercises staged in the Canal area on December 15, 1989 and declared 'a state of war' with America, war was exactly what they got.

Almost 57,000 American troops were sent into combat immediately after midnight on December 20, 1989, backed by 300 aircraft. Though the Panamanian defence forces could supposedly field 46,000 troops, the result was (in retrospect) inevitable. At a cost of twenty-four fatalities, the US government was able to put Guillermo Endara – the presumed victor in the voided spring election – on the presidential throne. Noriega himself took refuge in the Vatican embassy in Panama City but was eventually hounded out – ironically, by loud American music – and arrested on January 3, 1990 to stand trial in America on drug-trafficking charges.

In a free vote, the United Nations condemned the invasion as an act of rank imperialism, as did most of the civilized world, especially in view of the several thousand innocent civilian casualties incurred. However, it was difficult to claim sympathy for General Noriega himself, or to argue that the country was not better off without him (as proved to be the case). Above all, American troops were withdrawn into the Canal Zone or to the American mainland within weeks. The invasion thus passed into history as a model modern

American military intervention – if creating, as it did so, a worrying precedent. Noriega himself was unmourned. But what if a similar US invasion was to be inspired by more rabid, ideologically driven American militarists in the vein of Barry Goldwater? What if such an invasion proved less surgically swift and efficient, involving higher casualties among innocent civilians? And what if it got bogged down, either in a long conventional war, or, despite initial success, what if it met a consequential insurgency – thus saddling the United States with a classic imperial conquest that required huge expenditures in men and materiel to maintain? At what point, in such a case, should American troops be withdrawn?

Only six months later, these questions would be raised for real, when another military dictator, Saddam Hussein, marshalled his forces by the border between Iraq and tiny Kuwait.[59]

Hussein had invaded Iran in 1980, compelling the Iraqi Army to fight a futile, eight-year war which ended in the loss of an estimated half a million Iranian and Iraqi lives. Now Hussein appeared to be on the warpath once more. Or was he merely grandstanding, in order to wring territorial and oil concessions from defenceless neighbouring Kuwaitis? No one, apart from Hussein himself, seemed quite sure.

Complaining vociferously of Israel's continuing military occupation of the West Bank (seventeen years since the October War and the UN resolution demanding Israeli withdrawal), Hussein was able to garner considerable Arab support for his Middle East sabre-rattling, even though Kuwait had no connection with Israel. Moreover, American intelligence services were deceived, as were the Russians, who had more than 8,000 oil, arms and other personnel in the country. When Hussein's army crossed the Kuwait border on August 2, 1990 – conducting its own version of the invasion of Panama – there was consternation in Washington and Moscow. The head of US Central Command, General Norman Schwarzkopf, had predicted Hussein might possibly seize a Kuwaiti island, but would go no further. When Hussein's forces swept on into Kuwait City, the West was faced with a fait accompli. Or seemingly so.

Panama might have emboldened Saddam Hussein, as an example of *coup de main* warfare, but the lightning success of American forces in Panama had also served to restore the confidence of the Pentagon – and voters. 'In breaking the mindset of the American people about the use of force in the post-Vietnam era,' Bush's Secretary of State, James Baker, later noted, 'Panama established an emotional predicate that permitted us to build the public support so essential for the success of Operation Desert Storm.'[60]

Brilliantly executed six months after Hussein's own territorial strike, Operation Desert Storm would demonstrate the new ability of the American Empire to act effectively not only at its own back door, but also far away in the Middle East, and as the leader, moreover, of a huge Allied force assembled under the aegis of the UN. The reason for its effectiveness as a counterstrike was not just the modernization of American military command, performance and weaponry, but the diminishing ability, even willingness, of the Soviet Union to contest American diplomatic or military decisions. With economic conditions deteriorating within the Soviet Union – the Central Committee was unable even to raise the artificially low price of bread lest there be a popular revolt – Gorbachev's latitude for manoeuvre was becoming daily more restricted as he sought to be seen as an equal partner rather than opponent of American hegemony in the looming post-Cold War world. The result, in the Middle East, was farce, as Gorbachev's Foreign Secretary, Eduard Shevardnadze, attempted to act as the West's negotiator-in-chief with Saddam Hussein and avert a world war. Since Hussein was mad and Russia not only near to bankruptcy but powerless to protect its thousands of advisers and engineers in Iraq – who could be held hostage by Hussein – the Soviets merely resembled amateurs on the new global democratic stage.

Astute participants and observers were aware that not only the fate of oil ownership and production in the Middle East but also the future of the world order now hung in the balance. A prime participant was General Colin Powell, who had been Reagan's national security adviser and was now Bush's chairman of the Joint Chiefs of Staff.

As a Vietnam veteran, General Powell would become famous for the Powell Doctrine, based on Field Marshal Montgomery's campaign doctrine in World War II: soldiers should never be committed to combat unless their objectives were established in clear terms, and sufficient forces were assembled and applied not only to start, but also to finish the job. There was, however, a less well-known part of the Powell Doctrine: asking whether military intervention was, in all honesty, the best policy to achieve political and economic ends. When

Powell asked President Bush and the cabinet whether it was worth going to war to liberate Kuwait, rather than moving troops to protect Saudi Arabia and applying sanctions and the threat of war to Hussein, 'I detected a chill in the room' he recalled.[61]

It was clear that Bush, after initially maintaining his composure with reporters asking whether the US would respond militarily ('I am not discussing intervention . . . I'm not contemplating such action'), was angling for another war. After the meeting, the Secretary of Defense, Dick Cheney, took Powell aside. 'Colin, he said, you're chairman of the Joint Chiefs. You're not Secretary of State. You're not the national security adviser anymore. And you're not Secretary of Defense. *So stick to military matters.*'[62]

Chastened, Powell was even more stunned when he learned that Cheney had taken directly to President Bush a wacky, secret plan to seize Baghdad from the desert rear, without consulting with Powell as head of the combined US military. Clearly, as an alleged Vietnam draft dodger (five deferments, without completing his further degree), Cheney had no conception of military command or logistics and was worryingly myopic.

Though gagged by Cheney over the expediency of military action, Powell afterwards recalled asking himself how far – even if he did go ahead and order military action – Bush would want to take the American counterstrike, given Cheney's secret machinations. 'Do we want to go beyond Kuwait to Baghdad? Do we try to force Saddam out of power? How weakened do we want to leave Iraq?' And if Hussein was removed, 'Do we necessarily benefit from a Gulf oil region dominated by an unfriendly Syria and a hostile Iran?'[63]

These were crucial questions in relation to the impending post-Cold War world order. The direct use of American military power in a combat role for the first time in the history of the Middle East – rather than the threat of force – raised huge questions for the future stability of the world's most volatile region. Would the United States then be seen by Muslim countries as the bullying protector not only of its puppet oil state, Saudi Arabia, but of Israel, which had still not complied with UN resolutions for it to withdraw from the territories it had seized in the October War? Was such an outcome beneficial for long-term American interests? Would war simply beget further war down the road?

Mikhail Gorbachev vainly attempted to act in concert with George

Bush, warning Saddam Hussein to negotiate a withdrawal of Iraqi forces and appealing for an Israeli–Palestinian peace conference to tackle the primary problem in the Middle East. The Soviet leader was ignored by the mad dictator in Baghdad, however, while his attempt to turn the Iraqi malfeasance into a Soviet–US triumph of concerted diplomacy fell foul of lobbyists for Israel in Washington. Bush later said that 'There will be, and is, no linkage to the West Bank question',[64] and rejected Gorbachev's plea at the Helsinki talks in September 1990 for an 'international conference' on a solution to the Israeli–Palestinian problem.[65]

With 200,000 US troops dispatched to Saudi Arabia, as well as warships and a huge air force capability, plus UN pressure building on him to withdraw from Kuwait, Saddam Hussein had nowhere to go save to reverse engines. Had Hussein been rational, the Israelis less intransigent, and had the Soviet Union not been in freefall, the Kuwait debacle might well have led to an improvement in the Middle East situation rather than war. But Saddam Hussein was not rational, and with the Baltic States increasingly restless, the two Germanies uniting as the Federal Republic of Germany on October 3, 1990, as well as rising unemployment and inflation across the Soviet Union and fifty million Soviet Muslims who would 'rise up in fury against the Kremlin' if Gorbachev assigned Russian troops to the impending Desert Storm Coalition counterstrike, there was no ideal outcome.

In conversation with Brent Scowcroft, his national security adviser, Bush had reflected on the way the crisis in the Gulf had encouraged him to see both the UN and the Soviet Union in a new way – a chance for 'real cooperation' between the US and the USSR in enforcing peace and stability in the world, with the backing of the UN. But with Hussein first refusing Gorbachev's effort in February 1991 to negotiate an Iraqi withdrawal except on a six-week timetable, with numerous caveats and linkage to an international conference to address the Israeli–Palestinian problem, then spinning out the endgame to the point where no one believed Hussein's word any longer, Bush felt that for good or ill, egged on by Cheney, he had no option but to issue the order to begin military action.

In his memoirs, Gorbachev metaphorically shook his head at Hussein's tactics. In Moscow, Hussein's foreign minister Tariq Aziz declared he was 'not afraid of confrontation with the Americans', despite knowing full well 'that confrontation could lead to a wide-scale conflict, the consequences of which would affect not only the Arab region but the entire world. That prospect does not frighten us, though.' Gorbachev was appalled. 'The Iraqi leaders were "not frightened" by the possibility of global catastrophe! Such were the kind of people with whom the world community had to deal' he commented sadly.[66]

Following the Hussein–Aziz version of Russian roulette, and the US decision to launch Operation Desert Storm on February 24, 1991, Gorbachev saw his reputation as a world statesman shattered. His political survival was as threatened, in fact, as Hussein's. Hussein surrendered only four days later, as Coalition Forces numbering 540,000 made mincemeat of his men in Kuwait. Hussein now agreed not only to the immediate unconditional withdrawal of all his troops but to all UN conditions, prompting President Bush to halt the Allied counteroffensive, and agree a ceasefire.

With its Coalition allies, the US had won the swiftest major war in modern history (one hundred hours of ground combat). America had demonstrated not only its renewed military prowess, moreover, but also the sagacity of its emperor, who wisely refused to countenance the recommendations of those members of his administration who wanted him to ignore the UN resolutions and send his troops on to Baghdad. If Saddam Hussein was to fall, Bush reasoned, the dictator should fall as the result of Iraqi discontent, not American interference – which could only inflame anti-American feelings in the Arab world.

Instead, of course, it was Gorbachev who fell, later that year.

Was it illness, in the meantime, that assailed President Bush at the seeming height of his presidency, and affected his mind? No other Caesar save President Johnson had suffered a crisis of nerve at the very point of acclamation, as when he baulked at running for nomination in the summer of 1964, just as his great civil rights bill passed Congress. Now, in the spring of 1991, with his Gallup polls running at an extraordinary 87 per cent public approval and a ticker-tape parade slated for June in New York, similar to that of General Eisenhower after World War II, Bush felt the very ground beneath him slipping away.

Bush's father had suffered a similar affliction in 1962, when in exhaustion and depression at age sixty-seven he had decided not to run for re-election as senator for Connecticut – a decision he had afterwards regretted.[67] George Bush was now the same age, and in his diary he confessed he not only felt depressed after his historic victory in Kuwait, but also little if any interest in running for re-election as president the following year.

Bush vainly attempted to quieten his anxiety in patriotic gore, revelling in the victory tributes, American 'flags, patriotism . . . music' and 'praying' – but he was continually haunted by something else: the imminent death of his Mephistopheles, Lee Atwater, and the price he himself would have to pay for his Faustian bargain in 1988: vengeance by Democrats for his egregious vaporization of Governor Dukakis. 'I feel the build-up now on the domestic side' the president noted in his diary. 'When will Bush stumble; what about the domestic agenda; can he handle it? . . . I don't know whether it's the anticlimax or that I'm too tired to enjoy anything, but I just seem to be losing my perspective.'[68] Maybe, he pondered, he should step down. 'I don't seem to have the drive,' he confided to his journal, sickened at the thought of 'the political stuff' he'd have to face if he ran: not only fund-raising, but also campaigning on behalf of a Republican Party that had no respect for statesmanship, and seemed hell-bent on neoconservative Goldwaterland.[69]

Bush's vice president, Dan Quayle, was busy spreading mischief, complaining that American forces should have invaded Iraq – 'a new right-wing theme', Bush noted – while deploring the National Rifle Association's lobbying against the Senate bill in Congress to restrict automatic weapons in America. Even in international affairs the right wing was rampant, saying that the president and his Secretary of State, James Baker, were being too soft on Gorbachev and should unilaterally recognize Lithuania's independence. ('Fuck you!' Baker had snarled at the Secretary of Housing, Jack Kemp, who was attempting to interfere in Baker's patient diplomacy.[70]) Meanwhile Israel's government, under Yitzhak Shamir, had proven as myopic and intransigent as ever.

'Israel rolled us', Bush lamented in his diary in March 1991, as disappointed as presidents Carter and Reagan had been. 'They are very, very difficult.' Despite the fact that the US had 'kicked Saddam Hussein and solved their problem in the area', they were demanding more weaponry but refusing to offer 'land for peace' and delaying the international peace conference that Gorbachev had vainly pleaded to tie to Desert Storm, insisting instead on expanding their illegal West Bank settlements which could only make eventual reconciliation with the Palestinians impossible.[71] 'They are never going to get peace in the Middle East without solving the Palestinian question' Bush wrote. 'I know it; they know it; the Arabs know it; the French and Europeans know it; and we're standing alone against reason a lot of times' in supporting Israel. He even swore he would do what 'no president has done since Ike': forgo Jewish support for his election campaign, preferring to 'stand up for what is fair and right'.[72] But would he even stand?

'Sometimes I really like the spotlight,' Bush confided, 'but I'm tired of it. I've been at the head table for many years, and now I wonder what else is out there.' He felt dead tired, and acknowledged he didn't 'really care' any more for politics. He'd lost fifteen pounds, and even his handwriting, his doctor noted, had altered. Could the Republicans not get someone else to lead them, he wondered – someone better equipped for the 'rough and tumble', moreover someone 'who likes it better'.[73]

The chief of staff, John Sununu, was instructed to keep the majority of problems away from the president's desk, while Bush made the fateful decision not to begin his campaign for re-election until the following year, relying on his credentials as a victorious war president. With unemployment exceeding 8.5 per cent, and interest rates so high that house mortgages were unobtainable save for the rich, this was potentially fatal to his chances for re-election – if, indeed, he decided to run. 'I haven't made up my mind' he told his eldest son George Jr, who in turn told the deputy chief of staff 'there is a good chance that he won't' – a concern they must keep quiet about, since 'if we told anybody else that, we were dead meat'.[74]

Graves' disease was diagnosed after an attack of arrhythmia, but even after treatment the president did not appear to recover his former elan. As the ticker tape drifted away in the summer of 1991, Bush seemed uncharacteristically distant, listless and unwilling to make decisions. He was going to bed in August at the family dacha at Kennebunkport, Maine, bracing for Hurricane Bob to hit the New England coast, when he was told there was another storm coming: CNN was reporting a putsch at Gorbachev's dacha on the Black Sea, claiming he had been overthrown and replaced by his deputy, Gennadi Yanayev, in what became known as 'the putsch of fools'. Bush, who had been warned in June this might happen, had personally warned Gorbachev of the danger during his own trip to London, Moscow and Ukraine.

Upset and anxious, the president hastened back to Washington. He had wisely, if cold-heartedly, left Saddam Hussein in power in Iraq, lest the United States be encumbered with the burden of imperial responsibility for the country, with its myriad internal ethnic and religious problems dividing Shiites, Sunnis and Kurds. A complete collapse of the Soviet Union, however, posed far greater problems, given the vast nuclear arsenals and the economic black hole facing a moribund Communist system, as well as the pent-up aspirations for independence among the Soviet republics.

In March 1990, Mikhail Gorbachev had got himself retitled 'president' by the new Congress of People's Deputies, for a term of five years – but president of what? For his part, Bush hoped the USSR could cast off its Communist past and yet be preserved as a political, governing structure, in the interests of stability in eastern Europe – but such divestiture was never going to be easy. This was not, after all, a case like Europe after the fall of Napoleon's empire, or after World War I, or even the Allies winding up World War II and establishing the United Nations in the hope once again of arbitrated peace in the world: masking the desperate arms race between the two ideologically driven superpowers that emerged from the ruins of a global anti-fascist struggle. Now was different. The only other competing major world empire to that of the US was spinning increasingly out of control and towards its possible doom, leaving the American Empire the world's sole superpower, but without a clear doctrine espoused by its president, beyond pragmatism.

The news of the Russian putsch, if it was true, raised an uncomfortable new challenge for the American leader. A review of US policy towards the USSR which he had commissioned immediately after his inauguration had been disappointing – 'mush', as Secretary of State Baker had called it. Trusting his instincts Bush had decided to back Gorbachev with rhetoric, summits and diplomatic respect, but no money or real partnership over Iraq and the future of the Middle East. Now that Gorbachev was seemingly gone, what would happen in Russia, and what should be the agenda and role of the United States? The right-wing Secretary of Defense, Dick Cheney, had long proposed

American rearmament in anticipation of Soviet right-wingers seizing control from Gorbachev. Bush had overruled Cheney, in the hope that Gorbachev would succeed in reforming the Soviet economy and down- sizing its military. But if the military was now in the ascendant, should Bush therefore recognize the Soviet coup, and face up to Cheney's vision of a resurgent Soviet 'iron first', with all its nuclear implica- tions for America and the world?

Bush's dilatory state of mind, whether the result of his illness or his fear of having to campaign again, now ironically came to his rescue. At his dacha, Gorbachev had refused to sign the transfer of power to his vice president, which the cabal of plotters presented to him. They thus flew off empty-handed, and into the dustbin of history. In Moscow the new populist president of the Russian Republic, Boris Yeltsin, was more than a match for them – but his victory, though welcomed with relief by President Bush several days later, raised new worries for the stability of the world. Yeltsin was only interested in Russia, not the Union.

More than 70 per cent of Soviet citizens had voted in a referendum in the spring for keeping the USSR as an overarching federal system of government, similar to the federal system of the United States; indeed Boris Yeltsin had put his signature to the continuation of the Soviet Union as a supranational body. But the putsch exposed Gorbachev's helplessness and lack of electoral support. By the time Gorbachev was freed at his dacha and returned to Moscow, his star had fallen. He had already resigned from the Communist Party (which was soon banned as a party of putschist traitors). This left Gorbachev as an emperor without clothes: an appointed but unelected president of the Soviet Union, his standing fatally diminished by the putsch, and Yeltsin's heroism. Though Gorbachev subsequently attempted to act as President Bush's equal in Madrid at the belated Middle East peace conference in October 1991, it was a charade. The USSR, born like the United States out of revolution and civil war, was, unlike the USA, dissolving.

The Soviet military had stayed out of the struggle between Yeltsin and the plotters in August. With Yeltsin's emergence as the big man on the Russian campus, the military threw in their lot with him when he proposed a Commonwealth of Independent States, not a Soviet Union. It would mean the end of Mikhail Gorbachev's history-making.

On Christmas Day 1991, as the Bush family opened their presents at Camp David, protected by the secret service, a call came through to President Bush from the Kremlin. Gorbachev had already announced that the USSR would cease to exist the next day. Meanwhile, Gorbachev told Bush on the telephone, he was resigning his meaningless presidency to become a private citizen.

For George Bush it was an extraordinary moment, at the end of more than four decades of Cold War. A couple of hours later Gorbachev went on television in Moscow to tell the people of a now moribund empire the truth. He refused to be blamed for the collapse of the Soviet Union, or the economic and political chaos of the past several years. 'All the half-hearted reforms – and there were a lot of them – fell through, one after another. This country was going nowhere, and we couldn't possibly live the way we had been living. We had to change everything' – but 'dismembering this country and breaking up the state' was not what he'd had in mind.[75] He was distraught.

On the telephone at Camp David, President Bush had been compassionate and dignified. Speaking later the same night on television from the Oval Office, he again decided not to rub salt in Gorbachev's wound, announcing merely that the historic 'confrontation' with Communism 'is over'. Several weeks later, however, as the New Year began, he dropped diplomatic niceties. He would be facing re-election in November, if he won the Republican nomination. America, he therefore announced to Congress and many millions of voters watching on television, had 'won the Cold War'. Gorbachev shuddered but could say nothing, for it was true.

In three years, Bush had thus won three wars – two by the application of surgical force, the third by patience and cautious diplomacy, overriding the hawks in his administration. He had every reason to feel proud, despite his sense of psychic exhaustion.

Had the president now announced he would stand down at the end of his successful first term and join Gorbachev in retirement, he might have gone down in history as one of the most effective transitional presidents of modern times, inaugurating a new era.

The gene that makes people want to win the presidency, however, does not make it easy for them to relinquish the office, once attained. Haunted by the memory of Atwater's evil but effective tactics in his last campaign and its consequences, Bush had held off making a final decision, but in the end, he felt, it had to be done – and on February 12, 1992, he formally announced his candidacy for re-election.

Twelve months previously, Bush's approval rating had hit an astonishing 84 per cent in opinion polls, prompting George Jr to boastfully predict victory at the next election: 'Do you think the American people are going to turn to a Democrat now?'[76] The ancient Greeks had always mistrusted hubris, however – and with reason. Bush's stratospheric numbers had tumbled, cascading into a worrying slide, and by February 1992 he was down to an ominous 42 per cent in polls – a number that did not guarantee re-election. The very man who, with Atwater's help, had stopped America from electing an effective modern, managerial governor in 1988 was now seen, ironically, to be a disappointingly incompetent manager of the economy, prompting millions of people, especially the unemployed, to look for a possible national saviour, either in the young, five-times elected Democratic governor of Arkansas, Bill Clinton, or a paranoid but successful independent, billionaire businessman Ross Perot.[77]

'Our whole political problem is the recession,' warned one of Bush's aides only a month after the president's announcement of his candidacy. 'We face a twenty-month recession, a 78 per cent [on the] "wrong track" [poll] number, and likely a southern conservative Democrat [Clinton]. The situation is about as bad as it could be.'[78]

Like Mikhail Gorbachev, then, President Bush was faced by menacing failure not as a statesman, since he had proved himself a master steward of America's interests on a global stage, but by his inability to master the domestic challenges that faced him. Lacking a clear vision of what he wanted to achieve at home, as well as the rhetoric to back such a vision, he was seen more and more as a 'flip-flopper' – too much like a Democrat by right-wing conservative Republicans, too conservative by Democrats – and by all as too willing to respond to lobbying pressure rather than his own convictions, whatever they might be.

A 1988-style personal-attack campaign might just have saved the president. However, Lee Atwater had died of a brain tumour and Roger Ailes, Atwater's chief accomplice, had resigned long ago. With all too little fund-raising done, the president now found himself bereft, with no political weaponry, or strategy, or even driving desire. The result was visible when Pat Buchanan, a right-wing Republican journalist and former speechwriter for Richard Nixon, almost toppled him in the New Hampshire primary.

Winning the Republican nomination but lagging in the polls that summer, Bush's fortunes seemed briefly to rise when Ross Perot, having left the race once, re-entered it, and threatened as an independent to split the vote of the Democratic nominee, Governor Bill Clinton. But in the all-important presidential debates, Perot was dismissed as a weirdo, President Bush appeared out of touch with ordinary Americans' lives, and it was Governor Clinton of Arkansas who came across as a centrist, southern politician with an IQ off the charts, yet full of optimism, compassion, energy, goodwill and good domestic ideas – especially in dealing with the recession.

A last-minute attempt to use Atwaterian tactics – raiding Clinton's passport files at the State Department, labelling him and his running mate, Senator Al Gore, as covert Marxists and 'Those Bozos' – failed to destroy the Democratic challenge. Bush lost the election in November, 38 per cent to Clinton's 43 per cent, with Ross Perot winning 19 per cent as an independent.[79] Bill Clinton, not George Bush, would be the forty-second US president.

Bush was as devastated as President Carter had been to lose after a single term. Though he went on to sign the North American Free Trade Agreement which he and James Baker had negotiated in December 1992 with Canada and Mexico – his final example of statesmanship – and though he sent troops to Somalia to ensure humanitarian aid to the starving population, he seemed a broken man. His mother had died shortly after his defeat.

At Camp David he confided to Colin Powell, who had come up with his wife to commiserate: 'Colin, it hurts. It really hurts.'[80] Referring to the president-elect, he wailed: 'I just never thought they'd elect him.'[81]

## Part Three: Private Life

JFK once said his mother, Rose Fitzgerald Kennedy, was the 'glue that held the family together'. In the Bush family, Dorothy Walker Bush performed the same role: another tiny American matriarch, whose longevity and moral expectations profoundly influenced her son, as in so many cases of the American Caesars. It was not that their sons necessarily met their exacting standards of honesty, courage or behaviour. For good or ill, however, their sons were moulded in that crucible, answering – and at times denying or subverting – the powerful maternal aspirations held up for them.

At age sixteen Barbara Pierce, a beautiful girl with brownish-red hair, met the seventeen-year-old George H. W. Bush at a Christmas dance while he was still a schoolboy at Andover Academy. They became secretly engaged, and in 1943 publicly so, when the USS *San Jacinto* was commissioned at Philadelphia and an expensive diamond ring was held up in evidence before the family. Barbara played tennis and 'could talk to absolutely anybody', Dorothy Walker Bush pronounced, giving her blessing. 'The Bush family liked my mom from the start' their daughter Doro later wrote in her family memoir.[82] She fitted right in to a family of do-ers, with little time or inclination for books, history or music. As Doro Bush related, her father couldn't 'play the piano or carry a tune', indeed suffered what he himself called a 'genetic power outage' in relation to music – an outage that extended to the public-speaking gene, too, which made electoral politics ever tougher, especially in the age of the twenty-four-hour media news cycle.[83]

Failing twice to win election to the Senate, and warned he had no chance of winning office as Texas governor, Bush's path to the White House thus followed a different course from his nine predecessors in its non-electoral course – a path based upon networking, fund-raising and the series of political appointments and job offers he secured. His ascent was not, however, without arduous personal demands, in patience, loyalty and in fortitude. The death of his daughter Robin from leukaemia almost destroyed his marriage; Barbara's beautiful brown-red hair, at age twenty-eight, turned white overnight, and she refused to colour it, lest it signify she was forgetting little Robin's tragic fate. In grief she 'kind of smothered' her eldest boy, George Jr.[84]

More children (Neil, Marvin, Doro) helped, as did a growing sense of family destiny: that of Senator Prescott Bush's four sons it would be the second son, not George's elder brother Bucky or younger brothers Johnny or Pres, who had been singled out by God to be the anointed Bush family standard-bearer: the war hero and self-made oil millionaire who would continue the family's prominence, and hopefully raise it still further.

That high expectation had its downside, however; friends became anxious when George took on a new secretary at the Republican National Committee, and then asked her to come to China as his personal assistant in 1974.

For years, even after he was forced by James Baker to sideline her, Bush would be tormented by rumours that he and Jennifer Fitzgerald, the English-born divorcée and martinet who ruled his office schedule as executive assistant with a rod of iron, had a romantic relationship – much as speculation never ceased over Eisenhower's relationship with his English driver and office assistant, Kay Summersby. Bush travelled everywhere with Jennifer, but as with Eisenhower there was no real danger he would end his marriage to wed her, if only because such a decision, made in a moment of madness or passion, would have ended his presidential ambitions, and his family's hopes for him. Besides, he had no wish to divorce Barbara.

Bush, who had been genuinely infatuated with Barbara when a young man – even painting her name on his warplane – continued to love 'Bar' loyally as the mother of his five surviving children. Barbara, however, left Beijing to spend Thanksgiving and then Christmas with her children back home, thus leaving George to his own devices: and to Jennifer Fitzgerald. George's mother Dorothy came out on a special mission to China, there to guard the chicken coop. 'Mother arrives tomorrow' Bush wrote in his diary. 'I have that kind of high school excitement – first vacation feeling.'[85] Alarmed by what she found, Dorothy warned Barbara to start dying her hair, the better to compete with Jennifer.

Whether this would have helped is doubtful. As one congressman's wife noted, 'George and Barbara married young and had those kids when the hormones were working well.' Gradually Barbara had turned into a devoted-mother figure, indeed many people initially thought she *was* George's mother, so debonair did he seem, so dowdy did she. 'He came into the Green Room', noted a CBS television staffer, 'with a gray-haired woman who I thought was his mother. Someone told me she was his wife, and I became fascinated by their dynamic because they were not a matched pair . . . He engaged women immediately. He's not a lecher, but he makes eye contact with sexual energy. He's polite and does not behave improperly – he's no Bill Clinton – but the sexual message is there. She [Barbara] is oblivious to it all. She's supremely confident and in charge of him like a mother who totally wears the pants . . . and it's also clear that he relies on her.'[86] Another congressman's wife, who visited Bush in China, noted that Barbara 'adored George. Pure love . . . I think she saw that her biggest strength was to imitate his mother, almost become his mother.' And in terms of her hair and her clothes, 'Barbara let herself look the way she did on purpose. If George had wanted her to look any other way, she would have' – and whatever disappointment there might have been, romantically, 'with Barbara her kids made up for everything'.[87]

Short, blonde, loyal, available when he needed her and in love with George, the forty-two-year-old Jennifer Fitzgerald, by contrast, suited the chameleon in Bush in a different way. He took her with him on travels, and to the CIA when he became head spy. Even after he quit the CIA, he got her a job as special assistant to the US ambassador to Britain, Kingman Brewster, and continued to see her. Though Brewster was irritated by her 'frequent absences' flying back to the US 'to see George', there was little the ambassador could do. 'Their relationship was no secret to the embassy staff', Ambassador Brewster's biographer claimed, though without offering proof. 'Everyone knew that she was George's mistress.'[88]

True or not, Barbara had only herself to blame. She had, after all, made her own marital bed: not only imbibing, but herself enforcing the Bush family imperative that, if accepted into the family, wives of the Bushes must stay at home, raise children and not compete with their husbands. 'I went through sort of a difficult time' Barbara later admitted, when her children became adults and she suffered midlife depression; 'suddenly women's lib had made me feel that my life had been wasted . . . But I got over it, thank heavens.'[89] She watched over her children's lives and marriage choices, attempting vainly to stop her son Jeb from marrying a Mexican teenager, and watching stonily as her husband thrived on Jennifer Fitzgerald's undistracted feminine adulation at his office.[90] Anxious lest the relationship cause a scandal, James Baker insisted Fitzgerald be removed from the abortive 1980 campaign for the presidency. Bush consented, but paid out of his own pocket for her to work for him privately in New York.

When Bush became vice president to Ronald Reagan, Barbara Bush got the vice president's imposing huge white official mansion on Massachusetts Avenue, and a distinguished interior designer (Mark Hampton) to upgrade its decor. But at his office Bush got Jennifer back – in a mink coat. When Bush's top aide, Rich Bond, objected, Bush fired Bond, not Fitzgerald. 'Jim Baker made me make that choice once before,' he told Bond, 'and I made the wrong choice.'[91]

The press ignored the relationship, as did the Bush family. Bush's sister Nancy remarked: 'Dumpy little Jennifer! She's like the most reliable, good person you know. We've all known her forever. She just absolutely adores George.'[92] 'She became in essence his other wife,' another intimate reflected, 'his office wife.'[93] There was 'no denying the connection between them' one staffer commented. 'Jennifer was a doter. She made George feel that he was God's gift to mankind. She'd bat her eyes and gush all over him. She'd poof her hair, put on lipstick, and spray perfume every time she walked into his office in her high stiletto heels. She was a courtesan, but not that gifted', the assistant sniffed, deriding Fitzgerald's middle age and lack of fashionable style. 'Still, she was a treat from Bar[bara], who is no gusher. Bar would just as soon say, "George, cut the crap," as "Open the door." Jennifer was an ego trip for him.'[94]

Fitzgerald's quasi-courtship flattered the 'femme' in Bush, a perceptive female friend also reflected. The person who seemed to object the most, ironically, was the First Lady, Nancy Davis Reagan, who hated both Bushes for their Yankee rather than Californian manners, but derided Barbara Bush especially for her size sixteen, overweight figure, and her complete lack of dress sense. By contrast, Nancy – a fashion devotee, reminiscent of Mrs Simpson, the Duchess of Windsor – wore a size four dress, spent a fortune on designer clothes, and was suspicious to the point of paranoia of other women, as well as men who might compete with her 'Ronnie' for the limelight. To Nancy, George was a 'wimp' and a 'Whiner'. She positively revelled in the incident of 'George and his girlfriend' – the widow of a former congressman – when the car Bush was driving in was involved in an accident, and the secret service had to be called in to airbrush the episode.[95] 'I always knew Nancy didn't like me very much,' Bush later noted in his diary, when president, 'but there is nothing much we can do about all that.'[96]

Not even Nancy Reagan, however, had dared leak the supposed secrets of George Bush's love life, which could damage the public image of the White House. Moreover, the serious press still abided by an unwritten rule over scandal-mongering, until in 1987, handsome senator and Democratic contender Gary Hart dared the press to report his dalliance with Donna Rice – and paid the price.

The consequences for Vice President George Bush and all who wished to run for public office in the republic, after Hart, were dire. Republican candidates especially were now expected to pass muster not only on political issues, such as their anti-abortion stance or anti-tax and anti-government posture, but in terms of squeaky-clean family conduct, a demand that also drew enthusiastic support from feminists sick of patriarchal behaviour. Donna Brazile, a senior aide to Governor Dukakis, thus challenged Bush in the 1988 campaign with the words 'The American people have every right to know,' in view of the rumours about Jennifer Fitzgerald, 'if Barbara Bush will share that bed with him in the White House.'

To his lasting credit, Governor Dukakis promptly fired Ms Brazile, never wavering in the correctness of his decision in later years. 'To hell with all that' he told Bush's daughter Doro. 'When you decide you're going to go into this business, you've got to decide who you are, what standards you're going to set for yourself and the people around you. If folks get out of line, you can't accept that.'[97]

To his lasting discredit Bush did not return the favour. By pioneering the use of personal and racial smear strategy by Lee Atwater to destroy Dukakis over Willie Horton, Bush reversed his losing campaign and won the post he had craved during the preceding eight years, failing thereby to live up to the moral precepts his father had lived and died by. His daughter later blamed the press: 'one more example of how people who run for office become public property, and how some people in the media will stop at nothing to bring them down', she excoriated the Fitzgerald stories. But in truth it was her own, beloved father – like Julie Nixon's father – who had made his pact with the Devil, in the form of Lee Atwater and his squad of character-assassins.

Four years later George Herbert Walker Bush lost the office he had spent a lifetime pursuing, and the Bush family, saddened by the death of Dorothy Walker Bush ('Ganny'), went into double mourning. Retiring to Texas on January 20, 1993, the forty-first President had only himself to blame for his failure to be re-elected, yet blamed the media instead. He was determined neither to write his memoirs nor to say anything in public, lest he give vent to his bitterness. He was resolved, as he put it, to 'stay out of Dodge'. 'He stayed out of Dodge', the journalist Bob Woodward subsequently noted, but in retirement 'he never seemed to reach a state of peace, relaxation or happiness' as Reagan did.[98]

More significantly, however, was the effect that Bush's unhappy retirement had on his sons. He had brought them up to tell the truth, yet he allowed his resentment to overshadow the positive aspects of his legacy – the peaceful collapse of the Soviet Union, and the liberation of Kuwait – as well as failing to express remorse for the campaign tactics he'd employed to destroy Governor Dukakis in 1988. His legacy to his sons became not pride and honesty, but a haunting sense of unfair failure: a failure for which his sons could and should, if they were truly loyal – like the Kennedys when making up for their father Joe Kennedy's fiasco as ambassador to Britain – make amends. Thus would arise one of the greatest ironies in the history of the American Caesars: that the man who had guided his empire's fortunes with great responsibility and flexibility in a transitional world, would, with his wife Barbara, live to see his own son do the opposite.

# CHAPTER ELEVEN

# BILL CLINTON

Democrat

42nd President

(January 20, 1993–January 20, 2001)

## Part One: The Road to the White House

Bill Clinton was born a Baptist, in Hope, Arkansas, on August 19, 1946, not as a Clinton, but as William Jefferson Blythe IV. His supposed father, Bill Blythe III, was a bigamous salesman who died in an automobile accident before his son's birth.

Bill Clinton's mother, Virginia, was the only daughter of a Hope ice deliverer and storekeeper with no education, and his wife, an auxiliary nurse. While his widowed mother went away for two years to New Orleans to train as a nurse-anaesthetist, little Billy Blythe IV was looked after by his grandparents in Hope.

Who Billy Blythe IV's real father was would never be known, but the boy's astonishing intelligence revealed itself once his widowed mother remarried and moved along with her flamboyant, reckless second husband, Roger Clinton – a divorced car dealer – and her little son to Hot Springs: the 'dunghill' of Arkansas, as one local ideologue called it.

In 1959, when Billy was twelve, Virginia filed for divorce, but withdrew the application. A witness to continuing domestic, male-dominated family violence, Billy finally grew tall enough to challenge his drunken stepfather to stop beating his mother – and won, temporarily, when Roger Clinton was again hauled off to spend the night in a police cell. The drunkenness, threats and beatings did not, however, cease, and Virginia finally re-filed for divorce in 1962, this time definitively.

Delighted, Billy changed his family name from Blythe to Bill Clinton, at age fifteen. Throwing himself into his schoolwork, he grew to be exceptionally tall (6' 3"). He excelled at the saxophone, maths, English and general studies – and was mortified when his mother, in a fit of compassion, remarried Roger Clinton.

Virginia's remarriage proved a mistake, Roger Clinton remaining an abusive drunk, and their son Roger Clinton Jr becoming a wastrel like his father, eventually landing in jail for drug dealing and addiction.

Bill Clinton was of a different calibre, however, blessed with a phenomenal intelligence, photographic memory, deep compassion – and a determination, after meeting President Kennedy as a high-school senior on a visit to Washington in the summer of 1963, to see the world and make a difference. He applied for a place at Georgetown University's School of Foreign Service, a predominantly Catholic academy in the capital, set up in the 1930s to educate would-be diplomats and political scientists, and was accepted.

Working as a university student intern in the DC office of Democratic Senator William Fulbright, chairman of the Senate Foreign Relations Committee during the first years of the Vietnam War, Clinton became, like his mentor, an increasingly bitter opponent of the conflict and was personally reluctant to fight there, if drafted. Awarded a Rhodes Scholarship to Oxford, he continued his postgraduate studies and took part in peace protests in London. Finally, however, after what amounted to a mental breakdown, he changed his mind. All presidents since Harry Truman had served in the military. Abandoning further possible deferments or the National Guard service he had been offered, Clinton formally re-registered for the draft, come what might.

Clinton proved – as he'd secretly hoped – lucky, his number, in 1969, too low to be called-up (311th out of 365). Freed of that obligation he was thus eligible to apply to Yale, attending in the autumn of 1970.

Returning to Arkansas as a law professor in 1973, after being awarded a top-grade law degree at Yale, Clinton exhibited both brilliance as a teacher and a precocious ambition to represent the district in Congress as a Democrat.

After indefatigable personal campaigning, during which the twenty-eight-year-old attempted to shake the hand of every living constituent, Clinton failed to unseat the incumbent Republican congressman – shy of only 3,000 votes he was certain had been purloined. Disappointed but unbowed by his defeat, he then married his loyal girlfriend from Yale Law School, Hillary Rodham, and in 1976 ran for state Attorney General, a post he won without difficulty, aged only thirty. Two years later, when the popular governor ran for the Senate, Clinton took aim at the vacant governor's mansion and won, becoming the youngest governor in America.

Two further years later, however, after a rocky first term characterized by indiscipline, competing objectives and no chief of staff, Clinton became the youngest ex-governor. He was, in the words of his best friend, 'really very upset, in tears', unable to admit to himself what he'd done wrong.[1]

This failure to admit to personal error would prove a serious defect in an otherwise extraordinarily talented young politician. His friend begged him to enlarge his resumé by earning a living in another field, for a time. 'You need to go out and make some money!' he advised. 'You know, do something out in the real economic world.'[2] Clinton, however, was obsessed with politics, and had no interest in learning a new trade or earning money, leaving that to his wife, who had joined the prestigious Rose Law Firm in Little Rock. 'He looked me straight in the eyes,' his friend recalled, 'and he said, "There's nothing else I want to do." I thought, man! You're a sick butt!'[3]

Sick butt or not, Clinton was serious. He unashamedly invited a Republican strategist from New York, Dick Morris, to work for his campaign, and appointed a new chief of staff, Betsey Wright, to run his team, winning back the governor's mansion in 1982 and again in 1984.

In 1987, the now four-times governor of Arkansas, still aged only forty-one, gave serious thought to running for the presidency. President Reagan remained immensely popular, but the core Republican Party was moving further and further to the right, leaving the centre unmanned. Clinton's wife urged him to try, if only to achieve national name recognition, but Betsey Wright, who knew the skeletons in the governor's cupboard, confronted him with their names. 'What Bill thought he was getting away with for a number of years', she later recalled of his philandering, now 'caught up with him.'[4] Senator Gary Hart had already been compelled to abandon his intended campaign for the presidency when exposed as a Kennedy-style philanderer in a post-Kennedy political age. There was no way, Wright made clear, the governor could avoid his private life being investigated by the national press, and his being eviscerated like Hart if he ran. Reluctantly, with his wife weeping at the decision, Clinton announced he would not be a candidate.

Given Governor Mike Dukakis' treatment at the hands of Lee Atwater in 1988, it was just as well. In 1990, Clinton contented himself with a fifth term as governor of Arkansas, population 2.3 million, as opposed to the 248 million of the US.

Left to his own devices, however, Clinton was in danger of becoming self-destructive. Convinced he was the smartest Democratic politician of his generation, the most charismatic and the most energetic, Clinton finally decided to fire Betsey Wright. It was at this point, in July 1991, that he received a telephone call from one of President George H.W. Bush's White House advisers, Roger Porter, asking the governor if he was going to run.

When Clinton said he was unsure but lectured Porter – a Harvard business professor – on the crucial issues facing the nation, Porter cut him off. 'Cut the crap, Governor,' Porter snarled, warning that, if he did run, 'they would have to destroy [him] personally'. 'Here's how Washington works', Porter explained, likening America's system to that of the Coliseum in amusing the mob in ancient Rome. 'The press has to have somebody in every election, and we're going to give them *you*.' The media 'would believe any tales they were told about back-water Arkansas. "We'll spend whatever we have to spend, to get whoever we have to get to say whatever they have to say to take you out. And we'll do it early." I tried to stay calm,' Clinton recalled later, 'but I was mad.'[5]

Porter's challenge now swept away Betsey Wright's earlier warnings regarding collateral damage. By fighting on a national stage for the things he believed in, he would banish his demons, please Hillary, and engage in the fight of his life against an Atwater-trained enemy out to destroy him.

Even Clinton's own staff would be minded to throw in the towel during the ensuing campaign for the Democratic nomination, as revelation after revelation was – just as Porter had predicted – fed to a voracious press to gratify a greedy-for-scandal public. Porter's parallel with Rome was, in fact, extraordinary.

A supermarket tabloid began the assault, in the all-important first primary in New Hampshire, by claiming Clinton had enjoyed a twelve-year dalliance with a pretty nightclub singer, Gennifer Flowers. The story instantly migrated into the serious press. As if this was not enough, allegations over financial malfeasance relating to a long-buried, loss-making real estate deal, Whitewater, were bruited, while the back-story of Clinton's slippery evasion of military service during the Vietnam War also emerged. When George Stephanopoulos, Clinton's young communications director and a former Greek Orthodox Church altar boy, read the letter Clinton had sent to the Arkansas National Guard ROTC chief, thanking him 'for saving me from the draft', he initially said to himself: 'That's it. We're done.'[6]

Stephanopoulos, however, had no idea how tough was the governor's hide, or how prepared Clinton was to dissemble in order to confound the Republican trashing machine. 'Ted,' Clinton snapped at the television presenter of *Nightline*, on which Clinton had agreed to appear, 'the only times you've invited me on the show are to discuss a woman I never slept with and a draft I never dodged.'[7]

Given that seemingly authentic audiotapes of Clinton's phone conversations with Ms Flowers were played at a specially convened press conference in New York, and Clinton's draft-avoidance letter was made public, the majority of viewers found it hard to believe the governor's denial. To Stephanopoulos' delight, however, voters seemed willing to excuse Clinton because, in the end, such allegations were irrelevant to his potential stewardship of the White House in a time of economic adversity. Governor Jimmy Carter had, after all, promised he would 'never lie' to the American public; it had not made him a better president, indeed in some respects – as in his 'malaise' speech – it had made him a worse one. In a poor field of candidates, Bill Clinton stood out as a larger-than-life personality, possessing rhetorical skills that could help inspire the country to embrace the new, global era of trade, finance and technological innovation, while seeking peace abroad. Thus, Stephanopoulos later conceded, he also became, like Hillary and his campaign colleagues, an 'enabler'.[8]

Stephanopoulos was later ashamed. But could the young Arkansas governor have won the Democratic presidential nomination and the subsequent election if he *had* admitted the truth? In truth there was probably only one Democratic presidential candidate in America with the necessary intellect, charisma, cunning, shamelessness and sheer willpower to overcome the cynical red tide of Republican hawks in elections: 'Slick Willie', as he was affectionately known in Arkansas.

Clinton's tough childhood, and especially his two electoral defeats in Arkansas, were crucial elements in his political maturation. Few, if

any, bested Governor Bill Clinton on the campaign trail. He talked
articulately, had total recall, was a born teacher, exuded energy and
idealism, hugged and glad-handed, felt people's pain, never tired –
and raised prodigious amounts of campaign finance by showing no
inhibition in asking for funding support. Thus when, in the wake of
the damaging allegations in the New Hampshire primary in February
1992, he placed second, the governor was over the moon. He had
weathered a veritable hurricane of revelations meant to destroy his
candidacy, and had survived. His positive, articulate, centrist message,
looking ahead to an exciting future for the American Empire, made
President Bush's campaign, based as it was on negativism, seem all
too deficient in ideas, especially after the long Reagan years preceding
it. In the weeks thereafter Clinton won primary after primary. By the
late spring he had sewn up the Democratic nomination to become
the official party candidate. He also made a much-admired choice of
vice-presidential candidate in selecting Senator Al Gore, two years
younger than himself. The two baby boomers then stormed the
country pounding out an upbeat message of responsibility and renewal,
making the billionaire independent candidate, Ross Perot, look odd,
and the president passé. By the time Bush recognized the danger and
sought new revelations by raiding Clinton's passport files at the State
Department, it was too late: the Clinton-Gore team was unstoppable.

In the Electoral College, in the November 1992 presidential election, Governor Bill Clinton trounced President Bush 370 to 168; in the
popular vote he bested Bush by almost six million votes, and Ross
Perot by more than twenty-five million. To the delight of Democrats,
Bill Clinton was the undisputed victor.


## Part Two: The Presidency


What became lamentably clear as the Clintons moved into their new
home at 1600 Pennsylvania Avenue following the inauguration on
January 20, 1993, was that Bill Clinton was the cleverest man ever to
win the presidency, but had done no thinking about the Oval Office.

Bill Clinton loved ideas and discussion. Proud of the three-day
conference on economics he'd held in Little Rock during his transition the new president pulsed with initiatives, but proceeded to make

every conceivable mistake in terms of presidential leadership. White House appointments had been left to the last moment, in favour of cosmetic obsession with selecting a multiracial 'rainbow' cabinet. His appointment of a kindergarten friend as chief of staff sent shivers of apprehension through Washington; then, instead of using his vice president, Al Gore, he stunned the capital by announcing that his own wife, Hillary, would head up a Health Care Reform Task Force, charged with delivering a solution to America's health care woes in a hundred days.

Since Hillary confessed she knew next to nothing of health care, and since reforming health care was the most intractable problem in American politics which no previous president had been able to tackle since FDR, it was the assignment from hell. Not only would Hillary's Task Force take almost 1,000 days, but its eventual proposal would be rejected by both houses of Congress, and delay health care reform in America by more than a decade.

Without an experienced chief of staff to guide him and without any idea as to the command, operations and culture of the military, young President Clinton meanwhile turned half the nation against him by announcing, on his first full day in office, that he would press for 'gays in the military' as his first presidential priority.

Without preparation or prior public debate (since the issue was at the bottom of gay people's agenda), the announcement – by a draft dodger who had been 'saved from service in Vietnam' – provoked immediate opposition from an already sceptical Joint Chiefs of Staff Committee, and a menacing backlash in Congress. Clinton found himself facing a barrage of fury across the nation, at the very moment he was seeking to deal with a spiralling national deficit and an ailing economy, with unemployment the highest in ten years – and the world abroad in post-Communist transition.

Almost everything he touched or tackled in his first year in office turned into a similar disaster or near-disaster. The bombing of the World Trade Center in New York by disaffected Muslim terrorists, in February 1993, pointed to a new threat to western civilization. Clinton's deliberately cautious, lawyerly response certainly kept public outrage at the death toll (five people) to a minimum, but the lack of experience and clear lines of authority at the White House worried those charged with national, indeed international, security.

After George H. W. Bush's steady hand at the American tiller, the new White House's missteps alarmed even Clinton's most ardent supporters. The handling of the Waco stand-off in Texas was watched with especial alarm. In a heavily armed compound a mad, self-appointed messiah calling himself David Koresh had barricaded himself and more than a hundred adherents to await Armageddon. Government officers who attempted to enter the compound were slaughtered by Koresh, who welcomed death. It came in due course, on April 19, 1993, when Koresh and almost a hundred men, women and their innocent children were torched to death by federal agents. The president, having authorized the government assault, passed the buck, however, leaving his Attorney General, Janet Reno, to take responsibility. It was clear he was no John F. Kennedy.

In the White House Rose Garden, the President had hosted the signing of the historic, Norwegian-brokered Oslo Peace Accord between Israel and Palestine by Yasser Arafat and Yitzhak Rabin, on September 13, 1993 – but any hopes that the tall, photogenic president was maturing as a leader were dashed in Somalia three weeks later. On October 3, an attempt was made to take out two top lieutenants of the chief warlord, Mohamed Aideed, who had been disrupting UN humanitarian operations. Like President Carter's abortive attempt to rescue the American embassy hostages in Iran in 1975, however, Operation Gothic Serpent went disastrously wrong. The raid failed and nineteen American Rangers died. Worldwide horror was expressed as their naked bodies were dragged through the streets of Mogadishu, in ridicule at the efforts of the world's last remaining superpower.

For Clinton, the Battle of Mogadishu was bad enough for his freshman standing as president and commander-in-chief, but it was soon followed by yet another disaster for American prestige. Transporting the elected president of Haiti, Jean-Bertrand Aristide, back to his Caribbean island following a UN agreement with the military junta there on October 8, 1993, the USS *Harlan County* tank-landing warship was forced to retreat when faced by mere stick-waving thugs at Port au Prince, shouting 'Somalia! Somalia!'

Clinton's national security adviser, Tony Lake, was appalled, anxious lest such humiliations 'put a bull's eye on the backs of American soldiers around the world'.[9] Lake was not alone, the chief of staff of the US Army, General Sullivan, saying to NATO's naval chief, Admiral Miller, 'we can't live with this'.[10] After the long years of muscular American responsibility in maintaining peace and security across the globe, and with the Soviet Union having recently collapsed, the vacuum in the Oval Office was viewed with alarm as much by diplomats as servicemen, nervous lest the lack of world leadership at the White House encourage further factionalism abroad at the very moment when Reagan's vision of the triumph of democratic capitalism, however simplistic, had proven itself so stunningly successful.

Clinton's travails were made worse, moreover, by a series of past scandals that – as Betsey Wright had foretold – came back to bite him: Whitewater, Troopergate and Paula Jones. Each new revelation – whether true or false – diminished the young president's frail standing. The First Lady's massive health care reform bill was trashed and finally voted down in Congress on August 26, 1994, as right-wing millionaires like Richard Mellon Scaife lined up eagerly to force Clinton's resignation as a failed emperor.[11] In television advertising, Clinton's face was morphed on to the faces of Democratic candidates standing for midterm re-election. As a result, in what Clinton's media director (who resigned) called 'a negative referendum on the Clinton presidency', the Democratic Party suffered one of the biggest electoral defeats in its history, not only losing eight Senate and forty-four House seats, but their majorities in both chambers.[12] The whole country was stunned. The big Arkansan with the silvery tongue looked as if he was finished.

For several weeks the wounded president went into a 'funk', his press secretary later described. The election result was a 'full-blown disaster', even the First Lady admitted, bursting into tears in front of her all-female staff in the White House, the so-called 'Chix'. Her much-vaunted attempt at health care reform having foundered, she was left openly wondering 'whether I had gambled on the country's acceptance of my active role and lost'.[13] Out on the road, campaigning for her health care plan, she'd been shocked by the personal animosity she evoked, becoming, as she put it later, 'a lightning rod for people's anger'.[14] 'Everything I do seems not to work' she cried in a phone call to Clinton's old Republican pollster and strategist, Dick Morris. 'Nothing goes right, I just don't know what to do.'[15]

The first thing, Morris recommended to the president, was to get

rid of Hillary as 'co-president'. Then, Morris strategized, Clinton
should co-opt the new Republican Speaker's capitalist manifesto in
Congress, drawn up by Representative Newt Gingrich and called the
'Contract With America' – a call to Republican arms in which the rich
had nothing to lose but their taxable chains. In short, Clinton should
become like Morris, a Republican.

Hillary, beaten down, agreed to vacate her West Wing office and
abandon her effort at co-presidency, but Clinton obstinately refused to
accept personal responsibility for the electoral catastrophe, as was his
wont. He did, however, admit to collective Democratic guilt. As he put
it, 'we got the living daylights beat out of us'.[16] However, he suddenly
saw what no one else, including Morris, seemed to realize: the Republican
tsunami had removed from office all internal competition within the
Democratic Party, from Governor Mario Cuomo of New York to the
Speaker of the US House of Representatives, Jim Wright. The president
was almost literally the last Democrat standing, offering him the chance
not to become a Republican, as Morris recommended, but by virtue of
his phenomenal intelligence and public speaking ability, to become the
Moses of his generation: leading his beaten tribe of Democrats, trashed
and trampled by Newt Gingrich and his fellow travellers of the right,
out of the land of misery and back towards the Promised Land.

Mercifully, to make this epic journey easier, the president had finally
been persuaded to dismiss his ineffective kindergarten friend Mack
McLarty as his chief of staff, and to take instead, upon Al Gore's
advice, Leon Panetta, a former nine-times congressman and currently
the director of the White House Office of Management and Budget.
Knowing Gingrich and his mercenaries at first hand, Panetta – the son
of Italian immigrants and a politician who had served in the military
– was certain the Republicans would overreach. Without the First
Lady interfering, Clinton empowered Panetta to run the government
while he, as the Democrats' Last Hope, travelled the country with a
new vision of the presidency. No longer would he be the easily traduced
mad, bad, dangerous-to-know liberal, pushing progressive agendas
from gays in the military to ambitious health care and environmental
reform. Instead, he would be like Winston Churchill in June 1940 after
the evacuation of Dunkirk: the last defender of civilized, centrist
values, and armed, moreover, with the most potent weapon in the US
Constitution: the power of presidential veto.

For his part the new Speaker of the House, Newt Gingrich – fat, short, mop-haired and self-important – strutted the halls of the Capitol, imagining himself to be Napoleon. He was in for a rude awakening. The retiring Secretary of the Treasury, Lloyd Bentsen, had warned that Bill Clinton was not called 'The Comeback Kid' for nothing – he was 'a Comeback fellow'.[17] And so it proved. Dick Morris was used as a sort of double agent, reporting to the Republican Deputy Senate Majority Leader in secret on the White House's plans, but also secretly reporting back on Republican plans to the president.[18] Clinton fashioned a strategy of 'triangulated' defence, allowing Gingrich to win trophy victories to appease the lunatic right, such as the firing of the black Surgeon General, Joycelyn Elders.[19] Meanwhile he ring-fenced those issues over which Democrats would never surrender: Medicare, Medicaid, education and social security.[20]

Thus unfolded one of the most extraordinary reversals of presidential political fortune in American political annals, as Clinton's 1994 *annus horribilis* gave way to his *annus mirabilis*: a year in which he not only confronted, on behalf of the nation, the mass murder of innocents by an American terrorist, but brought the nightmare of genocidal civil war in Bosnia to an end.

At first, news of a massive explosion bringing down the main federal government building in Oklahoma City like a pack of cards suggested another Islamic terrorist outrage, like the attempted destruction of the World Trade Center. More thoughtful analysts, however, noted the date: April 19, 1995 – two years to the day since the storming of Koresh's 'Branch Davidian' complex at Waco. Could the mass murder be the work of right-wing *Americans*, responding to the drumbeat of Newt Gingrich's endlessly anti-government rhetoric and antics in Washington?

'Go for a head shot; they're gonna be wearing bulletproof vests' recommended Gordon Liddy, Nixon's jailed 'Plumber' who had been released and now offered his expertise in how to 'resist' the Bureau of Alcohol, Tobacco and Firearms if its officers came to confiscate listeners' weapons, as at Waco. First and foremost, Liddy urged, they should to shoot to kill: 'Head shots, head shots.'[21] Rush Limbaugh, another right-wing syndicated radio talk-show host, was similarly irresponsible, with the result that anti-government militias were springing up and increasing across the nation. One such member of the Michigan

Militia was Timothy McVeigh, a gun enthusiast who was arrested by a traffic cop less than ninety minutes after the Oklahoma City explosion for driving a vehicle without registration plates. With another white supremacist militiaman, Terry Nicholls, the unrepentant McVeigh was soon charged with committing the deadliest hate crime on American soil in US history, in which almost 1,000 people were wounded and 168 innocent victims died, including nineteen small children in the building's Day Care Center.

Against the backdrop of nationwide grief and outrage, the president finally became presidential. 'The bombing in Oklahoma City was an attack on innocent children and defenseless citizens' he immediately declared on national television, flanked by the Attorney General, Janet Reno, promising that he would not 'allow the people of this country to be intimidated by evil cowards'. Flags flew at half mast across the country, and in the White House, the president gathered together and addressed the children of his staff.

No longer was Bill Clinton the widely ridiculed former governor with a woman problem, but a parent himself: incredulous at such cold-blooded mass murder, yet anxious to calm the fears of millions of fellow parents. 'I know it is always – or, at least, it's often difficult', he began, 'to talk to children about things that are this painful' (the photograph of a city firefighter carrying the dead body of a small child emblazoned across newspaper pages and television screens). 'But at times like this, nothing is more important for parents to do than to simply explain what has happened to the children and then to reassure your own children about their future . . . This is a frightening and troubling time. But we cannot let the actions of a few terrible people frighten us any more than they already have. So reach out to one another and come together. We will triumph over those who would divide us. And we will overcome them by doing it together, putting our children first.'[22]

In Oklahoma City the next day Clinton seemed to channel the grief of the nation as he vowed to bring to justice 'those who did this terrible evil. This terrible sin took the lives of our American family: innocent children, in that building only because their parents were trying to be good parents as well as good workers; citizens in the building going about their business; and many who served the rest of us, who worked to help the elderly and the disabled, who worked to support our farmers and our veterans, who worked to enforce our laws and to protect us ... To all my fellow Americans beyond this hall, I say: one thing we owe those who have sacrificed is the duty to purge ourselves of the dark forces which gave rise to this evil. They are the forces that threaten our common peace, our freedom, our way of life. Let us teach our children that the God of comfort is also the God of righteousness. Those who trouble their own house will inherit the wind. Justice will prevail. Let us let our children know that we will stand against the forces of fear. When there is talk of hatred, let us stand up and talk against it. When there is talk of violence, let us stand up and talk against it. In the face of death, let us honor life. As St Paul admonished us, let us not be overcome by evil but overcome evil with good.'[23]

The president's handling of the mass murder in Oklahoma proved healing and inspiring – 'a moment he was born to be president for', Stephanopoulos afterwards commented.[24] Leon Panetta saw it as 'a real turning point' in Clinton's presidency, not only in putting a damper on the vitriolic Gingrich rhetoric of the right, but in establishing Clinton's 'traction with the American people about who he was'.[25]

Ronald Reagan had maintained that government was not the solution to America's problem, government *was* the problem – a mantra Gingrich had mercilessly repeated. The Oklahoma City bombing, however, showed that Speaker Gingrich, not the government, was the problem, and people like him: anti-government, anti-gun control, anti-birth control, anti-tax, anti-everything that might regulate society rather than promoting free enterprise and personal profit.

For all his personal faults, President Clinton emerged as the real voice of centrist America. Qualities that had seemed so bumbling and ineffectual the year before now looked, as he found his embattled feet, remarkably caring and wise. While Speaker Gingrich's polls plunged, Clinton's rose, giving him, along with his power of veto, a second string to his presidential bow. Whatever Speaker Gingrich might railroad through the House of Representatives, even if rubber-stamped by Republicans in the Senate, the president could simply strike down – and did. Assault weapons would not be permitted back on the streets, whatever pressure the NRA exerted on congressmen. One by one, the ten vaunted items of Gingrich's proposed 'Contract With America' crumbled.

As Clinton's authority increased in relation to domestic issues, so too did his willingness to act abroad. He had successfully evicted the military junta from Haiti in the late summer of 1994 by launching, after due warning, an invasion of the island by sea and air, causing the junta to surrender without a shot being fired. He had celebrated the anniversary of the ending of World War II in Red Square, Moscow – having got the Russian president, Boris Yeltsin, to join the Partnership For Peace programme, ensuring its cooperation with NATO. Using the threat of NATO intercession, moreover, he had caused the Serbs to suspend their attack on Sarajevo in Bosnia; but when the Serbs renewed their ethnic-cleansing in the summer of 1995, Clinton finally decided to act, not only in his role as commander-in-chief of the US, but as the effective captain of NATO.

The Serb massacre at Srebrenitsa of more than 7,000 Bosnian males in the second week of July, and mass rape of Muslim women, proved the point of departure, like Oklahoma City, for a transformed emperor. With Vice President Gore at his side, and his national security adviser Tony Lake pursuing an endgame strategy that would force the Serbs to the negotiating table to hammer out a peace treaty, the president ignored Gingrich's calls to stay out of Europe and fused his NATO allies in the biggest and most concentrated application of military force as deterrent in its post-war history. Tens of thousands of NATO troops assembled in south-east Europe while NATO aircraft, on August 30, 1995, pummelled Serb artillery positions. 'Shouts of joy could be heard from balconies all over Sarajevo' the *Washington Post* reported, following yet another Serb mortar attack that had killed thirty-seven innocent civilians in a marketplace. 'My God, the Serbs are bombing us' a resident had exclaimed as she heard the planes come overhead. 'When I realized it was NATO, I was literally jumping through my flat with joy.'[26]

Flying the leaders of Bosnia, Croatia and Serbia to Dayton Air Force Base in Ohio on November 1, 1995, President Clinton then used the threat of further NATO force to get the parties to agree a peace accord in a matter of weeks. It would hold for more than a decade.

Poor Gingrich, who had earlier that year basked in the widely touted moniker 'Prime Minister of America', was distraught, and in his frustration now committed the biggest error of his life. He wanted automatic weapons back on the streets, to curry favour with the NRA;

moreover, with power having gone to his head, earlier that summer he had threatened Clinton with what he called a 'train wreck' if the president did not agree to his legislative proposals to abolish the federal departments of education, commerce and housing, and to curtail Medicare and Medicaid. Clinton had said no, however, warning he would use his veto. Gingrich had then made history by carrying out his threat.

Gingrich's shutdown of the US government, halfway through the Dayton negotiations, began on November 14, 1995, causing almost a million federal workers to be sent home, forcing the government to default on its loans, US embassies and consulates worldwide to close, and tens of millions to go without cheques. All federal museums closed, as well as national parks and institutions. Gingrich's right-hand man and House Majority Leader, Congressman Dick Armey of Texas, warned the president in a midnight meeting that it was going to be the end of his presidency.

Instead it would mark the end of Gingrich's posturing. When the Speaker then complained that he had not been allowed to exit Air Force One by the front ramp, beside the president, on his way back from the funeral of the terrorist-assassinated Yitzhak Rabin in Tel Aviv ('You just wonder, where is their sense of manners? Where is their sense of courtesy?') and gave this as his reason for continuing the government shutdown, his infantile whining struck a risible note. A cartoon was published in the *New York Daily News* showing Gingrich dressed in nappies, captioned: 'CRY BABY'.

Gingrich's stock plummeted while Clinton's, in the wake of the historic Dayton Peace Accords, rocketed. Even the Majority Leader of the Senate, Bob Dole, was ashamed. When Gingrich, having temporarily ended the shutdown for a few weeks, reimposed it over the Christmas holiday, Republican defectors finally forced him to back down on January 5, 1996. The 'train wreck' had been an unmitigated disaster, not only for the country, but also for any hopes of 'Prime Minister' Gingrich – or Senator Dole – becoming president.

President Clinton, so belittled in his first year in office and knocked to the canvas in his second, now began to emerge as the master politician of the age. Even journalists began to look at him differently. In London, journalist Hamish McRae had warned those of his colleagues who had written Clinton off after the midterm tsunami not to underestimate the American president. Two years before the election of Tony Blair as prime minister of Great Britain, McRae pointed out that the old politics of union solidarity and entitlements were out of date in a global economy, and that a new, practical liberalism could only arise from the ashes if leaders sought a fresh compact between politicians and the people. Clinton's makeover 'should be studied carefully by all politicians in Europe. For it signposts a way down the path they are likely to have to travel themselves' – a 'roadmap that will be useful to us all'.[27]

Young, indefatigable, smart, well read, willing to listen and determined to do good in the world, Bill Clinton was coming into his own, his nation's best ambassador both in pursuing peace, and where necessary applying force to obtain it. From Turkey to Japan, political leaders were wowed by his sheer energy and positive outlook; indeed he achieved rock-star status wherever he travelled abroad, pressing for improvement in trade, greater environmental protection, and reduction in ethnic and nationalist violence. His ability to articulate the different sides and aspects of any problem, and review solutions, was unique among world leaders. Moreover, with an American economy undergoing an information technology revolution as profound as the Industrial Revolution more than a century before, he wore something of FDR's mantle in foreign eyes: a president with benevolent, compassionate feelings, as well as an extraordinary curiosity about other cultures. It was small wonder his popularity abroad exceeded even that of John F. Kennedy.

At home, the president's increasing self-confidence was best demonstrated in his State of the Union address on January 23, 1996. In the course of a spellbinding, eighty-minute *tour d'horizon*, he pointed to a Vietnam veteran in the gallery who had entered the bombed wreckage of the Murrah Federal Building in Oklahoma City to save the lives of three women. As the audience rose to applaud Richard Dean's courage, Clinton thundered 'I challenge all of you in this chamber. Never – ever – shut the federal government again.'[28]

Viewers and commentators expressed amazement at Bill Clinton's extraordinary journey, from fumbling naivety to mastery of the presidential office. Why had it taken him so long, people wondered? Certainly there was no one on the Republican benches who had a hope of beating him if he stood for re-election in 1996, as polls made savagely clear to the ragbag of Republican wannabes, from Lamar Alexander and Steve Forbes to Newt Gingrich and Bob Dole.

Only one man could have given Clinton a fight: the former chairman of the Joint Chiefs of Staff, General Colin Powell, and he removed himself from contention, citing domestic reasons. The way for Clinton was clear.

Had Bill Clinton decided at this, his proudest and most successful moment as president, to stand down in favour of his stalwart, rock-steady vice president, Al Gore, he would – like Lyndon Johnson in 1964, after passing his civil rights bill – undoubtedly have gone down in history as one of the most effective of American Caesars, after a rocky start. At home the national deficit had already been halved since he took office, thanks to his 1993 economic bill; ten million new jobs had been added; new businesses were starting up at a record rate; unemployment was at its lowest level for twenty-eight years; the minimum wage had increased to $4.75 per hour, and portability of medical insurance was ensured from job to job. Moreover, these achievements had been won in direct refutation of the Reagan-Republican mantra against tax hikes. Disproving Reagan's dictum, the president had increased the highest tax bracket to 36 per cent, with a 10 per cent surcharge on the highest earnings – making a tax bracket of 39.6 per cent. Moreover he had raised the corporate income tax rate to 36 per cent, as well as increasing the federal tax on gas – and the American economy had flourished, not dwindled as Republicans had predicted. Abroad he had not only brought Serbian genocide in Bosnia to an end, but he had, using the US as an independent arbitrator, helped the move towards peace in Northern Ireland and an Israeli–Jordan Peace Accord. Like Lyndon Baines Johnson in 1964, however, Bill Clinton could not say no to the lure of another term in the White House, whatever attacks might be unleashed by his enemies.

Second Acts had rarely proven successful in the history of the American Caesars, after FDR; indeed in many ways they contradicted the feature that best characterized America: its constant self-reinvention and renewal. But Bill Clinton, having finally found his feet as American president, had no wish to hand over his hard-won spurs to his deputy marshal, Al Gore. Not only did he see himself as the most intelligent person he knew, but – as when he was defeated as governor of Arkansas after a single term – he had no idea what he would do with himself outside of politics. Jimmy Carter had taken up carpentry and Habitat for Humanity, as well as service to peacemaking, from North Korea to Haiti. But Carter had perhaps the deepest well of humility of any Caesar, whereas Bill Clinton's hubris had since his student years made it impossible for him to play second fiddle to another human being, let alone multiple beings. He *had to* shine, to wow, to win over, to seduce, lest the demons in his psyche take him over and bring him down – as they had his drug-addicted, imprisoned brother Roger. For the president, this was a powerful argument for staying put in the White House.

His decision to run for re-election thus looked, on the surface, a no-brainer; indeed he told his aides that, if he campaigned well enough, he might even reverse the Republican landslide in the House of Representatives, thus felling the egregious Speaker, Newt Gingrich. Against that, however, as would emerge in due course, he had a very personal, and highly secret, reason *not* to run.

Despite the efforts of the Republican nominee, Senator Dole, to sink his opponent with a missile aimed at the president's 'character' and financial probity, the presidential debates resulted in three resounding victories for the patient, endlessly positive, articulate Clinton. The independent candidate, Ross Perot – who had not been permitted to participate in the debates – garnered ten million votes fewer than in 1992, while Dole, who had resigned his seat in the Senate to devote himself to the campaign, came nowhere close, winning only 159 to Clinton's 379 Electoral College votes on November 3, 1996. William Jefferson Clinton would get to stay in the White House, becoming the first Democrat since Franklin Roosevelt to win and serve a second elected term.

Instead of welcoming the president's belated learning curve in the Oval Office, Republican opponents continued to see him as the prime target of their resentment; indeed the more he succeeded in rallying the nation after the Oklahoma City bombing and the Dayton Peace Accords, the more determined their diehards became to find some way to take the Democratic polymath down. The fact that his Omnibus economic bill, on the wheel of which they had almost broken him in the spring and early summer of 1993, had proven an historic turning point in steering the American economy back into sustained growth and reduction in national debt only maddened such opponents more. They had blocked health care reform in 1994, and had forced the president to sign a welfare reform bill in the summer of 1996 (preferring lower welfare rolls to a healthier country), but otherwise they were unable to point to anything constructive that they had proposed – in part because Clinton seemed to co-opt in advance every issue they addressed, from urban crime (where the president got federal funding to provide 100,000 more police on the streets of American cities) to V-chips on televisions to safeguard children from violence and pornography.

In the view of diehard anti-Clintonistas, then, the president had to be brought down not for the good of America, but for the good of the Republican Party. That such a conspiracy might amount to near-treason, at a moment when the nation required the legislature and security officials to unite and concentrate on dealing with the growing threat of Islamic terrorism, was not something, lamentably, that worried them – as shown by the behaviour of the director of the FBI, Louis Freeh.

Freeh would later boast that, from the spring of 1993, when he was made FBI director, he met with the president 'one time, maybe two, maybe three times in the entire seven-plus years I worked under Bill Clinton'.[29]

Historians rubbed their eyes in disbelief. How, when plot after plot was being hatched against America at home and abroad, by terrorists concerted by al-Qaeda – an organization formed and financed by a Yemeni-Saudi millionaire, Osama Bin Laden – was it conceivable that the director of the FBI, a Republican, refused to meet with his own president – and would later *boast* of this?

Freeh's hatred for the president reflected the blinkered venom that Clinton seemed to stir in a minority of Americans, even as his popularity with the majority reached record levels of approval. Certainly, thanks to his upbringing and political career in one of the most bigoted states in the nation, President Clinton was no stranger to the hatred he inspired as a 'liberal' in the minds of bigots and right-wing fanatics. Nonetheless he tried, again and again, to hold out an olive branch to his opponents. His last act before his second inauguration had been to award the Presidential Medal of Freedom to his defeated opponent, Bob Dole, a hero of World War II, in which he had served as an infantry officer. 'I liked Dole' Clinton later wrote. 'He could be mean and tough in a fight, but he lacked the fanaticism and hunger for personal destruction that characterized so many of the hard-right Republicans who now dominated his party in Washington.'[30]

The president also decided not to press for criminal charges against the Speaker, Newt Gingrich, who was found guilty by the House Ethics Committee of violating tax and ethics laws, for which he was fined $300,000 by Congress. Instead, in his second inaugural address on January 20, 1997, Clinton called for 'a new spirit of community for a new century'. He pointed to the 'divide of race' which had been 'America's constant curse', as well as other evils. Each 'new wave of immigrants gives new targets to old prejudices' he stated. 'Prejudice and contempt, cloaked in the pretense of religious or political conviction, are no different. These forces have nearly destroyed our nation in the past. They plague us still. They fuel the fanaticism of terror. And they torment the lives of millions in fractured nations all around the world. Those obsessions cripple both those who hate and, of course, those who are hated, robbing both of what they might become. We cannot, will not, succumb to the dark impulses that lurk in the far regions of the soul everywhere. We shall overcome them', he promised – leading, in the next century, to renewed opportunity, thanks to 'our rich texture of racial, religious and political diversity'. After all, he pointed out, 'Ten years ago the Internet was the mystical province of physicists; today it is a commonplace encyclopedia of schoolchildren.' And in that increased level of communication, he foresaw a situation in which 'the voice of the people' would 'speak louder than the din of narrow interests', redeeming the promise of America to its citizens. It was time, he declared, to end 'acrimony and division' at home, the better to be able to spread 'America's bright flame of freedom' throughout the world.

These were famous last words. Whatever Clinton might do to disarm his opponents, and whatever he now did to prove himself a worthy, bipartisan president, he could neither change his own dark urges nor the minds of those who had hated him for his early incompetence, but who now seemed to hate him all the more for his success. Shortly before the election he had signed the Comprehensive Test Ban Treaty, together with Russia, China, France and the UK. In the twelve months following his second inauguration he signed off on a balanced budget passed by Congress, a primary supposed objective of Republicans, and an important step in achieving federal fiscal responsibility. Abroad he

ensured, in a personal meeting with Boris Yeltsin, Russia's acquiescence to the expansion of NATO to include the Czech Republic,
Hungary and Poland. These were signal achievements, but his signature was, literally, on hundreds of other initiatives, from Internet
funding to cancer research and clean water initiatives. Like Lyndon
Johnson he was a force of nature, as he met with foreign leaders from
Britain's new prime minister, Tony Blair, to China's leader, Jiang Zemin,
visited American troops in Bosnia, travelled across South America, got
the Chemical Weapons Convention Treaty ratified by Congress over
the sworn opposition of Caspar Weinberger and Donald Rumsfeld, yet
seemed as knowledgeable and involved in domestic initiatives as their
progenitors, from children's health care to middle-class tax cuts – which
he persuaded the Republican-controlled House of Representatives to
pass, in return for a reduction in capital gains tax. Asked by the *Wall
Street Journal* 'at what point', given the depth of animosity he inspired
in his detractors, 'do you consider that it's just not worth it, and do
you consider resigning the office?' he responded sharply: 'Never. I
would never walk away from the people of this country and the trust
they have placed in me.'[31]

Begged by right-wing fanatics not to give up on the Whitewater
investigation regarding possible culpability by the Clintons, Kenneth
Starr, the Independent Investigator appointed by the Republican House
of Representatives to examine allegations of malfeasance in the
imbroglio, decided *not* to terminate his investigation of the Clintons'
role, as he had promised. Instead, with the help of Louis Freeh, on
February 21, 1997 Starr renewed his detective inquiry, this time focusing
on the keyhole to the president's boudoir.

Never in American presidential history had such a sex-investigation
taken place while a president was in office. The notion of executive
privilege was now cast to the four winds by Republican right-wingers
– often the very people who had objected to Nixon being investigated
while in office – as the Supreme Court awarded Paula Jones, who was
attempting to sue Clinton for previous sexual harassment in Arkansas
in 1991, the right to have her civil case heard in court while Clinton
was still president.

Alarmed, Clinton eventually offered what he should have offered four
years before: a financial settlement, more than $700,000. Even Jones'
own lawyers acknowledged that, according to the then-operative

Arkansas law under which she had brought her case, she could point to no monetary or professional suffering incurred by the alleged harassment. Her lawyers thus urged her to accept the money and to run. When she refused, her lawyers resigned, leaving the right-wing 'Rutherford Institute' to fund new lawyers for her case.

Ms Jones demanded from Clinton an admission of guilt and an apology. 'I couldn't do that because it wasn't true,' Clinton would later maintain. Few, however, believed him then, or later. Assuming Ms Jones' allegations of sexual harassment were true, there were, chroniclers could see in retrospect, only two possible reasons why the president was unable to bring himself to issue an apology. The first was entirely rational.

No other president in modern times possessed Clinton's ability to calculate political expediency in advance. Since childhood, he had used his brains to stay ahead of others, however aggressive. He was, in effect, a modern Houdini, able not only to contort himself to accommodate every political belief, from capital punishment to compulsory recitation of the pledge of allegiance, but to escape from every net thrown over him by his political enemies. Believing that such an open apology to Ms Jones would only encourage other women from his exotic past to come forward with similar, perhaps even worse, examples of his sexual self-indulgence, he calculated it would be political suicide – in the media and possibly the courts – to agree to her demand.

Besides this, though, there was the matter of pathology.

Despite his extraordinary ability to empathize, indeed a legendary ability to 'feel your pain', Bill Clinton had always suffered from the opposite, too: namely sexual sociopathy, or bipolar behaviour. In Clinton's case this took the form of an initial inability to say no to high-risk sexual misconduct, however much it might threaten to ruin him, followed afterwards by an inability to acknowledge his guilt. Only his wife Hillary, possibly, could have got him to confess to his addiction, but even she, who was an intensely private person, could not now get him to issue a public apology, since her own distrust of the media and right-wing fanatics went deeper even than his: a distrust so pronounced that, whatever her private feelings (fury, disappointment, lamentations at yet another example of her husband's bad behaviour), she simply could not countenance such a public *mea culpa*.

Thus, inexorably, the tragedy unfolded as Paula Jones' new legal team began, in the absence of an apology from the president, and in the hope of establishing a pattern of sexual misbehaviour, to seek to unearth other examples from the past – never dreaming they would find examples from the present. It was this 'fishing expedition' that Kenneth Starr and the director of the FBI, Louis Freeh, decided to join.

Pointing to Clinton's stellar polls for a second-term president, the White House staff did not take the news of Starr's sex-trawling seriously; but they did not know what the president was hiding from them, indeed from his own wife. Only Clinton himself knew that at the very moment his enemies were seeking to corral evidence of past sexual impropriety against him in the spring of 1997, he had yet again indulged in an 'inappropriate' extramarital liaison: to wit, a 'friendship with benefits' in the hallowed confines of the Oval Office, conducted with a young former intern.[32]

His conduct – or misconduct, given that it involved a government employee in the president's official, government-funded work quarters – defied subsequent belief. It was true that previous presidents had indulged in far more egregious extramarital practices while in the White House, especially John F. Kennedy and Lyndon Johnson, but those practices had been unknown by the general public in their day, thanks to patriarchal attitudes and self-censorship by (male) editors in the serious American press. Times had changed since then, as Clinton well knew. Public expectations of presidential morality had, if anything, become all the more idealistic, the further that public mores – whether in the entertainment industry or in ordinary people's lives – declined, relative to supposed earlier standards. The president, however briefly in that imperial role, was in an almost sacred position of trust. Why would anyone in that role in the late twentieth century put not only his career but the very office of the presidency at risk, to gratify a fleeting sexual impulse?

The word hubris, then, could not begin to describe Clinton's departure from his senses as a man *already* facing a major lawsuit over earlier sexual misbehaviour when Arkansas governor. It suggested more than the power to misbehave, as emperor; indeed it seemed so deliberately self-destructive that many subsequent chroniclers ascribed it to a sort of metaphorical death wish, when details of the alleged liaison finally emerged.

The 'victim' chosen by Starr and Freeh to illustrate Clinton's pattern of misconduct was unfortunate: a plump, twenty-two-year-old Jewish intern who had previously been the willing mistress of a married teacher at her college in California, before coming to Washington for an internship at the White House arranged through her divorced mother. She then boasted to her companions that she was setting her beret, as well as 'presidential knee-pads', for the president. Once successful in that quest – her innocent seduction of Clinton taking place during the Gingrich government shutdown, when only a skeleton White House staff was operating – Monica Lewinsky would not thereafter let go. Nor, however, would Ms Jones' team or Ken Starr's, once they got wind of the affair. The more the investigation delved, the more it took on the form of a cat-and-mouse contest: Jones, Starr and Freeh determined to entrap the president, and, Clinton, like Richard Nixon before him, determined to prove himself cleverer than his accusers.

Blessed with an ability to multitask that no president in American history had evinced, Clinton was amazingly successful. He was observed to complete in minutes the *New York Times* crossword puzzle, sign letters, read documents and take telephone calls, all simultaneously. As a narcissistic genius and former law professor trained at Yale, he knew he could not admit to his closest friends or family the truth of what he had done, in case they were subpoenaed.[33] He therefore stopped all but phone sex and chaste meetings with the former intern, to keep her from turning against him; meanwhile, knowing her gossipy, loose-tongued, childlike personality, he braced himself, throughout the second half of 1997, for the impending legal challenge, without ever asking himself whether it was right and proper for the American people to be put through another wrenching drama, once Starr got evidence of the 'affair'.

Finally, on January 18, 1998, news broke on the very medium the president had extolled in his State of the Union address, the Internet: a '23-year-old, former White House intern' had had a 'sex relationship with president. World Exclusive.'[34]

The news reverberated across the world like an earthquake, fulfilling the worst nightmares of Democrats as they continued their efforts to rebuild the party following the 1994 meltdown. The last thing they needed was *another* Clinton sex scandal.

Telling the truth, however, seems never to have entered the president's calculating brain. Clinton had already used his friendship with a successful outside lawyer, Vernon Jordan, to get the former intern a job in New York, thereby whisking her away from the prying eyes of Washington journalists and mischief-makers. He had also colluded with Ms Lewinsky in drawing up an affidavit to sign, lest she be formally deposed and cross-examined by the Jones team. (In this she denied, on oath, that there had been a sexual or improper relationship.) Meanwhile Clinton had responded to a subpoena from the Jones team by giving them a six-hour deposition at the offices of his lawyers in downtown Washington on January 16, 1998, in which he denied virtually all allegations about sexual misbehaviour in his past, and denied any recollection of having met, let alone lewdly exposed himself to an Arkansas employee, Paula Jones. With reference to Ms Lewinsky, he had, by shrewd use of the past and present tenses, been able to deceive the team about the nature of his White House relationship, and the extent of his connection with the former intern.

Any relief, or Yalie pride, in having evaded the Jones legal team's most searching questions evaporated, however, when less than thirty hours later the Internet news story broke in the *Drudge Report*, indicating that Ms Lewinsky – and thus the president – had been entrapped by Starr's men using illegally recorded telephone tape recordings and concealed body-wires, supplied by the FBI, as in a Hollywood movie. It was thus no rumour, but a story backed by FBI evidence. All hell broke loose.

The Clinton administration would in effect be shut down again, by yet another arm of the Republican-controlled Congress: its so-called Independent – though unashamedly Republican – Counsel. Having already wasted $28 million of American taxpayers' money in pursuit of Whitewater, Starr's fruitless efforts would now make presidential history.

In a televised press conference in the White House on January 26, 1998, the president attempted to tamp down media speculation, given that he had not in fact had sex with Ms Lewinsky, if sex meant sexual intercourse, as defined by the law. After lengthy remarks on children's reading and after-school programmes, he declared 'I want to say one thing to the American people. I want you to listen to me. I'm going to say this again. I did not have sexual relations with that woman. I never told anybody to lie, not a single time – never. These allegations are false. And I need to go back to work for the American people.'[35]

Starr could only smile. Day by day, week by week, month by month, leaking evidence and rumours as they went along, the members of his team now took up the baton of the Jones team, threatening the former White House intern with twenty-eight years in penitentiary if she did not cooperate in bringing down the president with whom she had become besotted. Like the Dreyfus case in France in the final decade of the nineteenth century the matter became a cause célèbre, pitting liberals against conservatives, puritans against tolerants and seniors against the younger generation, in a strangely symbolic *fin de siècle* struggle.

That the world's most powerful empire, attempting to maintain Pax Americana across a fractious globe, should become so embroiled in the minutiae of its president's most private parts and the legal defin-ition of 'sexual relations' was not only demeaning but dangerously distracting, given the rise of 1990s Islamic terrorism. Yet as long as Clinton refused to resign and instead made it his mission to slay the 'vast right-wing conspiracy' seeking to bring him down, the United States – and the world – was doomed to watch while the two sides slugged it out. All hope of constructive, bipartisan legislation in 1998 was abandoned, and in foreign affairs America's leading role became fatally tarnished.

As Clinton's counter-terrorism czar Richard Clarke would later write, he found himself seething with fury that the serving president could have put himself, and thus the nation, into such a ridiculous situation, owing to his lack of 'discretion or self-control'. But Clarke was even 'angrier, almost incredulous, that the bitterness of Clinton's enemies knew no bounds, that they intended to hurt not just Clinton but the country by turning the president's problem into a global, public circus for their own political ends'.[36]

Several days after the scandal erupted, the group calling itself al-Qaeda – named after the foundation stone or base of a building, and having merged with its counterpart in Egypt, Egyptian Islamic Jihad – declared official 'war' on the American Empire. In March, the presi-dent summoned his cabinet and senior officials from the State Department, Department of Defense, CIA, FBI, Health, the Federal

Emergency Management Agency (FEMA), Energy, OMB and other agencies, under Clarke, to plan for a possible nuclear, chemical or biological terrorist attack in the US.[37] In June, Osama Bin Laden was indicted *in absentia* by a federal grand jury in New York, and the president issued his third Counter-terrorism Directive (PDD-62, 63 and 67). Soon after that – just as had been feared – the next massive terrorist attack on America took place, aimed this time at American sovereign territory and personnel in Africa.

On August 7, 1998, the American embassies in Kenya and Tanzania were simultaneously blown up by al-Qaeda mass murderers. In Nairobi, 257 people were killed and 5,000 wounded. This was deliberate Islamist slaughter and maiming of innocents, forbidden in the Koran, but excused by a disputed interpretation of jihad on a new, global scale. Though the bombings aroused shock and condemnation in the US, the American press and news channels on radio, television and the Internet simply ignored the tragedy and concentrated on the president's sex life, as Clinton was compelled by Starr to go before a grand jury and fight for what was left of his reputation. On August 17, 1998, the FBI, working for Starr's Republican Whitewater team, arranged to record, then deliberately leak to the media, yet another deposition by the serving president. This time the interrogation was given in the Map Room of the White House and on videotape, owing to an absent juror. In almost surreal comic opera, Clinton was grilled not on the subject of national security and the measures being taken to combat Islamist terrorism, but the exact nature of his consensual trysts with Ms Monica Lewinsky in the White House during and after Gingrich's government shutdown in 1995, when she succeeded in entering the otherwise off-limits area of the West Wing. Starr's prosecutor and the president battled not over sarin and other threats to the homeland, but over the definition of the word 'sex' and even 'what the meaning of the word "is" is'.[38]

The Lewinsky business had now become tragic farce. That night Clinton again went on television to address the nation. Not even his wife knew whether he would resign or what he would say in his speech, let alone his lawyers and staff.

In the event, Clinton's announcement to the nation was not, as many assumed, to resign honourably and spare the country further shame and embarrassment. Instead, the former Rhodes Scholar and

Yale Law School graduate decided to see whether he could extricate himself by turning the tables on Starr. The president still denied having committed perjury or an obstruction of justice, claiming he had put no pressure on his former intern to lie to the Jones and Starr teams. He still insisted that he and Ms Lewinsky had not, in any biblical sense, had full 'sexual relations' since sexual intercourse had not taken place, and only heavy petting had been involved. However, Clinton did admit he had obfuscated the truth of his relationship, in understandable embarrassment. 'I misled people, including even my wife' he now admitted. 'I deeply regret that.' Nevertheless, he asserted, the matter was strictly a private matter 'between me, the two people I love most – my wife and our daughter – and our God', not with Ken Starr or the people of the United States who had elected him. 'It's nobody's business but ours' Clinton insisted. 'Even presidents have private lives.'[39] And with that he promised to dedicate the rest of his presidency to his job – 'the challenges and all the promise of the next American century'.

By turning the tables on Starr, Clinton demonstrated yet again why he was called 'The Comeback Kid', daring the prosecutor to escalate yet further a sordid but relatively benign sex scandal that had consumed the attention of the country's media for the past seven months. As 60 per cent of respondents believed he was doing a good job as president, Clinton felt convinced of his own essential goodness, compassion, competence, and his elected right to remain in the job until officially removed by Congress. Thus, he made clear, he would *not* stand down just to appease Republican assassins. He had figured out the way to deal with diehards such as Newt Gingrich and Dick Armey, Gingrich's odious henchman in Congress, and now saw himself in the same embattled light as Nixon, determined to focus on idealistic causes and foreign affairs in order to distract the media from its obsession with his own private affairs.

Tirelessly he sought to get Yasser Arafat to negotiate peace with Benjamin Netanyahu, the Israeli prime minister; worked with the new British prime minister, Tony Blair, on the historic 'Good Friday' settlement in Northern Ireland; sent military forces to the Gulf to threaten Saddam Hussein, when the dictator got out of line; visited China, where he pressed for more open trade and mutual investment; and on August 20, 1998, authorized a cruise-missile strike on a training camp in Afghanistan where Osama Bin Laden was reported to be, just as President Reagan had sought to take out Muammar Qaddafi after the bombing of Pan Am Flight 103 over Lockerbie.

To Clinton's disappointment, Bin Laden was not hit – Clinton was. Where Reagan had not been faulted for seeking the demise of an evil, mass-murdering enemy of the US, the fallout from Clinton's failure demonstrated how wounded he was. He looked not only incompetent to Americans at home, but also, thanks to the continuing Lewinsky scandal and his refusal to resign, deceitful, accused by the media not of seriously attempting to keep America safe by killing Bin Laden, but of wanting to distract attention from his continuing woes over the Lewinsky sex saga – and impending impeachment.

The crippling effect of the Lewinsky farce on Bill Clinton's ability to carry out his duties as president is almost impossible to overstate. Faced with impeachment Richard Nixon had maintained he was 'not a quitter'; in the same manner, Clinton swore to friend and foe alike he would fight Starr and his men 'till the last dog dies' – regardless of the consequences for his beloved country. Moreover, standing behind him, the First Lady hardened his resolve. She had told a succession of reporters in January that her husband's 'relationship' with Ms Lewinsky 'was not sexual', had denied it was an 'improper relationship', had insisted the scandal would disappear ('I have seen how these charges evaporate and disappear as they're given the light of day'), and on January 27, 1998, she had famously spoken of a 'vast right-wing conspiracy'.[40] Emboldened by her loyalty – even after she had heard from his own tainted lips, in August, the truth of his relationship with Ms Lewinsky – the president stood firm as Starr delivered his 452-page report and its official recommendation to Congress on September 9, 1998: namely that the president should be impeached.

Two days later, the House voted to release the Starr Report in its entirety to the public, including a long, sexually explicit autobiographical memoir of transgression by Ms Lewinsky, forced from her under threat of imprisonment by one of Starr's female prosecutors.

The world now gulped, as in fastidious, fully footnoted pornographic prose, Starr's dissertation on the serving president's private life and his deplorable sexual mores, even the use of his cigars, was made public. As one of the best chroniclers of the impeachment noted, in the 'first weekend after the release of the Starr Report, the Clinton presidency teetered' – and not because of a right-wing conspiracy.[41] Even honourable, God-fearing and ethical Democrats were, along with Republicans, appalled by the revelations. Just as the Nixon tapes had scandalized a nation used to thinking of the president as an almost sacred personage, and were then shocked by transcripts of his mafia-like gutter-language, so now both Democrats and Republicans alike were outraged at the implicit scorn for presidential dignity displayed by the nation's chief executive in the Oval Office. One liberal Democrat, Congressman David Obey, declared to the Democratic Minority Leader as the House voted: 'We have to get rid of this guy. He will destroy the Democratic Party for a generation', and recommended that the Democratic Minority Leader and his colleague in the Senate, Tom Daschle, would 'have to go tell [the President] to get out'.[42]

For a third time, however, the president refused to budge. Millions downloaded the text of the Starr Report from the Internet, even before it was bound and widely published in paper form. The 'facts', as cajoled from Ms Lewinsky, seemed incontrovertible, as well as disgusting in their intimate details, but as Clinton had calculated, they hardly comprised grounds for impeachment, given Alexander Hamilton's original view, in helping to draw up the Constitution, that impeachment was to guard against a genuine threat to America. Was Speaker Gingrich once again overreaching, as he had been in shutting down the US government in 1995? Asked why he was pushing for impeachment of the President over the Lewinsky scandal Gingrich replied, simply, 'because we can'.[43]

Given that the effective administration of America and its empire had been seriously hobbled by the Lewinsky business for almost a year, if an impeachment of the serving President was authorized by Speaker Gingrich things could only get worse. They did. Instead of getting support for the president's executive order 13099 to halt funding to al-Qaeda, the Taliban and other terrorist organizations, obstructionism now ruled in Washington.[44] The personal had truly become the political – with a vengeance. In Congress and elsewhere, especially the media, the impeachment saga became a sort of metaphorical Gettysburg, with charges and counter-charges, artillery barrages and counter-battery fire. By refusing to resign, and instead framing the issue as *Clinton* vs *A Right-Wing Conspiracy*, the president had deftly managed to reorientate the national debate from 'doing the right thing' to 'doing in' the right wing.[45]

The longer he could stretch out the process, Clinton reckoned, the more likely the public would eventually tire of it and turn against the Republicans, who seemed to fatally underestimate his Darwinian ability to survive when cornered. How long could it go on, people wondered?

Rather than gaining seats in the midterm elections in November 1998, as Gingrich had hoped, the Republicans lost yet more, ratifying the president's decision to mount his version of Custer's Last Stand. Republican hypocrisy now came under the spotlight, as investigations were made regarding legislators' own private lives. As Gingrich's marital infidelity came to light, the Speaker wisely decided not to seek re-election but to resign at the end of the session. The wisdom of this was soon demonstrated when, amid a flurry of new revelations, his elected successor, Bob Livingstone, the Republican Speaker-designate of the House of Representatives, was also compelled to resign. To the fury of Republicans, however, Clinton refused to follow suit.

Relentlessly, implacably, the impeachment process was therefore pressed by the Republican-controlled House of Representatives. On December 19, 1998, in Resolution 611, the House unwisely rejected the simpler alternative of censure. Instead it voted by 228 to 206 to have the president put on trial by the Senate for 'perjury committed before a grand jury', and by 221 to 212 for his 'obstruction of justice' – both claims relating to Clinton's attempt to mislead investigators over his relationship with Ms Lewinsky, a private matter that was of no concern to Congress or to the law, which Clinton had not broken.

For only the second time in American history (and the first time ever for an elected president) a full impeachment trial in the Senate was now prepared against the president. Presided over by the Chief Justice of the Supreme Court, the comic opera opened on January 7, 1999, and stretched across five weeks during which the business of the state, as well as the Supreme Court, was yet further disrupted. America became the laughing stock of the world.

Finally, on February 12, 1999, the trial ended with acquittal (just) on all counts. William Jefferson Clinton had won, but had America? After owning up to Hillary in August 1998, Clinton had begun 'a serious counseling program, one day a week', while being exiled for months to sleep on the couch 'in the small living room that adjoined our bedroom' in the White House, in a renewed effort to 'unify my parallel lives', the first of which he saw as noble, the other as deeply self-destructive – a trait he attributed to unaddressed anger and grief, stemming from his abused childhood. His acquittal he saw as the consequence of majority public support among ordinary Americans, as evidenced by his approval ratings in opinion polls. 'It would have been much harder' to maintain his sanity, he afterwards claimed, 'if the American people hadn't made an early judgement that I should remain president and stuck with it.'[46]

Once again, however, Bill Clinton was parsing history, since the majority of voters had no quarrel with the president's performance in running the country, especially the economy – but they had less and less faith in his honesty, his ethics, his integrity, his dignity or his moral character. In a nation where the president is the embodiment not only of American power but also of self-respect, this was a grave shortcoming that could only have been addressed by his resignation – which he refused to concede.

Ever the narcissist, Clinton wanted the public's love and forgiveness rather than banishment, and to his credit was prepared to work harder than ever to merit it, in a spirit of 'reconciliation and renewal for America'. The final two years of the Clinton presidency thus took place in a strange political twilight: the public was relieved the Lewinsky saga was finally over and pleased at the continuing strength of the economy as it continued its longest sustained boom ever, yet also ashamed of its president whom few now respected.

Clinton might – and did – proudly point to statistics showing how the country was moving towards a historic surplus and the paying-down of the once spiralling national debt; might – and did – pride himself on showing strong leadership in NATO's intervention in the former Yugoslavia, when Serbs were compelled to halt their ethnic cleansing in Kosovo and, on June 3, 1999, to accept NATO administration of the enclave; and might – and did – take credit for seeing the country safely into the new millennium without another Islamic terrorist outrage, or millennium-induced computer meltdown. These were, however, hardly matters which President Gore, had he been appointed, would have been unable or unwilling to manage; indeed by the autumn of 2000 it became ever more evident that a new American president was needed, one who would have the trust and authority to meld together the FBI, CIA, defence and security agencies, given the ongoing refusal of the director of the FBI, Louis Freeh, to meet with

President Clinton for a single meeting in his second term, or to resign in favour of a new FBI director. ('I spent most of the eight years as director investigating the man who appointed me' Freeh later said.[47] Then he admitted he stayed on 'longer' at the FBI because he 'didn't want to give Clinton a chance to name his successor', 'I was going to stay there and make sure he couldn't replace me' he confessed.[48])

The fact was, America needed a tough, respected president, for the threat to America was not going away – indeed it was magnified, to Richard Clarke's chagrin, by the president's reduced stature and authority. Despite titanic efforts between Israeli and Palestinian negotiators at Camp David in July 2000, Yassar Arafat rejected Clinton's compromise peace agreement: a two-state solution in which the Palestinians would eventually get back 91 per cent of the West Bank, all of Gaza, and control of East Jerusalem, including custodianship, though not sovereignty, of the Temple Mount. Once Ariel Sharon blithely insisted on walking across the Temple Mount, on September 28, to rub in Israeli sovereignty in his bid to oust Ehud Barak as prime minister, the Middle East exploded. Protest begat violence. A second intifada or Palestinian uprising commenced – leading to thousands of deaths, suicide bombings, reprisals and targeted assassinations, and arousing yet more Muslim hostility towards the 'Great Satan', America, which was perceived as Israel's military protector and primary funder, yet lacked the power or will to rein its expansionist policies in, or compel Israel to compromise.

Clinton refused to give up on his peace proposals, knowing how America's security depended on the outcome. He took pride in the fact that every attack planned against Americans on American soil since the World Trade Center bombing shortly after his first inauguration had been successfully disrupted. But with the Palestinian intifada fanning the flames of Islamist terror groups, he knew time was running out. On October 12, 2000, three weeks before the presidential election, two suicide bombers approached the anchored USS *Cole* in Aden, Yemen, and blew themselves up, killing seventeen American sailors as they did so. It was clear the clash of civilizations was growing ever more earnest, and with Osama Bin Laden still at large in southern Afghanistan, and unless there was a peace agreement between the Israelis and the Palestinians under Yasser Arafat, the future of the American Empire under its next president would be severely tested.

Who that president would be was a moot point. At the beginning of August, Republicans had nominated as their candidate for the White House – after a bruising fight with competitors – the eldest son of former president George H. W. Bush, Governor George W. Bush. Two weeks later, on August 17, 2000, Democrats nominated as their candidate Vice President Al Gore. Secret polls indicated a disturbing groundswell of residual public anger, 'still mad as hell over the Year of Monica' and at President Clinton's moral failings, however much they abhorred the tactics which Ken Starr had adopted.[49] In view of this alarming information, Gore decided it would be unwise to ask the president to campaign for him – indeed that he must take as his running mate a 'squeaky clean' but little-known vice-presidential running mate, Senator Joe Lieberman, an observant Jew from Connecticut.

The result, for Gore, was not encouraging. The country was deemed by the public to be on the right track politically and economically, but on the wrong track in terms of ethics and ethical leadership. By a five-to-one margin, voters felt that the born-again Christian, Governor Bush, was more 'honest' than the vice president who was tainted by his loyal service to Clinton. In the closest election in American history, on November 7, 2000, Vice President Gore won the majority of votes cast, but after a Supreme Court ruling of five votes to four on December 12, lost in the Electoral College (266 to 271) thanks to a number of disputed paper chads in Florida. Clinton's refusal to resign had ensured his own survival in the Oval Office, but had ruined Gore's chances of succeeding him.

Just as President Carter had worked to the last hours of his presidency to secure the release of the American embassy hostages in Tehran, so President Clinton worked to get an Israeli–Palestinian settlement while the centrist Israeli prime minister, Ehud Barak, was still in power. Clinton even passed up the possibility of flying to North Korea to get an agreement banning long-range missiles, in a last-ditch attempt to get Arafat to accept an American-brokered Middle East peace deal. To his chagrin Arafat declined the deal, thereby surrendering the best opportunity for an Israeli–Palestinian settlement since 1948. In one of their last conversations, as Clinton recalled, Arafat 'thanked me for all my efforts and told me what a great man I was. "Mr Chairman," I replied, "I am not a great man. I am a failure, and you have made me one." I warned Arafat that he was single-handedly electing Sharon and that he would reap the whirlwind.'[50] Arafat did – but so too did America.

That Clinton, for all his brilliance as a politician, was simply too shameless and self-centred to put the dignity of the office and the good of the nation first seemed to be symbolized as he left the White House. In the final hour of his presidency he chose to grant a controversial pardon to Mark Rich, the ex-husband of a major donor promising to give more than $150,000 to Clinton's Presidential Library and museum project in Little Rock – but a man still wanted for massive IRS tax fraud and evasion.[51]

Many of Clinton's staffers and subordinates had already left his administration in disgust at the Lewinsky scandal. Even the most loyal remaining Friends of Bill, however, wondered if the departing president had taken leave of his senses. Despite his weekly counselling, months spent on the marital couch and two post-impeachment years trying to demonstrate his still-remarkable skills as president, Clinton had shown yet again that personal interest had triumphed.

The Rich pardon thus marred the by now traditional departure of the former president from Washington. In an emotional speech at Andrews Air Force Base on January 20, 2001, the charismatic, indefatigable but narcissistic arch-egoist of the United States lauded his time and achievements in the White House as 'the ride of my life' and flew into retirement – not to Arkansas, but to Chappaqua, New York, where his wife had won a thrilling election that had put her in the Senate, and on track for her own eventual bid for the imperial crown.[52]

## Part Three: Private Life

From earliest infancy Bill Clinton wanted to please. His absolute determination to be liked and admired masked, however, deep inner turmoil, something he later described as 'the difficulty I've had in letting anyone into the deepest recesses of my internal life. It was dark down there.'[53] His lack of a real father, his abusive, alcoholic stepfather, his mother's divorce and remarriage all contributed to this black hole; indeed it was remarkable the boy from Hope was in most respects so normal.

At elementary school in Hot Springs one of his Catholic teachers jokingly told his mother he was so smart he would land either in jail or in the White House.

Over time this need to please, and his propensity to over-promise, became a serious moral hazard. He was, in his way, too gifted to be true, especially given his underlying demons. As the 6' 3" All State saxophone-player prodigy from Hot Springs High School went out into the wider world, he was like an accident waiting to happen, at once brilliant and yet, in his overweening ambition, lacking a reliable core moral fibre. Somehow, he continued to hope, his positives – a genuine compassion for the underprivileged, a determination to improve the conditions of life in which most people struggled, an ability to synthesize smart thinking, and a promise of betterment to those in need of hope – would outweigh his inability to say no to temptation. As his neighbour Carolyn Staley, the daughter of a Baptist minister, put it, he wore 'good on one shoulder, and bad on the other'.[54] For many – indeed ultimately for tens of millions, who came to see him as a political rock star – the good would outweigh the bad. But for many others, the bad aroused contempt and even hatred, sometimes of a distinctly malevolent kind, suggesting that Clinton's transgressions – his occasionally callous behaviour, his over-promising, and his lying – were experienced as a betrayal of their high expectations, like scorned lovers.

In some cases, this was no more than the truth. Bill Clinton's private life abounded with such cases. In Hot Springs his best female friend, Carolyn Yeldell, loved him and expected him to propose to her, so close did she feel to him. One night, on her way to meet him, she saw him on his doorstep, on vacation from Georgetown University, kissing another woman. She assumed it was a fellow Georgetown undergraduate whom Bill had been seeing – only to find it was Miss Arkansas.[55]

Wherever he went, Bill Clinton seemed to arouse – and disappoint – such dreams; indeed when he became president, a whole book, *Dreams of Bill*, was published, recording actual nocturnal dreams people had experienced and recorded in which they found themselves – men as well as women – seduced by the Man From Hope: romantically, companionably, erotically, sexually.[56] He was, some claimed, a sort of throwback to the great studio stars of Hollywood, about whom millions had also dreamed: big, bushy-haired, hugely intelligent, fun-loving like his mother, rippling with energy and in his positivism promising more than he could possibly deliver – especially once he met Hillary Rodham at Yale Law School and became engaged to her.

The fact was, among women in a 1970s American culture of women's lib, Bill Clinton's unusually open nature, at once inquisitive and compassionate, invited friendship and easy intimacy. For men who hewed to a more moral line in their behaviour, or were less successful in attracting women, Bill Clinton's ability to 'have it all' aroused fearsome envy, even in his twenties. It didn't seem fair that a man from such a humble background should have such mega-intelligence, such an abundant love of life, such a confident ability to network and promote himself, and such success with the fairer sex. 'Did I feel he was exploiting her?' one friend asked rhetorically, learning that Bill was having sex with one of his congressional campaign aides, despite his engagement to Hillary Rodham. 'I did, I did! I mean this was just one example that happened to involve a female, an example that happened to involve sex. But he does it with men, too! He seduces men – and when I say seduce, I mean the minds, the commitments, the emotions – yes, the affections. He demands a kind of loyalty, complete, consummate loyalty, while giving nothing in return!'[57]

This objection, amounting to moral outrage, had little to do with politics, and everything to do with envy, though envy of an interesting kind. Clinton's friend, over time, would become his nemesis – and lawyer for the Arkansas Troopers whose scandalous story of unending sexual conquests, which they were expected to facilitate, led to the Paula Jones harassment case, setting in motion a process that would lead to impeachment.

Politics, as such, did not figure in this equation. What it boiled down to, in essence, was the spectacle of a hugely charismatic, idealistic individual whose amoral conduct defied and thus threatened the moral code that others were trying to live up to in their own lives. That Bill Clinton not only indulged himself, but *got away with it* – his Gingerbread Man, catch-me-if-you-can casualness – infuriated such observers, some of whom became determined to try and take him down, not as Republicans but as moral human beings struggling in their own lives to be good. It was not for nothing that Clinton sneeringly referred to the director of the FBI, Louis Freeh, as the 'Boy Scout'.

As if to make the syndrome more galling still, Hillary Rodham's refusal to take Bill's surname upon their marriage in 1975 aroused yet more ire, in Arkansas, since this too took the matter of enviable success and amorality to a fourth dimension: not only was the super-gifted Attorney General, then governor, committing adultery with nightclub singers such as Gennifer Flowers with marital impunity, but his wife was meanwhile benefiting as a corporate lawyer from his political eminence, without even having to pay the traditional dues by surren-dering her name. Indeed those who did not know the Clintons assumed it must be nothing short of a marriage of convenience.

They were wrong, however convenient the bond between such ambitious, self-seeking individuals, besotted by the nobility of their mutual enterprise. Bill Clinton *did* genuinely love Hillary, his friends agreed – but then, Bill Clinton genuinely loved everybody, from his grandma to his neighbour. What was different, they noted, was that he also *needed* Hillary. In the intimate company of the Gennifer Flowers-type women he bedded (or who bedded him), he might complain that Hillary – the eldest daughter of a tough, self-made Republican million-aire from Chicago – was too hard, too anti-erotic, too workaholic, too humourless. But from the moment he had stared at her in the Yale Law School library in 1971 and the fateful conversation they'd had on the steps outside after she deliberately accosted him, the Arkansas prodigy from the wrong side of the tracks had known Hillary was the only woman who could possibly share his political goals, keep him focused, and rein him in for his own good. This was not convenience, it was necessity. As one aide later reflected, without Hillary, Bill Clinton could easily have ended up a convicted drug addict like his younger half-brother Roger, pumping gas on prison furlough in Arkansas.

The marriage to Hillary Rodham in 1975 was, in short, a lifesaver for Bill Clinton, however much he thereafter strayed and thereby strained Hillary's patience, loyalty and perseverance. Without Chelsea, the daughter Hillary gave birth to in 1980, the union might well have collapsed, but as in many marriages, parental responsibility trumped dreams of flight. It was never easy, however: Bill's self-indulgence, his narcissism and his love of sexual adventure led him to acts of lunacy for a politician aspiring to a larger stage than that of landlocked little Arkansas, with its two million souls. As chairperson for Northwest Arkansas Democrats, Ann Henry later recalled how her daughter had telephoned her, sobbing. 'She was so angry, so upset!' Ann explained. 'She'd been to dinner at a friend's house – one of my friend's houses, who was then Bill's big supporter – and there was a woman there talking about *her affair with Bill Clinton!*' Going to Diane Blair, a political science professor and close friend of the Clintons, Mrs Henry said: 'I can't support him . . . Chelsea is eight years old, and this is going to devastate her – I mean he *cares* about his daughter.'[58]

Bill did, but the urge to play off-reservation was simply too enticing, and Hillary's leash too elastic for a state governor with a whole security detail willing to pimp and lie for him, as long as he controlled their jobs.

Thus, though Bill Clinton withdrew from a possible presidential run in the 1988 election, the leopard in him could not, and did not, change its spots. Clinton reasoned that his country needed him, despite his failings. For Hillary it was often a form of purgatory knowing that every so often a new scandal would arise, which they would have to deal with as best they could, unable to protect their daughter from the shame. That a man of such unique talents – the most gifted politician of his generation – should be so much a prey to his sexual, self-gratificatory urges, was a cross Hillary continued to bear, hoping others would bear it too, since they were, after all, not even *married* to him. What they both declined ever to address, though, was the effect that an adult lifetime of deceit and inevitable lying, however white the lies, and however well intentioned, would have on the trust that electors place upon those they empower – especially presidents.

The net result, then, of Hillary turning a blind eye to her husband's private failings, and her unquestioned conviction that others should ignore them too – the First Lady loudly contesting every allegation until her husband was eventually forced, each time, to confess his guilt – was to prolong the agony of a nation crippled by a sex scandal. Only Hillary, perhaps, could have persuaded Bill to resign. Concerned that she should have his fund-raising and politicking skills behind her when she began to eye a seat in the Senate for herself, she did not do so.

Thus did the tragedy of Bill Clinton's presidency unravel, a reign at once so positive and yet so negative for America. As the national exchequer filled, public trust in the silver-tongued Democratic president diminished, creating a deep public yearning in America for a more disciplined, authoritative leadership, such as that being offered by an unseasoned, seemingly simple-minded Republican: the born-again Christian son of the forty-first president.

# CHAPTER TWELVE

# GEORGE W. BUSH

Later Reviled

Republican
43rd President
(20 January, 2001–20 January, 2009)

## Part One: The Road to the White House

George Walker Bush was born on July 6, 1946, in New Haven, Connecticut, the first child of Lieutenant George Herbert Walker Bush, a distinguished navy flier who was taking his undergraduate degree at Yale, postponed by his service in World War II.

George W. – nicknamed 'Dubya' or 'Junior' once the Bush family moved to Odessa and then Midland, Texas – proved a tormented child. He suffered learning disabilities and attention deficit disorder at school which left him with a lifelong inadequacy, a deficit he masked in a variety of ways, from hellraising to sneering contempt for those more intellectually gifted. His father's long absences as an oil prospector and entrepreneur, his mother Barbara's rocky, peremptory attempts to bring up the growing family largely on her own, and the early death of his young sister Robin from leukaemia when he was seven, left him flailing as eldest son, wanting to do what was responsible, yet by nature a rebel: insecure, provocative, a jester, but often angry with himself, sullen, and driven to flight.

Doing what was responsible involved emulating his father's record – a high bar for any child of George H. W. Bush to vault. At Andover boarding school George W.'s teachers despaired of him, and assumed he would not be accepted at Yale on his grades. The records of his grandfather – senator for Connecticut – and his father at the university, however, along with his father's run for the Senate that year (1964), ensured his acceptance.

Leaving Yale, W. told his family he hadn't 'learned a damn thing'.[1] Ineligible for graduate school deferment due to his poor grades, he was only able to avoid service in Vietnam by his acceptance, thanks to his father, in the Texas Air National Guard as a part-time fighter-interceptor pilot trainee, but without a regular job.[2] His father then bailed him out when he was arrested and charged for possession of cocaine in 1972. Instead of going to prison, the Houston judge arranged for him to do community service, and the legal record to be expunged.[3] Thus ended George W. Bush's National Guard authorization to fly nuclear-capable F-102 Interceptors.[4] Leaving Texas, he did not complete the final two years of his ANG air force service in any capacity, or indeed any of the work projects to which he was assigned by his father.

Though many partied with 'Junior' (a name he hated), few liked the bullying George W. Bush – including himself. His permanent sneer or smirk, his insecurity vis-à-vis his father, his love of alcohol, his awkward, antagonistic relationship with his siblings, his use of nicknames for people – as if he could only cope with others in his own cartoon-like world – conspired to produce an often obnoxious and resentful figure, at odds with the world around him and the expectations placed upon him. He was turned down by the University of Texas Law School and seemed locked in a downward, binge-drinking spiral. However, his father's reputation as a loyal public servant and rising figure in the Republican Party once again came to his rescue, and to widespread astonishment W. was accepted into Harvard University's MBA programme in the autumn of 1973 ('I got lots of help', as he put it).[5]

W. was 'dumber than dumb', one of his classmates recalled, 'so inarticulate it was frightening'.[6] In a class discussion of the Great Depression, George W. announced: 'People are poor because they are lazy' – words he would rue twenty-four years later, when Wall Street imploded.[7] His macroeconomics professor was sickened by his arrogance and deliberately closed mind – a young man 'totally lacking in compassion, with no sense of history, completely devoid of social responsibility, and unconcerned with the welfare of others . . . I gave him a low pass.'[8]

George W. was arrested and charged with drink-driving in Maine in September 1976; even his Harvard MBA did not lead to success in the oil prospecting business in Texas.[9] In 1977 he therefore tried an alternative route to success, by entering politics as a Republican. Despite his father's best efforts – including the help of one of George

Sr's political action committee aides, of Karl Rove, and of Bush's brother Neil – he lost his bid for the seat of a retiring Texas Democratic congressman in the 1978 elections by over 6,000 votes. Bush's sneer lengthened. Repeated attempts at business in the 1980s fared as badly as in the 1970s, his energy companies soaking up investment from rich family friends and others, but teetering always on the edge of bankruptcy. It was then that the sudden advent of evangelical Christianity changed W.'s life.

W.'s 'conversion', or submission to the saving grace of Jesus Christ, intrigued those watching the Bush dynasty. Though for campaign purposes it was later ascribed to the intercession of the Revd Billy Graham, who visited the Bush family at their summer home in Kennebunkport, Maine, in 1986, George W.'s epiphany took place in Texas, and was the triumph of an evangelical preacher, Arthur Blessitt, who brought W. to 'know Jesus' in 1984. Famous for ministering to dropouts and drug addicts in San Francisco, and for carrying a twelve-foot-high, forty-five-pound cross around the world, Blessitt was proselytizing on Midland local radio when George W. asked for a private meeting at the Midland Holiday Inn. 'A good and powerful day', Blessitt noted triumphantly in his diary that night, April 3: 'Led vice president's son to Jesus today. George Bush Jr! This is great! Glory to God!'[10] Holding hands with Blessitt and an oilman friend, Jim Sale, Bush prayed and received Blessitt's benediction: 'You are saved!'[11]

Jesus alone was not enough to get the vice president's son to quit drinking, however. Rather, it was finding himself under threat of divorce by his long-suffering, pretty, librarian wife for his binge drinking and neglect of their twin daughters that, on W.'s fortieth birthday on July 6, 1986, finally caused him to give up alcohol completely, and start his life on a new basis of paternal responsibility and temperance.[12]

Evangelical Christianity did not make George Bush Jr into a good person, but it incontrovertibly made him into a less bad one, as he himself was the first to admit. 'I wasn't pleasant to be around', he said, describing his drinking bouts. 'All you have to do is ask my wife.'[13] His wife joked that 'it was when he got the bar bill' that the penny dropped.[14] The truth, however, was more prosaic. 'His marriage was falling apart,' a friend confided, 'and he cared about his girls. That's what turned him around.'[15] 'George is pretty impulsive,' Laura Bush observed, 'and does pretty much everything to excess. Drinking is not one of the good things to do to excess.'[16] As W.'s doctor explained, he just couldn't stop drinking, once he started.[17]

The vice president was delighted by his son swearing off alcohol, though he denied in public that George W. was ever 'an alcoholic. It's just he knows he can't hold his liquor.'

Alcohol, W. confided, had begun to 'compete with my energies', causing him to 'lose focus'.[18] He had never bothered to learn the oil business from the ground up, as his father had done, or to nurture relationships based on goodwill, trust and earned respect. What he offered investors and partners, however, was access to his father, the vice president, and to his father's Rolodex.

With commercial success in the oil industry still eluding him, W. moved in 1987 to Washington DC to work for George Sr as he prepared his run for the presidency, acting as the campaign's family 'enforcer', side by side with the egregious Lee Atwater and Roger Ailes.

The success of Lee Atwater's tactics in destroying Governor Dukakis in the 1988 presidential campaign exhilarated the younger members of the Bush team, even if it rewarded the destructive aspect of his character that W. had, in embracing born-again Christianity, sought to overcome. 'If we lose this one, we're dead' George W. warned Atwater before the all-important New Hampshire primary in February 1988. 'Get out a dirty tricks book, Lee, and start reading.'[19]

Atwater did – and George H. W. Bush was elected president. At the climax of the campaign, however, George W. organized a quite different, personal coup from the campaign office: the purchase of the Texas Rangers baseball team.

W.'s financial gamble of a mere $600,000 towards the $86 million purchase price for the team turned out a windfall, since the investors – culled from his father's Rolodex – gave W. a full 10 per cent stake as the 'rainmaker'. When taxpayers then financed the building of a new $135 million stadium in Arlington for the Rangers, he became a multimillionaire overnight. More significantly, it gave W., at last, his *own* claim to fame, irrespective of his father – despite the disappointing subsequent performance of the baseball team. 'This is as good as it gets' he later recalled thinking. 'Life cannot be better than this.'[20]

But it could be, he was assured by his cronies – by entering politics again, on his own behalf. He was asked by his mother not to run for the governorship of Texas in 1990, however, or for a seat in the

Senate in 1992, given the huge funds his father would need for his 1992 re-election. Instead, W. once again offered his paid services as war-room 'enabler' to the president in the 1992 campaign.

W.'s father, to the chagrin of his staff, was not re-elected that year. For W. himself, it was a bitter blow, since he attributed his father's demise to his refusal to use dirty tricks in the campaign against Governor Bill Clinton until it was too late. The failure of his father thus became a turning point in W.'s life trajectory, since he saw himself as tougher and more streetwise and yearned to demonstrate his own skills. He thus announced he would stand for the governorship of Texas against the incumbent, Ann Richards, in the 1994 election.

W.'s younger brother Jeb did likewise, in Florida, challenging the incumbent Democratic governor Lawton Chiles. Where Jeb did so, however, on a clearly articulated right-wing Republican platform, W. decided to employ a strategy recommended by the political aide who'd worked closely with Lee Atwater in the 1970s: Karl Rove.

Karl Rove was short, ugly, prematurely balding and ambitious. He had been instantly drawn to the ruggedly good-looking political wannabe with the big family pedigree and money, George W. Bush. 'He was the kind of guy political hacks like me wait a lifetime to be associated with' explained Rove, who considered himself hitherto a 'diehard Nixonite'.[21] Rove, a non-believer, told his new idol that the support of evangelists would trump all other political advantages and issues, if properly marshalled. 'This is just great!' Bush responded. 'I can become governor of Texas just with the evangelical vote.'[22]

Having formally hired Rove as his 'brain', W. now went into electoral battle with Governor Richards, having carefully lined up the support of evangelical Christian leaders in the state. Guns, too, provided a platform. Reclining by his swimming pool and smoking a cigar, W. threw in a tennis ball for his dog to fetch. 'Sip, my man,' he said to Don Sipple, his media consultant, 'don't underestimate what you can learn from a failed presidency.'[23] His father, W. maintained, had permitted 'Bill Clinton [to] decide what issues the two of them were going to talk about' – a 'major mistake' that he, George W. Bush, wasn't going to make, at least not when he could bang the twin drums, God and guns.

Bush's Texas gubernatorial campaign in 1994 represented the culmination of disciplined modern partisan political campaigning in America:

cynical, relentlessly focused, manipulative, largely dishonest, negative
– and hugely funded. Claiming he had never once been unfaithful to
his porcelain-pretty wife (who had asked him not to run), but was a
born-again Christian and successful Texas businessman now that he
owned the Texas Rangers baseball team, Bush was able not only to
separate himself from his East Coast father, but to contrast himself
against his baby-boomer contemporary in the White House: the
scandal-dogged, incompetent-looking President Bill Clinton, who in
the summer of 1994 was the proverbial elephant in the room.[24] Thus,
to Governor Richards' chagrin, in a triumphant year for Republicans
as they captured control of both the Senate and House of
Representatives for the first time in forty years, Bush won the Texas
gubernatorial battle that autumn by an astonishing 352,000 votes. The
'black sheep of the family', as his mother had ribbed him in conversation with the Queen of England, had redeemed himself as the
Prodigal Son. He would now be governor of the second largest and
second most populous state of the union.

To the amazement of those like Ann Richards who had predicted
disaster for the state if 'the jerk' (as she called him) was elected, George
W. Bush proved, thanks to the checks and balances of the Texas polity
in the 1990s, a popular and remarkably effective governor in the public's
perception. He had promised he would permit Texans the right to carry
concealed weapons, and he did – persuading a sceptical legislature, in
defiance of the recent passing of the Brady Background Check and
Assault Weapons Ban bills in Congress, to pass his pro-gun bill, which
he then signed into law. In a period of otherwise diminishing violent
crime, over time it would prove a Texas nightmare. Yet for the moment
he basked in his achievement, gaining the same bipartisan success in
pushing through three other primary platform promises he'd made:
ending automatic parole for prisoners, instituting civil court tort reform,
and reforming welfare. Though each measure was considerably altered
by the Democratic legislature, the governor was lauded for his clear
agenda, tight focus, and the way he worked with the state's Democratic
lawmakers. Best of all, from Texans' perspective, was the fact he did
not seem to be, as former Governor Richards had claimed, an out-
of-depth greenhorn in politics, or a poor copy of his privileged,
sugar-daddy East Coast father. Eating peanut-butter sandwiches and
Mexican food, visiting with every legislator in their own offices rather

than the governor's mansion, drinking beer with ordinary folk, befriending journalists and insisting on a ceaseless schedule of public events as governor, Bush soon earned the moniker 'the Energizer Bunny' – casually dressed in jeans and cowboy boots, sincere, simplistic and willing to listen to opponents, even to compromise.[25] In 1998, after four years in office, he was re-elected governor by a landslide. Given his pedigree, people began to talk of a presidential run in 2000, when Clinton's scandal-ridden second term would come to an end.

With his wavy, wiry hair, the blue-eyed ease with which he joshed people, and his ability to memorize their names and faces, the Texas governor seemed a paragon of simple, homey virtues. He rose at dawn and cycled three to six miles before breakfast. He neither chased women nor allowed them to chase him. And he went to bed with his pretty wife ritually at 9 p.m., even before his daughters retired.

Texas was booming thanks to the NAFTA free trade agreement with Mexico that had led to surging growth, especially in high-tech and maquiladora cross-border manufacturing assembly areas. Hand in hand with W.'s confidence in his growing political leadership skills went another, darker piece of knowledge: he had cracked the secret code of success in modern American campaigning – character assassination.

It was W.'s ability to sleep soundly every night, knowing this and not being ashamed of it, that finally convinced him he had the necessary toughness to be president. Though capable of surprising empathy with less privileged, ordinary individuals in Texas, he had displayed no qualms or compassion when approving some 152 executions as governor, even where doubts lingered as to the culpability or mental health of the criminal.[26] With the help of his strategist Karl Rove and his communications director Karen Hughes, he felt he was ready to face his rivals if he ran.

The Bush Tragedy, as it came to be called, was that however popular he was in his home state, he had no business seeking to be leader of the free world. His wife begged him not to do it. He had virtually never travelled abroad. As his national security adviser Dr Condoleezza Rice, a Stanford University professor, put it, he was conversant only with Mexico across the border. 'He has on-the-ground experience there,' she explained, 'which I would say is much more valuable than if he had been attending seminars at the Council on Foreign Relations for the last five years.' Guffaws of laughter contested her view.[27]

When Senator McCain won the first Republican primary in New

Hampshire by a huge margin of nineteen percentage points, Bush was distraught. McCain had campaigned in a bus he called 'The Straight Talk Express' while Bush had travelled in a private jet and, nervous lest his ignorance show, had not given a single in-depth interview to the hundred reporters following his campaign.

Bush's response, as it had been when helping his father defeat Governor Dukakis, was to get out the dirty tricks book. In the case of McCain, this required trashing the senator's war record and his character, spreading rumours that he had fathered an illegitimate child who was black.[28]

The accusations defied belief in their viciousness, pillorying Senator McCain 'with lies that he was a liberal reprobate who abandoned a crippled wife to father black children with black prostitutes. Preposterous charges of extramarital affairs, abortion, wife beating, mob ties, venereal diseases, and illegitimate children were flung at him, while his wife Cindy was tarred as a wayward woman and drug addict who had stolen to support her habit, his children were vilified as bastards' – the 'poison drip' saturating South Carolina 'for eighteen days and nights of slaughterhouse politics'.[29]

Had Atwater lived, he would have been proud of Karl Rove, but McCain – who lost the second primary – was so disgusted he never forgave Bush. 'Don't give me that shit,' the senator snarled when, after their one televised debate, Bush apologized and claimed 'We've got to start running a better campaign.'[30]

'The deeply personal, usually anonymous allegations that make up a smear campaign are aimed at a candidate's most precious asset: his reputation', McCain's campaign director said when watching Bush and Rove repeat their tactics in 2004. 'The reason this blackest of the dark arts is likely to continue is simple: It often works.'[31] It did. Though McCain countered by resorting to bare-knuckle tactics in the Michigan primary, and won it by seven percentage points, his heart wasn't in such methods. Nor, more significantly, could he raise the tens of millions of dollars W. was assembling. On March 9, 2000, Senator McCain dropped out of the race, and Bush's path to nomination as the Republican candidate was cleared.

There remained just one major decision to make, in the summer of 2000, as the Republican National Convention approached: who Governor Bush should invite to be his Republican vice-presidential nominee.

With a Harvard MBA but no administrative experience outside Texas,

Bush looked for an older man to be his vice-presidential partner. All polls showed the revered four-star general, Colin Powell, to be the most popular choice he could make. When asked if he would serve, however, Powell declined, though he left his door open to a possible cabinet post.

George H. W. Bush, Powell's former boss, begged him to reconsider, but Powell struck to his decision – which doomed both Governor Bush and America. The only other nominee for the vice presidency with major public approval was Senator McCain, who would not even speak to Bush after the primary campaign, let alone serve under him. Bush therefore entrusted the selection process to his father's former Secretary of Defense, Richard B. Cheney.

Cheney gave a thumbs down to all contenders – save himself. To Governor Bush the idea of Dick Cheney as vice president seemed a welcome, unthreatening idea, one that would appeal not only to those Republicans who revered W.'s father but also to those pundits who claimed the governor of Texas was an inexperienced lightweight. On July 25, 2000, the announcement was made and the Bush–Cheney ticket was born. On November 7, the dead heat that polls predicted actually transpired. It was the tightest presidential election since 1876.

Early results in Florida caused the Democratic candidate, Vice President Gore, to concede the presidential election to Bush, but then to retract his concession when a recount looked necessary. Thirty-five excruciating days of tallying, recounting, legal objection, appeals to state Supreme Court jurisdiction, and finally Republican appeals to the US Supreme Court, ensued.

Despite Gore having won the popular vote by an estimated 200,000 (later certified to be more than half a million) out of a total 105 million votes cast, the Supreme Court overthrew the Florida Court's decision to continue the recount process.[32] By virtue of Florida's twenty-five Electoral College votes, Governor Bush was thus declared the president-elect on December 12, 2000, in a split vote of the nine Justices, five to four.


## Part Two: The Presidency


Given the controversial nature of the election result, most pundits expected the forty-third president to be humble, and to seek to unify the country through compromise and goodwill. After all, he gave a 'solemn pledge' in his inaugural address to 'build a single nation of justice and opportunity', especially in tackling reform of American public education, the social security system and Medicare sectors of the economy. Abroad he promised to 'show purpose without arrogance'. Seldom were a president's inaugural vows so neglected.

In the White House, the new president was determined to make his mark, both in dress and in speech, and thereby provide a contrast to his predecessor. He insisted on new standards of behaviour and clothing, ordering that everyone wear shirts, ties and jackets at all times, and be punctual to the minute. (Unpunctuality had been Clinton's second name.) Within that professional formality for others, however, Bush sought to etch his own image not only as commander-in-chief, but also a 'regular guy'. He thus continued his practice of calling people by nicknames he bestowed on them, such as 'Pablo' for the astonished new Treasury Secretary, Paul O'Neill, or 'Fredo' for his new Attorney General, Alberto Gonzales. In this way he asserted his distinctive new Bush leadership style: friendly, personal, yet strictly focused and expeditious.

It did not, however, fool those who were significantly cleverer, especially the former president. 'He doesn't know anything', commented Clinton in frustration, after meeting Bush during the transition and attempting to warn him of the grave dangers posed by Islamic terrorism. 'He doesn't *want* to know anything.'[33]

Sensing the intellectual void at the heart of the imperial presidency, Bush's new chief of staff Andrew Card (who had served under George Sr as a deputy chief of staff) redoubled his efforts to protect the prince from scrutiny while he found his feet. Presidential press conferences and interviews were therefore not permitted, lest Bush stumble or reveal his lacunae. Visits to the inner sanctum were carefully screened and kept to a minimum.

If the press was thereby held at bay, however, Bush's shallowness of intellect and limited understanding were not easy to conceal from his close colleagues. In meetings with the cabinet it was almost impossible to hide the President's lack of knowledge, or even interest, in most subjects discussed, beyond the wish to get decisions made, whatever the consequences.

There were some issues the president seemed genuinely to care about, Card was relieved to know. For example, Bush wanted to promote education reform through new national testing – a subject the First Lady, as a trained librarian, felt strongly about. He also wished to push through a major tax cut for the wealthy, who would – he hoped – use the money to invest in the economy, which was faltering at the end of a sustained boom. But beyond that he seemed remarkably . . . vacant. When a Texas friend had asked during the campaign what would happen if he lost the election, W. had shrugged. 'Oh, I don't know, Jimmy. That wouldn't be the worst thing that could happen. I guess I'd just go back to Dallas, watch a lot of baseball games, spend time with my friends and Laura and the girls, make a living, enjoy life. Do what other people do.' 'Simple as that?' the friend had pressed. 'Yep, that simple.'[34]

In Austin, Texas, where the legislature only met once every two years for 140 days, and where the lieutenant governor was arguably more powerful than the governor, Bush's empty-headedness hadn't really mattered. But in Washington, at the citadel of the world's mightiest empire, power was the meat and drink of daily life. People fought for it, used it, abused it, manipulated it, and had done so long before the nation became an empire. If the president saw his role merely as a mediator-manager, a chairman of the board of America Inc., would there not then be a struggle for power among the directors of the board?

Meeting for a full hour with the president in the Oval Office shortly after the coronation, Treasury Secretary Paul O'Neill – who had served under presidents Ford and George H. W. Bush – was stunned by Bush's inability to ask a single question. 'Strange', O'Neill reflected.[35] Over subsequent weeks, he recognized Bush had already ceded control of economic policy and tax cuts to his new presidential adviser, Karl Rove. Moreover, in the very first National Security Council meeting he attended, on January 30, 2001, O'Neill was astonished to hear the Secretary of Defense, Donald Rumsfeld, and the vice president, Dick Cheney, talking about invading Iraq.[36]

To O'Neill's near-disbelief the president then announced, in confidence, that America was pulling out of further attempts to obtain peace in the Middle East through an Israeli–Palestinian accord. 'Clinton overreached', Bush declared simply. 'If the two sides don't want peace, there's no way to force them.' And W. went on to extol the new prime minister of Israel, Ariel Sharon – who had a black

name for intransigence, provoking the Palestinian intifada, and expanding Jewish settlements in the West Bank. 'I'm not going to go on
past reputations when it comes to Sharon' the president said. Sharon
had taken Bush on a helicopter flight over Palestinian camps in 1998,
on one of his handful of trips outside the United States. That seemed
to be enough. 'Just saw him that one time', Bush explained. 'Looked
real bad down there. I think it's time to pull out of that situation.'[37]

Astonished, the new Secretary of State, General Colin Powell,
warned that an American withdrawal from Clinton's Middle East peace
process would offer a green light for Sharon and the Israeli Army to
use force, undeterred. 'The consequences of that could be dire,' Powell
cautioned, 'especially for the Palestinians.' To which the president
responded with a shrug, followed by the fateful words that 'a show
of strength by one side can really clarify things'.[38] And with that, the
meeting was invited by the national security adviser, Dr Condoleezza
Rice, to discuss an alternative way of imposing democracy on the
Middle East – via the ousting of Saddam Hussein, and the colonization of Iraq! To this end, the president instructed Rumsfeld and the
chairman of the Joint Chiefs, General Shelton, to 'examine our military options'.[39]

O'Neill and Powell were dumbfounded. Neither Gerald Ford nor
George H.W. Bush had been men of the highest intellect, but both
had learned to listen, and to process competing interpretations of the
facts, consider carefully the consequences of a proposed action, and
make an informed ultimate decision as president and commander-in-
chief. Now, behind the mask of tight-lipped, leak-proof, disciplined,
crisp new management style, O'Neill began to realize a palace coup
seemed already to have taken place under Karl Rove, who proceeded
to set up no less than four new Republican Political Offices on the
second floor of the White House, and insisted he have a point-man
on every White House committee. Moreover, Rove had a twin: the
vice president.

Cheney had also immediately set up his political store in the White
House. He insisted that his chief of staff, Scooter Libby, not only hold
the job of national security adviser to the vice president but also the
position of presidential assistant to Bush – entitled, like Rove's capos,
to see all documents before they reached the president. Cheney, Libby
or the vice president's legal adviser, David Addington ('the most

powerful man you've never heard of'), thus not only sat in on every committee and panel in the White House, but ensured that every presidential letter, email or document be copied to them – yet that no vice-presidential document be copied to the president.[40]

Treasury Secretary Paul O'Neill was not the only official worried by the Rove–Cheney palace takeover. Counter-terrorism czar Richard Clarke, for example, had already felt concern during the election campaign at the Bush team's apparent indifference to the growing threat of terrorism. Very soon Clarke was reprimanded by the national security adviser. 'You know,' Dr Rice said to him, 'don't give the president a lot of long memos, he's not a big reader.' Clarke was amazed. 'Well shit. I mean,' Clarke said later, '*the president of the United States is not a big reader?*'[41]

The vice president was, though.

John Nance Garner had described the office of vice president as 'not worth a pitcher of warm piss', since it carried no constitutional responsibilities beyond certifying the election result, and then presiding over the Senate with a deciding vote in the event of a tie. The position *did* offer a literal and metaphorical side door to the presidency, though – however much Cheney assured Governor Bush he had no intention of ever running for the office himself.

At the core of Cheney's agenda, from the very start, was a determination to make himself as indispensible to the new monarch as Thomas Cromwell had been to King Henry VIII – only in Cheney's case, the throne would be his should the president be assassinated or incapacitated.

From the start of the Bush presidency, Cheney, sensing the ignorance and naivety of the new president in the Oval Office, was deferential to Bush in person, but a law unto himself outside. 'Bush's staff is terrified of Cheney's people', one White House staffer confided.[42] Another commented: 'They are too smart, too powerful for Bush and his team.' A third, a colonel who had admired Cheney earlier as Secretary of Defense, found himself appalled by the calculating way Cheney went about his task as vice president. Under George H.W. Bush, Dick Cheney had been brought back to earth whenever he moved out of line, such as the occasion when he openly criticized Mikhail Gorbachev in 1989 without presidential approval. 'Dump on Dick with all possible alacrity', had been Secretary of State James Baker's classic order at the time.

But now, with a callow, inexperienced, outmanoeuvred, outstaffed, and fatally incurious president in the Oval Office, there was a void – and it did not take Cheney long to fill it, Colonel Wilkerson reflected later. 'What in effect happened was that a very astute, probably the most astute, bureaucratic entrepreneur I've ever run into in my life became the vice president of the United States.' Seeing his opportunity, Cheney then waded 'into the vacuums that existed around George Bush – personality vacuum, details vacuum, experience vacuum'.[43]

To those around him, Bush insisted that his agenda was still 'compassionate conservatism', as his speechwriter, David Frum, recalled, especially with regard to public education. Cheney, however, did not care a fig for public schooling; indeed as a congressman he had voted to close down the nation's Department of Education completely. What he wanted was less federal interference in people's daily lives, and more imperial power in the White House to advance America's interests abroad: securing its energy supplies and requisite raw materials, disarming those who threatened it in any way, and maintaining military superiority. To achieve these aims would require beating back the inroads he felt Congress had made on presidential power since Watergate. So strongly did he feel about this, and so contemptuous of the Senate as an institution, he was willing to drive the White House off a cliff – as he did when persuading Bush not to compromise with the Republican senator Jim Jeffords over funding of the Disabilities Education Act. Even Karl Rove felt the president should make a concession to Jeffords, who wanted more budget money for special education programmes rather than giving it away in tax reduction. Rove memorably remarked that Senator Jeffords could be 'fucked over' later.[44] Cheney, however, got his way. Appalled, Senator Jeffords then carried out his threat to vote with the Democrats, causing the Senate to change hands in what was called a 'political earthquake'.[45]

This was not how Governor Bush had operated in Texas, insiders complained. But much worse was to follow.

Although Cheney had, as he himself put it, 'flunked' his further degree at Yale, whereas Dr Rice was a tenured professor at Stanford, she was no match for him. Cheney saw the same national intelligence information as Rice, and all her communications, but did not allow her to see *his* communications. Cheney would rise at 4.30 a.m. and hold his own intelligence briefing before Rice convened her morning security panel, prior to briefing the president. He dogged her every meeting, and oversaw her every recommendation. He even attended every meeting of the National Security Council Principals, and relentlessly demanded, from day one, that despite the deadly suicide attack on the USS *Cole* the previous autumn, they focus not on terrorism or al-Qaeda, but on Iraq.

Richard Clarke had no doubt that Osama Bin Laden had been behind the *Cole* bombing in Aden. Day after day, week after week, month after month, Clarke attempted to convince his new colleagues there was going to be another attack, either on American installations abroad or at home. Clarke, however, could make no headway with Cheney, Rice or Donald Rumsfeld, nor with Rumsfeld's number two, Paul Wolfowitz; indeed in the entire first eight months of the Bush presidency, Clarke was not permitted to brief President Bush a single time, despite mounting evidence of plans for a new al-Qaeda outrage.

To her subsequent shame, Rice first refused to agree to a meeting of Principals on the subject, then insisted the matter be handled only by a more junior Deputy Principals meeting, in April 2000, at which Wolfowitz announced he could not understand 'why we are beginning by talking about this one man Bin Laden'. Even after Clarke explained the al-Qaeda network, Wolfowitz protested: 'You give Bin Laden too much credit', and claimed Bin Laden could not achieve his ends without the aid of a state sponsor – namely Iraq, which Wolfowitz blamed for the 1993 World Trade Center bombing.

Clarke was dismayed. 'I could hardly believe it' he later wrote, given the utter discrediting of any Iraqi connection to the attack in New York. Attempting to keep his temper, Clarke prophesied: 'Al-Qaeda plans major acts of terrorism against the US' – indeed Osama Bin Laden and his terrorist group had actually published their plans. Sometimes, he said, 'as with Hitler in *Mein Kampf*, you have to believe that these people will actually do what they say they will do'.[46]

Clarke regretted the words as soon as they were out of his mouth, for Wolfowitz immediately declared he resented 'any comparison between the Holocaust and this little terrorist in Afghanistan'.[47]

For Clarke, the sheer obtuseness and sneering contempt of Bush's senior advisers and colleagues towards officials who had served in the Clinton administration was galling. It was as if a sort of wilful blindness seemed to afflict the new president, the vice president, the national security adviser and her deputy, and the Secretary of Defense and his deputy – leaving only Secretary of State Colin Powell and his deputy, Richard Clarke and a sceptical Treasury Secretary in a lonely battle to waken a seemingly deranged new administration, obsessed with Iraq, and with ending the ABM missile treaty with Russia, which was about to expire.

In vain Clarke sent out word that 'al-Qaeda is planning a major attack on us'; ordered all agencies on to high-alert status; asked the FBI and CIA to report to the downgraded Counterterrorism Group everything they could find out about suspicious individuals or activity inside and outside the United States.[48] Then, in a final challenge to Rice at the Principals meeting which she belatedly convened on September 4, 2001, Clarke asked her to picture herself at a moment 'when in the very near future al-Qaeda has killed hundreds of Americans', and to imagine asking herself what 'you wish then that you had already done'.[49]

Neither the president, Rice, nor other senior members of the Bush administration would ever admit afterwards to their somnambulance. Nor would any of them be brought to account. It made Clarke's blood boil.

On the morning of September 11, 2001, four small teams of al Qaeda suicide bombers, armed with simple boxcutters, boarded without hindrance four commercial US airliners: American Airlines flights 11 and 175 at Boston's Logan airport; American Airlines flight 77 at Dulles International, outside Washington DC; and United Airlines flight 93 at Newark Airport, outside New York. Using the very simplest of weapons to kill the pilots and fly the aircraft as guided missiles on to carefully chosen targets, they sought to create the maximum symbolic effect, killing thousands of innocent American citizens.

Though one team's effort was aborted in mid-flight, when passengers attacked the hijackers, the outrage achieved its object: the United States suffered more deaths that sunlit morning, in New York and Washington, than at Pearl Harbor in 1941.

As film and video of the collapsing Twin Towers at New York's World Trade Center were broadcast across the world, America went into shock. The president himself, sitting in on a class of second-graders in a school in Sarasota, Florida, seemed as stunned as ordinary people. He appeared unable to comprehend the footage of an aircraft flying into a high-rise building in Manhattan playing on a television screen as he went into the classroom, or the news whispered to him some minutes later that another plane had crashed into the second tower. Vice President Cheney was equally stunned.

The news came as no surprise, however, to the demoted counter-terrorism czar Richard Clarke, who knew immediately the organization behind the attack.

The president's message to the nation and the world, written by Karen Hughes and videotaped on board Air Force One, was forceful in asserting that the United States would not be intimidated by terrorists. Yet when Bush finally spoke, for the very first time in his presidency, to Richard Clarke the next evening in the Situation Room, it was to make what seemed an amazing presidential request: 'Look, I know you have a lot to do and all, but I want you, as soon as you can, to go back over everything, everything. See if Saddam did this. See if he's linked in any way.'[50]

Clarke, who had scarcely slept or eaten in two days as he grounded the nation's air traffic and attempted to thwart possible follow-up terrorist attacks, was 'taken aback, incredulous', he recalled. 'But Mr President, al-Qaeda did this' he protested. 'I know, I know,' Bush said, 'but . . . see if Saddam was involved. Just look. I want to know.'[51]

Dutifully, Clarke did so, suspecting that in the space of a few hours, Bush must already have been 'gotten at' by the madmen controlling National Security: Cheney, Rumsfeld and Wolfowitz, men who had, on the very night of the attack, held meetings not to avert further terrorism, or pursue al-Qaeda, but to have 'discussions about Iraq'.

Vice President Cheney had advised the president to stay out of Washington in a 'secure location' – a euphemism for cowardice. To his credit, Bush insisted on returning to the White House, joined by the First Lady. Cheney, who hid away for the next weeks, would not allow his obsession with Iraq to be defused or sidelined. As in surreal-ist science fiction, Cheney continued to participate in all discussions via 'secure video' communications, encouraging Bush to see the 9/11 attack not as the premeditated plot of demented Islamic terrorists answering to Osama Bin Laden, but as a global *casus belli*. George W. Bush could then become the war leader of the American Empire.

The president needed little persuasion. Without consulting his Secretary of State,[52] Bush announced to assembled reporters in the

Roosevelt Room at the White House on September 12, 2001, that the 'deliberate and deadly attacks' on New York were 'more than acts of terror. They were acts of war.' America would respond with full-scale war, a 'monumental struggle between good and evil' in which, if other countries did not join the US, 'we'll go it alone'.[53]

Had the last half-century of American experience as the leader of the free, democratic nations of the world, with decades of diplomacy and careful nurturing of allies, been discarded overnight? Half an hour later, when Bush again used the word 'war', the Senate Majority Leader, Democratic senator Tom Daschle, cautioned that 'War is a powerful word.' The president ignored him – and it was left to eighty-three-year-old Senator Robert Byrd, president *pro tempore* of the Senate, to warn that Congress would not give the blank cheque it had given Lyndon Johnson over the Tonkin incident, pulling from his pocket a copy of the Constitution to prove his point. To obtain congressional approval under the Constitution, any riposte would have to be targeted on al-Qaeda, not take America to war on a massive, open-ended scale like Vietnam.

Undeterred, Bush attended a fateful National Security Council meeting at 4 p.m. that day. 'Why shouldn't we go against Iraq, not just al-Qaeda?' Rumsfeld asked the president.

Cheney emphatically agreed, concerned that it might take time to 'get' the 'little terrorist' Bin Laden in Afghanistan, whereas a massive US invasion of a Muslim country like Iraq would make a powerful 'statement' of American imperial power and resolve. It was left to Secretary Powell to bring the meeting, which was advocating something very close to treason in its indifference to the need for Congress to approve such a war, back to its senses. Not only was there no evidence Iraq had anything to do with 9/11 or al-Qaeda, but 'Any action needs public support', Powell reminded his colleagues, in addition to congressional approval. 'It's not just what the international coalition' – should he be able to put together such a coalition – 'supports, it's what the American people want to support.' And lest there be any misunderstanding, he spelled it out again: 'The American people want us to do something about al-Qaeda.'[54]

The president seemed not hear his Secretary of State. Indeed, if ever there was a wrong man for the job of Caesar of the world's most powerful nation, it was the 'toxic Texan', as Bush proudly called himself after his withdrawal from the Kyoto Protocol. Hitherto he had seen his role as being that of a crisp, decisive chairman of the board of America, Inc, 9/11, however, changed him into a buffoon – to the delight of Cheney, who urged him to talk in public not just of locating and removing Bin Laden, but of launching a hopefully long and profitable war. Stepping down from his Marine One helicopter on September 16, 2001, Bush announced that 'this crusade, this war on terrorism is going to take a while'.

Rather than marginalizing al-Qaeda terrorists as freakish Islamic hotheads, was it not more likely that talk of a 'crusade' would raise the spectre of a new Judaeo-Christian military campaign against the Muslim world – and thus inflame such radicals, driving fringe groups to join with al-Qaeda as their inspiration, their strategic and ideological brain? Congress remained cautious. On September 18, 2001, a joint assembly of Congress authorized the president to 'use all necessary and appropriate force', but only 'against those nations, organizations, or persons he determines planned, authorized, or aided the terrorist attacks that occurred on September 11, 2001'.[55] Beyond that, Congress insisted on retaining its constitutional War Powers authority.

Rather than dampening Bush's zeal, Congress' cautionary language only seemed to galvanize him and Cheney. Addressing Congress in person on September 20, 2001, for the second time in his presidency, the president initially backtracked, assuring Muslims in America and across the world that they were not to blame, and would not be blamed, for their faith. Nevertheless, he made clear, the attack on the World Trade Center and the Pentagon constituted, like Pearl Harbor, a declaration of 'war' and the United States was thus a nation *at* war, one unlike any previous war America had waged. 'Americans are asking, "How will we fight and win this war?" We will direct every resource at our command – every means of diplomacy, every tool of intelligence, every instrument of law enforcement, every financial influence, and every necessary weapon of war – to the destruction and to the defeat of the global terror network.'

Diplomats across the world found this worrying. Bush's demeanour and language suggested that of a hastily deputized town marshal in a Wild West movie, rather than the heir of George Washington. 'It will not look like the air war above Kosovo two years ago, where no ground troops were used and not a single American was lost in combat', the president asserted. This time there would be blood – for America's new 'war on terrorism' would be war with a capital W – and without foreseeable end. 'Americans should not expect one battle, but a lengthy campaign unlike any other we have ever seen. It may include dramatic strikes visible on TV and covert operations, secret even in success. We will starve terrorists of funding, turn them one against another, drive them from place to place until there is no refuge or no rest. And we will pursue nations that provide aid or safe haven to terrorism. Every nation in every region now has a decision to make: either you are with us or you are with the terrorists.'

What did these words really mean, viewers and diplomats across the world wondered? Was not Congress, constitutionally, the only body entitled to declare war – especially such a vague 'war on terror' rather than on al-Qaeda, as the plotters specifically responsible for 9/11? What exactly would it mean to 'pursue' whole nations that aided terrorism? 'Our war on terror begins with al-Qaeda,' the president had declared, 'but it does not end there. It will not end until every terrorist group of global reach has been found, stopped and defeated.'

Every terrorist group found, stopped, defeated – not simply al-Qaeda? In the context of a president who had only once referred to the problem of terrorism in the eight and a half months since being inaugurated, and had now been given only specific, limited authorization by Congress, it seemed vague, messianic, emotional and ill-considered. Also – something that could not be said of Osama Bin Laden – not a little stupid, since it would be the very response Bin Laden wanted, energizing jihadists across the Muslim world.

As Colin Powell, would later remark, 'Bush had a lot of .45-caliber instincts, cowboy instincts.'[56] The president certainly seemed overexcited, or on mood-enhancing medication. In his address to the joint session of Congress he had added, ominously and almost sotto voce, 'tonight a few miles from the damaged Pentagon I have a message for our military: be ready. I have called the armed forces to alert, and there is a reason. The hour is coming when America will act, and you will make us proud.'

The president's first 'act' of war took place four weeks later – in Afghanistan, not Iraq, to Rumsfeld's and Wolfowitz's chagrin. Blitzed by US and British air power, the Taliban forces that had harboured Bin Laden's jihadists ran away. Kabul fell on November 13, 2001, and Kandahar on December 7 as more than 1,000 Marines joined CIA, paramilitaries and US Commandos supporting the anti-Taliban forces of the Northern Alliance on the ground.

Casualties among innocent Afghan civilians (referred to as 'collateral damage') mounted, however; indeed by Christmas 2001 they exceeded those killed in the 9/11 attacks in America. Neither the president nor Rumsfeld, nor Cheney, nor Rice, took heed. The US was magnificently 'winning' – so far. Bin Laden and the Taliban leader, Mullah Omar, fell back towards the Pakistani border, resolving to fight a guerilla, mujahidin-style campaign, just as they had done against the Russians. Retreating to the well-known caves of Bora Bora, Bin Laden seemed cornered in December, 2001. As Gary Berntsen, the CIA intelligence commander at Bora Bora later recounted, the Eastern Alliance blocked any escape route back into Afghanistan – but not into Pakistan. A 15,000 lb 'daisy cutter' was dropped, but though it wounded Bin Laden, it did not kill him. Hundreds of innocent villagers were hit by stray bombs. Berntsen requested American boots on the ground – 800 Rangers – to make sure Bin Laden did not escape, but Secretary Rumsfeld, anxious to avoid American casualties and insisting that Afghan anti-Taliban forces take them instead, denied the request – and President Bush, the commander-in-chief, declined to overrule him.

'Unfortunately,' Berntsen recalled, 'the decision was made at the White House to use the Pakistani Frontier Force' for the job of capturing or killing the arch-terrorist. 'What the White House didn't understand', he explained, 'was that the frontier force had cooperated with the Taliban' and had no desire to see it exterminated.[57]

The result was that both Bin Laden and Omar evaded the American dragnet.

Neither Bush nor his courtiers Cheney, Rumsfeld, Wolfowitz and Rice, recognized the enormity of their mistake at the time. 'The great Don' Rumsfeld, self-preening and arrogant, was proud he had toppled the Taliban, the harbourers of Bin Laden, in a matter of weeks without a single American soldier's death, and only a tiny number of American 'boots on the ground'. But beyond shock and awe, what had really been achieved, if Bin Laden, architect of the 9/11 attack, escaped?

'We proceeded systematically, village by village, and we destroyed the houses, filled up the wells, blew down the towers, cut down the great shady trees, burned the crops and broke the reservoirs in punitive devastation', Second Lieutenant Winston Churchill had described the Malakand Field Force's campaign against the 'Mad Mullah of Swat' and his 12,000 Pathan tribesmen a century before, in 1897. 'Whether it was all worth it I cannot tell.'[58] Beyond the weaponry, little seemed to have changed.

The entire Islamic world watched, mesmerized and often with admiration, as their Jesse James, Osama Bin Laden, escaped – leaving egg on Marshal Bush's face, and unending combat in the forbidding mountains of Afghanistan ahead. As one Russian officer warned the head of the US Counter-terrorism Center when told in advance of American plans to go to war in Afghanistan, the mountainous region they would encounter was guerilla heaven: 'With regret, I have to say you're really going to get the hell kicked out of you.'[59]

Bush's next war would prove an even greater calamity. Fevered madness once again infected him and his war cabinet as Kabul fell. On November 21, 2001, only ten weeks after 9/11, Bush 'took Rumsfeld aside', having, in Bob Woodward's triumphal account at the time, 'decided it was time to turn to Iraq'.[60]

Previous leaders of empires had come unstuck for just such thoughtless, obsessional hubris. 'I'm not a textbook player, I'm a gut player', the president described himself to the admiring *Washington Post* journalist. In Condoleezza Rice's even more admiring eyes, Bush was less a player than 'the coach', urging his all-star team to 'victory'.[61] Offence, not defence, was the president's creed, which sounded fine in football, but masked the saddest truth: with regard to war he was a gambler, with a 'devil take the consequences' attitude, when other men's lives were at stake.

The head of US Central Command, General Tommy Franks, was certainly appalled once Cheney passed on the president's instruction that he investigate 'what it would take' to 'remove Saddam Hussein if we have to'. In the midst of a difficult logistical challenge in sending more forces to bring order to Afghanistan, Franks let loose 'a string of obscenities'.[62] Then he obediently did as instructed, with a possible D-Day of June 2002, cognizant of the president's orders that not only did the invasion have 'the highest priority', but also that planning was to be kept entirely secret.[63] As Bush later explained to Woodward, he did not 'want others in on the secret because a leak would trigger "enormous international angst and domestic speculation. I knew what would happen if people thought we were developing a potential or a war plan for Iraq."[64]

The president was right; instead of angst, however, the country would get seven years of affliction. At the end of December 2001, with Cheney, Rumsfeld, Rice, George Tenet of the CIA and Powell participating via secure video link, General Franks duly briefed Bush in person at the president's ranch in Crawford, Texas. Under pressure, the general had reduced the anticipated requirement of 500,000 troops to just 230,000 in an effort not to alarm the American public – still a huge army for the US to field, however, while simultaneously attempting to stabilize the situation in Afghanistan, where complex security and logistics problems remained and Bin Laden was still at large.

At first, Colin Powell did not believe the president was serious. Saddam Hussein had few supporters in the world, given his ruthless Ba'ath Party regime. But taking America, without allies, into full-scale war in Iraq, when al-Qaeda had still not been dealt with, and Afghanistan posing huge problems in reconstruction and the restoration of civil order? Congress' 9/11 War Resolution did not currently authorize such an undertaking. Nor did the United Nations Security Council, which had backed Desert Storm a decade before, but which could not be counted upon to license regime change in a sovereign country, just for the sake of regime change.

Powell, who as chairman of the Joint Chiefs of Staff had masterminded the Gulf War in 1991, thus opposed the president's hare-brained imperial venture, knowing it was viewed with the utmost suspicion in the capitals of what Rumsfeld would call 'old Europe'. There was no evidence or serious suspicion that Saddam Hussein had any ties to al-Qaeda. Nor was there was any evidence that he was currently developing either biological or nuclear materials. What, then, was the justification for a proposed massive US invasion, involving a quarter of a million troops? What would be the exit strategy? Who would run a post-Hussein Iraq? A handful of unreliable Iraqi exiles? And why was the proposed attack so secret, on orders of the president? Was Bush afraid that, if discussed nationwide, the public would stay his warrior hand?

Those who heard, or overheard, members of the administration and the president himself on the subject, were not only alarmed that a second Bush war was being planned while the first was incomplete, but that the *raison d'être* was so puerile. 'Fuck Saddam!' the president told a group of senators at the White House in March 2002. 'We're going to take him out' – but with no serious examination of who would take Saddam's place.[65]

Powell vainly attempted to dissuade his colleagues, but Cheney, in particular, seemed gripped by a 'fever', as Powell later commented. Powell's reluctance to rush to war restrained, but did not stop, the president. Addressing Congress in a State of the Union speech on January 29, 2002, Bush now used a new term, 'axis of evil', to describe America's enemies – by which he meant, he explained, Iraq, Iran and North Korea.[66] (His speechwriter, David Frum, had suggested the phrase 'axis of hatred', but was overruled by Bush.)

Moral courage seemed to go out the window as the 'Vulcans' in the administration – named after the statue of the god of fire in Rice's home town of Birmingham, Alabama – now clamoured for another war.

A *casus belli* was, however, still required – and could best be manufactured if Saddam Hussein could be found to be developing weapons of mass destruction (WMD). The President thus insisted Saddam Hussein re-admit UN inspectors into Iraq, which Hussein reluctantly agreed to. When no evidence of WMD was found, Bush refused to back down. With the president's approval, Cheney's office ordered the false authentication of suspect secret intelligence, suggesting that an agent of Saddam Hussein had tried to buy uranium concentrate powder, or 'yellowcake', in Niger for Saddam's secret nuclear arms programme, and that the dictator was also sponsoring al-Qaeda plots against America.

The Bush administration's rush to a second war became unstoppable. At a meeting called by the prime minister in London on July 23, 2002, the head of British intelligence reported on his recent visit to Washington: 'Military action was now seen as inevitable' he confided, as noted in the minutes. 'Bush wanted to remove Saddam, through military action' to which end 'the intelligence and facts were being fixed around the policy'. Even more sobering was that 'there was little discussion in Washington of the aftermath after military action'.[67]

Even Blair's backing (he was soon dubbed 'Bush's poodle') was not enough, however, to convince Britain's European partners and enough members of UN Security Council, in the absence of any evidence of WMD, that the US should invade. Fatefully, therefore, President Bush decided to go to war without UN backing.

War hysteria now began to sweep America. Analogies with 1914 and myriad other wars that had begun with popular excitement were drawn, especially the example of Hitler's blitzkrieg in the spring of 1940, and then his doomed occupation of western Europe and invasion of the Soviet Union in 1941. Powell, in particular, had warned Bush in August 2002 that if he followed through with such a madcap plan, he would then 'own' Iraq and its '25 million people' – a people who had never known democracy, and were traditionally divided between Sunni and Shia clans, with a hostile Kurdish region in the north. A messy occupation could destabilize Saudi Arabia, Egypt and Jordan, and potentially ignite a firestorm of loathing for the United States throughout the Islamic world. And this at the very time when most Muslims still disapproved of al-Qaeda's dedication to violence, and deplored the 9/11 attacks on innocents, which went against the divinely inspired teachings of Mohammed as set down in the Koran.

Once again the president thanked Powell for the warning, but went ahead with his war plans. On March 19, 2003, he publicly announced that war with Iraq had 'reluctantly' begun. He had, he said, given the green light to the invasion out of sheer necessity, since 'the people of the United States will not live at the mercy of an outlaw regime that threatens the peace with weapons of mass destruction'.

Like Roman military campaigns in the time of the original Caesars, the initial Battle of Iraq proved another demonstration of American mastery of modern aerial, ground and logistical blitzkrieg warfare – its legions disciplined, well armed, well commanded, and focused. On April 9, 2003, only three weeks after the invasion began, Iraqis in the main square of Baghdad saw the great statue of Saddam Hussein being toppled from its column. Soon after, President Bush co-piloted a Navy S-3B Viking attack fighter on to the flight deck of the aircraft carrier USS *Abraham Lincoln* off the California coast. Wearing a green combat suit, the president stood under a vast banner prepared by the White House: 'Mission Accomplished'.

Relief among ordinary Americans soon turned to anxiety, however, as they heard worrying stories from their loved ones in the armed forces. No public acclamation had greeted the 'liberators' in Iraq; indeed they were almost instantly seen as infidel 'occupiers'. In Baghdad itself Donald Rumsfeld, reading an advance copy of the president's speech, was distraught: 'I just died, and I said my God, it's too conclusive.'[68] Though Rumsfeld recommended removing any mention of 'mission accomplished', Karl Rove's political team at the White House, who had produced the banner, had been too exultant to order it to be taken down – thus piling hubris upon hubris.

In subsequent weeks, everything in Iraq that could go wrong did go wrong. A quarter of a million American soldiers, backed by 40,000 British, Australian, Polish and Danish troops, found no weapons of mass destruction. Nor did they find evidence of an al-Qaeda connection. Mesopotamia had been one of the great centres of early civilization; in the absence of instructions from Washington, its historic treasures were openly pilfered from the National Museum by looters undeterred by the overstretched American troops who, under orders from the White House that would haunt them afterwards, disbanded the one organization capable of keeping order: the Iraqi Army.

Far from being a mission accomplished, the invasion of Iraq turned into a monumental debacle. The orgy of bloodletting and sectarian violence in Iraq soon escalated into civil war, exceeding the wildest warnings issued before the invasion, not only in numbers murdered and maimed, but in the utter inhumanity exhibited by human beings towards each other. US soldiers and 'contractors', however well-meaning, were seen neither as peacekeepers nor as philanthropists, simply as occupation forces. As the numbers of American body bags rose and the extent of the fiasco deepened, even 'embedded' journalists who had extolled the brilliance of the blitzkrieg invasion began to speak up and to report reality: a quagmire of internecine civil strife, suicide bombings, roadside bombings, assassinations, beheadings and sectarian-cleansing that reduced the world's oldest surviving civilization to mayhem.

As casualties mounted not only reporters but former generals spoke up. By 2004, a year after the invasion began, casualties exceeded 20,000 US soldiers wounded, with more than 1,000 American servicemen dead. 'We are now being viewed', lamented General Zinni, the former chief of US Central Command, 'as the modern crusaders, as the modern colonial power in this part of the world', and he called for

Rumsfeld, and Rumsfeld's fanatical deputy Wolfowitz (who had set up a rogue political unit, the Office of Special Plans at the Pentagon, to bypass normal chains of command), to tender their resignations, along with the other neocons: 'Undersecretary of Defense Douglas Feith; former Defense Policy Board member Richard Perle; National Security Council member Elliot Abrams; and Vice President Cheney's chief of staff, Lewis "Scooter" Libby.'[69]

Zinni's passionate call for heads to roll, and for the president to revert to his original, Congress-approved mission after 9/11 – to pursue al-Qaeda – went nowhere. Instead, Rove's political team went into action, trashing the four-star general – a distinguished Vietnam veteran – as an anti-Semite.

The treatment of Zinni symbolized not only the moral depravity of Rove's huge team, operating at the heart of the White House, but the double bind in which George Walker Bush found himself. By virtue of his chosen advisers and his own ignorant and 'gut player' personality, Bush was hoist with his own petard. It was he who had made a deliberate, emotion-driven choice to rush to war, using the most powerful military in the world, egged on by a gung-ho war cabinet of neoconservatives who had almost all avoided military service themselves. Even sceptics in his administration had been forced to choose between loyalty to their president and their own wisdom. 'Are you with me?' Bush had asked General Powell on the eve of the invasion of Iraq. To his distress later, Powell had loyally said yes to his commander-in-chief.[70]

In the midterm election of November 2002, the Senate had been won back by the Republican Party, along with the Republican-dominated House. Once the invasions of Afghanistan and Iraq proved pyrrhic victories, however, Rove's job became much more difficult. Scott McClellan, the president's press secretary, would later describe Rove's role in the US government under Bush as 'political manipulation, plain and simple'.[71] As the Iraq War spiralled into ever worsening violence, the president's re-election in 2004 could only be secured by further spin, obfuscation, deceit and cover-up.

Without 'transparency', noted McClellan – who had to fend off and manipulate the press each day – the White House was doomed to become a House of Lies. Had the president admitted his error and cleaned his stables by firing the 'Vulcans', exiling the vice president from the White House, and denying Cheney and his henchmen access to his presidential communications, he might just have rescued his presidency – and America's prestige in the world – before it was too late, even if it ended up costing him a second term.

George W. Bush, however, was no Jack Kennedy. Retaining his loyal team, he dug himself yet deeper into a morass of deception, secrecy and cover-up, all excused on the grounds of national security, but in reality done to conceal and protect the guilty from being exposed. 'That secrecy', McClellan wrote afterwards, 'ended up delaying but not preventing the consequences.'[72]

Refusing to set up an independent investigation into the 9/11 disaster, then making sure the commission, once set up, would not deliver its report until *after* the 2004 election, was only one of an increasing number of manipulations, misdemeanours and even crimes that would have merited impeachment of the president and vice president, had not the country remained, conveniently, 'at war'.[73] The head of the Office of Legal Counsel, Jack Goldsmith, recorded the effect of such high-level lack of accountability – indeed refusal to be held accountable – as it gradually permeated almost every area of government in the Bush administration, fusing lack of transparency and outright political skullduggery, as the embattled president – using Dick Cheney as his malevolent Lord Protector – attempted to ward off congressional oversight.[74]

For his part, the vice president relished his role. As President Nixon had once targeted whistle-blowers such as Daniel Ellsberg and Seymour Hersh, so now Cheney's staff swung into action against anyone of consequence who criticized the president or dared expose White House falsifications. When former US ambassador Joe Wilson debunked, from personal knowledge, claims that Iraq had been buying 'yellow-cake' from Niger, Cheney's office deliberately leaked the name of the ambassador's wife as a serving, covert CIA officer: a criminal, even treasonable act. Once Valerie Wilson's career had been ruined – endangering her life but sending a stern 'message' to would-be whistle-blowers – Cheney and his staff covered up their actions for as long as possible, ensuring that the ostensible culprit (Scooter Libby) was not indicted until after the 2004 presidential election.[75]

With each further deception Bush authorized or deliberately ignored, he not only empowered his subordinates' move towards the cynical abuse of power, but surrendered his own authority as chief executive. Osama Bin Laden's mad jihad and Saddam Hussein's notorious cold-blooded, vindictive savagery as dictator were condemned by all, but an America out of control – with revelations of American torture at Abu Ghraib, Guantanamo Bay and in secret foreign locations – could only lessen the righteousness of America's cause.[76]

The issue came to a head on March 11, 2004, when the president's authority to conduct surveillance of foreign communications came up for renewal by the Justice Department. Without informing Congress, Cheney had already, in 2001, set up a secret operation to monitor all domestic American communications – by telephone, cellphone, email and others[77] – and to torture suspects as he directed.[78] 'It is unlikely that the history of US intelligence includes another operation conceived and supervised by the office of the vice president'[79] Cheney's biographer would later write, in awe – for Cheney refused to inform the president's own counter-terrorism adviser of the programme. Not even the head of Homeland Security or Congress Intelligence Committee members were allowed to know what Cheney was doing, let alone be permitted to arrange congressional oversight or an extension of the law to cover it. Known only to a handful of people, the illegal programme smacked of the KGB at its worst. Shortly before March 11, 2004, it resulted in a stand-off when the acting Attorney General, refusing to sign off on further illegal acts, offered his resignation, along with seventeen senior members of the Justice Department.

To Cheney's fury, Bush backed down; the US would abide by the Geneva Convention in Iraq, and the programme itself was altered until the Justice Department could sign off on it. Meanwhile the drama was kept from the press and public until after the election.

As the dust settled in the White House, however, insiders wondered why the president so often gave in to Cheney's shadow presidency, when it brought him so much grief. At times the overweight Cheney appeared to be not only ill from heart disease (he had required implantation of a cardioverter-defibrillator in 2001), but also seemed mentally unbalanced. When a targeted anthrax mailing was discovered that killed five people in 2002, for example, Cheney had suspected (wrongly, and with no evidence) foreign terrorists rather than a domestic culprit. He had thereupon insisted that the *entire population of America* be

immediately vaccinated against an anthrax attack by foreign terrorists;[80] only the president's refusal to issue such an order (which would
have resulted in many allergic-reaction deaths) had stopped him.
Meanwhile Cheney's legal counsel, David Addington, terrorized the
Washington legal bureaucracy as Cheney's 'eyes, ear and voice', –
ensuring no decision was made without his permission, and treating
even the president's legal counsel, Alberto Gonzales, as a puppet.[81]
'Of probably a hundred meetings in Gonzales' office to discuss national
security,' Jack Goldsmith later wrote, 'I recall only one when Addington
was not there.'[82]

Instead of dropping the all-too-powerful Cheney from the 2004
re-election ticket, however, Bush kept him as his co-president. The
greatness of America as an open society, honest with itself and reliant
upon Congress to provide the necessary checks and balances to
monarchical-style presidency, had been abandoned, citing the
constraints of war – a war the president himself had manufactured; a
war being waged on three fronts without a clear vision; a war without
exit strategies; and a war which, in many people's eyes, had turned the
United States, in terms of torture and the rule of law, into a failed state.

Impetuous, impulsive, shallow and insecure, Bush had no one to
blame but himself. However, the tragedy did not end there, for on
November 2, 2004, he was re-elected.

Benefiting from a group masquerading as 'Swift Boats For Truth',
Karl Rove and the Bush campaigners had removed their gloves and –
as they had with Senator McCain four years before, and again with
the triple-amputee Senator Max Cleland in 2002 – had destroyed the
character and reputation of the Democratic nominee, Senator John
Kerry, whose courage in Vietnam should have put the president and
vice president to shame.

Triumphantly re-elected, Bush thanked Karl Rove as the 'brilliant
architect' of his victory.[83] It was a victory not even his father had been
able to win without a Rove or Atwater to 'push the envelope to the
limit of what is permissible ethically or legally', as McClellan later
commented, thinking of the way Rove – a 'savvy, shrewd and devious
strategist'[84] – had manipulated even national terror alerts during the
campaign to heighten domestic insecurity.[85]

It was now, in November 2004, that Bush had one final opportunity to secure his legacy as a 'compassionate conservative', however,

and reinsert the United States into the international fold alongside its allies and in step with the UN. Had he asked Dick Cheney to step back into an advisory rather than co-presidential role, and had he made Colin Powell the 'new face' of the administration in what promised to be difficult years of bridge-building or -rebuilding – thereby embarking on a four-year term in which he could be seen to be pursuing a course of moderation and peace, not unilateralism and contempt for international law – he might still have avoided the bottom tier of the pantheon of US presidents.

The next day, November 3, 2004, all eyes turned to the vice president at the midmorning cabinet meeting. There, Cheney told his colleagues how, in a conversation 'about whether to trim the sails' following the contested victory and long drawn-out election result in November 2000, the president had said compromise 'was not an option' – and it had 'paid off' in 2001. 'This time', the vice president claimed, the mandate was 'clear': to continue with their right-wing domestic and foreign agenda.[86]

McClellan later described them as living in a fool's paradise. The war in Iraq was still a sickening quagmire of violence, terrorism, corruption, ethnic cleansing and bloodshed, yet *still* the neocons contemptuously dismissed the United Nations, and the need for allies and congressional support. Several days later Bush fired Colin Powell for not having been a neocon 'team player'. In the months that followed, moreover, he nominated for promotion his most incompetent loyalists: Condoleezza Rice to replace Powell as Secretary of State, Alberto Gonzales to be Attorney General, and his legal counsel Harriet Miers to be a Supreme Court judge.[87] He also promoted Karl Rove to be Deputy Chief of Staff for Policy.

Not only Powell but American journalists and observers went into shock. Democrats went into depression. America's standing abroad plummeted to an all-time low.

The overriding – and cynical – influence of Karl Rove on the president was demonstrated in March 2005 when Bush rushed back to Washington from his ranch in Texas to sign 'critical' Republican legislation: a special bill pushed through Congress to keep a patient, Terri Schiavo, alive in Florida by federal fiat, against the wishes of her husband, after seven years in a brain-dead, vegetative state. At a time when thousands of American soldiers had died in Iraq, tens of thousands had been wounded and troops were complaining of poor body armour and insufficiently armoured vehicles to protect them in what had become a civil war and protracted new battleground for al-Qaeda insurgents, the Schiavo affair seemed to typify what had gone wrong with the Bush administration in its desperation to appease its 'base'.

Sickened by reports and imagery of the orgy of violence in towns such as Falluja and Mosul, the majority of respondents in opinion polls declared the war in Iraq to have been, as Senator Kerry had declared, 'a mistake'. As the tide turned against the president that year, so too did Congress, despite its Republican majorities. One by one the Bush team's sins of commission and omission were now revealed. On June 7, 2005, documents were published showing the source of the decision to abandon the Kyoto Protocol on climate change had been an Exxon-sponsored group; the chief of staff of the president's Council on Environmental Policy then resigned, only to be reported taking a job at Exxon.[88] On June 22, Karl Rove was widely condemned for traducing those who opposed the war in Iraq as liberals who 'saw the savagery of the 9/11 attacks and wanted to prepare indictments and offer therapy and understanding for our attackers'.[89] Days later, in July, not only Rove but Vice President Cheney and their staffs were investigated on behalf of a grand jury, with a view to indictment. Although Rove and Cheney managed to avoid indictment, Cheney's chief of staff Scooter Libby was arrested, charged, found guilty, and eventually sentenced to prison for his part in deliberately revealing the role of Ambassador Wilson's wife as a CIA operative to America's enemies.

More damning still, however, was the final release, on July 22, 2005, of the bipartisan 9/11 Commission Report, confirming its announcement the previous summer that, despite Cheney's insistent claims to the contrary, there was 'no credible evidence' there had been a link between al-Qaeda and Saddam Hussein's Iraq before 9/11.[90] Indeed the report quoted a secret investigation given to the then national security adviser, Condoleezza Rice, only a week after the 9/11 attack, that had found '"no compelling evidence" that Iraq either planned or perpetrated the attacks'.[91]

As if to mirror the turning of the tide against the 'Vulcans', a terrifying 175 mph hurricane hit New Orleans and the Louisiana Gulf coast on August 30, 2005. The Corps of Engineers' levees were breached, inundating the city and marooning scores of thousands of New Orleans residents, almost 2,000 of whom were then allowed to die.

When the president, returning to the Oval Office from his Texas ranch three days later, asked Cheney 'if he'd be interested in spear-heading' a cabinet-level task force to deal with the crisis, he was told no. 'Let's just say I didn't get the most positive response', Bush mocked the vice president in front of his crisis team: Andy Card, Condoleezza Rice, Karl Rove, and the deputy press secretary, Dan Bartlett. Yet still the president did not order Cheney to take charge. Meekly he asked him: 'Will you at least go do a fact-finding trip for us?' The vice president again demurred.

Rove suggested the president himself fly over the flooded city in Air Force One, and a widely published photo was taken of the nation's commander-in-chief peering out of a porthole window thousands of feet above the devastation, having failed to federalize the emergency response. Any hope of saving the president's second term was extinguished. As Bush's own pollster and chief campaign strategist reflected afterwards, 'Katrina was the tipping point. The president broke his bond with the public. Once that bond was broken, he no longer had the capacity to talk to the American public. State of the Union addresses? Legislative initiatives? PR? Travel? It didn't matter.' Nothing could now help. 'I knew when Katrina – it was like, man, you know this is it man. We're done.'[92]

Pictures of Condoleezza Rice shopping for expensive shoes in New York only added to public outrage at the administration. Bush had promoted Michael D. Brown, a feckless Republican lawyer and long-time director of the Arabian Horse Association, of all people, to run the Federal Emergency Management Agency (FEMA) in 2002. Brown's utter mishandling of the Katrina disaster resulted in further outrage on all sides, compounded by the president's deplorable remark during the crisis, as he turned to the hapless FEMA director – the most incompetent in American annals – and said 'Brownie, you're doing a heck of a job!'[93]

Brown was forced to resign in ignominy several weeks later. Bush's failure to prepare for the disaster, despite warnings by the National Hurricane Center, his tardiness in responding to it, and his cronyism in promoting a horse breeder to such a crucial post, shocked the nation. For the president's press secretary, Katrina represented 'the defining turning point for Bush and his administration. It left an indelible stain on his presidency'.[94] In fact it came to 'define Bush's second term. And the perception of this catastrophe', McClellan added, 'was made worse by previous decisions President Bush had made, including, first and foremost, the failure to be open and forthright on Iraq and rushing to war with inadequate planning and preparation for its aftermath.'[95]

That aftermath, meanwhile, had grown worse and worse. Why, even jingoistic veterans wondered, had the president fired General Zinni for saying that at least 300,000 to 400,000 troops would be required to keep order after the invasion of Iraq? Why had the president not ordered a draft, if the military was overstretched and the need to avoid immediate chaos was so crucial? Why was the vice president allowed to secretly eavesdrop on conversations by US diplomats abroad, using the National Security Agency, in order to make sure no American officials strayed from his unilateralist line?[96] Orwell's nightmare of *Nineteen Eighty-Four* had come true, in America, with Big Brother watching and even the most senior American officials warned by well-meaning intelligence officers to be careful.[97]

The violence in Iraq, which Cheney claimed had already peaked, only grew worse. The famed Golden Mosque in Samarra was destroyed by Sunnis in February 2006; a *Lancet* medical journal report in June 2006 claimed that more than 600,000 Iraqis had died in the post-invasion violence, with millions more 'ethnically cleansed', displaced and living as refugees in camps or abroad. It seemed a heavy price for invading and ridding the country of a dictator, however much the president boasted of having 'done the absolute right thing in removing him from power', despite the lack of WMD.[98] In the *New York Times*, even Thomas Friedman, the war's biggest champion as a Middle East gamechanger, now admitted the US was 'not midwifing democracy in Iraq' but 'babysitting a civil war' – a civil war for which America, by virtue of its blitzkrieg invasion and failure to restore order in the aftermath, was wholly responsible.[99] With Israel, armed and unchecked by the United States, invading Lebanon for a second time, on July 12, 2006, to do battle with Hezbollah adherents – killing over 1,000 civilians and displacing over a million Lebanese – hopes for peaceful democracy in the Middle East looked bleaker than ever.[100]

On September 3, 2006, it was announced officially that 2,974 US servicemen had died since the start of the president's 'war on terror'.

More than 40,000 American soldiers had been either wounded or evacuated sick.[101] Osama Bin Laden still remained uncaptured, while al-Qaeda openly boasted of fielding 12,000 fighters now in combat in Iraq, with perhaps another 20,000 armed Iraqi insurgents attacking the 'infidel' US occupying forces for religious or nationalist reasons.

In what was called a 'referendum on Iraq', voters in the United States finally registered their assessment of the presidency on November 7, 2006: Democrats were elected back into control of the House of Representatives (233–202) and the Senate (fifty-one to forty-nine) in the midterm elections for the first time since 1992.

Six years into his presidency, Bush now had to reassess his own performance – and to his credit, he did. Bowing to pressure from Congress and members of his administration, he ignored the furious opposition of Dick Cheney and finally fired Donald Rumsfeld as Secretary of Defense the day after the elections. Then on December 6, 2006, he was faced with the sequel to the 9/11 Commission Report.

The new document, entitled *The Way Forward – A New Approach*, it was the work of an independent, bipartisan commission headed by his father's former Secretary of State, James Baker, to analyze what had gone wrong in Afghanistan and Iraq – and how to fix it. Far from 'winning' the 'war', the commission's authors concluded, the mire America had produced in Iraq was now 'grave and deteriorating' with no exit strategy beyond undefined 'victory'. 'The gist of what we had to say was a responsible exit. He [Bush] didn't like that', related the report's co-author, former congressman Lee Hamilton, afterwards. 'I don't recall, seriously, that he asked any questions', confided another of the authors, former Secretary of State Lawrence Eagleburger. Instead, the president 'ignored it so far as I can see', Hamilton sighed.[102]

In truth the president *did* read the report, however reluctantly, noting the authors' recommendation that he 'significantly increase the number of US personnel, including combat troops, imbedded and supporting Iraqi units' – which would thus allow US forces gradually to leave Iraq to the Iraqis. In this respect the Iraq Survey Group supported a short-term 'surge of American combat forces to stabilize Baghdad'.

It was close to midnight in terms of American failure, with the outgoing American commander in Iraq so pessimistic, in the face of an ever worsening orgy of bloodshed that he was recommending

American troops simply withdraw to safe havens and hand over responsibility to the provisional Iraqi government to deal with the chaos. Was he right, or were the authors of *The Way Forward*?

In the days and weeks that followed, Bush finally recognized he must listen to those commanders, statesmen and critics who had alternative ideas of how the US could get out of Iraq without too much shame, loss of face, and humiliation.

Six *years* to read, listen and ask searching questions? The president's father broke down in tears when launching the USS *Bush* and when interviewed on *Larry King Live*. Secrecy, contempt for democratic public debate and Congress ('Fuck yourself', Cheney had been heard to snort at Senator Patrick Leahy of Vermont, the ranking Democrat on the Judiciary Committee), and a bureaucracy of fear and intimidation had been the vice president's chief contribution to the twenty-first century American presidency – or co-presidency.[103] With Cheney's chief of staff formally indicted for deliberate felony, however, and his replacement denied the post of adviser or assistant to the president, Cheney's star had fallen. Rumsfeld, Wolfowitz, Perle, Feith, John Bolton and other outspoken proponents of unilateral American power, had gone – and both McLellan and the president's ineffective chief of staff, Andy Card, had resigned. The way was clear to reconstitute the chief executive.

In an interview with the press, Andy Card's successor, Josh Bolten, thus made clear that Cheney's co-presidency was over. 'The president took him as a *counselor*, not as a deputy', he explained. To be sure, the president might be seen as more 'courteous' to the vice president, but he was not, and would not be, 'more deferential' to Cheney than to others. Moreover, with regard to any presidential decision, 'the president will make it' – no one else. 'If it is not presidential,' Bolten added, 'it is going to be one of the cabinet officers [who] would make it – or me' – i.e. not the vice president.[104]

Bush was finally growing up, and in his careful weighing of the arguments for withdrawal, prolongation or change of direction in the military occupation of Iraq he finally donned the true mantle of the presidency. 'I am listening to a lot of advice to develop a strategy', he told reporters in December – who appeared stunned by the change in his vocabulary. Gone was the cowboy braggadocio. 'I will be delivering my plans after a long deliberation . . . I'm not going to be rushed into making a decision.'[105]

'Is he lucky?' Napoleon had famously asked when reviewing the recommendation of a new commander. Belatedly the president recognized the one man who could, perhaps, turn defeat into victory – or if not victory, then a successful exit from Iraq: Lieutenant General David Petraeus, author of the army's *Field Manual on Counterinsurgency*, whom Bush nominated to be the new American commander-in-chief in Iraq. Congress, impressed by Petraeus' testimony before the Senate Armed Services Committee on January 27, 2007, approved. Against a background of scepticism and conflicting views – especially from the new Democratic Majority Leaders of both House and Senate, Speaker Nancy Pelosi and Senator Harry Reid – the president authorized the temporary 'surge' the ISG had recommended, involving 30,000 more troops being sent to Iraq – as well as major funding to back Petraeus' strategy: to *pay* Iraqi militias to stop attacking American occupiers, and instead to turn their weapons on al-Qaeda insurgents.

Petraeus certainly proved lucky, and an inspired choice by Bush. With the Shiite warrior cleric Muqtada al-Sadr ordering his Mahdi Army militias to stand down, and the American-paid Sunnis, the Sons of Iraq, taking on al-Qaeda, the American surge – concentrated on combat operations in Baghdad – slowly but surely worked. By the autumn of 2007, sectarian violence began to diminish, and the road to gradual withdrawal of occupying forces from Iraq looked open.

Meanwhile Dick Cheney, who had suffered four heart attacks by the time he was fifty-nine, was treated for deep vein thrombosis in March 2007 and diagnosed with atrial fibrillation in November 2007, requiring electric shock treatment. Everywhere they went Vice President Cheney and Karl Rove – who resigned as deputy chief of staff on August 31, 2007 – were booed. On a visit to Afghanistan, Cheney even became the target of an assassination attempt which killed twenty-three innocent people outside a US air base. His approval rating dropped below 30 per cent, while his disapproval rating rose to 60 per cent. With rumours that he was urging a missile attack on Iran before it became a nuclear power, public anxiety grew even more pronounced. When asked on ABC News in the spring of 2008 whether he 'cared what the American people think', he answered bluntly: 'No.'[106]

President Bush, by contrast, cared – but found that, despite the improving situation in Iraq, it was too late to rehabilitate himself at home. The long housing bubble he had deliberately nurtured to distract from the war's negatives burst, and, as Republican and Democratic candidates for the 2008 presidential election argued over how best to end Bush's misguided wars, Wall Street began to totter – and collapse.

For this, the blinkered president had only himself to blame. As with the Hurricane Katrina fiasco, he seemed to be a man out of his depth, with no idea how to avoid what was soon predicted to become the worst recession since the Great Crash and Depression of the 1930s – the crisis that had brought the first American Caesar, Franklin D. Roosevelt, to power.

On the day of the presidential election in November 2008, Bush's approval rating, in a CBS tracking poll, dipped to 20 per cent – 'the lowest ever recorded by a president', as newspapers reported – while his disapproval rating soared to 72 per cent.[107] It was a sorry finale to a disastrous presidency, the crowds jeering at his departure, and hoping against hope that a new American Caesar could get their proud empire back on track.[108]

## Part Three: Private Life

Of the American Caesars, George W. Bush resembled John F. Kennedy the most, at least in childhood – both men born into large, wealthy, competitive families, irreverent and content to cultivate their 'bad boy' images, especially with women.

Bush became engaged to a stunning blonde student at Rice University, Cathryn Wolfman, at age twenty. Plans were made for a wedding in 1967. 'Everybody agreed that she and George made a great couple', a friend recalled – the studious, mature but outgoing step-daughter of a wealthy clothier, and the wayward son of a Texas congressman. 'George, of course, prided himself in being a bad boy. But Cathy always seemed to be having an awful lot of fun whenever they were together. He made her laugh the way he made everybody laugh. Maybe she lived vicariously through him a little.'[109]

Wedding plans, however, were delayed, and then, over time, dropped. After college, Bush went into his 'nomadic years', as he later called them: restless, partying, smoking, binge drinking, drug-using, lost. When his father famously called him to account for driving drunk into a garbage can outside their house, W. challenged him to a fight, '*mano a mano*'.[110] Unable to stay in any job or assignment, he seemed bewildered by adult life: spoiled, purposeless, self-destructive, a James Dean in the making. As such, he was dangerously attractive to women who wished to rescue him, but who found his family, congregating at Kennebunkport every summer, too formidable to handle. 'I don't want to go to Maine' his fiancée Cathryn Wolfson had said when ending their relationship. 'And I don't think this is going to work out.'[111] Crushed, W. had burst into tears, but Cathryn was not taken in. 'He can have any woman he wants – and he knows it', she said later.[112]

Though in fun-loving, reckless behaviour the similarities between the two playboy sons of rich, high-profile fathers were striking, there were also fundamental differences between Kennedy and Bush. Kennedy was smart, with an IQ that stunned even his teachers, and a voracious reader – a habit which repeated illness and hospitalization in childhood and youth only deepened. His fourth-year undergraduate thesis at Harvard, *Why England Slept*, was published as a book in 1940, when Kennedy was twenty-three – and two years later the FBI, tapping his phone and listening to secretly installed tape-recorders, heard him talking world politics with his mistress, Inga Arvad, telling her he was determined one day to be president of the United States.

Political ambition, then, was in John F. Kennedy's blood from the start, as was courage. With the onset of World War II, Kennedy finagled his way from clear unacceptability on medical grounds into heroic combat service in the US Navy as a PT boat captain. By contrast, George W. Bush's problem, from the start, was his limited IQ, lack of military courage and refusal to study in order to succeed.

The fateful odyssey that was Bush's rise to the presidency we have outlined, together with its tragic denouement, as the once popular, bipartisan Texas governor turned into his opposite – with terrible consequences for the country. Within that sorry tale, affecting so many millions of people's lives across the globe, there was, however – as in the story of Tsar Nicholas and Empress Alexandra – an affecting inner saga which, though it could never make amends for the damage done to the United States and other nations, did touch people's hearts at a human level.

In 1977 Laura Lane Welch, thirty-one-year-old librarian and registered Democrat, was introduced to the wastrel thirty-one-year-old son of the then US ambassador to the United Nations. Finding him both funny and tantalizingly unfulfilled, she consented to his dating her. Three months later, in a small ceremony after a lightning courtship, they were married. Where he was impetuous, Laura was cautious; where he was gregarious, she was private; where he was ill-read to the point of near-illiteracy, 'I read and I smoke' Laura had told her astonished future mother-in-law.

Calm, quiet, principled, an only daughter and the survivor of a terrible car crash at age seventeen (when inadvertently she ran a stop sign and killed her former high-school boyfriend), Laura Welch became George Walker Bush's lodestar. She turned his life around, threatened to leave him unless he stopped drinking, gave birth to twin daughters, and provided what he craved: trust in his essential worth, beneath the wastrel exterior. Though she didn't encourage him to run for the governorship of Texas and declined to give stump speeches or interviews, she stood by him, and became proud of his accomplishments in the governor's mansion. She brought out, people said, the best in W. and by her constancy banished the worst. He never strayed, and indeed hated to spend a night apart. If marriage is co-dependency, they were deeply, and movingly, co-dependent.

Why, then, did Laura Lane Bush not stop her beloved husband, the twice-elected and most popular governor of Texas since records began, from reaching for a yet higher political post, one he was not qualified to take? Bush saw himself at times as Reagan's disciple – folksy, humorous, and opposed to big government – but had no idea of Reagan's serious side, and the decades-long, arduous political path Reagan had taken, honing his skills as a speaker and spokesman for Republican causes. All W. had was a cheeky, friendly glamour, without political or intellectual depth. He had been at sea academically at both Yale and Harvard Business School, and would be overwhelmed by the complexity of economic, legal, congressional and diplomatic issues he would have to face if elected president. Laura had not enjoyed living in Washington when W. had worked for his father's 1988 presidential election campaign. She had no desire to live there again. She loved Texas; she loved the life that they had made there, and she worried what effect the White House – if Bush won the race – would have on their teenage daughters.

Sadly, fatefully, Laura did not stop her husband. Worse still, she innocently recommended that her husband take Dick Cheney, the man who was vetting vice-presidential candidates, as his number two, thinking the unvetted Cheney would lend 'gravitas' to the ticket. It was a decision she would come to deeply regret, once George W. Bush won the election, and the co-presidency turned into a haunting refutation of all that had characterized her husband's governorship in Texas.

Thanks to Cheney and Rove, George W. Bush quickly changed back to the bullying, snide, wilful and obstinate person he had been at school and at college. 'That's the interesting thing about being president,' W. said later in an unguarded moment, 'I don't feel like I owe anybody an explanation.'[113] Nothing Laura was able to do, as his wife and First Lady, seemed able to rescue him from the nefarious vice president or the manipulative Rove, the two men wheedling, urging, pressing, protecting and manoeuvring her naive, insecure and fatally ignorant spouse into imagining himself as a modern Cincinnatus, called to be dictator in troubling times.

Given the dynamic of the Bush dynasty and the quadrennial torrent of Republican Party money thrown at likely candidates for supreme power, was it inevitable that George W. Bush, a man of prankster charm but weak intellect, would be hauled to the apex of the political pyramid as a faux pharaoh of his nation, and then cast to the wolves when he failed to lead the American Empire wisely? Could it have been different, observers wondered, at the end of Bush's eight years in office, as they watched their beleaguered president fly into domestic exile, pursued by rumblings of possible international lawsuits calling him to account for torture and crimes against humanity? Looking at the slim, still delectably pretty woman in her pale grey coat holding the former president's hand as the couple strode to the helicopter that would take them away, those who knew them best could not help but ponder the role of the First Lady in the history of the American Empire. Eleanor, Bess, Mamie, Jackie, Lady Bird, Pat, Betty, Rosalind, Nancy, Barbara, Hillary, Laura . . . all had played their part, with varying success, in keeping their husbands sane as they carried ultimate executive responsibility for the world's most powerful hegemony; none had stopped them from accepting the challenge.

Within the Oval Office, the tragedy had then unfolded. The Cheney–Rove stranglehold had proved simply too powerful, and by the time Republican control of Congress was lost and bipartisanship became critical, it was too late. For all his African AIDS initiative, Prescription Drug, No Child Left Behind and other well-meaning programmes, the president's legacy would, like that of Lyndon B. Johnson, forever be his ill-considered, unilateral rush to war in Afghanistan and Iraq, and the quagmires they produced.

True to his image as Dr Strangelove, Dick Cheney attended the inauguration of the forty-fourth President in a wheelchair (he had hurt his back, packing more boxes of documents stolen from the government and the prying eyes of posterity, wags explained), and did everything possible in subsequent months to scorn the new Caesar's efforts to deal with the massive problems he was inheriting. By contrast a chastened George W. Bush not only refused to pardon Cheney's chief of staff, but said how delighted he was to have 'a front-row seat' at the impending 'historic event' on January 20, 2009, as the first black president mounted the inauguration podium.[114] When, after the swearing-in ceremony by the Capitol, the two men then embraced, arms around each other and cheek to cheek, it was as if a torch was truly passing from one generation, one race, and one approach to the responsibility of empire in the modern world, to another. Bending to say goodbye to Obama's little daughters, George W. Bush reminded watchers in Texas of what he had once been: a caring father, devoid of racial prejudice, blessed with a simple human touch.

As the two Caesars strode with their wives from the bottom of the Capitol steps towards the waiting helicopter, the compassionate hand of Obama laid across the shoulder of the departing former president seemed to symbolize the start of a new era for America: one in which humility and goodwill would mix with articulate idealism not seen for almost half a century, when President John F. Kennedy electrified the world.

# Acknowledgements

*American Caesars* originated in 2007, when I was approached by Dan Hind of The Bodley Head, part of the Random House publishing group in London.

For several years I had taken time out from presidential biography to write two short books on biography – *Biography: A Brief History*, and *How To Do Biography: A Primer*. However, having spent more than ten years writing multi-volume, large-scale presidential biographies (*JFK: Reckless Youth*; *Bill Clinton: An American Journey*; *Bill Clinton: Mastering the Presidency*), I was actively exploring the idea of a group biography of US presidents I admire – in part because I so deprecated the performance of George W. Bush as 43rd President, as I explained in the Prologue to *Bill Clinton: Mastering the Presidency*.

Dan's idea of a book about modern American presidents in the manner of Suetonius' *The Twelve Caesars* – a book I have cherished (and quoted) for four decades – thus struck me as serendipitous. And intriguing. No author since Suetonius has, after all, emulated his portraits of the first Roman emperors by seeking to look at a succession of such world-historical rulers.

What I particularly liked about the Suetonian approach, when I examined it structurally, was the separation of his lives into first the public career, and only then the personal life, or love-life, of his subjects. I had never used this biographical paradigm, since every modern biographer is *de rigeur* a disciple of Freud, and must lace a modern understanding of the subject's psychology into the gradual unravelling of the subject's lifestory, from the start, to satisfy public expectation. A trial chapter addressing President Truman, however, demonstrated to me, and to Dan, that by focusing first on the public career of the President, and only then on the life of his heart, so to speak, it was possible to see the politician initially in the context of his historic imperial role, and then, by contrast, as a man with a private life story.

Would that *American Caesars* had followed such a straightforward trajectory! The number of excellent individual biographies of the presidents, over recent decades, made it unnecessary to seek out unpublished material for the new work – but it did pose a substantial challenge of printed digestion. Beyond that, my task became one of 'selection and design', as Lytton Strachey put it in the preface to his masterpiece *Eminent Victorians*: using the framework of modern American empire, or hegemony, as the backcloth to the Caesars' lives. In this respect, at least, it promised to be less forbidding for me to tackle, perhaps, than for a number of my fellow American historians. Not only because of my detailed previous work on Presidents John F. Kennedy and Bill Clinton (and, earlier, on Dwight D. Eisenhower as a general, when writing my official biography of Field Marshal Montgomery), but because of the years I had spent in Great Britain – which made the concept of empire perfectly normal for me. Britain had, after all, established the world's largest territorial empire in the nineteenth century. In my own lifetime it had then ceded that role as guardian of international order and prosperity to the United States. Nevertheless, the sheer epos – political and personal - of the presidents' lives within the imperial context soon ran away with me. By the time the manuscript was ready, after two years' research and writing, it was twice too long.

Dan's successor at the Bodley Head, Jörg Hensgen, rightly refused to publish the book *en gros* – indeed felt it to be unpublishable at such length (and digressiveness). There thus began the heartbreaking task of self-editing, or self-mutilation. Only by picturing myself back in the cutting room studios of the BBC's Film and Documentaries Department in the 1980s was I able to overcome my aversion to the sight of so much lexical blood (First Cut, Second Cut, Final Cut). In the end the necessary surgery was completed, however, and I was able to see how wise Jörg had been. The lives of the twelve American Caesars had become shorter, omitting many a crucial event or aspect, but were now significantly more focused in my narrative. And, perhaps most important to me – and hopefully the reader – the portraits were still *moving*. To my editor Jörg Hensgen, then, I owe a huge debt of gratitude.

All my writing life I have sought to examine the nature, vagaries and conduct of leadership: literary, military, and political. In large part, I suppose this is due to my late father, who from humble circumstances rose to become a decorated infantry battalion commander in World War II, and later Editor-in-Chief of the London *Times* and *Sunday Times*. He had arranged for me to intern at age nineteen on the *Washington Post* in the summer of 1963 – an experience which, though it did not make me a journalist, did make me into a lifelong student of American history and politics, spurred by that great American patriot and editor, Russ Wiggins. Over the years, in researching my military biographies, I gradually learned my way around myriad American archives – and in 1988, after my father's death, I moved to Boston, Massachusetts, to start work on a fresh life of President John F. Kennedy. Save for a stint teaching biography and history in England in the late 1990s, I have been at work in the US ever since, with my intellectual home located in the state's diverse and beautifully situated University of Massachusetts Boston, next to the Massachusetts State Archives and Kennedy Library. I want to thank therefore my many colleagues at UMass Boston, especially Professors Paul Bookbinder, Padraig O'Malley, William Percy, Robert Weiner, Carter Jefferson and Ed Beard, as well as the Director, Steve Crosby, the staff and all my colleagues in the John W. McCormack Graduate School of Policy Studies. I am particularly grateful to Steve Crosby for help in providing a student research trainee, Lisa Cathcart, who worked diligently and tirelessly to assemble relevant documentation for each chapter, following initial research assistance by Danielle Thompson. Bill Baer and the staff of UMass' Healey Library, likewise, were, once again, of invaluable assistance. The directors and archivists of the National Archives' John F. Kennedy, Richard M. Nixon, Gerald R. Ford, Jimmy Carter and Ronald Reagan Presidential Libraries were invariably hospitable and helpful on my visits; also my sojourn as a Visiting Scholar at George Washington University and at Georgetown University in 2005 proved immensely helpful – especially since, at the latter, my office was located in the Classics Department, where Greek and Roman parallels with modern America were constantly discussed! I am particularly grateful to those members of the Clinton Administration I was able to interview for my Clinton biography, from Rahm Emanuel to Leon Panetta and Larry Summers, but also to the historians of the US Senate, Richard A. Baker and Donald A. Ritchie, as well as distinguished authors belonging to the Washington Writers Group, led by Dan Moldea, for their constant kindnesses and encouragement.

The fact is, no serious historian can write a biography without the help of his or her literary peers. I was fortunate to be alerted by James McGrath Morris, the editor of thebiographerscraft.com, to the existence of the Boston Biographers Group – and to them I would like to extend my heartfelt gratitude for moral, emotional and intellectual support during the genesis of this work. To my fellow biographers, authors and professional colleagues Herbert Parmet, Carlo D'Este, David Kaiser, Clive Foss, Larry Leamer, David Chanoff, Mark Schneider, Timothy Naftali, Craig Howes, Andrew Phillips, David Sparks, John Gartner, Mel Yoken, and others who read or listened to parts of the manuscript, my deep gratitude. My lifelong friend and classmate from Cambridge University days, Robin Whitby, read each chapter of the original manuscript for readability and general interest, as did my brother Michael Hamilton, following his retirement from Briggs & Stratton, Milwaukee. Audience responses at Suffolk University in Boston, UMass Boston, UMass Dartmouth, Roxbury Latin School and the Cambridge Boat Club to preliminary readings from the evolving manuscript proved greatly encouraging. My wife, Dr Raynel Shepard, ESL Curriculum Developer of the Boston Public Schools, kept me focused and happier than perhaps I have ever been while undertaking a major book project. Bruce Hunter, of David Higham Associates, acted as not only my literary agent but, as always, my stalwart adviser, friend and reassurer-in-chief. I have much to be grateful for – and I am, especially for the faith of the Publishing Director of The Bodley Head, Will Sulkin, and his colleagues, in the merit of the project. I can only hope the book, for all its faults, is worthy of so much help and support across two continents.

Nigel Hamilton
Somerville
Massachusetts
October 2009

# Select Bibliography

*American Empire*

Ambrose, Stephen, *Rise to Globalism: American Foreign Policy since 1938* (1971) (New York: Penguin Books, 1993)

Bacevich, Andrew, *American Empire: The Realities and Consequences of US Diplomacy* (Cambridge, MA: Harvard University Press, 2004)

— *The Limits of Power: The End of American Exceptionalism* (New York: Macmillan, 2008)

Bender, Peter, *Weltmacht Amerika: Das Neue Rom* (Munich: Deutscher Taschenbuch Verlag, 2005)

Beschloss, Michael R., and Strobe Talbott, *At the Highest Levels: The Inside Story of the Cold War* (Boston: Little Brown, 1993)

Brands, H. W., *The Devil We Knew: Americans and the Cold War* (New York: Oxford University Press, 1993)

— *Into the Labyrinth: The United States and the Middle East, 1945–1993* (New York: McGraw-Hill, 1994)

de Grazia, Victoria, *Irresistible Empire: America's Advance through 20th Century Europe* (Cambridge, MA: Harvard University Press, 2005)

Ferguson, Niall, *Colossus: The Price of America's Empire* (New York: Penguin Press, 2004)

—*The War of the World: Twentieth-Century Conflict and the Descent of the West* (New York: Penguin Press, 2006)

Gelb, Leslie H., *Power Rules: How Common Sense Can Rescue American Foreign Policy* (New York: HarperCollins, 2009)

Hardt, Michael, and Antonio Negri, *Empire* (Cambridge: Harvard University Press, 2001)

Hedges, Chris, *Empire of Illusion: The End of Literacy and the Triumph of Spectacle* (New York: Nation Books, 2009)

Herring, George C., *From Colony to Superpower: US Foreign Relations since 1776* (New York: Oxford University Press, 2008)

Hobson, J. A., *Imperialism: A Study* (1938) (Ann Arbor: University of Michigan Press, 1965)

Hoff, Joan, *A Faustian Foreign Policy: From Woodrow Wilson to George W. Bush – Dreams of Perfectibility* (New York: Cambridge University Press, 2008)

Johnson, Chalmers, *The Sorrows of Empire: Militarism, Secrecy, and the End of the Republic* (New York: Metropolitan Books, 2004)

Kagan, Robert, *Of Paradise and Power: America and Europe in the New World Order* (New York: Knopf, 2003)

Kennedy, Paul, *The Rise and Fall of the Great Powers* (New York: Random House, 1987)

Lapham, Lewis H., *Pretensions to Empire: Notes on the Criminal Folly of the Bush Administration* (New York: The New Press, 2006)

Lundestad, Geir, *Empire by Integration: The United States and European Integration, 1945–1997* (New York: Oxford University Press, 1998)

McMahon, Robert J., *The Cold War: A Very Short Introduction* (Oxford: Oxford University Press, 2003)

Maier, Charles S., *Among Empires: American Ascendancy and Its Predecessors* (Cambridge, MA: Harvard University Press, 2006)

Murphy, Cullen, *Are We Rome? The Fall of an Empire and the Fate of America* (Boston: Houghton Mifflin, 2007)

Robinson, Jeffrey, *The End of the American Century: Hidden Agendas of the Cold War* (London: Hutchinson, 1992)

Ross, Dennis, *Statecraft: And How to Restore America's Standing in the World* (New York: Farrar Straus and Giroux, 2008)

Turchin, Peter, *War and Peace and War: The Rise and Fall of Empires* (New York: Plume, 2006)

Tyler, Patrick, *A World of Trouble: The White House and the Middle East – From the Cold War to the War on Terror* (New York: Farrar Straus and Giroux, 2009)

Vidal, Gore, *The Decline and Fall of the American Empire* (1992) (Tucson, AZ: Odonian Press, 2004)

— *Imperial America: Reflections on the United States of Amnesia* (New York: Nation Books, 2004)

— *The Last Empire: Essays 1992–2000* (New York: Doubleday, 2001)

## US Presidency

Andrew, Christopher, *For the President's Eyes Only: Secret Intelligence and the American Presidency from Washington to Bush* (New York: HarperCollins, 1995)

Anthony, Carl Sferrazza, *First Ladies: The Saga of the Presidents' Wives and Their Power, 1789–1961* (New York: William Morrow, 1990)

Bohn, Michael K., *Nerve Center: Inside the White House Situation Room* (Washington: Brassey's, 2003)

Caroli, Betty Boyd, *First Ladies: An Intimate Look at How 38 Women Handled What May Be the Most Demanding, Unpaid, Unelected Job in America* (New York: Oxford University Press, 1995)

Dallek, Robert, *Hail to the Chief: The Making and Unmaking of American Presidents* (New York: Hyperion, 1996)

Degregorio, William A., *The Complete Book of US Presidents* (New York: Avenel, 1993)

Doyle, William, *Inside the Oval Office: The White House Tapes – From FDR to Clinton* (New York: Kodansha America, 1999)

Edwards, George C., and Stephen J. Wayne (eds), *Studying the Presidency* (Knoxville: University of Tennessee Press, 1983)

Hess, Stephen, *Organizing the Presidency* (Washington, DC: Brookings Institution, 2002)

Jones, Charles O., *Passages to the Presidency: From Campaigning to Governing* (Washington, DC: Brookings Institution, 1998)

Milkis, Sidney M., and Michael Nelson, *The American Presidency: Origins and Development, 1776–1998* (Washington, DC: CQ Press, 1999)

Moore, Kathryn, *The American Presidency: A Complete History* (New York: Barnes & Noble, 2007)

Patterson, Bradley H., *The White House Staff: Inside the West Wing and Beyond* (Washington, DC: Brookings Institution, 2000)

Schlesinger, Arthur M., Jr, *The Imperial Presidency* (New York: Popular Library, 1974)

Smith, Carter, *Presidents: Every Question Answered* (Irvington, New York: Hylas Publishing, 2004)

Wilson, Robert A. (ed.), *Power and the Presidency* (New York: PublicAffairs, 1999)

## Franklin D. Roosevelt

Black, Conrad, *Franklin Delano Roosevelt: Champion of Freedom* (New York: PublicAffairs, 2003)

Brands, H. W., *Traitor to His Class: The Privileged Life and Radical Presidency of Franklin Delano Roosevelt* (New York: Doubleday, 2008)

Dallek, Robert, *Franklin D. Roosevelt and American Foreign Policy, 1932–1945* (New York: Oxford University Press, 1979)

Davis, Kenneth S., *FDR: The War President, 1940-1943 – A History* (New York: Random House, 2000)

Freidel, Frank, *Franklin Roosevelt: A Rendezvous with Destiny* (Boston: Little Brown, 1990)

Jenkins, Roy, with Richard E. Neustadt, *Franklin Delano Roosevelt* (New York: Times Books, 2003)

Lash, Joseph P., *Eleanor and Franklin* (New York: Norton, 1971)

— *Roosevelt and Churchill 1939-1941: The Partnership That Saved the West* (New York: Norton, 1976)

Meacham, Jon, *Franklin and Winston: An Intimate Portrait of an Epic Friendship* (New York: Random House, 2003)

Perkins, Frances, *The Roosevelt I Knew* (New York: Viking Press, 1946)

Persico, Joseph E., *Franklin & Lucy: President Roosevelt, Mrs Rutherfurd, and the Other Remarkable Women in His Life* (New York: Random House, 2008)

Roosevelt, Eleanor, *The Autobiography of Eleanor Roosevelt* (1961) (New York: Da Capo Press, 1992)

Smith, Jean Edward, *FDR* (New York: Random House, 2007)

Ward, Geoffrey C., *Before the Trumpet: Young Franklin Roosevelt, 1882–1905* (New York: Harper & Row, 1985)

— *A First Class Temperament: The Emergence of Franklin Roosevelt* (New York: Harper & Row, 1989)

— (ed.), *Closest Companion: The Unknown Story of the Intimate Friendship between Franklin Roosevelt and Margaret Suckley* (Boston: Houghton Mifflin, 1995)

## Harry S. Truman

Acheson, Dean, *Present at the Creation: My Years in the State Department* (New York: Norton, 1969)

Clifford, Clark, *Counsel to the President* (New York: Random House, 1991)

Donovan, Robert, *Conflict and Crisis: The Presidency of Harry S. Truman, 1945–1948* (New York: Norton, 1977)

— *Tumultuous Years: The Presidency of Harry S. Truman, 1949–1953* (New York: Norton, 1982)

Ferrell, Robert H., *Harry S. Truman, and the Modern American Presidency* (Boston: Little Brown, 1983)

— (ed.), *The Autobiography of Harry S. Truman* (Boulder, CO: Colorado Associated University Press, 1980)

— (ed.), *Dear Bess: The Letters from Harry to Bess Truman, 1910–1959* (New York: W. W. Norton, 1983)

— (ed.), *Off the Record: The Private Papers of Harry S. Truman* (New York: Harper & Row, 1980)

Hamby, Alonzo M., *Man of the People: A Life of Harry S. Truman* (New York: Oxford University Press, 1995)

Isaacson, Walter, and Evan Thomas, *The Wise Men: Six Friends and the World They Made – Acheson, Bohlen, Harriman, Kennan, Lovett, McCloy* (New York: Simon & Schuster, 1986)

Jenkins, Roy, *Truman* (New York: Harper & Row, 1986)

McCullough, David, *Truman* (New York: Simon & Schuster, 1992)

Miller, Merle, *Plain Speaking: An Oral Biography of Harry S. Truman* (New York: Berkley / G.B. Putnam's Sons, 1973)

Offner, Arnold A., *Another Such Victory: President Truman and the Cold War, 1945–1953* (Stanford: Stanford University Press, 2002)

Pemberton, William E., *Harry S. Truman: Fair Dealer and Cold Warrior* (Boston: Twayne Publishers, 1989)

Perret, Geoffrey, *Commander in Chief: How Truman, Johnson, and Bush Turned a Presidential Power into a Threat to America's Future* (New York: Farrar, Strauss and Giroux, 2007)

Poen, Monte M. (ed.), *Strictly Personal and Confidential: The Letters Harry Truman Never Mailed* (Boston: Little Brown, 1982)

Pogue, Forrest C., *George C. Marshall: Statesman 1945–1959* (New York: Viking, 1987)

Truman, Harry S., *Memoirs, Volume One: Year of Decisions* (New York: Doubleday, 1955)

— *Memoirs, Volume Two: Years of Trial and Hope* (New York: Doubleday, 1956)

Truman, Margaret, *Harry S. Truman* (New York: William Morrow, 1972)
— (ed.), *Where the Buck Stops: The Personal and Private Writings of Harry S. Truman* (New York: Warner Books, 1989)

## Dwight D. Eisenhower

Adams, Sherman, *First Hand Report: The Inside Story of the Eisenhower Administration* (New York: Harper, 1961)

Ambrose, Stephen, *Eisenhower: Soldier, General of the Army, President-elect, 1890-1952* (New York: Simon & Schuster, 1983)

— *Eisenhower: The President* (New York: Simon & Schuster, 1984)

— *Ike's Spies: Eisenhower and the Espionage Establishment* (1981) (Jackson: University of Mississippi, 1999)

Beschloss, Michael R., *May-Day: Eisenhower, Khrushchev and the U2 Affair* (New York: Harper & Row, 1986)

Brendon, Piers, *Ike: His Life and Times* (New York: Harper, 1986)

Carlson, Peter, *K Blows Top: A Cold War Interlude, Starring Nikita Khrushchev, America's Most Unlikely Tourist* (New York: PublicAffairs, 2009)

David, Lester, and Irene David, *Ike and Mamie: The Story of the General and His Lady* (New York: G.B. Putnam's Sons, 1981)

D'Este, Carlo, *Eisenhower: A Soldier's Life* (New York: Holt, 2002)

Eisenhower, Dwight D., *The White House Years: Mandate for Change, 1953–1956* (New York: Doubleday, 1963)

— *The White House Years: Waging Peace, 1956-1961* (New York: Doubleday, 1965)

Ferrell, Robert H. (ed.), *The Eisenhower Diaries* (New York: Norton, 1981)

Fursenko, Aleksandr, and Timothy Naftali, *Khrushchev's Cold War: The Inside Story of an American Adversary* (New York, Norton, 2006)

Khrushchev, Nikita, *Khrushchev Remembers: The Last Testament* (Boston: Little Brown, 1974)

Pach, Chester J., and Elmo Richardson, *The Presidency of Dwight D. Eisenhower* (Lawrence: University Press of Kansas, 1991)

Perret, Geoffrey, *Eisenhower* (New York: Random House, 1999)

Powers, Thomas, *The Man Who Kept the Secrets: Richard Helms and the CIA* (New York: Knopf, 1979)

Taubman, William, *Khrushchev: The Man and His Era* (New York: Norton, 2003)

Taubman, William, et al. (eds), *Nikita Khrushchev* (New Haven: Yale University Press, 2000)

## John F. Kennedy

Beschloss, Michael, *The Crisis Years: Kennedy and Khrushchev, 1960–1963* (New York: HarperCollins, 1991)

Blair, Joan, and Clay Blair, *The Search for JFK* (New York: Putnam, 1974)

Bradlee, Ben, *Conversations with Kennedy* (New York: Norton, 1997)

Dallek, Robert, *An Unfinished Life: John F. Kennedy 1917–1963* (Boston: Little Brown, 2003)

Giglio, James N., *The Presidency of John F. Kennedy* (Lawrence: University Press of Kansas, 1991)

Hamilton, Nigel, *JFK: Reckless Youth* (New York: Random House, 1992)

Hersh, Seymour, *The Dark Side of Camelot* (Boston: Little Brown, 1997)

Kaiser, David, *American Tragedy: Kennedy, Johnson, and the Origins of the Vietnam War* (Cambridge, MA: Harvard University Press, 2000)

Leamer, Laurence, *The Kennedy Men, 1901–1963* (New York: William Morrow, 2001)

May, Ernest R., and Philip D. Zelikow, *The Kennedy Tapes: Inside the White House during the Cuban Missile Crisis* (Cambridge, MA: Harvard University Press, 1997)

Parmet, Herbert, *JFK: The Presidency of John F. Kennedy* (New York: Dial Press, 1983)

Perret, Geoffrey, *Jack: A Life Like No Other* (New York: Random House, 2001)

Reeves, Richard, *President Kennedy: Profile of Power* (New York: Simon & Schuster, 1993)

Reeves, Thomas C., *A Question of Character: A Life of John F. Kennedy* (New York: Macmillan, 1991)

Rubin, Gretchen, *Forty Ways to Look at JFK* (New York: Ballantine, 2005)

Smith, Sally B., *Grace and Power: The Private World of the Kennedy White House* (New York: Random House, 2004)

Sorensen, Theodore C., *Kennedy* (New York: Bantam, 1966)

## Lyndon B. Johnson

Beschloss, Michael R. (ed.), *Taking Charge: The Johnson White House Tapes, 1963–1964* (New York: Simon & Schuster, 1997)

— (ed.), *Reaching For Glory: Lyndon Johnson's Secret White House Tapes, 1964–1965* (New York: Simon & Schuster, 2001)

Bornet, Vaughn Davis, *The Presidency of Lyndon B. Johnson* (Lawrence: University Press of Kansas, 1983)

Caro, Robert, *The Years of Lyndon Johnson: Master of the Senate* (New York: Knopf, 2002)

— *The Years of Lyndon Johnson: Means of Ascent* (New York: Knopf, 1990)

— *The Years of Lyndon Johnson: The Path to Power* (New York: Knopf, 1982)

Christian, George, *The President Steps Down: A Personal Memoir of the Transfer of Power* (New York: Macmillan, 1970)

Dallek, Robert, *Flawed Giant: Lyndon Johnson and His Times, 1961–1973* (New York: Oxford University Press, 1998)

— *Lone Star Rising: Lyndon Johnson and His Times, 1908–1960* (New York: Oxford University Press, 1991)

— *Lyndon B. Johnson: Portrait of a President* (New York: Oxford University Press, 2004)

Gardner, Lloyd C., *Pay Any Price: Lyndon Johnson and the Wars for Vietnam* (Chicago: Ivan R. Dee, 1995)

Goldman, Eric F., *The Tragedy of Lyndon Johnson* (New York: Knopf, 1969)

Herring, George C., *LBJ and Vietnam: A Different Kind of War* (Austin: University of Texas, 1994)

Johnson, Lyndon Baines, *The Vantage Point: Perspectives on the Presidency, 1963–1969* (New York: Holt, Rinehart and Winston, 1971)

Johnson, Sam Houston, *My Brother Lyndon* (New York: Cowles, 1970)

Kearns, Doris, *Lyndon Johnson and the American Dream* (New York: Harper, 1976)

Kotz, Nick, *Judgment Days: Lyndon Baines Johnson, Martin Luther King Jr., and the Laws That Changed America* (Boston: Houghton Mifflin, 2005)

Miller, Merle, *Lyndon: An Oral Biography* (New York: G.B. Putnam's Sons, 1980)

Perlstein, Rick, *Before the Storm: Barry Goldwater and the Unmaking of the American Consensus* (New York: Hill and Wang, 2001)

Phipps, Joe, *Summer Stock: Behind the Scenes with LBJ in '48* (Fort Worth: Texas Christian Press, 1992)

Reedy, George, *Lyndon B. Johnson: A Memoir* (New York: Andrews and McMeel, 1982)

Schwartz, Thomas Alan, *Lyndon Johnson and Europe* (Cambridge, MA: Harvard University Press, 2003)

VanDeMark, Brian, *Into the Quagmire: Lyndon Johnson and the Escalation of the Vietnam War* (New York: Oxford University Press, 1991)

Vandiver, Frank E., *Shadows of Vietnam: Lyndon Johnson's Wars* (College Station: Texas A&M University Press, 1997)

Woods, Randall B., *LBJ: Architect of American Ambition* (New York: Free Press, 2006)

### Richard M. Nixon

Aitken, Jonathan, *Nixon: A Life* (Washington DC: Regnery, 1993)

Ambrose, Stephen, *Nixon: The Education of a Politician, 1913–1962* (New York: Simon & Schuster, 1987)

— *Nixon: The Triumph of a Politician, 1962–1972* (New York: Simon & Schuster, 1988)

— *Nixon: Ruin and Recovery, 1973–1990* (New York: Simon & Schuster, 1991)

Black, Conrad, *Richard Milhous Nixon: The Invincible Quest* (New York: PublicAffairs, 2007)

Dallek, Robert, *Nixon and Kissinger: Partners in Power* (New York: HarperCollins, 2007)

Dean, John, *Blind Ambition: The White House Years* (New York: Simon & Schuster, 1976)

Ellsberg, Daniel, *Secrets: A Memoir of Vietnam and the Pentagon Papers* (New York: Viking Penguin, 2002)

Hahnimaki, Jussi, *The Flawed Architect: Henry Kissinger and American Foreign Policy* (New York: Oxford University Press, 2004)

Hersh, Seymour M., *The Price of Power: Kissinger in the White House* (New York: Summit Books, 1983)

Kutler, Stanley I., *Abuse of Power: The New Nixon Tapes* (New York: Free Press, 1997)

Macmillan, Margaret, *Nixon and Mao: The Week that Changed the World* (New York: Random House, 2007)

Morris, Roger, *Richard Milhous Nixon: The Rise of an American Politician* (New York: Holt, 1989)

Nixon, Richard, *RN: The Memoirs of Richard Nixon* (New York: Grosset & Dunlap, 1978)

— *Six Crises* (New York: Doubleday, 1962)

Parmet, Herbert, *Richard Nixon and His America* (Boston: Little Brown, 1990)

Reeves, Richard, *President Nixon: Alone in the White House* (New York: Simon & Schuster, 2001)

Small, Melvin, *The Presidency of Richard Nixon* (Lawrence: University Press of Kansas, 1999)

Summers, Anthony, *The Arrogance of Power: The Secret World of Richard Nixon* (New York: Viking, 2000)

Woodward, Bob, and Carl Bernstein, *The Final Days* (New York: Simon & Schuster, 1976)

### Gerald R. Ford

Brinkley, Douglas, *Gerald R. Ford* (New York: Times Books, 2007)

Cannon, James, *Time and Chance: Gerald Ford's Appointment with History* (New York: HarperCollins, 1994)

DeFrank, Thomas M., *Write It When I'm Gone: Remarkable Off-the-Record Conversations with Gerald R. Ford* (New York: G.B. Putnam's Sons, 2007)

Ford, Gerald R., *A Time to Heal* (New York: Harper & Row, 1979)

Greene, John Robert, *The Presidency of Gerald R. Ford* (Lawrence: University Press of Kansas, 1995)

Mieczkowski, Yanek, *Gerald Ford, and the Challenges of the 1970s* (Lexington: University of Kentucky Press, 2005)

Mollenhoff, Clark, *The Man Who Pardoned Nixon* (New York: St. Martin's Press, 1976)

Werth, Barry, *31 Days: The Crisis That Gave Us the Government We Have Today* (New York: Doubleday, 2006)

### Jimmy Carter

Bourne, Peter G., *Jimmy Carter: A Comprehensive Biography from Plains to Postpresidency* (New York: Scribner, 1997)

Carter, Jimmy, *An Hour Before Daylight* (New York: Simon & Schuster, 2001)

— *Keeping Faith: Memoirs of a President* (New York: Bantam, 1982)

— *Palestine Peace Not Apartheid* (New York: Simon & Schuster, 2007)

Carter, Rosalynn, *First Lady from Plains* (Boston: Houghton Mifflin, 1984)

Jones, Charles O., *The Trusteeship Presidency: Jimmy Carter and the United States Congress* (Baton Rouge: Louisiana State University Press, 1988)

Jordan, Hamilton, *Crisis: The Last Year of the Carter Presidency* (New York: Berkley Publishing, 1982)

Kaufman, Burton I., *James Earl Carter, Jr.* (Lawrence: University Press of Kansas, 1993)

Lasky, Victor, *Jimmy Carter: The Man and the Myth* (New York: Richard Marek, 1979)

Mazlish, Bruce, and Erwin Diamond, *Jimmy Carter: A Character Portrait* (New York: Simon and Schuster, 1979)

Meyer, Peter, *James Earl Carter: The Man and the Myth* (Kansas City: Sheed Andrews and McMeel, 1978)

Morris, Kenneth E., *Jimmy Carter: American Moralist* (Athens: University of Georgia Press, 1996)

Schramm, Martin, *Running for President: A Journal of the Carter Campaign* (New York: Pocket Books, 1978)

Strong, Robert A., *Working in the World: Jimmy Carter and the Making of American Foreign Policy* (Baton Rouge: Louisiana State University Press, 2000)

Stroud, Kandy, *How Jimmy Won: The Victory Campaign from Plains to the White House* (New York: Morrow, 1977)

Thompson, Kenneth W. (ed.), *The Carter Presidency: Fourteen Intimate Perspectives of Jimmy Carter* (Lanham, MD: University Press of America, 1990)

Witcover, Jules, *Marathon: The Pursuit of the Presidency, 1972–1976* (New York: Viking, 1977)

## Ronald Reagan

Brown, Edmund G., *Reagan and Reality: The Two Californias* (New York: Praeger, 1970)

Cannon, Lou, *President Reagan: The Role of a Lifetime* (New York: PublicAffairs, 2000)

Colacello, Bob, *Ronnie and Nancy: Their Path to the White House – 1911–1980* (New York: Warner Books, 2004)

Dallek, Robert, *Ronald Reagan: The Politics of Symbolism* (Cambridge, MA: Harvard University Press, 1999)

Deaver, Michael, with Mickey Herkovitz, *Behind the Scenes* (New York: Morrow, 1987)

Diggins, John Patrick, *Ronald Reagan: Fate, Freedom, and the Making of History* (New York: Norton, 2007)

Donaldson, Sam, *Hold on, Mr President!* (New York: Random House, 1987)

D'Souza, Dinesh, *Ronald Reagan: How an Ordinary Man Became an Extraordinary Leader* (New York: Free Press, 1997)

Edwards, Anne, *Early Reagan* (New York: William Morrow, 1987)

Gorbachev, Mikhail, *Memoirs* (New York: Doubleday, 1995)

Kelley, Kitty, *Nancy Reagan: The Unauthorized Biography* (New York: Simon & Schuster, 1991)

Kengor, Paul, *The Crusader: Ronald Reagan and the Fall of Communism* (New York: HarperCollins, 2006)

Morris, Edmund, *Dutch: A Memoir of Ronald Reagan* (New York: Random House, 1999)

Noonan, Peggy, *When Character Was King: A Story of Ronald Reagan* (New York: Viking, 2001)

Pemberton, William E., *Exit with Honor: The Life and Presidency of Ronald Reagan* (Armonk, NY: M. E. Sharpe, 1997)

Reagan, Nancy, with William Novak, *My Turn: The Memoirs of Nancy Reagan* (New York: Random House, 1989)

Reagan, Ronald, *An American Life* (New York: Simon and Schuster, 1990)

— *The Reagan Diaries*, ed. Douglas Brinkley (New York: HarperCollins, 2007)

Reeves, Richard, *President Reagan* (New York: Simon & Schuster, 2005)

Troy, Gill, *Morning in America: How Ronald Reagan Invented the 1980s* (Princeton: Princeton University Press, 2005)

Wilentz, Sean, *The Age of Reagan: A History 1974–2008* (New York: Harper, 2008)

## George H. W. Bush

Baker, James, with Thomas DeFrank, *The Politics of Diplomacy: Revolution, War and Peace, 1989–1992* (New York: G. B. Putnam's Sons, 1995)

Bush, Barbara, *A Memoir* (New York: Scribner, 1994)

Bush, George, *All the Best, George Bush: My Life in Letters and Other Writings* (New York: Scribner, 2000)

Bush, George, and Brent Scowcroft, *A World Transformed* (New York: Knopf, 1998)

Engel, Jeffrey A., *The China Diary of George H. W. Bush: The Making of a Global President* (Princeton: Princeton University Press, 2008)

Green, FitzHugh, *George Bush: An Intimate Portrait* (New York: Hippocrene Press, 1991)

Greene, John Robert, *The Presidency of George Bush* (Lawrence: University Press of Kansas, 2000)

Halberstam, David, *War in a Time of Peace: Bush, Clinton, and the Generals* (New York: Scribner, 2001)

Koch, Doro Bush, *My Father, My President: A Personal Account of the Life of George H. W. Bush* (New York: Grand Central Publishing, 2006)

McGrath, Jim, *Heartbeat: George Bush in His Own Words* (New York: Scribner, 2001)

Mervin, David, *George Bush and the Guardianship Presidency* (New York: St Martin's Press, 1996)

Naftali, Timothy, *George H. W. Bush* (New York: Times Books, 2007)

Parmet, Herbert, *George Bush: The Life of a Lone Star Yankee* (New York: Scribner, 1997)

Phillips, Kevin, *American Dynasty: Aristocracy, Fortune, and the Politics of Deceit in the House of Bush* (New York: Viking, 2004)

Powell, Colin, with Joseph E. Persico, *An American Journey* (New York: Random House, 1995)

Tarpley Webster G., and Anton Chaitkin, *George Bush: The Unauthorized Biography* (Washington, DC: Executive Intelligence Review, 1992)

Woodward, Bob, *The Commanders* (New York: Simon & Schuster, 1991)

— *Shadow: Five Presidents and the Legacy of Watergate* (New York: Simon & Schuster, 1999)

## Bill Clinton

Blumenthal, Sidney, *The Clinton Wars* (New York: Farrar, Straus and Giroux, 2003)

Conason, Joe, and Gene Lyons, *The Hunting of the President: The Ten-Year Campaign to Destroy Bill and Hillary Clinton* (New York: St Martin's Press, 2000)

Clinton, Bill, *My Life* (New York: Knopf, 2004)

Clinton, Hillary Rodham, *Living History* (New York: Simon & Schuster, 2003)

Fick, Paul, *The Dysfunctional President: Understanding the Compulsions of Bill Clinton* (Secaucus, NJ: Carol Publishing, 1995, 1998)

Freeh, Louis B., *My FBI: Bringing down the Mafia, Investigating Bill Clinton, and Fighting the War on Terror* (New York: St Martin's Press, 2005)

Gartner, John D., *In Search of Bill Clinton: A Psychological Biography* (New York: St Martin's Press, 2008)

Gergen, David, *Eyewitness to Power: The Essence of Leadership – Nixon to Clinton* (New York: Simon & Schuster, 2000)

Hamilton, Nigel, *Bill Clinton: American Journey – Great Expectations* (New York: Random House 2003)

— *Bill Clinton: Mastering the Presidency* (New York: PublicAffairs, 2007)

Harris, John, *The Survivor: Bill Clinton in the White House* (New York: Random House, 2005)

Johnson, Haynes, *The Best of Times: America in the Clinton Years* (New York: Harcourt, 2001)

Johnson, Haynes, and David S. Broder: *The System: The American Way of Politics at the Breaking Point* (Boston: Little Brown, 1996)

Maraniss, David, *The Clinton Enigma: A Four-and-a-half Minute Speech Reveals the President's Entire Life* (New York: Simon & Schuster, 1998)

Morris, Dick, *Behind the Oval Office* (New York: Random House, 1997)

Renshon, Stanley A., *High Hopes: The Clinton Presidency and the Politics of Ambition* (New York: New York University Press, 1996, 1998)

Schmidt, Susan, and Michael Weisskopf, *Truth at Any Cost: Ken Starr and the Unmaking of Bill Clinton* (New York: HarperCollins, 2000)

Stephanopoulos, George, *All Too Human* (Boston: Little Brown, 1999)

Stewart, James B., *Blood Sport: The President and His Adversaries* (New York: Simon & Schuster, 1996)

Starr, Kenneth, *The Starr Evidence*, ed. *Washington Post* (New York: PublicAffairs, 1998)

Toobin, Jeffrey, *A Vast Conspiracy: The Real Story of the Sex Scandal That Nearly Brought down a President* (New York: Random House, 1999)

Woodward, Bob, *The Agenda: Inside the Clinton White House* (New York: Simon & Schuster, 1994)

— *The Choice* (Simon & Schuster, 1996)


## George W. Bush


Anderson, Christopher, *George and Laura: Portrait of an American Marriage* (New York: William Morrow, 2002)

Bovard, James, *The Bush Betrayal* (New York: Palgrave Macmillan, 2004)

Bruni, Frank, *Ambling into History: The Unlikely Odyssey of George W. Bush* (New York: HarperCollins, 2002)

Cannon, Lou, and Carl M. Cannon, *Reagan's Disciple: George W. Bush's Troubled Quest for a Presidential Legacy* (New York: PublicAffairs, 2008)

Clarke, Richard A., *Against All Enemies: Inside America's War on Terror* (New York: Free Press, 2004)

Dean, John, *Worse than Watergate: The Secret Presidency of George W. Bush* (Boston: Little Brown, 2004)

Dubose, Lou, and Jake Bernstein, *Vice: Dick Cheney and the Hijacking of the American Presidency* (New York: Random House, 2006)

Feith, Douglas J., *War and Decision: Inside the Pentagon at the Dawn of the War on Terrorism* (New York: Harper, 2008)

Freiling, Thomas M., *George W. Bush: On God and Country* (Fairfax, VA: Allegiance Press, 2004)

Frum, David, *The Right Man: The Surprise Presidency of George W. Bush* (New York: Random House, 2003)

Gellman, Barton, *Angler: The Cheney Vice Presidency* (New York: Penguin Press, 2008)

Goldsmith, Jack, *The Terror Presidency: Law and Judgment inside the Bush Administration* (New York: Norton, 2007)

Hatfield, J. H., *Fortunate Son: George W. Bush and the Making of an American President* (New York: Soft Skull Press, 2001)

Kean, Jack, Lee H. Hamilton et al., *The 9/11 Commission Report: Final Report of the National Commission on Terrorist Attacks upon the United States* (New York: Norton, 2004)

Kelley, Kitty, *The Family: The Real Story of the Bush Dynasty* (New York: Doubleday, 2004)

Kessler, Ron, *A Matter of Character: Inside the White House of George W. Bush* (New York: Sentinel, 2004)

Mann, James, *Rise of the Vulcans: The History of Bush's War Cabinet* (New York: Viking, 2004)

McClellan, Scott, *What Happened: Inside the Bush White House and Washington's Culture of Deception* (New York: PublicAffairs, 2008)

Mayer, Jane, *The Dark Side: The Inside Story of How the War on Terror Turned into a War on American Ideals* (New York: Doubleday, 2008)

Miller, Mark Crispin, *Cruel and Unusual: Bush/Cheney's New World Order* (New York: Norton, 2004)

Moore, James, and Wayne Slater, *Bush's Brain: How Karl Rove Made George W. Bush Presidential* (Hoboken, NJ: John Wiley, 2003)

Suskind, Ron, *The Price of Loyalty: George W. Bush, the White House and the Education of Paul O'Neill* (New York: Simon & Schuster, 2004)

Unger, Craig, *American Armageddon: How the Delusions of the Neoconservatives and the Christian Right Triggered the Descent of America – and Still Imperil Our Future* (New York: Scribner, 2007)

Weisberg, Jacob, *The Bush Tragedy* (New York: Random House, 2008)

Woodward, Bob, *Bush at War* (New York: Simon & Schuster, 2002)

— *Plan of Attack: The Definitive Account of the Decision to Invade Iraq* (New York: Simon & Schuster, 2004)

— *State of Denial: Bush at War, Part III* (New York: Simon & Schuster, 2006)

# Notes

*Preface*

1. Ron Suskind, 'Faith, Certainty and the Presidency of George W. Bush', *New York Times Magazine*, October 17, 2004. • **2.** At the end of President George W. Bush's final term in office, in January 2009, the US Government officially administered only six colonies or US Territories across the world: American Samoa, the Federated States of Micronesia, Guam, Midway Islands, Puerto Rico, and the US Virgin Islands. However, the US was still fighting two major wars, in Iraq and Afghanistan, and operating more than 900 officially acknowledged military bases overseas, in 130 countries (other than its official US Territories), as well as more than a hundred secret or disguised installations – up from only 14 overseas bases in 1938. Catherine Lutz, 'Obama's Empire,' *New Statesman*, July 30, 2009.

*Chapter One: Franklin Roosevelt*

1. Jean Edward Smith, *FDR*, p. 23. • **2.** Ibid., p. 50. • **3.** Ibid., p. 63. • **4.** Ibid., p. 61. • **5.** Ibid., p. 59. • **6.** Ibid., p. 102. • **7.** Ibid., p. 140. • **8.** H. W. Brands, *Traitor to His Class: The Privileged Life and Radical Presidency of Franklin Delano Roosevelt*, pp. 129–30. • **9.** Ibid., p. 137. • **10.** Ibid. • **11.** *New York Times*, September 16, 2001, in Smith, *FDR*, p. 192. • **12.** Smith, *FDR*, p. 211. • **13.** Ibid. • **14.** Brands, *Traitor to His Class*, p. 206. • **15.** Smith, *FDR*, p. 225. • **16.** Ibid., p. 251. • **17.** Ibid., p. 258. • **18.** Ibid., p. 263. • **19.** Ibid., p. 316. • **20.** Ibid., p. 299. • **21.** Ibid., pp. 350–1. • **22.** Initially, only 60 per cent of workers were covered, as firms employing less than ten people were exempt from contributions. • **23.** Smith, *FDR*, p. 359. • **24.** Ibid., p. 371. • **25.** Ibid., p. 419. • **26.** Ibid., p. 426. • **27.** Ibid.,

p. 445. • **28.** Conrad Black, *Franklin Delano Roosevelt: Champion of Freedom*, p. 290. • **29.** Smith, *FDR*, p. 441. • **30.** Ibid., p. 458. • **31.** Ibid., p. 466. • **32.** Ibid., p. 476. • **33.** Conrad Black, *Franklin Delano Roosevelt*, p. 595. • **34.** Smith, *FDR*, p. 477. • **35.** Ibid., p. 448. • **36.** Hamilton, *JFK*, p. 396. • **37.** Smith, *FDR*, pp. 485–6. • **38.** Ibid., p. 487. • **39.** Ibid., p. 490. • **40.** Joseph P. Lash, *Roosevelt and Churchill 1939–1941*, p. 391. • **41.** Ibid., p. 403. • **42.** Jon Meacham, *Franklin and Winston*, p. 122. • **43.** Lash, *Roosevelt and Churchill*, p. 401. • **44.** Meacham, *Franklin and Winston*, pp. 122–3. • **45.** Max Domarus, *Hitler: Speeches and Proclamations 1932–1945, and Commentary by a Contemporary*, Vol. 4 (Wauconda, IL: Bolchazy-Carducci Publishers, 2004), p. 2542. • **46.** Ibid., p. 2551. • **47.** FDR to Knox, in Smith, *FDR*, p. 537. • **48.** Ibid., p. 541. • **49.** Domarus, *Hitler: Speeches and Proclamations*, p. 2593. • **50.** Nigel Hamilton, *The Full Monty* (London: Allen Lane, 2001), p. 584. • **51.** Meacham, *Franklin and Winston*, p. 185. • **52.** Smith, *FDR*, p. 568. • **53.** Ibid., p. 567, quoting de Gaulle memoirs. • **54.** Morgan, *FDR*, pp. 656 and 723. • **55.** Mark A. Stoler, *The Politics of the Second Front* (Westport, CT: Greenwood Press, 1977) p. 158. • **56.** Ibid., p. 150. • **57.** Ibid. • **58.** Brands, *Traitor to His Class*, p. 701. • **59.** Bohlen, *Witness to History*, p. 140. • **60.** Frank Freidel, *Franklin Roosevelt: A Rendezvous with Destiny*, p. 481. • **61.** Keith Sainsbury, *The Turning Point*, p. 227. • **62.** Smith, *FDR*, p. 622. • **63.** Ibid., p. 623. • **64.** Ibid., p. 625. • **65.** Ibid., p. 627. • **66.** Frances Perkins, *The Roosevelt I Knew*, p. 393. • **67.** For an excellent historiographical survey of the 'supposed blunders and naïveté of President Franklin D. Roosevelt' theses and their rebuttal, see Mark Stoler, 'World War II', in Robert D. Schulzberger (ed.), *A Companion to American Foreign Relations* (Oxford: Blackwell, 2003), pp. 188–214. • **68.** Smith, *FDR*, p. 629. • **69.** Freidel, *Franklin Roosevelt*, p. 595. • **70.** Smith, *FDR*, p. 632. • **71.** Edward M. Bennett, *Franklin D. Roosevelt and the Search for Victory*, pp. 166. • **72.** Freidel, *Franklin Roosevelt*, p. 597. • **73.** The other two were Frances Dana, granddaughter of H. W. Longfellow, and Dorothy Quincy: Smith, *FDR*, p. 35. • **74.** Ibid., p. 36. • **75.** Joseph E. Persico, *Franklin & Lucy*, p. 60. • **76.** Ibid., p. 93. • **77.** Ibid., p. 124. • **78.** Ibid., p. 130. • **79.** Ibid., p. 131. • **80.** Ibid. • **81.** Ibid., p. 184. • **82.** Smith, *FDR*, p. 150. • **83.** Ibid., p. 207. • **84.** Persico, *Franklin & Lucy*, p. 227. • **85.** Ibid., p. 249. • **86.** Ibid., p. 250. • **87.** Ibid., p. 263. • **88.** Ibid. • **89.** Ibid., p. 264. • **90.** Ibid., p. 315. • **91.** Ibid., p. 316. • **92.** Ibid. • **93.** Ibid., p. 326. • **94.** Ibid., p. 335. • **95.** Ibid., p. 339.

## Chapter Two: Harry Truman

1. David McCullough, *Truman*, p. 41. • 2. Alonzo M. Hamby, *Man of the People*, p. 19. • 3. Ibid., p. 27. • 4. Robert H. Ferrell (ed.), *The Autobiography of Harry S. Truman*, p. 29. • 5. Hamby, *Man of the People*, p. 30. • 6. Robert H. Ferrell (ed.), *Dear Bess: The Letters from Harry to Bess Truman, 1910–1959*, p. 167. • 7. Letter of October 11, 1918, in ibid., p. 275. • 8. Hamby, *Man of the People*, p. 160. • 9. Ibid., p. 191. • 10. Ibid., p. 233. • 11. Ibid., p. 235. • 12. McCullough, *Truman*, p. 251. • 13. Hamby, *Man of the People*, p. 262. • 14. Ibid., p. 254. • 15. Ibid., p. 258. • 16. Letter of October 27, 1939, in Robert H. Ferrell (ed.), *Dear Bess*, p. 426. • 17. Hamby, *Man of the People*, p. 283. • 18. Frank Freidel, *Franklin Roosevelt: Rendezvous with Destiny*, p. 537. • 19. McCullough, *Truman*, p. 327. • 20. Hamby, *Man of the People*, p. 293. • 21. Robert Donovan, *Conflict and Crisis*, p. 15. • 22. Letter of June 6, 1945, in Robert H. Ferrell (ed.), *Dear Bess*, p. 514. • 23. Martin Gilbert, *Winston Churchill* (New York: Holt, 1991), p. 6. • 24. July 7, 1945, in Robert H. Ferrell (ed.), *Off the Record: The Private Papers of Harry S. Truman*, p. 49. • 25. July 16, 1945, in ibid., p. 52. • 26. Ibid., pp. 52–3. • 27. July 17, 1945, in ibid., p. 53. • 28. July 25, 1945, in ibid., p. 56. • 29. July 26, 1945, in ibid., p. 57. • 30. July 30, 1945, in ibid., p. 58. • 31. March 15, 1957, in ibid., p. 348. • 32. March 15, 1957, in ibid., p. 349. • 33. March 15, 1957, in ibid., p. 348. • 34. July 25, 1945, in ibid., p. 56. • 35. McCullough, *Truman*, pp. 440 and 437. • 36. July 25, 1945, in Ferrell (ed.), *Off the Record*, pp. 55–6. • 37. William Rees-Mogg, 'The American empire, a fine old British tradition' (review of Niall Ferguson's UK Channel 4 television series, *Empire*), *The Times*, January 12, 2003. • 38. Harry S. Truman, *Memoirs*, Vol. 2, p. 105. • 39. Ibid., p. 101. • 40. Ibid., p. 106. • 41. Ibid. • 42. John T. Woolley and Gerhard Peters (eds), *The American Presidency Project*, http://www.presidency.ucsb/edu/?pid=12859. • 43. Truman, *Memoirs* Vol. 2, p. 111. • 44. Merle Miller, *Plain Speaking*, p. 245. • 45. Truman, *Memoirs*, Vol. 2, p. 111. • 46. Ferrell (ed.), *Off the Record*, p. 145. • 47. Truman, *Memoirs*, Vol. 2, p. 131. • 48. Robert Fisk, *The Great War for Civilisation* (New York: Knopf, 2005), p. 365. • 49. Robert Donovan, *Conflict and Crisis*, p. 319. • 50. Hamby, *Man of the People*, p. 408. • 51. Donovan, *Conflict and Crisis*, p. 319. • 52. Hamby, *Man of the People*, p. 405. • 53. Dean Acheson, *Present at the Creation: My Years in the State Department*, p. 175. • 54. Donovan, *Conflict and Crisis*, p. 382. • 55. Miller, *Plain Speaking*,

p. 216. • **56**. Donovan, *Conflict and Crisis*, p. 413. • **57**. Ibid., p. 423. • **58**. Ibid., p. 413. • **59**. Miller, *Plain Speaking*, p. 291. • **60**. Ibid., p. 292. • **61**. Forrest C. Pogue, *George C. Marshall: Statesman 1945–1959*, p. 47. • **62**. Donovan, *Conflict and Crisis*, pp. 286–7. • **63**. Geoffrey Perret, *Commander in Chief*, p. 169. • **64**. Arnold A. Offner, *Another Such Victory*, p. 398. • **65**. Robert Donovan, *Tumultuous Years*, p. 314. • **66**. Miller, *Plain Speaking*, p. 305. • **67**. Donovan, *Conflict and Crisis*, p. 294. • **68**. Miller, *Plain Speaking*, p. 366. • **69**. McCullough, *Truman*, p. 813. • **70**. Hamby, *Man of the People*, p. 429. • **71**. Rovere, *Senator Joe McCarthy*, pp. 123–4. • **72**. John Hersey, 'Truman Would Answer With Truth', *St Petersburg Times*, August 6, 1973. • **73**. John Hersey, *Aspects of the Presidency* (New Haven: Ticknor and Fields, 1980), p. 138. • **74**. Clark Clifford, *Counsel to the President*, p. 290. • **75**. Ibid., pp. 290–1. • **76**. Joseph Goulden, *The Best years: 1945–1950*, p. 427. • **77**. Acheson, *Present at the Creation*, p. 366. • **78**. Ibid., p. 369. • **79**. Clifford, *Counsel to the President*, p. 290. • **80**. Ferrell (ed.), *Off the record*, p. 178. • **81**. Margaret Truman, *Harry S. Truman*, pp. 551–2. • **82**. Letter of December 28, 1945, in Monte M. Poen (ed.), *Strictly Personal and Confidential*, p. 173. • **83**. Letter of December 7, 1950, in McCullough, *Truman*, p. 829. • **84**. Roy Jenkins, *Truman*, p. 15. • **85**. Letter of November 10, 1913, in Robert H. Ferrrell (ed.), *Dear Bess*, pp. 140–1. • **86**. Ibid., p. vii. • **87**. McCullough, *Truman*, p. 435. • **88**. Lord Moran, *The Struggle for Survival*, p. 298. • **89**. McCullough, *Truman*, p. 886. • **90**. Hamby, *Man of the People*, p. 473. • **91**. McCullough, *Truman*, p. 435. • **92**. Donovan, *Conflict and Crisis*, p. 148. • **93**. Ibid. p. 147. • **94**. Acheson, *Present at the Creation*, p. v.

*Chapter Three: Dwight Eisenhower*

1. Carlo D'Este, *Eisenhower: A Soldier's Life*, p. 39. • **2**. Ibid., p. 34. • **3**. James C. Humes, *Confessions of a White House Ghostwriter* (Washington DC: Regnery, 1997) p. 39. • **4**. D'Este, *Eisenhower*, p. 222. • **5**. Ibid., p. 224. • **6**. Ibid., p. 229. • **7**. Ibid., p. 235. • **8**. Ibid., p. 315. • **9**. Ibid., p. 375. • **10**. Stephen Ambrose, *Eisenhower: Soldier, General of the Army, President-elect, 1880–1952*, p. 273. • **11**. D'Este, *Eisenhower*, p. 467. • **12**. Piers Brendon, *Ike: His Life and Times*, p. 194. • **13**. Stephen Ambrose, *Eisenhower: Soldier, General of the Army, President-elect*, p. 409. • **14**. Geoffrey Perret, *Eisenhower*, p. 368. • **15**. Ambrose, *Eisenhower: Soldier, General of the Army, President-elect*, p. 441. • **16**. Ibid., p. 523. • **17**. Perret,

*Eisenhower*, p. 391. • **18**. Ambrose, *Eisenhower: Soldier, General of the Army, President-elect*, p. 523. • **19**. Robert Donovan, *Tumultuous Years: The Presidency of Harry S. Truman, 1949–1953*, p. 394. • **20**. Ambrose, *Eisenhower: Soldier, General of the Army, President-elect*, p. 53. • **21**. Ibid., p. 96. • **22**. Conrad Black, *Richard Milhous Nixon*, p. 185. • **23**. Ibid., p. 206–7. • **24**. Perret, *Eisenhower*, p. 426. • **25**. Stephen Ambrose, *Eisenhower: The President*, p. 42. • **26**. Perret, *Eisenhower*, p. 436.' • **27**. Andrew Goodpaster, introduction to Robert R. Bowie and Richard H. Immerman, *Waging Peace: How Eisenhower Shaped an Enduring Cold War Strategy* (New York: Oxford University Press, 1997), p. vi. • **28**. Perret, *Eisenhower*, p. 456. • **29**. Brendon, *Ike*, p. 245. • **30**. Robert H. Ferrell (ed.), *The Eisenhower Diaries*, p. 234. • **31**. Ambrose, *Eisenhower: The President*, p. 55. • **32**. Ibid., p. 167. • **33**. Ibid., p. 60. • **34**. Ibid., p. 162. • **35**. David M. Oshinsky, *A Conspiracy So Immense: The World of Joe McCarthy* (New York: Free Press, 1983), pp. 462–5. • **36**. Perret, *Eisenhower*, p. 504. • **37**. Ambrose, *Eisenhower: The President*, p. 220. • **38**. Ibid., p. 200. • **39**. Ibid., pp. 220–1. • **40**. Ibid., p. 202. • **41**. Ibid. • **42**. Ibid., p. 184. • **43**. Conrad Black, *Nixon: The Invincible Quest*, pp. 323–4. • **44**. See Chester J. Pach, Jr., and Elmo Richardson, *The Presidency of Dwight D. Eisenhower*, pp. 123–4. • **45**. Dwight D. Eisenhower, *Waging Peace*, p. 34. • **46**. Ambrose, *Eisenhower: The President*, p. 332. • **47**. Ibid. • **48**. Ibid., p. 333. • **49**. Ibid., p. 339. • **50**. Ibid., p. 352. • **51**. Ibid. • **52**. Ibid., p. 353. • **53**. Ibid., p. 356. • **54**. Ibid., p. 358. • **55**. Ibid., p. 360. • **56**. Ibid., p. 361. • **57**. Ibid., p. 364. • **58**. Ibid., p. 367. • **59**. Ibid., p. 368. • **60**. Brendon, *Ike*, p. 319. • **61**. Ambrose, *Eisenhower: The President*, p. 406. • **62**. Senator Paul Douglas, in Robert Dallek, *Lone Star Rising: Lyndon Johnson and His Times, 1908–1960*, p. 526. • **63**. Dwight D. Eisenhower, *Waging Peace*, p. 166. • **64**. Ambrose, *Eisenhower: The President*, p. 421. • **65**. Ibid., p. 420. • **66**. Ibid., p. 422. • **67**. Ibid. • **68**. Ibid., p. 440. • **69**. Khrushchev, *Khrushchev Remembers: The Last Testament*, p. 374. • **70**. Ibid., p. 375. • **71**. Ibid., pp. 374–5. • **72**. Dwight D. Eisenhower, *Waging Peace*, p. 440. • **73**. Ambrose, *Eisenhower: The President*, p. 456. • **74**. Dwight D. Eisenhower, *Waging Peace*, p. 440. • **75**. Khrushchev, *Khrushchev Remembers: The Last Testament*, p. 411. • **76**. Ibid., p. 536. • **77**. Ibid., pp. 412–13. • **78**. Oleg Troyanovsky, 'The Making of Soviet Foreign Policy', in William Taubman et al. (eds), *Nikita Khrushchev*, p. 226. • **79**. Ambrose, *Eisenhower: The President*, p. 578. • **80**. Troyanovsky, 'The Making of Soviet Foreign Policy', p. 227. • **81**. Ambrose, *Eisenhower: The President*, p. 579. The Sputnik, which sent back extended telemetry, subsequently malfunctioned and eventually disintegrated on re-entry into the earth's atmosphere two years later; a chunk was supposedly found in a street in Wisconsin. • **82.** In his memoirs Khrushchev claimed he had demanded at the summit an apology from Eisenhower, and a promise that there would be no more U-2 flights, which Eisenhower repudiated, on the advice of Dulles's successor, Christian Herter. This was untrue – in fact Eisenhower assured him 'these flights were suspended after the recent incident and are not to be resumed.' Khrushchev, *Khrushchev Remembers: The Last Testament*, editor's note on p. 455. • **83.** Khrushchev, *Khrushchev Remembers: The Last Testament*, p. 455. • **84.** Ibid., p. 449. • **85.** Ambrose, *Eisenhower: The President*, p. 612. • **86.** Michael R. Beschloss, *May-Day: Eisenhower, Khrushchev and the U2 Affair*, p. 388. • **87.** D'Este, *Eisenhower*, p. 86. • **88.** Ibid., p. 88. • **89.** Ibid., p. 109. • **90.** Ibid., p. 101. • **91.** Ibid. • **92.** Ibid., p. 99. • **93.** Ibid., p. 110. • **94.** Ibid., p. 111. • **95.** Merle Miller, *Plain Speaking*, pp. 339–40. • **96.** Robert H. Ferrell and Francis H. Miller, 'Plain Faking', *American Heritage*, June 1995. • **97.** Ambrose, *Eisenhower: Soldier, General of the Army, President-elect*, p. 417. • **98.** Ambrose, *Eisenhower: The President*, p. 29. • **99.** Brendon, *Ike*, p. 288. • **100.** Samuel Lubell, *Revolt of the Moderates* (New York: Harper and Brothers, 1956), pp. 4–5. • **101.** Poll of seventy-five historians conducted by Arthur M. Schlesinger Sr in 1962, published in William A. DeGregorio, *The Complete Book of US Presidents*. By 1999, however, a C-Span viewer survey had raised Eisenhower to 8th place in American presidential history.

## Chapter Four: John F. Kennedy

**1.** Nigel Hamilton, *JFK: Reckless Youth*, p. 130. • **2.** Ibid., p. 127. • **3.** Ibid., p. 391. • **4.** Ben Bradlee, *Conversations with Kennedy*, p. 33. • **5.** Geoffrey Perret, *Jack: A Life Like No Other*, p. 269. • **6.** Ambrose, *Eisenhower: The President*, p. 604. • **7.** Ibid., p. 606. • **8.** Ibid., p. 583. • **9.** Ibid., p. 608. • **10.** Barry Goldwater, *Goldwater* (New York: Doubleday, 1988), pp. 135–6. • **11.** Perret, *Jack*, p. 309. • **12.** E. B. Potter, *Admiral Arleigh Burke* (New York: Random House, 1990), pp. 437–8. The only formal air attack that President Kennedy finally authorized, to cover Cuban rebel B-26 bombers supporting the invasion force, proved a fiasco – the US naval pilots getting the time-zone in Cuba wrong. • **13.** Richard Reeves,

*President Kennedy: Profile of Power*, p. 101. • **14**. Ibid., p. 106. • **15**. James Reston, *Deadline: A Memoir* (New York: Random House, 1991), p. 290. • **16**. Michael Beschloss, *The Crisis Years: Kennedy and Khrushchev, 1960–1963*, p. 224. • **17**. William Taubman, *Khrushchev: The Man and His Era*, p. 496. • **18**. Ibid., p. 766. • **19**. Beschloss, *The Crisis Years*, p. 234. • **20**. *FRUS, 1961–1963*, Vol. 5 (Washington, DC: US Government Printing Office, 1991), pp. 229–30. • **21**. Taubman, *Khrushchev*, p. 495. • **22**. Ibid., p. 500. • **23**. Beschloss, *The Crisis Years*, p. 234. • **24**. Sergei Khrushchev, *Nikita Khrushchev and the Creation of a Superpower*, trans. Shirley Benson (University Park: The Pennsylvania State University Press, 2000), p. 436, and Taubman, *Khrushchev*, p. 493. • **25**. Taubman, *Khrushchev*, p. 766. • **26**. Richard Reeves, *President Kennedy: Profile of Power*, pp. 361–2. • **27**. 'Radio and Television Report to the Nation on the Situation at the University of Mississippi', September 30, 1962, www.jfklibrary.org/Historical+Resources/Archives. • **28**. Herbert Parmet, *JFK: The Presidency of John F. Kennedy*, p. 262. • **29**. Reeves, *President Kennedy*, p. 362. • **30**. Taubman, *Khrushchev*, p. 541. • **31**. Aleksandr Fursenko and Timothy Naftali, *Khrushchev's Cold War* (New York: Norton, 2006), p. 459. • **32**. Reeves, *President Kennedy: Profile of Power*, p. 370. • **33**. Robert, Dallek, *An Unfinished Life: John F. Kennedy 1917–1963*, p. 544. • **34**. Taubman, *Khrushchev*, p. 551. • **35**. Reeves, *President Kennedy*, p. 370. • **36**. Oleg Troyanovsky, 'The Making of Soviet Foreign Policy', in William Taubman et al. (eds), *Nikita Khrushchev*, p. 234. • **37**. Taubman, *Khrushchev*, p. 559. • **38**. Ibid., p. 551. • **39**. Beschloss, *The Crisis Years*, p. 456. • **40**. Taubman, *Khrushchev*, p. 561. • **41**. Ibid. • **42**. Ibid. • **43**. Beschloss, *The Crisis Years*, p. 498. • **44**. Taubman, *Khrushchev*, p. 581. • **45**. Ibid., p. 578. • **46**. Reeves, *President Kennedy*, p. 437. • **47**. Ibid., p. 438. • **48**. Ibid., p. 462. • **49**. Ibid., p. 522. • **50**. Ibid., p. 584. • **51**. Ibid., p. 585. • **52**. Ibid., p. 547. • **53**. Ibid., p. 149. • **54**. Dallek, *An Unfinished Life*, p. 666. • **55**. Reeves, *President Kennedy*, p. 309. • **56**. Geoffrey Perret, *Commander in Chief*, p. 188. • **57**. Dallek, *An Unfinished Life*, p. 672. • **58**. Ibid., p. 668. • **59**. Ibid., p. 682. • **60**. Ibid., p. 683. • **61**. Charles Spalding, NH Papers, Massachusetts Historical Society; Perret, *Jack*, p. 393. • **62**. Dallek, *An Unfinished Life*, p. 684. • **63**. Oswald was murdered by a Dallas nightclub operator, Jacob Rubenstein, who had legally changed his name to Jack Ruby. Whether or not Oswald was prompted, or funded, by others to assassinate President Kennedy has never been definitively established. Ruby died of aggressive lung, liver and brain cancer on January 3, 1967, at Parkland Hospital, Dallas, where Oswald had died and President Kennedy had been pronounced dead. In a last statement Ruby declared, 'There is nothing to hide. There was no one else'. ('A Last Wish,' *Time*, December 30, 1966). • **64**. Hamilton, *JFK*, p. 155. • **65**. Ibid., p. 440. • **66**. Ibid., p. 443. Inga, who married Hollywood actor Tim McCoy, lived to see JFK win the presidency, but also his assassination; she herself died of cancer ten years later, in 1973.• **67**. Ibid., p. 547. • **68**. Ibid., p. 617. • **69**. Ibid., p. 637. • **70**. Ibid., pp. 658–61. • **71**. Charles Spalding, interview with the author. • **72**. Laurence Leamer, *The Kennedy Men, 1901–1963*, p. 250. • **73**. Alistair Forbes, interview with the author. • **74**. James Reed, interview with the author. • **75**. James Reed, interview with the author. • **76**. Seymour Hersh, *The Dark Side of Camelot*, p. 22. • **77**. Beschloss, *The Crisis Years*, p. 473. • **78**. Richard N. Goodwin to author. • **79**. *New York Times*, June 3, 1961. • **80**. Gretchen Rubin, *Forty Ways to Look at JFK*, p. 185. • **81**. Ben Bradlee, interview with the author. • **82**. Anna 'Chiquita' Cárcanos, interview with the author. • **83**. Charles Spalding, interview with the author. • **84**. Rubin, *Forty Ways to Look at JFK*, p. 239. • **85**. Ibid. • **86**. Sally B. Smith, *Grace and Power: The Private World of the Kennedy White House*, p. 143. • **87**. Reeves, *President Kennedy*, p. 291. • **88**. Smith, *Grace and Power*, p. 143. • **89**. Hersh, *The Dark Side of Camelot*, p. 19. • **90**. Ibid., p. 18. • **91**. Ibid., p. 442–6; also Paul Corbin to author. • **92**. Rubin, *Forty Ways to Look at JFK*, p. 241. • **93**. Hersh, *The Dark Side of Camelot*, p. 238. • **94**. Perret, *Jack*, p. 397. • **95**. Ibid.

### Chapter Five: Lyndon Johnson

**1**. Robert Caro, *The Years of Lyndon Johnson: The Path to Power* (New York: Knopf), 1982, p. 52. • **2**. Dallek, *Lone Star Rising: Lyndon Johnson and His Times, 1908–1960*, p. 143. • **3**. Robert Caro, *The Years of Lyndon Johnson: The Path to Power*, p. 448. • **4**. Ibid., p. 449. • **5**. Ibid., p. 742. • **6**. Robert Caro, *The Years of Lyndon Johnson: Means of Ascent*, p. 29. • **7**. Robert Dallek, *Lyndon B. Johnson: Portrait of a President*, p. 65. • **8**. Robert Caro, *The Years of Lyndon Johnson: Means of Ascent*, p. 214. Having worn out the Sikorski engine, Johnson then used a smaller, five-foot-long Bell 47-D helicopter, barely powerful enough to lift the candidate and his loudspeaker equipment, for the final weeks: Caro, pp. 247–8. • **9**. Ibid., p. 219. • **10**. Robert Dallek, *An Unfinished Life: John F. Kennedy,*

*1917–1963*, p. 189. • **11**. Ibid. • **12**. Michael Beschloss, *The Crisis Years: Kennedy and Khrushchev, 1960–1963*, p. 513. • **13**. Michael R. Beschloss (ed.), *Taking Charge: The Johnson White House Tapes, 1963–1964*, p. 30. • **14**. Ibid., p. 67. • **15**. *Public Papers of the Presidents: Lyndon B. Johnson, 1963–64*, Book I (Washington, DC: US Government Printing Office, 1965), p. 114. • **16**. Robert Dallek, *Flawed Giant: Lyndon Johnson and His Times, 1961–1973*, p. 63. • **17**. Doris Kearns, *Lyndon Johnson and the American Dream*, p. 178. • **18**. Dallek, *Flawed Giant*, p. 112. • **19**. Ibid., p. 120. • **20**. Ibid., p. 123. • **21**. Beschloss (ed.), *Taking Charge*, p. 388n. • **22**. Ibid. • **23**. Nineteenth-century populist. • **24**. Lyndon Baines Johnson, Tuesday, January 28, 1964, in Beschloss (ed.), *Taking Charge*, p. 190. • **25**. Lyndon Baines Johnson, Saturday, February 8, 1964, in ibid., 231. • **26**. Lyndon Baines Johnson, Saturday, March 7, 1964, in ibid., p. 271. • **27**. Lyndon Baines Johnson, Thursday, June 4, 1964, ibid., p. 382. • **28**. Barry Goldwater, Acceptance Speech, July 16, 1964, http://www.americanrhetoric.com/speeches/barrygoldwater1964rnc.html. • **29**. Lyndon Baines Johnson, Saturday February 8, 1964, in Beschloss (ed.), *Taking Charge*, passim. • **30**. Lyndon Baines Johnson, Thursday June 11, 1964, in ibid., p. 401. • **31**. Lyndon Baines Johnson, Wednesday, May 27, 1964, in ibid., p. 367. • **32**. Lyndon Baines Johnson, Wednesday, May 27, 1964, in ibid., p. 364. • **33**. Lyndon Baines Johnson, Wednesday, May 27, 1964, in ibid., p. 368. • **34**. Lyndon Baines Johnson, Wednesday, May 27, 1964, in ibid., p. 369. • **35**. Lyndon Baines Johnson, Tuesday, August 4, 1964, in ibid., p. 496. • **36**. Lyndon Baines Johnson, Saturday, December 7, 1963, in ibid., p. 95. • **37**. Dallek, *Flawed Giant*, p. 123. • **38**. Ibid. • **39**. Ibid. • **40**. Jack Valenti interview, *American Experience*, Vietnam Online, Transcript, PBS: www.pbs.org/wgbh/amex/vietnam/series/pt_03.html. • **41**. Lyndon Baines Johnson, *Vantage Point: Perspectives on the Presidency, 1963–1969*, p. 125. • **42**. David Kaiser, *American Tragedy: Kennedy, Johnson, and the Origins of the Vietnam War*, p. 398. • **43**. Frank E. Vandiver, *Shadows of Vietnam: Lyndon Johnson's Wars*, p. 30. • **44**. http://www.hawaii.edu/powerkills/SOD.TAB6.1A. • **45**. http://www.pbs.org/battlefieldvietnam/timeline/index2.html. • **46**. Dallek, *Flawed Giant*, p. 255. • **47**. Ibid., p. 249. • **48**. Brian VanDeMark, *Into the Quagmire: Lyndon Johnson and the Escalation of the Vietnam War*, p. 123. • **49**. Dallek, *Flawed Giant*, p. 361. • **50**. George C. Herring, *LBJ and Vietnam: A Different Kind of War*, p. 19. • **51**. Dallek, *Flawed Giant*, p. 427. • **52**. Ibid. • **53**. Ibid., p. 429. • **54**. Ibid., p. 430. • **55**.

'Chinese Checkers', *Time*, January 31, 1964. • **56**. Dallek, *Flawed Giant*, p. 494. • **57**. Clark Clifford, *Counsel to the President*, p. 485. • **58**. Dallek, *Flawed Giant*, p. 500. • **59**. Clark Clifford, *Counsel to the President*, p. 495. • **60**. Ibid., p. 518. • **61**. Sam Houston Johnson, *My Brother Lyndon*, p. 4. • **62**. George Reedy, *Lyndon B. Johnson: A Memoir*, 1982, p. 150. • **63**. Randall B. Woods, *LBJ: Architect of American Ambition*, p. 834. • **64**. Lloyd C. Gardner, *Pay Any Price: Lyndon Johnson and the Wars for Vietnam*, p. 463. • **65**. George Christian, in Dallek, *Flawed Giant*, p. 573. • **66**. Dallek, *Flawed Giant*, p. 573. • **67**. Ibid., p. 580. • **68**. Ibid. • **69**. Ibid., p. 583. • **70**. Ibid. • **71**. Ibid. • **72**. Ibid., p. 584. • **73**. Ibid., p. 591. • **74**. Ibid., p. 588. • **75**. Ibid., p. 590. • **76**. Ibid., p. 586. • **77**. Woods, *LBJ*, p. 290. • **78**. Caro, *The Years of Lyndon Johnson: The Path to Power*, p. 173. • **79**. Ibid., p. 162. • **80**. Sam Houston Johnson, *My Brother Lyndon*, p. 29 and Doris Kearns, *Lyndon Johnson and the American Dream*, p. 57. • **81**. Woods, *LBJ*, p. 80. • **82**. Caro, *The Years of Lyndon Johnson: The Path to Power*, p. 299. • **83**. Ibid. • **84**. Ibid. • **85**. Ibid., p. 300. • **86**. Ibid., p. 301. • **87**. Ibid., p. 302. • **88**. Ibid., p. 303. • **89**. Woods, *LBJ*, p. 105. • **90**. Ibid., p. 640. • **91**. Ibid., p. 132. • **92**. Ibid., p. 205. • **93**. Ibid., p. 290. • **94**. Dallek, *Lone Star Rising*, p. 189. • **95**. Ibid., p. 191. • **96**. Ibid. • **97**. Woods, *LBJ*, p. 247. • **98**. Ibid., p. 288. • **99**. Ibid., p. 481. • **100**. Ibid., p. 288. • **101**. Dallek, *Lone Star Rising*, p. 537. • **102**. Ibid., p. 189. • **103**. Ibid. • **104**. Eric F. Goldman, *The Tragedy of Lyndon Johnson*, p. 531. • **105**. Thomas Alan Schwartz, *Lyndon Johnson and Europe*, p. 237.

## Chapter Six: Richard Nixon

**1**. Herbert Parmet, *Richard Nixon and His America*, p. 58. • **2**. Ibid., p. 113. • **3**. Ibid., p. 90. • **4**. Ibid., p.104. • **5**. Ibid., p. 94. • **6**. Ibid., p. 133. • **7**. Ibid., p. 141. • **8**. Ibid., p. 107. • **9**. Conrad Black, *Richard Milhous Nixon: The Invincible Quest*, p. 159. • **10**. Ibid., p. 149. • **11**. Parmet, *Richard Nixon and His America*, p. 182. • **12**. Black, *Richard Milhous Nixon*, p. 162. • **13**. Ibid., p. 149. • **14**. Ibid., p. 157. • **15**. Stephen Ambrose, *Nixon: The Education of a Politician, 1913–1962*, p. 282. • **16**. Black, *Richard Milhous Nixon*, p. 229. • **17**. Richard Nixon, *Six Crises*, p. 110. • **18**. Black, *Richard Milhous Nixon*, p. 248. • **19**. Quoted in ibid., p. 249. • **20**. Anthony Summers, *Arrogance of Power: The Secret World of Richard Nixon*, p. 225. • **21**. Ibid., p. 226. • **22**. Jonathan Aitken, *Nixon: A Life*, p. 305. • **23**. Ibid., p. 306. • **24**. Ibid., p. 323. • **25**. Ibid., p. 357. • **26**. Robert Dallek, *Nixon and*

*Kissinger: Partners in Power*, p. 91. • **27**. Ibid., p. 92. • **28**. Stephen Ambrose, *Nixon: The Triumph of a Politician*, p. 66. • **29**. Dallek, *Nixon and Kissinger*, p. 104. • **30**. Ibid., p. 107. • **31**. Richard Reeves, *President Nixon: Alone in the White House*, p. 33. • **32**. Ambrose, *Nixon: The Triumph of a Politician*, p. 309. • **33**. Dallek, *Nixon and Kissinger*, p. 107. • **34**. Ibid., p. 154–5. • **35**. Ambrose, *Nixon: The Triumph of a Politician*, p. 309. • **36**. Taylor Owen and Ben Kiernan, 'Bombs over Cambodia: New Light on US Air War', *The Walrus* (Canada), October 2006. • **37**. 'The problem is, Mr. President, the Air Force is designed to fight an air battle against the Soviet Union. They are not designed for this war . . . in fact, they are not designed for any war we are likely to have to fight.' Owen and Kiernan, 'Bombs over Cambodia'. • **38**. December 9, 1970. The Kissinger Telcons, National Security Archive, Washington, DC, accessed May 29, 2004 www.gwu.edu/~nsarchiv/NSAEBB/NSAEBB123/. Owen and Kiernan, 'Bombs over Cambodia'. • **39**. Ambrose, *Nixon: The Triumph of a Politician*, p. 285. • **40**. November 1971, in David Reynolds, *One World Divisible: A Global History Since 1945* (New York: Norton, 2001), p. 350. • **41**. Dallek, *Nixon and Kissinger*, p. 144. • **42**. Ibid., p. 91. • **43**. Ibid. • **44**. Reeves, *President Nixon*, p. 64. • **45**. Dallek, *Nixon and Kissinger*, p. 280. • **46**. Ibid. • **47**. Ibid., p. 288. • **48**. Ambrose, *Nixon: The Triumph of a Politician*, p. 516. • **49**. Ibid., p. 459. • **50**. Reeves, *President Nixon*, p. 363. • **51**. Nixon tapes, May 4, 1972, quoted in Daniel Ellsberg, *Secrets: A Memoir of Vietnam and the Pentagon Papers*, p. 419. • **52**. Arthur M. Schlesinger Jr, *The Imperial Presidency*. • **53**. Reeves, *President Nixon*, p. 368. • **54**. Ibid., p. 411. • **55**. Ibid., p. 506. • **56**. Ibid., p. 507. • **57**. Dallek, *Nixon and Kissinger*, p. 446. • **58**. Ibid., p. 455. • **59**. Ibid., p. 487. • **60**. Ibid., p. 539. • **61**. Reeves, *President Nixon*, p. 578. • **62**. Ibid. • **63**. Ibid. • **64**. Ibid., p. 590. • **65**. Dallek, *Nixon and Kissinger*, p. 512. • **66**. Ibid., p. 521. • **67**. Reeves, *President Nixon*, p. 604. • **68**. Jussi Hahnimaki, *The Flawed Architect: Henry Kissinger and American Foreign Policy*, p. 303. • **69**. Ibid. • **70**. Dallek, *Nixon and Kissinger*, p. 545. • **71**. Ibid. • **72**. Ibid., p. 546. • **73**. Ibid., p. 547. • **74**. Ibid., p. 556. • **75**. Ibid., p. 600. • **76**. Ibid., p. 601. • **77**. Ibid., p. 604. • **78**. Aitken, *Nixon*, p. 14. • **79**. Ibid., p. 29. • **80**. Ibid., p. 13. • **81**. Ibid. • **82**. Ibid., p. 14. • **83**. Ibid., p. 29. • **84**. Roger Morris, *Richard Milhous Nixon: The Rise of an American Politician*, p. 126. • **85**. Aitken, *Nixon*, p. 61. • **86**. Black, *Richard Milhous Nixon*, p. 31. • **87**. Aitken, *Nixon*, p. 61. • **88**. Ibid., p. 63. • **89**. Ibid. • **90**. Ibid., p. 64. • **91**. Summers, *Arrogance of Power*, p. 92. • **92**. Aitken, *Nixon*, p. 86.

• **93**. Ambrose, *Nixon: The Education of a Politician*, p. 350. • **94**. Summers, *Arrogance of Power*, p. 4. • **95**. Ibid., p. 40. • **96**. Stephen Ambrose, *Nixon: The Triumph of a Politician*, p. 111. • **97**. Summers, *Arrogance of Power*, p. 40. • **98**. Ibid., p. 88–99. • **99**. Ambrose, *Nixon: The Education of a Politician*, p. 244. • **100**. Summers, *Arrogance of Power*, p. 3. • **101**. Ibid., p. 2. • **102**. Ellsberg, *Secrets*, p. 419. • **103**. Ibid., p. 418. • **104**. William Taubman, *Khrushchev: The Man and His Era*, p. 620. • **105**. Ellsberg, *Secrets*, p. 418. • **106**. Dallek, *Nixon and Kissinger*, p. 609.

## Chapter Seven: Gerald Ford

**1**. Ford's University of Michigan transcript showed he earned 74 hours of Bs, 28 hours of Cs, 14 hours of As, and 4 hours of Ds. Domestic Intelligence Report on Gerald Ford, né Lynch, Office of Naval Intelligence file, January 10, 1942, Ford Library, Michigan. • **2**. Gerald R. Ford, Personal Files, Ford Library, Michigan. • **3**. Douglas Brinkley, *Gerald R. Ford*, p. 26. • **4**. Thomas DeFrank, *Write It When I'm Gone: Remarkable Off-the-Record Conversations with Gerald R. Ford*, p. 103. • **5**. Brinkley, *Gerald R. Ford*, p. 36. • **6**. Alexander Hamilton's Federalist Papers No 74, published under the pseudonym Publius, in 1788. The essay argued, 'But the principal argument for reposing the power of pardoning in this case to the Chief Magistrate is this: in seasons of insurrection or rebellion, there are often critical moments, when a well-timed offer of pardon to the insurgents or rebels may restore the tranquillity of the commonwealth; and which, if suffered to pass unimproved, it may never be possible afterwards to recall. The dilatory process of convening the legislature, or one of its branches, for the purpose of obtaining its sanction to the measure, would frequently be the occasion of letting slip the golden opportunity. The loss of a week, a day, an hour, may sometimes be fatal.' As president, Nixon could not conceivably be seen as an insurgent, however. • **7**. Cannon, *Time and Chance*, p. 299. • **8**. Ibid., p. 308. • **9**. Ibid. • **10**. Ibid., p. 310. • **11**. Brinkley, *Gerald R. Ford*, p. 59. • **12**. Cannon, *Time and Chance: Gerald Ford's Appointment with History*, p. 316. • **13**. Ibid. • **14**. Ibid. • **15**. Ibid. • **16**. Ibid., p. 330. • **17**. Ibid., p. 333. • **18**. Ibid. • **19**. Ibid., p. 338. • **20**. Ibid. • **21**. Audiotaped diary entry, August 8, 1976, John W. (Bill) Roberts Papers, Ford Library, Michigan. • **22**. Audiotaped diary entry, August 11, 1976, ibid. • **23**. Memorandum, September 9, 1974, Benton

L. Becker Papers, Ford Library, Michigan. • **24**. Audiotaped diary entry, August 18, 1976, John W. (Bill) Roberts Papers, Ford Library, Michigan. • **25**. Ibid. • **26**. Bunny Buchan (wife of Philip Buchan, Counsel to the President), 'Diary' Notes, August 28, 1976, Ford Library, Michigan. • **27**. Cannon, *Time and Chance*, p. 373. • **28**. Barry Werth, 31 *Days: The Crisis That Gave Us the Government We Have Today*, p. 294. • **29**. Benton L. Becker Memorandum, September 9, 1974, Benton L. Becker Papers, Ford Library, Michigan. • **30**. Ibid. • **31**. Ibid. • **32**. Jonathan Aitken, *Nixon: A Life*, p. 531. • **33**. Benton L. Becker Memorandum, September 9, 1974, Benton L. Becker Papers, Ford Library, Michigan. • **34**. John Robert Greene, *The Presidency of Gerald R. Ford*, p. 42; Alexander M. Haig Jr, *Inner Circles: How America Changed the World*, (New York: Grand Central Publishing, 1992), p. 513. • **35**. Cannon, *Time and Chance*, p. 381. • **36**. Ibid., p. 383. • **37**. Ibid. • **38**. Brinkley, *Gerald R. Ford*, p. 81. • **39**. Audiotaped diary entry, September 8, 1976, John W. (Bill) Roberts Papers, Ford Library, Michigan. • **40**. Bunny Buchan, 'Diary' Notes, October 12, 1976, Ford Library, Michigan. • **41**. DeFrank, *Write It When I'm Gone*, p. 46. • **42**. Cannon, *Time and Chance*, p. 385. • **43**. *Washington Post* and *New York Times*, September 9, 1974. • **44**. Cannon, *Time and Chance*, p. 391. • **45**. Brinkley, *Gerald R. Ford*, p. 67. • **46**. Karen M. Hult and Charles E. Walcott, *Empowering the White House: Governance under Nixon, Ford, and Carter* (Lawrence: University Press of Kansas, 2004), p. 37. • **47**. Shirley Ann Warshaw, *Powersharing: White House-Cabinet Relations in the Modern Presidency* (Albany, NY: State University of New York Press, 1996), p. 67. • **48**. Yanek Mieczkowski, *Gerald Ford, and the Challenges of the 1970s*, p. 140. • **49**. Ibid. • **50**. Ibid., p. 148. • **51**. Ibid., p. 146. • **52**. DeFrank, *Write It When I'm Gone*, p. 46. • **53**. Mieczkowski, *Gerald Ford*, p. 290. • **54**. Ibid. • **55**. Greene, *The Presidency of Gerald R. Ford*, p. 137. • **56**. Ibid. • **57**. Brinkley, *Gerald R. Ford*, p. 91. • **58**. Mieczkowski, *Gerald Ford*, p. 289. • **59**. Greene, *The Presidency of Gerald R. Ford*, p. 141. • **60**. Ibid., p. 150. • **61**. The USS *Pueblo*, an American spy ship, had been boarded in international waters and taken into custody by North Korea in 1968; it had taken ten long months and a torture-induced confession of guilt by its captain to get back its 82-man naval crew – by which time the 1968 election was lost by Hubert Humphrey, the Democratic presidential nominee. • **62**. Greene, *The Presidency of Gerald R. Ford*, p. 151. Although a major conflagration was avoided, the incident was not without tragedy. Just as the *Mayanguez* crew were released, an abortive US helicopter-lifted attack on the island of Koh Tang was launched. Heavily defended against the North Vietnamese, who disputed its ownership, the Cambodians beat off the misguided assault, which resulted in the loss of 41 American lives. • **63**. Yves Berthelot, *Unity and Diversity in Development Ideas: Perspectives from the UN* (Bloomington: Indiana University Press, 2004). • **64**. Wesley Clark, 'Broken Engagement: The strategy that won the Cold War could help bring democracy to the Middle East – if only the Bush hawks understood it', *Washington Monthly*, May 2004 issue. • **65**. John Lewis Gaddis, *The Cold War: A New History* (New York: Penguin Press, 2005), p. 205. • **66**. Mieczkowski, *Gerald Ford*, p. 298. • **67**. Gerald R. Ford, *A Time to Heal*, p. 297. • **68**. Ibid., p. 300. • **69**. Ibid. • **70**. Ibid. • **71**. Ibid. • **72**. Barbara Frum, interview with Sandra Good, CBC Radio, September 10, 1975. • **73**. Eileen Keerdoja, 'Squeaky and Sara Jane', *Newsweek*, November 8, 1976. • **74**. Tom Matthews et al., 'Ford's Brush with Death', *Newsweek*, September 15, 1975. • **75**. 'Those gunslinging ladies of California', *The Economist*, September 27, 1975. • **76**. 'Trials: Life for Sara Jane', *Newsweek*, December 29, 1975. Moore was finally released in 2007, at age 77, having renounced her earlier views. • **77**. Ford, *A Time to Heal*, p. 238. • **78**. Ibid. • **79**. Greene, *The Presidency of Gerald R. Ford*, p. 128. • **80**. Ford, *A Time to Heal*, p. 240. • **81**. Ibid. • **82**. Avi Shlaim, *The Iron Wall: Israel and the Arab World* (New York: Norton, 2001), p. 339–40. See also Kenneth W. Stein, *Heroic Diplomacy: Sadat, Kissinger, Carter, Begin and the Quest for Arab-Israeli Peace* (New York: Routledge, 1999), pp. 178–81. • **83**. Mieczkowski, *Gerald Ford*, p. 311. • **84**. DeFrank, *Write It When I'm Gone*, p. 93. • **85**. Cannon, *Time and Chance*, p. 407. • **86**. Ibid. • **87**. Ford, *A Time to Heal*, p. 322. • **88**. Ibid. • **89**. Mieczkowski, *Gerald Ford*, p. 312. • **90**. Ibid., p. 315. • **91**. From the spring of 1975 Cheney explored ways to increase presidential power, avoid Congressional oversight, and hobble the investigatory role of the Fourth Estate in democracy, especially the *New York Times* itself, whose star reporter, Seymour Hersh, had aroused his ire. Cheney's notes, revealed thirty years later, posited an 'FBI investigation of the *Times*', a 'Grand Jury indictment of Hersh and the *Times*', and 'a search warrant to "go after Hersh papers in his ap[artmen]t"'. Lowell Bergman and Marlena Telvick, 'Dick Cheney's Memos from 30 Years Ago' (5/28/75, in Gerald R. Ford Library. http://www.pbs.org/wgbh/pages/frontline/newswar/preview/

documents.html, accessed April 1, 2008). • **92**. Mieczkowski, *Gerald Ford*, p. 161. • **93**. Ibid., p. 318. • **94**. Ibid., p. 316. • **95**. Ibid., p. 323. • **96**. Greene, *The Presidency of Gerald R. Ford*, p. 177. • **97**. In ballots cast, Carter won by 40.83 million to Ford's 39.14 million votes. • **98**. Air Force One and Angel are used when the President is aboard the aircraft. Air Force 2600 is used at all other times. • **99**. DeFrank, *Write It When I'm Gone*, p. 62. • **100**. In total, Ford served 896 days, until Carter's inauguration. Nineteenth-century presidents William Harrison, Zachary Taylor and James Garfield all died (or were assassinated) in office, having served shorter terms. • **101**. Ford, *A Time to Heal*, p. 46. • **102**. Ibid., p. 43. • **103**. Ibid., p. 44. • **104**. Ibid., p. 55. • **105**. Ibid., p. 63. • **106**. Ibid., p. 55. • **107**. Ibid. • **108**. DeFrank, *Write It When I'm Gone*, p. 181. • **109**. Ford, *A Time to Heal*, p. 52. • **110**. Jane Howard, 'The 38th First Lady: Not a Robot at All', *New York Times*, December 8, 1974. • **111**. Betty Ford, *Betty: A Glad Awakening* (New York: Doubleday, 1987), p. 30. • **112**. Ibid. • **113**. Ibid., p. 32. • **114**. Howard, 'The 38th First Lady'. • **115**. Sandra Salmans and Thomas DeFrank, 'A Family Affair', *Newsweek*, August 25, 1975. • **116**. CBS, January 7, 2007. • **117**. Salmans and DeFrank, 'A Family Affair'. • **118**. Howard, 'The 38th First Lady': • **119**. Salmans and DeFrank, 'A Family Affair'. • **120**. DeFrank, *Write It When I'm Gone*, pp. 181–2.

## Chapter Eight: Jimmy Carter

**1**. Jimmy Carter, *An Hour Before Daylight*, p. 26. • **2**. Ibid., p. 121. • **3**. Ibid., p. 71. • **4**. Bruce Mazlish and Erwin Diamond, *Jimmy Carter: A Character Portrait*, p. 101. • **5**. Mazlish and Diamond, *Jimmy Carter*, p. 100. • **6**. Carter, *An Hour Before Daylight*, p. 75. • **7**. Ibid., p. 259. • **8**. Ibid. • **9**. Peter G. Bourne, *Jimmy Carter: A Comprehensive Biography from Plains to Postpresidency*, p. 81. • **10**. Bourne, *Jimmy Carter*, p. 86. • **11**. Mazlish and Diamond, *Jimmy Carter*, p. 100; Carter, *An Hour Before Daylight*, p. 118. • **12**. Bourne, *Jimmy Carter*, p. 82. • **13**. Ibid., p. 81. • **14**. Ibid., p. 123. • **15**. Ibid., p. 131. • **16**. Mazlish and Diamond, *Jimmy Carter*, p. 181. • **17**. Ibid., p. 193. • **18**. Kandy Stroud, *How Jimmy Won: The Victory Campaign from Plains to the White House*, p. 16. • **19**. Ibid. • **20**. Bourne, *Jimmy Carter*, p. 250. • **21**. Stroud, *How Jimmy Won*, p. 21. • **22**. Peter Meyer, *James Earl Carter: The Man and the Myth*, p. 3. • **23**. Bourne, *Jimmy Carter*, p. 347. • **24**. The final tally was 297 electoral votes to President Ford's 241. In the popular vote, Carter won 40.2 to 38.5 million. • **25**. Bourne, *Jimmy Carter*, p. 366. • **26**. Kenneth E. Morris, *Jimmy Carter: American Moralist*, p. 243. • **27**. Ibid. • **28**. Bourne, *Jimmy Carter*, p. 361. • **29**. Ibid. • **30**. Morris, *Jimmy Carter*, p. 244. • **31**. Bourne, *Jimmy Carter*, p. 360. • **32**. Burton I. Kaufman, *James Earl Carter, Jr.*, p. 22. • **33**. Jimmy Carter, *Keeping Faith: Memoirs of a President*, p. 91. • **34**. Ibid., p. 97. • **35**. Ibid., p. 135. • **36**. Meyer, *James Earl Carter*, p. 196. • **37**. Victor Lasky, *Jimmy Carter: The Man and the Myth*, p. 11. • **38**. James Schlesinger, Miller Center Oral History, July 1984, courtesy of Carter Library, Atlanta, Georgia. • **39**. Lasky, *Jimmy Carter*, p. 14. • **40**. James Schlesinger, Miller Center Oral History, July 1984. • **41**. Meyer, *James Earl Carter*, p. 4. • **42**. Robert A. Strong, *Working in the World: Jimmy Carter and the Making of American Foreign Policy*, p. 178. • **43**. Carter, *Keeping Faith*, p. 275. • **44**. Ibid., p. 315. • **45**. http://en.wikipedia.org/wiki/1947_UN_Partition_Plan#cite_note-5. • **46**. http://www.donteverstop.com/files/apn/upl/assets/pressconf 191005.ppt#256,3,Slide 3. • **47**. Bourne, *Jimmy Carter*, p. 411. • **48**. Carter, *Palestine Peace Not Apartheid*, p. 52. • **49**. Bourne, *Jimmy Carter*, p. 411. • **50**. Carter, *Palestine Peace Not Apartheid*, p. 52. • **51**. Bourne, *Jimmy Carter*, p. 441. • **52**. Ibid., p. 443. • **53**. Thirteen were released in November 1979, and one more in July 1980, leaving fifty-two. • **54**. Bourne, *Jimmy Carter*, p. 455. • **55**. Ibid., p. 460. • **56**. Ibid. • **57**. National Security Archives interview with Zbigniew Brzezinski, http://www.gwu.edu/ ~nsarchiv/coldwar/interviews/episode-17/brzezinski1.html. • **58**. Vincent Jauvert, 'Oui, la CIA est entrée en Afghanistan avant les Russes . . .' (interview with Zbigniew Brzezinski), *Le Nouvel Observateur*, January 15, 1998. • **59**. Ibid. • **60**. National Security Archives interview with Zbigniew Brzezinski. • **61**. Bourne, *Jimmy Carter*, p. 458. • **62**. National Security Archives interview with Zbigniew Brzezinski. • **63**. Ibid. • **64**. Bourne, *Jimmy Carter*, p. 459. • **65**. Ibid. • **66**. Ibid., p. 461. • **67**. Ibid., p. 462. • **68**. Ibid., p. 428. • **69**. Hamilton Jordan, *Crisis: The Last Year of the Carter Presidency*, p. 357. • **70**. Ibid., p. 358. • **71**. Ibid., p. 361. • **72**. Ibid., p. 362. • **73**. Mazlish and Diamond, *Jimmy Carter*, p. 104. • **74**. Kandy Stroud, *How Jimmy Won*, p. 47. • **75**. Bourne, *Jimmy Carter*, p. 428. • **76**. William Safire, 'On Language', *New York Times*, May 7, 2000. • **77**. Jimmy Carter and Rosalynn Carter, *Everything to Gain: Making the Most of the Rest of Your Life* (New York: Random House, 1987), p. 9. • **78**. Morris, *Jimmy Carter*, p. 293. • **79**. Dr. M. S. Swaminathan, agriculture scientist known as 'Father of the Green Revolution in India', Peter G. Bourne, *Jimmy Carter*, p. 490.

## Chapter Nine: Ronald Reagan

1. Ronald Reagan, *An American Life*, p. 21. • 2. Ibid. • 3. Ibid., p. 35. • 4. Bob Colacello, *Ronnie and Nancy: Their Path to the White House – 1911–1980*, p. 70. • 5. Ibid., p. 118. • 6. Ibid., p. 176. • 7. Ibid., p. 171. • 8. Ibid., p. 252. • 9. Ibid., p. 279. • 10. Ibid., p. 316. • 11. Ibid. • 12. Edmund Morris, *Dutch: A Memoir of Ronald Reagan*, p. 321. • 13. 'Flying Scared', *Time*, November 8, 1968. • 14. Morris, *Dutch*, p. 348. • 15. Ibid., p. 351. • 16. Ibid., p. 349. • 17. Ibid., p. 375. • 18. Edmund G. Brown, *Reagan and Reality: The Two Californias*, p. 32. • 19. Martin Anderson, *Revolution*, pp. 289–90. • 20. Colacello, *Ronnie and Nancy*, p. 492. • 21. Michael Deaver, with Mickey Herkovitz, *Behind the Scenes*, p. 96. • 22. Colacello, *Ronnie and Nancy*, p. 505. • 23. Richard Reeves, *President Reagan*, p. 34. • 24. Ibid., p. 40. • 25. Ibid., p. 42. • 26. Ibid., p. 38. • 27. Ibid., p. 35. • 28. Ibid., p. 36. • 29. Morris, *Dutch*, p. 451. • 30. Reeves, *President Reagan*, p. 45; *Washington Post*, April 1, 1981. • 31. Reeves, *President Reagan*, p. 71. • 32. Ibid., p.60. • 33. Ibid., p. 62. • 34. Ibid., p. 75. • 35. Ibid., p. 78. • 36. Ibid., p. 104. • 37. Since the early 1960s Reagan had declared in speeches that the way to force the Russians to 'recognize' the superiority of the western 'way of life' over Soviet communism was to 'let their economy come unhinged so that the contrast is apparent'. Paul Kengor, *The Crusader: Ronald Reagan and the fall of Communism*, p. 118. • 38. Ibid., p. 120. • 39. Friday, March 26, 1982, in Ronald Reagan, *The Reagan Diaries*, ed. Douglas Brinkley, p. 75. • 40. Reeves, *President Reagan*, p. 105. • 41. Ibid., p. 102 and 105. • 42. Ibid., p. 109. • 43. Ibid., pp. 108–9. • 44. Ibid., p. 110. • 45. Ibid. • 46. Ibid., p. 143. • 47. Wednesday, March 23, 1983, in Reagan, *The Reagan Diaries*, p. 140. • 48. Reeves, *President Reagan*, p. 146. • 49. Ibid. • 50. John Patrick Diggins, *Ronald Reagan: Fate, Freedom, and the Making of History*, p. 348. • 51. Reeves, *President Reagan*, p. 205. • 52. Ibid. • 53. Ibid., p. 228. • 54. Ibid., p. 258. • 55. Ibid., p. 310. • 56. Reagan, *The Reagan Diaries*. • 57. Reeves, *President Reagan*, p. 69. • 58. Ibid.; Reagan, *The Reagan Diaries*, p. 25. • 59. Morris, *Dutch*, p. 462. • 60. Reeves, *President Reagan*, p. 114. • 61. Monday, June 21, in Reagan, *The Reagan Diaries*, p. 90. • 62. Reeves, *President Reagan*, p. 123. • 63. Ibid. • 64. Reagan, *The Reagan Diaries*, p. 98. • 65. Ibid. • 66. Reeves, *President*

*Reagan*, p. 124. • **67**. Ibid., p. 127. • **68**. The Marines were evacuated in February 1984, five months after the Beirut truck bombing. • **69**. Reeves, *President Reagan*, p. 183. • **70**. Ibid., p. 191. • **71**. Ibid., p. 234. • **72**. Ibid., p. 266. • **73**. From 'High Flight', a poem by Pilot Officer John Gillespie Magee Jr, who died on December 11, 1941, over Lincolnshire, England. Reagan's planned State of the Union address to Congress was delivered a week later. • **74**. Paul Kengor, *The Crusader*, p. 236. • **75**. Ibid., p. 234. • **76**. December 17, 1984, in Reagan, *The Reagan Diaries*, p. 287. • **77**. November 5, 1985, ibid. • **78**. Mikhail Gorbachev, *Memoirs*, pp. 405–6. • **79**. November 19, 1985, in Reagan, *The Reagan Diaries*. • **80**. November 20, 1985, ibid. • **81**. Reeves, *President Reagan*, p. 285. • **82**. CIA Study, State Department Intelligence and Research Report, and National Intelligence Estimate, in Reeves, *President Reagan*, p. 283. • **83**. Reeves, *President Reagan*, p. 286. • **84**. Gorbachev, *Memoirs*, p. 191. • **85**. Reeves, *President Reagan*, p. 285. • **86**. Ibid., p. 345. • **87**. Ibid., p. 433. • **88**. Ibid., p. 401. • **89**. Gorbachev, *Memoirs*, p. 452. • **90**. Reeves, *President Reagan*, p. 467. • **91**. Ibid., p. 475. • **92**. Ibid. • **93**. National Security Planning Group Minutes, 'Subject: Central America', SECRET, June 25, 1984, National Security Archive, George Washington University. • **94**. Robert McFarlane, Iran-Contra Hearings, May 14, 1987, in Holly Sklar, *Washington's War on Nicaragua* (Cambridge, MA: South End Press, 1988), p. 251. • **95**. Reagan, *The Reagan Diaries*, p. 374. • **96**. William E. Pemberton, *Exit with Honor: The Life and Presidency of Ronald Reagan*, p. 175. • **97**. Diggins, *Ronald Reagan*, p. 295. • **98**. Sklar, *Washington's War on Nicaragua*, p. 393; Lou Cannon, *President Reagan: Role of a Lifetime*, p. 309. • **99**. Reeves, *President Reagan*, p. 431. • **100**. The son was Arturo Cruz Jr: see Keith Schneider, 'Fawn Hall Steps into the Limelight', *New York Times*, February 26, 1987. • **101**. Reeves, *President Reagan*, p. 400. • **102**. Ibid., p. 408. • **103**. Ibid., p. 461. • **104**. Ibid., p. 486. • **105**. Cannon, *President Reagan*, p. 17. • **106**. Diggins, *Ronald Reagan*, p. 63. • **107**. Morris, *Dutch*, p. xi. • **108**. Ibid., p. 696. • **109**. Tom Vallance, 'Jane Wyman' (obituary), *The Independent* (London), September 11, 2007. • **110**. Colacello, *Ronnie and Nancy*, p. 106. • **111**. Lawrence J. Quirk, *Jane Wyman* (New York: Norton, 1987), p. 113. • **112**. Colacello, *Ronnie and Nancy*, p. 222. • **113**. Ibid., p. 223. • **114**. Kitty Kelley, *Nancy Reagan: The Unauthorized Biography*, p. 87. • **115**. Ibid., p. 88. • **116**. Ibid.; Morris, *Dutch*, pp. 282, 750; Anne Edwards, *Early Reagan*. • **117**. Kelley, *Nancy Reagan*, p. 91. • **118**. Cannon, *President Reagan*, p. 192. • **119**. Nancy Reagan,

*My Turn: The Memoirs of Nancy Reagan*, p. 106. • **120**. Cannon, *President Reagan*, p. 193. • **121**. Ibid., p. 82. • **122**. Ibid., p. 193. • **123**. Colacello, *Ronnie and Nancy*, p. 471. • **124**. Nancy Reagan to Richard Reeves, in Reeves, *President Reagan*, p. 492.

### Chapter Ten: George H. W. Bush

**1**. Herbert Parmet, *George Bush: The Life of a Lone Star Yankee*, p. 30; Doro Bush Koch, *My Father, My President: A Personal Account of the Life of George H. W. Bush*, pp. 5–6. • **2**. Parmet, *George Bush*, p. 32. • **3**. Koch, *My Father, My President*, p. 19. • **4**. Parmet, *George Bush*, pp. 30–1. • **5**. Ibid., p. 96. • **6**. Ibid., p. 109. • **7**. Ibid., p. 113. • **8**. Ibid., p. 114. • **9**. Ibid., p. 115. • **10**. Ibid., p. 132. • **11**. Ibid. • **12**. Timothy Naftali, *George H. W. Bush*, p. 21. • **13**. Ibid., pp. 21–2; Parmet, *George Bush*, pp. 170–1. • **14**. Jack Steel, quoted in Parmet, *George Bush*, p. 145. • **15**. Parmet, *George Bush*, p. 144. • **16**. Fitzhugh Green, *George Bush: An Intimate Portrait*, p. 113. • **17**. Parmet, *George Bush*, p. 150. • **18**. Ibid., p. 157. • **19**. Ibid., p. 159. • **20**. Ibid. • **21**. Barbara Bush, *A Memoir*, p. 109. • **22**. Ibid., p. 111. • **23**. Ibid. • **24**. Parmet, *George Bush*, p. 165. • **25**. Ibid. • **26**. Ibid., p. 172. • **27**. Ibid. • **28**. Bush, *Peking Diary*, p. 294; Parmet, *George Bush*, p. 176. • **29**. Stanley I. Kutler, *Abuse of Power*, p. 553. • **30**. Parmet, *George Bush*, p. 191. • **31**. Victor Gold, *Invasion of the Party Snatchers: How the Holy-Rollers and the Neo-Cons Destroyed the GOP* (Chicago: Sourcebooks Trade, 2007), p. 92. • **32**. James Mann, *Rise of the Vulcans: The History of Bush's War Cabinet*, (New York: Viking, 2004). • **33**. 'Intelligence Community Experiment in Competitive Analysis: Soviet Strategic Objectives: An Alternative View, Report of Team 'B', December 1976,' 1 and 9, released by the CIA to the National Archives. See Anne H. Cahn, *Killing Detente: The Right Attacks the CIA* (University Park: Pennsylvania State University Press, 1998), p. 163. • **34**. Adam Curtis, *The Power of Nightmares*, Documentary series, BBC television, October 20–November 3, 2004, quoted in Thom Hartmann, 'Hyping Terror for Fun, Profit – and Power', December 7, 2004. www.common dreams.org. Retrieved November 26, 2008. • **35**. Parmet, *George Bush*, p. 200. • **36**. Webster G. Tarpley and Anton Chaitkin, *George Bush: The Unauthorized Biography*, Chapter XV. • **37**. David Keene to George Bush, in Parmet, *George Bush*, p. 220. • **38**. Barbara Bush, *A Memoir*,

p. 197. • **39**. Parmet, *George Bush*, p. 301. • **40**. Diary entry, May 28–30, 1988, in Parmet, *George Bush*, p. 333. • **41**. Starting in September 1988 with a month-long airing of an attack ad by 'Americans for Bush', the ads related the story of a black Massachusetts murderer, Willie Horton, who had been furloughed as part of a state programme, only to commit battery and rape in Maryland. This was then followed by official Bush campaign ads, known as 'The Revolving Door'. In this, prisoners in uniform went in and out of a revolving door – with an announcer declaring Governor Dukakis had vetoed the death penalty in Massachusetts and approved furloughs for prisoners, including those who had committed 'first-degree murder' – i.e. Willie Horton. Taken apart, Bush could not be accused of directly stirring racism, but taken together, they proved devastating to the Dukakis campaign. • **42**. Parmet, *George Bush*, p. 336. • **43**. Ibid. • **44**. Ibid., p. 341. • **45**. Ibid., p. 352. • **46**. Ibid., p. 349. • **47**. Ibid., p. 351. • **48**. Richard Stengel, 'The Republicans', *Time*, August 22, 1988. • **49**. Parmet, *George Bush*, p. 355. • **50**. Atwater's 'negative politics' were contagious, and rooted in the era. 'We both cut our teeth at the same time' recalled Karl Rove of the 1970s and 80s, on becoming chief strategist to Bush's eldest son in 1999 – proud to be compared with the chief smearer in America. 'He rose much faster, much farther than I did' Rove said of Atwater, while Texas Republican Party Chairman Tom Pauken remarked of Rove: 'Karl's very capable and wants to be the next Lee Atwater.' Rove had already been investigated in 1973 by the Republican National Committee for dirty tricks, and never gave up. Dan Balz, 'Team Bush: The Iron Triangle', *Washington Post*, July 23, 1991. • **51**. John Robert Greene, *The Presidency of George Bush*, p. 93. • **52**. Naftali, *George H. W. Bush*, p. 77. • **53**. Colin Powell, *An American Journey*, p. 376. • **54**. Bill Keller, 'Gorbachev, in Finland, Disavows Any Right of Regional Intervention', *New York Times*, October 26, 1989. • **55**. Michael Beschloss and Strobe Talbott, *At The Highest Levels: The Inside Story of the End of the Cold War*, p. 134. • **56**. Ibid., p. 135. • **57**. Ibid., p. 137. • **58**. Ibid., p. 165. • **59**. Kuwait had a population in 1990 of 2 million. • **60**. James Baker, *The Politics of Diplomacy: Revolution, War and Peace, 1989–1992*, p. 194. • **61**. Powell, *An American Journey*, p. 464. • **62**. Ibid., pp. 465–6. • **63**. Ibid., p. 470. • **64**. Beschloss and Talbott, *At the Highest Levels*, p. 262. • **65**. Ibid. • **66**. Gorbachev, *Memoirs*, p. 553. • **67**. Parmet, *George Bush*, p. 89. • **68**. Ibid., p. 488. • **69**. Ibid. • **70**. Ibid., p. 487. • **71**. Ibid.,

p. 499. • **72.** Ibid., p. 500. • **73.** Ibid., p. 488. • **74.** Ibid., p. 490. • **75.**
Beschloss and Talbott, *At the Highest Levels,* p. 463. • **76.** Ibid., p. 434.
• **77.** Nigel Hamilton, *Bill Clinton: An American Journey,* p. 681. • **78.**
Greene, *The Presidency of George Bush,* p. 164. • **79.** In the Electoral College
Clinton took 370 votes to Bush's 168. • **80.** Doro Bush Koch, *My Father,
My President,* p. 417. • **81.** Colin Powell, *An American Journey,* p. 561. • **82.**
Doro Bush Koch, *My Father, My President,* p. 17. • **83.** Ibid., p. 5. • **84.**
Naftali, *George H. W. Bush,* p. 11. • **85.** Quoted in Kitty Kelley, *The Family:
The Real Story of the Bush Dynasty,* p. 330. • **86.** Nadine Eckerts, in Kelley,
*The Family,* p. 331. • **87.** Marian Javits, ibid. • **88.** Geoffrey Kabaservice,
author of *The Guardian: Kingman Brewster, His Circle and the Rise of the
Liberal Establishment* (New York: Henry Holt, 2004), interview in Kelley,
*The Family,* pp. 353 and 653. Other interviewees claiming an affair included
Roy Elson and Anne Woolston: ibid., pp. 329 and 435. The *New York
Post* scandalously headlined a report 'The Bush Affair' on August 11,
1992, quoting Susan Trento's new book, *The Power House.* Again, no
factual evidence was adduced beyond the account of a deceased US
Ambassador, Louis Fields, who had arranged for Vice President Bush
and Mrs Fitzgerald to share on romantic grounds a guest house in
Switzerland. • **89.** Quoted in Kelley, *The Family,* p. 351. • **90.** Ibid., pp.
354–5. • **91.** Ibid., p. 375. • **92.** Parmet, *George Bush,* p. 241. • **93.** Kelley,
*The Family,* p. 326. • **94.** Ibid., p. 435. • **95.** Parmet, *George Bush,* p. 273.
• **96.** Ibid. • **97.** Koch, *My Father, My President,* p. 224. • **98.** Bob Woodward,
*Shadow: Five Presidents and the Legacy of Watergate,* p. 223.

### Chapter Eleven: Bill Clinton

**1.** Nigel Hamilton, *Bill Clinton: American Journey,* p. 362. • **2.** Ibid.,
p. 364. • **3.** Ibid., p. 370. • **4.** Ibid., p. 475. • **5.** Bill Clinton, *My Life,*
p. 368. • **6.** George Stephanopoulos, *All Too Human,* p. 74. • **7.** Ibid., p. 77.
Clinton finally admitted, in a legal deposition in 1998, that he had in
fact slept with Gennifer Flowers. • **8.** Stephanopoulos, *All Too Human,*
p. 61. • **9.** Hamilton, *Bill Clinton: American Journey,* p. 192. • **10.** Ibid., p.
195. • **11.** Joe Conason and Gene Lyons, *The Hunting of the President,* p.
173 et seq. • **12.** David Gergen, *Eyewitness to Power,* p. 314. • **13.** Hillary
Rodham Clinton, *Living History,* p. 257. • **14.** Ibid. • **15.** Gail Sheehy,
*Hillary's Choice* (New York: Random House, 1999), p. 253. • **16.** Clinton,
*My Life,* p. 629. • **17.** Nigel Hamilton, *Bill Clinton: Mastering the Presidency,*

p. 421. • **18**. Ibid., p. 413. • **19**. Ibid., pp. 386–7. • **20**. Ibid., p. 415. • **21**. Hamilton, *Bill Clinton: Mastering the Presidency*, pp. 451–5 • **22**. Ibid., pp. 443–4. • **23**. Ibid., p. 445. • **24**. Stephanopoulos, interview with Chris Bury, 'The Clinton Years', PBS Television. • **25**. Leon Panetta interview, in Hamilton, *Bill Clinton: Mastering the Presidency*, p. 448. • **26**. Hamilton, *Bill Clinton: Mastering the Presidency*, p. 515. • **27**. Ibid., p. 424. • **28**. Ibid., p. 575. • **29**. Louis B. Freeh, *My FBI: Bringing down the Mafia, Investigating Bill Clinton, and Fighting the War on Terror*, p. 246. • **30**. Clinton, *My Life*, p. 741. • **31**. Ibid., p. 778. • **32**. Conason and Lyons, *The Hunting of the President*, p. 275. • **33**. Ibid., p. 343. • **34**. Matt Drudge, *The Drudge Report*. • **35**. 'Remarks to the After-School Child Care Initiative', January 26, 1998, in William J. Clinton, *Public Papers of the Presidents of the United States*, 1998, Book I (Washington, DC: US Government Printing Office, 1999), p. iii. • **36**. Richard Clarke, *Against All Enemies*, p. 186. • **37**. Ibid., p. 163. • **38**. Sidney Blumenthal, *The Clinton Wars*, p. 463. • **39**. Ibid., p. 465. • **40**. Jeffrey Toobin, *A Vast Conspiracy: The Real Story of the Sex Scandal That Nearly Brought down a President*, pp. 254–6. • **41**. Ibid., p. 336. • **42**. Ibid., p. 332. • **43**. Clinton, *My Life*, p. 835. • **44**. Clarke, *Against All Enemies*, pp. 190–5. • **45**. Clinton, *My Life*, p. 834. • **46**. Ibid., p. 845. • **47**. Freeh, *My FBI*, p. viii. • **48**. Daniel Schorn, 'Louis Freeh talks about Terrible Relationship with Clinton', CBS *60 Minutes*, October 6, 2005. • **49**. 'Clinton and Gore Have It Out', Associated Press, February 8, 2001. • **50**. Clinton, *My Life*, p. 944. • **51**. John Harris, *The Survivor: Bill Clinton in the White House*, p. 429; Blumenthal, *The Clinton Wars*, p. 783. • **52**. 'Former President Clinton's Farewell Remarks', Saturday, January 20, 2001, http://www.australianpolitics.com/usa/Clinton/speeches/01-0120 farewell.shtml. • **53**. Clinton, *My Life*, p. 149. • **54**. Hamilton, *Bill Clinton: An American Journey*, p. 44. • **55**. Ibid., pp. 168–70. • **56**. Hamilton, *Bill Clinton: Mastering the Presidency*, pp. 217–18. • **57**. Hamilton, *Bill Clinton: An American Journey*, p. 293. • **58**. Ann Henry interview, ibid., p. 474.

## Chapter Twelve: George W. Bush

**1**. Jacob Weisberg, *The Bush Tragedy*, p. 42. • **2**. 'My dad fixed it so I got into the Guard', Bush told Harvard professor Yoshi Tsurumi. Kitty Kelley, *The Family: The Real Story of the Bush Dynasty*, p. 310. • **3**. J. H. Hatfield, *Fortunate Son: George W. Bush and the Making of an American*

*President*, p. 313. • **4**. Ibid., pp. 316–17. • **5**. Kelley, *The Family*, p. 310. • **6**. Steve Arbeit, in Kelley, *The Family*, p. 309. • **7**. Professor Yoshi Tsurumi, in ibid., p. 309. • **8**. Ibid., p. 310. • **9**. Christopher Anderson, *George and Laura: Portrait of an American Marriage*, p. 109. • **10**. Weisberg, *The Bush Tragedy*, p. 76. • **11**. Ibid., p. 77. • **12**. Andersen, *George and Laura*, p. 146. • **13**. Hatfield, *Fortunate Son*, p. 73. • **14**. Ibid., p. 72. • **15**. Andersen, *George and Laura*, p. 150. • **16**. Hatfield, *Fortunate Son*, p. 73. • **17**. Ibid. • **18**. Ibid. • **19**. Ibid., p. 80. • **20**. Kelley, *The Family*, p. 489. • **21**. Ibid., p. 543. • **22**. Weisberg, *The Bush Tragedy*, p. 87. • **23**. Ibid., p. 63. • **24**. Hatfield, *Fortunate Son*, p. 122. • **25**. Ibid., p. 173. • **26**. Kelley, *The Family*, pp. 585–6; Hatfield, *Fortunate Son*, pp. 190–212 . • **27**. James Traub, 'The Bush Years: W.'s World', *New York Times Magazine*, January 14, 2001. • **28**. Richard H. Davis, 'The Anatomy of a Smear Campaign', *Boston Globe*, March 21, 2004. • **29**. Kelley, *The Family*, p. 595. • **30**. Ibid., p. 598. • **31**. Davis, 'The Anatomy of a Smear Campaign'. • **32**. Gore's final majority over Bush was 543,895 votes, out of a total 105,405,100 applicable votes cast. The electoral college, however, voted 271 to 266 for Governor Bush, with one abstention. • **33**. Weisberg, *The Bush Tragedy*, p. 67. • **34**. James Moore and Wayne Slater, *Bush's Brain: How Karl Rove Made George W. Bush Presidential*, p. 5. • **35**. Ron Suskind, *The Price of Loyalty: George W. Bush, the White House and the Education of Paul O'Neill*, p. 58. • **36**. Ibid., pp. 70–5. • **37**. Ibid., p. 71. • **38**. Ibid., p. 72. • **39**. Ibid., p. 75. • **40**. Chitra Ragavan, 'Cheney's Guy', *U.S. News & World Report*, May 29, 2006; Barton Gellman, *Angler: The Cheney Vice Presidency*, p. 376. • **41**. Cullen Murphy and Todd S. Purdum, 'Farewell to All That: An Oral History of the White House', *Vanity Fair*, February 2009, p. 93. • **42**. Lou Dubose and Jake Bernstein, *Vice: Dick Cheney and the Hijacking of the American Presidency*, p. 179. • **43**. Murphy and Purdum, 'Farewell to All That', p. 90. • **44**. Gellman, *Angler*, p. 78. • **45**. Ibid., p. 79. • **46**. Richard A. Clarke, *Against All Enemies: Inside America's War on Terror*, p. 232. • **47**. Ibid. • **48**. Ibid., p. 236. • **49**. Ibid., p. 237. • **50**. Ibid., p. 32. • **51**. Ibid. • **52**. Bob Woodward, *Bush at War*, p. 47. • **53**. Ibid., p. 45. • **54**. Ibid., p.49. • **55**. 'Authorization for Use of Military Force', Public Law 107-40, September 18, 2001. • **56**. Murphy and Purdum, 'Farewell to All That', p. 160. • **57**. Ibid., p. 99. • **58**. Winston S. Churchill, *My Early Life* (1930) (New York: Scribner, 1996), p. 147. • **59**. Woodward, *Bush at War*, p. 103. • **60**. Bob Woodward, *Plan of Attack: The Definitive Account of the Decision to Invade Iraq*, p. 30. • **61**. Woodward, *Bush at War*, p. 246.

• **62**. Associated Press, April 16, 2004. • **63**. Bob Woodward, *State of Denial: Bush at War, Part III*, p. 35. • **64**. Woodward, *Plan of Attack*, p. 3. • **65**. Daniel Eisenberg, 'We're Taking Him Out', *Time* magazine, May 5, 2002. • **66**. Technically, Bush's February 2001 Address was a 'Budget Message' to the Joint Session of Congress. • **67**. 'Iraq: Prime Minister's Meeting, 23 July', David Manning Memo, S 195/02, published in the *Sunday Times* (London), May 1, 2005. • **68**. DefenseLink News Transcript, Secretary of State Donald Rumsfeld interviews with Bob Woodward, July 6 and 7, 2006. • **69**. Rebecca Leung, 'Gen. Zinni: "They've Screwed Up", Former Top Commander Condemns Pentagon Officials Over Iraq', *60 Minutes*, CBS Television, May 21, 2004. • **70**. Woodward, *State of Denial*, p. 106. • **71**. Scott McClellan, *What Happened: Inside the Bush White House and Washington's Culture of Deception*, p. 117. • **72**. Ibid., p. 118. • **73**. Jane Meyer, *The Dark Side: The Inside Story of How the War on Terror Turned into a War on American Ideals*, p. 328. • **74**. Jack Goldsmith, *The Terror Presidency: Law and Judgment inside the Bush Administration*. • **75**. McClellan, *What Happened*, pp. 3–4. • **76**. Gellman, *Angler*, pp. 132–3, 174–5. • **77**. Ibid., pp. 144–9. • **78**. Ibid., pp. 177–9. • **79**. Ibid., p. 282. • **80**. Meyer, *The Dark Side*, p. 4. • **81**. Ibid., p. 77, quoting Ted Olson, Solicitor General. • **82**. Ibid., p. 76. • **83**. McClellan, *What Happened*, p. 237. • **84**. Ibid., p. 76. • **85**. Ibid., p. 77. • **86**. Ibid., p. 237. • **87**. Miers' nomination ultimately failed. • **88**. Philip Cooney: see Murphy and Purdum, 'Farewell to All That', p. 155. The Bush administration also directed that any references to the National Assessment of Climate Change Impacts effort of 1997–2000 should be excised from government agency documents: ibid. • **89**. 'White House defends Rove over 9/11 remarks', Associated Press, June 24, 2005. • **90**. Hope Yen, '9/11 Commission: No Link between al-Quaida and Saddam', Associated Press, June 16, 2004. • **91**. Jack Kean, Lee H. Hamilton et al., *The 9/11 Commission Report: Final Report of the National Commission on Terrorist Attacks upon the United States* (New York: Norton, 2004), p. 334. • **92**. Dan Bartlett, in Murphy and Purdum, 'Farewell to All That'. • **93**. McClellan, *What Happened*, p. 288. • **94**. Ibid., p. 290. • **95**. Ibid., p. 291. • **96**. Gellman, *Angler*, p. 243. • **97**. Ibid. • **98**. Hope Yen, '9/11 Commission'. • **99**. Thomas Friedman, Op-ed page column, *New York Times*, August 4, 2006. • **100**. Craig Unger, *American Armageddon: How the Delusions of the Neoconservatives and the Christian Right Triggered the Descent of America – and Still Imperil Our Future*, p.

341. • **101**. James Ridgeway, 'American Casualties in Iraq More than 44,000', *Mother Jones*, November 2, 2006. • **102**. Murphy and Purdum, 'Farewell to All That', p. 157. • **103**. Helen Dewar and Dana Milbank, 'Cheney Dismisses Critic with Obscenity', *Washington Post*, June 25, 2004. • **104**. Gellman, *Angler*, p. 365. • **105**. 'Bush says he won't be rushed on Iraqi changes', CNN, December 14, 2006. • **106**. Gellman, *Angler*, p. 391. • **107** 'Countdown to Crawford: As voters go to polls to pick his successor, George W. Bush hits new low in approval rating', *Los Angeles Times*, November 4, 2008. • **108**. Maria Recio, 'Bush, his approval in tatters, flies home to Texas', McClatchy Newspapers, January 20, 2009. • **109**. Christopher Andersen, *George and Laura*, p. 65. • **110**. Ibid., p. 109. • **111**. Ibid., p. 73. • **112**. Ibid., p. 74. • **113**. Woodward, *Bush at War*, p. 146. • **114**. Andrew Malcolm, 'The Long Farewell of George W. Bush', *Los Angeles Times*, January 12, 2009.

# Picture Credits

Bettmann/Corbis: 1, 13, 14, 16, 20, 22, 25, 26; Régis Bossu/Sygma/Corbis: 32; George Bush Presidential Library: 28, 29; Jimmy Carter Library: 23, 24; Corbis: 21; Larry Downing/Reuters/Corbis: 34; Dwight D. Eisenhower Presidential Library: 7; Lyndon Baines Johnson Presidential Library: 17 (Yoichi R. Yokamoto), 18 (Jack Knightlinger), 19 (Yoichi R. Yokamoto); Saul Loeb/Pool/Corbis: 35; Michael Probst/epa/Corbis: 27; Franklin D. Roosevelt Library: 2, 3; Ron Sachs/CNP/Sygma/Corbis: 33; Mike Stewart/Sygma/Corbis: 31; George Tames/*New York Times*: 15; Time & Life Pictures/Getty Images: 10; Peter Turnley/Corbis: 30; US Army and Dwight D. Eisenhower Presidential Library: 8, 9; US Army Signal Corps, courtesy of Harry S. Truman Library: 4, 5, 6; US Navy and John F. Kennedy Presidential Library: 11, 12.

The official inaugural medals have been reproduced courtesy of H. Joseph Levine of the Presidential Coin & Antique Company.

# Index

**DOGON COUNTRY (p513)**
World-class trekking amid villages clinging to the cliffs of the Bandiagara Escarpment

**GOROM-GOROM THURSDAY MARKET (p163)**
West Africa's most colourful market and a magnet for all the peoples of the Sahel

**AÏR MOUNTAINS (p608)**
An oasis of brooding black peaks, Tuareg villages and palm-fringed wells

**ABOMEY (p110)**
A city alive with the ghosts and glories of one of West Africa's greatest ancient civilisations

**LAGOS (p629)**
Nigeria's pulsating heart with more great markets museums, music and noise than you ever thought possible

**COASTAL FORTS (p354)**
As rich in Ghana's modern buzz as it is home to evocative reminders of Africa's tragic past

**LOMÉ (p778)**
Crazy nightlife and some of Africa's most intriguing and clamourous markets

**MT CAMEROON (p192)**
The highest mountain in West Africa with an unrivalled, mist-shrouded world to explore

# Destination West Africa

There's nowhere on earth quite like West Africa. This is a destination with cachet, a frontier territory where the unspoiled Africa of your imagination awaits, a challenging destination that promises endless opportunities to venture into the unknown.

For some it's the call of the wild, the lure of landscapes that provide some of Africa's signature moments, from the deep-green rainforests of Cameroon to the otherworldly solitude of a Cape Verdean volcano. For others it's the Sahara with pristine sand dunes and magical oases, or the Niger River, which plots a course through the Sahel like an evocation of a fairytale. Or perhaps it will be the extraordinary escarpment villages of Mali's Dogon Country that will live longest in the memory or the beaches that you'll never want to leave.

But West Africa is, more than anything else, defined by its people. Here, indigo-clad Tuareg nomads mingle with some of Africa's most extraordinary cultures – Ashanti, Dogon, Hausa and Malinké. Together they make the music that has taken the world by storm and meet in the vibrant markets that bring alive Africa's rich and colourful past.

Wherever you find yourself, West Africa is an assault on the senses. It's in-your-face, full-volume Lagos, or the silent gravitas of a camel caravan silhouetted against a blood-red Saharan sunset. It's Atlantic sand or red Sahel dust between your toes. It's a smile of friendship from some of the world's poorest people. It's a beat, a rhythm, an idea of Africa that has somehow survived the ravages of time.

Dive in. Return the smiles. Dance to the music. But above all, immerse yourself in a journey that will change your life forever.

# Highlights

Gasp at the heavy Fula earrings (p507) made of gold in Mali

Get in touch with your roots at the International Roots Festival (p324), The Gambia

Pass the time on the faded streets of Saint-Louis (p712), Senegal

Surf the sand wave in magical, mysterious Mauritania (p547)

Paddle your way through the stilt village of Ganvié (p102), Benin

JANE SWEENEY

THOR VAZ DE LEON

The Basilique de Notre Dame de la Paix (p279), Yamoussoukro , Côte d'Ivoire

Visit one of the oldest stone mosques in Senegal, on Île de Gorée (p696)

ARIADNE VAN ZANDBERGEN

Explore the unique Ashanti dwellings of Ghana (p378)

ARIADNE VAN ZANDBERGEN

Chill out in idyllic Paúl (p244), on Santo Antâo, Cape Verde's most spectacular island

Marvel at the volcanic landscape of Rhumsiki (p212), Cameroon

Float your troubles away on a Niger River cruise (p510)

JANE SWEENEY

Hauling in the catch of the day in Aného (p787), Togo

Jump aboard a *pinasse* (motorised boat) to journey to the legendary Timbuktu (Tombouctou; p521), Mali

PATRICK BEN LUKE SYDER

CRAIG PERSHOUSE

Watch fishermen at work in the scenic, Fanti fishing village of Sassandra (p275), Côte d'Ivoire

Take in the hustle and bustle on the beach at former slave-trading post, Cape Coast (p359), Ghana

ARIADNE VAN ZANDBERGEN

# Contents

# Regional Map Contents

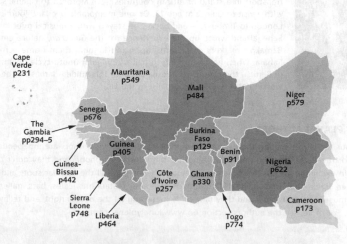

# The Authors

## ANTHONY HAM
### Coordinating Author

Anthony's first trip for Lonely Planet was to West Africa where he ate rat, was held up at knifepoint and fell irretrievably in love with the region. In the six years since, he has often returned to the region (collecting a formidable array of parasites en route) to indulge his passions for West African music, days of Saharan solitude and long, slow trips up the Niger, not to mention visiting old friends. He is also writing a book about his Tuareg friends and the Sahara. When he's not in West Africa, Anthony lives in Madrid from where he writes and photographs for numerous newspapers around the world.

## My Favourite Trip...

For me it just has to be the Sahara where the silence, solitude and night-time companionship of the campfire has no equal. In particular, I'd return to **Chinguetti** (p565), **Timbuktu** (p521) and **Agadez** (p604). From the latter, I'd explore the **Aïr Mountains** (p608) and **Ténéré Desert** (p609) with my Tuareg friends. I could also happily sail up and down the **Niger River** (p510) to the end of my days, leaving it only to trek the **Dogon Country** (p513) and catch the world's best live-music scene in **Bamako** (p499). I also find myself returning again and again to **Bobo-Dioulasso** (p148) and would love to revisit the **Mandara Mountains** (p211) of Cameroon, despite what the crab sorcerer of Rhumsiki told me.

## JAMES BAINBRIDGE
### Benin & Togo

James has grooved to the amazing music and grimaced on the appalling transport in a string of African countries from Morocco to Ghana, starting with a visit to Guinea at age 13. On one memorable overland journey from London to Timbuktu – and back – he stayed with a musical griot family in Senegal and wrote up the experience for the *Guardian*, before emptying Bamako's markets of cassette tapes and lugging them home across the Sahara. When he's not trying to hail a *zemi-john* (motorcycle taxi) in Togo or Benin – the countries he researched for this guide – James can be found working as a freelance journalist in the UK.

---

### LONELY PLANET AUTHORS

Why is our travel information the best in the world? It's simple: our authors are independent, dedicated travellers. They don't research using just the Internet or phone, and they don't take freebies in exchange for positive coverage. They travel widely, to all the popular spots and off the beaten track. They personally visit thousands of hotels, restaurants, cafés, bars, galleries, palaces, museums and more – and they take pride in getting all the details right, and telling it how it is. For more, see the authors section on www.lonelyplanet.com.

### TIM BEWER                               Côte d'Ivoire, Guinea & Sierra Leone

While growing up, Tim didn't travel much except for the obligatory pilgrimage to Disney World and an annual summer week at the lake. He's spent most of his adult life making up for this, and has since visited nearly 50 countries. After university he worked briefly as a legislative assistant before quitting capitol life in 1994 to backpack around West Africa. It was during this trip that the idea of being a freelance travel writer and photographer was hatched, and he's been at it ever since, returning to Africa several times. He lives in Minneapolis.

### JEAN-BERNARD CARILLET                                            Mauritania

Jean-Bernard got his first taste of Mauritania while on a romantic tour of the Adrar with his significant other in 2000. It would have been wiser to choose an idyllic island in the South Pacific because the romance ceased soon afterwards...but at least his love affair with the desert is still ardent. A Gallic author based in Paris, he was all too happy to cover a country where he could discuss in French with nomads under a traditional tent the virtues of strong tea. Jean-Bernard is an Africa aficionado – he's visited 13 African nations and has also co-authored Lonely Planet's *Ethiopia & Eritrea* and *Africa on a Shoestring* – the first Lonely Planet guidebook he bought.

### PAUL CLAMMER                                            Cameroon & Nigeria

Once a molecular biologist, Paul has long since traded his test tubes for a rucksack, and the vicarious life of a travel writer. Overlanding in Africa was his first significant travel experience, and he has returned to the continent many times since. He is fascinated by the interface between Muslim and black Africa (he's also written a book about Sudan), and so particularly relished the chance to explore Nigeria, that most maligned of West African countries.

### MARY FITZPATRICK                                                    Liberia

Originally from Washington, DC, Mary set off after graduate studies for several years in Europe. Her fascination with languages and cultures soon led her further south to sub-Saharan Africa, where she has spent much of the past decade living and working, including several years as a freelance writer in Liberia, Sierra Leone and Guinea. Mary has authored and co-authored numerous guidebooks on Africa, and currently works as a full-time travel writer from her home base in Cairo.

### MICHAEL GROSBERG                                                    Ghana

After a childhood spent stateside in the Washington, DC area and a valuable philosophy degree in hand, Michael took a job doing something with developing a resort on an island in the Pacific after which he left for a long overland trip through Asia. He later found his way to South Africa where he did journalism and NGO work and found time to travel all over southern Africa. He returned to New York for graduate school in comparative literature and he has taught literature and writing in several NYC colleges in addition to Lonely Planet assignments that have taken him around the world.

### KATHARINA KANE                                      The Gambia & Senegal

When Katharina Kane heard the haunting sound of a Fula flute during a London concert, her fate was sealed. She headed straight to Guinea in West Africa, where she ended up studying the instrument for a year before writing a PhD on its origins. She then decamped to Senegal, a country that she'd fallen in love with during one of her many travels to West Africa in her role as a music journalist. Katharina has worked on other Lonely Planet titles, writes for various world music magazines, including *Roots* and *Songlines*, and produces radio features on world music for stations including the BBC and WDR. She currently lives in Dakar, or on a plane to yet another new place.

### ROBERT LANDON                              Cape Verde & Guinea-Bissau

Robert has degrees in literature from two different California universities, but his best education continues to be travel, especially yearlong stints in Italy, Paris and Rio de Janeiro. For more than a decade, Robert has been able to finance his trips with his writing, and his work has appeared in the *San Jose Mercury-News*, Bloomberg.com and countless other websites (most now defunct). His time in Brazil introduced him to the far-flung Portuguese-speaking world and was his gateway to West Africa's Cape Verde and Guinea-Bissau – two of the most extraordinary places he's visited.

### MATT PHILLIPS                                                       Niger

Matt got his first taste of Niger (literally a mouthful of sand – ughh!) while liberating Mr Harry, a loveable 1982 Landrover, from the Sahara's grip. Although that sand wasn't too tasty, Matt acquired a taste for Niger and stayed for his fill. He's travelled the country three times, by three different means: Mr Harry, bus and bush taxi. Highlights include finding seashells in the Saharan sands and standing atop Agadez's mosque. Lowlights include 'sleeping' overnight in a Peugeot at Gouré's *autogare* (bush-taxi station) and projectile vomiting from a moving bush taxi. Matt's crossed 21 African nations and has also co-authored Lonely Planet's *Kenya* and *Ethiopia & Eritrea* guides.

## CONTRIBUTING AUTHORS

**Jane Cornwell** is an Australian-born, UK-based journalist, author and broadcaster, who wrote the Music in West Africa chapter. After graduating with a Masters degree in anthropology, she left for London where she worked, variously, at the Institute of Contemporary Arts and for Peter Gabriel's Real World company. She currently writes about arts, books and music – most notably world music – for a range of UK and antipodean publications, including the *Times*, *Evening Standard* and *Telegraph* newspapers, *Songlines* magazine and the *Australian* newspaper. She travels about the planet regularly, interviewing world musicians.

**Dr Caroline Evans** wrote the Health chapter. Caroline studied medicine at the University of London, and completed General Practice training in Cambridge. She is the medical adviser to Nomad Travel Clinic, a private travel health clinic in London, and is also a GP specialising in travel medicine. She has been an expedition doctor for Raleigh International and Coral Cay expeditions.

# Getting Started

West Africa is a great destination to plan, with a wealth of resources to track down – books that capture the region's unmistakable whiff of the exotic (opposite), excellent movies that get little airtime elsewhere (p21) and a host of unique festivals that can act as your route planner to the region (p21). The region's world-renowned music (p58) is also worth tracking down to provide a soundtrack for your visit.

On the practical side, West Africa can be a challenging destination so think carefully about what sort of trip best suits you.

Most travellers use buses, bush taxis and trains. This mode of transport is a lot slower than with a private vehicle, and you probably won't reach as many places, but it's cheap and a great way to experience local life.

That said, if you've never travelled in Africa before you may want to take an organised tour (p840). Although more expensive than travelling solo, a tour takes the hassle out of organising everything from transport to hotels. Another benefit is travelling with a guide whose local knowledge can offer countless invaluable insights.

For a range of possible itineraries to whet your appetite, see p23.

## WHEN TO GO

See p813 for climate charts.

It's best to visit West Africa in the drier and generally cooler period from November to February. Any time up to April (in southern coastal countries) or May (in Sahel countries) is also dry; from then on it gets progressively hotter and more humid. From January to May, the dusty harmattan winds of the Sahel can reduce visibility and cause respiratory complaints.

Hotels along the coasts of Senegal and The Gambia are packed with European sunbathers on package tours from December to March. The Dogon Country, Timbuktu and Djenné in Mali are very crowded at this time, especially in December and January.

The rainy season is from May/June to September/October and is not ideal for travel. The wettest areas are Guinea, Sierra Leone and Liberia, where annual rainfall often tops 4000mm. In the Sahel countries, rain falls for a few hours per day, keeping temperatures down and the skies clear of dust. In all areas, rainy periods get shorter and levels decrease as you move further north and away from the ocean. Most people find dry heat, such as that found in the Sahel, easier to handle than the humidity of the coast.

Avoiding the rainy season is about more than not getting your feet wet. Although many major roads in the region are tar, the overwhelming majority of minor roads are dirt and can become impassable after heavy rains. Many wildlife reserves are also closed from June to November. For specific details, see the climate charts in the country chapters.

Regional festivals (see the Directory in all individual country chapters and p21) can be a highlight of travel in the region, and it's worth considering timing your trip to coincide with some of the major ones. In the Sahel countries especially, note when Ramadan and major Islamic holidays will take place (see p818).

## COSTS & MONEY

Travel in West Africa doesn't come as cheap as you might expect, with prices generally around 50% and up to 75% of what you pay in developed countries. Mali and Senegal are particularly expensive. Exceptions to the generally high prices include local food, beer and transport.

**DON'T LEAVE HOME WITHOUT...**

- sealable plastic bags – to protect your belongings from moisture and dust
- the requisite vaccinations (p853) and proof of yellow fever vaccination (most countries won't let you in without it)
- travel insurance (p819) – accidents do happen
- waterproof jacket – essential during the rains
- one smart set of clothes – advisable for visa applications, crossing borders or if you're invited to somebody's house
- basic medical kit (see p853)
- mosquito net and repellent – free-standing nets are heavier than regular ones, but often more practical
- light sleeping bag (for cold desert nights) or a sleeping sheet (for less-than-clean hotels)
- sunglasses, hat and sunscreen (as essential in the Sahara as on the beach)
- torch (flashlight) and spare batteries
- sturdy water bottle, water purifier and filter
- universal washbasin plug and length of cord for drying clothes
- sanitary towels or tampons
- condoms
- an emergency stash of toilet paper
- photocopies of your important documents (and leave a copy somewhere safe back home)
- English-language books – they're very rarely available in West Africa
- a small (size-three) football – a great way to meet local kids and their families
- contact-lens-cleaning-and-soaking solutions and a pair of prescription glasses as a back-up
- patience – most bush taxis do leave eventually

In addition to accommodation, food and transport, you should also factor in things such as visa fees, national park admission charges and the cost of hiring local guides.

If you're staying in the most basic accommodation (from US$5 a night), eating only local food (as little as US$2 a day), getting around on local transport (around US$2 per 100km), take no tours and buy few souvenirs you can count on spending US$10 to US$15 per day.

Those looking for a little more comfort (midrange hotels can range from US$15 to US$70 per night) and preferring to eat in reasonable restaurants (from US$2 to US$10 for a sit-down meal) could get by on US$30, but US$55 is a more reasonable budget.

At the upper end, the sky's the limit – top-end hotels start at around US$80 and can be three times that, organised tours are scarcely cheaper than taking a tour in Europe and car rental averages about US$100 per day and sometimes more, plus petrol.

For advice on local accommodation costs, see the Accommodation section in the Directory for each individual country.

## READING UP
### Books
*The Gates of Africa: Death, Discovery & the Search for Timbuktu*, by Anthony Sattin, is a beautifully written text about the time when Africa drew an eclectic range of travellers, from fortune-seekers to serious explorers.

*The Lost Kingdoms of Africa,* by Jeffrey Taylor, is a highly readable account of a modern journey through the Sahel; it was published in the US as *Angry Wind.*

*The Shadow of the Sun,* by Ryszard Kapuściński, is a masterpiece by one of Africa's most insightful observers who always places Africans at the centre of their own history.

*African Silences,* by Peter Matthiessen, is a classic on African wildlife and the environment in Africa; the passages on Senegal, The Gambia and Côte d'Ivoire are so beautifully written that you'll return to them again and again.

*Journey Without Maps,* by Graham Greene, is a wonderful narrative by one of the 20th century's best writers as he travelled through the forests of Liberia and Sierra Leone in 1935.

*The State of Africa,* by Martin Meredith, is so accessible that it doesn't read like a history book and its searing retelling of Africa's transition to independence contains some fascinating sections on West Africa's best-known rulers.

*Sahara: A Natural History,* by Marq de Villiers and Sheila Hirtle, is one of the most comprehensive English-language histories of the natural and human world of the Sahara that is wonderfully easy to read.

*The Strong Brown God,* by Sanche de Gramont, is lively, beautifully written and still the best overview of the Niger River's human and geographical history.

## Websites

For specific country overviews and hundreds of useful links, head to Lonely Planet's website (www.lonelyplanet.com), including the Thorn Tree, Lonely Planet's online bulletin board.

Background information on West Africa can also be found at the following websites:

**African Studies Center** (www.africa.upenn.edu//Home_Page/Country.html) Extensive links from the University of Pennsylvania's Africa programme.

**Contemporary Africa Database** (www.africaexpert.org) This growing online database contains general information on Africa.

---

### WEST AFRICA'S WORLD HERITAGE SITES

Sites in West Africa considered to be of global significance by Unesco include the following:

**Benin** Royal palaces of Abomey (p112)

**Cameroon** Réserve de Biosphère du Dja (p215)

**Côte d'Ivoire** Parc National de Taï (p278) and Parc National de la Comoé (p263)

**Gambia** James Island (p318)

**Ghana** Coastal forts and castles (p354) and Ashanti traditional buildings in Kumasi (p377)

**Guinea** Nimba Mountains (p430; also extending into Côte d'Ivoire)

**Mali** Djenné old town (p505), Timbuktu (p521), Tomb of the Askia (Gao; p531) and Falaise de Bandiagara (Dogon Country; p513)

**Mauritania** Parc National du Banc d'Arguin (p561) and the *ksour* (fortified areas, or old quarters) of Ouadâne (p567), Chinguetti (p565), Tichit (p569) and Oualâta (p570)

**Niger** Réserve Naturelle Nationale de l'Aïr et du Ténéré (p583) and Parc Regional du W (p596)

**Nigeria** Osun Sacred Forest & Groves (p641) and Sukur Cultural Landscape

**Senegal** Île de Gorée (p696), Saint Louis (p712), Parc National des Oiseaux du Djoudj (p717) and Parc National de Niokolo-Koba (p721)

**Togo** Koutammakou, the Land of the Betamaribé

**Ecowas** (www.ecowas.info/index.htm) The official site of the Economic Community of West African States (Ecowas) is a useful, if limited, introduction to the countries of the region with a few useful links.
**Norwegian Council for Africa** (www.afrika.no) This is a comprehensive site with extensive information and links for each country, chat forums and more.
**Sahara Overland** (www.sahara-overland.com) The best practical guide for travellers to the Sahara, it has useful forums, route information and book reviews.

For good news sites on the region, try **AllAfrica.com** (www.allafrica.com), **BBC** (http://news.bbc.co.uk/2/hi/africa/default.stm), **IRINNews** (www.irinnews.org) and **West Africa News** (www.westafricanews.com). For country-specific websites, see the individual country chapters.

## MUST-SEE MOVIES

West African directors are world-renowned, in part because of the prestigious Fespaco film festival (p133), held biannually in Ouagadougou.

*Mooladé*, by Ousmane Sembene, is a moving story about female circumcision and the most recent offering by this prolific and talented Senegalese director, who is considered to be the father of African cinema.

*Yeleen*, by the Malian director Souleymane Cissé, is a lavish generational tale set in 13th-century Mali, which won the Special Jury Prize at the Cannes Film Festival in 1987.

*Tilä*, by the Burkinabé director Idrissa Ouédraogo, is an exceptional cinematic portrayal of life in a traditional African village; it won the 1990 Grand Prix at Cannes and the top prize at the 1991 Fespaco festival.

*Buud Yam,* by Gaston Kaboré from Burkina Faso, won Fespaco's top prize in 1997 for its tale of childhood identity, superstition and a 19th-century African world about to change forever.

*Dakan,* by Mohamed Camara of Guinea, daringly uses the issue of homosexuality to challenge prevailing social and religious taboos.

*Clando,* by the Cameroonian director Jean-Marie Teno, addresses the timely issue of Africans choosing between fighting corrupt regimes at home and seeking a better life in Europe.

*The Blue Eyes of Yonta,* by Flora Gomes, is one of few feature films ever made in Guinea-Bissau and captures the disillusionment of young Africans who've grown up in the postindependence era.

For more information see p49, and each individual country chapter.

## RESPONSIBLE TRAVEL

In regions such as West Africa where the global inequities of wealth distribution are so pronounced, it's particularly important to ensure that your travel enjoyment is not at the expense of locals and their environment. For advice on travel in Islamic areas see p47, ettiqutte p54 and meeting locals p42.

'Ensure that your travel enjoyment is not at the expense of locals...'

At one level, the impact of tourism can be positive – it can provide an incentive for locals to preserve environments and wildlife by generating employment, while enabling them to maintain their traditional lifestyles.

However, the negative impacts of tourism can be substantial and contribute to the gradual erosion of traditional life. Please try to keep your impact as low as possible by considering the following tips:

- Please don't give cash, sweets, pens etc to children. It encourages begging and undermines existing social structures. Also, doling out medicines can encourage people not to seek proper medical advice. A donation to a recognised project, eg a health centre or school, is more constructive.
- Try to give people a balanced perspective of life in developed countries and point out the strong points of local culture (eg strong family ties, openness to outsiders).
- Make yourself aware of the human rights situation, history and current affairs in the countries you travel through.
- Try not to waste water. Switch off lights and air-conditioning when you go out.
- When visiting historical sites, consider the irreparable damage you inflict upon them by taking home an unattached artefact (eg pottery shards or arrowheads).
- Many precious cultural objects are sold to tourists (eg the traditional doors of granaries in the Dogon Country of Mali) – you should only buy newly carved pieces to preserve West Africa's history and stimulate the carving industry.
- Question any so-called eco-tourism operators for specifics about what they're really doing to protect the environment and the people who live there.
- Support local enterprise. Use locally-owned hotels and restaurants and support trade and craft workers by buying locally made souvenirs.
- Resist the local tendency of indifference to littering.

UK-based organisation **Tourism Concern** ( ☎ 020-7133 3330; www.tourismconcern.org .uk; Stapleton House, 277-281 Holloway Rd, London N7 8HN) is primarily concerned with tourism and its impact on local cultures and the environment. It has a range of publications and contacts for community organisations, as well as further advice on minimising the impact of your travels.

# Itineraries
## CLASSIC ROUTES

### THROUGH THE HEART OF THE SAHEL  Six to Eight Weeks / Dakar to Agadez

If you're wondering why Africa gets under the skin, begin in **Dakar** (p683); a cosmopolitan city that's a great place to start your West African odyssey. While there, head offshore to tranquil **Île de Gorée** (p696), before taking the train to vibrant **Bamako** (p490) with its world-class nightlife and unmistakably African feel. **Djenné** (p504) boasts a beautiful mud-brick mosque and a clamorous Monday market, so pause here en route to the **Dogon Country** (p513) with its outstanding trekking and intriguing cultural traditions. No trip to West Africa is complete without an excursion north to fabled **Timbuktu** (Tombouctou; p521) on the Sahara's fringe. As the great explorers discovered, Timbuktu is on the road to nowhere so retrace your steps to the lovely, riverside town of **Ségou** (p501). From there make for Burkina Faso and **Bobo-Dioulasso** (p148), an infectiously languid town. Continue on to the gloriously named **Ouagadougou** (p134) and then east. After a detour to Togo's otherworldly **Tamberma Valley** (p799), head for **Niamey** (p584), Niger's capital which rests quietly on the banks of the Niger River. A long bus ride north takes you to **Agadez** (p604), an evocative former caravan town of the Sahara.

From Dakar to Agadez (around 4800km) can be reasonably done in six weeks (a week in Senegal, two to three weeks in Mali, a week in Burkina Faso and another week for Niger) using public transport. Two months would, however, be ideal.

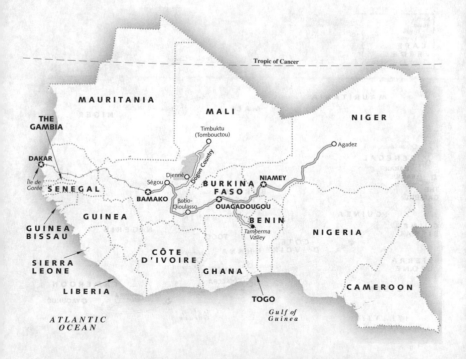

## ATLANTIC ODYSSEY                              Six Weeks / Dakar to Limbe

West Africa's dusty, thorn-strewn interior is not for everyone, so just as well there's the palm-fringed Atlantic Coast. All flights lead to **Dakar** (p683), Senegal's capital, which combines tropical ambience with African sophistication. To the north, **Saint-Louis** (p712) is like stepping back into precolonial Africa. The Gambia may be small, but its beaches, especially those around **Serekunda** (p303) make it a good (English-speaking) rest stop for taking time out from the African road. Cape Verde is one of West Africa's greatest surprises, with its soulful musical soundtrack, unspoiled beaches, mountainous interior and laid-back locals. The islands of **Santiago** (p235), **São Vicente** (p240), and **Santo Antão** (p243) are particularly beautiful; if you can be here for Mardi Gras (p251), you'll love it. Consider flying to agreeable **Accra** (p339) in Ghana, from where excursions to the old **coastal forts** (p354), **Cape Coast Castle** (p360) and stunning beaches at **Kokrobite** (p354) and **Gomoa Fetteh** (p356) never disappoint. Don't fail to detour north to **Kumasi** (p377) with its wonderful market in the heartland of the fascinating Ashanti culture. There's plenty of onward transport to the fascinating markets of **Lomé** (p778) and on to the decadent colonial charm of **Aného** (p787). Not far away is Benin, with **Ouidah** (p106), the evocative former slaving port and home of voodoo, the history-rich town of **Abomey** (p110) and the stilt-villages of **Ganvié** (p102). **Cotonou** (p95) has all the steamy appeal of the tropics; from here fly to **Yaoundé** (p179) in Cameroon, which has a distinctive Central African feel. **Kribi** (p217) and **Limbe** (p188), from where you can climb **Mt Cameroon** (p192) for stunning Atlantic views, are places to laze on the sand and consider just how far you've travelled.

**Dakar to Limbe (around 2500km by land, plus flights) should take about six weeks (one week in Senegal, two in Cape Verde, two travelling from Ghana to Benin and a further week in Cameroon).**

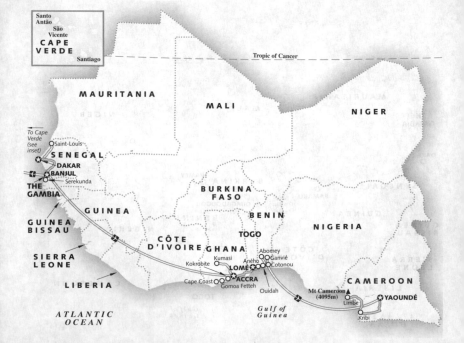

# ROADS LESS TRAVELLED

## FORBIDDEN WEST AFRICA        One Month to Forever / Dakar to Sassandra

The westernmost extremity of Africa's bulge has recently been off-limits to travellers but tentative peace processes have opened up some destinations that you could well have all to yourself. Begin in **Dakar** (p683) and catch the ferry to **Ziguinchor** (p727), the capital of **Casamance** (p725), which is culturally distinct from the rest of Senegal and home to fine beaches, labyrinthine river systems and lush forests. Just across the border, Guinea-Bissau is battle-scarred but its return to peace has allowed travellers to enjoy the architectural remnants of Portugal's colonial occupation, not to mention the village-like capital, **Bissau** (p445). The **Arquipélago dos Bijagós** (p450) is isolated, rich in wildlife and like nowhere else on the coast. Continuing south, Guinea is a great destination, with **Conakry** (p409), a good place to start for its night-life and the vaguest whiff of emerging sophistication. Guinea's interior is lush and beautiful, nowhere more so than in the **Fouta Djalon highlands** (p418), which offer trekking and **Mali-ville** (p423), a beautiful base. To really get off the beaten track, head into the forests of Guinea's **Forest Region** (p428) where Graham Greene's *Journey Without Maps* will resonate. Just across the border, Sierra Leone is another country on the up, with stunning beaches and **Freetown** (p753), the oddly beautiful capital and a city that seems to contain all the country's optimism and drive. Liberia is probably off-limits, but if the situation stabilises in Côte d'Ivoire, **Sassandra** (p275), a fishing village with great beaches, will be the first to welcome back visitors.

Getting as far as Freetown involves around 3300km of dodgy roads and infrequent transport – count on anywhere between a month and forever. If you fly to Abidjan, count on an extra week kicking back in Sassandra.

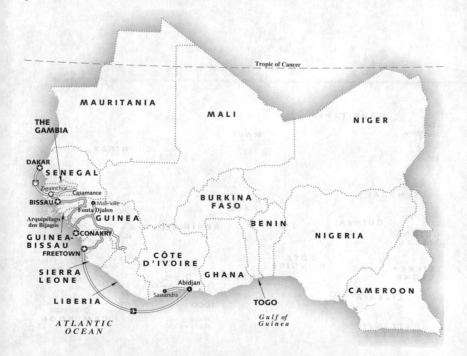

## NIGERIA & CAMEROON

**Two Months / Lagos to Foumban**

Nigeria is one of those destinations that suffers from bad press, although it must be said that most of the horror stories are told by those who've never set foot in the country. **Lagos** (p629) may be in-your-face, high volume and logistically confronting, but it's also Africa's most energetic city, awash with pulsating nightlife, clamorous markets and a terrific museum. **Osun Sacred Forest** (p641) in Okumu Sanctuary, and the Oba's Palace in **Benin City** (p644) are worthwhile stopovers as you head across the south en route to **Calabar** (p647), which is likeable for its old colonial buildings, fish market and lovely setting. From the steamy climate of the south head for the cooler mountain setting of **Jos** (p652), set amid stone-strewn rolling hills and a good base for visiting the excellent **Yankari National Park** (p655). **Kano** (p659), West Africa's oldest city and one of the Sahel's most significant cultural centres, is a fascinating place with a strongly Islamic character. The long journey east takes you across the border to **Maroua** (p208), a pleasant base for exploring the weird-and-wonderful landscapes of the **Mandara Mountains** (p211) and **Parc National de Waza** (p213). From **N'Gaoundéré** (p205), you can either head deep into the utterly untouristed rainforests (p213) of the southeast, which offer a verdant taste of Central Africa, or take the train through the country's heart, through forests and skirting isolated rivers all the way to Yaoundé. **Bamenda** (p196) is your gateway to the villages of the **Ring Road** (p198), a deeply traditional area of Cameroon that feels untouched by time. **Foumban** (p203), with its markets and royal palace, is another important cultural centre and a great place to end your journey.

This route will see you covering at least 5100km (much more if you detour down into Cameroon's remote southeast) and will take a minimum of two months by public transport.

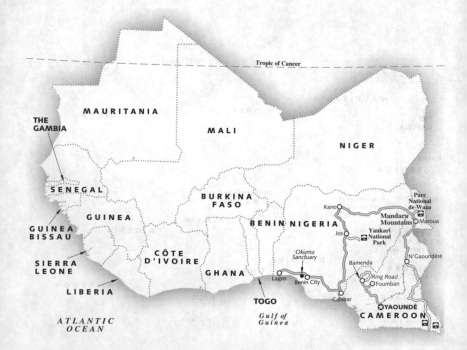

# TAILORED TRIPS

## INTO THE SAHARA

If the sculpted perfection of sand dunes, the isolated serenity of former caravan towns and the immensity of solitude to be found in the Sahara's vast open spaces appeal, this itinerary is for you, although you'll either need your own or a rented 4WD or, in some places, a camel.

Begin by entering West Africa from the Western Sahara (p839) to **Nouâdhibou** (p559) in Mauritania, before making for the wonderful oasis towns of **Chinguetti** (p565), surrounded by sand dunes, and **Ouadâne** (p567) with its stone-ruin sense of abandonment. Rather than returning to civilisation, continue to **Tidjikja** (p569), **Tichit** (p569) and **Oualâta** (p570), each of which has beautifully painted houses. In Mali, **Timbuktu** (Toumbouctou; p521), perhaps the greatest of all desert cities, is a gateway to lonely **Araouane** (p528) and the remote salt mines of **Taoudenni** (p528), an epic of deep desert immersion. En route east, look out for Mali's desert elephants (p534) and pause in **Gao** (p529), another once-great desert city and gateway to the **Adrar des Ifôghas mountains** (p533). Evocative **Agadez** (p604) in Niger enables you to explore the **Aïr Mountains** (p608), a massif once described by Heinrich Barth as 'the Switzerland of the Sahara' and a desert home of the Tuareg, and the exquisitely remote **Ténéré Desert** (p609), which is known as the 'desert beyond the desert'.

## THE STRONG BROWN GOD

The Niger River is one of Africa's grand old rivers and its strange course through West Africa, which fascinated European geographers for centuries, can guide your footsteps to some of the best the region has to offer.

It's a challenge to reach the **source of the Niger** (p425) in the highlands of Guinea, but there's something special about standing at the sacred spot where the river's 4000km course begins. **Kankan** (p426), the spiritual home of the Malinké people, is one of the most interesting towns of Upper Guinea, while Mali's sights are all close to the Niger's path, including **Bamako** (p490) with its wonderful live music; sleepy **Ségou** (p501), which stretches along the riverbank; and **Djenné** (p504), a beautiful old island town on the Bani River. **Mopti** (p508) has a raucous river port where you can arrange the ultimate river experience – a slow boat (p510) up the Niger River to **Timbuktu** (Toumbouctou; p521). En route, if you're here in December, head to **Diafarabé** (p504) for the amazing annual Fulani cattle crossing. Anywhere along the Niger Bend, where the river turns its face away from the Sahara, sand dunes line the riverbank, most accessibly around **Gao** (p529). Where Niger meets Benin, **Parc Regional du W** (p596 and p120) is one of the best spots in West Africa to see wildlife.

## WEST AFRICA'S BEST MARKETS

West Africa's markets are where the peoples of the region meet and trade, where music blaring from speakers competes for attention with aromas fair and foul and where all the colours of Africa will brighten your day.

In Ghana, Kumasi's **Kejetia Market** (p378) is enormous and awash with the colours of Ashanti culture. In neighbouring Togo, the **Marché des Féticheurs** (p779) in Lomé may just appeal if you're in need of a monkey's skull. Moving on to Benin, the huge **Grand Marché du Dantokpa** (p97), Cotonou, is also for those who get turned on by talismans. Lagos' **Balogun Market** (p633) is the best of many in the Nigerian capital and carries the vaguest hints of a medieval bazaar amid the Lagos clamour. To the north, in Nigeria, Kano's **Kurmi Market** (p661) is, at 16 hectares, one of the largest markets in Africa. In Niger, the **Tuareg camel market** (p606) in Agazdez is full of Tuareg men in turbans and anything but a desert stillness. Gorom-Gorom's **Thursday spectacular** (p163) in Burkina Faso is a who's who of the Sahel's ethnic groups, while in Mali, Djenné's **Monday market** (p505) has the town's spectacular mud-built mosque as a backdrop. The **Makola Market** (p344) in Accra, Ghana, **Bamako market** (p495) of Mali, the **Grand Marché** (p150) of Bobo-Dioulasso in Burkina Faso and the **Marché Sandaga** (p694) in Dakar, Senegal threaten to take over the cities, while **Kaolack** (p711), also in Senegal, has the second-largest covered market in Africa.

## IN SLAVERY'S FOOTSTEPS

Slavery ravaged practically all of West Africa and a visit to the sites where slaves left African shores for the last time is at once poignant and essential to understanding the shadow slavery cast over the region.

Ghana has perhaps the greatest concentration of slavery sites. Accra's **National Museum** (p344) has an evocative exhibition that provides historical context before you set out for the many forts and castles where slaves were held in dire conditions and then loaded onto equally dire ships. They're all worth visiting, but **Cape Coast Castle** (p360), Elmina's **St George's Castle** (p363) and **Fort Amsterdam** (p358) in Abanze are must-sees. East along the coast, **Ouidah** (p106) in Benin is another essential and emotion-filled reminder of slavery's horrors with a well-marked **Route des Esclaves** (p106) with its moving 'Point of No Return' memorial. The ports of Senegal were also used by slaving ships, with slaves from the interior brought to the coast. Île de Gorée's **La Maison des Esclaves** (p697) is famous as a grim holding centre for slaves, although historians dispute whether many slaves were shipped from here. In Guinea is the lesser-known **Îles de Los** (p417) where countless Africans saw their last view of their continent. In Sierra Leone, **Bunce Island** (p760) was a major shipping port for slaves, while **Freetown** (p753) was originally founded as a refuge for ex-slaves.

# Snapshot

There was a time when Côte d'Ivoire was the exception to the grim realities of a rough neighbourhood. Now, West Africa's one-time success story has become a poster boy for race-driven conflict, and for every step it takes forward, it takes two steps in the wrong direction. Elsewhere, the tide has turned for the better and Côte d'Ivoire has been left behind by its neighbours. Sierra Leone, Liberia (which in 2005 elected Africa's first female head of state) and, to a lesser extent, Guinea-Bissau, are showing genuine signs of a lasting return to civilian rule. Look elsewhere and there are more reasons to be optimistic, with Senegal, Ghana, Cape Verde, Niger and Mali the real stars of West Africa's democratic revival. Former military rulers continue to hold power in Benin, Burkina Faso and Nigeria, but now do so under the guise of democratic legitimacy, while the coup in Mauritania in 2005 shows early signs of heralding a more open era. The death of the world's longest-serving leader, Gnassingbe Eyadéma in Togo in 2005, brought his son to power, but for once the African Union and Ecowas (the Economic Community of West African States) bared their teeth, refused to recognise the dynastic succession, and forced the long-entrenched leadership of the country to finally subject itself to the will of the people. In a sign of how times have changed, Guinea's Lansana Conté and Cameroon's Paul Biya, in power since 1984 and 1982 respectively, now stand out as dinosaurs.

West Africa's movement towards political liberalisation has not, however, put food on the table, and West Africa remains the world's poorest region. In the UN Human Development Index for 2005, which ranks countries on a range of socio-economic indicators, Niger, Sierra Leone, Burkina Faso and Mali occupied the four lowest positions, with Guinea-Bissau not far behind in the table of the world's worst places to live. Of the 17 countries covered in this book, only Cape Verde (which ranked an acceptable 105th out of 177), Ghana (138th) and Togo (143rd) were deemed to be among the countries which could be said to enjoy 'Medium Human Development'. Programmes of debt relief for many West African countries, given momentum and popularised by Bono and Bob Geldof and the Live8 concerts in 2005, suggest that there is both popular goodwill in developed countries for helping the region lift itself out of poverty, and the possibility that such change could become a reality. The **New Partnership for Africa's Development** (Nepad; www.nepad.org) suggests that African governments are starting to take their own responsibility for finding a way out of the morass seriously. It's not that Africa doesn't have riches – Nigeria and, increasingly, Mauritania have oil, Sierra Leone has diamonds in abundance (the illegal mining of so-called 'blood diamonds' by rebel groups and unscrupulous diamond traders fuelled the country's devastating civil war), and Ghana and Mali have ample gold. But West Africa's natural environment is in crisis and until Western agricultural policies cease to undercut impoverished African farmers, and the corruption, sadly still prevalent, among many West African elites comes to an end, life for ordinary people in West Africa will continue to be the harshest of struggles.

Burkina Faso has the lowest adult literacy rate in the world (12.8%), followed by Niger (14.4%) and Mali (19%). Cape Verde is the star with 75.7% of adults able to read and write, followed by Cameroon (67.9%), Nigeria (66.8%), Ghana (54.1%), Togo (53%) and Mauritania (51.2%).

In Niger, there are just 3.3 doctors for every 100,000 people, while Burkina Faso (4) and Mali (4.4) fare little better. Mauritania has the highest proportion with 47, followed by Nigeria (26.9). Comparable Western countries include Australia (249.1), the UK (164) and the US (548.9).

The highest infant mortality rates are in Sierra Leone (166 per 1000 live births), Niger (154) and Guinea-Bissau (126). The lowest are in Cape Verde (26), Ghana (59), Senegal (78) and Togo (78). The figures for Western countries include Australia (6), the UK (5) and the US (7).

# History

West Africa may be the poorest region on earth, but it wasn't always that way. The now-dusty plains of the Sahel and southern Sahara were home to some of the richest and most extravagant empires in the world during the Middle Ages, empires which were centres as much of world-renowned scholarship as of wealth. As these empires crumbled, weakened by greed and foreign conquest, West Africa fell under the sway of Islam, and to the European colonial invaders who followed in the footsteps of explorers, slave traders and adventurers – all drawn by rumours of the region's riches. West Africa, whose modern political borders bear little relation to the territories of its many ethno-linguistic groups, has been in decline ever since.

This section provides an overview of the history of the region, focusing on the period before European influence significantly penetrated the interior. For accounts of the colonial and postcolonial periods in each country, see the individual country chapters.

*Africa: The Biography of the Continent*, by John Reader, is ambitious in its sweep but has good sections on the early history of the continent, which other writers often bypass.

## FIRST FOOTPRINTS ON THE SAHEL

Some archaeological evidence has been found of early human occupation in West Africa. Tools and other artefacts found in Senegal, Guinea, Mali, Mauritania and elsewhere, date back to 200,000 BC and are attributed to *Homo erectus*, the predecessor of *Homo sapiens* (modern man).

The picture starts to become a little clearer somewhere between 6000 and 10,000 years ago, when agricultural development began in the regions now occupied by the Sahara desert. At the time, most of West Africa (including what is now the Sahel and the Sahara) was the earth's idyll, home to lakes, rainforests and a pleasant Mediterranean climate. Rock art in the Aïr Mountains of northern Niger (see the boxed text, p609) from the period depicts giraffes, elephants and leopards being hunted by what are assumed to be hunter-gatherer societies.

The historical context of Saharan rock art is informatively discussed and beautifully illustrated in *African Rock Art*, by David Coulson and Alec Campbell.

From around 5000 BC, global climate changes caused the savanna to begin to dry out, thereby beginning the long process of turning the Sahara into a desert. Agriculture became difficult and farmers were forced to migrate to areas south of the savanna (the area today known as the Sahel), where the vegetation was also thinning but soils were still fertile.

As the land dried out and the animals that sustained hunting societies became more scarce, most of West Africa's peoples forsook transient life and settled in communities. By between 4000 and 3000 BC, people had domesticated cattle and were also cultivating and harvesting indigenous plants, including millet (a cereal crop), yam (root tubers) and rice. The shift to more sedentary communities was further confirmed by later Saharan rock art and finds of pottery shards, stone hoes, digging tools and hand-scythes used for cutting grasses.

## VILLAGES OF STONE

The shift to farming had far-reaching implications for the region. The land – suddenly able to support larger populations – became more intensively inhabited, with people living in much closer proximity than

| 200,000 BC | 5000 BC |
| --- | --- |
| Human beings make their first appearance in West Africa | Rains become infrequent and the Sahara begins to be transformed into a desert |

ever before. With village life and growing populations came the need for systems of administration, cooperation and control.

It has been said that the history of Africa resides in the belly of the termite, and remarkably little evidence has been found to chart this momentous period in the history of the region. Nonetheless, the earliest signs of organised society in West Africa date from around 1500 BC, in present-day Mauritania, where the remains of stone villages and domestic animals have been found. Similar remains have been found in what is now northern Nigeria. Centuries of subsequent building have buried such remains elsewhere, but it seems likely that settlements of this kind existed across the Sahel, which was much more densely vegetated than it is today.

Of the early societies that inhabited the Sahel during this period, two dominant groups emerged, the first along the Niger River, and the second around Lake Chad – both areas where soils were fertile and well suited to agriculture. These groups built large stone villages and even towns, and were in contact with other African peoples, particularly those living on the southern shores of the Mediterranean.

> Saharan rock art contains sophisticated but curious depictions of horse-drawn chariots driven by the forerunners to today's trans-Sahara overlanders, leading some to speculate that the Romans reached further south than was previously thought.

## THE IRON REVOLUTION

In the same way that climate change once transformed West Africa, the introduction of iron ushered in sweeping changes for the peoples of the region.

The earliest evidence of iron-working in West Africa is found in central Nigeria and dates from around 450 BC. Iron tools were much more efficient than those made from stone or bronze. It became possible to clear forests, which at once enabled people to dramatically expand the amount of land under cultivation (especially for cereal production), and therefore feed more people, and commenced the process of denuding the landscape. Although population numbers at the time suggest that an

> Knowledge of iron-working is thought to have been introduced to the region from Egypt via the Nile Valley and Lake Chad, although some authorities believe that the use of iron actually originated in West Africa, and that the knowledge went the other way, to Egypt.

---

### AFRICA ON THE MOVE

The changes set in motion by West Africa's increasingly widespread use of iron didn't just plant the seeds for future environmental pressures, it also began the process of remapping West Africa's human landscape.

As lands were cleared and settlements arose, people began to expand or migrate into new territories. These were not sudden mass movements of people, but rather gradual expansions over hundreds of years. At first, they consisted of many short moves – from valley to valley, or from one cultivation area to the next. Slowly, dominant peoples began to absorb other, weaker groups through intermarriage and assimilation.

The most successful migratory group in Africa were the Bantu people, whose current territory is almost a continent away from where they began. Originally from what is now Nigeria and Cameroon, the Bantu began to slowly make their way eastward and southward through the forests of Central Africa. The migration, which began around 2000 BC, gathered momentum after the introduction of iron, and by 100 BC the Bantu had reached the East African plateau. Over the next thousand years they moved down the continent as far as present-day Zimbabwe and South Africa. Today, the vast majority of indigenous peoples in Africa south of the equator are of Bantu origin. The only West African countries with significant Bantu populations are Nigeria and Cameroon – those who stayed behind.

---

| 450 BC | 300 BC |
|---|---|
| Iron starts being used in West Africa, ultimately changing the human and natural map of the region | Jenné-Jeno, West Africa's first-known urban settlement is founded |

Empires of Medieval
West Africa: Ghana, Mali,
and Songhay, by David
Conrad, covers the
sweep of West Africa's
three greatest historical
empires in one accessible
tome.

equilibrium was maintained between human needs and environmental preservation, the advent of iron began the conflict between the two, and provided the origins for some of West Africa's most pressing modern threats; for more information on this see p86.

Jenné-Jeno, in present-day Mali (p506), established around 300 BC, is believed to have been one of the earliest urban settlements in West Africa, and one where iron was used. Similar settlements were most likely established elsewhere around this time and, by AD 500, towns and villages were dotted across the region. The father of West African cities, Jenné-Jeno continued to grow, however, and by AD 800 was home to an estimated 27,000 people.

## WEST AFRICA'S GOLDEN AGE

By the end of the 1st millennium AD, Saharan trade routes were among the most lucrative in the world, with salt, gold, silver, ivory and slaves all being transported across the desert. The result was that the early settlements on the desert fringe grew into city-states which became increasingly large, wealthy and influential.

Into Africa: A Journey
through the Ancient Em-
pires, by Marq de Villiers
and Sheila Hirtle, looks at
Africa's past through the
prism of modern journeys
through the region – it's
a book you'll dip into
again and again.

### Empire of Ghana

The Empire of Ghana (which has no geographic connection with the present-day country) was the first major state of its kind established in West Africa. Founded in AD 300, Ghana was, by the 5th century, an established centre of the Soninké people. By the 8th century, Ghana profited not only from control of trans-Saharan trade, but also from exploiting the massive gold deposits that fed its legends – rumour had it that the streets were paved with gold, that Ghana's gold mines supplied two-thirds of the world's gold, and that the emperor of Ghana routinely tied his horse to a nugget of pure gold.

The capital of Ghana was Koumbi Saleh, in present-day Mauritania, about 200km north of modern Bamako (Mali). At its height, the empire covered much of present-day Mali and parts of eastern Senegal.

---

**THE BLACKSMITH – MASTER OF THE BLACK ARTS**

Not only did the increasing availability of iron propel a redrawing of Africa's human dispersal and have massive ramifications in terms of agricultural possibility, it also spawned one of Africa's most curious phenomena – the aura around the blacksmith. In almost all societies of West Africa, blacksmiths occupy a special role, at once feared and respected due to their daily and almost mystical communion with the basic elements of iron and fire. This status still places them at the heart of traditional ceremonies, bequeaths them the inherited and privileged role of intermediaries, and provides an unbroken connection to West Africa's past.

Among the Tuareg, for example, blacksmiths (known as *inaden*) produce numerous items essential to daily life (such as weapons and jewellery), but they're also healers, herbalists, poets, singers, skilled sacrificers of animals, advisers in matters of tradition and the custodians of oral traditions. Noble women confide in the *inaden*, use them as go-betweens in marriage negotiations and as mediators in love affairs. So important are they that no Tuareg festival could be complete without *inaden* participation, and anyone who tries to prevent them from attending is shunned by the whole community.

---

| AD 300 | 900 |
| --- | --- |
| The Empire of Ghana begins its 800-year rule | Islam first reaches the Sahel |

---

**THE EPIC OF SUNDIATA**

In the annals of West African history and legend, few tales have endured like the story of Sundiata Keita. In the 13th century, a sacred hunter prophesied to a Malinké king, who was best known as 'Maghan the Handsome' and who possessed no great power, that if he married an ugly woman, she would one day bear him a son who would become a great and powerful king, known to all the world. Maghan followed the seer's advice, but when his son Sundiata was born, he was disabled and unable to walk. When Maghan's successors battled for the throne, Sundiata was bypassed and forced into exile, only to return one day as king. When he defeated his more powerful Sosso rivals in 1240, he was crowned 'Mansa', or 'King of Kings', whereafter he founded the Empire of Mali, with its capital at his village of Niani, close to the Guinea-Mali border. He drowned in 1255 but his legend lives on in the tales of *griots* and in songs that drew heavily on his story, recorded by most of West Africa's best modern musicians.

---

Islam was introduced by traders from the north, and although it was adopted by local merchants and some members of the political elite, its half-hearted application sowed the seeds of Ghana's destruction. The empire was destroyed in the late 11th century by the better-armed Muslim Berbers of the Almoravid Empire from Mauritania and Morocco.

## Empire of Mali

In the middle of the 13th century, Sundiata Keita, leader of the Malinké people, founded the Empire of Mali in the region between the present-day countries of Senegal and Niger. By the beginning of the 14th century, the empire had expanded further, controlling almost all trans-Saharan trade. This brought great wealth to the rulers of Mali, who embraced Islam with enthusiasm.

During this period the trans-Saharan trade reached its peak, and the wealth created meant that Mali's main cities became major centres of finance and culture. The most notable was Timbuktu, where two Islamic universities were founded, and Arab architects from Granada (in modern-day Spain) were employed to design new mosques, such as Timbuktu's Dyingerey Ber mosque (p522).

*If the story of Sundiata has captured your imagination, Sundiata: An Epic of Old Mali, by DT Niane, is the best and most easily accessible version around today.*

## Empire of Songhaï

While Mali was at the height of its powers, the Songhaï people had established their own city-state to the east, around Gao in present-day Mali. As Mali descended into decadence and royal squabbles, Gao became powerful and well organised. At its height, the empire stretched from close to Lake Chad in the east to the hinterland of the Atlantic Coast in the west. Its emperors were reported to have travelled to Mecca with 300,000 gold pieces.

A hallmark of the Empire of Songhaï was the creation of a professional army and a civil service with provincial governors. The state even subsidised Muslim scholars, judges and doctors. By the mid-15th century, the Empire of Songhaï was at its most powerful and presided over most of West Africa, and by the 16th century, Timbuktu was an important commercial city with about 100,000 inhabitants. The golden period ended with an invasion by Berber armies from Morocco in 1591.

*By the middle of the 15th century, the Empire of Songhaï was the great power of the region and, after capturing Timbuktu, its forces finally took Djenné after a siege that lasted for seven years, seven months and seven days.*

| Late-11th century | 1240 |
|---|---|
| The Empire of Ghana is destroyed by the Berber armies of the Almoravid Empire | Sundiata Keita is crowned 'King of Kings' and founds the Empire of Mali |

## MALI – LAND OF KINGS

Mali's heyday in the 14th century was characterised by ambitious and extravagant kings, whose deeds caught the attention of the world. One such monarch, King Abubakari II, sent an expedition across the Atlantic in an attempt to discover the Americas. When only one ship returned, with stories of a great river running through the ocean's heart, the king was undeterred. He himself led a second expedition of 200 ships. Not a single ship returned.

King Abubakari's anointed successor was King Kankan Musa (the grandnephew of Sundiata Keita), who has a strong case to be called one of the most legendary of all African kings. In 1324 he made his pilgrimage to Mecca, accompanied by an entourage of more than 60,000 people and needing 500 slaves to carry all the gold. Along the way he gave away so much of his gold as gifts, that the world price of gold did not recover for 12 years, some say a generation. His actions attracted the attention of European merchants in Cairo and news spread quickly about a land of fabulous wealth in the desert's heart. King Kankan Musa was even depicted on a 1375 European map of Africa in which he was shown holding a gold nugget.

Generous as he was, King Kankan Musa was not the world's shrewdest financial manager. During his return journey from Mecca, he was so poor that he had to depend on the charity of towns along the way.

## Later States & Empires

As the Empire of Mali declined, the Wolof people established the Empire of Jolof (also spelt Yollof) near the site of present-day Dakar in Senegal. Meanwhile, on the southeastern fringe of the Songhaï realm, the Hausa people created several powerful city-states, such as Katsina, Kano and Zinder (still important trading towns today), but they never amalgamated into a single empire.

Further east again, on the shores of Lake Chad, the Kanem-Borno Empire was founded in the early 14th century. At its height it covered a vast area including parts of present-day Niger, Nigeria, Chad and Cameroon, before being loosely incorporated into the Songhaï sphere of influence; it nonetheless remained a powerful force in the region until the 19th century.

To the south, between the 13th and 16th centuries, several smaller states arose in areas where gold was produced. These included the kingdoms of Benin (in present-day Nigeria), Dahomey (Benin), Mossi (Burkina Faso) and Akan-Ashanti (Ghana); see the individual country chapters for more information.

> Mali's ancient kings were at the forefront of efforts to abolish slavery, most notably the legendary Sundiata Keita, founder of the Empire of Mali, who included a clause prohibiting slavery in his Charter of Kurukanfuga.

> BBC World Service's 'The Story of Africa' (www .bbc.co.uk/worldservice /africa/features/storyof africa) is a good introduction to West Africa's ancient kingdoms and contains links to research sites on the subject.

## EUROPEAN FOOTHOLDS

Trans-Saharan trade had carried gold from the coastal regions, via the Mediterranean, to the courts and treasuries of countries such as England, France, Spain and Portugal. As early as the 13th century the financial stability of several major European powers depended largely on the supply of West African gold. European royalty became obsessed with rumours of fabulously wealthy kingdoms south of the Sahara, although no European had yet visited the region.

Prince Henry of Portugal (Henry the Navigator, 1394–1460) was the first to act, encouraging explorers to sail down the coast of West Africa, which soon became known as Guinea. His intention was to bypass the

| 1443 | Mid-15th century |
|---|---|
| Portuguese ships reach the mouth of the Senegal River | The Empire of Songhaï is at the height of its powers and rules over much of West Africa |

Arab and Muslim domination of the trans-Saharan gold trade and reach the source by sea. The prince's goal would ultimately come to fruition and change the course of West African history.

In 1443 Portuguese ships reached the mouth of the Senegal River. Later voyages reached Sierra Leone (1462) and Fernando Po (now Bioko in Equatorial Guinea, off the coast of Nigeria) in 1472. As the Portuguese made contact with local chiefs and began to trade for gold and ivory, West Africa turned on its axis, the focus of its trade (and power) shifting from the Sahara to the coast as the great empires of the Sahel lost their monopoly.

In 1482 the Portuguese built a fortified trading post at Elmina (p363), on the coast of today's Ghana, which was the earliest European structure in sub-Saharan Africa. By 1500, Portuguese ships had also sailed some distance upstream along the Senegal and Gambia Rivers. But West Africa had few other large rivers that allowed access to the interior, and most trade remained on the coast.

> Some historians believe that the Gambia River's name (and indeed the name of the country) derives from the Portuguese word *cambio*, meaning 'exchange' or 'trade'.

## ISLAM IN THE SAHEL

Islam first reached the Sahel around AD 900, via trans-Saharan traders from present-day Morocco and Algeria. Perhaps not surprisingly, for a religion born in the desert, Islam quickly became the religion of the rulers and the wealthy in West Africa. Although ordinary people generally preferred to retain their traditional beliefs, rulers skilfully combined aspects of Islam and traditional religion in the administration of the state, thereby creating the fusion of beliefs that remains a feature of West African life today.

Islam cemented its position as the dominant religion in the Sahel in the 17th and 18th centuries, filling the vacuum left by the now defunct Sahelian empires. Spiritual power was fused with political and economic hegemony, and Islamic jihads (holy wars) were declared on nonbelievers and backed up by the powers of the state. In time, several Muslim states were established, including Futa Toro (in northern Senegal), Futa Djalon (Guinea), Masina (Mali) and the Sokoto state of Hausaland (Niger and Nigeria).

## EUROPE DECIDES TO STAY

While Islam was becoming firmly established, Europeans began to penetrate the interior. One explorer, Mungo Park – a Scottish doctor who travelled from the Gambia River to reach the Niger River in present-day Mali, and determined that the Niger flowed from west to east – was enslaved for a time by Moors, and later died in an attack on his boat. Later explorers included Frenchman René Caillié, the first European to reach the fabled city of Timbuktu, in 1828, and return home alive; the prolific Heinrich Barth, who stayed for a time in Agadez, Kano and Timbuktu in the 1850s and also lived to tell the tale; Scotsman Hugh Clapperton, who reached Kano in northern Nigeria; and the English brothers Richard and John Lander, who finally established that the Niger River flowed into the Atlantic, thereby solving one of the great geographical questions of the age.

As European influence grew in the first half of the 19th century, jihads were fought less against 'infidel' Africans, and more against Europeans –

> *Travels in the Interior of Africa*, by Mungo Park, is an epic tale of exploration on the Niger River; you'll find yourself asking how he stays so cheerful in the face of overwhelming hardship.

| 16th century | 17th century |
|---|---|
| Timbuktu has become a great centre of scholarship and wealth, and is home to 100,000 people | Islam becomes the dominant religion across the Sahel |

## SLAVERY IN WEST AFRICA

Slavery had existed in West Africa for many centuries, but it gained momentum with the arrival of Islam, despite the fact that the Qur'an prohibits the enslavement of Muslims. The Moors, Tuareg and Soninke in particular were known as slave traders. Later, the Portuguese escalated the trade, taking slaves to work on the large sugar plantations in Portuguese colonies on the other side of the Atlantic (including present-day Brazil) between 1575 and 1600.

By the 17th and 18th centuries, other European nations (particularly England, Spain, France and Holland) had established colonies in the Americas, and were growing sugar, tobacco, cotton and other crops. Huge profits could be made from these commodities, and the demand for slaves to work the plantations was insatiable.

In most cases, European traders encouraged Africans on the coast to attack neighbouring tribes and take captives. These were brought to the coastal slaving stations and exchanged for European goods such as cloth and guns, perpetuating a vicious cycle that enabled more tribes to be invaded and more slaves to be captured. A triangular trans-Atlantic trade route developed – the slaves were loaded onto ships and transported to the Americas, the raw materials they produced were transported to Europe, and the finished goods were transported from Europe to Africa once again, to be exchanged for slaves and to keep the whole system moving. The demand for slaves was maintained because conditions on the plantations were so bad that life expectancy after arriving in the Americas was often no more than a few years.

Exact figures are impossible to come by, but it is estimated that from the end of the 15th century until around 1870, when the slave trade was abolished, as many as 20 million Africans were captured. Up to half of these died, mostly while being transported in horribly overcrowded and unhealthy conditions, and 'only' around 10 million actually arrived in the Americas. The trade only came to an end when a liberalisation of attitudes brought on by the Enlightenment changed attitudes and, more expediently, the Industrial Revolution led to a demand for stable, compliant colonies supplying raw materials and providing a market for finished goods.

Although the trade in slaves became, for the most part, a thing of the past, there remains evidence – hotly disputed by governments – that people continue to be born into, and live their whole lives in slavery, especially in Mali, Mauritania and Niger. A local NGO in Niger, Timidria, issued a damning report in 2003, which suggested that slavery remained widespread in the country. The report, produced in conjunction with **Anti-Slavery International** ( ☎ 020 7501 8920; www .antislavery.org; The Stableyard, Broomgrove Rd, London SW9 9TL, UK) and available on its website, makes for sober reading, and suggests that slavery is yet to be consigned to history.

particularly against the French, who were pushing deeper into the West African interior. The most notable leader of the time was Omar Tall (also spelled Umar Taal), who led a major campaign against the French in the interior of Senegal from around 1850 until he was killed in 1864. After his death, the jihads known as the 'Marabout Wars' persisted in Senegal until the 1880s.

Despite growing penetration of the West African interior, the main European powers were largely confined to pockets of territory on the coast, among them the French enclave of Dakar (Senegal), and the British ports of Freetown (Sierra Leone) and Lagos (Nigeria). Portugal was no longer a major force, but had retained some territory – notably, Bissau, capital of today's Guinea-Bissau.

As these colonies became established, and with the major European powers apparently in for the long haul, often brutal military expeditions

To better understand the forces that drove the British campaign to abolish slavery in the 18th century, *Bury the Chains: The First International Human Rights Movement*, by Adam Hochschild, is masterful.

| 1828 | 1850–80s |
|---|---|
| Frenchman René Caillié becomes the first European to reach the fabled city of Timbuktu and return home alive | The 'Marabout Wars' are fought between Islam's holy warriors and the Europeans in Senegal |

were sent to the interior (the French marched into the Sahel while the British confined themselves to Ghana, Nigeria and Cameroon). Various minor treaties were made with local chiefs, but Europe's African domains were more a matter of unspoken understandings between European powers, than formal agreements or treaties.

## THE SCRAMBLE FOR AFRICA

Europe's wholesale colonisation of Africa was triggered in 1879 by King Leopold of Belgium's claim to the Congo. The feeding frenzy that followed saw Africa parcelled out among the French, British, Germans and Belgians, with the Portuguese refusing to let go of the colonies they already occupied.

Togo and Cameroon fell under German rule, Portugal held fast to Guinea-Bissau and Cape Verde, Britain staked a claim in 1883 to Gambia, Sierra Leone, the Gold Coast (Ghana) and Nigeria, while the Sahel (and most of Cameroon) was largely the preserve of the French. These claims – at once military realities and colonial fantasies as many Africans had not seen a European from the country to whom his or her land now supposedly belonged – were confirmed at the Berlin Conference of 1884–85. France was awarded almost one-third of the entire continent, including much of West Africa which became known as Afrique Occidentale Française (French West Africa), or the French Soudan.

Thus armed with the imprimatur of their fellow colonisers, the European powers consolidated their presence in the new colonies. Although anti-European feelings ran high among Africans, local resistance was sporadic and easily quashed by well-armed European soldiers.

Despite lip service to the idea of introducing 'civilisation' to the 'heathen natives' – which had officially replaced trade as the *raison d'être* of the colonial mission – the main aim of European governments was to exploit the colonies for raw materials. In West Africa, gem and gold mining was developed, but the once gold-rich region disappointed the occupiers. Consequently, labour-intensive plantations were established, and cash crops such as coffee, cocoa, rubber, cotton and groundnuts (peanuts) soon came to dominate the economies of the fledgling colonies, and to be a major source of employment – not always voluntary or paid – for local people.

After the German defeat in WWI, Togo and Cameroon were divided between France and Britain, with the divisive effects still evident today, especially in Cameroon.

During the first half of the 20th century, France controlled its West African colonies with a firm hand, and through a policy of 'assimilation' allowed Africans to become French citizens if they virtually abandoned their African identity. Britain made no pretence of assimilation and was slightly more liberal in its approach towards its colonies. Portugal ruled its empire in Africa with a rod of iron.

In all the West African economies, however, money was spent on building infrastructure (such as the Dakar–Bamako rail line) which benefited the colonial economy, with little or no attempt to improve living standards or expand education for West Africans, let alone build the institutions on which their future depended.

*Travels & Discoveries in North and Central Africa 1849–1855*, by Heinrich Barth, is a fascinating insight into what is now Niger, Nigeria and Mali, from arguably West Africa's greatest explorer.

*The Scramble for Africa*, by Thomas Packenham, can be a bit dry in patches, but it's a seminal text on the 1884–85 Berlin Conference and the European lust for African territory.

An outstanding piece of travel literature, Kira Salak's *Cruelest Journey: Six Hundred Miles to Timbuktu* follows in the footsteps of Mungo Park, and contains a moving account of her own bid to free two Bella slaves in Timbuktu.

| 1870 | 1884–85 |
| --- | --- |
| The slave trade is officially abolished | The Berlin Conference of European powers divides Africa into colonial spheres of influence |

## INDEPENDENCE

After WWII, the irresistible tide of nationalism and increasingly loud cries for independence were at first fiercely resisted by France and (to a lesser extent) Britain, but the colonial rulers eventually accepted the inevitable. In 1957 Ghana became the first country in West Africa to gain independence, followed by Guinea in 1958. In 1960 independence was granted to Benin, Côte d'Ivoire, Nigeria, Togo, Senegal and several other countries. Most other countries in the region became independent in the following few years, ending in 1965 with Gambia. Only recidivist Portugal held firm, not granting independence to Guinea-Bissau until 1973, and only after a bloody war.

France encouraged its former colonies to remain closely tied in a trade-based 'community', and most did; Guinea was a notable exception. In contrast, Britain reduced its power and influence in the region. The French maintained battalions of its own army in several former colonies, while the British provided more discreet military assistance.

Regardless of the approach of the former colonial powers, the first intoxicating rush of optimism after independence quickly gave way to dictatorship, corruption, an epidemic of coups d'état and massive economic problems. Independence offered West Africans greater freedom, but could not conceal the fact that colonialism had created fragile economies based on cash crops prone to huge price fluctuations, and had equipped few Africans to deal with such crises. To make matters worse, ethnic tensions created by artificial boundaries and divide-and-rule policies manifested as border disputes, separatist uprisings, military takeovers and civil wars, which continued into the 1980s. Basically, life for ordinary people became increasingly difficult.

The end of the Cold War – during which Africa became a theatre for meddling by the superpowers as the West propped up anticommunist dictators and the Soviet bloc buttressed those claiming to be Marxist – led to dramatic changes throughout West Africa, as the popular demand for democracy gained strength and multiparty elections were held in several countries. But even as democracy spread during the 1990s, West Africa's hopes of a new dawn were, not for the first time in its history, tempered somewhat by the descent into brutal civil war in Sierra Leone, Liberia, Guinea-Bissau and, to a lesser extent, Côte d'Ivoire.

For a snapshot of West Africa today, see p29.

It is believed that up to 200,000 African soldiers served in the French army during WWI and a further 200,000 in WWII; during the latter, Africans accounted for 9% of the French army and at least 50,000 were killed defending France, many on French soil.

There is no finer, more readable, or up-to-date history of Africa than *The State of Africa*, by Martin Meredith, which evocatively captures the pre-independence optimism and the problems that have beset the continent ever since.

| 1957 | 2000 |
|---|---|
| Ghana becomes the first West African country to gain independence | Côte d'Ivoire, the former poster boy for West African development, begins its descent into anarchy and civil war |

# The Culture

You'd be hard pressed to find any other region of the world with such a diversity of peoples. Cameroon alone has around 280 ethnic groups in its population and Guinea-Bissau, a country of less than one million people, has at least 20. West Africa is also a fascinating study of how traditional societies are coping with the assaults of the modern world. For more information on the major ethnic groups in West Africa and their traditions, see p73.

## DAILY LIFE

West Africans are adept at juggling multiple layers of identity, with family, ethnic group and gender among the most important.

Family life is the bedrock for most West Africans. In traditional society, especially in villages, homes were arranged around a family compound and life was a communal affair – the family ate, took important decisions, celebrated and mourned together in a space that was identifiably theirs and in a family group which spanned generations. Although family remains a critical source of support for many West Africans (those who earn a salary frequently distribute it among members of their family) and such family structures remain strongly evident in many villages, things are changing.

Vast numbers of Africans have migrated to cities, where ethnic identity takes on added significance, as recent arrivals in cities gravitate towards those with whom they share a tribal or ethnic tradition. Most (but by no means all) form friendships with people from their own ethnic groups. This is particularly true of minorities.

If family and ethnic identity are fundamental foundations of a West African's existence and serve to define them in their relations within their home countries, the nation to which they belong serves to announce who they are to the rest of the world. Most West Africans proudly identify themselves as being, for example, Malian or Nigerian, suggesting that one success of post-colonial West Africa has been the building of national identity in countries whose borders often cut across longer-standing ethnic boundaries. That said, the tragic descent into conflict in Côte d'Ivoire suggests that origins remain hugely significant and a calling card that is never forgotten.

### Traditional Culture

Many West African people organise their society along hierarchical lines, with status determined by birth. At the top are traditional noble and warrior families, followed by farmers, traders and persons of lower caste, such as blacksmiths (see p32), leather-workers, woodcarvers, weavers and musicians. Slaves were once at the bottom of the social hierarchy and although this status no longer officially exists (slavery is thought to continue in Mauritania, Mali and especially Niger), many descendants of former slaves still work as tenant farmers for the descendants of their former masters.

In traditional societies, older people (especially men) are treated with deference. Teachers, doctors and other professionals (usually men) often receive similar treatment. However, modernity is increasingly eroding traditional hierarchies. The government official who shows contempt for a rural chief may actually be a member of a lower caste who went away to the city and now has an office job.

Remittances to families from West African immigrants to Europe and the United States play a huge role in West African economies and amounted to US$1.759 billion in 1999.

*African Ceremonies*, by the finest photographic chroniclers of African traditional culture, Carol Beckwith and Angela Fisher, is a lavish, must-have coffee-table book with informative text and incomparable photos.

The average Niger woman will give birth to 7.9 children in her lifetime, maternal mortality is one of the highest in the world (1600 deaths per 100,000 live births), life expectancy hovers around 40 and only 9% of Niger's women can read and write.

## DO YOU HAVE SOMETHING FOR ME?

### Begging

In Africa, there's no government welfare cheque for the unemployed, crippled, homeless, sick or old; the only social security system is the extended family, meaning that many people are forced to beg. Because helping the needy is part of traditional African culture, and one of the pillars of Islam, you'll see even relatively poor people giving to beggars. If you want to give, even a very small coin is appreciated. If you don't have any change, just say 'next time' and at least greet the person and acknowledge their presence. If you're considering a larger donation, it's best to channel this through one of the many aid organisations working in the region.

### Cadeau

Far more pervasive than begging are the endless requests of *'Donnez-moi un cadeau'* (literally 'Give me a gift'), usually from children, but also from youths and adults. Part of this expectation comes from a belief that anyone to whom God has been good (and all foreigners are thought to be rich) should be willing to spread some wealth around.

Lest you get too paranoid, remember this. Considering the wealth of most tourists, and the unimaginable levels of poverty suffered by most West Africans, the incidence of robbery or theft in most countries in the region is incredibly low. Even a shoestring traveller's daily budget of US$15 a day is more than the average local labourer makes in a month and the vast majority of local people are decent and hard working, seeking only the chance to make an honest living. Many requests are just 'worth a try' situations, and your polite refusal will rarely offend.

It is sometimes appropriate to give a small gift in return for a service. Simply being pointed in the right direction is not a significant service, whereas being helped for 10 minutes to find a hotel probably is. If you're not prepared to offer a tip, don't ask for significant favours. Do remember, however, that some people will help you out of genuine kindness and will not be expecting anything in return.

Things sometimes work the other way. West Africans are frequently very friendly towards foreigners, and, after just a few minutes of talking, may offer you food or a bed for the night. You may want to repay such kindness with a gift such as tea, perfume or kola nuts, but money is usually the easiest thing to give.

### Bribery

A gift or tip becomes a completely different matter when you have to pay an official to get something done (also called a *cadeau* in Francophone countries or a 'dash' in English-speaking countries). The best approach is to feign ignorance, smile a lot, be patient and simply bluff your way through. Be personable and calm, and give the official plenty of room to back down and save face. Never simply offer to pay and remember that threats or shows of anger won't get you anywhere.

There are occasionally cases where a small dash or *cadeau* is unavoidable. If you really have no choice, remember that the 'fee' is always negotiable.

At the other end of the spectrum, children rate very low on the social scale and are expected to defer to adults in all situations. Unfortunately for half the region's population, the status of women is only slightly higher.

Village festivals (*fêtes* in French), which are fundamental to traditional life, are held to honour dead ancestors, local traditional deities and to celebrate the end of harvest. They are of particular importance in traditional culture. Some festivals include singing and dancing; some favour parades, sports or wrestling matches. In some areas you may see puppets used to tell stories, or elaborate performances with masks, which play an important part in traditional life. For more information on festivals, see p21.

## Women in West Africa

Women in West Africa face a formidable array of barriers to their participation in public life on an equal footing with men. In much of the region, social mores demand that a women is responsible for domestic work (cooking, pounding millet, child-rearing, gathering firewood), while many women also work (often as market or street vendors) to supplement meagre family incomes. Indeed it's a depressingly common sight to see women pounding millet or otherwise working hard while men lounge in the shade 'working' on their social relationships. Education of girls also lags significantly behind men, as evidenced by often appalling female literacy rates. Little wonder, therefore, that West African women are greatly under-represented in most professions – this is starkly evident for tourists in Mali, for example, where of the hundreds of accredited guides working with tourists, only one is a woman – let alone in government or at the upper levels of industry.

*Africa Through the Eyes of Women Artists*, by Betty La Duke, takes a sideways glance at the African world as viewed by some of the continent's best female artists.

### MARRIAGE & POLYGAMY

In many parts of West Africa, marriage is an expensive affair. Gifts from the groom to the bride's family can easily cost several hundred dollars in a region where annual incomes of US$200 are typical. Many men cannot afford to get married before their late 20s or 30s.

Despite the financial constraints, in traditional society (among Muslims and some non-Muslim people), men who can afford more than one wife (and many who can't) sometimes marry two, three or even four women (the Qur'an allows up to four). You will be told (by men) that women are not averse to polygamy, and that the wives become like sisters, helping each other with domestic and child-rearing duties. In reality, however, fighting and mistrust between wives is more common than marital bliss. However, there's not much women can do. Leaving a marriage simply because a husband takes another wife can bring shame to the woman and her family. She might be cast out of the family home or even physically beaten as punishment by her own father or brothers.

Musow (www.musow .com) is a slick and thoroughly modern online women's lifestyle magazine (French-language) that offers a mainly Malian antidote to the grim struggles faced by most West African women.

### FEMALE GENITAL MUTILATION

Female genital mutilation (FGM), often euphemistically termed 'female circumcision' or 'genital alteration', is widespread throughout West Africa. The term covers a wide range of procedures, from a small, mainly symbolic, cut, to the total removal of the external genitalia (known as infibulation). In West Africa, the procedure usually involves removal of the entire clitoris. The World Health Organisation's estimates range from about 15% to 20% of women altered in Togo, Ghana, Niger, Cameroon and Senegal, to up to 90% in Guinea, Sierra Leone, Mali and Gambia. It's a particularly common practice among the Fulani.

Although outsiders often believe that FGM is associated with Islam, it actually predates the religion (historical records of infibulation date back 6000 years). The procedure is usually performed by midwives on girls and young women. They sometimes use modern surgical instruments, but more often it's done with a razor blade or even a piece of glass. If the procedure is done in a traditional setting the girl will not be anaesthetised, although nowadays many families take their daughters to clinics to have the procedure performed by a trained doctor. Complications, especially in the traditional setting, include infection of the wound, leading to death, or scarring which makes childbirth and urination difficult.

In West Africa, FGM is seen among traditionalists as important for maintaining traditional society. An unaltered woman would dishonour

*Female Genital Mutilation: Legal, Cultural And Medical Issues*, by Rosemarie Skaine, tackles head-on the debate about this controversial practice, canvassing in detail traditional arguments in favour and well thought-out arguments to counter them.

## TIPS ON MEETING LOCALS

Although the rush to modernisation is irretrievably changing West Africa and attitudes are becoming more liberal, especially in cities, social mores remain quite conservative. You'll make a much better first impression if you avoid public nudity, open displays of anger or affection, and vocal criticism of the government or country; with the latter, people often take such criticism personally.

### Greetings

Great importance is placed on greetings in West Africa. Muslims usually start with the traditional Islamic greetings, *'Salaam aleikum'* and *'Aleikum asalaam'* ('Peace be unto you', 'And peace be unto you'). This is followed by more questions, such as 'How are you doing?', 'How is the family?' and 'How are the people of your village?'. The reply is usually *'Al humdul'allah'* (meaning 'Thanks be to God'). In villages, highly ritualised greetings can seem to last for an eternity. In cities, the traditional greetings may give way to shorter ones in French or English, but they're never forgotten. As such, it's important to use greetings whenever possible. Even for something as simple as exchanging money or asking directions, start with 'Good day, how are you? Can you help me please?' Launching straight into business is considered rude. Learning some greetings in the local language will smooth the way considerably. Even a few words make a big difference (see p861 for some useful phrases).

Handshaking is also an important part of greetings. Use a soft – rather than overly firm – handshake. Some Muslim men prefer not to shake hands with women, and West African women don't usually shake hands with their male counterparts.

### Deference

Another consideration is eye contact, which is usually avoided, especially between men and women in the Sahel. If a West African doesn't look you in the eye during a conversation, remember that they're being polite, not cold. When visiting rural settlements, it's a good idea to request to see the chief to announce your arrival and request permission before wandering through a village. You'll rarely be refused. When you meet people holding positions of authority, such as police officers, immigration officials or village chiefs (usually men), it is important to be polite.

### Conduct

How you conduct yourself can have a lasting impact on the people you meet in West Africa. Remember also that respect for local etiquette earns you respect.

- If you're in a frustrating situation, be patient, friendly and considerate. A confrontational attitude may make you feel better but it can easily inflame the situation and offend local sensibilities. Remember, you are a guest.
- Be respectful of Islamic traditions and don't wear revealing clothing; loose lightweight clothing is preferable.
- Public displays of affection are usually inappropriate, especially in Muslim areas.
- Try and learn some of the standard greetings (p861) – it will make a very good first impression.
- Ask permission to photograph people and always respect the wish of anyone who declines.
- If you agree to send someone a photo, make sure you do so.

### Dress

West Africans place great importance on appearance, and generally dress conservatively, especially in the Sahel and inland areas. Hardly surprising, therefore, that clothes worn by travellers (eg singlets, shorts or tight trousers) are often considered offensive and may mean you get treated with a certain contempt. In general, the more professional you look, the better you will be received and treated. For women, in addition to respecting local sensibilities, dressing modestly also helps minimise hassles. This is especially important in rural areas and when in the presence of chiefs or other esteemed persons.

her family and lower its position in society, as well as ruining her own chances for marriage – a circumcised woman is thought to be a moral woman, and more likely a virgin. Many believe that if left, the clitoris can make a woman infertile or damage, and even kill, her unborn children.

Although FGM is deeply ingrained in West African societies, there are moves to make it illegal. Guinea, Ghana and Burkina Faso have banned the procedure and Côte d'Ivoire is planning such a law. The governments of Benin, Ghana, Senegal, Guinea and, to a lesser extent, Burkina Faso, Guinea-Bissau and Mali have mounted public awareness campaigns against the practice.

However, there remain doubts about how effective these efforts are. Practitioners are afraid of being arrested, but find it hard to go against tradition.

## IMMIGRATION & EMIGRATION

The majority of immigrants trying to enter Europe illegally in recent years come from West Africa. Most are driven to emigrate by persecution and authoritarian governments, poverty or conflict, and their departure leaves gaping holes in the structure of traditional societies. Among the Tuareg of northern Niger, for example, entire villages have emptied of young men who have been driven to cities and neighbouring countries in search of subsistence, leaving behind, (probably forever) the nomadic lifestyle that once defined their people.

Another major problem facing West African countries is a shortage of skilled labour, especially doctors and nurses, who emigrate in search of a better life. In particular, doctors and nurses from Ghana and Nigeria help to keep the UK health system operational, while back home health services are crying out for skilled staff.

On the other side of the equation, the benefits derived from those who do reach Europe and find employment are considerable. Some traditional chiefs (especially in southern Mali) actually gather funds to pay for the fittest young man to try his luck, as those who stay behind profit hugely from remittances from Europe.

Within West Africa, Côte d'Ivoire's one-time economic miracle drew immigrants from across the region, providing much-needed labour for a booming economy and a livelihood for millions of citizens of neighbouring countries. However, the conflict in the country since 2000 has laid bare the veneer of tolerance with which many Ivorian viewed the immigrants. Second-generation immigrants – some of whom have known no country but Côte d'Ivoire – have been told that they are no longer welcome and blamed for all the country's ills.

## SPORT

West Africans love their football (soccer) and the incredible success of players in the European leagues and the emergence of Africa as a future world footballing power has served to take this passion to new heights.

The African Cup of Nations, held every two years in January, generates great enthusiasm across the continent. In the preliminary rounds, 34 national teams compete, with the 16 best teams then gathered together in one place for the final rounds. The 2002 African Cup of Nations was held in Mali with Cameroon defeating Senegal in the final to become the first team since 1967 to win successive titles. It also joined Ghana and Egypt as the only four-time winners in the cup's history (Nigeria has won two cups and Côte d'Ivoire one). In 2006 the tournament was held in Egypt and Côte d'Ivoire lost out to the home side in the final.

Amnesty International's webpage on female genital mutilation (www .amnesty.org/ailib /intcam/femgen/fgm9 .htm) has a detailed rundown on the prevalence of the practice in 16 West African countries (only Cape Verde is excluded).

The Sussex Centre for Migration Research (www .gdrc.org/icm/remittance /mwp15.pdf) has detailed analysis of the importance of remittances to West Africa, which is hugely informative but makes for somewhat dry reading.

For the latest results and news on African football, fans can check out the website of the Confédération Africaine de Football (CAF; www.cafonline .com), Africa's football governing body.

**THE DAKAR RALLY**

The Dakar Motor Rally, also known simply as 'Le Dakar', is considered to be one of the world's longest, hardest and most dangerous driving events. It was the brainchild of French racing driver Thierry Sabine and was first held in 1979, although adventurous motorists have been crossing the Sahara since the 1920s. The race is held annually in January, usually starting in Paris (in recent years it has begun in Barcelona and Lisbon) and finishing in Dakar. The race always crosses the Sahara Desert, although the route changes every year. The route distance is around 10,000km and takes about 20 days to complete.

The pace, heat and terrain are so tough that of the 400 or so vehicles that start each year, less than half (and sometimes only around a quarter) cross the finish line. Categories include motorbikes, cars and trucks, and international auto manufacturers such as Citroën and Yamaha spend millions of dollars on drivers, machines and support teams to ensure top rankings. Of equal interest are the 'privateers' – individuals or amateur teams who compete on shoestring budgets and keep the spirit of the original adventurers alive.

Some commentators have questioned the morality of a million-dollar orgy of Western consumerism blasting its way through the poverty-stricken Sahel. The sponsorship money the rally generates, for example, equals 50% of Mauritania's total aid budget and each rally stage burns 10% of Mali's total annual fuel consumption. In fact, so much petrol is needed by the competitors that 'host' countries run short and some aid and relief operations report being unable to move their trucks for weeks. Competitors get killed most years, but when innocent villagers (who account for 75% of the overall numbers of deaths) get run over by speeding cars with a value many times the lifetime earnings of an entire town, the contrast is brought even more sharply into focus.

The organisers of the race have begun to react to criticism by teaming up with French aid agency SOS Sahel. Since the partnership began in September 2002, the majority of the Dakar's donations have gone towards environmental protection (eg waste management, tree planting and education) and projects providing safe drinking water in Senegal, Mali, Mauritania and Burkina Faso.

An offbeat and thoroughly worthwhile alternative is the Plymouth–Banjul Challenge, which often runs at the same time as its more illustrious counterpart. To enter, competing cars must cost less than UK£100, the maximum budget for preparation is UK£15 and all vehicles that reach Banjul (or Dakar) must be handed over to the race organisers who auction them off to support Gambian and Senegalese charities.

But it was at the 1990 World Cup in Italy that West Africa finally emerged as a football powerhouse on the world stage. Cameroon stunned the world by defeating the reigning champions Argentina in the opening match of the tournament and went on to become the first African team to reach the quarter finals. Senegal also defeated the defending champions France in 2002 and reached the quarter finals and Cameroon won the football gold medal at the 2000 Sydney Olympics. Although Cameroon, Nigeria and Senegal have been the major players in recent years, all three dramatically failed to qualify for the 2006 World Cup, where West Africa will be represented by Ghana, Togo and Côte d'Ivoire.

The Dakar Motor Rally website (www.dakar .com) has everything you need to know about the world's most famous desert rally. The website of the Plymouth–Banjul Challenge (www.ply mouth-dakar.co.uk) doesn't take itself quite as seriously.

All West African countries have football leagues and tournaments in which teams from different towns and cities compete on a national or regional basis. The winners of local league and cup competitions qualify for continent-wide club competitions, which include the African Champions League and the Confédération Africaine de Football (CAF) Cup, both held annually.

## RELIGION

Generally speaking, roughly half of all West Africans are Muslim, particularly those living in the desert and Sahel countries. Although you'll also find Christians living in some of the larger cities of the Sahel,

Christianity is more widespread in the southern coastal countries. For information on the religious make-up of individual countries, see the relevant country chapters.

## Traditional Beliefs

Before the arrival of Islam and Christianity, every race, tribe or clan in West Africa practised its own traditional religion. While many people in the Sahel converted to Islam, and those in the south converted to Christianity, traditional religions remained strong in many parts of the region and still retain a powerful hold over the consciousness of West Africans, even co-existing with established aspects of Islam or Christianity; firm lines between one set of values and another can often be difficult to draw. When discussing traditional beliefs, terms such as 'juju', 'voodoo' and 'witchcraft' are frequently employed. In certain specific contexts these may be correct, but they cannot be applied to all traditional African religions. For more information on some of these terms, see p93.

*The Encyclopedia of African and African-American Religions,* edited by Stephen Glazier, is encyclopaedic in scope and certainly the best resource on Africa's traditional religions.

There are hundreds of traditional religions in West Africa, with considerable areas of overlap, but there are no great temples (more modest local shrines often served the same purpose) or written scriptures (in keeping with West Africa's largely oral tradition). Beliefs and traditions can be complex and difficult to understand, but several common factors can be outlined. The description here provides an overview only, and is necessarily very simplified.

Almost all traditional religions are animist, meaning that they are based on the attribution of life or consciousness to natural objects or phenomena. Thus a certain tree, mountain, river or stone may be sacred because it represents, is home to, or simply *is* a spirit or deity. The number of deities of each religion varies, as does the phenomena that represents them. The Ewe of Togo and Ghana, for example, have more than 600 deities, including one that represents the disease smallpox.

*Egypt,* by Youssou N'Dour, Senegal's most famous international star, pays musical tribute to Senegal's rich and tolerant Sufi tradition, which blends perfectly with the sounds of Egyptian orchestral arrangements.

Several traditional religions accept the existence of a supreme being or creator, as well as the spirits and deities, although this figure usually figures in creation myths and is considered too exalted to be concerned with humans. Communication is possible only through the lesser deities or through the intercession of ancestors. Thus, in many African religions, ancestors play a particularly strong role. Their principal function is to protect the tribe or family and they may on occasion show their ancestral pleasure or displeasure (eg in the form of bad weather or a bad harvest, or when a living member of the family becomes sick). Many traditional religions hold that the ancestors are the real owners of the land, and while it can be enjoyed and used during the lifetime of their descendants, it cannot be sold.

Communication with ancestors or deities may take the form of prayer, offerings (possibly with the assistance of a holy man, or occasionally a holy woman) or sacrifice. Requests may include good health, bountiful harvests and numerous children. Many village celebrations are held to ask for help from, or in honour of, ancestors and deities. The Dogon people from the Bandiagara Escarpment in Mali, for instance, have celebrations before planting (to ensure good crops) and after harvest (to give thanks). Totems, fetishes (talismans) and charms are also important features of traditional religions; for more details, see p70.

## Islam

### ISLAM & WEST AFRICA

Between AD 610 and 620 in the city of Mecca, Saudi Arabia, the Prophet Mohammed, after a series of revelations from Allah, called on the people to turn away from pagan worship and submit to Allah, the one true god. His teachings appealed to poorer levels of society and angered the wealthy merchant class. In AD 622 Mohammed and his followers were forced to flee to Medina. This migration, the Hejira, marks the beginning of the Islamic calendar, year 1 AH (anno Hegirae). By AD 630 (8 AH), Mohammed had gained a larger following and returned to Mecca.

Mohammed died in AD 632, but within two decades most of Arabia was converted to Islam. Over the following centuries, Islam spread through North and West Africa and down the coast of East Africa. En route to West Africa, Islam adapted to local conditions by evolving features that would not be recognised by purists in Cairo or Mecca. Most notable of these are the marabouts – holy men who act as a cross between priest, doctor and adviser for local people. In some countries, especially Senegal, marabouts wield considerable political power.

Islam spread so quickly partly because it provided a simpler alternative to the established faiths, which had become complicated by hierarchical orders, sects and complex rituals, offering instead a direct relationship with God based only on the believer's submission to God ('Islam' means submission). Sufism, which emphasises mystical and spiritual attributes, was one of the more popular Islamic forms in West Africa; some scholars speculate that the importance that Sufis ascribe to religious teachers may have found favour in West Africa as it mirrored existing hierarchical social structures.

For more information on the history of Islam in West Africa, see p35.

## THE FIVE PILLARS OF ISLAM

The five pillars of Islam (the basic tenets that guide Muslims in their daily lives) are as follows:

**shahada** (the profession of faith) 'There is no god but Allah, and Mohammed is his Prophet' is the fundamental tenet of Islam.

**salat** (prayer) Muslims must face Mecca and pray at dawn, noon, mid-afternoon, sunset and nightfall. Prayer times are marked by the haunting call to prayer, which emanates from mosques and rings out across the towns and villages of the Sahel.

**zakat** (alms) Muslims must give a portion of their income to the poor and needy.

**sawm** (fasting) Ramadan commemorates Mohammed's first revelation, and is the month when all Muslims fast from dawn to dusk.

**haj** (pilgrimage, usually written hadj in West Africa) Every Muslim capable of affording it should perform the haj, or pilgrimage, to the holiest of cities, Mecca, at least once in his or her lifetime. The reward is considerable: the forgiving of all past sins. This can involve a lifetime of saving money, and it's not unusual for families to save up and send one member. Before the advent of air travel, the pilgrimage often involved an overland journey of a year or more. In West Africa, those who complete the pilgrimage receive the honorific title of Hadj for men, and Hadjia for women. If you meet someone with this prefix, you may appreciate the honour this bestows on them in the community.

For information on Islamic holidays, including a table of dates, see p818.

## ISLAMIC CUSTOMS

In everyday life, Muslims are prohibited from drinking alcohol and eating carrion, blood products or pork, which are considered unclean, the meat of animals not killed in the prescribed manner and food over which the name of Allah has not been said. Adultery, theft and gambling are also prohibited.

Islam is not just about prohibitions but also marks the important events of a Muslim's life. When a baby is born, the first words uttered to it

---

**TIPS FOR THE TRAVELLER IN ISLAMIC AREAS**

When you visit a mosque, take off your shoes; women should cover their heads and shoulders with scarves. In some mosques, women are not allowed to enter if prayers are in progress or if the imam (prayer leader) is present; in others, there may be separate entrances for men and women. In others still, non-Muslims are not allowed to enter at all.

If you've hired a guide or taxi driver for the day, remember that he'll want to say his prayers at the right times, so look out for signs that he wants a few moments off, particularly around noon, late afternoon and sunset. Travellers on buses and bush taxis should also be prepared for prayer stops at these times.

Despite the Islamic proscription against alcohol, some Muslims may enjoy a quiet drink. Even so, it's impolite to drink alcohol in their presence unless they show approval.

During Islamic holidays, shops and offices may close. Even if the offices are officially open, during the Ramadan period of fasting, people become soporific (especially when Ramadan falls in the hot season) and very little gets done.

---

are, in many places, the call to prayer. A week later follows a ceremony in which the baby's head is shaved and an animal sacrificed in remembrance of Abraham's willingness to sacrifice his son to Allah. The major event of a boy's childhood is circumcision, which normally takes place between the ages of seven and 12. When a person dies, a burial service is held at the mosque and the body is buried with the feet facing Mecca.

# ARTS

West Africa has a rich artistic heritage that extends from arts and handicrafts (see p67) and music (p58) to literature, architecture and a thriving film industry.

## Literature

African society has long revolved around storytelling, which took either oral or musical form. The greatest and most famous tale is the Epic of Sundiata (see p33), the story of the founder of the Empire of Mali and whose story is still recounted by modern griots, musicians and writers.

Modern-day West African writers have adapted this tradition, weaving compelling tales into the great issues facing modern West Africa, most notably the arrival and legacy of colonial powers and the role of women within traditional society. For a good introduction to the literature of the region, the most useful anthology is the *Traveller's Literary Companion – Africa*, edited by Oona Strathern, which contains more than 250 prose and poetry extracts from all over Africa, an introduction to the literature of each country, author biographies and a list of 'literary landmarks' (features that appear in novels written about the country). Poetry anthologies include *The Heinemann Book of African Poetry in English*, edited by Adewale Maja-Pearce, and *The Penguin Book of Modern African Poetry*, edited by Moore and Beier.

Listed here is a brief selection of classic works by African authors of international renown. All are highly recommended and many are published as part of the Heinemann African Writers series. For more titles by regional authors see the individual country chapters.

*The Epic of Sundiata is at its most accessible in* Sunjata: Gambian Versions of the Mande Epic, *by Bamba Suso and Banna Kanute, which retells West Africa's most famous story as told in the tradition of Gambian griots.*

## NIGERIA

Nigeria has a particularly strong literary tradition and is largely credited with producing the first African novels of international quality. Amos Tutuola's *The Palm-Wine Drunkard* was published in the early 1950s and brought African writers to the world's attention by providing a link between traditional storytelling and the modern novel. Dylan Thomas, poet and critic, described it as 'brief, thonged, grisly and bewitching'. It's about an insatiable drunkard who seeks his palm-wine tapster in the world of the dead.

Chinua Achebe is even better known and his *Things Fall Apart* (1958) is a classic; it has sold over eight million copies in 30 languages, more than any other African work. Set in the mid-19th century, this novel studies the collision between pre-colonial Ibo society and European missionaries. Achebe's more recent work, *Anthills of the Savannah*, is a satirical study of political disorder and corruption. It was a finalist for the 1987 Booker Prize.

Taking the art form to new heights, Wole Soyinka won the Nobel Prize for Literature in 1986 (the first author from Africa to achieve this accolade) for his impressive body of work, which includes the plays *A Dance of the Forest, The Man Died, Opera Wonyosi* and *A Play of Giants*. He has also written poetry (including *Idane & Other Poems*), novels (including *The Interpreters*), political essays and the fantastical childhood memoir *Ake*. Soyinka's works are noted as expressions of his social vision and strong beliefs, and are praised for their complex writing style.

Another Nigerian author is the exceptionally talented Ben Okri, whose novel *The Famished Road* won the Booker Prize in 1991. When critics grumbled that to appreciate the book's style and symbolism the reader had to 'understand Africa', Okri recalled reading Victorian novelists such as Dickens as a schoolboy in Nigeria. He continues to fuse modern style with traditional mythological themes in his later novels *Songs of Enchantment, Dangerous Love, Infinite Riches* and *Astonishing the Gods*.

Buchi Emecheta is one of Africa's most successful female authors. Her novels include *Slave Girl, The Joys of Motherhood, Rape of Shavi* and *Kehinde*, and focus with humour and irrepressible irony on the struggles of African women to overcome their second-class treatment by society.

A particularly exciting collection of Nigerian writers has emerged in the last few years to build on the successes of the earlier generation. Those who have received glowing critical acclaim include Chimamanda Ngozi Adichie *(Purple Hibiscus)*, Helen Oyeyemi *(The Icarus Girl)*, Uzodinma Iweala *(Beasts of No Nation)* and Helon Habila *(Waiting for an Angel)*, each of which vividly portrays modern Nigeria in all its vigour and complexity.

### ELSEWHERE IN WEST AFRICA

The strength of the West African oral tradition is such that the phrase, 'the death of an old man is like the burning down of a library' is now known across the world. What few people know is that it was first penned by Mali's greatest writer, Amadou Hampaté Bâ, who was, until his death in 1991, one of the most significant figures in West African literature, as well as a leading linguist, ethnographer and religious scholar. Bâ wrote prolifically, although only three of his books are readily available in English – *The Fortunes of Wangrin* (which won the 1976 'Grand Prix littéraire de l'Afrique noire'); *Kaidara* and *Radiance of the Great Star*. His critically acclaimed autobiography, *Amkoullel, l'enfant peul*, has yet to be translated into English.

Sembène Ousmane, from Senegal, is better known as an acclaimed movie director (see p679), but he has also published short story collections and *God's Bits of Wood*, an accomplished novel set in colonial Mali and Senegal. It's one of the few Francophone novels that is well known

---

*Magical Realism in West African Literature: Seeing with a Third Eye*, by Brenda Cooper, is a tad academic but is essential for those eager to learn more about West African literature in the wider literary context; it's especially good on Ben Okri and Kojo Laing.

*West African Folktales*, which is edited by Steven H Gale, is a good introduction to the myths and stories of West Africa, many of which form the underpinning of the region's modern literary forms.

and readily available in English. Another Senegalese writer is Mariama Bâ, whose novel *So Long a Letter* won the Noma Award for publishing in Africa. The late Leopold Senghor, former Senegalese president and a literary figure of international note, is the author of several collections of poetry and writings. For more information on Senegalese writers, see p679. Of the next generation of Senegalese women writers, Nafissatou Dia Diouf is attracting attention. Her work includes *Retour d'un long exil et autres nouvelles* (2001) and *Sables Mouvants* (2000), although she's still new on the African literary scene, ensuring that her novels are yet to be translated from the French.

Côte d'Ivoire's finest novelist, Ahmadou Kourouma, is widely available in English. His *Waiting for the Wild Beasts to Vote* is a masterpiece that evocatively captures both the transition to colonial rule and the subsequent corruption of power by Africa's leaders. *The Suns of Independence, Monnew* and *Allah Doesn't Have To* are also great reads.

Cameroon's best-known literary figure is the late Mongo Beti. *The Poor Christ of Bomba* is Beti's cynical recounting of the failure of a missionary to convert the people of a small village. Other works by Beti include *Mission to Kala* and *Remember Ruben*.

Ghana's foremost writer is Ayi Kwei Armah. His *The Beautiful Ones Are Not Yet Born* (1969) is a classic tale of corruption and disillusionment in post-independence Africa and undoubtedly the best in a fine body of work. Ama Ata Aidoo, one of Ghana's few well-known female writers, wrote *Changes: A Love Story,* a contemporary novel about a modern Ghanaian woman's life in Accra. Her other books, *Our Sister Killjoy* and *Dilemma of a Ghost and Anowa,* are also excellent. Kojo Laing (*Woman of the Aeroplanes, Search Sweet Country, Major Gentl and the Achimota Wars* and *Godhorse*) is another Ghanaian novelist of modest international renown.

Other acclaimed writers include Gambia's William Conton, whose 1960s classic *The African* is a semiautobiographical tale of an African student in Britain who later returns to his homeland and becomes president, and Camara Laye (Guinea), who wrote *The African Child* (also called *The Dark Child*), which was first published in 1954 and is one of the most widely printed works by an African.

## Cinema & TV

West African music (p58) may be making a lot of noise in international circles, but the region's film industry has for decades been quietly gathering plaudits from critics. Where major non-Western movie industries elsewhere (eg India and Egypt) have captured attention for the volume of their output and their song-and-dance, cops-and-robbers populism, West African film is high quality and a regular presence at the world's best film festivals. West Africa also has one such festival of its own – Fespaco (see p133) – which takes place biannually in Ouagadougou in Burkina Faso and has placed quality film-making at the centre of modern West African cultural life.

A small but significant West African film industry has existed in the region since the heady post-independence days of the 1960s. At that time, some countries in the region nurtured cultural links with the Soviet Union, and several directors trained in Moscow, returning home to make films – often with state support or funding – based on overtly Marxist themes.

Common themes explored by the first wave of postcolonial film makers included the exploitation of the masses by colonialists and, later,

A particularly incisive account of the clash between modern and traditional views on polygamy is given in *So Long a Letter,* an especially fine novel written in the voice of a widow by Senegalese author Miriama Bâ.

California Newsreel (www.newsreel.org) is a resource on African film with extensive reviews and a Library of African Cinema, where you can order many of the best West African films, especially those that have won at Fespaco.

www.lonelyplanet.com

corrupt and inefficient independent governments. Another theme was the clash between tradition and modernity. Films frequently portrayed African values – usually in a rural setting – suffering from Western cultural influence.

The 1970s was the zenith of African film making, and many films from this era still inspire the new generation of directors working today. However, through the 1980s and 1990s and into the 21st century, directors have found it increasingly difficult to find the necessary finance, production facilities and – most crucially – distribution that would give West African directors the wider recognition they deserve. The lack of a good distribution network for African films also makes it difficult for travellers to see them, even though most of the continent's directors (outside South Africa) are from West Africa, particularly the Francophone countries.

West African film is dominated by three countries: Senegal, Mali and Burkina Faso. For a list of West Africa's finest movies, see p21.

*Butabu: Adobe Architecture of West Africa*, by James Morris, is a stunning photographic study of West Africa's traditional architecture with informative text; a great reminder of your visit.

Ousmane Sembène from Senegal is arguably West Africa's best-known director. His body of work includes *Borom Sarret* (1963), the first commercial film to be made in post-independence Africa, *Xala, Camp Thiaroye* and, most recently, the critically acclaimed *Moolade*, which tackles the taboo subject of female genital mutilation. Other important Senegalese directors include Ahmed Diallo, Mansour Wade, Amadou Seck and Djibril Diop. For more information on Senegalese films, see p679.

Mali's leading director is Souleymane Cissé, whose 1970s films include *Baara* and *Cinq Jours d'Une Vie*. Later films include the wonderful

**THE BEST OF WEST AFRICAN ARCHITECTURE**

West Africa is more known as a destination where people, cultures and landscapes provide the major attractions. However, there are some stunning examples of architecture dotted around the region.

The king of traditional mosques is the extraordinary Djenné Mosque (Mali; p506) with its forest of turrets and mud flourishes. Other especially fine traditional mosques include the Grande Mosquée of Bobo-Dioulasso (Burkina Faso; p150), the seven mosques of Bani (Burkina Faso; p163), the Dyingerey Ber Mosque and Sankoré Mosque in Timbuktu (Mali, p522) and the Grande Mosquée of Agadez (Niger; p606), all of which are built, at least in part, of mud, straw and wood with pyramidal minarets.

The villages of the Dogon Country (Mali; p489) huddle up against the cliffs of the Bandiagara escarpment, while the fortified villages of the Tamberma Valley (Togo; p799) in northern Togo are similarly otherworldly. Elsewhere, the villages of southern Burkina Faso, especially the multistorey, fortresslike family compounds of the Lobi (Burkina Faso; p158) and the geometrically painted windowless homes of the Gourounsi in Tiébélé (Burkina Faso; p160), are definitely worth the effort to get there. The same could be said of the old quarters of the Saharan oasis towns of Ouadâne (Mauritania; p567), Chinguetti (Mauritania; p565), Tichit (Mauritania; p569) and Oualâta (Mauritania; p570). Timbuktu (Mali; p521), Agadez (Mali; p604) and Djenné (Mali; p504) also have evocative, if crumbling, old towns built entirely of mud. The traditional mud-and-thatch homes in the area around Bamenda (Cameroon; p198) are also some of the finest in the region.

Cameroon is particularly rich in traditional palaces, especially at Foumban (Cameroon; p203) and Bafut (Cameroon; p201), while Abomey (Benin; p110) also boasts a fine royal palace. Africa's only stilt villages (Benin; p102) are not far away at Ganvié. In Ghana, there are also traditional Ashanti buildings (Kumasi, Ghana; p378) and fine, if blood-stained colonial forts (Ghana; p354) all along the coast.

For elegant colonial-era buildings, the Portuguese left their mark throughout Guinea-Bissau and Cape Verde; in the latter Cidade Velha (Cape Verde; p238) is undoubtedly home to the richest collection.

*Yeelen,* a prize-winner at the 1987 Cannes festival, and *Waati.* Cheick
Omar Sissoko has won prizes at Cannes and his *Guimba, un Tyran, une
Epoque Guimba,* won the Étalon d'Or de Yennega, Africa's 'Oscar', at the
1995 Fespaco. Other highly regarded Malian film makers include Assane
Kouyaté, Adama Drabo, Falaba Issa Traoré and Abdoulaye Ascofaré. For
more information on Malian films, see p489.

From Burkina Faso, Idrissa Ouédraogo, who won the 1990 Grand
Prix at Cannes for *Tilä,* is one of very few West African film-makers to
find genuine commercial success in the West. His other movies include
*Yaaba, Samba Traoré, Kini* and *Adams.* Gaston Kaboré is another fine
director whose film *Buud Yam* was the 1997 winner of the Étalon d'Or
de Yennenga. Other Burkinabé directors include Djim Mamadou Kola,
Dany Kouyate and Daniel Kollo Sanou. For more information on films
from Burkina Faso, see p132.

Television in West Africa is pretty dire, dominated as it is by
government-run channels and poorly resourced production. In most
countries of the region. Its saving grace may be the music performances
by amateur local musicians or local drama serials that are folksy rather
than high quality. Satellite news channels from France, England and the
US are sometimes available in top hotels.

Fespaco (www.fespaco
.bf) is an English- and
French-language site
that has comprehensive
information about Africa's
premier film festival,
including past winners
and upcoming events. It's
updated daily during the
festival.

## FOOD & DRINK

Although poverty means that food in West Africa is often monotonous
and is a functional rather than enjoyable feature of life for ordinary
West Africans, the combination of influences – including local, French
and even Lebanese – has resulted in some delicious cuisine. The key is
knowing where to find it (you won't find much variety outside larger
cities), trying not to let the rather generous amounts of oil used in cooking bother you and learning to appreciate the atmosphere – an essential
ingredient in the region's cooking – as much as the food. The quality
of food tends to vary considerably from country to country. Culinary
highlights of the region include Côte d'Ivoire, Senegal and Cameroon,
although you'll find tasty dishes in many other places as well. In desert
countries such as Mauritania or Niger, ingredients are limited. In general,
the countries with the best range of food tend to be those along the coast,
where rainfall is plentiful and the crops are varied.

### Staples & Specialties

Rice, rice and more rice is the West African staple that you'll encounter
most on your travels. Millet is also common, although this grain is usually
pounded into flour before it's cooked. The millet flour is steamed and
then moistened with water until it thickens into a stiff porridge that can
be eaten with the fingers. Sorghum is a similar grain crop, although it's
not used as much as millet. In the Sahel, couscous (semolina or millet
grains) is always on the menu.

*"My Cooking"* West-
African Cookbook, by
Dokpe L Ogunsanya, is
an exuberantly presented
cookbook that's ideal for
researching before you go
to get an idea of what to
look for.

In the countries nearer the coast, staples may be root crops such as
yam or cassava (also called manioc), which are pounded or grated before
being cooked. They're served as a near-solid glob, called *fufu* or *foufou*
(which morphs into *foutou* further north) – kind of like mashed potatoes
mixed with gelatine and very sticky. You grab a portion (with your right
hand) form a ball, dip it in the sauce and enjoy. In the coastal countries,
plantain (green banana) is also common – either fried like French fries,
cooked solid or pounded into a *fufu.*

If you don't find much variety in terms of rice and other grains or
roots, that's because the secret's in the sauce. The combination is most

---

**KOLA NUTS**

Kola nuts are yellow or purple nuts, about half the size of a golf ball, which are sold in streets and markets everywhere in West Africa and are known for their mildly hallucinogenic effects. West Africans traditionally give kola nuts as gifts, and they're also a good option for travellers to carry and give to people in exchange for their kindness (or if you want to endear yourself to your fellow passengers in a bush taxi). The nuts last longer if you keep them moist but will become mouldy in a day or two if kept in a plastic bag. Despite the nuts' popularity among West Africans, most foreigners find them too bitter to chew and anyone looking for a high is usually disappointed.

---

*South of the Sahara: Traditional Cooking from the Lands of West Africa,* by Elizabeth A Jackson, brings the flavours of West Africa to your kitchen; the writer lived for a time in Africa and loves her food.

often called *riz sauce*. In some Sahel countries, groundnuts (peanuts) are common, and a thick brown groundnut sauce (usually called a variation of *arachide*) is often served, either on its own or with meat or vegetables mixed in with the nuts. When groundnut sauce is used in a stew, it's called *domodah* or *mafé*. Sometimes deep-orange palm oil is also added. Sauces are also made with vegetables or the leaves of staple food plants such as cassava.

Okra is popular, particularly in coastal countries – the result is a slimy green concoction that tastes a whole lot better than it looks. Other vegetables used in meals include *pommes de terre* (potatoes), *patates* (sweet potatoes), *oignons* (onions), *haricots verte* (green beans) and *tomates* (tomatoes). For flavouring, chillis may be used, or *jaxatu* (ja-ka-too) – similar to a green or yellow tomato but extremely bitter.

Some of the enduring favourites can be found throughout the region but are specialities from particular countries. These include: the ubiquitous *jollof rice* (rice and vegetables with meat or fish and called '*riz yollof*' in Francophone countries); *kedjenou* (Côte d'Ivoire's national dish of slowly simmered chicken or fish with peppers and tomatoes); *poulet yassa* (a Senegalese dish consisting of grilled chicken in an onion and lemon sauce); you'll also come across *poisson yassa* (fish), *viande yassa* (meat) and just *yassa*; and *tiéboudienne* (Senegal's national dish of rice baked in a thick sauce of fish and vegetables).

Stock cubes or sachets of flavouring are ubiquitous across the region (Maggi is the most common trade name) and are often thrown into the pot as well. Where it can be afforded, or on special occasions, meat or fish is added to the sauce; sometimes succulent slices, sometimes grimly unattractive heads, tails and bones.

*Troth Wells' New Internationalist Food Book is more than just a recipe book – it tells vignettes from a whole host of countries and puts food at the heart of the Africans' daily struggle for survival.*

The availability of fruit depends on the season, but choice is always good and increases as you head south from the Sahel into the coastal countries. Fruits you're likely to see include oranges, mandarins and grapefruits (all often with green skin despite being ready to eat), bananas (many different colours and sizes), mangoes (also many varieties), papayas, pineapples, guavas and passionfruit.

See individual country chapters for more details on regional specialities, while for other dishes you'll come frequently come across, see opposite.

## Drinks
### NONALCOHOLIC DRINKS

International and local brands of soft drinks are sold virtually everywhere. A tiny shop in a remote village may sell little food, but chances are they'll have a few dusty bottles of Coca-Cola or Pepsi for sale. (Coke is called 'Coca' in Francophone countries.) Bottled mineral water is widely available in cities, towns and tourist areas.

Home-made soft drinks include ginger beer and *bissap,* a purple mixture made from water and hibiscus leaves. These drinks are usually sold in plastic bags by children on the street. Although they are refreshing, the water may not be clean, so they're usually best avoided.

In the Sahel countries, tea comes in two sorts. There's the type made with a tea bag (its local name is 'Lipton tea' even if the brand is actually something else), and there's the type of tea drunk by the local population – made with green leaves (often imported from China) and served with loads of sugar in small glasses. Mint is sometimes added, or the tea may be made from mint leaves alone. Half the fun of drinking local-style tea is the ritual that goes with it, taking at least an hour. Traditionally, the tea is brewed three times and poured from a small pot high above the glass.

Coffee is almost exclusively instant coffee (Nescafé is the usual brand). At street-side coffee stalls it's mixed with sweetened condensed milk, and in some areas the water may be infused with a local leaf called *kinkiliba,* which gives it a woody tang – unusual but not unpleasant once you get over the shock.

The Africa Guide's cooking webpage (www.africa guide.com/cooking.htm) is not as detailed as most cookbooks but it's good on basic ingredients and does have some tasty recipes.

### ALCOHOLIC DRINKS
You can sometimes find imported beers from Europe and the USA, but about 45 brands of beer are brewed in West Africa, with Nigeria alone producing about 30. Some beers are European brands, brewed locally, others are specific to the region. The quality is often very good. Brands to look out for include: Club (Ghana, Nigeria and Liberia), Flag (Côte d'Ivoire, Mali and Senegal), Star (Sierra Leone, Ghana and Nigeria), Harp and Gulder (Nigeria and Ghana). Guinness is found in several countries, too.

In the Sahel a rough, brown and gritty beer made from millet (called *chakalow* or *kojo*) is common, but West Africa's most-popular brew is palm wine. The tree is tapped and the sap comes out mildly fermented. Sometimes yeast is added and the brew is allowed to ferment overnight, which makes it much stronger. In Nigeria, it's even bottled in factories.

## Celebrations
Ceremonies are very important in traditional societies, as they reinforce social structures, connect people to their traditions, mark important rites of passage (baptisms or naming ceremonies, circumcisions, weddings and funerals) and generally provide an excuse for a big feed. Most of these family or village ceremonies involve gifts and, invariably once the formal rituals are completed, a meal of slaughtered sheep or goat.

Some travellers have been lucky enough to stay with local people, where a great way to repay their hospitality is to pay for a special meal for the entire family. This way you'll also be able to see how meals are put together. For the full picture, visit the market with the lady of the house (it's always the women who do the cooking in domestic situations) and see the various ingredients being bought.

Betumi (www.betumi .com) is dedicated to traditional and contemporary cuisine, where a useful feature is the online forum where people write in with ideas and places to track down ingredients; it's especially helpful for American readers.

## Where to Eat & Drink
The best place to eat, if you're lucky enough to be invited, is at somebody's house. Most days, though, you'll be heading for a restaurant or eating on the street.

### STREET FOOD
Street food is ideal if you're on the move, trying to save money or if you prefer to eat little but often. It tends to be absurdly cheap and is often delicious – especially the grilled fish.

---

**MINDING YOUR MANNERS**

If you're invited to share a meal with locals, there are a few customs to observe. You'll probably sit with your hosts on the floor and it's usually polite to take off your shoes. It may be impolite, however, to show the soles of your feet, so make sure you observe what your hosts do.

The food is served in one or two large dishes, and is normally eaten by hand. Beginners will just pick out manageable portions with their fingers, but experts dig deep, forming a ball of rice and sauce with the fingers. Everybody washes their hands before and after eating. As an honoured guest you might be passed choice morsels by your hosts, and it's usually polite to finish eating while there's still food in the bowl to show you've had enough.

While eating with your hand is a bit of an art and takes some practice, it should soon start to feel natural. At the outset, you probably won't offend anybody by asking for a spoon. The most important thing, however you eat, is to use only the right hand (as the left hand is traditionally used for more personal, less delicious, matters).

---

On street corners and around bus stations, especially in the morning, you'll see small booths selling pieces of bread with fillings or toppings of butter, chocolate spread, yogurt, mayonnaise or sardines. In the Francophone countries, the bread is cut from fresh French-style loaves or baguettes, but in the Anglophone countries the bread is often a less-enticing soft, white loaf. Price depends on the size of the piece of bread you want, and the type of filling.

One of the region's finest institutions (found mainly in the French-speaking countries) are the coffee stalls where clients sit on small benches around a table and drink glasses of Nescafé mixed with sweetened condensed milk, served with French-style bread, butter or mayonnaise – all for around US$0.50. Some also offer Lipton tea or even Milo, while more enterprising stallholders fry up eggs or serve sardines. Many coffee stalls are only open in the morning.

In the Sahel countries, usually around markets, you'll see women with large bowls covered with a wicker lid selling yogurt, often mixed with pounded millet and sugar. This sells for around US$0.15 a portion – you can eat it on the spot, or take it away in a plastic bag.

In the evenings you can buy brochettes (small pieces of beef, sheep or goat meat skewered and grilled over a fire) or lumps of roast meat sold by guys who walk around pushing a tin oven on wheels. Around markets and bus stations, women serve deep-fried chips of cassava or some other root crop.

In Francophone countries, grilled and roast meat, usually mixed with onions and spices, is sold in shacks (basically an oven with a few walls around it). These are called *dibieteries* in some places, and you can eat on the spot (a rough bench might be provided) or take away. To feed one or two, ask for about CFA1000 worth (about US$2).

Another popular stand-by in the larger cities are Lebanese-style shwarmas, thin slices of lamb grilled on a spit, served with salad (optional) in Lebanese-style bread (pita) with a sauce made from chickpeas. These cost about US$1.

**SIT-DOWN MEALS**

West Africa abounds with restaurants – from fine and varied cuisine in capital cities to one-wooden-bench tin shacks in smaller towns. The smallest, most simple eating houses usually have just one or two meals available each day and if you spend most of your time eating in these places, your meals will be pretty straightforward – bowls of rice or an-

*Spices of Life: Piquant Recipes from Africa, Asia and Latin America for Western Kitchens*, by Troth Wells, has recipes, social and cultural information and some fascinating ideas for your next dinner party.

other staple served with a simple sauce. For information on the art of eating in a *maquis* (open-air restaurant), see p264.

In slightly smarter places your choice may also include fried chicken or fish served with *frites* (hot chips). Cooked vegetables, such as green beans, may also be available. Up a grade from here, mainly in cities, you'll find midrange restaurants catering to well-off locals and foreigners. They may serve only 'international' dishes such as steaks or pizzas (although some also do African dishes), and these meals are usually expensive, particularly if some of the ingredients have been imported from Europe. Ironically, local specialities, such as fish and rice, may cost the same in this kind of place.

*Cooking the West African Way*, by Bertha Vining Montgomery and Constance Nabwire, is another fine cookbook and one of only a handful that dedicates itself solely to West Africa.

## Vegetarians & Vegans

Being a vegetarian in West Africa is challenging, though possible, and decidedly unexciting when it comes to choice – you'll end up eating the same things again and again. Indeed, the concept of vegetarianism is rarely understood in West Africa, and vegetarian restaurants are rare. Your best bet is often Asian or (less common) Indian restaurants in capital cities, which always have some vegetarian dishes. The main challenge is likely to be keeping some variety and nutritional balance in your diet, and getting enough protein, especially if you don't eat eggs and dairy products.

If you do eat eggs and dairy products, pizzas and omelettes make a change from the ubiquitous bean-and-vegetable dishes. The French may have bequeathed a love of coffee and good bread to its former colonies, but cheese never quite caught on. Expensive imported cheese is usually available in capital cities. Otherwise, cheese is seldom available except for the ultra-processed triangular varieties, which are often sold in larger supermarkets.

Vegetarian street food possibilities include cassava, yam and plantain chips, bread with mayonnaise, egg or chocolate spread, and fried dough balls. Alternatively, head for the markets and do your own catering. There is always plenty of fresh fruit and vegetables (usually sold in piles of four or five pieces), as well as bread and tins of margarine or tomato paste. Banana and groundnut (local-style peanut butter) sandwiches made with fresh bread are a nutritious option, while it's sometimes possible to find take-away spaghetti and tomato sauce served in banana leaves.

Keep in mind that even the most simple vegetable sauce may sometimes have a small bit of meat or animal fat in it, and chicken or fish are usually not regarded as 'real' meat. The ubiquitous Maggi cubes also often contain chicken. Another factor to consider if you're invited to someone's home for dinner is the fact that meat – a luxury for most local residents – is often reserved for special occasions or honoured guests (such as yourself). This means that the beast in the cooking pot bubbling away on the fire may well have been slaughtered in your honour, so give some thought as to how you might deal with this situation in advance.

## Food & Drink Glossary

| | |
|---|---|
| *afra* | grilled meat, or grilled-meat stall |
| *agouti* | a rodent of the porcupine family, known as grasscutter or cane rat in Anglophone countries; it's popular in stews |
| *aloco* | fried bananas or plantains with onions and chilli |
| *attiéké* | grated cassava |
| *benchi* | black bench peas with palm oil and fish |
| *bissap* | purple drink made from water and hibiscus leaves |
| *brochette* | cubes of meat or fish grilled on a stick |

| | |
|---|---|
| buvette | small bar or drinks stall |
| caféman | man serving coffee (usually Nescafé), sometimes tea, and French bread with various fillings; found in Francophone countries mainly, usually only in the morning |
| capitaine | Nile perch (fish) |
| carte | menu |
| cassava | a common starch staple eaten as an accompaniment; the leaves are eaten as a green vegetable; also called *gari* or manioc |
| chakalow | millet beer |
| chop | meal, usually local style |
| chop shop | a basic local-style eating house or restaurant (English-speaking countries); also called a rice bar |
| cocoyam | starch-yielding food plant, also called taro |
| couscous | semolina or millet grains, served as an accompaniment to sauce |
| dibieterie | grilled-meat stall |
| domodah | groundnut-based stew with meat or vegetables |
| épinard | spinach |
| felafel | Lebanese-style deep-fried balls of ground chickpeas and herbs, often served with chickpea paste in sandwiches |
| feuille sauce | sauce made from greens (usually manioc leaves) |
| foutou | sticky yam or plantain paste similar to *fufu;* a staple in Côte d'Ivoire |
| frites | hot potato chips or French fries |
| fufu | a staple along the southern coast of West Africa made with fermented cassava, yams, plantain or manioc which is cooked and puréed; sometimes spelt foufou |
| gargotte | simple eating house or stall in Senegal, parts of Mali and Gambia; also spelt gargote or gargot |
| gari | powdered cassava |
| gombo | okra or lady's fingers |
| groundnut | peanut; sometimes called arachide |
| haricot verte | green bean |
| jaxatu | bitter flavouring |
| jollof rice | common dish throughout the region consisting of rice and vegetables with meat or fish; called riz yollof in Francophone countries |
| kedjenou | Côte d'Ivoire's national dish but available elsewhere; slowly simmered chicken or fish with peppers and tomatoes |
| kinkiliba | leaf that is sometimes used in coffee, giving it a woody tang |
| kojo | millet beer |
| koutoukou | a clear, strong alcohol home-made in Côte d'Ivoire |
| mafé | groundnut-based stew; also spelt mafay |
| Maggi | brand name for a ubiquitous flavouring used in soups, stews etc throughout the region |
| maquis | rustic open-air restaurant, primarily serving braised fish and grilled chicken with *attiéké,* and traditionally open only at night |
| menu du jour | meal of the day, usually at a special price; often shortened to menu |
| palaver sauce | usually made from spinach or other leaves plus meat/fish; also spelled palava |
| palm wine | a milky-white low-strength brew collected by tapping palm trees |
| patate | sweet potato |
| pâte | starch staple, often made from millet, corn, plantains, manioc or yams, eaten as an accompaniment to sauce; also called akoumé |
| pito | local brew in northern Ghana |
| plantain | a large green banana, which has to be cooked before eating |
| plasas | pounded potato or cassava leaves cooked with palm oil and fish or beer |
| plat du jour | the dish of the day, usually offered at a special price |
| poisson | fish |
| pomme de terre | potato |
| poulet | chicken |

| *poulet yassa* | grilled chicken in onion and lemon sauce; a Senegalese dish that's found in many countries throughout the region; similarly you get *poisson yassa* (fish), *viande yassa* (meat) and just *yassa* |
| *pression* | draught beer |
| *riz sauce* | very common basic meal (rice with sauce) |
| *rôtisserie* | food stall selling roast meat |
| *salon de thé* | literally 'tearoom'; café |
| *shwarma* | a popular and ubiquitous Lebanese snack of grilled meat in bread, served with salad and sesame sauce |
| *snack* | in Francophone Africa this means a place where you can get light meals and sandwiches, not the food itself; you'll often see signs saying 'Bar Snack', meaning you can get a beer or coffee too |
| *sodabe* | a spirit made in Togo |
| *spot* | simple bar |
| *sucrerie* | soft drink (literally 'sweet thing') |
| *suya* | Hausa word for brochette |
| *tiéboudienne* | Senegal's national dish, rice baked in thick sauce of fish and vegetables; also spelt thieboudjenne |
| *tô* | millet or sorghum-based *pâte* |
| *viande* | meat |
| *wigila* | Songhaï speciality from Gao (Mali) of sun-dried dumplings dipped in a meat sauce made with cinnamon and spices |
| *yam* | edible starchy root; sometimes called igname |

# The Music of West Africa

Music put West Africa on the map. Years ago, even if no one knew exactly where Senegal was, they knew that Youssou N'Dour lived there, and the great Baaba Maal. They could tell you that Salif Keita came from Mali, and Mory Kanté from Guinea. That Nigeria was home to Fela Kuti and *juju* music emperor, King Sunny Ade. Reggae-star Alpha Blondy defined the Ivory Coast. Saxophonist Manu Dibango was Cameroon, just as Cesária Evora was Cape Verde and Angélique Kidjo, Benin. All of these West African stars fuelled the global Afropop boom. Once filed under 'A' for Africa, they lent the world music genre much needed individuality, commerciality and cred.

Cassette piracy is a huge problem in West Africa and many high profile names have devoted themselves to the task of its eradication.

The international success of these West African elders has paved the way for an apparently bottomless pot of talent. Desert rebels Tinariwen; dreadlocked Senegalese mystic Cheikh Lo; and his hotly tipped compatriot, Daby Baldé. The fresh prince of the Ivory Coast, Tiken Jah Fakoly, and its fresh princess, Dobet Gnahoré. Golden-voiced Mauritanian Daby Touré, and afrobeating politicos such as Nigeria's Femi Kuti (in looks, sound and sentiment, very much his father's son). Lura from Cape Verde, with her contemporary *morna* style, and Malians including ethereal songbird Rokia Traore, *kora* maestro Toumani Diabaté and husband-and-wife team Amadou and Mariam – whose Manu Chao-produced album, *Dimanche á Bamako*, went to the top of the global charts and stayed there.

Oumou Sangare is the owner of Bamako's Hotel Wasulu, a purpose-built 35-room hotel whose rooms are named after famous Malian musicians. There's an Ali Farke Touré room and, of course, an Oumou Sangare suite. Oh, and she is also the resident headliner.

Mentioning these names is only scratching the surface. Music is everywhere in West Africa, coming at you in thunderous, drum-fuelled polyrhythms, through the swooping, soaring voices of griots (traditional musicians or minstrels; praise singers) and via socially-aware reggae, rap and hip-hop. From Afro-beat to pygmy fusion, highlife to *makossa*, *gumbe* to Nigerian gospel, genres are as entrenched as they are evolving, fusing and re-forming. Little wonder that here – in this vast, diverse region, with its deserts, jungles, skyscrapers, and urban sprawl – myriad ethnic groups play out their lives to music. Here are traditional songs that celebrate weddings, offer solace at funerals, keep work rhythms steady in the fields. Here are songs and rhythms that travelled out on slave ships to Cuba and Brazil. Songs that retell history and, in doing so, foster inter-clan and inter-religious respect.

In West Africa, too, are the roots of Western music (along with guitars, keyboards, Latin influences and other legacies of colonialism). Not for nothing did Senegalese rap crew Daara J title their 2003 international debut *Boomerang*. 'Born in Africa, raised in America,' says member Faada Freddy, 'rap has come full circle.' As has the blues. A host of American blues musicians – Ry Cooder, Corey Harris, Taj Mahal, Bonnie Raitt – have found inspiration and affirmation in West Africa, in Mali in particular. 'I never heard American blues music before I started playing,' said the famed Malian guitarist, Ali Farke Touré, 'but when I did, I recognised it as African music, the music from my region.'

Kora maestro Toumani Diabaté and his traditional-meets-modern big band the Symmetric Orchestra play Bamako's outdoor Hogon Club most Friday nights.

Even Blur and Gorillaz frontman Damon Albarn embarked on a love affair with West Africa, recording his hi-tech *Mali Music* album after a visit in 2000. His Honest Jons record label has since released a series of intriguing West African albums, including 2005's *Lagos Chop Up* and drummer Tony 'Afrobeat' Allen's 2006 offering, *Lagos Shaking*. 'The amazing thing about West Africa,' Albarn has said, 'is that you can hear all the components of Western music there.'

---

**TEN MUST-HAVE WEST AFRICAN ALBUMS**

- *Dimanche à Bamako* (Because) by Amadou and Mariam
- *M'Bemba* (Universal Jazz France) by Salif Keita
- *In the Heart of the Moon* (World Circuit) by Ali Farke Touré and Toumani Diabaté
- *Worotan* (World Circuit) by Oumou Sangare
- *The Best Best of Fela Kuti* (MCA) by Fela Kuti
- *Nothing's In Vain* (Nonesuch) by Youssou N'Dour
- *Firin in Fouta* (Mango) by Baaba Maal
- *Juju Music* (Island) by King Sunny and his African Beats
- *Miss Perfumado* (Lusafrica) by Cesária Evora
- *Amassakoul* (Independent Records) By Tinariwen

---

You could, if you like, seek out the thriving West African scene in London or Paris, where many of the aforementioned West African acts have forged their international careers. But just as Salif Keita relocated to Bamako in 2005 after 20 years in Paris, it is better, really, to soak it up *in situ*. 'A trunk never turns into a crocodile, no matter how long it stays in the water', says Keita.

Trust us. Your musical tastes, attitude and perceptions will – like your iPod – never be the same again.

*Radio Liberte (www .comfm.com/musique) is a Bamako-based station with a global outlook.*

## A POTTED HISTORY OF WEST AFRICAN MUSIC

The musical history of West Africa is closely linked to its diverse and long-established empires, such as Ghana's (6th to 11th centuries), where court music was played for chiefs, music accompanied ceremonies and chores, and was played for pleasure at the end of the day. In the vast Mande Empire (13th to 15th centuries), music was the province of one social caste, the *jelis*, who still perform their folk styles today. Correspondingly in Senegal, griots – Wolof culture's *kora*-strumming, praise-singing caste – trace genealogies, recount epics and span generations. There are myriad musical styles in West Africa, courtesy of its hundreds of ethnic groups and various Islamic and European influences, but the *jeli/griot* tradition is arguably the best known.

Senegal, Gambia, Guinea, Mali, Mauritania, Burkina Faso and Côte d'Ivoire all share the same *jeli* tradition, though each linguistic group calls it something different and each has its own subtly different sound. They are acknowledged as oral historians – nearly all children know the epic of Sundiata Keita, the warrior who founded the Mande Empire – and often as soothsayers but, although they top the bill at weddings and naming ceremonies, *griots* occupy a lowly rank in their hierarchical societies. Many big West African stars faced parental objections to their choice of career. Others, such as Salif Keita – a direct descendent of Sundiata and as such, not a *jeli* – made their reputations in exile.

Oral tradition is equally strong in Nigeria, where stories of ancient Yoruba, Ashanti, Hausa and other kingdoms flourish. Like many a West African style, Yoruba music has its roots in percussion. Indeed, if there is any element common to the huge, diverse region that is West Africa, it is drumming. From the Ewe ensembles of Ghana – similar in style to those of Benin and Togo – to Senegal's sabar drummers, beating their giant instruments with sticks, drumming kick-started West Africa's

*In Griot Time: An American Guitarist in Mali (2002) is an acclaimed account of Malian musicians and culture, written by a fellow musician who spent seven months in Bamako playing guitar with Djelimady Tounkara, formerly of the legendary Super Rail Band.*

## YOUSSOU N'DOUR

Dressed in white, arms spread wide, Youssou N'Dour stands on stage and unleashes his startling tenor. 'Africa…all…my…people', he sings, unaccompanied, his voice curling sensuously skywards, his eight-piece band, Le Super Étoile, ready for action. As the crowd roars its response, N'Dour launches into the funky, riotous sound he's famous for. Hits come in Wolof, French and English, including his 1994 smash duet with Neneh Cherry, 'Seven Seconds'. West Africa's greatest musical hero is, as ever, on message. His pride in his culture is obvious.

'Africa needs new, positive images', says the 47-year-old afterwards. 'For too long it has been seen as a place where war, poverty and sad things happen. But it is also a place of beauty and poetry, colour and music,' he sighs. 'It is up to African artists,' he adds, 'to bring these images to the West.'

For a long time it seemed to be up to Youssou N'Dour. One of a long line of Tukulor griots, N'Dour grew up singing alongside his mother at religious ceremonies. His swooping, soaring voice won him live slots on national radio and a boy-wonder status he exploited by hustling for gigs outside nightclubs like the Thoissane, the Copacabana-style venue in Dakar that he now owns. By 16 he was in the line-up of Ibra Kasse's Star Band and, soon after, Étoile de Dakar. Aged 18 he formed Le Super Étoile de Dakar, throwing in Latin influences, adding guitars and keyboards and reclaiming the big Senegalese sabar drum. The sound, *mbalax*, spawned a phenomenon.

N'Dour set about straddling the commercial and traditional worlds. He introduced funk and fusion into his sound, then achieved world renown in the 1980s when he supported Peter Gabriel in concert and starred alongside Gabriel, Sting and Bruce Springsteen on the celebrated 1988 Amnesty International Tour. A series of glossy crossover albums followed, but it was 2002's acoustic *Nothing's In Vain* and 2004's inspired, Grammy-winning *Egypt* (a paean to Islam composed on Senegalese instruments and recorded with an Egyptian Orchestra) that had critics doing backflips. Having cancelled a US tour in March 2003 in protest at the invasion of Iraq, the Egypt album was the album that he always wanted to make. A new album is scheduled for 2007.

Among other projects, N'Dour owns a record label, Jololi, a cassette factory, a radio station, a newspaper and Xippi, the country's best recording studio, from where he produces rap artists for the local market ('Wolof rap will never be popular outside Senegal', he says). He enjoys his role at the top, from where he channels his wealth into community projects. When he's not touring, and he tours often (scandalously, he was the only African star to play at the 2005 Live8 concert in Hyde Park). N'Dour regularly gigs at the Thoissane where, though he's rarely onstage before 3am, he always gets a stomping, shouting hero's welcome.

'I have a message to deliver to the world,' says N'Dour, 'and that message is in the music.'

---

Youssou N'Dour is the host of the Great African Ball, a Senegalese-style shindig that takes place in New York, Paris and Milan each year, attracting glammed-up expats from a variety of African countries. These five-hour extravaganzas offer the same sort of collective spectacle as laid on at the Thoissane.

musical heart. Often accompanied by ululation, vocal repetition, call-and-response vocals and polyrhythms, drums beat out a sound that immediately says 'Africa'.

As West African music travelled out on the slave ships (and brought other influences back with it later), so the music of the colonisers travelled in. The Portuguese presence in Cape Verde created *morna*, music of separation, and *saudade*, and creole-style *gumbe* in Guinea-Bissau. Western-style dance orchestras had the colonial elite fox-trotting on the Gold Coast. Francophone Africa fell in love with Cuban dance music, a genre, in rhythm and structure, remarkably close to Mande music. Cuban music (and guitar-based Congolese rumba) introduced modern instruments to the region, creating a swathe of dance bands such as Guinea's legendary Bembeya Jazz (a signifier of modern music, 'Jazz' was commonly tagged on a band's name), who played local styles with Latin arrangements.

Post-independence, the philosophy of 'negritude' – or cultural redis-covery – arose among some 1960s-era West African governments. Popular Latin sounds were discouraged in favour of folkloric material. Electric Afropop began to incorporate traditional rhythms and instruments, such as the *kora* (a harp-like musical instrument with over 20 strings), balafon (xylophone), and *ngoni* (stringed instrument). State-sponsored dance bands won big audiences and spawned even bigger stars. The first president of Senegal (poet Leopold Senghor) fostered the young Orchestra Baobab band, whose phenomenal 21st-century comeback continues. Mali's Le Rail Band du Bamako (sponsored by the Malian Railway Company) became an African institution that launched the careers of two of Africa's greatest singers: Salif Keita and Mory Kanté.

When the young Maninka singer Salif Keita defected to their foreign-style rivals, Les Ambassedeurs du Motel, there was uproar. Fierce, Oasis-vs-Blur-style competition ensued throughout the 1970s, making Bamako the dance music capital of West Africa (see p499). Meanwhile, in Nigeria, the poppy highlife sound of the 1940s, '50s and '60s gave way to genres with a strong percussive element, such as *juju* and *fuji*. The West's popular music genres – rock, soul, jazz, funk, pop – made their mark, each spawning its own 'Afro' equivalent. Today the likes of 1960s' Sierra-Leonean Afro-soul king Geraldo Pino and Ghanaian Afro-rock collective Osibisa are being rediscovered by a new generation of Western hipsters.

The recording studios of Lagos offered commercial opportunities for Nigerian performers, as did those of 1980s' Abidjan in Coté d'Ivoire – a musical Mecca for artists from across the continent. But by the mid-1980s all eyes were on Paris, the city where Mory Kanté recorded his seminal club floor track 'Yeke Yeke', and where innumerable West African musicians lived. Big names moved back and forth between Paris and London and West Africa, recording cassettes for the local market and albums for the international one, as remains the case today. With the 1990s' world-music boom, many stars – Youssou N'Dour, Salif Keita, Cesária Evora, King Sunny Ade – established their own record companies, and signed up local talent.

Some savvy Western record labels pre-empted mainstream interest in West African music. London-based World Circuit signed the likes of Ali Farke Touré, Cheikh Lo, Oumou Sangare and Orchestra Baobab, arguably doing for West Africa what it did for Cuba with the Buena Vista Allstars. West African artists are now staples of international festivals including Womad and Glastonbury. Club producers have remixed Cesária Evora, Femi Kuti and Rokia Traore. West African albums make it into mainstream charts, West African musicians sell out Western venues and Western musicians look to West Africa for inspiration.

In West Africa, big-name artists attract hordes of followers wherever they go. The politicians who try to hijack such popularity are usually shrugged off. Youssou N'Dour, Baaba Maal et al are international ambassadors in their own right, stars who use their position (and their lyrics) to campaign against poverty, disease and illiteracy. Oumou Sangare sings, however obliquely, about women's rights. The rap movement in Senegal promotes peace and love. But freedom of expression is still curtailed, and Femi Kuti's pro-democracy narratives are censored in Nigeria, just as his father's were.

Latin music remains popular in Mali. Guitar-based highlife is still a staple of Ghana, where hip life – the country's very own hip-hop – is also huge. Nigerian music isn't as popular in the West as it was; Mali, Guinea and Senegal and The Gambia are currently ahead in the popularity stakes. Traditional acoustic albums from that region have been enjoying a renaissance and Salif Keita, Youssou N'Dour, Baaba Maal and Mory Kanté have all recently unplugged. Everywhere, musicians are creating, collaborating, experimenting. New, exciting performers are constantly emerging.

West African music has never been healthier. Styles may change, but one thing, at least, is certain: the drums will beat forever.

Afropop (www.afropop.org) aims to be the premier destination for web denizens interested in the contemporary music of Africa and the African diaspora; highlights include streaming audio and a searchable database.

The great bluesman Ali Farke Touré, who passed away from cancer in March 2006, was the mayor of his hometown, Niafunké, a village near his farm on the the Niger River in Timbuktu (Tombouctou) province. 'Your job on earth is to share what gifts God has given you', he says. Check out his posthumously released album, *Savane*.

## TINARIWEN

Tinariwen loosen their turbans when they play away from home. Sand is never a problem outside of the Sahara. Back home it gets into ears and mouths, making it hard to sing, and under the fretboards of their Fender Stratocasters, making them hard to play. Not that this most rugged of guitar bands, a collective of Tuareg nomads from Kidal, a dusty town way out past Timbuktu, are bothered. Even their name means 'desert'. The sound conjured by their chants, ululations and call-and-response vocals, hand claps, hand-drums and wall of guitars, is all space and spirit. Their attitude – reflective, angry, resilient – is pure desert blues.

And if anyone has the right to play the blues, it's the Tuareg. Once upon a time these nomadic pastoralists roamed the Sahara with their cattle, camels and goats, but African independence left them exposed to old enmities in the 1960s, and their living was devastated by drought in the following decades. Conflict with the Malian authorities was ongoing – eventually leading to a bloody rebellion (see p529) – and in the 1980s many Tuareg ended up in Libyan President Gadafi's training camps, where they fought unrelated battles and – in Tinariwen's case – learned how to play guitar. Legend has it they went to battle with Kalashnikovs in one hand and guitars slung across their backs.

'Desert life is hard,' says bandleader Ibrahim Ag Alhabib, 45, through a cloud of cigarette smoke, 'our own music, our own poetry is vital.' Tinariwen's songs tell the lives of their dispossessed kinsmen; passed on by generations of cheap cassette recordings, they have become as anthemic in the Sahara as those of, say, the Rolling Stones or White Stripes – bands with whom they've been compared.

'I have had sadness from an early age,' says Ibrahim. 'I saw my father killed by Malian soldiers. I grew up in exile in Algeria, fending for myself.' Music offered an escape. In the camps he met other musically minded freedom fighters. They threw out the traditional lute and one-stringed fiddle, and set their traditional rhythms to the electric guitar. 'At first we improvised with tin cans, sticks and string. Then somehow we got hold of guitars and taught ourselves how to play.'

They became so popular that the Malian government outlawed possession of their cassettes. 'But we were singing about hardship, about the desert, about taking pride in your heritage,' Ibrahim insists. In 2000 a rejigged Tinariwen recorded their debut album, the Radio Tisdas Sessions, in Kidal's electricity-starved local radio station. In 2001 they hosted the first annual Festival in the Desert in Essakane (see p540 and p525), an interclan get together so unique and exotic that the likes of Damon Albarn and Robert Plant have suffered the three-day slog to get there.

'The Tuareg have always placed a great importance on gatherings,' offers Ibrahim. Which is why, perhaps, Tinariwen's seven-strong touring line-up – six tough men and one demure but feisty woman, all in pale, flowing robes – have become a staple of the international festival circuit. They won a BBC World Music Award (Africa) for their second album, 2004's *Amassakoul* and, with their mesmeric sounds and effortless left-field cred, have become *the* world music name to drop. A new album is out in 2006.

'Life has improved for the Tuareg people,' says Ibrahim, 'and I know Tinariwen have helped. Our message is being heard further away.' He dusts some imaginary sand off his shoe. 'We just want to take people with us,' he says, 'and the place we are going is back home.'

# WEST AFRICAN INSTRUMENTS

West Africa's traditional instruments tend to be found in its rural areas and are generally fashioned from local materials – everything from gourds, stalks and shells to goat skin, cow horns and horse hair. Discarded objects and nature also have multiple musical uses; in Sierra Leone, empty Milo tins filled with stones were the core instrument for the genre called Milo-jazz. Hausa children in Nigeria beat rhythms on the inflated belly of a live pufferfish. The Pygmies of Cameroon beat rhythms on river water.

There are bells made of bronze in the Islamic orchestras of northern Nigeria, and scrapers made of iron in the south. In Cape Verde women place a rolled-up cloth between their legs and beat it as part of their *batuco* music (the singer Lura does this live, with silver lamé). Everywhere, there is men's music and women's music, men's instruments and women's instruments: in Mauritania, men play the *tidinit*, a four-stringed lute, and women the *ardin*, a sort of back-to-front *kora*. Accordingly there are men's dances and women's dances. And most of these, like most instrumental ensembles, are fuelled by drums.

West Africa has a phenomenal variety of drums. Kettle, slit and talking drums; water, frame and hourglass-shaped drums; log, goblet and double-headed barrel drums. Drums used for ritual purposes, like the *dundun* drums of the Yoruba, which communicate with the *orishas*; drums made from tree trunks and used for long distance messages; drums that mark the major events of one's life – baptism, marriage, death – and drums for entertainment. 'Talking' drums, such as the Wolof *tama*, a small, high-pitched instrument clamped under the armpit and beaten fast with a hooked stick, or the *djembe*, the chalice-shaped drum ubiquitous from Ghana to Senegal, and in the West's endorphin-inducing African drum circles.

There's a diverse array of string instruments too, from the one-stringed viol of the Niger Tuareg and the 13-string *obo* zither of the Igbo in Nigeria, to the 21-string *kora* – the harp/lute of the *griots* and one of the most sophisticated instruments in sub-Saharan Africa. *Kora* players are usually virtuosos, having studied their craft from childhood. Mory Kanté's amplified rock-style *kora* helped establish its reputation as a formidable solo instrument, while *kora* master Toumani Diabaté, son of the virtuoso Sidiki Diabaté, displayed its crossover potential by collaborating with everyone from flamenco musicians to bluesmen Ali Farke Touré and Taj Mahal.

Regarded by some as the precursor to the banjo, the *ngoni* (*xalam* in Wolof, *hoddu* in Fula, *konting* in Mandinka) is also popular with *griots*. A feature in the 14th-century courts of Mali, it has between three and five strings which are plucked, and is tricky to play. Another well-known *griot* instrument is the *balafon*, a wooden xylophone with between 18 and 21 keys, suspended over a row of gourds to amplify the sound. The *balafon* is often played in pairs, with each musician – one improvising, one not – striking the keys with wooden mallets. The Susu people of Guinea are renowned *balafon* experts.

There are other xylophones with different names in West Africa, xylophones fashioned from huge logs, or xylophones amplified by boxes and pits. There are wind instruments (Fula shepherds play melodies on reed flutes) and brass instruments (the Niger Tuareg favour the *alghaita shawm* trumpet) and voices used as instruments – such as the timeless vocals of the *griots*, the polyphonic singing of the Pygmies and the sung poetry of the Tuareg.

Across the region, percussion vies and blends with brass and wood and wind instruments. In urban areas, traditional instruments complement and ground modern instruments. West Africa is, indeed, a hive of musical activity, thrumming to its own collective orchestra.

## WEST AFRICAN MUSICAL STYLES

While mega-successful artists like Mory Kanté, Angélique Kidjo, Salif Keita, Kandia Kouyaté, Cheikh Lo, Baaba Maal, Youssou N'Dour, Oumou Sangare, the late Ali Farke Touré and Rokia Traoré et al (and it's a big et al) might be classified as 'Afro-pop', thanks to commercial sales at home and/or in the West, the region boasts a gamut of distinctive musical styles. The following are just a few of them.

*Songs of West Africa* (2000) contains over 80 traditional African folk songs and chants in six languages, along with extensive translations, music fundamentals, a pronunciation guide and introductions to West African society. Oh, and a sing-along CD.

*Martin Scorsese presents the Blues: Feels Like Going Home* (Martin Scorsese; 2003) follows musician Corey Harris' travels through Mississippi and West Africa, exploring the roots of blues music. Includes performances by Salif Keita, Habib Kolté, Taj Mahal and Ali Farka Touré.

## Afrobeat

Co-created by the late, great Fela Anikulapo Kuti, Afrobeat is a hybrid of Nigerian highlife, Yoruba percussion, jazz, funk and soul. Fela, a singer, saxophonist and bandleader, and one of the most influential 20th-century African figures, used Afrobeat to give voice to the oppressed. His onstage rants, tree-trunk-sized spliff in hand, were legendary. A succession of governments tried to shut him up. When he died of AIDS in 1997, a million people joined his funeral procession through Lagos (see p627 for more). His son, Femi, has picked up the baton, releasing fine albums such as *Shoki Shoki* and reopening his father's Lagos night club, the Shrine. A host of Fela imitators – Tony Allen, the masked Lagbaja, and Fela's youngest son, Seun – keep the flame alight. A recent surge in interest has seen Afrobeat crossover into dance mixes, hip-hop and reggae collaborations.

*Fela Kuti: Music is the Weapon* (1982) is a hard-hitting documentary filmed in Lagos, mixing interviews with Kuti with footage of life at his Kalakuta Republic, and performances at his Shrine nightclub. Comes with a double CD of Kuti's best-known songs.

## Cape Verdean Music

Cape Verdean music came late to the West. The undisputed star of the bluesy, melancholy songs (known as *morna*) is the 'barefoot diva' Cesária Evora, a ciggie-puffing grandmother erroneously thought to appear onstage without shoes in support of the disadvantaged women in her country ('No,' she says, 'I just don't like wearing shoes.'). European influences are obvious in *morna*, the equivalent to Portugal's *fado*, while Africa is at the fore in other genres such as the dance-oriented *coladeira*, accordion-led *funana* and percussive women's music, *batuco*. Look out for recordings by *morna* tenor Bana, the Lisbon-based Lura and Tcheka, a singer/songwriter and guitarist who plays beats that are normally played on percussion.

## Gumbe

Closely associated with Guinea-Bissau, *gumbe* is an uptempo, polyrhythmic genre that fuses about ten of the country's folk music traditions. Lyrics, sung in Portuguese creole, are topical and witty; instruments include guitars and the water drum, an upturned calabash floating in a bucket. Civil unrest rendered *gumbe* a latecomer to the West, until the Lisbon-based Manecas Costa brought out his acclaimed 2004 album *Paradiso di Gumbe*. In Sierra Leone, *gumbe* evolved from the breezy, calypso-style guitar music called palm-wine. The late SE Rogie and London-based Abdul Tee-Jay are probably the best-known exponents. In Nigeria, palm-wine gave rise to *juju* and in Ghana, to highlife.

African Music Encyclopedia (www.africanmusic.org) offers a country-by-country, artist-by-artist breakdown for lovers of music from Africa and the African diaspora.

## Highlife

Ghana's urban, upbeat highlife, which started off in the dancehalls of the colonial Gold Coast, has had a ripple effect throughout West Africa. Trumpeter and bandleader ET Mensah was the post-war, pan-African king of this sound, a blend of everything from Trinidadian calypso, brass band music and Cuban son, to swing, jazz and older African song forms. Osibisa were *the* 'Afro-rock' pop/highlife group of the 1970s. Today's hybrids include gospel, hip-hop (hip-life) and the ever-popular guitar highlife. The Western Diamonds, Amekye Dede and Jewel Ackah are popular artists. Highlife is also a staple of Sierra Leone, Liberia and (with a Congolese influence) Nigeria. Check out early recordings by Dr Victor Olaiya, Nigerian highlife's 'evil genius' and his band, Cool Cats.

## Juju

*Juju* music evolved from a mix of traditional Yoruba talking drums and folklore, and popular palm-wine guitar music. *Juju's* best known ambassador, King Sunny Ade, has been deploying his relentless blend of ringing guitar lines, multilayered percussion, tight harmonies and booty shaking for four decades now. In Nigeria he's known as KSA, the Minister for Enjoyment. Competition with his main rival, Chief Commander Ebenezer Obey, continues, with the likes of Sir Shina Peters close behind. *Juju* is not to be confused with the Arabesque percussion frenzy that is *fuji*: main players here include elder statesman Sir Ayinde Barrister and innovators Pasuma Wonder and Adewale Ayuba, whose recent award-winning collaboration with Adé Bantu, *Fuji Satisfaction*, added Afrobeat, ragga, rap and hip-hop.

Conakry's Radio Kankan (www.radio-kankan.com) is a French-language station devoted to news and music from the region.

## Makossa

A fusion of highlife and soul, influenced by Congolese rumba and characterised by electric guitars, Cameroon's distinctive pop-*makossa* music remains one of West Africa's most vibrant dance genres. It's biggest star is still the jazz-minded sax player and singer Manu Dibango (track down his 1973 release, *Soul Makossa*), who has worked in related genres such as *mangambe, assiko* and *bikutsi* and regularly sells out London venues such as Ronnie Scott's. The ever-adventurous Francis Bebey is another big name, while Sam Fan Thomas has popularised *makassi,* a sort of *makossa*-lite. Other names include Toto Guillaume, Ekambi Brilliant and the guitarist Vincent Nguini.

## Mbalax

Taken from the Wolof word for rhythm, *mbalax* is Senegal's primary musical genre, an intensely polyrhythmic sound that evolved in the 1970s from Afro-Cuban dance bands such as the Star Band and Orchestra Baobab, and then fiercely reclaimed its African roots. Youssou N'Dour was the first to introduce more traditional elements, including *tassou* (a form of rap), *bakou* (a kind of trilling) and instruments such as the *tama* and *sabar* drums. Popular *mbalax* artists include females Khar M'Baye Maddiagaga, Kine Lam and N'Dour's Britney-esque sister-in-law, Vivianne.

*I'll Sing for You* (Je Chanterai Pour Toi; 2001) is an award-winning, life-affirming documentary featuring legendary Mali bluesman Boubacar 'KarKar' Traoré returning to his homeland after decades of self-imposed exile in France.

## Reggae, Rap & Hip-Hop

Afro-reggae, rap and hip-hop are huge throughout West Africa. Elder Ivorian statesman Alpha Blondy has enjoyed a 20-year career, spawning hits like the classic 'Jerusalem', recorded in Jamaica with the Wailers. His younger, equally political, compatriots include Serge Kassy and Tiken Jah Fakoly. Ivorian hip-hop includes the gangsta-style rap *dogba*, which contrasts with the socially aware, anti-bling Wolof rap of Senegalese outfits such as Daara J and Positive Black Soul. There is a growing Mandinka rap scene in Mali (check out the album *Mandinka Rap From Mali* (Naxos World) by the rapping *griot* duo Les Escrocs). Majek Fashek is the best known Nigerian reggae artist, and Nigerian hip-hop musicians include Eedris Abdulkareem – he of the much-hyped spat with 50 Cent – along with JJC and the 419 Squad. Rap Nigerien (sic) is a melange of different languages spoken in Niger – as deployed by groups such as Was Wong, Gogro G and Metaphor – and covers such topics as forced marriages, child labour and corruption.

Africanhiphop.com (www.africanhiphop .com) has been mapping the development of African hip-hop culture since the '90s; features links, new productions and contributions from the artists themselves.

## Wassoulou

Wassoulou music is named after the region of the same name, south of Bamako in Mali (p490), and the Fula people who inhabit it. Wassoulou is not *jeli* music – they have no castes – but is based on hunting songs. The women usually sing, and the men dance. The music is based on the *kamalengoni* or youth's harp – a sort of funky, jittery bass guitar invented in the 1950s – and is augmented by the thwack and slap of the *fle*, a calabash strung with cowrie shells and thrown and spun in the air. Having shot to fame with her 1989 release, *Moussoulou*, Oumou Sangare is still the biggest Wassoulou star, singing, however obliquely, in her native Bambara about the injustices of life in West Africa: polygamy, arranged marriages, the price of a bride. 'There is still much work to be done,' she says. A new album is due out in 2007.

# Arts & Craftwork

West Africa's rich and famous artistic heritage is one of the most vibrant found anywhere in the world. The fascinating traditional sculptures (in wood, bronze and other materials), masks, striking textiles and jewellery are one of the enduring threads of the region's unique cultures that remain, in some cases, largely unchanged from the days when fabulously wealthy empires ruled the land. At the same time, what brings West African art alive is that it remains at the centre of cultural life and still carries powerful meaning for Africa's diverse peoples.

## MASKS

In West Africa there is a staggering range of shapes and styles of mask, from the tiny 'passport' mask of the Dan to the snake-like Dogon *iminana* mask, which can tower up to 10m in height.

Masks, which are usually created by professional artisans, can be made of wood, brass, tin, leather, cloth, glass beads, natural fibres and even (in the case of the Ashanti) gold. They are also made in a number of forms, including face masks, helmet masks (which cover the whole head), headdresses (which are secured to the top of the head), the massive *nimba* masks of the Baga tribe in Guinea (which are carried on the dancer's shoulders) and the famous ivory hip masks from the Kingdom of Benin (present-day Nigeria), which are worn around the waist.

West African masks are usually classified as anthropomorphic (resembling the human form) and zoomorphic (the representation of deities in the form of animals). Anthropomorphic masks are often carefully carved and can be very realistic. Many tribal groups use masks representing beautiful maidens, whose features reflect the aesthetic ideal of the people. The zoomorphic masks mostly represent dangerous and powerful nature spirits, and can be an abstract and terrifying combination of gaping jaws, popping eyes and massive horns. Some masks combine human and animal features. These convey the links between humans and animals, in particular the ability to gain and control the powers of animals and the spirits they represent.

The mask is only part of a complex costume that often covers the dancer's entire body. Made of plant fibre or cloth, often with elaborate appliqué, the costume is usually completed with a mane of raffia surrounding the mask. Most masks are associated with dance, although some are used as prestige symbols and are worn as amulets. For more information on the masks and statues of Côte d'Ivoire – where West Africa's woodcarving tradition is at its richest – see p262.

## TEXTILES

Few places in the world can match West Africa for the beauty, vitality, colour and range of its textiles. Contrary to what many travellers expect, men are the main producers of textiles (the *bogolan* cloth of Mali is an exception), weaving wool, cotton, nylon, rayon and silk on a variety of looms. Most of West Africa's textiles follow the strip-cloth technique, whereby cloth is woven in narrow strips which are then sewn together. As many West Africans now wear Western clothes and traditional textiles are largely reserved for ceremonial occasions, the skills required to produce the finer textiles are disappearing, a trend that sales to collectors and tourists can only partly ameliorate.

*African Masks*, by Iris Hahner-Herzog, catalogues more than 200 masks from a private collection from West and Central Africa, and is essential reading for those who plan to start their own, albeit more modest, collection.

Some art historians believe that one of Picasso's most famous paintings – *Les Demoiselles d'Avignion*, which is often cited as the first work of the cubist form for which he later became famous – depicts women wearing ceremonial Dogon masks.

The New York-based Museum for African Art (www.africanart.org) has good general information on African masks.

## THE MASK COMES ALIVE

In West Africa, masks were rarely produced for purely decorative purposes. Rather they were highly active signifiers of the spirit world and played a central role in local ceremonies that served to both accompany important rites of passage and to entertain.

When masks and costumes are worn for a dance, which is accompanied by percussive music and song, they come alive and convey their meaning to the audience. Masked dances are used in initiation and coming-of-age ceremonies; in burial rituals, when dancing and celebrations assist the spirit of the dead to forsake the earth and reside with ancestors; in fertility rituals, which are associated with agriculture and the appeasement of spirits to ensure a successful harvest; and in the rituals surrounding childbirth. Masks fulfil the function of entertainment, with community-based dances and theatrical plays being created for social education and enjoyment.

The role of the mask is, however, changing. Christianity, Islam and the 20th century have had a big impact on the animist masked dances of West Africa. Many dances are no longer performed, and sometimes those that are have transformed from sacred rituals to forms of entertainment. Since the arrival in Africa of tourists and collectors, artisans have also begun to produce masks for widespread sale. This serves to keep artisans employed in their traditional art at a time when demand from traditional sources is endangering the future of such traditions. Indeed the masks' (and artisans') changing role in society may merely be the latest evidence that masking traditions were never static and continue to transmute over time.

It is still possible to see masked dances in West Africa, although they may be specially arranged 'tourist' performances. Getting to see the real thing is often a matter of being in the right place at the right time. For information on Dogon masks, see p517.

## Kente Cloth

Probably the best-known West African fabric is the colourful kente cloth from Ghana, made by the Ashanti people. Clothing is one of the most visual and important marks of distinction in Ashanti society and the people clearly have a flair for exuberance, as expressed in the brightest of colours. The basic traditional garment for men is a long rectangular piece of *ntoma* (cloth) passed over the left shoulder and brought around the body like a toga. The earliest kente cloth was cotton, but from the 18th century Ashanti weavers began incorporating designs using unravelled, imported Dutch silk. Silk has since gone on to be the fabric of prestige and the most expensive kente cloths contain silk (or imported rayon).

For some interesting history about kente, Ghana's most famous textile, as well as a discussion of the different kente designs, visit www.ghana.co.uk/history/fashion/kente.htm.

The weaving is done exclusively by men (usually working outdoors) who weave narrow, brightly coloured strips with complex patterns and rich hues. Kente cloth is worn only in the southern half of Ghana and is generally reserved for prestigious events.

The colourful cloth worn by women all throughout West Africa, often in two or three pieces, owes little to traditional craftsmanship – it is usually imported or locally produced 'Dutch wax', a factory-made material using stencils and a batik process.

The Ewe also weave kente cloth, but their designs are somewhat different and include motifs of geometric figures. Every design has a meaning and some designs are reserved exclusively for royal families.

## Adinkra Cloth

Just as impressive as the better-known kente cloth, *adinkra* cloth (a colourful cotton material with black geometric designs or stylised figures stamped on it) is also from Ghana. The word '*adinkra*' means 'farewell', and Ghanaians consider this fabric most appropriate for funerals.

Originally the printing was done on cotton pieces laid on the ground. Today, the cotton fabric is cut into long pieces, spread on a raised padded board and held in place by nails. The symbolic designs are cut on calabash stamps, and the dye is made from the bark of a local tree called *badie*. The printer dips the calabash into the hot dye and presses it onto the fabric.

The rich colours are about far more than aesthetics – each colour has a special significance: vermilion (red) symbolises the earth, blue signifies love, and yellow represents success and wealth.

## Bogolan Cloth

From the Sahel region of Mali comes *bogolan* cloth (called *bokolanfini* in Bambara, and often simply referred to as 'mud cloth'). This textile can be found in markets throughout much of West Africa, but its true home is Djenné.

The cloth is woven in plain cotton strips, sewn together and dyed yellow using a solution made from the leaves of a local tree. If you thought mud was mud, think again – after weaving, the cloth is covered in designs using various types of mud from different sources: mud from sandstone outcrops is used for reds and oranges; mud from riverbeds is used for blacks and greys. The cloth is left to dry in the sun, and the mud designs are then removed, leaving their imprint – the effect is very striking.

Designs are traditionally geometric and abstract, but *bogolan* cloth made specifically for tourists is more representational, showing animals, markets or village scenes. Some designs are very complex and involve many hours of work by the artists, who are all women. *Bogolan* cloth is usually used for wall hangings and bedcovers, and is also sometimes used for making waistcoats, caps and bags.

*Bogolan: Shaping Culture through Cloth in Contemporary Mali*, by Victoria L Rovine, is splendidly photographed and is a fine study of how Malian textile art has changed along with the outside influences which Mali has been increasingly subjected to.

## Indigo Cloth

Another classic West African fabric is the indigo-dyed cotton worn primarily by the Tuareg as robes and headdresses. The indigo colour comes from the indigofera plant and the indigo vine; the plant is crushed and fermented, then mixed with an alkaline solution to produce the dye. The dyed cloth is often beaten with a mallet to produce a sheen. Other West African tribes noted for their use of indigo include the Hausa, Baoulé, Yoruba and Soninké.

The Yoruba produce an indigo-dyed cloth, *aderi*, which has designs that are applied using the tie-dye technique, or by painting motifs with a dye-resistant starch. The Dogon also produce an indigo cloth, which has characteristic geometric patterns.

The Tuareg were once famously known as the 'Blue People of the Sahara' because the indigo of their clothing rubs off on their skin – an effect that they admire. Indigo cloth is, however, used less often now and usually only for special occasions.

## Other Textiles

The Fula have a caste of weavers, called Maboub, who produce blankets known as *khasa*. These are usually made from camel hair, although the term is sometimes used to describe cotton blankets as well. The Maboub also make rare and expensive wedding blankets. These large and elaborately detailed textiles are traditionally displayed around the marriage bed.

The Fon and the Fanti are known for their appliqué banners and flags. Shapes of people and animals are cut from colourful material and are carefully sewn onto a cloth panel.

The Hausa are known for their embroidery, which was once hand-stitched onto their robes and caps. Although now machine-stitched, the designs remain unchanged. In keeping with Islam, Hausa designs are nonfigurative.

*African Elegance*, by Ettagale Blauer, is a magnificently photographed chronicle of African art forms and their role in modern Africa – the sections on masks and jewellery are of particular interest.

## JEWELLERY

West Africans love their jewellery, which is important to both men and women, and wherever you go you're likely to see a fascinating variety of designs.

The humble bead is elevated to high art in this part of the world and they serve as more than simple adornments – they are often used as objects representing spiritual values, and can play a major role in community rituals such as birth, circumcision, marriage and death. Like most major art forms, bead-making has changed over time, particularly since the arrival of Europeans. Beads are now more likely to be made of glass, after local jewellers started copying the highly decorative *millefiori* trading beads from Venice, which featured flowers, stripes and mosaic designs. Discarded bottles and medicine jars were pulverised into a fine powder to be remade into glass beads and the Krobo in Ghana still melt powdered glass in terracotta moulds. In a slight variation, the Nupe in central Nigeria wind molten glass on long iron rods to make beads and bracelets. Referred to as *bakim-mutum* by bead traders (most of whom sell glass beads by weight, hence their other name, 'pound beads'), beads are commonly worn by village chiefs and elders as a sign of power and wealth.

A variety of other materials are used in Africa for making beads, including coral, shell, copal, amazonite, silver, gold and brass. In Mali you'll see large amber beads worn by Fula women. The Dogon also treasure amber, and use it in their necklaces, bracelets and pendants. They also use beads made of stone and terracotta incised with geometric patterns.

Rings in West Africa are sometimes stunning. In Burkina Faso, look out for Bobo bronze rings, which often have intricate designs, including a tick bird, a warrior on horseback or a chameleon. In Mali, older Dogon men wear large bronze rings as a sign of status. All over the region you'll find beautiful dark-green malachite jewellery, which usually comes from Congo (Zaïre). Cowrie shells are often used to decorate jewellery; for a long time these shells were used as money in many areas of Africa.

The Ashanti are famous for their goldwork in jewellery, ornaments and staffs, and in most areas of the region the preferred metal for jewellery is gold. In and near the Sahara, however, the Tuareg and Moors prefer silver. The Tuareg are renowned for their intricate filigree silverwork in jewellery and in the decoration on the handles of their daggers. Tuareg men and women often wear silver crosses as pendants around their necks. These come in various designs, characterised by protective symbolism. Some incorporate circle and phallus designs, or fertility symbols; those representing a camel's eye or jackal tracks are symbolic of power and cunning.

## TOTEMS & TALISMANS

An important feature of traditional religions is the totem, which is an object (usually representing an animal) that serves as an emblem for a particular tribe, and is usually connected with the original ancestor of that group. It is taboo for a member of the clan whose totem is, for example, a snake, to harm any snake, as this would be harming the ancestor. Other common totems include lions, crocodiles and birds.

Talismans (sometimes called fetishes) are another important feature in animism. These are objects (or charms) that are believed to embody a spirit, and can take many forms. For example, bird skulls and other animal parts may be used as charms by a learned elder for helping people communicate with their ancestors. The elders (usually men) that are responsible for these sacred objects are sometimes called fetish-priests or *féticheurs*.

The most common charms found throughout West Africa are the small leather or metal amulets, often containing a sacred object, which are worn by people around the neck, arm or waist. These are called grigri and are usually worn to ward off evil or bring good luck. Many West African

*Africa Adorned, by Angela Fisher, is an extravagantly beautiful coffee-table book that could just be the finest of its kind, with some exceptional and detailed sections on African jewellery.*

The use of crosses in Tuareg culture (in jewellery and the shape of pommels on their camel saddles) led early European explorers to speculate that they were once Christians. The crosses are actually fashioned by Muslim blacksmiths who believe themselves to be of Jewish origin.

Muslims (including the Tuareg) also wear grigri, which are called *t'awiz* in other Islamic countries; there is often a small verse from the Qur'an inside and they are only considered effective if made by a marabout.

## FIGURATIVE SCULPTURE

African sculpture is now considered one of the most dynamic and influential art forms around. Once relegated to curio cabinets and dusty museum storerooms, and labelled as crude, barbaric and primitive, African carving finally gained credibility in the early 20th century when Picasso, Matisse and others found inspiration in its radical approach to the human form.

Most West African sculpture is carved in wood, but some superb bronze and iron figures are produced, and some funerary figures are created in terracotta and mud. The strange and uncompromising forms found in West African sculpture are rarely the unique creations of an inspired artist – the sculptures have always been made to fulfil specific functions within the tribe, using centuries-old designs redolent with meaning.

In West Africa, sculpture is mostly used in connection with ancestor or spirit worship. Many tribal groups believe that the spirits of the dead can have a major impact, both positive and negative, on a person's life. Ancestral figures are carved and placed in shrines and altars where they receive libations and sacrificial blood. Some tribes carve figures that are cared for by women to ensure fertility and in the hope that the resulting child will inherit the fine looks represented in the sculpture. The famous *akuaba* 'doll' of the Ashanti is the best-known example of this. Prestige objects are also carved, such as figurative staffs of office, commemorative statues and other regalia used by kings, chiefs, traditional healers and diviners as emblems of power.

West African sculpture is usually created by a professional artist, who is almost always male and who has learned his craft through an apprenticeship. Mostly a family- or caste-specific occupation, the forms and skills are passed down from generation to generation, resulting in highly refined styles.

Like in any nonstatic cultural tradition, the process is does change – occasionally a virtuoso carver will introduce new elements that may then be incorporated by other artists. In many cases a carver will be commissioned to create a work. After payment has been arranged, the carver selects the wood required, which can involve lengthy rituals. He then blocks out the form using an adze, completes the finer details with a knife and, traditionally, sands the carving with a species of rough leaf.

Across the many tribal-specific styles produced in West Africa, some common characteristics can be identified. The figure is usually symmetrical and faces forward, the features are impassive and the arms are held to the side with the legs slightly bent at the knees. Certain features may be exaggerated, and the head is almost always large in proportion to the body.

The surface of the carving will often have tribal marks carved or burnt into the blackened face and torso, and there may be crusty deposits of sacrificial material, even though such rituals are less often practised now. Sometimes the carving is highly polished or painted with ochre or imported enamel paint.

## BRONZE CASTING

West Africa's best-known castings were created for the Kingdom of Benin in present-day Nigeria. Plaques, statues and masks were produced to decorate the palaces and compounds of the kings and chiefs, and their

*Tribal Arts of Africa, by Jean-Baptiste Bacquart (the former head of Sotheby's tribal arts section), combines superb photos with informative text about Africa's (mostly) pre-colonial masks and statutes.*

*African Art of the Dogon, by Jean Laude, is a seminal 1970s' text that explores the meaning of the highly ritualised art forms that distinguish one of West Africa's most intriguing cultures.*

discovery (and plundering) by Western governments and collectors did at least serve to challenge the prevailing view that African cultures were primitive.

West African brass and bronze is often cast using the *cire perdue* (lost wax) technique. The casting process involves creating a sculpture out of wax, which is then dipped in a solution of silt and mud. When the sculpture is dry, clay is built around the form to create a strong mould. The mould is then heated and the wax is melted out. Molten bronze is then poured into the empty mould and, when cool, the mould is broken away to reveal the bronze sculpture. Each cast is therefore unique. This process is thought to have produced the 1000-year-old beautifully intricate bronzes of the Ibo-Ikwu, which can be seen today in the National Museum in Lagos (p632). Today, latex is often used instead of wax, which creates even finer detail.

The Yoruba cast ritual staffs called *edan*. These comprise male and female figures in bronze, surmounting an iron tip and joined together by a chain. Figurative weights for weighing gold were cast by the Ashanti, and often symbolised the colourful proverbs for which those people are known.

The Guggenheim Museum's African collection is displayed in all its glory on its informative and visually enticing website: http://artnetweb.com /guggenheim/africa/.

# Peoples of West Africa

More than anything else, it is West Africa's people and the richness of their cultural traditions that lure travellers to the region and provide the highlight of any visit. The diversity you'll encounter is astounding; there are hundreds of different groups, each with their own customs and language.

Following are brief profiles of some of the larger or better-known groups (ordered alphabetically).

## ASHANTI

Inhabiting the heart of the now-thinning forest of southern Ghana are the Ashanti, whose kingdom was famed for its gold, its royalty and its traditional state organisation. As the political role of the state declined under colonial rule, a new source of wealth emerged. Cocoa underpinned the prosperity of town and village life, and traditional crafts such as stool carving, kente cloth weaving and goldsmithing continued to embellish the proud rituals and ceremonies of traditional life. Today, it is the aesthetic of traditional life and its chiefly ceremony that give Ashanti culture its appeal to the traveller. Some of the best-known African artefacts and symbols in Europe and North America are Ashanti, including kente cloth, carved stools and *Adinkra* symbols.

One of the most famous Ashanti war leaders against the British was Yaa Asantewaa, queen mother of Ejisu, who in 1900 shamed the Ashanti army into entering battle by leading them herself (see p384).

## BAMBARA

The Bambara (also known as Bamana) are the largest ethnic group in Mali, comprising about 33% of the population. Although they are Muslim, many have retained their traditional beliefs and customs. One of the most important of these is an occupational caste system, which includes farmers, leather-workers, poets and blacksmiths. Blacksmiths are particularly significant – not only do they make hoes for producing food, but also door locks that protect women and children, and guns that arm the village. All of these are furnished with spiritual power as well as utility. Door locks often have a water-lizard symbol to protect the house from thieves, or a long-eared creature similar to a bat that is said to hear every sound, thus protecting the household.

The Bambara are known for their artwork, especially woodcarvings and masks. Each of the occupational groups or castes has its own initiation rituals, for which particular masks are required, and it is only blacksmiths who inherit the capacity to tap into the spiritual power, or *nyama,* that enables them to transform wood and iron into masks and other religious objects. Because *nyama* is inherited, blacksmiths must marry within their own occupational group.

According to Bambara legend, the Creator sent an antelope to teach the Bambara how to cultivate grain, which is why the *chiwara,* a stylised antelope with long arched neck and horns, is the best-known symbol of the Bambara.

## BAOULÉ

The Baoulé, who separated from Ghana's Ashanti in bygone years, live in eastern and central Côte d'Ivoire. They are known for their belief in the *blolo* (meaning 'elsewhere' or 'the beyond') – another world, parallel to our own. The *blolo,* although invisible, is believed to be inhabited by people. A man may even have a *blolo bla,* a wife from beyond, and a woman a *blolo bian,* or other husband. Both can influence a partner's wellbeing, marital stability and sex life, usually negatively.

To counteract problems such as these, a soothsayer is called, who usually recommends that the *blolo* partner be 'called in' or 'brought down' to prevent further havoc. This can be done either by moulding a cone of fine kaolin clay mixed with secret herbs, or by fashioning a clay or wooden statue of the *blolo* partner, thus controlling the parallel-world partner and limiting further damage.

## BOBO

The Bobo, who escaped subjugation by the Mossi, live in western Burkina Faso around Bobo-Dioulasso, although some also live across the border in Mali. They are renowned for their mask traditions, involving many different types of masks, including the famous butterfly and helmet masks.

The large horizontal butterfly masks are typically about 1.5m wide and painted red, black and white. They are worn during funeral rites, and when invoking the deity known as 'Do' in planting-time ceremonies asking for rain and a good harvest. The dancer twists his head so rapidly that the mask almost appears to be spinning. Other animals represented in Bobo masks include owls, buffaloes, antelopes, crocodiles and scorpions. The masks are usually tall, and have bold-coloured patterns similar to those adorning the butterfly masks.

## DAN

The Dan (also known as the Yacouba) inhabit the mountainous area around Man in Côte d'Ivoire. Masks are an important part of Dan culture. Each village has several great masks that represent its collective memory and which are glorified during times of happiness and abundance. Masks are regarded as divinities and as repositories of knowledge. They dictate the community values that give the clan cohesiveness and help to preserve its customs. For example, harvest-time yields, or whether a woman will give birth to a son or a daughter, are believed to depend on masks, and no important action is undertaken without first addressing a mask to request its assistance.

## DOGON

The Dogon, who live in the area around Mali's Falaise de Bandiagara (Bandiagara Escarpment), are among the region's most intriguing people, and are also known for their masks. There are various types, including the famous *iminana*, which can be up to 10m high, the bird-like *kanaga*, which protects against vengeance (of a killed animal), and the house-like *sirige*, which represents the house of the *hogon*, who is responsible for passing on Dogon traditions to younger generations. For more on the Dogon, see p517 and p516.

The Dogon are traditionally farmers. Both men and women are very industrious, as work is a central feature of Dogon society. Crops such as millet are planted in the fields below the escarpment and on terraces created on the lower slopes (where water and soil must be brought up from the plains below). In some areas dams have enabled the creation of irrigated market gardens on the solid rock of the plateau.

Unsurprisingly, many Dogon now choose to farm down on the plains, where traditionally there had been conflict with the Fula and Mossi. Now Fula groups bring their cattle to graze on harvested Dogon fields, thus providing fertiliser for the following year's crop.

## EWE

The Ewe people of Ghana and Togo are known for hard work, tidy villages, their love of education, their spirituality, and the power of their traditional shrines and priests. The supreme deities of the Ewe are Mawu-Lisa, the female-male moon-sun twins.

The form of a butterfly is used in Bobo masks because butterflies appear in great swarms immediately after the first rains and are thus associated with the planting season.

The Ethnologue website (www.ethnologue.com) is a comprehensive and fascinating database of the world's languages, listing the languages, the linguistic families to which they belong and the number of speakers in each country.

A Dogon man must spend time working hard in fields belonging to his intended wife's parents before permission to marry will be granted.

The Ewe are also known for their subtly coloured kente cloth and for their *vu gbe* (talking drums). The tonality of the Ewe spoken language and the rhythm of particular phrases and proverbs are combined in drumming to produce messages that range from the commonplace, which everyone understands, to a specialised repertoire known only to the master drummers. Drum language is used for communication, especially in times of crisis. It is also an integral part of religious song and dance. Ewe dances are widely appreciated for their fast and intricate movements, especially of the shoulders and feet. For more information on the Ewe, see p776.

## FULA

The Fula (also called Fulani, Peul or Foulbé in French-speaking countries) are tall, lightly-built people who have been settling across the West African savanna for centuries. They are estimated to number more than 12 million, and are found from Senegal to as far east as Cameroon, and sometimes beyond. The Tukulor (Toucouleur) and the Wolof of Senegal, as well as the Fulbe Jeeri of Mauritania, are all of Fula origin.

Although the Fula were originally nomadic cattle herders, many are now settled farmers, while others continue to follow their herds in search of pasture, living in grass huts resembling large beehives. Those Fula with no cattle of their own often work as herdsmen, looking after other peoples' cattle. Cattle occupy a central position in society, with Fula often putting the welfare of their animals above their own. Islam also plays a central role. Town-dwelling Fula (referred to as Fulani Gida in some areas) adopted Islam as early as the 12th century and were major catalysts in its spread.

The nomadic Fula, or Wodaabé, are known for their public initiation ceremony in which young boys are lashed with long rods to the accelerating rhythm of drums, as part of their passage into manhood. There are many onlookers, including potential brides, and the boys must show no fear, though their ordeal leaves them scarred. At the annual Gerewol festival (p613), where the young Wodaabé meet prospective marriage partners, men pay great attention to their appearance, adorning themselves with shining jewellery, feathers, sunglasses and elaborate make-up – anything to create an impression, and to look their best for the women.

## HAUSA

Hausaland extends over much of northern Nigeria (where the Hausa make up the largest ethnic group) and into Niger. Hausa culture is closely intertwined with Islam; you may see Quranic script, together with symbols of modern technology such as bicycles and aeroplanes, in the mud-relief patterns on house walls in the old quarters of Nigerian towns such as Kano and Zaria.

The emirs of the Hausa states are known for the pomp with which they live and travel. Their bodyguards traditionally wear chain mail, carry spears and ride strikingly caparisoned horses, while attendants on foot wear red turbans, and brilliant red and green robes. These days, however, it's more likely that you'll see an emir riding slowly through town in a large American car, with the horn sounding.

Many rural Hausa farm grains, cotton and groundnuts, and sacks of groundnuts stacked in pyramids are one of the distinctive sights of many Hausa markets.

Hausaland is one of the few places where cloth is dyed with natural indigo, and if you travel in this region, you'll probably see the drying cloths, patterned in shades of blue on blue, in contrast with the surrounding mud-red urban landscape.

The traditional Ewe institution of *Trokosi*, in which young girls are given as virtual slave-wives to priests in order to appease the spirits, has come under increasing criticism in recent years.

The Africa Guide website (www.africaguide.com) has a great People and Culture section, which includes information on festivals, ceremonies and the traditions of various ethnic groups.

Traditionally, Hausa women rarely step from behind the walls of their compounds – many trade home-processed foods, crafts and other goods from home, while children are sent to run errands between compounds.

## IGBO

The Igbo (also known as Ibo) occupy a large, densely settled farming area in southeastern Nigeria. They form Nigeria's third-largest ethnic group, are predominantly Christian, and have a reputation for hard work, ambition and a love of education. Traditional-minded Igbo will not eat the new season's yam until Ikeji, the annual new yam festival, when thanks are given to the gods for a productive year. The most important Ikeji festival takes place in September at Arochukwu. Judges select the best village presentation of dance, parade and music.

An Igbo receives his destiny or *chi* directly from Chukwu, the benign god of creation. At death, a person returns his *chi* and joins the world of ancestors and spirits. From this spirit world, the deceased watches over living descendants, perhaps returning one day with a different *chi*. A traditionalist's daily preoccupation is to please and appease the *alusa* – the lesser spirits who can blight a person's life if offended and bestow rewards if pleased.

In Igbo tradition, those who died a bad death (such as in childbirth or suicide) were denied proper burial and entry into the realm of the ancestors. Instead, they were thrown into the forest where they became harmful wandering ghosts.

## LOBI

The Lobi live in southwestern Burkina Faso, as well as northern Côte d'Ivoire and Ghana, in distinctive mud-brick compounds resembling small fortresses. They follow ancestor-based beliefs and their traditions are very well preserved.

The Lobi don't use masks. Most of their woodcarvings are of human figures, typically 35cm to 65cm high, which represent deities and ancestors. The woodcarvings are used for ancestral shrines, and traditionally were found in every home. The Lobi also carve staffs and three-legged stools with human or animal heads, as well as combs with human figures or geometric decorations. Lobi carvings are distinguished by their rigid appearance, with arms generally positioned straight down, along the sides of the body. They are also notable for their realistic and detailed renderings of certain body parts, particularly the navel, eyes and hair.

*Faces of Africa*, by Carol Beckwith and Angela Fisher, is a stunning coffee-table book of photos of people from different ethnic groups, by the two photographers who've done more than anyone to bring African cultures to the world.

## MALINKÉ

The Malinké (in some areas synonymous with, or closely related to, the Mandinka or Mandingo) are part of the larger Mande group, which also includes the Bambara and the Soninké and is believed to have originated as early as 4000 years ago. It was at this time that various agricultural peoples of the southern Sahara merged with the indigenous hunter-gatherers of the Niger River basin. Today, the Malinké are found in southern Mali as well as northern Guinea, Côte d'Ivoire, Senegal and Gambia. They are famed hunters and warriors, and were prominent converts to Islam from around the 11th century. In the mid-13th century the Malinké founded the powerful Empire of Mali. Thanks to their central position, they were able to control almost all trans-Saharan commerce – from the gold trade on the coast to the commodities trade coming south across the desert from the Mediterranean states.

Originally the Malinké were divided into 12 clans, each with its own king and highly stratified castes. The heads of these 12 clans formed a royal council, which elected a single leader, known as a *mansa*. The traditional hunter societies of the Malinké, with their secret initiation rites, still thrive today.

*Lords of the Savanna: The Bambara, Fulani, Igbo, Mossi and Nupe*, by Philip Koslow, is aimed at young teenagers, but adults will also learn a thing or two from the simply told histories of West Africa's more populous peoples.

## MOSSI

The Mossi, who are concentrated in the central plateau area in and around Ouagadougou, are the largest ethnic group in Burkina Faso. In the 14th century they established powerful kingdoms in this area after

**WHAT WAS YOUR NAME AGAIN?**

One result of the European language influence in West Africa is that the same African word or sound may be spelt differently according to the interpretation of the original colonial recorder. Travelling through the region, you'll soon realise that many groups of people have more than one name.

The Jola people in Gambia (a former British colony) spread over the border into Senegal (a former French colony), where they are known as the Diola. The Fula people, who are spread across much of northern West Africa, were identified by the French as Peul and by the English as Fulani, the former being the singular and the latter the plural of the word used by these people to identify themselves. Their language is known as Fula or Pulaar.

Similarly, spellings of names can vary, either according to the language of the country's original colonial power, or as linguistic studies become more phonetically precise. For example, Peul can be spelt Peulh; Tamashek (the language of the Tuareg) is generally spelt Tamachek by French speakers; and the Toucouleur of northern Senegal are now often called the Tukulor.

To add to the confusion, the definitions of ethnic groups don't always correlate with those of language groups. Usually a common tongue is the most fundamental aspect that links people together, but linguists and anthropologists sometimes classify as a single ethnic group several subgroups (or sub-subgroups) which speak mutually unintelligible languages, even though they share a common root. Thus the Malinké people of Senegal and Guinea and the Mandinka people of Gambia are sometimes regarded as the same ethnic group. Linguists, however, point out that their languages differ in significant ways and therefore the two peoples should be categorised separately – even though their languages are both part of the wider Manding language group. Both the Malinké and the Mandinka are also sometimes called the Mandingo.

leaving their original homeland around the Niger River. The Mossi are known for their rigid social hierarchies and elaborate rituals, and they still exert considerable political influence in Burkina Faso today. Historically, they resisted invasion by the Muslim Empire of Mali, and today many continue to follow traditional beliefs.

Artistically, the Mossi are best known for their tall wooden antelope masks, often more than 2m high and painted red and white. Male and female antelope masks are distinguished from each other by their top sections. Female masks feature a human female figure, while male masks consist of a nonhuman plank-like structure. At the bottom of these masks is a small oval face, bisected by a serrated vertical strip, with triangular eyeholes on either side. The masks were worn primarily at funerals.

> Blacksmiths are believed to possess special powers in many West African societies (especially Bambara, Senoufo, Tuareg and Wolof), in part because their relationship with iron and fire renders them immune to evil spirits.

## SENOUFO

The Senoufo, who live in Côte d'Ivoire, Burkina Faso and Mali, are renowned as skilled farmers. Animals are held in high regard in Senoufo culture, and when someone dies it is believed that they are transformed into the clan's animal totem.

As a result, many Senoufo dances are associated with animals. One of these is the dance of the leopard men, which is performed in Natiokaba-dara, near Korhogo, as well as in other Senoufo areas when young boys return from their Poro (part of the secret Lô association) initiation-training sessions. In this and other dances, masks – often of animal heads – are instrumental in making contact with the gods and driving away bad spirits.

When someone dies in traditional Senoufo society, the corpse is carried through the village in a procession, while men in grotesque masks chase away the soul. It is the blacksmiths who dig the grave and place the corpse inside, after which they present a last meal to the deceased, and then feast and celebrate.

## SONGHAÏ

The Songhaï live predominantly in Niger (where they are the fourth-largest grouping) and in northern Mali, between Timbuktu and Gao. Historically they trace their roots back to the 7th or 8th century, when Aliman Za (or Dia) arrived at the upper Niger River from Mandinka (Malinké) lands further west and forced out the local fisherpeople. Other theories claim that it was the Tuareg that founded the original Songhaï state, while yet another hypothesis states that the ancestors of the Songhaï were the original inhabitants of the Upper Niger. The truth is probably a mixture of all three theories, but in any case, it's generally agreed that the Songhaï are of Nilo-Saharan stock. Some Songhaï make a distinction between the Songhaï of Gao (supposedly of pure blood) and those of Timbuktu (who have mixed with Tuareg and Moors).

Songhaï villages are divided into neighbourhoods, each of which elects a head. These heads then come together to elect a village chief, who typically is of noble descent. Most Songhaï consider themselves Muslim, although their religious practices are often mixed with strong traditional elements, including ancestor worship and witchcraft. Large communities often have both a mosque as well as a *troupe* that specialises in mediums for spirit intervention.

Songhaï are traditionally farmers, who often have strong bonds with their Tuareg neighbours. There is even an affectionate term in the Songhaï language that refers to the nomadic Tuareg as 'our Tuareg'.

## TUAREG

The Tuareg are a nomadic, camel-owning people, who traditionally roamed across the Sahara from Mauritania to western Sudan. Although originally the Tuareg were a Berber group from North Africa (their language, Tamashek, has Berber roots), who migrated to the desert after the Arab-Islamic invasions of the 7th and 11th centuries. In recent times they have had to abandon their traditional way of life, primarily because of droughts, and many of the Tuareg have moved southwards to settle near cities.

The Tuareg traditionally follow a rigid status system, with nobles, blacksmiths and slaves all occupying strictly delineated hierarchical positions, although the importance of caste identity has diminished in recent years.

The veils, or *taguelmoust*, that are the symbols of a Tuareg's identity and extend from a man's turban, are both a source of protection against the desert wind and sand, and a social requirement; it is considered improper for a Tuareg man to show his face to a man of higher status. Traditionally, Tuareg men rarely remove their shawl to expose the lower half of the face in company and, when drinking tea, pass the glass under their *taguelmoust* so as not to reveal the mouth.

Tuareg women – who are not veiled and who enjoy an unusual degree of independence – weave artificial strands into their plaits and attach cowrie shells. They also can be recognised by their large pieces of silver jewellery.

The *croix d'Agadez* is one of the best-known Tuareg symbols, together with intricately decorated dagger handles. The crosses are in silver filigree, and the Tuareg believe they are powerful talismans offering protection against 'the evil eye'; some serve as fertility symbols. The designs vary slightly, depending on which desert town they were made in. Tuareg men use the crosses as a form of currency to buy cattle; between trades the crosses are worn by Tuareg wives as a sign of wealth.

*Niger: Epopées Zarma Et Songhay*, by Jibo Baje – a Songhaï *griot* from Niger who sings the epic tales of his people in the ancient Songhaï language, accompanied by a three-stringed lute – is strangely mesmeric.

*The Pastoral Tuareg: Ecology, Culture, and Society*, by Johannes and Ida Nicolaisen, is a comprehensive two-volume study of the Tuareg with good photographs. Subjects range from traditions to the challenges faced by the Tuareg today.

## WOLOF

The Wolof heartland is in Senegal, where these people comprise about 36% of the population, and are active in the Muslim brotherhoods.

Wolof society is hierarchical, with hereditary castes determining traditional occupations and status. Today, though, family status is only important for marriage and traditional occupations, such as blacksmiths and *griots* (praise singers).

Although Islam has been an influence in Wolof areas since the 11th century, many traditional beliefs persist. For example, there is a belief in a snake monster so terrible that to look upon it causes death. In order to guard against witches and other forms of evil, many Wolof wear leather-bound amulets containing written verses of the Qur'an.

The Wolof, who are of Fula origin, tend to be tall and striking in their traditional flowing robes of white, dark blue or black. The women wear a series of loose, layered gowns, each a little shorter than the one underneath. Men wear long gowns over loose white pantaloons that overhang the knee.

*Folktales from the Gambia: Wolof Fictional Narratives*, by Emil A Magel, offers revealing insights into the Wolof people through the medium of traditional stories, which are as enjoyable for adults as for children.

## YORUBA

Yorubaland extends from southwestern Nigeria to neighbouring Benin. Most Yoruba traditionally prefer to live in towns, migrating seasonally to their more-distant farmlands. The urban culture of the Yoruba has facilitated the development of trade and elaborate arts, including the famous Benin bronzes. The old quarters of Yoruba cities contain large household compounds of extended families. Every town has an *oba* (crowned chief). The traditional head of all Yorubas is the *alafin,* who lives at Oyo, in Nigeria, while the *oni* (chief priest) lives at Ife. Formality, ceremony and hierarchy govern Yoruba social relations, and ostentation in dress and jewellery is a social requirement for women at traditional functions.

*The Religion of the Yorubas*, by Olumide Lucas, gives the detailed story behind the spirit world of the Yoruba – it can be a little dry in places but there's no finer text on this fascinating people.

# Environment

West Africa spans some of the great landscapes of the African continent, with lush, tropical rainforests yielding to savanna before the Sahel provides an introduction to the Sahara. With such a rich environmental bounty at its disposal (and also at the disposal of a resource-hungry world), West Africa is facing some of the most pressing environmental issues of our time in a territory where the world's poorest people and most rapidly diminishing wildlife scratch about in the dust for the means to survive.

For more information on travelling responsibly throughout the region, see p22.

*The Sahara* (part of the World's Wild Places series by Time-Life Books) captures the lure of the Sahara with its evocative prose, but is also hugely informative; it'll have you dreaming of a desert campfire.

## THE LAND

The geography of West Africa is a story of three horizontal lines: a northern band of desert, a southern band of woodland and forest, and a semidesert zone in between known as the Sahel (see opposite).

West Africa largely consists of a gently undulating plateau and has very few mountains. However, there are some important highland areas in the region: the borderlands between Nigeria and Cameroon rise to Chappal Wadi (2418m); the Jos Plateau (1781m) and Shebsi Mountains (2418m) are in Nigeria; Mt Bintumani (1945m) in Sierra Leone; the rocky Aïr Mountains in Niger, rising to Mt Bagzane (2022m); the hill country around Mt Nimba (1752m), in the border area between Guinea, Côte d'Ivoire and Liberia; and the hills of the Fouta Djalon in western Guinea (1538m), which extends down into southeastern Senegal. The peaks of the volcanic Cape Verde islands are also notable with the highest one being Mt Fogo (2839m). Mt Cameroon (4095m) is the highest point in West Africa.

The Sahara covers more than nine million sq km (approximately the size of the United States) but is home to just 1400 plant species, 50 species of mammals and 18 species of birds.

Although West Africa's highland areas are limited, they create headwaters for several rivers, including the Niger (see the boxed text, p82). Other major rivers include the Senegal River, which forms the border with Mauritania; the Gambia River, again giving its name to the country it flows through; the Casamance River in southern Senegal; the Volta River in Ghana and Burkina Faso; and the Benue River (a major tributary of the Niger) in Nigeria and Cameroon.

---

### THE HARMATTAN – SCOURGE OF THE SAHEL?

Harmattan (from a Hausa word meaning 'north wind') refers to the dry, dust-laden winds that originate in the Sahara and blow throughout much of West Africa during the dry season, January (sometimes December) to March. The harmattan can cause respiratory complaints, spread diseases such as meningitis, and reduce visibility to a few hundred metres, often cloaking the landscape in a spectral orange glow. Aircraft delays are commonplace during the harmattan and photographs taken on hazy days will often have a disappointingly overcast and colourless hue. Even when the wind stops blowing, conditions often remain hazy until the first May rains.

But the harmattan is not just a bearer of bad tidings. Some locals look forward to the harmattan season as a cooler respite from the searing heat, and also as a signal that the year has turned the corner towards the rainy season. In many of the countries, the peak tourist period coincides with the harmattan's arrival and some travellers even await the harmattan with relish – most notably the decidedly singular late-18th-century explorer Mungo Park, who welcomed the wind as a curer of all ills and proclaimed it to be definitely the best time to travel in West Africa.

**THE SAHEL**

The Sahel – a horizontal band stretching from the Atlantic coast to the Nile – is the transition zone between the forested lands of the south and the Sahara desert to the north, but for its detractors it possesses the redeeming features of neither. At face value, the Sahel is indeed one of the direst stretches of inhabited geography on earth, beset by drought, erosion, creeping desertification, periodic locust invasions and increasingly infertile land.

That said, within its boundaries are many different subregions. Among these are zones which are variously described as semidesert savanna, Guinea savanna, Sudanese savanna, dry savanna or dry woodland savanna. In the north, near the true desert, the Sahel is dry, dusty, sparsely vegetated and barely distinguishable from the Sahara, but in the south, nearer the forests, it is greener and contains areas of light woodland fed by more plentiful rains.

The countries covered in this book that are considered to be all or partly in the Sahel are Senegal, Gambia, Guinea, Mali, Burkina Faso, Niger and Nigeria. However, the boundaries are not fixed, and southern Nigeria and southeastern Guinea are actually in the forest zone. In the same way, the northern parts of the coastal countries of Côte d'Ivoire, Ghana, Togo, Benin and Cameroon are relatively dry, and so are sometimes described as having a Sahelian climate or vegetation.

If West Africa is overshadowed by the looming Sahara desert to the north, it is barricaded by the equally formidable Atlantic Ocean to the south. Many major cities – Dakar, Banjul, Bissau, Conakry, Freetown, Monrovia, Abidjan, Accra, Lomé, Cotonou, Porto Novo, Lagos and Douala – are strung out along the coast like beads in a chain, in some areas forming an almost constant linear urban sprawl, cut only by national frontiers.

# WILDLIFE
## Animals
### MAMMALS

Although West Africa comes a distant third behind East and Southern Africa when it comes to wildlife viewing, it's still home to an impressive variety of animals. Some of the region's national parks (see p85) contain classic African mammal species – including elephants, lions and leopards – but your chances of seeing them are much smaller than elsewhere in Africa. There are also significant wildlife populations, including elephants, in rainforest areas, although animals are generally hidden by the dense vegetation. Another problem is that, unlike East African mammals which are accustomed to large-scale safari tourism, West Africa's species are much more wary of humans.

Mammals more readily seen include several beautiful antelope species, such as bushbucks, reedbucks, waterbucks, kobs, roans, elands, oribis, sitatungas and various gazelles and duikers. The Sahel-dwelling dama gazelle is the largest gazelle species in Africa, but is now close to extinction, as its grazing lands have been taken over by cattle and reduced by desertification. Wild pig species include giant hogs and bush pigs (the West African species is often called the red river hog), which inhabit forest areas, and warthogs, frequently seen in drier savanna areas. Buffalos in West Africa inhabit forest regions, and are smaller and redder than the East African version.

Possibly the best-known and most easily observed mammals of West Africa are monkeys. These include several types of colobus and green or vervet monkeys. Other primates include mangabeys, baboons, galagos (bushbabies), as well as chimpanzees and the rare and endangered drill.

In the Niger Inland Delta in Mali, the fisherpeople of the Bozo are known in Bambara as *gui-tigui*, the 'Masters of the River', and are believed to possess a mystical affinity with the river and its creatures.

*African Silences*, by Peter Matthiessen, is a profoundly moving, beautifully written book about surveying wildlife in West and Central Africa.

## THE NIGER RIVER

The Niger River is one of Africa's grand old rivers and its curious course has fascinated travellers since the 18th century. Africa's third-longest river, the Niger begins its journey just over 200km from the Atlantic, but then flows for over 4100km in its search for an outlet to the sea. From its source in the Fouta Djalon highlands of Guinea, close to the border with Sierra Leone, the Niger flows deep into Africa's heart, passing Bamako and Mopti and on through the vast Niger Inland Delta and Lac Debo of central Mali. From there, the Niger narrows and comes within touching distance of Timbuktu before it comes up against the impenetrable barrier of the Sahara, from which it turns its face away, as if unable to bear the solitude. In its attempts to avoid the desert, it performs a long, laborious curve south (which is known as the Niger Bend or Boucle du Niger) and courses down into Niger, then crosses a slice of Benin before finally emptying into the Atlantic via a maze of swamps and channels (in Nigeria, west of Port Harcourt) called the Niger Delta.

Until the intrepid Mungo Park reached the Niger River close to Ségou on 21 July 1796, European mapmakers were convinced that the river flowed east–west and originated in the Nile or Lake Chad.

Cameroon also hosts an endangered population of western lowland gorilla.

In the rivers, including the upper reaches of the Niger and Gambia Rivers, hippos can sometimes be seen, but numbers are low. Some hippos have adapted to live in salt water and exist in coastal areas, while a few forest areas of West Africa, including in Liberia, are home to very small populations of pygmy hippos, which are less aquatic than their larger cousins.

Other marine mammals found in the region include dolphins, especially where the region's main rivers meet the ocean, and manatees (sea cows) – giant seal-like relatives of the elephant that inhabit mangrove and delta areas along the coast.

### BIRDS

African Birdclub (www .africanbirdclub.org) is ideal for those who love their birds, with plenty of interesting reading and West African bird-watching links.

West Africa is a world-class birding destination, with more than 1000 species recorded. Many are endemic, others are passing migrants, flying down the Atlantic coast to and from their wintering grounds, while some are African nomads moving within the continent in pursuit of seasons of plenty. Among those you're likely to see are flamingos, storks and pelicans (around waterways), beautiful gannets and fish-eating cormorants (in coastal areas), turacos – including the striking violet turaco – and African grey and red-billed hornbills.

One of West Africa's best bird-watching destinations is tiny Gambia, with more than 560 species recorded and several easily accessed bird-watching sites. Abuko Nature Reserve (p315) is closest to Banjul and hosts a surprising diversity of birds, especially forest species. Tanji Bird Reserve (p313), on the Atlantic coast, protects a patchwork of habitat on the flyway for migrating birds. Although it covers only 600 hectares, close to 300 species have been recorded here. Kiang West National Park (p319), one of the country's largest protected areas, is also good.

Senegal also offers excellent birding, particularly in Parc National de la Langue de Barbarie (p717) and Parc National des Oiseaux du Djoudj (p717). Both are famous for vast pelican and flamingo flocks, and Djoudj is a Unesco World Heritage site, where almost 400 bird species have been recorded. In Parc National du Niokolo-Koba (p721), also a World Heritage Site, about 350 bird species have been recorded. There are several other good sites in northern Casamance near Kafountine (p735).

Mali is an underrated birding destination with more than 655 recorded species. In the Niger Inland Delta (see the boxed text, p510), Egyptian plovers, hammerkops (which make an enormous nest), jaçanas (lily trotters), pied kingfishers, cattle egrets and majestic crowned cranes can be seen year-round, but February is the best time to visit, when over-wintering species such as greenshanks, black-winged stilts, marbled teal and ferruginous duck are resident. The sandstone cliffs of the Falaise de Bandiagara (see p513) are good for large raptors, while in the wooden savanna at the base are Abyssinian and blue-bellied rollers among others.

In Ghana's Mole National Park (p389) more than 300 species have been recorded, while Nigeria's Yankari National Park (p655) has a stunning array of about 600 species and the Hadejia-Nguru Wetlands (p628), 200km northeast of Kano, is an important resting place for migratory birds and endemic species.

Public access to Mauritania's remote Parc National du Banc d'Arguin (p561) may be restricted during the breeding season, but it's a busy crossroads for birds migrating between Europe and Southern Africa.

Sierra Leone's Tiwai Island Wildlife Sanctuary (p763) is again safe to visit and hosts more than 120 bird species, including hornbills, kingfishers and the rare white-breasted guinea fowl. Around Mt Bintumani (p767), the endangered rufous fishing-owl has been sighted, while Outamba-Kilimi National Park (p766) supports kingfishers, hornbills, herons, hawks and the spectacular great blue turaco.

In Cameroon, the lushly vegetated Korup National Park (p195) has more than 300 species.

> *Birds of West Africa*, by W Serle, is a must for birders who want to know what species are present and where you're most likely to see them.

> It is estimated that 5000 million birds from Europe and Asia migrate to tropical Africa every year, a journey of up to 11,000km – less than half make it home, either dying en route or preferring to remain in Africa.

## REPTILES & AMPHIBIANS

West Africa's most notable reptile is the Nile crocodile, which was once abundant all over the region. Hunting and habitat destruction has taken its toll, however, and few remain. Your best chance to see them is along

---

### SOME CURIOUS RELICS AND WHERE TO SEE THEM

The Sahara desert and the Sahel were once lands of lakes, rivers, rolling savanna and abundant water and wildlife. Giraffes, elephants, leopards, wildebeest and lions once roamed far into North Africa. When the Sahara began to dry out and turn to desert 6000 years ago, the larger mammals died out or retreated south. Elsewhere, wildlife in more fertile areas has been driven to the brink of extinction by hunting, human encroachment, habitat destruction, poaching and the trade in bush meat. Just a few pockets remain, including the following:

**Chimpanzees & gorillas** (p215) Remote and difficult to reach, the rainforests around Lobéké in southeastern Cameroon have nonetheless been discovered by commercial loggers; gorillas and chimpanzees are considered at particular risk.

**Giraffes of Kouré** (p594) Decimated by road accidents and by a government who, in 1996, shot a dozen of them as gifts for friendly foreign leaders, the last giraffes in the West African wild number less than 100.

**Hippos, manatees and red-fronted gazelles** (p533) The Réserve d'Ansongo-Ménaka is next to the Niger River in an isolated corner of Mali near Gao. Much of the wildlife has gone, but you can still see red-fronted gazelles, manatees and hippos.

**Mali's desert elephants** (p534) Mali's desert elephants are long-legged and short-tusked, and migrate according to the season through the Gourma region between the Niger River and the border with Burkina Faso.

**Monk seals** (p560) Possibly the world's last colony of monk seals survives along Mauritania's remote Atlantic Coast.

**Olive trees, olive baboons and spurred tortoises** (p608) The remote Aïr Mountains of northern Niger have a remarkable array of species, including thousand-year-old Mediterranean wild olive trees, a stranded population of about 70 olive baboons and the Sahara's only amphibian, the African spurred tortoise.

**Rescued primates** (p189) At the Limbe Wildlife Centre in Cameroon, you'll find a hugely impressive project to rescue and rehabilitate chimpanzees, gorillas, drills and other primates. Other similar projects are run at Bélabo (p214) and Calabar Nigeria (p649).

## WILD WILDLIFE

If you set out in search of wildlife, remember that West Africa's wildlife is just that – wild. *Always* keep a healthy distance between you and any elephant, lion, rhino or other wild animal that you may be lucky enough to encounter. *Never* get between a mother and her calves or cubs, and invest in a telephoto lens instead of approaching an animal at close range. On safaris, heed the advice of your guide, and respect park regulations, especially those that require you to stay in a vehicle. Exercise care when boating or swimming, and be particularly aware of the dangers posed by crocodiles and hippos.

the larger rivers such as the Gambia, Senegal and Niger. Two lesser-known species, the dwarf crocodile and slender-nosed crocodile, also occur.

Turtles survive along the coast of West Africa and on some of the offshore islands. The females come to the beaches to lay eggs in the sand, sometimes several hundred at a time. The threats faced by turtles are considerable, and include damage by humans to nesting areas, hunting, and the effects of water pollution – turtles often mistake floating plastic bags for food.

West Africa has a full complement of both venomous and harmless snakes, but most fear humans and you'd be 'lucky' to even see one. The largest snake is the nonvenomous python, which grows to more than 5m in length. It kills by coiling around and suffocating its prey – not the nicest way to go, but fortunately it doesn't usually fancy humans. The venomous puff adder, which reaches about 1m in length and enjoys sunning itself, isn't aggressive but, being very slow, it's sometimes stepped on by unwary people before it has had time to wake up and move out of the way. When stepped on, it bites. Take special care when hiking in bush areas, especially in the early morning when this snake is at its most lethargic.

Lizards are ubiquitous in West Africa, from the desert to the rainforest and from the bathroom ceiling to the kitchen sink. The largest of these is the monitor (up to 2m in length), which spends a lot of time lying around rivers and water holes, perhaps dreaming of being a crocodile. You're more likely to see agama – lizards about 20cm long with purple bodies and orange heads, energetically doing press-ups on walls and boulders. And in any house or small hotel you'll inevitably see geckos running around on the walls or hiding behind pictures, with their sucker-like feet and near-transparent skin. They can appear alarming, but they're your friends – they love to eat mosquitoes. Other insect-eaters include frogs, which inhabit riverside reeds and mangroves, and toads, which are happier out of water than their froggy relatives.

*In several countries, including Mali, Burkina Faso and Côte d'Ivoire, crocodiles are regarded as sacred, and although travellers must take care, locals believe that the crocodiles recognise villagers and would never attack them.*

*Seeds of Famine, by Richard Franke and Barbara Chasin, is as dry as the Sahel dust, but essential reading for anyone keen to learn more about the connection between colonial policies and the droughts that still face the region.*

## Plants

### FOREST & WOODLAND

Much of West Africa's coastal area is between 5 and 10 degrees north of the equator, where rainfall is heavy. Dense rain-fed lowland forest (or just 'rainforest') contains trees which can reach heights of 45m. The upper branches form a continuous canopy, blocking light from the forest floor, which hinders the growth of smaller plants, although vines flourish.

Forests or dense woodland can only be found in parts of Liberia, Sierra Leone, southwestern Côte d'Ivoire and southern and eastern Cameroon. Smaller areas of woodland exist in Benin, Ghana, Guinea, Nigeria and Togo.

An especially rich bounty of rainforests, set amid volcanic mountains, straddles the border between Nigeria and Cameroon. In 2005

British scientists from the Royal Botanic Gardens in Kew surveyed over 2400 plant species in this Kupe-Bakossi region, with 10% of them completely new to science (for more information see p177). In the east, Cameroon's rainforests connect West Africa to the vast Congo Basin in Central Africa.

### SAVANNA & SEMIDESERT
In the northern parts of the coastal countries the climate is drier, and forest and woodland yield to savanna and semidesert. Here, the landscape consists primarily of well-dispersed trees, especially acacia, and low scrub bush, although ribbons of dense gallery forest occur along river courses. Gallery forest is similar to rainforest but is fed by ground water rather than rain, so many of the vines characteristic of rainforest are absent.

### DESERT
North of the Sahel is the true desert (which engulfs northern Mali and Niger, plus most of Mauritania), where rainfall and vegetation growth are minimal. Apart from desert grasses and small flowers, which can carpet the desert in colour after rains (even after having lain dormant for years), the most striking plant is the Calotropis procera, otherwise known as the Apple of Sodom. Its prolific (but poisonous) green leaves should be no invitation to taste. Wild colocynth melons (think watermelons in the sand) produce brittle, gourd-like fruits that burst open in the sun and scatter their seeds on the wind, but should not be eaten.

*Sahara: A Natural History,* by Marq de Villiers and Sheila Hirtle, covers the natural and human history of the Sahara like no other recent book, and the lively text makes it a pleasure to read.

## NATIONAL PARKS
Most of West Africa's national parks are either remote (such as the parks of southeastern Cameroon), not particularly well set up for tourists, or inaccessible by public transport. This often means that a serious and

---

### THE BAOBAB TREE – KING OF THE AFRICAN BUSH

There is nothing quite like the baobab *(Adansonia digitata)*, whose thick, sturdy trunk and stunted root-like branches are an instantly recognisable symbol of Africa. So otherworldly and utterly distinctive is the baobab, that many traditional cultures believe that the tree displeased a deity who promptly plucked it in anger and thrust it back into the ground upside down – hence the root-like branches. Or as that great writer on Africa, Ryszard Kapuściński, wrote: 'Like elephants among other animals, so are baobabs among trees: they have no equals.'

Despite the apparent misdemeanours of its ancestor, today's baobab is revered by local people. Its wizened appearance, combined with an ability to survive great droughts and live for many hundreds of years, ensures that the baobab is believed to possess magical powers. Old trees often develop cavities, which are sometimes used to inter a revered griot.

Another reason why the baobab occupies such an important position in local life is that they grow in savanna zones, where rainfall is limited. The baobab can be found in most parts of West Africa, not to mention many other areas of the continent, and serves a variety of practical, often essential, purposes. The hollow trunk sometimes holds rainwater, making it a useful reservoir in times of drought. The tree's large pods (which resemble pendulous Christmas decorations and are sometimes called 'monkey bread') contain seeds encased in a sherbet-like substance that can be eaten or made into a juice-like drink. The pods themselves are used to make cups or bowls (often for drinking palm wine) and as fuel; they burn slowly and are especially good for smoking fish. The leaves of the baobab can be eaten when chopped, boiled and made into a sauce; they can also be dried and ground into a paste to use as a poultice for skin infections and joint complaints. Even the flowers are used as decoration at ceremonies.

---

**WEST AFRICA'S TOP FIVE NATIONAL PARKS**

■ Parc National de Waza (p213) In Cameroon, this is one of the best and most accessible parks of the region, and home to elephants, hippos, giraffes and lions.

■ Parc Regional du W (p596) Straddles the three countries of Niger, Benin and Burkina Faso, and takes its name from the shape of the Niger River. This fine park has leopards, lions, cheetahs, elephants, baboons, Nile crocodiles and hyenas, plus over 300 bird and 500 plant species.

■ Parc National de la Pendjari (p118) Elephants, leopards, buffaloes, hippos and lions are the main attractions at this well-organised park in Benin. The national park is only open from mid-December to mid-May.

■ Mole National Park (p389) Ghana's best park boasts elephants, olive baboons, and 90 other mammal and 300 bird species.

■ Yankari National Park (p655) Home to 600 elephants (one of the largest populations in West Africa), this excellent Nigerian park also has bushbucks, waterbucks, lions, hippos, monkeys and crocs.

---

expensive expedition is required to indulge your passion for wildlife. Once there, walking safaris, as found in East and Southern Africa, are virtually unheard of. On the plus side, once you've made the effort to get there, you may have a national park to yourself.

*Sahel: The End of the Road,* by Sebastião Salgado, is a grim photographic journey across the Sahel during the 1984–85 drought by one of the world's best photographers, who's adept at capturing people in the landscape they call home.

The peak viewing months are invariably from March to early May when water is scarce and animals congregate at watering holes. For information about specific national parks see the individual country chapters, but following are five which stand out and are not too far off the beaten track.

## ENVIRONMENTAL ISSUES

There's no way to put this politely – West Africa is one of the world's environmental basket cases, with rampant deforestation and uncontrolled logging, desertification, soil erosion, air and water degradation, urban encroachment, and habitat and wildlife destruction.

Deforestation is the most visible problem, with just a tiny fraction of West Africa's original forest cover remaining. The extent of the problem is evident from the causes – increased population growth, commercial logging, clearing of trees for farming and slash-and-burn farming techniques – the effects of most of which are either irreversible or require massive investment from impoverished governments. Even assuming the best political will in the world, meagre government resources and aid funds are, understandably, directed to more pressing human needs, with long-term environmental protection seen as a luxury few can afford, even as such policies of short-term necessity merely serve to make the region more vulnerable to famine in the future. Potential earnings in global timber markets, for example, are infinitely more attractive (and lucrative) than preserving wildlife for the trickle of tourists who come to see it. Deforestation is particularly acute in Côte d'Ivoire; see p264 for more.

Sahara Conservation Fund (www.saharaconserva tion.org) is one of few sources of information on the wildlife of the Sahara, and the efforts being undertaken to protect it.

The results of deforestation can be devastating – many bird and animal species lose vital habitats, local human populations lose their lifeblood, soil erosion sets in, fewer areas are cultivable, water catchments are reduced, and the availability of traditional building materials, foodstuffs and medicines is decreased. In Cameroon, especially, the incursion of humans ever deeper into the forest is fuelling the trade in bush meat, which is exacting a terrible price on the country's wildlife.

Fortunately, it's not all bad news. In Cameroon and Liberia (home to about 40% of the last remaining 'Upper Guinean' rainforest that once stretched from Sierra Leone eastward to Ghana), several international environmental organisations have pledged resources to help improve forestry and environmental management.

## Global Links

West Africans are often blamed for the destruction of their own environment, but the reality is far more complex. Many of the problems began in colonial times, when farmers were encouraged to plant thirsty cash crops (such as the peanut) that require intensive farming – traditional methods involved fallow periods, which allowed the soil to regenerate. Thus deprived of essential nutrients, the soil required fertilisers to recover, but these were often too expensive for poor farmers to afford. The soil began to unravel.

This process was exacerbated by well-intentioned animal husbandry and well-building schemes funded by the European Union (EU) in the 1960s and '70s, which helped to increase herd sizes without any accompanying growth in pasturelands. In the absence of fodder, the additional cattle and goats ate the grasses and thorns that bound the soil together.

*Squandering Eden,* by Mort Rosenblum and Doug Williamson, is a highly readable, scathing indictment of Western aid policies in Africa, and their impact on the environment (sadly, little has changed since it was written in 1987).

---

### COMMUNITY-BASED CONSERVATION – SOME SUCCESSES

Sustainable environmental protection usually works only by involving local communities and providing them with the material benefits (tourism, sustainability of resources for future generations) which derive from preserving pristine environments. For those who live hand-to-mouth, as many do in West Africa, long-term planning is often impossible and the pretty forests that Westerners are desperate to protect are actually a necessary and time-honoured resource for locals.

Several forestry projects in Gambia, for example, recognise this delicate balance, fusing environmental protection with traditional sources of livelihood. Natural woodland areas are not simply fenced off, but rather used in a sustainable way for the benefit of local communities, with the emphasis on sustainable resource management. In Gambia's Kiang West National Park, limited cattle grazing and (more controversially) rice cultivation is permitted in the park. Dead wood can be used for timber, fruits and edible leaves can be collected, and grasses can be harvested for thatch. These products can be used or sold, but all activities take place without destroying the growing trees. In this way, local people view the forest as a source of produce, income or employment, and have a real incentive to protect it in the long term. Local inhabitants also take a leading role in environmental planning – at Niumi National Park, also in Gambia, community groups have been established to give local people a formal voice in the park's management structure.

The Gambian government has also identified key areas of ecological importance as potential sites for ecotourism projects. In Côte d'Ivoire, a similar approach protects one of West Africa's largest stands of rainforest in Parc National de Taï. Thanks to the efforts of a village tourism project, forest clearing and poaching have decreased significantly, although the conflict in Côte d'Ivoire is threatening to undo all the good work.

In Burkina Faso, small-scale NGO projects encourage farmers to return to traditional methods of cultivation, in particular the laying of *diguettes* or stone lines along field contours, which slow water run-off, maximise water penetration and reduce erosion.

Across the border in Niger, the community-based Guesselbodi National Forest Project was launched not far from Niamey in 1980, in an attempt to enable reafforestation by encouraging villagers to build windbreaks and establish nurseries. The project may have been a success at a micro level in reducing soil depletion, but the dire state of Niger's soil means that it probably comes too late for widespread application throughout the country.

For information on ecotourism projects in Ghana and Côte d'Ivoire, see the boxed texts, p338 and p278 respectively.

Patches of desert began to appear around villages which once lay many kilometres south of the desert's southern boundary. As populations increased and enticements by Western seed companies prompted ever-more farmers to increase the land under cultivation, the few remaining trees and forests were cut down, thereby accelerating a process which began centuries ago. The situation is especially grim in Niger, where less than 3% of the land can now support agriculture.

*Africa in Crisis,* by Lloyd Timberlake, is a damning chronicle of Africa's environmental history, with clear-headed solutions offered; written in 1986, its examples of Côte d'Ivoire are somewhat outdated.

Even the fraught issue of poverty alleviation can carry a considerable cost. Many international bodies favour alleviating poverty through large-scale economic development initiated by loans. However, such development often brings with it severe environmental damage; heavy industry creates air and water pollution, and inevitably requires the use of natural resources.

It is often also said that Westerners are so intent on saving Africa's wilderness because we have none left of our own. Indeed, the figures are stark: a citizen of urban Britain, Australia or the USA, for example, consumes more than 50 times more of the earth's resources than a rural inhabitant of Niger or Guinea-Bissau. All of which may just mean that the most effective way to preserve West Africa's environment is to ensure that efforts are made to reduce Western consumption and encourage *everyone* (and not just poor West African farmers) to use resources sustainably.

# Benin

If you're heading to West Africa to unearth lost treasure, look no further than Benin. This club-shaped country, on the western edge of Nigeria, was once one of the most powerful empires in Africa – the Dahomey kingdom. The ruins of the Dahomeyans' palaces and temples can be seen in Abomey, while Ouidah is a poignant reminder of where their riches came from: the slave trade. The Route d'Esclaves in Ouidah was the last walk on African soil for slaves bound for Brazil and the Caribbean. Museums here and in Porto Novo, Benin's lagoon-side capital, examine the resultant Afro-Brazilian society and culture.

But regardless of the ill-gotten Dahomeyan gains glittering in the Musée Historique d'Abomey, there are plenty of treasures on Benin's dusty streets and palm-fringed beaches. This is the birthplace of voodoo, the country's national religion, exported by the slaves and distorted by Hollywood. Voodoo is an important part of everyday life and most towns bear signs of it, such as the fetish markets stocked with the heads and skins of every animal imaginable.

Elephants, lions and crocodiles can be seen in more animated form in the northern wildlife parks, Pendjari and W, two of the best in West Africa. Then there are the stilt villages, home to thousands in the southern lagoons, and the northern *tata somba*, mud fortresses built by the insular Somba people. Not only is Benin a richly historical and cultural country, this politically stable nation is one of the most tourist-friendly parts of West Africa.

## FAST FACTS

- **Area** 112,622 sq km
- **Capital** Porto Novo
- **Country code** ☎ 229
- **Famous for** Voodoo; slavery; the Kings of Dahomey; adopting Marxism; Angélique Kidjo
- **Languages** French, Fon, Yoruba, Dendi, Bariba and Ge
- **Money** West African CFA franc; US$1 = CFA544.89; €1 = CFA655.96
- **Population** 7.4 million
- **Visa** CFA10,000 at border, 30-day extension CFA12,000

## HIGHLIGHTS

- **Ghézo's throne** (p110) Shiver in front of this throne mounted on human skulls, one of the dark relics from the slave-trading Dahomey kingdom in Abomey.
- **Route des Esclaves** (p106) Retrace the last steps of millions of slaves to the Point of No Return memorial in Ouidah.
- **Fetish market** (p93) Shop for essential voodoo items such as monkey testicles and bat wings.
- **Stilt villages** (p102) Where tens of thousands of people go about their daily business 2m above the surface of Lake Nokoué.
- **Malanville market** (p120) Watch the nomadic Fula traders drift into town, produce piled on their heads, in the arid far north of the country.

## ITINERARIES

- **One Week** A classic example of urban Africa **Cotonou** (p95) is worth a brief look, but the other southern cities have more charm. **Porto Novo** (p103), the tranquil capital, and **Ganvié** (p102) the lacustrine stilt village, are both within two hours taxi journey of Cotonou. A little further along the country's two main roads are a couple of must-sees that ooze a sense of culture and history: **Abomey** (p110), home to the ruined palaces of the Kings of Dahomey, and **Ouidah** (p106) once a capital of the slave trade and now the centre of voodoo worship.
- **Two Weeks** Relax after all that sightseeing with a few days of lounging on the empty beaches at **Grand Popo** (p108). This elegantly decaying beach resort is a handy base for excursions to the peaceful fishing villages around **Lake Ahémè** (p109). Inland, the stand-out towns are **Natitingou** (p116), gateway to the intriguing fortified compounds in Somba country, and **Malanville** (p120), where the weekly market draws Fula nomads from the neighbouring countries.
- **One Month** With this much time on your hands, you should be able to delve into every corner of this small country. In addition to the above, linger in Somba country and stay with a family in their compound, then explore the two wildlife parks, **Pendjari** (p118) and **W** (p120). **Parakou** (p113) and **Djougou** (p115) are pleasantly sleepy towns to while away a few days.

### HOW MUCH?

- **Traveller's fetish** CFA3000
- **Mashed yam** CFA200
- **Appliqué hat** CFA1500
- **Zemi-john** CFA100
- **National park entry** CFA10000

### LONELY PLANET INDEX

- **1L of petrol** CFA300-600
- **1L of bottled water** CFA500
- **Bottle of La Béninoise** CFA250
- **Souvenir T-shirt** CFA2000
- **Yam chips** CFA100

## CLIMATE & WHEN TO GO

In southern Benin, there are two rainy seasons: April to mid-July, and mid-September to late October. The rains in the north fall from June to early October. In the north temperatures can reach 46°C, while the coastal south is cooler, with temperatures ranging from 18°C to 35°C. Harmattan winds billow out of the Sahara between December and March, and the hottest time of the year is from February to April. The coolest, driest time to visit is between November and February.

Parts of the northern Atakora region occasionally receive heavy rainfall, and smaller roads throughout Benin may be impassable during the rainy seasons; notably those in the wildlife parks, particularly Parc Regional du W.

## HISTORY

More than 350 years ago, the area now known as Benin was split into numerous principalities. One of the chiefs quarrelled with his brother for the right to succession and, around 1625, settled in Abomey. He then conquered the neighbouring kingdom of the Dan, which became known as Dan-Homey, meaning 'in Dan's belly' (see p112). The name was later shortened by the French colonisers.

Each king pledged to leave his successor more land than he inherited, a pledge kept by waging war with his neighbours, particularly the Yoruba of Nigeria. Meanwhile, the Portuguese, and later other Europeans,

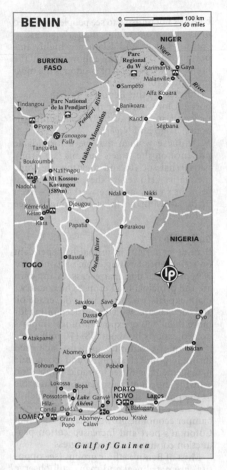

**BENIN**

established trading posts along the coast, most notably at Porto Novo and Ouidah. The Portuguese, French, Dutch and English, whose forts can still be seen in Ouidah, spelled the town's name four different ways but pronounced it the same.

The Dahomeyan Kings grew rich by selling slaves to traders, who then gave them the guns that let them pillage their neighbours for slaves and land. For more than a century, an average of 10,000 slaves per year were shipped to the Americas (primarily Brazil and the Caribbean, in particular Haiti), taking voodoo with them. As a result southern Dahomey was dubbed the Slave Coast.

Early in the 19th century, the French colonised the kingdom of Dahomey, making it part of French West Africa (see p103). During the 70-year colonial period, progress was made in education, and many Dahomeyans were employed as government advisers in French West Africa. The country's intellectual nature led the French to nickname it 'the West African Latin Quarter'.

## Independence & Le Folklore

When Dahomey became independent in 1960, Hubert Maga was elected the country's first president. Almost immediately, other former French colonies started deporting their Dahomeyan populations. Back home without work, they were the root of a highly unstable political situation. Three years after independence, having seen how easily some disgruntled soldiers in neighbouring Togo had staged a coup, the military did the same in Dahomey.

During the next decade, Dahomey saw four more military coups, nine more changes of government and five changes of constitution: what the Dahomeyans called in jest *le folklore*.

## Revolution

In 1972 a group of officers led by Lieutenant Colonel Mathieu Kérékou seized power in a coup that initiated almost two decades of military dictatorship. The country then took a sharp turn to the left as he embraced Marxist-Leninist ideology and aligned the country with superpowers like China, the Soviet Union and North Korea. To emphasise the break from the past, Kérékou changed the country's flag and renamed it Benin. He informed his people by radio on 13 November 1975, a date still etched into the memories of most Beninese.

The government established the schools it required to teach Marxism, along with collective farms, state enterprises, a central trade union, and a more militant spirit in the army. However, the revolution was always more rhetorical than real. The economy fell into a shambles: inflation and unemployment rose, salaries remained unpaid for months. People soon tired of living in West Africa's answer to Eastern Europe, and there were ethnic tensions between the president, a Natitingou-born northerner, and the Yoruba population in the south. There were six attempted coups in one year alone. Then in the late 1980s, workers and students went on strike.

In December 1989, as a condition of French financial support, Kérékou ditched Marxism and held a conference to draft a new constitution. Dissidents used the occasion to blame the government for bankrupting the country, and for corruption and human rights abuses. The 488 delegates then engineered a coup, relegating Kérékou to head of the army, and formed a new cabinet under former dissident Nicéphore Soglo.

## The 1990s: Multiparty Elections

The first free multiparty elections were held in March 1991 and Soglo swept to power. However, his austere economic measures – following the 1994 devaluation of the CFA – came under fire, as did his autocracy and nepotism. Top jobs went to Soglo family members such as his son Liadi. Kérékou was voted back into power in March 1996, although he stuck to the desperately needed economic measures implemented by his rival.

Five years later, in the March 2001 presidential elections, Kérékou and Soglo faced each other again. Soglo and fellow opposition candidate Adrien Houngbédji withdrew from the race, alleging electoral fraud, leading to a landslide victory for the incumbent president.

## Benin Today

Kérékou's second and final five-year term in office finished with the presidential elections in March 2006, bringing an end to his 33 years at the top. The USA and France had replaced China et al on his speed dial, and Benin has become one of the most stable, and responsible, democracies among the Ecowas members; a trend that is set to continue under the new president, Yayi Boni. The former head of the West African Development Bank beat Adrien Houngbédji in a run-off. In his campaign, based around the slogan of 'change', he pledged to fight corruption and revive an economy suffering from depressed cotton prices. 'If you want to change the future, change yourselves,' he said when he was sworn in.

## THE CULTURE
### The National Psyche

Nicknamed 'the West African Latin Quarter' by the French for its intellectualism, Benin has a strong culture of discussion and de-

bate. It's not unusual to see people engrossed in a book or one of the country's papers.

Catholicism and Islam are highly important to their many followers, but the home-grown religion of voodoo is the most influential force.

Politically, the Beninese feel they have borne a lot to achieve their stable democracy and are wary of their troubled neighbours, Togo and Nigeria.

Beninese women may be a formidable presence on the streets but this is a firmly patriarchal society and they tolerate some inequality. However, they do have vital roles in society and the workforce – even in the Muslim north of the country (see below).

### Daily Life

Benin's economy is primarily dependant on subsistence farming, which accounts for 38% of GDP. Yams, maize, cassava and corn are the principal food crops. The country's main exports are cotton, palm oil, crude oil and cocoa beans, with cotton accounting for more than 75% of export earnings. Imports exceed exports by about US$170 million.

Benin's economic growth, achieved through political stability and economic management, is offset by rapid population growth. The country also remains vulnerable to the political turmoil in Nigeria, which it depends on for fuel. While high fuel costs hamper economic growth, the expansion of Cotonou's port and increased cotton production continue to drive progress.

Most of Benin's ethnic groups (see opposite) are patrilineal and many still observe polygamy, although the practice is becoming increasingly rare among urban and educated Beninese. Marriages are still arranged by families and divorce is rare.

Most families support themselves through agriculture. Women control the local food distribution system, including the transport of produce to market and the subsequent barter and sale.

Average life expectancy is around 53, with an AIDS rate of about 2% and some 70,000 people living with the virus. Women have 5.9 children each on average and almost 50% of the population is aged 14 or under.

There is evidence of wealth, particularly in the south, but much of it comes from external sources such as tourism or young

Beninese men working in Europe. Young men in Benin can typically expect a roof over their heads, enough food to live on and, in many cases, a scooter to sit on.

## Population

There is an array of different ethnic groups within Benin's narrow borders, although five of them account for 50% of the population: Fon, Yoruba, Bariba, Betamaribé and Fula.

The Fon, who comprise 40% of the Beninese population, migrated from southwestern Nigeria in the 13th century and established a kingdom in Allada in southern Benin.

The Yoruba (called Nagot locally), who also migrated from Nigeria, occupy the southern and mideastern zones of Benin and comprise 12% of the population.

The Bariba, who make up 9% of the population, live mostly in the Borgou region. According to legend, they migrated from the Bussa and Ife areas of Nigeria. Their most famous kingdom in Benin was centred at Nikki, and because of distance and earlier slave raids they have remained aloof towards southern Benin.

The Betamaribé (often called the Somba) comprise 8% of the population and live in the northwest, around the Atakora mountains. Having lived for hundreds of years in relative seclusion from modern influences, they have managed to keep much of their traditional culture intact.

The nomadic Fula (also called Fulani or Peul) live primarily in the north and comprise 6% of the population.

Despite the underlying tensions between the southern and northern regions, the various groups live in relative harmony and have intermarried.

## RELIGION

Some 30% of the population is Christian, 20% is Muslim, and 50% retains traditional beliefs, such as animism and voodoo.

Most people practice voodoo, whatever their religion. The practice mixed with Catholicism in the Americas, where the Dahomeyan slaves took it and their Afro-Brazilian descendants brought it back. Christian missionaries also won over Dahomeyans by fusing their creed with voodoo.

The northern peoples practice voodoo under the name of fetishism, as evidenced by the fetish shrines outside the *tata somba* houses around Natitingou.

---

### GRIGRI CHARMS & JUJU MEN

Voodoo, or *vodou*, got its current name in Haiti and Cuba, where the religion arrived with Fon and Ewe slaves from the Dahomey Kingdom and mixed with Catholicism. It was originally called *vodun* in Benin and Togo – a word that means 'the hidden' or 'the mystery'. Unfortunately, it has suited Hollywood to put a sinister spin on this.

In fact, voodoo is, for millions of Beninese and Togolese, a skullduggery-free part of everyday life. It does have a dark side – it's hard to miss the voodoo dolls riddled with nails – but this is only one aspect of it.

The practice conforms to the general pattern of West African religions, with a supreme god, Mawu, and a host of lesser spirits that are ethnically specific to their followers and to the part of the spiritual world inhabited by a person's ancestors. Traditional priests, or *juju* men, are consulted for their power to communicate with particular spirits and seek intercession with them. This communication is achieved through spirit possession and ritual that often involves a gift or 'sacrifice' of palm wine, gin or food such as eggs, chickens or goats. The grace of the spirits is essential for protection and prosperity, and some spirits can be harnessed for malicious and selfish ends.

A fetish is an object or potion imbued with the spirits' power. Fetish markets are like voodoo pharmacies. The buyer has a prescription of the items the priest needs to make the required concoction – such as a parrot's tail, a cobra's head and, often, perfume.

Benin's own government has been as damaging to voodoo as Hollywood. Kérékou's Marxist government outlawed it as being inimical to a rational and socialist work ethic. Since a democratic government was installed here in 1989, traditional religious practice has been permitted. Vodoo was formally recognised as a religion by the government in February 1996.

## ARTS

### Art & Craftwork

Benin has a rich cultural heritage, and its traditional art has brought international attention to the legendary kingdom of Dahomey.

Traditionally, art served a spiritual purpose, but under the Fon kings, artisans and sculptors were called upon to create works that evoked heroism and enhanced the image of the rulers. They became the historians of the era, creating richly coloured appliqué banners that depicted past and present glories. Banners are still being made, particularly in Abomey, depicting animals, hunting scenes and deities using cut-out cloth figures.

### Cinema & TV

The Quintessence film festival (www.festivalouidah.org) takes place in Ouidah at the same time as the voodoo festival. The annual festival, which also tours the country, aims to promote films made in sub-Saharan Africa.

Expect badly dubbed Brazilian soaps on the commercial TV channels such as LC2 and Golfe TV. Television Nationale is the state-run channel.

### Music

Angélique Kidjo, a major international star, is Benin's most famous recording artist (see below). Other well known Beninese artists include Gnonnes Pedro, Nel Olivier and Yelouassi Adolphe, and the bands Orchestre Poly-Rythmo and Disc Afrique.

### Architecture

Don't miss the bas-reliefs on the walls of the Musée Historique d'Abomey in Abomey. These are polychrome bas-reliefs in clay that were used to decorate the palace, temples and chiefs' houses. The palace has been restored and designated a Unesco World Heritage Site.

The Lake Nokoué stilt villages and the *tata somba* houses around Natitingou are remarkable examples of traditional architecture.

### Sculpture

The *cire perdue* (lost wax) method used to make the famous Benin bronzes comes from Benin City in present-day Nigeria. (President Kérékou adopted the once-great kingdom's name when he relaunched Dahomey as a socialist nation in 1975.) However, the method spread west and *cire perdue* figures can be bought in Benin, particularly Abomey and Cotonou.

Figures called *bochio* are carved from the trunk of a tree and placed at the entrance of a village to discourage malevolent spirits. Some voodoo wood figures are combined with a variety of materials, such as bottles, padlocks and bones, to imbue them with power. Moulded figures of unfired clay represent Legba (a Fon god) and receive daily libations for the protection of the home.

---

**ANGÉLIQUE KIDJO**

The posters for her many performances worldwide have proclaimed her 'the African funk diva' and 'West Africa's finest singer', but the truth is that Angélique Kidjo is a world musician in the true, boundary-busting sense of the phrase.

Born in Ouidah in 1960 to a choreographer and a musician with Portuguese and English ancestry, Kidjo remains influenced by the town's Afro-Brazilian heritage. Her recent trilogy of albums explores the links between Africa and Latin America, culminating in *Oyaya!,* her latest record, which sees Kidjo singing in four languages on tracks that dabble in Caribbean rhythms such as salsa, calypso and mambo.

Most famous for the 1994 hit 'Agolo' – from the album *Ayé,* which means 'life' in the Fon language – Kidjo has also held onto the voodoo beliefs she first developed in Ouidah. She believes music can't exist without spirituality and regards voodoo as bringing energy and spirituality to everyday life.

Now a special representative for Unesco and resident in New York, Kidjo has been criticised for losing touch with her 'African-ness'. She answered this criticism with 1995's *Fifa,* for which she and her bassist husband spent several months travelling around Benin recording traditional singers and musicians. Check out www.angeliquekidjo.com.

## ENVIRONMENT

Sandwiched between Nigeria and Togo, Benin is 700km long and 120km across in the south, widening to about 300km in the north. Most of the coastal plain is a sand bar that blocks the seaward flow of several rivers. As a result, there are lagoons a few kilometres inland all along the coast, which is being eroded by the strong ocean currents. Inland are a densely forested plateau and, in the far northwest, the Atakora mountains.

Significant vestiges of wildlife are found in Parc National de la Pendjari (p118) and in Parc Regional du W (p120), including herds of elephants and several species of cat and antelope.

Deforestation and desertification are the major environmental problems. In the north, droughts continue to severely affect marginal agriculture, while poaching is threatening the small remaining wildlife populations.

## FOOD & DRINK

Beninese grub is unquestionably among the best in West Africa. *Igname* (yam) is the staple food. Mashed yam, which must be eaten fresh, tastes as good in the humblest roadside stall as it does in a restaurant. Yam chips are a great snack.

The Beninese also eat a lot of couscous, rice, *pimane* (pepper) and *arachide* (groundnut) sauce with chicken and fish, such as Dourade. There is normally a vegetarian sauce on offer.

The local beer, La Béninoise, is a passable drop. The adventurous could try palm wine, the millet-based brew *tchapallo,* or *sodabe* (moonshine).

# COTONOU

**pop 761,900**

Spending a day in Cotonou, which officially plays second fiddle to Porto Novo but is Benin's capital in everything but name, is like being locked in car with a chain-smoking speed freak. The *zemi-johns* swarm down the boulevards like kamikaze pilots, filling the air with fumes that only briefly clear at night, when the streets seem eerily quiet.

Benin's most populous city does have its positives of course – the country's best hotels, nightlife and shops, and the sprawling Grand Marché du Dantokpa.

Cotonou means 'mouth of the river of death' in Fon – a reference to the Dahomeyan kingdom's role in the slave trade. In 1868 the city was ceded to the French, but this was challenged in 1892 by the Dahomeyan king Béhanzin, leading to the Franco-Dahomeyan campaigns and the formation of the French protectorate of Dahomey.

Place de l'Etoile Rouge is an imposing reminder of former President Mathieu Kérékou's dalliance with socialism.

## ORIENTATION

The heart of town is the intersection of Ave Clozel and Blvd Steinmetz. Going northeast along Ave Clozel, one of the two main thoroughfares, you pass over the Pont Ancien and the road eventually turns into the highway to Porto Novo and Lagos. The new bridge, Pont Martin Luther King (Nouveau Pont) is further to the north; the wide Blvd St Michel (which becomes Ave du Nouveau Pont), the other main road, passes over it and eventually connects with Ave Clozel. Rue des Cheminots in the centre is also known as the Jonquet strip.

### Maps

The 1:15000 *Cotonou* map (Institut Géographique National de Bénin), which lists the city's hotels, cinemas, banks and markets, is available at bookshops.

## INFORMATION
### Bookshops

**Librairie Nôtre-Dame** ( ☎ 21 31 40 94; Ave Clozel; 9am-12.30pm & 4-7pm Tue-Sat, 4-7pm Mon) Next to the cathedral, with an excellent selection of books on Benin (in French), including a practical guide to Parc National de la Pendjari (CFA5500) and maps of Cotonou (CFA4255) and Benin (CFA7560).

**Sonaec** ( ☎ 21 31 22 42; Ave Clozel; 8.30am-12.30pm & 3.30-7pm Mon-Fri) Smart bookshop with the latest periodicals and some photography books on West Africa. Takes Visa and has maps of Cotonou (CFA7500) and Togo (CFA7500).

### Cultural Centres

**Centre Culturel American** ( ☎ 21 30 03 12; fax 21 30 03 84) Adjoining the US embassy.

**Centre Culturel Chinois** ( ☎ 21 31 31 74; fax 21 31 48 33; Ave Jean Paul II; 9am-12pm & 3.30-6.30pm) Shows films (see p101) and runs Tai Chi and martial arts courses (see p98).

## COTONOU

**Centre Culturel Français** ( ☎ 21 30 08 56; fax 21 30 11 51; Route de l'Aéroport; www.ambafrance-bj.org/ccf; 9.30am-12pm & 3-7pm Tue-Sat, closed am Thu) This exciting centre has a gallery, outdoor theatre, library, cinema and bar.

## Internet Access

Blvd Steinmetz and the Jonquet strip have the most Internet cafés.

**Cyber Café Le Teranga** ( ☎ 21 30 29 29; Haie Vive; per hr CFA1000; 10am-midnight) In front of the English International School.

**Cyber des Arts** ( ☎ 21 30 60 05; Centre de Promotion de l'Artisinal; per hr CFA500; 7am-7pm Mon-Sat) Breezy place with a café.

**Cyberpôle** ( ☎ 21 32 72 07; Blvd Steinmetz; per hr CFA300; 8am-midnight) The connection is a little

temperamental. Cheap food is also available on the quiet balcony round the back.

**Star Navigation** ( ☎ 21 31 81 28; per ⅓ hr CFA500/1000; 24hr Tue-Fri, 8am-midnight Sat-Mon) The fastest Internet connection we found in Benin.

## Medical Services

**Pharmacie Camp Ghezo** ( ☎ 21 31 55 52; Rue 240) The best-stocked pharmacy, just around the corner from the US embassy.

**Pharmacie Jonquet** ( ☎ 21 31 20 80; Rue des Cheminots) A *pharmacie de garde* (all-night pharmacy) in the Jonquet district.

**Polyclinique les Cocotiers** ( ☎ 21 30 14 20; Rue 373) A private and efficient clinic at the Carrefour de Cadjehoun, across from the PTT Cadjehoun.

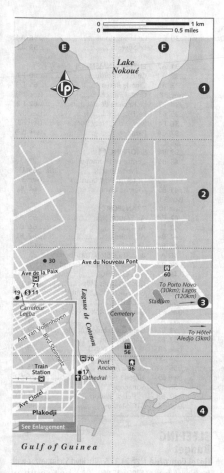

## Money

Financial Bank, Bank of Africa and Ecobank change cash and travellers cheques. Financial Bank gives advances on Visa cards (but applies exorbitant fees). Societe Generale de Banques au Benin has an ATM.

**Bank of Africa** ( ☎ 21 31 32 28; Ave Jean Paul II)

**Ecobank** Blvd Steinmetz ( ☎ 21 31 66 36; Blvd Steinmetz); Rue 657 ( ☎ 21 31 40 23; Rue 657) Behind Marché Ganhi.

**Financial Bank** ( ☎ 21 31 31 00; Rue 637) Just south of Ave Clozel.

**Societe Generale de Banques au Benin** ( ☎ 21 31 83 00; Ave Clozel)

There's a thriving black market for currencies including the Nigerian Niara around the Jonquet district and Gare du Dantokpa.

## Post

**Main post office** (off Ave Clozel; ⏲ 7am-7pm Mon-Fri, 8am-11.30pm Sat)

## Telephone

**Telecom (OPT) building** (Ave Clozel; ⏲ 7.30am-midnight Mon-Sat, 9am-1pm Sun) You can make overseas telephone calls and send faxes.

## Tourist Information

**Direction du Tourisme et de l'Hôtellerie** ( ☎ 21 32 68 24; tourisme@elodia.intnet.bj; Place de l'Étoile Rouge) Inconveniently located out of the centre, behind Pharmacie de l'Étoile Rouge and of limited use.

## Travel Agencies

**Agence Africaine de Tourisme** ( ☎ 21 31 54 14; fax 21 31 54 99; Ave Proche) One of the best agencies. Offers a wide range of information and tours, including pirogue trips to Ganvié.

## Visa Extenions

**Direction Emigration Immigration** ( ☎ 21 31 42 13; Ave Jan Paul II; ⏲ 8am-11am, 3-6.30pm Mon-Fri) Issues 30-day visas.

## DANGERS & ANNOYANCES

Cotonou is a dangerous city where muggings at knife-point are not uncommon, but tourists will be fine if they follow a few rules. Stay away from the beach, a lawless zone that even the locals avoid. Watch your wallet in the Grand Marché du Dantokpa. Avoid the Jonquet and Ganhie business districts and the port area from late afternoon onwards, and stick to thoroughfares throughout the city. Taxis are safer at night than walking or *zemijohns* – which are hair-raising at the best of times, and plain suicidal during rush hour.

## Scams

Plausible in both appearance and manner, they have all sorts of stories to lure tourists to a secluded area where they have a gang of accomplices waiting. They may say they are in a band and they want to give you a CD, or they want you to meet a Western colleague from the aid agency they work for. If someone offers to take you to the beach, that should definitely set alarm bells ringing.

## SIGHTS
### Grand Marché du Dantokpa

The seemingly endless **Grand Marché du Dantokpa** is Cotonou's exhilarating, exhausting

BENIN

**INFORMATION**
Agence Africaine de Tourisme.....**1** A1
American Embassy......................**2** C4
Bank of Africa...........................**3** A3
British Community Liason
  Officer....................................(see 7)
Centre Culturel American...........**4** B4
Centre Culturel Chinois.............**5** D4
Centre Culturel Français..........(see 14)
Commissariat Central................**6** D3
Cyber Café Le Teranga..............**7** A4
Cyber des Arts.........................(see 63)
Cyberpôle................................(see 19)
Direction du Tourisme et de
  l'Hôtellerie.............................**8** C2
Direction Emigration
  Immigration.............................**9** D4
Ecobank..................................**10** C3
Ecobank (Main Office)..............**11** E3
English International School......(see 7)
Financial Bank........................**12** B2
French Consulate.....................**13** B3
French Embassy.......................**14** C4
German Embassy.......................**15** C4
Ghanaian Embassy....................**16** A4
Librairie Nôtre-Dame................**17** E4
Main Post Office......................**18** B3
Marche St Michel.....................**19** E3
Nigerian Embassy.....................**20** B4
Nigerien Embassy.....................**21** B3
Pharmacie Camp Ghezo.............**22** C4
Pharmacie Jonquet...................**23** B2
Point Afrique...........................**24** A4
Polyclinique
  les Cocotiers.........................**25** B4
Societe Generale de Banques au
  Benin....................................**26** B2
Sonaec...................................**27** B2
Star Navigation.......................**28** B2
Telecom
  (OPT) Building.......................**29** B2

**SIGHTS & ACTIVITIES**
Grand Marché du Dantokpa.....**30** E3

**SLEEPING** 🛏
Alex's Hotel............................**31** A2
Benin Marina Hotel..................**32** A4
Hôtel Babo..............................**33** A1
Hôtel Benin Vickinfel...............(see 38)
Hôtel Concorde........................**34** B2
Hôtel de la Plage......................**35** B3
Hôtel du Lac............................**36** F4
Hôtel du Port...........................**37** C4
Hôtel le Crillon........................**38** C2
Novotel Orisha.........................**39** B4
Pension des Familles.................**40** B1

**EATING** 🍴
American 24.............................**41** B2
Cafeterias................................(see 33)
Cafeterias................................(see 40)
Chez Clarisse...........................**42** C4
Chez Mama Benin.....................**43** D3
Faim Gourmet..........................**44** B4
Hai King..................................**45** B4
Indiana...................................**46** A4
La Gerbe d'Or...........................**47** B2
La Ponte.................................**48** B2
La Verdure...............................**49** C2
Le Costa Rica...........................(see 63)
Le Petit Four............................**50** C2
Le Sorrento..............................(see 63)
L'Oriental................................**51** A3
Maquis Le Lagon......................**52** B2
Maquis le Mandingue...............**53** B2
Omelette Stall..........................(see 38)
Pili Pili...................................**54** D3
Restaurant l'Amitié...................**55** A1
Restaurant Mandarine..............(see 65)
Restaurant Romantica..............**56** F3
Sandwich Ladies......................**57** B3
Street Food..............................(see 52)

**DRINKING** 🍸
Le Livingstone.........................**58** A4
Le Soweto...............................**59** B2

**ENTERTAINMENT** 🎭
Ciné Concorde.........................**60** F3
Ciné le Benin...........................**61** D3
Cristal Palace...........................(see 31)
Le Repaire de Bacchus..............**62** B2
Le Téké...................................(see 32)
New York, New York..............(see 63)
Paradise..................................(see 57)

**SHOPPING** 🛍
Centre de Promotion de
  l'Artisanal.............................**63** D3
Hôtel du Port boutique...........(see 37)
Marche Ganhi...........................**64** B2

**TRANSPORT**
Air France...............................**65** A4
Air Gabon................................**66** B1
Air Ivoire................................**67** B1
Air Togo..................................**68** A4
Bush-Taxi Stop (for Abomey,
  Abomey-Calavi, Grand Popo
  & Ouidah)..............................**69** D3
Confort Lines Stop..................(see 19)
Gare de l'Ancien Pont (for the
  East).....................................**70** E4
Gare du Dantokpa (for Porto
  Novo)....................................**71** E3
Gare Guinkomé (for the North)..**72** B2
Gare Jonquet
  (for the West)........................**73** B2
Gare Missébo (for Abomey).....**74** B1
Ghana Airways.........................**75** B2
Nigeria Airways.......................**76** B1
Sonacop
  Petrol Station........................(see 19)
STC Station.............................(see 3)

heart, bordered by the lagoon and Blvd St Michel. Everything under the sun can be purchased in its labyrinthine lanes, particularly if 'everything' happens to be a dodgy Lucky Dube CD or a pair of plastic sandals. More traditional fare, such as batiks and Fon jewellery, can be found in the market building. There is also a **fetish market**, located near the pirogues arriving from the lagoon. Look out for the so-called 'Mama Benz', the haughty matriarchs of the market who are named after their favourite make of car.

## COURSES

For Fon-language classes, call **Vinawamon** ( ☎ 21 30 08 56), also contactable via the Centre Culturel Français (p95). There are **Tai Chi and martial arts courses** ( ☎ 21 31 31 74; Ave Jean Paul II; course CFA20000; 😊 7pm-8.30pm Tue & Sat, 5pm-6.30pm Wed & Sat) at the Centre Culturel Chinois.

## SLEEPING
### Budget

**Hôtel Concorde** ( ☎ 21 31 55 70; Blvd Steinmetz; r with fan/air-con from CFA7000/15,000; ❄ ) Just south of the now-defunct Ciné Vog, this is one of the friendlier and cleaner of the central budget hotels, but it is often booked out.

**Hôtel le Crillon** ( ☎ 21 31 51 58; Rue 105; s with fan/ air-con CFA6500/12,500; ❄ ) With sparse rooms and dark landings, these cheap central digs off Blvd Steinmetz have the feel of a 1950s boarding house – right down to the cockroaches unfortunately. Breakfast is CFA700.

**Pension des Familles** ( ☎ 21 31 42 01; Ave Proche; s/d CFA5500/6500) Both cleaner and cheaper than the nearby Pension de l'Amitié, this friendly pension has 14 spartan rooms with fan. The main drawback is it's right on the main road.

**Hôtel Babo** ( ☎ 21 31 46 07; Rue Agbeto Amadoré; s with fan/air-con CFA6000/10,000; ❄ ) This tenement-like place of peeling paint and laundry hanging on five floors of balconies is for hardcore budget travellers only. Request a room on the top level as they are more spacious and airy, not to mention having great views. Meals are CFA500 to CFA1500.

## Midrange

**Hôtel du Port** ( ☎ 21 31 44 44; fax 21 31 43 26; hotel-duportcotonou@yahoo.fr; Blvd de la Marina; s/d from CFA38,500/43,500, bungalow s/d CFA46,500/53,500; ⓟ ⓧ ⓡ 🖳 ) The carpeted rooms and, overlooking the popular pool, spacious bungalows, restaurant (meals CFA3800 to CFA6500) and bar make this Cotonou's best midrange hotel. It's in a bad area of town though.

**Hôtel du Lac** ( ☎ 21 33 19 19; r CFA35,000-40,000; ⓧ 🖳 ⓡ ) Excellent midrange choice in an unrivalled location at the east end of Pont Ancien. Rooms are sunny, spacious and exceptionally clean, with TVs and telephones. Ask for a sea view. The Lebanese restaurant (meals CFA2500 to CFA4800) has views across the lagoon to the port. Robberies have occurred on the bridge at night.

**Hôtel de la Plage** ( ☎ 21 31 34 67; Blvd de la Marina; s/d from CFA22,500/25,000, s/d apartment 35,000/40,500; ⓧ ⓡ ) The antiquated Hôtel de la Plage, opposite the Nigerien embassy, is a colonial throwback, with breezy rooms, swimming pool and laundry service. In addition to the restaurant (meals CFA800 to CFA4500), there is a bar and a fast-food joint overlooking the beach.

**Alex's Hotel** ( ☎ 21 31 25 08; Rue 108; r from CFA41,500; ⓧ ) Cotonou's Hotel California, with mildly erotic art decorating the corridors, a cosy restaurant (meals CFA3500 to CFA4000) with a colonial feel, and sweetly scented rooms. There are city views from the roof and an excellent karaoke bar and nightclub, Cristal Palace.

**Hôtel Benin Vickinfel** ( ☎ 21 31 38 14; vkfhotel@intnet.bj; off Blvd Steinmetz; r from CFA25,000; ⓧ ) Don't be fooled by the grim exterior. This 33-room hotel is one of the most comfortable and professional hotels in the city centre, though the rooms are a little pokey. Meals are available for CFA3000.

**Hôtel Aledjo** ( ☎ 21 33 05 61; fax 21 33 15 74; r CFA35,500-56,500, ste CFA100,500; ⓟ ⓧ ⓡ ) If you're looking for a beach hotel and won't be going into the city very often, try the ageing four-star Aledjo, 3km east of the centre.

There are 55 lavish rooms in 11 bungalows; tennis courts, a small pool and bowls. The restaurant serves good but expensive food (meals CFA4500 to CFA5000).

## Top End

**Novotel Orisha** ( ☎ 21 30 41 77; novotel.orisha@intnet.bj; Blvd de la Marina; s/d CFA70,500, tr CFA80,500, ste CFA110,000; ⓟ ⓧ 🖳 ⓡ ) While not as impressive as the grandiose driveway implies, this Accor hotel delivers comfortable rooms and good service. Serves Sunday brunch (CFA9500; open 11am to 4pm) by the pool and other meals are available (CFA3500 to CFA11,500).

**Benin Marina Hotel** ( ☎ 21 30 01 00; fax 21 30 11 55; Blvd de la Marina; r with city/ocean view CFA120,500/133,500, bungalow CFA154,500, ste CFA245,500-355,500; ⓟ ⓧ 🖳 ⓡ ) A regular pleasure garden of a place, the monstrous ex-Sheraton offers Cotonou's most luxurious accommodation, although some people prefer the Novotel Orisha. Daily happy hour in Bar Nokoué (6pm to 8pm) and poolside buffet on Friday night. Meals are available for CFA5500 to CFA10,000.

## EATING
### African

**Restaurant l'Amitié** (Rue 118; menu du jour CFA1000) About 100m southwest of Hôtel Babo, this Senegalese lunchtime joint is one of the best places in town for a spot of fish and rice.

**Maquis le Mandingue** ( ☎ 21 31 37 61; off Ave Proche; meals CFA3800-6000) Dishes such as fish of the season, in *gombo* (green vegetable), *yassa* (lemon, onion and mustard) and *arachide* sauces, are available in this popular but tranquil place with a garden and, on some nights, a harmonica player.

**Chez Maman Bénin** ( ☎ 21 32 33 38; Rue 201A; meals CFA500-3000) This long-standing restaurant, behind Ciné le Bénin, has a large selection of West African dishes scooped from steaming pots. Upstairs is a more expensive air-con section with a TV showing big sports matches.

**Pili Pili** ( ☎ 21 31 29 32; Rue du Révérend Père Kitti; meals CFA2500-3800; ⏱ 12.30-5pm & 7.30-11pm) This slightly upmarket restaurant with a great ambience, behind Hôtel de l'Union, gets going from 8pm.

**Restaurant Romantica** ( ☎ 97 06 15 66; Rue 1885; meals CFA4000-7000) A limited menu but a mellow atmosphere and a great location next to Hôtel du Lac, in view of the *zemi-johns* hurling themselves over Pont Ancien.

## Asian

**Hai King** ( ☎ 21 30 60 08; Route de Lomé; meals CFA3500-4000; ☺ 10am-2.30pm & 6-11.30pm) Not far from the airport, this popular place offers classic Chinese food, has snappy service, and a covered terrace overlooking the bustling Carrefour de Cadjéhoun.

**Indiana** ( ☎ 21 30 03 20; Haie Vive; meals CFA3500-5000) This Indian-run restaurant with garden seating, on the same street as Le Livingstone, does a delicious curry.

## European

**La Verdure** ( ☎ 21 31 31 75; off Ave Clozel; meals CFA1500-10,000) Tucked away, just west of Blvd Steinmetz, is this great little French seafood restaurant, which also has a bar with a pool table.

**Chez Clarisse** ( ☎ 21 30 60 14; Camp Guézo; meals CFA1500-3500) This small French restaurant, next to the US embassy, rates highly with readers. If you are feeling ambitious try the *brochette des escargots* (snails cooked on a skewer).

**Le Sorrento** ( ☎ 21 31 57 79; Blvd St Michel; mains CFA2500-4500) This is the only authentic Italian restaurant in Cotonou, serving decent pizza, pasta and other Mediterranean dishes. It's at the back of the Halle des Arts complex.

**Maquis Le Lagon** ( ☎ 21 31 55 53; Blvd Steinmetz; meals CFA1500) Tasty but stingy portions of grilled chicken and chips and the like. You eat on the boulevard and get a front-row view of one of Cotonou's quieter thoroughfares.

**Faim Gourmet** ( ☎ 21 30 98 62; Blvd de la Marina; meals CFA4500-5000) Right across the road from the Novotel Orisha, this place serves delicious steaks and fish in a pleasant garden.

## Lebanese

**Restaurant Mandarine** ( ☎ 21 30 14 57; Route de l'Aéroport; meals from CFA1500) Turkish cakes and coffee in the morning, kebabs later on. Next to the Air France office on the southwestern edge of town.

## Cafés & Patisseries

**Le Petit Four** ( ☎ 21 31 20 11; Blvd Steinmetz; ☺ 7am-10pm, until 11pm Fri & Sat) A classy, air-conditioned café for croissants and coffee, and beers at night.

**La Gerbe d'Or** ( ☎ 21 31 42 58; Ave Clozel; ☺ 6am-10pm) The best shop for fresh bread, croissants and pastries, yogurt, ice cream, cheese and wine.

## Quick Eats

Superb brochettes can be found all over Cotonou, for around CFA400 to CFA500, from late afternoon onwards – look for the smoking grills piled with meat on sticks. The stalls in front of Maquis Le Lagon Grill on Blvd Steinmetz are perennial favourites, as are the **sandwich ladies** (off Ave Clozel) on the same street as Paradise nightclub. They allow you to create your own rolls with sausages, hot pepper sauce and loads more.

There are also omelette men who set up shop around dusk and work through the night. Their tables, covered in hot chocolate, coffee and tea containers, are everywhere, offering an entire breakfast here for around CFA400. The all-day stall opposite Hôtel le Crillon is good. The side streets around Hôtel Babo and Pension des Familles are dotted with caféterias.

## Self-Catering

In the centre, around Marché Ganhi, are a number of good supermarkets, including **La Ponte** ( ☎ 21 31 69 45; off Ave Clozel; ☺ 8.30am-1pm & 3.30-8pm), and **American 24** ( ☎ 21 31 52 57; Ave Clozel; ☺ 24hr).

## DRINKING

**Le Livingstone** ( ☎ 21 30 27 58; livin@leland.bj; Haie Vive; meals CFA3500-4500; ☺ 11am-late) Expect reassuring guitar riffs – at least when the rock-loving English owner's wrested control of the hi-fi – and an expat crowd kicking back on the terrace. Hearty food too.

**Le Costa Rica** ( ☎ 30 20 09; Centre de Promotion de l'Artisanal; meals CFA2400-4500) Don't be scared off by the paintings at the entrance of those formidable Gauls, Asterix and Obelix – this French-owned joint is the coolest city-centre spot to sink a draft beer. Its pizza, steak and seafood dishes are also popular.

The Jonquet strip is bristling with wild and wicked bar-hoppers and bars, such as **Le Soweto** ( ☎ 97 44 17 49; Rue des Cheminots; ☺ 10am-5am).

Haie Vive, near the airport, is a good, safe area by night, with many of the city's best bars and restaurants.

## ENTERTAINMENT
### Cinemas
Good cinemas are **Ciné le Bénin** ( ☎ 21 32 12 50; Blvd St Michel; ☺ from 7pm) and **Ciné Concorde** ( ☎ 21 33 39 72), east of the new bridge. Both show Western and African films in French. Tickets are around CFA500. You can also see films at the Centre Culturel Français, which issues monthly pamphlets with upcoming programme details, and at the Centre Culturel Chinois on Saturdays at 8pm.

### Nightclubs
The decadent bars on Jonquet strip are generally open through the night, often without a cover – try Le 2001, Le Soweto, Playboy, Le Must and L'Ancien Pattaya.

**New York, New York** (Halle des Arts; admission CFA4500) A glitzy hall of mirrors, frequented by some of the friendliest young ladies you'll encounter this side of Lomé.

**Paradise** ( ☎ 97 44 66 44; off Ave Clozel; admission CFA3000) CFA5000 whisky, sleazy expats, and techno.

**Cristal Palace** ( ☎ 21 31 25 08; admission CFA3500; ☺ 11pm-dawn Tue-Sun), at Alex's Hotel, has a karaoke bar and is a lot of fun. Benin Marina Hotel's **Le Téké** ( ☎ 21 30 01 00; Blvd de la Marina; free for Benin Marina Hotel guests) is also fun on holidays and special occasions, any time there's a crowd; otherwise it's usually pretty dead.

### Live Music
**Le Repaire de Bacchus** ( ☎ 21 31 75 81; lerepairedeb @yahoo.fr; Ave Proche; ☺ 11am-midnight, to 2am Thu, to 4am Fri & Sat) This funky jazz bar also has a food menu, although it's shorter than the list of cocktails, which start at CFA2000. With live jazz on Thursday from 10.30pm, and music such as rumba and Côte d'Ivoire sounds on Friday and Saturday, this place is the hideout of choice for Cotonou's beatniks in berets. C'est cool.

## SHOPPING
**Centre de Promotion de l'Artisinal** (Blvd St Michel; ☺ 9am-7pm) There are more beckoning hands than quality work in this large centre, but it's worth a look to get your cultural bearings. The boutiques sell woodcarvings, bronzes, batiks, leather goods, jewellery and appliqué banners.

**Marché Ganhi** is smaller and less intense than Grand Marché de Dantokpa. On the road behind the market you can pick up

bags, snakeskin wallets, *tam tam* (small hand drum) and CDs of African music.

In addition to the Centre, try the **Hôtel du Port boutique** ( ☎ 21 31 44 44; Blvd de la Marina; ☺ 10am-noon & 3-7pm), which is expensive but not as bad as the boutiques at the two top-end hotels.

## GETTING THERE & AWAY
### Air
The international airport is on the western fringe of town. The airport is rudimentarily equipped with an information centre, phone booths and a pharmacy.

If flying out of Cotonou, arrive early, as checking in is a predictably long-winded process. Departure tax is included in tickets. For fliers, there is a duty-free shop and a café-bar: a good place to fortify yourself for an encounter with the grisly officials at the entrance to the departure lounge.

For more information on airlines flying to Cotonou see p124.

### Bush Taxi, Minibus & Bus
Cotonou has a rather confusing number of stations for minibuses, buses and bush taxis. It's easiest to ask a taxi or a *zemi-john* to take you to the right one.

**Gare Jonquet** (Rue des Cheminots), a couple of blocks west of Blvd Steinmetz, services western destinations such as Lomé (CFA3000, three hours) and Ouidah (CFA600, one hour). **Gare Guinkomey** (Rue des Dako Donou) has services to the northern centres including Parakou (CFA6500, eight hours). **Gare de l'Ancien Pont** (cnr Ave Clozel & Rue des Libanais), services eastern destinations such as Lagos (CFA3000, three hours).

Bush taxis for Porto Novo (CFA500, 45 minutes) leave from **Gare du Dantokpa** (Ave de la République) at the new bridge; those to Abomey (CFA2000, two hours) leave from **Gare Missébo** (Ave van Vollenhoven). However, for Abomey, Abomey-Calavi (for Ganvié), Grand Popo and Ouidah it's far better to wait at the unofficial bush-taxi stop about 100m southwest of Église St Michel on Blvd St Michel.

Confort Lines runs daily buses between Cotonou and Natitingou. The north-bound bus leaves from the **Sonacop station** (Carrefour Legba, Cotonou) at 7am. Benin Routes' daily buses between Cotonou and Parakou leave in both directions at 7.30am. For more information on buses within Benin, see p125.

STC runs buses between Cotonou and Abidjan via Accra. West-bound buses leave from the station in Cotonou, just off Rue de Ouidah, on Monday, Wednesday and Friday at midday. STN is among the coach lines that ply the route between Cotonou and Niamey. For more on international buses to/from Cotonou, see p125.

### Train

The train station is in the heart of town one block north of Ave Clozel and several blocks southwest of Blvd Steinmetz. See p126 for more details of train services.

## GETTING AROUND

### To/From the Airport

A private taxi from the city centre to the airport costs around CFA2000, although drivers will demand double this amount *from* the airport. You can cut costs, if you don't have much to carry and you arrive during the day, by walking or catching a *zemi-john* from the airport.

### Taxi

A *zemi-john* will whiz you around town for CFA100 to CFA300 depending on the distance, though this is a dangerous way to travel on Cotonou's crowded roads.

Fares in regular taxis and minibuses are CFA150 for a shared ride (double that for fairly long trips). Taxis can be hired for CFA2000 per hour; rates increase from early evening on. Tariffs are often written on the dashboard. Gare du Dantokpa is a good place to pick up taxis.

# AROUND COTONOU

## GANVIÉ

The main attraction near Cotonou is Ganvié, where 27,000 Tofinu people live in bamboo huts on stilts several kilometres out on Lake Nokoué. All the houses, restaurants, shops, auberges and even the post office are on wooden stilts 2m above water level. The town has become a tourist magnet but a tour of its waterways is still worthwhile, especially if you have a knowledgeable guide.

The Tofinu fled to this swampy region in the 17th century from the Dahomey slave-hunters, who were banned by a religious custom from venturing into the water. They live almost exclusively from fishing, which they do by planting branches on the muddy lagoon bottom. When the leaves on the branches begin to decompose, the fish congregate there to feed.

The best times to see Ganvié and the other, quieter stilt villages are early in the morning or late in the afternoon, when the sun is weaker.

While many people, especially the women, object to having their pictures taken, children will beg you to photograph them in exchange for a *cadeau* (present).

### Sleeping & Eating

**Hôtel Carrefour Chez M Ganvié** (☎ 21 49 00 17; r CFA5000) This quaint hotel in the middle of the village next to the craft boutique has 11 rooms with balconies, mosquito nets, communal showers and flush toilets. Guests get free transport back to Abomey-Calavi. Meals are available for CFA2500 to CFA3000.

**Chez M** (☎ 21 36 03 44; r CFA5000) Formerly called Hôtel du Lac, this grubby place doesn't have much going for it other than being close to the jetty in Abomey-Calavi. Meals available for CFA1000 to CFA3000.

### Getting There & Away

From Cotonou catch a bush taxi at Gare du Missébo or near Église St Michel (see p101) or a Confort Lines bus (see p101) to Abomey-Calavi (CFA300, 35 minutes), not to be confused with Abomey.

The embarkation point in Abomey-Calavi is 800m downhill from the pirogue moorings. At the **official counter** (☎ 95 05 27 01; 🕐 9am-6pm), return fares to Ganvié for one person in a regular/motorised pirogue are CFA6050/7050; CFA4050/5050 each for two to four people; CFA3050/4050 for five to nine; CFA2550/3050 for 10 or more. Prices, which can be cut by travelling with locals or other tourists, include a circuit of the village with stop-offs. The whole trip takes about 2½ hours.

# THE SOUTH

Leaving Cotonou's traffic and Ganvié's touts, life soon starts to look up. Not only does Benin's coastal region offer some top beach action in the resort town of Grand Popo, it is brimming with intriguing culture and history. Porto Novo could be West Africa's most laid-back capital city, packed with museums and restaurants. Ouidah and Abomey contain the remains of the riches accrued by the European slave traders and their fearsome allies, the Dahomeyan Kings. Evidence of voodoo, which originated here, can be spotted all over the region.

## PORTO NOVO

**pop 234,168**

Nestling on the shores of Lake Nokoué, 30km east of Cotonou and 15km from the Nigerian border, Porto Novo is Benin's administrative centre. The refined, hilly city, home of functionaries, ministerial buildings, museums and colonial architecture, is a more rewarding place to stay than Cotonou.

Porto Novo has been Benin's official capital since it was used as such by the French, whose colonisation followed the Wars of Resistance that began here in 1890. The Portuguese named the city after Porto when they established a slave-trading post here in the 16th century. Local results of the freed slaves' return from the Americas can be seen in the Musée da Silva, which examines Afro-Brazilian culture, and the statue in Place Jean Bayal celebrating co-operation between the Yoruba and Creole peoples.

## Information

There is a hospital west of the Assemblée Nationale.

**Centre Songhai** (☎ 20 22 50 92; Route de Pobè), a popular community centre, has a supermarket and web access (per hour CFA400). Basic information about the city can be found online at www.porto-novo.org.

There are three banks and a post office in the city centre.

## Sights & Activities

### MUSÉE ÉTHNOGRAPHIQUE DE PORTO NOVO

This colonial building houses an **ethnographic museum** (☎ 20 21 25 54; Ave 6; admission CFA1000; 🕙 8am-6pm Mon-Fri, from 9am Sat, Sun & holidays, closed 1 May 1 & 1 Jan). Announced by the imposing carved doors from the palace of Kétou, the museum is one of the country's best, thanks to the knowledgeable guides. The top floor is organised thematically around birth, life and death, with

everything from costumes to carved drums. Downstairs is an impressive display of the Yorubas' inventive Gelede ceremonial masks, some dating back 200 years.

### MUSÉE HONMÉ

Formerly known as the Palais Royal du Roi Toffa, this **museum** (☎ 20 21 35 66; Rue Toffa; admission CFA1000; 🕙 9am-6pm, until 5pm Sat & Sun) is housed in the walled compound of King Toffa, who signed the first treaty with the French in 1863. The kingdom of Porto Novo was one of the longest lasting in sub-Saharan Africa, running from 1688 to the 25th king in 1976, when the five dynasties had a disagreement and let the kingdom die.

Although last remodelled in 1890, the complex has the feel of a Roman bath house, with bare chambers used for regal purposes such as initiation and suicide. The guide, François, speaks some English and will likely ask for a *cadeau*.

### MUSÉE DA SILVA

This privately owned **museum** (☎ 20 21 50 71; silvamus@leland.bj; Ave Liotard; admission CFA1000; 🕙 9am-5.30pm) is a wonderfully eccentric African establishment. It begins with a tour of an Afro-Brazilian house dating back to 1870, veers into a room filled with photocopied portraits of world leaders and jazz icons, and ends in a garage containing a Rolls Royce and a Harley Davidson hotrod.

### MOSQUE

The multicoloured building near the market is a **mosque**. Originally a Brazilian-style church, built in the late 19th century, its crumbling façade painted in pastels makes it a flamboyant example of southern Benin's many buildings of that period.

### GRAND MARCHÉ D'ADJARA

The **market** in the small town of Adjara, 10km north of Porto Novo on a back road to Nigeria, is one of the most colourful in Benin. Held every fourth day, it's stocked with fetishes, grigri charms, unique blue and white tie-dyed cloth, some of the best pottery in Benin, and *tam tams* and other musical instruments. Shared taxis to Adjara leave Porto Novo *gare routière* on market day – or take a *zemi-john*.

**BENIN**

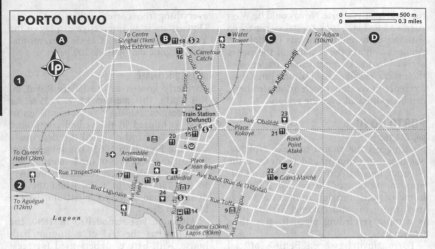

## PORTO NOVO

### PIROGUE RIDES

The 12km pirogue trip to the stilt village of Aguégué is a less touristy option than Ganvié. Among the guides and hotels offering to oblige are Hilaire and his company **Iroko Tours** ( ☎ 97 44 53 87), also contactable through **Hôtel La Détente** ( ☎ 20 21 44 69; off Blvd Lagunaire), with reasonable prices starting at CFA6000 per person.

## Festivals & Events

In mid-January Porto Novo celebrates the city's Afro-Brazilian heritage with its own version of Carnival. Contact the Musée da Silva (p103) for more information.

## Sleeping
### BUDGET

**Hôtel La Détente** ( ☎ 20 21 44 69; off Blvd Lagunaire; r CFA6500; **P** ) A popular budget option, this centrally located hotel's rooms are run-down but it has a great lagoon-side *paillote* (thatch-roofed) restaurant.

**Casa Danza** ( ☎ 20 21 48 12; Place du Gouvernement; r CFA5500-12,500; **X** ) The ground-floor rooms at the back of this restaurant one block south of the Musée Éthnographique de Porto Novo are a better, if kitschier, option than those in the tower block.

**Musée da Silva** ( ☎ 20 21 50 71; fax 20 21 26 99; silvamus@leland.bj; Ave Liotard; r CFA8500; **X** ) The museum has four large, airy rooms with baths in some of the bathrooms. Ask for a room on the inside of the complex, as the outside ones overlook a busy street and can be noisy.

**Centre Songhaï** ( ☎ 20 22 50 92; Route de Pobè; r CFA4000-12000; **P** **X** **▯** ) This lively community centre, reached by heading straight on at the two roundabouts north of Carrefour Catchi, has 70 basic but clean rooms.

## MIDRANGE

**Hôtel Beaurivage** ( ☎ 20 21 23 99; Blvd Lagunaire; r CFA15,500-25,500; 🅧 ) Tired but spacious rooms with the town's best lagoon views and a wonderful terrace bar and restaurant.

**Hôtel Dona** ( ☎ 20 22 30 52; www.hoteldona.com; Blvd Extérieur; s/d/tr CFA16,500/18,500/21,500; 🅿 🅧 ) Rooms have hot water and are like those at Beaurivage in this shockingly pink building with two restaurants and a nightclub.

**Queen's Hotel** ( ☎ 01 16 01, 90 27 60; queenhot 2005@hotmail.com; off Route de Louho; r CFA9000-12000; 🅿 🅧 ) This low-key hotel 2km west of town has some of Porto Novo's smartest rooms and an excellent restaurant.

## Eating

### RESTAURANTS

**Java Promo** ( ☎ 20 21 20 54; Place du Gouvernement; meals CFA1500-3000) Get down to this popular haunt for a yummy steak or *dourade* (fish) and chips with a carafe of wine.

**Restaurant Akango** ( ☎ 20 69 42 59, 93 15 58; meals CFA2000-3000) Lavish dishes such as *coq au vin* are the order of the day in this restaurant on a quiet side street opposite a ministerial building.

**Le JPN** ( ☎ 20 21 38 66; Jardin des Plantes et de la Nature, site 2; 🕑 10am-9pm Tue-Thu, to 11pm Fri-Sun; meals CFA1800) Set in a leafy park southwest of the Assemblée Nationale, this place offers breakfast, lunch and the odd stream of ants.

**Centre Songhai** ( ☎ 20 22 50 97; Route de Pobè; menu du jour CFA3500) The posher of the centre's two restaurants offers mouth-watering cuisine and CFA500 carafes of wine.

Alternatively try the restaurants at Casa Danza (CFA1000 to CFA3500) and the three midrange hotels (meals CFA2500 to CFA4500).

### CAFÉS

**Chez Mahi** (Ave 6; meals CFA300-600; 🕑 lunch only, closed Sun) Locals swear by this restaurant, just south of Place Kokoyé; hearty meals include mutton, *igname* and sauce.

**Buvette Escale du Pont** (Gare Routière) Has cheap drinks and Beninese tucker.

**Maquis Katchi Ambiance** (Carrefour Catchi; meals CFA350-500) Features many local specialities.

### QUICK EATS

**Cafeteria Place Catchi** (Carrefour Catchi) A popular and well-organised spot that churns out coffee and omelettes in the morning.

**Cafeteria La Pirogue** (Gare Routière) This unmarked omelette joint next to Buvette Escale du Pont is a little fly-blown but handy for early-morning taxis.

Just northeast of the Musée Éthnographique de Porto Novo and opposite the school, a street stall serves fish sauce with yam chips or mashed yam. More stalls are found around the market and Rond-Point Ataké.

### SELF-CATERING

**La Peniche Pâtisserie** ( ☎ 20 22 46 59; Carrefour Catchi) Sells passable croissant and yogurt. There is another patisserie, **Esperance** (west end of Gare Routière), and a supermarket at Centre Songhai.

## Drinking

The restaurants Casa Danza, Java Promo and Le JPN are also popular watering holes.

**Festival Plus** ( ☎ 20 22 39 79; Rue Obalédé) Set in a pleasantly ramshackle courtyard and *paillote*, this lively bar also has a small restaurant.

**Mess-Mixte** (Blvd Lagunaire) A mellow place to watch the world roll down the boulevard. Serves brochettes during the week.

## Entertainment

**Casa Danza** ( ☎ 20 21 48 12; Place du Gouvernement) is the place to be on Sunday nights, with live music and dancing from 7pm. The town's most popular club is **Feelings Night Club** (Blvd Extérieur; admission CFA3000; 🕑 Wed & Fri-Sun), 500m north of Hotel Beaurivage. There is also **Quartz Club** (Blvd Extérieur; admission CFA3000; 🕑 Fri, Sat & holidays) at Hôtel Dona.

The **outdoor cinema** (CFA500) at Musée da Silva sporadically shows French films.

## Getting There & Away

Plenty of minibuses and bush taxis leave for Cotonou (minibus/bush taxi CFA300/500, 45 minutes) from the *gare routière*. To Abomey from Porto Novo is CFA1900.

There are also frequent taxis to Lagos (CFA2700).

## Getting Around

If Cotonou hasn't scared you off *zemijohns*, they are the best way to see Porto Novo. A full town tour with the driver waiting should cost no more than CFA5000 for

BENIN

the day. Alternatively all the major sites and facilities are within half an hour's walk of each other.

## OUIDAH

### pop 87,200

Some 42km west of Cotonou is Ouidah, a relaxed, relatively prosperous town and a must-see for anyone interested in voodoo or Benin's history of slave-trading. Until a wharf was built at Cotonou in 1908, Ouidah had the only port in the country. Its heyday was from 1800 to 1900, when slaves from across West Africa left Ouidah for the Americas.

Good preliminary reading is Bruce Chatwin's evocative *The Viceroy of Ouidah*, which tells the story of the ill-fated slave-trader Francisco da Silva's arrival from Brazil and subsequent relationship with the war-mongering Kings of Dahomey.

A visit to the beach, where the slaves once left from, is well worthwhile. The 4km journey there from town takes you past a lagoon with fishermen and a small stilt village.

There are voodoo ceremonies every weekend during the dry season and the annual Voodoo Festival is celebrated here in January (see opposite). There is a **film festival** (www.festival-ouidah.org) here at the same time, and a festival honouring twins in October.

## Information

Slow Internet access can be found at **Socofas** ( ☎ 21 34 14 76; Rue Olivier de Montaguerre; per hr CFA400; ☽ 7am-midnight).

There are no banks in Ouidah. Post cards are available in the post office on the south side of Rue F Colombani in the centre of town.

## Sights & Activities

### MUSÉE D'HISTOIRE D'OUIDAH

This **museum** ( ☎ 21 34 10 21; Rue van Vollenhoven; admission CFA1000; ☽ 9am-noon & 3-6pm), two blocks east of the market, is housed in Fortaleza São João Batista, a Portuguese fort built in 1721. Perhaps the best museum in the country, with exhibits focusing on the slave trade and the resulting links between Benin, Brazil and the Caribbean. You'll be shown voodoo artefacts, skulls, photos showing the influence of Dahomeyan slaves on Brazilian culture, and traces of Brazilian architecture that the repatriated slaves brought back to Africa.

## OUIDAH

0 ——— 500 m
0 ——— 0.3 miles

| INFORMATION | |
|---|---|
| Hospital | 1 B5 |
| Post Office | 2 A5 |
| Socofas | 3 A4 |

| SIGHTS & ACTIVITIES | |
|---|---|
| Basilica | 4 B5 |
| Casa do Brazil | 5 A5 |
| Musée d'Histoire d'Ouidah | 6 B5 |
| Sacred Forest | 7 B5 |
| Temple des Serpents | 8 B5 |

| SLEEPING ⌂ | |
|---|---|
| Hôtel Gbena | 9 A4 |
| Oasis Hôtel | 10 B5 |
| Oriki Maquis Hôtel | 11 A5 |

| EATING ⊓ | |
|---|---|
| Cafeteria le Kilombo | 12 B5 |
| Eureka Café | 13 B5 |

| DRINKING ⊔ | |
|---|---|
| Buvette La Marmite D'Or | 14 A4 |
| Buvette Relais Du Sportif | 15 B5 |
| Evivi | 16 A5 |
| Le Belier | 17 A5 |
| Le Karakoo | 18 A3 |
| Liberty's | 19 A5 |
| Maquis Benin | 20 A3 |

| TRANSPORT | |
|---|---|
| Bush Taxi & Zemi-john Stop | 21 B5 |
| Gare Routière | 22 B5 |
| Shared-Taxi Stop (to Grand Popo & Togo) | 23 A3 |

### ROUTE DES ESCLAVES

The 4km **Route des Esclaves**, now the main road to the beach, starts near the Musée d'Histoire d'Ouidah. This is the route the slaves took to the coast to board the ships. Lining the sandy track are fetishes and monuments such as the Monument of Repentance and the Tree of Forgetfulness.

---

### THE VOODOO FESTIVAL

Benin's most vibrant and colourful celebration is the annual Voodoo Festival held on 10 January. While celebrations take place all over the country, those in Ouidah, the historic centre of voodoo, are the best.

Since 1997, one year after the government officially decreed voodoo a religion, thousands of believers have flocked to Ouidah to reclaim and rejoice in their faith. The main festivities take place on the beach near the Point of No Return monument at the end of Route des Esclaves.

The celebrations begin when the supreme voodoo priest slaughters a goat to honour the spirits, and are marked by much singing, dancing, beating of drums and drinking of gin. However, while this is certainly eye-opening, those expecting to see *The Night of the Living Dead* will be sadly disappointed.

---

Slaves were forced to circle the tree that once stood here, to forget the land they were leaving.

There is a poignant memorial on the beach, the **Point of No Return**, in honour of those departed slaves. Walk through this grand arch, with its bas-relief depicting slaves in chains, to the water. Imagine the slaves climbing into lighters to go out to the 'slavers', where they would descend into dark holds for the journey to the Americas.

A short walk east are a monument marking the millennium and the Door of Return, which houses a **museum** ( ☎ 21 33 74 14; admission CFA1000; ☽ 9am-6pm).

If you don't want to walk, you can always find a *zemi-john* for under CFA1000.

### CASA DO BRAZIL

Sometimes called La Maison de Bresil, this **museum** ( ☎ 21 34 18 63; admission CFA1000; ☽ 9am-6pm) gives an overview of the African Diaspora. The sculptures and photographic displays, with explanations in English and French, have a particular focus on women in African society. The house itself is the former residence of the Brazilian governor and was later occupied by a Portuguese family until they were ousted in the early 1960s.

### TEMPLE DES SERPENTS

The voodoo **python temple** ( ☎ 95 40 08 90; admission CFA1000, photos CFA5000; ☽ 8am-7pm) is now more of a tourist trap than a sacred site. The guide explains some of the beliefs and ceremonies associated with the temple, ushers you into a room containing 40 sleepy pythons, drapes one round your neck, and asks for a *cadeau*.

### SACRED FOREST

This **park** ( ☎ 97 68 89 22; admission CFA1000 incl guide; ☽ 8am-6pm Mon-Sun) contains the huge and rare iroko tree that King Kpassé, founder of Ouidah, is reputed to have turned himself into while fleeing enemies. To make a wish, touch the tree and leave an offering among its roots. The forest is dotted with sculptures that symbolise all sorts of voodoo and animist deities and beliefs.

### CASA DEL PAPA

Nonguests can use the facilities at this resort (see below): swimming pool (per hour CFA3500), volleyball and tennis courts (per hour CFA3500), canoes, pirogues, and kayak tours of the lagoon (half-/full-day CFA6500/17,000).

## Sleeping

**Le Jardin Brasilien Auberge de la Diaspora** ( ☎ 21 34 10 11/; r CFA7500-20000; P ☒ ) On the beach near the Point of No Return, this tranquil place is an excellent choice. There are three categories of rooms in the 34 bungalows among the windswept palms. The restaurant (meals CFA3000 to CFA9000) is pricey but has a beautiful view and a good selection of fish.

**Casa Del Papa** ( ☎ 21 49 21 01; matbenin@serv.eit.bj; Ouidah Plage; r CFA30,500-51,000; P ☒ ) This beach resort has 57 bungalows between the beach and the lagoon. The plushest accommodation in the area, though it is 7km beyond the Door of No Return on a road that is unsafe at night. Meals are available for CFA4000 to CFA6000.

**Oasis Hotel** ( ☎ /fax 21 34 10 91; Rue van Vollenhoven; r CFA9000-18000 ☒ ) The best and most central of the hotels in town. The 25 rooms are nothing special for the price but the restaurant (meals CFA2000) is one of Ouidah's best and the rooftop bar has a superb view. The friendly management are open to negotiation on prices.

**Oriki Maquis Hôtel** ( ☎ 21 34 10 04; Rue Marius Moutel; r CFA4000-8000) Ouidah's best budget option is the quiet, friendly Oriki, about 1km south of the crossroads on Route de Togo. The comfortable rooms have fans and there is a good restaurant/bar (meals CFA2500) attached.

**Edelweiss Les Retrouvailles** ( ☎ 21 34 12 86; Rue du Général Dodd; r with fan/air-con CFA6500/15,500; P ) About 1km east of the Musée d'Histoire d'Ouidah, near the French military cemetery and the memorial to the arrival of Christian missionaries, this excellent budget choice is set in leafy grounds with a *paillote* restaurant (meals CFA2000 to CFA3500) and a children's playground.

**Le Retour de la Diaspora** ( ☎ 21 34 10 47; Route des Esclaves; r CFA5000) The best of an uninspiring bunch of hotels and *buvettes* (bars) gathered around the Village Artisinal de Ouidah on the way to the beach. The rooftop restaurant (meals CFA1800 to CFA2500) serves a small selection of dishes such as pizza and quiche.

**Hôtel Gbena** ( ☎ 21 34 12 15; Route de Togo; r CFA14,000-16,000; ❄ ) This midrange hotel on the bypass 2km north of the town centre is past its prime. The gloomy bedrooms are well maintained, but the rates are expensive and some rooms overlook the noisy road. Meals for CFA2500 to CFA3000.

**Hôtel DK** ( ☎ 21 34 11 97; Route de Togo; r CFA15,500-20,500, ste CFA35,500) With its decaying façade and its dysfunctional swimming pool, this hotel near the bypass east of town has a ghostly air. Its 50 air-conditioned rooms make it a possible choice for large groups. Meals for CFA4000 to CFA8000.

## Eating

For cheap eats try the open-air **Cafeteria de Kilombo** (meals from CFA400), across from the Musée d'Histoire d'Ouidah, or **Eureka Café** (Rue van Vollenhoven; meals from CFA400). Head to the market for fish stands, omelette joints and the Fan Milk depot, and to Carrefour Benin for brochettes and other meat treats.

## Drinking

The town centre is peppered with small bars, notably **Evivi** (Rue F Colombani), opposite the post office; **Liberty's** (Rue d'Orgre), one block northeast

of Oriki Maquis Hôtel; **Buvette Relais du Sportif** (Rue F Colombani), overlooking the Basilica; and **Le Belier** (off Rue F Colombani), at the market.

**Buvette La Marmite D'Or** (Rue Olivier de Montaguerre) Located south of Socofas Internet café, this is a sociable spot to watch the *zemi-johns* racing into town.

**Maquis Benin** (Route de Togo) Is an atmospheric place in earshot of the lorries approaching Carrefour Benin.

**Le Karakoo** (admission CFA3000, free for women; ☽ Fri & Sat) PAMFL Hotel's nightclub.

## Getting There & Away

Bush taxis and occasional buses to Cotonou (CFA600, one hour) leave from the two stations in the centre of town and from Gare de Kpassé, at the market on Route de Togo, near the Sacred Forest. For Grand Popo, Abomey and Togo, wait at Carrefour Benin.

## GRAND POPO

Some 82km from Cotonou and 20km from the Togo border at Hila-Condji, Grand Popo is Benin's best getaway spot for travellers to spend a few idle days on the sand – although swimming is limited due to strong currents. It's Benin's most tourist-focused location, but this hasn't lessened its sleepy charm. If you do tire of lounging by the pool, nearby are some fascinating landscapes and voodoo culture. In the small villages lining the coastal highway, the white flags flying from poles identify voodoo practitioners.

### Sights & Activities
#### VILLA KARO
On the main road through the village is this Finnish-African **cultural centre** ( ☎ 22 43 03 58; www.villa-karo.org) with a small **gallery** ( ☽ 8am-11am & 4-6pm Mon-Fri, 8-11am Sat). There's also a library with books in French, Finnish and English, a free open-air cinema from 8pm on Friday evenings, and a free concert on the first Saturday of the month.

#### PIROGUE TRIPS
Local fishermen can be persuaded to take you to the **Bouche du Roy**, where the Mono River meets the ocean. These trips can also be organised through Awale Plage (see opposite), which runs excursions to villages, markets, voodoo sites, and a turtle beach.

### Sleeping & Eating
**Auberge de Grand Popo** ( ☎ 22 43 00 47, central reservations ☎ /fax 21 31 38 62; www.hotels-benin.com; camping

per person CFA1500, tent hire CFA5000, r CFA13,000-23,000; (P) (≋) ) The mothership of the dependable 'Auberge de…' chain, this long-standing and highly recommended hotel is right on the beach. Rooms are split between a beautiful colonial building and quaint garden bungalows. The attractive terrace restaurant (meals CFA3800 to CFA9000) has an impressive menu and wine selection. The pool is CFA1000 for non-guests.

**Awalé Plage** ( ☎ /fax 22 43 01 17; awaleplage@yahoo .fr; Route de Togo; camping per person CFA1500, tent hire CFA3000, bungalows CFA14,500-28,500; (P) (≋) ) This lively resort, on the main highway west of the Grand Popo turn-off, has been given the thumbs up by LP readers. There is an excellent beach bar, the restaurant (meals CFA2900 to CFA5000) is good, and you can hire boogie boards. Staff are dressed as pirates and they throw fortnightly full- and new-moon parties, with poolside live music.

**Etoile de Mer** ( ☎ 22 43 04 83; Route de Togo; r CFA10,500-25,000; (≋) ) This cheap alternative to Awalé Plage, with a garden restaurant (meals CFA3500 to CFA5000) and beach bar, located on the highway at the Grand Popo turn-off, was seeking new management at the time of writing.

**Doue Plage** (camping per person CFA1500, r CFA6000-7000) One of three basic auberges in the centre of the village, this three-roomed hotel was building six more rooms at the time of writing – along with a toilet and shower. A quiet spot for a beer and a bite to eat (meals CFA2500 to CFA4000).

**Saveurs d'Afrique** (meals CFA2500-3000) This beachfront restaurant, which serves brochettes, fish and other typical fare, has the best location of the cluster of touristy eateries in the middle of the village.

### Getting There & Away
From Cotonou, take a bush taxi from Gare de Jonquet (CFA1300, two hours) and have it drop you off at the Grand Popo junction on the main coastal highway, 20km east of the Togo border crossing at Hila-Condji. The beach and village are 3.5km off the main road and are easily accessible via *zemi-john* (CFA200).

## LAKE AHÉMÈ & AROUND
Possotomè, Bopa and the other fishing villages on the western shores of Lake Ahémè, 40km southeast of Lokossa, are voodoo

strongholds and you'll spot fetishes in their shops and houses. There are also regular voodoo ceremonies, which tourists are generally welcome to attend. In Possotomè, ask around on the beach near the *gare routière* to meet a fetish priest, who can prepare you a talisman.

Possotomè is famous for its thermal springs, the country's primary source of mineral water. The springs themselves are an anticlimactic trickle but you can visit the bottling factory that has been set up nearby, and the tiny **Centre de Tissage** ( ⏱ 7am-6pm Mon-Wed). Pirogue trips to the fishing villages can be organised at Village Club Ahémè or, for a cheaper trip, by asking around the village.

Lokossa, midway between Grand Popo and Abomey, is a convenient spot to find taxis east to Possotomè and Bopa, as well as north and south along the Abomey-Comé highway. If you stop here, check out the market, which takes place every five days.

### Sleeping & Eating
Possotomè has the best facilities in the area.

**Auberge Palais des Jeunes** ( ☎ 95 96 12 87; r CFA5000-10,000; (P) (≋) ) Good value and central. The *paillote* bar-restaurant (meals CFA1300 to CFA1500) serves French and American cuisine and turns into a nightclub on Saturday nights.

**Village Club Ahémè** ( ☎ 43 00 29; village aheme@yahoo.fr; r CFA12,000-25,000; (P) (≋) ) This 20-room hotel on the water's edge has seen better days. The more-expensive upstairs rooms are considerably sunnier. As well as picking up from Cotonou airport, the hotel organises excursions around southern Benin. Breakfast is CFA1500, and other meals CFA5000 to CFA6500.

**Hôtel Chéz Theo** ( ☎ 22 43 08 06; r CFA10000-18000; (P) (≋) ) Newer and better value than Village Club Ahémè, though its beach is not as good and it has a monkey chained to a tree. Meals are CFA2500.

**Café Bar La Source** (meals CFA350) Scruffy but charming *buvette* on the beach in the centre of the village.

### Getting There & Away
From the coastal highway take the turn-off north to Lokossa (20km) and Comé (700m), from where a dirt road heads east to Possotomè (18km) and Bopa (26km). Taxis and

**BENIN**

*zemi-johns* to Possotomè and Bopa can be found at Comé and Lokossa *gare routières*. Shared taxis between Lokossa and Comé do occasionally take the lake road, but they generally stick to the main road.

## ABOMEY

pop 114,600

Abomey, 144km northwest of Cotonou in Fon country, is a remarkable town. Its winding lanes are dotted with *banco* (mud brick) houses and the palaces and temples built by the kings of Dahomey. The main attractions are the 'Dahomey Trail' tour of these ruins and the restored royal palace, where a museum contains artefacts such as a throne mounted on human skulls.

### Orientation & Information

There are few main roads in Abomey – dirt streets radiate from the central market. Use the water tower as a point of reference.

There is a web café, **Cyber Goho** ( ☎ 22 50 08 10; Place de Goho; per hr CFA1000r; ☒ 7pm-midnight).

### Sights

The kings of Dahomey were a bloody lot, and their litany of slave-trading, human sacrifice and war is illustrated by the bold appliqué banners hanging in the **Musée Historique d'Abomey** ( ☎ 21 50 03 14; www.epa-prema.net/abomey; admission CFA2500; ☒ 8.30am-6pm Mon-Fri, to 5pm Sat & Sun). One of the tapestries shows Glélé using a dismembered leg to pound his enemy's head, another shows a head being crushed in a vice.

The same is true of the many exhibits on display in the museum, such as Ghézo's throne, which is mounted on the skulls of four enemies. The museum is housed in two palaces – all that remains of what was once one of the most impressive structures in West Africa, with a 4km perimeter and a 10m-high wall enclosing 44 hectares and a court of 10,000 people. There were originally 12 palaces, as every king built a new one.

The final king of Dahomey, Béhanzin, torched the place while fleeing the French in the late 19th century. His forces had been fighting the invaders using their own guns – bought from the Germans in Togo – but the French got the last laugh when they turned the palace into their administrative centre.

The bas-reliefs on the exterior, which illustrate the gory history of Dahomey, were a major factor in Unesco's decision to classify the structure as a World Heritage Site.

The admission fee includes a guide, who will take about an hour to show you round the courtyards, ceremonial rooms and burial chambers. The tour finishes at the Centre des Artisans, where you can buy appliqué banners and bronze figurines made using the *cire perdue* method: items once made especially for the kings of Dahomey.

### Sleeping

Accommodation in Abomey is skewed towards the bottom of the market.

**Chez Monique** ( ☎ 22 50 01 68; camping per person CFA3000, r CFA7500-12,000; ℗ ) A regular pleasure garden, where antelopes, crocodiles, tortoises, monkeys and murals of Amazons can be found between the trees and the wood carvings. The breezy rooms have tiled floors, blue walls and insect screens. Meals are available for CFA2500.

**Motel d'Abomey** ( ☎/fax 22 50 00 75; Route de l'Hôpital; r CFA12,500-60,500; ℗ ☒ ) The largest and best hotel in Abomey, with 33 rooms and 19 bungalows. The thatched bungalows, painted on the outside with murals in the local style, are decked out with TVs and comfortable furniture. European and Beninese food is available in the restaurant (meals CFA2200 to CFA4000), one of Abomey's best.

**Hôtel Guedevy 1** ( ☎ 22 50 03 04; s with fan CFA6500, s/d CFA10,500-15,500, bungalow CFA20,500; ℗ ☒ ) Despite the decrepit façade and eastern bloc ambience, the 50 rooms in this hotel 2km north of town are some of the best in Abomey, with TV installed. The decent restaurant (meals CFA1200 to CFA3800) serves European dishes and snacks.

**Hôtel Marie Josée** ( ☎ 22 50 02 89; off Route de Lokossa; r CFA6500-25,500; ☒ ) This professional hotel's nine rooms range from basic rooms with fan and insect screen to the plush suite with TV and stereo. There is an attractive terrace restaurant (meals CFA2500), and a hire car firm on the premises.

**Vulcan** ( ☎ 97 07 30 64; Quartier Adjahito; r CFA6000) This cool budget choice is set in gardens dotted with funky sculptures and canvases. Best found by *zemi-john,* it's located in the back streets between the hospital and Motel d'Abomey. Meals are CFA2500.

**Hôtel la Lutta** ( ☎ 42 16 83; s/d CFA4000/4500) This rundown hotel is lost among a maze of sandy streets 300m southwest of the

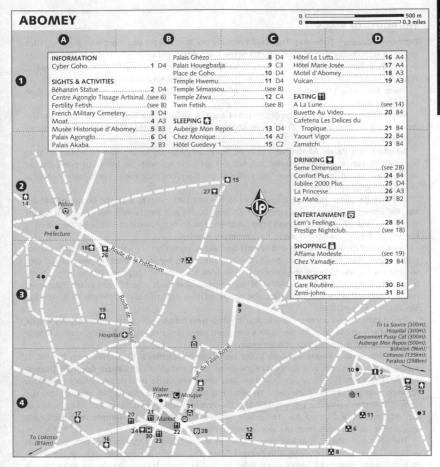

## ABOMEY

0 — 500 m
0 — 0.3 miles

**INFORMATION**
Cyber Goho...........................1 D4

**SIGHTS & ACTIVITIES**
Béhanzin Statue.....................2 D4
Centre Agonglo Tissage Artisinal..(see 6)
Fertility Fetish.......................(see 8)
French Military Cemetery.........3 D4
Moat....................................4 A3
Musée Historique d'Abomey.....5 B3
Palais Agonglo......................6 D4
Palais Akaba.........................7 B3

Palais Ghézo.........................8 D4
Palais Houegbadja..................9 C3
Place de Goho......................10 D4
Temple Hwemu.....................11 D4
Temple Sémassou...............(see 8)
Temple Zéwa.......................12 C4
Twin Fetish.......................(see 8)

**SLEEPING**
Auberge Mon Repos.............13 D4
Chez Monique......................14 A2
Hôtel Guedevy 1..................15 C2

Hôtel La Lutta.....................16 A4
Hôtel Marie Josée................17 A4
Motel d'Abomey..................18 A3
Vulcan...............................19 A3

**EATING**
A La Lune........................(see 14)
Buvette Au Video..................20 B4
Cafeteria Les Delices du
   Tropique..........................21 B4
Yaourt Vigor.......................22 B4
Zamatchi............................23 B4

**DRINKING**
5eme Dimension.................(see 28)
Confort Plus.......................24 B4
Jubilee 2000 Plus.................25 D4
La Princesse.......................26 A3
Le Mato.............................27 B2

**ENTERTAINMENT**
Lem's Feelings....................28 B4
Prestige Nightclub.............(see 18)

**SHOPPING**
Affama Modeste................(see 19)
Chez Yamadje.....................29 B4

**TRANSPORT**
Gare Routière......................30 B4
Zemi-johns.........................31 B4

Police

Préfecture

Route de la Préfecture

Route de l'Hôpital

Hospital

Rue du Palais Royal

Water Tower

Mosque

Market

To Lokossa
(81km)

To La Source (300m);
Hospital (300m);
Campement Pussy Cat (300m);
Auberge Mon Repos (500m);
Bohicon (9km);
Cotonou (135km);
Parakou (298km)

market – take a *zemi-john*. Run by local legend Monsieur 'La Lutta' (Adjolohoun Jean-Constant) and his French-novel–reading teenage daughter, it's an endearingly eccentric establishment, with voodoo dolls grinning in the gloomy parlour and extraordinary plumbing in the rooms. Meals are available for CFA1200 to CFA2500.

**Auberge Mon Repos** ( ☎ 22 50 17 66; Route de Bohicon; r CFA5500) Staff bend over backwards to welcome visitors to this respectable budget hotel, signposted on the right as you head towards Bohicon. There is a decent restaurant (meals CFA1000 to CFA1800), and plans to install air-con in the rooms.

**Campement Pussy Cat** ( ☎ 22 50 02 02; off Route de Bohicon; r CFA4500) Turn off the road heading to Bohicon between La Source and the garage for this characterless but comfortable budget choice, where the rooms themselves are adequate despite the large, dingy TV room.

## Eating

**La Source** ( ☎ 22 50 19 96; Route de Bohicon; meals CFA2000) As well as being one of the smarter bars in town, La Source serves hearty helpings of chicken and chips or couscous.

**A La Lune** (meals CFA2500) Fans of Chez Monique's restaurant reckon it serves the best West African cuisine around, but we weren't that impressed with our chicken and *pâté rouge* (corn flour with peppers and seasonings) in tomato sauce.

BENIN

## THE ROUTE OF KINGS

Exploring Abomey's **Dahomey Trail** could provide the best insight you'll get into Benin's gothic history. This half-day tour of the remnants of the Dahomey civilisation, which was as important as Benin City in Nigeria and Dogon country in Mali, is best attempted by *zemi-john* (CFA2500). Ask at Hôtel La Lutta for a driver – if you're lucky you'll get the knowledgeable proprietor himself.

There are some 14 sites to be seen, all of which have an air of faded majesty about their crumbling walls.

Begin the tour at the remains of the **moat** built in 1645 by the first king, Houégbadja. The moat, 42km around and 60m deep, gave Abomey its name – *abo* means 'moat' in Fon and *mey* means 'inside'.

Nearby is the **Palais Akaba**, who goaded his enemy Dan by telling him he would build in his belly. In classic Dahomey style, Dan did indeed wind up with his belly cut open, buried beneath a tree outside the palace. The name of the kingdom thus mixes Dan's name with the words *ho* (belly) and *mey*.

At **Place de Goho**, the story leaps ahead to the late 19th century with the **statue of Béhanzin**. He agreed to sign a treaty here with Colonel Dodds and the French forces – *goho* means 'meeting' – but his soldiers instead fired on them. The French casualties of the battle, which is known as 'the last six hours', are in the **cemetery** nearby.

The ruins of the **Palais Ghézo** and **Temple Sémassou** show that life was just as tough for earlier rulers. When Sémassou was born prematurely in the street, before he died he prophesised that terrible events would befall the kingdom. After Glélé's henchmen disposed of the baby's body in a bush, Dahomey suffered 21 days of war, plague, and destruction. When Glélé discovered his henchmen's' disrespectful action, the oracle advised him to build a temple to encourage Sémassou's annunciation.

Among the many curiosities in this quarter are a **twin fetish** and a large white **fertility fetish**. Local women would straddle the latter's oversized erect penis to ensure fertility, until a female tourist snapped it off to keep as a souvenir.

The 18th century **Palais Agonglo** is the best kept of Abomey's 12 palaces, with bas-reliefs inside listing the names and symbols of the great kings and chiefs. At **Centre Agonglo Tissage Artisinal** ( 8am-7pm), you can buy bags and costumes made in styles originally taught to Agonglo's weavers by his Portuguese slave-trading allies. Agonglo also had an unusual son, the midget Hwemu. Saying he was returning to the voodoo world, Hwemu walked into the sea at Cotonou and turned into a fish. The oracle advised Agonglo to build **Temple Hwemu** for his son, whose name comes from the words *hwe* (fish) and *mu* (raw).

The palace of Ghézo, who had over 200 wives and established the army of female Amazon warriors, can still be seen, along with **Temple Zéwa**. The temple was built to appease the spirits of a traitorous group of Ghézo's wives, who he had executed by covering in red palm oil and leaving them for the ants to eat. Zéwa was the last to die.

---

Good budget choices near the *gare routière* include **Zamatchi** and **Cafeteria Les Delices du Tropique**. **Buvette Au Video**, to the northwest, is more traditional than the name suggests, serving *pâté*- and rice-based dishes at rock-bottom prices. The market is the place to head for street stalls, along with the **Yaourt Vigor** (Route de l'Hôpital) yogurt depot.

## Drinking

Good bars include **5ème Dimension** (Route de l'Hôpital), attached to Lem's Feelings; **La Princesse** (Route de l'Hôpital), opposite Motel d'Abomey; **Jubilee 2000 Plus**, at the southeast end of Place de Goho; **Confort Plus**, near the *gare routière*; and **Le Mato**, opposite Hôtel Guedevy 1.

## Entertainment

**Prestige Nightclub** (admission CFA2500, free for guests of Motel d'Abomey;  Fri-Sun & holidays) This club at Motel d'Abomey is one of the fanciest places in town.

**Lem's Feelings** (admission CFA2500;  Fri) A more animated crowd is found at this air-conditioned club, not far east of the market. Entry includes a drink, and from then on drinks are CFA1000.

## Shopping

Abomey is one of the best places in Benin to buy craft work. As well as the stalls at Musée Historique d'Abomey and Palais Agonglo, try **Chez Yemadje** ( ☎ 95 40 66 97; Rue du Palais Royal ❤ 7am-7pm), run by the family that used to embroider for the Dahomeyan kings. Next to the Vulcan auberge is the studio of the talented pop-art sculptor **Affama Modeste** ( ☎ 95 05 31 86).

## Getting There & Away

Plenty of bush taxis depart from Cotonou (CFA2000, three hours), sometimes with a connection at Bohicon (9km east of Abomey).

Bush taxis and *zemi-johns* run between Abomey and Bohicon (around CFA300) during the day and in the early evening. Vehicles continuing to Parakou leave frequently from the *gare routière* in Abomey and stop off in Bohicon. In Bohicon, to hail a taxi headed north towards Parakou, just stand along the main road and wave.

**Confort Lines** ( ☎ 21 32 58 15) buses leave for Bohicon from Cotonou (CFA1500, three hours) and Natitingou (CFA6500, five hours) at 7am daily.

Alternatively, you could take the train to Bohicon (see p126). It takes four hours from Cotonou and costs CFA1400/1100 for 1st/2nd class.

## DASSA ZOUMÉ
pop 21,900

What makes Dassa Zoumé, the 'city of 41 hills', so interesting are the awesome rock formations overshadowing the town's sleepy streets. Every August, Catholic pilgrims pay a visit to **La Grotte** (cave), which is where the Virgin Mary is said to have to appeared. Behind the cave, a short walk leads to the thirteen shrines hidden among the rocks.

There is an evenings-only Internet café and a Bank of Africa in town, and plenty of cheap food stalls lining the main road.

**Auberge de Dassa Zoumé** ( ☎ /fax 22 53 00 98; www.hotels-benin.com; camping per person CFA2500, s/d with fan CFA10,000/11,000, with air-con CFA14,000/16,000) The best hotel in town, opposite the *rond-point* (roundabout) on the major highway. The camping pitches and excellent restaurant (meals CFA3800 to CFA4000) overlooking an ostrich farm.

**Auberge Le Cachet** ( ☎ 22 53 02 11; r shared bathroom CFA4500, r with bathroom CFA5000) Situated near the hospital, this small, rustic hotel has bog-standard rooms and a great restaurant (meals CFA1500).

## Getting There & Away

Bush taxis from Cotonou to Dassa Zoumé (CFA3000, four hours) depart from under the new bridge next to the Grand Marché du Dantokpa.

Daily Confort Lines buses cost the same and take the same time (see p125).

You can also get to Dassa Zoumé by train, which costs CFA2900/2500 for 1st/2nd class. See p126 for timetable.

# THE NORTH

Northern Benin's arid, dusty landscape is a far cry from the south's beaches and lagoons. Easier going than their Fon cousins on the coast, the northerners – mainly composed of the Betamaribé, Djende, Fula and Bariba groups – can often be found escaping the sun in the shade of a mango tree. Islam replaces Christianity as the dominant religion, apart from among the animist Betamaribé people in Somba country. The area's main sights are the two wildlife parks, particularly Pendjari, and the castellated *tata somba* houses.

## PARAKOU
pop 198,000

Once a major slave-market town, Parakou still has a prosperous, busy atmosphere, with the most facilities you'll find in northern Benin and a prime position on both the highway and railway line. There isn't much to keep you here, but with the many *buvettes* lining the town's dusty streets, Parakou makes a relaxing stop-over en route to the northern wildlife parks.

The centre of town is the area around the cinema at the intersection of Route de l'Aéroport, Rue des Cheminots and Route de Transa, three blocks northwest of the Grand Marché.

The Bank of Africa has a 24-hour ATM.

## Sleeping

**Le Majestic Hotel** ( ☎ 23 61 34 85; nablia25@yahoo .fr; Route de l'Hôtel Canaries; r CFA12,500-30,000; ❎ ) Clean, stylish and the best value in town.

BENIN

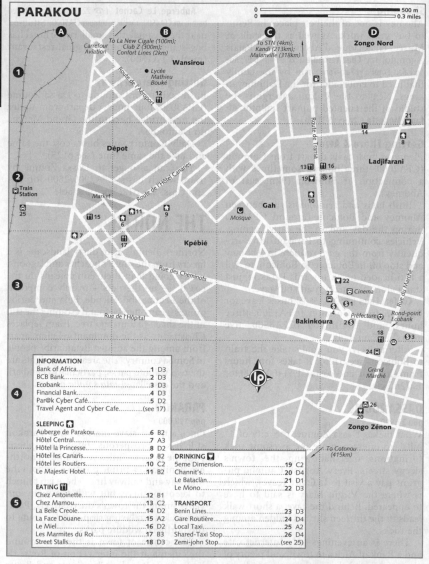

# PARAKOU

0 — 500 m
0 — 0.3 miles

Ask for a room with a balcony overlooking the market. Meals are available for CFA3000 to CFA4000.

**Hôtel les Routiers** ( ☎ 23 61 04 01; Route de Transa; s/d from CFA25000/28000, ste CFA41,000; **P** ⚄ ) This establishment, 500m north of the heart of town, has long been the most popular top-end hotel in Parakou. You can't help but

relax in the garden setting with its clean pool (CFA1500 for nonguests). There's also a good, but expensive, French restaurant (*menu du jour* CFA7000, meals from CFA5000).

**Auberge de Parakou** ( ☎ 23 61 03 05; www.hotels -benin.com; Route de l'Hôtel Canaries; s/d with fan CFA10,000/12,000, with air-con CFA14,000/16,000) This delightful auberge has large, spotless rooms with tiled floors and mosquito nets. Its excellent French restaurant serves delicious meals (CFA2600 to CFA3500).

**Hôtel la Princesse** ( ☎ 23 61 01 32; fax 23 61 32 86; s CFA6000-15,500, d CFA8000-18,500, bungalow s/d CFA25,000/27,000) The prices in this Parakou institution reflect past glories but it's a dependable choice nonetheless, with spacious, carpeted bungalows complete with phones and TV. The hotel has an attractive thatched restaurant (meals CFA2000 to CFA2500) across the street, and Le Bataclàn nightclub.

**Hôtel Central** ( ☎ 23 61 01 24; fax 23 61 38 51; r CFA19,500-25,500; P ✕ ) If you can get over the screamingly kitsch décor, this hotel is all ship-shape, with a pleasant pool open to non-guests (CFA1000). Rooms upstairs are bigger and more expensive. Meals are CFA2500 to CFA5000.

**Hôtel les Canaris** ( ☎ 23 61 11 69; Route de l'Hôtel Canaries; r with fan/air-con CFA6000/11,000) The friendly management of this long-standing hotel, about 400m east of the train station, were dusting down a new block at the time of writing, with a restaurant on the roof.

## Eating

Street stalls north of the market serve hunks of meat and corn on the cob.

**Le Miel** ( ☎ 23 61 00 67; Route de Transa; meals CFA1000-2500) Upstairs from the excellent bakery – which sells vegetarian savouries as well as cakes, croissant and yogurt – this restaurant serves good pizzas and sandwiches.

**Chez Mamou** (Route de Transa; meals CFA250) Friendly buvette serving good, cheap food such as wagassi (cow's milk cheese) and macaroni.

**La New Cigale** ( ☎ 97 89 11 98; off Carrefour Aviation; meals CFA2500-4500) Pleasant restaurant serving pizza and French food.

**La Face Douane** (meals CFA500) No-frills African restaurant with a busy kitchen doling out huge servings of rice and sauces.

**Chez Antoinette** ( ☎ 23 61 05 73; Route de l'Aéroport; meals CFA500) A reasonable place for omelettes in the morning and spaghetti at night, just south of the school.

**Les Marmites du Roi** ( ☎ 23 61 25 07; off Route de l'Hotel Canaries; meals CFA3500-4000) A relatively upmarket spot to sample African cuisine. You dine outdoors under paillotes.

**La Belle Creole** ( ☎ 23 61 40 32; off Route de Transa; meals CFA1500-3500) This hip-hop–playing pizzeria attracts a young crowd to its covered garden and pool table.

## Drinking

**Le Bataclàn** (admission Thu/Fri/Sat CFA1500/2500/4000; ☾ Thu-Sat) Opposite Hôtel la Princesse, this club is a Parakou favourite. The place fills up after midnight, especially on Saturdays.

**Channit's** (Rue du Marché) The newest and hippest club in Parakou, a block south of the market.

Buvettes abound – try **Le Mono** (Route de Transa) and **5ème Dimension** (Route de Transa); and **Club Z** (Route de Malanville), 200m northeast of La New Cigale.

## Getting There & Away

### BUSH TAXI, MINIBUS & BUS

From the gare routière, north of the Grand Marché, bush taxis and minibuses go regularly to Cotonou (CFA6500, eight hours), Kandi (CFA3000, 3½ hours), Malanville (CFA4500, five hours) and Djougo (CFA3000, two hours). It's extra for luggage.

Bush taxis east to the Togo border take at least three hours because the road is not sealed.

Benin Lines runs daily buses between Cotonou and Parakou (see p125). The southbound bus leaves from outside Parakou Financial Bank at 7.30am.

EHGM, STN and SNTV run buses between Cotonou and Niamey via Parakou (see p125). The northbound STN bus stops 4km north of Parakou at 10am daily.

### TRAIN

Save money by taking the train (see p126), which leaves for Cotonou (1st/2nd class CFA5600/4000) at 8.42am on Wednesday, Friday and Sunday and arrives at 7.30pm.

## DJOUGOU

Djougou is a lively crossroads town 134km northwest of Parakou, bustling with people passing through on the way to Natitingou and Togo. You are now entering Djende country, where Bertoolay replaces Yovo as the nickname of choice for white folk.

For hiking opportunities, the Tanéka villages around Badjoudè, near the Togo border, are very picturesque.

There is a Bank of Africa, and Internet access south of the town centre at **Cyber** ( ☎ 97 68 72 63; per hr CFA500).

**Motel du Lac** ( ☎ 23 80 15 48; Route de Savalou; r CFA10,500-14,500; P ⊗ ) The beds have seen better days in this French-owned hotel 3km from town, but the rooms have balconies and there's a great *paillote* restaurant (meals CFA2500 to CFA4000).

**Motel de Djougou** ( ☎ 23 80 01 40; r CFA5000-12,500; ⊗ ) Situated in grounds with the odd burnt-out car and the vague feel of a *Mad Max* film set, the hotel's round bungalows are shabby but tick the basic boxes. Meals are available for CFA2000 to CFA3500.

**Le Quasar** ( ☎ 23 80 00 49; meals from CFA1700) Beninese food served with a touch of class.

For cheap food, try Royal Verdue, next to Cinema Sabini, or the streets coming off the roundabout. For a cheap omelette in the morning, head to Chez Basile, in front of Motel de Djougou.

Good nightspots include Royal Verdue, nearby Buvette La Flamboyant and New Jacks nightclub, west of town.

If travelling to Kara, there are connections to the border. Bush taxis travelling between Parakou and Natitingou generally stop in Djougou. You may have to change a few times if you plan to travel down the quiet Savalou road by bush taxi – Confort Lines buses are a better option on this route (see p125).

## NATITINGOU
### pop 105,000

About 200km northwest of Parakou and pleasantly located at an altitude of 440m in the Atakora mountains, Natitingou is the most vibrant town in northern Benin thanks to funding from President Kérékou, who was born here. It's the starting point for excursions into Somba country and the Parc National de la Pendjari.

The **Musée d'Arts et de Traditions Populaires** ( ☎ 95 95 93 63; admission CFA1000; ⊗ 8.30am-12.30pm & 3.30-6.30pm Mon-Fri, 9am-noon & 4-6.30pm Sat & Sun), behind Hôtel de Bourgogne, gives an overview of life in Somba communities. The exhibition includes various musical instruments, jewellery, crowns and artefacts from dances, circumcision ceremonies and other Somba rituals. Most interesting is the habitat room, which has models of the different types of *tata somba* (Somba houses; see opposite).

You could also visit **Kota Falls**, 15km southeast of Natitingou, off the main highway on a well-maintained dirt road. It's a great spot for a picnic, and for at least half the year during the rainy season, you can swim in the pool at the bottom of the falls. It's also worth checking out the Fula **botanic gardens** ( ⊗ 8am-noon & 3-6.30pm) in Papatia, half way between Djougou and Natitingou.

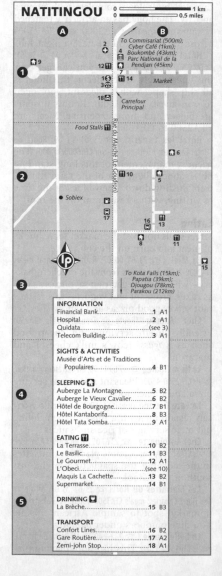

| INFORMATION | | |
|---|---|---|
| Financial Bank | 1 | A1 |
| Hospital | 2 | A1 |
| Quidata | (see 3) | |
| Telecom Building | 3 | A1 |

| SIGHTS & ACTIVITIES | | |
|---|---|---|
| Musée d'Arts et de Traditions Populaires | 4 | B1 |

| SLEEPING 🏠 | | |
|---|---|---|
| Auberge La Montagne | 5 | B2 |
| Auberge le Vieux Cavalier | 6 | B2 |
| Hôtel de Bourgogne | 7 | B1 |
| Hôtel Kantaborifa | 8 | B3 |
| Hôtel Tata Somba | 9 | A1 |

| EATING 🍴 | | |
|---|---|---|
| La Terrasse | 10 | B2 |
| Le Basilic | 11 | B3 |
| Le Gourmet | 12 | A1 |
| L'Obeci | (see 10) | |
| Maquis La Cachette | 13 | B2 |
| Supermarket | 14 | B1 |

| DRINKING 🍸 | | |
|---|---|---|
| La Brèche | 15 | B3 |

| TRANSPORT | | |
|---|---|---|
| Confort Lines | 16 | B2 |
| Gare Routière | 17 | A1 |
| Zemi-john Stop | 18 | A1 |

## Sleeping

**Hôtel Tata Somba** ( ☎ 23 82 11 24; fax 82 15 84; r CFA28,000-30,500; P ⊠ ☑ ) Natitingou's top hotel, a large pink version of a *tata somba* house, helps guests set up trips to the national park. It has a pool and tennis court, both of which are open to non-guests (CFA3000 and CFA1000). The *menu du jour* is CFA6500.

**Hôtel de Bourgogne** ( ☎ /fax 23 82 22 40; www .natitingou.org/bourgogne; s CFA20,500; ⊠ ) This two-storey hotel, on the main road at the northern end of town, is a good, cheap alternative to Hôtel Tata Somba. The *menu du jour* is CFA5500

**Auberge le Vieux Cavalier** ( ☎ 23 82 13 24; fan/air-con CFA5500/8000; ⊠ ) With amicable staff and a courtyard decorated with murals and sculptures, this is the most fun of Natitingou's hotels. Its restaurant (meals CFA1500 to CFA1800) and small, clean rooms with mozzie nets are an excellent budget choice.

**Hôtel Kantaborifa** ( ☎ 23 82 17 66; s/d with fan CFA6500/8500, with air-con CFA12,500/14,500; ⊠ ) This dependable midrange option is handy for Confort Lines buses, which leave from here. Meals are CFA1500.

**Auberge la Montagne** ( ☎ 23 82 11 16; r CFA5500-6500) Up the hill from La Terrasse, the rooms in this basic auberge are good value and it has a restaurant (meals CFA1500 to CFA3500).

## Eating & Drinking

**La Brèche** ( ☎ 90 92 43 20; menu du jour CFA4000) A strong contender to be the most culturally enlightening bar in the world, this *buvette* is in no less than a *tata somba* house with views of the Atakora mountains.

Natitingou has a fine array of places to grab a beer and a bite. Try **Le Gourmet** (Rue du Marché; meals CFA1700-2000), a good place to meet Somba guides; the 24-hour **Le Basilic** (meals CFA2800-3500), up the hill from Hôtel Kanta-borifa; **La Terrasse** (Rue du Marché) and **L'Obeci** (Rue du Marché), both next to Ciné Atacora; and **Maquis La Cachette**, 500m south of Auberge la Montagne.

Food stalls line Rue du Marché and there is a supermarket, Quidata, opposite the Financial Bank.

## Getting There & Away

From the *gare routière* on the main road, bush taxis and minibuses go to Parakou (CFA4000, five hours), although it is often quicker to get a connection in Djougou. There are also daily minibuses to Cotonou (CFA8500, 10 hours) and bush taxis to the Togo and Burkina Faso borders.

More comfortable is the daily Confort Lines bus from Natitingou to Cotonou (CFA7500, 10 hours), leaving at 7am from outside Hôtel Kantaborifa, its representative in Natitingou.

## BOUKOUMBÉ

On the Togo border, 43km southwest of Natitingou, Boukoumbé is the capital of Somba country. The drive there is stunning, bumping along red *piste* (rough track) roads past corn fields and baobab trees as wide as the nearby *tata somba* houses. About 15km

---

**THE SOMBA**

Commonly referred to as the Somba, the Betamaribé people are concentrated to the southwest of Natitingou in the plains of Boukoumbé on the Togo border, and to the southeast around Perma. They live in the middle of their cultivated fields, rather than together in villages, so their compounds are scattered over the countryside. This custom is a reflection of their fierce individuality, which has seen them resist both Dahomey slave hunters and the advance of Christianity and Islam.

The Dutamari-speaking Betamaribé's principle religion is animism – as seen in the rags and bottles they hang from the trees. Once famous for their nudity, they began wearing clothes in the 1970s, but they still hunt with bows and arrows.

What's most fascinating about the Betamaribé is their *tata somba* houses – round, tiered huts that look like miniature forts with clay turrets and thatched spires. There are some 10 types of them, including the *otchaou*, which is the same as the houses built by the Betamaribé's Tamberma relations nearby in Togo (see p800). The ground floor of the house is mostly reserved for livestock and defence mechanisms. A stepladder leads from the kitchen to the roof terrace, where there are sleeping quarters and grain stores.

before town you'll pass the sheer cliffs of Mt Koussou-Kovangou (589m), one of Benin's highest mountains. About 3km further on is the **Belvédère de Koussou-Kovangou** observation point.

Boukoumbé feels like a village at the end of the world but it has a lively market, where the Somba people gather for a few calabashes of *tchoukoutou* (sorghum beer). Every four years or so in late October or early November, there is a whipping ceremony, in which the young men belt each other black and blue to demonstrate their manliness. Boukoumbé is one of the few areas in Benin where you can buy the rare traditional smoking pipes.

The incredible **Auberge Villegoise de Tourisme de Koussou-Kovangou** ( ☎ 23 82 13 27; r CFA3500-4500) has 11 rooms in a *tata somba* house and in some less basic, *tata somba*-style bungalows. Signposted on the left 16km before Boukombé. Bring a torch. Meals are CFA2000.

**Chez Pascaline** ( ☎ 23 83 02 02; meals CFA1000-1500), near the rond-point in the middle of the village, is the best place to eat. Ask here to find a guide or to stay the night with a Somba family (CFA3000).

Accommodation can also be arranged at the Maison de Jeune – contact the **town hall** ( ☎ 23 83 01 02).

It's easiest to find a taxi from Natitingou to Boukoumbé (CFA2000, two hours) on market day, which happens every four days. Taxis do go on other days, or you can grab a *zemi-john* (CFA5000 return).

## PARC NATIONAL DE LA PENDJARI

This 275,000-hectare **national park** (admission per person CFA10,000, per vehicle CFA3000; ☒ 15 Dec-15 May), 45km north of Natitingou, is the wildlife park *par excellence* in this part of West Africa. Visitors may spot lions, leopards, elephants, baboons and hippos. The best viewing time is near the end of the dry season when the animals start to hover around the water holes.

With waterfalls, a woody landscape and good tracks, it is a pleasure to drive around.

The park adjoins the Parc National d'Arli in Burkina Faso and is bordered to the west, north and east by the Pendjari River. It's much more developed for tourism than the Benin section of Parc Regional du W, so receives more visitors.

The entrance fee is valid for 30 days. In reality, you may have to pay a lot more by the time you've factored in additional charges such as the photography fee (per day CFA3000) and the compulsory guide (per day CFA5000), who will expect to be provided with food and water.

There is an **office** ( ☎ 23 83 00 85; www.pendjari .net) in Tanguiéta. A guidebook, *Guide Pratique de la Pendjari* (CFA5500), is available from bookshops in Cotonou (see p95) and boutiques at the better hotels.

### Sleeping & Eating

Many visitors stay in Natitingou and make excursions from there, but you'll have a better chance of seeing animals if you stay at the park itself. Due to the presence of lions, there are only certain areas, including Mare Yangouali and Pont d'Arli, where camping is permitted. Park wardens show you where.

There are some rustic campements in Tanguiéta, at the southern tip of the park near the river and a waterfall. The town's best option is the well-run Hôtel Baobab, which has a good restaurant.

**Campement Relais de Tanougou** (bungalows Dec-May CFA9000) At the Tanougou Falls, well located for an early-morning walk and swim. The circular bungalows have a bathroom behind a dividing wall. Prices are 25% cheaper during low season. Meals are CFA3500. Some 15km southwest of the Batia park entrance. Book with **Hôtel Tata Somba** ( ☎ 23 82 11 24) in Natitingou.

**Hôtel Campement de Porga** (r with air-con CFA28000; ☒ ) Right at the main entrance to the park, it's a larger place with a restaurant, bungalows and basic rooms available. Again, book with **Hôtel Tata Somba** ( ☎ 23 82 11 24).

### Getting There & Away

The main entrances to Pendjari are roughly 100km north of Natitingou. To get to the park from Natitingou, take the *goudron* (bitumen road) 97km northwest to Porga near the Burkina Faso border. This village is the main entrance to the park.

Alternatively, turn off the sealed road at Tanguiéta, 45km from Natitingou, and take the *piste* (rough track) 41km northeast to Batia, the other entrance. Many people prefer this because the route is shorter.

As hiking is not permitted in the park, backpackers without vehicles can try to hitch

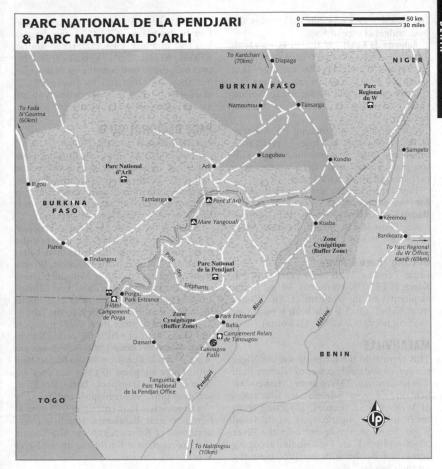

## PARC NATIONAL DE LA PENDJARI & PARC NATIONAL D'ARLI

a lift at the hotels in Natitingou, Porga and Batia. It is possible to hire a vehicle – inquire at the park office or at hotels including **Hôtel Tata Somba** ( ☎ 23 82 11 24). Travel agencies in Cotonou organise trips, but they are expensive.

## KANDI & AROUND

Kandi, 213km north of Parakou on the way to Niger, is worth a stop for its market. The Bariba and Fula people – originally from Nigeria and Niger respectively – and the voluptuous mango trees give this town its distinctive northern character.

Some 40km north of Kandi on the road to Malanville, just north of the village of Alfa Koura, is an accessible wing of the Parc Regional du W, where you can view elephants and many species of antelope. Readers have reported seeing up to 50 elephants in one day bathing and drinking in the water hole. The beautiful area is also worth a look during the wet season – you might see a crocodile.

It's CFA2500 for a day's entry to the park, including camping, and CFA500 for a guide. There are some basic rooms (CFA5000) and a restaurant (meals CFA3500), open during the wet season.

### Sleeping & Eating

**Auberge la Recontre** ( ☎ /fax 23 63 01 76; r with fan/ air-con incl breakfast CFA7500/14,500; ✱ ) The rooms are stuffy, and the cheaper ones share a bathroom, but the rooftop restaurant (*menu du jour* CFA4500) makes this the best budget choice in Kandi.

**Auberge de Kandi** ( ☎ 23 63 02 43; www.hotels -benin.com; camping per person CFA2500, r with fan/air-con CFA10,500/15,000; ☒ ) This auberge 2km north of Kandi has sizeable rooms, attractive gardens and its French restaurant (meals CFA3800 to CFA4000) is the best in town.

A barbecue at the turning for Auberge le Recontre dishes out bags of meat with onion and spices. Ask near the Sonapra cotton plant at lunchtime for a woman who prepares sublime mashed yam.

Popular places to drink include **Oasis Bar** (Route de Ndali), south of the market, and **Maquis C'est Ca Meme** (Route de Ndali), south of town. There is a nightclub, **Tropicana** (admission CFA2000), behind the maquis.

### Getting There & Away

From Parakou, bush taxis head north to Kandi (CFA3000, 3½ hours). To get to the elephant viewing platform at Alfa Koura from Kandi, catch a ride with a bush taxi heading north (CFA1000, 1½ hours).

## MALANVILLE

This town is in the far north on the Niger border, considerably closer to Niamey than it is to Cotonou, 733km away. Market day, held on Friday and Saturday, is a who's who of West African peoples, attracting traders from Togo, Nigeria, Burkina Faso and Niger. Stand on the bridge over the River Niger and you'll see Fula women trudging across the border with produce teetering on their heads.

**La Sota** ( ☎ 97 64 97 48; r with fan/air-con & TV CFA12,500/15,500, ste CFA17,500; ☒ ☒ ☒ ) Malanville's smartest hotel, formerly called Hôtel de Luxe, is 2km south of town on the banks of the River Sota. Meals are CFA2500 to CFA4800.

**Rose des Sables** ( ☎ 23 67 01 25; r with fan/air-con/ air-con & TV CFA5500/10,500/18,500; ☒ ) One kilometre south of town, is slightly battered but has reasonable facilities. Group discounts available. Meals are CFA2500.

Near the market, **Sous les Neems** (meals CFA300) serves *wagassi* (cow's milk cheese), *pâté* and cold beers. *Buvettes* and food stalls, selling everything from mashed yam to sugared pancakes, line the main road through town.

Malanville is well connected with Parakou by bush taxi (CFA4500, five hours), bus and minibus (CFA3000, seven hours). EHGM, STN and SNTV buses travel between Cotonou and Niamey via Malanville, but they are often full up (see p125). A *zemi-john* to Gaya in Niger, where you can get taxis to Niamey, is about CFA1000.

## PARC REGIONAL DU W

**Parc Regional du W** (admission CFA10,000; ☒ 1 Dec-15 Jun) covers 10,242 sq km in Burkina Faso, Niger and Benin, where the largest section of the park is. It was one of the first Unesco-recognised biospheres worldwide. You may see several species of cat and antelope, buffalos, hippos, crocodiles and elephants.

Although W is twice as large as Pendjari, it has traditionally been the less popular park, partly because the latter had better access and infrastructure. However, W now has a bridge over the River Mékrou, plans to tarmac the road between Kandi and Banikoara, and lodges with restaurants in locations including Koudou, right next to the falls.

Visitors need their own 4WD transport and guide, both of which the park's Kandi-based **Bureau de Liaison** ( ☎ 23 63 00 80; www.parc -w.org; ☒ 8am-12.30pm & 2pm-late Mon-Fri) can help with. There are plans to make the park accessible to other transport – horse, foot, bike, car, even pirogues for hippo-watching.

The park has four entrances in Benin: at Kérémou near Banikoara, which is 69km northwest of Kandi; Sampéto, Alfa Kouara and Kofonou, near Karimama on the Niger border.

# BENIN DIRECTORY

## ACCOMMODATION

Basic rooms with a fan cost about CFA6000, while comfortable air-conditioned mid-range rooms are around CFA10,000. Bathrooms are generally en suite. Tariffs should include the tourist tax of CFA500, and be listed prominently at the hotel entrance. Top End prices range from CFA70,000 to over CFA100,000.

The 'Auberge de' chain has consistently good hotels in Grand Popo, Dassa Zoumé, Savalou, Parakou and Kandi. Central reservations can be made on ☎ 21 31 38 62 or www.hotels-benin.com.

## ACTIVITIES

The beaches around Cotonou are fairly ordinary, and prone to muggings. For better sunbathing and swimming, head to Grand Popo (p108), although the currents are strong right along the coast. Many of the large hotels have swimming pools and tennis courts open to nonguests.

If you get the chance, hire a bicycle (but don't expect 18-speed mountain bikes) and cycle around Porto Novo (p103) or Abomey (p110).

There are few organised hikes but there is nothing to prevent you walking from village to village on the shores of Lake Nokoué (p102) or Lake Ahémè (p109), taking pirogue rides for some stretches; or along quiet back roads in the north of the country.

A good area for rock climbing is Dassa Zoumé (p113) and Savé.

You can kayak on the lagoon at Casa Del Papa (p107) in Ouidah. Other hotels that organise activities for guests include Awale Plage (p109) in Grand Popo and Village Club Ahémè in Possotomè (p109).

## BOOKS

*The Viceroy of Ouidah,* by Bruce Chatwin, is a biographical sketch of the notorious Brazilian slave trader Francisco da Silva and how he and the kings of Dahomey built the trade. The vivid novella begins with a 20th-century reunion of the da Silva clan and moves back to the original Afro-Brazilian himself via his descendents, their dreams and disappointments.

*Instruments of Darkness,* by Robert Wilson, is the debut of this award-winning thriller writer, following an English 'fixer' through the Cotonou underworld as he searches for a fellow expat who has mysteriously disappeared.

*Show Me the Magic,* by Annie Caulfield, is a slightly glib but entertaining account by this English comic writer, who has collaborated with the comedian Lenny Henry, of travelling around Benin in a taxi. She and her driver repeated the journey with Spice Girl Mel B for the documentary *Mel B Vodou Princess.*

## BUSINESS HOURS

Businesses are open from 8am to 12.30pm and 3pm to 6.30pm Monday to Friday. The banks are generally open 8am to 12.30pm and 3pm to 5pm Monday to Friday. Shops are open from 9am to noon and 3pm to 7pm Monday to Friday and until noon on Saturday.

## COURSES

There are Fon, Tai Chi and martial arts courses available in Cotonou (p98).

## DANGERS & ANNOYANCES

Tourists should be on their guard in southern Benin, which suffers from the crimes normally associated with tourism.

Muggings are a real danger on Cotonou's shoreline, even during the day (see p97). Never walk on the beach alone, and even when walking with someone, don't carry or wear valuables. At night, take a taxi if you want to travel in Cotonou, and in Ouidah avoid the roads to and along the coast.

Benin's beaches are plagued by dangerous currents – seek local advice before swimming.

## EMBASSIES & CONSULATES
### Beninese Embassies & Consulates

In West Africa, Benin has embassies and consulates in Côte d'Ivoire, Ghana, Niger, Nigeria and Senegal. For details, see the relevant country chapter.

In Africa, Benin also has representation in Algeria, Democratic Republic of the Congo, Gabon and Libya.

Elsewhere, Beninese embassies and consulates include the following:

**Belgium** ( ☎ 02-35 9471; 5 Ave de l'Observatoire, 1180 Brussels)

**Canada** ( ☎ 613-233 4429; www.benin.ca; 58 Glebe Ave, Ottawa K1S 2C3)

**France** ( ☎ 01-45 00 98 82; www.ambassade-benin.org; 87 Ave Victor Hugo, 75016 Paris)

**Germany** ( ☎ 0228-34 40 31; Rüdigerstrasse 10 Post-Sech, 228-5300 Bonn)

**UK** ( ☎ 020-8954 8800; fax 44 20 8954 8844; Dolphin House, 16 The Broadway, Stanmore, Middlesex HA7 4DW)

**USA** ( ☎ 202-232 6656; fax 202-239 6500; 2737 Cathedral Ave, Washington, DC)

### Embassies & Consulates in Benin

Embassies in Cotonou include the following, open Monday to Friday:

**France** Consulate ( ☎ 21 31 26 38; Rue 651A); Embassy ( ☎ 21 30 02 25; Route de l'Aéroport)

**Germany** ( ☎ 21 31 29 68; Ave Jean Paul II; ⊙ 9am-12pm)

**Ghana** ( ☎ 21 30 07 46; Route de l'Aéroport; ⊙ 8am-2pm)

**Niger** ( ☎ 21 31 56 65; Rue 651A; ⊙ 8am-noon & 3-6pm)

**Nigeria** ( ☎ 21 30 11 42; Blvd de la Marina; ⊙ 10-11.30am)

**UK** ( ☎ 21 30 12 74; Haie Vive) Officially, British Nationals must deal with the British Deputy High Commission in Lagos (p666). However, the Community Liaison Officer for the British community in Benin, Pauline Collins, based at the English International School, can be of some help.

**USA** ( ☎ 21 30 06 50; cotonou.usembassy.gov; Rue Caporal Bernard Anani)

## FESTIVALS & EVENTS

Apart from the colourful annual Muslim celebrations in the northern towns – Djougo and Natitingou are especially good places to see them – the main event is the annual Voodoo Festival, held in Ouidah on 10 January (see p107).

Every four years or so, in late October or early November, there is the coming-of-age 'whipping ceremony' in Boukombé, which seems to go on until the young men are satisfied that they have literally beaten each other black and blue.

There are frequent minor voodoo celebrations in Ouidah, Abomey and on the shores of Lake Ahémè.

## HOLIDAYS

Public holidays include the following:

**New Year's Day** 1 January
**Vodoun** 10 January
**Martyr's Day** 16 January
**Liberation Day** 28 February
**Labour Day** 1 May
**Independence** 1 August
**Armed Forces Day** 26 October
**Republic Day** 4 December
**Harvest Day** 31 December

Benin also celebrates the usual Christian and Muslim holidays. See p818 for a table of dates of Islamic holidays.

## MAPS

The best map by far is the 1:600,000 *République du Benin Carte Générale*, produced by the Institut Geographique National. With good country detail and insert city maps of Porto Novo and Cotonou, it costs about CFA7500 in Cotonou bookshops.

## MONEY

The unit of currency in Benin is the West Africa CFA (Comunauté Financiere Africaine) franc. Cash advances against credit cards (Visa only) are possible at the major banks in Cotonou. The best banks for changing money are Financial Bank, Bank of Africa, Ecobank and BTCI, which also often have ATMs.

Benin's neighbours all use CFAs apart from Nigeria, where the currency is the Nairi. There is no official way to get hold of Nairi in Benin but Cotonou has a healthy black market around the Jonquet district and Gare du Dantokpa.

Banks accept travellers cheques in most major currencies, although these can only be reliably changed in Cotonou.

## PHOTOGRAPHY & VIDEO

A photo permit is not required, but be careful when taking shots of cultural and religious buildings and ceremonies. Rules are not clear-cut, so it's best to ask first. A *cadeau* may be requested. For general information see p823.

## SOLO TRAVELLERS

Lone travellers should be on their guard in Cotonou as they may be more susceptible to muggings than groups.

# TELEPHONE

International telephone calls and faxes can be made at telecom offices and private telephone agencies throughout Benin. The cost per minute is about CFA1350 to France, CFA1850 elsewhere in Europe, CFA1400 to North America, and CFA2640 to Australasia.

## Phone Codes

The phone codes had recently been updated at the time of writing. Numbers in the Ouémé and Plateau areas (including Porto Novo) are now prefixed with 20; the Littoral and Atlantique areas (including Cotonou and Ouidah) with 21; the Mono, Couffo, Zou and Collines areas (including Grand Popo, Lake Ahémè, Abomey and Dassa Zoumé) with 22; and the Atakora, Donga, Alibori and Borgou areas (Parakou and the north) with 23. Libercom mobile phone numbers are now prefixed with 90, BBCom (Bell Benin) with 93, Telecel with 95, and Areeba with 97.

# TOURIST INFORMATION

There is a lacklustre tourist office in Cotonou, and, in northern Benin, offices of the two wildlife parks. Hôtel Tata Somba (p117) in Natitingou is also a good place to inquire about Parc National de la Pendjari.

# VISAS

Visas are required for all travellers except nationals of the Ecowas. If flying into Cotonou you will require a visa before arrival. A 30-day, single-entry visa costs UK£55 from the Beninese consulate in the UK; the embassy in the USA charges less.

If crossing overland, it's far easier to get a visa at the border, where the 24-hour posts issue 48-hour, single-entry transit visas (CFA10,000).

You can then obtain a 30-day, single- or multiple-entry visa (CFA12,000) in Cotonou. The **Direction Emigration Immigration** ( ☎ 21 31 42 13; Ave Jan Paul II, Cotonou; ☯ 8am-11am, 3-6.30pm) accepts applications between 8am and 11am Monday to Friday. These can be collected at 6pm the following working day, though it may be possible to speed the process up if you ask. You will need one passport photo. The office also offers the five-country Visa Touristique Entente for CFA25,000 (see p828).

## Visa Extensions

Only available in Cotonou at the **Direction Emigration Immigration** ( ☎ 21 31 42 13; Ave Jan Paul II, Cotonou; ☯ 8am-11am, 3-6.30pm).

## Visas For Onward Travel

For onward travel to Burkina Faso, Côte d'Ivoire and Togo, the French consulate issues three-month visas (CFA20,000) and transit visas (CFA6000) in 24 to 48 hours, with two photos required. However, it may be preferable, if more expensive, to get the five-country Visa Touristique Entente (CFA25,000) at the Beninese Direction Emigration Immigration (see p828).

### GHANA

Ghanaian visas take two days to issue and cost CFA12,000/30,000 for single/multiple entry. Four photos are required.

### NIGER

For Niger, it is, again, worth considering the Visa Touristique Entente (see p828). It costs about the same as the three-month visas issued by the Niger embassy, which takes 24 hours to process applications and requires two photos.

### NIGERIA

The Nigerian embassy issues only two-day transit visas to travellers with a Nigerian embassy in their home country. You need two photos, along with photocopies of your passport and, if you have one, your ticket for onward travel from Nigeria. The expensive visas vary according to nationality (CFA30,000 for UK, CFA68,000 for US, CFA20,000 for Australia) and are issued on the same day.

### TOGO

Seven-day visas for Togo (CFA10,000) are also issued at the border (see p804).

# WOMEN TRAVELLERS

Travelling in Benin presents few problems for women. Beyond the usual 'Where is your husband?' curiosity, the greatest annoyance is unwanted attention, especially from officials. The best tack in these situations is to say you are waiting for your husband.

As with anywhere in the world use common sense – don't wander around solo at night, especially in Cotonou, where the beach is a definite no-go area during the day.

While it is not necessary to cover yourself from head to toe, it is advisable to dress in a modest fashion. If in doubt, look at what the local women are wearing and follow suit. For more advice, see p828.

# TRANSPORT IN BENIN

## GETTING THERE & AWAY
### Entering Benin

Benin's immigration regulations and officials are awkward. If flying into the country, you cannot obtain a visa on arrival. However, you can if entering by land, but the visa is only valid for 48 hours, and can only be extended in Cotonou. Officially you need a yellow fever certificate, but you rarely have to show it.

### Air

The main airport is on the western fringe of Cotonou, in Cocotiers.

Air France has the most reliable and frequent services between Benin and Europe.

For flight information, ticket sales and reconfirmations, the following airlines have offices in Cotonou:

**Air France** (AF; ☎ 21 30 18 15; www.airfrance.com/bj; Route de l'Aéroport) Hub: Paris.

**Air Gabon International** (GN; ☎ 21 31 21 87; Blvd Steinmetz) Hub: Libreville.

**Air Ivoire** (VU; ☎ 21 31 86 14; Blvd Steinmetz) Hub: Abidjan.

**Air Togo** (YT) Hub: Lomé.

**Ghana International Airlines** (GH; ☎ 21 31 42 83; Blvd Steinmetz) Hub: Accra.

**Point-Afrique** (6V/DR; ☎ 95 84 85; www.point-afrique .com; Quartier Cocotiers) Hub: Paris.

**Virgin Nigeria Airways** (VK; ☎ 21 31 58 24; Blvd du Gouverneur Ballot) Hub: Lagos.

### Land
#### BURKINA FASO

There's at least one bush taxi a day along the 97km of tarred road from Natitingou to Porga (CFA1500, two hours), where you can cross to Tindangou in Burkina Faso. Monday, Porga market day, is a good day to find a ride.

#### NIGER

From Malanville, 733km from Cotonou on tarred road, a *zemi-john* or shared taxi can take you across the River Niger to Gaya in Niger (*zemi-john*/shared taxi CFA1000/500). The border is open 24/7 and it is quite straightforward to pick up visas there for both countries.

From Gaya, it's easier to find a Peugeot bush taxi to Niamey (CFA4500, five hours) or a minibus (CFA4100, 5½ hours) than it is to squeeze onto one of the Cotonou–Niamey coaches, which are usually full.

Heading south, there are no longer Peugeots or minibuses from Niamey to Malanville, Parakou or Cotonou. Instead, get to Gaya and walk or *moto-taxi* it to the border and Malanville, from where bush taxis head south.

#### NIGERIA

In Cotonou, bush taxis and minibuses leave for Lagos throughout the day from the Gare de l'Ancien Pont (CFA3000, three hours), as well as from the Gare de Dantokpa. You could save money by taking a taxi to the border crossing at Kraké and changing there, as Nigerian taxis are cheaper than those in Benin. If you do this, you will need to get some Naira at the border or on the black market in Cotonou (see p97). There are also taxis to Lagos from Porto Novo (CFA2700, 2½ hours), which is both closer to Nigeria and less hectic than Cotonou.

Avoid arriving or leaving Lagos at rush hour (the 'go slow' between 6am and 10am, and 3pm and 7pm) – it's a mess. If you're heading to Ibadan, Lagos can be bypassed by crossing at Kétou, though there is less public transport.

You may have to grease a few palms at Kraké (see p670), although asking for a receipt is a good way to discourage corrupt officials. If hiring a taxi across the border, check whether the price includes bribes.

#### TOGO

Cotonou and Lomé are connected by frequent bush taxis (CFA3000, three hours), which regularly leave the Gare de Jonquet in Cotonou for Lomé through the day and the early evening. Alternatively, pick up a taxi to the border point at Hilla-Condji and grab another taxi on the Togolese side of the frontier. There is also a daily STIF bus service from Cotonou to Lomé (CFA3000, three hours).

Other crossings are at Kémérida, northeast of Kara in Togo, and between Nadoba in Togo and Boukombé in Benin. The latter crossing takes you through spectacular countryside but you would need to be well organised, with your own 4WD vehicle.

**BUS**

**STC** ( ☎ 21 32 66 69) runs buses between Cotonou and Abidjan (CFA34000, 28 hours) via Accra (CFA15,000, seven hours).

**EHGM** ( ☎ 227 74 37 16), **STN** ( ☎ 227 74 03 69) and **SNTV** ( ☎ 227 73 30 20) are among the Niger-based coach lines that ply the route between Cotonou and Niamey. SNTV's buses leave Niamey daily at 4am (CFA20,000, 13 to 15 hours) and EHGM's leave on Tuesday, Thursday, Saturday and Sunday at 4am (CFA18700, 13 to 15 hours).

Buses stop in major towns such as Parakou and Malanville, but they are hard to get on as they fill up when they set off.

Burkina Faso–based TVC (see p170) has a Sunday bus from Ougadougou to Cotonou (CFA20,000) which continues to Lagos (CFA30,500).

## GETTING AROUND
### Bush Taxi, Minibus & Bus

Minibuses and bush taxis are the principal means of transport between towns, and are faster than in many West African countries. A bush taxi from Cotonou costs CFA600 to Ouidah, CFA2000 to Abomey, CFA3000 to Lagos or Lomé and CFA6500 to Parakou, while minibuses cost about 25% less and take much longer. There is sometimes a negotiable surcharge for luggage.

There are few domestic bus companies. **Confort Lines** ( ☎ 21 32 58 15) runs daily buses between Cotonou and Natitingou via Savalou (CFA7500, 10 hours), stopping in all major towns en route. There are free sandwiches and the conductors are faithful to the company's boast that there are no hidden charges. Benin Routes has daily buses between Cotonou and Parakou (CFA5500, five hours).

It is best to book ahead, particularly on buses between Cotonou and Niamey. The buses are, as usual in Africa, overloaded with passengers and luggage, but they are still more comfortable, and often cheaper, than bush taxis.

### Car & Motorcycle

Petrol costs between CFA300 and CFA600 per litre, with prices generally rising as you travel north. The price fluctuates because

of instability in Nigeria, on which Benin depends for petrol. In Nigeria petrol is cheaper, so much of it is carried illegally across the border into Benin and sold on the black market at prices slightly below the official rate. Just look for the guys along the roads with 1L to 5L bottles.

For private transport, organise a taxi through one of the major hotels in Cotonou, though this can prove costly. The taxis outside the Hôtel du Port are better value than those outside the Novotel Orisha and Benin Marina Hotel.

If you're driving, you need an International Driving Permit. Roads are in good condition throughout Benin.

### Local Transport
**TAXI**

Fares for regular journeys in taxis and minibuses in Cotonou are CFA150 for a shared ride. Taxis can be hired for CFA2000 per hour; rates increase from early evening on. Tariffs are often written on the dashboard. Gare du Dantokpa is a good place to find taxis.

**ZEMI-JOHNS**

In nearly all towns, you'll find *zemi-johns* (scooter taxis). While they are by far the fastest and most convenient way of getting around the cities, they are not as safe as regular taxis. Cotonou sees *zemi-john* crashes everyday – often fatal ones. Tell your driver to drive slowly.

You'll recognise them by the driver's yellow and green shirt (green and purple in some regional centres). Hail them just as you would a taxi, and be sure to agree on a price before the journey. The typical fare is CFA150 to CFA250. They are also an easy way to get to remote destinations.

### Tours

Two- and seven-day tours are available in restored colonial railroad cars on **La Train d'Ebene** ( ☎ 21 31 38 62). The shorter tour (CFA50,000 or CFA40,000 per person for groups of 12 or more) departs Cotonou on Thursday morning for Dassa Zoumé, where you can walk in the hills and visit an ostrich farm. Meals are served onboard. The longer tour (CFA250,000/200,000) also takes in towns not on the railway – Ganvié, Ouidah, Grand Popo, Abomey and Natitingou.

For ecotourism, **CPN Les Papillons** ( ☎ 22 54 07 13; cpnlespapillons@yahoo.com), an NGO based in the village of Camaté-Shakaloké, 10km from Dassa Zoumé, hosts groups of tourists and offers trips to other parts of Benin.

A recommended guide is Cotonou-based **Franck Tok** ( ☎ 95 05 61 04; tokfranck@yahoo.fr). A language facilitator for the Peace Corps, he is fluent in both English and French.

## Train

Run by **L'Organisation Commune Benin-Niger des Chemins de fer et Transports** ( ☎ 21 32 22 06), Benin's one railway line links Cotonou with Parakou via towns including Bohicon (for Abomey) and Dassa Zoumé. Cheap and spacious but frustratingly slow, the train leaves Cotonou at 8.30am on Tuesday, Thursday and Saturday, arriving in Parakou at 7pm and returning south at 8.42am the following day. Get to the station before 8am to buy tickets.

Second-class seats on the train are significantly cheaper than taking a bush taxi but the carriages tend to be crowded with humanity and produce. First class is about as comfortable as you'll find on any train in West Africa. It has a rudimentary bar, and food is available at stations along the way.

Tickets in 1st/2nd class from Cotonou to Bohicon (about four hours) cost CFA1400/1100, to Dassa Zoumé (about five hours) cost CFA2900/2500, and to Parakou (about 11 hours) cost CFA5600/4000.

# Burkina Faso

Standing at the geographical heart of West Africa, Burkina Faso (formerly Haute or Upper Volta, or just Burkina to the locals) is likely to appear on most travellers' itineraries, but it's so much more than a staging post en route to somewhere else. It's the sort of place that captures the imagination – how many of your friends back home even know that Burkina Faso exists? – and wins the hearts of travellers with its relaxed pace of life, friendly people and wealth of interesting sights.

From the deserts and unrivalled Gorom-Gorom market in the north, to the green countryside and strange rock formations of the country's southwest, Burkina spans a rich variety of landscapes. The country is also home to a fascinating cultural mix, with the Burkinabé (as people from Burkina Faso are called) almost as diverse as the terrain.

This may be one of the world's poorest countries, but it's also one of the most stable in the region and runs with an efficiency that's the envy of many of its neighbours. Throw in Africa's most important film festival, the delightful small-town atmosphere of Bobo-Dioulasso, wildlife safaris in the south, the enjoyable and gloriously named capital, Ouagadougou (pronounced waga-doo-goo), and there's enough here to transform Burkina from the country that no-one knows to an experience you'll never forget.

---

**FAST FACTS**

- **Area** 274,122 sq km
- **Capital** Ouagadougou
- **Country code** ☎ 226
- **Famous for** The coolest name for a capital city in the world; Thomas Sankara, Africa's Che Guevara
- **Languages** French, Moré, Fulfulde and Lobi
- **Money** West African CFA franc; US$1 = CFA544.89; €1 = CFA655.96
- **Population** 11.9 million
- **Visa** Available at borders (CFA10,000) or Burkina Faso embassies (up to CFA30,000)

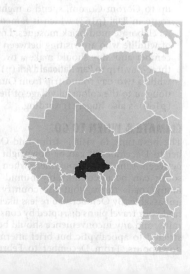

## HIGHLIGHTS

■ **Gorom-Gorom's Thursday market** (p163) Lose yourself in one of West Africa's most colourful experiences.

■ **Bobo-Dioulasso** (p148) Kick back in the languid charm of the old quarter and check out the beautiful Grande Mosquée.

■ **Sindou Peaks** (p158) Track down hippos and explore the other-worldly landscape here, near Banfora.

■ **Bani** (p163) Marvel at the intricate decoration of the seven mud-brick mosques in this small town.

■ **Parc National d'Arli** (p159) Search for wildlife in the country's remote southeast.

## ITINERARIES

■ **One Week** If you only have a week at your disposal, charming **Bobo-Dioulasso** (p148) is worth at least two days, and the country around **Banfora** (p155) merits a couple more. Pause for a day in **Ouagadougou** (p134), an unusually friendly and relaxed capital city with an active nightlife, before heading north for the Thursday market of **Gorom-Gorom** (p163) for another two days.

■ **Two Weeks** With two weeks to spare, plan on spending more time in the southwest, especially in Bobo-Dioulasso and around Banfora in the country's 'green' belt; allow at least two extra days. **Gaoua** (p158), in the heart of Lobi country, is also worth a few days. If you're heading up to Gorom-Gorom, spend a night en route in **Bani** (p163) which is famed for its elaborate mud-brick mosques. Lovers of wildlife who are visiting between December and May should make a two- or three-day trip to **Parc National d'Arli** (p159), while a two-day round-trip from Ouagadougou to the colourful village of **Tiébélé** (p160) is also hugely rewarding.

## CLIMATE & WHEN TO GO

The best time to visit is from mid-October to December. It can be downright wet between June and September, when the south can be uncomfortably humid and many roads throughout the country are impassable. By October you're less likely to find your travel plans disrupted by constant rains, and any inconvenience should be restricted to apocalyptic but brief afternoon downpours. From December to February

---

### HOW MUCH?

■ **Ouagadougou–Bobo-Dioulasso bus ride** CFA6000

■ **Museum admission** CFA1000

■ **Guide per day** CFA10,000-15,000

■ **Internet connection (per hour)** CFA300–750

■ **4WD rental (per day)** CFA40,000 plus petrol

### LONELY PLANET INDEX

■ **1L of petrol** CFA600

■ **1L of bottled water** CFA500

■ **Bottle of beer** CFA750

■ **Souvenir T-shirt** CFA5000

■ **Serve of Riz sauce** CFA500

---

the weather is marginally cooler (although if you've come from colder European climes you're unlikely to think so), with daily maximums only occasionally exceeding 35°C. During this period, the dry heat is more bearable, although dusty harmattan winds can produce hazy skies and sore throats in January and February. The hot season is from March to early June, when the mercury can rise well above 40°C in the capital.

Film enthusiasts won't want to miss Fespaco, Africa's premier film festival, which will run from 24 February to 3 March 2007, and again in 2009. For more information, see the boxed text Fespaco, p133. For other festivals which you may want to attend, see p140.

## HISTORY

By the 14th century, the territory of present-day Burkina Faso was occupied by the peoples who still inhabit the land. The earliest known inhabitants were the Bobo, the Lobi and the Gourounsi, who were in the area by the 13th century. A century later, the Mossi peoples (now almost half of Burkina Faso's population) had begun to move westward from settlements near the Niger River.

The first Mossi kingdom was founded more than 500 years ago in Ouagadougou. Three more Mossi states were subsequently established in other parts of the country,

BURKINA FASO

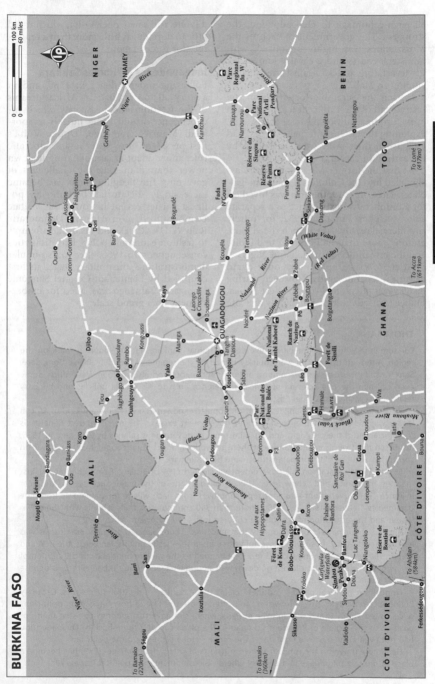

all paying homage to Ouagadougou, the strongest. The government of each of the Mossi states was highly organised, with ministers, courts and a cavalry known for its devastating attacks against the Muslim empires in Mali.

During the Scramble for Africa in the second half of the 19th century, the French broke up the traditional Mossi states, and, exploiting the latter's internal rivalries, had established their sway over the region by the early 20th century.

At first the former Mossi states were assimilated into the Colonie du Haut Sénégal-Niger. Then, in 1919, the area was hived off for administrative expedience as a separate colony, Upper Volta. In 1932, for purely commercial reasons, the French sliced it up, grafting more than half onto Côte d'Ivoire and the remainder onto Mali and Niger.

After WWII, Upper Volta once again became a separate entity. However, during its 60 years of colonial rule in West Africa, France focused its attention mainly on Côte d'Ivoire and saw Upper Volta, which it did little to develop, as little more than a repository for forced labour.

## Independence & Thomas Sankara

Following independence in 1960, and in a story all too familiar in Africa, dreams of the freedom and prosperity which independence would bring quickly evaporated. Maurice Yaméogo, Upper Volta's first president, proved to be an autocratic ruler more adept at consolidating his own power than managing the challenges of governing the fledgling state. He became increasingly dictatorial, banning all political parties except his own, the Voltaic Democratic Union-African Democratic Rally (UDV-RDA), and his crude attempts to fashion economic policy had disastrous consequences. In 1966, after mass popular demonstrations, the military staged its first coup, led by Lieutenant-Colonel Sangoulé Lamizana. Yaméogo was jailed for embezzlement on a grand scale.

### THOM SANK

For someone who ruled for barely five years, Thomas Sankara left an enduring mark on the region. Although his policies were quickly buried by the regime of President Blaise Compaoré, Sankara still inspires reverence among ordinary Burkinabés and elsewhere in West Africa. Some even call him the Che Guevara of Africa, a reference both to his radical policies and his cosy relationship with Cuba's Fidel Castro.

What marked out Thom Sank (as he is still popularly known) as a very different kind of African leader was his determination to stamp out government excess – he made modest Renault 5s the official car of the president and his ministers, cut government salaries by 25% and, in 1985, dismissed most of his cabinet and sent them to work on agricultural cooperatives – his war on corruption and the blitz campaigns that were his trademark.

In one 15-day marathon, his government vaccinated 60% of Burkina Faso's children against measles, meningitis and yellow fever. Unicef called it 'one of the major successes of the year in Africa'. The government also sent representatives from each village for training as front-line paramedics. Between 1983 and 1986, more than 350 communities built schools with their own labour and the education of school-age children increased by one-third to 22%.

But the charisma and blunt honesty that endeared Thom Sank to ordinary Burkinabés was less well received by those with powerful vested interests – trade unions, landlords, the USA and France. His decrees ordering that all rents be handed to the government and his description of rich people as thieves, also did not go down well among Ouagadougou's urban elites. His demise in 1987 came as little surprise.

Opposition political parties routinely claim to be Sankara's rightful successors. Ordinary Burkinabés remain sceptical, however, and often quote the tale of how opposition politicians once visited Thom Sank's wife in exile in Paris, where she gave them money to assist their opposition to the regime of President Compaoré. The plane carrying them back to Ouagadougou had not even arrived before fights over the money broke out among the politicians.

His simple grave on the rubbish-strewn outskirts of Ouagadougou (see p139) has become a place of discreet pilgrimage in a country where disillusionment with political leaders runs high.

In 1970, the military stepped down, allowing a civilian government led by Gérard Ouédraogoto take over under a constitution approved by referendum. In 1974 the army, led again by Lamizana, staged another coup. This time the military rulers suspended the constitution and banned all political activity by getting rid of the opposition, which was driven by one of the most powerful trade unions in Africa. Following a nationwide strike in 1975, the unions, by now the de facto opposition, forced the government to raise wages and, in 1978, got the new constitution and general elections they had been demanding.

Over the next five years there were three more coups. The last and most notable was in November 1982, when Captain Thomas Sankara, an ambitious young left-wing military star, staged a bloody putsch and seized power in the name of the People's Salvation Council.

When, in 1984, Sankara renamed the country Burkina Faso – meaning 'Land of the Incorruptible', or more prosaically, the 'Country of Honest Men' – he set about restructuring the economy to promote self-reliance in rural areas. The economy improved, financial books were kept in good order, debt financing was kept to a minimum, budgetary commitments were adhered to and Burkina Faso was one of few countries in Africa to enjoy per capita GNP growth during the 1980s. Most importantly, during that time people developed a genuine pride in their country.

In December 1985, Sankara engaged the country in a five-day war with Mali, which merely enhanced his popularity. However, he did not live to see the realisation of his policies. In late 1987, a group of junior officers seized power; Sankara was taken outside Ouagadougou and shot.

### The Compaoré years

The new junta was headed by Captain Blaise Compaoré, Sankara's former friend and co-revolutionary, and son-in-law of the late Houphouët-Boigny, Côte d'Ivoire's long-standing leader. Compaoré attempted, unsuccessfully, to discredit Sankara with a 'rectification' campaign, designed to correct the 'deviations' of the previous government. Every 15 October, the anniversary of his assassination, the regime mounts a stilted celebration, while the 'Sankaristes' pay their own more spontaneous, genuine homage.

In late 1991 Compaoré achieved a modicum of legitimacy when, as sole candidate and on a low turnout, he was elected president. This legitimacy was compromised, however, when Clément Ouédraogo, the leading opposition figure, was assassinated a couple of weeks later.

In legislative and presidential elections in 1997 and 1998, the President and his supporters won more than 85% of the vote. Since 2000 President Compaoré has been accused of involvement in the trade of illegal diamonds, and of meddling in the conflicts in Sierra Leone, Liberia and Côte d'Ivoire.

### Burkina Faso Today

The country remains one of the more stable in the region, although rumblings of discontent continue. Street demonstrations in April 2000 forced the government to draft a constitutional amendment that limits presidents to two terms. Arguing that the two-term limit did not apply to terms served before the amendment was passed, and with the opposition divided, President Compaoré won re-election on 13 November 2005 with 80% of the vote.

## THE CULTURE
### The National Psyche

Burkinabés are a laid-back lot, or, as they would say themselves, tranquil. Would-be guides can be persistent, but most are polite and friendly rather than annoying. If you breach local etiquette, most locals will be too polite to say anything.

Burkinabés have a genuine pride in their country, which manifests itself in a desire to embrace the modern world but at the same time remain unchanged by it. This is wedded to a belief that traditional ways of doing things remain important. If you're with a Burkinabé when he encounters a chief from his ethnic group, the displays of deference can be quite moving. Although ethnic identity (along with religion) is the bedrock of identity, you'll see little if any antagonism between members of different ethnic groups.

People are also proud that in a troublesome region riven with conflict, they have become known as a beacon of stability.

That doesn't mean that they love their president (they grumble about him as much as people do about politicians anywhere), but they acknowledge that, for all his faults, he has brought a measure of stability to the country – a quality that, in the absence of economic advancement, is extremely important to the Burkinabé. Many also express quiet anger that so many of their countrymen and women have been made scapegoats in the conflict across the border in Côte d'Ivoire.

## Daily Life
For all of their friendliness and relaxed nature, life for the Burkinabé is as tough as it gets. In 2005 the UN ranked Burkina Faso 175th out of 177 countries across a range of quality-of-life indicators, ranging from income and infant mortality to literacy and life expectancy. Almost 50% of the population survives, barely, on less than US$1 a day. Adult literacy stands at 13% and one in every five Burkinabé is malnourished. Just 2% of the government's budget is spent on health. Over one-third of Burkinabés will not live to 40.

As such, lifestyle is dictated by the daily need to survive. Families are large (the idea being that the more children you have, the more workers you will have to provide for the family) and usually live together in small houses (in urban areas) or family compounds (in rural places). As crops fail (as they did spectacularly in the aftermath of the 2004 drought and locust invasion), and Burkinabé continue to cross the border to escape the conflict in Côte d'Ivoire, cities in Burkina Faso are growing with new arrivals, who tend to seek out areas where members of their religion or ethnic group live.

In rural Burkina Faso, traditional life remains largely unchanged by the passing years with traditional religions, subsistence agriculture and village hierarchies still at the centre of rural life.

## Population
Burkina Faso, which occupies an area about half the size of France, is extremely diverse, with its almost 12 million people scattered among some 60 ethnic groups. The largest of these is the Mossi (48%) who are primarily concentrated in the central plateau area,

including Ouagadougou. The Bobo (7%) live in the west around Bobo-Dioulasso, while the southwest around Gaoua is home to the Lobi (7%). East of the Lobi, and straddling the border with Ghana, are the Gourounsi (5%). In the Sahel areas of the north are the Hausa, the Fulani (also known as Peul-Fulani or Fula; 8%), the Bella and the Tuareg peoples, many of which are still semi-nomadic. The Gourmantché predominate in the east around Fada N'Gourma. Around 80% of Burkinabés live in rural areas.

## RELIGION
Around 90% of Burkina Faso's population observe either Islam (about 50%) or traditional animist beliefs based mainly on the worship of ancestors and spirits (40%) – although there is often considerable overlap. Muslims are concentrated particularly in Ouagadougou and the north, while the 10% of Burkinabés who are Christian live predominantly in the south.

## ARTS
### Arts & Craftwork
While each ethnic group in Burkina Faso has its own artistic style, the work of the Mossi, the Bobo and the Lobi are the most famous; in the museums of Ouagadougou and Bobo-Dioulasso, you'll see examples of all three. The tall antelope masks of the Mossi and the butterfly masks of the Bobo are perhaps the most recognisable, but the Lobi are also well known for their figurative sculptures. See also p67.

### Cinema
Burkina Faso has a thriving film industry which receives considerable biennial stimulation from the Fespaco film festival held in Ouagadougou (see the boxed text, opposite).

Two Burkinabé filmmakers who have won prizes here and developed international reputations are Idrissa Ouédraogo, who won the 1990 Grand Prix at Cannes for Tilä and Gaston Kaboré, whose film Buud Yam was the 1997 winner of the Étalon d'Or. In addition to these well-known names, there are plenty of up-and-coming Burkinabé directors to watch. In 2001 the Burkinabé filmmaker Dany Kouyate came second at Fespaco with Sya – The Dream of the Python for which he also won the Special

**FESPACO**

Burkina Faso may, as one of the world's poorest countries, be an unlikely venue for a world-renowned festival of film, but the biennial nine-day Pan-African Film Festival, **Fespaco** (Festival Pan-Africain du Cinema; ☎ 50 39 87 01; www.fespaco.bf; Ave Kadiogo/Route de Bobo, Ouagadougou), goes from strength to strength.

Fespaco began in 1969, when it was little more than a few African filmmakers getting together to show their short films to interested audiences. Hundreds of films from Africa and the diaspora in the Americas and the Caribbean are now viewed every year, with 20 selected to compete for the prestigious Étalon D'Or de Yennenga – Fespaco's equivalent of the Oscar – as well as prizes in other categories (including TV). In 2005 the coveted prize for best film at Fespaco was won by the South African director Zola Maseko for his film *Drum*.

Fespaco has become an essential pillar of Burkina Faso's cultural life. Since its early days, it has helped stimulate film production throughout Africa and built on the passion for films among Burkina Faso's film-literate population. It has also become such a major African cultural event that it attracts celebrities from around the world.

Ouagadougou is invariably spruced up for the occasion and everyone seems to get in a festive mood. All the city's cinemas are used, each screening different films starting in the late afternoon. Although you can buy individual tickets to screenings, they sell out fast and you're advised to purchase either a 'festival-goer's badge' (CFA25,000), which gives access to all screenings and official Fespaco ceremonies, or the 'Étalon Pass' (CFA10,000) which grants access to screenings. Hotel rooms are hard to find, so advance booking is essential.

Fespaco is held in Ouagadougou every odd year, in the second half of February or early March (in even years it is held in Tunis). The next Fespaco will be held from 24 February to 3 March 2007. For more information about Fespaco, visit the festival's year-round office or check out the excellent website (in French and English).

Jury Prize. In 2005 Daniel Kollo Sanou took third place for the critically acclaimed *Tassuma*. Other prizes were won by Burkinabé directors across the categories, including Fanta Regina Nacro for *La Nuit de la Verite*, Apolline Traoré for *Sous la Clarte de la Lune*, Tahirou Tasséré Ouédraogo's *L'Autre Mal* and *Safi La Petite Mere* by Rasmané Ganemtoré.

## Music

Burkina Faso's modern musicians draw on influences from across the continent (especially Mali, Congo and Côte d'Ivoire), Jamaican reggae and Europe. It's not unusual to come across budding musicians in backyard jam sessions, usually in the late afternoon, which are often exuberant and pretty heavy on the drums.

In Ouagadougou and Bobo-Dioulasso, outdoor venues (usually cafés or bars) offer live music with both traditional troupes and modern ensembles on show. Music is also the mainstay of many traditional festivals and ceremonies across the country. In addition to hearing traditional music, you can also find out more about the instruments

and traditional forms by visiting the excellent Musée de la Musique in Ouagadougou (p139) and Bobo-Dioulasso (p150).

Established local stars include the reggae performers Black So Man, Nick Domby, Traoré Amadou Ballaké and Kaboré Roger, the Cuban-inspired Thomas Tiendrebeogo and Tidiane Coulibaly, and the soul and funk man Georges Ouédraogo. In Ouagadougou, listen out for Sonia Carré d'As, who's something of a local favourite. The most famous group internationally is Farafina, originally from Bobo – although the long years they've spent in Europe have somewhat diminished the following they enjoy at home.

For more information, see also p58.

## ENVIRONMENT
### The Land

Landlocked Burkina Faso's terrain ranges from the harsh desert and semidesert of the north, to the woodland and savanna of the green southwest. Around Banfora rainfall is heavier, and forests thrive alongside irrigated sugar-cane and rice fields; it's here that most of Burkina Faso's meagre 13% of arable land is found. The country's dominant feature, however, is the vast central laterite plateau of the Sahel, where hardy trees and bushes thrive.

The French named the country Upper Volta after its three major rivers – the Black, White and Red Voltas, known today as the Mouhoun, Nakambé and Nazinon rivers. All flow south into the world's largest artificial lake, Lake Volta, in Ghana.

### Wildlife

Parc National d'Arli, close to the border with Benin, is home to Burkina Faso's few remaining species of large animals, among them elephants, hippos, warthogs, baboons, monkeys, lions, leopards, crocodiles and various kinds of antelope.

### National Parks

Burkina Faso's two main protected areas – Parc National d'Arli (p159), which allows access to the contiguous national parks of Benin just across the border, and Ranch de Nazinga (p159) – are in the far southeast of the country. Parc National des Deux Balés (p148), south of Boromo, is less set up for tourists, but does host elephants. Parc Regional du W (p159) straddles Burkina Faso, Niger and Benin, but the best sections are across the border. Unfortunately, hunting (including by tourists) is still a problem around the parks' perimeters.

### Environmental Issues

Burkina Faso suffers acutely from two related forms of environmental damage: deforestation and soil erosion. Some sources attribute an annual GNP loss as high as 9% to such degradation.

Nowadays, Ouagadougou is surrounded by a 70km stretch of land virtually devoid of trees. Firewood accounts for more than 90% of the country's energy consumption, and then there is commercial logging, slash-and-burn agriculture and animal grazing. When these ravages are added to the perennial threat of drought and the locust invasion of 2004, Burkina Faso's ecological future looks decidedly fragile.

But it's not all that gloomy. Some small-scale projects supported by nongovernmental organisations (NGOs) have been successful at the micro level at addressing these issues. For example, farmers have been encouraged to rely on groundwater rather than unpredictable rains, and to return to traditional methods of cultivation, in particular the building of *diguettes*, or stone lines, laid along field contours which slow water run-off, maximise water penetration and reduce erosion. A highly successful World Health Organization (WHO) river blindness (onchocerciasis) eradication programme has also led to the repopulation and recultivation of large fertile areas.

### FOOD & DRINK

Burkina Faso's culinary tradition has little to mark it out as distinctive from its neighbours (p51). Sauces are the mainstay and are always served with a starch – usually rice or the Burkinabé staple, *tô*, a millet- or sorghum-based *pâte* (a pounded dough-like substance).

Stewed *agouti* (or grasscutter, a large rodent which is a whole lot easier to stomach if you don't see its rat-like resemblance) is a prized delicacy, as is *capitaine* (Nile perch). Grilled dishes of chicken and fish are available on seemingly every street corner and are often the cheapest foods on offer.

Lunch is the main meal; at night, grilled dishes are popular.

Castel, Flag, Brakina and So.b.bra (pronounced *so-bay-bra*) are popular and palatable lager-type beers. As one Burkinabé told us: if you learned to drink beer in Bobo-Dioulasso, you drink Brakina, if it was in Ouaga, then it just has to be So.b.bra.

## OUAGADOUGOU

pop 1,086,505

Many end up liking Ouagadougou without really knowing why. While it could just be that the city's name rolls off the tongue in a wonderfully rhythmical African way, there's no mistaking the fact that, for the capital of the world's third poorest country, Ouagadougou is surprisingly upbeat and agreeable. It's not that you'll find much to turn your head here, but it's a relaxed and compact place, home to friendly people. Plus it's easy, even pleasant, to get around on foot. Add some good hotels, restaurants and nightspots, and a few sights worth seeking out, and you'll most likely spend

BURKINA FASO

## THE REMAKING OF OUAGA

African cities are normally alive with people and movement, but resolutely static when it comes to cartography. Any radical change tends to occur on the outskirts of cities as birth rates soar, villagers arrive in search of opportunity, and shanty towns radiate out into the countryside. In recent years, however, Ouagadougou has bucked the trend.

In May 2003 the Grande Marché burned down. A concrete eyesore at the best of times, the charred and ruined shell that was left behind is a strangely disconcerting scar on central Ouaga. The market's demise has at once made the surrounding streets more chaotic and, devoid of traders who have dispersed throughout the city, left the central area deprived of much of its economic energy.

Of far more enduring significance, the government has embarked upon one of the most ambitious and radical projects of town planning anywhere in the world.

Dozens of entire city blocks have been bulldozed, and people and businesses resettled elsewhere. Cheap hotels, earthy bars and low-income shacks have all disappeared without a trace. So extensive has the demolition work been that if you wander south of Ave Houari Boumedienne, you'll find yourself surrounded by rubble-strewn green fields stretching to the horizon. Although former residents and businesses were compensated, grumbling continues about whether money was adequate recompense for moves which have left many stranded, far from the city centre.

The wholesale demolition of entire districts is part of the plan to transform the southern city centre into a commercial district that one local told us, somewhat hopefully, will be: 'the new Wall Street of Africa'. Although plans are yet to be finalised, one idea suggests that only buildings at least six-storeys high will be granted permission to build, thereby transforming Ouagadougou from a low-slung capital to an improbable refuge of high-rise architecture. The only sure thing is that it will take a lot longer to build up than it took to tear down.

But Ouaga's makeover doesn't stop there. Some 8km south of the centre, the 'Ouaga 2000' development is rapidly becoming a separate little world, home to ordered streets, luxury villas, a presidential palace larger than the White House, and with luxury hotels under construction. With most of the homes owned by African presidents, Burkinabé politicians and the Moroccan royal family, it's an exclusive dream that has little in common with the daily life of ordinary Burkinabés. Now if only they resettled in Ouaga 2000 those people whose houses were razed...

a few days here, and end up agreeing that Ouaga – as locals call it – is one of West Africa's more enjoyable large cities.

## HISTORY

Ouagadougou became the capital of the Mossi empire in 1441 and, 250 years later, was chosen as the permanent residence of the Moro-Naba, the Mossi king. The town grew up around the imperial palace, and was extended during colonisation. The Mossi traditional chief remains Burkina Faso's most powerful, and the Mossi dynasty's 500-year presence in Ouagadougou marks the city out as unusual in a region where capitals were more often creations of colonial convenience than seats of ancient power. The completion of the railway from Abidjan (Côte d'Ivoire) in 1954 resulted in the city expanding rapidly.

## ORIENTATION

Central Ouagadougou is built on a grid pattern and the streets are well signed. Take your bearings from the unmistakable globe at the centre of the busy Place des Nations Unies, from which the city's five main boulevards lead. The centre of town – where the streets are relatively ordered and the majority of shops, hotels, restaurants and other services are located – lies west and southwest of this crossroads. North of the railway line, around Marché Sankariaré and Ave de la Liberté, is lively and more chaotic.

## INFORMATION
### Bookshops

**Librairie Diacfa** (Map p138; ☎ 50 30 65 47; Rue du l'Hôtel Ville; ⊗ 8.30am-12.30pm & 3.30-6.30pm Mon-Sat) Sells a wide range of magazines and newspapers – including a few in English – and stationery items.

# OUAGADOUGOU

0 — 1 km
0 — 0.5 miles

**INFORMATION**
American Embassy......................1 D5
Côte d'Ivoirian Embassy.............2 D5
French Embassy.........................3 D4
Ghanaian Embassy.....................4 D3
Hôpital Yalgado........................5 D3
Institut Géographique du Burkina
(IGB)...................................6 C4
Italian Embassy.........................7 D3
Nigerian Embassy......................8 D3
Vacances OK Raids....................9 C6

**SIGHTS & ACTIVITIES**
Fespaco Office.........................10 A5
Moro-Naba Palace...................11 B6

**SLEEPING**
Hôtel Mercure Silmandé...........12 D2
Hôtel Ricardo...........................13 B2

**EATING**
Baratapas...............................14 A4

**DRINKING**
Baratapas.........................(see 14)
Le Festival..............................15 A4

**ENTERTAINMENT**
Ciné Neerwaya........................16 A4
Le Monde...............................17 A3

**TRANSPORT**
Ghana Airways........................18 C6
STMB Bus Station....................19 A4
Transport Confort Voyageurs
(TCV)................................20 B6

BURKINA FASO

To Manéga
(50km);
To Ouahigouya
(182km)

To Kaya (98km);
Dori (260km);
Gorom-Gorom
(320km)

Barage 1

Barage 2

Barage 3

Route de Kaya

Gardens

Gardens

Canal

Rue Nongremasson

To Gare de l'Est (10km);
Boudtenga (32km);
Laongo (50km);
Fada N'Gourma (234km);
Niamey (Niger; 514km)

See Central Ouagadougou Map (p138)

Ave de la Liberté

Rue Commerce

Ave Niandé Ouédraogo

Marché
Sankariaré

Ave Dimdolobson

Rue des Écoles

Canal

Ave d'Oubritenga

Ave Ho Chi Minh

Ministries

Blvd du Burkina

Rue 4.69

Train Station
(Sitarail)

Ave Kouanda

Rue Diongolo Traoré

Ave de l'Indépendance

Palais
Présidentiel

Blvd Charles de Gaulle

To Espace
Gondwana (2km);
Thomas Sankara's
Grave (5.5km);
Musée National
(9km)

Ave Yalenga

Camp
Militaire

Ave de la Nation

Rue du l'Hôtel Ville

Rue Agostino Neto

Rue Maurice Bishop
Ave Raoul Follereau
Ave JF Kennedy

Canal

Place du
2 Octobre

Ave Kadiogo

Rue Maurice Bishop

Ave Houari Boumedienne

Ave Houan Boumedienne

Ave Thévenoud

Ave Bassawarga

Ave Moro-Naba

Rue Joseph Badoua

Rue de la Chance

Ave Houari Boumedienne

Rue de la Mosquée

Rue Yennenga

Rue Loudun

Ave Kwame Nkrumah

Ave Léo Frobenius

Rue du
Dr Gournisson

Ave de la Resistance du 17 Mai

Camp
Militaire

To Centre de Formation
Féminine Artisanale (5km);
Gounghin (5km);
Koudougou (97km);
Bobo-Dioulasso (355km)

Stade
Municipal

St Léon

To Jardin de l'Unité
Africain (500m);
Mali Embassy (500m);
Gare Routière (2.5km);
Hôtel OK Inn (2.5km);
Café des Pros (3.5km);
Village Artisanal
de Ouaga (3.5km);
Ouaga 2000 (7km)

Ave Coulibaly

Square
Yennenga

Ave de l'Aéroport

To Le
Québécoise
(350m)

Aéroport International
d'Ouagadougou

## Cultural Centres

**Centre Culturel Français Georges Méliès** (Map p138; ☎ 50 30 60 97, ccf@fasonet.bf; Ave de la Nation; ⏱ 9am-noon & 3-6.15pm Tue-Sat) In addition to the library, where you can catch up on *Le Monde*, they've a full programme of concerts, exhibitions and movies here – pick up one of their detailed monthly programmes for details.

## Emergency & Medical Services

**Commissariat Central** (Map p138; ☎ 50 30 62 71; Ave Loudun) The first port-of-call for police-related matters.
**Emergency** ( ☎ 17 or 18)

## Internet Access

**Cyber K** (Map p138; Ave Dimdolobsom; per hr CFA500; ⏱ 24hrs Mon-Fri)
**Cyber K2** (Map p138; Ave de la Liberté; per hr CFA400; ⏱ 8am-11pm Mon-Sat, 10am-8pm Sun)
**Éspace Internautes** (Map p138; Ave Kwame N'Krumah; per hr CFA750; ⏱ 7.30am-4am) Net access is cheaper elsewhere, but these are the fastest connections in Burkina.

## Medical Services

**Hôpital Yalgado** (Map p136; ☎ 50 31 16 55; Ave d'Oubritenga)
**Pharmacie de la Concorde** (Map p138; ☎ 50 31 29 49; Ave Kwame N'Krumah)

## Money

**Biciab** (Map p138; 1st fl, Ave Kwame N'Krumah) There's an efficient exchange office here; Biciab ATMs (Visa only) are found here, and on Ave Loudun (Map p138) and Ave Yennenga (Map p138).
**Ecobank** (Map p138; cnr Rue Maurice Bishop & Ave de la Résistance) Excellent, has efficient service. There's another branch on Ave Kwame N'Krumah.

## Post

**Main post office** (Map p138; off Ave de la Nation; ⏱ 7.30am-12.30pm & 3.30-5.30pm Mon-Fri) Poste restante service charges CFA500 per collected letter and will hold mail for one month.

## Telephone & Fax

**Fax office** (Map p138; fax 50 33 81 30; per received page CFA750; ⏱ 7.30am-noon & 3-5.30pm Mon-Sat) In the post office building.
**Onatel** (Map p138; ⏱ 7am-10pm) Near the main post office, this is good for international calls.

## Tourist Information

**ONTB** (Map p138; Office Nationale du Tourisme Burkinabé; ☎ 50 31 19 59, Ave de la Resistance du 17 Mali; ⏱ 7am-12.30pm & 3-5.30pm Mon-Fri) They are more concerned with the business side of the tourism industry than tourist information here – give it a miss.

## Travel Agencies

For budget travellers, both the Hôtel les Manguiers (p141) and Le Pavillon Vert (p140) can organise tours at a reasonable price.

For more expensive (and professional) tours around Burkina Faso and further afield, try the following:
**Armelle Voyages** (Map p138; ☎ 50 31 17 60; Ave Léo Frobenius) Recommended for buying airline tickets.
**L'Agence Tourisme** (Map p138; ☎ 50 31 84 43; www.agence-tourisme.com; Hôtel les Palmiers, Rue Joseph Badoua)
**Meycom Voyages** (Map p138; ☎ 50 33 09 83; meycom@fasonet.bf; Ave Kwame N'Krumah 1435)
**Satguru Voyages** (Map p138; ☎ 50 30 16 52; Ave Kwame N'Krumah) Recommended for buying airline tickets.
**Vacances OK Raids** (Map p136; ☎ 50 30 03 52; okraid@cenatrin.bf; Ave Kwame N'Krumah)
**Zindi Voyages** (Map p138; ☎ 50 31 39 05; Ave Loudun) Recommended for buying airline tickets.

## Visa Extensions

**Commissariat central** (Map p138; ☎ 50 30 62 71; Ave Loudun)

## DANGERS & ANNOYANCES

Ouagadougou is one of the safer cities in the region but avoid walking around alone at night, as there are occasional, if persistent, reports of muggings. Take particular care along Ave Yennenga, the southern reaches of Rue Joseph Badoua, and the Ave Kwame N'Krumah nightclub strip (p144), and never carry valuables with you. That said, a crackdown by the capital's police in recent years – characterised by a shoot-on-sight approach to thieves – has considerably reduced the risks (albeit at the expense of human rights protections). Perhaps for this reason, the overwhelming number of visitors experiences no problems.

## SIGHTS

### MUSÉE NATIONAL

After its long-awaited move to new premises, the **national museum** ( ☎ 50 39 19 34; Blvd Charles de Gaulle; admission CFA1000; ⏱ 9am-12.30pm & 3-5.30pm Tue-Sat) has been left a little out on a limb, almost 10km east of the town centre. The

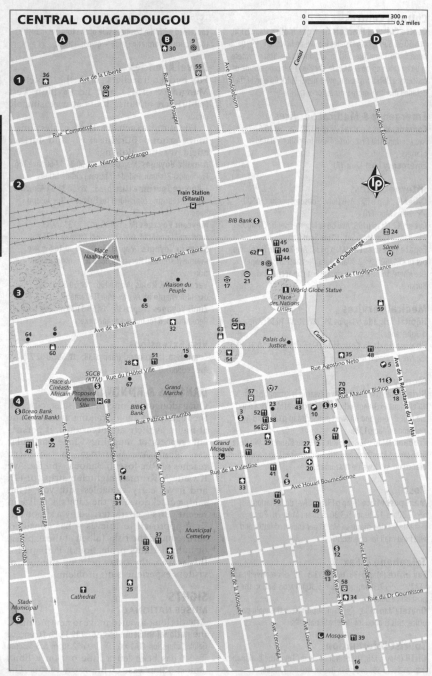

# CENTRAL OUAGADOUGOU

0        300 m
0        0.2 miles

Canal

Ave de la Liberté

Rue Zongola Prosper

Rue Commerce

Ave Niandé Ouédraogo

Ave Dimdolobsom

Rue des Écoles

Train Station
(Sitarail)

BIB Bank

Place
Naaba-Koom

Rue Diongolo Traoré

Ave d'Oubritenga

Sûreté

Ave de l'Indépendance

Maison du
Peuple

World Globe Statue

Place
des Nations
Unies

Canal

Ave de la Nation

Palais du
Justice

Rue Agostino Neto

Ave de la Résistance du 17 Mai

Place du
Cinéaste
Africain

SGCB
(ATM)

Rue du l'Hôtel Ville

Grand
Marché

Rue Maurice Bishop

Proposed
Museum
Site

Bceao Bank
(Central Bank)

Ave Thévenoud

BIB
Bank

Rue Patrice Lumumba

Rue Joseph Badoua

Grand
Mosquée

Rue de la Chance

Rue de la Palestine

Ave Houari Boumedienne

Ave Léo Frobenius

Ave Basswaréga

Ave Kwame N'Krumah

Municipal
Cemetery

Ave Moro-Naba

Rue de la Mosquée

Rue du Dr Gournisson

Stade
Municipal

Cathedral

Mosque

Ave Yennenga

Ave Loudun

**BURKINA FASO**

displays of the various masks, ancestral statues (especially from Lobi country) and traditional costumes of Burkina Faso's major ethnic groups are the highlights. The museum is still a work-in-progress – the various dusty pavilions (one for each region of the country) are marooned and somewhat bereft in the expansive grounds, and the labelling (French-only) is haphazard. To get there, a taxi should cost no more than CFA5000, or take Sotrao bus 1 (CFA100) which runs from the city centre along Ave de la Nation.

### MUSÉE DE LA MUSIQUE

This is a good **museum** (Map p138; ☎ 50 31 09 27; Ave d'Oubritenga; admission CFA1000; ⏲ 9am-12.30pm & 3-5.30pm Tue-Sat) to spend an hour if you have an interest in traditional music. The uncluttered displays in an imaginatively designed exhibition space include *tambours* (drums), flutes, xylophones and *luth* (harps) from around the country. Among the highlights are the impressive *lan* or *castagnettes de pieds* (foot castanets). There are informative labels in French throughout, and a guide will show you around (a tip is appreciated) but it's only worthwhile if you

speak French; otherwise he'll simply point and say 'drum'.

### THOMAS SANKARA'S GRAVE

This **grave** is on the depressing and ill-kept eastern outskirts of Ouagadougou, and is one of a number in the area belonging to high-profile supporters of his government (see the boxed text on p130). There's not a lot to see, but it's a poignant reminder of a more hopeful time in Burkina Faso's recent history and a site of enormous political significance. The grave is about 6km east of the city centre. To get there, charter a taxi for the hour (CFA5000), although some drivers won't take you because roads close to the grave are in a dire state.

## TOURS

Ouagadougou is an easy city to navigate on your own, but to see more than just the tourist sites, contact Eugene Compaoré, an excellent **guide** ( ☎ 76 62 58 98), who speaks French, English and Spanish. He is experienced at finding everything from buzzing Ouaga nightlife away from the expat crowd to the ideal place for getting your

## MORO-NABA CEREMONY

Such is the influence of the Moro-Naba of Ouagadougou, the emperor of the Mossi and the most powerful traditional chief in Burkina Faso, that the government will still make a show of consulting him before making any major decision. The portly present Moro-Naba (the 37th) is, typically for his dynasty, an imposing figure.

The Moro-Naba ceremony (la cérémonie du Nabayius Gou), takes place at 7.15am every Friday at the **Moro-Naba Palace** (Map p136). It's a very formal ritual that lasts only about 15 minutes. Prominent Mossis arrive by taxi, car and moped (also known as *mobylettes*), greet each other and sit on the ground according to rank: in the first row sit the Moro-Naba's spokesman and his chief ministers and, behind them, other dignitaries sit in descending order of seniority. The Moro-Naba appears, dressed in red, the symbol for war, accompanied by his saddled and elaborately decorated horse. There's a cannon shot, his most senior subjects approach to give obeisance and His Majesty retires, while his horse is unsaddled and beats the boundaries of his palace at a brisk trot.

The Moro-Naba reappears, dressed all in white (a sign of peace) and his servants invite his subjects to the palace for a drink; millet beer for the animists and a Kola nut concoction for the Muslims. It's much more than an excuse for an early morning tipple as, within the palace, the Moro-Naba gives audience and hands down his verdict on local disputes and petty crimes. The preceding ritual serves to reinforce the Mossi social order.

The story behind the ceremony? As so often in Africa, there are several conflicting versions. The predominant one recounts how the Ouahigouya Mossi had stolen the Ouagadougou people's main fetish. As the king made ready for war, his ministers persuaded him to desist and undertook to recover the fetish.

To be able to view the ceremony, approach the compound from the east. It's a traditional ceremony, not something put on for tourists. Photos during the ceremony are not permitted.

---

hair braided. Prices are negotiable, but a full day costs around CFA15,000.

## FESTIVALS & EVENTS

Ouagadougou is one of the cultural centres of West Africa. Apart from its lively nightlife, it is the undisputed capital of African film, hosting the biennial **Fespaco**, Africa's premier film festival (p133).

In even-numbered years in late October or early November, Ouagadougou hosts the **Salon International de l'Artisanat de Ouagadougou** (www.siao.bf), which attracts artisans and vendors from all over the continent.

## SLEEPING
### Budget

**Centre d'Accueil des Soeurs Lauriers** (Map p138; Mission Catholique; ☎ 50 30 64 90; off Rue Joseph Badoua; dm CFA4000) This place, within the cathedral compound, promises the only budget beds that we can safely recommend for lone women travellers. You'll leave the hassles of big-city life at the gate and accommodation is in simple, spotless rooms with a mosquito net, shower and fan. Copious meals start from CFA1500.

**Fondation Charles Dufour** (Map p138; ☎ 50 30 38 89; Rue de la Chance; dm CFA3000, s/d with shared bathroom CFA5000/6000) An alternative to your usual budget hotel, this place offers a dark dorm (get there early to snaffle the only standing fan) with mosquito nets, basic doubles, a kitchen for use by guests, and a laid-back ambience. Proceeds from the rooms go to support the 20 local orphans whom Adama Yameogo feeds, lodges and educates. Downsides include stiflingly hot rooms, the occasional hawker, and surrounding streets where car workshops abound. That said, it attracts plenty of repeat visitors.

**Le Pavillon Vert** (Map p138; ☎ /fax 31 06 11; pavillonvert@liptinfor.bf; Ave de la Liberté; s/d with fan & shared bathroom CFA6000/6500, with private bathroom CFA10,000/11,000, with air-con CFA15,000/16,000; 🕱 ) The closest Ouaga comes to a travellers' hang-out, Le Pavillon Vert is laid-back and highly recommended. The rooms (especially those with air-con) are spacious and all the facilities, from the rooms to the shared bathrooms, are spotless. The courtyard bar and restaurant are refuges from the clamorous African streets just outside the gate.

Staff are also friendly, professional and able to provide bicycles to explore Ouaga.

**Hôtel Yennenga** (Map p138; ☎ 50 30 73 37; Ave Yennenga; s with fan & shared/private bathroom CFA6200/7380, d CFA7200/8380, s/d with private bathroom & air-con CFA11,500/12,500; ⊠) Hôtel Yennenga represents top budget value and gets the thumbs-up from travellers. The rooms are simple, well-maintained and all come with mosquito nets. The location, just south of the city centre, is also a winner.

## Midrange

If you're willing to pay a little more, Ouagadougou has some high-quality upper midrange choices.

**Hôtel les Palmiers** (Map p138; ☎ 50 33 33 30; hotel lespalmiers@cenatrin.bf; Rue Joseph Badoua; d CFA29,500-38,500; P ⊠ ⊠) This place is something special, an oasis blending the best of understated African style with European levels of comfort. All the rooms, which are ranged around a leafy compound, are adorned with local prints and traditional wooden masks, and the more expensive rooms have satellite TV and an Internet connection for laptops. The garden is compact, but easily the nicest in Ouaga, with a small pool and a shady bar and restaurant. The location – on a quiet street but just a short walk from the centre – is another bonus. For this price, you won't find more charm in Burkina Faso. Not surprisingly, it's often full, so book ahead.

**Hôtel les Manguiers** (Map p138; ☎ 50 30 03 70; fax 50 30 03 75; Rue Zomodo Propser; s with fan/air-con CFA10,000/15,000, d CFA11,000/16,000; ⊠) Removed from the centre and in a fascinating African quarter, Hôtel les Manguiers, off Ave de la Liberté, is terrific. The clean rooms bear hints of local character, and are set around a large, sheltered and shady courtyard. The staff are friendly and there's also a bar and restaurant.

**Hôtel Ricardo** (Map p136; ☎ 50 30 70 72; ricardo@ cenatrin.bf; North of Barrage 2; s/d CFA30,000/35,000; P ⊠ ⊠) If you look at the overall package – lovely, leafy and bird-filled grounds, a pleasant pool which you may share with local ducks, a restaurant, disco, quiet location and satellite TV in all rooms – it's not hard to see why the colonial-style Ricardo is popular. The rooms are a touch spartan for the price, but are spacious enough. The staff can arrange a metered taxi into the city centre, which is a considerable distance away.

**Hôtel Yibi** (Map p138; ☎ 50 30 73 70; ypi@cenatrin .bf; cnr Ave Kwame N'Krumah & Rue du Dr Gournisson; s/d CFA28,000/31,000; ⊠ ⊠) In the government's rush to raze southern Ouagadougou, it's a good thing they spared Hôtel Yibi. The carpet may be peeling in the public areas but the rooms (with TV) are lovely, with some attractive decorative touches. There's also a pleasant garden and even a small pool with a palm-tree island.

**Hôtel OK Inn** (☎ 50 37 00 20; hotelok-inn@cenatrin .bf; Route de Pô; s/d CFA27,500/32,000, 2-/4-bed bungalows CFA39,600/49,500; P ⊠ ⊠) If you can ignore the truck park through which you have to pass to reach the hotel, you'll quickly discover why this terrific French-run place is so popular. Staff are friendly and professional, the rooms are colourful and nicely adorned, and there's a delightful pool and high-quality restaurant. The four-bed bungalows are ideal for families. The hotel organises regular minibuses for guests throughout the day.

**Hôtel Belle Vue** (Map p138; ☎ 50 30 84 98; fax 50 30 00 37; hbv.hotel-bellle-vue2000@caramail.com; Ave Kwame N'Krumah; s/d CFA17,760/18,760; ⊠) This is your standard midrange African hotel – simple rooms (which are a bit cell-like), friendly staff overflowing from the public spaces, and a good central location. For those who favour an African (as opposed to imitation European) ambience, this is the best option for the price in Ouaga. Don't, however, be seduced by the name – many rooms have no windows and the rooftop terrace was closed when we visited, amid plans to build upwards.

**Hôtel Relax** (Map p138; ☎ 50 31 32 31; relax .hotel@cenatrin.bf; Ave de la Nation; s/d from CFA34,500/38,500; ⊠ ⊠) If you like your rooms carpeted and a good central location, the Relax promises a pleasant stay. The service is good, if a little slow, and the views over central Ouaga from the 3rd floor rooms are among the best in town. The swimming pool is large, there's the usual bar and restaurant and a large-screen TV in the lobby.

**Hôtel Central** (Map p138; ☎ 50 30 89 24; h.central@cenatrin.bf; Rue de la Chance; d from CFA15,000, larger s/d from CFA22,500/25,000; ⊠) Although this hotel still stands in the centre of Ouaga, the energy has moved elsewhere since the Grande

Marché (directly opposite) burned down. It's still a reasonable option, with tiled floors and decent bathrooms. The more you pay, the more spacious the room, but if you're going to pay top dollar (CFA40,000/45,000) there's better value elsewhere.

**Hôtel Continental** (Map p138; ☎ /fax 50 30 86 36; fax 50 30 69 19; Ave Loudun; d CFA10,000-16,000; ⊠ ) Hôtel Continental is depressing on the outside and uninspired within, but the rooms are enormous, clean and the most expensive rooms on the third floor (no lift) have good views out over central Ouaga.

## Top End

**La Palmeraie** (Map p138; ☎ 50 30 48 90; lapalmeraie@cenatrin.bf; Rue Agostino Neto; d/ste CFA52,000/72,000; P ⊠ ⊠ ) Whereas most of Ouaga's top-end hotels mimic a European apartment-style aesthetic, La Palmeraie has a more African ambience, with spacious rooms arranged around a shady courtyard. Rooms have wrought-iron furniture, African masks looking down from the walls, and traces of the classy but relaxed atmosphere that pervades the hotel's public spaces, bar and restaurant. Service is also professional and the central location is hard to beat.

**Hôtel Mercure Silmandé** (Map p136; ☎ 50 35 60 05; www.mercure.com; Route de Kaya; d €75-100; P ⊠ ⊠ ) The owners of this former Sofitel have yielded to the inevitable and downgraded the hotel to a more reasonable four stars. As such, it no longer suffers from disappointed expectations and – until Accor's new Sofitel is completed in the Ouaga 2000 development south of town – is the city's most luxurious hotel. In addition to semi-luxurious rooms (some were being renovated when we visited), there are ample grounds, a swimming pool, tennis courts, Internet access, a good restaurant and bar, and traces of former luxury throughout.

# EATING
## African

**La Forêt** (Map p138; Ave Bassawarga; mains from CFA2800; ⊙ lunch & dinner) One of Ouaga's longest-standing restaurants with African specialities, this upmarket place ranges around a pleasant shady garden. It's not the most extensive menu in town but they do offer a few selections each day, all well prepared.

**Restaurant Akwaba** (Map p138; Ave Kwame N'Krumah; starters CFA1500-2500, mains CFA2500-4000; ⊙ lunch & dinner) Friendly service, decent African food and spectacularly kitsch ceiling fans (they even turn them on sometimes but only when you ask) are the order of the day here. The mainly Ivorian dishes take a while to prepare but the *foutou* (sticky yam or plantain paste) is strangely addictive and goes perfectly with the *poulet de kedjenou* (slowly simmered chicken with peppers and tomatoes, CFA3000). The *brochette de capitaine* (CFA3500) also stands out.

**Maquis Le Pouvoir** (Map p138; Ave Dimdolobsom; mains CFA1000-2000; ⊙ 11am-1am) This central and popular outdoor place offers a selection of good and well-priced African staples, with plenty of *foutou* and grilled meats, and a few nods to European tastes in the form of hamburgers. It's a slightly classier atmosphere than your average *maquis* and is as popular with expats as with locals. Highly recommended.

**Monopole Plus** (Map p138; off Rue Agostino Neto; mains mostly CFA3000-4500; ⊙ 9am-10pm) This pleasant outdoor bar-restaurant has salads, brochettes and sandwiches for starters, and a range of African-flavoured beef, chicken and fish dishes for mains. The *yassa poulet riz blanc* (CFA3500) is especially good. There's also a swimming pool (CFA1000 for nonguests) around which are pleasant straw paillotes and, in the evening, wealthy locals looking to pick up.

**Éspace Gondwana** (Rue13-14, off Blvd Onatel, mains mostly CFA3000-4500; ⊙ 6pm-late) Wow! Tucked away to the east of Ouaga, this stunning restaurant is the city's most atmospheric. The restaurant has a courtyard where music is often played, and the three dining rooms are richly adorned with masks (all for sale) and traditional furniture. Each room is themed in a different style – Gourounsi, Mauritanian and a Tuareg tent. The food is also splendid, from the *brochette de capitaine*, sauce Hollandaise (CFA6000) and bite-sized tapas (six for CFA5500) to the banana cake for dessert (CFA3000). There's also a children's menu (CFA4000) and service comes with a smile. To get here, you'll need to take a taxi (around CFA1500 from the city centre) but it's worth every ceefah.

## Asian & European

**Restaurant de Chine** (Map p138; Ave Houari Boumedienne; mains CFA2800-6000; ⊙ lunch & dinner Wed-Mon) If you believe expats and wealthy locals (and there's no reason not to) this is Ouaga's best Chinese restaurant. After spending time in Ouaga's markets you'll wonder where they get the fine cuts of meat and the freshest of ingredients. Not surprisingly, it's a popular place, especially on weekends when the extensive and varied menu and the attentive service draw the crowds.

**Le Verdoyant** (Map p138; Ave Dimdolobsom; mains CFA2800-4500; ☻ lunch & dinner Thu-Tue) If you ask expats for their favourite Ouaga restaurant, chances are a good number will choose the Italian Le Verdoyant. It's best known for its pasta (the lasagne here is the best you'll find in Africa) and wood-fired pizzas, but the outdoor tables are pleasant, the service good and the menu (mostly fish and meat) varied enough to cater to most tastes.

**Baratapas** (Map p136; Rue Commerce; salads CFA800-1500, tapas CFA500-3000, pizza CFA2500-5000; ☻ 10am-midnight Tue-Sun) Baratapas, just around the corner from the STMB bus station, comes very close to being our new favourite place in Ouaga. The courtyard is filled with the innovative work of local artists and occasional exhibitions, the food is excellent and creative, and Alain, the owner, is a delight. The salads in particular are enormous. In short, we can't recommend this place highly enough.

**Restaurant l'Eau Vive** (Map p138; Rue de l'Hôtel Ville; starters CFA1300-3800, mains mostly CFA3800-5900; ☻ lunch & dinner Mon-Sat) This Ouagadougou institution is run by an order of nuns and promises an air-conditioned haven from the clamour outside; there's also a garden dining area out the back. The menu is mainly French but has the occasional nod to African flavours. Profits go to the order's charitable works and, for the truly surreal bit, don't be surprised if you're there at 9.30pm and the nuns burst into song.

**Le Coq Bleu** (Map p138; cnr Rue Patrice Lumumba & Ave Kwame N'Krumah; mains from CFA3500; ☻ lunch & dinner Wed-Mon) You get what you pay for here. The menu is pricey but the French cooking is of the highest order. It's the sort of place to consider when you've been on the African road for a while and you're looking to stimulate jaded taste buds with a touch of class. The blue décor is tasteful and soothing, but the schmaltzy background music will have you scraping off the wallpaper. It also has a well-stocked bar.

**Hôtel OK Inn** ( ☎ 50 37 00 20; Route de Pô; mains from CFA3200) Of all the hotel restaurants, our favourite is this one, a regular haunt of discerning French expatriates who know good French cooking when they taste it.

## Quick Eats

**Sindabal's** (Map p138; Ave Loudun; starters CFA1000-3000, sandwiches & hamburgers CFA750-1500, mains CFA1500-3750; ☻ lunch & dinner) Most travellers who come to Ouaga on a budget end up here at some point. It's a low-key place with a varied menu (including spaghetti bolognese and some Lebanese dishes) and the only downside – vaguely disconcerting street smells at the outdoor tables if the wind's blowing the wrong way – could easily apply to any outdoor place in town. It's not a brilliant place but it's one of a kind in Ouaga.

**Café des Pros** (Blvd Tengsoba, known as Blvd Circulaire; mains from CFA750; ☻ 7.30am-10pm) Inside the Village Artisanal, Café des Pros allows you to combine eating and shopping, and is therefore convenient if you're down this way. The food (spaghetti or *riz sauce*) is simple, and takes a while to cook, but it's quiet, pleasant and reasonably priced.

Some of the more rustic places stay open as late as there are customers, and serve little that costs more than CFA500. These include **Chez Tante Propre** (Map p138; Ave Loudun), a wildly popular hole in the wall where they turn out yogurt sandwiches and simple rice dishes; **Kiosque Nabonswende** (Map p138; Ave Dimdolobsom), which is also good for yogurt baguettes; and **Maxi Café** (Map p138; Ave Léo Frobenius) where the brochettes are good.

If you're staying at Fondation Charles Dufour, try **Top Senegalaise Restaurant** (Map p138; Rue Joseph Badoua) or **Balmaya Snack Café Restaurant** (Map p138; Rue Joseph Badoua), which both belong in the same no-frills but cheap-and-cheerful genre.

For a more Western experience, try the oddly named **Happy Donald of Hamburger House** (Ave Kwame N'Krumah) or **Le Québécoise** (Ave de l'Aeroport), which is Canadian-run and probably does Ouaga's best hamburgers, plus other North American specialities.

## Self-Catering

**Marina Market** (Map p138; Ave Yennenga; ☻ 8am-1pm & 3.30-9pm Mon-Sat, 9am-1pm & 5.30-8pm Sun) Opposite the Grand Mosquée, Marina Market has a wide selection (from Magnum ice creams to Special K breakfast cereal) and long opening hours.

**Le Cave à Vins** (Map p138; cnr Ave Loudun & Rue de la Palestine; ☺9am-1pm & 4-7.30pm Tue-Sat, 4-7.30pm Mon) Stepping inside this sophisticated, French-run wine boutique is like momentarily escaping Ouaga for the south of France. Although it's aimed more at the expat market, prices for French wines are surprisingly reasonable.

## DRINKING

**Zaka** (Map p138; drinks from CFA500; ☺noon-1am) Right in the heart of Ouaga, Zaka is a hybrid live performance venue and cultural centre, with groups playing traditional or modern music from around 8.30pm (sometimes there's a small cover charge but usually it's free). At other times it's a pleasant open-air watering hole, something that is an oasis for this part of town.

For late-night drinking, one of the best areas is north of the centre, around Ave de la Liberté, where there are outdoor bars, whose tables are at a premium until the nightclubs kick into gear around 11pm. Our favourites include **Le Festival** (Map p136; Ave Kouanda) and the more sophisticated **Baratapas** (Map p136; Rue Commerce); at the latter you might hear some live music on Friday nights and a variety of rums are the starting point of the owner's plans for a Latino Bar. South of the centre, **Jardin de l'Unité Africaine** (cnr Ave de l'Aeroport & Ave Bassawarga) is laid-back and recommended.

## ENTERTAINMENT
### Concerts

Your best (and possibly only) chance of catching a concert featuring some of the best musicians from Burkina Faso or elsewhere in Africa, is at the **Centre Culturel Français Georges Mélies** (Map p138; Ave de la Nation).

### Live Music & Nightclubs

**Jimmy's Discotheque** (Map p138; Ave Kwame N'Krumah; admission CFA2500) For a more DJ-driven experience, plus well-heeled patrons, drinks that start at CFA2500 and Western dance music with occasional African rhythms, try this place. It gets going by 11pm on weekends and doesn't close until the last punters stagger home.

For soulful blues music, it's hard to beat **Maquis Pili-Pili** (Ave Kwame N'Krumah; admission free), although some nights the musicians simply don't turn up. If this or the other more mel-

low live music venues – such as **Zaka** (left), **Éspace Gondwana** p142 or **Baratapas** (p143) – are a bit tame for your dancing needs, the following places all offer live dance bands and plenty of sweaty, tightly pressed energy on Friday and Saturday nights:

**Palladium** (Map p138; Ave Yennenga; admission CFA500) A large dance floor and good snacks if you get the munchies.

**Bar Matata Plus** (Map p138; off Ave de la Liberté; admission free) Good and energetic from 9pm.

**Le Monde** (Map p136; off Ave de la Liberté; admission CFA500) Long-standing and still super-cool.

### Cinemas

**Ciné Burkina** (Map p138; Ave Loudun) Built for Fespaco in the late 1960s, this has a wide screen and good seats. It regularly shows African-produced films, as well as recent international releases and a diet of kung fu and Bollywood hands-in-the-air extravaganzas.

**Ciné Neerwaya** (Map p136; off Ave Kouanda) and **Ciné Oubri** (Map p138; Rue Patrice Lumumba; CFA100-1000) are pleasant alternatives.

## SHOPPING

Ouagadougou is an excellent place to look for masks and woodcarvings. There are also artisan stalls dotted around town, including along Ave Dimdolobsom, Ave de la Nation and Ave de la Résistance

**Nuance** (Map p138; ☎50 31 72 74; nuancebf@yahoo.fr; Ave Yennenga; ☺8.30am-12.30pm & 3.30-7pm Mon-Sat, 9am-1pm Sun) It's hard to beat this boutique for its combination of eclectic African art, textiles, clothing and carvings, all at reasonable (and fixed) prices. It supports local artists with occasional exhibitions, and its setting back from the street lends it a tranquil air.

**Zaka Boutique** (Map p138; Galerie Zak'apoto; ☎mobile 76 68 82 49; Rue du l'Hôtel Ville; ☺8am-10pm) This fine boutique showcases African textiles, as well as a few carvings, homeware and jewellery, in a low-key setting. Prices are fixed and surprisingly reasonable.

**Sortilèges** (Map p138; ☎50 31 60 80; Ave de la Nation; ☺8.30am-1pm & 4-7pm Mon-Sat) If you love wood carvings, you'll love this small, but high quality, place with price tags to match – apart from some of the jewellery, you won't find many masks or statues under CFA200,000.

**Centre National d'Artisanat et d'Art** (Map p138; ☎50 30 68 35; Ave Dimdolobsom; ☺8am-noon & 3-

6pm Mon-Fri) Profits here go directly to the artisan and, although the quality of the products is mixed, take some time to look over the bronze statues, wooden sculptures and colourful batiks, for there are some gems among the standard items you'll find elsewhere.

**Village Artisanal de Ouaga** ( ☎ 50 37 14 83; village.artisanal@cenatrin.bf; Blvd Tengsoba, known as Blvd Circulaire; ◷ 7am-7pm) This government-run cooperative has, arguably, the widest range of products – clothing, textiles, leatherwork, painting, wood- and metal-carving, and jewellery – and is ideal for getting a fix on prices and quality without the hard sell.

**Centre de Formation Feminine Artisanale** ( ◷ 8am-noon & 3.30-5.30pm Mon-Fri, 8am-noon Sat) Embroidered tablecloths and napkins, and woven rugs are the speciality of this women's cooperative, which is in Gounghin, off the road to Bobo-Dioulasso on the western outskirts of town.

**Éspace Gondwana** ( ☎ 50 36 11 24; Rue 13-14, off Blvd Onatel; ◷ 6pm-late) Better known as a restaurant (see p142), Éspace Gondwana has the widest selection of masks that we found in Ouaga, and prices are agreeable. Everything's for sale here (including the furnishings) except, as one waiter pointed out, the staff.

## GETTING THERE & AWAY
### Air
For details of international flights to/from Ouagadougou (some of which go via Bobo-Dioulasso), see p168.

### Bus
Leaving Ouagadougou can be confusing, as most buses leave from the bus companies' depots rather than from the *gare routière*. Although there are loads of private companies, there are only three that you're likely to need for destinations within the country.

Undoubtedly the newest and most comfortable buses are those of **Transport Confort Voyageurs** (Map p136; TCV; ☎ 50 39 87 77; Rue de la Mosquée) which run services between Ouaga and Bobo-Dioulasso (CFA6000, five daily).

Of the others, **STMB** (Map p136; ☎ 50 31 34 34; off Rue Commerce) has the best buses and the most extensive network of routes through-

out Burkina Faso (including those shown in the table).

| Destination | Fare (CFA) | Duration (hours) | Frequency |
|---|---|---|---|
| Bobo-Dioulasso* | 6000 | 5 | 5 daily |
| Dori | 5000 | 5 to 7 | Mon, Fri, Sun |
| Fada N'Gourma | 4000 | 5 | one daily |
| Ouahigouya | 3000 | 2 to 3 | six daily |
| Pô | 2000 | 3 | 5 daily |

\* The 10am and 4pm departures are buses with air-con, costing CFA7000

The best company for Koudougou (one way/return CFA1500/2500, two hours) is **Rayi's Transport** (Map p138; ☎ 50 33 27 13; Rue Joseph Badoua). It has nine daily departures from Monday to Saturday, with a further four on Sunday.

For Gorom-Gorom (CFA6000, seven to ten hours), services were in a state of flux at the time of research, but try STMB or the old clunkers of **Sogebaf** (Map p138; ☎ 50 33 27 13; off Ave de la Liberté), although it's easier to travel to Dori and arrange transport from there.

For details of services to Benin, Côte d'Ivoire, Ghana, Mali, Niger and Togo, see p169.

### Bush Taxi & Minibus
Most bush taxis and minibuses leave in the early morning from the *gare routière*, 4km south of the centre. To get there, a shared taxi costs CFA300.

## GETTING AROUND
### To/From the Airport
The 2km taxi journey from l'Aéroport International d'Ouagadougou to the city centre costs about CFA1000 (50% more to Hôtel Mercure Silmandé in the north). A shared taxi from central Ave Kwame N'Krumah should cost CFA200. It's also possible to walk; Ave Yennenga, with its many hotels, is only 1km away.

### Bicycle & Moped
The going rate to hire bicycles is CFA2000 a day, and for mopeds it could be anywhere from CFA3000 to CFA5000, depending on your negotiating skills; ask at your hotel. You can leave both bikes and mopeds safely for CFA50 to CFA100 at one of the myriad two-wheeler parks around town.

**BURKINA FASO**

## Bus

Sotrao city buses run throughout Ouaga with well-marked bus stops along major routes. Fares cost CFA100.

## Taxi

Shared taxis, mostly beaten-up old green Renaults, cost CFA250 for a ride within town. The basic rate for a private taxi (orange or green), which you commission just for yourself, is CFA500 – more for longer journeys. If you bargain hard, one by the hour will set you back at least CFA2500. Rates double after 10pm.

If you're tired of bargaining, the yellow **Taxi Urbain** ( ☎ 50 34 36 36) have meters; you're most likely to find them along Rue Maurice Bishop, close to the corner with Ave Léo Frobenius. If you're chartering a taxi for an hour or another set time period, agree on a price in advance rather than relying on the meter.

# AROUND OUAGADOUGOU

## LAONGO

At Laongo there's a rich outcrop of granite, varying from grey to pink. Here, the Ministry of Culture had the inspired idea of inviting Burkinabé and international sculptors to meet, relate and carve the rock. The results of this and subsequent workshops are chiselled in the pell-mell of rocks and boulders.

To get here, take the Fada N'Gourma road to the village of Boudtenga (32km), then head northeast on a dirt road to the village of Laongo.

## MANÉGA

The Manéga complex, about 50km north of Ouagadougou on the Kongoussi road, was established in the early 1990s by the Burkinabé lawyer and poet, Frédéric Pacéré Titinga, as a repository of Mossi culture. In the grounds, which teeter on the kitsch, are plaster statues of Mossi kings and a small museum with life-size dioramas depicting the major Mossi rites of passage. There's also a fine collection of masks at the **Musée des Masques** (www.musee-manega.bf/fr/), as well as *yokougas* (traditional tombstones).

## KOUDOUGOU

pop 87,347

Koudougou, 97km to west of Ouagadougou, may be Burkina Faso's third-largest settlement and home to a large cotton mill that keeps the area afloat, but it's one of those African towns that exists seemingly on the periphery, just off major roads, falling quietly to sleep. The main reason to visit is to see its market, which is bigger, calmer and more interesting than anything Ouagadougou can offer. The distinctively Sahelian style **Grande Mosquée** in the centre of town is also worth a look. We recommend that you visit as a day-trip from the capital, not least because Koudougou's hotels are nothing to get excited about. The only reason to stay here is as a base for exploring nearby picturesque villages such as Goundi (8km) or Sabou (p148) and its crocodile lake (25km).

## Sleeping

**Hôtel le Toulourou** ( ☎ 50 44 01 70; salamkabre@yahoo .fr; off Route de Ouagadougou; d with shared/private bathroom CFA12,500/18,000; 🌣 ) The best choice in town for its tidy rooms, central but quiet location, and pleasant courtyard. Hôtel le Toulourou was built by Maurice Yaméogo, a local boy made good and Burkina Faso's first president. It's starting to fade around the edges but it has weathered the years better than any other Koudougou hotel. Guests can hire a hotel car (without/with driver CFA25,000/30,000) to visit Sabou. The hotel is 50m south off Route de Ouagadougou but is not signposted until you reach the gate.

**Hôtel Photo Luxe** ( ☎ 50 44 00 87; fax 50 31 32 59; cnr Route de Ouagadougou & Route de Dédougou; s with fan/air-con & shared bathroom CFA6200/8600, s/d with air-con & private bathroom CFA9700/10,900; 🌣 ) Koudougou's second-best hotel, the Photo Luxe, at the eastern entrance to town, is a fair hike from the centre (the bus to Ouaga passes by the front door) and is ageing noticeably, but the rooms are big, simple, and kept reasonably clean.

**Hôtel Yelba Annexe** ( ☎ 50 44 11 16; d with fan/air-con & private bathroom CFA5750/8500) Yelba Annexe, overlooking the northwestern corner of the market, is ageing – and not especially gracefully. You enter from the rubbish-strewn courtyard at the back and climb to the rooms through a building site that hasn't got much further than obstructing the entrance. For all

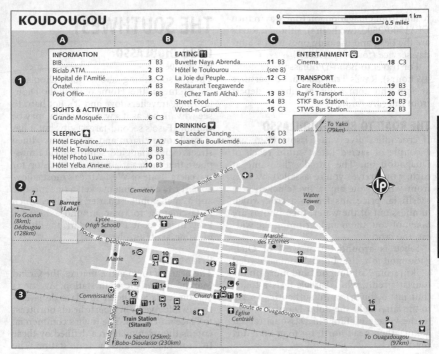

### KOUDOUGOU

0 — 1 km
0 — 0.5 miles

**INFORMATION**
BIB.....................................1 B3
Biciab ATM..........................2 B3
Hôpital de l'Amitié................3 C2
Onatel.................................4 B3
Post Office...........................5 B3

**SIGHTS & ACTIVITIES**
Grande Mosquée....................6 C3

**SLEEPING**
Hôtel Espérance.....................7 A2
Hôtel le Toulourou.................8 B3
Hôtel Photo Luxe...................9 D3
Hôtel Yelba Annexe................10 B3

**EATING**
Buvette Naya Abrenda...........11 B3
Hôtel le Toulourou .............(see 8)
La Joie du Peuple..................12 C3
Restaurant Teegawende
   (Chez Tanti Aïcha)..............13 B3
Street Food..........................14 B3
Wend-n-Guudi.....................15 C3

**DRINKING**
Bar Leader Dancing................16 D3
Square du Boulkiemdé............17 D3

**ENTERTAINMENT**
Cinema................................18 C3

**TRANSPORT**
Gare Routière.......................19 B3
Rayi's Transport.....................20 C3
STKF Bus Station....................21 B3
STWS Bus Station...................22 B3

BURKINA FASO

To Yako
(79km)

Route de Yako

Cemetery

Water
Tower

To Goundi
(8km);
Dédougou
(128km)

Barrage
(Lake)

Lycée
(High School)

Route de Dédougou

Church

Route de Trésor

Marché
des Femmes

Mairie

Market

Church

Route de Ouagadougou

Commissariat

Train Station
(Sitarail)

Église
Centrale

To Sabou (25km);
Bobo-Dioulasso (230km)

To Ouagadougou
(97km)

that, the rooms themselves are, fortunately, the best feature – simple but spacious, and almost clean. The bathrooms, however, lack important features (eg toilet seats and half of the basin in one room). You couldn't get any closer to the market.

**Hôtel Espérance** ( ☎ 50 44 05 59; esperance-hotel@ yahoo.fr; Route de Dédougou; d with fan/air-con & shower CFA5750/8500) This old hotel, 1km northwest of the centre, looks overgrown and abandoned, and may well be in the not-too-distant future – although the owners promised that a makeover was imminent. The rooms are fine (basic and spacious) but the shared toilets are not for the faint-hearted. Price would have to be everything to stay here.

## Eating & Drinking

The choice of places is limited – think greasy spoon rather than fine dining. The best option for a meal is the restaurant at **Hôtel le Toulourou** ( ☎ 50 44 01 70; off Route de Ouagadougou) where meals cost around CFA5000.

Otherwise, basic but friendly African street food is on offer from **Wend-n-Guudi** (rice or brochettes around CFA500), one block south

of the Grande Mosquée, or in any of the streets surrounding the market.

For similar food but in slightly more pleasant sit-down surroundings, **Restaurant Teegawende** (Chez Tanti Aicha; meals CFA500-2000), near the train station, is good. **Buvette Naya Abrenda**, across the same street, promises a musical ambience and delivers in decibels. It can get lively in the evening, as can **La Joie du Peuple** (meals from CFA500; ⏱ 11am-late) which is a spacious open-air place with funky paintings on the walls and recorded music; it has three or four African sauces to choose from. At night, it's also one of the best places for drinks and dancing.

If you don't mind straying from the centre, **Bar Leader Dancing** (Route de Dédougou) gets down to some serious dancing on weekends, while **Square du Boulkiemdé** (Route de Ouagadougou) has outdoor tables which are ideal for a drink on a warm summer's evening.

## Getting There & Away

**Rayi's Transport** ( ☎ 50 44 08 32), **STWS** ( ☎ 50 44 03 04) and **STKF** ( ☎ 50 44 17 06) all have at least seven buses a day from Monday to Saturday to and from Ouagadougou (one way/return CFA1500/2500, two hours), although Rayi's are the best, and the only ones with a Sunday service (four departures).

For travel to Bobo-Dioulasso (CFA4000, 4½ hours), Rayi's Transport has departures at 8am and 2pm daily. Minibuses depart from the *gare routière*.

## THE ROAD TO BOBO-DIOULASSO

If crocodiles give you frisson, there are a couple of sacred lakes within reach of Ouagadougou. The ritual's the same at each: you arrive, you're assailed by kids from whom you buy a live chicken at a sacrificial price, it's fed to a croc which lumbers out of the water, then photos are taken of you, them and, grinning the widest, the croc.

**Sabou** is around 90km west of Ouagadougou on the Bobo-Dioulasso road (25km from Koudougou) and more on the tourist circuit, while **Bazoulé** feels a touch (but just a touch) more authentic. To get to the latter, take the Bobo-Dioulasso road to the village of Tanghin Dassouri (about 30km), then head north for 6km on a dirt road.

**Boromo**, halfway between Ouagadougou and Bobo, has little to detain you itself, but serves as the gateway to the **Parc National des Deux Balés**. Although the main section of the park is some distance from the town, there are several areas within the park that are close to Boromo, and which are great places to see elephants. On the road to the national park, 7km from Boromo, is the newish and well-run **Campement Le Kaicedra** ( ☎ 76 62 17 78; http://kaicedra.waika9.com/camp.htm; 2-/4-bed bungalow CFA18,000/22,000; meals CFA5500). Accommodation here is in nice bungalows in a peaceful setting right by the river, where elephants often come to drink. The staff can arrange guides (CFA2000), three-hour 4WD elephant safaris (CFA30,000 per 4WD) or pirogue trips (CFA1000). They may even pick you up from the bus station in Boromo if you ask nicely.

Around 10km southwest of the camp, the charming small village of **Ouroubono** is home to blacksmiths and other craftsmen, who make masks for sale in Ouagadougou. Prices here are a lot cheaper and the sales pitch non-existent. This is also a good place to try millet beer.

# THE SOUTHWEST

## BOBO-DIOULASSO
pop 360,106

There's something about Bobo-Dioulasso (which means the 'Home of the Bobo Dioulas') that travellers love and it's not hard to see why. Bobo, as it's widely known, may be Burkina Faso's second-largest city, but it has a small-town charm and its quiet tree-lined streets exude a languid, semi-tropical atmosphere that makes it a favourite rest stop for travellers – one of West Africa's most enjoyable. It has a thriving market, a fine mosque and a small popular quarter, Kibidwe, which is fascinating to roam around. There's a lively music scene and, after dark, the district of Balomakoté throbs.

### Orientation

The heart of town is the market, the Grand Marché. From the train station, Ave de la Nation leads southeast to Place de la Nation, while Ave de la Liberté heads northeast to Place du Paysan. The town's commercial core is the triangular area defined by these two roundabouts and the train station. The area south and east of the market houses many of the hotels, restaurants and banks.

### Information
#### BOOKSHOPS
**Librairie Diacfa** ( ☎ 20 97 10 19; Rue Joffre; ☒ 8am-12.30pm & 3-6pm Mon-Fri, 8.30am-noon Sat) Not as well-stocked as its Ouagadougou counterpart, but it has a small selection of newspapers, postcards, books and stationery.

#### CULTURAL CENTRES
**Centre Culturel Français Henri Matisse** ( ☎ 20 97 39 79; cnr Ave Général de Gaulle & Ave de la Concorde; ☒ 9am-12.30pm & 3-7pm Mon-Sat) Has a library, cinema and a booklet outlining a monthly programme of concerts and exhibitions.

#### EMERGENCY
**Emergency** ☎ 17 or 18

#### GUIDES
Although a guide is not really necessary for exploring Bobo, you'll benefit from having one if you're planning on venturing further afield in the southwest of the country. Costs start from CFA5000 per day within Bobo, or CFA10,000 if you're travelling beyond.

# BOBO-DIOULASSO

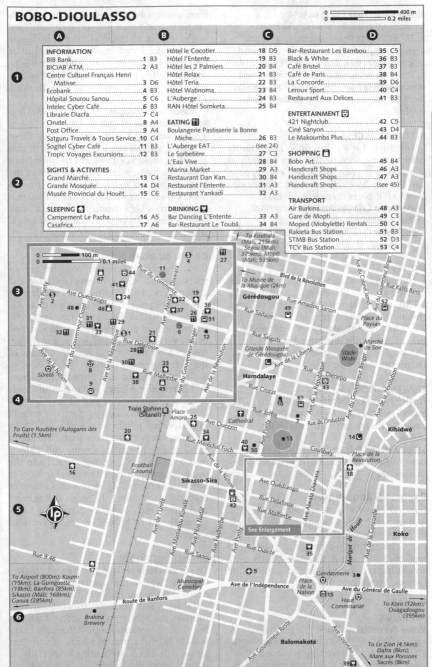

| | | |
|---|---|---|
| **INFORMATION** | Hôtel le Cocotier.....................**18** D5 | Bar-Restaurant Les Bambou.......**35** C5 |
| BIB Bank................................**1** B3 | Hôtel l'Entente......................**19** B3 | Black & White........................**36** B3 |
| BICIAB ATM...........................**2** A3 | Hôtel les 2 Palmiers.................**20** B4 | Café Bristel...........................**37** B3 |
| Centre Culturel Français Henri | Hôtel Relax...........................**21** B3 | Café de Paris.........................**38** B4 |
|   Matisse...............................**3** D6 | Hôtel Teria...........................**22** B3 | La Concorde..........................**39** D6 |
| Ecobank...............................**4** B3 | Hôtel Watinoma.....................**23** B4 | Leroux Sport.........................**40** C4 |
| Hôpital Sourou Sanou...............**5** C6 | L'Auberge.............................**24** B3 | Restaurant Aux Delices............**41** B3 |
| Intelec Cyber Café...................**6** B3 | RAN Hôtel Somketa.................**25** B3 | |
| Librairie Diacfa......................**7** C4 | | **ENTERTAINMENT** |
| Onatel................................**8** A4 | **EATING** | 421 Nightclub........................**42** C5 |
| Post Office............................**9** A4 | Boulangerie Pastisserie la Bonne | Ciné Sanyon..........................**43** D4 |
| Satguru Travels & Tours Service..**10** C4 |   Miche.................................**26** B4 | Le Makoumba Plus..................**44** B3 |
| Sogitel Cyber Café..................**11** B3 | L'Auberge EAT.....................(see **24**) | |
| Tropic Voyages Excursions.........**12** B3 | Le Sorbetière........................**27** C3 | **SHOPPING** |
| | L'Eau Vive............................**28** B4 | Bobo Art..............................**45** B4 |
| **SIGHTS & ACTIVITIES** | Marina Market.......................**29** A3 | Handicraft Shops.....................**46** A3 |
| Grand Marché.......................**13** C4 | Restaurant Dan Kan.................**30** B4 | Handicraft Shops.....................**47** A3 |
| Grande Mosquée....................**14** D4 | Restaurant l'Entente.................**31** A3 | Handicraft Shops...................(see **45**) |
| Musée Provincial du Houët........**15** C6 | Restaurant Yankadi..................**32** A3 | |
| | | **TRANSPORT** |
| **SLEEPING** | **DRINKING** | Air Burkina...........................**48** A3 |
| Campement Le Pacha...............**16** A5 | Bar Dancing L'Entente..............**33** A3 | Gare de Mopti.......................**49** C3 |
| Casafrica.............................**17** A6 | Bar-Restaurant Le Toubâ...........**34** B4 | Moped (Mobylette) Rentals.......**50** C4 |
| | | Rakieta Bus Station..................**51** B3 |
| | | STMB Bus Station...................**52** D3 |
| | | TCV Bus Station.....................**53** C4 |

**BURKINA FASO**

**Abdoul Karim Kone** ( ☎ 76 66 46 14; karimabdoul21@yahoo.fr) Speaks passable English.
**AGTB** ( ☎ 76 59 03 87; sawadogoboureima@yahoo.fr) A private association of 20 guides, offering tours around Bobo (including to the workshop for people with a disability with whom the association works) and further afield.
**Mamadou Cisse** (mamadou@yahoo.fr) Can be found at Bobo Art (p154), opposite the Hôtel Watinoma; speaks a little English.

### INTERNET ACCESS
Surprisingly for its size, Bobo has Internet cafés that are so slow that they'll have you wondering if your inbox will ever appear, and the machines are so old that questions about USB ports inspire blank looks.
**Intelec Cyber Café** (Ave Ouédraogo; per hr CFA300; ☽ 8am-midnight)
**Sogitel Cyber Café** (Rue du Commerce; per hr CFA300) Claims to be open 24 hours but don't count on it.

### MONEY
Biciab, Ecobank and BIB all have offices in Bobo, and Biciab has Visa-friendly ATMs dotted around the centre of town (including on the corner of Ave Ponty and Ave Ouédraogo). Banks in Mali and further west within Burkina Faso are more challenging, so if you're headed that way, change money here.

### TRAVEL AGENCIES
**Tropic Voyages Excursions** ( ☎ 20 97 60 94; tropicvoyages@fasonet.bf; Ave Ouédraogo) For tours around Burkina Faso, especially to Gaoua and the southwest.
**Satguru Travels & Tours Service** ( ☎ 20 98 32 10; kumar_sakhrani@yahoo.com; Rue Crozat) The best in town for airline tickets.

## Dangers & Annoyances
Bobo-Dioulasso is generally a safe city. Avoid, however, the small river – more a trickle – where travellers report there's a risk of being mugged by night. You'll need resilience to outlast the particularly persistent hangers-on who lounge around the Grande Mosquée.

## Sights
### MUSEUMS
**Musée Provincial du Houët** (Place de la Nation; admission CFA1000; ☽ 9am-12.30pm & 3-5.30pm Tue-Sat) This small but interesting museum showcases masks, statues and ceremonial dress

from all over Burkina Faso. In the grounds are three traditional houses, each furnished in the style of its inhabitants: a Bobo house in red *banco* (mud-brick); a Fulani hut of branches and woven straw; and a small Senoufo (a Voltaic people who settled in northern Côte d'Ivoire and southern Burkina Faso 400 years ago) compound.

**Musée de la Musique** ( ☎ 20 98 15 02; Blvd de la Revolution; admission CFA1000; ☽ 8.30am-6pm Tue-Sun) This is small but recommended for those with an emerging passion for African music, as well as those keen to learn the difference between a balafon and djembe. Most of the instruments on display (labels in French only) come from western Burkina Faso (especially from Lobi country). There's a small shop selling CDs of local traditional music which you won't find elsewhere.

### GRAND MARCHÉ
Bobo-Dioulasso's centrepiece, the expansive Grand Marché, is hugely enjoyable and atmospheric, and a wonderful (and largely hassle-free) place to experience a typical African city market. Occupying the inner circle are the fruit and vegetable stalls, watched over by colourfully clad women and surrounded by the overwhelming odours of the fish and meat sections. From here to the market's outer rim, impossibly narrow and labyrinthine lanes and makeshift stalls stock household wares and an excellent selection of African cotton prints – as well as reasonably priced tailors who can make clothing from them in a flash. There's a small choice of masks, drums and objects in bronze and gold among the stalls in the southeastern quarter. The market spills over onto the surrounding streets in a chaos of mopeds, wandering tradesmen and general clamour, which together provide a lively counterpoint to Bobo's otherwise tranquil streets.

### GRANDE MOSQUÉE
The **Grande Mosquée** (admission to grounds CFA1000), built in 1893, is an outstanding example of Sahel-style mud architecture, with conical towers and wooden struts (which both support the structure and act as scaffolding during replastering). Although entry is forbidden for non-Muslims, it's the exterior that is so captivating, especially at sunset when the façade turns golden and

---

### FÊTES DES MASQUES

In the Bobo-Dioulasso region, whenever there's a major funeral – such as that of a village chief, which takes place six months or so after his death – it's accompanied by a late night *fête des masques* (festival of masks) which features Bobo helmet masks, as well as other types.

Masked men dance to an orchestra of flute-like instruments and narrow drums beaten with curved canes. Sometimes they're dressed in bulky black-and-brown raffia outfits, resembling scarecrows; attached to the mask is a mop of brown raffia, falling over the head and shoulders to the waist. Often the dancers carry long pointed sticks with which they make enormous jumps. Each dancer, representing a different spirit, performs in turn, leaping, waving his stick and looking for evil spirits that might prevent the deceased from going to paradise. The onlookers, especially the children, are terrified and flee as the dancer becomes increasingly wilder, performing strange acrobatic feats and waving his head backwards and forwards until he catches someone and strikes them. The victim, however, mustn't complain. That chase over, another begins and the whole wild ceremony can last for hours.

---

the faithful pass by on their way home or to the neighbouring well, often pausing for prayer in the mosque en route. A powerful sense of community life revolves around the mosque. The quiet and shady grounds in the immediate vicinity are interspersed with shelters and prayer mats for worshippers, and add to the charm of one of Burkina Faso's most memorable sites.

If you take one of the guides who hang around the vicinity, expect to pay CFA5000 for explanations about the mosque and a short tour of the Kibidwe district; permission to take photos in the latter should be included in the price.

#### KIBIDWE

Just across the street to the east of the mosque is Kibidwe, the oldest part of town. You won't get around alone, so give in gracefully, make a contribution 'for the elders', and let yourself be guided. The best of the guides know their neighbourhood well, though their English is minimal. You'll see blacksmiths, potters, weavers, and **Sya** – the house of the ancestors, traditionally the oldest building in Bobo.

### Festivals & Events

The best time to be here is during Bobo's **Semaine Nationale de la Culture** (www.snc.gov.bf), a week of music, dance and theatre. It's held every even year in March or April.

### Sleeping

Staying in the city centre is convenient, but there are some imaginative choices in the quieter surrounding suburbs.

#### BUDGET

The two places on the west side of town are highly recommended (a shared taxi from the centre to either costs CFA200, more after 8pm).

**Campement le Pacha** ( ☎ 20 98 09 54; lepachabo@ yahoo.fr; Rue Malherbe; camping per person/moto/car/ campervan CFA1500/1500/2000/3000, s/d with fan & shared bathroom CFA4500/8000, d with air-con CFA11,000; P ⊠ ) A terrific choice beyond the rail line, the Franco-Swiss owned Campement le Pacha is arrayed around one of Bobo's nicest courtyards, with a veritable forest of palms and potted plants. The rooms are among the nicest budget beds in Burkina Faso – spacious, occasional hints of character, and spotlessly clean. Although there are no mosquito nets, the windows, unusually, have wire netting. When we visited the two jovial local women overseeing the place were wonderfully welcoming. They also cook pizza in the evening in the great garden restaurant.

**Casafrica** ( ☎ 20 98 01 57; Rue 9.46, off Route de Banfora; camping per person CFA1500, s/d with fan & shared bathroom CFA4000/5000, s/d with fan, shower & shared toilet CFA5000/6000; P ) Casafrica is recommended, and is watched over by the friendly Ajuma, who provides a warm welcome. The simple rooms come with mosquito nets, the courtyard is attractive, and there's a decent cheap bar and restaurant. The surrounding streets are quiet and very African with their laterite roads and overhanging trees.

**Hôtel le Cocotier** ( ☎ 70 75 90 09; Place de la Revolution; d with fan & shared bathroom CFA5000, with fan & shower CFA6500, with fan, TV & private bathroom CFA7500) Opened in 2003, this is Bobo's best budget hotel in the city centre. It has a good mix of bare but tidy rooms (all with mosquito nets), friendly staff and a rooftop bar-terrace, from where the nearby minarets of the Grande Mosquée are visible. The shared bathrooms are super-clean and it's easy walking distance from the Grande Marché, but just far enough away to ensure a quiet stay.

**Le Zion** ( ☎ 78 86 27 25; cbodelet@voila.fr; rooms CFA3000-6000) Now here's a place that will change your experience of Africa. Run by a French and Burkinabé couple, Camille and Wassa, this place cannot be recommended highly enough. On the outskirts of town and very much a part of the local community, they offer simple comfy rooms, built using traditional materials (and with mosquito nets). But it's the whole package that stands out – live music most weekends, a courtyard with shady mango tree, home-cooked meals, *mobylette* rental, an artisan's workshop, a recording studio for local performers, loads of advice on the surrounding area, and a wonderfully chilled ambience. You'll feel like you're staying in an African village, which is reason enough to come here. It can be difficult to find, so give them a call and they'll come and pick you up from the town centre.

### MIDRANGE

**L'Auberge** ( ☎ 20 97 17 67; hoberge@fasonet.bf; Ave Ouédraogo; s/d/ste CFA28,438/30,798/48,498; 🅿 🐼 🌊 ) Bobo's best hotel, L'Auberge is a well-run place with large and comfortable rooms, many of which have balconies overlooking the good-sized pool and fragrant palm-filled garden. Where other top-end hotels in Burkina Faso have worn down since we were last here, L'Auberge has kept its standards high. Rooms have mosquito nets and there's an excellent restaurant.

**Hôtel les 2 Palmiers** ( ☎ 20 97 27 59; fax 20 97 76 45; off Rue Malherbe; d from CFA32,000; 🅿 🐼 ) Run by the same people who own two similarly named and similarly excellent hotels in Ouagadougou, this fine hotel has traditional masks in all the public spaces and in the rooms, which are spacious, nicely decorated and quiet. The location is better than it looks on the map – an easy walk into town but in a nice quiet street.

**Hôtel Teria** ( ☎ 20 97 19 72; Ave Alwata Diawara; s/d with fan CFA8000/9000, with air-con CFA16,000/17,500; 🐼 ) This simple little place is good lower

midrange value, with surprisingly good rooms (it doesn't look much from the outside) which are sheltered from the busy streets just outside the door. Rooms with air-con are larger and air-tight, but don't have mosquito nets.

**Hôtel Watinoma** ( ☎ 20 97 20 82; fax 20 97 57 30; Rue Malherbe; small/large d CFA16,300/21,600; 🐼 ) You won't be inspired by this place, but the clean rooms (with mosquito nets) and a good location – quiet but central – are just about worth the price. Staff can seem alternately bewildered and indifferent at first, but are quite friendly once you get to know them. The smaller rooms are fine for a couple of days but a tad claustrophobic for any longer than that.

**RAN Hôtel Somketa** ( ☎ 20 97 09 00; hotran@fasonet .bf; Ave de la Nation; s/d/ste CFA33,000/42,900/64,480; 🐼 🌊 ) Amid the uncertainty regarding the future of passenger rail services, the RAN soldiers on, maintaining high standards with very large and comfortable rooms, most with balcony, satellite TV and tiny bathtubs. It's an easy walk into the town centre and there's a restaurant and pool, plus small handicrafts shops and a quietly professional air. It doesn't have a lot of character but it's highly recommended nonetheless.

**Hôtel Relax** ( ☎ 20 97 22 27; fax 20 97 13 07; Ave Alwata Diawara; small d CFA17,110, s/d with TV CFA33,630/36,580; 🐼 🌊 ) While still one of Bobo's best hotels, and a favourite of tour groups, the Relax is overpriced. The staff are friendly, the swimming pool is large, and you can get CNN on most of the TVs, but the rooms are a bit scruffy around the edges and mosquitos can be a problem. On the plus side, it's in the heart of Bobo but one or two blocks removed from the hangers-on that gather around L'Auberge. One strange feature is the pillow selection – square and with the consistency of overcooked *foutou*.

## Eating

### RESTAURANTS

**Restaurant Dan Kan** (Rue Malherbe; starters & soups CFA750-1500, mains CFA500-3000; 🕒 8.30am-3.30pm & 6-10.30pm) With agreeable outdoor (but covered) tables, very reasonable prices and a varied menu, Restaurant Dan Kan is an excellent deal. It's kept spotlessly clean and service is attentive. If you just eat *riz sauce* or couscous and drink tamarind juice, you'll be well-fed for around CFA1500. Highly recommended.

**Le Zion** ( ☎ 78 86 27 25; starters CFA500-1000, mains CFA600-3000, brunch CFA500-2000; ◷ lunch & dinner) At this homely place you can get everything from homemade pasta to *tajine de mouton au miel avec riz parfumé* (mutton cooked in a clay pot with honey and perfumed rice; CFA1400) or *pain de capitaine* (fish cakes, CFA1000). Camille, the French cook, blends fresh local ingredients with a French flair for creativity. There's also a different *plat du jour* every day, *bissap* (a refreshing local drink made from hibiscus-like flowers, CFA100) and mango milkshakes (CFA500) from the resident mango tree.

**Restaurant l'Entente** (Rue Delafosse; mains from CFA1200; ◷ 7.30am-10pm) This simple restaurant has a wide-ranging menu of African and European staples, but it's a rare day that all menu items are available. Waiters are laid-back and friendly, but the best thing about this place are the street-facing tables on the veranda – a wonderfully chilled place to watch the streetlife of Bobo passing by. It's also one of the few restaurants to do breakfast.

**L'Auberge** ( ☎ 20 97 17 67; Ave Ouédraogo; 3-course menu CFA5500; ◷ lunch & dinner) Far and away the best of the hotel restaurants. The three-course menu here is outstanding, with everything from sardine salads to crêpes and flourishes like fresh basil and a garlic-and-chive butter to accompany your entrecôte. If you've been on the road for a while, it'll all taste like paradise.

**L'Eau Vive** (Rue Delafosse; mains CFA2500-5000; ◷ lunch & dinner Mon-Sat) The sister venue to the restaurant of the same name in Ouagadougou, and also run by nuns, L'Eau Vive offers imaginative French cooking and a varied menu. Main dishes all come with potatoes or vegetables and the dining area offers a star-filled canopy of the night sky.

For a quick and cheap meal (mostly rice staples with sauce), try **Restaurant Yankadi** (Rue Delafosse; ◷ lunch & dinner).

**PÂTISSERIES**

**La Sorbetière** (Ave du Gouverneur Binger; ◷ 8am-10pm) This fine pâtisserie may lure you in with promises of ice cream, but there's rarely any available. There is, however, a spick-and-span dining room where they serve up excellent pastries (the croissants are good

for breakfast) or reasonable sandwiches, pizza slices and hamburgers.

**Boulangerie Pâtisserie la Bonne Miche** (Ave Ouédraogo) A little bit cheaper and less spick-and-span, this pâtisserie two blocks southeast of the market has excellent bread and a range of pastries.

**SELF-CATERING**

**Marina Market** (Ave de la République; ◷ 8am-1pm &3.30-9pm Mon-Sat, 9am-1pm & 5.30-8pm Sun) Ideal for stocking up for long bus or train rides, Marina Market has a good range of grocery items.

## Drinking

Bobo-Dioulasso only really comes to life at the weekend. One exception is the popular quarter of Balomakoté, which is rich in traditional music and is the area from where the internationally acclaimed group Farafina emerged. Here you'll enjoy great music in small, unpretentious *buvettes* (small cafés that double up as drinking places serving cheap meals), where you can drink *chopolo*, the local millet-based beer. Elsewhere – unless you're there very late on Friday or Saturday night – the bars are all pretty similar, with outdoor tables under straw paillotes and atmospheres filled with inertia and innuendo.

**Bar-Restaurant Les Bambou** (Ave du Gouverneur Binger; admission CA600; ◷ 6am-2.30pm & 6pm-midnight Mon-Sat, 6pm-midnight Sun) Definitely the most enjoyable of the outdoor bars in central Bobo, Les Bambou is a terrific outdoor venue with a lovely garden area and traditional live music (especially traditional djembé music) from around 8pm from Wednesday to Saturday.

**Le Zion** ( ☎ 78 86 27 25) Another lively, but more intimate, place for live music (both modern and traditional), with plenty of local artists on Friday and Saturday nights. It's very much a local bar, but is also popular with expats.

**Leroux Sport** (cnr Rue Maréchal Foch & Ave Faidherbe; ◷ 7.30am-10pm) While this place is OK for food, you really come here for the European-style outdoor terrace (Bobo's answer to café culture) and the real espresso coffee (CFA200).

Also worth visiting are the following:
**Bar Dancing L'Entente** (Rue Delafosse)
**Bar-Restaurant Le Toubâ** (Rue Maréchal Foch)
**Black & White** (Ave du Gouverneur Binger)

**BURKINA FASO**

**La Concorde** (Ave Louveau)
**Restaurant aux Delices** (Ave de la République)

**Café de Paris** (Rue Malherbe; ☺ 7.30am-10pm) is another good choice for a streetside coffee, while **Café Bristel** (cnr Ave Alwata Diawara & Ave Ouédraogo) is ramshackle, but popular for an afternoon drink.

## Entertainment
### NIGHTCLUBS
Although most of Bobo's garden bars turn into dance venues late on Friday and Saturday nights, **Le Makoumba Plus** (Ave de la République), near the market, is a dedicated nightclub that pumps out loud music most nights of the week, and really gets going by the weekend. You could also try **421 Nightclub** (Rue Malherbe), at the hotel of the same name, although the atmosphere can be a bit hit-or-miss.

### CINEMAS
The modern **Ciné Sanyon** (Ave de la République) is an excellent cinema (with air-con) that shows good films, including runs and reruns of Burkinabé productions which have won international acclaim, as well as dated Hollywood blockbusters and Jackie Chan flicks.

## Shopping
Bobo-Dioulasso is a good place to pick up wooden masks and other carvings – especially Lobi and Bobo items – and there are some good handicraft shops dotted around the town centre and in the southwestern quarter of the market.

One small shop that stands out for its variety of masks, statues and light sales-pitch is **Bobo Art** (Rue Malherbe; ☺ 8am-7pm Mon-Sat).

For clothing, the Grand Marché is your best bet; for a tailor-made shirt expect to pay CFA1500 for cloth, plus CFA1500 for labour.

## Getting There & Away
### AIR
**Air Burkina** ( ☎ 20 97 06 97; Ave du Gouverneur Clozel) Has three flights per week to/from Ouagadougou (one way/return, CFA30,000/ 60,000). For details of international flights from Bobo, see p168.

### BUS
**STMB** ( ☎ 20 97 08 78; Blvd de la Revolution) and **TCV** ( ☎ 20 97 23 37; Rue Crozat) have the best buses to Ouagadougou (CFA6000; 5 hours), with five daily departures each. STMB's 10am and 4pm departures cost CFA7000 as the buses are better and have air-con and snacks.

For getting around the southwest, **Rakieta** ( ☎ 20 97 18 91; Ave Ouédraogo) is a good local company that has regular departures for Banfora (CFA2300, 1½ hours, 10 daily) and Gaoua (CFA4000, around five hours, two daily).

For details on transport to Ghana and Mali, see p169.

### BUSH TAXI & MINIBUS
Nearly all bush taxis and minibuses leave from the *gare routière* (also known as the Autogare des Fruits) about 3km west of the city centre.

### CAR
The staff at **Hôtel l'Entente** (Rue du Commerce) can organise a 4WD vehicle for CFA50,000 per day, regardless of the number of people; petrol is extra. For shorter trips, **Laurent Sanou** ( ☎ 76 49 68 84) charges CFA2500 an hour for a 4WD with driver.

## Getting Around
### TO/FROM THE AIRPORT
Expect to pay CFA300/1500 for a shared/ private taxi between the airport and the city centre.

### BICYCLE & MOPED
To hire a bicycle for the day, ask at your hotel or around the market. A reasonable price is CFA2000 per day.

For a moped, expect to pay at least CFA4000 a day, and CFA6000 for a motorbike. You'll find some for hire opposite the Grand Marché on Ave Ponty.

During the rainy season, visiting the surrounding villages by bicycle or moped can be a sticky experience.

### TAXI
Shared taxis are plentiful and most trips within town cost between CFA150 and CFA250. Prices increase after 10pm and luggage costs extra.

## AROUND BOBO-DIOULASSO
The traditional houses in the villages around Bobo-Dioulasso are characterised by their tall conical roofs and narrow storehouses

linked by earth walls, which give the compounds the look of squat medieval castles.

## La Guinguette & Koumi

La Guinguette (admission CFA1000) is a crystal-clear bathing area, 18km from Bobo-Dioulasso in Forêt de Kou, a lush forest. Although it's popular at weekends, you'll probably have the place to yourself during the week. Camping is possible, but it's safer to ask the locals for a place to sleep in the village.

On the way, pause at the village of Koumi, which has some fine ochre two-storey adobe houses, typical of the area.

From Bobo, take the Sikasso road to Koumi (15km). Just after the village, turn right and then take a left fork along a narrow, rough dirt track. After passing two villages, take a sharp right alongside the forest and follow the track to the river.

## Koro

The village of Koro (admission CFA1000) is 14km east of Bobo, just off the main Ouagadougou road. Perched on the hillside, its houses – hewn into the natural rock – are unique in the area, and there are fine panoramic views over the countryside from the top of the village.

## Mare aux Hippopotames

Some 66km northeast of Bobo, access to this lake isn't easy and the hippo population doesn't compare with that of Tengréla (see p157). The local fishermen (tough bargainers) will take you in a pirogue. A fact to ponder as you glide across the lake: more people are killed in Africa every year by hippos than by any other animal. The lake has bilharzia (see p858), so don't dive in.

Getting here is very difficult without a vehicle as there's no public transport beyond Satiri, which leaves you with a 22km walk. If you have wheels, head for Satiri, 44km northeast of Bobo-Dioulasso on the dirt road to Dédougou. From there, take a rough dirt road northwest which, after about 15km, forks off to the left (south) towards the lake. From July to September this road can be impassable.

## Mare aux Poissons Sacrés

This sacred fish pond is around 8km southeast of Bobo, in the village of Dafra. The surrounding hills and the pond, at the base of a cliff and a 20- to 30-minute walk from the nearest parking spot, are memorable; the fish less so. Chickens, which you can buy on the spot, are sacrificed and thrown to the over-gorged *poissons sacrés* (sacred fish). It's all rather gruesome, with chicken feathers everywhere. Don't wear gold jewellery or anything red; both are prohibited at this sacred spot.

From Place de la Nation in Bobo, head southeast on Ave Louveau. After about 8km, ask for the turn-off to the right for Dafra. A taxi there and back from Bobo-Dioulasso will cost at least CFA5000.

## BANFORA
pop 60,288

Banfora is a dusty, sleepy little town in one of the more beautiful areas in Burkina Faso. As such, it serves as a good base for exploring the lush green surrounding countryside, not to mention the hippos of Tengréla Lake, the cascading waters of Karfiguéla Waterfall and the otherworldly Sindou Peaks. It's also a necessary gateway to the Lobi country further east.

In Banfora itself, the perimeter of the market, with its women fruit and vegetable traders, is more interesting than the actual market – especially on the north side. There are also some good hotels and places to eat.

### Information

As you wander around town, you're likely to be accompanied by guides keen to show you the neighbouring sights. Your best bet is to ask at Hôtel La Canne à Sucre or Hôtel le Comoé (see p156) for a recommendation. One taxi driver who has been recommended by readers is **Oumar Ouédraogo** ( ☎ 20 91 10 69 or 76 60 37 23) who charges CFA10,000 per halfday. The softly spoken **Boukary** ( ☎ 76 47 94 42; sombouka@yahoo.fr) is one of the less pushy guides and is adept at tracking down local traditional music; he speaks enough English to get by and charges CFA10,500 per site plus transport. As a rule, don't pay your guide until you return to Banfora.

Internet is still hard to find in Banfora. **Calypso Bar** (off Rue de la Poste; per min CFA40) is probably the best, but its prices are extortionate and its connections slow – ask at Hôtel le Comoé for directions.

**Pharmacie Nadon** ( ☎ 20 91 01 66; off Rue de la Préfecture) is reasonably well stocked.

BURKINA FASO

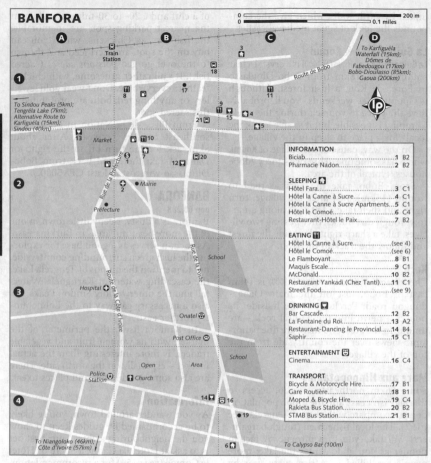

**BANFORA**

0 — 200 m
0 — 0.1 miles

To Karfiguéla
Waterfall (15km);
Dômes de
Fabedougou (17km);
Bobo-Dioulasso (85km);
Gaoua (200km)

Route de Bobo

To Sindou Peaks (5km);
Tengréla Lake (7km);
Alternative Route to
Karfiguéla (15km);
Sindou (40km)

Market

Rue de la Préfecture

Mairie

Préfecture

Rue de la Poste

School

Route de la Côte d'Ivoire

Hospital

Onatel

Post Office

School

Open        Area

Police
Station    Church

To Niangoloko (46km);
Côte d'Ivoire (57km)

To Calypso Bar (100m)

**INFORMATION**
Biciab...................................................1 B2
Pharmacie Nadon.................................2 B2

**SLEEPING**
Hôtel Fara.............................................3 C1
Hôtel la Canne à Sucre........................4 C1
Hôtel la Canne à Sucre Apartments...5 C1
Hôtel le Comoé....................................6 C4
Restaurant-Hôtel le Paix.....................7 B2

**EATING**
Hôtel la Canne à Sucre....................(see 4)
Hôtel le Comoé...............................(see 6)
Le Flamboyant......................................8 B1
Maquis Escale.......................................9 C1
McDonald............................................10 B2
Restaurant Yankadi (Chez Tanti)......11 C1
Street Food.......................................(see 9)

**DRINKING**
Bar Cascade........................................12 B2
La Fontaine du Roi..............................13 A2
Restaurant-Dancing le Provincial......14 B4
Saphir..................................................15 C1

**ENTERTAINMENT**
Cinema................................................16 C4

**TRANSPORT**
Bicycle & Motorcycle Hire..................17 B1
Gare Routière......................................18 B1
Moped & Bicycle Hire.........................19 C4
Rakieta Bus Station.............................20 B2
STMB Bus Station................................21 B1

For changing money, the **Biciab** (Rue de la Préfecture) facing the market, only accepts euros in cash.

## Sleeping

**Hôtel la Canne à Sucre** ( ☎ 20 91 01 07; hotel cannasucre@fasonet.bf; off Rue de la Poste; d with air-con CFA18,900, 4-bed apt CFA49,000; 🗙 🔊 ) Welcome to one of Burkina Faso's most charming hotels; an unexpected touch of class in Banfora. The immaculate rooms are attractive, the bathrooms enormous and the two apartments across the road are supremely stylish, with wooden beams, curtains and bedspreads cut from Bogolan cloth, and African woodcarvings throughout the six rooms. The apartments also have a large swimming pool just

for them. The leafy garden is home to Banfora's best restaurant. Jean, the Breton owner, distils his own rum from sugar cane, which is available for CFA6000 per bottle.

**Hôtel le Comoé** ( ☎ 20 91 01 51; Rue de la Poste; d/tw with fan & private shower CFA7000/7500, d with air-con & private bathroom CFA14,000; 🗙 ) If you don't mind being south of the centre – it's a 10- to 15-minute walk from the Rakieta bus station or a CFA200 taxi ride – Hôtel le Comoé is excellent. The rooms have a dusty smell, as if they haven't been opened in a while, but they're larger than most in town, have mosquito nets and are clean. The big selling point, however, is the lovely swept and shady courtyard, which is a great place to relax and hosts a bar and restaurant.

Restaurant-Hôtel le Paix ( ☎ 20 91 00 16; off Rue de la Préfecture; d with fan & shared bathroom CFA6000) Banfora's cheapest hotel is not a bad option for those counting their ceefahs. Rooms are minimalist, for reasons of economy rather than style (ie they're completely bare), but they're clean, come with mosquito nets and the shared bathrooms are also kept clean.

Hôtel Fara ( ☎ 20 91 01 17; off Route de Bobo; d with fan/air-con from CFA6845/10,500; ❄ ) Appearances can be deceptive – this central place seems bleak because of the dusty, lifeless compound that it inhabits, but the basic rooms aren't bad and come with mosquito nets and OK bathrooms. Staff are friendly once they warm up.

## Eating
Banfora has two stand-out places to eat.

Hôtel la Canne à Sucre (off Rue de la Poste; starters CFA1500-3500, mains CFA1900-3900; ❄ lunch & dinner) The restaurant at this fine hotel is high quality, with delightful open-air dining, a well-chosen wine list, good service and a varied menu that spans European and African flavours. A highlight among many is crevettes flambees ail-persil-rhum-maison (fried shrimp cooked in the house rum; CFA3500). You don't find quality like this every day in Burkina Faso.

McDonald (off Rue de la Préfecture; starters CFA500-1000, mains mostly CFA500-1900; meals CFA500-1000; ❄ 7am-10pm Thu-Tue, 7am-1pm Wed) A Banfora favourite, McDonald is friendly, sheltered from the street and exceptionally good. Servings are enormous – one traveller assured us that their steak consisted of half a cow – and there's everything, from brochettes and fresh fruit juices to fish and hamburgers. The most expensive thing on the menu is an entire chicken for CFA3000.

Other places which are less inspired, but OK nonetheless, include the following:

Le Flamboyant (Route de Bobo) A fairly typical maquis-style African restaurant, serving predominantly rice.

Maquis Escale (off Rue de la Poste) Is pleasant and serves sandwiches for CFA500 and cheap drinks.

Restaurant Yankadi (Chez Tanti; Route de Bobo) Close to the entrance to town if you're coming from Bobo-Dioulasso.

Hôtel le Comoé (Rue de la Poste) Service is slow but the brochette de capitaine (CFA2000) is delicious.

## Drinking
There are a number of small buvettes in Banfora, which are all good for a drink. The paillote of Bar Cascade (Rue de la Poste) is a relaxing place for a sundowner. La Fontaine du Roi (off Rue de la Préfecture), on the west side of the market, is a modest restaurant and dancing place, although you'll be lucky to find much going on outside weekends. Saphir (off Rue de la Poste) is a cosy and pleasant watering hole, while Restaurant-Dancing Le Provincial (off Rue de la Poste) also has a nice ambience.

## Getting There & Away
Rakieta ( ☎ 20 91 03 07; Rue de la Poste) has regular departures for Bobo-Dioulasso (one way/return CFA1200/2300, 1½ hours, 10 daily) and Gaoua (CFA3000, 3½ hours, two daily). STMB ( ☎ 20 91 05 81; Rue de la Poste) also leaves five times a day for Bobo-Dioulasso.

## AROUND BANFORA
You'll need wheels to visit the wonderful attractions surrounding Banfora. If you take a guide, they can help you make the arrangements – for information on guides see p155; alternately ask at your hotel. Daily rates start at CFA2000 per day for a bicycle, CFA4000 for a moped and CFA6000 for a motorcycle; the latter is advisable if you're making the longer journey to the Sindou Peaks.

### Tengréla Lake
This 100 hectare lake (Lac de Tengréla; admission CFA2000), around 7km west of Banfora on a good dirt road, makes a pleasant bicycle ride and is easy to find. You'll see fisherfolk, a variety of birdlife and, if you're lucky, hippos. The admission price includes a pirogue trip.

To get to the lake, take the dirt road that forks right at the Total petrol station in Banfora, then, after about 6km, turn left for the village of Tengréla. The lake is a further 1km beyond the village.

### Karfiguéla Waterfall
Some 15km northwest of Banfora, these waterfalls (Cascades de Karfiguéla; admission CFA1000) are at their best during and just after the rainy season when, unfortunately, the dirt tracks leading to the falls can be impassable. But, whatever the season, it's worth the journey. From below, you approach the falls through a magnificent avenue of mango trees, and the chaotic jumble of rocks over which the water splays are a sight in themselves.

From the waterfalls, you can walk or ride the 2km to the Dômes de Fabedougou (CFA500), an escarpment-type formation good for rock climbing, by following the main irrigation pipe eastwards (take the stairs to the right of the falls).

To get to the Domes from Bobo, take the road to Sindou and then turn right at a sign near the Karfiguéla falls turn-off. When you reach the T-junction at the main irrigation canal that leads from the head of the falls, follow it to the left (upstream).

### Sindou Peaks

The Sindou **rock formations** (Pics de Sindou; admission CFA1000) are a narrow, craggy chain which extends northwest from the dirt road, which you follow from Banfora for about 50km. The tortuous cones of these structures, sculpted and blasted by the elements, were left behind when the surrounding softer rocks eroded away.

This area is ideal for a short steep stroll, a day hike, or even a couple of days' trekking, for which you'll need to bring all your own food, gear and water.

### GAOUA

Gaoua is a good base for exploring Lobi country, an area that's culturally distinct. There's a vital Sunday market and, if you like your music traditional and untainted, Gaoua has plenty of great *boîtes* (informal nightclubs) with live music. There's also the small **Musée de Poni** ( ☎ 20 87 01 69; admission CFA1000) devoted to Lobi culture.

**Hôtel Hala** ( ☎ 20 87 01 21; d from CFA10,000) is Gaoua's only habitable hotel and, thankfully, it's a reasonable if unexciting place. It also serves excellent Lebanese fare. It's just outside of town on the road to Banfora.

For cheap food, your best bet is **La Porte Ouverte**.

### Getting There & Away

**Rakieta** ( ☎ 20 87 02 18) has a twice daily service to Bobo-Dioulasso (CFA4000, five hours) via Banfora (CFA3000, 3½ hours).

## AROUND GAOUA
### Loropéni

Loropéni, 39km west of Gaoua on the road to Banfora, is the site of some **ancient ruins** whose origins remain unknown. The local Gan people call the complex *la Maison de Refuge*. The structures themselves are far from overwhelming; their interest lies in their being among the very few stone remains in West Africa.

A further 8km northwest of Loropéni is the village of **Obiré** and the **Sanctuaire de Roi Gan** – the remains of a sanctuary of the Gan kings – which includes 12 statues representing the long-dead monarchs.

A taxi from Gaoua should cost around CFA15,000 for three hours plus petrol. Alternatively you could take any transport headed for Banfora and then take your chances finding onward transport from the main road.

---

#### LOBI TRADITIONS

Lobi traditions are some of the best preserved in West Africa. Perhaps because of this, Lobi art (in particular the wooden carvings which play an essential role in protecting the family) is highly regarded by collectors.

For travellers, the most obvious manifestation of enduring traditions is the architecture of rural Lobi homes. The compounds are rectangular and – rare for constructions of mud – sometimes multistorey. Each structure, with high mud-brick walls and scarcely slits for windows, is like a miniature fortress. Unlike most Africans, who live in villages, the Lobi (like the Somba and the Tamberma in northern Benin and Togo), live in their fields; a family compound may be several hundred metres from its nearest neighbours.

The Lobi are also known for holding fast to their cultural rituals. For example, the *dyoro* initiation rites, which take place every seven years, are still widely observed. As part of this important rite of passage, young men undergo three to six months of severe physical tests of their manhood, and learn the clan's oral history and the dos and don'ts of their culture.

In rural areas the Lobi often don't warm easily to foreigners. Don't take photos without express permission. In towns such as Gaoua, however, the Lobi can be very friendly, and if you're invited to have some *chopolo*, the local millet beer, by all means accept. For more on the Lobi, see p76.

# THE SOUTH & SOUTHEAST

## FADA N'GOURMA

pop 33,910

If you're headed for Niger or the parks of southeastern Burkina Faso and Benin, you'll most likely pass through Fada N'Gourma (or Fada as it's known as) some 219km east of Ouagadougou. It's a sprawling, shady town, with a moderately interesting market, but not enough to detain you any longer than the time it takes to change bush taxis.

Fada N'Gourma is known for its locally produced honey, *le miel de Gourma*, which is dark and tangy and is readily available at many roadside stalls. It's also, somewhat incongruously, the sister city of Epernay in France (home of champagne).

### Sleeping & Eating

**Auberge Yemmamma** ( ☎ 40 77 00 39; s/d with fan CFA6000/7000, with air-con CFA8000/10,000; ✖ ) This is the best hotel in town, which is not really saying much, but the simple rooms are kept reasonably clean. It has paillotes with comfortable chairs and a popular outdoor bar-restaurant where meals start at CFA1500.

There are usually several vendors selling inexpensive local food around the *gare routière*. **Restaurant de la Paix** (meals CFA1500), next to the Auberge Yemmamma, has an attractive shaded eating area and offers standard fare.

### Getting There & Away

**STMB** ( ☎ 40 77 06 94) has one daily bus between Fada N'Gourma and Ouagadougou (CFA4000, five hours). If you miss it, other companies occasionally coax their ageing fleets to life and sometimes even reach the capital without breaking down.

Transport for Niger and (especially) for the national parks of the southeast and Benin, is scarce and fills up slowly.

## PARC NATIONAL D'ARLI

In the southeast, on the border with Benin, **Parc National d'Arli** (admission per person CFA5000, plus obligatory guide CFA1500; ✖ 15 Dec-15 May) is Burkina Faso's major national park. It adjoins (and belongs to the same ecosystem as) Benin's Parc National de la Pendjari (p118). It's a long journey to get here from anywhere, but as the repository of Burkina Faso's only concentration of large mammals, it could just be worth it.

Animal species common to the parks on both sides of the border include hippos, elephants, warthogs, baboons, monkeys, lions, leopards, crocodiles and various kinds of antelope. Bird species are also varied.

If you have wheels, it's also possible to cross the Beninese border to visit Parc National de la Pendjari and the Benin section of Parc Regional du W. At the frontier, you can buy a 48-hour visa for CFA10,000.

With your own vehicle, you can also see the Burkina Faso side of **Parc Regional du W** ( ✖ usually 15 Dec-15 May) to the east of Arli on the Nigerien border; the entrance is via Diapaga. This park straddles Burkina Faso, Niger and Benin; see p596 for more details.

### Sleeping & Eating

**La Kompienga** (L'Agence Tourisme; ☎ 50 31 84 43; www .agence-tourisme.com; d with fan & bathroom CFA18,000, with air-con CFA20,000; ✖ ✖ ) This supremely comfortable complex has an attractive lodge, thatched-roof bungalows with tasteful local furnishings, and a bar-restaurant with air-con overlooking a clean pool; the fixed menu is CFA5000. At La Kompienga, you can arrange to hire a 4WD. Camping near the lodge is also possible.

### Getting There & Away

The only option for reaching the park by public transport from Ouagadougou is to take TCV's Sunday bus to Cotonou and ask to be let out at Tindangou (CFA6000, six hours); check when booking your ticket that the bus does indeed take this route. Otherwise, the only realistic options are to hire a 4WD (at least CFA40,000 per day plus petrol), or you can take an organised tour (see p137 for more details). **L'Agence Tourisme** ( ☎ 50 31 84 43; www.agence-tourisme.com) is probably the best; its prices may seem expensive, but the company is highly professional, and once you tot up park charges, lodging, the hire of a compulsory guide and tracker, and car rental, it's scarcely cheaper to go it alone.

## RANCH DE NAZINGA

The 97,000 hectare **Ranch de Nazinga** (Réserve de Nazinga; Nazinga ☎ 50 41 36 17; www.ranchdenazinga .com; admission per vehicle CFA1500, per person CFA8500, guide CFA2500, camera permit CFA1000; dm CFA5000, 2-bed apt CFA10,000, bungalows CFA12,500), south of Ouagadougou, near Pô and the Ghanaian border, is a work-in-progress. Established with Canadian assistance, the park has antelopes, monkeys, warthogs, crocodiles and a variety of birds. The park's custodians are, however, seeking to restock the area by raising the number of species of deer and antelope, and releasing them into the wild. Although there are 39 species of mammal, 600km of tracks and 11 watering holes within its boundaries, most of the ranch's elephants have migrated westwards to the contiguous Forêt de Sissili, which is richer in animals. As such, although Ranch de Nazinga may be more accessible than the park's further east, we're not convinced that it's yet worth the considerable expense of visiting here.

For information on the project and the reserve itself, visit the **Ranch de Nazinga office** (Map p138; ☎ 50 30 84 43; Rue Patrice Lumumba) in Ouagadougou. The ranch's overseers can arrange three/six-day photo safaris for €800/1300.

Driving time from Ouagadougou to Ranch de Nazinga is three hours; a 4WD is essential. Take the sealed road south to Pô (176km), then a dirt road west towards Léo. After 15km you'll come to a sign pointing south to Nazinga, some 40km further.

## TIÉBÉLÉ

Tiébélé, 40km east of Pô via a dirt track, is a wonderful detour if you're travelling up from Ghana, but it's also well worth visiting from Ouagadougou. Set in the heart of the green and low-lying Gourounsi country, Tiébélé is famous for its colourful and fortress-like windowless traditional houses. These are decorated by women, who work with guinea-fowl feathers, in geometrical patterns of red, black and white, which offer an antidote to the monochrome mud-brick villages found elsewhere in Burkina Faso. Once a Gourounsi capital, Tiébélé has an exceptional **chief's compound** (CFA1500) as well as other beautiful structures throughout the town. You can also go another 10km to the border village of Boungou, famous for its potters.

### Sleeping & Eating

**Auberge Kunkolo** ( ☎ 50 36 97 38 or 76 53 44 77; dm CFA4000, s/d with fan & shared bathroom CFA8000/10,000) This is French-run and is a wonderful

Tiébélé haven, with meals, a pleasant courtyard and nice rooms which borrow from local traditional designs.

### Getting There & Away

From Ouagadougou, STMB has five daily buses to Pô (CFA2000, three hours). Buses travelling between Kumasi and Ouagadougou also pass through Pô, from where there are semi-regular bush taxis to Tiébélé on its market day (every third day). Otherwise you'll have to charter a taxi.

# THE NORTH

## OUAHIGOUYA

**pop 61,096**

Ouahigouya (pronounced waee-gee-ya), 182km northwest of Ouagadougou by sealed road, may be the country's fourth-largest city, but it's either tranquil or deathly quiet, depending on your perspective. There's a market and an interesting chief's compound (the Maison du Naba Kango) but most people stay here only long enough to find onward transport to Mali.

During the Eid al-Fitr holiday (see p818), which marks the end of the fasting month of Ramadan, there's a famous pilgrimage to the mosque in Ramatoulaye, 25km east of town, between Baghélogo and Rambo.

### Information

The two banks in town, **Biciab** (Ave de Mopti) and **BIB** (Ave de Mopti), change euros in cash, but US dollars inspire worrying looks of bewilderment from the banks' tellers. The Biciab branch has an ATM that gives cash advances on Visa. For Internet access, try **Éspace Internautes** (Ave de Mopti; per hr CFA400; ⏱ 7.30am-9pm).

### Sights

A short walk northeast from Ouahigouya's market, the expansive but modest **Maison du Naba Kango** dates back to the days of the Yatenga kingdom, a pre-colonial rival of the principal Mossi kingdom, centred in Ouagadougou. The compound – home to the Naba, king of the predominantly Mossi Yatenga province and second only in importance to his Ouagadougou counterpart (see p140) – is a traditional mud construction. It contains numerous houses for the Naba's wives, sev-

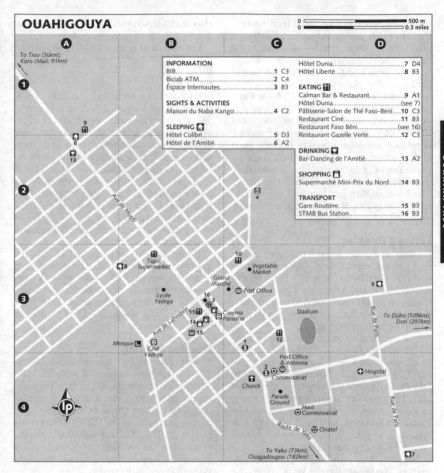

# OUAHIGOUYA

0 — 500 m
0 — 0.3 miles

**INFORMATION**
BIB.................................................1 C3
Biciab ATM......................................2 C4
Éspace Internautes...........................3 B3

**SIGHTS & ACTIVITIES**
Maison du Naba Kango......................4 C2

**SLEEPING** 🏠
Hôtel Colibri....................................5 D3
Hôtel de l'Amitié..............................6 A2

Hôtel Dunia.....................................7 D4
Hôtel Liberté....................................8 B3

**EATING** 🍴
Caïman Bar & Restaurant..................9 A1
Hôtel Dunia...............................(see 7)
Pâtisserie-Salon de Thé Faso-Béni....10 C3
Restaurant Ciné..............................11 B3
Restaurant Faso Béni..................(see 16)
Restaurant Gazelle Verte.................12 C3

**DRINKING** 🍸
Bar-Dancing de l'Amitié...................13 A2

**SHOPPING** 🛍
Supermarché Mini-Prix du Nord.......14 B3

**TRANSPORT**
Gare Routière.................................15 B3
STMB Bus Station...........................16 B3

BURKINA FASO

To Tiou (36km);
Koro (Mali; 91km)

Ave de Mopti

Tagui
Supermarket

Lycée
Yadega

Mosque

Ciné
Yadega

Ave de Lahinstein

Grand
Marché

Post Office

Cinema
Paradise

Vegetable
Market

Post Office
& Antenna

Commissariat

Church

Parade
Ground

Haut
Commissariat

Route de Yako

Onatel

Stadium

Rue de Paris

To Djibo (109km);
Dori (297km)

Hospital

Rue de Paris

To Yako (73km);
Ouagadougou (182km)

eral granaries, a small, plain reception room for guests, and a fetish house – forbidden even to the Naba's children. To be granted an audience with the Naba, you must bring a present; money is most appreciated. If he's unavailable, one of his young sons, *les princes*, may show you around for a tip.

## Sleeping

Ouahigouya has a small, but excellent range of accommodation, although most places are a fair hike from the centre.

**Hôtel Dunia** ( ☎ 40 55 05 95; Rue de Paris; s/d with fan CFA6000/8000, d with air-con from CFA15,000; ❄ ) This is one of those gems that seem to exist in the most unlikely places. Staying here is like stepping into someone's home, and the

friendly Syrian owners are a delight. There's a sitting room with satellite TV and a shady area in front, pleasant for a meal or drink. Madame's cooking is homely, plentiful and quite the best in town; meals cost CFA3000, and you'll need to order in advance.

**Hôtel Colibri** ( ☎ 40 55 05 72; d with fan/air-con CFA4920/8925; ❄ ) Staff at the Colibri are charming, and the spick-and-span rooms around a shady courtyard are of the sort (and at the price) that appeals to everyone from tour groups to budget travellers. It's about 1km east of the centre, but the warmth of the welcome compensates for the distance.

**Hôtel Liberté** ( ☎ 40 55 21 34; d with fan & shared bathroom CFA4500, d with air-con & private bathroom from

CFA8000) Budget travellers need look no further than this simple but tidy and well-run place, a few blocks northwest of the town centre. The rooms with fan are quite small, but fine for a night, and the chilled courtyard is a great place to hang out.

**Hôtel de l'Amitié** ( ☎ 40 55 05 21; Ave de Mopti; s/d with fan & shared bathroom CFA5000/6500, s/d with air-con & private bathroom CFA10,000/12,000; mains around CFA2500; 😢 ) Put this government-owned hotel in many other towns in Burkina Faso and it would be among the best, here in Ouahigouya it lacks the charm and personal touches that you'll find elsewhere. The hotel is 1km northwest of the centre, so it's handy that there's a good restaurant on site.

### Eating & Drinking

Ouahigouya is one town where we suggest that you eat in your hotel. Of the hotel restaurants, **Hôtel Dunia** ( ☎ 40 55 05 95; Rue de Paris) is the finest and promises home-cooked meals, although you'll need to order in advance and if Madame's too busy, meals may be restricted to hotel guests.

For inexpensive food, the tiny and central **Restaurant Ciné** has standard fare such as *riz sauce* for CFA350 and a small steak for CFA450, while **Pâtisserie-Salon de Thé Faso-Beni**, opposite the vegetable market, is good for breakfast, pastries and ice cream, expressed from a genuine Italian machine. **Restaurant Faso Béni**, next to the STMB bus station, is a typical African chop bar where you can eat simply and plentifully.

Slightly (but only slightly) more upmarket, **Restaurant Gazelle Verte**, near the stadium, is relatively new and well worth a visit.

In the evening, you can get grilled chicken and brochettes at **Caïman Bar & Restaurant**, just behind Hôtel de l'Amitié. On Saturday evening, it's a good place to hang out until the nearby **Bar-Dancing de l'Amitié** (admission CFA400) livens up, typically around midnight.

### Getting There & Away

Between the various private bus companies which serve Ouahigouya, there are almost hourly departures for the capital (CFA3000, two to three hours), but only **STMB** ( ☎ 40 55 00 59; six daily) has buses that you can be sure will arrive without breaking down. STMB also has departures to Bobo-Dioulasso (CFA8000, up to nine hours, two daily).

For details of getting to Mali, see p169.

## DORI

pop 27,380

Most people come to Dori, 261km northeast of Ouagadougou, as a means of reaching Gorom-Gorom, two hours further north. On one level that's understandable as Dori is dusty, has few charms of its own, and its small daily market isn't a patch on Gorom-Gorom's Thursday spectacular. And yet, once the Gorom-Gorom buses have departed and the touts tugging at the coat-tails of their more famous neighbour's popularity have given up on you, Dori can be appealing as a quintessentially somnambulant and dusty Sahel town.

If you do stay long enough to visit the market, one speciality is the prized Dori blankets, woven from wool provided by the seminomadic pastoralists who camp around the town's large pool. Take their popularity as a warning – Dori nights can be cold in winter.

### Sleeping & Eating

**Hérbergement de Dori** (private bathroom CFA8000; 😢 ) In the time-honoured style of West African campements, this place provides simple rooms and sees a steady stream of travellers passing through. Our only criticism is that some of the shared toilets could be cleaner. It's a fair old walk east from the centre, but the outskirts-of-town location does mean a multitude of stars in the night sky and quiet, quiet nights.

**Hôtel Oasis** ( ☎ 40 66 03 41; small s/d CFA9000/11,000, large s/d CFA16,000/18,000) Standards continue to slide, but the Oasis still represents good value for those who like their comforts. All cabins have air-con and bathroom. The smaller cabins are called, with some exaggeration, bungalows, while the larger ones, styled in an even greater flight of fancy as minivillas, include a spacious sitting area.

**Auberge Populaire** (Chez Tanti Véronique; d without/with shower CFA3500/4500) This barracks-like place on the northern side of town, on the road to Gorom-Gorom, has no-frills rooms with shared facilities and wins our prize for the most unfriendly hotel staff in the country. Not all the rooms have secure locks, and its large adjacent bar can either be a

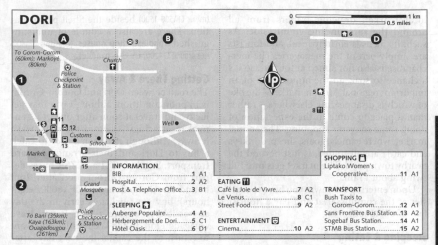

DORI

0 ——————— 1 km
0 ——————— 0.5 miles

| INFORMATION | |
| --- | --- |
| BIB.........................................1 | A1 |
| Hospital.................................2 | A2 |
| Post & Telephone Office.....3 | B1 |

| SLEEPING 🛏 | |
| --- | --- |
| Auberge Populaire.............4 | A1 |
| Hérbergement de Dori.......5 | C1 |
| Hôtel Oasis........................6 | D1 |

| EATING 🍴 | |
| --- | --- |
| Café la Joie de Vivre..........7 | A2 |
| Le Venus............................8 | C1 |
| Street Food.......................9 | A2 |

| ENTERTAINMENT 🎬 | |
| --- | --- |
| Cinema...............................10 | A2 |

| SHOPPING 🛍 | |
| --- | --- |
| Liptako Women's | |
| Cooperative.................11 | A1 |

| TRANSPORT | |
| --- | --- |
| Bush Taxis to | |
| Gorom-Gorom...........12 | A1 |
| Sans Frontière Bus Station..13 | A2 |
| Sogebaf Bus Station..........14 | A1 |
| STMB Bus Station.............15 | A2 |

**BURKINA FASO**

lively place to spend the evening, or an irritating sleep inhibitor – depending upon your mood and the hour. On the plus side, it's right in the heart of town.

You can eat simply at **Café la Joie de Vivre** (riz gras CFA250, spaghetti CFA350). If you're staying at the eastern end of town, the outdoor **Le Venus** (meals CFA500), a few doors from the Hérbergement de Dori, serves filling and simple meals. There's plenty of street food at the main intersection.

### Shopping
At the small **Liptako Women's Cooperative**, you can see members weaving the blankets as well as cloth for napkins, aprons and tablecloths.

### Getting There & Away
Numerous companies run between Dori and Ouagadougou (CFA5000, five to seven hours). **STMB** ( ☎ 40 66 98 67) is generally the best, but readers have reported that **Sans Frontière** ( ☎ 40 67 67 54) is also good. The best days to find transport headed for Dori (and sometimes onwards as far as Gorom-Gorom) is Wednesday.

For Gorom-Gorom it's shake, rattle and roll on a rough track all the way. Bush taxis (CFA2000, two hours) are plentiful on market day; most pull out by 8am from opposite the Sogebaf Bus Station. Locals often only pay CFA1000, so it's worth bargaining.

There are also intermittent services to Markoyé (CFA3000).

## AROUND DORI
### Bani
Bani, about 35km south of Dori on the road to Ouagadougou, is home to seven exceptional mud-brick mosques. You'll know you've arrived at this small, predominantly Muslim village when you see the minarets, the only structures over one storey high, stabbing like fingers at the sky. Begin at the large mosque in the centre of the village and continue up the hill to the outlying structures. The façades are extravagantly decorated with relief carvings; these unique structures are among the finest in Burkina Faso.

Local guide Cissé Souabou provides an informative commentary (in French only) on the town's mosques. He charges a negotiable CFA10,000 for his services, which include one night's accommodation at Hôtel de Fofo; he's easy to find in Bani.

The simple **Hôtel de Fofo** (r CFA2500) has basic rooms with bucket showers, and simple meals are available. There are also plans for a similar guesthouse nearby.

All transport between Ouagadougou (CFA4500) and Dori (CFA700) stops here.

### GOROM-GOROM
Gorom-Gorom's Thursday market is the most colourful in Burkina Faso, and one of the best in all West Africa. It is one of Burkina Faso's main highlights and is not to be missed while you're in the country. Its charm lies in the fact that it's an authentic

local market, drawing traders from all around the surrounding countryside. As such, its focus is entirely local, and tourists are simply part of the menagerie. The merchandise is also not aimed at tourists, so it's a chance to soak up the atmosphere of an important regional African market – the like of which is disappearing elsewhere – rather than a place to come in the expectation of doing some souvenir shopping. The animal market, where camels, goats, sheep, donkeys and cattle are all traded, is just beyond the nearby town pond. The market gets into full swing about 11am.

Upon entering the town, you have to register at the commissariat and pay a 'tourist tax' of CFA1000.

### Sleeping & Eating

**Le Campement Rissa** ( ☎ 40 46 93 96; r from CFA4000) What this fine campement lacks in luxury it more than makes up for with atmosphere. Beds are in mud huts or under the stars, and the family who own it serve as cooks, guides and general organisers of most things you can do in and around Gorom-Gorom. The food is good and hearty. Everyone around town knows Rissa, so finding the campement is never a problem.

**Auberge Populaire** (r CFA5000) This ageing place, with basic and vaguely depressing rooms with no fans, and roofs of corrugated iron, is nowhere near as good as the Campement Rissa. The dusty courtyard is the highlight of this place. There are cold bucket showers, which are definitely easier to bear at midday than on a cold desert night.

The best of the small eateries dotted around town is the friendly **Restaurant Inssa**

(meals CFA500-1500) beside the Shell petrol station. There are also a couple of undistinguished **Togolese chop houses** (couscous CFA400, rice around CFA200) in the market.

### Getting There & Away

The road between Dori and Gorom-Gorom is in poor condition, although you may get lucky and travel it soon after one of its annual resurfacings – before the rains wash it away. Although it's often easier to catch a bus to Dori and then arrange onward transport, Sogebaf, CTI and ZSR buses depart from Gorom-Gorom soon after 2pm bound for Ouagadougou (CFA6000, eight hours); buy your ticket as early in the day as possible to ensure a seat. If you leave Ouagadougou on the Wednesday and want to return to the capital the next day, after visiting the market, these buses are your only option. Bush taxis head back to Dori (CFA2000, two hours) around 7pm after the market's all said and done.

## AROUND GOROM-GOROM

You can hire a 4WD with driver (at least CFA40,000 per day, plus petrol) from Campement Rissa to visit some of the nearby Tuareg villages, or to go to Oursi, some 35km northeast of Gorom-Gorom. There are some spectacular sand dunes here, **Les Dunes d'Oursi**; if you can tear yourself from your bed, set off at 4am to catch the sunrise gilding their crests.

Another worthwhile excursion is to the pretty small town of **Markoyé**, 45km northeast of Gorom-Gorom, reached via a sandy track towards the Nigerien border. In the heart of Fulani country, Markoyé has a vi-

---

**THE PEOPLE OF GOROM-GOROM MARKET**

You'll see a variety of Sahel and Sahara ethnic groups at the market. The Tuareg are easily identified by their long flowing robes (boubous), indigo turbans and elaborate silver swords, and can often be seen riding proudly on their camels or haggling in the animal market over the price of camels and goats. The Tuareg's former slaves, the Bella, have taken over many of their erstwhile masters' skills in leatherwork, and both the men and the women favour black or grey gowns with wide belts of richly decorated leather.

You'll also see Songhaï farmers and Fulani herders (who wear the distinctive, conical straw hats). But it is the Fulani women who most catch the eye. Elaborately dressed, you can recognise them by their vivid, multicoloured dresses and complex hairstyles – usually braided and decorated with silver threads, tiny chains and colourful beads. These women carry their wealth with them in the form of beads, bracelets, heavy earrings or necklaces, many of solid silver with dangling Maria Theresa dollars.

brant camel and cattle market every Monday. If you don't have a 4WD, a minibus leaves Gorom-Gorom early on Monday morning and returns at 6pm.

It's also possible to explore the surrounding desert by camel, which should cost around CFA20,000 per person per day for a well-provisioned trip, including food. Make sure you know exactly what you're getting for the price, which should include sleeping bags (you'll be sleeping in the open air) and ample food. There are some decent sand dunes around 12km from Gorom-Gorom.

# BURKINA FASO DIRECTORY

## ACCOMMODATION

Ouagadougou, Bobo-Dioulasso and, to a lesser extent, Banfora and Ouahigouya have an excellent range of accommodation to suit most budgets, with some imaginative and comfortable choices in each town. Elsewhere, you may need to take what you can find, as choice is extremely limited and places often quite run-down and/or basic.

Throughout this chapter, budget listings for dorms are CFA3000 to CFA4000 while singles/doubles range from CFA3500/5000 up to CFA8000/10,000. Midrange hotels range from CFA10,000/12,000 for a single/double, up to CFA33,000/40,000 (for real quality and comfort in Ouagadougou and Bobo-Dioulasso you'll be paying in the upper end of that range), while top-end hotels can go as high as CFA65,000 for a double.

While staying in Ouagadougou and Bobo-Dioulasso you have to pay a *taxe de séjour* at each place you stay, also known as a *taxe communale*. It's a once-off payment, irrespective of the number of nights you stay at a hotel, and is calculated at CFA500 per person.

## ACTIVITIES

Burkina Faso is more for seeing than for doing, although there are opportunities for hiking, climbing and cycling around Banfora (p157). You can also do camel expeditions around Gorom-Gorom in the north (opposite) or go on safaris to the national parks in the country's southeast (p159).

---

### PRACTICALITIES

- Electricity supply is 220V and plugs are of the European two-round-pin variety.

- International versions of French- and (a few) English-language publications are available in Ouagadougou and Bobo-Dioulasso.

- BBC World Service (www.bbc.co.uk/worldservice) is on 99.2 FM in Ouagadougou. For French-language FM services, tune in to Horizon FM (104.4) and RFI (94).

- Burkina Faso uses the metric system.

## BOOKS

Tracking down books on Burkina Faso can be a frustrating task, although many books that are unavailable elsewhere can be found at **Abebooks** (www.abebooks.com).

*African Cinema and Europe: Close-Up on Burkina Faso*, by Teresa Hoefert de Turegano, is a wonderful primer for Fespaco and one of the few studies devoted to the country's most unlikely industry.

*Thomas Sankara Speaks: The Burkina Faso Revolution, 1983-87*, by Thomas Sankara (edited by Samantha Anderson), charts the rise and fall of the man known as Africa's Che Guevara through his charismatic speeches.

*The Mossi of Burkina Faso: Chiefs, Politicians and Soldiers*, by Elliott P Skinner, can be hard to find, but it's the only book to cover the history behind the largest group in precolonial Burkina Faso.

*The Parachute Drop*, by Norbert Zongo, is an eerily prescient novel by the journalist who was killed in 1998, sparking demonstrations in Ouagadougou. Recently republished, it's highly readable.

## BUSINESS HOURS

Banks are typically open between 7am and 11am, and 3.30pm to 5pm Monday to Friday, although Ecobank is a bit different (7.30am to 4.30pm Monday to Friday, and 8am until noon Saturday). Bars normally serve from noon until late, and nightclubs generally go from 9pm into the wee hours. Restaurants usually serve food between 11.30am and 3pm, then open again 6.30pm to 10.30pm. As a rule, shops and businesses operate 7.30am to noon and 3pm to 5.30pm Monday to Friday, and 9am to 1pm Saturday.

## DANGERS & ANNOYANCES

Burkina Faso is one of the safest countries in West Africa, although that's partly because of questionable police tactics (see p137). Crime isn't unknown, particularly around big markets, cinemas and *gares routières* (bus stations), but it's usually confined to petty theft and pickpocketing.

## EMBASSIES & CONSULATES
### Burkinabé Embassies

In West Africa, Burkina Faso has embassies in Côte d'Ivoire, Ghana, Mali and Nigeria. For more details, see the relevant country chapter. Embassies include the following:

**Belgium** ( ☎ 02-345 99 12; www.ambassadeduburkina .be; 16 Place Guy-d'Arezzo, Brussels 1180)

**Canada** ( ☎ 613-238 4796; www.burkinafaso.ca; 48, Chemin Range Ottawa, Ontario, K1N 8J4)

**France** ( ☎ 01-43 59 90 63; www.ambaburkinafrance .org; 159 Blvd Haussmann, 75008 Paris)

**Germany** ( ☎ 030-301 05 990; Karolingerplatz 10-11, 14052 Berlin)

**USA** ( ☎ 202-332 5577; www.burkinaembassy-usa.org; 2340 Massachusetts Ave NW, Washington, DC 20008)

In the UK, Burkina Faso has an **honorary consul** ( ☎ 020-8710 6290; fax 8770 7448; St Nicholas Rd, Sutton, Surrey, SM1 1EL).

### Embassies & Consulates in Burkina Faso

Embassies and consulates in Ouagadougou include the following:

**Canada** (Map p138; ☎ 50 31 18 94; ouaga@dfait -maeci.gc.ca; 586 Ave Agostino Neto) Represents Australia in consular matters.

**Côte d'Ivoire** (Map p136; ☎ 50 31 82 28; cnr Ave Raoul Follereau & Blvd du Burkina Faso)

**France** (Map p136; ☎ 50 30 67 74; www.ambafrance -bf.org; Ave de l'Indépendance)

**Germany** (Map p138; ☎ 67 30 67 31; amb.alle magne@fasonet.bf; Rue Joseph Badoua)

**Ghana** (Map p136; ☎ 50 30 76 35; Ave d'Oubritenga) Opposite the Unesco office.

**Mali** ( ☎ 50 38 19 22; 2569 Ave Bassawarga) Just south of Ave de la Résistance.

**Nigeria** (Map p136; ☎ 50 30 66 67; Ave d'Oubritenga) 1km northeast of Place des Nations.

**UK** (Map p138; ☎ 50 73 23; fax 50 30 59 00; Hôtel Yibi, cnr Ave Kwame N'Krumah & Rue du Dr Gournisson) British honorary consul at Ouagadougou's Hôtel Yibi.

**USA** (Map p136; ☎ 50 30 67 23; www.ouagadougou .usembassy.gov; 622 Ave Raoul Follereau)

## FESTIVALS & EVENTS

Fespaco is the biennial festival of African cinema, which takes place in Ouagadougou in odd-numbered years during February or March. For further information on the festival, see the boxed text, p133. In even-numbered years, Ouagadougou hosts the Salon International de l'Artisanat de Ouagadougou (p151) during October or November, and Bobo-Dioulasso stages the Semaine Nationale de la Culture (p151) in March or April.

For more information on the traditional festivities (or *fêtes*) in the Bobo-Dioulasso area, see the boxed text p151.

## HOLIDAYS

**New Year's Day** 1 January
**Women's Day** 8 March
**Good Friday & Easter Monday** March/April
**Labour Day** 1 May
**Ascension Day** 4-5 August
**Anniversary of Sankara's overthrow** 15 October
**All Saints Day** 1 November
**Christmas Day** 25 December

Burkina Faso also celebrates Islamic holidays, which change each year. See p818 for details of Islamic holidays.

## INTERNET ACCESS

Beyond the capital, Burkina Faso has been slow to embrace the Internet revolution. Although you'll find Internet cafés (per hour CFA300) in Bobo-Dioulasso, they're painfully slow, while elsewhere (apart from Ouahigouya), they're slow and often charge by the minute (CFA40 to CFA100). Far and away the best connections are in Ouagadougou (p137), where you'll pay CFA400 to CFA750 per hour.

## INTERNET RESOURCES

**Burkina By Matt** (www.burkinabymatt.com) A good photo site by a former US Peace Corps volunteer in Burkina Faso.

**Fespaco** (www.fespaco.bf) Website of Africa's favourite film festival.

**Ministry of Culture, Arts & Tourism** (www.culture .gov.bf) It's a bit clunky, but this government site has good (French-only) information on dance, cinema, music and literature in Burkina Faso.

# LANGUAGE

The country's official language is French. Of some 60 local languages, the most significant is Moré, the language of the Mossi and others living on the central plateau, which is spoken by more than half the population. Dioula is the lingua franca, the language of the market, even though within Burkina Faso it's nobody's mother tongue (it's closely related to Bambara, the major language of neighbouring Mali). Other significant local languages include Fula, Gourmantché and Gourounsi.

See p861 for a list of useful phrases in French, Moré, Dioula and Fula.

# MAPS

*Burkina Faso* (1:1,000,000), a map published by the French-based Institut Géographique National (IGN), is the most widely available. It's available at the **Institut Gèographique du Burkina** (Map p136; IGB; ☎ 50 32 48 23; fax 50 32 48 27; Ave de l'Indépendance) in Ouagadougou, or in many European bookshops. IGB and Librairie Diacfa in Ouagadougou sell detailed city maps (CFA5900 each) for Ouagadougou and Bobo-Dioulasso.

For more information on maps, see p820.

# MONEY

The unit of currency in Burkina Faso is the West African CFA franc.

Banks which will change money (usually euros in cash only) with a minimum of fuss include Banque Internationale du Burkina (BIB), Ecobank and Banque Internationale pour le Commerce, l'Industrie et l'Agriculture du Burkina (Biciab).

Biciab's ATMs in larger cities issue easy cash advances against Visa (but not MasterCard), although transaction fees are prohibitive (more than €10 per withdrawal); take out as much as the machine lets you each time.

# PHOTOGRAPHY & VIDEO

You no longer need a photo or video permit in Burkina Faso. Don't, however, point your camera at airports, government, police or military buildings or personnel. Other things which were once on the official off-limits list, in the days of photo permits, included bridges, reservoirs, banks, post offices, train stations, bus and bush-taxi *(taxi brousse)* stations, TV/radio stations, petrol stations, grain warehouses, water towers, industrial installations and poor people, so take special care around such subjects. For more general technical information and advice, see p823.

The only place where you can even think about burning photos onto CD is at Éspace Internautes (p150) in Ouagadougou, and only in the capital will you find USB-friendly computers.

# TELEPHONE & FAX

You can make international phone calls at Onatel offices from 7am to 10pm daily. A three-minute call costs CFA2650 (CFA750 for each additional minute) to Europe or the USA, and CFA4150 (CFA1260 for each additional minute) to Australia. The only place where you may be able to make Internet-connected calls is at Éspace Internautes (p150) in Ouagadougou.

The main post office in Ouagadougou has a **fax restante service** (fax 50 33 81 30).

Most mobile phones from European countries work in Burkina Faso; local SIM cards start from CFA20,000. Local mobile companies include Telemob, Celtel or Telecel.

There are no telephone area codes in Burkina Faso, although in 2004 all phone numbers (including mobiles) were changed from six to eight digits. You still see the old numbers from time to time, so if you're in Ouagadougou or the elsewhere in the centre add a '50' prefix. In the West, add '20', and the old numbers in the east require a '40' prefix. Mobile numbers are also now eight digits but you'll need to know whether it's Telemob (70), Celtel (76) or Telecel (78).

# VISAS

Everyone except Economic Community of West African States (Ecowas) nationals needs a visa. You can buy a tourist visa at Ouagadougou airport for CFA10,000 (paid in local currency; there's an exchange booth at the airport). The visa is not issued until the following day – the police will give you an authorisation until the passport is returned. Travellers also report that visas are issued at Burkina Faso's land borders for the same price, although they're invariably issued on the spot.

Burkina Faso embassies require at least two photos and may ask for proof of yellow fever vaccination. Visas cost US$75/100 for three/six months in the USA, while single-/multiple-entry three-month visas cost €20/30 in Europe. In Mali you'll pay CFA25,000/30,000 for single-/multiple entry three-month visa. In countries where there is no Burkina Faso embassy, French embassies sometimes issue 10-day visas on their behalf.

### Visas for Onward Travel

Apart from visas for Ghana and Mali, Burkina Faso is not the best place to stock up on visas. Benin, Niger and Togo do not have embassies in Burkina Faso. See the chapters for these countries for details of visa requirements and embassy addresses.

If you just want to slip over the border to Benin to explore Parc National de la Pendjari, you can get a 48-hour visa at the border post. Visas cost CFA10,000.

#### CÔTE D'IVOIRE

In theory, the embassy issues single-entry, 30-day visas for CFA10,000, and multiple entry visas valid for three months cost CFA20,000 (you'll also need two photos). However, the visa may only work if you fly to Abidjan, as the northern land borders are, at the time of writing, under rebel control or closed.

#### GHANA

The Ghanaian embassy issues one-month visas within 24 hours for CFA15,000; you'll need four photos (make sure they're identical).

#### MALI

One-month visas cost CFA20,000 and are issued within the hour if things are quiet.

# TRANSPORT IN BURKINA FASO

## GETTING THERE & AWAY
### Entering Burkina Faso

If you've travelled in Africa for a while, entering Burkina Faso is a pleasure. You'll almost never encounter anything other than quick efficiency at Burkina Faso's borders, with not a single suggestion that a bribe may be necessary to speed up the process or

smooth over 'misunderstandings'. Burkina Faso may have many problems but their border officials deserve a pat on the back for bucking the African trend.

Proof of yellow fever vaccination is, however, mandatory and is often checked.

### Air

Burkina Faso's two international airports are Aéroport International d'Ouagadougou and Aéroport International Borgo (Bobo-Dioulasso).

The following airlines have offices in Ouagadougou:

**Afriqiyah** (8U; ☎ 50 30 16 52; www.afriqiyah.aero) Hub: Tripoli.

**Air Algérie** (Map p138; AH; ☎ 50 31 23 01; www.airalgerie.dz) Hub: Algiers.

**Air Burkina** (Map p138; 2J; ☎ 50 30 76 76 or 50 31 53 25; www.air-burkina.com) Hub: Ouagadougou.

**Air France** (Map p138; AF; ☎ 50 30 63 65; www.airfrance.com) Hub: Paris.

**Air Ivoire** (VU; ☎ 50 30 11 95; www.airivoire.com) Hub: Abidjan.

**Air Sénégal International** (V7; ☎ 50 31 39 05; www.air-senegal-international.com) Hub: Dakar.

**Ghana Airways** (Map p136; GH; ☎ 50 30 41 46; www.ghana-airways.com) Hub: Accra.

**Point Afrique** ( ☎ 50 33 16 20; www.point-afrique.com) Hub: Paris.

#### WEST AFRICA

Air Burkina (CFA133,600) and Air Ivoire (CFA122,700) fly from Ouagadougou to Abidjan a couple of times a week each. Flights with Air Burkina go via Bobo-Dioulasso (CFA96,000).

There are flights from Ouagadougou to Bamako with Air Burkina (CFA109,200), Afriqiyah (CFA102,600) and Air Sénégal International (CFA120,000).

Afriqiyah (CFA80,000) has the cheapest flights connecting Ouagadougou and Niamey, although Air Burkina also flies the route for a similar price. Air France (CFA130,000) is another option.

For Dakar, Air Burkina (CFA211,400) and Air Sénégal International (CFA227,700) each fly from Ouagadougou at least once a week.

Other destinations served by Air Burkina include Lomé (Togo; CFA137,000), and Cotonou (Benin; CFA142,000), while Ghana Airways flies to Accra (Ghana) twice weekly (CFA199,000/287,600 one way/return).

## Land

The main border crossings are at Niangoloko for Côte d'Ivoire; Tanguiéta for Benin; 15km south of Pô or Hamale for Ghana; Sinkasse for Togo; east of Kantchari for Niger; and Koloko or west of Tiou for Mali. Borders tend to be closed by 5.30pm or 6.30pm at the latest. Remember that there is a time change of one hour going from Burkina Faso into Benin or Niger (both ahead of Burkina Faso).

### BENIN

A TCV bus runs every Sunday from Ouagadougou to Cotonou (CFA20,000). The alternative is to take a bus (eg STMB) to Fada N'Gourma (CFA4000, five hours, 225km), from where bush taxis and minibuses lie in wait (sometimes all day because transport to the border – CFA4000 – is scarce and fills up slowly). Minibuses occasionally leave for Natitingou from around the Total petrol station immediately north of Zaka on Ave Yennenga in Ouagadougou.

### CÔTE D'IVOIRE

Passenger train services between Burkina Faso and Côte d'Ivoire were suspended at the time of writing, cross-border traffic was minimal and the border frequently closed. To get an updated picture, take one of Rakieta's three daily buses from Banfora to Niangoloko (CFA800, one hour) from where onward transport may be possible. Remember, however, that travel to Côte d'Ivoire was unsafe at the time of writing.

### GHANA

A Ghanaian Intercity STC bus leaves the main *gare routière* in Ouagadougou three mornings per week (Monday, Wednesday and Friday at the time of research) heading towards Accra (CFA16,000, 1000km) via Tamale (CFA11,000, 363km) and Kumasi (CFA12,500, 720km). Note that some travellers have reported having to pay the fare to Kumasi even though they were only travelling as far as Tamale. Tickets should be purchased at least a day in advance.

STMB has five daily buses from Ouagadougou to Pô (CFA2000, three hours), 15km from the border, from where there's infrequent transport to the border (CFA1500) and on to Bolgatanga in Ghana (CFA1250). If you're coming the other way, Burkinabé bush taxis wait on their side of the border to take you to Ouagadougou.

The other frequently used border crossing is at Hamale in the southwest of Burkina Faso. Coming from Ghana, you may have to stay at Hamale's cheap hotel and catch the 8am bus to Bobo-Dioulasso the next morning, although travellers who took the first bus in the morning from Wa to Hamale reported reaching Bobo-Dioulasso the same day. From Bobo-Dioulasso, Rakieta has a daily bus at 2.30pm to Hamale (CFA6200) which passes through Banfora (CFA5000 to Hamale) en route.

### MALI

Almost every bus company in Bobo-Dioulasso offers a daily service to Bamako (CFA9000, 15 hours). The best buses are the TCV ones, which leave Bobo-Dioulasso at 1pm or Ouagadougou (CFA15,000) at 8am and STMB from Bobo-Dioulasso (12.30pm). Remember that all travel via Sikasso and Segou (rather than the more direct route) and arrive after midnight.

If you're heading from Bobo-Dioulasso to Mopti, Peugeot taxis (CFA9500, 15 hours) leave from Bobo's Gare de Mopti from about 7am or in the early evening; Sunday seems to be the best day.

If you're heading for Dogon country, the road from Ouahigouya to the border is in good condition, but usually deteriorates on the Malian side. STMB buses leave Ouahigouya to Koro (CFA2500, two to four hours) late morning (usually coinciding with the arrival of the bus from Ouagadougou). From Koro you'll need to connect by bush taxi to Bankass and then Mopti; on Saturday, market day in Koro, you stand a better chance of finding onward transport.

### NIGER

The Niger-registered SNTV bus runs between Ouagadougou and Niamey (CFA10,000, nine to 11 hours) a couple of times a week from the *gare routière*. Otherwise take any bus to Fada N'Gourma, then onward transport to Kantchari, from where there's intermittent transport across the frontier.

Minibuses from Ouagadougou to Niamey (CFA8100, 10 to 12 hours) leave from the petrol stations immediately north of the Zaka in Ouagadougou.

### TOGO

Sogebaf has a daily service between Ouagadougou and Lomé (CFA12,500 to CFA15,000, 18 hours), while at least three Togolese companies offer a similar service from Ouagadougou's *gare routière*. It may, however, be easier to travel via Accra in Ghana (see p169), and then change there.

There are direct bush taxis from Ouagadougou's *gare routière* to Lomé (CFA15,000, 36 hours), but consider breaking up the journey en route. Minibuses to the Togolese border often leave in the morning from the Total Petrol Station near Zaka in Ouagadougou. Alternatively, take any transport heading east and change in Koupéla. Expect heavy searches at the **border** (6am-6pm).

## GETTING AROUND
### Air
Air Burkina has at least three flights a week between Ouagadougou and Bobo-Dioulasso (CFA35,000).

### Bus
Buses are the most reliable and comfortable way to get around. There are a multitude of companies from which to choose, although STMB buses are generally better maintained and more reliable than other companies – apart from TGV, which has the best buses, but they only travel between Ouagadougou and Bobo-Dioulasso. Buses invariably leave from their own stations, rather than the *gares routières*. Bus companies seem to reserve their worst buses for the road between Ouagadougou and Dori or Gorom-Gorom.

Buses almost always operate with guaranteed seating (those who reserve earliest get choice of the best seats so buying a couple of days in advance is always a good idea) and fixed departure times.

### Bush Taxi & Minibus
Minibuses and bush taxis, mostly ageing Peugeot 504s, cover major towns, and also outlying communities that large buses don't serve. Most leave from the *gares routières*, and morning is the best time to find them. Minibuses are usually a third cheaper than Peugeot taxis, but can take an age to fill up.

### Car & Motorcycle
Burkina Faso's road network is excellent, with the sealed roads connecting major cities driveable year-round. The road from Kaya to Dori and beyond is an exception, and deteriorates the further north you travel. During the rainy season, you may find your progress impeded by rain barriers, which are lifted once temporary flooding further down the road has abated.

### Local Transport
Sotrao operates a good intracity bus service (CFA100) in Ouagadougou. All reasonable-sized towns have taxis which can be shared (usually for CFA250) or chartered (rates start at CFA500 for short trips). Only Ouagadougou has metered taxis (p146).

### Tours
Consider taking a tour or hiring a 4WD (CFA40,000 per day, plus petrol) to visit the wildlife parks and reserves in the country's southeast where public transport ranges from infrequent and inconvenient to non-existent. For details see p146. Tours are also necessary for exploring the desert regions north of Gorom-Gorom (p164).

### Train
Until things return to normal across the border in Côte d'Ivoire, there are no passenger train services along the main line from Ouagadougou to Abidjan.

# Cameroon

If a list were made of possible attractions that an African country might hold, then Cameroon would surely come close to the top. Sitting at the crossroads of West and Central Africa, it is one of the most culturally diverse countries on the continent. From ancient tribal kingdoms in the west to 'pygmy' villages in the south and Muslim pastoralists in the north, Cameroon has a rich tapestry of indigenous cultures.

Those interested in the natural world will be well rewarded. Parc National de Waza is one of the best in the region, with abundant mammal and birdlife, and large herds of elephants gathering at water holes in the dry season. The rainforest at Korup is thought to be the oldest on the continent, and is certainly one of the most biologically diverse. Cameroon's rainforests stretch east and south into the Congo basin, a truly wild area to tempt the most adventurous.

Trekkers will be attracted by Mt Cameroon, the highest peak in West Africa. A still-active volcano, it rises almost straight from the sea in a spectacular manner. The Mandara Mountains in the north are a complete contrast – dry and rocky, home to isolated villagers eking out a living. And if all this adventure leaves you exhausted, there are some fine palm-fringed beaches, complete with fantastic seafood, where you can recharge your batteries. Put all these elements together, throw in a lively soundtrack of home-grown *makossa* music, and you'll just find yourself wondering how this country has been overlooked by travellers for so long.

## FAST FACTS

- **Area** 475,442 sq km
- **Capital** Yaoundé
- **Country code** 237
- **Famous for** International footballing success
- **Languages** French, English, Bamiléké, Fulfude, Fulani and Ewondo
- **Money** Central African CFA franc; US$1 = CFA564.55; €1 = CFA681.77
- **Population** 16.4 million
- **Visa** Arrange in advance, US$60

# HIGHLIGHTS

- **Mt Cameroon** (p192) Don your hiking boots to climb the mist-shrouded slopes of West Africa's highest peak.
- **Kribi** (p217) Chill on the white beaches and practise your French with the locals over grilled fish.
- **Ring Road** (p198) Explore the cool green scenery and rolling countryside near Bamenda.
- **Mandara Mountains** (p211) Head into the remote landscape and trek from village to village.
- **Parc National de Waza** (p213) Watch elephants at the waterholes of one of the region's best national parks.

# ITINERARIES

Travel in Cameroon can be slow, especially off main routes, including in the Ring Road area and in the far north around Maroua. Allow plenty of time and keep your schedule flexible.

- **One Week** With just a week of travel, starting from either Douala (p184) or Yaoundé (p179), head to Limbe (p188) for a night or two to get your bearings. Then – if you have a bit of an adventurous bent – head either to Mt Cameroon (p192) or to Korup National Park (p195) for a few days exploring (in the dry season only), finishing again in Douala. Alternatively, if you're more interested in culture and history, go from Douala to Foumban (p203) (via Bafoussam, p201). After a night there, head to the Ring Road area (p198), ideally fitting in a day in Bafut (p201) and another on the stretch between Sagba (p199) and Kumbo (p199). Finish back in Douala or Yaoundé.
- **Two or Three Weeks** With two weeks, spend the first week exploring the Ring Road area (p198) and visiting Foumban (p203). Then you could head to Yaoundé (p179), from where you can fly north to Maroua (p208) and venture into the Mandara Mountains (p211) for a few days trekking. With three weeks or more, you would have time to go from Yaoundé to N'Gaoundéré (p205) by train, and from there to make your way north by road to Maroua – either flying or returning by road and train to Yaoundé or Douala.

---

**HOW MUCH?**

- **Ingredients for juju fetish** CFA500
- **100km bus ride** CFA850
- **Moto-taxi ride across town** CFA100
- **Bottle of palm wine** CFA1000
- **Carved mask** CFA15,000

**LONELY PLANET INDEX**

- **1L of petrol** CFA315
- **1.5L of bottled water** CFA450
- **Bottle of '33' beer** CFA600
- **Souvenir football shirt** CFA3500
- **Stick of brochettes** CFA100

---

- **One Month** With a month or more you'll have time to expand this itinerary, perhaps starting with a night or two in Limbe (p188), followed by a climb of Mt Cameroon (p192) or a visit to Korup (p195), before making your way up to Bamenda (p196) and the Ring Road area (p198). During the dry season, you could then go from Kumbo (p199) on the Ring Road direct to Foumban (p203); otherwise head to Foumban via Bafoussam (p201). From here, make your way to Yaoundé (p179) to rest up for a day or two, before heading north by train to N'Gaoundéré (p205) and beyond. Spend the remainder of the time exploring northern Cameroon (p205).

# CLIMATE & WHEN TO GO

The north has a single wet season from April/May to September/October. The hottest months here are March to May, when temperatures can soar to 40°C, although it's a dry (and therefore generally bearable) heat. The south has a humid, equatorial climate, with rain scattered throughout the year and almost continual high humidity. The main wet season here is June to October, when secondary roads often become impassable. From March to June are the light rains.

Throughout Cameroon, November to February are the driest months, though dust from harmattan winds greatly restricts visibility. These are the best months to visit,

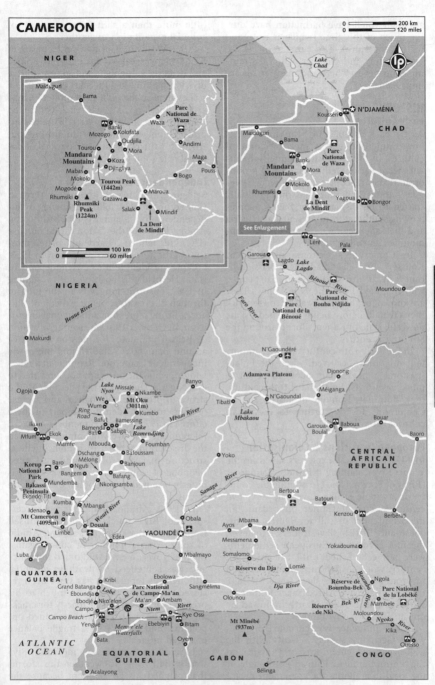

# CAMEROON

0 — 200 km
0 — 120 miles

although you'll have harmattan haze during much of this time (which is not good for photography). The worst months are between July and October, when it's raining almost everywhere and many roads are impassable.

## HISTORY
### Early Cultures
As far back as 8000 BC, the area that is now Cameroon was a meeting-point of cultures. In the south the original inhabitants were various ethno-linguistic groups of short stature, collectively known as 'Pygmies'. About 2000 years ago, they gradually started to be displaced by Bantu peoples moving southeast from present-day Nigeria and the Sahel region, although large communities do still remain.

In Cameroon's extreme north, near Kousséri and Lake Chad, the most significant early culture was that of the Sao people, who migrated from the Nile Valley. They are known for the pottery and bronze-work they created, before being absorbed by the powerful state of Kanem-Borno around the 8th or 9th century.

In the early 15th century another important migration occurred, when the Fulani (pastoral nomads from Senegal) began to move eastwards. By the late 16th century, they dominated much of north central Cameroon, adding further to the area's cultural heterogeneity.

### European Intrusions & Colonisation
In 1472 Portuguese explorers sailed up the Wouri River, naming it Rio dos Camarões (River of Prawns) and christening the country in a single stroke. Over the next two centuries, coastal Cameroon became an important port of call for Dutch, Portuguese and British slave-traders. However, the first permanent European settlements were not established until the mid-19th century, when British missionaries arrived in protest against the slave trade. In 1845 British missionary Alfred Saker founded a settlement in Douala, shortly followed by one at Victoria (now Limbe).

British influence was curtailed in 1884, when Germany signed a treaty with the well-organised chiefdoms of Douala and the central Bamiléké Plateau – although for the local inhabitants the agreement meant little more than a shift from one form of colonial exploitation to another.

After WWI the German protectorate of Kamerun was carved up between France and Britain – a linguistic and administrative division that marked the start of a fault line still evident in the politics of modern Cameroon. Local revolts in French-controlled Cameroon in the 1950s were brutally suppressed, but the momentum throughout Africa for throwing off the shackles of colonial rule soon took hold.

### Independence & Federalism
Self-government was granted in French Cameroon in 1958, followed quickly by independence on 1 January 1960. Ahmadou Ahidjo, leader of the Union Camerounaise (UC) independence party and prime minister of the autonomous regions from 1958, became president of the newly independent state. He held this position until resigning in 1982, ensuring longevity in the interim through the cultivation of expedient alliances, brutal repression and regional favouritism. In October 1961, the southern section of British-mandated Cameroon (the area around Bamenda) voted to join the newly independent Cameroon Republic in a referendum, while the northern portion voted to join Nigeria. During the next decade, Ahidjo strove to promote nationalism and a sense of Cameroonian identity. As part of these efforts, in 1972 the government sponsored a referendum that overwhelmingly approved the dissolution of the British-French federal structure in favour of the unitary United Republic of Cameroon – a move which is bitterly resented in Anglophone Cameroon to this day.

In 1982, Ahidjo's hand-picked successor, Paul Biya, quickly distanced himself from his former mentor, accusing Ahidjo of sponsoring a number of coups against the new government. Ahidjo fled to France and was sentenced to death *in absentia,* although his reputation has since been restored. In reality, Biya owed much to his predecessor, including a capacity for cracking down hard on real and imagined opponents, and preserving a fragile balance of vested interests.

In addition to repressive measures, Biya was initially able to weather the storms that plagued his government because the economy was booming. Prior to 1985, per capita GNP was one of the highest in sub-Saharan Africa, due largely to plentiful natural resources (oil, cocoa and coffee) and favourable commodity prices. When these markets collapsed and prices plunged, Cameroon's economy went into freefall. It has never really recovered and the shock-waves are still being felt by the country in today's globalised economy.

In 1986 Cameroon made a rare appearance in world headlines when 2000 people were killed by an eruption of poisonous gases from Lake Nyos in the northwest. International sympathy distracted attention from a clampdown on calls for genuine political pluralism, and Biya rode a further wave of international attention following the national football team's stunning performance at the 1990 World Cup.

### Elections & Emergencies
The clamour for freedom couldn't go ignored indefinitely. In 1991 Biya was forced to legalise opposition parties and multiparty elections were grudgingly held the following year – the first for 25 years. The Cameroonian Democratic People's Movement – led by Biya – hung on to power, despite widespread allegations of vote-rigging and intimidation. The main opposition party, the Social Democratic Front (SDF) boycotted subsequent parliamentary elections amid claims that their presidential candidate had been denied a legitimate victory – claims backed up by many international observers. That the SDF were the dominant Anglophone party rang alarm bells among the political elite.

In the 1990s, Biya's uneasy rule was often at an arm's length, as the president spent increasing amounts of time in France. At home, Cameroon lurched on in its customary state of uneasy stability and political stagnation. A small war with Nigeria over ownership of the oil-rich Bakassi Peninsula flared up in 1994 and again in 1996, deflecting attention from domestic problems. In December 1999 further domestic clampdowns followed the shock (if short-lived) declaration of independence for Anglophone Cameroon by the Southern Cameroons National Council (SCNC) on Buea radio, again exposing the country's deep political problems.

### Cameroon Today
In October 2004, with the opposition movement fractured, presidential elections returned Biya to power, for his 'second' seven-year term – the constitutional limit. International observers again complained that the process lacked credibility, in part due to the number of dead people who apparently turned up to vote for the status quo.

The economy continues to face severe difficulties. In 2004, Transparency International rated Cameroon 129th out of 146 countries on its corruption index, and corruption remains a cancer that gnaws away at the foundations of the country. Cameroon's failure to qualify for the World Bank's debt relief programme in the same year was blamed primarily on institutionalised corruption.

Cameroon's hard currency reserves have recently received a fillip from transit fees for Chad's oil pipeline, which terminates at Kribi (controversially chosen over Anglophone Limbe, which has its own oil refinery). While this has boosted the country's GDP on paper, the benefits have been slow to trickle down to the populace at large, and have had no impact on job creation, one of Cameroon's most pressing problems. While many officials have continued to grow fat on state revenues, over 50% of Cameroonians have complained that they have had to pay bribes to get government services. Until this malaise is seriously addressed and genuine political openness is permitted, Cameroon will continue to limp along for the foreseeable future.

## THE CULTURE
### The National Psyche
Cameroon is home to around 280 distinct ethno-linguistic groups. The dominant groups are the Bamiléké (around Bafoussam, and in Douala and Yaoundé), the Fulani (Foulbé or Fula) in the north and northwest, and Tikar communities northeast of Foumban. In the south and east are various so-called 'Pygmy' tribes, primarily Baka. The south and west are the most populous parts of the country.

Most Cameroonians are involved in agriculture, and the country is a major regional exporter of food, as well as being the seaport for Chad and Central African

Republic. While Cameroonians often have a reputation as hustlers, it's a skill they often need to navigate a faltering economy and corrupt bureaucracy.

## Daily Life

Traditional social structures dominate life. Local chiefs (known as *fon* in the west, or *lamido* in the north) still wield considerable influence, and when travelling in places that don't receive many tourists, it's polite to announce your presence. You'll also need to get the chief's permission to enter tribal lands, including various mountains and crater lakes. In many cases, a small gift is expected – a bottle of whisky is common currency.

There's a distinct cultural and political gap between the Francophone and Anglophone parts of Cameroon, albeit one felt predominantly by the Anglophone minority. The country is far from being truly bilingual, and Anglophones complain of discrimination in education (most universities lecture in French only) and in the workplace. The siting of the Chad oil pipeline was a particular bone of contention – rather than having it terminate in Anglophone Limbe, which has an oil refinery, it was directed to Kribi, in President Biya's home province, in what some activists claim was a deliberate act of marginalisation.

## SPORT

Cameroon exploded onto the world's sporting consciousness at the 1990 World Cup, when the national football team, the Indomitable Lions, became the first African side to reach the quarterfinals, led by the legendary Roger Milla, the oldest player to score in the World Cup.

Football is truly the national obsession, and the one thing that unites the country. Every other Cameroonian male seems to own a copy of the team's strip, and go into any bar and there'll be a match playing on TV. When Cameroon narrowly failed to qualify for the 2006 World Cup, the country's grief was almost tangible. Nevertheless, the Lions hold a proud record in the continent-wide Cup of Nations, winning the trophy four times – most recently in 2002. Cameroon's (and Africa's) current top player is the revered Barcelona striker Samuel Eto'o.

## RELIGION

Christianity is the most followed religion in Cameroon, with its adherents making up around 40% of the population. About a quarter of Cameroonians are Muslim, which is the predominant faith in the north. The remainder of the population follow indigenous religions, including the Kirdi – fiercely non-Muslim animists in the north – and the

---

### 'PYGMIES'

The term 'Pygmies' has long been used by outsiders to refer to a diverse group of people – many of whom are short in stature – living in the forested areas of southeast Cameroon and Central Africa. Traditionally, these people have lived by hunting and gathering wild forest resources which they either use themselves or trade in exchange for cultivated foods. Although 'Pygmy' is used generically, the 'Pygmies' do not view themselves as one culture (nor do they identify themselves as Pygmies). Rather, they belong to various distinct ethno-linguistic groups. In Cameroon, the most numerous are the Baka. Other groups include the Kola, the Medzan, the Aka and the Bofi.

Since early in the 1st millennium, these peoples and their traditional way of life have been under threat – first by Bantu groups, who forced them to consolidate and withdraw as they migrated southeastwards through traditional Pygmy areas; later by colonial masters, who forced the Pygmies into more easily 'managed' roadside settlements where they were often exploited; and, more recently, by forces such as multinational logging companies, mining interests, and government policies to encourage a more sedentary lifestyle. Now, while most Pygmies remain at least partially nomadic, many live in interdependent relationships with neighbouring Bantu farming peoples, although their exploitation continues.

Most Pygmies follow traditional religions, which typically centre around a powerful forest spirit, with the forest viewed as mother, father and guardian. Among the Baka, this forest god is known as Jengi – which is also the name given to celebrations marking the rite of passage of young Baka men into adulthood.

spirit faith of the Baka. Even where Christianity dominates it's often influenced by traditional practices, and many town markets have dedicated sections for fetishes and witchcraft.

## ARTS
### Literature
In addition to Mongo Beti (see p48), well-known literary figures include Kenjo Jumban, whose novel *The White Man of God* deals with the country's colonial experience, and Ferdinand Oyono, who's *Houseboy* and *The Old Man and the Medal* also deal with colonial themes. *The Crown of Thorns* by the prolific Linus Asong is well worth reading for insights into tribal society in northwestern Cameroon.

### Music
You'll hear music everywhere you go in Cameroon, pouring out of the radio, or with its videos distracting your receptionist as you check in to a hotel. Manu Dibango is the king of *makossa,* a fusion of highlife and soul that sprang from the clubs of Douala. He brought international fame to Cameroon in the 1980s with his hit *Soul Makossa.* Moni Bilé is another great exponent of the style. In competition is the more danceable *bikutsi* style, originally from Yaoundé. With its martial rhythms and often sexually charged lyrics, it's guaranteed to get the hips moving – listen out for Les Têtees Brulées.

### Craftwork
In a country so rich in forests, it comes as no surprise that wood carving makes up a significant proportion of traditional arts and crafts. The northwestern highlands area is known for its carved masks. These are usually representations of animals, and it's often believed that the wearer of the mask can transform himself and take on the animal's characteristics and powers. Stylised representations of spiders, which symbolise wisdom, are common on carvings from the Grassfields area, especially on items belonging to the chief.

Cameroon also produces some highly detailed bronze- and brass-work (including figurative art and pipes), particularly in Tikar areas north and east of Foumban. Carved wooden stools are generally round, except around Douala, where you'll see rectangular stools similar to those found elsewhere along the West African coast.

The areas around Bali and Bamessing (both near Bamenda), and Foumban, are rich in high-quality clay, and some of Cameroon's finest ceramic work originates here.

## ENVIRONMENT
### The Land
Cameroon is as diverse geographically as it is culturally. The south of the country is made up of low-lying coastal plain, covered by swathes of equatorial rainforest extending east towards the Central African Republic and the Congo Basin. Heading north, the sparsely populated Adamawa Plateau divides the country in two. Beyond this, the country begins to dry out, into a rolling landscape dotted with rocky escarpments. These are fringed to the west by the barren, but beautiful, Mandara Mountains, which make up the northern extent of a chain of volcanic mountains that form a natural border with Nigeria down to the Atlantic coast, often punctuated with stunning crater lakes. Most are now extinct, but one active volcano remains in Mt Cameroon – at 4095m the highest peak in West Africa.

### Wildlife
Cameroon's rainforests, especially those in the rich volcanic mountains bordering Nigeria, enjoy exceptional biodiversity. In 2005, British scientists from the Royal Botanic Gardens in Kew surveyed over 2400 plant species in the Kupe-Bakossi region, with a tenth of them completely new to science – making this Africa's top location for plant biodiversity. The range of animal species is no less spectacular. Cameroon's forests host populations of lowland gorillas and chimpanzees, as well being home to the drill – the most endangered primate species in Africa – which is restricted to Cameroon and Nigeria.

Larger mammal species include reasonable populations of elephants, buffaloes and lions, which are best observed at Parc National de Waza in the dry season. Elephants and buffaloes also still exist in reasonably healthy numbers in the rainforests, but these are rarely seen, due to the dense vegetation. Bénoué and Bouba Ndjida parks, near Garoua, also host populations of large

CAMEROON

animals – including a small number of black rhinos – but wildlife concentrations are not as high as in Waza.

Waza is the main wildlife-viewing park and the only one readily accessible to visitors. Korup National Park has the best visitor facilities of Cameroon's protected rainforest areas, but rainy season access can be a problem. In the east the rainforest holds no less diversity – Dja has been declared a World Heritage Site – but infrastructure is practically nonexistent, and a visit is for only the most adventurous.

### Environmental Issues

Dense forests cover about 22 million hectares in southern and eastern Cameroon, forming one of Africa's largest forest areas. Like many in Africa, Cameroon's government has had only limited success in balancing the interests of commercial logging and environmental protection. Timber exploitation is big business, and it's no surprise that the most common bank note – the CFA1000 – shows heavy machinery cutting down the forests. The bushmeat trade, once a subsistence activity, follows the driving of roads into the forest. Urban demand for bushmeat is massive, and it's thought that Yaoundé and Douala have the largest consumption of bushmeat in West Africa. New logging roads also act as conduits for HIV infection, with truckers bringing the disease into local communities.

Against this backdrop there are a few bright spots. The Worldwide Fund for Nature (WWF), in collaboration with the government, has expanded Cameroon's network of protected areas. In addition to benefiting the forest, these efforts are also focused on lessening the impact of commercial logging on the Baka and other communities that depend on the forests for their livelihood. The most notable progress in recent years has come in the southeast, where Lobéké – formerly a forest reserve and heavily damaged by logging activity – was awarded national-park status, with Boumba-Bek and Nki reserves following soon after. In the south, the Réserve de Campo has also been gazetted as a national park – largely to ensure adequate environmental and community protection for areas through which the Chad–Cameroon oil pipeline passes. In Limbe, the once nightmarish zoo is now run in conjunction with the pioneering conservation organisation, Pandrillus, rehabilitating captured primates and educating locals about environmental issues.

### FOOD & DRINK

Cameroonian cuisine is wide ranging. The staple dish is some variety of sauce with meat or fish, flavoured with pepper and served up with a plate of heavy bland starch – usually rice (*riz*) or *fufu*, a generic term for mashed yam, corn, plantain or couscous. Plantains may also be fried into delicious chips, or dishes accompanied with *batons* of steamed manioc, also called *feuilles*. One of the most popular sauces is *ndole*, made with bitter leaves similar to spinach and flavoured with smoked fish.

Cameroonians eat huge quantities of fish. This is most popularly bought off the street from women cooking them over charcoal grills, and comes with a starch accompaniment, all topped with a chilli or peanut sauce. It's quite common to order your fish and then retire to a nearby bar and have the dish delivered to your table. Grilled meats (brochettes or *suya*) are equally ubiquitous, although this time the grilling is done by men.

For sit-down meals there are chop houses, often with just a table and bench, which serve food throughout the day, but

---

**BEER MONEY**

If there's one thing Cameroonians love as much as football, it's drinking beer: the country has one of the highest rates of alcohol consumption in Africa. Competition between breweries is fierce, and this recently spilled over into a series of promotional offers, luring punters with free prizes hidden under the tops of beer bottles. Cars, phones or just more free booze were all on offer. More promotional bottle tops were produced than the population of Cameroon, to the extent that for a short time the tops became an unofficial form of currency – the value of a free beer being roughly equivalent to a taxi fare. Even the traffic police got in on the game, accepting bottle tops instead of the usual bribes for minor infractions.

there are usually only one or two dishes on offer. Major towns will have at least one restaurant where you can get Western-style cuisine, with Chinese and Lebanese dishes also commonly available.

Breakfast usually consists of coffee and bread – the French colonial influence means that you should never be too far away from somewhere selling baguettes and some sweet pastries. *Beignet* – sweet fried dough – is a popular street snack to eat on the hoof first thing in the morning.

Beer is available everywhere and drunk at any time, even in the Muslim north. Castel and 33 are the most popular brands – billboards for the latter make handy road signs on bus trips – announcing when you're '33'km from your destination. Guinness is also consumed in huge quantities. Palm wine is popular in the south and west – don't be fooled by its innocuous milky demeanour, it's lethal stuff.

Mineral water is sold in all major towns, with Tangui being the most commonly encountered brand.

# YAOUNDÉ

**pop 1.1 million**

Yaoundé is unique among West African capitals thanks to its green and hilly setting. Sat at an altitude of 750m, this gives the city a slightly more pleasant air than sweaty Douala. If its rival to the south is livelier, Yaoundé is better placed for travellers – anyone heading from north to south will pass through, and it's a good place to pick up onward visas, to rest from the road, and to recharge your batteries.

## ORIENTATION

Its hilly geography means that Yaoundé's street plan has evolved without any discernible pattern, and it can take a while to get your bearings. The focal point of the lower-lying Centre Ville is Place Ahmadou Ahidjo. From here, Blvd du 20 Mai runs northwest to the landmark Hilton hotel and the administrative district (Quartier du Lac). North from here, the road winds uphill to Carrefour (Rond-point) Nlongkak, a major roundabout. About 1.5km further up is Carrefour Bastos and the upscale Bastos residential quarter, where many embassies

are located, as well as some good restaurants. Overlooking town to the northwest, about 5km from the centre, is cool and green Mt Fébé, with a Benedictine monastery and museum at the top, a hotel on its slopes, and wide views over the city.

## INFORMATION
### Cultural Centres

**British Council** (Map p180; ☎ 220 3172; Ave Charles de Gaulle)

**Centre Culturel Français** (Map p182; ☎ 222 0944; Ave Ahidjo)

### Internet Access

Expect to pay CFA400 to CFA500 per hour for Internet access.

**ADT Cybercafé** (Map p182; Rue de Narvik, Bastos)

**Cometé Internet** (Map p182; Rue de Narvik) One of several near the US embassy.

**Espresso House** (Map p180; Carrefour Bastos; per 30 min CFA1000) Has broadband.

### Medical Services

**Pharmacie Bastos** (Map p180; ☎ 220 6555; Carrefour Bastos) A well-stocked pharmacy.

**Polyclinique André Fouda** ( ☎ 222 6612) For medical emergencies; in Elig-Essono southeast of Carrefour Nlongkak.

### Money

As always in Cameroon, travellers cheques are problematic to change in banks.

**Bicec** (Map p182) Near Place Ahmadou Ahidjo.

**Crédit Lyonnais** (Map p182) Near Place Ahmadou Ahidjo.

**Express Exchange** (Map p182; Ave Kennedy) Changes travellers cheques and US dollars.

**SGBC** Ave Monseigneur Vogt (Map p182; Ave Monseigneur Vogt); Ave de Gaulle (Map p180; Ave de Gaulle) Have ATMs.

### Post

**Central Post Office** (Map p182; Place Ahmadou Ahidjo; ☒ 7.30am-3.30pm Mon-Fri, 7.30am-noon Saturday) With another branch on Ave Foch (Map p182).

### Travel Agencies

**Inter-Voyages** (Map p182; ☎ 222 0361, 223 1005) One block north of the US embassy.

**Safar Tours** (Map p182; ☎ 222 8703; safar@safartours .com; Blvd du 20 Mai) At the Hilton.

### Visa Extensions

**Ministry of Immigration** (Map p182; ☎ 222 2413; Ave Mdug-Fouda Ada) Issues visa extensions. Bring one photo plus CFA15,000.

CAMEROON

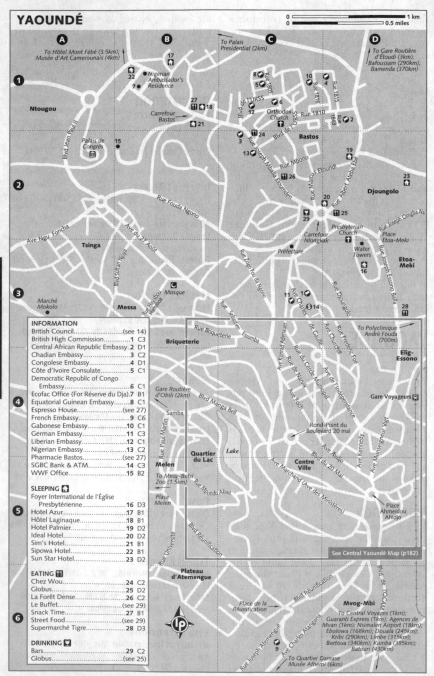

# YAOUNDÉ

To Palais Presidential (2km)
To Hôtel Mont Fébé (3.5km); Musée d'Art Camerounais (4km)
To Gare Routière d'Étoudi (3km); Bafoussam (290km); Bamenda (370km)
To Polyclinique André Fouda (700m)
To Gare Routière d'Obili (2km)
To Mvog-Betsi Zoo (1.5km)
See Central Yaoundé Map (p182)
To Central Voyages (1km); Guaranti Express (1km); Agences de Mvan (1km); Nsimalen Airport (18km); Ebolowa (168km); Douala (245km); Kribi (290km); Limbe (315km); Bertoua (340km); Kumba (385km); Batouri (430km)
To Quartier Damase Musée Afhemi (6km)

0                    1 km
0              0.5 miles

**INFORMATION**
British Council.....................(see 14)
British High Commission..............**1** C3
Central African Republic Embassy..**2** D1
Chadian Embassy......................**3** C2
Congolese Embassy....................**4** D1
Côte d'Ivoire Consulate..............**5** C1
Democratic Republic of Congo
  Embassy.............................**6** C1
Ecofac Office (For Réserve du Dja).**7** B1
Equatorial Guinean Embassy..........**8** C1
Espresso House.......................(see 27)
French Embassy.......................**9** C6
Gabonese Embassy.....................**10** C1
German Embassy.......................**11** C3
Liberian Embassy.....................**12** C1
Nigerian Embassy.....................**13** C2
Pharmacie Bastos.....................(see 27)
SGBC Bank & ATM......................**14** C3
WWF Office...........................**15** B2

**SLEEPING**
Foyer International de l'Église
  Presbytérienne.....................**16** D3
Hotel Azur...........................**17** B1
Hôtel Laginaque......................**18** B1
Hotel Palmier........................**19** D2
Ideal Hotel..........................**20** D2
Sim's Hotel..........................**21** B1
Sipowa Hotel.........................**22** B1
Sun Star Hotel.......................**23** D2

**EATING**
Chez Wou.............................**24** C2
Globus...............................**25** D2
La Forêt Dense.......................**26** C2
Le Buffet............................(see 29)
Snack Time...........................**27** B1
Street Food..........................(see 29)
Supermarché Tigre....................**28** D3

**DRINKING**
Bars.................................**29** C2
Globus...............................(see 25)

Ntougou

Palais de Congrès

Blvd Jean Paul II

Nigerian Ambassador's Residence

Carrefour Bastos

Blvd de l'URSS

Orthodox Church

Blvd de Bastos

Rue 1805
Rue 1816
Rue 1815
Rue 1810
Rue 1843

Rue Joseph Mballa Houmden

Rue Mbono

Rue Marc Vivien Foe

Rue Albert Ateba Ebe

Djoungolo

Rue Joseph Omgba Ns

Place Etoa-Meki

Presbyterian Church

Carrefour Nlongkak

Préfecture

Water Towers

Etoa-Meki

Rue Joseph Essono Balla

Rue Fouda Ngono

Ave Ngu Foncha

Ave du 27 Août

Tsinga

Blvd Sultan Njoya

Messa

Marché Mokolo

Mosque

Rue Nachtigal Ramosa

Rue Zogo Fou da Ngono

Rue Schlenter Essomba

Ave Churches

Ave Churchin

Rue Djoungolo

Ave Chutes

Briqueterie

Rue Briqueterie

Rue Konrad Adenauer

Rue du Crede Municipal

Ave Charles de Gaulle

Ave de l'Indépendance

Ave Frédéric Foe

Elig-Essono

Gare Voyageurs

Gare Routière d'Obili

Samba

Rue Paul Martin

Rue de Narvik

Ave Foch

Blvd Manga Bell

Quartier du Lac

Lake

Melen

Rue Mbondo Akwa

Place Melen

Rond-Point du Boulevard 20 mai

Ave Kennedy

Ave Monseigneur Vogt

Centre Ville

Blvd du 20 Mai

Ave Marchand (Ave des Ministères)

Place Ahmeidou Ahidjo

Rue Université

Blvd Réunification

Plateau d'Atemengue

Place de la Réunification

Blvd Réunification

Mvog-Mbi

Blvd de TOCAM

Rue Charles Atangana

Rue Joseph Atemengue

## DANGERS & ANNOYANCES

Yaoundé is more relaxed than Douala, but there's still a small risk of street crime. Be particularly wary around the central market, and don't carry too many valuables with you. Take a taxi if you're out at night.

## SIGHTS & ACTIVITIES
### Musée d'Art Camerounais

This **museum** (Quartier Fébé; donation requested; ⊙ 3-6pm Thu, Sat & Sun) forms part of Yaoundé's Benedictine monastery in the lea of Mt Fébé. It has a wonderful collection of masks, bronzes, wooden bas-reliefs and pottery. Look out for the brass sculpture of the 'Great Maternal Figure', from the area northeast of Foumban – similar sculpture is still produced at Foumban's Village des Artisans (p204). The museum has a really handy English/French guidebook (CFA2000) available at the entrance. The monastery's chapel (underneath the main church) is decorated with Cameroonian textiles and crafts, and *kora* are sometimes used to accompany the singing at Mass (11am Sunday). Take a shared taxi to Bastos and then change for Mt Fébé; chartered taxis from the city centre cost CFA2000.

### Musée National

Disappointing in comparison to the Musée d'Art Camerounais, this **museum** (Map p182; off Ave Marchand; CFA1000; ⊙ 9am-4pm Mon Sat) is small and dusty, counting masks and sculptures from across Cameroon in its exhibits. Some effort is being made to improve labelling, so it might be worth a look in the future.

### Musée Afhemi

This **museum** ( ☎ 994 4656; Quartier Nsimeyong; CFA3000; ⊙ 9am-8pm Tue-Fri, 10am-8pm Sat & Sun) is actually not a museum, but it's more of a gallery than a home. The collection of Cameroonian and regional artwork reflects the owner's eclectic tastes. Call in advance to arrange a tour in English and, possibly, lunch. It's 6km southeast of the centre.

### Mvog-Betsi Zoo

This **zoo** (Mvog-Betsi; CFA2000, camera CFA500; ⊙ 9am-6pm daily) is one of the better ones in West Africa. Co-run by the UK-based **Cameroon Wildlife Aid Fund** (CWAF, www.cwaf.org) it has a sizeable collection of native primates, including gorillas, chimps and drills, mainly rescued from poachers and the bushmeat trade. Well worth a visit, the zoo also houses a few lions, hyenas and a smattering of birds, snakes and lizards. A shared taxi to Mvog-Betsi should cost CFA200.

### Open-Air Mass

Although it's not put on for tourists, the Ewondo-language open-air mass outside the Paroisse de N'Djong Melen in Quartier Melen attracts many visitors. It's well worth a visit, but put on your Sunday best like everyone else. It begins at 9.30am on Sunday and features drums, dancing and a women's chorus. It's on the western side of town, and reached by shared taxi.

## SLEEPING
### Budget

**Foyer International de l'Église Presbytérienne** (Map p180; ☎ 985 236 mobile; off Rue Joseph Essono Balla; dm CFA3000, tw CFA5000, tent CFA2000; Ⓟ) Favoured by overlanders, this no-frills guesthouse is tucked behind the water towers looming over Nlongkak. Rooms and (communal) facilities are simple but clean, and the grounds have enough trees to laze under or kick a ball between. It's unsigned – look for the orange brick building trying to appear grand.

**Ideal Hotel** (Map p180; ☎ 220 9852; Carrefour Nlongkak; r CFA6000-8000; Ⓟ) Tucked behind a six-storey building on lively Rond Point Nlongkak. Some rooms are a bit dark, but balconies make up for this, and the hotel is a well-located budget option, particularly if you're in town hunting for visas.

**Hotel Palmier** (Map p180; ☎ 220 4593; Nlongkak; r CFA6800; ✼) In a lively area with a thronging market street outside, this hotel seems to define the word threadbare – check for missing tiles and broken air-con. It's a shame, as rooms are otherwise large and decent, and the carved statues and artwork show that they've made the effort elsewhere.

**Sun Star Hotel** (Map p180; ☎ 951 3327; Quartier Eig-Edjoa; r CFA7500; ✼) Better maintained than the Palmier, this is a low-slung place with a terrace bar out the front. Rooms are fine, but could do with a dust. Single female travellers might not feel comfortable here at night.

### Midrange

**El Panaden Hotel** (Map p182; ☎ 222 2765; elpanaden@yahoo.fr; Place de l'Indépendance; r CFA15,500-28,000; ✼) This centrally located hotel is

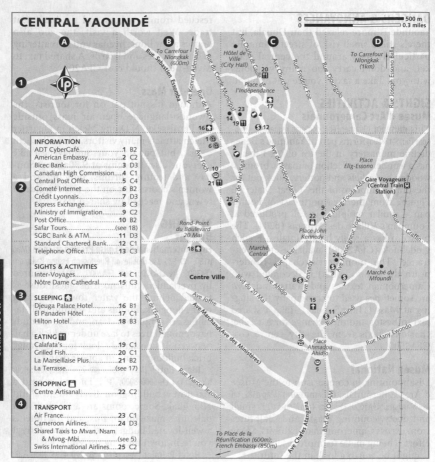

**CENTRAL YAOUNDÉ**

0 — 500 m
0 — 0.3 miles

To Carrefour
Nlongkak
(600m)

Hôtel de
Ville
(City Hall)

To Carrefour
Nlongkak
(1km)

Place de
l'Indépendance

Place
Elig-Essono

Gare Voyageurs
(Central Train
Station)

Rond-Point
du Boulevard
20 Mai

Place John
Kennedy

Marché
Central

Centre Ville

Marché du
Mfoundi

Place
Ahmadou
Ahidjo

To Place de la
Réunification (600m);
French Embassy (850m)

**INFORMATION**
ADT CyberCafé......................**1** B2
American Embassy.................**2** C2
Bicec Bank...........................**3** D3
Canadian High Commission....**4** C1
Central Post Office................**5** C4
Cometé Internet....................**6** B2
Crédit Lyonnais.....................**7** D3
Express Exchange..................**8** C3
Ministry of Immigration.........**9** C2
Post Office...........................**10** B2
Safar Tours.........................(see 18)
SGBC Bank & ATM................**11** D3
Standard Chartered Bank......**12** C1
Telephone Office..................**13** C3

**SIGHTS & ACTIVITIES**
Inter-Voyages.......................**14** C1
Nôtre Dame Cathedral...........**15** C3

**SLEEPING**
Djeuga Palace Hotel.............**16** B1
El Panaden Hôtel..................**17** C1
Hilton Hotel.........................**18** B3

**EATING**
Calafata's............................**19** C1
Grilled Fish..........................**20** C1
La Marseillaise Plus..............**21** B2
La Terrasse........................(see 17)

**SHOPPING**
Centre Artisanal...................**22** C2

**TRANSPORT**
Air France...........................**23** C1
Cameroon Airlines................**24** D3
Shared Taxis to Mvan, Nsam
  & Mvog-Mbi....................(see 5)
Swiss International Airlines....**25** C2

an old traveller's favourite. Helpful staff complement clean and generously sized rooms, most with balconies. La Terrasse bar next door is a handy late night stagger away.

**Sipowa Hotel** (Map p180; ☎ 221 9571; contact@sipowahotel.com; opposite Saudi Embassy, Bastos; r CFA15,000-30,000, ste CFA35,000; ☒ ) A clean, if slightly clinical, option. Small rooms here are good value and the suites are well-appointed with fridge and squashy sofas. Security shouldn't be a problem – even the windows have bars.

**Sim's Hotel** (Map p180; ☎ 220 5375; Carrefour Bastos; r CFA13,000-25,000) One of the cheaper options in Bastos, this hotel tries to straddle the budget/midrange divide but doesn't quite succeed

in being either. Rooms are a bit dark and dreary, and all have seen better days.

**Hôtel Laginaque** (p180; ☎ 221 0554; mang wachuisse@yahoo.fr; Carrefour Bastos; r CFA20,000-35,000; ☒ ) Just off the main road, this place has soft beds in very comfortable rooms, some with good views over the city. The management could be more efficient; room service makes up for the lack of restaurant, but order in good time.

**Hotel Azur** (Map p180; ☎ 221 1639; hotalfic@iccnet .cm; Bastos; r CFA35,000-45,000; ☒ ) A modern hotel in a quiet and secluded location. The cheaper rooms feel a bit pinched for the price, but the more expensive rooms are big enough to get lost in. Most have balconies, and those at the back have gorgeous views over the hills.

## Top End

**Hôtel Mont Fébé** ( ☎ 221 4002; Mont Fébé; r CFA48,000-56,000; P 🅿 ⛶ 🏊 ) High on the slopes of Mont Fébé, this hotel has commanding views over Yaoundé. It's a cool getaway from the frenetic city, with well-turned out rooms (many with balcony), bar and a restaurant with a good poolside buffet. The hotel also operates a shuttle bus to the airport for guests.

**Djeuga Palace Hotel** (Map p182; ☎ 222 6469; www.djeuga-palace.com; Rue de Narvik; r from CFA72,000; ⛶ 🏊 ) Yaoundé's newest four-star offering, the Djeuga Palace is well-located and steals some thunder from the international chains in town. Rooms are spacious and tastefully decorated, with good views, and there's the expected complement of swanky bars and restaurants, and a small pool.

## EATING

**La Terrasse** (Map p182; Place de l'Indépendance; mains from CFA3000; 🕑 7am-midnight) Ever popular, the laid-back atmosphere here is accentuated by mellow live music every evening. Dishes are a mix of Cameroonian and continental standards, but choose the draught beer over the bottles, it's a lot cheaper. As we went to press, rumours were that the restaurant was moving to Ave Churchill.

**Chez Wou** (Map p180; Rue Joseph Mballa Eloumden; mains from CFA4000; 🕑 lunch & dinner) One of Yaoundé's older Chinese restaurants, this has nice tables set under a wide porch, and a comprehensive menu. The starters (from CFA2000) are worth picking at.

**Globus** (Map p180; Carrefour Nlongkak; dishes from CFA700; 🕑 7am-11pm) A good watering hole as well as a restaurant, Globus has Cameroonian dishes and a few trusty standards like chicken with rice. The big draw is the location: raised above Nlongkak, it's great for watching the world go by, and catching some gorgeous sunsets.

**Snack Time** (Map p180; Carrefour Bastos; mains from CFA2700; 🕑 10am-11pm) This bright place serves up a menu straight from an American diner, with a few Lebanese and Italian dishes thrown in for good measure. The bean burritos (CFA3000) are real winners, and the vegetarian pasta a treat for those suffering from a surfeit of meaty Cameroonian stews.

**La Forêt Dense** (Map p180; Rue Joseph Mballa Eloumden; meals from CFA5500) This is a pricey place, with traditional Cameroonian dishes in an upscale setting. If you've ever wondered what crocodile *mbongo* tastes like, this is the place to find out.

**Le Buffet** (Map p180; Carrefour Nlongkak; mains from CFA500; 🕑 11am-9pm) The name gives this place away – there's a long, heated servery where you can help yourself to various stews, chicken, fish and as much rice and plantain as you can eat.

## Quick Eats

**La Marseillais Plus** (Map p182; Ave Foch; 🕑 12-3pm & 7-10pm) If it weren't for the posters of President Biya, this would be a good approximation of a provincial French café. Good breakfast, sandwiches and snacks.

**Calafatas** (Map p182; Rue Nachtigal; pastries from CFA200; 🕑 8am-6pm) People cross the city to get their pastries from Calafatas, and you should too. Although it's open all day, all the best choices are gone by late morning, leaving little but baguettes.

Around Carrefours Bastos and Nlongkak you can find grills serving *suya* throughout the day. On Place de l'Indépendance, near El Panaden Hotel, there are women grilling delicious fish, served with chilli or peanut sauce from CFA1000.

## DRINKING

The best bars are in Carrefours Bastos and Nlongkak, most with open-air seating facing the street – great for people-watching. Globus and La Terrasse (see left) serve equally well as places for a beer as a meal. Solo female travellers might find the atmosphere in some uneasy once the sun dips. It's difficult to recommend anywhere in particular – there are plenty, so just follow your nose to find one you like.

## SHOPPING

Yaounde isn't a great place for lots of souvenir shopping.

**Centre Artisanal** (Place John Kennedy) This large government-run establishment is a good place to get an idea of what handicrafts are available in Cameroon, although prices are a little high. Wood carving figures highly in what's on offer

## GETTING THERE & AWAY
### Air

For international flight connections to Yaoundé see p224. **Cameroon Airlines** (Map p182; ☎ 223 0304; Ave Monseigneur Vogt) operate a daily

**CAMEROON**

flight from Douala to Yaoundé (CFA65,000, 45 minutes). Other internal flights are to N'Gaoundéré, Garoua and Bertoua – all allegedly several times a week, but check with the airline, as timetables are a mix of fact and fiction.

### Bus

To Douala, Central Voyages and Guaranti Express have services (CFA3800, three hours) leaving regularly during the day. The former has a 'prestige' service costing CFA7500. Its office is south of the centre in Mvog-Mbi; unlike most companies, you can book 1st-class tickets a day before and they leave on time. Guaranti Express is recommended for Limbe (CFA5000, five hours), Bamenda (CFA5000, six hours), Bafoussam (CFA2500, three hours) and Kumba (CFA4000, four hours). Its office is in Quartier Nsam, 3km south of the centre.

Otherwise, all other transport for Kribi, Bertoua, Batouri and other destinations in southern, central and eastern Cameroon, departs from Blvd de l'Ocam, 3km south of Place Ahmadou Ahidjo (direct taxi drivers to Agences de Mvan). For Kribi (CFA3000, 3½ hours) look for La Kribienne or Jako Voyages, running throughout the day. For Bertoua and points east, the main line is Alliance Voyages, departing early daily to Batouri (CFA6000, at least eight hours). There is also plentiful transport from here to Ebolowa, Limbe, Buea and Kumba.

Transport to Bafoussam (CFA3000, five hours) and points north, departs from Gare Routière d'Etoudi, 5km north of Centre Ville, and is where most agencies have their offices; the best one is Binam. You can find vehicles to Bamenda here – though it's often quicker to get something to Bafoussam and another vehicle from there to Bamenda. Transport to Bamenda also departs from Gare Routière d'Obili on the western edge of town.

### Train

There is a daily train to N'Gaoundéré, departing at around 6pm from (☎ 223 50 03). For more information on train travel see p228.

### GETTING AROUND
### To/From the Airport

A taxi to Nsimalen Airport from central Yaoundé (40 minutes) should cost CFA3000 to CFA4000. There is no public transport.

### Taxi

Shared taxis are the only public transport option. There are no minibuses and surprisingly, Yaoundé doesn't permit *moto-taxis*. Fares are set at CFA175 for short to medium length rides – flag them down on the street and shout out the name of the *quartier, rond-point* or landmark near to where you wish to go; the driver will sound his horn if he's not going your way. Charter taxis start from CFA1000.

# DOUALA & THE SOUTHWEST

Cameroon's lush southwest and Littoral provinces are the most fertile parts of the country. Everywhere you go there is a riot of vegetation and a colourful selection of produce in the markets. For visitors the region is similarly bountiful with attractions. Douala, the country's pulsing economic heart, is the most popular gateway to Cameroon, and from here it's a short hop to the lazy beaches of Limbe and Kribi. The more energetic can hike up Mt Cameroon, or head further afield to the ancient rainforests of Korup National Park.

## DOUALA
### pop 1.7 million

Yaoundé might be Cameroon's capital, but Douala thinks the title is claimed unfairly. Founded during the German colonial period (and initially christened 'Kamerunstadt'), this sticky, hectic port is actually the largest city in the country, and main air hub. Douala has little in the way of tourist attractions and a brief visit doesn't do much to show off its charms – you're more likely to be struck by the bad roads and bad air – but give it some time and you may begin to appreciate the city's good restaurants, lively nightlife and decaying tropical ambience.

### Orientation

Akwa district, at the heart of Douala, is bisected by Blvd de la Liberté, where you'll find many hotels, Internet cafés, banks and restaurants. South of here, along and near Rue Joss in Bonanjo, is the administrative quarter, with airline offices, government buildings and the central post office.

# Information

## INTERNET ACCESS

Places open and close with the drop of a hat. The following are reliable:

**Cyberaljo** (per 3 hrs CFA1000) Near Cinema Wouri.

**Cyberbao** (Blvd de la Liberté; per hr CFA400)

## MEDICAL SERVICES

**Pharmacie du Centre** (Blvd de la Liberté)

**Pharmacie de Douala** (Blvd Ahidjo)

## MONEY

Hôtel Akwa Palace has plenty of touts outside for changing cash out of hours. Be on your guard.

**Bicec** (Blvd de la Liberté, Akwa) Recommended for changing money; the Akwa branch has an ATM.

**Crédit Lyonnais** Bonanjo (Rue Joss); Akwa (Rue Sylvani) Recommended for changing money.

**Ecobank** (Blvd de la Liberté) With ATM.

**Express Exchange** (Blvd de la Liberté) Conveniently changes travellers cheques and US dollars.

**SGBC** (Rue Joss) With ATM.

**Standard Chartered Bank** (Akwa) Recommended for changing money.

## POST

**Central Post Office** (Rue Joss)

## TRAVEL AGENCIES

**Saga Voyages** ( ☎ 342 3317; Rue Joss) A well-organised, professional agency.

**Trans Africa Tours** ( ☎ 342 8307; Blvd de la Liberté, near Rondpoint Deido) Good for flight connections within Africa.

# Dangers & Annoyances

Douala has a poor reputation for muggings and you need to be streetwise. Taxis are always a good idea after dark, and leave your valuables in your hotel. The beggars near the Hôtel Akwa Palace can sometimes be aggressive.

# Sights & Activities

The trick with Douala is not to anticipate formal attractions – getting into the city's vibe is what's needed here. You can best do this at any of the clamorous markets, most notably the sprawling **Marché de Lagos** (cnr Rue de New Bell & Rue Congo Pariso). All human life seems to be here, but watch out for pickpockets.

If it's too much, relax at one of Douala's pools. The best is at **Hôtel Akwa Palace** (Blvd de le Liberté; nonguests CFA4000); alternatively try the **Hotel Beausejour Mirabel** (Rue Joffre; nonguests CFA1500); both are in Akwa.

# Sleeping

## BUDGET

**Centre d'Accueil Missionaire** ( ☎ 342 2797, progemis .douala@camnet.cm; Rue Franceville; r with/without shower CFA7000/8000; P ⚡ ⚡ ) Sat back from Douala's frantic main drag, this is a real oasis. There are clean twin rooms, a pleasant veranda and a pool to cool off in. Part of the Catholic Mission, it's poorly signed – it's next to the pink Axa building.

**Église Évangelique de Cameroun** ( ☎ 342 3611; eec@wagne.net; Rue Alfred Saker; s/d/tr CFA6500/8000/ 11,000) This is an adequate option as church missions go, but it's a bit tired and in need of love. Rooms are basic for the money, with shared bathroom facilities; there's also a kitchen.

**Hotel Hila** ( ☎ 342 1586; Blvd de l'Unité; s/d CFA10,000-12,000/15,000; ⚡ ) Ideally located for the Yaoundé bus agencies, the Hila sits on a very busy road, so get a room at the back if you can. Rooms are a little threadbare, but fair value for the price. A deposit of CFA20,000 is required on checking in.

## MIDRANGE

**Foyer du Marin** ( ☎ 342 2794; douala@seemannsmission .org; Rue Gallieni; s/d CFA15,000/28,000; P ⚡ ⚡ ⚡ ) Otherwise known as the German Seaman's Mission, tidy comfortable rooms are kept ship-shape for visiting sailors – and other travellers – coming into port. It's equally popular as a drinking spot with Douala's expat community, who visit for the nightly sausage and meat grill from 7pm. You can play pool or swim in the watery one, and pick up something to read at the eclectic multilingual book exchange. Douala's bargain, it's regularly full, so advance booking is essential.

**Parfait Garden** ( ☎ 342 6357; hotel.parfait-gar den@globalnet2.net; Blvd de le Liberté; r from CFA35,000; ⚡ ) Rooms here are spacious and plush. There's a nice bar and restaurant, and the liveried bell boys inject a little class.

**Piano Hotel** ( ☎ 343 0825; piano_hotel@yahoo.fr; Rue Drouot Akwa Bonamouti; r CFA27,500-31,500, P ⚡ ) Rooms here are clean and comfortable, but with the hotel coming straight out of the business traveller model, there's not much character. Still, it's a reliable option; pricier rooms have both bathtub and balcony.

CAMEROON

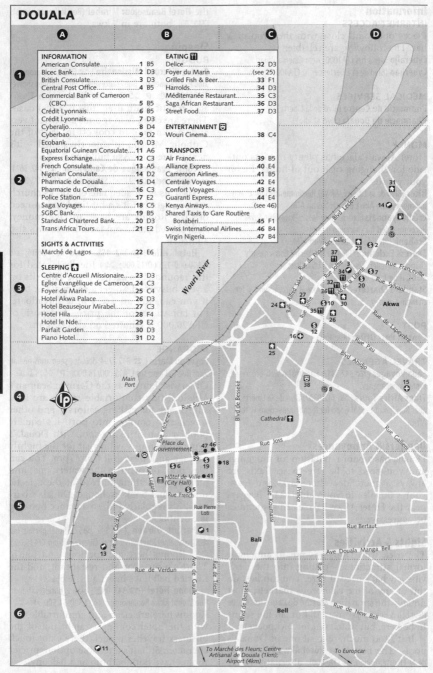

# DOUALA

## INFORMATION
| | |
|---|---|
| American Consulate...................1 | B5 |
| Bicec Bank...............................2 | D3 |
| British Consulate......................3 | D3 |
| Central Post Office...................4 | B5 |
| Commercial Bank of Cameroon | |
| (CBC)...................................5 | B5 |
| Crédit Lyonnais.......................6 | B5 |
| Crédit Lyonnais.......................7 | D3 |
| Cyberaljo...............................8 | D4 |
| Cyberbao................................9 | D2 |
| Ecobank................................10 | D3 |
| Equatorial Guinean Consulate...11 | A6 |
| Express Exchange...................12 | C3 |
| French Consulate....................13 | A5 |
| Nigerian Consulate..................14 | D2 |
| Pharmacie de Douala...............15 | D4 |
| Pharmacie du Centre...............16 | C3 |
| Police Station.........................17 | E2 |
| Saga Voyages........................18 | C5 |
| SGBC Bank............................19 | B5 |
| Standard Chartered Bank..........20 | D3 |
| Trans Africa Tours...................21 | E2 |

## SIGHTS & ACTIVITIES
| | |
|---|---|
| Marché de Lagos....................22 | E6 |

## SLEEPING
| | |
|---|---|
| Centre d'Accueil Missionaire......23 | D3 |
| Eglise Évangélique de Cameroon..24 | C3 |
| Foyer du Marin .....................25 | C4 |
| Hotel Akwa Palace..................26 | D3 |
| Hotel Beausejour Mirabel.........27 | C3 |
| Hotel Hila..............................28 | F4 |
| Hotel le Nde..........................29 | E2 |
| Parfait Garden.......................30 | D3 |
| Piano Hotel............................31 | D2 |

## EATING
| | |
|---|---|
| Delice...................................32 | D3 |
| Foyer du Marin ...................(see 25) | |
| Grilled Fish & Beer..................33 | F1 |
| Harrolds................................34 | D3 |
| Méditerranée Restaurant..........35 | C3 |
| Saga African Restaurant...........36 | D3 |
| Street Food...........................37 | D3 |

## ENTERTAINMENT
| | |
|---|---|
| Wouri Cinema........................38 | C4 |

## TRANSPORT
| | |
|---|---|
| Air France..............................39 | B5 |
| Alliance Express......................40 | E4 |
| Cameroon Airlines...................41 | B5 |
| Centrale Voyages....................42 | E4 |
| Confort Voyages....................43 | E4 |
| Guaranti Express....................44 | E4 |
| Kenya Airways.....................(see 46) | |
| Shared Taxis to Gare Routière | |
| Bonabéri..............................45 | F1 |
| Swiss International Airlines........46 | B4 |
| Virgin Nigeria.........................47 | B4 |

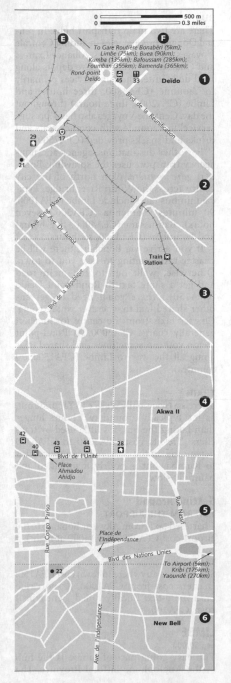

**Hotel le Nde** ( ☎ 342 7034; Blvd de le Liberté; s/d CFA18,000/21,000; ❄ ) The royal crest and Union Jack above the door try to make this hotel a place that is forever England. Rooms are tidy and decent, doing much to dispel the boarding school gloom of the lobby and corridors.

**Hotel Beausejour Mirabel** ( ☎ 342 3885; info@beausejour-mirabel.com; Rue Joffre; r CFA25,000-27,000; ❄ ☞ ) This hotel's bright exterior puts forward a warm welcome. The corner location can make the interior seem like it's all corridors, but at the end of them you'll find large tidy rooms with balconies. Non-residents can use the pool for CFA1500 per day.

**Hôtel Akwa Palace** ( ☎ 342 2601; akwa.palace@ camnet.cm; Blvd de le Liberté; s/d CFA38,000/45,000; ℗ ❄ ▣ ☞ ) There are two parts to this hotel. In the older annexe you get very large, airy rooms at midrange prices, while enjoying all the top-end facilities of the newer (Pullman) section, where rooms weigh in at CFA95,000. In the lobby you can find a travel agent, car hire, shops and a bar-restaurant. Plus there's a decent pool to cool off in.

## Eating & Drinking

There are plenty of good restaurants along Blvd de le Liberté, selling a spectrum of international cuisine.

**Méditerranée Restaurant** (Blvd de la Liberté; mains from CFA2500; ☯ 8am-midnight) With an open terrace – but still cleverly sheltered from the busy road – the Méditerranée is perennially popular. As the name suggests, the menu has a good mix of Greek, Italian and Lebanese dishes. Curiously, the restaurant also has a newsagent selling international papers.

**Foyer du Marin** (Rue Gallieni; kebabs from CFA1000; ☯ 7-10pm) The nightly grill at this hotel is worth making a diversion for. They serve great kebabs, chicken and – best of all – juicy German sausage. It's a Douala expat institution.

**Saga African Restaurant** (Blvd de la Liberté; mains from CFA1200; ☯ noon-10pm) Opposite the Parfait Garden Hotel, the Saga offers up an interesting mix of continental dishes and some local classics such as *ndole*. It's a nicely decked out place, with a bar out the front and a restaurant behind.

**Delice** (Blvd de la Liberté; snacks from CFA500; ☯ 7am-9.30pm) A great early morning stop for pastries and a shot of coffee; there are also some good toasted sandwiches. The 'delice' surely refers to the cool air-con and comfy seating.

**Harrolds** (Blvd de la Liberté; snacks from CFA500; ☻noon-10pm) A handy place for a quick bite or lunch on the run – sit down with a draught beer or eat on the hoof. The tasty shwarmas are CFA1500.

### STREET EATS

**Grilled fish & beer** (Rue de la Joie; fish from CFA1000; ☻10am-late) This street of bars off Blvd del la Réunification is punctuated at regular intervals by women with stalls selling grilled fish. Order the catch of the day, then retire to a drinking hole to sink a cold one while your meal is barbequing. It's served to your table with plantains and *baton* – delicious!

**Street Food stalls** (Rue Joffre; meals from CFA800; ☻10am-9pm) This market street has plenty of options for filling Cameroonian food – mostly simple stalls with little more than a bench and table. Food is served throughout the day, fresh and tasty.

## Entertainment

Douala is known for its nightlife, which is far more charged than Yaoundé. Asking locals is the best way to find the current hotspots, but when we visited, **Rue de la Joie** (near Rond-Point Dëido) was one of the happening streets, with bars and nightclubs dancing until dawn on the weekend.

## Shopping

**Centre Artisanal de Douala** (Marché des Fleurs, Ave Charles de Gaulle) This is a good place to stock up on Cameroonian handicrafts, including carvings, metal and leather work and fabrics. Bargain hard.

## Getting There & Away

### AIR

Douala is the main entry point for international flights into Cameroon. The airport can be pretty chaotic, with plenty of hustlers, so brace yourself when you get off the plane. For connections see p224. **Cameroon Airlines** ( ☎ 342 2525; off Rue de Trieste) flies daily to Yaoundé (CFA65,000, 45 minutes) and Garoua (CFA125,000, three hours), and three times a week to N'Gaoundéré, sometimes stopping at Maroua, according to the pilot's whim.

### BUS

There are two main transport hubs. In central Douala, bus agencies including Centrale Voyages, Confort Voyages, Alliance Express and Guaranti Express all have depots along Blvd de l'Unité, and run services primarily to Yaoundé (CFA3800, three hours) and Limbe (CFA2000, three hours) throughout the day. Centrale Voyages also has a 'prestige service' to Yaoundé with comfier seats and drinks and snacks provided (CFA7500).

For other destinations, agency and non-agency transport uses the sprawling Bonabéri *gare routière*, 6km north of the city centre across the Wouri River bridge. Typical minibus fares include Limbe (CFA1000, 90 minutes) Bamenda (CFA5000, seven hours), Bafoussam (CFA4000, five hours) and Foumban (CFA4500, six hours).

If you arrive via Bonabéri, there will be charter taxis waiting to take you to town. Otherwise, walk out to the main road and get a share taxi to Rond-point Dëido (CFA150), where you'll need to get another shared taxi to wherever you're going. Charter taxis from the centre to Bonabéri generally charge CFA3000. At Rond-point Dëido you can sometimes find shared taxis going all the way to Limbe (CFA1500, 70 minutes).

### TRAIN

There's a twice-daily service to Yaoundé but, as it's typically around two hours longer than taking the bus, it's little used by travellers. Tickets cost CFA3000 to CFA6700 depending on the class. A daily service runs to Kumba, but is poorly maintained and painfully slow.

## Getting Around

### TO/FROM THE AIRPORT

Chartered taxis from Akwa or Bonanjo to the airport cost CFA2500 (CFA3000 at night).

### TAXI

Shared taxis anywhere in town cost CFA150; charters cost from CFA1000. A short ride on a *moto-taxi* (locally called 'bendskins') costs CFA100.

## LIMBE

pop 50,000

The easy-going port of Limbe is the hub of the Anglophone Littoral Province. The

British missionary, Alfred Saker, founded the town in 1857, initially naming it after Queen Victoria. The town sits in the shadow of Mt Cameroon, surrounded by banana and coconut plantations. These days Limbe is best known as a weekend getaway from Douala, with people coming to enjoy the languid air and fresh seafood. If you're doing the same, arrive early to arrange accommodation or book in advance. On a very clear day you can look out across the bay to Equatorial Guinea's distant Bioko Island.

## Information

The banks change money, but don't rely on travellers cheques.

**Bicec** (Ahidjo Rd)

**Bifunde Computer Centre** (Bota Rd; per hr CFA800) Very fast Internet access.

**Computer World** (Banley St; per hr CFA400; ☒ closed Sun)

**Fako Tourist Board** ( ☎ 333 2861; Banley St; ☒ 7.30am-5pm Mon-Sat) A very helpful office which can arrange local tours, hotels and bookings with the Mt Cameroon Ecotourism Organisation.

**SGBC** (Beach Rd) Has an ATM.

## Sights & Activities

### LIMBE WILDLIFE CENTRE

Most zoos in Africa are depressing places, but this **wildlife centre** (www.limbewildlife.org; CFA3000; ☒ 9am-5pm) is a shining exception. Jointly run by the Ministry of the Environment

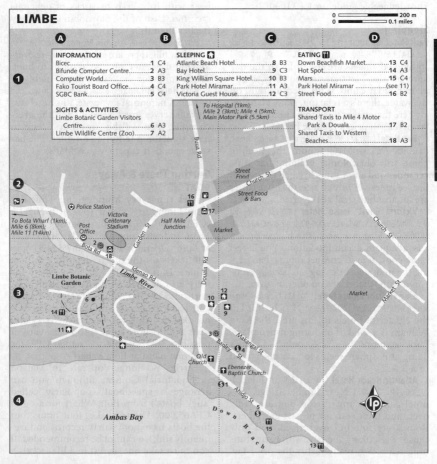

**LIMBE**

| 0 | 200 m |
| 0 | 0.1 miles |

| INFORMATION | |
| --- | --- |
| Bicec | **1** C4 |
| Bifunde Computer Centre | **2** A3 |
| Computer World | **3** B3 |
| Fako Tourist Board Office | **4** C4 |
| SGBC Bank | **5** C4 |

| SIGHTS & ACTIVITIES | |
| --- | --- |
| Limbe Botanic Garden Visitors Centre | **6** A3 |
| Limbe Wildlife Centre (Zoo) | **7** A2 |

| SLEEPING ⌂ | |
| --- | --- |
| Atlantic Beach Hotel | **8** B3 |
| Bay Hotel | **9** C3 |
| King William Square Hotel | **10** B3 |
| Park Hotel Miramar | **11** A3 |
| Victoria Guest House | **12** C3 |

| EATING ⌂ | |
| --- | --- |
| Down Beachfish Market | **13** C4 |
| Hot Spot | **14** A3 |
| Mars | **15** C4 |
| Park Hotel Miramar | (see 11) |
| Street Food | **16** B2 |

| TRANSPORT | |
| --- | --- |
| Shared Taxis to Mile 4 Motor Park & Douala | **17** B2 |
| Shared Taxis to Western Beaches | **18** A3 |

To Hospital (1km); Mile 2 (3km); Mile 4 (5km); Main Motor Park (5.5km)

Buua Rd

Street Food

Church St

Street Food & Bars

Police Station

Victoria Centenary Stadium

Half Mile Junction

Market

Garden St

To Bota Wharf (1km); Mile 6 (8km); Mile 11 (14km)

Post Office

Bota Rd

Idenao Rd

Limbe River

**Limbe Botanic Garden**

Douala Rd

Church St

Market

Market St

Makangal St

Banley St

Old Church

Ebenezer Baptist Church

Ahidjo St

**Ambas Bay**

*Down Beach*

CAMEROON

and the primate charity Pandrillus, it contains rescued chimpanzees, gorillas, drills and other primates – all housed in large enclosures – with heaps of information about local conservation issues. Staff are well-informed, and are heavily involved with community education. Interested visitors may even 'adopt' a primate, to help pay for their care, from CFA20,000 per year.

### LIMBE BOTANIC GARDENS
These **gardens** (www.mcbcclimbe.org; CFA1000, camera CFA2000; ☒ 8am-6pm) are a pleasant place to while away an afternoon. There's a small visitors centre and an area with Commonwealth War Graves. Those with particular botanic interests will profit from hiring a knowledgeable guide for CFA1000.

## Sleeping
**Park Hotel Miramar** ( ☎ 332 2332; Botanic Garden Rd; s/d CFA13,650/18,400, camping CFA5000; P ☒ ☒ ) Individual chalets are the order of the day here, but don't let that summon images of a plain holiday camp. With a terrace right on the water, there's a relaxing, almost languid air here that makes this Limbe's most popular hotel. All prices include breakfast.

**Bay Hotel** ( ☎ 773 3609 mobile; off Makangal Street; r CFA7000-7000, ste10,000) Ignore the peeling paint, this old colonial building has wide verandas and airy rooms to catch the best of the sea breeze. A tidy choice, the huge suites are an absolute steal at the price.

**Victoria Guest House Hotel** ( ☎ 333 2446; off Makangal Street; r with fan CFA6000-9000, air-con CFA12,000-16,000; ☒ ) Fine in a pinch, this budget option has adequate accommodation. You'll feel more content in its cheaper rooms than paying the midrange price tag – especially compared with what else is on offer in town.

**King William Square Hotel** ( ☎ 333 2529; Makangal Street; s/d CFA10,000/11,500-12,500; ☒ ) The third of the cluster of hotels in this area, the King William is a solid, if undistinguished place. Look at more than one room – Limbe's damp atmosphere seems to have taken hold in a few.

**Atlantic Beach Hotel** ( ☎ 332 2689; r CFA16,500-23,500; P ☒ ☒ ) Near Limbe Bridge, this hotel's days as town's top dog are sadly over, and there's an air of past glory here. Rooms are fine but overpriced, and only those overlooking the bay, with their stunning sea views, really justify the price tag.

Bizarrely, the more expensive rooms come with two breakfasts, even if you're travelling solo.

## Eating
You can find good street food around Half-Mile Junction, along with a good selection of grocery shops and bakeries.

**Mars** (Ahidjo Rd; mains from CFA2000) This decent place has the usual range of Cameroonian dishes, but come here for the seafood and the terrace sticking out into the bay – a great place for a sundowner.

**Down Beach Fish Market** (Down Beach; dishes from CFA1000) You'll find this cluster of shacks where the fishing boats haul up on the beach, grilling the day's catch. Soak up your beer with fish, crab or sticks of delicious *crevettes*. Dish of the day doesn't come any fresher than this.

**Hot Spot** (off Botanic Garden Rd; mains from CFA2000) On a low hill, there are great views here overlooking the water, and good meals to boot. Take a torch for the walk home at night.

**Park Hotel Miramar** (Botanic Garden Rd; mains from CFA2800) A perennial favourite, this hotel restaurant serves great seafood, and the ever-changing menu of the day always seems to have something tempting on offer. The bar serves good, if expensive, cocktails.

## Getting There & Away
### BOAT
Ferries run every Monday and Thursday from Limbe to Calabar (p647) in Nigeria (CFA35,000, 10 hours), departing around 11pm and returning on Tuesday and Friday at 6pm. Operator **Destiny** ( ☎ 755 3435 mobile) sell tickets on the day of departure at Bota Wharf, 1km west of town, from where the ferry also departs. You give up your passport on boarding, which is returned when you reach Nigerian immigration. There is no food or drink for sale on the ferry and seats are in short supply, so board early if possible. It's possible to change CFA for Nigerian naira at Bota Wharf.

Ferries no longer operate to Malabo in Equatorial Guinea, although you can arrange a speedboat (popularly called 'stick-boats') from Bota Wharf for around CFA65,000. The trip takes four hours, but the boats have poor safety records and frequently sink, so cannot be recommended. If you must take one, invest in a life jacket.

## BUS & TAXI

The main motor park is at Mile 4, about 5km from town on the Buea road. When arriving, you'll be dropped here, and will need to take a share taxi to Half Mile Junction in the centre of Limbe (CFA100). Minibuses depart throughout the day from Mile 4 to Buea (CFA500, 25 minutes), Douala (CFA1000, 90 minutes) and Kumba (CFA1500, 2½ hours). Share taxis also depart to Douala (CFA1500, 70 minutes) and Buea (CFA750, 20 minutes) from Half-Mile Junction. Chartering a taxi to Douala costs around CFA9000.

To Yaoundé, Guaranti Express and Patience, both on the Buea road (Mile 2), have one departure each around 8am daily (CFA5000, five hours). Guaranti Express also has a service to Bamenda (CFA4000, around 8 hours).

Shared taxis to the beaches at Mile 6 (CFA100, 10 minutes) and Mile 11 (CFA150, 15 minutes) depart from Idenao Road near the stadium. To Mile 11 they can take a while to fill – expect to pay CFA2500 for a charter.

## AROUND LIMBE
### Beaches

Beaches of dark brown volcanic sand stretch north from Limbe. The best are at Mile 8 (especially at Batoke village) and Mile 11. There's also a beach at Mile 6, although it isn't quite as nice, and inquisitive monkeys can be a problem here. Take local advice before swimming – currents are strong and can produce dangerous riptides. On the road just before Mile 11 you can see the lava flow from Mt Cameroon's 1999 eruption. Take transport heading for Mile 11.

### SLEEPING

All of these places are near the beach, but none have rooms on the water. There's no accommodation north of Mile 11.

**Fini Hotel** ( ☎ 333 2576; fini@finihotel.com; Mile 6 Rd; r CFA18,000–35,000; bungalow CFA25,000–80,000; P ⚡ ) The fanciest option in the Limbe area, with rooms in all shapes and sizes. Those in the main hotel are the best, but if there are several of you then the self-contained bungalows could be the bargain of your trip.

**Coast Beach Hotel** ( ☎ 333 2927; Mile 6 Rd; r CFA20,000–25,000; ste CFA40,000; P ⚡ ) Although

there's not quite as much beach here as the hotel's name suggests, some rooms are so close to the sea that you can almost dip your toes in from the balcony. Rooms are comfy, many with separate sitting room attached.

## BUEA

On the lower slopes of Mt Cameroon, Buea (pronounced *boy-ah*) is a large sprawling town, and the starting point for climbing the mountain. The rise in altitude gives Buea a much cooler air than sticky Limbe. From 1901, it was briefly the German colonial capital. The climate is well suited to growing tea, and the Tole Tea Plantation south of the town is a major local employer.

### Information

**Express Exchange** (Molyko Rd) A very useful branch that changes euros, dollars and travellers cheques.

**Mt Cameroon Ecotourism Organisation** ( ☎ 332 2038; mountceo@yahooo.uk; Buea Market; ⏰ 8am-5pm Mon-Fri, 7am-noon weekends) Can arrange tours of the Tole Tea Plantation.

**Nigerian Consulate** ( ☎ 332 2528; Nigeria Consulate Rd; ⏰ 8am-4pm Mon-Fri) Convenient for visas for onward travel.

### Sleeping & Eating

**Paramount Hotel** ( ☎ 382 2074; Molyko Rd; s/d with cold water CFA7000/10,000, with hot water CFA14,000/17,000; P 💻 ) This hotel should be credited for trying to bring some upscale pomp to Buea; for the most part it pulls it off. Rooms are comfortable and clean, and come with TV; the budget options are a little simpler.

**Parliamentarian Flats** ( ☎ 332 2459; Nigeria Consulate Rd; s/d CFA5000/10,000; P ) There's a stripped-down feeling at this hotel, although rooms are good value for the price. There are no showers, but if you've slogged up Mount Cameroon you'll appreciate the deep baths – and the hot water heater to help fill them.

**Presbyterian Church Synod Office** ( ☎ 332 2336; Market Rd; s/d with shared bathroom CFA2500/4000, private bathroom CFA3000/5000, camping CFA1000; P ) As church missions go, this one is a gem. Conveniently located and kept spotless, rooms are comfy, with a tidy communal sitting room and cooking facilities.

There are several cheap eating places on Molyko Road around the Paramount Hotel.

## Getting There & Away

The motor park for onward transport is at Mile 17, about 6km from town along the Limbe Road. Minibuses run throughout the day to Limbe (CFA500, 25 minutes), and less frequently to Douala (CFA1400, two hours) and Kumba (CFA1500, two hours). A shared taxi from Mile 17 to Buea Market is CFA150.

## MT CAMEROON

Known locally as *Mongo-mo-Ndemi* (Mountain of Thunder) by the Bakweri people, Mt Cameroon is West Africa's highest peak at 4095m. It is an active volcano and it's thought that a fleet of Phoenician explorers witnessed an eruption in 450 BC. The last eruption was in 2000. Scientifically, it's of great interest for its endemic plants and birds, and for the unique climatic conditions that make it a biodiversity hotspot.

November to April is the main climbing season. Although it's possible to climb the mountain year-round, you won't get much in the way of views during the rainy season. Late spring offers the best views – if not to the valley below, then at least for glimpses of the stars at night.

## Routes

There are several routes to the top and numerous trails on the mountain's lower slopes. None require technical equipment, but warm clothes are essential near the

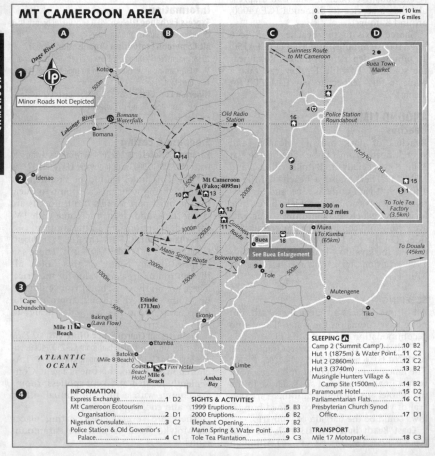

**MT CAMEROON AREA**

| SLEEPING |
|---|
| Camp 2 ('Summit Camp')..........10 B2 |
| Hut 1 (1875m) & Water Point...11 C2 |
| Hut 2 (2860m)........................12 C2 |
| Hut 3 (3740m)........................13 B2 |
| Musingile Hunters Village & |
| Camp Site (1500m)...............14 B2 |
| Paramount Hotel....................15 D2 |
| Parliamentarian Flats...............16 C1 |
| Presbyterian Church Synod |
| Office..................................17 D1 |

| TRANSPORT |
|---|
| Mile 17 Motorpark.................18 C3 |

| INFORMATION |
|---|
| Express Exchange....................1 D2 |
| Mt Cameroon Ecotourism |
| Organisation.........................2 D1 |
| Nigerian Consulate..................3 C2 |
| Police Station & Old Governor's |
| Palace..................................4 C1 |

| SIGHTS & ACTIVITIES |
|---|
| 1999 Eruptions........................5 B3 |
| 2000 Eruptions........................6 B2 |
| Elephant Opening....................7 B2 |
| Mann Spring & Water Point.......8 B3 |
| Tole Tea Plantation..................9 C3 |

summit and waterproof gear is a must. The quickest is the 'Guinness Route', a straight up-and-down climb that can be easily done in 1½ days, though it's quite steep in parts. Along this route are three poorly maintained huts (at 1875m, 2860m and 3740m), with plank beds and little else.

It's better to take at least two nights on the mountain, to experience its ecosystems and explore less-travelled routes; if you have the time, there are also set hikes of five days and more. One popular two-night, three-day combination ascends via the Mann Spring route and descends via the Guinness Route. With more time, it's possible to descend via Musingile on the mountain's northern side, and from there go through the forest to Koto (northeast of Idenao). Alternatively, the steep Radio Station route ascends from Bonakanda village through scrub and grassland to a hunter's camp at Nitele, and on to the summit from there.

Otherwise you'll need camping equipment, and for all routes you should be self-sufficient with food and water. The only water points on the mountain are at Hut 1 on the Guinness Route, and at Mann Spring.

### Guides & Permits

Treks are arranged in Buea through the very professional **Mount Cameroon Ecotourism Organisation** ( ☎ 332 2038; mountceo@yahooo.uk; Buea Market; ⏱ 8am-5pm Mon-Fri, 7am-noon weekends). The organisation works closely with the 12 villages around the mountain, employing many villagers as guides and porters. All trekkers pay a flat 'stakeholder fee' of CFA3000, which goes into a village development fund and is used for community projects such as improving electricity and water supply. The organisation's office also has a small shop selling locally produced handicrafts.

Guides, well trained in the local flora and fauna, cost CFA6000 per day (maximum five trekkers per guide), and porters CFA5000 per day. Equipment can also be hired on a daily basis, including tents (CFA5000), sleeping bags (CFA2000), sleeping mats (CFA300) and raincoats (CFA300). Expect to spend around CFA2000 per day on food for the trek – Buea market has a decent selection of basics.

It's usually possible to arrive in Buea in the morning and arrange everything on the spot to start trekking in the afternoon, but it's advisable to make advance bookings – particularly if you need to hire equipment. Treks can also be booked through the Fako Tourist Board in Limbe (p189) who act as agents for the Mount Cameroon Ecotourism Organisation. The organisation can also arrange day hikes, and tours of Buea and the Tole Tea Plantation.

## Mt Etinde

Small but steep Mt Etinde (also known as Petit Mt Cameroon), a 1713m sub-peak on Mt Cameroon's southern slopes, is an extinct volcano and is actually geologically older than its larger neighbour. Climbs can be arranged through the Mt Cameroon Ecotourism Organisation, either at its office in Buea (p191) or, at the Fako Tourist Board in Limbe (p189). It costs CFA6000 per guide plus a CFA3000 per person 'stakeholder' fee, and CFA1000 to CFA2000 for the local chief, whose permission you need to climb. You'll also need to bring a bottle of whisky along for the ancestral spirits.

It's possible to walk from Limbe to the mountain, in which case you should allow one long day for the entire trip. Otherwise take a shared taxi to Batoke, from where you can charter a taxi to either Ekonjo or Etumba (Etome), two villages at the mountain's base. From either of these, the ascent should take about half a day. The idea with the whisky is that half is poured out at the summit as a libation for the spirits, while

> ### RACE OF HOPE
>
> The Mt Cameroon Race, or 'Race of Hope', has been held annually around the last weekend of January since 1973, attracting an international group of competitors and many spectators. During a gruelling mountain marathon of 40km, competitors use the Guinness Route to reach the summit. Considerably faster than the leisurely trek most people opt for, winners usually finish in a staggering 4½ hours for men, and 5½ hours for women. For more information contact Fako Tourist Board in Limbe or the **Fédération Camerounaise d'Athlétisme** ( ☎ 222 4744) in Yaoundé.

CAMEROON

the other half is consumed, which can make for a fun walk down! Bring along insect repellent, sturdy shoes and waterproofs, along with whatever food and water you will need. Clarify before starting who is supplying food for the guide.

## KUMBA

The Anglophone town, Kumba, is an important transport junction and the site of one of Cameroon's largest markets. It's a major cocoa-producing area, with workers coming from across the country to harvest the crop. About 5km northwest is the gorgeous Barombi Mbo crater lake. Kumba is a huge, sprawling place, so you may need a shared taxi (CFA100) to get around.

### Barombi Mbo Lake

This beautiful spot makes a lovely side trip from Kumba. Steep, heavily wooded slopes surround the lake. There is a CFA200 entrance fee, and a small restaurant which is currently open during the dry season only. Although there are plans to build a small hotel, for now you can camp and enjoy the serene calm all to yourself. It's sometimes possible to hire canoes from the local fishermen, and paddle out to the villages on the opposite side of the lake.

To reach Barombi Mbo, take any shared taxi (CFA300) from the western side of Kumba towards 'Upstation' and ask the driver to drop you at the junction, about 3km from town. From here, it's about 2km further and a pleasant walk up a track – a new road should be finished during the life of this book. Otherwise, you can hire a taxi for the whole way.

### Sleeping & Eating

**Kanton Hotel** ( ☎ 335 4382; Buea Rd; r CFA6000-8000; P ✷ ) Centrally located, too much concrete gives this hotel a slightly brutal feel, reflected in rooms that aren't bad but aren't overly comfy either. Still, it's clean and the attached restaurant is good. Cheaper rooms have fan only.

**Golden Bull Hotel** ( ☎ 744 8324 mobile; Mundemba Rd; r CFA3000-5000, camping CFA 2000; P ) A short taxi ride from the southwest motor park is this decent budget choice. Rooms are large (and many are rented by the hour) but the showers are cold, along with the beers in the bar.

**Metropole Hotel** ( ☎ 335 4064; off Customary Court Rd; r CFA8000-11,000; P ✷ ) With huge well-kept rooms, this place is the closest that Kumba gets to a midrange hotel. There's a restaurant, but order early – it closes just in time for dinner.

### Getting There & Away
#### BUS

Tonton Express and Mondial Express have depots on Commonwealth Ave near the market, and run regular daily services to Yaoundé (CFA4500, six hours), Douala (CFA2000, two hours), Bamenda (CFA4000, around six hours), Bafoussam (CFA2000, three hours), Limbe (CFA1500, 2½ hours) and Buea (CFA1500, two hours). Tonton Express has the most departures, but get there early.

Non-agency transport to Douala, Limbe and Buea departs form the Buea Rd motor park on the southeastern edge of town.

Transport to Ekondo Titi (where you can find vehicles to Mundemba and Korup National Park) goes from Mundemba Rd motor park, and costs CFA2500 in the dry season. Fares double during the rains, and the 2½ hour journey can triple in duration.

#### TRAIN

There's a train four times daily between Douala and Kumba, though it's faster to take the bus from Douala to Mbanga, then the train from there to Kumba (CFA400, one to 1½ hours). Trains pass Mbanga every few hours from about 9am to 4pm.

## MANENGOUBA LAKES

The beautiful Manengouba Crater Lakes are set in a grassy caldera southeast of Bangem town. The lakes, known locally as Man Lake and Woman Lake, are the subject of various local superstitions. Camping and swimming is permitted at Woman Lake, but not at Man Lake. A visit costs CFA1000, which you're supposed to pay at the police station in Bangem (get a receipt), though it's often easier to just pay the guy near the lakes who will approach you to collect it.

The lakes are about three hours uphill on foot from Bangem; locals will point the way. Once you reach the rim, you'll need to hike through the caldera, past grazing cattle and Fulani herdsmen, to reach the lakes on the far side. The whole area is paradise for hikers.

CAMEROON

The most direct way from Kumba to Bangem is via Tombel, but the road becomes atrocious at even a hint of rain, so it's faster to go first to Melong (about halfway between Kumba and Bafoussam), from where it's just CFA1500 and 45 minutes in a shared taxi to Bangem. At Melong, Hotel La Forêt has basic rooms.

## KORUP NATIONAL PARK

Korup protects an exceptionally biologically diverse patch of rainforest, reported to be one of the oldest and richest in Africa. Within its 1259 sq km are more than 300 species of birds, 50 species of large mammals, more than 620 species of trees and over 100 medicinal plants. The vegetation is very dense and – apart from monkeys – you're unlikely to see many animals, but visiting is a superb way to experience a rainforest ecosystem. Korup is also the easiest of Cameroon's protected rainforest areas to reach, and the one with the most developed infrastructure. There are more than 100km of marked walking trails within the park, and knowledgeable guides who often work with field researchers. Two days is the ideal length for a visit.

The starting point for a visit is Mundemba village, about 8km before the park gate. There's an **Information Centre** ( ☎ 710 9175; ⏰ 7.30am-5.30pm Nov-May, 7.30am-3.30pm Mon-Fri, 7.30-8.30am & 4.30-5.30pm Sat & Sun Jun-Sep). Phoning ahead of your visit is strongly advised to discuss your requirements with the tourist officer. Park fees of CFA5000 per day are paid at the centre, where you must also hire a guide (CFA4000 per day, plus CFA1000 per night). Porters can also be arranged (CFA2000 per day plus CFA1000 per night, maximum load 25kg), as can rental of sleeping bags, foam mats and cookware. Pay all fees direct to the tourist officer, and ignore requests from anyone else for extra 'stakeholder' fees. Bring plenty of insect repellent.

### Sleeping & Eating

There are three camp sites (CFA3000 per person) in the park's southern section: Iriba Inene, about 2km from the entrance; Rengo (9km); and Chimpanzee (10km). Each has simple huts with wooden beds and mosquito screens, water for drinking and bathing, and a cooking area. You'll need to bring your own food, and a sleeping mat. You're not expected to supply food for guides and

porters, but it's best to clarify this before setting off. Basic supplies are available in Mundemba.

**Sure to Sure Guesthouse** ( ☎ 754 5009, r CFA5000-6000) At the southern end of Mundemba, this place has simple rooms with fan.

Martha's Sure serves good basic 'meat sauce and rice' dishes and the like for around CFA500.

### Getting There & Away

There's usually at least one taxi brousse daily in the dry season between Mundemba and Ekondo Titi (CFA1800, two hours), from where you arrange transport to Kumba. Rainy season transport is more ad hoc, takes longer and costs more.

From Mundemba to the park gate at Mana Footbridge, you can either walk, or go with a park vehicle (CFA8000 per vehicle return, 10 people maximum including guide and porters). An amazing suspension bridge crosses the Mana River here – almost worth the park entrance fee alone.

If you have the money, a great way to depart or arrive in Korup is by boat (carrying six people) along the Mana River. Staff can arrange pick-ups or drop-offs from as far south as Idenao, through the disputed Bakassi Peninsula area (CFA250,000 one way). The boat can also be rented for shorter excursions along the river to explore the mangrove swamps (CFA90,000 for three hours) or visit nearby Pelican Island (CFA150,000). All boat trips need to be arranged in advance through the Korup Information Centre.

There's another entrance to Korup at Baro, west of Nguti, which can be reached by taxi brousse from Mamfe during the dry season.

## MAMFE

On the bank of the Cross River, Mamfe is the last major town before the Nigerian border at Ekok, 60km further west. Together with nearby Kembong village, it's also a regional centre for witchcraft and traditional medicine.

There's no bank at the border, so you'll need to ask at shops in Mamfe or at the market if you're looking for Nigerian naira. Bicec bank in Mamfe is occasionally willing to change cash euros (no travellers cheques), but shouldn't be relied upon.

If you're heading to Nigeria, it's worth stopping by the Office for Immigration and

CAMEROON

Emigration to make friends with the officer and ask for some names at Ekok. It's in the town centre between the main roundabout and Bayang Garage; locals can point you in the right direction.

### Sleeping & Eating

**Data Club Guest House** ( ☎ 334 1399; r from CFA10,000; ☒ ) Easily the best lodging in Mamfe, on the northeastern edge of town, it also has a decent restaurant.

**African City Hotel** (r CFA5000) For something cheaper, but a lot more basic, try this place near the motor park.

There are several places to eat near the motor park, and there are also *suya* and fish vendors scattered around town during the evening.

### Getting There & Away

Transport connections in all directions are good, but the roads are not. Travelling during the rains can be a horrible, devilish experience. The main motor park is 500m southwest of Mamfe's central intersection.

Transport goes throughout the day to the border at Ekok, 60km away. The main lines are Ali Baba and Tonton Express, and the price is CFA1500 in the dry season, though this can reach CFA4000 during the rains, when you'll frequently have to get out and push. A better alternative is to take a pirogue down Cross River, direct to Ekok.

The mountainous road from Mamfe to Bamenda (around CFA9000) is beautiful, but has perilous drop-offs and is only an option in the dry season. It's better to take the longer southern route via Kumba (CFA5000, six hours) and travel on from there.

There's usually at least one vehicle daily between Mamfe and Nguti (for Korup National Park), although there's almost no traffic from Nguti into the park

# NORTH-WEST PROVINCE

The Anglophone North-West Province is one of the country's most rewarding areas for travellers. Its green hills provide a cool contrast to the sticky coast, and are covered with a patchwork of local chiefdoms and traditional practices, including witchcraft.

A tour of the Ring Road through the beautiful Grassfields area should a highlight of any trip to Cameroon, but bring an extra layer of clothing – evenings at altitude can verge on the chilly, especially between October and February.

## BAMENDA

**pop 235,000**

The capital of North-West Province is a slightly unkempt sprawling place, tumbling down a hill at over 1000m altitude. While not holding any particular drawcards for travellers in itself, it has decent amenities and is a good jumping-off point for exploring the countryside nearby, most notably the Ring Road circuit. Bamenda is the centre of political opposition to President Biya.

### Orientation

Most transport arriving in Bamenda will drop you at Upstation, overlooking Bamenda town proper. From here the road winds steeply down to Nkwen District, which has a good market, follows Cow St and Sonac St and eventually reaches City Chemist's Roundabout and the main drag – the aptly named Commercial Ave. Another important spot for getting your bearings is Hospital Roundabout, which leads on to Ntarikon Motor Park and the road to Bafut.

### Information

**Express Exchange** (City Chemist's Roundabout) Changes travellers cheques as well as US dollars cash and euros.
**Maryland Cybercafé** (Commercial Ave; per hr CFA300) Also has Internet phone for CFA250 per minute.
**Polyclinic** (Bali Rd)
**SCBC Bank** (Commercial Ave) Has an ATM.
**Tourist office** ( ☎ 336 1395) Can provide basic maps and dates of local festivals.
**World Trade Center** (Commercial Ave; per hr CFA3000) Internet access.

### Sleeping

**Presbyterian Church Centre** ( ☎ 336 4070; off Longla St; dm CFA4000, r CFA6000; ℗ ) Hidden away from the bustle of the centre, this is a good budget option. Private rooms are self-contained, but even the four-bed dorms have sinks. The generous grounds are a good place to relax.

**Baptist Mission Resthouse** ( ☎ 336 1285; Finance Junction; dm CFA2500; ℗ ) A bit far from

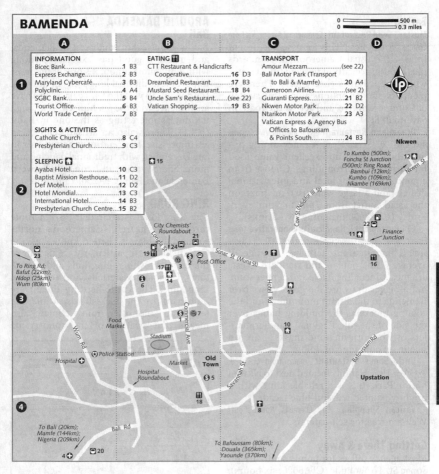

# BAMENDA

0 — 500 m
0 — 0.3 miles

### INFORMATION
Bicec Bank..........................1 B3
Express Exchange................2 B3
Maryland Cybercafé............3 B3
Polyclinic...........................4 A4
SGBC Bank........................5 B4
Tourist Office.....................6 B3
World Trade Center............7 B3

### SIGHTS & ACTIVITIES
Catholic Church.................8 C4
Presbyterian Church..........9 C3

### SLEEPING
Ayaba Hotel.....................10 C3
Baptist Mission Resthouse....11 D2
Def Motel........................12 D2
Hotel Mondial..................13 C3
International Hotel............14 B3
Presbyterian Church Centre...15 B2

### EATING
CTT Restaurant & Handicrafts
  Cooperative.................16 D3
Dreamland Restaurant.......17 B3
Mustard Seed Restaurant...18 B4
Uncle Sam's Restaurant....(see 22)
Vatican Shopping.............19 B3

### TRANSPORT
Amour Mezzam.................(see 22)
Bali Motor Park (Transport
  to Bali & Mamfe)...........20 A4
Cameroon Airlines.............(see 2)
Guaranti Express..............21 B2
Nkwen Motor Park............22 D2
Ntarikon Motor Park..........23 A3
Vatican Express & Agency Bus
  Offices to Bafoussam
  & Points South..............24 B3

CAMEROON

---

Bamenda's centre but, aside from that, this is a great cheap place to lay your head. Rooms are immaculate, with spotless shared bathroom facilities proving that cleanliness is indeed next to godliness.

**Def Motel** ( ☎ 366 3748; off Nkwen St; r CFA6000-10,000) Right in the middle of the lively Nkwen district, this place is decent value. Prices increase as you go up each floor – those climbing all the stairs get rewarded with a TV and hot water heater.

**International Hotel** ( ☎ 336 2527; off Commercial Ave; r CFA15,000-18,000) This multistorey option fits solidly into the Cameroonian business-man's class. Usually busy, rooms are big and come with balconies, while the restaurant serves a great breakfast. The higher tariff gets you a TV and 'guaranteed' hot water.

**Hotel Mondial** ( ☎ 336 1832; off Hotel Rd; s/d CFA12,500/14,000; P ) The Hotel Mondial feels a little more modern than its equivalents elsewhere in Bamenda – positively plush even. Comfortable rooms come with water heater and satellite TV – and there are a few decent cheaper options without (CFA7500), for those with slimmer budgets.

**Ayaba Hotel** ( ☎ 336 1356; ayabahotel@refinedct .net; Upstation; r from CFA18,000; P ⊠ ⊡ ) Near the Hotel Mondial, and looking over Bamenda town, the Ayaba is trying hard to recapture its glory days as the Bamenda's top hotel. Rooms are fine, if not spectacular for the price, but the restaurant has a decent menu.

## Eating

**Mustard Seed Restaurant** (Commercial Ave; mains from CFA800; ✓ 8am-10pm) This joint serves decent local – the usual Cameroonian standards plus a local speciality, *amajama* (meat sauce with chopped huckleberry leaf). There are plenty of similar options along this stretch of Commercial Ave, and across the road on Savannah St.

**Dreamland Restaurant** (Commercial Ave; mains from CFA1300; ✓ 7am-11pm) A fancy dining option this, dishing up excellent value food for such swish surroundings. Choose from a good selection of local and international dishes (and a large wine list), or graze on the salad buffet from 7pm to 9pm every Friday (CFA2000 including two drinks).

**CTT Restaurant & Handicrafts Cooperative** (near Finance Junction, upstairs; mains from CFA1000; ✓ 8am-9pm) The restaurant here has a range of average Cameroonian and standard Western meals, including *ndole* and pepper soup, but a bigger draw are the great views over Bamenda to the distant mountains, and the cooling breeze as the building hangs over the side of the hill. Regional handicrafts – lots of wood carving and masks – are on sale in an adjoining building.

**Uncle Sam's Restaurant** (mains from CFA1000; ✓ 10am-11pm) Handily located next to Nkwen Motor Park, this is a reliable joint with a brightly painted red-and-blue façade.

**Vatican Shopping** (City Chemists' Roundabout) Well-stocked for self-caterers.

## Getting There & Away

Most agency offices for points south are on Sonac St. To Yaoundé (CFA5000, six hours), Vatican Express and Guaranti Express are the best. The same agencies operate daily services to Douala (CFA5000, seven hours). Sonac St is also the departure point for Bafoussam (CFA1200, 90 minutes), from where you'll find more transport heading south.

Nkwen Motor Park has transport to the east stretch of the Ring Road including Ndop (CFA1000, 90 minutes) and Kumbo (CFA3000, five hours). Amour Mezzam Express has the most departures. The west stretch of the Ring Road is served by Ntarikon Motor Park, with minibuses to Wum (CFA2000, two hours). Transport also leaves for Bafut from here (CFA300, 20 minutes). Shared taxis to the farther motor parks shouldn't cost more than CFA150.

## AROUND BAMENDA

### Bali

Bali is about 20km southwest of Bamenda, and makes a good day excursion. Along with Bafut and Kumbo, it's one of the most important traditional kingdoms in the area. It's possible to visit the *fon's* palace, and have an audience with the *fon* himself – although it's not as interesting as the one in Bafut (p201). There's also an artisan centre, and an impressive *lela* (end-of-year festival) in late December, with traditional dancing and more. Shared taxis run frequently between Bamenda and Bali (CFA250, 15 minutes).

### RING ROAD

The Ring Road is a circular 367km route through the heart of Cameroon's north-western highlands, better known as the Grassfields. It's a particularly scenic part of the country, with rolling hills and mountains, lakes and waterfalls, and traditional kingdoms. The cattle-herding Fulani are dominant in the Grassfields, while the temperate and often rainy climate also means that swathes of the countryside

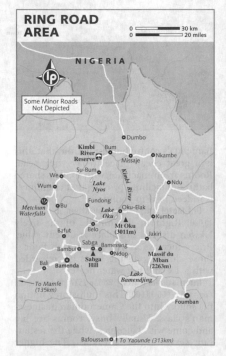

are given over to tea plantations. Some of Cameroon's most fascinating artwork also originates from the area, and it's possible to buy direct from artist's cooperatives.

There's very little in the way of organised tourism here, but the potential for hiking is huge. You could easily spend a couple of weeks trekking or cycling. Camping is generally safe, but always ask the permission of the local chief. For those heading east (anti-clockwise) by vehicle, the road is descent from Bamenda via Kumbo to Nkambe. Downed bridges mean that it's not currently possible to continue from here on to Wum by vehicle, although the rough tracks shouldn't stop hikers. From Wum, a rough dirt road leads south to Bafut, from where it's a short skip back to Bamenda. Transport links along the Ring Road are reasonable, but not always particularly frequent, usually leaving in the early morning.

Kumbo is the Ring Road's largest town, and apart from here (and to a lesser extent Nkambe), there's little infrastructure in the area, and nowhere to change money, so stock up on CFA before leaving Bamenda.

## Sagba, Bamessing & Ndop

From Bamenda, the eastern section of the Ring Road climbs quickly into some gorgeous mountain scenery. Stretching from the villages of Sabga to Ndop, this is one of the most beautiful stretches in the whole region, lush and green, particularly at the end of the rains. This section of the Ring Road makes an ideal day trip from Bamenda if you're short on time.

At Sabga, it's worth breaking your trip to climb Sabga Hill on the eastern side of the village. Ask to be dropped off about 500m after the village by the 10% gradient sign. It takes about 20 minutes to climb the hill (120m), where upon you'll be rewarded with glittering views over the mountains to the Mbam Massif, taking in pretty villages, red earth roads and a handful of waterfalls. There's a path of sorts, but it can be slippery under foot in places.

From Sabga, the route continues to Bamessing, which stretches along the road without ever quite settling into a single village. Bamessing is a good place to buy handicrafts, and there are several cooperatives along the road that sell carved wood. The **Prespot Centre** ( ☺ 9am-5pm Mon-Sat) has

fascinating tours of their pottery centre, where you can watch the whole process, from digging the clay from the local riverbed, to firing the finished articles. There's a small shop, but zero hard sell. The centre is badly signed 1km off the main road, so ask for directions.

The tar road from Bamenda finishes at Ndop, after which it's dirt roads all the way to Nkambe. Ndop is a thriving market town, large enough to have a petrol station and post office, and has the only sleeping options on this stretch of the Ring Road. Try the **Ndop Guest Home Hotel** (r CFA7000) which has self-contained rooms with their own water heater. Further from the main road is **Green Valley Resort** ( ☎ 336 3400; r CFA5000), with decent rooms and secure parking, but a meagre restaurant. There are several chop houses around the market area. Amour Mezzam, on the north side of Ndop, has daily minibuses to Bamenda (CFA1000, 90 minutes).

A two-hour drive north of Ndop is the dreary hamlet of Jakiri, which serves as a junction for the rough but stunning road southwest to Foumban. The **Trans-Afrique Hotel** (r CFA4000) will do in a pinch of you get stuck here waiting for transport.

## Kumbo

Sitting at a cool 2000m altitude, Kumbo is the largest town in the Grassfields. It's home to the Banso people, one of the major traditional kingdoms in the northwest. In mid-November, Kumbo hosts a horse racing festival, with cultural activities and markets. A huge Catholic cathedral dominates the town centre, at the junction leading west to Oku. You can also visit the *fon's* palace; there's no set fee, but CFA1000 to CFA2000 is expected for whoever shows you in. It's also worth visiting the market, especially the section devoted to traditional medicine.

Kumbo is an important junction town with a relaxed air – a good place to base yourself for exploring the Ring Road in more depth. There are plenty of bars and cheap eats, along with a post office and an Internet café opposite the cathedral. Lolika Handicrafts Training Centre, near the market, is good for souvenir shopping.

### SLEEPING & EATING
**Merryland Hotel** ( ☎ 348 1077; s/d CFA4000/5000; ℗ )
A good budget option just off the road from

---

### CLIMBING MT OKU

Mt Oku (3011m), in the centre of the Ring Road area, is Cameroon's second-highest mountain. Although not nearly as popular as Mt Cameroon, it makes a rugged but satisfying climb. On its western slope is a crater lake, which is considered sacred, and the mountain is a centre for witchcraft. More mundanely, the Oku area is known for its honey.

The starting point for the climb is the village of Oku-Elak, reached by taxi brousse from Kumbo (CFA1000). Once there, you'll need to first go to the *fon's* palace to get permission. There's no charge, but it's not a bad idea to bring a bottle of whisky or some other gift. The people at the palace will also help you to arrange a guide; expect to pay between CFA2000 and CFA5000. If you get stuck for the night, there's basic accommodation in Oku-Elak.

The climb itself takes about six hours return, and includes some steep, rough sections. You'll need a good windproof jacket, as well as sufficient water. It's possible to descend via the mountain's western side, finishing near Belo, from where there's sporadic transport south to Bambui, and then to Bamenda. There is basic accommodation in Belo.

---

Bamenda. Most, but not all, rooms have a water heater – pick one of these to take the edge off damp Kumbo days, but beware the ridiculously squashy mattresses.

**Fomo 92** ( ☎ 348 1616; s/d CFA7500/8500) Just north of the cathedral, there are lots of stairs and corridors in this hotel, which seems to tumble down the hill, but all paths lead to comfy carpeted rooms. It's nicely presented and has a decent restaurant to boot.

**Ring Road Travellers Inn** ( ☎ 348 1480; r with shared/private bathroom CFA3000/5000) Right on the town square, this place could hardly be better located. Rooms are basic though, and the management was extremely reluctant to show us the rooms with shared bathrooms. Draw your own conclusions.

**BB91** (mains from CFA1200; ☻ 10am-11pm) Next to the cathedral, this restaurant-bar has a good ambience. The meat with sauce and perfumed rice is a reliable and tasty standard.

### GETTING THERE & AWAY

Amour Mezzam Express, south of the market, runs daily to Bamenda (CFA3000, five hours), stopping at all points along the way and occasionally to Yaoundé (CFA8000, 24 hours via Foumban). Minibuses also run north to Nkambe (CFA2000, two hours) from just north of the square and to Oku (CFA1200, one hour), the latter leaves from Oku Rd, past the petrol station.

## Nkambe & Missaje

Nkambe is the only town of any size between Kumbo and Wum. Like Kumbo, it is at altitude and has a cool climate. The road from Kumbo passes through open grass-land and large tea plantations, centred on the village of Ndu. Heading north along to Nkambe, the earth road steadily deteriorates in quality. Nkambe has a reasonable selection of amenities for travellers.

**Millennium Hotel** (s/d CFA5000/10,000) is at the end of a very long (1.5km) road at the southern end of town. Doubles are big and decent, but make the singles look disappointing in comparison. A taxi here from town will set you back a steep CFA1000. There's a restaurant and 'occasional' nightclub.

Otherwise try the **Holy War Complex** (r with shared/private bathroom CFA1500/3000), a rock-bottom option with an irresistible name – the Holy War chain seem to own half the shops on this stretch of the Ring Road. Rooms aren't great, but at least they're cheap. Minibuses run from Nkambe to Bamenda most days (CFA5000, 10 hours).

At Missaje, about 20km west of Nkambe, the driveable road ends, and you'll need to continue on foot or mountain bike if you want to complete the circuit (it's all downhill from Nkambe to Wum). Allow a full day on foot between Missaje and We (13km northeast of Wum) – that's assuming you don't get lost, but it's better to bring provisions to last two days. For much of this stretch the road is nothing more than a rough track, and you might need to hire a Fulani herdsman to accompany you and point out the way, although many speak only Fulfulde. If you get stuck in Missaje, the only place to stay is in one of the very unappealing rooms behind the local bar.

## Wum

This is the only town of any size along the western side of the Ring Road, and the end of public transport if you're travelling in a clockwise direction. About 20km south of Wum are the lovely Metchum Falls. The waterfalls are not visible from the road, so you'll need to ask someone to point out the spot. Don't lean on the makeshift rail, as several visitors plunged to their deaths here some years ago

There are several undistinguished guesthouses in Wum, the best of which is probably **Morning Star Hotel** (r about CFA4000), with a restaurant. It's at the southern end of town along the main road.

Symbol of Unity has daily buses between Wum and Bamenda (CFA2000, two hours). It's possible to go in a loop from Wum to We (13km north) and from there turn south back to Bamenda via Fundong and Belo. In Fundong, there's inexpensive accommodation at Tourist Home Hotel. Guaranti Express usually has a minibus daily between Fundong and Bamenda.

North of We, the road takes another downturn in quality. Continuing northeast, you'll reach Lake Nyos, just off the Ring Road, south of the eponymous village. This volcanic crater lake gained notoriety in 1986 when it was the site of a natural gas eruption, which resulted in around 1700 deaths. Some local conspiracy theories still blame the disaster on Western misadventure. The seldom-visited Kimbi River Reserve is just north of Nyos, though you'll need your own vehicle to explore, and a tent if you plan to overnight. Public transport is infrequent on this stretch of the Ring Road.

## Bafut

About 20km north of Bamenda is the large Tikar community of Bafut, traditionally the most powerful of the Grassfields kingdoms. The *fon's* palace here is home to a 700-year-old dynasty and is a fascinating insight into traditional culture. In late December, Bafut holds a huge four-day celebration to mark the end of the year's ancestor worship with masked dancing and drumming. Bafut also holds a large market every eight days (every 'country Sunday').

The **palace compound** (admission CFA1000, camera fee CFA1500, museum CFA2000) has numerous buildings, including the houses of the *fon's* 150-

or-so wives (not all of whom are presently in residence), and the sacred Achum building, which is off-limits to everyone except the *fon* and his close advisors. The Achum is also a focus for several secret societies, which still play an important role in Tikar society. Its roof is rethatched every April in a large grasscutting festival. In front of the palace compound are several stones marking the burial sites of nobles who died while serving the *fon*, and the Takombang House which holds the *fon's* ceremonial drum.

The imposing colonial building above the palace is now a museum. It holds many interesting (and slightly scary) carvings, traditional costumes and weapons. Leopards, pythons, elephants and buffaloes are well-represented, as these are symbols of the *fon* – according to traditional belief, the *fon* can turn himself into these animals, acquiring their particular protective characteristics. Look out for the wooden statues of the first Europeans (German explorers) to visit the Tikar kingdom.

There's no accommodation at Bafut, but there are a couple of very basic eateries by the town square. About 5km from the palace along the Bamenda road is **Savanna Botanic Gardens** (Saboga; ☎ 336 3870; r CFA7000), which has adequate self-contained rooms and a restaurant.

A shared taxi to Bamenda is CFA300 (20 minutes). A daily minibus north to Wum passes through Bafut, but transport is easier to arrange in Bamenda.

# WEST PROVINCE

The Bamiléké people dominate Cameroon's Francophone West Province. Local traditions play an important role in day-to-day life: chiefs rule from distinctive *chefferies* (chiefs' compounds) with their triangular pointed gateways, and ancestor veneration sits alongside evangelical Christianity. Bafoussam is the commercial centre of the agriculturally rich highlands. In the east, the mainly Muslim town of Foumban is a centre for local handicrafts.

## BAFOUSSAM

A thriving business centre, Bafoussam is a Bamiléké stronghold in the middle of a coffee- and cocoa-producing area. The

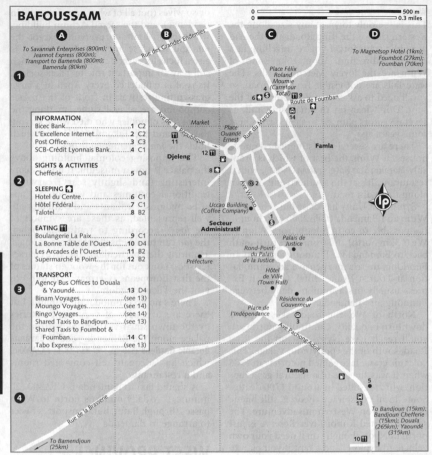

**BAFOUSSAM**

To Savannah Enterprises (800m);
Jeannot Express (800m);
Transport to Bamenda (800m);
Bamenda (80km)

To Magnetsop Hotel (1km);
Foumbot (27km);
Fouman (70km)

**INFORMATION**
Bicec Bank.................................1 C2
L'Excellence Internet..................2 C2
Post Office.................................3 C3
SCB-Crédit Lyonnais Bank.........4 C1

**SIGHTS & ACTIVITIES**
Chefferie...................................5 D4

**SLEEPING**
Hotel du Centre.........................6 C1
Hôtel Fédéral............................7 C1
Talotel......................................8 B2

**EATING**
Boulangerie La Paix...................9 C1
La Bonne Table de l'Ouest.......10 D4
Les Arcades de l'Ouest.............11 B2
Supermarché le Point...............12 B2

**TRANSPORT**
Agency Bus Offices to Douala
   & Yaoundé............................13 D4
Binam Voyages.....................(see 13)
Moungo Voyages...................(see 14)
Ringo Voyages......................(see 14)
Shared Taxis to Bandjoun.....(see 13)
Shared Taxis to Foumbot &
   Foumban.............................14 C1
Tabo Express........................(see 13)

To Bamendjoun
(25km)

To Bandjoun (15km);
Bandjoun Chefferie
(15km); Douala
(265km); Yaoundé
(315km)

town has outgrown its farming routes too quickly, and there is little of great interest for travellers as a result. There is, however, a large **chefferie** (admission CFA2000; www.museum cam.org; ☺ 10am-5pm), about 15km south at Bandjoun. The *chefferie's* main building is an excellent example of traditional Bamiléké architecture, with its square base, tall conical roof, and carved pillars resembling totem poles. It's primarily used for meetings, but there's an interesting museum attached. The *chefferie* is in Dja near the Yaoundé intersection, about 15 minutes walk from the main road.

There's also a less-interesting *chefferie* in Bafoussam, just off the main road at the southern end of town.

## Information

For changing cash try **Bicec** (Ave Wanko) at the southern end of the street, or **SBC-Crédit Lyonnais** (near Carrefour Total) along the Foumban road – a good landmark; as always, travellers cheques are a hassle.

For web access, call into **L'Excellence Internet** (per hr CFA400).

## Sleeping

**Hôtel Fédéral** ( ☎ 344 1309; Route de Foumban; r CFA6000-9000) Good value, and with a decent bar to boot, rooms here are neat and tidy. Take one at the back, choosing the balconied options over those with no external window.

   **Hotel du Centre** ( ☎ 344 2079; Carrefour Total; s/d CFA12,000/15,000) As well-located as the name suggests, and a useful landmark, the rooms here are bright and airy. They have balconies too, but choose one away from the noisy road. Some tidy negotiations can bring this hotel comfortably into the budget category.

**Magnetsop Hotel** ( ☎ 344 3061; Route de Foumban; r CFA10,000-15,000; **P** ✖ ) The paint was still wet when we visited this new place on the edge of town. Rooms are comfy and clean, the management helpful and the local street food is great.

**Talotel** ( ☎ 344 4185; hoteltalotel@camnet.cm; Place Ouandé Ernest; s/d CFA25,000/30,000; **P** ✖ ☐ ) Slightly grand, this is Bafoussam's top-of-the-range hotel. It's popular with business travellers looking for comfort at the end of the road – and when they arrive they even get to soak in a tub for their woes.

### Eating
Rue de Marché and Route de Foumban are good for street food and cheap eats.

**La Bonne Table de l'Ouest** (off Route de Douala; mains from CFA1500; ☺ 10am-11pm) At the southern end of town along the main highway, this restaurant is excellent value, with a pleasant atmosphere and local and Western cuisine.

**Boulangerie La Paix** (pastries from CFA150; ☺ 8am-10pm) This patisserie sells good bread and sticky sweet treats in the mornings, and acts as a handy general food shop during the rest of the day. **Supermarché le Point** (Ave de la Républiqe), at the opposite end of Rue de Marché, fulfils the same function.

**Les Arcades de l'Ouest** (off Ave de la République; ☺ 9am-late) Opposite the market, this is good for cheap Cameroonian food. Wash it down with copious amounts of beer deep into the night. There's occasional live music on weekends.

### Getting There & Away
Binam Voyages, Tabo Express and other agency buses to Yaoundé (CFA2500, three hours) and Douala (CFA4000, five hours) have their offices at the southern end of town along the main road. Shared taxis to Bandjoun (CFA300, 15 minutes) also leave from here throughout the day.

Transport to Bamenda leaves from the Bamenda Rd, 2km north of the centre (CFA150 in a shared taxi). Agencies include Savannah Enterprises and Jeannot Express and take 90 minutes (CFA1200).

Minibuses to Foumban (CFA800, one hour) depart from near the petrol station, downhill from Carrefour Total, along with shared taxis. Agency vehicles doing this route include Moungo Voyages and Ringo Voyages. Many nonagency vehicles only go as far as Foumbot (CFA500, 30 minutes), where you'll need to change to reach Foumban (CFA500, 45 minutes).

## FOUMBAN
Predominantly Muslim, Foumban is a great contrast to the rest of southwestern Cameroon. If you're heading north, this is the first place you'll hear the call to prayer. Home to the Bamoun people, it's also a great centre for Cameroonian handicrafts. Tabaski (see p818) is a great time to be in Foumban, when horse races and parades mark the end of Ramadan.

The Grand Marché is a warren of narrow stalls and alleys, which is great fun to explore and leads out to a square where the Grande Mosquée faces the palace. Wednesday and Saturday are the biggest market days. CPAC bank on the southern side of the market may change euros in cash if you're lucky, but it's best to do your changing in Bafoussam.

### Sights & Activities
#### PALAIS ROYAL (ROYAL PALACE)
Unlike the Bamiléké, who are grouped by allegiance to the chief in whose chiefdom they cultivate land, the Bamoun show allegiance to a sultan, who is part of a dynasty dating to 1394. The **palace** (admission incl museum CFA2000, camera fee CFA1500; ☺ 8.30am-6pm) was built in the early 20th century by the 16th sultan, Ibrahim Njoya, and modelled on the German governor's palace in Buea. Njoya developed his own alphabet, Shumon, which is still taught today, one of only a handful of indigenous West African alphabets. Njoya also authored *Histoires et Coutumes Bamoun*, which continues to be one of the main repositories of knowledge about Bamoun traditions, and started his own religion in an effort to combine Christian, Islamic and animist beliefs.

The palace has a fascinating and well-organised museum containing previous sultans' possessions, including royal gowns, musical instruments, war garments and jewellery. A trophy calabash decorated

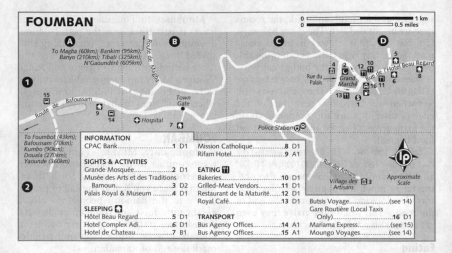

FOUMBAN

**INFORMATION**
CPAC Bank..............................1 D1

**SIGHTS & ACTIVITIES**
Grande Mosquée......................2 D1
Musée des Arts et des Traditions
Bamoun................................3 D2
Palais Royal & Museum ..........4 D1

**SLEEPING**
Hôtel Beau Regard..................5 D1
Hotel Complex Adi..................6 D1
Hotel de Chateau....................7 B1

Mission Catholique..................8 D1
Rifam Hotel............................9 A1

**EATING**
Bakeries.................................10 D1
Grilled-Meat Vendors..............11 D1
Restaurant de la Maturité........12 D1
Royal Café.............................13 D1

**TRANSPORT**
Bus Agency Offices.................14 A1
Bus Agency Offices.................15 A1

Butsis Voyage.....................(see 14)
Gare Routière (Local Taxis
Only).............................16 D1
Mariama Express.................(see 15)
Moungo Voyages................(see 14)

with human jawbones is the most macabre exhibit. Sadly, everything is labelled in French, and English-speaking guides are in short supply.

A statue of Njoya stands proudly halfway between the palace and the Grande Mosquée.

### VILLAGE DES ARTISANS

A long street packed with workshops, about 1.5km south of the market, this place seems to produce more handicrafts than the rest of Cameroon combined. As such, it's an ideal place to pick up just about anything, from woodcarvings and leatherwork to life-size bronze statues of royal lions. The village is one of the few places in the country where you can expect some tourist hustle – don't be afraid to haggle.

At the end of the road, the small **Musée des Arts et des Traditions Bamoun** (admission CFA1000; 9am-5pm) houses the private collection of Mosé Yeyap, a wealthy Bamoun during Ibrahim Njoya's time, who collected art and historical artefacts. Tours are in French and are included in the admission.

## Sleeping

**Hôtel Beau Regarde** ( ☎ 348 2183; Rue de l'Hotel Beau Regarde; r with shared bathroom CFA3000-4000, with private bathroom CFA6000) Thirty years ago this would have been a cracking hotel, with its grand wood panelling and once-tidy rooms. With a bit of care it could be again, but meanwhile it's a decent cheap option with

a lively bar. Rooms at the back overlook the town to good effect.

**Hotel Complexe Adi** ( ☎ 743 1181 mobile; Rue de l'Hotel Beau Regarde; r CFA7000-9000) One of the nicer budget options in Foumban, rooms here are simple but good value. Eat in the restaurant, or enjoy the grilled meat from vendors just a stone's throw away.

**Mission Catholique** (Rue de l'Hotel Beau Regarde; dm CFA2500) Head here if you're out of options – it's pretty spartan and you'll have to ask to be brought water. If you ask even more nicely, they might let you pitch a tent.

**Hotel de Chateau** ( ☎ 348 3155; off Route de Bafoussam; s/d CFA8000/12,000) A lack of hot water makes this place feel a bit over-priced, but the rooms are fair and for your money you also get to take in some lovely sunsets from the veranda.

**Rifam Hotel** ( ☎ 348 2878; Route de Bafoussam; s/d CFA15,000/25,000; ) Near the bus agency offices, this hotel is easily Foumban's plushest. The doubles are huge and come with balconies large enough to play football on. Very comfortable, with satellite TV and deep baths.

## Eating

The area just east of the *gare routière* is good for grilled meat; go to the nearby bakeries to make up a quick sandwich. The streets along the Grand Marché are also good for quick eats on the hoof.

**Royal Café** (meals from CFA2000; 8am-10pm) On the southern side of the Grand Marché, this has good meals and a patio with views. It's down a flight of steps and is easy to miss; look for the white building and red signboard.

**Restaurant de la Maturité** (meals from CFA2000; 🕐 8am-10pm) Opposite the *gare routière* at the eastern end of the market, is this other decent option, with good salads and omelettes.

### Getting There & Away

All agencies running transport to Bafoussam (CFA800, one hour) have their offices on Route de Bafoussam at the entrance to town, west of the town gate and about 3km from the market (CFA100 in a shared taxi). Moungo Voyages and Butsis Voyage have a few daily direct departures to Yaoundé (CFA3000, five hours) and Douala (CFA4500, six hours); otherwise you'll need to change vehicles in Bafoussam. Non-agency minibuses departs from the *gare routière* near the market.

Transport between Foumban and Kumbo (CFA3000, around six hours) runs all year, although travel times vary according to the rains. Although the road is very poor, it's easily one of the most beautiful in the country, skirting along the edge of the spectacular Mbam Massif. Ask for Mariama Express.

It's also possible during the dry season to find vehicles going northeast to Banyo, from where you can continue to N'Gaoundéré via Tibati; you should allow several days for this journey (see p207 for more).

# NORTH & EXTREME NORTH PROVINCES

Travelling to Cameroon's northern provinces can feel like visiting a different country. Separated from the south by the Adamawa Plateau, the north is a land where rolling grassland gives way to barren rocky outcrops of striking beauty, dotted with picturesque villages. The sense of difference is heightened by access issues – roads to the south are barely existent, so getting there means taking an overnight train or hopping on an internal flight. The north is also where you'll find most of Cameroon's Muslim population, herding cattle or cultivating millet and other crops. For tourists,

the north is one of Cameroon's most popular destinations and it's highly rewarding if you're able to get off the beaten track.

## N'GAOUNDÉRÉ

Leafy N'Gaoundéré is the terminus of Cameroon's main railway line and the first major town in northern Cameroon. It makes a relaxing stop, particularly if you've taken the overnight train, and at an altitude of 1100m the evenings are pleasantly cool.

Some parts of N'Gaoundéré have bad reputations for safety at night, including the area around the stadium, and north of the cathedral. If in doubt, take a *moto-taxi*.

### Information

The **Ministry of Tourism Office** ( ☎ 225 1138; Ave Ahidjo) is worth visiting for information on the surrounding area.

Bicec and Crédit Lyonnais, in the town centre, change cash and possibly travellers cheques.

The most reliable Internet in town is found at **Complexe Lin Business Center** (Rue De la Grande Mosquée; per hr CFA300), although you might need to queue.

### Sights

#### PALAIS DU LAMIDO

This **palace** ( 🕐 9am-5pm; admission CFA2000, guide CFA1000, photo fee CFA1000) is where the local chief (also known as the *lamido*) resides with his numerous wives. Although the exterior isn't hugely appealing, the traditional buildings inside are more rewarding. Next door is the Grande Mosquée. Among other things at the Palais, you can see where the *lamido* holds court and conducts marriages, and where the royal barber plies his trade (the present *lamido* apparently follows a rigorous twice-weekly barbering routine). Friday (especially) and Sunday are the best days to visit, as you'll be able to see many nobles from the surrounding area who come to pay their respects, and the procession from the palace to the mosque for midday prayers.

### Sleeping

N'Gaoundéré's cool climate renders air-con unnecessary in hotels.

**Hôtel Transcam** ( ☎ 225 1252; r CFA25,000-35,000) N'Gaoundéré's best hotel, with fine, well-kept rooms and a posh restaurant. More

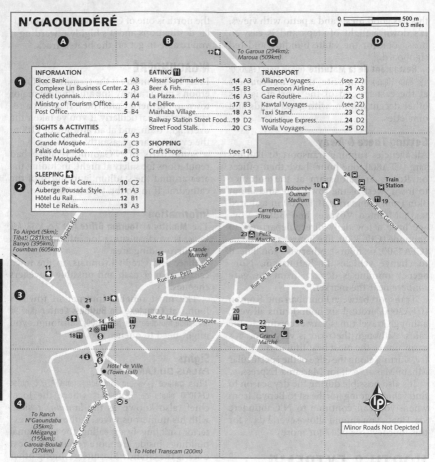

### N'GAOUNDÉRÉ

**INFORMATION**
Bicec Bank.............................1 A3
Complexe Lin Business Center.2 A3
Crédit Lyonnais......................3 A4
Ministry of Tourism Office.......4 A4
Post Office..............................5 B4

**SIGHTS & ACTIVITIES**
Catholic Cathedral.................6 A3
Grande Mosquée....................7 C3
Palais du Lamido...................8 C3
Petite Mosquée......................9 C3

**SLEEPING**
Auberge de la Gare..............10 C2
Auberge Pousada Style.........11 A3
Hôtel du Rail........................12 B1
Hôtel Le Relais.....................13 A3

**EATING**
Alissar Supermarket..............14 A3
Beer & Fish..........................15 B3
La Plazza.............................16 A3
Le Délice.............................17 B3
Marhaba Village...................18 A3
Railway Station Street Food...19 D2
Street Food Stalls.................20 C3

**SHOPPING**
Craft Shops.......................(see 14)

**TRANSPORT**
Alliance Voyages...............(see 22)
Cameroon Airlines................21 A3
Gare Routière.......................22 C3
Kawtal Voyages................(see 22)
Taxi Stand...........................23 C2
Touristique Express..............24 D2
Woïla Voyages.....................25 D2

---

expensive rooms have nicer décor but not much else in terms of facilities. It's in a quiet setting, 1.5km southwest of the centre.

**Auberge Pousada Style** ( ☎ 225 1703; r CFA4000-5000) A basic but friendly resthouse. There was a reassuringly clean smell of bleach throughout when we visited. Take a *moto-taxi* late at night in this area.

**Auberge de la Gare** ( ☎ 225 2217; r CFA5000-7000) Rooms here are basic but reasonably clean and tidy. It's convenient for the train station and bus agencies, and has an attached restaurant.

**Hôtel Le Relais** ( ☎ 225 1138; r without/with TV CFA9000/12,000) Well located, near the intersection of Rue du Petit Marché and Rue de la Grande Mosquée, rooms here are clean,

if sometimes a little musty. All are good-sized, the more expensive ones are even larger. There's a small bar.

**Hôtel du Rail** ( ☎ 225 1013; Rue de Garoua; r from CFA13,500) This is a good place with large rooms, but, although it's handy for the train station, it's some way from the action in town. Luckily there's a restaurant, and (French-language) TV in all rooms.

**Ranch de N'Gaoundaba** ( ☎ 225 2469; Route de Meiganga; s/d CFA9000/12,000, ste from CFA20,000, camping CFA2000) Staying at this lovely old stone hunting lodge, 35km southeast of N'Gaoundéré, is almost like a mini-break in itself. Accommodation is in *boukarous* overlooking a crater lake. There is horse riding on offer and plenty of hiking and bird watching opportunities in the surrounding countryside. There's a good restaurant and the bar mixes a mean gin and tonic. If you're using public transport to get here, the ranch is about a 3km walk off the main road. The ranch is only open from November to May.

## Eating

The best street food is easily found at the row of shops, stalls and bars opposite the train station, and is worth the detour even if you don't have a train to catch. A generic row of **bars** (fish from CFA1000; ♡ 10am-late) runs behind Rue Petit Marché, interspersed with women grilling fish over coals. Order the fish, then sink a beer waiting for your meal to arrive – a recipe for a great Cameroonian evening.

**La Plazza** (Rue de la Grande Mosquée; meals from CFA3000; ♡ 9am-midnight) Something of an N'Gaoundéré institution, this place has dining inside or outdoors, live music every evening and serves cold draught beer from the thatched bar. The Lebanese and pasta dishes are excellent, but don't miss the perennially popular Sunday buffet from noon (CFA5000).

**Marhaba Village** (mains from CFA1200; ♡ 9am-11pm) An open-air restaurant, with a snack bar and a more formal eating area. Its central location makes it a good place to hang out and people-watch.

**Le Délice** (meals from CFA1500; ♡ 9am-11pm) A friendly place off the western end of Rue de la Grande Mosquée, this is one of several in the immediate area serving Western and Cameroonian dishes.

Alissar supermarket is well-stocked for essentials and imported goods. The main market is the Petit Marché; the Grand Marché only sells vegetables.

## Shopping

For reasonably priced, quality crafts, try the shops next to Alissar supermarket. For textiles, go to Carrefour Tissu.

## Getting There & Away

### AIR

**Cameroon Airlines** ( ☎ 225 1295; Route de Foumban) has flights most days, connecting N'Gaoundéré with Garoua, Maroua, Yaoundé and Douala. The airport is about 5km west of town (CFA1000 in a taxi).

### BUS

For Garoua (CFA3500, five hours) and Maroua (CFA6000, eight hours), Touristique Express and Woïla Voyages are best, with several buses daily from about 6am. Both have depots near the train station.

The adventurous, with plenty of stamina and time, can consider going southeast to Garoua-Boulaï (CFA4000, 12 hours). Kawtal Voyages operates a service most days from the *gare routière* by the Grande Mosquée. The travel time is approximate, the vehicles are battered and you should think twice before attempting this during the rains.

Only marginally less strenuous is the road southwest to Foumban. Kawtal Voyages also operate this route, as far as Banyo (CFA5000, around 10 hours). Otherwise, travel as far as Tibati with Alliance Voyages and change there. There are a couple of basic auberges at Banyo, from where it's a six hour ride to Foumban. The roads are particularly bad all along this route, switching between broken tar and rough earth. The route from N'Gaoundéré to Yaoundé via Yoko is rarely used.

### TRAIN

The train is the best budget option if you're heading to Yaoundé, or to eastern Cameroon via Bélabo. Tickets are bought on the day of departure from the town's futurist concrete train station; the train leaves every evening at 6.30pm – see p228 for further details.

## Getting Around

N'Gaoundéré is spread out, making *moto-taxis* (CFA100) the main way of getting around. They're beefy Honda bikes instead of the weedy Chinese numbers found elsewhere in Cameroon, so hold on tight. Yellow taxis can be found at the Petit Marché and *gare routière*.

## GAROUA

On the Benue River, the port-town Garoua is the commercial hub of the north. There's little to hold the interest of travellers, but, as it's a transport junction, you might find yourself passing through. Garoua has a large Chadian population, direct flights to N'Djaména (see p208) and a **Chadian Consulate** ( ☎ 227 3128) that occasionally issues visas.

CAMEROON

## Sleeping & Eating

**Auberge Hiala Village** ( ☎ 227 2407; r CFA5000-7000; P ✗ ) Near the port, this has decent self-contained rooms, and is probably the best bet in the lower price bracket. There's a good bar and restaurant.

**Relais St-Hubert** ( ☎ 227 3033; Rue d'Yves Plumey; boukarous CFA18,000-23,000, r in the 'Grand Bâtiment' CFA25,000; ✗ ✗ ) A grander option, stay either in the pleasant *boukarous* or the *Grand Bâtiment* (main hotel building). There's a restaurant, and nonguests can use the pool after buying a drink.

**Super Restaurant** (Route de Maroua; mains from CFA1000; ✆ 9am-11pm) A breezy place in a busy location. The local food is good, and is best washed down with the delicious fruit juices.

## Getting There & Away

**Cameroon Airlines** ( ☎ 227 1055; Rue Centrale) flights connect Garoua daily with Douala (CFA125,000, two hours) and Yaoundé (CFA125,000, 90 minutes) – the airline's most reliable routes. Flights stop at N'Gaoundéré and Maroua according to the pilot's whim, usually twice a week. There is also a flight to N'Djaména in Chad every Tuesday (CFA155,000, 90 minutes). The airport is 5km northwest of the centre.

Woïla Voyages and Touristique Express have several buses daily to Maroua (CFA2500, 2½ hours) and N'Gaoundéré (CFA3500, five hours), departing from their depots near the market. Touristique Express can also book tickets for the N'Gaoundéré–Yaoundé train.

*Moto-taxis* are the main way to get around town (CFA100).

## MAROUA

**pop 214,000**

Dusty Maroua, Cameroon's northern-most major town, is popular with travellers. It's a good starting point for exploring the nearby Mandara Mountains, or to catch your breath before tackling the nearby borders with Chad and Nigeria. Neem trees line the streets, and there's an easy-going feel in the air. With its good range of accommodation and facilities, you can easily spend a little longer here than you had anticipated.

## Information

### INTERNET

**Braouz** (near Relais de la Porte Mayo; per hr CFA750) The fastest, most reliable connections.

**Marouanet** (Rue Mobil; per hr CFA400) A cheaper, but slower, option.

### MONEY

Maroua's banks can be reluctant to change even cash euros.

**Bicec** (Route de Maga)

**CCA Bureau de Change** (Route de Djourgou) Worth trying if the main banks won't help you change money.

**SGBC** (Route de Djourgou) Has an ATM.

### MEDICAL SERVICES

**Meskine Hospital** (off Garoua Rd) Try this hospital, west of town, for emergencies.

### POST

**Post office** (Ave de Kakataré)

### TOUR OPERATORS

There are numerous operators who can arrange trekking in the Mandara Mountains, visits to Parc National de Waza and can hire 4WDs with drivers. Better ones include the following:

**Extrême Nord Safaris** ( ☎ 229 3356; deliteri@hotmail .com)

**Porte Mayo Voyages** ( ☎ 984 1573 mobile; Pont Rouge) Based in Relais de la Porte Mayo (opposite).

**Fagus Voyages** ( ☎ 986 1871 mobile; www.fagus voyages.com)

## Sights

Maroua's **Marché Centrale** ( ✆ daily) is worth a visit – it's at its busiest every Monday when people from the surrounding region converge on the town to sell their wares. You can pick up some good local crafts here, or go to the **Centre Artisanal** at the end of the market. The leatherwork, tanned locally, is particularly good, as are the woven baskets.

The **Musée d'Art Local de Diamaré** (Marché Centrale; admission CFA500; ✆ 9am-6pm) is mildly diverting. It's small and cluttered, but has a few good pieces describing the diverse local cultures.

## Sleeping

### BUDGET

**Relais Ferngo** ( ☎ 229 2153; off Blvd de Diarenga; r CFA6000; P ✗ ) This is a delightful budget choice. Simply furnished but quite spotless *boukarous* sit between shady trees, ideal for whiling away the hours. It's well-located for buses and is near some great *suya* stalls.

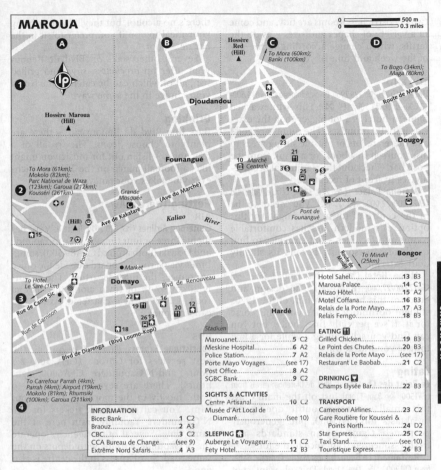

**MAROUA**

0 .............. 500 m
0 .............. 0.3 miles

To Mora (60km);
Banki (100km)

To Bogo (34km);
Maga (80km)

Route de Maga

Hossère Red (Hill)

Djoudandou

Hossère Maroua (Hill)

Dougoy

Founangué

10 Marché Centrale

To Mora (61km);
Mokolo (82km);
Parc National de Waza
(123km); Garoua (212km);
Kousséri (261km)

Grande Mosquée

(Ave du Marché)

Cathedral

Pont de Founangué

Kaliao River

Ave de Kakatare

(Hill)

Pont Rouge

To Mindif (25km)

Bongor

Market

To Hotel
Le Saré (1km)

Domayo

Blvd de Renouveau

Rue de Camp Sic

Rue de Garrison

Hardé

Stadium

Blvd de Diarenga (Blvd Loumo-Kopi)

To Carrefour Parrah (4km);
Parrah (4km); Airport (19km);
Mokolo (81km); Rhumsiki
(100km); Garoua (211km)

| INFORMATION | |
|---|---|
| Bicec Bank....................................**1** C2 | |
| Braouz..........................................**2** A3 | |
| CBC................................................**3** C2 | |
| CCA Bureau de Change........(see **9**) | |
| Extrême Nord Safaris..............**4** A3 | |

| SIGHTS & ACTIVITIES | |
|---|---|
| Marouanet....................................**5** C2 | |
| Meskine Hospital.....................**6** A2 | |
| Police Station.............................**7** A2 | |
| Porte Mayo Voyages...........(see **17**) | |
| Post Office...................................**8** A2 | |
| SGBC Bank...................................**9** C2 | |

| SIGHTS & ACTIVITIES | |
|---|---|
| Centre Artisanal......................**10** C2 | |
| Musée d'Art Local de | |
| Diamaré.................................(see **10**) | |

| SLEEPING | |
|---|---|
| Auberge Le Voyageur............**11** C2 | |
| Fety Hotel.................................**12** B3 | |

| Hotel Sahel...............................**13** B3 | |
|---|---|
| Maroua Palace.........................**14** C1 | |
| Mizao Hôtel..............................**15** A2 | |
| Motel Coffana..........................**16** B3 | |
| Relais de la Porte Mayo........**17** A3 | |
| Relais Ferngo...........................**18** B3 | |

| EATING | |
|---|---|
| Grilled Chicken.......................**19** B3 | |
| Le Point des Chutes...............**20** B3 | |
| Relais de la Porte Mayo ......(see **17**) | |
| Restaurant Le Baobab.............**21** C2 | |

| DRINKING | |
|---|---|
| Champs Elysée Bar.................**22** B3 | |

| TRANSPORT | |
|---|---|
| Cameroon Airlines...................**23** C2 | |
| Gare Routière for Kousséri & | |
| Points North...........................**24** D2 | |
| Star Express.............................**25** C2 | |
| Taxi Stand..............................(see **10**) | |
| Touristique Express...............**26** B3 | |

CAMEROON

**Auberge le Voyageur** ( ☎ 229 2100; Rue Mobil; r CFA5525-8500; ❄ ) This standard-issue hotel is handy for the town centre. Some rooms are a bit dreary, and you need to pay extra to get air-con. It's nothing special, but is still a decent option.

**Motel Coffana** ( ☎ 970 9643 mobile; off Blvd de Diarenga; r CFA6000-10,000; P ❄ ) You'll find nicely turned out *boukarous* here, freshly painted and welcoming. Cheaper rooms in the main block have fan only, but are airy enough with their high ceilings.

**MIDRANGE & TOP END**
**Relais de la Porte Mayo** ( ☎ 229 2692; Pont Rouge; s/d CFA13,900/15,000; apt CFA17,500 ❄ 💻 ) There's a lovely relaxed ambience at this French-run

establishment, with well-planted grounds and freshly uniformed staff. Rooms in *boukarous* are well presented, but sometimes a little small for the price. The restaurant-bar is good, and there's a fancy souvenir shop-cum-boutique.

**Fety Hotel** ( ☎ 229 2913; fetymatos@yahoo.fr; Blvd de Diarenga; s/d CFA10,000/12,000; P ❄ ) This hotel, opposite Stade Lamido, happily straddles the budget/midrange divide. The hotel and rooms alike are pleasantly spacious, and there's a useful bar and restaurant.

**Hotel le Saré** ( ☎ 229 1294; www.hotellesare.com; Quartier Pitoire; r from CFA15,000; P ❄ 💻 📺 ) Set amid quiet seclusion, this is a classy place in large, shady grounds, which hide sculptures by local artists, a pool and, rather bizarrely, two pet ostriches. Rooms are tidy, and come in a variety of shapes and sizes – as do the tariffs, which change according to the day of the week and time of year.

**TOP END**

**Hotel Sahel** ( ☎ 229 2960; Blvd de Diarenga; s CFA14,500-18,000, d CFA21,500; P 🞸 ) This whitewashed modern hotel is a lot bigger than the exterior initially promises. The rooms are good and there are lots of outside sitting areas to lose yourself in a book, or a drink from the posh bar. Check out the traditional beehive-houses in front of reception.

**Maroua Palace** ( ☎ 229 3164; Centre Ville; s/d CFA20,000/22,000; P 🞸 ) If you need to be in the centre of town, you might try this option. It's modern and has comfortable rooms and facilities – but struggles to find much of a personality beyond its slightly dour exterior.

**Mizao Hôtel** ( ☎ 229 1300; Quartier Sonel; s/d CFA22,600/27,000; P 🞸 🞸 ) The design and décor of this hotel has a hint of the 1970s student dormitory, but it's none the worse for it. It's a perfectly fine choice, but you can find yourself waiting a while for a taxi to take you into town.

## Eating

**Le Point des Chutes** (off Blvd de Diarenga; meals from CFA1500; 🕗 8am-11pm) Just off the main drag, this small one-room outfit does great breakfasts for CFA1000, plus generously portioned Cameroonian standards and freshly-squeezed fruit juice to die for.

**Restaurant Le Baobab** (near Marché Centrale; dishes from CFA2000; 🕗 7am-11pm) This pleasant spot has outdoor seating under thatch, a good atmosphere and good food. Check what's available – the lunchtime menu can be a bit limited.

**Relais de la Porte Mayo** (dishes from CFA4500; 🕗 7am-11pm) For good, upscale dining, this is Maroua's best option, and is very popular with the local French community. The restaurant has great French and Italian options, while there's a cheaper snack-menu available from the bar.

**Grilled Chicken** (dishes from CFA1000; 🕗 10am-midnight) Opposite the Champs Elysée Bar, this place does fantastic whole chickens, cooked over coals and served up with bread and a green salad (ask them not to put any sugar in the dressing though). As it's Muslim-run

there's no alcohol, but they'll happily bring your meal to you if you prefer to sit in the bar next door.

Several other stalls on Blvd de Renouveau offer up *brochettes, suya* and grilled fish, all of which can be eaten in the bar of your choice in the same way.

## Drinking

Bars line Blvd de Renouveau – there are plenty to choose from. They're all of a muchness – listen out for music you might like, a football match on the TV, or whichever vibe takes your fancy.

## Getting There & Away
### AIR

**Cameroon Airlines** ( ☎ 229 2019; Route de Maga) has flights three or four times a week to Yaoundé and Douala (both around CFA89,500), sometimes via Garoua. A board outside the office announces the next departure. The airport is 20km south of town along the Garoua road (CFA3000 in a chartered taxi, if you can find one).

### BUS

**Touristique Express** (Blvd de Diarenga) has the best services for Garoua (CFA2500, 2½ hours) and N'Gaoundéré (CFA6000; eight hours). There are several buses daily to both, mostly in the mornings from about 6am. You can also book tickets for the N'Gaoundéré–Yaoundé train here at the same time. Several other agencies operate the N'Gaoundéré route, with depots on the same road; Star Express in the centre is also good.

Plentiful transport to Mokolo (CFA1000, 90 minutes) and less frequently to Rhumsiki (CFA2000, around three hours) departs from Carrefour Parrah in Djarangol at the southern end of town.

Transport to Kousséri for the Chad border (CFA3500, five hours) departs from the *gare routière* on Maroua's eastern edge. Minibuses to Banki for the Nigerian border (CFA2000, two hours) also depart from here.

## Getting Around

There are very few taxis in Maroua – even to the airport – so you'll need to hop on the back of a *moto-taxi*. Most destinations in town are a flat CFA100.

# MANDARA MOUNTAINS

The Mandara Mountains, running west of Maroua to the Nigerian border, define one of the most enjoyable areas in Cameroon, and they're rich in tribal culture, natural wonders and beautiful scenery. Grassland gives way to a jumble of conical peaks, Monument Valley-style crags and hidden valleys, all sprinkled with thatched huts and boys herding animals. It's a very picturesque and varied landscape, alternately rugged and rolling, but never less than inviting. It's no surprise that the area offers Cameroon's best trekking.

There are many fascinating villages, including Rhumsiki, with its striking mountain scenery; Djingliya and Koza, set against steep terraced hillsides; Tourou, known for the calabash hats worn by local women; Maga, with its unique domed houses made entirely of clay; and Mora, which has a particularly notable weekly market. Hiking between villages is one of the best ways to appreciate the scenery and culture alike.

Rhumsiki is the main entrance point for visitors to the Mandara Mountains, and is the one place where there is a tangible feeling of a tourist scene, with over-attentive children and 'impromptu' traditional dances – although, being Cameroon, the idea of mass tourism is something of a relative term.

There is accommodation in Rhumsiki, Mokolo, Mora, Waza, Maga and a few other villages, but no infrastructure otherwise. Roads are rough and public transport infrequent, so if you're travelling independently allow plenty of time and plan to be self-sufficient with food and water. Local minibuses usually set off around 6am. *Moto-taxis* are sometimes the only option for getting around.

For those with limited time, travel agencies in Maroua can organise visits, although it's just as easy to arrange things on the spot in Rhumsiki or Mokolo, which will ensure that more of the money you spend is pumped directly into the local economy. Expect to pay around CFA30,000 per day (plus petrol) for a vehicle with driver. Petrol is available in Maroua, Mokolo and Mora, although prices frequently rise during the rains due to transportation problems. Change enough CFA to see you through before leaving Maroua.

One popular circuit goes from Maroua to Mora (with possible detours to Parc National de Waza and to Oudjilla), and then southwest via Koza, Djingliya and Mokolo to Rhumsiki, finishing back in Maroua. This can easily be broken down into two- or three-day treks, giving a great taste of the region.

## Mokolo

Mokolo, centre of the Mafa people, is about 80km west of Maroua along a bitumen road. There's not much here, but it's an important transport hub.

### SLEEPING & EATING

**Hotel Touristique le Flamboyant** ( ☎ 229 5585; r CFA12,000-14,000; ☒ ) Near the Total petrol station, this is the most comfortable place in town, with clean *boukarous* and a nice restaurant.

**Metcheme Bar** (r CFA3000) This bar has some grubby rooms in an annexe with shared bathroom. As budget options go, it's passable for a night's stay.

**Restaurant L'Incomparable** (meals from CFA1000) By the market, this place doesn't quite live up to its name, but serves up reasonable food nonetheless. For something fancier to eat, head to Le Flamboyant.

### GETTING THERE & AWAY

Most transport departs from the market, in the town centre. Tsanaga Voyages go several

---

### MARKET DAY

Getting to and from villages in northern Cameroon (and elsewhere) via public transport is always easier on market day, as there are many more vehicles. Some local market days are as follows:

| Town | Market day |
| --- | --- |
| Bogo | Thursday |
| Koza | Sunday |
| Maroua | Monday |
| Mogodé (north of Rhumsiki) | Friday |
| Mokolo | Wednesday |
| Mora | Sunday |
| Pouss (northeast of Maga) | Tuesday |
| Rhumsiki | Sunday |
| Tourou | Thursday |

CAMEROON

times a day to Maroua (CFA800, one hour). Transport onward to Rhumsiki is much less frequent; your best bet is the bus from Maroua which passes through mid-morning. Otherwise, it's a bumpy 55km ride by *moto-taxi*. There's a daily bus to Koza (CFA1500, two hours).

## Rhumsiki

Rhumsiki is on all the tourist itineraries, and it's setting tells the reason why – the village is framed by dramatic columns and whalebacks of rock set amid quite beautiful hill country. Just outside Rhumsiki is the much-photographed Rhumsiki Peak.

You'll get fair bit of attention in the village, with people after your custom. Plenty of people will offer their services as guides – get a recommendation if you can. Hiking rates start at about CFA10,000 per day, including simple meals, accommodation in local homes, camping (with your own tent or on mats in the open) and a guide. If you're self-sufficient, it's perfectly feasible to strike out on your own.

Most routes are between half a day and four days, and some cross briefly into Nigeria, just 3km away; no visa is necessary as long as you don't continue further into the country.

One thing worth doing in Rhumsiki is to have your fortune told by the local *feticheur*, who will divine your future by looking into his bucket of crabs. If you feel over-run, it's easy to leave the village behind and strike out into the countryside by foot.

### SLEEPING & EATING

Except as noted, all places are along the main road, listed here in the order you reach them when arriving from Mokolo. All arrange trekking.

**Kirdi Bar** (camping per person CFA1000, r per person CFA2500-5000) Kirdi Bar is a good shoestring choice. No-frills *boukarous* have bucket showers, and there are meals for about CFA2500, including decent pizzas. The manager is a good source of information on the area, and organises well-regarded treks, as well as *moto* hire. It's at the town entrance, to the left of the road.

**Auberge Le Kapsiki** ( ☎ 229 3356; s/d CFA5000/ 75000) The *boukarous*-style accommodation here is spartan but adequate. There's also a good restaurant with meals costing from

about CFA2500. As well as the usual hikes, the auberge also arranges horse trekking.

**Auberge Le Petit Paris** ( ☎ 229 5173; r CFA10,000-20,000) More *boukarous* are the order of the day here. They're clean and tidy, and there's a restaurant. Alternatively, dine at Le Casserole, opposite.

**La Maison de l'Amitié** ( ☎ 229 2113; r CFA8500-12,000) This place is a nice option, with comfortable, modern *boukarous* and a restaurant. It's at the far end of town, about 150m off the main road.

### GETTING THERE & AWAY

Transport to and from Rhumsiki is best on Sunday, Monday and Wednesday – get up early for the 6am starts, but always check what's running the day before travel. There's a minibus most days to Maroua (CFA2000, around three hours), passing through Mokolo. Except on market day, transport dries up by around 2pm. A *moto-taxi* to Mokolo costs around CFA2500; rucksacks are better balanced between the handlebars than on your back.

## Djingliya & Koza

Djingliya, 15km north of Mokolo, is a tiny village perched on a hill with good views over the surrounding terraced countryside. Société Cooperative Artisanale de Djingliya sells local crafts, and offers basic rooms with bucket bath for CFA3000; meals can also be arranged. Ask the caretaker for a tour of a typical local housing compound. Vehicles between Mokolo and Koza will drop you off, or take a *moto-taxi* from Mokolo.

Koza, 4km further north, marks the end of the scenic uphill route from Mokolo; from here to Mora the terrain levels out. There's nowhere to sleep, but places to eat.

There's at least one vehicle daily in each direction between Koza and Mokolo. On Monday there's also an early morning minibus vehicle direct to Maroua returning in the afternoon (CFA1500, two hours). A *moto-taxi* to Mokolo costs around CFA750.

## Mora

Mora is in the heartland of the Wandala (Mandara) people and is the last settlement of any size before reaching the Nigerian border. Try to time your visit for the large Sunday market, one of the best tastes of local culture in the region. About 11km west is Oudjilla, a touristy Podoko village. Apart from the scenery, the main attraction is the **compound** (saré; donation CFA1000) of the village chief and his many wives.

**Auberge Mora Massif** (camping per person CFA1000, r CFA3000) is the best place in Mora. There's fair rooms in the main building, but better *boukarous*. The restaurant serves simple starchy dishes. It's 400m west of the main junction.

**Campement Sanga de Podoko** (r CFA4000) has acceptable *boukarous* rooms, and there's a bar and restaurant. It's east of the main road near the Total petrol station.

Minibuses go daily between Mora and Maroua (CFA800, one hour). The main way to reach Oudjilla is by *moto-taxi*.

## PARC NATIONAL DE WAZA

**Waza** (admission CFA5000, plus CFA2000 per vehicle, camera fee CFA2000; �
6am-6pm 15 Nov-15 May) is the most accessible of Cameroon's national parks and the best for viewing wildlife. While it can't compare with East African parks, you're likely to see elephants, hippos, giraffes, antelopes and – with luck – lions. Late March to April is the best time for viewing, as the animals congregate at water holes before the rains. Waza is also notable for its particularly rich birdlife. The park is closed during the rainy season.

A guide (CFA3000 per day) is obligatory in each vehicle. Walking isn't permitted.

### Sleeping

Waza can easily be done as a day trip from Maroua if you start early (bring a packed lunch). Otherwise, there are three places to stay near the park entrance.

**Campement de Waza** ( ☎ 229 1646, 229 1165 in Maroua, 765 7717 or 765 7558 in Waza; s/d CFA14,800/16,000; ☒ ) This is the most luxurious option here, with accommodation in reasonably comfortable *boukarous* and an attached restaurant. There are a few cheaper rooms with fan only. It's on a small hill about 700m from the park entrance, on the opposite side of the main road.

**Centre d'Accueil de Waza** ( ☎ 229 2207; camping per person CFA2500, r CFA7000) This simple place at the park entrance has accommodation in no-frills two-person *boukarous* with shared toilet facilities. Meals can be arranged (CFA2000) and it has a small kitchen.

**GIC-FAC Café-Restaurant du IIme Millénaire** (r around CFA4000) The local women's group has a few very simple rooms in a basic guesthouse. Meals can be arranged. It's just off the main road along the park access road.

There's also basic accommodation in Waza village, just north of the park entrance.

### Getting There & Away

The park entrance is signposted and lies about 400m off the main highway. Unless you have your own wheels, the best way to visit is to hire a vehicle in Maroua (about CFA30,000 per day plus petrol). See p208 for listings of tour operators. A 4WD vehicle is recommended.

Accessing the park by public transport is difficult – any bus between Maroua and Kousséri should be able to drop you at the park turnoff, but after that you'll be reliant on hitching a lift into the park itself, which is likely to involve a long wait.

During the dry season, it's possible to drive through the park and exit at Andirni, about 45km southeast of Waza village. The road from Andirni to Maroua via Bogo is only partially paved, and is sometimes impassable during the wet season.

# EAST PROVINCE

Cameroon's remote east is wild and untamed. Seldom visited by travellers, it's very much a destination for those with plenty of time and the stamina to back up an appetite for adventure. There's little infrastructure and travel throughout is slow and rugged, although the landscape is archetypal Central Africa: dense green forest and red laterite earth roads. The rainforest is the main attraction – Cameroon's sweep of the Congo Basin, which takes in Parc National de la Lobéké, Boumba-Bek and Nki forest reserves, and the Reserve du Dja. While a few towns have experienced a boom in the last decade, development has exposed real fault lines in the area, with the country's natural bounty colliding with uncontrolled logging, HIV infection and the bushmeat trade.

## GAROUA-BOULAÏ

If you're looking for a picture of a rough African frontier town, Garoua-Boulaï is it. On the Central African Republic (CAR) border, it's a place of bars, trucks and prostitutes. The town's unwanted claim to fame is its alarmingly high HIV infection rate.

There are several unappealing and not recommended *auberges* with rooms for about CFA2000. Better is the **Mission Catholique** (dm for a donation, r about CFA5000) with dorm beds and a few rooms. It's near the military checkpoint coming from the north.

The road is in tolerable condition from Garoua-Boulaï to N'Gaoundéré during the dry season, there's one bus daily (CFA4000, 12 hours) and many police checkpoints. Ask around before travelling – sporadic banditry persists along the CAR border, although you're equally likely to get robbed by the police.

Vehicles go several times daily on a fair road to Bertoua. For details on getting to CAR, see p225; the border is on the edge of town next to the motor park.

## BERTOUA

The capital of East Province, Bertoua is a genuine boomtown, born out of logging and mining. Here you'll find all the facilities lacking elsewhere in the region – bitumen roads, banks and even a choice of what to eat in the evening.

### Sleeping & Eating

**Hôtel Mansa** ( ☎ 224 1650; Mokolo II; r CFA25,000; ✖ ) The Mansa is Bertoua's best place, complete with a restaurant, and is worth a splurge if you've been lost in the forest.

Hôtel Montagnia, near the *gare routière*, and Hôtel Mirage, near the main post office, both have basic rooms for around CFA6000.

**Café Moderne** (meals from CFA500) is found at the *gare routière*. Other similarly inexpensive places include Grille de la Ménagère (near the Orange phone mast) and Chez Odette, just off the road near La King textile store.

### Getting There & Away

**Cameroon Airlines** flies every Monday, Wednesday and Friday between Bertoua and Douala (CFA75,000, two hours), sometimes stopping at Yaoundé.

To Yaoundé, the main lines are Alliance Voyages and Djerem Express (CFA5000, about seven hours); most transport uses the southern route via Abong-Mbang and

Ayos. The road is unpaved to Ayos (bad in the rains), and bitumen from there to Yaoundé.

Minibuses go daily to Garoua-Boulaï, and on to N'Gaoundéré (CFA7500, one day); the road is paved as far as Garoua-Boulaï. There's also daily transport to Batouri (CFA1200, three hours), along a reasonable road, and to Bélabo (CFA1000, one hour), where you can catch the Yaoundé–N'Gaoundéré train.

Most transport departs from the main *gare routière* near the market. Alliance Voyages' office is just west of here.

## BÉLABO

The halfway point on the Yaoundé–N'Gaoundéré train line, Bélabo is the rail entry point for the east. There's not much to the place except a pumping station for the Chad–Cameroon oil pipeline. Bélabo has an edgy feel to it, and unfortunately taking the train means hanging around at the station at midnight, when the train arrives (from both directions), assuming it's on time. On arrival, hire a taxi or *moto* to take you to your hotel; walking alone isn't safe. If you're departing Bélabo with a 1st-class train ticket, you can wait in the VIP lounge, rather than out on the street.

About 25km west of town, off the road to Nanga Eboko, is the privately run Sanaga-Yong Chimpanzee Rescue Centre (donations welcome), which offers sanctuary to about 20 chimpanzees and promotes local education efforts.

For accommodation, try **La Girafe** (r from CFA8000) on the edge of town. There are a couple of cheaper places, including the very basic **Hôtel de l'Est** (r from CFA2000). The best food is at Mama Etémé, behind the health clinic.

Transport goes several times daily along the paved road between Bertoua and Bélabo (CFA1000, one hour). To get to the chimpanzee centre, you'll need to charter a taxi or *moto*.

## BATOURI

Batouri, 90km east of Bertoua on a poor road, is a useful enough place to break your journey if you're going to the southeastern forest reserves. For those going to CAR, it's the last town of any size before Berbérati across the border.

Budget accommodation is available at **Auberge Coopérant** ( ☎ 226 2300; r CFA5000) in the town centre. **Hôtel Belle Etoile** ( ☎ 226 2518; r CFA10,000) is a step up, with **Hôtel Mont Pandi** ( ☎ 226 2577, r CFA11,000; ☒ ) an even better bet if you're in need of a treat; there's a restaurant attached.

There are several buses daily to Bertoua, with the first leaving at about 8am, and usually at least one bus daily to Yaoundé. Local agencies include Atlantic Voyages and Narral Voyages. To Yokadouma, there's daily transport departing in the morning; allow half a day, more in the wet season. There is also transport at least once daily to Kenzou and the CAR border, departing Batouri at about 5am.

## YOKADOUMA

Logging has brought Yokadouma a fast-paced Wild West feel, with its attendant bushmeat markets and displaced 'Pygmies'. The **WWF branch office** can help with arranging visits to Parc National de la Lobéké, and Boumba-Bek and Nki forest reserves.

The best place to stay is **L'Elefant** ( ☎ 224 2877; r from CFA8000; ☒ ). Otherwise, there are numerous cheaper and more basic choices, including Auberge Libértate.

All transport departs early. To Moloundou, apart from hitching a ride in a comfortable Land Cruiser, the best bet is Alliance Voyages, with one bus daily in the dry season (CFA5000, about eight hours). During the wet season, the journey can take several days.

## MOLOUNDOU

You'll need to pass through this border town if you're heading for Réserve de Nki or Ouesso (Congo).

There are two basic places to stay, **La Forestière** (r from CFA3000) and **Jardin du Rose** (r from CFA3000).

Alliance Voyages has one bus daily in the dry season to/from Yokadouma (CFA5000, about eight hours).

## RÉSERVE DE BIOSPHÈRE DU DJA

The Réserve de Biosphère du Dja, as recognised by Unesco, protects about 526,000 hectares of primary rainforest. As with Lobéké and the other southeastern forest reserves, visiting here is a serious undertaking, and you'll need to be completely self-

sufficient. Although there are few people in the reserve area, there are Baka communities around its borders, particularly along the old road rimming Dja's northern edge.

The reserve is managed by **Ecofac** (Map p180; ☎ 220 9472; www.ecofac.org; Bastos) in Yaoundé, and you should visit their offices for information and to arrange a visit.

The best starting point for a visit is Somalomo village, on the reserve's north edge. There's a training centre here with basic rooms for CFA5000 per night. Accommodation must be arranged in advance, along with meals (unless you plan to be self-sufficient). There's no food other than basic foodstuffs available in Somalomo. You'll also need a good water filter. Guides (CFA3000 per day) are obligatory and can be arranged at Somalomo, as can porters (CFA2000 per day).

The main route from Somalomo into the reserve is a 30km hike south to Bouamir, where you can camp at the site of an old research base and then hike out again along the same path. Allow close to a week for a visit from Yaoundé, including a day each way to/from Somalomo, a day's hike in and out to Bouamir, and several days' camping in the forest. You'll need your own tent. At Bouamir, you're likely to see buffaloes and many birds, including the rare *Picathartes oreas* (grey-necked rockfowl), which nests here in May and June.

It's also possible to enter Dja from Lomié, to the east, although guides aren't as well organised there as in Somalomo. Also, because of heavy poaching in the reserve's eastern section, it's more difficult to see animals. The best time to visit Dja is during the drier season between December and February, although visits are possible into June.

## LOBÉKÉ, BOUMBA-BEK & NKI

These three designated areas protect large sections of southeastern Cameroon's rainforests. They are also the focus of a joint initiative between the Cameroon government and the WWF to halt timber exploitation and poaching, and to protect the forests as well as local Baka communities (who depend on the forests for their livelihood) against further threat. Lobéké, with more than 2000 sq km, was declared a national park in 2001. It is part of the Sangha

CAMEROON

---

**A GUEST IN THE RAINFOREST**

If you plan to visit the southeastern reserves, here are a few tips:

■ Budget a minimum of a week for a visit; travel from Yaoundé takes at least two days each way.

■ Be prepared to be totally self-sufficient for food, drink and lodging. A good water purifier/filter is essential.

■ Be sure all your vaccines and immunisations are up to date, take precautions for malaria and travel with a good first-aid kit.

■ Bring a mosquito net and plenty of insect repellent, and wear clothing that covers your arms and legs, and a hat.

■ Snake bites are a risk; wear sturdy, high-topped boots, and long trousers.

■ Given the lack of infrastructure, you'll probably need to request assistance from conservation project staff, which they are usually more than willing to give. Keep in mind, however, that their primary responsibility is the protection of nature.

■ Tread lightly; be patient; and wait for the rainforest to come to you.

---

Tri-National Park area, encompassing Dzanga-Sangha National Park (CAR), and Nouabalé-Ndoki Forest Reserve (Congo). Boumba-Bek and Nki are forest reserves, though they're slated to achieve national park status in the near future within a single 7500 sq km protected area.

Lobéké is the most accessible of the three areas, but all are difficult to reach, and you should only contemplate coming here if you have lots of time, as well as the patience and endurance necessary for discovering the rainforest. December to March are the best times to visit – the dry weather means better accessibility and lighter vegetation, which can increase your chances of spotting wildlife.

### Lobéké

Lobéké has large populations of forest elephants, chimpanzees and gorillas, although the dense vegetation means that sightings can be hard to come by. The best option is to use some of the *miradors* (viewing platforms) which have been constructed in more open areas, and let the wildlife come to you.

A visit to Lobéké starts in Yokadouma. Park fees (CFA5000 per person per day) and guide fees (CFA3000 per guide per day) are payable at the Ministry of Finance office; get a receipt to show at the park gate. You should also check in at the WWF office to get current information on accessibility and logistics. WWF can often help with transport (CFA3000) into the park through

their sub-office at Mambele, 160km south of Yokadouma. You'll need to be self-sufficient for food in the park.

If you get caught in Mambele for the night, there's accommodation at Le Bon Samariten, which has basic rooms for about CFA2000. You can also find food and bottled water in town.

### Boumba-Bek & Nki

Réserve de Nki – the most pristine of the three areas – is accessed via Moloundou, then by boat westwards along the Dja River, and finally on foot into the forest. WWF project staff can assist with boat arrangements; plan on about CFA150,000 per five-person boat.

Boumba-Bek can be accessed via Ngola (north of Mambele on the Yokadouma road), from where you head west by vehicle and foot to reach the Boumba River and the reserve.

If you get to either of these forest reserves, you'll be as remote in deepest Cameroon as it's possible to get.

# SOUTH PROVINCE

South Province is Cameroon at its most equatorial, with rampant vegetation and thick rainforest, hidden 'Pygmy' villages and pristine beaches facing the white waves of the Atlantic. Visitors here can rough it in the jungle, explore some of the country's newest national parks looking for wildlife, or break for the border and continue the adventure south, in neighbouring Gabon or Equatorial Guinea. For those who prefer a more relaxing time, the sand and surf at Kribi – a quick and easy hop from both Yaoundé and Douala – offers an ideal solution for easing the aches of the road.

## KRIBI

It's easy to see why Kribi is Cameroon's most popular beach resort. Its proximity to the country's two main cities make it an ideal weekend getaway for government ministers, tourists and expats alike, who are all attracted to the sweep of white sandy beaches fringed with palm trees. They're ideal for lazing around on, but you should take care when swimming – the oceanic waters can have strong currents and rip tides, so check locally before plunging in. After a quick dip, you can tuck in to Cameroon's best and freshest seafood.

Most of Kribi's hotels (usually with their own beach fronts) start at the southern end of town. There are also a few attractive beaches to the north, including at Londji, about 15km from Kribi, but not so many accommodation options. Pre-booking is a good idea for weekends and holidays, when the town fills up quickly; during the rest of the week, however, Kribi can be quite sleepy. Camping on the beach is not advised, and you should exercise caution walking on the beaches alone at night.

## Information

Stock up on CFA before coming to Kribi. **Bicec bank** (Rue des Banques) will only change cash euros under duress. **Club Internet de Kribi** (Rue des Banques; per hr CFA500) has the most reliable Internet connections. The **Ministry of Tourism** ( ☎ 346 1080) is occasionally useful, and may help with trips to Campo-Ma'an.

## Sleeping

If you're visiting in the rainy season, it's always worth asking for a discount.

**BUDGET**
**Hotel Panoramique** ( ☎ 346 1773; hotelpanoramique @yahoo.fr; Rue du Marché; r CFA6000-14,000; 🌀 ) Away

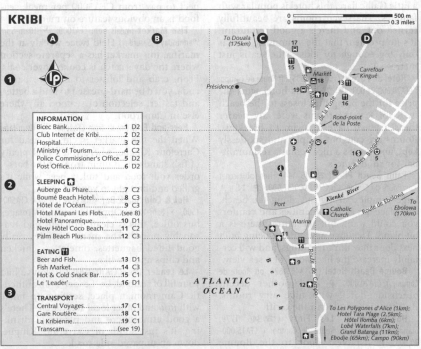

**KRIBI**

0 ————————— 500 m
0 ————————— 0.3 miles

To Douala (175km)

Présidence ●

Market

Carrefour Kingué

Rond-point de la Poste

Kienké River

Port

Catholic Church

Marina

ATLANTIC OCEAN

To Ebolowa (170km)

To Les Polygones d'Alice (1km);
Hotel Tara Plage (2.5km);
Hôtel Ilomba (6km);
Lobé Waterfalls (7km);
Grand Batanga (11km);
Ebodje (65km); Campo (90km)

**INFORMATION**
Bicec Bank.............................1 D2
Club Internet de Kribi..........2 D2
Hospital.................................3 C2
Ministry of Tourism..............4 C2
Police Commissioner's Office..5 D2
Post Office............................6 D2

**SLEEPING**
Auberge du Phare.................7 C2
Boumé Beach Hotel..............8 C3
Hôtel de l'Océan..................9 C3
Hotel Mapani Les Flots.........(see 8)
Hotel Panoramique.............10 D1
New Hôtel Coco Beach........11 C2
Palm Beach Plus..................12 C3

**EATING**
Beer and Fish.....................13 D1
Fish Market........................14 C3
Hot & Cold Snack Bar.........15 C1
Le 'Leader'.........................16 D1

**TRANSPORT**
Central Voyages..................17 C1
Gare Routière.....................18 C1
La Kribienne.......................19 C1
Transcam...........................(see 19)

CAMEROON

from the beach, but handy for town amenities, rooms come in all shapes and sizes at this decent budget option. Prices vary according to size and whether or not you choose air-con.

**Auberge du Phare** ( ☎ 346 1106; off Route de Campo; r without/with air-con CFA12,000/16,000-25,000; P ⚡ ) A long-standing favourite, this has a good beachside location, a great restaurant and is conveniently placed for the town centre. Cheaper rooms are a little spartan and don't face the sea, but the rest are good, with lots of wood-panelling. The hotel is usually closed in October, so call ahead.

**Hotel Tara Plage** ( ☎ 346 2038; Route de Campo; r without/with air-con CFA12,000/CFA16,000; P ⚡ ) A popular beachside option with a mellow vibe. A good place to get away from town, and luckily the restaurant serves great food. Frequently full, advance booking is recommended.

**MIDRANGE**

**New Coco Beach Hôtel** ( ☎ 346 1584; off Route de Campo; s/d/tr CFA25,000/32,000/46,000; P ⚡ ⚡ ) Small, but very nicely formed and run with a little Gallic flare, this hotel is popular with families. The seven rooms are beautifully turned out, and there's a good restaurant. It's no problem that the swimming pool is only big enough for kids – the sea is just metres away

**Hôtel de l'Océan** ( ☎ 346 1635; off Route de Campo; r CFA20,000-24,000; P ⚡ ) This hotel wins the prize for the being the closest to the beach in Kribi – if the rooms were any nearer the sea you'd have to swim to breakfast. Rooms are cute but simple, and spotlessly kept, and there's a nice veranda restaurant-bar for sundowners.

**Palm Beach Plus** ( ☎ 346 1447; hotelpb@iccnet .cm; Route de Campo; s/d CFA32,000/37,000; P ⚡ ) A large complex strung out along the beach, this place has all the amenities and comfort you could want, but the atmosphere is a bit bland. The huge new annexe being built next door may improve things, and will certainly increase the likelihood of a sea view.

**Boumé Beach Hotel** ( ☎ 346 1620; off Route de Campo; r CFA20,000; P ⚡ ) Another decent beachside hotel, with nice airy rooms. Breakfast is included in the tariff.

**Hotel Mapani Les Flots** ( ☎ 346 1779; manapani80@yahoo.fr; Route de Campo; r CFA15,000-20,000; P ⚡ ) Next door to the Boumé

Beach Hotel. The cheapest rooms are a bit small for the price, but the CFA20,000 options have four beds in two rooms – excellent value if you're in a group.

**Les Polygones d'Alice** ( ☎ 346 1504; Route de Campo; r CFA25,000; P ⚡ ) This hotel stands out for its octagonal shape and an exterior apparently covered in white bathroom tiles. But look past that and you'll find exceedingly comfortable and modern rooms, and the obligatory beachside restaurant.

**Hotel Ilomba** ( ☎ 346 1744; Route de Campo; s/d CFA25,000/30,000; P ⚡ ⚡ ⚡ ) Some way out of Kribi, this is quite the loveliest hotel in the area. Well-furnished and tastefully decorated rooms are in *boukarous*; mosquito nets are even included, a rarity in Cameroon. The hotel's Baobab Restaurant serves up a good variety of dishes, and there's a lazy beachside bar too. The Ilomba is just a short walk along the beach from the Lobé Waterfalls (opposite).

## Eating

All the beach hotels have restaurants, and are the nicest dining options in Kribi. Expect to pay from CFA3000 per meal; seafood is an obvious feature on menus.

**Fish Market** (meals from CFA1000; ☺ 10am-5pm Wednesday & Saturday) Held twice weekly at the marina, this market has a separate section where the day's catch is cooked over coals. From crab and lobster to massive barracuda, you'd be hard-pressed to find a better, and tastier, selection of seafood anywhere else in Cameroon.

**Beer and Fish** (meals from CFA1000; ☺ 10am-late) When the fish market is closed, head for Carrefour Kingué, where you'll find plenty of fish stands lined up in front of the bars – order your food and sink a beer while it's grilled and brought to your table.

**Hot & Cold Snack Bar** (snacks & fast food CFA500-1500; ☺ 8am-10pm) Opposite Central Voyages bus office, this is clean, efficient and reasonably priced. The menu includes really good filled baguettes, omelettes, chicken and chips and the like.

**Le 'Leader'** (meals CFA1000-2000) If you've had your fill of seafood, Le 'Leader' is an authentic Cameroonian place, serving up *ndole* with *fufu* and other local standards. There's a good atmosphere and plenty of drinking; it's just south of Carrefour Kingué, down an unpaved side road.

## Getting There & Away

Bus agencies have offices on Rue du Marché in the town centre. Nonagency transport leaves from the main *gare routière*, on the same street.

To Douala (CFA1800, three hours), Central Voyages is best, with buses throughout the day from about 5.30am.

To Campo, Transcam and La Kribienne have several buses daily (CFA2000, three hours). All agencies have daily buses to Yaoundé (CFA3000, 3½ hours). Ebolowa transport (CFA3500, four hours) only runs November to May due to the poor roads.

If you don't fancy the long walk along the beach to Lobé Waterfalls, you can charter a taxi (CFA2000) or hop on the back of a *moto-taxi* (CFA500). There's little public transport, so pay extra to the driver to wait for you.

## AROUND KRIBI
### Lobé Waterfalls

Besides the beaches, Kribi's main attraction is the Lobé Waterfalls (Chutes de la Lobé), 8km south of the town. Set in a very pretty location in a curved bay, the waterfalls are one of the few in the world that plunge directly into the sea. There's a small restaurant serving grilled fish and drinks. Touts will approach you offering pirogue trips upstream to a 'Pygmy village', which is disappointing, but the boat trip itself is an enjoyable and scenic slice of river and forest. Expect to pay around CFA5000 for a 90-minute round-trip, or just opt for a 10 minute trip past the rapids to the larger falls behind.

## EBOLOWA

Ebolowa, capital of Ntem district, is a bustling place, and a possible stopping point en route between Yaoundé and Equatorial Guinea or Gabon. It's main attraction is the artificial Municipal Lake in the centre of town.

The best accommodation is at **Hôtel Porte Jaune** ( ☎ 228 4339; Route de Yaoundé; r CFA10,000) in the town centre, with decent rooms and meals – although the management can be funny about two people of the same sex sharing a room. Of a similar standard is **Hôtel Le Ranch** ( ☎ 228 3532; Centre Ville; r CFA8000-12,000) near the police station. There are several cheaper, undistinguished *auberges* near the main roundabout, including **Hôtel Âne Rouge** (Place Ans 2000; r CFA4000).

During the dry season, there's at least one vehicle daily along the rough road between Ebolowa and Kribi. There are also several vehicles daily to Yaoundé (CFA3000, three hours).

Several vehicles, including those of Arc-en-Ciel, depart in the morning for Ambam (CFA1000, one hour). From there you can find transport towards Ebebiyin (Equatorial Guinea) or Bitam (Gabon). If you get stuck in Amban, **Hôtel La Couronne** (r CFA10,000-15,000) is fair quality, or try the more basic **Auberge de l'Amitié** (r CFA4000).

## CAMPO

Campo is the last town before the Equatorial Guinea border. It is a jumping off point for visiting Parc National de Campo Ma'an, as well as a community tourism project in nearby Ebodjé. The best accommodation is at **Auberge Bon Course** (r CFA5000) at Bon Course Supermarché at the main junction. There are three simple but decent rooms, and meals are available.

A small fishing village 25km north of Campo, Ebodjé is home to a sea turtle conservation project run by the Netherlands Development Organisation (SNV). Accommodation is in local homes – costs are CFA2000 per person for accommodation, CFA2000 per meal, and CFA1000 per person environmental protection fee. A proportion of all fees goes into the village development fund. Locals have also been trained as guides to the area. It's a good low-key way to get away from the standard tourist sites and gain an insight into Cameroonian village life. You'll need to bring your own water or filter, mosquito net and sleeping sheet.

### Getting There & Away

There are daily minibuses between Campo and Kribi (CFA1500) which also stop at Ebodjé. *Moto-taxis* to Campo Beach (for Equatorial Guinea) cost CFA500. For information on crossing the border, see p225. Taxis to Ebodjé from Campo cost CFA500.

### PARC NATIONAL DE CAMPO-MA'AN

Campo is the starting point for visiting the Parc National de Campo-Ma'an (2608 sq km), which protects rainforest, many plants and various animals, including buffaloes, elephants and mandrills. The animals are

CAMEROON

rarely seen because of the dense vegetation, but the park is being developed by WWF as an ecotourism destination, with plans for canopy walks and river trips on the drawing board. Before planning a trip, check with the **WWF office** (Map p180; ☎ 221 6267; www .wwfcameroon.org; Bastos) in Yaoundé to see what progress is being made.

Currently there's little infrastructure in place and you'll need your own 4WD to get here. The CFA5000 entry fee can be paid at the tourist office in Campo; get a receipt to show at the park entrance at the village of Nko'elon. Staff at the office can also help you arrange a guide (obligatory, CFA3000 per day). You'll need to be self-sufficient with equipment and supplies. The road between Campo and Ma'an (west of the park) is being rehabilitated. For now it's only possible to drive as far as Memve'ele Waterfalls, just outside the park's eastern boundary.

# CAMEROON DIRECTORY

## ACCOMMODATION

Cameroon has a fairly decent range of accommodation. In the budget range, basic auberges are the order of the day. Expect a no-frills room with a narrow double bed and attached bathroom, usually with a cold-water shower only, and either a ceiling fan or air-con. Some church missions take travellers and can be excellent value, as they are usually clean, cheap and well run. Most larger towns have at least a couple of comfortable midrange options, sometimes a bit faded, but with better fixtures, more reliable

---

**PRACTICALITIES**

- The *Cameroon Tribune* is the government-owned bilingual daily. The thrice-weekly *Le Messager* (French) is the main independent newspaper.

- Most broadcast programming is government-run and in French, through Cameroon Radio-TV Corporation (CRTV). TVs at top-end hotels often have CNN or French news stations.

- Electricity supply is 220V and plugs are of the European two-round-pin variety.

- Cameroon uses the metric system.

---

hot water and French satellite TV. Outside Yaoundé and Douala, international standard top-end accommodation is hard to find.

Most hotels quote prices per room, a practice followed in the text – genuine single and twin rooms are the exception rather than the norm. Breakfast is rarely included in the tariff. Throughout this chapter, we've considered budget accommodation as costing up to CFA12,000, midrange CFA12,000 to 40,000, and top end from CFA40,000 and up.

Camping is not generally recommended, except in the remote countryside. You should always ask permission from the village headman before pitching a tent.

## ACTIVITIES

Hiking is a big drawcard in Cameroon. The two most popular areas are Mt Cameroon near the coast (p192) and the Mandara Mountains in the north (p211). It's possible to organise treks with guides in both areas. On Mt Cameroon you'll either camp or stay in mountain huts; in the Mandara Mountains you generally stay with villagers. The Ring Road near Bamenda also offers great hiking possibilities, but there's nothing organised so you'll need to be self-sufficient.

## BOOKS

*Cameroon with Egbert* by Dervla Murphy is another outing with the trusted travel writer, here with a recalcitrant horse – the eponymous Egbert – and teenage daughter in tow. Great to get you in the mood for a trip

*An Innocent Anthropologist* by Nigel Barley speaks of the culture clash that can ensue between an anthropologist and 'his' subjects – here the Dowayo of northern Cameroon. It's very engagingly written.

Gerald Durrell's *A Zoo in My Luggage* and *The Bafut Beagles* are two gloriously told accounts of the naturalist's animal collecting trips to Cameroon in the 1950s and '60s.

*Culture and Customs of Cameroon*, by John Mukum Mbaku, is an academic but still highly accessible ethnological guide to Cameroon – a must-read for those wanting to really get under the skin of the country.

## BUSINESS HOURS

Government offices are officially open from 7.30am to 3.30pm Monday to Friday. Businesses are open from 7.30am or 8am until

6pm or 6.30pm Monday to Friday, generally with a one- to two-hour break sometime between noon and 3pm. Most are also open from 8am to 1pm (sometimes later) on Saturday. Banks are open from 7.30am or 8am to 3.30pm Monday to Friday.

## CUSTOMS

There are no limits on importing currency or on exporting CFA to other Central African CFA countries (Chad, CAR, Congo, Equatorial Guinea and Gabon). When departing the Central African CFA zone, you are permitted to export a maximum of CFA25,000.

## DANGERS & ANNOYANCES

Cameroon is generally a safe country to travel around in. Parts of Yaoundé and Douala, like big cities the world over, carry bad reputations for casual street crime. Be particularly wary around bus and train stations, and outside banks and expensive hotels. By day you're unlikely to encounter may problems, but taking a taxi at night is often recommended. The same caution should also be applied late at night in N'Gaoundéré and Bafoussam. Avoid carrying valuables on the street.

Travel to the Bakassi Peninsula, disputed between Cameroon and Nigeria, should be avoided (check in advance if you're planning on taking a boat from Kourp National Park to Idenao). Some parts of the north and east – most notably the area bordering the Central African Republic – are prone to armed banditry. Minibuses sometimes travel in convoys to avoid problems, although some Cameroonians complain this is more so police can earn an extra 'protection fee' as much as to prevent trouble.

Corruption is a large problem in Cameroon. The form most often encountered by travellers is at the interminable roadside police checkpoints. Although most attention is focused on locals, always keep your passport (or certified copy – see the boxed text, right) and vaccination certificate *(carte jaune)* handy. Police often seek out the most minor infraction, and aren't above inventing a few themselves. Those with their own vehicles may be asked to show their complete service history and ownership papers. Always remember to smile and be patient and polite, and most 'problems' will quickly

evaporate without having to put your hand in your pocket.

For all this, the most serious problem you are likely to encounter in Cameroon is through dangerous driving. Minibus drivers in particular pay little heed to road safety or speed limits, which can make for nervous travelling – see p226 for more information.

## EMBASSIES & CONSULATES
### Cameroon Embassies & Consulates

In West Africa, Cameroon has embassies in Côte d'Ivoire, Nigeria and Senegal. Check the appropriate country chapter. Embassies and consulates for other countries include the following:

**Australia** ( ☎ 02-9876 4544; www.cameroonconsul.com; 65 Bingara Rd, Beecroft, NSW)

**Belgium** ( ☎ 02-345 1870; Ave Brughmann 131-133, Brussels)

**Canada** ( ☎ 613-236 1522; 170 Clemow Ave, Ottawa, Ontario)

**Central African Republic** ( ☎ 611687; Ave de la France, Bangui)

**Chad** ( ☎ 512894; Rue des Poids Lourds, N'Djaména)

**Congo** ( ☎ 833404; Rue Général Bayardelle, Brazzaville)

**Equatorial Guinea** ( ☎ 2263; 19, Calle Rey Boncoro, Malabo)

**Ethiopia** ( ☎ 448116; Bole Rd, Addis Ababa)

**France** ( ☎ 01-47 43 98 33; Rue d'Auteuil, 75016 Paris)

**Gabon** ( ☎ 732910, 732800; Blvd Léon Mba, Libreville)

**Germany** ( ☎ 0228-356 038; Rheinallee 76, Bonn)

**Italy** ( ☎ 06-4429 1285, 3558 2234; Via Syracusa 4/6, Rome)

**Netherlands** ( ☎ 70-346 9715; www.cameroon -embassy.nl; Amalistraat 14, The Hague)

**Switzerland** ( ☎ 022-736 2022; 6 Rue Dunant, Geneva)

---

**IDENTIFY YOURSELF**

In Cameroon it is a legal requirement to always carry identification. If you're not happy with always keeping your passport on you – understandable if going out at night in Yaoundé or Douala – it's possible to get an officially certified copy. Photocopy the title and visa pages (with your entry stamp) of your passport, and go to the main police office in any large town during office hours and ask to be 'legalised'. The process is quick and easy, leaving you with a passport copy with enough official stamps to satisfy even the surliest of checkpoint police. The certification costs CFA1000.

**UK** ( ☎ 020-7727 0771; www.cameroon.embassy homepage.com; 84 Holland Park, London)
**USA** ( ☎ 202-265 8790; www.ambacam-usa.org; 2349 Massachusetts Ave NW, Washington, DC)

## Embassies & Consulates in Cameroon

The following embassies and consulates are in Yaoundé, except as noted. Australians and New Zealanders should contact the Canadian embassy in an emergency. Opening hours noted are for visa applications.

**Canada** (Map p182; ☎ 223 2311; Immeuble Stama-tiades, Ave de l'Indépendance, Centre Ville)
**Central African Republic** (Map p180; ☎ 220 5155; Rue 1863, Bastos; ☽ 8am-3pm Mon-Fri)
**Chad** Garoua ( ☎ 227 3128); Yaoundé (Map p180; ☎ 221 0624; Rue Joseph Mballa Eloumden, Bastos; ☽ 7.30am-noon & 1-3.30pm Mon-Fri)
**Congo** (Map p180; ☎ 221 2458; Rue 1815, Bastos; ☽ 8am-noon Mon-Fri)
**Democratic Republic of Congo** (Map p180; ☎ 220 5103; Blvd de l'URSS, Bastos; ☽ 9.30am-3.30pm Mon-Fri)
**Equatorial Guinea** Douala ( ☎ 342 2729; Rue Koloko; ☽ 9am-3pm Mon-Fri); Yaoundé (Map p180; ☎ 221 0804; Rue 1805, Bastos; ☽ 9am-3pm Mon-Fri)
**France** Douala ( ☎ 342 6250; Ave des Cocotiers, Bonanjo); Yaoundé (Map p180; ☎ 223 6399; Rue Joseph Atemengué, near Place de la Réunification)
**Gabon** (Map p180; ☎ 220 2966; Rue 1816, Bastos; ☽ 9.30am-3pm Mon-Fri)
**Germany** (Map p180; ☎ 221 0056; Ave de Gaulle, Centre Ville)
**Liberia** (Map p180; ☎ 221 1296; Blvd de l'URSS, Bastos)
**Nigeria** Buea ( ☎ 332 2528; Nigeria Consulate Rd; ☽ 8am-4pm Mon-Fri); Douala ( ☎ 343 2168; Blvd de la Liberté); Yaoundé (Map p180; ☎ 221 3509; Rue Joseph Mballa Eloumden, Bastos; ☽ 9.30am-3.30pm Mon-Fri). Visas not issued in Douala.
**UK** Douala ( ☎ 342 3612; Immeuble Standard Chartered, Blvd de la Liberté); Yaoundé (Map p180; ☎ 222 0796; Ave Churchill, Centre Ville)
**USA** Douala ( ☎ 342 0303; Immeuble Flatters, off Ave de Gaulle, Bonanjo); Yaoundé (Map p182; ☎ 223 0512; Rue de Nachtigal, Centre Ville)

## FESTIVALS & EVENTS

Tabaski (p819) is the biggest festival celebrated in Cameroon. If you're in the country at the time, head for Foumban, which holds the largest celebration, with a great procession led by the Bamoun sultan (p203). Every February, Cameroonian and international athletes gather for the Race of Hope to the summit of Mt Cameroon (p193), attracting crowds of spectators.

Finally, it's always worth checking if the national football team is playing when you're in Cameroon – there'll be impromptu festivals in bars across the country if they score the winning goal.

## HOLIDAYS

Public holidays include the following:
**New Year's Day** 1 January
**Youth Day** 11 February
**Easter** March/April
**Labour Day** 1 May
**National Day** 20 May
**Assumption Day** 15 August
**Christmas Day** 25 December

Islamic holidays are also observed throughout Cameroon (see p818).

## INTERNET ACCESS

Internet access can be found in any town of a reasonable size, usually with pretty good connections. Costs average CFA300 to CFA600 per hour, and most places can also burn photo CDs.

## INTERNET RESOURCES

**www.cameroon.fifa.com** All things to do with Cameroonian football, in French.
**www.cameroononline.org** A Cameroonian news portal website.
**www.ecofac.org** A Central African conservation organisation, heavily involved with projects in Cameroon.
**www.mcbcclimbe.org** A useful online tourism guide to the Limbe and Mt Cameroon area.

## MONEY

The unit of currency is the Central African CFA franc, which is pegged to the same exchange rate as the West African CFA (p171), but is not interchangeable. Bring your money in euros, as other currencies can be hard to change even in the cities, and attract poor exchange rates and high commissions. The main banks for changing money are Bicec, SGBC, Crédit Lyonnais and Standard Chartered Bank. Always stock up on CFA when you can, as foreign exchange can be difficult in small towns.

Deciding which form to bring your money in can be tricky in Cameroon. This is a country where cash is king. Although the major banks will frequently advertise the fact that they change travellers cheques, this isn't always the case in reality. You'll need to bring the original purchase receipts for the cheques, and be prepared to take around a 5% hit on commission. Even then, there's no guarantee the bank will accept the cheques – most cashiers tend to look with extreme distaste at anything other than euros cash. A new chain of private moneychangers, Express Exchange, is the traveller's saviour, with their readiness to change cheques and US dollars cash; there are branches in Yaoundé, Douala, Bamenda and Buea, with further plans for expansion.

Most towns now have at least one ATM, always tied to the Visa network. SGBC is usually the most reliable when using foreign cards. Banks won't generally offer cash advances on credit cards. Western Union have branches throughout Cameroon for international money transfers; the fee is only paid by the person sending the money.

There's no black market to speak of in Cameroon, but you can often find men with bundles of cash outside major hotels willing to change cash quickly. This can be convenient out of business hours, but the usual caveats on changing money on the street apply. Large denomination notes attract better rates.

## POST

Yaoundé and Douala have reliable poste restante services at their central post offices, with letters held for about two weeks (CFA200 per each letter collected). International post is fairly reliable for letters, but international couriers should be preferred for packages – there are branches in all large towns.

## TELEPHONE

International calls cost around CFA1000 per minute at IntelCam centres at post offices. Receiving an incoming call also attracts a small fee. Much cheaper are Internet phone calls, increasingly offered by Internet cafés – expect to pay around CFA250 per minute worldwide, although you often won't get much privacy. For calls within Cameroon, the quickest option is to use a streetside phone stand – usually a lady sitting at a table under a sun umbrella with a mobile phone. National calls are normally CFA150 per minute.

Mobile phones are everywhere in Cameroon, which has two GSM networks – MTN and Orange. A local sim card costs from CFA5000, depending on the amount of credit purchased.

## VISAS

All visitors to Cameroon require visas. Prices range from around US$60 for a one-month single-entry visa, to around US$110 for a three-month multiple-entry visa. Issuing time varies from 24 hours to a week. Applications made in West Africa are generally straightforward, applications at embassies in Europe and the USA often require a confirmed flight ticket, hotel reservation and proof of funds for the trip (a copy of a recent bank statement should suffice).

### Visa Extensions

You can obtain visa extensions at the **Ministry of Immigration** (Map p182; Ave Mdug-Fouda Ada) in Yaoundé, where one photo plus CFA15,000 is required.

### Visas for onward travel

For contact details of embassies and consulates in Cameroon, see opposite. Visas listed below are obtained in Yaoundé unless noted, and costs may vary according to nationality.

#### CENTRAL AFRICAN REPUBLIC (CAR)

A one-month single-entry visa costs CFA35,000, requires two photos, and is processed within 24 hours.

#### CHAD

A one-month single-entry visas costs CFA30,000, requires two photos and a passport photocopy, and is issued on the same day (for morning applications). Visas are sometimes also issued at the consulate in Garoua (see p207).

#### CONGO

One-month single-entry visas for Congo cost CFA70,000, require two photos, and are issued in 24 hours.

#### DEMOCRATIC REPUBLIC OF CONGO

While they don't share a border, Cameroon is a popular place for overlanders to get DRC visas. A one-month single-entry visa costs CFA45,000, requires three photos and a passport photocopy, and is issued on the same day.

CAMEROON

## EQUATORIAL GUINEA

One-month single-entry visas cost CFA37,000 for most nationalities, and require two photos and a passport photocopy. Applications are processed in 24 hours, and may also be made at the consulate in Douala.

## GABON

A one-month visa for Gabon costs CFA37,000, requires one photo and takes one day to issue.

## NIGERIA

A one-month single-entry visa costs CFA52,500 and takes 24 hours to process at the Yaoundé embassy, with two photos, a passport photocopy, proof of funds and letter of invitation from a Nigerian resident or business required (see p668). The consulate in Buea (p191) is a better place to apply, waiving the proof of funds, and issuing the same visa for CFA39,000 in a couple of hours. The Douala consulate only accepts applications from residents of Cameroon.

## WOMEN TRAVELLERS

Women can expect few problems in the north. In the south, especially in Francophone coastal areas, you may encounter hissing or comments, but rarely anything threatening. For more information, see p828. Tampons are available in Douala, Yaoundé and occasionally in larger towns.

# TRANSPORT IN CAMEROON

## GETTING THERE & AWAY
### Entering Cameroon

A valid yellow fever certificate is required for all those entering Cameroon, even if arriving by air from a country where the disease is not endemic.

## Air

Douala is Cameroon's air hub, with daily flights to Europe and connections to all neighbouring countries. Intercontinental carriers include Cameroon Airlines (the national airline), Air France, KLM and Swiss. See p188 for regional airline listings. There are also international airports at Yaoundé (with connections several times weekly to

---

> **DEPARTURE TAX**
>
> A departure tax of CFA10,000 is charged for all flights leaving Cameroon. Domestic flights incur a departure tax of CFA2500.

Europe), and Garoua (which currently has no intercontinental flights), but the airline offices following are all in Douala.

**Air France** (AF; ☎ 342 1555; Place du Gouvernement) Hub: Paris.
**Cameroon Airlines** (UY; ☎ 342 3222; Ave Charles de Gaulle) Hub: Douala.
**Kenya Airways** (KQ; ☎ 343 4725; off Rue Joss) Hub: Nairobi.
**Swiss International Airlines** (LX; ☎ 342 2929; Rue Joss) Hub: Zurich.
**Virgin Nigeria** (VK; ☎ 342 7628; Rue Joss) Hub: Lagos.

### AFRICA

Cameroon Airlines flights connect Douala and Yaoundé three or four times weekly with N'Djaména in Chad (there is also a weekly flight from Garoua), Lagos (Nigeria) and Abidjan (Côte d'Ivoire), and once or twice weekly with Cotonou (Benin), Ouagadougou (Burkina Faso), Dakar (Senegal), Bamako (Mali), Conakry (Guinea), Bangui (CAR), Nairobi (Kenya) and Johannesburg (South Africa).

Other regional connections to/from Douala include daily to Lagos on Virgin Nigeria or Bellview; five times weekly with Libreville on Air Gabon and weekly to Brazzaville (Congo) on Toumai Air. Kenya Airways flies twice weekly between Douala (weekly via Yaoundé) and Nairobi. Royal Air Maroc have a weekly service to Casablanca, and Ethiopian fly thrice weekly to Addis Ababa.

Some sample regional one-way fares are: Douala–Lagos on Virgin Nigeria (CFA172,000), Douala–Nairobi on Kenya Airways (CFA536,000) and Douala–Addis Ababa on Ethiopian (CFA537,000).

### EUROPE & NORTH AMERICA

Return fares between Cameroon and Europe are usually CFA550,000 or more. Cameroon Airlines and Air France have daily flights between Paris and Douala, and fly several times weekly between Paris and Yaoundé. It should be noted that in recent years, the French authorities have sometimes banned

Cameroon Airlines flights due to safety concerns. Swiss has flights twice weekly between Zürich and Douala, and goes weekly to and from Yaoundé. Another option is Royal Air Maroc, with flights connecting Douala with many European capitals via Casablanca. All connections to and from North America are via Europe.

## Land

With the exception of Nigeria, all of Cameroon's neighbours use the Central African CFA, so when crossing most of these borders you won't need to switch currencies.

### CENTRAL AFRICAN REPUBLIC

There are two main crossing points, each guaranteeing bumpy rides on poor roads – fun work in the rainy season. The standard route is via Garoua-Boulaï, which literally straddles the border (p213). It's the best route if you're travelling from north Cameroon. Semiregular buses and trucks go from Garoua-Boulaï to Bangui, taking two days with an overnight in Bouar.

An alternate, and equally rough, route is to go to Batouri further south (p214). Once in Batouri, there's usually one vehicle daily at dawn to Kenzou. At the border, you'll need to walk across and catch a vehicle on the other side to Berbérati.

### CHAD

Minibuses run daily from Maroua to Kousséri, from where *moto-taxis* will take you the 10-minute ride to the border at Nguelé. A bridge marks the border. Travellers and locals alike can get hit hard by corrupt officials here – Chadian immigration usually insist on an arrival or departure 'tax' of around CFA3000, while on the Cameroon side yellow-fever certificates are scrutinised for perceived infractions to attract a 'fine'. From Nguelé, it's a short hop by minibus to N'Djména (CFA300, 15 minutes).

A more obscure crossing is possible into southern Chad, via the towns of Bongor or Léré, and through a combination of taxis brousses and, in the case of Bongor, a pirogue (dugout canoe) across the Logone River – one for the adventurers.

### CONGO

The overland route to Congo is strictly for the hardcore – it's a long, rough journey through dense rainforest on rutted dirt tracks, best tackled in the dry season. The nearest town to the border on the Cameroonian side is Yokadouma (p215). From here, take any transport going to Moloundou, and on to the border crossing at Sokambo (near Ouesso) on the Ngoko River. Pirogues carry you across the river into Congo; there is also a ferry which can carry motorbikes and cars. Expect greedy officials to have their hands out here. There is onward transport to Pokola, where you must register with the Congolese police. From Pokola there is a barge (which can carry vehicles) to Brazzaville about three times a month, which takes around one week depending on the height of the river. A logging road from Pokola to Brazzaville is apparently under construction.

The Congo border has frequently been closed in recent years, so check in advance – it's a long trip back if no one will let you through.

### EQUATORIAL GUINEA & GABON

The main border crossings into Equatorial Guinea and Gabon are a few kilometres from each other, and are accessible from the Cameroonian town of Amban. In Ambam the road splits, the easterly route heading for Bitam and Libreville (Gabon) and the westerly route heading for Ebebiyin and Bata (Equatorial Guinea).

For Gabon, taxis brousses go from Amban to Aban Minkoo (CFA500, 45 minutes), where a bridge across the Ntem River leads into Gabon. Immigration is at the town of Bitam, a further 30km away (CFA500, 30 minutes). From Bitam, there are regular buses to Libreville. The road quality on this route is good, sealed all the way from Yaoundé to Libreville (barring a dirt stretch from Mitzic to Njolé, currently being upgraded).

For Equatorial Guinea, take a *taxi brousse* to the border at Kye Ossi (CFA1000, one hour). Getting stamped out of Cameroon is no problem, but officials on the other side may hit you for *'un cadeau'*. From Kye Ossi, it is a short taxi ride to Ebebiyin (CFA500, 10 minutes), where you can arrange onward transport to Bata (try to cross the border early to make the connection).

There is also a border crossing into Equatorial Guinea on the coast near Campo, but it is frequently closed and should not be relied on. If it is open, *moto-taxis* make the short hop to Campo Beach, from where pirogues quickly cross the Ntem River into Equatorial Guinea. Once across the river and stamped in, there's generally at least one pick-up daily to Bata.

### NIGERIA

There are two main border crossings into Nigeria, one each in the south and north. The busier is at Ekok, 60km west of Mamfe. There's frequent transport in the dry season between Mamfe and Ekok, alternatively pirogues ply the river between the two (see p196). Immigration procedures are pretty relaxed if your papers are in order. Once over the border, catch a shared taxi from the Nigerian border village of Mfum to Ikom (N50, 30 minutes), from where you can arrange transport to Calabar. On the Cameroonian side the road is in poor condition during the dry season and is quite atrocious once the rains hit.

In the north, it's straightforward to travel from Maroua to Maiduguri. Minibuses run daily from Maroua to the border at Banki. There are frequent police checkpoints on this road. Banki is a dusty village straddling the border; Cameroonian immigration is opposite the bus stand, and there are plenty of moneychangers. Border formalities are no nonsense. On the Nigerian side, a short N20 *moto-taxi* ride will take you to the bus stand, where you can catch a minibus or bush taxi to Maiduguri (N370 or N500 respectively, 2½ hours).

### Sea

#### EQUATORIAL GUINEA & GABON

There are no organised passenger services by boat to Equatorial Guinea or Gabon, although ad hoc transport can sometimes be arranged to Malabo from Limbe (p190). It might be worth checking at Douala port if there are any ships sailing to Libreville that will accept passengers.

#### NIGERIA

A twice-weekly ferry sails from Limbe to Calabar on Mondays and Thursdays, and in the opposite direction every Tuesday and Friday – see p190. There is an occasional service from Douala, but no timetable – ask at the Douala port. These services stay clear

of the disputed Bakassi Peninsula between the two countries. 'Stick boats' – fast speed boats – also run this route, often piloted by smugglers. Although cheaper than the ferry, they have poor safety records and what you save on the fare you'll shell out on bribes to Nigerian immigration and navy officials.

## GETTING AROUND
### Air

Cameroon Airlines flights connect Yaoundé and Douala daily, and go three times weekly to Garoua, Maroua N'Gaoundéré and Bertoua from both major cities. There are also occasional flights to Bafoussam. Of all these, the flights between the two main cities, and to Garoua are the most reliable – Cameroon Airlines timetables are a moveable feast, and schedules are often written on blackboards outside the offices for good reason. The harmattan can make the service to the north prone to cancellation. Always reconfirm your flight before attempting to travel. Sample one-way fares include Douala to N'Gaoundéré (CFA125,000) and Yaoundé to Maroua (CFA89,500).

### Bus

Agency *(agences de voyages)* buses run along all major and many minor routes in Cameroon. The major exception is across the Adamawa Plateau between Yaoundé and N'Gaoundéré, to cross which the train

---

**ROAD HAZARDS**

"Drivers! Your vehicle is a means of freedom, not of death!" warns a sign at one bus station in Cameroon – and with good reason. Road accidents are probably the biggest safety risk you'll meet while travelling in the country. Speeds are high, drivers are often tired from long hours at the wheel, and overtaking on blind corners is a badge of honour.

Avoid night travel, try not to get vehicles which are loaded so high on top that their balance is off, and try to stick with reputable agencies. It's also a good idea not to sit in the front seat next to the driver – not only is this the 'death seat' in the event of a crash, but you'll avoid the frightening temptation to keep glancing at the odometer to see what speed you're hurtling along at.

is the best option (p228). On the busier intercity routes, vehicles are often large and reasonably comfortable; otherwise expect minivans or 30-seater 'Coastal' buses. The main agencies operating in the south and west include Central Voyages, Guarantee Express (with a variety of spellings), Vatican Express and Mondial Express. In northern Cameroon, Touristique Express is reliable. Alliance Voyages battle it out on the poor eastern roads.

Each agency has its own office in the towns it serves, and arrivals and departures are from this office, rather than from the main motor park or *gare routière*. When you're ready to travel, the best thing to do is ask staff at your hotel which agency is best for your destination, and get a taxi to take you to that agency – all drivers know the agency offices. For main routes, such as Douala to Yaoundé, agency buses often adhere to a schedule, and leave approximately when they say they will. They also generally abide by the one-person-per-seat rule. It's a good idea to arrive at the agency office at least one hour prior to the anticipated departure to get a decent seat. On routes without many vehicles, try to book a seat the night before.

In addition to the agencies, there are nonagency vehicles – usually minivans or small Peugeots – that service the same routes, as well as off-the-beaten-track destinations that the agencies don't reach. These vehicles are also known as *clandos*, and usually charge about the same price as the agencies, but tend to be more overcrowded and leave when full. If you have a choice, it's better to go with an agency, as vehicles tend to be in marginally better condition and you'll probably have fewer hassles at police checkpoints.

On some shorter routes, there are also taxis brousses – basically the same as *clandos*, but a bit more 'official'. Taxis brousses and *clandos* use the main, and invariably chaotic, *gare routière* for departures/arrivals. In many towns, there will be several *gares routières*, so you'll need to find the one for the direction in which you're travelling – they're often named after their main destination. Whenever you get there, it's likely you'll have a wait, although transport is almost always best and quickest in the early morning.

If you're transiting through a city (from Limbe to Kribi via Douala for example), you'll need to catch local transport to get you from the agency office or *gare routière* of your incoming bus, to the agency office for your connecting bus. If you know your way around, shared taxis are cheapest, but generally, and especially if your luggage is unwieldy, it's better to charter a taxi. For more details, see below.

Major routes are sealed, including Douala–Yaoundé–Bafoussam–Bamenda, Douala–Limbe, Bafoussam–Foumban, and N'Gaoundéré–Kousséri. Otherwise, much of the country's road network is unpaved – secondary routes are quite often an endurance test during the rains.

## Car & Motorcycle

A small but significant number of people bring their own vehicle to Cameroon, usually as part of a larger trans-Africa trip. If you're prepared for the rigours of driving on African roads (see p845), then Cameroon shouldn't bring too many surprises. The main problem you'll encounter is likely to be the vast number of police checkpoints, many of whom will be curious to look inside a foreign vehicle. Don't be surprised if you're asked to show lots of paperwork. There are also frequent official toll points on many roads – usually costing CFA500. Look for the officials wearing orange uniforms. During the rainy season, some roads (notably on the Ring Road and in the south and east) operate rain gates to prevent large vehicles – which can include many 4WDs – passing.

## Taxi

Shared taxis are the main form of local transport for getting around within a town – even in a city like Yaoundé there are no local buses. Stand on the roadside in the direction you want to go and shout out your destination when a shared taxi passes. If the driver is going your way, he'll toot the horn. Once you get the hang of it, it's a great system. The standard fare is a bargain CFA150, more for far-flung destinations or after 10pm.

While the vast majority of shared-taxi rides are without incident, there have been a few cases of robberies in Douala and Yaoundé, and it pays to keep your wits about you. If you're female, avoid getting

CAMEROON

in a vehicle with only men as passengers, especially at night.

To charter a taxi for yourself (taxi course or depo), the base rate for town rides is CFA1000. If there aren't already other passengers in the taxi, make it clear to the driver whether you want a depo, or not. Note that at motor parks (gares routières), most taxis waiting for incoming buses are for hire only, so if you take them you'll pay charter prices.

Motorcycle taxis (moto-taxis or motos) are also a popular way of getting around town in much of Cameroon, particularly in the north. They charge CFA100 within town, more at night or for anything away from the central area. Just hail the driver and tell him your destination. In some areas (eg around Maroua), motos are also used for longer journeys when there is no vehicle transport. This is fun for the first few kilometres, but gets uncomfortable for the long haul. If you've got a rucksack, ask the driver to put it between his handlebars, rather than unbalancing yourself by keeping it on your back.

## Train

Cameroon's rail system (Camrail) operates three main lines: Yaoundé to N'Gaoundéré, Yaoundé to Douala, and Douala to Kumba. In practice, only the first is of interest to travellers, as it's the main way to get between the southern and northern halves of the country. The other routes are quicker by road.

Trains go daily in each direction, departing Yaoundé at 6pm, and N'Gaoundéré at 7pm. Arrivals are about 11am the next morning if all goes according to schedule, which it often doesn't. It's not unknown for the train to jump the rails, which can turn the overnight trip to three days. At least you'll get to see the scenery en route.

For seating, there's a choice of comfortable 1st class couchettes (sleeping compartments) for CFA25,000/28,000 per person in a four-/two-bed cabin; 1st-class airline-style seats (CFA17,000); and crowded 2nd-class benches (CFA10,000). The couchettes are the only recommendable option, in part because you'll be in an enclosed cabin. Seats in 1st and 2nd class are in open wagons, with no way to secure your bag. Even in couchettes, be alert for thieves.

The train has a restaurant car where you can buy surprisingly good meals (dinner CFA2500, breakfast CFA1000). If you're in 1st class, someone will come and take your order and deliver to your couchette. At every station stop, people will offer street food at the windows.

Couchettes can be reserved 24 hours in advance, but are paid for on the day of travel, which is useful as, if the train is delayed, you'll have some flexibility to change your plans. You'll need to purchase the ticket no later than about 9am on the morning of departure, as thereafter all unpurchased seats are put back up for sale. If you're going from north to south, Touristique Express in Maroua and Garoua also sell advance train tickets at their depots.

# Cape Verde

Most people only know Cape Verde through the haunting *mornos* (mournful songs) of Cesária Évora. To visit her homeland – a series of unlikely volcanic islands some 500km off the coast of Senegal – is to understand the strange, bittersweet amalgam of West African rhythms and mournful Portuguese melodies that shape her music.

It's not just open ocean that separates Cape Verde from the rest of West Africa. Cool currents, for example, keep temperatures moderate, and a stable political and economic system help support West Africa's highest standard of living. The population, who represent varying degrees of African and Portuguese heritage, will seem exuberantly warm if you fly in straight from, say, Britain, but refreshingly low-key if you arrive from Lagos or Dakar.

Yet life has never been easy here. For centuries, isolation and cyclical drought have resulted in famine. Generations of Cape Verdeans have been forced to emigrate, leaving those at home wracked by *sodade* – the deep longing that fills Cesária Évora's music. While hunger is no longer a threat, you need only glance at the terraced hillsides baking in the sun to understand that every bean, every grain of corn, is precious.

Though tiny in area, the islands contain a remarkable profusion of landscapes, from Maio's barren flats to the verdant valleys of Santo Antão. And Fogo, a single volcanic peak whose slopes are streaked with rivers of frozen lava. The beaches of Sal and Boa Vista increasingly attract package-tour crowds, but Cape Verde remains a destination for the connoisseur – the intrepid hiker, the die-hard windsurfer, the deep-sea angler, the *morno* devotee.

**CAPE VERDE**

## FAST FACTS

- **Area** 4035 sq km
- **Capital** Praia
- **Country code** ☎ 238
- **Famous for** Cesária Évora
- **Languages** Portuguese, Crioulo
- **Money** Cabo Verde escudo (CVE); US$1 = CVE91, €1 = CVE112.16
- **Population** 450,000
- **Visa** All non-Cabo Verdean citizens require a visa.

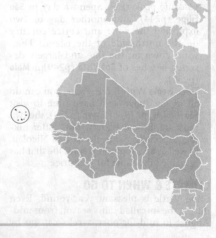

# HIGHLIGHTS

- **Mt Fogo** (p244) Huff to the top of this stunning, cinder-clad mountain, the country's only active volcano and, at 2829m, its highest peak.
- **Mardi Gras** (p241) Down quantities of *grogue*, the rumlike national drink, and dive into the colour and chaos in Mindelo.
- **Santo Antão** (p243) Hike over the pine-clad ridge of the island, then down into its spectacular canyons and verdant valleys.
- **Windsurfing** (p249) Head to the beaches of Boa Vista, and fill your sail with the same transatlantic winds that pushed Columbus to the New World.
- **Traditional music** (p234) Watch musicians wave loved ones goodbye with a *morno*, or welcome them back with a *coladeira*.

# ITINERARIES

- **One Week** Fly into **Sal** (p246), unwind for a few days on the beaches at **Santa Maria** (p247), which is a windsurfer's mecca and take a side trip to the salt mines of **Pedra da Lume** (p246). Next, head to **Mindelo** (p240), located on São Vicente, the country's cultural centre and prettiest town, and spend a day exploring the island's interior. From Mindelo, an hour-long ferry ride lands you in mountainous **Santo Antão** (p243), where stunning hikes cap off your trip.
- **Two Weeks** From Santo Antão, head over to **Fogo** (p244) to climb Mt Fogo or just simply to explore Chã das Caldeiras, the ancient crater out of which the 2829m volcanic peak rises. Spend a day in **São Filipe** (p244), and another day or two exploring the wine and coffee country on the north side of the island. Then wind down on the fine and largely deserted beaches of **Boa Vista** (p249) or **Maio** (p250).
- **Three Weeks** With three weeks, you can do all of the above, and have time to visit **São Nicolau** (p248) or **Brava** (p248), the two most traditional islands. Both offer hiking, especially the peaks of São Nicolau, as well as an insight into rural life that has remained the same for centuries.

# CLIMATE & WHEN TO GO

Cape Verde is pleasant year-round. Even during the so-called rainy season from mid-August to mid-October, weeks can go by

---

**HOW MUCH?**

- Taxi ride in Praia CVE200
- Berth on the overnight ferry from Sal to Mindelo CVE4200
- Espresso coffee CVE50
- Woven basket from São Vicente CVE500
- Fresh grilled tuna with rice and chips CVE650

**LONELY PLANET INDEX**

- 1L of petrol CVE80
- 1L of bottled water CVE80
- Bottle of beer CVE100
- Souvenir T-shirt CVE1000
- Plate of cachupa (bean and corn stew) CVE250

---

without a downpour. Thanks to cooling ocean currents and offshore winds, Cape Verde has the lowest temperatures of any country in West Africa, and also some of the most moderate, ranging from a minimum night-time average of 19°C in February to a maximum daytime average of 29°C from May to November.

Summer temperatures, especially in the northern islands, can be cooler than in Europe, though the southern islands, especially Fogo, can get hot and sticky. From December to March you may need a sweater in the evenings, especially at higher altitudes. Winter months are also marked by gusty winds, which blow in dust all the way from the Sahara.

See Climate Charts p813.

# HISTORY
## Slavery, Drought & Neglect

When Portuguese mariners discovered Cape Verde in 1456, the islands were uninhabited but fertile enough to attract the first group of settlers six years later. They founded Ribeira Grande (now Cidade Velha), the first European town in the tropics, on the island São Vicente. To work the land, settlers almost immediately began to import slaves from the West African coast. Plans by Genoese investors to create large sugar plantations never paid off, especially after the Caribbean proved so productive. However, the islands' remote yet strategic position made them a perfect clearinghouse and victualling station for the transatlantic slave trade. Within a century, the islands had grown wealthy enough to attract pirates, including a 1585 raid by England's Sir Francis Drake.

In 1747, changing weather patterns, aggravated by deforestation and overgrazing, resulted in Cape Verde's first recorded drought. In the 100 years from 1773, three droughts killed some 100,000 people – more than 40% of the population each time. It was only the beginning of a cycle that lasted well into the 20th century. At the same time, the island's

economic clout fell as Britain, France and the Netherlands challenged Portugal's control over the slave trade. As a result, Lisbon invested little in Cape Verde during the good times and offered almost no help during bad times. To escape hunger, many men left the islands, principally to work as hired hands on American whaling ships. Even today, Cape Verdean communities along the New England coast rival the population of Cape Verde itself, and foreign remittances account for as much as 20% of GNP.

Cape Verde's fortunes revived with the advent of the ocean liner at the end of the 19th century. It became an important stopover for coal, water and livestock, and Mindelo, with its deep, protected harbour,

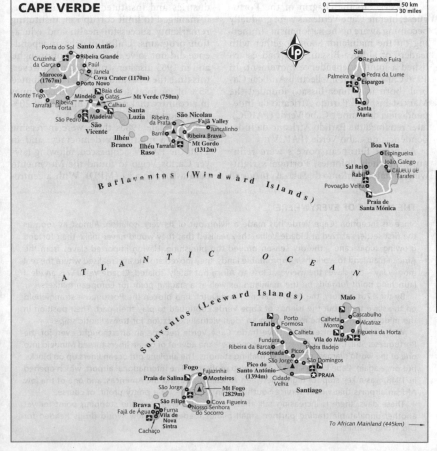

CAPE VERDE

0 ———— 50 km
0 ———— 30 miles

Ponta do Sol  **Santo Antão**
Cruzinha da Garça   Ribeira Grande
  Paúl
Marocos (1767m)   Janela
  Cova Crater (1170m)
  Porto Novo
Monte Trigo   Baía das Gatas   Mt Verde (750m)
Ribeira Torta   **Mindelo**   Calhau
Tarrafal   **Madeiral**   **Santa**
São Pedro   **São**   **Luzia**   Ribeira da Prata   **São Nicolau**
  **Vicente**   Fajã Valley
  **Ilhéu**   Barril   Juncalinho
  **Branco**   **Ilhéu Tarrafal**   Ribeira Brava
  **Raso**   Mt Gordo (1312m)

**Sal**
  Reguinho Fuira
Palmeira   Pedra da Lume
  Espargos
  **Santa Maria**

**Boa Vista**
  Espingueira
  João Galego
Sal Rei   Cabeço de Tarafes
Rabil
Povoação Velha
  **Praia de Santa Mónica**

**Barlaventos (Windward Islands)**

**ATLANTIC OCEAN**

**Sotaventos (Leeward Islands)**

**Maio**
  Porto Formosa   Cascabulho
**Tarrafal**   Calheta   Alcatraz
  Calheta   Morro
  Fundura   **Vila do Maio**   Figueira da Horta
Ribeira da Barca   Pedra Badejo
  **Assomada**   Picos
  São Jorge   São Domingos
**Fogo**   Pico do   **PRAIA**
  Fajãzinha   Santo António (1394m)
Praia de Salina   **Mosteiros**   Cidade
São Jorge   Velha   **Santiago**
  Mt Fogo (2829m)
São Filipe   Cova Figueira
**Brava**   Nossa Senhora do Socorro
Fajã de Água   Furna
  **Vila de Nova Sintra**
  Cachaço

To African Mainland (445km) →

**CAPE VERDE**

became the island's new commercial and cultural centre. When the airplane replaced the ocean liner, Cape Verde responded in kind, opening an international airport on Sal in 1948. Designed to service long, transatlantic flights, it remains a mainstay of the country's economy.

### Independence

Because much of Cape Verde's population was mixed race, they tended to fare better than fellow Africans in other Portuguese colonies. Beginning in the mid-19th century, a privileged few even received an education, many going on to help administrate mainland colonies. By independence, 25% of the population could read (compared with 5% in Guinea-Bissau).

However, to the chagrin of the Portuguese, literate Cape Verdeans were gradually becoming aware of the nationalism simmering on the mainland. Soon, together with leaders of Guinea-Bissau, they had established a joint independence movement. In 1956 Cape Verdean intellectual Amílcar Cabral (born in Guinea-Bissau) founded the Marxist-inspired Partido Africano da Independência da Guiné e Cabo Verde (PAIGC), later renamed the Partido Africano da Independência de Cabo Verde (PAICV).

As other European powers were relinquishing their colonies, Portugal's right-wing dictator, António de Salazar, propped up his regime with dreams of colonial greatness. From the early 1960s, one of Africa's longest wars of independence ensued. However, most of the fighting took place in Guinea-Bissau, and indeed many middle-class Cape Verdeans remained lukewarm toward independence.

Eventually, Portugal's war became an international scandal and lead to the nonviolent demise of its dictatorship in 1974, with Cape Verde finally gaining full independence a year later. Cape Verde and Guinea-Bissau seriously considered uniting the two countries, but a 1980 coup in Guinea-Bissau ended talks.

### Cape Verde Since Independence

Although the PAICV nationalised most industries and instituted a one-party state, it managed to limit corruption, instituting remarkably successful health and education programs. Unfortunately, independence did not solve the problem of drought, and in 1985 disaster struck again. However, this time the USA and Portugal contributed 85% of the food deficit; their aid continues in a country that produces only about 20% of its food supply.

By the late 1980s there were increasing calls for a multiparty democracy, and in 1990 the PAICV acquiesced, allowing lawyer Carlos Veigo to found the Movimento para a Democracia (MPD). With a centre-

---

**THE MIDDLE OF EVERYWHERE**

Since its inception, Cape Verde has made a living out of its very isolation. Almost as soon as the first settlers arrived at Cidade Velha, they realised that they would never make their fortune growing sugar cane – the dry season proved too punishing. Having imported slaves from the African mainland to work their unprofitable lands, they looked around and realised where the real money lay – the slaves themselves. Close to Africa but safely isolated, Cidade Velha was an ideal launching point for raids on the mainland, as well as a staging point for European markets.

By the 17th century, the English, French and Dutch had broken the Portuguese stranglehold on the slave trade, but the islands of Cape Verde continued to play their part. Their position in the middle of the Atlantic made them an ideal victualling station for transatlantic ships.

With the slow demise of the slave trade, Cape Verde became an afterthought even for the Portuguese. Still, the islands got another chance – the advent of ocean liners turned Mindelo into one of the world's largest coal and victualling stations. The airplane put ocean liners up on blocks, but once again, Cape Verde's isolation proved profitable. The international airport, which opened in 1948, was a key stop for flights between Africa, Europe and the Americas, and one of the few African airports that would service South African airlines – for a pretty profit, of course.

These days, there is increasing talk that the islands serve as a fine stopping point for yet another unpalatable trading partner: small planes loaded with New World drugs headed for Old World markets.

right policy of political and economic liberalisation, the MPD swept to power in the 1991 elections. Privatisation and foreign investment – especially in tourism – brought only slow results however, and in 2001, the PAICV reclaimed power. This time it promised to adhere to more a centrist policy of prudent fiscal and economic management – largely the result of International Monetary Fund (IMF) mandates.

## Cape Verde Today

With elections set for early 2006, the choice is very much between shades of grey, especially under the IMF's watchful eye. Tourism is the nation's main growth industry, and the country remains prosperous by West African standards. Famine is certainly no longer an imminent threat, yet improvements in the lives of the average Cape Verdean remain incremental, and for those without family abroad, conditions remain difficult.

## THE CULTURE
### The National Psyche

If you arrive from mainland Africa, the lack of hustle among Cape Verdeans will likely come as a welcome relief. While they are gregarious, you may catch whiff of a certain distance, even clannishness – partly a result of the islands' isolation (from the mainland as well as each other) and perhaps partly because of a history of Sicilian style vendettas among Portuguese landlords. However, patience and a well-timed smile can smooth most paths.

The European legacy is more marked here than in most parts of Portuguese-speaking Africa, yet Cape Verdeans will tell you their Crioulo culture is, at its core, African, citing especially their food and music. More recently, the huge expatriate community in the USA has also had its affect on attitudes, including a growing evangelical community.

One thing is certain: the people possess a great love of their native soil, despite, and perhaps in part because of, the hardships that it entails.

## Daily Life

Except for a small class of business owners and professionals who live like their Western counterparts, life in Cape Verde is not easy. Terraced farms require enormous effort and arid weather keeps yields small. While the infrastructure, from roads to water, is rapidly modernising, you regularly see women toting water from common wells. A high percentage of households consist of single mothers with children, a legacy of slavery and male-only emigration patterns that dates to the 18th century.

Cape Verdeans love their *grogue* and alcoholism is a major social problem. At the same time, the islands have eradicated other health problems that are a constant drain on their mainland neighbours, from malaria and cholera to high levels of infant mortality.

Based on the UN's quality-of-life index, Cape Verde comes out on top in West Africa. From 1975 to 2005, life expectancy leapt from 46 years to 70 years, far higher than the sub-Saharan African average. Cape Verde also boasts by far the highest GNP per capita (US$1400). Cape Verde's literacy rate of 76% is also the highest in West Africa. Virtually all children of primary school age attend school, though attendance at secondary schools is considerably less.

## Population

Cape Verde's population of 445,000 enjoys the longest life expectancy in West Africa, as well as one of the lowest growth rates. It's also the only country in West Africa with a population of primarily mixed European and African descent. About 40% of the population lives on Santiago, with about half again in or around Praia, the nation's capital. Mindelo, on the island of São Vicente, is the second-largest city, with a population of about 75,000. The rest of the population lives largely in small towns, most of which are clustered in the agriculturally productive valleys of São Antão, São Nicolau, Santiago and Brava. As tourism grows, so do the once-tiny populations of arid Sal, Boa Vista and Maio.

## RELIGION

The vast majority of Cape Verdeans are Roman Catholic, though the roots of the religion have never penetrated as deep in the culture as, for example, in Latin America. Evangelical Protestantism is making inroads, accounting for some 10% of the population. Traces of African animism remain in the beliefs of even devout Christians.

CAPE VERDE

## ARTS
### Craftwork
Traditional crafts include weaving, ceramics (mainly from Boa Vista, Maio, Santiago and Santo Antão), baskets (mainly from Santiago), mat making (from Brava, Fogo, Santiago and Santo Antão) and batik (mainly from São Vicente). Be aware that most craft shops sell objects from the African mainland rather than Cape Verde itself.

### Literature
While Cape Verde has the smallest population of any country in West Africa, its literary tradition is one of the richest. Prior to independence, a major theme in Cape Verdean writing was the longing for liberation. Poet, musician and national hero Eugénio Tavares (1867–1930) composed lyrical *mornos* in Crioulo rather than Portuguese. In 1936, a small clique of intellectuals founded a literary journal, *Claridade,* whose goal was to express a growing sense of Cape Verdean identity. Themes of contemporary literature, best expressed by poet Jorge Barbosa's *Arquipélago,* remain constant: *sodade* (longing and/or homesickness), mysteries of the sea and an attempt to come to terms with a history of oppression.

### Music
Much of Cape Verdean music evolved as a form of protest against slavery and other types of oppression. Today, two kinds of song dominate traditional Cape Verdean music: *mornos* and *coladeiras,* both built on the sounds of stringed instruments like the fiddle and guitar.

As the name suggests, *mornos* are mournful expressions of *sodade* – an unquenchable longing, often for home. With faster, more upbeat rhythms, *coladeiras,* in contrast, tend to be romantic love songs or else more active expressions of protest. Cesária Évora (p240) is hands down the most famous practitioner of both these forms. The ensemble group Simentera are the self-appointed guardians of traditional music, though they work to make it appealing to contemporary ears.

A newer style of music called *funaná* is built on fast-paced, Latin-influenced rhythms and underpinned by the accordion – great for dancing. Current practitioners include Ildo Lobo, Exitos de Oro and Ferro Gaita.

## ENVIRONMENT
### The Land
Cape Verde consists of 10 major islands (nine of them inhabited) and five islets, all of volcanic origin. Though none is more than about 50km from its closest neighbour, they represent a wide array of climates and landscapes. All are arid or semiarid, but the mountainous islands of Brava, Santiago, Fogo, Santo Antão and São Nicolau – all with peaks over 1000m – catch enough moisture to support grasslands, as well as fairly intensive agriculture, particularly in windward-facing valleys. Still, only 20% of the land is arable. Maio, Boa Vista and Sal are flatter and almost entirely arid, with long, sandy beaches and desertlike interiors.

### Wildlife
Cape Verde has less fauna than just about anywhere in Africa. Birdlife is a little richer (around 75 species), and includes a good number of endemics (38 species). The frigate bird and the extremely rare razo lark are much sought after by twitchers. The grey-headed kingfisher is more common though with its strident call.

Divers can see a good range of fish, including tropical species such as parrot fish and angelfish, groupers, barracudas, moray eels and, with luck, manta rays, sharks (including the nurse, tiger and lemon) and marine turtles. Five species of turtles visit the islands on their way across the Atlantic. Nesting takes place throughout the year, but in particular from May to October.

### Environmental Issues
The greatest threats to the environment remain cyclical drought and soil erosion, exacerbated by deforestation and overgrazing – mostly by goats. To combat these problems, the country has constructed more than 15,000 contour ditches and 2500km of dams, and since the 1970s has been implementing a major reforestation program.

## FOOD & DRINK
While Cape Verdean cuisine may include Portuguese niceties such as imported olives and Alentejo wines, it's built on a firm African base, with *milho* (corn) and *feijão* (beans) the ubiquitous staples. To these they add relative luxuries such as *arroz* (rice), *batatas fritas* (fried potatoes) and

*mandioca* (cassava). From the sea come excellent *atum* (tuna), *garoupa* (grouper), *serra* (sawfish) and, most famously, *lagosta* (lobster). Other protein sources include *ovos* (eggs) and, in increasing rarity, *cabrito* (goat), *frango* (chicken), *porco* (grilled pork) and *carne de vaca* (beef). Vegetables – often *cenoura* (carrots), *couve* (kale) and *abóbora* (squash) – come in *caldeirada* (meat or fish stews), or simply steamed.

Meals tend to be very simple wherever you go: a piece of grilled or fried meat or fish, accompanied by rice or *xerém* (cornmeal) and your choice of steamed vegetables or French fries. Practically nowhere will you pay less than CVE500, yet even the fanciest place will rarely charge more than CVE800 (except for beef and shellfish, which cost significantly more). The classic dish is the ubiquitous *cachupa*, which consists of beans and corn mixed with whatever scraps of fish or meat that might be around. In the evening, it's served as *cachupa fresca* (stew), while in the morning it's often sautéed and typically served with a fried egg and sausage (*cachupa guisada*). For sweet tooths, there are concoctions of *cóco* (coconut), *papaia* (papaya) and banana, as well as flanlike *pudim* of either *leite* (milk) or *queijo* (soft goat cheese).

For drinks, there's *grogue*, the local sugarcane spirit; *ponch* (rum, lemonade and honey); Ceris, a decent bottled local beer, and of course, Portuguese beers and wines.

# SANTIAGO

The largest member of the archipelago and the first to be settled, Santiago is a recapitulation of all the other islands, with sandy beaches, desertlike plains, verdant, windward valleys and a mountainous interior. It's also home to nearly half of the country's population, most of whom live in or near Praia, its capital.

## Getting There & Away
### AIR
Praia's airport is, together with Sal's, the main air hub for the islands. It has international flights to Dakar via both TACV and Air Sénégal, as well as to Amsterdam and Lisbon. There are daily flights to Boa Vista, two daily to Fogo, three weekly to Maio, one flight weekly to Santo Antão, daily flights to São Nicolau and up to 10 flights daily to Mindelo and Sal. No domestic flight lasts longer than 45 minutes. For more information see p253.

### BOAT
**Polar** ( ☎ 2-615223; Av Unidade Guiné-Cabo Verde) offers regular service to Fogo and Brava, Sal and Boa Vista. **STM** ( ☎ 2-321179; Av Unidade Guiné-Cabo Verde) heads twice weekly to Mindelo via São Nicolau. For more ferry information, see p253.

## Getting Around
### CAR
**Alucar** ( ☎ 2-614520; fax 2-614900), near the Hotel Marisol has reasonable cars at good prices (see p254).

### MINIBUS
Private *aluguer* (for hire) minibuses to most towns leave from Sucupira Market, just down the northwest side of Platô, Praia's town centre. Those headed to Tarrafal depart daily starting at around 9.30am and cost CVE350.

# PRAIA
pop 78,000
Cape Verde's capital and largest city, Praia, is a good place to finish your business quickly and then move on. Neither attractive nor particularly clean, it does have a few saving graces. The town's centre, on a large fortresslike plateau (hence the name Platô) overlooking the ocean, has a number of colonial buildings in various states of restoration. There are also two decent town beaches, around which most of the city's upscale restaurants and hotels are clustered.

## History
Praia became the Portuguese military and administrative headquarters in the 18th century after Cidade Velha, the island's first settlement, proved vulnerable to pirates. Praia's Platô, by contrast, was protected by steep cliffs on all sides, yet stood next to a serviceable port. The city has undergone considerable growth since independence, with an infrastructure that has not always kept pace. Today the city is the economic as well as the political centre and home to more than a quarter of the nation's population.

CAPE VERDE

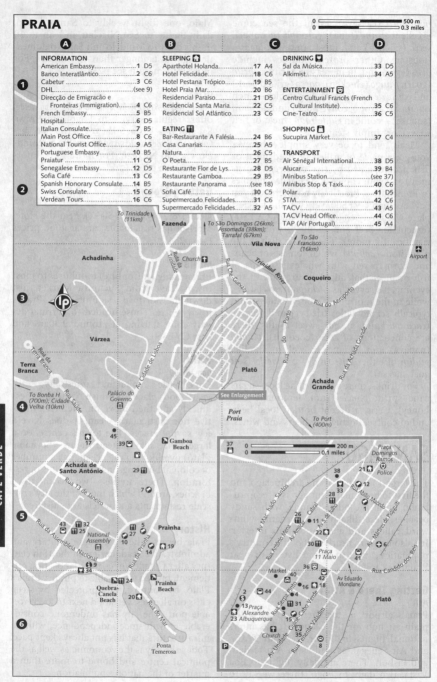

# PRAIA

**INFORMATION**
American Embassy...................1 D5
Banco Interatlântico.................2 C6
Cabetur ...................................3 C6
DHL.....................................(see 9)
Direcção de Emigracão e
  Fronteiras (Immigration).........4 C6
French Embassy.......................5 B5
Hospital...................................6 D5
Italian Consulate.....................7 B5
Main Post Office......................8 C6
National Tourist Office.............9 A5
Portuguese Embassy..............10 B5
Praiatur..................................11 C5
Senegalese Embassy..............12 C6
Sofia Café..............................13 C6
Spanish Honorary Consulate...14 B5
Swiss Consulate.....................15 C6
Verdean Tours........................16 C6

**SLEEPING**
Aparthotel Holanda................17 A4
Hotel Felicidade.....................18 C6
Hotel Pestana Trópico............19 B5
Hotel Praia Mar......................20 B6
Residencial Paraíso.................21 D5
Residencial Santa Maria..........22 C5
Residencial Sol Atlântico........23 C6

**EATING**
Bar-Restaurante A Falésia.......24 B6
Casa Canarias.........................25 A5
Natura....................................26 C5
O Poeta..................................27 B5
Restaurante Flor de Lys..........28 D5
Restaurante Gamboa..............29 B5
Restaurante Panorama .......(see 18)
Sofia Café..............................30 C5
Supermercado Felicidades.......31 C6
Supermercado Felicidades.......32 A5

**DRINKING**
5al da Música.........................33 D5
Alkimist..................................34 A5

**ENTERTAINMENT**
Centro Cultural Francês (French
  Cultural Institute).................35 C6
Cine-Teatro............................36 C5

**SHOPPING**
Sucupira Market......................37 C4

**TRANSPORT**
Air Sénégal International.........38 D5
Alucar....................................39 B4
Minibus Station..................(see 37)
Minibus Stop & Taxis.............40 C6
Polar......................................41 D5
STM.......................................42 C6
TACV......................................43 A5
TACV Head Office..................44 C6
TAP (Air Portugal)..................45 A4

## Orientation

Around Platô, the town tumbles onto the land below: to the north is the commercial district of Fazenda; to the east Achada Grande and the port; and to the southwest, the more affluent, residential area of Achada de Santo António, where the parliament building and some embassies are also found. Due south of Platô is the beachfront area known as Prainha, with pricier hotels and restaurants, as well as a number of embassies.

## Information

### BOOKSHOPS
**Sofia Café** (Praça Alexandre Albuquérque) Has a small but good Portuguese-language bookstore on the ground floor.

### EMERGENCY
**Fire** ( ☎ 131)
**Medical assistance** ( ☎ 130)
**Police** ( ☎ 132)

### INTERNET ACCESS
Internet cafés are springing up around the city, and cost CVE150 to CVE200 per hour.
**Sofia Cafés** (Praça 11 Maio & Praça Alexandre Albuquérque) The two most pleasant Internet cafés are these two in Platô.

### MEDICAL SERVICES
**Hospital** ( ☎ 2-612462; Av Mártires de Pidjiguiti) The city's main hospital is located in Platô, east of Praça 11 Maio.

### MONEY
There are ATMs throughout the city, especially around Praça Alexandre Albuquérque. You can change travellers cheques at the following banks, both in Platô:
**Banco Interatlântico** ( ☎ 2-618430; Av Amilcar Cabral)
**Caixa Económica do Cabo Verde** ( ☎ 2-603560; Av Amilcar Cabral)

### POST
The post office is situated three blocks east of the main *praça* (park or square).
**DHL** ( ☎ 2-623124; Av Oua) Across from the National Assembly.

### TOURIST INFORMATION
The **national tourist office** ( ☎ 2-624110; cvinvestment@cvtelecom.cv; Rua da Assembleia Nacional) may be able to answer some questions, though for practical information and reservations, your best bet is a travel agency.

**Cabetur** ( ☎ 26 1 55 51; Rua Serpa Pinto)
**Praiatur** ( ☎ 2 61 57 46; Av Amilcar Cabral)
**Verdean Tours** ( ☎ 2 60 82 80; Rua Serpa Pinto)

## Sleeping

Accommodation in Praia is expensive – expect to pay up to 50% more than similar digs in the rest of the country.

### BUDGET
**Aparthotel Holanda** ( ☎ 2-623973; fax 2-623710; Rua Saúde; s/d with bathroom CVE2700/3500; ✕ ) Though located in an unpleasant section of Achada de Santo António, this Dutch-run hotel has the most pleasant rooms in this price range. Breakfast extra.

**Residencial Paraíso** ( ☎ 2-613539; Rua Serpa Pinto; s/d with bathroom CVE2300/3500) At the leafy north end of Platô, this place is clean, pleasant, and surprisingly removed from the bustle.

**Residencial Sol Atlántico** ( ☎ 2-612872; Praça Alexandre Albuquérque; s/d without bathroom CVE1400/2200, with bathroom CVE2000/2700; ✕ ) Well located and as cheap as Praia gets, but rooms are cramped and not well maintained. No breakfast available.

### MIDRANGE
**Residencial Santa Maria** ( ☎ 2-614337; Rua Serpa Pinto; r CVE4200; ✕ ) Good value by Praia standards, this '60s-style place is clean and well maintained; some rooms have verandas and sea views.

**Hotel Felicidade** ( ☎ 2-600246; hotelfelicidade@hotmail.com; Av Unidade Guiné-Cabo Verde; r CVE6000) Rooms are small and expensive, but newly renovated – including new bathrooms. Some rooms have sea views.

### TOP END
**Hotel Praia Mar** ( ☎ 2-613777; praiamar@cvtelecom.cv; Rua do Mar; s/d CVE10,800/13,500; P ✕ 🖳 🛋 ) Set right on the water, this is the city's top address, with large, luxurious rooms, almost all with large balconies and ocean views.

**Hotel Pestana Trópico** ( ☎ 2-614200; www.pestana.com; Rua do Mar; s/d from CVE9800/12,100; P ✕ 🖳 🛋 ) Another luxury option just above Prainha Beach with all amenities, including a courtyard with a large pool and ocean views.

## Eating

The food scene in Praia is limited, and prices tend to be higher than the national norm of around CVE600 per dish. For a

**CAPE VERDE**

cheap quickie, try kiosks on Praça Alexandre Albuquérque, which sell toasted sandwiches and hamburgers for CVE100 to CVE200.

**Restaurante Gamboa** (Rua 19 de Maio; mains from CVE800; ☺ noon-3pm, 7-11pm) Excellent service (a rarity in Praia) and the freshest, best ingredients make this the city's top choice.

**Casa Canarias** (Achada de Santo António; mains from CVE750) Simple but delicious cuisine from the Canary Islands.

**Sofia Café** (Praça 11 Maio; mains from CVE750) The menu here is quite limited and rather expensive, but this café has pleasant outdoor seating, good espresso, and you can always get a heaping plate of *cachupa guisada*, the classic Cape Verdean dish of sautéed maize with eggs and sausage, for around CVE300.

**Restaurante Flor de Lys** (Av 5 de Julho; mains from CVE600) Good pastries, decent meals, attractive enough décor, and good value by Praia standards.

**O Poeta** (Rua da Assembleia Nacional; mains from CVE850) With renowned seafood and a cliffside terrace overlooking the sea, O Poeta is the place to see and be seen. Beware that service can be indifferent.

**Restaurante Panorama** (Rua da Assembleia Nacional; mains from CVE850) On the top floor of Hotel Felicidade, this place serves good if pricey Cape Verdean and international dishes. The terrace overlooking Praia Gamboa and the ocean makes a fine spot for an evening beer.

**Bar-Restaurante A Falésia** (mains CVE800-1200) Attractive, upmarket restaurant with a seaside terrace – another good spot for an evening beer.

**Natura** (Platô; ☺ Mon-Sat 9am-6pm) A pleasant café attached to a natural food store. No lunch or dinner, but *cachupa* (CVE250) is served most mornings.

For self-catering, go to Supermercado Felicidade in Achada de Santo António and Platô (Rua Serpa Pinto) – it's the best supermarket in town.

## Drinking

The terraces of Restaurante Panorama, O Poeta and Bar-Restaurante A Falésia are excellent places for an evening beer, as is the outdoor patio of Sofia Café. **Alkimist** (Rua da Prainha), just up from Quebra-Canela Beach, is a low-key but popular hangout.

---

### SÃO FRANCISCO BEACHES

The best beaches on the southern side of the island of Santiago are at São Francisco, 16km northeast of Praia. You reach them by bus from Sucupira Market (CVE200), though the return trip can involve long waits. You can also hitch (easiest on weekends) or take a taxi (CVE3000 return, with at least two hours on the beach). At writing, a large, British-run hotel is in the works, but at present you'll still need to bring your own refreshments.

---

## Entertainment
### LIVE MUSIC
**5al da Música** ( ☎ 2-617282; Av Amilcar Cabral) For the best local music, head here most nights for live music from around 10.30pm.

### CINEMAS
**Cine-Teatro** (Praça 11 de Maio) Usually shows Hollywood films (with Portuguese subtitles). Tickets cost CVE250/400 for normal/balcony seats.

**Centro Cultural Francês** ( ☎ 2-611196; Av Unidade Guiné-Cabo Verde) Hosts French-language film series as well as live performances. Check current schedules.

## Getting There & Away
For more information, see p235.

## Getting Around
### TO/FROM THE AIRPORT
A taxi from the airport to Platô (5km) costs around CVE400. There is no regular bus service.

### BUS
Small Transcor buses connect Platô with all sections of the city; short journeys cost from CVE70. Destinations are marked on the windshields.

### TAXI
Taxies are plentiful and inexpensive – you can go from Platô to Achado de Santo António, for example, for about CVE200.

## CIDADE VELHA
Dramatically situated on the sea, 15km from Praia, Cidade Velha (literally 'Old City') has won Unesco World Heritage sta-

tus as the first European settlement in the tropics. Founded in 1462, the city became wealthy as a clearinghouse and key victualling station for the transatlantic slave trade. Raids by pirates – including a particularly destructive visit from Sir Francis Drake in 1585 – eventually forced the Portuguese to move shop to Praia.

Remains from its heyday include the ruins of the **cathedral**, constructed in 1693, and the **pillory** on the old town square where enslaved captives were chained up and displayed. Perhaps more impressive is the town's position between the sea and the mouth of a canyon that, thanks to irrigation, remains green even in the driest months. For sweeping views, take the trail up to the dramatic, cliffside fort, **Fortaleza Real de São Filipe**.

Buses from Praia (CVE80, 20 minutes) leave from Sucupira Market. However, service is not regular, and the return trip can involve a long wait. Taxis charge about CVE3000 for a return trip, including an hour or two to visit the sites.

## ASSOMADA

Heading inland from Praia, the desertlike plains gradually give way to the mountainous interior, home to fertile valleys and the sharp, volcanic peaks of the Serra do Pico de Santo António. The town of Assomada, though not particularly beautiful, occupies a narrow plain with fine views onto Pico de Santo António (1394m), making a good base to hike through the surrounding mountains.

Picos, the town just south of Assomada, is home to the **Jardim Botanico Nacional** (botanical gardens). Situated about 2.3km off the main road, it is a good place to learn about the plant and bird life of the islands. Just north of town is a monstrously large silk cotton tree thought to be some 500 years old. Head for Boa Entrada, a short walk north from town, then turn right and head down into the valley.

**Asa Branca** ( ☎ 2-651195; r CVE1500) has clean, basic rooms and a downstairs restaurant that serves the usual fare (mains from CVE700). **Hotel Avenida** ( ☎ 2-653468; s/d CVE3000/3200) is a new hotel with comfortable rooms (some with mountain views) and a rooftop terrace with vistas onto Pico de Santo António. In Praia, minibuses for Assomada (CVE250) leave from Sucupira Market

starting around 9.30am. For buses heading back to Praia, wave down a minibus on the main highway. Note that return service is most frequent before 8.30am.

## TARRAFAL

With a small but fine white-sand beach and cooling breezes, Tarrafal is a favourite getaway from Praia, some 70km to the southeast. The town itself has a pleasant, hibiscus-lined main square, whose south side serves as an open market; you'll also find ATMs and a few Internet cafés here. The beach is short but lovely, and a cliff-side trail to the north makes for a fine stroll. In town, packs of boys are likely to hit you up for a few escudos; be ready with a litany of firm noes. For watersports, including boat and snorkel rental, head to the Italian-run **Hotel Sol Marina** ( ☎ 2-661219).

About 2km before the town centre is the former **prison**, where Portuguese authorities used to hold and interrogate political prisoners during the 1940s; business was especially brisk during the independence struggles in Guinea-Bissau and Cape Verde. It's now a **museum** (admission CVE100; ◔ 9am-6pm), and although not well maintained, it remains a haunting reminder of colonial abuses.

### Sleeping & Eating

**Baía Verde** ( ☎ 2-661128; fax 2-661414; r incl breakfast CVE3200) Simple but attractive bungalows, each with bathroom and small porch, are clustered under a grove of palms just back from the main beach. A hearty breakfast is included.

**Hotel Sol Marina** ( ☎ 2-661219; r CVE2200) Rooms are basic but large, clean and good value, particularly if you get one with a balcony and views onto the beach.

**Hotel Tarrafal** ( ☎ 2-661785; fax 2-661787; r CVE5000; ◔ ☻ ) Tarrafal's high-end option has a pleasant courtyard with bar and pool, plus comfortable rooms with TV, telephone and minibar; some have balconies and/or sea views.

Dining options are limited. **Hotel Baía Verde** (mains from CVE800) serves up generous quantities of simple but delicious local cuisine, as well as pleasant views onto the beach. However, prices are high. **Hotel Sol Marina** (mains from CVE450) serves up similar grub at significantly lower prices.

## Getting There & Away

Minibuses from Praia (CVE350; around two hours) depart from Sucupira Market; service is most frequent from about 10am to noon – otherwise waits can be long. From Tarrafal, minibuses leave from the western end of the central park. Again, after about 8am, you may be in for a long wait.

# SÃO VICENTE

Small, stark and mountainous, São Vicente is the unlikely home to Mindelo, Cape Verde's prettiest city. Looming over Mindelo is Monte Verde (750m), the island's highest peak and only touch of green. Its summit affords sweeping views over the entire island, from the lunar interior to the fine beaches of Baia das Gatas and Calhau, as well as across to the peaks of neighbouring island, Santo Antão.

## Getting There & Away
### AIR
**TACV** ( ☎ 2-321524) has six to 10 flights daily to and from Praia and two to three flights daily to Sal. Taxis to and from the airport cost CVE800.

### BOAT
Ferries connect Mindelo with most islands, including daily boats to Santo Antão. **STM** (Av 5 de Julho) also offers regular, twice-weekly boats to/from Praia via São Nicolau. For service to other islands, check at the ferry port, a short walk from downtown. See also p253.

## Getting Around
The most convenient way around the island is by taxi, including trips to Monte Verde (CVE1200 return) and Calhau (CVE 1500 each way). Alternatively, there are *aluguers*

to Baia das Gatas that leave from the roundabout at the eastern end of Av 12 Septembro, and to Calhau that leave from near the Praça Estrela. Both cost around CVE250. Note that service is irregular and can involve long waits.

# MINDELO
pop 50,000
Set around a moon-shaped port and ringed by barren mountains, Mindelo is Cape Verde's answer to the Riviera, complete with cobblestone streets, candy-coloured colonial buildings and yachts bobbing in a peaceful harbour. Safely around a bend is the country's deepest industrial port, which in the late 19th century was a key coaling station for British ships and remains the source of the city's relative prosperity.

Mindelo has long been the country's cultural centre, producing more than its share of poets and musicians, and it's still a fine place to hear *morno* while downing an espresso. Savvy locals, plus a steady flow of travellers (many sailing down from Europe on their way to the Caribbean), support a number of sophisticated bistros and watering holes.

## Information
### INTERNET ACCESS
**GlobalNet** (Rua de Tejo; per hr CVE150; ✆ 8am–midnight)

### MONEY
**Banco Comercial do Atlântico** (Rua de Libertad d'Africa) Has an ATM.
**Caixa Económica** (Av 5 de Julho) Has an ATM.

### POST & TELEPHONE
The phone and post offices are combined in a single site on Praça Amilcar Cabral.

---

### CESÁRIA ÉVORA

Undisputed queen of the *morno* (mournful songs) and Cape Verde's most famous citizen, Cesária Évora continues to wow the world with a voice that is at once densely textured and disarmingly direct. She began to gain an international audience in the mid-1990s, but vaulted to stardom in 1997 when, at the second annual all-African music awards, she ran away with three of the top awards, including top female vocalist. Suddenly people around the world were swaying to the rhythms of Cape Verde's music, even if they couldn't point it out on a map. She has left her native Mindelo in favour of Paris, but the 'bare-foot diva' refuses to put on airs, and has been known to appear onstage accompanied by a bottle of booze and a pack of ciggies.

## TOURIST INFORMATION

There is a small tourist kiosk near the harbour, just off Av Marginal.

## Sights & Activities

The colonial heart of the city is centred around Rua da Libertad d'Africa, which runs from the harbour to the **Palácio de Presidente**, a pink colonial confection that now serves as the island's governing council. Nearby is the recently restored **mercado municipal**, a great place to see the produce that Cape Verdeans manage to bring forth from seemingly barren lands. At the harbour is the **Centro Cultural do Mindelo** ( ☎ 2-325840; admission free), which houses changing exhibitions of local arts and culture, a café,

a craft shop and a good book and music store. Jutting out into the harbour is the fortresslike **Torre de Belem** – a kitschy, 1920s version of the 15th-century tower that guards Lisbon's port. Just past the tower is the city's photogenic **fish market**. Heading about 1km north via the coastal road, you reach **Prainha Laginha**, the very pleasant town beach. It may be ringed by industrial-looking silos, but its waters are clean and crystal clear.

## Festivals & Events

In February and March, Mindelo puts on Cape Verde's most extravagant **Mardi Gras** (see p242). Every August, the **Festival de Música** attracts musicians of all styles from

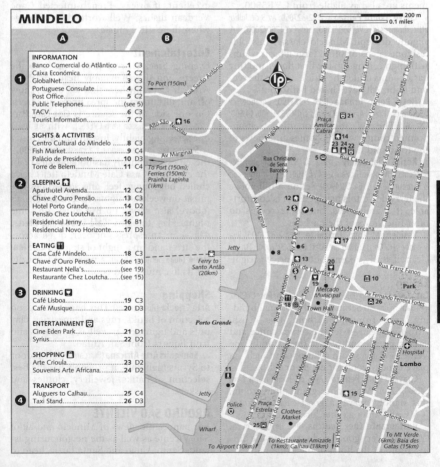

**MINDELO**

0 ——— 200 m
0 ——— 0.1 miles

| INFORMATION | |
| --- | --- |
| Banco Comercial do Atlântico | ....1 C3 |
| Caixa Económica | ....2 C2 |
| GlobalNet | ....3 C3 |
| Portuguese Consulate | ....4 C2 |
| Post Office | ....5 C2 |
| Public Telephones | (see 5) |
| TACV | ....6 C3 |
| Tourist Information | ....7 C2 |

| SIGHTS & ACTIVITIES | |
| --- | --- |
| Centro Cultural do Mindelo | ....8 C3 |
| Fish Market | ....9 C4 |
| Palácio de Presidente | ..10 D3 |
| Torre de Belem | ..11 C4 |

| SLEEPING | |
| --- | --- |
| Aparthotel Avenida | ..12 C3 |
| Chave d'Ouro Pensão | ..13 C3 |
| Hotel Porto Grande | ..14 D2 |
| Pensão Chez Loutcha | ..15 D4 |
| Residencial Jenny | ..16 B1 |
| Residencial Novo Horizonte | ..17 D3 |

| EATING | |
| --- | --- |
| Casa Café Mindelo | ..18 C3 |
| Chave d'Ouro Pensão | (see 13) |
| Restaurant Nella's | (see 19) |
| Restaurante Chez Loutcha | (see 15) |

| DRINKING | |
| --- | --- |
| Café Lisboa | ..19 C3 |
| Café Musique | ..20 D3 |

| ENTERTAINMENT | |
| --- | --- |
| Cine Eden Park | ..21 D1 |
| Syrius | ..22 D2 |

| SHOPPING | |
| --- | --- |
| Arte Crioula | ..23 D2 |
| Souvenirs Arte Africana | ..24 D2 |

| TRANSPORT | |
| --- | --- |
| Aluguers to Calhau | ..25 C4 |
| Taxi Stand | ..26 C3 |

CAPE VERDE

around the islands, offering a heady mixture of dancing, singing and grog.

## Sleeping

**Pensão Chez Loutcha** ( ☎ 2-321636; fax 2-321635; Rua de Coco; s/d CVE2400/3000; ❄ ) With a good restaurant and attractive, well-appointed rooms, this place makes a great base camp in Mindelo. On Sunday, the hotel arranges half-day excursions (including transport, buffet lunch and traditional music) to the beach at Calhau (18km from Mindelo) for around CVE1500 per person.

**Aparthotel Avenida** ( ☎ 2-323435; aparthtlavenida @cvtelecom.cv; Av 5 de Julho; s/d CVE3200/4300) Offers small but comfortable rooms with verandas and harbour views. Self-catering apartments are also available from CVE5500.

**Chave d'Ouro Pensão** ( ☎ 2-327050; Av 5 de Julho; attic rooms s/d CVE1000/1300, s/d CVE1700/2000) A slightly decrepit Mindelo classic, this old-fashioned pension offers large if basic rooms with high ceilings on the first floor, and tiny basic rooms under the attic eaves on the second floor. All have shared bathrooms.

**Hotel Porto Grande** ( ☎ 2-323190; pgrande@cv telecom.cv; Praça Amilcar Cabral; s/d CVE11,600/14,500; ❄ ⓖ ) The city's top option offers well-appointed rooms with balconies and views of the town and harbour.

**Residencial Jenny** ( ☎ 2 32 8969; hstaubyn@cv telecom.cv; Alto São Nicolau; s/d CVE3100/3700, with air-con & harbour views CVE4200/4900) Set on a hill above the ferry dock, this new pension is comfortable, if characterless, but some rooms do offer fine views of the harbour.

**Residencial Novo Horizonte** ( ☎ 2 32 3915; Rua Senador Vera Cruz; s/d incl breakfast CVE1600/2000) Basic clean, if stuffy, rooms but the price is right.

## Eating

**Casa Café Mindelo** (Rua Santo António; mains from CVE500; ◷ 8am-midnight) Set in a lovely colonial building across from the harbour, this stylish, Afro-European–style café serves coffee and sweets, *grogue* and *cerveja* (beer), and Cape Verdean classics with a European touch – a place equally good for eating or idling.

**Chave d'Ouro Pensão** (Av 5 de Julho; mains from CVE500) Occupying a once-grand dining room, this standby serves a good *cachupa fresca* (CVE500) among other local favourites.

**Restaurante Chez Loutcha** (Rua de Coco; mains CVE350-400) Very good food served in the dining room of the hotel of the same name.

---

### MINDELO'S MARDI GRAS

Mardi Gras (usually in February) is a great time to be in Cape Verde (though it's also when the islands are most crowded). While celebrations and parades are held all over the islands, those at Mindelo are the best. Preparations begin several months in advance and on Sundays you can see the various groups practising for the procession. The fanciful costumes, however, are worn only on the celebration days.

---

**Restaurant Nella's** (Rua Libertad d'Africa; mains from CVE750) Set upstairs in a charming colonial building, the restaurant serves up excellent, if pricey, French-infected Cape Verdean dishes. Well worth the surcharge when there's live music.

## Entertainment

Evening breezes bring people out into the streets, and they inevitably head for Praça Amilcar Cabral, where they sit, stroll, show off and flirt under the spreading acacia trees. On one side of the square is **Cine Eden Park** ( ☎ 2-325354; admission from CVE200), with at least one screening nightly. Just around the corner is **Syrius** (Rua Patrice Lumumba; admission from CVE300), the city's perennially fashionable disco. In the evenings, Casa Café Mindelo (left) has a chilled-out lounge feel, and sometimes live music on weekend nights. Restaurant Nella's (above) also serves up live music on some nights. Try the tiny **Café Lisboa** (Rua Libertad d'Africa) for an espresso or beer, or go across the street and up a flight of stairs to **Café Musique** (Rua Libertad d'Africa), a perennial favourite for its live music and bonhomie.

## Shopping

**Arte Crioula** (Rua Camões) This has quite a good selection of batiks, rugs and tapestries, clay pots and figurines, as well as postcards and fruit liquors from San Antaõ.

**Souvenirs Arte Africana** (Rua Camões) Next door to Syrius nightclub, it probably has the best selection of batiks, jewellery, clothes and baskets.

## AROUND SÃO VICENTE

For panoramic views of Mindelo and all of São Vicente as well as the neighbouring islands Santo Antão and Santa Luzia, head to

**Mt Verde** (750m). São Vicente's highest peak, it earns its name (literally 'green mountain') because of the cloud-fed lichen that cling to its rocky sides. There are no buses; a taxi from Mindelo is your best bet (around CVE1200 return).

The island's best beaches are at **Calhau**, a weekend getaway 18km southeast of Mindelo. Irregular *aluguers* leave from Praça Estrela (CVE200, ask around for exact stop). Or you can arrange a taxi (around CVE1200 each way); consider arranging a time with the same driver for your return.

# SANTO ANTÃO

Cape Verde's greenest island, and arguably its most spectacular, Santo Antão, encompasses a dizzying array of landscapes, from barren, volcanic flats to cedar- and pine-covered peaks to lush, tropical canyons. Many hills have been turned into gravity-defying farms that, thanks to varying altitudes and moisture levels, yield everything from apples to sugar cane.

Many visitors come on day trips from Mindelo, though it's perennially popular with hikers (see below) who spend a week or more on the well-developed network of trails. Just the spectacular 36km car ride from the ferry landing at Porto Novo over the island's central ridge to Ribeira Grande is worth the trip.

## Getting There & Away
**TACV** (☎ 2-211184) has weekly flights to/from Praia and weekly flights to São Vicente.

There are ferries daily between Mindelo and Santo Antão. While subject to change, the comfortable *Mar Novo* leaves Mindelo at 8am, returning 10.30am. Then it leaves Mindelo again at 3pm, returning 5pm. The trip costs CVE600 and lasts one hour. You must buy tickets 30 minutes before departure at the offices at the ferry docks on both islands. Note that services may be more limited on Wednesday and Sunday. Crossings are short, but can be rough during December and January.

## Getting Around
If you want to see a lot of the island in a single day, your best bet is to hire your own *aluguer*, though expect to pay at least CVE6000 for a full day. You can usually arrange one when you land at Porto Novo. Alternatively, you can join locals on an *aluguer* headed toward Ribeira Grande (CVE300, one hour). There are also *aluguers* that leave Ribeira Grande at around 3pm to return to Porto Novo in time for the afternoon boat.

---

### HIKING SANTO ANTÃO

Dramatic canyons, high central peaks and a dizzying variety of microclimates make Santo Antão a hiker's paradise. If possible, get hold of the *Glodstadt Wanderkarte* hiking map. You may also consider hiring a guide; the going rate is around CVE2000 per day. Hikes tend to begin or end on the trans-island road. From here you can hitch a ride on a passing *aluguer*, or arrange for a taxi to wait for you ahead of time (around CVE2500).

The classic hike is up the stunning **Ribeira Grande valley**, which begins several kilometres southeast of the town Ribeira Grande. Initially, the slope is gentle and takes you through cultivated fields and past traditional stone farmhouses. Soon enough it turns steep as you puff for an hour or more to reach the island's mountainous spine, which recompenses you with cooling breezes and spectacular views (if you aren't clouded in). Eventually, a dirt road will lead you to the transisland road, where you can hitch to Ribeira Grande or Porto Novo. The hike takes at least half a day.

Behind the town of Paúl looms the narrow but spectacular **Valé do Paúl.** The road passes through verdant stands of bananas and fields of sugar cane until you reach Passagem, a pretty village where much of Cape Verde's *grogue* (spirit made from sugar cane) is distilled. Eventually you reach Cova Crater (1170m), with its fascinating patchwork of farms. Nearby is the trans-island road.

Another popular hike is along the northeast coastal road from Ribeira Grande to Paúl and Janela. The coast along here is dramatic, with sheer cliffs and crashing sea. The leg between Paúl and Janela (6km) is especially impressive.

CAPE VERDE

## RIBEIRA GRANDE

Except for a small colonial heart, Ribeira Grande, the island's administrative centre, is not beautiful, though its position between steep cliffs and the roaring Atlantic is impressive. Located on a distinctly Portuguese street next to the main church, **Residencial 5 de Julho** ( ☎ 2-211345; d with/without bathroom CVE1500/1200) is basic but cheap. **Residencial Tropical** ( ☎ 2-21 1129; fax 2-212126; s/d CVE2600/3400; 🔀 ) has more comfortable digs with TVs and minibars, a good restaurant and an Internet café (CVE300 per hour).

## PAÚL

Located about 10km southeast of Ribeira Grande, idyllic Paúl is made up of two distinct components: a strip of pretty pastel houses along the ocean and the agricultural valley just behind it. At the top of the valley is **Cova crater**, an extinct volcanic crater whose floor is a patchwork of farms. Located on the water, **Residencial Vale do Paúl** ( ☎ 231319; s/d CVE800/1300) offers basic rooms with shared bathroom and hot meals (CVE700).

## PORTO NOVO

Santo Antão's port town has a few decent places to stay if you've missed a connection. Just east of the dock, **Residencial Restaurante Antilhas** ( ☎ 2-221193; s/d without bathroom CVE1000/1400, with bathroom CVE1500/1800) offers simple but clean, bright rooms that are good value. **Residencial Restaurante Pôr do Sol** ( ☎ 2-222179; fax 2-221166; s/d CVE3200/3600) has bright, spacious rooms. Both hotels have restaurants (mains from CVE700).

# FOGO

Essentially a single, giant volcano that sometimes rumbles to life (it last erupted in 1995), the island of Fogo (meaning 'fire') certainly deserves its name. Most people come to climb, or at least gawk at cinder-clad **Mt Fogo**, which at 2829m is the country's highest peak (see p246).

**São Filipe**, the attractive capital and home to both the ferry port and airport, has cobblestone streets, a well-preserved colonial centre, and sweeping views across to Ilha Brava. Consider the pretty drive around the east side of the island to the small town of **Mosteiros**, which takes you past terraced hill-sides that yield both wonderful produce as well as winningly game red wines, muscadets and, to sober up, mild arabica coffee.

### Getting There & Away

**TACV** ( ☎ 2-811228) has two daily flights to/from Praia, with connections to other islands. A taxi from the airport into São Filipe (2km) costs CVE200. Boats arrive at the tiny port 3km from town, and a taxi into town costs CVE300. There are usually two to three boats weekly to Praia and Brava. For schedules and tickets, visit **Agenamar** ( ☎ 2-811012) in São Filipe.

To travel to Mt Fogo, a taxi there and back will cost around CVE6000. For a car (CVE3500 to CVE4000 a day), try **Discount Auto Rental** ( ☎ 2-811480).

### Getting Around

Minibuses around the island are relatively scarce. Most are based around the central market in São Filipe. That means they head to São Filipe in the early morning, and then back home later in the day; plan accordingly. Fares depend on distance but shouldn't cost more than CVE350. For a car (CVE3500 to CVE4000 a day), try **Discount Auto Rental** ( ☎ 2-811480), though beware that both cars and service can be dodgy. A return taxi ride to Mt Fogo costs CVE6000. See p246 for more information on getting to Chã das Caldeiras.

## SÃO FILIPE

Set commandingly on cliffs above a long, black-sand beach, São Filipe is among Cape Verde's most pleasant towns, with colonial buildings, cobblestone streets and pretty squares and plazas – many with views across turbulent straits to Brava.

Strong currents make the town beach unsafe for swimming, but you can join the locals at the lovely **Praia da Salina**. Protected by strange, volcanic rock formations, the beach is located 17km to the north of town on the route to Mosteiros. On 1 May, the town celebrates **Nhô São Filipe**, its yearly city-wide festival. Its Mardi Gras celebration is also raucous.

Visitors interested in history and culture should consider visiting **Dja'r Fogo** ( ☎ 2-812879). Run by a local artist, it serves as an art gallery as well as a launching point for informal trips around the island.

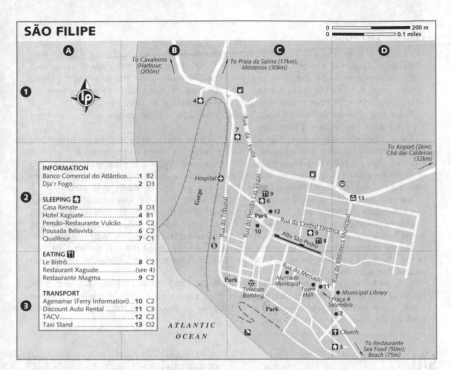

SÃO FILIPE

| | |
|---|---|
| 0 | 200 m |
| 0 | 0.1 miles |

To Cavaleiros (Harbour; (200m)

To Praia da Salina (17km); Mosteiros (30km)

To Airport (2km); Chã das Caldeiras (32km)

**INFORMATION**
Banco Comercial do Atlântico......**1** B2
Dja'r Fogo..............................**2** D3

**SLEEPING** 🏠
Casa Renate.............................**3** D3
Hotel Xaguate.........................**4** B1
Pensão-Restaurante Vulcão......**5** C2
Pousada Belavista....................**6** C2
Qualitour................................**7** C1

**EATING** 🍴
Le Bistrô.................................**8** C2
Restaurant Xaguate.............(see 4)
Restaurante Magma..................**9** C2

**TRANSPORT**
Agenamar (Ferry Information)...**10** C2
Discount Auto Rental .............**11** C3
TACV.......................................**12** C2
Taxi Stand ..............................**13** D2

Hospital

Rua da posta

Rua do Pensão Las Vegas

Rua do Tribunal

Gorge

Park

Alto São Pedro

Rua da Central Eléctrica

Praça 4 Setembro

Rua da Biblioteca Municipal

Rua do Mercado

Mercado Municipal

Telecom Building

Town Hall

Municipal Library

Park

ATLANTIC OCEAN

Church

To Restaurante Sea Food (50m); Beach (75m)

CAPE VERDE

## Sleeping

**Pousada Belavista** ( ☎ 2-811734; s/d CVE2000/3000; 🏠 ) An elegant, understated, impeccably run hotel built around an old colonial home. Rooms are well-furnished, bathrooms are new, and breakfasts are hearty. Air-conditioning is CVE500 extra.

**Casa Renate** ( ☎ 2-812518; renatefogo@gmx.de; r CVE3500) In a beautiful colonial building opposite the main church, this German-run inn offers large, spotless rooms, some with ocean views. Inquire at Le Bistrô if the hotel is locked. Reservations recommended.

**Qualitour** ( ☎ 2-811089; www.qualitour@cvtelecom .cv; r with/without bathroom CV3200/2500) Decent rooms, pleasant common areas, and friendly staff that also organises group fishing and hiking excursions.

**Pensão-Restaurante Vulcão** ( ☎ 2-811896; r without bathroom CVE1500) A decent cheapie, though current renovations could boost prices.

**Hotel Xaguate** ( ☎ 2-811222; hotelxaguate@yahoo .com; s/d CVE7100/8600; 🏠 🛏 ) On the cliffs just out of town, Hotel Xaguate is the most luxurious option, with large, well-appointed rooms, with verandas and sweeping ocean

views. There's also a pleasant cliffside pool (available to nonguests for CVE300).

## Eating & Drinking

São Filipe is one of the best (and most reasonable) places in Cape Verde to try seafood.

**Le Bistrô** (mains from CVE600) German owner Renate serves up simple but delicious fare based on local seafood and produce. The cleverly decorated terrace has sweeping views of the sea and Brava. Renate is also a great source of information about the islands. Highly recommended.

**Restaurante Magma** (mains from CVE450) Great, fresh, traditional cuisine in a pleasant dining room. Prices are reasonable, too.

**Restaurante Sea Food** (mains from CVE600) Most people come here for the pleasant, cliffside terrace seating; the food is only OK.

**Restaurant Xaguate** (mains from CVE750) Local and international dishes served in the pleasant, white-tablecloth dining room on the ground floor of the Hotel Xaguate.

## Getting There & Away

For more information, see opposite.

**CLIMBING MT FOGO**

The conical Pico do Fogo volcano, shrouded in black cinder, rises dramatically out of the floor of an ancient crater known as Chã das Caldeiras ('Chã'). Bound by a half-circle of precipitous cliffs, Chã was born when, sometime in the last 100,000 years, some 300 cu km of the island collapsed and slid into the sea to the east. The main cone has been inactive for more than 200 years, though there've been regular eruptions in Chã. The latest, in 1995, threatened the village of Pedra Brabo, whose famously friendly residents manage to grow grapes, coffee, beans and even apples in this forbidding landscape.

There's fascinating hiking along the crater floor, but most people come to climb the peak. While not technically difficult, it requires good physical condition, a hearty pair of boots, and a guide. There are plenty in Pedra Brabo, and the going rate is around CVE2000. The taxing ascent – a climb of 1000m up a 30- to 40-degree slope – takes three to four hours, with some challenging scrambles near the top, but the views are magnificent. Afterwards, you can run down in 45 minutes!

Start climbing early to avoid the noon heat. Leave São Filipe by 5am by taxi (90 minutes, one way/return CVE4000/6000). There is no guaranteed transportation back down, so it's best to arrange a round trip. The driver should be able to locate a guide. Otherwise, you will have to spend two nights in Chã. Come by aluguer (CVE250), which leave from São Filipe around 11am. Spend the afternoon exploring the crater, and then make the ascent the next morning. Recover in the afternoon and then head back to São Filipe the next morning by aluguer, which leave around 7am from Pedra Brabo.

In Pedra Brabo you can stay at **Pensão Pedra Brabo** ( ☎ 2-618940; r CVE2000/3000), with basic rooms around an arcaded, plant-filled courtyard. There's also a cooperative that offers very basic rooms (no electricity or running water) in local homes for around CVE1000. Ask at the tourist kiosk on the main road in Pedra Brabo.

# SAL

Though flat and desolate, Sal boasts more tourists than any other island. They fall into three categories: hardcore windsurfers, the package holiday crowd and those in transit to more interesting islands. The largest town is **Espargos**, located right next to the international airport, but most people stay near the fine beach in **Santa Maria**, 18km to the south.

The island gets its name from its salt mines, which formed a link in Portuguese trade with both Africa and Brazil and supported the islanders until the mid-20th century. Don't miss the surreal lunar **Pedra da Lume**, the crater of an ancient volcano where seawater is transformed into shimmering salt beds. It's located 2km west of Espargos; walk or take a taxi (CVE700 round trip). Rehydrate on the beachfront terrace of **Cá da Mosta** (pizza CVE500-800; ☼ 9am-6pm), an Italian-run pizzeria next to the old salt refinery.

## Getting There & Away
### AIR
**TACV** ( ☎ 2-411268) has six to 10 flights daily to/from Praia, two to three daily to/from São Vicente, and two to three flights weekly to Boa Vista.

The airport has left-luggage facilities (CVE100 per bag per 24 hours), an ATM, bureau de change (open 24 hours) and a tourist booth. Taxis to Espargos (2.3km) charge around CVE200 during the day and CVE300 at night. Taxis to Santa Maria run CVE700 and CVE1000 at night. Or, you can hail a minibus on the highway in front of the airport in either direction (CVE100).

### SEA
Interisland ferries call at Palmeira, the port about 4km northwest of Espargos. Schedules are irregular. Inquire at both **Anaú Sal** ( ☎ 2-411349), located near the taxi stand in Palmeira, and **Polar** ( ☎ 2-414245) also in Palmeira. For more details about interisland ferries, see p253. A taxi to the port from the airport or Espargos costs about CVE400

## Getting Around
Minibuses ply the road between Santa Maria and Espargos (CVE100, 25 minutes); all stop on the main road just in front of the airport. Taxis along the same route cost CVE700/1000 during the day/night .

## SANTA MARIA

Sitting at the southern tip of the island, Santa Maria is a dusty, largely graceless resort town that is growing too fast for its own good. Still, it boasts a long, lovely beach with clear, blue-green waters. The standouts here are windsurfing and kitesurfing, which is superb (from CVE20,000 weekly rental). There are also good opportunities for deep-sea fishing, surfcasting and scuba diving.

The default main square, which you hit when you first enter town, has a cinema, bank and the main minibus stop. There are several bureaux de change as well as ATMs that accept Visa and debit cards.

### Activities

**Funsystem** ( ☎ 49-89 20 23 21 80 in Germany; www.fun-system.com), on the beach in front of Hotel Morbeza, rents the latest equipment for surfing, windsurfing and kitesurfing (including F2/Naish boards). For more information and reservations (recommended in August, December and January), contact the head office in Germany. Lessons are also available.

**Nautic Fishing Club** ( ☎ /fax 2-421617) can arrange trawling (for wahoo, tuna and dorade) and deep-sea fishing (for shark and blue marlin). The travel agency at the **Hotel Morbeza** ( ☎ 2-421020) offers day trips to Boa Vista (from CVE13,400 per person) as well as sailing trips (half-day/full-day from CVE4620/7260 per person). You can also check into other excursions at **Barracuda** ( ☎ 2-422033) and **CVTS** ( ☎ 2-421220), both off the beach just west of the sagging pier.

There are a number of scuba schools, including the French-run Mares Dive Center (contact through the Hotel Morbeza); the Portuguese-run **Manta Diving** ( ☎ 2-421540), just beyond Hotel Belorizonte; the Italian-run **Blueway Diving Center** ( ☎ 2-421339) at Hotel Djadsal Holiday Club along the beachfront, which offers PADI courses; and the German-run **Stingray Dive Center** ( ☎ 2-421134) inside the Odjo d'Água Hotel complex.

### Sleeping

**Residencial Nhá Terra** ( ☎ 2-421109; nhaterra@hotmail.com; s/d from CVE3700/4700) Around the corner from the cinema, Nhá Terra offers good value, with large, spotless rooms, some with ocean views. The restaurant is very good too. Beds could be cushier, however.

**Residencial Alternativa** ( ☎ 2-421216; fax 2-421165; s with/without bathroom CVE3600/3100, d with/without bathroom 3600/2600) The cheapest place in town (though not a bargain) offers clean, decent – if gloomy – rooms three blocks from the cinema.

**Les Alizés** ( ☎ 2-421446; lesalizes@cvtelecom.cv; s/d CVE4400/6300) Opposite Restaurante Piscador, this French-owned guesthouse is simple but classy. Rooms have verandas, and breakfast is served on a rooftop terrace with ocean views.

**Hotel Morabeza** ( ☎ 2-421020; www.hotelmorabeza.com; s/d from CVE9910/13,200) Right on the beach just west of the pier, this classy, stone-faced resort hotel has spacious rooms arranged around a leafy common area.

**Aqui Sal** ( ☎ 2-421325; www.aquisal.com) For longer stays, the friendly staff here rents studio apartments by the month for €250 to €300.

### Eating

**Restaurante Nhá Terra** (mains CVE600-1100; ☺ 8am-10pm) Classic Cape Verde dishes made with the freshest ingredients and served in the hotel's pleasant dining room.

**Restaurante Côte Jarain** (mains CVE1000-2500; ☺ 7pm-10pm Mon-Sat) The chef-owner serves up French-inflected Creole dishes in a small, palm-filled courtyard just down from the cinema.

**Tam Tam** ( ☺ 8am-midnight) Friendly, Irish-owned pub-restaurant serves egg breakfasts (around CVE2500) and a fine *cachupa* (CVE300), as well as beer and cocktails.

**Mateus** (mains CVE600-1000) Live music and terrace seating on a pleasant square make up for the just OK food.

**Restaurante Piscador** (mains CVE750-1250) Two blocks down from Nhá Terra, this well-established fish restaurant also has a small grocery store for self-catering.

### Entertainment

The town's main disco **Pirata Pizzaria Disco Pub** ( ☺ until 4am Mon-Sat) is located just outside of town on the road to the airport. Chill Out Bar, next to Residencial Nhá Terra, attracts windsurfers after the sun goes down.

### Getting There & Around

Taxis between Santa Maria and the airport cost CVE700 during the day and CVE1000 at night. Plenty of minibuses ply the road between Espargos and Santa Maria (CVE100), and all stop on the main road in front of the airport.

## ESPARGOS

Located near both the airport and the ferry dock, Espargos – the island's capital – is a small, dusty town that proves more convenient than attractive. Still, it feels more like a real Cape Verdean town than touristy Santa Maria, and in the evenings Praça 19 de Septembro grows quite lively.

### Sleeping & Eating

Both food and accommodations are cheaper here than in Santa Maria.

**Pensão Restaurante Violão** ( ☎ 2-411720; Rua Abel Djassi; s/d CVE3000/3500) Large clean rooms, a rooftop terrace, and a bar-restaurant that serves up good food (mains from CVE700) and great traditional music make this the top choice in town. It's located about five blocks north of Praça 19 de Septembro.

**Casa da Angela** ( ☎ 2-411327; casaangela20@hotmail.com; s/d CVE1900/2800) Clean, basic rooms – some with fans. Located several blocks north of Praça 19 de Septembro.

**Residencial Central** ( ☎ 2-411366; ccentral@mail.cv telecom.cv; s/d incl breakfast CVE2000/3000) Basic but pleasant rooms, some with verandas, around a courtyard just off Praça 19 de Septembro.

**Esplanada Bom Dia** ( ☎ mains from CVE460; ☯ 7am-midnight) Café fare as well as simple meals served on an attractive terrace a few blocks behind the town hall and taxi stand.

For groceries, try Supermercado Central, located just across from Praça 19 de Septembro.

### Getting There & Away

Minibuses ply the road every 10 to 15 minutes between Espargos and Santa Maria (CVE100, 25 minutes); all stop at the airport. The main minibus and taxi stop is in front of the town hall at the southern entrance of the town.

# OTHER ISLANDS

## BRAVA

**pop 5000**

Except for the occasional car that braves the cobblestone, cross-island roads, Brava seems to reside firmly in the 19th century. Its terraced hillsides are farmed with the aid of mules, and even new construction imitates the simple, Portuguese-style farmhouses that still dominate the landscape. First settled in the 17th century by Portuguese fleeing an eruption on nearby Fogo, the island became a key source of whalers for American ships. To this day, more natives live in the US than on the island itself.

**Vila de Nova Sintra** ('Vila'), the tiny capital, sits on a little plateau regularly engulfed in clouds; it's reputed to have some of the finest *morno* in Cape Verde. From Vila, there are some short but lovely hikes: eastward down to Vinagre via Santa Barbara and westward to Cova Joana and then on to Nosso Senhora do Monte or Lima Doce, both nearby. **Fajã d'Agua** ('Fajã') is set dramatically between a rocky cove and impressive cliffs. Beyond Fajã lies Porteto, with its small but pleasant black-sand beach.

In Vila, there's a Banco Comercial do Atlântico with ATM. *Aluguers* ply the road between Fajã, Vila and the ferry port at Furna (CVE250). You can get one to yourself for CVE800 between Vila and both Furna and Fajã. Plan ahead if you have a morning boat, as transport can be scarce.

### Sleeping & Eating

With one exception, accommodations in Brava are basic.

In Fajã, **Pensão Sol na Baia** ( ☎ 2-852070; pensao_sol_na_baia@hotmail.com; r from CVE3500), run by a French-Cape Verdean couple, offers tastefully appointed rooms, excellent French-inspired meals (three courses for CVE2000), and delightful gardens. Nearby, **Manuel Burgo Ocean Front Motel** ( ☎ /fax 2-851321; s/d CVE1500/2000) has basic rooms, though they open onto the ocean.

In Vila de Nova Sintra, **Pensão Restaurante Paul Sena** ( ☎ 2-851312; r per person CVE1200) offers small, basic rooms that are clean, if musty-smelling.

### Getting There & Away

TACV is not currently flying to Brava. Boats from Praia normally arrive twice a week in Brava, generally stopping in Fogo on the way. For ferry routes and details, see p253.

## SÃO NICOLAU

**pop 5000**

Formed by three scenic ridges that meet at **Mt Gordo** – at 1312m the island's highest peak – São Nicolau is a hiker's delight. While the southern slopes are dry and largely barren, northern slopes are remarkably green – in years when rains cooperate, at least; drought is a perpetual threat that deeply marks the island's culture.

Near the mouth of the fertile **Fajã valley** lies **Ribeira Brava**, the island's capital. Long Cape Verde's religious centre, it was built inland to protect its treasures from pirates. Its narrow, hillside streets and tiled roofs are still reminiscent of 17th-century Portugal. Ribeira Brava's **Carnival** celebration is second only to Mindelo's.

You can go to Ribeira Brava by minibus (CVE200) or taxi (around CVE1200) from the unbeautiful town of Tarrafal, the island's port. The 26km drive is spectacular. A great option is to get off halfway at Cachaço and hike down through the Fajã valley to Ribeira Brava. Any driver will be able to show you the way. The trail up to Mt Gordo also goes through Cachaço, passing through a protected pine forest before reaching the summit.

### Sleeping & Eating

In Tarrafal, options include **Residencial Alice** ( ☎ /fax 2-361187; s/d CVE1200/1400), just down the beach from the port, and **Residencial Natur** ( ☎ /fax 2-361178; r CVE1400), further down the beach and behind the soccer field. The former serves meals (around CVE600). Both are very basic.

In Ribeira Brava, the spotless **Pensão Jardim** ( ☎ 2-351117; s/d CVE2000/3000), located on a hill overlooking town, has quaint, comfortable rooms (some with views), plus a very good rooftop restaurant (meals CVE800, order ahead). **Pensão Jumbo** ( ☎ 2-351315; d CVE1600), just across the riverbed, is good value, with clean, decent rooms. The new **Pensão Santo António** ( ☎ 2-352200; fax 2-352199; r CVE3800), on the town's main square, has simple but large, comfortable and tastefully appointed rooms, some with views. **Pensão da Cruz** ( ☎ 2-351282; s/d without bathroom CVE1000/1200), opposite the post office, has clean if tattered rooms. Restaurant Bela Sombra Dalila, near the main square, serves good tuna steaks.

### Getting There & Away

**TACV** ( ☎ 351161, 351162) has daily flights to and from Praia and weekly flights to Sal. The airport is 5km southeast of Ribeira Brava

(CVE500 by taxi). While other ferries sometimes bypass the island, the *Tarrafal* reliably stops at least twice a week on its way between Praia and São Vicente. See p253 for more details.

## BOA VISTA

pop 5000

With long, sand beaches, Italian-run resorts, and breezes favourable to windsurfing, Boa Vista is another Sal in the making. And like its neighbour to the north, the island is largely flat and arid, with the exception of three mountains to the east and a hint of vegetation along the northern coast. Much of the interior undulates with shifting sand dunes.

Sal Rei, the capital and largest town, is home to most of Boa Vista's tiny population – and virtually all its accommodations. The town beach is attractive, but the longest and most beautiful, **Praia da Santa Monica**, is located about 25km away on the island's south coast. Closer in (about an hour's hike from Sal Rei) is the pretty Praia de Chaves.

There's plenty to do for water enthusiasts: snorkelling, fishing, diving, whale- and turtle-watching (mostly humpbacks) and of course windsurfing and kitesurfing. **Hotel Dunas** ( ☎ 2-511225) and **Boa Vista Wind Club** ( ☎ 2-511392; www.boavistawindclub.com) both rent boards for around CVE25,000 per week. For diving as well as windsurfing, contact **Boa Vista Watersport System** ( ☎ 2-511392; www .bwscv.com) on the main square in Sal Rei, or **Submarine Dive Center** ( ☎ 9927866 mobile; alitros@hotmail.com).

*Aluguers* (from CVE100) ply the island's roads, but they're scarce. Taxis are readily available but costly – an excursion from Sal Rei to Praia da Santa Monica runs around CVE5000 to CVE6000. There are several car rentals – expect to pay CVE5000 to CVE6000 per day. Hotel Dunas rents bikes for around CVE1500 per day – a good option on this largely flat island.

### Sleeping & Eating

Accommodations are a relatively good value in Sal Rei. Restaurants are mostly limited to hotel dining rooms, though in town, the Riba d'Olte serves up very good pasta.

**Residencia A Paz** ( ☎ 2-511078; www.a-paz.com; r CVE4500) While not inexpensive, a friendly Italian owner, tastefully appointed rooms and a lovely rooftop terrace add up to a good value.

**Bed & Breakfast Criola** ( ☎ 2-511373; r CVE3000) This coral-pink cottage right on the water offers small but pleasant rooms. There's also a café with good espresso.

**Residencial Bom Sossego** ( ☎ 2-511155; s/d CVE1300/2000) Basic but well-maintained rooms make this place a good value.

**Migrante Guesthouse** ( ☎ 2-511143; r CVE7500) With comfortable, brightly painted rooms, this upscale, Italian-run inn is more reminiscent of Marrakesh than Cape Verde.

**Hotel Dunas** ( ☎ 2-511225; fax 2-511384; r CVE9000) Sunny, well-appointed rooms, many with fine views onto the water.

**Cá Nícola** ( ☎ 2-511793; r CVE4000) Simple but tasteful rooms with small kitchens; just 50m from the beach.

### Getting There & Away

**TACV** ( ☎ 2-511186) has daily flights to/from Praia (one hour) and five to six flights weekly to Sal (25 minutes). Ferries sail to Boa Vista from Praia and Sal. For ferry details and routes, see p253.

## MAIO

pop 5900

Maio's interior may be flat and forbidding, but travellers and real estate speculators alike are slowly discovering the western coastline, with its turquoise waters and long, beautiful and largely deserted beaches. Besides a strand to yourself, you can expect one of the warmest welcomes in Cape Verde – the island is reputedly the nation's friendliest.

Maio was once an important salt-collecting centre and, though hard to believe today, wealthy enough to attract a wave of high-seas pirates. The British controlled the salt trade, which is why the main city and port, Vila do Maio, is commonly called Porto Inglés. There's a good beach, **Bitche Rotche**, just outside town. There are no buses, but **Maio Car** ( ☎ 2-551700) rents cars for around CVE4000 per day.

**Hotel Bom Sossego** ( ☎ 2-551365; fax 2-551327; s/d CVE2900/3800) is pricey, but with clean and well-maintained if simple rooms. There's also a decent restaurant. Or, **Ilha do Maio Imobiliária** ( ☎ 2-551312; r CVE3300-4200) offers small apartments, with the office a short walk from the airport.

**TACV** ( ☎ 2-551256) has three flights weekly to/from Praia (15 minutes). There's a ferry service that runs at least once a week between Praia and Vila do Maio.

# CAPE VERDE DIRECTORY

## ACCOMMODATION

By West African standards, accommodation is expensive in Cape Verde, especially on Sal and the city of Praia, where prices are some 50% more than the rest of the country.

Most places, you can expect to pay under US$16 (CVE1500) for a basic but decent double with shared bathroom. For around US$30 to US$40 (CVE2800 to CVE3800), you can expect a modest but quite comfortable midrange double with hot water and air conditioning. At the top end, there are mostly just resort hotels that cater to package tours, especially on Sal and Santiago. For all the amenities, from pool to gym to business centre, they charge US$75(CVE8000) and up. There are no camp sites, but camping on remote beaches is possible and generally safe.

## ACTIVITIES

For active types, the main draws are windsurfing and kitesurfing, scuba diving and deep-sea fishing on Sal (p246) and Boa Vista (p249), plus trekking in the mountains of São Nicolau (p248), Brava (p248), Fogo (p246) and especially Santo Antão (p243).

Prices for diving are around CVE3500 for one dive (cheaper for a series) plus CVE1000 extra per dive for full equipment rental. Courses cost from CVE35,000 to CVE65,000 (PADI Open Water Diver). Diving in Cape Verde is well known for

---

**PRACTICALITIES**

- *A Semana* and *Expresso das Ilhas* are the weekly newspapers.

- Radio and TV is mostly limited to Portugal's, with Portuguese and Brazilian shows as well as Cape Verde news.

- Voltage is 220V with European-style twin-pronged plugs.

- Cape Verde uses the metric system.

its diversity of species. Dolphins, whales, sharks and rays are all occasionally seen. Because of currents, not all sites are suitable for beginners or inexperienced divers. Note that there is currently no decompression chamber in Cape Verde. The best months are from March to November.

An F2 windsurfer costs from around CVE20,000 per week. If you come in the high season, book boards in advance. Six hours of kitesurfing tuition costs around CVE15,000. The best months are between mid-November and mid-May (and particularly January to March when winds are strong and constant). Because the winds can be strong and blow off-shore, conditions are not ideal for beginners.

April to November (especially June to October) is good for fishing (rays, barracudas, marlins, wahoos, sharks), and trekking and cycling are good year-round.

## BOOKS

Publications in English about Cape Verde are scarce but include: *Historical Dictionary of the Republic of Cape Verde* by Richard Lobban, *Cape Verde: Politics, Economics and Society* by Colm Foy, *Atlantic Islands* by Anne Hammick and Nicholas Heath, and *The Fortunate Isles* by Basil Davidson. If you read Portuguese or Italian, or just want glossy photos for souvenirs, look out for *Cabo Verde Cruzamento do Atlântico Sul* by Federico Cerrone. If you're keen on birds, the *Aves de Cabo Verde*, a fairly basic BirdLife International brochure available at some tourism kiosks, contains around 12 pages of illustrations.

## BUSINESS HOURS

Business hours are generally 8am to noon and 3pm to 6pm, Monday to Friday, and 8am to noon or 1pm Saturday. Banking hours are from 8am to 3pm Monday to Friday. Note that on posted hours, time is usually measured with the 24-hour system, and days are often numbered according to the Portuguese system from 1° to 7° (ie 1° is Sunday; 7° Saturday).

## DANGERS & ANNOYANCES

While Praia (on the island of Santiago) is among the safest cities in West Africa, violent crime is not unknown here or in Mindelo. Follow the same common sense

rules you would in any city. The rest of the country is very safe, though petty crime like pick-pocketing is always a possibility.

## EMBASSIES & CONSULATES
### Cape Verdean Embassies & Consulates

In West Africa, Cape Verde has an embassy in Senegal. For more details, see p739. Cape Verde has no diplomatic representation in the UK. Elsewhere, Cape Verdean embassies include the following:

**Belgium** ( ☎ 2-646 9025; fax 2-646 3385; Rue Antonie Laborre 30, 1050 Brussels)

**Canada** ( ☎ 416-252 1082; fax 416-252 1092; The Queensway, Suite 103, Etobicoque, Ontario M8Z 1 N5) Honorary Consulate.

**France** ( ☎ 01 42 12 73 54; fax 01 40 53 04 36; Rue Jouffroy d'Abbans 80, 75017 Paris)

**Germany** ( ☎ 30-2045 0955; fax 30-2045 0966; 43 Dorotheenstrasse, D-10117 Berlin)

**Italy** ( ☎ 06-474 4678; fax 06-474 4764; Viale Giosué Carduci 4, 00187 Rome)

**Netherlands** ( ☎ 70-346 9623; fax 70-346 7702; 44 Kninginnegracht, 2514 AD The Hague)

**Portugal** ( ☎ 21-301 9521; fax 21-301 5308; www .embcv.pt/index.asp; Av do Restelo 33, 1400 Lisbon)

**Spain** ( ☎ 91-570 2568; fax 91-570 2563; Calle Capitán Haya 51, 28020, Madrid) Consulate.

**USA** ( ☎ 202-965 6820; fax 202-965 1207; 3415 Massachusetts Ave, NW, Washington, DC 20007)

### Embassies & Consulates in Cape Verde

**France** ( ☎ 2-615589; Rua da Prainha, Achada de Santo António, Praia, Santiago)

**Portugal** Santiago ( ☎ 2-623032; Rua da Assembleia Nacional, Achada de Santo António, Platô, Praia); São Vicente ( ☎ 2-323130; Av 5 de Julho, Mindelo)

**Senegal** ( ☎ 2-615621; Rua Abilio Macedo, Praia, Santiago)

**USA** ( ☎ 2-615616; 81 Rua Abilio Macedo, Platô, Praia, Santiago)

## FESTIVALS & EVENTS

Cape Verde's main festivals include Mardi Gras, which is held all over Cape Verde in February or March, the largest occurring in Mindelo (São Vicente); Nhô São Filipe (Fogo), held on 1 May; and the Festival de Música, held in Baia das Gatas (São Vicente) in August.

## HOLIDAYS

Public holidays include the following:
**New Year's Day** 1 January
**National Heroes' Day** 20 January

CAPE VERDE

**Labour Day** 1 May
**Independence Day** 5 July
**Assumption Day** 15 August
**All Saints' Day** 1 November
**Immaculate Conception** 8 December
**Christmas Day** 25 December

## INTERNET ACCESS

The main towns of each island, and even good-sized towns, have Internet cafés. In general, though, connections are rather slow.

## INTERNET RESOURCES

**www.caboverde.com** Comprehensive tourism listings in English, Portuguese and Italian.
**www.caboverdeonline.com** For news and current events in Portuguese.
**www.umassd.edu/specialprograms/caboverde /cvgeog.html** For information about history and culture.
**www.umassd.edu/specialprograms/caboverde /cvhist.html** For a good introduction to Cape Verde's geography and plant and animal life.

## LANGUAGE

Portuguese is the official language, but most Cape Verdeans speak Crioulo, an African-inflected version of medieval Portuguese, as their first language. In rural areas and even sometimes in towns and cities, you may have trouble communicating in standard Portuguese. For some useful words and phrases in Portuguese and Crioulo, see p861.

## MAPS

A good map of the islands is the German-produced AB Karten-Verlag *Cabo Verde* (1:200,000; 2001). An excellent hiking map for Santo Antão is the (also German) *Goldstadt Wanderkarte* (1:50,000; 2001) with around 40 suggested walks.

## MONEY

The unit of currency is the Cape Verde escudo (CVE), divided into 100 centavos. It's not a hard currency, but it's stable; in January 2002, it was pegged to the euro. Most businesses also accept US dollars and euros.

Banks are found in all the main towns and even some of the smaller ones, and most have ATMs that accept bankcards and Visa. Many also change travellers cheques and cash in all the main currencies (except the West African CFA). Many also give cash advances with a Visa card.

Changing money on the black market is illegal and carries risks (US dollars and Portuguese escudos are often fakes), so avoid it unless you're desperate. Be careful not to get stuck with Cape Verdean escudos (not legal tender outside the islands). The bank at Sal's airport and Banco Interatlântico in Praia should change escudos back into other currencies, but bring moneychanging receipts, your passport and air ticket, which may be requested.

Credit cards are accepted only in very upmarket establishments.

## PHOTOGRAPHY & VIDEO

In general, Cape Verdeans are less likely to object to their photos being taken than people elsewhere in West Africa, but you should always ask permission first. Avoid photographing military installations.

## POST

The postal service is reliable and reasonably quick. A 20g letter or postcard costs CVE60 to anywhere outside the islands. *Correios* (post offices) are open from 8am to noon and 2.30pm to 5.30pm Monday to Friday, and Saturday mornings in some towns.

## TELEPHONE

Every number for a fixed telephone line in Cape Verde has seven digits; all start with '2.' No area code is necessary. Public telephone booths are fairly plentiful but you'll need a phonecard (available in CVE50/150 cards at any post office and many small shops). Post offices often have call centres as well, which can be more convenient for expensive, international calls, which start at around CVE200 per minute. For better deals, keep an eye out for Internet-based calling centres, which are starting to appear around the country.

To buy a local GSM chip for your mobile phone, head to the post office, where there is usually also a representative of the national mobile service provider.

## VISAS

All visitors, except Cape Verdean nationals, require a visa. In the USA, mail your passport, one photo and US$40 to the Cape Verdean embassy in Washington, DC. Visas are issued routinely for stays of up to five years. Within West Africa, Dakar, in

Senegal, is one of the few places where you can get a visa. If there's no Cape Verdean embassy, inquire at the nearest Portuguese embassy.

That said, a tourist visa can be obtained on arrival at the airports and ports of Praia and Sal, and will cost CVE4000. Your allowed stay may be short, however, so after arriving, you may need to go to a police station on any island, or the **Direcção de Emigrãçao e Fronteiras** (Rua Serpa Pinto, Platô, Praia, Santiago), and renew it (a maximum of 180 days). In practice, visas are usually issued on the spot (particularly if you're polite and smiling!). Note that there's a fine of CVE15,000 if you let your visa expire.

### Visa Extensions
For an extension of more than a week, you need, in theory, to fill in a form, supply a photo and lodge the application at the **Direcção de Emigrãçao e Fronteiras** (Rua Serpa Pinto, Platô, Praia, Santiago), which will take a few days.

### Visas for Onward Travel
Visas for Senegal can be obtained at that country's embassy in Praia. They cost around CVE500 and take up to 48 hours to process. If you need a visa upon arrival in West African countries, you may need to head to Dakar, in Senegal, first.

## WOMEN TRAVELLERS
Cape Verde is one of the safest countries in West Africa for solo women travellers – no special precautions are required. For more general information and advice, see p828.

# TRANSPORT IN CAPE VERDE

## GETTING THERE & AWAY
### Entering Cape Verde
Proof of yellow fever vaccination is only required if you are coming from an infected area (see p852 for more details).

### Air
Most international flights land on Sal, though Praia is seeing an increasing amount of international activity.

TACV has flights three to four times weekly from Lisbon, and once or twice per week from Boston, Amsterdam, Basel, Fortaleza, Madrid, Munich and Paris. TAP Air Portugal has daily flights from Lisbon. South African Airways flies to Sal from New York and Atlanta, Johannesburg, and Buenos Aires,

From West Africa, TACV flies between Praia and Dakar (Senegal) three to four times weekly. Air Sénégal International has three flights weekly to/from Dakar, with connections to most major West African cities.

Airlines servicing Cape Verde include the following:

**Air Sénégal International** (V7; ☎ 2-617529; www.air-senegal-international.com; Av Amilcar Cabral, Praia, Santiago) Hub: Dakar.

**South African Airways** (SA; ☎ 2-411358; www.flysaa.com) Hub: Johannesburg.

**TACV** (VR; ☎ 2-608200; www.tacv.cv; Av Amilcar Cabral, Praia, Santiago) Hub: Praia.

**TAP Air Portugal** (TP; ☎ 2-411195; www.flytap.com) Hub: Lisbon.

## GETTING AROUND
### Air
TACV serves all the inhabited islands except Brava. Internal flights are slightly cheaper if you buy tickets in Cape Verde. If you're taking two or more internal flights, you may want to purchase TACV's Cabo Verde AirPass (available from travel agencies abroad but not in Cape Verde). You have to arrive by TACV to qualify. In addition, savings are small, and may not be worth the sacrifice in flexibility.

Note that if flights are full, it's well worth flying standby as no-shows are very common. Also, be prepared to purchase you ticket in cash as most travel agencies and even some TACV offices don't accept credit cards or traveller's cheques.

### Bicycle
Cycling is a good way to get around the islands, but there are few places to rent them; think about bringing your own. See p843 for general information.

### Boat
There are ferry connections to all nine inhabited islands, and prices are reasonable. However, be prepared for delays. Seas can be rough, and most boats also carry cargo, so unloading time can be unpredictable. Sometimes departures are delayed by a day

or more. There are cafés onboard, but it's always a good idea to bring a reserve of water and snacks.

The most reliable – and comfortable – service is via SMT's *Tarrafal*, which connects Mindelo and Praia via Saõ Nicolau. Twice a week, boats leave Mindelo in the early afternoon, arrive in Saõ Nicolau in the evening, and then head to Praia overnight, arriving the following morning. In the other direction, the *Tarrafal* leaves in the evening from Praia, arriving the following morning at São Nicolau and in Mindelo around midday.

The twice-daily service between São Vicente and Santo Antão is also very reliable. The trip lasts one hour and costs CVE600.

**Polar** ( ☎ 2-615223; Av Unidade Guiné-Cabo Verde, Santiago) operates a ferry that generally connects Praia, Fogo, Brava, and Maio, but also sometimes hits all the islands, including Boa Vista, Sal, São Vicente and São Nicolau. Prices vary. The short one- to two-hour trip from Fogo to Brava costs about CVE7000. The overnight trip from Praia to Sal costs CVE2100 in the second-class lounge and CVE3400 for an overnight berth.

In the town of Espargos on Sal, the Anaú agency also handles boats to São Vicente. The eight- to 12-hour trip costs around CVE2500 (CVE4200 per person for a fairly comfortable overnight berth with four beds).

## Car & Motorcycle
You can rent cars on many islands, but the only three that make the expense worth it are Santiago, Boa Vista and possibly Fogo.

Consider a four-wheel drive, as conditions are rough once you get off the few main roads. The largest company is **Alucar** (alucarst@mail.cvtelecom.cv; Praia ☎ 2-615801; Sal ☎ 2-421187; São Vicente ☎ 2-325194). Cars cost from about CVE4500 per day, including tax and insurance all-inclusive, with the first 100km free (CVE0.10 per kilometre thereafter). As tourism grows, international car rental agencies are also opening shop. Check at airports upon arrival.

## Minibus & Taxi
Ranging from comfortable vans to pick-up trucks with narrow wooden benches, the *aluguers* provide regular connections between even relatively small towns on most islands. They pick up people at unmarked points around town (ask locals for directions), set off from their initial stop when they're more or less full, and drop passengers off anywhere on the way, on request. They usually charge around CVE100 to CVE200 per passenger, and no more than CVE350 for even the longest trip

Taxis are generally plentiful and cheap in major towns, with fares rarely topping CVE500 and often CVE100 to CVE200. However, you could be stung fairly hard for excursions. Expect to pay around CVE3000 for a few hours, and CVE6000 or more for a full day's services, depending on distances.

Hitching is easy, though payment is sometimes expected. It's usually safe but see p845 for a general warning on the possible risks of hitching.

# Côte d'Ivoire

Côte d'Ivoire was once the economic miracle of Africa and a role model for stability on the continent. Never completely breaking with their colonial masters, the post-independence leaders wooed French capital to build a modern infrastructure and considerable prosperity. The long-serving and charismatic first president, Houphouët-Boigny, managed to promote the notion of a happy amalgam of pragmatic Western capitalism with benign African values. The society he presided over, however, was far from liberal and the dream ended with his death.

A consequent string of coups and popular insurgencies shook the country and a northern-led rebellion in 2002 violently split it in half. Most of the huge French expat community jumped ship and the economy has since crumbled. However, the country abounds in some of the best natural attractions in West Africa, such as Parc National de Taï's vast patch of rainforest and the string of beaches along the Atlantic coast. It's also a land rich in tradition due to a diverse tribal mix that includes Dan, Lobi, Baoulé and Senoufo peoples.

But it's really the modernity that sets Côte d'Ivoire apart from other West African nations. Abidjan is decidedly dog-eared these days, no longer justifying monikers such as the 'Paris of West Africa', but its shimmering skyscrapers will still astound. Yamoussoukro is famous for its basilica, an astonishing replica of Rome's St Peter's, which epitomises the Houphouët-Boigny era and in a way Africa's current place in today's world, since the Big Man philosophy shows few signs of fading.

## FAST FACTS

- **Area** 322,465 sq km
- **Capital** Yamoussoukro
- **Country code** ☎ 225
- **Famous for** Cocoa
- **Languages** French, Mande, Malinké, Dan, Senoufo, Baoulé, Agni, Dioula
- **Money** West African CFA franc; US$1 = CFA544.89; €1 = CFA655.96
- **Population** 17.3 million
- **Visa** Required of most nationalities; not available at borders or the airport.

**WARNING**

The British Foreign & Commonwealth Office advises against all travel to only two countries: Somalia and Côte d'Ivoire. The situation on the ground can change rapidly, and most of the threats and rumours turn out to be false alarms – but history clearly shows you can not dismiss such talk. A few people still travel to Abidjan and the nearby beaches, but seek up-to-the-minute information if you decide to join them. Due to violent street protests and additional threats in Abidjan and elsewhere, we were unable to do on-the-ground research for this edition. Instead, we relied on friends and journalists residing in the country.

## HIGHLIGHTS

- **West Coast beaches** (p275) Soak up the sun at these rainforest-clad strands.
- **Parc National de Taï** (p278) Commune with chimpanzees.
- **Yamoussoukro** (p279) Cast your eyes upon the awe-inspiring basilica.
- **Grand Bassam** (p273) Wander the town and bask in the faded colonial charm.
- **Man** (p281) Take in a live performance of exhilarating music and masked dance.

## CLIMATE & WHEN TO GO

In the south of the country, annual rainfall is 1500mm to 2000mm, and there are two wet seasons: May to July and October to November (see p813). In the drier northern half of the country, the wet season extends from June to October with no intermediary dry spell. The south is very humid, with temperatures averaging 28°C. In the less-humid north, the average temperature is 26°C from December to February with midday maximums regularly above 35°C. Temperatures can drop to 10°C in the highlands.

Since the intercity roads are all sealed, the rains shouldn't impede general travel too much; however, they will affect visits to beaches and national parks, especially the heaviest downpours in May, June and July. Come December the harmattan winds, blowing in from the Sahara, greatly reduce visibility.

## HISTORY

The major tribal groups in Côte d'Ivoire all migrated relatively recently from neighbouring areas. Around 400 years ago, the Krou (or Kru) people moved eastward from Liberia while the Senoufo and Lobi moved southward from Burkina Faso and Mali. It was not until the 18th and 19th centuries that the Akan people, including the Baoulé, migrated from Ghana into the eastern area and the Malinké (also called Mandingo) from Guinea moved into the northwest.

The Portuguese were the first Europeans to arrive. Compared with neighbouring Ghana, Côte d'Ivoire suffered little from the slave trade. European slaving and merchant ships preferred other areas with better harbours. France took no interest until the 1840s when they enticed local chiefs to grant French commercial traders a monopoly along the coast. Thereafter, the French built naval bases to keep out non-French traders and began a systematic conquest of the interior. They accomplished this only after a war in the 1890s against Malinké forces headed by the illustrious Samory Touré. But guerrilla warfare by the Baoulé and other eastern tribal groups continued until 1917.

Once the French had complete control and established their capital, initially at Grand Bassam then Bingerville, they had one overriding goal – to stimulate the production of exportable commodities. Coffee, cocoa and palm trees (for palm oil) were soon introduced along the coast, but it wasn't until a railway was built that the interior was opened up. To build the railway and work the cocoa plantations, the French conscripted workers from as far away as Upper Volta (present-day Burkina Faso). Cocoa was the country's major export; although by the late 1930s coffee ran a close second.

Côte d'Ivoire was the only country in West Africa with a sizable population of *colons,* or settlers. Elsewhere in West and Central Africa, the French and English were largely bureaucrats. But here, a good third of the cocoa, coffee and banana plantations were in the hands of French citizens.

The hated forced-labour system was the backbone of the economy. Under this system, known as *la corvée,* young males were rounded up and compelled to work on private estates or public sector projects, such as the railway.

## Houphouët-Boigny

Born in 1905, the son of a wealthy Baoulé chief, Félix Houphouët-Boigny became Côte d'Ivoire's father of independence. After studying medicine in Dakar, he became a medical assistant, prosperous cocoa farmer and local chief. In 1944 he turned to politics and formed the country's first agricultural trade union – not of labourers but of African planters. Opposing the colonial policy, which favoured French plantation owners, the planters united to recruit migrant workers for their own farms. Houphouët-Boigny soon rose to prominence and within a year converted the union into the Parti Démocratique de Côte d'Ivoire (PDCI). A year later, he al-

lied the PDCI with the Rassemblement Démocratique Africain (RDA), becoming the RDA's first president. That year the French abolished forced labour.

In those early years, Houphouët-Boigny was considered a radical. The RDA was closely aligned with international Marxist organisations and staged numerous demonstrations in Abidjan, resulting in many deaths and arrests. It wasn't long, however, before Houphouët-Boigny adopted a more conciliatory position. France reciprocated, bringing two representatives, including Houphouët-Boigny, to Paris as members of the French national assembly. Houphouët-Boigny was the first African to become a minister in a European government.

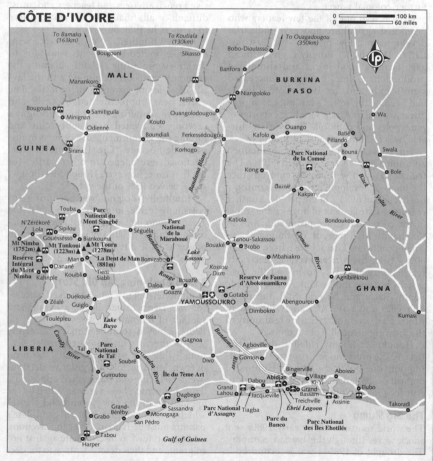

Even before independence, Côte d'Ivoire was easily French West Africa's most prosperous area, contributing more than 40% of the region's total exports. Houphouët-Boigny feared that, with independence, Côte d'Ivoire and Senegal would find themselves subsidising the poorer ex-colonies if all were united in a single republic. His preference for independence for each of the colonies coincided with French interests.

## Independence

In 1960, Houphouët-Boigny naturally became the country's first president. While leaders throughout Africa offered varying strategies for development, Houphouët-Boigny favoured continued reliance on the former colonial power.

He was also one of the few leaders who promoted agriculture and gave industrial development a low priority – at least initially. Houphouët-Boigny's government gave farmers good prices and stimulated production. Coffee production increased significantly and, by 1979, Côte d'Ivoire had become the world's leading cocoa producer, as well as Africa's leading exporter of pineapples and palm oil. The Ivorian 'miracle' was foremost an agricultural one.

For 20 years, the economy maintained an annual growth rate of nearly 10%. The fruits of growth were widely enjoyed since the focus of development was on farming – the livelihood of 85% of the people. Another reason was the absence of huge estates; most of the cocoa and coffee production was in the hands of hundreds of thousands of small producers. Literacy rose from 28% to 60% – twice the African average. Electricity reached virtually every town and the road system became the best in Africa, outside South Africa and Nigeria. Still, the many Mercedes and posh African residences in Abidjan's Cocody quarter were testimony to the growing inequality of incomes.

Houphouët-Boigny ruled with an iron fist and the press was far from free. Tolerating only one political party, he eliminated opposition by largesse – giving his opponents jobs instead of jail sentences.

## The Big Slump

The world recession of the early 1980s sent shock waves through the Ivorian economy. The drought of 1983–4 was a second body blow. From 1981–4 real GNP stagnated or declined. The rest of Africa looked on gleefully as the glittering giant, Abidjan, was brought to its knees for the first time with constant power blackouts. Overlogging finally had an impact and timber revenue slumped. Sugar had been the hope of the north, but world prices collapsed, ruining the huge new sugar-refining complexes there. The country's external debt increased 300% and Côte d'Ivoire had to ask the IMF for debt rescheduling. Rising crime in Abidjan made the news in Europe. The miracle was over.

Houphouët-Boigny slashed government spending and the bureaucracy, revamped some of the poorly managed state enterprises, sent home one-third of the expensive French advisers and teachers and, most difficult of all, finally slashed cocoa prices to farmers in 1989 by 50%.

In 1990 hundreds of civil servants went on strike, joined by students who took to the streets protesting violently, blaming the economic crisis on corruption and the lavish lifestyles of government officials. The unrest was unprecedented in scale and intensity, shattering Houphouët-Boigny's carefully cultivated personality cult and forcing the government to accede to multiparty democracy. The 1990 presidential elections were opened to other parties for the first time; however, Houphouët-Boigny still received 85% of the vote.

Houphouët-Boigny was becoming increasingly feeble, intensifying the guessing game of who he would appoint as his successor. Finally, in late 1993, after 33 years in power as Côte d'Ivoire's only president, 'le Vieux' (The Old Man) died aged 88.

## A New Beginning, An Old Story

Houphouët-Boigny's hand-picked successor was Henri Konan-Bédié, a Baoulé and speaker of the national assembly. In 1995, Bédié achieved some legitimacy, receiving 95% of the vote in open presidential elections, while his party, the PDCI, won an overwhelming victory in legislative elections over a bickering and fragmented opposition. True democracy, however, was stifled by the application of the new 'parenthood clause', which stipulated that both a candidate's parents must be Ivorian. After the elections, Bédié continued to discriminate against immigrants and their descendants who for decades had fuelled the country's agricultural expansion. This persecution was focused, in particular, on foreign Muslim workers in the north, but extended to all northern Muslims regardless of their origin.

In December 1999, Bédié's unpopular rule was brought to an end by a military coup led by General Robert Guéi; however, having deposed Bédié on the basis of his discriminatory policies, Guéi only pursued them further. The coup was quickly followed by military rebellion, violence and elections in 2000 in which Guéi was able to have his main opponent, Alasanne Ouattara, a former prime minister and IMF official, disqualified by the Supreme Court on the grounds that his mother was from Burkina Faso and papers proving otherwise were forgeries. When Guéi tried to steal the subsequent result from winner Laurent Gbagbo, he was deposed by a popular uprising.

The first two years of Gbagbo's presidency were marked by attempted coups and tensions. Scores of Ouattara's supporters were killed in the wake of their leader's call for a new election, though his party won the most seats in the 2001 municipal elections. On 19 September 2002, a failed coup led to a full-scale rebellion and troops from the north gained control of much of the country. Former president Guéi was killed early in the fighting and his death has never been investigated. A month later the government agreed to a cease-fire with the rebels, now known as the Patriotic Movement of Côte d'Ivoire (MPCI), who had the full backing of the mostly Muslim northern populace. France sent in troops to maintain the cease-fire boundaries, but this truce was short-lived, and fighting over the prime cocoa-growing areas resumed, with both sides employing Liberian militias who pillaged much of the western border region. The rebels tired of their new friends and executed those they couldn't kick out. The loyalists have maintained ties with the militias to this day.

In January 2003, President Gbagbo and leaders of the rebel factions met in Paris and signed the Linas-Marcoussis Peace Accord, creating a 'government of national unity' with representatives of the rebels taking places in a new cabinet. This was slowly but peacefully implemented, curfews were lifted and French troops cleaned up the lawless western border. On 4 July 2003 both sides officially declared the war over and vowed to work for demobilization, disarmament and reintegration; but the harmony was short-lived. The MPCI, now called the 'New Forces', pulled out of the government in September, citing President Gbagbo's failure to honour the peace agreement. Three months later, the north and south shook hands again.

## Côte d'Ivoire Today

No improvement in the country's situation was seen in 2004 and neither side drew any closer to its ultimate goal. The government hadn't regained control of the north and Ouattara's backers still had no guarantees of new elections, with their candidate eligible to run. In fact, things grew less stable and more violent. In March, the PDCI accused Gbagbo of 'destabilising the peace process' and quit the government. A few weeks later, after security forces in Abidjan opened fire on an opposition demonstration demanding Gbagbo implement the peace deal (killing 120 unarmed civilians), the New Forces followed suit. UN peacekeepers, under the UN Operation in Côte d'Ivoire (Unoci) banner, arrived soon after to help keep things rolling forward; or at least stop them from slipping back. New talks held in Accra in July resulted in yet another peace agreement, and once again, the government fell short of meeting its end of the bargain, so the New Forces rebels refused to disarm.

On 4 November Gbagbo broke the cease-fire and began bombing rebel strongholds including Bouaké. Two days later, jets struck a French military base killing nine French peacekeepers. The French destroyed the Ivorian air force in retaliation, and then all hell broke loose in the streets of Abidjan. Government soldiers clashed with peacekeepers while state-run TV and radio broadcasts whipped citizens into a frenzy, imploring them to take revenge against French soldiers and citizens. The Young Patriots, a nationalist militia closely linked to President Gbagbo, which had already been torching opposition newspapers and political party offices, led the mobs on sprees of looting and targeted violence. Thousands of foreigners were evacuated by their governments and dozens of Ivorians died in clashes with French soldiers. The government called off the mayhem after a few days, but for many, the anti-French sentiment behind it lingers even today.

The UN Security Council quickly imposed an arms embargo against the government and threatened to freeze the assets of individual leaders. In December, the African Union asked South African President Thabo Mbeki to get the peace process back on track and his intervention prompted parliament to enact key proposals from the 2003 peace agreement. Though the issue of Ouattara's ballot eligibility remained muddled, further talks in Pretoria in 2005 led to a cease-fire and a specific timetable for August disarmament and October presidential election. All this happened amidst continued violence, including a tribal massacre in Duekoué leaving over 100 dead, and suspicious attacks on police stations in Abidjan and Agboville that some suggested had been carried out by government forces in order to disrupt the peace process.

Predictably, neither side followed through on disarmament and when the government failed to properly prepare for the elections, they were cancelled. Though his constitutional mandate expired 31 October, Gbagbo declared he would remain president until elections were held, while the rebels called for the appointment of an independent transitional government. Amidst credible reports that Gbagbo was rebuilding his air force, a UN resolution backed his bid to stay in office for another year. In December, African mediators named Charles Konan Banny interim prime minister and charged the respected economist with organising elections by October 2007. Both sides hailed the appointment, but a split between rebel groups in the north and anti-UN rioting in the south further complicates the picture. Côte d'Ivoire remains trapped in an untenable status quo.

# THE CULTURE
## The National Psyche

Everyone in Côte d'Ivoire worries about the war and dreams of peace, but after riding a five-year rollercoaster of peace deals brokered and broken, many are losing hope. The government has never made any serious efforts at compromise and the rebels, having enriched themselves, through extortion and black market trade, have lost their moral authority.

But despite the various groups – Muslim and Christian, northern and southern, immigrant and indigenous – falling into the same dire straights, there is little reconciliation among them and old tribal conflicts that have nothing to do with the current crisis have been enflamed. The country only came together after the Ivorian Elephants qualified for football's 2006 World Cup for the first time ever. But when the all-night partying finished, the goodwill evaporated.

---

**THE CHILD JUGGLERS**

No, we don't mean precocious Indian-club swingers, but men of superhuman strength of the Guéré, Wobé and Dan (Yacouba) peoples, who literally juggle young girls.

The preparation for both juggler and juggled is long and demanding. The juggler retires to the sacred forest, where he undergoes tests of endurance and learns the arcane secrets of his skill, which are handed down from father to eldest son. During his training he remains isolated from the village. His food, prepared by a group of specially nominated young girls, is left at the edge of the forest. The girls, selected when they're only five years old, are kept apart from the rest of the village children and wear a special headdress to emphasise their separateness.

When the juggler returns from isolation, he offers two sheep and four chickens to the families of the girls who will be his accomplices. In preparation for the ritual performance, the girls are washed in a liquid with secret medicinal properties and also drink secret concoction of roots and herbs to make them supple and light. Their faces are painted white and their lips are coated with a black substance, which, it's believed, encourages silence, for they mustn't utter a word or cry.

Four adolescent drummers and a sidekick, whose role is to highlight the skill of his superior, warm up the crowd. And then, as the girls roll their heads, trance-like, to stimulate the spirits, it begins. They're tossed in the air, the juggler brandishes knives on which they seem certain to be impaled and the crowd becomes more frenzied. But all the while, the countenances of the girls remain as still as death masks. Child juggling can be seen in Diourouzon and also in Bloleu.

**STILT DANCERS**

In the mountain villages around Touba, a group of young Dan men perform heart-stopping masked dances atop three-metre-high stilts. It's an exciting spectacle well worth going out of your way to experience, as much for the cultural setting as the dance itself. One such village is Silacoro, where circular mud-brick houses with conical thatched roofs are surrounded by a sacred forest. There are fetish houses with sacred yucca plants and interesting-shaped sacred rocks.

The dance takes place as the sun is setting, when houses and compound walls are bathed in radiant ochre light. Most of the villagers participate in the cooperatively run performances. As kola nuts are passed around, proceedings begin with a chorus of young women singing and swaying to the beat of five young drumming men.

Eventually a beturbaned young woman, the village beauty, appears swinging a pair of tail-like brushes to the uplifted voices and drums. She represents the beauty of girls in traditional society. Individual dances by young men follow as the drumming becomes more and more frantic. By this stage the chief and other dignitaries have arrived and have seated themselves in the best vantage points. It's at this point that the stilt dancers make their appearance. Their costume is otherworldly; on their high stilts they don't resemble the human form in any way. Their frightening masks are of woven raffia dyed a dark indigo with tassels cascading from their mouths. Around their heads they wear cowrie shells and bells and their bodies are hidden beneath ballooning straw overcoats. As their swirling dance progresses the acrobatic feats become more and more outrageous, until they are spinning at a terrific speed and hurtling themselves into the air, throwing their stilts over their heads then miraculously landing on them. The crowd goes wild. After each dangerous whirl the dancer approaches the chief and dignitaries howling like a demented wounded jungle bird until gifts of money are surrendered to their clutch.

Before they can dance publicly the dancers undertake three to five years of training. They tell no-one, not even their wives, what they're doing. Once initiated, they become empowered to communicate with the spirits who, during the dancing, direct their elaborate stunts.

## Daily Life

Before the war, despite the economic wonders the country was famous for, the literacy rate was below 50% and life expectancy was only 45 years. No one is able to take statistics on such things these days, but, needless to say, things have deteriorated dramatically. Business owners are struggling or closing up shop, farmers are barely breaking even, and many people are giving up and getting out. People understand that, even when peace comes, there will still be problems.

## Population

The 60-plus tribal groups in Côte d'Ivoire can be divided, on the basis of cultural unity, into four principal groupings, each of which has tribal affiliations with members of the same group living in bordering countries.

The Akan (Baoulé and Agni primarily) live in the eastern and central areas and constitute about 42% of the indigenous population. The Baoulé, which separated from the Ashanti in Ghana around 1750 (following a dispute over the chieftaincy) and migrated west into the central area under the leadership of Queen Awura Pokou, is the country's largest tribal group.

The Krou (15% of the indigenous population) originated from present-day Liberia. The Bété are its most numerous subgroup and the second-largest tribal group in the country.

The savanna peoples can be divided into the Voltaic and Mande groups. The Voltaic group (17% of the indigenous population) includes the Senoufo, animists and renowned artisans who live in the north around Korhogo, and the Lobi, who straddle the borders with Burkina Faso and Ghana. The Mande (27%), who live in the north and west, include the Malinké (numerous around Odienné) and the Dan (renowned for their impressive masks and stilt dancers), who inhabit the mountainous region around Man.

See the Peoples chapter (p73) for more information on the Dan, Senoufo and other tribal groups of Côte d'Ivoire.

Before the fighting, up to five million residents were non-Ivorian; of this, one-third to a half were Burkinabé, 100,000 Lebanese and 14,000 French. It's unclear how many people have fled, but most of the French evacuated in November 2004.

## RELIGION

Although the country has two of the largest Catholic cathedrals in the world, only about 35% of the people are Christian, including some Protestants. Some 40%, mostly the Malinké and Dioula (plus most West African immigrants), are Muslims, living primarily in the north. Discrimination, both real and perceived, against the mostly Muslim north by the mostly Christian south has played a significant role in the current crisis. The remaining people practice traditional religions based upon ancestral worship, which can be loosely termed animist.

## ARTS

### Arts & Craftwork

The art of Côte d'Ivoire is among the most outstanding in West Africa. Three groups stand out – the Baoulé, the Dan and the Senoufo. The definitive Ivorian craft is Korhogo cloth, a coarse, cream-coloured cotton painted with either geometrical designs or fantastical animals. It's made in the northeast, but sold all over. Also prized are Dan masks of wood or copper from the Man region and Senoufo wooden statues, masks and traditional musical instruments from the northeast. For more details see below.

### Music & Dance

Reggae is one of the most popular musical styles in Côte d'Ivoire, and the country's best-known export, Alpha Blondy, has achieved considerable international success following the footsteps of Bob Marley. An early great, and probably his best recording, is *Apartheid is Nazism*. Other reggae stars are Serge Kassy, Ismael Isaac and Tiken Jah Fahkoly. Top female vocalists include Aïcha Koné, Monique Seka and Nayanka Bell. Gadji Celi plays more traditional Ivorian music. For more about the music scene see Music of West Africa chapter, p58.

Côte d'Ivoire is renowned for its masked dances and there are numerous opportunities to watch them, particularly in the

---

### WOODCARVINGS OF CÔTE D'IVOIRE

Côte d'Ivoire has a greater variety of masks and woodcarvings than any other country in West Africa. Dan masks show a high regard for symmetry and balance, and are often highly expressive. Traditionally, they were carved spontaneously, inspired perhaps by a beautiful face. The most common mask is that of a human face, slightly abstract but with realistic features; a smooth surface, protruding lips, slit or large circular eye holes and a calm expression. These masks often have specific uses; a mask representing a woman, for example, is used to prevent women from seeing uncircumcised boys during their initiation into adulthood. Other common Dan carvings include large rice-serving spoons that typically rest on two legs carved in a human form.

 Baoulé masks often represent an animal or a human face. The latter are intended to portray particular individuals who can be recognised by the mask's facial marks and hairstyles. Other Baoulé masks, however, are wholly works of the imagination. The *kplekple* horned mask, for example, represents a forest demon and is very stylised. The same is true of the painted antelope and buffalo masks called *goli*, which have large open mouths and are intended to represent bush spirits.

The Baoulé also carve figures. These often incorporate fine details and a shiny black patina. Baoulé *colon* carvings of people in European-style clothing are sold all over West Africa. Current opinion is that, far from portraying a colonial official, such figures represent a person's other-world mate – *blolo bian*, a wife from beyond, and *blolo bla*, a husband from beyond. Of course, these days most are carved for the tourist trade, and not necessarily by a Baoulé carver.

Senoufo masks are very stylised, like the animal masks of the Baoulé. The most famous, perhaps, is the 'fire-spitter' helmet mask, which is a combination of antelope, warthog and hyena. Powerful and scary, it is said to represent the chaotic state of things in primeval times. The human face masks, on the other hand, can often have a very serene expression. One that you'll see everywhere in the tourist markets is the *kpelie* mask that features a highly stylised hairdo, thin eyes, small round mouth, various facial markings and two horns. The Senoufo also carve a great variety of statues, mostly female, which are used in divination and other sacred rituals.

Man region. Dan stilt dancing is detailed on p261.

## Literature

The doyen of Côte d'Ivoire literature is Bernard Dadié, who is credited with writing the country's first play, first poetry anthology and first collection of short stories in French. He has a warm, simple style, even when expressing his dissatisfactions. One of his first novels, published in 1970, is *Climbié*, an autobiographical account of his childhood. Other works translated into English include *The Black Cloth* (1987) and *The City Where No One Dies* (1986).

Aké Loba is best known for *Kocoumbo* (1970), an autobiographical novel of an impecunious, uprooted African in Paris being drawn toward militant communism. Ahmadou Kourouma's first hit novel was *The Suns of Independence* (1981), the wry and humorous story of a disgruntled village chief, deposed following independence. His second novel, *Monné, Outrages et Défi*, written in 1990 after 22 years of silence, took that year's Grand Prix Littéraire d'Afrique Noire – Francophone Africa's premier literary prize.

Among younger writers, Bandama Maurice won the same honour in 1993 for his novel *Le Fils de la Femme Mâle*. Two Ivorian novelists and poets who are also widely read throughout Francophone Africa are Véronique Tadjo and Tanella Boni.

## Cinema

Côte d'Ivoire was one of the first African countries to promote a film industry, establishing the Ivory Coast Cinema Company, in 1962. Some noteworthy releases, all in French, include Roger Gnoan M'Bala's *Adanggaman* (2000), a courageous look at the role of Africans in the slave trade, and the feminist *Faces of Women* (1985), directed by Désiré Ecaré.

# ENVIRONMENT
## The Land

Côte d'Ivoire covers an area about the size of Germany. The central area, where most of the coffee and cocoa grows, is generally flat. A pair of impoundments here have created lakes Buyo and Kossou, two of the largest lakes in West Africa. In the west and northwest the interior rises to a plateau averaging around 300m. Here, Man, with its rolling hill country, is punctuated by several peaks over 1000m. Mount Nimba (1752m), on the Guinean and Liberian borders, is the country's highest peak. In the drier north, the land becomes savanna grassland interspersed with acacia and other bushes and trees.

Little remains of the dense rainforest that once covered most of the southern half of the country. The residue is mostly confined to the southwest, inland from the coast and toward the border with Liberia; the largest tract is protected within the spectacular Parc National de Taï (p278).

A coastal lagoon with a unique ecosystem stretches from the Ghanaian border westward for nearly 300km.

## Wildlife

While Côte d'Ivoire has a large range of fauna, poaching and tragic habitat destruction mean numbers are small and the possibility of sightings limited; however, there are chimpanzees, at least 11 species of monkey, and 17 species of carnivore, including lions and leopards. There are giant pangolins, aardvarks, rock hyraxes, hippopotamuses, elephants, sitatungas, buffaloes, duikers, waterbucks, kobs, roan antelopes, oribi and warthogs.

Côte d'Ivoire has superb bird-watching potential, particularly in Comoé (with over 500 species) and the Parc National de Taï. Notable species include the white-breasted guineafowl, Nimba flycatcher, western wattled cuckoo-shrike and the yellow-throated olive greenbul. There are 10 species of heron, as well as yellow-billed egrets, ducks, raptors, plovers, francolins, hammerkops, black-winged stilts, four of the six West African stork species and five of the six West African vulture species.

## National Parks

Côte d'Ivoire has some of West Africa's best parks, though for the time being only four are feasible for visits: Parc National d'Assagny, a rainforest park east of Grand Lahou with good birdwatching; Parc National des Îles Ehotilés, a marine park protecting six islands in the Abi Lagoon near Assinie; Parc National de la Marahoué, a savanna and woodland park northwest of Bouaflé, and Parc National de Taï (p278), a

Unesco World Heritage site protecting one of the largest remaining virgin rainforests in West Africa. Parc National de la Comoé, in the savanna country of the northeast is another World Heritage site, but it's off limits until the crisis ends; and even then it won't be what it once was. Poaching and cattle grazing are putting it's long term future at risk. For additional information try the **Directorate of National Parks** ( ☎ 20-225366).

## Environmental Issues

Between 1977 and 1987, when hardwood exports exceeded Brazil's, a country over 20 times larger, 42% of Côte d'Ivoire's woodland was felled: the highest rate of destruction in the world. During the 1990s the deforestation rate slowed to 3.1%, but this was still the fifth worst in Africa and nearly three times the continental average. Wood exported includes mahogany, samba, sipo, bété and iroko. Along with logging, the expansion of agricultural lands (from 3.1 million hectares in 1965 to nearly eight million hectares in 1995) has taken a devastating toll on the forests, and thus the diverse flora and fauna. The south was once covered in dense tropical rainforest, but is now largely given over to coffee and cocoa production and massive groves of native palm, tapped for palm oil.

Even before the deforestation crisis began, elephant poaching was a serious problem and, along with the loss of habitat, it dropped their numbers to an estimated few hundred. It is now conceivable that the country's namesake will be completely wiped out in the not so distant future. For years the government, in flagrant violation of the UN Convention on International Trade in Endangered Species, has done nothing to stop the sale of ivory. While most of it ends up being sold illegally overseas, you can find carvings in many markets and gifts shops – don't listen when they tell you it came from elephants that died naturally. Tusks aren't the only coveted body part: many Ivorians still have a taste for elephant steak.

The country's large hydroelectric projects, such as those on the Sassandra River at Buyo and the Bandama River at Kossou, produce about a third of the country's electricity production, but also considerable ecological damage. There are also problems with water pollution from industrial and, in particular, agricultural effluent.

## FOOD & DRINK

There are three staples in Ivorian cooking: rice, *fufu* and *attiéké*. *Fufu* is a dough of boiled yam, cassava or plantain, pounded into a sticky paste similar to mashed potato and so glutinous that it sticks to your palate. *Attiéké* is grated cassava with a subtle taste and texture similar to couscous. They're invariably served with a sauce, such as *sauce arachide*, which is made with groundnuts (peanuts); *sauce graine*, a hot sauce made with palm oil nuts; *sauce aubergine*, made with eggplant; or *sauce gombo* and *sauce djoumgbré*, both with a base of okra (ladies' fingers). In the sauce there will usually be some sort of meat, from chicken, pork or fish to more exotic offerings such as *hérrison* (hedgehog) or *biche* (antelope), which you should choose to avoid on environmental grounds.

*Aloco*, a dish of ripe bananas fried with chilli in palm oil, is a popular street food. *Kedjenou* – chicken, or sometimes guineafowl, simmered with vegetables in a mild sauce and usually served in an attractive earthenware pot – is almost a national dish. Many restaurants will serve you a whole chicken unless you specify that you only want half. While vegetarians are on the whole not well catered for, it is possible to find a variety of bean dishes and spicy vegetable stews containing yam, pumpkin and baby cabbage. Spinach stew is quite common and very delicious.

Fizzy drinks are widely available. Youki Soda, a slightly sweeter version of tonic

---

### EATING OUT IN A MAQUIS

The *maquis* is Côte d'Ivoire's contribution to eating in West Africa. Much copied by the country's Francophone neighbours, a typical *maquis* is a reasonably priced open-air restaurant, often housed under a *paillote* (a pole-and-thatch roof of varying degrees of sophistication). Usually open for lunch and dinner, they generally offer one or two of the standard sauces (aubergine, peanut, okra and *kedjenou*) containing chunks of meat or fish accompanied by rice, bread or *attiéké* (grated cassava). In the evenings, charcoal grills sizzle with meat, fish or poultry, normally served in an onion and tomato salad. On the coast the fish is superb and comes either whole or as brochettes.

water, is a good thirst quencher. *Bandji* is the local palm wine, which is very palatable when freshly tapped. Distilled, it makes a skull-shattering spirit known as *koutoukou*.

The standard beer is Flag, which locals order by asking for *une soixante-six*, a 660ml bottle. If you've a real thirst, go for *une grosse bière,* a hefty 1L bottle. For a premium beer, call for a locally brewed Tuborg.

# ABIDJAN

**pop 3.5 million**

Abidjan, the capital in all but name, was an unimportant town until it became a major port in 1951 when the French finished the Vridi Canal connecting the Ébrié Lagoon with the ocean. Since then, its population has skyrocketed from 60,000 to 3.5 million.

If you've just flown in from the USA or Europe, you won't fully savour the uniqueness of Le Plateau, the business district. But if you arrive after a few weeks of bus- and bush-taxi travel around West Africa, you'll gasp.

Your first glimpse of the city will probably be from across the lagoon; water in the foreground, offset by daring high-rises which puncture the sky. If you can ignore the dispossessed, the beggars, the street hawkers and the gun-toting soldiers who've slipped in from another world, the impression's sustained; smart hotels and boutiques, chic Ivorian ladies clacking along in high heels, on their way to restaurants of four-star Parisian quality – and prices to match – with their smooth escorts, talking in French. You'll sense the same atmosphere in the leafy residential areas of Cocody and Les Deux Plateaux, though many of the villas here are '*a louer*' (for rent) and the people who have stayed are building taller fences.

But Abidjan has always had two faces. Adjamé, on the north side of town, plus Marcory and Treichville to the south of Le Plateau, linked by two major bridges, are areas in which rural immigrants have settled – these neighbourhoods remain pure Africa in all its vitality and urban poverty.

## ORIENTATION

Abidjan spreads around the inlets and along the promontories of the large Ébrié Lagoon. Le Plateau, with its boulevards and skyscrapers, is the hub of the business and government districts. These days it's nearly a ghost town at night. Across a finger of the lagoon, east of Le Plateau, is the exclusive residential district of Cocody. North of Cocody lies the residential and restaurant district of Les Deux Plateaux. To the north of Le Plateau is Adjamé and the main bus station, the frantic Gare Routière d'Adjamé. South of Le Plateau, across two busy bridges is Treichville. The international airport and main marine port are at Port Bouët, further south, on the Atlantic Ocean.

## INFORMATION
### Bookshops
**Librairie de France** (Map p268; ☎ 20-306363; Ave Chardy, Le Plateau) Very good for French titles, but it also has a small collection of English-language classics. There are other smaller branches around the city.

### Cultural Centres
**Goethe-Institut** (Map p266; ☎ 22-400160; Rue 27, Cocody; ✆ 9am-noon & 2.30-6pm Tue-Fri) Shows European films and hosts local art exhibits.

### Emergency
☎ 147

### Internet Access
Cybercafés, most with good connections, are found virtually everywhere. Rates average CFA400 per hour.

### Medical Services
**Polyclinique Internationale St Anne-Marie** (Pisam; Map p268; ☎ 22-445132; off Blvd de la Corniche, Cocody) The only hospital with a 24hr intensive care unit.

### Money
Euros can be changed at main branches of banks in Le Plateau, most hotels and many Lebanese-owned stores, including Hayat supermarkets.

**Bicici Bank** (Map p268; Ave Delafosse) Has an ATM.
**Cobaci** (Airport; ✆ 8.30am-7.30pm) Changes euros, dollars and Swiss francs, but does not take travellers cheques.
**Sgbci Bank** (Map p268; Ave Anoma) Has an ATM.

### Post
**Post office** (Map p268; opposite Place de la République; ✆ 7.30am-noon & 2.30-5pm Mon-Fri) Post restante letters cost CFA1000 each to collect and are held for one month.

CÔTE D'IVOIRE

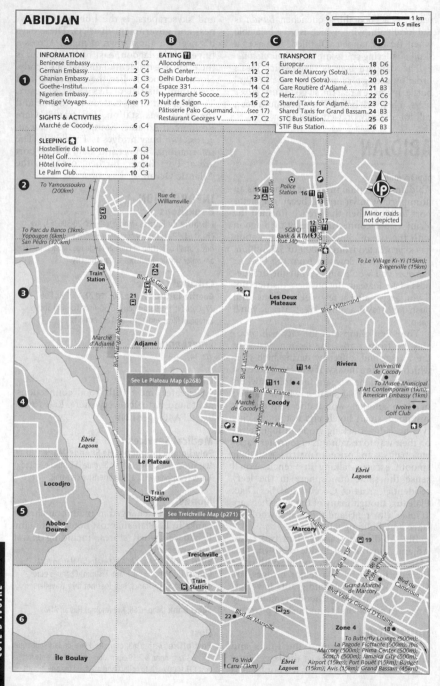

# ABIDJAN

0 ——————— 1 km
0 ——————— 0.5 miles

**INFORMATION**
Beninese Embassy................1 C2
German Embassy....................2 C4
Ghanian Embassy..................3 C3
Goethe-Institut......................4 C4
Nigerien Embassy..................5 C5
Prestige Voyages..............(see 17)

**SIGHTS & ACTIVITIES**
Marché de Cocody..................6 C4

**SLEEPING**
Hostellerie de la Licorne........7 C3
Hôtel Golf..............................8 D4
Hôtel Ivoire...........................9 C4
Le Palm Club.......................10 C3

**EATING**
Allocodrome........................11 C4
Cash Center........................12 C2
Delhi Darbar........................13 C2
Espace 331..........................14 C4
Hypermarché Sococe............15 C4
Nuit de Saigon....................16 C2
Pâtisserie Pako Gourmand......(see 17)
Restaurant Georges V..........17 C2

**TRANSPORT**
Europcar............................18 D6
Gare de Marcory (Sotra)......19 D5
Gare Nord (Sotra)................20 A2
Gare Routière d'Adjamé......21 B3
Hertz................................22 C6
Shared Taxis for Adjamé......23 C2
Shared Taxis for Grand Bassam24 B3
STC Bus Station..................25 C6
STIF Bus Station..................26 B3

Minor roads
not depicted

To Yamoussoukro
(200km)

Rue de
Williamsville

To Parc du Banco (3km);
Yopougon (6km);
San Pédro (320km)

Police
Station

SGBCI
Bank & ATM
Rue J40

To Le Village Ki-Yi (15km);
Bingerville (15km)

Train
Station

Blvd de Gaulle

Les Deux
Plateaux

Blvd Mitterrand

Marché
d'Adjamé

Adjamé

Blvd Nangui Abrogoua

Blvd Latrille

Ave Mermoz

Riviera

Université
de Cocody

To Musée Municipal
d'Art Contemporain (1km);
American Embassy (1km)

Blvd de France

Cocody

Marché
de Cocody

Ave Aka

Rue Washington

Ivoire
Golf Club

See Le Plateau Map (p268)

Ébrié
Lagoon

Le Plateau

Locodjro

Train
Station

Ébrié
Lagoon

Abobo-
Doume

See Treichville Map (p271)

Marcory

Blvd Achalmé

Ave de la TSF

Ave de la
Côte d'Ivoire

Blvd du
Cameroun

Treichville

Train
Station

Grand Marché
de Marcory

Blvd Valéry Giscard d'Estaing

Blvd de Marseille

Zone 4

Île Boulay

To Vridi
Canal (3km)

Ébrié
Lagoon

To Butterfly Lounge (500m);
La Pagode Flottante (500m); Ibis
Marcory (500m); Prima Center (500m);
Scotch (500m); Jamaica City (500m);
Airport (15km); Port Bouët (15km); Budget
(15km); Avis (15km); Grand Bassam (45km)

## Tourist Information

**Côte d'Ivoire Tourisme** (Map p268; ☎ 20-251610; dg@tourismeci.org; Place de la République, Le Plateau; ⏰ 7.30am-6pm Mon-Fri) They have welcome centres at the airport and opposite the post office in Le Plateau where you can get a good, free map of Abidjan.

## Travel Agencies

**Net Voyages Côte d'Ivoire** (Map p268; ☎ 20-336121; info@voyager-en-afrique.com; Immeuble Borija, Ave Noguès, Le Plateau)
**Osmosis Akan** (Map p268; ☎ 07-801518; osmosisak @yahoo.fr; Rue du Commerce, Immeuble le Mali, Le Plateau)
**Prestige Voyages** (Map p266; ☎ 22-417673; prestige voyages@yahoo.fr; Rue Des Jardins, Centre Commercial Louis Panis, Les Deux Plateaux)

## Visa Extensions

**La Sureté Nationale** (Police de l'Air et des Frontieres; ☎ 20-222030; Police de l'Air et des Frontieres, Blvd de la République, Immeuble Douane; ⏰ 8am-noon, 3-5pm Mon-Fri) Near the main post office in Le Plateau in Abidjan. An extension, valid for up to three months, costs CFA20,000 (plus two photos) and is ready the same day if you apply early.

# DANGERS & ANNOYANCES

Crime is a serious problem in Abidjan, though the increased UN and French troop presence and swell of security guards have significantly cut down on the incidence of armed robbery. Still, take a taxi after dark. While most people remain friendly, there is a general suspicion of white faces because of all the rumours flying around about spies and mercenaries, so it helps to move around with an Ivorian if you can.

Despite its reputation for crime, Treichville is relatively safe up to 15th Ave, but for the time being, Marcory and Adjamé are best avoided as much as possible since the chance of travellers getting mugged there remains relatively high. The bridges between Treichville and Le Plateau have long been notorious for theft, so don't walk over them, day or night. You might not even want to drive over Pont du Général de Gaulle during rush hour when many taxi passengers get robbed.

Getting around the city can be frustrating because police regularly stop vehicles, especially shared taxis, demanding bribes from the drivers, and sometimes passengers. Those presumed to be French often get a little extra hassle.

# SIGHTS

## Le Plateau

Step back and look up at some of the buildings of Le Plateau; they're as breathtaking up close as from a distance. **La Pyramide** (Map p268; cnr Ave Franchet d'Esperey & Rue Botreau-Roussel), designed by the Italian architect Olivieri, was the first daring structure.

Looming over the cathedral are the towers of the **Cité Administrative** (Map p268; Blvd Angoulvant), featuring giant copper-coloured slabs with fretted windows. The shimmering **Ministry of Post & Telecommunications** (Map p268; cnr Ave Marchand & Rue Lecoeur), all rounded angles and curves soaring skyward, contrasts with its cuboid, right-angled neighbours.

## Musée National

About 1km north of Le Plateau market is the **Musée National** (Map p268; ☎ 20-222056; Blvd Nangul Abrogoua, Le Plateau; admission CFA1000 ⏰ 9am-5pm Tue-Sat). It has a very dusty collection of over 20,000 objects, including wooden statues and masks, pottery, ivory and bronze.

## Musée Municipal d'Art Contemporain

This **art museum** ( ☎ 22-471686; off Route de M'Pouto, Riviera; admission free; ⏰ 11am-5pm Tue-Sat) beyond the Hôtel Golf has a thought-provoking collection of works by contemporary Ivorian and other African artists and regularly mounts exciting, temporary exhibitions.

## Cathédrale St-Paul

Designed by the Italian Aldo Spiritom, this is a bold and innovative **cathedral** (Map p268; Blvd Angoulvant, Le Plateau; admission free; ⏰ 8am-7pm). The tower is a huge stylised figure of St Paul, with the nave sweeping behind him like trailing robes. Inside, the stained-glass tableaux are as warm and rich as those of the basilica in Yamoussoukro. Make a point of seeing these three in particular: the one behind the altar depicting God blinding St Paul on the road to Damascus; the storm on Lake Galilee with Jesus pointing the way ahead as the disciples jettison the cargo; and, opposite, the tableau of the first missionaries stepping ashore to a scene of African plenty – elephants, gazelles, luxuriant palms and smiling villagers.

## Hôtel Ivoire

Visiting the colossal **Hôtel Ivoire** (Map p266; ☎ 22-408000; Blvd Latrille, Cocody), once West Africa's premier hotel and a small city in

# LE PLATEAU

0 ——————————— 300 m
0 ——————————— 0.2 miles

To Adjamé (1km)

To Cocody (1.5km); Les Deux Plateaux (2.5km)

Ave 13

Blvd Nangui Abrogoua

Ave Pope Jean Paul II

Ave Jamot

Blvd Carde

Blvd Roume

Ave Angoulvant

Ave Crozet

Blvd Clozel

Stadium

Rue Jesse Owens

Ave Marchand

Ave Terrasson de Fougères

Ave Chardy

Blvd Angoulvant

Blvd Clozel

Blvd de la République

Rue Gourgas

Rue Lecoeur

Ave Chardy

Ave Franchet d'Esperey

Marché Plateau

Ave Delafosse

Citibank

Le Plateau

Le Plateau

Ave Anoma

BIAO Bank

Ave Lamblin

Grande Mosquée

Ave Crosson Duplessis

Presidential Palace

Ave Houdaille

Blvd Botreau-Roussel

Rue du Commerce

Ave Noguès

Blvd Général de Gaulle

Place de la République

Train Station

See Treichville Map (p271)

To Treichville (500m)

Pont Houphouët-Boigny

Treichville

Blvd Général de Gaulle

Ébrié Lagoon

Pont du Général de Gaulle

CÔTE D'IVOIRE

## INFORMATION
| | | |
|---|---|---|
| Belgian Embassy | 1 | B4 |
| Bicici Bank | 2 | B4 |
| British Embassy | 3 | A2 |
| Burkina Faso Embassy | 4 | A4 |
| Cameroonian Embassy | 5 | C5 |
| Canadian Embassy | 6 | C5 |
| Côte d'Ivoire Tourisme | 7 | B5 |
| French Embassy | 8 | B3 |
| Guinean Embassy | 9 | C5 |
| Liberian Embassy | 10 | B4 |
| Librairie de France | 11 | B4 |
| Malian Embassy | 12 | D5 |
| Net Voyages Côte d'Ivoire | 13 | C5 |
| Nigerian Embassy | 14 | B3 |
| Osmosis Akan | (see 12) | |
| Police Station | 15 | B5 |
| Polyclinique Internationale St Anne-Marie (PISAM) | 16 | C1 |
| Post Office | 17 | B5 |
| Senegalese Embassy | 18 | C5 |
| SGBCI Bank & ATM | 19 | B5 |
| Togolese Embassy | (see 18) | |

## SIGHTS & ACTIVITIES
| | | |
|---|---|---|
| Cathédrale St-Paul | 20 | A2 |
| Cité Administrative | 21 | A2 |
| La Pyramide | 22 | C4 |
| Ministry of Post & Telecommunications | 23 | B4 |
| Musée National | 24 | A2 |

## SLEEPING
| | | |
|---|---|---|
| Grand Hôtel | 25 | C5 |
| Hôtel des Sports | 26 | B6 |
| Hôtel Tiama | 27 | B3 |
| Ibis Plateau | 28 | A3 |
| Novotel | 29 | C6 |

## EATING
| | | |
|---|---|---|
| Café Restaurant Oasis | 30 | B4 |
| Cash Center | 31 | B5 |
| Food Vendors | 32 | C5 |
| Food Vendors | 33 | C5 |
| Food Vendors | (see 21) | |
| La Cascade | 34 | B4 |
| La Croisette | 35 | B4 |
| La Taverne Romaine | 36 | C4 |
| Nour-al-Hayat | 37 | B4 |
| Pizzeria Bruno | 38 | B3 |
| Restaurant des Combattants | 39 | B3 |
| Tuan | 40 | C4 |

## DRINKING
| | | |
|---|---|---|
| Bar des Sports | (see 26) | |

## ENTERTAINMENT
| | | |
|---|---|---|
| La Java Disco | 41 | C5 |
| Place Vendôme | (see 30) | |

## TRANSPORT
| | | |
|---|---|---|
| Afriquiyah Airways | (see 9) | |
| Air Algérie | (see 42) | |
| Air Burkina | 42 | B5 |
| Air France | 43 | C5 |
| Air Gabon | (see 10) | |
| Air Ivoire | (see 7) | |
| Air Mauritanie | (see 12) | |
| Air Sénégal International | (see 45) | |
| Bellview Airlines | 44 | C5 |
| Cameroon Airlines | (see 44) | |
| Ethiopian Airlines | 45 | B4 |
| Gare Lagunaire | 46 | B6 |
| Gare Sud (Sotra) | 47 | B6 |
| Kenya Airways | (see 50) | |
| Middle East Airlines | 48 | C4 |
| Royal Air Maroc | 49 | C4 |
| South African Airways | 50 | B4 |
| Tunisair | (see 18) | |

itself, was always an odd experience, but the lack of guests these days makes it almost surreal. The complex has 11 tennis courts, swimming pools, a cinema, casino, restaurants, grocery store, nightclub, sauna and bowling alley.

## Parc du Banco

On the northwest edge of town is the **Parc du Banco** (Autoroute de Nord) rainforest reserve. It has very pleasant walking trails, majestic trees and a lake, but little in the way of wildlife. Stay away for the time being as many of the convicts who escaped prison in November 2004 are rumoured to hide out here. Near the park entrance is Africa's largest outdoor laundrette (see below).

## Markets

The **Marché de Treichville** (Map p271; Ave Victor Blaka) is an ugly Chinese-built building, but inside it's African to the core and well stocked. There is little you can't find. The top floor of the **Marché de Cocody** (Map p266; Blvd de France) is geared for tourists with all the usual trinkets. **Marché Plateau** (Map p268; Blvd de la République) has been razed, but will be rebuilt.

## FESTIVALS & EVENTS

The **Marché des Arts et du Spectacle Africains** (MASA Festival) is ostensibly a pan-African trade fair to promote dance, drama and music, but the highlight is the week of live performances. It used to take place in March and April of odd years, but recently dates have varied considerably.

## SLEEPING
### Budget

**Hôtel Terminus** (Map p271; ☎ 21-241577; Blvd Delafosse, Treichville; r CFA15,000; P ⊠ ) Treichville's most comfortable option is in a good, busy location; though it's not great value for money.

**Hôtel l'Ariegeois** (Map p271; ( ☎ 21-249968; Blvd de Marseille, Treichville; s/d CFA15,000/22,000; P ⊠ ) This hotel, 400m north of Treichville train station, has unassuming rooms, but it's a convenient location.

**Hôtel International** (Map p271; ☎ 21-240747; Blvd Valéry Giscard d'Estaing, Treichville; s/d CFA12,000/18,000; P ⊠ ) When they finish the ongoing renovation, this hotel should be pretty good.

### Midrange

**Hôtel Ivoire** (Map p266; ☎ 22-408000; Blvd Latrille, Cocody; s CFA30,000, d from CFA56,000; ⊠ P ⊒ ⊑ ) More than just a nearly empty hotel, the 750-room Ivoire is a monument of Abidjan's bygone glory. See p267 for a list of the hotel's many entertainment options.

**Grand Hôtel** (Map p268; ☎ 20-332109; Rue du Commerce, Le Plateau; r CFA25,000-45,000; ⊠ P ) The Grand is good value and the staff is accommodating.

**Hostellerie de la Licorne** (Map p266; ☎ 22-410730; Rue des Jardins, Les Deux Plateau; r CFA30,000-40,000; ⊠ ⊒ P ⊑ ) Immaculate and friendly. It is down a side street behind the Total petrol station and has a great ambience, a garden and a swimming pool.

**Le Palm Club** (Map p266; ☎ 22-444450; Blvd Latrille, Les Deux Plateau; r CFA20,000-25,000; ⊠ P ⊑ ) Formerly the Palme Industrie guesthouse, the rooms are drab but it remains popular. There are pleasant garden surrounds, two pools, a tennis court and an attractive *paillote*, which has a menu that changes daily.

**Hôtel des Sports** (Map p268; ☎ 20-836404; Rue du Commerce, Le Plateau; ⊠ ) The cheapest place to stay in Le Plateau was undergoing a

---

### THE OUTDOOR LAUNDRETTE

Every day some 375 *fanicos* (washermen), mostly Burkinabé and none Ivorian, jam together in the middle of a small stream near the Parc du Banco, frantically rubbing clothes on huge stones held in place by old car tyres. Afterward, they spread the clothes over rocks and grass for at least 500m (never getting them mixed up) and then iron them. Any washer not respecting the strict rules imposed by the washers' trade union, which allocates positions, is immediately excluded.

The black soap is sold by women who make it from palm oil in small wooden sheds on the hills surrounding the stream. The *fanicos* begin arriving with their loads around 6.30am, but it's best to come between 10.30am and noon when the action is at its peak. You'll get some superb photos, although payment is expected. In the afternoon all you'll see is drying clothes.

much-needed restoration at the time of research. Enquire about prices.

## Top End

**Novotel** (Map p268; ☎ 20-318000; 10 Blvd Général de Gaulle, Le Plateau; r CFA85,000-90,000; ⓟ ⌘ ▯ ▥) This superswish, lagoon-side complex will have you wanting for nothing. You pay more for a good view.

**Hôtel Golf** (Map p266; ☎ 21-431044; golfhotel@ golfhotel-ci.com; Blvd de France, Riviera; s/d CFA50,000/60,000; ⓟ ⌘ ▯ ▥) This relaxing hotel, on Ébrié Lagoon in the Riviera neighbourhood and a 15-minute taxi ride from the centre, has a pool and tennis courts. The **Ivoire Golf Club** (☎ 22-430844), one of Africa's best courses, is across the street.

**Ibis Plateau** (Map p268; ☎ 20-301600; 7 Blvd Roume, Le Plateau; r CFA40,000-45,000; ⌘ ⓟ ▯) A comfortable and popular hotel. Some of the rooms have views of adjacent bat-infested trees which, if you like bats, is quite entertaining.

**Ibis Marcory** (☎ 21-756300; Blvd Valéry Giscard d'Estaing; r CFA42,000-49,000; ⌘ ▯ ⓟ ▥) Sister to its clone in Le Plateau, this one is handy to the airport and has a pool. It has grown in popularity because of its location near a French military camp.

**Hôtel Tiama** (Map p268; ☎ 20-313333; com@hotel .tiama.ci; Blvd de la République; r CFA72,000-85,000, ste CFA190,000; ⌘ ▯ ⓟ ▥) It has a piano bar and exercise room and sauna, but some find the Tiama more sterile than plush.

## EATING

*Abidjan Gourmand*, available around town, is an excellent bilingual directory of Abidjan and Grand Bassam restaurants.

## Restaurants

### AFRICAN

**Espace 331** (Map p266; Rue 12, Cocody; dishes CFA2000-6000; ☯ lunch & dinner) This is a happening, tree-shaded outdoor joint with lunch time sauce dishes and evening grills such as *brochette d'escargots* (grilled snail kebabs).

**Maquis Le Sole Plus** (Map p271; Ave 27, Treichville; meals CFA3000-5000; ☯ lunch & dinner) The best sole in town. Just order from the lady in back and take a seat outside.

**Restaurant des Combattants** (Map p268; Ave Marchand, Le Plateau; meals CFA2000-5000; ☯ breakfast, lunch & dinner) A huge colonial building with a wide-ranging African menu featuring *es-*

*cargot, sauce feuille* (manioc leaf sauce with beef tail, fish and crab) and other dishes not often found in sit-down restaurants.

**Maquis Chez Fifine** (Map p271; Ave 26, Treichville; meals CFA3000-5000; ☯ lunch & dinner) This place serves African dishes during the day and delicious grills at night.

**Café Restaurant Oasis** (Map p268; Blvd de la République, Le Plateau; meals less than CFA3000; ☯ breakfast, lunch & dinner Mon-Sat) The Oasis is, as its name suggests, a good place to take refuge from the busy streets outside. Afro-European food is served in a diner-style atmosphere.

### ASIAN

**La Pagode Flottante** (Blvd de Marseille, Zone 4; meals CFA15,000; ☯ lunch & dinner) High-priced but very tasty Vietnamese is served on a barge on the Ébrié Lagoon. There is indoor and outdoor seating.

**Delhi Darbar** (Map p266; Rue des Jardins, Les Deux Plateaux; meals CFA4500-12,000; ☯ lunch & dinner Tue-Sun) Delhi Darbar has very good, authentic Indian dishes – most notably seafood – served in tasteful surrounds.

**Nuit de Saigon** (Map p266; Rue des Jardins, Les Deux Plateaux; meals CFA3000; ☯ lunch & dinner) This is arguably the best Vietnamese restaurant in Abidjan; the food is first rate and the décor swish. It specialises in duck and has an excellent French wine list.

**Tuan** (Map p268; Blvd du Général de Gaulle, Le Plateau; meals CFA2000-5000; ☯ lunch & dinner) Tuan serves good but expensive food in a relaxing atmosphere.

### FRENCH & ITALIAN

Most Italian restaurants offer both Italian and French cuisine.

**La Cascade** (Map p268; Ave Chardy, Le Plateau; meals CFA10,000; ☯ lunch & dinner Mon-Sat) The cuisine at Cascade is superb so it's usually packed. Try the *feuilleté de foie gras* (pâté in puff-pastry) for a not-quite-African experience. A gushing waterfall and pond add to the ambience.

**La Croisette** (Map p268; Rue Botreau-Roussel, Le Plateau; meals CFA8000-14,000; ☯ lunch Mon-Fri, dinner Mon-Sat) The food is excellent, especially the fish, and it is served in airy, nautically inspired surroundings.

**Pizzeria Bruno** (Map p268; Blvd de la République, Le Plateau; meals CFA5000-8000; ☯ lunch & dinner Mon-Sat) This popular pizzeria does big, wood-fired pizzas in apt surroundings, and real coffee to boot.

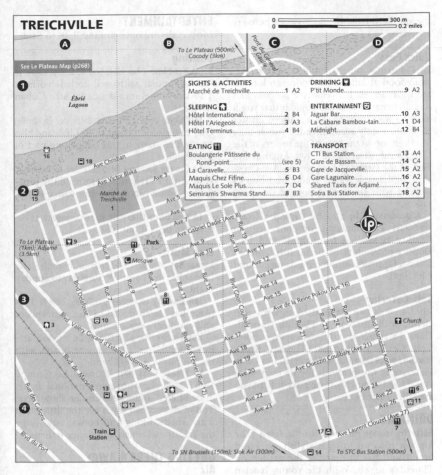

**TREICHVILLE**

See Le Plateau Map (p268)

*Ébrié Lagoon*

To Le Plateau (500m); Cocody (3km)

Pont du Général de Gaulle

To Le Plateau (1km); Adjamé (3.5km)

Marché de Treichville

Park
Mosque

To Le Plateau Map (p268)

To SN Brussels (150m); Slok Air (300m)    To STC Bus Station (500m)

| SIGHTS & ACTIVITIES | | DRINKING | |
|---|---|---|---|
| Marché de Treichville.........................1 A2 | | P'tit Monde.................................9 A2 | |
| **SLEEPING** | | **ENTERTAINMENT** | |
| Hôtel International.........................2 B4 | | Jaguar Bar.................................10 A3 | |
| Hôtel l'Ariegeois.........................3 A3 | | La Cabane Bambou-tain.............11 D4 | |
| Hôtel Terminus.........................4 B4 | | Midnight.................................12 B4 | |
| **EATING** | | **TRANSPORT** | |
| Boulangerie Pâtisserie du | | CTI Bus Station.........................13 A4 | |
| Rond-point.........................(see 5) | | Gare de Bassam.........................14 C4 | |
| La Caravelle.........................5 B3 | | Gare de Jacqueville.....................15 A2 | |
| Maquis Chez Fifine.........................6 D4 | | Gare Lagunaire.........................16 A2 | |
| Maquis Le Sole Plus.........................7 D4 | | Shared Taxis for Adjamé..............17 C4 | |
| Semiramis Shwarma Stand..........8 B3 | | Sotra Bus Station.........................18 A2 | |

**La Taverne Romaine** (Map p268; Blvd du Général de Gaulle, Le Plateau; meals CFA5000-15,000; ☽ lunch & dinner Mon-Sat) This place does great wood-fired pizzas for around CFA6000 and focaccias, the house speciality, for CFA7000.

**LEBANESE**
You'll find Lebanese restaurants and shwarma outlets all over town.

**Restaurant Georges V** (Map p266; Rue des Jardins, Les Deux Plateaux; meals CFA750-5000; ☽ breakfast, lunch & dinner) This is a friendly, inexpensive diner/takeaway with free Internet.

**Semiramis Shwarma Stand** (Map p271; Ave 13, Treichville; meals CFA1000-5000; ☽ lunch & dinner) Semiramis is great for fresh shwarmas and takeaways.

**La Caravelle** (Map p271; Ave 8, Treichville; meals CFA200-3000; ☽ breakfast, lunch & dinner) This place has copious, all-inclusive meals including hamburgers and pizza (lunch only). Its adjacent sweet shop produces delicacies as good as any sold in Beirut.

**Patisseries**
**Pâtisserie Pako Gourmand** (Map p266; Rue des Jardins, Les Deux Plateaux; ☽ breakfast, lunch & dinner) This popular place does sweet French fare superbly – cakes, pastries, buttery croissants and brilliant, real coffee – plus there is ice cream and African food. Strongly recommended.

**Boulangerie Pâtisserie du Rond-point** (Map p271; Ave 8, Treichville; ☽ breakfast & lunch) Despite

CÔTE D'IVOIRE

the simple surrounds, the pastries here are superb.

## Quick Eats

Le Plateau is superb for inexpensive African food at lunchtime. Food vendors on the short streets between Ave Noguès and Rue du Commerce are so popular that you'll have to wait in line. There's also a cluster of small, highly recommended lunch-time food vendors at the base of the towers of the Cité Administrative on Blvd Angoulvant. East of the Grande Mosquée, on Ave Crosson Duplessis, a walled compound houses women with simmering pots of delicious sauces.

**Allocodrome** (Map p266; Rue Washington, Cocody; ☻ dinner) This fantastic outdoor grill in Cocody is sizzling from 4pm until late. Dozens of vendors barbecue fish, chicken and beef, providing filling meals for around CFA2000.

## Self-Catering

Abidjan has two established supermarket chains with stores in Le Plateau: Nour-al-Hayat (Map p268) and the cheaper, gaudier Cash Center (Map p268). The vast **Hypermarché Sococé** (Map p266; Blvd Latrille) in Les Deux Plateaux is worth a visit for its own sake: you'll need to pinch yourself to confirm you are still in Africa.

## DRINKING

**Butterfly Lounge** (off Blvd de Marseille, Zone 4) The hippest place in town is stylish, cool and bright and has live jazz in the garden on Thursday nights. With the young Ivorian elite spending freely on cocktails and Johnnie Walker, it pulls off a New York vibe. It's right near the Notre Dame church.

**Scotch** (Rue Paul Langevin, Zone 4) The latest 'in' venue sports a swimming pool in the courtyard. There is no cover charge, but dress smart or you won't get in.

**Bar des Sports** (Map p268; Rue du Commerce, Le Plateau) The bar below Hôtel des Sports is a favourite watering hole for French expats and old-school Ivorian professionals. With its bustle and French football-league tables posted on the wall it could have been transplanted from Marseille. It's the ideal place to watch the world go by.

**P'tit Monde** (Map p271; Blvd Delafosse, Treichville) This is a tastefully decorated, cheery little bar.

## ENTERTAINMENT

Most clubs are open around 9pm to 6am.

## Dancing

**Place Vendôme** (Map p268; Blvd de la République, Le Plateau) Popular with well-heeled Ivorians. You can sometimes dance to Afro-Cuban rhythms.

**Midnight** (Map p271; Blvd Delafosse, Treichville) One of the oldest clubs in Abidjan and also one of the many in this happening part of Treichville.

**Le Cabane Bambou** (Map p271; Ave 27, Treichville) A long-time favourite, despite all the prostitutes. Some nights you can dance to live bands.

**La Java Disco** (Map p268; Rue du Commerce, Le Plateau) Java belts it out till late.

## Live Music

**Jaguar Bar** (Map p271; Blvd Delafosse, Treichville) The Jaguar has live bands Wednesday to Sunday night.

**Jamaica City** (opposite Prima Center, Zone 4) This place has cheap drinks, a fun atmosphere and excellent reggae bands.

**Hôtel Ivoire** (Map p266; Blvd Latrille, Cocody) Starting around 7pm the lobby resonates with the sounds of a lively band.

**Le Village Ki-Yi** (Blvd Mitterrand) Le Groupe Ki-Yi M'bock, who enjoy national fame, once offered a fantastic dinner show here. Today all you can do is see the little shop with woodworking and books…and hope the traditional music and dance returns.

## GETTING THERE & AWAY
## Air

Port Bouët International Airport is on the south side of town. For details on international flights see p288 or p290 for domestic travel.

## Bus & Bush Taxi

The main bus station is the shambolic Gare Routière d'Adjamé, some 4km north of Le Plateau. Most buses and bush taxis leave from here and there's frequent transport to all major provincial towns.

Bush taxis and minibuses for destinations east along the coast, such as Grand Bassam, Aboisso and Elubo at the Ghanaian border, leave primarily from the Gare de Bassam at the corner of Rue 38 and Blvd Valéry Giscard d'Estaing, south of Treichville. Transport for Grand Bassam also departs from Gare Routière d'Adjamé, but takes longer.

## GETTING AROUND
### To/From the Airport

Walk out, turn sharp left and continue for about 20m to a long line of waiting orange taxis. Try to get the driver to switch on his meter; when he refuses, establish a price, which shouldn't exceed CFA4000 (rates double between midnight and 6am), to Le Plateau or Cocody. If he won't accept this, make a show of getting out; you'll quickly reach an agreement and, if not, there are plenty more behind him. The fanciest hotels have free shuttle services.

### Boat

Abidjan has a good ferry service on the lagoon. It goes from Treichville to Abobo-Doumé (across the lagoon, west of Le Plateau) to Le Plateau to Treichville again (in that sequence; it's a long ride from Treichville to Le Plateau). Taking a *bateau-bus* (boat-bus) is a great way to the see the city from a different perspective. The *gare lagunaire* (ferry terminal) in Le Plateau is 100m east of Pont Houphouët-Boigny. The fare from there across the lagoon to the Treichville ferry terminal, also east of Pont Houphouët-Boigny, is CFA200. There are several departures every hour from around 6am to 8pm.

### Bus

The city's Sotra buses tend to be crowded, but they're cheap – CFA200 for regular service and CFA400 for Express. They display their route number, which also features on bus-stop signs, but only rarely their destination. The people waiting for a bus with you should know which ones go where.

The major Sotra bus station in Le Plateau is the Gare Sud, south of Place de la République. Other stations are the Gare Nord in Adjamé, 500m north of the train station, and a Sotra bus station on Ave Christian in Treichville. The buses on most lines operate from about 6am to between 9pm and 10pm daily.

### Car

Hiring a car is expensive if you use one of the multinational agencies: **Avis** ( ☎ 20-328007), **Budget** ( ☎ 21-751616), **Europcar** ( ☎ 21-20-313333) or **Hertz** ( ☎ 21-751105). All of the companies have branches at the airport and in Le Plateau. Prices and terms vary, but in general a small car starts around CFA31,000 per day, including tax and compulsory insurance, plus CFA225 per kilometre. The price will rise if you want to leave the city. A 4WD is CFA48,000 per day, plus CFA500 per kilometre. You are generally better off arranging a car and driver with the many men who wait in front of the fancy hotels. You should be able to arrange one for the day for around CFA15,000 to CFA20,000. Most journalists hire cars from **Mr Konan** ( ☎ 07-675508) who keeps his Mercedes in front of Hôtel Tiama.

### Taxi

Private taxis in Abidjan are reasonably priced, but drivers probably won't switch on their meter without prompting. Make sure it's set to tariff No 1. The more expensive No 2 rate only applies between midnight and 6am. Fares from Le Plateau to Treichville and Cocody should cost around CFA1000. If you want to hire a taxi driver for a day plan on paying about CFA30,000.

*Woro-woro* (shared taxis) cost between CFA250 and CFA700, depending on the length of the journey. They vary in colour according to their allocated area (although drivers are now beginning to ignore this convention). Those between Plateau, Adjamé, Marcory and Treichville, for example, are red, while those in Les Deux Plateaux and Cocody are yellow and Yopougon's are blue.

## THE EAST COAST

The beaches east of Abidjan are still the playground of wealthy Ivorians and expats; there are just far fewer of them soaking up the sun than there once was. A dramatic increase in petty criminals and muggers means that most visitors now weekend at Assinie, which is much safer.

### GRAND BASSAM
☎ 21

Grand Bassam, some 45km east of Abidjan, retains a fascinating colonial heritage; though most come for the beach. The narrow strip of land between ocean and lagoon, known as Ancien Bassam, is where the French first settled, distancing

## COLONIAL BUILDINGS

Confident structures with spacious balconies, verandas and shuttered windows were the style of the day. Of the colonial-era buildings, mostly constructed between 1894 and 1920, the elegant former post office and the *mairie* (town hall) have been beautifully restored. The former governor's palace, with its imposing outer staircase, is now the **Musée National du Costume** (admission CFA1000). It has a nice little exhibit of the housing styles of various tribal groups. Most of the remainder, including the old *palais de justice* (law courts), tax office, customs house, prison and hospital, are vacant and in various stages of decay.

themselves from the locals, whose own settlement across the lagoon expanded as servants' quarters. Grand Bassam was declared capital of the French colony in 1893, but a mere six years later a major yellow-fever epidemic broke out prompting the French to move their capital to Bingerville. Bas-

sam, it seemed, was headed for oblivion. Construction of a wharf two years later, however, brought new life and substantial new construction. In 1931, when the French built another wharf in Abidjan, three golden decades came to an end. The *coup de grace* was the opening of the Vridi Canal, connecting the lagoon and the ocean.

Dugout canoe trips to see traditional crab fishers, mangroves and birdlife can be arranged with local boatmen. There are also artisan stalls on the road into town so you can get some souvenir shopping out of the way. The best time to visit is in late October or early November during the colourful week-long Fête de l'Abissa, when the N'Zima people honour their dead.

## Sleeping & Eating

**Taverne la Bassamoise** ( ☎ 301062; r/bungalow incl breakfast CFA25,000/29,000; 🏊 🅿 🍴 ) This lovely lodge mixes African design with old-world charm, and adds tennis courts and a swimming pool.

**Hôtel Boblin la Mer** ( ☎ 301418; r with fan CFA10,000, with air-con CFA15,000-20,000; 🏊 🅿 ) This

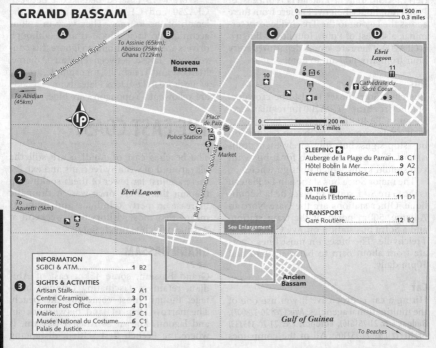

**GRAND BASSAM**

To Assinie (65km);
Aboisso (75km);
Ghana (122km)

Route Internationale (Bypass)

To Abidjan
(45km)

Nouveau
Bassam

Ébrié
Lagoon

Cathédrale du
Sacré Coeur

Place
de Paix

Police Station

Market

Ébrié Lagoon

To
Azuretti (5km)

Blvd Gouverneur Angoulvant

See Enlargement

Ancien
Bassam

Gulf of Guinea

To Beaches

| INFORMATION | |
| --- | --- |
| SGBCI & ATM...................................**1** B2 | |

| SIGHTS & ACTIVITIES | |
| --- | --- |
| Artisan Stalls.................................**2** A1 | |
| Centre Céramique........................**3** D1 | |
| Former Post Office......................**4** D1 | |
| Mairie...........................................**5** C1 | |
| Musée National du Costume......**6** C1 | |
| Palais de Justice..........................**7** C1 | |

| SLEEPING 🛏 | |
| --- | --- |
| Auberge de la Plage du Parrain...**8** C1 | |
| Hôtel Boblin la Mer.....................**9** A2 | |
| Taverne la Bassamoise.................**10** C1 | |

| EATING 🍴 | |
| --- | --- |
| Maquis l'Estomac.........................**11** D1 | |

| TRANSPORT | |
| --- | --- |
| Gare Routière...............................**12** B2 | |

CÔTE D'IVOIRE

Italian-owned hotel, west of town, has a great ambience and small, but good-value rooms overlooking the ocean.

**Auberge de la Plage du Parrain** ( ☎ 301541; r CFA8000; P ) The attractive *paillote* bar is the best part of this hotel.

**Maquis l'Estomac** (lagoon-side road; meals from CFA2000; ☽ lunch & dinner) Along with the hotels listed above, all of which serve good food, the best dining options are the many welcoming *maquis*, such as l'Estomac, serving African food at African prices on the lagoon-side of Ancien Bassam.

### Getting There & Away
Bush taxis (CFA500) from Abidjan's Gare de Bassam arrive faster than from Gare Routière d'Adjamé. UTB has busses from Gare Routière d'Adjamé (CFA500). In Grand Bassam, the *gare routière* is beside the Place de Paix roundabout, north of the lagoon.

### ASSINIE
Some 85km east of Grand Bassam, Assinie, near the tip of a long sand spit where the Canal d'Assinie meets the mouth of the Abi Lagoon, has magnificent beaches. The pre-serve of rich weekenders from Abidjan and formerly package tours from Europe, it has little to do with Africa.

Accommodation is largely top end but **Blue Cargo** ( ☎ 07-539276; huts with shared bathroom CFA12,000; P ☒ ) has funky wooden huts with fans on the lagoon. There is a swimming pool and their brochettes are fantastic. Also good value, for the area, is **Beach Lodge** ( ☎ 07-872040; r CFA30,000-35,000; P ☒ ) in nearby Assouindé. The French owner knows nearly everything about Côte d'Ivoire.

From Abidjan, head first for Grand Bassam, from where there are irregular bush taxis to Assinie (CFA1500).

# THE WEST COAST

The rainforest-clad beaches in the western half of the country are some of Africa's most beautiful. There aren't many people roaming the sands these days due to the crisis, but many of the rivers and forests still teem with wildlife. So does Parc National de Taï, which is well known for its chim-

panzees. And when you're not commun-ing with nature, there are many fascinating fishing villages to explore.

### TIAGBA
About 100km west of Abidjan is Tiagba, a fascinating village on the Ébrié Lagoon where many of the houses are on stilts. Hir-ing a pirogue for a trip around the lagoon is well worth the haggle. Reportedly, the **Hôtel Aux Pilotis de l'Ébieyé** ( ☎ 07-182791; r CFA4500), near the boat dock on the mainland, is still in business, though it closes in the rainy season. Its terrace bar facing the lagoon is a good place for a drink. It is also possible to stay in villagers' homes.

There is one minibus per day from Dabou (CFA1000), which leaves late in the afternoon and returns early the next morning. To make it a day trip, you can charter a taxi in Dabou.

### SASSANDRA
☎ 34
Sassandra is a great base for visiting the spectacular beaches to its west. It's also an interesting Fanti fishing village on a scenic river estuary. (The Fanti, renowned as fishing people, are recent arrivals from present-day Ghana.) Sassandra was origin-ally established by the Portuguese in 1472, who named it São Andrea. Settled succes-sively by the British and the French, who developed it mainly as an outlet for timber from Mali, it went into swift decline once the port at San Pédro was constructed in the late 1960s to the west. Although the lack of travellers has precipitated another decline, the town is small enough to explore on foot and you can still see several old colonial buildings, such as the governor's house.

### Sleeping & Eating
**Hôtel la Côtière** ( ☎ 720120; s with fan CFA6000, d with air-con CFA10,000; P ☒ ) The small bungalows sit on the estuary beneath coconut palms and a giant flame tree. You might have to wait awhile to be served, but Mademoiselle Tantie Youyou's delicious African fare (fish dishes CFA3000) is worth it. Some rooms have mosquito nets.

**Hôtel le Pollet** ( ☎ 720578; r CFA17,000; P ☒ ) Near the lighthouse, this place is rather sterile, but a friendly French owner and

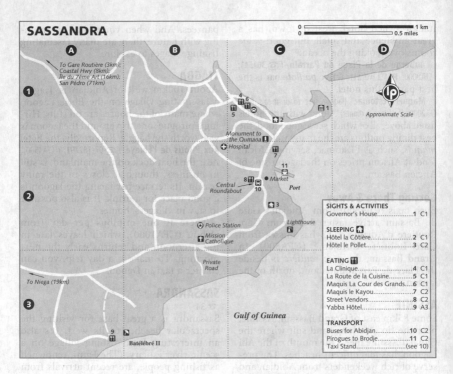

**SASSANDRA**

0 _____ 1 km
0 _____ 0.5 miles

To Gare Routière (3km);
Coastal Hwy (8km);
Île du 7ème Art (16km);
San Pédro (71km)

Approximate Scale

Monument to
the Oumana
Hospital

Central
Roundabout

Market
Port

To Niega (19km)

Police Station
Mission
Catholique

Private
Road

Lighthouse

*Gulf of Guinea*

Batélébré II

**SIGHTS & ACTIVITIES**
Governor's House.....................1 C1

**SLEEPING**
Hôtel la Côtière.......................2 C1
Hôtel le Pollet........................3 C2

**EATING**
La Clinique............................4 C1
La Route de la Cuisine...............5 C1
Maquis La Cour des Grands....6 C1
Maquis le Kayou......................7 C2
Street Vendors.......................8 C2
Yabba Hôtel..........................9 A3

**TRANSPORT**
Buses for Abidjan..................10 C2
Pirogues to Brodje.................11 C2
Taxi Stand...........................(see 10)

exceptional views over Sassandra and the ocean more than make up for it. It has the most reliable kitchen in town.

There are plenty of street food vendors at the central roundabout plus some good *maquis* like **La Clinique** (meals from CFA1000) and **La Route de la Cuisine** (meals from CFA1000) near the post office, grilling up the day's catch, which often includes swordfish and barracuda. (Help the survival of an endangered species and skip the turtle steak.) **Maquis La Cour des Grands** (meals from CFA1000), which has dancing on weekends, is the most popular *maquis* at the moment.

## Getting There & Around

STP and AMT both run two buses a day between Abidjan and Sassandra (CFA4000), leaving Sassandra from the central roundabout. Bush taxis and minibuses, departing from the small *gare routière*, some 3km north of town, connect Sassandra and San Pédro (CFA3000); buses cost CFA2000. Shared taxis around town cost CFA150, even for the longish journey to the *gare routière*. A new motorboat service crosses

the Sassandra River several times a day to the small Neyo village of Brodje.

## AROUND SASSANDRA
### Beaches

Except for Dagbego, all these beaches are along a dirt road west of Sassandra. Most of the hotels have closed, but you can still find a few Robinson Crusoe–style huts at some beaches. Otherwise, talk to village chiefs about spending the night. To reach all but the nearest, you'll have to hire a taxi. The trip to Niega, the furthest beach, costs at least CFA6000. For the return journey, make firm arrangements in advance.

You can walk from Sassandra to **Batélébré II**, the nearest beach. The Yabba Hôtel no longer rents rooms, but does serve simple meals and drinks on weekends and holidays. Look for crocodiles beneath the water lilies in the small lake here. Another 2km westward is the stunning **Plage Niezeko**.

About 8km down the coast from Sassandra is the small fishing port of **Drewen** (*dray*-van) and its ruined cocoa-oil factory, possibly the first factory in West Af-

CÔTE D'IVOIRE

rica. Just beyond Drewen at **Wobuko**, the former owners of the Helice de Sassandra hotel (destroyed during the crisis) offer five-hour **hippopotamus-watching trips** ( ☎ 05-119790; CFA45,000) and will also take you out fishing on the ocean. They also rent gear (CFA5000) if you'd rather do some surf casting. There is a simple *campement* here with cheap rooms.

The final and brightest jewel in this necklace of beach paradises is **Niega**, where the road ends. With its curling breakers, it's a popular surfing venue. Its other great attraction is the dense forest stretching inland. For a modest fee, the village boys will guide you along the narrow trails.

About 35km east of Sassandra, at Dagbego, is **Best of Africa** ( ☎ 34-720606; best@bestofafrica.org; bungalows CFA40,000-60,000; P ☒ 🖳 ), a gorgeous and luxurious resort. The food is fantastic and the facilities are top-notch, from the library right down to the foam in the settees. The beach is riptide free and a variety of on-site activities and nearby nature tours are available. They are working with local villages to create the Trepoint Mask Festival, intended to be held biannually on 7 August and 31 December. Just 1km away, a former 'Best of' employee has opened the **Tribunal** (huts CFA2500), a *campement* with a few simple huts.

## Île du 7ème Art

This little island oasis up the Sassandra River, owned by film director Yéo Kozoloa, is a good wildlife-watching spot. You might see hippo and manatee on a boat tour (CFA8000) and there are two simple rooms and a **bungalow** ( ☎ 22-424394; r CFA16,000; P ) if you want to spend the night. Take the road to the north opposite the Sassandra turn-off. It's about 8km to the park.

## SAN PÉDRO
☎ 34

Built from nothing in the late 1960s, San Pédro, 330km west of Abidjan, is the country's second-major port. Much of the country's timber, palm oil, rubber, coffee and cocoa is exported from here; although business has dropped considerably in recent years because bribes demanded by soldiers and police make it cheaper to truck the goods to Abidjan.

If you get stuck here en route to Sassandra, Grand-Béréby or Parc National de Taï

your night won't be wasted. The Cité area in the heart of San Pédro throbs after dark, with *beaucoup maquis* and dance clubs. The latter cluster around what locals call Le Triangle. The main public beach is 1km west of the commercial port, which itself is of no interest, but the small, reeking area where the fishing boats moor is well worth a browse.

## Sleeping & Eating

**Hôtel Bahia** ( ☎ 712733; Rue Akossika; r CFA8000-12,000; P ☒ ) In the centre of town, this is one of the city's cheaper hotels.

**Hôtel La Caravelle** ( ☎ 05-715507; Blvd Houphouët-Boigny; r CFA15,000-20,000; P ) Down on the beach, small and beautifully decorated, this hotel

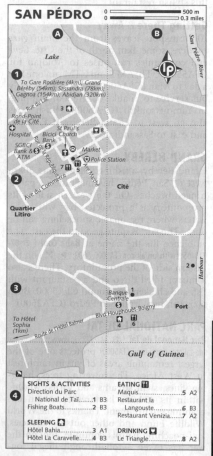

SAN PÉDRO

| SIGHTS & ACTIVITIES | EATING 🍴 |
| --- | --- |
| Direction du Parc | Maquis.....................5 A2 |
| National de Taï........1 B3 | Restaurant la |
| Fishing Boats..............2 B3 | Langouste.................6 B3 |
| | Restaurant Venizia......7 A2 |
| SLEEPING 🛏 | |
| Hôtel Bahia................3 A1 | DRINKING 🍷 |
| Hôtel La Caravelle......4 B3 | Le Triangle................8 A2 |

CÔTE D'IVOIRE

serves excellent African food, including the best grilled pigeon you'll ever taste.

**Hôtel Sophia** ( ☎ 34-713434; Rue a la Plage; s/d CFA36,000/46,000; P ✷ ✷ ) Just out of town, this hotel has a large swimming pool and offers sport fishing trips.

San Pédro is great for eating out. The Cité has an animated strip of cheap *maquis* and drinking places wedged one beside another next to the market.

**Restaurant la Langouste** (Blvd Houphouët-Boigny; meals CFA3500-12,000) Specializing in *langouste* (lobster), this place has an attractive terrace overlooking the ocean.

**Restaurant Venizia** (Ave du Commerce; sandwiches CFA1000; ✷ breakfast, lunch & dinner) For salads and sandwiches, as well as first-rate coffee, try this stylish restaurant.

### Getting There & Away

All transport leaves from the main *gare routière*, some 4km north of the Cité. Several companies run buses to Abidjan for CFA5500. UTB, AMT and CTM run one bus a day to Man (CFA6000) and UTB has daily bus service to Boauké (CFA8000) stopping in Yamoussoukro (CFA6000). Bush taxis also go west to Grand-Béréby (CFA2500) and east to Sassandra (CFA3000).

## GRAND-BÉRÉBY

Grand-Béréby, a fishing village some 50km west of San Pédro, has magnificent palm-fringed beaches. On the western side of its promontory is a protected bay with calm waters where reasonable snorkelling can be done. The surf is quite good to the east. The ambience fits the name at **Baba Cool** ( ☎ 07-710465; r with fan/air-con CFA5000/8000; P ✷ ) on the eastern side of the promontory. There's also a mirror-filled disco and a restaurant with fish and chicken for around CFA5000. Bush taxis run here from San Pédro (CFA2500).

## PARC NATIONAL DE TAÏ

**Parc National de Taï** ( ☎ 34-712353; www.parc-national -de-tai.org; per person CFA5000) protects one of the largest remaining areas of virgin rainforest in West Africa. The towering trees, hanging vines, swift streams and varied wildlife within its 454,000 hectares create an enchanting environment. Thanks to the World Wildlife Fund and other outside agencies, anti-poaching patrols continue, though the war has taken a toll through illegal log-

> **CONSERVATION & ECOTOURISM: THE TAÏ EXAMPLE**
>
> The Parc National de Taï team has had remarkable success in preserving West Africa's largest rainforest from further destruction. The key has been to give a stake in its development to those who made their living from the forest. A proportion of the revenue from tourism is used to improve the quality of life in the villages bordering the park by, for example, opening health care centres, improving drinking water and providing veterinary support for livestock. One program trains people to raise agoutis (rabbit-sized rodents) in captivity to reduce the demand for poaching. As a result of these projects, logging and poaching were diminished significantly; before the war that is.

ging and gold mining. For more information about the park's special conservation scheme, see above.

At press time, the park wasn't fully operational, but visits could be arranged through the park office in San Pédro. There was a hotel and restaurant and they hope to reopen again, but for the time being, overnight visitors are lodged in nearby villages. Guided walks through the forest cost CFA15,000 per person and visiting a habituated group of chimpanzees is CFA20,000. You can opt for all-inclusive, full board packages. A two-day chimpanzee expedition is CFA65,000 per person; a two-day ascent of Mont Niénokoué (396m), the highest point in the park and a sacred mountain for the local Krou population, is CFA95,000 and a four-day visit including chimpanzees, a mountain climb, and pirogue trip is CFA125,000. This is a very rainy, humid area, so the best time to visit is from December to February, when there's a dry season. In these months, you can get there by car; at other times, travelling by 4WD is strongly recommended.

# THE CENTRE

Yamoussoukro has suffered right along with the rest of the country, but the amazing Basilique de Notre Dame de la Paix is such a point of pride that it was spared during the November 2004 riots. Though it is still possible to travel to the capital, the nearby national parks are off limits until the crisis ends, and even then, unfortunately, it's hard to believe there will be much forest or wildlife left.

## YAMOUSSOUKRO

Yamoussoukro has no embassies, ministries or significant commercial life, even though it has been the country's capital since 1983. Originally a village called Ngokro with no more than 500 inhabitants, it has grown because of the whim of Félix Houphouët-Boigny, who happened to be born hereabouts and who wanted to glorify himself, his family and ancestors. With its six-lane highways (bordered by more than 10,000 streetlights) leading nowhere, and its grandiose monuments set just far enough apart to be inconvenient for walking, it's a lasting testament to Africa's greatest curse – the Big Boss, who can get away with anything.

But let's not be churlish. Some of the overweening monuments are architecturally stunning, even if they owe little to Af-

rica: the Basilique de Notre Dame de la Paix with its many superlatives, Hôtel Président and the complex of structures that constitute the Institut National Polytechnique Houphouët-Boigny are worth a look. Plus, the Reserve de Fauna D'Abokouamikro, which might still have elephants, is just a day trip away; though at the time of research it was closed.

### Information

**Sgbci bank** (Ave Houphouët-Boigny) Has a 24hr Visa card–friendly ATM.

**Tourist office** ( ☎ 30-640814; Ave Houphouët-Boigny; ☼ 8am-noon, 3-6pm Mon-Fri) Arranges Baoulé dancing performances in nearby villages for around CFA50,000.

### Sights

#### BASILIQUE DE NOTRE DAME DE LA PAIX

One of Africa's most astonishing sites is the **basilica** (Route de Daloa; admission CFA1000; ☼ 8am-noon & 2-5.30pm Mon-Sat, 2pm-5pm Sun), which remains in tiptop shape, with English-speaking guides on duty. Don't forget to take your passport, which the guard holds until you leave. See p280 for more details.

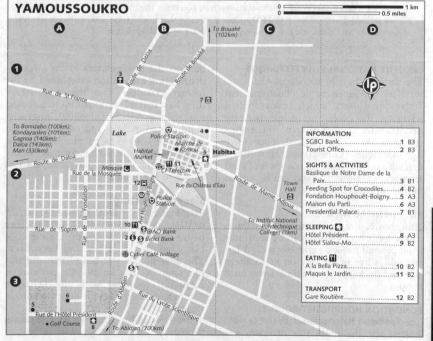

YAMOUSSOUKRO

To Bouaké (102km)

To Bomizabo (100km); Kondayakoro (101km); Gagnoa (140km); Daloa (143km); Man (330km)

To Abidjan (200km)

To Institut National Polytechnique Colleges (1km)

**INFORMATION**
SGBCI Bank..................................1 B3
Tourist Office...............................2 B3

**SIGHTS & ACTIVITIES**
Basilique de Notre Dame de la
  Paix........................................3 B1
Feeding Spot for Crocodiles........4 B1
Fondation Houphouët-Boigny.....5 A3
Maison du Parti...........................6 A3
Presidential Palace......................7 B1

**SLEEPING** 🛏
Hôtel Président............................8 A3
Hôtel Sialou-Mo..........................9 B2

**EATING** 🍴
A la Bella Pizza...........................10 B2
Maquis le Jardin.........................11 B2

**TRANSPORT**
Gare Routière..............................12 B2

CÔTE D'IVOIRE

**YAMOUSSOUKRO'S AMAZING BASILICA**

A visit to Yamoussoukro's Basilique de Notre Dame de la Paix is an emotion-provoking experience not to be missed. You will struggle to reconcile this wondrous construction with its time and place. For miles around, it broods on the humid skyline like a giant, pearl-grey boiled egg.

Its statistics are startling. Completed in 1989, it was built in three years by a labour force of 1500, working day and night in great secrecy. The price tag was about US$300 million and annual maintenance costs US$1.5 million. It bears a striking and deliberate resemblance to St Peter's in Rome. Although the cupola is slightly lower than St Peter's dome (by papal request), it's topped by a huge cross of gold, making it the tallest church in Christendom. Inside, each of its 7000 seats is individually air-conditioned, a system only used on the two occasions when it has been full: at its controversial consecration by a reluctant Pope John Paul II and at the funeral of the man responsible for its creation. The basilica can fit a further 11,000 standing worshippers and as many as 300,000 pilgrims in the 3-hectare plaza – an area slightly larger than St Peter's. There are only one million Catholics in the country and no more than a few hundred attend Sunday mass!

Except for its architect, Pierre Fakhoury, an Ivorian of Lebanese descent, and its toiling construction workers, it owes nothing to Africa. Stop in front of the second bay to the left of the entrance. There, frozen in stained glass, are the architect, the French lady who chose the furnishings, the French foreman and the French stained-glass master craftsman. And, at Christ's feet is the only African face in all of the glass, the conceiver, one Félix Houphouët-Boigny.

The president was reluctant to discuss the details of its financing. He had done a 'deal with God' and to discuss God's business publicly would be more than indiscreet. Proponents of the basilica will rhetorically ask, were there no poor in France when Chartres Cathedral was lovingly built? And was England affluent when the spires of Canterbury Cathedral first stabbed the sky?

What's certain is that you'll catch your breath as you cross the threshold and see the 36 immense stained-glass windows, all 7400 square metres of them, with their 5000 different shades of warm, vibrant colour. It's like standing at the heart of a kaleidoscope.

**INSTITUT NATIONAL POLYTECHNIQUE**

The institute has three colleges: the Institut National Supérieur de l'Enseignement Technique (Inset), which trains applied scientists, the École Nationale Supérieure des Travaux Publics (Enstp) for engineers and the École Normale Supérieure Agronomique (Enmsa) for agricultural specialists. Each building is a jewel of contemporary architecture and can be visited during business hours.

**PRESIDENTIAL PALACE**

Houphouët-Boigny's massive palace, where he is now buried, can be seen only from beyond its 5km perimeter wall. A few crocodiles live in the lake on its southern side and the keeper tosses them some meat at 5pm.

**FONDATION HOUPHOUËT-BOIGNY**

The **Fondation Houphouët-Boigny** (Rue de l'Hôtel Président), on the south side of town, was built as the headquarters of the largesse-distributing association established by the former president. The impressive structure has several auditoriums (including one with a capacity of 4500), huge air-conditioned public spaces and marble floors. All it lacks is people. Nearby, the **Maison du Parti**, the old headquarters of the country's first political party, the PDCI, is closed to the public.

**Sleeping & Eating**

**Hôtel Président** ( ☎ 30-641582; Route d'Abidjan; s/d/ste CFA31,000/36,000/65,000; P ✗ ⊛ ) The city's better hotels were looted during the 2004 riots, but the city's best has been fixed. The 284-room tower has plenty of extras like tennis courts, an 18-hole golf course, nightclub (popular with the Lebanese community) and the 14th-floor Restaurant Panoramique.

**Hôtel Sialou-Mo** ( ☎ 36-641364; r & paillotes CFA5000-6000; P ) Like an African village within the lively Habitat *quarter*, this a fun place to stay. The Sialou-Mo (which means 'thanks, mother' in Baoulé) has attractive *paillotes* with fan and bathroom for the same price as the undistinguished, shower-only rooms in the main block.

Shacks around the Marché de Kossou on Rue du Château d'Eau in Habitat and the *gare routière* across the lake sell dishes such as *sauce graine* for around CFA600 plus snack food and brochettes. **Maquis le Jardin** (across from Habitat market; meals CFA3000-5000; lunch & dinner), is more upmarket and expensive than the others clustered by the lake, but the quality justifies the price. French-owned **A la Bella Pizza** (Ave Houphouët-Boigny; meals CFA3500-5000; lunch & dinner) serves great pastas, crêpes and local fare as well as its namesake pies.

### Getting There & Away

Onward travel in all directions is, in principal, easy from Yamoussoukro, which is a transit hub; however, some buses roll through full so you may have to wait a while. Bush taxis and minibuses leave from the main *gare routière*, which is basically the first 100m of Ave Houphouët-Boigny south of the lake. MTT and UTB, whose stations are south of town, run buses frequently to Abidjan (CFA4000), with the latter also going frequently to Bouaké (CFA3500) and once daily to Man (CFA5000) and San Pédro (CFA6000).

When the security situation improves, you'll again be able to catch buses direct to Bamako, Mali and Bobo-Dioulasso and Ouagadougou in Burkina Faso.

# THE NORTH

The rebel-held half of Côte d'Ivoire, once one of the most fascinating cultural destinations in West Africa, is suffering. The infrastructure is crumbling, the banks are gone, jobs are scarce, and gun-toting soldiers expect handouts. Even if you have all your papers in order, travel here is risky, especially beyond Man and Bouaké.

## MAN
☎ 33

Man, known as *la cité des 18 montagnes* (city of 18 mountains), has the most beau-

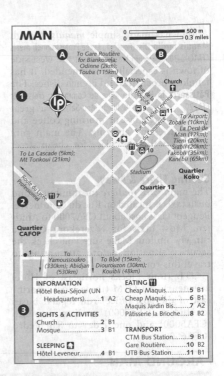

**MAN**

**INFORMATION**
Hôtel Beau-Séjour (UN Headquarters).......1 A2

**SIGHTS & ACTIVITIES**
Church.....................2 B1
Mosque...................3 B1

**SLEEPING**
Hôtel Leveneur..........4 B1

**EATING**
Cheap Maquis............5 B1
Cheap Maquis............6 B1
Maquis Jardin Bis.......7 A2
Pâtisserie la Brioche....8 B2

**TRANSPORT**
CTM Bus Station........9 B1
Gare Routière...........10 B2
UTB Bus Station........11 B1

tiful location of any inland Ivorian town; unfortunately illegal logging is destroying the lush hills that envelop it. War damage is visible at the entrance and around the mayor's office, while the rest of Man is now falling apart due to neglect. The city's famous charm, however, hasn't completely faded.

Man is a good base for exploring the Dan villages nearby, though wandering out of town on foot is a bad idea. Don't leave Man without getting a *laissez-passer* (travel permit) from the rebel chief. He is no pushover; expect to be interrogated thoroughly.

### Sleeping & Eating

All of Man's midrange hotels have either closed or now serve as headquarters for NGOs and the UN. The centrally located **Hôtel Leveneur** ( ☎ 791481; Rue de l'Hôtel Leveneur; r CFA8000; P ) is the best place still standing, though it is in sorry shape. It has a decent restaurant and everybody from rebel commanders to stranded legionnaires gather here for drinks on the terrace.

CÔTE D'IVOIRE

Man has many simple *maquis*, though **Maquis Jardin Bis** (Route du Lycée Professionnel; meals CFA1000-3000; ☺ lunch & dinner) on the west side of town is especially recommended. It has fabulous brochettes and French dishes. The **Pâtisserie la Brioche** (Rue du Commerce; croissants CFA220; ☺ breakfast & lunch Mon-Sat) is a great place for breakfast or morning coffee and the pastries are amazing. The main *gare routière* is the best place for cheap street food.

## Getting There & Away

The main *gare routière* for minibuses and bush taxis is located on Rue du Commerce. Peugeot taxis cost about CFA7000 to Abidjan. Most taxis for N'zérékoré Guinea run via Sipilou. Make sure you check the security situation before attempting to travel this route.

UTB (four blocks northeast of Hôtel Leveneur) and CTM (three blocks northeast of the post office) run regular buses to Abidjan (CFA7000) via Yamoussoukro (CFA5000) and one a day to San Pédro (CFA6000).

# AROUND MAN
## Natural Attractions

Some 5km west of town is **La Cascade** (CFA300), a waterfall within a bamboo forest. August to November are the months of fullest spate, but the site is still beautiful in the dry season. Ask your guide to take you to see the monkeys nearby.

**Mt Tonkoui** (1223m) is the second-highest peak in Côte d'Ivoire and a further 16km of steep, winding road beyond La Cascade. The views from the summit are quite breathtaking and extend to Liberia and Guinea, although not during the harmattan season.

Hikers will love **La Dent de Man** (The Tooth of Man), a steep molar-shaped mountain (881m) 12km northeast of town. The climb begins in the village of Zobale, 4km from Man. There, the inhabitants ask for a CFA500 village tax and children will offer to show you the way. A guide isn't necessary, but they make good company. Allow at least four hours for the round trip, including a breather at the summit, which you'll need after the final gruelling ascent.

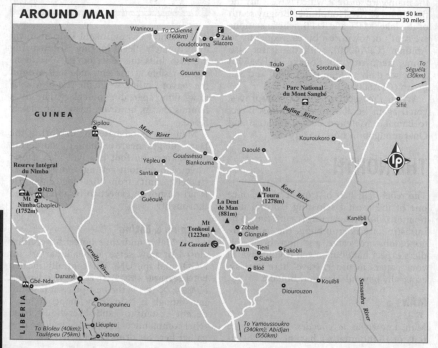

**AROUND MAN**

## Villages

The villages around Man are well used to visitors, not that they get many these days. All of these are accessible by car and, much less conveniently, minibus. Arranging dances (this used to cost about CFA20,000) must be done with the chief in the morning to give the village enough time to prepare for a later performance.

The nearest to Man is **Bloé**, where a Yacouba dance is performed by girls wearing Goua masks. **Biankouma**, north of Man, is known for its acrobatic Goua dances, which usually take place on Sunday, and the village's traditional houses with decorative paintings in kaolin clay. The fetish houses are sacred, so ask permission before taking any pictures. In **Kanébli** you can hire a pirogue for a trip to view hippos and crocodiles, or, perhaps, see the Tematé dance performed by Wobé girls at the end of the rice harvest. **Diourouzon** is one of the places where child juggling (see p260) is performed.

The most celebrated village around is **Silacoro**, about 110km north of Man, which is famous for its stilt dancing (see p261). It's also a very attractive village, consisting entirely of mud houses with thatched, conical roofs. A spring-fed pond is teeming with large, whiskered fish which will slide onto dry land and eat bread from your hand.

## BOUAKÉ

☎ 31

Sprawling and filthy, Bouaké is the country's second-largest city and the capital of the New Forces. Before the war it had around half a million inhabitants; there's probably less than half that today. The Dioula are dominant now, having chased most of the Boualé away when the fighting began. Rag-tag soldiers shouldering Kalashnikovs are everywhere (keep plenty of coins handy) and damage from the November 2004 bombings remains. Even before the war, there was little reason to come here other than **Le Carnaval de Bouaké**, one of Africa's largest carnivals, previously held every March. You can't come here without a *laissez-passer* from the rebels, and they don't just hand them out to anyone. Despite all this, Bouaké is a much safer city than Abidjan.

## Sights

Bouaké's **Grand Marché** was one of the most diverse markets in the country, though few crafts and fabrics are sold here now. A couple of stalls next to the Ran Hôtel, now the rebel headquarters, sell masks and bronze statuettes. Like a vast hangar when empty, the modern **Cathédral St-Michel** (Ave Houphouët-Boigny) is brightened by abstract stained-glass windows. Also notice the black Madonna in bronze to the left of the altar.

## Sleeping & Eating

The **Hôtel Printemps** ( ☎ 07-845632; Rue de la BCAO; r CFA10,000-14,000; P ✷ ) is a pleasant hotel inside the Moroccan-controlled UN compound. Also safe is the nearby **Hôtel du Centre** ( ☎ 633278; Ave Mamadou Konaté; r CFA12,000; P ✷ ) which has large, well-appointed rooms and a nice terrace in front. The staff is friendly and the service still good. The adjoining restaurant is pleasant plus cheap steak and fries are available across the street. You could also call **Madame Delon** ( ☎ 06-349749; CFA20,000-25,000; P ✷ ), a well-known French woman who offers B&B-style accommodation and serves the best French food in the city.

The area around the *gare routière* and market abounds with cheap, simple stalls. **Maquis Walé** (Ave Houphouët-Boigny; meals CFA1500-3500; ✷ lunch & dinner) is a friendly, value-for-money place with a pleasant street-side terrace. The food and service are impressive. The French-run **Pâtisserie les Palmiers** (Ave Gabriel Dadié; breakfast CFA1500; ✷ breakfast, lunch & dinner) is unbeatable for breakfast and coffee. It also does inexpensive pastries and baguettes. The **Restaurant Black & White** (Ave Jacque Aka; meals CFA4000-6000; ✷ lunch & dinner, closed Mon) has an intimate outdoor thatched terrace and an ambitious French menu. It is popular with rebel leaders for drinks at night.

## Getting There & Away

Most buses and bush taxis leave from Gare Routière du Grand Marché. UTB has several buses a day to/from Abidjan (CFA7000) and one to San Pédro (GF8000) – both via Yamoussoukro (CFA3500) – from its station south of the market. Peugeot taxis serve the same routes and charge about the same.

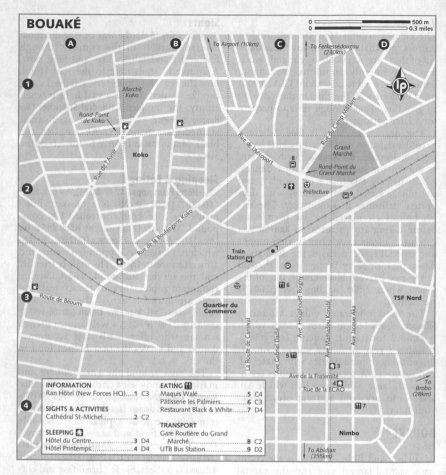

**BOUAKÉ**

| INFORMATION | |
| --- | --- |
| Ran Hôtel (New Forces HQ)....**1** C3 | |
| **SIGHTS & ACTIVITIES** | |
| Cathédral St-Michel...............**2** C2 | |
| **SLEEPING** | |
| Hôtel du Centre....................**3** D4 | |
| Hôtel Printemps...................**4** D4 | |
| **EATING** | |
| Maquis Walé.........................**5** C4 | |
| Pâtisserie les Palmiers...........**6** C3 | |
| Restaurant Black & White........**7** D4 | |
| **TRANSPORT** | |
| Gare Routière du Grand Marché...**8** C2 | |
| UTB Bus Station....................**9** D2 | |

# CÔTE D'IVOIRE DIRECTORY

## ACCOMMODATION

Many of the country's hotels have shut down and most that remain are going to pot. Most cheapies double as brothels. Before the war, accommodation was generally expensive and poor value for money, but now places are so desperate for guests that you can bargain over the already low rates in some four-star hotels. Note that there is no running water in the north. In this chapter budget accommodation is CFA15,000 and below, while top end is

over CFA40,000 and midrange is in between the two.

## ACTIVITIES

The area around Man is good for hiking, while for swimming, there are unlimited possibilities all along the coast. Several spots on the coast, most notably Bassam, Dagbego and Drewen, have decent surfing. **Kamesurf** ( ☎ 21-256401) in Abidjan's Prima Center shopping mall can provide information.

Côte d'Ivoire also has a lot to offer bird-watchers. It's worth polishing your binoculars before visiting the Parc National de Taï (p278) or the last remaining coastal rainforest around San Pédro (p277). See p263 for more details.

## BOOKS

A trio of beautifully written books offer insight into Ivorian village life. Sarah Erdman, a Peace Corps health worker, began her two year stint in a Senoufo village in 1998, just as AIDS and other trappings of modern life were arriving. She recounts the highs and lows of her stay in *Nine Hills to Nambonkaha*. Both *In the Shadow of the Sacred Grove* by Carol Spindell and *Parallel Worlds* by Alma Gottlieb and Philip Graham, date back to around 1980, but their year-long experiences still ring true today. If you read French, look for *La Crise en Côte d'Ivoire* by Thomas Hofnung, which offers an up-to-date overview of the current crisis.

## BUSINESS HOURS

Business hours are 8am to noon and 2.30pm to 6pm Monday to Friday, and mornings only on Saturday. Government offices are open 7.30am to noon and 2.30pm to 5.30pm Monday to Friday. Banking hours are from 8am to 3pm Monday to Friday and 8am to noon Saturday.

## CUSTOMS

Travellers may not take more than CFA500,000 out of the country. You'll also need a permit (inquire at the Musée National; p267) to export Ivorian artefacts.

## DANGERS & ANNOYANCES

Côte d'Ivoire can be visited safely, but overall it is still not a safe country. There has only been sporadic violence since the attacks of November 2004 and most of the rumours of violence turn out to be false, but the situation remains volatile and the possibility of further unrest – or a resumption of all-out war – can't be discounted. Additionally, the north–south divide is strong and even elections might not end the crisis.

But, unless fighting breaks out again, the biggest concern is crime. Poverty and unemployment are rampant and there is no shortage of guns. Armed robberies and carjackings are common, as are grab-and-run street crimes. Do not display jewellery, cash or cameras and always take a taxi at night.

Security checkpoints are frequent in the north and south, particularly near the Zone of Confidence and on the outskirts of cities. Soldiers inspect documents and frequently demand money or cigarettes. These encounters can be friendly or tense. Either way, just remain calm, talk with them, and hand over what they ask for – usually CFA500.

Travelling around the north without proper paperwork from rebel leaders (the Abidjan rebel headquarters is at the Hôtel du Golf) is foolish. Even when their documents are in order, Westerners are greeted with suspicion, especially in Bouaké.

Finally, take care at the beach. The Atlantic has fierce currents and a ripping undertow and people drown every year; often strong, overly confident swimmers. Heed local advice.

For assessment of Abidjan's security risks, see p267.

## EMBASSIES & CONSULATES
### Ivorian Embassies & Consulates

In West Africa, Côte d'Ivoire has embassies in Ghana, Mali, Guinea, Senegal, Nigeria, Liberia and Burkina Faso. For details see the relevant country chapter. Elsewhere, Côte d'Ivoire has the following embassies:

**Belgium** ( ☎ 02-661 34 50; mailbox@ambacibnl.be; 234 Ave Franklin-Roosevelt, Brussels 1050)

**Canada** ( ☎ 613-236 9919; www.ambaci-ottawa.org; 9 Marlborough Ave, Ottawa, Ontario, K1N 8E6)

**France** ( ☎ 01-53 64 62 62; bureco-fr@cotedivoire.com; 102 Ave R-Poincaré, Paris 75116)

**Germany** ( ☎ 0228-26 30 45; Clausewitz St 7, Berlin 10629)

**UK** ( ☎ 020-7201 9601; 2 Upper Belgrave St, London SW1X 8BJ)

**USA** ( ☎ 202-797-0300; 2424 Massachusetts Ave, Washington DC, NW, 20008)

## Embassies & Consulates in Côte d'Ivoire

The following embassies and consulates in Abidjan are mostly in Le Plateau, unless otherwise indicated:

**Belgium** (Map p268; ☎ 20-219316; abidjan@diplobel .org; Immeuble Alliance, Ave Terrasson des Fougéres 01; ☾ 8.30-11.30am & 2-5pm Mon-Fri) Assists Dutch nationals.

**Benin** (Map p266; ☎ 22-414413; Rue des Jardins, Les Deux Plateaux; ☾ 8am-2pm Mon-Fri)

**Burkina Faso** (Map p268; ☎ 20-211501; Ave Terrasson de Fougères; ☾ 8.30am-1pm Mon-Fri) Also a consulate in Bouaké.

**Cameroon** (Map p268; ☎ 20-212086; 3rd fl, Immeuble le Général, Rue du Commerce; ☾ 8.30am-2.30pm Mon-Fri)

**Canada** (Map p268; ☎ 20-300700; www.dfait-maeci .gc.ca/abidjan; Immeuble Trade Centre, 23 Ave Noguès; ☾ 7.30am-1pm & 2-5.30pm Mon, Tue, Thu, to 1pm Wed, to 12.30pm Fri) Assists Australian nationals.

**France** (Map p268; ☎ 20-200404; www.ambafrance -ci.org; 17 Rue Lecoeur; ☾ 8am-12.30pm & 2.30-5.30pm Mon-Thu, to 1pm Fri)

**Germany** (Map p266; ☎ 22-442030; www.abidjan.diplo .de; 39 Blvd Hassan II, Cocody; ☾ 9am-noon Mon-Fri)

**Ghana** (Map p266; ☎ 22-410288; Rue des Jardins, Les Deux Plateaux; ☾ 8.30am-1pm Mon-Fri)

**Guinea** (Map p268; ( ☎ 20-329494; Immeuble Crosson Duplessis, Ave Crosson Duplessis; ☾ 9am-4pm Mon-Thu, 9am-1pm Fri)

**Liberia** (Map p268; ☎ 20-324636; Immeuble Taleb, Ave Delafosse; ☾ 9am-3:30pm Mon-Fri)

**Mali** (Map p268; ☎ 20-311570; Maison du Mali, Rue du Commerce; ☾ 7.30am-noon Mon-Fri) Also a consulate in Bouaké.

**Niger** (Map p266; ☎ 21-262814; Blvd Achalma, Marcory; ☾ 8am-3pm Mon-Fri)

**Nigeria** (Map p268; ☎ 20-211982; Blvd de la République; ☾ 9.30am-12.30pm & 2.30-4.30pm Mon-Fri)

**Senegal** (Map p268; ☎ 20-332876; Immeuble Nabil, off Rue du Commerce; ☾ 8.30am-1pm Mon-Fri)

**Togo** (Map p268; ☎ 20-320974; Immeuble Nabil, off Rue du Commerce; ☾ 8.30am-3pm Mon-Fri)

**UK** (Map p268; ☎ 20-226850; Immeuble les Harmonies, Blvd Carde) Operations were suspended on 1 April 2005. Services are now provided from Accra.

**USA** ( ☎ 22-494000; http://abidjan.usembassy.gov; Riviera Golf; ☾ 8am-12.30pm & 1.30-5pm Mon-Fri)

## FESTIVALS & EVENTS

Côte d'Ivoire is rich in traditional festivals, though not all are being celebrated during the crisis. Some particularly exuberant ones include the following:

**Fête de l'Abissa** Held in Grand Bassam in October or November. A week-long, traditional carnival in which N'Zima people honour their dead and publicly exorcise evil spirits. Travellers can join in some parts of the celebration.

**Fête des Harristes** Held in Bregbo near Bingerville, 15km east of Abidjan, on 1 November, this is a major annual Harrist festival. Harrists have a 'born again' amalgam of Christianity and traditional beliefs. Their founder was William Wade Harris, who in 1913 began a preaching journey, walking barefoot from Liberia, through the Ivory Coast and on into the Gold Coast (modern Ghana).

**Fêtes des Masques** Masks are an integral part of Dan society, serving as the community's collective memory and embodying a divine energy. The annual Fêtes des Masques in February, held in the villages around Man, brings together a great variety of masks and dances from the area.

**Fête du Dipri** Held in Gomon in April, 100km northwest of Abidjan. At midnight, naked women and children carry out nocturnal rites to rid the village of evil incantations. Before dawn the village chief appears to the sound of drums, and villagers are sent into a trance. An animated frenzy carries on throughout the following day.

**Le Carnaval de Bouaké** This weeklong celebration of friendship and life in March is one of Africa's largest carnivals.

## HOLIDAYS

For more information on Islamic holidays, see p818. Public holidays in Côte d'Ivoire include the following:

**New Year's Day** 1 January
**Easter** March/April
**Labour Day** 1 May
**Independence Day** 7 August
**Assumption Day** 15 August
**All Saints' Day** 1 November
**Fête de la Paix** 15 November
**Christmas Day** 25 December

## INTERNET ACCESS

Most cities in government territory have cybercafés, though outside Abidjan, connections can be slow and unreliable.

## INTERNET RESOURCES

A good news source, if you read French, is www.abidjan.net.

CÔTE D'IVOIRE

# LANGUAGE

French is the official language and widely spoken. In Abidjan and other towns that used to get tourists, some people speak English. Principal African languages include Mande and Malinké in the northwest; Dan/Yacouba in the area around Man; Senoufo in and around Korhogo; Baoulé and Agni in the centre and south; and Dioula, the market language, everywhere. See p861 for useful phrases in French, Dioula, Senoufo and Dan.

## MAPS

The Michelin 1:800,000 map gives the best coverage of Côte d'Ivoire.

## MONEY

Endeavour to bring a Visa card and euros, otherwise you'll find obtaining CFA costly and time consuming in Abidjan, and nearly impossible most other places. Change as much as you can in Abidjan because rates are better than anywhere else. Banks for changing money include Bicici (Banque Internationale pour le Commerce et l'Industrie en Côte d'Ivoire), BIAO (Banque Internationale pour l'Afrique Occidentale), Sgbci (Société Générale de Banques en Côte d'Ivoire), Cobaci (Compagnie Bancaire de l'Atlantique – Côte d'Ivoire) and Citibank. You can also change euros commission-free at most hotels and many shops. There are no banks in rebel territory.

You won't be able to pay with credit cards very often (and when you can, make sure the transaction is completed electronically in front of you – fraud is a growing problem), but Sgbci and Bicici have ATMs in Abidjan, San Pédro and Yamoussoukro that reliably provide holders of Visa cards with CFA. Commission charged on travellers cheques varies significantly from bank to bank.

In Abidjan there is a black market for changing US dollars; however, you shouldn't use it unless a local friend makes the introduction as most of these guys are hustlers and there is a lot of counterfeit money floating around these days. Moneychangers in the north prefer dollars over euros.

## TELEPHONE

There are CI Telecom offices in major towns, but calls from private *télécentres* and cyber-cafés are cheaper – calls to USA/Europe/

Australia can be as low as CFA75/100/200 per minute in Abidjan. Phonecards are also handy and if you have a GSM mobile phone, you can buy a SIM card for as low as CFA5000.

## VISAS

Everyone except nationals of Ecowas (Economic Community of West African States) and US citizens need a visa. Visas are usually valid for three months and are good for visits of up to one month. The cost varies quite substantially depending on your nationality and where you are applying for it. You can't get a visa at the border or the airport.

### Visa Extensions

Visas can be extended at **La Sureté Nationale** (Police de l'Air et des Frontieres; ☒ 8am-noon & 3-5pm) near the main post office in Le Plateau in Abidjan. An extension, valid for up to three months, costs CFA20,000 (plus two photos) and is ready the same day if you apply early.

### Visas for Onward Travel

In Côte d'Ivoire, you can get visas for the following neighbouring countries.

#### BURKINA FASO

Three-month single-/multiple-entry visas cost CFA25,000/30,000 and require two photos. They are usually issued the same day. A consulate in Bouaké also issues visas.

#### GHANA

Four photos, CFA15,000 and 24 hours are required of most nationalities for one-month single-entry visas.

#### GUINEA

One-month single-entry visas cost CFA32,000 for most nationalities, though Americans pay CFA55,000. Everyone pays CFA96,000 for three-month multiple-entry. You need three photos and visas might be ready the same day if you get there early.

#### LIBERIA

One-month single-entry visas, issued the same day, cost CFA27,000 for most nationalities. Multiple-entry visas are good for a year and cost CFA57,000. You need two photos.

#### MALI

For most nationalities, one-month single-entry visas cost CFA20,000, three-month multiple entry visas cost CFA40,000, and one-year multiple-entry visas cost CFA60,000. Americans are charged $100. You must bring one photo and a letter detailing your reason for visiting Mali and can pick up your visa within 24 hours. A consulate in Bouaké also issues visas.

## WOMEN TRAVELLERS

With the possible exception of persistent men at the few coastal resorts, women travellers are unlikely to meet with special hassles. For more general information and advice, see p828.

# TRANSPORT IN CÔTE D'IVOIRE

## GETTING THERE & AWAY
### Entering Côte d'Ivoire

A yellow fever vaccination certificate is mandatory and will be requested when applying for a visa and on arrival.

### Air

Port Bouët is Côte d'Ivoire's only international airport. Ignore the touts who offer to speed you through passport control and customs, and if someone is picking you up, make sure the person holding the sign with your name is really who they say they are.

Airlines servicing Côte d'Ivoire and with offices in Abidjan include the following:

**Afriqiyah Airways** (8U; Map p268; ☎ 20-338785; www.afriqiyah.aero; Abidjan Universel Voyages, Crosson Duplessis, Le Plateau) Hub: Tripoli.

**Air Algérie** (AH; Map p268; ☎ 20-325651; www.airalgerie.dz; Ave Houdaille) Hub: Algiers.

**Air Burkina** (2J; Map p268; ☎ 20-328919; www.air-burkina.com; Ave Houdaille, Le Plateau) Hub: Ouagadougou.

**Air France** (AF; Map p268; ☎ 20-202424; www.airfrance.com; Immeuble Kharrat, Rue Noguès, Le Plateau) Hub: Charles de Gaulle, Paris.

**Air Gabon** (GN; Map p268; ☎ 20-215506; Ave Delafosse) Hub: Leon M'ba International Airport, Libreville.

**Air Ivoire** (VU; Map p268; ☎ 20-251561; www.airivoire.com; Immeuble Le République, Place de la République) Hub: Abidjan International Airport, Abidjan.

**Air Mauritanie** (MR; Map p268; ☎ 20-320991; www.airmauritanie.mr; Immeuble du Mali, Rue du Commerce) Hub: Nouakchott.

**Air Sénégal International** (V7; Map p268; ☎ 20-302380; www.air-senegal-international.com; Ave Chardy) Hub: Dakar.

**Bellview Airlines** (B3; Map p268; ☎ 20-320714; www.flybellviewair.com; Immeuble l'Amiral, Rue du Commerce) Hub: Lagos.

**Benin Golf Air** (A8; ☎ 20-338887; www.beningolfair.com) Hub: Cotonou.

**Cameroon Airlines** (UY; Map p268; ☎ 20-211919; www.cameroon-airlines.com; Immeuble l'Amiral, Rue du Commerce) Hub: Douala.

**Ethiopian Airlines** (ET; Map p268; ☎ 20-215284; www.flyethiopian.com; Ave Chardy, Le Plateau) Hub: Addis Ababa.

**Kenya Airways** (KQ; Map p268; ☎ 20-320767; www.kenya-airways.com; Immeuble Jeceda, Blvd de la République, Le Plateau) Hub: Nairobi.

**Middle East Airlines** (ME; Map p268; ☎ 20-226282; www.mea.com.lb; Blvd Delafosse) Hub: Beirut.

**Royal Air Maroc** (AT; Map p268; ☎ 20-212811; www.royalairmaroc.com; Immeuble Le Paris, Blvd Botreau Roussel) Hub: Casablanca.

**Slok Air** (SO; Map p271; ☎ 21-248867; www.slokairinternational.com; Immeuble les Dunes, Blvd Valéry Giscard d'Estaing, Treichville) Hub: Banjul.

**SN Brussels** (SN; Map p271; ☎ 27-232345; www.flysn.com; behind Supermarché Cap Sud, off Blvd Valéry Giscard d'Estaing, Treichville) Hub: Brussels.

**South African Airways** (SA; Map p268; ☎ 20-218280; www.flysaa.com; Immeuble Jeceda, Blvd de la République, Le Plateau) Hub: Johannesburg.

**Tunisair** (TU; Map p268; ☎ 20-224542; www.tunisair.com; Immeuble Nebil, Rue du Commerce, Le Plateau) Hub: Tunis.

**Weasua Air Transport** (XA; ☎ 21-586981) Hub: Monrovia.

### AFRICA & MIDDLE EAST

Elsewhere in Africa and the Middle East you can get direct to Addis Ababa (Ethiopia), Algiers (Algeria), Beirut (Lebanon), Casablanca (Morocco), Johannesburg (South Africa), Libreville (Gabon), Nairobi (Kenya), Tripoli (Libya) and Tunis (Tunisia).

### EUROPE

The cheapest flights from Europe are out of Paris and can come as low as €350/€600 one-way/return. Air France and Air Ivoire fly nonstop from Paris though the best price usually comes with a change of planes in Marseille. Other airlines, including Air Sénégal International, Royal Air Maroc and Tunisair, have convenient connections between Paris and Abidjan through their African hubs. SN Brussels fly nonstop from Brussels for around €850 return.

**REGIONAL FLIGHTS FROM ABIDJAN**

| Destination | Flights per week | Airline | One-way/ return fare (CFA) |
|---|---|---|---|
| Accra (Ghana) | 18 | Air Ivoire, Air Sénégal International, Bellview Airlines, Ethiopian Airlines, Kenya Airways | 99,000/132,000 |
| Bamako (Mali) | 14 | Air Ivoire, Air Mauritanie, Air Sénégal International, Benin Golf Air, Cameroon Airlines, Slok Air, Tunisair | 112,000/189,000 |
| Banjul (The Gambia) | 1 | Slok Air | 213,000/272,000 |
| Conakry (Guinea) | 7 | Air Ivoire, Bellview Airlines, Slok Air | 123,000/147,000 |
| Cotonou (Benin) | 15 | Afriqiyah Airways, Air Ivoire, Air Mauritanie, Air Sénégal International, Benin Golf Air | 91,000/133,000 |
| Dakar (Senegal) | 15 | Air Gabon, Air Ivoire, Air Mauritanie, Air Sénégal International, Bellview Airlines, Benin Golf Air, Cameroon Airlines, Slok Air | 117,000/183,000 |
| Douala (Cameroon) | 9 | Air Ivoire, Cameroon Airlines, Kenya Airways | 226,000/290,000 |
| Freetown (Sierra Leone) | 3 | Bellview Airlines, SN Brussels | 278,000/392,000 |
| Lagos (Nigeria) | 9 | Bellview Airlines, Cameroon Airlines, Middle East Airlines | 94,000/164,000 |
| Lomé (Togo) | 10 | Air Ivoire, Benin Golf Air, Air Sénégal International | 88,000/135,000 |
| Monrovia (Liberia) | 4 | Bellview Airlines, Weasua Air Transport | 117,000/186,000 |
| Niamey (Niger) | 3 | Air Burkina, Air Ivoire | 183,000/273,000 |
| Nouakchott (Mauritania) | 3 | Air Mauritanie | 209,000/254,000 |
| Ouagadougou (Burkina Faso) | 6 | Air Burkina, Air Ivoire, | 129,000/284,000 |
| Yaoundé (Cameroon) | 1 | Cameroon Airlines | 289,000/423,000 |

Prices are approximate.

## NORTH AMERICA & AUSTRALASIA

There are no direct flights from North America or Australia. A return flight from New York via Paris with Air France or via Casablanca with Royal Air Maroc in the low/high season is about US$1250/1450. If you can find a deal on the trans-Atlantic leg of the trip, it's usually cheaper to buy a ticket to Europe and then a separate discounted ticket onward from there. Doing it this way might cost as little as US$1000 from the east coast. Best bet from Australia is through Johannesburg with South African Airways: a return will cost around A$3000.

The table above details regional flights.

## Land

At the time of research all borders were open, though this is subject to change based on the situation on the ground at any particular time.

### BURKINA FASO

The route to Burkina Faso through Ouangolodougou is sealed all the way, and there is still regular bus and bush taxi traffic to/from Bobo-Dioulasso and Ouagadougou, but it would be foolish to take any of them until the crisis ends. The train still runs to Ouagadougou, but only for cattle and cargo.

### GHANA

The coastal road connecting Abidjan to Ghana is sealed and still in pretty good condition. The most reliable bus service to Accra is STC which has its own bus station south of Treichville and charges CFA18,000. Also decent are STIF and UTB, departing from Gare Routière d'Adjamé and charging CFA20,000. Each company charges CFA300 per kilogram for luggage (the final total is subject to bargaining) and possibly a CFA1000 whip-round at the border (at Noé) to cover bribes to border officials. Tickets should be purchased a day in advance because the buses are usually full and you should get to the station at least 45 minutes before departure to guarantee your seat.

It is faster to go to by bush taxi from the Gare de Bassam in Abidjan, even though it

CÔTE D'IVOIRE

will involve walking across the border and changing cars. A seat to Noé costs CFA5000 and then it is about another 100,000 cedi to Accra.

The border crossings further north near Agnibilékrou and Bouna should be considered off limits to travellers for the time being.

### GUINEA

The most frequently travelled route to Guinea is between Man and N'zérékoré, either through Danané and Nzo or Biankouma and Sipilou. By bush taxi it is quicker to use the later route. Roads on both are bad. Do not set off on this trip without first getting clearance from the rebel authorities in Man. Though it is off limits to travellers, bush taxis also link Odienné and Sinko, which is where most traffic headed to Kankan goes because the more direct route through Mandiana is nearly impassable.

### LIBERIA

The main route is from Danané to Ganta via Sanniquellie. Minibuses sometimes make the quick hop from Danané to the border at Gbé-Nda (border fees will set you back about $20), but you may have to hitch. On the Liberian side there is a daily bush taxi (charging about CFA3000) on to Sanniquellie. A bus takes this route from Abidjan to Monrovia (around CFA25,000) several times a week.

The coastal route, between Tabou and Harper, is impractical, though adventurous. Bush taxis travel to the border at the Cavally River (crossed by boat) in both directions daily, but beyond Harper the journey to Monrovia is difficult enough (it takes two to three days with a 4WD in the dry season) that residents of Harper going to the capital sometimes cross into Côte d'Ivoire and use the Danané route.

### MALI

The routes to Bamako via Ferkessédougou or Odienné are sealed all the way, and buses and bush taxis still run from Abidjan, Yamoussoukro and Bouaké; but until the crisis is over, it would be unwise for a traveller to be on any of them.

## GETTING AROUND

Because of all the hassles, locals aren't travelling as much as they used to, and consequently there is less transport available; however, all sizable towns, even those in the north, are still connected. But, unless things change, travel to the north by public transport is unwise. Also note that security checkpoints make estimating travel times impossible. A bush taxi from Abidjan to Sassandra, for instance, can take anywhere from five to ten hours depending on how the stops go.

### Air

**Sophia Airlines** ( ☎ 34-713434) flies daily except Sunday between Abidjan and San Pédro for CFA75,000/140,000 one-way/return.

### Bus

The country's large, relatively modern *cars* (buses) are around the same price and are significantly more comfortable than bush taxis or minibuses. Most have fixed departure times and don't charge extra for luggage. Before all the security checkpoints were initiated, they used to take the same time as bush taxis, but are now usually much slower.

### Bush Taxi & Minibus

Bush taxis (ageing Peugeots or covered pickups, known as *bâchés*) and minibuses cover major towns and outlying communities not served by the large buses. They leave at all hours of the day, but only when full so long waits may be required. While they are usually not as comfortable as the buses, they generally cover the same routes faster.

### Car & Motorcycle

Côte d'Ivoire used to have one of the best road systems in Africa, but most paved roads are deteriorating, in particular the highway between Sassandra and San Pédro which now takes three hours to traverse. The highway linking Abidjan to Yamoussoukro remains good. But checkpoints, rather than potholes are the biggest hassle.

### Tours

The Abidjan travel agencies listed (p267) lead personalized tours throughout government territory.

# The Gambia

The tiny sliver of The Gambia is wedged into surrounding Senegal, and is either seen as a splinter in its side, or the tongue that makes it speak, depending on who you talk to. For most travellers, it's an easily negotiated country with a magnificent shoreline that invites visitors to laze and linger. But there's more to Africa's smallest country than sun and surf. Small fishing villages, nature reserves and historical slaving stations are all within easy reach from the clamorous resort zones at the coast, and Gambia's vibrant culture is always there to be taken in by open-eyed visitors. Traditional wrestling matches regularly take place in Serekunda's arenas and the striking performances of griots can be experienced during weddings, baptisms or public concerts.

Bird lovers will easily be seduced by this compact country. On a tour upriver, the cries of over 300 species will follow you as your pirogue charts a leisurely course through mangrove-lined wetlands. Even if your ornithological skills don't go beyond identifying an inner-city pigeon, you'll be tempted to wield binoculars here, and can rely on an excellent network of trained guides to help you tell a pelican from a flamingo.

## FAST FACTS

- **Area** 11,300 sq km
- **Capital** Banjul
- **Country code** ☎ 220
- **Famous for** Being the smallest African country; the *kora*; birds and beaches
- **Languages** Mandinka, Wolof, Fula, English
- **Money** dalasi (D); US$1 = D50; €1 = D34
- **Population** 1.6 million
- **Visa** Not needed for nationals of Commonwealth countries, Belgium, Germany, Italy, Luxembourg, the Netherlands, Ecowas or Scandinavian countries. One-month visas of around US$45 for all others. Best purchased before travel – can be difficult to obtain at the border.

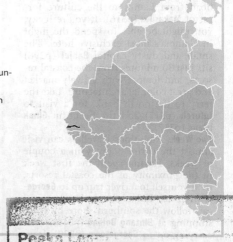

# HIGHLIGHTS

- **Atlantic Coast resorts** (p303) Watch the sun slide into the Atlantic from a hammock on the beach.
- **Georgetown** (p320) Tour upriver, past islands, tiny *campements* and nature reserves.
- **Abuko Nature Reserve** (p315) Spot birds, monkeys and crocodiles in Gambia's tiniest national park.
- **Banjul** (p306) Negotiate a bargain in crammed Albert Market.
- **Gunjur & Kartong** (p313) Taste tranquil village life in tiny fishing communities.

# ITINERARIES

- **Three Days** Over a long weekend, you can explore quite a good part of the Gambian coastal area. Spend a good amount of time at the beaches of the **Atlantic Coast** (p303), and tie in the occasional day trip to the surrounding areas. The busy market of **Serekunda** (p303) is close by, and the pretty museum and bird reserve of **Tanji** (p313), as well as the small fishing villages of **Gunjur** (p313) and **Kartong** (p314), which are only a short distance further along the coast. **Abuko Nature Reserve** (p315), Gambia's smallest stretch of protected nature, is only a short drive away from the Atlantic Coast. A trip here can also be combined with a meal at **Lamin Lodge** (p315), a creaking wooden restaurant nestled in the mangroves.
- **One Week** Start your trip as above, then head from Lamin to the culture forest of **Makasutu** (p316). If you're lucky, you might be able to spend the night in Gambia's most exclusive hotel. The small and dusty capital **Banjul** (p298) sits just 30 minutes from the coastal resorts, and tempts with a lively market and great colonial architecture. Take the ferry to the north bank, for a visit to **Jufureh** (p317) and the beautiful **Ginak Island** (p317).
- **Two Weeks** Ambitious travellers can visit almost the entire country in a couple of weeks. Having spent the first week in the proximity of the coastal resorts, treat yourself to a river trip up to **Georgetown** (p320). If that's beyond budget, you can follow the southern shore by road, stopping at **Bintang Bolong** (p319), then carrying on to **Georgetown** (p320), from

where you can take pirogue excursions to **Gambia River National Park** (p321) and visit **Basse Santa Su** (p321).

# CLIMATE & WHEN TO GO

By far the most popular time for tourists to visit The Gambia is the period from November to February, when conditions are dry and relatively cool, with average day time maximum temperatures around 24°C (75°F). This is also the best time to watch wildlife and birds. From mid-February to April, the average day time maximums rise to 26°C (79°F).

The wet season starts around late June and lasts until late September. During this time, temperatures rise to around 30°C (86°F). It's the time most tourists avoid. The rains wash away some of the roads, rendering certain journeys upcountry impossible. Malaria is widespread and the stifling and humid heat can become uncomfortable. But there's a positive side to this, too. Everything is greener, independent travellers will enjoy the absence of large tourist groups, and many places reduce their prices by up to 50%.

October and November are fairly dry, though very hot – if you can take the temperatures, this is a great time to come. You can still enjoy the sight of lush greens, swelling rivers and large waterfalls, while staying dry yourself. The beaches aren't packed yet, and you're bound to find a hotel room.

---

**HOW MUCH?**

- **Soft drink** D15
- **Newspaper** D10
- **Sandwich** D50
- **French bread** D8
- **1hour Internet** D30

**LONELY PLANET INDEX**

- **1L of petrol/gas** D30
- **1L of bottled water** D30
- **Bottle of Julbrew** D20
- **Souvenir T-shirt** D200-500
- **Shwarma** D50

### THE GAMBIA

The Gambia's official name always includes 'The', but this is often omitted in everyday situations. In this book we have usually omitted 'The' for reasons of clarity and to ensure a smooth-flowing text.

## HISTORY

Ancient stone circles, such as the famous Wassu group in Eastern Gambia, and burial mounds indicate that this part of West Africa has been inhabited by ancient civilisations for at least 1500 years.

By the 13th century, the area had been absorbed into the Empire of Mali, which stretched between present-day Senegal and Niger. Mali's influence began to wane in the mid-15th century, when it was eclipsed by the more powerful Empire of Songhaï. The gradual disintegration of the Empire of Mali caused a significant migratory movement of the Malinké towards the valley of the Gambia River. They brought Islam with them, and became known as the Mandinka – a Malinké branch with distinctive culture.

The first Europeans to reach Gambia were Portuguese explorers in 1455. By 1650, they had been eclipsed by the British, who established Fort James on an island 25km upstream from the mouth of the Gambia River. Twenty years later, the French built a rival fort at nearby Albreda, and during the 17th and 18th centuries, the French and British vied for control of the region's trade.

While the Europeans traded tobacco and gunpowder for ivory and gold, it was the purchase of slaves for shipment that most upset the traditional balance. Encouraged by European traders, local chiefs invaded neighbouring tribes and took captives, selling them to the Europeans. In 1783, Britain gained all rights to trade on the Gambia River, and Fort James became one of West Africa's most infamous slave shipment points.

### The Colonial Period

When the British abolished slavery in 1807, Royal Navy ships began capturing slave ships of other nations, and Fort James was converted from a dungeon into a haven. As part of this crusade, in 1816, the British built a fort on Banjul Island, and established a settlement that was named Bathurst.

The Gambia River protectorate was administered from Sierra Leone until 1888, when Gambia became a full colony. For the next 75 years though, Gambia was almost forgotten, and administration was limited to a few British district commissioners and the local chiefs they appointed. Britain actually tried to trade Gambia for other colonial territories, but no one was interested.

In the 1950's, Gambia's groundnut plantations were improved as a way of increasing export earnings, and other agricultural schemes were implemented. But there was little else in the way of services; by the early 1960's, Gambia had fewer than 50 primary schools and only a handful of doctors.

### Throwing off the British Yoke

In 1960, when other West African nations had already gained independence, Dawda Jawara founded the People's Progressive Party (PPP). The political landscape was hardly developed apart from that, and, given the colony's small size, Britain doubted that an independent Gambia could be economically self-sustaining.

Still, Gambia became independent in 1965. Jawara became prime minister, and Britain's Queen Elizabeth II remained titular head of state. Bathurst, now renamed Banjul, became the country's capital.

A viable future still seemed unlikely, but during the next 10 years, the world price for groundnuts increased and Gambia became a popular tourist destination, both factors which boosted the local economy.

In 1970, Gambia became a fully independent republic, with Jawara as president. Opposition parties were tolerated, though not encouraged, and the Jawara government was accused of neglect and mismanagement.

The first signs of discontent came in 1980, when disaffected soldiers staged a coup. In accordance with a mutual defence pact, the Senegalese army helped oust the rebels and, acknowledging his debt, Jawara announced that the armies of Gambia and Senegal would be integrated. In 1982, the Senegambian Confederation came into effect. Although politicial unity seemed a good idea, relations were never completely relaxed and, by 1989, the confederation was dissolved.

Meanwhile, groundnut prices began to fall and restructuring by the International

## THE GAMBIA

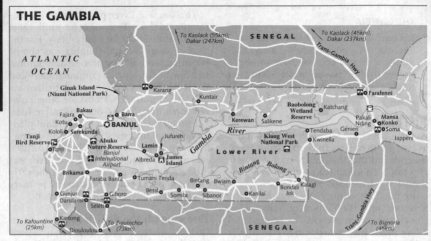

Monetary Fund (IMF) resulted in reduced agricultural subsidies and even more dissatisfaction in rural areas. Despite this, and in the face of frequent allegations of incompetence and corruption, Jawara remained popular throughout the 1980s.

### The 1990s

In April 1992 President Jawara and the PPP were re-elected for a sixth term. To the outside world, Jawara appeared to remain popular. It came as a surprise, therefore, when he was overthrown on 22 July 1994 by young military officers in a reportedly bloodless coup. The coup leader, 29-year-old Lieutnant Yahya Jammeh, announced a new government, to be headed by the Armed Forces Provisional Ruling Council (AFPRC). Jammeh initially promised that the AFPRC would be back in the barracks within a few months, but when this promise went unfulfilled, aid donors and the World Bank threatened to cut their support, and Gambia's tourist industry was badly affected.

In early 1995, Jammeh pragmatically switched tack and announced that elections would be held the following year. In March 1995, the British Foreign Office advised tourists that Gambia was safe again, and tourism picked up.

The 1996 elections were won by the APRC (now neatly renamed the Alliance for Patriotic Reorientation and Construction), and Jammeh was made president, completing his smooth transition from

minor army officer to head of state in just over two years.

To consolidate this support, Jammeh announced a series of ambitious schemes to rebuild the country's infrastructure and economy. A new airport was constructed, a national television station opened and new clinics and schools were promised for the upcountry provinces. Despite a series of human rights abuses that included the shooting of several protesting students in 2001, many people came to regard Jammeh as a force for good, and in October 2001, voted him into a second five-year term.

### Gambia Today

At the time of writing, the country was again preparing for elections, this time against a rather sinister background. The assassination of prominent journalist Deyda Heydara in 2004, which came only days after he had expressed his opposition to a controversial media law, reinforced feelings of oppression. In March 2006, international observers were once again alerted to the political situation in The Gambia when several high ranking military officers were arrested on claims of an attempted coup d'état – one of several such claims Jammeh has made during his time in power. Only a few months before the presidential polls, this was widely interpreted as a way of 'cleansing' the government of rivals, and seems indicative of the way elections might be handled.

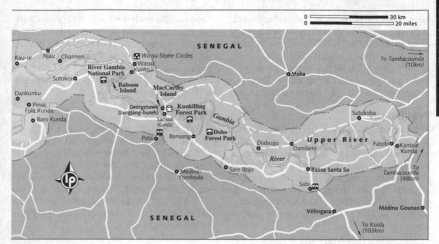

# THE CULTURE
## The National Psyche

Holiday brochures like to describe Gambia as the 'Smiling Coast', a welcoming 'gateway to Africa', where local culture is easily accessible. Wiping the gloss off those descriptions, some of the smile still remains, though real hospitality is easier found upcountry, away from the coastal resorts where mass tourism has somewhat distorted social relations and the respectful interaction otherwise typical of the country.

Years of authoritarian rule and the increasing repression exerted by Gambia's government have also resulted in a certain climate of distrust. Conversations are often conducted with care, and few people will express their views on governmental politics openly – you never know who might be listening. Short-term travellers might not readily notice this, seeing that the government is keen to present a gleaming holiday image to the tourist community, whose dollars are vital to the local economy. Yet being aware of the troubles that plague the population will help you to understand silences in conversation or the avoidance of topics, and gradually grant you an insight into the real Gambia, the one that lies beyond the polished smiles and tourist hustling.

## Daily Life
### FAMILY LIFE

In Gambia, as anywhere else in Africa, the extended family plays an important role in a person's life. The network of relatives widens even more in polygamous families, which still account for the majority of marriages in Gambia. Even relatively poor men sometimes marry a couple of wives, and with an average childbirth rate of around five, this means that a 'small' household can quickly number up to 10 offspring.

Unmarried children, particularly women, stay at their parents' home until they are married, which is when men found their own household, and women join that of their husband. After a divorce, women usually join the home of their parents. Single-women or single-mother households are virtually unheard of, with the exception of a growing number of households whose heads of family have left the country for Europe, sending money home to support their wives, children and parents at home.

### EDUCATION

Despite some measures taken by the government, Gambia still suffers fairly low literacy rates. 40% of boys are estimated to be able to read and write, and for girls this drops by another 15% to 20%. In theory, primary education is available to all children. In reality, it's family income, rather than academic performance, that determines which children go to school and how far up the ladder they progress. While numbers are still fairly equal in the early years of primary school, many girls don't even complete their primary exams, and even fewer carry on to the secondary level. If there's not enough money to send every child to school, boys will usually be the first to benefit, while the girls keep helping out in the household. At secondary or university level, girls often drop out if they are getting married and or having children.

## Population

With around 115 people per sq km, Gambia has one of the highest population densities in Africa. The strongest concentration of people is around the urbanised zones at the Atlantic coast, the area many people migrate to from the upcountry towns to try and make a living from the tourist industry. 45% of Gambia's population are under 14 years old.

The main ethnic groups are the Mandinka (comprising around 42%), the Wolof (about 16%) and the Fula (around 18%). Smaller groups include the Serer and Jola. With the exception of the Jola, these ethnic groups are structured in a hierarchical fashion that has its origins in West Africa's precolonial empires. The freeborn (rulers and traders) are traditionally at the top of society, followed by professional occupational groups, including griots and blacksmiths, and formerly, slaves. These structures still determine much of social life, though other aspects, such as economic success and education are also relevant.

## RELIGION

Islam is the dominant religion – about 90% of Gambia's population is Muslim. The Wolof, Fula and Mandinka people are almost exclusively Muslim, while the Christian faith is most widespread among the Jola and to a lesser extent the Serer. Traditional religious forms (sometimes called animism) are most commonly practiced in the predominantly Christian areas. Elements of traditional religious practice have found their way both into Islam and Christianity.

## ARTS
### Architecture

Banjul has several grand homes once occupied by the colonial elite, as well as unpretentious Krio-style homes, some still occupied by the descendants of freed-slave families who moved to Banjul from Sierra Leone in the early 1800s. Not far from Banjul you can see the remains of Fort James (James Island) and Fort Bullen (Barra); British colonial fortifications. For contemporary architecture, visit Arch 22 and Banjul Airport, both designed by Senegalese architect Pierre Goudiaby.

## Literature

Gambia doesn't exactly have a thriving literature scene – the fact that the works of Gambia's best-known novelist, William Conton, date from the 1960s is indicative of this. The 1960s classic *The African* is his most famous work. Authors such as Ebou Dibba (*Chaff on the Wind;* 1986) and Tijan Salleh (*Kora Land;* 1989) are leading writers of the new generation.

## Music

Gambia is a major centre of the *kora*, an icon of African music throughout the world whose history is deeply connected to The Gambia. This tiny country became a veritable centre of *kora* playing, when Malinké groups settled in the region after the gradual collapse of the mighty Empire of Mali. For its small size, Gambia proudly boasts a wide variety of styles, notably the dry patterns of the eastern regions around Bansang and Basse Santa Su, and the softer Casamance style more common in the west of the country. Famous *kora* players include Amadou Bansang Jobarteh, Jali Nyama Suso, Dembo Konte and Malamini Jobarteh.

In the 1960s, Gambia was hugely influential in the development of modern West African music. Groups like the Afro-funky Super Eagles and singer Labah Sosse had a huge impact in Gambia, Senegal and beyond. Today, Gambia's music scene is mainly dominated by Senegalese artists and Jamaican reggae. Renowned local musicians include the *kora*-playing brothers Pa Bobo and Tata Dindin Jobarteh, singer Jelibah Kuyateh and reggae artists such as the Dancehall Masters and Rebellion the Recaller.

## Painting & Sculpture

Banjul's national museum has a few good examples of traditional statues and carved masks on display. Also fascinating is the art of batik making, which contemporary artists such Baboucar Fall and Toimbo Laurens push into new creative directions.

# ENVIRONMENT
## The Land
Gambia's shape and position epitomise the absurdity of the colonial carve-up of Africa. About 300km long, but averaging only 35km wide, Gambia is entirely surrounded by Senegal, with the small exception of an 80km coastline. With only 11,295 sq km, it is the smallest country in Africa (half the size of Wales, or less than twice that of Delaware) and its territory is entirely dominated by the Gambia River.

Gambia is so flat that the Gambia River loses less than 10m in elevation over 450km between the far eastern border and Banjul, the capital, at the river's mouth.

## Wildlife
### ANIMALS
Gambia doesn't tempt tourists with huge mammals, though warthogs, various antelope species, monkeys, hippos and crocodiles can sometimes be seen in the national parks. But while it can't show off with mighty elephants or rhinos, Gambia beats most other destinations when it comes to birds. More than 560 species have been recorded, including many migratory species that use the coast as a flight path between Europe and the tropics. Of particular interest to ornithologists are Egyptian plovers, swallow-tailed and red-throated bee-eaters, Abyssinian rollers, painted snipes and Pel's fishing owls. Good sites for bird-watching include all the protected areas listed under national parks, but also much humbler areas, such as hotel gardens in Kololi, Gunjur and Kartong, sewage ponds in Kotu and mud flats in Banjul. Upcountry, Georgetown and Basse Santa Su are particularly rewarding.

### PLANTS
Vegetation is largely determined by the land's proximity to the coast and the Gambia River, which is lined with mangroves in the saline areas and dense gallery forest further upstream. Away from the river, Gambia's position in the southern Sahel means that natural vegetation consists mostly of dry grassland and open savanna woodland.

## National Parks
The Gambia has six national parks and reserves, covering 3.7% of the national land area. All, except the River Gambia National Park (p321; also known as Baboon Island) are open to the public. Abuko Nature Reserve (p315) is a tract of gallery forest, while Kiang West National Park (p319) protects several habitats including mangroves, mud flats and dry woodland. Baobolong Wetland Reserve is north of the Gambia River, and Niumi National Park (p317) and Tanji River Bird Reserve (p313) are coastal, with dunes, lagoons, dry woodland and coastal scrub.

Several forest parks have been established to provide renewable timber stocks. Bijilo Forest Park (p306) is well-known, primarily as a nature reserve and bird-watching spot. Kunkiling and Dobo Forest Park upcountry are administered by the Central Division Forestry Project in Georgetown, and are interesting examples of community-involved protection schemes.

## Environmental Issues
The main environmental issues faced by Gambia are overfishing, deforestation and coastal erosion. Caused mainly by illegal sand mining, erosion became so bad that the wide sandy beaches of the Atlantic coast literally started disappearing. A US$20 million beach rejuvenation project, using Dutch technology to trap sand near the shore as it was washed in on the tide, brought some temporary relief. Yet sand mining continued apace, and only a few years after the beaches had been 'sprayed back on', they are once again diminishing at a rapid rate.

Away from the coast, deforestation is the biggest problem. Woodlands are cleared to match a growing demand for farmland, but trees are also felled to make firewood and charcoal, much of which is used to smoke fish (caught through overfishing). On a larger scale, forests are cleared to make room for cash crops, notably groundnuts. The Central Division Forestry Project (CDFP) tries to address the problem through educational projects that directly involve the local population in the protection efforts eg as tourist guides.

## FOOD & DRINK
## Staples & Specialities
National dishes include *domodah,* rice with a thick, meaty groundnut sauce and *benechin,* rice cooked in tomato sauce and decorated

with carefully arranged chunks of fried fish, carrots, cassava and other vegetables.

Gambia has a rich array of locally produced juices. The most famous of those are the hibiscus drink *bissap*, ginger beer and *bouyi*, a thick, sweet juice made from the fruits of the baobab. For breakfast, the sweet herbal tea *kinkiliba* is often served. Or, for a real caffeine punch, try a glass of *ataaya*, served with the free offer of an afternoon's socialising. A local alcoholic drink is the thick and sour palm wine.

### Where to Eat & Drink

Gambia's Atlantic Coast is blessed with an excellent restaurant scene. You'll find anything here, from refined local to international cuisine. If you're on a budget, you'll probably search for tiny local eateries, called chop shops. Most of those only have one dish available at any time, so you just ask what they've got, rather than to see the menu. They rarely open all day, but only serve food during lunch and dinner – and when the pots are empty at night, the place simply shuts, or serves beers only. Choose your chop shop carefully – some are of rather dubious hygienic quality.

### Vegetarians & Vegans

Vegetarian food is hard to find in restaurants, and what's worse, there's little understanding why someone who can afford it won't eat meat – vegetables are for the poor. This means that when you order a dish without meat, you'll still often notice a suspicious chicken or fish flavour, just no 'bits'. Prepare for a rather limited variety of food choices during your stay.

### Habits & Customs

Meals are traditionally eaten squatting on the floor, grouped around a large platter of rice and sauce. People eat the traditional rice dishes with a spoon or the hand. If you try the hand version, make sure you use your right only – the left is the hand you wipe your bum with and is strictly out at meal times.

It's usually polite to finish eating while there's still food in the bowl to show you have had enough. The shocked comments of 'you haven't eaten anything, dig in' are more an acceptance of you finishing, rather than actual invitations to eat more.

# BANJUL

pop 35,000

It's hard to imagine a more unlikely, more consistently ignored capital city than the sleepy seaport Banjul. Yet despite the shadow of neglect that haunts its sand-blown streets, Banjul is truly worth a visit. Its colourful markets and hectic harbour show urban Africa at its busy best, while the old museum and fading colonial structures are imbued with a sense of history that Gambia's plush seaside resorts lack.

## HISTORY

The island settlement Banjul was founded in 1816 by Captain Alexander Grant, and was first named Bathurst, after Henry Bathurst, the secretary of the British Colonial Office. It was established as an operational base from which to impede illegal human traffic, after the British Slave Trade Act of 1807 prohibited the slave trade (at least on paper).

When Gambia achieved independence in 1965, Bathurst was granted city status, became the capital of the young nation, and was soon after renamed Banjul (the Mandinka word for 'bamboo' and the island's original, local name).

## ORIENTATION

The July 22 Square is the centre of town. From here, several main streets run south, including Russell St, which leads past the bustling Albert Market into Liberation St. West of the October 17 Roundabout is the old part of Banjul – a maze of narrow streets and ramshackle houses rarely visited by tourists.

July 22 Dr runs west from July 22 Square, becoming the main road out of Banjul. On the edge of the city, it goes under the vast structure of Arch 22 and turns into a dual carriageway, which, after about 3km, crosses Oyster Creek on Denton Bridge to reach the mainland proper.

## INFORMATION
### Internet Access

Reliable Internet services include the following:

**Gamtel Internet Café** (July 22 Dr; per hr D30; ☯ 8am–midnight)

**Quantumnet** (Nelson Mandela St; per hr D30; ☯ 9am–10pm)

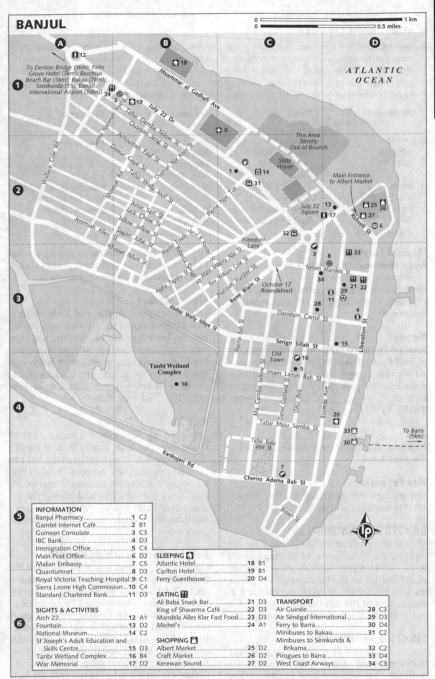

# BANJUL

THE GAMBIA

## STREET NAME CHANGES

Most of Banjul's streets were renamed in the late '90s, and now carry the names of Gambia's heroes of independence rather than those of colonial personalities. However, local residents, including taxi drivers, tend to continue using the old names, and you'll usually get a more reliable answer asking for directions to the old names of places. The Banjul map displays the new names. Please refer to the list below for the corresponding old name.

| Old name | New name | Old name | New name |
| --- | --- | --- | --- |
| Bund Rd | Kankujeri Rd | Hope St | Jallow Jallow St |
| Clarkson St | Rene Blain St | Independence Dr | July 22 Dr |
| Cotton St | Cherno Adamah Bah St | Liberation St | Wellington St |
| | | MacCarthy Sq | July 22 Sq |
| Dobson St | Ma Cumba Jallow St | Marina Pde | Muammar al Gadhafi Ave |
| Grant St | Rev William Cole St | Orange St | Tafsir Ebou Samba St |
| Hagan St | Daniel Goddard St | Picton St | Davidson Carrol St |
| Hill St | Imam Lamin Bah St | Wellington St | Liberation St |

## Medical Services

**Banjul Pharmacy** ( ☎ 4227470; ☽ 9am-8.30pm) Across the road from the hospital.
**Royal Victoria Teaching Hospital** ( ☎ 4228223; July 22 Dr) Gambia's main hospital has an A&E Department, but facilities aren't great.

## Money

**Standard Chartered Bank** ( ☎ 4222081; Ecowas Ave) and **IBC Bank** ( ☎ 4428145; Liberation St) both have ATMs that accept Visa cards and change travellers cheques. They open from 8am to 1.30pm Monday to Thursday, and from 8am to 11am Friday.

## Post

**Main post office** (Russell St; ☽ 8am-4pm Mon-Sat) Near Albert Market.

## Visa Extensions

**Immigration Office** ( ☎ 4228611; OAU Blvd; ☽ 8am-4pm) Visa extensions cost D250.

## DANGERS & ANNOYANCES

Violent crime is rare in Banjul, but there are pickpockets. Their favourite hunting ground is the Barra ferry; be vigilant around the terminal and Albert Market as well. Don't enter the area behind the State House (marked as Strictly Out of Bounds on the map), or you risk difficulties with the military and police.

## SIGHTS & ACTIVITIES

Banjul feels more like a very large village than a national capital, and this sleepy atmosphere has a quaint kind of charm. The city's attraction lies not in grand sights, but in intimate details, and these are best taken in on a casual stroll around town.

## Albert Market

Since its creation in the mid-19th century, **Albert Market** (Russell St), an area of frenzied buying, bartering and bargaining, has been Banjul's hub of activity. From shimmering fabrics and false plaits, fresh fruits and dried fish to tourist-tempting souvenirs at the **Craft Market**, you can find almost anything here and then some.

## Arch 22

Designed by Senegalese architect Pierre Goudiaby, the **arch** (July 22 Dr; admission D35; ☽ 9am-11pm) is a 35m-high gateway built to celebrate the military coup of 22 July 1994. Its publicly accessible balcony grants excellent views over the city and coast. There's also a cosy café, souvenir shop and a small museum that enlightens visitors about the coup d'état.

## Royal Victoria Teaching Hospital

Gambia's main health facility, the **Royal Victoria Teaching Hospital** ( ☎ 4226152; www.rvth.dosh .gm; July 22 Dr) not only offers emergency treatment, but also tours around its complex of late 19th century and modern buildings. A hospital visit might not sound like a seductive holiday idea, but the daily two-hour tours (free, though donations are welcome) are surprisingly interesting. They offer excellent explanations of its research projects into malaria and hepatitis, and worthwhile, though painful, insight into the dire situation medical services face in The Gambia.

## St Joseph's Adult Education and Skills Centre

Tucked away in an ancient Portuguese building, this **centre** ( ☎ 4228836; stjskills@qanet .com; Ecowas Ave; ☣ 9am-2pm Mon-Thu, 9am-12pm Fri) has provided training to disadvantaged women for the last 20 years. Visitors can take a free tour of sewing and tie-dye classes, and purchase their beautiful craftwork at reasonable prices in the on-site boutique.

## Old Town

Heading west from the Ferry Port, towards the wide Ma Cumba Jallow St and beyond, you reach the 'old town' – a chaotic assembly of decrepit colonial buildings and Krio-style clapboard houses (steep-roofed structures with wrought-iron balconies and corrugated roofs). It's no coincidence they resemble the inner-city architecture of Freetown in Sierra Leone, as many of them still belong to families who came to Banjul from there, some as early as the 1820s.

## National Museum

The **museum** (July 22 Dr; admission D25; ☣ 8am-4pm Mon Thu, 8am-1pm Fri & Sat) has some dog-eared and dated exhibits that are worth a look. Explanations are generally good, and there's a dusty but fascinating display of photos, maps and historical papers.

## July 22 Square

The **square** (MacCarthy Sq), a recently greened colonial creation, was once the site of cricket matches, and is now mainly used for governmental pomp and public celebrations. Look out for the **War Memorial** and the (now dried up) **fountain** to commemorate the coronation of King George VI of Britain in 1937.

## Tanbi Wetland Complex

The stretch of mangrove either side of Kankujeri Rd is known as the **Tanbi Wetland Complex**, and is a popular and easily accessible bird-watching area.

## SLEEPING

Not many tourists stay in Banjul, preferring the beach and comforts of the Atlantic coast instead. However, if you want a more African environment, you're likely to find it here.

**Ferry Guesthouse** (Ami's Guesthouse; ☎ 4222028; 28 Liberation St; s/d/tr D350/500/610; ☒ ) This simple guesthouse above a busy shop is not glamorous, but your best budget bet. It has a great balcony for watching the busy trading stalls and ferry terminal. Single room prices double if you want air-con.

**Carlton Hotel** ( ☎ 4228670; fax 4227214; 25 July 22 Dr; s/d D500/550, with air-con D800/850; ☒ ) This is a little more upmarket, with luxuries like running water and indoor toilets. A good-value option.

**Atlantic Hotel** ( ☎ 4228601; atlantic@corinthia.com; www.corinthiahotels.com; Muammar al Gadhafi Ave; s/d D3007/3937; ☒ ☒ ☒ ☒ ) This vast, plush resort hotel has numerous bars, restaurants and plenty of leisure facilities including a nightclub, massage centre and a garden created by ornithologist Clive Barlow to please the bird-watchers.

**Palm Grove Hotel** ( ☎ 4201620; www.gambia -palmgrovehotel.co.uk; s/d incl breakfast D1150/1840; ☒ ☒ ) About 3km from Banjul towards Serekunda, this hotel is smaller, more personal and better value than the Atlantic. It has a decent swimming beach and all the usual activities you'd expect from a resort.

## EATING & DRINKING

Banjul is hardly a culinary haven, offering little beyond fast-food joints. Around the north end of Liberation St and Albert Market, you'll find several cheap chop shops and streets stalls where plates of rice and sauce start at about D25.

**Ali Baba Snack Bar** ( ☎ 4224055; Nelson Mandela St; snacks from D50, meals D150-200; ☣ 9am-5pm) More than just a kebab shop, this place is an institution with a deserved reputation for its shwarmas and felafel.

**Michel's** ( ☎ 4223108; 29 July 22 Dr; meals D150-250; ☣ 8am-11pm) This is about the only restaurant in town that can be called classy. From the breakfast menu all the way to after-dinner drinks, it offers excellent choices at decent rates.

**Mandela Alles Klar Fast Food** (Ecowas Ave; snacks from D30) The name is as great as the food is greasy. Sometimes nothing but a burger grilled in old fat will do, right?

**King of Shwarma Café** ( ☎ 4229799; Nelson Mandela St; meals D150-250; ☣ 9am-5pm Mon-Sat) This friendly place serves excellent Lebanese food, and what's even better, large glasses of freshly pressed juice.

**Bacchius Beach Bar** ( ☎ 4227948; meals D150-300) Next to the Palm Grove Hotel, this busy little beach bar is a great place to sip a drink and dig into a platter of grilled fish.

## SHOPPING

In Banjul, the best place to go shopping is Albert Market (p300). If you enter via the main entrance, you will pass stalls selling clothes, shoes, household and electrical wares and just about everything else you can imagine. Keep going and you'll reach the myriad colours and flavours of the fruit and vegetable market. Beyond here you'll find stalls catering mainly for tourists, usually called the Craft Market.

Near the main entrance, you'll also find **Kerewan Sound** (Russell St), Gambia's best place to buy CDs and cassettes, and one of the very few boutiques that sell recordings by Gambian artists.

## GETTING THERE & AWAY
### Air

For details of international flights to Banjul, see p326. Airline offices in and around Banjul include the following:

**Air Guinée** ( ☎ 4223296; www.mirinet.com/airguinee; 72 OAU Blvd)

**Air Sénégal International** ( ☎ 4472095; www.air-senegal-international.com; Ecowas Ave)

**SN Brussels Airlines** ( ☎ 4496301/2; www.flysn.com; 97 Kairaba Ave, Fajara)

**West Coast Airways** ( ☎ 4201954; 7 Nelson Mandela St)

### Boat

**Ferries** ( ☎ 4228205; Liberation St; passengers D10, cars D150-200) travel between Banjul and Barra, on the northern bank of the river. They are supposed to run every one to two hours from 7am until 7pm and take one hour, though delays are frequent and one ferry is often out of action.

The ferries take vehicles, but car space is limited, and you might have to wait for a couple of hours (if it's any consolation – trucks can sometimes be there for days). You buy your ticket before going through to the waiting area; keep it until getting off, as it'll be checked on the other side. If you're coming from the north side by car, you need to purchase your ticket at the office near the border (just after the junction where

the northbank road to Farafenni turns off), about 3km from Barra.

If the wait for the ferry is too long, you can also jump onto one of the large pirogues that do the same journey (D50 for a seat on a public pirogue or around D600 if you hire the whole boat). Be warned though – they can be dangerously overloaded. Fares rise sharply after dark (as does the risk).

### Bush Taxi

Minibuses and Mercedes buses to Brikama and upcountry towns, and to places in southern Senegal, all go from the Serekunda garage. For details, see p312.

## GETTING AROUND
### To/From the Airport

A green tourist taxi from Banjul International Airport to Banjul, Serekunda, Kairaba Ave or the Atlantic coast resorts (Bakau, Fajara, Kotu and Kololi) costs around D300 to D400, depending on your destination. Fixed rates are usually printed on a board at the taxi rank, so bargaining is not required. With yellow taxis, the price you pay depends entirely on your haggling skills; expect to pay D150 to D200 to Banjul. There is no airport bus.

### Minibus & Shared Taxi

Minibuses run between Banjul, Serekunda and the other coastal towns, while shared taxis run between Serekunda, Fajara and Bakau.

From Banjul, minibuses to Bakau leave from the stand opposite the Shell station on July 22 Dr. Minibuses to Serekunda and Brikama leave from a roadside corner opposite July 22 Sq. See p312 for more information.

### Private Taxi

In a taxi to yourself (known as a 'town trip'), a short ride across Banjul city centre will cost about D50, after bargaining. From Banjul it costs about D150 to D200 to Bakau, Serekunda, Fajara, Kotu or Kololi.

Hiring a taxi for the day starts at D1000, and will be more if you venture beyond Banjul and the coastal resorts. For a tour out of the city, most drivers charge by the destination – the worse the roads they'll have to drive on, the steeper the price.

The best place to find a taxi at night is at the Atlantic Hotel.

# ATLANTIC COAST RESORTS & SEREKUNDA

The 10km stretch of coast from Bakau and Fajara to Kotu and Kololi is the beating heart of Gambia's tourist industry. The bustling area has all the makings of a thriving holiday zone: rows of hotels and guesthouses, a wide selection of restaurants, a vibrant nightlife and packed beaches.

While it's perfectly possible to pass your days here, spread-eagled on white sand, you can also get a feel for African culture without having to venture too far from the strand. Bakau has retained the strongest local character of the four places. The 'old town', a lively concentration of clapboard, corrugated iron and colourful market stalls, begins only a few steps away from the gleaming hotel fronts. Kololi, by contrast, known to most Gambians as 'Senegambia' after the hotel of the same name, is Gambia's greatest monument to tourism. Hotels, bars, clubs, tour agencies, casinos, banks and, naturally, hustlers, operate on a crammed space stretching barely beyond a couple of streets. Don't go looking for the 'real Africa' here – that lies a short drive eastwards in Serekunda. This hot and heaving town is bursting at the seams with traffic and people. A stroll around its market (in reality the town is one big market) is highly recommended for a taste of unrelenting, in-your-face urban West Africa.

## ORIENTATION

The main road from Gambia's upcountry towns goes past Banjul International Airport and reaches Serekunda, where it divides: straight ahead is the dual carriageway for about 14km to Banjul; and to the left is Kairaba Ave, which leads to Bakau, Fajara, Kotu and Kololi.

In Bakau and Fajara, the main drag is Atlantic Rd, which runs parallel to the coast, linking Kairaba Ave and Old Cape Rd. Just south of Atlantic Rd, and running parallel to it, is Garba Jahumpa Rd (formerly, and still better known as New Town Rd). Badala Park Way branches off Kairaba Ave at the Fajara end and leads to the hotel/beach areas of Kotu and Kololi. It crosses Kairaba Ave at the country's only set of traffic lights.

## INFORMATION

### Bookshops

**Timbooktoo** ( ☎ 4494345; cnr Kairaba Ave & Garba Jahumpa Rd, Fajara; ☾ 10am-7pm Mon-Thu, 10am-1pm & 3-7pm Fri, 10am-8pm Sat) An excellent shop with a good range of fiction, non-fiction, mainstream fiction, maps and local and international papers.

### Cultural Centres

**Alliance Franco-Gambienne** ( ☎ 4375418; www .alliancefrance.gm; Kairaba Ave, Serekunda; ☾ 9.30am-5pm Mon-Fri) At the southern end of Kairaba Ave, it runs French and Wolof courses, and has regular concerts, films, shows and exhibitions. There's a good, cheap restaurant at the back.

### Internet Access

Getting online isn't a problem at this well organised part of the coast. Many of the large hotels have Internet cafés, and Kairaba Ave is well served. The following usually have good connections:

**Gamtel** Kololi ( ☎ 4377878; Senegambia Strip; ☾ 9am-11pm); Serekunda (Westfield Junction; ☾ 8am-11pm)
**Quantumnet** ( ☎ 4494514; ☾ 8.30am-10pm) Next to Timbooktoo bookshop.

### Medical Services

**Medical Research Council** (MRC; ☎ 4495446; Fajara) If you have a potentially serious illness, head for this British-run clinic, off Atlantic Rd.
**Stop Steps Pharmacy** ( ☎ 4371344; Serekunda; ☾ 9am-10pm Mon-Sat) One of the best-stocked pharmacy chains around, with branches all along the coast.
**Westfield Clinic** ( ☎ 4398448) Another option, at Westfield Junction in Serekunda.

### Money

The main banks, Standard Chartered, Trust Bank and IBC have branches all across the resort zone. Banks open in the morning from 8.30am or 9am to noon or 2pm, in the afternoon from 4pm to 6pm, and for a few hours on Saturday morning. There are also a few exchange bureaus scattered around the busy tourist miles, some part of supermarkets, but you're unlikely to get a better rate.

Police have seriously cracked down on Gambia's once flourishing black market, and though you can usually find someone to change some cash after hours, it's too risky to be worthwhile. Chances of fraud are high, and the rates aren't better than the official ones.

**THE GAMBIA**

# ATLANTIC COAST RESORTS & SEREKUNDA

**A**     **B**     **C**     **D**

**INFORMATION**
Afri-Swiss Travels..................................1 F4
Alliance Franco-Gambienne....... 2 G5
American Embassy...............................3 F4
Belgian Consul.............................(see 36)
Bellview Airlines....................................4 G5
British High Commission.................5 E3
Danish Consul..............................(see 10)
French Embassy...................................6 H2
Gambia River Experience.................7 F3
Gamtel Office................................(see 19)
Gamtel Office........................................8 B6
Gamtel Office........................................9 C6
German Consul...................................10 G3
Guinea-Bissau Embassy..............(see 16)
IBC Bank Serekunda........................11 G6
Mauritanian Consulate...................12 C6
Medical Research Council..............13 F3
Norwegian Consul.......................(see 10)
Olympic Travel..............................(see 18)
Post Office............................................14 G5
Quantumnet....................................(see 18)
Senegalese High Commission.....15 F4
Standard Chartered Bank Bakau.16 G2
Standard Chartered Bank
  Serekunda.......................................17 A5
Stop Steps Pharmacy....................(see 59)
Swedish Consul.............................(see 10)
Timbooktoo........................................18 F3
Tropical Tour & Souvenirs........(see 36)
Trust Bank Bakau.............................19 G2
Trust Bank Kololi..............................20 C6
Westfield Clinic................................21 B6

**SIGHTS & ACTIVITIES**
Batafon Arts.......................................22 G5
Bijilo Forest Park Headquarters....23 C6
Botanic Gardens...............................24 G2
Fajara Golf Club.................................25 E4
Kachikaly Crocodile Pool...........26 H3

**SLEEPING** 🛏
Bakau Lodge......................................27 G2
Bakotu Hotel......................................28 E4
Balmoral Appartments..................29 C6
Cape Point Hotel.........................(see 42)
Coconut Residence..........................30 C6
Effu's Villa............................................31 G3
Fajara Guesthouse...........................32 E3
Francisco's Hotel...............................33 E3
Holiday Beach Club Hotel..............34 C6
Jabo Guesthouse..............................35 H2
Kairaba Hotel.....................................36 C6
Kanifeng YMCA.................................37 G4
Kombo Beach Hotel.........................38 D4
Leybato.................................................39 E3
Mannjai Lodge...................................40 E5
Ngala Lodge........................................41 F3
Ocean Bay Hotel & Resort..............42 H2
Praia Motel..........................................43 G6

Roc Height's Lodge..........................44 H2
Romana Hotel....................................45 G2
Safari Garden Hotel..........................46 E3
Sarge's Hotel......................................47 C6
Senegambia Hotel.......................(see 36)
Teranga Suites...................................48 D5

**EATING** 🍴
Aisa Marie Cinema............................49 F6
Al Basha...............................................50 C6
Ali Baba's.............................................51 C6
Atlantic Bar & Restaurant...............52 G2
Butcher's Shop...................................53 E3
Chapman's..........................................54 G2
Clay Oven.............................................55 F3
Come Inn..............................................56 F5
Crystals Ice Cream Parlour and
  Gallery...........................................(see 62)
Eddie's Bar & Restaurant................57 E3
Francisco's Restaurant...............(see 33)
Harry's Supermarket........................58 F4
Kairaba Supermarket.......................59 F5
Kora......................................................60 C6
La Pailotte......................................(see 2)
La Rive Gauche............................(see 38)
Le Palais du Chocolat......................61 F4
Luigi's Italian Restaurant...............62 D5
Mama's Restaurant..........................63 E3
Maroun's.............................................64 A6
Ocean Clipper...............................(see 42)
Pepper's Tropical Restaurant....(see 81)
Ritz........................................................65 E3
Safe Way Afra King..........................66 F5
Sailor's Beach Bar.............................67 E4
St Mary's Food & Wine....................68 F4
St Mary's Food & Wine....................69 H2
Solomon's Beach Bar..................(see 79)
Sunshine Bar......................................70 H2
Weezo's................................................71 E3
Yok...................................................(see 83)
Youth Monument Bar &
  Restaurant.....................................72 B6

**DRINKING** 🍷
Aquarius...........................................(see 60)
Chapman's......................................(see 54)
Churchill's........................................(see 62)
Come Inn.........................................(see 56)
Lana's Bar............................................73 F6
Paparazzi.........................................(see 50)
Weezo's............................................(see 71)

**ENTERTAINMENT** 🎭
Arena Babou Fatty (Wrestling
  Arena)..............................................74 F6
Destiny..................................................75 C5
Jazziz....................................................76 D5
Jokko.....................................................77 B6
Lama Lama..........................................78 G2
Teranga Beach Club..........................79 C5
Totties Nightclub...........................(see 81)
Tropicana Nightclub.........................80 C6
Waaw Nightclub...............................81 C6

**SHOPPING** 🛍
African Heritage Centre..................82 G2
African Living Art Centre................83 F3
Batik Factory......................................84 F6
Salam Batik.........................................85 F6
Village Gallery & Restaurant......86 D5

**TRANSPORT**
AB Rent-A-Car.................................(see 36)
Bus & Taxi Stop..................................87 F6
Cars4Rent............................................88 D4
Green Taxi Rank.................................89 D5
Hertz.................................................(see 97)
Minibuses to Banjul..........................90 F6
Minibuses to Banjul..........................91 A6
Minibuses to Banjul &
  Serekunda.......................................92 G2
Shared Taxis to Fajara & Bakau..93 B6
Slokair..................................................94 F3
SN Brussels..........................................95 C5
Taxi Stand............................................96 G2
Tippa Garage.......................................97 F6

*38* 🔼

Kotu
Point

*88* ●

Kololi
Point

Kololi

🔲 *79*
*62* ⓘ
*76* *89*

🔲 *48*

*75*
🔲 *95*

🔲 *86*

Badala Park Way

Kololi Rd

Palma Rima Rd

**SLEEPING** panel inset:
17 ⓘ    0 ————— 200 m
    0 ———— 0.1 miles
🔲 8
🏠 93
64 🍴    🍴 72
91 🔲    Westfield
   ⊕ 21   Junction
Sayer Jobe Ave Sukuta Rd
🔲 77

*36* 🔲
Senegambia Strip
*9* 🔲 *80*
*20* ⓘ
*50*
*34* 🔲 *51* 🔲
*47* 🔲 *81*
*12*
*29*
*60*
*23* ●
*30*

**Bijilo Forest
Park**

To Gambia Tours (1km);
Tanji (8km); Kartong (38km)

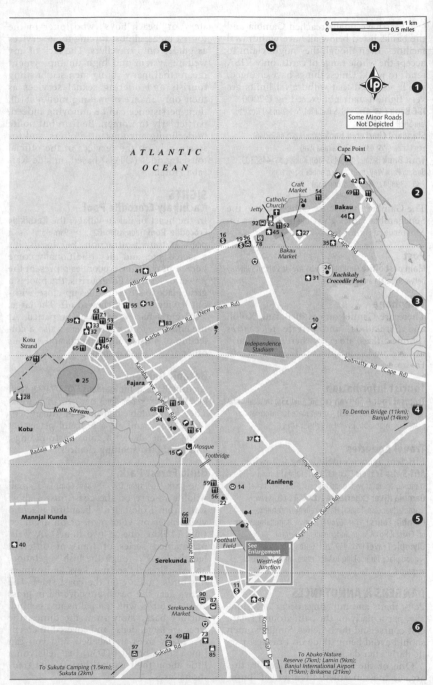

ATMs have finally reached Gambia and the banks listed below all have withdrawal facilities. Even though they might claim to accept the whole range of cards, only VISA tends to work. Unless things have changed, you'll also find that withdrawal limits are very tight, usually not exceeding D2000.

**IBC Bank** ( ☎ 4377878; Sukuta Rd, Serekunda) Next to the Shell Petrol Station.

**Standard Chartered Bank** Bakau ( ☎ 4495046); Serekunda ( ☎ 4396102; Kairaba Ave)

**Trust Bank** Bakau ( ☎ 4495486); Kololi ( ☎ 4465303; Badala Park Way, near 'Senegambia'); Serekunda ( ☎ 4398042; Westfield Junction)

The Gambia Experience Office next to the Senegambia Hotel gives cash advances on Mastercards for a fee.

### Post
**Main post office** (just off Kairaba Ave) It's about halfway between Fajara and Serekunda.

### Telephone
There are Gamtel offices in Bakau, Kololi and Serekunda, and private *télécentres* (phone offices) are everywhere, particularly in Serekunda and just off Kairaba Ave in Fajara.

### Tourist information
**Tropical Tour & Souvenirs** ( ☎ 4460536; tropicaltour@ gamtel.gm; Kairaba Hotel) A great place for information materials, maps, books and insightful advice.

### Travel Agencies
Efficient agencies include the following:
**Afri-Swiss Travels** ( ☎ 4371762; Fajara) A long-standing operator with good reports. Also does ticketing.
**Gambia River Experience** ( ☎ 4494360; www .gambiariver.com; Fajara) Has excellent river tours.
**Gambia Tours** ( ☎ 4462601/2; www.gambiatours.gm; off Coastal Rd) A large, independent operator.
**Olympic Travel** ( ☎ 4497204; Garba Jahumpa Rd) A good place for booking tickets, tours, and all general enquiries.

## DANGERS & ANNOYANCES
Petty thefts and muggings occur occasionally, particularly on the path around Fajara golf course and the beaches. Single women should avoid being alone on beaches, particularly after dark.

One of the major annoyances in this area is the unwanted attention of 'bum-sters' or 'beach boys', who loiter in the tourist areas, almost forcing their services as guides onto travellers. The lack of any welfare system and high unemployment means that many young men see hustling tourists and offering sexual services as their only chance of making money. Still, their persistence can be annoying indeed, particularly to women. Be firm but polite in declining any unwanted offers, and for safety, rely on the services of the official tourist guides (OTGs) based outside Kairaba Hotel.

## SIGHTS
### Kachikaly Crocodile Pool
In the heart of Bakau village, the **Kachikaly Crocodile Pool** (admission D25; ⏰ 9am-6pm) is a popular tourist attraction. For locals, it's a sacred site, and they traditionally come here to pray, as the crocodiles represent the power of fertility. For tourists, the pool is a great place to see crocodiles up-close, without having your leg chewed off. The large, lethargic 'Charley' can even be patted. At the entrance to the pool, there's also a collection of musical instruments and various other artefacts on display.

### Botanic Gardens
Also in Bakau, the **gardens** ( ☎ 7774482; adult/ child D50/free; ⏰ 8am-4pm) are worth a look. They were established in 1924, during colonial times, and are a peaceful place that offers some shade in calm surroundings, and good bird-spotting chances.

### Bijilo Forest Park
The **park** (admission D30; ⏰ 8am-6pm) is a small wildlife reserve on the coast, just a short walk from Kololi. It's a beautiful place to visit, either on your own, or on a guided walk (4.5km, one to two hours). A well-maintained series of trails of different lengths leads through the lush vegetation, and you'll easily see monkeys and numerous birds (mainly on the coast side). The dunes near the beach are covered in grass and low bush, with tall palms just behind. Further back, away from the dunes, the trees are large, dense and covered in creepers. Many trees are labelled, and you can buy a small booklet (D30) that tells you a little about their natural history and traditional uses.

## ACTIVITIES
### Fishing
The **Sportsfishing Centre** ( ☎ 7765765) at Denton Bridge is the place to organise your fishing tours. The two following companies are based there.

**Gambia Fishing** ( ☎ 7721228; www.gambiafishing .com) Specialises in lure and anchored bottom fishing. They're very friendly and able to accommodate both experienced anglers and those new to the game.

**Greenies Gamefishing** ( ☎ 9907073; greenies@ gambiafishing.freeserve.co.uk) Malcolm 'Greenie' Green specialises in blue water fishing.

### Golf
**Fajara Golf Club** ( ☎ 4495456) is the country's main golf course. The club also has a pool and courts for tennis, squash and badminton. Temporary membership is available by the day. Enquire about rates.

### Swimming
Most beaches in this area are relatively safe for swimming, though currents can sometimes be strong. Always check conditions locally before plunging in – people do drown every year in the zone. The entire coastline suffers badly from erosion, and the sand strands that lure tourists here are gradually disappearing. The best beaches are in Fajara and Kotu.

If the Atlantic doesn't appeal, all the major hotels have swimming pools. If you're not a guest, you might have to pay, or buy your swim with a sandwich and a soft drink.

### Watersports
Some of the large hotels, notably Ocean Bay, Atlantic and Combo Beach, offer various water sports to guests. Most of their activities are run by the **Watersports Centre** ( ☎ 7765765) at Denton Bridge, so you might as well go straight to them to organise your jet-skiing, parasailing, windsurfing or catamaran trips.

## COURSES
Drumming and dancing courses are popular. The Safari Gardens Hotel has classes in **African Dance** (per person D50; ☎ 6pm to 7pm Tue) and **African Drumming** (per person D150; ☎ 5.30pm to 6.30pm Wed). Half or all day batik courses (D400) can be arranged on request.

**Batafon Arts** ( ☎ in UK 01273 605791, in Gambia 4392517; www.batafonarts.co.uk; Kairaba Ave, Serekunda)

offers excellent African percussion and dance tuition, from one-off lessons to drumming holidays.

## SLEEPING
You'll find everything from plush resorts to grotty dives on the Atlantic coast. Competition is so intense that if you're here out of the peak season you'll almost always be able to negotiate a better deal, even at the top places.

The list here is not exhaustive, but gives a good cross-section of options, especially for independent travellers. All rooms have bathrooms unless otherwise specified.

### Budget
#### BAKAU
**Jabo Guesthouse** ( ☎ 4494906, 7777082; 9 Old Cape Rd; d D500) This down-to-earth place has surprisingly large, clean rooms, some with self-catering facilities.

**Bakau Lodge** ( ☎ /fax 4496103; d from D650; 🖳 ) This small place with spotless, two-room bungalows set around a swimming pool comes as a real surprise, right in the heart of the Bakau 'hood. Excellent value.

**Romana Hotel** ( ☎ 4495127; aframsromanahotel@ yahoo.co.uk; Atlantic Rd; r D350) Rooms are basic, but if you close the door and sit in the pretty garden space, you'll probably make your peace with this place.

#### FAJARA
**Kanifeng YMCA** ( ☎ 4392647; www.ymca.gm; Kanifeng; B&B D175) The huge building has just about passable rooms for the budget-bound. Ask for the self-contained ones on the top floor.

#### KOTU
**Teranga Suites** ( ☎ 4461961; off Kololi Rd; s/d/ste D500/750/1000; 🖳 ) This jewel of a guesthouse has airy rooms and large, self-catering suites with bright, wooden décor and that rarity of really comfortable mattresses. Perfect for families (cots can be arranged).

#### SEREKUNDA
**Sukuta Camping** ( ☎ 9917786; www.campingsukuta .de in German; camping per person D100, per vehicle D14, s/d D235/340, d with bathroom D465) This well-organised camping site in Sukuta (southwest of Serekunda) also offers comfortable rooms. The friendly owners Joe and Claudia are experienced overland travellers, and

have thought of everything a desert-driver might need, including long-term parking, repair shops and car sales advice.

**Praia Motel** ( ☎ 4394887; Mame Jout St; r D300; ✗ ) A few minutes' walk off Sayer Jobe Ave, these simple but clean rooms in a very local part of Serekunda are worth your consideration. Amiable manager, Mr Ceesay, is full of advice and serves cheap beer, too.

## Midrange

Several of the hotels in this range are small, owner-managed, and more used to dealing with individual travellers than the larger, top-end establishments. All rooms have their own bathroom and most hotels accept credit cards.

### BAKAU

**Cape Point Hotel** ( ☎ 4495005; Cape Point; d D1000; ✗ ✉ ) At the east end of Atlantic Rd, this family-run place is set in attractive gardens, and is pleasantly low-key compared to the mighty tourist palaces next door.

**Roc Height's Lodge** ( ☎ 4495428; www.rocheights lodge.com; Samba Breku Road; s/d D1000/1500) Places this nice are a rare treat anywhere. This three-storey villa sits in a quiet garden, and has stylish rooms and apartments with fully equipped kitchen.

**Effu's Villa** ( ☎ 4494699; d/apt D600/650) Lovely Effu has turned a few rooms in her compound into quite impressive self-catering lodgings. Rooms are spacious, clean, and even have hot water. Run by a woman and in a hassle-free zone, this is perfect for lone female travellers. Find your way to Tina's Grill (below the Swedish Embassy) and ask for directions, it's five minutes from there.

### FAJARA

**Safari Garden Hotel** ( ☎ 4495887; www.gamspirit.com; s/d incl breakfast D950/1600; ✗ ✉ ) This peaceful, popular place in the heart of Fajara has pleasingly decorated rooms that make you look forward to spending the night here – should you be able to tear yourself away from the animated conversations to be had in Flavour's restaurant, the hotel's centre piece. Management is friendly and exceptionally well-informed.

**Leybato** ( ☎ 4497186; www.leybato.abc.gm; Fajara Beach; d D800-900, with kitchen D1200) This calm and cosy guesthouse overlooks the ocean from one of the best locations anywhere on the

coast. Rooms are variable, the kitchen-types tend to be better, but you're unlikely to find better beachfront value.

**Fajara Guesthouse** ( ☎ 4496122; fax 4494365; r with breakfast D650-950; ✗ ) This cosy place exudes family vibes, with its leafy courtyard and welcoming lounge. Rooms are basic but clean, and some are big enough to house couples with children.

**Francisco's Hotel** ( ☎ /fax 4495332; Atlantic Rd; s/d D650/850; P ✗ ) The leafy restaurant enjoys a good reputation, and has plenty more character than the rather ordinary rooms, but the value is about right.

### KOTU

**Mannjai Lodge** ( ☎ 4463414; manlodge@gamtel.gm; Mannjai Kunda; s/d/apt incl breakfast from D500/750/1000; ▯ ✉ ) This pretty-in-pink place has large rooms and self-catering apartments grouped around a lively bar and a dodgy pool.

### KOLOLI

**Balmoral Apartments** ( ☎ 4461079; www.balmoral-apartments.com; Kololi Rd; s/d D925/1680; ✗ ✉ ) East off Badala Park Way, these slick self-catering apartments are excellent value.

**Holiday Beach Club Hotel** ( ☎ 4460418; www.holidaybeachclubgambia.com; Senegambia; s/d 1500/2000; ✗ ✉ ) Slightly removed from the busiest hectare of the Senegambia tourist mile, this place has comfortable bungalows set in a lush tropical garden.

**Sarge's Hotel** (Tafbel; ☎ 4460510; www.sargesho tel.gm; s/d incl breakfast D1260/1750; ✗ ✉ ) This well-equipped hotel is something of a classic on the Gambian scene. It sits right in the heart of Kololi, so don't expect much sleep at night.

## Top End

If some of these seem unreachable in price, try negotiating. During the low season, many of these places are willing to offer sizeable reductions in rates. Most of these places deal mainly with tour groups and accept credit cards.

### BAKAU

**Ocean Bay Hotel & Resort** ( ☎ 4494265; www.ocean bayhotel.com; Cape Point; s/d D3105/3425; P ✗ ▯ ✉ ) Just like its sister, the Kairaba Hotel, this is government-owned, plush luxury hotel. A sparkling palace with all the amenities you'd expect, including an on-site clinic, baby sitting and car rental, though service doesn't live up to the 5 stars.

### FAJARA

**Ngala Lodge** ( ☎ 4494045; www.ngalalodge.com; 64 Atlantic Rd; ste D3750; 🍽 🖵 🌊 ) This stylish red-clay structure houses lovingly decorated rooms; think African materials and sculptures teased into modern designs. During high season, it's usually booked up by Gambia Experience clients.

### KOTU

**Bakotu Hotel** ( ☎ 4465555; fax 4465959; Kotu Beach; s/d D1250/1500; 🍽 🌊 ) Compared to its resort neighbours, this is pleasantly understated, and has comfy terrace apartments in a pleasant garden.

**Kombo Beach Hotel** ( ☎ 4465466; www.kombobeachhotel.gm; Kotu Beach; s/d from D1530/2040; 🍽 🖵 🌊 ) A favourite with young Europeans on group tours, facilities here include a nightclub and one of the most renowned (and most expensive) restaurants around. The upstairs rooms are particularly nice.

### KOLOLI

**Coconut Residence** ( ☎ 4463377; info@coconutresidence.com; Badala Park Way; ste from D5500; 🍽 🌊 ) There isn't a nicer hotel in the country than this classy five-star palace. It's one of the few top hotels where luxury hasn't been traded for soul. All amenities and services come wrapped in sophisticated chic, and character flavours the air of the lush tropical gardens and carefully designed rooms.

**Kairaba Hotel** ( ☎ 4462940; www.kairabahotel.com; Senegambia; s/d D4352/5235; 🅿 🍽 🖵 🌊 ) This government-owned hotel is the kind of vast, labyrinthine, anything-can-be-arranged place you might be tempted not to leave during your whole holiday. The right address for a holiday break wrapped in cotton wool.

**Senegambia Hotel** ( ☎ 4462717; www.senegambia.com; Senegambia; s/d D2205/2695; 🅿 🍽 🖵 🌊 ) Next to the Kairaba, the Senegambia Hotel looks a little pale, but in less glamorous surroundings, this would be considered the top of tops.

## EATING

Mass tourism has made the area around the Atlantic coast resorts one of the best areas to dine in West Africa. There is no shortage of places to eat, though many restaurants offer a similar menu, composed of a handful of dishes from all four corners of the globe. Between the culinary grey, you can find some real gems to tickle your tastebuds.

### Bakau

**Atlantic Bar and Restaurant** ( ☎ 4494083; Atlantic Rd; dishes from D60; 🕑 10am-2pm) This local-style place run by a couple of enterprising youngsters was just starting out when we visited. Gambian meals and snacks were as decent as they were cheap, and the kitchen spotless.

**Sunshine Bar** ( ☎ 9931800; dishes D75-150; 🕑 until 8pm) This simple, relaxed bar right on the beach often gets lively with a young bikini-clad crowd.

**Chapman's** ( ☎ 4495252; Atlantic Road, Bakau Beach; meals around D150-250; 🕑 11am-10pm Thu-Tue) People call this 'the place where everyone seems to go'. It's usually packed with a mixed crowd, the menu is varied and drinks flow.

**Ocean Clipper** ( ☎ 4494265; Ocean Bay Hotel, Cape Point; 🕑 6pm-midnight) Part of the Ocean Bay Hotel complex, this lush place serves Mediterranean and Asian food with a dose of exclusivity.

For self-catering options, try **St Mary's Food & Wine** (Cape Point) or any of the other small supermarkets in the heart of Bakau.

### Fajara

**Butcher's Shop** ( ☎ 4495069; www.thebutchersshopgambia.com; 130 Kairaba Ave; dishes D169-285; 🕑 8am-11pm) This Moroccan place has gradually morphed from one of the best butchers in the area into one of the best butchers with one of the best restaurants attached. Everything here – from the rich local juices to flavour-dripping three-course dinners – comes with personal attention from owner and star-chef Driss, and and is rounded off to full, tasty perfection. They also do a mean Sunday brunch (D200) from 10am to 4pm.

**Mama's Restaurant** (cnr Atlantic Rd & Kairaba Ave; dishes around D100; 🕑 11am-10pm Tue-Sun) One of the most established places serving Gambian and international food, this vibrant place is as much renowned for its delicious buffet dinners as for the raw charm of Mama the manager.

**Yok** ( ☎ 4495131; African Living Arts Centre; 🕑 12:30pm-midnight) Getting to this restaurant puts you in the mood for fairytale flavours; you get here via a winding wooden staircase, a leafy, glass-roofed gallery, and then a walk through an impressively-stacked antique and arts shop. This striking Oriental restaurant serves excellent meals fusing Singaporean, Thai and Chinese cuisine to the gentle flow of waterfalls and the rustling of palm trees. Oh, and the best cocktails on the coast.

**Clay Oven** ( ☎ 4496600; dishes D175-195; ☺ 7-11pm) For Indian food, this place is one of the best in the whole of West Africa. No exaggeration. And with its scrubbed white walls, leafy garden and personalised service, the surroundings are right, too.

**Eddie's Bar & Restaurant** (dishes D60-100; ☺ 8am-2am) This tiny local restaurant can look a little desolate during the day, but it serves excellent *afra* (grill food) and other Gambian dishes.

**Ritz** ( ☎ 4496754; meals from D150-250; ☺ 8am-midnight) The standard European fare of this small place doesn't quite live up to the restaurant's aspirational name, nor to its prices.

**Francisco's Restaurant** ( ☎ 4495332; cnr Atlantic Rd & Kairaba Ave; grills D150-300; ☺ lunch & dinner) There are few places where mixed seafood platters and grills taste better than in the tranquil setting of Francisco's garden.

**Weezo's** ( ☎ 4496918; 132 Kairaba Ave; mains D250-350; ☺ 11am-3.30pm & 7pm-3am) This classy place serves a range of excellent food, snacks and tapas all day and cocktails in a trendy setting in the evenings. It was taking a slight downhill slope when we visited – check if it's recovered.

**Le Palais du Chocolat** ( ☎ 4395397; 19 Kairaba Ave; cakes around D30; ☺ lunch & dinner) It's all in the name – a chocolate palace this is indeed, the perfect place for an indulgent breakfast.

**La Paillote** ( ☎ 4375418; www.alliancefrance .gm; dishes from D25; ☺ noon-4pm) The choice at the restaurant of the Alliance Franco-Gambien is between the African dish at a mind-boggling D25 and the European three-course-meal at D90. Both are usually delicious – you'd have to try very hard to find better value anywhere.

**Come Inn** ( ☎ 4391464; meals D100-200; ☺ 10am-2am) For a hearty meal, a good draught beer and a solid dose of local gossip, there's no better place than this German-style beer garden. It's popular with overlanders and

pretty much anyone else who likes big portions at decent rates.

For supermarkets, head for Kairaba Ave where there's plenty of choice. Kairaba Supermarket is usually well stocked, while **Harry's Supermarket** ( ☺ 9am-10pm Mon-Sat) has the best hours. **St Mary's Food & Wine** ( ☺ 9am-7.30pm Mon-Sat, 10am-1.30pm Sun) has a branch here.

## Kotu
**Sailor's Beach Bar** ( ☎ 4464078; meals D100-200; ☺ 9am-midnight) This is one of the best beach bars along the coast. The food tastes great, from cheesy pizza to grilled barracuda, and drinks can be sipped while lounging on sunbeds.

**La Rive Gauche** ( ☎ 4465466; dishes from D250) So what if it's a hotel restaurant! The Kombo Beach Hotel's own eatery enjoys a reputation for good food that reaches far across the Atlantic resorts. You pay for it, though.

## Kololi
There are plenty of generic tourist restaurants in Kololi; following is a selection of the more interesting ones.

### PALMA RIMA AREA
**Solomon's Beach Bar** ( ☎ 4460716; meals D100-200; ☺ 10am-midnight) At the northern end of Kololi beach, this cute round house with a light reggae feel is famous for its grill food and youthful atmosphere.

**Luigi's Italian Restaurant** ( ☎ 4460280; luigis@gambianet.gm; Palma Rima Rd; dishes D200-300) Luigi knows his job – the pasta is al dente and the pizzas crisp. Above the shiny restaurant are also a couple of excellent self-catering apartments and an Internet café.

**Crystals Ice Cream Parlour & Gallery** ( ☎ 7774567; Palma Rima Rd; ☺ 11am-7pm Tue-Sun) A tranquil patio and colourful gallery invite you to linger over delicious ice creams, homemade from local ingredients and seasonal fruit. A highpoint on the coast's snacking agenda.

### SENEGAMBIA STRIP
**Ali Baba's** ( ☎ 4461030; Senegambia strip; meals around D200; ☺ 11am-2am) Everyone knows Ali Baba's, so it's as much a commendable restaurant as a useful meeting point. There's occasionally live music.

**Peppers Tropical Restaurant** ( ☎ 4464792; Senegambia Strip, meals around D150-250; ☺ 24hr) In the heart of the Senegambia strip, you'll find the best Caribbean food, and excellent Gambian dishes here. On Fridays and Saturdays, there's a live salsa band.

**Al Basha** ( ☎ 4463300; Senegambia Strip; meals from D300; 🕑 11am-2am) At the time we visited, this was an ice-cool Lebanese place with suit'n'tie attitude and occasional belly dancing shows, but management was about to change. Check it out.

**Kora** ( ☎ 462727; dishes D200-375; 🕑 lunch & dinner) This plush place does a tasty range of meals from around the world. Their enormous mixed platters for four people (per person D500) seem to contain some of everything on the menu.

## Serekunda

There are several cheap eateries around the market and taxi station entrance, and several others scattered through the streets of Serekunda.

**Youth Monument Bar & Restaurant** (Westfield Junction; meals around D100; 🕑 lunch & dinner) This local favourite is impressively named and as much loved for cheap food and drinks as for matches on screen.

**Safe Way Afra King** (dishes CFA50-150; 🕑 5pm-midnight) Shoestringers have descended onto this greasy joint for years for *afra*, sandwiches, *fufu* (a dish made from pounded cassava, similar to polenta) and other African dishes.

**Aisa Marie Cinema** (Serekunda Market) You can sip a beer and buy a snack in a great people-watching zone, while waiting for your B-movie to start.

**Maroun's** (Westfield Junction; 🕑 9am-7.30pm Mon-Sat, 10am-1.30pm Sun) For the basics, such as local and imported food and toiletries, go to this local supermarket.

## DRINKING

All the major hotels have bars and most restaurants turn the lights down and the music up at night. In Bakau, **Chapman's** ( ☎ 4495252; Atlantic Road; 🕑 11am-10pm Thu-Tue) is the best beer option, while **Churchill's** (Palma Rima Rd; 🕑 11am-1am) is an English-style pub near Kololi beach. At **Weezo's** (Atlantic Rd) in Fajara, the cocktails taste sweeter with every passing hour, and the **Come Inn** ( ☎ 4391464; Kairaba Ave; 🕑 10am-2am) is a proper, German-style beer house.

The bars in Serekunda are more local in character. Lana's Bar, near Serekunda

market, is a small all-day affair on a corner of Sukuta Rd.

Around the tourist areas of Kotu and Kololi, you will find several upmarket bars, including **Aquarius** ( ☎ 4460247; Senegambia; 🕑 10am-3am) and **Paparazzi** (Senegambia; 🕑 10pm-3am), a chic wine bar. Both turn up the dance beats after 10pm.

## ENTERTAINMENT
### Live Music

The vast **Teranga Beach Club** ( ☎ 9982669; abdul kabirr@hotmail.com; Palma Rima Rd; 🕑 10am-2am), run by a renowned Gambian musician, holds occasional jazz afternoons, large-scale concerts by visiting artists, and full-moon beach parties (D100) with seafood buffet and acoustic music.

**Jazziz** ( ☎ 4462175; 🕑 10pm-late) A young and colourful salsa place that gets swinging on Fridays and Saturdays. The music is live and the atmosphere unbeatable.

Several of the nightclubs listed below also feature occasional live bands on weekends.

### Nightclubs

You don't have to search too hard to find a heaving dance floor on the Atlantic Coast, whether it's a rootsy, rowdy shack or a slick temple of dance you're after. Just like Gambia's restaurants, the nightclubs present punters with a global mix that tries to cater to everyone – a mixture of hip-hop, R&B, *mbalax* (percussion-driven, Senegalese dance music), reggae and a whole lot more. Clubs usually open their doors around 9pm, but don't even think about arriving before 11pm.

At the time of writing, the **Lama Lama** ( ☎ 4494747) was Bakau's club of choice for the dance floor creatures that determine whether a place is in or out. The hugely popular **Tropicana Night Club** (off Badala Park Way), still known to locals as Spy Bar, gets hot and sweaty late at night, as does the techno-heavy **Waaw Nightclub** ( ☎ 4460668; Senegambia). Next door to Waaw, **Totties Nightclub** (Senegambia) is a club with a chic dance floor, while the open-air **Jokko** (Westfield Junction) in Serekunda is a raucous local affair that makes a convincing claim of being the most entertaining club of all. **Destiny** (off Badala Park Way, Kololi) was sparkling new at the time of research, and drawing glittering crowds on weekends.

## Spectator Sports

The Gambia's main stadium is Independence Stadium in Bakau – the site for major football and traditional wrestling matches. The more exciting place to watch wrestling, however, is the **Arena Babou Fatty** (off Sukuta Rd), a couple of hundred metres south of Sukuta Road in Serekunda. Matches take place in the late afternoon, usually on Sunday, though it's notoriously difficult to hear about them beforehand. Your best chance is during the months of November and December – ask a taxi driver or Serekunda barmen, or check local radio and posters for events.

## SHOPPING

Bakau Market sells fruit and vegetables, and has an adjacent crafts section stuffed to the rims with carvings, traditional cloth and other souvenirs. Opposite the market, next to the church, you'll find the beautiful African Heritage Centre, a great little boutique with a range of original stock (as well as a good restaurant and a few pretty guest rooms down the back). Another excellent option is **Tropical Tour & Souvenirs** ( ☎ 4460536; tropicaltour@gamtel .gm), a hassle-free place with a good range of information materials, books, maps, arts and fashion. While there, ask them about their Tropical Gardens project. It had just taken off at the time we visited, and is likely to grow into an impressive business. The **Village Gallery & Restaurant** ( ☎ 4463646; ☺ 10am-midnight) sells original works by renowned and upcoming local artists. It also has a small café where a busy chef tries hard to match the exquisiteness of his food to that of the works on display.

Serekunda is the place to hunt for good-quality batiks. Musu Kebba Drammeh's **batik factory** ( ☎ 4392258) is hidden deep in the back streets of Serekunda, and tracking down the small workshop is almost as much fun as watching the batiks being made (most taxi drivers and locals can give you directions). **Salam Batik** (Amadou Jallow ☎ 4395103, Sheikh Tijan Secka ☎ 982 0125; salam_batik_mp_art@yahoo.co.uk; London Corner, Serekunda) is the place to get your personalised clothes dyed and tailored.

**African Living Art Centre** ( ☎ 4495131; Garba Jahumpa Rd, Fajara) is something of an institution – a place to rummage for quality artworks, antiques and original souvenirs, as well as home to Gambia's best European hairdressers.

## GETTING THERE & AWAY

Bush taxis depart from the garages of Serekunda, the main transport hub for the whole country. Serekunda to Soma is D60, and to Farafenni it's D75. If you're heading for the south coast you can get bush taxis to Brufut (D12), Tanji (D15) and Sanyang (D18). A bush taxi to Gunjur is D30, whether via Brikama or directly along the coastal road. Direct bush taxis to the south of the river leave from the Tippa Garage in Serekunda or from Senegambia, and vehicles for Brikama leave from Westfield Junction. Bush taxis (mainly Peugeots) go from Serekunda to Kafountine and Ziguinchor in southern Senegal via the border at Séléti.

## GETTING AROUND
### To/From the Airport

A green tourist taxi from Banjul international airport to Serekunda is D300, and to any Atlantic coast resort is D400. Yellow taxis cost about D150, or even less, depending upon your powers of negotiation.

### Car & Motorcycle

Car hire starts around D800, exclusive of mileage and 15% sales tax, and goes up to around D2000 for 4WDs. Drivers must be 23 years or over, refundable deposits are required (around D25,000) and discounted rates are available for seven days or more. Some of the most reliable car hire companies include the following:

**AB Rent-a-Car** ( ☎ 4460926; abrentacar@gamtel .gm; Hotel Kololi, Senegambia) Has had consistently good reviews for years.

**Cars4Rent** ( ☎ 7782848; cars4rentgambia@hotmail.com; Elton Badala Oasis, Kotu) A smaller, but equally recommended operation.

**Hertz** (hertz@gamtel.gm); Airport ( ☎ /fax 4473156); Boketh Total Station ( ☎ 4390041) Slightly more expensive. 4WDs can only be hired with a driver.

### Shared Taxi

Shared taxis around the Atlantic resorts cost D5, to Banjul D6. From Bakau, at the junction of Saitmatty and Atlantic Rds, you can get shared taxis and minibuses to Banjul city centre or Serekunda. In Serekunda, shared taxis to Bakau go from outside the Gamtel office on the south end of Kairaba Ave. For Fajara, it's usually necessary to be dropped at the Garba Jahumpa Rd junction on Kairaba Ave. Shared taxis and minibuses to Kololi leave from the northwest corner of Serekunda market and go to the Kololi taxi park.

### Private Taxi

Green 'tourist taxis' usually wait outside the larger hotels. In some of the dense tourist areas, such as the Senegambia strip, they are the only taxis that have permission to enter. Fares are fixed, usually more than twice the rate charged by yellow taxis. For a tourist taxi from Fajara to Banjul, you'll pay around D350 by tourist taxi, D150 in a yellow cab.

Yellow taxis generally don't have fixed rates, except the 'town trip', any trip between Bakau, Fajara, Kololi and Kotu, which is usually charged at D25. Hiring a taxi for a day around the Atlantic resorts and Banjul should cost around D1000 to D1500.

# WESTERN GAMBIA

Heading inland or southward from the bustling resort zones, the big-business side of tourism gives way to a slightly more intimate experience of Gambian nature and culture. Small fishing villages, still fairly sheltered from mass tourism, line the southern strip of white-sand coast, inviting visitors to experience local life. On the northbank, the villages Jufureh and Albreda tempt with a fictionalised slice of history.

## SOUTH COAST & INLAND
### Tanji & Around

Moving on southwards from Serekunda and Kololi, a smooth tarmac road takes you past the villages of the South Coast, right to the Senegalese border at the river Hallahein, some 50km further south. Tanji is a major attraction, thanks to the charming **Tanji Village Museum** ( ☎ 9926618; tanje@dds.nl; adult/child D100/25; ☇ 9am-5pm) and the **Tanji River Bird Reserve** ( ☎ 9919219; admission D31.50, guided walks D200 ☇ 8am-6pm), an area of dunes, lagoons, dry woodland and coastal scrub. The wide range of habitats here attracts an excellent selection of birds, including indigenous species and European migrants; more than 300 species have been recorded. Although waders and waterbirds are the most prolific, there are also 34 raptor species. The nearby

Bijol Island is an important breeding site of the Caspian tern and the grey-headed gull. Outside breeding season, the wildlife department organises occasional boat tours (D500) here. Don't visit this bird sanctuary with other guides – it's illegal for anyone but the wildlife department to take tourists there. A trip to Tanji could be combined with a visit to the rapidly urbanising fishing village **Brufut** – the Tanji reserve office is a 2km walk from Brufut beach.

In Brufut, a couple of multi-star lodgings were being built at the time of research, and Tanji Village, 3km south of the reserve office, has some good accommodation options. The most attractive is the **Paradise Inn Lodge** ( ☎ 8800209; www.paradiseinngarden.com; r per person incl breakfast D660), which is stunningly located amidst mangroves and forest, and runs excellent birding excursions and music courses. A little further south in Tujering, the rootsy **Bendula Lodge** ( ☎ 7717481; www.bendula.com; s/d D510/680) has accommodation in simple, pretty huts placed between a lush tropical forest and a long stretch of white beach. They offer drumming or dancing courses and excursions to herbalists and artisans.

Further south is the white band of Sanyang Beach, with a scattering of crowded beach bars and a couple of hotels, including **Sanyang Nature Camp** ( ☎ 9902408; per person incl breakfast D400), a secluded but slightly neglected place. A better option is **Kobokoto Lodge** ( ☎ 9984838; www.salla.se/kkl; r per person D250) where rooms are simple but attractive.

### Gunjur & Gunjur Beach

One of Gambia's largest fishing centres, bustling Gunjur beach tempts with the impressive sight of pirogues rolling in, unloading their glistening catch on the shore. You can watch the busy scene from a number of informal workers' beach bars. There's a surprising choice of places to stay, including the excellent **Footsteps Eco Lodge** ( ☎ 7706830; www.natureswaygambia.com; camping D250, d D1750) – an attractive place complete with compost toilets, solar power, a freshwater pool and an extensive garden that grows organic food and attracts over 100 bird species. In the village, the **African Lodge** ( ☎ 4486143; fax 4486026; per person incl breakfast D400) is a peaceful, friendly hotel with a local feel. Five kilometres further south, **Balaba Nature Camp**

THE GAMBIA

**WESTERN GAMBIA**

0 — 10 km
0 — 6 miles

To Kaolack (83km);
Dakar (275km)

SENEGAL

Karang
Amdallai

Madiyana Lodge
Ginak Island

Ginak
Niji

Duniajoe
Fass

Maka Bala
Mana

ATLANTIC
OCEAN

Mbangkama
Njongon

Lohen

Ndungu
Kebbe

Denton
Bridge

Niumi
National
Park

Chamen

Ker Samba Njabeh

Cape
Point

Bakau

Wardner
Beach

Barra
Point

Kanuma

Berending
Buniadu

Medina
Seringe Mass

Madina
Bafuloto

Fajara

Kotu

Tanbi
Wetland
Reserve

Barra

Essau

Kanifing

BANJUL

Bakendik

Bijilo
Forest
Park

Kololi

Serekunda

Oyster
Creek

Bakalarr

Jurunku

Brufut
Beach

Ghana
Town

Latri Sabiji

Dog Island
(Charles Island)

Sittanunka

Pakau
Penku

Tanji River
Bird Reserve

Sukuta

Abuko
Nature Reserve

Lamin Lodge

Sika
Baduma

Bijol
Island

Brufut

Brufuts Woods

Lamin

Mandinari

Dog Island
Point

Lamin

Jufureh

Tanji River

Banjul Nding

Albreda

James Island

Tanji
Tujering
Point

Tanji Village
Museum

Yundum

Banjul
International
Airport

Gambia River

Tujering

Bendula Lodge

Jambur

Makasutu
Culture
Forest

Sansankoto
Island

Sanyang
Point

Sanyang
Nature
Camp

Jambanjali

Kuloro

Pirang

Taibatu

Jakoi
Sibrik

Sanyang
Beach

Sanyang

Brikama

Mandinaba

Faraba
Banta

Tumani
Tenda Camp

Brefet

Kachuma

Faraba Banta

Kiti

Marakissa

Basori

Sotokoi

To Soma (93km);
Basse Santa Su (305km)

Gunjur
Beach

Gunjur

Sifoe

Busura

Giboro

Douassu

Kafuta

Bessi

Ndemban
Chapechum

Somita

Gikis

Footsteps
Eco Lodge

Darsilami

Dimbaya

Omortoh

Bulok

Bator Sateh

Balaba
Nature
Camp

Dombondir

Séleti

Boboi Beach Lodge

Kartong

Allahein River

SENEGAL

Kartong Beach

Allahein

To Kabadio (10km);
Kafountine (24km)

To Ziguinchor
(78km)

( ☎ 9919012; huts per person from D550) is a laid-back, environmentally friendly camp, sat amid dense savanna woodland, that offers drumming and dancing courses and bird-watching excursions.

## Kartong

Picturesque Kartong is gradually turning into one of Gambia's most attractive spots for tourism, due to its stunning location near the Allahein River, a growing range of quality accommodation choices and the inspiring local tourist organisation **KART** (Kartong Association for Responsible Tourism; ☎ 4495887; www.safarigarden.com). Their range of initiatives includes the rootsy **Kartong Festival** ( ☎ 8900411, 7730535; www.kartongfestival.com).

## SIGHTS & ACTIVITIES

Kartong is a great place for pirogue and bird-watching tours – ask at the **Riverside Café** ( ☎ 9957694), a low-key place next to the Italian Restaurant. They arrange one-hour tours for D500. Or, if you prefer snakes to birds, stop by the **Reptile Farm** (admission D100), which has some small cages with snakes and lizards. If you like your reptiles in the wild, ask your hotel or KART for tours to the sacred **crocodile pool** of Mama Bambo Folonko.

A real Kartong gem is the **Lemon Fish Art Gallery** ( ☎ 4394586; www.lemonfish.gm), an excellent contemporary art gallery with a couple of pretty rooms for rent, and a boutique where you can purchase quality batiks, paintings and sculptures at fixed prices.

## SLEEPING & EATING

The prettiest place to stay is **Boboi Beach Lodge** ( ☎ 7776736; www.gambia-adventure.com; camping per person D150, tree house D250, d incl breakfast D600), which sits amid palm trees 10 steps from the beach. You can stay in bungalows with shared toilets or sleep under a starlit sky (mosquito-nets provided). Another good option is **Tamba Kuruba** ( ☎ 9851857; r per person D350), a basic, but very friendly place that donates its profits to the local hospital. Right on the river, the fishing and birding camp **Stiching Stala** ( ☎ 9915604; www.stala-adventures.com) was getting ready to open when we visited. It should by now be a cosy eco-lodge.

A 300m sand track west of Kartong, **Morgan's Grocery** (snacks and meals from D50 to D200; ☽ lunch & dinner) is a great place for local information and bird tours as well as food and beer. In town, **Umpacola Bar** ( ☎ 4419111; meals around D150) is a good place to meet locals, while the **Italian Restaurant** ( ☎ 9957694, 00221 616 43 82 in Senegal; dishes D60-150; ☽ 11am-midnight) near the Fishing Centre (3km south of town) has excellent pizza, pasta and espresso.

## GETTING THERE & AWAY

On the map, Kartong looks like a great launch pad into Senegal, but that's deceiving. You can cross the border here, but you need to take a pirogue across the river, then prepare for a 10km hike as there's no public transport on the Senegalese side. If you do decide on the adventure, get your passport stamped at the police post just south of town, then head towards the river and negotiate a pirogue (around D10). There's no border post in Senegal, so you need to make arrangements to get your passport stamped in Abéné or Kafountine.

## Abuko Nature Reserve

For a park of only 105 hectares, the **Abuko Nature Reserve** ( ☎ 7782633; drumohq@qanet.gm; www.darwingambia.gm; admission D31; ☽ 8am-7pm) has amazingly diverse vegetation and wildlife. Bird-watchers will love this place – more than 250 species have been sighted in the gallery forest, Guinea savanna and along the calm waters of Lamin Stream. Species include African goshawks, oriole warblers, yellowbill, leaflove, green and violet turaco, white-spotted flufftails and western blue-

bills. Birds can be observed pretty much anywhere, though the trail of the birding extension is particularly good. Several photo hides also reveal mammal varieties, including bushbucks, duikers, porcupines, bushbabies and three monkey types: green or vervet monkeys, endangered western red colobus monkeys, and patas monkeys.

The reserve is also famous for its Nile crocodiles, and has a small animal orphanage, where animals are looked after before being released into the wild.

Abuko is an important hub of preservation work in The Gambia, largely thanks to the **Makasutu Wildlife Trust** (drumohq@qanet.gm; www.darwingambia.gm), a busy research centre that studies Gambia's biodiversity, trains wildlife guides and runs various education projects. They also take on volunteers and can provide them with accommodation next to the reserve.

If you're a bird-watcher, you can enter the reserve from 6.30am, otherwise mid-morning, before the heat, is the best time to visit.

A thin book about the reserve can be bought at the ticket office, and several publications on the reserve and Gambian flora and fauna are for sale at the **Darwin Field Station** ( ☽ 8am-4pm).

A private taxi to Abuko from the Atlantic coast resorts costs about D400, including two hours of waiting time. Alternatively, take a minibus from Serekunda towards Brikama (D10). The reserve entrance is on the right (west) of the main road.

## Lamin

The village of Lamin is unremarkable, but **Lamin Lodge** ( ☎ 4497603; www.gambiariver.com), a rugged, handmade log cabin on stilts, overlooking a mangrove creek, makes for a great day out. The food here is good, the views fantastic, and, best of all, the lodge's eccentric owner is also head of the **Gambia River Experience** ( ☎ 4494360; www.gambiariver.com), which organises plenty of imaginative boat trips on the Gambia River. At the lodge, you can hire pirogues and small motorboats by the hour (D700), or for day trips (D10,000), and arrange drop-offs to Denton Bridge (D1600) and Banjul (D1500). Best-loved of all is their famous birders breakfast trip – think oysters and pancakes, binoculars clenched.

Most people get here by an organised boat tour. By road it's best to hire a taxi (D150), or combine Lamin Lodge with time at Abuko (D300). Or, from Banjul or Serekunda you can take a minibus to Brikama (D10), get off in Lamin and then follow the dirt road for about 3km to the lodge.

## Brikama

Brikama, The Gambia's third-largest settlement, is a typical junction town; extensive, noisy and busy. People and goods moving in and out and up and down the country pass through this dusty upcountry place, though few choose to stay here.

There's little to see, apart from the bustle itself and the famous **crafts market** (also known as the Woodcarvers' Market) at the edge of town on the right as you come in from Banjul or Serekunda. It's a hectic corner of covered stalls crammed with souvenir-style sculptures, improvised ateliers and hordes of eager salesmen.

There's a hospital, post office, Western Union Branch, a couple of Internet cafés (the best ones are Bojank K Net and the Gamtel office), and a Trust Bank branch that's supposed to take Visa cards, though you shouldn't wholly rely on it.

---

### KORA COURSES

For anybody interested in African music, Brikama should be an obligatory stop on the itinerary. The dusty town is home to one of the most renowned families of *kora* players in the country, a griot clan that reaches back several generations and has brought forth such mighty talents as Dembo Konte, his son Bakari Konte, and Malamini Jobarteh and his sons Pa and Tata Dindin Jobarteh. Forget about 'instant drumming courses' at the coast – this is one of Gambia's best places to learn traditional instruments, such as *kora, djembe, bolon, balafon* or *sabar*, watch them being made, and get an introduction to the griot's métier. Prices are entirely negotiable, and depend on duration and whether you stay and eat at their compound (which is possible). The best way of contacting them is by phoning ( ☎ 7710015; www.kairakundaarts.org). If you can't get them on the phone, ask any kid in town to show you the way to their home.

---

### SLEEPING & EATING

Brikama's hotels are certainly no enticement to stay here. The best of the worst is the nameless place known to locals at **Chief's Place** ( ☎ 9845959; off Basse Highway; r D200), right behind the mayor's home. Ask for chief Bojang's house and you'll be led to an iron compound door that hides a cluster of well-maintained bungalows.

Food options are mainly limited to greasy local eateries. The **Lucky Palace** (meals D15-45) is a fairly decent option, the **Kambeng Restaurant** (meals D15-45) has a pretty garden, and the **Gilanka Restaurant** ( ☎ 9851857; meals D15) serves enormous bowls of tasty rice and fish. More exotic things like chicken and chips are slightly pricier (D40).

### GETTING THERE & AWAY

Many minibuses (D10) pass through Brikama from Serekunda, about once every 10 minutes during the day.

If you're headed eastwards, there is frequent transport to Soma (D80), where you change for any other upcountry destinations. There are also frequent bush taxis to Gunjur (D10), where you change for transport to Kartong.

Brikama is the best junction from which to reach the Casamance region in Senegal. A bush taxi to the Senegalese border in Séléti costs D40 (CFA800), and then Séléti to Ziguinchor is CFA2200.

## Makasutu

Makasutu means 'sacred forest' in Mandinka, or 'cultural theme park' in the language of tourist enterprise. The **Makasutu Culture Forest** ( ☎ 4483335; www.makasutu.com; admission adult/child D700/400) occupies about 1000 hectares of land along Mandina Bolong, land that's dedicated to display a pretty, lush and smiling Gambia, just a bit more perfect than the one beyond the forest boundaries.

A day in the forest includes a mangrove tour by pirogue, guided walks through a range of habitats, including a palm forest where you can watch palm wine being tapped, demonstrations of traditional dancing and a visit to a crafts centre. For a half-day visit, take D200 off the price and the food out of the programme. Next to the forest, tucked away in the mangroves, is the **Mandina River Lodge** ( ☎ /fax 4484100; www

.makasutu.com; r per person with half board D5440), an exclusive eco-retreat that's world-famous for its successful marriage of lavishness and respect for nature, and for its stunning architecture, including floating, solar-powered luxury lodges. Bookings are made through Gambia Experience or the Makasutu website, and surprise visitors aren't even allowed near the site.

Most people come on a tour arranged through one of the ground operators. If you're making your own way, it's best to hire a taxi (D300). Alternatively, you can ask a bush taxi to drop you at Tuti Falls Rd (D12) and walk the last 3km.

## Tumani Tenda

The **Tumani Tenda Camp** ( ☎ 9903662; tumani tenda@hotmail.com; per person D200) is another eco-tourism venture situated about an hour from the coast on a *bolong* (creek) near the Gambia River. It's owned and operated by the residents of the neighbouring Taibatu village, who use the profits to fund community projects within the village. There are five traditional-style huts, each maintained by a different family from the village, where you can stay, with rates including breakfast. Other meals are D30. This is basic living, but for a taste of village life in a great location it's hard to beat. Bird-watchers venture here to try their luck spotting the rare brown-necked parrots.

Take a bush taxi from Brikama (D10) and ask to be dropped off at the turn-off to Taibatu (look for the sign). From here it's a 2.5km walk.

## NORTH COAST & NORTH BANK

Gambia's north coast stretches all of 10km from Barra at the mouth of the Gambia River to the border with Senegal. Those with an interest in history should have a look at **Fort Bullen** (admission D25; ☺ 9am-5pm), built by the British in the 1820s to help control slave shipping.

### Ginak Island (Niumi National Park)

**Niumi National Park** (Map p314) spreads across a small corner of northwest Gambia, including the long narrow island of Ginak (also spelled Jinak), where the range of habitats (beach, mud flats, salt marshes, dunes, mangrove swamps, lagoons and woodland) makes for excellent bird-watching.

Dolphins are occasionally spotted from the shore. In theory, the park protects small populations of manatees, crocodiles, bushbucks and duikers, plus various monkey species, but many animals have been hunted down, making chances of spotting them rather slim.

Ginak is a pretty stretch of land, by all means, though claims to celestial beauty made by various tour operators are a touch exaggerated. Over the last years, the heart of Niumi National Park has been eroded and replaced by large marijuana fields, which aren't quite as fascinating as the lush tropical forest that used to grow here.

The modest and charming **Madiyana Lodge** ( ☎ 4494088, 9920201; r per person D600) sits in a pretty spot on the western seafront and has accommodation in simple huts, with kerosene-lamp lighting and shared toilets. There's also a breezy bar-restaurant serving excellent food (meals D150). If you phone the lodge before arrival, you can organise pick-up from your front door (CFA1500 one way).

Another good option of getting here is joining an organised tour. The trips by the small operator Hidden Gambia (p327) get consistently good reviews. For D3000, they include transport, accommodation at Madiyana Lodge and full board.

Otherwise, a private taxi from Barra to the mainland opposite Ginak costs around D400. From there, you take a dug-out canoe across the river (D5), and a 20-minute walk west across the island to reach the lodge.

### Jufureh & Albreda

Jufureh became world famous in the 1970s following the publication of the book *Roots*, in which African-American writer Alex Haley describes how Kunta Kinte, his ancestor, was captured here and taken to America as a slave some 200 years ago.

His story has turned the tiny community into a popular tourist destination, though there's actually very little to see except the overblown village action that ensues as soon as the tourist boats arrive. Women pound millet at strategic points, babies are produced to be admired and filmed, and one of Haley's supposed descendants, the sister of the deceased Binde Kinte, makes a guest appearance at her compound.

Five hundred metres from Jufureh, Albreda is a little more peaceful. The main

THE GAMBIA

---

**THE ROOTS DEBATE**

Alex Haley based his research for his novel *Roots* on recollections of elder relatives who knew their African forebearer's name was Kinte and that he'd been captured by slavers while chopping wood for a drum outside his village. This later tied in with a story Haley was told by a griot at Jufureh.

Critics have pointed out (quite reasonably) that the story is flawed in many areas. Kinte is a common clan name throughout West Africa, and the griot's story of Kunta Kinte's capture would hardly have been unique. Also, as the slave stations of Albreda and James Island had been there for some decades, very close to Jufureh, it's unlikely that a villager from here would have been taken by surprise in this way. While the story of Alex Haley's ancestor is almost certainly true, it's exceedingly unlikely that he actually came from Jufureh. Despite the inconsistencies, Haley seemed happy to believe he was descended from the Kintes of Jufureh, and the myth remains largely intact.

Detractors may delight in exposing fabrication, but there is a danger that the debate on the accuracy of Haley's story may obscure a much more serious, and undeniable, fact: the slave trade was immoral and inhuman, and had a devastating effect on Africa. Millions of men and women were captured by European traders, or by other Africans paid by Europeans, and taken to plantations in the Americas. Many historians also hold that their labour, and the slave trade itself, was fundamental to the economic development of Europe and the USA in the 18th and 19th centuries.

---

thing to see here is the ruined 'factory' (fortified slaving station) originally built by French traders in the late 17th century, and the **museum** ( ☎ 710276; admission D100; ⊗ 10am-5pm Mon-Sat), which has a simple but striking exhibition tracing the history of slavery on the Gambia River.

The best place to stay is the **Kunta Kinte Roots Camp** ( ☎ 9905322; baboucarrlo@hotmail.com; s/d D500/1000) in Albreda – an ambitiously sized hotel with spotless accommodation in colourfully decorated bungalows. If you phone before arriving, they can also organise excellent meals. The **Jufureh Resthouse** ( ☎ 5710276; amadou.juffure@yahoo.fr; r per person incl breakfast D300) is a slightly lethargic drumming camp that mainly works with French groups, but can accommodate independent travellers if there's space in the shabby bungalows.

**GETTING THERE & AWAY**
The usual way to visit Jufureh and Albreda is by organised river tour. All the tour operators along the Atlantic Coast and several hotels have the 'Roots Tour' in their catalogue.

Alternatively, take the ferry across to Barra, then find a shared taxi to Jufureh (around D50) or hire a taxi (around D700 including a couple of hours waiting time). If you want to do the trip in a day, you'll have to catch the first ferry from Banjul. But, if you are making the effort to come all this way, you should consider staying overnight; both Jufureh and

Albreda are at their best in the evening, when the tourist groups have left.

### James Island
James Island is in the middle of the Gambia River, about 2km south of Jufureh and Albreda. On the island are the remains of Fort James, built in the 1650s and the site of numerous skirmishes in the following centuries.

Today, the fort is largely in ruins, the only intact room being a food store, which is often called the slave dungeon because it sounds more interesting. The island is rapidly eroding, and at some points the water is lapping the battlements. Only the baobab trees seem to be holding the island together.

Most people take in James Island as part of a boat trip from Banjul to Jufureh, but you might be able to arrange a pirogue to take you over from Albreda. Admission to the island including a visit to the museum of Jufureh costs D100.

# CENTRAL & EASTERN GAMBIA

Gambia being such a tiny sliver of land, nothing is really remote – yet once you've spent 12 hours on the tyre-busting road that leads upcountry, you'll probably feel as though you've crossed the continent. The route winds through crop fields, rice paddies, palm groves and patches of natural forest. Every 10km or so there's a junction where a dirt track leads north towards the Gambia River, which is never far away, but always frustratingly out of view. If you want to see the waterway, or go on a pirogue trip, just hop off the taxi and make a couple of overnight stops at the few brilliantly located camps sprinkled along the riverside – or do the whole journey by boat, by far the most enjoyable way of travelling.

## BINTANG BOLONG

Tucked away among the maze of shrubs lining the shores of the Bintang River is the spectacular **Bintang Bolong Lodge** ( ☎ 4488035, 9867615; www.bintang-bolong.com; r per person D400; 🏊 ), an intimate, eco-friendly camp made almost entirely from local mangrove woods and clay bricks. Stunning huts sit on stilts right on the river – you can leap from your balcony into a pirogue for a boat tour (per hour D800).

Twice a day, there's a bus from Brikama to Bintang (one hour, D25). If you can't face the wait for the bus to fill-up, you can hire a taxi (around D1700 to D2000). The driver needs to follow the main road east through the village of Somita, and turn left (north) at Killy along the dirt road to reach Bintang village and the lodge. Or, just phone the place and arrange to be picked up (D750).

## TENDABA

Tendaba is a small village on the southern bank of the Gambia River, 165km upstream from Banjul. It's mainly famous for the enduring **Tendaba Camp** ( ☎ 4541024, 4465288; tendaba@qanet.gm; bungalows without/with bathroom D225/245; luxury r D270), a classic on the travellers' scene. Tendaba's attraction lies in its position – opposite the Baobolong Wetlands and in close proximity to Kiang West National Park – in short, it's a birdwatcher's dream destination.

Accommodation ranges from small bungalows to VIP rooms, fully equipped with a river-edge veranda and TV. The restaurant gets consistently good reviews, too.

From Tendaba, you can arrange 4WD excursions to Kiang West and boat rides around the creeks of the Baobolong Wetland Reserve. If you don't want to take a vehicle trip, there are lots of options for walking in this area.

Most hotels around the Atlantic coast resorts arrange tours here – prices differ widely, so do some shopping around. Hidden Gambia and the Gambia River Experience both include Tendaba in their tours (see p327). If you prefer to come by road, it's best to hire a taxi. Otherwise, take a bush taxi from Banjul or Serekunda along the main road towards Soma. Get off at the village of Kwinella – the camp is 5km north along the dirt road.

## KIANG WEST NATIONAL PARK

The mangrove creeks and mud flats, dry woodland and grassland of Kiang West, The Gambia's largest national park, are home to an extraordinary variety of species, including bushbabies, baboons, colobus monkeys, warthogs, marsh mongooses and bushbucks. Rarely sighted species include hyenas, dolphins and crocodiles. Birds are also plentiful, with more than 300 species recorded, including Abyssinian ground hornbill, osprey, fish eagle, martial eagle and the rare brown-necked parrot. The 20m-deep escarpment that runs parallel to the riverbank is a good place for spotting animals – or for enjoying the scenery, if the beasts are proving too shy. A popular viewing site is Toubab Kollon Point, a river promontory to the northeast of the park. Behind the point, the escarpment runs close to the riverbank. About 2km west is a viewing hide overlooking a water hole which attracts a good range of animals, especially in the dry season.

Entry is D31.50, payable at the park headquarters in Dumbuntu, although this is included in the price of tours from Tendaba.

## SOMA & MANSA KONKO

Soma is a dusty junction town where Gambia's southbank artery crosses the Trans-Gambia Hwy. About 10km north of Soma is Yelitenda, where you catch the ferry across the Gambia River to Bambatenda, and then continue to Farafenni.

Nearby is Mansa Konko, originally an important local chief's capital (the name means 'king's hill'), and an administrative centre during the colonial era. Today it's a sleepy ghost town with a few reminders of the glory days, such as the district commissioner's residence and his crumbling colonial villa.

The lively **Moses Guesthouse** ( ☎ 4531462; r per person D125) is the only place worth considering if you get stuck – it's popular, hence noisy, and holds little appeal beyond 24-hour electricity.

## Getting There & Away

Bush taxis from the coast stop at the garage in the town centre, where you can change for a taxi to Georgetown or Basse Santa Su. If you're heading north, take a local bush taxi to the Gambia River ferry at Yelitenda (D6), go across as a foot passenger (D5), and take one of the vehicles waiting on the northern bank at Bambatenda to Farafenni (D6), where you can find transport to Kaolack or Dakar.

## FARAFENNI

On the north bank, the market town Farafenni is much more pleasant than Soma. The main *lumo* (weekly market) is on Sunday, when people come from surrounding villages and merchants from as far as Mauritania and Guinea to sell their wares. If you're low on cash visit the Trust Bank; it's the only bank for many miles. The border with Senegal is only 2km to the north and is open from 7am to midnight.

If you do get stuck here, it's worth taking the 10km dirt road trail towards **Kataba Fort**. Though reduced to its dusty foundations, this 1841 Wolof construction tells a half-forgotten story of old African kingdoms.

To spend the night, head for **Eddy's Hotel & Bar** ( ☎ 7735225; s/d with bathroom D200/250; ✷ ), a quirky place with a leafy courtyard that enjoys enduring popularity. It's also the best place to eat in town.

## Getting There & Away

Direct minibuses from Farafenni go to Serekunda most mornings for D90. For most other places, you have to go to Soma and change. If you're heading for Dakar there are bush taxis for CFA4000; some go from Farafenni itself, but most go from the Senegal side of the border.

## GEORGETOWN (JANGJANG-BUREH)

Under the British, the island settlement Georgetown was a busy administrative centre and trading hub full of grand buildings. Today it's got a new (or should that be old?) name, a host of crumbling monuments to history and the sort of sluggish atmosphere that discourages all but the most necessary work – the perfect place to relax for a couple of days.

The traditional, and now officially reintroduced, name for the town and island is Jangjang-bureh, but most people still call it Georgetown. The island is 10km long and 2.5km wide, covered with fields of rice and groundnuts. It has ferry links to both riverbanks, but there is little in terms of infrastructure – no banks and no hospital. There is though plenty to please those with a weak spot for birds and history.

## Sights

On the waterfront, either side of the northern ferry landing, are two crumbling colonial warehouses, which local youth will try to 'sell' you as 'Slave Prison', also talking up a 'Freedom Tree' and 'Slave Market'. This is fictionalised history – though slaves were transported through Georgetown, these buildings were constructed much later. Nearby is the old **Commissioner's Quarters** now inhabited by the district governor, and a **monument** outside the police station that recalls the building of Fort George in 1823 by the British after the local king asked for protection against a neighbouring tribe. West of town is the colonial **Armitage High School**.

Another place to visit is the **Lamin Koto Stone Circle**. At only 1.5km away from the north bank ferry ramp, it is far more accessible than the larger, and more famous, stone circles at **Wassu**, which can also be reached by tours from Georgetown. Those with a historical bent should visit **Karantaba Tenda** village, 20km from town, where an obelisk marks the spot where Scottish explorer Mungo Park started his journey to trace the course of the Niger River.

In town, the **Central River Division Forestry Project** (CRDFP; ☎ 5676198; www.crdfp.org), which battles against deforestation, is a great place to visit, mainly for their tours along the ecotrails of various forest parks.

## Sleeping

Most of the camps below have tours to Wassu, Gambia River National Park and bird-watching excursions on offer.

**Bird Safari Camp** ( ☎ 5676108; www.bsc.gm; r with half-board per person D1000; ✷ ) In a secluded location, this place has accommodation in bungalows or luxury tents and runs excellent bird-watching excursions accompanied by a resident ornithologist.

**Baobolong Camp** ( ☎ 5676133; fax 5676120; Owens St; s/d D300/400) Set in lush gardens at the eastern end of town, this camp has well-maintained rooms, friendly staff and the luxury of a generator.

**Alaka-bung Lodge** ( ☎ 5676123; alakabung@qanet .gm; Owens St; r per person D100) This low-key hostel is Georgetown's cheap and cheerful option. It mainly attracts a local clientele, and has email access (though not always reliable generator power).

**Jangjang-bureh Camp** ( ☎ /fax 5676182, 9920618; www.gambiariver.com; r per person D200) This rootsy place on the north bank consists of an eclectic collection of rustic bungalows set in a maze-like garden. Lighting is by oil lamps, and a drink at the bar overlooking the river is a fine way to spend the evening. You reach the place by boat from **Dreambird Camp** ( ☎ /fax 5676182; r per person D200).

### Eating & Drinking

Few options exist outside the camps and lodges, especially after dark. The popular **Maradona Roadside Pub** (Findlay St; meals D50-100; ✆ lunch & dinner) opposite Alaka-bung Lodge, is a good place for drinks and snacks and **Talamanca Restaurant** ( ☎ 9921100; Findlay St; meals from D50; ✆ 11am-8pm) is a relaxed address that's gradually growing from a decent restaurant into a humble 'hotel'. Otherwise, it's down to the eateries near the market.

### Getting There & Away

Georgetown is only reached by ferry. Most bush taxis turn off the main road between Soma and Basse Santa Su to drop off passengers at the southern ferry ramp – you should request this when entering the taxi. The ferry costs D5 for passengers and D50 for cars.

## GAMBIA RIVER NATIONAL PARK

South of Kuntaur, five islands in the Gambia River are protected as a national park. The heart of the park is the so-called Baboon Island, whose name is sometimes used to refer to the entire park. Baboon Island is the site of a project (privately initiated but now government owned) that helps once-captured chimpanzees to live in the wild again. Boat trips are available in the area,

but visitors are not allowed to land or get close to the islands. This is partly because it interferes with the rehabilitation process, but mainly because the chimps (there are more than 60) are nervous when humans get too close.

Because of the dense cloak of gallery forest on the banks of the island, it is unusual to see chimpanzees, so it's best to go with the aim of having a good day out on this beautiful stretch of river. You'll quite likely see baboons and monkeys, and possibly crocs and hippos too, plus an excellent selection of birds. And if you do happen to see any chimps – while keeping a responsible distance – it will be a bonus.

### Getting There & Away

The easiest option is by boat tour from Georgetown. Alternatively, you can go to Kuntaur by road and hire a boat there. Several people provide the service; the going rate is about D250 for a three or four-hour trip, after some bargaining.

Boats are only permitted on the main channel between the islands and the east bank of the mainland, and are not allowed to approach the islands nearer than midstream.

## BASSE SANTA SU

Set on a beautiful waterfront, this eastern-most town is the last major ferry-crossing point on the Gambia River and a transport hub for the surrounding area. It's a traditional trading centre, and as crammed and busy, run-down and forever deal-making as any West African junction town, especially if you come on a Thursday when the market is in full swing.

Both Trust Bank and Standard Chartered Bank have branches in Basse Santa Su that can advance money to Visa cardholders, and there's an Internet café. You can make calls at the Gamtel office.

By the waterfront, an old colonial warehouse has been converted into the cultural centre and café **Traditions** ( ☎ 5668533; sulaymanj allowtraditions@yahoo.com; ✆ 9am-6pm). It exhibits and sells locally made crafts, including handmade clothes, mats and wall hangings. Since the place's founders have left, it has started gathering dust, and the café as well as the display spaces were slightly haunted by neglect when we visited. But the remaining staff are immensely enthusiastic, and optimistic that this major stopping point of any tour to Basse Santa Su will shine once again.

Even if you find Traditions devoid of activity, a trip here is rewarding. The balcony gives a great view across the river and ferry point, and between June and February, it's also a good place to see the rare Egyptian plover. Boat rides to see this and other birds can be arranged with locals on the waterfront.

### Sleeping

Staying the night in Basse Santa Su can feel like a punishment if you're not used to roughing it a bit.

**Basse Guesthouse** ( ☎ 5668283; r D150) This place has dingy rooms with shared toilets, but at least you can spend some entertaining hours people-watching from the first-floor balcony above a tailor shop.

**Jem Hotel** ( ☎ 5668356; off the road to Vélingara; s/d D300/600) When we visited, it was managed by a mere boy trying his best to prevent this large place from drowning in dust. He's doing a pretty good job, though running this hotel-restaurant-nightclub machine on teenage adrenalin alone is tough.

**Traditions** ( ☎ 5668533; sulaymanjallowtraditions@ yahoo.com; apt D250) The staff here can dust off the former manager's apartment for unexpected visitors.

**Fulladu Camp** ( ☎ 5668743; r per person D300) This is undoubtedly the best place to stay on the north bank. Accommodation is in comfortable bungalows and they can organise pirogue trips.

### Eating & Drinking

Food is pretty much limited to hotels – Fulladu Camp and Jem Hotel are particularly good – the café of Traditions and the *gargottes* (simple eating house) and roast-meat stalls near the market. The nightclub of the **Jem Hotel** (meals D50-150) promises 'London sounds', but the manager admitted that the sign was a little old. The **Kassoumai Bar** (opposite the market; ❤ 7pm-2am) and **Plaza Nightclub** ( ❤ 8pm-3am) are both a little run down, but still good for beers.

### Getting There & Away

Bush taxis and minibuses go to the eastern outpost of Fatoto (D20, 40 minutes); the ferry ramp for Georgetown (D75, one hour); Soma (D150, four hours); and Serekunda (D300, eight hours).

The ferry to the Gambia River's northern bank takes one car at a time, and the journey is fairly quick. The charge for a car is D50, and for passengers, D5.

If you're heading for Senegal, you can go by bush taxi to Tambacounda via Vélingara (see p326). Even further afield, a Peugeot taxi goes more or less daily (passengers depending) to Labé in northern Guinea. The fare is CFA30,000 (D1500) and the trip takes at least 24 hours (or longer if there are delays at roadblocks).

# GAMBIA DIRECTORY

## ACCOMMODATION

In the Atlantic coast resorts, there's plenty of choice in places to stay, from basic guesthouses and self-catering apartments to palatial hotels. Upcountry, your options are severely limited, mainly to camps with accommodation in bungalows and round huts. Beware of the rapidly proliferating 'eco-lodges', only very few actually do justice to their name. If you want to travel responsibly, check their claims to eco-friendliness carefully. In this chapter budget accommodation is under US$30, top end is over US$75 and midrange is somewhere between the two.

## ACTIVITIES

Most tourist activities in Senegal and Gambia tend to be related to the sea, beach tourism being the most important slice of the holiday industry. Some beaches aren't safe for swimming though, due to strong undertows. Upcountry, it's all about the scenery and wildlife, with bird-watching, tours around the national parks and hiking among favourite pursuits. Pirogue and fishing trips can be arranged at Denton Bridge near Banjul (p307) and at the coast, and watersports equipment can be hired (see p307).

## BOOKS

The most famous work relating to The Gambia is probably *Roots* (1976) by Alex Haley. A mix of historical fact and imaginative fiction, the hugely influential book describes the African-American author's search for his African origins.

---

**PRACTICALITIES**

- *Africa Today* (Afro Media) has good political and economic news, plus business, sport and tourism.

- *Focus on Africa* (BBC) has excellent news stories, accessible reports and a concise run down of recent political events.

- *West Africa* (West Africa Publishing) is a long-standing and respected weekly with a focus on political and economic news.

- The electricity supply in The Gambia is 220V. Plugs either have two round pins, as those in continental Europe, or three square pins, as used in Britain.

- The Gambia uses the metric system.

---

For historical insights into the region, try Mungo Park's 19th-century classic *Travels in the Interior of Africa*. The written version of the Kelefa Saane epic, a famous recitation of Gambia's griots, affords excellent insights into the history of the Mandinka in Gambia. Mark Hudson's *Our Grandmother's Drum* is an entertaining fiction with moving insights into Gambia's music scene.

## BUSINESS HOURS
Government offices are open from 8am to 3pm or 4pm Monday to Thursday, and 8am to 12.30pm Friday. Banks, shops and businesses usually open 8.30am to noon and 2.30pm to 5.30pm Monday to Thursday and 8am to noon Friday and Saturday. Restaurants tend to serve lunch from around 11am to 2.30pm and dinner from 6pm onwards. Most restaurants in the cities stay open until the last guest leaves, though in smaller towns and villages many close around 10pm or whenever the food runs out. Bars usually open around 8pm, tend to get going from 11pm onwards, and close around 3am or 4am.

## CHILDREN
Children are generally welcome, though there's little in the way of child-centred activities. Most hotels offer the facility of adding an extra bed to a room. Children under 12 usually get a 50% discount or even stay free of charge.

Child-minding facilities are only available in a few hotels, most of them in the upper midrange or top-end bracket, and there's little in the way of professional babysitting agencies. Nappies and baby food are found in the big supermarkets, but up-country you might encounter problems.

## DANGERS & ANNOYANCES
On a world scale, Gambia is a fairly safe place to visit. Pickpocketing is rife though, and there are occasional muggings. Perhaps most annoying are the 'bumsters' near the coast, who try to make a living from hustling tourists. Firm but polite refusals to their offers of services should keep them away. Gambia's police checkpoints are notoriously irritating, being staffed with officials keen to extract some dalasi. Stay polite and friendly when faced with such behaviour – anger will only get you tied up in red tape. Women should be careful at beaches and on the road after dark – some readers have reported mild to very serious hassle.

## EMBASSIES & CONSULATES
### Gambian Embassies & Consulates
**Belgium** ( ☎ 02 640 1049; 126 Ave Franklin-Roosevelt, Brussels 1050)
**France** ( ☎ 01 42 94 09 30; 117 Rue Saint-Lazare, 75008 Paris)
**Germany** ( ☎ 030 892 31 21; fax 030 891 14 01; Kurfurstendamm 103, Berlin)
**Guinea-Bissau** ( ☎ 0203928; Av de 14 Novembro, Bissau) Located 1km northwest of Mercado de Bandim.
**Nigeria** ( ☎ 0682 192; 162 Awolowo Rd, Ikoyi, Lagos)
**Senegal** ( ☎ 821 44 76; 11 Rue de Thiong, Dakar)
**Sierra Leone** ( ☎ 225191; 6 Wilberforce St, Freetown)
**UK** ( ☎ 020 7937 6316; 57 Kensington Court, London W8 5DH)
**USA** ( ☎ 0202-785 1399; gamembdc@gambia.com; Suite 1000, 1155 15th St NW, Washington, DC 20005)

### Embassies & Consulates in Gambia
For details of embassies in Gambia not listed here, check in the phone book (most Gamtel offices have one).
**Guinea** (Map p299; ☎ 4226862, 909964; top fl, 78A Daniel Goddard St, Banjul; ⏰ 9am-4pm Mon-Thu, 9am-1.30pm & 2.30-4pm Fri)
**Guinea-Bissau** (Map pp304-5; ☎ 4494854; Atlantic Rd, Bakau; ⏰ 9am-2pm Mon-Fri, 9am-1pm Sat)
**Mali** (Map p299; ☎ 4226942; VM Company Ltd, Cherno Adama Bah St, Banjul)

**Mauritania** (Map pp304-5; ☎ 461086; off Badala Park Way, Kololi; ◷ 8am-4pm Mon-Fri)

**Senegal** (Map pp304-5; ☎ 4373752; fax 373 750; off Kairaba Ave, Serekunda; ◷ 8am-2pm & 2.30-5pm Mon-Thu, to 4pm Fri)

**Sierra Leone** (Map p299; ☎ 4228206; 67 Daniel Goddard St, Banjul; ◷ 8.30am-4.30pm Mon-Thu, 8.30am-1.30pm Fri)

**UK** (Map pp304-5; ☎ 495133/4; fax 496134; 48 Atlantic Rd, Fajara; ◷ 8am-3pm Mon-Thu, 8am-1pm Fri)

**USA** (Map pp304-5; ☎ 4392856/8, 391971; fax 392475; Kairaba Ave, Fajara)

Several European countries have honorary consuls in Gambia, including Belgium (at the Kairaba Hotel, Kololi), Germany, Denmark, Sweden and Norway (above Tina's Grill, Saitmatty Rd, Bakau).

## FESTIVALS & EVENTS
Two of Gambia's most interesting festivals include the following:

**International Roots Festival** Biannual festival held all across Gambia in June, with a focus on the 'Roots' village, Jufureh. Features mainly traditional music, as well as debates.

**Kartong Festival** ( ☎ 8900411, 7730535; www.kartong festival.com) Village festival in Gambia, featuring local, largely traditional dance and music groups.

## GAY & LESBIAN TRAVELLERS
Strictly speaking, being gay or lesbian is illegal in Gambia, and for many people, gay sexual relationships are a cultural taboo. It is probably best to avoid public displays of affection (which are also frowned upon in straight couples). Actual aggression is quite rare, though you might encounter some hostility.

## HOLIDAYS
Apart from the state holidays below, Muslim holidays, such as Korité, Tabaski, Tamkharit and Moulid are celebrated. Their dates are determined by the lunar calendar, and occur on different dates each year. See p818 for more information.

Holidays include:
**New Year's Day** 1 January
**Independence Day** 18 February
**Good Friday** March/April
**Easter Monday** March/April
**Workers' Day** 1 May
**Anniversary of the Second Republic** 22 July
**Christmas** 25 December

## INTERNET ACCESS
There are plenty of Internet cafés in Banjul and around the Atlantic coast, and most upcountry towns have at least one sluggish cybercafé. The two main operators are **Quantumnet** (www.qanet.gm) and **Gamtel** (www .gamtel.gm). All charge about D30 an hour as a base rate.

## INTERNET RESOURCES
**ASSET** (www.asset-gambia.com) The homepage of the Gambian Association of Small Scale Enterprises in Tourism lists plenty of interesting, one-man businesses.

**Gambia Tourism Authority** (www.visitthegambia .gm) Gambia's official tourist website, it covers the basics of travel information, though not in any great detail.

**One Gambia** (www.onegambia.com) Tells you all about Gambia's vibrant reggae scene, complete with its own radio station 'West Coast Radio'.

## MONEY
The Gambia's unit of currency is the dalasi, which is divided into 100 bututs. Notes in circulation are D5, D10, D25, D50 and D100. Over the years, the dalasi has drastically decreased in value and had recently stabilised when this book was written. You need to check the situation when you travel, and bear value-decrease in mind when considering prices listed in this book.

### ATMs
ATMs exist at several banks (notably Standard Chartered) and a couple of petrol stations in Banjul and around the Atlantic coast. In theory, ATMs accept credit and debit cards from banks with reciprocal agreements, but in reality, Visa tends to be the only reliably accepted card. Withdrawal limits can be tight, with some banks only allowing withdrawals of up to D2000.

### Black Market
The government has clamped down on The Gambia's once flourishing black market, which means that changing money with moneychangers is now risky, without giving you better value than at a bank. If you travel overland from Senegal, moneychangers will probably crowd around your taxi as you enter The Gambia. Don't feel pressured – many places and most taxis in The Gambia also accept CFA, so that you can get by without changing before reaching Banjul or the coastal resorts.

## Cash

In Senegal and Gambia, major international currencies such as euros, US dollars and British pounds can be changed in banks and hotels in the capital cities, major towns and tourist areas. Upcountry, changing might be difficult.

## Credit Cards

The use of credit cards is mainly limited to midrange and top-end hotels and restaurants, car rental, air tickets and some tours, but there's a real risk of fraud. Amex and Visa are the most widely accepted.

## Moneychangers

All the major banks change money, as do exchange bureaus, which are found in the tourist zones. Bureaus tend to give a slightly better rate for cash than banks, and a slightly worse rate for travellers cheques, but as rates and commissions can vary, it might be worth shopping around.

## Tipping

Tipping is usually expected in upmarket places – cheap hostels would be surprised to receive a tip. At the better restaurants, you're expected to tip around 10%, though many places include this in the bill. No one tips taxi drivers.

## Travellers Cheques

Changing travellers cheques can be tricky, even at banks, which invariably charge high commissions. Forget about changing them upcountry and don't bring anything but American Express.

## POST

The Gambia has a fairly reliable postal service, with letters from Banjul and the Atlantic resorts usually arriving in Europe within a week, and in North America and Australasia in 15 days. The poste restante service, which is available in the main post office in Banjul, is reportedly slow.

## TELEPHONE & FAX

There are plenty of public telephone offices, from where you can make local, national and international calls, and send faxes. Even the tiniest towns tend to have at least one, either privately owned or run by the national company Gamtel.

There are no area codes. Calls are charged by the unit, and add up fast on a call abroad. National calls are cheap, but to call abroad, you'll pay around D50 per minute. A 33% discount applies between 11pm and 7am.

For directory assistance dial ☎ 151.

## Mobile Phones

Mobile coverage is generally good. The main operators are Gamcell and Africell. A Gamcell SIM card costs D500. You can top up with prepaid cards, which are available in units of D50, D100, D150 and D300. Calls from mobile to mobile are fairly cheap, while mobile–landline costs almost the same as an international call.

## TIME

Gambia is at GMT/UTC. The country has no daylight savings. When it's noon in Gambia, it's 7am in New York, noon in London, 1pm in Paris and 10pm in Sydney.

## TOURIST INFORMATION

The Gambia is represented in Britain by the **Gambia National Tourist Office** ( ☎ 020 7376 0093; www.gambiatourism.info), based at the Gambian high commission.

In The Gambia, the **Association of Small Scale Enterprises in Tourism** (ASSET; www.asset-gambia.com) is a great umbrella organisation, trying to help small businesses. In Kartong, the local **Kartong Association for Responsible Tourism** (KART; ☎ 4495887; www.safarigarden.com) is a good source, especially for independent travellers.

## VISAS

Visas are not needed by nationals of Commonwealth countries, Belgium, Germany, Italy, Luxembourg, the Netherlands, Ecowas or Scandinavian countries for stays of up to 90 days. For those needing one, visas are normally valid for one month and are issued in two to three days for about US$45; you'll need two photos.

### Visa Extensions

Visa extensions are usually dealt with swiftly at the **Immigration Office** ( ☎ 4228611; OAU Blvd, Banjul; ☒ 8am-4pm). They cost D250.

### Visas for Onward Travel

For onward travel, get your visa from the relevant embassy. Most deal with requests within 24 hours.

## WOMEN TRAVELLERS

While it's not exactly dangerous to travel on your own as a woman in The Gambia, unwarranted interest is a pretty steady travel companion. Guys won't hesitate to approach you, and see how far they can go. It's up to you to set the boundaries. Inventing a husband is a pretty good strategy, and can help ward off suitors. On the same note, it's always better to refer to your boyfriend as husband in order to see your relationship respected.

Beaches are prime hassle zones, and the areas where female readers report the most irritating, sometimes downright threatening, advances.

It's often suggested that dress code can make a crucial difference to how you are regarded. That's true, though only to a certain extent. In urban areas, tight jeans and tops are perfectly acceptable, but in villages and when visiting people stick to long skirts or trousers (skirts are better in Muslim areas). You'll make your own life very hard if you walk around in miniskirts.

# TRANSPORT IN GAMBIA

## GETTING THERE & AWAY
### Entering The Gambia

A full passport is essential for entering The Gambia. If you cross by land from Senegal, you might experience difficult officials. Stay polite, and make sure that your papers are in complete order; meaning you've got a passport with a valid visa (if you need one) and your vaccination certificate.

### Air

The Gambia's main airport is **Banjul International Airport** (BJL; ☎ 4473117; www.gambia.gm /gcaa) at Yundum, about 20km from the city centre.

Most people travel to Gambia by charter flight. Regular airlines include the following:

**Air Guinée** (Map p299; 2U; ☎ 4412907; www.mirinet .com/airguinee; OAU Blvd cnr Davidson Carrol St, Banjul) Hub Conakry.

**Air Sénégal International** (Map p299; V7; ☎ 4202117; www.air-senegal-international.com; Ecowas Ave, Banjul) Hub: Dakar.

**Slok Air** (Map pp304–5; ☎ 4377782; www.slokair.com; Kairaba Ave, Fajara) Hub: Banjul.

**SN Brussels** (Map pp304–5; ☎ 027232323; www.flysn .be; Kololi) Hub: Brussels.

**West Coast Airways** (Map p299; WCG; ☎ 7767666; Nelson Mandela St, Banjul) Hub: Accra.

### Land

If you travel by land, you'll invariably enter from Senegal. The virtual disappearance of Gambia Public Transport Corporation's (GPTC) bus service has left the bush taxi as the only reliable option.

There are frequent connections between Dakar and Banjul. Most pass through the border crossing at Karang. You need to change vehicles twice – first into a minibus to cross the 'no-man's land' between the Senegalese and Gambian border post, then into a taxi of the nation you're entering – Senegalese taxis don't continue all the way to Banjul, neither do Gambian taxis take you into Senegal. To get to Banjul, you'll have to take the ferry in Barra. If you're coming from Dakar and think you might miss the last ferry across to Banjul (it leaves at 7pm), accommodation in Barra is limited to a couple of sleazy hotels. You'd be far better off staying in Toubacouta and getting the ferry from Barra to Banjul the next morning.

A second option takes you eastwards from Banjul to Soma, where you cross the Gambia River to Farafenni, then along the Trans-Gambia Hwy to Kaolack and Dakar. It's an interesting journey, but you'll have to put up with some terrible roads. The stretch from Brikama to Soma counts among the worst roads of the region.

There are a few border crossings between Gambia and the Casamance in Senegal. To get to Ziguinchor, you take a taxi from Brikama or Serekunda to the Senegalese border post at Séléti, where a bush taxi to Ziguinchor is CFA2200.

If you're heading for Kafountine, you could get yourself to Diouloulou via Giboro, then change for Kafountine. It's also possible to go from Brikama to Kafountine via the tiny border town Darsilami. This route isn't frequently used by public transport, but perfectly possible to do in a hired taxi.

The short hop from Kartong to Kafountine you see on the map isn't that timesaving, if you consider a pirogue crossing of the Hallahein River, a 10km walk on the Senegalese side, and the absence of border posts to complete your formalities.

From Basse Santa Su bush taxis go to Vélingara (D20, 45 minutes, 27km). Another tiny crossing is the one at Pata, from where a smooth dirt road takes you to Kolda. This isn't very frequented, and there isn't always a post at the Senegalese border, but it's the most direct route from Georgetown to Kolda.

## GETTING AROUND
### Boat
There's no regular transport upriver, though a couple of tour operators, including **Gambia River Experience** ( ☎ 4494360; www.gambiariver .com) and **Hidden Gambia** ( ☎ in UK 01527 576239; www.hiddengambia.com) run excellent river excursions and cruises. Denton Bridge near Banjul (see p307) is the starting point for many pirogue excursions around the coast and western end of the river. The main ferries across the Gambia River are at Barra, Farafenni, Georgetown and Basse Santa Su.

### Bus
The GPTC bus network was once the envy of many West African nations, but has now almost completely disintegrated. There are occasional buses that go to upcountry, all the way to Basse Santa Su, but they are not reliable, and can take an extremely long time (more than 12 hours) to arrive.

### Bush Taxi
There are two main routes though Gambia: the potholed dirt road along the northern bank of the river, and the potholed tar road along the southern bank. At the time of writing, the north bank was in a slightly better state than the south bank, but most bush taxis take the southern route. Bush taxis upcountry leave from Serekunda. They usually go to Soma, where you have to change for transport to Georgetown and Basse Santa Su. Bush taxis can take up to 12 hours for the 360km to Basse Santa Su.

There are two types of taxis, the yellow ones and the green 'tourist taxis'. Both can be hired for particular journeys or daytrips. Yellow taxis are just hailed down and tourist taxis usually park at hotels to pick up customers. Their prices are fairly fixed, and usually at least twice as expensive as yellow taxi rates (though these are entirely up for negotiation). Costs rise enormously the further you go upcountry. Day-hire of a yellow taxi for trips around the coast costs between D1000 and D1500, and going up to Basse Santa Su will set you back at least D6000.

### Car & Motorcycle
It's possible to hire a car or motorbike in Gambia's resort areas, but it's often advisable to hire a taxi with a driver, as driving on Gambia's dilapidated roads shouldn't be taken lightly, and in case of mechanical problems, it's the driver who'll be responsible and not you.

Despite the British heritage, traffic in Gambia drives on the right.

# Ghana

In Ghana life is public. People evacuate their homes and apartments every day to escape the stifling heat. And much like the kente cloth worn by market women, the disparate parts and peoples somehow mix and weave together into a cohesive whole. Ghana is home to a number of diverse peoples and cultures, all finding ways to coexist in a rapidly modernizing country. You'll see men and women in traditional clothes text messaging friends and suited businessmen taking offerings to tribal chiefs.

Compared to other countries in the area, Ghana is stable and prosperous, but this valuation is in part founded on hopes for the future. The country is often labelled 'Africa for beginners' and while you'll be welcomed by the people in a hot, sweaty clinch, the same way the sun grabs hold of you the second you go outside, getting around is by no means easy.

Ghana has no iconic calling card like Victoria Falls or Kilimanjaro, but one look at a map reveals a geographic blessing: hundreds of kilometres of coast shared by beautiful beaches, ruined European forts, the poignant reminders of the country's importance as a way station for African slaves, and the battered shacks of lively fishing villages. Accra is the commercial and cultural motor of the country, while Kumasi is the traditional home of the Ashanti, and is famous for its crafts. In the Volta region to the east, where the geography was given a facelift by the Akosombo dam, you can still find substantial swaths of forest crawling up mountains along the Togo border. And finally the north, which offers opportunities for wildlife viewing up close and personal, stretches across the horizon like an overcooked pancake to the Burkina Faso frontier.

## FAST FACTS

- **Area** 238,537 sq km
- **Capital** Accra
- **Country code** ☎ 233
- **Famous for** UN Secretary General, Kofi Annan; kente cloth; Ashanti culture
- **Languages** English, Twi, Ga and Ewe
- **Money** Cedi (see-dee); US$1 = C9525; €1 = C11,761
- **Population** 21 million
- **Visa** US$50 in advance or US$100 upon arrival at airport

## HIGHLIGHTS

- **Beachlife** (p354) Soak up the rays and Rasta vibe at a beach resort in Axim, Busua, Anomabu or Kokrobite.
- **Past Life** (p359 and p363) Tour the castles at Cape Coast and Elmina to learn about the history of slavery.
- **Wildlife** (p389) Engage in a staring contest with a bus-sized elephant in Mole National Park.
- **Hiplife** (p350) Take in Accra's club scene, the birthplace of some of the region's most popular music.
- **Village Life** (p370) Rough it in one of the community tourism projects like the stilt village at Nzeluzu.

## ITINERARIES

**Two Weeks** Without private transportation two weeks is really only enough time to do the triangular route bounded by Accra, Takoradi to the west, and Kumasi at the top. Start in **Accra** (p339; three days), then head to the beach at **Anomabu** (p358; two nights), then on to **Cape Coast** (p359; three nights) with day trips to **Kakum** (p362) and **Elmina** (p363). If you want to mix things up take the night train from **Takoradi** (p365) to **Kumasi** (p377; three nights) to explore the surrounding area, then head back to Accra.

**Four Weeks** With four weeks to spare, you can do all of the above plus throw in visits to the coastal resorts at **Busua** (p368) and **Axim** (p370) and also explore some of the north. If possible fly from **Accra** (p339) to **Tamale** (p386; one night) – if not take your time bussing it to **Kumasi** (p377) and then further north – and on to **Mole National Park** (p389) and **Larabanga** (p389; two nights). Continue west to **Wa** (p390; one night) and the hippo sanctuary at **Wechiau** (p391), if time permits, and return to Kumasi. From there you can head south to Accra and then visit the east: **Ada Foah** (p371; two nights), **Akosombo** (p372; one night), on to **Ho** (p373) and **Hohoe** (p376; three nights) and back to Accra. Alternatively, head directly to the coastal resorts of your choice from Kumasi.

## CLIMATE & WHEN TO GO

Ghana has a tropical equatorial climate, which means that it's hot year-round with seasonal rains. In the humid southern coastal

region, the rainy seasons are from April to June, and during September and October; the dry months, November to March or July and August, are easier for travelling.

Throughout the year, maximum temperatures are around 30°C, dropping three or four degrees during the brief respite between rainy seasons. The humidity is constantly high, at about 80%. In the central region, the rains are heavier and last longer. In the hotter and drier north, there is one rainy season, lasting from April to October. Midday temperatures rarely fall below 30°C, rising to 35°C and higher during December to March when the rasping harmattan wind blows in from the Sahara. At this time, dust particles hang heavily in the air, making it constantly hazy, and temperatures plummet at night.

The tourist high season is from June to August, which coincides with the summer vacation in the US. The country sees few tourists from September to December.

## HISTORY

Present-day Ghana has been inhabited since at least 4000 BC, although little evidence remains of its early societies. Successive waves of migration from the north and east resulted in Ghana's present ethnographic composition. By the 13th century, a number of kingdoms had arisen, influenced by the Sahelian trading empires north of the region, such as that of Ancient

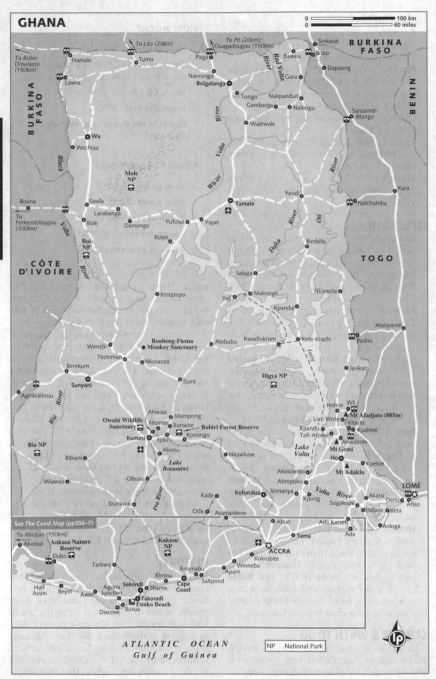

## GHANA

| | 0 | 100 km |
| 0 | | 60 miles |

To Bobo-Dioulasso (150km)

To Léo (20km)

To Pô (20km); Ouagadougou (150km)

BURKINA FASO

Hamale
Tumu
Paga
Navrongo
**Bolgatanga**
Sinkassé
Bitou
Bawku
Garu
Dapaong

Lawra
Wechiau
**Wa**
Tongo
Gambarga
Nakpanduri
Nalerigu
Sansanné-Mango

BURKINA FASO

Bouna
Sawla
Larabanga
Bole

BENIN

Walewale

Mole NP

White Volta

Red Volta

Yendi
Natchamba

Kara

To Ferkessédougou (300km)

Damongo
Fufulso
Yapei
**Tamale**

Daka River

Oti River

Bui NP

CÔTE D'IVOIRE

Buipe

Bimbilla

TOGO

Salaga

Kintampo
Yeji
Makongo
Kpandai

Nkwanta

Atakpamé
Badou

Boabeng-Fiema Monkey Sanctuary
Atebubu
Kwadiokrom
Kete-Krachi

Wenchi
Techiman
Nkoranza

Ejura

**Digya NP**

Jasikan

Berekum
Agnibilékrou
**Sunyani**

Ahwiaa
Mampong

Hohoe
Wli
**Mt Afadjato (885m)**
Liati Wote
Klouto
Kpalimé

Owabi Wildlife Sanctuary
Ntonso
Bonwire
**Bobiri Forest Reserve**
Kpandu
Tafi-Atome
**Amedzofe**

Bia NP

Kumasi
Ejisu
Konongo
Abonu

Lake Bosumtwi

Nkawkaw

**Mt Gemi**
Ho

Bibiani

Obuasi

Lake Volta

Akosombo
**Mt Adaklu**
Kpetoe

Wiawso

Pra River

Kade
Asamankese
Oda

**Koforidua**
Somanya
Atimpoku
Kpong

**LOMÉ**

Volta River

Akatsi
Denu
Sogakope
Dabala
Keta
Aflao

Dunkwa

Aburi
Ada Kasseh
Anloga

**See The Coast Map (pp356–7)**

To Abidjan (150km)
Aboisso
Ankasa Nature Reserve
Elubo

Tema
Ada

**Kakum NP**

**ACCRA**
Kokrobite
Winneba
Apam

Half Assini
Beyin
Axim
Tarkwa
Agona Junction
**Sekondi**
Elmina
Shama
**Cape Coast**
Anomabu
Saltpond

Dixcove
Busua
**Takoradi**
**Funko Beach**

**ATLANTIC OCEAN**
**Gulf of Guinea**

| NP | National Park |

Ghana (which incorporated western Mali and present-day Senegal). Fuelled by gold (of which Ghana has substantial deposits), trading networks grew, stimulating the development of Akan kingdoms in the centre and south of present-day Ghana. The most powerful of these was that of the Ashanti, who by the 18th century had conquered most of the other kingdoms and taken control of trade routes to the coast. This brought them into contact, and often conflict, with the coastal Fanti, Ga and Ewe people – and with European traders.

The Portuguese arrived in the late 15th century, initially lured by the trade in gold and ivory. However, with the establishment of plantations in the Americas during the 16th century, slaves rapidly replaced gold as the principal export of the region. The fortunes to be earned in the slave trade attracted the Dutch, British and Danes in the late 16th century. The Akan kingdoms grew rich on the proceeds of delivering human cargoes to collection points in coastal forts built by the Europeans, among whom competition for trading concessions was fierce.

By the time slavery was outlawed in the early 19th century, the British had gained a dominant position on the coast. The Ashanti continued to try to expand their territory and protect their interests and the coastal Ga, Ewe and Fanti peoples came to rely on the British for protection. Conflict between the British and the Ashanti sparked a series of wars that culminated in 1874 with the sacking of Kumasi, the Ashanti capital. However, the Ashanti remained defiant and in 1896 the British launched another attack, and this time occupied Kumasi and exiled the Ashanti leader, Prempeh I, to the Seychelles. The British then established a protectorate over Ashantiland, which was expanded in 1901 to include the northern territories.

Under the British cocoa became the backbone of the economy, and in the 1920s the Gold Coast became the world's leading producer. By WWI, cocoa, gold and timber made the Gold Coast the most prosperous colony in Africa. By independence in 1957 the Gold Coast was also the world's leading producer of manganese. It had the best schools and the best civil service in West Africa, a cadre of enlightened lawyers and a thriving press.

## Independence

In the late 1920s a number of political parties dedicated to regaining African independence sprang up. However, these parties were identified with the intelligentsia and failed to recognise the grievances and aspirations of most of the population. In response, Kwame Nkrumah, secretary-general of the country's leading political party, the United Gold Coast Convention, broke away in 1949 to form his own party, the Convention People's Party (CPP). With the slogan 'Self Government Now', it quickly became the voice of the masses.

A year later, exasperated by the slow progress towards self-government, Nkrumah called for a national strike. Seeking to contain the situation, the British responded by imprisoning him. While he was there, the CPP won the general election of 1951 and he was released to become leader of the government. Ghana finally gained its independence in March 1957; it was the first West African country to do so. At independence, Nkrumah cast aside the name Gold Coast in favour of that of the first great empire in West Africa, Ghana, famed for wealth and gold.

Much remained to be done to consolidate the new government's control over the country. Factional and regional interests surfaced and there was powerful opposition from some traditional chiefs. Repressive laws were passed in an attempt to contain this opposition, and the CPP became a party that dispensed patronage and encouraged corruption. Meanwhile, Nkrumah skilfully kept himself out of the fray and became one of the most powerful leaders to emerge from the African continent. He was handsome, charismatic and articulate, and his espousal of Pan-Africanism and his denunciations of imperialism and neocolonialism provided inspiration for other nationalist movements in the region.

Nkrumah borrowed heavily to finance grandiose schemes, the most ambitious of which was the Akosombo Dam. This project to dam the Volta River was to be financed by the World Bank, other international banks and Valco, a US aluminium company. However, Nkrumah, abandoned by other backers, was obliged to shortchange his country by accepting Valco's offer of the dam in return for all the electricity it needed, virtually at cost (see p374).

With a steadily deteriorating economy, the expected private-sector demand never materialised, and the electrification and irrigation programmes were shelved for more than a decade.

In the end, unbridled corruption, reckless spending on ambitious schemes, his anti-Western stance and unpaid debts to Western creditors were Nkrumah's undoing. Worst of all, he alienated the army by setting up a private guard answerable only to him. In 1966, while the president was on a mission to Hanoi, the army ousted him in a coup. Exiled to Guinea, Nkrumah died of cancer six years later.

## The Rawlings Era

Neither the military regime nor the civilian government, installed three years later and headed by Dr Kofi Busia, could overcome Ghana's corruption and debt problems. In 1972 there was another coup, headed by Colonel Acheampong, under whose inept leadership the economy worsened still further. As the cedi became increasingly worthless, food staples and other basic goods became scarce. In 1979, in the midst of serious food shortages and demonstrations against army affluence and military rule, a group of young revolutionaries seized power. Their leader was a charismatic, half-Scottish 32-year-old air-force flight lieutenant, Jerry Rawlings, who quickly became the darling of the masses.

As he had promised, the Armed Forces Revolutionary Council (AFRC) handed over to a civilian government several months later, after general elections. But first some major 'house cleaning' was done, resulting in the sentencing and execution of some senior officers, including Acheampong, and the conviction of hundreds of other officers and businessmen. The new president, Hilla Limann, unable to halt the country's downward spiral and uneasy with Rawlings' enormous grassroots support, accused him of attempting to subvert constitutional rule. This provoked a second takeover by the AFRC in January 1982, and this time Rawlings stayed for two decades.

Although Rawlings never delivered on his promised left-wing radical revolution, under his colourful leadership life became better for most Ghanaians. He yielded to World Bank and IMF pressure and carried out some tough free-market reforms, which included floating the cedi, removing price controls, raising payments to cocoa farmers and disposing of some unprofitable state enterprises. In return, the World Bank and the IMF rewarded Ghana amply with loans and funding. For a while, in the 1980s, Ghana was lauded as an economic success story, with an economic growth rate that was the highest in Africa.

In 1992, yielding to pressures from home and abroad, Rawlings announced a hastily organised referendum on a new constitution and lifted the 10-year ban on political parties. Opposition groups formed along traditional lines but divisions were deep. Without a united opposition front, Rawlings triumphed at the November 1992 presidential election, winning 60% of the vote. Humiliated, the main opposition parties withdrew from the following month's parliamentary elections, so Rawlings' National Democratic Congress (NDC) won and Rawlings was sworn in as president. Since 1992, Ghana has been a multiparty democracy with elections held every four years. Under the 1992 constitution, the government is headed by an elected president and a 200-member national assembly, which is also elected.

During the 1990s, Ghana made mixed progress. On the one hand, Rawlings seemed to have achieved a respectable democratic mandate, economic growth was maintained and Ghana continued to attract praise from the IMF. On the other hand, however, austerity measures, lack of improvement in social services, rising inflation, increasing corruption within the NDC and a hurried attempt by the government to launch an unpopular value-added tax in 1995 led to major civil unrest.

Rawlings' personal popularity was relatively unaffected and in December 1996 he was again elected as president. At much the same time, the appointment of Ghanaian Kofi Annan as UN secretary general boosted national morale. In 1998, in an effort to improve tax collection and spread the burden more equitably, VAT was successfully introduced. However, a drought in the late 1990s led to morale-sapping electricity and water rationing throughout the country, while a fall in the world price of cocoa and gold diminished Ghana's foreign-exchange earnings.

## Ghana Today

Ghana is one of the few politically stable countries in the region. Observers however say the 2008 presidential election will be the true test of the country's democratic maturity. After eight years of Rawlings and the NDC – the constitution barred Rawlings from standing for a third term in the 2000 presidential elections – his nominated successor and former vice-president, Professor John Atta Mills, lost to Dr John Kufuor, leader of the well-established New Patriotic Party (NPP), which also won a slim majority in the parliamentary elections. Kufour and the NPP won again in 2004, meaning that each party will have had eight years in power by the time the next national elections roll around. Some predict the election will be a referendum on the NPP's more economically liberal policies versus the NDC's more state-controlled or socialist approach.

Kufuor and the NPP inherited some tough economic and political challenges. Falling prices of gold and cocoa compounded by rampant corruption and stalled reforms in the 1990s caused a massive devaluation of the cedi and precipitated an economic crisis as Ghana entered the 21st century. One of the Kufuor's government first acts was to raise the price of fuel, previously heavily subsidised, and to loosen restrictions on the currency, allowing it to stabilise. Long-standing attempts to reduce Ghana's dependency on gold and cocoa have led to increasing interest in exports such as shea-nut butter, tobacco, cotton and pineapples. Manganese, diamonds and bauxite are also mined for export.

Politically, Kufuour and the NPP have had to tread carefully; the party's slogan, 'So Far So Good', is perhaps an uncannily accurate reflection of the confidence they and the country hold. Rawlings was in power for nearly 20 years, and in many parts of the country the state is still synonymous with the NDC, which isn't surprising considering the fact that many local leaders are indebted to their positions through political patronage. Both parties continue to be criticised for practicing cronyism and only awarding lucrative government contracts to fellow party members.

For the past century there's been large-scale mining in Ghana, but Australian giant Newmont's recent billion-dollar investment in two new mines in the middle of a forest preserve is not without controversy. With US$75 million from the World Bank, Newmont says it hopes to show that mining and social development can go hand in hand; it points to the fact that thousands of displaced people were compensated, new job training was offered and new homes were built. However, in the end only 450 full-time jobs will be created and nearby Obuasi, where AngloGold Ashanti operates, looks like the prototypical squalid mining town and is a somewhat dismal example of how vast underground wealth doesn't necessarily translate into better lives for those who live nearby; only half of the homes have an indoor bathroom and 20% have running water.

Some economists and political observers see as a fundamental problem the relationship between the large mining concerns and the tribal chiefs who control 80% of the land and receive most of the money – in what are still called 'drink commissions' – for the related land concessions. Because the chiefs are under no legal obligation to distribute the funds in any particular way and because there is little transparency in the process, ordinary Ghanaians may not be benefiting from the sale of their country's abundant resources as much as they should. Others argue that the funds are used in at least as socially beneficial a way as they would if the national government were solely in charge.

Ghana's economy continues to grow and attract investment, and the outlook is better than in many other parts of Africa. That being said, in 2002 the per-capita income was an estimated US$270 and Ghana is classified by the UN as a low-income, food-deficit country. To the average visitor from the US or Europe, most Ghanaians appear to live in terribly difficult conditions, and suffer from the consequences of poverty and unemployment. The majority of the very poor live in rural areas, and Northern Ghana is the poorest part of the country. The bulk of the country's labour force is employed in agriculture, which accounts for 37% of its GDP and 35% of its export earnings.

## THE CULTURE
### The National Psyche

To the average Ghanaian, World Bank or IMF optimism or pessimism about their country's macroeconomic position seems as relevant as the weather on the moon. Most people, apart from the residents of a handful of leafy residential neighbourhoods in Accra or Kumasi, live in fairly primitive conditions and aren't necessarily confident that their children's lives will look much different from their own.

Ask about the government's ability to make positive changes, and people will generally respond sceptically, no doubt a fairly common sentiment all over the world, but they do so without pointing to other social institutions that can or will do so in its place. On a local level, the church, the tribal chief or foreign NGOs supply the social safety net and many Ghanaians, not surprisingly, dream of emigrating to the US or Europe. Strike up a conversation and you'll often be told of relatives now living in New Jersey or Hamburg and how as soon as the speaker saves up enough money they plan to join them overseas.

Though the majority of foreigners living in Ghana work for international and religious development organisations devoted to good works, their relative prosperity and influence certainly rubs some people the wrong way. The average 'obroni' is viewed rightly or wrongly as a visitor from a more prosperous planet. Some Ghanaians who have lived abroad argue that real change will only come about when Ghanaian businessmen and politicians feel confident they are at least the equal of any Westerner who sits across from them in the boardroom or at the negotiating table.

Maybe the most famous and arguably the most important Ghanaian is Otunfu Osei II, the king of the Ashanti. He's considered at least as influential as the president, in part because he rules with no term limits and because of his relative youth; he's only in his 50s. Some Ghanaians living abroad send remittances to the king, some money comes from allowances paid by the government, and some of his wealth comes from taxes or tributes given by the people themselves.

Malaria, the leading cause of hospitalisation, is accepted as a fact of life. A hopeful sign of the government's commitment to dealing with the disease is the oft-aired TV commercial with a catchy jingle publicising the dangers of malaria and introducing a new drug to replace chloroquine. Ghana was the first country to receive a grant from the Global Fund to fight AIDS – an estimated 3% of the population is infected.

## Daily Life

The majority of Ghanaians work in agriculture, tending small subsistence plots, and the majority of these workers are women. The Ashanti, Ghana's richest and most self-confident culture, have a matrilineal social system and trace descent through the female line. Ashanti women are known for their independence, business acumen and influence in traditional politics. The *asantehene* (king) can have as many wives as he likes, although the present incumbent has just one. The Queen Mother, who can be the sister, niece, aunt or mother of the *asantehene*, exerts considerable power. She is the only person who can criticise the *asantehene*.

Funerals, rather than marriages or naming ceremonies, are the occasions that bring together family, townspeople and distant relatives. This is consistent with the ancestor-focused nature of Ashanti traditional religion. The streets of Ashanti towns teem with mourners and sympathisers wearing the distinctive funeral colours of black, red and shades of reddish brown. Expenditure is lavish and there's plenty of socialising and drinking.

Wealth is important in Ashanti culture; when Ashantis make money they build a fine house in their home town or village, however remote that may be. Many small Ashanti towns boast a few houses of a magnificence that is almost incongruous in simple villages ill served with basic facilities.

The extended family is the foundation of Ghanaian society. The Akan people are unusual in that they are matrilineal – you belong to your mother's clan. Clans are grouped under a chief, who in turn is answerable to a paramount chief, who is the political and spiritual head of his people.

Age, education and wealth are afforded great respect, and visitors are generally welcomed with friendliness. You'll probably be struck by how courteous Ghanaians are. Greetings are extremely important and an essential prelude to social interaction of any kind. It's usual to shake the hand of anyone you meet. The Ghanaian handshake involves a fairly limp grasp of the hand followed by a snap of your index finger with the index finger of the person whose hand you're shaking. Religion is extremely important in Ghana; blasphemy or swearing of any sort is unacceptable.

## Population

Ghana's population of 21 million makes it one of the most densely populated countries in West Africa. Of this, 44% are Akan, a grouping that includes the Ashanti (also called Asante), whose heartland is around Kumasi, and the Fanti, who fish the central coast and farm its near hinterland. The Nzema, linguistically close to the Akan, fish and farm in the southwest. Distant migrants from present-day Nigeria, the Ga are the indigenous people of Accra and Tema. The southern Volta region is home to the Ewe.

In the north, the Dagomba heartland is around Tamale and Yendi. Prominent neighbours are the Gonja in the centre, Konkomba and Mamprusi in the far northeast, and, around Navrongo, the Kasena. The Sisala and Lobi inhabit the far northwest.

For more details on the Ashanti and Ewe people, see p73 and p74.

## SPORT

Not surprisingly, the qualification of the national team, the Black Stars, for the 2006 World Cup only increased the profile of football, already the country's most popular sport. Three of the country's most prominent players are: Michael Essien, who plays for Chelsea in Britain's Premier League; Prince Tagoe, who plays in Ghana; and Freddy Adu, who plays for DC United in the US professional league. Boxing is the second most popular sport, and fights are periodically held Friday and Saturday nights from November to April in the Accra Sports Stadium and the Azuma Complex in Accra. Ringside seats cost C100,000. There are three golf clubs in the country. Cricket, basketball and the NBA are also popular.

## RELIGION

Churches of every imaginable Christian denomination are found in Ghana, some in the most far-flung, off-the-beaten-track villages. Christianity was introduced by European missionaries, who were also the first educators, and the link between religion and education persists. About 70% of Ghanaians are Christian; they're concentrated in the

south. Pentecostal and charismatic denominations are particularly active, as are the mainline Protestant and Catholic churches. About 15% of the population is Muslim; the majority are in the north, although there are also substantial Muslim minorities in southern cities such as Accra and Kumasi.

The rest of the people practice traditional religions, which generally include a belief in a supreme being as well as in spirits and lesser gods who inhabit the natural world. Ancestor veneration is an important part of traditional beliefs. Most people retain traditional beliefs alongside Christian or Muslim beliefs.

## ARTS
## Music
### TRADITIONAL

Certain types of music are customarily associated with specific social occasions and even more so with certain social and ethnic groups, even though similar musical instruments and types are found throughout Ghana. Some categories of music are exclusive to royalty and are performed only on state occasions, such as installation ceremonies and royal funerals or simply for the entertainment of the chief. This is more common in northern Ghana, where royal musicians perform at court weekly as a tribute to the chief.

### MODERN

Some of the country's more successful exports, at least to other African countries and increasingly to other parts of the world, are the musical fusion genres of highlife and hiplife. The latter is a more recent invention that takes a page from the American hip-hop world.

Popular highlife recordings include those by ET Mensah, Nana Ampadu and The Sweet Talks. Ko Nimo, now in his late 60s, is Ghana's foremost exponent of acoustic guitar highlife (or palm-wine music) and still performs with his band, the Adadam Agofomma Group, throughout Ghana. Hiplife stars to look out for include VIP, Castro, Reggie Rockstone, Kojo Antwi, Ofori Amponsah, Genesis Gospel Singers, Daddy Lumba and George Darko.

Gospel music is also big in Ghana, as is reggae; gospel rap is an immensely popular fusion of styles. Founded by visionary Nana Danso Abiam, the Pan African Orchestra has recorded an album of neoclassical, Afrocentric symphonic music.

It's a sign of the times that the Ghanaian song that is probably most familiar to Western ears is *Run* by singer Selassie – it was made famous as the theme music for *FIFA 2006*, a best-selling football video game with over 6 million units sold.

## Arts & Crafts

Ghana has a rich artistic heritage. Objects are created not only for their aesthetic value but as symbols of ethnic identity or to commemorate historical or legendary events, to convey cultural values or to signify membership of a group. The Akan people of the southern and central regions are famous for their cloth, goldwork, woodcarving, chiefs' insignia (such as swords, umbrella tops and linguist staffs), pottery and bead-making.

### TEXTILES

The Ashanti in particular are famous for their kente cloth, with its distinctive basketwork pattern. It was originally worn only by royalty and is still some of the most expensive material in Africa. The colour and design of the cloth worn is yet another way of indicating status and clan allegiance. Different cloth is worn depending on the occasion. It is traditionally worn by high-ranking men at ceremonies to display their wealth and status. Kente is woven on treadle looms, by men only, in long thin strips that are sewn together. Its intricate geometric patterns are full of symbolic meaning while its orange-yellow hues indicate wealth.

In contrast, *adinkra* cloth is worn primarily on solemn occasions by both men and women. The symbolic designs are printed in black on cotton cloth that is usually dark grey, dark red or white.

The Ewe people of the southeast, who claim to have originally passed on the method of kente weaving to the Ashantis, produce both the Ashanti kente and their own Ewe kente, which is even more intricately woven.

### STOOLS

Akan stools are among the finest in West Africa and incorporate designs that are rich in cultural symbolism. There's an Ashanti saying: 'There are no secrets between a man and his stool', and when a chief dies his people say 'The stool has fallen'. Ashanti stools are among the most elaborate in Africa. They are carved from a single piece of wood and the basic form is the same – a curved seat set on a central column with a flat base. Historically, certain designs, such as the seat supported upon the image of a leopard or elephant, were restricted to particular ranks within Ashanti society. The higher a person's status, the larger and more elaborate the stool.

Stools have a variety of functions and meanings. In official ceremonies, stools act as symbols of authority; on the death of their owner, consecrated stools are worshipped as homes to ancestral spirits; in most households, stools are articles of everyday use. A stool is the first gift of a father to his son, and the first gift bestowed by a man on his bride-to-be. Women's stools are different from men's. After death, the deceased is ritually washed upon a stool, which is then placed in the room for ancestral worship. Chiefs consider stools to be their supreme insignia. There are as many stool designs as there are chiefs, and the symbols are infinite.

### OTHER OBJECTS

The *akuaba* doll is carved from wood and used as a household fetish to protect against infertility; these are easily identified by the extra-large round head. The Akan are skilled in the lost-wax method of metal casting, used to make exquisite brass objects, including weights used for measuring gold dust. Glass beads are made by grinding up glass of different colours and layering it in a mould to produce intricately coloured patterns. Around Bolgatanga in the north, fine basket weaving and leatherwork are traditional crafts. Drums and carved *owara* boards – the game of *owara* has various names throughout West Africa – are also specialities.

## Cinema & TV

Miracle Films and HM are two Ghanaian film production companies. However, most of the films you'll see (on VanefSTC buses, in one of the few makeshift theatres or sold as bad pirated copies on the street) are Nigerian, or B-grade, straight-to-video movies from the US.

In 2005, the Oprah Winfrey–produced documentary *Emmanuelle's Gift* received a limited release outside the country. The film chronicles a young, handicapped Ghanaian man's bicycle ride across the country and his attempt to address the problems faced by the two million people (or almost 10% of the population) with disabilities in Ghana.

There are four TV channels in Ghana; the government-owned channel is GTV. Most of the series are produced in Nigeria or South Africa, though *District Colonial Court*, a widely watched programme is Ghanaian. Strangely enough, one of the more popular shows is *The Promise*, a soap opera from the Philippines dubbed in English. TV, like the radio, turns religious on Sundays.

## Literature

There's only a handful of fiction from Ghana available to Western readers. Highly recommended is the recently published, *The Prophet of Zongo Street* by Mohammed Naseehu Ali, a Ghanaian living in New York City; the stories explore life in the author's hometown of Kumasi and the dislocation of living in the West. *The Seasons of Beento Blackbird*, a novel by Akosua Busia (an actress who was in the film *The Color Purple*) and *No Sweetness Here and Other Stories*, by Ama Ata Aidoo, also deal with how Africans come to terms with traditional culture in an increasingly cosmopolitan world.

*The Two Hearts of Kwasi Boachi* by Arthur Japin, based on a true story, is a novel about the 19th-century tragic exile of an Ashanti prince. *Ama: A Story of the Atlantic Slave Trade* by Manu Herbstein, winner of 2002 Commonwealth Writers Prize for best first book, is a novelistic imagining of a young Ghanaian woman's tortured journey from slavery to freedom.

Ayi Kwei Armah's *The Beautiful Ones Are Not Yet Born* and *Fragments* are recommended. Both were written in the '60s and '70s before Armah gave up the trappings of literary success and moved to an island off the coast of Senegal.

## ENVIRONMENT
### The Land

Ghana is about the size of Britain. It's generally flat or gently undulating, consisting of low-lying coastal plains punctuated by saline lagoons in the south, wooded hill ranges in the centre and a low plateau in the northern two-thirds. All of the country lies

below 1000m. Keta Lagoon east of Accra, near the Togolese border, is Ghana's largest lagoon. Dominating the eastern flank of the country is Lake Volta, formed when the Volta River was dammed in the mid-1960s. It's the world's largest artificial lake, about twice the size of Luxembourg. The highest hills are part of the Akwapim range in the east, which runs from just north of Accra, then east of Lake Volta and into Togo.

### Wildlife

Ghana's national parks and reserves protect a variety of large mammals, including elephants, antelope species such as roan, kob, hartebeest, water buck, duiker and the endangered bongo, and primate species such as olive baboons, colobus and Mona monkeys and chimpanzees. The Black Volta River has a resident population of hippos; the best place to see them is at Wechiau Hippo Sanctuary (p391) near Wa. Nile crocodiles can be seen in various parts of the country but the crocodile ponds at Paga (p394) on the border with Burkina Faso are the best known. To see primates at close quarters, visit the sanctuaries at Boabeng-Fiema (p385) and Tafi-Atome (p375), where villagers have traditionally venerated and protected the resident populations of black-and-white colobus and Mona monkeys.

Forested areas contain numerous species of butterflies. Kakum National Park (p362), where some 400 species of butterflies have been recorded, and Bobiri Butterfly Sanctuary (p385) are some of the best places to see them.

The Volta estuary and coastal areas west of Accra (such as Kokrobite and around Winneba) are important turtle-nesting sites for green, leather-back and Olive Ridley turtles.

Bird-watchers will find Ghana has much to offer. In forested areas, birds such as hornbills, turacos, African grey and Senegal parrots and the rare white-fronted guinea fowl can be seen. The coastal wetlands around the Volta estuary and coastal lagoons are important resting and feeding grounds for some 70 species of indigenous and migratory water birds.

### National Parks & Reserves

Ghana has five national parks and nine protected areas. Mole National Park (p389) in the northwest of the country protects

GHANA

---

**COMMUNITY-BASED CONSERVATION**

Besides the big three sights of Mole, Kakum and Cape Coast Castle, tourism in Ghana is really driven by community-based ecotourism projects. There are over 30 dotted around the country, and they are the best ways to experience Ghana's natural attractions and traditional culture, while at the same time benefiting the local community. These projects are being established by traditional councils and district assemblies with the support of the Ghana Tourist Board and the Peace Corps and, most importantly, Ghana's Nature Conservation Research Centre (NCRC).

These projects are typically in small villages and have a visitors centre where you can arrange activities such as guided walks, village tours, bicycle hire and basic accommodation in a guesthouse or with families. Projects that are up and running include the Tafi-Atome (p375) and Boabeng-Fiema (p385) monkey sanctuaries, Wechiau Hippo Sanctuary (p391), Bobiri Butterfly Sanctuary (p385), Mt Adaklu (p375), Liati Wote Waterfalls (p377) and Domama Rock Shrine (p363). For more details of these and other ecotourism sites, check out the NCRC website (www.ncrc .org.gh) or contact the regional tourist office.

---

savanna woodland and is the best place to see wildlife, including elephants, baboons and antelope species. Kakum National Park (p362), just inland of Cape Coast, is known for its canopy walkway and is a good place to see rainforest habitat and birdlife. The three remaining national parks, Bui, Bia and Digya, aren't set up for visitors and aren't feasible to visit without your own transport. Of the protected areas, Ankasa Nature Reserve (p371) near Elubo in the southwest is noted for its rainforest habitat and forest elephants. Owabi Wildlife Sanctuary (p384), near Kumasi, is one of several designated Ramsar wetlands conservation sites in Ghana.

## FOOD & DRINK

A typical Ghanaian meal consists of a starch staple such as rice, *fufu* (mashed cassava, plantain or yam), *kenkey* or *banku* (fermented maize meal) eaten with a sauce or stew. Common sauces (called soups) include groundnut, *palaver* (made from greens) and light soup (egg and tomato sauce with fish or meat). Other menu regulars are fried rice with chicken or vegetables, *jollof* rice (the West African paella) and *red red*, bean stew with meat or fish, often served with fried plantains. The meat used is usually chicken, goat or beef; guinea fowl replaces chicken in the north of the country. Grasscutter, a large rodent, is also popular. Fish, usually dried and smoked, is a common component of meals. *Omo tuo*, a special dish served only on Sunday, is mashed rice balls with a fish or meat soup.

Breakfast is usually iced *kenkey*, a sort of liquid porridge made from fermented maize, with a hunk of bread, or bread and an omelette. Ghanaian bread is soft and white; varieties include sugar bread (very soft and sickly sweet), tea bread (less sweet), milk bread (slightly richer) and cinnamon bread.

## Where To Eat

The cheapest food is sold at street stalls. Look out for women doling out rice, pasta and sauce from huge covered bowls set up on a wooden table. You can either eat it at the stall or take it away in a plastic bag or plantain-leaf parcel. Other food-stall staples include egg salad with rice, roast yam with spicy sauce, roast plantain with groundnuts, omelette in bread, and spicy kebabs. Inexpensive food is also available from chop bars, which serve up a selection of dishes, usually with daily specials. Cheap places to eat are also referred to as 'catering services' and 'canteens'.

In Accra and other major centres you'll find a variety of cuisines, commonly Lebanese, Chinese and West African, but also Italian, French and Indian. Western fast food is hugely popular and there are plenty of outlets in Accra and other centres in the south. Most restaurants offer a choice of Western and Ghanaian dishes.

Regardless of where you eat, service is slow – sometimes incredibly frustratingly slow. If you can it's almost always a good idea to order in advance and give an estimate of when you will return. The average wait for food after ordering at almost anywhere but the highest-end place in Accra is 30 minutes. An additional tax of 15% (12.5% for VAT and 2.5% for NHIL) is added to almost every bill.

## Drinks

Cold water is sold everywhere in plastic sachets or plastic bags for about C250. The stuff in sachets (called 'pure water') has been filtered, whereas the stuff tied up in plastic bags (called 'ice water') is just ordinary water. Bottled water in 1.5L containers costs around C6000. A delicious homemade ginger ale is sold in some areas. As well as the usual brand-name soft drinks, bottled pure pineapple juice is available in some places. Generally, though, fresh fruit juice is difficult to find and expensive compared with the bottled drinks. Ghanaian tea is drunk from a huge mug with lots of evaporated milk and heaps of sugar.

Bars in Ghana are often referred to as a 'spot'. Decent, locally made beer is widely available. Popular brands include Star, Club, Gulder and Guinness.

Among home-brew alcoholic drinks, *pito* (millet beer) is the drink of choice in the north. Palm wine, which is more subtle, is the preferred tipple in the south. 'Tap before seven, drink before eleven' is the local saying. As the day grows older the wine becomes less refreshing, more sour – and more seriously alcoholic. *Akpeteshie* is a fiery local spirit.

# ACCRA

☎ 021 / pop 2 million

Nobody loves Accra. Much like family, it's sometimes only best appreciated at a distance or after a long separation. With its back mostly turned to the Gulf of Guinea, taking little advantage of its waterfront location, Accra crawls up and over a modern landscape, gobbling up real estate and producing a chaotic lowrise skyline. As the writer Ryszard Kapuscinski wrote in *The Shadow of the Sun* (2001), it's like an 'overgrown small town that has reproduced itself many times over.' Originally a scattering of villages controlled by Ga chiefs, today it's a sprawling city that extends eastwards almost 25km to the neighbouring city of Tema. Its congested and pockmarked sidewalks, baking streets that in the midday heat can make a block feel like a kilometre, shanty towns and genteel leafy suburbia, chop bars and gourmet restaurants, hiplife and highlife, combine to make Accra at once exhausting and exhilarating.

## ORIENTATION

The centre of Accra is bounded by a semicircular road called Ring Rd West, Ring Rd Central and Ring Rd East. Its four major circles and interchanges are, from west to east, Lamptey, Nkrumah, Sankara and Danquah. Accra's jam-packed commercial heart is Makola Market. South of Makola, High St runs along the seafront. West of the city centre are the shantytown areas of James Town and Ussher Town, bordered by Korle Lagoon. East of the city centre is the beachside suburb of La. North of Makola, the commercial district extends along Nkrumah Ave and Kojo Thompson Rd, two parallel north–south highways that connect High St with the Nkrumah Circle area. The district of Adabraka, south of Nkrumah Circle, is where you'll find budget hotels and inexpensive bars and restaurants. East of Adabraka, the leafy residential areas of Asylum Down and North Ridge have some good accommodation options, and this area is another popular base for travellers. Easily Accra's most happening area is Osu, south of Danquah Circle, which has lots of fast-food joints, restaurants, Internet centres and more expensive hotels. On the northern and eastern side of Ring Rd East are the upmarket residential areas of Cantonments, Labone and Airport, with embassies and upmarket hotels.

## MAPS

The best map available outside Ghana is a 1:750,000 version of the country produced by International Travel Maps of Vancouver, Canada. In Accra, the Survey Offices (Giffard Rd) produces a series of four 1:500,000 maps (C65,000 each) that cover the entire country. Other maps available in Ghana include the KLM-Shell map (C80,000) with Accra on one side and, on the other, a rather out-of-date but adequate map of Ghana, and there's also the Tourist Map of Ghana (C80,000), which makes a nice souvenir. Both maps are available from bookshops at the major hotels and from the tourist office in Accra.

## INFORMATION
### Bookshops

The University of Ghana in Legon (p353) has an excellent bookshop, although Accra traffic means it's a hassle to get there. A limited selection of foreign paperback novels, books on Ghana, magazines and newspapers

GHANA

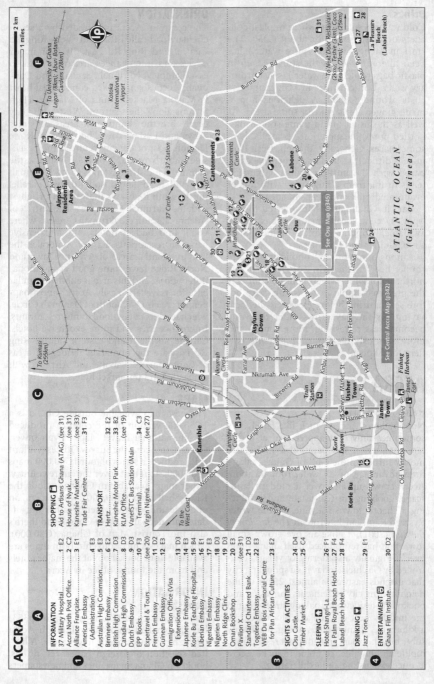

# ACCRA

**INFORMATION**

| | |
|---|---|
| 37 Military Hospital | 1 E2 |
| Accra North Post Office | 2 C2 |
| Alliance Française | 3 E1 |
| American Embassy (Administration) | 4 E3 |
| Australian High Commission | 5 E3 |
| Beninese Embassy | 6 E2 |
| British High Commission | 7 D3 |
| Canadian High Commission | 8 D3 |
| Dutch Embassy | 9 D3 |
| EPP Books | 10 F3 |
| Expertravel & Tours | (see 20) |
| French Embassy | 11 D2 |
| Guinean Embassy | 12 E3 |
| Immigration Office (Visa Extensions) | 13 D3 |
| Japanese Embassy | 14 E3 |
| Korle Bu Teaching Hospital | 15 B4 |
| Liberian Embassy | 16 E1 |
| Nigerien Embassy | 17 E3 |
| Nigerian Embassy | 18 D3 |
| North Ridge Clinic | 19 D3 |
| Omari Bookshop | 20 E3 |
| Pavilion X | (see 31) |
| Standard Chartered Bank | 21 D3 |
| Togolese Embassy | 22 E3 |
| WEB Du Bois Memorial Centre for Pan African Culture | 23 E2 |

**SIGHTS & ACTIVITIES**

| | |
|---|---|
| Osu Castle | 24 D4 |
| Timber Market | 25 C4 |

**SLEEPING**

| | |
|---|---|
| Hotel Shangri-La | 26 F1 |
| La Palm Royal Beach Hotel | 27 F4 |
| Labadi Beach Hotel | 28 F4 |

**DRINKING**

| | |
|---|---|
| Jazz Tone | 29 E1 |

**ENTERTAINMENT**

| | |
|---|---|
| Ghana Film Institute | 30 D2 |

**SHOPPING**

| | |
|---|---|
| Aid to Artisans Ghana (ATAG) | (see 31) |
| House of Nyak | (see 31) |
| Kaneshie Market | (see 33) |
| Trade Fair Centre | 31 F3 |

**TRANSPORT**

| | |
|---|---|
| Hertz | 32 E2 |
| Kaneshie Motor Park | 33 B2 |
| KLM Office | (see 19) |
| Omari Bookshop | |
| VanefSTC Bus Station (Main Terminal) | 34 C3 |
| Virgin Nigeria | (see 27) |

are available at bookshops at upmarket hotels and supermarkets in Osu.

**Books for Less** (Map p345; 17th Lane, Osu) Large selection of second-hand novels.

**Cosmopolitan Books for Less** (Map p345; 11th Lane, Osu) English-language paperback novels.

**EPP Books** (Map p340; Burma Camp Rd, Labadi) Random selection of non-fiction and novels and books on Ghana; opposite the Trade Fair.

**Omari Bookshop** (Map p340; Ring Rd East) Interesting books on Ghana plus a limited range of fiction.

## Cultural Centres

**Alliance Française** (Map p340; ☎ 773134; alliance@ghana.com; Liberation Link, Airport Residential Area) Lectures and cultural events.

**British Council** (Map p342; ☎ 244744; Liberia Rd; www.britishcouncil.org/ghana) Air-con library open to the public. English newspapers and magazines, and lectures and cultural events.

**Public Affairs Section, US Embassy** (Map p342; ☎ 229179; African Liberation Sq) Off Independence Ave.

## Emergency

**Ambulance** ( ☎ 193)
**Fire** ( ☎ 192)
**Police** ( ☎ 191)

## Internet Access

All of the top-end hotels have small business centres but charge ridiculously high rates for Internet, usually around C2500 per minute. Several have wi-fi across, including the La Palm Royal Beach Hotel for US$10 per day.

**Busy Internet** (Map p342; Ring Rd, Asylum Down; per hr C10,000; ☉ 24hr) Everything is modern and hi-tech at this popular and hip Internet cafe and entertainment centre.

**Internet Café** (Map p342) Across from the White Bell restaurant, on the left. There's another Internet Café on the second floor of a building across the street, on Akasanoma Rd.

**Mega Internet** (Map p342; Ring Rd, Asylum Down; per hr C10,000; ☉ 4.30am-1.30am) Flat-screen computers, all office-related services.

**Pavilion X** (Map p340; ATAG complex, Trade Fair Centre) Modern office centre with high-speed Internet and flat-screen computers.

**Osu Internet Café** (Map p345; Mission St, Osu; per hr C7000; ☉ 24hr)

**Sharpnet** (Map p345; Ring Rd East, Osu; per hr C10,000; ☉ 24hr) Flat-screen computers, all office-related services.

## Laundry

Public laundromats are few and far between. Midrange and top-end hotels tend to charge exorbitant rates. It's best to ask at a budget hotel, where three kilos can be washed, dried and ironed for around C40,000.

## Media

*No Worries! The Indispensable Insiders' Guide to Accra*, published by the North American Women's Association, is a mine of practical information about Accra. It's available from upmarket hotels and major supermarkets, though at C300,000 it's obviously geared towards resident expats.

## Medical Services

Ask your embassy for a list of recommended doctors and specialists. The main public hospitals in Accra are included here. Pharmacies are everywhere, or try the supermarkets in Osu.

**37 Military Hospital** (Map p340; ☎ 776111; Liberation Ave) Near 37 Circle, recommended for traumatic injuries.

**Korle Bu Teaching Hospital** (Map p340; ☎ 665401; Guggisberg Ave, Korle Bu)

**North Ridge Clinic** (Map p340; ☎ 227328, 024-355366; Ring Rd Central) Near the KLM office at the eastern end of Ring Rd Central.

**Ridge Hospital** (Map p342; ☎ 228382; Castle Rd)

**Trust Hospital** (Map p345; ☎ 776787; Cantonments Rd, Osu) Recommended private hospital where you can see a general practitioner. Also has a laboratory if you need a medical test.

## Money

The head offices of Barclays and Standard Chartered are both on High St and there are several branches, including one on Nkrumah Ave in Adabraka and Cantonments Rd in Osu. All the branches have ATMs. There is also a plethora of forexes around town, especially in the area around Makola Market and off Kojo Thompson Rd in Adabraka and along Cantonments Rd in Osu.

**Afro Wings Ltd** (Map p342; Farrar Ave) In the Trust Towers complex. Amex representative.

**Forbes Forex Bureau** (Map p345; Cantonment Rd, Osu)

**Jibrin Forex Bureau** (Map p342; Kojo Thompson Ave, Adabraka)

**Star Forex Bureau** (Map p342; High St) For whatever reason this place in the entrance to the Centre for National Culture has some of the best rates in town.

## Post

**Accra North post office** (Map p340; Nsawam Rd) Just north of Nkrumah Circle.

**Main post office** (Map p342; Ussher Town) On the Lutterodt intersection.

GHANA

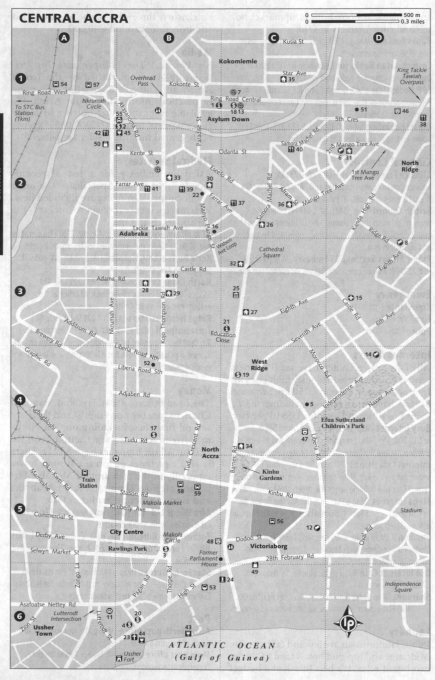

# CENTRAL ACCRA

0 — 500 m
0 — 0.3 miles

| | | |
|---|---|---|
| **INFORMATION** | Kwame Nkrumah Memorial | **DRINKING** |
| Accra Visitor's Centre................1 B1 | Park..............................24 C6 | Akuma Village.........................43 B6 |
| Afro Wings Ltd....................(see 37) | National Museum...................25 C3 | Champs Sports Bar.............(see 35) |
| Barclays Bank.............................2 B1 | | Osekan...................................44 B6 |
| Barclay's Bank...........................3 B5 | **SLEEPING** | Vienna City Entertainment |
| Barclays Bank (Head Office)........4 B6 | Beverly Hills Hotel...................26 C2 | Complex...............................45 B2 |
| British Council...........................5 C4 | Calvary Methodist Church | |
| Burkina Faso Embassy...............6 D2 | Guesthouse........................27 C3 | **ENTERTAINMENT** |
| Busy Internet.............................7 C1 | Date Hotel.............................28 B3 | Bass Line................................46 D1 |
| Doscar Travel & Tours............(see 38) | Hotel Avenida........................29 B3 | National Theatre.....................47 C4 |
| German Embassy........................8 D3 | Hotel President.......................30 B2 | Rex Cinema............................48 B5 |
| Internet Café.............................9 B2 | Korkdam Hotel.......................31 D2 | |
| Jibrin Forex Bureau..................10 B3 | Millenium Guesthouse.............32 C3 | **SHOPPING** |
| Main Post Office......................11 A6 | Niagara Hotel.........................33 B2 | Centre for National Culture......49 C6 |
| Malian Embassy.......................12 C5 | Novotel Hotel........................34 C4 | Loom....................................50 A2 |
| Mega Internet.........................13 C1 | Paloma Hotel & | |
| Public Affairs (US Embassy)......14 D4 | Restaurant.........................35 C1 | **TRANSPORT** |
| Ridge Hospital.........................15 D3 | Times Square | Alitalia Office...........................51 D1 |
| Speedway Travel & Tours..........16 B2 | Lodge..............................36 C2 | Avis......................................(see 16) |
| Standard Chartered Bank..........17 B4 | | British Airways Office..............52 B4 |
| Standard Chartered Bank..........18 C1 | **EATING** | Europcar...............................(see 34) |
| Standard Chartered Bank..........19 C4 | Choos Eatery.........................37 C2 | Labadi Lorry Station.................53 B6 |
| Standard Chartered Bank (Head | Edvy Restaurant..................(see 25) | Neoplan Motor Park................54 A1 |
| Office)................................20 B6 | Le Petit Paris..........................38 D1 | Taxi Station (for La, Osu & |
| Star Forex Bureau...................(see 49) | Orangery...............................39 B2 | Airport)................................55 B1 |
| Tourist Office..........................21 C3 | Spicy Chicken.........................40 C2 | Tema Station..........................56 C5 |
| WB Travel & Tours...................22 B2 | Trafix Courtyard | Tro-Tro Park...........................57 A1 |
| | Restaurant.......................(see 47) | Tudu Bus Station.....................58 B5 |
| **SIGHTS & ACTIVITIES** | White Bell.............................41 B2 | VanefSTC Bus Station (to Ho |
| Holy Trinity Cathedral..............23 B6 | Wok Inn................................42 A2 | and Aflao)............................59 B5 |

## Telephone

There are plenty of card phones for direct dialling and every street corner seems to have a communication centre, but it's probably more convenient and cheaper (if you're calling within the country) to visit one of the informal calling tables – literally a phone on a table – that are everywhere.

## Tourist Information

**Accra Visitor's Centre** (Map p342; ☎ 252186; bentsifi@ighmail.com) Near Mega Internet on Ring Rd Central. Has maps, and is reasonably helpful.

**Tourist information counter** ( ☎ 776171 ext 1314; Airport) A small counter in the international arrivals hall at the airport.

**Tourist office** (Map p342; ☎ 231817; ☒ 8am-4pm Mon-Fri) This is 50m down Education Close, off Barnes Rd. Some leaflets are free, others are for sale. Can't help with lots of practical information.

## Travel Agencies

**Doscar Travel & Tours** (Map p342; ☎ 239229; fax 248328; Sedco House, 5 Tabon St) Next to Le Petit Paris Café.

**Expertravel & Tours** (Map p342; ☎ 775498; fax 773937; Ring Rd East)

**M&J Travel & Tours** (Map p345; ☎ 773153; fax 774338; 11th Lane, Osu)

**Speedway Travel & Tours** (Map p342; ☎ 227744; fax 228799; Tackie Tawiah Ave)

**WB Travel & Tours** (Map p342; ☎ 245900; wbtravel@wwwplus.com; 29 Farrar Ave) Opposite Hotel President.

## Visa Extensions

**Immigration office** (Map p340; ☎ 221667 ext 215; ☒ 8.30am-noon for applications) Near the Sankara interchange. You need two photos, a letter stating why you need an extension, and an onward ticket out of Ghana. Your passport is retained for the two weeks it takes to process the application.

## DANGERS & ANNOYANCES

Accra is not plagued by crime and in fact it is generally a safe city to visit. The biggest hazard you'll face as a pedestrian is making sure you don't step off the curb into a ditch or a sewer or another hazard that will cause an ankle sprain. When crossing the street, look both ways several times and keep an eye out for taxis and tro-tros being driven like Formula One race cars.

As in any big city, it makes sense to take the usual precautions against pickpockets, especially in busy areas such as the markets and bus stations. Other areas that it's worth taking care around are Independence Square, James Town and Nkrumah Circle. Petty theft and even the occasional mugging are real possibilities at some of the area

**GHANA**

beaches, where you should avoid solitary strolls after dark.

## SIGHTS & ACTIVITIES
### National Museum

This gently decaying **museum** (Map p342; ☎ 221633; Barnes Rd; adult/student C20,000/45,000; ☒ 9am-6pm Tue-Sun), set in shady grounds, has interesting displays on various aspects of Ghanaian culture and history. The displays on royal stools, state umbrellas, swords and linguist's staffs *(akyeamepoma)* are enlightening. There is some fine brass work, including weights used by Ashanti goldsmiths for measuring gold and the spoons they used for loading the scales with gold dust. There are informative displays explaining local iron-smelting techniques, the lost-wax method for casting metal sculptures and how glass beads are made. Smaller displays feature masks, drums, wooden statues and the artifacts of other African cultures, such as the Baoulé and Senoufo peoples.

In the museum grounds is a shady open-air restaurant (see p349).

### Makola Market

There is no front door or welcoming sign to Accra's central market. It's a gradual transition from the usual sidewalks clogged with vendors hawking shoes and second-hand clothes to the market itself, which only becomes obvious once you can't take a step without tripping over a pile of Chinese-made locks or tube socks and you're sucked into the vortex of the swirling crowds. The food vendors have some of the most fascinating displays – pungent-smelling smoked fish, mountains of bread, painstakingly arranged piles of tomatoes and shallots, pyramids of rice, maize and millet, roast plantain and vast arrays of sweets, toffees and chewing gum. It's an intense – and perfectly safe – introduction into Ghanaian street life which by its sheer chaos forces you to keep your eyes, ears and even nose open and always aware. The goods sold here are for everyday household use and run the gamut from portable radios to underwire bras.

### Independence Square & Osu Castle

As a symbol of a young country's ambitions, grandiose architectural follies are fairly common. **Independence (Black Star) Square** (Map p340) is exceptional only in that there must be a better use of a large swath of beachfront property than a vast, baking expanse of concrete dominated by a ginormous McDonalds-like arch beneath which the Eternal Flame of African Liberation, lit by Nkrumah, still flickers. Opposite the arch, in the square, is the memorial to the Unknown Soldier.

The square can hold 30,000 people but it's almost always empty except for a sleeping guard or two who, if woken, may hit you up for some cedis. It marks the spot where, in colonial times, three ex-servicemen were shot while attempting to present grievances to the governor in a peaceful demonstration.

From the square, looking east along the coast towards La, you can see **Osu Castle** (Map p340). Built by the Danes around 1659 and originally called Christiansborg Castle, it's now the seat of government and is off limits to the public.

### Kwame Nkrumah Memorial Park

Pointing the way forward with arm outstretched, towering over a huge marble pile, is an effigy of Kwame Nkrumah, the founder of Ghana. About 250m west of the Arts Centre is this **park** (Map p342; High St; ☒ 10am-6pm) and final resting place laid out in the early 1990s as a gesture of rehabilitation. With the playing fountains, the swath of grass and the twin ranks of musicians at his feet, it's all on the monumental scale that he favoured and would have appreciated. There's also a small air-conditioned museum, with photos and artefacts from Nkrumah's life.

### James Town & Ussher Town

The residents of James Town and Ussher Town, two of the oldest neighbourhoods in Accra, don't live in conditions remarkably different from those anywhere else in the city. However, because it's fairly concentrated and walkable it's a chance to witness how ordinary Ghanaians go about their everyday lives.

These aren't shantytowns like you'd find in Johannesburg or Nairobi, but the people are undoubtedly poor and it may feel uncomfortably voyeuristic just walking around on your own. While this is probably safe enough, it's recommended that you find a local to take you around to find the more interesting spots and because it's easy enough to lose your way – negotiate a fee in advance. You should generally ask for permission before photographing people.

There are several boxing gyms – really nothing more than a makeshift ring in a concrete patio – that have nurtured a long line of neighbourhood kids who have become champions. For a great view of the city and the busy and colourful fishing harbour (haze and pollution permitting), climb to the top of the old **lighthouse** (Map p340; admission C3000) near James Fort.

If you're walking back to the centre along Cleland Rd, which becomes High St, you could take a detour along Hansen Rd to see the **Timber Market** (Map p340; it's hard to find so you'll need to ask someone to

show you where it is). The fetish section is fascinating, with its animal skulls, live and dead reptiles, strange powders, charms, bells, shakers, leopard skins, teeth, porcupine quills and juju figurines.

Head on to the Holy Trinity Cathedral, opposite Barclays on High St, which has a shady garden and, inside, a magnificent wooden barrel-vaulted roof.

## WEB Du Bois Memorial Centre for Pan African Culture

Dr Du Bois was an academic who championed civil rights and African unity. Towards the end of his life, he was invited to Ghana by Kwame Nkrumah to begin work on an encyclopaedia of Pan-Africanism.

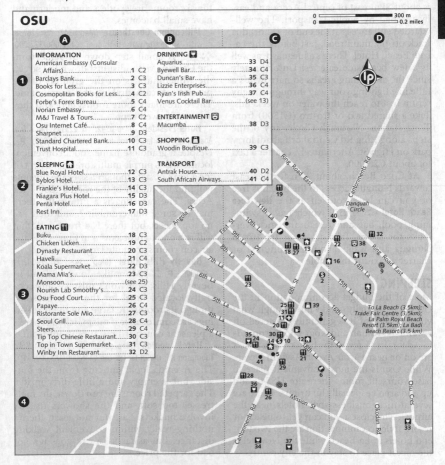

GHANA

### OSU

0     300 m
0     0.2 miles

**INFORMATION**
American Embassy (Consular Affairs).....................1 C2
Barclays Bank.............................2 C3
Books for Less............................3 C3
Cosmopolitan Books for Less........4 C2
Forbe's Forex Bureau....................5 C4
Ivorian Embassy..........................6 C4
M&J Travel & Tours......................7 C3
Osu Internet Café........................8 C4
Sharpnet.................................9 D3
Standard Chartered Bank..............10 C3
Trust Hospital...........................11 C3

**SLEEPING**
Blue Royal Hotel........................12 C3
Byblos Hotel............................13 C3
Frankie's Hotel..........................14 C3
Niagara Plus Hotel......................15 D3
Penta Hotel............................16 D3
Rest Inn................................17 D3

**EATING**
Buku..................................18 C3
Chicken Licken.........................19 C2
Dynasty Restaurant.....................20 C3
Haveli.................................21 C4
Koala Supermarket......................22 D3
Mama Mia's............................23 C3
Monsoon..............................(see 25)
Nourish Lab Smoothy's.................24 C3
Osu Food Court........................25 C3
Papaye................................26 C4
Ristorante Sole Mio....................27 C4
Seoul Grill............................28 C4
Steers................................29 C4
Tip Top Chinese Restaurant............30 C3
Top in Town Supermarket..............31 C3
Winby Inn Restaurant..................32 D2

**DRINKING**
Aquarius..............................33 D4
Byewell Bar...........................34 C4
Duncan's Bar..........................35 C3
Lizzie Enterprises.....................36 C4
Ryan's Irish Pub.......................37 C4
Venus Cocktail Bar....................(see 13)

**ENTERTAINMENT**
Macumba..............................38 D3

**SHOPPING**
Woodin Boutique......................39 C3

**TRANSPORT**
Antrak House..........................40 D2
South African Airways..................41 C4

This **centre** (Map p340; ☎ 776502; 1st Circular Rd, Cantonments; adult/child C20,000/10,000; 🕒 8.30am-4.30pm Mon-Fri), where Du Bois spent the last two years of his life, houses a research library for students of Pan-Africanism and memorabilia from his life, including a photographic display of leading black personalities and political leaders. In the grounds is the burial place of Du Bois and his wife, built in the form of a traditional chief's compound.

## Beaches

It's easy to forget that Accra includes kilometres of oceanfront real estate. While most is rocky and undeveloped, there are several sandy beaches. **La Pleasure Beach** (Map p340; admission C20,000), also known as Labadi Beach, is about 8km east of central Accra and easily reached by public transport. The well-guarded entrance is at the end of a short dirt track off the main road, just before the Labadi Beach Hotel. There's a lifeguard, as well as a few beachside eateries. Unfortunately since the swimming area is so narrow it's a little like fighting your way through a rugby scrum just to reach the water on weekends. Take a shared taxi or tro-tro (C1500) from Tema station, Nkrumah Circle, any of the stops along Ring Rd Central or Labadi lorry park on High St. Alternatively, charter a taxi for about C25,000.

At Coco Beach, about 7km further east towards Nungua, access to the beach is free or you can base yourself at the **New Coco Beach Hotel** (☎ 717237), which has a swimming pool, bar and restaurant and overlooks the shore. Take a taxi or tro-tro to Nungua and walk (about 20 minutes) or charter a taxi for the whole way.

## SLEEPING

Most of the budget accommodation in the city isn't especially good value, though what you will find of it is generally clustered off Kwame Nkrumah and Kojo Thompson Rds in Adabraka. A few of the better-value hotels are on or near Farrar Ave in Asylum Down. While Osu is the most convenient place to base yourself, rooms there are US$40 and up and aren't especially luxurious. There are several nice, business-style hotels near the airport. The closest you can get to beach or resort-style accommodation are the two top-end hotels at La Beach while the Novotel is the nicest place to stay in the city centre.

## Adabraka
### BUDGET
**Date Hotel** (Map p342; ☎ 228200; Adama Rd, Adabraka; r from C80,000) A long time favourite with budget travellers the Date Hotel is coasting on a now undeserved reputation. It's not so tranquil since the concrete courtyard is a drinking spot during the day and the fan rooms are bare-bare bones. Bring your own bath towel.

### MIDRANGE
**Calvary Methodist Church Guesthouse** (Map p342; ☎ 234507; Barnes Rd, West Ridge; s/d C220,000; P 🞨 ) Even the uneclessiastically inclined will find the rooms on the top floor of a building in this compound divine for the price. Each of the six rooms are spotless and modern and have small balconies.

**Millennium Guesthouse** (Map p342; ☎ 226738; r with shared/private bathroom C172,000/322,000; 🞨 P ) A small step down in value from the Calvary Methodist just down the street, the Millennium is on the grounds of the prominent cathedral of the same name. There are many more rooms here and they are equally well kept.

**Hotel President** (Map p342; ☎ 223343; Farrar Ave, Adabraka; r with fan/air-con from C140,000/180,000; P ) Despite a grandiose name and a convenient location, this purple multistorey hotel isn't fit for a head of state though less exalted people will find the quality of the rooms good – for Accra. The carpeting is a little ratty, there may be some wall crumbling, and there are no top sheets, but there is a front desk that will respond to problems – in time – and the air-con rooms are quite large.

**Beverly Hills Hotel** (Map p342; ☎ 224042; r C300,000; P 🞨 ) More like down and out in Beverly Hills; you won't mistake this centrally located hotel for the Four Seasons, though its rooms are large and the furnishings are comfortable if mismatched. There's a pleasant courtyard restaurant out front.

**Hotel Avenida** (Map p342; ☎ 221354; 94 Koko Thompson Rd; r with fan/air-con C146,000/183,000; P ) The Avenida looks enticing from the outside, but is empty and a little dirty inside. The carpeted rooms are run down, the mattresses too soft, and the showers usually involve buckets. Last but not least, there's nothing really within convenient walking distance. But as far as Accra goes it's not bad for the price.

## TOP END
**Paloma Hotel** (Map p342; ☎ 228700; paloma@africa online.com.gh; Ring Rd Central; s/d US$50/70; P ⌨) A rare find in Accra, the Paloma pays attention to the details and the attractive rooms are simple but tastefully furnished. It's part of a complex popular with expats that includes a restaurant, courtyard café and bar (see p350). Well located for tro-tros to Osu or the city centre, on the northern side of busy Ring Rd Central.

**Niagara Hotel** (Map p342; ☎ 230118; fax 230119; Kojo Thompson Rd, Adabraka; s/d US$66/88; P ✂) The plush leather couches in the lobby promise so much, but the rooms are a little disappointing at this price. While they're large and comfortable and have a painting or two they're a little frayed at the edges. On the hectic corner of Farrar and Kojo Thompson Rds. Offers car-hire services and has a good Lebanese restaurant.

## Osu
### MIDRANGE
**Rest Inn** (Map p345; ☎ 785543; www.therestinn.com; 14th Lane; r US$45; P ✂) As far as Osu goes, this is as good value as you'll find. Right around the corner from the Koala supermarket, and behind the art gallery in front, are several small, clean and modern rooms.

**Niagara Plus Hotel** (Map p345; ☎ 772428; 14th Lane; s/d C460,000/598,000; P ✂) Under the same management as the Niagara in Adabraka, this friendly hotel is down a quiet lane about 200m from Cantonments Rd. Rooms are large and comfortable in this especially attractive whitewashed villa with a cobblestone courtyard.

**Frankie's Hotel** (Map p345; ☎ 773567; www.frankies -ghana.com; Cantonments Rd; s/d US$65/85; ✂ ⌨ P) Above the excellent eatery of the same name, Frankie's has little atmosphere though everything is immaculate, including the basic, modern rooms.

**Blue Royal Hotel** (Map p345; ☎ 783075; 18th Lane; s/d from US$60/70; P ✂) The African paintings and crafts signals some attempt at decoration, which is rare thing indeed in Ghana. The rooms are modern and clean but still seems a tad overpriced. Has a third floor restaurant and bar.

**Penta Hotel** (Map p345; ☎ 774529; Cantonment Rd; s/d US$60/70; P ✂) This hotel in the heart of the Osu craziness is professionally run though at the expense of warmth or character. The small, modern rooms aren't especially good value. Tycoon restaurant and Hemingway's Bar attached.

**Byblos Hotel** (Map p345; ☎ 782250; byblos hotels@hotmail.com; 11th Lane; s/d US$50/60; P ✂) The Byblos attracts a loyal following as much for the Venus cocktail bar attached to it as for its simple but clean rooms with cable and good TVs.

## Asylum Down & North Ridge
### BUDGET
**Times Square Lodge** (Map p342; ☎ 222694; cnr Mango Tree Ave & Afram Rd, Asylum Down; d C200,000; P) You might have to wake the front-desk staff and you might have to switch rooms till you find one with adequate water pressure and lights that work, but other than that this hotel in a quiet residential area is an adequate first-night choice.

**Korkdam Hotel** (Map p342; ☎ 226797; korkdam@ africaonline; 2nd Mango Tree Ave, Asylum Down; s/d with fan C115,000/185,000, r with air-con C250,000; P) A slightly better choice than the next-door Lemon Lodge, the rooms are run down and the water pressure is lousy. Only a thin wall separates your cell from your neighbour's.

### MIDRANGE
**North Ridge Hotel** ( ☎ 225809; nrhotel@hotmail.com .gh; s/d US$50/60; P ✂) Easily the best value in this price range in the neighbourhood, the friendly North Ridge is a large building on a quiet residential street. The tile-floored rooms have some character even though the furniture is old.

## City Centre, Airport Area & Elsewhere
### TOP END
**La Palm Royal Beach Hotel** (Map p340; ☎ 771700; www.gbhghana.com; La Beach; r US$200-350; P ✂ ⌨ ♨) God forbid there should ever be a disaster in Accra, but if there were everyone would probably go to the La Palm. A little like a city-state unto itself, complete with large conference centre, casino, several restaurants, a pool complex (the nicest in the city), a lounge with a big-screen TV, an ice-cream shop etc, almost every expat in town on the weekend heads here at some point. There are rooms of varying size and quality.

**Novotel Hotel** (Map p342; ☎ 667546; www.novotel .com; Barnes Rd, Accra North; r from US$158; P ✂ ⌨ ♨) Stepping into the Novotel, is like crossing the threshold into another world. Right in the crazy, chaotic heart of the city, it's a refuge of modernity and quiet, worth a stop at the pool or café if only to break up a day of sightseeing. All the rooms are modern and up to business-class quality; be sure to ask for one with a view.

**Labadi Beach Hotel** (Map p340; ☎ 772501; www .labadibeach.com; Labadi Bypass, La; s/d US$185/200; P ❄ ▯ ▨) Queen Elizabeth and Tony Blair stayed here. That should be enough to guarantee a certain level of comfort, and the rooms here are a little more sumptuous than those at La Palm, though the pool area isn't as nice. It does have direct beach access and more old-world character than others in this price range.

**Hotel Shangri-La** (Map p340; ☎ 762590; www .shangri-la.gh.com; Liberation Ave, Airport Residential Area; r from US$85; P ❄ ▯ ▨) Unless you have an early flight to catch there isn't much reason to stay out here past the airport. The low-slung Shangri-La does have a following with Ghanaians, and is decorated with traditional crafts, but it's looking a little worse for wear. The basic, bungalow rooms are set in a garden as is a nice swimming pool (nonguests C35,000). There is a restaurant and café.

## Coco Beach

**MIDRANGE**

**Akwaaba Beach Guesthouse** ( ☎ 717742; www.ak waaba-beach.de; Nungua; r incl breakfast from US$50; P ❄ ▯) It's easy to forget you're only around 15km east of Accra at this wonderfully tranquil place with private beach access. The Akwaaba looks a little like a Mediterranean-style villa and has seven bright and attractive rooms. The spectacular penthouse studio is great value (US$80).

**New Coco Beach Hotel** ( ☎ 717237; newcoco beach@yahoo.com; Nungua; s/d US$70/90; ❄ ▨) This internationally owned hotel can't compete with the Akwaaba's charm and is standard and institutional where the former is creative and personal. Facilities include a gym and a swimming pool.

## EATING

Accra has the best choice of restaurants in the country, and the food will seem like *haute cuisine* if you're returning to the city after time spent elsewhere in Ghana. Cedi savers can eat cheaply at chop bars and food stalls, especially around the transport terminals and major circles such as Nkrumah

and Danquah. Several good, inexpensive restaurants are on Farrar Ave in Asylum Down. Osu is China Town, Little Italy and your mall food court rolled into one long clogged road. Some of the upmarket restaurants where you'll spend at least C80,000 are found off the main road, down one of the residential streets.

Most of the midrange and all of the top-end hotels have restaurants and are especially recommended for breakfast splurges. The Ghanaian Village and Bali Hai at the La Palm Royal Beach Hotel deserve special mention.

If you're self-catering, for basic provisions such as biscuits, bread, margarine, bananas, tinned sardines and baked beans, there are plenty of food stalls and small shops around town. For imported goods, the supermarkets in Osu are best, especially **Koala Supermarket** (Map p345; Cantonments Rd), which might as well be called 'expat central', just off Danquah Circle at the top of Cantonments Rd. **Top in Town Supermarket** (Map p345; Cantonments Rd) is another.

## Adabraka

**Orangery** (Map p342; Farrar Ave; mains C25,000-75,000) Part furniture shop, part charming restaurant, the Orangery is definitely the best restaurant in the neighbourhood. It's a pretty-looking place decorated with potted plants and specialising in sweet and savoury pancakes, muffins, waffles, and crepes. Non-breakfast specialities include moussaka (C45,000) and seafood bouillabaisse (C75,000). The curious can try the peanut-butter soup (C25,000).

**White Bell** (Map p342; Farrar Ave; mains C35,000) The 2nd-floor dining area catches some cooling breezes and is deservedly popular with those staying in the area. The White Bell serves up burgers, sandwiches and chicken and rice dishes. Music and dancing in the evening.

**Choos Eatery** (Map p342; 2nd fl, Trust Bldg, Farrar Ave; mains C30,000) There aren't many eating options within walking distance of Adabraka and Asylum Down hotels, and Choos is one of the better ones. Mostly a lunch spot for local business people, the open-air dining area gets a cool breeze and it has a large selection of Ghanaian dishes and burgers too (C20,000). There's a bar as well.

**Wok Inn** (Map p342; Nkrumah Ave; mains C35,000) Mostly a takeout place, this Chinese restaurant with an extensive menu of meat and noodle dishes a block from Nkrumah circle does have a small air-con dining room.

**Edvy Restaurant** (Map p342; Barnes Rd; mains ¢30,000; ☺ 9am-4pm) For a post-museum bite, sit at one of the trellis-covered tables in the grounds of the National Museum. The menu is a small selection of Ghanaian basics.

**Trafix Courtyard Restaurant** (Map p342; Independence Ave; mains ¢30,000) An outdoor eatery within the National Theatre complex grounds, Trafix gets lots of traffic at lunchtime. There's a selection of Ghanaian, Chinese and Western dishes.

## Osu

**Monsoon** (Map p345; ☎ 782307; Oxford St; mains ¢100,000; ☒ ) There's few more incongruous locations than above a fast-food court for what could be Accra's most upscale restaurant. The décor is understated fancy, simple white and black and there is a more casual cigar lounge and sushi bar (sushi and sashimi ¢30,000 to ¢75,000) attached as well as tables outside on the patio for drinks. The menu includes interesting items like ostrich filet (¢90,000), crocodile tail (¢130,000) and warthog filet (¢120,000). Reservations are recommended weekend nights, and you may get snooty looks if you're dressed for tro-tros.

**Mama Mia's** (Map p345; ☎ 264151; 7th Lane; pizza ¢65,000-90,000) Expats swear by the pizza here. From this author's own pizza survey of Accra, the thin-crusted, wood-oven-cooked pies do indeed come out on top. The pleasant outdoor garden dining area makes everything taste better. Spaghetti and kid-friendly chicken fingers also served.

**Buku** (Map p345; 10th Lane; mains ¢35,000-90,000) African food *Bon Apetit* could love. Ghanaian, Nigerian, Togolese and Senegalese specials are lovingly prepared at Buku, where the stylish 2nd-floor open-air dining area is reason alone for coming. Cable TV here gets overseas sports.

**Haveli** (Map p345; 18th La; mains ¢50,000-80,000; ☒ ) There's no bells and whistles and in fact little decoration at this friendly Indian restaurant in the heart of Osu. It has a big menu serving Indian standards, all kinds of naan and good veggie dishes.

**Dynasty Restaurant** (Map p345; ☎ 775496; Cantonments Rd; mains ¢55,000-110,000; ☒ ) A fancy place as far as Accra restaurants go, the

Dynasty specialises in Peking cuisine, but the large menu includes specialities like frog legs (¢62,000), lobster (¢110,000) sea cucumbers and squid. Dim sum every Sunday afternoon.

**Frankie's** (Map p345; Cantonments Rd; mains ¢30,000-60,000) An Accra institution, this well-established place has a takeaway outlet, an ice-cream shop and a bakery and patisserie, while upstairs is an air-con restaurant. You can get burgers, pizzas and fried chicken, as well as salads, baguettes and sandwiches.

**Ristorante Sole Mio** (Map p345; 11th Lane; mains ¢70,000; ☒ ) 'Standard' describes this restaurant well; from the furnishings to the service to the menu of basic Italian fare, Sole Mio does nothing unusually well. The pasta dishes are the kind you make yourself at home but the fish and meat are better choices and there's a selection of wines.

**Tip Top Chinese Restaurant** (Map p345; Cantonment Rd; mains ¢35,000) A less expensive alternative to Dynasty, if you're craving Chinese food. Tip Top is in front of the Star World building, and has casual outdoor seating.

**Seoul Grill** (Map p345; Mission St; mains ¢60,000-180,000; ☒ ) One of the few Korean restaurants in Accra, the Seoul Grill does traditional barbeque at the table and sushi and sashimi and noodle dishes as well.

**Winby Inn** (Map p345; mains ¢75,000; ☒ ) This restaurant just off Danquah Circle shares a building with Egypt Air and is fairly elegant indoors, all white tablecloths and dim lighting. You can also eat more informally outside if the heat isn't a bother. The menu is a mix of Lebanese, continental, seafood and Ghanaian dishes, and good pizzas.

**Chicken Lickin** (Map p345; mains ¢40,000; ☒ ) A block from Ring Rd East in one direction and the American Embassy in the other, Winby is a step up from the fast-food joints on Cantonments Rd and is popular with lunching businesspeople. Menu includes chicken dishes, some Lebanese and Ghanaian standards.

**Nourish Lab Smoothy's** (Map p345; 3rd Lane; smoothies ¢20,000; ☺ 8am-10pm) In an ideal Accra there'd be a Nourish Lab Smoothy's every several blocks. These refreshing drinks, a combination of fruit and soft yogurt, aren't especially unusual in the US or Europe but throw in the oppressive heat and they're practically addictive here. Also serves iced-coffee drinks, sandwich wraps and salads.

GHANA

**Osu Food Court** (Map p345; Cantonments Rd; 🔀 ) A mini mall with Nando's, a South African chain doing spicy Portuguese-style chicken, a coffee shop and bakery, a pizza joint and a couple of fried-chicken places. Sit at the upstairs terrace bar and watch the mayhem in the street below.

Other fast-food options are **Papaye** (Map p345; Cantonments Rd) and **Steers** (Map p345; Cantonments Rd). Papaye provides a takeaway service and features what many claim to be the best charcoal-grilled chicken in Accra.

## Asylum Down & North Ridge

**Paloma Restaurant** (Map p342; Ring Rd Central; mains C50,000; 🔀 ) Part of the hotel and bar complex, the Paloma serves a variety of food, including pizzas, Lebanese and Ghanaian food, and has a garden bar and restaurant area. You can also eat inside in the bare, unlit dining room.

**Le Petit Paris** (Map p342; Kanda High Rd; croissants C12,000; 🔀 ) An excellent spot for a morning coffee and croissant, Le Petit Paris is a simple bakery selling excellent baked goods. Grab a coffee for a nice sit-down breakfast.

**Spicy Chicken** (Map p342; Samora Machel Rd, Asylum Down) Fast food and fried chicken.

## La & Coco Beach

**Next Door Restaurant & Bar** (mains C40,000) One of the few places to take advantage of Accra's seaside locale, Next Door is a large, popular place, especially on weekends. It has an eclectic menu but seafood is the speciality. Friday and Saturday nights it's a club with music and dancing. It's off the Tema road about 2km east of Labadi Beach Hotel; any tro-tro heading down this road to Teshie should be able to drop you here, or you can get a taxi.

## DRINKING

Most drinking spots in Accra are nothing more than a few plastic tables and a Star beer sign. There's no shortage of these, though more congenial bars are fewer and farther between. Osu has the highest concentration, and includes restaurants that transform into lively bars with music and dancing at night, as well as a number of drinking-only establishments. Several other worthwhile spots are scattered throughout the city and all of the top-end hotels have comfortable and generally subdued bar scenes.

**Osekan** (Map p342; High St) Those in the know say there's no better place for a beer than Osekan. Spend a sunset nursing a cold Star at one of the cliffside tables and you'll probably agree. Spicy kebabs and other snacks are available. To get here, walk through the large, empty lot, down the steep steps to the bar.

**Champs Sports Bar** (Map p342; Ring Rd Central; 🔀 ) Part of the Paloma Hotel complex, this expat-friendly pub beams in sports from abroad. Thursday is quiz night, Friday is karaoke night, Saturday is live music night and Sunday movie night. One of the few places that serves Mexican food in Accra.

**Bywel Bar** (Map p345; Cantonments Rd, Osu) Live music Thursday and Saturday nights transforms this otherwise cool hangout at the southern end of Cantonments Rd into a fun party.

**Ryan's Irish Pub** (Map p345; Osu; 🔀 ) More Irish pub than an Irish pub, this large green-and-yellow colonial building off Cantonments Rd in the south of Osu serves draught Guinness and hearty food like ostrich filet (C80,000) and Irish beef stew (C60,000). Live music at the weekends.

**Venus Cocktail Bar** (Map p345; 11th Lane, Osu) This spot with a nice little bamboo bar, attached to the Byblos Hotel, is popular with Peace Corps types and other long-term volunteers.

**Duncan's Bar** (Map p345; 3rd Lane, Osu) Nothing more than a few plastic tables out on the street, Duncan's is nevertheless a popular drinking spot with locals.

**Lizzie Enterprises Bar** (Map p345; Cantonments Rd) While the name is more suitable for a massage parlour or a mechanics than a bar, Lizzie is just that and only that, at about a half-block of plastic tables.

**Akuma Village** (Map p342) A better drinking spot than hotel, the Akuma has ocean views, cool breezes and cheap beer. Live music Friday nights.

**Aquarius** (Map p345; Osu Crescent, Osu) This place is tucked down one of Osu's winding residential streets, and has German beer on tap, German food on the menu and pub games like pool, pinball and darts.

## ENTERTAINMENT
### Nightclubs

Accra is Ghana's biggest city and the birthplace of highlife, hiplife and other hybrid music genres, so it's not surprising there's a lively club scene. Thursday, Friday and

Saturday are the big nights and although clubs open from about 8pm, the action rarely starts before 10pm or 11pm. Osu is where most of the trendiest clubs are but there are also some popular, inexpensive places around Nkrumah Circle. Most clubs have a cover charge.

**Jazz Tone** (Map p340; Third Close, Airport Residential Area) A popular place with good live jazz music.

**Indigo** (Map p345; Ring Rd East) Near Danquah Circle, this stylish place is housed in an old embassy building and attracts Accra's trendsetters. Friday and Saturday are the best nights.

**Macumba** (Map p345; Ring Rd East) One of Accra's nightlife institutions, Macumba is just off Danquah Circle and is popular with European discophiles.

**Bass Line** (Map p342; Ring Rd Central) Another good hip jazz club, the Bass Line just west of Kanda High Rd, gets smoky and stays open late

**Vienna City Entertainment Complex** (Map p342; Kwame Nkrumah Ave) A massive bar, game room, and club in the heart of Adabraka near Nkrumah Circle.

## Cinema

Every Tuesday is movie night at the Alliance Française (p341).

Surprisingly, one of the nicest places to watch a movie in Accra is the Busy Internet Café (p341), which shows recent Hollywood releases Thursday through Sunday nights from 6pm to 10.30pm. Champs Sports Bar (opposite) shows films on Sunday nights.

The **Ghana Film Institute** (Map p340; ☎ 763462), across from the French embassy, shows the latest Ghanaian films and foreign releases nightly, and the **Rex Cinema** (Map p342; Barnes Rd) shows recent Western films in English in the city centre.

## Theatre

The Chinese-built **National Theatre** (Map p342; ☎ 666986; Liberia Rd) looks like the base for an enormous eternal flame. There are performances by West African playwrights – check the billboards for future activities. One regular weekly event is the Saturday afternoon Concert Party, a Ghanaian music hall or vaudeville, with sketches, songs and stand-up comedians. Even if you don't understand Twi, Twi humour needs no translation.

The British Council also offers regular concerts and exhibitions.

On Thursday to Sunday afternoons performances are often held at the Centre for National Culture (Arts Centre; below), including music, drumming, traditional dance and theatre. Check the chalkboard at the main entrance for what's on.

## SHOPPING

The **Centre for National Culture** (Map p342; Arts Centre; ☎ 664099; 28th February Rd; ⏰ 9am-5pm), a warren of stalls selling arts and crafts and known simply as the Arts Centre, is the place to shop in Accra and the most visited site in the country. Once you step on the grounds the level of aggressive hassling may make you want to keep your cedis in your pocket. If you don't mind the grabbing and the constant importuning calls to 'just have a look' and have the patience and wherewithal to bargain after the initial absurd offer, you can come away with good-quality handicrafts from all over Ghana, including batik, kente and other fabrics, beads, masks, woodcarvings, drums, brass and leatherwork. There's talk of altering the layout so that shop owners in the back don't feel compelled to highjack tourists once they enter, and of trying to convince them that their hard-sell style is not the best in terms of getting foreigners to part with cash. The small **art gallery** (⏰ 9am-5pm Sun-Fri), to the right as you enter, displays and sells paintings by local artists. There's also a small post office and a forex with good rates within the complex.

For altogether more sedate shopping the **Trade Fair Centre** (Map p340; off Burma Camp Rd, La) has several stores selling high-quality goods at fixed prices or try **Aid to Artisans Ghana** (Map p340; ATAG; ☎ 771325; atag@ataggh.com; Trade Fair Centre, off Burma Camp Rd, La; ⏰ 8am-5pm Mon-Fri, 10am-4pm Sat), an NGO that offers practical assistance to Ghanaian artisans for crafts and furniture. The **House of Nyak** (Map p340; Trade Fair Centre, off Burma Camp Rd, La) has a huge selection of textiles and batiks and tailors here can whip up a Western or traditional Ghanaian-style suit or dress for you in only a few days.

**Woodin Boutique** (Map p345; Cantonments Rd) in Osu is a chic and modern fabric shop that sells some of the most attractive textiles in the city. The **Loom** (Map p342; ☎ 224746; 117 Kwame Nkrumah Ave), 200m south of Nkrumah

Circle, sells moderately to expensively priced paintings as well as woodcarvings, fabrics and statues.

Look out for roadside stalls selling crafts, such as pottery and cane chairs near 37 Circle, tie-dye clothes, paintings, prints, shoes, leather bags and woodcarvings around Danquah Circle and along Cantonments Rd in Osu, and woodcarvings near La Beach.

Makola Market and the area around is particularly rich in fabrics, including batik and tie-dye. Zongo Lane, not far from the post office, has rows of small shops offering colourful prints. Expensive Dutch wax cloth is everywhere, but you can also find almost identical cloth made by Akosombo Textile Co that is almost as good and much cheaper. The market is also good for glass beads, and you'll find second-hand clothing everywhere, sold for a few cedis.

Accra's second major market, **Kaneshie Market** (Map p340; Winneba Rd) on the western side of the city, is also a good place to look for beads and textiles as well as basic goods and foodstuffs. Music CDs, some original, some bad copies – ask before buying – of Ghanaian and other African pop stars are sold around both markets, as are mostly poor-quality pirated knock-offs of Nigerian and Hollywood films. Shoes are another staple of Accra markets – for that matter anywhere in the country – though most come with names like 'Babidas' and upside-down swooshes which look eerily similar to another well-known trademark; better quality, handmade leather shoes are also sold.

On or near the Tema road in Teshie are several **coffin workshops**, where trippy-looking coffins are fashioned in the shape of lobsters, Mercedes, guns, aeroplanes – whatever is meaningful for the client. These surreal-looking final resting places have been produced for the last 35 years or so and take around two weeks to carve and paint.

## GETTING THERE & AWAY
### Air
Kotoka international airport (Map p340) is served by several major airlines, including Alitalia, British Airways, KLM-Royal Dutch Airlines, Lufthansa and South African Airways and the newly formed Ghana International Airways. There are several small private regional carriers, however, the age and quality of the planes may be suspect.

For a list of airline offices in Accra see p399.

### Bus & Tro-tro
There are two VanefSTC bus stations in Accra. There are also two classes of bus: ordinary and luxury. The latter have air-con and are newer and more comfortable. The main **VanefSTC bus station** ( ☎ 227373) is just east of Lamptey Circle and serves destinations to the west and north. Buses leave hourly from early morning to early evening for both Kumasi (ordinary/luxury C46,000/65,000, four hours) and Takoradi (C38,000/50,000, four hours), and four times a day to Cape Coast (C25,000/38,000, three hours) and Tamale (C90,000/150,000, 12 hours). Other destinations include Wa, Bolga and Bawku with trips three days a week. There are fewer trips on all routes on Sundays. If you want to be assured of a seat on a bus leaving at a specific time it's probably best to purchase the ticket a day in advance.

The second, smaller VanefSTC terminal is next to Tudu Station, at the northern end of Makola Market. From there buses head east, serving Ho (C40,000, 3pm, four hours), Hohoe (ordinary/luxury C30,000/C48,000, 3½ hours, ☽ 3pm), Kpando (C28,000/45,000, ☽ 3pm) and Aflao (C45,000, four times a day), on the Togo border. Buses leaving from this station are generally much more unreliable and may leave hours after their scheduled departure time or simply not at all.

Private buses and tro-tros leave from four main motor parks. Those for Cape Coast, Takoradi and other destinations to the west leave from Kaneshie motor park, 500m northwest of Lamptey Circle. Neoplan motor park, 250m west of Nkrumah Circle, has buses to north points such as Kumasi and Tamale. From Tema station east of Makola market, tro-tros leave for local destinations as well as Tema and Aburi. From the chaotic **Tudu station** (Map p342; ☎ 662523) at the northeast corner of Makola Market, tro-tros leave for destinations such as Aflao, Ada, Keta, Hohoe and Akosombo. In addition, there's a small station tucked in behind Tema station from which tro-tros go to Ho and Hohoe. Kingdom Transport Services (KTS) runs shockingly comfortable minivans with leather seats and air-con to Ho (C45,000, two hours) from here.

## Train

There are train services between Accra and both Kumasi and Takoradi but these take forever and are really only for train enthusiasts. For more details, see p402.

## GETTING AROUND
### To/From the Airport

When you step outside Accra's Kotoka international airport, you'll be set upon by drivers and quickly ushered to the taxi rank for the journey into central Accra. Drivers may claim a set fare but there isn't one, and depending on your negotiating abilities and patience the fare can range from C20,000 to C70,000. Anything under C40,000 for the city centre is fair. Tro-tros and shared taxis (around C5000) also leave from the small, well-organised station in the airport compound. From the city centre to the airport, a private taxi costs around C25,000. Alternatively, get a shared taxi from the taxi parks at Nkrumah Circle or Sankara Interchange or a tro-tro from Tema station.

### Line Taxi & Tro-Tro

Line taxis and tro-tros travel on fixed runs from major landmarks or between major circles, such as Danquah, 37 and Nkrumah (usually just called 'Circle'). Fares are fixed and are typically about C1000. Major routes include Circle to Osu via Ring Rd; Circle to the central post office via Nkrumah Ave; Tudu station to Kokomlemle; 37 Circle to Osu; Makola Market to Osu; and Circle to the airport. Major shared taxi and local tro-tro parks include Tema station and the ones at Nkrumah Circle and 37 Circle. In addition, transport to La leaves from the taxi park at Nkrumah Circle or from Labadi lorry station on High St.

At the stations, tro-tros and shared taxis often have the destination written on a placard. Elsewhere, flag one down and shout your destination – if they're going your way, they'll stop and pick you up. For Nkrumah Circle, point the index finger of your right hand towards the ground and make a circular motion.

### Private Taxi

Taking taxis in Accra is convenient but since there are no meters the unavoidable haggling can get tiring. You will probably first be quoted a ridiculous amount. If you reply with an even more ridiculous lowball you should be able to find your way to something fair. Any ride within the city shouldn't cost more than C10,000. Rates rise slightly to around C15,000 to C20,000 at night.

Drivers don't seem to know the city well. When providing directions, include as many large landmarks as possible to pinpoint your destination.

# AROUND ACCRA

## UNIVERSITY OF GHANA

Probably the country's premier university, the University of Ghana in Legon was founded in 1948 on the northern fringes of Accra and 14km from the city centre. Its **Balme Library** ( 8am-4.30pm Mon-Sat) has a rich collection dating from the colonial era. Its botanical gardens are run down, but they're a pleasant place for a stroll. The university bookshop is probably the best in the country. Tro-tros (C6000) leave from Tema station in Accra or from the Sankara interchange.

## ABURI BOTANICAL GARDENS & AKWAPIM HILLS

Built as the classic British hill station, a cool mountain retreat from the oppressive heat of the lowlands, Aburi still retains a hint of its former therapeutic appeal, at least as far as temperatures and views go. On clear days you can see Accra in the plains below, only 34km away. The entrance to the **botanical gardens** (adult/student C10,000/20,000; 8am-6pm), about 200m up from the tro-tro station, are framed by two rows of towering palm trees. The gardens themselves make for a peaceful stroll though they're not of the finely manicured variety. Established in 1890 with seedlings from all over the British Empire, they are home to an impressive variety of tropical and subtropical plants and trees. The oldest tree, more than 150 years old, is a huge kapok tree facing the headquarters building. It's the only indigenous one the British didn't cut down.

The botanical gardens are the obvious tourist focus, though it's really the surrounding beautiful Akwapim Hills that warrant anything more than a day trip out here. The area is one of the best places in the country to explore by pedal power thanks to the friendly and enthusiastic **Aburi Bike**

GHANA

**& Hike Tours** ( ☎ 024-267390; www.ghanabike.com); the small office is on the second floor of a home at the southern entrance of the gardens. A mountain bike, helmet, backpack, maps and repair kit plus a shower on return will cost you a paltry C39,000. Day-long or overnight guided biking and hiking tours are also offered.

### Sleeping & Eating

**Aburi Botanical Gardens Resthouse** ( ☎ 0876-22022; r C100,000, bungalows C200,000) Unfortunately the resthouse here probably hasn't changed much since the colonial days, and while the surroundings are leafy the rooms are run down. Some of the upstairs rooms have good views and therefore may be a better option than the bungalows.

The **Little Acre Hotel** ( ☎ 0876-22078; r C300,000; 🏋 ), **May Lodge & Restaurant** ( ☎ 0876-22025; r C80,000) and **Sweet African Guesthouse** (r from C80,000) are all a little over 2km before Aburi on the road from Accra.

**Rose Plot Restaurant** (mains C30,000) is attached to the resthouse and prepares basic fare while the **Royal Botanical Gardens Restaurant** (mains C45,000) just down the hill has a better selection and pretty views.

### Getting There & Away

Tro-tros to Aburi (C7000, 1½ hours) leave regularly from the far eastern end of Tema station, behind the Makola Market in Accra, though the wait can be a half-hour or longer. You may have to wait a while

for transport back to Accra on a Sunday. Regular shared taxis run north from Aburi to towns such as Mampong, Adukrom and Somanya, from where you can get connections to Kpong (for Akosombo and Ho) and Koforidua.

# THE COAST

Stretching 500km from the Ivory Coast to Togo, the coastline is Ghana's premier attraction. It's dotted with wonderful palm-lined beaches and the imposing remains of European coastal forts that once serviced the gold and later the slave trade.

Tuesday and Friday are the primary market days in Elmina and Cape Coast, and Tuesday is also the traditional day off for fishermen.

## KOKROBITE
☎ 027

This beach has developed an enthusiastic following. Those who swear by Kokrobite point to the long stretch of white sand, the laid-back backpacker–style accommodation and the fact that it couldn't feel further from the bustle of Accra, only 32km away. Others more tepidly say it's too close to the capital, the lodging isn't luxurious enough and there's not much else to do besides be lazy and soak up the sun. But no doubt this sleepy village will continue to welcome foreigners looking for a little R&R.

---

**BE BEACHWISE**

Ghana has around 500km of Atlantic coastline, an almost continuous palm-fringed, sandy stretch of beach. However, there's a sting to Ghana's tropical paradise beaches – offshore, the Atlantic has fierce currents and a ripping undertow and there are several drownings every year. Ask the locals for advice, respect what they tell you and stay well within your depth.

There's another sting – theft and the occasional muggings at knifepoint occur on and around beaches frequented by tourists. Most fishing villages along the coast are extremely poor and local people don't benefit from tourism, as resorts tend to be run by outsiders, so tourists are a tempting target for some elements in the community. It makes sense not to take any valuables onto the beach with you and to avoid being alone on isolated stretches. If you're walking along the beach or a coastal path, do what the locals do and take a guide with you – not only to show you the way but also as protection against possible muggings. As a way of helping to make a difference, try to patronise community-run businesses as far as possible.

Most beaches near settlements are working beaches from which the important business of fishing is carried out. They also function as the village toilet. If you don't want to feel a squelch underfoot, stick either to resort beaches, for which you usually pay a small fee, or to beaches away from settlements.

## THE COASTAL FORTS

The chain of forts and castles (the terms are used interchangeably) along Ghana's coast is an extraordinary historical monument, unique in West Africa. Most of the forts were built during the 17th century by various European powers, including the British, Danes, Dutch, French, Germans, Portuguese and Swedes, who were vying for commercial dominance of the Gold Coast and the Gulf of Guinea. Competition was fierce and the forts changed hands like a game of musical chairs. By the end of the 18th century, there were 37 along the coastline. The forts were concentrated along this relatively short (around 500km) stretch of coast because access to the interior was relatively easy compared with the more swampy coastlines elsewhere along the West African coast, and because the rocky shore provided building material. They were fortified not against the locals, with whom they traded equitably, but against attack from other European traders.

The forts were originally established as trading posts to store goods bought to the coast, such as gold, ivory and spices. Later, as the slave trade took over, they were expanded into prisons for storing slaves ready for shipping. Slaves were packed into dark, overcrowded and unsanitary dungeons for weeks or months at a time. If you tour some of the forts, you'll leave with a deep impression of just how brutally the captives were treated. When a ship arrived, they were shackled and led out of the forts to waiting boats through the Door of No Return.

If your time is limited, make sure you visit at least Cape Coast Castle (p360), which houses a superb museum, and St George's Castle (p363) at Elmina, both of which are deservedly Unesco World Heritage sites. With a bit more time, you could also visit Fort Metal Cross (p368) at Dixcove, Fort Amsterdam (p358) at Abanze and Fort Princess Town (p369) at Princess Town, all of which are atmospheric and have great settings. Fort Good Hope (p356) at Senya Bereku and Fort Patience (p358) at Apam are also worth a look if you have time to spare; both overlook busy fishing harbours.

Most forts are open to the public, usually 9am to 5pm daily, and most charge an admission fee of around US$0.70, apart from a few such as Cape Coast Castle and St George's Castle, which charge more. The admission fee usually includes a guided tour by the custodian. If you don't have any qualms about staying in a fort where slaves were held captive, Fort Good Hope, Fort Patience and Fort Princess Town offer very basic accommodation for around US$4.

The renowned Academy of African Music & Arts (AAMAL), founded by legendary drummer Mustafa Tettey Addy, offers courses (from two hours to three months) in traditional African music, drumming and dance. It is a 20-minute walk along the beach. On Saturday and Sunday afternoons you can groove to the beat by listening to live music and drumming performances.

Theft and the occasional mugging, once a problem, has largely been eradicated since hotel owners have partnered with villagers to help patrol the beach. Still, it's not advised to walk on the beach with valuables at night.

Between August and March turtles nest on the beach

## Sleeping & Eating

Just past the beach at AAMAL a huge concrete structure with an amphitheatre was going up at the time of research and is supposed to be functioning as a hotel by 2008.

**Big Milly's Backyard** (Wendy's; ☎ 607998; www .bigmilly.com; camping with own/rented tent C25,000/35,000, s/d with shared bathroom C65,000/100,000, r with private bathroom C145,000; P ) The Big Kahuna of Kokrobite, Big Milly's is something of an institution to West Africa overlanders and volunteers who all seem to consider the place their home away from home. The basic concrete and thatched roof cottages with shared bathrooms are fine though a little besides the point since most people spend their time whiling away the day and night at the 24 hour bar and restaurant or the beach, which extends almost to your front door. A beautiful Moroccan-style suite (US$65) is available as well. Drumming, dancing and music happen most weekend nights.

**Sobamba Coastal Resort** ( ☎ 683084; r C180,000; P ) A low key alternative to Big Milly's, friendly Sobamba has four basic tiled rooms with modern bathrooms. The attached bar/restaurant overlooks the beach and discounts are available for extended stays. Breakfast included.

**Andy's Akwaaba Lodge** ( ☎ 277261; www.akwaaba lodge.com; r with shared/private bathroom C70,000/130,000;

## THE COAST

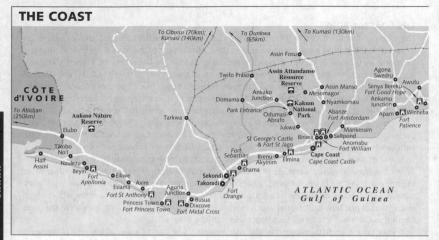

GHANA

(**P**) This lodge is just across the dirt road from Sobamba. The five concrete rooms are basic but set in a pleasant, small grassy compound where you can camp with your own tent for C30,000. The restaurant serves up good German food.

**Kokrobite Beach Resort** (AAMAL; ☎ 380854; s/d C95,000/110,000; **P**) A beautiful 20-minute walk along the beach and up and over rocky outcroppings from Big Milly's – a road goes here as well – takes you to this rustic, seemingly abandoned resort famed for the attached music school. The large rooms are old but the warped wooden floors charming and there's a simple restaurant and bar on the premises.

**Bojo Beach Resort** ( ☎ 2325169; afamefuna14@ hotmail.com; **P**) Future plans call for rooms, but at the time of research Bojo is a welcoming and professionally run day resort. Small boats shuttle guests across the freshwater lagoon to a beautiful stretch of sandy beach where you can order drinks and food and hire boogie or surf boards or just luxuriate in the quiet.

**Franco's** (Kokrobite Garden; pizza C50,000) An Italian restaurant behind Big Milly's, Franco's is especially popular for its pizzas; the chef reputedly rides his bicycle to Accra for fresh ingredients daily.

### Getting There & Around
Tro-tros (C5500, 45 minutes) to Kokrobite go from the western end of Kaneshie motor park (Donsoman Station) in Accra. Depend-

ing on your ability to negotiate, a taxi from Accra will cost from C50,000 to C100,000.

## GOMOA FETTEH & SENYA BEREKU
☎ 027

The main reason to visit Gomoa Fetteh, an attractive fishing village set on a hill on the coast between Accra and Winneba, is for its magnificent beaches. Senya Bereku, about 5km west, is the site of the impressive **Fort Good Hope** (admission US$0.70), built by the Dutch in 1702. Originally intended for the gold trade, the fort was expanded in 1715 when it was converted into a slave prison. Well restored, it sits on the edge of a cliff above the beach and has good views. Shared taxis (US$0.20) regularly ply between the villages or you could walk (with a guide).

### Sleeping & Eating
**White Sands Beach Club** ( ☎ 550707; www.white sandsbc.com; r US$100; **P** **X**) The large, individually designed Moroccan-themed villas at the White Sands are some of the nicest accommodation in Ghana. They're located on a spectacular beach with three superb restaurants. Bear left as you enter Fetteh and follow the main road down through the village until you reach the resort gates.

**Till's No 1 Hotel** ( ☎ 559480; tillsbeach@yahoo.com; s/d US$45/55; **X**) Though not as luxurious as the White Sands, Tills also occupies prime beachfront property and is an excellent, less-expensive alternative. This German-owned resort has comfortable rooms with

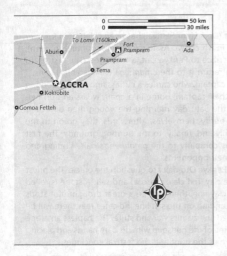

balconies and sea views and a veritable Olympics worth of equipment for water and other games. It's signposted as you enter Fetteh. Breakfast included.

**Fort Good Hope** (r with fan US$7) Despite once holding slaves in its dungeon, this fort has been developed into a guesthouse. You can sleep here in basic rooms with shared bathrooms (bucket showers); it has a nice, breezy sitting area upstairs and a restaurant and bar on the premises.

### Getting There & Away
From Kaneshie motor park in Accra, there are direct tro-tros to Senya Bereku (one hour). Tro-tros also ply the scenic but bumpy cross-country route between Winneba and Senya Bereku (40 minutes). For Gomoa Fetteh, take a Winneba-bound tro-tro from Accra and stop at Awutu junction on the main road, from where you can get a tro-tro direct to the village.

## WINNEBA
☎ 0432
To Ghanaians, this town is synonymous with the University College of Education (UCEW), fishing and the famous Aboakyer festival (see p358). The town itself (the largest between Accra and Cape Coast) has little appeal and sees few foreigners. There is a good, undeveloped beach and a pleasant hotel within walking distance of it.

Near the now-defunct tourist centre on the outskirts of town, fishing boats pull in

from early morning to around midday, and dozens of fisherman haul in their nets while singing a rousing tune. A lovely, palm-fringed beach stretches west from here for a couple of kilometres, though the slope is steep and swimming isn't recommended. Inland of the beach, the lagoon is an important wetlands area for birds.

There's a Ghana Commercial Bank and a post office on Commercial St.

### Sleeping & Eating
**Lagoon Lodge** ( ☎ 22435; s/d C80,000/C150,000;  P ) This lodge alone is almost reason enough to come to Winneba. It's rare in Ghana to find such a well-run, professional yet hospitable hotel and at budget prices no less. The Lagoon has 19 small, modern, perfectly kept rooms with enormous bathrooms and a pleasant courtyard restaurant (mains C30,000) and bar that catches a great breeze in the evenings. It's reached by heading down a winding track through the fields, signposted off the beach road past the turn-off to the (closed) Sir Charles Tourist Centre.

**Ghana Armed Forces Resthouse** ( ☎ 22208; r C60,000) After the Lagoon Lodge everything else is a very distance second, and as you'd expect from a place with military associations, this resthouse won't win any medals for design. It's strictly utilitarian concrete, though it's a peaceful enough setting on a hill overlooking the lagoon. Follow the road up past the UCEW South Campus and, where it forks, take the road on the right.

The Lagoon Lodge restaurant is the best place to eat, though for a change of pace there are several basic eateries serving cheap Ghanaian food on Commercial St and the road leading towards the UCEW South Campus.

**Halo Halo** is a typical spot for icy beers, though the food here gets mixed reviews and the music is loud. **Hut de Eric** (mains C30,000) at the highway junction is the most comfortable restaurant you'll find in the area; it's a modern, large pavilion with outdoor seating serving Ghanaian staples and grilled meats.

### Getting There & Away
There's a bus station in Winneba town but the main transport hub is at the junction on the coastal road. Regular shared taxis (C2000) run between the junction and Winneba town. Tro-tros to Winneba leave from

---

**DEER HUNTER**

Held on the first weekend in May, the **Aboakyer** (Deer Hunt Festival) has been celebrated for over 300 years. The main event is a competitive hunt in which two Asafo (companies or guilds of men), the Tuafo and Dentsifo, hunt an antelope to sacrifice to Penkye Out, a tribal god. The first Asafo to capture one alive with their bare hands and return it to the *omanhene* (village chief) wins.

The Tuafo, in blue and white, are led by their captain, who carries a cutlass and rides a wooden horse; the Dentsifo dress in red and gold and their captain, borne in a chair, wears an iron helmet and carries a sword and cutlass. Early on the Saturday morning the young men don their traditional battle dress and go to the beach to purify themselves. Afterwards, they go on to the palace of the *omanhene* to greet the royal family and, finally, to the hunting grounds. The first man to catch an antelope alive rushes with his company to the *omanhene's* dais, singing and dancing along the way and hurling taunts at their opponents.

Next day the companies assemble before the Penkye Otu deity to question the oracle. The priest draws four parallel lines on the ground, in white clay, red clay, charcoal and salt. A stone is rolled down from the fetish. If it falls upon the white clay line, there will be a great drought. If it stops at the charcoal lines, this portends heavy rains. Landing on the salt line indicates that there will be plenty of food and fish, while settling upon the red line augurs war and strife. The hapless antelope is then sacrificed and cooked, the priest taking some of the hot soup with his bare hands and placing it on Penkye Otu. This offering is the *raison d'être* of the hunt and the festival concludes.

---

Kaneshie motor park in Accra (C8000, 1¼ hours) or from the Accra station in Cape Coast (C8000, 1½ hours). From the junction, plenty of transport runs in both directions.

## APAM
☎ 0432

A lively fishing harbour and fantastic views from the ramparts of **Fort Patience** (admission C10,000), make Apam, 20km west of Winneba, worth a visit. The fort, built by the Dutch in 1697, is set on a hill overlooking the village and picturesque fishing harbour at one end of a wide sandy bay. Near the harbour is a great three-storey *posuban* (shrine), with mounted horsemen overlooked by a white-robed Jesus.

The fort also functions as a **guesthouse** (r C35,000). Very basic rooms with shared bathroom (bucket shower) are available. Simple meals can be prepared on request or there are food stalls along the main street.

Apam is about 9km south of Ankamu junction on the coastal road, from where regular shared taxis and tro-tros run down to the village. Any tro-tro running between Cape Coast and Winneba or Accra will be able to drop you at the junction.

## ABANZE

The atmospheric **Fort Amsterdam** (admission US$1.40; ☺ 9am-5pm), also known as Fort Kormantin, is clearly visible from the coastal road, about 32km northeast of Cape Coast.

It has a fantastic location high on a hill above Abanze village, and the views from the ramparts are wonderful. Established in 1598 by the Dutch, it was rebuilt by the English in 1645 as their first settlement along the coast of the Gulf of Guinea and named Fort York. When the Dutch recaptured it in 1665, they renamed it Fort Amsterdam as a stylish thumbing of the nose at the English who, the previous year and on the other side of the Atlantic, had taken possession of New Amsterdam and re-christened it New York. The fort is only partially restored, giving it a poignancy that many of the whitewashed castles elsewhere along the coast lack.

Transport going west to Cape Coast can drop you at Abanze. From Cape Coast, take a tro-tro (20 minutes) from Kotokuraba station as you head towards Mankessim and get off when you see the fort up on the hill to your right, just before Abanze. Returning to Cape Coast you may have to wait a while for an empty seat.

## ANOMABU
☎ 042

As far as tourists are concerned, Anomabu means an excellent resort on a beautiful beach. However, residents of this very unpicturesque, cramped fishing village about 18km northeast of Cape Coast live in fairly makeshift squalor. Fort William, on the seafront in the centre of town, was built by the British in 1753 and is now an unphotographable prison. More interesting are Anomabu's seven *posubans*. The easiest to find is Company No 3's, which features a collection of animals, and is about 50m from the main road, opposite the Ebeneezer Hotel. The most spectacular shrine is the one in the form of a large painted ship; it's in the area just west of the fort.

## Sleeping & Eating

**Anomabu Beach Resort** ( ☎ 91562; www.anomabo .digitafrica.com; camping own/rented tent US$4/13, hut without/with air-con US$20/38; **P** ) This is the perfect weekend getaway from Accra. One of the few places in Ghana to embrace low-key native architecture rather than big concrete eyesores, it has cosy bungalows set within a sandy and shady grove of coconut palms. But you'll spend most of your time lounging on the beautiful white-sand beach or chowing down on seafood at the exquisite wood pavilion restaurant. Rates are higher Friday and Saturday nights. A breakfast buffet is included. Nonguests can cross the beach from the road for C20,000.

**Weda Lodge** ( ☎ 806958; r with fan/air-con C245,000/ 305,000; **P** ) For a bird's eye view of the ocean and town below, Weda Lodge, perched high at the top of a hill, is a nice alternative to the beach resort. There are spectacular views from some of the rooms and all are quite large and modern and nicely furnished. The Weda has a homey feel, from the friendly staff to the living room with TV and the cliffside garden. It's off the same road and within walking distance of the Anomabu Beach Resort.

**Ebeneezer Hotel** ( ☎ 33673; s/d C57,000/80,000, r with air-con C200,000; **P** ) There's no beach access or mountain views but the Ebeneezer actually makes sense for the budget-minded. Its highway location means it's convenient for tro-tros and you can always commute to the beach at the Anomabu Beach Resort. Carpeted doubles are large and comfortable and even have small separate sitting rooms and balconies. Rooms are in the building behind the roadside restaurant and are quiet.

## Getting There & Away

From Cape Coast, take a tro-tro (C5000, 15 minutes) from Kotokuraba station heading for Mankessim and ask to be dropped at the Ebeneezer Rest Stop for Anomabu town or at the turn-off for the beach resort, which is

about 2km west of the Ebeneezer. From the turn-off, it's about 500m to the resort gates. The main tro-tro and shared taxi stop in Anomabu is just east of the Ebeneezer and plenty of vehicles run in both directions along the coastal road.

## CAPE COAST

☎ 042

The centre of Cape Coast, the former British colonial capital, is lined with neglected buildings whose ages are irrelevant in this now-vibrant town and whose history – Cape Coast was the largest slave-trading centre in West Africa – only becomes apparent after a visit to the castle on the waterfront, one of the more interesting sights in Ghana. Today, Cape Coast is the capital of the Central Region, the home of one of the country's best universities and a logical base for trips to other destinations in the surrounding area, including Kakum National Park. Maybe the best time to truly appreciate the city is after dark, when small groups take to the sidewalks to escape the still baking heat and eat, chat, dance and often sleep under the stars.

## Information

### BOOKSHOPS

**Black Star Bookshop** (Commercial St) A surprisingly good mix of high-quality contemporary fiction in English and a more obscure and random collection of nonfiction.

### INTERNET ACCESS

**Cornell Internet** (Commercial St)
**Ocean View Internet** (Commercial St; ☒ 24hr) A few dozen computers. Printing, scanning, CD burning.
**Odas Internet** (Commercial St) Across the street from Cornell Internet.

### MONEY

There aren't many forexes in town. Coastal Forex on Jackson St is reliable.
**Barclays Bank** (Commercial St) Can change travellers cheques and cash; has an ATM.
**Standard Chartered Bank** (Chapel Sq) Near the tourist office. Can change travellers cheques and cash; has an ATM.

### POST

**Post office** (Attebury St)

### TOURIST INFORMATION

**Tourist office** ( ☎ 30265; ☒ 8am-5pm Mon-Fri) Even if there's someone around, the office isn't much help. On the 1st floor of Heritage House, a restored colonial-era building.

GHANA

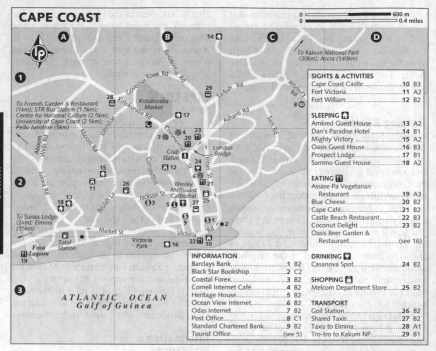

## CAPE COAST

**SIGHTS & ACTIVITIES**
Cape Coast Castle.................10 B3
Fort Victoria.........................11 A2
Fort William..........................12 B2

**SLEEPING**
Amkred Guest House.............13 A2
Dan's Paradise Hotel............14 B1
Mighty Victory.....................15 B2
Oasis Guest House................16 B3
Prospect Lodge....................17 B1
Sammo Guest House.............18 A2

**EATING**
Assase Pa Vegetarian
  Restaurant........................19 A3
Blue Cheese.........................20 B2
Cape Café............................21 B2
Castle Beach Restaurant.......22 B3
Coconut Delight...................23 B2
Oasis Beer Garden &
  Restaurant.....................(see 16)

**INFORMATION**
Barclays Bank.......................1 B2
Black Star Bookshop...............2 C2
Coastal Forex........................3 B2
Cornell Internet Café.............4 B2
Heritage House......................5 B2
Ocean View Internet..............6 B2
Odas Internet........................7 B2
Post Office............................8 C1
Standard Chartered Bank........9 B2
Tourist Office...................(see 5)

**DRINKING**
Casanova Spot.....................24 B2

**SHOPPING**
Melcom Department Store......25 B2

**TRANSPORT**
Goil Station.........................26 B2
Shared Taxis........................27 B2
Taxis to Elmina....................28 A1
Tro-tro to Kakum NP.............29 B1

## Sights

### CAPE COAST CASTLE

This majestic **castle** (adult/student US$7/4, still/video camera fee C5000/10,000; 9am-5pm) is in the heart of town overlooking the sea. First converted into a castle by the Dutch in 1637 and expanded by the Swedes in 1652, the castle changed hands five times over the 13 tumultuous years that followed until, in 1664, it was captured by the British. During the two centuries of British occupation, the castle was the headquarters for the colonial administration until the capital was moved to Accra in 1877. Extensively restored, the whitewashed castle now houses a superb museum. The introductory video shown at the museum is a little cheesy but the displays on the history of Ghana, the slave trade and the culture of the Akan people are excellent. The castle buildings, constructed around a trapezoidal courtyard facing the sea, and the dungeons below, provide a horrifying insight into the workings of a Gold Coast slaving fort. A guided tour is offered with your admission and should not be skipped; allow a minimum of an hour for the tour.

### FORT WILLIAM & FORT VICTORIA

It's worth the short but steep hikes up to Fort William, which dates from 1820 and now functions as a lighthouse, and Fort Victoria, originally built in 1702 and heavily restored in the 19th century, for the spectacular views. The castle and the two forts originally formed a triangular lookout system between which signals could be passed. You can't go inside either of the forts.

## Courses

**African Footprint International** ( 024-4615294; www.africanfootprint.dk) is an NGO that arranges dancing and drumming classes from 8am to noon Monday to Friday. Attached to the Cape Café is **Global Mamas** (www.globalmamas.org), a shop selling handmade batiks and clothes – it's connected to Women in Progress, a nonprofit group encouraging the growth of women-owned enterprises in Africa. It arranges batik workshops (four hours, C190,000), Ghanaian cuisine courses (three hours, C160,000) and drumming classes (three hours, C170,000).

## Festivals & Events

Cape Coast's **Fetu Afahye Festival**, a raucous carnival, takes place on the first Saturday of September. The highlight is the slaughter of a cow for the gods of Oguaa (the traditional name for Cape Coast). The biennial **Panafest** celebration is held in Cape Coast.

## Sleeping

### BUDGET

**Oasis Guest House** ( ☎ 35958; ali_d@gmx.da; s/d with shared bathroom C80,000/120,000, bungalows with private bathroom C200,000; P ) Formerly only a restaurant and bar, Oasis has expanded into a fully fledged backpacker resort and the only beachfront place in Cape Coast. It has several comfortable rondavels set in a grassy compound; some are quite large and attractively designed with coloured tiles and linens. Dancing and drumming classes are held, and the restaurant and bar areas are some of the best places to meet other travellers in town.

**Sammo Guest House** ( ☎ 33242; Jukwa Rd; r C75,000) Backpackers flock to Sammos, a compound within walking distance of the city centre to the east. There are simple but clean fan rooms of various sizes, and a rooftop terrace restaurant popular for the sunset views and social scene. Food here is fine but service is slow.

**Amkred Guest House** ( ☎ 32868; r with fan/air-con C98,000/C119,000; P ) The Amkred, down a lane behind Sammo, is less institutional and you're less likely to mix with other travellers. The carpeted rooms are a little frayed around the edges but they're comfortable enough. Guests can order food in advance. Smaller rooms are available for C76,000.

### MIDRANGE

**Prospect Lodge** ( ☎ 31506; prospectlodge2005@hotmail .com; s/d US$25/35; P ) This new hotel is easily the nicest place in the city centre. You can't miss the green-and-yellow building perched on a hill up a steep driveway off Commercial St. Rooms here are small but modern and have cable TV. Also has a cosy restaurant (mains C40,000 to C60,000) and tables set up outside with good views of town.

**Mighty Victory** ( ☎ 30135; gh72@aol.com; Aboom Cl; s/d with fan C160,000/190,000, r with air-con C220,000; P ) The Mighty Victory, set on a hill just below Fort Victoria, has a tranquil garden out front and is far removed from the noise of the centre. While the rooms have private bath-rooms and are well kept they're not a big step up quality-wise from Sammo or Amkred. There's a simple indoor restaurant.

**Dan's Paradise Hotel** ( ☎ 32942; d with air-con C140,000; P ) Like your uncle who wears a toupee and still goes to discos, Dan's Paradise won't admit it's getting old and take steps to slow down the inevitable wear and tear. Its dotage is further compounded by the remarkably chintzy décor. It's on the top of a steep hill off Sarbah Rd north of the Accra bus station. On Saturday nights it hosts a popular nightclub.

### TOP END

**Sanaa Lodge** ( ☎ 32570; sanaalcape2@yahoo.com.uk; s/d US$65/70; P ) On a hill overlooking the beach near the westernmost entrance to town, the Sanaa Lodge, Cape Coast's most upscale hotel, enjoys a wonderfully tranquil location and rooms with all the modern amenities. The pool and poolside grill are worth the price alone.

## Eating & Drinking

There are several hole-in-the-wall eateries and stalls selling street food around Kotokuraba Market, the intersection of Commercial St and Ashanti Rd and along Intsin St.

**Oasis Beer Garden & Restaurant** (mains C35,000) Part of the hotel compound of the same name, the Oasis is sometimes just that, a quiet place to eat, drink and while away a few hours, which you might have to do because the service can be lethargic. It has probably the largest and most eclectic menu in town serving everything from kebabs to grilled seafood and curry dishes and several tables are directly on the beach. Live music on Wednesday night, and Friday and Saturday nights the treehouse turns into a nightclub with local bands. There are cultural performances, dancing classes and beach bonfires on some weekend nights.

**Castle Beach Restaurant** (mains C30,000) There's no more pleasant spot to hang out and grab some food and drinks than this wooden pavilion overlooking the beach next to the Cape Coast Castle. Though your sandwiches, seafood or Ghanaian food may be slow in coming it's hard to be impatient with such cooling breezes and peaceful views.

**Assase Pa Vegetarian Restaurant** (mains C30,000) Assase Pa has a fantastic location, on a promontory overlooking the sea just across the bridge over the lagoon. Has a varied menu that includes vegetarian versions of Ghanaian dishes. Most afternoons there are live-music and dance sessions at the practice ground next door.

**Cape Café** (mains C20,000) The centrally located Cape Café is a big, bare, empty dining room, hardly an inviting place to eat and you can count the Ghanaian dishes available on half a hand. The charitably inclined should keep in mind that proceeds from here and the batik shop on the premises go to help needy women in the community.

**Coconut Delight** (Ashanti Rd) This tiny chop bar, near London Bridge, does wonderful fresh fruit juices as well as snack food. A couple of doors along is another tiny place selling home-made ice cream.

The **Blue Cheese** (mains C20,000), opposite the crab statue and the **Cassanova Spot** (Commercial St) are popular bars that also serve basic food.

### Getting There & Away

The VanefSTC bus station is in the Goil petrol station at Pedu junction, about 5km northwest of the town centre. There are buses twice a day to and from Accra (ordinary/luxury C25,000/38,000, three hours) and Takoradi (C12,000, one hour) and once a day to and from Kumasi (C65,000, four hours). Passenger taxis to Pedu junction leave from Commercial St, opposite the Cape Café.

There are two main motor parks in Cape Coast. The Accra bus station, at the junction of Sarbah and Residential Rds, serves long-distance routes, such as Accra and Kumasi. Kotokuraba station, on Governor Rowe Rd, near the market, serves destinations around Cape Coast, such as Abanze, Anomabu, Kakum National Park and Takoradi. Shared taxis to Elmina (C3700, 15 minutes) leave from the station on Commercial St, opposite the Cape Café.

## KAKUM NATIONAL PARK

☎ 042

Gingerly sliding across a rope bridge at dizzying heights is not for the agoraphobic. But for an easily earned adrenaline rush, the canopy walkway at this **national park** ( ☎ 33278; admission C2000; ☺ 8am-4pm), 33km north of Cape Coast, shouldn't be missed. Of course the park is more than only this much-hyped attraction. Together with the neighbouring Assin Attandanso Resource Reserve,

it protects 357 sq km of diverse and dense vegetation, a mixture of true rainforest and semideciduous forest. It's home to 40 species of larger mammals (including elephants, colobus monkeys and antelopes), about 300 species of birds and a staggering 600 varieties of butterfly. The park is an important refuge for several endangered species, including forest elephants, bongos and yellow-backed duikers. However, don't come expecting great wildlife viewing, since you'll almost certainly be disappointed. Most of the wildlife understandably chooses to stay well away from the action areas. Your best shot to see any wildlife is to get here when the park opens at 8am or take a night hike.

The 350m rope and cable **canopy walkway** (adult/student C90,000/50,000) was constructed in 1996. It consists of seven viewing platforms linked by a circuit of narrow suspension bridges, along which you sway, 30m above the forest floor. It gives you a bird's-eye view of the forest, although as you bounce along it's hard to concentrate on anything except how flimsy the ropes seem and what a vast distance it is from the forest floor.

Although the hype can make it seem as if the walkway *is* the park, there are other activities. A guided hike costs C40,000/20,000 per hour for adults/students and is a good way to learn about the rainforest flora and its traditional uses. Guided night walks need to be arranged in advance; call ☎ 30265 or fax 33042. In the park's visitor centre, there's a superb, ecologically sensitive display.

An interesting alternative option is to visit the park from Mesomagor on its eastern outskirts. You can arrange guided walks and there's a good chance of seeing wildlife such as forest elephants. Mesomagor is also the home of the famous **Kukyekukyeku Bamboo Orchestra** and it may be possible to hear a performance. For details, contact the park or ask at the tourist office in Cape Coast.

### Sleeping & Eating

Most people visit Kakum as a day trip from Cape Coast, but if you want to stay you can sleep on a tree platform at the camp site near the park headquarters for C80,000 per person; equipment hire (sleeping mat, sleeping bag, flashlight and mosquito net) costs C50,000. No camp fires are allowed. Simple homestay accommodation is also available in Mesomagor, on the eastern outskirts of the park.

**Hans Cottage Botel** ( ☎ 33621; hcottage@yahoo.com; s/d with fan US$10/15, s/d with air-con US$20/30; P ✕ ), on the road to Kakum, only 10km north of Cape Coast, feels like something your crazy uncle would cook up. But you can't argue with spending at least a few hours lounging in the two-storey wood pavilion restaurant perched over an artificial crocodile pond where birds and monkeys compete for your attention. Rooms are simple and clean. Any tro-tro heading along the Jukwa road towards Kakum can drop you at the hotel.

The **Kakum Rainforest Café** (mains ¢40,000) serves basic continental breakfast and Ghanaian dishes for lunch.

## Getting There & Away

From Cape Coast, tro-tros (¢6000, 45 minutes) that go past the entrance to the park leave from Kotokuraba station on Governor Rowe Rd. It's a five-minute walk from the main road to the park headquarters. Or, you could charter a taxi for about ¢150,000 round trip. To get to Mesomagor, take a tro-tro from Cape Coast to Nyamkomasi and a shared taxi from there to the village.

## DOMAMA ROCK SHRINE

The real reason to make the journey out to the village of Domana, almost 34km northwest of Kakum National Park, is for the guided trek and canoe trip on the Pra River. A tour that includes a visit to a cool **natural rock formation** ( 8am-5pm) costs around ¢30,000; it takes about five hours on foot and three hours if you have your own transport. Simple accommodation (¢40,000 for doubles with bucket showers and no electricity) and food is available at the guesthouse in Domama. Most visitors stay overnight so that they can get an early start in the morning. No tours are available on Wednesday, when it's taboo for the villagers to work.

From Cape Coast, take a tro-tro from Kotokoraba station to Ankako junction on the road to Twifo Praso, past the entrance to Kakum National Park. From Ankako, it's 17.5km down a bumpy but scenic dirt road to Domama village. Tro-tros run sporadically from the junction to Domama. Transport from Domama back to the junction can be a problem. A charter taxi from Cape Coast should cost around ¢225,000 round trip.

## ELMINA

☎ 042 / pop 20,000

Much more picturesque than Cape Coast, its neighbour 15km to the east, the small town of Elmina is the site of St George's Castle, the oldest European structure still standing in sub-Saharan Africa, and a lively fishing harbour. On a narrow peninsula between the Atlantic Ocean and Benya Lagoon, Elmina has one of the best natural harbours on the coast, which was what attracted first the Portuguese and later the Dutch and the British. The name Elmina, known as Edina in the local language, is likely derived from Mina d'Ouro (Gold Mine), the Portuguese name for this stretch of the coast.

## Sights

### ST GEORGE'S CASTLE

It's an uncanny feeling to look at this imposing and even beautiful building and think about its lurid history. At the end of a rocky peninsula, **St George's Castle** (adult/student US$7/4, still/video camera fee ¢5000/10,000; 9am-4.30pm) was built by the Portuguese in 1482, and captured by the Dutch in 1637. From then until they ceded it to the British in 1872, it served as the African headquarters of the Dutch West Indies Company. It was expanded when slaves replaced gold as the major object of commerce, and the storerooms were converted into dungeons. The informative tour takes you around the incredibly grim dungeons, punishment cells and the turret room where the British imprisoned the Ashanti king, Prempeh I, for four years. The Portuguese Catholic church, converted into slave auctioning rooms by the Protestant Dutch, now houses a museum with excellent displays on the history and culture of Elmina.

### FORT ST JAGO

Facing the castle across the lagoon is the much smaller **Fort St Jago** (admission ¢10,000; 9am-5pm), also a Unesco World Heritage site, built by the Dutch between 1652 and 1662 to protect the castle. The views of the town and St George's Castle from the ramparts of this partial ruin are superb.

### FISH MARKET

Watching the colourful pirogues pull in and out and listening to the cacophony of shouts at the crowded Mpoben port is like having front-row theatre seats. The vast fish market on the lagoon side is also fascinating to wander around, particularly when the day's fishing catch is being unloaded in the afternoon.

### DUTCH CEMETERY

There are a few interesting *posubans* in town and a well-kept Dutch cemetery. To get to the cemetery from the castle take a left turn over the bridge and follow the road around which takes you past some of the *posubans*.

## Festivals & Events

Elmina's colourful **Bakatue Festival** takes place on the first Tuesday in July. It's a joyous harvest thanksgiving feast, and one of its highlights is watching the priest in the harbour waters casting a net to lift a ban on fishing in the lagoon.

The first Thursday in January is **Edina Buronya** time, a sort of Christmas signifying Ghanaian-Dutch friendship with fishing, drinking and slaughtering – of a lamb.

## Sleeping

**Coconut Grove Beach Resort** ( ☎ 33650; www.coconutgrovehotels.com.gh; s/d US$92/110; P ⚡ ) The resort of choice for various heads of state, this luxurious resort has a beachside location 4km west of Elmina and offers a variety of well-appointed rooms as well as a nine-hole golf course. Substantial discounts when reservations are made online.

**Almond Tree Guesthouse** ( ☎ 37365; www.almond3.com; r from C280,000; P ⚡ ) You'll feel at home staying at this highly recommended guesthouse just past the Elmina beach resort. It has several large rooms with wicker furniture and yellow bed linen, and the ones with wood floors and balconies are especially attractive. The more expensive room has air-con. Breakfast included.

**Coconut Grove Bridge House** ( ☎ 34557; Liverpool St; d US$30-50; ⚡ ) Looking like a pirogue out of water amid the disorder and chaos just opposite St George's Castle, this converted old mansion is a neat stone building that would blend in on a narrow London street. Run by the Coconut Grove Beach Resort, it has comfortable and modern rooms. Restaurant attached.

**Elmina Beach Resort** ( ☎ 33105; www.gbhghana.com; r from US$72; P ⚡ ⚡ ⚡ ) Bringing new meaning to the term 'white elephant', the Elmina Beach Resort sprawls behind a walled compound about 2km east of the centre towards Cape Coast. Blandness and bad aesthetic decisions aside, the rooms are modern and clean and it has its own artificial swept beach above the real rocky one. Ocean view rooms are more expensive. The restaurants and lounges built to impress can't be offset by service no better than at budget hotels. Shuttle service to nearby Brenu beach.

**Nyansapow Hotel** ( ☎ 33955; Lime St; r C80,000) The only centrally located budget-priced hotel, the Nyansapow has a pleasant courtyard surrounded by simple and clean rooms with private bathrooms. It's signposted off the main road into town.

## Eating

There are several basic eateries and food stalls near the harbour and Liverpool St.

**Coconut Grove Bridge House** (mains C50,000; ⚡ ) There's no better place in Elmina to escape than this restaurant in front of the castle, part of the hotel of the same name. The menu includes Ghanaian standards and fresh-caught seafood like fried calamari. You can also sit on the small stone terrace outside overlooking the crazy boat action a few feet away.

**Castle Restaurant** (mains C35,000) This pleasant wood-floored restaurant is within the castle walls and serves Ghanaian dishes – slowly. Access it through a separate entrance in the wall to the left after you cross the bridge.

**Gramsdel J** (High St; mains C25,000) A bright red-and-yellow spot on the beach road about 1.5km from town on the way to the Elmina Beach Resort. Serves basic and cheap meals.

## Getting There & Away

The main taxi and tro-tro station is outside the Wesley Methodist Cathedral. From here you can get tro-tros to Takoradi (C10,000) or passenger taxis to Cape Coast. In Cape Coast, shared taxis (C2700, 15 minutes) to Elmina leave from the station on Commercial St, a block north of Barclays Bank.

# BRENU-AKYINIM

A fabulous stretch of sandy beach is the feature of the village of Brenu-Akyinim, about 10km west of Elmina. Part of the beach has been cordoned off to form the **Brenu Beach Resort** ( ☎ 36620; admission US$0.50; r about US$10), where the sand is clean and there's a good restaurant and other facilities. A small fee is charged for admission to the resort. You can stay in basic rooms at the resort, or in the village for about US$4. At the junction on the main road is a simple eatery called the Ocean Style Restaurant.

From Elmina or Cape Coast, take a tro-tro west towards Takoradi and ask to be let off at the junction for Brenu-Akyinim. From here you should be able to get a passenger taxi to the village (5km).

## SHAMA
☎ 031

Few foreigners stop in Shama, a ramshackle town where the Pra River joins the ocean, and even though you'll likely receive celebrity-like attention, it can be a tranquil place to experience typical fishing village life.

Originally built as lodge for Dutch traders in 1526, **Fort Sebastian** (admission C10,000) in Shama really didn't become Fort Sebastian until it was redesigned by the Portuguese in 1590. Later recaptured by the Dutch, then briefly by the British, then the Dutch again, today the fort stands guard over the town.

The colourful **fish market** is alive and bustling every day but Tuesday and there's a beautiful sandy beach nearby. Boatmen on the town side will ferry you across a little inlet for a small fee or take you on longer excursions up the river.

Another hotel too big for its britches, or at least it doesn't quite fit in with its surroundings, is the **Hotel Applause** ( ☎ 23941; r from C60,000) which has simple rooms with fans, bathrooms and balconies, and a rooftop restaurant with views that call for a little clapping.

Shama junction is about 18km east of Takoradi, off the main coastal road. The town is 4km south of the junction. Any vehicle travelling between Takoradi and Cape Coast or Elmina can drop you at the junction, from where there are regular shared taxis into Shama. Alternatively, you can get a tro-tro direct to Shama from the Cape Coast station in Takoradi.

## SEKONDI-TAKORADI
☎ 031

Takoradi is definitely the big sister of these twin cities. While it lacks any tourist sights and the beach is narrow, rocky or nonexistent, there are several good hotels and restau-

rants, and it's the transport hub west of Cape Coast. Takoradi was just a fishing village until it was chosen as Ghana's first deep-water seaport; since then it has prospered. Sekondi, the older of the two settlements, is about 10km northeast of Takoradi. The only reason you might venture into Sekondi is to take a quick look at Fort Orange, built by the Dutch in 1640 and now a lighthouse.

At the far (northeastern) end of John Sarbah Rd, across the Cape Coast road, is a wooded hill that is home to a quickly diminishing population of colobus and spot-nosed monkeys.

## Orientation
The heart of Takoradi is the busy Market Circle, around which you'll find the motor parks, most of the cheap hotels and eateries, and banks and forexes. The port is about 2km southeast of Market Circle. Near it is the train station and head offices of banks. West of the port area is a green residential area where you'll find many of the hotels, bordered to the south by a golf course and the beach.

## Information
### INTERNET ACCESS
**2-Gees Internet** (Collins Rd)
**Heaven's Gate Internet** (Old Ashanti Rd; ☷ 7.30am-10pm)
**JW Andrews Internet** (John Sarbah Rd) Best connection in town.

### MEDICAL SERVICES
**Kenrich's Pharmacy** (John Sarbah Rd)

### MONEY
**Barclays Bank** (Market Circle) Southeastern side of the circle. Has an ATM.
**Esam Forex Bureau** (John Sarbah Rd)
**Ghana Commercial Bank** (Market Circle) Southeastern side of the circle. Has an ATM.
**Idemahl Forex Bureau** (Liberation Rd)

### POST
**Post office** Axim Rd (Axim Rd); John Sarbah Rd (John Sarbah Rd)

## Sleeping
### BUDGET
**Golden Queen Palace Hotel** ( ☎ 23463; r from C130,000; P ᠁ ) Right off the Axim Rd roundabout south of the centre, the Golden Queen is the only budget hotel in this quiet part of

**TAKORADI**

0 _____ 700 m
0 _____ 0.4 miles

**INFORMATION**

| | |
|---|---|
| 2-Gees Internet.....................1 | B2 |
| Barclays Bank........................2 | B2 |
| Barclays Bank........................3 | C4 |
| Esam Forex ..........................4 | A2 |
| Ghana Commercial Bank.........5 | B1 |
| Ghana Commercial Bank.........6 | C4 |
| Ghana Commercial Bank.........7 | B2 |
| Ghana Commercial Bank (Head | |
| Office).............................8 | B2 |
| Heaven's Gate Internet..........9 | B2 |
| Idemahl Forex Bureau...........10 | B2 |
| JW Andrews Internet............11 | A2 |
| Kenrich's Pharmacy..............12 | A2 |
| Post Office (Axim Rd)...........13 | A2 |
| Post Office (John Sarbah Rd)...14 | B2 |

**SLEEPING**

| | |
|---|---|
| Africa Beach Resort...............15 | A4 |
| Animens Hotel......................16 | A3 |
| Golden Queen Palace Hotel....17 | B3 |
| Hillcrest Hotel......................18 | B4 |
| Hotel de Mexico...................19 | A4 |
| Hotel Melody.......................20 | A2 |
| Raybow International Hotel.....21 | A4 |
| Super Star Hotel & Restaurant..22 | B1 |
| Taadi Hotel..........................23 | B2 |
| Trust Lodge.........................24 | A2 |
| You 84 Hotel & Restaurant.....25 | B2 |
| Zenith Hotel........................26 | B2 |

Fishing
Harbour

**EATING**

| | |
|---|---|
| Akroma Plaza Restaurant.........27 | B3 |
| Captain Hook's Bar & | |
| Restaurant......................28 | B3 |
| Max Mart............................29 | B2 |
| Memories Restaurant.............30 | B3 |
| Northsea Restaurant..............31 | A2 |
| Silver Pot Restaurant.............32 | A1 |
| SOS Restaurant & Bar............33 | B2 |

**TRANSPORT**

| | |
|---|---|
| Accra Motor Park..................34 | A2 |
| Minibuses to Axim.................35 | A2 |
| Taxi Park (Destinations within | |
| Takoradi)........................36 | B2 |
| Taxi Rank............................37 | B2 |
| Tro-tros to Agona Junction, | |
| Princess Town & Elubo ......38 | A1 |
| Tro-tros to Sharma, Cape Coast | |
| & Winneba.......................39 | B1 |
| VanefSTC Bus Station............40 | A2 |

town. Some of the rooms are actually too
big and the concrete and lack of light aren't
exactly pleasant.

**You 84 Hotel & Restaurant** ( ☎ 22945; Market Circle; d with fan/air-con C80,000/130,000) This intriguingly named hotel is upstairs on the western
side of Market Circle. Despite the rather
grim reception area, the rooms, some of

which open onto a balcony, are good value
(private bathrooms).

**Zenith Hotel** ( ☎ 22359; Kitson Rd; r C80,000) A
run-down colonial-era building east of
Market Circle, the Zenith is nicely arranged
around a central courtyard but the ratty
and bare rooms are about what you'd expect at this price.

**GHANA**

## MIDRANGE

**Taadi Hotel** ( ☎ 31104; Wiawso Rd; r C180,000; P ⊠ ) Well located at the edge of central Takoradi, the Taadi stands out because of its friendly and attentive service. Some of the rooms even have sitting rooms, small balconies and cable TV.

**Super Star Hotel & Restaurant** ( ☎ 23105; Ashanti Rd; r with fan/air-con C165,000/216,000) This centrally located hotel is an oasis of air-conditioned calm amid the hot and dusty market area. It has clean, carpeted rooms and professional service though noise is a potential problem. There's a good modern restaurant on the ground floor, the best place to eat around the market area.

**Animens Hotel** ( ☎ 24676; r C200,000; P ⊠ ) This hotel on a quiet residential street next to the Raybow is a high-rise as far as Takoradi is concerned. Carpeted rooms are small but comfortable and sometimes get cable TV. A basic restaurant is attached.

**Hotel de Mexico** (r C250,000; P ⊠ ) Opposite the Animens and the Raybow and sharing their peaceful, residential setting, the Mexico is a low-slung concrete building with modern and clean rooms.

**Hotel Melody** ( ☎ 24109; Axim Rd; r C270,000; P ⊠ ) Though you can't beat the location as far as bus travel is concerned, spacious rooms at the Melody are no nicer than less expensive ones found elsewhere. There's a good restaurant.

## TOP END

**Hillcrest Hotel** ( ☎ 22277; hillcrest@africaonline.com .gh; r US$70; P ⊠ 🖳 🔊 ) A favourite for foreign business travellers in the area, the Hillcrest has the nicest rooms – large, sunny and modern – in Takoradi and the most professional staff. Some rooms have big balconies looking out on the pool (nonguests C40,000) in the garden courtyard. A quality restaurant is attached.

**Raybow International Hotel** ( ☎ 25438; raybow hotel@yahoo.com; r C450,000; P ⊠ 🖳 ) For those seeking modern comforts, the whitewashed Raybow compound is another good option. Each of the chalets has high-quality amenities and the charming bamboo-and-wicker restaurant serves some of the best food in town. Breakfast included.

**Trust Lodge** ( ☎ 23923; fax 23918; r US$50; P ⊠ ) Better value than the two hotels closer to the beach, this low-slung building on a quiet tree-lined street has large, comfortable and modern rooms and friendly, personable staff.

**Africa Beach Resort** ( ☎ 25148; africa_beach@yahoo .com; s/d US$45/55; P 🔊 ) What it has going for it, a beachside location, is offset by the fact that there's not much of a beach here. Perched on a hill with the water below and relatively nice pool area means it's more like resort than anything else Takoradi has to offer. The decaying cottages have seen better days though. Live music Saturday nights in the bar and restaurant area.

## Eating & Drinking

There are several good-value eateries and lively drinking spots along Axim Rd, around Market Circle and on Liberation Rd. **Max Mart** (Liberation Rd), only a block from the market, is an oasis, a modern, air conditioned grocery store. See the previous Sleeping section for several recommended hotel restaurants.

**Captain Hook's Bar & Restaurant** (Africana Roundabout; mains C70,000-200,000) Not surprisingly seafood is the speciality at this nautically themed restaurant, probably the best and certainly the most expensive in Takoradi. Besides lobster, calamari and the like, pizza and European-style meat dishes round out the menu. The shady backyard beer garden is popular.

**Akroma Plaza Restaurant** (Accra Rd; mains C35,000) A cross between a large banquet hall and an institutional cafeteria, the Akroma Plaza is something of a local institution, especially on weekends when the vast dining room is at least partially filled as are some of the tables outside under the bamboo pavilions. Has a big menu with Ghanaian and continental dishes.

**Memories Restaurant** (Chapel Hill Rd; mains C30,000) Just down the road from the Hillcrest Hotel, Memories may look closed and abandoned from the outside but it's actually quite a pleasant little restaurant serving Chinese, Ghanaian and continental dishes plus pizza (C60,000) that can be recommended.

**Silver Pot Restaurant** (Liberation Rd; mains C25,000) One of the few places to eat comfortably in the market area, the Silver Pot is a clean and calm oasis good for a drink or meal of Ghanaian and continental cuisine.

**Northsea Restaurant** (Axim Rd; mains C60,000) Conveniently located next to the VanefSTC station and attached to the Mosden Hotel, the

Northsea looks like a diner that wants to be a dive bar. The booths are tearing at the seam and the air-con is weak though the menu is a respectable mix of seafood (C70,000), pizza (C45,000) and Ghanaian and continental food. Live jazz Friday nights.

**SOS Restaurant & Bar** (cnr Ashanti Rd & Market Circle; mains C20,000) A basic local's eatery serving snacks and drinks on the southern side of Market Circle, the SOS is notable only for its breezy upstairs balcony.

## Getting There & Away
### BUS & TRO-TRO
The **VanefSTC bus station** ( ☎ 23351; Axim Rd) is opposite the junction with John Sarbah Rd. It has regular departures for Accra (ordinary/luxury C38,000/C50,000, four hours) between 3am and 5.30pm. There are three buses per day to Kumasi (C65,000, six hours, 4am, 10am and 4pm); only two at 8am and 2pm on Sunday. The Accra bus can drop you at Pedu junction (for Cape Coast) or Anomabu, but you will have to pay the full Accra fare. If you're heading for Abidjan, it's possible to pick up the bus from Accra as it passes through but you'll need to arrange this in advance; it's easier get transport to Elubo and continue from there. There's also a Monday-morning bus to Tamale and Sunday-evening bus to Aflao.

Opposite the VanefSTC bus station is the Accra motor park, from where you can get OSA and City Express buses and GPRTU minibuses to Accra. At the top of Axim Rd, near the traffic circle, is a tro-tro park serving destinations west of Takoradi, including Agona junction (30 minutes, for Busua and Dixcove), Axim, Beyin and Elubo (three hours). This is also where you can get tro-tros and Peugeot taxis to Abidjan. Tro-tros to destinations east of Takoradi leave from the Cape Coast tro-tro station north of Market Circle. Destinations include Shama, Cape Coast and Winneba .

### TRAIN
There are passenger trains from Takoradi to Kumasi and Accra. For more details, see p402.

## BUSUA & DIXCOVE
☎ 031
These two fishing villages, only 30km or so west of Takoradi and an easy drive from

Accra, boast some of the nicest beaches in Ghana. Busua, the more developed of the two as far as tourism goes, is blessed with a long, sandy stretch and water ideal for swimming and even a little surfing. Now there's even more reason to head this way with the addition of two low-key bungalow hangouts near Dixcove.

## Sights & Activities
On the shore of a rocky cove, Dixcove is an animated fishing village. Its natural harbour is deep enough for small ships to enter – one of the reasons why it became the site of the picturesque **Fort Metal Cross** (admission C10,000, camera fee C5000; ☾ 9am-5pm), which overlooks the port. Built in 1696 by the British, it got its name from the metal brand used on the slaves who passed through here. The post office in the first courtyard has been here since the British occupation and is still the only post office for the entire Busua-Dixcove area. From the ramparts there are magical views over the harbour and the village.

If you head east along the beach from Busua, after about 2km you'll reach the settlement of Butre, site of the ruined **Fort Batenstein**.

Dixcove is about 2km around the coast west of Busua, an undemanding 20- to 30-minute walk over the headland to the west. Locals warn against walking the track alone; follow their advice and take a local guide (for a small fee) and don't take any valuables with you. Alternatively, you can get a shared taxi back to Agona junction then another from there to Dixcove. There's no direct transport between Dixcove and Busua.

## Sleeping
The more established accommodation is in Busua but two new resorts near Dixcove are extremely attractive options.

### BUDGET
**Ellis Hideout** ( ☎ 290456; www.ellishideout.com; camping with own tent C25,000, dm C50,000, bungalows C180,000) Owned and operated by a Swedish family dedicated to drawing people in and making them never want to leave. A few minutes from Butre, separated by a short canoe ride, this beachfront mini-village has beautifully crafted bungalows with colourful tiled floors, and budget rooms with five beds in a small

room. A restaurant serves up good Ghanaian and continental dishes. You can arrange drumming classes and all manner of tours including crocodile safaris up the Butre river. There are discounts for students and volunteers.

**Green Turtle Lodge** ( ☎ 893566; www.greenturtle lodge.com; camping with own tent C25,000, dm C50,000, r with shared/private bathroom C100,000/200,000) Another new resort, equally committed to the environment and community, the Green Turtle uses solar power, recycles shower water and is built entirely from local, natural materials. It's on a palm-lined beach and has spacious, clean bungalows with showers open to the sun and stars. There's a restaurant, and the young British owners can organise day and overnight tours including hikes, canoe trips and surfing safaris. Green Turtle is 10km west of Dixcove near the village of Akwidaa. It discounts for students and volunteers.

**Alaska Beach Club** (rondavels with shared/private bathroom C85,000/C200,000; P ) The oddly named Alaska (considering it's on a beach and it's always hot) is the best value in Busua. Each of the simple round huts with thatched roofs comes with a mosquito net and desk and the shared bathroom facilities are kept clean. The only hassle is that the beachside restaurant and bar attracts a fair number of hangers-on and tourist leeches. Rents surfboards and boogie boards.

**MIDRANGE**

**African Rainbow Resort** ( ☎ 32149; www.african rainbow.net; s/d with fan US$45/50, s/d with air-con US$60/65; P ) Certainly more charming than the Busua Beach Resort, this hotel across the street from the beach has large, clean rooms with balconies, plus a rooftop bar and lounge area, a nicely decorated restaurant and a ground-floor bar with pool table. Breakfast included.

**Busua Beach Resort** ( ☎ 21210; www.gbhghana .com; r from US$50/60; P 🍴 💻 🏊 ) Though it gives white elephants a bad name, this large complex does boast a superb beachside location and all the amenities you'd expect, though architecturally it doesn't exactly blend in. The budget accommodation (room with fan US$12) was being refurbished at the time of research. There's a beachside pavilion restaurant as well as one indoors, and a bar. Has the only (semi) reliable Internet access in Busua.

**Eating**

The three resorts in Busua have their own restaurants: the Alaska Beach Club is the most laid back and least expensive, the African Rainbow has the most welcoming dining area plus a rooftop, and the Busua Beach; well the service is slow and it's overpriced.

There's no shortage of locals who will catch and cook seafood for you upon request. Take a walk down the beach or simply hang out at the Alaska Beach Club and you'll likely be propositioned by an entrepreneurial chef or two. There are several makeshift restaurants set up along the beach as well, really nothing more than a sign and a table, but whatever eating option you choose, you should try to order around an hour in advance.

At the far western end of the beach at Busua is the Black Mamba Corner, a restaurant owned and operated by a German woman who lives on this rocky promontory set apart from the rest of town. Order well in advance for the seafood and pizza that's served. Walk to the end of the beach and look for the sign across the water. There is one round cottage on the property that comfortably sleeps four, available for C100,000.

**Getting There & Away**

Busua and Dixcove are each about 12km from the main coastal road. There's no direct transport to and from either Busua or Dixcove; you have to get to Agona junction on the main road and then take a tro-tro or shared taxi from there. From Takoradi, regular tro-tros (C6000, 45 minutes) leave for Agona junction from the station at the top of Axim Rd. From Agona junction there is frequent transport (C2500) to Busua and Dixcove. A private taxi between Busua and Takoradi will cost around C80,000.

## PRINCESS TOWN

Despite the relative difficulty getting here, or perhaps because of it, Princess Town draws travellers to its abandoned beach and **Fort Princess Town** (admission C5000, still/video camera fee C5000/10,000; ☻ 9am-5pm), a castle perched magnificently at the top of a hill on the eastern edge of the village. Originally called Gross Friedrichsburg by the Prussians who built it in 1683, the partly restored fort is made from greyish local stone and this, together with the lush vegetation surrounding it, makes it one of the most attractive forts on the coast. There are superb views from the ramparts over the sandy bay and towards Cape Three Points, Ghana's southernmost point. The fort's caretaker can help arrange excursions in the area, such as canoe trips on the nearby lagoon, and trips up the River Kpani to visit a palm-wine distillery.

The only accommodation in Princess Town is at the fort, where simple rooms with shared bathroom (bucket showers) cost C25,000; you can also camp with a tent for C15,000. At the start of the short trail up to the fort is a terrace bar and restaurant where you can get cold drinks and cheap seafood meals. Odds are you'll be approached by self-appointed guides, though they're not necessary.

The junction for Princess Town is about 15km west of Agona junction; any tro-tro heading west from Agona can drop you there. From here, it's about 18km to Princess Town along a scenic but rough dirt road. Shared taxis run reasonably regularly between the junction and the town. There are also direct tro-tros from Agona to Princess Town but they take forever to fill up.

## AXIM
☎ 0342

Closer to Abidjan than Accra, Axim is just about the end of the road as far as Ghanaian beach resorts go, and it's this relative isolation plus an exceptional resort that makes the journey more than worthwhile. The town itself, the largest on the coast west of Takoradi, is fairly unexceptional except for the whitewashed **Fort St Anthony** (admission C10,000, camera fee C5000). It was built by the Portuguese in 1515, making it the second-oldest fort on the Ghanaian coast. From the top of the fort there are excellent views of the coastline in either direction. Though the official status of accommodation is a little ambiguous, the caretaker says a bed in the fort minus bathroom can be had for C45,000. Whales can be seen from October to March in the waters around Axim.

### Sleeping & Eating
**Axim Beach Hotel** ( ☎ 22260; www.aximbeach.com; bungalows with fan/air-con US$33/43, s/d with fan/air-con US$8/16, budget r US$6; P ⊠ ⬚ ) This hotel, perched on a cliff with sea views a couple of kilometres east of the town centre, is one of

the nicest places to stay in all of Ghana. The traditional-style bungalows have a single flower placed on every immaculately made bed and even the bathrooms (private for the bungalows, shared for the rooms) are done lovingly with attention to detail. Two restaurants, one on top of the hill and the other on the fantastic beach below, serve excellent seafood, Ghanaian and continental food. Staff can arrange canoe trips to Princess Town and Cape Three Points, drumming and dancing courses, and tours to Nzulezu and Ankasa Nature Reserve. Hosts a full-moon party at the end of May.

**Ankobra Beach Hotel** ( ☎ 22400; ankobra_beach@hotmail.com; r US$11, bungalows US$25-29) The Ankobra is another highly recommended resort with an unbeatable location set within a grove of palms on a stunning beach. The bungalows don't have as much character as those at the Axim but they're comfortable and the restaurant is equally good. Activities such as canoe trips up the nearby Ankobra River and tours to Nzulezu and Ankasa can be arranged. Ankobra Beach is signposted off the main Elubo road, about 5km from the turn-off to Axim. From the main road, it's about 500m to the resort.

### Getting There & Away
Axim is 69km west of Takoradi, off the main Elubo road, which bypasses it. Axim's motor park is in the centre of town, across from the football pitch in front of the fort. There are regular tro-tros to Takoradi (1½ hours), which can drop you at Agona junction (for Busua and Dixcove) or the Princess Town junction. Heading west, for Elubo and Ankasa you may have to get a tro-tro to Esiama, a big transport hub on the coastal road about 10km from Axim, and get onward transport from there. To Beyin, you'll have to get a tro-tro to Eikwe and then transport on from there.

## BEYIN & NZULEZU
About 65km west of Axim, is the village of Beyin. It's the site of Fort Apollonia, the last of the coastal forts west of Accra, and it's the departure point for visits to the Amansuri Lagoon and the stilt village of Nzulezu. This village is reached by canoe, which takes about an hour each way. At the Ghana Wildlife Society office on the outskirts of Beyin, you register and pay a fee of C40,000 per per-

son, which includes the canoe trip and entry to the village. (Contact the project manager Mr James Parker on ☎ 233 20 81 60 996, cell phone 233 31 92 310 or email him at pmckeown100@yahoo.co.uk.) There's no shade on the lagoon so the earlier in the day you leave the better, and take plenty of water and a hat with you.

You can stay overnight in Nzulezu in a tranquil room over the water for C35,000. Simple meals can be arranged. Let them know you want to stay over when you are arranging your trip.

Beyin is on a rough dirt road that leaves the main Elubo road about 20km west of Esiama. From there it's about 15km to Eikwe and then the road follows the coast to Beyin. From Takoradi, you may be able to get a direct tro-tro from the station at the top of Axim Rd but it's probably quicker to get a tro-tro to Esiama and then transport on from there. From Axim, there are a few tro-tros to Eikwe, from where you can get onward transport to Beyin. Alternatively, Axim Beach Resort and Ankobra Beach Hotel can charter a taxi to take you there and back for about C250,000. Heading to Elubo, you can get transport east from Beyin to Tikobo No 1 and onward transport from there.

## ANKASA NATURE RESERVE

One of the few untouched tropical rainforests, this **reserve** (admission C25,000), near the border with Côte d'Ivoire offers reasonable wildlife-viewing opportunities, although facilities are very basic. Together with the neighbouring Nini-Suhien Reserve, Ankasa covers 490 sq km of wet rainforest. Mammals such as forest elephants, leopards, bongos and several monkey species have been identified and the area is particularly rich in birdlife, including parrots, hornbills and the rare white-fronted guinea fowl.

The park headquarters is at the main Ankasa Gate, where you pay the entrance fee and can arrange guided hikes including night-time ones. Overnight accommodation is available in the park in camps (C25,000) within walking distance of the main Ankasa Gate. You'll need to bring your own mosquito net or tent, sleeping bag and food.

Ankasa Gate is about 6km north of the main Elubo road, about 20km southeast of Elubo. Direct transport can be difficult so it may be better to take any transport along the main road and ask to be dropped at the junction.

# THE EAST

Once part of German Togoland and now known as the Volta region, appropriately enough since the huge lake of the same name dominates its geography, this part of the country offers the best opportunity for hiking. The three waterfalls at Wli, Tagbo and Amedofe are surrounded by some of the most beautiful countryside in Ghana.

VanefSTC buses leave from Accra's Tudu station north of Makola market for Aflao, Ho, Hohoe and Kpando daily, but, it's common for departure times for these destinations to be delayed significantly. Crossing to or from Togo will take you along the coastal highway and through the border at Aflao.

## ADA

☎ 0968

Don't be confused by the fact that there are three Adas: Ada Kasseh at the junction on the main Accra to Aflao highway, Big Ada about 15km south and Ada Foah on the estuary. It's only Ada Foah, with its languorous air of decay, riverfront setting and superb beach, that is worth visiting. Turtles come ashore here to nest between November and February.

There's a small community-run **tourist centre** near the motor park in Ada Foah. Boat trips on the river can be arranged at the tourist centre or more expensively from the Manet Paradise Beach Hotel. Swim in the ocean, as there's a chance of picking up bilharzia in the estuary.

### Sleeping & Eating

**Manet Paradise Beach Hotel** ( ☎ 22398; info@manet paradise.com; s/d US$75/88; ☒ ) Easily the best place to stay in Ada, the Manet Paradise has an exquisite location near the mouth of the estuary about 1.5km east of the town centre and set amid palm-shaded, well-kept grounds. The rooms are modern but unspectacular. You can cool off in the nice pool and watersport activities are offered; it also has tennis courts. There's a nice restaurant and terrace bar that catches sunset views.

GHANA

**Estuary Beach Club** (huts C85,000) Hard to get to, but worth the slog because of its location on an otherwise deserted stretch of beach, the Estuary has only a few simple huts but may expand in the future. Don't attempt the drive here in anything but a good 4WD, or it's over a half-hour walk from the Manet Paradise. Alternatively you can charter a boat here.

There are several basic guesthouses in and around the market area and just north of Ada Foah.

### Getting There & Around

Any transport heading in either direction along the Accra to Aflao highway should be able to drop you at the junction, Ada Kasseh, from where regular passenger taxis run to Ada Foah (C2000). From Accra, tro-tros (C10,000, two hours) direct to Ada leave from Tudu station. To get to Ho from Ada, you'll need to change vehicles at Sogakope or, possibly, Akatsi junction. If you're headed to Akosombo, it's probably easiest to take any vehicle to Tema and change there.

From the lorry park in Ada Foah, private taxis go to the Manet Paradise.

## KETA
☎ 0966

Birdwatchers will want to flock to Keta, one of the least touristed parts of the country, and one of the last stops before reaching the Togolese border at Aflao. The Keta Lagoon, the largest in the country, is separated from the encroaching sea by a narrow strip of land and a sandy beach which in places is quite pretty. Keta itself seems to be in a perpetual state of ruin, at least in part because some of the town has in fact been washed away. You can visit the ruins of Fort Prinzenstein, built in 1784 by the Danes. Just on from the fort is the beach; other beaches are at Tegbi, Woe and Anloga on the road south of Keta.

### Sleeping & Eating

**Lorneh Lodge** ( ☎ 42160; r from US$25; ✳ ▢ ▨ ) Several kilometres south of Keta near Tegbi on the ocean side of the road, the Lorneh has a row of concrete bungalows on a good swimming beach. Less expensive rooms are a few hundred metres away. There's a restaurant and Internet access.

**Keta Beach Hotel** ( ☎ 21288; r with fan/air-con C85,000/150,000) This once-popular place, on the beachside of the road 2km south of Keta, has fairly run-down accommodation but a pleasant bar and restaurant area.

**Abutia Lodge** ( ☎ 22239; r from C75,000) On the edge of the lagoon in Woe, about 8km south of the Keta Beach Hotel and clearly sign-posted off the main road, this is a tranquil and laid-back place best appreciated for its garden setting and not for the low quality of its rooms. Meals can be provided.

### Getting There & Away

Tro-tros to Keta leave from Tudu station in Accra (C20,000, three hours). From Ada, you may need to change vehicles in Soga-kope and again at Dabala. From Ho, infrequent tro-tros head to Keta but it's quicker to go to Akatsi junction and on from there. East of Keta towards Aflao and the Togo border, the sea has encroached on the road. Occasionally 4WDs make the trip when the water is especially low; otherwise there are frequent boats across and onward transport from there. Although there is a motor park near the fort in Keta, the main transport hub is at Anloga, about 15km southwest. Tro-tros and shared taxis connect the settlements between Anloga and Keta.

## AKOSOMBO
☎ 0251

Once a boom town housing thousands of workers building the dam that now holds back the world's largest artificial lake, known as Lake Volta, today Akosombo deserves a visit only to take in this engineering marvel, preferably from the vantage of a canoe or ferry on the Volta River. It's also the terminus for a passenger-boat service north to Yeji.

Akosombo is about 7km north of the Accra to Ho road, 2km before the dam and 6km before the port. There's a Ghana Commercial Bank, post office and small visitor centre on the main road near the motor park in town. A wider selection of accommodation and eating options are available in Atimpoku, to the south of Akosombo, where the Ho road crosses the Volta at the impressive Adome Suspension Bridge.

### Sights & Activities

To view the dam, take a shared taxi to 'Mess' and get off at the foot of the drive to the Volta Lake Hotel; the lookout is halfway up the drive. The Volta River Authority arranges tours of the dam (ask at the visitor centre or the Volta Hotel).

More like a booze cruise than the Love Boat, the infelicitously named *Dodi Princess* chugs out to nearby Dodi Island on Saturday, Sunday and holidays (adult/child C160,000/100,000); the price includes lunch and a drink. Leaving at around 11am, the trip takes five hours, with two hours on the island, but you can stay on board if you want. Contact the Volta Hotel for reservations. It leaves from a well-signposted jetty beyond the dam, before the port. Any shared taxi heading for the port from the motor park can drop you at the jetty.

## Sleeping

### BUDGET

**Adomi Hotel & Restaurant** ( ☎ 20095; r with fan/air-con C120,000/200,000) Overlooking Atimpoku roundabout opposite the suspension bridge, the Adomi has comfortable, modern rooms, some with cable TV. The terrace restaurant has especially good views.

**Benkum Motel** ( ☎ 20050; r C70,000) It's not as bad as it looks. This isn't exactly a compliment since the basic, fan-cooled rooms at this budget hotel in Atimpoku, south of the suspension bridge, are only a slight step up in quality from the crumbling building. Bathrooms are shared.

**Zito Guesthouse** ( ☎ 20474; r with fan/air-con C120,000/190,000) Still the only acceptable budget choice in Akosombo. Zito is up the hill from the motor park past the market, and has fairly spacious bare bones rooms. There's a small garden on the property.

### MIDRANGE

**Aylo's Bay** ( ☎ 20901; www.aylosbay.com; r US$30) Near the Volta Bridge and next to the Continental, this laid-back hotel has several small cottages on shady riverside frontage as well as a garden bar and restaurant. Canoe trips and all kinds of workshops can be arranged.

**Akosombo Continental Hotel** ( ☎ 20091; r US$60; ❄ ⚑ ) The Continental doesn't have the character of Aylo's Bay or the relative luxury of the Volta, but it does have an excellent riverfront location just beyond the suspension bridge, and bland but modern accommodation. There's a swimming pool and a good but moderately expensive restaurant.

### TOP END

**Volta Hotel** ( ☎ 251731; s/d US$95/105; ❄ ⚑ ) Even without the panoramic views of the dam, the lake and the Akwamu highlands, the Volta Hotel is superb hotel just on its own merits: top-flight service, quality, modern rooms and a good restaurant. The bar has live music on most weekend nights. Look for signs to the hotel in town.

## Eating

Street food in Akosombo and Atimpoku include specialities like fried shrimp sold in plastic bags and 'one man thousand' (minute-fried fish). In Akosombo town, try the Kokoo-Ase Spot near the motor park for a drink or bite to eat. Aylo's Bay and the Volta Hotel have good restaurants. The **Maritime Club** (Volta Transport Club; mains C35,000), about 500m beyond Akosombo port, has a relaxing bar and restaurant.

## Getting There & Around

The main transport hub is at Kpong, on the Accra to Ho road 10km south of Atimpoku. Regular tro-tros travel between Kpong, Atimpoku and Akosombo. From Accra, tro-tros for Kpong/Akosombo (C30,000) leave from Tudu station. Alternatively, get any transport to Ho from Accra or to Accra or Kpong from Ho and get off at the suspension bridge at Atimpoku.

For details about the boat between Akosombo and Yeji, see p400.

Regular shared taxis leave the motor park in Akosombo for places in and around town. For the port, get one to 'Marine'.

## HO

☎ 091

Capitals sometimes aren't all they're cracked up to be; provincial ones near the border with Togo…well, even more so. While Ho, about 75km northeast of Akosombo, is the political and administrative seat of the Volta region, its appeal lays solely in its proximity to other more interesting and attractive destinations in the region. The city's backdrop, a range of hills with the distinctive Mt Adaklu to the south, is pleasant enough, and there are a few good hotels, but it's Ho's status as a transport hub that makes it the obvious base for exploring this region.

Ho's streets are long and things are spread fairly far apart, although the VanefSTC

## AKOSOMBO DAM

In 1915 an engineer, Albert Kison, realised that the Kwahu plateau was a rich bauxite deposit, that damming the Volta River at Akosombo could generate enough electricity for a huge foundry and that Tema could be converted into a deep-water port to export the aluminium. His conclusions gathered dust for 40 years until Nkrumah, keen to industrialise Ghana, picked up the idea. To finance the project, he had to accede to the harsh terms of Valco, the US company most interested in the project. Under these terms, in return for building the dam, Valco would receive over two-thirds of the electricity generated, at cost price, for its aluminium smelter at Tema for the foreseeable future.

The project proved so expensive that it was decided to import the necessary raw material for the foundry rather than to extract it from the Kwahu Plateau. Costs immediately escalated. Some 84,000 people had to be relocated – some of these people are still yet to be fully compensated today – and, at Tema, a new port and town had to be constructed. The dam was eventually inaugurated in 1966; a month later Nkrumah was gone, ousted by the military.

For years, the economy spiralled downward and Valco's savage terms allowed little potential for the country to earn money from power generation, realise the dam's potential for electrifying the country or irrigate nearby farmland. Only now, partly due to Valco's terms being renegotiated, is the country truly beginning to benefit, but the dam's full potential is still far from realised.

In 2005, after six of years of work funded by the Volta River Authority, the World Bank and the European Development Fund, the turbines at the dam were upgraded. Despite this work power outages throughout the country, including in Accra are by no means infrequent and while demand grows exponentially, the level of the lake continues to fall.

There's talk of a deal to harvest timber buried in the lake which is the cause of boating accidents and, maybe of more interest to potential investors, possibly worth tens of millions of dollars. Some also speculate that the lake is a treasure trove of other valuable minerals and even gold.

The dam is 124m high and 368m wide and can now generate (after upgrades) 1,012,000 KW. In theory there should be enough electricity to power most of Ghana plus export the remainder to Togo and Benin but ironically Ghana has even had to import power from Côte d'Ivoire during particularly severe droughts. Because of the earthquake risk, the dam is not built of solid concrete but has a central nucleus of clay covered by a layer of crushed rock and outer walls covered with huge boulders. Lake Volta, which flooded 850,000 hectares of land (7% of Ghana's land surface), stretches north from Akosombo for 402km.

---

bus station and main lorry park and the central market are next to one another, not too far from the Freedom Hotel.

## Information

There's a small **tourist office** ( ☎ 26560) on the fourth floor of an office complex next to the Goil petrol station on the Accra road. Barclays Bank is just down the road from here and has an ATM. For Internet access, try the New Image centre just down the road from Mother's Inn, or the business centre at the Freedom Hotel or Chances Hotel.

## Sleeping

**Freedom Hotel** ( ☎ 28158; www.freedomhotel-gh.com; r/chalets C250,000/450,000; P ⊠ 🔲 🛋 ) Because it's within walking distance of the market and lorry station, the Freedom Hotel on the Kpalimé road is the best choice in Ho.

The large and modern chalets are probably the best accommodation in town and the less expensive rooms in the main block are clean and well kept. There's a great pool and lounge area and bar out back. A restaurant is attached though the service is extremely slow. The best place in town to hang out is the rooftop lounge and bar with views over the road.

**Chances Hotel** ( ☎ 28344; r/chalets US$40/48; P ⊠ 🔲 🛋 ) On the Accra road about 3km before the centre, Chances is Ho's most upmarket hotel and worth the price if you get a room in one of the new annexes. The older rooms that surround a central courtyard are nothing special. There's a beautiful pool, a good restaurant (mains C40,000) and an Internet centre.

**Fiave Lodge** (r C70,000) On the Kpalimé road between the market and the Freedom Hotel, this is a small family-run guesthouse with a few rooms of varying quality, some with their own bathrooms. Meals are available upon request.

## Eating & Drinking

Around the motor park and the VanefSTC bus station on the main street are plenty of stalls selling tasty food. The Freedom and Chances hotels have the two best restaurants in Ho. Mother's Inn, on the southern outskirts of town just down the road from the Shell station, is a popular drinking spot and serves cheap, simple local food, as does Lord's Restaurant just off the main street near the junction with the Accra road, and the White House, a short way up the hill from the Hotel de Tarso.

## Getting There & Away

Ho's busy main lorry park is well organised. From here, regular tro-tros run between Ho and Hohoe (two hours) throughout the day. Other destinations include Accra, Amedzofe, Akatsi and Keta.

VanefSTC runs one ridiculously early bus a day (C40,000, four hours) between Ho and Accra, leaving from the VanefSTC station on the main street in Ho at 4am. In Accra, buses for Ho leave from the smaller VanefSTC bus station near Tudu station. Tro tros for Ho depart from the small terminal near Tema station.

Possibly the most comfortable public transport available in Ghana are the KTS minivans connecting Ho and Accra (C45,000, two hours). If only all the transportation in the country was like this… They leave when full from a little clearing on the left side of the Kpalimé road coming from the central market.

OSA has a daily bus from Ho to Kumasi via Koforidua, leaving from opposite the lorry park early in the morning.

## AROUND HO
### Mt Adaklu

The views from the top of this impressive mountain, about 12km south of Ho, are spectacular. Surrounded by nine villages, the Adaklu area is part of a community-based tourism project. At the visitor centre in the village of Helekpe at the foot of the mountain, you pay a fee of US$2 and are assigned a guide. It's a challenging two- to four-hour

climb return and you need appropriate footwear and plenty of water with you. There's a basic **guesthouse** (r US$1.70) in Helekpe or you can camp on the mountain. Tro-tros leave sporadically (but not on Sunday) for Helekpe (30 minutes) from the motor park in Ho; another place to pick up transport is on the Adaklu road just south of the town. Finding return transport can be difficult.

### Amedzofe

This mountain village is the main centre in the Avatime Hills, an area that offers breathtaking vistas, a waterfall, forests, cool climate and plenty of hiking opportunities. In Amedzofe there's a community-run **visitor centre** where you pay a flat fee of US$2 and can arrange hikes. Popular hikes include a 45-minute walk to Amedzofe Falls and a 30-minute walk to the summit of Mt Gemi (611m), one of the highest mountains in the area, where there is a 3.5m iron cross and stunning views. There's basic accommodation at the **Sun Lodge** (r C70,000) where you can also hire mountain bikes or you can arrange a homestay for about C40,000. Sun Lodge also has a campsite directly facing Mt Gemi.

Infrequent tro-tros head for Amedzofe (one hour) from the motor park station in Ho but transport of any kind is unlikely on a Sunday. If you're planning to head to Amedzofe from Hohoe, note that the route between Fume and Amedzofe (about 8km) is passable by foot only.

### Kpetoe

Kpetoe, a 15-minute tro-tro ride to the southeast of Ho, near the Togo border, is a major kente-weaving centre. The Ga-Adangbe people of this area claim to have introduced the art of kente weaving to the Ashanti. Two types of kente are woven: the Ashanti version and the Ewe version, which is more difficult to make.

### Tafi-Atome Monkey Sanctuary

At Tafi-Atome, about 25km north of Ho, the villagers have created a sanctuary around the village to protect the sacred Mona monkeys that live in the surrounding forest. The monkeys are used to humans and roam around the village like teenagers just released from school in the early morning and late afternoon. Admission and a guided tour of the sanctuary costs around C30,000.

You can hire a bicycle to visit other sites in the area or stay for drumming, dancing and storytelling sessions in the evening. Basic accommodation and meals are available at the guesthouse (C40,000 per person) or at the homestays for a negotiated fee.

Tafi-Atome is about 5km west of Logba Alakpeti on the main road between Ho and Hohoe. Any tro-tro running between Ho and Hohoe can drop you at Logba Alakpeti, from where you can either walk or wait for transport – infrequent except on market day.

## HOHOE
☎ 0935

The sound of silence you hear in Hohoe is people going about their everyday lives. For whatever reason, maybe because fewer foreigners make it here, there are no shouts of 'obroni', which is a welcome relief from other parts of the country. In this pleasant district capital you're likely to elicit nothing more than a friendly nod or smile, and it's this pleasant, laid-back vibe, the nearby Wli Falls and several good hotels in town that make Hohoe a preferable base to Ho for exploring the Volta region. It's also a staging point for travel across the border into Togo and north to Tamale via Bimbilla and Yendi.

### Orientation & Information
The action area of Hohoe (ho-we) is the Accra road, which becomes the road to Jasikan and Bimbilla as it heads north out of town. Along here, south to north, you'll find the motor park, market and **Ghana Tourism office** (Hohoe District Assembly building), a Mobil and Shell station, a Ghana Commercial Bank, Ghana Telecom and the post office. The road to Wli and the Togo border turns off the main road at the Bank of Ghana about 1km from the motor park; there's a Barclays Bank for changing money a short distance down this road. **Emmason Internet** (✉ 9am-9.30pm) is just around the corner from the post office on your left on the road to the Taste Lodge.

Better than the tourist office is **Tourcare International** (☎ 44735732; tourcare@freeghana.com) at Taste Lodge. They arrange day and overnight guided tours anywhere in the region.

### Sleeping & Eating
**Taste Lodge** (☎ 22023; fax 22025; r from C180,000; P 🛇) Highly recommended in part because of the friendly and helpful owner,

Florence Yaadra, this comfortable place has five rooms, all with their own small balconies opening onto a shady courtyard. A good restaurant is attached. To get to the Taste Lodge, walk north up the main street from the main lorry station for about 500m until you get to the post office and take the turn-off on the right. The Taste is just on the left, about 250m from the intersection.

**Evergreen Lodge** (☎ 22254; r C230,000; P 🛇) The Evergreen, a short way off the road heading north from town to Bimbilla, has the nicest and most modern rooms in town but little character. A nice restaurant with cable TV is attached.

**Pacific Guesthouse** (☎ 22146; r C150,000; 🛇) Down the same dirt road past the Taste Lodge, the Pacific is also a warm and friendly place comfortable with foreign travellers. Cheaper fan rooms are available and there's a nice lounge area and bar. Breakfast is included and other meals can be arranged.

**Geduld Hotel** (☎ 22177; r C100,000; 🛇) It's a bit of a walk into town but the Geduld, located further down the same road as the Taste Lodge and Pacific Gueshouse, has pleasant rooms in a two-storey home and a garden bar and restaurant.

**Matvin Hotel** (☎ 22134; r with fan and shared/private bathroom C69,000/92,000, r with air-con and private bathroom C150,000; P) This lonely complex on the northern outskirts of town, just before the Evergreen, possesses all the charm of a military checkpoint. Several life-size human statues dot the unkempt grounds and the rooms of various shapes and sizes are uniformly bad choices.

**Grand Hotel** (☎ 22053; r from C60,000) The Grand is the cheapest option in town and also the most central across from the Bank of Ghana. Basic rooms (shared bathrooms) are set around a concrete central courtyard and restaurant.

At night, you'll find a selection of food stalls along the main street, especially around the post office. There are also several good-value chop bars (all closed on Sunday) and lively evening drinking spots on the road to the Taste Lodge, near the Pacific Guesthouse and in the area around the Grand Hotel.

### Getting There & Away
VanefSTC buses leave Hohoe for Accra at the ungodly hour of 3am (C30,000, four hours) and from Accra at 3pm daily. Tro-

tros leave regularly throughout the day for Accra (C28,000, four hours), Ho (C15,000, one hour) and Akosombo (C20,000, 2½ hours). Tro-tros and shared taxis go to Wli Falls and the Togo border at Wli (C5000, 30 minutes). Heading north, tro-tros to Jasikan and Nkwanta (for Bimbilla and Tamale) leave from a stop on the Jasikan road, north of the post office. Tro-tros to Liati Wote (see right) leave from Fodome station in front of the post office.

## AROUND HOHOE
### Wli (Agumatsa) Falls
Nowhere else in Ghana will you feel so far from Accra and so close to sublime nature, even if there are benches and an outhouse nearby. After a scenic, undemanding 40-minute walk along a bubbling stream, it's hard not to gawk at the 40m-high cascade. Those aren't birds but an estimated half a million bats swirling around near the top of the horseshoe-shaped cliff. If the icy water isn't an obstacle you can swim in the shallow pool at the bottom of the falls. A hike to the upper falls is a more demanding 1½-hour climb and a guide is necessary.

These spectacular falls about 20km east of Hohoe are within the Agumatsa Wildlife Sanctuary. At the Wildlife Office in Wli (pronounced vlee) village, you pay a fee (adult/student C33,000/16,000, camera fee C3000); a guide is optional but not needed since it's fairly impossible to lose your way. Wli is an easy day trip from Hohoe, but if you want to stay overnight, you can camp near the falls (C15,000) or stay in Wli village at one of two hotels.

The **Waterfall Lodge** ( ☎ 0935-20057; www .ghanacamping.com; r C110,000), owned by Germans, is only a few hundred metres from the Wildlife Office, and is a great place to sleep after a day at the falls. There are only a few nice, modern rooms so do your best to make a reservation in advance, although this is difficult since the phone line rarely works. Tasty food is served indoors or in the pavilion on the lawn.

**Wli Water Heights Hotel** ( ☎ 833855; r C100,000) is past the turnoff for the falls and the Waterfall Lodge. It has comfortable and basic rooms and a restaurant, though it's not as well set up for travellers.

Regular tro-tros (40 minutes) and share taxis (C4500, 25 minutes) make the scenic run between Wli and Hohoe throughout the day. If you're heading for Togo, the Ghanaian border post is on the eastern side of Wli (turn left at the T-junction as you enter the village). From there, it's a 10-minute walk to the Togolese side.

### Liati Wote & Mt Afadjato
This pretty village, 21km south of Hohoe, lies on the foothills of Ghana's highest mountain, Mt Afadjato (885m; nearby Aduadu peak is really the highest point in Ghana, but isn't considered a mountain because the height difference between the base and the peak is too small). Liati Wote is part of another community-based ecotourism initiative – check in at the visitor centre when you arrive to pay your fees and arrange a hike. It's a reasonably challenging two-hour climb to the summit of Mt Afadjato, which offers stupendous views of Lake Volta and the countryside below. There are also a couple of easier walks, including to Tagbo Falls, a 45-minute hike from the village through coffee and cocoa fields. The surrounding forest is filled with fluttering butterflies. There's a small guesthouse and eatery in town. Tro-tros leave for Liati Wote (one hour) from Fodome station in Hohoe.

# THE CENTRE

This region is more than just the cultural heartland of the country and the historic centre of the Ashanti. Besides Kumasi, which is the historic seat of royalty, a major urban centre and the transport hub of the region, there are rural areas, villages and forests, handicrafts, butterflies and monkeys all within striking distance. Kumasi marks the tip of the triangle linking Takoradi and Accra in a popular travel circuit. There are several flights daily linking it with Accra.

## KUMASI
☎ 051 / pop 1 million
Most people who spend time in Ghana hold a certain amount of affection for Kumasi. Once the capital of the rich and powerful Ashanti kingdom, today it's a bustling multiethnic metropolis. Founded in 1695, little remains of the original city that was razed by the British in 1874 during the Fourth Ashanti War. Unlike Accra, Kumasi, which

GHANA

spills over a series of hills, has a clearly demarcated centre, ground zero being an enormous throbbing daily market. The demographic complexity of the city may not be obvious at first glance but the city is a patchwork of ethnic neighbourhoods. Almost half the residents are Muslims and almost half speak Hausa, a language originating in Nigeria; some speak Dagwamba, from the north near Tamale.

## Orientation

Kumasi sprawls over a vast hilly area. The heart of town is Kejetia Circle, a vast traffic-clogged roundabout. On the eastern side of the circle is Kejetia Market, which spills over onto the roads around it. West of the circle is the vast Kejetia motor park, the city's main transport park. South of the circle, the parallel Guggisberg and Fuller Rds lead past the train station. The district of Adum, just south of the circle, is the modern commercial district, where you'll find the major banks and shops. The VanefSTC bus station is on the southern edge of this district, a 10-minute walk from Prempeh II Roundabout.

## Information

### INTERNET ACCESS
**Easylink Internet** ( 9am-11pm) Across from the Alliance Française.
**Internet Link** (Prempeh II Rd) Just down the street from Vic Baboo's Café.
**Shell Internet** (per hr C10,500; 7am-9pm) Entrance around back of station.
**Unic Internet** (per hr C6000; 7.30am-8.30pm) Next to the British Council.

### MEDICAL SERVICES
Pharmacies are dotted around town.
**Okomfo Anokye Teaching Hospital** (Bantama Rd) A large complex near the National Culture Centre; Kumasi's main public hospital.

### MONEY
All banks listed here change traveller's cheques and have ATMs. There are also several forexes for changing cash.
**Barclays Bank head office** (Prempeh II Roundabout)
**Ecobank** (Harper Rd)
**Garden City Forex Bureau** (Harper Rd) Has the best rates around.
**Ghana Commercial Bank** (Harper Rd)
**Stanbic Bank** (Harper Rd)

**Standard Chartered Bank head office** (Prempeh II Roundabout)

### POST
**Main post office** (Stewart Ave; 8am-5pm Mon-Fri) Opposite the Armed Forces Museum. Poste restante shuts at 4.30pm.

### TOURIST INFORMATION
**Tourist office** ( 26243; 7am-5pm Mon-Fri) In the National Cultural Centre complex. Staff can help arrange guided tours of the city and surrounding villages.

## Sights
### KEJETIA MARKET
From afar, the Kejetia Market looks like an alien mothership landed in the centre of Kumasi. Closer up, the rusting tin roofs of this huge market, often cited as the largest in West Africa, look like a circular shantytown. But once you take a breath and step down into its interior, it's infinitely disorienting but also throbbing with life and commerce. Watch your step, often over unused railroad tracks, in the narrow alleyways selling everything from foodstuffs, second-hand shoes, clothes and plastic knick-knacks to kente cloth, glass beads, Ashanti sandals, batik and bracelets. You may also see fetish items, such as vulture heads, parrot wings and dried chameleons.

Kente cloth, made locally, is a particularly good deal here. It's usually sold in standard lengths of 12m and price varies according to the composition of the material (cloth containing a mixture of cotton, silk and rayon is more expensive than all-cotton, for example) and weave (double weave is, naturally, more expensive than single). You can get cloth made up cheaply and expertly into whatever you want by dressmakers in the market.

### NATIONAL CULTURAL CENTRE
This **complex** (admission free; 8am-5pm) is set within spacious grounds and includes a model Ashanti village; craft workshops where you can see brassworking, woodcarving, pottery making, batik cloth dyeing and kente cloth weaving; a gallery and crafts shop; the regional library; the tourism office; and the small Prempeh II Jubilee Museum. The craft workshops aren't always active, especially on Sunday, and it's all rather low-key, but the grounds are shady and it's an agreeable place to spend a few hours including lunch at the restaurant in the complex.

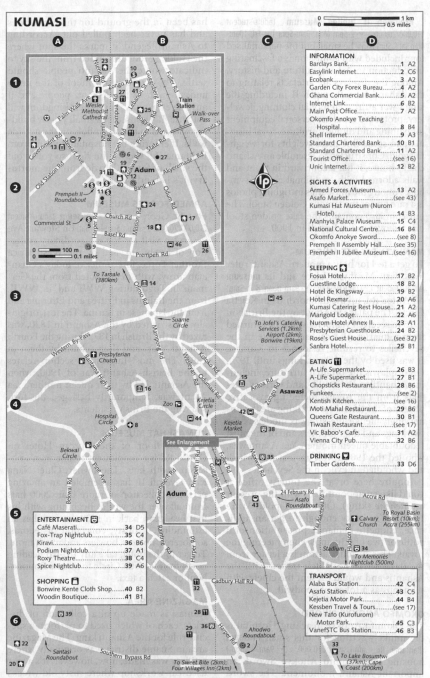

# KUMASI

0 ───── 1 km
0 ───── 0.5 miles

**INFORMATION**
Barclays Bank.....................1 A2
Easylink Internet.................2 C6
Ecobank............................3 A2
Garden City Forex Bureau.....4 A2
Ghana Commercial Bank.......5 A2
Internet Link......................6 B2
Main Post Office.................7 A2
Okomfo Anokye Teaching
  Hospital..........................8 B4
Shell Internet.....................9 A3
Standard Chartered Bank.....10 B1
Standard Chartered Bank.....11 A2
Tourist Office.................(see 16)
Unic Internet.....................12 B2

**SIGHTS & ACTIVITIES**
Armed Forces Museum..........13 A2
Asafo Market..................(see 43)
Kumasi Hat Museum (Nurom
  Hotel)............................14 B3
Manhyia Palace Museum.......15 C4
National Cultural Centre.......16 B4
Okomfo Anokye Sword......(see 8)
Prempeh II Assembly Hall....(see 35)
Prempeh II Jubilee Museum..(see 16)

**SLEEPING**
Fosua Hotel......................17 B2
Guestline Lodge................18 B2
Hotel de Kingsway............19 B2
Hotel Rexmar...................20 A6
Kumasi Catering Rest House....21 A2
Marigold Lodge................22 A6
Nurom Hotel Annex II.........23 A1
Presbyterian Guesthouse......24 B2
Rose's Guest House.........(see 32)
Sanbra Hotel....................25 B1

**EATING**
A-Life Supermarket............26 B3
A-Life Supermarket............27 B1
Chopsticks Restaurant........28 B6
Funkees........................(see 2)
Kentish Kitchen.............(see 16)
Moti Mahal Restaurant........29 B6
Queens Gate Restaurant......30 B1
Tiwaah Restaurant..........(see 17)
Vic Baboo's Cafe...............31 A2
Vienna City Pub.................32 B6

**DRINKING**
Timber Gardens.................33 D6

**ENTERTAINMENT**
Café Maserati...................34 D5
Fox-Trap Nightclub............35 C4
Kiravi............................36 B6
Podium Nightclub..............37 A1
Roxy Theatre...................38 C4
Spice Nightclub................39 A6

**SHOPPING**
Bonwire Kente Cloth Shop....40 B2
Woodin Boutique..............41 B1

**TRANSPORT**
Alaba Bus Station..............42 C4
Asafo Station...................43 C5
Kejetia Motor Park............44 B4
Kessben Travel & Tours.....(see 17)
New Tafo (Kurofurom)
  Motor Park.....................45 C3
VanefSTC Bus Station.........46 B3

GHANA

0 ───── 100 m
0 ───── 0.1 miles

To Tamale
(380km)

To Jofel's Catering
Services (1.2km);
Airport (2km);
Bonwire (19km)

Suame
Circle

Western By-Pass

Presbyterian
Church

Zoo

Kejetia
Circle

Asawasi

Kejetia
Market

Hospital
Circle

Bekwai
Circle

See Enlargement

Adum

24 February Rd
Asafo
Roundabout

Accra Rd

Calvary
Church

To Royal Basin
Resort (10km);
Accra (255km)

Stadium

To Memories
Nightclub (500km)

Cadbury Hall Rd

Ahodwo
Roundabout

Santasi
Roundabout

Southern Bypass Rd

To Sweet Bite (2km);
Four Villages Inn (2km)

To Lake Bosumtwi
(37km); Cape
Coast (200km)

**Prempeh II Jubilee Museum** (adult/student C10,000/20,000; 2-5pm Mon, 9am-5pm Tue-Fri, 10am-4pm Sat & Sun) may be small but the personalised tour included with admission is a fascinating introduction to Ashanti culture and history. Among the displays are artefacts relating to the Ashanti king Prempeh II including the king's war attire, ceremonial clothing, jewellery, protective amulets, personal equipment for bathing and dining, furniture, royal insignia and some fine brass weights for weighing gold. Constructed to resemble an Ashanti chief's house, it has a courtyard in front and walls adorned with traditional carved symbols. Among the museum's intriguing photos is a rare one of the famous Golden Stool. The museum also contains the fake golden stool handed over to the British in 1900.

### MANHYIA PALACE MUSEUM

To get a feel for how a modern Ashanti ruler lives, visit Manhyia Palace and its **museum** (adult/student C20,000/10,000; 9am-noon & 1-5pm) off Antoa Rd, up the hill north from Kejetia Circle. The palace was built by the British in 1925 to receive Prempeh I when he returned from a quarter of a century of exile in the Seychelles to resume residence in Kumasi. It was used by the Ashanti kings until 1974. On display is the original furniture, including Ashantiland's first TV, and various artefacts from the royals, including evocative photos of the time. More striking are the unnervingly lifelike, life-size wax models of the two kings and their mothers and of the most redoubtable queen mother, Yaa Asantewaa, who led the 1900 revolt against the British and who died in exile in the Seychelles.

Inquire here or at the tourist office if you'd like an appointment with the present *asantehene* (king), Otumfuo Opoku Ware II. If you're lucky enough to get an audience, etiquette demands presentation of a bottle or two of schnapps when meeting the royals. This curious custom is a legacy from the days when the Dutch traded with the Ashantis and would present the chiefs with schnapps as a token of goodwill.

### OKOMFO ANOKYE SWORD

The Okomfo Anokye Teaching Hospital is the unlikely setting for this small **museum** (Bantama Rd; admission C10,000; 9am-4.30pm) housing the Okomfo Anokye Sword, an important Ashanti monument. The sword has been in the ground for three centuries and has never been pulled out. According to Ashanti legend, it marks the spot where the Golden Stool descended from the sky to indicate where the Ashanti people should settle. The sword is a symbol of the unity and strength of the Ashanti people and if anyone ever pulls it out, their kingdom will collapse. It's housed in a small yellow building with red Ashanti symbols on the outside walls. If entering the hospital grounds from Bantama Rd, veer to the right so you avoid the smell of formaldehyde from the mortuary; it's behind Block C.

### ARMED FORCES MUSEUM

Fort St George and its **museum** (adult/student C10,000/20,000; 8am-5pm Tue-Sat) on Stewart Ave deserve a visit for the extraordinary collection of booty amassed by the West Africa Frontier Force, forerunner of today's Ghanaian army, with items looted from the Germans in Togo during WWI and, in WWII, from the Italians in Eritrea and Ethiopia and from the Japanese in Burma. The fort, originally constructed by the Ashanti in 1820, was razed by the British in 1873 during the Fourth Ashanti War, and then rebuilt by them in 1896. The most interesting section relates to the British-Ashanti war of 1900, when the Ashanti, led by their queen mother, Yaa Asantewaa, temporarily besieged the fort, starving the British residents.

### KUMASI HAT MUSEUM

The top floor of the Nurom Hotel on Ofinso Rd is a monument to one man's obsession with hats. The owner, Chief Nana Kofi Gyemfi II, has assembled an amazing personal collection of more than 2000 hats from all over the world. Beginning with his first headgear, back in 1928, he now has an astounding, if dusty, collection of fedoras, sombreros, boaters, bowlers and much more. To get to the hotel, take any tro-tro heading north from Kejetia Circle to Suame Roundabout or catch a taxi.

### MAGAZINE AREA

Kumasi is made up of a collection of districts, each of which used to perform a specific role for the Ashanti king. The Magazine area in Suame district was originally where artillery was made; now, however, it's a vast used-car workshop where rusty old wrecks are miraculously brought back to life. Piles and piles of rusting engine parts line the sides of the roads and the air is filled with the chinking sound of metal hitting metal. It's an amazing sight, worth a look as you pass through on your way north.

## Festivals & Events

The 42-day cycle of the Ashanti religious calendar is marked by Adae festivals, a public ceremony involving the *asantehene*. The tourist office has a list of exact dates. The **Odwira festival** is an important annual celebration. For more details, see the boxed text, below.

## Sleeping

### BUDGET

**Guestline Lodge** ( ☎ 23351; mahesh161us@yahoo.com; r C150,000-270,000; ⊠ ▣ ) There's no better place in Kumasi for independent travellers on a budget. The VanefSTC station is a block away, there's Internet access and there's a relaxing and sunny courtyard where you can read and order meals to be delivered from Vic Baboo's café, which is owned by the same friendly Indian family. Look first before deciding on a room since they vary in quality, size and appeal. Some are carpeted, some have tiles and others have concrete floors. Dorm rooms are available. It's a three-storey old white building with star decorations along the side.

**Sanbra Hotel** ( ☎ 31256; Bogyawi St; r C160,000-270,000; ⒫ ⊠ ) Even with the daytime chaos on this street, the Sanbra is easy to spot because of the flags from countries around the world flying from the first floor. Popular with Ghanaians because of its restaurant as much as for its clean but basic tiled-floor rooms; some of the more expensive rooms even have small balconies.

**Hotel de Kingsway** ( ☎ 26228; r with fan/air-con from C108,000/125,000) This slightly depressing hotel occupies most of an entire block in the centre of Kumasi. The old rooms and bathrooms are remarkably large.

**Presbyterian Guesthouse** ( ☎ 23879; Mission Rd; r C80,000; ⒫ ) This two-storey colonial-style guesthouse is all deep wooden balconies

---

### ADAE & ODWIRA FESTIVALS

On the day before Adae, horn-blowers and drummers assemble at the chief's house and play until late at night. Early next morning, the chief's head musician goes to the stool house where the sacred stools are kept and he drums loudly. Eventually the chief arrives and he and his elders go into the stool house to ask their forefathers for guidance. Ritual food of mashed yam, eggs and chicken is then brought into the room; the chief places portions on each of the sacred stools inside. A sheep is sacrificed and the blood is smeared on the stools. The sheep is then roasted and offerings of meat are placed on each stool. The queen mother prepares *fufu* (mashed cassava, plantain or yam) and places some on the stools.

A bell is sounded, indicating that the spirits are eating. Gin or schnapps is poured over the stools and the rest is passed around. When the ritual is over, the chief retires to the courtyard and the merrymaking begins; drums beat and horns blast. The chief dons his traditional dress with regalia and sits in court, receiving the homage of his subjects. On some occasions, he is then borne in public in a palanquin shaded by a huge canopy, and accompanied by lesser chiefs.

On Monday, the path to the royal mausoleum is cleared. On Tuesday, the ban on eating the new yam is lifted and tubers are paraded through the streets while the chief sexton proceeds to the royal mausoleum with sheep and rum to invoke the Odwira spirit. He then returns to the chief and is blessed. Wednesday is a day of mourning and fasting. People wear sepia-coloured attire and red turbans and there's lots of drinking and drumming all day long. Thursday is for feasting. Ritual food, including yam *fufu*, is borne in a long procession from the royal house to a shrine where it's presented to the ancestors. That night, when the gong strikes, everyone must go indoors; no-one but the privileged few may see the procession of the dead, when the sacred stools are borne to the stream for their yearly ceremonial cleansing.

The climax is Friday, when the chief holds a great durbar, a grand meeting, at which all the sub chiefs and his subjects come to pay their respects. The highlight is a great procession of elegantly dressed chiefs, the principal ones being borne on palanquins and covered by multi-coloured umbrellas.

and high ceilings. The huge rooms are basic but quiet and you get use of a kitchen. It's possible to camp here if the rooms are full. One room with bathroom costs C150,000.

**Nurom Hotel Annex II** ( ☎ 32324; Nsene Rd; r C70,000) This hotel close to the Kejetia Market and lorry station can be noisy, and the rooms are only about as nice as at the Presbyterian, but it's clean and friendly.

### MIDRANGE

**Fosua Hotel** ( ☎ 37382; www.fosuahotel.com; r C350,000; P ☒ ☐ ) This is the highest quality place to stay in the city centre. Occupying the top floor of the Aseda Complex a block from the VanefSTC station, the rooms here are clean and comfortable though each has a strange, small-glassed in space facing out in lieu of a balcony. There's a forex bureau, travel agency, bar and restaurant in the same complex.

**Marigold Lodge** ( ☎ 38756; www.marigoldlodge .com; s/d incl breakfast C360,000/450,000; ☒ P ) This lodge is in a quiet compound in the south of town. It has simple well-kept rooms with cable TV.

**Kumasi Catering Rest House** ( ☎ 26506; Government Rd; r with fan/air-con C200,000/450,000; P ) This charming guesthouse set within shady grounds a short walk from the centre seems engaged in a single-handed attempt to bring '70s-style furniture back into fashion. The rooms are huge and the bathrooms need their own zip code. Also on site is a popular restaurant with a large menu (mains C35,000).

**Rose's Guest House** ( ☎ 32594; Harper Rd; r C300,000; P ☒ ) Within stumbling distance of the Vienna City Pub on the same grounds, Rose's offers several large and clean tiled-floor rooms. More expensive executive rooms have carpeting and cable TV.

### TOP END

**Hotel Rexmar** ( ☎ 29111; rexmar@idngh.com; s/d incl breakfast US$76/90; P ☒ ☐ ☒ ) Considering the price, rooms at this low rise hotel complex south of the Ahodwo Circle, aren't exactly luxurious but you do get a private porch and access to one of Kumasi's nicest pools. There's a good restaurant attached.

**Four Villages Inn** ( ☎ 22682; www.fourvillages .com; Old Bekwai Rd; s/d US$60/70; P ☒ ) Several kilometres south of the centre is this bed and breakfast, equally popular for its four comfortable individually designed rooms each with high ceilings and homey décor, as

for the guide and transport services offered. Throw in a garden, a terrace, an indoor atrium and breakfast with real brewed coffee and you'll feel like family.

**Royal Basin Resort** ( ☎ 60144; www.royalbasin resort.com; s/d US$60/70; P ☒ ☒ ) Next to the US Peace Corps compound 10km east of the city, the Royal Basin is nothing special in terms of design or furnishings but it has clean, modern simple rooms and the pool area (nonguests C35,000) in the back is a pleasant place to escape the heat. Restaurant attached.

## Eating

For food stalls, good areas are near the train station, around Kejetia Circle and on the Hudson Rd side of the stadium. There are several small chop bars along Prempeh II Rd, including the aptly named Quick Bite Fast Food.

**Vic Baboo's Cafe** (Prempeh II Rd; mains C20,000-50,000; ☒ from 11am; ☒ ) Almost every foreigner in Kumasi ends up at this café on one of the busiest intersections. It has the biggest cocktail menu in the city, milkshakes, and Indian, Chinese and Ghanaian dishes plus sandwiches and pizza, with several veggie options. It also has ice cream, cashew nuts and popcorn. Last order taken around 9pm. There are plans to open an Internet café here.

**Queens Gate Restaurant** (Prempeh II Rd; mains C40,000) There's no better spot for people watching in Kumasi than the third floor balcony at the Queens Gate. The indoor dining room with big screen cable TV usually tuned to African soaps is equally pleasant and one of the few city centre dinner options. Everything from omelettes to soups, salads, burgers and Ghanaian dishes are served.

**Sanbra Hotel Restaurant** (Bogyawi Rd; mains C45,000; ☒ ) As far as the centre of Kumasi goes, this restaurant in the hotel of the same name deserves several Michelin stars. The waiters are uniformed and it has a huge menu with European, Chinese, Ghanaian, seafood, pizza, lobster, sandwiches etc.

**Moti Mahal Restaurant** (mains C40,000-90,000; ☒ ) One of the most expensive restaurants in Kumasi, with a large selection of Indian cuisine; because everything is a la carte the bill can add up. It's off the Southern Bypass Rd – some taxi drivers know where it is.

**Vienna City Pub** (Harper Rd; ⚹) This place, formerly Ryan's Irish Pub, is home sweet home for many expats who can wash away their nostalgia with the pool table, foosball, darts, Guinness and other imported beers, wines and mixed drinks. Snacks, sandwiches and pizza (C40,000) too. On the grounds of Rose's Guest House.

**Sweet Bite** (Ahodwo Main Rd; mains C30,000-90,000; ⚹) It's worth a trip out to Sweet Bite, several kilometres south of Ahodwo Circle, for good Lebanese food like shwarma, falafel, hummus and tabbouleh. Other options like burgers and seafood are on the menu.

**Funkees** (mains C35,000) This little place with outdoor seating is in the minimall across from the Alliance Française and is known for its woodfire pizza and kebabs. There's a good wine shop above the restaurant.

**Tiawaah Restaurant** (mains C30,000-65,000; ⚹) You may catch the staff sleeping at this modern restaurant on the third floor of the Aseda Complex, a block from the VanefSTC station. It has a wide selection of Ghanaian, Chinese and continental cuisine. KPS World Enterprise Coffee Shop is on the second floor of the same complex.

**Chopsticks Restaurant** (Harper Rd; mains C35,000) Looking like the remains of a restaurant, Chopsticks is only a few outdoor tables with plastic chairs serving standard Chinese dishes and delicious large pizzas (C10,000).

**Kentish Kitchen** (mains C15,000-30,000; ⚐ breakfast-6pm) Really only worth a visit if you're already at the National Cultural Centre complex, Kentish is a small outdoor eatery serving a small selection of basic Ghanaian fare.

### SELF-CATERING
Self-caterers can find basic provisions at the food shops along Prempeh II Rd. The best supermarket is the A-Life chain, which has three stores in town, including a branch on Prempeh II Rd and another only two blocks from the STC station.

## Drinking
Popular drinking spots include **Vienna City Pub**, especially on weekend nights; **Jofel's Catering Services** (Zongo Rd), which has live music on Saturday; **Vic Baboo's Café**, where foreign travellers go for its extensive cocktail menu; and **Timber Gardens**, at the junction of Lake Rd and Southern Bypass Rd, which is a lively outdoor spot for a drink or a bite to eat.

## Entertainment
Several clubs still endure like the **Podium Nightclub** (Nsene Rd) in the centre, a nightclub on Wednesday to Saturday evening. The **Fox-Trap Nightclub** (Maxwell Rd), next to Prempeh Assembly Hall and attached to the studio of a local radio station, has a DJ and disco, and the classy **Kiravi** (Harper Rd) near Chopsticks is a disco Saturday nights. The DJ at **Café Maserati** (Hudson Rd) plays hip-hop and R&B on Wednesday and Friday nights, otherwise you can always get a drink at the outdoor tables, and **Memories Nightclub** is open Wednesday to Sunday nights as is **Spice Nightclub** (Bantama Rd) just north of the Santasi Roundabout.

For a real taste of local Kumasi head to the **Roxy Theatre**, an old cinema showing schlock near Zongo St in the Muslim section of the city.

## Shopping
For high-quality locally produced textiles try the **Bonwire Kente Cloth Shop** (Bank Rd), a little hole-in-the wall near Prempeh II Roundabout or **Woodin Boutique** a block from the train tracks and Kejetia Market.

## Getting There & Away
### AIR
Kumasi airport is on the northeastern outskirts of town, about 5km from the centre Citilink and Antrak have flights between Kumasi and Accra twice a day (one way around C570,000). For information and reservations, go to the airport or to **Kessben Travel & Tours** ( ☎ 37350; kessbenlcc.co.uk) on the second floor of the Aseda Complex. Antrak and American Airlines share an office on Harper Rd though opening hours are unreliable.

### BUS & TRO-TRO
The huge Kejetia motor park is the city's main transport hub, from where you can get tro-tros to most regional destinations as well as non-VanefSTC buses to Accra and other points south. Despite major renovations, the motor park is still confusing to navigate; try to look for signs with destinations posted. In addition, transport for Accra (again), Sunyani, Cape Coast, Takoradi and local destinations such as Lake Bosumtwi leave from Asafo station east of Asafo Roundabout.

Large buses to Tamale, Bolgatanga, Bawku and Ouagadougou (Burkina Faso) leave from

GHANA

New Tafo (Kurofurom) station in Dichemso, about 2km north of Kejetia market. Smaller buses to Tamale (again) and destinations in the Upper West region leave from Alaba bus station off Zongo Rd, on the northwestern side of the market. The **VanefSTC bus station** ( ☎ 24285) is on Prempeh Rd. Buses to Accra (ordinary/luxury C46,000/65,000, four hours) leave regularly between 3.30am and 5pm. VanefSTC buses also pass through Cape Coast (C65,000, four hours, ☺ 4am, 10am and 4pm) on their way to Takoradi (C65,000, five hours). There are two buses a day to Tamale (C90,000, eight hours, ☺ 7am and 5pm). There are less frequent services to Alfao and Tema. STC services Ouagadougou (C195,000, ☺ 5pm Monday, Wednesday, Saturday and Sunday) from Kumasi. Includes an additional charge in CFAs.

**TRAIN**

For details of the train service to Takoradi and Accra, see p402.

### Getting Around

Most taxi lines start at Kejetia motor park and across the street at the intersection of Prempeh II and Guggisberg Rds. From Ntomin Rd, shared taxis head south along Harper Rd, serving the areas of town beyond Ahodwo Roundabout. The standard fare is about C2000. A 'dropping' taxi normally costs about C8000 within town; to the airport around C20,000. Taxis are often reluctant to cross Kejetia Circle (because the traffic is so bad) so consider breaking a long journey into shorter stages.

To visit a number of villages surrounding Kumasi it makes sense to charter a taxi for a half day (C75,000) or full day (C200,000).

An alternative to hiring a taxi for the day, **Dodi Travel & Tours** ( ☎ 20421; www.dodighana.com; Hudson Rd, Kumasi) based at the Hotel de Texas, is a dependable place to hire a car. Small to medium vehicles are US$55 per day.

## AROUND KUMASI
### Craft Villages

Because of their proximity to Kumasi, the craft villages in the region offer a convenient if also touristy way to experience how some of Ghana's traditional workshops operate.

There are two villages just on the outskirts of Kumasi, on the Mampong road beyond Suame Roundabout. Pankrono, 8km away, is a major pottery centre. One kilometre further is Ahwiaa, known for its woodcarving and an aggressive sales approach. Ntonso, 15km further, is the centre of *adinkra* cloth printing. Bonwire, 18km northeast of Kumasi, is the most famous of several nearby villages that specialise in weaving kente cloth. At the visitor centre here weavers demonstrate their craft and sell their wares.

Other less visited kente villages include Wonoo and Adanwomase, near Bonwire, and, further north, Bepoase. Several villages northwest of Kumasi on the Barekese road specialise in bead-making, including Asuofia and Pasoro.

The easiest way to visit these villages is probably to hire a private taxi (about US$25 for a full day) with or without the additional services of one of the 'guides' who mostly hang out in front of Vic Baboo's Café. Some of these young men are sincere and knowledgeable, some aren't. **Nasir Abubakar** ( ☎ 0243-978270) is a freelance guide who comes recommended. You can also arrange a tour through the Kumasi tourist office. Less convenient, especially if you want to make a number of stops in one day, you can get a tro-tro from Kejetia motor park for the villages on the Mampong road or from Antoa station for Bonwire.

### Owabi Wildlife Sanctuary

For butterflies and birds, maybe a Mona monkey or two, visit this small **sanctuary** (admission C20,000; ☺ 9am-5pm) 16km northwest of Kumasi, just off the Sunyani road. It's a pristine forest crossed with several footpaths around the Owabi reservoir. You have to be accompanied by a guide, which you can arrange at the entrance gate. Take a tro-tro from Kejetia motor park to Akropong on the Sunyani road, from where it's a 3km walk.

### Ejisu

The small junction town of Ejisu, about 20km east of Kumasi on the Accra road, is home to the **Nana Yaa Asantewaa Museum** (admission C10,000; ☺ 9am-5pm), built in the form of a traditional queen mother's palace. It houses a fascinating display of artefacts from the life of Yaa Asantewaa, the queen mother and chief of Ejisu. She's most remembered for resisting British rule and for preventing the revered Golden Stool from falling into their hands. Also recommended is a visit to the **shrine** (admission C10,000; 9am-5pm) at nearby Besease. This was the shrine Yaa Asantewaa consulted before launching her attack against the British. Inside is an excellent display on traditional Ashanti shrines. There are a number of other harder-to-get-to shrines in the area that see few tourists.

Regular tro-tros to Ejisu (30 minutes) leave from Asafo motor park in Kumasi. The museum is about 1.5km from the motor park in Ejisu and Besease is about 2km further along the Accra road. You can either walk or get a dropping taxi.

## Lake Bosumtwi

For a break from the bustle and choking pollution of Kumasi, take a trip to tranquil Lake Bosumtwi, 38km southeast of Kumasi. A crater lake, it's ringed by lush green hills in which you can hike, visiting some of the 20 or so small villages around its perimeter. The lake is a popular weekend venue for Kumasi residents, who come here to relax, swim (the water is said to be bilharzia-free), fish and take boat trips. You can cycle around the lake's 30km circumference. One downside is the high level of hassle in Abonu, the lakeside village.

Not only is Bosumtwi the country's largest and deepest natural lake (86m deep in the centre), it's also sacred. The Ashanti believe that their souls come here after death to bid farewell to their god Twi. One interesting taboo is any form of dugout canoe, which is believed to alienate the lake spirit. Instead the fishermen head out on specially carved wooden planks, which they paddle either with their palms or with calabashes cupped in their hands.

### SLEEPING & EATING

It's possible to stay in basic rooms in Abonu – you'll likely be accosted by locals offering you accommodation as soon as you set foot in town. If you ask the local chief for permission in advance you can camp beside the lake.

**Lake Point Guesthouse** ( 220054; r C170,000) This highly recommended guesthouse, owned by a Ghanaian and Austrian couple, is set on landscaped grounds that lead down to the lakeshore a few kilometres from Abona. The spacious and clean rooms are in freestanding bungalows. Bicycle tours and meals can be arranged.

**Paradise Resort** ( 20022; frontdesk@lakeboso mtweresort.com; s/d US$45/50; ) You're mostly paying extra for air-con and cable TV at this resort, also set on the lake's edge. The rooms are modern and have nice views and there's a restaurant and bar area on the lakefront.

### GETTING THERE & AWAY

Occasional tro-tros run direct to Abonu (C10,000) from Asafo motor park in Kumasi; alternatively, take a tro-tro to Kuntanase (C5000, 45 minutes) and a passenger taxi from there (C15,000, 15 minutes).

## Bobiri Forest Reserve

This reserve protects a parcel of virgin, unlogged forest about 35km east of Kumasi. The main goal for visitors is **Bobiri Butterfly Sanctuary** (admission C10,000), home to more than 300 species of butterfly and an arboretum. Even if you don't see any butterflies, this is a serene and beautiful place to relax. Guided walks of varying length are available or you can hike unaccompanied on some of the trails. The guesthouse at the sanctuary is better than many and each fan room with wood floors (C50,000) has a painted wall mural. Simple meals are available.

From Kumasi or Ejisu, take any vehicle going to Konongo or further south, and ask to be dropped at Kubease, from where Bobiri is a pleasant 3km walk.

## BOABENG-FIEMA MONKEY SANCTUARY

This **sanctuary** (admission C40,000), a superb example of community-based conservation, is between the twin villages of Fiema and Boabeng, 165km north of Kumasi. The villagers have traditionally venerated and protected the black-and-white colobus and Mona monkeys that live in the surrounding forest, and in 1975 passed a law making it illegal to harm them. Maybe conscious of their status outside the law, the monkeys shamelessly roam the streets scavenging for food from the villagers.

You can go on guided walks through the forest and there's a simple, concrete six-room **guesthouse** (d C60,000) in Fiema; camping is also possible here.

From Kumasi, take a tro-tro to Techiman from Alaba station. From there, take a shared taxi to Nkoranza, 25km east. There are regular passenger taxis from Nkoranza to Fiema, about 20km away.

## YEJI

One of the main port towns on Lake Volta and the last stop for the Lake Volta ferry, Yeji is 216km northeast of Kumasi on the old Tamale road. There's nothing to keep you here but if you have to stay overnight, you can get basic accommodation in town for about C40,000.

Tro-tros run between Yeji and Antoa station in Kumasi (four hours). For Tamale, take the twice-daily ferry (45 minutes) across to Makongo on the east bank. Tro-tros run between Makongo and Tamale (five hours).

For details of the ferry service to Akosombo, see p400.

# THE NORTH

This region, the largest in the country, rewards those with time and patience. It includes Mole National Park, the best place to see large wildlife in the country and several other community projects offering off-the-beaten-track experiences. The traditional round huts that most villagers live in, and the well-ordered geometric plots of cultivated land, are quite beautiful from the air but on the ground things are fairly flat, monotonous and sparsely vegetated. While it's generally drier than the south of the country there's still enough rainfall to make it the breadbasket of the country.

Antrak currently flies between Accra and Tamale, which saves you the long 611km car journey. Some overlanders cross over from Burkina Faso.

## TAMALE

☎ 071

What distinguishes this hot, dusty regional capital from others of its ilk is that bicycles are everywhere and add another feature to the ubiquitous games of vehicular chicken. Tamale, 380km north of Kumasi, is the fourth-largest city in Ghana and the major transport hub for the north. It tends to be a stopover for travellers on their way to Mole or overland to Burkina Faso but the presence of several good-value hotels make it a good base to explore other spots in the

area. The water supply and electricity can be erratic.

The heart of town is the cramped and bustling central market and motor park, marked by the tall radio antenna near the VanefSTC bus station. The **National Cultural Centre**, off Salaga Rd, has an echoing auditorium where music and dance performances are occasionally put on; there are a bunch of craft shops around the back that rarely see shoppers.

## Information

### INTERNET ACCESS

**Agric Internet Café** (per hr C6000) Conveniently located close to several guesthouses.

**CVL Internet** (per hr C8000; ☾ 6am-10pm) On the second floor in the back of the building.

**First Class Link Internet Café** (Bolgatanga Rd)

**Forsumel Internet Café** (Salaga (Hospital Rd)

**My.com Internet Café** ( ☾ 8am-11.30pm) Directly across from Relax Lodge.

### MONEY

Man Forex Bureau is one of the only ones in town although the exchange rate at the Gariba Lodge is better.

**Barclays Bank** (Salaga Rd) Near the Giddipass Restaurant. Has an ATM.

**Standard Chartered Bank** (Salaga Rd) Opposite the market. Has an ATM.

### TOURIST INFORMATION

**Tourist office** ( ☎ 24835; ☾ 9am-5pm Mon-Fri) About 1.5km east of the centre, in the administration buildings.

### TRAVEL AGENCIES

**M&J Travel & Tours** ( ☎ 26529) Next to offices for Uniglobe Travel & Tours and DHL, can book Antrak flights.

## Festivals & Events

The **Dagomba Fire Festival** takes place in July. According to legend a chief lost his son and was overjoyed when he found him asleep under a tree. Angry that the tree had hidden his son, he punished it by having it burnt. On the night of the festival young men rush about with blazing torches.

## Sleeping

### BUDGET

**Catholic Guesthouse** ( ☎ 22265; Gumbihini Rd; r C70,000; P ☒ ) This is the kind of find backpackers tell other backpackers about. There are no top sheets, no bath towels and no luxury, but who needs it at this price. The

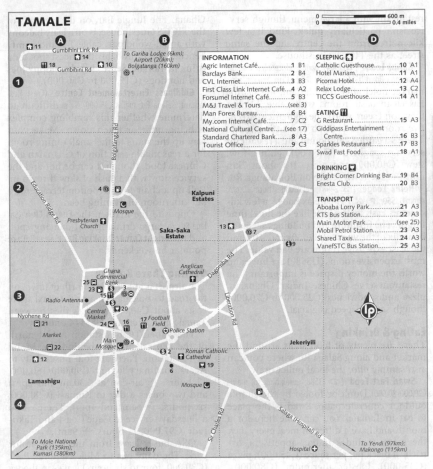

**TAMALE**

0 — 600 m
0 — 0.4 miles

**INFORMATION**
Agric Internet Café.................1 B1
Barclays Bank.........................2 B4
CVL Internet...........................3 B3
First Class Link Internet Café...4 A2
Forsumel Internet Café............5 B3
M&J Travel & Tours.............(see 3)
Man Forex Bureau..................6 B4
My.com Internet Café.............7 C2
National Cultural Centre......(see 17)
Standard Chartered Bank.......8 A3
Tourist Office.........................9 C3

**SLEEPING**
Catholic Guesthouse.............10 A1
Hotel Mariam.......................11 A1
Picorna Hotel.......................12 A4
Relax Lodge.........................13 C2
TICCS Guesthouse................14 A1

**EATING**
G Restaurant........................15 A3
Giddipass Entertainment
  Centre..............................16 B3
Sparkles Restaurant..............17 B3
Swad Fast Food....................18 A1

**DRINKING**
Bright Corner Drinking Bar....19 B4
Enesta Club.........................20 B3

**TRANSPORT**
Aboaba Lorry Park................21 A3
KTS Bus Station....................22 A3
Main Motor Park...............(see 25)
Mobil Petrol Station..............23 A3
Shared Taxis........................24 A3
VanefSTC Bus Station...........25 A3

To Gariba Lodge (6km);
Airport (20km);
Bolgatanga (160km)

Kalpuni
Estates

Mosque

Presbyterian
Church

Saka-Saka
Estate

Anglican
Cathedral

Ghana
Commercial
Bank

Radio Antenna

Central
Market

Nyohene Rd

Market

Football
Field

Police Station

Main
Mosque

Lamashigu

Jekeriyili

Roman Catholic
Cathedral

Mosque

To Mole National
Park (135km);
Kumasi (380km)

Cemetery

Hospital

To Yendi (97km);
Makongo (115km)

GHANA

---

air-con is powerful – that is when there are no brownouts. Rooms surround a leafy garden bar and lounge area. Breakfast and other meals are available on request. It's about 2.5km north of the centre.

**TICCS Guesthouse** ( ☎ 22914; www.ticcs.com/res .htm; Gumbihini Link Rd; r with fan C80,000, s/d with air-con C120,000/140,000; P ) Good for groups and students, this guesthouse run by a Catholic institution has the feel of a summer camp. The concrete bungalows are clean and simple and guests have use of the living room, TV and kitchen. Breakfast is included and the recommended Jungle Bar is here.

**Picorna Hotel** ( ☎ 22672; picornahotelgh@yahoo .com; r C150,000; P ) The Picorna is the best value in the centre, though the competition

isn't too fierce. Rooms are comfortable but run down and the whole place seems to be decaying before your very eyes. Also on the premises are a restaurant, a popular bar and nightclub, and an open-air cinema, active at the weekends.

**TOP END**
All hotels in this category are outside the centre, though they are easily reachable by private or line taxis.

**Hotel Mariam** ( ☎ 23548; www.mariamhotel.com .ph; Gumbihini Rd; r US$50-80; P ) A favourite with international aid workers and business travellers, the Mariam is the nicest place to stay in Tamale. The rooms are modern, clean and well kept, and there's a good restaurant with a large menu, though service isn't particularly quick. Find it a few kilometres from the centre, up the same street as the TICCS Guesthouse.

**Gariba Lodge** ( ☎ 23041; gariba@africaonline.com.gh; Bolgatanga Rd; d US$60-80; P 🞥 ) The most upmarket hotel after the Mariam, the Gariba has clean basic rooms with cable TV but they don't seem worth the high price. Executive rooms have bathtub and sitting room. There's a garden compound and a restaurant serving spaghetti (C45,000), guinea-fowl stew (C40,000) and more. It's about 7km north of the town centre on Bolgatanga Rd.

**Relax Lodge** ( ☎ 24981; relaxlodge@hotmail.com; r from US$50; P 🞥 ) The Relax Lodge, a few kilometres east, feels a little like the hotel time forgot. The furniture and buildings seems to be a mix of the worst of the '50s and '70s, and the least expensive rooms are bad value. The most expensive rooms (US$80) are huge and worth the money if space is important. The restaurant serves Chinese, Indian, Ghanaian, pizza and sandwiches (C25,000 to C70,000) though service speed is glacial.

## Eating & Drinking

There are plenty of food stalls around the market and along Salaga Rd where you can also sample *pito*, the local millet brew.

**Swad Fast Food** ( ☎ 23588; Gumbihini Rd; mains C20,000-80,000) Don't be fooled by the simple outdoor concrete patio, Swad is the place to eat in Tamale. You can dine here for a month and have a different meal every day: the menu includes Indian appetisers, ostrich in black pepper sauce (C45,000), pizza (C35,000), lobster thermidor (C80,000), breakfast and takeaway lunchboxes. Just around the corner from the Mariam Hotel.

**Sparkles Restaurant** (mains C25,000; 🕑 8am-8pm) This restaurant in the back of the National Cultural Centre behind the football field has a variety of Ghanaian and Chinese dishes and pizza (C40,000). It's a pleasant place to cool off with a drink as well.

**G Restaurant** (mains C25,000; 🞥 ) A petrol station may not be the loveliest of settings, but the Ghanaian food served here is good and it's conveniently located in the Goil parking lot directly across from the market. It's nothing more than a few tables in a clean, modern, fan-cooled room.

**Jungle Bar** (TICCS Guesthouse, Gumbihini Link Rd) There should be more places like this in

Ghana. The Jungle Bar, on the grounds of the TICCS Guesthouse, is on a leafy balcony with an all-wood bar, cable TV and comfy benches and is probably the nicest spot for a drink in Tamale. Serves kebabs, sloppy Joes and hot dogs (C15,000 to C50,000).

**Giddipass Entertainment Centre** (Crest Restaurant; Salaga Rd; mains C35,000) It's difficult to determine whether this rambling complex is being built or taken down. Make your way up the stairs to the small dining room for a reasonable selection of Ghanaian and Chinese food, though it can be hot and the service slow with a dash of slow thrown in. Pull up a chair to the rooftop terrace for a late-afternoon or evening beer.

Opposite the market, the **Enesta Club** (Salaga Rd), a large drinking and dancing spot, and the **Bright Corner Drinking Bar** (Salaga Rd) are popular on weekends.

## Getting There & Away

The airport is about 20km north of town, on the road to Bolgatanga; a private taxi there costs about C40,000. Antrak flies between Tamale and Accra for US$144 one way.

The VanefSTC bus station is just north of the central market, behind the Mobil petrol station. There are four buses daily to Accra (ordinary/luxury C90,000/150,000, 12 hours, 🕑 air-con at 6.30am and 2pm) and two buses a day to Kumasi (C90,000, six hours, 🕑 6am and 4pm). There's also a Tuesday service to Cape Coast and Takoradi (C97,000, 12 hours, 🕑 9am).

OSA buses leave from the main motor park. The daily bus to Mole National Park (C30,000, four to six hours) leaves in theory at 2.30pm but in practice one later. Get to the bus station well before its scheduled departure time to be sure of a seat. There's also a daily service to Wa (C45,000, eight hours), leaving at 5.30am. The KTS bus station is opposite the Picorna Hotel; KTS has services to Accra, Kumasi, Sunyani and Takoradi.

Tro-tros leave the motor park during the day heading to Bolgatanga (C23,000, 2½ hours). For details of services to the Volta Region via Yendi and Bimbilla, see opposite.

## Getting Around

You won't have to wait more than a few minutes for a line taxi running along the Bolgatanga road to take you into town from one of the hotels.

## TAMALE TO HOHOE

Adventure-seekers and masochists – sometimes they're one and the same – will find the route between Tamale and the Volta Region via Yendi and Bimbilla is rough, and there are few facilities for travellers, but it offers a rewarding off-the-beaten-track experience and some magnificent scenery. This route can be done in either direction and takes a minimum of two days but if you've got time, it's worth breaking the journey up. Transport is generally infrequent so be prepared for long waits. Apart from a short tarred section just outside Tamale and again before Hohoe, the road is dirt and very bumpy.

### Yendi

Home to the paramount Dagomba chief, the Ya-Na, Yendi is a traditional town notable for its palace and an interesting fusion of Moorish and Sahelian architectural styles. Most travellers stop here only briefly on their way somewhere else but Yendi, like Tamale, is a good place to see the Dagomba Fire Festival. The Greenwich meridian passes through here.

If you want to break up your journey here, you can stay at the **Yayaidi Guesthouse** (r C150,000; 😢) which has basic rooms and meals upon request. Street food is available around the motor park and petrol station in Yendi.

Tro-tros and GPRU buses to Yendi (C11,000, two hours) leave regularly from the main motor park in Tamale, 97km to the east, and there's a 5am and noon OSA bus that covers the same route; at least one tro-tro heads daily from Yendi to Bimbilla.

### Bimbilla

This flat, dusty district capital is about 100km from Yendi and a convenient place to break your journey. It too has an interesting palace, home to the chief. Just off the main drag, clearly signposted, is the **Hilltop Guesthouse** (r C50,000), where basic rooms come with shared bathrooms (bucket shower). Meals can be prepared for you here or at one of the basic eateries on the main road. The lorry station is on the southern edge of town. From here, there's a daily bus to Tamale via Yendi (four hours) and Accra via Hohoe (seven hours), although transport can be scarce on Monday. Tro-tros to Accra leave at around 11am but get there a little after 6.30am to be sure of a seat. **Nkwanta**, a pretty little village with a

scenic mountain backdrop, halfway between Bimbilla and Hohoe, is another possibility for breaking your journey.

## LARABANGA

Whether it's a highlight or a frustrating experience, Larabanga is more than simply the turn-off to Mole National Park. Known mostly for its unusual looking mud-and-pole mosque, originally built in the 15th century (making it the oldest of its kind in Ghana), the village provides a good opportunity to see what traditional village life is like.

You can register for a guided tour (C10,000) of the mosque at the information post next to it, although you can't actually go inside. An additional small donation (C5000) to the imam is expected. In the village you'll see some fine examples of the mud-walled domestic compounds decorated with geometric two-tone patterns that are a feature of northern Ghana.

Look for the Salia Brothers in a small replica of the mosque doubling as a tourist office on the eastern outskirts of the village. They have established a community-based project where you can hire bicycles, binoculars, bird-identification kits and stay overnight in their small but well-maintained guesthouse (C40,000). Or you can sleep on the roof for star viewing. Meals are available on request. Some travellers have complained about other villagers who aggressively compete for their business and don't deliver on promises.

Transport from Larabanga is limited. To Tamale, there's the daily bus from Mole and a daily bus from Wa, both of which pass through town early in the day; heading east, there are two daily buses to Bole, in the early afternoon and a daily bus to Wa at around 9.30am. Tro-tros from the junction town of Sawla on the Kumasi to Wa road occasionally pass through on the way to Tamale. To get to Mole, you can walk (not advisable in the heat of the day), hire a bicycle or try to hitch (a long wait). There have been reports of robberies on this road, and so it's best to err on the side of caution when considering this route, especially alone or in the dark.

## MOLE NATIONAL PARK

☎ 0717

It's not everywhere you can get up close and personal with bus-sized elephants. Face-to-face encounters with these beasts, plus roving gangs of baboons, warthogs, water bucks and antelopes – 90 species of mammals in total – are possibilities at this **national park** (adult/student C40,000/25,000, still/video camera fee C5000/20,000), Ghana's largest at 4660 sq km and best as far as wildlife viewing goes. It consists for the most part of flat savanna, with gallery forests along the rivers and streams. There's one main escarpment, on which the motel and park headquarters are situated. More than 300 bird species have been recorded here. The best time for seeing wildlife is during the harmattan season from January to March, but it's worth a visit any time of the year, even if it's just to admire the green landscape during the rains (July to September).

The park entrance gate is about 4km north of the turn-off in Larabanga. The park headquarters and the motel are a further 2km into the park. Guided walks are offered twice daily, at 6.30am and 3.30pm, and cost C15,000 per person for one hour (the walks usually last two hours). The walks are excellent value – the guides are informed and you'll see plenty of wildlife at close quarters, although the electricity generator by the main waterhole spoils the ambience somewhat. You are not permitted to walk (or drive) in the park unless you're accompanied by an armed ranger. You are, however, allowed to walk unaccompanied along the road back to Larabanga – apparently the park isn't liable for people attacked outside its domain.

## Sleeping & Eating

**Mole Motel** ( ☎ 22045; camping own/rented tent per person C20,000/C40,000, d C170,000, chalets C200,000; ☲ ) A strictly utilitarian boxy structure that does nothing to take advantage of its location, the Mole Lodge could benefit from a little competition. But as for now there's nowhere else to stay within the park, which means you should try to book ahead since it gets busy in the dry season. The run-down rooms and indifferent service aside, the views overlooking a waterhole where animals gather is worth the sacrifice. Water and electricity are sometimes in short supply. The camp site is cheap and has even more spectacular views. Alternatively, you can stay in Larabanga and cycle into the park for the day.

If you're hungry, you can either chance the very slow service at the motel restaurant (meals around C40,000) or bring your own provisions.

## Getting There & Away

The reserve is 135km west of Tamale, off the dirt road that connects Fufulso on the Kumasi to Tamale road with Sawla on the Kumasi to Wa road. The turn-off to the park is in Larabanga, 15km west of Damongo, a busy transport and market centre.

A daily OSA bus runs from Tamale (C40,000, four to six hours), leaving some time after 2.30pm, once it's packed to the gunwales, and arriving at the park motel around 7pm if all goes well. You really need to get your ticket a day in advance or early the morning of the departure to be assured a seat. The same bus returns to Tamale the next day, leaving the park at around 5.30am. The alternative is to take any early-morning bus from Tamale heading to Bole or Wa and get off at Larabanga, then walk, cycle or try to hitch (very difficult). Leaving Mole, your options are to take the OSA bus from the motel to Tamale or to make your way to Larabanga, from where there is infrequent transport in either direction.

## WA

☎ 0756

Few visitors make it to Wa, in the far northwestern corner of the country near the Burkina Faso border, but it's worth the slog getting here; not only as it's a departure point for visits to the Wechiau hippo sanctuary, but to check out the palace of the Wa Na (as the chief is called). This palace, found behind the post office and Ghana Telecom complex, was built in the traditional Sahelian mud-and-pole style and you can take a quick tour of the crumbling remains inside.

Also worth a look are the relatively new and impressive Great Mosque and, behind it, an older mud-and-pole mosque. First pay your respects (and a small donation) to the imam, who will expect you to sign his visitor's book.

About 5km past the Upland Hotel is the small village of Nakori, which has an impressive mud-and-pole mosque. There's no public transport; you'll have to either take a private taxi from the motor park or it makes a pleasant walk (allow a good hour one way from the Upland Hotel).

The **tourist office** ( ☎ 22431) is in the Admin Block near the fire station at the roundabout. On the main drag, near the roundabout, is the post office and Ghana Telecom. Further down, on the same side, is the Ghana Commercial Bank.

## Sleeping & Eating

**Upland Hotel** ( ☎ 22180; r C180,000; ❄ ) About 3km west of the town centre is Wa's best hotel, not only for the DSTV in some of the rooms and reception area and the pleasant restaurant and garden area, but because the rooms are spacious and clean and the staff unusually helpful.

The other hotels, the **Seinu Hotel** ( ☎ 22010; r C55,000), **Numbu Hotel** (r C50,000) and **Hotel du Pond** ( ☎ 20018; r C80,000; ❄ ) are all located near one another close to the market and are similar in quality and amenities (that is, basic and under-maintained).

There are plenty of food stalls and chop bars in and around the market area.

## Getting There & Away

OSA has a daily service to and from Tamale (C55,000, seven hours, ⏱ 4am) via Larabanga (for Mole National Park). If you're coming from Mole it's possible to catch the same bus passing through Larabanga at around 6am on the way to Wa. OSA buses leave from the empty lot next to the post office and Ghana Telecom. City Express has daily buses to Bolgatanga (C40,000, six hours) via Tumu. VanefSTC has services that pass through Kumasi on their way to Accra (C65,000, ⏱ 2pm Sunday, Tuesday and Thursday). The VanefSTC and City Express buses leave from the main roundabout, opposite the police station. Other transport, includes GPRTU buses to Kumasi (C60,000) that leave daily around 6pm and arrive in Kumasi at dawn the following morning. Tro-tros to Bole, Sawla, Hamale, Lawra and Tumu leave from around the motor park. For Wechiau, tro-tros leave from within the motor park. If you're headed for Burkina Faso, border crossings can be reached via Hamale, Lawra and Tumu.

## WECHIAU COMMUNITY HIPPO SANCTUARY

One of the more remote ecotourism projects in the country, this sanctuary along the Black Volta River, which marks the border with Côte d'Ivoire, is home to hippos as well as a variety of bird species. Basic guesthouse accommodation (pit toilet and bucket shower) is available and you can arrange canoe trips

to see the hippos; November through June is the best time to see these prehistoric-looking beasts. Meals can be prepared if you bring your own provisions. Wechiau village is reached by tro-tro (C6500, one hour, 46km) from the main lorry park in Wa. The sanctuary is about 20km from Wechiau. Transport uncertainties (roads sometimes become impassable in the rainy season from July to September) mean you really should plan to spend one night at the sanctuary itself rather than try to do it as a day trip from Wa.

## BOLGATANGA
☎ 072

To truly appreciate Bolga, as it's known to locals, you probably have to leave Bolga for the surrounding villages. It's the capital of the Upper East Region and the major town between Tamale and the border with Burkina Faso but it's best considered as a base for exploring the surrounding area.

Bolga's market is known in Ghana as a centre for crafts, including textiles, leatherwork (sandals, handbags, wallets and day packs), multicoloured baskets woven from raffia prized throughout Ghana, and the famous Bolga straw hats. For baskets, you could also try the shop on Commercial Rd near the intersection with Bazaar Rd.

The small **museum** (admission C10,000; ⏱ 9am-5pm), off Navrongo Rd behind the Catholic mission, has a small display on the ethnology and culture of the northeast.

## Information

There's a **tourist office** ( ☎ 23416; Navrongo Rd; ⏱ 9am-5pm Mon-Fri) across from SSNIT House. Your best bet for changing money is the Ghana Commercial Bank. Internet access is available at **Globe Express Internet** (Albilba Rd) and there is a bookshop, **Readwide Bookshop** (SSNIT House, Navrongo Rd).

A group of enterprising and enthusiastic boys, Joseph, Awal, Nick, Sumaila, Jessy and Musah (josephadugbire@yahoo.com) can be recommended as guides for Bolga and the surrounding area. Ask around or contact them in advance.

## Sleeping

**Tienyine Hotel** ( ☎ 22355; Starlet 91 St; r C235,000; ❄ ) This hotel has the most expensive and probably most modern rooms in Bolga. The bungalows are arranged traditionally in a

**GHANA**

GHANA

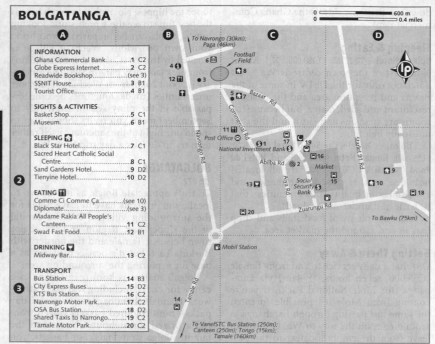

## BOLGATANGA

0        600 m
0        0.4 miles

**INFORMATION**
Ghana Commercial Bank...........1 C2
Globe Express Internet............2 C2
Readwide Bookshop...........(see 3)
SSNIT House.........................3 B1
Tourist Office........................4 B1

**SIGHTS & ACTIVITIES**
Basket Shop..........................5 C1
Museum...............................6 B1

**SLEEPING**
Black Star Hotel.....................7 C1
Sacred Heart Catholic Social
 Centre................................8 C1
Sand Gardens Hotel................9 D2
Tienyine Hotel.....................10 D2

**EATING**
Comme Ci Comme Ça.........(see 10)
Diplomate..........................(see 3)
Madame Rakia All People's
 Canteen............................11 C2
Swad Fast Food....................12 B1

**DRINKING**
Midway Bar.........................13 C2

**TRANSPORT**
Bus Station..........................14 B3
City Express Buses................15 D2
KTS Bus Station....................16 C2
Navrongo Motor Park............17 C2
OSA Bus Station...................18 D2
Shared Taxis to Narrongo.......19 C2
Tamale Motor Park...............20 C2

To Navrongo (30km);
Paga (46km)

Football Field

Bazaar Rd

Commercial Rd

Navrongo Rd

Post Office

National Investment Bank

Abilba Rd

Ajya Rd

Social Security Bank

Market

Starlet 91 Rd

To Bawku (75km)

Zuarungu Rd

Mobil Station

Tamale Rd

To VanefSTC Bus Station (250m);
Canteen (250m); Tongo (15km);
Tamale (160km)

circular compound and have air-con and TV. Restaurant attached.

**Sand Gardens Hotel** ( ☎ 23464; r with fan ₵130,000, s/d with air-con ₵150,000/225,000; ✹ ) Rooms surround a large dirt compound, part bar, part restaurant, sometimes loud, but the concrete bungalows are clean and comfortable. To find it head east down Zuarungu Rd until you reach the fire station and turn left down the dirt road.

**Black Star Hotel** ( ☎ 22346; fax 23650; Bazaar Rd; s/d with fan and shared bathroom ₵60,000/120,000; r with air-con and private bathroom ₵172,000; ✹ ) This long-standing hotel can feel a little abandoned, especially if you have to search the concrete compound for someone to help you, but the rooms were probably once nicer than any in Bolga.

## Eating & Drinking

There are plenty of food stalls on the stretch of Zuarungu Rd east of the intersection of Navrongo and Commercial Rds. There's a canteen at the VanefSTC bus station.

**Swad Fast Food** (Navrango Rd; mains ₵35,000) Lovers of the Tamale Swad won't be disap-

pointed as this eatery has the same eclectic menu of Indian, Chinese, Ghanaian and continental dishes.

**Comme Ci Comme Ça** (Starlet 91 St; mains ₵30,000) This restaurant in the Tienyine Hotel compound is nothing more than a few plastic tables and chairs in a concrete patio. Chicken and beef dishes are delivered at a snail's pace.

**Madam Rakia All People's Canteen** (Commercial Rd; dishes ₵20,000) Nothing more than a basic canteen dishing up local staples like millet-based dishes just north of the post office.

**Diplomate** (cnr Bazaar & Navrongo Rds; mains ₵25,000) At SSNIT House, this popular restaurant has something of the look of an English tearoom. It's comfortable and pleasant and serves good solid Ghanaian food.

**Midway Bar** (Commercial Rd) For a drink, head for this lively outdoor bar facing the street with decent music and grilled meat.

## Getting There & Away

Tro-tros to Tamale (₵23,000, 2½ hours) leave from the motor park on Zuarungu Rd east of the intersection with Navrongo and

Tamale Rds. Tro-tros to Navrongo (C5000, 30 minutes) and buses to Kumasi and Accra leave from the Navrongo motor park on Bazaar Rd. Passenger taxis to Navrongo leave from the taxi station diagonally opposite the National Investment Bank. The VanefSTC bus station is on Tamale Rd, about 800m south of the intersection with Navrongo and Zuarungu Rds. From here, buses leave daily for Accra (C150,000, 15 hours) and Kumasi (C70,000, six hours). Behind the market, in the block between Zuarungu and Bazaar Rds, is a vast motor park. In the far northwest corner is the KTS bus station, with buses to Accra and Kumasi. In the southeast corner is the City Express bus station. From here, there's an early morning (5.30am) service to Wa via Tumu on Monday to Saturday.

If you're headed for Ouagadougou in Burkina Faso, take a tro-tro tō the border at Paga (C6000, 40 minutes). To cross into Togo, take a tro-tro from the motor park behind the market to Bawku from where you can catch vehicles to the border (30km) and on to Dapaong (Togo), 15km further east.

## AROUND BOLGATANGA

A worthwhile side trip is to the **Tongo hills** southeast of Bolga, known for their balancing rock formations, panoramic views and the whistling sound the rocks make during the harmattan season. A popular goal is the village of **Tengzug**, about an hour'o hike (a steep 4km) from **Tongo** village and 9km from Bolgatanga, above which are numerous sacred shrines. The most famous is the *ba'ar Tpmma'ab ua' nee* or Nana Tongo shrine. Tro-tros run regularly to Tongo (C5000) from the main motor park behind the market in Bolgatanga. Travellers can arrange homestays or even sleep on the roof of a traditional mud home. Beds are also available at the Tongo Community Centre.

The **Red Volta River Valley**, between Bolgatanga and Bawku, is potentially a fascinating area to explore, with opportunities for learning about the distinctive local culture and architecture, hiking, canoeing and wildlife viewing (it's a migration corridor for elephants and other wildlife).

## GAMBARGA ESCARPMENT

Southeast of Bolga, the Gambarga Escarpment extends towards the Togolese border. Along it is **Gambarga**, ancient capital of the Mamprusi kingdom; **Nalerigu**, the modern district capital; and **Nakpanduri**, the goal of most travellers to the area. A sleepy, unspoilt village of neatly thatched huts, perched on the edge of the escarpment, Nakpanduri has magnificent views and offers some fine hiking. You can stay at the **Government Rest House** (r C40,000), which has basic rooms.

Nakpanduri and the other towns along the escarpment can be difficult to get to by public transport. Your best bet is to do the journey in stages: from Bolga, get any transport heading to Tamale and drop at Walewale, where the road to Gambarga turns off the Tamale road. From there, you should be able to get a tro-tro to Nalerigu, and from there to Nakpanduri, but it may take a while.

## NAVRONGO

From a traveller's perspective, the mostly shady and tranquil town of Navrongo, about 30km northwest of Bolgatanga and near the Burkina Faso border, is remarkable only for the **Our Lady of Seven Sorrows Cathedral**, which dates from 1906. It was constructed of *banco* (clay or mud) in the traditional Sahel style and colourful frescoes decorate the interior.

From December 17 to 18 in Sandema, a small village near Navrongo, is the **Feko festival** celebrating the people's resistance against slave traders from Nigeria and the northern region. Villagers put on buffalo antlers and others hunt them with bows and arrows. Naba Azantilow Ayeta, 100-plus years old and one of the oldest chiefs in all of West Africa, was installed here in 1931.

If you decide to stay overnight, try the **Hotel Mayaga** ( ☎ 22327; Sandama Rd; r C50,000), about 500m west of the bus station, off the road to Wa. The Catholic mission, near the cathedral, has a **guesthouse** (r C50,000) with clean, cool rooms with bathroom, but doesn't offer meals. The University of Development Studies (UDS), one of the tallest buildings in Navrongo also has a **guesthouse** (r C50,000). Stalls around the bus station have a small selection of street food or there are a couple of chop bars on the main drag.

### Getting There & Away

Regular shared taxis during the day make the short journey to Paga (C4000, 15 minutes) for the border with Burkina Faso, and to Bolgatanga (C5000, 30 minutes). If you're heading south, you're better off getting to Bolgatanga, which has much better transport connections. If you're heading west towards Tumu and Wa, the bus from Bolga to Wa passes through Navrongo but it's usually jam-packed by the time it reaches here, so it's better to pick it up from Bolga instead.

## PAGA

Most people stopping in Paga are on their way to or from Burkina Faso but if you're in the general vicinity it's worth a visit even if you're not crossing borders. The town has become synonymous with its **crocodile ponds**, now part of a formally organised community ecotourism project. Chief Pond is visible from the road, about 1km from the main motor park towards the Burkinabé border, while Zenga Pond is signposted off the main road, just after the motor park. At Chief Pond, you'll find official guides and a good informative booklet on the ponds. It costs around C30,000 per person to see the crocs, plus a little extra for the crocs' chickens. More interesting, and highly recommended, is a tour of the chief's compound, the Paga Pio's Palace, a traditional homestead of the local Kasena people. There's no set fee for the tour but a donation is expected. You can also arrange bicycle tours by of villages in the surrounding area through Alhassan Village Tours, opposite Chief Pond. Alhassan offers the only accommodation in Paga; you can sleep on the roof of mud huts for a negotiated price and meals can be arranged.

You can take a guided tour of the remains of the Pikworo Slave camp and cemetery two kilometres west of Paga.

Regular shared taxis and tro-tros run between Paga and both Navrongo and Bolgatanga. From the motor park in Paga, you can either walk the 2km to the border post or you can pay the going rate for a private taxi.

# GHANA DIRECTORY

## ACCOMMODATION

In general, accommodation in Ghana is not especially good value, better suited to people on an expense account. For this book budget refers to rooms US$30 and under, midrange US$30 to US$65 and top end US$65 and up. In Accra especially, rooms under US$40 are generally not well kept or maintained and bring a bit of sticker shock for those reasonably expecting more for their money. Most rates around the country already include 15% tax (12.5% VAT and 2.5% NHIL) and many midrange and top end hotels include breakfast though this is usually a very basic coffee, eggs and toast.

Before putting down any money it's a good idea to make sure everything works; check the air-con, try the water, turn the TV on if that's important to you (it really doesn't make any sense to pay extra for the TV if there isn't cable), flip the light switches, and be sure there's a bath towel and soap before getting in the shower and toilet paper before you, well, you know.

You'll almost always be offered an air-con, deluxe or superior room first; ask if there are standard rooms available. Despite the heat, fan-cooled rooms are sometimes preferable since some air-cons are so loud as to make sleep near impossible. Unfortunately, owners and staff are usually indifferent and aren't in the habit of going out of their way to make your stay more comfortable.

Prices are generally higher in Accra than elsewhere in the country. Off the tourist trail there are few hotels and guesthouses, but it's usually possible to arrange to sleep on a floor or roof somewhere. Most of the ecotourism projects offer overnight stays in simple guesthouses or homestays. Along the coast, there are some nice beach resorts, many of which are within reach of a midrange budget. Camping is a possibility at some of these resorts and also at national parks and reserves. A few of the coastal forts offer extremely basic guesthouse accommodation.

Many Ghanaian hotels don't have single rooms as such but offer the choice of double or twin rooms. Double rooms have one double bed and can sleep one or two people; twin rooms are usually more expensive and have two single beds. Midrange and top-end hotels sometimes quote prices in US dollars but you can pay in cedis or US dollars.

## ACTIVITIES

With its long coastline, one of the main things to do in Ghana is head to the beach where you can surf and boogie-board or simply do nothing, which should be considered an activity. However, ask before swimming since currents and undertow

---

**PRACTICALITIES**

▪ The national *Daily Graphic* is probably the best of the English-language newspapers available, with reasonably good coverage of Ghanaian, African and international news. The broadsheet *Ghanaian Times* is also worth picking up. There's a wide selection of tabloids, many of which feature lurid headlines.

▪ GTV is the national channel, available throughout the country. In Accra and Kumasi, you can also get TV3, which is very similar. GTV has nightly news in English at 7pm, and shows a selection of educational programmes, slapstick comedy shows (in Twi) and American soaps. On Sunday, sermons and gospel singing take centre stage. DSTV is the main satellite channel.

▪ Most radio programmes are at least partly in English. Talk radio rules here, and the shows make fascinating listening. The national radio (FM 95.7) has world news in English on the hour, every hour. Other popular stations include Joy FM (99.7), Luv FM (99.5; in Kumasi), Gold FM (90.5), Groove FM (106.3) and Vibe FM (91.9).

▪ Most electrical outlets are UK-style, with three square prongs, though adapters are easy to find.

---

make conditions unsafe. Good hiking can be found in the Volta Region around Ho (p373) and Hohoe (p376) in the east and in the Tongo Hills near Bolgatanga (p391) in the north. For drumming and dancing lessons, contact Big Milly's (p355) or the Academy of African Music & Arts (AAMAL; p354) in Kokrobite, the Oasis Guest House (p361) in Cape Coast, or almost any of the community-based tourism projects around the country.

## BOOKS
Albert van Dantzig's *Forts and Castle of Ghana*, although first published in 1980, remains the definitive work on the early European coastal presence. The Ghana Museums & Monuments Board's *Castles & Forts of Ghana* has less text but some beautiful pictures. *Asante: The Making of a Nation* by Nana Otamakuro Adubofour, widely available in Kumasi, gives an insight into Ashanti history and culture. *Two Hearts of Kwasi Boachi* by Arthur Japin explores the experiences of two Ashanti brothers who were sent to be educated in Holland in the early 19th century.

*African Voices of the Atlantic Slave Trade* by Anne C Bailey reveals Africans' roles in slavery through oral accounts and the stories of elders; *Empires of Medieval West Africa: Ghana, Mali, and Songhay*, by C Conrad, relies on oral accounts and other scholars to tell the history of this era, which has had little written about it; *Kwame Nkrumah, The Father of African Nationalism* by David Birmingham is a comprehensive biography of the first African statesman; *Onions Are My Husband: Survival and Accumulation by West African Market Women* by Gracia Clark draws on years of field research studying the women who work in the Kumasi market.

## BUSINESS HOURS
Most stores are open between 9am and 6pm Monday to Friday, with some from 9am to 2pm on Saturday. Very few stores are open on Sunday.

Banks are generally open daily from 8am to 3pm, and are closed on weekends. Most forex bureaus are open limited hours on Saturday. Major hotels have forex facilities open daily.

## DANGERS & ANNOYANCES
One of Ghana's competitive advantages, as far as tourism in the region goes, is that it's a stable and generally peaceful democracy. Having said that, ethnic violence does sporadically flare up in the far northeast around Bawku. Take care of your valuables on the beaches west of Accra (see p354) and always try to be aware of your surroundings especially if you're walking alone at night. Otherwise, reckless tro-tro drivers, heat exhaustion and open sewers are probably the main hazards you will encounter.

## DISCOUNT CARDS
With an international student card you can get discounts on admission to national parks, ecotourism projects and museums.

## EMBASSIES & CONSULATES
### Ghanaian Embassies & Consulates
Ghana has embassies in Benin, Burkina Faso, Côte d'Ivoire, Guinea, Mali, Nigeria, Sierra Leone and Togo. For details, see the relevant country chapter.

Elsewhere, diplomatic missions include the following:

**Australia** ( ☎ 02-9283 2961; Suite 1404, Level 14, 370 Pitt St, Sydney 2000)
**Canada** ( ☎ 613-236 0871; 1 Clemow Ave, The Glebe, Ottawa, Ont KLS 2A)
**France** ( ☎ 01 71 10 14 02; 8 Villa Said, 75116 Paris)
**Germany** ( ☎ 0228-35 20 01; Rheinalle 58, 53173 Bonn)
**Japan** ( ☎ 03-409 3861; Azabu, PO Box 16, Tokyo)
**Netherlands** ( ☎ 70-362 5371; Molenstraat 53, 2513 The Hague)
**UK** ( ☎ 020-8342 8686; 104 Highgate Hill, London N6 5HE)
**USA Consulate** ( ☎ 212-832 1300; 19 East 47th St, New York, NY 10017)
**USA Embassy** ( ☎ 202-686 4520; 3512 International Dr NW, Washington, DC 20008);

### Embassies & Consulates in Ghana
All of the embassies and consulates listed are in Accra (area code ☎ 021). Most are open 8.30am to 3.30pm Monday through Friday.

**Australia** (Map p340; ☎ 777080; www.ghana.embassy .gov.au; 2 Second Rangoon Close, Catonments) Australian High Commission.
**Benin** (Map p340; ☎ 774860; Switchback Lane, Cantonments)
**Burkina Faso** (Map p342; ☎ 221988; 2nd Mango Tree Ave, Asylum Down; ⏰ 8am-2pm Mon-Fri)
**Canada** (Map p340; ☎ 228555; fax 773792; 46 Independence Ave, Sankara interchange)
**Côte d'Ivoire** (Map p345; ☎ 774611; 9 18th Lane, Osu; ⏰ 9am-2.30pm Mon-Thu)
**Denmark** ( ☎ 226972; 67 Isert Rd, 8th Ave Extension) Near World Bank office.
**France** (Map p340; ☎ 228571; www.ambafrance -gh.org; 12th Rd, Kanda) Off Liberation Ave.
**Guinea** (Map p340; ☎ 777921; 4th Norla St, Labone)
**Germany** (Map p342; ☎ 221311; geremb@ghana.com; 6 Ridge Rd, North Ridge)
**Ireland** ( ☎ 772866; 5th Circular Extension)
**Japan** (Map p340; ☎ 775616; fax 775951; 8 Josef Broz Tito Ave, Cantonments)
**Liberia** (Map p340; ☎ 775641; Odoikwao St, Airport Residential Area)
**Mali** (Map p342; ☎ 775160; Liberia Rd, West Ridge)
**Netherlands** (Map p340; ☎ 231991; nlgovacc@ncs .com.gh; 89 Liberation Ave, Sankara Circle)

**Niger** (Map p340; ☎ 224962; E104/3 Independence Ave, Ringway Estate)
**Nigeria** (Map p340; ☎ 776158; fax 774395; 5 Josef Broz Tito Ave, Cantonments)
**Togo** (Map p340; ☎ 777950; Togo House, Cantonments Circle, Cantonments)
**UK** (Map p340; ☎ 221665; fax 221745; 1 Osu Link, Ringway Estate) British High Commission.
**USA** (Map p345; ☎ 776601; www.usembassy.org.gh; cnr 10th La & 3rd St, Osu)

## FESTIVALS & EVENTS
Ghana observes the Muslim festivals of Eid al-Fitr, at the end of Ramadan, and Eid al-Adha, both of which are determined by the lunar calendar. See p818 for a table of Islamic holidays.

Ghana has many festivals and events, including Cape Coast's Fetu Afahye Festival (first Saturday of September; see p361), Elmina's Bakatue Festival (first Tuesday in July; see p364), the Fire Festival (p386) of the Dagomba people in Tamale and Yendi (dates vary according to the Muslim calendar), the Feko festival in Sandema (17 to 18 December; see p393) and various year-round Akan celebrations (p381) in Kumasi. Ghana's most famous festival, Aboakyer (Deer Hunt; see p358), is celebrated in Winneba on the first weekend in May. Accra's tourist office sells a booklet on festivals. Panafest is celebrated annually in Cape Coast, Accra and Kumasi.

## HOLIDAYS
Public holidays include the following:
**New Year's Day** 1 January
**Independence Day** 6 March
**Easter** March/April
**Labour Day** 1 May
**Africa Day** 25 May
**Republic Day** 1 July
**Farmers' Day** 1st Friday in December
**Christmas Day** 25 December
**Boxing Day** 26 December

## INTERNET ACCESS
There are Internet cafés in all major towns. Connection speeds vary but not surprisingly they tend to be slower outside the larger urban areas. Average rates per hour are C6000 to C10,000.

## INTERNET RESOURCES
**africaonline Ghana** (www.africaonline.com/site/gh) Starting point for general info about Ghana.

**Daily Graphic** (www.graphicghana.com) Homepage for Ghana's best daily newspaper.

**Ghana Tourist Board** (www.ghanatourism.org.gh, www.ghanatourism.gov.gh) An excellent resource for information on the country's attractions and festivals, and transport information.

**Ghana.co.uk** (www.ghana.co.uk) This UK-based site has plenty of good information about Ghana, from tourist attractions to history, culture and the latest news.

**Ghanaweb** (www.ghanaweb.com) This site has links to the major Ghanaian newspapers, including the *Daily Graphic*, as well as useful background information on the country.

**Ghana Review International** (www.ghanareview .com) All the latest news and politics from Ghana.

**Nature Conservation Research Centre** (NCRC; www .ncrc-ghana.org) Information on all of the community-based tourism projects in the country.

**No Worries Ghana** (www.noworriesghana.com) Listings and practical information from the North American Women's Association.

## LANGUAGE

English is the official language. There are at least 75 local languages and dialects. The most widely spoken language is Twi, which belongs to the Akan language group and is spoken in different versions throughout most of the central and southern parts of the country. The Ashanti version of Twi is not only spoken throughout the Ashanti homeland but also serves as a lingua franca for much of the country and especially in Accra. Fanti is spoken along much of the coast to the west of Accra. Other prominent languages are Ga in the Accra-Tema area, Ewe in the southeast and Mole-Dagbani languages in the north. See the Language chapter for useful phrases in Ga (p872) and Twi (p876).

## MONEY

The unit of currency is the cedi (C). There are C1000, C2000, C5000, C10,000 and C20,000 notes, as well as C100, C200, C250 and C500 coins. Prices in this chapter reflect the way prices are quoted in Ghana; that means all but some of the top-end hotels and park admission fees are given in cedis.

The best currencies to bring are US dollars, UK pounds or euros. Barclays and Standard Chartered Banks exchange cash and well-recognised brands of traveller's cheques such as American Express (Amex) or Thomas Cook without a commission.

Foreign-exchange (forex) bureaus are dotted around most major towns, though there are fewer in the north. They usually offer a slightly better rate than the banks and stay open later. Higher denomination bills receive higher exchange rates. However, they don't generally change travellers cheques.

Bear in mind that you'll need something to put your wads of cedis in when you leave the bank or forex, as they won't fit in a money belt.

### ATMs

Most Barclays and Standard Chartered Banks throughout the country have ATMs where you can get a cash advance in cedis (up to about C800,000 or US$80) with Visa or MasterCard.

### Credit Cards

Credit cards, generally only Visa and MasterCard, are accepted by major hotels and travel agencies.

### Tipping

A service charge is rarely added to restaurant bills. A tip of 5% to 10% is normal in high-end restaurants and it's usually a good idea to add a few thousand cedis to the bill rather than wait for change.

## STUDYING

Ghana is one of the more popular options for foreign students wishing to study in Africa, at least in part because courses are offered in English. Many universities in the US and Europe have collaborative programmes with University of Ghana Legon (p353; www .ug.edu.gh) in Accra, the University of Cape Coast (www.ucc.edu.gh), and development studies programmes in Tamale. The University for Development Studies (uds@ug .gn.apc.org) based in Tamale studies rural poverty and the environment combining academic work with practical hands-on training in rural communities. The Tamale Institute of Cross-Cultural Studies (TICCS; www.ticcs.com/index.htm) offers two Masters Degree programs – the MA in Cross-Cultural Development, and the MA in Cross-Cultural Ministry.

## TELEPHONE

Every town and city has plenty of private 'communication centres' where you can make national and international calls and send and receive faxes. They're slightly more expensive than calling from a card phone. Little streetside tables festooned with signs announcing which cell-phone providers they can call are everywhere, from Accra to small villages. These generally cost from C1500 to C2500 per minute and are the most convenient phoning option.

Several companies, most prominently Buzz, Areeba (formerly Spacefon) and One-Touch are in a race to become the dominant player in the Ghanaian cell-phone industry. Cell phones are becoming more and more common and are the best way to communicate within the country. Inquire in advance if your phone is compatible with one of these networks and buy a SIM card in Ghana (C60,000), or you can purchase a phone there. The south and centre of the country has adequate coverage; the north is serviced in spots but expect erratic service throughout in the near future.

## TIME

Ghana is on Greenwich mean time and does not apply daylight-savings time.

## TOURIST INFORMATION

The website of the **Ghana Tourist Board** (www .ghanatourism.gov.gh) has some useful information, or try the Ghanaian diplomatic mission in your country. Within Ghana, the tourist board has a network of offices in the major regional capitals. The amount of information available is limited. Opening hours tend to be somewhat erratic and most offices are closed on Saturday and Sunday.

The **Nature Conservation Research Centre** (NCRC; www.ncrc-ghana.org), one of the main players behind the country's burgeoning community-run tourism efforts has information on all of its projects.

## VISAS

Everyone except nationals of Ecowas (Economic Community of West African States) countries needs a visa, which until recently could only be obtained before arriving in Ghana. Now, however, nationals of most countries can receive a tourist visa on arrival at the Kotaka airport in Accra for US$100, though it's not a convenient option if you're arriving late at night. Visas allow a stay of 60 days and can be single or multiple entry. They must be used within three months of the date of issue.

You can get visas in many countries in West Africa (see p828) or elsewhere. Visa applications usually take three days to process, and four photos are required. You often also need an onward ticket. In the UK, single/multiple entry visas cost UK£30/40. In the USA, they cost US$50/80.

### Visa Extensions

If necessary, visas can be extended at the **immigration office** (Map p340; ☎ 021-221667 ext 215) in Accra near the Sankara interchange. Applications are accepted between 8.30am and noon Monday to Friday. You need two photos, a letter stating why you need an extension, and an onward ticket out of Ghana. Your passport is retained for the two weeks it takes to process the application.

### Visas for Onward Travel

You need a visa for the following neighbouring countries.

#### BURKINA FASO

The embassy issues visas for three months on the same day if you get there early. You need three photos and it costs US$40 or CFA15,000 (not payable in cedis).

#### CÔTE D'IVOIRE

The embassy issues visas in 48 hours and you need two photos. A visa valid for up to a month costs US$4 (payable in cedis) for Australians and Americans or US$10 for British nationals.

#### TOGO

The embassy issues visas for one month on the same day. You need three photos and it costs US$20. Alternatively, you can get a visa for the same price at the border at Aflao, but it's only valid for seven days.

## WOMEN TRAVELLERS

Because there are plenty of women who work, study or volunteer in the country, Ghanaians in general are certainly not surprised to see foreign women travelling on their own or in groups. While women are less likely to receive semi-aggressive catcalls of 'obroni', they are more likely to be chatted up by solo young men whose intentions are usually perfectly friendly but who may be slow to respond to signals that their attention is unwanted.

## WORK & VOLUNTEERING

There are probably at least as many international and religious aid and development organisations operating in Ghana as any country in the world. Take a look at any passing 4WD and odds are there's a decal on it with an acronym identifying it as the property of one of these. The US Peace Corps programme also has a significant presence.

Many organisations welcome volunteers for short-term to long-term stints. The list here is by no means comprehensive.

**Cross Cultural Collaborative Inc** (www.culturalcollaborative.org/Ghana.htm) Educational and nonprofit, promotes cultural exchange and understanding through the arts.

**Cross Cultural Solutions** (www.crossculturalsolutions.org) Volunteer programmes.

**Experiential Learning International** (www.eliabroad.com)

**FLAME** (Free Learning and Merit Education; www.flameghana.org) Arranges study opportunities in Ghana.

**Kids Worldwide** (www.kidsworldwide.org)

**Travel Active** (www.travelactive.nl) Dutch volunteer organisation.

**Travellers Worldwide** (www.travellersworldwide.com/04-ghana/04-ghana-about.htm)

**Volunteer in Africa** (www.volunteeringinafrica.org) Offers short- and long-term volunteer placements in health, education, environmental preservation and socioeconomic development.

# TRANSPORT IN GHANA

## GETTING THERE & AWAY
### Entering Ghana

In theory you need a yellow-fever vaccination certificate to enter Ghana, although it is rarely checked. It's more important to have it for onward travel to other countries.

## Air

Ghana's only international airport is Kotaka international airport in Accra. The national carrier, Ghana Airways, was replaced by Ghana International Airways in late 2005. At the time of research it was only flying between London and Accra. Other airlines that regularly link Accra with Europe include Alitalia, British Airways, KLM and Lufthansa. South African Airways links Ghana with Perth in Australia, via Johannesburg. There are several other national carriers of African countries that service Accra plus several smaller, private African airlines. North

American Airlines has one nonstop flight a week between New York City and Accra. Charter flights from Europe, especially to and from Germany are becoming more frequent and are generally less expensive than flying with a major carrier.

Airlines servicing Ghana include the following:

**Afriqiyah Airways** (8U; ☎ 252465) Hub: Tripoli. Flights to Europe with stopover in Tripoli, Libya; office at Accra airport.

**Air Ivoire** (VU; ☎ 241461) Hub: Abidjan. Office at Accra airport.

**Alitalia** (Map p342; AZ; ☎ 239315; Ring Rd Central, Asylum Down, Accra) Hub: Rome.

**American Airlines** (www.aa.com)

**Antrak** (Map p345; ☎ 769458; Antrak House, Danquah Circle, Accra) Domestic airline that also flies to Ouagadougou, Burkina Faso and Lagos, Nigeria.

**British Airways** (Map p342; BA; ☎ 240386; Kojo Thompson Rd, Adabraka, Accra) Hub: London Heathrow.

**EgyptAir** (MS; ☎ 773537; Ring Rd East, Osu, Accra) Hub: Cairo.

**Emirates** (EK; ☎ 238921; Meridian House, Ring Road Central, Accra) Hub: Dubai. Four flights a week connecting Accra and Dubai with a stopover in Lagos.

**Ghana International Airways** (GH; ☎ 221000; www.fly-ghana.com; Silver Star Tower, Airport City, PMB 78, Kotoka International Airport) Hub: Accra. At time of research only flew to London.

**Ivory Coast Airways** Office at Accra airport.

**Kenya Airways** (KQ; ☎ 444301) Hub: Nairobi. Office at Accra airport.

**KLM–Royal Dutch Airlines** (Map p340; KL; ☎ 224020; Ring Rd Central, Accra) Hub: Amsterdam.

**Lufthansa Airlines** (LH; ☎ 243893; Fidelity House, Accra) Hub: Frankfurt. Off Ring Rd Central.

**Slok Air International** ( ☎ 3166206; No 3 Aviation Rd, Accra) Flies to Monrovia, Freetown, Banjul and Dakar; office at the airport.

**South African Airways** (Map p342; SA; ☎ 230722; Ring Rd Central, Asylum Down, Accra) Hub: Johannesburg.

**Virgin Nigeria** (Map p340; VK; ☎ 771700; www.virginnigeria.com; La Palm Royal Beach Hotel, Accra) Hub: Lagos.

## Land

Ghana has land borders with Côte d'Ivoire to the west, Burkina Faso to the north and west, and Togo on the east. The main border crossing into Côte d'Ivoire is at Elubo; there are less-travelled crossings between Sunyani and Agnibilékrou and between Bole and Ferkessédougou. Into Burkina the main crossing is at Paga, with other crossings at Tumu, Hamale and Lawra. The main crossing into Togo is at Aflao, just

GHANA

outside Lomé. Note that Ghana's borders all close promptly at 6pm.

### BURKINA FASO

Between Accra and Ouagadougou, the usual route is via Kumasi, Tamale, Bolgatanga, Paga and Pô. A direct VanefSTC bus runs to Ouagadougou from Accra (C260,000, 24 hours) once daily (except Sunday) and from Kumasi (C195,000, 20 hours) every Wednesday night. Though going the entire distance at once can be painful and most people do the trip in stages. From Bolgatanga, there are frequent tro-tros to the border at Paga (C10,000, 40 minutes), from where you can get onward transport to Pô, 15km beyond the border, and Ouagadougou.

You can also enter Burkina Faso from the northwest corner of Ghana, crossing between Tumu and Léo or from Hamale or Lawra and onto Bobo-Dioulasso. You can reach Tumu most easily from Bolgatanga, Hamale from Bolgatanga or Wa, and Lawra from Wa. However, traffic is relatively scarce on all these routes.

### CÔTE D'IVOIRE

VanefSTC buses run between Accra and Abidjan (C111,000, 12 hours) via Elubo once daily Monday to Friday, leaving in the early morning. The Ecowas Express, run by STIF, a company from Côte d'Ivoire, does three runs a week between Neoplan motor park in Accra and Abidjan. From Takoradi, Peugeot bush taxis make a daily trip to Abidjan. Otherwise, make your way to Elubo in stages, cross the border on foot and take onward transport from there.

Other less commonly used crossings are from Kumasi via Sunyani and Berekum to Agnibilékrou (you'll have to do this in short stages as there are no direct buses) and between Bole and Bouna to Ferkessédougou. However, on this route you have to cross the Black Volta River (the border) by canoe and readers report being at the mercy of dash-hungry border officials. Onward transport from Bouna to Ferkessédougou takes eight to 12 hours.

### TOGO

Tro-tros and buses regularly ply the coastal road between Accra and Aflao (all about C30,000, three hours). VanefSTC buses leave from the smaller Tudu bus station in Accra

(C45,000, four times a day). The border at Aflao is open from 6am to 10pm daily but you should cross between 9am and 5pm if you need a Togolese visa at the border. Public transport from Ghana doesn't cross the border, which is only 2km from central Lomé. Other crossings are at Wli near Hohoe and between Ho and Kpalimé, though the former is strictly a pedestrian crossing and it's not easy to find onward transport from here. In the north, you can cross from Tamale via Yendi to Sansanné-Mango or Kara but transport is scarce on this route.

## GETTING AROUND
### Air

Two domestic airlines, **Citylink** ( ☎ 312001; www .citylink.com.gh) and **Antrak** Accra ( ☎ 21-765337; Antrak House, Danquah Circle); Kumasi ( ☎ 51-41296); Tamale ( ☎ 71-91075) operate in Ghana. Both have two flights daily between Accra and Kumasi (one way US$60 to US$80, 45 minutes), and Antrak has flights on Wednesday, Friday and Sunday between Accra and Tamale (one way US$144, 1½ hours). Several travel agencies in Accra and Kumasi sell Citilink and Antrak tickets (see listings in their respective sections).

### Boat

A passenger boat, the Yapei Queen, runs along Lake Volta between Akosombo and Yeji, stopping at the town of Kete-Krachi and a few villages along the way. The journey winds past beautiful hills and is an experience in itself as well as an alternative to the travails of road travel. In theory it leaves the port at Akosombo at 4pm on Monday and arrives in Yeji on Wednesday morning; in practice the departure and arrival times are more fluid. The southbound service leaves Yeji around 4pm on Wednesday and arrives in Akosombo on Friday morning. Tickets cost C100,000/C50,000 in 1st/2nd class, and food and drinks are available on board. If you want one of the two 1st-class cabins (recommended), you have to reserve at least two weeks in advance – call ☎ 0251-20686 in Akosombo to make a booking.

### Bus

The best bus service in the country is provided by VanefSTC, the old State Transport Corporation now owned by Greyhound. Compared to other transport in the region it's fairly reliable, though late departures are all too common. Expect significant delays leaving from the Tudu station in Accra and on any of the less regular routes. Buses link the major centres, including Accra, Kumasi, Takoradi, Cape Coast, Tamale and Bolgatanga. Seats can generally be booked one day in advance, which is essential for long-haul routes especially during busy holiday periods. Other operators, which may have the only buses on some routes (such as between Tamale and Mole National Park), include OSA, Kingdom Transport Services (KTS), City Express and GPRTU. Where they share routes, fares are less than with VanefSTC, but the buses tend to be older and less comfortable.

You have to pay extra for luggage. On VanefSTC buses, your luggage is weighed and you're charged about C300 per kilogram. Avoid the flip-down aisle seats which can be real backbreakers on a long journey.

## Car & Motorcycle

Driving is on the right in Ghana. Most main roads in Ghana are in quite good condition though there are some extensive stretches of severely potholed road between Kumasi and Tamale and between Accra and Aflao. Almost all secondary roads are unsealed. The frequent police checkpoints along the road are usually angling for a dash. Self-drive car rental is available in Accra and Kumasi but is not recommended unless you are used to driving the West African way.

An international driver's license and many foreign countries' licenses are recognised. Insurance is expensive.

### FUEL
Petrol is a significant expense and should be taken into consideration when budgeting for transportation. At the time of research it cost around C7000 per litre but prices are particularly vulnerable to inflation. Petrol stations are easy to find throughout the country.

### HIRE
Car hire with a driver is a good option if you have limited time; it costs anything from US$70 to US$100 per day. The estimated cost is generally payable in advance in cash or by major credit card. Rental companies in Accra include the following:

**Avis** (Map p342; ☎ 021-761751; avis@ghana.com; Speedway Travel & Tours, 5 Tackie Tawiah Ave)

**Europcar** (Map p342; ☎ 021-667546; Novotel Hotel, Barnes Rd)

**Hertz** (Map p340; ☎ 021-223389; Golden Tulip Hotel, Liberation Ave, Airport Residential Area)

**Vicma Travel & Tours** ( ☎ 021-232294; fax 234843; Liberia Rd North)

### ROAD HAZARDS
Ghana's main road hazards are other Ghanaian drivers. Accidents and injuries or even fatalities are all too common; there were almost 15,000 accidents with 650 fatalities in 2004 alone. One of the contributing factors is that so many vehicles stop suddenly to pick up or drop off passengers. Poor roads are of course an issue, and unpaved and potholed roads threaten the condition of your vehicle.

### ROAD RULES
Driving in Ghana is a little like driving in Rome with a strong dose of New York – it's crazy. There seem to be few rules except 'use your horn' and 'the most aggressive driver wins', if by win one means survives. Accra is challenging since besides other kamikaze drivers you have to avoid hitting pedestrians who liberally translate crosswalk and other safety guidelines. Timid drivers should probably give it a pass. Things are more subdued outside of Accra and Kumasi.

## Taxis
Within towns and on some shorter routes between towns, shared taxis (called passenger or line taxis) are the usual form of transport. Line taxis run on fixed routes, along which they stop to pick up and drop off passengers. Passenger taxis run on routes between towns and will set you down wherever you want to go. Shared taxis are more expensive than tro-tros but still very cheap. If time is short it's always possible to pay for two or three seats rather than wait for the full load. Basically any taxi that stops for you and already has passengers is a line taxi.

Private or 'dropping' taxis don't have meters and rates are negotiable. It's best to ask a local in advance for the average cost between two points. You'll soon have a handle on what is fair and what is gouging. Taxis can be chartered for an agreed period of time from one hour to a day for a negotiable fee. Drivers will often try to renegotiate after a deal has been struck and you've started moving, saying things like 'it's really not enough' or 'you just give xxx more.' Stick to your guns though and you will have no problems.

Most taxis don't have air-con, which is only really problematic if the windows don't open, which is not unusual. Doors also can be difficult to open.

## Train

Ghana's railway links Accra, Kumasi and Takoradi. The rolling stock is good and, like so many tro-tros and buses, was imported second-hand from Germany. But the trains are much slower and no cheaper than motorised transport. There are daily passenger services in either direction between Accra and Kumasi (C40,000/C25,000 in 1st/2nd class, about 12 hours) and a nightly service between Accra and Takoradi, which costs about the same and takes at least 12 hours, but these are really only for masochists and train enthusiasts. However, the line between Kumasi and Takoradi is worth considering, both as a change from road transport and for the experience in itself. On this line, there are two trains daily, leaving at 6am and 8.30pm. Fares are C40,000/C25,000 in 1st/2nd class and on the night train this gets you either a two- or four-person sleeper. The journey in theory takes eight hours but it's usually more like 12 in practice, especially on the night train. No food is available

on the train, although you can get food at stops along the way.

## Tro-tros

Tro-tro is a catch-all category that embraces any form of transport that's not a bus or taxi. They cover all major and many minor routes and, without them, Ghana would come to a standstill. Except on real backcountry routes, tro-tros are minibuses of all shapes, sizes and degrees of roadworthiness. They don't work to a set timetable, but leave when full, having squeezed in as many passengers as they can. The beauty of tro-tros is that you can pick them up anywhere along a route and they're extremely cheap (about US$0.01 per kilometre). Most fares are under a dollar or two but frequently change by small amounts, and for that matter the fares on many routes are not given. For long journeys, though, buses are more comfortable and safer. Many tro-tro drivers demand a negotiable luggage fee though this seems to be applied fairly arbitrarily and is more commonly requested of foreigners than Ghanaians. If others don't have to pay then neither should you.

Most towns have an area where tro-tros and buses congregate, usually in or near the market. These are called lorry park or motor park (the terms are used interchangeably) or, quite often, station. You may hear the term tro-tro used, but taxis and minibuses are often just called 'cars'.

# Guinea

Guinea's landscape is spectacular. The country has some of the world's few remaining tropical dry forests, and the rainforests that remain in the south are lush and verdant and full of wildlife. The waterfall-rich Fouta Djalon plateau in the west has breathtaking scenery and some of the best hiking in West Africa. Guinea is not well endowed with beaches, but those it has are superb; and often empty.

Matching the country's beauty is its vibrant culture. Across Guinea, there's a strong tradition of music and dance and visitors have many opportunities to see performances. Also, thanks largely to Sekou Touré's impassioned defiance of the French, most Guineans are as proud of their nationality as they are of their ethnicity. They have stood together through the difficult decades of independence instead of turning on each other.

Guinea is not as prepared for tourism as some other West African countries, and beyond the capital, creature comforts are sparse. You won't always have to rough it upcountry, but as long as you are prepared for the possibility, a visit here can be very rewarding.

## FAST FACTS

- **Area** 245,855 sq km
- **Capital** Conakry
- **Country code** ☎ 224
- **Famous for** Bauxite; Camara Laye; Circus Baobab; Les Ballets Africains
- **Languages** French, Malinké, Pulaar (Fula) and Susu
- **Money** Guinean franc (GF); US$1 = GF4310; €1 = GF5120; CFA1 = GF7.8
- **Population** 9.5 million
- **Visa** Required in advance

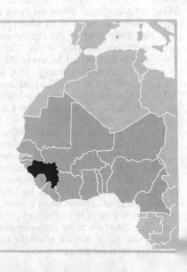

# HIGHLIGHTS

- **Fouta Djalon** (p418) Hiking in the green heartland of the Peul people.
- **Sobané** (p431) and **Îles de Los** (p417) Lazing on palm-fringed sands.
- **Bossou** (p431) Coming face to face with chimpanzees.
- **Conakry** (p415) Listening to live music.
- **Forêt Classée de Ziama** (p428) Tracking elephants in the virgin rainforest.

# ITINERARIES

- **One week** Spend a day or two in **Conakry** (p409) and the rest of your time exploring the mountains, waterfalls and villages of the **Fouta Djalon** (p418). If beaches are more your thing, head to **Îles de Los** (p417) and **Sobané** (p431) instead of the mountains.
- **Two weeks** Add **Upper Guinea** (p424) or the **Forest Region** (p428) to the one-week itinerary, perhaps roaming **Parc National du Haut Niger** (p425) for a few days. If you hustle, you could see the highlights of both regions. Or stay in the **Fouta Djalon** (p418) and strike out on an extended village-to-village trek.
- **One month** This is enough time to venture through all four of the country's regions if travelling by public transport, or start in the capital and circle the Fouta Djalon by bike (see p438).

# CLIMATE & WHEN TO GO

Guinea is one of the wettest countries in West Africa. Rainfall along the coast averages 4300mm a year, half of which falls in July and August, while the central mountainous region receives about 2000mm, more evenly distributed between May and October. Temperatures average 30°C along the coast, where it is always humid, and can fall to 10°C and below at night in Mali-ville and other highland areas during the winter (see climate charts p813).

The best time to visit is November and December, after the rains but before the dusty harmattan winds (December to March) spoil the views. The rains sometimes make minor roads impassable, though there's something to be said for visiting the Fouta Djalon when it's wet. The rains, which generally don't last very long, make the waterfalls more explosive and the countryside more verdant while the clouds lower the daytime temperatures.

## HOW MUCH?

- Raffia backpack GF3000
- 100km bush taxi ride GF13,000
- World Cola GF1000
- Two pagnes (about 2m) of hand-woven indigo cloth GF30,000
- A night at a music show GF5000

## LONELY PLANET INDEX

- 1L of petrol GF3800
- 1.5L of bottled water GF1500
- Bottle of Skol GF2300
- Souvenir T-shirt GF25,000
- Bag of groundnuts GF100

# HISTORY

Rock paintings found in the Fouta Djalon show Guinea was inhabited 30,000 years ago. By 2000 years ago, the Coniagui, Baga and other small tribes had established farming and fishing settlements in the northwest. These were slowly pushed aside by influxes of Susu and Malinké following the fall of the Ghana Empire. From the 13th century AD, the Malinké established dominance over much of Upper Guinea and by the 14th century all of Guinea had been incorporated into the powerful Mali Empire. (For more information about early empires, see p33.) Around the 15th century – about the same time that Portuguese navigators first reached the Guinean coast – Peul (or Fula) herders started migrating into the area and settled in the mountainous Fouta Djalon region where they established an influential theocracy.

In the 19th century, the Guinean hero Samory Touré led the fight against French colonialists. He was captured in 1898 and resistance gradually withered. Once the railway from Conakry to Kankan was completed, France began serious exploitation of the area, which by then had become part of French West Africa.

The most famous Guinean of all was Sekou Touré, a descendant of Samory Touré who was born into a poor Malinké family. After becoming the foremost trade unionist in French West Africa he led the fight for independence. In 1956 he led a breakaway movement from the French parent union to form a federation of African trade unions.

## Independence

In 1958 Charles de Gaulle offered the French colonies in West Africa a choice between autonomy as separate countries in a Franco-African community or immediate independence. Sekou Touré declared that Guinea preferred 'freedom in poverty to prosperity in chains' and was the only leader to reject de Gaulle's proposal. Thus, Guinea became the first French colony to gain independence. Sekou Touré became an African legend in his own time and, as leader of Guinea's only viable political party, the country's first president.

De Gaulle, infuriated, immediately withdrew the French colonial administration. French private citizens fled with massive amounts of capital, precipitating an economic collapse in Guinea.

Wanting nothing more to do with the CFA franc, which was linked to the French franc, Touré introduced a new currency, the syli. But with French economic assistance gone, the new country badly needed foreign aid. Touré turned to the USSR, but the link was short-lived.

The government continued on a socialist road, however, and in 1967 commenced a campaign of cultural revolution, with state-run farms and weekly meetings of revolutionary units. It was an unmitigated disaster.

GUINEA

As many as one million Guineans fled into neighbouring countries, while remaining farmers were able to work only one-quarter of the country's cultivable land.

## Reign of Terror

Sekou Touré appointed Malinké to all major government positions and treated his political opponents with cruelty. Following an unsuccessful Portuguese-led invasion in 1970, he became paranoid, often speaking of a plot against his regime. Waves of arrests and executions followed; torture became commonplace. In 1976 Touré charged the entire Peul population with collusion in an attempt to overthrow the government. Thousands of Peul went into exile.

Toward the end of his presidency, Touré changed many of his policies. A major influence was the 1977 Market Women's Revolt, in which several police stations were destroyed and three governors killed, as part of the fight against state plans to discourage private trade.

Sekou Touré died of heart failure in 1984. Days later a military coup was staged by a group of army colonels, including Diarra Traoré, who became prime minister, and Lansana Conté, the new president. They denounced Touré and promised an open society and restoration of free enterprise.

## The Second Republic

The change of government opened up Guinea, but tensions among leaders created problems. Following Traoré's failed coup in 1985, Conté was forced to face the urgent matter of reforming the economy. He introduced austerity measures to secure International Monetary Fund (IMF) funding and a new currency, the Guinean franc.

A new constitution in 1991 created a multiparty political system. Within months there were 34 legalised parties and eight presidential candidates for the 1993 election, which Conté won with just over 50% of the ballot against a divided opposition and despite accusations of fraud.

Conté's control was challenged in 1996, when an army mutiny, instigated by soldiers protesting poor salaries, threatened become a full-blown coup. With political vy, Conté quelled the uprising, but not ore several dozen civilians were killed the presidential palace was torched.

The 1998 presidential elections were considered freer than those of 1993, but proceeded in much the same vein: the campaign period was marred by widespread violence, military interference of opposition party rallies, and arrests of opposition supporters. On election day the country's borders were closed and irregularities (generally favouring Conté) were evident in polling stations. The following day, Alpha Condé, candidate of the leading opposition party, was arrested in Lola and charged with a slew of offences – including, ironically, attempting to overthrow the government. Two other opposition candidates were placed under house arrest while the results were announced: Conté had won again with 56% of the vote. The results were disputed by most observers.

## Instability in the Neighbourhood

Guinea was plagued with violence in 1998 and 1999, when cross-border raids by Sierra Leonean and Liberian rebels (and possibly Guinean dissidents) in the southeast resulted in dozens of deaths. Tension continued into 2000, when unidentified men from across the border in Liberia attacked the Guinean border town of Massadou, killing almost 50 people.

The world took notice days later when a UNHCR employee was killed, along with several others, in a raid on Macenta. By December, Guéckédou was a battle zone, and attacks on Macenta, Kissidougou and other small towns near the border were frequent. The crisis was compounded by the fact that refugee camps in the area were either destroyed in the process or else deliberately targeted by Guineans in retribution for the attacks. Thousands of refugees were trapped in the bush, while others fled further north in Guinea or to other countries. Things gradually quietened down in 2001, but over 1000 people had died in the fighting.

## Guinea Today

In November 2001 a nationwide constitutional referendum, also marred by irregularities, repealed the two-term limit for presidents and lengthened the term from five to seven years, effectively setting up Conté as president for life. Not surprisingly, he won the December 2003 election. Key opposition leaders, citing government obstruction, boycotted both this and the earlier parliamentary election. Conté, a chain-smoking diabetic, appeared in public just once during the campaign and has been rumoured to be on his death-bed several times since.

In January 2005 shots were fired at the presidential motorcade, though Conté was unhurt. Alpha Condé, who spent two years in prison before being pardoned, returned from exile in France in July. Three months later, he and other opposition leaders, united under the Front Républicaine pour l'Alternance Démocratique (FRAD) banner, called for the ailing Conté's resignation, for the sake of the nation, and proposed a transitional government. Conté ignored their advice, though he did allow local elections in December.

Today Guinea faces an unknown future. The economy is faltering and Conté appears not to have planned for his succession. Some observers, including the international, nonprofit International Crisis Group, say Guinea is in danger of becoming a failed state. Others cite the Guineans' unity and abhorrence of violence and predict that whatever happens will be peaceful.

## THE CULTURE
When Guinean women get together they complain about the rapid rise of prices in the market. With men, the conversation invariably turns to football. Both topics reflect the harsh reality of life in Guinea these days. While men have always talked about football, there was once also plenty of debate about politics and corruption. It's not the fear of the police state that has silenced them; they've just grown tired of the topics.

Despite a wealth of resources (over 30% of the world's bauxite supply, for instance), 40% of the population lives below the poverty line. Nobody expects life to change much when a new dictator (democracy is just a dream) takes over, though many figure it just has to get better. Guineans await their new future eagerly, anxiously…and silently.

### Population
Guinea's main tribal groups are Peul (about 40% of the population), Malinké (about 30%) and Susu (about 20%). Fifteen other groups, living mostly in the Forest Region, constitute the rest of the population. Susu

predominantly inhabit the coastal region, Peul the Fouta Djalon and Malinké the north and centre. About 50,000 Liberian refugees remain, mostly in the southeast and Conakry, and repatriation continues apace. Non-Africans, mostly French and Lebanese, total about 10,000.

## RELIGION
About 85% of the population are Muslims, 8% are Christians, and the remainder follow traditional religions. Most of the Christians are in Conakry and the Forest Region while the animists are mostly in the Forest Region and, to a lesser degree, Upper Guinea. While devoted followers of traditional beliefs continue to decline in number, the magic of the past is still respected by many Muslims and Christians: traditional medicines are common and sacred forests respected.

There is little religious discord in the country and mixed families are common. Some Muslims have even begun to celebrate Christmas.

## ARTS
### Arts & Craftwork
In the Fouta Djalon there are many textile cooperatives where you can see the production of a variety of indigo cloths. In the south you can watch women making mud-cloth, as most travellers call it. (Actually there is no mud involved: the earthy browns come from kola nuts and tree bark. Guineans call it forest cloth.) Masks and statues are vital to traditional religions but rarely seen by outsiders except in museums, especially since Sekou Touré was an ardent iconoclast. Modern artists have little opportunity to make a living from their work, though this is slowly changing. Painting is becoming more popular and a new breed of sculptors working with scrap metal has emerged in some cities.

### Music & Dance
Traditional music and dance have flourished in Guinea, partly due to government subsidies during the Sekou Touré era. This cultural heritage is accessible to visitors in Conakry, where performances are often held at the Palais du Peuple (p415) and Centre Culturel Franco-Guinéen (p415) as well as restaurants and nightclubs. One of the best known exports from Guinea is Les Ballets Africains, acclaimed as much for its music

as its movement. Earning its own international reputation is the energetic Circus Baobab. Early musical groups like Bembeya Jazz, Super Boiro and the all-female Les Amazonas de Guineé recorded on the state-owned Syliphone record label and were among the most popular groups in Africa. For more about Guinea's music scene see the Music of West Africa chapter (p58).

## Literature

Guinea's most famous cultural figure, Camara Laye, has been described as 'the first writer of genius to come out of Africa'. Several of his books are available in English including his autobiographical first effort, *The Dark Child* (AKA *The African Child*): it offers fascinating insights into Malinké traditions. A couple of Tierno Monenembo's books have been translated into English, such as *The Oldest Orphan*, but not *Cinema*, his best-known work.

## Cinema

Guinea has a limited cinematic oeuvre, though it features two of Africa's most controversial films. Mohamed Camara's *Dakan* (1997) is the first feature film about homosexuality from sub-Saharan Africa. Director David Achkar's search for answers about his father, executed by Sekou Touré, is documented in *Allah Tantou* (1991). Both are in French, but available on tape with English subtitles. French Director Laurent Chevalier adapted *The Dark Child* for the screen using members of the author's family.

## ENVIRONMENT
### The Land

Guinea has four distinct zones: a narrow coastal plain, the Fouta Djalon plateau, northeastern dry lowlands and the Forest Region of the southeast. The Fouta Djalon plateau, rising to over 1500m, is the source of the Gambia and Senegal Rivers and of much of the Niger (although the actual source of the Niger River lies to the south, near the Sierra Leone border). Southeastern Guinea is hilly and heavily vegetated, although little virgin rainforest remains.

## Wildlife

Large animals are rarely sighted, though waterbucks, bongos, buffalos, baboons, leopards and lions wander the forests while crocodiles, manatees and hippopotamuses swim the rivers. The abundant birdlife includes brown-cheeked hornbills, long-tailed hawks, grey parrots and Nimba fly-catchers. Two amphibians of note, both of which live on Mont Nimba, are the goliath frogs, which can weigh three kilograms, and the Nimba toads, which bear live young.

Guinea is one of West Africa's last strongholds for chimpanzees. One group living near Bossou got a lot of press in 2005 after a Japanese researcher documented that they not only knew how to detect and destroy traps but taught this skill to others. Because Guinea shares borders with Côte d'Ivoire and Senegal, two countries that permit ivory sales, its already small elephant population is especially endangered.

## National Parks & Reserves

Guinea has many designated protected areas *(forêts classée)*, although there is little enforcement of environmental regulations. The Mount Nimba Nature Reserve in the far southeast, on the Côte d'Ivoire border, is a Unesco World Heritage Site, but this didn't stop the government from opening an iron mine on the mountainside. Nearby is Forêt Classée de Ziama, where the rainforest remains pristine (for now, anyway) and elephants are often spotted. The future of the two national parks, Parc Transfrontalier Niokolo-Badiar, near Koundara, and Parc National du Haut Niger, northeast of Faranah, is unclear due to lack of funding. Inquire at the **Direction Nationale des Forêts et de la Faune** (Map pp410-11; Route de Donka, Conakry) before making a trip to either.

## Environmental Issues

Guinea's environmental record is atrocious. Most animal populations are declining and even basic data on much of the flora and fauna has never been gathered. The primary concern is deforestation. The departure of most refugees has eased the problem of unsustainable slash-and-burn agriculture, though logging continues largely unchecked and has proceeded so rapidly in the south that the Forest Region really ought to adopt a new name. On the coast, much of the mangrove forest has been cleared for rice production and overfishing is a growing problem. Large mining companies have pledged to improve their practices and there is some evidence this is happening.

## FOOD & DRINK

Guinean food is not the best of the west. Despite the abundance of peppers for sale in the markets, most cooks spare the spice. Thankfully, if the food is a little bland for your tastes you can usually get a pepper sauce or some crushed pepper to add to your bowl. Outside Conakry there are few proper restaurants (except those at hotels and they mostly serve European-style dishes) though most towns have one or two basic eating houses doing cheap meals of rice and sauce and lots of street food vendors. Rice is reserved for breakfast and lunch while nights are all about grilled meat. The most common sauces are made of manioc leaves (*feuille de manioc*) and groundnuts (*patate*).

Although Nescafé is available everywhere, Guinea is fortunate enough to have a real coffee tradition: *café noir* is a bit like espresso, and is served in small cups with lots of sugar. Guinea has two main beers – Skol, a light lager, and Guiluxe, a darker brew. European beers are available at most Conakry bars and restaurants.

# CONAKRY

**pop 2 million**
Historically, Conakry was one of colonial France's major ports in West Africa, but it has been a very long time since it wore the 'Paris of Africa' label. Today, even with an ongoing facelift, it's still a long way from regaining it and many travellers head up-country as fast as they can.

There is nothing really wrong with Conakry – it's calmer, cleaner and safer than many other West African capitals and getting around is easy because most traffic is limited to a few main roads – but it is certainly short of must-sees and must-dos; unless you consider the palm-fringed beaches of the Îles de Los a part of the city.

But Conakry's many good restaurants, live music and vibrant neighbourhood life make it well worth spending a few days here before you explore the rest of Guinea. These more subtle charms are likely to grow on you and many people end up loving the city by the time they leave.

## ORIENTATION

*La ville* (downtown; Map pp410–11), an island until the late 19th century, centres on Ave de la République: banks, airline offices and several restaurants are on or around this street. About 10km northeast, the colourful Taouyah *quartier* (neighbourhood), is livelier than the centre at night. Further out (Map p412) are the well-to-do Ratoma, Kipé and Kaporo *quartiers* with many hotels and restaurants.

The city is divided into five main communes: Kaloum covers downtown; Dixinn runs from Cameroun to Minière; Ratoma, a sprawling district that includes the Taouyah, Ratoma, Kipé and Kaporo *quartiers;* Matam, on the south side, contains Coléah and Madina; and Matoto is out by the airport and continues far inland.

The main streets are the Autoroute, Route du Niger and Route de Donka. Route du Niger runs into Ave de la République in town and into the Autoroute at the airport, and Route de Donka branches off the Autoroute at the Centre Culturel Franco-Guinéen and then continues into Ratoma. Conakry's location on a narrow peninsula means the city – now home to 20% of Guinea's population – suffers horrible rush hour traffic.

### Maps

Libraries, *papeteries* and Ave de la République street vendors sell Conakry maps for about GF15,000.

## INFORMATION
### Bookshops

**Soguidip** (Map pp410-11; 4th Ave, La ville) Has books in French, including works by Guinean authors as well as many French magazines and some in English. Their newsstand by the Hyper-Bobo Supermarket carries the *International Herald Tribune*.

### Cultural Centres

**American Center** (Map pp410-11; ☎ 454486; Corniche Sud, Coléah; ☒ 7.30am-5pm Mon, Tue & Thu, 7.30am-1pm Fri)
**Centre Culturel Franco-Guinéen** (Map pp410-11; ☎ 013-409625; Corniche Nord, Tumbo; ☒ 9am-6pm Mon-Fri, closed Aug) The centre also runs a library (Map pp410-11) on Ave de la République.

GUINEA

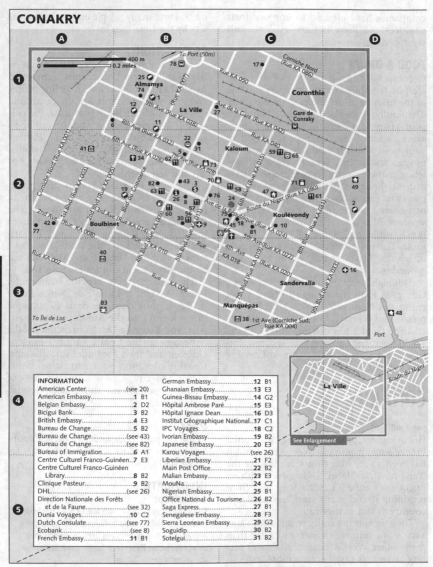

**CONAKRY**

## Internet Access

Cybercafés are all over the city, and connections are fast. The following are large with modern computers, open daily and have air-conditioning.

**Cyber Ratoma** (Map p412; Route de Donka, Ratoma)

**MouNa** (Map pp410-11; Ave de la République, La ville)

## Medical Services

There are many good pharmacies along Ave de la République.

**Clinique Pasteur** (Map pp410-11; ☎ 747576) This clinic in the centre is good, though for anything serious you'll probably need to get to Dakar or Europe.

**Hôpital Ambrose Paré** (Map pp410-11; ☎ 011-211320; Dixinn) Considered the best in Guinea.

**SLEEPING**
| | |
|---|---|
| Hôtel Camayenne | 44 E3 |
| Hôtel Central | 45 C2 |
| Hôtel du Golfe | 46 G1 |
| Hôtel du Niger | 47 C2 |
| Hôtel Petit Bateau | 48 D3 |
| Maison d'Accueil | 49 D2 |

**EATING**
| | |
|---|---|
| A-Z | (see 29) |
| Al Forno | 50 E3 |
| Belvédère | 51 G2 |
| Chez Sylvie | 52 E3 |
| Family Choice | 53 G1 |
| Hyper-Bobo | 54 E3 |
| Indochine | 55 G1 |
| Jbara | 56 B2 |
| La Gondole | 57 B2 |
| La Petit Bateau | (see 48) |
| Le Cèdre | 58 C2 |
| Le Gentilhommière | 59 C2 |
| Le Soft | 60 B2 |
| Pâtisserie Centrale | (see 45) |
| Pâtisserie le Damier | 61 C2 |
| Restaurant Chinois | 62 B2 |
| Rice Women | 63 B2 |

**SIGHTS & ACTIVITIES**
| | |
|---|---|
| Botanical Garden | 32 E3 |
| Camp Boiro | 33 E3 |
| Cathedrale Sante-Marie | 34 B2 |
| Gamal Abdel Nasser University of Conakry | 35 F2 |
| Grande Mosquée | 36 F3 |
| Jardin 2 Octobre | 37 E3 |
| Musée National | 38 C3 |
| Oppo Atelier | 39 E4 |
| Palais des Nations | 40 A3 |
| Palais Présidentiel | 41 A2 |
| Woodcarvers | 42 A2 |
| Woodcarvers | 43 B2 |

**ENTERTAINMENT**
| | |
|---|---|
| Atlantis | 64 E3 |
| Circus Baobab | 65 C2 |
| Fourchette Magique | 66 C2 |
| La Paillotte | 67 E3 |
| Palais du Peuple | 68 E4 |
| Siège des Ballets Africains | 69 F3 |

**SHOPPING**
| | |
|---|---|
| CAAF (Women's Cloth Coop) | 70 B2 |
| Marché du Niger | 71 C2 |
| Marché Madina | 72 G3 |
| Papeterie Centrale | 73 B2 |

**TRANSPORT**
| | |
|---|---|
| Air France | 74 B1 |
| Air Ivoire | 75 C2 |
| Air Sénégal International | 76 B2 |
| Avis | 77 A2 |
| Bellview Airlines | (see 76) |
| Bus Stop | 78 B1 |
| Europcar | (see 44) |
| Gare Voiture Matam | 79 H2 |
| Gare Voiture Siguiri | 80 G3 |
| Hertz | 81 C2 |
| Mondial Tours | 82 B2 |
| Pirogues to Îles de Los | 83 A3 |
| Slok Air | (see 18) |

## Money
Men offering to change money line Ave de la République, though it is best to go to one of the bureaus de change. There are several along 4th Blvd.

**Bicigui** (Map pp410-11; Ave de la République) The main branch changes travellers cheques and has an ATM (available 24 hours) that works with Visa cards.

**Ecobank** (Map pp410-11; Ave de la République) Just across the street, from Bicigui, this bank has better hours (open Saturday) and better exchange rates, but they still fall below what you will get from private money-changers.

## Post
**DHL** (Map pp410-11; 4th Blvd, La ville)

GUINEA

**Main post office** (Map pp410-11; 4th Blvd, La ville; ⊗ 8am-5pm Mon-Fri, until 3pm Sat) To collect a letter from the disorganised poste restante you must open an account (GF12,000).

**Saga Express** (Map pp410-11; 4th Blvd, La ville) The agent for FedEx.

## Telephone & Fax

Downtown you'll probably be approached by guys who run illicit phone services with international prices around GF1000 per minute.

**Sotelgui** (Map pp410-11; fax 453670; ⊗ 8am-8pm Mon-Sat) Faxes can be received for GF2000 per page and sent for GF8000 per page at this office, though they no longer handle phone calls.

## Tourist Information

**Office National du Tourisme** (Map pp410-11; ☎ 455163; ontour@sotelgui.net.gn; 2nd fl, Karou Voyages Bldg, Ave de la République, La ville) It's an office rather than a welcome centre, but the folks are friendly.

## Travel Agencies

The following agencies, all on Ave de la République, are long established and very professional.

**Dunia Voyages** (Map pp410-11; ☎ 454848, mlkaloga@yahoo.fr)

**IPC Voyages** (Map pp410-11; ☎ 455662; www.ipctravel.net/ipcgn.htm)

**Karou Voyages** (Map pp410-11; ☎ 452042, karouvoyagegn2003@yahoo.com)

## Visa Extensions

**Bureau of Immigration** (Map pp410-11; ☎ 441339; 8th Ave) Visas can be extended for up to three months for GF80,000.

## DANGERS & ANNOYANCES

Conakry is pretty safe by African standards, but the usual big-city precautions apply. The places you're most likely to have trouble with petty street crime are the airport and the markets, especially Madina. At night, the whole Madina *quartier* has a bad reputation for crime, though things have gotten better as of late. Conakry's frequent traffic jams make it easy for bag snatchers to reach in vehicle windows, so keep hold of your belongings.

After midnight, checkpoints are set up at Place du 8 Novembre (Map pp410–11) and the Japanese embassy (Map pp410–11), the two routes to and from downtown, and it's common for the soldiers manning them to

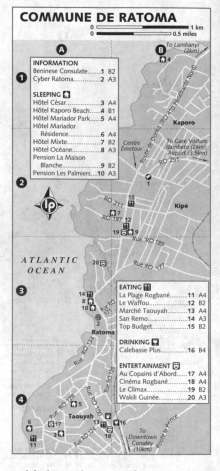

**COMMUNE DE RATOMA**

INFORMATION
Beninese Consulate.......1 B2
Cyber Ratoma.............2 A3

SLEEPING
Hôtel César...............3 A4
Hôtel Kaporo Beach......4 B1
Hôtel Mariador Park.....5 A4
Hôtel Mariador
Résidence...............6 A4
Hôtel Mixte.............7 B2
Hôtel Océane............8 A3
Pension La Maison
Blanche................9 B2
Pension Les Palmiers....10 A3

EATING
La Plage Rogbané..........11 A4
Le Waffou.................12 B2
Marché Taouyah..........13 A4
San Remo..................14 A3
Top Budget................15 B2

DRINKING
Calebasse Plus..............16 B4

ENTERTAINMENT
Au Copains d'Abord......17 A4
Cinéma Rogbané.........18 A4
Le Climax.................19 B2
Wakili Guinée.............20 A3

seek bribes. As long as you have your papers in order, you shouldn't have to pay if you're riding in a taxi. In your own car, most people simply pay GF1000 or GF2000 up front to avoid protracted discussion. If the soldiers are drunk the going rate is GF5000.

## SIGHTS

**Musée National** (Map pp410-11; ☎ 415060; 7th Blvd, La ville; admission GF1000; ⊗ 9am-5.30pm Tue-Sun) is the country's largest collection of masks, statues and musical instruments. It's modest, but interesting. Woodcarvers and drum-makers ply their trades on the museum grounds.

Financed primarily by Saudi Arabia and inaugurated in 1984, the impressive **Grande Mosquée** (Map pp410-11; Autoroute, Camayenne) has an inner hall capable of accommodating 10,000 worshippers. Although visitors are not usually allowed inside, you can inquire at the Islamic Centre next door about arranging a tour. Sekou Touré's grave is in a small gazebo on the grounds.

Not as impressive as the mosque, Conakry's yellow and red **Cathédrale Sainte-Marie** (Map pp410-11; Blvd du Commerce, La ville) is nevertheless a beautiful building. Behind the Cathedral is the Palais Présidentiel.

Intended to be the venue for the Organisation of African Unity conference in 1984, which was cancelled when Sekou Touré died, the grand **Palais des Nations** (Map pp410-11; quartier de Boulbinet, La ville) served as the president's office until being destroyed in the February 1996 army rebellion. It's in ruins. Near the palace are 50 Moorish-style villas, built to house African presidents during the conference and now used as residences and offices.

**Oppo Atelier** (Map pp410-11; Corniche Nord, Tumbo; 8am-6pm) is an association of welders that makes funky sculptures from scrap metal near the Palais du Peuple. You can watch the statues being made and if you bring a picture they will do custom work.

The two large and interesting mosaics at the **Gamal Abdel Nasser University of Conakry** (Map pp410-11; Route de Donka, Dixinn) are worth a look.

Many families gather in **Jardin 2 Octobre** (Map pp410-11; Corniche Nord, Tumbo) on weekends.

Surrounding the Direction Nationale des Forêts et de la Faune, the **Botanical Garden** (Map pp410-11; Route de Donka, Camayenne) is the coolest place in the city, though not the cleanest.

## COURSES
The **Centre Culturel Franco-Guinéen** (Map pp410-11; ☎ 013-409625; Corniche Nord, Tumbo) arranges drum and dance lessons.

## FESTIVALS & EVENTS
If you are here during the week-long **Guinea Festival** (see p438) you will have the chance to see Les Ballets Africains and other top groups perform.

## SLEEPING
### Budget
Inexpensive lodging is scarce in Conakry, and most of what exists is in Ratoma, a 30-minute taxi ride from the city centre.

**Maison d'Accueil** (Map pp410-11; ☎ 343655, traore _celestine@yahoo.fr; Route du Niger, La ville; s/d with fan from GF30,000/45,000, s/d with air-con GF50,000/75,000; P 🛇 ) With rooms so clean you could eat off the floor, the Catholic Mission is the best of the budget accommodation and, unusually, it is right in the centre of town, but you are unlikely to get in without booking well in advance. Rooms at the back face a tranquil yard.

**Pension La Maison Blanche** (Map p412; signposted off Route de Donka, Kipé; r with fan GF40,000; P ) This simple hotel is in a quiet location and is excellent value. You'll often hear the Amoussou drum and dance troupe practicing next door – they welcome visitors.

**Hôtel du Niger** (Map pp410-11; ☎ 414130; 6th Blvd, La ville; r with fan GF35,000, r with air-con 45,000-50,000; 🛇 ) Rooms at this, the only other cheap accommodation in the centre, are musty and

**GUINEA**

---

**CAMP BOIRO**

Although over 20 years have passed since Sekou Touré's death, his legacy continues. Some knowledge of his era is important if you want to understand present-day Guinea.

A good place to start is Camp Boiro (Map pp410–11), in the centre of Conakry on Route de Donka. Called Garde Républicaine on some maps, this military base rapidly became synonymous with the worst atrocities carried out during Touré's 'reign of terror'. From 1960 until Touré's death in 1984, thousands of prisoners were tortured or killed at Camp Boiro, including many prominent figures. Every sector of society was affected, and most Guineans you meet can tell of a family member or friend who was there. Many prisoners were held for years in isolation; others were kept in a horrifying cement holding-pen open to the elements until they died.

Boiro was not the only camp of this kind in Guinea; there was another notorious one in Kindia, as well as smaller camps throughout the country. The bodies of many of those who died at Boiro have been lost. Others are buried in unmarked graves at the overgrown Nongo cemetery on the outskirts of town beyond Kaporo. The present government is not eager to discuss this part of Guinea's history, but in 1998 a group of organisations associated with family members of victims succeeded in walling off a cemetery in Boiro to commemorate those who died.

ragged, but generally clean. The bar can get pretty noisy.

**Hôtel Mixte** (Map p412; ☎ 280644; Rue RO 197, Kipé; r with fan GF30,000; P ) Like most of the cheap places hidden off Route de Donka in Ratoma, the clientele here generally rents by the hour, but its okay for a night or two. Single women, however, may want to look elsewhere.

### Midrange

**Pension Les Palmiers** (Map p412; ☎ 421103; Route de Donka, Ratoma; s/d GF100,000/120,000; P X ) Known to most as Pension Ghussein, after the delightful French owner, Les Palmiers is as homey as they come. The seaside patio is great for breakfast and sunsets.

**Hôtel Kaporo Beach** (Map p412; ☎ 527978; signposted off Route de Donka, Kaporo; r GF90,000; P X X ) Not only are rooms bright and spotless, but they come with a swimming pool and a view that will make you forget you're in a city. The restaurant is good too.

**Hôtel Petit Bateau** (Map pp410-11; ☎ 013-406275, www.hotelpetitbateau.com; port de plaisance; s/d GF155,000/220,000, ste 245,000-280,000; P X X X ) Nice rooms with nice views; Petit Bateau takes full advantage of its seaside location.

**Hôtel Mariador Résidence** (Map p412; ☎ 011-333535, residence@mariador.com; off Rue RO 128, Taouyah; s GF120,000-140,000, d GF140,000-160,000; P X X ) This popular hotel has a seaside terrace, a pool (GF15,000 for nonguests) and comfortable rooms. The most expensive rooms have sea views.

**Hôtel Mariador Park** (Map p412; ☎ 229740, park@mariador.com; Rue RO 128, Taouyah; r GF132,000-180,000; P X ) Despite the higher prices, the Mariador Park is a small step down from the Résidence, but still good. Rooms are spacious and clean and the higher priced ones have sitting rooms and kitchens.

**Hôtel Océane** (Map p412; ☎ 422022; Route de Donka, Ratoma; s/d incl breakfast GF150,000/175,000; P X X ) This is a nice-looking place on the ocean, where waves crash up to the large swimming pool, but make sure everything in your room works before handing over your francs.

**Hôtel César** (Map p412; ☎ 221067; off Rue RO 124, Taouyah; r GF100,000; P X ) The César is a homey little place and decent enough for the price.

**Hôtel du Golfe** (Map pp410-11; ☎ 421394; off Route de Donka, Minière; s GF65,000-75,000, d 70,000-80,000, ste GF125,000; P X ) Nothing fancy, but the rooms

here are good value and the place is as professionally run as more expensive hotels.

**Hôtel Central** (Map pp410-11; ☎ 431250; 6th Blvd, La ville; s GF160,000-200,000, d 180,000-220,000; P X X ) The large rooms at this downtown hotel have balconies and plenty of fixings, though the price is a little high for what you get.

### Top End

**Hôtel Camayenne** (Map pp410-11; ☎ 012-664848, info@camayenne.net; Corniche Nord, Camayenne; s GF560,000-720,000, d GF640,000-800,000; P X X X ) All 96 of the Camayenne's comfortable, fully equipped rooms overlook the ocean, and the pleasant pool and bar area catch sea breezes and sunsets. Besides the swimming pool, fitness centre and tennis courts, Camayenne has a little beach.

## EATING & DRINKING
### La Ville

Places with good street food for less than GF3000 include Marché du Niger (Map pp410-11) and the stalls at the intersection of Corniche Nord and Blvd du Commerce. At lunch time, you'll find a slew of women serving rice at several (often hidden) spots just south of Ave de la République.

**Le Gentilhommière** (Map pp410-11; Rue KA 040; meals GF15,000-30,000; ☽ lunch & dinner) Gentilhommière doesn't look like much from the outside, but the bamboo, thatch and calabash interior invites you to stick around a while; as does the wide variety of African dishes.

**Pâtisserie le Damier** (Map pp410-11; Route du Niger; meals GF12,000-40,000; ☽ breakfast & lunch Mon-Sat) This place serves some of the best French cuisine in the city and successfully pulls off a Parisian vibe. The handmade chocolates are expensive, but worth it, as is the all-you-can-eat Saturday brunch.

**Le Cèdre** (Map pp410-11; 7th Ave; meals GF17,000-27,000; ☽ lunch & dinner) With the best Middle Eastern food in town, Le Cèdre is always busy.

**Le Petit Bateau** (port de plaisance; meals GF15,000-30,000; ☽ breakfast, lunch & dinner) Famous for seafood, naturally, but you can also eat Asian and Italian favourites under the thatch roofs while enjoying the cool ocean air.

**La Gondole** (Ave de la République; meals GF2500-30,000; ☽ breakfast, lunch & dinner) La Gondole has a full menu, but it's really all about the ice cream, which comes in 20 flavours including banana and chewing gum and is fairly good: at GF5000 per scoop it ought to be.

**Pâtisserie Centrale** (Map pp410-11; Ave de la République; meals GF5000-30,000; ☯ breakfast, lunch & dinner) This place has lots of sweets as well as fast food like shwarma and pizza slices.

**Le Soft** (Map pp410-11; 4th Blvd; meals GF5000-10,000; ☯ lunch & dinner) Crowded little Le Soft serves large plates of Guinean, Ivorian and Senegalese dishes and packs them in for the flavour, not the décor.

**Restaurant Chinois** (Map pp410-11; 6th Ave; meals GF5000-30,000; ☯ lunch & dinner) This pleasant restaurant has a monstrous menu and a mostly Asian clientele. It's the best Chinese food downtown.

### Dixinn

**Chez Sylvie** (Map pp410-11; fronting Hôtel Camayenne; meals GF4000-6000; ☯ dinner) Chez Sylvie is one of several little simple rice bars on this end of the street that prepare the best-quality *attiéké* (cassava couscous) in town.

**Al Forno** (Map pp410-11; ☎ 011-589482; Rue DI 011, Camayenne; meals GF10,000-26,000; ☯ lunch & dinner Wed-Mon) This cute little place has crepes and brick-oven pizzas; and they deliver.

**Indochine** (Map pp410-11; Rue DI 777, Minière; meals GF23,000-34,000; ☯ lunch Tue-Sun, dinner daily) Indochine serves delectable dishes from China, Thailand and Vietnam and features one of the classiest dining rooms in Conakry.

**Belvédére** (Map pp410-11; Route de Donka, Bellevue; meals GF8000-32,000; ☯ dinner) The food – sandwiches, steak, pizza – is nothing special, but this brightly lit open-air place is a lot of fun at night. The playground equipment entertains the kids and there is sometimes live music on weekends for the adults.

### Ratoma

Plenty of good street food vendors front the Marché Taouyah (Map p412), especially in the evening. Hôtels Océane, Kaporo Beach and Mariador Residence all draw diners as much for the seaside settings as the food.

**Le Waffou** (Map p412; off Route de Donka, Kipé; meals GF5000-20,000; ☯ lunch & dinner) Le Waffou, a colourful spot with tables under thatch-roofed huts, serves delicious Ivorian food, including banana *fufu* (pounded cassava). The Amoussou drum and dance troupe performs at 8pm on Friday nights.

**San Remo** (Map p412; Route de Donka, Ratoma; meals GF15,000-30,000; ☯ dinner Wed-Sun) A quiet little

place in Ratoma with a brick oven that just might make Guinea's best pizza.

**La Plage Rogbané** (Map p412; near Rue RO 128; Taouyah; meals GF10,000-20,000; ☯ lunch & dinner) This stretch of beach at the end of an unmarked alley was cleaned up (well, sort of) so people could use it, though the water is pretty dirty. The bar is aimed right at the sunset and they serve surprisingly good seafood.

**Calebasse Plus** (Map p412; Rue de Donka, Taouyah) No longer a live music hotspot, this animated bar is still a good place for a drink.

### Supermarkets

Well-stocked (but expensive) supermarkets include **A-Z** (Map pp410-11; Carrefour Bellevue), **Family Choice** (Map pp410-11; Minière), **Hyper-Bobo** (Map pp410-11; Camayenne), **Jbara** (Map pp410-11; downtown) and **Top Budget** (Map p412; Kipé).

## ENTERTAINMENT

Conakry has *beaucoup de* night spots, most out in Ratoma, that get busy around 11pm. Saturday is the busiest night. Cover charges start around GF5000, more on weekends.

You chance of seeing a performance by Les Ballet Africains, the national dance company, or the renowned Circus Baobab are pretty slim, but when they aren't touring the world you are welcome to drop by their practice spaces. You can watch them practice on weekday mornings at **Siège des Ballets Africains** (Map pp410-11; off Corniche Sud, Coléah). **Circus Baobab** (Map pp410-11; Rue KA 040) has its home base downtown. They rehearse Monday to Saturday mornings and share their space with the Fatou Abou drum and dance troupe who practice in the afternoon.

### Live Music

**Wakili Guinée** (Map p412; signposted off Route de Donka, Ratoma) Opened by local musicians, Wakili plans to feature drum, balafon (xylophone) and *kora* (a harp-like instrument) players on Thursday, Friday and Saturday nights. They also intend to open some budget-priced guestrooms with air-conditioning.

**Fourchette Magique** (Map pp410-11; 6th Blvd, La ville) An intimate place downtown with live jazz Wednesday through Sunday night.

**Centre Culturel Franco-Guinéen** (Map pp410-11; Corniche Nord, Tumbo) Every Wednesday is Café Concert night, with free live music and there are sometimes performances by local and visiting artists on other nights.

**Au Copains d'Abord** (Map p412; Rue RO 128, Taouyah) The live music, sometimes played by blind musicians, goes well with the pizzas at this lively spot.

**La Paillotte** (Map pp410-11; Corniche Nord, Camayenne) Once the stage of choice for Guinea's old-school stars, Paillotte now has a mix of old and new artists most Saturdays.

**Palais du Peuple** (Map pp410-11; Corniche Nord; Tumbo) The place for special events, whether it's a Guinean women's rap festival or a touring act down from Paris.

### Dancing

**Atlantis** (Map pp410-11; Corniche Nord, Tumbo) The Hôtel Riviera Royal's flashy nightclub is an expat favourite.

**Le Climax** (Map p412; Route de Donka, Kipé) A long-running night spot that once appealed to the younger set, but is now trying to reinvent itself for an older crowd.

### Cinemas

Near the Marché Taouyah, the recently renovated **Cinéma Rogbané** (Map p412; Route de Donka, Taouyah) has shows most evenings. The Centre Culturel Franco-Guinéen and the American Center (see p409) also frequently show films, both Western and African.

## SHOPPING

**Marché Madina** Map pp410-11; Madina) is one of West Africa's largest markets and there is little you can't find, including some talented thieves. A walk through the **Marché du Niger** (Map pp410-11) is an experience.

The **Centre d'Appui à l'Autopromotion Féminine** (CAAF; Map pp410-11; 5th Blvd, La ville) women's co-operative outlet has a huge selection of interesting tie-dyed cloth. The numerous vendors opposite Hôtel Camayenne sell all the usual crafts while the shops around the CAAF have a smaller selection but higher quality. In general, it's better to buy baskets, textiles and other crafts upcountry, as quality is as good or better and prices are lower. Several woodcarving shops are found around town.

**Papeterie Centrale** (Map pp410-11; 8th Ave, La ville) has the city's best postcards.

## GETTING THERE & AWAY
### Air

Conakry has the only functioning airport in the country, though at the time of research there was talk of resuming flights to Kankan, Labé, N'zérékoré and Siguiri. When available, domestic flights use the *aérogare nationale* near the international airport. For details of international flights to/from Conakry see p436.

### Bush Taxi, Minibus & Bus

Domestic destinations, and some foreign ones, are served by two *gares voitures*: Bambeto and Matam (Map pp410–11). In terms of destinations served, they're nearly the same (big buses to Kankan, Boké and N'zérékoré only use Matam). The big difference is that Bambeto is paved and orderly while Matam is a bit busier so cars often fill faster. Bush taxis coming into Conakry drop passengers off along the main roads and don't necessarily go to the *gare voiture*. For a few thousands francs (it's best to arrange this at your point of departure when everyone else in the car will keep the driver honest on the price) you can usually convince your driver to take you right to your hotel.

Leaving Guinea, there are several taxis daily from each *gare voiture* for Freetown, Sierra Leone (GF55,000, seven hours) and Diaoubé, Senegal (GF100,000, two days). A bus also goes to Freetown (GF60,000) from Matam on Tuesday and Friday. For Bamako, Mali (GF110,000, 24 hours), cars use the Gare Voiture Siguiri (Map pp410–11) in the Madina market (see also left) and the three-day marathon to Monrovia (GF150,000) begins at the Gare Voiture de Matoto. See also p436.

## GETTING AROUND
### To/From the Airport

Chartering a taxi between downtown and the airport shouldn't cost more than about GF15,000 (GF20,000 to GF25,000 at night). You can also catch a shared taxi from just outside the airport to most destinations in the city.

### Bus

Though the bus (GF400) is the slowest way to get around and there aren't very many of them, when every taxi that has passed you by for the last 20 minutes is full you may want to jump on. Buses run along Route de Donka in Ratoma as well as up the Autoroute past the airport. You can catch buses for both places downtown at the roundabout opposite the port.

## Car

Prices and terms between these companies vary widely though you can expect Hertz to be the lowest. Be sure to inquire about what is and is not included in the price.

**Avis** (Map pp410–11; ☎ 445021; Novotel)
**Europcar** (Map pp410–11; ☎ 215060; Hôtel Camayenne)
**Hertz** (Map pp410–11; ☎ 433778; Ave de la République)

## Taxi & Minibuses

A seat in a shared taxi around town costs GF700 per zone, with the downtown zone ending at Dixinn (on the Route de Donka) and Madina (on the Route du Niger and Autoroute). Believe it or not, you can almost always trust drivers to charge you the right price. To catch one, stand on the appropriate side of the road and yell your destination as the taxi passes. There's also a clever hand-signal method by which you point in the direction that the taxi takes at the major roundabouts. Drivers sign back the number of seats available. The slightly cheaper mini-buses *(magbanas)* work like taxis, only they are a lot slower. They cost GF500 per zone.

If you want to charter a taxi (called *dé-placement*) you'll need to find an empty one and then bargain hard. From downtown to Taouyah, for example, should cost around GF15,000 during the day and GF20,000 to GF25,000 at night.

# AROUND CONAKRY

## ÎLES DE LOS

The Îles de Los are a group of small islands about 10km southwest of Conakry, once used as a way station for the slave trade and later by the British (who controlled the islands during much of the 19th century) to resettle freed slaves. They're now popular for weekend excursions. Besides the hotels, some locals rent out rooms in their homes, but keep your belongings locked up if you choose this option.

Tiny **Île Room** has a tranquil beach, which is good for swimming, and a pretty hotel, **Le Sogué** ( ☎ 215959; s GF160,000, d GF195,000; ☯ Oct–mid-Jun; ☒ ) which can organise return transport for CFA30,000. **Foré-Foté** (r around GF15,000) in the village has basic rooms, the price is negotiable. Ask at the beach for Sinny or Kalla, who run the place along with their drumming school.

**Île de Kassa** is closer to Conakry and a beautiful place to walk around. Near **Soro** (admission GF1000), the attractive main beach, are some cheap **bungalows** (Mon–Fri around GF35,000) and a restaurant. **Le Magellan** ( ☎ 422022; r GF212,000; ☯ Oct–mid-Jun; ☒ ☒ ) is a fancy place on the other side of the island owned by the same people as Hôtel Océane in Conakry. They can organise return transport for GF20,000.

**Île Tamara**, used by the French and later by Sekou Touré as a penal colony, is not as popular, as its beaches aren't particularly good, although it offers some interesting hikes. Fotoba, with its small Anglican church, is the main village.

### Getting There & Away

Overcrowded *pirogues* (traditional canoes, up to GF3000) leave regularly for Soro, Fotoba and Room from Port Boulbinet, near Palais du Nations. Alternatively, several of Conakry's fanciest hotels run their own weekend boats.

You can also hire your own *pirogue* (which holds up to 30 people) for any of the islands at Port Boulbinet or over by the Novotel. The price depends more on where you want to go than how long you want to stay out: bargain hard and don't pay the full amount upfront.

## DUBRÉKA

Dubréka is President Lansana Conté's home town and the starting point for excursions to several natural attractions. Near the town are mangrove swamps with a rich variety of bird and animal life. You can hire a large *pirogue* at Port Soumba (where you can also see some captive crocodiles) for about GF150,000, but be sure it's in good condition as it takes over an hour to really get into the swamps.

**Les Cascades de la Soumba** (admission GF7500; r with breakfast GF180,000; meals GF10,000-28,000; ℗ ☒ ) make a good outing; except from February to May, when they dry up to a trickle. The falls were held sacred by locals and were once a site for sacrifices. Beneath the falls is a refreshing pool where you can swim. There's a nice restaurant here and, nearby, six fully equipped bungalows. The owner can organise hikes into the surrounding area. The signposted turn-off to the falls is 11km after Dubréka junction on the Boké highway; the falls are 5km further down a

GUINEA

dirt road. To charter a taxi for the day from Dubréka junction costs about GF20,000.

About 10km east of Dubréka **Mt Kakoulima** (1011m) offers some good day hikes. Ask someone at Dubréka junction to point out the famous **Le Chien Qui Fume** rock formation.

## KINDIA

After Conakry, Kindia is Guinea's most crowded and hectic town. It's a good place to look for indigo cloth and if you ask around somebody will lead you to one of the cooperatives, where you can watch it being made. About 5km north of town is the decaying **Institut Pasteur** (7.30am-4pm), which locals calls Pastoria, once an important medical research centre. Today it hosts a horrific little zoo. A shared taxi costs GF1500, though you'll probably wait a long time to get back.

**Voile de la Mariée** (Bridal Veil Falls; admission GF1000), 12km out of town, are worth a visit during the rainy season. A taxi to Bendougou (GF2000) will drop you off right there or you can walk 3km from the highway.

### Sleeping & Eating

There's little reason to stay here since the sights can be quickly seen on your way to or from Conakry, though there are plenty of options if you choose to.

**Bungalows** (r GF25,000; P) Best located are these bungalows at Voile de la Mariée. They're getting old, but the setting more than makes up for it. Meals are available by request.

**Le Flamboyant** ( 610212; signposted off the Conakry Hwy; r GF60,000; P ⌧ ⌨ ) This place, west of town, is in a tranquil setting and has beautiful rooms and shady grounds. They can advise you on hikes in the surrounding hills.

**Hôtel 3 Avril** (r GF10,000) This hotel is pretty dingy, but it's in the centre of town and the staff is friendly.

Kindia has a number of good hole-in-the-wall cafés in town.

**Café de l'Amitié** (snacks from GF1000) South of the market is this place with good coffee and a warm atmosphere.

**Le Mont Gangan** (meals GF3000-7000) Serves up simple comfort food like spaghetti and chicken plus good people watching.

### Getting There & Away

Taxis leave daily for Télimélé (GF17,000, five hours), Mamou (GF13,500, three hours) and Conakry (GF10,000, three hours). For Kamakwie (GF25,000, seven hours) in Sierra Leone there is a departure about every other day. See also p437.

All taxis run from the *gare voiture* and town taxi stand, except taxis for Conakry, which leave from the stand further west.

# FOUTA DJALON

The Fouta Djalon plateau – an area of green rolling hills, 1000m peaks, orchards and farmland – is one of the most scenic areas of Guinea and the heartland of the country's Peul population (the language spoken is Pulaar). It's also one of the best hiking places in West Africa, especially from November to January, when temperatures are cooler and the sky is not too dusty.

## MAMOU

Mamou, sometimes called the gateway to the Fouta Djalon, is a dusty junction town with an interesting hilltop mosque. Mamou offers little reason to stop, but there are some worthy sights nearby. Several vine bridges span area rivers, including one at **Soumayereya**, 30 minutes by motorcycle from Marella, southeast of Mamou, on a very bad road. It's some hassle to get here, but worth it. Not only is it a good vine bridge, but the village is very traditional and beautiful and the men might drive their cattle across the river for you.

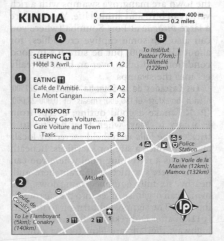

**KINDIA**

| 0 | 400 m |
| 0 | 0.2 miles |

**SLEEPING** 🏠
Hôtel 3 Avril...................1 A2

**EATING** 🍴
Café de l'Amitié................2 A2
Le Mont Gangan..............3 A2

**TRANSPORT**
Conakry Gare Voiture.......4 B2
Gare Voiture and Town
  Taxis...........................5 B2

To Institut
Pasteur (7km);
Télimélé
(122km)

Police
Station

To Voile de la
Mariée (12km);
Mamou (132km)

Market

Route de
Conakry

To Le Flamboyant
(5km); Conakry
(140km)

---

### HIKING IN THE FOUTA DJALON

The Fouta Djalon is excellent for hiking (and mountain biking) as – unlike many other places in West Africa – you can essentially go at will. It's suitable either for an extended series of day trips based in one of the towns, or for village to village walking (the villages are closely spaced). The terrain is hilly, but not overly strenuous for the most part, and the landscape is pastoral with wide views over rolling hills and small mountains.

Lodging is basic (with villagers) and cheap, and limited food is available en route; you should carry your own supplies as well as water-purifying tablets. Bring a jacket, as it gets surprisingly chilly at night. It's advisable to use topographical maps from the IGN in Conakry (see p434 for more details).

Outside the major towns there is no infrastructure and the area is not much visited, although tourism is increasing. Even so, you'll probably be the only traveller on the back paths.

---

Twenty-five kilometres west of town, at the village of **Konkouré**, is a beautiful waterfall and 15km the north is **Lake Bafing**, a Sunday getaway for picnics and swimming. Also near Mamou is **Timbo**, former capital of the Fouta Djalon and, together with Fougoumba near Dalaba, an important religious centre for Guinea's Peuls. Just west of town is **École Forestière** (Enatef), a forestry school perched on the edge of a wooded reserve; trails through the woods are open to visitors.

### Sleeping & Eating

**Hôtel Rama** ( ☎ 011-570757; signposted off the Dalaba road; r GF25,000-35,000; P ) Rama, a long walk northwest of downtown, has clean and comfortable rooms and the staff is a wealth of knowledge about the area. The nightclub next door can get loud.

**Hôtel Balys** ( ☎ 011-573070; Dalaba road, Quartier Pétel; s/d with fan GF40,000/45,000; r with air-con GF55,000; P ✗ ) Rooms at this new place 4km from the centre (GF750 in a shared taxi) have separate sitting rooms and all the fixings. A disco is under construction, but it's being built underground so it shouldn't get very loud. With dishes like cow's liver with lemon juice averaging GF13,000, this is also the best kitchen in town.

**École Forestière** ( ☎ 680634; Conakry road; dm GF15,000, r GF25,000; P ▣ ) The forestry school has rooms with three beds each and clean shared bathrooms, as well as rooms in 'villas' with a sitting area and kitchen.

**Hôtel Luna** ( ☎ 680739; Luna Carrefour; r GF15,000-20,000; P ) This grubby hotel has no generator. Its only plus is that it is located in town.

### Getting There & Away

Mamou is a major transport junction. Frequent bush taxis to Conakry (GF22,000, six hours), Kindia (GF13,500, three hours), Dalaba (GF7000, one hour), Labé (GF17,000, three hours), Faranah (GF22,000, three hours) and Kissidougou (GF35,000, six hours) depart from the *gares voiture*, on the main drag, as do a few morning buses to Conakry (GF16,000). Vehicles for Dabola (GF17,000, three hours) and sometimes Kankan (GF40,000, seven hours) leave from the *gare voiture* near the Hôtel Rama.

## DALABA

With its pretty pine groves and interesting nearby villages, Dalaba makes a superb base for hiking or biking in this region. Before independence, the town, perched at a pleasant 1200m, was a therapeutic centre for colonial administrators and many buildings from the era remain. Market day is Sunday.

There's an excellent **tourist office** ( ☎ 011-269348; Quartier des Chargeurs; ⏱ 8.30am-6.30pm). Informative booklets with maps, photos and descriptions (in English and French) detail dozens of area attractions. Use these to plan your own adventure or let the director, Mr Mamadou Diallo, get you a guide (GF45,000 per day for up to three people). He also has motorcycles for hire (GF30,000 per day) and arranges village stays (GF35,000 for up to three people).

### Sights

#### IN TOWN

The old French governor's residence, **Villa Sili**, built 1936, is fascinating in its decay. Next door, the **Case de Palabres**, decorated with Fula bas-relief designs, was used as a meeting hall. The caretaker will show you around both for a small tip. The odd little **Williams-Bah Museum** ( ⏱ 9am-6pm) has a few Fula artefacts plus posters about eminent African-Americans. You can also get on the Internet here, though the connection is very slow.

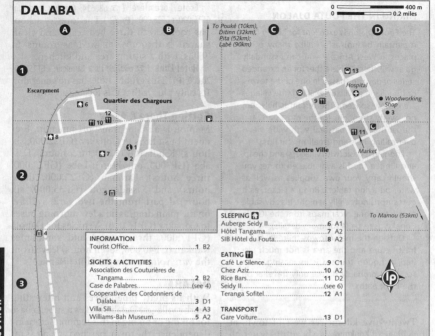

**DALABA**

0 / 400 m
0 / 0.2 miles

To Pouké (10km),
Ditinn (32km);
Pita (52km);
Labé (90km)

Escarpment

Quartier des Chargeurs

Hospital

Woodworking
Shop ● 3

Centre Ville

Market

To Mamou (53km)

**SLEEPING** 🏠
Auberge Seidy II................6 A1
Hôtel Tangama.................7 A2
SIB Hôtel du Fouta...........8 A2

**EATING** 🍴
Café Le Silence................9 C1
Chez Aziz.......................10 A2
Rice Bars.......................11 D2
Seidy II.........................(see 6)
Teranga Sofitel...............12 A1

**TRANSPORT**
Gare Voiture...................13 D1

**INFORMATION**
Tourist Office..................1 B2

**SIGHTS & ACTIVITIES**
Association des Couturières de
Tangama.......................2 B2
Case de Palabres............(see 4)
Cooperatives des Cordonniers de
Dalaba.........................3 D1
Villa Sili........................4 A3
Williams-Bah Museum.......5 A2

## CRAFTS

The Dalaba region is good for crafts. Places worth visiting include the **Association des Couturières de Tangama** for fabrics, **Cooperatives des Cordonniers de Dalaba** for leather and the village of **Pouké**, 10km from town, for baskets. You can place custom orders for crafts at the tourist office.

## AROUND TOWN

One of Guinea's tallest waterfalls, the **Chutes de Ditinn**, takes a remarkable 80m drop straight down off the cliff. Bush taxis run from Dalaba to the namesake village (they're easiest to find on Thursday, market day), 32km away and the parking area is 5km further on. From here it's a 20-minute walk and it helps to take one of the local children as a guide.

Much closer is the impressive **Chutes de Garaya**. Monkeys are often spotted here and also by the **Pont de Dieu**, a natural rock bridge. Shady **Chevalier Gardens** was started in 1908 to determine which European plants could grow in Guinea. The waters of **Lake Dounkimagna** nourish strawberries and other vegetables in the dry season.

## Sleeping

**Hôtel Tangama** ( ☎ 691109; r with shared bathroom GF20,000, s/d with bathroom GF30,000/40,000, villa GF60,000; P ) This cosy place has good rooms and a fireplace in the lounge.

**Auberge Seidy II** ( ☎ 691063; r GF25,000; P ) This homey place has four large rooms and the two upstairs have great views.

**SIB Hôtel du Fouta** ( ☎ 695036; s/d GF50,000/60,000; P ) Dalaba's luxury option has fully equipped rooms and something resembling a golf course. Even if you don't stay here, swing by for a drink at sunset; the views of the valley from the terrace are wonderful.

## Eating & Drinking

On the west side of the market are several good rice bars and you can find *attiéké* in the neighbouring alleys at night.

**Seidy II** (meals from GF10,000; ◷ dinner) All three hotels have good restaurants, but this is the most noteworthy. The *plat du jour* is usually just chicken and chips, but if you order in advance Mr Koffi will whip up almost any West African dish you can name.

**Chez Aziz** (meals from GF5000; ☾ dinner) Little Chez Aziz has inexpensive local fare and satellite TV.

**Café Le Silence** ( ☾ breakfast & lunch) A petit spot with *café noir* and cheap sandwiches.

**Teranga Sofitel** ( ☾ dinner) This friendly bar often has drumming and dancing late in the evening.

## Getting There & Away

Bush taxis go to Pita (GF7000, one hour), Labé (GF14,000, two hours), Mamou (GF7000, one hour) and Conakry (GF28,000, seven hours).

## PITA

Pita's major attraction, **Chutes du Kinkon**, is below the hydroelectric plant. To get there, take the main road north out of town for 1km, then head left 10km down a dirt road to the falls. It's a good walk or an easy bike ride. You are supposed to get a permit at the police station though this is a hassle; it's easier and probably cheaper to just pay the police at the entrance.

A much better excursion is the three-tiered **Chutes de Kambadaga** about 35km from Pita, though you'll need your own transport. Follow the dirt road from Pita to Kinkon and then branch right. It's a steep hike to the bottom. There's a small **bungalow** (r GF10,000) where you can overnight; bring your own food and water.

## Sleeping & Eating

**Auberge de Pita** (signposted off the Dalaba road; r GF20,000; 🅿 🕸) The rooms are clean and spacious, while the bar/lounge has a TV and a friendly atmosphere. Out front is an outdoor weaving centre with looms lined up in the shade of the trees.

**Centre d'Accueil** (rondavels GF10,000, r with shared/private bathroom GF15,000/20,000; 🅿 ) The *rondavels* (huts) are a bit rundown, but the rooms in the main building are alright. It's behind the *préfecture* (police headquarters).

**Soyez le Bienvenus** (meals from GF1300; ☾ breakfast & lunch) Pita has many good small cafés with cheap sandwiches and omelettes, but only this one, across from the Rex Cinéma, is also a hardware store.

**Petit Nirvana** (meals from GF5000; ☾ breakfast, lunch & dinner) Meals are only available with prior notice, but it's worth visiting for the *café noir* and a chat with Oury, who speaks

English and has information on the area. Petit Nirvana is on the northwest side of town, ask for directions on the main street.

## Getting There & Away

Bush taxis for Labé (GF5000, one hour) and Dalaba (GF7000, one hour) leave from the Rex Cinéma, and on a nearby side street for Doucki (GF9000, 1½ hours).

## DOUCKI

About 45km from Pita on the Télimélé road is the village of Doucki where the one-of-a-kind Hassan Bah (who speaks English, French and Spanish) runs a guesthouse of sorts. Twelve dollars gets you lodging in a traditional Fula hut, three meals and guided hikes to slot canyons and waterfalls in and around what many call Guinea's Grand Canyon. The scenery is amazing and otherworldly. Hiking with Hassan is an unforgettable experience, and, for many, the highlight of the trip. Bush taxis to Donghol-Touma will drop you at his brother's shop where you walk 2km to the village.

## LABÉ

The largest town in the Fouta Djalon, Labé is the area's administrative capital. It's a pleasant town with restaurants and nightlife.

Lying on a wide plain, Labé isn't the best base for hiking, though when you do get out to the hills, the scenery is excellent. **Chutes de Saala**, about an hour's drive down a rugged road off the Route de Koundara, is a good destination. Be sure to visit the falls at both the main entrance – where you can picnic and swim – and at the lookout (veer right at the fork in the road as you approach). Expect to pay about GF65,000 for a chartered taxi. Also worth a trip is **Mont Kolima**. Hotel Tata has a map and information about these and other sights and can arrange guides and village stays. **Fouta Trekking Ventures** ( ☎ 011-231048) leads hikes from one to nine days across the Fouta Djalon. They are building *campements* (hostels), using traditional designs, in three area villages.

## Information

The banks won't change travellers cheques, but one of the moneychangers at the market will. For Internet visit Cofoprec next door to the Hôtel de l'Indépendance or Cyber Ismailo Diallo and Cyber Fafaya near the post office. They charge around GF6000 per hour and connections can be good.

## Sights

Narrow, covered passageways give the **Marché Central** an Arab feel. In the north end is an area full of indigo cloth (for the finished product try **Tienture-Promotion Labé** south of the *gare voiture*) and a leather workshop turning out sandals and handbags.

**Le Petit Musée de Fouta** (admission by donation; ⏱ 8am-6pm) has crafts and other regional items. The mock-up of a Peul woman's home is illuminating. Just behind the museum is **Alpha Bah's Garden** where you can discuss environmentalism and buy organic coffee and flowers from the enthusiastic owner.

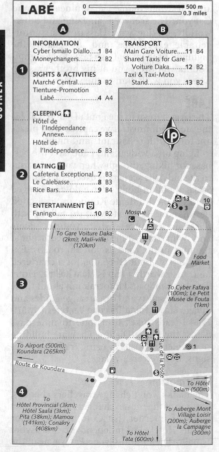

**LABÉ**

0 — 500 m
0 — 0.3 miles

| INFORMATION | |
| --- | --- |
| Cyber Ismailo Diallo.....1 | B4 |
| Moneychangers...........2 | B2 |

| SIGHTS & ACTIVITIES | |
| --- | --- |
| Marché Central...........3 | B2 |
| Tienture-Promotion Labé.....4 | A4 |

| SLEEPING 🏠 | |
| --- | --- |
| Hôtel de l'Indépendance Annexe..................5 | B3 |
| Hôtel de l'Indépendance......6 | B3 |

| EATING 🍴 | |
| --- | --- |
| Cafeteria Exceptional....7 | B3 |
| Le Calebasse..............8 | B3 |
| Rice Bars.................9 | B4 |

| ENTERTAINMENT 🎭 | |
| --- | --- |
| Faningo...................10 | B2 |

| TRANSPORT | |
| --- | --- |
| Main Gare Voiture.....11 | B4 |
| Shared Taxis for Gare Voiture Daka........12 | B2 |
| Taxi & Taxi-Moto Stand..................13 | B2 |

Mosque

Food Market

To Gare Voiture Daka (2km); Mali-ville (120km)

To Cyber Fafaya (100m); Le Petit Musée de Fouta (1km)

To Airport (500m); Koundara (265km)

Route de Koundara

To Hôtel Salam (500m)

To Hôtel Provincial (3km); Hôtel Saala (3km); Pita (38km); Mamou (141km); Conakry (408km)

To Auberge Mont Village Loisir (200m); Auberge la Campagne (300m)

To Hôtel Tata (600m)

## Sleeping

**Hôtel de l'Indépendance** ( ☎ 511000; r in annexe/main bldg GF10,000/25,000) Labé's cheapest and most centrally located lodging has decent rooms right at the *gare voiture*. Rooms in the annexe are clean, but the toilets often aren't.

**Hôtel Salam** ( ☎ 512472; r with shared bathroom GF20,000, s/d with private bathroom 30,000/35,000; 🅿 ) The Salam needs a paint job, but is otherwise fine. It's in a quiet *quartier* on the south side of town and many rooms have balconies.

**Auberge Mont Village Loisir** ( ☎ 574445; r GF25,000; 🅿 ) Though the rooms are a tad spartan, they are the best you will find at this price. The hard-to-find green and white building is behind the football field on the south side of town.

**Auberge la Campagne** ( ☎ 571702; s/d GF45,000/65,000; 🅿 ) The Mont Village Loisir's upscale neighbour has six brand new rooms and eager staff.

**Hôtel Tata** ( ☎ 510540; r & huts GF75,000; 🅿 ) The hotel of choice for Peace Corps volunteers, both the rooms and the *cases* (huts) are cosy and spotless. Madame Raby, the owner, has lots of information on the area.

**Hôtel Saala** ( ☎ 011-520462; r with/without bathroom GF25,000/15,000; villas GF30,000; 🅿 ) The Saala, 3km south of town, is convenient for nightlife. The rooms with shared toilet are smelly, but the rest are good.

## Eating & Drinking

Labé has good street food. You'll find stands everywhere selling rice and beans, fried sweet potatoes and *brochettes* for under GF1000. There are rice bars along the length of the *gare voiture* and a few good small restaurants down the street as you head into town.

**Le Calebasse** (meals GF3000-15,000; ⏱ lunch & dinner) This cosy place is tucked downstairs, away from the street noise and serves some exceptional shwarma and *riz gras* (rice and sauce).

**Hôtel Salam** (meals GF5000-10,000; ⏱ breakfast, lunch & dinner) The restaurant here doesn't look like much, but Chef Barry works wonders in the kitchen and will whip up whatever you request if you ask early enough in the day.

**Cafeteria Exceptional** (meals from GF1500; ⏱ breakfast & lunch) This little snack counter is good for coffee, sandwiches and people-watching.

GUINEA

**Hôtel Tata** (pizzas GF10,000; ☽ breakfast, lunch & dinner) The pizzas are fantastic, though you take your chances with anything else.

## Entertainment

The most popular dance spots are **Salaa Plus** (Hôtel Salaa), and **Bain de Kouré** (Hôtel Sofiton), both on the road out of town. Faningo, by the market, is the busiest nightclub in the centre.

Behind Hôtel Salaa is **Hôtel Provincial**, a tranquil garden with live music on Sunday. Mouctar Paraya, among other well-known Guinean musicians, often performs here.

## Getting There & Away

Labé is an important transport junction. Bush taxis for Mali-ville (GF18,000, four hours), Koundara (GF35,000, eight hours) and Kamsar (GF35,000, 15 hours) leave from Gare Voiture Daka, 2km north of town. There is one car a day to Diaoubé (GF75,000) in Senegal, except Monday and Tuesday when many go. There is also a daily taxi to Basse Santa Su (GF95,000) in Gambia. For all of these trips, the roads are so bad on the Guinean side that taxis leaving in the morning rarely make it to the border before it closes, meaning you need to sleep there. Many cars depart at night to avoid this hassle. Shared taxis (GF800) for Gare Voiture Daka leave from near the mosque in the town centre. See also p437.

Bush taxis for Labé (GF5000, one hour), Dalaba (14,000, two hours), Mamou (GF17,000, three hours) and Conakry (GF35,000, eight hours) leave from the main *gare voiture* in the centre. There is also a big bus to Conakry (GF20,000) daily and Bamako (GF120,000) a few times a week.

When local airlines are in business they usually have flights between Conakry and Labé.

## MALI-VILLE

Mali-ville sits on the edge of the spectacular Massif du Tamgué, just before its precipitous drop toward Senegal and the plains below. Officially, the town is called Mali, but it usually has the 'ville' added to distinguish it from Mali the country. At over 1400m Mali-ville is the highest town in the Fouta; the climate is cool – sometimes downright cold – and the scenery superb. It makes an excellent base for hiking and mountain bik-ing excursions into the surrounding area. There's no electricity or running water in town, and only basic provisions.

On Sunday, Mali-ville has a good market. Look for the **honey vendors**; they gather the honey from the baskets you see in the trees lining the road to Labé. Opposite the market is the **Centre d'Appui à l'Auto-Promotion Féminine** (CAAF), a cloth-weaving cooperative with a small boutique that also sells pottery. Just around the corner is the **Bureau de Tourisme** ( ☎ 511739), staffed by the enthusiastic Monsieur Souaré who runs Campement Bev and knows about local waterfalls, caves, mountains and artisan villages. He'll get you a guide (GF30,000 per day) or detailed directions so you can visit the sights on your own.

Mali-ville's best-known attraction is **Mt Loura**, which has the **La Dame de Mali** rock formation on its side. The top (look for the radio antenna) is 7km from town by bike (shorter if you hike), and offers unparalleled views over the surrounding countryside. On a clear day you can see the Gambia River and Senegal. It's a three-hour hike to the top of **Mt Lansa** for more excellent views. You'll need a guide on the upper section; ask him to point out the stone platform used for drumming messages to the villages below.

The gorgeous **Chute de Guelmeya**, 15km away, is the largest waterfall in the area and a good day-trip, as are the pottery and weaving villages **Toqué** and **Kolossi**.

## Sleeping & Eating

**L'Auberge Indigo** ( ☎ 510274; s/d GF15,000/20,000; Ⓟ ) The only place in town with electricity (solar powered) has cute little rooms and a peaceful garden. The staff has all sorts of information on the area. You can cook your own meals in the kitchen or have them find someone to cook for you (otherwise there are a few rice bars in town).

**Campement Bev** ( ☎ 511739; huts GF10,000, r GF10,000 per person; Ⓟ ) You'll definitely want to stay in one of the four huts here, each of which has a comfy double bed. It is set in the friendly village of Donghol-Teinseire, 7km away, and is perfectly aligned with La Dame de Mali's profile. Meals are available. Solo women may not want to stay here.

**La Dame de Mali** (s/d GF7500/10,000; Ⓟ ) The building, near the library, is crumbling and most guests are short-term visitors from the adjoining bar, but rooms are pretty clean.

A fancy place, tentatively named Windy Kana, is supposed to open in 2006.

## Getting There & Away

There are a few taxis between Mali-ville and Labé (GF18,000, four hours) every day and one to Conakry (GF50,000, 12 hours) on Monday and Thursday. Transport from Mali-ville to Koundara is only feasible on Saturday, market day in Madina Woura, where you change taxis.

Generally there are three vehicles per week to Kedougou, Senegal (GF50,000) in the dry season. Many people choose to travel this route on foot, not because the road is so horrible (which it is), but because the scenery is so good. The tourist office has all the details on the six-to-12 hour downhill hike (it's much more difficult in the other direction) and can arrange boys to guide you and carry your bags.

To get from Mali the city to Mali the country you can take the seldom travelled road west toward Kita and Bamako. There's no public transport. For more details, see p436.

## KOUNDARA

Koundara, a fairly sleepy town with some lovely mountains nearby, is the starting point for visits to Parc Transfrontalier Niokolo-Badiar, which consists of Guinea's Parc Regional du Badiar and Senegal's Parc Regional du Niokolo-Koba. Together they encompass a 950,000-hectare protected area, of which about 50,000 hectares are in Guinea. Unlike the Senegalese side, there is little development here other than a simple *campement* near the park headquarters in Sambaïlo. You can't walk or ride mopeds in the park so if you don't have a car, you'll have to charter one in Koundara. Animals you might see include bushbucks, roan antelopes, wart hogs and patas monkeys. There are also chimpanzees and hippopotamuses in the region. Your chance of seeing large mammals is slim (it's much better on the Senegalese side), but there are some interesting birds here and the landscape alone makes for a nice drive. The park is officially closed during the rainy season, from June to November. In Conakry, information on the park is available from the **Direction Nationale des Forêts et de la Faune** (Map pp410-11; Route de Donka, Conakry).

There are many tribal groups in this area, including the Badiaranké, Bassari, Peul and Coniagui, and the colourful mixture makes Koundara an interesting place to visit. The little **museum** at the *préfecture* is open weekdays, whenever the caretaker is around. About 25km from Koundara, near the Guinea-Bissau border, is **Saréboïdo**; it has a good Sunday market.

## Sleeping & Eating

All of Koundara's hotels are near the radio antenna.

**Hôtel Nafaya** (r GF10,000-15,000; **P**) Nafaya has basic rooms with shared bathrooms. There's a decent restaurant here and a nightclub that can get noisy on Thursday and Saturday nights.

**Hôtel Gangan** (r GF15,000) This hotel is quieter and about the same quality as Nafaya, but there's only electricity at night if enough people are staying here.

There are several rice bars near the *gare voiture*. In the mornings, look for *gosseytiga*, a rice porridge with ground peanuts and sugar that is a speciality of the region. The **Niokolo-Badiar Café** near the Saréboïdo taxis has good coffee and the unsigned **Café Theino**, behind where the trucks park, makes good omelettes.

## Getting There & Away

Bush taxis run frequently to Saréboïdo (GF5000, one hour) and daily to Labé (GF35,000, eight hours). For Boké go to Saréboïdo to find a car bound for Conakry (GF59,000, 13 hours); only a sure thing on Friday, Saturday and Sunday. For those driving their own vehicle, note there are ferry crossing on both of these routes.

A bush taxi generally heads daily for Diaoubé (GF35,000, six hours), Senegal along a horrible road. For Gabú, Guinea-Bissau, also a rough journey, you'll need to take three taxis, changing at Saréboïdo and the border. See also p437.

# UPPER GUINEA

In Upper Guinea (Haute Guinée), the hills and greenery of the Fouta Djalon give way to the reds and browns of the country's grassy, low-lying savanna lands. Although few travellers make it to this region, it's an area well worth exploring, even if it does get hot as hell in the dry season.

# DABOLA

Dabola is a peaceful town set amid hills. The main attraction is the **Barrage du Tinkisso**, which supplies electricity for Dabola, Faranah and **Dinguiraye**, an influential religious centre with the country's most famous mosque. At the bottom of the dam is a picnic area, which is popular on weekends. You can also cross over the stream, where there's a beach and a small waterfall. The dam is 8km from town, signposted on the Conakry road.

## Sleeping & Eating

**Hôtel Tinkisso** (Conakry road; bungalows/r GF20,000/40,000; P ✂) Just out of town, this is Dabola's top hotel, with spotless rooms. The thatch-roofed bungalows have electricity and bathrooms, but are in an isolated area far behind the main building.

**Hôtel Le Mont Sincery** (s/d 25,000/30,000; P ✂) This friendly and peaceful place is 2km south of Tinkisso and nearly as nice.

Most people eat at their hotel (Tinkisso has a bigger menu; Le Mont Sincery has a prettier dining area; both have satellite TV), but it's much more fun to join the crowds at the row of busy open-air restaurants branching off the main junction downtown. *Brochettes* (cubes of meat or fish grilled on a stick), salads and other simple meals cost GF1500 to GF3000.

## Getting There & Away

Dabola is a junction town, but it's small, so it can take a long time for taxis to fill. There is at least one departure daily to Faranah (GF15,000, two hours), Mamou (GF17,000, three hours), Kankan (GF25,000, four hours) and Conakry (GF37,000, nine hours).

# FARANAH

President Sekou Touré came from Faranah and the city still bears his marks. There's a conference centre, airstrip built to accommodate a Concorde, oversized presidential villa and street lights: all now abandoned. It's also the highest point on the Niger River that is easily accessible, just 150km from the source. The main reason to come here is to visit Parc National du Haut Niger (see below). Behind the old Cité de Niger conference centre is the house of renowned Guinean drummer **Fadoua Oularé**. Serious students can arrange lessons for a fee; or just stop by to see if there are any performances scheduled.

## Sleeping & Eating

**Hôtel Bibisch** ( ☎ 011-276599; r with fan/air-con GF40,000/50,000; P ✂) Brand new and the best in town, Bibisch is about 2km from the centre on the way to Sidakoro and has a decent restaurant.

**Hôtel Firya** ( ☎ 581682; r GF25,000, villas with aircon GF35,000; P ✂) Firya, in a quiet, pastoral

---

### PARC NATIONAL DU HAUT NIGER

The Parc National du Haut Niger covers one of West Africa's last remaining tropical dry forest ecosystems. The park's 1200-sq-km core areas (there are another nearly 6000 sq km of inhabited buffer zones) have an interesting assortment of wildlife that is, unfortunately, not very easy to spot, including waterbucks, bushbucks, buffalos, duikers, crocodiles, hippos, chimpanzees, leopards and lions.

The park headquarters and an interesting botanical garden are in Sidakoro, 50km from Faranah on a rough road. There are some nice rooms available for around GF15,000 per person, though you'll need to bring your own food and water.

In Somoria, the gateway to the core area, about 30km into the park on a very rough track that barely qualifies as a road, you can arrange with local fishermen for a *pirogue* ride on the Niger. The small **campement** (per person GF20,000) here has a few huts with bathroom. There's running water, but no restaurant. Somoria is also home to the **Chimpanzee Conservation Center** (CCC; www.projectprimate.org) where confiscated or donated chimps are prepared for release into the wild. They are hoping to have a habituated group ready to meet visitors in coming years.

To visit the park, you'll need your own 4WD. Permits for entering the park cost GF15,000 per person per day, with a GF10,000 additional charge for the mandatory guide. The CCC, though a separate entity from the park, works hard to protect it and is the best source of information, though you could also inquire at the **park office** ( ☎ 810482; Faranah) or the **Direction Nationale des Forêts et de la Faune** (Map pp410-11; Route de Donka, Conakry).

GUINEA

setting across the Niger from town, has a shady yard and the villas have two rooms.

**Hôtel Camaldine** ( ☎ 581598; r GF15,000; P ) Rooms are aging, though the lakeside setting is nice. The nightclub gets loud on Thursday and Saturday nights. Camaldine is unmarked, 2km from the centre off the Dabola road.

**Hôtel Bati** (r with shared/private bathroom GF8000/ 10,000) Stuffy and scruffy, but clean enough. It's one of the few places in the centre.

**Restaurant Bantou** (meals GF1000-10,000; ☯ lunch & dinner) This loud and lively outdoor bar-restaurant is near the Bati and is as good as any restaurant in the centre.

Best bet for street food is around the *gare voiture*.

### Getting There & Away

The *gare voiture* is on the main street next to the petrol station. Vehicles go daily to Kissidougou (GF15,000, two hours), Mamou (GF22,000, three hours), Dabola (GF15,000, two hours) and Conakry (GF40,000, nine hours). The road to Kabala (GF38,000, seven hours) in Sierra Leone is very bad and so there is little traffic, but taxis do go a couple of times a week. See also p437.

## KANKAN

Guinea's second city and a university town, Kankan is a pleasant place with a Sahelian feel. It sits on the banks of the Milo River (a large tributary of the Niger River). The capital of the ancient Empire of Mali was at Niani, 130km northeast, and today Kankan has become an unofficial 'capital' for Guinea's Malinké people. Nearly every Malinké you meet, even as far away as Senegal, regards Kankan as their spiritual home. Kankan is big enough to have some cybercafés.

### Sights

Kankan's **Grande Mosquée** is as beautiful inside as it is outside, and you're welcome to visit between prayer times. Women should cover their heads before entering. The old presidential palace, **Villa Syli**, overlooking the Milo, is undergoing restoration, though supposedly you'll still be able to walk the grounds when the work is done. Just over the river is **Samory Kourou**, the hill from which Samory Touré's famed siege of Kankan and later standoff against the French colonialists took place. It offers nice views of the city.

To see **traditional dancing** in one of the nearby villages talk with the delightful Millimouno 'Robert' Saa at **Makona Photocopy Centre** ( ☎ 583128) across from Hôtel Uni. He can usually arrange things, for a small fee, with two days' notice.

**Kouroussa**, about 65km from Kankan on the Dabola road, is the birthplace of Guinean author Camara Laye (see p408). You can visit the family compound here and there are a few decent hotels if you want to overnight. Catch a bush taxi (see opposite).

### Sleeping

**Centre d'Accueil Diocesain** (r GF20,000 P ) The Catholic mission guesthouse has some of the cleanest rooms in the city. They have showers and sinks (toilets are down the hall), mosquito nets, ceiling fans and electricity at night.

**Hôtel Baté** ( ☎ 712368, hotelbate@yahoo.fr; s GF70,000, d GF80,000, annexe r with fan GF40,000; P 🔀 ) The large rooms here have all the fittings (though make sure everything works), and rates include breakfast. The cheaper rooms in the annexe aren't nearly as good. It is the first choice of NGO workers.

**Hôtel Uni** ( ☎ 011-580414; r GF60,000; P 🔀 ) Rooms are just as nice and well equipped as the Baté.

**Le Calao** ( ☎ 712797; r GF45,000; P 🔀 ) It doesn't look like much at first sight, but the good-value rooms are clean and well appointed.

### Eating

**Restaurant Sénégalais, Chez Mme Neass** (meals GF2000-5000; ☯ lunch & dinner) Mme Neass makes a great *riz gras au poisson* (rice and sauce with fish) and will prepare just about any West African dish, including *yassa* (onion and lemon sauce), with advance notice.

**Leader Alimentation** (meals from GF1000; ☯ breakfast, lunch & dinner) This place, facing Hotel Baté, is a well stocked supermarket with plenty of expensive imported goods. They sell cheap shwarma out front while the restaurant upstairs has the biggest menu in town – hamburgers, *riz sauce* (rice with sauce), chicken, pizza and much more – though it's not all available every day.

Kankan has good street food and many rice bars. One of the best spots to look at night is around the Marché Diaka where simple places like **Moderne Restaurant Sénégalais** (meals from GF1500; ☯ dinner) serve tasty *riz sauce*.

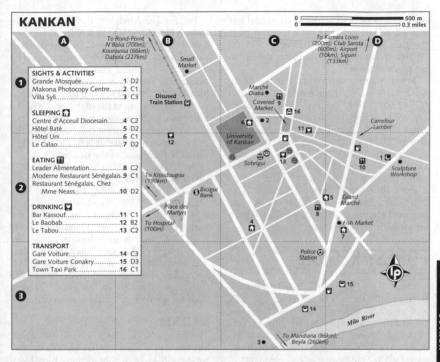

KANKAN

SIGHTS & ACTIVITIES
Grande Mosquée.....................**1** D2
Makona Photocopy Centre.......**2** C1
Villa Syli.............................**3** C3

SLEEPING
Centre d'Acceuil Diocesain........**4** C2
Hôtel Baté.........................**5** D2
Hôtel Uni...........................**6** C1
Le Calao...........................**7** D2

EATING
Leader Alimentation................**8** C2
Moderne Restaurant Sénégalais.**9** C1
Restaurant Sénégalais, Chez
    Mme Neass.....................**10** D2

DRINKING
Bar Kassouf........................**11** C1
Le Baobab..........................**12** B2
Le Tabou...........................**13** C2

TRANSPORT
Gare Voiture.......................**14** C3
Gare Voiture Conakry..............**15** D3
Town Taxi Park....................**16** C1

To Rond-Point N'Balia (700m); Kouroussa (66km); Dabola (227km)

To Kamara Loisir (200m); Club Sarota (600m); Airport (10km); Siguiri (133km)

Small Market

Marché Diaka

Covered Market

Disused Train Station

University of Kankan

Sotelgui

Carrefour Lamber

Sculpture Workshop

To Kissidougou (190km)

Place des Martyrs

Bicigui Bank

To Hospital (100m)

Grand Marché

Fish Market

Police Station

Milo River

To Mandiana (86km); Beyla (260km)

GUINEA

## Entertainment

Le Baobab, in the field behind the university – look for the two baobab trees – is popular with students for conversation in the afternoon and dancing at night. Bar Kassouf is a long-time Kankan favourite and usually crowded and lively.

Kankan's most popular nightspot, **Club Sarota** (Fri & Sat cover GF5000), is hidden away on the north side of town (take a *taxi-moto*). Besides the bar and dance floor, you can cool off in the swimming pool. **Le Tabou** is near the university, and thus a popular dance floor for students.

Odds are the double feature at **Kamara Loisir** will feature guns or Bollywood song and dance.

## Getting There & Away

Bush taxis for most places, including places like Conakry (GF65,000, 13 hours), Kissi-dougou (GF25,000, five hours), Siguiri (GF20,000, two hours) and N'zérékoré (GF48,000, 12 hours), leave from the twin *gares voiture* near the bridge. A big bus goes daily to Conakry (GF40,000). With the

road paved nearly the whole way, Bamako can be reached in seven hours by bush taxi (GF65,000) while the big buses (GF40,000) going several times a week take longer. The best way to get to Côte d'Ivoire (when that becomes safe again) is via Bamako because the road to Odienné via Mandiana is so bad that taxi drivers don't use it. See also p436.

There's also a smaller bush taxi stand near Rond-point N'Balia for Kouroussa (GF10,000, one hour) and Dabola (GF25,000, four hours).

When local airlines are in business they usually have flights between Conakry and Kankan.

## SIGUIRI

Siguiri is the last major town en route to Mali. If you find yourself with some time to kill you can check out the scant ruins of a 19th-century **French fort** atop a little hill just a few minutes from the *gare voiture* or head out further for a stroll along the Niger and Tinkisso Rivers.

The best option is **Hôtel Tam Tam** ( ☎ 582272; r with fan GF30,000, with air-con GF40,000-60,000; P ) on the Kankan road, which is clean and has a good restaurant. The only lodging near the *gare voiture* is the **Hôtel Niani** (r GF25,000; P ) which is a real pit, though not the filthiest place in town.

From Siguiri, two roads lead to Mali. Bush taxis go via Kourémalé to Bamako (GF42,000, five hours). The secondary route along the Niger River makes a great bike trip during the dry season. See also p437. Bush taxis also leave daily for Kankan (GF20,000, two hours) and Conakry (GF75,000, 15 hours). During the rainy season there is usually a boat or two a week down the Niger to Bamako. The trip takes a day and costs GF5000. Get your passport stamped before departing. There are sometimes flights from Conakry.

# FOREST REGION

Guinea's Forest Region (Guinée Forestière), in the southeast, is a beautiful area of hills and streams, although deforestation has taken a heavy toll and there are only pockets of primary forest left. What little remains, however, offers excellent wildlife watching, especially for chimpanzees and elephants.

## KISSIDOUGOU

Kissidougou, running seemingly forever along the Conakry highway, is a good place to break your journey south. The **Musée Préfectoral de Kissidougou** (admission GF1000; ⊗ 9am-5pm Mon-Fri, 9am-4pm Sat) across from the police station is small but has great masks and other supposedly magical objects. The surrounding area, with gently rolling hills and many villages, is perfect for exploring by bicycle. The seldom visited village of **Koladou**, 30km down a rough, nearly nonexistent road, has a vine bridge above some rapids. If you go, take some kola nuts for the village chief and check in at the police station along the way. Just 3km east of Kissi is a metal bridge built in vine-bridge style. From the roundabout, head down the Kankan road, take the second right and ask often for the *pont artisanal*.

Between Kissidougou and Faranah a dirt road branches about 70km south toward the village of Forokonia (no hotel, but you'll be able to find a place to sleep) from where you can walk the 7km to the **source of the Niger River**, which is considered sacred by locals.

For food and lodging, the nicest place in town is **Hôtel Savannah** ( ☎ 981040; r with fan/air-con & breakfast GF35,000/45,000; P X ) on the Faranah side of town. The restaurant, surrounded by flowers, is beautiful and the food superb; pizzas and seafood cost around GF15,000. **Hôtel Béléfé** ( ☎ 981234; r GF20,000; X ), signposted 500m south of the highway, is a funky little place with a rooftop patio. Friendly staff and a pleasant restaurant compensate for the cell-like rooms at **Hôtel de la Paix** (r GF8000; P ), which is 300m east of the market.

Bush taxis go daily to Faranah (GF15,000, two hours), Kankan (GF25,000, five hours), Guéckédou (GF11,000, 2½ hours) and Macenta (GF23,000, five hours). For Conakry (GF55,000, 12 hours) many taxis depart around 6pm. Every Thursday a 4WD (GF12,000, four hours) departs for Forokonia, returning late on Friday, market day. The scenic Kankan road is very potholed: for cyclists, Tokounou, which despite its size still consists mostly of traditional houses, makes a good stop. Friday is market day.

## MACENTA

The Forest Region begins in Kissidougou, but the area's beauty (what's left of it, anyway) really kicks in at Macenta, a busy town ringed by hills and streams. Inside the market is a **theatre** which puts on occasional dance performances.

About 40km south of Macenta the 116,000-acre **Forêt Classée de Ziama**, one of Guinea's few remaining virgin rainforests, blankets the mountains. Elephants are often spotted here, and you don't need a car to enter the forest. Guides and information are available at the headquarters in Sérédou, though they request that you call the **Centre Forestier** ( ☎ 910389) in N'zérékoré first so the staff can prepare for your visit. Admission is GF50,000 and the mandatory guide is another GF15,000. Simple rooms that can be arranged at the office cost GF10,000 per night.

**Hôtel Bamala** ( ☎ 011-585227; r with fan GF20,000-25,000, r with air-con GF30,000; P X ), 3km from the centre off the N'zérékoré road, is old but clean. The cheap rooms at **Hôtel Palm** ( ☎ 526113; r GF5000-25,000; P ) smell bad while the best aren't that far behind the Bamala. It's near the N'zérékoré *gare voiture*.

Bush taxis head daily to Kissidougou (GF23,000, five hours) and to N'zérékoré (GF18,000, 2½ hours). Several taxis a day take the rough road to Voinjama, Liberia (GF14,000, two hours) via Daro; however, if you're heading to Monrovia it's better to go from N'zérékoré. See also p436.

## N'ZÉRÉKORÉ

N'zérékoré, the major city in Guinea's Forest Region, is a busy and fast-growing place and a good base for exploring the surrounding area. This is Guinea's NGO central so you'll find many foods and services unavailable in most other cities. Market day is Wednesday.

The **Musée Ethnographique** ( 8.30am-5pm Sat-Thu, 8.30am-1pm Fri; admission GF1000) has a small but fascinating collection of masks, fetishes and other objects of traditional forest culture. The museum director is a spritely old man who tells good stories about the forest. You can watch women dyeing mud-cloth at the **artisan village** in the small 'sacred' forest as you enter town. A variety of other crafts are also made and sold here, including masks and the region's distinctive raffia basketry.

Many local villages have vine bridges, particularly those along the Oulé River. Ask at the museum for advice and directions. There's a more accessible one near the hamlet of Koya, just north of Koulé, about 40km north on the Macenta road. Give the chief a small tip and he will get you a guide for the Pont de Liana (not to be confused with Pont Diana, a highway bridge nearby). Forty-five minutes and forty-five thousand butterflies later you're there.

## Information

Bicigui and Ecobank change cash only, but some of the moneychangers at the market and *gare voiture* take travellers cheques; and with better rates than in Conakry. You can get online (sometimes) at both Cyber Café Espoir and Sotelgui.

## Sleeping

**Chez Aïda** ( 910747; r with fan/air-con GF35,000/40,000; P ) Aïda, on the north side of town, has four clean and spacious rooms with fan and an excellent restaurant that draws many NGO workers (most dishes cost around GF9000). The air-con rooms are in another nearby building; though larger and more modern, they're not as cosy.

**Auberge Golo** ( 911719; r with fan/air-con GF35,000/45,000; P ) A friendly and quiet choice near most of the NGO offices. All rooms have separate sitting areas and the air-con rooms have satellite TV. Golo also serves good food with steaks and pizzas costing around GF11,000.

**Catholic Mission** ( 910897; r GF20,000; P ) The Catholic Mission, on the east side of town, has simple but spotless rooms with shared toilets and mosquito net. It's a nice, quite location downhill behind the church.

**Hôtel Bakoly** ( 910734; r GF5000-10,000; P ) This hotel near the market is the cheapest place to stay. The basic rooms have a bucket shower; toilets are shared.

**Hôtel Le Mont Nimba** ( 911557; s GF120,000-200,000, d 160,000-240,000; P ) If you have

GUINEA

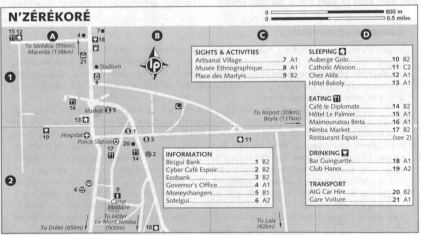

**N'ZÉRÉKORÉ**

| | 800 m |
| 0 | 0.5 miles |

| SIGHTS & ACTIVITIES | |
| Artisanal Village | 7 A1 |
| Musée Ethnographique | 8 A1 |
| Place des Martyrs | 9 B2 |

| SLEEPING | |
| Auberge Golo | 10 B2 |
| Catholic Mission | 11 C2 |
| Chez Aïda | 12 A1 |
| Hôtel Bakoly | 13 A1 |

| EATING | |
| Café le Diplomate | 14 B2 |
| Hôtel Le Palmier | 15 A1 |
| Maimounatou Binta | 16 A1 |
| Nimba Market | 17 B2 |
| Restaurant Espoir | (see 2) |

| DRINKING | |
| Bar Guinguette | 18 A1 |
| Club Hanoi | 19 A2 |

| TRANSPORT | |
| AIG Car Hire | 20 B2 |
| Gare Voiture | 21 A1 |

| INFORMATION | |
| Bicigui Bank | 1 B2 |
| Cyber Café Espoir | 2 B2 |
| Ecobank | 3 B2 |
| Governor's Office | 4 A1 |
| Moneychangers | 5 B1 |
| Sotelgui | 6 A2 |

To Sérédou (95km); Macenta (138km)

Stadium

Market

Hospital

Police Station

To Airport (20km); Beyla (131km)

To Lola (42km)

To Diéké (65km)

To Hôtel Le Mont Nimba (500m)

Camp Militaire

money to burn there's this fancy, but over-priced place owned by President Conté. Nonguests can use the pool for GF15,000.

## Eating

There are some excellent street food vendors near the *gare voiture.*

**Hôtel Le Palmier** (meals GF3000-8000; ☯ breakfast, lunch & dinner) Dishes at Le Palmier are simple but fresh – the *poulet avec sauce curry* (chicken with curry sauce) is amazing.

**Mouminatou Binta** (meals GF2000-5000; ☯ lunch & dinner) This friendly woman whips up a mean rice with *arachide* (peanut) sauce at her simple place, which is hidden with several others directly behind Sougué Boutique.

**Restaurant Espoir** (meals GF5000-10,000; ☯ lunch & dinner) Espoir, attached to N'zérékoré's best cybercafé, serves dishes from Guinea and its neighbours.

**Café le Diplomate** ( ☯ breakfast, lunch & dinner) You'll get a good *café noir* at the Diplomate, and many of the men who hang here love to share their knowledge of the Forest Region.

**Nimba Market** ( ☯ daily) This little supermarket has instant ramen, chocolate bars and other imported goods.

## Drinking

**Bar Guinguette** ( ☯ lunch & dinner) This simple watering hole at the entrance to town is a good people-watching spot. At night, women sell grilled fish right out front.

For dancing, NGO workers tend to gravitate toward **Club Hanoi** (admission GF5000) on Friday and **Hôtel Le Mont Nimba** (admission GF5000)

on Saturday, but both are busy both nights. Cover charges are often waived for women.

## Getting There & Away

Bush taxis depart daily from the well-organised *gare voiture* for Lola (GF6000, 30 minutes), Macenta (GF18,000, 2½ hours), Beyla (GF20,000, four hours), Kankan (GF48,000, 12 hours) and Conakry (GF80,000, 20 hours).

Travel to Monrovia, Liberia, is a rough, all-day trip with many checkpoints: seek local advice before heading there. Bush taxis go to the border at Diéké (GF19,000, three hours) frequently and there you get another car to complete the trip. If Côte d'Ivoire becomes safe again, you can get taxis to Man via Sipilou. See also p436.

**AIG** ( ☎ 911430) hires 4WDs for GF200,000 per day with driver plus GF2000 per kilometre.

Flights are sometimes available to/from Conakry.

## LOLA

Lola, near the borders of Liberia and Côte d'Ivoire, is the starting point for hiking up Mt Nimba (see the boxed text, below). There are several mud-cloth cooperatives in town and if you ask around someone will lead you to one. Lola is also home to the endangered grey parrot, which, because it can imitate sounds, is often sold into captivity. There are some places (called *dortoits*) around town where the birds sing daily at dawn and dusk. On Tuesday the market overwhelms the town.

---

**HIKING ON MOUNT NIMBA**

Mount Nimba, Guinea's highest peak at 1752m, is part of the mountain range straddling Guinea, Côte d'Ivoire and Liberia. The summit, best reached from the village of Gbakoré, 18km southeast of Lola, offers phenomenal views of surrounding peaks in all three countries. It's a steep, winding four-hour trek to the top and a guide (the friendly Guillah Bamuh who lives in Gbakoré comes highly recommended) is mandatory.

Getting the required permit at the *préfecture* in Lola is a royal pain in the ass and will likely put plenty of francs in some official's pocket (reportedly this is not the case at the governor's office in N'zérékoré), so it's best to go straight to Gbakoré and let your guide get the permit for you. Come in the afternoon and you can climb the next day; come early enough in the morning and you might be able to summit the same day. The price is negotiable, but count on GF100,000 for everything. There is no guesthouse in Gbakoré (one is planned) but food and lodging can be arranged.

The Nimba mountains host a rich variety of plant and animal life. Nearly a dozen vertebrate species are endemic to the area, including some notable amphibians (see p408). The range is protected as a World Heritage Site, but this didn't stop the government from granting a license for an iron mine. Because of this, Unesco has also inscribed it on their List of World Heritage in Danger.

**Hôtel Heinoukoloa** (r GF15,000; **P** ), signposted 1km off the main road, has basic but acceptable rooms. En route is the newer **Hôtel Nouketi** (r with shared bathroom GF10,000, r with private bathroom GF20,000-25,000; **P** ) which has a friendly staff and a good restaurant.

Bush taxis head to N'zérékoré (GF6000, 30 minutes), Bossou (GF4000, 30 minutes) and Gbakoré (GF4000, 45 minutes). To Yekepa (GF6000, 45 minutes) in Liberia the road is pretty good. Heading toward Man in Côte d'Ivoire it's a bad road whether you go via Danané or Sipilou. See also p436.

## BOSSOU

The **Bossou Environmental Research Institute** ( ☎ 584761; gban@nifty.com) attracts researchers from around the world to study the famous chimpanzees (see p408 ) living in the surrounding hills. There's not a lot of primary forest left, though the area remains scenic and, because the chimps are tracked daily, your chances of finding them are excellent. (Note that they take an early afternoon nap.) A guide for a couple hours in the forest costs GF50,000, with half the money going to the village.

The **Monkey Nest Guesthouse** (r GF5000) at the base of Mont Gban has surely the cleanest, most comfortable rooms at this price in the country. If space is available you can also sleep at the research centre for GF10,000.

Instead of heading straight back to Lola, consider taking the seldom-travelled rocky track east to Gbakoré where you'll enjoy gorgeous views of Mt Nimba. About 4km before Gbakoré the road crosses a natural bridge cut through the rock by the Cavally River. It's a magical little spot, ideal for a picnic and a swim.

# LOWER GUINEA

While much of Guinea's coast is rocky or marshy and inaccessible, there are beautiful spots worth discovering. Lower Guinea (Basse Guinée) also has some interesting caves and other geological formations, though most visitors are here for the beaches.

## FRIA

Fria is a bustling town in an attractive area, marred only by the enormous bauxite mining compound that dominates views on ap-

proach. The main reason to come here is to explore the geologically fascinating surrounding countryside. About 15km from Fria, beyond Wawaya village, are the **Grottes de Bogoro**, a good place for a swim. The **Grottes de Konkouré** can be reached by continuing out of town on the airport road and then down about 4km on a very rough road (best on bike or foot) to the Konkouré River where fisherman will take you in their boat to the caves. The trip is best done in the dry season when the river is calmer. There are also interesting caves in **Tormélin**, between Fria and the Boké highway; they're about a 6km walk from the Tormélin mosque.

Fria's fanciest hotel (and nightclub too) is **Le Bowal** ( ☎ 240490; airport road; r GF80,000-100,000; **P** 🏵 ), but the best choice for people coming to explore the area is **Hôtel Yaskadi** ( ☎ 240984; signposted off Route Unite; r with fan/air-con GF15,000/30,000; **P** 🏵 ). It has clean, decent rooms and the affable staff know all about the area and can arrange guides. **Restaurant-Nightclub Le Kamsoum** (meals GF10,000; 🕙 breakfast, lunch & dinner), a colourful place behind the mineworkers' apartments, is one of Fria's best restaurants. It's open early to late, and as midnight approaches the dancing starts.

Bush taxis go daily to the Boké highway junction (GF5000, one hour), Conakry (GF12,000, three hours) and Télimélé (GF14,000, four hours), from where you can continue on to Pita.

## BEL AIR & SOBANÉ

About 40km north of Boffa is the signposted turn-off leading to Plage de Bel Air, Cape Verga, the fishing village of Koukoudé and a beautiful coastline. Bel Air beach, 25km from the highway, was once a great place to relax in simple beach huts, but now it's dominated by President Conté's flash **Grand Hôtel de Bel Air** ( ☎ 434840; r GF200,000-250,000; ste GF800,000; **P** 🏵 🏵 ).

Three kilometres before Bel Air is the signposted turn-off for Conté's wife's **Village Touristique Sobané** ( ☎ 011-545129; bungalows GF80,000; closed Jul-Oct; **P** ), a much better choice whether you're a backpacker or a billionaire. Big beautiful thatch-roofed bungalows sit below palm trees just off a gorgeous stretch of sand or you can sleep on the beach for GF10,000. The restaurant is pretty good and the nightclub has

GUINEA

dancing on weekends. Beach access for nonguests us GF2000.

In between the other two, a short walk to the beach, is the simple **Hôtel Soumatel** (r & huts with shared bathroom GF30,000; **P** ). It's overpriced, but you should be able to bargain.

Without your own transport, you'll need to charter a taxi in Boffa (GF75,000) or Boké (GF100,000) or be prepared for a long wait at the junction for the occasional pick-up truck plying this route (GF5000), but you'll probably still have to walk the 5km to Sobané.

## BOKÉ

Boké is a clean and orderly town with views over the surrounding countryside. You might find yourself stopping here if you are heading to Guinea-Bissau or Senegal. If you spend the night, ask if there are any concerts taking place; there often are. If you'd rather do the performing, inquire about drum and dance lessons with **Batafon Arts** ( ☎ 011-291116), which offers all-inclusive stays at their simple huts in the nearby village of Tamakéné for anything from a few days to a few months.

Near the *gare voiture* is the **Fortin de Boké** (admission negotiable; ☼ 8am-6pm), now a museum with a small collection of artefacts. You can also see the prison cells downstairs where rebellious slaves were kept before being taken downriver to the coast. You can sometimes check email at the unnamed shop next to Sotelgui.

**Hôtel Filao** ( ☎ 310202; r with fan GF25,000, r with air-con GF35,000-40,000; **P** 🏊 ), about a kilometre east of Boké, isn't the most expensive hotel in town, but it is the best value. The restaurant is good and the bar relaxed. The **Maison des Jeunes** (GF10,000) near the *gare voiture* has clean rooms with shared bathroom. **Restaurant Bibine** (meals GF2500-12,000; ☼ breakfast, lunch & dinner) near Sotelgui is homey and friendly and the *riz gras* and roast chicken are good. They open very early and serve until very late.

There are direct bush taxis to Conakry (GF23,500, three hours). For Labé you'll need to go to Kamsar where a taxi departs most mornings. Minibuses run to Québo (GF30,000, six hours) in Guinea-Bissau on Tuesday and Saturday. Trucks sometimes go on other days. The road is very bad. See also p437.

# GUINEA DIRECTORY

## ACCOMMODATION

Conakry has lots of luxury properties and even more dives, plus plenty of choices in between, though nothing truly priced in the budget category. The budget category covers places under GF50,000 and the top end encompasses places that cost over GF200,000. Upcountry, where most towns have at least one cheap hotel with rooms from around GF10,000, the more expensive places to stay are usually excellent value. You can often get a lovely, comfortable room with private bathroom and air-con for the same price as a grubby brothel in the capital.

Outside Conakry most hotels are on the outskirts of towns to offer peace and quiet, or, in the case of the cheap places, privacy. The roar of traffic is sometimes replaced by the music of the attached nightclubs.

A tourism tax of GF5000 per person applies to top-end and some midrange hotels.

## ACTIVITIES

The Fouta Djalon region (p418) is great for hiking and biking and the Forest Region (p428) also has good possibilities. Anglers should bring a rod; there are streams and rivers everywhere and deep-sea fishing is possible off the coast by Conakry. Guinea has many wild and scenic rivers to paddle; the biggest adventure is on the remote upper reaches of the Niger. The trip from Faranah to Kouroussa through Parc National du Haut Niger (p425) is highly recommended, but not for the inexperienced.

If you have more time, you can easily find teachers of traditional dance and music across the country. Faranah (p425) and Boké (left) have established schools.

## BOOKS

*Guinea Today* by Mylène Rémy has a good historical background. You can pick up a copy for GF25,000 in Conakry at Soguidip and from vendors on Ave de la République.

## BUSINESS HOURS

Government offices are open from 8am to 4.30pm Monday to Thursday and 8am to 1pm Friday. Most businesses are open from 8am to 6pm Monday to Saturday, except Friday, when many close at 1pm.

---

**PRACTICALITIES**

■ Guinea uses the metric system.

■ Electricity is 220V/50Hz and plugs have two round pins.

■ Guinea's best-selling newspaper is the satirical weekly *Le Lynx*.

■ The only TV station is the government-owned RTG, which shows a lot of sports and speeches.

■ The BBC World Service is broadcast in French on FM and English on short wave.

---

Businesses also close for an hour or so at lunch. Banking hours are from 8.30am to 12.30pm and 2.30pm to 4.30pm Monday to Thursday, and 8.30am to 12.30pm and 2.45pm to 4.30pm Friday.

## CUSTOMS

You're not allowed to export more than GF100,000 in local currency or US$5000 in foreign currency. You must have a licence to export precious stones. To export art objects (interpreted to include anything made of wood), you'll need a permit from the Musée National in Conakry (p412). The cost varies, but averages 15% of the value for items worth less than GF50,000, and 25% of the value for more expensive pieces. It's best to do this a day before departure and to bring purchase receipts.

## DANGERS & ANNOYANCES

Overall, travel in Guinea is safe; but there are several things to keep in mind. Some towns in the Forest Region suffer occasional tribal fighting. While these incidents are usually small scale and don't directly affect travellers, it would be wise to inquire locally before visiting the region. There are also occasional armed robberies of bush taxis and private cars in the south, so don't travel at night.

Many bush taxi drivers are maniacs; disregarding lanes and passing other vehicles on blind corners. The many wrecks and mangled rails lining the roads offer ample evidence that this is bravado, not skill. Don't be afraid to ask your driver to slow down. No matter how good your driver is, the vehicle is bound to be crap and breakdowns are common.

Electricity, running water and phones (even mobiles) are all intermittent. Most hotels have generators, though they don't usually run all night at cheap hotels.

## EMBASSIES & CONSULATES
### Guinean Embassies & Consulates

Within West Africa, Guinea has embassies in Côte d'Ivoire, Ghana, Mali, Gambia, Guinea-Bissau, Senegal, Sierra Leone, Nigeria and Liberia. For details see the relevant country chapter. Elsewhere, Guinea has the following:

**Belgium** Brussels ( ☎ 02-771 0126; ambassadedeguinee .bel@skynet.be; 108 Auguste Reyers Blvd, 1030)

**Canada** Ottawa ( ☎ 613-789-8444; 483 Wilbrod St, K1N 6N1)

**France** Paris ( ☎ 01-47 04 81 48; 51 rue de la Faisanderie, 75116)

**Germany** Berlin ( ☎ 030-20 07 43 30; berlin@embaguinee.de; Jägerstraße 67-69, 10117)

**UK** London ( ☎ 020-7078 6087; 83 Victoria St, SW1H 0HW)

**USA** Washington DC ( ☎ 202-986-4300; 2112 Leroy Place NW, 20008)

### Embassies & Consulates in Guinea

All of the following are in Conakry.

**Belgium** (Map pp410-11; ☎ 412831; Corniche Sud, Kouléwondy; ⏲ 9am-12.30pm & 3-4pm Mon-Thu, 9am-1pm Fri)

**Benin** (Map p412; ☎ 292688; cbc-gn@yahoo.fr; Rue RO 251, Kipé; ⏲ 9am-1pm & 3-5.30pm Mon-Fri)

**Côte d'Ivoire** (Map pp410-11; ☎ 451082; Blvd du Commerce; ⏲ 8.30am-3pm Mon-Thu, 8.30am-2pm Fri)

**France** (Map pp410-11; ☎ 411655; Blvd du Commerce; 7-11am Mon-Fri) Processes visas for Burkina Faso and Togo.

**Germany** (Map pp410-11; ☎ 411506; www.conakry .diplo.de; 2nd Blvd; ⏲ 7.30am-noon Mon-Fri)

**Ghana** (Map pp410-11; ☎ 409560; Corniche Nord, Camayenne; ⏲ 9am-3pm Mon-Fri)

**Guinea-Bissau** (Map pp410-11; ☎ 422136; Route de Donka, Bellevue; ⏲ 8am-2.30pm Mon-Thu, 8am-1pm Fri)

**Japan** (Map pp410-11; ☎ 468510; Corniche Sud, Coléah; ⏲ 8am-5pm Mon-Thu, 8am-1pm Fri)

**Liberia** (Map pp410-11; ☎ 012-676526; Rue DI 258, Landreah; ⏲ 9am-4pm Mon-Thu, 9am-1pm Fri)

**Mali** (Map pp410-11; ☎ 461418; Corniche Nord, Camayenne; ⏲ 7.30am-4pm Mon-Thu, 7.30am-1pm Fri)

**Netherlands** (Map pp410-11; ☎ 415021; Novotel, Rm 121) ⏲ 8am-11pm Mon-Fri)

**Nigeria** (Map pp410-11; ☎ 411681; Ave de la Gare; ⏲ 11am-1pm Mon, Wed & Fri)

**Senegal** (Map pp410-11; ☎ 409037; Corniche Sud, Coléah; ⏲ 8am-12.30pm & 1.30-5pm Mon-Thu, 8am-12.30pm & 2.30-5pm Fri)

**GUINEA**

**Sierra Leone** (Map pp410-11; ☎ 464084; Carrefour Bellevue; ☑ 9am-3pm Mon-Fri)
**UK** (Map pp410-11; ☎ 434715; britcon.oury@biasy.net; Corniche Sud, Residence 2000, Villa 1; ☑ 8am-4.30pm Mon-Fri, 8am-1pm Fri) Assists Australian and Canadian citizens.
**USA** (Map pp410-11; ☎ 411520; http://conakry .usembassy.gov; 9th Ave; ☑ 7.30am-noon Mon-Fri) A new embassy is under construction in *quartier de* Lambanyi.

## FESTIVALS & EVENTS
During May, the **Fish Festival**, in the village of Baro (near Kouroussa, p426) draws big crowds. People try to catch (and release) sacred fish to get good luck. There is also plenty of drumming and dancing. The **Hunting Festival** held annually in the Kankan area (p426, the time and location changes) lets Malinké men show off their shooting prowess. During September's **Potato Festival**, the city of Mali-ville (p423) throws a party for the farmers of the surrounding villages.

## HOLIDAYS
Public holidays include:
**New Year's Day** 1 January
**Easter** March/April
**Declaration of the Second Republic** 3 April
**Labour Day** 1 May
**Assumption Day** 15 August
**Market Women's Revolt** 27 August
**Referendum Day** 28 September
**Independence Day** 2 October
**Christmas Day** 25 December

Islamic holidays are also observed, and Eid al-Fitr is one of Guinea's biggest celebrations; see p818.

## INTERNET ACCESS
Internet services are easy to come by in Conakry, though outside the capital only a few towns have Web connections. In the capital, costs are rarely more than GF6000 per hour.

## INTERNET RESOURCES
**Friends of Guinea** (www.friendsofguinea.org) A useful little site created by a group of returned Peace Corps volunteers.
**Guinea Forum** (www.guinea-forum.org) A good site for current news.
**National Tourist Office** (http://ontguinee.free.fr) Still a work in progress.

## LANGUAGE
French is the official language, and it is widely spoken throughout the country to varying degrees of proficiency. Major African languages are Malinké in the north, Pulaar (also called Fula) in the Fouta Djalon and Susu along the coast. Learning some phrases in these local languages is helpful if you'll be spending time off the main routes. See p861 for a list of useful phrases in French, Malinké, Pulaar and Susu.

## MAPS
Institut Géographique National's (IGN) 1992 map of Guinea is outdated, though a new version is due in 2006. It's available at some stationary stores in Conakry, and on the street (GF15,000). The IGN also sells black-and-white or colour copies of topographical maps (scales 1:50,000 to 1:500,000) covering individual regions of the country for GF10,000 to GF20,000.

## MONEY
Banks outside Conakry exchange only cash. If you're arriving overland carry some US dollars, euros or CFA, as they're easily changed almost everywhere. Black-market dealers are widely used throughout Guinea and some even take travellers cheques. Their rates are generally about 5% better than the bank rate. They work in the open, but you should still be discreet when dealing with them, especially in Conakry: not all are honest and there are occasional police crackdowns. No matter who you change with, rates are best in Conakry.

Only a few fancy hotels take credit cards, (and the numbers are sometimes stolen), though the Banque Internationale pour le Commerce et l'Industrie de la Guinée (Bicigui) branches in Conakry, Kindia, Labé and N'zérékoré will advance cash from Visa cards. By sometime in 2006, they say, all of their branches (Boké, Fria, Kamsar, Kankan, Kissidougou, Macenta, Mamou and Sangaredi) will offer this service. The ATM at Bicigui's Ave de la République branch in Conakry also works with Visa cards.

The exchange counter at the airport is rarely open and offers bad rates. Neither this bank nor any other will change Guinean francs back into hard currency when you leave Guinea, even if you have your exchange receipts.

## PHOTOGRAPHY & VIDEO

Photo permits are not required, although don't snap government buildings, airports, bridges, military installations or anything that might be deemed embarrassing to Guinea's image or you could be in for some trouble. In fact, it's best not to use a camera at all in cities and towns unless you're sure the police aren't watching and locals don't object: unfortunately many will. Copies of a government decree expressly permitting tourist photos are available at the tourist office and it's worth picking one up because officials outside the capital will be impressed by the stamps on the last page. The same restrictions apply to video.

Konica and Tudorcolor film are available in Conakry. For developing, the best place is Labo Photo with several locations on Ave de la République in Conakry, although quality is erratic. For more general information, see p823.

## POST

Outside Conakry the post cannot be trusted for anything other than postcards, and even in the capital there is a good chance a letter or package won't get through. If you are sending something valuable, use the private shipping services in Conakry (p411).

## TELEPHONE

For domestic and international calls there is a government-owned Sotelgui office in all large- and medium-sized towns, though most people use the many telecentres. Sotelgui phonecards are another possibility, but it's not always easy to find a phone you can use them on.

Telecentres usually charge GF500 per minute for local calls and around GF3000 for international. Be sure to shop around because some charge nearly double for the same call as their neighbours. In Conakry, many telecentres will offer illicit international lines for as low as GF1000 per minute. Internet phone connections (GF1500 to GF2000 per minute) are another choice, but the quality isn't always good.

## TOURIST INFORMATION

The Office National du Tourisme in Conakry (see p412) can provide some general information. There are Ministére du Tourisme, de l'Hôtellerie et de l'Artisanat offices in many upcountry towns, but the staff are just as likely to hinder as help you.

## VISAS

All visitors, except nationals of Economic Community of West African States (Ecowas) countries, Morocco and Tunisia, need a visa. Visas, usually valid for three months, are not available at airports or land borders.

### Visa Extensions

Visas can be extended for up to three months at the **Bureau of Immigration** (Map pp410-11; ☎ 441339; 8th Ave) in Conakry for GF80,000.

### Visas for Onward Travel

#### CÔTE D'IVOIRE

One month single-entry visas cost GF84,000 to GF168,000, depending on nationality, plus two photos, and are issued in two days.

#### GUINEA-BISSAU

One-month single-entry visas cost GF70,000 (GF120,000 for three-month multiple-entry visas). You need two photos and visas are issued within three hours.

#### LIBERIA

Three-month single-entry/multi-entry visas cost GF200,000/250,000 for most nationalities and six-month multiple-entry visas are GF350,000. US citizens must buy a US$100 one-year multiple-entry visa. You need two photos and a letter of request. Visas are ready within two days.

#### MALI

One-month single-entry visas cost GF16,200; except for Americans, who must get a one-year multiple-entry visa for US$100. Two photos are required and the visas can be ready the same day if you go early. Reportedly you can also get a *laissez-passer* (travel permit) valid for up to a month for GF10,000 in Kankan. Take two photos and photocopies of your passport front page and the Guinean visa to the *gendarmerie* near the market in the morning and pick up the pass in the afternoon.

#### SENEGAL

Visitors from Canada, the USA and EU do not need a visa for stays up to 90 days. Most other nationals, including Australians pay

GUINEA

GF14,600/33,600 for a one-month single-entry/three-month multiple-entry visa and they should be issued right away.

### SIERRA LEONE

A one-month single-entry/three-month multiple-entry visas costs up to CFA430,000/650,000. You need one photo and they are ready within 72 hours, or you can pay CFA85,000 for rush service.

## WOMEN TRAVELLERS

Women travellers are unlikely to experience any special problems in Guinea. For more general information and advice, see p828.

# TRANSPORT IN GUINEA

## GETTING THERE & AWAY
### Entering Guinea

A certificate with proof of a yellow fever vaccination is required of all travellers.

## Air

Guinea's only international airport is Conakry-G'bessia, 13km from the centre of Conakry. It remains one of the most chaotic and exasperating in West Africa. Direct flights from Europe are available with Air France (Paris) and SN Brussels (Brussels) for as little as £660 return.

The table on below lists flights between Conakry and West African destinations. Regional flights leave from the *aérogare nationale*, next to the international airport. For Southern and East Africa, you can connect to Johannesburg via Abidjan (Côte d'Ivoire) and Dakar (Senegal); Nairobi via Abidjan and Dakar; and to Addis Ababa via Abidjan.

---

> **DEPARTURE TAX**
>
> Departure tax for international flights is usually included in the ticket; otherwise it's GF20,000.

The following airlines service Guinea and have offices in Conakry:

**Air France** (AF; Map pp410-11; ☎ 413657; www .airfrance.com; 9th Ave, Conakry) Hub: Paris.

**Air Ivoire** (VU; ☎ 434526; www.airivoire.com; Ave de la République, Conakry) Hub: Abidjan.

**Air Sénégal International** (V7; Map pp410-11; ☎ 212120; www.air-senegal-international.com; Ave de la République, Conakry) Hub: Dakar.

**Bellview** (B3; Map pp410-11; ☎ 434340; www.flybell viewair.com; Ave de la République, Conakry) Hub: Lagos.

**Slok Air** (SO; Map pp410-11; ☎ 295676; www.slokair international.com; 6th Blvd, Conakry) Hub: Banjul.

**SN Brussels** (SN; ☎ 413610; www.flysn.com; Ave de la République, Conakry) Hub: Brussels.

## Land

Though Guinea is small, it shares borders with six countries.

### CÔTE D'IVOIRE

Transport continues to run to and from Côte d'Ivoire, but until the situation changes, you shouldn't be on it. The most frequently travelled route is between Lola and Man either via Nzo and Danané or via Sipilou and Biankouma. By public transport, the latter is the fastest choice. From Kankan it is easiest to go via Bamako as the road to Odienné via Mandiana is so bad. There's also a seldom-travelled route between Beyla and Odienné (via Sinko). The roads here are also horrible, but taxis run from Kankan and N'zérékoré to Beyla where you can connect onward.

---

### REGIONAL FLIGHTS FROM CONAKRY

| destination | flights per week | airline | approximate one-way/return fare (GF) |
| --- | --- | --- | --- |
| Abidjan (Côte d'Ivoire) | 9 | Air Ivoire, Bellview | 900,000/1,400,000 |
| Accra (Ghana) | 5 | Air Ivoire, Bellview | 1,000,000/2,000,000 |
| Bamako (Mali) | 3 | Air Ivoire, Slok Air | 800,000/1,200,000 |
| Banjul (The Gambia) | 3 | Slok Air | 550,000/830,000 |
| Bissau (Guinea-Bissau) | 5 | Air Sénégal International | 1,600,000/1,900,000 |
| Dakar (Senegal) | 10 | Air Sénégal International, Slok Air | 600,000/1,050,000 |
| Praia (Cape Verde) | 2 | Air Sénégal International | 1,840,000/2,300,000 |

## GUINEA-BISSAU

Most people travelling by taxi get to Bissau via Labé, Koundara and Gabú. You have to taxi hop between Koundara and Gabú and the road beyond the border is horrible (especially in the rainy season), but it can be done in a day if you start in the morning. Traffic picks up considerably on the days around Saréboïdo's Sunday market.

Minibuses go a couple times a week (you might find a truck on other days) from Boké and Kamsar up the horrible road to Québo. Going to Koundara (to get to Gabú) via Boké is only feasible on weekends and even then involves long waits for taxis to fill. With your own vehicle you can shave some distance, though not necessarily time, off this journey by going direct from Koumbia to Pitche.

## LIBERIA

Because of the large number of refugees in Guinea there is a lot of traffic to Liberia, but check the security situation before heading there. The primary route is from N'zérékoré to Ganta via Diéké. Bush taxis go frequently from N'zérékoré to the border where you can get a *taxi-moto* or walk the remaining 2km to Ganta where you can get a Monrovia-bound taxi.

From Macenta, bush taxis go via Daro to the border and on to Voinjama, although the Voinjama road is terrible. The route south from Guéckédou to Foya is similarly difficult. It's probably better to go from Macenta to Koyama, where you can find transport to Zorzor and on to Monrovia, because this road is reportedly being upgraded. Still, plan on a full day to reach the capital.

Another route goes from Lola via Bossou to Yekepa but traffic is sporadic beyond here. For all of these routes you buy a single ticket, but change cars at the border.

## MALI

Taxis and buses travel direct to Bamako from Kankan, Siguiri, Labé and Conakry. The road is sealed and in excellent shape, except for a 50km-stretch in Mali that is due to be upgraded soon. If you have your own 4WD you can also go from Kankan via Mandiana to Bougouni, or Mali-ville via Kita.

## SENEGAL

Taxis to Senegal going via Koundara, the busiest route, stop at Diaoubé, a small town with a huge market, where you can connect to almost everywhere, including Dakar. Because the roads on the Guinean side are so bad, you often end up getting to the border so late you need to sleep there, though some taxis leave at night to avoid this hassle.

There is also a rough road between Maliville and Kedougou, though many people travel this route on foot. See p424 for more details.

## SIERRA LEONE

Bush taxis run regularly from Conakry to Freetown. The road is sealed most of the way and at the time of research work had already begun to finish the job. Alternatively, you can take a bush taxi to the border at Pamelap and connect with vehicles on the other side to all other large towns in Sierra Leone.

From Kindia to Kamakwie there are regular taxis to the border at Medina-Oula, but little transport further south. The road on the Sierra Leone side is quite bad and sometimes during the rainy season the Little Scarcies River runs so high the ferry shuts down. The road from Faranah to Kabala is also in bad shape and so sparsely travelled, but taxis do go a couple times a week.

The crossings in Guinea's parrot's beak, the point of land west of Guéckédou, are probably best avoided for the time being. Not only are the roads bad, but we've heard reports of Sierra Leone border officials demanding travellers purchase visas even though they already have one. If you do cross this way and are travelling by bush taxi, go to Kailahun rather than Koindou because there is much more traffic there.

## River

During the rainy season (July to November) barges run once a week or so from Siguiri to Bamako in Mali. It's a one-day journey downstream and at least two days coming back up.

## Sea

Boats go from Kamsar (southwest of Boké) to Bissau (GF30,000) stopping in Cacine and Kamkhonde, where many passengers catch bush taxis to complete their trip to the capital. The boats follow no set schedules.

The ferry service to Freetown is expected to begin again, so it's worth asking around at the port if you are interested.

GUINEA

## Tours

**Batafon Arts** ( ☎ 01273 605791, www.batafonarts
.co.uk) This English (Sussex-based) drum-and-dance school
offers a four-week accompanied trip to Boké, the artistic
director's hometown, in February, or individualised trips
the rest of the year.

**Guinea Festival** (www.festagg.com) Created to promote
tourism, particularly among African-Americans, this week-
long packaged tour event, usually held in February of even
years, features music and dance performances, hands-on
cultural workshops and guided tours upcountry. Book
through **Brock Travel** ( ☎ 404-244-1980) in the US and
**Mondial Tours** (Map pp410-11; ☎ 433550; Ave de la
République, Conakry).

## GETTING AROUND

With few good roads, travel can be long and
hard. You won't always have to rough it
upcountry, but as long as you are prepared
for that possibility a visit here can be very
rewarding.

## Air

At the time of research there were no internal
flights. Many local airlines – usually flying to
Kankan, Labé, N'zérékoré and Siguiri – have
come and gone in recent years so it's always
worth asking what is available.

## Bicycle

Although Conakry is too congested for cycling, many areas upcountry, particularly the
Fouta Djalon, are excellent for mountain biking. Villages are spaced closely enough that
lodging and food are seldom a problem on
longer trips. You'll need to be fully equipped
with spare parts, as you won't find fittings for
Western-made cycles anywhere, though most
towns have at least one shop that can mend
flat tyres and take care of other basics.

## Bus

A big bus (*grand car*) usually runs daily between Conakry and Boké, Kindia, Mamou,
Labé, Kankan and N'zérékoré. Although
buses are fairly comfortable and less expensive than bush taxis, they're slow and
break down often.

## Bush Taxi & Minibus

Bush taxis are the main form of transport
in Guinea. They're always overcrowded and
breakdowns are common, though the driv-

ers usually manage to fix things before too
long. The standard Peugeot station wagons
usually carry ten or eleven passengers (plus
more on the roof). In general, transport is
faster and more frequent in the morning
and on or around market days. Please note
that all of the travel times given are just
rough approximations.

Although minibuses are cheaper than
taxis, they are just as overcrowded and take
far longer to fill up. They also usually travel
slower, especially on bad roads; however,
a new minibus will cover the same route
faster than a decrepit old taxi.

The post office in Conakry has its own
minibuses departing twice a week (the days
often change) to and from Dabola, Kankan,
Faranah and Kissidougou. Post buses, which
generally cost a little more than bush taxis,
are a good choice because you get a seat to
yourself, though you'll need to book at least
a day in advance.

In Guinea, the term *gare voiture* is used
for taxi and bus stations.

## Car & Motorcycle

If you're driving your own or a hired vehicle in Guinea, be sure the insurance and
registration papers are in order, as they will
likely be checked. They'll also sometimes be
held for bribes – remember that amounts
are always negotiable. See p417 for details
of car-hire agencies in Conakry.

### ROAD CONDITIONS

The main road east from Conakry to Lola
via Mamou and Kissidougou is sealed and
in good condition, except for the stretch
between Kissidougou and Sérédou.

From Mamou north, the road is sealed
and excellent as far as Labé. Continuing on
to Mali-ville it is in fair shape; to Koundara
it is worse. There's a ferry crossing between
Labé and Koundara.

In Upper Guinea, the roads from
Mamou and Kissidougou to Kankan are
sealed but riddled with potholed. From
Kankan north to Siguiri the road is excellent while south to Beyla is one of Guinea's
worst.

The coastal road from Conakry is sealed
and in excellent condition as far as Boké;
from there it's dirt.

# Guinea-Bissau

Like most sub-Saharan nations, Guinea-Bissau as we know it is an arbitrary, European construct, yet it has two qualities that make this country stand out from its neighbours. First and foremost are the people. They're disarmingly friendly, yet you'll almost never hear the disingenuous '*bonjour, mon ami*' that signals the beginning of an unwelcome sales pitch. If you're arriving from Dakar, you'll be happy to learn that helpful gestures and friendly conversation are almost always just that rather than a means to extract cash.

The country's other big draw? The remarkable Arquipélago dos Bijagós. These delta islands are lined with powdery, white-sand beaches, washed by azure waters, and populated by a fascinating people whose culture, long protected by hidden sandbanks and treacherous tides, is unlike any found in West Africa.

The mainland provides a fine recapitulation of many of West Africa's attractions. There are mangrove-lined rivers, home to crocodiles and shy hippos. The beaches of Varela rival those of Cap Skiring just across the border in Senegal. The tropical rainforests of the south serve as the westernmost habitat of the chimpanzee. And Bissau, the friendly capital and largest city, has a sleepy historic centre of Portuguese colonial buildings shaded by giant mango trees.

Always poor, the country's economy and infrastructure were severely damaged by civil war in the late 1990s. As a result, transport and communications are trying at best and, ironically, hotels and even food – especially in the capital – are no bargain. The good news is that national reconciliation seems to have finally arrived with peaceful elections in 2005, and the people have a cautious optimism about the country's future.

**FAST FACTS**

- **Area** 36,120 sq km
- **Capital** Bissau
- **Country code** ☎ 245
- **Famous for** Cashews
- **Languages** Portuguese, Crioulo
- **Money** West African CFA franc;
  US$1 = 544.89; €1 = 655.96
- **Population** 1,416,000
- **Visa** All visitors except citizens of Ecowas nations require a visa. They are available upon arrival at Bissau airport. Otherwise, arrange for a visa before arrival.

**WARNING**

The peaceful presidential elections in 2005 and the nonviolent resolution of a serious constitutional crisis that followed have been hailed as signs of movement towards long-term stability. That said, fundamental problems of corruption, poverty and lingering rivalries among the political and military elites could destabilise the current peace. Be sure to check the latest situation before entering Guinea-Bissau. The region around São Domingos and along the Senegalese border is particularly prone to instability, since it is considered by Senegal's Casamance separatists to be part of their natural territory. Violent flare-ups still continue.

Also, beware that there are still land mines in some rural and remote areas, left over from both the 1998–9 civil war and the war of liberation from Portugal. If you plan to travel far off the beaten path, be sure to research your route and consider bringing a trusted guide.

## HIGHLIGHTS

- **João Vieira** (p453) Discover the island's powdery sand beaches and disarmingly friendly people.
- **Orango** (p453) Stalk rare, salt-water hippos after visiting the tombs of Bijagós kings and queens.
- **Bolama** (p451) Witness the crumbling colonial grandeur of the antique Portuguese capital.
- **Sacred forests** (p457) Disappear into the dense jungle around Catió and Jemberem – the westernmost habitat of the African chimpanzee.
- **Bissau** (p445) Sip your way through blackouts at the capital's amiable cafés.

## ITINERARIES

- **One Week** Most travellers with only a week to spare spend a day or two in the capital **Bissau** (p445), which has few 'sights' but a pleasant, relaxing feel. This could be combined with a few days visiting the country's major attraction, the **Arquipélago dos Bijagós** (p450), southwest of Bissau. The island of **Bubaque** (p452) is the easiest to reach, with good beaches and a range of places to stay.

- **Two Weeks** If you have a second week to spare, consider further explorations of the Bijagós. Head to **Orango** (p453), with its rare, saltwater hippos, and **Bolama** (p451), home to the once-grand Portuguese capital. Then check out one of the small but paradisiacal islands like **Acunda** (p454) or **João Vieira** (p453) for serious decompression.

- **Three Weeks** A third week would give you enough time to explore some of the rich mainland ecosystems in-depth. Consider the mangrove swamps of the **Parque Natural dos Tarrafes do Rio Cacheu** (p454) in the north or the **Cantanhez forest** (p457) in the south, home to chimps and elephants.

## CLIMATE & WHEN TO GO

The rainy season is from June to October; it rains almost twice as much along the coast as inland. Conditions are especially humid in the months before the rains (April and May), when average maximum daytime temperatures rise to 34°C. Although daily maximums rarely fall below 30°C, this is quite bearable in the months after the rains, especially on islands that catch the sea breeze.

The best time to visit is from late November to February, when conditions are dry and relatively cool. February/early March is also Carnival time in Bissau, although smaller festivals take place in many towns to celebrate the end of the harvest in November and December.

See Climate Charts p813.

## HISTORY

The great Sahel Empire of Mali, which flourished between the 13th and 15th centuries AD, included parts of present-day

**GUINEA WHO?**

Causing no end of confusion to visitors, people from Guinea-Bissau refer to themselves as *guinenses* and to the country as Guiné, while that southerly neighbour known to the rest of the world as Guinea is here demoted to Guiné-Conakry. You may also hear people from Guinea-Bissau referred to as Bissau-Guinean. In this chapter, we refer to citizens of Guinea-Bissau simply as Guineans.

Guinea-Bissau. For more information on the precolonial history of this part of West Africa, see p33.

## European Arrival

Portuguese navigators began exploring the coast of West Africa in the early 15th century, reaching what's now Guinea-Bissau around 1450. They found the region particularly attractive, with navigable rivers that facilitated trade with the peoples of the interior. Soon, the Portuguese were extracting gold, ivory, pepper and, above all, slaves. For centuries though, the Portuguese presence was limited to coastal trading stations.

In the 17th century, the New World's thirst for slave labour grew astronomically. France and the Netherlands, watching Portuguese merchants grow rich, began to challenge their monopoly on the nefarious trade. Although, Portugal eventually lost control of much of the African coast, it managed to hang onto its valuable Guinean ports.

## Colonial Period

With the decline and eventual end of the slave trade in the 19th century, the Portuguese had to win control of Guinea-Bissau's interior if they wanted to continue to extract wealth from their possession. To do so, they often allied themselves with Muslim ethnicities, including the Fula and Mandinko,

in order to subdue the territory's animist tribes. Without the means to win hearts and minds with educational or economic incentives, Portuguese Guinea descended into one of the most repressive and exploitative colonial regimes in Africa. When right-wing dictator António Salazar came to power in Portugal in 1926, he imposed punishing tariffs on foreigners in order to re-establish direct Portuguese rule. The rules were simple: peasants planted groundnuts, like it or not.

## War of Liberation

By the early 1960s, African countries were rapidly winning independence from their European colonial rulers. Britain and France made fairly smooth transitions from colonial to neocolonial countries, continuing to profit from trade with their former colonies. But Salazar, fuelled as much by weakness as by his own nationalist rhetoric, refused to relinquish his hold on his African colonies. The result: one of the longest liberation struggles in Africa's history.

The leader of the independence movement was writer and engineer Amilcar Cabral, who in 1956 helped found the Partido Africano da Independência da Guiné e Cabo Verde (PAIGC). In 1961, the PAIGC started arming and mobilising peasants. Though outnumbered, PAIGC troops won control of half the country within five years. Portugal, meanwhile, was becoming increasingly isolated internationally. Foreign politicians and journalists visited the liberated area, and the struggle became front-page news during the early 1970s.

Even though Fula agents assassinated Amilcar Cabral in Conakry, Guinea, in 1973, the momentum for freedom was too strong. The PAIGC organised nationwide elections in the liberated areas and proclaimed independence, with Amilcar Cabral's half-brother, Luiz, as president. Eighty countries quickly recognised the new government, but it took the overthrow of Portugal's dictatorship the following year for Portugal to do the same.

## Independence

Once in power, the new PAIGC government faced staggering problems. Only one in 20 people could read, life expectancy was 35 years, and 45% of children died before the age of five. During the war of independence,

GUINEA-BISSAU

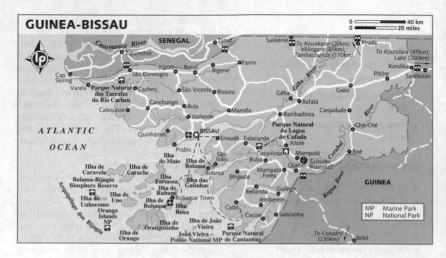

GUINEA-BISSAU

rice production had fallen by 71% and rice had to be imported for the first time ever.

Politically, the PAIGC wanted a unified Guinea Bissau and Cape Verde. However, this idea died in 1980 when President Luis Cabral (Amilcar's half-brother) was overthrown in a coup while he was visiting Cape Verde to negotiate the union. João Vieira took over as president.

Despite the change of leadership, Guinea-Bissau continued to follow a socialist path. The state controlled most major enterprises, Marxist literature was everywhere and political dissent was banned, although behind the dogma, Vieira encouraged pragmatism and political neutrality. The Soviet Union provided arms and advisers while the West provided nonmilitary aid.

Life remained hard for most people. Bissau's shops were almost empty and in rural areas, foreign products were even more scarce. Vieira realised that Guinea-Bissau was making no progress under Marxism, and in 1986, following a serious coup attempt the previous year, the government completely reversed its policies, devalued the currency and began selling off state enterprises.

## The 1990s

Vieira proved to be a shrewd politician, surviving three coup attempts while keeping the PAIGC in power. He won the 1994 presidential elections, although 52% of the vote was hardly a landslide victory. Even though many Guineans questioned the results, op-

position leader Koumba Yala accepted defeat and appealed for national unity.

Economic conditions were gradually improving for most people. Unusually for an African nation, rural inhabitants had been enjoying a slight improvement in standards since the 1970s. Overall, however, Guinea-Bissau's social and economic situation remained dangerously poor. Cracks began to show in 1997 when teachers, health workers and other state employees went on strike to protest, among other things, embezzlement of foreign aid money.

Things suddenly came to a head on 7 June 1998 with an attempted coup led by General Ansumane Mane, former head of the army. Vieira had sacked Mane the day before, accusing him of supplying arms to the Mouvement des Forces Démocratique de la Casamance (MFDC), the separatist rebel group in neighbouring Senegal. Mane's coup was backed by a majority of Guinean soldiers and, reportedly, by the MFDC. Senegal and Guinea became involved in the conflict, sending soldiers to help defend Vieira and loyal government troops. As the two sides shelled and bombed each other's positions in and around Bissau, residential districts were caught in the crossfire, and many people were killed. News reports from mid-July told of towns and villages being attacked, with many civilians killed and atrocities committed. By late July, 300,000 people were displaced.

Despite attempts by Portugal and several Ecowas states to negotiate peace, fighting continued. In May 1999, the military junta led by General Ansumane Mane at last conquered all of Bissau and personally escorted Vieira to the Portuguese embassy. With the junta's claim that they had no interest in power, the president of the national assembly became interim president.

## Unstable Peace

Transparent presidential and legislative elections were held in November, and a presidential run-off in January 2000 made Koumba Yala the president of the new civilian government. He successfully quashed a coup attempt by General Ansumane Mane, who was eventually killed in a shoot-out at Quinhámel, 40km from the capital.

Yala's problems with the military had been temporarily solved, but it wasn't long before his relations with other sectors of the government, as well as with civic groups and the media, became strained. In 2001 and 2002, Yala seemed to seek out controversy, arresting journalists, defying court rulings, and sacking half the civil service.

In September 2003, a coup headed by General Veríssimo Correira Seabra finally removed the erratic Yala. Legislative elections were held in 2004, with Seabra as caretaker head of state. But, in October 2004, Seabra was killed by a faction of soldiers who, according to some, were protesting unpaid wages. The country held its collective breath until presidential elections in 2005.

## Guinea-Bissau Today

Despite widespread fears of continued factional violence, the 2005 presidential elections were held as planned and have been generally deemed free and fair. The winner?

Deposed president João Vieira, who had returned from exile in Portugal to run a successful campaign based on national reconciliation. People remembered his regime as, if not free of corruption, then at least as a time of stability and a modicum of economic growth.

Still, an obstacle to peace remained. Prime Minister Carlos Gomes Júnior, long Vieira's rival in the PAIGC, refused Vieira's calls to resign. After a tense fall, the stand-off was finally decided in the country's Supreme Court – Gomes had to go. While fundamental problems of corruption and poverty could yet destabilise the current peace, Guineans generally express cautious optimism about their country's future.

## THE CULTURE
### The National Psyche

Despite grinding poverty, a severely damaged infrastructure and wide religious and ethnic differences, Guineans are united by a neighbourly goodwill that is genuinely remarkable. Even in the capital city where blackouts keep streets pitch black most nights, you can walk the streets with only a modicum of care. Violence and even aggressive salesmanship are rare. Visitors of European descent may be peppered with the epithet *branco* (white), especially outside the capital. However, it's almost always an expression of curiosity and surprise rather than a putdown. You will feel welcome just about anywhere you go.

The mainland people share many cultural aspects with similar groups in neighbouring Senegal and Guinea. However, the Bijagós people from the islands of the same name have very distinct customs (see p451).

---

**REVOLUTION, NOT REVOLT**

Three decades after the liberation of Guinea-Bissau, the Partido Africano da Independência da Guiné e Cabo Verde (PAIGC) is viewed as a model for revolutionary armies in many parts of the world. Realising that society had to be completely reorganised if the people were ever to be genuinely free, party founder Amilcar Cabral insisted on genuine revolution rather than an armed revolt that traded colonialism for home-grown oppression.

As each part of the country was liberated, the PAIGC helped villagers build schools, provided medical services and encouraged widespread political participation. As a result, the PAIGC quickly built popular support in a country of deep ethnic, social and linguistic differences. At the same time, the movement gained wide international support that helped isolate Portugal's right wing dictatorship. The result of the PAIGC's political efforts: they were able to improve the lives of their fellow citizens and at the same time defeat a better armed enemy.

## Daily Life

On paper, Guinea-Bissau is one of the world's poorest countries, though regular rains and relatively fertile land make outright hunger rare. In rural areas, most people scratch out a living from fishing and subsistence farming. Villages consist of mud-brick houses roofed with thatched grasses, and at night families gather around wood fires that are both the stove and, after dark, the only source of light.

Except for a lucky few, life is hardly easier in cities and towns. In a nation with virtually no industry, most people eke out a living as small-time merchants, hawking foodstuffs or cheap imports, mostly from China. The good news is that urban dwellers, while poor, do not face the kinds of threats, from pollution to violence, that wrack many African cities.

## Population

Current estimates put the population at about 1.4 million, divided among some 23 ethnic groups. The two largest are the Balante (30%) in the coastal and southern regions and the Fula (20%) in the north. Other groups include the Manjaco (or Manjak), Papel, and Fulup (closely related to the Diola of Senegal) in the northwest, and the Mandingo (Mandinka) in the interior. The offshore islands are mostly inhabited by the Bijagós people (see p451).

Cities, particularly Bissau, are home to a significant minority of people of mixed European and African ancestry. Largely descendants of Cape Verdean immigrants, they form a kind of urban elite. There are also a number of more recent immigrant groups, including Mauritanian and Lebanese merchants. French entrepreneurs dominate the fledgling tourist industry in the Bijagós. And there is still a scattering of Portuguese colonials who have chosen to stay on after independence, running shops, restaurants and hotels.

For more information on Fula and Mandingo cultures, see p73.

## RELIGION

About 45% of the people (mainly Fula and Mandingo) are Muslims; they are concentrated more upcountry than along the coast. Christians make up less than 10% of the population. Most are Catholic, though evangelical Christians are making small but significant inroads. Animist beliefs remain strong along the coast, in the south, and on the Bijagós islands. Animism still has a strong influence even on the practices of those who espouse Christianity or Islam.

## ARTS

While mainland Guinea-Bissau is not noted for the use of sculpted figures and masks, the Bijagós people continue to maintain these traditions. Statues representing *irans* (great spirits) are used in connection with agricultural and initiation rituals. The Bijagós also carve initiation masks, the best known being the Dugn'be, a ferocious bull with real horns. One of the best times to see masks is in Bissau at Carnival time (usually February).

On the mainland, traditional dance and music are influenced by the Mandingo and Diola people of neighbouring Gambia and Senegal. The harplike *kora* and the xylophone-like *balafon* are played, while women take turns dancing in front of a circle of onlookers. The traditional Guinean beat is *gumbé*.

Modern music shares the same roots, though the Portuguese colonial legacy has given it a Latin edge, especially among the larger orchestras. On the street and in bush taxis you'll hear little Sahelian-style music and more salsa and Latin sounds. One of Guinea-Bissau's most popular groups is Super Mama Djombo, along with Dulce Maria Neves, N'Kassa Cobra, Patcheco, Justino Delgado, Rui Sangara, and Ramiro Naka. These singers perform occasionally in some of Bissau's nightclubs.

## ENVIRONMENT

### The Land

Guinea-Bissau has an area of just over 36,000 sq km (about the size of Switzerland), making it one of West Africa's smaller countries. The coastal areas are flat, with estuaries, mangrove swamps and patches of forest. Inlets indent the coast and high tides periodically submerge the lowest areas. Inland, the landscape remains flat, with the highest ground, near the Guinean border, just topping 300m above sea level. Off the coast is the Arquipélago dos Bijagós, consisting of 18 main islands and dozens of smaller ones.

## Wildlife

### ANIMALS

Guinea-Bissau's rivers are home to freshwater hippos, while the island of Orango supports a small population of rare, saltwater hippos. The Bijagós are also an important nesting ground for aquatic turtles. The rainforests of the southeast are the most westerly home of Africa's chimpanzee population. There is also a stunning variety of birds, especially along the coastal wetlands, including cranes and peregrine falcons.

### PLANTS

The natural vegetation of the inland areas is lightly wooded savanna, but much of it is under cultivation. You'll see rice fields and plantations of groundnuts, maize and other crops. The coastal zone is very low-lying and indented by many large creeks and estuaries, where mangrove swamps dominate.

## National Parks

Guinea-Bissau has a number of protected areas, including the flagship Bolama-Bijagós Biosphere Reserve, which contains the Orango Islands National Park (p453) and the João Vieira–Poilão National Marine Park (p453). On the mainland, the Parque Natural dos Tarrafes do Rio Cacheu (p454), near the border with Senegal, protects a vast area of mangroves. In the south of the country, near Buba, the Parque Natural de Lagoa de Cafatada (p457) protects a freshwater wetland area. South of here the Parque Natural de Cantanhez (p457) is planned to protect estuarine mangroves and several sacred forests that have cultural significance.

Despite this impressive collection, parks can be difficult to visit because of poor national roads as well as limited park infrastructures. And because of a long history of unpaid salaries, park staff tend to see visitors as potential income sources. That said, a new management structure holds out promise for improved facilities and scheduled rates, though at writing, plans were still being worked out. If you plan to visit any of the parks, check with the friendly people at the Bissau headquarters of **IBAP** ( ☎ 207106; Rua São Tomé), the institute that oversees all the parks.

## Environmental Issues

A major environmental issue is the destruction of mangroves – some of the most important in Africa – on the coast, due to the expansion of rice production in seasonally flooded areas. The increase in groundnut production also creates problems – the plants rapidly exhaust soil nutrients and farming methods lead to erosion. Offshore, Guinea-Bissau has rich fishing waters, but overfishing may become an issue if controls are not introduced. The UICN (World Conservation Union) and several other bodies are working to protect Guinea-Bissau's natural environment.

## FOOD & DRINK

Seafood is the highlight of Guinean cuisine, from oysters and shrimp to the meaty *bica* (sea bream). Fish is generally either grilled or sautéed in a delicious white sauce based on onions and limes. Rice is the ubiquitous staple, sometimes supplemented with other starches like French-fried potatoes, yams, beans and *mandioca* (cassava). Vegetables generally include okra, often served as a puree, carrots and squash. Rich, reddish-orange palm oil, called *chabeu,* is another important staple. In rural areas, meat dishes may be *macaco* (monkey), so ask before ordering if you don't fancy chimp. Vegetarian options are limited indeed, though eggs are plentiful.

Canned soft drinks, bottled water and beer imported from Portugal are widely available. Local brews include palm wine, as in many other West African countries. You may also come across *caña de cajeu* (cashew rum), equally strong and made not from the nuts, but from the fruit of the cashew-nut tree. However, beware that homemade distilled products can have high levels of toxins.

# BISSAU

Despite ruined monuments, cavernous potholes and regular blackouts, Bissau manages to have its charms. The sleepy colonial heart, while largely crumbling, has wide, mango-shaded streets and attractive, pastel-coloured buildings. There are several attractive cafés and restaurants where the country's elite and intelligentsia reliably

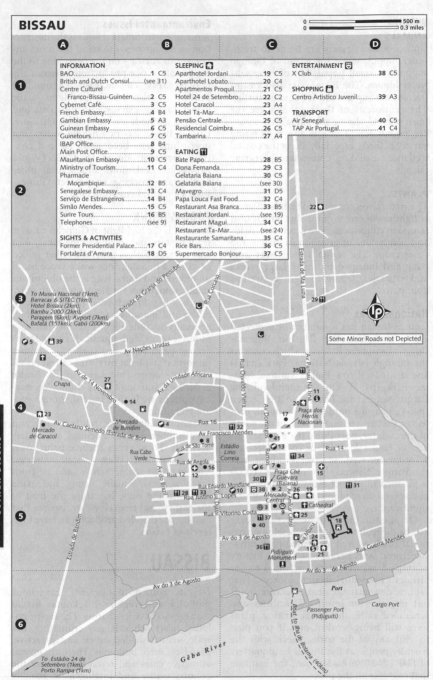

# BISSAU

0    500 m
0    0.3 miles

**INFORMATION**
BAO.............................................1 C5
British and Dutch Consul........(see 31)
Centre Culturel
  Franco-Bissau-Guinéen........2 C5
Cybernet Café...............................3 C5
French Embassy.............................4 B4
Gambian Embassy.........................5 A3
Guinean Embassy..........................6 C5
Guinetours.....................................7 C5
IBAP Office....................................8 B4
Main Post Office...........................9 C5
Mauritanian Embassy..................10 C5
Ministry of Tourism.....................11 C4
Pharmacie
  Moçambique...........................12 B5
Senegalese Embassy....................13 C4
Serviço de Estrangeiros..............14 B4
Simão Mendes.............................15 B5
Surire Tours.................................16 B5
Telephones...........................(see 9)

**SIGHTS & ACTIVITIES**
Former Presidential Palace.......17 C4
Fortaleza d'Amura....................18 D5

**SLEEPING**
Aparthotel Jordani....................19 C5
Aparthotel Lobato....................20 C4
Apartmentos Proquil.................21 C5
Hotel 24 de Setembro..............22 C2
Hotel Caracol...........................23 A4
Hotel Ta-Mar...........................24 C5
Pensão Centrale.......................25 C5
Residencial Coimbra.................26 C5
Tambarina................................27 A4

**EATING**
Bate Papo.................................28 B5
Dona Fernanda.........................29 C3
Gelataria Baiana.......................30 C5
Gelataria Baiana .................(see 30)
Mavegro...................................31 D5
Papa Louca Fast Food..............32 C4
Restaurant Asa Branca..............33 B5
Restaurant Jordani.............(see 19)
Restaurant Magui.....................34 C4
Restaurant Ta-Mar...............(see 24)
Restaurante Samaritana............35 C4
Rice Bars..................................36 C5
Supermercado Bonjour............37 C5

**ENTERTAINMENT**
X Club......................................38 C5

**SHOPPING**
Centro Artistico Juvenil............39 A3

**TRANSPORT**
Air Senegal..............................40 C5
TAP Air Portugal.....................41 C4

To Museu Nacional (1km);
Barracas & SITEC (1km);
Hotel Bissau (2km);
Bambu 2000 (2km);
Paragem (6km); Airport (7km);
Bafatá (151km); Gabú (200km)

Some Minor Roads not Depicted

Port

Passenger Port
(Pidjiguiti)

Cargo Port

To Estádio 24 de
Setembro (1km);
Porto Rampa (1km)

Gêba River

GUINEA-BISSAU

gather day after day. Best of all, you'll feel a distinct lack of hustle in the streets that will seem a blessing if you arrive from, for example, Lagos or Dakar.

## ORIENTATION

Bissau's main drag is the wide Av Amilcar Cabral, running between the port and Praça dos Heróis Nacionais. A block west on Av Domingos Ramos is the main market, the Mercado Central, and Praça Ché Guevara (better known as Baiana), which has some bars and restaurants. On the northwestern edge of the centre is the Mercado de Bandim. From here, Av de 14 Novembro leads northwest to the main *paragem* (bus and taxi park), the airport and all inland destinations.

## INFORMATION

### Cultural Centres

**Centre Culturel Franco-Bissao-Guinéen** ( ☎ 206816; Praça Ché Guevera; ☻ 9am-10pm Mon-Sat) This newly re-built centre has a library, art gallery, theatre and an interior courtyard with a pleasant café.

### Emergency

**Fire** ( ☎ 118)
**Police** ( ☎ 117)

### Internet Access

**Cybernet Café** (Rua Vitorino Costa; per hr CFA1200; ☻ 9am-10pm) Slow but dependable connections, open evenings and Sundays.
**SITEC** (Av de 14 Novembro; per hr CFA1500; ☻ until 10pm Mon-Sat, to 6pm Sun) Decent connections in air-con outside the city centre.

### Medical Services

**Pharmacie Moçambique** ( ☎ 205513) The best pharmacy in town is well-stocked and has a helpful pharmacist. If you need to see a doctor, ask here for Dr Kassem Dahrouge, who speaks French and some English.
**Simão Mendes** ( ☎ 212861; Av Pansau Na Isna) Bissau's main hospital, but facilities are limited, to say the least.

### Money

At writing, there were no ATM machines in Guinea-Bissau, and credit cards were not accepted anywhere. You must plan to arrive with all the money you need in the form of traveller's cheques or, preferably, cash. BAO near the port is the only bank in the country that reliably exchanges cash. They

strongly prefer euros but will sometimes exchange US dollars.

If you have only traveller's cheques, try the **Supermercado Mavegro** ( ☎ 201224, 201216; Rua Eduardo Mondlane; ☻ 3.30-6pm Mon, 9am-12.30pm & 3-6pm Tues-Fri, 9am-12.30pm Sat), though be warned that rates are not good. The store also exchanges cash – including US dollars – at slightly better rates.

There are a number of small moneychangers around the Mercado Central, including some who work on the streets themselves. Some may exchange traveller's cheques, though at poor rates. Rates for cash, on the other hand, can be good. Beware, though – there are definitely scammers mixed in amongst the honest brokers.

### Post

**Main post office** (Correio; Av Amilcar Cabral)

### Telephone

For local calls, keep an eye out for signs for a '*posto publico*'; they are located in corner grocery stores and other shops around the city centre. They allow you to make local calls and international long-distance calls, though the latter can be punishingly expensive – between CFA2200 and CFA5000 per minute, depending on the country. There is also a call centre at the main post office.

### Tourist Information

**Ministry of Tourism** ( ☎ 245643; Av Pansau Na Isna) The people here are friendly enough, but not equipped with much useful information for travellers. For information on hotels and private transport, you're better off at a travel agency or tour operator.

### Travel Agencies

**Guinetours** ( ☎ 214344; Rua 12) This is the best agency for international or domestic flights, and for information about hotels around the country.
**Surire Tours** ( ☎ 214166; Rua de Angola) Also recommended.

## DANGERS & ANNOYANCES

Walking around at night is safer in Bissau than in just about any other African capital city. Nevertheless, crime is slowly increasing, so take the usual precautions. Where possible, avoid unlit streets and the port area at night.

GUINEA-BISSAU

## SIGHTS

The **former presidential palace** dominates Praça dos Heróis Nacionais at the northern end of Av Amilcar Cabral. With a bombed-out roof and shrapnel in its once graceful, neoclassical façade, it's an ever-present reminder of the country's devastating civil war.

Off the southern end of Av Amilcar Cabral are the narrow streets of the old Portuguese quarter. The quarter houses colourful if often crumbling Mediterranean-style buildings. The old neighbourhood is guarded by the **Fortaleza d'Amura**. Surrounded by imposing stone walls, it's still used by the Guinean military and strictly off-limits to visitors.

On the campus of the national university on the outskirts of town is the **Museu Nacional** (Av de 14 Novembro; admission CFA500; 8am-noon & 3-6pm Mon-Fri). Looted during the war, it is slowly rebuilding a small but interesting collection of tribal art. Don't miss the collection of Carnival floats located in the upstairs gallery.

## FESTIVALS & EVENTS

Guinea-Bissau's main event is **Carnival**, which takes place in Bissau every February/early March. Music, masks, dancing, parades and all-round good times are the order of the day.

## SLEEPING

Accommodations in Bissau are expensive and generally of poor quality, especially given the high prices. Be prepared for power blackouts in budget and even some midrange hotels.

### Budget

**Pensão Centrale** ( 213270; Av Amilcar Cabral; r with shared bathroom CFA20,000) Occupying a once-grand building with wide verandas and huge, high-ceilinged rooms, this is the traditional backpacker choice Beware though: mattresses are thin, rooms are not terribly clean and security can be lax. The hotel is run by Dona Berta, a popular figure in Bissau who may share tales of her city and the various wars she and it have survived.

**Hotel Caracol** (Av Caetano Semedo; r CFA10,000) This seedy place offers small rooms with a bucket of water and a piece of foam on the cement floor, yet manages to be one of Bissau's 'best' (read 'only') budget options.

### Midrange

**Aparthotel Jordani** ( 201719; Av Pansau Na Isna; s/d CFA25,000/35,000; ) The Jordani is a friendly hotel and offers digs with running water, TV, small fridge, and a generally dependable power supply. Although, there is only cold water, and rooms are neither very attractive nor particularly clean or well-maintained, yet still manage to be some of the best in Bissau.

**Hotel Ta-Mar** ( 206647; r from CFA25,000; ) Located in the old Portuguese quarter, this hotel has definitely seen better days – think rickety fixtures and crumbling plaster. That said, it has newish beds and air-conditioning. All rooms have their own shower and sink; in-room toilets cost an extra CFA10,000 per night.

**Hotel 24 de Septembro** ( 221033; r from CFA35,000; ) This state-run hotel offers pleasant-looking bungalows set on peaceful, leafy grounds a little removed from the town centre. Unfortunately, rooms were looted during the war, and so are neither comfortable nor particularly clean.

**Apartmentos Proquil** ( 204980; r with fan/aircon CFA20,000/25,000; ) Located near the port, above an export business of the same name, this place has slightly decrepit rooms with furnishings that date to the 1960s. This is as good as it gets for this price range.

**Aparthotel Lobato** ( 201719; Av Pansau Na Isna; s/d CFA35,000/45,000; ) Rooms are newish and comfortable enough, though stuffy; prices are high.

### Top End

**Residencial Coimbra** ( 213467; fax 20 14 90; Av Amilcar Cabral; s/d CFA55,000/78,000; ) With tastefully appointed rooms featuring interesting local art, as well as an attractive rooftop garden, the Coimbra is the only genuinely decent hotel in the city – though you'll pay dearly for the privilege of staying here. A high-quality breakfast buffet is included.

**Hotel Bissau** ( 251251; fax 255552; Av de 14 Novembro; s/d CFA50,000/60,000; ) Taken over by rebels during the recent civil war, this graceless concrete monolith has definitely seen better days. Rooms are large and have balconies, but are definitely frayed. However, the leafy grounds are attractive enough; the swimming pool is available to nonguests for CFA5000 per day.

## EATING

If your budget is tight, check out the rice bars near the port, where you can expect to pay around CFA500 for a heap of rice mixed with meat or fish. Unfortunately, the street stalls that are so common in West Africa are practically absent from Bissau.

### Restaurants

Unless otherwise indicated, the following restaurants are open for lunch (around noon to 3pm) and dinner (around 7pm to 10pm) daily.

**Restaurant Magui** (Av Amilcar Cabral; meals CFA2500) The charming Magui serves up spot-on Senegalese dishes in her simple eatery above the now-defunct cinema.

**Dona Fernanda** (meals CFA2500-5000; ☯ dinner) Hidden down a dirt road east of Estrada de Santa Luzia, Dona Fernanda serves up excellent Guinean dishes. Her *bica* (sea bream) is considered one of the best in the city.

**Gelataria Baiana** (Praça Ché Guevara) Serving espresso, drinks and baked goods on an outdoor terrace in the city's most attractive *praça* (park or square), Baiana is a favourite of politicians, artists and expats alike.

**Restaurant Samaritana** (off Av Pansau Na Isna; meals CFA2500) Another restaurant serving up simple, fresh and delicious Senegalese food in humble surroundings. Next door, there's also a decent Chinese restaurant with wide-screen TVs playing music videos.

**Papa Louca Fast Food** (Av Francisco Mendes) A decent option for 'fast food' such as shwarmas (CFA1000), hamburgers (CFA1500) and pizza (CFA2000) that is popular with expats.

**Restaurant Ta-Mar** (mains CFA4000) A favourite of the city's movers and shakers, this newly refurbished restaurant in the hotel of the same name has a distinctly European feel. Food is generally decent if pricey. On Friday nights, they close off the street, set up tables outside and often feature live music.

**Bate Papo** (Rua Eduardo Mondlane; meals CFA4000) At night, this upmarket place has the best pizza in town (CFA3500), and in the morning, it has good pastries and coffee.

**Restaurant Jordani** (Av Pansau Na Isna; mains CFA4000-5000) Come here for the festive, red-tiled dining room rather than the food, which is only sometimes good. It's a great spot on Thursdays when people come to eat, drink and listen to live music by some of the country's leading musicians.

**Restaurant Asa Branca** (Rua Justino Lopes; meals CFA4000-6000) Asa Branca serves traditional Portuguese fare and is particularly noted for its seafood.

### Self-Catering

You can get fresh produce in and around the Mercado Central or at the Mercado Bandim, though be prepared to bargain – the ladies will rob you blind if you don't know your papayas. For imported foodstuffs, head to one of the city's higher-end supermarkets. **Supermercardo Mavegro** (Rua Eduardo Mondlane) sells all kinds of imported items, from tents and car tyres to shampoo, plus a decent selection of packaged foods. **Supermercado Bonjour** (Rua Vitorino Costa) near the Air Sénégal office also has a decent selection of packaged food.

## DRINKING

Perhaps the best thing about Bissau is its easy sociability, and there are a number of places to while away an afternoon or evening over beer or coffee.

French speakers may prefer the café in the inner courtyard of the Centre Culturel Franco-Bissao-Guinéen (p447) on the other side of the square.

A number of restaurants also double as bar-cafés, including the Restaurant Jordani and the Restaurant Ta-Mar. On Thursday nights the Jordani hosts some of the best musicians in the country without even charging a cover and on Friday nights, the Ta-Mar closes off the street in front, set up tables outside and often features live music.

## ENTERTAINMENT

**X Club** (Rua Osualdo Vieira) For late-night partying, this club caters to everyone from idealistic UN workers to shady businessmen on the prowl. Décor is Euro-trendy and there are two free snooker tables.

**Bambu 2000** (Av de 14 Novembro) On weekends, this more rustic locale overflows with locals willing to drop a few thousand CFA to dance till dawn.

## SHOPPING

**Centro Artistico Juvenil** (Av de 14 Novembro) Not only a great place to shop (prices are actually marked and there is no pressure to buy!),

GUINEA-BISSAU

this is also a fine introduction to the arts and crafts of the Guinea-Bissau's many ethnicities. Purchases help young trainees learn traditional artisanship.

Check out the beaded jewellery and wood carvings on sale on the sidewalk in front of Pensão Centrale (p448), though here you will have to bargain. Just north of the main post office, vendors sell a variety of textiles (beautiful but mostly machine made). For cheap wares, from hats and sunglasses to used clothing, try Mercado de Bandim.

### GETTING THERE & AWAY
### Air
Bissau is home to the country's only airport with regularly scheduled flights, with services by TACV Cabo Verde Airlines, Air Sénégal International, TAP Air Portugal, and Air Luxor. See p460 for more information.

### Boat
Currently there is no ferry service in Bissau, but there is talk of restarting service to Bubaque in the Bijagós. For information about boat travel to the Bijagós, see opposite.

### Bush Taxi & Minibus
You can get bush taxis and minibuses to just about anywhere in the country, as well as to Senegal, at the outdoor *paragem* (stop), hidden about 500m south of Av de 14 Novembro, about 5km outside town. It's always best to get transport in the morning. For more information about travel by bush taxi and minibus, see p461.

To get to the *paragem*, take a *toca-toca* (minibus) from the Mercado de Bandim (CFA100) or a taxi (about CFA1000) from anywhere in town.

### GETTING AROUND
### To/From the Airport
The airport is about 9km from the town centre. Taxis meet most flights, and it should cost no more than CFA2000 to get into town. To get a minibus (CFA100), walk 200m to the roundabout at the start of Av de 14 Novembro, the main road into the city.

### Taxi
Shared taxis – generally well-worn Mercedes, and always painted blue and white – are plentiful and ply all the main routes. Prices vary according to distance and whim, but never

cost more than CFA300 for trips within the city centre.

### Toca-Toca
These are small minibuses painted blue and yellow that run around the city. Most rides cost CFA100. The most useful route for visitors goes from Mercado de Bandim along Av de 14 Novembro towards the *paragem* and airport.

# ARQUIPÉLAGO DOS BIJAGÓS

At first, the Bijagós – Africa's only archipelago – may seem simply a pleasant escape from the problems of the mainland, with swaying palms, cooling breezes and powdery, white-sand beaches. Stay a little while though, and you'll begin to fall under the islands' singular spell.

Protected by swift tides and treacherous sandbanks, the islands have long been a world apart. They eluded Portuguese control until the 1930s, and the fiercely independent Bijagós people still retain a large degree of autonomy from the federal government.

Most visitors to the islands seem to be either biologists who come to study the unique and rich variety of marine life, or else sports fishermen who come to catch and eat it. When you see the islands' turquoise waters quiver with fish, you can understand what attracts both groups. The entire archipelago has been declared a biosphere reserve, and two island groups have also been declared national parks: the southern Orango group, home to saltwater hippos; and the eastern João Vieira group, breeding ground to a number of endangered sea turtles.

Travellers should note that transportation to and between the islands is difficult. See opposite for more information. Also, low tides often reveal mud flats that reach kilometres out to sea, limiting beach-going to high tide – unless you like to wade thigh-deep in mud. Finally, telephone service on the islands – including mobile service – is very unreliable.

### Dangers & Annoyances
Because of the higher density of tourism, the Bijagós are one of the few places in the country were you will hear a litany of

---

### QUEENS OF THE BIJAGÓS

Protected by the shallow channels and treacherous tides that wash their islands, the peoples of the Arquipélago dos Bijagós have, over the centuries, developed a largely matriarchal culture that is remarkably distinct from that of mainland Guinea. The islanders are ruled by a king and queen (they're not married) who serve as co-regents – the king managing men's affairs and the queen managing women's affairs. Women often serve as chiefs of individual villages, and they're also the sole homeowners – only fair since they are entirely responsible for homebuilding, from brick-making to actual construction.

Marriage is also a matriarchal affair. On some islands, when a girl reaches puberty, the young men venture forth with as much rice and other goods as they can afford in the hope of buying their way into her favour. She chooses a suitor, but if she's not pregnant within a year, or if someone else makes a better offer, she can ditch her man and choose another. The man usually only stays around until she gives birth, then returns home and becomes eligible for other liaisons. Children take their mother's name and are often unable to identify their father.

The majority of the people remain almost virtually untouched by modern civilisation. They're exceedingly open and friendly, though they'll also ask you to give them anything you might be carrying, up to and including the shirt off your back – literally. But however welcoming they are, remember that their culture's survival depends exactly on its isolation. If you travel to the more remote islands, tread very, very lightly.

---

requests, mostly by children and always in French, for *cent francs* (CFA100).

### Getting There & Away

Transportation to the islands is, simply put, difficult. There is no longer a ferry service or regularly scheduled flights. That leaves two options. First are *canoas* – large, motorised, occasionally leaky and nearly always overloaded canoes – that leave Bissau from either the port at the foot of Av Amilcar Cabral, or Port Rampa, the fishermen's port near the Estádio 24 de Setembro. Expect to share the boat with farm animals, bags of rice and cement, and quantities of powerful-smelling, not-quite-dried fish. There are several Bissau–Bubaque *canoas* (CFA2500 per person, four to six hours) that follow a regular weekly schedule, though departure times vary according to tides and winds. It's always worth asking around for unscheduled departures, but do check the boat's conditions (and your own instincts) carefully.

At the other extreme, a number of higher-end fishing camps on the islands hire out speedboats to Bubaque or the other islands. However, you can expect to pay more than CFA100,000 for the trip from Bissau to Bubaque. If your hotel doesn't arrange transport, your best bet for fast, safe transport is the **Hotel Marazul** ( ☎ 6-626277) in Quinhámel. It has a range of boats.

At writing, a small cruise ship called the *African Queen* was expected to return to Bissau, with regular, multiday excursions to the islands. The schedule, prices and details were still to be determined; check with travel agencies in Bissau for current schedules, prices and itineraries.

### Getting Around

Travel between the islands is just as difficult as travel from the mainland. For *canoas*, ask around at the port on each island to find out if anyone is going where you'd like to go. Alternatively, you may be able to hire a boat and driver from one of the top-end hotels, though you should expect to pay about CFA50,000 to CFA100,000 per day plus fuel.

## ILHA DE BOLAMA

Located just off the mainland, about 40km south of Bissau, the island of Bolama was long home to the Portuguese capital. Deprived of its status in 1941, the once-grand town (also called Bolama) has been decaying ever since, with sagging colonnades and papaya trees sprouting from stately living rooms. The effect is one of eerie beauty, though the damage is so advanced in some cases that it causes more regret than reverie.

The island is virtually devoid of a tourist infrastructure, though the NGO Prodepa, an international group devoted to preserving traditional fishing techniques, rents basic rooms (CFA12,000) and serves food (three meals for around CFA5000 per person). The closest beach is about 4km south of Bolama town, but the best beaches are along the far southwest end of the island, about 20km from town via a poorly maintained road.

Currently there is a regularly scheduled *canoa* that leaves Bissau for Bolama on Saturday (CFA2000, about three hours), returning Sunday. See p451 for more information about boat travel to the Bijagós.

## ILHA DE BUBAQUE

At the centre of the Bijagós, Bubaque is home to the archipelago's largest town, as well its major transport hub. If you can't make it to remoter islands, Bubaque makes a fine place to unwind. There is a range of accommodation in and around the main town and a small beach at the island's northern tip. Or, a better option is Praia Bruce, a wide expanse of powdery white sand at the southern end of the island. It's about 30km from Bubaque town along a paved, if pitted road. Some hotels arrange transport to the

beach (up to CFA10,000 round trip), or you can ask around to hire a bicycle (around CFA5,000 per day). If you make the trip, make sure you're there for high tide.

## Sleeping & Eating

There is a range of good accommodation in Bubaque, all of which also serve meals if you order ahead. Prices are significantly lower – and standards of cleanliness significantly higher – than in Bissau. For cheap eats, head to the port area, where there are several workers' bar-restaurants serving cheap beers and rice plates. Note that the island only has power in the evenings (and this not always).

### BUDGET

All the rooms in this category have shared bathroom with bucket shower.

**Chez Titi** (r CFA5000) Very basic rooms, but they're ideally perched on a small bluff just above the water. Good Senegalese food is served.

**Chez Raoul** (s/d CFA4000/6000) Another good budget option run by a Senegalese couple, with a dining room attached that is con-

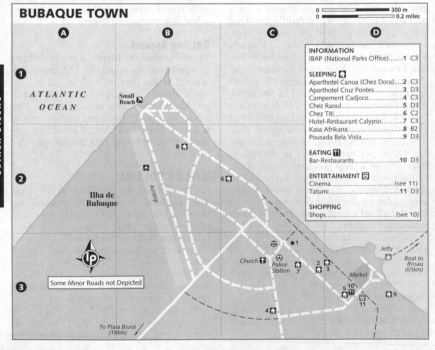

**BUBAQUE TOWN**

0 —————— 300 m
0 —————— 0.2 miles

**INFORMATION**
IBAP (National Parks Office)........1  C3

**SLEEPING**
Aparthotel Canoa (Chez Dora).....2  C3
Aparthotel Cruz Pontes...............3  D3
Campement Cadjoco..................4  C3
Chez Raoul...............................5  D3
Chez Titi..................................6  C2
Hotel-Restaurant Calypso...........7  C3
Kasa Afrikana...........................8  B2
Pousada Bela Vista....................9  D3

**EATING**
Bar-Restaurants........................10  D3

**ENTERTAINMENT**
Cinema...............................(see 11)
Tatumi...................................11  D3

**SHOPPING**
Shops...................................(see 10)

ATLANTIC OCEAN

Small Beach

Ilha de Bubaque

Airstrip

Some Minor Roads not Depicted

Church
Police Station

Market

Jetty

Boat to Bissau (65km)

To Praia Bruce (18km)

GUINEA-BISSAU

sidered the best in town (mains CFA500 to CFA2500).

**Campement Cadjoco** (r CFA7000) This French-run *pensão* (pension) offers good value, with well-maintained rooms at the back of a pleasant garden. The owner also has a good, fast boat and offers fishing trips as well as transport to and from the islands.

**Pousada Bela Vista** (r CFA7500) Located in the heart of town, this Franco-Senegalese run place offers small but clean, newly furnished rooms. Beware, though, that the owners tend to think prices are flexible (upwards, of course) even after you're sure you've settled on a figure, and the food is iffy.

**MIDRANGE**

**Chez Dora** (r CFA12,000) Officially called Aparthotel Canoa, Chez Dora offers simple, but tasteful, impeccably maintained cottages with private baths and running water ranged around a lush garden. The gracious Dora does all the cooking (meals around CFA3000), which is a delicious amalgam of local ingredients – including her own pigs and papayas – and techniques from her native Portugal. She's also relentlessly clean, so if you're going to eat raw greens anywhere in West Africa, this is the place to do it. Highly recommended.

**Aparthotel Cruz Pontes** ( ☎ 821135; r CFA10,000) Another good option, with simple but clean cottages with a private bathroom and running water. The friendly owner also serves meals (CFA2500 to CFA3000) and is a good person to ask about boat transport.

**Hotel-Restaurant Calypso** ( ☎ 821131; s/d CFA12,000/15,000; ☒ ) This French-run place offers simple but attractive bungalows with private bathrooms, ranged around a little garden and swimming pool.

**TOP END**

**Kasa Afrikana** ( ☎ 821144; develayg@yahoo.fr; r CFA50,000; ☒ ☒ ) The island's newest and cushiest hotel caters to rich fishermen. It's a French-run establishment with tastefully decorated and fully equipped rooms plus attractive grounds with a bar, a pool, and views of the water.

**Entertainment**

While the food is iffy, Pousada Bela Vista has a terrace set on the water, making it a popular place for an evening beer. If you're

determined to party, check out **Tatumi** (admission CFA1000-2000), the island's only full-fledged nightclub, catering mostly to locals. Next door is a 'cinema' that plays mostly French-language DVDs on a large screen TV.

**Getting There & Away**

There are unscheduled *canoas* to and from Bissau almost every day. In addition, there are regularly scheduled (and generally more reliable) *canoas* that leave Bissau for Bubaque on Tuesday and Friday, returning Wednesday and Sunday (CFA2500 per person, four to six hours). There is also fairly regular service to Orango (CFA2000, two to four hours), and occasional services to other islands. Just head to the port and ask around for times and destinations. See p451 for more information about boat travel to the Bijagós.

If you plan to visit either of the national parks, it's worth checking with the IBAP office (national parks office) in Bubaque to see if you can join the staff on one of the park's boats for the price of fuel (though this can run as high as CFA50,000 return).

## ORANGO ISLANDS NATIONAL PARK

Home to rare saltwater species of hippo and crocodile, Ilha de Orango and the surrounding islands together make up the Orango Islands National Park. The island is also the burial site of the Bijagós kings and queens.

The island's only hotel, **Orango Parque Hotel** ( ☎ satellite phone 00871-761 273221; per person incl 3 meals CFA30,000) has attractive, well-maintained rooms with pretty tile bathrooms, and sits right on the beach. The Italian-Portuguese owners also serve up excellent food. The hotel is a short walk to the royal burial grounds, though you'll have to hire a boat to visit the shy hippos and crocs.

## JOÃO VIEIRA – POILÃO NATIONAL MARINE PARK

At the far, southwest end of the archipelago, the João Vieira – Poilão National Marine Park consists of four islands and surrounding waters that together form a key nesting area for three species of endangered sea turtles. Ilha João Vieira is the only island with accommodations – two adjoining fishing camps run by Frenchmen who have been friends since childhood in Brittany.

Set on a paradisiacal beach, **Chez Claude** (per person per night with full board CFA40,000) offers simple but spotless cabins and Franco-African cuisine that is based on the catch of the day and served up with a hospitality that is at once down-to-earth and distinctly French-inflected. Just up the beach is **Tuburon Club** (per person per night with full board CFA50,000), which caters to higher-end fishing tours.

Between the two lodges is the IBAP office, which has French-language displays illustrating the local ecosystem and at writing was also in the process of building basic rooms for visitors. Check in with park officials before visiting the turtle nesting sites on nearby islands.

## OTHER ISLANDS

Just across from Bubaque is **Ilha de Rubane**, which has a number of high-end, French-owned lodges catering to sports fishermen. At writing, a new eco-hotel promoting low-impact travel was also under construction. Another option is the tiny but paradisiacal **Ilha Acunda**, just off the Unhocomo and Unhocomozinho islands – the most westerly of the Bijagós. The rustic but attractive **Hotel Acunda** (per person per night incl 3 meals CFA25,000) offers cabins just up from a lovely stretch of white sand. To make reservations and arrange transportation, contact the **Hotel Marazul** ( ☎ 6-626277 in Quinhámel).

# THE NORTHWEST

Northwest Guinea-Bissau offers two distinct experiences for the traveller. Varela, which sits just across the border from Senegal's Cap Skiring, shares its neighbour's gorgeous, wide beaches yet remains almost completely undeveloped. The region is also home to remarkably well-preserved mangrove swamps and the Cacheu river, with its hippos and crocodiles. A word of caution: poor road conditions throughout the region make travel in northwest Guinea-Bissau an exercise in patience.

## QUINHÁMEL

Located about 30km west of Bissau, Quinhámel has a small but lively town centre, and also serves as capital of the Biombo region, which is the traditional home of the Papel people. If you are arriving from Bissau, you'll see a local collective just before the centre of town on the left that, with support from international groups, is devoted to preserving traditional weaving techniques. There are no formal tours, but it's well worth a stop to see the men and boys at work on the traditional looms. Down a dirt road to the left, past the town, lies the **Hotel Marazul** ( ☎ 6-626277; s/d CFA30,000/35,000; ✗ ☙ ). It offers attractive bungalows set amid a pretty grove of palms, plus the country's best-maintained swimming pool. The hotel also rents boats for fishing trips or transfers to the Bijagós islands. Minibuses run regularly to/from Bissau (CFA500).

## CACHEU

The small riverside town of Cacheu (cash-ay-ou) was once a major Portuguese slave-trading centre from which the infamous English pirate Sir Francis Drake was repulsed in 1567. You can visit the reconstructed fort, with cannons and some large bronze statues stacked in a corner and seemingly forgotten. Most visitors, though, come to visit the nearby park. Minibuses run regularly to/from Bissau (CFA2000).

## PARQUE NATURAL DOS TARRAFES DO RIO CACHEU

Established to protect large areas of mangrove, the Parque Natural dos Tarrafes do Rio Cacheu is home to a diverse array of wildlife, including alligators, hippos, monkeys, manatees, panthers, gazelles and hyenas. There are also more than 200 bird species, among them flamingos, Senegal parrots and African giant kingfishers.

The park's infrastructure is limited. However, the park office (on the left before you reach the town of Cacheu if you're coming from Bissau) offers rooms with shared bath with running water, and solar-powered electricity for CFA3000 per person. They'll also prepare meals for guests. At writing, there were no fixed prices for meals – be prepared to bargain. Park officials can organise boat trips on the Cacheu and surrounding swamps, or perhaps arrange for a motorbike. For more information, contact the **IBAP office** ( ☎ 207106; Rua São Tomé) in Bissau.

A cheap way to view wildlife is to take the *canoa* that plies the river daily between

Cacheu and São Domingos; the trip costs CFA1500 and takes around two hours. Schedules depend on tides.

## SÃO DOMINGOS

While there is not much reason to linger in São Domingos, this town on the Senegalese border is a regional transport hub, sitting on the main route to/from Ziguinchor (Senegal). If you get stuck here (not impossible as the border post is often closed at night), there are food stalls and several hotels around the main square. If you're headed to Varela by public transport, you may be able to find a bush taxi outside the border post. There are plenty of bush taxis to/from Bissau (CFA2700, two to three hours).

## VARELA

With wide sand beaches as beautiful as those of Cap Skiring just across the Senegalese border, Varela is the favourite getaway of Guineans – at least those with four-wheel drives. The road from São Domingos is, at writing, in terrible condition, though there is a lot of talk about repaving. Even with a good vehicle, the 50km drive can take several hours.

Once you arrive, you can pitch a tent along the beach without a problem. Or you can stay at **Chez Helene** (r CFA12,000) which offers simple but well-maintained rooms and excellent meals (CFA2500; at least if the Italian chef decides to stick around). Consider packing food as well, since shops in this isolated town often run out of many items.

There is usually at least one minibus daily that runs to/from São Domingos (two to three hours).

# THE NORTHEAST

Travelling northeast from Bissau, the flat, wet coastal regions give way to drier and hillier land that serves as the transition into the Sahel. There is little to detain the traveller, although the forests and rivers are popular with hunters and fishermen, and the road between the Gabú and the Guinean border winds through pretty hills as high as 300m – the highest point in the country.

## Getting There & Away

Transport from Bissau to Gabú via Bafatá is plentiful and ranges from bush taxi to toca-tocas. Roads are mostly good as far as Gabú, though annual flooding can change conditions quickly

## BAFATÁ

Bafatá is the birthplace of Amilcar Cabral and the region's largest city. Bafatá retains a small but interesting colonial centre, which is located on a bluff above the Gêba River. Travellers should check out the old public market, with its odd, arabesque façade, and stroll down by the peaceful area around the riverbank.

The nicest place to stay in Bafatá is **Hotel Maimuna Capé** (r with fan/air-con CFA12,000/17,000; ⊠ ), which offers comfortable, spotless rooms in an attractive building in the old colonial centre. The hotel also offers meals for CFA2800 to CFA5000. Hidden on an unnamed street off the main Bissau–Gabú road is **Apartmento Fao** (r CFA5000), which offers small, basic rooms with shared bathroom with bucket water. The best place to eat is **Restaurante Ponto de Encontro** (dishes around CFA3500). Run by a friendly Portuguese family, it serves simple but hearty Portuguese food made from fresh local ingredients. There are also plenty of food stalls along the main Bissau–Gabú road.

Minibuses to Bissau (CFA1800), Gabú (CFA700) or Buba (CFA1800) depart from the petrol station area.

**BAFATÁ**

0      500 m
0      0.3 miles

Ⓐ           Ⓑ

SLEEPING 🏠
Apartmento Fao.................................1 B2
Hotel Maimuna Capé.........................2 A2

EATING 🍴
Food Stalls.........................................3 B2
Restaurante Ponto de Encontro.........4 A2

TRANSPORT
Minibus & Bush Taxi Park...................5 B2
Petrol Station.................................(see 5)

Gêba River

Cabral Monument   Stadium   To Gabú (50km)

❶

❷ Main Market   4   2   Hospital   3   Pharmacy   Market Stalls   5

1

Some Minor Roads not Depicted     To Bissau (151km)

GUINEA-BISSAU

## GABÚ

It may not be beautiful, but Gabú is definitely lively, especially in the evening as the shops and food stalls along the main road to Bafatá come to life. A range of accommodation makes it a good place to stay if you're travelling to/from Guinea.

If you're determined to get to know this part of the country, you can head to Canjadude, 40km south on the poorly maintained road to Boé. From here, you can hike up several rocky hillocks rising from the plain and get good views of the area.

### Sleeping & Eating

**Hotel Visiom** ( ☎ 511484; r with fan/air-con CFA8000/ 15,000; 🗷 ) Out in a quiet spot north of town, the Visiom is good value, with clean rooms with bathroom, a friendly staff, and a small garden.

**Residencial Djaraama** ( ☎ 511302; r with shared bathroom CFA12,500) Occupying the 2nd floor of a colonial building and ringed by a wide veranda, this place may be overpriced, but it's the only place with character. Kitschy décor includes a 4m-long snakeskin and an inflatable reindeer.

**Jomav** (r CFA5000) This bar-restaurant-disco offers small but spotless rooms with fan and tiny bathrooms with bucket water. Be aware that you won't get much sleep here when the disco's open.

**Restaurant Binta** (meals from CFA500) Binta is a feisty Dakar lady who makes one hell of a peanut sauce.

**Pó di Terra** (meals CFA1000-2000) The Pó di Terra has outdoor seating in a pleasant garden on the north side of town.

### Getting There & Away

Minibuses go to Bissau regularly (CFA2500, five to six hours). If you're heading for Guinea or Senegal, see p460 for details of transport options from Gabú. You can easily change CFA into Guinean francs at the bush taxi and minibus park.

# THE SOUTH

Moving into southern Guinea-Bissau, you leave the Sahel well behind and enter a beautiful region of tropical forests penetrated by countless waterways. The bird and monkey populations are impressive, and this is the home of Africa's most westerly chimpanzee populations.

### Getting There & Away

Currently, the only way to get to the region is by minibus or with your own vehicle – preferably a very sturdy four-wheel drive. Roads are very poor, so even short distances can be slow. There's a minibus that plies the Bissau–Catió route most days (CFA3000, all day), though you may have to switch vehicles in Buba. You can also get a minibus from Bafatá. Either way, you should ask around the day before to confirm schedules.

At writing there were no longer any regularly scheduled *canoas* or ferries between Bissau and Catió or Enxude.

### Getting Around

Without a very sturdy four-wheel drive vehicle, getting around the region is very difficult. Regular cars can make it to Buba but not to Catió. Minibuses ply most roads, but service can be infrequent and erratic.

## SALTINHO

The main Bissau-Buba road crosses the Corubal River right over the Saltinho waterfalls. The **Pousada do Saltinho** ( ☎ 202901; s/d CFA20,000/25,000; 🗷 ) has fine views of the falls, though they're largely obscured by a metal bridge. The hotel is popular with European hunters. Even if you don't stay here, come for a drink or just for a swim in the falls.

**GABÚ**

0 — 200 m
0 — 0.1 miles

SLEEPING 🏠
Hotel Visiom..............................1 B1
Jomav........................................2 A2
Residencial Djaraama...............3 A2

EATING 🍴
Pó di Terra.................................4 B2
Restaurant Binta.......................5 B2
Street Food Stalls......................6 B2

TRANSPORT
Bush Taxi & Minibus Park............7 B2

To Bafatá (50km);
Bissau (200km)

Guiné
Telecom

Market

To Guiné
(66km)

Some Minor Roads not Depicted

## BUBA

Buba is a small junction town on the way to points further south and east. The most pleasant place to stay (and best value) is **Pousada Bela Vista** ( ☎ 6-647011; r CFA10,000; 🖫 ), which has spotless, attractively fitted-out bungalows and lovely vistas of the river. To find it, head all the way to the port and turn left along a dirt road for about 500m. Another option is the **Foroya Club** ( ☎ 611120; r CFA15,00), a hunting and fishing club that offers bungalows with bathroom on a pleasant spot just above the river. There's also a restaurant (meals CFA3000). In town, there are a number of places to get cheap bowls of fish and rice (around CFA500). A minibus from Bissau (CFA2500, all day) leaves most mornings.

About 5km before you reach the town of Buba, you will see signs for **Parque Natural da Lagoa de Cafatada**. While there was no infrastructure for visitors at writing, it is an important habitat for both bird and aquatic life. For more information about arranging a visit, contact the **IBAP office** ( ☎ 207106; Rua São Tomé) in Bissau.

## CATIÓ

Catió is the most remote area in the south that still has regular transport connections with Bissau. There is not much reason to linger, but it's a necessary stop on the way to Jemberem and the Cantanhez Forest. You can reach Catió by minibus (CFA3000, all day) from Bissau (though you may have to switch vehicles in Buba).

## JEMBEREM & THE CANTANHEZ FOREST

Jemberem is a small village 22km east of Catió, and the centre of a community-based conservation scheme connected with the proposed Parque Natural de Cantanhez, which is a good place to see birds and, with luck, chimpanzees and elephants. The local women's association has set up the small and inexpensive Raça Banana guesthouse. Through them or the local chief you can arrange a guide (essential) to show you through the nearby sacred forest.

There's a daily *kandonga* (truck or pickup) in the morning between Catió and Jemberem. You may also check in at the **IBAP office** ( ☎ 207106; Rua São Tomé) in Bissau for more information about the park, including transport.

# GUINEA-BISSAU DIRECTORY

## ACCOMMODATION

Accommodation in Bissau is not only expensive but also poor value. The budget doubles are primitive and not very clean but still cost around CFA10,000. Expect to pay upwards of CFA35,000 for a midrange double with running water, electricity and air-conditioning. Outside the capital, the situation is, fortunately, very different. For CFA10,000 to CFA15,000 you can expect a clean, comfortable room with running water, private bath and, at the higher end of the scale, air-conditioning. Budget digs outside Bissau cost around CFA5,000. Specialist hunting and fishing camps are scattered around the country, catering to upmarket visitors flying in from France and Portugal. They generally charge CFA30,000 to CFA50,000 per person for room and full board.

## ACTIVITIES

The Arquipélago dos Bijagós (p450) and especially Varela have great sandy beaches, and the waters around the Bijagós also offer some of the best deep-sea fishing in the world. Cycling is an excellent way to get around Guinea-Bissau, as roads are quiet and generally flat. There are no formal hire outlets, but you can usually arrange something just by asking around. For more serious exploration, consider bringing your own bike (for more information, see p843).

---

**PRACTICALITIES**

- The national radio and TV stations broadcast in Portuguese. Most interesting for travellers is Radio Mavegro FM (100.0MHz), which combines music with hourly news bulletins in English from the BBC.

- Newspapers come and go quickly in Bissau. If you sit at one of the city's cafes or restaurants, a vendor will quickly be offering you the latest offerings.

- Electrical voltage is 220V with European plugs (2 round prongs).

- Guinea-Bissau uses the metric system.

---

GUINEA-BISSAU

## BOOKS

Patrick Chabal's *Amilcar Cabral: Revolutionary Leadership and People's War* is a fine antidote to current cynicism about African politics, documenting the way the leader of Guinea-Bissau's revolution combined idealism, sharp analytical powers and political acumen.

Walter Hawthorne's *Planting Rice and Harvesting Slaves: Transformations along the Guinea-Bissau Coast, 1400–1900* examines the way European slavery radically changed the way of life of the stateless Balanta people of Guinea-Bissau.

Jonina Einarsdottir's *Tired of Weeping: Mother Love, Child Death, and Poverty in Guinea-Bissau* explores the unexpected ways women of Guinea-Bissau's matrilineal Papel tribe cope with high rates of infant mortality.

## BUSINESS HOURS

Opening hours for banks and government offices vary quite a bit, but are usually 8am to noon and 3pm to 6pm Monday to Friday, or from 8am to 2pm Monday to Friday. The post offices are generally open Monday to Friday mornings only, but the main post office in Bissau is open 8am to 6pm Monday to Saturday. Larger shops are generally open from 8am or 9am until 6pm Monday to Friday and 8am until 1pm or 2pm Saturday. Some shops also close for an hour or two in the early afternoon. In most towns there are usually corner grocers that will stay open until 10pm or even later.

## EMBASSIES & CONSULATES
### Guinea-Bissau Embassies & Consulates

In West Africa, you can get visas for Guinea-Bissau in The Gambia, Guinea, Mauritania and Senegal. For more details see the relevant country chapter. Outside Africa, Guinea-Bissau has very few embassies or consulates. These are more or less limited to the following:

**Belgium** ( ☎ 02-647 08 09; 70 Av Franklin-Roosevelt, Brussels 1000)
**France** ( ☎ 01 45 26 18 51; 94 Rue Saint Lazare, 75009 Paris)
**Portugal** ( ☎ 21 303 04 40; Rua Alcolena, 17, Lisbon 1400)
**USA** ( ☎ 301-947 3958; 15929 Yukon Lane, Rockville, MD 20855)

## Embassies & Consulates in Guinea-Bissau

All embassies and consulates are in Bissau, some in the centre, others along the road towards the airport.

**France** ( ☎ 201312; cnr Av de 14 Novembro & Av do Brazil)
**Gambia** ( ☎ 203928; Av de 14 Novembro; ⏰ 8.30am-3pm Sat-Thu, to 12.30pm Fri) Located 1km northwest of Mercado de Bandim.
**Guinea** ( ☎ 201231; Rua 12; ⏰ 8.30am-3pm Sat-Thu, to 1pm Fri) East of the central stadium.
**Mauritania** ( ☎ 203696; Rua Eduardo Mondlane) South of the central stadium.
**Senegal** ( ☎ 212944; off Praça dos Heróis Nacionais; ⏰ 8am-5pm)

The consul for the UK and the Netherlands is **Jan van Maanen** ( ☎ 201224, 211529; fax 201265; Supermercardo Mavegro, Rua Eduardo Mondlane, Bissau). Contact the French embassy for information about visas for Benin, Côte d'Ivoire and Togo.

## FESTIVALS & EVENTS

Guinea-Bissau's main event is Carnival, which takes place in Bissau every year in February or early March. Music, masks, dancing, parades and all-around good times are the order of the day. Small festivals are held in other towns around the country at about the same time of year, although you need to ask locally for details as dates are not fixed.

## HOLIDAYS

Public holidays include:
**New Year's Day** 1 January
**Anniversary of the Death of Amilcar Cabral** 20 January
**Women's Day** 8 March
**Easter** March/April
**Labour Day** 1 May
**Pidjiguiti Day** 3 August
**Independence Day** 24 September
**Christmas Day** 25 December

Islamic feasts such as Eid al-Fitr (at the end of Ramadan) and Tabaski are also celebrated. See p818 for a table of dates of Islamic holidays.

## INTERNET ACCESS

There are several Internet cafés in Bissau. They charge CFA1000 to CFA1500 per hour for slow, dial-up connections. Outside of the capital, there is virtually no public Internet access.

## LANGUAGE

Portuguese is the official language, but no more than a third of the people speak it. Each group has its own language, but the common tongue is Crioulo – a mix of medieval Portuguese and local words. As Guinea-Bissau is increasingly drawn into the Afro-Francophone world, more and more people understand French. See p861 for some useful phrases.

## MONEY

At writing, there are no ATM machines in Guinea-Bissau, and credit cards are not accepted anywhere. You must plan to arrive with all the money you need in the form of traveller's cheques or, preferably, cash. Euros are the easiest to exchange. US dollars are more difficult, and sometimes impossible outside Bissau.

The unit of currency is the West African CFA franc. The principal bank of Guinea-Bissau is the Banco da Africa Ocidental (BAO), although they don't change travellers cheques. In Bissau you can change cash at BAO or with the moneychangers around the Mercado Central (some may also accept travellers cheques, though at ruinous rates). You can also change cash and travellers cheques at Supermercado Mavegro. Outside Bissau, there are few banks, so most travellers change money in Bissau.

Outside of Bissau you may have luck changing euros, and in rare cases US dollars, just by asking around any public market. However, plan to carry all the local currency you think you might need.

Tipping is optional.

## PHOTOGRAPHY & VIDEO

Photo permits are not required, but the usual restrictions apply. For more information see p823.

## POST

The postal service is reliable but slow – you're probably better off posting mail home from Senegal or Gambia. If you decide to make a go of it, airmail letters cost CFA450. Travellers report that the poste restante in Bissau is unhelpful and unreliable.

## TELEPHONE

For local calls, keep an eye out for signs 'posto publico'; they are located in corner grocery stores and other shops around the country. They allow you to make local calls, and sometimes international long-distance calls, though the latter can be punishingly expensive – between CFA2200 and CFA5000 per minute, depending on the country. There is also a call centre at the **main post office** (Av Amilcar Cabral) in Bissau.

It is relatively easy to buy a mobile phone with a prepaid plan. You can also buy a SIM card and put it in your own mobile phone. The best company is Areeba, which charges about CFA5,000 for a SIM card, about CFA100 per minute for calls within the country and as little as CFA500 for international calls. Service is fairly reliable on the mainland, but not in the Arquipélago dos Bijagós.

There are no city phone codes in Guinea-Bissau. All fixed-line numbers have six digits. Mobile phones have seven digits.

## VISAS

All visitors, except nationals of Ecowas countries, need visas. These are normally valid for one month and are issued for around US$40 at embassies. They are not issued at land borders, but may be issued at the airport if you come from an African country where visas are not available. To avoid hassles, get one before you arrive.

### Visa Extensions

Extensions are easy to obtain at **Serviço de Estrangeiros** (Av 14 de Novembro, Bissau), behind the main immigration building across from the Mercado Bandim. For virtually all nationalities, 45-day visa extensions cost around CFA4000 and are ready the same day if you apply early.

### Visas for Onward Travel

Visas for the following neighbouring countries can be obtained at their embassies in Bissau.

**Gambia** Three-month single-entry visas cost CFA15,000 and require one photo; they're ready the same day if you go early.

**Guinea** Two-month multiple-entry visas cost US$40 plus two photos and take a day or two to issue.

**Senegal** One-month multiple-entry visas cost CFA5000 with four photos and are issued in two days.

## WOMEN TRAVELLERS

The combined legacy of Portuguese assimilation and the role of women fighters in the liberation war, plus limited Islamic influence, means local women enjoy a certain degree of freedom. If you've travelled through Senegal or Mali, the sight of women in trousers, couples holding hands in public, or men and women simply socialising comfortably together, makes a refreshing change. Although the atmosphere is relaxed, in rural areas female visitors may be more comfortable behaving and dressing conservatively. For more information, see p828.

# TRANSPORT IN GUINEA-BISSAU

## GETTING THERE & AWAY
### Entering Guinea-Bissau

A certificate with proof of a yellow fever vaccination is required of all travellers.

### Air

Guinea-Bissau's only international airport is on the outskirts of Bissau. The main airlines flying to/from Guinea-Bissau are TAP Air Portugal, TACV Cabo Verde Airlines, Air Sénégal International and budget airline Air Luxor. Departure tax for international flights is US$20, but this is usually included in the ticket price.

TAP Air Portugal and Air Luxor are the only airlines with direct flights from Europe to Bissau. Between them, Air Sénégal and TACV Cabo Verde Airlines operate seven flights per week between Bissau and Dakar. To fly between Bissau and anywhere else in Africa, you'll have to get a connecting flight in Dakar.

The following airlines service Guinea-Bissau:

**Air Luxor** (LK; ☎ 206422; www.airluxor.com; Av 24 de Setembro) Hub: Lisbon.
**Air Sénégal International** (V7; ☎ 205211; www/air
-senegal-international.com; Rua Osualdo Vieira) Hub: Dakar.

---

**DEPARTURE TAX**

There is a US$20 airport departure tax, which is usually included in your ticket.

---

**TACV Cabo Verde Airlines** (VR; ☎ 206087; www.tacv
.com; Av Amilcar Cabral) Hub: Praia.
**TAP Air Portugal** (TP; ☎ 201359; www.flytap.com;
Praça dos Heróis Nacionais) Hub: Lisbon.

### Land

The busiest crossing point to/from Senegal is at São Domingos, on the main route between Ingore and Ziguinchor. There are also crossing points between Tanaf and Farim, and near Pirada, north of Gabú on the route to/from Vélingara and Tambacounda.

To/from Guinea, most traffic goes via Kandika and Saréboïdo on the road between Gabú and Koundara. A less-travelled route, open only in the dry season, links southeastern Guinea-Bissau and western Guinea via Quebo and Boké.

#### GUINEA

Bush taxis usually go to the border daily from Gabú and Koundara (CFA2500). It can take all day to cover this 100km stretch, although the winding road through the Fouta Djalon foothills is beautiful. If you have to change transport at Saréboïdo, tying in with the weekly Sunday market will improve your options.

During the dry season you may be able to take a four-wheel drive from Gabú to Boké (CFA8000); from here transport goes on to Conakry.

The adventurous may be able to get a *canoa* from Cacine in the far southeast to Kamsar (about a five-hour trip), from where you can find onward transport to Boké or Conakry.

#### SENEGAL

Most overland travel between Senegal and Guinea-Bissau passes through Ziguinchor, Senegal and the Guinean border town of São Domingos. The recently completed bridge at Joalande means that vehicles rely on only one ferry – the one that crosses Cacheu river. A bush taxi between Bissau and Ziguinchor costs CFA4700 per person, and each passenger must pay another CFA100 for the ferry.

You can also cross the border between Farim and Tanaf by bush taxi. You may also be able to get transport from Gabú to Tambacounda (via Vélingara), though road conditions are poor and journeys long.

## GETTING AROUND
### Air
At writing there were no domestic flights in Guinea-Bissau.

### Boat
*Canoas* connect Bissau with the Bijagós, with regularly scheduled boats to Bubaque and Bolama and occasional boats to other islands. In addition, top-end hotels rent boats, though costs are high. See p451 for more information about travel to the Bijagós.

### Minibus & Bush Taxi
The main roads between Bissau and the towns of Bafatá, Gabú, and São Domingos are all tar and at writing in good condi-

tion, except for some stretches of significant potholes. The roads to Buba, Catió, Cacheu and Varela have long stretches of several potholes, slowing travel to 10km to 20km per hour. Other roads are even slower going, and often become impassable in the rainy season.

Public transport around the country consists mainly of minibuses (almost always painted blue and yellow) and Peugeot 504 bush taxis, often called *sept-places* (sevenseater). *Kandongas* ply the rural routes. Mornings (before 8am) are always the best time to get transport. For an idea of fares across the country, from Bissau to Gabú (around 200km) is CFA2700 by Peugeot 504, CFA2000 by minibus and CFA1500 by *kandonga*.

# Liberia

Liberia seems at last to have found some breathing room. Prior to late 2003, this lush, rainforested country draped across West Africa's southern flank had been at war for almost two decades. Its towns were destroyed, families were scattered and, worst of all, an entire generation was robbed of its childhood, as peace accord after peace accord was shattered. Yet, this time around, perhaps peace is here to stay.

If Liberia does stabilise and open up for travel, it promises to offer intrepid adventurers a fascinating glimpse into what had previously been one of West Africa's most hospitable and enigmatic societies. The country's artistic traditions – especially carved masks, dance and storytelling – rivalled those of anywhere in the region, and traditional culture was strong. This was especially true in the interior, where secret initiation societies played a central role in growing up, and even today still serve as an important repository of traditional knowledge and life skills.

The country's natural attractions are equally impressive. In contrast with its ravaged infrastructure, Liberia's dense, humid rainforests – some of the most extensive in West Africa – are alive with the screeching and twittering of hundreds of birds, who are kept company by forest elephants, pygmy hippos and other wildlife padding around the forest floor.

For now though, most of this cultural and natural wealth remains inaccessible to independent travellers, as Liberians focus on the task of rebuilding their livelihoods. If you're contemplating a visit, get an update on local security conditions first. Also remember that the peace is still extremely fragile, and independent travel outside of Monrovia is not considered safe.

## FAST FACTS

- **Area** 111,370 sq km
- **Capital** Monrovia
- **Country code** ☎ 231
- **Famous for** Rainforests; traditional masks; rubber plantations
- **Languages** English (official) plus Bassa, Kpelle, Kru, Grebo & other local languages
- **Money** Liberian dollar (L$); US$1 = L$55; €1 = L$69
- **Population** 3.3 million
- **Visas** Required by almost everyone, and must be arranged in advance. Don't forget to stop by the Bureau of Immigration to extend beyond the initial 48-hour validity (see p478).

LIBERIA

**WARNING**

Liberia is finally at peace, but it's still a fragile peace, and the country is not yet geared for tourism. In general, independent travel outside of Monrovia is not yet possible. Before setting off, get a complete briefing first from people who know the situation; embassies and resident expats are the best sources.

Given the current travel restrictions, this chapter was updated as a 'desk update' from afar, with the generous assistance of various people in Liberia. We've tried to make it as accurate as possible, but the perishable information should be treated as a general guide, rather than hard and fast facts. (And if you get to Liberia, we'd love to hear back from you about your experiences!)

## HIGHLIGHTS

- **Silver Beach** (p474) Relax on this surf-pounded and palm-fringed stretch of sand just minutes from central Monrovia.
- **Sapo National Park** (p469) Wander under the lush, humid canopy of one of West Africa's last remaining rainforests.
- **Monrovia** (p469) Stroll through central Monrovia, seeing what sidewalk vendors have on offer and getting a feel for the beat on the street.
- **Liberians** (p467) Mingle with the locals over a plate of *fufu* and sauce and a cold Club beer, or cheering on the Lone Stars at a soccer match.

## ITINERARIES

Liberia's peace is still too fragile to contemplate classic travel itineraries. But, if you find yourself here, and security situation permitting, **Sapo National Park** (p469) is the obvious destination. There's currently nothing organised (and the park isn't even officially open yet to tourism), but if you should luck onto an excursion, allow at least five days round trip. Otherwise, both **Gbarnga** (p476) and **Buchanan** (p475) make intriguing day jaunts, affording glimpses of the countryside outside the capital. Closer to home, **Monrovia** (p469) is peppy and pleasant enough to enjoyably spend a weekend or longer poking around, with ample opportunities for relaxation available at the nearby beaches.

## CLIMATE & WHEN TO GO

Monrovia is one of the two wettest capital cities in Africa (Freetown in Sierra Leone is the other), with rainfall averaging more than 4500mm per year here and elsewhere along the Liberian coast. Inland, it's less – in some areas only about 2000mm annually. Temperatures range from 23°C to 32°C in Monrovia, and slightly higher inland. However, humidity levels of more than 85% in the dry season (November to April) and more than 90% in the rainy season (May to October) often make it feel much warmer. There is little seasonal temperature variation.

The best time to visit Liberia is during the dry season, between November and April.

## HISTORY

The area that is now Liberia has likely been populated for more than 2000 years, although little is known of its early history. Many present-day Liberians trace their ancestry to peoples who migrated southeast from the Sahel following the fall of the Empire of Mali in the 15th century. However, settlement of the area remained sparse because of the dense and inhospitable forests covering most of the country, and no great cities developed.

European contact with Liberia began in the 1460s with the arrival of Portuguese navigators, who named several coastal features, including Cape Mesurado (Monrovia) and Cape Palmas (Harper). Because

**HOW MUCH?**

- **Souvenir basket** US$2
- **Kilo of bananas** US$0.40
- **Fufu & soup** US$0.75
- **Short taxi ride** US$1
- **Soda** US$0.30

**LONELY PLANET INDEX**

- **Litre of petrol** US$3.45
- **Litre of bottled water** US$0.20
- **Bottle of Club beer** US$1
- **Souvenir T-shirt** You'll be lucky if you find one!
- **Street snack – cassava leaf** US$0.75

LIBERIA

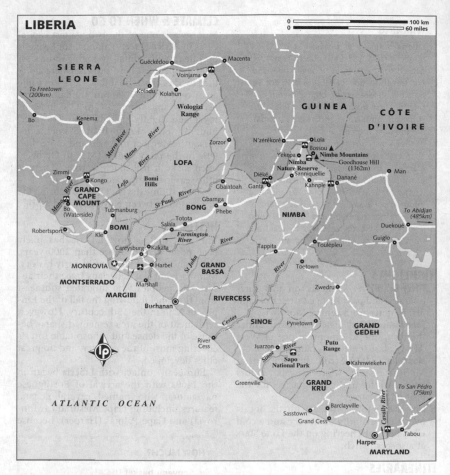

**LIBERIA**

of the trading success of a pepper grain, the area soon became known as the 'Grain Coast'.

### The Arrival of the Settlers

In the early 19th century, the Grain Coast rose to the forefront of discussions within the abolitionist movement in the USA as a suitable place to resettle freed American slaves. After several failed attempts at gaining the agreement of local chiefs, officials of the American Colonization Society (ACS) forced a treaty upon a local king at Cape Mesurado. Despite resistance by the indigenous people, settlement went ahead, and in April 1822, an expedition with the first group of Black American settlers arrived at Providence Island in present-day Monrovia. Within a short time, under the leadership of the American Jehudi Ashmun, the foundations for a country were established. Additional settlements were founded along the coast, notably at Greenville and Harper.

### A Shaky Independence

In 1839 Thomas Buchanan was appointed first governor of the new territory. He was succeeded in 1841 by Joseph Jenkins Roberts, who expanded its boundaries and encouraged cooperation among the various settlements. In 1846 the settlement at Cape Mesurado merged with others along the coast, and a declaration of independence and a constitution were drafted. Both were modelled on those of the USA. In 1847 Liberia declared itself an independent republic, although – fatally for its future history – citizenship excluded indigenous peoples. Roberts was elected the first president. Every successive president until 1980 was of American freed-slave ancestry.

By the mid-19th century, about half of the 5000 Black Americans who had originally migrated to Liberia had either died or returned to the USA. The remaining settlers, the citizens of the new republic, came to be known as Americo-Liberians. They saw themselves as part of a mission to bring civilisation and Christianity to Africa, and although constituting only a tiny fraction of Liberia's total population, they dominated the indigenous peoples. The Masonic Order, established in the country in 1851, came to be a symbol of Americo-Liberian solidarity and five presidents, starting with Roberts, were grand masters.

For nearly a century, Liberia foundered economically and politically while indigenous populations continued to be repressed, suffering under a form of forced labour that anywhere else would have been called slavery. In 1930 Britain and the USA cut off diplomatic relations for five years because of the sale of human labour to Spanish colonialists in what was then Fernando Po (now Bioko in Equatorial Guinea).

## The Golden Years?

The True Whig Party monopolised power from early in Liberia's history. Despite the country's labour-recruitment policies, the party was able to project an image of Liberia as Africa's most stable country. During William Tubman's presidency (1944–71), this led to massive foreign investment, and for several decades following WWII Liberia sustained sub-Saharan Africa's highest growth rate. Firestone and other American companies made major investments and Tubman earned praise as the 'maker of modern Liberia'. In the 1960s, iron ore–mining operations began near Yekepa by Lamco (Liberian-American Swedish Minerals Company), which became the largest private enterprise in sub-Saharan Africa.

The influx of foreign money soon began to distort the economy, resulting in exacerbation of social inequalities and increased hostility between Americo-Liberians and the indigenous population. Viewing this development with alarm, Tubman was forced to concede that the indigenous people would have to be granted some political and economic involvement in the country, including the franchise. Until this point (1963), 97% of the population had been denied voting rights.

William Tolbert succeeded Tubman as president in 1971. While Tolbert initiated a series of reforms, the government continued to be controlled by about a dozen related Americo-Liberian families and corruption was rampant. Tolbert established diplomatic relations with Communist countries such as the People's Republic of China, and at home clamped down harshly on opposition.

## Coup d'Etat & Years of Darkness

Resentment of these policies and of growing government corruption grew. In 1979 several demonstrators were shot in protests against a proposed increase in rice prices. Finally, in April 1980, Tolbert was overthrown in a coup led by an uneducated master sergeant, Samuel Doe. In the accompanying fighting, Tolbert and many high-ranking ministers were killed. For the first time, Liberia had a ruler who wasn't an Americo-Liberian, giving the indigenous population a taste of political power and an opportunity for vengeance. The 28-year-old Doe shocked the world by ordering 13 ex-ministers to be publicly executed on a beach in Monrovia.

Although the coup gave power to the indigenous population, it was condemned by most other African countries and by Liberia's other allies and trading partners. Over the next few years, relations with neighbouring African states gradually thawed. However, the post-coup flight of capital, coupled with ongoing corruption, caused Liberia's economy to rapidly decline. During the 1980s, real incomes fell by half, the unemployment rate in Monrovia rose to 50% and electricity blackouts became common.

Doe struggled to maintain his grip on power by any means available, including a sham election held in 1985, largely to appease his major creditor, the USA. By the late 1980s, however, it was clear that opposition forces had had enough. Following a foiled post-election coup attempt, members of Doe's Krahn tribe began killing and torturing rival tribespeople, particularly the Gio and Mano in Nimba County.

## Civil War

On Christmas Eve 1989, several hundred rebels led by Charles Taylor (former head of the Doe government's procurement agency) invaded Nimba County from Côte d'Ivoire. Doe's troops arrived shortly thereafter and indiscriminately killed hundreds of unarmed civilians, raped women and burned villages. Thousands fled into Côte d'Ivoire and Guinea.

Shortly after the invasion, Prince Johnson of the Gio tribe broke away from Taylor and formed his own rebel group. By mid-1990, Taylor's forces controlled most of the country, while Johnson's guerrillas had seized most of Monrovia; Doe was holed up with loyal troops in his mansion. Meanwhile, Liberia lay in ruins. Refugees were streaming into neighbouring countries, US warships were anchored off the coast and an Ecowas peacekeeping force (known as Ecomog or an Ecowas Monitoring Group) was despatched in an attempt to keep the warring factions apart.

It was all to no avail. Refusing to surrender or even step down as president, Doe and many of his supporters were finally wiped out by Johnson's forces. With both Johnson and Taylor claiming the presidency, Ecomog forces installed their own candidate, political-science professor Amos Sawyer, as head of the Interim Government of National Unity (IGNU). Meanwhile, Taylor's National Patriotic Front of Liberia (NPFL) forces continued to occupy about 90% of the country, while remnants of Doe's former army and Johnson's followers were encamped within Monrovia itself.

## Peace Accords But No Peace

After a brutal assault by Taylor on Monrovia in October 1992, Ecomog increased its forces and in August 1993 the protagonists finally hammered out the Cotonou Agreement peace accord. This called for installation of a six-month transitional government representing IGNU, NPFL and the third major player, Ulimo (United Liberation Movement for Democracy), Doe's former soldiers. When its mandate expired in September 1994 a new agreement, the

---

> ### GOVERNMENTAL AFFAIRS
>
> Liberia's government is modelled on that in the USA, with popularly elected executive and legislative branches and a court system, although a network of paramount chiefs still holds sway at the local level.

Akosombo Amendment, was signed, but then later rejected.

In August 1995, yet another peace agreement (the Abuja Accord) was signed by leaders of the main warring factions. This one lasted until April 1996, when fighting erupted in Monrovia between NPFL and Ulimo, resulting in widespread looting and damage.

August 1996 saw the negotiation of an amended Abuja Accord, providing for a cease-fire, disarmament and demobilisation, followed by elections. Despite serious cease-fire violations and an incomplete disarmament process, elections took place in July. Charles Taylor and his National Patriotic Party (NPP) won an overwhelming majority (75%) – in large part because many Liberians feared the consequences if he lost.

Following the elections, life began to resume its normal rhythms, yet the political scene remained tenuous. By late 1998, all former faction leaders except Taylor were living in exile and power became increasingly consolidated in the presidency. In 1999 dissident groups led by the Liberians United for Reconciliation and Democracy (LURD) launched armed incursions in Lofa County near the Guinean border, setting off a new round of low-level fighting. The peace was further shattered with devastating outbreaks of fighting in 2002 and 2003. Finally, in August 2003, with LURD and other groups controlling much of the country, and under pressure from the international community, Charles Taylor went into exile in Nigeria. A transitional government was established, headed by local businessman Charles Gyude Bryant and assisted by UN peacekeepers.

## Liberia Today

In late 2005 Liberians again went to the polls. In a hotly contested run-off vote between former World Bank economist Ellen Johnson-Sirleaf and international soccer star George Weah, Johnson-Sirleaf won the presidency, thereby also becoming the first woman to be elected president anywhere in Africa. As she steps into her new role, the tasks facing Liberia are massive – completion of the disarmament process, resettlement of vast numbers of displaced persons and refugees, solidification of the still-fragile peace and a complete rebuilding of the country's government, economy and infrastructure. Yet most Liberians and longtime Liberia watchers are upbeat. While optimism for the future is tempered by the tragic realities of the country's recent past, the future on the whole is looking brighter.

## THE CULTURE
### The National Psyche

If there's any word that characterises Liberians, it's resilience. Here, in this lush, war-ravaged land, almost one in two Liberians were displaced from their homes during the long years of conflict and many were brutalised or witnessed unspeakable atrocities. Yet, despite all the suffering, there's a remarkable air of peppiness, especially on the streets of Monrovia, and a sense of cautious hope that the time has finally come to rise up from the ashes and start rebuilding. In one recent display of this determination to move forward, thousands of Liberians stood in line for hours in the hot sun waiting for a chance to cast their votes in the 2005 national elections.

Apart from war, one of the most significant defining factors in Liberia's national psyche is the long-standing division between Americo-Liberians and the indigenous population. The inequalities and sense of separateness that have existed since the country's earliest days (see p463) continue to shadow political and economic life, although hopes are that the shared desire of all Liberians for peace will gradually work to overcome this.

### Daily Life

Want to take a peek inside a typical home? It's not such an easy task these days, as most Liberians are just starting to rebuild theirs. In a country where there's no electricity grid, national telephone network nor comprehensive road network, life for most focuses on survival. Families have been divided, and children traumatised and estranged from their communities. During the war years, schooling for most children was severely disrupted, and rebuilding educational networks is one of the most important tasks facing the new government. Yet slowly the rhythms of daily life are returning. Produce from rural areas is once again making its way to Monrovia's markets, returning residents are seeking zinc to roof their newly rebuilt houses, and the hospitality for which Liberians are renowned is alive and well.

---

### SECRET SOCIETIES

Liberia is famous for its secret societies, called *poro* for men and *sande* for women. They are found throughout the country, except in the southeast, and they are especially strong in the northwest. Each society has a wealth of rites and ceremonies that are used to educate young people in tribal ways, folklore and general life skills, and they continue to be a major force in preserving Liberia's traditional culture.

Many rituals centre around initiations into adulthood, which traditionally involved up to four years of training, though these days the time is usually shorter. If you're lucky enough to spend time in the countryside, you may see initiates, who are easily recognised by their white painted faces and bodies and their shaved heads.

Within the societies, there's usually a strong pecking order, with lower-ranking members forbidden from sharing in the special knowledge of higher-ranking members or attending their secret meetings. The most extreme example of these hierarchies is the *poro* among the Vai, with up to 99 levels. Ascending in the ranks depends on a combination of birth (with leadership sometimes restricted to certain families), seniority and savvyness in mastering traditional beliefs and rituals.

The secret societies shape not only religious rituals and education, but also community life, with *zoes* (*poro* society leaders) wielding significant political influence. The societies also control the activities of traditional medicinal practitioners, and are used to settle disputes or to levy punishments. A village chief who doesn't have the support of the *poro* on important decisions can expect trouble enforcing them.

## Population

With about 30 persons per sq km, Liberia is one of the least densely populated of West Africa's coastal countries. Monrovia is the only real city, with other population centres elsewhere along the coast, in the centre near Gbarnga and Ganta, in the northwest near the Sierra Leone border and in the southeast near Harper. Elsewhere, large tracts of the country are completely uninhabited or have only very scattered populations.

The population of about 3.3 million consists overwhelmingly of people of indigenous origin belonging to more than a dozen major tribal groups. These include the Kpelle in the centre, the Bassa around Buchanan, the Krahn in the southeast, the Mandingo (also called Mandinka) in the north and the Kru along the coast. The Kpelle and the Bassa together comprise just over one-third of the population, while Americo-Liberians account for barely 5% of the total. There's also a large Lebanese community in Monrovia, who wield a disproportionate share of economic power.

## SPORT

Liberian soccer – long a national passion – gained worldwide attention with the rise of George Weah to become Fifa world player of the year in 1995. Since retiring, Weah has kept himself busy as coach and sponsor of Liberia's national team, the Lone Stars, as well as by campaigning for president and serving as a UN goodwill ambassador. His personal following in the country is almost as great as that for the sport itself.

## RELIGION

Religious fervour is strong in Liberia. This is particularly evident on New Year's Eve, when many churches stay open throughout the night, filled with singing and praying Liberians, and on Sundays, when services are invariably packed. Close to half of the population are Christians and about 20% are Muslim, with the remainder following traditional religions.

## ARTS
### Sculpture

Liberia has long been famed for its masks, which hold religious as well as artistic significance, and traditionally were used for entertainment as well as to teach traditional

---

**TALKING DRUMS**

One of Liberia's best-known traditional instruments – although it's not uniquely Liberian – is the 'talking drum'. It looks like an hourglass, with the upper and lower ends connected by tension strings. When the drummer compresses the strings while holding the drum under one arm next to his body, the pitch of the drum increases, producing a variable tone and giving the drum its name. Talking drums are generally beaten with a stick, rather than with the hands.

---

values. The Gio in Nimba County in the northeast have some particularly rich traditions, including the *gunyege* mask, which shelters a power-giving spirit, and the *kagle* mask, which resembles a chimpanzee. The Bassa around Buchanan are renowned for their *gela* masks, which often have elaborately carved coiffures, always with an odd number of plaits.

## ENVIRONMENT
### The Land

Liberia, which occupies a very wet 111,000 sq km patch of the West African coastline, is just under half the size of the UK. Its humid and low-lying coastal plain is intersected by countless marshes and tidal lagoons, and bisected by at least nine major rivers, the largest of which is the St Paul. Inland is a densely forested plateau rising to low mountains in the northeast, in Lofa and Nimba counties. The highest point in the country is Goodhouse Hill (1362m), in the Nimba range on the borders with Guinea and Côte d'Ivoire.

### Plants & Wildlife

Liberia's rainforests host an amazing diversity of birds, plants and other wildlife, including forest elephants, pygmy hippos, various antelope species and even leopards, as well as West African chimpanzees and numerous other primates. Sapo National Park alone is home to over 500 different bird species.

### National Parks

Liberia's only fully protected area is Sapo National Park (opposite) in the far southeast of the country. In 2003 the Nimba Nature

Reserve was declared, near the borders with Guinea and Côte d'Ivoire, and contiguous with the Guinean-Côte d'Ivorian Mont Nimba Strict Nature Reserve (a Unesco World Heritage Site). There are no facilities, but it will ultimately be open for tourism.

## Environmental Issues

Liberia is one of the last West African countries with significant areas of rainforest, although these now cover only about 40% of land area, primarily near the Sierra Leone border and around Sapo National Park. Until recently, up to two-dozen logging companies were operating in the country, primarily in the southeast, and large swathes of forest were cleared. The recent international timber trade sanctions have significantly halted this decimation, although only about 4% of Liberia's total forest cover is currently under protection, and effective regulation is weak.

On the brighter side, Liberia's forests comprise a critical part of the Guinean Forests of West Africa Hotspot – an exceptionally biodiverse area stretching across 11 countries in the region – and have attracted significant international attention, spearheaded by Conservation International (www.conservation.org), and its local partner, the **Society for the Conservation of Nature of Liberia** (Map p470; SCNL; ☎ 227 058, 06-512 506; scnlib2001@yahoo.com; Monrovia Zoo, Larkpase). Among other endeavours, they have been working to bring at least 30% of Liberia's forest areas under protection, to curb poaching and to protect endangered species, including the critically endangered Western chimpanzee.

## FOOD & DRINK

Monrovia has a satisfying array of dining options; elsewhere, you'll have to rely on chop bars.

Traditional Liberian food consists of rice or a cassava-based staple (called *fufu, dumboy* or GB), which is eaten with a soup or sauce made with greens and palm oil, and sometimes also meat or fish. Other popular dishes include *togborgee* (a Lofa County speciality made with kittaly – a type of eggplant – or bitterbuoy – another local vegetable – and country soda), *palava* sauce (made with *plato* leaf, dried fish or meat and palm oil) and palm butter (a sauce traditionally popular in Maryland and Grand Kru counties and made from palm nuts).

# MONROVIA

Monrovia, sprawled across a narrow peninsula between the Mesurado River and the sea, has suffered badly during the past two decades. Most infrastructure was gutted during the fighting, and infrastructure

---

### SAPO NATIONAL PARK

Sapo, Liberia's only national park, is a lush 1808-sq-km tract containing some of West Africa's last remaining primary rainforest, as well as forest elephants, pygmy hippos, chimpanzees, antelopes and other wildlife, although these populations suffered greatly during the final years of fighting at the hands of both refugees and rebels who had moved into the park boundaries. Large swathes of nearby forest, as well as some forest areas within the park itself, were also felled.

With the recent eviction of the remaining squatters from Sapo, work is now getting started on rebuilding infrastructure, including park headquarters, and on enforcing its protected status. Agro-forestry projects are slowly being recommenced in the 1.6km-wide buffer zone surrounding the park, and efforts are ongoing to increase community involvement in park management.

Currently, there are no commercial tours into Sapo, although this is expected to quickly change once the new government is in place. If you are interested in visiting, the best contact for updated information is the Society for the Conservation of Nature of Liberia (SCNL; above). Allow a full day to reach Sapo from Monrovia by 4WD along the road paralleling the coast, and at least two days going via Zwedru. Following the coastal road, once at Greenville, head 60km north to Juarzon and then 5km southeast to Jalay's Town in the park's buffer zone. From here it's 1.5km further on foot to the park boundary, on the opposite side of Pahneh Creek (a tributary of the Sinoe River). Once at the park, you can arrange guided hikes and canoe rides.

In addition to SCNL, you can obtain information on Sapo through Conservation International's office in Monrovia or through fpi@forestpartnersinternational.org.

**MONROVIA**

0 — 1 km
0 — 0.5 miles

To Freeport (4km); Duala Motor Park (8km);
Sierra Leone (110km)

Waterside Market

Providence Island

Mamba Point

See Central Monrovia Map (p472)

Rally Time Market

Mesurado River

Mesurado River

Zoo

Old Executive Mansion

Capitol Hill

University of Liberia

Balli Island

Matadi

City Hall

Fiamah

Tubman Blvd

Russel Ave

Coleman Ave

Cheeseman Ave

Sinkor

ATLANTIC OCEAN

To St Joseph's Catholic Hospital (7km);
Elwa Junction & Stadium (12km);
Red Light Motor Park (15km); Silver Beach (15km);
Thinkers Beach (17km); St Martin's Beach (18km);
Marshall (45km); Firestone Plantation (50km);
Robertsfield (55km); Buchanan (150km)

**INFORMATION**
American Embassy.....................1 A1
Côte d'Ivoirian Consulate...........2 C3
European Union Office..............3 A1
Ghanian Embassy.....................4 C4
Guinean Embassy.....................5 D4
Nigerian Embassy.....................6 D4
SCNL Office...........................7 D2
Sierra Leonean Embassy............8 C4

**SIGHTS & ACTIVITIES**
Masonic Temple.......................9 A1

**SLEEPING**
Krystal Oceanview Hotel.........10 A1
Mamba Point Hotel.................11 A1
Royal Hotel..........................12 C3

**EATING**
China Great Wall Restaurant....13 C3
Heartbreak Restaurant..........(see 12)
La Pointe............................14 A1
Living Room........................(see 12)
Mamba Point Hotel Restaurant &
    Mezza House...................(see 11)
New Jack Café & Bar...............15 A1
Taaj Indian Restaurant............16 C3

**DRINKING**
La Pointe...........................(see 14)
Pepper Bush.........................17 B1

**SHOPPING**
Craft Vendors.......................18 A1
Craft Vendors.......................19 A1

largely destroyed. Yet, if you can overlook the drone of generators and the bullet-scarred building shells, the city has an unmistakable pep and an unbending determination to rebuild. It's also one of the friendliest capitals you are likely to visit in Africa and – thanks in part to the large UN presence – also has a surprisingly good restaurant and bar scene. Pick a day when it's not raining, find some Liberian friends, and soon you'll forget you're walking around in what was only recently a war zone.

## ORIENTATION

The heart of town is Benson and Randall Sts, and along Broad St, where you'll find most shops and businesses. Southwest of here

at Mamba Point is Monrovia's tiny diplomatic enclave, and 1.5km to the southeast is Capitol Hill, with government buildings, many quite damaged. Beyond that is Sinkor, which sprawls about 6km further southeast until reaching Elwa junction and Red Light Motor Park. On Monrovia's northern edge is Waterside Market, and beyond that, Freeport and Bushrod Island. In the Mesurado River just opposite Waterside Market is Providence Island, where the first expedition of freed American slaves landed in 1822.

## INFORMATION

There's a reasonable selection of Internet cafés in the town centre, including several on or around Broad St. This is also the best place to look for foreign exchange bureaus and banks.

**Charif Pharmacy** (Map p472; Randall St) Good selection of European and US items.

**Karou Voyages** (Map p472; ☎ 226 508; Broad St) Regional and international flight bookings.

**Liberia Telecom** (Map p472; Lynch St; ☻ 8am-10pm) International calls, three-minute minimum, deposit required.

**Main post office** (Map p472; cnr Randall & Ashmun Sts; ☻ 8am-4pm Mon-Fri, 10am-noon Sat)

**St Joseph's Catholic Hospital** (Map p472; ☎ 226 207) About 7km southeast of town on the extension of Tubman Blvd, and for dire emergencies only.

## DANGERS & ANNOYANCES

Use caution when going out in the evening, and get an update on security when you arrive from your embassy or resident expats.

## SIGHTS & ACTIVITIES

The **National Museum** (Map p472; Broad St; admission free; ☻ 8am-5pm Mon-Sat) is only a shadow of its former self, with a handful of dusty masks, drums and paintings, accompanied by some interesting descriptions.

The now ruined **Masonic Temple** (Map p470; Benson St) was once Monrovia's major landmark. Since most Masons were Americo-Liberian descendants of the original settlers, the Temple was a prominent symbol of previous regimes, and was vandalised after the 1980 coup when the Masonic Order was banned. A grand master's throne from the temple, once used by William Tubman, sits on dusty display at the National Museum.

The chaotic and colourful **Waterside Market** (Map p472; Water St) offers almost everything for sale, including some attractive textiles (which are sold by the *lapa* or 2m).

## SLEEPING

Breakfast is included in room prices, except as noted.

**Mamba Point Hotel** (Map p470; ☎ 06-544 544, 06-440 000; mambapointhotel@yahoo.com; UN Dr, Mamba Point; s/d/ste US$120/160/175; ☒ ▣) This cosy establishment has long been Monrovia's best, and is a favourite with journalists and business travellers. Its 64 rooms, while not luxurious, are comfortable and well-appointed – all with satellite TV and wi-fi – and some have sea views. There's also a casino.

---

### CHILD SOLDIERS & STREET CHILDREN

It's no secret that many of the guns shot during Liberia's years of war were wielded by young people. However, it has only been during recent disarmament phases that the extent to which children were used in the fighting has become apparent. Of the approximately 20,000 former combatants disarmed under the August 1996 peace accord, about 4000 were under 17, and about half of these were aged 15 or under. Statistics are similarly sobering for the more recent disarmament, and some reports place the number of child soldiers at more than triple these figures. Equally distressing is the fact that fewer than 10% of the former combatants (about 97% of whom are males) have more than an elementary level of schooling.

Many of these disenfranchised youths now find themselves on the streets – disillusioned and lacking sufficient education or skills to move to happier circumstances. Many are unwilling or unable to return to their families, either for fear of community retaliation and rejection, or because of the difficulty of fitting into an established routine after spending so much time in the bush. In addition to the former combatants, hundreds of other youths are on the streets, estranged from family and community through the near-total suspension of schooling during the war, coupled with massive community displacement and wartime deaths and family separations.

There are several groups working to assist these boys and girls, including the church-run Don Bosco Program, which provides temporary night shelters and skills training while working to reunify children with their families. For the girls, many of whom have turned to prostitution, health advice and counselling are offered, as well as basic small-business training to help them find an alternative livelihood. Many of the young boys you'll meet by the supermarkets and on the street in downtown Monrovia are enrolled in the program. If you want to give them some support, speak to staff at the Sinkor headquarters off Tubman Blvd in Monrovia, or just give them a few minutes of your time and attention.

LIBERIA

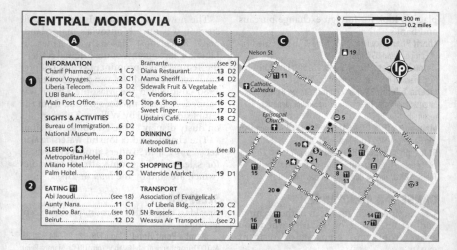

CENTRAL MONROVIA

INFORMATION
Charif Pharmacy...........1 C2
Karou Voyages.............2 C1
Liberia Telecom...........3 D2
LUBI Bank.................4 C2
Main Post Office..........5 D1

SIGHTS & ACTIVITIES
Bureau of Immigration....6 D2
National Museum..........7 D2

SLEEPING
Metropolitan Hotel.......8 D2
Milano Hotel.............9 C2
Palm Hotel..............10 C2

EATING
Abi Jaoudi............(see 18)
Aunty Nana.............11 C1
Bamboo Bar...........(see 10)
Beirut.................12 D2

Bramante...............(see 9)
Diana Restaurant........13 D2
Mama Sheriff...........14 D2
Sidewalk Fruit & Vegetable
    Vendors.............15 C2
Stop & Shop............16 C2
Sweet Finger...........17 C2
Upstairs Café..........18 C2

DRINKING
Metropolitan
    Hotel Disco........(see 8)

SHOPPING
Waterside Market........19 D1

TRANSPORT
Association of Evangelicals
    of Liberia Bldg.....20 C2
SN Brussels............21 C1
Weasua Air Transport...(see 2)

## Krystal Oceanview Hotel

**Krystal Oceanview Hotel** (Map p470; ☎ 07-776 7676, 06-510 424; UN Dr, Mamba Point; s/d US$130/180; ❄ 🖳 🕿) This 26-room hotel, well located overlooking the sea opposite La Pointe Restaurant, is one of the city's newest. Its rooms are homey – rates include Internet access and laundry service – and there's a pricey but very pleasant waterside restaurant-bar.

**Royal Hotel** (Map p470; ☎ 06-566 669; royalhotel liberia@yahoo.com; cnr 14th St & Tubman Blvd, Sinkor; s/ d/ste US$100/120/175; ❄ 🖳 ) The Royal is another popular choice, especially with UN staff, with 30 small but pleasant rooms, two restaurants and an Internet café.

**Metropolitan Hotel** (Map p472; ☎ 06-510 853; Broad St; r US$45-75; ❄ ) Located between Centre and Gurley Sts, this low-end alternative has 29 bland rooms of varying size and standard, though all come with continental breakfast and TV. Prices are often negotiable.

Also recommended:

**Milano Hotel** (Map p472; ☎ 06-454 068; hotel milano@yahoo.com; cnr Carey & Randall Sts; s/d/ste US$90/150/200; ❄ 🖳 ) A new, centrally-located place with 42 rooms – all with minibar, cable TV and Internet access – and a good restaurant.

**Palm Hotel** (Map p472; ☎ 05-618 618, 06-535 177; palmhotelmonrovia@yahoo.com; cnr Broad & Randall Sts; s/d US$100/150; ❄ ) Conveniently located in the heart of town, with 16 twin-bedded rooms with TV, and a popular rooftop restaurant-bar.

## EATING

Most places are open for lunch and dinner daily, except as noted.

## Liberian

**Aunty Nana** (Map p472; Robert St; meals US$7.50; ❧ noon-7pm Mon-Sat, to 3pm Sun) This upscale version of a chop house is a great place to get introduced to Liberian food, with everything from *fufu* soup and palm butter sauce to *jollof* rice and *dumboy*, plus inexpensive beers. It's between Ashmun and Front Sts.

**Mama Sheriff** (Map p472; cnr Carey & Lynch Sts; meals US$1.50-3) For an earthier experience, try this local haunt, with heaping portions of cassava leaf, groundnut soup and other favourites at rock-bottom prices, all served up in small, medium or large ('special') portions.

**Sweet Finger** (Map p472; cnr Carey & Lynch; meals US$2-3) Just around the corner from Mama Sheriff, with a daily-changing menu featuring potato greens, *palava* sauce, dry rice with fish and other specialities.

## Lebanese

**Diana Restaurant** (Map p472; ☎ 06-563 333, 06-623 333; Center St; meals US$3-10, pizzas US$9-13; ❧ 7.30am-11pm) This small, no-frills place favoured by Lebanese businessmen and expats is one of Monrovia's dining bargains. The menu features meat or chicken shwarma, felafel sandwiches, hummus, a large mixed grill platter and kofta, and there's also good pizza. It's between Carey and Broad Sts.

**Beirut** (Map p472; ☎ 227 299; Center St; meze US$3-8, meals US$10-26; ❄ ) This Lebanese institution has meze, plus salads, pastas, steaks, seafood (even lobster thermidor) and vegetarian platters. It's between Ashmun and Broad Sts.

**Upstairs Café** (Map p472; ☎ 06-438 718; Randall St; light meals US$1.50-5; meals US$6-12; ◷ 8am-8pm Mon-Sat) An unassuming place above Abi Jaoudi supermarket, and one of Monrovia's insider tips, with inexpensive Lebanese fare, plus omelettes, grilled platters, salads, pizzas and a Saturday afternoon buffet (US$8).

## Asian

**Bangkok Thai Restaurant** ( ☎ 06-590 455; Old Rd, Sinkor; meals US$4-12) A recent addition to the Monrovia restaurant scene, with a large selection of Thai dishes, plus a separate vegetarian menu. Outdoor seating is best if you want to get away from the blaring TV.

**China Great Wall Restaurant** (Map p470; ☎ 07-755 5666; 10th St, Sinkor; mains US$12-20) Monrovia's fanciest Chinese eatery with an authentic, if rather pricey, menu.

**Taaj Indian Restaurant** (Map p470; ☎ 07-777 6666; 5th St, Sinkor; mains US$5-10) The Taaj's extensive Indian and Chinese menu includes chicken, mutton, seafood and rice plates, plus vegetarian specialities, fruit shakes and mango lassis, and a Sunday buffet.

**Living Room** (Map p470; ☎ 05-672 375; Royal Hotel, cnr Tubman Blvd & 14th St, Sinkor; sushi US$3-6; ◷ lunch & dinner Mon-Sat) Monrovia's first sushi bar, with a gleaming sushi counter, and an appetising array of nigiri sushi, sashimi and more.

## Continental

**La Pointe** (Map p470; ☎ 06-510 587; UN Dr, Mamba Point; mains US$10-25) This pleasant eatery overlooking the ocean offers a great-value daily lunch buffet (US$10) featuring continental and Liberian cuisine, but arrive early, as appetizers and salads run out. The á la carte menu has chicken, meat, pasta and seafood dishes, plus some vegetarian selections.

**Bramante** (Map p472; ☎ 06-454 068; Milano Hotel, Carey St; meals US$15-20) The place to go for fine Italian dining, with everything from Parma ham to tagliatelle with shrimp. If you have room for more, the dessert menu includes tiramisu and chocolate mousse.

**Bamboo Bar** (Map p472; ☎ 05-618 618; Palm Hotel, cnr Broad & Randall Sts; appetizers US$3-6, sandwiches US$5-7, pizzas US$7-20, meals US$10-21; ◷ breakfast, lunch & dinner) This rooftop restaurant is ideal for people watching, while enjoying well-priced Lebanese appetizers, plus chicken, seafood and steak dishes, salads, burgers or pizzas.

**Mamba Point Hotel Restaurant** (Map p470; ☎ 06-440 000, 06-544 544; UN Dr, Mamba Point; light meals US$6-8, mains US$13-20; ◷ breakfast, lunch & dinner) The main hotel restaurant offers continental, Lebanese and Indian menus, plus a Sunday lunch buffet (US$12). There's also the smaller Mezza House, with burgers, salads and a tempting array of deserts and juices.

Other recommendations:

**Heartbreak Restaurant** (Map p470; ☎ 06-566 669; Royal Hotel, cnr Tubman Blvd & 14th St, Sinkor; meals US$10-25) A popular haunt, with a menu featuring everything from Lebanese appetisers to seafood, pasta and burgers, a Sunday lunch buffet (US$12) and music and dancing on Wednesday and Saturday evenings.

**New Jack Café & Bar** (Map p470; UN Drive, Mamba Point; meals US$5-15) On the seafront opposite Mamba Point Hotel, with shaded huts and delicious grilled lobster (US$14), plus ribs and more.

## Self-Catering

Self-caterers can try the well-stocked **Abi Jaoudi** (Map p472; Randall St; ◷ 8am-8pm Mon-Fri) between Sekou Touré and Benson Sts, which sells everything from French cheese and croissants to wine and liquors, or **Stop & Shop** (Map p472; Randall St), nearby, with a range of US products. Sidewalk vendors along Benson St sell a colourful array of fruits, vegetables and freshwater prawns.

## DRINKING

For drinks, the Bamboo Bar (left) is a favourite at any hour, and has live music Saturday evenings. For more local flavour, try Porch (off Benson St) or the lively but somewhat seedy La Point (Map p470; Mamba Point). Popular nightspots include Pepper Bush (Map p470; Warren St), near Carey St, and the disco at the Metropolitan Hotel (opposite).

## ENTERTAINMENT

Soccer games always draw a crowd. Liberia's Lone Stars play at the stadium near Elwa Junction, 12km southeast of town.

## SHOPPING

Vendors near the US embassy's Gate One – in tiny stalls lining a small alley bordering UN Drive – sell everything from wooden masks to baskets and textiles. Other places shop for crafts include the vendors opposite Mamba Point Hotel and in Waterside Market.

Textiles are sold by the *lapa* (2m) – the best place to look is Waterside Market (p471), near Gurley St. For custom-made

**LIBERIA**

African clothes, try the tailors along Benson St near the Randall St junction.

## GETTING THERE & AWAY
### Air
All flights arrive and depart from **Roberts International Airport** (Code ROB; Robertsfield), 60km southeast of Monrovia.

For details on flights to/from Monrovia see p480.

### Boat
**Sam Kazouh** (1st fl, Association of Evangelicals of Liberia Bldg, Randall St) runs a weekly boat to Greenville (US$30, deck seating only, 12 to 15 hours), sometimes continuing on to Harper (US$50 from Monrovia, 22 to 25 hours); schedules vary. There's also a sporadic speedboat between Monrovia and Harper (US$60, 36 hours). Inquire at the 'fishing pier' at the Freeport.

### Bush Taxi & Minibus
Bush taxis for Tubmanburg and the Sierra Leone border leave from Duala Motor Park, 9km northeast of the town centre. Transport for most other destinations, including the borders of Guinea and Côte d'Ivoire, leaves from the Red Light Motor Park, Monrovia's main motor park 15km northeast of the centre.

## GETTING AROUND
### To/From the Airport
**Roberts International Airport** (Robertsfield) is 60km southeast of Monrovia. Taxis charge about US$30 to central Monrovia, but it's best to arrange a pick-up in advance with your hotel.

### Taxi
Shared taxis are the main public transport. They operate on a zone system (US$0.20 from the centre to Duala Motor Park; US$0.50 to Red Light Motor Park).

# AROUND MONROVIA

## BEACHES
There are some beautiful beaches stretching south and north of Monrovia, which fill up with locals and foreign residents on weekends. Before jumping in, get local advice, as currents can be quite dangerous. One of

the most popular is **Silver Beach**, about 15km southeast of central Monrovia off the airport road. There's a restaurant here, small volleyball court, craft vendors, shower and toilet, and chairs and umbrellas for hire. About 2km further south is **Thinkers Beach**, also with a small restaurant, shower and toilets. **St Martin's Beach**, just beyond Thinkers Beach, is quiet and isolated, with no facilities, and is good for getting away from the crowds.

About 45 minutes further southeast is **Marshall**, where the Junk, Farmington and Little Bassa Rivers meet the sea. It boasts a lagoon and a deserted stretch of beach.

## FIRESTONE PLANTATION
Firestone – the world's largest rubber plantation – was established in 1926 when the Firestone tyre company secured one million acres of land in Liberia at an annual rent of only US$0.06 per acre. In its heyday, the company employed 20,000 workers, more than 10% of Liberia's labour force; Liberia was once known as the Firestone Republic.

After lying dormant during the war, Firestone is again operating, although at reduced capacity. There are no regular tours, but you can usually find employees on the grounds who can show you around and explain the tapping process. Stick to the beaten path, as Firestone is one of several areas in Liberia where land mines have been found.

The plantation is in Harbel, near Robertsfield International Airport. You'll need private transport to get here.

# THE COAST
Liberia's wild and heavily vegetated coastline is broken only by occasional towns and fishing villages, and numerous major rivers. Infrastructure is nonexistent. The coastal road is passable as far as Greenville, from where you'll need to head up and around along the rugged inland route to Harper.

## ROBERTSPORT
Once a relaxing seaside town, Robertsport was completely destroyed during the war. While there's no infrastructure and no-

where to stay, the beaches are still beautiful, and are rumoured to offer some of the
best surfing along the West African coast.
During WWII, Robertsport was used as an
Allied submarine base.

Lake Piso, separating Robertsport from the
mainland, often flows onto the road during
the rainy season; inquire first in Monrovia
about conditions before heading out here.

## BUCHANAN

Lively, laid-back Buchanan is Liberia's second port and the capital of Grand Bassa
County. While the town itself doesn't offer
much, it's an agreeable place, and makes
a good introduction to upcountry Liberia.
Southeast of the port are some attractive
beaches. To reach them, follow the port
road to the old Lamco Compound, then
ask locals the way.

Buchanan also hosts a large Fanti community, most of whom live in the lively
Fanti Town fishing village – a small piece
of Ghana in Liberia.

Wherever you wander, stick to the
beaten path, especially on the outskirts of

town and in the vegetated strip bordering
the beaches, as some areas were mined during the war.

### Getting There & Away

Bush taxis run daily to Monrovia (US$5,
three hours). From Monrovia, it's better to
get one at Elwa Junction than at the hectic
Red Light Motor Park.

During the dry season, at least several
vehicles travel weekly from Buchanan to
River Cess. It's also possible to take a fishing boat, although these are notoriously
unsafe. Boats leave from Fanti Town and
from near the fish market just west of the
town centre.

Bush taxis for all destinations depart
from the main taxi stand near the market;
some also leave from the junction on the
Monrovia road several kilometres northeast
of town.

## GREENVILLE

Greenville (also known as Sinoe) is the
capital of Sinoe County, and a former port
and logging centre. On the edge of town is a

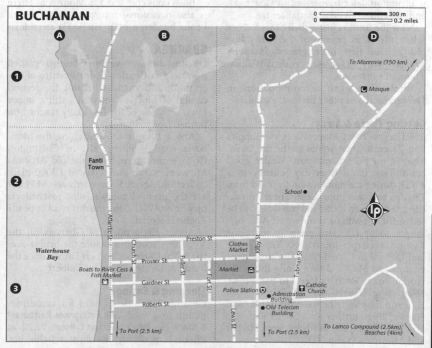

BUCHANAN

0                    300 m
0                    0.2 miles

To Monrovia (150 km)

Mosque

Fanti
Town

School

Waterhouse
Bay

Preston St
Clothes
Market

Atlantic St
Church St
Prosser St
Fuller St
Ford St
Kirby St
Tubman St

Boats to River Cess &
Fish Market

Market

Gardner St

Police Station

Catholic
Church

Admistration
Building

Roberts St

Old Telecom
Building

Lewis St

To Port (2.5 km)

To Port (2.5 km)

To Lamco Compound (2.5km);
Beaches (4km)

beach, but to reach the open sea you'll need to cross a shallow lagoon.

Greenville is also the jumping-off point for excursions to Sapo National Park, though you'll need your own vehicle as there's no public transport; see p469.

The main route between Monrovia and Greenville is via Buchanan along the rough coastal road. Otherwise, the only route is via Zwedru. There's also an occasional boat service from Monrovia (see p474).

## HARPER

Harper (sometimes referred to as Cape Palmas) is the capital of Maryland, which has long had a reputation as Liberia's most progressive county; until 1857 it was even a separate republic. In contrast with much of the rest of the country, where indigenous populations were severely repressed, settlers in Harper worked to cultivate a more cooperative relationship with the local residents. In the town centre is a monument commemorating the original accord between settlers and locals. Harper was also the seat of Liberia's first university (Cuttington, later transferred to Gbarnga), and the country's educational centre.

Now the town is just a shell of its former self. Only ruins remain of the many fine old houses that once graced Harper's streets, including former president William Tubman's mansion.

While there's no accommodation in Harper, food and other basics are available.

### Getting There & Away

Road access from Monrovia is via Tappita and Zwedru, then southeast to the coast. There's no public transport. Under good conditions, it's a three-day journey in a 4WD; during the rainy season the road from Zwedru becomes impassable. There's no accommodation en route, and you'll need to be self-sufficient with food and water. Although longer, many Liberians prefer to make the Monrovia–Harper journey via Sanniquellie and Danané in Côte d'Ivoire. From Danané continue to Man and then along the better Ivorian roads south and west to San Pédro, re-entering Liberia west of Tabou. Bush taxis run frequently between the border and Harper, 20km further west. See p480.

A boat runs sporadically between Harper and Monrovia (see p474).

# THE INTERIOR

Away from the Monrovia to Ganta corridor, Liberia's interior is covered with dense forests, gently rolling hills and small villages. Apart from the rough tracks leading to the handful of larger towns, there is no road network, and there are no tourist facilities.

## TUBMANBURG

Tubmanburg (which is also called Bomi), with an agreeable setting among the Bomi Hills, was once an important iron-ore and diamond mining centre. Although almost all of Tubmanburg's residents had to flee during the war. These days, as families make their way back, makeshift mud-and-thatch houses have replaced the sturdier zinc-roofed dwellings that once lined the streets, and the main activity in town is rebuilding.

For an inexpensive meal, try Sis Helen's Eye to Eye Bar & Restaurant on the main road.

Bush taxis cost US$3 to Monrovia. There is also occasional transport to the Sierra Leone border, usually via Bo (Waterside).

## GBARNGA

During the war years, Gbarnga gained notoriety as Charles Taylor's centre of operations, and virtually became the second capital of Liberia. Today it's still a major town, and one of the few easily reached on tarmac from Monrovia.

About 10km southwest along the Monrovia road is Phebe, site of Cuttington College and the ruins of the old Africana Museum, which once boasted a 3000-piece collection. About 30km northwest of Phebe are the pretty Kpatawe Falls, reached via bicycle or 4WD along the dirt road opposite Phebe Hospital.

About 40km north of Gbarnga on the Voinjama road, just before the bridge over the St Paul River, is Tolbert Farms, once the home of former President Tolbert.

### Sleeping & Eating

Gbarnga has little to offer for accommodation and food. **Jalk Enterprises Restaurant & Store** (Josephine's; r without bathroom US$20) in Phebe is probably the most reliable bet, with adequate rooms and a restaurant (closed Sunday lunch).

**CooCoo Nest** (Tubman Farms; r US$35, r with generator US$50) is an eccentric place, on the main road about 60km southwest of Gbarnga between Totota and Salala, was former president Tubman's private residence. Its name supposedly comes from Tubman's pet name for his young daughter. Rooms are reasonably spacious, and when the generator works, there's also a restaurant.

### Getting There & Away

Bush taxis go frequently from Gbarnga to Monrovia (US$10, six hours). Taxis from Gbarnga to Phebe Junction (US$0.60) leave from the taxi union parking lot at the top of the hill just off the highway. You need your own transport to get to CooCoo Nest.

### GANTA

Bustling and unassuming Ganta (officially called Gompa City) is just 2km from the Guinean border. For diversion, there's a small market, and an intriguing **mosque** (north of the main road), the design of which is said to be unique in Liberia. Otherwise, visit the small **craft shop** ( 8am-6pm Mon-Sat) on the edge of town along the Sanniquellie road.

### Sleeping & Eating

**Mid-Nite Fever Motel** (s/d US$7/9) This place on the Tappita road is the only hotel in town. Rooms are basic, but sheets are clean, and if the generator is working there's also a fan. Bring your own mosquito net.

For food, try **ABC African & European Food Garden** (meals from US$2.50), Anthony Buster Clinton's place, serving up good chicken or the more basic **Abuja's** (meals around US$1), next door, with rice and sauce.

For cold drinks and dancing try the Ritz, at the Tappita road junction. Opposite is Belgium Bar, also good for a drink.

### Getting There & Around

Bush taxis leave several times daily from the main taxi stand to Gbarnga (US$3, 1½ hours), Monrovia (US$13, five hours) and Sanniquellie (US$3, one hour). A few bush taxis go weekly to Tappita and Zwedru.

Bush taxis from the centre to the Guinean border cost US$0.30; from the border there's daily transport to Diéké (US$1).

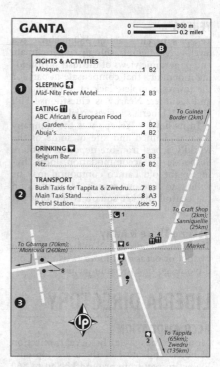

**GANTA**

0 — 300 m
0 — 0.2 miles

**SIGHTS & ACTIVITIES**
Mosque...................................................1 B2

**SLEEPING**
Mid-Nite Fever Motel.........................2 B3

**EATING**
ABC African & European Food
Garden...............................................3 B2
Abuja's...................................................4 B2

**DRINKING**
Belgium Bar..........................................5 B3
Ritz..........................................................6 B2

**TRANSPORT**
Bush Taxis for Tappita & Zwedru.......7 B3
Main Taxi Stand....................................8 A3
Petrol Station.................................(see 5)

To Guinea Border (2km)

To Craft Shop (2km); Sanniquellie (25km)

Market

To Gbarnga (70km); Monrovia (260km)

To Tappita (65km); Zwedru (135km)

### SANNIQUELLIE

Tiny Sanniquellie has a disproportionately big place in history as the birthplace of the Organisation of African Unity. Along the main road into town you can see the building where William Tubman, Sekou Touré and Kwame Nkrumah met in 1957 to discuss a union of African states – an idea that was formalised the next year with the drafting of a preliminary charter. The compound is now used to house official visitors.

Ordinary folk will need to content themselves with a room at the **Traveller's Inn Motel** (s/d without bathroom from US$4/7), 500m off the main road, and the only accommodation.

There are a few undistinguished chop houses along the main road and some reasonably well-stocked shops. Market day is Saturday.

### Getting There & Away

Bush taxis for the Côte d'Ivoire border (US$4) via Kahnple and sporadically onto Yekepa (US$3) congregate north of the market, while those for Ganta (US$3) and Monrovia (US$16) leave from the other end.

**LIBERIA**

## YEKEPA

Yekepa's perch – about 350m above sea level – gives it a refreshingly cooler climate and panoramic views of the lush surrounding mountains that compensate in part for the town's complete lack of infrastructure and facilities. Nearby is Guesthouse Hill (1362m), Liberia's highest peak.

In its heyday, Yekepa was the company town of Lamco and site of some of the world's richest iron-ore deposits. If you're desperate for accommodation, locals living in the old Lamco compound may be willing to hire out rooms. Ma Edith's on the central market square is the best bet for a meal.

### Getting There & Away

The Guinean border is 2km away, traversed by foot or occasional moto-taxis. For Côte d'Ivoire, go first to Sanniquellie.

# LIBERIA DIRECTORY

## ACCOMMODATION

Monrovia has a fairly decent selection of hotels and most of them are top end. Expect to pay from around US$40 to $60 for a decent 'budget' double, around US$80 to 100 for midrange, and from around US$150 for top end. Elsewhere, apart from the occasional guesthouse or basic budget establishment, there's no accommodation other than with missions or aid organisations, although these usually don't have sufficient facilities to accommodate independent travellers.

## BOOKS

*Journey Without Maps* is Graham Greene's classic tale of adventuring across Liberia on foot in the 1930s.

For a gripping take on the war, look for *The Final Days of Dr Doe* by Lynda Schuster (published in *Granta* 48, 1994).

*Rock of the Ancestors* by William Siegmann with Cynthia Schmidt is a catalogue based on museum exhibits, with fascinating information on traditional Liberian artwork.

History buffs should look for any of J Gus Liebenow's intriguing series of writings about Liberia, including *Liberia, 1969 through 1987*.

---

### PRACTICALITIES

- Voltage is 110V, and most plugs are US-style (two flat pins).
- There's no power outside the capital, and blackouts and power surges are common in Monrovia.
- Local dailies include the *Inquirer* and the *Monrovia Guardian*.
- Liberia uses the imperial system for weights and measures.

---

## BUSINESS HOURS

Government offices are open 8.30am to 4pm Monday to Friday. Most businesses operate from 9am to 5pm Monday to Friday (often with a break between noon and 2pm) and from 9am until 1pm on Saturday. Banking hours are 9.30am to noon Monday to Thursday and until 12.30pm on Friday.

## DANGERS & ANNOYANCES

The security situation in Liberia is fragile and there are still weapons around. In general, independent travel outside of Monrovia is not yet possible. Before setting off, get a complete briefing first from people who know the situation; embassies and resident expats are the best sources.

## EMBASSIES & CONSULATES

### Liberian Embassies & Consulates

In West Africa, Liberia has embassies or consulates in Cameroon, Côte d'Ivoire, Gambia, Ghana, Guinea, Nigeria and Sierra Leone. See the relevant country chapters for more details. Elsewhere, embassies and consulates include the following:

**Belgium** ( ☎ 02-414 7317, 02-664 1653; 50 Ave du Château, 1081 Brussels)

**France** ( ☎ 01-47 63 58 55; libem.paris@wanadoo.fr; 12 Place du General Catroux, 75017 Paris)

**Germany** ( ☎ 0228-923 9173; Mainzerstrasse 259, 53179 Bonn)

**UK** ( ☎ 020-7388 5489; 23 Fitzroy Square, London WIT 6EW)

**USA** ( ☎ 202-723 0437; www.embassyofliberia.org; 5201 16th St NW, Washington, DC 20011)

### Embassies & Consulates in Liberia

Diplomatic representations in Monrovia include the following. Canadians and Australians should contact their high commissions in Abidjan (see p286) and Ghana (see p396), respectively.

**Côte d'Ivoire** (Map p470; 8th St, Sinkor)
**Germany** ( ☎ 06-438 365; Tubman Blvd)
**Ghana** (Map p470; ☎ 06-518 269; 15th St, Sinkor)
**Guinea** (Map p470; cnr 24th St & Tubman Blvd, Sinkor)
**Nigeria** (Map p470; Nigeria House, Tubman Blvd, Congo Town)
**Sierra Leone** (Map p470; ☎ 06-515 061, 06-515 058; 15th St, Sinkor)
**UK** (chalkleyroy@aol.com; Clara Town, UN Drive, Bushrod Island) Honorary consul, emergency assistance only; otherwise contact the British High Commission in Freetown (p768).
**USA** (Map p470; ☎ 07-705 4826; http://monrovia .usembassy.gov/; United Nations Dr, Mamba Point)

## HOLIDAYS

Public holidays include the following:
**New Year's Day** 1 January
**Armed Forces Day** 11 February
**Decoration Day** 2nd Wednesday in March
**JJ Roberts' Birthday** 15 March
**Fast & Prayer Day** 11 April
**National Unification Day** 14 May
**Independence Day** 26 July
**Flag Day** 24 August
**Thanksgiving Day** 1st Thursday in November
**Tubman Day** 29 November
**Christmas Day** 25 December

## INTERNET RESOURCES

**Friends of Liberia** (www.fol.org) Started by former Peace Corps volunteers, with information on the activities and projects of the nonprofit Friends of Liberia group.
**Liberia News** (www.liberianews.com) Current events.
**Liberian Connection** (www.liberian-connection.com) General information and news.
**Onliberia.org** (www.onliberia.org/urls.htm) A comprehensive site with an excellent page of links.
**Perspective** (www.theperspective.org) Liberian news and opinions.

## LANGUAGE

More than 20 African languages are spoken, including Kpelle in the north-central region, Bassa and Kru along the coast, and Grebo in the southeast. English is the official language. The following will help you get started understanding the local version:

| | |
|---|---|
| *dash* | bribe |
| *coal tar* | tar road |
| *waste* | discard (*waste* the milk) or splash (*waste* water) |
| *I beg you* | please (with emphasis) |
| *carry* | give a ride to |

| | |
|---|---|
| *wait small* | just a moment please |
| *kala kala* | crooked, corrupt |

## MONEY

The unit of currency is the Liberian 'unity' dollar (L$). US dollars are also widely accepted.

Money can be changed at the airport, at one of the several foreign-exchange bureaus in Monrovia and at a bank. Avoid changing money on the street. The best rates are for the US dollar, though other major currencies are also accepted. Travellers cheques are virtually useless, although if you're stuck some shop owners may accept payment for purchases in travellers cheques and give you the change in local currency. Credit cards are not accepted anywhere, and there are no ATMs.

## PHOTOGRAPHY & VIDEO

Use a high degree of caution when photographing. Don't take photos of government buildings, airports, bridges, military installations or anything even remotely official, and always ask permission before photographing locals.

Kodak film is available in Monrovia.

## TELEPHONE

The country code is ☎ 231, and the international access code is ☎ 00.

There are no telephones upcountry, and no area codes. Rates are about US$3 per minute to the USA and US$4 to Australia and Europe. Telephone numbers are six digits, although the national telephone network is essentially defunct, with mobile phones the only way to connect. Mobile numbers are six to seven digits, preceded by 04, 05, 06 or 07.

## VACCINATION CERTIFICATE

A valid yellow fever vaccination certificate is required to enter Liberia.

## VISAS

Visas are required by all except nationals of Ecowas countries and cost US$54 (US$100 for US citizens) for three-month single entry, plus two photos, a medical statement of good health and proof of financial resources. Regardless of the duration of your visa, you'll be given 48 hours on arrival during which you must report for an extension to the **Bureau of Immigration** (Map p472; Broad St; ☾ 9am-5pm Mon-Fri, 9am-3pm Sat) in Monrovia.

**LIBERIA**

Once there, it's US$25 plus two more photos for an initial 30-day stay.

## Visa Extensions

The bureau of immigration is also where you'll need to go to extend your visa beyond this initial month's stay.

## Visas for Onward Travel

In Liberia, you can get visas for Côte d'Ivoire, Sierra Leone and Guinea. Embassies are open for applications from 9am to noon and visas are generally issued within two days.

# TRANSPORT IN LIBERIA

## GETTING THERE & AWAY

For information on getting to Liberia from outside West Africa, see p830.

## Entering Liberia

Although getting a visa for Liberia has become somewhat more bureaucratic these days, it's not particularly difficult. Once you have this, plus proof of yellow fever vaccination, entry is usually straightforward, though if you don't look like you're on official business, you can expect some questioning on arrival.

## Air

All flights arrive and depart from **Roberts International Airport** (Robertsfield), 60km southeast of Monrovia. Airlines include the following. Karou Voyages (see p470) can assist with bookings.

**Brussels Airline** (Map p472; SN; ☎ 06-590 991, 06-512 147; www.flysn.com) Hub: Brussels. Three flights weekly between Brussels and Monrovia via Freetown (Sierra Leone).

**Slok Air International** (SO; ☎ 06-590 178) Hub: Banjul. Three flights weekly to/from Dakar via Freetown and Banjul; three flights weekly to/from Accra

**SN Bellview Airlines** (BLV; ☎ 06-543-133, 06-553 928) Hub: Lagos. Three flights weekly to/from Lagos via Accra and Abidjan.

**Weasua Air Transport** (Map p472; WTC; ☎ 06-556 693) Hub: Monrovia. Three flights weekly to/from Abidjan.

---

**DEPARTURE TAX**

Departure tax for all flights is US$25. There's also a US$15 security tax. Both must be paid with exact change, US dollars cash only.

---

## Land

### CÔTE D'IVOIRE

Border crossings with Côte d'Ivoire are just beyond Sanniquellie, and east of Harper, towards Tabou.

There's a bus several times weekly from Monrovia to Abidjan and on to Accra via Sanniquellie (US$40 to Abidjan, US$60 to Accra, plus approximately US$20 for border fees).

Daily bush taxis go from Monrovia to Ganta and Sanniquellie, from where you can continue in stages to Danané and Man (12 to 15 hours).

In the south, a road connects Harper with Tabou; you'll need to cross the Cavally River in a ferry or canoe. Once across, there are taxis to Tabou, from where there's transport to San Pédro and Abidjan.

### GUINEA

For Guinea, the main crossing is just north of Ganta. There are also border points at Voinjama and Yekepa, though public transport is sparse on both routes.

Bush taxis run daily from Monrovia to Ganta (US$15), from where you'll need to walk or take a moto-taxi the remaining 2km to the border. Once across, there are frequent taxis to N'zérékoré. Allow a day for the journey, and expect many checkpoints. The Monrovia–Conakry stretch (US$35) takes two to three days.

It's possible to go in the dry season via Voinjama to Macenta, changing vehicles at the border. The road from Gbarnga north to Zorzor and Voinjama is in bad shape, though rehabilitation work is underway; allow two days for the entire stretch.

From Yekepa it's a few kilometres to the border, from where there are Guinean vehicles to Lola (US$1.50, one hour).

For information on boats between Conakry (Guinea) and Monrovia (at least 36 hours), inquire at Monrovia's Freeport. Fishing boats run sporadically between Harper and San Pédro (Côte d'Ivoire).

### SIERRA LEONE

The main Sierra Leone crossing is at Bo (Waterside), with other posts at Kongo and northwest of Kolahun (currently closed).

There are frequent daily bush taxis between Monrovia and the Bo (Waterside) border (two hours), from where it's easy to find onward transport to Kenema (about eight very rough hours further), and then on to Bo and Freetown.

The crossing at Kongo is rarely travelled by bush taxi; allow a full day from Tubmanburg, and confirm first that the border is open.

## GETTING AROUND
### Air
There are no regularly scheduled flights within Liberia. Weasua Air Transport (see opposite) does charters.

### Boat
Fishing boats link coastal cities, and while slow and often dangerous, are sometimes faster than road travel. There are also charter boats from Monrovia that sometimes have room for passengers; see p474.

### Bush Taxi & Minibus
Independent road travel is not currently recommended outside Monrovia. Once things settle down, the main form of public transport is bush taxis, which go daily from Monrovia to Buchanan, Gbarnga, Ganta, Sanniquellie and the Sierra Leone border. Several weekly bush taxis link Monrovia with almost everywhere else, although many routes (especially those connecting

Zwedru with Greenville and Harper) are restricted during the rainy season. Minivans (called 'buses') also ply most major routes, although they're more crowded and dangerous than bush taxis, and best avoided. Sample journey times and fares: Monrovia to Buchanan (US$5, three hours, 150km); Monrovia to Bo (Waterside; US$5, 2½ hours, 140km); Monrovia to Sanniquellie (US$16, six hours, 305km). The luggage surcharge shouldn't exceed US$1 for a standard backpack.

### Car & Motorcycle
Vehicle rental can be arranged through better hotels and sometimes through shop owners; prices (including driver) average about US$100 per day for 4WD.

#### ROAD CONDITIONS
Most roads are dirt and many are impassable during the rainy season. Exceptions include the tarmac routes connecting the capital with Bo (Waterside), Tubmanburg, Ganta and Buchanan, although there are some deteriorated stretches on the Buchanan road.

Driving is on the right. Road hazards here are similar to those elsewhere in West Africa; see p845. Expect frequent stops at UN security checkpoints.

LIBERIA

# Mali

Mali is the jewel in West Africa's crown, a destination that seems to have all the right ingredients.

The country occupies the heart of a territory that once supported Africa's greatest empires and is rich with historical resonance. This enormously significant history bequeathed to Mali some of its most dramatic attractions – the legendary city of Timbuktu, whose name has never lost its remote allure for travellers from afar, and the gloriously improbable mosque at Djenné are simply two among many.

Mali's history has always been a story of deserts and of rivers. The lucrative trade routes of the Sahara once made the region the world's richest, and the waterways still provide the country's lifeblood. The Niger, one of the grand rivers of Africa, still sustains the country, and to journey along it (preferably on a slow boat to Timbuktu) is one great journey.

Not too far from the riverbank, the extraordinary Falaise de Bandiagara rises up from the plains and shelters one of West Africa's most intriguing peoples – the Dogon, whose villages and complex cultural rituals still cling to the edge of rocky cliffs. If you can visit one place in Mali, go to the Dogon Country: it is utterly unforgettable.

But all of Mali is alive with a fascinating cultural mix of peoples, from the nomadic Tuareg people of the Sahara to the fishing societies of the Bozo, who are respected as the masters of the Niger River (*gui-tigui* in Bambara). It seems that everywhere you go there are fascinating ceremonies. And a world-famous musical tradition, with strong roots in the local soil, mean that the cultures of Africa have never been so accessible as they are in Mali.

## FAST FACTS

- **Area** 1,240,140 sq km
- **Capital** Bamako
- **Country code** ☎ 223
- **Famous for** Timbuktu; Dogon Country; the best in West African music
- **Languages** French, Bambara, Fula, Tamashek, Dogon, Bozo and Songhaï
- **Money** West African CFA franc; US$1 = CFA544.89; €1 = CFA655.96
- **Population** 10.6 million
- **Visa** Renewable five-day visa available at border CFA15,000 or one-month visas at any Malian embassy

# HIGHLIGHTS

- **Dogon Country** (p513) Trek down the Falaise de Bandiagara and into the timeless villages.
- **Djenné** (p504) Haggle with locals on market day (Monday) beneath the shadow of the incomparable mosque – the largest mud building in the world.
- **Niger River** (p510) Take a slow boat up the river and into the culturally rich inland delta.
- **Timbuktu** (p521) Discover the legendary city, and stand amid the solitude of the Sahara watching a salt caravan arrive.
- **Bamako** (p490) Dance to the infectious rhythms of Mali's world-famous musicians.

# ITINERARIES

- **One Week** If you've only got one week – what were you thinking? – make sure your Monday is spent at **Djenné's weekly market** (p505), where the great mud-mosque is a stunning backdrop. Continue northeast to the lively port town of **Mopti** (p508), an excellent base for short **Niger River boat trips** (p510) and forays into **Dogon Country** (p513) – three days is a minimum. Try also to pass through **Bamako** (p490) on a Friday or Saturday, when the Malian capital rocks.
- **Two Weeks** An extra week will allow you to break up the long journey north by pausing for a couple of nights in languid **Ségou** (p501), a wonderful introduction to the towns of the Niger riverbank. From **Mopti** (p508), you could also take a three-day slow-boat journey (p510) up the Niger River to **Timbuktu** (p521), the dusty and labyrinthine city of legend that resonates with Saharan caravans and has a become byword for the end of the earth.
- **One Month** In a one-month itinerary you could include extra days in **Djenné** (p505), which is lovely and quiet once the clamour of the market subsides, as well as up to 10 days of outstanding **Dogon Country trekking** (p518). Your boat journey to Timbuktu could even continue beyond, to the fascinating and remote outpost of **Gao** (p529) – a handy staging post on the road to Niger – while a longer **Saharan camel trek** (p525) from

## HOW MUCH?

- **Bamako–Mopti bus ride** CFA8000
- **Mopti–Timbuktu on Comanav ferry** CFA49,110 (1st class)
- **Sunset camel ride into Sahara** CFA10,000
- **Internet connection** CFA1000 to CFA1500 per hour
- **Guide to Dogon Country** CFA9000 to CFA15,000 per day

## LONELY PLANET INDEX

- **1L of petrol** CFA650
- **1l of bottled water** CFA750
- **Bottle of Castel beer** small/large CFA500/1000
- **Souvenir T-shirt** CFA8000
- **Portion of riz arachide (rice with peanut sauce)** CFA500

Timbuktu is another option for lovers of the desert.

## CLIMATE & WHEN TO GO

Mali is wettest between July and August, although the rainy season – when torrential downpours and thunderstorms are preceded by strong winds – runs from June to September. It's hottest between April and June, when temperatures frequently exceed 40°C. September and October are also extremely hot and Timbuktu in particular can be unpleasant. From November through January, the best time to visit, the *alize* wind blows cooler air from the northeast, keeping daytime temperatures in the 30s – Malians refer to this period as the cold season! From January to June, the hot and dusty harmattan blows, irritating throats and, on some days, reducing visibility to a few hundred metres. River trips are usually only possible until December, after which a lack of rain sees water levels drop.

Mali's most famous cultural event is the **Festival in the Desert**, a musical extravaganza of Mali's best musicians amid the sand dunes near Timbuktu which takes place in early January. For the timing of other festivals, see p525.

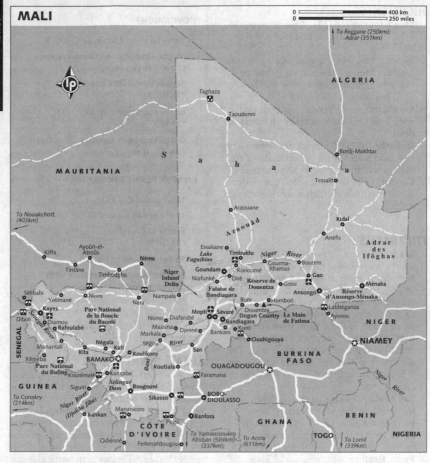

# MALI

To Reggarie (250km);
Adrar (351km)

ALGERIA

**Sahara**

MAURITANIA

To Nouakchott
(403km)

To Conakry
(214km)

Taghaza

Taoudenni

Bordj-Mokhtar

Tessalit

Araouane

Azaouâd

Kidal

Anéfis

Adrar
des
Ifôghas

Kiffa        Ayoûn-el-        Essakane
             Atroûs         Lake         Timbuktu   Niger River
                            Faguibine                          Bourem
     Tintâne   Néma       Goundam   Korioumé  Gourma-
              Timbédgha   Niger    Niafunké  Diré   Rharous   Gao
                          Inland            Réserve de  Gossi
Sélibabi                  Delta   Nampala   Douentza            Ménaka
     Yélimané   Nioro    Nara             Boni    Hombori    Réserve
Kayes   Parc National                   Mopti  Sévaré  Douentza  d'Ansongo-Ménaka
Diboli  de la Boucle            Niono  Diafarabé  Bandiagara  Ansongo  Labbéganza
     Diamou  du Baoulé        Markala  Djenné  Bankass  Koro           Ayorou   NIGER
     Bafoulabé                 Massina                           
Manantali  Négala                San   Ouahigouya         NIAMEY
     Kita   Kati   Koulikoro                      BURKINA
        BAMAKO            River              FASO
     Parc National   Kangaba
     du Bafing  Kourémalé            OUAGADOUGOU     Niger River
GUINEA   Siguiri   Sélingué  Bougouni        Faramana
              Dam
        Mankankoro   Sikasso           BOBO-        BENIN
     Kankan        Pogo           DIOULASSO
     CÔTE         Banfora   GHANA              NIGERIA
     D'IVOIRE   To Yamoussoukro   To Accra      TOGO
     Odienné  Ferkessédougou  Abidjan (584km);  (611km)   To Lomé
                    (337km)                    (339km)

# HISTORY

Rock paintings and carvings in the Gao and Timbuktu regions suggest that northern Mali has been inhabited since 50,000 BC, when the Sahara was fertile grassland across which roamed an abundance of wildlife. By 5000 BC farming was taking place, and the use of iron began around 500 BC. By 300 BC, large organised settlements had developed, most notably at Djenné (see p506). By the 6th century AD, the lucrative trans-Saharan trade in gold, salt and slaves had begun, facilitating the rise of Mali's three great empires.

The Empire of Ghana (unrelated to present-day Ghana) covered much of what is now Mali and Senegal until the 11th century.

It was followed by the great Empire of Mali, which in the 14th century stretched from the Atlantic Ocean to present-day Nigeria. Timbuktu was developed as a great centre of commerce and Islamic culture. The Songhaï Empire, with its capital at Gao, came next, but this empire was destroyed by a Moroccan mercenary army in the late 16th century.

At around the same time, European ships were arriving along the coast of West Africa, thus circumventing the trans-Saharan trade routes and breaking the monopoly and power of the Sahel kingdoms and northern cities.

Later the Bambara Empire of Ségou rose briefly to control huge swathes of Mali, before being usurped by two waves of Fula-led

Islamic jihad, the second originating from the Tukulor Empire of northern Senegal. The Tukulor were still around when the French expanded east into Mali during the mid-19th century. For more information about Mali's pre-colonial history see p30.

By the end of the 19th century, Mali was part of French West Africa. Remnants of this colonial era that are still visible today, include the huge Office du Niger irrigation scheme near Ségou, and the 1200km Dakar–Bamako train line, the longest rail span in West Africa; both were built with forced labour. Such vast infrastructure projects notwithstanding, Mali remained the poor neighbour of Senegal and Côte d'Ivoire. France's chief interest was in 'developing' Mali as a source of cheap cash crops (rice and cotton) for export.

## Independence

Mali became independent in 1960 (for a few months it was federated with Senegal). Its first president, Modibo Keita, embarked on an unsuccessful period of one-party state socialism. Newly formed state corporations took control of the economy, but all except the cotton enterprise soon began losing money. Ambitious planning schemes went awry, the economy wilted, and Keita was forced to ask the French to support the Malian franc – something of a humiliation for a country that had eagerly thrown off the shackles and symbols of colonialism. Eventually, in 1968, Keita was overthrown by a group of army officers led by Moussa Traoré.

Cold War rivalries were at fever pitch and Mali was firmly in the Soviet camp, with Moscow-style socialism the dominant economic model. Continual food shortages were conveniently blamed on droughts (which did devastate the north in 1968–74 and in 1980–85), but were largely due to government mismanagement. The situation was hardly helped by government instability and military intervention – from 1970 to 1990 five coup attempts were made against Traoré, and the early 1980s were characterised by strikes, often violently suppressed.

In 1979 Mali was officially returned to civilian rule, although it remained a one-party state with Moussa Traoré as its head. Thanks to market liberalisation (and adequate rainfall), by 1987 Mali had produced its first grain surplus.

However, even a leader as entrenched as Traoré could not resist the winds of change sweeping the world. The clamour for multiparty democracy elsewhere coincided with a growing restlessness among Mali's population about Traoré's autocratic rule. Democracy would come, but it was a bloodstained transition.

The Tuareg uprising (p529) began in 1990, and later that year a peaceful pro-democracy demonstration attracted about 30,000 people onto the streets of Bamako. This action was followed by strikes and further demonstrations. On 17 March 1991, security forces met students and other demonstrators with machine-gun fire. Three days of rioting followed, during which 150 people were killed. The unrest finally provoked the army, led by General Amadou Toumani Touré (General ATT as he was known), to take control. Moussa Traoré was arrested, and around 60 senior government figures were executed.

Touré established an interim transitional government and gained considerable respect from Malians and the outside world when he resigned a year later, keeping his promise to hold multiparty elections.

## The 1990s

Alpha Oumar Konaré (a scientist and writer) was elected president in June 1992, and his party – Alliance for Democracy in Mali (Adema) – won a large majority of seats in the national assembly. Though a widely respected and capable leader who oversaw considerable political and economic liberalisation, Konaré had to deal with a 50% devaluation of the CFA during the 1990s (which resulted in rioting and protest) and an attempted coup.

Presidential and national assembly elections were held in 1997, but were marred by irregularities and the withdrawal of opposition parties. Konaré and his party were duly re-elected, whereafter he appointed opposition figures to his cabinet and made genuine attempts to democratise and decentralise Mali.

In sharp contrast to many African leaders, Konaré stood down in 2002, as the new constitution he'd helped draft dictated – although many Malians believe that he did so reluctantly; he is now the Chairman of the African Union. The former general, Amadou

Touré, was rewarded for his patience and elected as president in April 2002.

## Mali Today

On many fronts Mali is a model West African democracy, one in which the overall health of the system has proven more enduring than the ambitions of individual leaders. It has become Africa's third-largest gold producer, which offers hope for a more prosperous future and the prospect of a long-overdue diversification of the economy – agriculture currently accounts for almost half of Mali's GDP, and cotton provides 40% of exports.

Malian-style democracy may have fostered stability and peace, and received international acclaim, but Mali is still one of the poorest countries on earth – almost one-third of Malians are malnourished, 90% of the population live on less than US$2 a day and adult literacy is just 19%. The locust invasion and drought of 2004 served as a reminder that Mali is still as dependent on international aid money as it is on good rains. Widespread corruption also remains a problem and, for all the international momentum for debt relief in Africa, more government money in Mali is still spent on debt servicing than on education, although it is hoped that may change after the July 2005 G8 agreement to slash the debts of indebted countries such as Mali.

## THE CULTURE
## The National Psyche

Malians are open and tolerant. For centuries the country's diverse peoples have shared a country that is not always bountiful, and they've learned to do it pretty well (competing kingdoms and slavery aside). Ethnic identity is still important, but where once there was enmity, in most cases a *cousinage* or 'joking cousins' relationship now exists. People from different groups commonly tease and poke fun at ethnic stereotypes and past deeds to everyone's enjoyment. The only possible exception is the Tuareg, who remain a people apart, the more so since the divisive conflict of the 1990s (p529).

In Mali, personal relationships are important, friendships are things of great value, families are the glue that holds everything together, and hospitality and generosity seem to increase in inverse proportion to a person's means. Malians worry about the dire state of the country and a perceived

---

**MALI – LAND OF GOLD**

Mali hasn't always been one of the world's poorest countries – it was once home to rich empires whose legends were the colour of gold.

The Empire of Ghana, which encompassed vast swathes of what is now Mali, was fabled as a kingdom where gold was so plentiful that it was visible on the ground, and its king was even said to tether his horse to a nugget of pure gold. Two-thirds of the world's gold came from the Empire of Ghana. After the empire yielded to that of Mali, King Kankan Musa distributed so much gold on his pilgrimage to Mecca that world gold prices did not recover for a generation (see p34 for more).

Not surprisingly, Mali's ancient rulers kept the source of their gold – primarily an area known as Bouré that surrounds present-day Siguiri in Guinea and stretches along the Niger River into Mali – as a closely guarded secret. Gold was traded for salt and other goods in a system of 'dumb barter', in which transactions were almost devoid of direct contact, meaning that very few people knew where the gold came from.

Rumours of West Africa's gold reserves helped drive Europe's clamour for parts of the continent's interior. Although, by the 16th century, invaders from Morocco, and later Europe, found that West Africa's gold had seemingly been exhausted. Gold mining was reduced to individual prospectors searching for nuggets.

Gold mining in Mali is no longer a matter of looking for nuggets. Economic and political liberalisation in the 1990s, and a revision of the mining code, has attracted a host of multinational mining companies (particularly from South Africa and Australia). The government is a stakeholder in all mines and levies taxes on revenues. All mines are open-cast operations where gold particles are leached from crushed rock using cyanide.

But some things don't change – the areas most interesting to the multinationals are still Bambouk and Bouré, from where the great empires grew.

loss of tradition, rail against corruption and long for a better life, but deep down they're a remarkably optimistic people who love to dance. They love it even more if you dance with them.

## Daily Life
Malian societies are highly stratified, with hereditary nobles at the top and castes of hunters and blacksmiths at the bottom. In former centuries slavery was universal and subtribes of former slaves (and even slavery itself) still exist in some societies.

Mali today is – like many traditional societies in the region – struggling to hold fast to old ways of living, while embracing modern culture. This conflict is particularly acute, because Mali is officially the fourth-poorest country in the world, and for most Malians daily life is a struggle. In this context, the role played by music in Malian life cannot be overestimated. Not only has Mali's music proven to be a reassuring bastion of traditional rhythms and a bulwark against the encroachment of the modern world, it has also provided a refuge and diversion from difficult economic circumstances, showcased the strength of traditional Malian culture, and highlighted the country's ability to take the modern world by storm. It is little wonder, therefore, that music accompanies everything in Malian life, providing the soundtrack for everything from important rites of passage to the obligatory dancing on a Saturday night.

Greeting people in Mali is very important, and you'll often see highly formalised ritual greetings which last for minutes. Indeed, one of the rudest things you can do to a Malian is ignore them. People think it very impolite to ask for directions to the nearest bank before saying hello or enquiring about their health.

Although Mali has a higher number of female government ministers than France, and progress towards equality is being made in the higher echelons of society, rural women have few rights over the fruit of their labours, must accept polygamy and female genital mutilation as their lot, and are generally marginalised.

## Population
Mali's population is growing by 2.9% per year, which means that the number of Malians doubles every 20 years. This figure would be even higher, but Mali has the fourth-highest child mortality rate in the world – around a quarter of children will die before their fifth birthday. By African standards the HIV infection rate is low (about 2% of the population).

About 80% of Malians are tied to the land, directly or indirectly, so it's hardly surprising that most of the population live in Mali's fertile south. The vast northern desert and semidesert (60% of Mali) contains just 10% of the population (the same percentage of the population live in Bamako).

Concentrated in the centre and south of the country, the Bambara are Mali's largest ethnic group (33% of the population) and they hold much political power. Together with the Soninké and Malinké (who dominate western Mali) they make up 50% of Mali's population.

Fula (17%) pastoralists are found in Mali, wherever there is grazing for their livestock, particularly near Massina in the Niger Inland Delta. The farmlands of the Songhaï (6%) are concentrated along the 'Niger Bend', the stretch of river between Niafunké and Ansongo, while the Sénoufo (12%) live around Sikasso and Koutiala. The Dogon (7%) live on the Falaise de Bandiagara in central Mali. The lighter-skinned Tuareg (6%), traditionally nomadic pastoralists and traders, inhabit the fringes of the Sahara. Other groups include the Bozo fisher people of the Niger River and the Bobo (2.5%) farmers, who live close to the border with Burkina Faso.

There is considerable intermarriage between people of different ethnic groups, the common tie being Islam. However, it's taboo for some groups to intermarry (such as between Dogon and Bozo).

## RELIGION
Between 80% and 90% of Malians are Muslim, and 2% Christian. The remainder retain animist beliefs, which often blur with Islamic and Christian practices, especially in rural areas.

Mali is a secular state, but Islam here is conservative and reasonably influential. In recent years some powerful imams have called for more Islamic influence in the running of the country and less Westernisation. However, despite the odd Bin Laden T-shirt in the market, there is very little anti-Western sentiment in Mali.

## ARTS
### Music

Mali's cultural diversity affords it a wealth of great music, not only from the dominant Bambara, but also from the Tuareg, Songhaï, Fula, Dogon and Bozo people. Best known are the griots (also called *jalis*), a hereditary caste of musicians who fulfil many functions in Malian society. You can tell if a musician or singer comes from a griot family by their name: Diabaté, Kouyaté and Sissoko are the most common. Many of Mali's modern singers are members of the griot caste. The female griots of Mali are famed throughout West Africa for the beauty and power of their voices; some of the most famous singers include Ami Koita, Fanta Damba, Tata Bambo Kouyaté and Mariam Kouyaté.

Mali's wealth of talented female singers also includes the hugely popular Oumou Sangaré, whose songs deal with contemporary social issues such as polygamy and arranged marriages. Her music is influenced by the musical traditions of the Wassoulou region of southwestern Mali, and features the *kamelen-ngoni*, a large six-stringed harp-lute. If you like her music, also look out for recordings by Sali Sidibé and Kagbe Sidibé. Rokia Traoré has become one of Mali's most respected female singers in Europe, but has yet to attract a broad following at home. Kandia Kouyaté has a sublime voice but she rarely performs.

After independence, Malian cultural and artistic traditions were encouraged and several state-sponsored 'orchestras' were founded. The legendary Rail Band de Bamako (actual employees of the Mali Railway Corporation!) was one of the greatest, and one of its ex-members, the charismatic Salif Keita, has become perhaps the brightest in Mali's pantheon of stars.

The enigmatic, laid-back and much-loved Ali Farka Touré is perhaps Africa's best-known modern musician – look out for his albums *The River* and *Radio Mali*. His blues-influenced sound highlights similarities between the music of Africa and the Mississippi delta (some scholars believe that the roots of American blues lie with the Malian slaves who worked on US plantations). Other emerging blues performers include Lobi Traoré, Afel Bocoum, Boubacar Traoré and Tinariwen, a beguiling Tuareg group from Kidal that have taken the world by storm (see p62 for more on this band).

Lovers of the *kora* will adore the work of the master, Toumani Diabaté, who has collaborated with everyone from Roswell Rudd and Taj Mahal to Spain's Ketama. Ballake Sissoko and Sidiki Diabaté (Toumani's father) are two other masters of the art.

Other popular musicians include Kassy Mady Diabaté, Habib Koita, Djelimady Tounkara, and Amadou and Mariam, whose collaboration with Manu Chao was the sound of the 2005 summer across Europe.

To hear some of Mali's best musicians in action in Bamako, see p499. For a broader look at the wider West African music scene, see p58.

### Arts & Craftwork

Mali's famous sculptural traditions date back to the 12th century, when figures in terracotta, bronze and gold were created by the inhabitants of Djenné and surrounding towns. These sculptures usually depict a kneeling person with stylised eyes.

Woodcarvings made by the Bambara people are noted for their angular forms. Figures called *flanitokele* are carved in a rigid posture, with an elongated torso, arms held stiffly to the side – often with palms out – and conical breasts. Bambara masks are usually bold and solid, with cowrie shells and human and animal features incorporated into the design; they're often used in secret society ceremonies. The best known (and frequently used as a symbol of West Africa) is the *chiwara,* a headpiece

---

**MALI'S TOP TEN ALBUMS – THE AUTHOR'S CHOICE**

- Salif Keita, *The Best of the Early Years*
- Toumani Diabaté, *New Ancient Strings*
- Ballake Sissoko, *Tomora*
- Ali Farka Touré and Toumani Diabaté, *In the Heart of the Moon*
- Ali Farka Touré, *Niafunke*
- Tinariwen, *Amassakoul*
- Amadou et Mariam, *Dimanche a Bamako*
- Kandia Kouyaté, *Biriko*
- Oumou Sangaré, *Worotan*
- Rokia Traoré, *Bowmboï*

carved in the form of an antelope, and used in ritualistic dances.

The Bozo sculpt a mask representing a sacred ram, called *saga*, and are believed to have begun the tradition of marionette theatre, where human and animal figures are used to act out scenes from history and everyday life. The Bambara, Malinké and Soninké have adopted this tradition, and there are annual marionette festivals in Diarabougou (20km east of Koulikoro; p501) and Markala (p504).

The Bambara also produce striking *bogolan*, or mud cloth (p69), and the Dogon are also renowned for their masks (see the boxed text, p517).

## Architecture

When the Dogon first moved into central Mali, they took their lead from the Tellem (p514) and built their houses on the high cliffs of the escarpment of the Falaise de Bandiagara for protection. These houses were made of mud on a wooden frame, with a flat roof supported by wooden beams, while the smaller granaries had conical roofs. In recent times, many of the cliff dwellings have been abandoned, as more Dogon moved down to the better farmland on the plains.

The design of Dogon houses is unique. Each house is collectively built of rock and mud, and set in a compound that contains one or two granaries. Single-sex dormitories are constructed for those who have been circumcised, but are not yet married, and slight architectural variations occur across Dogon Country.

The granaries, with their conical straw roofs, stand on stone legs to protect the maize or other crops from vermin. At one time their most notable feature were the elaborately carved doors and shutters in some villages, but sadly, many have been sold to unscrupulous tourists and replaced with plain wooden doors.

The focal point of any village is the *toguna*, a low-roofed shelter which is the meeting place for older men, where they discuss the affairs of the village or simply lounge, smoke, tell jokes and take naps. Nine pillars support the roof, made from eight layers of millet stalks, and the outside pillars are sometimes carved with figures of the eight Dogon ancestors. Women are allowed into some *togu-na*, although by no means all.

The *taï* is a village's central square and is where most ceremonies take place; there's often an important *togu-na* close by.

Each clan in the village has a clan house, called a *guina*, which usually contains a shrine. The most impressive of these are characterised by rows of holes, like compartmentalised shelves, and geometric decoration.

## Literature

Mali's story-telling was once an almost exclusively oral tradition, but one of the few tales which has been committed to paper, and is now available to a wider audience, is that of one of ancient Mali's greatest kings, Sundiata (see the boxed text, p33), whose story delightfully blurs the lines between history and literature. An accessible version is *Sundiata: An Epic of Old Mali*, by DT Niane.

Mali's greatest writer of the modern era was the Bandiagara-born Amadou Hampaté Bâ, who died in 1991 (see p48 for more information).

## Cinema & Photography

Although Mali lacks the cinematic traditions of neighbouring Burkina Faso and Senegal, it does have some directors who have attracted attention beyond the region.

Souleymane Cissé is perhaps the best known, especially for the masterful *Yeleen*, which won the Special Jury Prize at the Cannes Film Festival in 1987. His other films include, *Den Muso* (1975), *Finye* (1981) and *Waati* (1995).

Other well-regarded Malian directors include: Assane Kouyaté (whose *Kabala* won the Special Jury Prize at the 2003 Fespaco film festival); Abdoulaye Ascofaré; Adama Drabo; Falaba Issa Traoré and Cheick Oumar Sissoko – whose *La Genése* and *Guimba, un Tyran, une Epoque* won prizes at Cannes (1999) and Fespaco (1995) respectively, and who is now Mali's Minister of Culture

Mali's photographers have also been attracting international acclaim in recent years, especially the self-taught Seydou Keita, whose eccentric but revealing portraits of his fellow Malians have been exhibited around the world. Malick Sidibe also does portraits, in addition to being known for his stirring images from Bamako in the heady days surrounding Malian independence. Books worth seeking out include *Seydou Keita;* the famous *You Look Beauti-*

*ful Like That: The Portrait Photographs of Seydou Keita and Malick Sidibe;* and *Malick Sidibe: Photographs.*

## ENVIRONMENT
### The Land
Mali, the largest country in West Africa, is home to five different environments. The north contains the Sahara, the south is relatively flat and well-watered agricultural land, the west is a hilly and well-wooded extension of the Futa Djalon highlands of Guinea, the central band is semi-arid scrub savanna (the Sahel) and the Niger Inland Delta is a maze of channels, swamps and lakes.

The Niger River, the country's lifeline, is the major geographical marvel of Mali. It flows 1626km through the country, sweeping up from Guinea, in the southwest, to Timbuktu and the edge of the Sahara, before heading southeast through Niger and Nigeria to the Atlantic.

### National Parks
Mali has four national parks and reserves, but its wildlife has been devastated by centuries of human encroachment and the parks are not easily accessible.

Northwest of Bamako, the vast Parc National de la Boucle du Baoulé reportedly has good bird-watching, while bordering the lake formed by Manantali dam, west of Kita, Parc National du Bafing protects a number of primate species, including chimpanzees.

The Réserve d'Ansongo-Ménaka lies southeast of Gao, next to the Niger River, and is extremely isolated. Much of the wildlife has gone but the Niger still has hippos. Of most interest to visitors, although difficult to reach, is the Réserve de Douentza, a vast area of semidesert north of the main road between Mopti and Gao inhabited by hardy desert elephants (p534).

### Environmental Issues
Mali's most urgent environmental issues are deforestation, overgrazing and desertification. The three problems are inextricably linked and, between them, threaten much of the country. In the Sahel, trees are felled for cooking fuel and building materials. Elsewhere, overgrazing is stripping the land of ground cover and root systems ensuring that the soil has little to bind it together and is unravelling, causing erosion.

The increasing population only exacerbates these problems.

## FOOD & DRINK
Food in Mali is generally similar to that found in Senegal, with *poulet yassa* (chicken in an onion and lemon sauce), *riz yollof* (rice with vegetables and/or meat) and *riz arachide* (rice with peanut sauce) featuring on many menus. All along the Niger River, restaurants also serve grilled or fried *capitaine* (Nile perch). Many tourist restaurants cater to more Western tastes. In Gao, look out for *wigila,* a local specialty of sun-dried dumplings dipped in a spice-laden meat sauce.

Street food is usually excellent and widely available. Look out for beef brochettes, fried fish, corn on the cob, fried bananas, egg sandwiches, sweet-potato chips and plates of rice and sauce.

Soft drinks are omnipresent, but local drinks such as ginger juice, or red *bissap* or *djablani* juice (which is brewed from hibiscus petals then chilled) and orange squash are sometimes available (but are not always sterile).

Although Mali is predominantly Muslim, most towns have at least one bar or hotel where you can buy Castel, a Malian lager. Flag, from Senegal, is also available in Bamako and Mopti.

# BAMAKO

**pop 1.3 million**
Bamako grows on you. Those who rush through will find Mali's capital to be a far cry from its origins as a small Bozo fishing village. Bamako today is sprawling and gritty, and can be a charmless place if you let the streets full of people, cars, buzzing flocks of *mobylettes* (mopeds) and its fair share of pollution get to you. And yet, expats who live here often end up loving the place; they're drawn in by great restaurants and a soundtrack provided by some of Africa's best music stars. Bamako's hotels are also excellent, while the National Museum is arguably the best in the region. If you're looking for a tranquil stay, you should probably look elsewhere, but if you like your markets colourful, clamorous and spilling into the surrounding streets, appreciate energy that illuminates the night and hanker for the opportunity to

### GUIDES IN MALI

Few topics occupy travellers' conversations in Mali quite as much as the question of guides. No matter where you go (Bamako, Djenné, Mopti and the Dogon Country are especially bad, although even sleepy Ségou is fast catching up), guides will sidle up and offer tours of the country, for which you pay a daily fee. They're persistent, regaling you with horror tales of thieves and the difficulty of travelling solo, which are simply not true.

If you don't want one, you certainly don't need a constant companion or intermediary to enjoy Mali. That said, in many places, such as Djenné or Timbuktu, a knowledgeable and informative local guide, hired on the spot for a few hours, can greatly enhance your visit. Guides are also highly recommended in the Dogon Country.

So, how to choose a guide? It used to be that every young Malian male could drop everything and become your guide to Mali, which meant that some were knowledgeable travel companions while others were charlatans. Thankfully, it has recently become a lot easier. Would-be guides have to take a comprehensive, one-year course organised by Mali's Ministry of Tourism, including written and oral exams. All accredited guides, who have completed the course and passed the exams, must now carry cards, which indicate whether they are accredited to guide nationally (blue) or only in their local district (yellow). To find such a guide, ask at the local tourist office, Mission Culturelle, hotel or tour operator, or ask other travellers for recommendations.

The system is not foolproof – not every guide who has passed the exam is necessarily good. Some guides can't read or write in French, meaning that they failed to sit the first-round of exams, and we have received unconfirmed reports of corruption allowing some budding guides to circumvent the exam process.

But overall, Mali's tourism authorities are to be commended on a system that has dramatically improved the situation.

---

befriend open and friendly locals, Bamako might just get under your skin.

## ORIENTATION

Bamako's city centre is on the north bank of the Niger River, focused on the triangle formed by Ave Kassa Keita, Blvd du Peuple and the train tracks. ACI 2000 is a new district, west of the centre, which will one day rival the downtown area as a commercial centre. The Quinzambougou and Hippodrome districts, northeast of the centre, are great places to find hotels, restaurants and nightclubs. Heading south from the centre, Pont des Martyrs leads across the river to Route de Ségou (also called Ave de l'Unité Africaine, OUA), the main road out of town – the Sogoniko *gare routière* is about 6km along this road. The Pont du Roi (west of Pont des Martyrs) carries a new highway that leads to Sénou International Airport (17km).

## INFORMATION

### Bookshops

Bamako suffers from a lack of good bookshops; check out the following.

**Azalaï Hôtel Salam** (Map p492; Next to Pont du Roi) The book shop here is also worth trying.

**Librairie Bah Grand Hôtel** (Map p494; ☎ 223 6705; Ave van Vollenhoven; ☽ 9.30am-1pm & 3-7pm Mon-Sat, 9.30am-12.30pm Sun) In the Grand Hôtel, has a decent selection of French books, magazines and newspapers; they also have occasional and hard-to-snaffle copies of *International Herald Tribune* and *Newsweek*.

### Cultural Centres

**Centre Culturel Américain** ( ☎ 223 6585; Badalabougou Est; ☽ 9am-4pm Mon-Wed, 1-4pm Thu, 8.30-11am Fri) South of town, carries US magazines and newspapers.

**Centre Culturel Français** (Map p494; ☎ 222 4019; www.ccfbamako.org; Ave de l'Indépendance; ☽ 9.30am-5.30pm Mon-Wed & Fri & Sat, 1.30-5.30pm Thu) Has a good library as well as a cinema and live performances; pick up their bimonthly programme.

### Emergency

**Ambulance** ( ☎ 15)
**Police** ( ☎ 17)

### Internet Access

**Ikatel** (Map p492; Route de Koulikoro; per hr CFA1000; ☽ 8am-11pm Mon-Fri, 9am-11pm Sat & Sun) Tech-savvy and with the fastest connections in town.

**Smint Cyber Café** (Map p494; Pl OMVS; per hr CFA500; ☽ 7.30am-10pm) Central but slower.

# BAMAKO

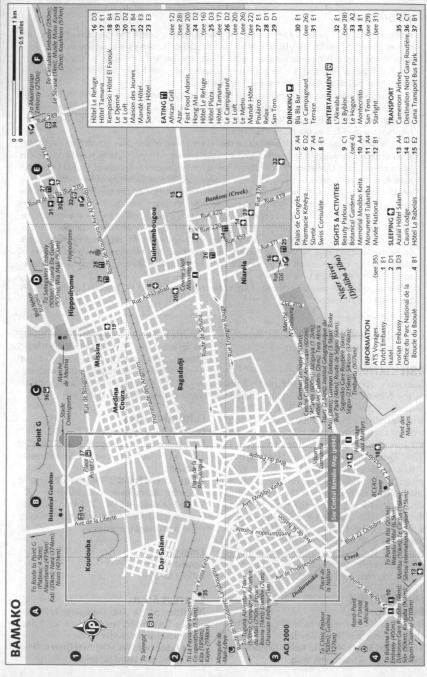

## Medical Services

**Clinique Pasteur** ( ☎ 229 1010; ☺ 24 hr) West of town, this is Mali's best hospital for African diseases, emergencies and other consultations; they have their own labs and handle insurance claims with a minimum of fuss.

**Hôpital Gabriel Touré** (Map p494; ☎ 222 2712; Ave van Vollenhoven)

**Pharmacie Kénéya** (Map p492; Rue Achkhabad, Quinzambougou)

**Pharmacie Officine Coura** (Map p494; Ave de la Nation)

## Money

**Banque de Développement du Mali** (BDM); Ave Modibo Keita (Map p494; Ave Modibo Keita); Rue de la Cathedral (Map p494; Rue de la Cathedral) Can exchange cash and travellers cheques, plus cash advances on Visa card.

**Bicim** (Map p494; Immeuble Nimagala, Blvd du Peuple) May do Visa transactions.

**BIM** (Map p494; Ave de l'Indépendance)

## Post

**Main post office** (Map p494; Rue Karamoko Diaby) Poste restante is fine for letters (CFA500 to collect), but unreliable for packages.

## Tourist Information

**Office Malien du Tourisme et de l'Hôtellerie** (Map p494; Omatho; ☎ 223 6450; www.tourisme.gov.ml; Rue Mohammed V) This is not set up for independent travellers, but has the occasional brochure and has list of guides.

Look out for *Le Dourouni*, a monthly listings magazine available free at some travel agencies and hotels, which has advertisements for local events, nightclubs and restaurants, plus listings for hotels and emergency services.

## Travel Agencies

Several agencies deal with international and domestic flights, for tickets consult the following:

**ATS Voyages** (Map p494; ☎ 222 2245; ats@ats.com.ml; Ave Kassa Keita)

**ESF** (Map p494; ☎ 222 5144; esf@cefib.com; Place du Souvenir) Long-standing and reliable.

**TAM Voyages** (Map p494; ☎ 221 9210; www.tamvoyage.com; Sq Lumumba)

For tours around Mali and further afield, the following companies are recommended, and can arrange English-speaking guides:

**TAM Voyages** (Map p494; ☎ 221 9210; www.tamvoyage.com; Sq Lumumba)

**Tara Africa Tours** ( ☎ 228 7091; www.tara-africatours.com; Baco Djicoroni ACI)

**Toguna Adventure Tours** ( ☎ /fax 2297853; toguna adventure@afribone.net.ml; ACI2000) West of town, Toguna are highly recommended.

## DANGERS & ANNOYANCES

Bamako is largely safe, although, like any city, it has its share of pickpockets and bag-snatchers, so take the normal security precautions and never carry valuables. Bamako train station, the trains themselves and Rue Baba Diarra are a popular haunts for thieves, especially at night. The streets around Sq Lumumba (especially close to the river) should also be avoided after dark.

## SIGHTS

### Musée National

The **Musée National** (Map p492; Ave de la Liberté; admission CFA2500, guide CFA3000; ☺ 9am-6pm Tue-Sun) is exceptionally good, with a stunning collection of masks, statues, textiles, archaeological artefacts and a fine model of the Djenné mosque. Since the renovations in 2003, it's beautifully presented and well-labelled, and the tranquil grounds, excellent bookshop and good restaurant make it an excellent place to spend an afternoon. French and English-speaking guides can be arranged.

### Musée Muso Kunda

This **museum** (Rue 161, Korofina Nord; admission free; ☺ 9am-6pm Tue-Sun) is a homage to Mali's women, with displays of traditional clothing and everyday household objects. Take a *sotrama* (battered green minibus; CFA150) or taxi (CFA1500) from the west end of Route de Koulikoro and ask for Fagigula (the museum is signposted from there).

### Musée de Bamako

**Musée de Bamako** (Map p494; Place de la Liberté, admission CFA500; ☺ 9am-6pm Tue-Sun) occupies a pleasant, if somewhat kitsch, garden in the centre of Bamako. The museum itself is still a work-in-progress, with some ethnographic exhibits (including a life-sized pirogue). Of greatest interest are the enlarged postcards of colonial Bamako; some still bear the original postmarks and date from the 19th century. Look especially for the photo of Bamako train station awash in crinolines and pith helmets – a far cry from the clamour today. There is also some local contemporary art upstairs.

MALI

# CENTRAL BAMAKO

0 ————————— 500 m
0 ————————— 0.3 miles

**INFORMATION**
American Embassy.....................1 C4
BDM........................................2 C5
BDM........................................3 C6
Bicim...................................(see 28)
BIM.........................................4 B6
Centre Culturel Français..............5 B6
DHL.........................................6 C6
ESF..........................................7 C5
French Embassy........................8 D6
Hôpital Gabriel Touré..................9 D3
Librairie Bah Grand Hôtel...........10 C3
Main Post Office......................11 C4
Nigerien Consulate...................12 B5
Office Malien du Tourisme et de
  l'Hotellerie.........................13 D5
Pharmacie Officine Coura...........14 B6
Smint Cyber Café.....................15 B6
TAM Voyages..........................16 D6

**SIGHTS & ACTIVITIES**
Fetish Stalls.........................(see 36)
Grand Marché.........................17 D4
Maison des Artisans...............(see 36)
Monument de l'Indépendance...18 B6
Musée de Bamako....................19 B4

**SLEEPING**
Hôtel Yamey...........................20 C6
L'Auberge Lafia.......................21 B6
Mission Catholique...................22 B5
Restaurant de la Paix................23 B5

**EATING**
African Grill............................24 B6
Appaloosa..............................25 C6
Café Restaurant la Casa...........26 B5
Food Stalls.............................27 B4
Food Stalls.........................(see 35)
Les Délices de Bamako.............28 D5
Pâtisserie le Royaume des
  Gourmands...........................29 C5
Restaurant Chinois Long Ma......30 B6
Restaurant de la Paix............(see 23)
Restaurant le Gourmet.............31 D5
Restaurant Sabunyuman 2.........32 B5
Soukhothai..............................33 C6

**DRINKING**
Appaloosa..........................(see 25)

**ENTERTAINMENT**
Buffet de la Gare.....................34 C3
Cinéma Vox............................35 C4

**SHOPPING**
Indigo...............................(see 24)
Maison des Artisans.................36 D4
Music Shop (Grand Hôtel)......(see 10)
Tokyo Color............................37 C5

**TRANSPORT**
Afriqiyah Airways..................(see 43)
Air Algérie.............................38 C4
Air Burkina........................(see 43)
Air France.............................39 D6
Air Ivoire..........................(see 43)
Air Mauritanie....................(see 39)
Air Sénégal International...........40 C5
Ethiopian Airlines.................(see 39)
Ghana Airways....................(see 16)
MAE Office.............................41 B6
Point Afrique..........................42 C6
Royal Air Maroc......................43 D6
Sotrama Stop......................(see 35)
Sotrama to Sogoniko Gare
  Routière..............................44 C4
Sotrama to Sogoniko Gare
  Routière..............................45 D6
Station Office.........................46 C3
Taxi Rank..............................47 D4

Stade
Omnisports

Place
Point G

To
Hippodrome
(1.8km)
Route de Koulikoro
(Ave Al Qoods)

Assemblé
Nationale

Place de la
République

Ave van Vollenhoven

Bamako Train
Station

Rue Baba Diarra

Rue de Rochester

Rue Archinard

36  Grande
    Mosquée
Route de Sotuba

To Niaréla (1km);
Quinzambougou
(1km)

Dabanani
Intersection

Ave de l'Artois

Rue Gouraud

Rue Laperrive

Ave Pasteur

Ave de la Marne

Ave de Verdun

Square
Lumumba

Ave Kassa Keita

Carrefour
des Jeunes

Place de
la Liberté

Rue Karamoko Diaby

Ave de la République

Place de
Bamako

Cathedral

Place du
Souvenir

Rue Caron

Blvd de la Paix

Rue de la Fosse (R328)

Rue 361

Ave de l'Indépendance

Rue 358

Rue 357

Rue 355

Rue Mamadou Konaté

Rue Bagayoko

Rue Diarra

Rue 351

Rue 322

Ave de Djako

Rue Ousmane Bagayoko

Bamako Coura

Rue Mohammed V

Rue Famolo Coulibaly

Rue 337

Rue Modibo Keita

Rue l'Enseigne Froger

Rue Poincarré

Quartier
du Fleuve

Ave Mamadou Sall

Diafarakanda (Creek)

Route 367

Rue de Dakar

Rue 136

Rue de la Nation

Place
l'OMVS

Place
du Fleuve

Rue Moussa Travelé

Blvd 22 Octobre

Ave Ruault

Ave de l'Yser

Rue 311

Rue 309

Rue 313

R306

To Pont du Roi (1.5km);
Sénou International Airport (14km)

Place
de la
Nation

To Pont des Martyrs
(150m); Sogoniko
Gare Routière (5.5km)

## Markets
The mother of all Bamako markets is the **Grand Marché** (Map p494), which spreads over an ever-expanding postcode of city blocks in the heart of town. It's a claustrophobic warren of streets, overtaken by traders of food, clothing and household goods, and can easily submerge into a crush of people and powerful smells. For those who've just arrived in Africa it can be a bit overwhelming, but it's an essential part of the Bamako experience. Mercifully, from 8.30am to around 5pm, vehicle traffic is diverted elsewhere.

The **fetish stalls** (Map p494; Blvd du Peuple), near the Maison des Artisans (see p500), is also not for the faint-hearted, offering up a stomach-turning array of bones, skins, dried chameleons and rotting monkey heads.

While the markets of central Bamako attract their fair share of touts, who gravitate towards travellers, the **Marché de Medina** (Map p492), northwest of the Hippodrome, is a large bustling place, where the locals do their shopping and traders are too busy making a living to bother hassling tourists. It's also a good place to buy second-hand clothes and, if you have a few hours, you can get your hair braided or your hands and feet decorated with henna in the **beauty parlour** (Map p492) section of the market.

**Marché de N'Golonina**, between Niaréla and the city centre, is another fascinating local market to visit.

## Point G
On the escarpment north of the city, **Point G** (Map p492) is great for a panoramic overview of Bamako (and, on a still day, its pollution). To get there, take a shared taxi from Place Point G (CFA200). Travellers report that there's a path up to it from the pleasant botanical gardens on Ave de la Liberté, although it can be easier to find coming down.

## SLEEPING
Bamako has a good range of places to sleep, although prices are generally expensive. Most of the midrange places have left behind the city centre to its chaos.

### Budget
**Mission Catholique** (Map p494; Foyer d'Accueil Bamako Coura; ☎ 222 7761; Rue Ousamane Bagayoko; per person CFA4000) This place gets high marks from travellers and could just be the best choice for those on a tight budget. Nun-run and set up for visiting church people, the Mission Catholique lets out the remainder (mattresses in the courtyard, dorms or private rooms) to travellers. It's a study in simplicity, but it's also clean, calm, secure and a haven from hassles in one of Bamako's busiest areas (the courtyard is kept locked and guests are given a key, for a deposit of CFA5000). Check-in is from 7am to 1pm and 4pm to 10pm Monday to Saturday, 5pm to 10pm Sunday.

**Maison des Jeunes** (Map p492; ☎ 222 2320; maisjeunes@yahoo.fr; off Sq Lumumba; dm with fan CFA2000, d with air-con & shared bathroom CFA6000; ⊠ ) The recently spruced-up Maison des Jeunes is fine budget value. Rooms are as simple as they come – so simple, in fact, that the management call them boxes, which is pretty accurate. Check the bed sheets for cleanliness in the larger dorms (they range in size from two to 12 beds). Shared bathrooms are cleaned daily, although the toilets are of the squat variety.

**L'Auberge Lafia** (Map p494; ☎ 636 6894; bocoume@yahoo.fr; Rue 367, Bamako Coura; dm CFA4000, d with fan from CFA9000) As far as cheapies go, the simple, bare and generally clean rooms with mosquito nets are pretty good value. The sleeping quarters are also back a little from the street and are ranged around a bare courtyard. It's not signposted but ask around, as it's well known in the surrounding streets.

**Jatiguiya** ( ☎ 223 9798; Rue 108, off Rue Abdel Gamel Nasser, Badalabougou l'Ouest; d with fan from CFA7000) This nicely somnambulant place has spare rooms with mosquito nets – some with showers – but it seems to make no difference when it comes to price. Simple meals are also available (CFA1500). It's a 20-minute hike into town across the river, but the area is good for those who like African streets to be home to local schoolchildren rather than guides.

**Restaurant de la Paix** (Map p494; ☎ 223 1118; Rue Bagayoko; rooms CFA4000) There's not much to be said about this place – rooms are bare and basic and won't have you running back at the end of the day – but it's cheap and has a good, simple restaurant. At the time of writing there were only three rooms but more were under construction.

### Midrange
**Hôtel Tamana** (Map p492; ☎ /fax 221 3715; www.hotel tamana.com; Rue 216, Hippodrome; d with shared/private bathroom incl breakfast CFA23,000/25,000; ⊠ ⊠ ⊡ )

This charming hotel out by the Hippo-drome is easily our favourite in Bamako. The rooms have character (though those with shared bathroom are overpriced), the staff are among Bamako's friendliest and most laid-back, the bathrooms are immaculate and the ambience of the leafy court-yard is wonderful to retreat into after a long Bamako day. There's also a swimming pool, a reasonably priced laundry service, a varied restaurant menu and the location – removed from the clamour of the city centre but close to good restaurants and bars – is also one that you'll soon appreciate. If you've spent any time researching Bamako hotels, you'll quickly realise what a great deal this is.

**Cauris Lodge** (Map p492; ☎ /fax 679 1438; hotelcaurislodge@yahoo.fr; Rue 220, Niaréla; s/d CFA20,000/25,000; ✖ ⚊ ) Although not quite as good as Hôtel Tamana, Cauris Lodge is in a similar vein. The seven rooms are simple, but nicely kept, and all have mosquito nets. African art abounds in the lobby and the paillote bar is one of Bamako's more intimate. There's an OK swimming pool and the surrounding streets are quiet and tree-lined – and have an unmistakeably African feel, without too much clamour.

**Sarama Hôtel** (Map p492; ☎ 221 0563; sarama@cefib.com; Rue 220, Niaréla; s/d CFA30,000/37,000; ✖ ⚊ ) Tucked away in the quiet streets of Niaréla, the Sarama is an interesting choice that sees fewer tourists than it deserves. Rooms are spacious, quiet and attractively furnished, and the super-friendly management is a plus. There's a small swimming pool and, although prices could be a notch lower, it represents terrific Bamako value.

**Hôtel les Colibris** ( ☎ 222 6637; hotelcolibris@yahoo.com; off Ave de l'OUA, Sogoniko; s/d from CFA20,000/25,000; ✖ ⚊ ) As far as Bamako prices go, Les Colibris is good value. It does have some of the stereotypical problems of an African hotel – staff who need to be roused in the afternoon and an attention to detail that could be sharper – but the rooms are well kept, spacious and worth every ceefah. The surrounding streets are quiet and leafy, and the hotel sprawls through a shady grounds (there's a pool) with bungalow-style accommodation and rooms in the main hotel building.

**Le Djenné** (Map p492; ☎ /fax 221 3082; djenneart@afribone.net.ml; off Route de Koulikoro; small d CFA21,000, larger s/d CFA30,000/35,000; ✖ ) If you're tired of hotels that mimic European ambience,

Le Djenné offers an antidote. Local and West African artists were given free rein to decorate this place – think masks, statues, African colour schemes and architectural flourishes that are rooted strongly in local culture. Some rooms are a bit dark, but all are highly original, well maintained and come with mosquito nets.

**Hôtel Le Refuge** (Map p492; ☎ 221 0144; lerefuge@arc.net.ml; Rue 326, Niaréla Sud; s/d CFA27,500/38,500; ✖ ⚊ ) This tranquil Lebanese-run hotel comes warmly recommended by travellers and by us. Rooms are cool, well-equipped, modern and spotless, if a little lacking in character. The surrounding streets are quiet and pleasant, the bar is good, the restaurant excellent and every room has satellite TV. There's also a small swimming pool.

**Le Loft** (Map p492; ☎ 221 6690; leloft@arc.net.ml; Rue Archkabad, Niaréla; s/d/ste CFA32,500/36,500/50,500; ✖ ⚊ ) We like this place. The building may not appear to be Bamako's most promising, but inside is another, completely renovated world. Rooms are light, airy and spacious, with an attention to style that's lacking in many Bamako hotels. Wrought-iron furnishings and European-standard bathrooms set the tone, with the occasional nod to African themes. Good service, satellite TV, double-glazed windows and an excellent restaurant are among the other highlights.

**Hôtel La Rabelais** (Map p492; ☎ 221 5298; touraine@afribonemali.net; Route de Sotuba, Quinzambougou; d/ste CFA38,000/57,000; Ⓟ ✖ ⚊ ) This excellent French-run hotel has much to commend it. Every room is different – some are brightly coloured, others have dark wooden beams – bathrooms are excellent and come with shampoos, soaps and fluffy towels, and there's also satellite TV, fridge and safes. The swimming pool wins our vote for Bamako's most inviting.

**Mandé Hôtel** (Map p492; ☎ 221 1993; mandehotel@afribone.net; Rue Niaréla, Cité du Niger; d/ste CFA42,000/55,000; Ⓟ ✖ ⚊ ) The Mandé wins the prize for having the nicest location of any hotel in Bamako. Yes, it's a long way from the city centre (a taxi should cost CFA1000), but its perch on a quiet stretch of the Niger River's bank is outstanding. The best views are reserved for the restaurant, while the bungalow-style rooms are set back behind the swimming pool. Rooms are good, if unspectacular, and the bathrooms are in need of a loving overhaul.

**MALI**

**Hôtel Yamey** (Map p494; ☎ 223 8688; gorainta datatech@toolnet.org; Rue 311, Quartier du Fleuve; d CFA17,500-25,500; 🔀) Hôtel Yamey is in a good location, close to the centre and adjacent to one of Bamako's restaurants and lively bars – which is just as well because the rooms, while fine, are a tad run-down. Price increases according to size – the cheapest rooms are pokey, the most expensive are large enough to leave your baggage lying around without falling over it whenever you get out of bed.

## Top End

**Azalaï Hôtel Salam** (Map p492; ☎ 222 1200; www.azalaihotels.com; next to Pont du Roi; d/ste from CFA75,000/125,000; P 🔀 🖥 🖳 🖳) One of Bamako's premier hotels, the Salam is a classy place, from the marble-lined lobby to the warmly furnished rooms, which are enormous, luxurious and equipped with everything to ensure a comfortable stay – satellite TV, Internet connection, minibar and safe. Add in the numerous gift shops, swimming pool, tennis courts, bars and restaurants, and there's everything you need here.

**Kempinski Hôtel El Farouk** ( ☎ 223 1830; www .kempinski.com; Blvd 22 Octobre; s/d/ste from CFA75,000/8 5,000/110,000; P 🔀 🖳) Opened in 2003, this is Bamako's most intimate and atmospheric top-end hotel. The public areas boast African art and the rooms are large, supremely comfortable and have all the bells and whistles. Unlike other riverbank hotels in Bamako, every room has a river-view, although the more you pay the better it is – the river suites have balconies overhanging the river, while the ambassador suite (CFA150,000) is like a large apartment with a sweeping balcony. The service is also good.

# EATING
## Restaurants

**San Toro** (Map p492; Route de Koulikoro; starters CFA2500, mains CFA4500; 🕑 lunch & dinner) This original place is run by the same people who brought you Le Djenné (opposite) and it shows. The décor is charmingly African and there are galleries of local art in the grounds. The specialties are quality Malian dishes (*the poulet au coco* is especially good) which can take a while to appear, but are always worth the wait. There's no alcohol, but there are tasty fruit juices. Best of all, in the evenings from around 8pm, there's

live kora music with djembe thrown in on Thursdays. Highly recommended.

**Soukhothai** (Map p494; ☎ 222448; Rue 311, Quartier du Fleuve; starters CFA3500-4500, mains CFA4500-7500; 🕑 lunch & dinner Mon-Fri, dinner Sat) Craving a *pad thai*? It's only CFA6000 away. You won't find more authentic Thai cuisine in Africa, and expats swear by this place as one of Bamako's best restaurants. We're inclined to agree. If you order a bottle of wine, you'll easily pay CFA20,000 per person, so you may want to save it for a special occasion, but it's a classy place. Reservations are recommended.

**African Grill** (Map p494; Pl OMVS; starters around CFA2000, mains CFA4000-5000; 🕑 lunch & dinner Mon-Sat) African Grill is a wonderful place to sample African specialties like *foutou* (sticky yam or plantain paste), *kedjenou* (slowly simmered chicken or fish with peppers and tomatoes) and *poulet yassa* (grilled chicken in onion and lemon sauce). There's a different *plat du jour* every day, a delightful oasis of a dining area, friendly service, and a steady stream of regulars. They also do sandwiches (CFA1500) and have a branch restaurant in the Musée National (p493), which opens the same hours as the museum. Warmly recommended.

**Le Compagnard** (Map p492; off Route de Sotuba, starters CFA3200-6000, mains CFA4200-6250; 🕑 6am-11pm) Top marks for this place. High quality French cooking, French wines and a switched-on ambience ensure plenty of regular customers among the expat community. The salad bar (CFA3900) is a nice touch and the wood-fired pizzas are as good as you'll find in Bamako.

**Pizzeria Da Guido** (Rue 250, off Blvd Nelson Mandela, Hippodrome; pizzas & pasta CFA4500-7500; 🕑 lunch & dinner Sat-Wed, dinner Fri) Expats swear this place in the northeast makes the best pizzas in town, but the Italian owners also do wonderful things with lasagne, ravioli, cannelloni, gnocchi and a different, but always tasty, *plat du jour* every day.

**Restaurant Chinois Long Ma** (Map p494; Ave de la Nation; starters from CFA1500, mains CFA3000-4000; 🕑 9am-11pm) One of the best of Bamako's many Chinese restaurants, Long Ma has tasty food, good service and a varied menu of the usual Chinese staples.

**Appaloosa** (Map p494; Rue 311, Quartier du Fleuve; starters CFA2000-4000, mains CFA3500-6500; 🕑 lunch & dinner) Spend any prolonged period of time in Bamako and you'll end up here at some stage; it's where Tex Mex meets Beirut

MALI

with the merest nod to Bamako. There are many highlights, including Lebanese meze, steaks and pizzas. There's also a popular bar (see right).

The best of the hotel restaurants are at **Mande Hôtel** (Map p492; ☎ 221 1993; Rue Niaréla, Cité du Niger), on a platform over the Niger River, **Le Refuge** (Map p492; ☎ 221 0144; Rue 326, Niaréla Sud), **Le Loft** (Map p492; ☎ 221 6690; Rue Archkabad, Niaréla), **Hôtel Tamana** (Map p492; ☎ /fax 221 3715; Rue 216, Hippodrome) and **Hôtel Plaza** (Map p492; Rue 326, Niaréla Sud; meals from CFA8000; ☽ lunch & dinner) which has good elevated views of Bamako.

## Cafés & Patisseries

**Pâtisserie le Royaume des Gourmands** (Map p494; Ave Modibo Keita; pastries & cakes CFA250-700; meals CFA1000-3000; ☽ 7am-11pm) It may not look much from the outside but this place is an air-con haven amid busy Bamako, with one of the nicest dining areas in downtown. More importantly, it's the best patisserie in town, with good croissants, coffee and fresh orange juice served with a smile.

**Les Délices de Bamako** (Map p494; Immeuble Nima-gala, Rue Famolo Coulibaly; meals CFA750-4000, pastries & cakes CFA250-600; ☽ 6am-midnight) This is a friendly and popular choice with cake eaters, although it's a bit down-at-heel.

**Relax** (Map p492; Route de Koulikoro; meals CFA2000-CFA3000, pastries CFA250-700 ☽ 24hrs) Relax, one of numerous patisseries in the Hippodrome area, this is popular at all hours, with rich cakes and some excellent pastries.

## Quick Eats

Snacks like brochettes (grilled pieces of meat on a stick) and chips are cooked on small barbeques all around town. At the *sotrama* ranks near the Cinéma Vox, as well as west of Place de la Liberté across from Carrefour des Jeunes, there are food stalls serving cheap rice and sauce.

In Bamako Coura, cheap and cheerful sit-down restaurants include **Restaurant de la Paix** (Map p494; Rue Bagayoko) and **Restaurant Sabunyuman 2** (Map p494; Rue 136, Bamako Coura), which both serve spicy Senegalese dishes for around CFA1000, and don't normally bother with printed menus. **Café Restaurant la Casa** (Map p494; Rue Ousmane Bagayoko; meals CFA750-1000) is a fine, relaxed backpacker hang-out opposite the Mission Catholique; their spaghetti, couscous and ragout dishes contain the freshest ingredients, but if you want meat you'll need to order in advance.

On the other side of Ave Modibo Keita, but still in the centre, **Restaurant le Gourmet** (Map p494; Rue Caron; meals CFA600-1000; ☽ 7am-6pm Mon-Sat) is another small and simple place, offering only two or three dishes per day (often rice with a stew or sauce).

For good Lebanese specialties, try **Poularco** (Map p492; Route de Bla Bla; starters CFA1250-3000, mains CFA3500-7500; ☽ 8am-midnight) which does decent shwarmas as well as grilled dishes and paninis; it's a great place to watch the passing parade in the evening. **Fast Food Adonis** (Map p492; Rue Achkhabad; meals CFA2500-3000), below Le Loft, offers more fast food, but it's one of the best in town.

**Hong Mai** (Map p492; Rue 220, Niaréla) does cheap and quick Vietnamese food, and is a Bamako institution.

## Self-Catering

For imported food and wine, try **Azar** (Map p492; Route de Koulikoro) or **Le Metro** (Map p492; off Route de Sotuba, Niaréla). There are good fruit and vegetable stalls at the *sotrama* rank near the Cinéma Vox and on Place OMVS.

## DRINKING

**Bla Bla Bar** (Map p492; Route de Bla Bla, Hippodrome; small beers CFA1000) This is Mali's most sophisticated bar, and is so well known that the road on which it sits is now named after the bar. Regulars lament that it has lost something since being glassed in and blasted with air-con, but it's still filled with the bold and the beautiful at weekends.

**Terrace** (Map p492; Route de Bla Bla, Hippodrome; small beers CFA1000; ☽ 8pm-late) Upstairs and open-air, Terrace is the place to go to gaze longingly into someone's eyes, if only because the high decibel music drowns out conversation streets away, let alone at the bar. It's a pretty upmarket crowd but the atmosphere, for all the noise, is agreeable.

If Bla Bla Bar and Terrace are too highbrow for you, there are plenty of earthy bars with an exclusively African clientele and outdoor tables between the Bla Bla and Route de Koulikoro.

**Le Campagnard** (Map p492; ☎ 221 92 96; www.le campagnard.com; off Route de Sotuba; small beers CFA1000; ☽ 11am-late) This is the sort of place where South African and Australian gold miners rub shoulders with Peace Corps volunteers, which should give some idea of the breadth of its appeal, although it's mainly a foreign crowd. In 1995, *Newsweek* voted this one of the best bars in Africa – it's not *that* good but it is terrific.

**Appaloosa** (Map p494; Rue 311, Quartier du Fleuve; beers CFA1500-3000) As good as the restaurant is here (see p497), the food's a sideshow for evening frisson with long-legged, blond-haired hostesses (who don't expect to pay for their drinks) rubbing shoulders (and other parts of the anatomy) with rich Malian men and world-weary escapists. Classily seedy, this is, for all its faults, a Bamako institution. Make of it what you will.

## ENTERTAINMENT
### Live Music
Bamako has some of the best live music in the world. Where else can you see some of the finest international performers just about every weekend? The problem is that they tend to change venues almost as soon as advertising banners go up, so either ring around, ask a savvy taxi driver, or pay a visit to check who's on the bill. For more information on Mali's musicians, see p488 and p58.

**Wassulu Hôtel** ( ☎ 228 7373; Route de l'Aeroport) When she's not in Paris or touring the world, Oumou Sangare plays at the hotel she owns at 9pm on Saturday evenings. Admission is free for guests of the hotel, or CFA2500 for nonguests.

**Éspace Bouna** ( ☎ 229 5468; Rue 360, ACI200) One of Bamako's most agreeable garden venues, Éspace Bouna sometimes plays host to the master kora player, Toumani Diabaté, as well as Djelimady Tounkara and the Super Rail Band. The big names are most likely to be on the bill on Friday or Saturday night at 10pm (admission CFA2500 if someone famous is playing), but otherwise the local salsa bands which fill in aren't half bad.

Moffou, a nightclub 10km southwest of Pont du Roi, is owned by the legendary Salif Keita, Moffou is really only worth it on the rare Saturday nights when he's playing. Otherwise you'll hear orchestras of varying quality.

**Le Hogon** (Map p492; off Ave Kassa Keita) Toumani Diabaté was playing here (CFA1500) when we were in Bamako, but this slightly seedy place always has traditional live music of some description from 9pm on Friday and Saturday nights.

**Buffet de la Gare** (Map p494; ☎ 228 7373; off Rue Baba Diarra) This is where the legendary Super Rail Band (which once included Salif Keita), made its name. Although they still play here from time to time, you're more likely to hear an up-and-coming local band on Friday and Saturday nights.

**Centre Culturel Français** (Map p494; ☎ 222 4019; www.ccfbamako.org) The CCF doesn't offer many concerts but, at least once a month, they do it in style – pairing anyone from Habib Koite, Kassy Mady Diabaté and Toumani Diabaté to Kandia Kouyate and Tartit. Check out their bimonthly programme for details.

Other places where live music is on the programme include **L'Akwaba** (Map p492; Route de Bla Bla); **Djembe** (Lafiabougou; admission CFA2000), west of town, where lots of Guinean musicians play; **Le Savanna** (Route de Koulikoro), east of town, which attracts Burkinabé stars; and **San Toro** (Map p492; Route de Koulikoro), a restaurant with live kora music from 8pm nightly.

### Nightclubs
Bamako is a city that comes into its own after dark, and on weekends it's a party town. Clubs don't get going before midnight and close around 6am. You won't hear a whole lot of African music, and male visitors will be propositioned by women hoping to be their expensive friend, but all of that is secondary to the feel-good vibe. On Friday and Saturday places really jump, and most clubs also open Thursday and Sunday. Cover charges (CFA5000) usually include a drink, and after that drinks cost CFA1000 to CFA3000. If you leave Bamako without visiting at least one of the following for some high-octane dancing, you haven't really understood what makes the city tick: **L'Atlantis** (Badalabougou Est) South of the river. **Le Byblos** (Map p492; Route de Koulikoro, Hippodrome) **Montecristo** (Map p492; Rue 249, off Route de Koulikoro, Hippodrome) **Starlight** (Map p492; Route de Bla Bla, Hippodrome)

## SHOPPING
**Mia Mali** ( ☎ 221 2442; www.miamali.com; 1528 Blvd Nelson Mandela; ⏰ 10am-6pm Tue-Sat) Far and away the most innovative and stylish boutique in Mali, Mia Mali has eminently reasonable prices and its commitment to working with over 175 artisans deserves to be supported. The array of items for sale – silver jewellery, masks, statues, textiles, artwork and home

furnishings – is endless and of the highest quality. In addition to traditional pieces, Elaine Belleza, the American owner, and her local craftspeople combine traditional themes with creative design twists. If you only visit one shop in Bamako, make it this one. To get here, head north along Route de Bla Bla, turn right (east) on Blvd Nelson Mandela, then look for the sign about 200m after you reach the mosque; Mia Mali is on the right.

**Maison des Artisans** (Map p494; Blvd du Peuple) Leather goods and woodcarvings are made and sold here, and there are several jewellers offering gold and silver objects, which are sold by weight (watch out for gold-plated brass). Bargaining is tough. Even if you don't plan to buy, it can be a good place to get an idea of price and selection.

**La Paysanne Women's Cooperative** (off Ave Kassa Keita) West of the city centre, this friendly place promises some great fabrics, designed and printed by women from the surrounding area.

**Indigo** (Map p494; ☎ 222 0893; www.indigo.com.ml; Place l'OMVS; ⏰ 9am-7pm Mon-Sat) A charming, if small, boutique in the city centre, Indigo has reasonable prices for a well-chosen selection of textiles, masks, statues, musical instruments, crafts and home decorations.

Although you can find handicrafts in most of Bamako's markets (for more details see p495), the Marché N'Golonina has the best selection.

For the latest CDs of Mali's international music stars, try the music shop in the lobby of the **Grand Hôtel** (Ave Van Vollenhoven; ⏰ 9.30am-1pm & 3-7pm Mon-Sat, 9.30am-12.30pm Sun). Prices are on a par with European prices (CFA20,000 per CD), but buying here means the musicians get royalties, unlike the bootleg copies you find around town, which do untold damage to Mali's music industry.

Bamako's best places for print film and processing is **Tokyo Color** (Map p494; ☎ 222 3498; Ave de la Nation), although if you're buying slide film, check the expiry dates.

## GETTING THERE & AWAY
### Air

Bamako's Sénou International Airport also serves a number of domestic routes which are shared between **MAE** (Map p494; ☎ 223 1465; Ave de la Nation) and **CAM** (Map p494; ☎ 229 9100; Ave Cheick Zayed, Hamdallaye). For more details on these two airlines, see p543.

| Bamako to | Fare (CFA one-way) | Departures | Airline |
|---|---|---|---|
| Gao | 120,900 | Saturday | CAM |
| Kayes | 57,850 | 4 weekly | MAE, CAM |
| Mopti | 57,860 | 3 weekly | MAE, CAM |
| Timbuktu | 90,360 | 3 weekly | MAE, CAM |

### Boat
The big boats leave from Koulikoro, some 50km downstream of Bamako. For details on the Niger River boat service see p545.

### Bus
Long-distance transport for destinations south of the Niger River leaves from the Sogoniko *gare routière*, 6km south of the city centre on the left-hand side of the road heading south (CFA2000 by taxi, CFA125 by *sotrama*). This is home to **Bani** (☎ 220 6081), **Bittar** (☎ 220 1205) and **Somatra** (☎ 220 9932). About 2km back towards town is the bus park for **Binke** (☎ 220 5683). These companies have dozens of services heading north along the Bamako–Gao road.

Transport for destinations north of the Niger River leaves from **Destination Nord gare routière** (below Place Point G) or around Marché de Medina. Truck-buses to Kita leave at least three times a day, while services to Nioro, Nara and Timbuktu (only in the dry season) leave a couple of times a week. Transport to Koulikoro (CFA1000) leaves when full.

Also handy for Koulikoro, Timbuktu and Kangaba is the **Gana Transport** (☎ 221 0978) bus park at Place Point G.

| Bamako to | Fare (CFA) | Duration (hrs) |
|---|---|---|
| Bandiagara | 9500 | 9-11 |
| Douentza | 10,500 | 10-12 |
| Gao | 16,000 | 16-20 |
| Kita | 3000 | 4 |
| Mopti | 8000 | 7-10 |
| Nioro | 11,000 | 24-28 |
| Ségou | 3000 | 3 |
| Sikasso | 4500 | 3 |
| Timbuktu | 17,000 | 24-30 |

### Train
Tickets can be bought in advance from the **station office** (Map p494; ☎ 222 8110) – come with the correct change and plenty of patience, as queues can be long and chaotic. Tickets

bought from touts may not be valid. Beware of thieves amid the crowds.

There's a service from Bamako to Kayes (2nd/1st class CFA6960/11,670, 10–14 hours) on Sunday, Monday and Friday, which returns the following day. You can also take the Wednesday morning service, which runs to Dakar via Kita (2nd/1st/ couchette class CFA4600/6370/9375) and Kayes (2nd/1st/couchette class CFA11,480/ 16,190/22,190).

For details on international train services, see p544.

## GETTING AROUND

The official rate from the airport to the city centre by private taxi is CFA7500, although it should cost CFA5000 going the other way.

The battered green *Sotramas* run from central Bamako to the *gares routières* and the outer suburbs for between CFA75 and CFA150. Important stops are marked on the Central Bamako map.

Most taxis in Bamako are yellow. Those with a 'taxi' sign on the roof are shared, while those without signs are for private hire (*déplacement*) only. The longest journey (such as Sogoniko *gare routière* to Hippodrome) in a private taxi should never cost more than CFA2000, although most journeys should cost half that.

# AROUND BAMAKO

## KOULIKORO

Koulikoro may have been an important place in colonial days, when the train from Dakar terminated here, but today most visitors only come here to catch the Comanav boat to Timbuktu. In November, there's an annual marionette festival at Diarabougou, roughly 20km east of town.

**Motel le Saloon** ( ☎ 226 2024; d CFA13,500; ⊠ ) is the most pleasant place to stay, while close to the river east of town **Centre d'Accueil Regional** ( ☎ 262261; d CFA10,000) has passable rooms.

Plenty of transport leaves from Koulikoro market for Bamako's Destination Nord *gare routière* (CFA1000, one to two hours). Gana Transport has four buses a day from Place Point G. The **Comanav office** ( ☎ 226 2095; fax 226 2009) is on the western outskirts of town. See p545 for more information.

# THE CENTRE

Central regions of Mali are dominated by the Niger River, Mali's lifeblood, a transporter of people, and the antidote to Mali's often bleakly arid countryside. As a traveller, the Niger River is also your guide to seeing the best that Mali has to offer – you may leave it behind at times, but generally you'll follow its path through the country, and each time you arrive on the riverbank you'll re-enter an African world that has changed little over the centuries.

## SÉGOU

**pop 92,500**

There's something about Ségou; while Mopti is an example of clamorous riverbased comings-and-goings, Ségou, strung out lazily along the riverbank 230km east of Bamako, has a languid slow-paced charm and there's an unmistakeable sense that it remains a village in disguise. With its wide avenues, faded colonial buildings and nearby river excursions, it's a wonderful place to slow down, rest from life on the African road and get a sense of the Mali that exists beyond its tourist sites.

### Information

**BDM** (Blvd de l'Indépendance) Changes cash and travellers cheques.

**Cybercafé Sotelma** (Blvd de l'Indépendance; per hr CFA1000; ⊗ 8am-9pm) Old computers but quite fast connections.

**Pharmacie Officine Adam** ( ☎ 232 0643; Blvd de l'Indépendance)

**Quai des Arts** (Quai Ousmane Djiri; ⊗ 8.30am-1.30pm & 2.30-6pm Tue-Sun) A private tourist office that's little more than a man and a map, but is more than the tourist office can muster; friendly and eager to help with information on hotels, transport, restaurants and sights.

### Sights & Activities

Ségou's tree-lined streets just back from the riverbank (especially along Blvd El Hadj Omar Tall and the eastern stretches of Blvd de l'Indépendance) are enjoyable, with plenty of former colonial buildings bearing traces of decaying colonial elegance. From the small but interesting pottery market on the riverbank, it's a pleasant stroll to the Quai Ousmane Djiri area, which is slowly being developed with replica traditional

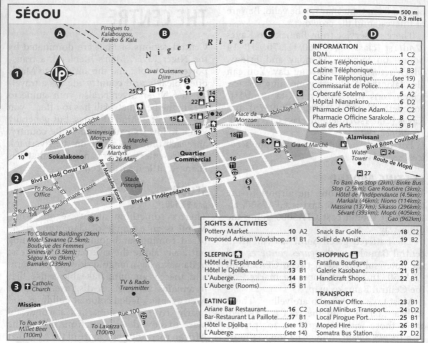

### SÉGOU

**INFORMATION**
| | |
|---|---|
| BDM | 1 C2 |
| Cabine Téléphonique | 2 C2 |
| Cabine Téléphonique | 3 B3 |
| Cabine Téléphonique | (see 19) |
| Commissariat de Police | 4 A2 |
| Cybercafé Sotelma | 5 A2 |
| Hôpital Nianankoro | 6 D2 |
| Pharmacie Officine Adam | 7 C2 |
| Pharmacie Officine Sarakole | 8 C2 |
| Quai des Arts | 9 B1 |

**SIGHTS & ACTIVITIES**
| | |
|---|---|
| Pottery Market | 10 A2 |
| Proposed Artisan Workshop | 11 B1 |

**SLEEPING**
| | |
|---|---|
| Hôtel de l'Esplanade | 12 B1 |
| Hôtel le Djoliba | 13 B1 |
| L'Auberge | 14 B1 |
| L'Auberge (Rooms) | 15 B1 |

**EATING**
| | |
|---|---|
| Ariane Bar Restaurant | 16 C2 |
| Bar-Restaurant La Paillote | 17 B1 |
| Hôtel le Djoliba | (see 13) |
| L'Auberge | (see 14) |

| | |
|---|---|
| Snack Bar Golfe | 18 C2 |
| Soliel de Minuit | 19 B2 |

**SHOPPING**
| | |
|---|---|
| Farafina Boutique | 20 C2 |
| Galerie Kasobane | 21 B1 |
| Handicraft Shops | 22 B1 |

**TRANSPORT**
| | |
|---|---|
| Comanav Office | 23 B1 |
| Local Minibus Transport | 24 D2 |
| Local Pirogue Port | 25 B1 |
| Moped Hire | 26 B1 |
| Somatra Bus Station | 27 D2 |

buildings (including an artisan workshop and exhibition area).

Market day in Ségou is Monday and, although it's not a patch on the Djenné spectacular, it's still an African experience with loads of atmosphere.

From the waterfront, pirogues can take you on excursions to some nearby sites, such as to Kalabougou, where pottery is produced (and fired at weekends), and Farako, a centre for mud-cloth making. Trips cost from CFA15,000 per boat. In Kalabougou, you'll also have to pay a CFA3500 tourist tax (per group, not per person as some unscrupulous guides are fond of saying). Opposite Ségou, the interesting fishing village of Kala can be reached by public pinasse (CFA200).

The historic and beautiful village of Ségou Koro lies 9km upstream, just off the main Bamako road. In the 18th century it was the centre of Biton Mamary Coulibaly's Bambara empire, and the great man is buried here. Its crumbling Bambara buildings are interspersed with three ancient mosques (including one right on the riverbank) which are compact and pleasing. Intro-

duce yourself to the chief, who collects the CFA2500 tourist tax. A taxi to/from Ségou costs at least CFA10,000, and a guided tour around CFA2500.

### Festivals & Events

Since 2005, Ségou has hosted the **Festival Sur le Niger** ( ☎ 232 1804; www.festivalsegou.org) in the first week of February. At this time, the riverbank comes alive with exhibitions, dance, theatre and puppet performances, storytelling and craft displays. As the festival gains reputation, it may even attract some of Mali's music stars for concerts.

### Sleeping

**Hôtel le Djoliba** ( ☎ /fax 232 1572; www.segou-hotel -djoliba.com; cnr Rue 21 & Blvd El Hadj Omar Tall; dm CFA4000, s/d with fan & shared bathroom CFA10,000/17,000, with air-con & satellite TV CFA20,000/25,000; ⊠ ) This is our choice for the best hotel in town, combining a great location, just back from the riverbank, with large and pleasant rooms and great service. There's also something to suit all budgets, a good restaurant, and an ambience in which European quality is wedded to an African air of tranquillity. For some, the lack of a swimming pool may be a drawback.

**L'Auberge** ( ☎ 232 1731; www.promali.org/aub-ind; Rue 21; s/d/ste CFA23,000/25,000/35,000; 🗙 🗩 ) Long Ségou's best hotel, L'Auberge is still a favourite for many travellers. It's one of those African hotels where 4WDs park out the front and travellers fill the bar and restaurant. The garden (with swimming pool) is delightful and the restaurant excellent. The only drawback is that the decent (if unspectacular) rooms are a short block away.

**Hôtel de l'Indépendance** ( ☎ 232 1733; hotel independence@cefib.com; Route de Mopti; s/d with fan CFA12,000/16,000, with air-con CFA18,000/22,000; 🅿 🗙 🗩 ) If this place wasn't 4.5km southeast of town (CFA300 in a shared taxi), it would come close to topping our list for its quality rooms (tastefully decorated and with some character), pleasant courtyard and service. Lebanese-run, its restaurant is terrific, plus there's secure parking and a large swimming pool.

**Motel Savane** ( ☎ 232 0974; savane@motelsavane .com; off Blvd de l'Indépendance; d with fan/air-con CFA10,000/18,000, bungalows CFA20,000-26,000; 🗙 ) If you don't mind being a pleasant 10-minute walk from the riverbank, Motel Savanne has spacious, sparkling rooms with splashes of colour and character. It's also wonderfully quiet, has a shady garden area, and they sometimes offer drumming classes.

**Hôtel de l'Esplanade** ( ☎ /fax 232 0127; esplanade@ afribone.net.ml; Quai Ousmane Djiri; s/d with fan & shared bathroom CFA10,000/12,500, with private bathroom from CFA17,000/19,500; 🗙 ) Position, position, position. Although most rooms don't take advantage of the riverside locale, walk out the door and there's the Niger in all its glory. The rooms may now be overhauled, as the hotel was recently brought under Italian management. Expect nice touches rather than major renovations.

If the dorm at Hôtel le Djoliba (the only highly recommended budget beds in town) is full, cheap beds can also be found at **Lavazza** (right; d from CFA7500) but they're big, bare and noisy.

## Eating & Drinking

**Soleil de Minuit** (cnr Rue 21 & Blvd El Hadj Omar Tall; starters CFA1300-2000, main CFA1700-2200, 3-course meal CFA4000; ☾ 6am-midnight) Highly regarded by travellers for its fresh ingredients and laid-back atmosphere, this place is warmly rec-

ommended. The *capitaine a la Bamakoise* (fried Nile perch with bananas and tomato sauce; CFA4000) is a highlight.

**Ariane Bar Restaurant** (Rue 21; starters CFA1000-2000, mains CFA800-3000, breakfast from CFA1200; ☾ 7.30am-midnight) They love the TV in this place (it often holds the waiters spellbound) so escape to the garden. The cooking's nothing special but they do *poulet yassa* and prices are reasonable.

**Bar-Restaurant La Paillote** (Quai Ousmane Djiri) This wonderful riverside location is about to be wedded to fine Italian cooking – in November 2005 it came under the guidance of the owners of the excellent Pizzeria Da Guido in Bamako, so expect high-quality Italian cooking. They have traditional djembe and balafon artists on Friday nights and a local orchestra at 9pm on Saturday.

There are a couple of cheap restaurants at the *gare routière* and **Snack Bar Golfe** (Route de Mopti) is good for a quick sit-down meal.

Of the hotel restaurants, **Hôtel le Djoliba** ( ☎ /fax 232 1572; cnr Rue 21 & Blvd El Hadj Omar Tall) is excellent, and they serve good pizzas on the terrace on Saturday nights. **Hôtel de l'Indépendance** ( ☎ 232 1733; Route de Mopti) does good local and Lebanese specialties which are well worth the trip south of the centre, and **L'Auberge** ( ☎ 232 1731; Rue 21) also does good pizzas. All three also have well-stocked and pleasant bars.

Away from the centre, **Lavazza** ( ☾ 9pm-late Thu-Sat) is an intimate garden venue where traditional and modern live music can be heard.

In the same area, locals brew thick, brown and bubbling millet beer that is worth trying; Rue 97 behind the cathedral is arguably the best.

## Shopping

You can find Bambara pottery at the **pottery market** (Route de la Corniche), 1km southeast of the centre. For Ségou strip cloth and blankets, try the **Grand Marché** (Route de Mopti). A large group of curio sellers (heavy on the woodcarvings) can be found opposite L'Auberge. Bargain hard.

**Farafina Boutique** (Rue 15; ☾ 8.30am-12.30pm & 3-6pm Mon-Sat, 8.30am-12.30pm Sun) sells a small range of clothes, textiles (including *bogolan* mud cloth) and jewellery. For a wider range of *bogolan* textiles, check out **Galerie Kasobane** (Rue 21; ☾ 9am-6pm Mon-Sat).

## Getting There & Away

Many buses leave from the *gare routière*, 3km east of town on Route de Mopti. Somatra has a separate bus park nearby and Binke Transport and Bani are based along or just off Route de Mopti.

Numerous buses to Bamako (CFA3000, almost hourly), Mopti/Sévaré (CFA6000) and Sikasso (CFA4500) pass through Ségou daily. A few buses head up to Gao (CFA14,000).

**Comanav** ( ☎ 232 0204) also has an office in Ségou; see p545 for details of boat services from Ségou to elsewhere in Mali.

Minibuses to local destinations collect passengers on the dirt road behind the Elf petrol station. There are frequent buses to Markala (CFA1000), while the noon bus continues on to Massina (CFA3000).

Mopeds can hired along Rue 21 for CFA6000 per day.

## AROUND SÉGOU

Markala, north of Ségou, is the gateway to the Office du Niger irrigation scheme, and has an amazing bridge/dam and an interesting market. In March it hosts a fascinating marionette festival. From the pleasant Fula village of Massina, you can start a trip along the Niger by public pinasse (large pirogue). A good first stop is Diafarabé (CFA1500). There are basic places to stay in all three villages.

## DJENNÉ

**pop 22,382**

One of the premier sites in West Africa, World Heritage–listed Djenné, which sits on an island in the Bani River, is worth as much time as you can give it. Its incomparable mosque – the largest mud-built structure in the world – is like a fairytale apparition from a child-like imagination and provides Djenné with a backdrop to its huge, lively and colourful Monday market, one of the best of its kind in West Africa. By Monday evening, most of the tourists and traders have left – if you buck the trend and stay a few more days, you'll enjoy the labyrinthine streets and sleepy atmosphere virtually undisturbed. Away from the crowds, you'll quickly discover that Djenné is one of West Africa's oldest towns, and that little has changed since its heyday during the 14th and 15th centuries, when it profited, like Timbuktu, from trans-Saharan trade, and was a revered seat of Islamic learning. All of which adds up to what is unquestionably one of the most interesting and picturesque towns in West Africa.

## Information

Visitors to Djenné must pay a CFA1500 tourist tax per person; it's collected at the checkpoint at the Djenné turn-off, soon after leaving the Bamako–Mopti road.

There are no banks in Djenné, but you may be able to change euros or dollars at **Le Campement** ( ☎ 242 0497) or **Auberge le Maafir** ( ☎ 242 0541). Phone calls can be made at the post office. The hospital is on the western edge of town and **Pharmacie Alafia** is central.

Guides are not essential in Djenné, although hiring a good one will open your eyes to aspects of Djenné you'd otherwise

---

**THE GREAT CROSSING**

All across central Mali from November, you're likely to see vast Fula herds closing in on the Niger River, readying themselves for one of West Africa's most picturesque annual rituals. Every late December or early January (the exact date of the crossing is not set until November because much depends on water levels), Diafarabé and other places along the Niger with large Fula populations are transformed into hives of activity, as hundreds of thousands of cows are driven southwards and across the Niger River to greener pastures. The crossing, known as *Dewgal*, dates back almost 200 years, and is a happy time for the Fula herders, who have been on the fringes of the Sahara for many months. The crossing means reunion with their families and a time to celebrate with music and dance. Fula women adorn themselves in all their ritual gold and amber finery, while the men paint and decorate their favourite animal to see who owns the finest and fattest beast.

Other smaller cattle crossings are held throughout the inland delta region in December or January, including in Sofara. This rarely visited small village, 2km west of the Bamako–Gao road just north of the Djenné turn-off, has two good-looking mosques and a large cattle market on Tuesday. Its cattle crossing is two weeks after the one at Diafarabé.

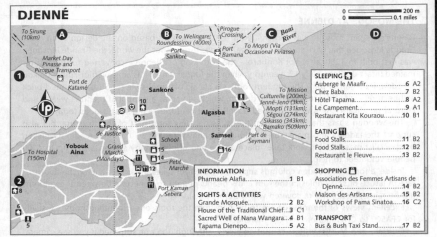

**DJENNÉ**

| SLEEPING |
| --- |
| Auberge le Maafir...................6 A2 |
| Chez Baba.............................7 B2 |
| Hôtel Tapama.......................8 A2 |
| Le Campement......................9 A1 |
| Restaurant Kita Kouraou.........10 B1 |

| EATING |
| --- |
| Food Stalls............................11 B2 |
| Food Stalls............................12 B2 |
| Restaurant le Fleuve.............13 B2 |

| INFORMATION |
| --- |
| Pharmacie Alafia......................1 B1 |

| SIGHTS & ACTIVITIES |
| --- |
| Grande Mosquée.......................2 B2 |
| House of the Traditional Chief...3 C1 |
| Sacred Well of Nana Wangara...4 B1 |
| Tapama Dienepo......................5 A2 |

| SHOPPING |
| --- |
| Association des Femmes Artisans de |
| Djenné..............................14 B2 |
| Maison des Artisans...............15 B2 |
| Workshop of Pama Sinatoa....16 C2 |

| TRANSPORT |
| --- |
| Bus & Bush Taxi Stand............17 B2 |

miss. Some guides speak English and fees are negotiable (aim for CFA3000 per person).

## Sights

### MISSION CULTURELLE

Before touring the town properly it's worth visiting the **Mission Culturelle** (admission free; ☯ 9am-4.30pm), which gives an excellent background to Djenné and the surrounding region. Apart from some photos and artefacts from Jenné-Jano (p506), there are some fine old photos of Djenné. The well-informed staff can recommend good guides. It's just before entering Djenné if you're coming from the ferry.

### MONDAY MARKET

Every Monday, the wide open area in front of the mosque is transformed into a clamorous market, which has barely changed since the days when Saharan camel caravans brought salt across the sands to the gates of Djenné. Thousands of traders and customers come from miles around, and many of these itinerant traders follow the calendar of local market days in the region's villages, their week culminating in Djenné. Most arrive the night before, and by 6am on market day traders are already staking out the best sites (ie those with shade). By mid- to late-morning (the best time to visit the market), the open square in front of the mosque is filled with traders selling everything from cloth to calabashes, spices to spaghetti and pottery to pungent local

foods and prize goats. It spills over into the surrounding streets, especially those to, the west. It's all the more atmospheric because it's a local's market, with little on sale for tourists, and stallholders are too busy hawking their wares to each other to worry about the intrusion of travellers. Put simply, this market experience is not to be missed.

### ARCHITECTURE OF OLD DJENNÉ

You'll struggle to find a modern building anywhere in Djenné where, unusually for Africa, many of the mud-brick houses are over a storey high; traditionally, the top part was for the masters, the middle floor for the slaves and the bottom floor for storage and selling. The porches of the houses are lined with wooden columns, and the wooden window shutters and doors are painted and decorated with metal objects. Several of the most impressive houses once belonged to Moroccan traders and are decorated in a Moorish style, with elaborate windows and doors; the skill required to build such adornments is today the preserve of just one family of Djenné artisans. You'll also see Fulani-style entrances, with their covered entrances.

On a stroll through the dusty streets you'll pass a few **madrassas** (schools where young children learn the Qur'an); there are more *madrassas* in Djenné than in any other town in Mali, which serves as a reminder of its days as a renowned centre of Islamic scholarship. With the help of a guide, you can also see the old **Sacred Well of**

MALI

---

## THE MOSQUE AT DJENNÉ

Djenné's elegant mosque was constructed in 1907, though it's based on the design of an older Grande Mosquée that once stood on the site. Famous throughout the world, the Grande Mosquée was first built in 1280, after Koi Konboro – the 26th king of Djenné – converted to Islam. It remained intact until the early 19th century when the fundamentalist Islamic warrior-king, Cheikou Amadou, let it fall to ruin. The modern form – a classic of Sahel-style (or Sudanese) mud-brick architecture – is faithful to the original design, which served as a symbol of Djenné's wealth and cultural significance, and which dazzled travellers for centuries – much as it does today.

The wooden spars that jut out from the walls not only form part of the structure, but also support the ladders and planks used during the annual repairs to the mud-render. Overseen by specialist masons, this work takes place at the end of every rainy season, when up to 4000 people volunteer to help.

Inside, a forest of wooden columns supporting the roof takes up almost half of the floor surface. A lattice of small holes in the roof allow beams of light to penetrate between the columns (in the rainy season they're covered with ceramic pots).

Excellent views of the mosque are to be had from the roofs of surrounding houses (usually for CFA500 to CFA1000) or the Petit Marché.

Officially non-Muslim visitors cannot go inside, although don't be surprised if you see camera-toting tourists high on a minaret. Bear in mind that, not only have they paid anywhere up to CFA10,000 to local opportunists keen to cash in on the tourist dollar, but they're also trampling on local sensibilities in the process.

---

**Nana Wangara** and the beautiful **house of the traditional chief**, whose role today is mainly as an adjudicator in local disputes. On the southern edge of town is **Tapama Dienepo**, the tomb of a young girl sacrificed here (she volunteered, according to locals) in the 9th century, after a local religious leader decided the town was corrupt.

### JENNÉ-JENO

About 3km from Djenné are the ruins of Jenné-Jeno, an ancient settlement that dates back to about 300 BC. Implements and jewellery discovered here suggest that it may have been one of the first places in Africa where iron was used, and exposed the myth that no organised cities existed in West Africa before trade began and external influences were brought to bear upon it. In the 8th century AD, Jenné-Jeno was a fortified town with walls 3m thick, but around 1300 it was abandoned. Today, there's nothing much to see – some mounds and millions of tiny pieces of broken pottery – so a visit is of greater historical rather than aesthetic interest.

## Sleeping & Eating

Djenné suffers from a severe shortage of hotel rooms, so for all but budget hotels, you should book ahead to beat the tour-group invasion.

**Le Campement** ( ☎ 242 0497; mattress on roof CFA4000, s/d with fan CFA10,000/12,500, with fan & bathroom CFA15,000/17,000, with air-con & bathroom CFA18,000/20,000; meals from CFA2000; 🔀 ) This sprawling, handily located place is Djenné's tourism centre, with dozens of rooms across a wide price range, a large and pleasant open-air restaurant, and clean and tidy rooms which have the bare essentials. The spartan annexe rooms are fine, but suffer from the unfortunate problem of mosquito nets which block the air generated by the fan – making for a hot night.

**Auberge le Maafir** ( ☎ 242 0541; sinintadiawoye@yahoo.fr; d fan/air-con CFA18,000/23,000, incl breakfast; 🔀 ) More intimate than the Campement, this pleasant place has attractively furnished rooms with some traditional design work (such as terracotta basins), but maintenance is not what it could be. The courtyard is pleasant and the views from the rooftop are good. Some quiet and fascinating Djenné streets lie just outside the door and you're within an easy walk to the mosque. No alcohol is served and dinner is CFA4000.

**Restaurant Kita Kouraou** ( ☎ 242 0138; mattress on roof CFA1500, r per person CFA2500) Rooms here are simple and clean, if cell-like (without windows), but it's a friendly place. The restaurant offers tasty, traditional Malian and

European staples from CFA1500. A nice, if basic, bolt-hole.

**Chez Baba** ( ☎ 242 0598; camping CFA2500, dm CFA3500) It's hard to know what to make of this place. The large, open courtyard could, at a stretch, resemble an old *caravanserai* or travellers' inn, but it also has all the comings-and-goings (guides and salesmen especially) of a bus station. Meals are available for CFA300. The rooms with mattresses on the floor are swept clean, and the mattresses on the roof have good views, but the shared toilets resemble the black hole of Calcutta.

**Hôtel Tapama** ( ☎ 242 0527; residencetapama @yahoo.fr; mattress on roof CFA2000, d with bathroom & fan from CFA10,000) Hôtel Tapama is showing its age, with bare neglected rooms, not averse to the occasional cockroach, and bathrooms that seem to be slowly falling apart. It's a pity, because the Moroccan-style internal courtyard and the surviving traces of the building's former elegance suggest that, with some renovations, it could be a terrific place with a nice feel. It's often full, more for reasons of Djenné's bed shortage than quality. Meals are around CFA2000.

There are a number of stalls serving food near the market in the early evening, while **Restaurant le Fleuve** (dishes CFA750-2000) offers simple Malian dishes which are best ordered in advance.

## Shopping
Djenné is famous for *bogolan*, or mud-cloth (see p69). Although the cloth is on sale all across town, the most famous female artisan is **Pama Sinatoa** ( ☎ 242 0610; almamydiaka@yahoo.fr), whose workshop is near the town entrance. The quality is top-notch, the selection enormous, and in the showrooms they do demonstrations on how the cloth is dyed. The sales pitch is more encouraging than hard-sell and they tend to be open daylight hours. You could also try the **Maison des Artisans** or the **Association des Femmes Artisans de Djenné**.

## Getting There & Away
### BOAT
Djenné is away from the main river routes, but when the Bani River is high enough (usually from July to December), it's possible to arrive by public pinasse (CFA4000) from Mopti. There's a semi-regular Sunday service as well as departures on other days.

For the rest of the year, everything goes by road.

### BUS & BUSH TAXI
Very little transport goes into Djenné except on Monday (market day). Most transport will drop you at the junction on the Mopti–Bamako road, 30km from Djenné itself, from where you may have a long wait for a lift into town.

Transport to Djenné is easiest from Mopti's *bâché gare – bâchés* (CFA2000) and Peugeot taxis (CFA2500) leave from here most mornings, and return in the afternoon. The journey takes about two hours.

Transport from elsewhere, such as Sikasso (CFA7000) and Ségou (CFA5000) arrives Monday morning and leaves in the afternoon.

Just before Djenné there's a short ferry crossing. Costs from CFA500 to CFA2000 depending on the vehicle size and the hour.

## AROUND DJENNÉ
Welingare and Roundessirou are two of the most interesting Fula villages a few hundred metres north of Djenné and well worth the walk. Most travellers cross by

---

**FULA EARRINGS**

In Djenné, Mopti and other towns along the Niger, you will occasionally see well-to-do Fula women dressed very elaborately – although there are very few who do so on a daily basis, with most reserving such attire for festive occasions. Adornments include large bracelets of silver and necklaces of glass beads. Most spectacular, however, are the huge gold earrings called *kwotenai kanye*, worn by the wealthiest women. They are so heavy that the top of each earring is bound with red wool or silk to protect the ear, and is sometimes supported with a strap over the top of the woman's head. Earrings are given as wedding gifts from the woman's husband, who will have had to sell off several cows to afford them, but Fula women remain financially independent of their husbands, so gold and jewellery is often passed down from mothers to daughters. If you don't get to see a women dressed in this way, some of Mali's postage stamps bear photos.

the bridge on foot (to the west) or hire a moped, but it costs CFA150 to cross by pirogue. Sirung, a beautiful Bozo village with a stunning mud mosque, is approximately a 20-minute moped ride southwest from Djenné. Bicycles (CFA3500 per day) and mopeds (CFA6000 per day including fuel) are available for hire and this can be arranged at most hotels in Djenné.

## MOPTI

pop 109,456

In Mopti, tourism is a contact sport, with more guides, pinasse owners and touts per square metre than anywhere else in Mali. That said, clamour is central to Mopti's charm – its port is Mali's most lively and interesting – and you'll have to pass through here if you want to take a pinasse trip to Timbuktu. It's also a major staging post for journeys into the Dogon Country, and has reasonable transport connections to Djenné. If it all gets too much, stay in Sévaré, 12km away – which has great hotels and better transport options – and just come into Mopti when you have to.

Like many other Malian settlements, Mopti – at the junction of the Niger and Bani Rivers – is an agglomeration of quarters made up of several ethnic groups (especially Bozo and Fulani) who have been coming here for centuries to trade. Surrounded by rice fields and the river that is the city's reason for existence, Mopti can be hard work, but it's a necessary stop-off, and can even be fun.

### Information
#### GUIDES
For a recommended guide, ask at your hotel, the tourist office, other travellers, or contact the local guides association **AGTM** ( ☎ 679 3916), who speak English.

#### INTERNET ACCESS
**Action Mopti Internet** (off Ave de l'Indépendance, Old Town; per hr CFA1500; ☯ 8am-1pm & 4-8pm Mon-Sat) Super-fast satellite connections.
**Librairie & Cybercafé de la Venise** (Ave de l'Indépendance; per hr CFA1000; ☯ 8am-1pm & 4-8pm Mon-sat) Central but slow.

#### MEDICAL SERVICES
**Hospital** ( ☎ 243 0441; Blvd de l'Indépendance) Offers basic health care.

**Pharmacie Officine du Carrefour** ( ☎ 243 0422; Ave de l'Indépendance)
**Pharmacie Officine de La Venise** ( ☎ 243 0377; off Ave de l'Indépendance)

#### MONEY
Some hotels and shopkeepers will change cash and travellers cheques; CFA650 to the euro is possible but CFA640 is more common. Remember that banks in Mopti close at 11am on Friday and don't open again until Monday.
**BCEAO** (Route de Sévaré) Changes euros.
**BDM** (off Ave de l'Indépendance) Might do cash advances on credit cards, but don't count on it.
**BIM** (Blvd de l'Indépendance) Changes euro (cash only) and is a Western Union agent.

#### POST & TELEPHONE
**Post office** (Rue 68; ☯ 8am-12.30pm & 1-4pm) Poste restante.
**Sotelma** (Rue 68; ☯ 8am-10pm) Has cardphones.

#### TOURIST INFORMATION
**Bureau Régional du Tourisme** ( ☎ 243 0506; mopti tourisme@hotmail.com; Blvd l'Indépendance) About 200m north of Hôtel Kanaga; services are improving all the time.

#### TRAVEL AGENCIES
The following two companies can assist with travel reservations, hire 4WDs and run a range of river trips and Dogon treks:
**Bambara Africa Tours** ( ☎ /fax 243 0080; bambara@bambara.com; Hôtel Kanaga)
**Satimbé Travel** ( ☎ 243 0791; www.satimbetravel .com; Ave de l'Indépendance) An excellent company run by Issa Ballo.

#### VISA EXTENSIONS
**Comissariat de Police & Sûreté** (Route de Sévaré; ☯ 8.30am-2pm & 5-8pm Mon-Thu, 8.30am-12.30pm Fri) One-month visa extensions cost CFA5000 and take about 15 minutes to process.

### Dangers & Annoyances
Mopti is the centre of Mali's tourist industry and your visit can be tarnished by local and hard-to-shake youths continually offering their services as guides, or simply trying to sell you postcards and souvenirs.

### Sights & Activities
Mopti's port is Mali's busiest and most evocative, it's a lively place where boats from up and down the river unload their

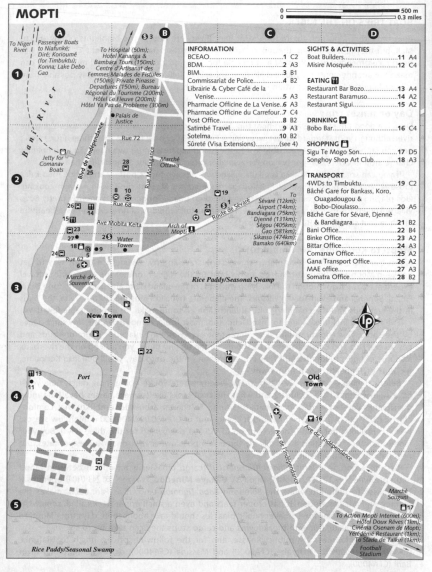

# MOPTI

0 _____ 500 m
0 _____ 0.3 miles

To Niger
River

Passenger Boats
to Niafunké;
Diré; Korioumé
(for Timbuktu);
Konna; Lake Debo
Gao

To Hospital (50m);
Hôtel Kananga &
Bambara Tours (150m);
Centre d'Artisanat des
Femmes Malades de Fistules
(150m); Private Pinasse
Departures (150m); Bureau
Régional du Tourisme (200m);
Hôtel Le Fleuve (200m);
Hôtel Ya Pas de Probleme (300m)

**INFORMATION**
BCEAO...........................................1 C2
BDM..............................................2 A3
BIM................................................3 B1
Commissariat de Police...............4 B2
Librairie & Cyber Café de la
   Venise.......................................5 A3
Pharmacie Officine de La Venise..6 A3
Pharmacie Officine du Carrefour..7 C4
Post Office...................................8 B2
Satimbé Travel.............................9 A3
Sotelma......................................10 B2
Sûreté (Visa Extensions)........(see 4)

**SIGHTS & ACTIVITIES**
Boat Builders..............................11 A4
Misire Mosquée..........................12 C4

**EATING** 🍴
Restaurant Bar Bozo....................13 A4
Restaurant Baramuso...................14 A2
Restaurant Sigui.........................15 A2

**DRINKING** 🍷
Bobo Bar....................................16 C4

**SHOPPING** 🛍
Sigu Te Mogo Son.......................17 D5
Songhoy Shop Art Club..............18 A3

**TRANSPORT**
4WDs to Timbuktu.......................19 C2
Bâché Gare for Bankass, Koro,
   Ouagadougou &
   Bobo-Dioulasso.......................20 A5
Bâché Gare for Sévaré, Djenné
   & Bandiagara............................21 B2
Bani Office..................................22 B4
Binke Office................................23 A2
Bittar Office................................24 A2
Comanav Office..........................25 A2
Gana Transport Office.................26 A2
MAE office..................................27 A3
Somatra Office............................28 B2

To
Sévaré (12km);
Airport (14km);
Bandiagara (75km);
Djenné (131km);
Ségou (405km);
Gao (581km);
Sikasso (474km);
Bamako (640km)

Rice Paddy/Seasonal Swamp

New Town

Port

Old
Town

Rice Paddy/Seasonal Swamp

Marché
Souguni

To Action Mopti Internet (600m);
Hôtel Doux Rêves (1km);
Cinéma Osenam de Mopti;
Yérédémé Restaurant (1km);
To Stade de Taïkiri (1km);

Football
Stadium

---

cargoes. You'll see slabs of salt from Timbuktu, plus dried fish, firewood, pottery,
goats, chickens and much more. You'll
also see a wonderful cast of characters,
from stylishly dressed local women taking
a pirogue back home and small boys diving
into the water, to grizzled fishermen who
regard it all with the disdain of the ancients.

Boat building happens next to Restaurant
Bar Bozo.

The classic Sahel-style **Misire Mosquée**
(Grande Mosquée; Ave de l'Independance), built in
1933, towers over the old part of town.
Just before the rains in May or June the
lower, mud-covered part of the mosque
is re-rendered. The mosque is off-limits

## BOAT TRIPS ON THE NIGER

Boat trips from Mopti on the Niger and/or Bani Rivers are one of the highlights of any trip to Mali, but they're also among the most daunting to organise. **Satimbé Travel** ( ☎ 243 0791) has been recommended as a pleasant and reliable local operator to deal with and most guides can make the arrangements on your behalf. Remember that longer boat trips are only possible from July or August to December when water levels are high.

### Day or sunset trips

Dusk is a good time to take a short boat trip. There are numerous Fula and Bozo villages along the river, although your standard sunset excursion (CFA25,000 per boat for less than three hours) won't get you far beyond Mopti – probably just to the island separating the two rivers. Tour companies charge around CFA15,000 per person for a smaller pirogue (without a motor) for half a day.

If you can spare a day, Kotaka is a Fula village well known for its pottery and a fine mud-brick mosque, and the Bozo village of Kakalodaga really comes alive at dusk, with women cooking, kids playing and men repairing their nets and building boats. Tongorongo is another pretty Bozo village known for its mosque and pottery. A little further afield is Konna, which has a beautiful mosque (but sits on the Bamako–Gao road).

### Mopti to Korioumé (for Timbuktu)

If you can spare the time (two nights, three days), travelling by pinasse is a terrific way to get between Mopti and Timbuktu. Indeed a slow boat up the Niger is one of the great African travel experiences. You'll go through the low-lying wetlands of the inland delta and pass fascinating Bozo, Fulani, Songhaï and even Tuareg villages. The elaborate riverside mosques of the Delta, the birds in the wetlands and the changing cultural landscape en route make for a memorable few days.

The first day includes sailing to Lake Debo and, most likely, camping on the low sand dunes by the shore. This enormous lake is an important over-wintering place for migratory birds and has several Fula and Bozo villages on its shores. By the second night, you'll sleep on the riverbank a couple of hours before Niafunké. By late afternoon on the third day, you'll pull into Korioumé, the port of Timbuktu, 18km from town.

Before signing up to any river trip, check exactly where you're going, how much time you'll have sightseeing, what's included, and what the boat looks like (some pinasses have little more than planks covered in thin foam mats to sit on). To charter a boat to Timbuktu that comfortably seats 10 people, you won't get much change out of CFA450,000/400,000 in high/low season; petrol is included but food is not (count on CFA15,000 per person for the three days). Buy your food in advance. Arranging a trip directly through a boat owner may get you cheaper rates, but negotiations can be difficult.

Getting a ride on a large *pinasse transporteur* (cargo pinasse) is an option between Mopti and Korioumé (CFA12,000, about two days). **Bakaye Minedou Traore** ( ☎ 243 0104) operates a big pinasse to Timbuktu, while the 80m-long *Baba Tigamba* (known as *Petit Baba*) makes the journey on Friday afternoon. It has proper seats and even a small upper deck called, somewhat ambitiously, the *cabine luxe*! Smaller public pinasses should take about three days from Mopti to Korioumé (CFA9000), but with breakdowns and cargo stops they can take up to six.

For shorter journeys by public pinasse, aim for the following prices: north to Niafunké (CFA4000) or south to Diafarabé (CFA3000) and Massina (CFA4000), or to Djenné along River Bani (CFA4000).

to non-Muslims, but money (CFA500 to CFA1000) can buy you a good view from a nearby rooftop.

East of the mosque is the old town, where tourists rarely venture. It's an interesting place to wander around, although the architecture is pretty modern by the standards elsewhere in Mali. There are separate Fula, Bella, Bobo and Mossi quarters.

At the **Marché Souguni**, to the southeast of town, traders sell fruit, vegetables, salt, fish and meat downstairs and art and crafts upstairs. A smaller market sells herbs, spices, traditional medicines and food stuff, and nearby is a small Bobo bar which features bellaphone music and millet beer (see right).

## Sleeping

Mopti has two top hotels, but many travellers prefer to stay in Sévaré (p512).

**Hôtel Ya Pas de Probleme** ( ☎ /fax 243 0246; www .yapasdeprobleme.com; off Blvd de l'Indépendance; mattress on roof with mosquito net CFA3500, dm CFA4500, s/d with fan & shared bathroom CFA10,000/13,500, with fan & shower CFA15,000/18,000, with air-con & private bathroom CFA22,000/25,000; 🌣 ) Mopti has been crying out for a place like this. A delightful French- and Dogon-run place, Ya Pas de Probleme has beautifully decorated rooms, an intimate and homely atmosphere and represents top value across a range of budgets. In addition to the spacious rooms, there's likely to be a terrace restaurant, larger dorm and more rooms to choose from by the time you arrive. The owners Olivier, Jean Marie and Ousman, are wonderful hosts.

**Hôtel Kanaga** ( ☎ 243 0500; kanaga@bambara .com; Blvd de l'Indépendance; d CFA53,000; P 🌣 🛋 ) They may have hiked their prices, and it may lack a personal touch, but this former Sofitel is the classiest place in town. Rooms are stylish and come with satellite TV and superb bathrooms with real shower receptacles. The swimming pool and restaurant are both excellent. It's 1km north of the centre on the banks of the Niger.

**Hôtel Doux Rêves** ( ☎ 243 0490; Rue 540; mattress on roof CFA3500, s/d with shared bathroom from CFA9000/12,000, with private bathroom from CFA12,000/ 15,000) Although it looks better from the outside than it actually is, the rooms here are simple (if a touch depressing) and the ambience in the surrounding streets is unmistakeably African. Some rooms are bigger than others and all have mosquito nets, although not all have toilet seats.

**Hôtel le Fleuve** ( ☎ /fax 243 1167; Rue 86; d with fan/ air-con CFA10,000/20,000; 🌣 ) These bog-standard Mali hotel rooms are bare, but clean, and the whole place suffers from not receiving many tourists (the service goes missing at times). Then again, when the tourists arrive, so too will the guides. The rooms in the newer annexe are slightly better.

## Eating & Drinking

**Restaurant Baramuso** (Rue 68; meals from CFA500) This is the place for a wonderful cheap lunch in the centre of town.

**Yérédémé Restaurant** (off Ave de l'Indépendance; meals CFA1500-3000) In the southeast of the Old Town, opposite Stade de Taï'kiri, Yérédémé offers reasonable food served in a nice shady courtyard. It also sells mango and bissap jam for CFA1000 and makes clothes to order.

**Restaurant Bar Bozo** (meals CFA1800-3000; 🕑 lunch & dinner) While the food is average tourist fare and the service is incompetent (a two-hour wait for your meal to arrive is not unusual), Restaurant Bar Bozo is superbly located at the mouth of Mopti harbour. The passing panorama of Mopti river life could easily occupy an afternoon, so even if you don't eat here, stop by for a drink, preferably at sunset. It's a shame it starts running out of *everything* by 8pm.

**Restaurant Sigui** (Blvd de l'Indépendance; meals CFA2500-3000; 🕑 lunch & dinner) This popular place gets the thumbs-up from travellers for its hybrid of European, Asian and Malian dishes, with a few vegetarian options thrown in. It's the best place to eat in town. They cook up a mean *capitaine a la Bamakoise* (fried Nile perch with bananas and tomato sauce) among other dishes.

**Hotel Ya Pas de Problem** (off Blvd de l'Indépendance; mains from CFA2000) and **Hôtel Kanaga** (Ave de l'Indépendance; meals CFA7500) are two good hotel restaurants; the latter does excellent smoked *capitaine* sandwiches.

Numerous food stalls cluster around the *gare routière*, port and entrance to town. In the Old Town is a small **Bobo bar** (cnr Rue 271 & Rue 282) where bellaphone music is sometimes played, continuing as long as people keep drinking millet beer.

## Shopping

There's a fantastic range of art and craft for sale in Mopti, but you'll need to negotiate with some of Mali's toughest traders. Although you'll find crafts from all over Mali, Mopti is famous for blankets, and with hard bargaining, you can get the all-wool variety (made by combining six or seven long thin bands) from around CFA5000, a wool-cotton mix for CFA7500, all-cotton ones with simple coloured squares for CFA10,000 or CFA12,500 for a more complex design. Ornate Fula wedding blankets can cost CFA50,000 or more.

There are numerous artisan stalls upstairs at **Marché Souguni**. **Sigu Te Mogo Son** and a group of disabled people who make handicrafts, are also based here. Opposite Hôtel Kanaga, just off Blvd de l'Indépendance, is **Centre d'Artisanat des Femmes Malades de Fistules** ( 🕙 8am-1pm & 4-8pm Mon-Sat), a local association helping handicapped women and selling textiles and weaving.

One of the best boutique-style shops in Mopti is the central **Songhay Shop Art Club** ( 🕙 8am-1pm & 4-8pm Mon-Sat) which is more expensive and largely fixed price, but its jewellery and textiles are good quality.

## Getting There & Away

### AIR

The airport is about 2km southeast of Sévaré and 14km from Mopti. **CAM** ( ☎ 243 1261) and **MAE** ( ☎ 679 4979; off Ave de l'Indépendance) each have at least two flights a week to Timbuktu (CFA43,360) and Bamako (CFA57,860). CAM also has one flight per week to Gao (CFA85,200, via Timbuktu). A private taxi from Mopti to the airport costs at least CFA6000.

### BOAT

From Mopti many travellers head for Korioumé (Timbuktu's port) by boat. **Comanav** ( ☎ 243 0006) has an office on the waterfront, though tickets can be hard to come by as this is the busiest sector on the boat's itinerary. For details on the Niger River boat service see p545.

For details on travelling by pirogue and public or private pinasse, see the boxed text p510.

### BUS & BUSH TAXI

Although some buses continue as far as (and originate in) Mopti, Sévaré is now the main transport hub for the region. Bus company offices in Mopti are marked on the map. For details on destinations and prices, see opposite.

*Bâchés* (CFA200) and Peugeot taxis (CFA250) cover the 12km between Mopti and Sévaré between 7am and 8pm daily (a private taxis costs CFA2500). They leave from the *bâché gare* at the town entrance. Transport also leaves here every morning for Djenné (CFA2000) and Bandiagara (CFA1750). Bâchés and Peugeot taxis leave from near the port some mornings for Bankass (CFA3000, two hours) and Koro (CFA5000, three hours).

To Timbuktu (CFA15,000, 12 hours on a good day), 4WDs leave most days from behind the *bâché gare*. It's a hard journey.

## SÉVARÉ

This bustling little town has not a single sight worth seeing, but it's much more relaxed than neighbouring Mopti, has terrific places to stay, and ample transport connections. Bandiagara and the Dogon Country are just 63km away.

## Information

**BNDA** (Route de Mopti) Charges 2% commission on travellers cheques and cash.
**Post office** (Route de Mopti) Does Western Union office transfers.

## Sleeping & Eating

All of the following places are either on or signposted off the main road through town.

**Mac's Refuge** ( ☎ 242 0621; malimacs@yahoo.com; Rue 124; camping without/with own equipment CFA6000/4500, s/d with fan & shared bathroom CFA12,000/18,000, with fan & private bathroom CFA18,000/21,000, with air-con CFA21,000/25,000; 🅿 🗷 🗷 ) One of the best places to stay in Mali, Mac's is indeed a refuge. Rooms are individually styled to reflect the culture of Mali's many ethnic groups – with Bobo masks, Bozo fishing nets and Tuareg leather cushions and so on. The food here is legendary (there's a banquet meal – CFA5000 – of a different cuisine at 7pm every night) and his buffet breakfasts (included in room and camping prices) are enough to make you want to stay longer. Add a small pool, bicycle hire (CFA1000 per day), a small reference library on Malian culture and Mac's talents as a qualified masseur (CFA15,000 per hour) and you'll soon see why it's so popular.

**Mankan Te Bed & Breakfast** ( ☎ 242 0193; www .mankan-te.de; off Route de Bamako; s CFA15,000-19,000, d CFA16,500-20,500; 🗷 ) Another outstanding choice, the intimate Mankan Te has lovingly maintained rooms with splashes of colour, super-clean bathrooms and mosquito wire (no holes) on the windows. In addition to the redoubtable Jutta, the owner and a fount of practical knowledge on the region (her website is excellent), there are also five tortoises in residence. It's warmly recommended, and a couple of blocks away from the B&B, Jutta also runs a restaurant,

**Mankan Te Restaurant** (www.mankan-te.de; Route de Bamako; mains CFA2000-5000, 3-course meals CFA4000-8500; ☺ lunch & dinner), that is quickly earning a reputation as one of the region's best. A garden setting and a wide variety of dishes (vegetarian, pasta, African specialties) make this an excellent place. It turns into a late-night bar after the kitchen closes.

**Hôtel Ambedjele** ( ☎ 242 1031; www.ambedjele hotel.com; off Route de Mopti; s/d CFA34,000/40,000; mains CFA200-4500; ☒ ☒ ℗ ) Styled like a Dogon village, just off the road between Mopti and Sévaré, this charming Spanish-run place has expansive gardens, a rock pool for swimming and bungalows shaped like a Dogon granary. They're not huge, but are beautifully decorated with terracotta basins, exposed stone walls and stylistic flourishes throughout. There are mosquito nets in the rooms and the grounds are sprayed twice daily. The restaurant (Spanish flair wedded to African flavours) is one of the best in Mali.

**Hôtel Flandre** ( ☎ 242 0829; www.hotelflandre.com; off Route de Bamako; s/d CFA20,000/22,500; ☒ ) While there are more stylish places in town, the well-run Flandre boasts super-clean and spacious rooms that are well-appointed and come with satellite TV (one of only two hotels in the Mopti region to have the latter, and the only one in this price range). There are also plans for a swimming pool, and some English is spoken.

**Hôtel Via-Via** ( ☎ 679 4841; www.viaviacafé.com; Route de Bandiagara; camping CFA3000, s/d with air-con & breakfast CFA12,500/15,000; ☒ ) Right next to the *gare routière*, but quiet and peaceful, the Via-Via is handy in a town with little to see and where all the hotels are a long way from anywhere. It's a newish place, and it needs a while for the trees to mature, but the rooms are tiled and spotlessly clean.

## Shopping

**Farafina Tigne** ( ☎ 242 0449; www.farafina-tigne.com; Route de Bamako; ☺ 8am-8pm) One of the best shops in the country, Farafina Tigna has an extensive selection of quality Malian handicrafts, including bogolan cloth and Tuareg jewellery. There's also zero sales pitch.

## Getting There & Away

### AIR

Although the regional airport is in Sévaré, travel agents talk about planes to Mopti. For details about flights between Sévaré/

Mopti and other Malian towns see opposite. For international flights to/from Mopti with Point Afrique, see p543.

### BUS

Sévaré is on a busy transport route with plenty of transport coming and going from the **gare routière** (Route de Bandiagara). Any transport going along the main Bamako–Gao highway stops at the main crossroads in the centre of town. Buses headed to Bamako (CFA8500, seven to 10 hours), Ségou (CFA5000, four to six hours), Gao (CFA7000, nine to 13 hours), Douentza (CFA3500, three hours), Hombori (CFA4500, four hours) are among the options.

Occasional minibuses go to Bandiagara (CFA1750) and Bankass (CFA3000). *Bâchés* head to/from Mopti (CFA200) between 7am and 8pm from close to the post office.

## AROUND SÉVARÉ

The ruins of Hamdallaye, the capital of Cheikou Amadou's 19th-century Fula empire, are 17km from Sévaré on the Route de Bamako. The site is about 3km across, but the mud walls that once encircled Hamdallaye have eroded down to small banks of earth, and this is all that now remains of the once grand buildings. The high stone wall that surrounded the mosque now encircles the simple tombs of Cheikou Amadou and his son Alaye Cheikou. A few nomadic Fula set up camp here from time to time, and there are plans to build a large new mosque at this important Fula pilgrimage site.

# DOGON COUNTRY

In this era of top-10-places-to-see-before-you-die lists, Dogon Country (Pays Dogon) features prominently, and deservedly so. Mali's stand-out highlight encompasses the homeland of the fascinating Dogon people, arrayed above and below the huge Falaise de Bandiagara, which extends some 150km through the Sahel to the east of Mopti. The landscape is stunning, and the Dogon people are noted for their complex and elaborate culture, art forms and unique houses and granaries – some clinging to the bare rock face of the escarpment.

The best way to see Dogon Country is on foot. Treks along the escarpment are possible for anything from between one day and three weeks. Ancient tracks link village with village and the plateau with the plains. In places, carefully laid stones create staircases up a fissure in the cliff face, while elsewhere ladders provide a route over a chasm or up to a higher ledge.

On standard treks, daily distances are often short, allowing plenty of time to appreciate the people and landscape while avoiding the heat in the middle of the day.

## History

Before the Dogon reached the escarpment, it was inhabited by the Tellem people. The origins of the Tellem are unclear – Dogon tradition describes them as small and red

skinned – and none are believed to remain today, although some Dogon say that the Tellem now live on the plains to the east. The vertical cliff is several hundred metres high, yet the Tellem managed to build dwellings and stores in the most inaccessible places. Most cannot be reached today, and the Dogon believe the Tellem could fly, or used magic powers to reach them. Another theory suggests that the wetter climate of the previous millennium allowed vines and creepers to cover the cliff, providing natural ladders for the early inhabitants. The Tellem also used the caves to bury their dead, and many are still full of ancient human bones.

The Dogon were first brought to the attention of the outside world through the

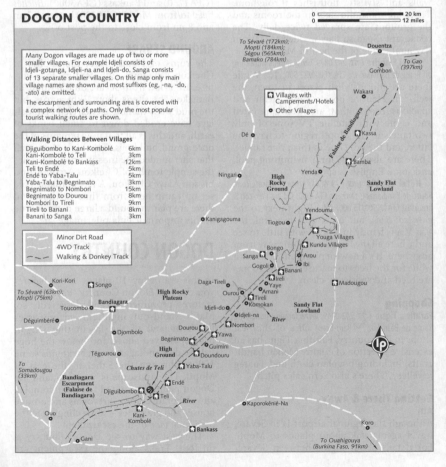

**DOGON COUNTRY**

0 _____ 20 km
0 _____ 12 miles

Many Dogon villages are made up of two or more smaller villages. For example Idjeli consists of Idjeli-gotanga, Idjeli-na and Idjeli-do. Sanga consists of 13 separate smaller villages. On this map only main village names are shown and most suffixes (eg, -na, -do, -ato) are omitted.

The escarpment and surrounding area is covered with a complex network of paths. Only the most popular tourist walking routes are shown.

| Walking Distances Between Villages | |
|---|---|
| Djiguibombo to Kani-Kombolé | 6km |
| Kani-Kombolé to Teli | 3km |
| Kani-Kombolé to Bankass | 12km |
| Teli to Endé | 5km |
| Endé to Yaba-Talu | 5km |
| Yaba-Talu to Begnimato | 3km |
| Begnimato to Nombori | 15km |
| Begnimato to Dourou | 8km |
| Nombori to Tireli | 9km |
| Tireli to Banani | 8km |
| Banani to Sanga | 3km |

Minor Dirt Road
4WD Track
Walking & Donkey Track

Villages with Campements/Hotels
Other Villages

To Sévaré (172km); Mopti (184km); Ségou (565km); Bamako (784km)

Douentza
To Gao (397km)
Gombori
Wakara
Falaise de Bandiagara
Dé
Kassa
Ningari
High Rocky Ground
Yenda
Bamba
Sandy Flat Lowland
Kanigagouma
Yendouma
Tiogou
Youga Villages
Kundu Villages
Bongo
Arou
Sanga
Ibi
Gogoli
Banani
Daga-Tireli
Ireli
Madougou
Kori-Kori
Songo
Ourou
Yaye
Amani
High Rocky Plateau
Tireli
Komokan
Sandy Flat Lowland
To Sévaré (63km); Mopti (75km)
Bandiagara
Idjeli-do
Idjeli-na
River
Toucombo
Déguimbéré
Djombolo
Dourou
Nombori
Yawa
Begnimato
Guimini
High Ground
Doundouru
Tégourou
Yaba-Talu
To Somadougou (33km)
Chutes de Teli
Bandiagara Escarpment (Falaise de Bandiagara)
Djiguibombo
Endé
Teli
River
Kaporokénié-Na
Ouo
Kani-Kombolé
Koro
Gani
Bankass
To Ouahigouya (Burkina Faso, 91km)

work of French anthropologist Marcel Griaule, whose influential book *Dieu d'Eau: Entretiens avec Ogotemmêli* (published in 1948) was the result of many years of living and studying near the village of Sanga. Griaule died in France in 1956, and a plaque near a dam he helped build marks the spot where the Dogon believe his spirit resides. Griaule's book was published in English under the title *Conversations with Ogotemmêli* in 1965, and is still available.

## Guides

Guides are not strictly necessary in a practical sense, but in a cultural sense they are vital. Ideally a guide will be your translator, fixer (for accommodation and food) and verbal guidebook, not to mention a window into the Dogon world. Without one you'll undoubtedly miss many points of interest, and could genuinely offend the Dogon villagers by unwittingly stumbling across a sacred site. All guides speak French and some also speak English or other European languages.

As a general rule, it's much better to hire your guide at one of the gateway towns than in Mopti or Bamako, although more importantly, your guide to the Dogon Country should be a Dogon. Non-Dogon guides may not speak Dogon or know anything about the culture or local paths, which can lead to problems – some non-Dogon guides have asked travellers to also pay for local guides to show them the way!

Choosing a guide can have a huge impact on your experience of the Dogon Country, so take your time and write down all the expenses, as this aids memory on both sides, and ask lots of questions about market days, history, festivals etc, to see if they know their stuff.

It's also worth spending an extra day or two asking around for recommendations from other travellers, rather than rushing off with the first guide you meet. Other places to ask around include good hotels (such as Mac's Refuge in Sévaré, p512), the Mission Culturelle in Bandiagara (see under p519), and the Bureau Regional du Tourisme in Mopti (p508), who can put you in touch with the only female guide to Dogon Country. Or, the guide associations in Bandiagara (p519) and Mopti (p508) have lists of accredited guides (see the boxed text p491); if a guide fails to produce their yellow or blue card, this should be a warning sign to look elsewhere.

Tour operators who can organise treks are listed on p546.

## Costs

Visitors to Dogon Country must pay for the privilege. Not only do various fees provide the local people with a much-needed source of income, they also go a small way towards compensating the Dogon people for the alienating impact of mass tourism. Standard costs include the following:

**Breakfast** (CFA500)
**Lunch or dinner** (without/with meat CFA1500/2500)
**Guide** (per day guiding only, from CFA9000; all-inclusive CFA15,000 to CFA20,000)
**Porter** (per porter, per day CFA2500)
**Village tourist tax** (per person CFA500 to CFA1000) Nothing if you're just passing through.
**Sleeping in village campement** (per person, per night CFA1000 to CFA1500)

The village tourist tax should allow you to take photos of houses and other buildings (but *not* people – unless you get their permission), and to visit nearby cliff dwellings. If possible, pay this fee directly to the village headman, not to your guide.

You should always agree in advance with your guide about what's included in his or her fee (some guides offer all-inclusive packages). Make sure you discuss everything, from the above fees to who'll be paying for the guide's food and lodging (the latter should be covered by the daily fee). Per-person fees for guides fall if you're a larger group.

Your only other cost is reaching the escarpment. From Bandiagara, a local taxi to any of the local trailheads will cost CFA10,000 to CFA20,000. If you're alone it might be cheaper for you and the guide to hire mopeds.

From Bankass to the escarpment at Endé or Kani-Kombolé (12km) by horse and cart is around CFA5000 (the track is too sandy for mopeds). Of course, you can save money by walking this section.

Optional costs include payments to take photos of people (with permission of course) or to visit a village's *hogon* (spiritual leader); it's usual to give him a small gift of around CFA500. Another good gift are kola nuts, which can be bought in Mopti or Bandiagara.

MALI

## DOGON CULTURE

### Dogon Religion & Cosmology

The Dogon believe that the earth, moon and sun were created by a divine male being called Amma. The earth was formed in the shape of a woman, and by her Amma fathered twin snake-like creatures called the Nommo, which Dogon believe are present in streams and pools. Later, Amma made two humans – a man and a woman – who were circumcised by the Nommo and then gave birth to eight children, who are regarded as the ancestors of all Dogon.

Amma is credited with creating the stars, and a feature of Dogon cosmology is the star known in Western countries as Sirius, or the Dog Star, which was also held to be auspicious by the ancient Egyptians. The Dogon are able to predict Sirius' periodic appearance at a certain point above the skyline, and have long regarded it as three separate stars – two close together and a third invisible. The movements of these stars dictate the timing of the Sigui festival, which takes place about every 60 years. Modern astronomers knew Sirius to be two stars, but it was only in 1995 that powerful radio telescopes detected a third body of super-dense matter in the same area.

Aspects of Dogon religion readily seen by visitors are the *omolo* or fetishes, sacred objects which are dotted around most villages. Most are a simple dome of hard-packed mud, and their function is to protect the village against certain eventualities. To strengthen their power, sacrifices are made to these *omolo* on a regular basis. This usually means pouring millet porridge over them, although sometimes the blood of a chicken is used.

### Hogon Etiquette

Meeting a *hogon* (Dogon spiritual leader) can be a fascinating experience, but travellers should be aware of certain rules and regulations to avoid any cultural faux pas:

- Always make initial approaches to the *hogon* through the *kadana* (guardian of the hogon).
- Always show respect and reverence to the *hogon* and never touch him.
- Take gifts, such as kola nuts or a little cash for millet beer, but don't thrust these into his hands.
- If you really want to wow the *hogon* of Arou, bring him an ostrich egg (they are always blowing off the top of his temple).
- Wait for instructions as to where to walk and where to sit – it's easy to wander into a sacred part of the sanctuary or upset a fetish (this will require you to pay for a sacrifice).
- Don't probe too deeply – many *hogon* are reluctant to explain the inner workings of Dogon religion.

### Dogon Villages – A Snapshot

Each Dogon village has its own charm, whether it be a stand-out geographical feature or an ambience you won't find elsewhere. The following snapshots (from southwest to northeast) may be helpful for choosing your route.

**Kani-Kombolé** Home to an interesting mosque.

**Teli** Very picturesque with waterfalls nearby.

**Endé** Pretty villages, nearby waterfalls and a good place to visit the village *hogon*.

**Begnimato** Spectacular views of the plains.

**Dourou** More good views from atop the escarpment.

**Nombori** Stunning views on the route here from Dourou. This is an untouristy village, and good place to visit the *hogon*.

**Komokan** Largely animist village with a fine *togu-na* (traditional Dogon meeting place or shelter where men sit and socialise).

**Ourou** Nestled in an alcove of the escarpment.

**Tireli** Known for its pottery, a touristy but good place to see Dogon mask ceremony.

**Amani** Home to a sacred crocodile pool.

**Yaye** Still clinging to the cliff.

**Ireli** A classic Dogon village with cylindrical granary towers at the foot of the cliffs, and a mass of ancient Tellem houses.

**Banani** Sits under an amazing overhanging cliff and full of wonderful Tellem buildings.

**Bongo** Spectacular views of the plains and an enormous natural tunnel.

**Arou** Home village of the most powerful *hogon* in Dogon Country; the temple is marvellous and there's a nice rock arch.

**Kundu villages** Stretch from top to the bottom of the escarpment making for an excellent walk.

**Youga villages** On a separate hill out on the plains, they're quite traditional, animist and beautiful.

**Kassa** Numerous springs and very attractive.

**Wakara** One of the highest villages in the area.

## Dogon Masks & Ceremonies

Masks are very important in Dogon culture, and play a significant role in religious ceremonies. The most famous ceremony is the Sigui, performed every 60 years (most recently during the 1960s), which features a large mask and headdress called the *iminana*, which is in the form of a prostrate serpent, sometimes almost 10m high. During the Sigui, the Dogon perform dances recounting the story of their origin. After the ceremony, the *iminana* is stored in a cave high on the cliffs.

The *iminana* is used during a major 'funeral' ceremony that takes place every five or so years. According to tradition, when a person dies their spirit wanders about looking for a new residence. Fearful that the spirit might rest in another mortal, the Dogon bring out the *iminana* and take it to the deceased's house to entice the spirit to live in the mask. The accompanying ceremony can last a week and celebrates the life of the dead person and the part they played in village life.

When important village members die, they are interred in a cave high on the cliffs (sometimes appropriating a Tellem cave), usually on the same day or the day after they die. The body is wrapped in colourful cloth and paraded head-high through the village, then lifted with ropes up to the cave. A smaller funeral ceremony takes place about five days later.

Other masks used by the Dogon include the birdlike *kanaga,* which protects against vengeance (of a killed animal), and the house-like *sirige,* which represents the house of the *hogon*, who is responsible for passing on traditions. Most ceremonies, where you may see masks, take place from April to May. These include Agguet, around May, in honour of the ancestors, and Ondonfile and Boulo (the rain welcoming festival), which takes place in the time leading up to the first rains.

If it's not possible to be here at this time, at least two villages – Tireli and Sanga – organise (with a day's advance notice) early-morning or late-afternoon re-enactments (CFA70,000) of the traditional mask ceremonies. It's not the real thing but it's taken seriously by the dancers and a rare insight into one aspect of Dogon culture. It's also enjoyed as much by local women and children (who are forbidden from seeing the real thing) as by tourists. Female tourists are sometimes allowed to watch the real thing but it varies very much from village to village.

## Weekdays & Markets

The traditional Dogon villages keep a five-day week, while those on the plateau tend to observe a seven-day week. Dogon markets are always lively affairs, although they don't get going until about noon. The following table of market days should help you attend one.

| Five-day week | Dourou cluster | Sanga cluster | Others |
| --- | --- | --- | --- |
| 1 | Dourou | Tireli | Ibi |
| 2 | Gimini, Nombori | Banani, Tiogou | |
| 3 | Idjeli, Pelou, Amani | Yendouma | |
| 4 | Konsongo, Komokan | Sanga | |
| 5 | Doundjourou (near Begnimato) | Ireli, Kama | |

| Seven-day week | | | Village |
| --- | --- | --- | --- |
| Monday (big) & Friday (small) | | | Bandiagara |
| Tuesday | | | Bankass |
| Thursday | | | Kani Kombolé |
| Saturday | | | Bamba |
| Sunday | | | Douentza, Endé, Songo |

## Equipment

The general rule is to travel as lightly as possible, because paths are steep or sandy in places. Footwear should be sturdy, but boots are not essential. It's vital to have a sunhat and a water bottle, as otherwise heatstroke and serious dehydration are real possibilities. You should always carry at least a litre of water. Re-useable bottles can be bought in villages along the way and you can get water from village pumps (always preferable to a well) en route – although it needs to be purified. Avoid carrying 'Western' products that have layers of packaging. Tents are not required, although a mosquito net is a good idea, especially after the rains. Nights are warm, although a lightweight sleeping bag will keep off the predawn chill from November to February. Dogon villages are dark at night, so a torch (flashlight) is useful, and you'll need toilet paper. Wearing shorts for trekking is OK, as they do not offend Dogon culture, although women will feel more comfortable wearing a skirt or long trousers when staying in a village.

## Dangers & Annoyances

We have received isolated reports of travellers having things stolen from their backpacks when left on the roofs of *campements*; the culprits are far more likely to be other travellers rather than locals. Stow your valuables away and securely lock your bag when you go off to explore the village.

## Starting Points

Three towns, Bandiagara (opposite), Bankass (p521) and Douentza (p534), provide gateways to Dogon Country. From these towns transport to the actual trailheads must be arranged (although Douentza is only about 5km from Dogon Country). Of the numerous possible trailheads, Kani-Kombolé, Djiguibombo, Endé, Dourou and Sanga are the most popular.

## Trekking Routes

Time and money usually decide the length and starting point for a trek, but also consider how much energy you want to exert. Simple routes will take you along the bottom (or top) of the escarpment, while more interesting routes head up and down the cliff itself, often scrambling on all fours, leaping from boulder to boulder or using ladders carved from logs to cover the steepest sections. People with no head for heights may feel shaky in places. You should factor local market days (p517) when planning.

### DAY TREKS

If you are very short of time there are three circular walks from Sanga, aimed at tour groups on tight schedules. The **Petit Tour** (7km) goes to Gogoli, the **Moyen Tour** (10km) goes to Gogoli and Banani, and the **Grand Tour** (15km) goes to Gogoli, Banani and Ireli.

### TWO DAYS

Spending a night in a Dogon village gives you a much better impression of life on the escarpment than you'll ever get on a one-day trip.

From Bandiagara, with a lift to Djiguibombo (pronounced, wonderfully, Jiggy-boom-bo) you can walk down to the plains, spend the night in either Kani-Kombolé, Teli or Endé and return by the same route. You could also do a circular route from Dourou to Nombori.

From Bankass, a short, but rewarding circuit takes you to Kani-Kombolé, through Teli to Endé (spending the night at either) and then back.

### THREE TO FIVE DAYS

A good three-day trek from Bandiagara starts with a lift to Djiguibombo. You descend to Teli for the first night and trek northeast to Begnimato (second night). On the third day continue to Yawa, then up the escarpment to Dourou, where you can arrange a lift back to Bandiagara. You can add an extra day by diverting northeast to Nombori. An easier trip from Bandiagara would be Djiguibombo, Teli and Endé, returning by the same route.

An excellent four-day alternative, and one of our favourites, is to start from Bandiagara, trek down the escarpment to Nombori (first night), head northeast to Ireli (second night), on to Tireli (third night), then up the escarpment to Sanga.

From Bankass, you can get to Teli or Endé and then walk northeast to Begnimato, Yawa or Nombori, and on to Dourou and Bandiagara.

From Sanga, a good four-day route descends first to Banani then heads north to Kundu (first night), Youga (second night) and Yendouma (third night). On the fourth day go up the cliffs to Tiogou and return over the plateau to Sanga. The escarpment is less well-defined north of Banani, but unlike areas further south, it's rarely visited.

### SIX DAYS OR MORE

If you have plenty of time, any of the routes described above can be extended or combined, and routes in from Douentza exploring the north are possible. For example, from Douentza to Sanga takes at least seven days and takes in Gombori, Wakara, Kassa and Bamba. From Sanga and Banani you can head southwest via Tireli and Yawa to reach Dourou (after three days) or Djiguibombo (after another two or three days), and then end your trek at Bandiagara or Bankass. This trek can also be done in reverse.

## Sleeping & Eating

These days almost every Dogon village has at least one *campement*, which invariably consists of one-storey buildings encircling a courtyard. Although some have rooms, sleeping on the flat roof under the stars can be a wonderful experience – the sights and sounds of the village stirring in the early morning light are unforgettable.

Evening meals are usually rice with a sauce of vegetables or meat (usually chicken). In the morning, you'll be given tea and bread with jam or processed cheese. Small shops and restaurants catering for tourists have been set up in the most-visited Dogon villages, while beers, bottled water and soft drinks are available almost everywhere. Millet beer is also widely available, and it's not bad.

## BANDIAGARA

**pop 6853**

This small, dusty town lies 63km east of Sévaré, and about 20km from the edge of Falaise de Bandiagara. Once a major administrative centre, tourism is now the main show in town, as it basks in the reflected glow of the smaller and more beautiful Dogon towns and villages closer to the escarpment. The attention of numerous would-be guides as soon as you arrive can be quite intimidating.

## Information

In the heart of town is the market (market day is Monday, although there's a smaller version on Friday) and supplies can be pur-

chased from here and a number of outlets nearby – try Alimentation Niang Ibrahim.
**Centre de Médecine Traditionnelle** ( ☎ 244 2006; crmt@afribone.net.ml) As well known for its *maisons sans bois* (houses without wood) architecture as it is for its work with medicinal plants. Visits are free, although donations are appreciated.
**Cybercafé Clic** (Route de Djiguibombo; per hr CFA1500; ☯ 9am-1pm & 3-7pm Mon-Fri, 9am-1pm Sat) Super-fast satellite connections.
**Guide association** ( ☎ 244 2128) Guides in Bandiagara have a reputation for aggressive salesmanship, but you can contact the guide association, which has no office.
**Mission Culturelle** ( ☎ /fax 244 2263) Staff can provide cultural information and recommend guides.

## Sleeping & Eating

**Hôtel Satimbe** ( ☎ 244 2378; amadoutinouologuem@ yahoo.fr; opposite gare routière; beds CFA2500) The garden here is nice, but privacy isn't a priority as the partitions separating the rooms are more window than wall. A stay here is all about price. It's also central, and simple meals are available if you order in advance.

**Auberge Kansaye** ( ☎ 625 0762; kansayebouba@ yahoo.fr; beds from CFA3000) Bare, blue concrete rooms are where you'll sleep (mosquito net and fan are available on request) but there's a mellow ambience here – the music wafting through the corridors ranges from Bob Marley to cool Ibiza chill-out. Their riverfront restaurant (meals CFA1000 to CFA3000), was nearing completion when we were there and will be *the* place to eat in Bandiagara. A great choice if you don't spend too much time in the room.

**Hôtel Toguna** ( ☎ 244 2159; Route de Sévaré; camping CFA3500, d CFA5000) After a recent overhaul, the Toguna is outrageously good value, boasting tidy rooms with private (but outdoor) shower and toilet. The garden's pleasant, the *toguna*-style restaurant (meals CFA500-2500) likewise, and it's super-quiet. The downside is that it's 4km west of town with not a lot of passing public transport.

**Le Kambary** (Cheval Blanc; ☎ /fax 244 2388; chevalblancmali@yahoo.fr; s/d with fan CFA18,000/20,000, with air-con from CFA25,000/27,000; ☯ ☯ ) Accommodation in this delightful Swiss-run place is in attractive stone igloos, with whitewashed and spacious interiors and portholes for natural light. The bathrooms also have character and are terrific. If you've just arrived from Dogon, you may wonder if you've been transported to heaven. The restaurant

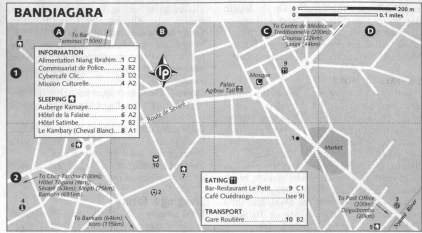

**BANDIAGARA**

INFORMATION
Alimentation Niang Ibrahim...**1** C2
Commissariat de Police.........**2** B2
Cybercafé Clic......................**3** D2
Mission Culturelle.................**4** A2

SLEEPING
Auberge Kansaye..................**5** D2
Hôtel de la Falaise................**6** A2
Hôtel Satimbe.....................**7** B2
Le Kambary (Cheval Blanc)....**8** A1

EATING
Bar-Restaurant Le Petit.........**9** C1
Café Ouédraogo.................(see 9)

TRANSPORT
Gare Routière.....................**10** B2

---

(mains from CFA2200) is outstanding (the food's great and the garden is beautifully designed) and there are sometimes musical evenings with buffet meals (CFA7700). There's also a swimming pool and mini-golf. They have a list of recommended guides.

**Hôtel de la Falaise** ( ☎ /fax 244 2128; napopapa2003@yahoo.fr; mattress on roof CFA1500; dm CFA4000; s/d with fan CFA14,000/16,000, with air-con CFA22,500/25,000; starters CFA600-1500, mains CFA1500-2800; ⚇ ) This new hotel in the centre of town is a welcome addition and, although the rooms are a touch overpriced, they're comfortable, well kept and awash with blue walls and tiled floors. If you're staying in the dorm, the toilet and shower is a fair walk across the compound. The restaurant does unremarkable African and European dishes.

Street food is available around the market and *gare routière* in the evening. For a sitdown meal, try **Bar-Restaurant Le Petit** (Route de Sévaré; starters CFA500-900, mains CFA1500-3250, breakfast CFA1500, small/large beer CFA500/900) which is as chilled as the steady stream of guides allows it to be. Take refuge from them with an espresso coffee (CFA500). **Café Ouédraogo** next door is similar, though more of a bar.

### Getting There & Away
Most transport leaves Bandiagara around 7am or 5pm. There's a lot of transport to Sévaré/Mopti (around CFA1500), but getting to Bankass (CFA1000) or Koro (minibus/bush taxi CFA2000/2500) means a longer wait. You might also find the odd

minibus heading to Sanga (CFA1500) and the occasional Somatra bus to Bamako, but for most onward transport it's almost always easier to go via Sévaré or Mopti.

## SANGA
Sanga (also spelt Sangha), 44km east of Bandiagara and close to the top of the escarpment, is one of the largest Dogon villages in the region. It's a fascinating place to explore with a guide, in particular the Ogol Da section, which is full of temples, fetishes and shrines. It's a favourite of tour groups and has become quite touristy in recent years, and for independent travellers it's expensive to get to, but it's worth it.

### Sleeping & Eating
**Hôtel Femme Dogon** (mattress on roof CFA3000, d CFA7500) Oddly, this place looks and feels slightly like a French refuge, though a little shabbier. However, it's a nice setup, with a popular bar and restaurant and running water. Treks and 4WD hire can be arranged here, but you'll need to bargain hard.

**Campement-Hôtel Guinna** (s/d with bathroom & fan CFA15,000/17,500; meals CFA1000-5000) This is a tourgroup favourite and it's certainly the best-equipped place to stay in any of the Dogon villages. Rooms are spick-and-span and have good bathrooms. After a week's trekking the garden's lovely, the food is good and the hot showers and cold beer fantastic.

The Protestant Mission also has plans to open up some guest rooms for travellers.

## Getting There & Away

Apart from the occasional minibus to Bandiagara (CFA1500), there's no regular public transport to Sanga; chances are higher on Sanga's or Bandiagara's market day (see p517). Otherwise hitching might be your best bet. Chartering a taxi costs at least CFA15,000, or getting a moped to drop you off costs CFA7500 (including petrol).

## BANKASS

Bankass is 64km south of Bandiagara, along the dirt road to Burkina Faso. The Falaise de Bandiagara is about 12km away, which makes it a good gateway to southern Dogon Country, particularly if you're coming from Burkina Faso.

### Information

Association Bandia represents Bankass' guides, many of whom hang out beside the *cabine téléphonique*. There's also a small hospital in town.

### Sleeping & Eating

**Campement & Hôtel Hogon** (camping/mattress on roof CFA2000, r CFA5500; mains CFA2500-3500) On the western edge of town, this is the best of the cheapies, although it's pretty run-down and basic. It's set up with tourists' quirks in mind, but the best assets are the guys who run it – friendly and helpful with everything from finding guides to transport to Burkina Faso.

### Getting There & Away

There are daily Peugeot taxis and minibuses to Bandiagara (CFA1000), Mopti (CFA3000, two hours) and Koro (CFA1250, one to two hours).

## KORO

Koro has a nice mosque but little else to offer apart from an impressive baobab tree, the Saturday market and a bus to Ouahigouya (CFA2500, two to four hours) which leaves Koro around 2pm daily. Passport and customs formalities must be completed in Koro and Tiou (in Burkina Faso). Peugeot taxis and minibuses ply the route between Koro and Mopti (CFA3500) daily. There are weekly buses to Bamako. If you find yourself stuck here overnight, it will give you time to discover **Aventure Dogon** ( ☎ 244 2191; www.aventure-dogon.com; camping CFA4000,

d from CFA8000; meals CFA4500), an excellent place to stay and plot your exploration of the Dogon Country.

# THE NORTH & EAST

Northern Mali is dominated by the vast empty plains and dunescapes of the Sahara Desert. It's also home to Timbuktu, one of the world's most important destinations down through history. Away to the east, it doesn't get much more remote than Gao – a great place to venture beyond well-worn tourist paths.

## TIMBUKTU (TOMBOUCTOU)

pop 32,460

Timbuktu, that most rhythmical of African names, has for centuries been synonymous with Africa's mysterious inaccessibility, with an end-of-the-earth allure that some travellers just have to reach. It's the name we all knew as kids, but never really knew where it was. More than just a name, Timbuktu's fame was derived from its strategic location, at once on the edge of the Sahara and at the top of the 'Niger bend', from its role as the fabulously wealthy terminus of a camel caravan route that has linked West Africa and the Mediterranean since medieval times, and from the vast universities of Islamic scholarship which flourished under the aegis of some of Africa's richest empires.

After it was 'discovered' by Western travellers, Timbuktu also became a byword for the West's disappointment with Africa. Even today, Timbuktu is a shadow of its former self, existing as a sprawl of low, often shabby, flat-roofed buildings which only hint at former grandeur, while all the time the streets fill up with sand blown in from the desert. And yet, still the travellers come and you'll get the most from your visit here if you give yourself time to understand the significance of this town – its isolation, its history and its continuing importance as a trading post on the salt-trade route.

### History

Timbuktu is said to have been founded around AD 1000 as a seasonal encampment for Tuareg nomads. An old woman was put in charge of the settlement while the men tended the animals. Her name was Bouctou, meaning 'large navel', possibly indicating a physical disorder. Tim simply means 'well' and the town became known as Timbouctou. Other accounts say that in Tamashek *tim* means 'that belonging to'. The well which Bouctou tended and which started the Timbuktu legend can still be visited (p524).

Timbuktu was only developed as a trading centre in the 11th century, but it went on to rival Gao to the east and Walata (in Mauritania) to the west. Gold, slaves and ivory were sent north and salt (from the mines of Taghaza and Taoudenni) came south.

Kankan Musa, the greatest king of the Empire of Mali (see p34), passed through the town in 1336, on his way back from Mecca, and commanded the construction of the Dyingerey Ber mosque. Islamic scholars were sent to study in Fez, thus beginning a great tradition of Islamic education, which increased when Sonni Ali Ber and the Empire of Songhaï took the town in 1468. Timbuktu also began to get seriously rich. In 1494 Leo Africanus, a well-travelled Spanish Moor, recorded in his *History and Description of Africa* that Timbuktu had 'a great store of doctors, judges, priests and other learned men, that are bountifully maintained at the king's expense'.

In 1591 Moroccan armies sacked Timbuktu, killing many scholars and sending others to Fez (along with much of the city's riches). Fifty years later the remnants of the invading army had been assimilated into the local population, but their invasion signalled the start of the city's decline, which continued as European ships began to circumvent the trans-Saharan trade routes. Over the next 300 years Timbuktu fell to the Songhaï (1780–1826), Fula (1826–63) and the Tuareg (1863–95). The French marched in during 1894, and found the place pretty much how it looks today.

After Mali gained independence, its governments were dominated by (and therefore Timbuktu ruled by) the Bambara of southern Mali, which led to simmering tensions. These came to a head during the 1990s when Timbuktu was badly hit by fighting between Tuareg rebels, the Bambara-dominated army and Songhaï militias. There was no actual fighting, but Tuareg civilians and suspected sympathisers from other groups were arrested and imprisoned. Many were reportedly executed in the sand dunes.

## Information

Officially every visitor to Timbuktu must pay a CFA5000 tourist tax, but in reality this only applies to those who want to visit Dyingerey Ber Mosque and the Ethnological Museum (the tax operates as a de facto admission fee). The fee is collected at the Bureau Régional du Tourisme (where they can put a 'Tombouctou' stamp in your passport) or at the entrance to the mosque or museum.

There are a number of places where local and international telephone calls can be made around town.

**BDM** (Route de Korioumé) Also south of town, does cash advances on Visa card and Western Union transfers.

**BDR** (Route de Korioumé) South of town, changes euro cash.

**Bureau Régional du Tourisme** ( ☎ 292 2086; Blvd Askia Mohamed; ⏰ 7.30am-4pm) Has a list of recommended guides and can advise on trips further afield.

**Commissariat de Police** ( ☎ 292 1007; Place de l'Indépendance)

**Hospital** ( ☎ 292 1169; off Route de Korioumé)

**Pharmacie Officine Jour et Nuit** ( ☎ 292 1333) Near the Ethnological Museum.

**Post office** (Route de Korioumé) Sells postcards and stamps – for that all-important postmark.

**TCP** (Route de Korioumé; per hr CFA1000; ⏰ 7.30am-1pm & 4-7pm Mon-Fri, 7.30am-1pm Sat) Slow Internet connections.

## Sights

### MOSQUES

Timbuktu has three of the oldest mosques in West Africa. While not as visually stunning as some in Mali, they're still extremely impressive and represent classic and well-preserved examples of the Sudanese style of architecture which prevails throughout much of the Sahel.

The oldest, dating from the early 14th century, is **Dyingerey Ber Mosque** (admission CFA5000 as part of town tourism tax). You can go into this mosque, west of Place de l'Indépendance, but sometimes only with a guide. The interior is a forest of 100 sturdy pillars, and there are a series of interconnecting rooms with holes in the wall at ground level – in the days before microphones, worshippers who could not hear the imam could look through into the main prayer hall to see when to pray. There's a separate women's section, from close to which stairs lead up onto the roof (ask permission before climbing up) for good views over the town and out towards the desert; don't point your camera south as

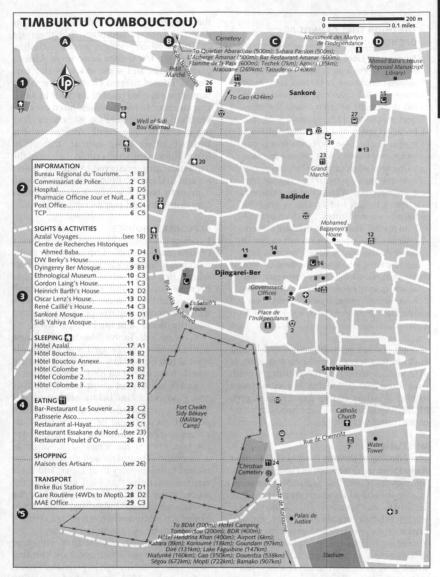

# TIMBUKTU (TOMBOUCTOU)

0       200 m
0       0.1 miles

**MALI**

To Quartier Abaradjou (500m); Sahara Passion (500m);
L'Auberge Amanar (500m); Bar Restaurant Amanar (600m);
Flamme de la Paix (600m); Techek (7km); Agouni (35km);
Araouane (269km); Taoudenni (740km)

Ahmed Bâba's House
(Proposed Manuscript
Library)

Cemetery

Monument des Martyrs
de l'Indépendance

Sankoré

To Gao (424km)

Well of Sidi
Bou Kasimad

Badjinde

Grand
Marché

Mohamed
Bagayoyo's
House

Djingarei-Ber

Es Saheli's
House

Government
Offices

Place de
l'Indépendance

Sarekeina

Fort Cheikh
Sidy Békaye
(Military
Camp)

Catholic
Church

Rue de Chemnitz

Water
Tower

Christian
Cemetery

Route de Korounké

Palais de
Justice

To BDM (100m); Hotel Camping
Tombouctou (200m); BDR (400m);
Hôtel Hendrina Khan (400m); Airport (6km);
Kabara (8km); Korioumé (18km); Goundam (97km);
Diré (131km); Lake Faguibine (147km);
Niafunké (160km); Gao (350km); Douentza (538km);
Ségou (672km); Mopti (722km); Bamako (907km)

Stadium

## INFORMATION
| | |
|---|---|
| Bureau Régional du Tourisme......1 | B3 |
| Commissariat de Police..............2 | C3 |
| Hospital....................................3 | D5 |
| Pharmacie Officine Jour et Nuit...4 | C3 |
| Post Office................................5 | C4 |
| TCP..........................................6 | C5 |

## SIGHTS & ACTIVITIES
| | |
|---|---|
| Azalaï Voyages.....................(see 18) | |
| Centre de Recherches Historiques | |
|   Ahmed Baba...........................7 | D4 |
| DW Berky's House.....................8 | C3 |
| Dyingerey Ber Mosque..............9 | B3 |
| Ethnological Museum...............10 | C3 |
| Gordon Laing's House..............11 | C3 |
| Heinrich Barth's House.............12 | D2 |
| Oscar Lenz's House..................13 | D2 |
| René Caillié's House................14 | C3 |
| Sankoré Mosque.....................15 | D1 |
| Sidi Yahiya Mosque.................16 | C3 |

## SLEEPING
| | |
|---|---|
| Hôtel Azalaï............................17 | A1 |
| Hôtel Bouctou........................18 | B2 |
| Hôtel Bouctou Annexe.............19 | B1 |
| Hôtel Colombe 1.....................20 | B2 |
| Hôtel Colombe 2.....................21 | B2 |
| Hôtel Colombe 3.....................22 | B2 |

## EATING
| | |
|---|---|
| Bar-Restaurant Le Souvenir.......23 | C2 |
| Patisserie Asco........................24 | C5 |
| Restaurant al-Hayat.................25 | C1 |
| Restaurant Essakane du Nord...(see 23) | |
| Restaurant Poulet d'Or.............26 | B1 |

## SHOPPING
| | |
|---|---|
| Maison des Artisans................(see 26) | |

## TRANSPORT
| | |
|---|---|
| Binke Bus Station ...................27 | D1 |
| Gare Routière (4WDs to Mopti)..28 | D2 |
| MAE Office..............................29 | C3 |

---

there is a police building in the vicinity. The muezzin still climbs to the summit of the pyramidal minaret, with its wooden struts, to call the faithful to prayer on those days when the electricity isn't working; otherwise it's done by microphone.

**Sidi Yahiya Mosque**, north of Place de l'Indépendance, is named after one of the

city's saints (it's said that 333 saints have lived in Timbuktu) and was constructed in 1400. Non-Muslims are not allowed to enter, and from the outside it's the least interesting of Timbuktu's main mosques.

Built (reportedly by a woman) a century later than Sidi Yahiya was the **Sankoré Mosque**, northeast of the Grand Marché. It

**THE DOOR THAT CANNOT BE OPENED**

Appropriately for a city of legend, Dyingerey Ber Mosque has a particularly fine and suitably mysterious one. At the back of the main prayer hall is a straw mat, which covers an old door made of palm wood. The story goes that, in the 12th century, a local man became famous as a practitioner of black magic. At the time, Timbuktu was a city which only Muslims were allowed to enter, so the local religious authorities, concerned over the man's popularity, expelled him from the town. After a day he returned, claiming to have had a dream in which he became a good Muslim. The imam told the man that he should come to Friday prayers, after which he would be allowed to stay in town. As the prayers began, the man suddenly turned into a lion and jumped into the small room behind the door in question. It was quickly closed behind him and has never been opened again, lest the man's spirit (and evil) be released into the world.

also functioned as a university, and by the 16th century was one of the largest schools of Arabic learning in the Muslim world, with some 25,000 students. It, too, is closed to non-Muslims, but its pleasing minarets, interesting location and aesthetic harmony make it well worth a visit.

**MUSEUMS**

The **Ethnological Museum** (admission CFA5000 as part of town tourism tax; ☻ 8am-5pm) occupies a hugely significant site near Sidi Yahiya Mosque, containing the well of Bouctou (see p521), where Timbuktu was founded. There's also a variety of exhibits including clothing, musical instruments, jewellery and games, as well as interesting colonial photographs and pictures of the ancient rock carvings at Tin-Techoun, which have since been stolen or destroyed.

An amazing collection of ancient manuscripts and books are kept at the **Centre de Recherches Historiques Ahmed Baba** (Cedrhab; ☎ 292 1081; cedrhab@tombouctou.org.ml; Rue de Chemnitz; admission CFA1000). Home to (at last count) 23,000 Islamic religious, historical and scientific texts from all over the world, the centre is the focus of a South African–funded project to protect, translate and catalogue

the manuscripts. The oldest manuscripts date from the 12th century, but there are countless other priceless works, including some of the few written histories of Africa's great empires, and works of scholarship carried to Timbuktu from Granada after Muslims were expelled from al-Andalus in 1492. Documented family histories (often over 400 years old) of Timbuktu's most famous clans are also held here. South African experts with whom we spoke estimate that up to five million manuscripts could survive in the Timbuktu area, preserved by the dry desert air and in the possession of families. Indeed, Timbuktu has a few other private libraries containing ancient manuscripts and books.

**EXPLORERS' HOUSES**

Between 1588 and 1853 at least 43 Europeans tried to reach this fabled city; only four made it and only three made it home. The houses where they stayed while in Timbuktu have been preserved (and marked with small plaques) although most remain in private hands; entering requires prior negotiations with the owners and can be expensive.

West of Sidi Yahiya Mosque, the house where Gordon Laing stayed is very small. He was the first European to reach Timbuktu, but was then murdered on his journey home.

René Caillié spent a year learning Arabic and studying Islam before setting off for Timbuktu disguised as a Muslim. Caillié's research paid off and he was the first European to reach Timbuktu and live to tell the tale, even if his honest description of a careworn Timbuktu well past its prime earned him less glory than anger, and there were accusations that he'd fabricated the story. West of Sidi Yahiya Mosque, the house where he did indeed stay in 1828 was under renovation when we visited, but it's unlikely to be opened to the public.

Heinrich Barth's incredible five-year journey began in Tripoli and took him first to Agadez, then through Nigeria and finally, in September 1853, he reached Timbuktu disguised as a Tuareg. He stayed for the best part of a year before narrowly escaping with his life and eventually returning to Europe. East of Sidi Yahiya Mosque, **Heinrich Barth's house** (admission CFA1000; ☻ 8am-6pm), where he stayed, is now a tiny museum containing reproductions of Barth's drawings and extracts of his writings.

There are other houses where a host of lesser-known explorers stayed while in Timbuktu, among them Oscar Lenz's old residence and the house of DW Berky, leader of the first American Trans-Saharan Expedition of 1912.

### MARKETS

The Grand Marché is the large covered building in the centre of town. It's not particularly grand, but it's busy and not a bad place to buy slabs of salt. The Petit Marché is further west by the old port, while the Maison des Artisans (where local artisans produce and sell their wares) is close by, at the end of Blvd Askia Mohamed.

### FLAMME DE LA PAIX

On the northwestern outskirts of town, the striking **Flamme de la Paix** (Flame of Peace) monument is worth visiting. It was built on the spot where 3000 weapons were ceremonially burnt at the end of the Tuareg rebellion (p529). The monument is where Timbuktu meets the desert, so continue on to enter the dunes.

## Activities

### TREKKING

Like a vestige from another age, salt caravans still travel between Timbuktu and Taoudenni. The return trip takes between 36 and 40 days. Trucks also make the journey – a fact which is lengthening the expedition for those who travel by camel, as the trucks sometimes exhaust salt supplies at the mines for a few days. But with fuel costs high and camels costing very little, it is extremely unlikely that the camels will be replaced by four-wheeled transport any time soon.

These are commercial operations and trips are extremely gruelling; they're not to be taken lightly – there's no escape if you find you can't hack it or get sick. Expect to spend between 15 and 18 hours a day on the move, with no rest days, and often with just four hours' sleep a night. The food can be pretty grim (dates, peanuts, dried goat meat and rice if you're lucky) and not always sufficient to keep hunger at bay. Most meals are taken on the move.

The trip costs between CFA650,000 and CFA700,000 per person. This gets you a guide, food and three camels. Guides are essential even if you travel with a caravan –

many guides will try to get you to leave the caravan behind to speed things up, so insist before leaving if you want the caravan experience all the way to Taoudenni. Many guides and camel drivers speak only Hasaniya, a Moorish dialect of Arabic, and interpreters can cost an extra CFA400,000.

November and December are the ideal months to travel – the desert is not too hot and the harmattan has not begun. Sand storms are a problem in January and February.

For an evocative account of the journey and of the salt mines themselves, read *Men of Salt: Across the Sahara with the Caravan of White Gold*, by Michael Benanav (p539).

## Festivals & Events

Every year in early January, Essakane, 50km from Timbuktu, hosts the outstanding **Festival in the Desert**, which attracts a host of Mali's best musicians (especially Tuareg groups) and the occasional international group. For more information on the festival, see p62. Tour operators listed in the following section or at p546 can also help you make arrangements.

## Tours

Local guides offer tours of the town and can set up camel trips, trucks to Gao or boats to Mopti. Their services are not essential, but can make your walk around town more interesting. For guides, the best bet is to choose one of the companies/guides listed below, or ask your hotel or the Bureau Régional du Tourisme for a recommendation.

The following can also arrange cars and long-distance camel trips:

**Abderhamane Alpha Maï'ge** ( ☎ 292 1681, 602 3406; alpha@timbuktu-touristguide.com; Hotel Hendria Khan) Experienced English-speaking guide.

**Azalaï Voyages** ( ☎ 292 1199; azalaivoyages@nomade .fr; Hôtel Bouctou)

**Azima Ag Mohamed Ali** ( ☎ 602 3547) An experienced English-speaking Tuareg guide, and a wonderful desert companion.

### CAMEL RIDES & 4WD TOURS

#### Sunset or overnight trips

You'll receive numerous offers of camel trips into the surrounding desert during your stay in Timbuktu. The most popular excursions include short sunset trips to nearby dunes and/or Tuareg encampments (CFA10,000

MALI

per person per camel), and overnight trips that take you to the dunes at sunset, followed by a night under the stars, often at a Tuareg encampment (from CFA20,000 per person, including a traditional meal).

**Longer expeditions**

For extended trips there are a number of interesting options. Techek (7km away) and Agouni (35km away) are popular destinations (salt caravans muster at Agouni before entering Timbuktu), while more far-flung destinations include Lake Faguibine (p528), Araouane (p528), and even the salt mines at Taoudenni, deep in the Sahara's heart.

Prices start at CFA20,000 per day by camel, or at least CFA50,000 per day in a 4WD (plus petrol) – up to CFA90,000 including guide, driver and food. No prices are cast in stone and opening prices can be 10 times higher than these! Always agree on what's included in the fee – food, sleeping bags etc – with your guide (and write it down) before setting out, and never pay the full amount until you return to Timbuktu.

## Sleeping

For a place that's so popular with tourists, Timbuktu lacks outstanding accommodation choices.

**Hotel Camping Tombouctou** ( ☎ 292 1433; Route de Korioumé; camping CFA2500, dm CFA3500, s/d CFA7500/10,000) This place is simplicity itself but the rooms have cool, thick walls, mosquito nets and fans, and there's a nice communal area. The long walk into town can be punishing in the afternoon.

**Sahara Passion** ( ☎ 604 1907; camping or mattress on roof CFA3500, dm CFA5000, s/d with fan & shared bathroom CFA10,000/12,500, with private bathroom CFA15,000/17,000; P ) Although not as good as its Gao equivalent, Sahara Passion, close to the Flamme de la Paix monument on Timbuktu's northern outskirts, has rooms with high ceilings – those with private bathroom are enormous. Some are a bit stark (including the 15-mattress dorm) but it's in a quiet part of town and food is available on demand.

**Hôtel Bouctou** ( ☎ /fax 292 1012; dm, camping or mattress on roof CFA6000, s/d with fan & shared bathroom CFA12,500/15,000, s/d with fan & private bathroom CFA15,000/18,000, with air-con CFA19,000/22,500; ✴ ) Arrive here at noon when things are quiet and you might find the place deserted, save for the staff sleeping in the restaurant. By

sunset, it swarms with tourists, guides and other hangers-on, but the rooms are large and spacious with tiled floors. The location, on the desert fringe but a short stroll from the centre, is ideal. The rooms in the annexe, north across the sandy track, are newer but even more bare.

**Hôtel Hendrina Khan** ( ☎ 292 1681; www.tomboctou.com; off Route de Korioumé; s/d from CFA19,500/23,500; ✴ ) The Hendrina Khan probably has the best rooms in town (the excellent bathrooms clinch it) and it's a very well-run place. The rooms have satellite TV and fridge, and are spacious and tiled, while other services include a laundry, excellent restaurant, a bar and a small reading library. The best rooms are in the annexe. The only drawbacks are the long walk into the centre of town and the fact that the surrounding desert fringe is not Timbuktu's most appealing.

**Hôtel Colombe 1** ( ☎ 292 1435; Blvd Askia Mohamed; s/d from CFA19,000/23,000; ✴ ) If you like to be in the centre this place is excellent, with enormous rooms and a terrace overlooking the street where meals and drinks are served. Service can be woeful, however, and the bathrooms need an overhaul. The same owners also run the nearby **Hôtel Colombe 2** ( ☎ 292 2132; ✴ ) and **Hôtel Colombe 3** ( ☎ 292 2554; ✴ ) which are newer (it shows in the much nicer bathrooms), but otherwise identical, and go for the same price.

**Hôtel Azalaï** ( ☎ 292 1163; s/d CFA25,000/32,000; P ✴ ) If we tell you that this used to be a Sofitel, you'll see how far standards have fallen. The rooms, while comfortable, are faded and overpriced – although the desert-fringe location and traces of traditional architecture will appeal to many.

## Eating

Here's an important hint for eating out in Timbuktu: never just turn up in a restaurant hoping to be fed. Ordering in advance is almost always necessary.

**Bar Restaurant Amanar** (meals CFA1500-3600; ☾ lunch & dinner) Our favourite restaurant in Timbuktu, Amanar has a mellow atmosphere with a soundtrack of Malian blues (think Ali Farke Touré and Tinariwen), chilled and friendly waiters and a small and intimate garden. They do all the travellers' staples, but the soups are outstanding. Right outside the door stands the Flamme de la Paix monument and the Sahara. From

Thursday to Saturday, they stay open late as a lively bar with a DJ from 10.30pm.

**Restaurant Poulet d'Or** (Maison des Artisans; meals CFA1000-2500; ☺ lunch & dinner) This is a popular (and recommended) travellers' restaurant, which does the usual chicken and chips, brochettes, rice, meat and sauce, but does them particularly well – also look out for some more adventurous dishes (like roast goat), which might need ordering in advance.

**Patisserie Asco** (Route de Korioumé; meals CFA3000; ☺ 6am-midnight) The friendly Patisserie Asco does a range of pastries, the croissants are dense and stodgy, but their local specialities are excellent. The *riz alabadja* (rice, cow butter, meat and lemon) is a highlight. The only drawback are the hangers-on who seem to appear whenever tourists do.

For cheap meals there are rotisseries all over town, while **Restaurant al Hayat** (Blvd Askia Mohamed; ☺ 6am-midnight) does breakfast (CFA600) and a range of couscous and spaghetti dishes (CFA750). On the roof of the Grand Marché, you'll find the pleasant **Bar-Restaurant Le Souvenir** (☺ 7am-midnight) and **Restaurant Essakane du Nord** (☺ 6am-midnight), both of which do couscous for CFA1500/2000 without/with meat.

## Getting There & Away

Getting out of Timbuktu is often harder than getting in. Start planning and negotiating your departure early.

### AIR

Both **CAM** (☎ 292 1345) and **MAE** (☎ 602 3929; Place de l'Indépendance) have at least two weekly flights between Timbuktu's flash new **airport** (☎ 292 1320), 6km south of town off Route de Korioumé, and Bamako (CFA90,360) via Mopti (CFA43,360). There's also one weekly flight to Gao (CFA42,140).

### BOAT

Between late July and late November, the large Comanav passenger boats stop at Korioumé, Timbuktu's port – for details on prices, see p545. The **Comanav ticket office** (☎ 292 1206) is in Kabara (the old port) although there's a smaller office at Korioumé. **Azalaï Voyages** (☎ 292 1199; azalaivoyages@nomade .fr) can reserve a ticket for a small fee. If you're waiting for the boat, Korioumé has some food stalls and basic eateries. Rooms can be found for the desperate.

The Comanav passenger boat stops from four to 12 hours at Korioumé, so if you're travelling between Gao and Mopti, it's possible to make a mad dash to Timbuktu, 18km north. The going rate for a round-trip tour in a chartered taxi is around CFA20,000 – there's no time to take a shared one.

Alternatively, you can travel between Mopti and Korioumé (the official port for Timbuktu) by public or private pinasse; for details see the boxed text p510. Public pinasses also go a few times a week to Niafunké (CFA3500).

Apart from the Comanav ferry, there's very little transport to and from Gao, although an occasional pinasse goes to Gourma-Rharous, where you might find another pinasse going to Gao or (more likely) a place in a truck. The same rules of chartering a private pinasse to Mopti also apply to Gao, although beware of guides charging you for a chartered pinasse and then putting you on a public one carrying cargo and dozens of other passengers.

### LAND

In the dry season, battered 4WDs run from Mopti to Timbuktu (CFA12,500 for a seat or CFA60,000 for the car to yourself) almost every day. The main route (via Douentza) is bad – waterlogged and muddy after the rains, sandy and dusty in the dry. It's a very uncomfortable journey, often with a night under the stars. The journey should take around eight hours, but can take double that after breakdowns, river crossings and other incomprehensible stops in the middle of nowhere.

A few days a week there's a Binke truck-bus (dry season only) to Douentza (CFA10,000, eight hours), from where a Binke bus waits to carry passengers on to Mopti and Bamako. The buses can take twice as long as the 4WDs. Gana Transport also runs a weekly dry season service from the *gare routière* between Timbuktu and Bamako (CFA19,500, 24 hours); the journey goes via Niafunké (CFA7500) and Ségou.

If you're heading east, trucks also run a couple of times each week between Timbuktu and Gao (CFA12,500 to CFA15,000) along the north side of the river. Occasionally, 4WDs also make the trip. Ask around the Grand Marché, be prepared to wait and steel yourself for a tough two-day trip.

## Getting Around

Timbuktu has only one official taxi and he doesn't work after 6pm. You may, however, find some unofficial taxis (ie local guys with underutilised vehicles). A private taxi/*bâché* to Kabara costs CFA6000/300 and to Kori-oumé, CFA6000/500, but you may be asked five times as much.

## AROUND TIMBUKTU
### Niafunké

Niafunké, a large, typically sleepy town on the west bank of the Niger River, is a pleasant riverside settlement with shaded streets and friendly, relaxed locals. The town is best-known as the home of Ali Farke Touré (who named one of his albums after the town), Mali's master bluesman and one of the country's best-loved stars; the locals love him so much that he is now the town's mayor. He also owns the **Campement** (r from CFA8000), which has pretty respectable rooms and is close to the market (market day is Thursday).

Trucks leave each week to Timbuktu (CFA7500) and elsewhere, and you'll find plenty of river transport heading to Timbuktu (CFA3500) and Mopti (CFA4000), especially around market day.

## Lake Faguibine

When the Empire of Ghana was at its height this lake, about 50km north of Goundam, was one of the most impressive in West Africa. However, it's now been dry since the end of the 1980s. The landscape and cliffs on the northern shore are very impressive, and cave paintings are found at Farach. For organising an expedition here and elsewhere in the Sahara, see p525.

## ARAOUANE
**pop 4026**

The sand-drowned oasis village of Araouane is a remote outpost over 250km north of Timbuktu. It was once a place of great learning; clan histories and Islamic texts dating back centuries are still kept by local families. It's still a major staging post on the camel caravan route from the salt mines of Taoudenni.

Araouane is about nine days from Timbuktu by camel, or 12 hours by 4WD. There are two routes to Araouane; the eastern route takes in an ancient mosque now almost completely buried (only the minaret now protrudes from the sand). Further along the route, rock paintings can be seen on a desolate outcrop.

---

### THE TIMBUKTU SALT TRADE

Throughout the cool season, from October to March, a camel caravan from the salt mines at Taoudenni (about 740km north of Timbuktu) arrives in Timbuktu every few days.

Each caravan consists of anywhere from 20 to 300 camels, with smaller caravans often joining up with larger ones en route. Every camel carries four to six slabs of salt, weighing about 60kg. The journey takes about 16 days, and because of the intense heat the caravans often travel at night, with camels unloaded and rested during the day. On arrival in Timbuktu the salt is sold to merchants who transport it upriver to Mopti, where it is sold again and dispersed all over West Africa. Salt is a valuable commodity which used to be traded weight for weight with gold. Nowadays, a good-quality slab will fetch up to CFA8000 in Timbuktu, with its value increasing as it heads south.

The salt comes from the beds of ancient lakes, which dried out many millennia ago. The salt starts about 2m below the surface and is reached by a system of trenches and tunnels up to 6m deep and 200m long. The salt is dug out in large blocks and split into slabs on the surface.

Work in the mines is appallingly paid and dangerous; each man earns up to CFA80,000 for six months' work, and is allowed to keep one in every four bars mined. Indeed, these salt bars, which are sold to supplement salaries, are how the salt workers really make their money. But they don't bring many back to Timbuktu where they can be sold; the nearest well to the mines is around 15km (a one-day camel journey) away, and camel drivers provide water to the miners in exchange for salt. Four *guerbas* of water (about 120L) costs two slabs.

The salt caravans unload on the northern side of Timbuktu, where the Bella live in temporary camps, but the Tuareg and Arab traders do not welcome visitors. If you really want to see more, go with a reputable guide who knows the traders.

*With thanks to Michael Benanav*

## SAVING ARAOUANE

Araouane, amongst the Sahara's most isolated settlements, was once the scene of
one of the more ambitious and unusual
desert stories. In 1988, a New York loft
renovator by the name of Ernst Aebi arrived in Araouane on a mission to prevent
the town disappearing under the Saharan
sands. Using his own money, and in association with eager locals, he planted trees
to keep the desert at bay, and gardens of
fruits and vegetables, which he taught the
villagers to tend. He even built a hotel. By
the early 1990s, however, and with the
Tuareg rebellion putting much of northern
Mali off-limits, Aebi left Araouane, whereafter his hotel fell apart and the gardens
quickly died. Although locals continue to
struggle against the inevitable through a
project called **Arbres pour Araouane** (Trees
for Araouane; ☎ /fax 292 1253), just a few tama-
risk trees are all that remain of this worthy
dream. Aebi's book, *Seasons of Sand* tells the
story in detail and is a great read.

## GAO

**pop 38,190**

Gao, one of the most important towns of
Mali's more illustrious past, doesn't carry
the resonance of the more evocatively
named Timbuktu, but it has a grand history
(Gao was the former capital of the Songhaï Empire – see p33) and, like its more
famous cousin, similarly appears stranded
amid frontier territory. Gao can feel like a
cluster of nomadic settlements (semiperma-
nent Songhaï and Tuareg encampments are
found across town) pushed onto the Niger
River's shores by the Sahara Desert that
dominates to the north. Expeditions into
the desert are a highlight of a visit here, as
is the lively port. There's a remote desert
ambience here, created by the sandy streets,
fascinating cultural mix and – the somewhat incongruous Point Afrique flights to
and from Paris (p830) notwithstanding –
the sense of finding yourself somewhere this
close to the end of the earth. Apart from
anything else, to say that you've been 350km
past Timbuktu earns pretty big traveller-
cachet points.

Gao's tourist season runs from mid-
December until mid-March.

## History

### EARLY HISTORY

Gao was probably founded in AD 650, and
by 1000 – before Timbuktu had even been
created – it was a well-established city-state
and a gateway to the eastern trans-Saharan
trade routes. Gao became the capital of the
Empire of Songhaï around 1020, shortly after
Dia Kossi, the then ruler, converted to Islam.
Over the next 300 years Gao became rich
and powerful and, although it eventually fell
to the mighty Mali empire in 1324, its people
were subjugated for less than 20 years.

One of the greatest leaders of the Songhaï
was Sunni Ali Ber, a ruthless military tacti-
cian more content with waging war than administering his empire, which soon included
Djenné and Timbuktu. Alas, his son wasn't
a patch on his father and was overthrown
by Askia Muhammad Touré. Askia was a
devout Muslim and immediately set about
restoring the prestige of Gao's Islamic institutions (he now lies in the Tomb of Askia in the
north of the city). Then in 1591, 53 years after
his death, Gao was smashed and looted by invading Moroccan armies. Gao subsequently
fell into decline and never recovered.

### THE TUAREG UPRISING

The Tuareg rebellion of the 1990s, which
was devastating as much for towns like Gao
(which were cut off from the rest of the
world by fighting and banditry) as it was
for the Tuareg themselves, was a conflict
with deep roots.

After Mali and Niger became independent in the 1960s, the governments of the
fledgling states inherited a deep Tuareg
mistrust towards those who wanted to con-
fine their nomadic lifestyle, and a reciprocal
enmity from the peoples of the south – who
dominated government – who remembered
the Tuareg as slave-owners who had preyed
on villages south of the Sahara. Persecution
of the Tuareg was widespread after independence and little government money was
spent in Tuareg areas.

The great droughts of 1968–74 and
1980–85 drove many Tuareg to cross borders in search of food. When their return
was negotiated by the governments of Mali,
Algeria and Niger, many found themselves
restricted to poorly resourced transition
camps. By the late 1980s, the camps had
become permanent.

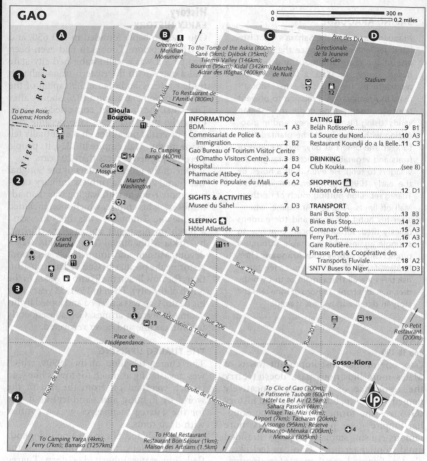

# GAO

0    300 m
0    0.2 miles

| INFORMATION | | EATING | |
|---|---|---|---|
| BDM..........................................1 A3 | | Belàh Rotisserie...........................9 B1 | |
| Commissariat de Police & | | La Source du Nord.......................10 A3 | |
|   Immigration..............................2 B2 | | Restaurant Koundji do a la Belle..11 C3 | |
| Gao Bureau of Tourism Visitor Centre | | | |
|   (Omatho Visitors Centre)...........3 B3 | | DRINKING | |
| Hospital.......................................4 D4 | | Club Koukia..............................(see 8) | |
| Pharmacie Attibey........................5 C4 | | | |
| Pharmacie Populaire du Mali.........6 A2 | | SHOPPING | |
| | | Maison des Arts.........................12 D1 | |
| SIGHTS & ACTIVITIES | | | |
| Musee du Sahel............................7 D3 | | TRANSPORT | |
| | | Bani Bus Stop...........................13 B3 | |
| SLEEPING | | Binke Bus Stop..........................14 B2 | |
| Hôtel Atlantide............................8 A3 | | Comanav Office.........................15 A3 | |
| | | Ferry Port.................................16 A3 | |
| | | Gare Routière............................17 C1 | |
| | | Pinasse Port & Coopérative des | |
| | |   Transports Fluviale.................18 A2 | |
| | | SNTV Buses to Niger.................19 D3 | |

In May 1990, just across Mali's border with Niger in Tchin-Tabaradane, young Tuareg men attacked the *gendarmerie*, killed two soldiers and made off with a cache of weapons. When they were captured in the Malian town of Menaka, local Tuareg stormed the prison and released them. Fighting quickly spread and a Tuareg group attacked government offices in the Gao region. Heavy-handed retaliation by Malian soldiers led to a widespread Tuareg uprising and a proliferation of groups advocating everything from an independent Tuareg state to a more equitable distribution of government money.

President Alpha Konaré agreed to allow more Tuareg representation in the army, civil service and government, but in 1994

there was a large Tuareg assault on Gao, which in turn led to bloody reprisals by the Malian army and the creation of the Ghanda Koi, a Songhaï militia. By the middle of the year, Mali was in a state of virtual civil war. Hundreds of people were killed and bandits exploited this unrest to cause further chaos in the north.

Things calmed in 1995, after moderate representatives from the Songhaï and Tuareg communities came together to push towards a lasting peace. This culminated in the ceremonial burning of 3000 weapons in Timbuktu on 27 March 1996 (where the Flamme de la Paix now stands).

Aid money has since been pumped into the region and Tuareg refugees have returned from Mauritania, Algeria and Libya (who had armed and trained many of the insurgents). However, for many the traditional nomadic lifestyle, pivotal to the Tuareg's cultural identity, is now a thing of the past.

## Information

### INTERNET
**Clic of Gao** (Route de l'Aéroport; per hr CFA1000; 8-11am & 4-9pm Mon-Thu & Sat, 6-9pm Fri, 8-11am Sun) At L'Institut de Formation des Maîtres.

### MEDICAL SERVICES
**Hospital** ( ☎ 282 0254; Route de l'Aéroport) A new hospital.
**Pharmacie Attibey** ( ☎ 282 0441; Rue Aldousseini O Touré)
**Pharmacie Populaire du Mali** (Ave des Askia)

### MONEY
**BDM** (Ave des Askia) Changes euro cash, organises Western Union transfers and, sometimes, provides cash advances on Visa cards.

### TOURIST OFFICES & GUIDES
**Association Askia Guide** ( ☎ 282 0130) Guides for exploring local sites and the Sahara.
**Gao Bureau of Tourism Visitor Centre** (Omatho Vistors Centre; ☎ 282 1182, 605 1559; Place de l'Indépendence; 7.30am-5pm Mon-Fri, by appointment Sat & Sun) The best tourist office in Mali, with savvy and helpful staff who have a full list of hotels, restaurants, accredited guides and a host of other services – well done, guys!

## Sights & Activities

Gao's premier tourist attraction is a sunset trip to **La Dune Rose** ('The Pink Dune', known locally as Koïma), a wonderful sand dune on the eastern bank of the Niger, visible from town. As it turns pink with the setting sun, there is magic in the air, not least because it was once believed by locals to be the home of magicians. If you're coming here (only possible from September to February when water levels allow), consider also hiring a pirogue (from CFA15,000 for three hours) to drift further along the river as the dunes come alive. Upstream at Quema and Hondo (a three-hour trip) there are more stunning dunes, while you're almost guaranteed hippo sightings at Tacharan.

Prices for longer river excursions are somewhat inflated, but hippo and manatee spotting is possible (CFA75,000 per day).

**Musée du Sahel** (Rue 224, Sosso-Kiora; admission CFA1000; 8am-noon & 3-6pm Tue-Sun) is a wonderful museum that tells the story of the Songhaï and Tuareg people, and the prehistoric sites in the surrounding region.

The **Tomb of the Askia** (admission CFA1000; Sat-Thu), north of town, was built in 1495 by Askia Muhammad Touré, whose remains lie within. It's an amazing building and a classic of Sudanese (Sahelian) architecture, with its combination of mud-brick, wooden struts and a tapering tower. It may be possible to climb the 10m-high tomb for good views of the city and river.

The **Grand Marché** and **port** are interesting and well worth checking out, especially on Sunday (market day), but it's always busy.

Five blocks east of the water tower, the **Maison des Artisans** ( 8am-dusk) has 60 artisan-owned shops and is a great place to browse.

## Sleeping

Advanced booking of accommodation (which is mostly far from central Gao) is a good idea between November and February.

**Hôtel le Bel Air** ( ☎ 282 0540; mattress on roof CFA4000, d with fan/air-con CFA12,500/17,500; ) A relatively new place that hasn't yet begun the long descent into decline, Bel Air is busy and bustling, and the good rooms are accompanied by an African ambience in the public areas. The rooms in the annexe are especially good.

**Sahara Passion** ( ☎ /fax 282 0187; spassion@malinet .ml; s/d with fan CFA10,000/12,500, with air-con CFA17,000/ 22,000; ) Off Rue 381 southeast of the town centre, Sahara Passion is nicely done and is Gao's most switched-on place. The courtyard is lovely, the restaurant is one of Gao's best (meals CFA1500 to CFA3000), although it's heavy on the oil, and this is one of the best places to organise your desert expedition. The only drawback is that they're often booked out weeks in advance during high tourist season.

**Camping Euro** ( ☎ 608 7827; nr Algerian Consulate, Aljanabandia; d/ste with fan CFA7500/10,000) Since we were in Gao, we've learned of this new and super-clean *campement*-style place, where English is spoken. It's winning good reviews from travellers.

**Hôtel Atlantide** ( ☎ 282 0130; d with fan/air-con CFA10,000/17,500) Around since the 1930s, this

MALI

once-grand colonial place has a past more glorious than its present. Renovations are promised but little seems to change each time we come, so not everything works and it's very frayed around the edges. Then again, it's central, clean and the decaying elegance does have a certain ramshackle charm.

**Camping Bangu** ( ☎ 619 7675; cnr Rues 227 & Tiemoko Fadiala Sangare, Sosso-Kiora; dm CFA3000-5000) has simple dorm accommodation, while **Camping Yarga** ( ☎ 624 2047; off Route de Bac; r CFA5000), 4km south of central Gao, is similar and has a low-key, laid-back atmosphere. **Village Tizi-Mizi** ( ☎ 282 0194; d with fan CFA7500-12,500, with air-con CFA17,500; 🌊 ), 4km along Route de l'Aéroport, is a step up in quality and a pleasant place to stay, although some rooms are overpriced; there's also a good bar.

**Hôtel Restaurant Bon Séjour** ( ☎ 282 0338; mattress on roof CFA1500, d with fan & shared bathroom CFA10,000, with air-con & shared/private bathroom CFA15,000/17,500; 🌊 ) No style or comfort awards here, but this ageing place, opposite the water tower, is one of the few places close to the centre, and the rooms are tidy if unremarkable. The food (meals CFA1500 to CFA2500) is pretty good, and it sells beer.

## Eating

While here, it's definitely worth seeking out the local Songhaï specialty, *wigila*, sun-dried dumplings which you dunk into a meat sauce made with cinnamon and spices. To eat this in a restaurant, you'll need to order it in the morning so you can have it for dinner.

**La Source du Nord** ( 🕐 7am-10pm; salads CFA500-1000, mains CFA750-1750) You can try *wigila* in this place, opposite the Shell petrol station in central Gao, and they also do a good braised *capitaine* (CFA1500).

**Restaurant de l'Amitié** ( 🕐 8-4am; cnr Rues 234 & 213, Sosso-Kiora; meals CFA500-3000) Does rice (CFA500) and steak and chicken dishes for CFA1000 and CFA2000 respectively. Both the Amitié and La Source du Nord are good, and they move up a gear come tourist season.

**Le Petit Restaurant** (3rd paved road, Sosso Koïra; 🕐 6am-8pm; meals CFA500) This is a very popular place with tourists and expats, who come for the cheap and hearty lentils, liver, couscous and macaroni. Oumar, the kindly Algerian owner, is another drawcard.

**Patisserie Le Taubon** (Chateau, Secteur 2; 🕐 5pm-2am; pastries CFA250-300, meals CFA1500-3000) A good range of snacks and lights meals are avail-

able here, including meat pockets (CFA300), chicken burgers (CFA2000) and *nêmes* (shredded beef in an egg roll; CFA500). It's on the road to the airport.

**Restaurant Koundji do a la Belle** (Rue 107, Saneye; meals CFA500-3500) Serves up the standard fare of brochette and rice and sauce, plus some other Malian specialities by prior arrangement.

Of the hotel restaurants, **Hôtel Restaurant Bon Séjour** ( ☎ 282 0338) is the best, followed by **Sahara Passion** ( ☎ /fax 2820187; off Rue 381) and **Hôtel Le Bel Air** ( ☎ 282 0540).

Around the Grand Marché you can get coffee and bread in the mornings, and street food in the evenings (check out the excellent local sausages). Rotisseries are found all over Gao – **Bellàh Rôtisserie** (Ave des Askias; meals from CFA500) is worth a try.

## Drinking

**Club Koukia** (admission CFA1500; 🕐 8-4am), behind Hôtel Atlantide, is a popular bar-cum-nightclub where a Castel will set you back CFA500.

Restaurant de l'Amitié and La Source du Nord are as much bars as restaurants during the tourist season.

## Getting There & Away

### AIR

Apart from international flights operated by Point Afrique (see p543), **CAM** ( ☎ 282 0960; Hôtel Atlantide) offer Gao's only plane connection with the outside world, with one flight per week to Bamako (CFA120,900) via Mopti (CFA85,200) and Timbuktu (CFA42,140).

### BOAT

Pinasses go most Wednesdays to Ansongo (market day on Thursday), but the rapids at Labbe inhibit direct pinasse traffic to Niger. Apart from the **Comanav ferry** ( ☎ 282 0466; p545) there's no regular transport upstream to Timbuktu; chartering your own private pinasse is possible, but expensive (from CFA300,000).

### BUS

Gao lies on the north bank of the Niger River, but the long bitumen road from Bamako terminates on the southern side; a ferry makes the crossing. A new bridge is under construction, however, which will be great news for those who arrive on a bus at night and will no longer have to wait until dawn for the ferry to start running.

Departures to Bamako (CFA16,000, 16 to 20 hours) via Sévaré (CFA7000, eight hours) and Ségou (CFA14,000, 12 hours) leave early in the morning (usually 5am) and mid-afternoon. The office of **Binke** ( ☎ 282 0558) is off Ave des Askia. **Bani** ( ☎ 282 0424) buses leave from Place de l'Indépendance.

A Binke truck-bus leaves for Kidal (CFA7500, eight hours) once a week, and returns the following day. There's also an occasional truck/4WD to Timbuktu (CFA12,500 to CFA15,000, 12 hours) from the *gare routière*. For information on SNTV's truck-buses to Niamey in Niger, see p544. Land Rovers for Ansongo (CFA2700), and occasionally Ménaka (CFA8000), leave when full from Place de l'Indépendance.

### Getting Around

There are no *bâchés* for getting around the sprawl of Gao, which usually means a hot, dusty walk. **Tiobou Maïga** ( ☎ 282 0424) runs two of Gao's few regular taxis.

**Sahara Passion** ( ☎ /fax 820187; spassion@bluewin .ch) is your best bet for 4WD hire (CFA70,000 per day).

## AROUND GAO

Before setting out into the desert north of Gao, check with the local Bureau of Tourism, or police in town, as to the security situation. Although infrequent, there have been reports of banditry.

There's a huge cattle market at Djébok on Monday (transport from Gao CFA750) and the archaeological remains of ancient Gao lie at Sané (though there's not much to see). The Tilemsi Valley is beautiful and Neolithic rock paintings and carvings can be seen in the Adrar des Ifôghas, a remote desert massif around Kidal (where the landscape is stunning). Stone tablets inscribed with historic and Quranic texts have been found near remote Ménaka. Just when you thought you'd reached the end of the road, there's Andéramboukane. This small border town hosts the **Festival of Andéramboukane** (January), one of the most important Tuareg festivals. Talk to the Bureau of Tourism Visitor Centre in Gao about how to get here.

The **Réserve d'Ansongo-Ménaka** is next to the Niger River and is extremely isolated. Much of the wildlife has gone but with considerable luck you may see red-fronted gazelles or manatees, and the Niger River

still contains hippos. Access (via Ansongo) is difficult. You'll require a well-equipped 4WD and an informed guide.

## HOMBORI

Hombori is a large village, on the main road between Mopti and Gao. The older, more picturesque quarter, climbs the hill to the south. Elephants pass close to Hombori in February and March (p534), and Hombori stands in the heart of some spectacular scenery and good climbing country.

Anyone wanting to climb here should contact a Spanish climber called **Salvador Campillo** (salva@maindefatma.com; http://empresas .iddeo.es/mascarell/maindefatma/pag/catal.html), who lives in the area for part of the year and arranges climbing tours.

### Sights & Activities

A series of magnificent sandstone buttresses, or mesas, punctuate the semidesert landscape in this area – some people call the 80km stretch of road between Hombori and Douentza Mali's monument valley. The rock formations and sheer cliffs of the Gandamia Plateau (with great trekking potential) are truly beautiful.

The huge towers of rock culminate north of town with Hombori Tondo, which rises from the plains to 1155m (the highest point in Mali). To reach the wide summit plateau you'll need some climbing ability and equipment, but La Clé de Hombori ('Key to Hombori'), a separate jagged spire at the southwestern end of the massif, can be climbed without ropes in about four hours.

About 13km south of town is La Main de Fatima (The Hand of Fatima) whose narrow, finger-like towers reach up 600m from the plains and provide world-class technical rock climbing. Several routes have been established, most of very high and demanding standard (British grades around E4, French grades around 7A).

A spectacular walking trail passes left (south) of Fatima's northern-most digit to a wonderful campsite, before descending to Garmi Tondo, a picturesque, stone-built village (with a water pump) close to the Gao–Bamako road and where all visitors to the rock should pay a CFA1500 tourist tax.

A 45-minute walk north of Hombori is an impressive dune system, Hondo Miyo. It's a great place to watch the sunset.

**DESERT ELEPHANTS**

Perhaps because the Sahel seems unable to produce enough food even for people and their livestock, it comes as a surprise to most visitors to learn that Mali is home to large herds of migratory elephants. Mali's elephants have longer legs and shorter tusks than their East African cousins and inhabit the Gourma region between the Niger River and the border with Burkina Faso. During the rainy season they fatten themselves up in the relatively lush southern area, and around November to January, as the vegetation withers, they move north to a chain of reliable water holes and survive on relatively little food for the duration of the dry season.

The easiest place to see them is near Gossi, where they drink at the large lake. They move south again in June, a welcome sign for local people of coming rain, often passing near the town of Boni. This annual 1000km circuit is the longest elephant migration in Africa.

For centuries the elephants have coexisted with Fula pastoralists, happy to share their water sources and have the elephants fertilise their lands. Nomadic pastoralists even trail the elephants in order to find the best pasture and water sources. But conditions in the Sahel have become very hard for farmers recently and as the population grows, so pressure on the land increases.

Seeing the elephants requires 4WD transport and a good local guide. For tour operators who can arrange such expeditions, see p546.

## Sleeping & Eating

**Campement Hôtel Mangou Bagni** (camping or mattress on roof CFA3000, s/d CFA4000/6000) The atmosphere makes this a simple, but really quite nice, place to stay and eat. Otherwise there's another very simple *campement* on the main road just west of Hombori's two surprisingly good Senegalese restaurants.

## Getting There & Away

Hombori lies along the Sévaré to Gao road, and all transport between these two towns passes through Hombori (by bus CFA3500 either way, five to nine hours).

## AROUND HOMBORI

Boni lies halfway between Hombori and Douentza, in a wide pass 5km south of the main road. It's a beautiful setting and on Thursday there's a huge cattle market.

Douentza, though an unappealing town, is home to a Sunday market and is the launching point for treks into northern Dogon Country. Douentza's best place to stay, **Campement de Douentza** ( ☎ 245 2052, 633 0301; beds around CFA10,000), is run by the endearingly eccentric Frenchman Jérôme Hurpoil, and is the first choice for arranging expeditions to the Dogon Country. Members of the **guide association** ( ☎ 245 2002) hang out at **Auberge Gourma** ( ☎ 245 2031; CFA3000 per person), a basic place to stay. Guides here can advise about exploring the nearby **Réserve de Douentza** (and provide 4WD hire; expect to pay around CFA50,000 per day plus petrol).

# THE SOUTH

Southern Mali sees relatively few tourists, other than those making their way between the attractions along the Niger River and Burkina Faso away to the south. There's not a whole to see, but you will experience a side to Mali entirely different from the tourist Mali that you encounter further north.

## SIKASSO

pop 144,786

Agreeable, if unexciting, Sikasso stands at the heart of a relatively lush region which is known as the 'market garden of Mali'. Physical evidence of Sikasso's fascinating history has eroded over time, although the mud-brick *tata* (town wall), that fell to French cannons in 1898 is still visible in places. Sikasso was the last Malian town to resist French colonialism, and King Babemba Traore chose to kill himself rather than surrender. The beautiful Palais du Dernier Roi still stands on the western side of town and in the centre is the Mamelon, a small hill that was sacred to the Kénédougou kings, and on which a French colonial tower now stands.

## Information

**Bank of Africa** (off Ave Mamadou) Changes euro cash.
**Hospital** ( ☎ 262 0001; Ave du Gouverneur Jacques Fousset)
**Pharmacie du Souvenir** ( ☎ 262 0119; Blvd Coffet)

## Sleeping & Eating

**Zanga Hôtel** ( ☎ 262 0431; s/d with fan CFA12,500/17,000, with air-con & bathroom CFA21,500/24,500; 🔀 ) Zanga, 100m north of the *gare routière*, is fairly flash (by Sikasso standards), has a pool and is easily the best place to stay in town. The rooms are fine, if uninspiring, but the cheaper ones with fans are not brilliant and are overpriced.

**Hôtel Lotio** ( ☎ 262 1001; Blvd Coiffet; s/d from CFA6000/8000) If you're coming from Burkina Faso, basic rooms here can be a depressing introduction to Mali, but it's a friendly place and the rooms have fans.

**Hôtel Mamelon** ( ☎ 262 0044; Ave Mamadou Konate; d with bathroom CFA8000-16,000) Some of the air-con at this once-lovely hotel seems to date from the colonial era, but it somehow keeps working. Like most people we encountered in Sikasso, the owners are a friendly lot.

Blvd Coiffet has several cheap eateries serving good filling meals (heavy on the rice) for around CFA500 to CFA1500. **La Vieille Marmite** (Blvd Coiffet) and **Restaurant Kene-dougou** (Blvd Coiffet) provide good Malian fare and the enormous Sunday market is a real bonus for street-food fans.

### Getting There & Away

The *gare routière* is a 15-minute walk (CFA200 in a shared taxi) from the town centre. There are daily buses to Bamako (CFA4500, three hours), Mopti (CFA6000, five hours) and Ségou (CFA4500, three hours).

## AROUND SIKASSO

Riddled with chambers and tunnels, the fascinating Grottes de Missirikoro, a lump of limestone roughly 12km southwest of Sikasso, is important to local animists *and* Muslims. A taxi tour from Sikasso costs around CFA8000.

The beautiful waterfalls, Les Chutes de Farako, lie about 27km east of Sikasso, and are easily accessible from the Route de Burkina Faso.

# THE WEST

Western Mali is hard work – transport is infrequent or nonexistent, tourist infrastructure likewise and most of the sights are few and very far between. The region's appeal lies, however, in these very facts. This is Mali largely untrammelled by tourists and

the modern world and losing yourself here is about deep African immersion.

## NATIONAL PARKS

Mali's western national parks are difficult to reach, but will be worthwhile for those who long to escape Mali's tourist crowds.

Bordering the lake formed by Manantali dam, west of Kita, **Parc National du Bafing** protects a number of primate species, including chimpanzees, which are the focus of a small NGO project. Access is from Kounjdan, 45km from Manantali on the route to Kéniéba. From Kounjdan, take the road south to Makandougou; the road is terrible and you may have to walk the 25km from Kounjdan. Once there, ask for Famakan Dembele, a forestry worker. Manantali makes a good base for exploring the region. There are several places to stay and good connections to Mahina (for the Kayes–Bamako train).

The vast Parc National de la Boucle du Baoulé once contained many of the species that you'd see on a Kenyan safari. However, most of the large herbivores have been hunted out, their demise in turn signalling the end for many large carnivores. Northwest of Bamako, the park lies between two large bends on the Baoulé River and is mostly wooden savanna with pockets of riverine forest. Bird-watching is reported to be good, but you'll see few animals. The park is probably of more interest to archaeologists than zoologists, as over 200 archaeological sites have been found here. Access to the park is best via Négala, a small village 60km northwest of Bamako. You'll need a 4WD and to be completely self-sufficient. For more information contact the **Office du Parc National de la Boucle du Baoulé** (Map p492; ☎ 222 2498), which is next to Bamako's botanical gardens.

## KAYES

**pop 97,464**

You wouldn't come here just to see Kayes (pronounced Kai), but as the principal settlement in the west of Mali, it can be a reasonable place to break up the long journey between Bamako and Dakar. Kayes is hot and dusty, and was the first place the French settled in Mali (several colonial buildings remain). There's a thriving, chaotic market, the town is largely hassle-free and a number of interesting excursions are possible.

MALI

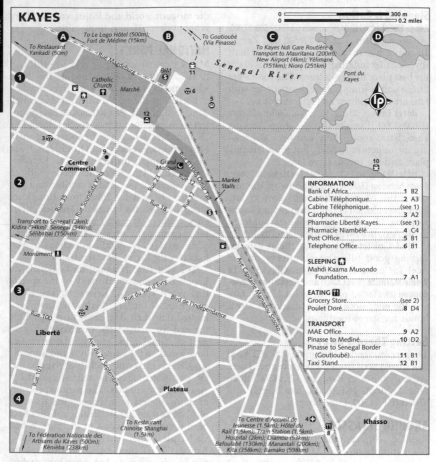

KAYES

0 ———————— 300 m
0 ———————— 0.2 miles

## Information

There are telephone call centres (cabines téléphonique) including on Ave du 22 Septembre and Rue 14.

**Bank of Africa** (Rue 14) Changes euro cash.
**Hospital** ( ☎ 252 1232) Is 2km south of town.
**Pharmacie Liberté Kayes** (Rue 14)
**Pharmacies Niambélé** (Ave du Capitaine Mamadou Sissoko)

## Sleeping & Eating

**Centre d'Accueil de Jeunesse** (camping or mattress on roof CFA3000, s/d CFA5000/7500) This hostel-style place is a real late-night, let's-just-crash sort of spot, with a bar.

**Hôtel du Rail** ( ☎ 252 1233; d with air-con CFA18,000-28,000; ❄ ) Opposite the train station, Kayes'

Rail Hotel is typical of such places across West Africa – always people coming and going, a lovely old colonial building, and interiors that fade noticeably with each passing year. The food here is good (three-course menu CFA6000), while the garden's an ideal place to wait for trains.

**Mahdi Kaama Musundo Foundation** (beds CFA6000) This foundation for the promotion of Soninke language and culture, is not really a hotel, but is an imaginative choice nonetheless. The rooms are simple and there's an atmosphere of quiet scholarship; not surprisingly the staff are a mine of information on local culture. It's next to the petrol station and opposite the market in the centre of town.

**Le Logo Hôtel** ( ☎ 252 1381; Rue 139 Légal Ségou; s/d with air-con & breakfast CFA12,500/17,500; ❂ ) Although not really convenient for much other than the riverbank, Le Logo, off Rue Madgeburg, is a friendly place with good food (meals CFA1500 to CFA4000) and a decent bar.

There are several cheap food stalls near the train station and in the market. Of the sit-down options (all open for lunch and dinner daily), **Restaurant Yankadi** (Rue 122; meals CFA250-700), near the junction with Rue Magdeburg, serves filling meals; **Poulet Doré** (Ave du Capitaine Mamadou Sissoko) does great roast chicken (whole chicken CFA3000); and **Restaurant Chinois Shanghai** (meals CFA1250-3750), at the southern end of Ave du 22 Septembre, offers authentic Chinese cuisine, freshly prepared in front of your eyes (the portions are tasty, but a little small).

## Shopping

The excellent market is busy on Saturday. **Fédération Nationale des Artisans du Kayes** ( ☎ 252 2445), beside the stadium, puts you in touch with local artisans producing excellent textiles.

## Getting There & Away

The best route to Bamako is currently via Bafoulabé, Manantali and Kita (the first quarter is pretty rough).

For cross-border transport to Senegal and Mauritania, see p543.

### AIR

**CAM** ( ☎ 672 7676) and **MAE** ( ☎ 252 1582; Rue Soundiata Keita) each have up to four weekly flights between Kayes and Bamako (CFA57,850). As few tourists come this way, seats fill up fast with Malians on business. The new airport is north of the Senegal River, on the road to Yélimané.

### BOAT

Pinasses to the Senegal border at Goutioubé (CFA3000) leave mid-afternoon. Some go on to Bakel (CFA11,000).

### BUSH TAXI

Transport leaves daily from Kayes Ndi *gare routière*, on the north side of the river, to Nioro (CFA7500 to CFA9000) and Yélimané (CFA5000). Old 4WDs go to Sélibabai (CFA10,000) in Mauritania, directly from Kayes Ndi.

### TRAIN

There's a service from Kayes to Bamako (2nd/1st class CFA6960/11,670, 10 to 14 hours) on Monday, Tuesday and Saturday (it travels the other way the previous day). You can take the weekly international service from Dakar to Bamako (2nd/1st/couchette class CFA11,480/16,190/22,190), although getting tickets can be difficult. For more details on services to Senegal, see p546.

## AROUND KAYES

The **Fort de Médine**, about 15km upstream from Kayes, was part of a chain of defence posts built along the Senegal River in French colonial times. The crumbling buildings hold a real sense of history and the old train station is particularly beautiful. You may be able to stay with a local family; ask either of the guides at Fort de Médine or at the mayor's office just beside it.

The Chutes de Felou are a set of rapids and waterfalls about 2km south from Médine.

Pinasses to Médine (CFA1000) leave from opposite the Total petrol station in Kayes around 6.30am and 1.30pm daily, and return around 8am the following morning. Pirogues to Médine (CFA750) leave around 3pm and return to Kayes the following morning. A taxi there and back costs around CFA12,500.

## YÉLIMANÉ

The new dirt road between Yélimané and Kayes makes the interesting journey to this little Sahelian town easy. The compact hilltop centre of Yélimané is worth exploring, but the real attractions are out of town.

After the wet, dozens of lily-covered seasonal lakes and flooded forests appear along the course of the Kolinbiné River, providing feeding grounds for migratory and endemic water birds.

Mare de Goumboko is the closest lake to Yélimané (10km west), while Mares de Garé, Lebé and Toya are harder to get to. The former two are best reached via Komolo (signposted from the Kayes road around 45km west of Yélimané). Mare de Toya is reached via Yaguine (22km west of Yélimané). You are advised to seek out the chief of both villages and take a guide to see you safely along the often-confusing 4WD tracks.

**MALI**

Maison de l'Amitié ( ☎ 252 2251; beds CFA2000) offers good, cheap accommodation. It's just north of the market.

## DIAMOU

This tiny rail-side town has nothing to offer travellers, but the surrounding landscape is stunning. The Senegal River flows through a cluster of large sandstone mesas, creating potentially great trekking country. One good objective is the Chutes de Gouina, a 200m-wide, 10m-high set of waterfalls located about 24km upstream from Diamou.

The road between Bafoulabé (a small town at the junction of Bafing and Bakoy Rivers) and Kayes provides a direct route to the falls, but there's no regular transport. Follow the old bitumen road 6km out of Diamou to a junction just past the defunct cement factory. Turn right onto the dirt road (signposted to 'Gouina and Bafoulabé') and after 18km, just after passing the ruins of a French Mission, you'll see the spray of the falls through the scrub.

Back in Diamou, Bar Le Khasso (across the tracks from the station) offers very simple accommodation, should you miss the train.

Trains between Bamako and Kayes stop here. There's little road transport to Kayes.

## KÉNIÉBA

This neglected town may be something of a dog's breakfast, but the surrounding escarpments and hills are dramatic and picturesque. Unusually for Mali, there's also a fair amount of wildlife in the region, so if you go walking (and you really should) your chances of actually seeing some are not bad. Just make sure that if you're with a guide they don't try to kill it.

The town was once the centre of a gold-producing area (see p486) and is the starting point for little-used routes into Guinea and Senegal.

The **Casa Ronde** (s/d CFA3000/4500) *campement* provides the only basic, grubby and rather depressing accommodation, but the simple food is OK. Restaurant Wassa, located beside Pharmacie Abdoul Wahab and just up from the Total petrol station, has better grub.

### Getting There & Away

There's usually one vehicle per day for Kayes (CFA7500) and other surrounding towns, with regular departures chalked up on a board in the square next to the mayor's office.

There are also cross-border options for Guinea (p544) and Senegal (p544).

# MALI DIRECTORY

## ACCOMMODATION

Mali has some outstanding hotels, although compared to other West African countries you pay a lot more for quality.

Everywhere, budget hotels (up to CFA8000/10,000 for a single/double) vary from basic and depressing to simple and tidy, but rarely have any character. Sleeping on flat roofs (mattresses are usually provided) is the cheapest accommodation option in Mali; prices range from CFA1000 in the Dogon Country (where it can be the only budget option) to CFA3000. Some hotels have dorms (CFA3000 to CFA4000); the best of these are in Ségou, Sévaré, Mopti and Bandiagara. Elsewhere, the best you can hope for is a *campement*, which are simple and range around a courtyard.

The standard of midrange hotels (from CFA10,000/12,000 for a single/double up to CFA33,000/40,000) is generally quite high across the country. Bamako, Ségou, Sévaré, Bandiagara and, to a lesser extent, Mopti have the best hotels, while tourist hotspots like Djenné and Timbuktu have good hotels, but few that stand out.

In Bamako there are dozens of top-end hotels (above CFA35,000/42,000 for a single/double and up to CFA75,000 for a

---

**PRACTICALITIES**

- Electricity supply is 220V, and two-pin Western European-style plugs are used.

- Local daily French-language newspapers include *Le Soir* and *Le Malien*; *Le Figaro* and *Le Monde* are available in Bamako, and *International Herald Tribune,* and *Newsweek* appear at just a few Bamako outlets.

- The BBC World Service is on 88.9FM in Bamako; elsewhere check www.bbc .co.uk/cgi-bin/worldservice.

- Mali uses the metric system for weights and measures.

double) to choose from, but the only other quality top-end place is in Mopti.

Some places add CFA500 per person tourist tax to room costs, and this has been included in the prices in this chapter.

## ACTIVITIES

Mali is one of the most active destinations in West Africa. Possibilities include exceptional trekking in Dogon Country (p513); evocative desert expeditions by camel or 4WD in the Sahara north of Timbuktu (p525), or Gao (p533); river journeys up the Niger between Mopti and Timbuktu (p510); and world-class rock climbing near Hombori (p533).

## BOOKS

*Ségu,* by Maryse Condé, is an epic generational tale of a late 18th-century family living in the Niger River trading town of Ségou.

*In Griot Time: An American Guitarist in Mali,* by Banning Eyre, is a great read, offering up-close pen portraits of many of Mali's world-renowned artists and a meditation on the role of music in modern Malian society.

*The Cruelest Journey: Six Hundred Miles to Timbuktu,* by Kira Salak, is one of the best books on Mali recently. Follow the author as, inspired by Mungo Park, she paddles up the Niger to Timbuktu where she exposes the continued existence of slavery in Mali.

*Dogon – Africa's People of the Cliffs,* by Stephenie Hollyman and Walter van Beek, is a beautifully photographed study of the Dogon, with informative anthropological text – it'll look nice on your coffee table but it's not for your backpack.

*Men of Salt: Across the Sahara with the Caravan of White Gold,* by Michael Benanav, is a highly readable account of an epic modern-day journey to the remote salt mines of Taoudenni, with plenty of fascinating anecdotes and historical detail.

*Banco: Adobe Mosques of the Inner Niger Delta,* by Sebastian Schutyser, is a beautifully presented collection of black-and-white photographs of Mali's weird-and-wonderful mosques – it's a great souvenir of your visit.

## BUSINESS HOURS

Banks open between 8am and noon, then 3pm to 5pm Monday to Friday, plus 8am til noon Saturday. Bars normally serve from

noon until late, while nightclubs hop between 10pm and the wee hours. You should be able to grab a bite in most restaurants between noon and 3pm, then 6.30pm to 11pm. Shops and businesses generally open from 8am to noon and 3pm to 5pm Monday until Friday, and 8am til noon on Saturday.

## CHILDREN

Mali's a terrific destination for children. While there are few sights or activities dedicated to kids, the improbable houses of the Dogon Country (p513), the sandcastle-like Djenné mosque (p506), the fascinating riverside villages of the Niger (p510) and a Tuareg encampment amid the sand close to the legendary city of Timbuktu (p525) will be experiences your children will never forget.

## COURSES

For French classes, enquire at the **Centre Culturel Français** (Map p494; ☎ 222 4019; www.ccf bamako.org) in Bamako, where they sometimes offer courses.

Sadly, courses in Mali's musical instruments and traditions are extremely rare. In Bamako try the **Carrefour des Jeunes** (Map p494; Ave Kassa Keita) or **Maison des Jeunes** (Map p492; ☎ 222 2320; maisjeunes@yahoo.fr; off Sq Lumumba), while **Motel Savane** ( ☎ 232 0974; savane@ motelsavane.com; off Blvd de l'Indépendance) in Ségou sometimes has drumming classes.

## DANGERS & ANNOYANCES

Crime is not a big problem in Mali, although in Bamako you should be careful about walking around at night in some areas (see p493 for more details). People travelling by train should take extra care, as the train stations in Kayes and Bamako are targeted by thieves who enjoy the chaotic scenes when the train pulls in. Be vigilant on the trains themselves, especially between Kati and Bamako, and before arriving at Kayes. Carry a torch (flashlight), keep nothing in your pockets, watch (and lock) your bags at all times, and be extra vigilant when embarking and disembarking.

Always check the local security situation if you're heading out into the desert north of Gao, as banditry has been reported.

The main annoyance for visitors are the young men who lurk outside hotels in Bamako, Mopti, Djenné, Ségou, Timbuktu and the gateway towns to the Dogon

Country offering their services as guides (see the boxed text, p491).

Some travellers have also reported respiratory complaints coming from dust-laden air, which can be a particular problem during the harmattan season from January to May.

## EMBASSIES & CONSULATES
### Malian Embassies & Consulates

All embassies issue visas and in West Africa, Mali has embassies in Burkina Faso, Côte d'Ivoire, Ghana, Guinea, Mauritania, Senegal, Sierra Leone and Niger. For details, see the relevant country chapters. In Paris, note that it is the Consulate-General which issues visas, not the embassy. Other Malian embassies or consulates include the following:

**Belgium** ( ☎ 02-345 7432; ambassade.mali@skynet.be; 487 Ave Molière, Brussels 1060)

**Canada** ( ☎ 613-232 1501, 232 3264; www.ambamali canada.org/english/a1.html; 50 Ave Goulburn, Ottawa, Ontario K1N 8C8)

**France** Consulat Général ( ☎ 01-48 07 85 85; www .consulat-mali-france.org; fax 45 48 55 34; 64 Rue Pelleport, Paris 75020); Embassy ( ☎ 01-45 48 58 43; fax 01 45 48 55 34; 89 Rue du Cherche Midi, Paris 75006)

**Germany** ( ☎ 030-319 9883; fax 319 9884; Kurfürstendamm 72, 10709 Berlin)

**Italy** ( ☎ 06-4425 4068; amb.malirome@tiscalinet.it; Via Antonia Boston 2, Rome)

**USA** ( ☎ 202-332 2249; www.maliembassy.us; 2130 R St NW, Washington, DC 20008)

### Embassies & Consulates in Mali

The following are all embassies in Bamako:

**Burkina Faso** ( ☎ 229 3171; off Route de Guinea; ☽ 7.30am-12.30pm & 1-4.30pm Mon-Fri)

**Canada** ( ☎ 221 2236; www.bamako.gc.ca; Route de Koulikoro) Opposite Luna Parc; also assists Australian and UK nationals.

**Côte d'Ivoire** (Map p492; ☎ 221 2289; Rue 220; ☽ 9am-12.30pm & 1.30-4pm Mon-Fri) Near Marché N'Golonina, above TAM Voyages.

**France** (Map p494; ☎ 221 2951, 221 3141; Sq Lumumba) Consulate; assists Austrian, Belgian, Spanish, Greek, Italian and Portuguese nationals.

**Germany** ( ☎ 222 3715; Badalabougou Est) South of Pont des Martyrs.

**Ghana** ( ☎ 229 6083; ACI2000; ☽ 8am-12.30pm & 1.30-4.30pm Mon-Thu, 8am-12.30pm Fri)

**Guinea** ( ☎ 221 0806; Rue 37, off Ave de l'OUA, Faso-Kanu; ☽ 8.30am-12.30pm & 1.30-4.30pm Mon-Thu, 8.30am-12.30pm Fri)

**Mauritania** ( ☎ 221 4815; Rue 213, off Route de Koulikoro, Hippodrome; ☽ 8am-3pm Mon-Fri)

**Netherlands** (Map p492; ☎ 221 5611; bam@minbuza .ml; Rue 437, off Route de Koulikoro, Hippodrome)

**Niger** ( ☎ 601 9239, 698 7828; Ave Mamadou Konaté; ☽ 8am-4pm Mon-Fri)

**Senegal** ( ☎ 221 8273; fax 221 1780; Rue 287, off Blvd Nelson Mandela, Hippodrome; ☽ 7.30am-1pm & 1.30-4pm Mon-Fri)

**USA** (Map p494; ☎ 222 5470; www.usa.org.ml; cnr Rue de Rochester & Rue Mohammed V)

## FESTIVALS & EVENTS

In addition to mask ceremonies in Dogon villages (April to May; p517), Bozo fishing celebrations (February), marionette festivals in Diarabougou (November; p501) and Markala (p504), and the great cattle crossings of the Fulani (December to January; p504), the following are worth checking out:

**Biennal** (Bamako; September in even years) A sport and cultural festival with live music groups from around Mali.

**Festival in the Desert** (www.festival-au-desert.org; January; Essakane, near Timbuktu; p62)

**Festival of Andéramboukane** (January; Andéramboukane on Mali–Niger border; p533)

**Festival Sur Le Niger** (February; Ségou; p502)

## HOLIDAYS

Public holidays include:

**New Year's Day** 1 January
**Army Day** 20 January
**For the Martyrs of the 1991 Revolution** 26 March
**Easter** March/April
**Labour Day** 1 May
**African Unity Day** 25 May
**Independence Day** 22 September
**Christmas Day** 25 December

For a table of Islamic holiday dates, see p818.

## INTERNET ACCESS

Internet access is widely available in Bamako and there are fast connections in Mopti, Bandiagara and, to a lesser extent, Ségou. Elsewhere you'll find at least one Internet café in most towns (including Timbuktu), but connections can be slow. Access usually costs between CFA1000 and CFA1500 per hour .

## INTERNET RESOURCES

**Afribone Mali** (www.afribone.com) General French-language information on Mali.

**Dogon-Lobi** (www.dogon-lobi.ch/index_1024.htm) Great photo site with an exceptional list of links to sites about Malian architecture and society.

**Journée Nationale des Communes** (www.journee
-nationale-communes.org) Dry government website (in
French) with some interesting statistics by region.
**Mali Pages** (www.malipages.com.com) Yellow pages
listings for Mali.
**Mali Photos** (www.maliphotos.de) Excellent photos of
Mali and good information about Mopti/Sévaré.
**OMATHO** (www.omatho.com) Government-tourist
office site which is surprisingly packed with information,
from full listings of tour operators to upcoming
events.

## MAPS

The French **IGN** (www.ign.fr) produces the
excellent *Mali* (1:2,000,000), but it's not
available in Mali itself. They also sell the
Carte Internationale du Monde series
(1:1,000,000), which is outdated for roads
but the best in the business for physical
geography. Michelin's 953 *Africa North and
West* (1:4,000,000) is large scale, but shows
Mali's minor roads accurately.

**Institute Geographique du Mali** ( ☎ 220 2840),
off Ave de l'OUA, Badalabougou Est in
Bamako, holds basic country and town
maps (CFA10,000) plus 1:200,000 topographical maps (CFA5000).

## MONEY

The unit of currency is the West African
CFA franc.

### Cash & Travellers Cheques

Most of Mali's banks change foreign
cash. Outside Bamako you may have difficulty with travellers cheques, and when
banks do change them commission rates
vary wildly. Bank of Africa, Ecobank and
Banque Internationale du Mali (BIM) usually charge around 2%.

Changing money in a bank (even cash)
can take up to an hour, but some Western-
orientated businesses, such as supermarkets
and big expensive cafés, will happily change
cash and sometimes travellers cheques.
Moneychangers also deal openly outside the
banks and at the airport. Most offer good
rates with no commission and the process is
quick. However, rip-offs do happen.

Euros are the best to carry. US dollars are
OK, but commissions are quite often higher
and nonbank exchange rates grim.

Western Union (for international money
transfers; see p820 for details) are found in
most banks and post offices.

### Credit Cards

At the time of writing, only Banque de Développement du Mali (BDM) was offering cash
advances for Visa cards. Banque Internationale pour le Commerce et l'Industrie du Mali
(Bicim) used to provide Visa cash advances
and there were rumours that they may do so
again. There were no functioning ATMs, but
Visa card is accepted in a few hotels, restaurants and businesses in Bamako. No bank
gives out CFAs against your MasterCard.

## POST

Letter and parcel post from Mali's cities
is reasonably reliable, but letters can still
take weeks to arrive. Parcels do go missing,
but usually only items sent from overseas.
Anything of real value should be sent by **DHL**
(Map p494; ☎ 222 6376; Ave Ruault, Bamako).

A postcard to Europe/North America costs
CFA395/405 and a letter CFA485/515.

Poste restante is available at all major
post offices. Some charge CFA500 per letter
upon collection.

## TELEPHONE

Sotelma, the national telephone company,
has installed cardphones and phonecards
are sold by vendors throughout Mali. Local
calls cost CFA100 per minute, national calls
CFA300 to CFA500, calls to Europe CFA1875
and to the USA CFA3050. However tariffs
are reduced significantly after 5.30pm. Most
towns have privately owned *télécentres* or
*cabines téléphonique,* which allow easy telephone and fax communication.

### Mobile Phones

Malians love their mobile (cell) phones, and
costs are coming down and coverage is expanding. **Malitel** (www.malitel.com.ml) and **Ikatel**
(www.ikatel.net) are the main providers; both
websites have maps showing each company's
coverage within Mali. Local SIM cards can be
a good investment if you plan on spending
a prolonged period in the country, and occasional offers usually work out cheaper than
international calls than calling from a fixed
line. Most GSM mobiles from European and
other Western countries work in Mali.

## TOURIST INFORMATION

Mali's **Office Malien du Tourisme et de Hôtellerie**
(Omatho; www.omatho.com) is something of a mixed
bag, but is improving all the time. Their

website is excellent, and some local offices (Gao is a stand-out example) have really got their act together in recent years. The recent Omatho-driven system of accrediting guides is a huge improvement on the past and the Omatho offices in Bamako, Timbuktu, Gao and Mopti can provide lists of accredited guides. Despite such improvements, in many towns there's no real reason to visit the Omatho office (often called Bureau Régional du Tourisme), where you won't find much more than the odd brochure.

## VISAS

Visas are required by everyone. If there's no Malian embassy in your home country, it's possible to get your visa on arrival at the border. It costs CFA15,000 and you'll need to bring passport photos for the purpose. The visa is valid for an initial period of five days and must then be extended at a police station (no charge), whereafter it will be valid for one month. However, we would still advise you to get your visa in advance (either in Paris, Brussels, Washington DC or while you're travelling through West Africa), because travellers who arrive without visas routinely report hassles from border officials keen to make a little extra money on the side.

The Malian embassy in Brussels charges €30 for a one-month visa, while the Consulate-General in Paris charges €28 for a 30-day single-entry visa, and €51 for the three-month multiple-entry variety; application forms for the latter can be downloaded at www.consulat-mali-france.org/services/texte/frame_base.htm.

The Malian embassy in the USA (www.maliembassy.us) requires payment in cashier's check or money order only (if paying by post), two copies of the application form, two photos, a yellow-fever vaccination certificate and printed flight itinerary; they sometimes also request a hotel reservation. Costs are US$80/110 for single-/multiple-entry three-month visas.

At Malian embassies in West Africa, you'll usually pay CFA20,000 for a one-month single-entry visa.

### Visa Extensions

One-month visa extensions cost CFA5000, require two photos and are only available at the Sûreté buildings in Bamako and Mopti. There's a fine of CFA15,000 per day for

every day you overstay, and border officials will delight in extracting this from you.

In Bamako, these are processed in 48 to 72 hours at the **Sûreté Nationale building** (Map p492), 200m northeast of Rond-point de l'Unité Africaine.

In Mopti, these are possible (after a 15-minute wait) at a small **office** ( ☎ 243 0020) next to the police station.

### Visas for Onward Travel

There is no Togolese embassy in Mali (see p804 for advice on getting Togolese visas), but you can get the following visas for neighbouring countries.

#### BURKINA FASO

Single-/multiple-entry three-month visas cost CFA25,000/30,000 and require three identical photos. If you leave your passport at the embassy in the morning you can pick it up in the afternoon.

#### CÔTE D'IVOIRE

In theory the embassy will issue visas (CFA30,000, two photos) in three days, but the security situation in Côte d'Ivoire means that rules and the state of mind of embassy officials change often.

#### GHANA

If you give the Ghanaian embassy CFA12,000 and four photos, they'll issue you with a one-month, single-entry visa in 48 hours (remember they close on Friday afternoon). Nine-month multiple-entry visas cost CFA30,000.

#### GUINEA

The embassy issues visas in 24 hours and requires two photos, but fees are high – for most nationalities it's CFA46,500/60,000/76,500 for one-month/two-month/multiple-entry visas, but US, UK, Canadian and Australian citizens pay CFA60,000/80,000 for single-/multiple-entry visas.

#### MAURITANIA

The embassy will issue visas (CFA16,000) in 48 hours. Three photos are required.

#### NIGER

The Niger consulate issues one-month visas for CFA20,000, asks for three photos, and takes two to three days to do so.

**SENEGAL**
One-/three-month Senegalese visas cost CFA3000/7000, require two photos and take two days to issue.

# TRANSPORT IN MALI

## GETTING THERE & AWAY
### Entering Mali
Be scrupulous in ensuring that you have *all* your papers in order (visa, yellow-fever vaccination) whenever you enter (or leave) the country, because Malian border officials are renowned for finding inconsistencies, whether real or invented. If your papers are in order, be patient, point out the entry stamp and visa duration, and resist requests to pay to clear up any 'misunderstandings'. Getting your visa on arrival can involve inflated visa prices (ie bribes) but will more often result in an hour or two extra of waiting.

### Air
Mali's main international airport is **Sénou International Airport** ( ☎ 220 4626), although Point-Afrique also flies into Mopti and Gao.

Numerous airlines fly into Bamako and those with offices there include the following:

**Afriqiyah** (Map p494; 8U; ☎ 223 1497; www.afriqiyah .aero; Ave de la Marne) Hub: Tripoli.

**Air Algérie** (Map p494; AH; ☎ 222 3159; www.air algerie.dz; Rue de la Cathedral; hub: Algiers)

**Air Burkina** (Map p494; 2J; ☎ 221 0178; www.air -burkina.com; Ave de la Marne) Hub: Ouagadougou)

**Air France** (Map p494; AF; ☎ 222 2212; www.airfrance .com; Sq Lumumba) Hub: Paris. You can check-in your luggage at the office between 11am and 1pm on the day of departure.

**Air Ivoire** (Map p494; VU; ☎ 223 9559; www.airivoire .com) Hub: Abidjan.

**Air Mauritanie** (Map p494; MR; ☎ 223 8740; www .airmauritanie.mr; Sq Lumumba) Hub: Nouakchott.

**Air Sénégal International** (Map p494; V7; ☎ in Bamako 223 9811; www.air-senegal-international.com; Ave Modibo Keita) Hub: Dakar.

**Cameroon Airlines** (Map p494; UY; ☎ 222 9400; www.cameroon-airlines.com; cnr Ave Kassa Keita & Ave de l'Indépendance) Hub: Douala.

**Ethiopian Airlines** (Map p494; ET; ☎ 222 2208; www .flyethiopian.com/et/; Sq Lumumba) Hub: Addis Ababa.

**Ghana Airways** (Map p494; GH; ☎ 221 9210; www .ghana-airways.com; Sq Lumumba) Hub: Accra.

**Interair** (Map p494; D6; ☎ 221 9210; www.interair .co.za; cnr Ave Kassa Keita & Ave de l'Indépendance) Hub: Johannesburg.

**Point Afrique** (Map p494; ☎ 223 5470; www.point -afrique.com; Ave de la Marne) Hub: Paris.

**Royal Air Maroc** (Map p494; AT; ☎ 221 6105; www .royalairmaroc.com; Ave de la Marne) Hub: Casablanca.

**WEST AFRICA**
Without a national carrier of its own, Mali relies on the carriers of neighbouring countries for flights to West African capitals.

There are almost-daily flights to Dakar in Senegal (CFA87,000), Abidjan in Côte d'Ivoire (CFA118,000), and Ouagadougou in Burkina Faso (CFA109,200). Flights leave three or four times a week to Lagos in Nigeria (CFA257,000), Nouakchott in Mauritania (CFA261,000), Accra in Ghana (CFA211,000), plus there's at least one weekly flight to Conakry in Guinea (CFA109,000) and Banjul in Gambia (CFA67,000). Air Sénégal International has arguably the biggest network, which includes three weekly flights to Niamey (CFA165,000) and a service to Lomé (CFA187,000). Air Burkina and Air Mauritania also do more than just fly home. For other regional capitals, you'll need to change in Dakar, Ouagadougou or Abidjan.

At the time of writing Bamako, Point Afrique were hoping to start a cut-price Ouagadougou–Bamako–Dakar service. If they do, expect prices on these routes to drop.

### Land
You can cross into Burkina Faso easily just south of Kouri (southwest of Koutiala) or along dirt roads east of Sikasso (to Koloko) or via Koro (east of Dogon Country).

Kourémalé is the main border crossing for Guinea, but some traffic takes the back roads via the border crossings at Bougouni, Sélingué or Kéniéba. The best way to drop into Côte d'Ivoire is along the bitumen road at Zégoua south of Sikasso.

The crossing to/from Senegal is at Kidira, west of Kayes. The main access points to Mauritania are north of Nioro or Nara, but it's possible to travel direct to Sélibabi from Kayes.

The Tanezrouft trans-Saharan route through Algeria is effectively closed to travellers. Go via Niger, crossing the border at Labbézanga, southeast of Gao.

MALI

## BURKINA FASO

Numerous buses leave Bamako's Sogoniko *gare routière* daily for Ouagadougou (CFA15,000, 20 hours) via Bobo-Dioulasso (CFA11,500, 15 hours). Note that most buses travel via Ségou and Sikasso, rather than via the more direct route. Buses also go to Bobo-Dioulasso from Mopti (CFA9000). A daily bus links Koro with Ouahigouya (CFA2500, up to four hours) from where there's onward transport to Ouagadougou.

## CÔTE D'IVOIRE

Travel to Côte d'Ivoire was unsafe at the time of writing and the volume of cross-border transport has dropped off. However, there are still daily buses to Abidjan (CFA22,500, 36 to 48 hours) from Bamako. Transport for Côte d'Ivoire also leave from Sikasso.

## GUINEA

Peugeot taxis or minibuses run most days from Bamako's Djikoroni *gare routière* to the border at Kourémalé (CFA3500, three hours) and then on to Siguiri (CFA6000). There's occasionally transport to Kankan (CFA8500) and Kissidougou (CFA14,500), while a once-weekly bus continues all the way to Conakry (CFA25,000).

From Kéniéba, there's only intermittent cross-border traffic (usually a motorcycle or two) to Labé in Guinea via the border town of Kali

## MAURITANIA

Battered 4WDs and trucks are the usual transport. There are daily departures from Kayes to Sélibabi (CFA12,000, eight hours) and from Nioro to Ayoûn el-Atroûs (CFA17,500). The latter option gets you onto the paved road leading to Nouakchott. All these routes are sandy in the October to May dry season, best travelled between November and February before the harmattan, and extremely difficult in the wet season from June to October.

## NIGER

**SNTV** ( ☎ 282 0395) depart for Niamey (CFA8600, 16 to 24 hours) on Wednesday and Saturday at 5.30am from their office east of the centre of Gao; coming the other way costs CFA11,500. The road between Ansongo and Gao is terrible. All passport formalities must be completed at the main police station in Gao the day before depar-

ture/upon arrival. If you want to split your journey and spend time in Ansongo make this clear to immigration officials.

There are also weekly slow boats that run between Gao and Ayorou (CFA14,000, two days).

## SENEGAL

Most travellers fly or take the train between Bamako and Dakar, although the road between Kidira and Dakar has improved in recent years.

The train service is one of Africa's great epics, although traveller opinion is divided; one reader described the journey as 'a mystical experience', while another saw it as 'more a chore than an adventure'. In theory the train departs Bamako for Dakar (2nd/1st/couchette class CFA25,500/34,620/53,145) at 9.15am Wednesday, and from Dakar at 10am. It could take forever but, if not, around 50 hours, and could conceivably depart any day of the week. You should take care as theft is frequent (see p539 for further details)

There's regular road transport from Kayes (Blvd de l'Indépendance, about 2km west of the town centre) to Diboli (CFA3000, two hours); some transport continues over the bridge to Kidira in Senegal, from where there's transport to Tambacounda. Alternatively, there's an overnight bus direct to Dakar from Kayes (CFA15,000, 24 hours) twice a week.

# GETTING AROUND
## Air

Mali's domestic air industry has undergone massive change in recent years, with a number of airlines falling by the wayside (though fortunately not from the sky). There are now two domestic carriers:

**Compagnie Aerienne du Mali** (CAM; ☎ 229 9100; o.nubukpo@cam-mali.com; Immeuble Tomota, Ave Cheick Zayed, Hamdallaye, Bamako) The newer operator, usually cheaper.

**Mali Air Express** (MAE; map p494; ☎ 223 1465; sae@cefib.com; Ave de la Nation, Bamako)

Both airlines fly from Bamako to Mopti (CFA57,860, three weekly flights), Timbuktu (CFA90,360, three weekly) and Kayes (CFA57,850, four weekly). CAM also operates a weekly flight to/from Gao (CFA120,900) which goes via Mopti and Timbuktu. Return fares are only a fraction under double one-way prices (eg Bamako-Timbuktu return costs CFA179,720).

## Boat

Most boat journeys on the Niger River are only possible from August to December when water levels are high.

For detailed information on travelling by pirogue and public or private pinasse, see p510.

### PASSENGER BOAT

Three large passenger boats (the *Kankan Moussa* is the best), operated by the Compagnie Malienne de Navigation (Comanav), ply the Niger River between Koulikoro (50km west of Bamako) and Gao, from August to November or December, stopping at numerous riverside towns including Mopti and Korioumé (for Timbuktu) en route. In theory, one boat heads downstream from Koulikoro at 10pm Tuesday, arrives in Mopti at 3pm Thursday, in Timbuktu at 7am Saturday and Gao on midnight Sunday. Another boat heads upstream from Gao at 8pm every Monday, reaching Timbuktu at 6pm on Wednesday, Mopti at 4pm Friday and Koulikoro at midnight Sunday. In practice, the journey can take twice as long.

Despite the vagaries of the timetable, the journey is a fascinating insight into village life along the Niger, but it's not for everyone. The boats are like floating villages – people and cargo are everywhere, the cabins are sweltering, the toilets flooded and the food, well it ain't cordon bleu – but it's a quintessentially African experience. Getting a group together, hiring a small cabin for everyone's kit and then going 4th class, which means sleeping on the roof (cabins can be hot and stuffy anyway), could be a good idea.

Of course, it's not essential to do the whole trip. The two-day section from Mopti to Korioumé (about 400km) is arguably the

most interesting, although from Koulikoro to Mopti is less crowded.

The 'luxe' cabins have a bathroom and air-con, 1st-class cabins have two bunk beds, toilet and washbasin, and 2nd-class cabins are four-berth with a washbasin and shared toilets. Third class is an eight-berth cabin and in 4th class you get to fight for a space on deck and don't get meals.

Booze, food and water are all available, but it's a good idea to take extra supplies as you may get stranded.

### PIROGUE & PUBLIC PINASSE

Pirogues are small canoes, either paddled by hand or fitted with a small outboard motor. They're usually the slowest form of river transport. Pinasses are larger motorised boats, carrying cargo and anything from 10 to 100 passengers. Some are large enough to have an upper deck and a couple of basic cabins; smaller pinasses make do with a reed mat roof to keep off the sun.

Public pinasses are generally faster than the Comanav passenger boat, but they're equally unpredictable and can be extremely crowded and overloaded. To avoid getting seriously stranded, use the various market days (when there's more river transport).

The table below lists some of the bigger markets along the Niger River.

| Market day | Town |
| --- | --- |
| Monday | Danga, Diafarabé, Ségou |
| Tuesday | Diré |
| Wednesday | Gourma-Rharous |
| Thursday | Mopti, Niafunké, Ténenkou |
| Friday | Massina |
| Saturday | Youvarou |
| Sunday | Gao, Markala, Tonka |

### PRIVATE PINASSE

The only way to bend flexible river schedules to your itinerary may be to hire a private

| PASSENGER BOAT FARES (CFA) | | | | | |
| --- | --- | --- | --- | --- | --- |
| route | luxe | 1st | 2nd | 3rd | 4th |
| Koulikoro to Ségou | 43,984 | 25,856 | 17,139 | 10,127 | 2706 |
| Ségou to Mopti | 70,397 | 36,349 | 26336 | 15,529 | 3418 |
| Mopti to Korioumé | 90,915 | 49,110 | 34,805 | 20,535 | 5025 |
| Korioumé to Gao | 99,500 | 57,500 | 35,750 | 21,000 | 5375 |

pinasse. They come in a range of sizes but expect to pay around CFA450,000 (including petrol) for a boat that comfortably seats 10 people, plus CFA15,000 per person for food. If you can get enough travellers together, per-person costs fall considerably.

## Bus
Journey times vary hugely, depending on the gung-ho nature of the driver (most are pretty 'keen'), the fitness of the vehicle, and the time taken at police and customs. As a rough guide, bank on at least 2¼ hours per 150km on sealed roads.

Sadly, no bus company consistently uses high-quality buses. One day you'll be on a seminew bus, only to find yourself the next day on a near-wreck that belongs to the same company. In our experience, the better companies are **Bani** ( ☎ 220 6081), **Binke** ( ☎ 220 5683), **Bittar** ( ☎ 220 1205) and **Somatra** ( ☎ 220 9932), all of which run regular services between the main towns south of the Niger River. Sample fares from Bamako include Ségou (CFA3000, 235km), Mopti (CFA8000, 640km) and Gao (CFA15,500, 1200km).

At major towns, new passengers are sometimes called by name from a list. Booking a ticket in advance puts you further up the list and thus ensures a good seat.

North of the Niger River, the roads can be terrible and 4WDs, fortified truck-buses and standard trucks are used as public transport.

## Bush Taxi
Bush taxis and minibuses, which are slightly pricier than buses (you're likely to be charged a CFA500 luggage fee), are handy on shorter, less frequented routes, where they may be the only option. These are either Peugeot 504s, carrying nine people, or *bâchés* (pick-ups) with about 16 passengers. *Bâchés* are slower, but about 25% cheaper than 504s. General bus and bush taxi stations in Mali are called *gares routières*.

## Car & Motorcycle
Self-drive car rental is rare, and not recommended because accident insurance for foreigners can be ineffective (even if you're not at fault) and the correct roadblock/bribe etiquette takes a while to master. However, 4WDs with drivers are easy to arrange through tour operators in all major cities.

Rates begin at CFA50,000 per day for a 4WD with unlimited mileage, plus petrol; but prices can often be double that, and some companies also levy a charge per kilometre.

## Tours
Although independent travel through Mali is easy, and is the cheapest way to go, taking a tour will add another dimension to your trip and take out the hassle of guides and long waits for slow transport. Tailor-made tours of Mali are easily arranged in Bamako or other cities, but can be expensive; it's worth enquiring if you can join an existing trip. Local companies which we recommend for tours around Mali include:

**Satimbe Travel** ( ☎ 243 0791; www.satimbetravel .com) Excellent Mopti-based company that's especially good for pinasse trips to Timbuktu and other trips; contact Issa Ballo.

**TAM Voyages** (Map p494; ☎ 221 9210; www.tam voyage.com; Sq Lumumba) Professional Bamako-based company, with an English-speaking owner and guides; contact Amadou Maiga.

**Tara Africa Tours** ( ☎ 228 7091; www.tara-africatours .com; Baco Djicoroni ACI, Bamako) Dogon–Dutch-owned and one of Mali's best companies; contact Marja or Amadou.

**Toguna Adventure Tours** ( ☎ /fax 2297853; togunaadventure@afribone.net.ml; ACI2000, Bamako) Terrific American-owned company which is professional and prides itself on a personal touch; contact Karen Crabb.

For a list of international tour companies offering tours to Mali and elsewhere in West Africa, see p840.

Even if you don't take a tour for the whole time in Mali, you'll benefit from having a local guide in at least some places, among them river trips on the Niger (p510) the Dogon Country (p515) and the desert around Timbuktu (p525).

## Train
The train is the best way to travel through western Mali (ie between Bamako and Kayes) although it's never on time and is not without its insecurities (see p539 for details). For details of prices and schedules, see the relevant sections for Bamako (p500) and Kayes (p537).

Second-class travel is cramped, chaotic and makes the journey seem eternal. For longer trips, 1st class is recommended and taking a couchette is likewise worthwhile for overnight journeys.

# Mauritania

For many travellers Mauritania is a revelation, a place of such natural beauty that it can substantially change your way of thinking. Spiritual seekers swear by the humungous sand dunes, giddily deep canyons and eye-popping plateaus of the Adrar or the Tagânt. History buffs rave about the World Heritage–listed caravan towns of Chinguetti, Ouadâne and Oualâta, all testifying to former flourishing civilisations. Sure, there may be similar landscapes in other parts of West Africa, but few are on the same scale or as overpowering as those in Mauritania. But wait! There's more to Mauritania than grandiose sand fields, millenarian cities and enchanting oases. The country is blessed with a wild stretch of coastline, with Parc National du Banc d'Arguin ranking as one of the best bird-watching venues in the world.

Culturally, Mauritania is a place apart. The population is almost equally divided between Moors of Arab descent and Black Africans. It's a Muslim country with a Black African twist. Although it's a transition between the North African Arab world and Black Africa, it doesn't really belong to either. This striking combination is part of its appeal.

A lot to love, a whole lot to see and do. Mauritania is much more than a gentle introduction to sub-Saharan Africa – it's a magnetic playland for mystical types.

## FAST FACTS

- **Area** 1,030,700 sq km
- **Capital** Nouakchott
- **Country code** ☎ 222
- **Famous for** Sand storms; bird-watching; *zrig* (camel milk)
- **Languages** Hassaniya, French, Fula, Soninké and Wolof
- **Money** ouguiya (UM); US$1 = UM270; €1 = UM320
- **Population** 3 million
- **Visa** In advance €25, at Moroccan border €20

## HIGHLIGHTS

- **Chinguetti** (p565) Get up at the crack of dawn to catch a glorious sunrise from the labyrinthine lanes of the old city.
- **4WD tours or camel trips** (p562) Experience the magic of the Sahara and sleep beneath the star-studded skies at the saffron dunes in the Adrar region.
- **Banc d'Arguin** (p561) Pack on your binoculars and observe vast flocks of birds from a traditional pirogue.
- **Oualâta** (p570) Admire the elaborate decorative paintings that grace traditional houses in one of Mauritania's best-kept secrets.
- **Iron-ore train** (p576) Hop on the world's longest train, and be ready for the most epic journey in your life!

## ITINERARIES

- **One Week** For most travellers the lure of the desert is irresistible. **Atâr** (p562) is the best launching pad for exploring the mystifying Adrar region – a good combination of fantastic landscapes and stunning architecture. Spend two days exploring the ancient, earth-toned desert towns of **Chinguetti** (p565) and **Ouadâne** (p567), and another three days trekking in the nearby incomprehensible dunefields. Then laze a couple of days away in an idyllic *palmeraie* (palm grove) – **Terjit** (p565) is an enchanting spot blessed with refreshing pools.
- **Two Weeks** Follow the one-week itinerary and, once you've had your fill of sand dunes, forge west to the Atlantic coast. From Atâr, take a bush taxi to Choûm where you'll hop on the iron-ore train that will bring you to **Nouâdhibou** (p559) the next day – an exciting, albeit arduous, ride. Seafood lovers will have a feast in Nouâdhibou. Consider taking a three-day tour to **Parc National du Banc d'Arguin** (p561), one of the best bird-watching areas in West Africa. Journey on to **Nouakchott** (p553), Mauritania's sprawling capital, with its striking melange of chaotic markets and modern buildings.
- **Three Weeks** Follow the two-week plan and then head to the far-flung corners of eastern Mauritania – it's a long drive but your patience will be amply rewarded. From Nouakchott, strike northeast to **Tidjikja** (p569), the gateway to the Tagânt area.

### HOW MUCH?

- **Cup of tea in a nomad's tent** free
- **Taxi ride in Nouakchott** UM300
- **Camel ride in the desert** about UM6000 per day
- **Bush taxi fare Nouakchott–Nouâdhibou** UM5600
- **Auberge room** about UM2000 per person

### LONELY PLANET INDEX

- **1L of petrol** UM209
- **1L of bottled water** UM250
- **Bottled beer** UM400
- **Souvenir T-shirt** UM600
- **Plate of couscous** UM600

Get a decent eyeful of the panoramic Tagânt plateau before backtracking to the Route de l'Espoir and veer due east to rough-around-the-edges **Néma** (p570), not far from Mali. Striking north, it's an easy ride to **Oualâta** (p570), one of the most spellbinding desert towns in Mauritania.

## CLIMATE & WHEN TO GO

In the Sahara region of the country, annual rainfall is usually less than 100mm. In the south, rainfall increases to about 600mm per year, mostly occurring during the short rainy season from July to September.

The most pleasant time to visit Mauritania is from November to March. Daytime temperatures hover in the mid-20°Cs with great regularity and the sky is invariably blue. Note that it can get quite cool at night, especially in the desert.

The heat is searing from April to October, especially from June to August when the *rifi* (hot winds) from the north send temperatures soaring to 45°C and above. However, along the coast, the *alizé* (trade winds) blow from the ocean, causing average highs to be 5°C lower.

## HISTORY

From the 3rd century AD, the Berbers established trading routes all over the Western Sahara, including Mauritania. By the

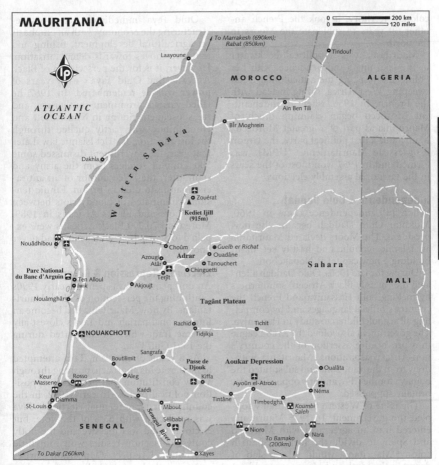

# MAURITANIA

9th and 10th centuries the gold trade, as well as slavery, had given rise to the first great empire in West Africa, the Soninké Empire of Ghana (the capital of which is believed to have been at Koumbi Saleh in southeastern Mauritania).

After the spread of Islam in the 7th century, the Almoravids established their capital in Marrakesh (Morocco), from where they ruled the whole of northwest Africa, as well as southern Spain. In 1076 they pushed south and, with the assistance of Mauritanian Berber leaders, destroyed the Empire of Ghana. That victory led to the spread of Islam throughout Mauritania and the Western Sahara. The Mauritanian part of the empire was subjugated by Arabs in 1674, after which virtually all Berbers adopted Hassaniya, the language of their conquerors.

## The Colonial Period

As colonialism spread throughout Africa, France stationed troops in Mauritania to protect the rest of French West Africa from raids by neighbours and ambitious European powers, but did nothing to develop the area. They also used the region as a place of exile for political prisoners.

In 1814 the Treaty of Paris gave France the right to explore and control the Mauritanian coast, but it wasn't until 1904 that, having played one faction off against another, the French managed to make Mauritania a colonial territory; it took the French another 30 years to subjugate the Moors in the north.

Mauritania was a political backwater in the lead up to independence, with her politicians resisting the anticolonial trend sweeping West Africa, siding instead with the French. In 1956, when an independent Morocco began claiming much of Mauritania as part of a 'greater Morocco', Mauritania's first political party, the Union Progressiste Mauritanienne (UPM), was formed and in 1957 won most of the seats in the territorial assembly elections.

## Independence & Ould Daddah

When full independence came in 1960, Mokhtar Ould Daddah became the new president. The Moors declared Mauritania an Islamic republic and hastily set about building a new capital at Nouakchott.

During the late 1960s, Ould Daddah alienated the (mainly Black African) southerners by making both Hassaniya and French the country's official languages and by compelling all schoolchildren to study in Hassaniya. The government also joined the Arab League in a provocative assertion of the country's non-African aspirations. Mauritania withdrew from the franc zone and substituted the ouguiya for the CFA, and any opposition was brutally suppressed.

The issue of Western Sahara finally toppled the government. In 1975 Mauritania entered into an agreement with Morocco and Spain to divide the former Spanish colony: Mauritania would take a slab of desert in the south and Morocco would get the mineral-rich northern two-thirds. But the Polisario Front launched a guerrilla war to oust both Morocco and Mauritania and many towns in northern Mauritania came under attack; iron-ore exports plummeted.

A bloodless coup took place in Mauritania in 1978, bringing in a new military government that renounced all territorial claims to the Western Sahara. For more details on the Western Sahara, see p838.

## Ould Taya & the 1980s

After a series of coups, the new government, ruled by a committee of high-ranking military officers, finally settled on the present ruler Colonel Maaouya Sid'Ahmed Ould Taya as leader in 1984.

Ould Taya immediately set about restructuring the economy, with an emphasis on agricultural development, fishing and tentative moves towards democratisation. However, it is for the persecution of Black Africans that Ould Taya's early years of power will be remembered. In 1987 he jailed various prominent southerners and the subsequent rioting in Nouakchott and Nouâdhibou was partly quelled through the introduction of strict Islamic law. Later that year, the government dismissed some 500 Tukulor soldiers from the army and soon after, the jailed author of an antiracist manifesto died in prison. Ethnic tensions culminated in bloody riots between the Moors and Blacks Africans in 1989. More than 70,000 Black Africans were expelled to Senegal, a country most had never known.

## Elections, Repression & Reforms

An unrepentant Taya spent the early 1990s continuing the persecution of Black Mauritanians. By now, Mauritania had become an international pariah and Taya's closest ally became Iraq, which he supported during the 1991 Gulf War.

As a result of criticism, Taya attempted to moderate his approach, pushing through a new constitution that permitted opposition political parties. In early 1992, in the country's first presidential elections, Taya was re-elected with 63% of the vote, but electoral fraud was massive and the hotly contested election results won him little international respect. Opposition parties consequently boycotted the general elections later in the year.

Bread riots in 1995, stemming from a new tax on bread, led to the arrest of Taya's principal political opponents, Ould Daddah and Hamdi Ould Mouknass – another sign that the crossover to a civilian government had yet to materialise.

In late 2000 electoral reforms were introduced under which political parties were to receive funds according to their electoral performance. Such changes will remain largely cosmetic as long as the harassment and arrest of opposition figures continues. To no-one's surprise, in October 2001 the ruling Parti Républicain Démocratique et Social (PRDS) won 64 out of the 81 National Assembly seats in elections.

## Mauritania Today

In June 2003 there was an attempted coup and two days of violent riots in the capital. Rebels were led by disaffected army leaders. It's thought that the war in Iraq partly provoked the uprising – the government had arrested numerous suspected Islamic extremists a couple of months before, and this served as a trigger. To everybody's surprise (and relief), Ould Taya's repressive regime came to an end in August 2005 when the president was toppled in a bloodless coup. This marked a symbolic turning point in the country.

Today, there are signs of hope and improvement. The new government, led by Ely Ould Mohamed Vall, is intent on putting the country back on its feet and on stamping out corruption. Vall has engaged in a 'transition period' that should end with a presidential election scheduled in 2007. The government maintains a moderate stance on the international stage, maintaining close ties to the West, including France and the USA, while introducing a couple of token measures to appease Islamic movements, such as temporary crackdowns on sales of alcohol in clubs or restaurants. But what could really give a new impetus to the country is the oil boom that began in 2006 with the exploitation of offshore fields off Nouakchott. This bonanza could foster growth and impact positively on the country, one of the poorest in the world. Unsurprisingly, Mauritania has become the focus of much international attention in a few years and other oil fields await exploration.

## THE CULTURE
## National Psyche

Mauritanian society is changing fast – with tourism development in the heart of the desert, Internet and mobile phones playing a crucial role in the last decade. You'll be surprised to see two parallel societies: the modern, Western-leaning society of Nouakchott and the main tourist areas, and the traditional society of the smaller towns and villages. But despite the profound social changes, the extended family, clan or tribe, remains the cornerstone of society, especially with the Moors. Deeply rooted traditional loyalties remain of the utmost importance.

As in many Muslim countries, religion continues to mark the important events of

> ### THE HARATIN & THE BIDAN
>
> The Moors have one of the most stratified caste systems in Africa. The system is based on lineage, occupation and access to power, but colour has become an increasingly popular determinant of status. At the top are the upper classes, the typically light-skinned Bidan Moors descended from warriors and men of letters. Below them are commoners, mostly of Berber-Negroid stock. The lowest castes traditionally consisted of four groups: the Haratin Moors, artisans and griots who have very few rights, and slaves, who have none at all. The Haratin do most of the menial work.
>
> Only in 1980, when there were an estimated 100,000 Haratin slaves in Mauritania, did the government finally declare slavery illegal. International human rights agencies continue to express concern that pockets of slavery still exist in the country.

life. The 1991 constitution legalised political parties but prohibited them from being opposed to Islam. Although slavery was declared illegal in 1980, the caste system (see above) still impregnates society's mentality.

## Daily Life

The iconic image of nomadic Moors sipping a cup of tea under a tent in the desert belongs to the past. Over the past three decades, drought has resulted in a mass exodus of traditionally nomadic Moors from the desert to Nouakchott. This doesn't mean that they have abandoned their cultural habits. Moors living in cities often feel the need to leave their concrete houses in Nouakchott for a couple of days spent under tents in the desert.

The men characteristically wear *draa* (long light-blue robes). Many have the name Ould (son of), eg Ahmed Ould Mohamed. For women it's Mint (daughter of). Women are in a fairly disadvantaged position. Only a third as many women as men are literate and few are involved in commercial activities other than selling food and crafts. Female genital mutilation and the forced feeding of young brides are still practised in rural communities. However, Mauritanian women have the right to divorce and exert it routinely.

MAURITANIA

**TEA, ANYONE?**

Elaborate greetings are traditional in Moorish society. Social activities revolve around tea, which is invariably strong and sweet. It's almost obligatory to accept the first three glasses, but declining the fourth is not impolite.

## Population

Of Mauritania's estimated three million inhabitants, about 60% are Moors of Arab and Berber descent. Moors of purely Arab descent, called 'Bidan', account for 40%.

The other major group is Black Africans, ethnically split into two groups. The Haratin, or Black Moors, the descendants of people enslaved by the Moors, have assimilated the Moorish culture and speak Hassaniya, an Arabic dialect. Culturally, they have little affinity with Black Mauritanians living in the south along the Senegal River, the 'Soudaniens'. The Soudaniens constitute 40% of the population and are mostly Fula (also known as Peul) or the closely related Tukulor. These groups speak Pulaar (Fula). There are Soninké and Wolof minorities.

## RELIGION

Over 99% of the population are Sunni Muslims. Islamic fundamentalists are growing in number but remain a minority.

## ARTS

Mauritania has a strong tradition of arts and craftwork, especially silverwork. Most prized are wooden chests with silver inlay, but there are also silver daggers, silver and amber jewellery, earth-tone rugs of camel and goat hair from Boutilimit, hand-painted Kiffa beads, hand-dyed leatherwork including colourful leather cushions and leather pipe pouches, camel saddles and sandals.

The traditional music of Mauritania is mostly Arabic in origin, although along its southern border there are influences from the Wolof, Tukulor and Bambara. One of the most popular Mauritanian musicians in Mauritania is Malouma. She has modernised the Moorish traditional music, blending it with more contemporary rhythms. She has created what is called the 'Saharan blues' and is to Mauritania what Cesária Évora is to Cape Verde.

There's superb traditional architecture in the ancient Saharan towns in the Adrar as well as in Oualâta. The adobe houses in Oualâta are enhanced with elaborate paintings.

## ENVIRONMENT
### The Land

Mauritania is about twice the size of France. About 75%, including Nouakchott, is desert, with huge expanses of flat plains broken by occasional ridges, rocky plateaus and sand dunes. Moreover, the desert is expanding southward. One of the highest plateau areas (over 500m) is the Adrar, 450km northeast of Nouakchott, with its towns of Chinguetti and Ouadâne. These plateaus are often rich in iron ore, and there are especially large deposits at Zouérat about 200km north of Chinguetti. The highest peak is Kediet Ijill (915m) near Zouérat. Mauritania has some 700km of shoreline, including the Banc d'Arguin. The south is mostly flat scrubland.

### Wildlife

In the desert regions, the camel is the most common animal that visitors will come across. Giraffes and lions have long gone – victims of desertification and the bullet. One endangered species that you might see if you're lucky is the monk seal, off Cape Blanc near Nouâdhibou (see p560).

Mauritania is a paradise for twitchers. Between Nouâdhibou and Nouakchott is Parc National du Banc d'Arguin, where hundreds of thousands of birds migrate from Europe in the winter. It is one of the world's major bird-breeding grounds and is on Unesco's list of World Heritage sites.

### Environmental Issues

Pollution, desertification, overgrazing – put them together and you have a glimpse of Mauritania's urgent environmental threats. Nearly 75% of Mauritania's land surface is desert or near-desert and this is increasing. Wood has become so scarce that most cooking is now done on kerosene stoves. Negligent garbage disposal is also a critical issue, but tourism development has fostered a growing awareness in the Adrar region.

Overfishing is another concern, with hundreds of tonnes of fish caught every day off the Mauritanian coastline.

## FOOD & DRINK

The desert cuisine of the Moors is rather unmemorable and lacks variety. Dishes are generally bland and limited to rice, mutton, goat, camel or dried fish. *Zrig* (unsweetened, curdled goat or camel milk) often accompanies meals served in private homes. Mauritanian couscous, similar to the Moroccan variety, is delicious. A real treat is to attend a *méchui*, (traditional nomad's feast), where an entire lamb is roasted over a fire and stuffed with cooked rice.

Mauritania's Atlantic coastline is an abundant source of seafood, and this has influenced local cuisine, especially in Nouakchott and Nouâdhibou. Fruit is pretty hard to find, except in the capital.

The cuisine of southern Mauritania, essentially Senegalese, will appeal more to your taste buds, with much more variety, spices and vegetables. Two of the most popular dishes are rice with fish and Senegalese *mafé* (a peanut-based stew).

The restaurant scene is pretty dull, except in Nouakchott, where you'll find a good range of eateries serving a great variety of dishes.

There's not a lot of choice when it comes to beverages. Soft drinks and bottled water are available everywhere. Mauritanian tea is also ubiquitous. In principle, alcohol is available at some hotels and restaurants in Nouakchott and Nouâdhibou.

# NOUAKCHOTT

**pop 800,000***

First impressions of Nouakchott are certainly not edifying. Hastily constructed in 1960 this sprawling city lacks charisma. Don't expect majestic monuments or cultural landmarks. Its location is discombobulating: it's unusually built 5km inland from the coast and, reflecting the desert origins of Mauritania's dominant Moors, its orientation is more towards the desert than the Atlantic. The shambolic suburbs are unbelievably filthy – piles of rubbish litter the streets.

It's not all that bad, however, with its phenomenal fish market (one of the most active in West Africa) and eye-catching mosques, it's also colourful and exotic. And you'll feel at ease wandering the streets: Nouakchott is laid-back and amazingly safe compared with many African capitals. It also has modern amenities, a couple of hip restaurants and comfortable hotels in which to pamper yourself – bliss after the rigours of the desert.

## ORIENTATION

The main streets are Ave Abdel Nasser running east to west and Ave du Général de Gaulle running north to south. The nicest district is to the north while to the south, near where Ave Abdel Nasser and Ave du Général de Gaulle cross, is the Grand Marché and, 2km further south, the Cinquième Quartier, a major shanty town with a busy market. The ocean is 5km west along Ave Abdel Nasser, while Le Ksar district (old town) and airport are 3km northeast of the centre.

### Maps

*Nouakchott – Centre-Ville* (about UM1500) is the only available street map. It is on sale at Libraire Vents du Sud (see below) and at some hotels, including the El Amane.

## INFORMATION
### Bookshops

**Librairie Vents du Sud** ( ☎ 525 26 84; Ave Kennedy; ✆ 8am-1pm & 4-7pm Mon-Sat) Has postcards, foreign newspapers, magazines and books, although little in English.

### Internet Access

There is no shortage of Internet cafés in Nouakchott but don't expect ultra-fast connections. Among the most convenient ones are the following:

**Confort Cybercafé** (Off Ave du Général de Gaulle; per hr UM300; ✆ 8am-midnight)

**Internet** (Off Ave du Général de Gaulle; per hr UM200; ✆ 8am-midnight Sat-Thu, 9am-noon Fri) It isn't signposted.

**Netland** ( ☎ 525 13 14; Ave du Palais des Congrès; per hr UM500; ✆ 8am-midnight Mon-Thu, 8am-noon & 4pm-midnight Fri, noon-midnight Sat & Sun) Has the best connection.

### Medical Services

**Cabinet Médical Fabienne Sherif** ( ☎ 525 15 71) Recommended by expats. Charges around UM6000 for a consultation.

### Money

There are bureaus de change on Ave du General de Gaulle and on Ave du Gamal Nasser, as well as in the Marché Capitale. Banks are also an option but they keep

MAURITANIA

# NOUAKCHOTT

0      500 m
0      0.3 miles

**A**    **B**    **C**    **D**

## INFORMATION
| | |
|---|---|
| American Embassy | 1 B4 |
| Asfaar | 2 B4 |
| BMCI Bank | 3 D6 |
| BNM Bank | 4 D6 |
| Cabinet Médical Fabienne Sherif | 5 A4 |
| Confort Cybercafé | 6 B4 |
| French Embassy | 7 B4 |
| German Embassy | 8 B4 |
| Internet | 9 D6 |
| Librairie Vents du Sud | 10 C6 |
| Main Post Office | 11 B5 |
| Moroccan Embassy | 12 B4 |
| Netland | 13 A3 |
| Regional Air - Rega Tours | 14 B4 |
| Senegalese Embassy | 15 B3 |
| Sûreté | 16 C5 |

## SIGHTS & ACTIVITIES
| | |
|---|---|
| Friday Mosque | 17 C5 |
| Grande Mosquée (Mosquée Saudique) | 18 D6 |
| Mosquée Marocaine | 19 A6 |
| Musée National | 20 B5 |

## SLEEPING
| | |
|---|---|
| Auberge La Bienvenue | 21 B4 |
| Auberge La Dune | 22 A4 |
| Auberge Menata | 23 B4 |
| Hôtel El Amane | 24 D6 |
| Hôtel Halima | 25 B4 |
| Hôtel Mercure Marhaba | 26 B5 |
| Hôtel Mouna | 27 B3 |
| JMC | 28 B3 |
| L'Escale des Sables | 29 D4 |
| Maison d'hôtes Jeloua | 30 B3 |
| Novotel | 31 B3 |

## EATING
| | |
|---|---|
| Bana Blanc | 32 B3 |
| Club B | 33 A3 |
| El Amane | (see 24) |
| La Palmeraie Pâtisserie Restaurant | 34 C6 |
| La Salamandre | 35 A4 |
| Le Bambou | 36 B3 |
| Le Jardin | 37 B3 |
| Le Méditerranéen | 38 B4 |
| Le Petit Café | 39 A4 |
| Le Prince | 40 C6 |
| Pâtisserie Les Princes | 41 A4 |
| Phenicia | 42 D6 |

| | |
|---|---|
| Pizza Lina | 43 A3 |
| Restaurant El-Bahdja | 44 A4 |
| Rimal | 45 D6 |
| Snack Irak | 46 D6 |
| Tata | 47 B3 |

## ENTERTAINMENT
| | |
|---|---|
| Modern KTV | 48 B3 |
| VIP Club | (see 37) |

## SHOPPING
| | |
|---|---|
| Artisans' Shops | 49 A4 |
| Centre Artisanal | 50 C6 |
| Cinquième Marché | 51 A6 |
| Marché Capitale | 52 C6 |
| MATIS | 53 D3 |

## TRANSPORT
| | |
|---|---|
| Air Algérie | 54 D6 |
| Air France | 55 A4 |
| Air Mauritanie | 56 C5 |
| Air Sénégal International | 57 D6 |
| Car & 4WD Rental Agencies | 58 C6 |
| Europcar | 59 C6 |
| National Tour Car | 60 D4 |
| Royal Air Maroc | 61 D6 |
| Transport to Kiffa & Néma (4WD's) | 62 B6 |
| Transport to Kiffa & Néma (bush taxis) | 63 D3 |
| Transport to Tidjikja | 64 B5 |
| Tunis Air | 65 C5 |

To Malian Embassy (250m)

Ave du Palais des Congrès

Stade Olympique

Ksar District

To Garage Atâr (2.5km); Atâr (436km)

To Auberge du Sahara (600m); Café-Restau Bruxelles (1km); Nouâdhibou (525km)

Rue de l'Ambassade du Sénégal

Rue de l'Hôtel Halima

Airport

Rue Abdallaye

Rue Abou Baker

Rue Alioune

See Enlargement

Rue Alioune

Ave Boubacar Ben Amer

Ave Bouriba

Rue Ghay

Rue Abdel Nasser

Ave Abdel Nasser

To Beach (5km); Port de Pêche (5km)

Rue Baker Ahmed

Rue Hennoune Ould Bouccif

Stade de la Capitale

To Garage Rosso (6km); Rosso (204km); Senegal (204km)

Rue Ely Ould Mohamed

Rue Mohamed el Habib

Rue Mohamed Temine

Ave Kennedy

Rue Bakary Hacha

Rue de l'Espoir

To Néma (1100km)

Rue de la Mosquée Marocaine

To Garage Nouâdhibou (200m)

Rue du Marché Cinquième

Cinquième Quarter

Rue de l'Indépendance

Ave Kennedy

Ave du Général de Gaulle

Rue Mamadou Konaté

Rue Alioune

Ave Abdel Nasser

0    200 m
0    0.1 miles

shorter hours than bureaus de change. They change only cash. At the time of writing, bank rates were slightly lower than those offered by bureaus de change.

The BNP bank has officially announced the construction of an ATM when this book went to print, and other banks should follow. However, it's wise not to rely on this option. Inquire at the reception of your hotel when you get there.

There are no cash advances on credit cards either. If you need a money transfer, your best is to head to a Moneygram or a Western Union office.

**BMCI** (Ave Abdel Nasser; ☼ 8am-3pm Mon-Thu, 8-11am Fri) BMCI is an agent for Western Union.

**BNM** (Rue Alioune; ☼ 8am-3pm Mon-Thu, 8-11am Fri) BNM is an agent for Moneygram.

### Post
**Main post office** (Ave Abdel Nasser; ☼ 8am-3pm Mon-Thu, to noon Fri)

### Telephone
There are heaps of private telephone offices in the centre where local and long-distance calls can be made.

### Travel Agencies
For purchasing domestic or international air tickets, these places come recommended:

**Asfaar** ( ☎ 529 04 06; fax 525 80 37; Ave du Général de Gaulle; ☼ 8am-5pm Mon-Thu, 8am-noon Fri)

**Regional Air – Rega Tours** ( ☎ 524 04 22, 632 87 35; fax 524 04 25; Ave du Général de Gaulle; ☼ 8am-5pm Mon-Thu, 8am-noon Fri)

### Visa Extensions
Visa extensions can be obtained at the **Sûreté** (Ave Abdel Nasser; ☼ 8am-3pm Mon-Thu).

## DANGERS & ANNOYANCES
Nouakchott is a relatively safe city, especially compared with other capital cities in the region. It's a late-night city, with many people walking around even at 11pm. Even at those hours walking is generally safe for men, but avoid the beach at night.

## SIGHTS & ACTIVITIES
### Musée National
Anyone with an interest in Moorish culture shouldn't leave Nouakchott without a visit to the **Musée National** (admission UM300; ☼ 8am-3.30pm Mon-Fri). On the first level is

a prehistoric gallery with archaeological exhibits while the second level is taken up with more recent ethnographic displays from Moorish society. Admission is officially UM300, but you may be charged UM500. The building is labelled as the Ministry of Culture.

### Mosques
Dominating the city's skyline, the **Grande Mosquée** (Rue Mamadou Konaté), better known as the Mosquée Saudique, is right in the centre. It's not exactly a model of architectural magnificence but it's worth a couple of pictures for its slender minarets.

South of Ave Abdel Nasser, towards the Cinquième Quartier, looms the large **Mosquée Marocaine** (Moroccan Mosque; Rue de la Mosquée Marocaine), another precious landmark in this bustling area. On the road to the airport, the **Friday Mosque** (Ave Abdel Nasser) is notable for its blindingly white façade. Visitors aren't allowed inside during prayer times.

### Port de Pêche
An absolute must-see, the fish market, or Port de Pêche, is by far Nouakchott's star attraction. It's incredibly lively and extremely colourful. You'll see hundreds of teams of men, mostly Wolof and Fula, dragging in heavy hand-knotted fishing nets. Small boys hurry back and forth with trays of fish, which they sort, gut, fillet and lay out on large trestles to dry. The best time is between 4pm and 6pm, when the fishing boats return. It's a fantastic experience and not to be missed. It's pretty safe as long as you're vigilant and sensible (wear a money belt).

Take a taxi to get there (around UM500 from the centre).

### Beaches
Fancy a dip? The nearest beach to Nouakchott is 5km west of the centre. OK, it ain't the Bahamas, but it can be fun for a couple of hours. There's no shade, so bring sunscreen. Beware of undertows.

## SLEEPING
### Budget
**Auberge du Sahara** ( ☎ 670 43 83; www.auberge -sahara.com in French; tent per person UM1500, dm UM2000, d UM4000; ℗ ) On the road to Nouâdhibou. Your cordial hosts, Sidi, Hermann and Katia will go the extra yards. Dorms

and rooms are plain but functional and shared bathrooms are kept in good nick. The other pluses are the outdoor areas, a kitchen for guests' use and the rooftop terrace where guests can relax and share their African experiences. Clearly a solid choice for discerning travellers, albeit a bit out of the action – you'll need a taxi to get to the centre.

**JMC** ( ☎ 641 76 24, 667 28 32; jmc_organisation@yahoo .fr; off Ave du Général de Gaulle; r UM5000-10,000; P ⬚ ) A godsend for savvy travellers, this *maison d'hôtes* (B&B) behind the Novotel has lots of personality. The rooms are exceedingly neat (some with private bathrooms) and are arranged around a courtyard. Other pluses include an art gallery that houses African crafts, a communal room where to unwind and a mellow atmosphere.

**Auberge Menata** ( ☎ 636 94 50; off Ave du Général de Gaulle; tent per person UM1500, dm UM2000, d UM4000; P ) This welcoming auberge is a good place to park your grungy backpack, with cheap but well-tended rooms. Auberge Menata and its shady garden are in a quiet street away from Ave du Général de Gaulle's hubbub. The friendly owner has a wealth of information about the country. Meals are available on request (about UM1200) and there's secure parking.

**Auberge La Bienvenue** ( ☎ /fax 525 14 21; ☎ 676 78 71; Ave du Général de Gaulle; s UM10,000-12,000, d 12,000-14,000; ⬚ ) An honest-to-goodness guesthouse, with only eight salubrious rooms, which ensures intimacy. All have private bathrooms. Although it's on the main drag, it's surprisingly peaceful and there's a pleasant leafy garden at the front. Meals are available on request (about UM1500). A good pick.

**Auberge La Dune** ( ☎ /fax 525 62 74; Ave Kennedy; dm UM2500-3500, s UM4000-7000, d 8000-9000; P ⬚ ⬚ ) They're a friendly bunch here, and although the accommodation is nothing to write home about it's still a popular haunt for frugal overlanders. There's a mixed bag of bare rooms, some with private bathrooms, some with aircon – ask to see a few. Precious perks include an on-site restaurant, Internet access, secure parking and a laundry service.

## Midrange

**Maison d'hôtes Jeloua** ( ☎ 636 94 50, 643 27 30, 525 09 14; maison.jeloua@voila.fr; r UM8000-10,000; P ⬚ ) The newest kid on the block, this

tidy *maison d'hôtes* (B&B) is run by helpful Olivia, who also owns Auberge Menata. It's housed in an imposing villa located in a tranquil neighbourhood. The seven rooms are well-appointed and relatively neat. The cheaper ones have shared bathroom.

**L'Escale des Sables** ( ☎ 525 23 75; www.escale -des-sables.com; Ksar District; d incl breakfast UM20,000-27,000; P ⬚ ⬚ ⬚ ⬚ ) Find heaven in this B&B-style nest in the Ksar district. Rooms are seductively cosy and a healthy size and the communal areas are embellished with various artistic touches. The atmospheric garden is a great place to chill out after a long day sightseeing. Fancy a dip? There's a small pool to cool off in when it's sweltering. You can order (expensive) meals (about UM5000). The only downside is that it's a flick out of the action, near the airport, but taxis are within easy reach.

**Hôtel Mouna** ( ☎ 524 13 30; fax 524 11 20; Ave du Général de Gaulle; s/d incl breakfast UM21,500/24,800; P ⬚ ) A mere skip and jump from the Novotel, this modernish abode is nothing flash, but it's calm, tidy and well managed. Rooms are spacious and come equipped with the requisite amenities, including satellite TV and air-con. Credit cards are accepted.

**Hôtel El Amane** ( ☎ 525 21 78; www.toptechnology .mr/elamane; Ave Abdel Nasser; s UM13,000, d 15,000-17,000; ⬚ ⬚ ) Don't expect a whole lotta lovin' when you're checking in or out – just a central location and an airy patio out back. This oldtimer is an OK runner-up if the rest are full, although the décor could do with a serious update – especially the dull corridors. The real draw is the restaurant (see opposite).

## Top End

Heave a sigh (of relief): all these hotels accept credit cards.

**Hôtel Mercure Marhaba** ( ☎ 529 50 50; www.mer cure.com; Ave Abdel Nasser; r UM33,000-37,000; ste UM58,000; P ⬚ ⬚ ⬚ ) After a much-needed renovation, the Mercure has regained some of its appeal. Think good-sized, well-appointed rooms and bathrooms in good working order but no extravaganza. Extras include a pool.

**Novotel** ( ☎ 525 74 00; www.novotel.com; Ave du Général de Gaulle; s UM45,000-58,000, d UM47,000-60,000, ste UM62,000-83,000; P ⬚ ⬚ ⬚ ). Feeling posh? Head straight to the Novotel. You can't miss the blinding orange and yellow façade of this four-star monolith on the main drag. Inside it feels pretty slick and the rooms come with all mod-cons. This is where foreign officials bunk down when in town.

**Hôtel Halima** ( ☎ 525 79 20; fax 525 79 22; Rue de l'Hôtel Halima; s/d UM26,500/29,500, ste UM49,000;  P 🔀 🖵 ) If the prices of the Novotel or the Mercure make you flinch, opt for the well-run Halima. Sure, it doesn't claim the glitz of its competitors but for the price it's a good bet in this bracket, with well-organised rooms, good facilities and a tough-to-beat location.

# EATING

Unless otherwise stated, all restaurants are open for lunch and dinner every day. In principle, alcohol is available at higher-end places.

## Restaurants

**Restaurant El-Bahdja** ( ☎ 630 53 83; off Route des Ambassades; mains UM1500-3000) One of Nouakchott's best choices, this cosy eatery wins plaudits for its excellent Moroccan-inspired menu at very reasonable prices. You can't really go wrong – everything's pretty good – but if you want a recommendation, go for a *tajine* (Moroccan stew featuring meat or poultry simmered with vegetables and olives).

**Café-Restau Bruxelles** ( ☎ 621 63 80; Route de Nouâdhibou; mains UM1500-2500) A laid-back restaurant with outdoor seating and a neat interior, this is a lovely place to eat. It's run by amiable Alex, a Belgian, and his Mauritanian wife. Expect savoury dishes that are well presented, including *brochettes de poisson* (fish kebabs), rump steak, a good range of crunchy salads and hearty omelettes. Make sure to leave room for the tasty pancakes. It's a bit far from the centre, on the road to Nouâdhibou, but it's well worth the taxi ride.

**Pizza Lina** ( ☎ 525 86 62; Route des Ambassades; mains UM1500-3500) Not far from the stadium, Pizza Lina has been flying the flag for tasty pizzas served bubbling hot from the oven for some years. The meat and fish dishes are also excellent, or you could order a scrummy plate of pasta. There's a pleasant modern dining room but the terrace is also agreeable.

**Le Jardin** ( ☎ 636 76 60; off Rue de l'Ambassade du Sénégal; mains UM3000-4000) It's the setting that's the pull here, with a mellow open-air terrace and a couple of elegant dining rooms. This upscale outlet is patronised by expats

and the local glitterati who want to dine in style. A full meal fetches about UM6000. The menu features meat and fish dishes, including beef Orloff, lamb skewers and African threadfin with coconut sauce.

**La Palmeraie Pâtisserie Restaurant** ( ☎ 642 02 12; Rue Alioune; mains UM1500-2500) This snazzy-but-not-sooty venue is a contender for the title of best restaurant in Nouakchott. Whatever your own verdict, you'll eat in genteel surroundings. The outdoor seating is particularly inviting. Signature dishes include *filet de dorade* (sea bream fillet) or *lotte grillée* (grilled monkfish). It's also recommended for breakfast (about UM1800).

**Le Bambou** ( ☎ 634 27 72; Ave du Général de Gaulle; mains UM1000-1500) If you fancy a change from European or African food, head to this humble Asian restaurant. The setting is positively old-fashioned and the dining quarters couldn't be more cramped, but there's a pleasant garden. Dig into staples such as Chinese soups, meat or fish dishes at puny prices.

**Phenicia** ( ☎ 525 25 75; Rue Mamadou Konaté; mains UM1000) You'll find no cheaper place for a sit-down meal in the centre. The setting is wonderfully modest with old paintings hanging on peeling walls. It's certainly not gourmet food but it's filling, with omelettes, steaks and sandwiches.

**El Amane** ( ☎ 525 21 78; Ave Abdel Nasser;  closed lunch Sat) French expats swear by this restaurant. Sure, the airy patio is refreshing and the char-grilled meat expertly cooked, but we found the reputation somewhat exaggerated.

**Le Méditerranéen** ( ☎ 660 96 65; off Ave du Général de Gaulle; mains UM2000-3000;  closed Sun & lunch Fri) Another reputable French (Corsican, to be accurate) restaurant, housed in a stylish villa. The camel kebab was average – fish dishes are reportedly better.

**Club B** ( ☎ 529 29 78; off Rue de l'Ambassade du Sénégal;  closed Sun) Another place well worth bookmarking if you want to dine in style. It's housed in a posh building off the main drag, a stone's throw from the Senegalese embassy – you can't miss the orange façade.

**Rimal** ( ☎ 525 48 32; Ave Abdel Nasser; mains about UM1000;  closed lunch Sun) It's not expensive, it's utterly without frills and the food is never going to win any Michelin awards, but we found the rustic look – bare tables, plastic tablecloths, peeling walls – suggestive and the time-warped ambience strangely

MAURITANIA

seductive. Stick to the classics such as omelettes or fried fish.

**La Salamandre** ( ☎ 524 26 80; off Route des Ambassades; mains UM1600-4000; ✆ Mon-Sat) Just off
Route des Ambassades, La Salamandre enjoys a deserved reputation for lip-smacking
French cooking. Here you can warm
yourself with *salade périgourdine* (salad),
shrimps, beef dishes and *côte d'agneau
grillée* (grilled lamb). The sleek setting, with
lashings of bright colours splashed all over
the walls, is another draw.

### Quick Eats

There are many fast-food establishments on
Rue Alioune between Ave Kennedy and Ave
du Général de Gaulle. Open until 11pm or
later, most have a Lebanese bent. Pick of the
bunch is **Le Prince** (Rue Alioune; mains UM500-1300).
Plonk yourself on a wobbly chair in the
room at the back and tuck into a plate of
well-prepared shwarma. A few doors down
to Le Prince, **Snack Irak** (Rue Alioune) is another
long-running favourite.

Near the French embassy, **Le Petit Café**
( ☎ 525 90 88; Route des Ambassades; mains UM1000-
2000) is a smart fast-food joint with good
snacks at moderate prices.

### Self-Catering

On Ave Kennedy and Rue Alioune are
shops with tinned goods and drinks and
stalls stacked with fresh fruit.

**Pâtisserie Les Princes** (Rue Kennedy) One of
the capital's most sweet-smelling bakeries. Stock up on baguettes and cakes of all
shapes and sizes.

**Tata** (Ave du Général de Gaulle) A well-stocked
supermarket, it has imported cheeses, vegetables and numerous tinned goods.

**Bana Blanc** (Ave du Général de Gaulle) Another
recommended store.

## DRINKING

The top-end hotels, as well as most
European-style restaurants, usually serve
alcohol. La Salamandre with its spiffy setting, and Le Jardin with its open-air terrace
and cosy interior, were the flavour of the
month when we visited.

## ENTERTAINMENT

Don't expect all-night carousing; Nouakchott is not Dakar. If you want to find dance
partners, two places to seek out are **Modern**

**KTV** (Ave du Palais des Congrés) and **VIP Club** ( ☎ 636
76 60; off Rue de l'Ambassade du Sénégal), with regular
live musicians and Senegalese DJs. Thurs-
day, Friday and Saturday are the liveliest
nights. Admission costs about UM1500. La
Salamandre is also worth checking out.

## SHOPPING

**Marché Capitale** (also called Grand Marché)
offers a bit of everything. Potential souvenirs
include brass teapots, silver jewellery, traditional wooden boxes with silver inlay, pipes,
leather bags, sandals, cushions, beads and
grigri. You'll find dress material, colourful
Soninké tie-dyed material, Senegalese batiks
and the inexpensive, crinkly *malafa* (fabric)
that Moor women use as veils.

**Cinquième Marché** is good for browsing and
people-watching, and has good vegetables,
household wares and tailors.

If you're after hand-woven carpets, head
to **MATIS** ( ☎ 525 50 83; Ave Abdel Nasser, Ksar District;
✆ 8am-4pm Mon-Thu & Sun), a short hop from
the airport.

For wooden boxes with silver inlay, daggers and jewellery, check the **artisans' shops**
northeast of the corner of Ave Kennedy
and Route des Ambassades. Also check
the **Centre Artisanal** (or silver market), south
on the highway to Rosso – it's beyond the
roundabout intersection for Boutilimit and
on your right.

## GETTING THERE & AWAY
### Air

Nouakchott's airport is on the eastern outskirts, about 2.5km from the centre. It has
very few facilities. If you want to change
money to pay for the taxi ride, ask at the
shops, but the rates offered are bad. There's
talk of extending and renovating the airport
in the forthcoming years.

For details of international and domestic
flights to/from Nouakchott, see p574 and
p575.

### Bush Taxi

There are specific garages for Mauritania's
various regions. For Nouâdhibou (about
UM5600, six hours), the Garage Nouâdhibou is close to Cinquième Marché;
for Rosso (about UM2000, 3½ hours), the
Garage Rosso is almost 10km south of
the centre; for Atâr (UM3500, six hours),
the Garage Atâr is on the road to Atâr,

about 3km north of the airport; for Kiffa (UM4300, ten hours), Ayoûn el-Atroûs (UM6000, 14 hours) and Néma (UM7500, up to two days), 4WDs leave from an open area at the corner of Rue de l'Indépendance and Rue de la Mosquée Marocaine, and 504 bush taxis from a parking lot close to the airport. For Tidjikja (UM5000, ten hours), infrequent bush taxis leave from a small shop on Rue Ely Ould Mohamed (ask for 'boutique 245').

## GETTING AROUND
### To/From the Airport
The airport is in the Ksar district. The standard taxi fare to the centre is about UM1000. It's cheaper to hail a taxi from the highway nearby (UM300).

### Car
If you want to hire a car with driver, try **Europcar** ( ☎ 525 11 36; fax 525 22 85; Ave du Général de Gaulle); or **National Tour Car** ( ☎ 525 97 34; fax 529 93 45; Rue Ghary), on the road to the airport.

The best place to start looking for 4WDs for hire is on the north side of Ave Abdel Nasser, about 50m west of the intersection with Ave Kennedy. The cheapest Toyota Corolla/Hilux (4WD) costs UM15,000/21,000 per day with driver. Costs quickly escalate once you add petrol.

### Taxi
Green-and-yellow taxis are plentiful. It costs UM300 for a ride within the centre, and about UM700 to Port de Pêche.

# THE ATLANTIC COAST

Wild coast meets Saharan dunes. This description should be enough to lure you here. This coastline, mostly occupied by Parc National du Banc d'Arguin – one of the world's greatest birdlife-viewing venues – is a rapturous place for tranquillity seekers, nature lovers and bird-watchers alike.

## NOUÂDHIBOU
**pop 80,000**
For Nouâdhibou, the good old days seem to have gone. With the new tar road connecting the Moroccan border to Nouakchott, most travellers give Nouâdhibou a wide berth and dash to the capital or to the

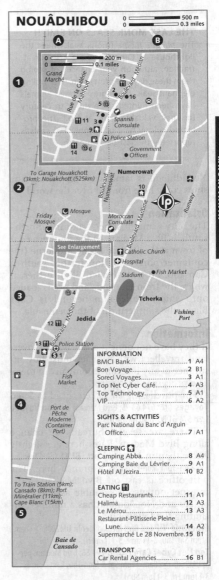

MAURITANIA

**INFORMATION**
BMCI Bank...........................................1 A4
Bon Voyage.........................................2 B1
Soreci Voyages...................................3 A1
Top Net Cyber Café..........................4 A3
Top Technology..................................5 A1
VIP.........................................................6 A2

**SIGHTS & ACTIVITIES**
Parc National du Banc d'Arguin
  Office..............................................7 A1

**SLEEPING** 🏠
Camping Abba.....................................8 A4
Camping Baie du Lévrier..................9 A1
Hôtel Al Jezira...................................10 B2

**EATING** 🍴
Cheap Restaurants..........................11 A1
Halima...............................................12 A3
Le Mérou...........................................13 A3
Restaurant-Pâtisserie Pleine
  Lune.............................................14 A2
Supermarché Le 28 Novembre....15 B1

**TRANSPORT**
Car Rental Agencies......................16 B1

Adrar region. Sure, there is little of specific interest to travellers, but it is a good base if you plan to visit Banc d'Arguin.

This unintimidating city is on the Baie du Lévrier, in the middle of a narrow 35km-long peninsula. The sea on both sides is chilled by the Canary current, and it has one of the world's highest densities of fish. As a result,

---

**THE LAST MONK SEALS ON EARTH**

The *phoque moine* (monk seals) near the lighthouse at Cape Blanc are a major attraction, although your chances of seeing them these days are pretty slim. Resembling elephant seals, these grey-skinned animals have been hunted since the 15th century for their valuable skins and oil. The protected colony here of roughly 100 seals is reportedly the last one on earth.

---

Nouâdhibou is famous for its fishing and ships come here from all over the world.

## Orientation

The city's main street, running north–south, is Blvd Médian. At the southern edge of town is the Port de Pêche Moderne (the container port) and 8km further south is Cansado. Port Minéralier, 3km further, is where the train line ends and ore is loaded onto ships, while 4km beyond is Cape Blanc, the southern tip of the peninsula.

## Information

If they have not done it at the border, overland travellers with vehicles must buy insurance at any insurance company in town. The process is hassle-free.

For purchasing air tickets, head to **Soreci Voyages** ( ☎ 574 63 25; Blvd Médian) or **Bon Voyage** ( ☎ 574 61 80; Blvd Médian).

There are several bureaus de change along Blvd Médian. Rates here are slightly lower than in Nouakchott. **BMCI** (Blvd Médian; ☽ 8am-3pm Mon-Fri) has a branch here. The post office is east off Blvd Médian. Most Internet outlets also double as telephone offices and Nouâdhibou has a number, including the following:

**Cybercafé VIP** (off Blvd Médian; per hr UM200; ☽ 8am-11pm Sat-Thu, 8-11am & 3-11pm Fri).

**Top Net Cyber Café** ( ☎ 574 91 88; Blvd Médian; per hr UM200; ☽ 8am-11pm Sat & Mon-Thu, 8am-1pm & 3-11pm Fri, 3-11pm Sun)

**Top Technology** ( ☎ 574 56 43; Blvd Médian; per hr UM200; ☽ 8am-midnight Sat-Thu, 2pm-midnight Fri)

## Sleeping

**Camping Baie du Lévrier** ( ☎ 574 65 36, 650 43 56 mobile; Blvd Médian; s/d UM3000/5000; P ) This highly recommended place is excellent value with a family feel. Ali, your hospitable host, is

a good source of local information. Accommodation is in clean four-bed rooms, there's a tent for relaxing and a kitchen.

**Camping Abba** ( ☎ 574 98 96; fax 574 98 87; Blvd Médian; tent per person UM1500, s/d UM2200/3400; P ) Another good haunt for overlanders. It has simple rooms – some with private bathrooms – and an inviting communal room with notice board.

**Hôtel Al Jezira** ( ☎ 574 53 17; fax 574 54 99; Blvd Maritime; s/d incl breakfast UM13,000/15,000; P ⛶ ) A clean, dependable midrange option north of the centre, with good amenities. With its incongruous carpet on the floor, it's almost cosy. The rooms are a tad sombre, but the surroundings are nice.

## Eating

In the centre, you'll find a slew of very cheap restaurants along Rue de la Galérie Mahfoud. They are nothing fancy, but they serve filling fare at unbeatable prices (around UM300 for a meal).

**Restaurant-Pâtisserie Pleine Lune** ( ☎ 574 98 60; off Blvd Médian; mains UM1000-1500) A mandatory stop for carb-lovers, right in the heart of town, this cute pastry shop also serves snacks and various mains. Scoff a plate of grilled fish or brochettes and finish off your meal with a delectable croissant, and you can walk away happy and buzzing for UM1500. It's also a good spot for breakfast.

**Le Mérou** ( ☎ 574 59 80; Blvd Médian; mains UM1500-2500) Make a beeline for this much-lauded restaurant on the main drag. Ignore the bland décor and focus on the eclectic range of tasty dishes, most of them with a Chinese bent. The octopus salad is divine.

**Halima** ( ☎ 574 54 28; Blvd Médian; mains UM1500-3000; ☽ closed lunch Fri) A serious competitor to the Mérou, Halima is a mix of stunning seafood and oddly kitsch interior design. Still, the food should do the talking and by any standards it screams. Feast on ultra-fresh fish dishes, lobster and shrimps. Bookings are essential.

**Supermarché Le 28 Novembre** ( ☎ 574 58 63; Blvd Médian; ☽ closed afternoon Fri) This well-stocked supermarket has the best selection of products in town.

## Getting There & Away

### AIR

**Air Mauritanie** ( ☎ 574 54 50) has four weekly flights to/from Nouakchott (UM16,000/

32,000 one way/return). For details of international flights, see p574.

### BUSH TAXI
Bush taxis ply daily between Nouâdhibou and Nouakchott. Since the opening of the tar road linking the two cities late in 2005, the ride is straightforward. The fare is UM5600 (six hours). Vehicles (Mercedes and Land Rovers) leave Nouâdhibou from the Garage Nouakchott, 5km north of the market.

### CAR
There's a number of car rental offices on the main drag, but the owners of the camps and hotels can also arrange this for you.

### TRAIN
The 'train station' is about 5km south of town, 3km before Cansado. There's a tiny building near the tracks where you can buy tickets. The iron-ore train with a passenger car leaves around 2.30pm daily, arriving in Choûm (UM1000, or UM3000 for a 'berth') around 2am, where 4WDs for Atâr will be waiting. It reaches Zouérat (UM1200) at around 7am. For more details, see p576.

### Getting Around
Chartered green-and-yellow taxis charge UM500 from the airport to the centre (less if you share). Within the centre, it costs about UM200.

## PARC NATIONAL DU BANC D'ARGUIN
Twitchers, rejoice! This must-see **park** (admission per person per day UM1200) is an important stopover and breeding ground for multitudes of birds migrating between Europe and Southern Africa. Over two million broad-billed sandpipers *(limicoles)* have been recorded here in the winter. Other species include pink flamingos *(flamant rose)*, white pelicans *(pélican blanc)*, grey pelicans, royal terns *(sternes royales)*, gull-billed terns *(spatula blanche)*, black terns *(sterne bridée)*, white-breasted cormorants, spoonbills and several species of herons, egrets and waders.

The park extends 200km north from Cape Timiris (155km north of Nouakchott). Most birds are found on sand islands in the shallow ocean. The best viewing time is December and January, which is also the mating season. The best way to see them is by tra-

ditional fishing boat, called a *lanche* – a recommended, ecofriendly excursion. The main island, 30km long, is **Tidra**, and just to the west of the northern tip are two tiny islands, **Niroumi** and **Nair**. The principal launching point is **Iwik**, a fishing village on the mainland 6km northeast of Tidra. You can find boats here; they cost UM15,000 (plus UM3000 for the guide) whether you stay out all day or only a few hours.

After, you could head to **Cape Tagarit**, 40km north of Tidra. The view from the cape is magnificent and the water is crystal clear.

Park permits (UM1200) are issued either at the entrance gates or in Nouâdhibou at the **park office** (Park office in Nouâdhibou, ☎ 574 67 44; Blvd Médian; ◷ office 8am-4pm Mon-Thu, 8am-noon Fri).

### Sleeping & Eating
Inside the park there are official camp sites equipped with traditional tents at Arkeiss, Ten Alloul, Iwik and Nouâmghâr. It costs UM3000 for a small tent (up to two people), UM6000 for a larger one (up to seven people). Meals can also be ordered (about UM1000).

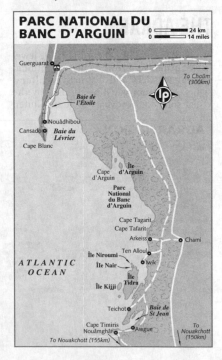

PARC NATIONAL DU BANC D'ARGUIN

## Getting There & Away

Your best bet to visit the park is to hire a 4WD with a knowledgeable driver, either in Nouakchott or in Nouâdhibou. Consider taking three days. Contact any travel or car rental agency for more information.

If you want to cross the park with your own 4WD, the trip from Nouakchott to Nouâdhibou (525km) takes at least two days. The first 155km from Nouakchott north to Cape Timiris is along the beach and passable only during low tide. Thereafter you enter the worst section, dunes for 300km. There are poles every 5km between Nouâmghâr, the fishing village at Cape Timiris, and just before the railway track in the north, but they won't keep you from getting lost if you don't have a guide. The last 70km southwest along the railway tracks is flat and easy but don't stray from the track, as mines abound.

For safety reasons (it's easy to get lost) go with at least one other vehicle and a guide (typically UM50,000 for three days); in Nouâdhibou, ask at your hotel. Make sure you take sufficient food, water and warm clothes.

# THE ADRAR

North of the country, the Adrar is the jewel in Mauritania's crown with exceptional natural wonders and distinctive cultural sights. No doubt you'll be stunned by the visual splendour of what you'll encounter.

The Adrar has it all: there are the ancient Saharan towns of Chinguetti and Ouadâne, mighty sand dunes that look sculpted by an artist, mellow oases where to unwind under a *khaima* (Moorish tent) and grandiose basaltic plateaus. For desert lovers, the Adrar is a must. Camel rides, trekking routes and even hot-air ballooning are on offer.

Don't expect to have the whole place to yourself, though. With regular flights direct from France during the European winter, the Adrar is no longer a sleeping beauty. Be prepared to come across groups of frazzled French executives in search of peace and harmony.

## ATÂR

### pop 25,000

Atâr is the major northern commercial centre and an obvious transit point for travellers. It probably won't leave you awestruck but it is an excellent place in which to organise camel or 4WD forays in the Adrar.

With the arrival of regular flights direct from France, the town has become quite a competitive place and, unlike the rest of Mauritania, you're likely to encounter your fair share of touts and hustlers.

A large *rond-point* (roundabout) marks the centre of Atâr and the market is just north of it. You'll find several bureaux de change, banks (US dollars and euros) including the **BMCI** ( 8am-3pm Mon-Thu, 8-11am Fri) and telephone offices on or around the main drag. The small mazelike Ksar

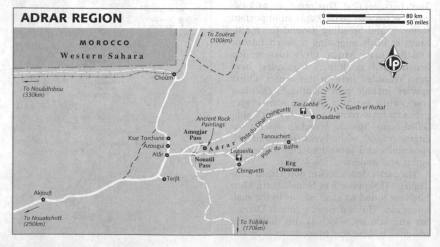

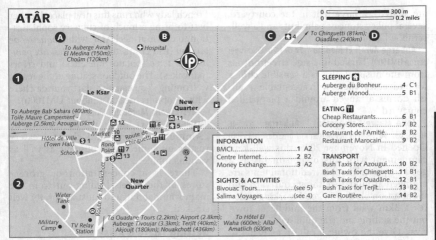

**ATÂR**

SLEEPING
Auberge du Bonheur............4 C1
Auberge Monod................5 B1

EATING
Cheap Restaurants.............6 B1
Grocery Stores................7 B2
Restaurant de l'Amitié........8 B2
Restaurant Marocain..........9 B2

TRANSPORT
Bush Taxis for Azougui......10 B2
Bush Taxis for Chinguetti...11 B1
Bush Taxis for Ouadâne.....12 B1
Bush Taxis for Terjît.........13 B2
Gare Routière................14 B2

INFORMATION
BMCI.......................1 A2
Centre Internet.............2 B2
Money Exchange............3 A2

SIGHTS & ACTIVITIES
Bivouac Tours...............(see 5)
Salima Voyages.............(see 4)

MAURITANIA

district, west of the market, is a good place to explore. It's the old residential quarter, with narrow winding streets, brick walls and carved doorways.

Atâr had only one Internet café at the time of writing. **Centre Internet** (per hr UM200; ☉ 9am-1pm & 4-11pm) is not far from the garage.

## Activities

At last count, more than 20 agencies were attempting to arrange **camel rides** or **4WD tours** from Atâr. The most popular 4WD trip is a five-day circuit called 'tour de l'Adrar' (round the Adrar), taking in Chinguetti, Ouadâne, Tanouchert, Terjît and various other fine spots. But you can arrange custom itineraries.

The main costs are the vehicle and driver, so trips are a lot cheaper if you're in a group. Four people is ideal. Count on paying up to UM21,000 per day for a Toyota Hilux plus petrol. Add about UM3000 per day per person for food.

Most travel agencies also organise custom camel rides in the Adrar but it's probably better to start your trip in either Chinguetti (p565) or Ouadâne (p567) where the most scenic dunes are almost on your doorstep. Prices start at UM12,000 per day with food and lodging.

The following agencies have been around for a few years and have good credentials:
**Allal Amatlich** ( ☎ 546 47 18; 647 88 68) Near Hôtel El Waha.

**Bab Sahara** ( ☎ 647 39 66) At Auberge Bab Sahara.

**Bivouac Tours** ( ☎ 546 45 95) At Auberge Monod.
**Ouadane Tours** ( ☎ 646 93 82, 634 72 73) Near the airport.
**Salima Voyages** ( ☎ 546 46 11) At Auberge du Bonheur.
**Tivoujar** ( ☎ 678 13 42, 625 51 82; www.vuedenhaut .com) At Auberge Tivoujar.

## Sleeping

These days Atâr has 20-plus places to stay but we were not overly impressed by the aesthetics of the infrastructures. If you're after a romantic hideaway, Atâr is certainly not the place. Most places serve meals.

**Auberge Bab Sahara** ( ☎ 647 39 66; justus_buma@ yahoo.com; tent per person UM1500, stone hut UM7000; P ) Off Route de Azougui, this longstanding backpacker haunt is well run by a Dutch/German couple, Justus and Cora, long-term residents of Atâr. *Tikits* (traditional stone huts) and tents are nothing thrilling but tidy enough and the courtyard is a pleasant place to mooch around. Justus can arrange alternative tours into the desert. It costs UM300 to park your car. Meals are available on request (about UM2000). It's a flick out of the action but it's quiet.

**Auberge du Bonheur** ( ☎ 546 45 37; fax 546 43 47; tent or hut per person UM1700, r UM6000; ☒ 🖳 ) Those wanting a reliable base could do worse than checking in at this welcoming outfit, a five-minute stroll from the centre. The owners have a reputable travel agency and are used to dealing with tourists. Facilities include five rooms with air-con (bathrooms are shared), a large tent in the courtyard, several pokey stone or palm huts and a well-scrubbed ablution block.

**Auberge Avrah El Medina** ( ☎ 671 26 05; dm per person UM1500) Tucked in a side street not far from the hospital, this is a sensible choice for budget travellers, with acceptable smallish dorms arranged around a plant-filled courtyard.

**Toile Maure Campement – Auberge** ( ☎ 546 40 85, 632 98 19; tent per person incl breakfast UM3500) Opened in November 2005, this well-kept campement with lots of personality is a good surprise. The five traditional tents are arranged around a soothing courtyard and the ablution block is in good working order. It's a 3km walk from the middle of town but the setting and tranquillity are hard to rival. Give the owner a call on arrival and he will pick you up.

**Auberge Monod** ( ☎ 546 42 36; Route de Chinguetti; s/d UM7000/8000; ✦ ) The rooms here are not exactly suitable for a honeymoon but are serviceable enough, with spacious bathrooms. The main selling point is its spiffing location, a short stagger from the market.

**Hôtel El Waha** ( ☎ 546 42 49; fax 546 42 73; Route de l'Aéroport; s/d UM9000/10,000; ste UM17,000; P ✦ 🖳 ) In a peaceful neighbourhood, this is a reassuring choice with 26 clean-smelling, well-equipped *tikits* scattered around a well-tended garden. Forget about the meals here as at UM4000, it's a joke.

**Auberge Tivoujar** ( ☎ 678 13 42, 625 51 82; www .vuedenhaut.com; tent/tikit per person with half-board UM5500/7000; P ✦ 🖳 ) Opened in January 2006, this professionally run venture is the closest that Atâr comes to having a top-end hotel. It's popular with tour groups, so don't expect much privacy. It boasts excellent amenities, including wheelchair-accessible *tikits* and scrupulously clean bathrooms. The only drawback is the location, about 4km from the centre on the road to Nouakchott.

## Eating

From the roundabout head east on the Chinguetti road for a block, then turn left. Most cheap restaurants are along this road. They are run by Wolof and Fula and serve basically the same fare, including spaghetti, rice, fish and Senegalese *mafé* for about UM300.

**Restaurant de l'Amitié** ( ☎ 610 71 50; Route de Chinguetti; set menu UM2500; 🕒 closed May-Aug) The

French lady who runs this neat place does her best to bring a touch of culinary sophistication to down-at-heel Atâr, with *croquettes de poisson* (fish croquettes), *omelettes aux pommes de terre* (potato omelettes) and *crêpes* (pancakes). The outdoor seating at the rear is welcoming. You can also start your day here with a copious breakfast (about UM1000).

**Restaurant Marocain** (Route de Chinguetti; mains UM500-700) Next door to Restaurant de l'Amitié, this cheap and cheerful eatery rustles up some good couscous as well as various nibbles.

There is a concentration of grocery stores in the streets leading out from the main roundabout, and most are pretty well stocked.

## Getting There & Away

### AIR

From October to April **Point Afrique** (www .point-afrique.com) has a weekly flight from Paris to Atâr via Marseilles. Return fares start at around €440.

### BUSH TAXI

The main *gare routière*, in the heart of town, is where you can get vehicles for Choûm (UM2000, two hours) and Nouakchott (UM3500, six hours).

Battered 4WDs headed for Chinguetti (UM2000, two hours) leave from near a shop located a block north of Auberge Monod (ask for directions). For Ouadâne (UM2500, four hours), they leave from a street north of the roundabout (ask for 'boutique Sonimex'). For both towns, services are infrequent – usually one in the morning and one in the afternoon, more during the Guetna season. For Azougui (UM1000) and Terjît (UM1000), infrequent 4WDs leave from near the roundabout.

### CAR

For details of the route from Atâr, see p567. If you wish to take the Amogjar Pass (it's easier and more spectacular coming the other way), the turn-off to the left is 10km out of Atâr.

## AZOUGUI

A good side trip from Atâr is to Azougui, 10km northwest. This charming oasis town makes for an excellent retreat if you need some hush.

It was from here in the 11th century that the Berber Almoravids launched their attacks on the capital of the Empire of Ghana, Koumbi Saleh, leading to the spread of Islam throughout West Africa. It was once an oasis of 20,000 palms, and one of the premier cities in the region, before the rise of Chinguetti and Ouadâne.

**Auberge Oued Tillige** ( ☎ 546 43 43; r, tents or tikits per person UM2000) is an excellent, quiet alternative to staying in Atâr and has wonderful views down the valley. It's pretty well maintained and there are whitewashed huts with blue doors, tents or the traditional *tikits* in which to sleep. The catch? There's no shade. Breakfast/meals cost UM600/2000.

Another worthy option is **Auberge de la Medina – Chez Khassem** ( ☎ 654 77 84, 649 40 03 in Atâr; tents or tikits per person UM1500), a more recent auberge further up, on the edge of the dunes. It's similar in standards to Auberge Oued Tillige and there's a homely, hospitable feel. You can get breakfasts/meals for UM600/1500.

A smarter auberge comprising several classy stone huts was being built at the entrance of Azougui when we visited. Ask around when you get there.

The easiest way to get to Azougui is by taxi (about UM3000). With plenty of time you could also wait for a bush taxi near the roundabout in Atâr (about UM1000).

## TERJÎT

Shade, shade, shade. Be sure to make a beeline for Terjît, an unusually verdant oasis, about 40km south of Atâr as the crow flies. This surprisingly lush place at the end of a narrow canyon is wonderful – you'll think you're in the tropics. What's special here is a natural pool in which you can swim – bliss after the aridity of the desert. You pay UM1000 to enter the site. A tip: avoid Terjît at weekends in season, as it's usually packed with tour groups.

The main spring has been taken over by **Auberge Oasis de Terjît** ( ☎ 644 89 67, 546 50 20 in Atâr; tents or huts per person UM1500), where a mattress in a tent by the trickling stream is on offer. A meal costs about UM1500. Facilities are sometimes dysfunctional.

The only other place to stay is the **Auberge des Caravanes** (r or tikits per person UM1500; P ), at the entrance of the village. The setting is less enticing but it's an honest-to-goodness

### THE GUETNA SEASON

'You would be nuts to travel in the Adrar in summer.' Don't pay attention to this hackneyed cliché. Sure, from June to August the heat is muffling, with temperatures reaching 45°C, but this is the much-awaited Guetna season. The Guetna refers to the harvest of dates in the palm groves. In spite of the heat, it's a very festive season and all oases get very lively. During the Guetna, many Mauritanians from the cities return to their tribes and take part to the harvest. There's a congenial, mellow atmosphere, with much socialising, tea and *zrig* (unsweetened, curdled goat or camel milk) drinking, playing games and dancing. Moreover, there are virtually no tourists – the perfect occasion to sample Mauritanian hospitality at its best.

place, with six uncluttered yet clean *tikits*, four rooms and well-maintained shared bathrooms. There's also a protected area for parking. Add UM4500 per day for meals.

To get here by private car, drive 40km south of Atâr on the road to Nouakchott, then turn left at the checkpoint and follow a sandy track for 11km. The trip takes 1½ hours. By public transport, take anything headed towards Nouakchott and hitch a ride from the checkpoint. There's also a bush taxi that leaves every morning from near the roundabout in Atâr (UM1000) but this option is not really convenient.

## CHINGUETTI
pop 4000

One of the more attractive of the ancient caravan towns in the Sahara, Chinguetti will appeal to spiritual seekers. The seventh-holiest city of Islam, it's shrouded with a palpable historic aura. The heavenly backdrop is another draw. You'll discover an outlandish landscape of mighty sand dunes upon which the light plays a daily show.

Once famous for its Islamic scholars, it was the ancient capital of the Moors, and some of the buildings date from the 13th century. In its heyday, Chinguetti had 12 mosques, 25 *madrassas* (Quranic schools) and was home to 20,000 people. Epic *azalais* (caravans) of 30,000 camels laden with salt once travelled between Chinguetti and

Morocco, St Louis in Senegal (each 30 days), Nioro in Mali (45 days) and Timbuktu (55 days).

The highlight of any visit is a wander through the labyrinthine lanes of Le Ksar (the old town). The modern town, which has a delightfully sleepy market (remarkable for how little produce is available), is separated from the old town by a broad, flat wadi where palm trees grow. Chinguetti is a place where the streets have no name and there is only generator-powered electricity.

## Sights & Activities

### LE KSAR

The old quarter's structures are mostly stone and most are in ruins and unoccupied. The principal attraction is the 16th-century stone mosque (no entry to non-Muslims). Also of great interest are the five old libraries, which house the fragile-as-dust ancient Islamic manuscripts of Chinguetti. In these libraries are the stories of Chinguetti's golden age. The libraries include the **Bibliothèque Ehel Hamoni** (admission UM300), **Bibliothèque Moulaye** (admission UM300), **Bibliothèque Habbot** (admission UM300), and **Fondation Ahmed al Mahmoud** (admission UM300) and each has an attached **museum** (admission UM200) containing items from the old caravans. None of the libraries keep regular opening hours and your best bet is to ask at your hotel for the man with the key.

### CAMEL TREKKING & 4WD EXPEDITIONS

The picture-postcard sand dunes around Chinguetti are the single most definitive image of Mauritania for many people. Each year, thousands of Europeans come here to experience the magic of the desert.

The best way to see this fascinating region is by camel. Numerous *méharées* (camel trips) are available. Plan on at least a full day's ride as you'll see little of the dunes in half a day. Possible trips include to the oases of Abeir (3km), Tendewalle (5km), Legueilla (12km) or a four-day return trip to Tanouchert (45km). With more time you could go as far as Ouadâne (five to six days), Terjît (six days) and even Tidjikja (13 to 15 days) in the Tagânt (see p569). Prices are reasonable – standard costs start from UM8000 per person per day for the camel, food and guide. Any reputable travel agency in Atâr (see p562) or auberge owner

can arrange camel rides. You don't really have to haggle much, because everyone charges more or less the same price.

If you don't want to sweat it out, you can hire a 4WD and driver. It costs from UM17,000 (Toyota Hilux) to UM31,000 (Toyota GX) per day, petrol not included.

### HOT-AIR BALLOONING

Fancy quietly sailing through desert skies at dawn? In the mood for jaw-dropping views? Well, don't miss the chance to try going up in a hot-air balloon in the Adrar. Auberge Tivoujar, a reputable outfit based in Atâr (see p562), can organise departures from Atâr or Chinguetti. It's not cheap (about €160 per person) but looking down on the dune fields and rock formations from the air is bound to be one of the highlights of your trip.

## Sleeping & Eating

All the places listed below have terraces on the roof overlooking town, all have shared shower and toilet unless stated otherwise. Breakfast and meals are available on request (about UM2000 per meal).

**Le Maure Bleu** ( ☎ 540 01 54, 546 51 30; www.maurebleu.com; Old Town; r or stone hut s/d UM5200/8400, tent per person UM2500) One of Adrar's most appealing places to stay. This French-run peach of a place has oodles of rustic charm and features well-arranged rooms and *tikits*, as well as *khaimas* (nomad's tents) for shoestringers. The soothing courtyard is a great place to unwind over a cup of tea. Meals (about UM2500) come in for warm praise, however, breakfast is included in the price. Rejoice: the shared bathrooms are sparkling clean. Avoid staying here at weekends in season – it can fill up with French tour groups, in which case privacy is at a premium.

**Auberge des Caravanes** ( ☎ 540 00 22; fax 546 42 72; New Town; r per person UM1500) With its eye-catching, traditional architecture, it's hard to miss this well-run place right in the centre of town. It's popular with tour groups and is thus a good place to meet other travellers, but it feels a wee bit impersonal. There's an equally pleasant extension at the western end of the old town.

**Auberge Abweir** ( ☎ 540 01 24; New Town; stone hut or tent per person UM2500) Next door to Auberge des Caravanes, this welcoming place will appeal to a more sedate crowd, with a bunch of simple yet well-organised stone huts and small tents set around a plant-filled courtyard. The well-scrubbed ablution block is an added bonus.

**L'Eden de Chinguetti** ( ☎ 540 00 14; New Town; r per person UM5500) 'Eden' might be pushing it a bit, but at least it's neat, well-tended and embellished with well-chosen knick-knacks. The owner, Mahmoud, is a local character and a mine of information. There are only eight rooms, with proper beds (read: not mattresses on the floor), which ensures intimacy. The ablution block was clean to boot when we visited. It's on the road to Atâr, not far from Auberge La Rose des Sables.

**Auberge La Rose des Sables** ( ☎ 540 01 48; New Town; stone hut or tent per person UM1500) Stumbling distance from Auberge Abweir, this auberge is run by the amiable Cheikh Ould Amar. It is a touch more run-down than its competitors but still fits the bill for shoestringers, with adequate stone huts arranged in a compact compound.

**Les Mille et Une Nuits** (Le Ksar; stone huts UM3000) Not your average auberge, Les Mille et Une Nuits is run by Leila, a Mauritanian lady, whose family owns the Bibliothèque Habbot. It's a very neat place, close to Le Maure Bleu, with impeccable bathrooms, well-designed stone huts, a manicured courtyard dappled in sunshine and some feminine touches. Recommended.

**Dar Salma** ( ☎ 630 18 74, 540 02 44; Le Ksar; d incl breakfast €60; ✉ ) The newest kid on the block, this ultracharming, riad-like *maison d'hôtes* (guesthouse) smack-bang in the old town exudes bucket-loads of personality, thanks to its cushy setting, professional service and tastefully decorated rooms. An excellent base if you want to kick back in style.

If you want to get away from it all, you can base yourself at **Jardin d'Eden** ( ☎ 540 00 14; stone hut per person UM1500) or at **Le Jardin du Bien Être** (stone hut per person UM1500), both located in a secluded oasis about 4km from Chinguetti, on the way to Ouadâne. Facilities are basic but the setting is really enchanting, with lots of shade and greenery.

### Getting There & Away
**CAR & BUSH TAXI**
There is at least one vehicle a day to/from Atâr (UM2000, about two hours). They leave from just behind the market; you'll need to ask around as the driver often goes off looking for his full complement of passengers. There are no bush taxis between Chinguetti and Ouadâne – you'll have to go back to Atâr.

For those with their own vehicles, there are two routes to Atâr. The faster route (81km, two hours) is via the Nouatil Pass and the lunar-like Adrar plateau; while the other (91km, three to four hours) leads up to the Amogjar Pass, which is slow going but offers spectacular views. If you're coming from Chinguetti, the turn-off for the Amogjar Pass is at the signpost to the faintly discernible Neolithic rock paintings.

There are also two routes to Ouadâne – via the plateau or, more picturesque, across the sand dunes to the east of town.

## TANOUCHERT
Don't miss this gem of an oasis, approximately halfway between Chinguetti and Ouadâne. This is your typical oasis, nestled around a freshwater source, complete with palm trees and surrounded by superb dune fields, miles from anywhere. You wanted an escape hatch? This is the one!

Another attraction is the welcoming **Auberge Chez Chighaly Ould Bigue – Oasis Tanouchert** (tents or tikits per person with half-board UM4200). Chighaly, your amiable host, is a local figure and will welcome you wholeheartedly in his unsophisticated but tidy auberge. The perfect *griot*, he is a pleasure to listen to if you can understand French. **Auberge Amoure Tanouchert** (tents or tikits per person with half-board UM4200) is another enchanting place to stay, with seven nicely laid-out *tikits* and a small garden.

Various camel rides can be organised in the area. Tanouchert is off the beaten track and you'll need to hire a 4WD with driver to get there. If you do a camel trek from Chinguetti to Ouadâne, you'll probably spend a night in Tanouchert.

## OUADÂNE
Gosh, the first glimpse of Ouadâne from the dirt track is arresting. The old quarter that stretches on top of the hill is one of the most enchanting semi-ghost towns of the Sahara. Pity about the telecom tower that was installed in 2005 – it *does* mar the great vista.

Ouadâne was founded in 1147 by Berbers, and sits on the edge of the Adrar plateau, 120km northeast of Chinguetti. For 400

**MAURITANIA**

years, it was a prosperous caravan centre and a transit point for dates, salt and gold. It was the last stopover for caravans heading to Oualâta in the southeastern corner of the country. The decline began in the late 16th century when the powerful Moroccan prince Ahmed el Mansour gained control of this trans-Saharan route and diminished Ouadâne's commercial role.

## Sights
### LE KSAR AL KIALI
As you arrive across the sands or plateau from Atâr or Chinguetti, the stone houses of **Le Ksar al Kiali** (old quarter) seem to tumble down the cliff like an apparition, and they change colour depending on the time of day. From the base of the town, the lush gardens of the oasis stretch out before the desert again takes hold. The top of the hill is dominated by the minaret of the **new mosque**, which is a mere 200 years old, while at the western end at the base of the town is the 14th-century **old mosque**. At the height of Ouadâne's power, the two mosques were connected by the **Street of 40 Scholars (savant)** and houses along either side were only allowed to be occupied by Ouadâne's considerable intelligentsia. In between, the crumbling structures seem to have been piled up higgledy-piggledy by some giant child playing with building blocks. From a distance, they can seem to blend to form a massive stone wall. Only 20 to 30 families still live in the old town.

Like Chinguetti, Ouadâne was a place of scholarship and is home to over 3000 manuscripts held in 23, mostly private, libraries. At the time of research, some of them were open to the public (about UM500 each). There's also a **small museum** (UM500) housing various artefacts from the ancient caravans.

The knowledgeable, French-speaking guide Mohamed Lemine Kettab (UM1000) can really enhance your visit. He will probably have found you long before you start looking for him.

## Sleeping & Eating
All places can prepare meals for their guests (about UM2000 for lunch or dinner). Try the *ksour*, a local delicacy. It's a thick pancake made of wheat. You dip it into a sauce and it makes a great accompaniment.

**Auberge Mayateg** (tents or tikits per person UM1700) This is one of the few places to stay atop the rocky bluff and is an easy walk to the top of the old town. It won't win any style awards but it's salubrious enough and there's a homely feel.

The following places are down on the plateau.

**Auberge Warane 1** ( ☎ 546 46 04 in Atâr; r or tents per person UM1600) The first place you'll encounter coming from Atâr. The rooms are a bit bunker-like but serviceable enough.

**Auberge Vask – Chez Zaida** ( ☎ 681 76 69; tikits or tents per person UM1500) This mellow auberge is run by Zaida, a congenial lady who goes out of her way to make your stay a happy one. There are five *tikits* and a couple of nomad's tents – it's nothing particularly glam but perfectly adequate for thrifty travellers.

**Auberge El Ghalaouya** (tents or tikits per person UM1500) Almost a carbon copy of the Vask, with pleasant stone huts and tents, as well as a clean ablution block.

**Auberge Agoueidir – Chez Isselmou** ( ☎ 525 07 91; Nouakchott; tikits or tents per person UM1700, d UM4000) If you want decent facilities without blowing a fortune, this is the place to go. It features orderly rooms (with proper beds) adorned with modest artistic touches, as well as a number of tents and *tikits*. Top marks go to the shared bathrooms with toilets that are clean enough to sit on and the well-tended sand-floored courtyard. It is at the entrance to town coming over the dunes from Chinguetti.

Ignore the incongruous Hôtel Oumou Maabed at the entrance of Ouadane. It's a botched attempt at creating a luxurious establishment.

## Getting There & Away
Finding transport to Ouadâne is not easy. Atâr is a much better place to look than Chinguetti, as vehicles go between Atâr and Ouadâne every few days (every day, if you're lucky), but next to never from Chinguetti. The trip (UM2500) normally takes about four hours.

If driving you have two alternatives: the southerly Piste du Batha, which passes through sand dunes and definitely requires a guide, and the northerly Piste du Dhar Chinguetti along the plateau, which is in very good condition. The latter departs the Atâr–Chinguetti road 18km before Chinguetti.

## AROUND OUADÂNE

The **Guelb er Richat** crater is 40km to the northeast. En route, stop at **Tin Labbé** (7km), a unique settlement where the large boulders prevalent in this area have been incorporated into the villagers' homes.

# THE TAGÂNT

No area in Mauritania possesses a more mystical pull than the Tagânt region. There's magic in the land, an irresistible force that tugs on those who dream about empty spaces and wild expanses. Compared with the Adrar, the Tagânt is much less touristy and remains virtually untouched.

This does not mean that it is not accessible. There's a picturesque, sealed road that branches off the Route de l'Espoir to Tidjikja, the main gateway. You could also cross the entire region from Chinguetti to the north down to Oualâta to the south via Tichit – allow at least six days by 4WD or three weeks by camel.

Whatever the option, the sense of adventure is ever palpable.

## TIDJIKJA

### pop 6000

Tidjikja is the capital of the Tagânt region and a major stopover for those who cross the Tagânt from Chinguetti down to Nema. Founded in 1680 and now surrounded by sand dunes, the town supports one of the country's more important palm groves (which dates from the 18th century), a busy market, a couple of eye-catching mosques, numerous shops and Fort Coppolani (an old French military fort used in subduing the Moors).

A good side trip can be made to Rachid, 35km north on the track to Atâr. High up a cliff, it's one of the most picturesque spots in Mauritania and was once used as a site for launching attacks on passing caravans.

### Sleeping & Eating

**Auberge des Caravanes de Tidjikja** ( ☎ 569 92 25; r with full board UM7000, tikits s/d 9000/10,000; ✘ ) Part of a small chain of homely auberges across Mauritania's desert region, this reputable place is good value. In addition to plain rooms, a dozen comfortable *tikits* (some with air-con and private bathrooms) were

under construction when we visited. It's in the new quarter of town on your left as you arrive from Nouakchott.

**Auberge Phare du Désert** ( ☎ 563 29 99; tikits UM5000-7000) Almost a carbon copy of Auberge des Caravanes, if a bit more intimate.

For food, there are also some small grocery shops and the market.

### Getting There & Away

A good, sealed road connects Nouakchott with Tidjikja. Occasional bush taxis leave from near a shop on Rue Ely Ould Mohamed in Nouakchott (look for 'boutique 245'). It costs UM6000.

It's possible to drive from Tidjikja to Atâr (470km). A guide is essential and attempting it with only one vehicle is inadvisable. Allow at least two days. There's petrol in Tidjikja.

## TICHIT

If you're adventurous and want to see a ghost town in the making, head for the isolated, ancient town of Tichit, 255km east of Tidjikja. Driving here, you'll pass through a barren landscape – the trees are bare, the scrub is twisted, and the ground is littered with the bleached bones of camels and goats. You should report to the police when you arrive.

The town once furnished water and precious supplies to desert caravans and boasted over 6000 people and 1500 houses. Today, fewer than 300 houses remain and only about half are inhabited. The main mosque is impressive, as are the old houses, which are made of local stone of different hues. They have decorative motifs on the exterior and solid, ornate doors with wooden latches.

A guide is essential and you'll need your own transport. The tracks frequently disappear and there are few landmarks, so you'll need enough petrol for a return trip, including unplanned detours. Bring some food.

# THE SOUTH

The south is mostly flat scrubland, with no great vistas and few remarkable towns. It pales into comparison with the north or the Atlantic coast, which offer more spectacular landscapes. Most travellers with their

MAURITANIA

own 4WDs head straight from Nouakchott to Ayoûn el-Atroûs or Néma and then journey on to Mali, or head to Rosso and on to Senegal.

But there's Oualâta. This uniquely unforgettable town is definitely worth the effort to get there and should be on every savvy traveller's itinerary.

## ROSSO

**pop 30,000**

Rosso is a the main Mauritanian–Senegalese border crossing. It's a grubby, haphazard town with a slightly sinister feel. Most travellers breeze through, as there aren't really any worthwhile sights or attractions here. For more details, see p574.

Mercedes bush taxis from Nouakchott cost UM2000. The trip takes at least three hours. The onward trip to Dakar costs CFA5500 by Peugeot taxi. From Rosso, you can also take a Peugeot bush taxi to Diamma/Keur Masséné (UM500) to the west and cross the border there.

## THE ROAD TO MALI

Good news for overlanders: the Route de l'Espoir (Road to Hope) from Nouakchott to Néma (around 1100km) is now entirely tarred. There's not really much to see on the way, so you can cover this monotonous stretch in two days. For more details on reaching this area by public transport, see p558.

The first major town on the road to the Malian border is **Kiffa** (population 30,000), an important regional trading centre and crossroads. Much of the activity of this vibrant place centres on the active market. The best places to stay are **Hôtel Emel** ( ☎ 563 26 37; fax 563 26 38; s/d UM7000/10,000; ❄ ), 7km west of the centre, with fusty but spacious and well-equipped bungalows, and the more recent **Auberge Le Phare du Désert** ( ☎ 563 28 88; tikits UM10,000; ❄ ), a nicely laid-out auberge, also on the outskirts of Kiffa. Meals are available at both places, but don't expect the Ritz.

You could also break up your journey at lively **Ayoûn el-Atroûs**, which is a good place to spend your last ouguiyas before crossing into Mali (see p574). For accommodation, try the unpretentious **Hôtel Ayoûn** ( ☎ 515 14 62; s/d UM5000/8000; ❄ ), which is in the centre (rooms come with bathroom),

or **Auberge Saada Tenzah** ( ☎ 515 13 37, 641 10 52; r UM5000-8000), about 3km east of the centre on the road to Néma. The beds in both places probably keep local chiropractors in business.

The tarred road ends at **Néma**, where you can already feel the flavour of neighbouring Mali. Néma doesn't have much to detain you but it's the main jumping-off point for Oualâta and the southern gateway to the Tagânt. At the time of research, there was talk of launching direct flights from Nouakchott to Néma (to serve the Tagânt) – if this happens, this little town could develop quickly. You'll find several petrol pumps, a BMCI branch (euros only), a couple of modest stores and a police station at which you can get your passport stamped. You can base yourself at **Complexe Touristique N'Gady** ( ☎ 513 09 00; fax 513 09 70; bungalows s/d UM7000/9000, r 12,000/15,000; P ❄ ), a few kilometres west of the centre. It's not ultracharming but convenient enough for a night or two.

## OUALÂTA

It's a darn gruelling ride to get to Oualâta but you'll instantly fall in love with this middle-of-nowhere community – at least we did. Possibly one of Mauritania's best-kept secrets, Oualâta, about 100km north of Néma, is another ancient Saharan town high on atmosphere and personality. It lacks facilities but it's hard not to be touched by the end-of-the-world, forgotten-city feeling that emanates from this poignant place. Dating from 1224, it used to be the last resting point for caravans heading to Timbuktu.

A hint: get there before it becomes too touristy. At the time of research, there was talk of re-opening the airport in nearby Néma, which would translate into an influx of tourists. Some say Oualâta could be the 'Chinguetti of the southeast' in the forthcoming years.

### Sights & Activities

Entering the town you'll be struck by the red **mud-brick houses** adorned with decorative paintings on the exterior and interior. Many houses were restored with the help of a Spanish organisation. The women paint geometric designs with dyes, typically red or indigo, making use of all materials found in the region. If you're lucky, you may get invited inside one of them. A small donation is recommended (about UM500). There's also a small **museum** (UM500) and a **library**, which houses ancient Islamic manuscripts. If you're in for some souvenirs, Oualâta women are renowned for their original and fanciful clay carvings. Try to meet Izzi, near Auberge Gamni – her works are really appealing.

The knowledgeable, French-speaking guide Sidi Ould De (UM2000) can enhance your visit. He is usually hanging around when tourists arrive in town.

If you have plenty of time, you could easily spend several days pottering about in the town and the area – watching nomads bring vast herds of goats or camels down the hills to the river and enjoying the natural splendour. There are also several rock paintings and **archeological sites** in the vicinity. Various **camel trips** can also be organised (ask your hosts).

### Eating & Sleeping
Fear not: although you're miles from anywhere, you'll find about six guesthouses to rest your weary limbs. Nothing flash, but they are exceedingly atmospheric, with traditional murals. Bathrooms are shared. They all serve meals (about UM1800 for lunch or dinner, UM800 for breakfast). Try the local delicacy, *pigeon farci aux dattes* (pigeon stuffed with dates).

**Auberge Tayib/Gamni – Auberge de l'Hôtel de Ville** (r per person UM3000) is a great place with a very homely feel, as is the more basic but still welcoming **Auberge de l'Amitié** (r per person UM1500), not far from the old mosque. Moulaye Ahmed De, the chirpy owner, is used to dealing with travellers and will do his best to ensure a memorable stay. A notch up from these two, **Auberge Ksar Walata** (r per person UM5000) is tucked away in a lane in the old city. It features a lovely patio and attractive rooms.

### Getting There & Away
There are two dirt tracks between Néma and Oualâta (approximately 110km). Land Rovers ply between the two towns (UM2000, 2½ hours) on an infrequent basis – usually every other day, sometimes more if there are enough people. Ask around in Néma market.

# MAURITANIA DIRECTORY

## ACCOMMODATION
In general, you can expect to spend less than US$15 per person in places we list as budget options; US$15 to US$50 in those we list as midrange; and more than US$50 in those as we list as top end. Finding budget accommodation is easy in cities and major towns. There's also a sprinkle of air-conditioned hotels meeting international standards in Nouakchott and, to a lesser extent, Nouâdhibou and Atâr. In the desert, you'll find numerous basic auberges or *campements*. They consist of a series of *tikits* or *khaimas* that come equipped with mattresses on the floor.

The last couple of years has seen a gradual improvement in the choice on offer, with a growing number of tasteful, midrange *maisons d'hôtes*.

## ACTIVITIES
Camel rides and 4WD expeditions in the desert are the most popular activities. Numerous tour companies can arrange custom trips in the desert (p563).

Alternatively, if bird-watching gets you in a flap, head for the Parc National du Banc d'Arguin (p561), along the Atlantic coast – this area is rated as one of the world's greatest birdlife-viewing venues.

## BUSINESS HOURS
Although it's a Muslim country, for business purposes Mauritania adheres to the Monday to Friday working week. However, Friday is the main prayer day, so many

---

**PRACTICALITIES**

- Mauritania uses the metric system for weights and measures.

- Electrical current is 220V AC, 50Hz and most electrical plugs are of the European two-pin type.

- Mauritania's only TV station is TVM, with programmes in Arabic and French, but top-end hotels have satellite TV.

- For the news (in French), pick up *Le Calame* or *Horizons*.

businesses have an extended lunch break on Friday afternoon.

Many shops are open every day. Government offices, post offices and banks are usually open from 8am to 4pm Monday to Thursday and from 8am to 1pm on Friday.

## CHILDREN

On the whole, Mauritania is a friendly and welcoming place for children. Possible activities might include camel riding and short hikes in the desert.

## CUSTOMS

It is illegal to bring any alcohol into the country and heavy fines are levied. There are no longer currency declaration forms and there is no restriction on the amount of foreign currency you can bring in. Local currency cannot be imported or exported.

## DANGERS & ANNOYANCES

Don't get paranoid in Mauritania – it remains one of the safest countries in Africa.

A word of warning though. There are thousands of land mines buried along the Mauritanian side of the border with the Western Sahara, even as close as a few kilometres from Nouâdhibou.

There have been isolated incidents of bandits attacking single cars travelling overland to Mali, especially on off-the-beaten tracks around Néma, so keep to the main roads.

## EMBASSIES & CONSULATES
### Mauritanian Embassies & Consulates

In West Africa, Mauritania has embassies in Côte d'Ivoire, the Gambia, Mali, Nigeria and Senegal, and a consulate in Niger. For more details, see the relevant country chapter.

Elsewhere, Mauritania has embassies and consulates in the following countries:

**Belgium** ( ☎ 02-672 47 47; Colombialaan 6, Brussels 1000)

**Canada** ( ☎ 613-237 3283; 121 Sherwood Drive, Ottawa K1Y 3V1)

**France** ( ☎ 01-45 48 23 88; 89 Rue du Cherche-Midi, 75006 Paris)

**Germany** ( ☎ 030-20 65 88 30; Axel Springer Strasse 54, 10117 Berlin)

**Morocco** ( ☎ 07-75 68 28 or 65 66 78; 1 Rue de Normandie, Souissi, Rabat)

**Spain** ( ☎ 91-575 7007; Velasquez 90, 28224 Madrid)

**UK** ( ☎ 020-7478 9323; 8 Carlos Palace, Mayfair, London W1K 3AS)

**USA** ( ☎ 202-232 5700; www.ambarim-dc.org; 2129 Leroy Place NW, Washington, DC 20008)

## Embassies & Consulates in Mauritania

The following countries are represented in Nouakchott:

**France** ( ☎ 525 23 37; Rue Ahmed Ould Mohamed)

**Germany** ( ☎ 525 17 29; Rue Abdallaye)

**Mali** ( ☎ 525 40 81, 525 40 78; Tevragh Zeina)

**Morocco** ( ☎ 525 14 11; Ave du Général de Gaulle)

**Senegal** ( ☎ 525 72 90; Rue de l'Ambassade du Sénégal)

**USA** ( ☎ 525 26 60; fax 525 15 92; Rue Abdallaye)

## HOLIDAYS

Public holidays include:

**New Year's Day** 1 January
**National Reunification Day** 26 February
**Workers' Day** 1 May
**African Liberation Day** 25 May
**Army Day** 10 July
**Independence Day** 28 November
**Anniversary of the 1984 Coup** 12 December

Mauritania also celebrates the usual Islamic holidays – see p818 for a table of estimated dates of these holidays.

## INTERNET ACCESS

Mauritania has joined the Internet revolution with cybercafés in (at the time of writing) Nouakchott, Nouâdhibou, Atâr and Ayoûn-el-Atroûs.

The quality of the connections varies – some are painfully slow, others reasonable, none are superfast. The normal cost of one hour's surfing is UM200.

## LANGUAGE

Arabic is the official language, but French is still spoken in all government sectors and is widely used in business. The everyday language of the Moor majority is a Berber-Arabic dialect called Hassaniya. In the south, other languages are spoken, including Fula (Pulaar), Wolof and Soninké. See p861 for a list of useful phrases in French, Hassaniya, Fula and Wolof.

## MONEY

'The unit of currency is the ouguiya (UM). Euros and US dollars are the cash to carry and wads of cash it must be, as travellers cheques and credit cards are pretty useless.

At the time of writing there was no ATM in Mauritania. Many banks in Nouakchott transfer money via Western Union. No banks give cash advances on credit cards.

There is no longer a huge difference between the black-market rate and those offered by bureaus de change and banks. There are banks and bureaus de change in most cities. The Banque Mauritanienne pour le Commerce International (BMCI) and Banque Nationale de Mauritanie (BNM) are your best bet. Rates outside Nouakchott are slightly lower than in the capital.

Credit cards are accepted only at top-end hotels in Nouakchott.

## TELEPHONE

You can make international calls and send faxes at post offices. The innumerable privately run phone shops in the major cities and towns cost about the same and are open late.

There are no telephone area codes.

## VISAS

Visas are required for all, except nationals of Arab League countries and some African countries, although check that these exceptions haven't changed. The standard visa is valid for three months and good for a stay of one month from the date of entry.

In most places, Mauritanian embassies require an onward air ticket (or at least an itinerary). This is the case at most embassies in Europe as well as Morocco. It is common practice for an overland traveller to buy an airline ticket in Rabat for the purpose of obtaining a visa and to sell (or refund) the ticket once the visa is issued. The visa will indicate that it's valid for entry at Nouakchott airport but border officials routinely ignore this. Visas can cost anywhere from US$20 to US$120.

In countries where Mauritania has no diplomatic representation, including Australia and many countries in West Africa, French embassies will issue visas with a minimum of fuss for around US$30.

### Visa Extensions

Visa extensions can be obtained at the **Sûreté** (Ave Abdel Nasser, Nouakchott; ⏰ 8am-3pm Mon-Thu). It costs UM5000 for one month.

### Visas for Onward Travel

In Mauritania you can get visas for the following neighbouring countries.

### MALI

Visas are issued the same day (UM6500) and are valid for one month. You need two photos and a photocopy of the information pages of your passport.

### MOROCCO

Single-/double-entry visas cost UM5800/ 8700 and are issued in 48 hours. You need two photos and photocopies of your passport and air ticket.

### SENEGAL

One-month visas (UM1500) are issued in 24 hours. You need to supply four photos.

## WOMEN TRAVELLERS

Mauritania is a conservative Muslim country but by no means the most extreme in this regard. It is not unusual to find women working in public offices and driving; most wear a headscarf rather than a veil covering the face. The best way to meet local women is to hope for an invitation home from a family or to spend some time talking with stallholders, most of whom are women, in local markets.

Women travellers can be subjected to sexual harassment, especially when alone or with other women, although most women encounter no problems. It's a good idea for women to dress modestly. Cover the upper legs and arms and avoid shorts or skimpy T-shirts.

# TRANSPORT IN MAURITANIA

## GETTING THERE & AWAY

Most people from Western Europe or further abroad will fly to Mauritania, most probably to Nouakchott or Atâr. However, if you're doing a grand tour across West Africa, road border posts are open between Mauritania and neighbouring countries.

### Entering Mauritania

Your passport must be valid for at least six months beyond your intended departure from Mauritania and stamped with a valid visa (see left). For travellers coming overland from Morocco, visas can also be issued at the border. You must also have proof of your vaccination against yellow fever.

Travellers arriving with the charter flight from Paris to Atâr from October to April don't need to bother about the visa; it's included in the price and is routinely issued upon arrival at Atâr airport.

## Air

Nouakchott, Nouâdhibou and Atâr have international airports. Nouakchott's airport handles most traffic.

Mauritania's national carrier is Air Mauritanie. It has offices in Nouakchott, Nouâdhibou, Kiffa and Ayoûn-el-Atroûs. The following airlines also fly to/from Mauritania:

**Air Algérie** (AH; ☎ 525 20 59; www.airalgerie.dz; cnr Ave du Général de Gaulle & Ave Abdel Nasser) Hub: Algiers.

**Air France** (AF; ☎ 525 18 08, 525 39 16; www.airfrance .com; Ave Kennedy) Hub: Paris.

**Air Mauritanie** (MR; ☎ 525 22 16, 525 80 98; www .airmauritanie.mr; Ave Abdel Nasser) Hub: Nouakchott.

**Air Sénégal International** (V7; ☎ 525 05 84; www .air-senegal-international.com; Ave du Général de Gaulle) Hub: Dakar.

**Point Afrique** (BIE; ☎ 00 33 4 75 97 20 40 in France; www.point-afrique.com) Hub: Paris.

**Royal Air Maroc** (AT; ☎ 525 35 64, 525 30 94; www .royalairmaroc.com; Ave Abdel Nasser) Hub: Casablanca.

**Tunis Air** (TU; ☎ 525 87 63; www.tunisair.com.tr; Ave Kennedy) Hub: Tunis.

For details on travelling from Australia, New Zealand, Europe and the USA please see p830.

### AFRICA

Air Mauritanie and Air Sénégal both operate between Dakar and Nouakchott. There are also twice weekly Air Mauritanie flights to Bamako in Mali. Abidjan in Côte d'Ivoire and Cotonou in Benin are also served by Air Mauritanie, via Bamako and via Abidjan respectively.

For other Saharan or sub-Saharan countries, you'll have to change in Dakar or Abidjan.

Mauritania is well connected to North Africa. Air Mauritanie and Royal Air Maroc operate between Casablanca and Nouakchott five times a week), while Tunis Air connects Tunis with Nouakchott (three times a week). Air Algérie flies to Algiers.

## Land

If driving into Mauritania, see opposite.

### MALI

At the time of research, the most straightforward route to Mali was from Ayoûn el-Atroûs to Nioro. You can also cross at Néma, Timbedgha (both connecting with Nara in Mali), Tintâne and Kiffa (both connecting with Nioro in Mali).

If crossing into Mali, have your passport stamped by police at the first town you reach after crossing the border. You must also clear customs, which is done in Néma or Ayoûn el-Atroûs.

From Nouakchott, you can catch bush taxis to Néma (about UM7500, two days) and Ayoûn el-Atroûs (about UM6000, 15 hours). From these places you can catch transport into Mali.

There are two routes between Nioro and Ayoûn el-Atroûs if you're travelling by car. The trip is roughly 230km and usually takes less than a day.

Petrol is available in Nioro, Nara, Néma, Ayoûn el-Atroûs and Kiffa.

### MOROCCO

The trans-Sahara route via Mauritania is now a very popular route from North Africa into sub-Saharan Africa.

The only border crossing between Morocco and Mauritania is north of Nouâdhibou. Crossing this border is straightforward; there is no longer any need to travel with a military escort from Dakhla (Morocco) and the road is now entirely tarred to Nouakchott, except for the 3km no-man's-land that separates the two border posts. Coming from Morocco, you can buy the Mauritanian visa at the border (€20). Expect to pay about €20 for various 'taxes' on top of the visa price. Although there are no longer currency declaration forms, some customs officials still ask for it and, of course, if you can't present it, they will expect a small bribe. See also p838.

Note that there's no public transport between Morocco and Mauritania.

### SENEGAL

The main border crossing for Senegal is at Rosso but it's also possible to cross at Diamma (Keur Masséne), west of Rosso.

When crossing into Senegal at Rosso, note that immigration is only open on the Mauritanian side from 8am to noon and 3pm to 6pm. The border crossing here is notorious for its hassles. Be prepared for some confrontation with customs officials who usually ask for 'exit taxes'. It's even worse for vehicle owners.

From Dakar to Nouakchott by public transport usually takes from 11 to 13 hours depending on the wait at the border. Most minibuses and bush taxis leave Dakar before 10am to be sure of arriving in Rosso well before the border closing time (6pm). At Rosso, most travellers without vehicles cross by pirogue (five minutes; UM200/CFA500) as the ferry crosses only four times daily. If you want to avoid the hassles at Rosso, you can take a bush taxi from Rosso to Diamma (Keur Masséne) and cross at Diamma. The border at Diamma is open 24 hours and the hassles are reportedly less problematic (although you'll probably be asked for an 'extra hours tax' if you cross at night).

With your own vehicle, you can either cross the Senegal River at Rosso, which takes only ten minutes by *bac* (ferry), or use the bridge at Diamma (open 24 hours). At Rosso, the ferry departs from the Mauritanian side at 9.30am, 11.15am, 3.30pm and 5pm, and from the Senegalese side some 45 minutes later. It costs UM4000 for a 4WD. During the dry season, most travellers with a car tend to opt for Diamma.

## GETTING AROUND
### Air
#### AIRLINES IN MAURITANIA
Air Mauritanie flies from Nouakchott to Nouâdhibou (UM16,000/32,000 one way/return, four times per week), Kiffa (UM13,000/25,000, once per week), Ayoûn el-Atroûs (UM14,500/28,000, once per week), Selibaby (UM16,000/31,000, twice per week) and Zouérat (UM17,500/34,200, once per week).

At the time of writing, there was talk of scheduling flights to Néma.

### Bush Taxi
Mercedes taxis (Mercedes 190), Peugeot taxis (Peugeot 504s), Land Rovers and minibuses, in descending order of cost, are the four types of public transport. Overcharging is rare except with the baggage fee, which requires bargaining. Bush taxis go to all the major towns daily, but finding one for small villages is challenging.

Mercedes or Peugeot bush taxis are uncomfortable because you're crammed in four to a row, so consider paying for two seats to avoid the misery. The front two seats are less cramped but they're also more expensive. Note that a *taxi course* is a taxi that you have all to yourself.

## Car & Motorcycle
### BRING YOUR OWN VEHICLE
You don't need a *carnet de passage en douane* in Mauritania (see p837 for more information). Mauritanian officials enter details of the car in your passport, which is then checked on departure from the country. An International Driving Permit (IDP) is not required.

### FUEL & SPARE PARTS
Petrol was UM209 per litre at the time of writing, slightly more in the Adrar and along the Route de l'Espoir. There are petrol stations in most cities, including Tidjikja and Néma.

### HIRE
If you don't have a vehicle and you want more freedom than a tour can offer (most companies won't run tours for less than four people), consider renting a 4WD and driver. The standard Toyota Hilux usually costs around UM21,000 per day for the vehicle, plus petrol.

### INSURANCE
Many European car-insurance companies will only issue policies for as far south as Morocco; in Mauritania you must buy a Mauritanian policy purchased at Nouâdhibou (and sometimes directly at the Moroccan border) or at Nouakchott. Expect to pay around US$20 for ten days.

### ROAD CONDITIONS
Roads are being steadily upgraded. A major improvement in late 2005 was the opening of a new tarred road connecting Nouakchott with Nouâdhibou, bypassing the Parc National du Banc d'Arguin. The Route de l'Espoir from Nouakchott to Néma (around 1100km) is also entirely tarred, as is the road from Nouakchott to Tidjikja.

The road to Atâr is excellent, so driving there from Nouakchott is now six hours nonstop. The unsealed road from Atâr to

MAURITANIA

**AN EPIC JOURNEY ON THE IRON-ORE TRAIN**

We will never forget the experience – neither will you. The Zouârat to Nouâdhibou train is the longest in the world – typically 2.3km long. When it arrives at the 'station' in Nouâdhibou, a decrepit building in the open desert, a seemingly endless number of ore wagons pass before the passenger carriage at the rear appears. Then the stampede to get on board begins. The lucky ones find a place on one of the two long benches; the rest stand or sit on the floor, or perch on the roof for free. There are also a dozen of 'berths' that are so worn out that you can see the springs. The atmosphere can be quite jovial, with people playing cards on the floor. In the late afternoon, many men find space on the floor to pray and at dusk when the cabin becomes totally dark, chanting begins. On board, a man sells tea and cheap snacks. Take enough clothes to keep warm, as it can get cold at night.

Choûm (about two hours) is reasonably good but requires a 4WD. You'll also need a 4WD to Chinguetti and Ouadâne, whichever road you take – the one that goes along the northern plateau is much better but less scenic than the sandy southern route.

Expect police checkpoints at the entrance and exit of each town.

## Tours

There are numerous travel agencies in Nouakchott that offer tours around the country but it's not a bad idea to arrange a tour with a more regional-focussed company – eg in Atâr for the Adrar or the Tagânt. Travel is usually by 4WD. Standard tours include an eight-day tour to Atâr, Chinguetti, Ouadâne, Guelb er Richat and Terjît, the Tagânt plateau, or five-day excursions to the Banc d'Arguin. If there are at least four travellers, prices should average around UM20,000 per person per day.

## Train

The Nouâdhibou–Zouérat train is a great adventure (see above). It's an iron-ore train with no passenger terminals, but it has become a passenger train for lack of better alternatives. The trip takes 16 to 18 hours, but most travellers get off at Choûm, 12 hours from Nouâdhibou. You can also put your car on board.

# Niger

With the Ténéré Desert boasting some of the Sahara's most beautiful dunes, the stark splendour of the Aïr Mountains being one of West Africa's most spectacular sights, and the intriguing ancient trans-Saharan trade-route towns of Agadez and Zinder playing home to magnificent mazes of mud-brick architecture and fascinating locals, the international appeal of Niger as a destination is undeniable.

Odd then, that the first question friends ask prospective travellers is 'Why Niger?'. Simply stated, press regarding Niger's plight with localised food shortages dominates headlines and paints the entire nation in the same poor light. Watching the news in 2005, you'd have been forgiven for thinking locusts and drought had destroyed the entire nation's food supply. In reality, crop production was only 10% lower than average, locust damage was limited to grasses used to feed livestock, and food was still available in most markets. The main problem was that nomadic herders lost much of their livestock (their only income) and couldn't afford the rising costs of food, putting 3.6 million of them at risk of starvation. There's no denying that Niger is one of the world's poorest countries, but taking your tourist dollars elsewhere because of that is only contributing to the problem.

The lucky ones who do visit Niger will witness its enduring physical beauty and meet a vibrant mix of people, who must be some of the planet's most stoic and resilient citizens. Whether you travel by bush taxi, 4WD or camel, you'll never forget your time in Niger.

**NIGER**

## FAST FACTS

- **Area** 1,267,000 sq km
- **Capital** Niamey
- **Country code** ☎ 227
- **Famous for** Aïr Mountains, Ténéré Desert; Cure Salée Festival
- **Languages** French, Hausa, Djerma, Fulfulde, Tamashek, Kanouri, Toubou and Gourmanchéma
- **Money** West African CFA Franc; US$1 = CFA544.89; €1 = CFA655.96
- **Population** 12.8 million
- **Visa** Required by almost everyone except West African citizens. Obtained easily in Algeria, Benin, Chad, Mali and Nigeria.

## HIGHLIGHTS

- **Aïr Mountains** (p608) Make tracks with camel companions through red sands and blue rocks in these mystical mountains, or buckle up and tackle the **Ténéré** (p609).
- **Agadez** (p604) Spiral up and squeeze out onto the spiky summit of the majestic mud mosque here, to captivating views over the surrounding Sahara.
- **Zinder** (p601) Backtrack through the banco houses of the Birni Quartier and soak up the Hausa history.
- **Ayorou** (p594) Savour Sunday market smells, before boarding a boat bound for bellowing hippos on a serene section of the Niger River.
- **Kouré** (p593) Walk in sublime silence with the gregarious giraffes nearby, the last wild herd of the gorgeous animals in West Africa.
- **Plateau du Djado** (p610) Dive in the deep end with a 4WD expedition to this remote spot, and visit the mystical honeycombed ruins of Djado's medieval citadel.

## ITINERARIES

- **One Week** While it's possible to make a whistle-stop tour of Niamey, Zinder and Agadez within a week (even using public transport), you're better off saving your backside and staying local. With a pleasant riverside location, some interesting sights and an array of fine restaurants, **Niamey** (p584) makes a great base for a few days. Possible excursions include the Sunday markets of **Ayorou** (p594) and **Filingué** (p595), and wandering with the giraffes near **Kouré** (p593). Round out the week with three to four days visiting **Parc Regional du W** (p596) in the south. Alternatively, base yourself in intriguing **Agadez** (p604) for a taste of the astounding **Aïr Mountains** (p608).
- **Two Weeks** Combine the two one-week itineraries above with a day or two discovering the old quarters and Hausa architecture in **Zinder** (p601). If the Sahara beckons and your wallet is bulging, bypass Niamey and delve deeper into the Aïr Mountains and **Ténéré Desert** (p608) on a 4WD expedition.
- **One Month** Toss out our advice so far, join a **camel caravan** (p610) and see the Sahara

how it should be seen. Or relax and explore Niger's towns at will – enjoy.

## CLIMATE & WHEN TO GO

December to February is the best time to visit, as temperatures are at their coolest and rainfall is nonexistent. The only drawbacks are the harmattan winds, which can reduce visibility to less than 1km and spoil photographic opportunities, and surprisingly cold evening temperatures in the desert.

The hottest part of the year is March to June, with April daytime temperatures reaching 45°C (113°F) or more, especially in the north, and heat so intense that rain evaporates before reaching the ground. Desert travel isn't feasible at these times.

Rains dampen the south between late May and September, with August being the wettest time. The south's annual rainfall is usually 550mm, while the north is lucky to receive 150mm.

Niamey's climatic chart is found on p813.

## HISTORY
### Early History

Some 6000 years ago, Niger's vast northern plateaus were verdant grasslands supporting hunters, herders and abundant wildlife. Around 2500 BC the Sahara began swallowing this region and its rivers whole, driving the population south. Little remains of this lush past, besides the splendid images captured in the Neolithic rock art of the Aïr Mountains (see the boxed text, p609). By the 1st millennium BC, the migrating peoples had learnt metalwork skills, developed complex social organisations and forms of trade.

## Great West African Empires

Lying at the crossroads of the lucrative trans-Saharan trade route (in gold, salt and slaves), Niger's arid landscape once supported some of West Africa's great empires. One was the Kanem-Borno Empire, which flourished around Lake Chad between the 10th and 13th centuries AD. It survived the arrival of Islam during the 10th and 11th centuries, and remained a significant force until the 1800s. Between the 14th and 15th centuries, western Niger was controlled by the Islamic Empire of Mali before falling to the powerful Empire of Songhaï in the early 1500s, which subsequently controlled much of central Niger until the late 16th Century.

Also playing important roles before the arrival of Europeans were the Tuareg, who migrated south into the Aïr Mountains during the 11th century, and the Hausa and Kanouri peoples, who founded the mighty Damagaram state around Zinder having fled Nigeria in the 1600s.

## Late Precolonial Niger

Although abolished in most of West Africa by the 1850s, the slave trade was still going strong in Niger and Chad. With 12,000 soldiers, the Sultan of Zinder had little trouble attacking villages in his own kingdom, capturing inhabitants and selling them as slaves to support his 300 wives and numerous children.

Agadez, once a great gold-trading centre, was hit as trade shifted from the Sahara to the Portuguese-controlled coastal ports; its population shrinking from 30,000 in 1450 to less than 3000 by the early 20th century.

As trade in gold declined, the value of salt rose. Mined at remote oases in the desert, salt deposits were the prerogative of the Tuareg nomads, and it was so rare that it was often traded ounce for ounce for gold. Salt sustained the huge trans-Saharan camel

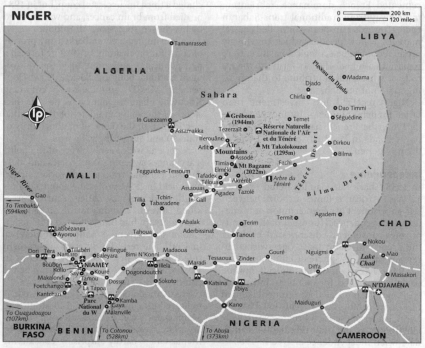

caravans, and, as recently as 1906, a 20,000-camel caravan left Agadez to collect salt at Bilma, an oasis 610km to the east.

## Colonial Era

The French strolled into the picture late in the 19th century and met stronger-than-expected local resistance. Decidedly unamused, they quickly dispatched the punitive Voulet-Chanoîne expedition, which laid waste to much of southern Niger in 1898–99. The Birni N'Konni massacre is one of the most shameful episodes in French colonial history. Although Tuareg revolts in the north continued, culminating in the siege of Agadez in 1916–17, French control over the territory was assured.

French rule wasn't kind to Niger. The colonial administration selectively cultivated the power of traditional chiefs, whose abuses were almost encouraged as a means of de facto control. The imposition of the French franc (in which taxes were paid) drove many agricultural workers to seek work in the cities. The enforced shift from subsistence farming to cash crops further cemented French dominance, reorienting trade away from traditional trans-Saharan routes towards European-controlled coastal markets. Fallow periods, which previously preserved a fragile ecological balance, were replaced with high-density farming, the effects of which still contribute to the ongoing march of the Sahara.

Niger received less investment than other French colonies – by independence in 1960, the French had built 1032km of paved roads in West Africa, only 14km of them Nigerien.

## Independence

In 1958 Charles de Gaulle offered France's 12 West African colonies a choice between self-government in a French union or immediate independence. Hundreds of thousands of votes conveniently disappeared, enabling the French to claim that Niger wished to remain within its sphere of influence.

Djibo Bakari and the radical Sawaba party campaigned for complete independence, and the infuriated government banned the party, exiling Bakari. This left Hamani Diori, leader of the Parti Progressiste Nigérien (PPN), as the only presidential candidate when independence arrived in 1960.

Diori's repressive one-party state maintained close French ties. Diori survived several unsuccessful coups before the great Sahel drought of 1968–74, when foodstocks were discovered in several ministerial homes. This was the final straw and Lieutenant Colonel Seyni Kountché overthrew Diori in a bloody coup. Kountché, then president, established a military ruling council.

## Post-Independence Period

Kountché and Niger hit the proverbial jackpot in 1968 when uranium was discovered near Arlit. Between 1974 and 1979 uranium prices quintupled, permitting some ambitious projects, including the 'uranium highway' to Agadez and Arlit. Yet not everyone was smiling: the cost of living rose dramatically and the poorest were worse off.

In the early 1980s government revenue from uranium plummeted, halting the construction boom. Tragedy then struck with the drought of 1983. For the first time in recorded history the Niger River stopped flowing. Kountché's reputation for honesty helped him weather the unrest, which included a third unsuccessful coup, but in 1987 he died from brain cancer, and was replaced by his chosen successor, Ali Saïbou.

Saïbou immediately embarked on a process of constitution-making. In 1989 he formed a new political organisation called the Mouvement National pour une Société de Développement (MNSD), simultaneously enforcing Kountché's ban on political parties. He then stood as the sole candidate for presidential election (all in the name of national unity of course!) and surprisingly, he won.

Nigeriens were keenly aware of the political changes sweeping West Africa and mass student demonstrations and worker strikes were held in 1990, protesting about Saïbou's fictitious democracy. After security forces killed several demonstrating at Niamey University, public outcry forced a reluctant Saïbou to convene a national conference in 1991. The resulting interim government ruled until the first multiparty elections in 1993, which made Mahamane Ousmane the country's first Hausa head of state.

His democratic reign was short-lived. A military junta, led by Colonel Ibrahim Bare Mainassara, staged a successful coup in January 1996. Elections held in July were won by Mainassara – hardly surprising considering

**TUAREG REBELLION**

Being a minority in Niger has put the Tuareg at a serious disadvantage when it comes to getting their fair share of the respective national budgets, and they have been marginalised politically and economically. Their difficulties were compounded by the droughts in the 1970s and 1980s, which decimated livestock and altered the lives of these traditionally nomadic herders. Meanwhile, increasing desertification and population growth thrust them into conflict with other pastoral groups such as the Arabs and Fulani.

In 1992 the Nigerien Tuareg raided a police post at Tchin-Tabaradene, an action reflecting their frustration over the lack of assistance given to Tuaregs recently returned from Algeria and the misappropriation of funds promised them following Saïbou's accession. They also sought the right for Tuareg children to learn Tamashek in schools. Brutal government reprisals followed, sparking a protracted conflict in which hundreds of rebels, police and civilians were killed.

The Tuareg demanded a federal country, with an autonomous Tuareg region in the north. During the conflict, the government banned travel in Niger's north and closed its main border with Algeria, halting the tourist flow across one of the Sahara's oldest routes and stifling tourism.

In early 1994, the Tuareg Front de Libération de l'Aïr et l'Azouack (FLAA) and Front de Libération Tamouist (FLT) reached an uneasy truce. A peace accord was signed in 1995 after the government and the Organisation de la Résistance Armée (ORA), representing the Tuareg groups, met in Ouagadougou. Although peace was signed with the last rebel group in 1998, discontent still simmers among the Tuareg today. Their biggest frustration is still the complete lack of government funding and education in Tuareg regions.

he'd dissolved the independent election commission and confined his main opponents to house arrest.

In 1999, during widespread strikes and economic stagnation, the commander of the presidential guard assassinated Mainassara. The prime minister described the death, without any apparent irony, as 'an unfortunate accident'. The coup leader, Major Daoud Mallam Wanke, quickly re-established democracy and peaceful elections were held in late 1999. Mamadou Tandja was elected with over 59% of the vote. In the 113-seat national assembly (with only one female MP), Mamadou forged a coalition majority with supporters of former President Ousmane.

**Niger Today**

To state the obvious, Niger is truly struggling. Even before the devastating food crisis of 2005, Niger ranked last on the UN's Human Development Index, a statistic based on life-expectancy, infant mortality, health and education. Sadly, Niger also ranked last on the UN's Human Poverty Index and Gender-Related Development Index.

The one bright spot in recent years is the impressive transition from military to democratic rule. On July 24 2004 the first-ever successful municipal elections were held to select members of 265 local councils. A part of the ongoing decentralisation process, these councils will assume many administrative powers from the government. The municipal elections were followed by the second presidential elections in November 2004. Mamadou was re-elected president with 65% of the vote and his coalition party took 88 of the National Assembly's 113 seats.

**THE CULTURE**
**The National Psyche**

Although arguably the poorest people in the world, Nigeriens are a proud bunch, quick with welcoming smiles and occasional spontaneous acts of generosity. Similarly refreshing is their willingness to stay and work to improve their nation, unlike citizens of some African countries, who admit they'd jump at the first chance to emigrate.

Although over 90% of the population is devoutly Muslim, the government is steadfastly secular and Islam takes on a more relaxed public persona here than in other countries with similar demographics. Women don't cover their faces, alcohol is quietly consumed by many and some Tuareg, recognising the harsh dictates of desert life, even ignore the annual Ramadan fast. The area around Maradi is the exception, with Muslims calling for Islamic conservatism and the imposition of Islamic Sharia law.

Slavery has long been part of Niger's culture and remarkably it was only outlawed in May 2003. However, human rights groups believe at least 43,000 Nigeriens still live in subjugation. Besides temporarily imprisoning those leading the fight against slavery, the government strictly denies the problem exists, claiming members of the lowest caste are simply mistaken for slaves.

## Daily Life

Above all, Islam plays the greatest role in Nigeriens' daily life, shaping beliefs and thoughts. Yet little of this is visible to the visitor. The one exception is at *salat* (prayer), when the country grinds to a halt at dawn, noon, afternoon, sunset and nightfall – buses and bush taxis will break their journeys to partake.

Religion aside, survival occupies the vast majority of Nigeriens' days. About 90% of the population make their tenuous living from agriculture and livestock, with the majority living on less than US$1 per day. Having numerous children to help with the burdening workload is a necessity for many families, a fact contributing to the rising population. For the majority of children, their youth is spent working and not studying – only 35% of boys and 21% of girls attend primary school, which leads to staggering adult illiteracy rates (only 7% of women and 21% of men are literate) and sentences further generations to a life in the fields.

Family life is further complicated by widespread polygamy and, more recently, urbanisation drawing men away from their families to seek work. The 2005 food crisis highlighted this phenomenon, when aid workers found numerous wives and children starving because their granaries, while stocked with sorghum and millet, were locked by long-absent fathers and husbands. Traditionally in polygamist families the head of the household controls the family produce, while his wives must each fend for themselves and their children using only a small plot of land received at marriage.

The Tuareg, meanwhile, are effectively monogamous, and women enjoy greater independence, owning their own livestock and spending the income on themselves, while men must provide for the home.

## Population

With a growth rate of around 3%, Niger's population has grown from 6.6 million in 1985 to 12.8 million in 2006, and is expected to reach a staggering 21.4 million in 2025. An astounding 49% of the population is less than 15 years of age. Currently, 23% of the population lives in urban areas,

---

### SUFFER THE CHILDREN...

Niger's statistics are suitably dire for what is arguably the world's poorest country. The indicators are particularly horrifying for children under five: the infant mortality rate is 131 per 1000 live births; 40% are stunted; 16% are badly malnourished; 40% are underweight; and one-fourth of Niger's children die before they reach the age of five. Studies in villages around Niamey have revealed that micronutrient deficiencies in pregnant women and school children are rife – 60% are anaemic (iron deficient) and iodine deficient. Vitamin A deficiency – the cause of xerophthalmia (night blindness) – is also widespread.

Further facts highlight the desperate situation – maternal mortality is one in 62, compared with one in 11,000 in developed countries; each woman has, on average, 7.9 children; only 16% of the births are aided by trained health workers (and only in Niamey); in rural areas there is little or no prenatal or postnatal care; some 40% of women have given birth by the age of 17; and only 7% of those most at risk for HIV use contraception.

The problems are compounded by the drought cycle that regularly ravages the region. Urban migration has also decimated rural communities and led to dislocated populations of urban poor living without adequate infrastructure on city fringes.

Meagre government resources, drained by the country's crippling foreign debt, have failed to cope. Hopefully the massive international debt-relief packages announced in 2005 will allow the government to start providing basic medicines and preventative health programs. Currently, the failure to take preventative measures against diseases such as measles, meningitis and malaria claims the majority of children.

though this number is steadily rising and is expected to reach 35% by 2025.

More than 90% of the population lives in the south, mostly in the southwest. The south's population is dominated by the Hausa, who make up 56% of the country's populace, and the Songhaï-Djerma, who are centred on the Niger River and comprise 22% of Niger's population. The next-largest groups are the traditionally nomadic Fulani (8.5%) and Tuareg (8%), both found in Niger's north, and the Kanuri (4.3%), located between Zinder and Chad. The remaining 1.2% is made up of the Gourmantché in the south and the Toubou and Arabs in the north.

## SPORT

Traditional wrestling, which intriguingly incorporates numerous Nigerien cultural elements like the use of prayers, poems and the wearing of grigri (charms), is overwhelmingly popular. Unfortunately it only occurs several times a year.

Camel racing is a favourite Tuareg sport. The usual routine involves a champion riding off into the desert with a woman's indigo scarf. Competitors ride in hot pursuit and whomever successfully grabs the scarf, wins. During the race, women decked out in their best silver jewellery cheer on the riders, singing and clapping to the sound of drums.

## RELIGION

Over 90% of the population is Muslim and a small percentage of urban dwellers are Christian. A few rural communities still practice traditional animist religions.

Due to the strong influence of Nigeria's Islamic community in southern Niger, there's a minority of Muslims in areas like Maradi calling for Islamic conservatism and the imposition of Islamic Sharia law.

## ARTS

The best-known artisans must be the Tuareg silversmiths, who produce a wide range of necklaces, striking square amulets and ornamental silver daggers, complete with leather hilts. In a Muslim country, the most unusual items are the stylised silver crosses, each with intricate filigree designs, that represent towns and regions boasting significant Tuareg populations. The most famous cross is the *Croix d'Agadez*. Tuareg see the crosses as powerful talismans that protect against ill-fortune and the evil eye.

The leatherwork of the *artisans du cuir*, found in Zinder, is also particularly well regarded. They produce traditional items such as saddle-bags, cushions and tasselled pouches (which hang from mens' necks and carry tobacco or money), along with attractive modern items like sandals, backpacks and briefcases.

Beautifully unique to Niger are the vibrant Djerma blankets, or *kountas*, produced from patterns of bright cotton strips.

Although most Nigerien music remains traditional, there are some artists breaking moulds. Quickly gaining an international reputation is Mamar Kassey, a nine-piece band playing what the BBC call 'the most infectiously breezy, life-affirming slice of Afropop you're likely to hear'.

## ENVIRONMENT
### The Land

Niger is West Africa's second-largest country and is landlocked 650km from the sea. The Niger River, Africa's third-longest river, flows through 300km of the country's southwest.

It's debatable whether Niger's most remarkable landscapes are the Aïr Mountains' dark volcanic formations, which rise more than 2000m and culminate in the Bagzane peaks, or the Ténéré Dessert's spectacularly sweeping sand dunes.

### Wildlife

In desert regions, camels are the most common animal visitors will see, but gazelle herds still exist in remote areas (dorcas gazelle being the most common) and nocturnal fennecs (small foxes with large ears) are occasionally glimpsed. If you spot a Saharan cheetah, buy a lottery ticket the minute you get home because you're one lucky…

Besides Kouré's graceful giraffes (p594) and the hippos bobbing in the Niger River, there are few other animals of note that you'll bump into. That is of course, only if you don't delve into Parc Regional du W (p596).

### National Parks

Niger hosts one of West Africa's better national parks, Park Regional du W (p596). Its dry savanna environment straddles the Niger River and welcomes everything from elephants, hippos and antelopes to lions, leopards and cheetahs.

The astounding Aïr Mountains (p608) and western section of the Ténéré Desert (p609) have also been designated as the Réserve Naturelle Nationale de l'Aïr et du Ténéré.

### Environmental Issues

Today, two-thirds of Niger is desert and the rest is Sahel (the semidesert zone south of the Sahara). Desertification, Niger's greatest environmental problem, is primarily due to overgrazing and deforestation. Adding to the woes is the abundant quartz-rich sand, which is unsuitable for high-yield crops and prevents anchoring of topsoil, causing erosion.

Community-based projects continue, with limited success, to facilitate reafforestation by encouraging villagers to build windbreaks and establish nurseries. Irrigation projects in the north have also brought life back to once-barren soil, with the village of Azad now among those supplying Agadez with fruit.

To help rebuild livestock herds (after they were decimated by the droughts in the early 1990s) and generate income, one aid scheme 'loans' young goats to farmers to tend until the animals mature and reproduce. The animals' offspring are then 'repaid' to the aid scheme. However, it's a fragile balancing act to prevent herds from growing beyond the land's carrying capacity.

### FOOD & DRINK

Niger's traditional food is not much to get excited about. Dates, yogurt, rice and mutton are standard northern fare among the Tuareg, while rice with sauce is the most common southern dish. Standard fare at restaurants is grilled fish or chicken with chips, or beef brochettes and rice. Couscous and ragoût are also popular. Niamey boasts Niger's best restaurants, with Chinese, French, Italian and even Japanese selections. Outside the capital vegetarian options are fairly limited.

Tapwater in the cities is generally safe, as are the bags of chilled water sold by children. If they don't float your boat, bottled water and soft drinks are everywhere. Sitting for a cup of Tuareg tea is as rewarding as it's thirst quenching.

To put a little wobble in your step, try the local Biére Niger. For a serious wobble dive into some palm wine.

# NIAMEY

**pop 795,000**

Set on the Niger River's lush shores and home to culinary delights unparalleled elsewhere in Niger, Niamey can be a breath of fresh air for those arriving from the Sahel's wilds and a laid-back place to recharge the batteries. Conversely, it can feel like the end of the earth – in summer the dust never settles and, as the capital of one of the world's poorest countries it can be a desperate place, where Africa's pain is everywhere on show.

Since becoming the capital, Niamey has experienced fantastic growth – from around 2000 people in the 1930s to almost 800,000 today. Although smart government buildings do rise from town's centre (a reminder of uranium's past sky-high prices), Niamey still has a traditional African ambience that gives the city its charm.

Dive into the markets, peruse the national museum, take a pirogue along the river or simply enjoy a riverside drink at sunset and watch silhouettes of loping, laden camels crossing Kennedy Bridge.

## ORIENTATION

Niamey is quite spread out, which means a bit more walking than in other Sahel capitals. The street pattern can be confusing, but thankfully street signs now aid navigation.

Crisscrossing through the hub of town like spokes on a wheel – and home to numerous restaurants, bars and banking facilities – are Rue du Président Heinrich Lubké, Ave de la Mairie and Rue du Commerce.

One of Niamey's major thoroughfares is Ave de l'Amitié/Route de l'Aéroport, which links Kennedy Bridge with the airport and the Niger's only highway heading east across the country. Another is Blvd de l'Indépendance, which heads northwest out of town towards Tillabéri, Ayorou and Mali. Cutting through the town centre, and linking the aforementioned thoroughfares, is the Rue de la Copro and Blvd de la Liberté.

## INFORMATION
### Cultural Centres

**American Cultural Center** ( ☎ 73 31 79; Rue de la Tapoa; ☺ 8am-4.30pm Mon-Fri) A comfortable place to catch US TV news and newspapers. They also screen movies at 4.30pm on Wednesday and Friday.

**Centre Culturel Franco-Nigérien** (☎ 73 48 34; www.ccfn.ne; Rue du Musée; ☿ 9am-12.30pm & 3.30pm-6.30pm Wed-Sat, 3.30-6.30pm Tue & 9am-noon Sun) Besides the library there's a busy schedule of lectures, exhibits, dance and theatre. It also screens excellent films on various days at 8.30pm (CFA500), and offers Internet access.

**Centre Culturel Oumarou Ganda** (☎ 74 09 03; Ave de l'Islam; ☿ hours vary) Often closed, this centre sponsors a variety of African cultural activities that include traditional wrestling, dancing, local films, concerts and art exhibitions.

## Internet Access

**Cyber @ Bebto** (Blvd de l'Indépendance; per hr CFA500; ☿ 8am-midnight) A handy option for those staying in west Niamey.

**Cyber Etoile** (Rue de Souvenir; per hr CFA600; ☿ 9am-10pm Mon-Sat & 3-10pm Sun) Located within the Immeuble Sonara II complex.

**Centre Culturel Franco-Nigérien** (Rue du Musée) Although closed during our visit, it's usually a good surfing option.

**Photo-adc** (off Rond-point Maourey; per hr CFA1000; ☿ 8am-9.30pm Mon-Sat & 10am-7pm Sun; ☒ ) Town's fastest connections. Using USB they burn images to CD (per session CFA1500).

**Pl@net Cyber Cafe** (Blvd de Mali Béro; per hr CFA500; ☿ 8am-midnight) Cheap, fast and handy for those staying in Niamey's northeast. Bring water – it gets rather toasty in here.

## Laundry

Most accommodation options happily transform stinky cardboard-stiff items into the clothes you remember and love. Prices start from CFA100 per T-shirt and CFA200 for trousers.

## Media

The widely available local French-language newssheet *Le Sahel* offers little real news, but details events taking place in town.

## Medical Services

**Clinique Alissa** (☎ 72 57 66; Ave du Président Kalt Casten; ☿ 24hr) A convenient, efficient and quality clinic with laboratory and emergency services.

**Clinique de Gamkalé** (☎ 73 20 33; Corniche de Gamkalé; ☿ 8.30am-12.30pm & 3.30-6.30pm Mon-Fri, 8.30am-12.30pm Sat) Consultations cost CFA11,000. Emergency services are open 24 hours.

**Nouvelle Poly-Clinic Pro-Santé** (☎ 72 26 50; Ave du Général de Gaulle; ☿ 24hr) A respected local clinic. Consultations cost between CFA3000 and CFA5000.

**Pharmacie El Nasr** (☎ 73 47 72; Rue du Président Heinrich Lubké)

**Pharmacie du Grand Marché** (☎ 73 40 78; Blvd de la Liberté)

**Tafadeck** (☎ 73 20 34; Rue du Président Heinrich Lubké) Behind the tooth-shaped entrance sits Niamey's best dentist.

## Money

**BIA-Niger** (Rue du Commerce) The best option for painlessly changing travellers cheques (1.6% commission), euros, US dollars and pounds sterling. Visa cash advances cost CFA10,000 per transaction. Western Union transfers are also available.

**Eco Bank** (Blvd de la Liberté; ☿ 8.30am-3.30 Mon-Fri, 9am-1pm Sat, 9am-3pm Sun) There's a painful CFA10,000 commission for changing a US$100 travellers cheque, but changing cash is free. There's also a branch in Hôtel Gaweye (Ave Mitterrand) which offers credit card advances (2% commission).

**Hôtel Gaweye** (Ave Mitterrand; ☿ 24hr) The hotel's front desk will change cash and travellers cheques for a hefty 5% commission.

## Post

**Grande Poste** (Rue de la Grande Poste) Home to Niamey's poste restante sevice.

**Plateau Poste** (Place de la République) Simply stamps and franks here.

## Telephone & Fax

Dozens of private telecentres now dot Niamey's streets. International calls cost CFA150 for each 10-second block. Some charge nothing for incoming calls.

**Grande Poste** (Rue de la Grande Poste) A three-minute call to Europe costs about CFA5000 (the minimum charge). Subsequent minutes cost CFA1600. There's a handy and free 'fax restante' service – have faxes sent to ☎ 73 44 70.

**Photo-adc** (off Rond-point Maourey; ☿ 8am-9.30pm Mon-Sat & 10am-7pm Sun) Offer cheap international calls of variable quality over the Internet. A call to a landline in Europe is CFA200 per minute.

## Tourist Information

**ONT** (☎ 73 24 47; Rue de Président Heinrich Lubké; ☿ 8am-noon & 3.30-6.30pm Mon-Fri) Besides dusty brochures, you'll get little help here.

## Travel Agencies

**Niger-Car Voyages** (☎ 73 23 31; nicarvoy@intnet .ne; Ave de l'Afrique) The best, albeit most expensive, agency in Niamey for tours. Their tours include Filingué and Baleyara, Ayorou, pirogue journeys, the giraffes at Kouré and Parc Regional du W. Prices plummet if there's six or more of you.

NIGER

# NIAMEY

## INFORMATION
| | |
|---|---|
| American Cultural Center | 1 C4 |
| Beninese Embassy | 2 B3 |
| BIA-Niger | 3 A5 |
| Canadian Embassy | 4 C2 |
| Centre Culturel Franco-Nigérien | 5 C4 |
| Centre Culturel Oumarou Ganda | 6 F4 |
| Chadian Embassy | 7 B4 |
| Clinique Alissa | (see 54) |
| Clinique de Gamkalé | 8 D6 |
| Cyber @ Bebto | 9 B3 |
| Cyber Etoile | 10 A6 |
| Danish Consulate | 11 B4 |
| Direction de la Surveillance du Territoire | 12 A6 |
| Eco Bank | 13 D5 |
| French Consulate | 14 C4 |
| German Embassy | 15 B4 |
| Grand Poste | 16 B6 |
| Nouvelle Poly-Clinic Pro-Santé | 17 B3 |
| ONT (Tourist Information) | 18 A6 |
| Pharmacie du Grand Marché | 19 B5 |
| Pharmacie El Nasr | 20 A6 |
| Photo-adc | 21 A5 |
| Pl@anet Cyber Cafe | 22 F4 |
| Plateau Poste | 23 C4 |
| Satguru Travels & Tours | 24 A5 |
| Tafadeck | 25 A6 |

## SIGHTS & ACTIVITIES
| | |
|---|---|
| Bat Colony | 26 C4 |
| Grand Marché | 27 B5 |
| Grande Mosquée | 28 E4 |
| Musée National du Niger | 29 C4 |

| | |
|---|---|
| Petit Marché | 30 A5 |
| Stade de la Lutte Traditionelle | 31 F4 |
| Zoo | (see 29) |

## SLEEPING
| | |
|---|---|
| AFVP Rest House | 32 B3 |
| Camping Touristique | 33 A2 |
| Chez Tatayi | 34 F4 |
| Grand Hôtel | 35 A6 |
| Homeland Hotel | 36 C4 |
| Hôtel du Sahel | 37 D5 |
| Hôtel Gaweye | 38 C4 |
| Hôtel Maourey | 39 A5 |
| Hôtel Ténéré | 40 D4 |
| Hôtel Terminus | 41 D5 |
| Mission Catholique | 42 C4 |
| Village Chinoise | 43 C3 |

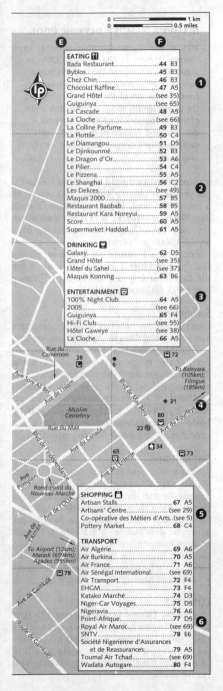

**EATING** 🍴
| | | |
|---|---|---|
| Bada Restaurant | 44 | B3 |
| Byblos | 45 | B3 |
| Chez Chin | 46 | B3 |
| Chocolat Raffine | 47 | A5 |
| Grand Hôtel | (see 35) | |
| Guiguinya | (see 65) | |
| La Cascade | 48 | A5 |
| La Cloche | (see 66) | |
| La Colline Parfume | 49 | B3 |
| La Flottile | 50 | C4 |
| Le Diamangou | 51 | D5 |
| Le Djinkounmé | 52 | B3 |
| Le Dragon d'Or | 53 | A6 |
| Le Pilier | 54 | C4 |
| Le Pizzeria | 55 | A5 |
| Le Shanghai | 56 | C2 |
| Les Delices | (see 49) | |
| Maquis 2000 | 57 | B5 |
| Restaurant Baobab | 58 | B5 |
| Restaurant Kara Noreyui | 59 | A5 |
| Score | 60 | A5 |
| Supermarket Haddad | 61 | A5 |

**DRINKING** 🍷
| | | |
|---|---|---|
| Galaxy | 62 | D5 |
| Grand Hôtel | (see 35) | |
| l Hôtel du Sahel | (see 37) | |
| Maquis Konning | 63 | B6 |

**ENTERTAINMENT** 🎭
| | | |
|---|---|---|
| 100% Night Club | 64 | A5 |
| 2005 | (see 66) | |
| Guiguinya | 65 | F4 |
| Hi-Fi Club | (see 55) | |
| Hôtel Gaweye | (see 38) | |
| La Cloche | 66 | A5 |

**SHOPPING** 🛍
| | | |
|---|---|---|
| Artisan Stalls | 67 | A5 |
| Artisans' Centre | (see 29) | |
| Co-opérative des Métiers d'Arts | (see 5) | |
| Pottery Market | 68 | C4 |

**TRANSPORT**
| | | |
|---|---|---|
| Air Algérie | 69 | A6 |
| Air Burkina | 70 | A5 |
| Air France | 71 | A6 |
| Air Sénégal International | (see 69) | |
| Air Transport | 72 | F4 |
| EHGM | 73 | F4 |
| Katako Marché | 74 | D3 |
| Niger-Car Voyages | 75 | D5 |
| Nigeravia | 76 | A6 |
| Point-Afrique | 77 | D5 |
| Royal Air Maroc | (see 69) | |
| SNTV | 78 | E6 |
| Société Nigerienne d'Assurances et de Reassurances | 79 | A5 |
| Toumaï Air Tchad | (see 69) | |
| Wadata Autogare | 80 | F4 |

**Point-Afrique** ( ☎ 73 40 26; www.point-afrique.com; Rue du Sahel) This charter airline now also offers reasonably priced packaged trips from Agadez into the Ténéré and Aïr Mountains.

**Satguru Travels and Tours Service** ( ☎ 73 69 31; stts-nim@intenet.ne; Rue de la Copro) Looking for air tickets? Look no further.

## Visa Extensions
**Direction de la Surveillance du Territoire** ( ☎ 73 37 43, ext 249; Rue de Président Heinrich Lubké). Niger visa extensions available, for further details see p615.

## DANGERS & ANNOYANCES
Thanks to Niger's bleak economy, crime levels have increased. That said, the difference between crime in Niamey and Nairobbery (Nairobi) is still vast. In the day, market pickpockets are your only worry. At night, as you would in most big cities, avoid carrying valuables openly and don't walk down dark and deserted streets. One area to avoid after dark is Kennedy Bridge and its surrounds, as there have been reported muggings. Seeing the ancient monster croc at Niamey's museum should be enough to keep you out of the Niger River! If that doesn't dissuade you, know that hippos kill more humans than any other wild animal in Africa.

## SIGHTS & ACTIVITIES
### Markets
#### GRANDE MARCHÉ
Wade through the chaos that is the exterior of the **Grand Marché** (Blvd de la Liberté; ⏰ 8am-6pm) and dive into the labyrinth of narrow lanes shaded by a kaleidoscope of tattered sheets. Although it's hard to ignore the heady aroma of spices, piles of colourful clothes, boisterous vendors and steady torrent of local shoppers, if you manage to find a good hiding spot the market is a wonderful place to observe Nigeriens interacting – peace amid the pandemonium. And when you jump back into the stream of shoppers, remember the trade-off for the lack of elbow room is the bustling African ambience!

#### PETIT MARCHÉ
The **Petit Marché** (Ave de la Mairie; ⏰ 8am-6pm) is right in the centre of town and also merits a visit. Shoppers can go mad, squeezing fruit and veg to their hearts content in this market. Watch where your wallet is when you're ogling the wares, as pickpockets are rife.

**NIGER**

## Musée National du Niger

This sprawling **museum** ( ☎ 73 43 21; Rue du Musée; admission CFA1000, camera/video fee CFA1000/5000; ☯ 9am-noon & 3.30-5.30pm Tue-Sun) is one of West Africa's standouts. Numerous themed pavilions, each tipping their hat to Hausa architecture, give visitors a peek into Niger's history. The Pablo Toucet pavilion displays the dress of Niger's different ethnic groups – a quick way to train the eye for differentiating these groups as you travel in Niger. While common sense and science dictate that there are no 2m-tall, 15m-long crocodiles wandering the earth today, one jaw-dropping glimpse of the Boubou Hana pavilion's 100 million-year-old *Sarcosuchus imperator*, or 'Super Croc', and you'll be second guessing everything – chilling indeed! Oddly, similarly aged dinosaur skeletons (with comparably sized teeth) in the Palaeontology/Prehistory pavilion don't elicit any similar irrational fears, only thoughts of these past creatures' majesty. Nearby, anchored in concrete, is the infamous Arbre de Ténéré (see p610).

At the museum's **artisans' centre** ( ☯ 8am-6.30pm Tue-Sun), you can watch the creative process and purchase silver, leather and other items direct from artists.

The least appealing aspect of the museum is the depressing **zoo** ( ☯ 8am-6.30pm Tue-Sun), where lethargic and neurotic animals are kept in appallingly cramped conditions.

## Grande Mosquée

Rising above eastern Niamey is this impressive **mosque** (Ave de l'Islam), with its massive minaret and bulbous green dome. Everything from the elaborately carved exterior wooden doors to the interior's 16 ornate pillars and grand tiled dome were financed by CFA500 million of Libyan money. If you linger outside, someone will offer you a short tour (CFA2000 is fair). The view and breeze atop the minaret are well worth the dizzying 171 steps to get there.

## Pirogue Trips

There's no better way to experience the Niger River than from aboard a peaceful pirogue skimming its surface at sunset. Although numerous 'guides' in town offer just such a trip, your cheapest option is to visit the piroguers themselves, on the riverfront between Palais du Congrés and La Flottile restaurant. After negotiating, four-passenger

---

### NIAMEY'S 'ALMOST' OLYMPIC POOL

Why is the Piscine Olympique D'Etat in Niamey known as the 'almost' Olympic pool? Well, it turns out the builders humorously and infamously forgot to take into account the width of the tiles, thus making the pool's length about a centimetre short of the compulsory 50m! Today the pool sits dejected and drained of its liquid assets... sadly another Olympic dream falls short.

---

punted pirogues should cost about CFA2000 per person per hour – triple that if you want a motorised boat. If negotiating isn't your bag, **Niger-Car Voyages** ( ☎ 73 23 31; Ave de l'Afrique; ☯ 7.30am-noon & 3.30-6pm) runs hour-long trips for CFA5000 per person.

For more adventure, and some hippo action, you can hire a pirogue in Boubon for the two-hour trip downstream to Niamey (see p593 for more details).

## Swimming

Beat the midday heat with some underwater action at **Hôtel Gaweye** (Ave Mitterrand; admission CFA2500), Niamey's best pool, complete with deck chairs to go with river views. **Grand Hôtel** (Rond-point Grand Hôtel; admission CFA2000) is a close second, while the tiny pool at **Homeland Hotel** ( ☎ 72 32 82; off Ave du Général de Gaulle; admission CFA2000) and the streetside pool at **Hôtel Ténéré** (Blvd de la Liberté; admission CFA1500) are a very distant third and fourth respectively.

## Bat Colony

Unless you're new to town, you'll have seen the huge fruit bats (looking like flying dogs) soaring in the sky each evening. To get a closer look at these massive bats in the daylight, head towards Place de la République along Ave de la Mairie – you'll find thousands of them hanging, snoozing and squeaking in the trees lining the compound of Banque Centrale de l'Afrique de l'Ouest. At sunset it's a hive of activity. Guano anyone?

## COURSES

The **Centre Culturel Franco-Nigérien** ( ☎ 73 48 34; www.ccfn.ne; Rue du Musée) occasionally offers short-term language courses. If no courses are running, it's still the best place to find tutors for your burgeoning French and Hausa skills.

## TOURS

Although there are no organised tours of the city itself, Niamey is the best place to arrange tours of Filingué (p595), Baleyara (p595), Ayorou (p594), the giraffes at Kouré (p593) and Parc Regional du W (p596). **Niger-Car Voyages** ( ☎ 73 23 31; Ave de l'Afrique) offer these tours, as do countless local 'guides' (they'll find you). Prices are steep and range from CFA40,000 to CFA90,000 per day (one to six people).

## FESTIVALS & EVENTS

Of Niger's many festivals, the only one centred in Niamey is Hangandi. See the boxed text on below for more weighty details.

## SLEEPING

Vacancies come at a premium in Niamey, especially at budget options, so make reservations early.

### Budget

**Chez Tatayi** ( ☎ 74 12 81; www.tatayi.com; Ave de l'Entente; dm CFA5000, s/d with shared bathroom from CFA12,000/15,000; P ☒ ) This peaceful haven near the Wadata Autogare has everything in spades. Behind the shady garden veranda are spotless rooms, a small stash of books (albeit in French), board games and free drinking water. Guests can even use the fridge. Shared bathrooms (the one in the dorm is amusingly quirky) and pesky mosquitos are the only downsides, though each and every bed has its own mozzie net. For air-con add CFA4000.

**Village Chinoise** ( ☎ 72 33 98; Blvd du Zarmaganda; tw with shared bathroom CFA5000-7000; P ☒ ) These bare-bones rooms are clean enough and the more expensive options have air-con. Bathrooms (get ready for some porcelain jockey action – no toilet seats) are shared between two rooms. It's nestled north of Stade Général Seyni Kountche.

**Camping Touristique** ( ☎ 75 44 89; Blvd des Sy et Mamar; camping per person CFA2500, plus per vehicle CFA1000; P ) This dusty site in western Niamey is the only option for campers. While it's a long walk (or CFA200 in a shared taxi) to town, it may be a very short walk to take a dip – during our visit a new complex being built next door was rumoured to have a cool pool.

The following two quality options are available only to volunteers and NGO employees:

**AFVP Rest House** ( ☎ 75 30 69; off Ave des Zarmakoye; dm CFA4000; P )

**Mission Catholique** ( ☎ 73 32 03; Ave du Gountou Yena; d with fan/air-con CFA7000/10,000; P ☒ )

### Midrange

**Hôtel Terminus** ( ☎ 73 26 92; hotermi@intnet.ne; Rue du Sahel; r/ste CFA32,000/45,000; P ☒ ☒ ) Just south of town centre, clean comfy bungalows here host large sunny rooms, with TVs and gargantuan bathrooms. There's a pleasant restaurant and separate bar whose TV is trained to follow French footy. It's popular with tour groups.

**Hôtel les Rôniers** ( ☎ 72 31 38; Rue Tondibia; s/tw CFA22,500/25,500; P ☒ ) Bright rooms, with cool tiled floors and oddly contemporary bathrooms, are found beneath the thatched conical roofs of Rôniers' great traditional cottages. The garden is lovely, the restaurant's great and the swimming pool is rather hip. The only setback is its location, 7km west of town (CFA1000 by taxi).

**Hôtel du Sahel** ( ☎ 73 24 31; fax 73 20 98; Rue du Sahel; s/d CFA25,550/28,500; P ☒ ) Le Sahel has comfortable and clean rooms, though at this price we'd hope all toilets had seats. The odd numbered rooms have great river views and don't cost a penny more. Renovations were underway when we visited (perhaps

---

**SUPERSIZE ME!**

During rare years of bountiful harvests, Niamey's Djerma population celebrate with the renowned Hangandi festival. Although the festivities are good fun, it's really the reputation of the festival's beauty contest that keeps on growing and growing, much like its competitors. For this is no ordinary beauty contest. You see, in the eye of the Djerma beholder, the larger a woman is the more magnificent she becomes. So in the months leading up to Hangandi, beautiful Djerma women who've been chosen to compete (some plucked right off buses!) train by ingesting as much millet, milk and water as they possibly can. The festival culminates with the heaviest, and thus most gorgeous, woman being crowned at the Palais du Congrés. Her reward? Much public admiration and…more food!

new toilet seats!), and some new bungalows were being built. The terrace overlooking the river is great at sunset. Unfortunately it's a 15-minute walk from town through an area noted for robberies.

**Hôtel Maourey** ( ☎ 73 28 50; Rond-point Maourey; s/tw/ste CFA25,000/30,000/35,000; 🗶 ) Although perfectly set in the heart of town, rooms are on the dark side and some are musty thanks to the old carpeting – check out a few.

**Hôtel Ténéré** ( ☎ 73 20 20; hotenere@intnet.ne; Blvd de la Liberté; s/d CFA30,250/37,550; 🗶 🗩 ) A large section of this place was being gutted by renovations during our visit, so hopefully the shabby rooms with ripe carpets and dog-eared bathrooms will now be a thing of the past. Rooms new and old contain satellite TVs and fridges.

## Top End

**Grand Hôtel** ( ☎ 73 26 41; www.grandhotelniger.com; Rond-point du Grand Hôtel; s/d/ste from CFA49,500/ 59,500/60,000; 🅿 🗶 🗩 ) While Hôtel Gaweye's socks fall down and its prices rise, Grand Hôtel continues to provide attentive service, value for money and top-notch rooms that boast satellite TVs and lovely river views. The swimming pool is great and the terrace is perfect for a meal, a beer or just taking in the sunset.

**Homeland Hotel** ( ☎ 72 32 82; homeland@intnet .ne; off Ave du Général de Gaulle; r/ste CFA45,500/75,500; 🗶 🗩 ) Opened in 2004, Homeland has moderately-sized, spotless rooms with gleaming tile floors, colourful throw rugs, satellite TVs and modern bathrooms. All that it's missing is a riverside location.

**Hôtel Gaweye** ( ☎ 72 27 10; gaweye@intnet.ne; Ave Mitterrand; r with city/river view CFA85,000/90,000, ste from CFA119,000; 🅿 🗶 🗩 ) Built next to the Palais du Congrés during the uranium boom, this towering riverside complex was long the jewel of Niamey's hotels. While it's still comfortable, the rising prices, slipping standards and indifferent service have made it a bit of a sad joke these days. It accepts Amex and Diners Club, but adds a surcharge of 5%.

## EATING

Whether wielding chop sticks in a fresh sashimi and sushi feeding frenzy, using your hands to devour a delicious pizza or using your pearly whites to pluck smoking meat off streetside brochettes, you and your stomach will enjoy your time in Niamey.

## African & Middle Eastern

**Byblos** (Blvd de l'Indépendance; meals CFA2500-5000; 🕓 lunch & dinner) This great Lebanese restaurant, with thatched garden pavilions and open-air ambience, has some of the best tabbouleh and hummus in Niger. It's on the pricey side, but its large set meals for two people (CFA10,000) are decent value.

**La Flottile** (Corniche de Yantala; meals CFA2500-3800; 🕓 lunch & dinner Tue-Sat) The shady garden confines of this friendly restaurant, west of Palais du Congrés, are a perfect place to indulge in some of the Niger River's tastiest fish. The *capitaine* (Nile perch) is excellent. It's not safe to walk here after sunset, so organise a taxi.

**Maquis 2000** (cnr St 19 & St 26; meals CFA2500-5800; 🕓 lunch Sun, dinner daily) This Ivorian-style open-air restaurant has a varied menu including *brochette de capitaine, crevette grillé* (grilled prawns) and, if you're game, *agouti braisé* (grilled grasscutter rat).

**Restaurant Kara Noreyui** (Rue du Festival; meals CFA700-1500; 🕓 lunch & dinner) This tiny eatery serves up some decent Senegalese dishes and is popular with locals.

**Le Djinkounmé** (Ave du Fleuve Niger; meals CFA1000-4000; 🕓 lunch & dinner Tue-Sat) A welcoming place for a simple, yet memorable, African meal.

## Asian

**Le Dragon d'Or** (Rue de Grand Hôtel; meals CFA1700-5400; 🕓 lunch & dinner) Slurp delicious Vietnamese *pho* (a noodle soup with coriander, bean sprouts and beef), sharpen your teeth on frog legs, or work your chopstick magic on tasty stir-fried chicken with cashew nuts and fresh ginger. The Saturday night buffet (CFA8000) is also superb.

**Bada Restaurant** (Ave du Général de Gaulle; meals CFA3000-15,000; 🕓 lunch & dinner) Put your chop sticks in the kung fu position and go to battle with everything from tempura vegetables and roasted eel to fresh sashimi and sushi. When we arrived, three of Niamey's temporary Japanese contingent were leaving, oh so happy and full as eggs.

**Le Shanghai** (Blvd de Mali Bero; meals CFA1700-5400; 🕓 lunch & dinner) While Le Shanghai's Chinese and Vietnamese cuisine is of a similarly high standard to that of Le Dragon d'Or, it lacks the same garden ambience.

**Chez Chin** (Blvd de l'Indépendance; meals CFA2000-6500; 🕓 lunch & dinner) With options like tender chicken in sesame paste and steaming dumplings, this is a great choice for Chinese cuisine.

**La Colline Parfume** (Blvd de l'Indépendance; meals CFA1500-3250; ☺ lunch & dinner) This diminutive place serves up a mix of Asian fare, ranging from flavourful beef curries to spring rolls and ginger chicken.

## European

**Le Pilier** (Rue de la Tapoa; meals CFA3000-6500; ☺ lunch & dinner Wed-Mon; ⌘ ) Hands down, this is *the* place for fine Italian fare. Enjoy a plethora of pastas, ranging from various raviolis to lasagne and even gnocchi dripping in gorgonzola. Dine in their air-con equipped lounge, within the vibrant courtyard terrace, or downstairs in the Taverne (evenings only), which serves great pizza.

**Hôtel les Rôniers** (Rue Tondibia; meals CFA2100-4100; ☺ dinner) This hotel's lovely pebble-floored garden dining area is as memorable as their fresh fish, fine French fare and Moroccan sausages.

**Le Pizzeria** (Rue du Commerce; pizzas from CFA3000; ☺ dinner; ⌘ ) The pizzas are excellent – a bit pricey, but they're much larger than what you'll get elsewhere. It's in the heart of town and is a good place to line the stomach before dancing the night away.

**Chocolat Raffine** (Rue NB 29; meals CFA1200-3000; ☺ breakfast, lunch & dinner) This cafés menu is laden with French treats like *croque monsieur*, *crêpes* and *chocolat mousse*. While most hit their mark, others remind you that you're in Niamey and not Paris. It's often closed for short periods during the day.

**La Cascade** (Rue NB 29; meals CFA1800-4500; ☺ lunch Tue-Sun, dinner daily; ⌘ ) With friendly service and great Italian, French and Lebanese fare, this restaurant is justifiably popular with expats, travellers and well-to-do locals. We'll let you decide which is cheesier, the delicious pizza or the artificial waterfall...

**Le Diamangou** (Corniche de Gamkalé; meals CFA2200-3000; ☺ lunch & dinner) Put aside your fear and grumbling insides to walk the plank out to this established boat restaurant. The views can't be beat, and the lemon chicken and other fare aren't bad either. Like La Flottile, this place isn't in the safest neck of the woods, so arrange a taxi after sunset.

**Grand Hôtel** (Rond-point du Grand Hôtel; buffet CFA7000; ☺ breakfast, lunch & dinner; ⌘ ) For a fabulous midday feast this hotel's renowned buffet can't be beat.

## Quick Eats

The best place for really cheap food on the go is around the Petit Marché, where street stalls and basic eating houses serve *riz sauce* (rice with meat or chicken) for around CFA500. Until 9am they also serve up Nescafé, bread and fried-egg sandwiches for less than CFA500. The food stalls on Rond-point Yantala are similar.

In the late evening along the disco strip of Rue du Commerce, there are some great *suya* stalls (*suya* is Hausa for brochette) opposite the nightclubs; brochettes go for CFA100 a pop.

**Restaurant Baobab** (Ave de Maourey; meals CFA600-2500; ☺ lunch & dinner) A short walk from the Grand Marché, this Senegalese place is perfect for a pre- or post-shopping feed. It's usually packed with locals, so share a table and practice your French.

**Les Delices** (Blvd de l'Indépendance; pastries from CFA350; ☺ 6am-midnight) This is Niamey's top patisserie. Sink your teeth into a fresh *pain au chocolat* (heavenly), croissant or baguette.

**La Cloche** (Ave Luebké; meals CFA1000-3000; ☺ lunch & dinner) When it's late and taste is secondary to hunger, the shwarmas do the trick nicely.

**Guiguinya** (Ave de l'Entente; meals CFA1000-2000; ☺ dinner) While more of a nightclub than a restaurant, there's always a free chair under the stars out the back for a decent dining session.

## Self-Catering

**Score** (Ave Luebké) Next to the Petit Marché, Score is large and loaded with French groceries like Bonne Maman jam. It also sells the cheapest chilled bottled water in town (1.5L for CFA350).

**Supermarket Haddad** ( ☎ 73 61 60; Rue de Commerce) Try to not leave nose marks on this well-stocked supermarket's cheese case, home to Edam, Brie and even Gouda with cumin seeds. Mmmmmm...cheese!

**Petit Marché** (Ave de la Mairie) The best bang for your buck in the produce department. It's also more of an experience than wandering the aisles with a shopping cart!

## DRINKING

**Grand Hôtel** (Rond-point du Grand Hôtel) Few places can beat this hotel's poolside terrace for a sunset beer – the river views are tremendous.

**Hôtel du Sahel** (Rue du Sahel) While lacking the posh feel of the Grand Hôtel, this hotel's

NIGER

riverside terrace is another great spot for a wobbly pop (beer).

**Hôtel Gaweye** (Ave Mitterrand; 🕱 ) Take a cold beverage by the riverside pool or while watching some African football on the large TV in their plush air-con–blessed bar.

**Galaxy** (Rue du Sahel) For a more African experience, head to this bar perched on the river behind the Piscine Olympique D'Etat (Olympic swimming pool).

**Maquis Konning** (cnr St 24 & St 19) This open-air bar has a great vibe and is a top spot to meet locals.

## ENTERTAINMENT
### Nightclubs

**Guiguinya** (Ave de l'Entente; no cover) Belting out African and European beats, this massive place is usually packed with locals (and the odd prostitute). Tear it up beneath the strobing red lights or stick your feet in the sand and chill out under the stars and trees in the courtyard.

**2005** (Ave Luebké; cover CFA1500 Wed, CFA2500 Fri & Sat) Reverberating with Western and African tunes, this lively club was the best place to cut loose on the dance floor when we were in town.

**La Cloche** (Ave Luebké; no cover) If you can get over the number of prostitutes and the glowing Christmas light–interior, this club (next to 2005) can be fun. There's a pool table and the music ranges from Arabic to Western.

**100% Night Club** (Ave de la Mairie; cover CFA1000; ☾ weekends only) This new club is trying to emulate the success of 2005 and its popularity is growing steadily.

**Hi-Fi Club** (Rue du Commerce; cover CFA3000 Fri & Sat) This place, which throws some reggae into the mix, can be hit or miss – have a peek inside before paying the cover.

### Cinemas

Your only options for cinematic distraction are the **Centre Culturel Franco-Nigérien** (Rue du Musée; admission CFA500; ☾ 8.30pm, days vary), which screens excellent French, American and African films, and the **American Cultural Center** (Rue de la Tapoa; admission free; ☾ 4.30pm Wed & Fri), which plays Hollywood flicks.

### Sport

You may be lucky enough to take in a traditional wrestling match at the **Stade de la Lutte Traditionelle** (Blvd de Mali Bero) or the **Centre Cul-**turel Oumara Ganda ( 🕿 74 09 03; Ave de l'Islam). We say lucky because they're quite the spectacle and only happen a handful of times a year. So keep your ear to the ground and you may just get – you guessed it – lucky!

## SHOPPING
### Art & Craftwork

If you're patient and peruse the nether regions of the **Grand Marché** (Blvd de la Liberté) you'll find a fine selection of goods, including Tuareg and Hausa leatherwork, silver jewellery, *batiks* and tie-dyed cloth. Look out for *les couvertures Djerma* (known locally as a *kountas*) – large, bright strips of cotton sewn together into a blanket, which are truly spectacular and unique to Niger. The largest and most extraordinary *kountas* shouldn't cost more than CFA10,000 to CFA15,000 – as always, friendly negotiations are in order!

Also recommended is the museum's **artisans' centre** (Rue du Musée; ☾ closed Mon) and **Coopérative des Métiers d'Arts** (Rue du Musée), which is just up the road. The **artisan stalls** (Rue de Président Heinrich Lubké) south of Petit Marché are bursting with wares, but their starting prices are ridiculous.

The hand-painted pottery found at the informal **pottery market** (Ave de la Mairie) is bulky but beautiful.

### Music

Original and bootlegged CDs of local and Western music can be bought at the **Grand Marché** (Blvd de la Liberté) or from stalls along Ave Luebké adjacent to the Petit Marché.

## GETTING THERE & AWAY
### Air

For details of international flights to/from Niamey, see p616.

### Bus

The government run bus company **SNTV** ( 🕿 73 30 20; sntv@intnet.ne; Ave de Gamkalé; ☾ 8.30-11.45am & 3.30-5.45pm) is still the most reliable transportation in Niger, but private companies are not far behind. Despite it being slightly more expensive than **EHGM** ( 🕿 74 37 16; Blvd de Mali Béro), and **Aïr Transport** (off Ave du Canada), which serve the same routes, SNTV is usually sold out first. Best to book at least a day in advance. All companies' buses leave between 4am and 6am. One way fares from Niamey on SNTV include the following.

| Destination | Fare (CFA) | Duration (hr) | Frequency |
|---|---|---|---|
| Agadez | 14,310 | 12 | Tue, Thu-Sun |
| Arlit | 17,500 | 15 | Tue, Thu-Sun |
| Birni N'Konni | 6600 | 6 | daily |
| Dogondoutchi | 4860 | 4 | daily |
| Dosso | 2440 | 2 | daily |
| Gaya | 5950 | 5 | daily |
| Maradi | 9565 | 9 | daily |
| Tahoua | 8750 | 8 | Tue, Thu-Sun |
| Zinder | 12,650 | 12 | daily |

## Bush Taxi

The **Wadata Autogare** (Ave du Kourfeye) is Niamey's main transport hub for bush taxis and several vehicles leave for each destination daily. The following is a list of one-way fares for Peugeots, there estimated durations and the level of patience required for each journey.

| Destination | Fare (CFA) | Duration (hr) | Patience of... |
|---|---|---|---|
| Agadez | 15,100 | 16½ | Mahatma Gandhi |
| Baleyara | 2000 | 1¼ | John McEnroe |
| Birni N'Konni | 5500 | 7½ | David Blaine |
| Dogondoutchi | 4400 | 4½ | Bill Bryson |
| Dosso | 2100 | 2½ | Paris Hilton |
| Filingué | 3250 | 2 | Russel Crowe |
| Gaya | 5000 | 5 | Michael Palin |
| Maradi | 9000 | 11 | Mother Teresa |
| Tahoua | 8000 | 10 | The Pope |
| Zinder | 12,400 | 14 | Shackleton's men |

Minibuses are generally more plentiful but are even slower (requiring one more level of patience than exactly the same trip in a Peugeot!). Minibuses service Agadez (CFA11,800), Birni N'Konni (CFA4400), Dogondoutchi (CFA3300), Gaya (CFA4000), Maradi (CFA8000), Tahoua (CFA7600) and Zinder (CFA11,800).

Minibuses to Ayorou (CFA3000, four hours) via Tillabéri (CFA1900, two hours) leave from **Katako Marché** (Blvd de l'Indépendance).

For details of getting to Burkina Faso, Benin, Mali and Nigeria, see p616.

## Car

**Niger-Car Voyages** ( ☎ 73 23 31; Ave de l'Afrique) hires Toyota Corollas for a whopping CFA60,000 per day. This includes insurance, 200 free kilometres, an obligatory chauffeur and tax. Petrol is extra (ouch!).

## GETTING AROUND
### To/From the Airport

A private taxi from the airport to the city centre (12km) costs between CFA5000 and CFA10,000, depending on your bargaining powers and the time of day; going the other way costs about CFA2500. During daylight hours you could also walk from the terminal to the nearby highway and catch a shared taxi to town (CFA200).

### Taxi

Taxis are abundant until about 10pm and most are shared. Share taxis simply head in the direction requested by the first passenger and troll for subsequent passengers en route. To catch one, simply hold out your arm and blurt your destination when the taxi slows. If it's going your way, you get the nod and you're only out CFA200. If not, you get the dreaded head shake and a face full of dust as it zooms on. Yes, the unofficial theme song of Niamey's shared taxis is *Are You Gonna Go My Way?* by Lenny Kravitz.

A taxi to yourself (*déplacement*) costs about CFA1000 for a trip across town.

# AROUND NIAMEY

## BOUBON

Although the best time to come to Boubon, 25km northwest of Niamey, is during its marvellous **Wednesday market** (keep an eye out for local pottery), its glorious riverside location means there's no wrong time to visit. Hire a pirogue for an enjoyable short excursion (around CFA5000) or pay about double that for an adventurous two-hour cruise down to Niamey's outskirts – the latter option almost guarantees you some up-close hippo action. There's no restaurant or hotel in Boubon, but accommodation and food are available at **Le Campement Touristique Boubon** ( ☎ 73 24 27; r CFA6000), on a nearby island, easily accessed by pirogue.

## KOURÉ

About 60km east of Niamey, West Africa's last remaining **giraffe herd** (see p594) quietly munch acacia trees and patrol the baking soils around the village of Kouré. The elegant

**NIGER**

**WEST AFRICA'S LAST GIRAFFES**

Don't let the gregarious giraffe herd wandering around Kouré fool you – most animal populations facing extinction are not so friendly or easy to find. Over the past few decades this herd has shrunk in size from more than 3000 giraffes down to an anaemic 50 in 1996. The threat to their existence has come from the destruction of their habitat through desertification and deforestation, as well as disease, poaching, road accidents and farmers killing them to protect their crops. It also didn't help that from April to August 1996, soldiers shot around a dozen of them while trying to carry out a presidential order to capture giraffes for presentation as gifts to friendly foreign leaders. In the late 1990s, the government of Niger and international conservation groups finally launched a campaign to save what were the last wild giraffes left in West Africa. Although the giraffe population today stands at around 150, vigilance and continued conservation efforts must continue to ensure these gorgeous and graceful giraffes live on another day.

long-necked beasts are rather tame and we spent 30 magical minutes walking in their midst. Even if you don't have a vehicle, it's an easy half-day trip from the capital in a taxi (good natured negotiations should cut the taxi price to around CFA30,000). The turn-off to the giraffes is well-marked with signs on the main highway, and there's a booth nearby where you can pick up your compulsory guide (around CFA2000) and entry ticket (CFA2000). Depending on the season, the giraffes can be right around the corner, or deep in the bush some 20km away.

# NORTH OF NIAMEY

Sunday rules the roost north of Niamey. It's the day Baleyara, Filingué, Tillabéri and Ayorou burst into colourful life with their weekly markets. Tillabéri and Ayorou have the added attraction of resting on the verdant path paved by the chocolate waters of the Niger River. Each of these villages can theoretically be visited as a day trip from Niamey using bush taxis, though you'd be better off to hire a car to visit Ayorou.

## TILLABÉRI
pop 19,200

Unless you have a keen interest in rice production or are here for the **Sunday market**, there's little more than **pirogue trips** on the Niger's waters to hold you in Tillabéri (also spelt Tillabéry). The village's only hotel has also long since closed. For the adventurous and patient, a passenger boat runs up to Ayorou on Friday (CFA8000; eight to 12 hours). Regular bush taxis run to Niamey's Kataka Marché (CFA1900, two hours).

## AYOROU

Ayorou, on the Niger's banks just 24km south of the Mali frontier, is renowned in for its multifaceted **Sunday market**. Head to the livestock portion, near the communications tower on town's east, and witness camels, cattle, mules, sheep and goats overrunning the place, along with their fascinating nomadic Bella, Fulani and Tuareg owners. It's especially frenetic between November and April. The market's western section near the river is more subdued, but just as intoxicating. Songhaï-Djerma and Mauritanian Moors gather here between the crooked acacia supports and beneath the woven mat roofs to sell everything from fruit and veg to traditional medicines and slabs of Saharan salt. Keep an eye out for colourful *Kountas* (Djerma blankets) and *sourgindis* (millet mats) as they are much cheaper here than in Niamey. The market warms up around noon, so if you arrive early watch cattle swimming across the Niger. Although guides and pirogueurs can be persistent around town, it's not a bad idea to hire a guide (CFA4000 per day) as they'll arrange photo permissions.

With the obvious beauty of the river, and hippos lurking nearby, a **pirogue trip** is a no-brainer. If your negotiations don't budge the boat owner's asking price of CFA5000 per person for a two-hour trip, you can always head 11km north to the village of Firgoun, where prices are much cheaper.

### Sleeping & Eating

The only official option is **L'Hôtel Amenokal** ( ☎ 71 14 24; abdoulkatia@yahoo.fr; s/tw from CFA8000/ 10,000; 🔀 ), which has old rooms with cement floors, stained walls and sporadic running water in the bathrooms. Rooms with air-con cost CFA4000 more per night, though prices are negotiable considering the rooms, the lack of electricity before 2pm and the absence of water in the pool. There's also a restaurant (set meals CFA5000) and anaemic bar on the premises.

## Getting There & Away

There are several daily bush taxis between Niamey's Katako Marché and Ayorou (CFA3000; four hours). Passenger boats run south to Tillabéri Sunday evening or early Monday morning (CFA8000, eight to 12 hours). Larger boats run north to Gao, Mali (CFA14,000, two days).

## FILINGUÉ
### pop 12,100

The 185km trip northeast to Filingué from Niamey is picturesque, with ochre mesas back-dropping endless traditional villages. For a petite village, Filingué offers up a surprisingly dynamic **Sunday market**. Wander town looking for traditional architecture, or head up the small hill for a bird's-eye view of the action and a glimpse of the parched valley, Dallol Bosso.

If you come on a Sunday, don't fail to stop in **Baleyara** (meaning 'where the Bella meet'), halfway between Niamey and Filingué. Its **Sunday market**, heavenly shaded by a canopy of trees, is equally pleasing – the animal bartering, which takes place on the town side of the market, is particularly worth seeing.

In Filingué, the rudimentary **Kourfey Bar Restaurant** ( ☎ 77 10 58; d with shared toilets CFA3000) is your only sleeping option. The cement rooms are a cell-like, but they are pretty clean and have fans and private showers. It's on your left as you enter town from Niamey – look for the sign across from the fort-like Red Cross building.

Regular Peugeot taxis run to Niamey's Wadata Autogare (CFA2000, two hours) along good tarmac roads. Oddly, the trip here from Niamey is CFA3250.

# THE SOUTH

Seeing that it embraces the borders of Burkina Faso, Benin, Nigeria and Chad, it would be a safe bet to assume southern Niger is a diverse region. Delve into Park Regional du W (one of West Africa's better

wildlife parks), have fun saying Dogond-outchi while deep in its raucous Friday market, absorb the influx of Islam in Maradi, or just get lost wandering the myriad of alleys in Zinder's Birni Quartier – it's all up to you. A reasonable tarmac road links the entire region from west to east and makes transportation relatively painless. For details on getting into Burkina Faso, Benin, Nigeria and Chad, see p616.

## DOSSO
### pop 50,000

Named after 'Do-So' a Djerma spirit, Dosso is the first major settlement along the main southern road, 136km southeast of Niamey. Dosso was once an important Islamic centre and home to Djermakoye, Djerma's most important religious leader. Being at the crossroads of Niamey, Zinder, Benin and Nigeria, Dosso is an important trading centre and its **Grand Marché** is worth peeking at.

The **Musée Regional de Dosso** ( ☎ 65 03 21; Route de Niamey; admission CFA500;  9am-5.30pm Tue-Sun) is now looking rather dishevelled, with most cabinets laying empty – the only collecting going on these days is of the dust variety. More interesting is the attached **Centre Artisanal** (admission free), which offers guests the chance to see artists in action.

## Sleeping & Eating

**Auberge Au Zenith** ( ☎ 50 38 80; Route de Niamey; d with shared toilet CFA6300-12,600;  ) The cement floored rooms are dark, but they're the tidiest in town and also have their own shower. Unfortunately the shared squat toilets are on the stinky side. There's also an attached **restaurant** (meals CFA400-1000;  breakfast, lunch & dinner) and bar, which can make it a little loud on weekends. It's about a 15-minute walk north from the *gare routière*.

**Hôtel Djerma** ( ☎ 65 02 06; Route de Gaya; d CFA12,500-16,500;  ) This aged, and occasionally unfriendly, hotel hides behind an old petrol station just south of the *gare routière*. While air-con is a pleasant option in all rooms, the glowing green lightbulbs and crude bathrooms aren't so endearing.

**Restaurant des Arts** (Route de Niamey; meals CFA500-1000;  breakfast, lunch & dinner) Art it isn't, but the museum's restaurant has some of the town's best food.

**Mamaki Club** (meals CFA500-1500;  lunch & dinner) This new garden restaurant hidden north of the Grand Marché, with decent meals, a bar, dance floor and swimming pool (CFA500) is a glorious revelation indeed.

Cheap street food can be found along the main road, particularly at the *gare routière*. Also, at night, the road running out from opposite Hôtel Djerma is alive with gas lanterns, diesel fumes and good street food.

### Getting There & Away
There are always plenty of bush taxis to Niamey (CFA2100, 2½ hours), Gaya (CFA2000, three hours) and Dogondoutchi (CFA2000, 2½ hours).

## GAYA
**pop 33,300**
Gaya is the only border town for Benin, and one of four for Nigeria – there's no reason to linger here. You'll find a **BIA-Niger** (Route de Dosso) directly across from the autogare on the main drag, though it only changes euros and US dollars.

**Hotel Hamdallah** (off Route de Dosso; ☎ 68 04 68; s/d CFA12,500/13,500; ✖) This is the best place to stay, but it's hard to find in the shadows off the main road.

**Hotel Dendi** (Gaya Hwy; ☎ 68 03 40; d CFA6500-10,000; ✖) The Dendi is easier to locate, as it sits on the main drag about a 15-minute walk south from the autogare, and it gives you the option of fan or air-con. It's friendly, but shabbier than Hamdallah.

You can dine at your hotel or try **Station Bar** (Route de Dosso; meals CFA1000-2000; ✖ lunch & dinner), which sits opposite Hotel Dendi. During the occasional evening, bugs have another reason to dance on the lights here, namely a local musician strumming in the courtyard.

Several minibuses/Peugeot taxis make daily runs to Niamey (CFA4100/4500, 5½/ five hours) via Dosso (CFA2000/2200, 2½/ three hours). For information on getting to Benin and Nigeria, see p616.

## PARC REGIONAL DU W
What this excellent **national park** (adult/child CFA3500/2000; ✖ Dec-late May) lacks in animal numbers, it makes up for in spades with the diversity of its wildlife. Antelopes, buffalos, elephants, hippos, lions, leopards, cheetahs, baboons, Nile crocodiles, hyenas, jackals, warthogs and over 300 species of migratory bird call this unique

environment home. The park rests on the west bank of the Niger River and is an area of dry savanna woodland, a transition zone between the Sahel and moister savannas to the south. The 'W' (pronounced du-blay-vay) in the name comes from the double bend in the Niger River at the park's northern border. The park is a massive 9120 sq km and straddles Niger, Benin and Burkina Faso. Niger's portion is 2200 sq km.

The best wildlife-viewing is March to May, when the migratory birds arrive and when the environment becomes incredibly barren, forcing animals to congregate around water holes. A favoured haunt of the elephants is the river near the Relais de la Tapoa (the lodge).

The entrance to the park is at La Tapoa, 145km south of Niamey, where a map and park guidebook (CFA5000) are available. Your obligatory guide should set you back CFA5000 per day.

### Sleeping & Eating
**Relais de la Tapoa** (bookings ☎ 73 40 26; pa@intnet .ne; s/d CFA17,500/27,000, with air-con CFA20,000/31,500; ✖ Dec-late May; P ✖ ⊕) This comfortable 35-room lodge is located next to the river in the village of Tapoa. The lodge is the only official park accommodation. Rates include half-board (bed, breakfast and dinner or lunch). There's also a bar and swimming pool.

Campers have to keep their fingers crossed that the unreliable **camp site** (camping CFA2500) near the lodge is open, as camping inside the park or in one of the adjoining protected reserves is prohibited. Enquire at the lodge for more information.

### Getting There & Away
Simply put, there's no point reaching the park independently without a vehicle. From Niamey by car, take the conversation-stopping washboard road 50km south to Say, and then 55km further to Tamou at the border with Burkina Faso, then 40km further south to La Tapoa.

Niger-Car Voyages (p585) runs two-day tours to the park for CFA140,000 per person for two people, or CFA70,000 per person if there are six or more people. The price includes accommodation, transport, admission to the park and food.

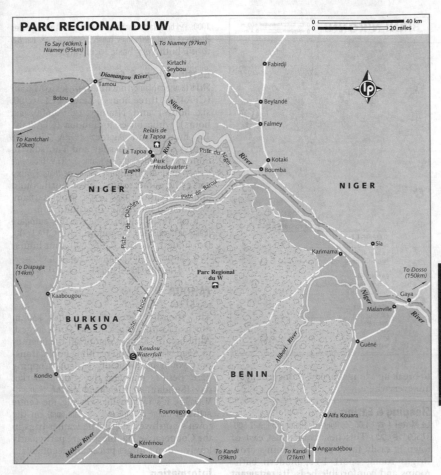

PARC REGIONAL DU W

## DOGONDOUTCHI
**pop 32,200**

'Doutchi' is a tiny village on the highway, about halfway between Dosso and Birni N'Konni. Everything but its **Friday market**, which swallows the *gare routière* whole, is outdone by the dramatic landscapes surrounding town. The ochre outcrops and rusty bluffs stand starkly out against the sky's blue backdrop and make for some interesting short hikes.

The well-signposted **Hôtel Magama** ( ☎ 65 03 48; s with shared bathroom CFA4300, d CFA9000-13,800; P 🞨 ) has pleasant rooms and all but the small single have air-con and private bathrooms. Rooms are found in a basic block of bungalows and a series of missile silo–looking structures. Larger two-bedroom 'family' rooms (CFA17,000 to CFA20,000) and meals are also available.

One of the shacks backing onto the *gare routière* has amazingly ice-cold yogurt for sale (CFA125) – look for the large fridges and enjoy!

Bush taxis depart every few hours for Dosso (CFA2000, 2½ hours) and Birni N'Konni (CFA1500, two hours).

## BIRNI N'KONNI
**pop 50,000**

About 420km east of Niamey, Birni N'Konni (or simply 'Konni') is one of four major border crossings with Nigeria. There's very little to see, but it makes a convenient place

**BIRNI N'KONNI**

SLEEPING 🏠
Hôtel Kado.......................................1 B2
Le Motel..........................................2 B1
Relais-Camping Touristique...........3 A1

EATING 🍴
Auberge des Routiers......................4 A1
Restaurant La Fleur.........................5 A1

TRANSPORT
Aïr Transport...................................6 A1
Autogare..........................................7 B2
EHGM...............................................8 A1
RTV....................................................9 A1
SNTV...............................................10 A1

to break up a long journey. Moneychangers are everywhere.

## Sleeping & Eating

**Le Motel** ( ☎ 64 06 50; Route de Niamey; d CFA22,500–37,500; P 🍴) This new comer just east of town is easily the cream of Konni's crop. Bright rooms sport TVs, modern bathrooms and comfortable beds. Its **restaurant** (meals CFA1000-4000; 🕙 breakfast, lunch & dinner) is also a step above the rest.

**Relais-Camping Touristique** ( ☎ 64 06 00; Route de Niamey; camping per person CFA1500, plus CFA1000 per vehicle, d CFA10,000-12,500; P 🍴) The spartan bungalows are large enough to make the sizeable double beds look lost inside. It's clean, friendly and its has a decent **restaurant** (meals CFA750-2750; 🕙 breakfast, lunch & dinner). There's even some shade in the dusty yard for tents.

**Hôtel Kado** ( ☎ 64 03 64; Route de Nigeria; d with fan/air-con CFA6800/9800; 🍴) This place is reasonable, though you'll see through the sheets, hover over the porcelain (no toilet seats) and have to kill the odd scurrying roach.

Besides eating at your hotel, you're limited to **Restaurant La Fleur** (Route de Niamey; meals CFA400-

1000; 🕙 breakfast, lunch & dinner) and **Auberge des Routiers** (Route de Niamey; meals CFA400-700; 🕙 lunch & dinner), both very basic local eateries.

## Getting There & Away

**SNTV** (Route de Niamey) have daily buses to Maradi (CFA4500, three hours), Zinder (CFA6300, six hours) and Niamey (CFA6600, six hours), while buses to Tahoua (CFA2000, 1½ hours) and Agadez (CFA7750, 5½ hours) only run Tuesday and Thursday to Sunday. **EHGM** (Route de Niamey), **RTV** (Route de Niamey) and **Aïr Transport** (Route de Niamey) also serve the same routes. Most northbound and eastbound buses arrive around 10am. Westbound buses pull in around 1pm.

Bush taxis regularly leave the **autogare** (Route de Nigeria) for Dogondoutchi (CFA1600, two hours), Maradi (CFA2600, four hours) and Tahoua (CFA1300, 1½ hours).

For transport to Nigeria, see p617.

## TAHOUA
pop 82,600

This friendly Hausa town, about 130km north of Konni, is the country's fifth-largest. Although it's a slight detour off the Niamey to Agadez road, if you're riding public transport you'll undoubtedly end up stopping here. Besides enjoying the vibrant market day (Sunday) at the **Grand Marché** (Route de Maternite), it's worthwhile visiting the **Centre Artisanal** (Route de l'Artisanal; 🕙 9am-6pm) on the town's northwest edge. The leather bags in the Cooperative Handicapie are particularly lovely – don't forget prices are negotiable!

## Information

**BIA-Niger** (Route de l'Artisanal) Change travellers cheques (1.6% commission) and cash.
**Pharmacie Populaire** ( ☎ 61 05 43; Route de l'Artisanal)

## Sleeping & Eating

**Hôtel de L'Amitié** ( ☎ 88 33 95; Route de Maternite; d CFA10,300-12,300; 🍴) If you bet the rooms here have toilet seats, air-con and a little bright sunshine, you'll hit the trifecta! Yes, this is Tahoua's best place to sleep. It's on the main drag, 400m east of the SNTV bus station – look for the wooden giraffes outside. There's also a friendly bar and reasonable **restaurant** (meals CFA1000-2000; 🕙 breakfast, lunch & dinner).

**Hôtel les Bungalows** ( ☎ 61 05 53; Jardin Publique; d with fan/air-con CFA7500/9500; 🍴) We're guessing the five empty cans of 'Rambo Insecticide' sitting at reception can't be a good omen. However, if you have a mozzie net, flip flops for insect killing action and don't mind riding porcelain (no toilet seats), this place will do for a night's kip – bargaining wouldn't hurt.

**Restaurant Milana** (Route d'Arène; meals CFA800-3500; ☺ breakfast, lunch & dinner) Just up the hill from the Centre Artisanal, this Italian eatery is *the* place to eat in Tahoua. Whether you're craving ravioli, lasagne, gnocchi, tagliatelle or aubergine on your pizza, you'll be seriously satisfied.

There are plenty of **food stalls** (sandwiches CFA250) opposite the entrance to the SNTV bus station.

## Getting There & Around

**SNTV** ( ☎ 61 00 06; Route de Maternite) buses stop here en route to Agadez (CFA6845, 4½ hours) daily except Monday and Wednesday, around noon. Southbound buses to Niamey (CFA8880, 7½ hours) arrive at a similar time on Wednesday and Friday through to Monday. EHGM, RTV and Aïr Transport have similar services on a daily basis.

Minibuses frequently leave for Konni (CFA1300, 1½ hours) from the autogare, which sits just east of Place Tassaoungoum on Route de Maternite.

Although banditry has decreased on the road to Agadez, it's still best to drive this section during daylight hours.

*Motos* patrol Tahoua's streets are charge no more than CFA150 for a cross-town trip.

## MARADI

**pop 179,000**

Maradi, the country's third-largest city, remains the administrative capital and commercial centre for agriculture. Its proximity to northern Nigeria has fostered staunchly conservative Islamic views and many Muslims here are calling for the introduction of Islamic Sharia law. It's not the most engaging place for visitors, but there's enough here to warrant stopping for a day.

## Orientation

Maradi's streets and most doorways have now been numbered in a system that baffles locals and visitors alike. For your help, we've left some of the more commonly understood old names on the map – happy hunting!

## Information

For changing naira (for Nigeria), try the *gare routière* 200m north of Sonibank.

**BIA-Niger** (1 SGI Rue 2) Change euros, US dollars and occasionally travellers cheques.

**Microsoft Windows** (BRJ Rue 1; per hr CFA6000) Internet prices drop to CFA4500 per hour on Saturday.

**Pharmacie Populaire** (39 SGI Rue 2)

**Post office** (off BRJ Rue 1)

**Regional Hospital** ( ☎ 41 02 20; off Rue de l'Hôpital)

**Sareli Informatique** (97 BRJ Rue 1; per hr CFA7500) A slightly faster option than MS Windows.

## Sights

As you might imagine, sinking into Maradi's **Grande Marché** (BRJ Rue 1) on market days (Monday and Friday) is a pleasurable assault on the senses. Vending of an entirely different variety goes on at the **Centre Artisanal de Maradi** ( ☎ 41 01 02; BRJ Rue 1; ☺ 8am-10pm), 2km north of town. It's worth a stop – wander the workshops, witness the workmanship and wonder where to start the negotiations.

We could tell you that walking east to Place Dan Kasswa will reward you with the sight of a lifetime, the magnificent **Maison des Chefs** (Place Dan Kasswa), but we won't because we'd be lying! Although it's rather unimpressive, it does possess traditional geometric designs and is a fine example of Hausa architecture. Nearby is the **Grande Mosquée** (Place Dan Kasswa), where you'll see children on the sidewalk studying the Qur'an and writing sections of it onto small wooden tablets.

## Sleeping

**Maradi Guest House** ( ☎ 41 07 31; s/d/tw from CFA31,500/33,600/42,000; P ⚡ ⚡ ) This new place is pricey, but worth every penny. The rooms are brilliant and massive, some even boasting king-size rod-iron canopy beds and verdant balconies. It's well-signposted and is 2km southeast from town centre. Prices stated include a 5% tax. Reservations are essential.

**Hôtel Larewa** ( ☎ 53 01 44; d with fan/air-con from CFA5500/10,600; P ⚡ ) Larewa is Maradi's best budget value and is found east of the EHGM station, north of town. Rooms are now in two complexes on opposite sides of the lane. The western side's rooms, with showers and shared toilets (don't cringe – they're clean and most have seats), are brighter and slightly less expensive than the eastern side's rooms, which have private bathrooms.

NIGER

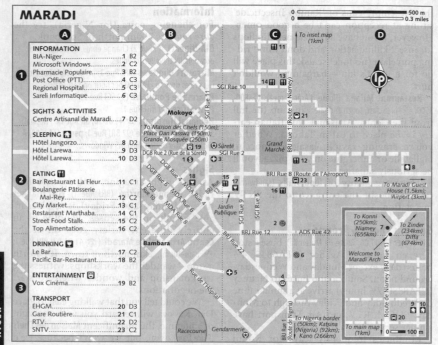

**MARADI**

| INFORMATION | |
| --- | --- |
| BIA-Niger.................................1 | B2 |
| Microsoft Windows...................2 | C2 |
| Pharmacie Populaire................3 | B2 |
| Post Office (PTT)......................4 | C3 |
| Regional Hospital......................5 | C3 |
| Sareli Informatique..................6 | C3 |

| SIGHTS & ACTIVITIES | |
| --- | --- |
| Centre Artisanal de Maradi......7 | D2 |

| SLEEPING | |
| --- | --- |
| Hôtel Jangorzo........................8 | D2 |
| Hôtel Larewa...........................9 | D3 |
| Hôtel Larewa.........................10 | D3 |

| EATING | |
| --- | --- |
| Bar Restaurant La Fleur.........11 | C1 |
| Boulangerie Pâtisserie | |
| Mai-Rey............................12 | C2 |
| City Market...........................13 | C1 |
| Restaurant Marthaba..............14 | C1 |
| Street Food Stalls..................15 | C2 |
| Top Alimentation...................16 | C2 |

| DRINKING | |
| --- | --- |
| Le Bar..................................17 | C2 |
| Pacific Bar-Restaurant...........18 | C2 |

| ENTERTAINMENT | |
| --- | --- |
| Vox Cinéma...........................19 | B2 |

| TRANSPORT | |
| --- | --- |
| EHGM...................................20 | D3 |
| Gare Routière........................21 | C1 |
| RTV......................................22 | D2 |
| SNTV....................................23 | C2 |

Map labels: Mokoyo; To Maison des Chefs (150m); Place Dan Kasswa (150m); Grande Mosquée (250m); Sûreté; Grand Marché; SGI Rue 10; SGI Rue 11; SGI Rue 2; BRJ Rue 1 (Route de Niamey); BRJ Rue 8 (Route de l'Aéroport); To Maradi Guest House (1.5km); Airport (3km); DGB Rue 2 (Rue de la Sûreté); DGB Rue 4; DGB Rue 6; MDA Rue 4; MDA Rue 6; MDA Rue 8; Jardin Publique; SGI Rue 9; SGI Rue 5; Bambara; BRJ Rue 12; ADS Rue 42; BRJ Rue 22; Rue de l'Hôpital; Racecourse; Gendarmerie; BRJ Rue 1 (Route de Nigeria); To Nigeria border (50km); Katsina (Nigeria) (92km); Kano (266km); To main map (1km); To Konni (250km); Niamey (655km); To Zinder (234km); Diffa (674km); Welcome to Maradi Arch; Route de Namey (BRJ Rue 1); To inset map (1km)

**Hôtel Jangorzo** ( ☎ 41 01 40; BRJ Rue 8; s with shared toilet CFA6000, s/d CFA16,500/18,500; P ✗ ) With sheets entirely too short, ensuring your toes play with the holey mattresses (lovely!), and bathrooms breeding mosquitos, all you're clearly paying for is this sloppy hotel's great location. The sight of mossies sailing on a log in the small singles' shared toilet (ughh!) continues to haunt us.

## Eating

**Maradi Guest House** (meals CFA1700-5000; ☿ breakfast, lunch & dinner; ✗ ) If your tummy has a pang for pizza, lasagne, hamburgers, wine or even chocolate ice cream, this hotel's bright dinning room is a serious stomach silencer.

**Restaurant Marthaba** (43 SGI Rue 10; meals CFA500-1000; ☿ breakfast, lunch & dinner) This sleepy outdoor place isn't bad for local dishes like *riz sauce* (rice with meat or chicken). This is provided the staff can find the cook!

**Boulangerie Pâtisserie Mai-Rey** (BRJ Rue 1; pastries CFA250) The selection and service here is fairly meagre, but it's still good for a snack, especially during Ramadan when it's one of the few places open during the day.

At night you can also find delicious grilled chicken and other snacks at **street stalls** (BRJ Rue 13) around the Jardin Publique. For self-caterers, **Top Alimentation** (6 BRJ Rue 1) and **City Market** (57 BRJ Rue 1) are two of the better stocked supermarkets, and they're both open late.

## Drinking

Thanks to the zeal of Islamic heavies, nightlife and alcohol are rather limited.

**Pacific Bar-Restaurant** (57 DGB Rue 4) This defiantly hedonistic place, west of Jardin Publique, is still the most popular place in town – though that isn't saying much. Live bands occasional strike up after 10pm.

**Le Bar** (BRJ Rue 13) Within the confines of the Jardin Publique, this can be an atmospheric place to take a beer or two.

More subdued drinking venues are the Hôtel Jangorzo and Maradi Guest House.

## Entertainment

Test your French or lip-reading skills at the diminutive **Vox Cinéma** (DGB Rue 2; CFA150), which shows French-dubbed versions of

NIGER

European and Hollywood films each night at 8.30pm.

## Getting There & Around
**SNTV** (81 BRJ Rue 1) has daily buses to Zinder (CFA4500, three hours) and also Niamey (CFA9565, nine hours). **RTV** ( ☎ 41 06 15; BRJ Rue 8) and **EHGM** ( ☎ 41 13 40; Route de Niamey) have similar services. On Wednesday and Saturday EHGM serves Diffa (CFA9700, 11 hours). All eastbound buses depart around 4pm, while westbound services leave about 9am.

Minibuses and Peugeots regularly depart the *gare routière* for Zinder (costing CFA2500/3000 and taking 4½/3½ hours respectively) and Konni (CFA3100/2500, five/four hours).

For transport to Nigeria, see p617.

A *moto* trip from the town centre out to the Centre Artisanal or EHGM costs about CFA150. Most trips within town are CFA100.

## ZINDER
pop 205,500

With its celebrated traditional Hausa houses, labyrinthine alleys of the old quarters, vestiges of Birni's old fortifications, an infamous prison within the Palais du Sultan and the classic French fort, Zinder clearly wears its history on its sleeve. And what a history it is. Zinder grew from a small resting spot for camels on the old trans-Saharan route, to a refuge for the Hausa and Kanouri people fleeing bloody 17th-century conflicts with the Fulani and Tuareg, before becoming the capital of the mighty Damagaram state, which thrived on everything from agriculture to the slave trade. The late 1890s brought the French, much blood letting, and Zinder's quarter-century reign as Niger's capital. While its economy is now in decline, thanks to a new highway routing most Nigerian goods through Maradi, Zinder is still the most fascinating place in southern Niger and a vibrant place to spend a few days.

## Information
For Nigerian naira, look for moneychangers around the *gare routière*. Moneychangers in Kano give better rates for US dollars.
**BIA-Niger** (Ave des Banques) Change travellers cheques (1.6% commission), euros and US dollars.
**Centre Culturel Franco-Nigérien** ( ☎ 51 05 26; Rue du Marché) French-language library and art gallery.

**Cybercafé Kandarga** (Rue du Marché; per hr CFA1500) Zinder's only reliable Internet.
**Hôtel Damagaram** (Ave des Banques) Changes euros and US dollars outside bank hours.
**National Hospital** ( ☎ 51 00 50; Ave De Maradi)
**Pharmacie Populaire** (Ave des Banques)
**Post office** (Ave de la République)

## Sights
### BIRNI QUARTIER
There are few things in Zinder as enjoyable as losing your bearings (and a few hours), within the innumerable narrow alleys of Birni, the old fortified quarter, south of the fort. The maze of old *banco* (mud brick) houses, some with colourfully painted geometric designs in relief, represents some of the best traditional Hausa architecture in existence – you won't see such a well preserved selection in Nigeria. Amazingly, a delicate sliver of Birni's massive original fortified *muraille* (tall wall) still stands at the southern section of the quarter.

### PALAIS DU SULTAN
Originally constructed in the mid-19th century, the **Palais du Sultan** (Place de la Grande Mosquée, Birni Quartier) is now home to the 23rd sultan, Elhadj Mamadou Moustapha, along with his three wives and some of his 23 children - you'll see some of his guards out the front in their bright red and green garb. The original door still hangs in the entrance and is covered with countless

---

**SULTANGATE**

In mid-2002 'Sultangate' rocked Niger and when the smoke cleared the 22nd Sultan of Zinder, Elhadj Aboubacar Sanda, was in jail and a former policeman was chosen to become the next sultan. So what did number 22, who made his living importing petrol and cars do wrong? Nothing, according to him and most of the nation's traditional chiefs (who elected him in the early 1980s). But Niger's government thought different and charged him with plotting a coup, cocaine trafficking, receiving stolen cars, involvement with killings and abductions, using counterfeit money, and worst of all, bringing immorality into Zinder!

And what does one get for such heinous crimes? Two years in prison!

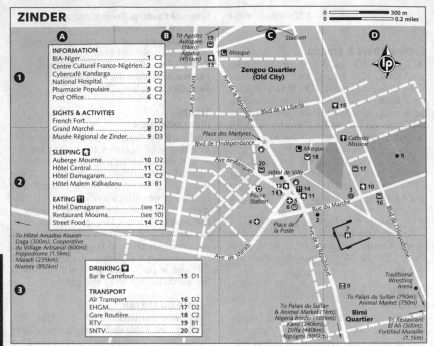

## ZINDER

**INFORMATION**
| | |
|---|---|
| BIA-Niger...............................**1** | C2 |
| Centre Culturel Franco-Nigérien...**2** | C2 |
| Cybercafé Kandarga.................**3** | D2 |
| National Hospital...................**4** | C2 |
| Pharmacie Populaire................**5** | C2 |
| Post Office.........................**6** | C2 |

**SIGHTS & ACTIVITIES**
| | |
|---|---|
| French Fort.........................**7** | D2 |
| Grand Marché.......................**8** | D2 |
| Musée Régional de Zinder..........**9** | D3 |

**SLEEPING**
| | |
|---|---|
| Auberge Mourna....................**10** | D2 |
| Hôtel Central......................**11** | C2 |
| Hôtel Damagaram...................**12** | C2 |
| Hôtel Malem Kalkadanu............**13** | B1 |

**EATING**
| | |
|---|---|
| Hôtel Damagaram................(see 12) | |
| Restaurant Mourna..............(see 10) | |
| Street Food.......................**14** | C2 |

**DRINKING**
| | |
|---|---|
| Bar le Carrefour...................**15** | D1 |

**TRANSPORT**
| | |
|---|---|
| Aïr Transport......................**16** | D2 |
| EHGM..............................**17** | D2 |
| Gare Routière.....................**18** | C2 |
| RTV...............................**19** | B1 |
| SNTV..............................**20** | C2 |

metal plates, each tacked on by a different chief over the years as a sign of support for the sitting sultan. Behind the door is a courtyard that once contained a small prison for slaves. One of the cells, known as the *chambre des scorpions* was scented with butter to lure the venomous creatures! If you linger outside the palace, you'll usually be offered a tour. A tip of CFA2000 should suffice.

### MUSÉE RÉGIONAL DE ZINDER

This **museum** (☎ 59 61 35; Ave de la République; admission CFA1000, camera CFA1000; ☑ 8am-noon & 3-6pm), has seen better days and seems to be more of a work in progress. However, the English-speaking (slight exaggeration) curator is wonderful and adds much to the experience, like telling you that the dusty, boring looking sword in the corner was actually used to lop off the head of a traitor to the sultan a century earlier!

### ZENGOU QUARTIER

Although the Zengou Quartier predates the Birni Quartier, most of its present-day

buildings are much younger, and cement structures outnumber classic *banco* homes. However, life within the quarter remains the same and a visit is still worthwhile.

### OTHER SIGHTS

The **Grand Marché** (Blvd de l'Hippodrome; ☑ dawn to dusk) is one of the liveliest in Niger – the big day is Thursday. Look for leather goods as Niger's best *artisans du cuir* are here. If you strike out, or just want to see goods being made, visit the **Cooperative du Village Artisanal** (Ave de Maradi; ☑ 8am-6.30pm), about 2km west of town. Thursday also brings the big **animal market** to Zinder's outskirts, near the Palais du Sultan. For something a bit less worthy, the horse races 3km west of town at the **Hippodrome** (Ave de Maradi; ☑ 4pm Sat & Sun) are a hotbed of healthy secular gambling. There's also a charming and stereotypical **French fort** that you'll see rising from a pile of massive rounded boulders just south of town centre. Sadly, it and its surroundings, looking much like a giant's abandoned game of marbles, is currently used by the Nigerien military and is off-limits.

## Sleeping

**Auberge Mourna** ( ☎ 99 03 06; off Rue du Marché; s/d/tw from CFA14,500/18,500/18,500; P X ) This mid-range place is leaps and bounds ahead of the competition. The smart, spotless and bright rooms all have TVs, air-con and modern bathrooms. The town's best restaurant is also on the terrace. There are only seven rooms, so reservations are crucial.

**Hôtel Damagaram** ( ☎ 51 00 69; Ave des Banques; s/d/tw CFA16,500/20,000/20,000; X ) A serious step up in cleanliness from Hôtel Central, but a long drop in quality and comfort from Auberge Mourna. The teeny-weeny mosquito nets hanging over the gargantuan beds would be funny if mossies weren't living in the loo.

**Hôtel Amadou Kouran Daga** ( ☎ 51 07 42; Ave de Maradi; s/tw from CFA13,500/18,500; P X ) Another shadow of Auberge Mourna, though its rooms are larger, brighter and less dog-eared than Damagaram. Unfortunately it's almost 2km west of town.

**Hôtel Malem Kalkadanu** ( ☎ 50 07 74; Ave de la République; s with shared bathroom CFA3100-6100; P ) West of the Zengou Quartier, this rambling budget place has crude but clean rooms, ranging from dark cells with no fans to larger options with fans, windows and private showers. Rooms surround a cute courtyard and the terrace gives you a glimpse over town. It's good value and now has a small restaurant.

**Hôtel Central** ( ☎ 51 20 47; Ave de la République; s/tw CFA6600/8500, s/d with air-con CFA9500/12,500; X ) Murdered cockroaches, victims of brutal flip-flop attacks, still hang from the walls of this budget place – police still have to dust for prints, so don't touch anything! Central yes. Pleasant no. The large rooms do boast clean bed sheets, but the bathrooms are grotty.

## Eating & Drinking

**Restaurant Mourna** (off Rue du Marché; meals CFA2000-3200; ☽ breakfast, lunch & dinner) This tiny, quiet Chinese-styled terrace serves up delicious meals, like *fillet de capitaine à la Basquaise* (Basque-style Nile perch), Cantonese rice and beef curry. Hold off salivating over the crêpes and chocolate mousse on the dessert menu until you've confirmed they have them.

**Restaurant El Ali** (meals CFA500-2000; ☽ breakfast, lunch & dinner) All your African favourites (especially rice and couscous with sauce) can be tasted underneath the pleasantly down-at-heel *paillotes* (thatched sun shelters). Fol-low Blvd de l'Hippodrome south and take the first left after the wrestling arena. There are no signs, but locals will point it out.

**Hôtel Damagaram** (Ave des Banques; meals CFA1000-3000; ☽ breakfast, lunch & dinner) The hotel's glowing garden courtyard is an atmospheric place for a meal or beverage in the evening. There are the usual suspects, like couscous and brochettes (CFA100), as well as Chinese dishes such as ginger chicken. A small Flag beer is a steep CFA650.

Some of the best **street food** (Ave de la République; brochettes CFA100, roast pigeons/chickens CFA900/1500; ☽ dinner) can be found in the square in front of Hôtel Central. There are several supermarkets around town for self-caterers, particularly between Place des Martyres and Hôtel Central.

For a local night out, hit the rough and ready **Bar le Carrefour** (beer from CFA400), known locally as L'Escalier, which sits north of the Catholic Mission.

## Getting There & Away

**SNTV** ( ☎ 51 04 68; Ave des Banques) buses run to Niamey (CFA12,650, 12 hours, daily), Agadez (CFA7700, 7½ hours, Monday and Thursday) and Nguigmi (CFA7900, 10 hours, Monday and Friday) via Diffa (CFA6200, seven hours). **EHGM** ( ☎ 51 00 97) also serves Niamey (CFA11,700, 6.30am daily), Agadez (CFA7200, 6.30am Tuesday and Saturday) and Diffa (CFA6000, Saturday). **Aïr Transport** ( ☎ 51 02 47; Blvd de l'Hippodrome) and **RTV** ( ☎ 51 04 16; off Ave de la République) only have daily services to Niamey (CFA12,500).

Minibuses/Peugeots depart the *gare routière* daily for Diffa (CFA6000/6500, nine/eight hours) and Maradi (CFA2500/3000, 4½/3½ hours).

Minibuses/Peugeots for Agadez (CFA7000/8000, nine/eight hours) depart daily from the Agadez autogare, which is 1km northeast of town on Ave de la République.

For transport to Nigeria, see p617.

## Getting Around

*Motos* are everywhere, providing a fast and cheap way to get across town (CFA150).

## DIFFA

**pop 30,600**

This diminutive and dusty town is only of interest to those travelling overland between Niger and Chad because it's the last place in Niger with decent facilities. Along the main drag you'll spot a Pharmacie Populaire, a **BIA-Niger** ( ☎ 54 03 06) that changes cash (euros only) and a petrol station serving *essense* and *gasoil* out of the barrel. For recent arrivals from Chad, there's a branch of Société Nigerienne d'Assurances et de Reassurances that sells vehicle insurance.

**Hôtel le Tal** ( ☎ 56 39 57; off Route de Nguigmi; d with fan/air-con CFA7500/13,500; ✹ ), behind the petrol station, is your only sleeping option. It's friendly and clean enough, but seriously overpriced.

If heading east, the market near the autogare is a good place to stock up on essentials – if you haven't already – as you'll find some pretty imaginative prices further down the road.

SNTV has buses departing in the late afternoon for Nguigmi (CFA1800, four hours, Monday and Friday) and in the early morning for Zinder (CFA6200, seven hours, Wednesday and Sunday). EHGM also services Zinder (CFA6000, Saturday).

Bush taxis run the potholed highway to Nguigmi (CFA2500, four hours).

## NGUIGMI
**pop 17,400**

Nguigmi is a small town at the end of the sealed road, some 45km from the Chad border. It's the last Niger settlement of any size and it's where you must get your passport stamped. The town has no hotels or eateries, but there's a lively market area to the south of town where you can buy brochettes.

There are a few bush taxis between Nguigmi and Diffa (CFA2500, four hours). For transport to/from Chad, see p617.

# THE NORTH

With the ever-so-sublime Aïr Mountains, the Sahara sea's most graceful and gargantuan dunes, remote oases and the ancient trans-Saharan trading town of Agadez, northern Niger is the highlight of any trip to this African nation.

## AGADEZ
**pop 95,100**

While some of the Sahara's great ancient trading towns, like Timbuktu, try to survive on international mystique alone, Agadez thrives by being the gateway to some of the most spectacular desert and mountain scenery in all of Africa.

That said, Agadez itself is still the most fascinating of Niger's cities and should not be ignored. When standing in the porcupine shadow of the famous Grand Mosquée, or weaving through the sandy streets and distinctive mud-brick architecture, it's not hard to imagine what it was like at its zenith some four centuries ago. Back then its population of 30,000 flourished off the caravans *(azalai)* plying between Gao (Mali) and Tripoli (Libya), some as large as 20,000 camels, laden with gold, salt and slaves.

The recent arrival of charter flights from Europe has had a big impact on Agadez. The remote, slightly depressed outpost has been turned into a buzzing hub of activity. Don't worry, it hasn't lost any of its charm. And there's plenty of space in the Sahara for a few hundred visitors a week!

## Information
### INTERNET ACCESS
**Agadez.com** (Route de l'Aéroport; per hr CFA2000; ☾ 8am-10.30pm; ✹ ) Agadez's only Internet option. Burn images to CD using USB connection.

### MEDICAL SERVICES
**Hospital** ( ☎ 44 00 84, 44 01 42; off Route de l'Aéroport; 24hr)
**Medical Clinic** ( ☎ 96 34 74; Route de l'Aéroport; ☾ 7.30am-12.30pm & 3.30-6.30pm)
**Pharmacie de l'Aïr** (Route de l'Aéroport)

### MONEY
**BIA-Niger** (Route de Bilma) Changes travellers cheques (1.6% commission), euros and US dollars. Availability of Visa cash advances is sporadic.
**VIP Bureau de Change** (Route de Bilma; ☾ 8am-11.30pm) Changes most currencies.

### TELEPHONE
There are numerous private offices along Route de l'Aeroport offering international telephone services over the nation's burgeoning mobile network. Calls to most nations cost CFA150 for each 10-second block. Conveniently, most offices charge nothing for incoming calls.

### TOURIST INFORMATION
**Centre d'Information Touristique** ( ☎ 98 78 81; Vieux Quartier; ☾ 8am-12.30pm & 3.30-6.30pm Fri-Tue)

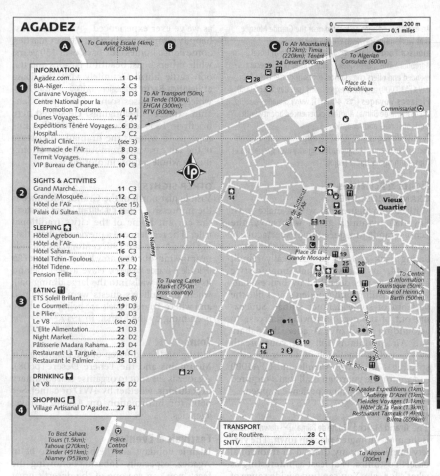

**AGADEZ**

0 —————— 200 m
0 —————— 0.1 miles

To Camping Escale (4km);
Arlit (238km)

To Aïr Mountains
(12km); Timia
(220km); Ténéré
Desert (500km)

To Algerian
Consulate (600km)

Place de la
République

Commissariat

**INFORMATION**
Agadez.com.............................1  D4
BIA-Niger................................2  C3
Caravane Voyages....................3  D3
Centre National pour la
  Promotion Tourisme..............4  D1
Dunes Voyages.......................5  A4
Expéditions Ténéré Voyages....6  D3
Hospital.................................7  C2
Medical Clinic......................(see 3)
Pharmacie de l'Aïr..................8  D3
Termit Voyages.......................9  C3
VIP Bureau de Change............10  C3

**SIGHTS & ACTIVITIES**
Grand Marché........................11  C3
Grande Mosquée....................12  C2
Hôtel de l'Aïr.....................(see 15)
Palais du Sultan.....................13  C2

**SLEEPING**
Hôtel Agreboun.....................14  C2
Hôtel de l'Aïr........................15  D3
Hôtel Sahara.........................16  C3
Hôtel Tchin-Toulous...........(see 3)
Hôtel Tidene.........................17  D2
Pension Tellit........................18  C3

**EATING**
ETS Soleil Brillant...............(see 8)
Le Gourmet...........................19  D3
Le Pilier................................20  D3
Le V8................................(see 26)
L'Elite Alimentation...............21  D3
Night Market.........................22  D3
Pâtisserie Madara Rahama......23  D4
Restaurant La Targuie............24  C1
Restaurant le Palmier............25  D3

**DRINKING**
Le V8....................................26  D2

**SHOPPING**
Village Artisanal D'Agadez....27  B4

To Aïr Transport (50m);
La Tende (100m);
EHGM (300m);
RTV (300m)

Route de Niamey

Rue de Sultanat
de l'Aïr

Vieux
Quartier

To Tuareg Camel
Market (750m
cross country)

Place de la
Grande Mosquée

To Centre
d'Information
Touristique (50m);
House of Heinrich
Barth (500m)

Route de l'Aéroport

Route de Bilma

To Agadez Expéditions (1km);
Auberge D'Azel (1km);
Pleiades Voyages (1.1km);
Hôtel de la Paix (1.3km);
Restaurant Tamgak (1.4km);
Bilma (609km)

To Best Sahara
Tours (1.5km);
Tahoua (270km);
Zinder (451km);
Niamey (953km)

Police
Control
Post

**TRANSPORT**
Gare Routière.......................28  C1
SNTV....................................29  C1

To Airport
(300m)

NIGER

---

The product of a failed attempt to unify Agadez's tourist operators. There's some helpful information, but you'll have to put up with some pressure sales for guides/desert trips.

**Centre National pour la Promotion Tourisme**
( ☎ 44 00 36; Route de l'Aéroport; ⌚ 8.30am-12.30pm & 3.30-6.30pm Mon-Fri) Basically a government version of Centre d'Information Touristique – a dash of help to go with a spoonful of self-promotion.

**TRAVEL AGENCIES**
There are more than 70 travel agencies in Agadez, all specialising in tours of the Aïr Mountains and Ténéré Desert. Agencies that we recommend, or which have been recommended to us, include the following:

**Agadez Expéditions** ( ☎ /fax 44 01 70; www.agadez -tourisme.com; Route de Bilma) Based at Auberge D'Azel,

this is arguably the most professional and most expensive agency in Agadez. Their prices get you new 4WDs, comfy tents, tables and Akly Joulia-Boileau, the experienced and enthusiastic leader.

**Best Sahara Tours** ( ☎ 97 86 66; www.best-sahara-tours .com; Route de Niamey) Boasting experience in Libya, Mali, Chad and Niger, this reasonably priced option is enthusiastically recommended by travellers who've used it.

**Caravane Voyages** ( ☎ 44 04 59; caravanevoyages@hotmail.com; Route de l'Aéroport) Based at Hôtel Tchin-Toulous, Caravane offers some decent prices for camel safaris to go with its 4WD options.

**Dunes Voyages** ( ☎ 44 05 83; www.dunes-voyages .com; Route de Niamey) A top-notch European-run outfit with high quality service and prices to match.

**Expéditions Ténéré Voyages** ( ☎ 98 32 60; www .expeditionstenere.com; Place de la Grande Mosquée)

An experienced agency, located near the Grande Mosqée, that works primarily with French tour groups.

**Moussa Touboulou** ( ☎ 28 86 93; inquire at Hôtel Agreboun) This independent guide comes highly recommended and offers cheap prices for both camel treks (per day CFA30,000) and 4WD expeditions (per day CFA80,000).

**Pleiades Voyages** ( ☎ 44 05 41; www.pleiades-agadez .com; Route de Bilma) Another experienced agency with loads of Ténéré and Aïr options.

**Termit Voyages** ( ☎ 42 02 47; http://niger.tribu.ch; off Place de la Grande Mosquée) This agency also specialises in trips south to the Zinder region.

## Sights & Activities

### GRANDE MOSQUÉE

With a slim figure that would make most Egyptian pyramids green with envy, the ochre Grande Mosquée climbs spectacularly into the blue skies over Agadez. Although dating back to 1515, it was totally rebuilt in 1844. Its classic Sahel/Sudanic-style architecture was described by Bruce Chatwin as 'bristling with wooden spires like the vertebra of some defunct fauna'. Squeezing out of the ever-narrowing staircase to astounding views over Agadez, the Sahara and Aïr Mountains will take your breath away – well, all that's left of it after the constricting 27m climb! A smile and CFA1000 *cadeau* for the guardian is all that's required to make this magical experience happen.

### MARKETS

The **Grand Marché** (Route de Bilma; ☼ dawn to dusk) is the most animated place in town. The variety of people, many dressed in traditional desert costumes, is at least as interesting as what's for sale. You can find a wide range of art and craftwork here, including rugs and Tuareg leatherwork.

The **Tuareg camel market** ( ☼ dawn to dusk) on Agadez's western outskirts is as colourful as the Grande Marché, but even more odoriferous. Slobbering camels are joined by sheep, donkeys, goats, massive cattle and dozens of fascinating nomadic Tuareg traders. Photographs here usually require the market chief's permission, oh, and about CFA2500. Sunrise and sunset are the best times to visit.

### VIEUX QUARTIER

This enchanting maze of small crooked alleys, tiny artisan shops, and fascinating mud-brick architecture of Tuareg and Hausa inspiration is as good a time machine as we've ever experienced – yes, hours just happily disappear within the Vieux Quartier. Some *banco* homes date back over 150 years, while others boast beautiful façades and the odd cattle horn! Definitely visit the **House of Heinrich Barth** (admission CFA1000; ☼ 8am-7pm), which now houses some of the great Saharan explorer's belongings. He stayed here briefly in 1850 and was one of the first Europeans to witness the dramatic departure of the salt caravans from Agadez, describing it as 'a whole nation in motion'.

### OTHER SIGHTS

Visible just north of the Grande Mosquée is the impressive **Palais du Sultan** (closed to visitors), the current home of the city's traditional ruler. The residence of a previous Sultan, dating back to the late 19th century, also stands near the mosque and now houses **Hôtel de l'Aïr** (Place de la Grande Mosquée). Have a peek behind its 1m-thick walls into the large dining hall, where the Sultan's guests were entertained and where Tuareg rebels are believed to have been hung by the French in 1917.

## Tours

Sitting on the doorstep of the inspiring Aïr Mountains and the Ténéré Desert (p608), Agadez is *the* spot to organise extraordinary expeditions, whether by 4WD or camel. See p605 for information on Agadez's travel agencies.

## Festivals & Events

Islamic holidays are the best time to be in Agadez, especially Tabaski. Following the feast, you can see one of the desert's great spectacles – the 'cavalcade', a furious camel race through the crowded narrow streets to the square in front of the Palais du Sultan. Similar races take place during Eid al-Fitr. See p818 for more Islamic holiday details.

## Sleeping

### BUDGET

**Hôtel Agreboun** ( ☎ 98 63 32; s/tw/tr with shared toilet CFA5000/7000/12,000; ℗ ) It's hard to beat this budget-friendly hotel, on the western edge of town. Rooms are rather rudimentary and bunker-like, but they're cheap, clean and surround two very pleasant courtyards for sitting out the day's heat.

**Hôtel Sahara** ( ☎ 98 61 15; r with fan/air-con CFA7000/15,000; ☷ ) The long black-lit corridor will stop most of you in your tracks. The brave will discover crumbling walls, no running water and dingy looking beds. Yes, this is a last resort.

**Camping Escale** ( ☎ 89 67 06; Route de Arlit; camping per person CFA2000, plus vehicle CFA1500) Perfect for overlanders, this sleepy campground 4km west of town has fresh well-water, simple bathrooms and leafy shade. Although the friendly family who run it are never far away, it's too deserted to leave any valuables out when you're in town. Campers without their own vehicles should head for La Tende.

**MIDRANGE**
The following hotels levy a tax of CFA300 to CFA500 per person per night. Prices below don't include this tax.

**Pension Tellit** ( ☎ 44 02 31; Place de la Grande Mosquée; tw CFA18,000-32,000, ste CFA36,000; ✖ ) Whether sitting on the rooftop terrace taking in the Grande Mosquée, or snoozing on your oh-so-comfortable bed, you'll love this place. Throw in charming traditional décor, hot-water showers and remote controlled aircon and you're laughing. The delicious suite (room No 4) boasts a mosque view. With only five rooms, reservations are essential.

**Hôtel Tidene** ( ☎ 44 04 06; off Route de l'Aéroport; s/tw CFA9500/15,000, tw with air-con CFA20,300; ✖ ) Tidene is another good choice, with tidy traditional rooms spread around several courtyards. Its only drawback are the small non-air-con equipped single rooms, which seem to trap the day's heat and bake at night.

**La Tende** ( ☎ 44 00 75; off Route de Niamey; s/tw with shared bathroom CFA10,000/12,500, s/tw CFA21,000/25,000; P ✖ ) This pretty place on the western fringe of town offers great value. Take a small, bright and clean room with a fan, or a larger one with air-con and private bathrooms. It's also possible to camp (CFA2000) or hire a simple Tuareg tent (CFA3000). If it lacks anything, it's the traditional charm of Tellit and Tidene.

**Hôtel de l'Aïr** ( ☎ 96 91 23; Place de la Grande Mosquée; tw CFA10,000-15,000; P ✖ ) You'd think that rooms in a hotel which was formerly a Sultan's palace would ooze historical ambience and cost a mint, but you'd be wrong on both accounts. Prices for these uninspired cement-floored rooms depend on whether you want a private bathroom, hot water and air-con.

**Hôtel Tchin-Toulous** ( ☎ 44 04 59; caravanevoyages@ hotmail.com; Route de l'Aéroport; s/tw with shared bathroom CFA10,000/15,000, s/tw CFA15,000/20,000; ✖ ) With pebble floors and Tuareg beds this place takes the quirky cake. Most of the cheaper rooms here are small and airless, but No 11 and 12 up on the terrace are exceptions.

**Hôtel de la Paix** ( ☎ /fax 44 02 34; Route de Bilma; s/tw/d CFA21,000/25,000/35,000; P ✖ ✿ ) Although this modern hotel is comfortable, clean and has many facilities, it doesn't even register a blip on the traditional charm radar.

**TOP END**
**Auberge D'Azel** ( ☎ 44 01 70; www.agadez-tourisme .com; Route de Bilma; tw/d CFA33,000/44,000; ✖ ) Thanks to striking domed brick ceilings and archways, massive rod-iron canopy beds, comfortable sitting areas, sparkling modern bathrooms and first-class service, Auberge D'Azel is Agadez's top hotel. The Tuareg/ French couple, Akly and Céline, are delightful hosts. It's about 1km east of town.

## Eating
**Le Pilier** (Route de l'Aéroport; meals CFA2000-4000; ✖ lunch & dinner) Savour *capitaine au grill* (grilled Nile perch), *côtelettes d'agneaux panées* (lamb chops fried in bread crumbs) or a range of fine Italian fare, all within the superb traditional architecture of this amazing eatery.

**Auberge D'Azel** (Route de Bilma; meals CFA3500-5500; ✖ lunch & dinner) The food here is fantastic – the *mouton targui* (Tuareg mutton) is particularly divine – though prices are a little steep. With a lovely terrace, leafy courtyard and two charming dining rooms, picking a place to sit is as tricky as choosing your meal!

**Restaurant Tamgak** (Route de Bilma; meals CFA2000-2700; ✖ lunch & dinner) While Le Pilier and Auberge D'Azel are aimed squarely at Westerners, Tamgak serves more of a local crowd. The food is quite good and you can snack on popcorn while you wait for your meal.

**Restaurant le Palmier** (Route de l'Aéroport; meals CFA1500-3800; ✖ breakfast, lunch & dinner) This is the perfect place to start the day with an omelette and coffee. Remember you're on the verge on the Sahara – seriously lower your expectations before diving into the Thai rice. The Tunisian couscous is closer to the mark.

**Le V8** (Route de l'Aéroport; meals CFA800-4000; ✖ lunch & dinner) Although more a bar than a restaurant, they serve up tasty local dishes and even pizzas here. The *riz sauce* does a good job of shutting your hungry tummy's cakehole.

**Le Gourmet** (Place de la Grande Mosquée; meals CFA500-1500; ☾ breakfast, lunch & dinner) Known for its heaped servings, high benches and low tables, Le Gourmet is a simple place for a simple meal. The *steak garni* is still a cut above the rest, but the spaghetti can be rather greasy.

**Restaurant La Targuie** (meals CFA800-1500; ☾ breakfast, lunch & dinner) Conveniently located next to SNTV, La Targuie serves up rice pilaff, *mouton targui* and some spicy omelettes. Snacking and watching English-language movies makes bus delays a little more enjoyable.

**Pâtisserie Madara Rahama** (Route de l'Aéroport; pastries from CFA250) Although you have to get your timing right to find pastries (around 10.30am), there's usually refreshing yogurt (CFA125) in the fridge.

The **night market** (Route de l'Aéroport; ☾ dinner) is great for ambience and a hearty selection of stews, *igname* (pounded yams baked in a doughy bread-like mix), brochettes and spaghetti ensure you'll be stuffed for under CFA400. The daring can try goat's head.

Besides perusing the Grand Marché, self-caterers can visit **ETS Soleil Brillant** (Route de l'Aéroport) and **L'Elite Alimentation** (Route de l'Aéroport).

## Drinking

Options for evening drinks are pretty limited. The best when we were in town was the recently reopened **Le V8** (Route de l'Aéroport; beer from CFA550), which had a friendly crowd to go with its atmospheric courtyard under the stars. Your only other real choice is to head to the sterile bar at **Hôtel de la Paix** (Route de Bilma; beer from CFA900).

## Shopping

For buying jewellery and seeing silversmiths at work, check out the **Village Artisanal D'Agadez** (off Route de Niamey; ☾ 8am-6pm) in the town's southwest. Within the Vieux Quartier you'll also find silversmiths, leatherworkers producing Tuareg *samaras* (sandals), *coussins* (cushions) and magnificent *selles de chameau* (camel saddles), and bronzesmiths making a variety of objects, including jewellery. There are also loads of small Tuareg boutiques around Place du Grande Mosquée. Bargaining is always required.

If you're after a Tuareg turban expect to pay CFA500 per metre in the market (indigo costs more); 3m should suffice.

## Getting There & Away

### AIR
Point-Afrique and Go-Voyages have weekly charter flights between Paris/Marseilles and Agadez during high season (October through April). See p616 for more.

### BUS
**SNTV** (☎ 29 61 80) serves Arlit (CFA3400, three hours, 4.30pm Thursday to Tuesday), Niamey (CFA15,100, 12 hours, 7am Wednesday, Friday to Monday) and Zinder (CFA7700, 7½ hours, 7am Tuesday and Saturday). Similar services to Arlit and Niamey are provided by **EHGM** (Route de Niamey), **Aïr Transport** (off Route de Niamey) and **RTV** (Route de Niamey). EHGM also has a Saturday service to Zinder.

### BUSH TAXI
Bush taxis leave from the *gare routière* on the north side of town. At least one Minibus/Peugot leaves daily for Arlit (CFA2600/3000, four/3½ hours), and Zinder (CFA7000/8000, nine/eight hours). If you're even thinking about Niamey in a bush taxi, head straight for the hospital's psychiatric department.

## Getting Around

As with most Niger towns, *motos* are ideal for getting across town quickly (CFA150).

# AÏR MOUNTAINS & TÉNÉRÉ DESERT

Who would have ever thought that rock, wind and sand could produce such magic?

## Aïr Mountains

Simply put, the Aïr Mountains are among the most spectacular sights in West Africa. Dark volcanic masses dramatically rise from the Saharan surrounds and culminate in grand peaks, the highest being Mt Bagzane (2022m), 145km from Agadez. In some areas marvellous deep-blue marble outcrops poke from rich red sands – just amazing. Lurking within this range – which covers an area the size of Switzerland – are some fascinating prehistoric sites (see opposite for more).

Besides the Neolithic art and general jaw-dropping scenery, some specific highlights of Aïr include a dip in the thermal hot springs at **Tafadek** (a slight detour off the main route north, some 60km from Agadez), and the oasis of **Timia**, which sits about 110km north of Elméki and 225km north of Agadez. The village of Timia, with its Tuareg residents, mud-brick homes, verdant gardens and wavering palms, is a sight indeed, as is the nearby waterfall during the rains. Almost 30km north of Timia are the intriguing vestiges of the former Tuareg capital, **Assodé**, founded around 1000AD – have a wander.

About 150km further north, or 160km east from Arlit, is the beautiful oasis of **Iferouâne**. Its sheer beauty makes Iferouâne a great place to stop, and there are also some interesting prehistoric rock paintings in the area. In 2000 Iferouâne hosted the unique **Festival de l'Aïr** to celebrate and preserve Tuareg culture, and it has taken place

every December since – inquire at Agadez's travel agencies for more details.

**Hôtel Tellit** ( ☎ satellite phone 0088216244722, in Agadez ☎ 44 02 31; r with shared bathroom CFA16,000-20,000; ☺ Jan-Apr) is run by the same owners as the Pension Tellit in Agadez and is of a similarly high standard. There's also now a nearby **campsite** (camping CFA8000) that has traditional Tuareg tents.

Northeast of Iferouâne, on the eastern boundary of the Aïr, the sand dunes at **Temet** are also well worth the journey.

## Ténéré Desert

The Ténéré, east of the Aïr Mountains, is the one of the world's most legendary deserts and plays home to some of the Sahara's most extraordinarily beautiful sand dunes. Other areas are rather harsh and bleak, monotonous miles of flat hard sand,

### ROCK ART OF THE AÏR

The Aïr Mountains are a treasure trove of Neolithic art. These enthralling images capture the lush region and some of its inhabitants – such as elephants, giraffes and rhinos – before the spreading Sahara started engulfing the area some 4500 years ago. Amazingly, few visitors are aware that they are visiting one of the world's most remote open-air galleries.

The art predominantly consists of petroglyphs, or carvings created with a sharp stone, a method known as 'pecking'. Another stone was sometimes used to bang the sharp stone like a pick. The outline was usually completed first, often by scratching and, occasionally, the rock face was smoothed first as a form of preparation. Upon completion, some of the lines were ground smooth. After metal was introduced to the Sahara around 1200 BC, a metal spike may have been used.

It's thought that the oldest rock art in the Aïr dates back to 6000 BC. The majority of the carvings date from the Pastoral Period (5500–2000 BC), a period characterised by depictions of domesticated cattle and dominant human figures, and the later Horse or Camel Periods (1000 BC to the arrival of Islam). This latter period of rock art is also known as the Libyan Warrior Tradition and typically features chariots and human figures represented by two triangles.

The most common subjects depicted in the Aïr are people, horses, cows, camels, giraffes, ostriches, gazelles, elephants and rhinos. The best sites are at Iwelene, Arakaou, Tanakom and Anakom, all of which are at the mouths of wadis running into the Ténéré. In the northern Aïr, there are some fine sites around Iferouâne while, to the west, Dabous is especially rich in carvings. Perhaps the most famous carving is the 5.4m-high giraffe at Dabous, discovered in 1999 and some 500km from the nearest similar work. A moulding of the giraffe is now on display at Agadez airport and in 2000 the site was listed by Unesco as one of the world's most threatened monuments.

If you're fortunate enough to see some of the art, remember a few simple rules. Whatever you do, please leave the carvings as you find them. Throughout the Sahara, travellers have chipped away sections of the rock wall or thrown water on the paintings to enhance the light for taking photographs, causing irreparable damage to these ancient sites.

If you want to learn more about Saharan rock art or about efforts being undertaken to preserve rock art across Africa, contact the **Trust for African Rock Art** (TARA; ☎ 254-20-884467; www.tara .org.uk). In addition to a wealth of historical information, it also has a nine-point Recommended Code of Conduct for viewing the art. A superb resource is also *African Rock Art* by David Coulson and Alec Campbell.

NIGER

**THE TUAREG'S FIRST BOARDING SCHOOL**

In 2005, after a few years of intensive fundraising, a unique boarding school for the children of Tuareg nomads opened in the remote area of Tezerzaït, on the fringes of the Aïr and Ténéré, about 100km northeast of Iferouâne. Centre de Éducation et de Santé de Tezerzaït (CEST) is the first school in the entire region and gives hope to many families hoping to improve their lives. It was the brainchild of the region's Kel Teddeley Tuareg tribe, who were fed up with being ignored by the central government, and of an energetic Canadian tourist. The school is placed near an oasis often visited by the nomadic herders, meaning that parents still see their children regularly. Besides hiring a teacher, the school has also hired two respected grandmothers to look after the children, giving much-needed reassurance to parents.

If you'd like to help support this important and novel school, contact Jacqueline Lanouette (jacquelinelanouette@yahoo.com; 483 B Grande Côte, Rosemere, Quebec, Canada J7A 1M1).

but, much like the Aïr Mountains hide their Neolithic artwork, the Ténéré holds its fair share of sublime secrets too – massive dinosaur graveyards and evocative, deserted medieval settlements.

If you head east from Agadez towards Bilma, you'll come to Tazolé after 100km. To the south is one of the Ténéré's **dinosaur cemeteries**, believed to be one of the globe's most important. Its fossils are spread over a belt 150km long. Continually covered and uncovered by the sand, they are silent witness to the fact that the whole Sahara Desert was once green and fertile. You may see fossils of a number of species, maybe even the Super Croc (see p588 for more on this monster).

Another 179km east and you'll pass the *Mad Max*-looking metal **Monument to the Arbre du Ténéré**, the only tree to have been marked on Michelin's Africa map (see boxed text, below).

Some 171km further east is the salt-producing oasis of **Fachi** and, 610km from Agadez, **Bilma** – which is truly the end of the earth. This town satisfies every thought

you ever had of an exotic oasis in the middle of a forbidding desert. It's fortified and surrounded by palm trees and irrigated gardens – everywhere are piles of salt destined for the market towns of southern Niger and northern Nigeria. You'll see how it is purified and poured into moulds made from large palm trunks, giving the salt its loaf-like form (in contrast, for example, to the door-like slabs from Mali).

**Amis du Kawar et Fils des Oasis** ( ☎ 73 55 45; mattress CFA3000) is a new, fairly basic, encampment we've recently been made aware of in Bilma. Meals cost CFA500 and the owner can apparently organise tours of the salt mines. There is a weekly SNTN bus which travels with a military escort from Agadez as far as Dirkou (30 hours), from where there are taxi brousses to Bilma (a further 15 hours).

If you go north to the **Plateau du Djado**, about 1000km from Agadez via Bilma, you'll see some of the prehistoric cave paintings of antelopes, giraffes and rhinos for which the area is noted – not to mention deserted old towns, medieval *ksars* atop rocky crags and forbidding mountain scenery. The honey-combed vestiges of Djado's citadel are truly stunning.

**Getting There & Away**

Exploring the Aïr Mountains or Ténéré Desert without an official guide and *feuille de route* issued from a licensed travel agency is now illegal in Niger. Information about Agadez and Niamey travel agencies (where trips can be arranged) can be found on p605 and p585 respectively.

The list of potential routes to the Aïr Mountains and/or Ténéré Desert is as vast as the Sahara itself, but standard excursions

**AFRICA'S LUCKIEST AND UNLUCKIEST TREE**

Why does the Arbre du Ténéré deserve such a title? Well, it was lucky to have been the last surviving acacia of the once-great Saharan forests – standing alone in the desert's core, some 400km from its nearest relative. Unlucky? Sitting in a sea of sand and open space, what were the odds of a collision with a truck? Oh to have been a fly on the wall when the Libyan truck driver explained the accident to his boss back in 1973!

include the following: an eight-day circuit of the Aïr Mountains (including the dunes at Temet); a tour of the Aïr and Ténéré (eight to 12 days); or a circuit of the Aïr/Ténéré and the ghost towns of the Plateau du Djado (14 to 15 days). An extra week will enable you to explore all of the above plus the heart of the Ténéré and the dinosaur fossils at Termit. While they cover less distance and involve a lot of walking, camel safaris are an amazing way to see parts of the region.

If you have your own 4WD, expect to pay at least CFA15,000 per day for a compulsory guide, or at least CFA20,000 for a driver/guide. However, many agencies are now hesitant to grant the mandatory *feuille de route* (official itinerary) to those travelling in their own vehicles. Also note that if you plan on visiting the Plateau du Djado or remote areas of the Ténéré, agencies won't grant you a *feuille de route* unless you're travelling in a pair of 4WDs. This may mean that you have to hire a second 4WD to accompany you.

Though significantly decreased, banditry can still be problem in these regions, as was illustrated by the murder of a French tourist in late 2005. Always check the latest before heading out.

## ARLIT
**pop 90,700**
Uranium was discovered here in 1965. Six years later, Somair, the uranium mining company, created Arlit, Niger's most northern major town. Since the original boom, Arlit's prosperity has risen and fallen with the price of uranium. With oil prices shooting skyward and several major governments leaning towards nuclear power, Arlit's future may be getting even brighter.

Very few travellers would bother passing through Arlit were it not for the fact that it's the first town of any size in Niger if crossing the Sahara from Tamanrasset (Algeria).

**Hôtel l'Auberge la Caravane** ( ☎ 89 29 49; d fan/air-con CFA5000/12,000; ✴ ) is just west of town centre and a short walk from the SNTV station. The rooms are spartan and all but six have shared, slightly stinky toilets. It's the best Arlit has to offer.

The only other option is the **Tamesna Club** (d CFA5000), which has large but rather dingy rooms above its loud bar.

The best place to eat is **Restaurant Le Train** (meals CFA1000-2000; ⓧ breakfast, lunch & dinner), which serves the usual stuff and is on the road entering town from Agadez. There's also a string of street stalls selling brochettes in front of the Tamesna Club.

SNTV buses run south to Agadez (CFA3000, three hours, 4am) and Niamey (CFA17,500, 15 hours, daily except Tuesday and Thursday). RTV, Aïr Transport and EHGM all have similar services.

# NIGER DIRECTORY

## ACCOMMODATION
Budget places are relatively expensive in Niger, with the cheapest single rooms ranging from CFA3000 (not surprised to see a cockroach) to CFA8000 (mildly surprised to see a cockroach) – yes, quality is a little on the low side. Camping (typically CFA2000 per person) is possible in Niamey, Birni N'Konni, Agadez and Parc Regional du W.

Midrange hotels aren't cheap either, but they usually offer more cleanliness and your own bathroom. Prices in smaller towns start from CFA11,000 for a double room with fan, and another CFA5000 if you want air-con. Expect to pay up to double that in Niamey and Agadez.

Niamey and Agadez have upmarket hotels, where rooms cost between CFA30,000 and CFA95,000.

---

**PRACTICALITIES**

- The only local newssheet is the anaemic French-language *Le Sahel,* which is available from a few roadside stalls and bookshops in Niamey.

- Besides some local music stations in Niamey, the government-run La Voix du Sahel is the only national radio station.

- Télé-Sahel, which broadcasts news and French-language films, is the only non-satellite TV channel available. Some of the TVs in Niamey's hotels and restaurants pick up French-based programs.

- Electricity supply is 220V and plugs are of the European two-round-pin variety.

- The metric system is used in Niger.

## ACTIVITIES

Coasting in a pirogue through hippos and the Niger River's moist environments, and lumbering through the Sahara's beautifully barren expanse with a camel train are two activities that are as different as they are rewarding.

## BOOKS

In *Eaters of the Dry Season: Circular Labor Migration in the West African Sahel,* David Rain uses his extensive research around Maradi to attack the stereotype that the nomads of the Sahel are unfortunate, powerless victims of drought, and proves them to be a resourceful and intelligent people.

Kathleen Hill's semi-autobiographical novel *Still Waters in Niger* tells of an Irish-American returning to Niger after a 17-year absence to visit her daughter, who's working as an aid worker. While the story is fictional, the lyrical descriptions of Zinder and its surrounds are beautifully true to life.

While rather limited in its scope, *Riding the Demon: On the Road in West Africa* by Peter Chilson, is an interesting attempt at painting a portrait of Niger using information gleaned during the author's time in and around bush taxis.

*Nomads of Niger* by Carol Beckwith is a gorgeous picture book depicting the lives of the Wodaabé people. Despite being published in 1983, Marion Van Offelen's text and Carol's pictures still captivate most readers.

## BUSINESS HOURS

Typical business hours are from 8am to noon and 3pm to 6pm Monday to Friday, and from 8am to noon Saturday, though large markets bustle daily between 8am to 6pm. Government offices are open from 8.30am to 12.15pm and 3.30pm to 6pm Monday to Friday. Banking hours are from 8am to 11.30am and 3.45pm to 5pm Monday to Friday, and from 8.30am to noon on Saturday. Simple local eateries open around 6am and don't shut the doors until 10pm, while fancier options serve breakfast from 7am to 10am, lunch from noon to 2pm and dinner between 6pm and 11pm.

## COURSES

Courses to improve your French or budding Hausa skills are available in Niamey (p588).

## CUSTOMS

The thoroughness of searches by customs officials varies, though foreign travellers are rarely targeted for a total going-over. Ignore requests for 'special taxes'. There's no limit on the import or export of foreign currencies.

## DANGERS & ANNOYANCES

Despite travel in the far north of Niger being more strictly regulated these days, banditry can be a problem. On 2 December 2005, a French tourist was killed 60km north of Agadez when bandits fired on his vehicle after it failed to stop at their roadblock. Although it was the first such attack in northern Niger for over a year, it's always wise to check the latest before setting out.

## EMBASSIES & CONSULATES
### Nigerien Embassies

In West Africa, Niger has embassies in Benin, Nigeria and Mali. Niger does not have diplomatic representation in the UK. For details see the relevant country chapter. Embassies elsewhere include the following:

**Algeria** ( ☎ 213-788921; 54 Rue du Vercors)

**Belgium** ( ☎ 02-648 6140; 78 Ave Franklin-Roosevelt, Brussels 1050)

**Canada** ( ☎ 613-232 4291; 38 Blackburn Ave, Ottawa, Ontario K1N 8A3)

**Chad** (off Ave Gourang, N'Djaména)

**France** ( ☎ 01-45 04 80 60; www.ambassadeniger.org; 154 Rue de Longchamp, 75016 Paris)

**USA** ( ☎ 227-483 4224; www.nigerembassyusa.org; 2204 R St NW, Washington, DC 20008)

### Embassies & Consulates in Niger

All embassies and consulates are in Niamey unless stated. There's no UK diplomatic representation in Niger.

**Algeria** Agadez ( ☎ 44 01 17; ◔ 8am-2.30pm Mon-Fri, 8.30am-noon Sat); Niamey ( ☎ 75 30 97; Blvd de la République; ◔ 8am-12.30pm & 4-6pm Mon-Fri) Embassy 6km west of city centre.

**Benin** ( ☎ 72 28 60; Rue des Dallois; ◔ 9am-4pm Mon-Fri)

**Canada** ( ☎ 75 36 86; niamy@international.gc.ca; off Blvd Mali Bero)

**Chad** ( ☎ 75 34 64; Ave de Presidence; ◔ 8.30am-3.30pm Mon-Thu, 8am-noon Fri)

**Denmark** ( ☎ 72 39 48; Ave du Général de Gaulle)

**France** Consulate ( ☎ 72 27 22; fax 73 40 12; Place Nelson Mandela; ◔ 8am-12.30pm Mon-Fri); Embassy ( ☎ 75 27 86; Rue des Ambassades).

**Germany** ( ☎ 72 35 10; Ave du Général de Gaulle; ⊙ 9am-noon Mon-Fri)

**Mali** ( ☎ 75 42 90; consmali@intnet.ne; off Blvd des Sy et Mamar; ⊙ 8am-3pm Mon-Thu, 8am-12.30pm & 3-5.30pm Fri)

**Nigeria** ( ☎ 73 24 10; Rue des Ambassades; ⊙ 10am-1pm Mon-Fri).

**USA** ( ☎ 72 26 61; usemb@intent.ne; Rue des Ambassades; ⊙ 8am-4.30pm Mon-Fri)

## FESTIVALS & EVENTS

The largest festival in all of Niger is the annual **Cure Salée** (Salt Cure) celebration held by the nomadic Fula and Tuareg peoples during September. While each group of herders has its own Cure Salée, the Wodaabé's celebration is renowned throughout all of West Africa (see the boxed text, below).

---

### LA CURE SALÉE

One of the most famous annual celebrations in West Africa is the Cure Salée (Salt Cure). It's held in the vicinity of In-Gall, particularly around Tegguidda-n-Tessoum.

Each group of herders has its own Cure Salée, but that of the Wodaabé people is famous through-out Africa. The festival lasts a week, usually during the first half of September, and the main event happens over two days.

The Wodaabé are a unique sect of nomadic Fulani herders. When the Fulani migrated to West Africa centuries ago, possibly from the Upper Nile, many converted to Islam. For the Fu-lani who remained nomads, cattle retained their pre-eminent position. Valuing their freedom, they despised their settled neighbours and resisted outside influences. Many called themselves 'Wodaabé', meaning 'people of the taboo' – those who adhere to the traditional code of the Fulani, particularly modesty. The sedentary Fulani called them 'Bororo', a name derived from their cattle and insinuating something like 'those who live in the bush and do not wash'.

Wodaabé men have long, elegant, feminine features, and believe they have been blessed with great beauty. To a married couple, it's important to have beautiful children. Men who are not good-looking have, on occasion, shared their wives with more handsome men to gain more at-tractive children. Wodaabé women have the same elegant features and enjoy sexual freedom before marriage.

During the year, the nomadic Wodaabé are dispersed, tending to their animals. As the animals need salt to remain healthy, the nomads bring their animals to graze in the area around In-Gall (known for its high salt content) at the height of the rainy season, when the grass can support large herds. During the Cure Salée, you'll see men on camels trying to keep their herds in order and camel racing. The event serves, above all, as a social gathering – a time for wooing the opposite sex, marriage and seeing old friends.

For the Wodaabé, the Cure Salée is the time for their Gerewol festival. To win the attention of eligible women, single men participate in a 'beauty contest'. The main event is the Yaake, which is a late-afternoon performance when the men dance, displaying their beauty, charisma and charm. In preparation they'll spend long hours decorating themselves in front of small hand mirrors. They then form a long line, dressed to the hilt with blackened lips (to make the teeth seem whiter), lightened faces, white streaks down their foreheads and noses, star-like figures painted on their faces, braided hair, elaborate headwear, anklets, all kinds of jewellery, beads and shiny objects. Tall, lean bodies, long slender noses, white even teeth, and white eyes are what the women are looking for.

After taking special stimulating drinks, the men dance for hours. Their charm is revealed in their dancing. Eventually, the women, dressed less elaborately, timidly make their choices. If a marriage proposal results, the man takes a calabash full of milk to the woman's parents. If they accept, he then brings them the bride price, three cattle, which are slaughtered for the festivities that follow.

Rivalry between suitors can be fierce, and to show their virility the young men take part in the *Soro*, an event where they stand smiling while others try to knock them over with huge sticks. At the end of the festival, the men remove their jewellery, except for a simple talisman.

In 2005 the government tried to organise some separate Cure Salée events specifically for tour-ists (complete with admission fees), but this just seemed to confuse matters and the festival was rather disjointed.

A beauty contest of a very different variety occurs at Niamey's **Hangandi festival** (p589).

Another interesting celebration is the Festival de l'Aïr (p609) in Iferouâne each December. It was started in 2000 to celebrate and preserve traditional Tuareg culture and to promote tourism in the far north.

The Muslim holiday of **Tabaski** (see p606) in Agadez is an event indeed, with the 'cavalcade' camel race passing through town's crooked and crowded streets.

The months of July and August are also rich ones for festivals in the Sahara, with a large feast being held in a different village almost every week. For information about these remote festivities you'll have to keep your ear to the ground in Agadez.

## HOLIDAYS

With over 90% of the population being Muslim, Islamic holidays dominate the calendar (see p818 for dates and details). Other public holidays include the following:

**New Year's Day** 1 January
**Easter** March/April
**Labour Day** 1 May
**Independence Day** 3 August
**Settlers' Day** 5 September
**Republic Day** 18 December
**Christmas Day** 25 December

## INTERNET ACCESS

Internet is readily available in Niamey, with only a few options in Maradi, Zinder and Agadez. Prices range from CFA500 per hour in Niamey, to CFA6000 per hour in Maradi.

## LANGUAGE

French is the official language. The principal African languages are Hausa, spoken mainly in the south, and Djerma (also spelt Zarma), spoken mostly in the west, including around Niamey. Other languages include Gourmanchéma in the south and Fulfulde, Tamashek, Toubou and Kanuri, the languages of the northern nomadic and seminomadic herders. See p879 for useful phrases in French, Hausa, Fulfulde and Tamashek.

## MONEY

The unit of currency is the West African CFA franc.

Carrying cash or travellers cheques in euros is best, though you'll rarely have trouble with

US dollar equivalents. The most convenient bank to change cash (no commission) or travellers cheques (1.6% commission) are the branches of Banque Internationale pour l'Afrique – Niger (BIA-Niger) in Niamey, Maradi, Tahoua, Zinder and Agadez. The branches of Ecobank can also be helpful, but they tend to have higher commission charges (especially for travellers cheques).

There are currently no ATMs in Niger and credit-card advances (Visa and MasterCard) are only a real option in the capital. Some of the top-end hotels, airline offices and travel agencies in Niamey also accept credit cards.

## PHOTOGRAPHY & VIDEO

A photo or video permit is not required, but you should avoid taking pictures of government buildings, military sites, bridges (especially Kennedy Bridge in Niamey) and people bathing in the river. For more details see p823.

## POST

Postal services outside the capital are slow and unreliable, so you should send everything from Niamey. As an example of rates, a postcard or 10g letter to Europe or North America costs CFA525/550 respectively.

## TELEPHONE

Throughout Niger you'll find private telecentres offering international calls for about CFA750 per minute. The quality is generally pretty good and most places will let you receive calls for free. A three-minute (the minimum) call to Europe from most post offices costs about CFA5000. Subsequent minutes cost CFA1600

Niger's new mobile phone network now covers most major cities, but people have only had mixed success setting up their foreign phones.

## VISAS

Visas are required by everyone who isn't a West African citizen. Requirements change all the time, however, so check with a Nigerien embassy.

Getting a visa outside West Africa is generally straightforward. You usually have to provide three photos, proof of yellow-fever vaccination (and cholera vaccination if entering from a country with a recent outbreak), a recent bank statement proving you have at least US$500, and a copy of your airline ticket proving onward travel (although this can usually be a ticket for departing some months later from another African country). Your passport must also be valid for at least six months after your planned exit date from Niger. You can find up-to-date information and printable visa application forms from the websites of Niger's embassies in Paris (www.ambassadeniger .org) and Washington DC (www.nigerem bassyusa.org). If applying in person, embassies usually process visas within 24 hours. Costs vary depending where you apply. For instance, a one-/three-month tourist visa in Washington DC costs US$34.58/88.94, while a one-month tourist visa in Paris is €50. See p612) for a list of Nigerien embassies outside of West Africa.

If you're travelling overland you'll find Niger visa information for the following countries on the following pages: Benin (p123), Mali (p542) and Nigeria (p669).

Visas are also available in Chad at the **Niger Consulate** (off Ave Gourang, N'Djaména). A one-month visa costs US$35, while a two-month option is US$70. Both require two photos and can be processed the same day. There's *no* Niger representation in Burkina Faso, but there is a **Niger Consulate** ( ☎ 213-788921; 54 Rue du Vercors) in Algiers. They issue one-month visas costing US$60 or €50. The service is same-day and you'll need three photos.

Some visitors entering from a country without any Nigerien diplomatic representation (eg Burkina Faso) have been known to get their passport stamped at the border and then get the full visa issued in Niamey. That said, if you don't want to risk getting turned back or having to pay a substantial bribe, you're better off arriving with a visa resting peacefully in your passport.

### Visa Extensions

For a one- to three-month visa extension, take two photos, your passport and CFA20,000 to the **Direction de la Surveillance du Territoire** ( ☎ 73 37 43, ext 249; Rue du Président Heinrich Lubké, Niamey; ✆ 8am-12.30pm & 3.30-6.30pm Mon-Fri). Extensions are typically processed the same day.

### Visas for Onward Travel

In Niger, you can get visas for the following neighbouring countries.

### ALGERIA

While the Algerian embassy in Niamey only issue visas to Niger residents, the consulate in Agadez told us they'd issue tourist visas if you have a letter from an Algerian travel agency (stating your plans with the agency), a photocopy of your vehicle's *carte grise* and three colour photos.

### BENIN

Transit visas cost CFA10,000, three-month single-entry tourist visas are CFA15,000 and three-month multiple-entry visas go for CFA20,000. You'll need to bring two photos and the process takes two working days. You can also get a transit visa (CFA4000) at the border in Malanville, but it's good only for 48 hours (though you can renew it in Cotonou).

### BURKINA FASO, CÔTE D'IVOIRE, GABON, SENEGAL & TOGO

The French consulate grants three-month visas for these countries. Each visa costs CFA23,000 and requires one photo and a photocopy of your passport. The service usually takes 24 hours.

### CHAD

For a single-entry one-month visa you'll need two photos, CFA15,000 and a pleasant demeanour (to try and avoid being one of the people refused a visa for little or no reason). Visas are usually ready the same day.

### MALI

A one-month single-entry visa costs CFA20,000, requires one photo and are issued in 24 hours.

### NIGERIA

Although the embassy previously didn't issue visas to non-Niger residents, they seemed to have changed their tone and now offer same-day visa services. You'll need two photos and somewhere between CFA21,000 and CFA27,400, depending on your country of origin. Note that visas can only be obtained on Tuesday and Thursday between 10am and 1pm.

## WOMEN TRAVELLERS

Whether in a group or alone, woman rarely face any different trouble than men when travelling in Niger. Solo travellers will face more than their fare share of suitors, but their advances are typically harmless and can be easily rebuked. Remember that dress is taken very seriously in Muslim countries and shorts or singlets are not advised as they show a lack of sensitivity. For more general information and advice, see p828.

# TRANSPORT IN NIGER

## GETTING THERE & AWAY
### Entering Niger
Despite needing to provide a yellow-fever vaccination certificate to obtain a visa, you'll still need to show it when entering the country. Proof of cholera vaccination is also occasionally asked for if you're entering Niger from a country with a recent outbreak. While all those arriving by plane must have obtained their visa ahead of time, rare travellers have managed to enter overland without a visa (if arriving from a country without Nigerien diplomatic representation). However, this is rare and never a smooth process – it's always best to have a visa prior to arrival.

If you have your ducks in a row, arriving by air or overland on public transport is pretty routine. Those in their own vehicles usually face more scrutiny and officials usually do their best to find/create problems with your *carnet*, international drivers licence or insurance papers.

### Air
Airlines with offices in Niamey include the following:
**Air Algérie** (AH; ☎ 73 32 14; www.airalgerie.dz; Rue du Gaweye) Hub: Algiers.
**Air Burkina** (2J; ☎ 73 70 67; www.air-burkina.com; Rue du Commerce) Hub: Ougadougou.
**Air France** (AF; ☎ 73 31 21; www.airfrance.com; Rue du Souvenir) Hub: Charles de Gaulle, Paris.
**Air Sénégal International** (V7; www.air-senegal -international.com) Hub: Dakar. Contact the Royal Air Maroc office for information.
**Nigeravia** ( ☎ 73 35 90; www.nigeravia.com; Rue du Président Heinrich Lubké)
**Point-Afrique** ( ☎ 73 40 26; www.point_afrique.com; Rue du Sahel) Hub: Paris. Also known as Point-Air Niger.
**Royal Air Maroc** (AT; ☎ 73 28 85; www.royalairmaroc .com; Rue du Gaweye) Hub: Casablanca.
**Toumaï Air Tchad** ( ☎ 73 04 05; Rue du Gaweye) Hub: N'Djaména.

### AFRICA
Several airlines fly in and out of Niamey and together they serve many of West Africa's major cities. Prices at each airline fluctuate wildly and can range from a low of CFA135,000 for a short hop to Ouagadougou, to CFA380,000 for a flight to N'Djaména or Casablanca.

Airlines serving Niamey and their African destinations include the following:
**Afriqiyah Airways** (8U; www.afriqiyah.aero) Hub: Tripoli. Links Niamey with Cotonou and Ouagadougou with weekly flights.
**Air Burkina** (2J; www.air-burkina.com) Hub: Ougadou gou. Weekly flights to Abidjan and Ouagadougou.
**Air Ivoire** (VU; www.airivoire.com) Hub: Abidjan. One flight a week to Abidjan.
**Air Sénégal International** (V7; www.air-senegal -international.com) Hub: Dakar. Connects Niamey with Dakar and Bamako with Monday, Wednesday and Friday flights.
**Royal Air Maroc** (AT; www.royalairmaroc.com) Hub: Casablanca. Flies between Niamey and Casablanca each Monday and Friday.
**Toumaï Air Tchad** ( ☎ 73 04 05) Hub: N'Djaména. Friday flights serve N'Djaména.

### EUROPE & THE USA
There's less choice when flying to Europe or the USA from Niger, however there are two charter companies providing great value.

Airlines serving Niger and their international destinations include the following:
**Air Algérie** (AH; www.airalgerie.dz) Hub: Algiers. Have reasonable one-way fares to Paris, Marseilles and Lyon from Niamey.
**Air France** (AF; www.airfrance.com) Hub: Charles de Gaulle, Paris. Two weekly flights between Niamey and Paris. One-way fares are extortionate while return fares are more reasonable.
**Go-Voyages** (www.govoyges.com) Hub: Paris. This char ter company has cheap flights to Agadez from Paris/Mar seilles during high season (October to April).
**Point Afrique** (www.point-afrique.com) Hub: Paris. Offering the best value from Europe, this charter company has year-round weekly flights from Paris/Marseilles to Nia mey. Between October and April they also serve Agadez.
**Royal Air Maroc** (AT; www.royalairmaroc.com) Hub: Casablanca. Has regular flights via Casablanca to Paris and New York.

### Land
#### ALGERIA
The classic crossing from Assamakka (Niger) to In Guezzem (Algeria) is open, though only a trickle of overlanders pass

this way thanks to the increased bureaucracy resulting from bandits and the area's past instability. Algerian visas and arrangements with an Algerian travel agency must be made prior to reaching the border. The same can be said for heading south, as no vehicles can travel in this region of Niger without a licensed guide and *feuille de route* (official itinerary) – both are available through Nigerien travel agencies.

### BENIN

The Gaya/Malanville border is now open 24 hours a day and few travellers have problems here. The road connecting Niamey and Cotonou is sealed all the way and **SNTV** ( ☎ 73 30 20; sntv@intnet.ne; Ave de Gamkalé, Niamey) runs daily buses between the two cities (CFA20,000, 13 to 15 hours). **EHGM** ( ☎ 74 37 16; Blvd de Mali Béro, Niamey) runs similar services four days a week for CFA18,700.

Bush taxis don't cross the border, so if you'll have to use a *moto* (CFA500) to link Gaya and Malanville. See the Gaya (p596) and Malanville (p120) sections for further transportation information.

### BURKINA FASO

The main crossing linking Niger and Burkina Faso is Foetchango, southwest of Niamey. It's pretty straightforward and now remains open around the clock. SNTV buses cover the 500km between Niamey and Ouagadougou (CFA10,000, nine to 11 hours, Tuesday to Sunday).

Minibuses leave Niamey's *gare routière*, which is 1km west of Kennedy Bridge, for Makalondi (CFA2100, 1¼ hours), Kantchari (CFA3100, two hours) and Ouagadougou (CFA8100, 10 to 12 hours). Note that times to Kantchari and Ouagadougou don't include border festivities at Foetchango. Despite what drivers tell you, Peugeot taxis don't cross the border and you must change at Kantchari.

An alternative crossing for those with their own vehicles is the northwestern route via Téra. It involves a short but enjoyable ferry crossing (CFA1000) at Farié (62km northwest of Niamey).

Remember that there's an hour's time difference between Niger and Burkina Faso.

### CHAD

There's no scheduled public transport travelling across the border, but there are a couple of Landcruisers that make the dusty day-long journey from Nguigmi to Mao, Chad (CFA15,000) each week. From Mao you may have to wait several days before you find something to get you to N'Djaména.

Don't forget to get your passport stamped in Nguigmi and Mao, and remember that, in Chad, they use Central African CFA francs.

### LIBYA

Currently the Libyan border is only open to traffic entering Niger. To enter you must be travelling with a licensed guide and have a *feuille de route* (official itinerary) – both are available through Nigerien travel agencies in Agadez (p605).

### MALI

SNTV has a bus (actually a truck with a cabin on the back) that goes between Niamey and Gao on Monday and Thursday (CFA11,500, up to 30 hours). The road from Niamey to Ayorou is sealed; from the border at Labbézanga it's sandy to Gao. From July to September, the route is muddy and the journey has been described by one reader as 'a horrific journey of hassles, bureaucracy, time-wasting and general lunacy'. Take plenty of water.

It's also possible to take a slow-boat from Ayorou to Gao (CFA14,000, two days) on Monday. There's no shade, so a hat, or better yet an umbrella, is as crucial as a large supply of water.

### NIGERIA

There are four border crossings between Niger and Nigeria: Gaya/Kamba, Birni N'Konni/Illela, Maradi/Katsina and Zinder/Jibiya. With Nigerian authorities having about five standard checks (customs, immigration, luggage, drugs and bribe), few travellers have a painless and timely crossing.

The quickest option from Niamey is the Gaya/Kamba crossing. Several minibuses/Peugeots make daily runs from Niamey to Gaya (CFA4100/4500, 4½/5½ hours), from where you can hop on a *moto* or grab a shared taxi to the Nigerian border (CFA100). From there you can get another *moto* to Kamba (200N).

Crossing at Birni N'Konni/Illela is also straightforward. Take a *moto* from Birni N'Konni to the border (CFA100), where you'll find minibuses/Peugeots running to/from Sokoto (300N/350N, 1½ hours).

---

**BUSH TAXI TRAVEL TIMES**

In *A Brief History of Time,* author Steven Hawking stated he was warned that his book's sales would be halved for each formula he included. Nonetheless, his inclusion of $E=mc^2$ didn't hurt sales, so we'll follow the famous physicist's lead and enlighten you with the Bush Taxi Time Formula: $T=(cb/2ns)t$.

If maths isn't your thing, don't worry, we've done our best to estimate bush taxi durations throughout this chapter. However, if you're a maths whiz and want to know the exact length of your upcoming journey, our formula is for you!

The formula is comprised of the following variables: $(c)$ is the number of windshield cracks; $(b)$ is the number of bald tyres; $(n)$ is the number of tools in the car; $(s)$ is the number of spare tyres; $(t)$ is this chapter's estimated duration of journey; and $(T)$ is what you're after – your journey's exact duration!

So, if you have six cracks in the windshield, three bald tyres, six tools in the boot, one spare tyre, and an estimated travel time of two hours, your journey time will be precisely three hours. You'll note that if there are no tools or no spare tyres, the formula results in an error (that dividing by zero demon). This only tells you one thing: without a spare tyre or tools there is no telling how long your journey will take!

If, after you're happy with the maths and settled in your seat, the taxi requires a push to get started, throw out the watch and accept the fact that your journey will be a not-so-brief history of time!

---

Peugeots link Maradi with the Nigerian towns of Katsina (CFA1200, 1½ hours) and Kano (CFA3000, four hours).

Zinder is also connected to Kano via the Jibya crossing. Several Peugeots (CFA3000, 3½ hours) ply this route each day.

None of the transportation times mentioned above include border procedures/hold-ups.

# GETTING AROUND
## Air
There are no scheduled flights within Niger. If you're short on time and flush with cash, **Nigeravia** ( ☎ 73 35 90; www.nigeravia.com; Rue du Président Heinrich Lubké) has a 10-seater plane for charter.

## Bus
With decent tarmac roads stretching the breadth of the country, bus transport in Niger is fairly comprehensive, reliable and efficient. With more experienced drivers than its private counterparts (EHGM, RTV and Aïr Transport), the government company, SNTV, is still the most popular – despite its slightly higher price tag.

All companies have reserved seating, so there shouldn't be anyone in the aisles, though private companies bend this rule. It's best to book your ticket early to ensure a seat.

Each company's buses leave from their respective offices in each town, not from the autogares.

## Bush Taxi
Bush taxis are cheaper and leave more frequently than buses, although they're always very crowded and can take twice as long for the same journey (exact durations of bush taxi journeys can be calculated using the boxed text above).

There are two types of bush taxi: Peugeot 504 seven-seater station wagons, which carry 10 people; and Japanese minibuses, which carry about 18 people. The Peugeots are preferable because they fill faster and stop less, though the most comfortable option is to pay about 10% more for the front window seat of a minibus (ask for cabin and point to the window). To get the same amount of room in a Peugeot you'd have to pay double.

Bush taxis cover all but the most remote villages, although there's next to no public transport in the Sahara. In rural areas you'll find converted trucks and pick-ups called *fula-fulas,* which are cheap, slow and terribly uncomfortable.

## Car & Motorcycle
### BRINGING YOUR OWN VEHICLE
While most information regarding bringing your own vehicle into West Africa is

on p836, there's one very important thing unique to Niger: private vehicles are not allowed to drive north from Agadez or north from Nguigmi without a licensed Nigerien guide and *feuille de route* (official itinerary) – both available through Nigerien travel agencies in Agadez (p605). If you want to visit very remote areas, like the Plateau du Djado, you'll even have to hire a second vehicle to escort you.

### HIRE

There are a few car-rental agencies in Niamey, the most reliable being Niger-Car Voyages (p585).

### INSURANCE

To legally drive your vehicle in Niger, you must posses third-party insurance. This regulation is rigorously checked at roadside stops throughout the country and at the borders. While there's nowhere to buy insurance immediately upon entering Niger, officials will let you proceed to the first town that sells it. Société Nigérienne d'Assurances de Réassurances has offices in Niamey, Diffa, Maradi, Zinder and Birni N'Konni. Their insurance costs less than CFA2500 per day.

### ROAD CONDITIONS.

Most main roads in Niger are tarmac and are in generally good condition, although some sections, like that between Zinder and Gouré, are rather cratered and dire indeed. Thanks to being engulfed by the desert, the Zinder–Agadez road is the only major road that isn't passable with a 2WD.

### ROAD HAZARDS

Although buses no longer feel the need to take on armed soldiers between Tahoua and Agadez, you still shouldn't drive this section of road at night, due to the risk of banditry.

### ROAD RULES

Driving is done on the right side of the road in Niger. Private cars must pay a toll *(péage)* to use the main routes. You buy a ticket before travelling from a checkpoint on the edge of each town, either for a whole trip, eg Niamey to Agadez (CFA1000), or in sections, eg Niamey to Tahoua (CFA500), then Tahoua to Agadez (CFA500). If you don't have a ticket when it's asked for at a checkpoint, you're fined on the spot.

As a courtesy while driving on the highway, you should always switch on your left-turn signal when you see a vehicle coming in the opposite direction. Don't turn it off until the vehicle has safely past you. This routine is to simply let the approaching driver know that you've seem them and that it's safe to pass on your left.

## Tours

Your only choice in order to visit Parc Regional du W, or to dive into the desert areas around Agadez, may be to take an organised tour. Tours to Parc Regional du W are discussed on p589, while desert tours are found on p606.

NIGER

# Nigeria

Nigeria is superlative in every sense. It's the most populous country on the continent – every fifth African is a Nigerian – it dominates the region economically, and its music and literature have made it a major cultural player far beyond its borders. It's also a country of extremes. Great wealth and great poverty sit cheek by jowl, and, while awash with oil, it suffers from chronic power shortages and decrepit infrastructure. The sprawling megalopolis of Lagos contrasts sharply with the ancient cities of the north and the river deltas and lush forests of the south and east.

Nigeria can feel like more than the sum of its parts – an unruly collection of regions pulling against each other with a centrifugal force that occasionally erupts into violence. While the three main ethnic groups – the Yoruba, Igbo and Hausa – may sometimes rub together uncomfortably, and strife between the Christian and Muslim communities simmers below the surface, the marvel is that amid all this disorder the country seems to work, and Nigerians have such obvious pride in where they come from.

Nigeria carries a fearsome reputation among travellers. Getting around can sometimes be tough, and it's not a destination for first-timers to Africa, but you shouldn't believe all the scare stories. While a few parts of the country remain problematic, the vast majority is as warm and welcoming to visitors as anywhere in Africa. Chaotic and exuberant yes, but never dull. If you don't visit Nigeria you can barely say that you've been to West Africa.

## FAST FACTS

- **Area** 924,000 sq km
- **Capital** Abuja
- **Country code** ☎ 234
- **Famous for** Corruption; email scams; writers Wole Soyinka and Chinua Achebe; football
- **Language** English, Hausa, Igbo, Yoruba
- **Money** naira (N); US1= N132; €1= N162
- **Population** 140 million
- **Visa** Get in advance, letter of invitation usually required

NIGERIA

## HIGHLIGHTS

- **Lagos** (p629) Plunge in and sample the adrenaline charge and social scene of Nigeria's wild beating heart.
- **Calabar** (p647) Meet rescued chimpanzees and monkeys at the conservation centres in the southeast's old colonial port.
- **Kano** (p659) Find a trace of the old Saharan trade routes in the old city and the indigo dye pits.
- **Osun Sacred Forest** (p641) Enjoy the cool green peace of this place in Oshogbo, dedicated to the old Yoruba gods.
- **Yankari National Park** (p655) Look for wildlife and finish your day with a soak in the delightful Wiki Warm Spring.

## ITINERARIES

- **One to Two Weeks** No one should visit Nigeria without at least a few days in **Lagos** (p629), trying to navigate the city's mindset and traffic jams, and spending late nights in the bars and clubs. When Lagos gets too much, head east to **Benin City** (p642) to see the ancient craft of brass sculpture, before carrying on to the old port city of **Calabar** (p647), where you can check out some pioneering primate conservation work and the country's best museum. You could also stop off at **Umuhaia** (p647) to see the National War Museum and learn about the Biafran conflict. Extend your time in the southeast to the lush forests of the **Afi Mountain Drill Ranch** (p650).
- **One Month** A longer trip allows you to further explore the south, but also to take in northern Nigeria. From Lagos, fly to **Abuja** (p650), and then continue by road to the old trading cities of **Zaria** (p658) and **Kano** (p659). An interesting detour would be via the cool plateau city of **Jos** (p652), with a side-trip to **Yankari National Park** (p655) and the delightful Wikki Warm Spring. A month-long trip can easily encompass all these areas and give an excellent taste of Nigeria's diversity.

## CLIMATE & WHEN TO GO

For travel to the south, March to August are the wettest months to visit, and best avoided if possible. Temperatures are hot year-round, peaking at about 35°C in the spring; the humidity is constant. Late spring to summer is the hottest part of the year in the north (sometimes topping out at an

**HOW MUCH?**

- **Okada ride across town** N50
- **Replica Benin brass sculpture** N12,000
- **Afrobeat CD** N500
- **Bribe at police roadblock** N20
- **One minute local phonecall** N20

**LONELY PLANET INDEX**

- **Litre of petrol** N65
- **Litre of bottled water** N80
- **Beer (bottle of Star)** N150
- **Souvenir football shirt** N800
- **Street snack (stick of suya)** N100

extreme 45°C). The mercury drops from October to January at the onset of the dusty harmattan winds.

As well as the weather, take note of political developments when planning your trip. Although the country is generally calm, local trouble can quickly flare up, so once you're in Nigeria keep an eye on the news and be prepared to change your plans at short notice if necessary.

## HISTORY

Northern and southern Nigeria are essentially two different countries, and their histories reflect this division. The first recorded empire to flourish in this part of West Africa was that of the Kanem-Borno, in the north around Lake Chad. Its wealth was based on control of the important trans-Saharan trade routes from West Africa to the Mediterranean and the Middle East. Islam arrived in the 12th century and was adopted as the state religion. A number of Islamic Hausa kingdoms also flourished between the 11th and 14th centuries, based around the cities of Kano, Zaria and Nupe.

Islam made little headway in the south, and the southwest became a patchwork of small states, often dominated by the Yoruba. One of the earliest kingdoms, Ijebu, arose in the 10th century, and built the earthworks at Sungbo's Eredo. This was followed in the 14th and 15th centuries by the Ife, Oyo and Benin Kingdoms, which became important centres of trade. The Benin, the most famous,

**NIGERIA**

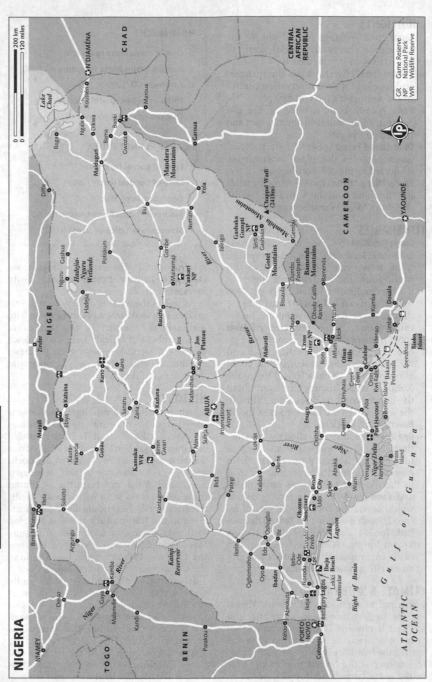

produced some of the finest metal artwork in Africa. The political systems of these states rested on a sacred monarchy, with a strong court bureaucracy. The *obas* (kings) of these states retain considerable influence. In the southeast, the Igbo and other agrarian peoples never developed any centralised empires, instead forming loose confederations.

## Colonial Contacts

The first contact between the Yoruba empires and Europeans was made in the 15th century, when the Portuguese began trading in pepper – which was later supplanted by the more lucrative slave trade. In contrast, the northern Islamic states continued to trade principally across the Sahara, and remained untouched by European influence until well into the 19th century.

While the slave trade flourished until the early 19th century, the Portuguese were eventually pushed out by other European powers. As the abolition movement grew, the British took a lead in suppressing slavery along the Niger Delta, where conflicts with Yoruba slavers led to the annexation of Lagos port – their first colonial toehold.

At the same time, Islamic revivalism was sweeping the north. The Hausa kings were overthrown by their Fulani subjects who, in the 1820s, set up a caliphate based in Sokoto, led by Osman Dan Fodio. The caliphate eventually stretched from Senegal to Cameroon, with its religious fervour inspiring Islamic revolutions across the region.

The British grab for Nigeria was a classic piece of imperial buccaneering, inspired by the palm oil trade which replaced slaving. The Royal Niger Company was formed in 1879, to cut out local middlemen and thwart the ambitions of the French, who were advancing along the Niger River. From here it was a short step to full annexation, and after the turn of the 20th century, British soldiers stormed Sokoto and Kano to create Nigeria.

Nigeria was divided in two – the southern Colony and the northern Protectorate. The British chose to rule indirectly through local kings and chiefs, a policy that worked well in the northern city-states, but much less so in the southwest, where none of the traditional Yoruba rulers had ever extracted taxes. In the southeast, where there had never been any centralised authority, the policy was even less successful.

## Independence & Other Struggles

Indirect rule stored up trouble for the future. The north remained economically underdeveloped, while in the south, Western education and Christian missionaries were promoted. As cries for independence grew louder after WWII, the British struggled to balance the interests of the regions whilst drawing up a new constitution. It was a tricky task. The Hausa north feared that the southerners' educational advantage would allow them to dominate politics and commerce, while mistrust between the Yorubas and Igbos divided the south. The British solution was to divide the country into three regions between these major ethnic groups.

Tensions arose over who was to dominate the federal parliament. After the hard-fought elections of 1959, Sir Abubakar Tafawa Balewa, a moderate northerner, was asked to form a government. Nigeria became an independent republic on 1 October 1960.

The coalition government of the First Republic was a disaster. Politics quickly degenerated into regional self-interest, corruption became rampant and the elite accumulated wealth by any means possible. The elections of 1965 were so outrageously rigged that protesting groups went on a rampage.

By early 1966, the stage was set for a development which would dominate Nigeria for years: the army got involved in politics. A group of Igbo officers staged a coup. Balewa and the premiers of the north and west were assassinated, and General Ironsi, the Igbo head of the army, took the reins of power.

Ironsi barely lasted four months. Anti-Igbo riots broke out in the north, and he was overthrown by a regime led by Yakubu Gowon, a Christian northerner. The violence grew, with anti-Igbo pogroms in the north and attacks on Hausas in the south. A state of emergency was announced, but in May 1967 the east's military governor, Lt Colonel Ojukwu, announced the secession of Biafra; the Igbo homeland which was awash with newly found oil. A bloody civil war began.

Independent Biafra was recognised by only a handful of African countries, who were often insecure in their own post-colonial borders; most international powers supported the federal government. The civil war dragged on for nearly three years, as the Igbo forces fought tooth and claw for every inch of territory which the federal forces took

**NIGERIA**

back. By early 1970, as a result of a blockade imposed by the federal government, Biafra faced starvation – this was the world's first 'TV famine', reported by a largely pro-Biafra international media. Biafra's forces finally capitulated, and Ojukwu fled the country. Up to a million Igbos had died in the war, mainly from hunger.

## Oil Boom and Bust

A policy of 'no victors, no vanquished' smoothed the path to reconciliation, which was aided in part by the sudden rocketing of world oil prices. Nigeria's oil production increased sevenfold between 1965 and 1973, and Gowon's military government became drunk on easy money. Foreign contractors chased oil dollars to Lagos, corruption exploded and crime was rampant. The chaos eventually became unbearable and, in July 1975, Gowon was overthrown in a bloodless coup led by General Murtala Mohammed.

The new government launched a clean-up of the civil service, the judiciary and the universities. However, despite his widespread popularity, Mohammed was assassinated by the army in early 1976. His successor, Biafran war hero Olusegun Obasanjo, drafted a US-style constitution and handed power back to a civilian government following elections in 1979. A northerner, Shehu Shagari, was sworn in as president.

Shagari followed earlier leaders by squandering Nigeria's wealth, a problem compounded when the price of oil crashed in the early 1980s. The country plunged into debt. Foreign workers packed up and left, and those who didn't (three million West Africans) were expelled as convenient scapegoats for the economic crisis. Shagari's end came with a coup on New Year's Eve 1983.

The new general in charge, Mohammed Bahari, tried playing the autocrat, but didn't have much time to enjoy his position. As regular as clockwork, another coup – Nigeria's sixth since independence – toppled him from power, to be replaced by General Ibrahim Babangida in 1985.

## Military Misrule

Babangida gained instant popularity by releasing political prisoners, and by lifting press controls. He also attempted something of an economic revolution, by devaluing the naira and privatising many

public enterprises, but these measures bore little fruit. Oil revenues dropped again and the country's debt rose to US$20 billion. Crime and corruption increased, with those on government payrolls often the worst culprits. The country was broke.

Babangida promised to return Nigeria to democracy with the Abuja Declaration, announced from the new capital. Under this, political parties were allowed, but a return to civilian rule was twice postponed. A multi-billion dollar oil windfall from the Gulf War disappeared before even reaching the government's coffers and, as the general population suffered fuel shortages, unrest spread.

The much-delayed presidential elections went ahead in June 1993. Chief Moshood Abiola, a wealthy Yoruba Muslim from the south, claimed victory, having gained unprecedented support across ethnic and religious lines. The result met with little favour among the Hausa-dominated military, and Babangida annulled the election result within a fortnight. Abiola fled and an announcement of new polls was greeted by widespread rioting. Babangida's army colleagues forced him out of power, to be replaced by the vice-president General Sani Abacha.

Abacha was a grotesque caricature of an African dictator. He offered no warm words about a return to democracy, and abolished any institutions that might suggest otherwise. Aware of his own route to power, he purged the army of potential coup plotters. Abiola, who had returned from exile to claim power, was arrested and charged with treason. Intellectuals, labour leaders, politicians and prodemocracy leaders were also arrested. Dozens of newspapers were shut down and strikes brutally suppressed.

Unrest in the oil-rich Delta brought a particularly tough clampdown. Ken Saro-Wiwa, an Ogoni activist and writer, was executed in November 1995 for allegedly plotting to overthrow the government – an action that led to Nigeria's expulsion from the Commonwealth and EU oil sanctions.

Abacha cared less about Nigeria's international isolation than siphoning off its wealth into Swiss bank accounts. But in June 1998, Nigerians were finally rescued by the 'coup from heaven'. Aged 54, and worth about US$10 billion in stolen money, Abacha died of a heart attack in the arms of two Indian prostitutes. His defence chief, Abdulsalam

Abubakar, was sworn in as his successor and immediately promised reforms. In a strange echo of Abacha's fate, Abiola died of a heart attack in prison within a month of the dictator, still claiming the presidency. While viewed as suspicious by many Nigerians, his death cleared the way for the military to hold elections, and many other political prisoners were subsequently released.

True to his word, Abubakar allowed elections to proceed, and in February 1999, Olusegun Obasanjo, the former military leader and southern Yoruba Christian, was returned as president.

## Nigeria Today

Obasanjo inherited a country in tatters. Free from the military yoke, the deep political and cultural differences between the north and south of the country began to play themselves out in an unruly manner. A major test came in 2000, when several northern states introduced sharia, or Islamic law, amid a climate of religious revivalism. Tensions between communities became inflamed and the federal government handled the situation badly, resulting in mass riots and bloodshed.

The flames were fanned again in 2002, when Nigeria was due to hold the Miss World contest, an event that caused fresh fighting. With democracy having had little chance to grow roots, local and national politicians repeatedly used ethnic and religious differences to build power bases, sometimes stoking unrest for their own gain. During Obasanjo's first term as president, over 10,000 people were killed in communal violence.

One major area where Obasanjo has had success, however, is in returning Nigeria to its status as a major player on the international stage. Nigeria now plays a lead role in the Commonwealth, and has been deeply involved in projects such as debt relief and the New African Partnership for Economic Development (NEPAD) and it has acted as mediator in several conflicts. His reelection in 2003 was generally regarded as a consolidation of civilian rule. Despite this, domestic critics have claimed Obasanjo's high international profile is a distraction from tackling Nigeria's problems at home.

Nigeria's economy has not prospered. A much-publicised anticorruption drive has had mixed results, claiming back some of Abacha's stolen millions, but it hasn't netted many high-profile officials on the make.

Nigeria's oil industry is in an even worse position. Governments have neglected the infrastructure, to the point where Nigeria was left needing to import refined fuel at a higher price than it sold its crude for, resulting in petrol shortages. Plans to remove fuel subsidies in 2004 were met with a general strike by Nigerians, who see cheap fuel as a birthright, having witnessed many of the other benefits of statehood pass them by. This sense of alienation is particularly acute in the oil-producing Delta, one of the most underdeveloped parts of the country. In 2005, the Niger Delta People's Volunteer Force put their case against marginalisation by launching guerrilla attacks on oil installations.

Presidential elections are due in 2007, and while Obasanjo is barred from standing for a third term, many of his supporters are urging a change to the constitution to allow it. This is already causing political turmoil, and huge potential damage to Nigeria's standing. Babangida is back on the scene, fancying another attempt at running the country, this time as a civilian. As Nigeria continues to lurch from crisis to crisis, whoever takes on the challenge will have a lot on their plate.

## THE CULTURE
### National Psyche

The economy lumbers on, but is a long way from keeping up with the rapidly growing populace, let alone reaching the bright potential it showed at independence. Oil has proved to be a curse on the country, with governments repeatedly pumping money straight out of the wells and into private bank accounts. In 2005, the government's anticorruption commission announced that over US$352 billion had been stolen or misused since the oil came on tap: four times the value of all western aid given to the whole of Africa in the last 40 years.

Ordinary Nigerians have been the ones to pay the price. Infrastructure has been neglected and agriculture, the mainstay of most of the population, has been largely ignored. Once a food exporter, Nigeria now imports most of its food, meaning higher prices for the majority of Nigerians living on just a few dollars a day. Healthcare is also in crisis. Nigeria is one of the few African countries where polio is still endemic,

---

**419**

If you're online, the chances are that at some point you've received a 419 email. A particularly pervasive form of spam, the email offers the recipient a cut of an implausibly huge sum of money in return for help getting it out of Nigeria. All you have to do is send your own bank details – together with a handling fee – and the money is yours. The name 419 comes from the section of the Nigerian criminal code that covers fraud – a crime rife in Nigeria. An average scammer can make around US$6000 a month from 419, targeting the greed of the victims, or *maghas* (Yoruba slang for fool). Scammers even have their own anthem – the single 'I Chop Your Dollars' was hugely popular in 2005.

Foreigners aren't the only victims of fraud. Inside Nigeria, a popular scam is to break into an empty property and then sell it on to an unsuspecting buyer – watch out for painted signs everywhere announcing 'This house is not for sale: beware 419'.

---

although to date the country seems to have avoided the worst of the AIDS pandemic.

Corruption is probably the worst problem facing Nigeria, as its corrosive effects have permeated every aspect of society. While roadside billboards plead with people to pay their taxes, federal and state budgets are constantly skimmed by dodgy officials and ordinary people have to pay cash for everything from government services to getting through police roadblocks. No country in Africa has such a vast gap between its super-rich and abject poor.

Against all this, it almost seems incredible that smiles come so readily to Nigerian faces. An international survey in 2003 announced that Nigerians were in fact the happiest people on earth. The important role that religion plays in everyday life is a major factor, along with the natural entrepreneurship of one of Africa's best-educated populations. Ill-served by repeated governments, Nigerians have had to learn to survive. As Fela Kuti sang, 'we suffer and we smile.' This resilience holds the best key to Nigeria's future.

## Population

With 140 million people already, Nigeria has a huge and expanding population. By the middle of the 21st century it's thought that as many as one in three people on the African continent will be a Nigerian.

## SPORT

Football is the only game that matters in Nigeria, and they regard themselves as virtually African footballing royalty. The country regularly produces fine players that make their way to Europe to play in the Premiership, La Liga and Serie A (notable recent players include Kanu and Obodo), and travellers should get used to being asked their opinions on the relative merits of Beckham and Ronaldinho. Unfortunately for Nigeria, their foreign-based players have a great tradition of being prima donnas, and of putting club before country. Used to good performances in successive World Cups since the mid-1990s, the country was shocked when the national side – the Super Eagles – failed to qualify for Germany 2006.

## RELIGION

Nigeria may just be the most visibly religious country in Africa, but there's a very clear divide between the Christian south and the Muslim north.

In the south, everything stops on a Sunday, as the population goes to church en masse. The more traditional churches imported during colonial rule are now being upstaged by an explosion of evangelism. You'll constantly see them publicised on huge billboards, usually announcing 'miracle crusades' and faith healing. Large gatherings can attract tens of thousands of worshippers, but there's tight – and not always particularly faithful – competition between the churches for new souls. Older Nigerian faiths, such as those involving the rich pantheon of Yoruba gods, are also increasingly threatened, but some traditions have been carried over – look out for adverts for schnapps, used for libations at prayers: 'Don't offend your ancestors with fakes: insist on the Original Prayer Drink', reads one.

This 'good time' religion collides hard and fast with the mosques and minarets of the north. Cities such as Kano have long pedigrees as centres of Islamic learning, but they haven't been immune to the politicisation sweeping the Islamic world. Since the return to democracy in 1999, many northern states have enacted laws based on Islamic Sharia law. Alcohol bans have been enforced (with mixed success) and education is increasingly segregated. While Nigerian Muslims are tolerant and welcoming to foreign visitors, relations with Christians in the north are under increasing strain. The introduction of Sharia law, and the issue of its application to non-Muslims is a political tinderbox, and one that has ignited with worrying frequency into communal violence. Sharia law has also brought international attention to Nigeria, particularly over the case of Amina Lawal in 2002, who was sentenced to death by stoning for adultery, despite her lover being acquitted. The sentence was eventually dropped after worldwide condemnation.

## ARTS

Nigeria's vast and rich art heritage is un-equalled anywhere in West Africa.

## Literature

Nigeria seems to have as many writers as the rest of the continent combined. Chinua Achebe is probably Nigeria's (and Africa's) most famous author, although he faces strong competition from Amos Tutuola, Nobel laureate Wole Soyinka and Booker Prize win-ner Ben Okri. For details of these writers, see p47. Nigeria also produced Africa's first major female novelist, Flora Nwapa.

More recently, a new generation of young Nigerian writers have been claiming a seat at the literary table. Internationally acclaimed novels by Chimamanda Ngozi Adichie (*Purple Hibiscus*), Helen Oyeyemi (*The Icarus Girl*) and Helon Habila (*Waiting for an Angel*) have demonstrated that Nige-rian literature is in rude health. Lagos has a thriving publishing scene, and is a great place to pick up African novels.

## Music

Some of Africa's best-known singers come from Nigeria. Foremost among them are the late Fela Kuti and King Sunny Ade. Along with Ebenezer Obey, Sunny Ade is the king of *juju* (from the Yoruba word for dance), one of Nigeria's most popular styles. Another famed Nigerian singer is Chief Stephen Osita Osadebe, a proponent of the Igbo-favoured highlife style. Sonny Okusun is a popular master of many styles, but currently records sermons as a pastor rather than a musician.

Massively popular in Lagos and through-out Yoruba-land is *fuji*, incorporating elements from *juju*, talking drums and praise singing. Sikiru 'Barrister' Ayinde and Ayinlu Kollington are *fuji*'s prime movers (for more details, see p58).

## Cinema

Hidden from the eyes of most of the world, Nigeria has the third-biggest film industry on the planet, after the USA and India. With typical local wit it is dubbed 'Nollywood',

### FELA KUTI – KING OF AFROBEAT

Fela Kuti, born in 1938 in Abeokuta, remains one of Africa's most famous musicians. Immensely popular in Nigeria, Fela was also highly vocal politically. When he travelled to Los Angeles in 1964, Fela met Malcolm X and the Black Panthers, who stirred black consciousness in him; on the musical front, James Brown was a huge influence. Returning to Nigeria, Fela mixed Brown's soul grooves with the many intricacies of Nigerian music to create Afrobeat.

During the 1970s, he formed the Kalakuta Republic, a commune for playing music. Government forces burnt it down in 1977, an action which resulted in the death of Fela's mother. Fela went into exile in Ghana during the late 1970s, but when he returned to Nigeria he continued to play music with lyrics critical of the regime. His views brought him repeated political trouble – briefly jailed on trumped-up currency-smuggling charges in 1985, he was later falsely accused of killing a man. Fela avoided the authorities throughout the 1990s and retired to a quiet life of performing twice a week at The Shrine, his Lagos nightclub. When he died of AIDS in 1997, his funeral prompted one of Lagos' greatest go-slows. His musician son, Femi Kuti, has stepped out from Fela's shadow and regularly tours internationally with his band Positive Force, pushing an even funkier line in Afrobeat than his father (to check them out at the new Shrine, see p636).

and turns out anything from 400 to 800 films a year. As cinemas are a rarity in Nigeria, films are shot to video and sold at shops and market stalls. They're great fun and hugely popular.

Nollywood's heartland is Surelere in Lagos. Movies are shot quickly and without fuss – it can take just two months to go from script to marketplace, with budgets as low as US$15,000. Plots are simple and melodramatic – spurned lovers, criminals and long-lost relatives are all staples – while fans buy magazines in the thousands to follow the (often no less dramatic) lives of the stars.

## Sculpture

Nigeria boasts some of the earliest and most acclaimed sculpture in Africa. The Jos Plateau's Nok Terracottas, featuring human figures 120cm tall and dating back over 2500 years, are the oldest sub-Saharan sculptures known. More famous still are the 16th-century Benin Brasses, ceremonial figures and masks produced for the court of the Benin Kingdom using the lost wax method, which were famously looted by the British army in 1897; those not in Lagos' National Museum are in the British Museum or Berlin.

Many tribal groups still produce fine sculptures and masks, most notably the wood carvings of the Yoruba. Most represent the gods of the Yoruba pantheon and its numerous cults, and are often used in rites of passage ceremonies; Oshogbo (p641) is good for Yoruba art. Masks are also common among the Igbo and Ekoi, and the northeastern Mumuye are renowned for their cubistlike figure carvings of ancestors.

## ENVIRONMENT

Nigeria occupies 15% of West Africa, but contains half of its people. In the north, the Sahel gives way to savanna and low hills, rising to a plateau in the centre of the country. From the west, the country is bisected by the Niger, Africa's third-longest river, which enters the Atlantic through a delta fringed with lagoons and swamps. Nigeria's second river is the Benue, which flows west from Cameroon and joins the Niger. Shared with Cameroon are Nigeria's mountains, the Adamawa Massif. Forest forms a thick line along the southern coast, inland from the delta.

Nigeria has extraordinary biological diversity, but the country's rapidly expanding population has put the environment under extreme pressure. An underfunded National Parks service does exist, but in practice very little land in Nigeria is protected. Deforestation is one of the largest problems, with Nigeria having logged around 95% of its original forests since independence. Where original forest exists, the local bush meat trade threatens mammal species further.

In the Delta, the oil industry has created a host of problems to match the wealth it generates. Oil spills are commonplace, with few ever cleaned up adequately. The local fishing industry, a mainstay of the delta economy, has suffered grievously. Air pollution caused by gas flaring (the burning of excess fuel during extraction) is also a serious problem, and continues unabated, despite being declared illegal in 1984.

## Wildlife

Despite the problems facing the Nigerian environment, it is possible to see wildlife in the country. **Yankari National Park** (p655) is the best-known area. It's home to elephants, buffaloes, waterbucks and several antelope species. The bird-watching is superb, but the fate of some mammal species, such as lions, is unknown. In the southeast, primates are well-represented in the forested **Cross River National Park** (p650). Chimpanzees, drills and guenons exist here in uncertain numbers, as do tiny populations of western lowland gorillas and forest elephants. **Gashaka-Gumti National Park** (p655) is the largest national park in Nigeria. It remains largely unsurveyed, but is very ecologically diverse and contains both savanna and forest species.

Nigeria's other national parks are largely devoid of game. Highlights for bird-watchers include Kamuku Wildlife Reserve, west of Kaduna, and the Hadejia-Nguru Wetlands near Nguru, about 200km northeast of Kano.

Two organisations based in and around Calabar, **Cercopan** (www.cercopan.org) and **Pandrillus** ( ☎ 234310; drill@infoweb.abs.net), are carrying out pioneering work in environmental education and primate rescue (see p647).

## FOOD & DRINK

Nigerians like their food – known as 'chop' – hot and starchy. Classic dishes are based on a fiery pepper stew or soup, made with meat and accompanied by pounded yam, cassava or manioc (*gari*). The Yoruba dish *isiewu*, or goat's head soup, is the closest thing to a national dish, while cow leg soup is also common on menus. Less spicy is *egusi*, made with meat, chopped greens and smoked fish. Cutlery isn't generally used – the yam or cassava is used to soak up the juices of the stew. As in most of Africa, you only eat with your right hand.

Another dish you'll eat a lot of is *jollof* – peppery rice with chicken. In the south, palm-nut soup – a thick stew made with meat, chilli, tomatoes, onions and palm-nut oil – is popular, along with groundnut soup, okra stew and, in the west, *ikokore*, a main course made with ground yams and various types of fish. Most dishes include meat, so vegetarians can have a hard time in Nigeria.

Chophouses serve food throughout the day, usually just cooking up one or two dishes and announcing when they're ready to eat by placing a sign saying 'food is ready' outside the door – look for these signs when you're hungry. Most hotels can rustle up 'tea bread eggs' for breakfast.

Street food is everywhere. *Moin-moin* are steamed bean cakes, while *suya* are simple kebabs served with a sprinkling of hot *pepe* spice. Also on offer are fried yam chips, fried plantains, meat pies, *akara* (a puffy deep-fried cake made with black-eyed peas and eaten with chilli dip), *kulikuli* (small deep-fried balls made of peanut paste), and lots of fresh fruit. Nigeria also has a few fast food chains, such as Mr Biggs, serving *jollof* and the like – they're worth noting for their clean toilets and air-con as much as for their food.

Nigerians drink a lot of beer. Star is the most popular but, as in much of West Africa, Guinness is drunk in vast quantities. In the north, Sharia law means that alcohol is often not available. Mineral water is widely available, although water is more commonly sold in sealed plastic bags – half a litre for N5. Labelled 'pure water', its provenance is not always guaranteed, so drink with care.

# LAGOS

☎ 01 / pop 16 million

Tell people that you're going to Lagos, and the reaction is quite likely to be one of concerned incredulity: 'You're going *where*?' The city carries an unenviable reputation before

it – crowded, polluted and dangerous; chaos theory made flesh and concrete. Exactly the kind of place you'd make a big detour to avoid. While all these problems do exist to lesser or greater extents, Lagos is also vibrant and exciting, with a good arts scene, great bars and restaurants, and all the raw energy of Nigeria distilled down into one city.

The city takes its name from the Portuguese word for lagoon. From the 16th century it was an important trading port between the Europeans and local Yorubas, before being subsumed into the Benin Kingdom. In 1861 the port became a British colony, later to become capital of the Nigerian Protectorate and, upon independence, of the new Nigerian nation. It lost the title to Abuja in 1991, but remains the economic and cultural powerhouse of the country, and the financial capital of West Africa itself.

Lagos' infrastructure has never kept pace with its growth. The modern city is an explosion of raised expressways hanging over mobbed streets of people and traffic. The electricity supply and garbage collection are hugely inadequate, and whole districts flood during the rainy season. Slums sit cheek by jowl with the richest addresses in Africa. The sprawl continues to grow irresistibly: already the biggest city in Africa, the UN estimate that by 2025 it will be the world's largest, with a mind-boggling 24 million people.

Lagos isn't going to be to everyone's taste, but its inhabitants frequently say they couldn't live anywhere else and if you're up for an urban adventure you'll begin to understand why. Unruly, exciting and compelling, Lagos is a true megacity, and the face of modern Africa as much as any picture postcard national park. Jump right in.

## ORIENTATION

Lagos is a series of islands, with Lagos Island the commercial heart of the city. The major road is Broad St, which passes Tinubu Sq, a major intersection near the centre of the island, and ends at Tafawa Balewa Sq. North of this is the market district, a warren of packed streets and shops. Running roughly parallel with Broad St is Marina St, which overlooks the harbour and is home to numerous large commercial establishments. The entire island is encircled by Ring Rd.

The island of Ikoyi to the east has now merged with Lagos Island; it's a mainly

NIGERIA

upscale residential area. Between the two areas is Obalende, with a useful motor park. On Ikoyi, the wide Kingsway Rd leads to the old Ikoyi Hotel. The liveliest street is Awolowo Rd, where there are many restaurants.

Most of the embassies and big houses are on Victoria Island (VI) to the southeast of Lagos Island – the most expensive part of Lagos. The towering 1004 Apartments building on the north of VI is a useful landmark. Ahmadu Bello Way skirts the south of VI, along sandy Bar Beach. VI is linked to Ikoyi by Falomo Bridge and to Lagos Island by Independence Bridge.

Most of the city's residential quarters are on the mainland, in the direction of the airport, and are connected to Lagos Island by three bridges. From east to west they are 3rd Axial Bridge, Carter Bridge and Eko Bridge. Heading north, Murtala Mohammed Way bisects the lively Yaba and Surulere districts. Two major expressways, Agege Motor Rd (leading to the airports) and Ikorodu Rd, intersect in Yaba. The latter passes through the major transport terminal of Ojota Motor Park in Ikeja. Ikorodu Rd eventually intersects with the Lagos–Ibadan Expressway, which leads to all points north.

## Maps

*Lagos Street Map* (West African Books) is the best available, followed by the *Satod Street Guide to Lagos*. Both cost around N600 in bookshops.

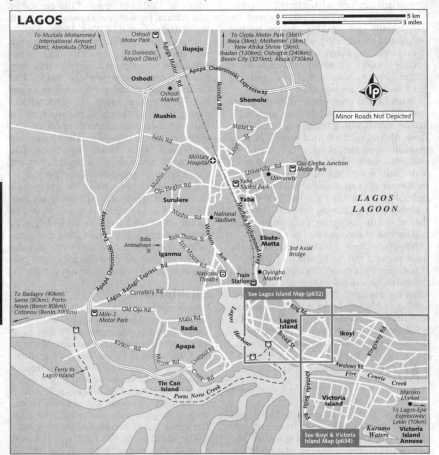

## INFORMATION

If you're spending any serious time in Lagos, pick up a copy of *Lagos Easy Access* by the American Women's Club of Lagos (N2500), which is a great guide, albeit aimed primarily at expats.

### Bookshops

Lagos has Nigeria's best bookshops by a country mile.

**Bookworm** (Map p634; Eko Hotel Shopping Complex, Ajose Adeogun St, VI)

**Glendora Bookshop** (Map p634; Eko Hotel, VI) Also good for international newspapers and magazines.

**Jazz Hole** (Map p634; Awolowo Rd, Ikoyi) Also good for Nigerian music.

### Cultural Centres

**British Council** (Map p634; ☎ 269 2188, 269 2192; 11 Kingsway Rd, Ikoyi; ☸ 9am-6pm) Day membership costs N500. Available are a library, magazines, free Internet access and café.

**Centre Culturel Français** (Map p634; ☎ 269 2365; Kingsway Rd; ☸ 10am-7pm) This library and café opposite the Ikoyi Hotel also has live music several nights a week.

**Goethe Institut** (Map p634; ☎ 261 0717; Maroko Rd, VI; ☸ 10am-5pm) Has regular art exhibitions.

### Internet Access

Internet places mushroom and then close on a weekly basis, usually charging N100 per hour. You're never likely to be far from one, but the following are three of the best:

**Cybercafé** (Map p634; Awolowo Rd, Ikoyi) Opposite the YMCA.

**Internet Planet** (Map p634; Ozumba Mbadiwe Rd, VI) In Mr Biggs Building.

**Mega Plaza Internet** (Map p634; Mega Plaza, Idowu Martin St, VI) On the top floor.

### Medical Services

While the following places are recommended, if you do have a medical problem, consider contacting your diplomatic representatives for a list of reputable medical practitioners.

**Chyzob Pharmacy** (Map p634; ☎ 269 4545; Awolowo Rd; ☸ 8am-8pm Mon-Sat)

**Medicines Plus** (Map p634; Mega Plaza, Idowu Martin St, VI; ☸ 10am-9pm Mon-Sat, 1-9pm Sun)

**St Francis Clinic** ( ☎ 269 2305; Keffi St, Ikoyi) Recommended general practitioners.

**St Nicholas Hospital** (Map p632; ☎ 263 1739; 57 Campbell St, Lagos Island) Has a 24hr emergency clinic.

### Money

Travellers should note that there is no foreign exchange at the airport, and that Lagos' banks are as useless as anywhere in Nigeria for changing money. Always check if your hotel will change money, otherwise the following are convenient moneychangers:

**Eko Hotel** (Map p634; Adetokumbo Ademola St, VI) Find Hausa moneychangers at the craft shops by the gatehouse.

**Ikoyi Hotel** (Map p634; Kingsway Rd, Ikoyi) There's a *bureau de change* office and Hausa moneychangers outside the (closed) hotel.

### Post

**GPO** Ikoyi (Map p634; Bourdillon Rd); VI (Map p634; Adeola Odeku St); Lagos Island (Map p632; Marina St; ☸ Mon-Fri)

### Travel Agencies

There are travel agencies on the southern side of Tafawa Balewa Sq on Lagos Island. Other good agencies include the following:

**Bitts Travel & Tours** (Map p634; ☎ 269 6095; Falomo Shopping Centre, Awolowo Rd, Ikoyi)

**Dolphin Travel & Tours** (Map p634; ☎ 262 4927; Federal Palace Hotel, Ahmadu Bello Rd, VI)

## DANGERS & ANNOYANCES

Contrary to popular perception, violent crime has decreased in Lagos in recent years. Most crime against foreigners targets expats in expensive cars, and travellers are unlikely to encounter any serious problems. That said, it always pays to take sensible precautions. Never carry any more money than is necessary and avoid flaunting valuables. Avoid walking at night where possible, particularly around hotels and restaurants frequented by foreigners, including on VI. Crowded areas carry a risk of pickpocketing. Listen out for the term Area Boy, Lagosian for a petty criminal or gang member, sometimes found holding up traffic or intimidating passengers or drivers in motor parks. The wide spaces under flyovers are common Area Boy hangouts, so give these a wide berth.

Rather than crime, the worst problem in Lagos is actually the traffic – the insane jams and drivers who treat the roads like a war zone. Take special care on the backs of *okadas* (motorcycle taxis; see p637).

## SIGHTS & ACTIVITIES

Look out in Lagos Island, along Kakawa and Odunfa Sts, for examples of old Brazilian architecture – distinctive houses built

**NIGERIA**

## LAGOS ISLAND

See Ikoyi & Victoria Island Map (p634)

**SIGHTS & ACTIVITIES**
Balogun Market.................7 A2
Catholic Church.................8 B3
Central Mosque.................9 B2
Isale Eko Market.................10 B1
Jankara Market.................11 B2
National Museum.................12 C4
St John's Church.................13 B2
Sandgrouse Market.................14 C3

**SLEEPING**
Ritz Hotel.................15 D4
Wayfarers Hotel.................16 B3
Zeina Hotel.................17 B2

**EATING**
Ghana High Buka.................18 D4
Mr Bigg's.................19 B3

**ENTERTAINMENT**
Muson.................20 C4

**TRANSPORT**
Ebute Ero Motor Park.................21 A1
Lufthansa.................22 A2
Obalende Motor Park.................23 D4

**INFORMATION**
British High Commission
(Consular Section).................1 A2
Ghanaian High Commission.2 D4
GPO.................3 B3
Nitel.................4 B3
Police Headquarters.................5 D4
St Nicholas Hospital.................6 C3

by former slaves and descendants who returned from Brazil. Sadly most are in need of rescue and renovation.

## National Museum

The **museum** (Map p632; Awolowo Rd; admission N100; 🕙 9am-5pm) is definitely worth seeing, but note no cameras are allowed. The stars are the brasses from Benin City, which get their own gallery. The Nok Terracottas are well represented. Another gallery dedicated to traditional symbols of power contains carved ivory and a royal host of crowns. A less fortunate symbol of power is the bullet-riddled car in which Murtala Mohammed was assassinated in 1976. The museum has a small crafts village with handicrafts for sale at fixed prices; you might also see a demonstration of *adire* – cloth-making from Abeokuta.

The museum is 150m southeast of Tafawa Balewa Sq, a huge arena adorned by statues of horses. In the square is Remembrance Arcade, with memorials to Nigeria's dead from two world wars and the Biafran conflict.

## Markets

On Lagos Island the many markets are by far the best attractions, but consider hiring a guide to show you around. They're safe enough to get lost in during the day but be circumspect with your camera, as photography isn't usually appreciated. The main market area is north of Broad St, and is divided into several distinct districts.

**Jankara Market** (Map p632; off Adeyinka Oyekan Ave) is a delight, with its closely packed stalls selling fabric and a witches' brew of juju ingredients. **Isale Eko Market** (Map p632; off Adeniji Adele Rd) has plenty of food and household goods on offer. The rambling maze of **Balogun Market** (Map p632; off Breadfruit St) is excellent for clothes and fabric from across West Africa. Finally, **Sandgrouse Market** (Map p632; off Lewis St) slightly further east, is the place for interesting food, much of it sold live.

On VI, **Bar Beach Market** (Map p634; off Ahmadu Bello Way) has fresh fish and a few handicrafts to attract the expats. Of course, thanks to the go-slow, every road in Lagos becomes an impromptu market, with hawkers making offerings to your vehicle as you wait in the stalled traffic.

## Beaches
You'll need to travel slightly outside Lagos to reach the best beaches. **Tarkwa Beach** is popular, as there's no undertow and it's safe for swimming. There are sun lounges and umbrellas, and a few stalls selling *suya* and chop. It's accessible by launch from along Walter Carrington Crescent in VI. The price is negotiable, with N800 per person (return) the maximum. Make arrangements to be picked back up in the afternoon.

The new favourite with fashionable Lagosians is **Eleko Beach**, a big 60km trip east of the city. You can rent a beach hut for the day here, and get someone to make a barbeque for you. There's also a small market selling interesting art. You'll need to hire a drop taxi to get there.

## SLEEPING
Lagos has some of the best hotels in Nigeria – and some of the worst. There's very little in the midrange bracket. Hotels either tend to be top of the range, or at the grubbier end of the budget spectrum. There is no real budget accommodation on Victoria Island.

### Budget
**Ritz Hotel** (Map p632; ☎ 263 0481; King George V Rd; r with/without air-con N2300/1400; ✗ ) The name's a bit of a misnomer, but this hotel is a reasonably decent budget option. Rooms are fine in a grubby 'by the hour' sort of way, but they're secure and management is friendly.

**YMCA** (Map p634; ☎ 773 3599; 77 Awolowo Rd; dm N500, r N1700-2700; ✗ P ) Very simple fare for men only, the YMCA is a busy hostel and is often full with other West Africans. It's decent, if not inspirational. Dorms have four beds and room prices drop by N200 after the first night; all share bathroom facilities.

**Zeina Hotel** (Map p632; ☎ 263 3254; 11 Smith St; r N2500; ✗ ) This hotel is tucked away in the heart of Ita Faji Market. A little battered, rooms are still comfy enough for a few nights. There's no hotel sign – look for the number 11 on the unassuming yellow door.

**Wayfarers Hotel** (Map p632; ☎ 263 0113; 52 Campbell St; s/d N2500/3000; ✗ ) Rooms here are good-sized and in fairly decent order. The reception doubles as a restaurant/bar and there are plenty of chophouses on the street outside. Rooms on the main road are noisy, but where in Lagos isn't?

### Midrange
**Bogobiri House** (Map p634; ☎ 270 7406; www.bogobirilagos.com; 9 Maitama Sule St, Ikoyi; s/d incl breakfast N18,000/23,100; ✗ ▨ ) A charming boutique hotel owned by the Nimbus Art Gallery opposite, Bogobiri House is an exhibition in itself. Beautifully decorated with paintings and sculptures by local artists, its side street location provides a calm escape from the Lagos buzz. There are just ten rooms, each exceedingly comfortable and more salon than sleeping place. Worth the budgetary blowout.

**Hotel Victoria Palace** (Map p634; ☎ 262 5901; hotelvp@alphalinkserve.com; 1623 Sake Jojo St; s/d N9660/12,075; P ✗ ) A genuine midrange hotel on VI is a rarity indeed, and luckily this place is good value. Rooms are generous and comfy, and there's a great Indian restaurant attached.

**Victoria Lodge** (Map p634; ☎ 262 0885; 5 Ologun Agbaje St; s/d N10,350/11,500; ✗ ▨ P ▨ ) A small and low hotel, with huge rooms – the feeling of space is added to by the acres of white tiles. A quiet, tidy option.

**Michael's** (Map p634; ☎ 461 6802; michael@hyperia.com; Plot 411 Adetokumbo Ademola St; r incl breakfast N13,800-17,250; ✗ P ▨ ) The pleasant compact rooms in this small guesthouse cluster around a small pool, overlooked by a mural of generously proportioned mermaids. It's a neat little choice.

### Top End
**B-Jays Hotel** (Map p634; ☎ 262 2902; bjayshotel24@yahoo.com; 24 Samuel Manuwa St; r from N32,500; ✗ ▨ P ) A plush guesthouse popular with expats,

# IKOYI & VICTORIA ISLAND

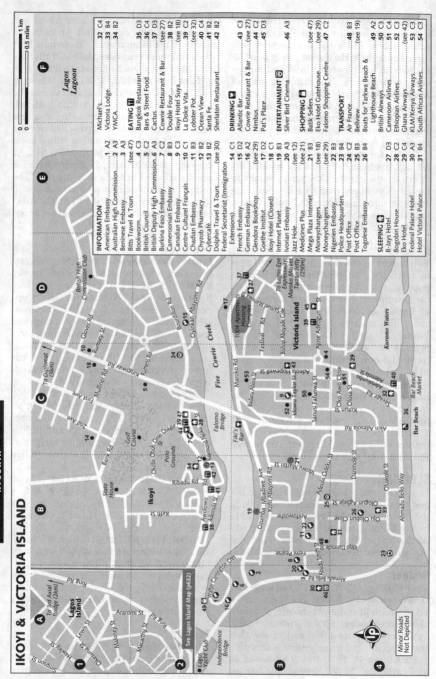

**INFORMATION**

| | |
|---|---|
| American Embassy | 1 A2 |
| Australian High Commission | 2 A3 |
| Beninese Embassy | 3 A3 |
| Bitts Travel & Tours | (see 47) |
| Bookworm | 4 C3 |
| British Council | 5 C2 |
| British Deputy High Commission | 6 A3 |
| Burkina Faso Embassy | 7 C2 |
| Cameroonian Embassy | 8 B3 |
| Canadian Embassy | 9 C3 |
| Centre Culturel Français | 10 C1 |
| Chadian Embassy | 11 B3 |
| Chyzob Pharmacy | 12 B2 |
| Cybercafé | 13 B2 |
| Dolphin Travel & Tours | (see 30) |
| Federal Secretariat (Immigration Extensions) | 14 C1 |
| French Embassy | 15 D2 |
| German Embassy | 16 A2 |
| Glendora Bookshop | (see 29) |
| Goethe Institut | 17 D2 |
| Ikoyi Hotel (Closed) | 18 C1 |
| Internet Planet | 19 B3 |
| Iranian Embassy | 20 A3 |
| Jazz Hole | (see 12) |
| Medicines Plus | (see 21) |
| Mega Plaza Internet | 21 B3 |
| Moneychangers | (see 18) |
| Moneychangers | (see 29) |
| Nigerien Embassy | 22 B3 |
| Police Headquarters | 23 B4 |
| Post Office | 24 C2 |
| Post Office | 25 B3 |
| Togolese Embassy | 26 B4 |

**SLEEPING**

| | |
|---|---|
| B-Jays Hotel | 27 D3 |
| Bogobiri House | 28 C2 |
| Eko Hotel | 29 C4 |
| Federal Palace Hotel | 30 A3 |
| Hotel Victoria Palace | 31 B4 |

| | |
|---|---|
| Michael's | 32 C4 |
| Victoria Lodge | 33 B4 |
| YMCA | 34 B2 |

**EATING**

| | |
|---|---|
| Bangkok Restaurant | 35 D3 |
| Bars & Street Food | 36 C4 |
| Cactus | 37 D3 |
| Cowrie Restaurant & Bar | (see 27) |
| Double Four | 38 B2 |
| Ikoyi Hotel Suya | (see 18) |
| La Dolce Vita | 39 C3 |
| Lobster Pot | (see 32) |
| Ocean View | 40 C4 |
| Santa Fe | 41 B2 |
| Sheraton Restaurant | 42 B2 |

**DRINKING**

| | |
|---|---|
| Atlantic Bar | 43 C3 |
| Cowrie Restaurant & Bar | (see 27) |
| Nimbus | 44 C2 |
| Pat's Place | 45 D3 |

**ENTERTAINMENT**

| | |
|---|---|
| Silver Bird Cinema | 46 A3 |

**SHOPPING**

| | |
|---|---|
| Batik Sellers | (see 47) |
| Eko Hotel Gatehouse | (see 29) |
| Falomo Shopping Centre | 47 C2 |

**TRANSPORT**

| | |
|---|---|
| Air France | 48 B3 |
| Bellview | (see 19) |
| Boats for Tarkwa Beach & Lighthouse Beach | 49 A2 |
| British Airways | 50 C3 |
| Cameroon Airlines | 51 C4 |
| Ethiopian Airlines | 52 C3 |
| Ghana Airways | (see 42) |
| KLM/Kenya Airways | 53 C3 |
| South African Airlines | 54 B4 |

**NIGERIA**

0 — 1 km
0 — 0.5 miles

*Lagos Lagoon*

See Lagos Island Map (p632)

Minor Roads
Not Depicted

this place was undergoing a refit when we visited. Rooms already have flat-screen TV and Internet connections, with further improvements planned. There's a delightful restaurant and a very stylish bar.

**Eko Hotel** (Map p634; ☎ 261 5118; reservation@ ekohotels.com; Adetokumbo Ademola St; lodge US$120-150, r with/without seaview US$340/300; 🏊 🖥 📶 🍴) Lagos' premier international business hotel, the Eko is a luxurious place indeed. Rooms are large and very well appointed, plus there's the expected complement of shops, restaurants, sports facilities and poolside bars.

# EATING

Many of the better restaurants are strung out along Awolowo Rd.

There are plenty of chophouses along Campbell St and Broad St on Lagos Island.

## European

**La Dolce Vita** (Map p634; Awolowo Rd; mains from N1200; 🕙 11am-11pm) It's no surprise to find pasta and pizza on the menu in a place like this, with the setting evoking an old Italian bistro. Wash down well-cooked and appetising food with a good drop of red.

**Cactus** (Map p634; Maroko Rd; mains from N1200; 🕙 8am-10pm) This new place labels itself primarily as a patisserie, and has cakes and some wonderful breads, but it also serves up proper meals throughout the day. Breakfasts of pancakes or bacon are good, and the club sandwiches with salad and chips are simply huge – excellent value at N1500.

**Ocean View** (Map p634; Adetokumbo Ademola St; mains from N1200 🕙 11am-11pm) Almost on Bar Beach – the name is a bit of a misnomer really – this airy restaurant has lots of glass and a long bar kept cool under delicious aircon. The menu offers a mix of international dishes; steaks are good from N2000.

**Lobster Pot** (Map p634; Adetokumbo Ademola St; seafood from N2000; 🕙 8am-11pm) Next to Michael's Guesthouse, the Lobster Pot is the place to come for seafood. There's a wide selection, with the house speciality – lobster of course – worth a splurge at N3000.

**Santa Fe** (Map p634; Awolowo Rd; mains from N1600; 🕙 12-5pm & 6pm-11pm) A splurge place by Ikoyi standards, Santa Fe sells Tex-Mex food and has décor that almost has you expecting a Nigerian John Wayne to walk in and slam his gun on the bar. The live band, sadly, doesn't play mariachi music.

**Cowrie Restaurant & Bar** (Map p634; Samuel Manuwa St; dishes from N1800; 🕙 6.30am-10pm) Part of B-Jays Hotel, the Cowrie is stylishly decorated, and has a mix of Italian and Nigerian dishes, with a few steaks and the like thrown in for good measure. The salads are particularly good.

## African

**Ghana High Buka** (Map p632; King George V Rd; mains from N300; 🕙 10am-9.30pm) Just outside the Ghanaian High Commission, this 'food-is-ready' place serves up great Nigerian dishes, such as *egusi* and *iwesu*, and as much pounded starch as you can eat. It's always busy and you'll likely come back for more.

**Ikoyi Hotel suya** (Map p634; Ikoyi Hotel, Kingsway Rd; suya from N100; 🕙 10am-10pm) Why make the effort to get to this hotel just for *suya*? Well, Lagosians do, as it's the best in town and offers not just beef and goat, but chicken, liver and kidney, plus some fiery *pepe* to spice it up.

**Double Four** (Map p634; Awolowo Rd; mains from N700; 🕙 11am-11pm) Offering mainly Lebanese dishes, the menu at Double Four tries to throw everything into the mix – Nigerian, Continental, Indian – so if you're unsure where to dine, this might be the place. It seems to work, as the place is always packed.

## Asian

**Sherlaton Restaurant** (Map p634; Awolowo Rd; mains from N600; 🕙 12-3pm, 7-10pm) Vegetarians suffer in Nigeria, but this Indian restaurant comes to the rescue. With tasty and filling portions at good prices, the Sherlaton is generally considered to be the city's best curry option.

**Bangkok Restaurant** (Muri Okunola St; mains from N1100; 🕙 11am-11pm) With the best Thai food in Lagos, the Bangkok is a treat. The cooks and waitresses are all Thai, and offer you a broad menu of fragrantly spiced dishes. Portions are very generous, and if you can't finish your meal, they're used to sending people home with a doggie bag.

# DRINKING

**Pat's Place** (Map p634; Ajose Adeogun St; 🕙 10am-late) A Lagos institution, this is an expat haunt, decorated with rugby shirts and serving up cold beer and Guinness with steak and kidney pie and other tastes of home, with the only visible Nigerians being the barmaids. The sort of place you'll either love or hate.

**Nimbus** (Map p634; Maitama Sule St; 🕙 8am-11pm) Part of the Nimbus art gallery, and

NIGERIA

cultivating the same slightly Bohemian air, this is a lovely place for a drink – mellow in the day and happening at night. At weekends there's usually live music, so there's a cover charge of around N1000 to get in.

**Cowrie Restaurant & Bar** (Map p634; Samuel Manuwa St; ☿ 8am-11pm) Immaculately put together, the bar at B-Jays hotel is a classy place for a drink. It's very laid back, with squashy sofas and low lighting, all the better for sampling the good array of whiskies. Only the terrace on the busy main road feels a bit out of place.

**Atlantic Bar** (Map p634; Adeola Hopewell St; ☿ 12pm-late) Head here if you want to hang with the fashionable Lagos kids. There's great music, a few bar snacks and live bands play at weekends. It's very cool.

The shacks along Bar Beach serve up cold beer throughout the day and into the small hours, with *suya* and other snacks on hand. They're authentically down at heel and enjoy a refreshing sea breeze, but keep to the well-lit areas after dark and don't carry valuables with you.

It's difficult to pick out bars on Lagos Island – every street has one or two local places serving drinks from early morning to late at night, and music blasting out – so follow your ears and dive right in.

## ENTERTAINMENT
### Nightclubs

The happening nightlife is on the mainland in Ikeja and Yaba, to the north of Lagos Island. There's usually a mix of live music and DJ's, all blasting out the best Nigerian tunes. Don't even think of turning up before 11pm.

**New Afrika Shrine** (Pepple St, Ikeja; admission N500, ☿ Thu-Sun) The spiritual home of Afrobeat, Fela Kuti's original Shrine was burned down, but this replacement is run by his son Femi, who plays on Fridays and Sundays when he's in town (cover charge N100). It's a huge shed, but the music blows the roof off (see p627 for more on the Kuti family).

**Motherlan'** (Opebi Rd; Ikeja, admission N1000; ☿ Thu-Sun) This place is owned by Lagbaja (see p64), who mixes groovy jazz with African drums, and is always hidden under a traditional Yoruba mask (the name simultaneously means anybody and nobody). Lagbaja plays the last Friday of the month (cover charge N1500). Motherlan' also hosts regular comedy nights, but the mix of Pidgin English and Yoruba slang can be hard to follow.

## Cinemas

**Silver Bird Cinema** (Map p634; Galleria Building, Ahmadu Bello Rd, VI; N750) For Hollywood, rather than Nollywood, blockbusters.

## Theatre

**Muson** (Map p632; Musical Society of Nigeria; ☎ 264 6670; Awolowo Rd, Ikoyi) Opposite the museum, Muson puts on regular plays and classical music concerts – call for details.

## SHOPPING

There are some good crafts on offer at the **Eko Hotel Gatehouse** (Map p634; Adetokumbo Ademola, VI), including carvings, calabashes and some unfortunate animals' skins. For batiks, Njoku St on the western side of Falomo Shopping Centre in Ikoyi is good. They're sold on the street and the selection is extensive.

The **National Museum** (Awolowo Rd) has a nonprofit crafts centre with batiks, calabashes, woodcarvings and textiles at fixed prices.

**Jankara Market** (Map p632; off Adeyinka Oyekan Ave) is the largest market in Lagos. You'll find tiedyed and indigo cloth, trade beads, jewellery and pottery. There is also a juju market here, where you can buy various medicines.

If you're going to the Lekki Conservation Centre (opposite), you should also check out the excellent handicrafts market there, which probably has the best selection in and around Lagos.

## GETTING THERE & AWAY
### Air

Murtala Mohammed International Airport is the main gateway to Nigeria. It has a scary reputation, but security has been greatly improved in the last few years. The airport is roughly 10km north of Lagos Island. For international connections see p669.

Domestic flights depart from a separate terminal next door. Tickets are bought on departure. Flights to Abuja depart virtually hourly (N9000, one hour); most domestic airlines operate this route. Every other major city in Nigeria is also connected to Lagos. Flights include Kano (N14,000, 90 minutes), Calabar (N12,000, one hour), Port Harcourt (N9000, one hour), Kaduna (N11,000, one hour) and Jos (N10,000, one hour).

It's worth calling the information desk to check on schedules before travelling. For details of airlines operating out of Lagos, see above.

## Minibus & Bush Taxi

Unsurprisingly, Lagos' motor parks are pictures of anarchy. Ojota Motor Park (with Ojota New Motor Park next door) on Ikorodu Rd is the city's main transport hub. Minibuses and bush taxis leave to just about everywhere in the country from here, but you'll have to ask repeatedly to find the vehicle you want – it's a crazy place. Sample fares are Benin City (N800, four hours), Ibadan (N250, 90 minutes), Oshogbo (N450, three hours) and Abuja (N1600, 10 hours).

**Mile 2 Motor Park** (Map p630) serves destinations east of Lagos, including the Benin border at Seme (N250, 90 minutes). You'll also find a few minibuses going as far north as Ibadan from here.

Arriving in Lagos can be more complicated as, depending on your point of departure, you'll be dropped at various motor parks, but probably not Ojota itself. **Oshodi** (Map p630), **Yaba** (Map p630) and **Oju Elegba** (Map p630) motor parks are the likeliest candidates – minibuses run from these to more central points, such as **Obalende Motor Park** (Map p632) on Lagos Island.

## GETTING AROUND

Might is right on the roads of Lagos, and driving is very much a contact sport. That's when it's moving: traffic jams, or go-slows, are an intrinsic part of travel in the city. Go-slows are worst at rush hours, or when you're trying to reach an important appointment.

### To/From the Airport

A taxi from the airport to Lagos Island or VI should cost around N3000 – allow an hour for the journey. Airport taxis are licensed, so ask to see the driver's ID if necessary. Alternatively, most hotels can arrange to meet you on arrival for a premium. Note that there is nowhere to change money at the airport, although you'll be approached by moneychangers. It's common practice to sit in your car and count out the naira before handing over your cash – a very Nigerian introduction to the country, it's not as bad as it sounds.

There are no airport buses. The public transport alternative is to walk 20 minutes from the airport and flag down a minibus – ideally to Obalende for Lagos Island or VI, but you'll probably have to change at Yaba Motor Park.

## Ferry

There are useful ferry services. One runs from Lagos Island to Apapa and on to Mile-2 in west Lagos. The terminal is to the southwest side of Lagos Island, just south of Ring Rd; each leg is N50. Smaller boats hop between VI and Ikoyi every few minutes for N30 from the Tarzan Jetty on VI's Maroko Rd.

## Minibus

Lagos is held together by an endless procession of battered yellow (or green and white on VI) minibuses, or *danfos*, each more beaten-up than the last. Short fares are around N30; long trips which involve crossing bridges ramp the price up considerably (for example a ride between Obalende and Mile 2 Motor Parks costs N200).

## Taxi & Okada

Yellow taxis are everywhere. Fares start from N200, while crossing half of Lagos will be closer to N2000. For short distances, *okadas* (motorcycle taxis) are a better bet, faster and nimbler in heavy traffic. Even a medium length trip shouldn't top N100, but you'll attract a hefty surcharge to persuade the driver to head out of his area and cross a bridge. If you're in a go-slow, jumping on an *okada* may be the only way out.

# AROUND LAGOS

## LEKKI CONSERVATION CENTRE

A mere 20-minute drive east from Lagos is **Lekki Conservation Centre** (Lagos-Epe Expressway; admission N50, camera fee from N700; ☉ 8am-6pm). Run by the Nigerian Conservation Foundation, it has 78 hectares of wetlands which have been set aside for viewing wildlife. Raised walkways enable you to see monkeys, crocodiles and birds; early morning is the best time. There is a visitors centre, library and simple café. Make time to visit the market, which is good for all sorts of handicrafts from metalwork and carvings to paintings and batiks.

The easiest way to get there is to flag down a passing bus on VI along Maroko Rd; the cost is around N100.

## BADAGRY

On the road to the Benin border, Badagry was once Nigeria's busiest slave port. Established in the 16th century, thousands of people a year were shipped from here, mainly to Brazil, before slavery's abolition in the 1880s. Modern Badagry is worth visiting to see its slave heritage. The town is the site of Nigeria's first church.

### Sights

**Chief Obee Slave Relic Museum** (N100, ☻ closed Sundays) is run by the family of the local chief, descended from the area's slavers. It's a room full of interesting artefacts, including fearsome slave chains and shackles that you can try on. You'll need to find someone to open the display. A short walk from here is the **Heritage Museum** (N100, ☻ closed Sundays), which has similar displays, including a model of a slave ship with the captives crammed into every space. On the waterfront, you'll pass the **Brazilian Baracoons** (N50 dash) once used to house slaves but now part of someone's house.

Near the barracoons, you can take a ferry (N20, 10 minutes) to the **Point of No Return**, on an island facing the Atlantic. It's a contemplative point, marked by a large arch, and the prettiness of the beach seems a shocking contrast to its dark history. The point is a well-marked (and very hot) 15-minute walk from the ferry. Halfway is a **Spirit Attentuation Well** – slaves were forced to drink from this to make them forget their homeland.

### Getting There & Away

Minibuses to Badagry leave from Mile 2 Motor Park in Lagos (N150, one hour), returning from 'roundabout'. You can also catch transport to the Benin border at Seme (N100, 30 minutes)

### ABEOKUTA

Abeokuta, 70km north of Lagos, translates as 'under the rock' in Yoruba. It's famous sons are a roll call of contemporary Nigeria – President Obasanjo was born here, along with the late musician Fela Kuti and Nobel laureate Wole Soyinka.

The city is dominated by **Olumo Rock** (admission N50). This huge chunk of granite is sacred in Yoruba religion and is used in various celebrations and rituals. Climbing the rock (140m) affords commanding views of city and surrounding countryside. There are several traditional shrines on the rock. Guides will approach you, and can give interesting insights into Yoruba religion and history for a small dash.

At the Itoku Market you can buy Abeokuta's renowned *adire* cloth and plenty of juju material.

Bush taxis leave from Ojota Motor Park in Lagos (N200, two hours).

# THE SOUTH

The South is the most populous part of Nigeria. Roughly bisected by the Niger River, to the west lie the lands of the Yoruba, and to the east live the Igbos, in the territory that declared itself independent Biafra in the 1960s (see p623). It's green and fertile, most

---

**SUNGBO'S EREDO**

It almost defies belief, but Africa's largest single man-made construction – bigger even than the Pyramids – lies just an hour away from Lagos, virtually unknown to the outside world. Sungbo's Eredo is a 160km-long 1000-year-old linear boundary rampart, sometimes as high as a seven-storey house, and dotted with guardhouses and barracks.

Its history is murky. It was built around 950AD in several stages, and its construction involved moving millions of tonnes of soil. It is believed that it was built for the Ijebu Kingdom, although tradition implausibly ascribes it to the Queen of Sheba, locally called Bilikisu Sungbo. The motives for construction are even hazier – the fact that it was built in a heavily forested area seems to defy normal military defensive tactics. Current theories suggest a spiritual role, or that it may even have been built to keep out marauding elephants. State-building in forests on this scale is simply unknown in Africa, and sadly few archaeologists are pursuing the topic.

The Eredo is still covered with the gloomy brooding forest that has kept it from the eyes of the modern world, and a foray into the deep 'ditch' can be quite eerie. It's difficult to take in its enormity in a day trip, but you'll certainly feel like an adventurer treading where few have gone before.

To reach Sungbo's Eredo, take a minibus from Ojota Motor Park in Lagos to Ijebu-Ode (N150, one hour). Locals should be able to direct you to the best sites.

notably around the troubled Niger Delta, although there's a fair degree of urbanisation – towns and freeways cut through the bush, and a multitude of billboards advertise the explosion of evangelical churches.

Calabar, near the Cameroon border, is a big draw for travellers, as are the brass sculptures of Benin City, and the unexpected peace of Oshogbo's Sacred Forest.

# IBADAN

☎ 022

A hundred years ago, hilly Ibadan could claim to be West Africa's largest city. It's easy to see why even today – the word sprawling could have been invented to describe the city. Congested and unattractive, it's a hard city to love. You're likely to pass through, as Ibadan is a major transport junction, but there's little else to amuse yourself with here before pushing on to more exciting destinations.

## Orientation

Ibadan doesn't have a centre as such. Oyo Rd runs north–south, turning into the Fajuyi Rd at the useful landmark of Mokola Roundabout (where it's bisected by Queen Elizabeth II Rd). Further south, it changes name again into Dugbe Rd around Dugbe Market – the high rise Cocoa House here is another handy landmark for taking bearings – before changing name again to Yaganku Rd.

## Information

The moneychangers around the mosque on Racecourse Rd are reliable and friendly.

**Bureau de Change** (Lebanon Rd, Dugbe Market)

**Kokodome Internet** (Cocoa House, Commercial St; per hour N100)

**Periscope Internet** (Mokola Roundabout; per hour N80) Also has Internet phone (per min N20).

**Post office** (Dugbe Rd)

## Sleeping

### BUDGET

**Lizzy Guesthouse** ( ☎ 241 3350; off Easy Life Rd; r N2875; ✖ ) At the top of a hill, the Lizzy has smallish but tidy rooms, with cold showers and satellite TV. Staff are helpful, plus there's a bar and a restaurant which rustles up breakfast and a few Nigerian standards.

**Ibro Guest House** ( ☎ 0805 2636559 mobile; Ring Rd; s/d N2625/3675; ✖ P ) This budget option is opposite D'Rovans hotel. The rooms are pretty compact, but OK for the price. A few

have unimpressive shared bathrooms – if these are the only choices available there's some room to negotiate a discount.

### MIDRANGE

**D'Rovans Hotel** ( ☎ 231 2907; drovans@skanet.com.ng; Ring Rd; s/d N6325/7475; ✖ 🖥 P ✖ ) This hotel is making a good attempt to break into the top end. Rooms are well turned-out, although try to avoid those next to the generator shed. There are a couple of shops, a restaurant, and a nightclub where the owner's highlife band plays every weekend.

**Premier Hotel** ( ☎ 240 0340; Mokola Hill; r from N6800; ✖ P ✖ ) With a commanding view over Ibadan, the Premier tries to lord it over lesser establishments. It's not entirely successful, but rooms are comfy nonetheless, the Chinese restaurant is good, and you can burn off some calories in the pool.

### TOP END

**Kakanfo Inn** ( ☎ 231 1471; reservation@kakanfoinn.com; Nihinlola St; r from US$126; ✖ 🖥 P ✖ ) A comfortable top-end option, with good rooms and an on-site masseur. Ask for the resident rate if you can, which should garner you a healthy naira discount.

## Eating

**Kokodome** (By Cocoa House, Commercial St; dishes from N400; ☽ 9am-11pm) An open terrace around a pool makes this a pleasant place to eat or just sink a few drinks. The menu has a definite Lebanese theme, but there's some trusty *jollof* on offer too. Upstairs, you can dine in slightly plusher surroundings.

**Bisi Restaurant** (Kakanfo Inn, Nihinlola St; dishes from N700; ☽ 8am-10pm) Along with the usual suspects this hotel restaurant does a line in Indian cuisine, with a selection of vegetarian dishes. If you make it there in the morning, the cooked breakfasts are good too.

**Dragon D'Or** (Premier Hotel, Mokola Hill; dishes from N800; ☽ 12-3pm & 7pm-10.30pm, closed Mon) The Chinese food here is quite excellent, with generous servings and plenty of noodles, rice and crackers.

**Tantalizers** (Mokola Roundabout, dishes from N200; ☽ 8am-10pm) Off-the-peg fast food. You might find yourself here if you have a craving for genuine chips, a rarity in Nigeria. Otherwise, the toilets are nice and clean.

There are plenty of 'food-is-ready' places around Dugbe Market.

NIGERIA

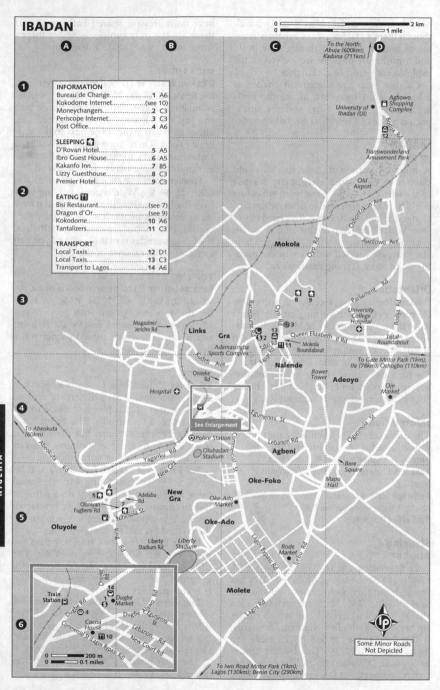

# IBADAN

**INFORMATION**
| | |
|---|---|
| Bureau de Change...................**1** | A6 |
| Kokodome Internet................(see 10) | |
| Moneychangers.......................**2** | C3 |
| Periscope Internet.....................**3** | C3 |
| Post Office...............................**4** | A6 |

**SLEEPING** 🏠
| | |
|---|---|
| D'Rovan Hotel.........................**5** | A5 |
| Ibro Guest House......................**6** | A5 |
| Kakanfo Inn.............................**7** | B5 |
| Lizzy Guesthouse......................**8** | C3 |
| Premier Hotel...........................**9** | C3 |

**EATING** 🍴
| | |
|---|---|
| Bisi Restaurant.......................(see 7) | |
| Dragon d'Or...........................(see 9) | |
| Kokodome..............................**10** | A6 |
| Tantalizers.............................**11** | C3 |

**TRANSPORT**
| | |
|---|---|
| Local Taxis.............................**12** | D1 |
| Local Taxis.............................**13** | C3 |
| Transport to Lagos...................**14** | A6 |

To the North;
Abuja (600km);
Kaduna (711km)

University of
Ibadan (UI)

Agbowo
Shopping
Complex

Bodija Rd

**12**

Transwonderland
Amusement Park

Old
Airport

Oshontokun Ave

Awolowo Ave

**Mokola**

Oyo Rd

Parliament Rd

Bodija Rd

University
College
Hospital

Total
Roundabout

Racecourse Rd

Oyo Rd

**8** **9**

@ **3**

**13**

Sabo Rd

**2**

Queen Elizabeth II Rd

Magazine/
Jericho Rd

**Links**

**Gra**

Adamasingba
Sports Complex

Kudeti Ave

Fajuyi Rd

🍴 **11**

Mokola
Roundabout

**Nalende**

To Gate Motor Park (1km);
Ife (78km); Oshogbo (110km)

Onireke
Rd

Hospital ✚

See Enlargement

Bower
Tower

**Adeoyo**

Oje
Market

Egunjenmi St

**Agbeni**

Ogunmola St

Bere
Square

★ Police Station

Olubadan
Stadium

Lebanon Rd

Mapo
Hall

To Abeokuta
(60km)

Abeokuta Rd

Yaganku Rd

New Gra

Commercial Rd

**Oke-Foko**

**6**

**5**

**7**

Adelabu
Rd

**New
Gra**

Oke-Ado
Market

**Oluyole**

Olaniyan
Fagbemi Rd

Nihiniola St

Ring Rd

**Oke-Ado**

Bode
Market

Iyebu Rd

Lagos Bypass Rd

Liberty
Stadium Rd

Liberty
Stadium

**Molete**

Lagos Rd

Some Minor Roads
Not Depicted

Train
Station

**14**

Dugbe
Market

Dugbe Rd

Oniroke Rd

Egunjenmi St

Dugbe Alawo Rd

Commercial St (Lagos Bypass Rd)

Cocoa
House

**4**

**10**

Lebanon
St

New Court Rd

To Iwo Road Motor Park (1km);
Lagos (130km); Benin City (290km)

**NIGERIA**

## Getting There & Around

Iwo Rd, to the south of the city, is Ibadan's major motor park; minibuses run to all points from here, including Lagos (N250, 90 minutes), Abuja (N1200, eight hours), Kaduna (N1700, 11 hours) and points north. The further you're travelling, the earlier you should get to the motor park. Transport to Lagos departs from Dugbe Market. For Oshogbo (N250, 90 minutes), go to Gate Motor Park in the east of the city.

Ibadan's sprawling nature makes *okada* trips more expensive than usual – around N50 for a typical ride. Pricier taxis are white with a thin blue stripe.

## OSHOGBO

☎ 035

This quiet Yoruba city has been a centre for contemporary Nigerian art since the 1950s, although some of the galleries are feeling a little tired these days, with artists relocating to more profitable climes in Lagos and New York. It's still worth a visit to see the Osun Sacred Forest, a shrine to Yoruba religion that's a real Nigerian highlight.

## Information

Change money before coming to Oshogbo. For Internet access try **Megatech Plaza Cybercafé** (Gbongan Rd; per hour N120).

## Sights

While here, wander through the **Oja Oba Market** (cnr Station & Sabo Rds) across from the Oba's Palace. It's packed with stalls selling juju material.

### OSUN SACRED FOREST & GROVES

This delightful **forest** (Osun Shrine Rd; admission N200, camera N500; ◷ 10am-6pm) is a cool green oasis away from the daily hustle of Nigerian life. An ancient centre for the Yoruba goddess Osun, the 'mother' of Oshogbo, its groves are filled with sculptures and shrines revering the traditional Yoruba gods – under increasing threat from the growth of evangelical Christianity. Many of the gods, some looking positively extraterrestrial, are overgrown and mossy, but somehow this adds further to their primal power.

Even without the shrines, the forest is a lovely place to walk, spotting monkeys and

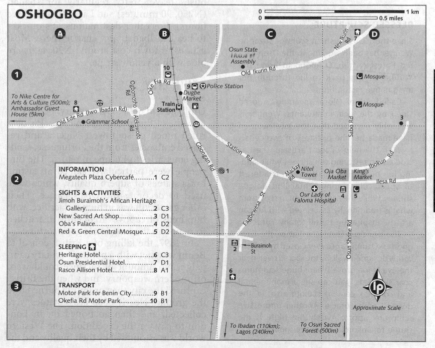

**OSHOGBO**

| INFORMATION | |
|---|---|
| Megatech Plaza Cybercafé | **1** C2 |

| SIGHTS & ACTIVITIES | |
|---|---|
| Jimoh Buraimoh's African Heritage Gallery | **2** C3 |
| New Sacred Art Shop | **3** D1 |
| Oba's Palace | **4** D2 |
| Red & Green Central Mosque | **5** D2 |

| SLEEPING | |
|---|---|
| Heritage Hotel | **6** C3 |
| Osun Presidential Hotel | **7** D1 |
| Rasco Allison Hotel | **8** A1 |

| TRANSPORT | |
|---|---|
| Motor Park for Benin City | **9** B1 |
| Okefia Rd Motor Park | **10** B1 |

To Nike Centre for Arts & Culture (500m); Ambassador Guest House (5km)

Osun State House of Assembly

Old Ikurin Rd

Police Station

Dugbe Market

Train Station

Grammar School

Mosque

Mosque

Station Rd

Nitel Tower

Oja Oba Market

King's Market

Ilesa Rd

Our Lady of Faloma Hospital

Buraimoh St

Osun Shrine Rd

To Ibadan (110km); Lagos (240km)

To Osun Sacred Forest (500m)

0 — 1 km
0 — 0.5 miles

Approximate Scale

NIGERIA

bright butterflies, with little more to disturb you than the sound of birdsong and running water. The forest was declared a World Heritage Site in 2006.

An *okada* from the centre of Oshogbo costs N50.

### ART GALLERIES

In its heyday, Oshogbo was the flourishing centre of the Oshogbo School of Art, a movement which started in the 1960s. To see some of the artists' work, you'll have to visit individual studios, as there is no central outlet for the sale of Oshogbo art.

Several galleries stand out: the **Nike Centre for Arts & Culture** (Old Ede Rd) run by Nike Davies-Okundaye, and strong on traditional and modern fabrics; **Jimoh Buraimoh's African Heritage Gallery** (1 Buraimoh St) selling abstract paintings; and the **New Sacred Art Shop** (41a Ibokun Rd).

### Sleeping & Eating

**Heritage Hotel** ( ☎ 241 881; hotelheritage@yahoo.com; Gbongan Rd; r N1265-2875; ✷ 💻 ℗ ) Owned by artist Jimoh Buraimah, rooms here are fair-sized with huge beds, although the mustard

walls make them seem gloomier than they should be. There's also a restaurant/bar, and a fairly anaemic generator.

**Rasco Allison Hotel** ( ☎ 240 705; Old Ede Rd; r N1500; ✷ ) Cheap as chips, rooms here reflect the price, but it's fine for a short stay if your funds are low.

**Osun Presidential Hotel** ( ☎ 232 299; Old Ikurin Rd; r from N9200; ✷ ℗ ) Once Oshogbo's grand old lady, this hotel is still adequate, but is almost ready to be pensioned off. Rooms are average for the price, which also sums up the restaurant.

**Ambassador Guest House** ( ☎ 242 254; Ido Osun Junction; r N15,000 ✷ ℗ ) This place, in large leafy grounds, is a real treat. More a home than a hotel, it's owned by artist Nike Davies-Okundaye and is decorated beautifully. Not all rooms have en suites, but otherwise the Ambassador does everything to treat you like a VIP. Reservations are accepted in advance.

Old Ede Rd is the main drag for chop-houses serving 'food-is-ready' fare.

### Getting There & Away

Okefia Rd is the main motor park. Minibuses leave pretty regularly for Ibadan (N250, 90 minutes) and Lagos (N450, three hours). For other destinations, it's quicker to head to Ibadan and change there. Most *okadas* in town cost around N30; taxis are blue with a yellow stripe.

## BENIN CITY

☎ 052

Until the end of the 19th century, Benin City was one of the great African cities. It's *obas* ruled much of southwest Nigeria and received embassies from the Portuguese, sending emissaries to Europe in return. The Bini people were particularly skilled at casting brass statues of superb quality, which were used to decorate the Oba's Palace. Their other great skill was in human sacrifice, with hundreds of captives frequently dispatched to maintain the kingdom's good fortune.

In 1897, the killing of a British consul to Benin was met with a punitive military campaign. No amount of sacrifice could ward off modern weaponry, and when the British captured the city they promptly burned it to the ground. Nearly 5000 brass statues were collected, and then auctioned off in London to pay for the expedition. The Western world was astounded by their quality and the

---

**BLESSED SCULPTURE**

Since the 1950s, Austrian sculptor Suzanne Wenger has been working in the Osun Sacred Forest outside Oshogbo to bring the Yoruba shrines back to life through her imaginative restorations.

Called Aduni Olosa (meaning 'Adored One') by the local inhabitants, Wenger is so highly regarded that the local women have made her the priestess of two cults.

With the help of local artisans she has worked on restoring the shrines while adding her own touches. The result is a forest of spectacular, monumental and unique shrines. While they are different in style from what is traditionally associated with African art, the inspiration is still totally Yoruba.

The principal shrine is that of the river goddess Osun, in a grove enclosed by an intricately designed wall. By the sacred river, near the Lya Mapa grove where huge sculptures soar skywards, you can see a monumental and complex cement sculpture to Ifa, the divine Yoruba oracle. Another impressive sculpture, approximately 5m high, is the shrine to Onkoro, the mother goddess.

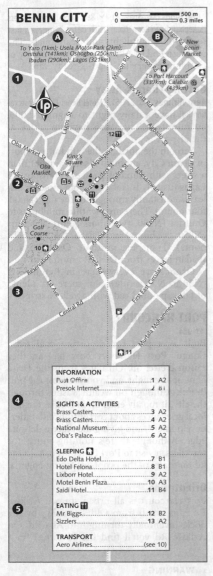

## BENIN CITY

0    500 m
0    0.3 miles

To Yaro (1km); Usela Motor Park (2km);
Onitsha (141km); Oshogbo (250km);
Ibadan (290km); Lagos (321km)

New Benin Market

To Port Harcourt (339km); Calabar (439km)

Oba Market St

King's Square

Oba Market

Ring Rd

Hospital

Golf Course

| INFORMATION | | |
|---|---|---|
| Post Office | 1 | A2 |
| Presok Internet | 2 | B1 |

| SIGHTS & ACTIVITIES | | |
|---|---|---|
| Brass Casters | 3 | A2 |
| Brass Casters | 4 | A2 |
| National Museum | 5 | A2 |
| Oba's Palace | 6 | A2 |

| SLEEPING | | |
|---|---|---|
| Edo Delta Hotel | 7 | B1 |
| Hotel Felona | 8 | B1 |
| Lixborr Hotel | 9 | A2 |
| Motel Benin Plaza | 10 | A3 |
| Saidi Hotel | 11 | B4 |

| EATING | | |
|---|---|---|
| Mr Biggs | 12 | B2 |
| Sizzlers | 13 | A2 |

| TRANSPORT | | |
|---|---|---|
| Aero Airlines | (see 10) | |

statues (often erroneously called the Benin Bronzes) became one of the first styles of African art to win worldwide recognition.

Today, Benin City, capital of Edo State, is a sprawling and undistinguished place. However, the art of brass statuary has recently been revived, and you can see craftsmen at work near the museum.

A good time to visit is December, when the seven-day Igue (Ewere) Festival – featuring traditional dances, a mock battle and a procession to the palace – and the nine-day New Yams Festival, celebrated with parades and dancing, giving thanks for a productive harvest, takes place around Edo State.

## Orientation

King's Square is at the centre of town, circled by Ring Rd. Running northeast from here is Akpakpava Rd, with Sapele and Sapoba Roads leading off to the southeast. You will find places to stay, plus restaurants, shops and local transport along these routes.

## Information

**Post office** (Airport Rd) Next to the hospital.
**Presok Internet** (Akpakpava Rd; per hr N80) Open 24 hours.

## Sights

### BRASS CASTERS

Part-funded by Unesco, **Brass Casters St**, near the centre, has been given over to reviving Benin brasswork. Craftsmen use the 'lost wax' technique, whereby a sculpture is made in wax, covered in clay and baked; the melted wax drains away, and the mould is poured with brass. As the mould must be smashed to retrieve the sculpture, every piece is unique (see p71 for more). The brassmakers are happy to show you their works, usually copies of the most famous Benin sculptures.

Everything is for sale – prices range from N300 for the smallest to over N50,000 for the big statues – and there's a blissful lack of sales pressure.

### NATIONAL MUSEUM

The **museum** (King's Sq; admission N100; 9am-6pm), surrounded by the ferocious traffic of Ring Rd, is the city's main landmark. The ground floor is dedicated to the Benin Kingdom, with a display of beautiful brasses. Photos represent the more important pieces now overseas. The more bloodthirsty aspects of Benin culture are neatly glossed over, but look out for the representations of Portuguese traders. The upstairs galleries are more ethnological in nature, providing a good survey of traditional cultures from across Nigeria.

The museum is dark when there's no National Electric Power Authority (NEPA), so a torch is a good idea.

NIGERIA

## OBA'S PALACE

The mud-walled **Oba's Palace** (cnr Adesogbe Rd & Airport Rd), a block southwest of the museum, is quite spectacular. The palace contains sculptures, brass relics and other art depicting historical events during Benin City's heyday. It also has an impressive array of traditional crafts and other works of art. It is still very much a working palace, and you'll see plenty of attendants and petitioners at the court.

You need the secretary's permission to visit, preferably arranged a day in advance; ask at the security post at the entrance. There's no fee but you'll be asked for a dash.

## Sleeping & Eating

**Edo Delta Hotel** ( ☎ 252 722; Akpakpava Rd; s 1500-2500, d from N3500; ❄ ) This is a friendly budget option, with a jumble of chalets and a hotel block proper. The cheapest rooms feel a little cramped and have fan only; other rooms are better value. The reception doubles as a small, impromptu bar, with decent sofas.

**Lixborr Hotel** ( ☎ 256 699; Sakopba Rd; s/d N2875/3450-4025; ❄ ) Formerly the Genesis Hotel, this is a great, well-run place with comfortable, tastefully decorated rooms. Look for the giant statue of the Benin woman outside; it's opposite the brass casters street.

**Hotel Felona** ( ☎ 256 699; Dawson Rd; s/d N3450/4025-5175; ❄ Ⓟ ) Rooms are decent and comfortable here, and there's a 24-hour generator. The restaurant serves good Nigerian and Continental dishes, and is worth visiting for nonguests to have the bacon and eggs breakfast (from N240), or the Nigerian dishes throughout the day.

**Saidi Hotel** ( ☎ 253 237; Murtala Mohammed Way; www.saidhotelsltd.com; r from N6900, apt from 12,075; ❄ ⚙ Ⓟ ) Never knowingly underdecorated, this huge compound mixes traditional Benin décor with Chinese theme park and 1970's kitsch. Get past that though, and rooms are large and plush with good amenities. If there are several of you, the two-bedroom apartments are excellent value. The restaurant has a good Chinese buffet every Sunday from 12pm to 3pm (N1200).

**Motel Benin Plaza** ( ☎ 254779; motelbeninplaza@info web.abs.net; Reservation Rd; s/d/ste from N5750/7425 /9775; ❄ ▭ ⚙ Ⓟ ) Easily Benin City's fanciest hotel, with immaculate rooms, a restaurant, a couple of shops, moneychangers and a great bar next to the pool (with live music each evening).

**Mr Biggs** (Akpakpava Rd, ☼ 8am-10pm) and **Sizzlers** (Sakopba Rd; ☼ 8am-10pm) both offer Nigerian fast food with bright lights and clean toilets. The southern end of Akpakpava Rd has plenty of chophouses serving 'food-is-ready' fare.

## Getting There & Away

**Aero Airlines** ( ☎ 271 512; Motel Benin Plaza, Reservation Rd) have a daily flight to Lagos (N8000, 40 minutes). They also have an office at the airport.

Yaro, in the north, is the hub for transport in Benin City, although it's less a depot than a street with minibus garages. Transport to Lagos (usually to Yaba or Ojota motor park) leaves constantly throughout the day (N800, four hours). There are plentiful minibuses to Onitsha (N350, two hours), Port Harcourt (N850, five hours) and Calabar (N1200, eight hours). Transport north to Oshogbo and Ibadan leaves from Usela Rd motor park.

*Okadas* are everywhere in Benin City (N30 to N50 a ride), plus there are plenty of taxis, painted red with a yellow stripe.

## PORT HARCOURT
☎ 084

Built as a port for exporting coal from Enugu, Port Harcourt now has another raison d'être: oil. Oil flares from the Delta light up the night, and you can taste the pollution. Although oil wealth washes through the city, it mostly ends up in Abuja, fuelling local grievances about corruption and underdevelopment, and giving the place a definite edge. Although there's nothing much for travellers, a visit to Port Harcourt can lift the lid on many of the problems facing Nigeria.

## Orientation

Port Harcourt is all urban sprawl. Azikwe Rd runs north from Old Township by the docks, eventually turning into Aba Rd. On Azikwe Rd you'll find the (defunct) train

---

### WARNING

Political instability meant that we were unable to visit Port Harcourt or the Niger Delta during research, so some information in this section may be unreliable. The threat of kidnap in the Delta region remains high – check the security situation carefully before considering travel to the area.

station, major banks, and the post office. Aggrey Rd in Old Township is another commercial centre, with food stalls and shops.

## Information

The expat-run website www.oyibosonline .com is an excellent guide for visitors to Port Harcourt, with everything from restaurant listings to weekly security briefings.

### AIRLINES

For information on domestic and international carriers based in Port Harcourt see p646 and p636.

### POST

**Post office** (Station Rd)

### TOURIST INFORMATION

**Rivers State Ministry of Tourism** ( ☎ 334 901; 35 Aba Rd) May help with advising on trips to the Delta.

## Sleeping & Eating

**Hotel Ferguson** ( ☎ 230 505; 1b Elelenwo St; s/d N3400/5000; ❄ ) The quiet, quirky Ferguson is one of the least-expensive and comfortable places you'll find in Port Harcourt, with clean rooms and an attached restaurant.

**Delta Hotel** ( ☎ 236 650, 1-3 Harley St; r N2500-5000; ❄ ) The Delta is a good choice, and although it's a bit away from the centre in the Gra district, this makes it quiet and relaxing. The nicely maintained rooms have air-con, TV and telephone. It has a decent bar and restaurant.

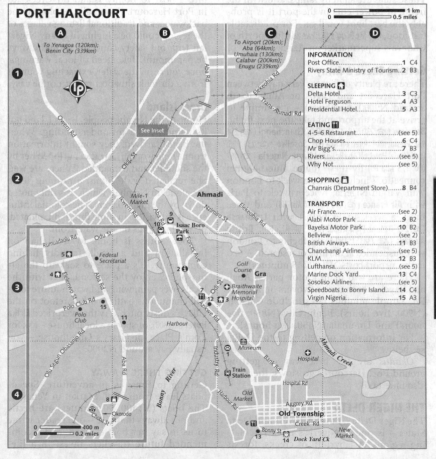

**PORT HARCOURT**

| INFORMATION | |
|---|---|
| Post Office | **1** C4 |
| Rivers State Ministry of Tourism | **2** B3 |

| SLEEPING | |
|---|---|
| Delta Hotel | **3** C3 |
| Hotel Ferguson | **4** A3 |
| Presidential Hotel | **5** A3 |

| EATING | |
|---|---|
| 4-5-6 Restaurant | (see 5) |
| Chop Houses | **6** C4 |
| Mr Bigg's | **7** B3 |
| Rivers | (see 5) |
| Why Not | (see 5) |

| SHOPPING | |
|---|---|
| Chanrais (Department Store) | **8** B4 |

| TRANSPORT | |
|---|---|
| Air France | (see 2) |
| Alabi Motor Park | **9** B2 |
| Bayelsa Motor Park | **10** B2 |
| Bellview | (see 2) |
| British Airways | **11** B3 |
| Chanchangi Airlines | (see 5) |
| KLM | **12** B3 |
| Lufthansa | (see 5) |
| Marine Dock Yard | **13** C4 |
| Sosoliso Airlines | (see 5) |
| Speedboats to Bonny Island | **14** C4 |
| Virgin Nigeria | **15** A3 |

NIGERIA

**Presidential Hotel** (☎ 310 400; off Aba Rd; r from N14,500; ⊠ ⊠) Once Port Harcourt's top hotel, the Presidential is a little down at heel these days, but still gets a good showing from the oil crowd. Sosoliso Airlines, Chanchangi and Lufthansa have their offices here, and you'll find it easy to change money. As a nonguest, you can use the pool for N100, visit the cinema or dine in the restaurants.

There are eateries on Aba Rd, three at Presidential Hotel alone: **4-5-6 Restaurant** (dishes from N1200) serving Chinese food; **Why Not** (mains from N800) with Lebanese and European fare; and **Rivers** (mains from N750) with Nigerian dishes.

For inexpensive chop, try any of the *suya* stalls scattered throughout the grid of Old Township, or the stalls at Old Market. These stalls are all lit by lamps, and with the frequent power cuts in the port it is probably the best light you'll get. For predictable fast food, try **Mr Bigg's** (Azikwe Rd), just north of Chanrais supermarket on Azikwe Rd.

### Getting There & Away

There are plenty of flights every day between Port Harcourt and Lagos or Abuja (both around N9000, one hour) – it's simple to arrive at the airport and take the next flight. **Bellview** (☎ 230 518; 47 Aba Rd), **Chanchangi** (☎ 234 937; Presidential Hotel, off Aba Rd), **Sosoliso** (☎ 231 908; Presidential Hotel, off Aba Rd) and **Virgin Nigeria** (☎ 467 000; 175 Aba Rd) fly these routes. International connections include twice a week to London with Virgin Nigeria, twice a week to Paris with **Air France** (☎ 486 901; 47 Aba Rd) and three times a week to Frankfurt with **Lufthansa** (☎ 232 014; at Presidential Hotel, off Aba Rd). **British Airways** (☎ 238351; 180 Aba Rd) flights to London were suspended at the time of research. A taxi to the airport costs N2000 (45 minutes).

There are two main motor parks, Abali and Bayelsa, both under flyovers on Azikwe Rd. Sample minibus fares include Calabar (N900, five hours), Benin City (N850, five hours) and Umuahia (N450, two hours).

For information on getting to the Delta, see below.

*Okadas* are the best way of getting around Port Harcourt's go-slows; there are also blue taxis.

### THE NIGER DELTA

The Niger Delta – Bayelsa, Rivers and Delta States – is one of Nigeria's most fascinating regions. A labyrinth of creeks, forests and mangrove, its history is one of great exploitation. Until the 19th century it was a major hub for the slave trade, which was eventually replaced by the British with palm oil exportation, and then, following independence, by the oil industry. Bonny Island in the Delta gives its name to Bonny Light, an important crude for making petrol.

Extreme care should be taken if planning a visit, as the Delta is infamous for kidnappings. Foreigners are often presumed to be oil employees and therefore worth holding for ransom. Warri, the capital of Delta state, is regularly out of bounds to foreigners. If security allows it, the most accessible part of the Delta is Brass Island, reached by boat from Yenagoa. Alternatively, it's possible to hire a boat to Bonny Island off Creek Rd in Port Harcourt. Potentially, exploring the backwaters and traditional fishing villages of the region could be a highlight of any Nigerian trip, but safety concerns should always be paramount. Take heed of local warnings; once you're on the water, extracting yourself from a difficult situation might not be easy.

### Brass Island

Home to the Nembe people, Brass Island got its name from a misunderstanding. When the British arrived, they sought information from a lone woman, an officer gripped her by the shoulder and demanded 'Where are we?' She retaliated with '*Barasi*' (meaning 'leave me alone' in Nembe), which was duly noted down by the map-makers. The colonial influence is still visible in some fine, if dilapidated, period buildings on the waterfront.

Today Brass is home to an Italian oil installation and a small, friendly fishing community. It's a place to soak up the atmosphere, enjoy the seafood, chat with the locals over palm wine and watch future football champions battle it out barefoot on the village's dusty pitch. Try the overpriced **Eirika Hotel** (r N6800), or stay in a local house – ask for Tom's Place, or Casey's Guesthouse – you usually pay around N2000.

#### GETTING THERE & AWAY

Getting to Brass is an adventure. Speedboats leave from Swali Market in Yenagoa. The boats (N1400, 90 minutes) are hectic and not always that safe – one reader wrote to us to say her boat crashed, and recommended future travellers invest in a life-

**OIL ON TROUBLED WATERS**

Oil accounts for over 95% of Nigeria's exports, but despite being the source of the country's wealth, the Niger Delta remains one of the most underdeveloped parts of the country. Oil money simply flows out of the Delta into the deep pockets of central government – and secret overseas accounts – leaving the locals with a neglected infrastructure and massive environmental damage – oil spills, gas flaring and even acid rain.

The first major attempt to confront the state and the western oil companies was by the minority Ogoni people in the 1990s. Led by the writer and activist Ken Saro-Wiwa, the Movement for the Survival of the Ogoni People (Mosop) mounted a vigorous campaign in Rivers State that was met with extreme violence by the Nigerian government. Saro-Wiwa was executed for treason by the Abacha regime in 1995, which led to Nigeria's suspension from the Commonwealth.

A decade on, the struggle for redistribution of oil wealth has been taken up by the Ijaws. The Niger Delta People's Volunteer Force (NDPVF), led by Mujahid Dokubo-Asari, has taken a militant line, demanding increased sovereignty for the Ijaws. It began a paramilitary campaign against oil installations, using arms paid for with the proceeds of smuggled oil. Threats to blow up oil platforms led to government talks; when they stalled, the NDPVF kidnapped Western oil employees. Following Dokubo-Asari's capture in 2005, the Movement for the Emancipation of the Niger Delta (MEND) has replaced the NDPVF, and stepped up the military campaign against the oil companies.

As we went to press, the governor of Bayelsa State was undergoing impeachment proceedings for corruption, a first in Nigerian history. Many western oil companies are now developing offshore oil platforms, and while this may bring a short-term solution to their security problems, the deeper issues surrounding Nigeria oil production can't be moved away so easily.

jacket. If you can, enjoy the green channels of the Delta, spotting plenty of birdlife and fishing canoes (and oil pipelines). Minibuses to Yenagoa (N300, 90 minutes) leave from Port Harcourt's main motor parks.

## UMUHAIA

An otherwise unremarkable slice of urban Nigeria, Umuhaia (pronounced *oh-MOY-ah*) was the headquarters of the Biafran army during the civil war in the 1960s (see p623), and has the interesting **National War Museum** (Museum Rd; N40; ☉ 9am-6pm Mon-Fri, 10am-5pm Sat & Sun) which commemorates the conflict.

The ingenuity of the blockaded Biafrans is on display in the grounds, with homemade armoured cars and the remains of their pitiful (but surprisingly effective) airforce, including a two-seater Cessna whose occupants literally dropped its bombs out of the window. There's also a 25m-long gunboat used by the Nigerian navy, now converted to a pleasant café serving drinks and simple meals. Inside the museum proper there's a fearsome array of traditional weapons, army uniforms and a photographic history of the Biafran war (inside the bunker that housed the Voice of Biafra radio station).

Umuhaia can be visited en route to other destinations, such as Calabar (N600, 2½

hours) or Port Harcourt (N450, two hours). Travelling west, it's easier to head to Onitsha (N700, four hours) and change there. Onward transport leaves from All Roads Motor Park. An *okada* to the museum costs N30.

## CALABAR

☎ 087

Tucked into Nigeria's southeastern corner, the capital of Cross River state is one of the most likeable cities in Nigeria for visitors. It's certainly the cleanest. It sits high on a hill overlooking Cross River, and its port has historically made the town a prosperous place – Calabar was one of Nigeria's biggest slave ports, and later a major exporter of palm oil. Even its name seems the picture of an equatorial trading post.

Many travellers pass through Calabar to or from Cameroon, and either way it is a great introduction or farewell to Nigeria. There's also plenty to do – an excellent museum, and two primate conservation centres that, along with the lush riverine vegetation, make this the greenest corner of the country.

### Orientation

Calabar is surprisingly hilly. Calabar Rd runs high above the river. On the waterfront is the older colonial quarter of Duke Town,

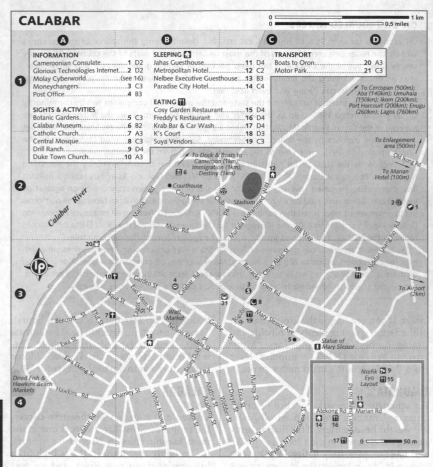

## CALABAR

**INFORMATION**
Cameroonian Consulate.............**1** D2
Glorious Technologies Internet....**2** D2
Molay Cyberworld....................(see 16)
Moneychangers......................**3** C3
Post Office...........................**4** B3

**SIGHTS & ACTIVITIES**
Botanic Gardens.....................**5** C3
Calabar Museum......................**6** B2
Catholic Church......................**7** A3
Central Mosque.......................**8** C3
Drill Ranch..........................**9** D4
Duke Town Church...................**10** A3

**SLEEPING**
Jahas Guesthouse....................**11** D4
Metropolitan Hotel...................**12** C2
Nelbee Executive Guesthouse......**13** B3
Paradise City Hotel..................**14** C4

**EATING**
Cosy Garden Restaurant............**15** D4
Freddy's Restaurant.................**16** D4
Krab Bar & Car Wash...............**17** D4
K's Court............................**18** D3
Suya Vendors.........................**19** C3

**TRANSPORT**
Boats to Oron........................**20** A3
Motor Park...........................**21** C3

where you'll find the town's first church and the tomb of the still-revered Scottish missionary Mary Slessor. At the centre of Calabar Rd is the warren-like Watt Market, where everything is for sale. To the east, Ndidan Usang Iso Rd runs north–south, which is where you'll find several of the better hotels and restaurants. The airport is 2km further to the east.

## Information

Hausa moneychangers can be found in the area around the central mosque on Mary Slessor Ave.

**ADC Airlines** ( ☎ 234 477; airport desk)
**Glorious Technologies Internet** (Ndidan Usang Iso Rd; per hr N100)

**Molay Cyberworld** (Atekong Rd; per hr N150)
**Post office** (Calabar Rd)

## Sights
### CALABAR MUSEUM

This **museum** (Court Rd; admission N100; ✆ 9am-6pm) housed in the beautiful old British governor's building, is Nigeria's best by some distance. It has a fascinating and impressive collection covering Calabar's precolonial days as the Efik kingdom (and is remarkably frank about the local slave trade), the palm-oil trade, the British Oil Rivers Protectorate and Nigerian independence. Take a torch – the upstairs galleries are very dark when there's no NEPA. The museum also has great views of the river and a good café.

NIGERIA

## DRILL RANCH

Run by the pioneering charity Pandrillus, this **primate rescue centre** ( ☎ 234 310; drill@infoweb .abs.net; Nsefik Eyo Layout, off Atekong Rd; ☉ 9am-5pm) is home to a colony of drill monkeys and orphaned chimpanzees, both found in the forests east of Calabar but increasingly endangered. Pandrillus has been at the forefront of primate conservation in Nigeria and places great emphasis on local education to combat poaching and the bushmeat trade. The ranch runs the most successful drill captive breeding programme in the world, with groups eventually taken to Afi Mountain Drill Ranch (p650) near Cross River National Park – visits can be arranged from here. Pandrillus also co-run the Limbe Wildlife Centre in Cameroon (p189). Donations are welcome.

## CERCOPAN & BOTANIC GARDENS

The second of Calabar's primate charities, **Cercopan** (www.cercopan.org; Ishie Lane; ☉ 9am-5pm) works with smaller monkeys, such as guenons and mangabeys, and has a visitor centre with rescued primates. Cercopan works closely with schools in teaching conservation. In 2006, Cercopan plans to relocate to the **Botanic Gardens** (www.irokofoundation.org; Mary Slessor Ave), which are under redevelopment. The gardens will draw attention to the biodiversity of the area. Donations are welcome.

## Sleeping

**Nelbee Executive Guesthouse** ( ☎ 232 684; Dan Achibong St; s/d N2300/2530; ✗ P ) Close to Watt Market is this handy budget option. Rooms are comfortable, the management friendly, and there's a terrifically formal dining room, but it can be gloomy when there's no NEPA.

**Jahas Guesthouse** (Marian Rd; r N3500; ✗ ) This clean and tidy budget option has a warm welcome, and is a pleasantly quiet option, off the main road. For those feeling weary from Nigeria's bustle, the health centre in the same compound offers restorative 'blood massages'.

**Marian Hotel** ( ☎ 220 233; Old Ikong Rd; s/d N3500/4600; ✗ P ) From the outside this hotel, east of town, looks to be aspiring to a little more than it can successfully carry off. Rooms are spacious and tidy, if a bit disappointing, with the usual creaky TV and optimistic plumbing.

**Paradise City Hotel** ( ☎ 235 726; Atekong Rd; r N2990-3450; ✗ ) Away from the centre, this

three-storey hotel is popular with conferences and evangelical meetings – none of which deters the bar girls in the hotel's lively Fountain Bar. Rooms are large, and there's a 24-hour generator.

**Metropolitan Hotel** ( ☎ 230 911; metrocal@hitecpro .com; Murtala Mohammed Way; s/d N6000/7200; ste from N15,000; ✗ ☒ P ) Calabar's poshest sleeping option, the Metropolitan has large well-appointed rooms, aimed at business travellers, plus a decent restaurant, a couple of shops and a popular pool.

## Eating

**Cosy Garden Restaurant** (Nsefik Eyo Layout, off Atekong Rd; mains from N300; ☉ 9am-8pm) If your mama was Nigerian, she'd cook like this. Choose hot and tasty pepper soup or delicately flavoured *egusi* with a mountain of pounded yam. It's poorly signed: look for the lime green building near the Drill Ranch.

**Freddy's Restaurant** (Atekong Rd; mains from N1200; ☉ 11.30am-3pm, 6.30pm-11pm, closed Sun lunch) Something of an institution for Calabar's tiny expat community, Freddy's serves Lebanese and continental dishes in well-presented surroundings, and has a large bar. The shwarmas (N1400) are ever-popular.

**K's Court** (Ndidan Usang Iso Rd; dishes from N300; ☉ 11am-late) An open-air chophouse, this place gets going better the later the day gets. It serves up fiery bowls of cow-leg soup with plantain, and once that's gone, pushes back the tables and cranks up the music to dance the weekend nights away.

**Krab Bar & Car Wash** (Ndidan Usang Iso Rd; dishes from N300; ☉ 10am-late) How Nigerian: drive to dinner, sink a few beers while your car gets washed and then drive home. During the day, meals don't run much past *jollof* rice, but in the evening the *suya* and grilled fish stands get going – there's cheap tasty meals either way.

There are some other good *suya* stands near the central mosque, and chophouses around the main motor park.

## Getting There & Away

**ADC Airlines** ( ☎ 234 477) fly every morning to Lagos (N12,000, one hour); the flight continues to Abuja (N15,000, two hours). Calabar's dark blue taxis will charge around N250 for an airport drop.

**Destiny** ( ☎ 085 514475 mobile; Calabar dock) sails every Tuesday and Friday to Limbe in

Cameroon (N5000, 10 hours). For more information see p671.

The main motor park is tucked between Mary Slessor Ave and Goldie St. Sample minibus fares include Port Harcourt (N900, four hours), Lagos (N3000, 10 hours), Umuhaia (N600, 2½ hours) and Ikom (N700, three hours).

An average *okada* ride around town should cost N30 to N40.

## AROUND CALABAR

Cross River National Park dominates the landscape to the east of Calabar – hilly, rugged and spectacular. Park facilities are severely dilapidated, so the best way to appreciate the area is to visit the Afi ranch on the edge of the park.

### Afi Mountain Drill Ranch

In the lush forests north of Cross River National Park, **Afi Mountain Drill Ranch** (N200 communitycharge, hut N2000, camping N1000, car/motorbike N500/250) is a satellite set-up of Pandrillus (p649) and houses six large drill groups (captive bred as well as rehabilitated) and orphaned chimps. The monkeys and apes live in separate huge natural enclosures, in as close a state to the wild as possible. Long-term plans will involve releasing drills back into the wild, but it is impossible to release chimps which have been habituated to humans.

The camp consists of a series of simple huts, a kitchen hut, basic shower and drop toilets. The views over the mountains are gorgeous and wild, and well worth the effort of getting here. Nearby are the Bano Waterfalls, where it's possible to swim. There are also plenty of birds and wild monkeys to spot.

The N200 charge goes directly to the local Boki villages, towards community development projects; the ranch is the area's largest private employer. There is no food at the ranch; you'll need to bring tinned goods with you, while beans, rice, eggs etc can be bought at local villages.

Visits to the ranch should be arranged in advance through Pandrillus in Calabar. A drop taxi from Calabar should cost around N8500; the road is under improvement to allow all-year access. From Calabar, the road leads past Ikom to Obudu, then turns west to Katabang village over the Afi River. It's a further 6.5km from the village to the ranch.

# THE CENTRE

Nigeria's centre is a transitional area, acting mainly as a hinterland between the northern and southern halves. It is home to the Federal Capital Territory of Abuja, the modernist capital, and the city of Jos, which sits cool and high on a temperate plateau. There are also a couple of national parks – Yankari and the remote and rugged Gashka-Gumti.

## ABUJA
☎ 09

Nigeria's made-to-measure capital, Abuja was founded in the booming 1970s. After the Biafran war, the decision was made to move the capital to the ethnically neutral centre of the country. Construction began as the price of oil crashed in the 1980s and, even today, it feels like a work in progress. The National Mosque, law courts and Presidential Palace are impressive, but the city has only slowly become the actual capital; many ministries and some embassies are in Lagos. Clean, quiet and with good electricity, sometimes Abuja hardly feels like Nigeria at all. There's not much to do, but it's a good place to catch your breath and do some visa shopping.

### Orientation

Abuja is criss-crossed by expressways and wide avenues – it's not built for pedestrians. Running parallel to each other southwest to northeast, the main roads are Constitution Ave, Independence Ave and Moshood Abiola Rd. These surround the Central Business District, and are crossed by the expressways Olusegun Obasanjo Way and Shehu Shagari Way, with the latter running near the Presidential Palace and Supreme Court. Maitama is to the north, where there are many embassies. The National Mosque and large Sheraton Hotel are good for getting your bearings.

### Information

The best place to change money is with the Hausa moneychangers outside the Sheraton Hotel.

**Anjo Cybercafé** (Borno St; per hr N100)

**Area 1 Internet** (Area 1 Shopping Centre, Moshood Abiola Way; per hr N100)

**British Council** (Plot 2395 Ibrahim Babangida Way; day membership N500; ☉ 10am-6pm) With a library, free Internet and rooftop café.

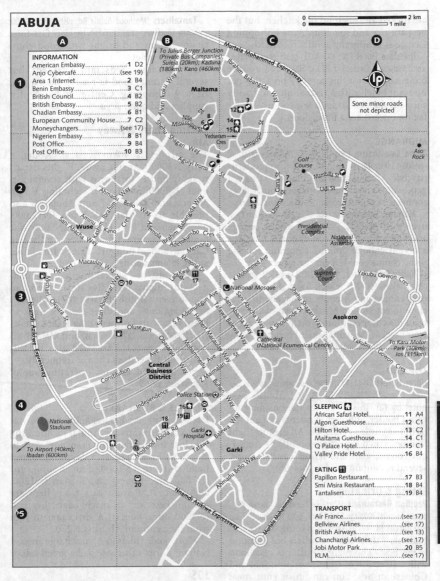

## ABUJA

**INFORMATION**
| | |
|---|---|
| American Embassy | 1 D2 |
| Anjo Cybercafé | (see 19) |
| Area 1 Internet | 2 B4 |
| Benin Embassy | 3 C1 |
| British Council | 4 B2 |
| British Embassy | 5 B2 |
| Chadian Embassy | 6 B1 |
| European Community House | 7 C2 |
| Moneychangers | (see 17) |
| Nigerien Embassy | 8 B1 |
| Post Office | 9 B4 |
| Post Office | 10 B3 |

**SLEEPING**
| | |
|---|---|
| African Safari Hotel | 11 A4 |
| Algon Guesthouse | 12 C1 |
| Hilton Hotel | 13 C2 |
| Maitama Guesthouse | 14 C1 |
| Q Palace Hotel | 15 C1 |
| Valley Pride Hotel | 16 B4 |

**EATING**
| | |
|---|---|
| Papillon Restaurant | 17 B3 |
| Smi Msira Restaurant | 18 B4 |
| Tantalisers | 19 B4 |

**TRANSPORT**
| | |
|---|---|
| Air France | (see 17) |
| Bellview Airlines | (see 17) |
| British Airways | (see 13) |
| Chanchangi Airlines | (see 17) |
| Jobi Motor Park | 20 B5 |
| KLM | (see 17) |

Some minor roads not depicted

**NIGERIA**

---

**Post office** ( Mon-Fri) Garki (Moshood Abiola Way);
Wuse Shopping Centre (**Wuse Shopping Centre**)

## Sleeping

Abuja tends to empty at weekends, with people leaving for more exciting destinations, so many hotels offer discounts for Friday/Saturday nights – always ask if

there's a deal when checking in. Budget hotels are thin on the ground.

### BUDGET

**African Safari Hotel** ( 234 1881; Plot 11, Benue Crescent; r from N2300; ) A nice quiet budget option, with a range of rooms which increase in size as the price does – the cheapest are tucked away behind the kitchen, but the best are airy and spacious. Area 1 Shopping Centre is nearby for good street food.

**Q Palace Hotel** ( ☎ 413 3021; qpalacehotel@yahoo .com; Yedseram Crescent; r N2500-5000; ❄ ) A rare budget option for this part of Abuja, this is a pleasant hotel, with a restaurant and handy shop on site. Ask to see a few rooms – those facing inward are a little gloomy.

### MIDRANGE

**Algon Guesthouse** ( ☎ 413 4798; Yedseram Crescent; r N6500-13,000; ❄ P ) Built in 'African modern-ist' style – lots of glass and marble – this is a good-value guesthouse with generously large rooms. Ask about weekend discounts here.

**Maitama Guesthouse** ( ☎ 413 0219; Yedseram Cres-cent; r N4000-7000; ❄ 🖥 P ) A bright orange and blue paint job welcomes guests here. It's a decent enough option, if nothing special; some rooms could be on the larger side.

**Valley Pride Hotel** ( ☎ 234 2401; Plot 1373, Borno St; r from N4500-7500 ❄ ) A well-located hotel with cosy rooms and friendly management, and close to eateries on Moshood Abiola. If you want the cheapest rooms you'll have to argue your case, as the management generally only considers them suitable for your driver.

### TOP END

**Hilton Hotel** ( ☎ 413 811; hilton.abuja@hilton.com; Aguiyi Ironsi; r from US$270; ❄ 🖥 P 🏊 ) Abuja's best hotel by far, this is one for the business ac-count holder, although residents can cut the tariff to as little as N23,000. All the top-flight facilities you'd expect are on offer – luxuri-ous rooms, gym and tennis courts, shops, several restaurants and a poolside bar.

## Eating & Drinking

**Papillon Restaurant** (Sheraton Hotel, Ladi Kwali Way; dishes from N1300; ⏰ 12-3.30pm, 6.30-10.30pm) The Sheraton Hotel is worth visiting for its res-taurants – there are two others but Papillon is the best. The nightly buffet is excellent, with a selection of Continental, Indian and Chinese dishes. You can finish your meal with drinks in the Elephant Bar until 1am.

**Smi Msira Restaurant** (Moshood Abiola Rd; dishes from N700; ⏰ 9am-midnight) You can get all your favourite Nigerian dishes here, but the main draw is being able to sit in the pleasant leafy surroundings – a genuine beer garden. Claims they never close are exaggerated, but the food is still good (especially in the evenings).

**Tantalisers** (Moshood Abiola Rd; dishes from N200; ⏰ 8am-10pm) A standard Nigerian fast-food chain – clean and bright with good chips and handy toilets.

In Maitama, Yedseram Crescent has several decent 'food-is-ready' places, and Area 1 Shopping Centre is handy for supplies and good *suya*.

## Getting There & Away

### AIR

The airport is 40km west of Abuja, a hefty N3000 taxi ride away. Flights depart roughly hourly for Lagos with several air-lines (N9000, one hour), including Virgin Nigeria and Bellview. From Abuja it's also possible to fly daily to Kano (N12,000, one hour) and Port Harcourt (N9000, one hour), and several times a week to Ibadan, Calabar and Maiduguri. Check timetables at the **information desk** ( ☎ 810 0001).

Abuja also has several international con-nections: flights leave five times a week to London with **British Airways** ( ☎ 413 9610; Hilton Hotel; Aguiyi Ironsi); and three times a week to Frankfurt with Lufthansa. **Air France** ( ☎ 461 0777; Sheraton Hotel, Ladi Kwali Way) and **KLM** ( ☎ 523 9966; Sheraton Hotel, Ladi Kwali Way) also fly this route, but timetables change frequently.

For a list of airlines operating out of Abuja see p669.

### MINIBUS & BUSH TAXI

**Jobi Motor Park** (Utoka; Nnamdi Azikiwe Expressway) is the main terminus for Abuja, on the Ring Rd close to the stadium. Transport goes to all points from here; sample minibus fares include Kano (N1000, four hours), Jos (N700, three hours) and Ibadan (N1200, eight hours). Private cars from here are the quickest way to reach Lagos by road (N3200, nine hours). A drop taxi to Jobi from the centre of Abuja is N250.

Most *okada* riders in Abuja charge around N40 for a trip, otherwise hail a green cab.

## JOS
☎ 073

The Jos Plateau, with its temperate climes, is one of the older inhabited parts of Nigeria, and the ancient Nok Terracottas originated here. At 1200m above sea level, Jos is notice-ably cooler than most other parts of the coun-try, and at night you might have the bracing sensation of having to put on an extra layer on.

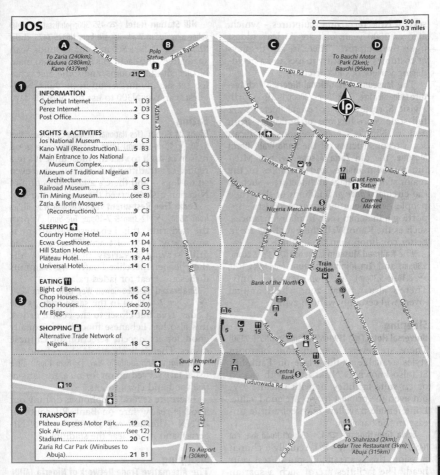

**JOS**

Modern Jos is a British creation which grew on tin mining, and popular tradition claims its name is an abbreviation of 'Jesus Our Saviour', from the first missionaries. It's a good story, but a corruption of a local name is a more likely and prosaic explanation.

The stone-covered rolling hills of the plateau make the area around Jos scenic, and in the city itself there's an unusual but worthwhile museum of Nigerian architecture.

## Orientation

The city has two main north–south drags. One is Bauchi Rd, along which you'll find the large covered market, the train station and some commercial establishments; it becomes Murtala Mohammed Way after

the major junction with Tafawa Balewa Rd (look for the giant woman statue). Roughly 1km to the west is Gromwalk Rd, known as 'The Beach', which runs parallel to the now-defunct railway line.

## Information

**Cyberhut Internet** (Murtala Mohammed Way; per hr N100)
**Perez Internet** (Murtala Mohammed Way; per hr N100)
**Post office** (Ahmadu Bello Way)

## Sights

The **Jos National Museum complex** (Museum Rd) is really four separate museums in one. The **Jos National Museum** (admission N10; 8.30am-5.30pm) has a superb collection of pottery, including several Nok Terracotta sculptures – which, at over 2500 years old, are Africa's oldest figurative sculptures. There are also displays of costumes, some scary masks and a bewildering variety of old currency.

The **Museum of Traditional Nigerian Architecture** (admission free; 🕙 8.30am-5.30pm) is also worth a visit. Spread out over several hectares are full-scale reproductions of buildings from each of Nigeria's major regions. You can see a reconstruction of the **Kano Wall**, **Ilorin Mosque**, the old **Zaria Mosque**, with a Muslim museum inside, and examples of the major styles of village architecture – such as the circular *katanga* buildings of the Nupe people, with beautifully carved posts supporting a thatched roof. In many instances, such as the Kano Wall, these replicas are in better condition than the originals.

The **Railroad Museum** (admission N20; 🕙 8.30am-5.30pm) and **Tin Mining Museum** (admission N20; 🕙 8.30am-5.30pm) are for devotees only. There's also a small zoo, which animal lovers will certainly want to avoid.

## Sleeping

**Universal Hotel** ( ☎ 459 166; Pankshin St; r N550-2150) There are several combinations of room styles available at this place on Pankshin St (also known as Nziki Ave), with shared or en suite facilities, or with satellite TV, but even the priciest rooms are good value. Lone female travellers may feel a little uneasy in the bar area.

**Ecwa Guesthouse** ( ☎ 454 482; off Noad Ave; dm N450, r N1000; 🌀 🖳 P 🔊) Actually a church mission, this is a tranquil spot to rest your head. The facilities are of such a spartan nature that you feel they must be good for the soul. No alcohol is allowed.

**Plateau Hotel** ( ☎ 455 741; Rest House Rd; r from N2875; 🌀 P 🔊) This government hotel is a bit run down, but the price has slipped as well, making it a decent budget option. Rooms are fairly modest, while the addition of water would improve the swimming pool immeasurably.

**Country Home Hotel** ( ☎ 462 479; Tudunwada Rd; r N4100-6350, ste from N8450; 🌀 P ) Smart green paint unifies this set of slightly sprawling blocks. Inside, rooms are cosy and all have water heaters. There's also a pleasant garden bar and a huge number of staff scurrying about everywhere. Good value for the price.

**Hill Station Hotel** ( ☎ 455 300; johillstationhotel@ yahoo.com; Tudun Wada Rd; s/d from N6325/7475, chalet N23,690; 🌀 P 🔊) Set in huge grounds with shady trees and cacti, this hotel has two main blocks with fine rooms, and some nicer chalets set slightly further up in the hills. Nonguests can pay N300 to use the pool all day.

## Eating

**Bight of Benin** (Jos National Museum Complex; dishes N250; 🕙 10am-5.30pm) This restaurant is a good reason in itself to visit the museums. It's in a replica of a traditional chief's hut – you even sit on logs – and there's a tasty selection of Nigerian dishes served throughout the day.

**Cedar Tree Restaurant** Yakubu Gowan Way; dishes from N500; 🕙 12-3pm & 7-10pm, Tue-Sun) Worth the taxi ride, this Lebanese restaurant is some way south of town. There's a good grill, serving a variety of kebabs, while the cheaper mezelike falafel and hummus dishes are great for jaded palates.

**Shahrazad** (Yakubu Gowon Way; dishes from N800; 🕙 12-3pm, 7-10.30pm) In the same style as the Cedar Tree but closer to the centre of Jos, this also has Lebanese food, but is equally good for its decent selection of Chinese dishes. There's lively music at weekends.

**Mr Biggs** (Ahmadu Bello Way; 🕙 8am-10pm) The usual fare served up on formica, for fans of fast food and clean toilets.

There are several chophouses dishing out 'food-is-ready' fare on Bank Rd south of ATNN (Alternative Trade Network of Nigeria), and more near the stadium.

## Shopping

The **Alternative Trade Network of Nigeria** (ATNN; Museum St) is a worker's cooperative selling attractive handicrafts such as baskets, leatherwork, and jewellery. It's part of the UK Fair Trade Network.

The Hill Station Hotel has a shop at the entrance selling Nok-style pottery.

## Getting There & Away

There is a daily flight between Jos and Lagos with **Slok Air** ( ☎ 455 300; desk at Hill Station Hotel). The airport is 30km south of Jos – N2800 by taxi.

Head for Bauchi Motor Park, northeast of town, if you're going north or east. Minibuses and bush taxis from here include to Kaduna (N600, four hours), Zaria (N500, four hours) and Kano (N600, five hours).

NIGERIA

From **Plateau Express Motor Park** (Tafawa Balewa Rd), minibuses leave for Abuja (N700, three hours) and points further south.

*Okadas* in Jos cost around N30–40 for a ride.

# BAUCHI

☎ 077

Bauchi city, capital of Bauchi State, is a convenient stop on your way to or from Yankari National Park. It was the home to Nigeria's first prime minister Tafawa Balewa, and you can visit his **mausoleum** (near Central Market Roundabout; admission free; ☉ 7am-6pm). Sharia law operates in Bauchi.

## Sleeping & Eating

**Horizontal Motel** (Jos Rd; r N1600; ✕ **P**) In the centre of Bauchi, the Horizontal is an adequate budget option, with reasonably well turned out facilities.

**Obuna Royal Hotel** ( ☎ 541 941; Murtala Mohammed Way; ✕ ) Near the football stadium, this is a good bright place, with nice rooms and a restaurant serving dependably tasty Nigerian food and alcohol.

**Zaranda Hotel** ( ☎ 543 814; Jos Rd; r N5870; ✕ 🖳 **P** 🖳 ) The Zaranda is several kilometres west of town. Rooms are comfortable, the hotel has a decent bar and two good restaurants, plus a booking office for Yankari National Park.

## Getting There & Away

The main motor park is just north of Bauchi Market. Minibuses depart to Maiduguri (N1000; five hours), Jos (N250, two hours) and Abuja (N900; five hours) from here. To get to Yankari, transport leaves erratically from Minivan motor park (N600, five hours) – the road is poor.

# YANKARI NATIONAL PARK

Open for wildlife viewing year-round, **Yankari** (admission N300, photo permit N100-1000 depending on type) is 225km east of Jos, and covers an area of 2244 sq km. It was once one of West Africa's best wildlife areas, but animal populations have suffered due to poaching. The park still holds reasonable numbers of buffaloes, waterbucks, bushbucks and plenty of baboons. The biggest draw is the 500-strong population of elephants, but these can be hard to see and remain threatened – during research we were

offered ivory from, it was claimed, Yankari. Hyenas and leopards can be found and it's possible that lions may also survive. The bird-watching is excellent.

The best time to see animals is from late December to late April, before the rains, when the thirsty animals congregate at the Gaji River. You're permitted to drive your own vehicle if you take a guide, otherwise the park has a **safari truck** (N300; ☉ 7.30am & 3.30pm daily) that takes two hour tours. It's a pretty basic affair, just a flatbed truck with benches in the back, but it gets the job done.

Yankari's other great attraction is the incredibly picturesque **Wikki Warm Spring** (admission N200), near the park campsite. The crystal-clear mineral water is a constant 31°C, forming a lake 200m long and 10m wide. Bring your swimming gear – even if you don't see much wildlife, the spring is a real highlight and shouldn't be missed.

## Sleeping & Eating

**Wikki Warm Spring Camp** ( ☎ 077 542 174; camping per person N500, bungalows N1730-3450; ✕ ) Yankari's only accommodation is 40km inside the park. It has slightly tatty circular bungalows, and a generator which keeps odd hours. We'd suggest giving the cheaper ones rooms a miss. Luckily, for its location, food in the restaurant is pretty good, and there's a bar. It's a short walk from the camp to the spring.

## Getting There & Away

You can get to the park gate at Mainamaji by minibus from Bauchi (N600, five hours). After paying the entrance fee, you'll need to arrange transport to the camp – around N2800 in a taxi, or N1000 by *okada* (if you've got the stamina). Remember to arrange a pick-up from the camp for when you want to leave – you could be waiting days for a lift otherwise.

# GASHAKA-GUMTI NATIONAL PARK

Nigeria's largest national park, Gashaka-Gumti, is also the remotest part of the country, and its least explored. Its 6700 sq km area contains rolling hills, savanna, montane forest and Nigeria's highest mountain, **Chappal Wadi** ('Mountain of Death'; 2418m). It is as wild and spectacular a corner of Africa as you could wish for.

It also holds incredible diversity and is one of West Africa's most important

NIGERIA

primate habitats. A new (to science) sub-species of chimpanzee was discovered here in 2003. The park is also supports lions, elephants, hippos and buffaloes. Much of the park remains unsurveyed, although human encroachment presents a clear threat.

Visiting Gashaka-Gumti is not a casual affair, as infrastructure is virtually nonexistent. The park headquarters are at Serti, eight hours from Jos. There is a small rest-house here, and you should be able to arrange a guide and vehicle hire. The area has no phone connections. It might also be worth visiting the WWF office 35km south in Gashaka, where they may be able to advise on current projects and accessibility. Inside the park, you'll need to be completely self-sufficient. With the proper planning, a trekking expedition here could be truly fantastic.

**Jemi-Alade Tours** (☎ 01 496 0297; jemi-alade@ alpha.linkserve.com) in Lagos have run a few expensive tours to the park.

# THE NORTH

Northern Nigeria feels like a completely different country to the south and, but for the accident of colonial borders, it would be. The green of the countryside becomes drier as the Sahel approaches, and there's a whiff of desert sand in the air. The profusion of churches also begins to disappear, and is replaced by mosques and the call to prayer. Most northerners are Hausa or Fulani.

Islam informs every aspect of life in the north. The ancient trading cities of Kano, Zaria and Sokoto carry echoes of the old Sokoto Caliphate, and still have ties to the old trading routes across the Sahara. And, while many of the political and religious issues which divide Nigeria – such as the introduction of Sharia law – find their centre in the region, visitors to the north are likely to find nothing more than traditional Muslim hospitality welcoming them on their visit.

## KADUNA
☎ 062
If you're travelling up from southern Nigeria, Kaduna is likely to be your first port of call. It was founded by Frederick Lugard, Nigeria's first colonial governor in 1913 (locals can still point out his residence) as a new political centre for the north. More re-

cently, Kaduna found unwanted fame as the centre of communal riots resulting from the aborted Miss World competition in Abuja in 2000. It's a small, modern city and, as the capital of a Sharia state, finds itself on one of Nigeria's political and religious fault lines.

Kaduna's main artery is the wide Ahmadu Bello Way, running north to south.

## Information
**Al-Ameen Bureau de Change** (Hamdala Hotel, Muhammed Buhari Way) A useful moneychanger. Hausa moneychangers also congregate outside the hotel gate.
**British Council** (☎ 236 033; Yakubu Gowon Rd) Near the post office and banks.
**Netpoint Internet** (Leventis Bldg, Ahmadu Bello Way; per hr N200)

## Sights
The **national museum** (Ali Akilu Rd; admission N100; � 9am-6pm), at the northern end of the city, on the road to Kano and across from the Emir's Palace, has local masks, carvings, pottery, brasswork and woodcarvings. Better is the replica Hausa Village on site, with traditional huts and, in the late afternoon, drumming and dancing. It's worth dashing one of the staff to give you a guided tour.

## Sleeping
**Budget Master Hotel** (☎ 372 915; www.nanet-hotels .com; 15 Abubakar Kigo Rd, r N1700-2200; ⚙) More than living up to its name, this hotel offers good quality, cheap lodgings. Rooms come with satellite TV and kettle, and there's a fast food restaurant and bar off the lobby.

**Gloria Moria Hotel** (☎ 240 720; 2 Ahmadu Bello Way; r incl breakfast N3000; ⚙) With cosy carpeted rooms, this is a tidy place to lay your head. All rooms have fridges, but try to choose one at the back, away from the noisy mosque on the main road.

**Excel Inn** (☎ 243 556; 23 Constitution Rd; r/ste N3450/6900; ⚙ 🖥) Large rooms here are comfortable, if characterless, with lots of sterile white tiles and marble in evidence, but each come with a handy fridge. The shop next to reception offers an eclectic selection of clothes and pocket calculators.

**Command Guesthouse** (☎ 242 918; 10 Mohammed Buhari Way; r from N11200; ⚙ Ⓟ) If the name has a slightly martial ring, then it should be no surprise to find this hotel being run with military precision: everything is spotless and the bed sheets are immaculately crisp.

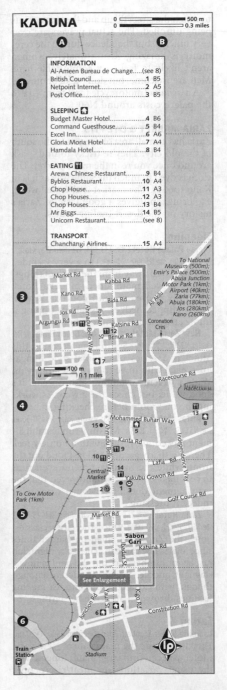

**KADUNA**

The atmosphere for guests is, thankfully, a little more relaxed, making this a great choice for a night or three.

**Hamdala Hotel** ( ☎ 245 440; 26 Mohammed Buhari Way; r US$69-98, ste from US$144; ❄ 🖥 🍴 🅿 ) Kaduna's large upscale establishment, with good, if occasionally bland, rooms. There's a restaurant and pleasant garden bar, plus a well-stocked bookshop (selling international press) and a moneychanger. Nonresidents pay in US dollars.

## Eating

**Byblos Restaurant** (Ahmadu Bello Way; mains from N1000, meze from N400; ⊗ 12-30pm & 7-11pm) Tucked behind a supermarket, Byblos has white linen and cheesy muzak as side orders to decent Lebanese and continental dishes. The meze platter for four (N10,500) is a good choice.

**Arewa Chinese Restaurant** (Ahmadu Bello Way; mains N650-1200; ⊗ 12-3pm & 7-10pm) Decorated with red Chinese lanterns, this is a classy place for dinner. Meals come in small, medium or large servings, whichever the dish, and, for a restaurant in a Sharia state, there's an impressive amount of alcohol served, and pork on the menu to boot.

**Unicorn Restaurant** (Hamdala Hotel; ☎ 245 440; 26 Mohammed Buhari Way) Offers similar fare to Arewa.

**Mr Biggs** (Yakubu Gowon Way; ⊗ 8am-10pm) Kaduna has a branch of the reliable Nigerian fast food outlet.

There are chophouses open all day on Ibrahim Talwo Rd and Ibadan St, and others serving up Nigerian dishes clustered around the Central Market and in Sabon Gari. Don't expect alcohol to be served.

## Getting There & Away
### AIR
**Chanchangi Airlines** ( ☎ 249 949, Ahmadu Bello Way) fly twice a day to/from Lagos (N11,000, one hour). The airport is 40km north of Kaduna; expect to pay N2800 for a taxi.

### BUS & BUSH TAXI
The main motor park is at Abuja Junction on the northern edge of Kaduna. Minibuses and bush taxis go from here to Abuja (N500, four hours), Jos, (N600, four hours), Kano (N400, three hours) and Zaria (N170, one hour). Zaria transport also goes from Cow Motor Park in the east – minibuses fill quickly from here.

**NIGERIA**

# ZARIA

While Kano is the north's biggest draw, it would be shame to miss this smaller walled city, just an hour from Kaduna. Another big player on the medieval Saharan trade routes, Zaria was one of the Hausa city states swept up by the tide of the Fulani jihad which formed the Sokoto Caliphate. Today, Zaria is a quiet and peaceful place, with its old walled centre surprisingly intact, sitting next to the tree-lined cantonments set up by the British in the early 20th century. Zaria's emir still lives in a grand palace, and leads the population in a grand ceremony at Friday prayers – an event worth seeing.

Sokoto Rd is the main road running through Zaria. At its northern end is Gra – the old British area with most of the hotels and the main motor park. As it crosses the Kubani river, it becomes Kaduna Rd, passing through Koko Dofa city gate and into the Old City.

## Information

Change money before travelling to Zaria. For net access, try **Grant Cybercafé** (Sokoto Rd, per hour N120) 250m north of Aiffas Motel.

## Sights

### EMIR'S PALACE & CENTRAL MOSQUE

The Emir's Palace and Central Mosque form the spiritual centre of Zaria's old city. Both are modern affairs, built on the sites of much older constructions.

The palace has a brightly painted carved plaster façade, covered with abstract Hausa designs which somehow manage to look both traditional and very modern. They sit above the public gateway, with its shaded benches for those waiting for an audience with the emir. The emir's gate is actually the duller brown gate 20m to the right – look for the green flag that indicates if he is in residence. Outside the royal gate is a green-roofed round building which houses the emir's war drums. The head drummer (who has been in the position for over 55 years) will show you inside for a small dash.

Every Friday at around 2pm, the emir walks from his palace to the mosque opposite to lead prayers, surrounded by his splendidly dressed royal guards. The entire area surrounding the compounds fills with up to 10,000 (male) worshippers. It's an impressive sight, and it's worth getting there early to watch the street fill up and the prayer mats being unrolled. The actual prayers are over very quickly, but the silence during the ceremony is amazing. Unfortunately, women aren't likely to feel very comfortable here. Men are welcome, but don't take photos.

An *achaba* (motorcycle taxi) from Gra to the palace costs around N60.

### ZARIA MARKET & DYE PITS

Zaria has a small area of dye pits in the south of the old city. They're tricky to find – ask around once you're in the main market. The cloth is dyed in much the same way as it is in Kano (p661). The market is also well worth exploring, and gives a good taste of Zaria's history on the desert trading routes.

## Sleeping

**Teejay Palace Hotel** ( ☎ 333 303; Western Way Close; r N3000-3800, ste N5000; ✷ ℗ ) In a very secluded location, well away from the thick of things, this is a well-maintained modern hotel, with tidy rooms around courtyards with neatly clipped hedges, just about tipping it into Zaria's top accommodation spot.

**New Zaria Motel** ( ☎ 332 451; Queen Elizabeth Rd; chalet N2300; ✷ ℗ ) Set in large grounds, this motel is a series of colonial-style bungalows, each with huge rooms and large beds. With a decent restaurant also on site, it's good value; but check the air-con is working in your room before checking in.

**Aiffas Motel** ( ☎ 332 033; Sokoto Rd; r N3450-5600, ste N5175; ✷ ) This Muslim-run establishment has comfy rooms with a homely feel. There's a shady garden and fast food out the front, while the breakfast menu even runs to cornflakes. Be advised, however, that the management doesn't welcome 'careless or indecent dressing'.

**Zaria Hotel** ( ☎ 333 092; Samura Rd; r N4025-5750, ste N9775; ✷ ✸ ℗ ) Once the city's classiest hotel, the Zaria has fallen on harder times since Sharia law came in. The tacky nightclub just about lumbers on, but the pool is now a stagnant puddle. Rooms are decent enough though, with extra cushions and tea-making facilities thrown in at the higher tariff.

## Eating

**La Reine** (Queen Elizabeth Rd; dishes from N500; ✷ 7am-11pm) Just inside the main gate of New Zaria Motel, you can find large plates topped with the usual variations on meat/rice/pepper sauce here. They also do a good, if greasy, chips with baked beans – curiously only for breakfast though, not dinner.

**Emanto** (Sokoto Rd; dishes from N750; 🕙 12-3pm, 7-10pm) Signed just off the main road, Emanto is a Lebanese-run restaurant, with meze and kebabs, along with a fair selection of pasta and continental dishes.

**Al Nasara Restaurant** (Sokoto Rd; dishes from N250; 🕙 8am-9pm) Between Dadi motor park and the Aiffas Hotel, the Al Nasara is a typical Nigerian 'food-is-ready' joint, with all the cow-leg soup, *egusi* and pounded yam which that entails.

**Tonia Restaurant** (Sokoto Rd) A few doors up from Al Nasara, this has more of the same.

For a fast food fix, there's a **Mr Biggs** (Kaduna Rd; 🕙 8am-10pm), just south of Gra. The **Zaria Hotel** ( ☎ 333 092; Samura Rd) is the only place to get a beer in this Sharia city.

## Getting There & Away

Dadi motor park is on Sokoto Rd next to the Kano–Zaria Highway flyover. Bush taxis and minibuses leave constantly for Kano (N300, two hours) and Kaduna (N170, one hour), as well as Sokoto (N500, four hours), Jos (N500, four hours) Abuja (N800, six hours) and further destinations. Bush taxis fight here for the same custom.

## KANO

☎ 064 / pop 4million
Largest of the ancient Hausa city states, Kano is the oldest surviving city in West Africa, and was founded around 1400 years ago. It was a major crossroads in the trans-Saharan trade routes and, from the Middle Ages, an important centre for Islamic scholarship. Today, it is still the economic centre of the northern Nigeria, and is the country's third biggest city. It's also the major draw for travellers in the region.

Kano's main attractions are found in the Old City. Indigo cloth has been made in dye pits here for hundreds of years, and the market remains atmospheric enough to evoke thoughts of Ibn Battuta and Mungo Park. Kano also has one of Nigeria's best museums, Gidan Makama.

Modern Kano is a huge place, with notoriously bad traffic. Fumes, coupled with the scouring harmattan wind, mean that on a bad day you'll have grit in your teeth and the sky will turn a dusty brown. Kano is

dry in other ways too – as capital of a Sharia state, alcohol was technically banned in 2004. The law is yet to be fully enacted, and you can still get a drink in upmarket restaurants, or in the bars of Sabon Gari, but this could change at a politician's whim.

## Orientation

Murtala Mohammed Way is one of Kano's most important roads, running east–west through the city. Travellers often base themselves near here, particularly around Bompai Rd, where there are good restaurants and other facilities. North of Murtala Mohammed is Sabon Gari, where you'll find most of Kano's Christian population, along with the majority of bars and the cheaper hotels.

The Old City is to the southwest, surrounded by the decrepit old walls. Some of the gates in the wall, however, are still intact; the main gate is Kofar Mata, which leads to the central mosque and the Emir's Palace. The warren of Kurmi Market is in the centre of the Old City; for amazing views, climb Dala Hill just to the north.

## Information

### CULTURAL CENTRES

**British Council** ( ☎ 626 500; Emir Palace Rd) Built in traditional Hausa style.

### INTERNET

**Friends Internet** (Murtala Mohammed Way; per hr N200) Possibly Nigeria's nicest Internet café.
**Sasilnet Cybercafé** (Inside Daula Hotel compound; per hr N150)

### MONEY

Try the moneychangers at the craft stalls outside the Central Hotel; they'll also exchange West African CFA. The tourist office has a bureau de change.

### POST

**DHL** ( ☎ 649752; 139 Murtala Mohammed Way)
**Post office** (Post Office Rd)

### TOURIST INFORMATION

**Kano State Tourist Board** ( ☎ 646 309, Tourist Camp, Bompai Rd) A rarity in Nigeria – a working tourist office. Has pamphlets and can arrange guides to the Old City (per hr N1500).

### TRAVEL AGENTS

**Visa Travel & Tours** ( ☎ 646 298; Bompai Rd)

# KANO

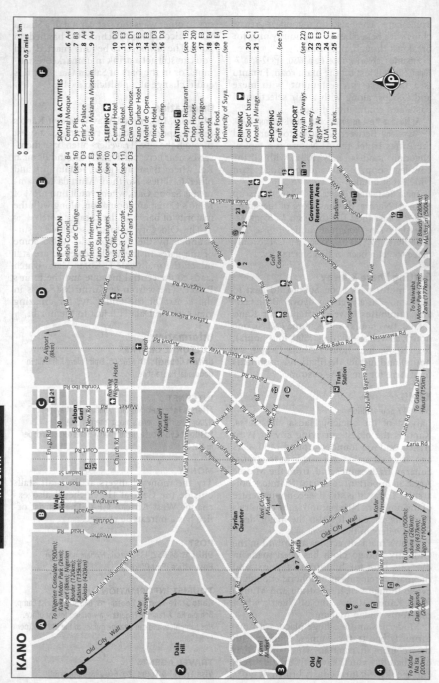

**INFORMATION**

| British Council | 1 B4 |
| --- | --- |
| Bureau de Change | (see 16) |
| DHL | 2 D3 |
| Friends Internet | 3 E3 |
| Kano State Tourist Board | (see 10) |
| Moneychangers | (see 16) |
| Post Office | 4 C3 |
| Sasilnet Cybercafe | (see 11) |
| Visa Travel and Tours | 5 D3 |

**SIGHTS & ACTIVITIES**

| Central Mosque | 6 A4 |
| --- | --- |
| Dye Pits | 7 B3 |
| Emir's Palace | 8 A4 |
| Gidan Makama Museum | 9 A4 |

**SLEEPING** 🛏

| Central Hotel | 10 D3 |
| --- | --- |
| Daula Hotel | 11 E3 |
| Eowa Guesthouse | 12 D1 |
| Kano Durbar Hotel | 13 E3 |
| Motel de Opera | 14 E3 |
| Prince Hotel | 15 D3 |
| Tourist Camp | 16 D3 |

**EATING** 🍴

| Calypso Restaurant | (see 15) |
| --- | --- |
| Chop Houses | (see 20) |
| Golden Dragon | 17 E3 |
| Locanda | 18 E4 |
| Spice Food | 19 E4 |
| University of Suya | (see 11) |

**DRINKING** 🍷

| Cool Spot bars | 20 C1 |
| --- | --- |
| Motel le Mirage | 21 C1 |

**SHOPPING**

| Craft Stalls | (see 5) |
| --- | --- |

**TRANSPORT**

| Afriqiyah Airways | (see 22) |
| --- | --- |
| Air Niamey | 22 E3 |
| Egypt Air | 23 E3 |
| KLM | 24 C2 |
| Local Taxis | 25 B1 |

## Sights

### KURMI MARKET & DYE PITS

With thousands of stalls in a 16-hectare area, Kurmi Market is one of the largest markets in Africa, and is the city's main attraction. It's a centre for African crafts, including gold-, bronze- and silver-work, and all types of fabrics – from ancient religious Hausa gowns and a huge selection of hand-painted African cloth to the latest imported suits. It can be a bit overwhelming; you might want to take up the offer of a guide, who will no doubt approach you.

Away from the throng are the **Kofa Dye Pits** (Kofa Mata Gate; ⏲ 7am-7pm daily), where indigo cloth has been dyed for hundreds of years. Each narrow pit is 6m deep, and is filled with 100kg of indigo, along with 30 buckets of ash and 5 buckets of potassium (usually from urine); the resulting mix lasts one year. The depth of colour varies according to the time the cloth is dipped – 90 minutes gives a pale blue, while the deepest indigo needs a six-hour soaking. Check out the room to one side where the finished cloth is hammered to give it a fashionable sheen. Finished cloth is for sale, starting from around N1200 for a couple of metres according to the design. A dash of around N100 is appropriate for a guided tour.

### GIDAN MAKAMA MUSEUM

This **museum** (Emir Palace Rd; N100; ⏲ 8am-6pm) is the best in northern Nigeria. It stands on the site of the original Emir's Palace (the oldest part is 15th century), and is a wonderful example of traditional Hausa architecture. In the entrance are two of Kano's original city gates, leading into a series of compounds. One of the first buildings is a mock-up of a Hausa bride's hut, followed by an interesting exhibition on the history of Islam (and particularly Sufism) in the region. Also on display is a fascinating photographic history of Kano, starting with the taking of the city by the British in 1902.

It's well worth taking one of the museum's guides, as they are very knowledgeable. A dash is appreciated.

### EMIR'S PALACE & CENTRAL MOSQUE

The modern **central mosque** (Kofar Mata Rd) hosts Kano's main Friday prayers at around 1pm, attracting up to 50,000 worshippers – which is an amazing sight. The original Hausa mudbrick mosque was torn down in the 1960s after Kano's emir had been on the Haj to Mecca, to be replaced with a Saudi design. There are good photos of the original in the Gidan Makama museum.

The **Emir's Palace** (Emir Palace Rd), next door, has a parade ground outside which is used for the annual Durbar.

### GIDAN DAN HAUSA

A great example of Kano's architecture is the **Gidan Dan Hausa** (Dan Hausa Rd; N50; ⏲ 8am-4pm, 8am-1pm Fri), blending Hausa and Arab styles. It's the former home of Hanns Vischer, the first British administrator, and was built in 1905. The house is now a museum, showing regional crafts and ceremonial costumes, but it's worth visiting for the building alone.

## Festivals & Events

The Kano Durbar is held annually just after the end of Ramadan, and is the biggest festival of its kind in Nigeria. Exact dates are variable (see p818) and check in advance if possible. There is a cavalry procession featuring ornately dressed men mounted on colourfully bedecked horses. The horsemen wear breastplates and coats of flexible armour and, on their scarlet turbans, copper helmets topped with plumes. The emir, draped in white and protected by a heavy brocade parasol embroidered with silver, rides in the middle of the cavalry. The procession finishes outside the Emir's Palace, where there is drumming, singing, and massed cavalry charges.

## Sleeping

For a city of its size, Kano's sleeping options feel a bit limited. Hotels usually add on a mysterious 1% tourist tax (included in all prices below).

### BUDGET

**Ecwa Guesthouse** ( ☎ 631 410; 1 Mission Rd; r N1500-2500; ✕) This church mission has spartan, but spotlessly clean rooms, to make it a good budget choice. Unusually for Nigeria, there are a few genuine twin rooms, with the cheapest having a fan only. There's a restaurant but alcohol is forbidden.

**Tourist Camp** ( ☎ 642 017; 11 Bompai Rd; r N2000) This state-run enterprise has a soporific air, and if you stay for too long you might end up as dusty and sleepy as the rooms and staff. Rooms are small and hot, but handy

**NIGERIA**

and cheap, with the novelty of a genuine working tourist office on site.

**Motel le Mirage** ( ☎ 311007; 27 Enugu Rd; r N1300-3200; ⚡ ) In the heart of Sabon Gari, le Mirage has small, slightly tatty rooms, which are nevertheless fair value for the price. There's a handy restaurant and bar, and dozens more within crawling distance.

### MIDRANGE

**Central Hotel** ( ☎ 630 002; Bompai Rd; r N3250-6960; ⚡ ⚡ P ) A huge concrete confection in pink and blue, with a crazy sci-fi dome in the courtyard, the Central's rooms are more staid than the exterior would have you believe. Accommodation is fair to good as the tariff rises, occasionally touching on the cosy.

**Daula Hotel** ( ☎ 640 010; 150 Murtala Mohammed Way; daulahotel@hotmail.com; r N3400-4200; ⚡ ⚡ ⚡ P ) Rooms are fair to middling in this large complex, but check for scary nests of wires poking from every plug. There are not one, but two, Internet cafés and a money-changer, while helpful signs remind guests not to spit on the walls.

**Motel de Opera** ( ☎ 316 347; 62 Hadejira Rd; r N4500-5500; ⚡ ) On a busy main road, rooms here are small but functional, with a few decorated by someone with a clear Disney obsession. All have fridges. There's a pleasant courtyard café-bar, but no alcohol is served.

**Kano Durbar Hotel** ( ☎ 641 139; 116 Ahmadu Bello Way; r N8120-9280; ⚡ P ) This hotel has large bright rooms, and bathrooms come with water heaters. It's a decent choice, although the acres of white tiles do much to preclude any outbreak of personality.

### TOP END

**Prince Hotel** ( ☎ 639402; Tamandu Rd; r N11,600-16,240, ste N24,360; ⚡ P ) Modern and exceedingly comfortable rooms, with gleaming bathrooms in a quiet close. It's often fully booked, but even nonguests should enjoy visiting the posh restaurant and bar.

### Eating

**Spice Food** (Magasin Rumfa Rd; dishes from N450; ⊙ 12-3.30pm & 6-11pm) If you've been craving some vegie food in Nigeria, this great Indian restaurant will answer your prayers (meat dishes are also served). The spices range from delicate to lively, with plenty of great naan bread and dhal as side orders. The N750 buffet every Sunday at 7.30pm is not to be missed.

**Golden Dragon** (Ahmadu Bello Way; mains N900-1200; ⊙ 10.30am-11pm) Liveried waiters and traditional Chinese decorations give this place a great ambience – there are even hot towels to freshen up. Dishes run the range of Chinese classics, but try not to fill up on the delicious spring rolls before your main course arrives.

**Locanda** (Sultan Rd; pasta from N750, ⊙ 10.30am-10.30pm Tue-Sun) Step inside here and you could be forgiven for thinking yourself transported to an old Italian bistro. Even the red-checked tablecloths look the part. The menu is stuffed with tasty pasta, pizza and meat options, and doesn't neglect the vegetarians either.

**Calypso Restaurant** (Prince Hotel; Tamandu Rd; meze from N400, mains from N1000; ⊙ 12-4pm & 7pm-midnight) The classiest presentation in town, you don't want to feel too scruffy eating here. The Lebanese meze are the highlight at Calypso, although there's a wide selection of good steaks. Only the muzak lets the atmosphere down.

**University of Suya** (Daula Hotel compound; suya from N100; ⊙ 10am-10pm) Claiming to be the 'Faculty of Meatology', you'd expect good things of the grilled meat here. It doesn't disappoint, with delicious chicken, liver and kidney supplementing the usual beef *suya*, plus some fiery *pepe* to garnish.

The best 'food-is-ready' fare is found in Sabon Gari, with plenty of *egusi* and pepper soup always on offer. Enugu Rd has plenty of **chophouses** (dishes from N250; ⊙ 8am-late), most also doubling up as bars.

### Drinking

Sabon Gari has heaps of bars – although a Sharia-crackdown could change all that during the life of this book. The best places are around Enugu Rd and Ibo Rd – any chophouse with 'Cool Spot' in the name is also a bar. There are also plenty of tavern stores where you can buy alcohol to take away. Don't drink in public outside Sabon Gari.

Most upscale and foreign restaurants also serve alcohol. The bar at the Prince Hotel is a particularly swish place to have a drink.

### Shopping

On Bompain Rd, opposite the Central Hotel, there's a small line of craft stalls, selling an interesting selection of goods and souvenirs from across north Nigeria. Beads, and wood or stone carvings are particularly well-represented.

## Getting there & Away

### AIR

Kano airport is 8km northwest of Sabon Gari – N150 on an *achaba*, three times that in a taxi. **Bellview** ( ☎ 311 462; Kano Airport) and **IRS** ( ☎ 637939; Kano Airport) fly daily to Lagos (N14,000, 90 minutes); IRS also has a daily flight to Abuja (N12,000, one hour).

Kano also has good international connections: once a week to Niamey with **Air Niamey** ( ☎ 316 904; Murtala Mohammed Way), twice weekly to Cairo with **Egypt Air** ( ☎ 630 759; Murtala Mohammed Way), and also twice weekly to both Tripoli and N'Djména with **Afriqiyah Airways** ( ☎ 977 255; Murtala Mohammed Way). There's also a useful European connection twice a week to Amsterdam with **KLM** ( ☎ 632 632; Sani Abacha Way).

### MINIBUS & BUSH TAXI

Kuka Motor Park, on the road to the airport on the west side of town, is the motor park for Sokoto and Katsina and to Maradi on the Nigerien border. Naiwaba Motor Park, possibly Nigeria's most disorganised transport depot (though there's some stiff competition) serves points south and west, including Zaria, Kaduna and Maiduguri, and is on Zaria Rd on the southern outskirts of town.

Sample fares and times include: Zaria (N300, two hours), Kaduna (N400, three hours), Maiduguri (N1000, six hours), Sokoto (N700, six hours) and Jos (N600, four hours). Stamina permitting, Lagos is reachable by bush taxi in 16 hours.

## Getting Around

Kano's *achabas* are fast and furious, charging N50 or thereabouts for a ride. They're the most practical option in the Old City, but Kano also has plenty of taxis if you don't fancy the adrenaline hit. In December 2005, a Sharia decree banned women from riding on *achabas*, a ruling that brought demonstrating drivers – and violence – to the streets, forcing a hasty legal retreat on the issue.

## AROUND KANO

### Katsina

Katsina is a backwater, but of all the cities in northern Nigeria it feels the closest to how the area must have been in its heyday as a medieval Hausa trading kingdom. Its Old City is still relatively intact, and you can wander the back streets and markets getting a real taste of the Sahel. Camels and mudbrick architecture abound.

The highlight of a trip to Katsina is the Gobarau Minaret, the best preserved example of traditional religious architecture in the region. Standing 15m high, it has an unusual spiral design, with steps on the outside. This is thought to be a Fulani concept, brought by pilgrims who would have seen similar minarets in Cairo and Samarra (Iraq). The minaret is in Kangiwa Sq, off Ibrahim Babangida Way, Katsina's main road. Also off this road is the Central Mosque and Emir's Palace.

The best accommodation option in Katsina is the **Katsina Motel** ( ☎ 065 430 017; Mohammed Bashir Rd; r N3000), with good inexpensive rooms, and an adequate restaurant. There's also street food along Ibrahim Babangida Way.

Katsina is an easy day trip from Kano (N300, two hours). It's also possible to travel from here to the Niger border at Maradi 30km away.

## SOKOTO
☎ 060

Tucked away in the hottest and dustiest corner of Nigeria, Sokoto is a scruffy city with a grand past. One of the ancient Hausa city states, in the early 19th century it was the seat of the Sokoto Caliphate, its Fulani masters administering an empire which stretched from Senegal to Cameroon. While Sokoto is now a pale shadow of its former glorious self, and concentrates primarily on trade with Niger, its sultan remains the spiritual head of Nigeria's Muslims today.

At the Sultan's Palace, between 9pm and 11pm on Thursday, you can hear Hausa musicians outside playing to welcome in the Holy Day, Friday. The Shehu Mosque is nearby. At the end of Ramadan, long processions of musicians and elaborately dressed men on horseback make their way from the prayer ground to the Sultan's Palace, a smaller version of Kano's Durbar.

The central market, well known for its handmade leather goods, is held daily except Sunday. Camels are sold just northeast of the market, near the city gate.

## Festivals & Events

Sokoto can be used as a base to visit the spectacular **Argungu Fishing & Cultural Festival** (every Feb), 100km to the southwest – for more details, see p667.

## Sleeping & Eating

**Sokoto Guest Inn** ( ☎ 233 205; Kalambaina Rd; r N1500) Rooms here are in basic but bright chalets; it's a good budget option.

**Shukura Hotel** ( ☎ 230 006; Gusau Rd; r N3500; ✖ ℗ ) This busy hotel, south of the centre, is decent value, with fair rooms.

**Double 7** (Abdullahi Fodio Rd; meals from N800; ✖ 8am-11pm) The best option if you're at the end of Nigeria and bored of pepper soup, Double 7 has a good range of Lebanese and continental food, as well as a convenient supermarket.

Chophouses serving 'food-is-ready' are dotted about the main roads, along with lots of *suya* stalls. Don't expect to find much alcohol.

## Getting There & Away

Sokoto feels a long way from anywhere. **ADC Airlines** ( ☎ 230 006; Shukura Hotel) fly five times a week to Kano (N7000, one hour), where you'll need to change for other destinations. Taxis to the airport (25 minutes) cost N1500.

The main motor park is next to the central market. Minibuses and bush taxis depart frequently to Kano (N700, six hours), Zaria (N500, four hours) and Kaduna (N650, five hours) and less frequently to further destinations. Transport also leaves from here to the Nigerian border at Ilela (N300, 90 minutes).

## MAIDUGURI

☎ 076

Maiduguri is the capital of Borno State, and is close to the Chad and Cameroon borders. Once a British garrison town (its railway station marks the farpoint of colonial influence in Nigeria), the city seems to be sleeping its time away. Even by Nigerian standards electricity is a problem here, so it's a case of early to bed, early to rise – not a bad idea given the scorching daytime temperatures.

Very few travellers make it to Maiduguri, and those who do are mostly on their way to or from Cameroon. The more adventurous might attempt a visit to Lake Chad.

**City Internet** (Shehidu Lamido Way) has Internet access for N130 per hour. For money, try **Barewu Bureau de Change** (Kashim Ibrahim Rd), near the Total petrol station.

Kashim Ibrahim Rd and Shehu Lamido Way, the main thoroughfares in Maiduguri, run north–south, roughly parallel to each other. There's a small, slightly dull, museum off Bama Rd, 1km east of the centre.

## Sleeping & Eating

**Deribe Hotel** ( ☎ 231 662; off Kashim Ibrahim Rd; r N3500; ✖ ℗ ☎ ) Cavernous and gloomy, the Deribe has large rooms and friendly staff. Everything works too – when there's electricity. Ask how many guests there are when checking in, as they won't run the generator if the place is near empty.

**Lake Chad Hotel** ( ☎ 232 400; Kashim Ibrahim Rd; r N4650; ✖ ℗ ☎ ) Another slightly tired but serviceable option, this hotel also has a decent restaurant, a shop selling old international newspapers and a desk for Albaraka Airlines.

**Chez Frenchies** (Kashim Ibrahim Rd; mains from N500; ✖ 9am-8pm) Around the corner from the Deribe Hotel, this small restaurant serves pepper soup and *jollof*. Further south, along Kashim Ibrahim Rd, you might also try Jil's Restaurant or, in a pinch, Mr Biggs.

## Getting There & Away

Border transport to Cameroon is the main reason to find yourself in Maiduguri. Minibuses to the border at Bama (N370, 90 minutes) leave from the busy Tishanbama Motor Park. Transport south also departs from here. Transport to Kano (N1000, six hours) leaves from Kano Motor Park, along with most other westbound vehicles.

There's a daily flight to Abuja with Albaraka Airlines (N10,000, two hours).

## AROUND MAIDUGURI
### Lake Chad

In recent years Lake Chad has receded northeast across the border, which means that Nigeria is no longer as good a vantage point for seeing the enormous lake as Chad or Cameroon. Given this, it is best to go when the water is at its highest, between December and February. Take a minibus to Baga (N600, two hours) from Baga motor park and arrange onward transport from there, most likely by *achaba*.

The bird-watching is excellent, and so is the people-watching – turbaned men leading camels and fisherman mending their nets by the water. It's very remote, but it's a special place and well worth the effort of getting there. If you want to stay, you'll need to be self-sufficient.

# NIGERIA DIRECTORY

## ACCOMMODATION

Throughout this chapter, we've considered budget accommodation as costing up to N2500, midrange N2500 to N5000, and top end from N5000 and up. Hotels are of a fair standard throughout Nigeria, although often poor value compared to neighbouring countries. Most towns and cities have something to suit all pockets. The big exception to this is Lagos, where rooms are either very cheap and not particularly wonderful or very expensive; there's not much middle ground.

Even at the cheaper end of the scale, rooms come with air-con and attached bathroom – the shower is usually a bucket-and-scoop affair in the bathtub, unless you're paying top whack. Bathrooms often have water heaters (useful in the event of an electricity failure), otherwise take promises of hot water with a pinch of salt. Rooms are subject to a hefty 15% tax, which has been included in all prices quoted in this chapter. When checking in, you'll also be asked to pay a deposit, which is usually somewhere between one and two night's room rate. This is refundable against your final bill. Many hotels, midrange and above, have a resident and nonresident rate; if you make it a habit of asking for the resident rate you can sometimes get lucky.

---

**PRACTICALITIES**

■ Privately owned English-language daily newspapers include the *Guardian*, *Daily News*, *Daily Times* and *Vanguard*.

■ There are over 30 national and state television stations, broadcasting in English and all major local languages. South African satellite DSTV is hugely popular.

■ Electricity supply is 220V. Plugs are an unpredictable mix of round European two-pin and square British three-pin.

---

Camping isn't really an option anywhere in Nigeria.

## ACTIVITIES

As countries in the region go, Nigeria isn't a great destination for specific 'activities', lacking the wildlife, mountains or beaches of its neighbours. Visiting Nigeria should perhaps be seen as an activity in itself – travelling by public transport, people-watching in local bars, checking out the nightlife and talking to Nigerians themselves. Nigerians love to talk (and shout and laugh – often all at the same time) and are constantly delighted to see foreigners travelling outside the expat bubbles of the major cities – perhaps the best activity of all.

## BOOKS

*This House Has Fallen,* by Karl Maier, is an excellent primer on modern Nigeria, and is essential reading for anyone visiting the country who wants to hold an informed conversation about the one topic everyone talks about: politics.

*A Month and a Day,* by Ken Saro-Wiwa – executed in 1995 – was written by the Ogoni activist in prison, and is part detention diary and part manifesto for a development in Nigeria. It is well recommended.

*Nigeria: Giant of Africa,* by Peter Holmes, is an excellent coffee-table book.

*The Art of Benin,* by Paula Girshick and Ben Amos, is a great introduction to the amazing art produced by the Benin Kingdom.

For more on Nigerian fiction, see p47.

## BUSINESS HOURS

Business hours are from 8.30am to 5pm Monday to Friday. Government offices are open from 7.30am to 3.30pm Monday to Friday, and 7.30am to 1pm Saturday. Banking hours are from 8am to 3pm Monday to Thursday, and 8.30am to 1pm Friday. Sanitation days – when the streets are cleaned and rubbish collected – are held on the last Saturday of the month and traffic isn't allowed on the streets before 10.30am.

## DANGERS & ANNOYANCES

There's no getting around the fact that Nigeria has a terrible reputation for safety. Corruption, fraud, civil unrest – it's all there in a big volatile mix. And yet, for the traveller, Nigeria really can seem like the

NIGERIA

**POWER CUTS**

Despite being in the world's top 10 oil exporting countries, Nigeria has chronic power shortages. The moribund National Electric Power Authority, NEPA, is more laughingly known as 'No Electricity Power Again' and other unflattering monikers, and for good reason – power cuts are long and frequent across the country, and you'll quickly get used to lights going out followed, a minute later, by the sound of generators striking up. When checking into hotels – particularly budget ones – always ask what time they 'off the gen'. That air-conditioning will be useless without it.

friendliest and most welcoming country in West Africa. Navigating these apparently contradictory states is the key to getting the most out of your visit.

It's a good idea to read the news before travelling; plenty of Nigerian newspapers have good websites (opposite). Consistently the most troubled region is the Niger Delta – Bayelsa, Rivers and Delta states – due to the long-running grievances between the local population and the big oil companies (for more on see p647). Kidnapping of Western oil employees is a continued threat here, and the Delta was the one part of Nigeria we were not able to visit to carry out research for this edition. In the north, communal disturbances between Muslims and Christians periodically spill over into bloody violence. Stay clear of demonstrations and areas where you suddenly see large numbers of police or army troops. Lagos has a terrible reputation for violent crime, not always undeserved. For more specific information, see p631.

Despite most preconceptions, as a traveller you are unlikely to have any trouble with corruption and bribery. Police roadblocks are common, but fines and bribes are paid by the driver. Some caution should be exercised on the major highways into Lagos, where armed robbery is a problem, although almost always at night. You should always travel in daylight – a good rule of thumb anyway, considering the terrible driving on Nigeria's roads.

Finally, while taking care to be sensible, it's important not to get too hung up on Nigeria's bad name. Many travellers fear the worst and avoid the country; those who

do make it here are more likely to come away with positive impressions rather than horror stories.

## EMBASSIES & CONSULATES
### Nigerian Embassies & High Commissions

In West Africa, Nigeria has embassies in all countries, except Cape Verde. For more details, see the relevant country chapter. Elsewhere, embassies and high commissions include the following:

**Australia** ( ☎ 02-6286 1222; 7 Terrigal Cres, O'Malley, ACT 2606) New Zealanders can also use their services.

**Belgium** ( ☎ 02-735 40 71; 3B Ave de Tervueren, Brussels 1040)

**Canada** ( ☎ 613 236 0521; www.nigeriahcottawa.com; 95 Metcalfe St, Ottawa K2P 1R9)

**France** ( ☎ 01 47 04 68 65; 173 Ave Victor Hugo, 75016 Paris)

**Germany** ( ☎ 30-477 2555; www.nigeria-online.de; Platanen Strasse 98a, 13156 Berlin)

**Ireland** ( ☎ 01-660 4366; 56 Leeson Park, Dublin 6)

**Netherlands** ( ☎ 070-350 1703; www.nigembassy.nl; Wagenaarweg 5, 2597 LL, The Hague)

**Switzerland** ( ☎ 022-7342140; 1 Rue Richard Wagner, 1211 Geneva)

**UK** ( ☎ 020-7839 1244; www.nigeriahighcommissionuk.com; 9 Northumberland Ave, London WC2N 5BX)

**USA** ( ☎ 202-986 8400; www.nigeriaembassyusa.org; 3519 International Court, Washington, DC 20008)

### Embassies & Consulates in Nigeria

Many embassies have yet to relocate from Lagos to Abuja. Opening hours listed are for visa applications.

**Australia** (Map p634; ☎ 261 8875; 2 Ozumba Mbadiwe Ave, VI, Lagos)

**Benin** Abuja ( ☎ 413 8424; Yedseram St; ⊗ 9am-4.30pm Mon-Fri); Lagos (Map p634; ☎ 261 4411; 4 Abudu Smith St VI; ⊗ 9am-11am Mon-Fri)

**Burkina Faso** (Map p634; ☎ 268 1001; 15 Norman Williams St, Ikoyi, Lagos)

**Cameroon** Calabar ( ☎ 222782; 21 Ndidan Usang Iso Rd; ⊗ 9am-3.30pm Mon-Fri); Lagos (Map p634; ☎ 261 2226; 5 Femi Pearse St, VI; ⊗ 8am-11am Mon-Fri)

**Canada** (Map p634; ☎ 262 2516, 4 Idowu Taylor St, VI, Lagos)

**Chad** ( ☎ 413 0751; 53 Mississippi St, Abuja; ⊗ 9am-3pm Mon-Fri)

**Côte d'Ivoire** (Map p634; ☎ 261 0963; 5 Abudu Smith St, VI, Lagos)

**European Union** ( ☎ 523 3144; 63 Usuma St, Abuja) Represents EU countries that don't have embassies in Nigeria, or those with representation in Lagos only.

**France** (Map p634; ☎ 260 3300; 1 Oyinkan Abayomi Rd, Ikoyi, Lagos)
**Germany** (Map p634; ☎ 261 1011; 15 Walter Carrington Crescent, VI, Lagos)
**Ghana** (Map p632; ☎ 263 0015; 23 King George V St, Lagos Island, Lagos)
**Niger** Abuja ( ☎ 413 6206; Pope John Paul II St; ☺ 9am-3pm Mon-Fri); Kano ( ☎ 080 6548 1152 mobile; Airport Roundabout; ☺ 9am-3pm Mon-Fri); Lagos (Map p634; ☎ 261 2300; 15 Adeola Odeku St, VI; ☺ 9am-2.30pm Mon-Fri)
**Togo** (Map p634; ☎ 261 1762; Plot 976 Oju Olobun Cl, VI, Lagos)
**UK** Abuja ( ☎ 413 2010; Aguyi Ironsi St); Lagos (Map p634; ☎ 261 9541; 11 Walter Carrington Cres, VI)
**USA** Abuja ( ☎ 523 0916; 9 Mambila St); Lagos (Map p634; ☎ 261 0150; 2 Walter Carrington Cres, VI)

## FESTIVALS & EVENTS

Of all the festivals in West Africa, the most elaborate are the celebrations in northern Nigeria (particularly in Kano, Zaria and Katsina) for two important Islamic holidays: the end of Ramadan, and Tabaski, 69 days later, which feature colourful processions of cavalry (see p661). Ramadan can be a tiring time to travel in the north – head for the Sabon Gari (Christian quarter) in each town, where food is served throughout the day.

Around mid-February, the three-day Argungu Fishing and Cultural Festival takes place on the banks of the Sokoto River in Argungu, 100km southwest of Sokoto. The fishers' customs and traditions are closely tied to Islamic religious practices. Several months before the festival, the Sokoto River is dammed. When the festival begins, hundreds of fishers jump into the river with their nets and gourds. Some come out with fish weighing more than 50kg. It's quite a sight.

Every August is the Pategi Regatta. Pategi is on the Niger River, halfway between Ibadan and Kaduna. There's swimming, traditional dancing, acrobatic displays, fishing and a rowing competition.

On the last Friday in August, the Oshun Festival takes place in Oshogbo, 86km northeast of Ibadan. It has music, dancing and sacrifices, and is well worth seeing.

The Igue (Ewere) Festival, held in Benin City, usually in the first half of December, has traditional dances, a mock battle and a procession to the palace to reaffirm loyalty to the *oba*. It marks the harvest of the first new yams of the season.

## HOLIDAYS

Public holidays include the following:
**New Year's Day** 1 January
**Easter** March or April
**May Day** 1 May
**National Day** 1 October
**Christmas** 25 December
**Boxing Day** 26 December

Islamic holidays are observed in Nigeria, even in the south – for a table of estimated dates for these holidays, see p818.

## INTERNET ACCESS

Nigerians are great lovers of the Internet. Cybercafés (as they are locally called) can be found in any town, usually prominently displaying requests that users don't send spam or scams. Costs average N100 toN150 per hour, and most places can also burn photos onto CDs. Never use Internet banking in a Nigerian cybercafé.

## INTERNET RESOURCES

**www.nigeriaworld.com** Huge portal site with news and current affairs, sport and business directory.
**www.kickoffnigeria.com** A good introduction to Nigerian football.
**www.remembersarowiwa.com** Campaigning website with background on the political and environmental problems in the oil-rich Delta.
**www.oyiboconline.com** Expat guide to Port Harcourt, but with useful travel and security information for visitors to Nigeria.
**www.nigeriavillagesquare.com** Generic guide to Nigeria, strong on music, culture and politics.

## LANGUAGE

English is the official language in Nigeria. The three principal African languages are Hausa in the north, Igbo in the south-east and Yoruba in the southwest, around Lagos. Nigerian English – Pidgin – has its own cadences and vocabulary, which take a while to get your ear into (see p861).

## MONEY

The unit of currency is the naira, with bills ranging from N5 to N1000. There are no coins.

In Nigeria, cash is king, and you shouldn't really bring anything other than US dollars. It is estimated that around 60% of the nation's currency is currently held outside the banking system. Although the

**DASH**

Used freely as both a noun and verb, dash is a word you'll hear a lot of in Nigeria. It can mean either a bribe or a tip. The most frequent form of dash you're likely to encounter is at roadblocks, which the driver pays. Although you're actually unlikely to be asked for dash as a bribe, dashing someone who performs a service for you, such as a guide, is often appropriate.

streets of towns are lined with banks, you are extremely unlikely ever to darken their doors, as none offer currency exchange. It is sometimes possible to find official exchange shops, otherwise you'll have to get used to changing on the street. Moneychanging areas are listed in the text – if you get caught short, head for an international hotel. They don't always let nonguests change money, but there are frequently moneychangers outside who will offer you business. Moneychangers are almost always Hausa, so if you're in the south, it's usually a safe bet to ask around at the town's mosque. In our experience, the moneychangers are among the most honest in Africa, but you should always be aware of potential scams (see p821). US$100 and US$50 bills attract better rates. Travellers cheques are useless in Nigeria.

Credit cards aren't much use either, and given the high levels of financial fraud, trying to use one anywhere in the country should be avoided. If you're worried about carrying large amounts of cash, even small towns usually have a Western Union branch to have money wired through. It is highly likely that ATMs will become commonplace in Nigerian cities during the life of this guide. Ecobank, First Bank of Nigeria and Standard Chartered should be the first to offer such facilities.

## POST

The internal mail service in Nigeria has improved in the last few years, most letters taking just a few days, but you are still almost certain to beat your postcards home (N80 to most destinations worldwide). Sending packages by courier is far preferable to entrusting it to the post office; the international couriers have offices in most towns.

## TELEPHONE

Nitel is the national phone company, but its poor connections and infrastructure have been greatly overtaken by the explosion in mobile phone use. It's quicker and easier to make a call at a phone stand on the street than track down a Nitel office. Phone stands are run by women with a mobile phone, a table and sun umbrella, timing your call with a stop watch. Calls inside Nigeria cost N15 to N30 per minute, depending on the network, and international calls around N60.

If you're taking your own phone, local GSM sim cards cost from N400, according to the amount of credit purchased. Operators include Glo, MTN and V-Mobile. Coverage is good in most parts of the country.

## VISAS

Everyone needs a visa to visit Nigeria, and applications can be quite a process. Nigerian embassies (including the high commissions in the UK and Australia, and the embassy in Benin) issue visas only to residents and nationals of the country in which the embassy is located, so it's essential to put things in motion well before your trip. Exact requirements vary, but as a rule of thumb, forms are required in triplicate, along with proof of funds to cover your stay, a round-trip air ticket, and possibly confirmed hotel reservations.

You also need a letter of invitation from a resident of Nigeria, or a business in the country. This must explain the purpose of your visit and, preferably, take immigration and financial responsibility for you during your trip. If the invitee is an expat, the letter should also attach a copy of their residence permit. Nigerian officialdom doesn't give the impression of encouraging tourism.

Fees vary. At the time of research, a one-month single entry visa cost £40 in London and US$100 in Washington, or £70/$200 for a three-month multiple entry visa. Applications at the High Commission in London were notably troublesome.

If you're travelling overland to Nigeria, the embassy in Accra (Ghana) is consistently rated as the best place in West Africa to apply for a visa, as no letter of introduction is required. The embassy in Niamey (Niger) also claims to issue visas the same way. The embassy in Cotonou (Benin) issues 48 hour transit visas if you can provide an onward plane ticket.

On arrival in Nigeria, immigration will ask the length of your stay and write this on your entry stamp – if your visa is one month then ask for this, even of you plan on staying for a shorter time. Several travellers have come unstuck having been stamped in for a week, then deciding they wanted to stay longer, but being unable to without either getting stuck in labyrinthine bureaucracy, or paying out lots of dash. Always check your passport stamp carefully before leaving immigration.

### Visa Extensions

Visas can reportedly be extended at the Federal Secretariat in Lagos, but it's a byzantine process of endless forms, frustration and dash, with no clear sense of success

### Visas for Onward Travel

#### BENIN

One-month visas cost CFA15,000, with one photo, and take 24 hours to issue. You can't pay in naira – although, as the embassy in Lagos carries a bad reputation for asking for dash, don't be surprised if greasing palms miraculously solves this 'problem'.

#### CAMEROON

A one-month single entry visa costs CFA50,000, with one photo, and is issued in a day. The consulate in Calabar is a good place to pick up a visa if you want to avoid Lagos, but it gives a poor exchange rate if you try to pay in naira – it's cheaper to change some cash into CFA on the street.

#### CHAD

Two photos and N5500 will get you a one-month single entry visa, which you can pick up the next day.

#### NIGER

Best obtained in Abuja, a one-month single entry visa costs N5300 with two photos, and is issued in 48 hours. The consulate in Kano, where the fee is CFA15,000 (payable in local currency), is also a good place to apply – take three photos.

### WOMEN TRAVELLERS

Nigeria is a nation where women have made more gains than in most African countries, but there is still a lot to achieve before any claims of gender equality can be made. Women

shouldn't encounter any specific problems, although an effort should be made to dress modestly in the northern Sharia states, covering the shoulders and legs. Women generally aren't allowed in mosques, and will feel conspicuous at open-air prayers.

For more general information and advice, see p828.

# TRANSPORT IN NIGERIA

## GETTING THERE & AWAY

### Air

The vast majority of flights to Nigeria arrive in Lagos, although there are also international airports in Abuja, Port Harcourt and Kano. Murtala Mohammed international airport in Lagos has traditionally been a nightmarish entry point into the country, and its chaos and con artists have been responsible for many peoples' bad impressions of the country. In recent years, however, the airport has sharpened its game considerably, and shouldn't present travellers with any undue horror. Nigerian airports have official porters, and notices urge passengers to ignore the services of touts. Since Nigeria Airways went bust, Virgin Nigeria and Bellview vie for the mantle of national carrier.

#### AIRLINES

Most domestic airlines just have desks at the airport. The following are airlines with service from Lagos (all offices are on Victoria Island unless stated):

**Aero** ( ☎ 496 1340; Airport desk)

**Air France** (Map p634; AF; ☎ 461 0461; www.airfrance .com; Idejo Danmole St) Hub: Paris Charles De Gaulle.

**Bellview** (Map p634; B3; ☎ 791 9215; www.flybellview air.com; Ozumba Mbadiwe Ave) Hub: Lagos.

**British Airways** (Map p634; BA; ☎ 262 1225; www .britishairways.com; 1st fl, C&C Tower, Sanusi Fafunwa St) Hub: London Heathrow.

**Cameroon Airlines** (Map p634; UY; ☎ 261 6270; Oko-Awo Close) Hub: Douala.

**Chanchangi Airlines** ( ☎ 493 9744; www.chanchangi -airlines.com; Airport desk) Hub: Lagos.

**Ethiopian** (Map p634; ET; ☎ 263 1125; www.flyethi opian.com/et/; Idowu Tayor St) Hub: Addis Ababa.

**Ghana Airways** (Map p634; GH; ☎ 266 1808; www .ghana-airways.com; 130 Awolowo Rd, Ikoyi) Hub: Accra.

**Kenya Airways** (Map p634; KQ; ☎ 461 2501; www .kenya-airways.com; Churchgate Tower, Badaru Abina St) Hub: Nairobi.

NIGERIA

**KLM** (Map p634; KL; ☎ 461 2501; www.klm.com; Churchgate Tower, Badaru Abina St) Hub: Amsterdam.
**Lufthansa** (Map p632; LH; ☎ 266 4227, www .lufthansa.com; Broad St, Lagos Island) Hub: Frankfurt.
**South African Airlines** (Map p634; SA; ☎ 262 0607; www.flysaa.com; Adetokumbo Ademola St) Hub: Johannesburg.
**Sosoliso** (SO; ☎ 497 1492; www.sosoliso.airline.com; Airport desk) Hub: Lagos.
**Virgin Nigeria** (VK; ☎ 461 2747; www.virginnigeria .com; Sheraton Hotel, Ikeja) Hub: Lagos.

The following are airlines with offices in Port Harcourt:
**Air France** (AF; ☎ 486 901; www.airfrance.com; 47 Aba Rd) Hub: Paris Charles De Gaulle.
**Bellview** (B3; ☎ 230 518; www.flybellviewair.com; 47 Aba Rd) Hub: Lagos.
**Chanchangi Airlines** ( ☎ 234 937; www.chanchangi -airlines.com; at Presidential Hotel, off Aba Rd) Hub: Lagos.
**KLM** (KL; ☎ 231 645; www.klm.com; 47 Aba Rd) Hub: Amsterdam.
**Lufthansa** (LH; ☎ 232 014; www.lufthansa.com; at Presidential Hotel, off Aba Rd) Hub: Frankfurt.
**Sosoliso** (SO; ☎ 231 908; www.sosoliso.airline.com; at Presidential Hotel, off Aba Rd) Hub: Lagos.
**Virgin Nigeria** (VK; ☎ 467 000; www.virginnigeria .com; 175 Aba Rd) Hub: Lagos.

The following are airlines with offices in Abuja:
**Aero Airlines** ( ☎ 810 0197; Abuja airport)
**Air France** (AF; ☎ 314 7419; www.airfrance.com; Plot 1267 Ahmadu Bello Way) Hub: Charles De Gaulle.
**Bellview Airlines** (B3; ☎ 523 0225; www.flybellview air.com; Sheraton Hotel) Hub: Lagos.
**British Airways** (BA; ☎ 413 9610; www.britishairways .com; Hilton Hotel; Aguiyi Ironsi) Hub: London Heathrow.
**Changchangi Airlines** ( ☎ 249 949, Ahmadu Bello Way) Hub: Lagos.
**KLM** (KL; ☎ 523 9966; www.klm.com; Sheraton Hotel, Ladi Kwali Way) Hub: Amsterdam.

### AFRICA

Virgin Nigeria operates daily flights from Lagos to Douala (Cameroon) and Accra (Ghana) and three flights a week to Johannesburg (South Africa). Kenya Airways operate four flights a week between Lagos and Nairobi; South African Airways have four flights a week from Johannesburg; while Ethiopian have a daily service from Addis Ababa. Bellview operate services to several West African cities, including Cotonou (Benin), Accra, Freetown (Sierra Leone),

Banjul (Gambia), Abidjan (Côte d'Ivoire) and Dakar (Senegal). Air Niamey fly weekly between Kano and Niamey (Niger). Egypt Air fly twice weekly to Kano from Cairo. Afriqiyah Airways has a twice weekly service between Kano and Tripoli (Libya) via N'Djaména (Chad).

### EUROPE & THE USA

There are frequent flights to Lagos from all major European hubs: British Airways and Virgin Nigeria fly daily from London, Air France daily from Paris, Lufthansa three times a week from Frankfurt, KLM daily from Amsterdam and Alitalia six times a week from Milan. Non-Lagos flights include London–Abuja (BA, five a week), Amsterdam–Kano (KLM, twice a week) and Paris–Port Harcourt (Air France, four a week). Lufthansa fly three times a week from Frankfurt to both Abuja and Port Harcourt. At the time of going to press, the Virgin Nigeria service from London to Port Harcourt was threatened with cancellation.

There are no direct flights between the USA and Nigeria. Continental Airlines have had a Newark–Lagos service planned since late 2004, but it has been repeatedly delayed by US air traffic authority restrictions.

## Land

### BENIN

The main border is on the Cotonou–Lagos highway. It's busy but slow, with lots of paper checks. Although Nigeria carries the worse reputation for corruption, it's actually the Beninese officials at this border that have the greediest appetite for bribes. Getting away with paying less than CFA3000 is a good day. The border point is Kraké in Benin and Seme in Nigeria. Transport to either Cotonou or Lagos is plentiful on either side, as are police checkpoints – Seme to Lagos probably has the highest density in Nigeria. If you're in rush, note that minibuses get stopped more frequently than taxis. If you're not in a rush, consider stopping at Badagry (p637), 30 minutes from Seme. Travelling from Lagos, border transport departs from Mile Two Motor Park.

An alternative border crossing is further north at Kétou, but there's not so much public transport. It's worth considering if you have your own vehicle and (understandably) can't face driving through Lagos, as the road takes you to Abeokuta and on to Ibadan.

### CAMEROON

There are two main border crossings, in the north and south. The northern border post is at Bama, 2½ hours from Maiduguri. You'll have to ask to have the immigration office pointed out to you, as it's not immediately clear – it's a short hop on an *okada* from the bus stand. Leaving Nigeria, you have to walk through a small market to find the Cameroon border post (Banki). This is conveniently next to the minibus rank for transport on to Mora (two hours, CFA2000). Border facilities and customs are pretty relaxed here. A remote alternative crossing is at Ngala, used mainly for transiting to Chad (see below).

The southern border crossing is at Mfum, 30 minutes from Ikom. Arrangements are straightforward on the Nigerian side, but the road infrastructure collapses pretty much as soon as you cross to Ekok in Cameroon. From Ekok, minibuses struggle on terrible roads to Mamfe, 60km away (CFA1500). An alternative route to Mamfe is by pirogue, up the Cross River. This border is problematic during the rainy season, and you might consider taking the Calabar–Limbe ferry instead during the wettest months (see right).

### CHAD

Although Nigeria and Chad share a short border, there are no official border crossings between the two countries. However, it is possible to make a quick transit across Cameroon, even without a Cameroonian visa. In Nigeria, the border crossing is at Ngala. You enter Cameroon here, but ask for a *laissez passer* to allow you to make the two-hour traverse to the Cameroon–Chad border point at Kousseri (see p226). Tell Nigerian immigration of your plan when getting stamped out. There's no fee for the paperwork on the Cameroon side, but this is a remote outpost with bored officials, so you're potentially a target for dash. During the research trip, we also saw *laissez passers* for Chad being issued at the Nigeria–Cameroon border further south at Banki.

### NIGER

There are four main entry points into Niger. From east to west they are Kano to Zinder,

Katsina to Maradi, Sokoto to Birni N'Konni and Kamba to Gaya. Of these, the busiest is the Sokoto route, as this is the main road for trade between the two countries. Minibuses and bush taxis run daily to the border, just past Ilela. Crossing to Birni you can get on a bus heading straight for Niamey.

From Niger, it is easiest to cross at Gaya, four hours from Niamey. You'll probably have to hire a bush taxi to take you from the Nigerian side at Kamba on to Sokoto; beware the potholes.

## Sea

### CAMEROON

A ferry sails from Calabar to Limbe every Tuesday and Friday evening, very occasionally continuing on to Douala. The boat sails in the opposite direction on Monday and Thursday (see p649 for more details). It's an overnight trip in each direction. It's a very atmospheric way of entering Nigeria, sailing up the delta past grey-green trees under leaden skies to a tropical port: perfect for imagining that you're in a Graham Greene novel. Immigration at Calabar is straightforward – your passport is collected before boarding and returned on arrival – and there are moneychangers at the docks. Try to keep hold of your luggage – if it gets stowed in the hold you'll be waiting hours to get it back.

On a more ad hoc basis it's possible, if risky, to catch a speedboat to Limbe. These are fast, highly dangerous, and leave you open to paying lots of dash. They leave from Oron, a N100 boat ride across the river from Calabar port.

## GETTING AROUND
### Air

Internal flights are a quick and cheapish way of getting around Nigeria. Flights range between N8000 and N14,000. Most cities are linked by air to Lagos; you'll usually have to change planes here if you want to fly between two smaller cities (buying separate tickets for each leg if you need to change airline).

Lagos–Abuja is the busiest route – Virgin Nigeria alone has eight flights a day – along with the Port Harcourt and (to a lesser extent) Kano routes. In these cases it's easy just to go straight to the airport, buy a ticket and be airborne pretty quickly. Lagos flights leave from the domestic terminal, where you should be aware of touts selling tickets.

On less busy routes, try to buy a ticket the day before departure. In some cities, airlines only have offices at the airport, and occasionally in the larger hotels.

Along with Virgin Nigeria, local airlines include Bellview, Aero, Sosoliso Airlines, IRS and ADC. Not all planes are perfectly maintained; in October 2005, a Bellview flight from Lagos to Abuja crashed on take-off, with the loss of over 170 people. The crash was blamed on catastrophic engine failure. Sample fares include Lagos to Abuja, N9000, Lagos to Calabar N12,000 and Lagos to Kano N14,000.

### Bus & Bush Taxi

Each town has at least one motor park full of minibuses and bush taxis which serves as the main transport depot. These places are Nigeria in microcosm – sprawling, chaotic and noisy. Vehicles have wooden signs on their roofs showing their destination, while touts shout out those that need filling. Minibuses don't run to any schedule – you pitch up at the motor park and wait until the vehicle is full. You'll do a lot of waiting during your trip. Luckily, motor parks are also huge markets, and there is a constant procession of hawkers and street food vendors, so you won't go hungry.

Minibuses are usually 'four across', referring to the number of passengers in each row – often a tight fit. 'Three across' is sometimes offered, at a premium comfort price. Bush taxis – big old Peugeots – somehow manage to squeeze in nine passengers. Bush taxis are faster than minibuses and cost about 25% more. You'll also sometimes find private cars at motor parks – the comfiest, fastest and most expensive option. Slower minibuses have the edge on the danger front, and account for most traffic fatalities on the roads. Nigerians call them 'maulers' for good reason.

There are a few companies operating large buses from their own depots, usually on long-distance intercity routes. These almost always travel at night, which can be dangerous, and they aren't recommended.

The main roads are littered with roadblocks, allowing the Nigerian police to supplement their meagre income with highway robbery. An accomplished minibus driver can pass through and pay the standard N20

dash without stopping. There seems to be no system to decree whether a driver stops or speeds past – the extent to which the police are armed often seems a deciding factor. There are fewer roadblocks in the north.

### Car & Motorcycle

Nigeria's road system is good, although for drivers this can bring problems in itself, as smooth tarmac allows Nigerians to exercise their latent talents as rally drivers. The accident rate is frighteningly high, and the only real road rule is survival of the fittest. Avoid driving at night at all costs.

Foreigners driving in Nigeria shouldn't get much hassle at roadblocks, particularly if your vehicle has foreign plates. If you get asked for a dash, a smile and some patience will often diffuse the request. Note however, that it's a legal requirement to wear a seatbelt; not doing so leaves you open to both official and unofficial fines. Petrol stations are everywhere, but keep your ear out for strikes than can cause fuel shortages. Diesel can sometimes be hard to come by, so keep your tank topped up.

### Taxi & Okada

In towns and cities, the quickest way to get around is to hop on the back of a motorcycle taxi or *okada* (*achaba* in the north). In a Lagos go-slow they're the only practical option. A trip shouldn't cost more than N50, slightly more at night. *Okadas* are absolutely everywhere – just flag one down and hold on tight. Many drivers seem to have a fatalist's view of their own mortality, so don't be afraid to tell them to slow down (say 'small, small').

Taxis generally operate set routes, and you pay a similar price to an *okada*. If you want the car to yourself, ask for a 'drop'. Small change is essential for both taxis and *okadas*.

### Train

Maps of Nigeria indicate that it has a rail network, but you'll be standing a long time on the platform waiting for a train – railway staff insist that passenger services still exist in the face of all available evidence. Should the decrepit locos ever run again, the main lines are Lagos–Kano (via Ibadan and Kaduna) and Port Harcourt–Maiduguri (via Jos).

# Senegal

Couched between the arid desert lands of the north and lush tropical forests in the south, Senegal boasts a stunning array of sights, sounds and flavours. The capital Dakar alone hands you the country in a capsule. Perched on the tip of a beach-lined peninsula, this dizzying city is composed elegance and street hustler rolled in one. Its busy streets, vibrant markets and glittering nightlife will easily draw you into their relentless rhythm, but the escape route is always open – be it to the meditative calm of the historical Île de Gorée or the golden sands of Yoff and N'Gor. And if Dakar's sensory overload really gets too much, the calm sway of the architectural beauty Saint-Louis, the first French settlement in West Africa, boasts a vibrant urban culture without the inner-city bustle.

Most visitors head to Senegal for its beaches, and for good reason. North and south of Dakar, wide strips of white sand invite swimming and sunbathing, whether in the built-up resort zones, where a lazy day at the beach can be followed by a cocktail trail at night, or in one of the coast's charming fishing villages, whose beaches are dotted with hundreds of colourful wooden pirogues. At the wide deltas of the Casamance and Saloum Rivers, the straight coastline is broken up into a maze of thick mangroves, tiny creeks, wide lagoons and shimmering plains. A pirogue trip through these striking zones reveals hundreds of bird species, from the gleaming wings of tiny kingfishers to the proud poise of pink flamingos. Whether you want to mingle with the trendsetters of urban Africa, or be alone with your thoughts and the sounds of nature – Senegal is the place to be.

## FAST FACTS

- **Area** 196,192 sq km
- **Capital** Dakar
- **Country code** ☎ 221
- **Famous for** Its hospitality; vibrant music scene; Dakar's urban culture
- **Languages** Wolof, Fula, Diola, Serer and French
- **Money** West African CFA franc; US$1 = CFA544.89; €1 = CFA655.96
- **Population** 11.1 million
- **Visa** Not needed for citizens of the EU, Canada, Norway, South Africa, Japan, Israel, USA and several other (mainly African) countries. For all others, one- to three-month visas cost about US$15 to US$20

SENEGAL

## HIGHLIGHTS

- **Casamance** (p731) Weave your way via tiny villages to Senegal's best beaches in Cap Skiring.
- **Saint-Louis** (p712) Follow in the footsteps of history in West Africa's first French settlement.
- **Dakar** (p683) Spend sleepless nights touring the capital's vibrant nightclub, bar and concert scene.
- **Siné-Saloum** (p705) Wind through the mangroves of the Siné-Saloum Delta in a pirogue.
- **Kedougou** (p723) Hike across the hills of the remote Bassari country.

## ITINERARIES

- **One Week** Spend a couple of days tasting the nightlife, arts and restaurant scene of **Dakar** (p683). From here, take day trips to the peaceful **Île de Gorée** (p696) and **Île de la Madeleine** (p697). Head north to visit the historical town of **Saint-Louis** (p712). And travel further north to visit the **Parc National des Oiseaux du Djoudj** (p717) and **Parc National de la Langue de Barbarie** (p717). On your way back to Dakar, take in the **Desert de Lompoul** (p712).
- **Two Weeks** Start as above, then head from Dakar south to the Petite Côte. Stop at the chilled-out fishing villages of **Toubab Dialao** (p701) and **Popenguine** (p702) before following the shoreline further south to **Mbour** (p704) and the unique seashell town **Joal-Fadiout** (p705), if you like your beach life local, or **Saly** (p703), if you're more at home in a holiday resort zone. From Mbour, trace the coastal road beyond to **Palmarin** (p705), the stunning entry port to the region of the Siné-Saloum Delta, then head via **Ndangane** (p706) and **Mar Lodj** (p706) for **Toubakouta** (p707), one of the prettiest spots in the Delta.
- **One Month** Follow the two-week itinerary as described, then cross The Gambia from Toubakouta to reach the Casamance. Head straight for the peaceful villages of **Kafountine** (p735) and **Abéné** (p736), then take the route towards Ziguinchor, with side trips to **Affiniam** (p734) and **Koulaban** (p734). Spend a couple of days in **Ziguinchor** (p727), the region's relaxed capital. Head west towards **Oussouye** (p731), with a detour via **Enampor** (p731), with its stunning *campement villageois* (village 'camps'

or guesthouses). From Oussouye, pass via **M'Lomp** (p731) and visit its traditional *cases étages* (two-storey mud-brick houses), then carry on towards **Elinkine** (p732) and take a pirogue to **Île de Karabane** (p732). Take a couple of pirogue excursions, then ask your driver to steer his wooden boat towards **Cap Skiring** (p732), where you can spend a few days chilling at Senegal's best beaches. Take a couple of days to visit **Boucotte** (p734) and **Diembéring** (p734). Return to Cap Skiring to take the plane to Dakar, or the long road back to the capital.
- **Six Weeks** In six weeks, you can visit pretty much the entire country. Continue from the Casamance towards **Tambacounda** (p720) and the **Parc National du Niokolo-Koba** (p721). Keep going south towards **Kedougou** (p723) and the **Bassari Country** (p723). In this part of the country you can go for long hikes in the mountains, take in the strong traditional culture of Bassari and Bédik villages and the stunning sights of plateaus, waterfalls and forests. From here, it's a long way back to Dakar. Stop at **Kaolack** (p711), **Diourbel** (p710), the holy town of **Touba** (p710) before re-entering the capital. Alternatively, travel from Tambacounda towards **Bakel** (p719), then follow the river route via **Matam** (p719), **Podor** (p719) and the amazing **Île à Morphil** (p719) towards Saint-Louis, then back to Dakar.

## CLIMATE & WHEN TO GO

Senegal's main tourist season is from November to February, during the dry season, and the 'coolest' months. Dakar average daytime maximums are around 24°C (75°F) from January to March. It's also the best time to spot wildlife (particularly migratory birds). If you are the partying kind, the urban centre of Dakar is a great place to spend Christmas and New Year. Several of Senegal's famous dance and music festivals take place between March and June, when temperatures are higher, though the climate is still dry. See Climate Charts, p813.

The wet months from late June to late September see far fewer visitors, as some national parks become inaccessible or even close, malaria is a major problem and the heat and humidity presses down on the country. But it's also the time everything

**HOW MUCH?**

■ **Soft drink** CFA300

■ **Newspaper** CFA200

■ **Sandwich** CFA1000

■ **French bread** CFA150

■ **One hour Internet access** CFA300

**LONELY PLANET INDEX**

■ **Litre of petrol/gas** CFA500

■ **Litre of bottled water** CFA400-600

■ **Bottle of Flag beer** CFA500-1000

■ **Souvenir T-shirt** CFA1500-5000

■ **Shwarma** CFA750

is green and beautiful, and many hotels reduce their prices by up to 50%.

Since you're travelling to a predominantly Muslim region, it's worth checking
the lunar calendar, particularly for the dates
of the fasting month Ramadan. Though it's
perfectly possible to visit during Ramadan,
and the month's special ambience is worth
experiencing, many restaurants close and
the entertainment scene is in hibernation.
See p818 for more information on Islamic
holidays.

## HISTORY

Evidence of organised societies from early
in the first millennium AD has been discovered in parts of Senegal (for instance
the ancient burial shell mound *diorom
bumag* near Toubakouta), and the area was
part of the great empires of Ghana (which
flourished between the 8th and 11th centuries), Mali (13th to 15th centuries) and
Songhaï (16th century). Smaller empires or
kingdoms were also established during that
period. Along the Senegal River, the Tukulor built the Tekrur empire in the 9th and
10th centuries; and as Mali's power began
to wane, the Wolof people united several
areas into the Jolof empire in the central
region of Senegal.

### European Arrival

In 1443, Portuguese explorers reached the
mouth of the Senegal River – a moment that
marked medieval Europe's first direct contact with West Africa. The following year

they landed at Cap Vert, near present-day
Dakar, and later settled on Île de Gorée – a
vital base for ships trading along the coast.

By the 16th century other European
powers had become increasingly active in
West Africa. For the next two centuries the
English and Dutch fought with the French
over the islands of Gorée and Saint-Louis,
and with it for control of the lucrative trade in
gold, ivory and, most importantly, slaves. In
1659 the French developed a trading station
in Saint-Louis at the mouth of the Senegal
River, and in 1677 finally secured Gorée.

During the 18th century, Saint-Louis grew
in size and importance, but after the slave
trade was banned in 1815, the French were
forced to look for new sources of wealth.
Louis Faidherbe was appointed governor in
1845, and forced the local people near the
Senegal River to grow groundnuts as a cash
crop. Over the next few decades, French
forces moved inland, and Senegal became the
gateway to the large territory of Afrique Occidentale Française (French West Africa).

Meanwhile, El Hajj Omar Tall, a marabout (Muslim holy man) who hailed from
the Fouta Toro region in northern Senegal,
had established a vast empire with Segou
(in today's Mali) as its centre. His soldiers
spread west into Senegal, where they clashed
with French forces. A chain of forts along
the Senegal River (including Bakel, Matam
and Podor) and Sudanese-style 'Omarian'
mosques still bear witness to the confrontation of cultures and interests of that era. Faidherbe also established a settlement opposite
Île de Gorée, which later became Dakar.

El Hajj Omar Tall's forces were defeated
by the French in 1864, but his missionary zeal inspired followers to continue
the 'Marabout Wars', as they were called,
for another three decades. Soldiers of the
Wolof king Lat Dior, for instance, repeatedly hindered French attempts to build a
railway between Dakar and Saint-Louis.
Another thorn in the French side was a
marabout called Cheikh Amadou Bamba
(p710), whose 1857 Islamic brotherhood of
the Mourides became a hugely popular focal
point of anticolonial sentiment.

### The Colonial Period

At the Berlin Conference of 1884–85, following the 'Scramble for Africa' (p37), the
continent was divided between powerful

SENEGAL

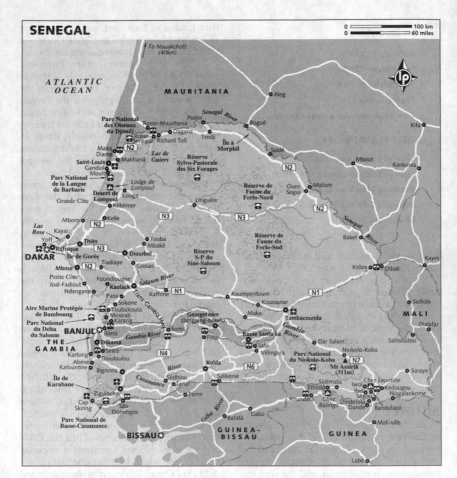

European states. While Britain, Germany and Portugal got most of East and Southern Africa, the greater part of West Africa was allocated to France. At the end of the 19th century, French West Africa stretched from the Atlantic to present-day Niger. In 1887, Africans living in the four main French settlements in Senegal (Dakar, Gorée, Saint-Louis and Rufisque) were granted limited French citizenship. Saint-Louis was the capital of the region until administration was shifted to Dakar in 1902.

In the early 20th century, things began to change. In 1914, Senegal elected its first black African delegate, Blaise Diagne, to the French national assembly in Paris. After WWI, an increasing number of Senegalese studied in France. One of them was Léopold Sédar Senghor. He became the first African secondary-school teacher in France, began writing poetry and founded *Présence Africaine,* a magazine promoting the values of African culture.

Senghor was an astute politician, and began building a personal power base that resulted in his election as Senegal's representative to the French national assembly. Meanwhile, the political influence of the marabouts had steadily increased, and through the 1950s Senghor made several secret deals with leading religious figures, allowing them limited autonomy and control of the groundnut economy in return for their public support.

## Independence

In the late 1950s, Senghor gained support from French Sudan (present-day Mali), Upper Volta (present-day Burkina Faso) and Dahomey (present-day Benin) to form a single union, the Mali Federation. But his plan failed when Upper Volta and Dahomey withdrew under pressure from France and Côte d'Ivoire. On 20 June 1960, Senegal and Mali became independent while remaining in the French union, and Senghor became the first president. But two months later, the Senegal–Mali union broke up, and French West Africa was divided into nine republics.

Senghor was a popular president, but the early years of independence did not always run smoothly. In 1968, student riots at the University of Dakar were answered with military pressure, though conflicts were only resolved when the students were promised reforms. The 1970s were less turbulent and Senghor held on to his position. In 1980, after 20 years as president, Senghor did what no other African head of state had done before – he stepped down voluntarily. His hand-picked successor Abdou Diouf took over.

One of Diouf's first major acts as president was to help the Gambian head of state Dawda Jawara regain power after he had been ousted in a coup, by sending in Senegalese military. Cooperation between the two countries was formalised through the establishment of the Senegambia Confederation later that year.

In 1983 and 1988, Diouf's Parti Socialiste (PS) defeated a loose opposition, led by Abdoulaye Wade, in elections widely thought to be rigged. During the latter election, Wade was arrested and charged with intent to subvert the government. He received a one-year suspended sentence and left for France. By this time, the Senegambia Confederation was in trouble, and in 1989 it was completely dissolved. But while Diouf was contending with this break-up and calls for political reform, he had two other major problems to deal with: a dispute with Mauritania and a separatist movement in the southern region of Casamance (see p725).

Wade returned from exile and stood again in the presidential election of 1993. Diouf won, but both Wade and his Parti Démocratique Sénégalais (PDS) had claimed a significant percentage of the vote.

## Wade's Sopi Campaign

Though the 1998 parliamentary elections were again won by Diouf, the growing power of the opposition became undeniable.

By the time voting began for the next election in 2000, Wade's *sopi* campaign (Wolof for 'change') had captured the imagination of the nation. Wade was elected and power was transferred peacefully. The people of Senegal were rightly proud of this affirmation of the strength of their democracy, and in January 2001 90% voted for the new constitution allowing the formation of opposition parties and giving enhanced status to the prime minister. Real change, however, was disappointingly slow.

## Senegal Today

In 2002, the country was shaken by a huge tragedy when the MS *Joola*, the ferry connecting Dakar and the Casamance capital, Ziguinchor, capsized due to dangerous overloading, leaving almost 2000 people dead. It is also thought that Wade's subsequent dismissal of his entire government is related to their handling of the catastrophe.

Also in the Casamance, separatist rebellion smouldered, despite a 2001 peace deal. Another accord signed between the MFDC and Wade's government in 2004 showed some results, and the situation in southern Senegal finally began to calm down, give and take occasional unrest that goes on to this day.

However, the president's controversial decision to arrest former prime minister Idrissa Seck on accusations of undermining state security and embezzling funds while working as mayor of the commune Thiès sparked clashes between Seck's supporters and police and sent the country into a flurry of political debate. In February 2006, Seck was released and all charges are dropped, probably in order to reunite their joint party PDS in good time before the next presidential and parliamentary elections in 2007.

## THE CULTURE
### The National Psyche

Senegal takes great pride in being the 'Land of Teranga' – meaning 'hospitality'. The national football team is called 'Lions of Teranga', and plenty of hotels and restaurants have adopted the name. Much of this is promotional hype, but as these things go, it's indeed rooted in that proverbial kernel of truth; people tend to be open and welcoming towards visitors.

In the busy tourist areas, it can be hard to tell the difference between true hospitality and a 'con job', devised to trick you into some unplanned spending. The further you get away from the resort zones, the more 'real' society gets, and you can relax your shoulders and practise your rudimentary Wolof or French – people will be keen to teach you their language.

In Senegal, conversation is the key to local culture, and the key to conversation is a great sense of humour and a quick-witted tongue. The Senegalese love talking, teasing and testing you out, and the better you slide into the conversational game, the easier you'll get around. Someone mocks your habits? Don't tense up, retaliate with a clever remark, and you're likely to be on your way to an entertaining evening. People don't mean harm laughing at you, and the ability to laugh at yourself is just as important an item in your luggage as your malaria pills and T-shirts.

## Daily Life

The majority of Senegalese households are polygamous, the Qur'an allowing men to take up to four wives (see below). Families are large and, as elsewhere in Africa, the extended family with its clearly defined rules of interrelations, responsibilities and respect, plays a vital role. Unmarried children, particularly women, stay at their parents' home until they are wed, which is when men establish their own household, and women join their husband. Marrying is a pricey business, and many men don't have the necessary means at their disposal to take this step until they are in their mid-20s. It's therefore not unusual (nor discreditable) for men of this age to still occupy a room in their parents' house. In the case of a divorce, the woman usually rejoins her family, bringing her children with her. Single women, or single-mother households (by choice), or even houseshares of young female students that are common in the Western world are virtually unheard of.

As to be expected, traditional family relations tend to remain more deeply preserved in rural regions than in the cities. There are exceptions, however, as many young men leave their villages to seek work in the cities or abroad, some rural communities show a worrying absence of men, and women raising a large number of offspring on their own are becoming increasingly common.

A second factor that determines daily life is religious faith. In most Senegalese homes, you'll notice the portraits of marabouts looking down earnestly from the walls. Men often join Senegal's influential Islamic brotherhoods for religious learning, while women tend to be the ones who mainly

---

### POLYGAMOUS MARRIAGES

When singer Youssou N'Dour (opposite) married a second wife in 2006, he set Senegal's paparazzi machine and boulevard press in motion, in a way only he can. In the following months, the debate around polygamy took up plenty of column space in Senegal's glossies. Young women were dismayed at the iconic singer's move, having seen in his monogamous status an influential example worth following by their male peers. The defenders of polygamy – you guessed it, mainly men – rejoiced, welcoming Youssou back into the more traditional fold.

The Holy Qur'an, which guides the lives of the vast Muslim majority of Senegal, allows men to take up to four wives, normally on the condition that they can equally provide for and love all of them. And that's really the crux of the issue – can one man equally love four women? Most women would say no, pointing an accusing finger at the many men who bring a pretty young wife into the family home once they've 'tired' of their first, aging, spouse.

Western women generally find it inconceivable to share their husband with another wife, and though Africa's women are generally resigned to this reality, few welcome it with joy, secretly praying that their partner will proudly spell the word 'monogamy' when asked about his choice at the civil wedding.

And a word of caution to the men who might dream of such rights – managing a polygamous household can be hard work. Wives tend to be jealous of one another, and resentment is often spread quite purposefully from the mothers to their children. All of this means a family home where tensions brew easily, and it's the head of the house that is expected to calm escalating situations.

consult them for advice in mystic matters, such as protection for their children and ways of keeping a husband faithful.

## Population

Senegal's population is young – around 42% people are under 14 years old. The greatest density is around the urban areas of Dakar – the rapidly growing, impoverished suburb of Pikine is a vivid example of the flight towards the cities and the problems this entails. However, the government is taking some decided measures to combat the country's strong centralisation, even contemplating moving the capital to a completely new location.

The main ethnic group of the country is the Wolof. They account for 43% of the population, and their language and culture is dominant. Smaller groups are the Fula (around 24%), Tukulor, a sub-branch of the Fula, who make up 10%, Serer (14%) and Diola (5%). Geographical distribution and cultural differences of these groups all lie with Senegal's precolonial history of empires. With the exception of the Diola, these ethnic groups are structured in a hierarchical fashion where the freeborn (rulers and traders) are at the top, followed by professional occupational groups, including griots (traditional musicians and oral historians) and blacksmiths, and formerly the slaves. These structures still determine much of social life, though other aspects, such as economic success and education are also important.

## RELIGION

About 90% of the population is Muslim. What's distinctive about Islam in Senegal, is the importance of Sufi brotherhoods, primarily that of the Mourides. Christian faith is most widespread among the Diola in Casamance, and to a lesser extent the Serer in the Siné-Saloum region and the Bassari around Kedougou. Traditional religious forms (sometimes called animism) are most commonly practised in the Christian areas. Elements of animism have also found their way into the practice of Islam and Christianity.

## ARTS
### Literature

Senegal is has a prolific literary output, but most works are only published in French.

Filmmaker Ousmane Sembène started out as a writer, and is still among the country's best-known authors. The most influential writer is probably Léopold Senghor, the country's first president. Studying in France during the 1930s, he coined the term 'negritude', which emphasised black-African ideas and culture, countering the colonial policy of 'assimilation'. Naturally, these beliefs influenced Senghor's own political thought.

Great female authors include Aminata Sow-Fall and Mariama Ba, whose short novel *So Long a Letter* is one of the most sensitive, intimate and beautiful contemplations of female lives in a polygamous society. Fatou Diome is a young author whose 2004 debut novel, *Le Ventre de l'Atlantique,* became an unexpected bestseller in France; it has since been translated into German. Perhaps her success will persuade publishing houses to work on an English translation, too.

The philosophical contemplation of religion and colonisation *An Ambiguous Adventure* by Cheikh Hamidou Kane has almost achieved the status of a Senegalese classic.

## Cinema

Senegal is one of the most productive nations in African cinema. The doyen of Senegalese cinema is Ousmane Sembène. From his first 1962 production *Borom Sarret,* a moving black-and-white tale about an inner-city horse-cart driver, through to the 2006 release *Moolaade,* which treats the sensitive subject of female circumcision, he has used cinema to shed a critical eye onto Senegalese society, history and culture.

Other famous directors include the illustrious Djibril Diop Mambety and the younger Joseph Kamaka Gaye whose acclaimed work *Karmen Geï* sets the classic story of Carmen in a Senegalese context.

Dakar's annual Festival International du Film de Quartier (see p740) is the place to spot future big names.

## Music

Senegal is one of Africa's most musical nations, and names such as Youssou N'Dour, Baaba Maal and Ismael Lô are famous worldwide. The beat that moves the nation is *mbalax*. Created from a mixture of Cuban beats and traditional, fiery *sabar* drumming in the late 1970s, *mbalax* was made famous by Youssou N'Dour, still the unrivalled leader of the scene. Since

SENEGAL

## MARABOUTS AND BROTHERHOODS

Take a tour around Dakar, and you are bound to notice the images of two veiled men, one dressed in white and the other in black, painted on numerous walls, cars and shop signs. They are the portraits of Cheikh Amadou Bamba, the 19th-century founder of the Mouride brotherhood, and Cheikh Ibra Fall, his illustrious follower and spiritual leader of the Baye Fall, a branch of Mouridism. *Télécentres* (telephone centres) and tailor shops are named after them, their names are written broadly across *cars rapides* (minibuses) and a vast number of pop songs, from *mbalax* (a mixture of Cuban beats and traditional, fiery sabar drumming) to hip-hop, praise the two revered personalities.

While orthodox Islam holds that every believer is directly in touch with Allah, Muslim faith in Senegal is more commonly channelled via saintly intermediaries who are ascribed divine powers and provide a link between God and the common populace. The concept of the marabout-led brotherhood was imported to Senegal from Morocco, where a spiritual leader is known as a *cheikh*, or khalif, terms that are also used in Senegal. The earliest brotherhood established south of the Sahara was the 16th-century Qadiriya. Today, most Qadiriya followers are Mandinkas, both in southern Senegal and in The Gambia.

The Moroccan-based Tijaniya brotherhood was introduced to Senegal by El Hajj Omar Tall in the mid-19th century, and remains powerful today, with large and important mosques in the towns of Tivaouane and Kaolack.

With over two million followers, the Mouridiya established by Cheikh Amadou Bamba is by far the most important brotherhood (see p710), and its power has consistently grown since the mid-19th century. The rise of Mouridism is closely connected to colonial expansion and popular resistance to the measures imposed by the French. Colonial administration weakened, or completely disabled traditional structures of governance, rendering the chiefs powerless, and leaving their subjects without respect-worthy leaders. The evolving structures of the brotherhoods were remarkably close to the societal organisation that had been lost, which made them extremely attractive to a population that sought to preserve its autonomy and oppose the colonial power.

For many years, Cheikh Amadou Bamba was a humble marabout, not more, perhaps even less, renowned than any other religious leaders of his time. Part of his rise to fame is due to the total adherence of his most famous *talibe* (student), Cheikh Ibra Fall. He was wholly devoted to the marabout, and demonstrated his commitment less through study than through hard, physical labour. 'Lamp' Fall, as he is often called, renounced Quranic study, and refused the Ramadan fast, stating that in order to serve God, he required all his time and bodily force to work hard. He soon gathered his own group of followers, the Baye Fall. Baye Fall adepts are traditionally recognisable by their long dreadlocks, heavy leather amulets containing pictures of their marabout, and patchwork clothing (not all follow the dress code), and to this day, the Baye Fall tend to be the hardest workers in the Touba region, building mosques and preparing fields for cultivation.

As the Mourides and Baye Fall gained immense popularity, the French began to fear their impact, and forced Cheikh Amadou Bamba into exile. His return in 1907 is still celebrated by the annual Magal pilgrimage (p710) to Touba.

Today, the Mourides, together with the ensemble of other brotherhoods, hold an almost worrying sway over politics and economics. About a quarter of the population hang on to every word of the khalif of the Mourides – a word that can thus easily decide the outcome of an election. The Mouride leaders also largely control the profitable groundnut trade, and see their immense wealth and subsequent economic impact further swell thanks to the donations they receive from their followers.

its inception, *mbalax* has evolved, always adapting to changing fashions without ever losing its essence. The always impeccably suited-and-tied Thione Seck has married the beat with Indian-style vocals. Senegal's 'street kid' Omar Pene and his band Super Diamono were the first to replace the con-gas of a standard *mbalax* outfit for a drum kit in 1974 – a move that has been copied ever since. Youssou N'Dour's sister-in-law Viviane N'Dour is one of Senegal's major style icons, mixing sexy *mbalax* beats with breathy, R&B–inspired vocals. And then there's a whole new generation that causes havoc on the region's dance floors, including such excellent performers as Abdou Guité Seck, Ablaye Mbaye, Aliou Mbaye N'Der and Titi.

In the 1960s, Cuban music was the most prominent influence, and Senegal still has a vibrant salsa scene. The most famous salsa orchestra is Orchestra Baobab, who reformed in 2001 and now tour regularly, luring audiences onto dance floors with their inimitable grandfather charm. The father of Senegalese music, however, is an artist that's lesser known today – Ibra Kasse, leader of the defunct Star Band de Dakar. In the line-up were Pape Seck and the illustrious Gambian-born singer Labah Sosseh. When the Star Band divided into glittering pieces, Etoile de Dakar emerged, which proved the rocket for Senegalese star Youssou N'Dour.

Influencing popular music are the griots (*gewel* in Wolof), West Africa's traditional praise singers, genealogists and oral historians (Youssou N'Dour is a griot on his mother's family lineage). The griots' soaring voice rings from modern recordings as well as traditional ceremonies, and their ancient repertoire forms the basis of many pop tunes.

Senegal has an exciting hip-hop scene, with leading names including: Positive Black Soul (who emerged in the mid-1980s), Daara J, Pee Froiss, Carlou D, Chronik 2H and Sen Kumpe. On a quieter side, Afrofolk is represented by artists such as Xalam, the Frères Guisse and Diogal Sakho.

And then there are of course the many artists that don't fit in any of the categories. Famous are Cheikh Lô, whose music is a moving mix of *mbalax* and Latin music; Turé Kunda, who stormed the world with their smooth Afro-pop in the '80s; and Baaba Maal, the voice of the Tukulor.

### Architecture
Prominent examples of historical architecture are the French colonial houses of Saint-Louis, Île de Gorée and Rufisque, as well as the ancient Faidherbian forts of Podor and Bakel. In northern Senegal, you will also find some late-19th-century 'Omarian' mosques in Sudanese style. Interesting local house constructions, range from the *banco* (mudbrick) architecture typical of the Tukulor and the stone huts of the Bassari to the *cases étages* (two-storey, mud-brick houses) and *cases à impluvium* (huge round huts with a

hole in the roof to collect rainwater) that are found in the Casamance.

The most famous contemporary architect is Pierre Goudiaby, who designed both Arch 22 (p300) and Banjul airport in The Gambia.

### Painting & Sculpture
Senegal has a vibrant contemporary arts scene. Well-known painters include Souleymane Keita and Kambel Dieng; leading sculptors are the world-famous Ousmane Sow and the emerging Gabriel Kemzo, who specialises in metal sculptures.

Senegal is particularly renowned for the unique art of *sous-verre* (reverse-glass painting). Outstanding artisans include Moussa Sakho (who has a workshop at the l'Institut Français in Dakar), Babacar Lô, Andy Dolly, Séa Diallo, Mbida and Gora Mbengue.

And don't forget to keep your eyes open for the everyday art that gives Dakar its particular character. The city's *cars rapides* and taxis are draped in decorative writings and images. Reproductions of the portraits of Cheikh Amadou Bamba and Cheikh Ibra Fall adorn walls around town, and painted profiles outside hairdressers' salons add spots of colour to ragged barbershops.

### ENVIRONMENT
#### The Land
Senegal is Africa's westernmost country; the continent's western tip, Le Point des Almadies, lies just north of Dakar. It comprises an area of just under 200,000 sq km, which compares in size to England and Scotland combined.

Senegal is largely flat, with a natural vegetation of dry savanna woodland. The country's western border, some 600km in length, is marked by the shores of the Atlantic Ocean.

Senegal has four major rivers, which flow east to west from the Fouta Jallon highlands in Guinea to the Atlantic Ocean. The Senegal River is the northernmost. The Gambia River flows through Senegal's only mountainous area (the lands surrounding Kedougou) before entering The Gambia itself. In the far south the Casamance River gives the surrounding region its name, and the Saloum River enters the ocean via a large delta to the south of the Petite Côte. This is a zone of labyrinthine mangrove swamps, salty plains, lagoons, small creeks and river islands.

## Wildlife

### ANIMALS

Main areas for bird-watching include the Parc National des Oiseaux du Djoudj, the world's third-largest bird sanctuary; the Parc National de la Langue de Barbarie; and the mangrove areas of the Casamance and the Siné-Saloum Delta. Inland, the dry Sahel landscape supports several arid-savanna species that are seldom seen elsewhere in Africa.

Easily recognised mammal species include baboons and three types of monkeys (vervet, patas and red colobus), while Parc National du Niokolo-Koba contains chimpanzee populations. The park also has drier grassland areas where antelope species (including cob, roan, waterbuck and Derby eland) roam, and there's a chance of seeing hyenas, buffaloes and hippos. Crossing the main road through the park in the early morning, you stand a reasonably good chance of spotting a lion near the roadside.

### PLANTS

Senegal lies in the Sahel zone, with a natural vegetation of well-dispersed trees (eg baobabs) and low scrub. Some northern areas come close to being desert, and the greenest zones are the Casamance in the south and the Siné-Saloum, where lush estuary vegetation, including mangroves, lines creeks and rivers.

## National Parks

Senegal has six national parks: Parc National du Niokolo-Koba (p721) in the southeast, the largest with a wide range of habitat types; Parc National du Delta du Saloum (p708; coastal lagoons, mangroves, islands and dry woodland); the Île de la Madeleine (p697) near Dakar; and in northern Senegal, Parc National des Oiseaux du Djoudj (p717) and Parc National de la Langue de Barbarie (p717), both noted for their bird life. Parc National de Basse-Casamance has been closed for years because of rebel activity and suspected landmines.

Other protected areas include the Ferlo wildlife reserves, the Réserve de Bandia (p701), the small reserves of Popenguine and La Somone (the latter a community reserve; see p703), and the Aire Marine Protegée de Bamboung, an area of protected sea, also managed by the local community.

## Environmental Issues

Overfishing, deforestation and coastal erosion are the main environmental issues the country faces. Coastal erosion is mainly caused by illegal sandmining. In Malika near Dakar, the problem has become so great that lines of trees, and the first tourist venues of a once vibrant holiday village are being claimed by the sea. In another bitter twist, the sand mined isn't even particularly suitable for building, as its high salt content ruins the metal skeletons of concrete constructions.

Overfishing is caused by both local fishermen and large European boats, and has reached such an extent that Senegal's characteristic fish, the *thiof*, is beginning to become rare. The community-run Aire Marine Protégée de Bamboung, established to protect endangered fish species, is showing an impressive rate of success in replenishing the species, but only covers a small area.

Deforestation is partly caused by a growing demand for farmland, mainly to cultivate groundnuts, but trees are also felled for firewood and to make charcoal, much of which is used to smoke fish.

## FOOD & DRINK
### Staples & Specialities

Senegal's national dish is the *tiéboudienne* (spelt in different ways, and pronounced chey-bou-jen). The word means fish and rice, and refers to a delicious dish of rice cooked in tomato sauce and served with chunks of fried fish, often stuffed with parsley and garlic paste, carrots, cassava and other vegetables. The festive variation is *tiebouyape* (or *yollof* rice), where fish is replaced by meat.

Another regional favourite is *yassa poulet*, grilled chicken marinated in a thick onion and lemon sauce. Occasionally chicken is replaced by fish or meat, changing the name to *yassa poisson* (fish) or *yassa bœuf* (beef).

*Mafé*, a meaty groundnut sauce served with rice, is another typical dish, and among the Fula and Tukulor, *lacciri* (millet couscous) is common, either eaten with a savoury sauce or *kosan* (milk).

### Drinks

Locally produced juices include the hibiscus drink *bissap*, *gingembre* (ginger beer) and *bouyi*, made from the fruits of the baobab.

For a caffeine kick, try a *café touba*, a spicy brew served in small cups at roadside stalls, or *ataaya*, concentrated, bittersweet green tea that's served with the free offer of an afternoon's socialising.

Palm wine is a popular home brew, particularly in the non-Muslim, and palm-tree blessed Casamance.

### Celebrations

The meals served for family celebrations are more refined versions of staples. For naming ceremonies, *lakh* (millet porridge) is served with milk or yogurt, and both for baptisms and weddings, *beignet* (small doughnuts) are fried and given to the guests. At Tabaski, every Muslim family slaughters a sheep to commemorate Abraham's willingness to sacrifice his son on God's demand (see p819).

### Where to Eat & Drink

Dakar's restaurant scene is excellent and varied – but meals in the best restaurants can be expensive. If you're on a budget, head for the *gargottes* (small, local eateries). Be careful, though, some are of rather dubious hygienic quality.

On the tiny side are the Senegalese *tanganas* (literally meaning 'hot stuff'), where you get your *café touba* and a sandwich with sauce. A *dibieterie* is a grilled-meat stall, usually only open in the evenings, and the place people head to before a night out, or before returning home in the wee hours of the morning. Dakar has fantastic patisseries, places to indulge in cakes and croissants, as well as a post-nightclub alternative to *dibieteries* for those who only leave at breakfast.

### Vegetarians & Vegans

Vegetarian food is hard to find and, what's worse, there's little understanding why someone who can afford it won't eat meat – vegetables are for the poor. This means that when you order a dish without meat, you'll still notice a suspicious chicken or fish flavour, just no 'bits'. Prepare for a rather limited variety of food choices during your stay.

### Habits & Customs

Meals are traditionally eaten squatting on the floor, grouped around a large platter of rice and sauce. People mostly eat the traditional rice dishes with a spoon or the hand. If you try the hand version, make sure you use your right only – the left is the hand you wipe your bum with and is strictly out at meal times.

It's usually polite to finish eating while there's still food in the bowl to show you have had enough, and the shocked comments of 'you haven't eaten anything, dig in' are more an acceptance of your finishing, rather than actual invitations to eat more.

# DAKAR

If Dakar only could, it would burst its beaches and lead its cacophonic parade of furious drumbeats, screeching traffic, exuberant nightlife, market shouting, street hustling and boundless creativity in ever-wider circles across the country. This is a feverish city that brims with life. It's got some of the best nightclubs, live venues and film, music and arts festivals in the whole of West Africa. You'll rarely have a boring day in Dakar, and the city charges only an occasional fee in unwanted hassle and sly con-jobs – easily negotiated once you've learnt a few tricks.

## ORIENTATION

Once a tiny settlement in the south of the Cap Vert Peninsula, Dakar now spreads almost across its entire triangle. The city's heart is the Place de l'Indépendance, from which Ave Léopold Senghor leads south in the direction of the Palais Présidentiel. Ave Pompidou goes west to the hectic area of Marché Sandaga, while Ave Albert Sarraut takes you east towards Marché Kermel.

The main arteries out of town are Ave du President Lamine Guèye, which runs north from Place de Soweto, reaching the Gare Routière Pompiers and the main *autoroute* (highway) out of the city. At the eastern edge, the Route de la Corniche-Est (Petite Corniche) winds above cliffs and small beaches, linking the main port to the north.

Ave Blaise Diagne takes you northwest, past the Grande Mosquée and La Médina, to become Ave Cheikh Anta Diop (known to locals as Route de Ouakam). This road runs between Fann and Point E, a pretty, middle-class *quartier* (suburb), before reaching Mermoz, Ouakam, and finally Pointe des Almadies and N'Gor. The Route de la Corniche-Ouest (Grande Corniche) runs along the Atlantic Ocean roughly parallel to Ave Cheikh Anta Diop; here you'll see the city's finest homes.

# DAKAR

0 — 500 m
0 — 0.3 miles

**Médina**

To Yoff (19km)

To Hann &
Pointe de Bel Air
Beaches (2km)

Port

To Marché
Tilène (500m)

To Point E (2km);
Ouakam (6km);
Les Almadies (11km);
N'Gor (12km)

To Île de
Gorée
(2.5km)

Rue 21

Autoroute

Ave Félix Éboué

Blvd du Général de Gaulle

Rue Worré

Ave du Président Lamine Gueye

Ave de l'Arsenal

22

20

13

Rue Wagane Diop

Rue de Reims

Ave Cheikh Anta Diop

Rue 11

Ave Malik Sy

Rue Marsat

11

17

Ave Faidherbe

19

Train
Station

Rue Coulibaly

Rue Escarfait

Marché
Malien

Rue Grasland

14

21

18

Ave Mangin

Ave Blaise Diagne

Rue Fall

Ave du Sénégal

Rue Angrand

Rue Galandou Diouf

Blvd de la Libération

To Soumbedioune
(2km); Fann (2.5km);
Magic Land
(2.5km); National
Park Office (2.5km)

Route de la Corniche-Ouest

Rue des Dardanelles

Rue N'Gouin

Rue el Hâji M'Baye Gueye

Ave Pompidou (Ponty)

Ave Albert Sarraut

23

16

Ave André Peytavin

Ave Jean Jaurès

Rue Carnot

Rue Jules Ferry

Ave Léopold Senghor

Rue Mohamed

Plage
Lagoon II

10

3

7

Ave Carde

Ave Jean XXIII

Blvd de la République

Ave Président Roosevelt

Rue Kléber

Place de Soweto

Rue Zola

See Central Dakar Map (p686)

Anse des Madeleines

Ave Nelson Mandela

Rue 18 Juin

Route de la Corniche-Est

8
9

6

12

Rue du Dr Guillet

4

Rue Mermoz

Rue Joffre

Ave Desbordes

2

1

**ATLANTIC
OCEAN**

5

15

Ave Pasteur

Plage de l'Anse
Bernard

Ave Pasteur

Lighthouse

Cap Manuel

**SENEGAL**

## Maps
By far the best city map is the colourful, detailed one by Editions Laure Kane (www .editionslaurekane.com; CFA3700). You can find it in most souvenir shops and hotels.

## INFORMATION
The free listings magazines *Dakar Tam Tam* and *l'Avis* and the pocket magazine *Clin d'Oeil* contain useful phone numbers, including those of embassies and hospitals and are available in hotels, restaurants and shops.

The tiny glossy *221* (CFA500) is an excellent source of information on cultural and sports events around the country, and includes Dakar concert listings.

### Bookshops
There's little available in English, the following have English books and magazines.
**Librairie aux Quatre Vents** (Map p686; ☎ 821 8083; Rue Félix Faure; ⏲ 8.45am-12.30pm & 3-6.45pm)
**Librairie Clairafrique** (Map p686; ☎ 822 2169; Rue el Haji M'Baye Guèye; ⏲ 8.45am-12.30pm & 3-6.45pm Mon-Sat)

### Cultural Centres
**British Council** (Map p691; ☎ 869 2700; www.british council.org/senegal; Rue Joseph Gomis, Amitié Zone A-B) Has a library with English magazines, books and newspapers.
**L'Institut Français Léopold Sédar Senghor** (Map p686; ☎ 823 0320; www.institutfr-dakar.org; 89 Rue Joseph Gomis) A cultural hub with regular exhibitions, concerts, events. Also has a pretty café, souvenir shop and glass-painters workshop in a leafy garden.

### Internet Access
There are plenty of Internet cafés in Dakar. Most charge between CFA300 and CFA500 per hour. Outside the centre, the university area is well covered with cybercafés.
**Cyber-Business Centre** (Map p686; ☎ 823 3223; Ave Léopold Senghor; ⏲ 8am-midnight)
**Espace Sentoo** (Map p686; Place de l'Indépendance; ⏲ 9.30am-8pm)
**Espacetel Plus** (Map p686; ☎ 822 9062; Blvd de la République; ⏲ 8am-midnight)

### Medical Services
Most embassies have a list of doctors used to dealing with nonresidents, particularly those speaking your language.
**Clinique Pasteur** (Map p686; ☎ 839 9200; 50 Rue Carnot) This privately run place is not the first choice for emergencies, but good for malaria tests.

**Hôpital le Dantec** (Map p684; ☎ 889 3800; Ave Pasteur) Has the best-trained staff, but terribly neglected infrastructure.
**Hôpital Principal** (Map p684; ☎ 839 5050; Ave Léopold Senghor) Fairly well-organised, with the main emergency department in Dakar.
**Suma Urgences** (Map p691; ☎ 824 2418; Fann Résidence, Ave Cheikh Anta Diop) Can give assistance in emergencies.

Dakar has many pharmacies. Most open from 8am to 11pm, and there's a rotational 24-hour stand-by system; you'll find details of the current 24 hour place outside every pharmacy.
**Pharmacie Mandela** (Map p684; ☎ 821 2172; Ave Nelson Mandela) Near the Hôpital Principal.

### Money
BICIS, CBAO, Citibank and SGBS have offices around Place de l'Indépendance. They all change money, though travellers cheques can sometimes be problematic. Except Citibank, they all have ATMs (withdrawal limit usually CFA250,000) The suburbs are equally well served with ATM-enhanced banks and petrol stations.
**BICIS** (Map p686; ☎ 839 0390; Place de l'Indépendance; ⏲ 7.45am-3.45pm Mon-Fri)
**CBAO** (Map p686; ☎ 839 9696; Place de l'Indépendance)
**Citibank** (Map p686; ☎ 849 11 11; Place de l'Indépendance)
**SGBS** (Map p686; ☎ 839 55 00; 19 Ave Léopold Sédar Senghor)

### Post
**Main post office** (Map p686; Blvd el Haji Djily Mbaye; ⏲ 7am-7pm Mon-Fri, 8am-5pm Sat) Near Marché Kermel. This is where you'll find the poste restante. Letters are held for up to 30 days, the cost is CFA250.
**Post office** (Map p686; Ave Pompidou) Smaller and at the eastern end of Ave Pompidou. Has a small *télécentre* and a Western Union service.

### Telephone
There are dozens of *télécentres*, mostly with similar rates. Post offices and Internet cafés often also have telephone facilities.

### Travel Agencies
Dakar has plenty of travel agencies. Good ones include the following:
**Dakar Voyages** (Map p686; ☎ 823 3704; dakarvoyages@sentoo.sn; 28 Rue Assane Ndoye) Tends to have the best ticket deals.

SENEGAL

CENTRAL DAKAR

200 m
0.1 miles

ATLANTIC OCEAN

Route de la Corniche-Est
Rue du Port
Rue des Messageries
A Lebon
Abdoulaye Fadiga
Blvd de la Libération
Blvd el Hadj Diily Mbaye
Rue Dagorne
Rue Parent
Rue Haut Malan
Rue de Thann
Marché Kermel
Rue le Dantec
Rue Caille
Rue des Essarts
Rue Huart
Ave Albert Sarraut
Rue Mage
Rue Salva
Rue Carnot
Rue Parchappe
Rue Amadou Assane Ndoye
Rue Bérenger Feraud
Rue P. Millon
Rue Masclary
Dily Mbaye
Ave Allés Delmas
Blvd el Hadj
Rue Malenfant
Place de l'Indépendance
Rue Colbert
Route de la Corniche-Est
High Tide Line
Plage Lagoon II
Rue de Médine
To Train Station (200m)
Rue Paul Holle
Rue du Docteur Thèze
Ave Léopold Senghor
Rue Wagane Diouf
Rue Vincens
Rue el Hadj Abdoulkarim Bourg
Rue Carnot
Rue Félix Faure
Rue Mohamed V
Rue Victor Hugo
Blvd de la République
Rue Calandou Diouf
Rue Moussé Diop
Rue Moussé Diop
Rue Joseph Gomis
Rue Raffenal
Rue Paul Holle
Rue el Hadj M'Baye Guèye
Rue de Thiong
Ave Pompidou
Rue Assane Ndoye
Rue Jules Ferry
Rue Kléber
Rue Zola
Ave du President Lamine Guèye
Marché Sandaga
Ave Emile Badiane
Cathedral
Ave Jean XXIII
Ave Nelson Mandela
Place de Soweto
R El Hadji Fall
Palais Présidentiel
Route de la Corniche-Est
Footbridge

| INFORMATION | | |
|---|---|---|
| American Embassy | **1** | A4 |
| BICIS Bank | **2** | C2 |
| Cape Verde Embassy | **3** | D1 |
| CBAO Bank | **4** | C2 |
| Citibank | **5** | C2 |
| Clinique Pasteur | **6** | B2 |
| Cyber-Business Centre | **7** | B3 |
| Dakar Voyages | **8** | C2 |
| Dutch Embassy | **9** | A4 |
| Espace Sentoo | (see 17) | |
| Espacetel Plus | **10** | A3 |
| French Embassy | **11** | D2 |
| Gambian High Commission | **12** | B2 |
| Librairie aux Quatres Vents | **13** | B3 |
| Librairie Clairafrique | **14** | C1 |
| L'Institut Français Léopold Sédar Senghor | **15** | B2 |
| Main Post Office | **16** | D1 |
| Mboup Voyages | **17** | C2 |
| Nouvelles Frontières | **18** | B4 |
| Post Office | **19** | B2 |
| Sahel Découverte Bassari | **20** | C1 |
| SDV Voyages | (see 70) | |
| Senegal Tours | **21** | C2 |
| SGBS Bank | **22** | C3 |
| VIA Senegal Voyages | **23** | C3 |

| SIGHTS & ACTIVITIES | | |
|---|---|---|
| Assemblée Nationale | **24** | A4 |
| Chambre de Commerce | **25** | C1 |
| Galerie le Manège | **26** | D2 |
| Galerie Nationale | **27** | D2 |
| Gouvernance | **28** | C1 |
| Hôtel de Ville | **29** | C1 |
| IFAN Museum | **30** | A4 |
| Lagon I | (see 53) | |

| | | |
|---|---|---|
| Palais Présidentiel | **31** | B4 |
| Pôle Linguistique de l'Institut Français | (see 26) | |

| SLEEPING | | |
|---|---|---|
| Hôtel Al Afifa | **32** | A3 |
| Hôtel Continental | **33** | B1 |
| Hôtel de l'Indépendance | **34** | C2 |
| Hôtel Farid | **35** | B1 |
| Hôtel Ganalé | **36** | A2 |
| Hôtel Lagon II | **37** | D2 |
| Hôtel le Miramar | **38** | B3 |
| Hôtel Océanic | **39** | D1 |
| Hôtel Provençal | **40** | C1 |
| Hôtel Saint-Louis Sun | **41** | A3 |
| Sofitel Teranga | **42** | C2 |

| EATING | | |
|---|---|---|
| Ali Baba Snack Bar | **43** | B2 |
| Caesar's | **44** | A3 |
| Chez Loutcha | **45** | B2 |
| Fili Fili Supermarket | **46** | C1 |
| Keur N'Deye | **47** | B1 |
| La Casa Créole | **48** | D1 |
| La Fourchette | **49** | D1 |
| La Metissacana | **50** | A2 |
| La Royaltine | **51** | A3 |
| La Villa Chez Yannick | **52** | C1 |
| Lagon I | **53** | D3 |
| Le Bambou | **54** | B3 |
| Le Méléa | **55** | B2 |
| Le Sarraut | **56** | D2 |
| Le Toukouleur | **57** | B3 |
| Ozio | (see 54) | |
| Restaurant VSD | (see 62) | |
| Saveur d'Asie | **58** | C1 |
| Score Supermarket | **59** | C2 |

| DRINKING | | |
|---|---|---|
| Café Indigo | **60** | B3 |
| Chez Grenelles | (see 36) | |
| Iguane Café | **61** | B3 |
| Le Mex | **62** | B2 |
| Le Seven | **63** | B3 |
| Snooker Palace | **64** | B1 |

| ENTERTAINMENT | | |
|---|---|---|
| Kadjinol Station | **65** | D2 |
| King's Club | **66** | B3 |
| Playclub | (see 32) | |

| SHOPPING | | |
|---|---|---|
| Cocktail du Sénégal | **67** | B3 |
| Galerie Antenna | **68** | C3 |
| Marché Sandaga | **69** | A2 |

| TRANSPORT | | |
|---|---|---|
| Afrique Location | (see 8) | |
| Air France | **70** | C2 |
| Air Guinée | **71** | B2 |
| Air Ivoire | **72** | C1 |
| Air Mali | **73** | B1 |
| Air Sénégal International | **74** | C2 |
| Alitalia | **75** | B2 |
| Dakar Location | **76** | B2 |
| DDD Bus Terminal | **77** | D1 |
| Ethiopian Airlines | **78** | B3 |
| Hertz | **79** | A2 |
| Iberia | (see 17) | |
| Noprola | (see 8) | |
| Royal Air Maroc | (see 17) | |
| Senecartours | **80** | A2 |
| SN Brussels | **81** | C2 |
| South African Airways | **82** | C2 |
| TACV Cabo Verde Airlines | **83** | B2 |
| TAP Air Portugal | (see 81) | |

**Mboup Voyages** (Map p686; ☎ 821 8163; mboup@telecomplus.sn; Place de l'Indépendance) One of the most enduring touring agencies.

**Nouvelles Frontières** (Map p686; ☎ 823 3434; fax 822 2817; 3 Blvd de la République) Often has cheap seats to Paris on charter flights.

**Pain de Singe** (Map p686; ☎ 824 2484; paindesinge@arc.sn) Unbeatable for ecotourism, off-the beaten track and original circuits. You can contact it at l'Océanium (p688).

**Sahel Découverte Bassari** (Map p686; ☎ 842 8751; bassari@bassarisenegal.com, carresahel@sentoo.sn; 7 Rue Masclary) This company yas a range of inspired tours around Senegal and caters for English, French and Spanish speakers.

**SDV Voyages** (Map p686; ☎ 839 0081; dkrsdvagv@sdvsen.net; 51 Ave Albert Sarraut) The Diners Club agent.

**Senegal Tours** (Map p686; ☎ 839 9900; fax 823 2644; 5 Place de l'Indépendance) One of the largest tour operators in the country. Good for trips throughout the country.

**VIA Senegal Voyages** (Map p686; ☎ 823 3300; www.viavoyages.sn; 13 Rue Colbert)

# DANGERS & ANNOYANCES

Beware of pickpockets, especially at the markets and on Ave Pompidou. Less worrying, but very annoying, are street traders and hustlers. Be firm but friendly to shake them off. A confident *bakhna* (it's OK), or *après* (later) usually gets rid of them. Don't fall prey to the inner-city scams. The 'remember me?' scam is particularly popular. Someone might call out 'my friend, long time no see!', pretending they know you, then cheat you out of money. The remedy: don't respond to random calls. If someone doesn't know your name, chances are they don't know you, and mistaken rudeness to someone you did actually know is still preferable to having your passport and purse snatched.

Muggings occur occasionally, particularly after dark, and as in most cities around the world, women should avoid walking around alone at night or waiting for taxis in empty areas.

Some vigilance and common sense should help you get around unharmed – inner-city

Dakar can be a pain to walk around, but Lagos it ain't, and none of the areas mentioned is a no-go zone.

# SIGHTS
## Historical Buildings

Central Dakar has a few impressive colonial buildings. The **Gouvernance** (Map p686) and the **Chambre de Commerce** (Map p686), both on Place de l'Indépendance, a remarkable space itself. The stately **Hôtel de Ville** (Town Hall; Map p686) sits right behind, and a short walk north takes you to the **train station** (Map p684), whose elegant façade inspires ideas of romantic train journeys (quickly wiped away once you enter the bleak interior).

A short walk east takes you to the roundhouse of **Marché Kermel** (Map p686), a reproduction of the original 1860 building. Further south, the awe-inspiring 1907 **Palais Présidentiel** (Map p686; Ave Léopold Senghor) is surrounded by sumptuous gardens and guards in colonial-style uniforms. The modern glass front of the parliament, the **Assemblée Nationale** (Map p686) on Place Soweto is in easy reach.

The impressive **Grande Mosquée** (Map p684), built in 1964, sits in the heart of the bustling neighbourhood of **Médina**, home to a busy market and birthplace of Senegalese superstar Youssou N'Dour. Further north, the 1864 lighthouse **Les Mamelles** (Map p693) sits on a small volcanic hill, from where you get great views across Dakar.

## Museums & Art Galleries

Though slightly dusty, Dakar's **IFAN Museum** (Map p686; Place de Soweto; adult/child CFA2000/200; ☻8am-12.30pm & 2-6.30pm) compares well to the national museums of other West African nations. There are imaginative displays of masks and traditional dress from the region (including Mali, Guinea-Bissau, Benin and Nigeria), as well as fabrics and carvings, musical instruments and agricultural tools.

Numerous small art galleries invite you to discover the city's vibrant contemporary arts scene. The **Galerie le Manège** (Map p686; ☎821 0822; 3 Rue Parchappe; ☻9am-5pm Tue-Sat), has excellent exhibitions in a beautifully restored 19th-century building. The space of the **Galerie Nationale** (Map p686; ☎821 2511; 19 Ave Albert Sarraut; admission free; ☻9am-6pm) is less enticing, but its exhibitions are usually very good.

In Point E, **Salon Michéle Ka** (Map p691; ☎824 7033; Tour de l'Oeuf) is not only the funkiest hairdresser in town, but also one of the most original art galleries. The salon is decorated with urban *sous-verre* (reverse glass painting) motives à la *car rapide*. In Hann, the fantastic gallery **Caracolo** (Map p693; ☎832 1590; www.caracolo .com; 7 Allée Marinas) exhibits and sells works made by local artisans, uniquely using materials 'found' in the immediate creative space.

# ACTIVITIES
## Diving

**L'Océanium** (Map p684; ☎822 2441; www.oceanium .org; Route de la Corniche-Est; ☻Mon-Sat), which is an environmental-protection agency, runs excellent diving excursions, ranging from introductory half-day dives to longer expeditions. Divers can stay at the l'Océanium for reasonable rates.

## Fishing

You can arrange deep-sea fishing at **West Africa Sport Fishing** (Map p684; ☎823 2858; fffs@sentoo .sn; Embarcadère de Gorée). The restaurant **Lagon I** (Map p686; ☎821 5322; Route de la Corniche-Est) also organises fishing trips and boasts several world-record catches.

## Swimming

Beaches within easy reach of the city include the **private beach** (Map p686) near Hôtel Lagoon II and **Plage de l'Anse Bernard** (Map p684) near Hôtel Le Savana. For swimming and sunbathing, the beaches of **N'Gor** (p698) and **Île de Gorée** (p696) are better. Other than that, there's always the chlorine option.

Dakar's best swimming pool is the sublime **Piscine Olympique** (Map p691; ☎869 0606; piscineolymp@sentoo.sn; Tour de l'Oeuf) in Point E, which is part of a huge sports complex. Most top-end hotels allow nonguests to access their pools for a small fee. The pool at Sofitel Teranga is free if you eat at the adjoining restaurant, otherwise it will cost you CFA4500 (CFA7000 on Sunday). The Hôtel de l'Indépendance charges CFA3000 for its rooftop pool with a great view of Dakar (free if you have a meal).

## Surfing

Dakar is great for surfing, ask at the **Tribal Surf Shop** (Map p693; ☎646 0914, 820 5400; tribal@arc .sn; Yoff Virage) for advice on good spots. This is also the best place to hire boards (per day CFA10,000), take courses, buy gear and get your board repaired.

## Wrestling
Dakar's main arena for traditional wrestling is in Médina, near the large **Stade Iba Mar Diop** (Map p684; Ave Blaise Diagne). Most matches are announced only on the radio, but important ones will be advertised around town, and talked about incessantly by the locals. Saturday and/or Sunday are the usual days for the fights, starting around 4.30pm or 5pm.

## COURSES
The **Pôle Linguistique de l'Institut Français** (Map p686; ☎ 823 84 83; 3 Rue Parchappe; ☼ Oct-May) runs recommended Wolof and French courses (four hours per week for 12 weeks; CFA90,000). Keen dancers should try the **Centre Culturel Blaise Senghor** (Map p691; Rue 10). Its bleak façade doesn't do justice to the creative bustle going on inside – just beware of the faux-drummers, out to hassle women.

## FESTIVALS & EVENTS
Dakar's cultural calendar is packed, and outside the wettest months (July and August), you're almost bound to stumble across a festival.

**Kaay Fecc** (☎ 826 4950; www.ausenegal.com/kaayfecc) is one of Africa's best events for contemporary and traditional dance. It usually happens in early June. Film lovers shouldn't miss the annual **Festival International du Film de Quartier** (www.festivaldufilmdequartier.com) featuring the best of contemporary film in cultural centres, restaurants and other spaces. The **Dak'Art Biennale** (☎ 823 0918; www.dakart.org) is the queen of Dakar's festivals. It drowns the city in colour, with art exhibitions all across town.

## SLEEPING
Dakar has a very wide range of accommodation from filthy dosshouses to palatial hotels – although everything is expensive and the steadily increasing prices are only justified in a few places. Outside the city centre, the suburbs of Yoff (p699) and N'Gor (p698) also have a number of good options .

### Budget
There's hardly such a thing as a budget hotel in Dakar. The cheapest places are usually brothels with a sure chance of theft. These two are acceptable.

**Hôtel Continental** (Map p686; ☎ 822 1083; 10 Rue Galandou Diouf; s/d from CFA13,000/15,000; ❄) The best of the cheapest. The basic rooms

even have a touch of character. For your own bathroom and air-con you pay some CFA5000 more.

**Hôtel Provençal** (Map p686; ☎ 822 1069; 17 Rue Malenfant; s/d CFA14,400/16,800) This isn't too bad for a place where rooms are often rented by the hour. Just make sure you get a room upstairs and you'll avoid most of the noise.

### Midrange
Most hotels in this range have rooms with private bathrooms. Prices do not include tax (CFA600 per person).

**Hôtel Saint-Louis Sun** (Map p686; ☎ 822 2570; fax 822 4651; Rue Félix Faure; s/d/tr CFA23,000/29,500/35,500; ❄ ❄) Pretty rooms with big, glass doors opening onto a peaceful, green courtyard. Right in the heart of Dakar, this allows for a mental escape from the crowds and fumes that wash past it.

**Hôtel Ganalé** (Map p686; ☎ 889 4444; hganale@sentoo.sn; 38 Rue Amadou Assane Ndoye; s/d CFA28,000/35,000, apt CFA38,000-48,000) This place is a gem. Rooms are bright and tastefully decorated, all equipped with TV and telephone and the restaurant is excellent.

**Hôtel Mamelles** (Map p693; ☎ 860 0000; www.lesmamelles.com; s/d CFA10,000/15,000, with bathroom CFA14,500/19,500) Tucked away in a side street in the *quartier* Les Mamelles, this tranquil place has colourfully decorated rooms set around a leafy patio.

**Hôtel Océanic** (Map p686; ☎ 822 2044; www.hoteloceanicdakar.com; 9 Rue de Thann; s/d/tr/q CFA21,600/25,800/33,000/36,800; ❄) With spotless rooms and a relaxed courtyard restaurant, this pleasant old-style place is fair value.

**Hôtel Faidherbe** (Map p684; ☎ 889 1750; faidherbe@sentoo.sn; cnr Ave Faidherbe & Raffenel; s/d/ste CFA36,000/42,000/70,000) This hotel has got plenty of the niceties of a top-end place – broadband connection in the rooms, swimming pool, ATM and a cosy bar – for a much better rate than the grand hotels.

**Hôtel le Miramar** (Map p686; ☎ 849 2929; miramard@hotmail.com; 25 Rue Félix Faure; s/d incl breakfast CFA25,600/31,200; ❄) Some call it funky, some call it scruffy. It's great for ambience, though a concerted effort at renovation wouldn't be lost on this gaudily coloured place.

**Hôtel Farid** (Map p686; ☎ 821 6127; www.hotelfarid.com; 51 Rue Vincens; s/d from CFA26,500/29,000) It looks modest, but has some of the best-maintained rooms in central Dakar. And the Lebanese restaurant is addictive.

**Auberge Marie-Lucienne** (Map p691; ☎ 869 0090; Rue A; Point E; s/d CFA28,920/36,000) It calls itself an *auberge* (inn or hostel), but it is actually quite a well-furnished, little hotel in a calm part of town. Rooms have TV and hot water.

## Top End

All hotels in this range have rooms with private bathrooms and accept major credit cards.

**Hôtel Al Afifa** (Map p686; ☎ 889 9090; gmbafifa@ telecomplus.sn; 46 Rue Jules Ferry; s/d/ste CFA37,000/ 40,000/45,000) This place is ageing a little, but it retains some of its lustre. Ask for room 103 – the only one with a terrace. The bar, restaurant and disco downstairs offer plenty of nightlife.

**Sofitel Teranga** (Map p686; ☎ 889 2200; fax 823 5001; Place de l'Indépendance; r from CFA136,000; ☒ ) Part of the Accor Hotel group, this is exactly what you'd expect from a luxury, businessmen's favourite. Facilities include tennis courts, sauna, shops and a nightclub.

**Hôtel Lagon II** (Map p686; ☎ 889 2525; www.lagon .sn; Route de la Corniche-Est; s/d/ste CFA72,000/80,000/12 0,000; ☒ ☐ ) If you can bear the kitsch seafarers décor, this is a great place to view the ocean from cabin-style rooms perched on stilts at the edge of the water.

**Hôtel le Savana** (Map p684; ☎ 849 4242; www .savana.sn; Route de la Corniche-Est; s/d CFA74,000/80,000; ☒ ☐ ☒ ) If you really want to relax in style, this ingenious construction overlooking the ocean is the place to go. Facilities include a business centre, fishing deck, private jetty, tennis courts, nightclub, sauna and gym.

## EATING

Dakar's restaurant scene is one of the capital's highlights. There are about 100 eateries in the town centre alone, and that's before you've even headed for the suburbs, where chic restaurants open all the time.

The French cuisine, a hangover from the colonial past, is a particular highlight, but the culinary range stretches from Cape Verdean over Vietnamese to Thai and Mexican. The seafood tends to be particularly good in Dakar. For flavoursome *yassa poulet* and *tiéboudienne* you're best off in one of the small places frequented by the locals. Restaurants are usually open for lunch and dinner, with some staying open all day. Most places are closed on Sundays.

## Restaurants

**Keur N'Deye** (Map p686; ☎ 821 4973; 68 Rue Vincens; dishes from CFA1500) Highly recommended, this place offers well-prepared Senegalese specialities. At most times, the tinkling of the *kora* (harplike instrument) accompanies your eager clattering of cutlery.

**Chez Loutcha** (Map p686; ☎ 821 0302; 101 Rue Moussé Diop; dishes CFA2500-3500; ☽ noon-3pm & 7-11pm Mon-Sat) Head straight for the air-conditioned garden, where the fountains embellish an aquatic theme. The Cape Verdean and 'Euro-African' cuisine is excellent and comes in enormous serves.

**Restaurant VSD** (Map p686; ☎ 661 3333; 91 Rue Moussé Diop; mains CFA3500; ☽ 7am-midnight) There's not much jazz at this intimate place any more, but the West African and international dishes are still good value.

**La Villa Chez Yannick** (Map p686; ☎ 823 2197; 4 Rue Malenfant; mains CFA5000; ☽ 11am-3pm & 7-11pm) French food and a few miscellaneous international dishes are served in an airy outdoor setting.

**Le Méléa** (Map p686; ☎ 502 8293; 90 Rue Moussé Diop; dishes CFA5000) This tiny French restaurant is all simple elegance, and the food tastes divine. The catch: it can get a little smoky.

**Le Sarraut** (Map p686; ☎ 822 5523; Ave Albert Sarraut; meals around CFA5000-8000; ☽ 8am-midnight Mon-Sat) This is a Dakar classic, and for good reason. The tasty French and international cuisine in this calm, central place is hard to beat.

**Le Bambou** (Map p686; ☎ 822 0645; 19 Rue Victor Hugo; mains CFA6000-10,000) If money is not a concern, then head to Le Bambou, the culinary equivalent of a day's pampering.

**Ozio** (Map p686; ☎ 823 8787; 21 Rue Victor Hugo; meals around CFA5000-9000) This uber-trendy restaurant has been a favourite of the glittering classes for years. The food is good, and is served with the ego-tickling sense that you belong to the in-crowd.

**Lagon I** (Map p686; ☎ 821 5831; Route de la Corniche-Est; mains around CFA7000) In this restaurant, the nautical theme is consistently pursued from cruise-ship décor to the cabin-style toilets, the terrace suspended on stilts in the ocean to the scrumptious platters of seafood.

**Saveur d'Asie** (Map p686; ☎ 821 4774; 21 Rue de Thann; dishes around CFA5000) Hugely popular, this takeaway restaurant makes a mysterious promise to serve Senegalese-Asian cuisine and sells most of the works of Youssou N'Dour in its adjacent boutique.

SENEGAL

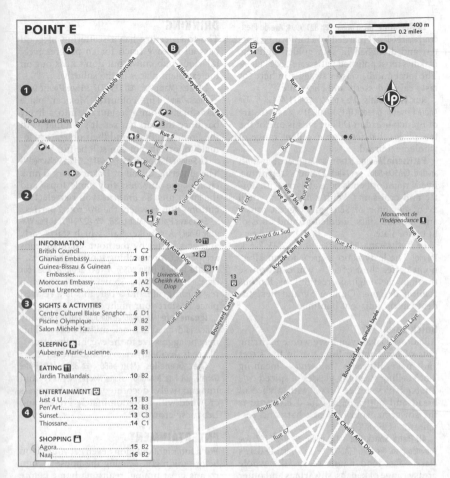

**POINT E**

0 — 400 m
0 — 0.2 miles

To Ouakam (3km)

Monument de l'Indépendance

**INFORMATION**
British Council.............................1 C2
Ghanian Embassy.........................2 B1
Guinea-Bissau & Guinean
    Embassies...............................3 B1
Moroccan Embassy.......................4 A2
Suma Urgences...........................5 A2

**SIGHTS & ACTIVITIES**
Centre Culturel Blaise Senghor....6 D1
Piscine Olympique........................7 B2
Salon Michèle Ka.........................8 B2

**SLEEPING**
Auberge Marie-Lucienne.............9 B1

**EATING**
Jardin Thailandais.....................10 B2

**ENTERTAINMENT**
Just 4 U....................................11 B3
Pen'Art.....................................12 B3
Sunset......................................13 C3
Thiossane.................................14 C1

**SHOPPING**
Agora.......................................15 B2
Naaj........................................16 B2

**Jardin Thailandais** (Map p691; ☎ 825 5833; 10 Blvd du Sud; meals around CFA8000; ☼ lunch & dinner Mon-Sat) There's no better Thai, perhaps no better Asian food altogether, in the whole of Senegal than that served at this pretty place in Point E.

**La Casa Créole** (Map p686; ☎ 823 4081; 21 Blvd Djily Mbaye; meals around CFA4000-6000; ☼ Mon-Sat) Don't be put off by the busy pub at the front – walk right through, and you get to a marvellous garden terrace where French and Creole food are served with a sprinkling of live jazz.

**La Fourchette** (Map p686; ☎ 821 8887; 4 Rue Parent; meals around CFA6000-10,000; ☼ Mon-Sat) The humble exterior betrays nothing of the polished food temple that hides behind the plain doors.

Impeccable sushi and dishes from around the world, prepared by two of Dakar's most renowned chefs, attract expats and trendy crowds. And don't leave without indulging in the heavenly *roti au chocolate* (a sinfully rich chocolate desert).

**Le Toukouleur** (Map p686; ☎ 821 5193; 122 Rue Moussé Diop; meals around CFA5000-8000; ☼ Mon-Sat) Divine. The setting oozes character and the cuisine is a refined mix of international flavours.

**Cafés & Patisseries**
In Dakar, a patisserie is not somewhere to buy your bread, but a gleaming place to take a special friend if you really want to make an impression.

**SENEGAL**

**La Royaltine** (Map p686; ☎ 821 9994; Ave du Président Lamine Guèye) Guarded by a uniformed porter, and drenched in soft, golden lighting, Dakar's most polished patisserie oozes class. The local middle classes swagger in here for tasty cakes, desserts and chocolates.

**Aux Fins Palais** (Map p684; ☎ 823 4445; 97 Ave André Petyavin; breads CFA150-700) It's easy to tire of French bread in Dakar. This is one of the few places that serve an excellent range of wholemeal bread.

**Patisserie Médina** (Map p684; Ave Faidherbe; pastries around CFA500-800; ☯ 24hr) Dakar's terminus. Every night out ends here at 5am, with coffee and croissants. With some luck, you'll even see some of Senegal's biggest music and football stars huddled around cups of hot chocolate.

**Le Metissacana** (Map p686; ☎ 822 2043; Rue de Thiong) The leafy patio is great for an afternoon coffee. Best of all – you can browse through the original creations by famous fashion designer Oumou Sy and her students in the adjacent boutique.

## Quick Eats

All across Dakar, you'll see women stirring pots of *mafé* and grilling fish in the street and makeshift cafés (*tangana* – meaning 'hot') selling steaming glasses of spiced *café Touba* (spicy coffee brew) with a slice of bread and butter. A fast-food favourite is the shwarma, sold in snack bars and restaurants (CFA800).

**Ali Baba Snack Bar** (Map p686; ☎ 822 5297; Ave Pompidou; snacks from CFA600; ☯ 8am-2am) Dakar's classic fast-food haunt serves the whole greasy range of kebabs, shwarmas and other quick snacks.

**Caesar's** (Map p686; ☎ 842 7879; 27 Blvd de la République; pizzas around CFA3000) Sometimes only greasy chicken wings, burgers and fries will do, and for those moments Caesar's is your place.

## Self-Catering

**Score Supermarket** (Map p686; 31 Ave Albert Sarraut) in the town centre is good for food, imported items, sanitary and baby products, and plenty of other nonfood items. **Fili Fili Supermarket** (Map p686; Ave Allés Delmas), three blocks north of Place de l'Indépendance, is a dusty little place with slightly cheaper prices but a much smaller range of stock. For fresh food, try the markets (see p694).

## DRINKING

The town centre has a scattering of good bars all in easy reach for an progressively hilarious pub crawl, but don't miss out on the excellent places in the suburbs.

**Le Mex** (Map p686; ☎ 823 6717; 91 Rue Moussé Diop; ☯ noon-2am) This colourful Mexican place transforms from a restaurant into a lively bar once the sun has set. It's popular with the French military and their obligatory female following, but can still be fun.

**Le Seven** (Map p686; ☎ 842 6911; 25 Rue Mohamed V) The glittering queen of Dakar's bars. Think champagne bubbles, tiny tank tops, and the latest hits. So *branché*, you risk electrocution – this is where the in-crowd parties.

**Snooker Palace** (Map p686; ☎ 822 9487; 44 Rue Wagane Diouf) A snooker hall, which starts early and gets hotter by the hour. Giant screens are perfect for watching football matches.

**Café Indigo** (Map p686; ☎ 842 2607; 26 Rue Félix Faure; ☯ 7am-midnight) Somewhere between a restaurant, café and a bar, this is a relaxed place to start your night out.

**Iguane Café** (Map p686; 26 Rue Jules Ferry) This tiny place is draped in mock-military décor. This may be aggressive to the eye, but the atmosphere is decidedly relaxed and friendly.

**Chez Grenelles** (Map p686; ☎ 889 4444; Hôtel Ganalé, 38 Rue Amadou Assane Ndoye) Classy and imaginatively decorated, this place gets crowded with a predominately French and Lebanese crowd.

## ENTERTAINMENT

For a fun night out, don't even get your kit on before midnight. Leaving the house at 1am means great timing, returning home before 4am is a sign of weakness. Now go party.

## Live Music

The live music scene was booming when we visited. More and more restaurants and bars feature small stages, and many nightclubs host live gigs. In restaurants, admission is often free, while clubs charge between CFA3000 and CFA5000.

**Just 4 U** (Map p691; ☎ 824 3250, 634 4801; km 2.5, Ave Cheikh Anta Diop; ☯ 11am-3am) This spacious bar-restaurant is the best address for live music in Dakar. There's a concert every night, sometimes even two. Senegalese greats like Cheikh Lô, Souleymane Faye and Orchestra Baobab, as well as visiting greats, proudly take their regular place on the small stage.

**Pen'Art** (Map p691; ☎ 864 5131; Blvd du Sud) Around the corner from Just 4 U, this is a cosy jazz club with good bands in a relaxed atmosphere.

**Kilimanjaro** (Map p693; ☎ 822 6991; Soumbédioune) The mighty Thione Seck plays here, at his personal club, every weekend. Fabulous. Men – don't forget your suit and tie...

**Thiossane** (Map p691; ☎ 824 6046; Sicap Rue 10) Youssou N'Dour's nightclub was once the hottest place in town, but is now frequently closed when the star is out of town. And even if he's there, he rarely appears on stage before 3am. Still, it's a hub of the hip-swaying, high-heeled *mbalax* scene.

**Sunset** (Map p693; ☎ 821 2118; Centre Commercial Sahm) Similarly popular with the Dakarois,

this *mbalax* club on the northeast corner of the intersection of Ave Blaise Diagne and Blvd de la Gueule-Tapée.

## Nightclubs

**Playclub** (Map p686; Hôtel Al Afifa, 46 Rue Jules Ferry) The club of the Hôtel Al Afifa is a classy affair for over 30s, hence the music is a little smoother and spiced with salsa beats.

**Koulgraoul** (Map p684; ☎ 505 6969; l'Océanium, Route de la Corniche-Est; admission CFA2500) This relaxed, once-monthly club night in the garden of the l'Océanium attracts a mixed, laid-back crowd.

**King's Club** (Map p686; 32 Rue Victor Hugo) This inner-city club is hugely popular for its heavy dance beats and good vibes.

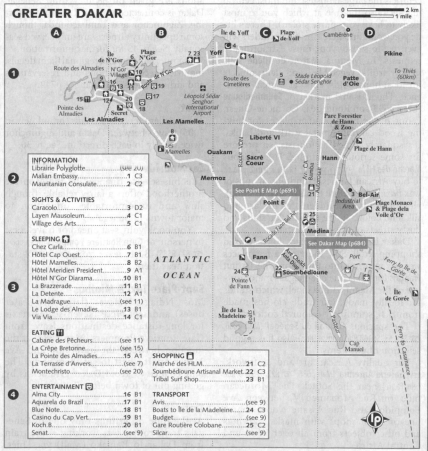

## Theatre

**Théâtre Daniel Sorano** (Map p684; ☎ 822 1715; Blvd de la République) The Ensemble Instrumental, the Ballet National du Sénégal and the Théâtre National du Sénégal frequently perform at Senegal's national theatre.

## Cinemas

**Kadjinol Station** (Map p686; ☎ 842 8662; www.kadjinol-edu.com; off Ave Albert Sarraut) This lounge bar and global-food restaurant has the most interesting film selection in town, including recent Hollywood flicks and world cinema.

## SHOPPING

Dakar has several markets that are worth exploring. **Marché Sandaga** (Map p686) in the centre is the largest, busiest and most central market (also the one at which you're most likely to have your purse stolen). There's little you won't find here, and eager traders will even try to satisfy your most extraordinary requests. In Médina, **Marché de Tilène** sells mainly fruits, vegetables, and daily objects for local households, and has a great ambience. The artisanal market of **Soumbédioune** (Map p693), on Route de la Corniche-Ouest, is one of the most popular places for buying wood carvings, metal work and batiks. It's squarely aimed at tourists, so prepare for some serious bargaining. The fabulous **Marché des HLM** (Map p693) is the best place to buy African fabrics. Hundreds of rolls of wax *bazin* (dyed cloth that's beaten to shine), vibrant prints, embroidered cloth, lace and silk lend colour to the ramshackle stalls and dusty streets of this popular *quartier*.

Dakar isn't really the place for a relaxed shopping stroll. Still, there are a few places worth venturing into town for. The **Institut Français** (p685) is one of Senegal's major outlets of the Maam Samba label, which stands for locally made, fair-trade clothes made from rich, stunningly coloured cottons.

The spacious **Cocktail du Sénégal** (Map p686; ☎ 823 5315; 108 Rue Moussé Diop) also has a good selection of gift items.

For quality African art and craftwork, try **Galerie Antenna** (Map p686; ☎ 822 1751; 9 Rue Félix Faure) near the Sofitel. The 'Moroccan mile' on Rue Mohamed V, between Ave Pompidou and Rue Assane Ndoye, has a line of small shops with masks, carvings and other objects from all over West and Central Africa.

The leafy suburb of Point E houses several chic shops, such as **Naaj** (Map p691; ☎ 825 7546; www.naaj.sn; Rue 1), where you can find tableware, decorated in traditional glass painting technique. The airy patio setting of **Agora** (Map p691; ☎ 864 1448; Rue D) displays beautiful Moroccan artwork and home décor at steep prices. Near Soumbédioune, the **Atelier Baba Diawara** (Map p693; Route de la Corniche Ouest) is a magic corner selling funky bags, toys, CD racks, lamps and other objects from recycled cans.

## GETTING THERE & AWAY

### Air

Léopold Sédar Senghor International Airport is in Yoff. Information on flights between Dakar and international or regional destinations are given on p830. Within Senegal, Dakar is connected to Saint-Louis, Cap Skiring, Ziguinchor and Tambacounda, though some upcountry airports are only served seasonally. See p743 for further information.

For international and regional flight details, inquiries, reconfirmations and reservations and airline offices in Dakar see p742.

### Boat

The excellent ferry boat *Wilis* (brand new in 2005) travels between Dakar and Ziguinchor twice weekly in each direction. See p730.

### Car Mouride

This bus service financed by the Mouride brotherhood offers a fairly reliable, though slow and uncomfortable connection to major towns in Senegal.

You book your seat ahead of travel, best in person, at **Gare Routière Pompiers** (Map p684; ☎ 821 8585). Buses leave from the petrol station near there.

### Sept-Place Taxi & Minibus

Most Ndiaga Ndiayes (large two-seater buses) and *sept-place* (seven-seater) taxis for long-distance destinations leave from Gare Routière Pompiers (Map p684) at the junction between the *autoroute* and Ave Malick Sy. It's best to get there early. The only chance to avoid Dakar gridlock is by getting out of town before 7.30am.

### Train

At the time of writing, only one of Senegal's train routes was working – the train from Dakar to Bamako (Mali) via Thiès,

**PUBLIC TRANSPORT FROM DAKAR**

Note that these prices (CFA) are indications only, you may encounter minor variations, luggage charges, and increases due to the rising cost of petrol.

| Destination | Sept-Place | Minibus | Ndiaga Ndiaye |
|---|---|---|---|
| Bakel | 11,500 | 9500 | 9000 |
| Karang (The Gambia) | 5500 | 4500 | 3500 |
| Kaolack | 2600 | 1650 | 1350 |
| Mbour | 1300 | 950 | 870 |
| Rosso | 5100 | 3880 | 3440 |
| Saint-Louis | 3500 | 2600 | 2200 |
| Tambacounda | 7500 | 6000 | 5000 |
| Thiès | 1200 | 900 | 800 |
| Touba | 3200 | 1900 | 1500 |
| Ziguinchor | 7500 | 6000 | 5000 |

Diourbel and Tambacounda. The service is unreliable and derailments are frequent. If you're keen on the adventure, check out the latest situation at Dakar's train station. For details on the train to Bamako, see p743.

## GETTING AROUND
### To/From the Airport
The journey from the airport to town is the only one with a fixed rate (CFA3000), though prices may well have risen by the time you read this. If you want to save a couple of hundred CFA, you can walk from the airport out onto the main road and flag down a taxi there.

### Bus
Dakar's DDD bus service is surprisingly good. DDD stands for Dakar Dem Dikk (meaning Dakar going and returning), and the large, blue DDD buses do go and come back with astonishing regularity. They have fixed stops and go about every 10 minutes. Short distances cost CFA150, longer ones CFA175, CFA200 or CFA250. Prices conform to a system of zones. You simply pay your ticket at the conductor's booth. You can view the full network, complete with maps and prices on www.demdikk.com. The main DDD terminal in Central Dakar is near the port, on Blvd de la Libération.

## Car
The major self-drive car-hire agencies in Dakar:

**Avis** (Map p693; ☎ 849 7757; www.cfaogroup.com) At the airport and the Hôtel Meridien President.
**Budget** (Map p684; ☎ 822 2513; cnr Ave du President Lamine Guèye & Ave Faidherbe) Agencies at the airport and the Hôtel Meridien President.
**Hertz** (Map p686; ☎ 820 1174; www.hertz.sn; Rue Gomis) Also at the airport.

Independent car-hire companies include the following:
**Afrique Location** (Map p686; ☎ 823 8801; 28 Rue Assane Ndoye)
**Dakar Location** (Map p686; ☎ 823 8610; 7 Rue de Thiong)
**Noprola** (Map p686; ☎ 821 7311; 29 Rue Assane Ndoye)
**Senecartours** (Map p686; ☎ 889 7777; www.senecartours.sn; 64 Rue Carnot)

### Car Rapide
These colourfully decorated, blue-and-yellow minibuses are Dakar's identity symbols, and while travelling in those pretty (though battered) vehicles is certainly an experience, their circuits are hard to understand if you don't know the city well. Destinations aren't marked, and the assistants perched dangerously on the back shout directions so fast, that untrained ears won't understand a thing. When you want to get off, just tap a coin on the roof. Journeys cost between CFA50 and CFA100.

### Ndiaga Ndiaye
These privately owned, white 30-seater minibuses (most of them have 'Alhamdoulilai' written across the front) roughly follow the same routes as the DDD buses. Fares are between CFA100 and CFA150 depending on the length of your trip. Destinations and routes are not marked, so you'll have to ask or listen for the call from the apprentice.

### Senbus
These white minibuses are assembled in Senegal. They were newly introduced in 2006 and are eventually supposed to replace the *cars rapides*. They are a lot more comfortable, and infinitely more user-friendly with clearly marked destinations and fixed stops. Rates are the same as *cars rapides*.

SENEGAL

## Taxi

Going by taxi is the easiest way to get around Dakar. Taxis are equipped with dusty old meters, but it's been years since any of them worked, so fares need to be negotiated. For a short ride across the city centre, the fare should be around CFA500. Place de l'Indépendance to Gare Routière Pompiers is around CFA750, and Dakar Centre to Point E around CFA1000. At night and on public holidays rates go up.

# GREATER DAKAR & CAP VERT PENINSULA

Once a busy harbour on the tip of the Cap Vert Peninsula, Dakar city is gradually clawing its way up this tongue of land, turning the area into a bustling centre of activity. Still the areas of Yoff and N'Gor, adorned with wide beaches, and the tranquil Île de Gorée just off the coast of Dakar are places to head for a breather, in case Central Dakar's relentless urban buzz gets too much.

## ÎLE DE GORÉE

The historical Île de Gorée is enveloped by an almost eerie calm. There are no sealed roads and no cars on this island, just narrow alleyways with trailing bougainvillea and colonial brick buildings with wrought-iron balconies. But Gorée's calm is not so much romantic as meditative, as the ancient buildings bear witness to the island's role in the Atlantic slave trade.

## Information

Gorée is tiny, and can easily be explored independently, though the **Syndicat d'Initiative** ( ☎ 823 9177; Rue du Port; ⏰ 9am-1pm & 2.30-5pm Tue-Sun) can arrange guides. For some quick, on-the-spot information, try the small tourist booth near the police station. This is also where you'll have to pay your CFA500 tourist tax – an obligatory payment for all non-Senegalese visitors. Gorée has a **post office** and an Internet café **Espace Multimedia** (per hr CFA500; ⏰ 10am-1pm & 3-10pm).

## Sights

There's plenty to see on the island, just don't come on a Monday, when all museums and historical buildings are closed.

The island's most famous building is **La Maison des Esclaves** (admission CFA500; ⏰ 10.30am-noon & 2.30-6pm Tue-Sun). No trip to the island is complete without a visit to this 1786 Dutch construction (see opposite), whose arched staircase opening to the ocean has become a symbolic image of the horrors of slavery.

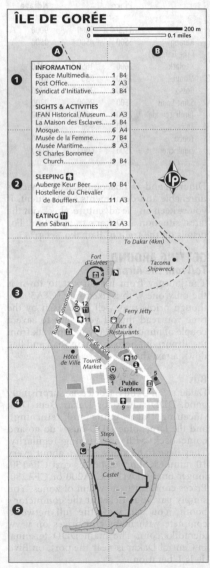

ÎLE DE GORÉE

| INFORMATION | |
| Espace Multimedia...........1 | B4 |
| Post Office....................2 | A3 |
| Syndicat d'Initiative........3 | B4 |

| SIGHTS & ACTIVITIES | |
| IFAN Historical Museum....4 | A3 |
| La Maison des Esclaves....5 | B4 |
| Mosque.......................6 | A4 |
| Musée de la Femme........7 | B4 |
| Musée Maritime.............8 | A3 |
| St Charles Borromee Church...............9 | B4 |

| SLEEPING | |
| Auberge Keur Beer.........10 | B4 |
| Hostellerie du Chevalier de Boufflers.............11 | A3 |

| EATING | |
| Ann Sabran...................12 | A3 |

The **Castel** at the southern tip of the island was erected in the 17th century, with other fortifications, including massive WWII guns, added over time. You get excellent views over the island from the top of the rocky plateaus.

Gorée's 1830 **St Charles Borromee Church** is usually open to visitors, and the **mosque**, built slightly later in 1892, is one of the oldest stone mosques in Senegal.

The **IFAN Historical Museum** (admission CFA200; ☺ 10am-1pm & 2.30-6pm Tue-Sat) in the ancient French **Fort d'Estrées** (1850) has interesting exhibits portraying Senegalese history up to the present day. The permanent exhibition at the **Musée de la Femme** (admission CFA500; ☺ 10am-5pm Tue-Sun), dedicated to the role of Senegalese women throughout history, really comes to life in the explanations by the enthusiastic museum guide (CFA350). The **Musée Maritime** (admission CFA500; ☺ 10am-5pm Tue-Sun) in an 18th-century West Indies Company building, isn't quite as interesting.

## Sleeping & Eating

**Auberge Keur Beer** ( ☎ /fax 821 3801; keurbeergie@ yahoo.fr; s/d CFA20,000/25,000) Gorée's most popular place has pristine rooms. Management is full of useful info, and can even arrange accommodation in private homes, should the place be full.

**Hostellerie du Chevalier de Boufflers** ( ☎ 822 5364; www.boufflers.com; r from CFA18,000) Best known for its terrace restaurant overlooking the harbour, this place has several rooms spread across a whole block. Prices vary depending on the view and floor – the best are the enormous rooms upstairs that sleep up to five.

For food, try the two hotels, or any of the stretch of restaurants opposite the ferry jetty. Near the post office, **Ann Sabran** ( ☎ 826 9429; dishes around CFA2500) is a cosy, portside restaurant serving simple meals.

## Getting There & Away

A **ferry** ( ☎ 24hr infoline 628 1111, 849 7961) runs regularly from the wharf in Dakar to Gorée (CFA5000 return for nonresidents, 20 minutes). See p744 for the timetable.

## ÎLE DE LA MADELEINE

Île de la Madeleine is west of Dakar, about 4km off the mainland. It was declared a national park in 1985, and consists of a main island (Sarpan), two other islets, plus several lumps of volcanic rock. The island is not inhabited, which makes its nature so much more interesting. Sarpan's dwarf baobab trees are worth looking at, and with a bit of luck you might spot dolphins or turtles. The best thing to do here is bird-watching.

---

### LA MAISON DES ESCLAVES

Île de Gorée was a busy trading centre during the 18th and 19th centuries, and many merchants built houses in which they would live or work in the upper storey and store their wares on the lower floor. La Maison des Esclaves is one of the last remaining 18th-century buildings of this type on Gorée. It was built in 1786 and renovated in 1990 with French assistance. With its famous doorway opening directly from the storeroom onto the sea, this building has enormous spiritual significance for some visitors, particularly African-Americans whose ancestors were brought from Africa as slaves.

Walking around the dimly lit dungeons, particularly after a visit to the historical museum, you will begin to imagine the suffering of the people held here, reinforced by the gruesome details provided by the curator. La Maison des Esclaves is an significant symbol and reminder of the horrors of the slave trade. Although an important slaving culture existed in Gorée, the island's role as a major slave-shipment point is sometimes overstated. Of the 20 million slaves that were taken from Africa, only 300 per year may have gone through Gorée, and even then, the famous doorway would not have been used – a ship could not get near the dangerous rocks and the town had a jetty a short distance away.

But the number of slaves transported from here isn't necessarily what matters in the debate around Gorée. The island, and particularly La Maison des Esclaves, stands as a terrible reminder of the immense suffering inflicted on African people through the Atlantic slave trade.

*Written with assistance from Chris de Wilde (specialist in 19th-century West African history)*

**SENEGAL**

If small trees and big birds don't make your heart beat faster, you can also come here for some snorkelling, diving or swimming in a natural pool.

Pirogues go from the **National Park Office** (Mr Seck or Mr Mbaye; ☎ 821 8182) on Route de la Corniche-Ouest, just a few metres north of Casino Terrou-Bi. A park ranger will organise your trip (admission adult/child under 10 CFA1000/free; pirogue CFA3000, 20 minutes). Groups from three to 10 people get CFA1000 discount per person.

## N'GOR & LES ALMADIES

Les Almadies is a plush Dakar neighbourhood where the polished villas of Senegal's richest look out onto private beaches. It's also home to a string of lively bars and restaurants and culminates in the Pointe des Almadies, West Africa's westernmost spot.

### Route des Almadies & Route de N'Gor

This northern continuation of Ave Cheikh Anta Diop is the area's lifeline. It's lined with several restaurants, and the major banks, which have ATMs.

#### SLEEPING & EATING

**La Detente** (Map p693; ☎ 820 3975; contact@hotel-ladentente.com; s/d from CFA39,000/47,000) has large rooms overlooking a pretty garden, while **Le Lodge des Almadies** (Map p693; ☎ 869 0345; hotellelodge@sentoo.sn; r CFA35,000) is a personalised hotel with tasteful rooms, bathrooms in which to enjoy a luxurious shower, and one of Dakar's best restaurants to boot.

#### ENTERTAINMENT

At the trendy **Koch.B** (Map p693; ☎ 820 8671; www.kochb.com; Route des Almadies; ☼ noon-3am), Dakar's in-set chills to live music in comfy armchairs. Across the road, the **Blue Note** (Map p693; Route des Almadies), with its myriad bar spaces, is also great for concerts.

Hidden in the *quartier* is the fabulous **Alma City** (Map p693; ☎ 820 2410). The complex houses a tiny restaurant, as well as a recording studio and concert space. The airy, brightly decorated bar-restaurant **Aquarela do Brazil** (Map p693; ☎ 536 17 70) follows the Brazilian theme to perfection from the *caipirinhas* (cocktails) and the mouthwatering menu to the samba music.

Clubbers are well catered for with the popular **Casino du Cap Vert** (Map p693; ☎ 820

0974) and the **Senat** (Map p693; ☎ 869 6969) at the Hôtel Meridien President.

## Pointe des Almadies

This understated cape is the *quartier*'s liveliest spot, framed by several restaurants and a shabby artisanal market.

Opposite the Club Med the palatial **Hôtel Meridien President** (Map p693; ☎ 869 6969; www.lemeridien-dakar.com; r from CFA90,000) overlooks the Pointe des Almadies. It's undeniably the finest hotel in and around Dakar, and has every facility (including its own golf club and heliport) and prices to match.

The bustling community of small restaurants huddled together at the point stands in complete contrast to such refined luxury. **La Pointe des Almadies** (Map p693; ☎ 820 0140; mains about CFA3500; ☼ Tue-Sun) is an enduring institution, with good food, including Vietnamese specialities, in a wide garden setting. For ambience, **La Crêpe Bretonne** (Map p693; crêpes from CFA1500) is unbeatable on Sundays, when Dakar's youth comes out to play.

### N'Gor

East of the point, the sheltered **Plage N'Gor** (N'Gor Beach) smacks of carefree beach-tourism. The **Hôtel N'Gor Diarama** (Map p693; ☎ 820 1005; fax 820 2723; r CFA45,000) is the monolith on the headland to the east. A touch more informal is **La Madrague** (Map p693; ☎ 820 0364; s/d CFA28,000/36,000; ☒ ), one of the nicest places to stay on Plage N'Gor, and **La Brazzerade** (Map p693; ☎ 820 0364; www.labrazzerade.com; d/ste CFA20,000/35,000; ☒ ☐ ) a cosy, affordable, sea-view hotel with a great grill restaurant. Seafood lovers mustn't miss a dinner at the **Cabane des Pêcheurs** (Map p693; ☎ 820 76 75; Plage de Ngor, meals around CFA5000-10,000), where freshly caught and heavenly spiced fish is served with real fishermen's insight.

A short pirogue ride away, **Île de Ngor** with its pretty beaches is popular with day-trippers on weekends. **Chez Carla** (Map p693; ☎ 820 1586; d with/without breakfast CFA20,000/15,000) is a friendly place to stay, with cosy rooms and fine Italian food (dishes about CFA3000).

### Getting There & Away

To reach Pointe des Almadies or N'Gor, you could catch bus 8 from central Dakar out towards the airport, and take a taxi from there for about CFA700. A taxi from central Dakar will cost about CFA2000.

## YOFF

The fishing town of Yoff has a completely different feel. The local residents are almost exclusively Lebu, renowned fishermen who have inhabited this area for many centuries and retain a vital spirit of independence. The town itself is self-administering, with no government officials, no police force and, apparently, no crime. In fact, it was regarded as a separate state by the French colonial authorities before Senegal itself became independent.

The Lebu of Yoff are nearly all members of the Layen, one of the brotherhoods that dominate life in Senegal. The founder of the brotherhood, Saidi Limamou Laye, is buried in the **Layen Mausoleum** (Map p693), a gleaming white building topped with a green onion-shaped dome, on the beach at the eastern end of town.

About 1km north from the mausoleum is the main fishing beach, where large pirogues are launched onto giant rollers and the day's catch is sold straight on the sand. Even if the waves weren't so dangerously large, and even if the beach wasn't covered in the town's rubbish, this is no place for swimming or sunbathing: skimpy clothing isn't inappropriate in the close-knit Muslim community. Forget about 'entertainment', too – there are no clubs or bars in Yoff Village, private drunkenness is frowned upon and smoking is prohibited. This is a place to come and wander around respectfully – dressed appropriately in long skirts or trousers.

### Sights & Activities

Yoff village life and the impressive Layen Mausoleum hold plenty of interest, though arts fans shouldn't miss a trip to the fabulous **Village des Arts** (Map p693; Route de l'Aeroport), squeezed between the Route VDN and the national stadium. Though slightly neglected, this is still a bubble of creativity, housing the *ateliers* (workshops) of some of Senegal's finest artists, including the sculptor Alpha Sow, painter Kebé and Moussa Mbaye.

### Sleeping & Eating

**Hôtel Cap Ouest** (Map p693; ☎ 820 2469; capouest@arc .sn; s/d CFA16,000/19,000) This cute place at Yoff Virage is possibly the best value on the whole peninsula. You can get a large, nicely furnished room here for the price of one

in a downtown brothel/hotel. The restaurant features changing displays of quality contemporary art and opens onto a small beach, perfect for a sunset drink. Plus, management are friendly and know their way around the country.

**Via Via** (Map p693; ☎ 820 5475; viavia@sentoo.sn; Route des Cimetières; s/d incl breakfast CFA9600/17,200) This backpackers' favourite at the eastern end of Yoff has been consistently friendly, clean and welcoming for years. It also has *djembe* drumming courses on offer.

**La Terrasse d'Anvers** (Map p693; ☎ 688 0000; Yoff Virage) The name evokes Belgium, and beer drinkers rejoice, this is indeed Dakar's most reliable address for Belgian brew, as well as an excellent restaurant.

### Getting There & Away

Yoff is near the airport, and is most easily reached from there by taxi (around CFA1500). From Dakar's city centre, a taxi to Yoff should cost around CFA2000. By public transport, take DDD bus 8.

## LAC ROSE

Lac Rose, also known as Lac Retba, is a shallow lagoon surrounded by dunes, mainly famous for being the final destination of the annual Dakar Rally.

Water here is 10 times saltier than the ocean, and the high concentration of minerals causes the lake to shimmer in a pink light when the sun is high. The spectacle isn't always visible, best chances are in the dry season, but even if nature lets you down, you can still swim here, buoyed by the salt. On the southern side of the lake, the small-scale salt-collecting industry is worth a glimpse.

The lake makes for an enjoyable day trip from Dakar, but the Dead Sea it ain't, whatever the tour operators try to tell you. The saleability of the faint hue together with the rally have caused the development of a massive tourist industry on the edges of the lake – be prepared for hassle.

Most of the hotels listed organise activities for similar prices (rates listed are approximate). They include 4WD tours around the lake (CFA15,000), beach-buggy tours (CFA25,000) and camel riding (per hour CFA15,000). **Chevaux du Lac** (☎ 630 0241) offers horse riding (CFA6000/400,000 for two hours/six days) for beginners to advanced riders.

SENEGAL

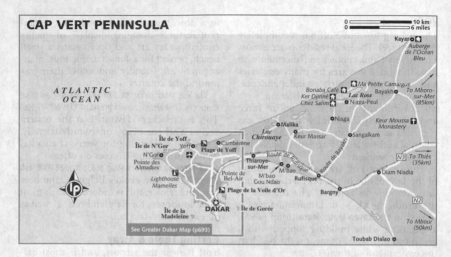

CAP VERT PENINSULA

## Sleeping & Eating

The cluster of hotels on the lake get busy with busloads of tourist groups, and the artisanal village that's developed can be a hassle to get through. There are slightly more secluded options near the salt village and at the opposite side of the lake.

**Bonaba Café** ( ☎ 638 7538; r per person CFA5000; 🖭 ) Hidden away on the far side of the lake, this has been a favourite with independent travellers for years. Rooms are simple and bathrooms shared, and the dunes invite walks and provide shelter from the more touristy zones. You get here either by walking 2km from the main hotel cluster through the dunes, or by pirogue from the salt village (CFA3000 to CFA5000).

**Ker Djinné** ( ☎ 634 0468; d CFA20,000; 🖭 ) The prettiest of the touristy places, this open-spaced *campement* has round-hut accommodation and a recommended restaurant where a griot usually strums his *kora*.

**Chez Salim** ( ☎ 638 1019; d/tr CFA20,000/25,000; 🅿 ⊠ 🖭 ) This large *campement* is one of the more upmarket, with accommodation in comfortable huts.

**Ma Petite Camargue** ( ☎ 511 2745; s/d CFA15,000/ 20,000) This cutesy *campement* on the road to Bombilor is a relaxing distance from the tourist hub. Accommodation is basic, with shared bathrooms. The French couple that manages this place had just taken over Le Jardin du Lac in Niaga Peul, and there's little doubt they'll turn it from a run-down shell into a stylish hotel-restaurant in no time.

## Getting There & Away

Trying to get here by public transport is near impossible, involving a journey by Ndiaga Ndiaye (CFA200), *car rapide* (CFA200) or DDD bus 11 to Keur Massar, from there a trip by taxi (CFA1000) or minibus (CFA100) to the village Niaga Peul, then a 5km walk to the lake.

Don't do it, hire a taxi (round trip with an afternoon waiting time around CFA20,000) or join an organised excursion from Dakar (see p685).

## RUFISQUE

Rufisque was one of the first and most important French settlements during colonial days, and the crumbling buildings along the transit town's dusty main road still tell the story of a former glory. It's worth stopping here for an hour or so, checking out the architecture and perhaps taking a ride on a horse cart, Rufisque's main mode of public transport. Otherwise do as the locals do – pass through.

If you want to spend the night, the cosy **l'Oustal de l'Agenais** ( ☎ 836 1648; r from CFA11,000) is a good option with clean, comfortable rooms, a cosy restaurant and friendly management.

Rufisque is on the main road out of Dakar and there's plenty of transport, including DDD bus 15, frequent Ndiaga Ndiaye and *cars rapides*. The road is notoriously congested, so the trip can take up to two hours during rush hour.

## KEUR MOUSSA MONASTERY

The Keur Moussa Monastery, situated southeast of Lac Rose and 50km from Dakar on the road to Kayar, is a great place to spend a reflective Sunday. The 10am mass is famous for its unique music – a stunning mixture of African music and Gregorian chants in Wolof. The monks sell CDs (CFA10,000) after the service, as well as homemade goat's cheese, prayer books and other various items. If you can't make it to the monastery, you can try Dakar's bookshops for copies of the CDs.

Take bus 15 to Rufisque and change for a minibus to Bayakh or Kayar (CFA100). Tell the driver where you're headed, and he'll drop you off at a junction, from where it's a 1.5km walk to the monastery. It's signposted and all the drivers know it. Alternatively, a taxi from Dakar should be around CFA15,000, including waiting time.

## KAYAR

The pretty fishing village Kayar marks the point where the coast swings north – the beginning of Senegal's Grand Côte. It is framed by a wide sand strand, where the whole cycle of a fisherman's day can be observed, from the rolling out to sea, to the homecoming, emptying of the nets and gutting of fish.

The northern beaches aren't really recommended for swimming – undertows are very strong. But the coastline makes an impressive sight, and is a great place to relax. Pirogue trips, as well as walks to the sand dune behind the village fill a day nicely, and watching pirogue makers at work is fascinating. Kayar isn't far from Lac Rose, and the two destinations can be combined in a weekend trip.

The **Auberge de l'Océan Bleu** ( ☎ 953 5058, 507 91 25; r CFA7000-10,000) is a relaxed, simple, solar-powered place right behind the beach (you can't drive here). Manager David can arrange excursions around the country, and also had a great plan to create a pirogue shuttle service between the airport at Yoff and Kayar. Phone to ask if that's already been implemented.

# PETITE CÔTE

South of Dakar, the Petite Côte is where Senegal greets the Atlantic with 70km kilometres of sandy coast. Safe swimming beaches attract large numbers of tourists, and cause the flashy holiday village Saly to

spill over its boundaries. If you like your holiday more low-key and your beach-body slightly less exposed, the villages Toubab Dialao, Popenguine and La Somone in the north, as well as Mbodiène, Nianing and Joal-Fadiout in the south have white strands that still swing to the local rhythm.

## TOUBAB DIALAO

The calm fishing village Toubab Dialao is an excellent hideout from the bustle of Dakar – a great place for walking, swimming and horse riding. **Les Cavaliers de la Savane** ( ☎ 836 7876) offers guided tours on horseback (CFA10,000 for two hours).

Perched on a cliff, the seashell-decorated **Sobo-Bade** ( ☎ /fax 836 0356; www.espacesobobade .com; dm per person CFA4000, s/d from CFA10,000/12,000) is something of a classic on the backpacker's scene, and the hub of much activity in the village. Its design has inspired two other places: **La Source Ndiambalane** ( ☎ 836 1703; ndiambalan@sentoo.sn; d/tr CFA12,000/15,000) and **Auberge La Mimosa** ( ☎ /fax 826 7326; mimosa@sentoo.com; d CFA10,000, ▨ ), which has an Internet café.

The grandest place in town is the **Iris Hotel** ( ☎ 836 2969; www.irishotel.net; s/d with half board CFA35,000/58,000; ▨ ▢ ▨ ), a luxurious address with tastefully decorated rooms and a spectacular sea-view terrace. A rough and muddy dirt track out of town, **La Pierre de Lisse** ( ☎ 957 7148; pierredelisse@sentoo.sn; s/d CFA20,000/30,000; ▨ ) is a welcoming place, run by the friendly and knowledgeable Bab Mbengue.

To get here from Dakar, take any transport headed for Mbour and get off at the Diam Niadia junction. Minibuses run from here to Toubab Dialao (CFA300). A taxi from Dakar should cost around CFA15,000.

## RÉSERVE DE BANDIA

This small **wildlife reserve** ( ☎ 685 5886; adult/child CFA7000/3500; ☉ 8am-6pm) sits 65km from Dakar on the road to Mbour, about 5km south of Sindia. The impressively well-managed reserve is crowded with wildlife, including colobus monkeys, crocodiles and other species indigenous to Senegal, as well as rhinos, giraffes, buffaloes, ostriches and other animals more at home in East Africa. In that sense, it's more of a zoo, but an amazingly beautiful one, with not a cage in sight. And unlike in the national parks, you're almost guaranteed animal sightings.

For those more interested in human tradition than beasts, the Serer burial mounds and giant baobab, once used to bury griots, may be an enticement to visit.

Walking isn't allowed here, but you can enter with your own car or taxi. During or shortly after the wet season you may have to hire one of the reserve's own 4WDs (CFA30,000), as many routes will be impassable for smaller vehicles. Tours take two to three hours.

Even if you don't want to visit the park, the fantastic restaurant, overlooking a pond is worth a visit. You can normally spot buffalos, monkeys, birds and crocodiles from here, and the food is good, too (dishes around CFA4000 to CFA6000).

Across the Dakar–Mbour main road lies the fantastic **Accrobaobab** (Xavier Larcher; ☎ 637 1428; www.accro-baobab.com; adult/child CFA15,000/10,000), where you can climb, glide, and clamber your way around mighty baobab trees – all with safety nets and trained staff to watch out. Great fun.

## POPENGUINE

This tranquil, friendly village is famous for its annual Pentecostal pilgrimage (check www.sanctuaire-poponguine.sn for details on the annual event) and a modern church that commemorates the apparition of the black Madonna in 1986.

## THE RESERVES OF POPENGUINE AND LA SOMONE

Less known than Senegal's large national parks, these two tiny reserves are home to some 150 different species of birds. The Réserve de Popenguine was declared a protected zone in 1986, after the blue rock-thrush was spotted here. Excursions to see this, and plenty of other species, can be organised by the Campement Keur Cupaam, whose women's collective looks after the reserve, and also has resident ornithological guides from the National Parks Authority. The adjacent Réserve de La Somone is very different in character. It was created by the local community in 1999, and is maintained independently. The park headquarters is situated at the edge of the reserve (ask locals to show you the way there), but for guided bird-watching tours you are better off booking a combined tour at Popenguine, which has the better trained staff. The protected zone of La Somone contains a stunning lagoon, where pelicans and flamingos are the most prominent feathered residents, though with a bit of patience, you'll spot rarer species, too. At Popenguine, you'll pay CFA5000 for a ½-day tour around both reserves.

Bird-watchers love it for its small nature reserve, and the adjacent community reserve of La Somone – a beautiful lagoon. More than 150 species of birds can be spotted in the two protected areas. The **Campement Ker Cupaam** ( ☎ 956 4951; dm CFA5000,d CFA12,000) sits right at the edge of the reserve, and the boisterous women's cooperative that runs it also organises recommended ornithological tours. Across the road, **Keur de Sable** ( ☎ 957 71 64; s/d CFA7500/12,000, house CFA20,000) is a wonderfully welcoming hotel, restaurant and cultural centre. The beach, where you find the small restaurant **L'écho-Côtier** ( ☎ 637 8772; meals CFA5000) lies a few stone steps further down. A short walk along the wave-kissed shore takes you back to the village proper, and the rustic beach bar **Chez Ginette** ( ☎ 957 7110; ☿ Wed-Mon).

From Dakar, head for Mbour and get off at Sindia, from where infrequent bush taxis run to Popenguine for CFA300.

## LA SOMONE

Eighty kilometres from Dakar, La Somone is the gentle medium between the mass tourism of Saly-Portugal and the village intimacy of Toubab Dialao. The town sits right on a stunning lagoon, whose extraordinary landscape and rich bird life are protected (see above).

### Sleeping & Eating

La Somone has several good accommodation choices – this is only a tiny selection of what's on offer. All of the places listed are along the main road that leads to the beach and the lagoon – Club Baobab sits right next to the lagoon.

**Canda** ( ☎ 958 5054; tening@sentoo.sn; d CFA18,500; ☒ ☒ ) The nicest place – a small family-style hotel with pretty rooms and Belgian beer on the menu.

**Hôtel Sorong** ( ☎ 958 5175; www.sorong.sn; s/d CFA21,000/30,000; ☒ ☒ ) A low-key hotel with a good restaurant.

**Le Phoenix** ( ☎ 957 7517; www.phenix-senegal .sn; villa CFA40,000) Has gleaming, spacious villas on the beach that accommodate whole families.

**Le Bassari** ( ☎ 957 7464; d/tr/q CFA17,000/ 25,000/34,000) A low-key, beach-view *campement* packed with masks and artefacts.

**Africa Queen** ( ☎ 957 7435; www.africaqueen.com; d CFA25,000; ☒ ☒ ) An unremarkable resort hotel catering mainly for groups.

**Club Baobab** ( ☎ 957 7402; h2131@accor.com) A luxurious option that only accepts independent travellers in the low season. Inquire for individual rates.

A recommended restaurant outside the hotels is the cute **Café Creole** ( ☎ 958 5191; dishes around CFA2500-3000), near the junction between Ngaparou and La Somone – the place for tasty Senegalese and European cuisine, with live music on Thursday evenings.

### Getting There & Away

To get to La Somone, take a Mbour-bound taxi, get off at Nguékokh where taxis leave for Ngaparou and La Somone (CFA300).

## SALY

The French call Saly Senegal's 'Cote d'Azur', and they're not far off. Once here it's easy to forget that you're in Africa. This is the sort of coastal holiday destination found all over the world: palm-lined beaches,

SENEGAL

dozens of big hotels, nightclubs, bars and souvenir shops. The main tourist mile is in Saly-Portugal. The northern part of town, Saly-Niakhniakhale, is much more local in character.

**BICIS** (☎ 957 3331; Saly Portugal; ◷ 3.30-5.30pm Mon, 9am-12.30pm & 3.30-5.30pm Tue-Fri, 9am-12.30pm Sat) and **SGBS** (☎ 957 37 03; Saly Portugal) have branches in Saly, and there are several Internet cafés.

## Sleeping

This is a tiny selection of the dozens of hotels and self-catering apartments in Saly.

**Les Bougainvillées** (☎ 957 2222; bougainvilleesaly@sentoo.sn; r CFA41,200; ⌗ ▯ ◲) With comfortable bungalows set in a spacious garden, this is prettier than your standard resort hotel.

**Les Flamboyants** (☎ 957 0770; www.hotelsenegal flamboyant.com; s/d from CFA24,600/25,000; ⌗ ◲) For Saly-Portugal, this is a nicely understated place. It's all about wrought iron it seems, from the room furnishings to the tables of the plant-adorned restaurant.

**Espadon** (☎ 957 1949; fax 957 2000; half board per person CFA36,600; ⌗ ▯ ◲) This smoothly decorated place provides luxury with an African flavour. The attached fishing centre enjoys a good reputation.

**Lamantin Beach Hotel** (☎ 957 0777; www.lelam antin.com; s/d/ste with half board CFA82,000/131,000/210,000; ⌗ ⌗ ◲) This five-star establishment calls itself paradise on earth, and if your idea of heaven involves being pampered in a spa, or relaxing on a private beach, then you'll probably agree with the hype.

**Au Petit Jura** (☎ 957 3767; www.aupetitjura.ch; d CFA19,500; Ⓟ ⌗ ▯ ◲) This pretty retreat in a calm corner of Saly-Niakhniakhale has spotless huts in a half-circle around a swimming pool.

**La Medina** (☎ 957 4993; lamedina@sentoo.sn; s/d 13,000/17,000; ⌗) This Mediterranean-style place stretches over three floors, surrounding a lush courtyard. A stunning oasis of peace in the heart of Saly village.

## Eating & Drinking

Saly-Portugal's restaurant scene leaves you spoilt for choice, though many serve similar fare. The following are among the most interesting.

**El Paséo** (Saly junction; meals around CFA5000) For scrumptious Spanish meals head to this lively place.

**Le Manguier** (Route de la Somone; dishes around CFA4000) This tastefully decorated restaurant is a gem, both for its excellent international cuisine, and the pleasant courtyard where giant mango trees watch over a collection of African masks and statues.

**Habana Café** (☎ 957 0724; dishes around CFA5000) Fast becoming one of Saly's mightiest magnets, thanks to its beautiful beach spot, excellent service and its delicious French cuisine.

**Chez Poulo** (☎ 659 6331; dishes around CFA1000) A small and informal eatery that is hugely popular, thanks to its mouthwatering Senegalese and European food.

## Getting There & Away

A taxi from Mbour is CFA1500.

## MBOUR

Five kilometres south of Saly, Mbour is a big fishing centre. The town's 200m-long fish market on the beach, the colourful dots of pirogues and the surrounding marine-related commerce is a sight to behold.

The *gare routière* (bus station) is near the exit towards Dakar, behind a wide gate. Mbour has a **BICIS** (☎ 957 1086) with ATM, several Internet cafés and a post office. All of those are found in the centre of Mbour, at the tree-lined alleyway that crosses town. Mbour hospital is on the route towards the beach and Tama Lodge.

## Sleeping & Eating

There are a few places to stay scattered around town, all of them south of the fishing market.

**Village Petit Eden** (☎ 957 4477; www.petit-eden .de; d CFA17,000) Has been a favourite with travellers for years, thanks to a leafy garden setting, clean rooms and friendly staff.

**Le Bounty** (☎ /fax 957 2951; bounty@sentoo.sn; d CFA9500; ⌗) Near the beach, the Bounty has rooms stuffed with souvenirs that try hard to look like apartments.

**Hôtel Club Safari** (☎ 957 1991; fax 957 3838; s/d incl breakfast CFA16,000/20,000; ⌗ ◲) A few blocks further down from Le Bounty, the seashell-decorated Safari has spacious, comfortable rooms set around a pool.

**Mbëgeel** (☎ 957 5177; www.mbegeel.com; hut/ste/house CFA39,500/59,000/98,000; ⌗ ◲) A few kilometres along the road to Nianing, this 'handcrafted' guesthouse is a softly lit, mosaic-decorated piece of art.

Tama Lodge ( ☎ /fax 957 0040; www.tamalodge
.com; s CFA30,000-40,000, d 60,000-80,000) The queen
of Mbour's hotels where amazing wooden
sculptures watch over modern mud-huts. A
dinner on the beach terrace by candlelight
is a fine night out indeed.

For cheap, filling and utterly delicious
Senegalese meals, head for **Chez Paolo** (dishes
from CFA2000) Anyone in town can show you
the way there.

## Getting There & Away

There's frequent public transport between
Mbour and Dakar (minibus CFA950, *sept-
place* CFA1300); Mbour to Joal is a little
less regular (minibus CFA600, *sept-place*
CFA750). Taxis cost around CFA15,000
from Dakar to Mbour.

## NIANING

Sleepy Nianing is one of the quieter
places along the coast, perfect if you like
to dip your toes without anyone stepping
on them. Youthful ambience and a spacious garden make **Le Ben'Tenier** ( ☎ 957 1420;
bentenier@telecomplus.sn; r per person CFA8630) a good
option. The **Auberge des Coquillages** ( ☎ /fax 957
1478; tjdiane@telecomplus.sn; s/d CFA26,000/28,100; ☒ ),
however, is much brighter and prettier. **Le
Girafon** ( ☎ 957 5266; s/d CFA10,000/15,000) is a tiny
*campement* with a relaxed family feel that
also organises local excursions.

Nianing is on the main road between
Mbour and Joal and all public transport
stops here.

## JOAL-FADIOUT

Joal is the birthplace of former president
Léopold Sédar Senghor, but it's the town's
'twin sister' Fadiout that attracts the people.
Fadiout sits on an island made entirely of
oyster and clam shells, and everything in
town is made of shells, from the houses and
car-free roads to the shared Muslim and
Christian cemetery. The island is reached
via a long wooden bridge from Joal.

The citizens of Joal and Fadiout are
rightly proud of their religious tolerance.
Christians and Muslims live in harmony
here, and Fadiout's impressive church and
shrines to the Virgin Mary are comple-
mented by a large mosque.

There are plenty of pirogue trips on offer,
taking you to the cemetery, a nearby oyster cultivation and a set of stilt-balanced

granaries. The trips make for a great day
out, but the pirogue owners are a hassle-
some lot. You're better off relying on the
badge-bearing employees of the Syndicat de
Tourisme. They hover around the bridge,
or can be found at the Hôtel le Finio.

## Sleeping & Eating

**Le Thiouraye** ( ☎ 515 6064; s/d/tr CFA10,000/12,000/
14,000) is a relaxed *auberge* right on the river.
You can leap straight from the brilliant terrace restaurant into a pirogue to Fadiout –
a useful way to avoid the hustlers near the
bridge. The quirky **Relais 114** ( ☎ 957 6178;
r incl breakfast without/with bathroom CFA7500/10,000)
is pretty run-down, though the larger-
than-life owner Mamadou Balde and his
performing pelicans give the neglect some
character. The fairly new **Hôtel de la Plage**
( ☎ 957 6677; hakim@yahoo.fr; d/tr CFA25,000/28,000;
P ☒ ) has bright, large rooms at reasonable rates, and a good restaurant.

## Getting There & Away

A minibus to/from Mbour is CFA600. If
you're heading on down the coast, from
Joal to Palmarin costs CFA1000. A *sept-
place* taxi goes directly to Dakar most
mornings (without changing at Mbour)
for CFA1800.

# THE SINÉ-SALOUM DELTA

Some 60km south of Mbour, the Petite Côte
is cut by the mouth of the Saloum River,
and sand strands give way to a maze of
mangrove swamps and creeks. This is the
180,000-hectare zone of the Siné-Saloum
Delta, with its shimmering flat lands, palm
groves, salt marshes and lagoons, which is
one of Senegal's most beautiful areas.

## PALMARIN

Palmarin is an expansive area encompassing four villages that lies 20km south of
Joal-Fadiout, where the beaches of the Petite
Côte merge with the labyrinthine creeks of
the Siné-Saloum Delta. It's a breathtaking
spot, where dots of bush grass and tall palm
groves, salty plains and patches of gleaming
water line a series of causeways. All places
are clearly signposted on the main road.

## Sleeping & Eating

Palmarin has a seductive choice of beautiful *campements*. Leading the pack is the original **Lodge des Collines de Niassam** ( ☎ 669 6343; www.nias sam.com; half board per person CFA37,000-57,000; 🗙 🗨 ) where you can sleep in classy treehouses that cling to the mighty branches of baobabs, or sit on stilts in the shallow waters of the delta. The **Yokam** ( ☎ 936 3974; yokam@teranga-horizon.com; r per person incl breakfast CFA7000) is run by a young and enthusiastic bunch and has accommodation in comfy straw huts. The red-mud bungalows of the **Lodge de Diakhamor** ( ☎ 644 9491, 957 1256; www.lesenegal.info; s/d with half board CFA23,000/41,000) are visible from afar. This is a stylish place where pirogue excursions, horse riding, bicycle and fishing trips are all included in the price. The basic **Campement Villageois de Sessene** ( ☎ 669 0365; r per person incl breakfast CFA6500) is run by the local population. If you wish to spend your holiday cash locally, this is the place to stay.

## Getting There & Away

Palmarin is most easily reached from Mbour, via Joal-Fadiout and Sambadia (where you may have to change). The fare from Joal to Sambadia is CFA500 in a Ndiaga Ndiaye, and from Sambadia to Palmarin it's CFA300.

## DJIFER

Fifteen kilometres south of Palmarin, Djifer is a good starting point for pirogue excursions around the Siné-Saloum Delta (half-day trips around CFA25,000). The filthy, litter-strewn village holds little appeal in itself, but the deserted sand bank **Pointe de Sangomar** and the tranquil islands of Guior and Guissanor are close by. A visit here can be combined with a pirogue tour through the maze of mangroves, and a stop at the villages of Dionewar and Falia.

In Djifer, **La Pointe de Sangomar** ( ☎ /fax 835 6191; d CFA8600, with bathroom CFA12,600) is popular, while the slightly shabby **Yokam** ( ☎ 936 3752; r per person CFA3000) is great for arranging pirogue excursions. In Dionewar, you can spend the night in the luxurious **Delta Niominka** ( ☎ 948 9935; www.deltaniominka.com; r per person incl breakfast CFA25,000).

## NDANGANE & MAR LODJ

Ndangane is a thriving tourist centre on the northern side of the Siné-Saloum Delta. From here you can get boats across the river to the village of Mar Lodj, on a peaceful island cut off from the mainland by the delta. There's no bank here, but Internet connections are available at a couple of places.

Beware of the overeager pirogue-owners on the departure point to Mar Lodj – you're best off arranging your trip through your *campement*.

## Sleeping & Eating
### NDANGANE

Most of the accommodation and eating options are located at the end of the road to Fimela, which is from where most boat trips depart. **Le Barracuda** (Chez Mbacke; ☎ 658 5794; s/d CFA9000/12,000) is a cheap and cheerful family-run place. Another good choice is the welcoming **La Palangrotte** ( ☎ 949 9321; lapalang@sentoo .sn; s/d incl breakfast CFA9750/13,000) at the exit of town where 10% of all profits are invested in local-development projects. The spacious **Les Cordons Bleus** ( ☎ 949 9312; cordons-bleus@sentoo.sn; s/d/tr CFA25,000/32,000/42,000; 🅿 🗙 🖵 🗨 ) is the classiest establishment in town.

Good restaurants include **Le Petit Paradis** (dishes from CFA800), **Le Tamarko** (dishes from CFA3000) and **Le Baobab** ( ☎ 653 4073; dishes around CFA4000), all of which serve mainly European food. For Senegalese food try **Le Picboeuf** and **La Maroise**.

### MAR LODJ

There aren't vast differences in quality between the *campements* on Mar Lodj, just in price and service. The friendly *campement* **Essamaye** (www.senegalia.com; r with full board CFA17,500) has excellent-value rooms with clean, shared bathrooms. **Le Limboko** ( ☎ 641 2253) has a good restaurant, a couple of rooms and a manager who's full of useful advice. Inquire for prices. **Mbine Diam** ( ☎ 636 9199; s/d/tr CFA9000/16,000/21,000) is one of the simplest *campements* on the island, which is reflected in the adequate prices. A little more upmarket are the bungalows of **Le Bazouk** ( ☎ 820 4125; lebazoudusaloum@sentoo.sn; per person CFA12,000) and **Nouvelle Vague** ( ☎ 634 0723; s/d/tr CFA15,600/ 23,200/25,800). All *campements* offer pick-up from Ndangane, some for free.

## Getting There & Away

Take any bus between Kaolack and Mbour, and get off at Ndiosomone, from where bush taxis shuttle back and forth to Ndangane. You can go directly by bush taxi from Dakar to Ndangane for CFA1800. From Mbour bush taxis go via Sambadia and Fimela.

You can charter a pirogue between Ndangane and Djifer for about CFA25,000. A pirogue to Foundiougne is about CFA40,000.

## FIMELA & SIMAL

The two villages Fimela and Simal lie just north of Ndangane, past the tourist trail. In Simal, 2km from Dioffor, the **Gite de Simal** ( ☎ 644 9491, 957 1256; www.lesenegal.info; s/d with half board CFA21,000/37,000) has accommodation in rootsy straw-huts. All activities, such as pirogue and fishing trips around the mangroves are included in the half-board rate.

There are fairly frequent bush taxis from Ndangane to Fimela (CFA200), from where you can hire a taxi to either place for about CFA1000 to CFA2000. Taxis from Fimela to Ndiosomone cost CFA400.

## FOUNDIOUGNE

Once a French colonial outpost, the expansive village of Foundiougne now mainly attracts keen anglers and is a good place to arrange pirogue trips. Most *campements* listed have boat tours on offer, and prices tend to be similar (pirogue day trips around CFA20,000 to CFA30,000, transfer to Djifer CFA40,000).

This area has notoriously bad drinking water – stick to bottled.

### Sleeping & Eating

West from the ferry pier, there's a string of *campements*. They're numerous, but overall quality standards are pretty low.

**La Pirogue** ( ☎ 516 7102; r per person CFA8000, with half/full board CFA13,000/16,000) This tiny hotel has spotless rooms and a bread oven onsite.

**Le Baobab sur Mer** (Chez Anne Marie; ☎ 948 1262; s/d/tr incl breakfast CFA8500/16,000/20,000) Right on the river and run by the boisterous Anne Marie, this place is booming. Meals are available (CFA3000 to CFA4000).

**Le Baobab sur Terre** (Chez Ismail; ☎ /fax 948 1108; s/d incl breakfast CFA6500/13,000) A relative of Baobab sur Mer, sur Terre is a more understated affair, with very basic, but cheap rooms.

**Les Bolongs** ( ☎ /fax 948 1110; www.lesbolongs .com; r CFA10,000) Spacious bungalows set in a lush garden.

**Indiana Club** ( ☎ /fax 948 1213; www.indianaclub .net; r per person with half/full board CFA15,000/19,000;

⊠ ⊠ ) Has a curious cowboy character and a very good restaurant.

**Saloum Saloum** ( ☎ 534 8370; saloumsaloum@ sentoo.sn; s/d/tr CFA8500/16,000/19,000; ⊠ ) Try the slightly rugged if you want to spend your money locally.

**Foundiougne Hôtel** ( ☎ 948 1212; fax 948 1310; s/d/tr incl breakfast CFA21,600/35,200/40,800; ⊠ ⊠ ) If you just want to spend, the overpriced Foundiougne might appeal – it offers a vast range of activities.

The Italian restaurant **La Cloche** ( ☎ 544 4242; meals CFA3500), right near the jetty, has an excellent reputation, both for the sparkling cleanliness of its kitchen and the fully-fledged Italian menu.

### Getting There & Away

By minibus, Kaolack to Foundiougne is CFA700. There aren't many direct buses, so you might have to change at Passi.

Alternatively, you can reach Foundiougne from Fatick. Take a bush taxi to Dakhonga, where you catch a ferry across to Foundiougne (passenger/car CFA100/1200). If there's no ferry waiting, you can take a pirogue across (around CFA3000).

## TOUBAKOUTA

Nestled among mazes of mangroves, the tiny town of Toubakouta is one of the most beautiful spots of the Siné-Saloum Delta. It's an excellent base for excursions to the nearby Parc National du Delta du Saloum and the stunning Air Marine Protegée, both of which teem with wildlife, including pelicans, flamingos, herons and egrets.

Toubakouta has a couple of cybercafés, *télécentres* and a post office, but no bank.

### Sleeping & Eating

Toubakouta has hotels for all budgets.

**Keur Youssou** ( ☎ /fax 9487728; d/tr CFA12,000/15,000; ⊠ ) One of the best-quality cheapies in the country. Rooms are beautifully furnished and the atmosphere friendly and relaxed.

**Les Coquillages du Niombatto** ( ☎ 645 3036; layoum@hotmail.com; d incl breakfast CFA12,500) Head here for basic, but impeccable rooms. It also has an excellent restaurant.

**Keur Bamboung** ( ☎ 510 8013; www.oceanium.org; r with half board/full board CFA17,000/22,000) The most fascinating place of all. A beautiful, village-run ecolodge, stunningly located on the edge

SENEGAL

of a mangrove-lined island, a pirogue journey and donkey-cart ride out of town. Transport and all activities (mangrove walks, pirogue trips, canoeing, bird-watching) are included in the price.

**Hôtel Keur Saloum** ( ☎ 948 7715; www.keursaloum .com; s/d with half board CFA36,000/58,000; ☒ ☙ ) This vast hotel is the most upmarket place where nicely furnished bungalows are scattered across a pretty garden.

### Getting There & Away

Toubakouta is just off the main road between Kaolack and Karang. Kaolack to Toubakouta is CFA3000 by *sept-place* taxi and CFA1300 by Ndiaga Ndiaye.

### PARC NATIONAL DU DELTA DU SALOUM

The 76,000 hectares of the **Parc National du Delta du Saloum** (admission CFA2000) encompass the dry savanna woodland of the Forêt de Fathala, wide stretches of mangrove swamps, and a maritime section that extends from the islands of Betanti to the Pointe de Sangomar. Wildlife in the forest section includes red colobus and patas monkeys, warthogs and hyenas. The sea sections allow for bird-watching, though sea turtles and dolphins can occasionally be spotted.

The main entrance to the park is in Missirah. You pay your admission charge at the office of the **eco guards** ( ☎ 936 3431; ☙ 9am-4pm), who can also show you around.

In Missirah, you can stay at the peaceful and welcoming **Gîte de Bandiala** ( ☎ 948 7735; www.gite.bandiala.com; r per person with half/full board CFA15,400/21,100), which lies about 2km east of Missirah, down a sand path that turns off the main road just before you get to the village. The place is full of character and a great base for exploring this part of the delta. It also has a water hole where monkeys, warthogs and other animals come to drink.

### Getting There & Away

A bush taxi from Toubakouta is CFA400, but they're few and far between. For around CFA5000, someone will usually drive you there. Another option is to get a private taxi all the way from Kaolack – this will cost anything between CFA20,000 and CFA40,000.

# CENTRAL & NORTHERN SENEGAL

This region covers a vast area, from the edge of the busy Cap Vert Peninsula, to the remote outer edges of northern Senegal. It includes some rarely visited spots, such as the magnificent Desert de Lompoul and the route through the arid lands along the Senegal River. These solitary spaces contrast sharply with the bustling towns of historical Saint-Louis, Thiès, Kaolack and Touba, Senegal's holy city.

## THIÈS

Thiès is the gateway to the region, a city destined to absorb Dakar's population overspill. The leafy town is of marginal interest to travellers apart from one major attraction – the world famous **Tapestry Factory** (see below).

### Information

CBAO, SGBS and BICIS all have branches with withdrawal facilities. There are several *télécentres*, cybercafés and a post office in the centre of town.

**BICIS** ( ☎ 951 8339; Place de France; ☙ 7.45am-12.15pm & 1.40-3.45pm)

---

**TAPESTRIES OF THIÈS**

The factory of the **Manufactures Sénégalaises des Arts Décoratifs** ( ☎ /fax 951 1131; admission CFA1000; ☙ 8am-12.30pm & 3-6.30pm Mon-Fri, 8am-12.30pm Sat & Sun) was one of the many artistic endeavours inspired by President Senghor during the 1960s. Today, the factory is run as a cooperative, with designs for the tapestries chosen from paintings submitted by Senegalese artists.

All the weaving is done on manual looms, and two weavers complete about 1 sq metre per month. Only eight tapestries are made from each design. Most their way around the world as gifts from the government to foreign dignitaries; there's a huge tapestry hanging in Atlanta airport and another in Buckingham Palace. Others are for sale, but at CFA500,000 per square metre, most of us will be content to admire them in the exhibition room.

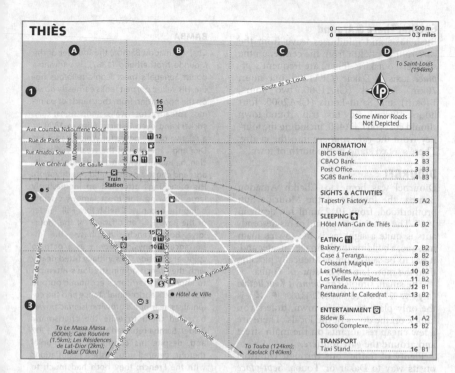

**THIÈS**

| | |
|---|---|
| To Saint-Louis (194km) | |

Some Minor Roads Not Depicted

Route de St-Louis

Ave Coumba Ndiouffene Diouf
Rue de Paris
Rue Amadou Sow
Ave Général de Gaulle

Train Station

Rue Houphouët-Boigny

Rue de la Mairie

Ave Aynatrall

Hôtel de Ville

Ave Léopold Sédar Senghor

Ave de Kombolé

To Le Massa Massa (500m); Gare Routière (1.5km); Les Résidences de Lat-Dior (2km); Dakar (70km)

To Touba (124km); Kaolack (140km)

**INFORMATION**
BICIS Bank.....................1 B3
CBAO Bank....................2 B3
Post Office....................3 B3
SGBS Bank....................4 B3

**SIGHTS & ACTIVITIES**
Tapestry Factory............5 A2

**SLEEPING** 🛏
Hôtel Man-Gan de Thiès.....6 B2

**EATING** 🍴
Bakery..........................7 B2
Case á Teranga..............8 B2
Croissant Magique...........9 B3
Les Délices...................10 B2
Les Vieilles Marmites.......11 B2
Pamanda......................12 B1
Restaurant le Cailcedrat...13 B2

**ENTERTAINMENT** 🎭
Bidew Bi.......................14 A2
Dosso Complexe..............15 B2

**TRANSPORT**
Taxi Stand....................16 B1

**CBAO** ( ☎ 952 05 05; Rue Nationale 2)
**SGDS** ( ☎ 951 82 25; Ave Léopold Sédar Senghor)

## Sleeping

There are several good sleeping options, including the excellent **Le Massa Massa** ( ☎ 952 1244; Cité Malick Sy; r with/without air-con CFA20,600/12,600), where rooms are simple and welcoming and the French and Belgian cuisine (dishes around CFA4000) divine. The simpler **Hôtel Man-Gan de Thiès** ( ☎ 951 1526; fax 951 2532; Rue Amadou Sow; s/d CFA15,000/18,000; 🐾) is more basic but has the added attraction of a pleasant courtyard garden. The most luxurious place is the multistar hotel **Les Résidences de Lat-Dior** ( ☎ 952 0777; residencelatdior@hotmail.com; s/d CFA27,600/35,200; 🅿 💻 🐾) equipped with a modern fitness centre, wi-fi access and even its own mosque.

## Eating

The local restaurant scene is mainly made up of Lebanese fast-food joints – but good ones. The **Croissant Magique** ( ☎ 951 1878; dishes around CFA2000) is popular, though pizzas are better at **Pamanda** ( ☎ 952 1550; Rue de Paris; dishes from CFA1000-5000; 🕒 9am-2am). **Les Délices** ( ☎ 931 7516; Ave Lópold Senghor; 🕒 7.30am-2am) serves good ice cream and pastries on a pretty terrace.

The **Restaurant le Cailcedrat** ( ☎ 951 1130; Ave Général de Gaulle; CFA1500-4000; 🕒 7am-midnight) leads the route upmarket, with kofta and other Lebanese dishes in pleasant surroundings. The excellent restaurant **Les Vieilles Marmites** ( ☎ 951 4440; dishes around CFA3000) has been popular for years and the **Case à Teranga** ( ☎ 611 5125; Ave Lépold Senghor; meals from CFA1000-5000) has a delicious choice of West Indian, Indian and French cuisine served with live music on weekends.

There's a good **bakery** (bread CFA150, croissants CFA700) for breakfast stuff, and several small boutiques for groceries and other items.

## Entertainment

The two mighty entertainment complexes **Bidew Bi** ( ☎ 639 8554; 🕒 7pm-4am) and **Dosso Complexe** ( ☎ 951 2640; www.dossonight.com; 🕒 Tue-Sun; 🐾) are where it all happens on weekends.

SENEGAL

## Getting There & Around

Bush taxis and minibuses leave from the *gare routière*, 1.5km from the centre, on the southern outskirts. There are frequent *sept-place* taxis to Dakar (CFA1200, one hour, 70km), Kaolack (CFA1900, two hours, 140km) and Saint-Louis (CFA2600, four hours, 196km). Any taxi trip around town should cost you CFA400, including the journey from the *gare routière* into the centre. There's a taxi stand in the north of town.

## DIOURBEL

Diourbel was home to Cheikh Amadou Bamba, the founder of the Mouride Sufi brotherhood, from 1912 until his death in 1927. The palatial compound of his descendants is quite a sight, as is the town's main mosque, a building that's smaller, neater and, it has to be said, more aesthetically pleasing than the more famous mosque of Touba.

The small, simple *campement* **Keur Déthié Caty** ( ☎ 971 5190; s/d CFA11,600/13,000; P 🞉 ) is the only place to stay in town, unless you knock on the doors of the locals. There are a few cheap restaurants on the main street and around the *gare routière*.

Plenty of traffic runs through Diourbel on its way to Dakar or Touba. *Sept-place* taxis go to Dakar (CFA1720, three hours, 146km), Thiès (CFA900, 80 minutes, 76km) and Touba (CFA700, one hour, 50km).

## TOUBA

Touba is the sacred focus of the Mouride Sufi brotherhood, the place where their spiritual leader Cheikh Amadou Bamba lived, worked and died. He is buried in the Grand Mosque of Touba, an awe-inspiring building whose minaret dominates the town. The constantly expanding building shows signs of various phases of construction, and has an impressive library containing the complete works of Cheikh Amadou Bamba.

But Touba is not only about spirituality, but about big business. The Mouride brotherhood is an influential economic and political force in the country, and much of Senegal's money is concentrated in Touba. Touba market is a huge sprawl of tax-free and illegal activity. Seeing the combined forces of religion, economy and politics work hand in hand is fascinating, though a bit confusing.

Once a year, 48 days after the Islamic New Year, around two million people

---

### BAMBA

Cheikh Amadou Bamba, the founder of the Mouride brotherhood (1887), is without a doubt Senegal's most iconic religious figure. His veiled portrait looks earnestly down on the population from thousands of paintings spread across walls, shop signs, cars, stickers and even T-shirts. Born in 1850 as a relative of the powerful Wolof leader Lat Dior and a member of the wealthy Mbacke clan, he initially renounced his noble heritage, and chose a path of religious devotion. His preachings attracted an increasingly large following, the most famous disciple being the eccentric Cheikh Ibra Fall, leader of the Baye Fall, an offshoot of the Mouridiya. Both branches emphasise the importance of physical labour as a path to spiritual salvation. This initially fitted neatly with the French administration's attempts to improve its territory's economic output, but Bamba's anticolonial stance and the colonialists' fear of his growing Islamic power base led them to exile the charismatic leader. Bamba returned to Senegal in 1907 and, despite his continued anticolonial rhetoric, entered into hushed negotiations with the French; they both had much to gain from keeping peasants working in the groundnut fields.

Long after his death, the influence of Bamba and his teachings keeps growing, the ever-increasing masses of people descending on Touba for the Magal being proof of the immense popularity the Mouridiya enjoys.

---

descend on Touba for the **Grand Magal**, a pilgrimage that celebrates Bamba's return from exile in 1907 where he was banished for 20 years by the French authorities. It's an impressive sight but you have to be early to find a place in a taxi and keep your wits about you once there.

There are no places to stay in Touba, but on the day of the Magal local residents open their homes for visitors. At any other time, your best bet is the **Campement Touristique le Baol** ( ☎ 976 5505; fax 976 7254; s/d CFA11,600/13,000; 🞉 ) in Mbaké (10km south of Touba), which has spartan rooms with their own bathrooms. There's an SGBS bank past the turn-off to Touba.

Touba to Dakar costs CFA3200 by *sept-place* taxi, CFA1500 by Ndiaga Ndiaye and CFA1500 by *car mouride*.

## KAOLACK

Kaolack is a city that sees a lot of visitors pass through, but only a few that stay. However, the town has a unique urban charm worth inhaling for a day or two, and its central position makes it a great base for exploring much of the country.

### Information

Banks include **CBAO** (Rue de la Gare) and **SGBS** (Rue de la Gare), both of which have Visa-welcoming ATMs. There are many places to connect to the net; the **Internet Café** (Rue Cheikh Tidiane Cherif; per hr CFA150) has a fairly speedy service. Kaolack has a relatively well-equipped and -staffed hospital.

### Sights & Activities

The town's round, covered **market** is one of the biggest in Africa, and fairly hassle-free compared to its Dakar relatives. The Moroccan-style building of the **Grande Mosquée** is the pride of the Baye Niass brotherhood. Interesting is also the **Alliance Franco-Senegalaise** ( ☎ 941 1061; Rue Galliene), either admire its fantastic décor, take in one of the frequent exhibitions and events, or just have a tranquil cup of coffee. If it's wood carvings and batiks you're after, check the **Village Artisanal** in the north of town, on the route to Thiès.

### Sleeping

There are several cheap places, but not all of them worth considering. The **Djolof Inn** ( ☎ 941 9360; r CFA10,000; ✷ ), near the *gare routière* to Dakar, is the friendliest and most welcoming of the lot. **Auberge de Carrefour** ( ☎ 941 9000; Ave Valdiodio Ndiaye; s/d CFA8500/13,000) is also pretty good, with clean, spacious rooms and enthusiastic management. You can also stay at the **Mission Catholique** ( ☎ 941 2526; Rue Merlaud-Ponty; dm CFA2000, s CFA5000), though rooms are nothing special.

More upmarket are the **Hôtel de Paris** ( ☎ 941 1019; fax 941 1017; Rue Galliéne; s/d CFA24,000/30,000; ✷ ⊠ ), which has a worn-out charm, and **Le Relais** ( ☎ 941 1000; fax 941 1002; Plage de Kundam; s/d CFA22,000/27,000; ✷ 💻 ⊠ 🐟 ), which surprises

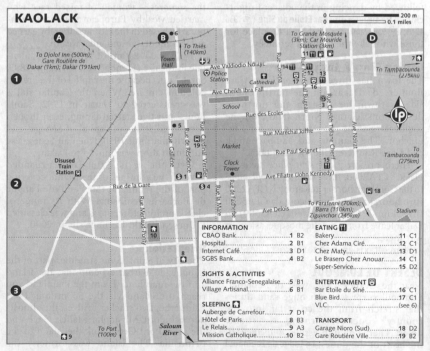

| KAOLACK | 0 — 200 m / 0 — 0.1 miles |
| --- | --- |

| INFORMATION | |
| --- | --- |
| CBAO Bank.................................1 B2 | |
| Hospital....................................2 B1 | |
| Internet Café...........................3 D1 | |
| SGBS Bank................................4 B2 | |

| SIGHTS & ACTIVITIES | |
| --- | --- |
| Alliance Franco-Senegalaise.....5 B1 | |
| Village Artisanal......................6 B1 | |

| SLEEPING 🛏 | |
| --- | --- |
| Auberge de Carrefour..............7 D1 | |
| Hôtel de Paris..........................8 B3 | |
| Le Relais..................................9 A3 | |
| Mission Catholique.................10 B2 | |

| EATING 🍴 | |
| --- | --- |
| Bakery.....................................11 C1 | |
| Chez Adama Ciré....................12 C1 | |
| Chez Maty...............................13 D1 | |
| Le Brasero Chez Anouar.........14 C1 | |
| Super-Service..........................15 D2 | |

| ENTERTAINMENT 🎭 | |
| --- | --- |
| Bar Etoile du Siné...................16 C1 | |
| Blue Bird................................17 C1 | |
| VLC.....................................(see 6) | |

| TRANSPORT | |
| --- | --- |
| Garage Nioro (Sud)................18 D2 | |
| Gare Routière Ville.................19 B2 | |

with style among the many unglamorous options around.

## Eating

If good-quality food is important to you, you should probably cook it yourself. Exceptions to Kaolack's dire *gargotte* scene include **Le Brasero Chez Anouar** ( ☎ 941 1608; Ave Valdiodio Ndiaye; meals about CFA3000; ☺ 7am-11pm), with an entirely deserved reputation for good food and lively ambience. For cheap shwarmas and simple meals, **Chez Maty** ( ☎ 941 9000; Rue Cheikh Tidiane Cherif; mains around CFA2500; ☺ Mon-Sat) is a good address.

Self-caterers are fairly well served, with the **Super-Service** (Ave Filiatre), a giant sprawl of a market selling fresh produce and a good **bakery** (Ave Valdiodio Ndiaye).

## Entertainment

The **VLC** (Village Loisir Club; Village Artisanal) is the closest Kaolack gets to urbane entertainment. The music is bass-heavy as it should be and the dance floors crammed. At **Blue Bird** ( ☎ 941 5350; Rue Maréchal Bugeau; ☺ 8am-3am Mon-Sat, 6pm-2am Sun), a dinner for two can be followed by dancing in the adjacent nightclub. The boisterous **Bar Etoile du Siné** ( ☎ 936 45 93; ☺ 9am-2am) is a grubby little place for those who take their drinks seriously.

## Getting There & Away

The town has three *gares routières*: Gare Routière de Dakar, on the northwestern side of town, for western and northern destinations; Garage Nioro (Sud), on the southeast side of the city centre, for Ziguinchor, The Gambia and Tambacounda; and Gare Routière Ville for local taxis.

There are frequent *sept-place* taxis to Dakar (CFA2600, three hours). A *sept-place* to the Gambian border at Karang is CFA2300 (two hours) and to Tambacounda CFA5000 (five hours). *Cars mourides* (CFA1500) to Dakar leave from near the mosque; ask your way there.

Shared taxis around town cost CFA500.

## DESERT DE LOMPOUL

Near the Grande Côte, west of Kébémer, Lompoul surprises with huge sand dunes that stretch from the coast far into the country's interior, forming a veritable desert. There's an impressive *campement* in the heart of the dunes, **Le Lodge de Loumpoul** ( ☎ 644 9194; 957 1256; www.lesenegal.info; s/d with half board CFA21,000/37,000), which offers accommodation in Mauritanian desert tents. Camel tours, picnic in the dunes and pick-up from Lompoul village are included in the price.

Most people get here by organised tour from Saint-Louis (see p714). If you're in your own car or hire taxi, take the route from Saint-Louis to Dakar, turn off at Kébémer and follow the smooth road to Lompoul village, from where *campement* staff can pick you up with 4WDs.

## SAINT-LOUIS
### pop 147,100

When you consider the enormous impact the French had on this continent it's fascinating to think that the place where it all began has barely changed for more than a century. Founded in 1659 by Louis Caullier on the easily accessible, flood-proof Île de Ndar, Saint-Louis was the first French settlement in Africa. By the 1790s, it had become a busy port and trading centre with a racially diverse population of 10,000. Most notable among the residents of Saint-Louis at this time were the *signares* – women of mixed race who married wealthy European merchants temporarily based in the city, and thereby earned aristocratic status and great wealth.

With the creation of l'Afrique Occidentale Française (French West Africa) in 1895, Saint-Louis became the capital of the French colonial empire. When the capital status was transferred to Dakar in 1902, Saint-Louis' prestige started fading, even though it retained status of capital of Senegal and Mauritania until 1958, when all Senegalese administration was moved to Dakar.

Over the years, Saint-Louis expanded beyond the confines of the island, covering part of the mainland (Sor) and the Langue de Barbarie Peninsula. With its range of classic architecture, the island was classified a Unesco World Heritage site in 2000.

### Orientation

The city of Saint-Louis straddles part of the Langue de Barbarie peninsula, the island and the mainland. From the mainland you reach the island via the 500m-long Pont Faidherbe; two smaller bridges, the almost-derelict Pont Mustapha Malick Gaye and the safer Pont Geole, link the island to the peninsula. The island was formerly the

# SAINT-LOUIS

0 _____ 300 m
0 _____ 0.2 miles

To Mauritanian
Border (Restrictd
Area; 2.5km)

**INFORMATION**
BICIS Bank.................................1 B4
CBAO bank.................................2 B3
Internet Café.............................3 B4
L'Institut Culturel et Linguistique
    Jean Mermoz........................4 C2
National Park Office...................5 C4
Post Office.................................6 C4
Sahel Découverte Bassari...........7 C3
Sentoo Office.............................8 B5
Syndicat d'Initiative...................9 C4
Télécentre.............................(see 3)

**SIGHTS & ACTIVITIES**
Cathedral.................................10 B5
Governor's Palace.....................11 B4
Grand Mosque..........................12 C2
Mame Thiouth..........................13 C3
Museum...................................14 B6
Rognât Casernes......................15 B4

**SLEEPING**
Auberge de Jeunesse................16 B2
Auberge de la Vallée............(see 29)
Auberge l'Harmattan................17 B4
Café des Arts...........................18 B2
Hôtel de la Poste......................19 C4
Hôtel de la Résidence...............20 C3
Hotel Sindone..........................21 C6
La Louisiane.............................22 B1
La Maison Rose........................23 C3
Sunu Keur................................24 B2

**EATING**
Aux Délices du Fleuve...............25 C4
Bou El Mogdad.........................26 C3
Coup de Torchon......................27 C3
Ecomarché...............................28 C3
La Linguère..............................29 C3
La Saigonnaise.........................30 B1
La Signare................................31 C2
Le Flamingo.............................32 C3
Libre-Service............................33 C4
Pointe Nord.............................34 C1

**DRINKING**
Iguane Café.............................35 B4
l'Embuscade...........................36 B4

**ENTERTAINMENT**
La Chaumière..........................37 A4
Le Laser..................................38 C3
Marco Jazz..............................39 C4
Quai des Arts & VIP Nightclub...40 C1

**TRANSPORT**
Le Routard.........................(see 39)

To Airport (7km);
Bango (8km);
Podor (220km)

To Gîte Walo (1km);
Gare Routière (3.5km);
Hôtel Mame Coumba Bang
(7km); Reserve de Guembeul
(12km); Gandiol (18km); Mouit
(20km); Dakar (260km)

N'Dar
Tout

ATLANTIC OCEAN

Langue de Barbarie Peninsula

Senegal River

Market

Guet
N'Dar

Muslim
Cemetery

To Hydrobase (4km); Parc
National de la Langue
de Barbarie (18km)

Police Station
Place
de Liège

Football
Field

Rue Adamson
Rue de France
Rue Brue
Rue Khalifa Ababacar Sy
Rue Abdoulaye Seck
Ave Jean Mermoz
Ave Blaise Diagne
Quai Roume

Senegal River

Rue Flamand
Rue Lt PH Diop
Rue Boufflers
Rue Aynima Fall
Watertower
Rue P Holle
Rue Seydou Tall
Rue Lanzun
Rue Blanchot
Rue Bisson
Rue du Général de Gaulle

Place
Faidherbe

Pont Geole

Pont Mustapha
Malick Gaye

Pont Faidherbe

Rue de l'Eglise
Rue AM Javouye
Rue Millis Lacroix

Blvd Abdoulaye Mar Diop
Rue Ibrahim Sarr
Rue Blaise Dumont
Rue Babacar Seye
Quai Henri Jay

Rue Thevenot
Rue Chassagnol
Rue Ribet
Rue A Fall

Train
Station

Old Gare
Routière

Sor

Route de la Corniche

Mainland

SENEGAL

European quarter, with many grand old houses, a few of which still retain their gracious wrought-iron balconies, while others are gradually crumbling away. The peninsula was the African quarter, previously inhabited by freed slaves; today it's a thriving fishing community called Guet N'Dar.

### MAPS

The map *Saint-Louis et la Region du Fleuve Senegal* (CFA3000), a cross between a cartoon and an aerial photograph, is available in bookshops and hotels.

## Information

### CULTURAL CENTRES

**L'Institut Culturel et Linguistique Jean Mermoz** ( ☎ 938 2626; www.ccfsi.sn; Ave Jean Mermoz; ⏰ 8.30am-12.30pm & 3-6.30pm Mon-Fri) Has a café and hosts films, concerts and art exhibitions.

### INTERNET ACCESS

**Internet Café** (Rue du Général de Gaulle; per hr CFA500; ⏰ 8am-11pm) Has decent terminals and several phone booths.

**Sentoo Office** (Blvd Abdoulaye Mar Diop; per hr CFA500; ⏰ 9am-1pm & 3-8pm)

### MONEY

Both banks change money and have ATMs.

**BICIS** ( ☎ 961 1053; Rue de France; ⏰ 7.45am-12.15pm & 1.40-3.45pm Mon-Thu, 7.45am-1pm & 2.40-3.45pm Fri)
**CBAO** ( ☎ 961 9639; Rue Khalifa Ababacar Sy; ⏰ 8.15-5.15pm Mon-Fri) Also has a Western Union office.

### POST

**Post office** (Rue du Général de Gaulle) The Art Deco–style building opposite the Hôtel de la Poste.

### TELEPHONE

**Télécentre** (Rue du Général de Gaulle; ⏰ 8am-midnight)

### TOURIST INFORMATION

**National Park Office** (Quai Henri Jay; ⏰ 8am-1.30pm, 3-7pm) Can also help with information about the national parks of northern Senegal.
**Syndicat d'Initiative** ( ☎ 961 2455; sltourisme@sentoo.sn) A haven of regional information and also organises tours.
**www.saintlouisdusenegal.com** This website contains plenty of useful of information and has links to all major hotels and restaurants.

### TRAVEL AGENCIES

**Sahel Découverte Bassari** ( ☎ 961 5689, 961 4263; www.saheldecouverte.com; Ave Blaise Diagne) Saint-Louis' best agency, with a range of tours on offer.

## Sights

Designed by Gustav Eiffel and originally built to cross the Danube, the **Pont Faidherbe**, linking the mainland and island, was transferred to Saint-Louis in 1897. The bridge is a grand piece of 19th-century engineering – 507m long with a middle section that can rotate to allow ships to pass through.

Across the bridge, you see the **Hôtel de la Poste**, the oldest hotel in town, and the place the colonial air-mail pilots used to stay in colonial times. The **Governor's Palace** is flanked north and south by the 1837 **Rognât caserns**. The nearby **Cathedral** (Rue de l'Eglise), built in 1828, is one of the oldest operating churches in Senegal. The **Grand Mosque** in the north was constructed in 1847 and features the oddity of an attached clock tower.

Saint-Louis has plenty of historical buildings, most of them in a semiruinous state, yet still recognisable with their typical balconies and two-storey layout surrounding a small courtyard. At the southern tip of the island is the historical **museum** ( ☎ 961 1050; Quai Henri Jay; admission CFA500; ⏰ 9am-noon & 3-6pm), but more interesting is the contemporary art gallery **Mame Thiouth** ( ☎ 961 3611; ⏰ 8am-7pm), housed in a restored old Saint-Louis building.

The mainland parts of Saint-Louis have less to offer in historical architecture, but more in contemporary life. **Guet N'Dar** is a fantastically busy fishing town. At the southern end of Guet N'Dar is the **Muslim cemetery** where each fisherman's grave is covered with a fishing net.

## Festivals & Events

The **Saint-Louis Jazz Festival** (see opposite) is an event of international renown that regularly attracts jazz greats from around the world. It takes place annually in early May.

If you pass through town in October, you might have the chance to watch the impressive **Regatta of Guet-Ndar**, a lively boat race that passes through the river arm between Saint-Louis and Sor. **Les Fanals**, the historic processions with decorated lanterns (not the handheld kind, but lanterns so big they resemble carnival floats), are a tradition unique to Saint-Louis. They were initiated

---

### SAINT-LOUIS JAZZ

Jazz is a big thing here – and it's not just the shared name with St Louis, Missouri, in the USA, where blues and jazz originated. Way back in the 1940s jazz bands from Saint-Louis (Senegal) were playing in Paris and elsewhere in Europe. Worldwide interest was revived in the early 1990s when the Saint-Louis Jazz Festival was first held, with mainly local bands performing. Now renamed the Saint-Louis International Jazz Festival, this annual event is held the second weekend of May, and attracts performers and audiences from all over the world. At most other times, the stages of the city's many concert venues and jazz bars remain empty. For more background, have a look at *St-Louis Jazz*, a book by Hervé Lenormond (French text, Editions Joca Seria), which outlines the history of jazz in Senegal and has some wonderful photos of musicians from Africa, America and Europe performing in Saint-Louis.

Programmes and dates can be checked on www.saintlouisjazz.com, or with the Syndicat d'Initiative.

---

by the *signares* – and are held around Christmas and sometimes during the jazz festival.

## Sleeping

### MAINLAND

**Gite Walo** ( ☎ 961 4407; clem.mathieu@voila.fr; d from CFA10,000) This understated place on the route from Dakar offers plenty for the amount you pay: a wide terrace, shaded courtyard and spacious, spotless rooms.

**Hôtel Mame Coumba Bang** ( ☎ 961 1850; www.hotelcoumba.com; s/d CFA28,000/35,000; ⊠ ⊠ ) It's named after a water spirit and calls itself 'lover's wood' – the large swimming pool and the tranquil riverside garden explain the choice of names. It's 7km from town just off the road to Dakar.

### ISLAND

**Auberge de Jeunesse** ( ☎ 961 2409; pisdiallo@yahoo .fr; Rue Abdoulaye Seck; dm/d CFA5500/10,000) Yes it's possible: a spotless, cheap, mosquito-netted, ventilated place to spend the night sleeping comfortably.

**Café des Arts** ( ☎ 961 6078; Rue de France; dm/d CFA4500/9000) Rooms are basic, but the fam-

ily atmosphere of this colourful little place more than makes up for it.

**Auberge l'Harmattan** ( ☎ 961 8253; auberge harmattan@yahoo.fr; Rue Abdoulaye Seck;d/tr CFA15,000/ 20,000; ⊠ ) Rooms in the historic building are enormous, but suffer slightly from neglect. The patio is a fine place to relax.

**Sunu Keur** ( ☎ 961 8800; chaffoisjeanjacques@yahoo .fr; s/d from CFA15,000/20,000) This calm guesthouse has beautifully decorated rooms overlooking the river in a carefully restored colonial building.

**La Louisiane** ( ☎ 961 4221; Point Nord; louisiane@ sentoo.sn; www.aubergelalouisiane.com; d/tr CFA18,400/ 24,300) Excellent value for money, this peaceful little place has spacious, ventilated rooms right on the river.

**La Maison Rose** ( ☎ 938 2222; www.lamaisonrose.net; Ave Blaise Diagne; s/d/ste from CFA45,000/55,000/77,500) Every room and suite in this beautifully restored house is unique, though they all exude a spirit of old-time comfort. The furniture is antique and the walls are decorated with wonderful art works.

**Hôtel Sindone** ( ☎ 961 4244; www.hotelsindone .com; Quai Henri Jay; s/d from CFA26,500/29,300; ⊠ ) A faint pink'n'fluffy honeymoon feel scents the air of this stylish and airy hotel on the south side of the island. River views cost CFA3000 extra.

**Hôtel de la Résidence** ( ☎ 961 1260; hotresid@sentoo .sn; Ave Blaise Diagne; s/d CFA27,600/34,200; ⊠ ) This is one of Saint-Louis' oldest hotels, and the owners (an ancient Saint Louisian family) have done a great job of evoking that sense of history. Rooms are pretty and comfortable, and the restaurant one of the town's best.

**Hôtel de la Poste** ( ☎ 961 1118; www.hotel -poste.com; Rue du Général de Gaulle; s/d/tr CFA30,000/ 36,000/43,000; ⊠ ) Another Saint-Louis classic; dating from the 1850s, the oldest hotel was the historical port of call for the pilots of the colonial air-mail service. You pay for the historic surroundings as well as for the plain rooms.

### LANGUE DE BARBARIE

**Hotel Dior** ( ☎ 961 3118; www.hotel-dior.com;s CFA12,600-18,700, d 18,100-24,200) This is a good-value option at the Hydrobase on Langue de Barbarie. You can also camp here (per person CFA2500).

**Hôtel Cap Saint-Louis** ( ☎ 961 3909; www.hotel capsaintlouis.com; s/d CFA10,400/14,800, with bathroom CFA12,600/32,200; P ⊠ ⊠ ) What looks like another resort hotel is in fact a friendly (and child-friendly) place. It's tastefully done, sits right on the sea, and has one of the best swimming pools around. Large groups or families can rent five-bed bungalows (CFA43,400).

**Hôtel l'Oasis** ( ☎ /fax 961 4232; http://hoteloasis .free.fr; s/d CFA15,000/21,000; 🔀 🔊 ) Small, unpretentious huts are decked out in busy African prints, and spotless bungalows house up to three people.

**Hôtel Mermoz** ( ☎ 961 3668; www.hotelmermoz .com; s/d/tr from CFA13,000/18,000/23,000; 🔀 🔊 ) This has more character than many of the large hotels. Huts and bungalows are spaced out in a large, sandy garden, and all buildings are connected by meandering, wheelchair-accessible paths.

## Eating & Drinking

There's a growing choice of good restaurants in Saint-Louis. Most hotels also do food – the Hôtel de Résidence leading the pack with a menu that leaves you spoilt for choice.

**La Linguère** ( ☎ 961 3949; Ave Blaise Diagne; meals around CFA2000) Never mind the shoddy interior, the *yassa poulet* of this place is almost unbeatable.

**Pointe Nord** ( ☎ 961 4221; Ave Jean Mermoz) This humble eatery in the far north of the island does an amazing grilled fish at very reasonable prices.

**Coup de Torchon** ( ☎ 518 5408; Ave Blaise Diagne; meals CFA3500-5000; 🕙 11am-1am) This friendly little restaurant is the perfect spot to spend long evenings chatting over huge plates of food.

**La Signare** ( ☎ 961 1932; Ave Blaise Diagne; meals CFA7000; 🕙 lunch & dinner Thu-Tue) Considered one of the best restaurants in Saint-Louis, La Signare offers a truly top-notch *menu du jour* in a beautifully decorated old-style building.

**Aux Délices du Fleuve** ( ☎ 961 4251; Quai Roume) Saint-Louis' famous patisserie serves delicious pastries, ice creams and milky coffees.

**La Saigonnaise** ( ☎ 961 6481; Rue Abdoulaye Seck; mains CFA5000; 🕙 noon-midnight) If you fancy a taste of Asia, this Vietnamese restaurant complements its great river location with tasty Saigon fare.

**Bou El Mogdad** ( ☎ 961 3611; Quai Roume; meals around CFA3000-6000) Here you can sample international cuisine in old-style surroundings overlooking the busy Quai Roume.

**Le Flamingo** ( ☎ 961 1118; Quai Roume; meals around CFA5000; 🔊 ) This classy restaurant turns into

an upmarket bar at night, and frequently has good live bands playing near the swimming pool.

**L'Embuscade** ( ☎ 961 7741; Rue Blanchot) A popular beer and tapas place that gets busy at weekends.

**Iguane Café** ( ☎ 558 0879; Rue Abdoulaye Seck) Stylish Dakar-vibes flow through this busy Cuban-themed bar.

Self-caterers can shop in the market just north of the bridge in Guet N'Dar. For European goods and French wine, head for the **Libre-Service** (Ave Blaise Diagne) or the **Ecomarché** (Ave Blaise Diagne).

## Entertainment

Saint-Louis has a fine selection of nightclubs and live-music bars. **Le Laser** ( ☎ 961 5398; www.casinolaser.com; admission from CFA2000; 🕙 Wed-Sun 7pm-3am), part of the Saint-Louis Casino complex, is popular. **La Chaumière** ( ☎ 961 1980; Pointe á Pitre, Guet N'Dar; admission around CFA2000) is Guet N'Dar's main haunt, and **Le Papayer** ( ☎ 961 8687; Carrefour de l'Hydrobase; 🕙 noon-midnight) has the best dance floor on the Langue de Barbarie.

For live concerts, try the intimate **Marco Jazz** ( ☎ 654 2442; benedettoma@yahoo.fr; Quai Roume), where the big jazz names tend to give impromptu concerts during the jazz festival. **Quai des Arts & VIP Nightclub** ( ☎ 961 5656; Ave Jean Mermoz) is where the main action happens during the jazz festival. The rest of the year, the place stays fairly calm, though the nightclub attracts a stylish crowd.

## Getting There & Away
### AIR
Saint-Louis has its own airport, 7km out of town; a taxi from there into Saint-Louis costs around CFA5000. Air Sénégal International operates a regular flight to Saint-Louis, which connects to Paris and Dakar every Wednesday. You can book directly, or through Sahel Découverte Bassari (p714).

### TAXI
The *gare routière* sits on the mainland at 4.5km from town, south of the Pont Faidherbe. A taxi from here to the city centre on the island costs CFA500. The fare to or from Dakar is CFA3500 by *sept-place*.

A *sept-place* to Gandiol, from where boats to the Parc National de la Langue de Barbarie leave, costs CFA500.

## Getting Around

### BICYCLE

Saint-Louis and its surroundings are good biking areas. **Le Routard** ( ☎ 608 9444; Quai Roume) opposite the Flamingo rents mountain bikes (in French VTTs) for CFA5000 per day.

### TAXI

Taxi prices in Saint-Louis are fixed (CFA350 at the time of writing). Prices to any destination in the surrounding regions depend on your negotiating skills.

## AROUND SAINT-LOUIS
### Gandiol & Mouit

Gandiol is a small village on the mainland, about 18km south of Saint-Louis. From the lighthouse north of the village, pirogues cross the estuary to the two *campements* on the southern end of the Langue de Barbarie.

About 2km south of Gandiol is Mouit, where you'll find the national park office and, on the edge of the river, the brilliant *campement* **Zebrabar** ( ☎ 638 1862; www.come.to/zebrabar; camping per person CFA2500, s CFA4000-7000, d CFA15,000-18,000). This spacious, child-friendly place has accommodation in simple huts (and the cut-off cabin of an old truck) and spacious bungalows. Guests can use kayaks for free, and arrange canoe tours and bird-watching trips with the local fishermen (CFA2500 per person). If you contact them before arrival, they can collect you from Saint Louis.

Hiring a taxi from Saint-Louis to Mouit and Zebrabar should cost you around CFA3000. Alternatively, there are a few daily bush taxis from Saint-Louis to Gandiol (CFA500). Sometimes this taxi continues to Mouit (CFA700), otherwise you'll have to walk the last 2km.

## Parc National de la Langue de Barbarie

The **park** (admission CFA2000; pirogue for 1 or 2 people CFA7500, each extra person CFA2500; ☯ 7am-7pm) includes the far southern tip of the Langue de Barbarie Peninsula, the estuary of the Senegal River and a section of the mainland on the other side of the estuary. Its 2000 hectares are home to numerous birds – notably flamingos, pelicans, cormorants, herons, egrets and ducks. From November to April these numbers are swelled by the arrival of migrants from Europe.

The park is best explored by pirogue, which can cruise slowly past the mud flats, inlets and islands where the birds feed and roost.

### SLEEPING

Two *campements* both provide meals, transfers and offer a range of activities, including sailboarding, kayaking and bird-watching.

**Campement Langue de Barbarie** ( ☎ 961 1118; s/d with half board CFA27,000) This large place that's run by the Hôtel de la Poste in Saint-Louis has pretty cottages, wonderfully positioned at the southern end of the peninsula.

**Campement Océan et Savane** ( ☎ 637 4790; r with half/full board CFA15,200/21,200) In this relaxed place run by the Hôtel de la Résidence in Saint-Louis you can stay in low-roofed, Mauritanian-style bungalows or, if you want a bit more comfort, in pretty log cabins that house one to five people (CFA30,000) and sit on stilts in the river. The place has got a fine restaurant under a huge Mauritanian tent.

### GETTING THERE & AWAY

Take a taxi from Saint-Louis to Gandiol lighthouse (around CFA7000). From there, you cross with a pirogue. Organised tours from Saint-Louis are another option.

## Parc National des Oiseaux du Djoudj

This 16,000-hectare **park** ( ☎ 968 8708; admission CFA2000, plus pirogue CFA3500; ☯ 7am-dusk Nov-Apr) is 60km north of Saint-Louis. With its channels, creeks, lakes, mud flats and woodland savanna, it's one of the best places on earth to view migratory birds from Europe. It is a bird sanctuary of global significance with Unesco World Heritage and Ramsar status.

Even if you're not a keen ornithologist, it's hard to escape the impact of seeing vast colonies of pelicans and flamingos in such stunning surroundings. Experienced bird-watchers will recognise many of the European species, and the sheer numbers that assemble here are impressive indeed. Around three million individual birds pass through the park annually, and more than 350 separate species have been recorded.

There are also a few mammals and reptiles in the park, most notably populations of warthogs and mongooses, serpents and crocodiles (you're unlikely to spot the latter though). Other mammals include jackals, hyenas, monkeys and gazelles.

Trips around the park are usually, and best, done by pirogue. The ideal time for

SENEGAL

**TOURING THE PARC NATIONAL DES OISEAUX DU DJOUDJ**

The Parc National des Oiseaux du Djoudj is a protected and internationally renowned bird sanctuary, and bird-watchers flock to the protected area to observe spur-winged geese, purple herons, egrets, spoonbills, jaçanas, cormorants, harriers and a multitude of European migrants that settle here during November and April. The park is, however, most famous for its impressive flocks of pelicans and flamingos, and all tours offered by agencies, hotels and guides focus on them.

Tours tend to leave Saint-Louis at 7am to reach the park by 8.30am. They start with a two-hour boat ride through the creeks, the highlight and sole purpose of which is to get a view of the enormous pelican colony. After lunch you drive to see flamingo flocks on the lake's edge.

You'll be able to spot other species, no doubt, but if it's the rarer varieties you're after, a tourist tour might not be so satisfying. Keen bird-watchers are better off coming with their own guide, or contacting the **Station Biologique** ( ☎ 542 4472; dpnsbpnod@sentoo.sn) and explaining their interest to park director Ablaye Diop or the head of the station Assane Ndoye. They can put you in touch with a trained ornithological guide, and will have up-to-date research findings about the park.

bird-watching is from December to January. During those months, you'll already be greeted by vast colonies of birds before you've even entered your boat.

### SLEEPING

**Hotel du Djoudj** ( ☎ 963 8702; fax 963 8703; huts d/tr CFA15,000/20,000, rooms d/tr CFA27,000/34,500; ⊙ 1 Nov-31 May; 🗟 ) This friendly, grand place sits near the main entrance. It has comfortable rooms and helpful staff. You can arrange boat rides around the park (adult/child over two CFA 3500/2500) and hire bicycles (half-/full-day CFA3000/6000).

**Station Biologique** ( ☎ 968 8708; dpnsbpnod@ sentoo.sn; r per person with full board CFA15,000) Situated at the park headquarters and main entrance, this low-key camp with clean rooms is intended for research groups, though

tourists can be accommodated if space is available.

### GETTING THERE & AWAY

There's no public transport to Djoudj, so it's best to go by hire taxi from Saint-Louis (around CFA20,000) or come on an organised tour. If you're driving from Saint-Louis, take the paved highway towards Rosso for about 25km. Near Ross-Béthio you'll see a sign pointing to the park, from where it's another 25km along a dirt road.

## SENEGAL RIVER ROUTE

From Saint-Louis, the route along the valley of the Senegal River traces the French conquest of the interior, as well as the signs of its opposition. Along the river, which marks Senegal's northern and eastern borders, you'll find a string of mid-19th century forts in Dagana, Podor, Matam and Bakel, some in nearly ruins, others in the early stages of restoration. The French fortifications were military and administrative centres and battle stations in the enduring clashes with the army of El Hadj Omar Tall, who put up fierce resistance to the colonial efforts.

The historical leader had plenty to defend – his expansive Islamic empire, which at its height reached all across West Africa to Timbuktu (in today's Mali). The few remaining Omarian mosques, dating from the second half of the 18th century, that are found in the river region (notably in Alwar), still seem to oppose the French forts in a silent, architectural battle.

Where other areas in Senegal lure visitors with lush vegetation and rich wildlife, the hot and arid north is all about history and cultural pride. Smooth *banco* (clay or mud) brick houses of the Tukulor seem to rise naturally from the soil, and would blend with their desertlike surroundings, were it not for the local custom of decorating the outer walls in bold stripes of red, brown and yellow.

### Rosso-Senegal

The fly-blown frontier town of Rosso-Senegal, around 100km northeast of Saint-Louis is the main ferry crossing point between Senegal and Mauritania. The boat service is also about the only reason you might want to visit Rosso.

If you get stuck, there's the **Auberge du Walo** (d CFA10,000) where basic double huts come with bathroom, and the restaurant can prepare meals on order.

The journey to Dakar costs CFA5100 by *sept-place* taxi, to Saint-Louis the fare is CFA2000. For more information on crossing the border see p743.

## Richard Toll

Richard Toll was once a colonial administrative centre and home to a French agricultural experiment, who tested the tropical adaptability of European plants (hence the name Richard Toll, meaning 'Richard's Garden'). Today, it's the centre of Senegal's sugar industry. A stroll or horse-cart ride to the **Château de Baron Roger**, a crumbling colonial château is a way to while away an hour or so.

**CBAO** ( ☎ 963 32 89; Route de Matam) and **BICIS** ( ☎ 963 3499; Route de Matam; ◷ Mon-Thu 7.45am-12.15pm & 1.40-3.45pm; 7.45am-1pm & 2.40-4.45pm Fri) banks have branches here, both equipped with Visa-friendly ATMs, and there are a couple of internet cafés.

**Hôtel la Taouey** ( ☎ 531 4010; s/d CFA13,600/16,800; P ⌘ ) on the river north of the main street, has adequate though bare rooms, a friendly bar and forthcoming management. The **Gîte d'Etape** ( ☎ /fax 963 3240; s/d CFA25,400/28,800; ⌘ ⌘ ), down a dirt road opposite the *gare routière*, is very well-appointed, though the food disappoints.

A direct *sept-place* from Dakar to Richard Toll costs around CFA10,000.

## Podor & Île à Morphil

The ancient town of Podor has been a busy trading centre since the first encounters between Arabs and the Tukulor of Fouta Toro. It's home to an ancient fort, first built in 1744, then reconstructed by Faidherbe in 1854. It was in the early stages of restoration when we visited. There's also a chain of colonial warehouses along the riverfront.

Podor is the gate to excursions along the **Île à Morphil**, which stretches for 100km between the Senegal River and a parallel channel. Rugged landscape, scenic Tukulor villages and the historical Omarian mosques of Guédé and Alwar, built in Sudanese style, makes this a great off-the-beaten track diversion. Nearby is **Wouro Madiyou**, home to the unique, mosaic-ornamented mausoleum of Cheikh Ahmadou Madiyou.

The **Maison de la Femme** ( ☎ 965 1234; r CFA5000), run by an enthusiastic women's collective is

a great place to stay. The **Catholic Mission** (Ave El Hajj Oumar Tall; r CFA5000) also has a couple of dusty rooms for stranded tourists that come with kind conversation by the talkative Pére Mohiss. The **Gîte d'Etape** ( ☎ 965 1642; d incl breakfast CFA6600), owned by famous singer Baaba Maal, is the only 'proper' guesthouse in Podor. Its Senegalese food is better than the bare rooms.

*Sept-place* taxis travel fairly regularly between Podor and Saint-Louis (CFA3000, four hours, 262km), sometimes continuing all the way to Dakar. *Sept-place* taxis go to Ouro Sogui (CFA4500, five hours, 222km); minibuses cost CFA2500 but take twice as long.

## Matam & Ouro Sogui

Matam was once a proud administrative centre 230km southeast of Podor, but has over the years lost in status to its neighbour Ouro Sogui, which is now a busy trading centre and transport hub for the Ferlo plains.

Ouro Sogui has two banks with ATMs (though it's not a good idea to rely too much on them), a hospital, post office and even an aerodrome. Matam has a waterfront lined with several colonial warehouses – testimonies of busy days gone by.

In Ouro Sogui, the cheapest accommodation is the **Auberge Sogui** ( ☎ 966 1198; s/d CFA8500/10,000; ⌘ ) opposite the market, which has just-passable rooms. Your best choice, however, is the **Oasis du Fouta** ( ☎ 966 1294; seftop@hotmail.com; s/d incl breakfast CFA13,500/15,000; ⌘ ⌘ ), which has comfortable rooms with TV, an Internet café and staff that tries to accommodate your every excursion wish, from pirogue journeys to trips into the mountains where El Hadj Omar Tall once battled French forces.

Food outside your hotel is pretty much limited to the cheap eateries in the same street and the *dibieteries* (grilled-meat stalls) spread across town. The best of those is probably **Le Teddungal**, where grilled-lamb skewers only cost a handful of CFA.

Battered *sept-place* taxis run to Dakar (CFA10,500, 10 hours, 690km) and Bakel (CFA2000, two hours, 148km).

## Bakel

Peacefully perched among a scattering of rocky hills, Bakel is a picturesque spot, though one that tourists rarely venture to. Like all of the northern towns it's hot, dry

SENEGAL

and sandy, but it's prettier than most. Its colonial architecture is still fairly intact. An 1854 **fort**, another ambitious Faidherbe endeavour, and the **Pavilion René Caillé**, once temporary home to the famous French explorer, have been fairly well maintained.

The barely held-together **Hôtel Islam** (r per person CFA10,000; ⚽ ) about 500m east of the *gare routière*, is about your only choice of accommodation. It has spartan rooms, and hardly inviting shared toilets.

For food, it's a trip to the market for fresh produce, or ready-made sandwiches and skewered meat at the *gargottes* next door.

If you come from Ouro Sogui on a vehicle bound for Kidira you might be dropped off at the junction 5km south of Bakel, from where local bush taxis shuttle into town. A *car mouride* goes daily (except Fridays) from Bakel to Tambacounda (CFA3500, five hours, 184km) via Kidira (CFA1500, one hour, 60km).

### Kidira

Kidira is the main border crossing between Senegal and Mali. Both the Dakar–Bamako train and bush taxis pass here. Note that the road on the Malian side has been severely washed out. For more details see p743.

# EASTERN SENEGAL

It takes some courage to brave the seemingly endless stretch of potholed tarmac that connects Dakar to Tambacounda in the east, but the road that leads through flat savanna lands specked with shrubs and baobabs takes you to one of Senegal's best-kept secrets – the mountainous Bassari lands of the southeast.

Eastern Senegal is also home to Senegal's main wildlife reserve, the gigantic Parc National du Niokolo-Koba, where you have a higher chance of seeing large mammals in their natural surroundings than anywhere else in the country.

## TAMBACOUNDA

Tambacounda is all about dust, sand, sizzling temperatures and lines of traffic heading in every direction. From here, routes lead eastwards to Mali, south to Guinea, west to Dakar and The Gambia, and south-

west to Ziguinchor. The town's hectic loading and unloading of taxis, and coming and going of people is well worth taking in for a day or so.

### Information

Tambacounda has an Internet café, a well-stocked **pharmacy** and a **SGBS** (Ave Léopold Sédar Senghor; ⊘ 7.45-noon & 1.30-3.45pm Mon-Thu, 7.45-noon & 2.45-4.15 Fri), which can exchange cash and give advances on credit cards. The Syndicat d'Initiative has a representative at **Hôtel Niji** ( ☎ 981 1250; nijihotel@sentoo.sn) and the **Headquarters of Parc National du Niokolo-Koba** ( ☎ 981 1097; ⊘ 7.30am-5pm) can help with inquiries about the park, and also has 4WDs for hire.

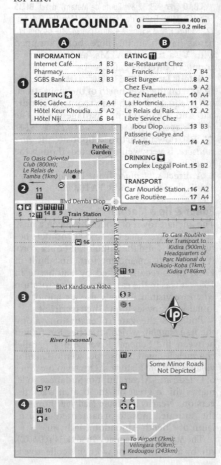

**TAMBACOUNDA**  0 ▭▭ 400 m / 0 ▭▭ 0.2 miles

**INFORMATION**
Internet Café.................1 B3
Pharmacy......................2 B4
SGBS Bank....................3 B3

**SLEEPING**
Bloc Gadec...................4 A4
Hôtel Keur Khoudia....5 A2
Hôtel Niji.....................6 B4

**EATING**
Bar-Restaurant Chez
 Francis........................7 B4
Best Burger..................8 A2
Chez Eva......................9 A2
Chez Nanette.............10 A4
La Hortencia...............11 A2
Le Relais du Rais........12 B3
Libre Service Chez
 Ibou Diop.................13 B3
Patisserie Guèye and
 Frères........................14 A2

**DRINKING**
Complex Leggal Point.15 B2

**TRANSPORT**
Car Mouride Station..16 A2
Gare Routière............17 A4

Public Garden

To Oasis Oriental Club (800m); Le Relais de Tamba (1km)

Market

Blvd Demba Diop

Police

Train Station

Ave Léopold Senghor

To Gare Routière for Transport to Kidira (900m); Headquarters of Parc National du Niokolo-Koba (1km); Kidira (186km)

Blvd Kandioura Noba

River (seasonal)

Some Minor Roads Not Depicted

To Airport (7km); Vélingara (90km); Kedougou (243km)

SENEGAL

## Sleeping

**Bloc Gadec** ( ☎ 531 8931; per person CFA3000) This friendly little hostel in the centre of town has spacious, clean rooms with shared toilets. There are double or quad rooms.

**Hôtel Keur Khoudia** ( ☎ /fax 981 1102; Blvd Demba Diop; s/d CFA11,700/16,000; ✖ ) With spotless bungalows at decent prices and helpful management, this popular *auberge* is an excellent choice for those travelling on a budget. The Hotel Simenti in Niokolo-Koba is run by the same family – so you're in perfect hands if you're intending to visit the park.

**Hôtel Niji** ( ☎ 981 1259; nijihotel@sentoo.sn; s/d/tr CFA11,200/14,00/16,700; ✖ ) This hotel has seen better days, though the adjacent Hôtel Niji Annexe, with its thatched, round houses in a shady garden compound isn't too bad, and a more upmarket section was being built when we visited.

**Le Relais de Tamba** ( ☎ 981 1000; www.relaisho rizons.net; s/d/tr CFA22,200/27,200/36,600; P ✖ 🛋 ) The Relais hotel chain has a reputation for classy simplicity, and this branch has all the niceties of its other places.

**Oasis Oriental Club** ( ☎ 981 1824; rgueguen@sentoo .sn; s/d/tr CFA25,000/32,000/40,000; P ✖ 🛋 ) Cheap it ain't, but the large huts of this top-level *campement* are nice, and perhaps even worth paying slightly exaggerated rates.

## Eating & Drinking

For good local food, the humble **Le Relais du Rais** (meals around CFA1000), near the train station, is almost unbeatable. **Chez Eva** (Blvd Demba Diop) and **Chez Nanette** (meals about CFA1500; ✖ 8am-midnight), near the *gare routière*, are two other good options. For greasy fast-food, try **Best Burger** ( ☎ 981 3203; Blvd Demba Diop), which is also a popular hang-out of Tamba's youth. **La Hortencia** (Blvd Demba Diop) and **Bar-Restaurant Chez Francis** ( ☎ 643 1231; Ave Léopold Senghor) have good, international menus.

For drinks and nights out on the dance floor, try **Complex Leggal Pont** ( ☎ 981 7756; Blvd Demba Diop; ✖ restaurant 8am-midnight, bar & nightclub 11pm-4am), a slightly run-down version of an entertainment complex that also has a few rooms down the back.

Self-caterers will find all the fruit, veg and bags of rice they need at the local market. In the centre of town, the **Libre Service Chez Ibou Diop** (Ave Senghor) is a good place to find European foods as well as a spot to mingle.

The **Patisserie Guèye and Frères** (Blvd Demba Diop) next to Best Burger is the place to get your bread and croissants in the morning.

## Getting There & Around

All taxi trips around town cost CFA300, no need to bargain.

### AIR

Air Sénégal International flies from Dakar to Tambacounda, in theory twice every Saturday from November to March. Contact the airline first, though, as flights can be quite irregular.

### BUS & BUSH TAXI

From the *gare routière* on the eastern side of town vehicles go to the Mali border at Kidira (CFA5000 by *sept-place*, CFA3500 by minibus, three hours). Vehicles to most other destinations go from the larger garage on the southern side of town.

Vélingara is well-served by minibuses (CFA1400) and *sept-places* (CFA1650). A *sept-place* journey Dakar–Tamba is CFA7500, by minibus CFA6000. Tamba-Kedougou is CFA4800 by *sept-place*, Vélingara–Kaolack CFA4000.

The *car mouride* bus leaves from outside the Car Mouride Station daily at 4.30am for Dakar (CFA5000, eight hours). You have to reserve your place in advance at the office. There are also *cars mourides* from here to Kedougou (CFA3000, three hours) and Bakel (CFA3500, five hours).

### TRAIN

The train between Dakar and Bamako (Mali) normally passes through Tambacounda on a Wednesday and Saturday, provided there hasn't been a derailment or other impediment (see p743).

## PARC NATIONAL DU NIOKOLO-KOBA

The World Heritage site Niokolo-Koba, a vast biosphere reserve spanning about 900,000 hectares, is Senegal's major national park. The landscape is relatively flat, with plains, marshes and a few hills – the highest is Mt Assirik in the southeast. Vegetation is spectacularly varied, with savanna woodland and grassland, patches of bamboo and gallery forest along the rivers.

The Gambia River and its two tributaries, the Niokolo-Koba and the Koulountou, cross

SENE

## PARC NATIONAL DE NIOKOLO-KOBA

the vast wilderness, and are crucial sources of water for the 80 species of mammals and 350 bird varieties that inhabit the park.

There are African classics such as lions, also waterbucks, bushbucks, kobs, duikers, baboons, monkeys (green and patas), warthogs, roan antelopes, giant Derby elands, hartebeests and buffaloes. There are hippos and three types of crocodiles (Nile, slender-snouted and dwarf), and chimpanzee troops inhabit parts of the eastern and southern areas, though you'll be lucky to see them.

Not all of Niokolo-Koba's enormous area is equally well maintained, and visitors to the more far-flung corners have reported woodcuttings and an eerie absence of wildlife. The best part for animal-spotting is the area of Simenti, the park's jewel.

If you take the Tambacounda–Kedougou route, you're likely to see monkeys, birds, porcupines and other animals cross the road and lie on the tarmac – so be careful if you're driving. Just before dawn the road is especially full of animals, and there's a good chance you might spot a lion stretching out on the roadside.

The park was neglected until the early 1990s, and poaching has also been a problem, but international funding for development as part of the Parc Transfrontalier Niokolo-Badiar transnational ecosystem (which includes areas in neighbouring Guinea) has improved the situation slightly. Several NGOs are also working directly with the surrounding populations to help conserve the resources found in the park, such as the ronier trees and bamboo.

A glossy visitor guide is available at the park entrance, with a park map and illustrations of some of the wildlife you might see. However, it's in French and costs CFA6000.

### Information

The park is officially open from 15 December to 30 April, though you can visit any time. You enter the park at Dar Salam, where you find a *campement* and the Biodiversity Centre, which has an exhibition. An hour's drive further on is Simenti, the park's main focus, where many animals are concentrated. There's also a park office, visitor information centre and the large Hôtel de Simenti.

Details about track conditions and other aspects of the park can be obtained from the park headquarters (p720) in Tambacounda.

You must have a vehicle to enter the park, and walking is not allowed, except near accommodation sites or in the company of a park ranger. Travellers without a car can visit the park using public transport, taxis or on an organised tour. All tracks, except those between the park gate and the Simenti area, require a 4WD, even in the dry season.

The entrance fee (adult/child under 10 CFA2000/free, vehicle CFA5000) gives you access for 24 hours. Trained and approved guides can be hired at the gate or in Simenti (per day CFA6000).

Several of Tambacounda's hotels can organise some 4WD tours (CFA70,000 to CFA90,000). Rates usually include fuel, driver/guide and admission for the car, while you pay for your park fees, food and accommodation.

### Sleeping & Eating

At the park entrance, the **Dar Salam Campement** ( ☎ 981 2575; camping per tent CFA3500, d/tr CFA7000/8000) has clean bungalows with bathrooms and a good restaurant (dishes CFA3500). Most people stay at **Hôtel de Simenti** ( ☎ 982 3650; s/d 15,000/20,000; ☒ ), a concrete monstrosity that may not look in touch with its surroundings, but sits in a prime spot overlooking the river. The busiest animal sites are close to here, and you can see many of them drinking and grazing from a nearby hide.

**Camp du Lion** (camping per person CFA3500, r CFA7000) is a tiny *campement* in a beautiful spot beside the Gambia River 6km east of Simenti. It has simple but adequate huts. You can also walk to the nearby Pointe de Vue, where hippos and other animals can be sighted drinking on the opposite bank of the river.

### Getting There & Away

You're best off hiring a taxi (around CFA35,000 to CFA40,000) or 4WD (around CFA60,000 to CFA70,000) in Tamba, for instance at the park headquarters. There's also an official transfer between Hôtel Keur Khoudia in Tamba and Hôtel de Simenti (CFA60,000).

If you do rely on public transport, take a Kedougou minibus from Tamba (CFA4500) and get off at the Dar Salam park entrance. From there, you can call Hôtel de Simenti, who'll pick you up (CFA25,000).

## BASSARI COUNTRY

The far southeast corner of Senegal is often called Bassari country after the largest ethnic group, whose traditional way of life gives this region its particular character. Also, this is the only place in Senegal where you can go mountain climbing. The striking landscape, with its craggy mountain paths, forests, plateaus and steep waterfalls has much in common with the adjacent Fouta Jallon region in neighbouring Guinea.

It's the perfect place for extended hiking tours along solitary paths through bushland, passing occasionally through a tiny village. It's advisable to walk with an experienced guide who knows the area and local people well. Don't forget to bring change and even better, kola nuts, as a gesture of appreciation for being allowed to visit the local villages.

### Kedougou

Kedougou is the largest town in southeast Senegal, though this seems hard to believe when you walk along the red, dusty roads lined by lush greenery and traditional huts.

It has a colourful market, famous for its indigo fabrics imported from Guinea, several *télécentres*, and Internet access (for a whopping CFA1500 per hour) at the Kedougou Multi-Service. There is no bank.

Alimentation de Dioubo in Kedougou centre is a well-stocked boutique and a popular evening gathering place for Kedougou's youth.

#### SLEEPING

There are plenty of *campements* to choose from. All arrange tours in the surrounding area and to Parc National du Niokolo-Koba. Note that in most places prices double for air-con rooms.

**Campement Bantamba** (Chez Moulaye; ☎ 558 0154; r CFA8300; ℗ ☒ ) A youth-run place that feels wonderfully remote, sitting at the edge of town in a large garden by the river.

**Chez Diao** ( ☎ 985 1124; d CFA5400; ☒ ) A relaxed spot with clean bungalows grouped around a leafy patio. Toilets are shared and breakfast is CFA1000, meals CFA3000.

SENEGAL

**Le Nieriko** ( ☎ 985 1459; d/tr CFA8600/12,600) At the edge of town this tranquil place is a good choice, with well-kept bungalows in a spacious garden setting, and satellite TV in the lounge for the bored.

**Le Bedik** ( ☎ 985 1000; s/d/tr incl breakfast CFA22,200/27,000/36,600; P ⊠ ⊑ ) A bit classier with comfortable, TV-equipped bungalows, a tennis court and friendly management.

### EATING & DRINKING

All *campements* serve food, though most only on request. Otherwise it's down to the cheap eateries around the market, such as **Keur Niasse**, near Chez Diao. The most up-market restaurant is the **Nieta** on the route to Tamba, with simple meals and drinks served in a spacious, round hut.

For an evening drink, try the **Tour de Babel** or **Black&White**, both lively bar-nightclubs.

### GETTING THERE & AWAY

There's plenty of traffic between Tamba and Kedougou (*sept-place* CFA4800, minibus CFA3500, four hours). There's no regular public transport to Mali, but occasional intrepid overland drivers go this way. Complete all your exit formalities in Kedougou,

---

**GUIDED WALKS**

The company of a clued-up guide is invaluable for exploring the myriad mountain paths of Bassari country. Two of the best guides in the region are **Noumou Diallo** and **Amadou Ba**, who have their base at the Le Bedik (see p723; phone the reception and ask for them) in Kedougou. They come from the area, know the best routes through the hills, and have a good relationship with the villagers, which will make you – the visiting stranger – much more welcome. (It remains up to you though to show the proper respect, and perhaps present kola nuts, money and small gifts to the *chefs de village* or village chiefs.)

They can arrange anything from leisurely day trips to strenuous hikes of several days through the forests, mountains and tiny Bedik and Bassari villages, with the possibility of sleeping in the homes of locals or at *campements*. They usually charge CFA10,000 per day, rates for longer excursions need to be negotiated.

---

as the border post on the route to Kéniéba is unreliable.

By contrast, Guinea is well-served by transport (*sept-place* to Labe CFA15,000, minibus CFA12,000, 24 to 48 hours). Taxis leave in theory every day, though the best day to set off is Friday.

### GETTING AROUND

Almost all *campements* have one or several 4WDs with driver for hire (per day CFA40,000 to CFA50,000, and some hire bicycles (CFA3000), which are good for town trips, but often too clapped-out for trips into the hills.

## Around Kedougou

The best way of exploring Kedougou's stunning surroundings is a combination of driving (in a 4WD) and hiking – best under the care of a good guide (see left).

### THE KEDOUGOU–SALÉMATA ROUTE

One of the nearest villages is **Bandafassi**, actually the capital of Kedougou district. The inhabitants are mainly Fula and Bassari, and the village is renowned for its basket-makers. In Indar, a part of Bandafassi, is the wonderfully welcoming *campement* **Chez Leontine** ( ☎ 554 9915; d CFA6000), with solar-powered lights and delicious meals prepared by the charming owner.

The Fula village of **Ibel** lies another 7km up the road from Bandafassi. Visits here are usually, and rewardingly, combined with a steep hike up to **Iwol**, a stunningly beautiful hamlet stretched out between a giant fromager tree and a sacred baobab. Plenty of legends are associated with this place, and the local teacher will share them with you for a donation (CFA1000). The local women make pottery, which you can buy (CFA300).

Continuing west from Ibel, you reach **Salémata**, 83km from Kedougou. This is a regional hub, with a health centre, small shops and the friendly *campement* **Chez Gilbert** ( ☎ 985 5009; d/tr CFA8000/9000). In April and May, the entire region surrounding Salémata is plunged into week-long festivities during the annual initiation ceremonies of the Bassari. Observers are accepted, but you might want to decline and leave the villagers to follow their custom undisturbed. The best day to visit is Tuesday, when the *lumo* (weekly market) brings the village to life, and with it a better chance of public transport (minibus from Kedougou CFA2250, four hours).

Don't leave Salémata without taking the 15km trip to **Ethiolo**, either on foot or by car. The road leads mainly through forest and bushland, and there's a good chance of spotting chimpanzees in the trees. Ethiolo's brilliant **Campement Chez Balingo** ( ☎ 985 1401) has accommodation in traditional Bassari stone huts, and is run by the enthusiastic and knowledgeable Balingo, who can take you on exciting tours to Ethiolo's surroundings.

### DINDEFELO

One of the most popular destinations from Kedougou is Dindefelo, famous for its impressive 100m **waterfall** with a deep, green pool suitable for swimming. It's a 2km hike through lush forest from Dindefelo village to the cascade. The starting point is the **campement villageois** ( ☎ 658 8707; r per person CFA3000), which has accommodation in well-kept huts. You pay CFA500 for admission to the waterfall at the *campement* (the money goes to the village, just check out the solar-powered street lamps). Much less visited is the village of **Dande**, on the hill above Dindefelo, but if you love steep climbs, don't miss out on this spectacular hike. From here, you can visit the source of the waterfall and stand scarily close to the edge (don't go here without a guide, the deep drop is hidden by some innocent-looking shrubs).

If you rely on public transport, go to Dindefelo on a Sunday, the day of the *lumo* (minibus CFA700, two hours). But a hired 4WD really is the best thing; the road is no fun, a punctured minibus wheel much less so.

# CASAMANCE

The Casamance is one of Senegal's most beautiful regions, with lush tropical landscapes, myriad waterways and the unique culture of the Diola, the largest ethnic group of the region. The Casamance River winds its way through the area in a labyrinth of picturesque creeks lined with abundant estuary vegetation – a pirogue is the ideal means of exploring the waterway. On the western coast, Senegal's finest beaches spread in a wide strip of white sand from Cap Skiring towards the 'hip' villages of Kafountine and Abéné, only broken by a mangrove-lined delta where the Casamance River spills into the Atlantic.

Over the last decades, the region has unfortunately become better known for an ongoing separatist rebellion than its attractive landscape. At the time of writing, a 2004 peace deal signed between the Senegalese government and insurgents had calmed things down, and tourists had started returning to the region. The most exciting sign of this was the renovation of several *campements villageois*, the rural, village-managed lodgings that are typical of the Casamance.

## History

In the 19th and early 20th centuries, the French colonial authorities controlled the territory through local chiefs. In Casamance, however, the Diola people do not have a hierarchical society and thus had no recognised leaders. The French installed Mandinka chiefs to administer the Diola, but they were resented as much as the Europeans, and Diola resistance against foreign interference remained very strong well into the 1930s.

In 1943, the last Diola rebellion against the French was led by traditional priestess, Aline Sitoe Diatta, from Kabrousse. The rebellion was put down and Aline Sitoe was imprisoned at the remote outpost of Timbuktu in Mali, where she eventually died.

The conflict that has plagued the region for nearly the last 25 years originated from a pro-independence demonstration held in Ziguinchor in 1982, after which the leaders of the Mouvement des Forces Démocratique de la Casamance (MFDC) were arrested and jailed. Over the next few years the army clamped down with increasing severity, but this only galvanised the local people's anti-Dakar feelings and spurred the movement into taking more action.

In 1990, the MFDC went on the offensive and attacked military posts. The army responded by attacking MFDC bases in southern Casamance and over the border in Guinea-Bissau, which had been giving covert support to the rebels following a coastal territorial dispute with Senegal. As always, it was local civilians who came off the worst, with both the Senegalese army and the MFDC accused of committing atrocities against people who were thought to be sympathetic to the opposite side.

# CASAMANCE

| 0 | 10 km |
| 0 | 6 miles |

THE GAMBIA

To Serekunda (30km);
Banjul (45km)

Darsilami

Séléti

Kartong

Néma

ATLANTIC OCEAN

Diouloulou

Kabadio

| Campements |
| 4WD Only |

Marigot de Baïla

Sindian

Abéné

Diannah

N5

Kagnarou

Kafountine

Baïla

Sanctuaire
Ornithologique
de Kassel

Tiobon

Kagnobon

Diégoune

Tendième

BIGNONA

N4

Casamance Nord

To Badiouré
(2km); Dakar
(425km)

Presqu'ile
des Oiseaux

Kalissaye

Tionk-Essil

N4

Sanctuaire
Ornithologique de la
Pointe de Kalissaye

Marigot

Tendouk

de

Diouloulou

Mangagoulak

Koubalan

Tobor

Casamance River

Pointe
St George

Affiniam

Barrage

Île des
Oiseaux

Djilapao

To Dakar
(500km)

Diogué

Bandial

Ziguinchor

N6

Carabane

Nikine

M'Lomp

Kagnout

Etama

Essil

Brin

To Sédhiou;
Kolda (188km)

Île de
Carabane

Séléki

N4

Elinkine

Loudia
Ouolof

Enampor

Kamoubeul

Toubacouta

Diembéring

Oussouye

Edioungou

Diohère

Nyassia

Mpak

Diakène
Ouolof

Oukout

Niambalang

Diakène
Diola

Basse Casamance

Kaguite

São Domingos

Boucoutte

Parc National
de Basse-
Casamance

To Ingore (40km);
Bissau (120km)

Cap Skiring

Santiaba
Mandjak

Youtou

Kabrousse

GUINEA-BISSAU

SEGAL

---

**TO GO OR NOT TO GO?**

It's the nature of news that you hear more about killing than about living, and in the case of Casamance good news is hard to find. This means that the vast majority of Senegalese know little more than yourself about the current situation in the Casamance and their view of the region's security may be as obscured as your own.

Anybody we spoke to in the Casamance assured us that travelling to the area was perfectly safe, but you do need to be extra vigilant. The most important thing is not to be travelling on the roads at night, particularly in the areas near Guinea-Bissau and the route from Ziguinchor via Bignona to Kafountine. There have been occasional carjackings and ambushes at roadblocks, usually put up by armed bandits, rather than separatists defending the rebel cause. Alarm bells rang when, in 2006, the deputy prefect of Diouloulou was assaulted at one of these roadblocks, and later lost his life. These attacks are rare, but they do occur, so make sure you give yourself enough time to arrive at your destination before nightfall.

At the time of writing, conflicts between rebels and Bissau-Guinean military had flared up in a small area near the border with Guinea-Bissau, resulting in the temporary suspension of public transport and the closure of the border in Sã Domingos. These kinds of confrontations have become rare since 2004, but you always need to check security advice, listen to the locals and give conflict areas a wide berth. In Ziguinchor you can ask at your hotel, but a more grass-roots picture may be gleaned by talking to bush-taxi drivers: if they are reluctant to go, you should be too.

During the two weeks we travelled through the Casamance, visiting remote villages as well as major tourist centres, we didn't experience any difficulties whatsoever. By contrast, the hospitality of the people and their eagerness to welcome foreign visitors back into their region and help tourists to travel safely were impressive and moving. Casamance used to be one of Senegal's major tourist destinations, and for most people, the suffering is greater for the lack of tourists and their dollars than any direct confrontation with separatist fighters.

The only real permanent no-go zone is the Parc National de Basse-Casamance, which has been closed for years because of suspected land mines. Rest assured that unless you just wander off on your own accord, people will simply not allow you to get too close to trouble.

---

As the '90s wore on, cease-fire agreements were signed and broken as periods of peace repeatedly ended in violence. In 1995, four French people touring Casamance disappeared. The Senegalese government blamed the MFDC, while Father Diamacoune Senghor, the MFDC's leader, accused the army of trying to turn international opinion against the rebels.

Peace talks continued, but following the government's refusal to consider independence for Casamance, a group of hardliners broke away from the MFDC and resumed fighting.

Meanwhile, Father Diamacoune urged his supporters to continue the search for reconciliation with the government. Another cease-fire was agreed in late 1997 but it did little to slow the mounting death toll, and during the following three years about 500 people were reportedly killed. His authority fading, Father Diamacoune unexpectedly signed a peace deal in March 2001. While the agreement provided for the release of

prisoners, the return of refugees and the clearance of landmines, it fell short of the full autonomy many rebels sought. Divisions within the MFDC deepened; a bloody battle was fought between two opposing factions and many in Casamance had begun referring to some of the rebels as bandits or common thieves. Things have become calmer since, and the 2004 peace deal appears to have been effective, though occasional uprisings and street ambushes still occur.

## ZIGUINCHOR

**pop 217,000**

Ziguinchor (pronounced *zig-an-shor*) is the largest town in southern Senegal, as well as the main access point for travel in the Casamance region. It's hard to imagine a more laid-back town than this regional capital – just don't call it sleepy. Unlike other 'junction towns', Ziguinchor has real atmosphere, couched among the majestic houses, leafy streets and busy markets of this old colonial administrative centre.

## Information

### BOOKSHOPS

The **bookshop** ( 9am-noon & 2.30-6pm) on the northern end of Rue Javelier has a few English-language magazines.

### CULTURAL CENTRES

**Alliance Franco-Sénégalaise** ( 991 2823; Ave Lycée Guignabo;  9.15am-noon & 3-7.15pm Mon-Sat) This stunning *case à impluvium* (large round hut) has regular exhibitions, a large concert hall and a café. Tourists are expected to make a donation of CFA750 when visiting the centre, and are given a postcard of the centre in exchange.

### INTERNET ACCESS

There are many *cybercafés* in town. Le Flamboyant hotel and Hôtel Kadiandoumagne are both wi-fi spaces, and the Alliance Franco-Sénégalaise has a speedy Internet café.

**Sud-Informatique** ( 991 1573; www.sudinfo.sn; per hr CFA1000;  9am-midnight)

**Web City** ( 991 1044; per hr CFA1000;  10am-midnight)

### MEDICAL SERVICES

Ziguinchor's regional **hospital** ( 991 1154) has an emergency department. Veronique Chiche at Le Flamboyant hotel can recommend other reliable doctors in town.

### MONEY

The following banks change money, give advances on credit cards and have ATMs taking Visa and MasterCard.

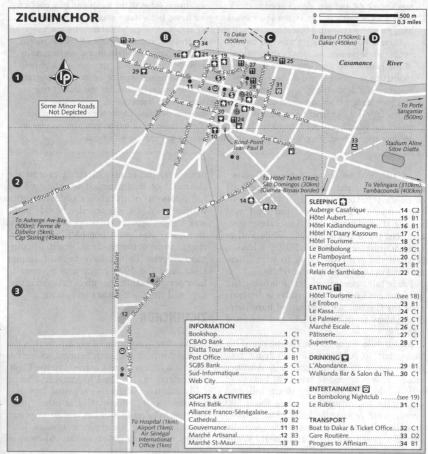

**ZIGUINCHOR**

0 — 500 m
0 — 0.3 miles

To Dakar (550km)

To Banjul (150km); Dakar (450km)

*Casamance River*

Some Minor Roads Not Depicted

Rue du Commerce
Rue du Général de Gaulle
Rue de Truch
Rue Emile Badiane
Rue de Boucotte
Rue de la Poste
Rond-Point Jean-Paul II
Ave Carvalho
Ave de France

To Porte Sangamar (500m)

Stadium Aline Sitoe Diatta

Blvd Edouard Diatta

To Auberge Aw-Bay (500m); Ferme de Djibelor (5km); Cap Skiring (45km)

Ave Chérif Bachir Aïdara

To Hôtel Tahiti (1km); São Domingos (30km) (Guinea-Bissau border)

To Velingara (310km); Tambacounda (400km)

Ave Emile Badiane

Route de l'Aviation

Ave Lycée Guignabo

To Hospital (1km); Airport (1km); Air Sénégal International Office (1km)

**INFORMATION**
Bookshop.................................1 C1
CBAO Bank..............................2 C1
Diatta Tour International.........3 C1
Post Office...............................4 B1
SGBS Bank...............................5 C1
Sud-Informatique....................6 C1
Web City..................................7 C1

**SIGHTS & ACTIVITIES**
Africa Batik.............................8 C2
Alliance Franco-Sénégalaise....9 B4
Cathedral...............................10 B2
Gouvernance.........................11 B1
Marché Artisanal...................12 B3
Marché St-Maur....................13 B3

**SLEEPING**
Auberge Casafrique...............14 C2
Hôtel Aubert..........................15 B1
Hôtel Kadiandoumagne.........16 B1
Hôtel N'Daary Kassoum..........17 C1
Hôtel Tourisme......................18 C1
Le Bombolong........................19 C1
Le Flamboyant.......................20 C1
Le Perroquet.........................21 B1
Relais de Santhiaba................22 C2

**EATING**
Hôtel Tourisme..................(see 18)
Le Erobon..............................23 B1
Le Kassa................................24 C1
Le Palmier.............................25 C1
Marché Escale........................26 C1
Pâtisserie...............................27 C1
Superette...............................28 C1

**DRINKING**
L'Abondance..........................29 B1
Walkunda Bar & Salon du Thé..30 C1

**ENTERTAINMENT**
Le Bombolong Nightclub....(see 19)
Le Rubis.................................31 C1

**TRANSPORT**
Boat to Dakar & Ticket Office...32 C1
Gare Routière........................33 D2
Pirogues to Affiniam..............34 B1

SEGAL

**CBAO** (Rue de France; ☼ 7.45am-noon & 1.15-2.30pm Mon-Thu, 7.45am-1pm & 2.45-3.45pm Fri)
**SGBS** (Rue du Général de Gaulle; ☼ 7.45am-noon & 1.15-2.30pm Mon-Thu, 7.45am-1pm & 2.45-3.45pm Fri)

**POST**
**Main post office** (Rue du Général de Gaulle)

**TRAVEL AGENCIES**
**Diatta Tour International** ( ☎ 991 2781; aessibye@ yahoo.fr; Rue du Général de Gaulle) A good agency, that arranges air tickets, tours, hotel and *campement* reservations.

## Sights & Activities
Ziguinchor has some colourful historical buildings, including the central **post office**, the office of **Diatta Tour International**, the **Gouvernance** (Rue du Général de Gaulle) and the stunning **Cathedral**. Still on the architectural side, the huge *case à impluvium* of the **Alliance Franco-Sénégalaise** offers plenty of interest – from the mosaic floors to the Ndebele patterns painted all across the walls and ceiling. Not far from there, the **Marché Artisanal** and the **Marché St-Maur**, both on Ave Lycée Guignabo, tempt with wooden carvings, fabrics and, more ordinarily, with fresh fruit and vegetables.

Heading 5km west out of town, you can walk through the vast greenness of the **Ferme de Djibelor** ( ☎ 991 1701; admission CFA2000; ☼ 9am-6pm), which has a tropical fruit and flower garden and a crocodile farm.

**Africa Batik** ( ☎ 9911 2689; near Rond-Point Jean-Paul II) offers batik-making courses of varying duration.

Most hotels offer pirogue excursions – day trips to Affiniam are particularly popular.

## Sleeping
**BUDGET**
**Le Bombolong** ( ☎ 938 8001; off Rue du Commerce; r CFA8000) This simple place with a leafy courtyard is best known for its nightclub – a relaxed place to stay, but not for light sleepers.

**Hôtel Tourisme** ( ☎ 991 2223; Rue de France; s/d CFA6600/8200) Four simple, clean rooms, in the heart of town, and above a great restaurant – it's a bargain. Managed by the owners of Le Flamboyant, it benefits from their vast regional knowledge.

**Relais de Santhiaba** ( ☎ 991 1199; off Ave Cherif Bachir Aidara; s/d CFA5000/8000, with bathroom CFA9000/13,000; ☒ ) It looks drab from the outside, but rooms are surprisingly welcoming and facilities are clean.

**Auberge Casafrique** ( ☎ 991 4122; casafrique@ yahoo.fr; off Ave Cherif Bachir Aidara; s/d CFA5000/7000, with bathroom CFA8000/10,000; ☒ ) The spartan rooms in a leafy garden seem to appeal mainly to young travellers.

**MIDRANGE**
**Le Perroquet** ( ☎ 991 2329; perroquet@sentoo.sn; Rue du Commerce; s/d CFA10,000/12,000) This simple place right on the river and beside the pirogue pier is excellent value. For 1st-floor rooms with river views you pay an extra CFA1000.

**Hôtel Tahiti** ( ☎ 991 5949; tahitimotel@sentoo.sn; s/d incl breakfast CFA15,600/18,200; ☒ ) It's placed in a strangely unattractive location in front of a military camp. But its well-kept rooms, equipped with TV, fridge and phone, make this a viable option.

**Hôtel N'Daary Kassoum** ( ☎ 991 1472; ndaary@ hotmail.com; Rue de France; d CFA12,000; ☒ ) With their dark décor and rattling air-conditioning, rooms don't exactly feel welcoming, but then again, they're fairly cheap, too.

**Le Flamboyant** ( ☎ 991 2223; flamboyant@ casamance.net; Rue de France; s/d CFA15,000/17,000; ☒ ▢ ☒ ) This classy place is possibly the best value in the country. The tranquil rooms with red-brick floors and comfy mattresses come with phone, satellite TV, bar fridge and soothing lighting, and are set in a quiet garden. The French couple who runs it are absolutely forthcoming and knowledgeable, and oh yes, the whole place is a wi-fi zone.

**TOP END**
**Hôtel Kadiandoumagne** ( ☎ 938 8000; www.hotel -kadiandoumagne.com; Rue du Commerce; s/d CFA22,000/ 25,000; ☒ ▢ ☒ ) Stunningly located right on the river, this top-quality place has good rooms, wi-fi access in the restaurant, and stunning views from the spacious terrace. It's wheelchair accessible.

**Hôtel Aubert** ( ☎ 938 8020; hotelaubert@sentoo.sn; Rue Fargues; d/tr CFA22,000/30,000; ☒ ▢ ☒ ) Part of Ziguinchor's upper class of hotels, this is a tastefully laid-out place, complete with a sports centre and jazz bar.

## Eating & Drinking
The best restaurants, and those with the widest range of choices, are part of the hotels, otherwise try one of these.

**Hôtel Tourisme** ( ☼ noon-2.30pm & 7-10pm; mains around CFA3000) This place doesn't actually look like much during the day but after sunset the subtle mood lighting lends this restaurant some style. Head here for some great seafood dishes and *al dente* spaghetti.

**Le Erobon** ( ☎ 991 2788; Rue du Commerce) This humble outdoor eatery serves a mean grilled fish in a relaxed environment.

**Le Palmier** ( ☎ 936 8181; Rue du Commerce; dishes from CFA1000; 🕑 24hr) Not the most attractive address, but this cheapie near the port serves good Senegalese, Guinean and Casamance specialities.

**Le Kassa** ( ☎ 936 8300; 🕑 8am-2am) This is the most inviting of the local-style places – a spacious restaurant-cum-bar, with a fairly wide menu and frequent live shows on weekends.

**Walkunda Bar & Salon du Thé** ( ☎ 991 1845; 🕑 9am-1am) This pretty place near the Rond-Point serves drinks at very reasonable rates, as well as filling meals.

**L'Abondance** (Rue du Général de Gaulle; 🕑 5pm-2am) Like any *dibiterie* worth its meat, this is the popular final stop after a night out dancing.

Self-caterers can buy all the fresh fruit and vegetables they can carry at the **Marché Escale** (Rue Javelier). There's a small **supermarket** (Rue Lemoine) and a good **patisserie** (Rue Javelier).

## Entertainment

**Le Rubis** (Rue de Santhiaba; admission CFA1000-2000) was Ziguinchor's most fashionable dance floor when we headed into town. They spin salsa music on Fridays and a global mix of hip-hop, R&B, *mbalax* and plenty more on Wednesdays and Saturdays. Another popular heaving choice in town is **Le Bombolong Nightclub** (Rue du Commerce; admission CFA1000-2000).

## Getting There & Away
### AIR
**Air Sénégal International** ( ☎ 991 1081) has an office at the airport and flies daily to Dakar (one way CFA80,000).

### BUSH TAXI, MINIBUS & BUS
Ziguinchor's extremely well-organised *gare routière* is 1km east of the centre. If you want to get all the way to Dakar, get there early, around 6am or even earlier. Some sample fares (in CFA):

| Destination | Sept-Place | Minibus | Ndiaga Ndiaye |
|---|---|---|---|
| Bissau | 6000 | - | - |
| Cap Skiring | 1400 | 1100 | 1000 |
| Dakar | 7500 | 6000 | 5000 |
| Elinkine | 1300 | 850 | 850 |
| Kafountine | 2500 | 1700 | 1600 |
| Kaolack | 5500 | 3800 | - |
| Kolda | 3500 | - | - |
| Séléti | 2200 | - | - |
| Soma | 2500 | - | - |
| Tambacounda | 7500 | - | - |

### BOAT
At the time of writing, a reliable and comfortable boat service had just started travelling between Dakar and Ziguinchor. There's a sad background for all this unexpected comfort though. The current boat (the *Wilis*, though it could well be a different one by the time you travel) resumed in 2005 the journey previously performed by the MS *Joola*, which tragically capsized in 2002, in the worst catastrophe Senegal had ever experienced. Almost 2000 people perished in the fatal accident (only 64 of the passengers were rescued), which was caused by dangerous overloading of the boat.

The accident was a shocking wake-up call and has now made the Joola's successor the *Wilis* one of the safest passenger boats of the region, where all essential measures are respected.

In Dakar, the **SOMAT ticket office** (Map p684; ☎ 889 8009, 889 8060/51), is located next to the Gorée Ferry; while in Ziguinchor, you'll find it at the port. The boat departs from Dakar every Tuesday and Friday at 7pm, returning from Ziguinchor every Sunday and Thursday at 2pm. In Dakar, you need to arrive at least 1½ hours in advance; in Ziguinchor at least one hour. Tickets cost CFA15,500 for an armchair, CFA23,500 for a sleeper seat and CFA28,500 for a cabin bed (cabins sleep four people). Residents pay CFA5000 less, children under 12 travel for half the price, and free if they're younger than four.

## Getting Around
### TAXI
The official rate for a taxi around town or to the *gare routière* (1km) is CFA400. The main taxi rank is at Rond-Point Jean-Paul II.

---

### VILLAGE CAMPEMENTS

Among Casamance's attractions are its *campements villageois* (village camps), traditional-style lodgings often in remote locations, that are built by local residents, integrated into the village and, best of all, benefit the local community directly. The *campements* have existed since the 1970s, when Adama Goudiaby and Christian Saglio initiated them as a way of counteracting the rural exodus and offering prospects to local youth. Ten were built originally, yet during the years of conflict, many were left in ruins. Over the last few years, the Fédération des Campements Villageois (FECAV) has, with financial help from the Alliance Française and German GTZ, been able to begin an ambitious renovation programme.

At the time this book was researched, the *campements* of Oussouye, Enampor, Baïla, Koulaban and Affiniam had been fully restored, so spectacularly, that some of them exceed any competing private ventures in quality and service. All of them are built in traditional architectural styles (the *case à impluvium* in Enampor and *case étage* in Oussouye are particularly impressive), and offer insightful excursions in the immediate surroundings led by knowledgeable local guides. Integrated and respectful rural tourism is rarely more enjoyable.

The prices of all Campements Villageois are standardised, with only small variations. A bed (with mosquito net) is CFA3000, breakfast CFA1500 to CFA1800, three-course lunch or dinner CFA2500 to CFA3500, beer CFA800 and soft drink CFA500.

For more information, particularly regarding renovation progress of other *campements*, contact Mr Sane at the **Fédération des Campements Villageois** (FECAV; ☎ 991 1268, 558 1421).

---

## BASSE CASAMANCE
### Enampor
The **Campement Villageois** ( ☎ 441 4484, 936 9160; r per person CFA3000) is a huge *case à impluvium*, a typical Casamance architectural style, where rainwater is funnelled into a large tank in the centre of the house through a hole in the roof. There are many such buildings around, but this is one of the most beautiful examples.

In theory, there are two minibuses per day from Ziguinchor to Enampor and nearby Séléki (CFA500). Hiring a taxi will set you back CFA7000 to CFA9000. Other than that, it's a bush taxi to Brin and a long walk or bicycle ride to Enampor.

### Oussouye
Roughly halfway between Ziguinchor and Cap Skiring, relaxed Oussouye is the main town in the Basse Casamance area. For the local Diola population this town is of significance, as it's home to an animist king who is often sought for advice.

At **Casamance VTT** (Chez Benjamin; ☎ /fax 993 1004; http://casavtt.free.fr) you can hire mountain bikes (half-day CFA4000, full-day CFA7500) and participate in tours.

#### SLEEPING & EATING
The **Campement Villageois d'Oussouye** ( ☎ 993 0015; http://campement.oussouye.org; s/d CFA4500/6000)

is one of the great success stories of the rekindling of the regional tourist industry. Accommodation is in a beautifully restored *case étage*, built entirely in the stunning, heat-busting mud-architecture once typical of the region. Another big plus: the resident guide Jean Baptiste, who is deeply familiar with the region and all too happy to share his knowledge. **Campement Emanaye** ( ☎ 993 1004; emanaye@yahoo.fr; s/d CFA4500/6000) is another striking two-storey, mud dwelling that houses good-quality rooms with bathrooms and great views over the local rice fields. At the more basic **Auberge du Routard** ( ☎ 993 1025; r per person CFA3000) you can sometimes see batiks being made, or even participate.

For food, **Le Kassa** (Chez Odette; ☎ 563 7186; dishes around CFA1000) and **Le Passager** ( ☎ 512 0243; meals around CFA1500) are good options, both serving deer.

#### GETTING THERE & AWAY
All bush taxis between Ziguinchor and Cap Skiring pass through Oussouye. Rates to the half-way point Oussouye are usually around CFA1000.

### M'Lomp
On what is allegedly a sealed road between Oussouye and Elinkine you'll pass through the village of M'Lomp, the best place to admire the local *cases étages* (two-storey,

mud-brick houses). An enormous fromager tree, at least 400 years old and sacred in the village, towers above the first case étage.

Decent food in a welcoming setting can be found at **Les Six Palmiers** ( ☎ 569 9058; meals CFA500-1000; ☒ 8am-11pm). To get here, ask for Chez Brigitte, and any local can give you directions.

## Elinkine

The busy fishing village Elinkine is the best jumping-off point for Île de Karabane. The simple but charming **Campement le Fromager** ( ☎ 525 6401; s/d CFA3000/6000) has been rebuilt after having been burnt to the ground a few years ago, and now offers good, basic accommodation and a vast range of excursions. Mammadou Ndiaye, the welcoming manager, has spent several decades in the local tourist industry – this is your chance to tap into his vast regional knowledge.

There are normally several Ndiaga Ndiayes each day from Ziguinchor to Elinkine, via Oussouye for CFA850, or from Oussouye for CFA300.

## Île de Karabane

It's hard to believe that the tranquil Île de Karabane was the first French trading station in the region (1836–1900). The French legacy is now ruins, but you can still see the crumbling remains of a tall Breton-style church and a school. Further along the beach lies the so-called Catholic cemetery with the graves of French settlers and sailors. The beach is good for swimming (and occasionally dolphin spotting), and the mangroves surrounding the island are great for bird-watching tours.

### SLEEPING & EATING

The following places are listed from east to west. All serve food. Always leave a message if you don't get an answer on any of the numbers given – mobile coverage isn't great.

**Campement le Barracuda** ( ☎ 659 6001; r CFA3000, with half board CFA7300) With its pretty rooms with bathrooms, forthcoming management and excellent restaurant, this is probably the most commendable place on the island. It's definitely the best address for bird-watching and angling excursions, whether you're experienced or first-time rod-holder.

**Hôtel Carabane** ( ☎ 569 0284; hotelcarabane@yahoo .fr; s/d CFA13,000/18,000) This delightful and well-maintained hotel is set in a lush and shady

tropical garden. You'll have the honour to stay in what used to be the colonial governance, and enjoy your drink in the former Catholic mission.

**Chez Helena** ( ☎ 654 1772; s/d CFA4000/6000) If the rooms were as pretty as the gleaming restaurant terrace, this would be a fantastic place to stay. But they're not, although boisterous manager Helena will try to make you forget the ugly lino floors and curious assembly of furniture by wrapping you up in sparkling conversation.

**Leliba** ( ☎ 544 5108; www.bamboocollege.ne; r per person CFA4000) Furthest along the beach, this busy little *campement* offers workshops in dance, music and crafts, and even houses a small recording studio. It's a place that'll appeal to those keen to learn about the local culture.

### GETTING THERE & AWAY

Île de Karabane is best reached by motorised pirogue from Elinkine. A fairly regular *navette* (boat) leaves Elinkine daily at 2.30pm and 5pm, reaching Île de Karabane half an hour later before continuing to the village of Diogé. It returns at 10am the next day. The fare is CFA1000. Alternatively you can charter a boat for about CFA10,000 each way, just ask at the harbour. If you know where you'll be staying, your *campement* can also arrange to pick you up for a fee. A hired pirogue from Cap Skiring will cost around CFA30,000 to CFA40,000.

## Cap Skiring

Considering the awesome beauty of Cap Skiring's beaches, the tourism industry of the area is still surprisingly low-key. A handful of resort-style hotels attract European package tours, but all along the beachfront you will also find small *campements* appealing to independent travellers. Off the beaten track this is not, but if you want a few easy days of sun and sand, with the option of a bit of partying after hours, this is the place.

### INFORMATION

Cap Skiring has a small hospital, a post office and several *télécentres* in the centre of the village. The **CBAO** bank in the village has an ATM that accepts Visa cards. **Diatta Tours** ( ☎ 991 2781; aessibye@yahoo.fr) is as close as you get to a local tourist-information office, and is the place to book tours around the area. **Net's Cap** ( ☎ 993 5371; net-s-cap@sentoo.sn; ☒ 9am-

10pm) is one of the fastest and best-equipped Internet cafés in the entire country.

## SLEEPING

You'll find accommodation for all budgets in Cap Skiring, most of it overlooking the beach and offering all the associated facilities and activities you'd expect, though with greatly differing quality and prices.

### Budget

Just south of the junction is a sandy track that stretches along the beach. All the *campements* listed here are situated there.

**Campement Paradise** ( ☎ 993 5129; r with/without bathroom CFA12,000/6000; 🔀 ) If you're spending your holiday on a beachfront, you're unlikely to spend much time in your room – so who cares if it's a little basic? The garden surrounding the bungalows invites lounging and gives access to the beach.

**Campement Chez M'Ballo** ( ☎ 936 9102; r with/without bathroom CFA7500/4000) Possibly the pick of the cheap places on this strip, M'Ballo is a good-value option with a relaxed and friendly atmosphere. Palm trees fight for space in this pretty plot of green, and the restaurant gives great views across the beach,

**Noopalou Coussene** (Chez Bruno Diatta; ☎ /fax 993 5130; www.casamance-peche.org; r per person with half board CFA15,000) This is a simple but excellent place, specialising in fishing excursions. Accommodation is in spotless rooms or self-catering bungalows.

**Auberge de la Paix** ( ☎ 993 5145; aubergedelapaix@ yahoo.fr; s/d CFA6000/10,000) A friendly place with a family feel and a chilled-out restaurant with hammocks to laze the day away.

### Midrange

**Villa des Pêcheurs** ( ☎ 993 5253; www.villadespecheurs .com; s/d from CFA13,000/15,000; 🔀 ) On the same beachfront strip as the *campements*, this place has stylish rooms and a renowned restaurant. Fishing trips, including surf casting and angling, can be arranged.

**Les Paletuviers** ( ☎ 993 5210; www.hotel-kaloa .com; r incl breakfast CFA15,000; 🔀 🐟 ) This freshly polished hotel offers great value for money. It looks out onto a beautiful stretch of mangroves, and has all the quality and comfort of a top-end place at a much better rate.

**Auberge le Palmier** ( ☎ 993 5109; d CFA10,000; 🔀 ) Opposite the Club Med, the Palmier masters the art of tasteful understatement.

Rooms are as welcoming as the friendly management, and for an extra CFA2000 per night you even get hot water.

**Les Bougainvilliers** ( ☎ 993 5129; d CFA20,000; 🔀 🖳 ) At the time of research, this was still a brilliant restaurant with eight nearly finished rooms at the back. If the character and quality of the eatery are anything to go by, this will be very nice indeed.

### Top End

**La Maison Bleue** ( ☎ 993 5161; www.lamaisonbleue.sn; r per person CFA30,8000) This luxurious place oozes sophistication, from the subdued colour scheme and Moroccan-style lounge to the mosaic-tiled swimming pool. Massages and beauty treatments are on offer, too. During the low season, prices drop by almost 50%.

**Hôtel la Paillote** ( ☎ 993 5151; www.paillote.sn; s/d CFA52,000/74,000; 🔀 🖳 🐟 ) This hotel has been here the longest, and spoils visitors the best. For a luxurious stay with access to a supreme range of activities and services (including tailoring, golf, tennis, beauty treatments, pirogue excursions and plenty more), this is your ideal holiday home.

**Les Hibiscus** ( ☎ 993 5136; hibiscus@sentoo.sn; s/d incl breakfast CFA19,900/28,800) Right on the border of Guinea-Bissau near Kabrousse is this classy hotel in lush gardens on the beach, where comfortable bungalows are decorated with stunning murals and local fabrics.

### EATING & DRINKING

Cap Skiring village has a whole range of quality eateries to choose from. **Le Terazza** (Chez Gnima; ☎ 993 5110) has tasty pizzas and plenty of character, thanks to the energetic owner Gnima and her mainly female staff. You pass the place on your way from the village to the beach. For Senegalese food, **Le Salima** ( ☎ 936 9127) and **Le Carpe Rouge** ( ☎ 993 5250) are both good. For something a little more upmarket, try the cosy restaurant **Le Djembe** (Chez Nadine & Patrick; ☎ 533 7692) where you can enjoy live jazz on Fridays while relishing mouth-watering French and Italian dishes. The lively *dibieterie* **Le Kassala** ( ☎ 653 0382; 🕑 8pm-4am) is the place danced-out clubbers head to for delicious roast meat (per kilo CFA5000) at 3am. Combine a visit with a night out at the stylish **Case Bambou** ( ☎ 993 5178; admission CFA1000; 🕑 10.30pm-4am), **Savane Café** (admission CFA3000; 🕑 9pm-3am) or the more down-to-earth **Kassoumaye** (admission

CFA500-1000; 10pm-4am) and **Les Paletuviers** (Les Paletuviers hotel; admission CFA1000; 9pm-3am).

### GETTING THERE & AWAY
### Air
**Air Sénégal International** has twice weekly flights to Dakar from November to April (return CFA110,600). **Air CM** ( in France 01 53 41 00 50; mail.aircom@wannadoo.fr) has a twice-weekly connection between Paris and the Cap.

### Bush Taxi & Minibus
Bush taxis (CFA1400) and minibuses (CFA1100) run regularly throughout the day between Ziguinchor and Cap Skiring, although there's more traffic in the morning.

### GETTING AROUND
It's quite a trek from the main *campement* area to Cap Skiring village. You can hail a taxi for around CFA600. Bicycles are another good option – most hotels, *campements* and Diatta Tours have them for hire. Day trips by pirogue start at around CFA25,000. Try the two reliable piroguers **Jean Baptiste** and **Philippe Gomis** ( 555 2415) opposite the Hôtel Katakalousse. **Auto Cap4** ( 993 5265; autocap4@sentoo.sn) has an eclectic mix of 4WDs for hire starting at CFA30,000 per day.

### Boucotte
This tiny village lies half-way between Cap Skiring and Diembéring, on the seemingly endless stretch of white sand that is Boucotte beach. Once in the village, you should absolutely pay a visit to the **Boucotte Museum** (ask any local to take you there). It's a low-key exhibition of Diola artefacts and objects among the roots of some giant fromager trees. The pretty, blue bungalows of the **Oudja Hôtel** ( 991 2781, 517 5895; s/d/tr CFA10,000/12,000/15,000) sit right on the shoreline.

Hiring a taxi from Cap Skiring to Boucotte should cost you around CFA2000 to CFA3000, if you call before setting out a pick-up can be arranged. Alternatively, you can walk along the beach, or do the polluting thing of driving along the seashore in your 4WD when the sea is low.

### Diembéring
Diembéring tempts independent travellers with a taste of village life and a quiet beach thrown in. The place to stay is **Campement Asseb** ( 993 3106; r per person CFA3000), a spacious, though slightly run-down place near the big fromager tree at the entrance to town. Check out the local *groupement des femmes* (women's collective) that makes cute toys and other souvenirs from colourful African fabrics and sells them at reasonable prices.

Rates for private taxis to/from Cap Skiring vary enormously depending on the season and state of the roads. Expect to pay between CFA4000 to CFA6000 each way. The daily minibus from Ziguinchor passes through Cap Skiring around 5pm and returns early next morning, the seat costs CFA600 to CFA700.

## CASAMANCE NORD
### Koubalan
Koubalan is a small village, 22km east of Ziguinchor. Its **campement villageois** ( 578 2091, télécentre 936 9473; badianepap@hotmail.com) was created in 1979, and has been restored. Accommodation is in a beautifully decorated, spacious round hut. Ask the staff to take you on excursions, there's plenty to do here: visit a sacred forest, pirogue trips through the mangroves (some just being reforested) to nearby bird habitats, trips to local artisans' workshops and much more.

You reach Koubalan by bush taxi from Ziguinchor (CFA500, 45 minutes). It's on a dirt road off the Ziguinchor–Bignona road.

### Affiniam
A few kilometres north of the river, Affiniam is stunningly located between forest and river, and easily reached from Ziguinchor by boat. The **campement villageois** ( 508 8025, télécentre 936 9619) is in a beautiful *case à impluvium* on the edge of the village, watched over by giant fromager trees, and close to the pirogue point. The village itself has an interesting artisanal centre, where you can buy locally produced soap, marmalade and juice, and sometimes watch batiks being made. Otherwise, Affiniam is in a good location for pirogue trips to bird habitats and the *case étage* in Djilapao.

The best way of visiting Affiniam is by pirogue. There's a public boat once a day between Affiniam and Ziguinchor (CFA400, 1½ hours, daily except Thursday and Sunday; departs from Ziguinchor 3.30pm, from Affiniam 9.30am). Hiring a boat will cost around CFA25,000, hiring a taxi from Ziguinchor CFA15,000 (one hour, 30km,).

## Bignona & Baïla

Bignona is a sleepy crossroads town with crumbling colonial buildings, where the main route to/from Banjul joins the Trans-Gambia Hwy 30km north of Ziguinchor.

A short drive out of town, the **Hôtel le Palmier** ( ☎ 994 1258; r CFA7000) has adequate facilities in an old, colonial-style building. In Badiouré, 11km from Bignona on the road towards Séléti, you'll find the **Relais Fleuri** ( ☎ 994 3002; fax 994 3219; s/d CFA12,000/14,000; ✖ ☎ ) ), which is as pretty as its name, but caters almost exclusively for hunters. Just avoid the main season (November to April).

Off the main road between Bignona and Dioulolou, Baïla tempts with another pretty **campement villageois** ( ☎ 544 8035; télécentre 936 9516). The area is great for walks and pirogue tours. It's best to go with a guide, and don't venture out on lonely paths late at night.

Ziguinchor to Baïla takes around 45 minutes along the tarmac main road. A bush taxi costs CFA1500, a hire taxi around CFA20,000.

## Kafountine & Abéné

Kafountine and Abéné are the hip face of tourism in Senegal. The two villages on the coast just south of The Gambia have spawned more than 20 guesthouses, often the sort of place where dreadlocked staff seem happy to drum the day away and everything is 'cool, mon'. The villages are separated from the rest of Casamance Nord by a large branch of the Casamance River called Marigot Dioulolou.

The area looks more to the north than to the south: if you travel here from The Gambia, the reggae-vibing tourist scene will seem familiar.

Several Senegalese and European artists have settled here, *djembe* drum clutched between their knees and tie-dye kit in hand, and have tuned in the area to the laid-back rhythms of 'baba cool' – a West African version of relaxed reggae culture. You don't have to look far for your introductory drumming, batik or dance workshop.

### KAFOUNTINE

Kafountine is a spread-out village near the end of the pot-holed tarmac leading in from Dioulolou. The village centre stretches along the main road. It's reasonably well equipped, with several *télécentres*, a slowish cybercafé,

---

**BIRD-WATCHING SITES AROUND KAFOUNTINE**

The creeks and lagoons around Kafountine are wonderful areas for watching birds, especially waders and shore birds. You can start your excursions right in town, at the small pool near the Campement Sitokoto, or at the bar of the *campement* Esperanto, where you can gaze across the *bolongs* (estuaries) while imbibing a soothing sunset drink. Esperanto, and several other lodgings organise trips to the famous bird-watching sites further afield, including the Sanctuaire Ornithologique de la Pointe de Kalissaye, a group of sandy islands (usually hidden by the waters), at the mouth of the Marigot Kalissaye, and the highly rated Sanctuaire Ornithologique de Kassel, some 5km southeast of Kafountine. Another place is the Presqu'île des Oiseaux, a narrow spit of land between the ocean and a creek, noted for its huge populations of Caspian terns. It lies south of the fishing village – most *campements* organise excursions.

---

a hospital and post office, but no bank. Most hotels and *campements* are scattered along a wide, sandy beach, which divides into two areas: the northern strip, reached by turning right on the sandy road as it leads west from the village; and the southern strip that lies on the main road south of Kafountine village. The beachfront is a taxi- or bicycle-worthy 2km from the village. To reach the southern strip, you pass the fishing village, a busy settlement with lines of shacks where fish are dried and smoked, and a beach from where boats are launched.

### Sleeping

**Esperanto** (Chez Eric & Antonella; ☎ 635 6280; esperanto@arc.sn; d CFA10,000, with half board CFA16,500) This relaxed place between the river and sea is a real gem, with bungalows (some family sized) set in a landscaped garden with palm trees and bamboo bridges.

**Le Fouta Djalon** ( ☎ 936 9494; www.casamance.net /foutadjalon; s/d CFA12,000/20,000) The hotel's extensive garden begins right behind a small dune that leads to the beach. The red-brick huts are comfortable and the cosy bar invites relaxed evening drinks.

**Le Kelediang** ( ☎ 542 5385; www.senegambia.net; r per person CFA3200) Enter the forest and soak up the free-spirited, close-to-nature atmosphere of this relaxed Dutch-run establishment. Accommodation is in deliberately basic, but comfy bungalows and the restaurant near the beach serves delicious lunch and dinner.

**Le Bolonga** ( ☎ 994 8515; s/d CFA7500/10,000) This quality place really is as warm and welcoming as the bar-reception in the brick building at the entrance suggests. The young staff go to great lengths to put you at ease and satisfy all your excursion or workshop wishes.

**Campement Sitokoto** ( ☎ 994 8512; r per person incl breakfast CFA4500) Kafountine's *campement villageois* has got basic rooms with clean, shared toilets right near the river.

**La Case de Marie Oldie** ( ☎ 936 9710, 539 2379; s/d CFA3000/4500) This red-brick *case à impluvium* construction is a treat close to Kafountine village. Sunny, clean and friendly – and the rates are unbeatable.

**Le Paradise** ( ☎ télécentre 936 9492; r CFA4000) 'Very Jah', is the going description of this phlegmatic little *campement*. Drumming, smoking, hanging about and philosophising – *voilà* the ambience of this self-declared paradise. The drumming courses get good reviews.

**Á la Nature** ( ☎ 994 8524; alanature@arc.sn; r per person incl breakfast CFA4500) Past the fishing village and pirogue-makers and just above the high-water line, this is Kafountine's famous beachfront venture with a rasta feel. Drumming workshops and hammock-lounging are obligatory.

**Le Saloulou** ( ☎ /fax 994 8514; r per person CFA6000) Fancy it ain't, but it's situated seconds from the surf and offers fishing trips in the sea or *bolongs*.

**Le Bandoula Village** ( ☎ 994 8511; s/d CFA13,000/15,000) A few steps down from the Saloulou, this place is slightly more upmarket, as the fair rates suggest. Not a bad option.

## Eating

Kafountine isn't a gourmet's paradise, and the hotel restaurants are still your safest bet. Esperanto, Fouta Djalon, Le Kelediang and Bandoula Village are among the most reliable. Other good options include **Le Bissap** ( ☎ 994 8512; dishes CFA2000-3000; ☽ 8am-midnight), where food is tasty. You can check your emails and buy your groceries there, too. Alternatively, there are a few cheap eateries in the market offering similar local fare for little money: **Chez Yandé**, **Le Cocotier Café** ( ☽ 8am-midnight) and **Couleur Café** ( ☎ 936 9520; ☽ 8am-midnight) are popular. **Pointe Nord** ( ☽ 11am-2am) is a lively bar. Simple Senegalese meals cost around CFA750 to CFA1500 in all three places.

Self-caterers can stock up in the centre of the village. The **Mini Marché** ( ☽ 9am-11pm) sells a good variety of foodstuffs and is a popular hang out for local youth.

## Entertainment

This is a town full of party-ready inhabitants. The nightclubs are usually packed with dreadlocked youngsters, and often get rowdy as the night wears on. The **Farafina** (admission CFA1500-2000) enjoys the reputation of being the most upmarket, and most expensive place of the lot. **Black and White** (admission CFA1000) and **Chez Pablo** (admission CFA500-1000) are the cheaper alternatives. Additionally, there's a set of bars that have live bands on rotation. They include the Le Kabekel and Le Flamant Rose.

## Getting There & Away

From Ziguinchor, *sept-place* taxis (CFA2500) and minibuses (CFA1700) run directly to Kafountine. Alternatively, take any vehicle to Diouloulou, from where local bush taxis take the rough tarmac road to Kafountine for CFA600.

You can also get bush taxis from Serekunda or Brikama in The Gambia, although direct traffic usually goes via the back roads and the sleepy Darsilami border crossing rather than the main one at Séléti. There's no Senegalese border post, so you might have to return to Séléti to get your passport stamped.

## Getting Around

It's quite a walk from the hotel-lined beachfront to the village centre, and while you can hope for a ride with a friendly local, you're unlikely to come across a taxi. Ask the hotel to call you a cab, it'll set you back around CFA1000 to CFA2000.

### ABÉNÉ

Abéné, a slightly quieter version of Kafountine, lies 6km north on the route to Diouloulou. From the village it's 2km along a sandy track to the beach, past a small craft villa…

SENEGAL

near the junction where a track goes off to the upmarket Le Kalissai Village-Hôtel .

If cycling is more your thing, try the Campement la Belle Danielle in the village centre, where bikes can be hired for CFA2000 per day. The friendly owner is full of suggestions for interesting day trips.

### Sleeping
**Campement la Belle Danielle** ( ☎ 936 9542; r per person CFA2500, with half board CFA6000) Contrary to what the name suggests, this isn't the most beautiful *campement* in town, but without a shadow of a doubt the one that offers the deepest insider knowledge. Manager Mammadou Konta is also the local representative of the tourist board, and can organise pretty much any pick-up and excursion in Casamance and beyond.

**Maison Sunjata** ( ☎ /fax 994 8610; info@senegambia .de; s/d CFA7500/15,000) Located in a well-tended garden, this small German-run place has clean, comfortable rooms with bathrooms shared between two bungalows.

**Le Kossey** ( ☎ 994 8609; r per person CFA5000) The beach begins where the lush garden with its inviting bungalows stops. This place is particularly famous for its rasta drumming parties on New Year's Eve.

**O'Dunbeye Land Ecole de Danse** (Chez Thomas; ☎ 524 9600; www.odunbeyeland.com/fr; r per person CFA2600) There are plenty of drumming and dancing courses in Abéné, this place offers some of the best-quality ones. The ambience is expectedly *artistique*, accommodation basic and the food delicious.

**Le Kalissai Village-Hôtel** ( ☎ 994 8600; www.kal issai.com; s/d CFA28,000/32,000; ✷ ⊜ ) You won't find anything more polished than this luxury establishment. Bungalows and surroundings are as welcoming as you want them to be for the price, and you can even fly here in your privately hired plane (see right). Class.

### Eating
**Chez Vero** ( ☎ 617 1714; meals around CFA3000) is the much-loved auntie of Abéné's restaurant scene. Food has been consistently good for many years now, and is served on a terrace, under the watchful eyes of gaudy Madonnas and griots on the walls. The unpretentious **Afad Snackbar** opposite the Village Artisanal and the nearby **Bistro Café** ( ☎ 634 3532) both serve reasonable fast food. Bistro Café is the more upmarket of the two, with decent pizzas

on the menu (CFA1000 to CFA2000), a well stocked boutique selling batiks and clothes, and the occasional drumming soirée.

### Getting There & Away
All public transport to and from Kafountine stops at the turn-off to Abéné, near a place called Diannah. The village is 2km off the main road, and the beach is a further 2km, which you'll have to walk. A private taxi will set you back CFA2500 to CFA3500. Abéné also has its very own aerodrome, with flights to and from Dakar. Hiring a three-seater aircraft will cost you around CFA280,000 one way. Plane hire is arranged at Le Kalissai Village-Hôtel.

## HAUTE CASAMANCE
### Sédhiou & Kolda
Some 100km east of Ziguinchor, Sédhiou is a tranquil place that sleep-walks through an existence that's rarely disturbed by visitors. From 1900 to 1909, this was the main trading post of the French colonial administration.

The **Hôtel la Palmeraie** ( ☎ 995 1102; philippe .bertrand@apicus.net; s/d CFA20,000/28,000; ✷ ) caters mainly for hunters, though its spectacular palm-grove setting distracts from the hunters' ambience. A short diversion off the smooth tarmac road from Kolda to Carrefour Diaroumé takes you to Sédhiou (bush taxi CFA3500); the turn-off is signposted. There are also bush taxis between Sédhiou and Bounkiling on the Trans-Gambia Hwy (CFA2000).

Kolda's glory lies in its past, the time when this second-largest city of the Casamance used to be the capital of Fouladou, the historical 19th-century Fula kingdom led by the illustrious kings Alpha Molo and his son Musa Molo. Today, it's an unspectacular place, mainly visited by hunters. The prettiest hotel is **Le Firdou** ( ☎ 996 1780; fax 996 1782; s/d CFA14,100/18,700; P ⊜ ), where attractive bungalows sit right on the river in a spacious palm-tree garden. In town, the impressively sized **Hôtel Hobbe** ( ☎ 996 1170; www.hobbe-kolda.com; s/d CFA18,100/22,000; ✷ ⊜ ) again caters mainly for hunters. Rooms are enormous and come with cable TV. **Hôtel Moya** ( ☎ 996 1175; fax 996 1357; s/d from CFA9,800/10,800; ✷ ) is drab, overpriced and run by uniquely unforthcoming management.

Kolda isn't exactly blessed with a thriving restaurant scene or nightlife. Simple meals an be found at **Chez Koumba**, **Chez Bintou**, **La Terasse** and **Darou Salam**. Culinary choices are mainly between your regular Senegalese dishes and brochettes with bread.

From Kolda, it's worth going on a day trip to the spectacular market of **Diaoubé** where traders from across Casamance, The Gambia and Guinea come on Wednesdays to peddle their wares.

Kolda is well-served by public transport. If you head to Ziguinchor, make sure you get into a *sept-place* that takes the route Kolda–Carrefour Diaroumé–Ziguinchor, rather than Kolda–Tanaf–Ziguinchor. The former is a bitumen dream, the latter a potholed promise of breakdowns. The CFA3500 price is the same. A *sept-place* to Vélingara costs CFA2300, to Tambacounda CFA3000. All bush taxis leave from the *gare routière* about 2km outside town on the road to Sédhiou.

# SENEGAL DIRECTORY

## ACCOMMODATION

In this chapter, rates are quoted exclusive of tourist tax. For larger towns, places are organised according to price range: budget hotels (less than US$30 per night), mid-range (between US$30 and US$75 per night) and top end (more than US$75 per night). Dakar has the biggest range of accommodation, though everything is expensive, and there are few budget options. Inland, there are several good rural *campements*, where accommodation is usually in round huts, including the *campements villageois* in the Casamance (see p731) and several upmarket options, particularly in the Siné-Saloum region.

---

**PRACTICALITIES**

- *Focus on Africa* (BBC) often has excellent news stories on Senegal, and is sold in the country.
- If you read French, *Jeune Afrique* and *l'Intelligent* are good sources of political and cultural news.
- The electricity supply in Senegal is 220V. Plugs have two round pins, as in France and continental Europe.
- Senegal uses the metric system.

---

All places charge a tourist tax of CFA600 per person, which usually isn't included in the price. In this book, rates are quoted exclusive of tourist tax.

Some hotels charge by the room, making no difference whether you're alone or sharing, and many have favourable rates for two people sharing. The high season for hotel rates is from around October to May, with extra hikes around Christmas and New Year. During the low season, rates can drop by up to 50%. Some hotels also offer half-board rates, which include breakfast and lunch.

## ACTIVITIES

Most tourists head to Senegal for the beaches, particularly those of the Petite Côte (p701) and Cap Skiring (p732). The main tourist centres have a range of sea-related activities on offer, including sailboarding, kayaking etc. Pirogue journeys are popular, particularly around the mangrove creeks of Siné-Saloum (p705) and Casamance (p725). The boat journeys are often combined with bird-watching – though there's no equivalent in Senegal to Gambia's well-organised network of ornithologists. Fishing, including deep-sea fishing, is possible along the coast, and in Dakar (p688). Along the Petite Côte (p701) diving and surfing are popular.

Some cautious wildlife spotting can be done in Senegal's national parks. In northern Senegal, 'desert tourism', including 4WD tours and windsurfing is possible around Saint-Louis, the Desert de Lompoul and the border areas with Mauritania.

## BOOKS

Most books on Senegal are in French and if you're capable of the tongue, you should read *Sénégal*, Christian Saglio's musings on the country. The author, currently head of Dakar's Institut Français, has spent the greater part of his life in Senegal, where he, among other things, helped conceive the fabulous network of *campements villageois* (see p731) in Casamance in the 1970s.

The stunning *Senegal behind Glass* by Anne-Marie Bouttianaux-Ndiaye contains reproductions of *sous-verre* paintings, from historical to contemporary examples, giving artistic insights into the country's religion and culture (as well as the arts scene). *A Saint in the City* by Allen and Mary Roberts takes a similar approach, discussing the ubiquitous presence of the images of Senegal's great Sufi leader Cheikh Amadou Bamba around urban Dakar. You'll spot them too on your travels – this book explains why. Music lovers should read the amusing *The Music in My Head* by Mark Hudson, which describes the power, influence and everyday realities of modern African music set in a mythical city that is instantly recognisable as Dakar.

## BUSINESS HOURS

Businesses and government offices open from 8am to noon and 2.30pm to 6pm Monday to Friday, and some open from 8am to noon on Saturday. Most banks are open from 8.30am to noon, and 2.30pm to 4.30pm Monday to Friday. Some banks also open until 11am on Saturday mornings. Shops are usually open from 9am to noon, and from 2.30pm to 7pm Monday to Saturday, and very few open from 9am to noon on Sunday.

Most restaurants offer lunch (noon to 2.30pm) and dinner (7pm onwards), and many are closed on Sundays.

For a night out in Dakar, don't even think of leaving the house before midnight, most clubs and bars only get going around 1am.

## CHILDREN

There's little in the way of child-centred activities, though Dakar has a few playgrounds and some children's entertainment, and the national parks and quiet beaches (beware of undertow) are good to visit with kids.

Children are generally welcome, and hotels and restaurants are usually accommodating, rustling up a kid's meal and arranging extra beds (at an extra cost). Babysitting services are rare, and only available in the more upmarket places.

Disposable nappies and baby food are found in the supermarkets and many smaller shops in the larger towns around the country; stock up before heading to the more remote regions. Babies are best carried in a baby-rucksack – it's near impossible to push a pram around anywhere in the country.

## DANGERS & ANNOYANCES

Dakar, particularly the inner city, markets and beaches, is a hotspot of pickpocketing, muggings and scams (see p687), though nowhere near the scale of, let's say, Lagos. Another risk is civil unrest in the Casamance – see p727 for more information).

## EMBASSIES & CONSULATES
### Senegalese Embassies and Consulates
**Belgium** ( ☎ 02 673 0097; senegal.ambassade@coditel .net; 196 Ave Franklin-Roosevelt, Brussels 1050)
**Canada** ( ☎ 613-0238 6392; www.ambassenecanada .org; 57 Marlborough Ave, Ottawa ON K1N)
**France** ( ☎ 01 44 05 38 69; www.ambassenparis.com; 22 Rue Hamelin, 75016 Paris)
**Germany** ( ☎ 022-821 80 08; Argelanderstrasse 3, 53115 Bonn)
**Guinea** ( ☎ 224-409037; Corniche Sud, Coléah, Conakry; 🕐 9am-12.30pm & 1.30-5pm Mon-Fri)
**Guinea-Bissau** ( ☎ 245-21 29 44; 43 Rue Omar Torrijhos, Bissau; 🕐 8am-5pm Mon-Fri)
**Japan** ( ☎ 0464 8451; fax 464 8452; 1-3-4 Aobadai, Meguro-ku Tokyo 153)
**Mali** ( ☎ 223-221 8273; fax 221 1780; off Blvd Nelson Mandela, Bamako; 🕐 7.30am-1pm & 1.30-4pm Mon-Fri)
**Mauritania** ( ☎ 222-525 72 90; Rue de l'Ambassade du Sénégal, Nouakchott)
**Morocco** ( ☎ 07754171; 17 Cadi Ben Hamadi Benhadj, BP 365 Rabat)
**UK** ( ☎ 020-7938 4048; www.senegalembassy.co.uk; 39 Marloes Rd, London W8 6LA)
**USA** ( ☎ 202-2340540; 2112 Wyoming Ave NW, Washington, DC 20008)

In West Africa, Senegal also has embassies in Banjul (The Gambia), Abidjan (Côte d'Ivoire), Freetown (Sierra Leone), Lagos (Nigeria), Niamey (Niger) and Praia (Cape Verde). See the appropriate country chapters for more information.

### Embassies & Consulates in Senegal
If you need to find an embassy that is not listed here, check the phone book, one of the listings magazines, or www.ausenegal.com /practique_en/ambassad.htm. Most of the following embassies are located in Dakar:
**Belgium** (Map p684; ☎ 822 4720; Route de la Corniche-Est)
**Burkina Faso** ( ☎ 827 9509/8; Lot 1, Liberty VI Extension; 🕐 8am-3pm Mon-Fri)
**Canada** (Map p684; ☎ 889 4700; Immeuble Sorano, 4th fl, 45-47 Blvd de la République)
**Cape Verde** (Map p686; ☎ 821 1873; 3 Blvd el Haji Djily Mbaye; 🕐 8.30am-3pm Mon-Fri)
**Côte d'Ivoire** ( ☎ 869 02 70; Rue 7 X G, Point E; 🕐 9am-12.30pm & 3-5pm Mon-Fri)
**France** (Map p686; ☎ 839 5100; 1 Rue Assane Ndoye)
**The Gambia** (Map p686; ☎ 821 7230; 11 Rue de Thiong; 🕐 9am-3pm Mon-Thu & 9am-1pm Fri)
**Germany** (Map p684; ☎ 889 4884; 20 Ave Pasteur)
**Ghana** (Map p691; ☎ 869 4053; Point E)

**Guinea** (Map p691; ☎ 824 8606; Rue 7, Point E; ☾ 9.30am-2pm Mon-Fri) Directly opposite Ker Jaraaf.

**Guinea-Bissau** Dakar ( ☎ 824 5922; Rue 6, Point E; ☾ 8am-12.30pm Mon-Fri); Ziguinchor ( ☎ 991 1046; Rue de France; ☾ 8am-2pm Mon-Fri)

**Italy** (Map p684; ☎ 822 0076; Rue Seydou Nourou Tall)

**Mali** (Map p693; ☎ 824 6252; 23 Route de la Corniche Ouest, Fann; ☾ 8am-11am Mon-Fri)

**Mauritania** (Map p693; ☎ 822 6238; Rue 37, Kolobane; ☾ 8am-2pm Mon-Fri)

**Morocco** (Map p691; ☎ 824 6927; Ave Cheikh Anta Diop, Mermoz) Near the Total petrol station where all the *cars rapides* wait.

**Netherlands** (Map p686; ☎ 849 0360; 37 Rue Kléber)

**Spain** (Map p684; ☎ 842 6408; 18-20 Ave Nelson Mandela)

**Switzerland** (Map p684; ☎ 823 0590; Rue René Ndiaye)

**UK** (Map p684; ☎ 823 7392; 20 Rue du Dr Guillet) One block north of Hôpital Le Dantec.

**USA** (Map p686; ☎ 823 4296; Ave Jean XXIII)

## FESTIVALS & EVENTS

There's always a festival on somewhere in Senegal; some so small and informal that you'll hardly hear about them, others huge, international events.

**Abéné Festivalo** This is an informal affair, mainly featuring drumming troupes of varying standard. Happens every New Year in Abéné.

**Dak'Art Biennale** ( ☎ 823 0918; www.dakart.org) This fantastic arts festival is held in Dakar every two years – one of Africa's best.

**Festival International du Film de Quartier** (www .festivaldufilmdequartier.com) Dakar's best film festival with excellent fringe shows.

**Kaay Fecc** ( ☎ 826 4950; www.ausenegal.com/kaay fecc). One of Africa's best dance festivals. Usually happens around June.

**Saint-Louis Jazz Festival** (www.saintlouisjazz.com) Renowned international jazz festival in a historical setting.

## GAY & LESBIAN TRAVELLERS

Gay sexual relationships are a cultural taboo and the gay scene, which certainly exists in Dakar and other urban centres, isn't very visible. Open displays of affection are generally frowned upon, whatever your sexual orientation, and can be met with downright hostility in the case of same-sex relationships.

## HOLIDAYS

Both Christian and Islamic events are celebrated. The Muslim holidays, such as Korité, Tabaski, Tamkharit and Moulid are determined by the lunar calendar, and occur on different dates each year. 48 days after Islamic New Year, Senegal celebrates the Grand Magal pilgrimage in Touba (p710).

The exact dates of Islamic holidays are only announced just before they occur, as they depend on the sightings of the moon. And occasionally, experts differ in their readings of the moon, which can result in a two-day celebration. See p818 for more information.

Other holidays include the following:

**New Year's Day** 1 January
**Independence Day** 4 April
**Easter Monday** March/April
**Whit Sunday/Pentecost** 7th Sunday after Easter
**Whit Monday** Day after Whit Sunday
**Ascension** 40th day after Easter
**Workers Day** 1 May
**Assumption** August 15
**Christmas Day** 25 December

## INTERNET ACCESS

Senegal is the third-best place in Africa for web services. Connections are usually fast and there are plenty of Internet cafés. The main operator is **sentoo** (www.sentoo.sn), which has a chain of speedy cybercafés around the country.

## INTERNET RESOURCES

**Au-Senegal** (www.au-senegal.com) A fantastically packed information site, with hotel booking facilities and up-to-date cultural and political information.

**Senegal Tourist Office** (www.senegal-tourism.com) Comprehensive tourist site listing attractions, and giving travel and accommodation tips.

**Stanford Site Guide** (www-sul.stanford.edu/depts/ssrg/africa/sene.html) Has links to hundreds of websites about Senegal, both in English and French.

**Senerap** (www.senerap.com) Comprehensive website with news on Senegal's hip-hop scene.

## MAPS

The locally produced *Carte du Senegal* (1:912,000) isn't bad. For Dakar, the colourful street map by **Editions Laure Kane** (www .editionslaurekane) is a must have. It was last updated in 2006.

## MONEY

The currency of Senegal is the West African CFA franc. CFA stands for Communauté Financière Africaine, and is also the official currency of Benin, Burkina Faso, Côte d'Ivoire Guinea-Bissau, Mali, Niger and Togo.

There are notes for CFA500, CFA1000, CFA5000 and CFA10,000. The value of the CFA is tied to the euro at a fixed rate of one euro to CFA655.967.

## ATMs

Banks with ATMs exist in most major towns throughout the country. Visa is the most widely accepted plastic. The withdrawal limit is supposed to be CFA300,000, though some bank branches only allow up to CFA150,000.

## Cash

Euros, US dollars, British pounds and other major currencies can be changed in banks, bureaux de change and hotels. Euros are most widely accepted, and the only currency dealt with outside Dakar. It's best to do all your changing in Dakar before heading into the country.

## Credit Cards

The use of credit cards is limited to top-end hotels, some restaurants, car hire and very few shops. American Express (Amex) and Visa are the most widely accepted. Some banks in the interior of Senegal can give cash advances on credit cards, though readers have reported this being too much hassle to try.

## Moneychangers

All major bank branches change money, and there are a few exchange bureaux in the tourist zones.

## Tipping

In good quality restaurants and hotels you're usually expected to tip, not so in most midrange and budget places. You wouldn't normally tip a taxi driver.

## Travellers Cheques

The major banks in the cities accept travellers cheques grudgingly, but tend to charge high commissions. Forget about changing them upcountry. Only American Express cheques tend to be considered, and the best currency for travellers cheques (as for cash) is euros.

## POST

Senegal's postal service is very reliable. Letters to and from Europe usually take about week, up to 15 days for Australasia. For speedier mail, there are DHL offices in Dakar and other major towns.

The main post office in Dakar has a poste restante facilities, though note that some travellers have reported problems with the service.

## TELEPHONE & FAX

There are plenty of public *télécentres* all around the country, where you can make national and international calls and send faxes. National calls cost CFA60 per minute, and international calls are around CFA500, depending on which country you call. After 8pm, prices fall by 20%.

Mobile coverage is excellent, with even the remotest villages having at least a tiny pocket of reception. Alizé, Sentel and Tigo are the main companies. An Alizé SIM card costs CFA25,000. You top up with prepaid cards, which are sold in units of CFA1000, CFA2500, CFA5000 and CFA10,000.

The country code is ☎ 221. For directory assistance dial ☎ 12.

## TIME

Senegal is at GMT/UTC, which for most European visitors means there is no or very little time difference. There is no daylight savings time.

## TOURIST INFORMATION

Senegal's Syndicat d'Initiative has an office in each of the regions. The main and best branch is in Saint-Louis.
Gorée ( ☎ 823 9177; methiourseye@hotmail.com)
Lac Rose ( ☎ 836 5517; kerkanni@tpsnet.sn)
Saint Louis ( ☎ 961 2455; sltourisme@sentoo.sn)
Saly ( ☎ 957 22 22; bgvsn@yahoo.fr)
Siné-Saloum ( ☎ 948 3140; www.tourismesinesaloum.sn)
Tambacounda ( ☎ 981 1250; nijihotel@sentoo.sn)
Ziguinchor ( ☎ 993 5151; paillote@sentoo.sn)

## VISAS

Visas are not needed by citizens of the EU, Canada, Norway, South Africa, Japan, Israel, USA and some other (mainly African) countries. Tourist visas for one to three months cost about US$15 to US$20. Australians and New Zealanders definitely need a visa.

## Visa Extensions

For extensions, submit a request to the **Ministère de l'Interieur** (Map p684; Place de l'Indépendance, Dakar), who'll give you a receipt, which already gives you right to extended stay. It takes about two weeks for the official letter confirming extension to arrive, which you then present to get your passport stamped.

### Visas for Onward Travel

For onward travel, it's best to get your visa beforehand at the relevant embassy (see p739). Most issue visas within 24 hours. For Mauritania, you can get visas at the border in Rosso. For The Gambia, it's always better to have your visa beforehand, as border officials can be difficult.

## WOMEN TRAVELLERS

While it's not exactly dangerous to travel on your own as a woman in Senegal, you do need to prepare for some low-key hassle and constant advances. If you travel on your own, inventing a husband is a good strategy, and you should also refer to boyfriends as husbands, to gain respect for your relationship.

It's always better to dress more modestly. Short skirts don't do anything to keep trouble away.

Downtown Dakar is a prime 'hunting ground' for *saï-saïs* – guys out to chat up women, either to get you into bed, or cheat you out of money and most probably both. Beware and shake them off with a firm but polite *bakhna* (meaning OK, it's alright) or by simply ignoring them.

Beaches are prime hassle zones, and the areas where female readers report the most irritating, sometimes downright threatening advances.

Very few women become the victims of physical harm or rape. And if you follow some common sense ground rules – don't stroll along deserted beaches or dark city roads alone, don't hitchhike or accept rides with cars full of drunken men – you're unlikely to get into serious trouble.

# TRANSPORT IN SENEGAL

## GETTING THERE & AWAY
### Entering Senegal

A full passport is essential for entering Senegal. If you enter from within the region, you'll also need to show a yellow fever vaccination certificate. Border checks are usu-

ally pain free, and the Dakar airport is very organised.

### Air

Senegal's main airport is the easily negotiated **Aéroport International Léopold Sédar Senghor** (DKR; ☎ 869 50 50, 24hr information line 628 1010; www.aeroportdakar.com) in Yoff, 30 minutes from central Dakar. The airports of **Saint-Louis** ( ☎ 961 14 90) and **Cap Skiring** ( ☎ 993 51 77) also have connections to Dakar and Paris.

The national carrier is **Air Sénégal International** ( ☎ 804 0404, in France 0820 202 123; www.air-senegal-international.com), one of the most reliable airlines in Africa.

Airlines servicing Senegal and with offices in Dakar include the following:

**Air Algérie** (AH; ☎ 823 2964; www.airalgerie.dz) Hub: Algiers.

**Air CM** ( ☎ in France 01 53 41 00 50; mail.aircom@wannadoo.fr) Has a twice-weekly connection between Paris and Cap Skiring and plenty of good package deals.

**Air France** (Map p686; AF; ☎ 823 2964; www.airfrance.fr; Ave Albert Sarraut) Hub: Paris, Charles de Gaulle.

**Air Guinée** (Map p686; 2U; ☎ 821 4442; www.mirinet.com/airguinee; 25 Ave Pompidou) Hub: Conakry.

**Air Ivoire** (VU; ☎ 889 0280; www.airivoire.com) Hub: Abidjan.

**Air Mali** (Map p686; XG; ☎ 823 2461; 14 Rue El Haji M'Baye Guèye) Hub: Bamako.

**Air Portugal** (Map p686; TP; ☎ 821 5460; www.tap.pt) Hub: Lisbon.

**Air Sénégal International** (V7; ☎ 804 0404; www.air-senegal-international.com; 45 Ave Albert Sarraut) Hub: Dakar.

**Alitalia** (Map p686; AZ; ☎ 823 3874; www.alitalia.com; 5 Ave Pompidou) Hub: Rome.

**Ethiopian Airlines** (ET; ☎ 821 32 98; www.flyethiopian.com/et/; 16, Ave Léopold Sédar Senghor) Hub: Addis Ababa.

**Iberia** (Map p686; IB; ☎ 889 0050; www.iberia.com; 2 Place de l'Indépendance) Hub: Madrid.

**Kenya Airways** (KQ; ☎ in Nairobi 020 3274747; www.kenya-airways.com) Hub: Nairobi.

**Royal Air Maroc** (Map p686; AT; ☎ 849 4747; www.royalairmaroc.com; 1 Place de l'Indépendance) Hub: Casablanca.

**SN Brussels** (Map p686; SN; ☎ 823 0460; www.flysn.com; Immeuble Fayçal, Rue Parchappe) Hub: Brussels.

**South African Airways** (Map p686; SA; ☎ 823 0151; www.flysaa.com; 12 Ave Albert Sarraut) Hub: Johannesburg

**TACV Cabo Verde Airlines** (Map p686; VR; ☎ 821 3968; www.tacv.cv; 105 Rue Moussé Diop) Hub: Praia, Cape Verde.

**TAP Air Portugal** (Map p686; ☎ 821 0065; Rue Amadou Assane Ndoye) Hub: Lisbon.

**Virgin Nigeria** (VK; ☎ 4600505; www.virginnigeria .com) Hub: Lagos.

## Land

### GAMBIA

See p326 for details.

### GUINEA

Nearly all traffic between Senegal and Guinea goes to/from Labé, a town in northwestern Guinea. The busiest route is via Koundara, but some transport also goes via Kedougou (in the far southeast of Senegal) and the small town of Mali (usually called Mali-ville, to distinguish it from the country of the same name). Tambacounda has connections almost every day. From Kedougou, your best chances to find transport are on a Friday, though at least one car might leave most other days. Another popular jumping-off point is Diaoubé near Kolda. Wednesday, the day of the Diaoubé *lumo* is the best day to get transport here. Fares to Guinea are around CFA15,000 from all these places, and the trip can take up to 48 hours as routes are bad and Guinean roadblocks tedious to pass.

### GUINEA-BISSAU

Bush taxis run several times daily between Ziguinchor and Bissau (CFA6000, 147km) via São Domingos (the border) and Ingore. The road is in fairly good condition, but the ferries on the stretch between Ingore and Bissau can make the trip take anything from four to eight hours. Occasionally the São Domingos border closes due to suspected rebel activity (see the boxed text, p727). Other options are to go from Tanaf to Farim or from Tambacounda via Vélingara to Gabú.

### MALI

You can take the train, or a *sept-place* from Dakar via Tambacounda to Kidira (CFA5000, three hours, 184km) where border crossings are reportedly hassle-free. In Kidira, you cross the bridge to Diboli, from where bush taxis go on a washed-out road to Kayes (CFA3000). From Kayes to Bamako, both train and taxi are equally good (or bad) options.

### MAURITANIA

The main border point is at Rosso, where a ferry (free for passengers, CFA2000 for a car and CFA3000 for a 4WD) crosses the Senegal River. It's been announced that a bridge is supposed to replace the boat service within the next few years, but work hadn't started when this book went to press.

Dakar–Rosso by *sept-place* taxi is CFA5100 (six hours, 384km), from Saint-Louis CFA2000 (two hours, 106km).

The only other option is the Maka Diama barrage, 97km southwest of Rosso and just north of Saint-Louis, but there's no proper road. The crossing here costs CFA5000/10,000 in winter/summer.

## River & Sea

If you're feeling brave, you can take a pirogue from the Siné-Saloum region to Banjul in The Gambia. Note that these aren't particularly safe and the ride can be very rocky.

The most common departure points are Djifer, where a place in an often overpriced pirogue costs CFA5000, and the trip takes around six hours. From Betenti, there's an almost daily pirogue to Banjul (CFA1500, three hours) that leaves around 8am.

A regular boat service between Banjul and Dakar had ceased at the time of writing, though it was rumoured that the route was supposed to be reopened.

## Train

The Dakar–Bamako train is something of a traveller's classic. In theory, trains run between Dakar and Bamako twice a week in each direction and the trip takes about 35 hours. In practice, this almost never happens – one train is often out of action, the trip usually takes 40 hours or longer, and derailments are frequent. Inquire about the situation at Dakar train station before setting of, and once on the train, watch out for pickpockets.

## GETTING AROUND
### Air

**Air Sénégal International** ( ☎ 804 0404; www.air -senegal-international.com) has flights from Dakar to Saint-Louis, Ziguinchor, Cap Skiring and Tambacounda, though only those to Ziguinchor (once or twice daily, return fare CFA80,600) operate with complete regularity. Flights to Cap Skiring (Friday and Sunday, return fare CFA110,600) and Saint-Louis (Wednesday, return fare CFA70,000) operate only from November to April, and the two flights that fly from Dakar to Tambacounda every Saturday seem pretty irregular.

To Ziguinchor or Cap Skiring, flights are particularly worth considering, as reaching the Casamance by road involves either tedious border crossings in The Gambia, or a seemingly endless tour via Tambacounda around The Gambia.

Other companies include the following:

**Air Saint Louis** ( ☎ 644 8629; www.airsaintlouis.com) Flights from Dakar to Saint-Louis.

**Le Kalissai Village-Hôtel** ( ☎ 994 8600; www.kalissai .com) Arranges flights from the aerodrome in Abéné to Dakar.

**Senegalair Avion Taxis** ( ☎ 821 3425) Flies mainly to Simenti in Parc National du Niokolo-Koba, though it can also arrange flights elsewhere.

## Bicycle

Senegal's flat savannah landscape is great for cycling, but there are a few things to consider. Roads are in poor condition, and often sandy. The bigger problem, however, is the drivers, who simply aren't used to cyclists, which makes cycling potentially very risky. The best place to hire bikes is Casamance VTT in Oussouye (see p731). Kedougou and the region around Saint-Louis are also particularly good for biking.

## Boat

By far the most important boat service in Senegal is the *Wilis*, which connects Dakar twice weekly to Ziguinchor in the Casamance, see p730.

In some areas, including Ndangane, N'Gor, Elinkine and Affiniam, pirogues are used as public transport. It's always possible to hire a pirogue for an excursion (particularly in the Casamance and Siné-Saloum regions), though it can get expensive. If you go to Île de Gorée or Foundiougne, you need to cross by ferry – these services are safe and reliable.

Major leisure boat options include the tours of the Bou El Mogdad from Saint-Louis to Podor, and the trips of the African Queen around the Petite Côte.

**Africa Queen** (West Africa Sportsfishing; ☎ 957 7435; Saly) Tours off the Petite Côte.

**Bou El Mogdad** ( ☎ 961 5689; www.saheldecouverte .com) One- to four-day cruise trips along the Senegal River can be booked through Sahel Découverte Bassari in Saint-Louis (see p714).

## GORÉE FERRY TIMETABLE

### DEPARTING FROM GORÉE

| Monday to Saturday | Sundays & Holidays |
| --- | --- |
| 6.45am | 7.30am |
| 8am | 9.30am |
| 10.30am | 10.30am |
| noon | 12.30pm |
| 2pm | 2.30pm |
| 3pm | 4.30pm |
| 4.30pm | 5.30pm |
| 6.30pm | 7pm |
| 7pm | 8pm |
| 8.30pm | 9pm |
| 11pm | 11pm |
| 11.30pm | midnight |

### DEPARTING FROM DAKAR

| Monday to Saturday | Sundays & Holidays |
| --- | --- |
| 6.15am | 7am |
| 7.30am | 9am |
| 10am | 10am |
| 11am | noon |
| 12.30pm | 2pm |
| 2.30pm | 4pm |
| 4pm | 5pm |
| 5pm (*) | 6.30pm |
| 6.30pm | 7pm |
| 8pm | 8.30pm |
| 10.30pm | 10.30pm |
| (*) except Sat | |

**Gorée Ferry** ( ☎ 24hr infoline 628 1111, 849 7961) Ferries travel 11 times daily between Dakar and Île de Gorée. The first ferry leaves at 6.15am, the last return from Gorée is at 11pm. The trip takes 20 minutes.

**Willis** ( ☎ 889 8009, 889 8060/51) Departs from Dakar every Tuesday and Friday at 7pm, returns from Ziguinchor every Sunday and Thursday at 2pm. Tickets start from CFA15,500.

## Bus, Bush Taxi & Minibus

Senegal's long-distance bus network is fairly good, punctual and cheap – though slow and not exactly comfortable. Buses are owned and operated by members of the Mouride brotherhood, hence they're known as *cars mourides*. These go from Dakar to most major towns in the country. In Dakar they leave from the Shell station at Ave Malick Sy near *gare routière* Sapeurs-Pompiers (just referred to as Pompiers), usually in the mid dle of the night. You have to book your seat in advance, best by going there in person.

'Bush taxi' is the generic term for all public transport smaller than a big bus. The most common forms include Ndiaga Ndiayes, large white Mercedes busses that usually have 'Alhamdoulilai' printed across the front, minibuses (usually Nissan Urvans) carrying 20 people, and *sept-place* taxis. These are seven-seaters, usually Peugeot 504s, that are also referred to as brake or *cinq-cent-quatre*. *Sept-place* taxis are always the most comfortable and fastest option. They cost around 20% more than Ndiaga Ndiayes. In some remote areas, however, Ndiaga Ndiayes, minibuses, or even pick-up trucks, might be your only option.

Bush taxis leave when they're full, and they fill up fastest in the morning, from 6.30am or earlier to 8.30am. In remote locations, your best chance for transport is on market days, when people will be heading to the market town (or village) in the early morning and returning in the evening.

## Car & Motorcycle

No cars older than five years may be imported to Senegal. You need an international driving licence to drive or hire a car in Senegal. Most hire companies request a minimum age of 23.

Car hire is generally expensive. By the time you've added up the costs, you can easily end up paying over US$1000 per week. In Senegal all the international names (Hertz, Avis, Budget etc) are represented, and there are also smaller independent operators. Dakar is the best place for car hire (see p695 for contact details).

It usually works out better hiring a *sept place* with its driver. To work out the cost of a journey, multiply the number of seats by the fare and add some extra, particularly for waiting times, and you've got your estimated price.

## Tours

Most places of interest in Senegal can be reached by public transport or car, but if you're short of time you could get around the country on an organised tour. A small selection of operators based in and around Dakar is included here.

**M'boup Voyages** (Map p686; ☎ 821 8163; mboup@telecomplus.sn; Place de l'Indépendance) One of the most enduring agencies with tours to the major destinations

**Origin Africa** (☎ 860 1578; origin@sentoo.sn; Cité Africa, Ouakam) One of the more interesting tour operators in Senegal, with plenty of tours to destinations less frequently covered.

**Pain de Singe** (Map p684; ☎ 824 2484; paindesinge@arc.sn) Absolutely original, this tiny operation runs excellent, eco-oriented tours, including trips to the marine reserve at Bamboung, Casamance and plenty of other off-the-beaten track destinations.

**Sahel Découverte Bassari** (Map p686; ☎ 842 8751; bassari@bassarisenegal.com, carresahel@sentoo.sn; 7 Rue Delmas) The tours in northern Senegal are particularly good. It caters well for Spanish speakers.

**Senegal Tours** (Map p686; ☎ 839 9900; fax 823 2644; 5 Place de l'Indépendance) One of the largest operators.

**TPA** (☎ 644 9491; 957 1256; tpa@sentoo.sn; www .lesenegal.info) A tour operator with a difference. The leading agency for 'bush tourism', with excellent tours around the lesser travelled routes, including trips to its remote *campements* in Lompoul, Simal and Palmarin (Siné-Saloum).

# Sierra Leone

Sierra Leone has largely stayed out of the news lately, which, considering how it earned most of its press in the 1990s, is a good thing. The decade-long civil war garnered regular headlines thanks to widespread atrocities committed by rebel soldiers; many of them not yet in their teens.

But oh, how things have changed. Peace was declared in 2002 and Sierra Leone has blossomed. Life has largely returned to normal and today it is one of West Africa's safest destinations. Reconstruction continues apace, investors are arriving in droves and travellers are trickling in.

With some of the most perfect palm-lined sands on the continent, it won't be long before Sierra Leone takes its place in Europe's packaged beach-holiday scene; but for now, visitors can have the surf outside the capital pretty much to themselves. And after a day in the sun, Freetown offers everything you need for a night out. Travel to the provinces, where roads are often abysmal and facilities usually basic, remains in the realm of the adventurous, but with vibrant culture and wonderful parks, the rewards are many.

To be sure, Sierra Leone still has problems. It ranked second last in the UN's most recent Human Development Index, unemployment remains high and the education system hasn't met expectations, but most locals hang on to their optimism.

## FAST FACTS

- **Area** 72,325 sq km
- **Capital** Freetown
- **Telephone code** ☎ 232
- **Famous for** Diamonds
- **Languages** English, Krio, Mende and Temne
- **Money** leone (Le); US$1 = Le2925; €1 = Le3475; CFA1 = Le5.3
- **Population** 6 million (2005)
- **Visa** Available at airport and borders, but best bought before arrival.

# HIGHLIGHTS

- **Beach bumming** (p760) Relax on the Freetown peninsula.
- **Tiwai Island** (p763) Primate-watching at the famous wildlife sanctuary.
- **Outamba-Kilimi National Park** (p766) Track big mammals at Sierra Leone's only national park.
- **Freetown** (p758) Discover the anything-goes nightlife.
- **Bonthe** (p763) Explore the remote coastal waters and islands.

# ITINERARIES

- **One week** Many people spend their whole week at the beaches. Although it might be hard to pull yourself off the sand, it's worth taking a few days upcountry to visit **Tiwai Island Wildlife Sanctuary** (p763) and a town or two. If you are here for the wildlife you can get to both Tiwai Island Wildlife Sanctuary and **Outamba-Kilimi National Park** (p766) and still have a day at the beach.
- **Two weeks** In two weeks you can see most of the country without travelling too fast. It also gives you enough time to add scaling **Mt Bintumani** (p767) to your itinerary.
- **One month** A month is enough time to see and do just about everything in this chapter.

# CLIMATE & WHEN TO GO

Sierra Leone is one of West Africa's wettest and hottest countries, with an average annual rainfall of 3150mm and temperature of 27°C (see climate charts p813). The rainy season stretches from mid-May to mid-November, with July and August the wettest months. The humidity can be oppressive along the coast, although sea breezes afford some relief. Inland, the days are even hotter, but it cools down much more at night, especially in Kabala and other northwest towns.

The best time to visit is November, after the rains and before the dusty harmattan winds blow in and paint the skies grey. During the rainy season, washed out roads make travel to some destinations difficult or impossible, though there are some sunny days at the beginning and end. The further you go into the dry season the more heat you'll have to endure and the less green you'll see in the countryside.

---

**HOW MUCH?**

- **Small Temne basket** Le5000
- **100km bush taxi ride** Le15,000
- **Bottle of palm wine** Le600
- **2 lapa (about 4 sq yds) of gara cloth** Le25,000
- **A night at a music show** Free

**LONELY PLANET INDEX**

- **1L of petrol** Le2500
- **1.5L of bottled water** Le2500
- **Bottle of Star beer** Le2000
- **Souvenir T-shirt** Le15,000
- **Fry fry with egg** Le800

---

# HISTORY

The region now called Sierra Leone was on the southern edge of the great Empire of Mali, which flourished between the 13th and 15th centuries (for more details on the early history of the region, see p30). Early inhabitants included the Temne, the Sherbro and the Limba, who were organised into independent chiefdoms. Mandingo/Malinké traders had also entered the region early on and integrated with indigenous peoples.

## European Contact

Contact with Europeans began in 1462 with the arrival of Portuguese navigators who called the area Serra Lyoa (Lion Mountain), which was later modified to Sierra Leone. Around 120 years later, Sir Francis Drake stopped here during his voyage around the world; however, the British did not control the area until the 18th century when they began to dominate the slave trade along the West African coast.

The American War of Independence in the 1770s provided an opportunity for thousands of slaves to gain freedom by fighting for Britain. When the war ended, over 15,000 ex-slaves made their way to London, where they suffered unemployment and poverty. In 1787 a group of philanthropists purchased 52 sq km of land near Bunce Island in present-day Sierra Leone from a local chief for the purpose of founding

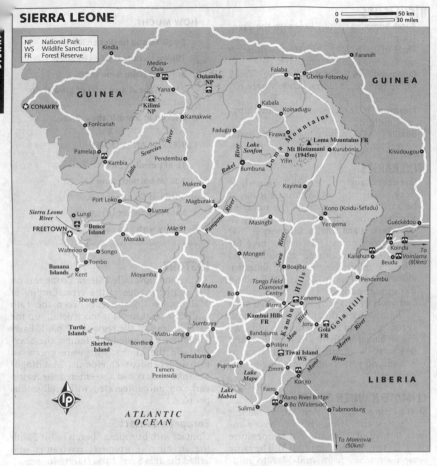

## SIERRA LEONE

| | | 0 — 50 km |
| | | 0 — 30 miles |

| NP | National Park |
| WS | Wildlife Sanctuary |
| FR | Forest Reserve |

a 'Province of Freedom' for the ex-slaves. This became Freetown. That same year, the first group of about 400 men and women (300 ex-slaves and 100 Europeans, mainly prostitutes) arrived.

Within three years all but 48 settlers had deserted or had died from disease or in fights with the local inhabitants. But in 1792 the determined British philanthropists sent a second band of settlers, this time 1200 ex-slaves who had fled from the USA to Nova Scotia. Later, they sent 550 more from Jamaica. To the chagrin of the philanthropists, some settlers, both white and black, joined in the slave trade. In 1808 the British government took over the Freetown settlement and declared it a colony.

## The Colonial Period

By the early 1800s, slavery had been abolished in Britain. Over the next 60 years British ships plied the West African coast, trying to intercept slave ships destined for America. Freetown became the depot for thousands of 'recaptives' from West Africa, as well as many migrants from the hinterland. By 1850 over 100 ethnic groups were represented in the colony. They lived in relative harmony, each group in a different section of town.

Like the previous settlers, the recaptives became successful traders and intermarried. All nonindigenous blacks became collectively known as Krios. British administrators favoured the Krios and appointed many to senior posts in the civil service.

Near the end of the 19th century, the tide began to turn against the Krios, who were outnumbered 50 to one by indigenous people, and in 1924 the British administrators established a legislative council with elected representatives, to the advantage of the more numerous indigenous people. Many Krios, who monopolised positions within the civil service, reacted by allying with the British. While other colonies clamoured for independence, they proclaimed loyalty to the Crown, and one group even petitioned against the granting of independence.

## Independence

At independence in 1961, it seemed that Western-style democracy would work. There were two parties of equal strength, but they became divided along ethnic lines. The Sierra Leone People's Party (SLPP) was the party of the Mendes (the dominant ethnic group in southern Sierra Leone) and represented the tribal structure of the old colony. The All People's Congress (APC), formed by trade unionist Siaka Stevens, became identified with the Temnes of the north and voiced the dissatisfaction of the small modernising elite. The Krio community threw its support behind the SLPP, whose leader, Milton Margai, became the first prime minister.

Following Margai's death in 1964, his brother Albert took over and set about replacing the Krios in the bureaucracy with Mendes. The Krios took revenge in the 1967 elections by supporting the APC, which won a one-seat majority. A few hours after the results were announced, a Mende military officer led a coup, placing Siaka Stevens under house arrest. Two days later fellow officers staged a second coup, vowing to end the corruption that was so widespread under the Margai brothers.

Stevens went into exile in Guinea and with a group of Sierra Leoneans began training in guerrilla warfare techniques for an invasion. This became unnecessary when a group of private soldiers mutinied and staged a third coup 13 months later – an African record for the number of coups in such a short period.

## The Downward Spiral

Stevens returned and formed a new government, but his first decade in office was turbulent. He declared a state of emergency, banned breakaway parties from the APC and put a number of SLPP members on trial for treason. Meanwhile, the economy continued to deteriorate. The iron-ore mine closed, diamond revenues dropped, living costs increased, students rioted and Stevens again declared a state of emergency. The 1978 election campaign almost became a civil war, and the death toll topped 100. Stevens won, and Sierra Leone became a one-party state.

Despite the one-party system, the 1982 elections were the most violent ever. Stevens was forced to give Mendes and Temnes equal representation in the cabinet, although this did not stop the deterioration of economic and social conditions. With virtually no support left, Stevens finally stepped down in 1985 at the age of 80, naming as his successor Major General Joseph Momoh, head of the army since 1970.

Under Momoh, the economy continued its downward spiral. By 1987 the inflation rate was one of the highest in Africa, budget deficits were astronomical, and smugglers continued to rob Sierra Leone of up to 90% of its diamond revenue.

Things worsened in late 1989 when civil war broke out in neighbouring Liberia. By early 1990, thousands of Liberian refugees had fled into Sierra Leone. The following year, fighting spilled across the border and the Revolutionary United Front (RUF), Sierra Leonean rebels who were opposed to Momoh, took over much of the eastern part of the country.

## The Difficult Decade

The Momoh government used the war in the east as an excuse to postpone elections, but finally, in September 1991, a new constitution was adopted to allow for a multiparty system. Before an election date could be announced, though, a group of young military officers overthrew Momoh in April 1992. The National Provisional Ruling Council (NPRC) was set up, and 27-year-old Captain Valentine Strasser was sworn in as head of state. Elections and a return to civilian rule were promised for 1995.

Soon, though, optimism began to fade. A major drain on resources was the continuing fighting in the east against the RUF, which expanded its control over the diamond-producing areas, robbing the government of a wealth of revenue. They were bolstered after

…e coup by supporters of the Momoh regime and by escaping rebels from Liberia. It soon became apparent that none of these groups was fighting for a political objective, but rather their goal was to control the diamond and gold fields. By late 1994 northern and eastern parts of the country had descended into near anarchy, with private armies led by local warlords, government soldiers, rebel soldiers and deserters from the Sierra Leonean and Liberian armies roaming the area at will and terrorising local communities.

In January 1996 Brigadier General Julius Maada Bio overthrew Strasser in a coup. Despite NPRC efforts to postpone them, previously scheduled elections went ahead, and in March, Ahmed Tejan Kabbah – the leader of the SLPP – was elected president. Kabbah's government continued peace talks with the RUF, which had been initiated by the previous military government, but his efforts bore little fruit.

## The Rise of the RUF

On 25 May 1997, a group of junior military officers sympathetic to the RUF staged a coup in Freetown. President Kabbah fled to neighbouring Guinea, and a wave of looting, terror and brutality engulfed the capital. Guerrilla warfare spread throughout much of the country, perpetrated by the RUF and the occupying junta. By early 1998 there were few areas that had not been affected. Food and fuel supplies were scarce almost everywhere, and thousands of Sierra Leoneans had fled the country.

In February 1998 a Nigerian-led West African peacekeeping force, Ecomog (Ecowas Monitoring Group), succeeded in ousting the junta and in taking control of Freetown and many upcountry areas – although not before fleeing rebels had looted and destroyed much in their path. President Kabbah was reinstated in March, but the situation refused to stabilise. On 6 January 1999, with nearly a quarter of the entire Nigerian military serving in Sierra Leone, the RUF staged its boldest assault yet on Freetown, code-named Operation No Living Thing. In the ensuing weeks the city was virtually destroyed and over 6000 people killed before Ecomog again forced the rebels from the capital.

The bloody battle prompted the government to sign the controversial Lomé Peace Agreement with the RUF on 7 July 1999. Under the agreement, the RUF leader Foday Sankoh was to become the country's vice-president and the cabinet minister in charge of diamond production, but over the next year the RUF repeatedly violated the agreement. In May, shortly after his soldiers shot and killed 19 anti-RUF demonstrators, Sankoh was arrested for plotting a coup.

## Sierra Leone Today

As part of the Lomé Peace Agreement, the UN deployed a peacekeeping mission, Unamsil, in Sierra Leone that became the largest and most expensive ever deployed by the body. Unamsil's disarmament of the RUF (over 40,000 firearms were destroyed) finished in February 2002, officially ending the war. Elections held that May garnered an 80% turnout and were deemed Sierra Leone's most fair and trouble-free in years. Kabbah was re-elected to a five-year term, while the RUF's political party didn't win a single seat in parliament. That summer an independent war crimes court and a Truth and Reconciliation Commission began and by autumn Unamsil began reducing its 17,500 personnel.

The only hitch in the country's new stability occurred on 13 January 2003, when Johnny Paul Koroma, a member of parliament and one of the 1997 coup leaders, organised an unsuccessful break-in at a Freetown armoury. He fled to Liberia, where unconfirmed reports claimed he died. Sankoh died of natural causes soon after. The first local elections in over 30 years were held in 2004 and the Special Court for Sierra Leone also issued its first indictments. The 11 people charged so far include leaders from all sides of the conflict, as well as former Liberian president Charles Taylor. The last Unamsil soldiers left Sierra Leone at the end of 2005 and were replaced by Uniosl, the United Nations Integrated Office for Sierra Leone, which will promote government accountability, reinforce human rights, oversee development, and prepare the nation for the 2007 elections.

## THE CULTURE
### National Psyche

When Sierra Leoneans get together, whether they're the best of friends or strangers thrown together in a *poda-poda* (minibus), talk always seems to turn to politics, development and corruption – the three largely being one and the same in Sierra Leone.

With elections coming up in 2007, people need to decide whether the ruling SLPP deserves more time to confront what everyone agrees are difficult problems, or if a changing of the guard will speed up the pace.

Though people will argue their points vigorously, they can still share a laugh with those taking the other side. The war did a lot to foster nationalism: everyone knows they are in the same boat and politicians of all stripes get chastised for the sluggish progress. But a line is being drawn between those who only see rough seas ahead and others who fear a sinking ship. Sierra Leone was awash with optimism coming out of the war, but four years on, people see few improvements in their country or their lives and a growing number are feeling tired and hopeless.

## Daily Life

The Mendes and Temnes operate a system of secret societies responsible for maintaining culture and tradition. If you see young children with their faces painted white, you'll know that they're in the process of being initiated. Masks are an important feature of some groups' ceremonies.

## Population

Sierra Leone is one of the more densely populated countries in West Africa. The two largest of the 18 indigenous tribal groups, the Temnes of the north and Mendes of the south, each comprise about one-third of the population. Other groups include the Limba and Koranko in the north, the Kissi in the east and the Sherbro in the southwest.

Krios, most living in Freetown, constitute less than 2% of the population but a large percentage of the intellectuals and professionals. There are significant numbers of Mandingo/Malinké and Fula/Peul in the north and east. For more information about the Fula and Malinké people, see p75 and p76. Nearly 50,000 Liberian refugees still live in the south. About 4000 Lebanese, 500 Indians and 2000 Europeans reside here permanently, while the profusion of aid workers has made Freetown a very multicultural city.

## SPORT

World football is more popular than the local club competition. Some even talk of erecting a giant TV screen at Freetown's stadium to show English Premiership games as a way to get more people to come watch their local teams.

Cricket matches have recently returned to the country's dusty pitches and many ex-combatants have been recruited to the teams as a way of bringing both sides together in 'gentlemanly conduct'. The national team occasionally plays other former British colonies in Africa.

Parasports, naturally, have come to Sierra Leone and the Single-leg Amputee Sports Club plays in many international football tournaments.

## RELIGION

The most recent figures available (which are very outdated) show that Muslims, who are concentrated in the north and east, comprise about 60% of the population. Christians, mainly Anglican, Methodist and a growing number of evangelicals, make up 30%, with the remainder adhering to traditional religions. But in recent years there have been many Muslim converts to Christianity, so the current breakdown is unclear. Additionally, traditional beliefs remain close to the heart of many Christians and Muslims.

## ARTS
### Textiles & Craftwork

Sierra Leone is known for its fabrics, especially country cloth and gara. Country cloth is a coarse material woven from wild cotton into narrow strips that are joined to make blankets and clothing, then coloured with natural dyes. Gara is a thin cotton material, tie-dyed or batik-printed, usually with bright synthetic colours. As you'll see in most hotels, it makes excellent bedding.

The Mendes produce the country's best-known masks. These are often used in initiation ceremonies of the women's bundu (secret societies). Another traditional craft is the distinctive Temne basketry, made in the north of Sierra Leone but available throughout the country.

### Music & Dance

Sierra Leone's main contribution to the world of music is palm-wine music, known locally as maringa, which merged the acoustic guitars introduced by Portuguese sailors with Caribbean Calypso brought back by freed slaves. Maringa strongly influenced West African music, but has been on the decline nce its best-known exponent, SE Rogie, who crooned with a country twang even before moving to the US, passed away in 1994. For more about the music scene see p58.

When they're not on tour in Europe, you can stop by to watch the Sierra Leone Dance Troupe practise at Freetown's Cultural Village on weekday mornings from 9am to about noon. On the village level, Sierra Leone's traditional dances are some of the most animated in West Africa, though opportunities for watching them are rare. Independence Day is your best bet. The Mende society is one of the few where women do masked dances.

### Literature

The narrator of *Moses, Citizen & Me*, by Delia Jarrett-Macauley, must deal with the fact that her cousin is an eight-year-old child soldier. Uzodinma Iweala's *Beasts of No Nation* is a more visceral look at child soldiers. Graham Greene's classic *The Heart of the Matter* goes back to colonial times, where Freetown is the setting for a tale of human weakness, waste and frustration. He wrote it while staying at the ruined City Hotel while working for the British Colonial Service in WWII. Richard Dooling's *White Man's Grave,* the story of the search for a missing Peace Corps worker, was a 1994 National Book Award finalist. On the local scene it is hard to find Sierra Leonean authors, even though many are published. The book vendors in downtown Freetown, on Garrison and Lightfoot Boston Sts, won't have any local books in stock, but can find some for you. Dozens of poets share their work at www.sierra-leone.org/poetry.html.

### Cinema

*Amistad* (1997) tells the story of Mende slaves, led by Sengby Pieh, who in 1839 revolted to obtain their freedom while being shipped from one Cuban port to another. The Amistad case so fuelled anti-slavery feelings in the USA that it became one of the catalysts of the American Civil War and, later, Sierra Leone's drive for independence. The Hollywood rumour mill says Leonardo DiCaprio will soon star in *The Blood Diamond,* a thriller set in 1999 Sierra Leone.

Two documentaries worth seeking out are *The Refugee All Stars* (2004), an inspiring story of the eponymous band, and the harrowing *Cry Freetown* (1999), featuring first-hand footage from Operation No Living Thing.

## ENVIRONMENT
### The Land

The coastal zone, consisting of mangrove swamps, beaches and islands, is flat except for the 40km-long Freetown peninsula – one of the few places in West Africa where mountains rise near the sea – where some peaks top 600m. Inland is an undulating, forested and extensively cultivated plateau. In the northeast are the Loma Mountains where Mt Bintumani (1945m) is one of the tallest peaks in West Africa.

### Wildlife

Much of the country's wildlife was killed or displaced to calmer regions during the war, but crocodiles, chimpanzees, bongos, buffalos, hippopotamuses, elephants, leopards and lions all hung on and are slowly recovering, especially the primates. Birdlife is much richer and grey parrots, great blue turacos, brown-cheeked hornbills, rufous fishing-owls and Sierra Leone prinias are some of over 650 recorded species. In October and November humpback whale sightings off the Freetown peninsula are reliable.

### National Parks

The government has established 21 parks and reserves, covering 4% of the country, though most are protected more by proclamation than practice. Tiwai Island Wildlife Sanctuary is one of the best places in Africa to see primates, while Outamba-Kilimi National Park is good for large mammals. Sierra Leone's last remaining virgin rainforest covers the Gola Hills in southeastern Sierra Leone. Some hope that the present Gola Forest Reserve, home to many chimpanzees, can become a national park. Protected by its remoteness, the highland rainforest of the Loma Mountains Forest Reserve, surrounding Mt Bintumani, is very pristine. Bird-watchers come to Kambui Hills Forest Reserve just outside Kenema for the near-guaranteed sightings of white-necked rockfowl.

### Environmental Issues

Most of Sierra Leone's original forest cover has been destroyed by logging, mining and unsustainable agricultural practices; only about 5% remains today. Population pressures, exacerbated by returned refugees, threatens what remains. Rapid development in the hills above Freetown has begun causing flooding problems down below. Diamond mining is polluting the Sewa River and gold mining is draining the sacred Lake Sonfon.

## FOOD & DRINK

Sierra Leone is known for its cuisine and every town has at least one *cookery* (basic eating house) serving tasty, filling chop (meals). Rice is the staple and *plasas* (pounded potato or cassava leaves, cooked with palm oil and fish or beef) is the most common sauce. Other typical dishes are okra sauce, palm-oil stew, groundnut stew, pepper soup and, for special occasions, jollof rice. Street-food favourites include roasted groundnuts and corn; fried chicken, plantains and dough balls; *suya* sticks (spiced beef or chicken on a kebab skewer); and fry fry (simple sandwiches). Every town of any size also has a choice of Lebanese restaurants, while Freetown has restaurants serving cuisine from around the globe. Seafood, often bought right off the boat, is a real treat in the capital.

Star is the top-selling beer, though Star Draft, Holsten and Heineken are preferred by those who can spend a little extra. *Poyo* (palm wine) is light and fruity, but getting used to the smell and the life forms floating in your cup takes a while.

# FREETOWN

☎ 022 / pop 1 million

Reminders of the recent violence are fading in the capital, but evidence of its growing pains is never far away. The city is crammed with war victims and refugees who have chosen not to return to their upcountry homes, traffic jams last from morning until night, the government seems to have given up on rubbish collection, and there hasn't been reliable power since the 1980s.

But, despite the difficulties, Freetown feels less threatening than other large West African cities and the beautiful setting and stunning beaches compensate for the chaos. Besides, if you spend all your time in the tourist-focused Lumley and Aberdeen areas you'll rarely encounter these problems anyway. But if you do head into the heart of town

to explore the markets and historical si..., you'll soon find there's more to the city th... first meets the eye. Freetown is filthy and frantic, but you can't help loving it.

## ORIENTATION

Central Freetown is set out on a grid pattern with Siaka Stevens St as the main thoroughfare. Halfway along is the huge Cotton Tree, a good landmark with which to orient yourself. Within a few blocks of the tree are the post office, banks, offices and several markets. Away from the central area, winding streets climb the surrounding hills.

The main route to the east is Kissy Rd, although some shared taxis and *poda-podas* go along Fourah Bay Rd through the dock area. Going west, the main route follows Sanders St and Main Motor Rd towards Aberdeen and Lumley, where most visitors spend their time. Note that Sir Samuel Lewis Rd is often called Aberdeen Rd because that is where it ends. Wilkinson Rd goes south all the way to Lumley Village.

## INFORMATION
### Cultural Centres

**British Council** (Map p756; ☎ 222223; www.british council.org/sierraleone; Tower Hill; ☼ 10am-6pm Mon, 9am-7pm Tue & Thu, 9am-6pm Wed & Fri, 10am-4pm Sat)

### Emergency
☎ 999

### Internet Access

**E-Zone** (Map pp754-5; 70D Wilkinson Rd; per hr Le4500; ☼ 10am-9pm Mon-Sat, 4-9pm Sun)
**Fidelity Globalcom** (Map p756; 19 Pultney St; per hr Le5000; ☼ 8.30am-10.30pm Mon-Thu, 24hr Fri & Sat)
**Lumley Beach Dot Com** (1 Lumley Beach Rd, Lumley Turntable; per hr Le4500; ☼ 24hr)

### Libraries

**Central Library** (Map p756; cnr Rokel & Gloucester Sts; ☼ 9am-6pm Mon-Fri, 9am-1pm Sat)
**Dr King Library** (Map p756; cnr Walpole & Siaka Stevens Sts; ☼ 10am-6pm Mon, Tue, Thu & 10am-3pm Wed) In the US Embassy building.

### Medical Services

**Central Pharmacy** (Map p756; ☎ 221735; 30 Wallace Johnson St; ☼ 9am-6pm Mon-Fri, 9.30am-3.30pm Sat)
**Choitram Memorial Hospital** (Map pp754-5; ☎ 232598; Hill Station) Freetown's best hospital, though for serious problems you'll need to go to Dakar or Europe.

## GREATER FREETOWN

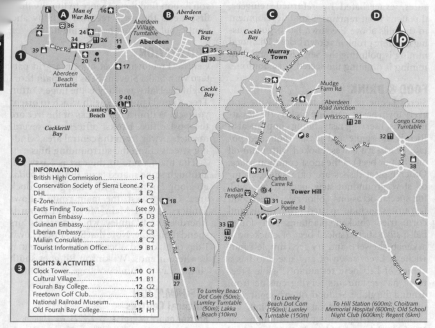

**INFORMATION**
British High Commission..................1 C3
Conservation Society of Sierra Leone..2 F2
DHL..................................................3 E2
E-Zone...............................................4 C2
Facts Finding Tours......................(see 9)
German Embassy................................5 D3
Guinean Embassy...............................6 C2
Liberian Embassy...............................7 C3
Malian Consulate...............................8 C2
Tourist Information Office...................9 B1

**SIGHTS & ACTIVITIES**
Clock Tower.....................................10 G1
Cultural Village................................11 B1
Fourah Bay College..........................12 G2
Freetown Golf Club...........................13 B3
National Railroad Museum................14 H1
Old Fourah Bay College....................15 H1

To Lumley Beach
Dot Com (50m);
Lumley Turntable
(50m); Lakka
Beach (10km)

To Lumley
Beach Dot Com
(150m); Lumley
Turntable (150m)

To Hill Station (600m); Choitram
Memorial Hospital (600m); Old School
Night Club (600km); Regent (6km)

---

**Kono Care Pharmacy** (Map p756; ☎ 229356; 11 Siaka
Stevens St; ⊕ 9am-5pm Mon-Sat)

### Money
Forex bureaus can be found throughout
the city: Rawdon and Wilberforce Sts have
several. Rates at the airport's exchange
bureau are usually better than the banks,
though a little below the forex bureaus in
town.
**Rokel Commercial Bank** (Map p756; 25/27 Siaka
Stevens St; ⊕ 9am-3pm Mon-Fri)
**Sierra Leone Commercial Bank** (Map p756; 29/31
Siaka Stevens St; ⊕ 9am-3pm Mon-Fri)

### Post
**DHL** ( ⊕ 8am-6pm Mon-Fri, 9am-5pm Sat); Central (Map
p756; ☎ 225215; 15 Rawdon St); Greater (Map pp754-5;
☎ 236156; 30 Main Motor Rd)
**Post office** (Map p756; 40 Siaka Stevens St; ⊕ 8am-
4.30pm Mon-Fri, 8am-noon Sat)

### Tourist Information
**Conservation Society of Sierra Leone** (Map pp754-5;
☎ 229716; cssc_03@yahoo.com; 2 Pyke St; ⊕ 9am-
5pm Mon-Sat)

**Tourist Information office** (Map pp754-5; ☎ 236620;
Lumley Beach Rd; ⊕ 10am-7pm) Run by the National
Tourist Board (whose head office is at Cape Sierra Hotel),
they answer questions and sell postcards.

### Travel Agencies
**IPC Travel** (Map p756; ☎ 221481; ipc@sierratel.sl; 22
Siaka Stevens St; ⊕ 8.30am-5pm Mon-Fri & 9am-1pm Sat)
**Lion Travel** (Map p756; ☎ 223211; 11 Siaka Stevens St;
⊕ 8am-6pm Mon-Sat)

### Visa Extensions
**Immigration Department** (Map p756; ☎ 223034;
15 Siaka Stevens St; ⊕ 10am-3.30pm Mon-Fri) Enter on
Rawdon St.

## DANGERS & ANNOYANCES
The postwar days of spontaneous demonstrations, violent crime and political instability are now largely gone and Freetown
is a reasonably safe city; though heed all
the usual big-city precautions. Crime in the
East End isn't as bad as the stories suggest,
but it's still best to watch your back in the
day and stay out of the area at night. Also,
watch your valuables in the markets down-

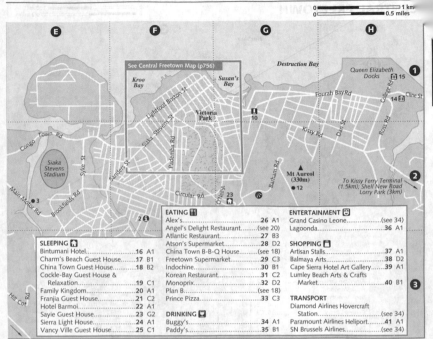

| SLEEPING | | |
|---|---|---|
| Bintumani Hotel | 16 | A1 |
| Charm's Beach Guest House | 17 | B1 |
| China Town Guest House | 18 | B2 |
| Cockle-Bay Guest House & Relaxation | 19 | C1 |
| Family Kingdom | 20 | A1 |
| Franjia Guest House | 21 | C2 |
| Hotel Barmoi | 22 | A1 |
| Sayie Guest House | 23 | G2 |
| Sierra Light House | 24 | A1 |
| Vancy Ville Guest House | 25 | C1 |

| EATING | | |
|---|---|---|
| Alex's | 26 | A1 |
| Angel's Delight Restaurant | (see 20) | |
| Atlantic Restaurant | 27 | B3 |
| Atson's Supermarket | 28 | D2 |
| China Town B-B-Q House | (see 18) | |
| Freetown Supermarket | 29 | C3 |
| Indochine | 30 | B1 |
| Korean Restaurant | 31 | C2 |
| Monoprix | 32 | D2 |
| Plan B | (see 18) | |
| Prince Pizza | 33 | C3 |

| DRINKING | | |
|---|---|---|
| Buggy's | 34 | A1 |
| Paddy's | 35 | B1 |

| ENTERTAINMENT | | |
|---|---|---|
| Grand Casino Leone | (see 34) | |
| Lagoonda | 36 | A1 |

| SHOPPING | | |
|---|---|---|
| Artisan Stalls | 37 | A1 |
| Balmaya Arts | 38 | D2 |
| Cape Sierra Hotel Art Gallery | 39 | A1 |
| Lumley Beach Arts & Crafts Market | 40 | B1 |

| TRANSPORT | | |
|---|---|---|
| Diamond Airlines Hovercraft Station | (see 34) | |
| Paramount Airlines Heliport | 41 | A1 |
| SN Brussels Airlines | (see 34) | |

town, especially in Victoria Park and along Lumley Beach.

## SIGHTS & ACTIVITIES
### Downtown
The massive **Cotton Tree**, perhaps 500 years old, in the heart of town, is the city's principal landmark. Thousands of bats fly out en masse at dusk and return in the morning. This beloved tree casts its shadow on the **Sierra Leone National Museum** (Map p756; ☎ 223555; Siaka Stevens St; ☺ 10am-4pm Mon-Fri), which has a small but fascinating collection of juju trinkets and historical artefacts, including Temne Guerrilla leader Bai Bureh's drum, clothes and sword.

The ornate **Law Courts** (Map p756; Siaka Steven St), beautifully restored following considerable war damage, are immediately east of the tree, while the **State House** (Map p756; Independence Ave) is just up the hill.

**St John's Maroon Church** (Map p756; Siaka Stevens St), a squat white building with big windows built around 1820, is two blocks southwest of the tree. The much larger **St George's Cathedral** (Map p756; Wallace Johnson St) was completed in 1828.

The ancestors of nearly all present-day Krios passed through **King's Yard Gate** (Map p756; Wallace Johnson St). Now the site of Connaught Hospital, this is where the British brought rescued slaves to begin their new lives. Many of these new arrivals climbed the **Old Wharf Steps** (Map p756), sometimes erroneously called the Portuguese Steps, that lead up from Government Wharf. The stones were set in 1818.

Many wood-framed **Krio houses** (Map p756) are scattered west of Tower Hill. A walk down Pademba Rd presents many good examples. Most date from the late 19th century and a few are even older.

### Up the Hills
Freetown's beauty, and potential, shows clearly when seen from above. The views are especially good from **Hill Station** (Map pp754–5) and **Leister Peak** (Map p761).

On Mt Aureol is **Fourah Bay College** (Map pp754–5; Barham Rd), founded in 1827. It later became one of the first universities in sub-Saharan Africa. On the edge of campus is a botanical garden and you can follow the

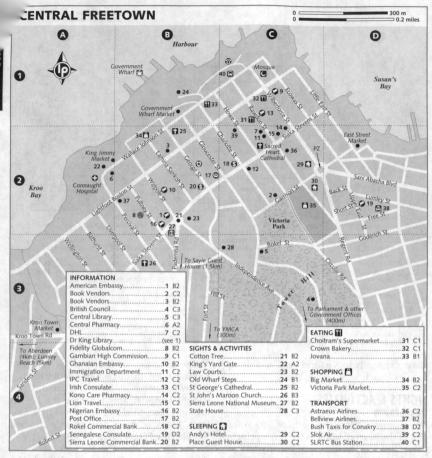

## CENTRAL FREETOWN

| INFORMATION | |
| --- | --- |
| American Embassy | 1 B2 |
| Book Vendors | 2 C2 |
| Book Vendors | 3 B2 |
| British Council | 4 C3 |
| Central Library | 5 C3 |
| Central Pharmacy | 6 A2 |
| DHL | 7 C2 |
| Dr King Library | (see 1) |
| Fidelity Globalcom | 8 B2 |
| Gambian High Commission | 9 C1 |
| Ghanaian Embassy | 10 B2 |
| Immigration Department | 11 C2 |
| IPC Travel | 12 C2 |
| Irish Consulate | 13 C1 |
| Kono Care Pharmacy | 14 C2 |
| Lion Travel | 15 C2 |
| Nigerian Embassy | 16 B2 |
| Post Office | 17 B2 |
| Rokel Commercial Bank | 18 C2 |
| Senegalese Consulate | 19 D2 |
| Sierra Leone Commercial Bank | 20 B2 |

| SIGHTS & ACTIVITIES | |
| --- | --- |
| Cotton Tree | 21 B2 |
| King's Yard Gate | 22 A2 |
| Law Courts | 23 B2 |
| Old Wharf Steps | 24 B1 |
| St George's Cathedral | 25 B2 |
| St John's Maroon Church | 26 B3 |
| Sierra Leone National Museum | 27 B2 |
| State House | 28 C3 |

| SLEEPING | |
| --- | --- |
| Andy's Hotel | 29 C2 |
| Place Guest House | 30 C2 |

| EATING | |
| --- | --- |
| Choitram's Supermarket | 31 C1 |
| Crown Bakery | 32 C1 |
| Jovana | 33 B1 |

| SHOPPING | |
| --- | --- |
| Big Market | 34 B2 |
| Victoria Park Market | 35 C2 |

| TRANSPORT | |
| --- | --- |
| Astraeus Airlines | 36 C2 |
| Bellview Airlines | 37 B2 |
| Bush Taxis for Conakry | 38 D2 |
| Slok Air | 39 C2 |
| SLRTC Bus Station | 40 C1 |

walking path through the forest down to the waterfall you passed on the drive up.

Sierra Leone's **Parliament** (Map p756) building sits atop Tower Hill, close to downtown. If MPs are in session the police might take you in for a look. Next to the entrance is the foundation of the Martello Tower, built in 1805 to defend Freetown against Temne attacks.

### Lumley Beach

With every patch of beachfront property purchased and many construction projects underway, it's not hard to imagine what Lumley Beach will look like in a few years, but for now development is pretty much limited to a few bamboo and thatch beer-

shacks. Life guards and beach wardens are on duty and the public toilets and showers are kept clean, but the beach is not.

Only desperate hackers will be satisfied, but visitors can rent clubs and play a round at the **Freetown Golf Club** (Map pp754-5; ☎ 272956; Lumley Beach Rd; 18 holes Le30,000).

### Cline Town

Visitors to the **National Railroad Museum** (Map pp754-5; Cline St; admission free; ☺ 10am-5pm Tue-Sat) are very rare, but the short tour through these restored train engines and cars is surprisingly interesting.

Gutted by fire in 1999, only the stone shell of the **Old Fourah Bay College** (Map pp754-5; College Rd) remains, but this 1848 building is graceful even in its decay. The World Monuments Fund lists it as one of the world's 100 most-endangered historic sites. There is talk of turning it into a community arts centre.

## FESTIVALS & EVENTS

The whole country goes kite crazy on Easter Monday and Lumley Beach is packed with free-flying families. Independence Day's Lantern Parade, an evening procession of illuminated floats, has recently been revived.

## SLEEPING
### Budget

**Place Guest House** (Map p756; ☎ 222608; 42 Rawdon St; s/d with shared bathroom Le30,000/35,000, s/d with private bathroom Le35,000/40,000, r with air-con Le50,000; ✼) Perhaps the best budget hotel in Sierra Leone, the Place is spotlessly clean and the generator runs all night. *Poda-podas* coming back from Aberdeen (though not those going via Circular Rd) can drop you off just a few doors down.

**Andy's Hotel** (Map p756; ☎ 222217; 31 Wilberforce St; r with fan/air-con Le45,000/75,000; ✼) A block over from the Place, Andy's is a bit scruffy, but the rooms are clean and big, and a restaurant is attached.

**Franjia Guest House** (Map pp754–5; ☎ 030 240426; 9K Carlton Carew Rd; r with fan & shared bathroom Le60,000, s/d with air-con & private bathroom Le80,000/120,000; Ⓟ ✼) Little Franjia, in a quiet neighbourhood, is very homey and the staff is eager to please. The rates include breakfast and they'll cook lunch or dinner on request.

**Cockle-Bay Guest House & Relaxation** (Map pp754–5; ☎ 272789; 36 Sir Samuel Lewis Rd; r with shared bathroom Le50,000, s/d with fan Le70,000/85,000, d with air-con Le95,000–110,000; Ⓟ ✼) Not the quietest place in town, but Cockle Bay is a good choice for beachgoers on a budget. Rooms are simple but clean and breakfast is included. Prices are discounted for midweek and long-term stays.

**Sayie Guest House** (Map pp754–5; ☎ 225550; 6 O'Neil St; r 40,000; Ⓟ) Though it's a little out of the way and only has bucket showers, Sayie, up a dirt road behind Tower Hill, is a bit cooler and quieter than hotels in the centre.

**YMCA** (32 Fort St; s/d with shared bathroom Le25,000/35,000) The Y has some of the cheapest rooms in town, and with good reason, though the views sort of make up for it.

### Midrange

These hotels, all convenient to Lumley Beach, have refrigerators, satellite TV and private bathroom, as well as breakfast, hot water and 24-hour power.

**China Town Guest House** (Map pp754–5; ☎ 236664; 84 Lumley Beach Rd; s/d Le195,000/255,000; Ⓟ ✼) These eight oriental-themed rooms lie just across the road from a quiet stretch of Lumley Beach.

**Charm's Beach Guest House** (Map pp754–5; ☎ 235716; 29 off Cape Rd; r Le105,000–180,000, ste 240,000; Ⓟ ✼ ☒) This big pink house on a quiet backstreet is just a few minutes' walk from the beach. The cheap rooms downstairs lack character, but the others are homey.

**Vancy Ville Guest House** (Map pp754–5; ☎ 076 636850; 7 Mudge Farm Rd; s Le105,000–150,000, d 135,000–165,000; Ⓟ ✼) This cosy British-style B&B is in a quiet location between downtown and the beach.

**Hotel Barmoi** (Map pp754–5; ☎ 234933; cape@sierratel.sl; 75C Cape Rd; s/d from Le223,500/319,000; Ⓟ ✼ ☒ ☒) Formerly the Cape Guest House, this small lodge has fine rooms and a great seaside location near the lighthouse. Some of the most expensive rooms virtually stick out over the ocean; prices for these rooms are higher. There is a small swimming pool and a good restaurant.

**Sierra Light House** (Map pp754–5; ☎ 273485; 5 Man Of War Bay; s/d Le255,000/315,000; Ⓟ ✼ ☒) All 38 of the large rooms have a balcony overlooking the bay and a separate sitting area. The restaurant has the same great views.

**Family Kingdom** (Map pp754–5; ☎ 236133; fking domresort@yahoo.com; Lumley Beach Rd; s Le180,000, d 240,000–270,000, 2-room ste Le360,000; Ⓟ ✼ ☒) The most colourful and bizarre lodging can be found at the Family Kingdom. The rooms are ordinary, and the cheapest could use a touch-up, but the real attractions are inside the compound, which has enough playground equipment for several schools worth of children, a wading pool, and duiker roaming the grounds.

### Top End

**Bintumani Hotel** (Map pp754–5; ☎ 233996; 11 Man Of War Bay; r Le414,000, ste Le560,000–780,000; Ⓟ ✼ ☒ ☒) This massive, hilltop tower is Freetown's largest and most exclusive hotel and each of the 200 rooms has at least a partial sea view. Facilities include a casino, sco, tennis court, two restaurants (Chinese and Western) and a pool large enough for a real swim.

# EATING
## Aberdeen & Lumley
**Alex's** (Map pp754-5; 64 Cape Rd; meals Le10,000-25,000; ☺ lunch Fri-Sun, dinner Tue-Sun) From under the palm trees you have a great view west over Man of War Bay at what is easily Freetown's loveliest dining room. Seafood is the speciality, but the large global menu includes enchiladas, lasagne, shepherds pie, *jollof rice* (rice and vegetables with meat and fish), falafel and Cajun chicken. The adjacent sports bar has a wide-screen TV and a pool table.

**Atlantic Restaurant** (Map pp754-5; 30 Lumley Beach Rd; meals around Le30,000; ☺ lunch Sun, dinner Tue-Sun) This restaurant at the southern end of Lumley Beach has good fish dishes and a terrace, which is great for drinks at sunset.

**China Town B-B-Q House** (Map pp754-5; 84 Lumley Beach Rd; meals Le8000-45,000; ☺ lunch & dinner) Eat Freetown's best Chinese food in the little open-air restaurant or under a thatch roof on the beach.

**Indochine** (Map pp754-5; 64 Sir Samuel Lewis Rd; meals Le15,000-30,000; ☺ lunch Tue-Sun, dinner daily) This classy spot with a patio overlooking Cockle Bay serves decent Chinese, Vietnamese and Thai food.

**Angel's Delight Restaurant** (Map pp754-5; Lumley Beach Rd; meals Le10,000-50,000; ☺ lunch & dinner) Angel's Delight, part of the Family Kingdom hotel complex, serves tasty Lebanese dishes, seafood and good pizzas. After the meal you can enjoy a hookah on the patio. Paddy's (right) serves good Indian food.

## Wilkinson Rd
**Prince Pizza** (Map pp754-5; 125 Wilkinson Rd; pizzas from Le 7000; ☺ lunch & dinner) This simple little snack bar not far from Lumley Village makes tasty brick-oven pizzas, plus other fast-food favourites.

**Korean Restaurant** (Map pp754-5; 34 Lower Pipeline Rd; meals Le10,000-30,000; ☺ breakfast, lunch & dinner) Attached to the Korean Guest House, the small Korean community gathers here for Korean, Chinese and European dishes.

## Downtown
Street-food vendors work their candlelit stalls around the PZ Turntable late into the night.

**Jovana** (Map p756; 16 Wallace Johnson St; meals Le4000-23,000; ☺ lunch & dinner Mon-Sat) Popular with business people, Jovana serves tasty African dishes, pizza and the usual meat and seafood choices. The patio is shady and the air-con is turned up inside.

**Crown Bakery** (Map p756; 5 Wilberforce St; meals Le13,000-45,000; ☺ lunch & dinner Mon-Sat) Besides being a delicious bakery, this expat favourite has a broad and expensive menu spanning pancakes to pizzas and curries to fajitas.

## Supermarkets
The flock of well-heeled UN and NGO workers living in Freetown keep many supermarkets, all full of expensive imported goods, in business, including **Atson's Supermarket** (Map pp754-5; 16 Wilkinson Rd), **Choitram's Supermarket** (Map p756; 7 Rawdon St), **Freetown Supermarket** (Map pp754-5; 137 Wilkinson Rd) and **Monoprix** (Map pp754-5; 4C Wilkinson Rd).

# DRINKING
**Paddy's** (Map pp754-5; 63 Sir Samuel Lewis Rd) No longer the den of iniquity it once was, Paddy's is still Freetown's most famous nightspot and the only place were everyone, no matter what their stripe, can really let their hair down at the bar or on the dance floor. The food is pretty good too. Paddy's never closes.

**Buggy's** (Map pp754-5; 74 Cape Rd; ☺ 8am-3am) This is a wild place on Man of War Bay that's more of what Paddy's used to be back in the day – though not quite that crazy. It has a dance floor and snooker tables. Many album launches by local artists take place here.

**Plan B** (Map pp754-5; 84 Lumley Beach Rd; ☺ dinner) Unusually tranquil for Freetown, Plan B, part of the China Town complex, is a jazz-infused wine bar.

# ENTERTAINMENT
Live music is rare, though bands sometimes take the stage at various spots around town. No place really gets hopping until midnight.

**Old School Night Club** (Map pp754-5; Hill Station; admission Le10,000-15,000, ladies free Wed; ☺ 11pm Wed-Sat) Owned by football star Mohamed Kallon, this is Freetown's hottest dance venue.

The slick disco at **Lagoonda** (Map pp754-5; 55 Cape Rd; admission Le10,000; ☺ Fri & Sat) is very popular with expats and there is a casino upstairs. Dress smart. You can also try to beat the odds at **Grand Casino Leone** (Map pp754-5; 74 Cape Rd; 🕐 8am-2am) and the Bintumani Hotel (p757).

## SHOPPING
The Lumley Beach Arts & Crafts Market (Map p756) and the artisan stalls near Aberdeen Beach Turntable are the main places people pick up woodcarvings, baskets and other tourist bric-a-brac. The top floor of the **Big Market** (Map p756; Wallace Johnson St), or Basket Market, downtown has a larger selection than Lumley, though what makes this the best place to shop for souvenirs is the traditional household goods on the ground floor. Lumley is tops for country cloth, and the hectic Victoria Park Market (Map p756) is the best place for *gara*.

**Balmaya Arts** (Map pp754-5; 32B Main Motor Rd) in Congo Cross has top-quality stuff from across West Africa (plus good sandwiches and salads), and the paintings at the **Cape Sierra Hotel's art gallery** (Map pp754-5; 🕿 272268; Cape Rd) are interesting.

## GETTING THERE & AWAY
### Air
Lungi Airport is about 25km north of Freetown across the river. For details of international flights to/from Freetown, see p770. There are no internal flights.

### Bus, Bush Taxi & Minibus
SLRTC buses leave around 7.30am from the **bus station** (formerly the train station; Map p756) on Wallace Johnson St, though not every day, so check the schedule before making plans. They are always full, so you'll need to arrive around 6am to be sure of getting a seat. Cities served are Bo, Kenema, Makeni, Kabala, Kono and Conakry in Guinea.

Bush taxis and *poda-podas* leave throughout the day from Shell New Rd Lorry Park on the far east side of town (from downtown catch a taxi on Goderich St), except those going to Conakry, which park along Free St near Victoria Park Market.

## GETTING AROUND
### To/From the Airport
The easiest ways to get to Lungi Airport are **Paramount's helicopters** (Map pp754-5; 🕿 076 621041; one way Le120,000) and **Diamond's hovercraft** (Map pp754-5; 🕿 076 624786; one way Le90,000). Both drop and depart from Cape Rd in Aberdeen and time their trips to coincide with flight arrivals and departures, though be sure to check a day in advance of your departure because they don't necessarily connect with every flight. Taxis stake out the landing sites in town.

The adventurous way from the airport is to take a shared taxi (Le2000) to the ferry terminal at Tagrin. A car ferry (Le1500 for passengers) crosses to the Kissy ferry terminal five or six times a day between 7.30am and 7.30pm. If you don't want to wait for it you can take one of the large *pam-pams* (big boats) for Le2000 or the less overcrowded speedboats for Le5000. These are wet landings, but men wait to carry passengers to the boats for a small tip. Chartering a taxi all the way to Aberdeen costs about Le50,000.

### Boat
Hiring a boat to go fishing or get to islands in the area is not cheap, though most hold 20 people. In Freetown you can find speedboats for around Le1,200,000 per day (try the Aqua Sports Club on 🕿 076 695455), while slower traditional boats can be found at Government Wharf and Kissy Ferry Terminal for around Le300,000 per day. Of course, the prices depend on the destination, your bargaining prowess and the cost of fuel. Most of the beach resorts down on the peninsula have their own boats.

### Car
Car hire is expensive (starting at around Le225,000; much more if you're heading upcountry), but don't base your choice of company only on the price; ask about the terms too. Miles will always be unlimited and a driver is usually included, but fuel costs and after-hours charges vary. Also, if going upcountry find out if the driver's food and lodging are your responsibility or his. IPC's prices are a little higher than the competition, but you'll get the vehicle for more hours and with few extra costs, so it might work out cheaper in the end.
**Cape Sierra Hotel** ( 🕿 272268)
**Dial A Ride** ( 🕿 241934)
**IPC Travel** ( 🕿 221481)

### Shared Taxi & Poda-Podas
Shared taxis and *poda-podas* cost Le700 per ride. Taxis generally make short hops while *poda-podas* run long distance, including

ing from downtown all the way to Lumley and Aberdeen. Pay no attention to the route numbers painted on the side of the cars. Not only do the drivers not use them, many don't even know what they're for. Just call out your destination to each passing vehicle. During the week there are few vehicles after midnight, while on weekends they run all night in Aberdeen and Lumley.

## Taxi

Freetown taxis don't have meters. Just find an empty one and bargain hard. A trip from downtown to Aberdeen will cost about Le15,000, while a short hop won't be less than Le3000.

# AROUND FREETOWN

## BEACHES

Some of West Africa's best beaches lie along the mountainous, 40km-long Freetown peninsula. Most beach resorts offer fishing and, in the autumn, whale-watching trips. *Podapodas* run to all points except Kent, but they are infrequent south of Lakka Village.

Shortly after **Goderich Village** and its animated afternoon fish market is **Lakka Beach**, home of **Pierre's Resort** ( ☎ 076 680737; s/d with fan Le120,000/165,000, s/d with air-con 200,000/250,000; P ⊠ ⊠ ). The bungalows need a serious spruce up, but remain popular. The swimming pool has its own bar and the restaurant is good, though try to have one meal at the simple Hard Rock restaurant on a petite island just offshore.

Lakka is followed promptly by so-so **Hamilton Beach** and, further down, by gorgeous **Sussex Beach** where you'll find **Franco's Dive Centre** ( ☎ 076 744406; r 180,000; P ⊠ ). Besides leading scuba trips to shipwrecks, Italian-born Franco offers seven large, well-equipped rooms and a restaurant with seafood and Italian dishes for around Le15,000. Have a meal here and you can sleep on the beach for Le2000.

About halfway down the peninsula at little **Bawbaw Village** is **Fivele Guest House**, with three simple rooms on a small but stunning stretch of sand. Prices are negotiable. Ask for directions to the natural whirlpool.

Many people rank **River No 2** as the choicest beach in the country, and scenery-wise it's hard to argue with that, though it's also one of the busiest. The community-run **River No 2 Development Association** ( ☎ 033 365934; camping Le5000, r incl breakfast Le120,000; seafood Le20,000; P ) offers new and large rooms right on the beach. Entry for the day (Le5000) gets you use of umbrellas, thatch huts and showers. Be sure to let them paddle you up to the waterfall on River No 2, passing monkeys and crocodiles on the way. The nearby **Guma Dam** is a popular picnic spot. You can either drive there or walk along the overgrown **Guma-No 2 Nature Trail**, passing a waterfall on the way.

Just down the shore is **Tokeh Beach** where you'll find **Baam Tokeh** (bungalows Le60,000; P ), a laid-back hang-out with nightly bonfires and superb seafood dinners. Hammocks front the three beachfront bungalows, or you can pitch a tent on the beach for next to nothing. A large luxury resort is under construction nearby.

**York** is an interesting Krio village. Ask someone to show you the caves where slaves stayed before being loaded onto ships. From nearby **York Beach** you can walk around the rocky bay to **Black Johnson Beach**. At the end of the peninsula is **Kent** village with its little horseshoe beach and ruined fort.

---

### BUNCE ISLAND

Bunce (rhymes with dunce) Island is at the mouth of the Sierra Leone River, 15km east of Freetown. With plenty of monkeys, it's a good wildlife-watching destination, but the major attraction is the ruined fortress. First built in 1663, it was levelled in 1702 by French warships. The ruins you'll see today are of a second fort built soon after.

After the original British and French occupations the fort was held by the Dutch, the Portuguese and the British (again) who made it one of the major collection points for slaves destined for Europe and the Americas. Before it was shut down in 1808 some 50,000 men, women and children were shipped off into exile, including the Gullah people of South Carolina.

To visit you're supposed to get a permit (Le15,000, Le9000 for students) from the National Tourist Board at the Cape Sierra Hotel (p759). They also lead tours, as does IPC Travel (p754), though neither is cost effective unless you have a large group.

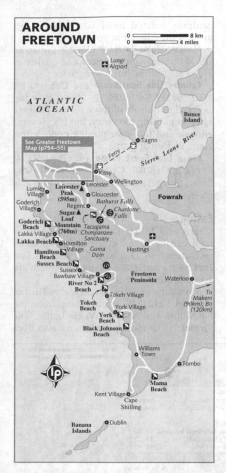

**AROUND FREETOWN**

of an 1881 church, and the old slave docks. Pay your respects to the chief before going off exploring and the locals will happily provide a guide.

The easiest way to get to the Bananas is to hire a local fishing boat at Tokeh Village: expect to pay around Le180,000, which includes a lavish seafood meal. It's a two-hour round trip and you should allow at least an hour to explore the ruins in Dublin. It's only a short hop from Kent, but you probably won't find the boats any cheaper and they aren't as used to taking travellers out there.

## REGENT AND AROUND

The village of **Regent** has many interesting Krio-style houses, including some that date from the early 19th century. St Charles Church, begun in 1809 and completed seven years later, is the third-oldest stone church built by Europeans on the continent. **Sugar Loaf Mountain** (760m) offers sweeping panoramas, though the paths to the summit are indistinct, so ask the chief to arrange a guide. Plan on three hours to the summit.

Three kilometres past Regent, uphill the whole way, is **Tacugama Chimpanzee Sanctuary** ( ☎ 224098; admission Le15,000; ⏰ 10am-5.30pm) where dozens of confiscated and abandoned chimps are being prepared for release. Most live semiwild inside large fenced enclosures. Just past the turn-off to the chimp sanctuary, at the bridge, you can see **Bathurst Falls** and a little further on is the path to **Charlotte Falls**, a good spot for a swim.

Taxis run from Freetown to Regent (Le1500). Chartering a taxi from Regent to the chimp sanctuary and back will cost around Le15,000.

# THE SOUTH & EAST

Southern Sierra Leone is humid, low-lying and forested. It also has the country's major diamond-mining areas, notably Tongo Field between Kenema and Kono (Koidu-Sefadu). Bo and Kenema are the largest and busiest towns outside the capital, but the region is still principally pastoral with some fantastic wildlife-watching opportunities, and remote islands and beaches ripe for exploration.

Around the bend and past **Mama Beach** you'll end up at the ramshackle fishing town of **Tombo**. From here there is a Saturday morning boat to Bonthe (Le10,000); it returns on Thursday. Another boat back-and-forths every other day to Shenge (Le8000), where you can have miles of white sand and palm trees all to yourself.

## BANANA ISLANDS

Diving and snorkelling are superb at the Banana Islands, which are off the southeastern tip of the peninsula. There is some coral and one of the shipwrecks left a pile of Portuguese cannons in shallow water. In **Dublin**, on the northern tip of the main island, there are more cannons, the remains

SIERRA LEONE

## BO

☎ 032 / pop 167,000

Sierra Leone's second-largest city, Bo is a lively, pleasant town in the heart of Mende country. Although it suffered much during the fighting with almost all residents at least temporarily uprooted, it's now bustling again with diamond merchants and other businessmen. There isn't really anything to see or do, except stroll the market or have a tailor sew you a smart shirt using kola-nut *gara*, but it's a pleasant place to while away some time.

## Information

**COMSU** (32 Dambara Rd; per hr Le12,000; ☒ 9am-6pm Mon-Sat) Has painfully slow Internet.

**Forex Bureaus** There are several of these on Fenton Rd.

**Rokel Commercial Bank** (10 Bojon St) Does foreign exchange and cash advances on credit cards.

**Union Trust Bank** (7 Bojon St) Across the street from Rokel, handles Western Union.

## Sleeping

**Hotel Sir Milton** ( ☎ 032493; 6 Kissy Town Rd; s/d Le38,000/49,000, r with air-con Le65,000; ℗ 🛏 ) This

centrally located hotel is a little rough around the edges, but good for the price.

**Madame Wokie Hotel** ( ☎ 032432; 25 Dambara Rd; ℗ 🛏 ) Same owners, prices and quality as Hotel Sir Milton, but fewer guests.

**Country Side Guesthouse and Club** ( ☎ 076 883527; s/d Le90,000/120,000; ℗ 🛏 🛰 ) Bo's top hotel, 2km outside of town on the Kenema Hwy, is nothing too fancy, but it's pleasant enough and has a swimming pool, tennis court and small gym.

**Green Leaf Guest House** ( ☎ 076 639817; 41 Fofanah St; r Le20,000) One of several sketchy hotels along Tikonko Rd – it has tolerable rooms.

## Eating

Cheap and filling Lebanese and African food can be found at a number of small restaurants on Dambara Rd, such as **Cool Zone** (meals around Le3000). Many street stalls are set up around here at night.

More substantial meat and seafood dishes (around Le12,000) are available from the Sir Milton and Madam Wokie hotels. The former is the most popular and also does

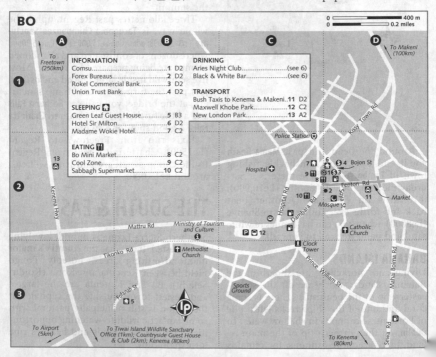

tasty pastas, while the latter has a smaller menu but a breezy 3rd-floor dining room.

Imported groceries can be bought at the **Bo Mini Market** (26 Dambara Rd) and **Sabbagh Supermarket** (7 Dambara Rd). The latter also serves fast food.

### Entertainment
After dusk many visitors camp out at their hotel's restaurant and watch the passing crowds. People watching is also good from the 2nd-storey **Black & White Bar** (8 Kissy Town Rd), one of the few watering holes not full of prostitutes.

**Aries Night Club** (2 Kissy Town Rd), next to Hotel Sir Milton, is loud and fun. Ask around before going to any other night club, as some are very rough and tumble.

### Getting There & Away
Bush taxis to Freetown (Le17,000, six hours) depart frequently each morning from Maxwell Khobe Park, as does the daily SLRTC bus. This is also the spot to catch taxis to Potoru (Le15,000, three hours), Matru-Jong (Le15,000, 2½ hours) and the Liberian border (Le35,000, six hours); though for the latter it is best to go from Kenema. To get to Freetown in the afternoon you'll probably need to go out to New London Park.

Bush taxis for Kenema (Le6000, one hour) and Makeni (Le15,000, four hours) depart from the market.

## TIWAI ISLAND WILDLIFE SANCTUARY
Tiwai is a beautiful reserve on a pristine, 1200-hectare island in the Moa River. Many animals that are rare elsewhere thrive here, including chimpanzees, pygmy hippos, river otters and white-breasted guinea fowl. It is not unusual to see over half of the island's 11 primate species on a two-hour walk. Besides strolling the well-maintained trails, a variety of boat trips are available and a beach is exposed in the dry season. They hope to restart white-water kayaking trips.

The **park headquarters** ( ☎ 076 755146, tiwai _island@hotmail.com) is in Lakka, near Freetown, and there are also offices in **Bo** ( ☎ 076 625277) and **Potoru** ( ☎ 076 922792). If you don't have a car, the friendly staff in Potoru, accessible by bush taxi from Bo and Kenema, will arrange transport at a fair price for the final 16km to Kambama village, where you take a boat to the island. Park entrance is Le15,000

(Le30,000 to stay the night) and the various guided tours range from Le10,000 to Le20,000. Overnight visitors sleep in tents and local women will cook meals.

## SULIMA
It's hard to believe when you see it, but Sulima was once a busy port town. Today this shady town at the mouth of the Moa River consists of mostly mud-and-thatch houses and a few crumbling colonial buildings. Siaka Stevens' old vacation home, a victim of the war, lies along the metal track leading to the lagoon, and Fanti fisherman, originally from Ghana, repair their nets down by the steep beach. It's a great place to chill a while – and you'll need to after roughing it over the road that brings you here.

The only hotel is the spartan but clean **Mamie Sambo Guest House Bar and Video Entertainment Centre** (r Le20,000). Ask permission from the paramount chief if you'd rather sleep on the beach.

There are taxis to Fairo on Friday and Saturday, but virtually no traffic at other times. Bargain hard and you might get a car for Le50,000 for the one-hour trip.

## BONTHE
pop 9,500
Bonthe, the only notable town on Sherbro Island, was used by the British as an anti-slaving post from 1861; later it grew into a prosperous port. Old British colonial buildings, like the town hall, still dot the sandy streets. Today fishing and farming are the primary livelihoods. Though Bonthe is small and remote, it's a district headquarters so there is a hospital and a police station and shops are pretty well stocked.

You can walk past the waterworks to visit some small beaches and fishing outposts or hire a boat to explore the surrounding mangrove forests. To get really remote bring a tent and trek along the south shore's unspoilt beaches to Cape St Ann. You could also ride along on the weekly boat to the idyllic **Turtle Islands**; it stops briefly at several villages to load fish.

The **Bontec Guest House** (r with shared/private bathroom Le15,000/25,000) has OK rooms and a generator. Eating is all about seafood, and wherever you are staying will prepare what you request, as long as someone caught it in their net that day.

Bush taxis go from Bo to Matru-Jong (Le15,000, 2½ hours) in the morning and from there you connect with a boat (Le20,000, four hours) heading down the beautiful Jong River to Bonthe. There is also a boat to Tombo (Le10,000) on the Freetown peninsula departing every Thursday and returning on Saturday.

## KENEMA

☎ 042 / pop 138,000

Kenema, the provinces' most prosperous town, is a busy trade centre for coffee, cacao, timber and, most visibly, diamonds. The main artery, Hangha Rd, is a crush of Lebanese diamond merchants. Befriend one and they may let you eyeball raw stones. It is possible to visit mines too, but don't show up without a guide. Again, Lebanese business owners might set you up, or ask at your hotel.

On the west edge of town is **Kambui Hills Forest Reserve**, a large woodland area and a good place for a walk, though you need to get pretty far out from the city to see much wildlife. Bambawo and Bayama villages are good starting points. Some 40km east of Kenema are the Gola Hills, the nation's largest remaining swath of virgin rainforest, parts of which are protected at the **Gola Forest Reserve**. Access is difficult, so there is little poaching and there are healthy populations of elephants, leopards, buffaloes, pygmy hippopotamuses, chimpanzees and hornbills. There are few facilities now, but a camping area is planned near Joru, the main access point. The **District Forestry Office** (☎ 420059) at the end of Maxwell Khobe St provides information for both reserves and can arrange guides, which are a must in Gola.

Kenema gets online at **African Information Technology Holdings** (18 Hangha Rd; per hr Le12,000; ☼ 8am-7.30pm Mon-Fri, 9am-5pm Sat).

## Sleeping

**Sinava Guest House** (☎ 076 770270; 9 Blama Rd; s/d Le100,000/120,000; ℗ ✖) Sinava is the best hotel in town, though it is overpriced for what you get.

**Ruby Motel** (☎ 076 784638; 20 Mambu St; r with shared/private bathroom Le15,000/35,000; ℗) This friendly place, down a lot of backstreets on the edge of town, was an anti-RUF militia base during the war. It's in good shape now.

**Sameday Guest House** (1 Sahara St; r with shared/private bathroom Le10,000/30,000) This is the best of the grubby guesthouses in the centre.

What is expected to be a fancy hotel is under construction on Hangha Rd.

## Eating

**Capitol Restaurant** (51 Hangha Rd; meals from Le5000; ☼ breakfast, lunch & dinner) A friendly restaurant with tasty African and Lebanese dishes. The front patio is a good people-watching place.

**Sinava** (☎ 076 770270; 9 Blama Rd; dishes around Le10,000) and **Reconcile** (Blama Rd; dishes around Le10,000) restaurants are popular places for drinks and basic fish- and chicken-and-rice dishes.

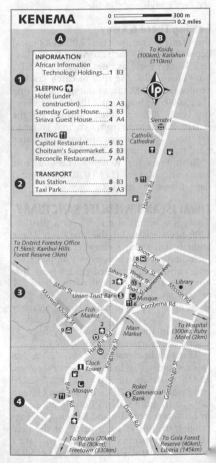

KENEMA

| INFORMATION |
| --- |
| African Information Technology Holdings....1 B3 |

| SLEEPING |
| --- |
| Hotel (under construction)................2 A3 |
| Sameday Guest House.....3 B3 |
| Sinava Guest House.....4 A4 |

| EATING |
| --- |
| Capitol Restaurant..........5 B2 |
| Choitram's Supermarket..6 B3 |
| Reconcile Restaurant......7 A4 |

| TRANSPORT |
| --- |
| Bus Station................8 B3 |
| Taxi Park................9 A3 |

## DIAMONDS FROM SIERRA LEONE

One of the tragedies of Sierra Leone is that despite being one of the poorest countries on earth it has one of the best sources of wealth. Hundreds of thousands of carats of diamonds wait under the jungle carpet to be mined, cut, polished and set into jewellery. Most mines have been dug around Kenema, Bo and Kono, but new fields are being found elsewhere and for the first time since independence, Sierra Leone might be able to harness the wealth of its diamonds for the benefit of its citizens.

When the RUF began its war in 1991, its sole aim was to control the country's diamond mines. It used forced labour to extract the wealth, and the receptive government of Charles Taylor in Liberia and ask-no-questions Western diamond dealers to put the gems on the world market. The money the RUF reaped from this enterprise – estimated at between US$25 million and US$125 million per year – was used to buy weapons to continue the brutal war. In the end, two million people (about one-third of the population) were displaced and at least 50,000 killed, while another 30,000 had their hands, lips, ears, or other body parts amputated by the rebels.

Diamonds are the most portable form of wealth known to man – 30g of gem-quality diamonds are equal in value to 18,000kg of iron ore – making smuggling them across borders very easy. They're also readily resold into the world market and practically impossible to trace. Osama bin Laden's Al-Qaeda terrorist network bought millions of dollars' worth of Sierra Leone diamonds prior to the 11 September 2001 attacks on the USA.

Although Sierra Leone's was not the only African war fuelled by 'blood diamonds' – they play a major role in Côte d'Ivoire's current crisis, see p259 – it was largely the atrocities committed by the RUF that brought the issue to international attention. In 2002 industry leaders and over 60 governments, with the backing of the UN, adopted the Kimberly Process Certification Scheme to regulate the trade in rough diamonds. The breakthrough deal, two years in the making, is a weakened version of the original proposal – monitoring is voluntary rather than mandatory – but it covers up to 99% of exported diamonds. The agreement also hinders establishing gem-polishing industries in the top producing nations, including Sierra Leone. Though far from perfect, the Kimberly Process is a significant silver lining from Sierra Leone's recent dark cloud.

---

**Choitram's Supermarket** (4 Hangha Rd) is well stocked with imported goods.

## Getting There & Away

SLRTC buses to Freetown depart every morning from the bus station in the centre. Bush taxis to Bo (Le6000, one hour), Potoru (Le8000, four hours), Kailahun (Le22,000, five hours), Kono (Le35,000, five hours), Freetown (Le21,000, seven hours) and the Liberian border (Le40,000, nine hours) depart from the taxi park on Maxwell Khobe St. The roads south to Monrovia and north to Kono are extraordinarily bad. Taxis for the latter go via Boajibu instead of the direct route.

# THE NORTH

Northern Sierra Leone is the homeland of the Temne people. The landscape is higher and drier than the southeast and the largest towns feel more like overgrown villages than cities. Where they haven't been culti-vated, the undulating hills are covered in light bush or savanna woodland, although ribbons of dense forest run along the major rivers. The hills become mountains in several places, with many peaks rising above 1500m.

## MAKENI

☎ 052 / pop 85,000

Makeni, the quiet capital of Northern Province, is a market town for the surrounding villages. Despite being the RUF headquarters for the final three years of the war, Makeni suffered little physical damage – there was plenty of human suffering though.

The crowded market is worth a wander, though you won't find any of the *blai* the area is known for. A few women sell the distinctive coiled baskets in the shade of the cotton tree in Independence Sq and across from Makeni Central Mosque, one of the most beautiful in the country. It is also the largest in the province, though not r long; another is under construction a short walk away.

Wusum Hill, rising to the west, can be climbed in about an hour. The route up the back (any small boy can show you the trail) isn't so steep and there is a small pool to cool off in on the way down. Other peaks north of town, along the road to Kabala, are just begging for rock hounds to break out the ropes.

**MJ Motel** ( ☎ 076 139945; 14 Freetown Hwy; s/d Le60,000/80,000; P ✕ ) is Makeni's best by far. Rooms have satellite TV and power all night. Across the street is **Buya's Motel** (25 Ladies Mile; r with shared/private bathroom Le15,000/25,000; P ), which is cheaper than Makeni's other bottom-end lodging and just as good, though that's not saying much. Both hotels will make dinner by request, plus there are several simple restaurants in the centre such as **Mem's** (8 Rogbane Rd; meals Le3000) serving cheap chop.

Bush taxis run frequently to Freetown (Le14,000, three hours) plus the SLRTC buses to Kono and Kabala will drop passengers here. There are also several taxis a day to Kabala (Le10,000 two hours), Kamakwie (Le12,000, four hours), Bo (Le15,000, four hours) and Kono (Le12,000, five hours).

## OUTAMBA-KILIMI NATIONAL PARK

Sierra Leone's only **national park** (admission Le7500) is a beautiful, peaceful place. The Wilderness Camp, as it is called locally, is easily reached by 4WD or motorcycle, though there are no roads inside, so visitors need to explore on foot or by canoe.

The 74,000-hectare Outamba ('hilly' in Susu) eastern section consists of rolling hills, grasslands, flood plains and rainforests intersected by several rivers. The headquarters is here. The 19,000-hectare Kilimi section to the west is flatter, less ecologically intact and has no facilities. Crocodiles, hippopotamuses, baboons, chimpanzees, elephants, buffaloes, bongos, leopards and perhaps lions all roam here. Black-casqued hornbills and great blue turacos are two of 260 bird species.

Footpaths cross the park – it's 8 miles to a waterfall – or you can track elephants on their own trails. By canoe you can look for hippos (sightings are almost guaranteed in the dry season) on the Little Scarcies River or go to Lake Idrisa and watch wildlife from observation towers. These excursions cost Le10,000 per person plus Le5000 for the

guide. The cosy thatch **huts** (Le10,000) right on the riverbank are reason enough to come. You need to bring your own food, though people there will cook it.

Without your own transport you'll need to hire a motorcycle (try for Le40,000) in Kamakwie, the nearest sizable town, for the 20-mile trip as the entrance road is too rough for taxis. Alternatively, you can catch any northbound vehicle (which are rare) and walk the 3.7 miles from the main road.

If you reach Kamakwie too late to get to the park you can sleep at the overpriced, but otherwise decent, **Sella Guest House** (r with shared bathroom Le40,000; P ) on the hill by the phone tower. Don't believe anyone here when they tell you there's no lodging in the park.

## KABALA

Kabala, the largest town in the north, is at the end of a sealed road and the last place of any size en route to Faranah, Guinea. It's quiet and friendly and well worth a visit. Gbawuria (*bow*-ree-ah) Hill provides a dramatic backdrop to the town and is easily climbed. A colourful New Year's Day

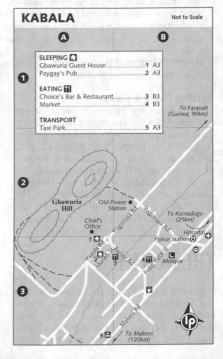

**KABALA**          Not to Scale

Ⓐ          Ⓑ

**SLEEPING** 🏠
Gbawuria Guest House..................1 A3
Paygay's Pub................................2 A3

**EATING** 🍴
Choice's Bar & Restaurant..............3 B3
Market.........................................4 B3

**TRANSPORT**
Taxi Park.....................................5 A3

To Faranah (Guinea; 90km)

Gbawuria Hill          Old Power Station
Chief's Office          Yogomaia Rd
To Koinadugu (25km)
Hospital
Police Station
Yagala Rd          North St
Burie Rd          Mosque
Fody Yalon St

Makeni Rd

5 🏠  To Makeni (120km)

LP

celebration is held at the top. Any *moto-taxi* driver can take you to see the women who dye the rust-coloured *ronko* cloth that Koinadugu district and the Kuranko people are known for.

**Gbawuria Guest House** (28 Yagala Rd; r with shared bathroom Le15,000; (P)), which resembles a Swiss chalet, is the most popular place to stay. If it's full of NGO workers try the louder **Pay-gay's Pub** (2 Moneh St; r with shared/private bathroom Le15,000/20,000). There are *cookery* shops at the market or try **Choice's Bar & Restaurant** (17 Barrier Rd; meals Le2000-5000; ⏰ breakfast, lunch & dinner) for the cassava leaves or other dish of the day.

Bush taxis travel to Freetown (Le20,000, five hours) and Makeni (Le10,000, two hours). There's also a SLRTC bus to Free-town three times a week. Both leave from the taxi park. To Faranah in Guinea, the road is bad and usually plied by very few taxis, but trucks go more often.

## MT BINTUMANI

Loma Mansa, as Sierra Leone's highest peak is also known, rises 1945m. In clear weather views from the summit are excellent. The Loma Mountains Forest Reserve protects the highland rainforest covering the lower slopes. There are chimpanzees and several species of monkey here and you have a fair chance of seeing elephants and bongos as you approach the mountain. In the rivers, you may be lucky enough to see pygmy hippopotamuses, dwarf crocodiles and rufous fishing-owls; all endangered species. Above 1500m the forest gives way to grassland where you can spot baboons, wart hogs, duikers, porcupines and even buffaloes.

The most scenic and wildlife-rich approach to the summit is from the west, either from Kabala via Koinadugu and Firawa or more commonly from Yifin village (from where it's at least a four-day walk), east of the dirt road between Kabala and Bumbuna. The western route from Kurubonla, north of Kono, can be done in two days if you move fast.

Pay your respects to the chief in either Firawa, Yifin or Kurubonla and he'll help you find a guide, which is necessary because many paths are overgrown. The climb isn't technical, but you need to be self-sufficient with camping gear and food.

# SIERRA LEONE DIRECTORY

## ACCOMMODATION

Freetown is full of classy, comfortable and costly hotels and more will open soon on the peninsular beaches. There are many budget choices in the capital, but few good ones; however, decent rooms can be found for around Le30,000. Generally budget rooms are under Le100,000 and top end over Le300,000.

Upcountry, most large towns have several hotels, though nothing that will satisfy those who need plenty of creature comforts. The cheapest are usually grubby and cater to short-term guests.

Always request discounts for stays of more than one night, as you'll often get them. Also note that a man and a woman can share a single room with no questions, but a same-sex couple, regardless of whether they are a 'couple', usually can not. Westerners are sometimes exempted from this rule if no doubles are available, but don't count on it.

---

**PRACTICALITIES**

- Sierra Leone uses British weights and measures.

- Electricity is 230V/50Hz and plugs have three large pins, like the UK, or sometimes three round pins.

- *Awoko* and *Concord Times* are two of the most respected newspapers, though the humorous *Peep* is more popular.

- Magazines like *Newsweek* and *Africa Week* are sold at supermarkets.

- Hardly anyone watches the government-owned SLBS TV station except when they show music videos: the American dramas and Nigerian soap operas on the privately owned ABC are far more popular.

- The BBC World Service is heard on 94.3FM, while Democracy (98.1FM) and SKYY (106FM) play the hits.

## ACTIVITIES

Hiking is excellent on the remote southern beaches and northeastern mountains. Climbers can scale Mt Bintumani (p767) and several other peaks, though getting to the mountains is more challenging than getting to the top. The Moa River will please white-water kayakers in the rainy season and Tiwai Island Wildlife Sanctuary (p763) is planning to offer trips. As soon as people learn the county is now safe, Sierra Leone is sure to become a bird-watching hotspot.

For swimming, the ocean is calm and warm and most beaches are rip-tide free, though always get local advice. The deep-sea fishing off the coast is some of Africa's best – twelve current world tarpon records in various line classes have been set here – and can easily be arranged in Freetown. To find a captain, ask around at the fancy hotels or at bars and restaurants popular with foreigners.

## BOOKS

The war spawned numerous harrowing books including Greg Campbell's *Blood Diamonds* and Daniel Bergner's *In the Land of Magic Soldiers*. *Fishing in Rivers of Sierra Leone* by Heribert Hinzen is a collection of local folk tales and songs.

In the first half of *The Devil That Danced on Water*, Aminatta Forna recounts her childhood in Freetown, during which her dissident father was executed, and then returns as a journalist 25 years later to investigate his death.

## BUSINESS HOURS

Business hours are 9am to 5.30pm Monday to Saturday, although many places close at 1pm on Saturday. Government offices are open 9am to 5pm Monday to Friday. Banking hours are Monday to Friday 9am to 3pm.

## CUSTOMS

You can not take more than Le50,000 out of the country. Exporting gold and diamonds without a licence is illegal.

## DANGERS & ANNOYANCES

These days Guinea's uncertain political future and Liberia's tenuous security situation present bigger challenges to Sierra Leone's newfound stability than anything internal.

Be sure to check on the condition near the borders if things in either neighbouring nation deteriorate.

Except for in Bo and Kenema, electricity is either sporadic or nonexistent, and even these towns suffer occasional shutoffs at the end of the dry season. Just about all hotels have generators, though most budget places will only run them from around 7pm to 1am.

## EMBASSIES & CONSULATES
### Sierra Leonean Embassies

Within West Africa, Sierra Leone has embassies in Ghana, The Gambia, Guinea, Senegal, Nigeria and Liberia. For details see the relevant country chapter. Elsewhere, Sierra Leone has the following embassies:

**Belgium** ( ☎ 0332-771 0053; sierraleoneembassy@brutele.be; 410 Ave de Terveuern, 1150 Brussels)
**Germany** ( ☎ 0228-352001; Rheinallee 20, 53173 Bonn)
**Netherlands** ( ☎ 35-6213504; G Van Amstelstraat 1, 1213 CG Hilversum)
**UK** ( ☎ 020-7287 9884; www.slhc-uk.org.uk; 245 Oxford St, W1D 2LX London)
**USA** ( ☎ 202 939 9261; www.embassyofsierraleone.org; 1701 19th St NW, 20009 Washington DC)

### Embassies & Consulates in Sierra Leone

All of the following are in Freetown:

**Gambia** (Map p756; ☎ 225191; 6 Wilberforce St; ❧ 9am-4pm Mon-Thu, 9am-12.30pm Fri)
**Germany** (Map pp754-5; ☎ 231350; germemb@sierratel.sl; 3 Middle Hill Station, Wilberforce; ❧ 9am-noon Mon-Fri)
**Ghana** (Map p756; ☎ 223461; 13 Walpole St; ❧ 9am-3pm Mon-Fri)
**Guinea** (Map pp754-5; ☎ 232496; 6 Carlton Carew Rd; ❧ 8am-3pm Mon-Fri)
**Ireland** (Map p756; ☎ 222017; 8 Rawdon St; ❧ 8.30am-noon & 2-4pm Mon-Fri, 9.30am-noon Sat)
**Liberia** (Map pp754-5; ☎ 230991; 2 Spur Rd, Wilberforce; ❧ 9am-3pm Mon-Fri)
**Mali** (Map pp754-5; ☎ 030 230284; 40 Wilkinson Rd; ❧ 9am-3.30pm Mon-Thu, 9am-12.30pm & 2.30-3.30pm Fri)
**Nigeria** (Map p756; ☎ 224229; 37 Siaka Stevens St; ❧ 10am-2pm Mon-Fri)
**Senegal** (Map pp754-5; ☎ 222948; Upper East St; ❧ 9am-4.30pm Mon-Fri, 9am-12.30pm Sat)
**UK** (Map p756; ☎ 232961; bhc@sierratel.sl; 6 Spur Rd; ❧ 8am-5pm Mon-Thu & 8am-1pm Fri) Assists French nationals.
**USA** (Map p756; ☎ 226481; http://freetown.usembassy.gov; cnr Walpole & Siaka Stevens Sts; ❧ 8.30am-4pm Mon-Fri) A new embassy is under construction at Hill Station.

## HOLIDAYS

Public holidays include the following:
**New Year's Day** 1 January
**Easter** March/April
**Independence Day** 27 April
**Christmas Day** 25 December
**Boxing Day** 26 December

Sierra Leone also celebrates Islamic holidays; see p818 for details.

## INTERNET ACCESS

Freetown has plenty of Internet cafés with good high-speed connections, most charging Le5000 per hour. Access in the provinces is rare and painfully slow.

## INTERNET RESOURCES

**National Tourist Board** (www.welcometosierraleone .org) The information is not kept up to date, but the site is still useful.
**Sierra Leone Web** (www.sierra-leone.org) Lots of good background information.
**Visit Sierra Leone** (www.visitsierraleone.org) Tons of travel advice and an active discussion forum where, no matter how obscure your inquiry, someone will probably have an answer.

## LANGUAGE

There are more than a dozen tribal languages, the most common of which are Mende and Temne. English is the official language and Krio is the most widely spoken. See p861 for a list of useful phrases in Krio.

## MAPS

*The Road Map of Sierra Leone and Freetown* by Oxford Cartographers is sold at the Tourist Information Office at Lumley Beach for Le35,000, and by street vendors around Crown Bakery (see p758) for less than half this. Outside Africa you can buy the International Travel Map series (2001; 1:560,000), which is slightly better for the country, but it doesn't have Freetown. Both are outdated.

## MONEY

The most easily exchangeable currencies are US dollars, UK pounds and euros. Large denominations get the best rates. You can't pay with a credit card anywhere in Sierra Leone, but some Sierra Leone Commercial Bank and Rokel Bank branches give cash advances on Visa cards. The handful of ATMs in the capital only work if you hav a local bank account.

Forex bureaus (and street traders, though you should avoid them unless you have a friend make the introduction) offer better rates than banks for cash and take travellers cheques for about 10% less than cash. There are banks and forex bureaus in Bo, Kenema, Makeni and a few smaller upcountry towns, but you'll get better rates in Freetown.

One hundred Leones is a 'block' and one thousand is a 'grand'.

## POST

Sierra Leone's regular post, including poste restante, is unreliable, though the separate express service seems to work. It is best to send everything from Freetown.

## TELEPHONE

The easiest way to make a phone call is at the countless small telecentres. Calls to the USA/UK/Australia cost Le2500 per minute. It's cheaper by about half to use the Sierratel phonecards, but finding a phone to use them on can be a chore.

Mobile phones are very common and the service is pretty good. If you have a GSM phone you can buy a SIM card for Le10,000 to Le15,000 and then use prepaid top-up cards. Mobile phone prefixes are Africel ☎ 077, Celtel ☎ 076, Comium ☎ 033 and Millicom ☎ 030.

## VISAS

All travellers, except those from Ecowas countries, need visas. While visas are available at the airport and land borders, it is strongly recommended that you get a visa before arrival to avoid any hassles, as this is a new policy.

### Visa Extensions

You can easily obtain visa extensions from the **Immigration Department** (Map p756; ☎ 223034; 15 Siaka Stevens St; ⏰ 10am-3.30pm Mon-Fri). Enter on Rawdon St.

### Visas for Onward Travel

**GUINEA**
One-month single-entry visas cost up to GF100,000 and a three-month multiple-entry visa as much as GF200,000, depending on your nationality. You need one photo and the visa is ready almost immediately.

BERIA
Three-month single-entry visas cost Le225,000 for most nationalities and six-month multiple-entry visas are Le300,000. You need one photo and the visa should be ready in 15 minutes.

## WOMEN TRAVELLERS

Sierra Leone does not present any specific problems for women travellers other than a handful of beach boys, though they are tame compared to The Gambia. For general information see p828.

# TRANSPORT IN SIERRA LEONE

## GETTING THERE & AWAY
### Entering Sierra Leone

You'll need a certificate of vaccination for yellow fever and cholera to enter Sierra Leone, though in practice they only check for yellow fever.

### Air

Lungi International Airport is efficient, though inconveniently located across the Sierra Leone River from Freetown. Return flights from London cost about £500 and often arrive/depart Freetown at ridiculous hours. SN Brussels charges a bit more for better service on flights from Brussels.

Airlines flying to and from Sierra Leone:

**Astraeus** (Map p756; 5W; ☎ 228405; www.flyastraeus .com; 24 Rawdon St) Hub: Gatwick Airport, London.
**Bellview Airlines** (Map p756; B3; ☎ 227311; www .flybellviewair.com; 31 Lightfoot Boston St) Hub: Murtala Muhammed International Airport, Lagos.

**Slok Air** (Map p756; SO; ☎ 076 770702; www.slokair international.com; 13 Howe St) Hub: Banjul International Airport, Banjul.
**SN Brussels** (Map pp754-5; SN; ☎ 236445; www.flysn .com; 72B Cape Rd) Hub: Brussels Airport, Brussels.

### Land
#### GUINEA

The main border crossing is at Pamelap. Bush taxis run between Freetown and Conakry, Guinea (Le30,000, seven hours), frequently and there is an SLRTC bus (Le40,000, seven hours) on Monday and Thursday. You can also get to the border from most large towns and easily continue to Conakry from there. The road is not yet paved north of the Makeni Hwy, but it should be completed soon. The trip usually takes about eight hours.

From Kamakwie to Kindia, Guinea, there is little transport on the Sierra Leone side, where the road is quite bad, and during the rainy season the Little Scarcies River sometimes runs so high the ferry shuts down. But once you get to Medina-Oula in Guinea moving on is easy. The road from Kabala to Faranah, Guinea, is also in bad shape and only has taxis a couple of times a week.

Get local advice before crossing from Kailahun on toward Guéckédou. Not only are the roads bad, but we've heard reports of hassles with Sierra Leone border officials. You'll need your own wheels to cross at Koindu as there is little traffic going this way. Both routes involve ferry crossings.

### REGIONAL FLIGHTS FROM FREETOWN

| Destination | No of flights per week | Airline | One way/return (Le) |
|---|---|---|---|
| Abidjan (Côte d'Ivoire) | 3 | Bellview Airlines, SN Brussels | 879,000/1,341,000 |
| Accra (Ghana) | 9 | Bellview Airlines, Slok Air | 1,020,000/1,530,000 |
| Banjul (Gambia) | 5 | Bellview Airlines, Slok Air | 393,000/552,000 |
| Dakar (Senegal) | 5 | Bellview Airlines, Slok Air | 555,000/984,000 |
| Lagos (Nigeria) | 6 | Bellview Airlines | 855,000/1,485,000 |
| Monrovia (Liberia) | 7 | Slok Air | 420,000/636,000 |
| | | | Prices are approximate. |

## LIBERIA

The main route between Freetown and Monrovia is via Kenema, Zimmi then Bo (Waterside). The journey takes two days in the dry season and no taxis go direct from Freetown to the border (where you need to change), so you first need to go to Kenema. It is a little quicker via Bo (if the ferry over the Moa River is working), but few taxis go this way. If you reach the border after it has closed there are some grubby guesthouses and plenty of *cookery* in the border town of Jendema.

The seldom-used crossings from Zimmi, Koindu and Buedu are also via horrible roads and have very little traffic. Check the security situation before using any of these crossings.

## Sea

Ferry service to Conakry is expected to begin again soon; inquire at Government Wharf in Freetown for details.

# GETTING AROUND
## Boat

Boats run from Tombo, on the Freetown peninsula, to Shenge and Bonthe. See p760 for details.

## Bus, Bush Taxi & Minibus

Bush taxis and *poda-podas* link all major and many minor towns, though, except for departures to and from Freetown (and between Bo and Kenema), traffic is usually pretty sparse, especially on Sunday. Please note that all of the travel times given are just rough approximations. The government-run Sierra Leone Road Transport Corpor-ation (SLRTC) buses charge the same as taxis and are more comfortable, but slower and at best have just one departure a day.

## Car

Several companies in Freetown hire cars, with driver included, though prices are high; see p759.

### ROAD CONDITIONS

The highway from Freetown to Kabala is paved and in excellent condition. From where it forks and heads to Bo is paved, but in horrible shape. Also surfaced and still smooth is the road between Bo and Kenema and the peninsular highway between Waterloo and Tokeh – south from Freetown it is very rough. The rutted dirt road between Kenema and the Liberian border is one of West Africa's worst, and though the route south from Bo to Zimmi is in better shape, don't head this way without ensuring the Moa River car ferry is working.

If you believe the government, all major roads will be paved in the next few years, but probably only the rest of the Peninsular Hwy, the Freetown–Bo road and the road to the Guinean border will be completed any time soon.

## Tours

**Facts Finding Tours** (Map pp754–5; ☎ 076 903675, factsfinding@yahoo.com; Lumley Beach Rd, Freetown) The knowledgeable Kenneth Gbengba leads personalised bird- and wildlife-watching tours across the country.

**IPC Travel** (Map p756; ☎ 221481; ipc@sierratel.sl; 22 Siaka Stevens St; ⏰ 8.30am–5pm Mon-Fri & 9am-1pm Sat) IPC offers several excellent city, peninsula and island tours and will be heading out to the provinces soon.

# Togo

While many African countries move slowly forward, Togo seems to be stumbling backwards. Once regarded as the pearl of West Africa for its tranquil beaches, exotic markets and friendly people, the tiny nation was overwhelmed by riots and human rights abuses in the 1990s, and sadly the saga continues. When the despotic president Gnassingbé Eyadéma died in February 2005, and his son Faure Gnassingbé seized power, hundreds were killed in street battles and thousands fled the country.

But with the new president gradually winning over the Togolese population, it's a great time to check out Togo's hilly landscape, warm people, diverse cultures, conquering football team and yam-based dishes.

Lomé, the capital, is one of the most beautiful cities in West Africa, with the grand Blvd du 13 Janvier sweeping away from the beach and into the heart of a ribald city, heaving with nightspots. To the east, past the resorts on Lake Togo and the Atlantic beaches, Aného exudes crumbling colonial charm and has a fetish market. Voodoo is also practised across the lake in Togoville, a fishing village with fetishes in the streets.

Inland, Kpalimé is the gateway to coffee country, where ruined chateaus, butterflies and mountain villages hide in the forests. Northern cities like Sokodé and Kara are appealingly slow-paced spots to take in rural Africa and, near the former, the animals are returning to Parc National de Fazao-Malfakassa. Close to Kara, the famous fortresslike mud-brick houses in the Tamberma Valley and the weekly markets in the Kabyé region show life being lived as it has been for centuries.

## FAST FACTS

- **Area** 56,790 sq km
- **Capital** Lomé
- **Country code** ☎ 228
- **Famous for** Emmanuel Adebayor; Prince Albert of Monaco's love child; political instability
- **Languages** French (official); Ewe; Mina; Kabyé
- **Money** West African CFA franc; US$1 = CFA544.89; €1 = CFA655.96
- **Population** 5.1 million
- **Visa** CFA10,000 at border; 30-day extension CFA10,000

**Le Kelediang** ( ☎ 542 5385; www.senegambia.net; r per person CFA3200) Enter the forest and soak up the free-spirited, close-to-nature atmosphere of this relaxed Dutch-run establishment. Accommodation is in deliberately basic, but comfy bungalows and the restaurant near the beach serves delicious lunch and dinner.

**Le Bolonga** ( ☎ 994 8515; s/d CFA7500/10,000) This quality place really is as warm and welcoming as the bar-reception in the brick building at the entrance suggests. The young staff go to great lengths to put you at ease and satisfy all your excursion or workshop wishes.

**Campement Sitokoto** ( ☎ 994 8512; r per person incl breakfast CFA4500) Kafountine's *campement villageois* has got basic rooms with clean, shared toilets right near the river.

**La Case de Marie Oldie** ( ☎ 936 9710, 539 2379; s/d CFA3000/4500) This red-brick *case à impluvium* construction is a treat close to Kafountine village. Sunny, clean and friendly – and the rates are unbeatable.

**Le Paradise** ( ☎ télécentre 936 9492; r CFA4000) 'Very Jah', is the going description of this phlegmatic little *campement*. Drumming, smoking, hanging about and philosophising – *voilà* the ambience of this self-declared paradise. The drumming courses get good reviews.

**Á la Nature** ( ☎ 994 8524; alanature@arc.sn; r per person incl breakfast CFA4500) Past the fishing village and pirogue-makers and just above the high-water line, this is Kafountine's famous beachfront venture with a rasta feel. Drumming workshops and hammock-lounging are obligatory.

**Le Saloulou** ( ☎ /fax 994 8514; r per person CFA6000) Fancy it ain't, but it's situated seconds from the surf and offers fishing trips in the sea or *bolongs*.

**Le Bandoula Village** ( ☎ 994 8511; s/d CFA13,000/ 15,000) A few steps down from the Saloulou, this place is slightly more upmarket, as the fair rates suggest. Not a bad option.

## Eating

Kafountine isn't a gourmet's paradise, and the hotel restaurants are still your safest bet. Esperanto, Fouta Djalon, Le Kelediang and Bandoula Village are among the most reliable. Other good options include **Le Bissap** ( ☎ 994 8512; dishes CFA2000-3000; 🕒 8am-midnight), where food is tasty. You can check your emails and buy your groceries there, too. Alternatively, there are a few cheap eateries in the market offering similar local fare for little money: **Chez Yandé, Le Cocotier Café** ( 🕒 8am-midnight) and **Couleur Café** ( ☎ 936 9520; 🕒 8am-midnight) are popular. **Pointe Nord** ( 🕒 11am-2am) is a lively bar. Simple Senegalese meals cost around CFA750 to CFA1500 in all three places.

Self-caterers can stock up in the centre of the village. The **Mini Marché** ( 🕒 9am-11pm) sells a good variety of foodstuffs and is a popular hang out for local youth.

## Entertainment

This is a town full of party-ready inhabitants. The nightclubs are usually packed with dreadlocked youngsters, and often get rowdy as the night wears on. The **Farafina** (admission CFA1500-2000) enjoys the reputation of being the most upmarket, and most expensive place of the lot. **Black and White** (admission CFA1000) and **Chez Pablo** (admission CFA500-1000) are the cheaper alternatives. Additionally, there's a set of bars that have live bands on rotation. They include the Le Kabekel and Le Flamant Rose.

## Getting There & Away

From Ziguinchor, *sept-place* taxis (CFA2500) and minibuses (CFA1700) run directly to Kafountine. Alternatively, take any vehicle to Diouloulou, from where local bush taxis take the rough tarmac road to Kafountine for CFA600.

You can also get bush taxis from Serekunda or Brikama in The Gambia, although direct traffic usually goes via the back roads and the sleepy Darsilami border crossing rather than the main one at Séléti. There's no Senegalese border post, so you might have to return to Séléti to get your passport stamped.

## Getting Around

It's quite a walk from the hotel-lined beachfront to the village centre, and while you can hope for a ride with a friendly local, you're unlikely to come across a taxi. Ask the hotel to call you a cab, it'll set you back around CFA1000 to CFA2000.

### ABÉNÉ

Abéné, a slightly quieter version of Kafountine, lies 6km north on the route to Diouloulou. From the village it's 2km along a sandy track to the beach, past a small craft village

## Bignona & Baïla

Bignona is a sleepy crossroads town with crumbling colonial buildings, where the main route to/from Banjul joins the Trans-Gambia Hwy 30km north of Ziguinchor.

A short drive out of town, the **Hôtel le Palmier** ( ☎ 994 1258; r CFA7000) has adequate facilities in an old, colonial-style building. In Badiouré, 11km from Bignona on the road towards Séléti, you'll find the **Relais Fleuri** ( ☎ 994 3002; fax 994 3219; s/d CFA12,000/14,000; ⚉ ⚏ ), which is as pretty as its name, but caters almost exclusively for hunters. Just avoid the main season (November to April).

Off the main road between Bignona and Dioulolou, Baïla tempts with another pretty **campement villageois** ( ☎ 544 8035; télécentre 936 9516). The area is great for walks and pirogue tours. It's best to go with a guide, and don't venture out on lonely paths late at night.

Ziguinchor to Baïla takes around 45 minutes along the tarmac main road. A bush taxi costs CFA1500, a hire taxi around CFA20,000.

## Kafountine & Abéné

Kafountine and Abéné are the hip face of tourism in Senegal. The two villages on the coast just south of The Gambia have spawned more than 20 guesthouses, often the sort of place where dreadlocked staff seem happy to drum the day away and everything is 'cool, mon'. The villages are separated from the rest of Casamance Nord by a large branch of the Casamance River called Marigot Diouloulou.

The area looks more to the north than to the south: if you travel here from The Gambia, the reggae-vibing tourist scene will seem familiar.

Several Senegalese and European artists have settled here, *djembe* drum clutched between their knees and tie-dye kit in hand, and have tuned in the area to the laid-back rhythms of 'baba cool' – a West African version of relaxed reggae culture. You don't have to look far for your introductory drumming, batik or dance workshop.

### KAFOUNTINE

Kafountine is a spread-out village near the end of the pot-holed tarmac leading in from Diouloulou. The village centre stretches along the main road. It's reasonably well equipped, with several *télécentres*, a slowish cybercafé,

---

**BIRD-WATCHING SITES AROUND KAFOUNTINE**

The creeks and lagoons around Kafountine are wonderful areas for watching birds, especially waders and shore birds. You can start your excursions right in town, at the small pool near the Campement Sitokoto, or at the bar of the *campement* Esperanto, where you can gaze across the *bolongs* (estuaries) while imbibing a soothing sunset drink. Esperanto, and several other lodgings organise trips to the famous bird-watching sites further afield, including the Sanctuaire Ornithologique de la Pointe de Kalissaye, a group of sandy islands (usually hidden by the waters), at the mouth of the Marigot Kalissaye, and the highly rated Sanctuaire Ornithologique de Kassel, some 5km southeast of Kafountine. Another place is the Presqu'île des Oiseaux, a narrow spit of land between the ocean and a creek, noted for its huge populations of Caspian terns. It lies south of the fishing village – most *campements* organise excursions.

---

a hospital and post office, but no bank. Most hotels and *campements* are scattered along a wide, sandy beach, which divides into two areas: the northern strip, reached by turning right on the sandy road as it leads west from the village; and the southern strip that lies on the main road south of Kafountine village. The beachfront is a taxi- or bicycle-worthy 2km from the village. To reach the southern strip, you pass the fishing village, a busy settlement with lines of shacks where fish are dried and smoked, and a beach from where boats are launched.

### Sleeping

**Esperanto** (Chez Eric & Antonella; ☎ 635 6280; esperanto@arc.sn; d CFA10,000, with half board CFA16,500) This relaxed place between the river and sea is a real gem, with bungalows (some family sized) set in a landscaped garden with palm trees and bamboo bridges.

**Le Fouta Djalon** ( ☎ 936 9494; www.casamance.net /foutadjalon; s/d CFA12,000/20,000) The hotel's extensive garden begins right behind a small dune that leads to the beach. The red-brick huts are comfortable and the cosy bar invites relaxed evening drinks.

## HIGHLIGHTS

- **Lomé** (p778) Hit the bars and boulevards to see the coastal capital in all its decaying glory.
- **Kpalimé** (p788) Hike in the surrounding hills, where exotic butterflies flutter in the lush forests.
- **Lake Togo** (p787) Stay at the tranquil resorts here and discover the area's voodoo culture.
- **Tamberma Valley** (p799) Seek out northern Togo's remote clay-and-straw fortresses: the *tata* compounds in Tamberma Valley and the cliffside silos south of Dapaong.
- **Lomé Grand Marché** (p785) Haggle with the formidable Mama Benz, female marketeers named after their favourite motors.

## ITINERARIES

- **One Week** Allow at least a week for exploring **Lomé** (p778) and its surrounds. Within easy reach of the coastal capital, the Friday market in **Vogan** (p787) is particularly interesting. Combine this trip with one to **Aného** (p787) and **Lake Togo** (p787).
- **Two Weeks** After investigating all that Lomé has to offer, head for the area around **Kpalimé** (p788) – a great place to go hiking – and the central towns north of the capital. From there, you could head to the Akloa waterfalls outside **Badou** (p793), then to **Sokodé** (p794) and as far as the vibrant Kabyé town of **Kara** (p796).
- **Three Weeks** For those with more time on their hands, the **Tamberma Valley** (p799) in the far north, home to the fascinating Tamberma people, is well worth a visit. Also worth short trips are Togo's two main national parks: **Fazao-Malfakassa** (p793) and **Kéran** (p800). If the fortified compounds in the Tamberma Valley have tweaked your interest in unusual indigenous architecture, head to the cliffside silos on **Mount Semoo** (p802). Nearby, **Dapaong** (p800) is a mellow market town not far from the Burkinabé border.

## CLIMATE & WHEN TO GO

This long, thin country stretches across six geographic zones and its climate ranges from tropical in the south to savanna in the north. Rain falls from May to October. In the south there's a dry spell from mid-July

to mid-September. In the north there is no such interlude, but on the whole the north is more arid than the south, which is fairly dry itself. Mid-February (after the harmattan wind lifts) to mid-April is the hottest period throughout the country, while November to February is the driest.

The two dry seasons are the best time to visit, although the July–September season coincides with the harmattan and is a rotten time for photographers. Major roads are dependable throughout the year, but unsealed roads, such as those in the national parks, can be unpassable during and after the rains. See climate charts p813.

## HISTORY

Togo's name comes from *togodo*, which means 'behind the lake' in Ewe – a reference to the body of water now called Lake Togo. The region was once at the edge of several empires, including the Dahomey and Akan–Ashanti kingdoms in present-day Benin and Ghana respectively. It played a few bit parts in the Dahomey story: the Alladahanou from Tado, southeast of Sokodé, established kingdoms in what would become known as Dahomey; and Togo was the toppled Dahomeyan kings' refuge of choice.

With the arrival of Europeans in the 16th century, the power vacuum in Togo allowed the slave-traders to use the country as a conduit. The Mina – who had immigrated from the west along with the Guin (while

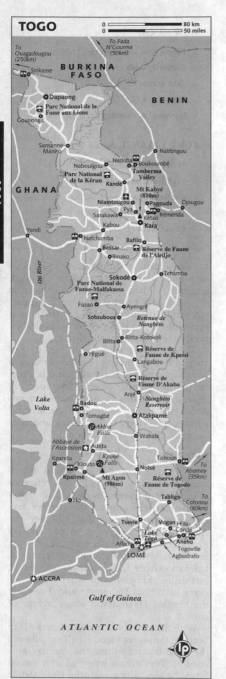

**TOGO**

the Ewe had arrived from the east) – became ruthless agents for the slave-traders.

## Germans in Togoland

With the abolition of slavery, the Europeans turned their attention to trade in commodities – palm and coconut oil, cacao, coffee and cotton. In 1884, Germany surprised its colonial rivals Britain and France, when it signed a treaty in Togoville with the local king, Mlapa, agreeing to 'protect' the inhabitants in return for German sovereignty.

Togoland, as the Germans called the area, underwent considerable economic development before WWI. The Togolese, however, didn't appreciate the Germans' forced labour, direct taxes and 'pacification' campaigns, in which thousands of locals were killed, and so they welcomed British forces in WWI. Encircled by British and French troops, the Germans surrendered at Kamina – the Allies' first victory in the war.

After the war, the League of Nations split Togoland, with France acquiring the eastern two-thirds of the country and Britain the remainder. This controversial move divided the populous Ewe, and political groups were still agitating for reunification following WWII.

## Independence & the Coup

Following a 1956 plebiscite, hopes of reunification were dashed, when British Togoland was incorporated into the Gold Coast (present-day Ghana). The division is still a source of discontent.

French Togoland became an autonomous republic and in 1960 gained full independence under the leadership of Sylvanus Olympio, who became the first president.

In 1963, Togo became the first African country to have a military coup after independence. Sylvanus Olympio, a Ewe from the south, disregarded the northerners, whom he called *petits nordiques* (small northerners), when he refused to integrate into his army 600 soldiers returning from the Algerian War (predominantly Kabyé northerners) they rebelled. Olympio was killed at the gates of the US embassy as he sought refuge.

His replacement, Nicolas Grunitzky, was deposed in turn – in a bloodless coup led by Kabyé sergeant Gnassingbé Eyadéma. The new leader set out to unify the country's tribal groups, insisting on one trade union and one political party, the Rassemblement du Peuple Togolaise (RPT). He established a cult of personality, surrounding himself with sycophantic staff and a chorus of cheering women in traditional dress.

When Eyadéma's private plane crashed near Sarakawa in 1974, he was convinced he had survived an assassination attempt and became increasingly irrational and unpredictable.

## Struggling for a Multiparty System

In 1990, France began pressuring Eyadéma to adopt a multiparty system. He resisted, and portrayed African multiparty systems negatively through TV broadcasts of scenes of violence and unrest in nearby countries. Early 1991 saw riots and strikes by pro-democracy forces, many of whom were killed in clashes with the army. In April 1991, 28 bodies were dragged out of Lomé-Bé Lagoon and dumped on the steps of the US embassy, drawing attention to the repressive nature of Eyadéma's dictatorship.

Finally bowing to international pressure, Eyadéma agreed to a conference in 1991, to decide the country's future. Delegates there stripped him of his powers and installed an interim government, headed by Joseph Koffigoh, pending democratic elections. Months later, however, troops loyal to Eyadéma attacked Koffigoh's residence and detained him, leaving Eyadéma, once again, in full control of the government.

Eyadéma now postponed the promised elections, prompting the trade unions to call a general strike in November 1992. This continued for months, paralysing Togo's economy – banks and businesses closed, exports lay stranded in Lomé port, tourism collapsed. In the ensuing violence, some 250,000 southerners fled the country.

In a contest boycotted by the opposition and denounced by international observers, Eyadéma won the August 1993 presidential elections. A coalition of opposition parties – the Committee for Renewed Action (CAR) and the Union Togolaise Démocratique (UTD) – won the 1994 parliamentary elections, which were boycotted by the Union des Forces du Changement (UFC) and marred by the killing of three opposition members.

Eyadéma reached a deal with UTD leader Edem Kodjo, and appointed him prime minister. This split the coalition, with CAR

leader Yao Agboyibo denied the role of prime minister and key posts going to Eyadéma supporters rather than CAR. Kodjo resigned in 1996 following a succession of opposition defeats in by-elections.

In the 1998 presidential elections Eyadéma triumphed again, although international observers criticised the conduct of the election. Fearing government manipulation, the opposition then boycotted the 1999 legislative elections, allowing the RPT to win 77 of the 81 seats in the national assembly.

## Togo Today

International pressure on Eyadéma increased at the same rate as aid from donors decreased. Amnesty International made allegations about executions and torture which had allegedly taken place around the 1998 elections, and Eyadéma responded by suing the organisation. He consistently reneged on promises, such as assuring Jacques Chirac he would step down before the 2003 elections, before changing the constitution to enable him to seek a third term.

Eyadéma finally left office the way many suspected he would – in a coffin. Following his death at 69 in February 2005, his son, Faure Gnassingbé, seized power in a military coup, then relented and held presidential elections, which he won. Amid allegations of fixing, some 500 people were killed in riots in Lomé, and thousands of refugees fled to Benin and Ghana.

Gnassingbé has appointed Edem Kodjo as prime minister and held talks with UFC leader Gilchrist Olympio. Although many Togolese see him as a perpetuation of the old regime, they accept that he is an improvement on his father and are willing to listen to his ideas.

## THE CULTURE
### The National Psyche

The Togolese ego corresponds to the country's small size and the dearth of tourists it sees as a result of its political problems. With the exception of the odd official and hustler in Lomé, Togolese people are friendly and easy to deal with.

Of course, visitors do encounter *yovo* (white person) surcharges, but these are negligible compared to those in other West African countries. The Togolese generally show foreigners great respect, and you will often be offered the front seat in bush taxis. They are proud and hospitable people – knowing a few words of their native languages is hugely appreciated.

Given the police state they have lived in for decades, Togolese people are understandably wary of political discussions. Although some pessimism remains about the country's political situation, the Togolese are as outgoing and vibrant as their Ghanaian and Beninese neighbours.

## Daily Life

Togo's Muslims are its keenest traders, particularly the Kotokoli, while the Mina produce the country's major exports. Overall, the Togolese population has an average age of 18 and a life expectancy at birth of 57. Literacy rates are 60% and over 100,000 people live with AIDS.

Most of the country's ethnic groups are culturally distinct, and are controlled by patrilineal heredity. Communities, which are headed by a chief, are well structured within a social, political and economic framework, with family at its heart and social-minded values encouraged.

Customs, rites and superstitions play a large part in everyday life, with milestones such as births, puberty, marriage and death celebrated through ceremonies. If you are invited to a ceremony, dress conservatively and be respectful of local customs.

Everyday conversations are often loud and animated, and minor disagreements can quickly escalate into heated arguments, then subside as quickly as they began. While such behaviour is quite common, it is unacceptable and ill-advised for visitors to emulate it.

John M. Chernoff's *Hustling is not Stealing: Stories of an African Bar Girl* is a must-read book on daily life in the societal underbelly of Togo and Ghana (see p802).

## Population

With about 40 ethnic groups in a population of some 5½ million people, Togo has one of Africa's more heterogeneous populations. The two largest groups are the southern Ewe and the northern Kabyé; the latter count President Gnassingbé among their number and are concentrated around Kara. Other significant groups include the Kotokoli, who live around Bassar and Bafilo,

> **EWE & THE AFTERLIFE**
>
> Togo's diverse cultural composition has given rise to a rich array of traditional practices. Many of the Ewe's funeral rites and conceptions of afterlife and death have a strong animist element.
>
> According to the Ewe, once a person dies their *djoto* (reincarnated soul) will come back in the next child born into the same lineage, while their *luvo* (death soul) may linger with those still living, seeking attention and creating havoc. Funerals are thus one of the most important events in Ewe society, involving several nights of drumming and dancing followed by rituals to free the soul of the deceased and encourage reincarnation.

and the Kabyé-related Tamberma, who live in fortified compounds east of Kara.

The Ewe-related people – including the Mina, Guin, Anlo, Adja and Pla-Peda – are concentrated on the plantations in the southwest. Although they call themselves Ewe, some of these groups are not ethnic Ewe. The Mina and the Guin are Fanti and Ga people respectively, both from the Ghanaian coast.

## ECONOMY

Togo's economy is reliant on agriculture, which contributes 42% of the GDP and is the livelihood of 65% of the population. Cocoa, coffee, and cotton form 40% of exports, with the industrial sector dominated by phosphate mining – Togo is the world's fourth-largest producer of phosphate.

Severely damaged in the 1990s by the 50% devaluation of the CFA and political unrest, the economy is now growing. The international donors and businesses that deserted Togo are returning; the country bagged a multimillion-dollar oil contract in 2001, when China also cancelled two-thirds of Togo's debt (some CFA18,800 million).

## SPORT

Togo's football team, Les Eperviers (the Sparrow Hawks), has been phenomenally successful given Togo's tiny size, having qualified for the 2006 World Cup at the time of writing. Striker Emmanuel Adebayor (who currently plays for the English team Arsenal) is a national icon, and the team's victories prompt street parties and public holidays.

## RELIGION

Christianity and Islam are the most evident religions in Togo – in the south and north respectively. However, about 59% of the population have animist beliefs, which are harder to spot. Voodoo is strongest in the southeast but there are traces of it throughout the country.

## ARTS
### Architecture

The country is well known for its French and German colonial buildings, and the fortified compounds in the Tamberma Valley are some of the most striking structures in West Africa.

### Arts & Craftwork

Togo's traditional arts and crafts are as varied as its people. Ironwork, pottery and weaving predominate in the northeast, while decorative wood burning (marking wood or calabashes with intricate geometric designs) is common in the northwest.

Batik and wax printing is popular throughout Togo, but the most well-known textile is the Ewe kente cloth, which is less brilliantly coloured than the Ashanti version. Cloth is sold by the *pagne* (2m strip).

### Music & Dance

Music and dance play an important part in Togolese daily life. Dances revolve around traditional life, incorporating subjects such as hunting, fishing, warfare, harvesting and love.

While drums play a pivotal role in all festivities, there are diverse musical styles. In the south you'll find percussion instruments, such as bells and gongs; in the central region, *lithophones* (stone percussion instruments); and in the north, flutes and the musical bow – played while holding an arrow.

Today, traditional music has fused with contemporary West African, Caribbean and South American sounds, creating a hybrid that includes highlife, reggae and soukous. Togo's most famous singing export was Bella Bellow, who, before her death in 1973, ruled the local music scene, toured internationally and released an album, *Album Souvenir*.

### Literature

The country's best-known author is Tété-Michel Kpomassie. His unlikely sounding autobiography, *An African in Greenland*, contains his unique perspective on life in the chilly land.

## ENVIRONMENT
### The Land

Togo's coastline measures only 56km, but the country stretches inland for over 600km. Lagoons stretch intermittently along the sandy coast, and further inland are rolling hills covered with forest, yielding to savanna plains in the north.

### National Parks

Togo's national parks are disappointing because the larger mammals have largely been killed or scared off. The country's remaining mammals, which include monkeys, buffaloes and antelopes, are limited to the north, while crocodiles and hippos are found in the rivers.

Since 1995, the Swiss Fondation Franz Weber has been working, with some success, to resurrect Parc National de Fazao-Malfakassa (see p793), but the other parks are in a dire condition, with deforestation and poaching continuing unhindered.

### Environmental Issues

Pressure for land, combined with lack of government commitment to conservation, lack of financial resources, and traditional practices such as slash-and-burn agriculture, have taken their toll on the environment.

Forestry managers are now attempting to involve communities in the care of reforested areas. In return for access to forests to get fruit and firewood, local farmers are asked to help prevent forest fires – in the past they started fires to show their resentment at being denied access to protected areas.

The coastline is also in a precarious state. Since the construction of a second pier at Lomé's port, several beaches have disappeared. Pollution compounds the situation.

## FOOD & DRINK

Togolese dishes, some of the best in West Africa, are typically based, as in much of the region, on a starch staple such as *pâte* (a dough-like substance made of millet, corn, plantains, manioc or yams) accompanied by sauce. Sauces include *arachide* (groundnut), *épinards* (spinach) and *aglan* (crab). Some Togolese specialities are *abobo* (snails cooked on a skewer) and *koliko* (fried yams). *Pintade* (guinea fowl) is a popular meat.

Togo has its fair share of local brews. *Tchoukoutou* (fermented millet) is the preferred tipple in the north, often found in the market areas. Elsewhere, beware of *sodabe*, a terrifyingly potent, clear-coloured moonshine distilled from palm wine, another popular southern tipple.

# LOMÉ

pop 675,000

Lomé was once one of the cities that claimed to be the Paris of West Africa, and, unlike many of the other claimants, it is easy to see how attractive the city was in its heyday. Although an air of desperation hovers over its decaying buildings, corrupt policemen and discontented inhabitants, there is real charm to its broad boulevards, palm-fringed beaches, craft markets and full-on nightlife.

The city's name comes from *alomé* – the Ewe name for the trees that produce chewing sticks, which once grew in abundance here.

## ORIENTATION

Orientating yourself is fairly easy in Lomé. Most places of interest are in the D-shaped central area within the coastal highway and the semicircular Blvd du 13 Janvier (often called Blvd Circulaire).

The heart of town is around the intersection of Rue de la Gare and Rue du Commerce, which becomes Rue du Lac Togo east of the market. The Grand Marché is a few blocks to the east of the intersection. About six blocks north of the market is Ave du 24 Janvier, which runs east–west. Ave Maman N'Danida leads north from the centre to meet Blvd de la Paix – which runs northeast to the airport – and turn into Blvd Gnassingbé Eyadéma. Having passed the university, the road changes its name again – to Route de Atakpamé, which heads north out of the city.

## Maps

The best map of Lomé is the *Lomé* city map (1998), available at most bookshops from CFA3000. The Direction de la Promotion Touristique also offers the pocket-sized fold-up *Plan de Lomé*.

The excellent *Guide Lomé*, found at most bookshops from CFA8000, has a detailed street directory, and is written in English and French.

## INFORMATION
### Bookshops

**Librairie Bon Pasteur** ( ☎ 221 36 28; cnr Rue du Commerce & Ave de la Libération; ✆ 8am-12.15pm & 3-6pm Mon-Fri) Lomé's best bookshop, a block west of the cathedral. It sells maps and, occasionally, English publications like the *International Herald Tribune* and *Time*.

### Cultural Centres

**American Cultural Center** ( ☎ 220 68 91; Rue du Lac Togo; ✆ 9am-12.30pm & 3-6pm, 9am-noon Sat) Located in the same complex as the US Embassy. Has a library and screens American TV and films.

**Centre Culturel Français** ( ☎ 221 02 32; www.ccf .tg.refer.org; 19 Ave du 24 Janvier) Offers regular films, concerts and exhibitions, and has a good selection of books and up-to-date newspapers.

### Emergency

**Centre Hospitalier Regional** ( ☎ 221 23 11; Blvd Notre Dame)
**Centre Hospitalier Universitaire de Tokoin** ( ☎ 221 25 01; Route de Kpalimé) The main hospital, 1.5km northwest of the city.

### Internet Access

There are numerous Internet cafés in Lomé. Expect to pay CFA400 to CFA500 per hour.

**La Pointe Cybercafé** (Blvd du 13 Janvier; per hr CFA400; ✆ 7.30am-2pm)
**Sunny-West Internet** ( ☎ 221 74 29; sunnyw@ifrance .com; 42 Ave du 24 Janvier; per hr CFA400)

### Media

Newspaper racks at major road intersections stock newspapers.

### Medical Services

If you need a doctor or a dentist, contact your embassy for a list of recommended practitioners.

**Dr Noel Akouvi** ( ☎ 221 32 46; Cabinet Dentaire NIFA 10, Rue Amouzou) For dental emergencies.
**Pharmacie Bel Air** ( ☎ 221 03 21; Rue du Commerce; ✆ 8am-7pm) Next to Hôtel du Golfe.

## Money

The major banks listed below are conveniently clustered in the centre, at or near the corner of Rue de la Gare and Rue du Commerce. All change cash and travellers cheques. Opening hours vary, but BTCI's are typical: 7.45am to 11.30am and 2.30pm to 4.30pm Monday to Friday.

Moneychangers congregate near Diaby Fast-Food on Rue du Commerce, but there is a good chance of being ripped off.

**BIA** ( ☎ 221 32 86; 13 Rue du Commerce; ☽ 8-11am & 2.30-4pm Mon-Fri)

**BTCI** ( ☎ 221 46 45; Rue du Commerce) Has an ATM, which issues up to CFA400,000 per transaction.

**BTCI Head Office** ( ☎ 221 46 41; Blvd du 13 Janvier) The best option. It gives cash advances on Visa over the counter and has an ATM, which issues up to CFA400,000 per transaction.

**Ecobank** ( ☽ 7.45am-4pm Mon-Fri & 9am-2pm Sat) Rue de Chemin de Fer ( ☎ 222 65 74; 1 Rue de Chemin de Fer); Rue du Commerce ( ☎ 221 71 14; 20 Rue du Commerce)

**SDV Togo Voyages** ( ☎ 221 26 11; fax 221 26 12; 2 Rue du Commerce) The American Express representative.

**UTB** ( ☎ 221 50 02; Rue du la Gare; ☽ 7.45-11.30am & 2.45-4.30pm Mon-Fri)

## Post

**Post office** ( ☎ 221 31 95; Ave de la Libération; ☽ 7.30am-noon & 2.30-5pm Mon-Fri, 7.30am-12.30pm Sat) Between Blvd du 13 Janvier and Ave du 24 Janvier; has an efficient poste restante service.

## Telephone

Local and international calls can be made from any of the multitude of private telephone agencies around the city.

**Telecom building** ( ☽ 7am-6pm Mon-Fri, 8am-noon Sat) Just behind the post office.

## Tourist Information

**Direction de la Promotion Touristique** ( ☎ 221 43 13; www.togo-tourisme.com; Rue du Lac Togo) Located in a dilapidated building near Marox Supermarché. Staff are helpful, if surprised to see tourists, and can give you a reasonable road map of Togo, which is more useful than their outdated Lomé maps.

## Travel Agencies

Lomé's many travel agencies are mostly in and around the Immeuble Taba on Ave Georges Pompidou. Many offer excursions to the interior, and to Ghana and Benin.

**Nouvelles Frontières-Corsair** ( ☎ 221 08 03; fax 221 07 83; 20 Rue de la Gare)

**SDV Togo Voyages** ( ☎ 221 26 11; fax 221 26 12; 2 Rue du Commerce) One of the best.

**Semper Travel** ( ☎ 221 73 33; fax 221 74 03; Immeuble Taba)

**Togo Voyages** ( ☎ 221 12 77; Rue du Grand Marché)

## DANGERS & ANNOYANCES

There are pickpockets around the Grand Marché and along Rue du Commerce, and muggings are frequent, some at knife-point. The worst thing you could do is walk on the beach alone, especially at night. Indeed, walking anywhere in the city at night is dangerous – take a taxi, also a safer option than the accident-prone *taxi-motos* (scooter taxis).

Avoid police roadblocks, as they act as an unofficial revenue-collection exercise.

There are occasionally violent riots in Lomé. If this happens, locals will generally suggest that you avoid certain districts – sound advice. Even in a street party, carry as little as possible with you, as muggers may take advantage of the general chaos.

If swimming, be aware of a very dangerous undertow (see p780).

## SIGHTS

The gilded bronze statue of President Eyadéma – and the one of his mother – were taken down from Place de l'Indépendance in 1991, during the civil disturbances. To the square's east is Palais du Congrès, previously Eyadéma's RPT headquarters.

To the square's southwest, the Presidential Palace is not worth taking a close look at because the fearsome guards will likely interrogate you (see p804). It's so decrepit that they are building a new one anyway.

The entrance to the **Musée National** (National Museum; ☎ 221 68 07; admission CFA1000; ☽ 7am-noon & 2.30-5.30pm Mon-Fri, hours vary Sat & Sun) is at the back of the Palais du Congrès in Place de l'Indépendance. It has historical artefacts, pottery, costumes, woodcarvings and traditional medicines, plus 'thunderstones' (large rocks shaped like eggs) and cowrie shells, both formerly used as legal tender.

The **Marché des Féticheurs** (fetish market; ☎ 227 20 96; Quartier Akodessewa; admission & guide CFA5000, plus per camera/video CFA5000/10,000; ☽ 6.30am-6pm), 4km northeast of the centre, stocks all the ingredients for traditional tonics and fetishes – porcupine skin, warthog teeth, donkey skull, serpent head, horse hair, parakeet tail, thunderstones and chameleons. You

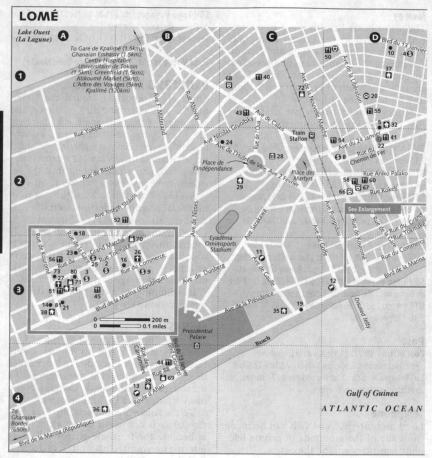

## LOMÉ

can also buy ready-made grigri charms, such as the lovers' fetish and the 'telephone' fetish for travellers. Stock is sourced all over Africa and some visitors may feel uncomfortable buying the parts of lions, panthers, antelopes and buffalo, or rare species.

The market is an overpriced tourist trap, but is still worth a visit. To get there charter a taxi (CFA1000) or a *taxi-moto* (CFA500).

## ACTIVITIES

The surf in Lomé is very dangerous because of a strong undertow, and drownings are common – be careful. Many of the beaches are also used as the local toilet. The beaches east of Lomé are better and more secluded (see p786).

Nonguests can use the swimming pools at **Hôtel 2 Février** ( ☎ 221 00 03; fax 221 62 66; Place de l'Indépendance; CFA3500) and – bigger and better – **Hôtel Mecure-Sarakawa** ( ☎ 227 65 90; www .accor-hotels.com; Route de Aného; CFA3000).

There are tennis courts at the large hotels and horse riding can be organised through **Club Hippique** ( ☎ 226 94 50; Route de l'Aéroport), located near the airport, or through Hôtel Mecure-Sarakawa.

For a bird's eye view of Lomé, go up with **Aeroclub Lomé** ( ☎ 226 21 01; Blvd de la Paix) in its two-seater plane (per hour CFA60,000) or four-seater (CFA75,000).

Keen cyclists can pick up a (poor quality) bike at the discouragingly named **Abattoir Bicycles** ( ☎ 911 48 51; Rue du Lac Togo; ⏰ 7am-5.30pm

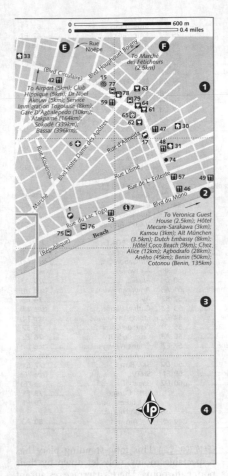

Mon-Sat), in front of Marox Supermarché, for about CFA40,000.

## COURSES

There is a **Prannic healing school** ( ☎ 220 58 64) near the town hall.

## LOMÉ FOR CHILDREN

Greenfield restaurant (p783) screens kids' films in its outdoor cinema on Saturdays at 3.30pm (CFA2500).

## TOURS

French biologist and lover of the *piste* (rough trails) **Henry Loïc** ( ☎ 927 52 03; africatoy@hotmail .com) offers 4WD tours to secluded local sights such as turtle beaches, and further

afield (€45 per person per day, or €150 for four people).

## FESTIVALS & EVENTS

Lomé grabs any excuse to take a day off and *faire la fête* (party). The street parties which take over Blvd du 13 Janvier are awesomely anarchistic events, but embassies normally advise against attending them. The parties see many accidents from dangerous driving, and pickpockets and muggers often use them to their advantage.

## SLEEPING

The following entries are accommodation options within 5km of the centre of town.

### Budget

**Hôtel le Galion** ( ☎ 222 00 30; togogalion@yahoo.fr; 12 Rue des Camomilles; s/d with fan CFA7000/8000, with air-con CFA12,000/14,000; ❀ ) This Swiss-owned hotel near the beach has an excellent restaurant – (meals CFA2000 to CFA3800) with fondue on the menu of course. There's a lounge upstairs with relaxing armchairs and shelves full of books, and the bar is popular with locals and travellers.

**Hôtel du Boulevard** ( ☎ 221 15 91; 204 Blvd du 13 Janvier; s with shared/private bathroom CFA5000/6000, d CFA10,000) The Boulevard is overpriced and run down, but in a great location, with views from the roof – though this noisy roadside position seems less of a boon in the middle of the night.

**Hôtel Mawuli** ( ☎ 222 12 75; 21 Rue Maoussas; r CFA4300-6000; ❀ ) The Mawuli has 25 rooms with fans or air-con. All are grotty but bearable, with the bathrooms veering towards the former. It's the pink building, two blocks south of the enormous Ecowas building and within ear-splitting distance of a mosque.

**Hôtel Lilly** (Blvd de la Marina; r with shared bathroom & fan CFA3000, r with private bathroom & fan/air-con CFA5000/10,000; ❀ ) A good fallback within walking distance of the Ghanaian border, this basic option has a loud and lascivious bar, but the rooms are respectable. Meals are available for CFA3000.

### Midrange

**L'Arbre des Voyages** ( ☎ 933 62 64; r with fan/air-con incl breakfast CFA10,000/15,000; ❀ Ⓟ ) Just off Route de Kpalimé, this large, comfortable guesthouse, run by a friendly young French-Togolese couple, has nine rooms

TOGO

| INFORMATION | | |
|---|---|---|
| American Cultural Center | | (see 1) |
| American Embassy | | 1 E2 |
| BIA-Togo Bank | | 2 A3 |
| BTCI Bank | | 3 A3 |
| BTCI Bank (Head Office) | | 4 D1 |
| Centre Culturel Français | | 5 D1 |
| Centre Hospitalier Regional | | 6 E2 |
| Direction de la Promotion Touristique | | 7 F2 |
| Ecobank | | 8 D2 |
| Ecobank | | 9 B3 |
| Ecowas Building | | 10 D1 |
| French Consulate | | 11 C3 |
| French Embassy | | 12 D3 |
| German Embassy | | 13 B4 |
| Immeuble Taba | | 14 A3 |
| La Pointe Cybercafe | | 15 E1 |
| Librairie Bon Pasteur | | 16 B3 |
| Moneychangers | | (see 45) |
| Nigerian Embassy | | 17 F1 |
| Nouvelles Frontières-Corsair | | 18 A2 |
| Occasional Police Roadblock | | 19 C3 |
| Pharmacie Bel Air | | (see 34) |
| Post Office | | 20 D1 |
| Prannic Healing School | | (see 24) |
| SDV Togo Voyages (AmEx) | | 21 A3 |
| Semper Travel | | (see 14) |
| Sunny-West Internet | | 22 D2 |
| Telecom Building | | (see 20) |
| Togo Voyages | | 23 A3 |
| Town Hall | | 24 C2 |
| UTB Bank | | 25 A3 |

**SIGHTS & ACTIVITIES**

| | | |
|---|---|---|
| Abattoir Bicycles | | (see 53) |
| Cathédrale du Sacré-Cœur de Jesus Lomé | | 26 B3 |
| Church | | 27 A3 |
| Musée National | | 28 C2 |
| Palais du Congrés | | (see 28) |

| SLEEPING 🏠 | | |
|---|---|---|
| Hôtel 2 Février | | 29 C2 |
| Hôtel Avenida | | 30 F1 |
| Hotel Copacabana | | 31 F2 |
| Hotel Digbawa | | 32 D1 |
| Hôtel du Boulevard | | 33 E1 |
| Hôtel du Golfe | | 34 A3 |
| Hôtel Ibis-le Bénin | | 35 C3 |
| Hôtel Lilly | | 36 A4 |
| Hôtel Mawuli | | 37 D1 |
| Hôtel Palm Beach | | 38 A3 |
| Le Maxime Hôtel | | 39 B4 |

| EATING 🍴 | | |
|---|---|---|
| Al Donald's | | 40 C1 |
| Bena Grill | | (see 53) |
| Boston Maquis | | 41 D2 |
| Brochettes sur la Capital | | 42 E1 |
| Brussels Café | | 43 C1 |
| China Town | | 44 B4 |
| Diaby Fast-Food | | 45 A3 |
| Golden Crown | | 46 F2 |
| Keur Rama | | 47 F1 |
| La Cigale | | 48 F2 |
| La Savane | | 49 F2 |
| L'Abeille d'Or | | (see 14) |
| Le Privilège | | (see 38) |
| Le Shanghai | | 50 D1 |
| Leader Price Supermaché | | 51 A3 |
| L'Okavango | | 52 B2 |
| Marox Supermaché | | 53 E2 |
| Ramco Supermaché | | 54 D2 |
| Relais de la Poste | | 55 D1 |
| Restaurant de l'Amitié | | 56 A3 |
| Restaurant la Pirogue | | 57 F2 |
| Restaurant Mini-Brasserie | | 58 D2 |
| Ristorante Da-Claudio | | 59 E1 |
| Vingt Sur Vins | | 60 D2 |

**DRINKING 🍷**

| | | |
|---|---|---|
| Bar Agou | | (see 29) |
| Bar d'Ambiance | | (see 66) |

| | | |
|---|---|---|
| Bronco City | | 61 F1 |
| Cafe Panini | | 62 F1 |
| Cristal Palace | | (see 68) |
| Le Palmiers | | 63 F1 |
| Restaurant la Terrasse | | 64 F1 |

**ENTERTAINMENT 🎭**

| | | |
|---|---|---|
| Byblos | | 65 F1 |
| Chess Nightclub | | (see 29) |
| Cinéma Concorde | | (see 29) |
| Cinéma Opera | | (see 34) |
| Domino | | 66 D2 |
| L'Abreuvoir | | 67 D2 |
| Millennium Nightclub | | (see 68) |
| Sunset Bar | | 68 C1 |
| Z Nightclub | | (see 66) |

**SHOPPING 🛍**

| | | |
|---|---|---|
| Bric à Brac | | 69 B4 |
| Grand Marché | | 70 B3 |
| Rue des Artisans | | 71 A3 |
| Village Artisanal | | 72 C1 |

**TRANSPORT**

| | | |
|---|---|---|
| Air France | | (see 14) |
| Air Gabon | | (see 14) |
| Air Ivoire | | (see 14) |
| Alitalia | | 73 A3 |
| American Airlines | | (see 14) |
| Avis | | 74 F2 |
| Cathay Pacific | | (see 14) |
| Ethiopian Airways | | (see 14) |
| Gare de Cotonou | | 75 E2 |
| Gare de STIF | | 76 E2 |
| Ghana Airways | | (see 14) |
| KLM | | (see 14) |
| SKV Buses | | 77 E1 |
| SNTV | | (see 76) |
| Sogabef | | (see 76) |
| Total Garage | | 78 F1 |
| TST Buses | | 79 F1 |
| Virgin Nigeria Airways | | 80 A3 |

with balconies and DVD which are popular with students from IAEC (the international business school next door). Located 5km north of town, near Atikoumé market, it's a breezy retreat from central Lomé.

**Hôtel Digbawa** ( ☎ 221 14 88; Rue de Paris; r with air-con CFA12,300-13,000, with air-con & hot water CFA16,000; 🏠 ) This hotel is Riad-like with its tiled floors, rooftop bar and balconies. The quiet rooms are of a good standard and the restaurant (meals CFA1500 to CFA3000) serves generous helpings of African and European food.

**Hôtel du Golfe** ( ☎ 221 02 78; fax 221 49 03; Rue du Commerce; r with fan CFA9500, s/d with air-con CFA18,500/23,500; 🏠 ) This comfortable central hotel with a courtyard bar is a little dilapidated, but not unattractively so. It's one of the best-value midrange places.

**Le Maxime Hôtel** ( ☎ 221 74 48; Route d'Aflao; r with fan CFA8300-9300, with air-con CFA13,300-14,300, ste CFA19,300; 🏠 ) This long-standing place has respectable rooms, only let down by their poor bathrooms. There's a terrace restaurant (meals from CFA3800) open from 10am to 10pm for lunch and dinner, serving delicious European fish and chicken dishes.

**Hôtel Avenida** ( ☎ 221 46 72; avenida@café.tg; 30 Rue d'Almeida; r CFA16,500-30,000; 🏠 ) Despite its unattractive exterior, the 23-year-old Avenida, a block east of the Nigerian embassy, has good, clean rooms with TV and hot water, and a decent restaurant (meals from CFA1500 to CFA3000). Guests are asked to pay in advance.

**Hôtel Copacabana** ( ☎ 221 64 57; Rue Litimé; r with fan CFA7000, with air-con & hot water CFA9000-18,000; 🏠 ) You'll find quiet, compact rooms with a faint whiff of polish, and an uninspiring restaurant (meals CFA500 to CFA2000) decorated with bad Futurist art, in this anonymous but well-located hotel east of Blvd du 13 Janvier.

## Top End

**Hôtel Mercure-Sarakawa** ( ☎ 227 65 90; www.accor -hotels.com; Route de Aného; r with city/sea view CFA71,000/ 79,000, deluxe r CFA85,000, ste CFA121,000; ✿ ☕ P ) The 164-room hotel, 3km east of the centre on the way to Benin, is one of the classiest in West Africa. It has an Olympic-sized pool (nonguests over/under 13 CFA3000/1500), horse riding (per 30 minutes adults/children CFA2500/1500), tennis courts, nightclub (entry CFA4500) and a hairdresser.

**Veronica Guest House** ( ☎ 222 69 07; veronica gh@bibway.com; Route de Aného; r CFA30,000-39,000; ✿ ☕ ) This charming 10-room hotel with a pint-sized pool is a more Togolese alternative to the chain hotels. Although it is on the busy highway, the rooms have thick double-glazing and views across the road to the beach. Meals are available for CFA4000.

**Hôtel Ibis-le Bénin** ( ☎ 221 24 85; fax 221 61 25; Blvd de la Marina; r with city/sea view CFA42,500/49,500; ✿ P ) Colonised by Ibis in 2003, the independence-era Hôtel le Bénin still represents the best value among the top-end hotels, even if the comfortable rooms now look a little bland.

**Hôtel 2 Février** ( ☎ 221 00 03; www.corinthiaho tels.com; Place de l'Indépendance; r from CFA70,000, ste CFA101,000-151,000; ✿ ☕ ) Once Lomé's best hotel, the 30-year-old Hôtel 2 Février has some 500 top-notch rooms, but is devoid of guests unless there's a political party meeting or a business conference. The swimming pool, with its attendant snack bar (meals from CFA6500), is CFA3500 for nonguests.

**Hôtel Palm Beach** ( ☎ 221 85 11; fax 221 87 11; 1 Blvd de la Marina; s/tw CFA46,000/53,500, ste CFA66,000-131,000; ✿ ☕ 🖳 ) This well-located high-rise hotel is not as smooth as Hôtel 2 Février but has better facilities, which include a rooftop swimming pool, a massage service and a nightclub. Meals are available from CFA5800 to CFA7000. Ask for an ocean-facing room for sweeping views down the beach.

## EATING

Blvd du 13 Janvier is bristling with restaurants of all descriptions.

## Restaurants

### AFRICAN

**L'Okavango** ( ☎ 221 05 75; Blvd du 13 Janvier; meals CFA5500-12,000; ✽ 12-2.30pm & 6.30-11pm, closed Mon)

Opposite UTB bank, not far from the beach, L'Okavango is a regular pleasure garden, with animals frolicking in the garden and a good selection of dishes and obscure beers.

**Restaurant la Pirogue** ( ☎ 221 40 97; cnr Blvd du 13 Janvier & Rue de l'Entente; meals CFA2000-4500; ✽ 8am-10.30pm) In the words of the head waiter at this friendly restaurant near the ocean, the food comes from Togo, from Vietnam, and from the sea. Try the agouti – a rodent called 'grasscutter' in English.

**Keur Rama** ( ☎ 221 54 62; Blvd du 13 Janvier; meals CFA2000-3000) This restaurant, on the eastern side of town near the Nigerian embassy, offers Senegalese and Togolese cuisine. Try the delicious *chep boudjen* (fish cooked with cabbage, eggplant and carrots).

**Restaurant de l'Amitié** (17 Rue du Grand Marché; meals from CFA1200; ✽ to 8pm) This popular place offers huge, inexpensive servings of dishes from both the West and across West Africa.

### ASIAN

The best Chinese restaurants are on Blvd du 13 Janvier.

**China Town** ( ☎ 222 30 06; 67 Blvd du 13 Janvier; meals CFA1800-4500; ✽ 11.30am-2pm & 6-10.30pm) This surprisingly unkitsch, air-conditioned Chinese restaurant, with a well-stocked bar, is at the southwest end of the boulevard.

**Golden Crown** ( ☎ 221 03 36; cnr Blvd du 13 Janvier & Route d'Aného; meals CFA4300-4900; ✽ 12-2pm & 7-11pm) This long-standing place offers dishes such as crab and lobster cooked with lashings of ginger and garlic.

**Le Shanghai** ( ☎ 222 26 28; Blvd du 13 Janvier; meals CFA2000-4000; ✽ Thu-Tue) Halfway along the boulevard is Le Shanghai, one of Lomé's best and most popular Chinese restaurants.

### EUROPEAN

There is an abundance of European restaurants in Lomé, most with a distinctly French flavour.

**Brochettes sur la Capital** (Blvd du 13 Janvier; meals CFA2500-3400) This Lomé institution is the city at its best – enjoy sitting outside eating lip-smacking kebabs and watching the boulevard hustle by.

**Greenfield** ( ☎ 222 21 55; Rue Akati; meals CFA3200-4500, pizza & tortillas from CFA2000; ✽ 6-11pm) Tucked away off Route de Kpalimé, near Tokoin Hospital, this funky French-owned garden bar–restaurant is decorated with dancing Keith Haring figures and colourful lanterns.

It is family-friendly, with a menu for children and teenagers, and films screened for youngsters on Saturdays, in addition to the adult films on Tuesdays and live jazz.

**La Savane** ( ☎ 906 17 48; Blvd du Mono; meals CFA3000-4500; ⏰ 11.30am-3pm & 6pm-midnight) This Italian-owned garden restaurant has cool African art on the walls, and serves African food as well as European dishes such as pizza.

**Vingt Sur Vins** ( ☎ 221 08 82; Rue Aniko Palako; meals CFA5000; ⏰ Mon-Sat) Near L'Aubreuvoir disco, this French restaurant serves up fine dishes made from top local produce, winning plaudits from among Lomé's expat community.

**La Cigale** ( ☎ 221 99 30; lacigale_lomé@hotmail.com; 198 Blvd du 13 Janvier; meals CFA3800-7500; ⏰ 10am-2pm & 6-11pm Mon-Sat) Salmon and T-bone steak are on the menu in this swish Tunisian-owned garden restaurant that, confusingly, specialises in Chinese and Italian food.

**Ristorante Da-Claudio** ( ☎ 222 26 65; Blvd du 13 Janvier; pizzas CFA3000, pasta CFA2000; ⏰ 6pm-12am Mon-Sat) This restaurant, owned by an Italian-Togolese couple, is a great place to sample traditional Italian fare, with both air-con dining and a relaxing terrace.

**Alt München** ( ☎ 227 63 21; Route d'Aného; meals CFA3000-7500; ⏰ 11am-2.30pm & 7-11pm Thu-Tue) A Bavarian restaurant just east of Hôtel Mercure-Sarakawa, offering a good selection of German beers and hearty European dishes such as goulash and knuckle of pork.

**Relais de la Poste** ( ☎ 221 46 78; 6 Ave de la Libération; meals CFA3000-3500) This charming restaurant, specialising in seafood and set in a quiet shaded courtyard, has long been a mainstay of locals and expats alike.

**Bena Grill** ( ☎ 222 41 38; Rue du Lac Togo; meals CFA2000-4700; ⏰ 7.30am-10pm) This is basically a supermarket restaurant, attached to Marox Supermarché, but it serves hefty German dishes in a pleasant outdoor setting.

**Restaurant Mini-Brasserie** ( ☎ 221 32 34; 44 Rue de le Gare; mains CFA3000-6000) This enduring favourite is a good spot to meet other travellers and have an ice-cold beer.

### LEBANESE

**L'Abeille d'Or** ( ☎ 904 07 77; Rue de Kouroumé; meals from CFA2500) This air-conditioned patisserie and restaurant, on the 1st floor of the Immeuble Taba, behind Hôtel Palm Beach, is popular with the Lebanese community.

## Quick Eats

Lomé is awash with cafeterias: good places to grab a cheap coffee with an omelette or spaghetti. They're typically open from 7am until midnight, and Rue de la Gare and Ave du 24 Janvier are good places to sniff them out.

**Al Donald's** (Blvd du 13 Janvier) Just for fun try the cheeky rip-off of the American fast-food giant.

**Brussels Café** ( ☎ 221 46 63; 8 Ave Nicolas Grunitsky; ice cream CFA800-2000; ⏰ evenings) For ice cream this is the best place to go. Its upstairs restaurant stocks Belgian beers.

**Boston Maquis** ( ☎ 222 26 06; Ave du 24 Janvier; meals CFA1500) You can get good, cheap food at this friendly restaurant opposite Centre Culturel Français.

**Diaby Fast Food** ( ☎ 221 75 12; Rue du Commerce; meals CFA750-2000) Head to this air-conditioned snack bar for nibbles such as shwarma, felafel, burgers and sandwiches, as well as a good choice of vegetarian dishes.

## Self-Catering

Local vendors sell a wide array of fresh fruit and vegetables outside the small **Marox Supermarché** (Rue du Lac Togo; ⏰ 8am-12pm), which itself is your best bet for meat products. Other supermarkets include the following:

**Leader Price Supermarché** (Rue du Commerce; ⏰ 8.30am-1pm & 3-7pm Mon-Sat, 9am-1pm Sun)

**Ramco Supermarché** ( ☎ 221 46 10; cnr Ave du 24 Janvier & Ave de la Nouvelle Marche; ⏰ 8.30am-12.30pm & 2.30-7.30pm Mon-Sat, 9am-1pm Sun)

# DRINKING

**Café Panini** ( ☎ 904 00 56; Blvd du 13 Janvier; ⏰ from 6pm) In the words of one French drinker we encountered here, Panini is 'the arse of the chicken' – the gloriously sleazy epicentre of Lomés nightlife. Avoid if you object to being hustled by multilingual prostitutes.

**Bronco City** (Blvd du 13 Janvier; ⏰ from 6pm) One of the unmarked bars across the boulevard from Café Panini, where you can watch the action from a safe distance.

**Cristal Palace** ( ☎ 920 20 00; cnr Blvd du 13 Janvier & Route de Kpalimé) Part of the popular Sunset Bar and Millennium nightclub complex, this beer garden is a good spot for a game of pool to a soundtrack of Togolese hip-hop.

**Bar Agou** ( ☎ 221 00 03; Hôtel 2 Février, Place de l'Indépendance; beer CFA1550) Appropriately named after Togo's highest mountain, this hotel bar has an unequalled view of Place de l'Indépendence and the city. Meals available from CFA6500.

**Restaurant la Terrasse** ( ☎ 906 60 66; Blvd du 13 Janvier; 9am-midnight, from 5pm Mon) This small bar, with pool tables and fruit machines, is a less hectic haunt than many of its rivals nearby on the boulevard. Meals available from CFA1800 to CFA3800.

**Le Palmiers** ( ☎ 220 66 22; Blvd Notre Dame; beer CFA400; 11am-10.30pm) The food here is nothing special (meals CFA1000 to CFA3200), but it's a great place to have a beer in view of the *taxi-motos* swarming down the boulevard like angry wasps.

**Bar d'Ambiance** (Rue de la Gare) A good place for a tipple before heading to the nearby Z Nightclub; also shows European football matches.

## ENTERTAINMENT
### Nightclubs
The European-style, discolike nightclubs are pricey and have cover charges, typically CFA3000. The area bounded by Restaurant Mini-Brasserie, Domino and L'Abreuvoir is known as the Bermuda Triangle – once you get inside you lose all bearings!

**Byblos** (Blvd du 13 Janvier; admission CFA5000; from 10pm Wed-Sun) Next to Café Panini is Byblos, a trendy nightclub that is a favourite haunt of rich young Togolese.

**Millennium Nightclub** ( ☎ 920 20 00; Ave de Calais) This hip hangout has a few different areas, including a beer garden with a barbecue and, often, live music.

**Z Nightclub** (Rue de la Gare; from 11pm) This jazzy nightclub, owned by Frenchman Philip, is next to Bar d'Ambiance.

**Kamou** ( ☎ 227 65 90; Hôtel Mecure-Sarakawa, Route de Aného) Beers are CFA1500 in the basement of the swanky Sarakawa.

**Chess** ( ☎ 221 00 03; Hôtel du 2 Février, Place de l'Indépendence; admission CFA3000 for nonguests; from 10pm) The Togolese football team went to this classy club to celebrate when they trounced the Congo and qualified for the World Cup.

**L'Abreuvoir** (Rue de la Gare) One of the hottest and best-known discos. Small beers are CFA2000, and there's a snack bar.

**Domino** (665 Rue de la Gare) Another popular bar-nightclub, this infamous pick-up joint plays rock and jazz from 10.30pm on Friday and Saturday.

**Le Privilège** ( ☎ 221 85 11; Hôtel Palm Beach, Rue de Kouromé; admission CFA4000; 10pm-4am) A barn-like place with expensive drinks that is popular with teenagers.

## Live Music
Hôtel le Galion (p781) and Greenfield (p783) put on live music from time to time.

**Chez Alice** ( ☎ /fax 227 91 72; chezalicetogo@hotmail .com; admission CFA6000) To party long into the night, take a bush taxi to Chez Alice in the village of Avéposo, about 12km from the heart of Lomé on the coastal highway to Aného. This German-owned joint, popular with overlanders, hosts barbecues or fondue feasts with traditional music and dancing on Wednesday from 8pm. Meals are available for CFA1500 to CFA3800.

## Cinemas
**Cinéma Concorde** ( ☎ 221 00 03; Hôtel 2 Février) Has air-conditioning and shows French-dubbed Hollywood films.

**Cinéma Opera** ( ☎ 221 85 12; Rue du Commerce; tickets CFA250-600) Opposite Hôtel du Golfe, shows Western blockbusters in French at 2pm, 6.30pm and 9pm.

**Cinéma Elysees** (Immeuble Taba, Rue de Kouromé; tickets CFA500-1000; Wed & Fri-Sun) Shows films at 3.30pm, 6.30pm and 9pm.

**Greenfield** ( ☎ 222 21 55; Rue Akati) Has an openair cinema on Tuesday at 7.30pm, screening Western films in French with English subtitles. The CFA2500 entry fee includes a drink and a medium Margherita pizza.

## SHOPPING
**Grand Marché** (Rue de Grand Marché; to 4pm Mon-Sat) This is the place to pick up everything from Togolese football tops to wax cloth (sold by the 2m *pagne* – the amount needed for a complete outfit – traders sometimes refuse to sell less than this as it's not always easy to shift the rest).

**Rue des Artisans** ( 7.30am-6.30pm Mon-Sat) Close to Grand Marché is this relatively low-pressure place to buy woodcarvings and brasswork – including some fetching malachite jewellery – from Burkinabé, Senegalese, Nigerian and Malian traders. The short street is east of Hôtel du Golfe, with some private art galleries at the north end. Come with your haggling cap firmly on.

**Village Artisanal** ( ☎ 221 68 07; Ave du Nouveau Marché; 7.30am-6.30pm Mon-Sat) At this centre you'll see Togolese artisans weaving cloth, carving statues, making baskets, lampshades,

**TOGO**

cane chairs and tables, sewing leather shoes – all for sale at reasonable fixed prices. Lomé is famous for leather sandals; they were originally all made at the Village Artisanal, but you can also buy them around the Grand Marché for about CFA3000.

**Bric à Brac** ( ☎ 221 02 45; messie@bibway.com; 71 Blvd de la Marina) Your best bet for high-quality art. The friendly owner has a showroom of good-quality West African pieces, and her fixed prices are very reasonable.

## GETTING THERE & AWAY
### Air
The international airport is 5km northeast of central Lomé. For details on flights to and from Lomé see p805.

### Bus, Bush Taxi & Minibus
Bush taxis and minibuses travelling east to Aného (CFA800, one hour), Cotonou (CFA3000, three hours) and Lake Togo/Agbodrafo (CFA500, 45 minutes) leave from **Gare de Cotonou** (Rue Holland), just west of the STIF bus station.

If you're going to Ghana it's best to catch a taxi (CFA500 shared, CFA1000 chartered) or taxi-moto (CFA500) to the border and cross on foot. Buses for Accra leave from just across the Ghanaian border in Aflao.

**Gare d'Agbalepedo** (Quartier Agbalepedo), 10km north of central Lomé, serves all northern destinations. Services include: Atakpamé (CFA2000, three hours), Bassar (CFA4000), Dapaong (CFA6000, 14 hours), Kara (CFA4000, seven hours), Sokodé (CFA3600, six hours) and Ouagadougou (CFA16,000, 24 hours). A few bush taxis and minibuses leave daily for these places, mostly in the morning. The earlier you get to a *gare* (station), the more chance you stand of finding a bush taxi without too long a wait and of reaching your destination in reasonable time.

Minibuses to Kpalimé (CFA1500 plus CFA500 baggage charge, three hours) leave from **Gare de Kpalimé** (Rue Moyana), 1.5km north of the centre on Route de Kpalimé.

Coaches run between Lomé and many other major West African cities – see p806.

## GETTING AROUND
### To/From the Airport
To the airport the taxi fare is about CFA1000 (but count on CFA1500 from the airport into the city).

### Car
**Avis** ( ☎ 221 05 82; 252 Blvd du 13 Janvier) Also has branches at Hôtel Mecure-Sarakawa. Among the garages in the city centre is the **Total Garage** (cnr Blvd du 13 Janvier & Blvd Notre Dame des Apotres).

### Taxi & Taxi-Moto
Taxis are abundant, even at night, and have no meters. Fares are CFA200 for a shared taxi (CFA300 after 6pm, more to the outlying areas) and CFA700 nonshared. A taxi by the hour should cost CFA2500 if you bargain well.

Zippy little *taxi-motos* are also popular, if rather dangerous. You should be able to go anywhere in the centre for CFA200.

# AROUND LOMÉ

## BEACHES
Past the Nioto oil plant, and the port and customs east of Lomé, is another world – a mellow land of beachfront auberges which are far preferable to similarly priced hotels in the city centre.

The first one you come to, 9km from the city centre on the highway to Aného, is Hôtel Coco Beach. The well-marked turn-off is 1km east of the large roundabout at the port. Taxis from the Gare de Cotonou cost about CFA1700.

**Hôtel Coco Beach** ( ☎ 271 49 35; cocobeachtogo@hotmail.com; d with air-con CFA28,000, d with air-con & sea view CFA32,000, 5-person bungalow CFA77,000; ✷ ) is the swishest hotel on this part of the coast, with boardwalks leading to a restaurant (meals CFA2500 to CFA4800) brimming with fish dishes, a seafront bar, and a private beach with deckchairs and *paillotes* (shaded seats) for hire. Rooms have hot water and funky blue-and-yellow colour schemes.

**Chez Alice** ( ☎ /fax 227 91 72; chezalicetogo@hotmail .com; camping per person CFA750, d/tr with fan & shared bucket shower CFA3500/4500, beachfront apt CFA7000) is a sleepy, slightly rundown place, featuring overlanders poring over maps in the shade and monkeys peering through the bars of their cage. This German-run auberge in the village of Avéposo is three minutes' walk from the beach and hosts a barbecue or fondue with traditional music and dancing on Wednesday from 8pm (CFA6000). Meals are available for CFA1500 to CFA3800.

## AGBODRAFO & LAKE TOGO

On the southern shores of this disease-free lake – part of the inland lagoon that stretches all the way from Lomé to Aného – Agbodrafo is a popular getaway for water sports fans and an easy place to find a pirogue to Togoville.

**Auberge du Lac** ( ☎ 904 72 29; bungalow with fan/air-con CFA7600/12,600; ☒ ) is a few kilometres west of Agbodrafo, a secluded cluster of thatched bungalows among palms on the lake shore. A guided pirogue trip from here to Togoville costs CFA2500 return. There is also jet skiing, pedal-boating and windsurfing. Meals are available from CFA3500 to CFA5500.

**Hôtel le Lac** ( ☎ /fax 331 60 19/09; d/tr with air-con CFA41,000/56,000; meals from CFA4200; ☒ ☒ ) is an old but pleasant establishment several kilometres east of Agbodrafo. It played host to Pope John Paul II when he visited Togoville, and has 22 sweetly scented rooms with lakeside patios. Facilities include jet skis (per 10 minutes CFA12000), pedal-boats (per 30 minutes CFA4000 to CFA6000), tennis, table tennis, guided pirogue trips to Togoville (CFA1500 return), a pool (CFA1000 for nonguests) and, separately, some crocodiles. Meals are available from CFA4200.

From the Gare de Cotonou in Lomé, bush taxis frequently travel along the coastal road to Aného, via Agbodrafo (CFA500).

## TOGOVILLE

On Lake Togo's northern shore is Togoville, the historical centre of voodoo in Togo. It was from here that voodoo practitioners were taken as slaves to Haiti, now a major centre for voodoo. And it was here in 1884 that Chief Mlapa III signed a peace treaty with the German explorer Gustav Nachtigal that gave the Germans rights over all of Togoland.

Having disembarked at the jetty, you'll come to the **Centre Artisanal** and the German-built **cathedral**. A shrine to the Virgin commemorates her reported appearance on the lake, which attracted Pope John Paul II to visit. Fetishes in the streets attest to the practice of voodoo here.

Inside the **Maison Royale**, 100m west of the church, a one-room museum houses the now-toppled Mlapa dynasty's throne and some interesting old photos of the former chiefs. A *cadeau* (gift) is expected

**Hôtel Nachtigal** ( ☎ 333 70 76; fax 221 64 82; r with fan/air-con CFA7000/11,500; ☒ ☒ (P) ), a surprisingly good hotel 100m west of the market

has clean, pleasant rooms and bungalows. There's also a tennis court, a pool and a large *paillote* bar-restaurant, where you can get breakfast (CFA2000) or a decent meal: 3-course meals are CFA3000.

Getting here from Lomé is a bit of a hassle. By road, catch a bush taxi to Aného (CFA800) then another along the back roads to Togoville (CFA700). A better option is to take a pirogue (CFA2000 return) from Agbodrafo, about 10km before Aného (see left), although this will deliver you to the guide-covered jetty.

## VOGAN & AGOÉGAN

The Friday market at Vogan is a must-see. It's one of the largest and most colourful markets in Togo, with a well-stocked fetish section featuring an impressive array of dead turtles and other essential fetish ingredients.

There's also a vibrant Monday market in the untouched town of Agoégan, on the intercoastal canal dividing Togo and Benin – 30 minutes by taxi from Aného.

The small **Hôtel Medius** ( ☎ 333 10 00; r with fan/air-con CFA4300/7300; ☒ ), near Vogan market, has clean rooms and a bar-restaurant serving good-sized meals for about CFA2000.

The trip from Lomé takes one hour and costs about CFA1500 by bush taxi. If you're driving, go to Aného and turn left, circling around the lake. From Togoville, bush taxis to Vogan (CFA800) leave on Friday morning.

# THE SOUTH

The cocoa and coffee triangle between Kpalimé, Badou and Atakpamé is an alluring area in this part of West Africa. Its hilly, forest-covered terrain is a hiker's paradise and feels far from the hectic cities and dusty savanna nearby. If you only have time to visit one place outside Lomé, head to chilled-out Kpalimé, a beautiful town that's sure to become a tourist hotspot when Togo issues more visitor visas. Aného is an intriguing Togolese town, where a sense of a murky past hangs in the silences between the cries of the mixed-race fetish marketers hawking animal parts.

## ANÉHO
### pop 28,100

Aného is a unique town within Togo and a taste of what's in store for travellers heading across the Beninese border, 2km away. The colonial capital until 1920, the town is overshadowed by crumbling buildings in peeling pastels, seemingly sliding into an ocean once used to ship slaves. The Afro-Brazilian heritage which resulted from this grisly trade can be seen in the relatively pale-skinned people drifting around Aného market.

Voodoo is strong here. The back of the market, which is busiest on Tuesdays, is packed with wooden dolls and snakes' heads, their blank eyes gazing towards the epicentre of voodoo in southeast Benin.

## Sleeping

**Hôtel de l'Oasis** ( ☎ 331 01 25; oasisaneh@hotmail.com; Route de Lomé-Cotonou; d with fan/air-con CFA8800/12,300, tr with air-con CFA15,300; 🗶 ) An unbeatable location east of the bridge, looking across the lagoon and the beach to the sea. The seven rooms are well maintained, the management is friendly, and the terrace is a prime place for a sunset drink. Meals are available for CFA4800.

**First Hôtel Night-Club** ( ☎ /fax 331 10 04; Route de Lomé-Cotonou; r with fan & shared bathroom CFA9500, with fan/air-con & private bathroom CFA11,500/21,500; 🗶 🗶 ) The most upmarket hotel in town, with clean, modern rooms, tennis courts, a magnificent swimming pool (CFA500 for nonguests) and a trendy nightclub.

**La Becca Hôtel** ( ☎ 331 05 13; Route de Lomé-Cotonou; r with/without fan CFA7000/6000) The cheap and cheerful La Becca, southwest of the market, is not as smart as its exterior suggests, but is Aného's best budget option nonetheless.

## Eating

On the southwestern side of the bridge, the market and SGGG supermarket are the places to find vendors and *buvettes* (small bars or drinks stalls) such as Anastasia, opposite the market. At night they sell omelettes, chicken, stews, brochettes, and *pâte* with sauce. Opposite Buvette Fontaine, 200m east of the *gare routière* (bus and taxi station), there's a food hut with cheap, simple fare.

**Hôtel de l'Oasis** ( ☎ 331 01 25; oasisaneh@hotmail .com; Route de Lomé-Cotonou; meals CFA4800) The hotel's restaurant above the lagoon is recommended, but you do pay for the view.

## Drinking

Les Trois Paillotes, next to the old market at the southwest end of town, is good for a drink in an outdoor setting. Near the new market, Bar Amite de la Gare is covered by a paillote.

Other bars are Buvette Fontaine and Pago Pago, both near the *gare routière,* and Bar 620, off Rue de l'Hôpital in the northeast.

But, **Hôtel Night-Club** ( ☎ /fax 331 10 04; admission CFA3000; 🕑 Saturday only) is the place to be in Aného on Saturday nights.

## Getting There & Away

From the *gare routière,* at the northeastern end of town, bush taxis and minibuses head to Lomé (CFA800, one hour) as well as to the Beninese border and Cotonou (CFA1500, 2½ hours).

## KPALIMÉ

pop 48,300

Kpalimé (pah-lee-may) is only 120km from Lomé, but feels like another world, hidden among the forested hills of the cocoa and coffee region, which offer some of Togo's best scenery and hiking ( p790). Noted for its mild climate, Grand Marché, Centre Artisanal and political symposium in August, Kpalimé is Togo's most alluring town.

Although many of Kpalimé's hotels are outside the centre, most commercial activity takes place between the Grand Marché and Rond-point Texaco. There are four major sealed roads out of town: northwest to Klouto, northeast to Atakpamé, southwest to Ho (Ghana) and southeast to Lomé.

## Information

There is Web access at **Centre Artisanal** ( ☎ 441 00 77; per hr CFA350; 🕑 8am-10pm Mon-Fri, 3-8pm Sun), 2km north on the road to Klouto, and **Cifaid** ( ☎ 441 07 38; Rue Kuma; per hr CFA400; 🕑 8am-9pm Mon-Sat), southwest of the church.

There are two banks, **UTB** ( ☎ 441 01 84) and **BTCI** ( ☎ 441 01 27), north of the market. UTB is better for changing money and neither has an ATM. If you want to buy or sell Ghanaian Cedis, money-changers can be found at the *gare routière* – but make sure you get an idea of the going rate first.

## Sights

Nearby attractions include Klouto, home to a wonderful variety of butterflies, and Mt Agou, Togo's highest peak at 986m. **Kpimé Falls** (admission CFA500), about 12km northeast of Kpalimé, are a good spot for a swim. Taxis are roughly the same to visit all the attractions:

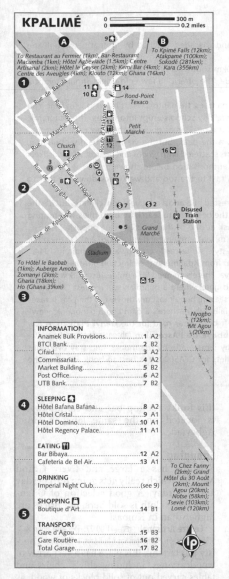

**KPALIMÉ**

0        300 m
0        0.2 miles

To Restaurant au Fermier (1km); Bar-Restaurant
Macumba (1km); Hôtel Agbeviade (1.5km); Centre
Artisanal (2km); Hôtel le Geyser (2km); Kemi Bar (4km);
Centre des Aveugles (4km); Klouto (12km); Ghana (16km)

To Kpimé Falls (12km);
Atakpamé (100km);
Sokodé (281km);
Kara (355km)

Rond-Point
Texaco

Petit
Marché

Church

Disused
Train
Station

Grand
Marché

Stadium

To Hôtel le Baobab
(1km); Auberge Amoto
Zomanyi (2km);
Ghana (18km);
Ho (Ghana 39km)

To
Nyogbo
(12km);
Mt Agou
(20km)

| INFORMATION | | |
|---|---|---|
| Anamek Bulk Provisions | 1 | A2 |
| BTCI Bank | 2 | B2 |
| Cifaid | 3 | A2 |
| Commissariat | 4 | A2 |
| Market Building | 5 | A2 |
| Post Office | 6 | A2 |
| UTB Bank | 7 | B2 |

| SLEEPING | | |
|---|---|---|
| Hôtel Bafana Bafana | 8 | A2 |
| Hôtel Cristal | 9 | A1 |
| Hôtel Domino | 10 | A1 |
| Hôtel Regency Palace | 11 | A1 |

| EATING | | |
|---|---|---|
| Bar Bibaya | 12 | A2 |
| Cafeteria de Bel Air | 13 | A1 |

| DRINKING | | |
|---|---|---|
| Imperial Night Club | (see 9) | |

| SHOPPING | | |
|---|---|---|
| Boutique d'Art | 14 | B1 |

| TRANSPORT | | |
|---|---|---|
| Gare d'Agou | 15 | B3 |
| Gare Routière | 16 | B2 |
| Total Garage | 17 | B2 |

To Chez Fanny
(2km); Grand
Hôtel du 30 Août
(2km); Mount
Agou (20km);
Notse (58km);
Tsevie (103km);
Lomé (120km)

CFA2000, or CFA300 shared, and CFA1500 for a *taxi-moto*. For more details, see p790.

## Sleeping

### BUDGET
**Hôtel Bafana Bafana** (Rue de l'Hôpital; s with shared/private bathroom CFA4000/5000) The terminally laid-back Bafana Bafana, near the church, offers cool, bare rooms with fan and a whitewashed courtyard bar.

**Auberge Amoto Zomanyi** ( ☎ 441 06 02; Rue de Kpadapé; r with fan & shared/private bathroom CFA4000/5500) A friendly place, 2km southwest of the centre, with clean spacious rooms, and the feel of a quiet colonial outpost. Meals are CFA2800.

**Hôtel Domino** ( ☎ 441 01 87; Rond-point Texaco; r with fan/air-con CFA4300/7800; ⚉ ) This long-standing establishment has small, fairly grubby rooms around a ramshackle courtyard.

### MIDRANGE
**Chez Fanny** ( ☎ /fax 441 00 99; hotelchezfanny@yahoo.fr; Route de Lomé; r CFA14,000; ⚉ **P** ) Run by a welcoming French-Togolese couple, this guesthouse in the countryside 2km south of town is a homely retreat. Meals are available from CFA3000 to CFA5000.

**Hôtel le Geyser** ( ☎ 441 04 67; hotellegeyser@hotmail.com; r CFA8500-15,000; ⚉ ⚉ ) The tranquil Hôtel le Geyser, 2km from the centre on the road to Klouto, has seven rooms, some with fan, air-con, hot water and TV. Set in a flowery garden, it also has a pool and an excellent restaurant. Meals from CFA2700 to CFA3500.

**Hôtel Cristal** ( ☎ /fax 441 05 79; hotelcristal2002@yahoo.fr; Rue de Bakula; s/d with air-con CFA9800/13,800; ⚉ ⚉ ) Behind its brutal grey façade, this hotel, signposted from Rond-point Texaco, is the best central accommodation. The well-kept rooms are reasonably priced and there's a pool with a restaurant – though nonguests must pay CFA1500 for a dip. Meals are CFA5000.

**Hôtel Regency Palace** ( ☎ 441 12 12; Rue Singa; r CFA10,000; ⚉ ) This pink building next to Hôtel Domino has quiet rooms in bungalows at the back of its attractive garden restaurant. Meals are available from CFA2000 to CFA3000.

**Hôtel Agbeviade** ( ☎ 441 05 11; r with fan/air-con/air-con & balcony CFA7000/12,500/15,500; ⚉ ) Signposted off the road to Klouto 1.5km northwest of town, the Agbeviade is a friendly, comfy and pebble-dashed option, with views of the surrounding hills. Meals are CFA2500.

## Eating
The Lebanese and Italian food at Hôtel Regency Palace and Chez Fanny's French restaurant are very good. Or head to the Grand Marché and Rue Singa, south of Rond-point Texaco, for street food.

**Bar Bibaya** (Petit Marché) This is among the great *buvettes* in the shacks around Cafeteria de Bel Air.

**TOGO**

## HIKING IN THE KPALIMÉ AREA

Kpalimé is surrounded by mountain villages and cascades, reached by footpaths through the lush forests.

The heartiest walk is up **Mt Agou** (986m), 20km southeast of Kpalimé. Catch a taxi from Kpalimé to Nyogbo, and get out at Hôpital Bethesda. The offer of a few cold drinks should tempt a local lad to guide you to the top.

The path climbs between backyards with cocoa trees, then into a forest heaving with fruit. You finally come to terraced mountain villages, where tiny schools erupt into waves. The panoramic view from the village of **Akibo**, one hour from the peak, is as good as the view from the top.

It is possible to see Lake Volta in Ghana from the peak, but the view can be disappointing, especially during harmattan season. The summit is scattered with fences and guards, who will likely demand to see your papers and mutter about authorisation before showing you the view.

The walk takes four hours return. Or, take a taxi to the top and walk back down – either to the village or to the Kpalimé–Lomé highway.

**Klouto**, 12km northwest of Kpalimé, offers forested hills and a relatively cool climate, but it's the butterflies that make it unique. Early morning is the best time to search for butterflies. Net-touting local guys will offer to guide you, or you can ask at one of the auberges (see opposite).

For views of Ghana, head up to **Mt Klouto** (741m) via Campement de Klouto (670m). On the other side of the village is **Château Viale**, a medieval-style stone castle built by a Frenchman in 1944.

Another option is to go to **Kpimé Falls**, 12km from Kpalimé in the direction of Atakpamé. The falls are signposted from the village of Kpimé-Séva. There's no need for a guide; just walk westward down the main track for 30 minutes to a closed gate, where a guardian will request CFA500.

The waterfalls are spectacular during the wet season, but almost dry the rest of the year. It takes about 90 minutes to carry on to the top of the falls, where there's a dam and a panoramic view.

At Adéta, 9km north of Kpimé-Séva, turn left onto a tar road for the **Danyi Plateau**. A few kilometres beyond the village of N'Digbé is **Abbaye de l'Ascension** (abzog@café.tg), a Benedictine convent and monastery where you can buy jams made by the monks, and stay overnight in a simple room with a shower and shared toilets for CFA5000. It is best to book ahead as the monastery is often full.

**Restaurant au Fermier** ( ☎ 902 9830; meals CFA2500-3000; ☺ Tue-Sun) For excellent European and African food, try this low-roofed, intimate spot on the northwestern outskirts of town.

**Bar-Restaurant Macumba** ( ☎ 441 09 68; meals from CFA2200; ☺ 8am-10pm) For an upmarket restaurant serving Togolese fare, you can't beat the open-air Macumba on the northern outskirts of town, signposted from the road to Klouto.

**Cafeteria de Bel Air** ( ☎ 441 03 61; Route de Lomé; meals CFA250-2000) This central eatery, where you sit at an outdoor counter, is overpriced but open 24 hours.

## Drinking

Restaurant au Fermier and the *buvettes* near the Petit Marché are good for drinking.

**Imperial Night Club** (Rue de Bakula; ☺ Fri & Sat; admission CFA3000) In Hôtel Cristal, this place is popular.

**Kemi Bar** ( ☎ 441 04 02; ☺ 9am-10pm Wed-Mon) Popular late in the week and at weekends, this funky rooftop bar and cultural space is located on the same lane as Hôtel Agbeviade.

## Shopping

Kpalimé has a large and lively Grand Marché, which really gets going on Tuesday and Saturday. A good selection of Ghanaian kente cloth is sold here, but prices are higher than in Kumasi.

**Centre Artisanal** ( ☎ 441 00 77; ☺ 9am-noon & 3-5.30pm Mon-Fri, 9am-4pm Sat & holidays, 1-5pm Sun) Touristy but tasteful, this place has a vast array of woodcarvings, including chiefs' chairs and tables carved out of solid blocks of wood, as well as pottery, macramé and batiks.

**Centre des Aveugles** ( ☎ 441 01 72; ☺ 8.30am-5pm Mon-Sat) Some 4km from Kpalimé, on the road climbing towards Klouto, this centre for blind artisans has a shop selling crafts made by residents.

**Boutique d'Art** (Rond-point Texaco; ☺ 9am-12.30pm & 2.30-6pm Mon-Fri, to 12.30pm Sat) This small place has a wide selection of arts and craftwork, such as djembe drums, masks and statues.

### Getting There & Away

The *gare routière* is in the heart of town, two blocks east of the Shell petrol station. Northbound bush taxis leave from Rond-point Texaco. Regular services include Atakpamé (CFA1200, two hours), Sokodé (CFA3500, four hours), Kara (CFA4200, seven hours) and Lomé (CFA1500, three hours).

You can also get minibuses direct to Notsé (CFA1200, 1½ hours), Tsévié (CFA1700, two hours), to the Ghanaian border (CFA700, 30 minutes) and to Ho in Ghana (CFA1400, 1½ hours).

## KLOUTO

The village of Klouto, 12km northwest of Kpalimé, is at the heart of the forested Kouma-Konda region.

### Sights & Activities

Some 7km from Kpalimé, the winding road passes the mineral-water spring **Kamalo Falls**.

The **Dzawuwu-Za harvest festival** takes place in Klouto in early August, featuring markets, feasts, traditional Apkesse music and dancing.

In addition to the ruined **Château Viale**, the big attraction in Klouto are the masses of colourful butterflies in the surrounding forests. **Guided butterfly walks** can be arranged at the following places:

**Adetop** ( ☎ 441 08 17; per half day/day CFA6000/12,000) Also offers evening lessons in singing, drumming and traditional medicine for CFA10,000.

**Auberge des Papillons** ( ☎ 441 00 97) The best option. Tours from 9am to 3pm, with a picnic, cost CFA7500, or shorter trips without a picnic CFA5000.

**Campement de Klouto** ( ☎ 441 00 97; per hr CFA1250)

### Sleeping & Eating

**Auberge Papillons** ( ☎ 441 00 99; prosnyanu@yahoo.fr; d CFA3000) This friendly auberge is run by the inimitable Monsieur Prosper – the 'Butterfly Man' – an entomologist whose finds adorn the walls. It has clean, colourful rooms with shared facilities, and a restaurant serving excellent local coffee and specialities. Meals are available from CFA2500 to CFA3000.

**Campement de Klouto** ( ☎ 441 00 97; s/d CFA6000/8000; **P** ) This former German hospital will appeal to hermits and bank robbers. It's up a mountain, 30 minutes' walk from Klouto

at the start of the paths to Mount Klouto and the falls. The 16 large, breezy rooms have mozzie nets but no fans and there's a restaurant. Meals are around CFA4000.

**Adetop** ( ☎ 441 08 17; dm CFA3000) The basic rooms here have balconies with forest views, outside toilets and a bucket shower. There are no fans as it is cold here at night. The evening entertainment (singing, lessons on traditional medicine etc) is CFA10,000 – though guests can listen for free. Meals are available from CFA2500 to CFA3500.

### Getting There & Away

Taxis from Kpalimé to Klouto are about CFA300 (see p788). From the Kouma–Konda checkpoint it's an easy walk to Klouto, and an uphill hike to Campement de Klouto or Château Viale. To return to Kpalimé, go to the checkpoint and wait for a taxi.

## ATAKPAMÉ

**pop 41,300**

Once the favourite residence of the German colonial administrators, Atakpamé today is a commercial centre that lacks the charm of other parts of the coffee country. However, the mountain town, which is famous for its stilt dancers, does have a colourful Friday market and is a handy stopover between Lomé or Kpalimé and the north.

The southern entrance to town is marked by a T-junction, the eastern leg of which continues on to Kara. The north-south leg is the highway from Lomé that continues into the centre of town.

### Information

There is Web access at the two branches of **Cib-Inta** ( ☎ 440 03 07; Rue de la Station de Lomé; per hr CFA300; ⊠ 8am-10pm).

There are three banks in the town centre, **UTB** ( ☎ 440 13 33; Rue du Grand Marché), **BTCI** ( ☎ 440 01 74; Rue du Commerce) and **BIA-Togo** ( ☎ 440 01 92; Rue du Commerce), and one south of the centre – **BTD** ( ☎ 440 01 17; Rue du Grand Marché). They don't have ATMs but can change money. There is a basic **hospital** ( ☎ 440 01 91; Rue de l'Hôpital) uphill northwest of the centre.

### Sleeping

**Hôtel Le Sahelien** ( ☎ 440 12 44; htelsahlien@yahoo.fr; Route Internationale; r CFA8800, with hot water CFA10,800, deluxe CFA14,300; ⊠ **P** ) The swish Hôtel Le Sahelien, one of the most professionally run hotels in Togo, has guarded parking, two restaurants, a terrace bar, mod cons in the rooms, a shop, a barbecue and even a booth selling CDs. Meals are available for CFA2800.

**Hôtel Roc** ( ☎ 440 02 37; fax 440 00 33; off Rue de la Station de Lomé; s/d/ste CFA11,000/13,000/20,000; 🞋 ) The government-owned Hôtel Roc has been here 30 years – and looks like it – but it's still one of the best places in Atakpamé. On a hill off the main road, its clean rooms have good bathrooms and balconies with views of green hills and rusty roofs. Meals are CFA4000.

**Hôtel de l'Amitié** ( ☎ 440 06 25; Agnonou; r with fan/air-con CFA3800/6300; 🞋 ) With the sunny feel of an Andalusian guesthouse, l'Amitié's only drawback is its location, out of town up a dirt track from the Route Internationale. Meals are available for CFA1500 to CFA2000.

**Hôtel Delices des Retraites** ( ☎ 440 04 37; Rue de la Station de Lomé; r CFA3500) Despite the basic facilities (no fans) and the large wasps buzzing in and out of the communal bathroom, the former Hôtel Miva is a great budget option with a reasonable restaurant (meals CFA1500).

**Hôtel Kapokier** ( ☎ 440 02 84; Rue de l'Hôpital; r with fan/air-con CFA5300/6300; 🞋 ) Kapokier's bare blue rooms are no better than those in cheaper hotels, but it's in a great location – it's the large building overlooking the schoolyard, just up from the post office. The terrace bar-restaurant has views of the hills, and meals are available from CFA1900.

## Eating

**Hôtel Le Sahelien** ( ☎ 440 12 44; htelsahlien@yahoo .fr; Route International; meals CFA2800) This hotel has two good restaurants.

**Le Pentagone** ( ☎ 440 09 06; Rue de Grand Marché; meals CFA2200-2500; 🕑 8am-10pm) Pleasant first-floor restaurant serving tasty fare such as stir fries laden with onion and garlic.

**Kfete** ( ☎ 440 03 61) This good 24-hour stop for omelettes and snacks is off Rue de Grand Marché, near the church

Near Kfete, Le Saint Louis, where you can eat and drink on the terrace, is a good example of Atakpamé's many *buvettes* and food stalls.

## Entertainment

**Hôtel Roc** ( ☎ 440 02 37; fax 440 00 33; off Rue de la Station de Lomé) The hotel's bar, a highly '70s

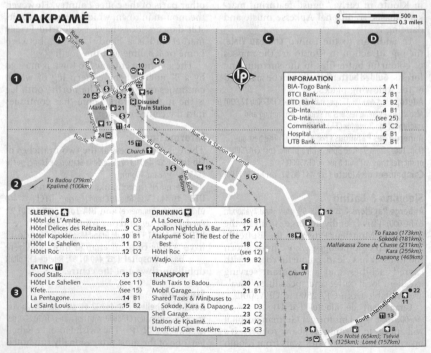

**ATAKPAMÉ**

0 _____ 500 m
0 _____ 0.3 miles

**INFORMATION**
BIA-Togo Bank.............................1 A1
BTCI Bank.....................................2 B1
BTD Bank......................................3 B2
Cib-Inta........................................4 B1
Cib-Inta.....................................(see 25)
Commissariat................................5 C2
Hospital........................................6 B1
UTB Bank......................................7 B1

To Badou (79km);
Kpalimé (100km)

**SLEEPING**
Hôtel de L'Amitie..........................8 D3
Hôtel Delices des Retraites............9 C3
Hôtel Kapokier............................10 B1
Hôtel Le Sahelien........................11 D3
Hôtel Roc....................................12 D2

**EATING**
Food Stalls..................................13 D3
Hôtel Le Sahelien.....................(see 11)
Kfete........................................(see 15)
La Pentagone..............................14 B1
Le Saint Louis.............................15 B2

**DRINKING**
A La Soeur...................................16 B1
Apollon Nightclub & Bar.............17 A1
Atakpamé Soir: The Best of the
   Best.........................................18 C2
Hôtel Roc.................................(see 12)
Wadjo.........................................19 B2

**TRANSPORT**
Bush Taxis to Badou.....................20 A1
Mobil Garage..............................21 B1
Shared Taxis & Minibuses to
   Sokode, Kara & Dapaong......22 D3
Shell Garage................................23 C3
Station de Kpalimé......................24 A2
Unofficial Gare Routière..............25 C3

To Fazao (173km);
Sokodé (181km);
Malfakassa Zone de Chasse (211km);
Kara (255km);
Dapaong (469km)

Church

To Notsé (65km); Tsévié
(125km); Lomé (157km)

hangout complete with mirrorball, has dancing at the weekends.

**A La Soeur** (off Rue de la Station de Lomé) Has seen better days, but draws the punters nonetheless.

**Apollon Nightclub & Bar** ( ☎ 440 00 99; Route de Kpalimé; � 9am-11pm) This rough and ready courtyard bar is announced by a mountain of Bonne Bierre crates at the entrance.

**Atakpamé Soir: The Best of the Best** ( ☎ 440 07 11; Rue de la Station de Lomé; � 8am-10pm) With its ultraviolet lights and psychedelic décor, this cavernous place near the Shell garage has the feel of a hangar awaiting an illegal rave.

**Wadjo** ( ☎ 400 06 21; Rue de Grand Marché; admission CFA1000) This nightclub and restaurant near the BTD bank is a plush and popular hangout.

### Getting There & Away

The T-junction about 200m south of Hôtel Delices des Retraites serves as the unofficial terminal for all public transport. Wait south of the junction for taxis to Lomé (CFA2000, three hours); and east of the junction on Route International, outside Hôtel Le Sahelien, for taxis to Sokodé (CFA2250, four hours), Kara (CFA3000, five hours) and Dapaong (CFA5900, eight hours).

Taxis to Badou (CFA1300, 2½ hours) and Kpalimé (CFA1200, 2½ hours) leave from Station de Kpalimé, just south of the market, and from northeast of the market.

### BADOU

Badou is lost somewhere in the northwest of coffee country, 88km west of Atakpamé on roads with a penchant for hairpin bends. The major attraction is **Akloa Falls** (also spelt Akrowa), 11km southeast of Badou, but the town itself has a pleasantly sleepy atmosphere and an unfeasible number of bars.

Access to the falls is 9km south of Badou at Tomagbé. You have to pay CFA500 to the villagers at Tomagbé, which includes a guide if you want one.

The hike up the hill from Tomagbé to the waterfalls takes 40 minutes. It's a pleasant walk and not too strenuous, except in the wet season. The trip is worth it as the falls are beautiful and you can swim beneath them.

**Hôtel Abuta** ( ☎ 993 85 25; r CFA6500-16,500; ☒ ) is past the post office on the road to Ghana, with 15 surprisingly plush rooms. The friendly staff can organise trips to the

falls and traditional dancing displays. Meals are from CFA2500 to CFA3500.

Popular bar **Au Carrefour 2000** ( ☎ 926 39 09; r with fan CFA2000-2500) has some uncomfortable beds and meals (CFA1500).

**Cascade Plus** ( ☎ 443 00 71; r with fan CFA2500) has basic but homely rooms, and meals are available from CFA500 to CFA1500.

Bush taxis head to Badou (CFA1300, 2½ hours) from the market area in Atakpamé. There are many on Thursday, Badou market day. Taxis (shared/hired CFA350/1000) and *taxi-motos* (CFA500) go from Badou to the waterfalls, but the walk there is pleasant.

### PARC NATIONAL DE FAZAO-MALFAKASSA

This 192,000-hectare **national park** ( � Nov-May), in central Togo's beautiful Malfakassa Mountains, is one of the most diverse West African parks in terms of landscape – with forest, savanna, rocky cliffs and waterfalls.

The Swiss **Fondation Franz Weber** ( ☎ 550 02 96; www.ffw.ch; � 7.30am-12pm & 2.30-5.30pm Mon-Fri, 7.30-12pm Sat), which has an office in Sokodé, is working to repopulate the park with animals, which were scared into neighbouring countries by rioters. This task has seen military personnel crack down on poachers, Peul (Fula) nomads and villagers, encouraging them to find alternative sources of agriculture and energy, such as solar power.

The park now boasts 30 species of bird and 91 species of mammal – including monkeys, antelopes and 60 elusive elephants.

Entry for private vehicles is CFA10,000, and CFA3000 per person. Four-hour **guided drives** (1 person CFA18,000, 2-3 people per person CFA13,000, 4-6 people per person CFA9000; 7-10 people per person CFA8000; 11 people & over per person CFA6000), leave Hôtel Parc Fazao at 5.30am and 2.30pm – contact the foundation 24 hours in advance.

Adjoining Fazao is Malfakassa Zone de Chasse, an excellent area for hiking with great views. If you want to hike, ask the foundation for permission and bring water. The park occasionally opens late if the tracks have suffered badly during the rainy season.

Malfakassa has many good animal trails; the best go along the mountain tops and south into the park. Orientation is easy, even when you're hiking off trails due to the broad views from the mountains. In the wet season, walking up the slopes through the tall grass takes considerable effort.

TOGO

Camping is not allowed in the park. **Hôtel Parc Fazao** ( ☎ 550 02 96; fax 550 01 75; ffw.fazzo@rdd .tg) was closed for renovation at the time of research but planned to reopen – check with the foundation.

There is a marked turn-off for the park in Adjengré, 38km south of Sokodé on the main highway. The trip takes 45 minutes and costs CFA600 shared. You may have to wait in Fazao for a ride to Hôtel Parc Fazao. There is also a northern entrance at Binako, 40km from Sokodé on the highway to Bassar.

To get to the Malfakassa Zone de Chasse, turn off the Sokodé–Bassar highway at Malfakassa – a semiabandoned village in a pass near the highest point of the small mountains – and hike south into the park.

# THE NORTH

As you head north, the pace of life slows down in the heat, Islam takes over from Christianity as the dominant religion, and the Kabyé replace the Ewe as the main ethnic group. Sokodé, Kara and Dapaong are short on sights but are good spots to watch the world splutter past on a dysfunctional *taxi-moto*. If you're searching for something more challenging, head to the Tamberma Valley on the Beninese border. Standing guard in front of the animist Tamberma people's castellated clay compounds, the skull-topped shrines are a mystery for the Western imagination.

## SOKODÉ
**pop 120,400**

Sokodé is Togo's second-biggest city but it doesn't feel like it, with no major sites beyond the odd colonial building. But, the people are friendly and the town has a relaxed atmosphere. In addition to dozing in the shade of a mango tree, it's worth checking out the markets: the Petit Marché, for squawking chickens and fetish stalls; and the less traditional Grand Marché, the province of *wagassi* cheese, plastic sandals and intestines.

The heart of town is the T-junction just south of the Grand Marché. This is the site of the **Adoss ceremony**, which takes place on the second day after the Prophet's birthday (for details see p818). During this spectacle, men engage in a series of violent, knife-flashing dances after drinking a special potion that supposedly makes their skin impenetrable.

## Information

There is a **cyber café** ( ☎ 550 02 69; Rue de Leara; per hr CFA300; ⌚ 7.30am-8pm Mon-Sat) on the first floor of the Ets Tchakala Papeterie et Informatique building, opposite the post office.

**UTB** ( ☎ 550 01 62) and **BTCI** ( ☎ 550 01 07) banks change money and UTB has Western Union.

## Sleeping
### BUDGET

**Hôtel Cercle de l'Amitié** ( ☎ 550 09 06; Route de Kara; r with fan & shared/private bathroom CFA4000/4500, d CFA5500, s with air-con CFA7500; 🅿 ) One of the most attractive hotels we saw, with colonial rooms, an outdoor bar-restaurant and snack bar. Ask for a room between 28 and 31.

**Campement Tchaoudjo** ( ☎ 550 15 17; Rue de la Préfecture; r with fan & shared/private bathroom CFA3500/4500; 🅿 ) The tranquil Campement is up the hill from the *douane* (customs post) on the southern edge of town, a walk from the centre. Its austere but spacious rooms have sheets and fans, and some have private bathrooms.

**New Hôtel Tchaoudjo** ( ☎ 925 89 94; Route de Bassar; r with fan CFA3500, with air-con CFA6000-7000, with air-con & TV CFA8500; 🅿 ) This cheap hotel is in a great central location, but there is an institutional feel to its gloomy rooms and crumbling corridors.

**Hôtel Relais de la Cigale** ( ☎ 914 72 50; Route de Lomé; r CFA2500-3000) An improvement on some nearby budget options, the Relais de la Cigale has spartan rooms with fans and shared bathrooms.

### MIDRANGE

**Hôtel Issofa** ( ☎ 550 09 89; off Route de Bassar; r with fan & shared/private bathroom CFA3800/4800, with air-con & bathroom CFA8800; 🅿 ) Popular with European travellers and workers for its pleasant bar and restaurant, the Issofa is tucked away down a quiet street. The rooms are clean and comfortable and those with air-con are carpeted, but the shared bathrooms leave a little to be desired. Meals are available from CFA1600.

**La Bonne Auberge** ( ☎ 550 02 35; Route de Kara; r with fan/air-con CFA3500/6500; 🅿 ) About 2km north of the centre, this friendly auberge has reasonable rooms and an attractive bar-restaurant (meals are from CFA1600 to CFA3000).

**Hôtel Ave Kedia** ( ☎ 550 05 34; Ave Kedia; r with fan & shared bathroom CFA4000, with air-con, private bathroom & TV CFA7500-12,000; meals CFA1900-3000; 🅿 ) This well-run place north of town is a good midrange

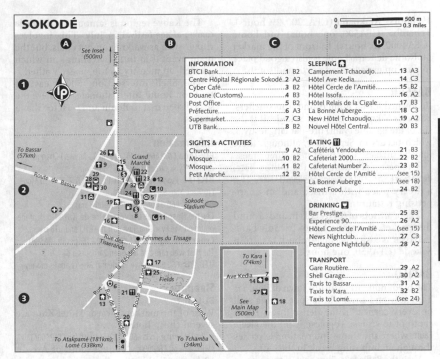

## SOKODÉ

**INFORMATION**
| | |
|---|---|
| BTCI Bank..............................1 | B2 |
| Centre Hôpital Régionale Sokodé..2 | A2 |
| Cyber Café............................3 | B2 |
| Douane (Customs)...................4 | B3 |
| Post Office............................5 | B2 |
| Préfecture............................6 | A3 |
| Supermarket..........................7 | C3 |
| UTB Bank.............................8 | B2 |

**SIGHTS & ACTIVITIES**
| | |
|---|---|
| Church.................................9 | A2 |
| Mosque...............................10 | B2 |
| Mosque...............................11 | B2 |
| Petit Marché.........................12 | B2 |

**SLEEPING**
| | |
|---|---|
| Campement Tchaoudjo............13 | A3 |
| Hôtel Ave Kedia.....................14 | C3 |
| Hôtel Cercle de l'Amitié...........15 | B2 |
| Hôtel Issofa..........................16 | A2 |
| Hôtel Relais de la Cigale..........17 | B3 |
| La Bonne Auberge..................18 | C3 |
| New Hôtel Tchaoudjo..............19 | A2 |
| Nouvel Hôtel Central...............20 | B3 |

**EATING**
| | |
|---|---|
| Cafétéria Yendoube.................21 | B3 |
| Cafeteriat 2000......................22 | B2 |
| Cafeteriat Number 2................23 | B2 |
| Hôtel Cercle de l'Amitié...........(see 15) |  |
| La Bonne Auberge..................(see 18) |  |
| Street Food..........................24 | B2 |

**DRINKING**
| | |
|---|---|
| Bar Prestige..........................25 | B3 |
| Experience 90.......................26 | A2 |
| Hôtel Cercle de l'Amitié...........(see 15) |  |
| News Nightclub......................27 | C3 |
| Pentagone Nightclub...............28 | A2 |

**TRANSPORT**
| | |
|---|---|
| Gare Routière........................29 | A2 |
| Shell Garage.........................30 | A2 |
| Taxis to Bassar......................31 | A2 |
| Taxis to Kara.........................32 | B2 |
| Taxis to Lomé........................(see 24) |  |

**TOGO**

option, with a bar-restaurant (meals from CFA1900 to CFA3000) and tidy rooms.

**Nouvel Hôtel Central** ( ☎ 550 01 23; Route de Lomé; s/d/bungalow/ste CFA11,000/13,000/16,000/22,000; meals CFA1700-3000; 🍽 🅿 ) Set in unkempt gardens at the quiet southern end of town, this large place has clean spacious rooms with air-con and tiled bathrooms with hot water. Meals are available for CFA1700 to CFA3000.

### Eating
For street food, try the area around the Grand Marché. Just north of the market are the no-frills 24-hour cafés **Cafeteriat Number 2** (off Route de Kara) and – behind a German colonial building – **Cafeteriat 2000** (off Route de Kara).

Nearby, **Hôtel Cercle de l'Amitié** ( ☎ 550 09 06; Route de Kara) has a small snack bar serving kebabs, sandwiches and roast guinea fowl (CFA200 to CFA750). The restaurant at **La Bonne Auberge** ( ☎ 550 02 35; Route de Kara) is also worth checking out.

**Cafétéria Yendoube** ( ☎ 550 17 69; Route de Lomé; meals CFA1000), a cheap, friendly café on the main road, serves mountains of guinea fowl and spaghetti at most hours.

There's a small **supermarket** (Ave Kedia; 🕑 8am-1pm & 3-11pm) near Hôtel Ave Kedia.

### Drinking
**Bar Prestige** ( ☎ 550 03 52; Route de Lomé) This lively open-air place, on the main drag south of the central area, has loud African music and CFA250 beers.

**News Nightclub** ( ☎ 550 11 30; Route de Kara) The former Riviera Club has an open-air bar and snack bar, and is the place to boogie at weekends.

**Pentagone Nightclub** ( ☎ 550 05 34; Route de Bassar; 🕑 10pm-midnight, until late Fri & Sat) In addition to loud music, Pentagone Nightclub, on the western side of town near the *gare routière*, has an outdoor café.

Other watering holes include the bar at **Hotel Cercle de l'Amié** ( ☎ 550 09 06; Route de Kara) and nearby **Experience 90** (Route de Kara).

### Getting There & Away
From the *gare routière* – one block west of the market, behind the Shell garage on Route de Bassar – minibuses go regularly to Bassar (CFA950, one hour), Kara (CFA1200,

1½ hours), Atakpamé (CFA2200, 2½ hours), Tchamba (CFA500, one hour) and Lomé (CFA4000, six hours). In front of the market on Route de Kara/Lomé is also a good place to pick up taxis headed north and south.

## BASSAR

Renowned for its hunters and iron smelters, Bassar is 57km northwest of Sokodé. It is the site of the Igname (yam) fire-dancing festival, which occurs in September, although there may be smaller versions of it at other times.

The best place to stay is the hilltop **Hôtel de Bassar** ( ☎ 663 00 81; bungalows from CFA6000; 🖭 ), a dreary place with a disco and an unappetising restaurant.

There are lots of food stalls in and around the market, and a number of friendly bars.

Bassar is easily reached by bush taxi from Sokodé (CFA950, one hour).

## BAFILO

The predominantly Muslim town of Bafilo is a friendly and smoky little spot, with a stall on every corner. In the dense forest 10km south of town is a Togolese icon, the **Aledjo Fault**, where the Route Internationale passes through an imposing break in the cliff.

Visit the **Bafilo falls**, 5km east of town, for a panoramic view of the surrounds. Swimming in the plunge pool is forbidden, but there's a wonderful 30-minute walk there, through fields, over streams and up overgrown stairs. Visit the chief in his compound, past the mosque, to get permission (CFA500).

At the **Groupement Artisanal Tisserands** ( ☎ 660 02 26; 🕘 7am-5pm Mon-Fri), you can see weavers in action and buy *pagnes* of cloth.

The 15-room **Hôtel Maza Esso** ( ☎ 660 02 54; Route de Kara; r with shared bathroom & fan/air-con CFA3500/6500; 🖭 ) is a popular, eccentric hotel with woeful facilities. Meals cost CFA1000 to CFA2000. Ask the manager, Abel, to take you to his sister's *sodabe* den next door – see p777 for appropriate health warnings!

## KARA

**pop 34,900**

Laid out by the Germans on a spacious scale, Kara is the capital of northern Togo and a good base for trips to the Tamberma Valley and Mt Kabyé (see p798). Because President Eyadéma came from Pya, a Kabyé village about 20km to the north, he pumped a lot of money into Kara.

The Kabyé region is famous for the **Evala coming-of-age festival** in July. This involves rituals such as walking on hot coals, but the main event is *la lutte* (wrestling), in which greased-up men try to topple each other.

The Shell intersection, 500m east of town on Route Internationale, is where the sealed road east to Benin and west to Ghana begins.

## Information

**BIA-Togo** ( ☎ 660 61 45; Ave du 13 Janvier) Changes money – you can also try Hôtel de Kara.

**BTCI** (Ave Eyadéma; 🕘 7.30-11.30am & 2.30-4pm Mon-Fri, 7am-1pm Sat) Has an ATM.

**BTD** ( ☎ 660 61 06; Rue de l'Hôtel Kara).

**Centre Hospitalier Universitaire de Kara** North of the centre on Ave Eyadéma, just past the BTCI and UTB banks.

**Cyber Café Agri-Info** ( ☎ 661 02 16; per hr CFA300) The best web café and it's open 24 hours a day.

**UTB** ( ☎ 660 60 10; Ave Eyadéma) Also changes money.

## Sleeping

### BUDGET

West of the market towards Hôtel Kara are several cheap hotels.

**La Détente** ( ☎ 660 14 22; s/d with fan CFA2300/3300, r with air-con CFA8000; 🖭 ) Just south of Ave du 13 Janvier is this proudly run auberge with quiet rooms and a lively bar. Reception is round the back.

**Hôtel le Relais** ( ☎ 660 01 88; r with fan/air-con CFA4500/10,500; 🖭 ) It's worth tracking down this hotel, north of Hôtel la Providence on dirt roads, for its clean comfortable rooms and bar-restaurant (meals CFA1900 to CFA2500) set around a lush garden. Despite what it says on the sign, there is no camping.

**Hôtel le Sourire** ( ☎ 926 13 55; Rue de l'Hôtel Kara; r with fan/air-con from CFA3000/6500, bungalow CFA12,000; 🖭 ) The best of the budget choices between the market and Hôtel Kara, le Sourire has homely rooms set around a leafy courtyard.

**Auberge la Lumiere** ( ☎ 660 03 25; Rue de l'Hôtel Kara; r CFA4000-6000) With its turquoise walls, la Lumiere is a basic, but quiet and breezy, hotel in a good location near Hôtel Kara.

**Hôtel Mini-Riz** ( ☎ 660 17 44; Ave Eyadéma; r with shared toilet & fan/air-con CFA5600/7600; 🖭 ) This central hotel, opposite Togotelecom, has musty rooms and a popular bar-restaurant where meals cost CFA1200 to CFA3500.

**Hôtel la Providence** ( ☎ 660 17 42; r with fan & shared toilet CFA5000, with air-con & private toilet CFA7000; 🖭 ) The former Hôtel Tombé, just off Route de Maman N'Danida, is a little moth-eaten, but has clean, quiet rooms.

**Centre Communautaire des Affaires Sociales** ( ☎ 660 61 18; Route de Maman N'Danida; s/d/tr with fan CFA2500/3500/5000, dm shared/alone CFA1500/2000, d with air-con CFA4500, bungalow CFA5500; 🞕 ) This large centre has a ghostly feel and is a little far from the centre, but the rooms are clean, the staff are friendly, and there's a popular bar-restaurant (meals CFA1500 to CFA3000).

### MIDRANGE
**Hôtel le Jardin** ( ☎ 660 01 34; r CFA9500; 🞕 ) This delightful hotel, off Rue de l'Hôtel Kara, has a pleasant garden and small but very attractive rooms, as well as Kara's top restaurant, where meals are CFA1750 to CFA3000.

**Hôtel la Concorde** ( ☎ 660 19 00; off Ave du 13 Janvier; r with fan/air-con CFA6000/12,000; 🞕 ) One of the slickest operations in town, with TVs and black and white furniture in the air-con-equipped rooms, a rooftop bar, pricey European dishes in the restaurant (meals from CFA1900) and a central location near the post office.

**Hôtel de France** ( ☎ 660 03 42; off Rue de Chaminade; r with fan CFA3800, r with air-con CFA7800, r with air-con & bath CFA10,800; 🞕 🅿 ) The quiet Hôtel de France, north of town, has large, attractive rooms and a rooftop terrace where you can watch the sun set over the town and the hills. Meals are available for CFA900 to CFA2500.

**Hôtel de l'Union** ( ☎ 660 14 88; Rue du 23 Septembre; r with/without air-con & hot water 15,300/CFA12,300; 🞕 ) This classy hotel offers small but

**TOGO**

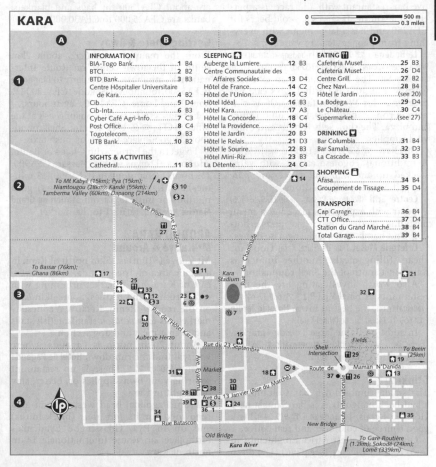

modern rooms and group discounts. Meals are CFA1500 to CFA3000.

**TOP END**

**Hôtel Kara** ( ☎ 660 05 16; fax 660 62 42; Rue de l'Hôtel Kara; s/d from CFA18,500/21,500, s/d bungalow CFA24,000/26,000; meals CFA6000; 🛒 🖾 P ) Kara's best and largest hotel, although it has seen better days. The stone bungalows are the most appealing, with TVs and minibars. Hôtel Kara has volleyball and tennis courts, shops, a nightclub and a swimming pool, which nonguests can use for CFA1000. Meals are CFA600.

## Eating

**Le Château** ( ☎ 660 60 27; Ave du 13 Janvier; meals CFA775-1975; 🕒 Tue-Sun) Le Château, an attractive bar-restaurant with a terrace, is a perennial favourite. It serves ice-cold beers for CFA250 and has a large menu with everything from pepper steak to yam chips.

**La Bodega** ( ☎ 919 54 47; la-bodega@hotmail.com; Route International; meals CFA700-3250; 🕒 10am-11pm, from 5pm Sat) The brainchild of an ex-Peace Corp worker, this is north Togo's café par excellence for Western faves such as cinnamon rolls, sandwiches, fries, onion rings and pizza. The shop sells Nutella and other vital supplies.

**Chez Navi** ( ☎ 660 19 02; Ave Eyadéma; meals CFA500) A traditional Togolese eatery, with yams stacked up the wall and sauce and *pâte* slopped out of metal cauldrons.

**Centre Grill** (Route de Prison; meals CFA975-1500) Popular with expats, this place has a menu including Western dishes like pizzas, hotdogs and hamburgers, and Togolese dishes.

**Cafeteria Muset** (Rue de l'Hôtel Kara) Good for cheap, filling meals. Another branch is found just south of the Shell roundabout.

Also worth investigating are the bar-restaurants at **Hôtel Mini-Riz** ( ☎ 660 17 44; Ave Eyadéma) and, the best in town, **Hotel le Jardin** ( ☎ 660 01 34; off Rue de l'Hôtel Kara).

In addition to the large Tuesday market, there is a well-stocked **supermarket** (Route de Prison) next to Centre Grill.

## Drinking

The small, tumbledown Bar Columbia is a laid-back hangout, as is Bar Samala near Hôtel le Relais. **La Bodega** ( ☎ 919 54 47) is a good source of cold beer and real coffee.

One of the hottest African nightclubs in town is at La Détente (see p796). The disco

at **Hôtel Kara** (admission CFA1000; 🕒 Sat & holidays) is the best place to dance.

Nearby, the open-air **Cascade** (Rue de l'Hôtel de Kara) is a lively local haunt.

## Shopping

**Groupement de Tissage** ( ☎ 660 12 92; 🕒 7am-12.30pm & 2.30-5pm) Sells high-quality fabrics and costumes made by local women. To get there, turn right at the sign, just east of Centre Communautaire des Affaires Sociales, and head south 250m on a dirt road.

**Afasa** (Rue Batascon; 🕒 8am-12.30pm & 2.30-5pm Mon-Fri) At the other end of town, this women's group sells great bags, blankets and batiks made of off-cuts from others. They send the money back to their local villages and prices are about CFA1500 for bags and blankets; batiks are CFA25,000 to CFA30,000.

## Getting There & Away

From the main *gare routière*, about 2km south of the town centre on Route Internationale, minibuses go regularly to Dapaong (CFA3800, four hours), Sokodé (CFA1200 1½ hours) and Lomé (CFA4600, seven hours).

For buses to Lomé and Sokodé, ask at the office of **CTT** ( ☎ 661 03 03) near the Shell roundabout; a good place to pick up bush taxis.

To get to the border with Ghana or Benin, and to local towns such as Bassar (CFA900, 1½ hours), Niamtougou (CFA550, 45 minutes) and Kandé (CFA900, 1½ hours), get a minibus or bush taxi from **Station du Grand Marché** (Ave Eyadéma) next to the market.

## AROUND KARA
### Mt Kabyé & Around

Mt Kabyé (810m) is 15km north of Kara, in a scenic area of Togo. Landa, 15km northeast of Kara, has a market brimming with local produce and textiles. Some 4km east, on the road to Benin, Kétao's Wednesday market has *tchoukoutou* stands, fetish stalls and even a meat and dog section.

About 20km north is Pagouda, where you will find the run-down **Hôtel de Pagouda** (chalets CFA5000; 🖾 ). There is no restaurant so bring your own supplies or, better, stay overnight in Kara.

From Pagouda, head west into an area renowned for its *forgerons* (blacksmiths) and on to Pya, Gnassingbé Eyadéma's birthplace, on Route Internationale 14km north of Kara.

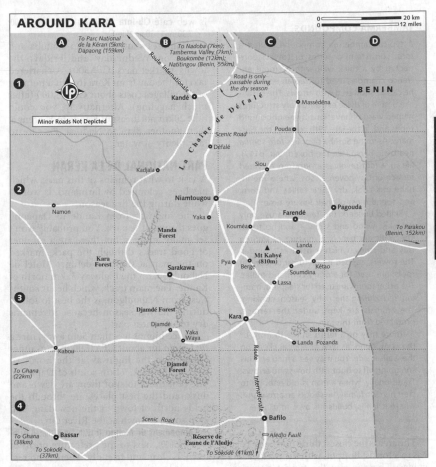

**AROUND KARA**

## NIAMTOUGOU

This sleepy town, 28km north of Kara on Route Internationale, has a Sunday market, where you'll find a selection of baskets and ceramic bowls, and **Codhani** ( ☎ 665 02 36; ⏱ 8am-1pm & 3-5.30pm, from 8.30am Sat & 9am Sun). This centre, 2km south, sells everything from T-shirts (CFA2500) to tablecloths (CFA8000) made by artisans with a disability. You can tour the workshop and watch them weaving, hammering, painting and boiling up wax.

Codhani has five attractive bungalows (shared bathroom CFA2500, or private bathroom CFA4000) and a bar-restaurant serving Togolese grub (CFA500 to CFA2400). A short walk south of Codhani, **Motel de Niamtougou** ( ☎ 665 02 41; s/d with air-con CFA5400/6700; ✖ ) has surprisingly plush, spacious rooms and meals are CFA2000.

## TAMBERMA VALLEY

The Tamberma Valley has a unique collection of fortified villages, founded in the 17th century by people fleeing the slave-grabbing forays of Benin's Dahomeyan kings (see the boxed text, p800).

To get to Nadoba – the region's capital, located on the Benin border – turn off the highway near the garage in Kandé, 27km north of Niamtougou, and head northeast for the same distance. If you have a 4WD, off-piste tracks into Benin pass through some of the most stunning mountain scenery in this part of West Africa.

TOGO

---

### TAMBERMA COMPOUNDS

A typical Tamberma compound, called a *tata*, consists of a series of towers connected by a thick wall with a single entrance chamber, used to trap an enemy so he can be showered with arrows. The castle-like nature of these extraordinary structures helped ward off invasions by neighbouring tribes and, in the late 19th century, the Germans. As in the Somba people's *tata somba* nearby in Benin (see the boxed text, p117), life in a *tata* revolves around an elevated terrace of clay-covered logs, where the inhabitants cook, dry their millet and corn, and spend most of their leisure time.

Skilled builders, the Tamberma use only use clay, wood and straw – and no tools. The walls are banco, a mixture of unfired clay and straw, which is used as a binder. The towers, capped by picturesque conical roofs, are used for storing corn and millet. The other rooms are used for sleeping, bathing and, during the rainy season, cooking. The animals are kept under the terrace, protected from the rain.

There may be a fetish shrine in front of the compound, as well as animal skulls on the walls inside. You may see a man and his son going off to hunt with bows and arrows. Traditionally, when a man is old enough to start his own family, he shoots an arrow and, where it lands, builds his own *tata*.

---

The area is the closest thing northern Togo has to a tourist hotspot, with the overzealous guides. There is also the tourist organisation **Ajvdc** ( ☎ 667 20 11), which can show you around *tata* houses in Nadoba and the less touristy villages of Bassamba, Warengo and Pimini, and runs a *tata*-style **auberge** (r CFA2000) in Nadoba, with meals from CFA1500.

Nadoba's Wednesday market, as much a *tchoukoutou*-fuelled gathering as a commercial event, is worth a visit in itself. Visitors must buy tickets (CFA1500) from the **police post** ( ☎ 909 08 14; 7am-4pm), 2km from Kandé on the Nadoba road.

On the southern outskirts of Kandé, the 18-room **Auberge Oxygene** ( ☎ /fax 667 01 19; r with fan/air-con CFA4500/6000; ), is a passable auberge with a lively bar. Meals are CFA1500.

Small shops and food stalls cluster opposite Kandé *gare routière*, and 300m north is web café **Cib-Inta** ( ☎ 667 01 31; per hr CFA400; 7.30am-11.30pm Mon-Sat).

Minibuses shuttle between Nadoba and Kandé on Wednesday and Friday, the towns' market days (CFA500). A chartered taxi for the day from Kara to visit a number of the villages costs about CFA15,000 (after much haggling). Alternatively, you could hike 20km northeast of Kandé to Warengo, then another 8km to Nadoba. Be sure to take plenty of water.

## PARC NATIONAL DE LA KÉRAN

A visit to what remains of this park, which has been colonised by farmland, is worthwhile during the dry season.

The highway from Kandé to Dapaong goes through the park. You probably won't see many animals, but there are a number of good tracks through the park, marked on the map at the now-defunct Motel de Naboulgou, on the highway 32km north of Kandé. The main track, which heads southwest from Naboulgou, is the best to follow during the wet season because it remains dry for the most part.

To see hippos less than 50m away, hire a *taxi-moto* for about CFA1800 in Sansanné-Mango, on the highway at the northern edge of the park, 71km south of Dapaong. The best times to spot them are dawn and dusk, and the best places are through the fields north of town at the new dam, and 2km south of town at the River Oti.

**Campement de Mango** (r with fan & shared bathroom CFA3000), next to the prefecture north of town, is clean and friendly. There is no restaurant but there are two *buvettes* opposite the *gare routière*.

## DAPAONG

**pop 31,800**

This lively little town is a West African melting pot, with the Burkinabé and Ghanaian borders both within 30km. Its attractive, hilly setting provides a welcome break in the otherwise flat landscape.

The Saturday market and the small **Museé des Savanes** (admission CFA1000; 9am-12.30pm & 3-6.30pm Tue-Fri) are worth a look, as is the **Coopérative Tissage** ( ☎ 770 86 05; 8am-5pm Mon-Sat) next to Radio Maria. It sells distinctive batiks, made by handicapped local women using Burkinabé and Beninese cotton.

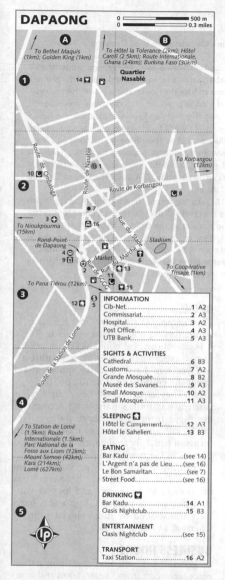

**DAPAONG**

To Bethel Maquis (1km); Golden King (1km)

To Hôtel la Tolerance (2km); Hôtel Caroli (2.5km); Route Internationale, Ghana (24km); Burkina Faso (30km)

Quartier Nasablé

To Korbangou (12km)

Route de Nasablé

Route de Korbangou

Route de Ombalaga

Rue du Stade

To Nioukpourma (15km)

Rond-Point de Dapaong

Market

Rue de SCOCC

Rue de Marché

To Pana Tiérou (12km)

Stadium

To Cooperative Tissage (1km)

Route de la Station de Lomé

To Station de Lomé (1.5km); Route Internationale (1.5km); Parc National de la Fosse aux Lions (12km); Mount Semoo (42km); Kara (214km); Lomé (627km)

| INFORMATION | | |
|---|---|---|
| Cib-Net | 1 | A2 |
| Commissariat | 2 | A3 |
| Hospital | 3 | A2 |
| Post Office | 4 | A3 |
| UTB Bank | 5 | A3 |

| SIGHTS & ACTIVITIES | | |
|---|---|---|
| Cathedral | 6 | B3 |
| Customs | 7 | A2 |
| Grande Mosquée | 8 | B2 |
| Musée des Savanes | 9 | A3 |
| Small Mosque | 10 | A2 |
| Small Mosque | 11 | A3 |

| SLEEPING | | |
|---|---|---|
| Hôtel le Campement | 12 | A3 |
| Hôtel le Sahelien | 13 | B3 |

| EATING | | |
|---|---|---|
| Bar Kadu | (see 14) | |
| L'Argent n'a pas de Lieu | (see 16) | |
| Le Bon Samaritan | (see 7) | |
| Street Food | (see 16) | |

| DRINKING | | |
|---|---|---|
| Bar Kadu | 14 | A1 |
| Oasis Nightclub | 15 | B3 |

| ENTERTAINMENT | | |
|---|---|---|
| Oasis Nightclub | (see 15) | |

| TRANSPORT | | |
|---|---|---|
| Taxi Station | 16 | A2 |

TOGO

Nearby hiking opportunities include the tiny **Parc National de la Fosse aux Lions**, 12km south of town, and the remarkable **cliffside fortress** (see the boxed text, p802).

For Western goods, go to Hope store at the market. **UTB** ( ☎ 770 81 46; Route de la Station de Lomé) has Western Union facilities; banks close on Monday and open Saturday morning.

## Sleeping & Eating

**Hôtel le Campement** ( ☎ 770 80 55; Route de la Station de Lomé; r with fan/air-con CFA8600/13,800; 😭 ) Dapaong's best accommodation. Rooms are pleasant and spacious, if rather '70s looking, with interior bathrooms and shared toilets. The excellent but pricey French bar-restaurant boasts a generous selection of extravagant desserts; meals are from CFA3500 to CFA4000.

**Hôtel le Sahelien** ( ☎ 770 81 84; Rue du Marché; s/d with fan CFA3700/4700, with air-con CFA5600/6600; 😭 ) Next to the market in the centre of town, the Sahelien has reasonable rooms and a bar. A woman at the gate sells cheap fish and rice.

**Hôtel la Tolerance** ( ☎ 770 89 48; r with fan/air-con CFA3800/5800; 😭 ) This place, 3km north of town, has 13 rooms with a stylish blue colour scheme and a terrace bar-restaurant.

**Hôtel Caroli** ( ☎ 770 81 61; r with fan/air-con from CFA4500/6500; 😋 ) This quiet place among the trees near Hôtel la Tolerance has laundry and car washing services, and rooms with balconies, hot water and satellite TV. Meals are available for CFA1500 to CFA3500.

**Bethel Maquis** ( ☎ 770 88 38) Behind Auberge Idriss north of the centre, this place serves delicious Western food (meals from CFA1500) in a tranquil garden.

Among the cafeterias and stalls on Route de Nasablé around the taxi station, **L'Argent n'a pas de Lieu** (Route de Nasablé) serves a fine omelette. **Mama Cap** (Route de Nasablé) runs a cracking street stall at the Cap garage.

## Drinking

Near the Cap garage, the rough-and-ready **Bar Kadu** (Route de Nasablé) also has cheap Togolese and European food. Otherwise, head to **Le Bon Samaritan** (Route de Nasablé), near customs, or the market area.

To dance, get down to the glitzy **Golden King** ( 😋 Fri & Sat), near Bethel Maquis, or **Oasis Nightclub** ( ☎ 770 82 22; off Rue de Marché; admission CFA500; 😋 from 10pm Sat).

## Getting There & Away

Taxis leave the station on Route de Nasablé for Sinkasse on the Burkinabé border (CFA750), from where transport heads to Ouagadougou.

From Station de Lomé on Route Internationale, 2km south of the centre, bush taxis head to Kara (CFA3800, four hours) and Lomé (CFA8000, 12 hours).

**CASTLE IN THE CLIFF**

Halfway up a cliff in the remote mountain ranges 42km southwest of Dapaong is an amazing minifortress.

During the 19th century the Chokossi Empire, centred around Sansanné-Mango, established a feudal empire over much of northern Togo. The Moba people, who lived on and around the plateau, resented this, and built cliffside stores on **Mt Semoo** to hide their possessions – and themselves – from Chokossi soldiers and tax collectors. The cliff's ledge provided perfect natural protection.

While the Moba people had to scale the cliff using tree roots and rocky ledges, there is now a protected steel ladder. At the long-since abandoned site you'll find a series of large conical clay containers, which were used to store food supplies, as well as the sleeping and cooking areas.

To reach the escarpment, follow Route Internationale south of Dapaong for about 16km. At the signs for Prefecture de Tanjouare and Aide et Action, turn right onto a dirt road and follow it 6km west to the village of Goundoga, where you can hire a guide (CFA2000). The hike to Chateau Semoo takes three hours return – bring plenty of water.

If you have a 4WD, it is possible to drive the 16km to the top of the escarpment along rough tracks from Nano (4km beyond Goundoga), where the chief will ask you to buy a ticket for the site (CFA2000). Visitors must also pay about the same amount to the chief of Nagou, near the site.

It's possible to find a shared taxi to Goundoga or Nano on Thursday, market day, but it's easier to hire a taxi to take you, wait while you walk, and then drive you back to Dapaong (CFA8000).

In Bogou, about 1km before Goundoga, is **Auberge Mont Djabir** (r without fan CFA2000), a friendly auberge where there are six rooms (with no electricity) and food is available.

# TOGO DIRECTORY

## ACCOMMODATION

Owing perhaps to its undeveloped tourist industry, Togolese accommodation is cheap even by West African standards. Expect to pay CFA3000 to CFA6000 for single or double budget rooms, CFA7000 to CFA13,000 for midrange and CFA15,000 to CFA25,000 for top end. In Lomé, prices are generally higher, with budget rooms costing up to CFA10,000, and the top end hotels, owned by international chains, charging Western rates – CFA70,000 to CFA120,000.

Top-end hotels with swimming pools and other amenities can be found in Lomé, at Lake Togo and in Kara.

## ACTIVITIES

There are plenty of hiking opportunities in Togo, particularly in the Kpalimé region (see the boxed text, p790) and around the national parks.

For swimming, there are some good beaches near Lomé and at Aného, but the currents can be dangerous (see p786). Several of the top-end hotels have swimming pools and tennis courts. Water sports can be arranged at Lake Togo, and horse riding can be organised in Lomé (see p780).

## BOOKS

*The Village of Waiting*, by George Packer, is an interesting observation on life in Togo. It is one of the best books yet on the Peace Corps experience, covering a volunteer's two years in Lavié, and it's quite candid about the country's autocratic politics.

*Do They Hear You When You Cry?* is Fauziya Kassindja's harrowing account of her flight from Togo, where she was facing female circumcision, to more Western forms of brutality in detention centres and prisons in Germany and the USA.

*Hustling is not Stealing: Stories of an African Bar Girl* follows the adventures of Hawa, a feisty hustler and 'pay-as-you-go wife', whose tales of Togo and Ghana were transcribed by musicologist John M Chernoff in the late '70s.

## BUSINESS HOURS

In general, you will find that information places are open from 7am to noon and from 2.30pm to 5.30pm Monday to Friday. Eating out is normally possible for lunch (12.30pm to 2.30pm) and dinner (6pm to 9pm), Monday to Sunday, while you can usually get a drink between 11am and midnight Monday to Saturday. Nightclubs are commonly open from 10pm until late Friday and Saturday. As a rule shops keep the following hours: 8am to

12.30pm and 2.30 to 7pm Monday through to Friday, and until 12.30pm Saturday.

## CHILDREN
In Lomé, activities such as horse riding are available through the top-end hotels, and Greenfield restaurant screens children's films in its outdoor cinema (see p783).

## COURSES
There is a Prannic healing school in Lomé (p781), and classes in singing, drumming and traditional medicine in Klouto (see p791).

## DANGERS & ANNOYANCES
Petty theft and muggings, sometimes violent, are rife in Lomé, especially on the beach and near the Grand Marché (see p779). *Taximotos* in the city may be convenient, but they are dangerous. Avoid large groups of people, and seek advice if you're planning to attend a street party. If you have to walk around Lomé after dark, stick to well-lit thoroughfares.

Police roadblocks in the countryside are common and tiresome, but generally harmless. Carry your passport with you. Togo's roads are a hair-raising experience, particularly north of Kara and at night.

## EMBASSIES & CONSULATES
### Togolese Embassies & Consulates
In West Africa, Togo has embassies in Ghana (p396) and Nigeria (p666).

Outside West Africa, Togolese embassies and consulates include the following:

---

**PRACTICALITIES**

- The government daily *Togo Presse* is in French, with some Kabyé and Ewe articles. Opposition weeklies include *Le Combat du Peuple*. Newspapers can be found in the racks at major road intersections in Lomé. Cultural centres and big hotels may have old international newspapers and magazines.

- Radio Lomé and Radio Kara are the state stations. Commercial stations include Radio Nostalgie and Radio Zephyr.

- The pay TV provider is Media Plus, and the state channel is TV Togolaise (TVT).

- The electricity supply is temperamental outside the main towns.

---

**Belgium** ( ☎ 32 770 17 91; 264 Ave de Tervuren, Brussels)
**Canada** ( ☎ 1 613 238 59 16; fax 1 613 235 64 25; 12 Chemin Range, Ottawa)
**Denmark** ( ☎ 45 33 93 84 74; fax 45 33 33 09 18, Nyhaun 31k, 1051 Copenhagen)
**Finland** ( ☎ 358 941 333 200; fax 358 941 333 222; Kanavaranta 7D, 00100 Helsinki)
**France** ( ☎ 33 1 43 80 12 13; fax 33 1 56 26 65 10; 8 Rue Alfred Roll, 75017 Paris)
**Germany** ( ☎ 49 30 49 31 34 43; Grabbealle 43, 13156 Berlin)
**Holland** ( ☎ /fax 31 36 5378 981; Reine Claudestraat 6, 1326 JE Almere)
**Sweden** ( ☎ 46 31 13 95 54; fax 46 31 13 48 23; Karl Gustavsgatan 4, 41125 Göteborg)
**Switzerland** ( ☎ 41 62 751 50 00; fax 41 62 751 60 00; Breitbachstrasse 8, 4802 Strengelbach)
**USA** ( ☎ 1 202 234 42 12; fax 1 202 232 31 90; 2208 Massachusetts Ave NW, Washington, DC 20008)

In Africa, Togo also has representation in the Democratic Republic of the Congo, Gabon and Libya. Visit www.republicoftogo.com for more details.

### Embassies & Consulates in Togo
Angola, the Democratic Republic of the Congo, Egypt, Gabon, Libya and Senegal have representation in Lomé. For more details, check out www.republicoftogo.com.
**France** Consulate ( ☎ 221 25 76; www.consulfrance-lome .org; Ave General de Gaulle; 🕑 8am-12pm); Embassy ( ☎ 221 25 71; www.ambafrance-tg.org; 13 Ave du Golfe, BP 337)
**Germany** ( ☎ 221 23 38; fax 222 18 88; Blvd de la Marina)
**Ghana** ( ☎ 221 31 94; 8 Rue Paulin Eklou, Tokoin; 🕑 8am-2pm)
**Nigeria** ( ☎ 221 34 55; 311 Blvd du 13 Janvier)
**UK** British Nationals should contact the British High Commission in Accra (p396).
**USA** ( ☎ 221 29 91; fax 221 79 52; cnr Rue Kouenou & Tokmake; 🕑 7.30am-5pm Mon-Thu, 7.30am-12.30pm Fri)

## FESTIVALS & EVENTS
Special events include Evala, the coming-of-age and wrestling festival in the Kabyé region around Kara, in July (p796); the political symposium in Kpalimé (p788) and the country's harvest festivals, notably Dzawuwu-Za in Klouto (p791) and Ayiza in Tsévié, in August; and the Igname (yam) festival in Bassar in September (p796). There are many others; contact the tourist office in Lomé for details. International

Women's Day (8 March) and World Aids Day (1 December) also see events taking place.

## HOLIDAYS
Public holidays include the following:

**New Year's Day** 1 January
**Meditation Day** 13 January
**Easter** March/April
**National Day** 27 April
**Labour Day** 1 May
**Day of the Martyrs** 21 June
**Christmas Day** 25 December

See p818 for a table of dates of Islamic holidays.

## INTERNET RESOURCES
**Republic of Togo** (www.republicoftogo.com) The best site, with plenty of country information as well as news and travel links.
**Togo Globe** (www.togodaily.com) A useful English language newspaper online.

## LANGUAGE
French is the official language. The main African languages are Ewe, Mina and Kabyé; the latter being the language of the current president.

## MAPS
The 1:500,000 *Carte Générale du Togo* (1991, L'Institut Géographique National) is the best and most recent country map; it's available at bookshops in Lomé for about CFA7500. The Direction de la Promotion Touristique in Lomé gives out an old-but-reasonable road map.

## MONEY
The unit of currency is the West African CFA franc.

Travellers cheques can be exchanged in Lomé and most major cities, but rates are about 3% to 5% lower than for cash. The main branch of BTCI, on Blvd du 13 Janvier in Lomé, offers cash advances on Visa, but it is quicker to use its ATM, which accepts Visa only. Nowhere accepts MasterCard. BTCI's branches in Lomé and the other cities generally have ATMs.

Money-changers can be found in most border towns. The black marketeers on Rue du Commerce in Lomé will likely short-change you.

## PHOTOGRAPHY & VIDEO
Do not photograph or film government buildings – travellers have been beaten by the police for photographing the presidential palace. See also p823.

## POST
Postcards and letters cost CFA550 to Europe, CFA650 to Australasia and CFA660 to North America. The poste restante service at the main post office in Lomé is reliable.

## SOLO TRAVELLERS
Lone travellers should be on their guard in Lomé as they may be more susceptible to muggings than groups.

## TELEPHONE & FAX
Make international calls (and faxes) at telecom offices, or the private telephone agencies in every town. The latter charge from CFA200 per minute to North America and Europe, and CFA300 to Australasia.

The Togocel and Telecel networks, owned by the same company, cover 80% of Togo. It is CFA12,000 to get an account and CFA5000 for a recharge. Other networks also work here. It costs CFA40 to send a local SMS, and CFA150 to send one internationally.

There are no telephone area codes in Togo.

## TIME
Togo is on GMT – one hour behind Benin, Niger, Nigeria and Cameroon, and the same as the rest of mainland West Africa.

## VISAS
Visas are required for everyone except nationals of the Economic Community of West African States (Ecowas) countries. Currently one-week extendable visas (CFA10,000) are issued at major border crossings with Ghana (Aflao/Lomé), Benin (Hillakondji) and Burkina Faso (Sinkasse).

Of these three countries, only Ghana has a Togolese embassy (p396), which issues visas for up to one year within hours, starting at CFA20,000 for one month; payment must be in CFAs or US Dollars. In Benin and Burkina Faso, it is easier obtaining a visa at the border than via the French embassy.

The **Service Immigration Togolaise** ( ☎ 250 78 56; Route d'Atakpamé; ☼ 7.30am-noon & 2.30-6pm), near the GTA building 8km north of Lomé centre, issues 30-day visa extensions in three days, though it may be possible to speed up this process. They cost about CFA10,000 (depending on the length and type of visa) and four photos are required. It's worth having a certified photocopy of your passport while your application is being processed, in case you encounter any awkward policemen.

Inquire at the French consulate in Lomé (see p803) about the five-country Visa Touristique Entente, which covers one entry to each of Benin, Burkina Faso, Côte d'Ivoire, Niger and Togo. The consulate also issues visas for Burkina Faso and Côte d'Ivoire.

There is no Beninese embassy in Lomé, but 48-hour transit visas (CFA10,000) are issued at the Hillakondji border. The Direction Emigration Immigration in Cotonou issues 30-day extensions (CFA12,000), which take 48 hours to issue (see p123).

The Ghanaian embassy in Lomé (see p803) issues one-month visas within 48 hours for CFA12,000 (less for Commonwealth citizens); four photos are needed.

## WOMEN TRAVELLERS
In the predominantly Muslim northern towns of Sokodé, Bafilo and Kara, long dresses and sleeves are recommended. As in most countries, avoid spots such as *tchoukoutou* bars if you don't take kindly to lewd offers of marriage and the like. For more information and advice, see p828.

# TRANSPORT IN TOGO

## GETTING THERE & AWAY
### Entering Togo
Getting into Togo is a breeze. You can pick up seven-day visas on the border, and embassies issue 30-day visas within 24 hours. Border guards and embassy officials are relatively friendly and communicative. Officially you need a Yellow Fever certificate, but it's rarely asked for. The only problem is that Togolese embassies are thin on the ground (p803).

### Air
Togo's international airport is 7km northeast of the centre of Lomé.

**Air France** (AF; ☎ 223 23 23; www.airfrance.com /tg; hub Charles de Gaulle Airport, Paris) has the most frequent and reliable services between Togo and Europe.

For confirming flights or ticket sales the following airlines have offices in Lomé:

**Air France** (AF; ☎ 223 23 23; Immeuble Taba) Also represents KLM.

**Air Gabon International** (GN; ☎ 221 05 73; Immeuble Taba) Hub: Libreville.

**Air Ivoire** (VU; ☎ 221 67 15; Immeuble Taba) Hub: Abidjan.

**Alitalia** (AZ; ☎ 222 01 08; cnr Rues de Kouromé & Tokmake) Hubs: Milan and Rome. Also represents Delta Air, Korean Air, Aeromexico and Czech Air.

**American Airlines** (AA; ☎ 221 10 16; Immeuble Taba) Hub: Fort Worth.

**Cathay Pacific** (CX; ☎ 221 67 15; Immeuble Tabla) Hub: Hong Kong.

**Ethiopian Airlines** (ET; ☎ 221 70 74; Immeuble Taba) Hub: Addis Ababa.

**Ghana International Airlines** (GH; ☎ 221 56 91; Immeuble Taba) Hub: Accra.

**Point-Afrique** (6V/DR; ☎ 220 57 47; www.point-afrique .com) Hub: Charles de Gaulle Airport, Paris. This is a budget alternative, a charter service that is opening up West Africa to European travellers. Flights are operated by Axis Airways and Air Mediterranee.

**Virgin Nigeria Airways** (VK; ☎ 221 58 26; Rue Tomaké) Hub: Lagos.

### Land
#### BORDER CROSSINGS
#### Benin
Bush taxis regularly ply the road between Gare de Cotonou in Lomé and Cotonou (CFA3000, three hours) via Hilakondji (CFA800, one hour), while **STIF** ( ☎ 221 38 48; Gare de SIIF) has daily buses to Cotonou (CFA3000, three hours). Beninese border officials are more bureaucratic and less approachable than their Togolese counterparts.

There are also border crossings at Tohoun (east of Notsé), Kétao (northeast of Kara) and Nadoba (in the Tamberma Valley), but public transport is infrequent and Beninese visas are not readily available at the borders.

#### Burkina Faso
The best way to get to Ouagadougou from Lomé is by bus. With four companies making the journey – and continuing to Bobo-Dioulasso and Bamako – there's a service leaving every day (see p170).

Minibuses and bush taxis to Ouagadougou go daily from Gare d'Agbalepedo in northern Lomé (CFA15,000, 24 hours). Given that it's 627km from Lomé to Dapaong, Benin's northern-most town, you may want to break up the journey. From Dapaong, it's cheapest and easiest to get a taxi to Sinkasse, 40km away on the border, or Bitou, 40km into Burkina Faso. From there it's CFA5000 to Ouagadougou by taxi. Sinkasse's market day, Sunday, is a good time to find taxis.

The border, open from 6am to 6pm, is beset on both sides by frequent police check points.

### Ghana
From central Lomé it is only 2km – CFA1000 in a hired taxi – to the border (open 6am to 10pm), where you cross to Aflao and can pick up tro-tros (minibuses) to Accra. STIF's Lomé–Abidjan buses go via Accra (CFA5000, three hours). In addition to the black marketeers, Global Forex in Aflao buys and sells Cedis and CFA.

There is a quieter crossing at Klouto, northwest of Kpalimé. A dearth of public transport and bad roads make the crossing difficult, but not impossible, at Badou, Natchamba (accessible from Sokodé and Kara) and northwest of Dapaong at Sinkasse.

### BUS
Many companies ply the route between Lomé and Bamako (from CFA20,000, 48 hours) via Ouagadougou (from CFA12,500, 18 hours) and Bobo-Dioulasso (from CFA15,000). These include the following:

**SKV** ( ☎ 220 03 01; 241 Blvd du 13 Janvier)

**SNTV** ( ☎ 220 81 21; Gare de STIF; Blvd de la Marina) Also goes to Niamey (CFA23200, 23 hours).

**Sogabef** ( ☎ 924 23 88; Gare de STIF; Blvd de la Marina)

**STIF** ( ☎ 221 38 48; Gare de STIF; Blvd de la Marina) Also has services to Cotonou (CFA3000, three hours) and Abidjan (CFA24,000, 15 hours), with an armed escort in the Côte d'Ivoire.

**TST** ( ☎ 929 01 90; Blvd du 13 Janvier)

## GETTING AROUND
### Bicycle
Abattoir Bicycles in Lomé sells bog-standard bikes (see p780).

### Bush Taxi & Minibus
Togo has an extensive network of six-, nine- and 15-place bush taxis and minibuses held together with rope. Travel is often agonisingly slow, less because of the police checkpoints and the poor roads than the drivers' inability to pass anyone without giving them a lift. During fee negotiations,

drivers often cite rising fuel prices – this is a genuine problem for Togo (see below).

Paying for two places gives you the front seat to yourself, as well as shortening the time you have to wait for the taxi to fill. The quickest and most comfortable, although most expensive, option are the 'express' taxis that travel between the major towns, leaving early in the morning.

There is occasionally a surcharge for luggage, based on size. From Lomé to Kpalimé, for example, a 65-litre rucksack is CFA500.

### Car & Motorcycle
The sealed Route Internationale is in quite good condition as far north as Kara, but thereafter it disintegrates. The roads linking Kpalimé, Badou and Bassar with the Route International are sealed. Road safety is not one of Togo's strong points, so be alert behind the wheel – especially at night, when you may meet vehicles without headlights.

Cars can be rented from Avis in Lomé (p786). If you're driving, you need an International Driving Permit. There are frequent police checkpoints.

Petrol stations are plentiful in the major towns. Unfortunately fuel prices are on the rise, thanks to the political turmoil in Togo's major supplier, Nigeria.

### Local Transport
#### TAXI
Taxis are abundant in Lomé, even at night, and have no meters. Fares in the city centre are CFA200 for a shared taxi and CFA700 nonshared (more after 6pm). A taxi by the hour should cost CFA2500.

#### TAXI-MOTOS
Taxi-motos, also called zemi-johns, are everywhere. A journey across town costs about CFA100 – more in Lomé. They are also a handy way to get to remote locations in the bush, but tell your driver to go slow – particularly in busy Lomé, where there are daily taxi-moto crashes.

### Tours
Lomé-based **Henry Loï'c** ( ☎ 927 52 03; africatoy@ hotmail.com), an enthusiastic French biologist and off-roader, offers 4WD 'raids' of the surrounding countryside and countries (€45 per person per day, or €150 for four people per day).

# West Africa Directory

## CONTENTS

This chapter provides a general overview of the essential things you need to know about West Africa, covering, in alphabetical order, everything from accommodation to women travellers. Each individual country chapter also has a directory which includes more specific information about these headings as they relate to each country. Please consult both when searching for information.

## ACCOMMODATION

In all the countries covered in this book, there's almost always some sort of accommodation available in most mid-sized and larger towns, although quality and price vary widely. For details of accommodation in each country, see the Directory section of each country chapter, while for details on the costs of travelling in the region, see p18.

Throughout this book, accommodation is divided into budget, midrange and top-end places. Within each category, listings are ordered according to the author's preference, with the best places listed first.

Although costs vary considerably across the region, expect to pay from US$5 a night for a bed in a basic dorm up to US$15 for a simple but relatively comfortable budget double. In the midrange category, such is the variety on offer that you could pay anywhere from US$15 a night up to US$70 for a double. Top-end hotels start at US$80 for a double and often go for considerably more.

In general, Mali and Senegal are the most expensive countries, while neither Nigeria nor Niger offer outstanding value for money when it comes to accommodation. Togo is one of the region's cheapest countries. In some countries, including Guinea, Mali, Burkina Faso and Nigeria, establishments charge a government tourist tax on top of the price they'll quote you. Sometimes (such as in Burkina Faso) this is a one-off payment regardless of the number of nights you stay, while in Nigeria or Mali it's a nightly surcharge added on to the quoted price.

In many parts of West Africa, particularly in the Sahel during the hot season, people often sleep outside their hut or on the flat roof of their house, as it's much cooler. In some hotels this is also possible, and carrying a mattress onto the roof – where you'll have some breeze and views of the stars – is usually allowed if you ask.

One other thing to note is that in Guinea, Sierra Leone and some other countries, a man and a woman may share a single room

---

**BOOK ACCOMMODATION ONLINE**

For more accommodation reviews and recommendations by Lonely Planet authors, check out the online booking service at www.lonelyplanet.com. You'll find the true, insider lowdown on the best places to stay. Reviews are thorough and independent. Best of all, you can book online.

with no questions asked, but a same-sex couple, regardless of whether they are a 'couple', usually cannot.

## Campements

Most towns and villages in Francophone countries have a *campement*. This can be translated as an 'inn', 'lodge', 'hostel' or even 'motel', but its primary purpose is not as a camp site in the traditional sense (ie a place for tents); however some *campements* do provide areas where you can pitch a tent and have access to shower facilities. *Campements* offer cheap and simple accommodation that is far less elaborate than hotels, containing the bare necessities and little else, but others are very good quality, with prices on a par with midrange hotels. Either way, they're often the best (and sometimes only) option in small towns. They're the sort of places where 4WDs fill the compound, and overlanders with their vehicles mingle with backpackers who've just arrived on the latest bush taxi.

In trekking areas such as Mali's Dogon Country (p513), it has become established practice for visitors to sleep on the roof of the *campements* in each village, as it is usually preferable to the stifling rooms that some offer.

## Camping

There are few dedicated camp sites in West Africa, and those that do exist cater mainly for overlanders in their own vehicle. However, some hotels and *campements* allow camping, or provide an area where tents can be pitched. Grassy knolls on which to pitch your tent are rare – you often have to force pegs through hard-packed gravel. Camping in the wild is a risky business in most countries as theft can be a problem, but if you do decide to camp, always seek permission from the local village chief before setting up.

## Hotels

Most hotels charge for a bed only, with all meals extra. If breakfast is included it's usually on a par with the standard of accommodation: a full buffet in the more-expensive places, instant coffee and bread further down the scale. Hotels are often called auberges.

Independent travellers on tight budgets are fairly well catered for, although there are almost no backpacker lodges. Most of what's on offer is basic, devoid of any discernible character, and ranges from the recently swept to downright grubby. The showers and toilets are usually shared and often bear the traces of the previous inhabitants; a broken window may provide fresh air. Many hotels in this price range double as brothels.

Midrange hotels tend to be at their best in the capitals or major towns where you're likely to find at least one place with lovingly maintained rooms, private bathrooms, splashes of local colour, satellite TV and even a swimming pool. Most midrange places, however, fall somewhat short of this ideal and, though fine, will hardly have you rushing back to your room at the end of the day. Most offer a choice between a fan and air-con.

At the luxury end of the scale, West Africa has very few top-end hotels outside the capitals, and offers little in the way of exclusive wildlife lodges or tented camps as found in East or Southern Africa.

## Missions

If you're travelling on a tight budget, mission accommodation can be a good alternative to cheap and nasty budget hotels, although rooms are usually reserved for mission or aid workers and are open to others only on a space-available basis. Usually called *missions catholique*, they're invariably clean, safe and good value, although these are not places to stagger home drunk at 4am – travellers will be allowed to stay at many missions only for as long as they respect the rules.

## Resorts

You'll find European-style resorts all along the West African coast, but the best facilities are at those which cater to Europeans looking for a two-week beach holiday without really having to look Africa in the eye. These are especially popular in Senegal, The Gambia and, to a lesser extent, Cape Verde where you'll find all-inclusive packages of meals, accommodation and airport transfers. Although it's occasionally possible to get a room by simply walking in off the street, most rooms (and the best deals) are reserved for those who book the whole package through a travel agency in Europe.

## ACTIVITIES

West Africa has plenty of opportunities for getting active, although infrastructure (eg detailed topographical maps, well-marked

## GETTING ACTIVE – WEST AFRICA'S TOP TEN ACTIVITIES

- Trekking Mali's **Dogon Country** (p513) through fascinating villages that cling to the Falaise de Bandiagara.
- Hiking in Guinea's **Fouta Djalon Highlands** (p418) in the off-road spirit of Graham Greene.
- Heading for the hills of the **Mandara Mountains** (p211) of northern Cameroon on foot.
- Climbing **Mt Cameroon** (p192), West Africa's highest peak, and accessible for experienced climbers and amateurs alike.
- Huffing and puffing all the way to the top of Cape Verde's **Mt Fogo** (see p246), an active volcano.
- Scaling the weird-and-wonderful landscapes around **Hombori** (p533) in Mali.
- Exploring the **Aïr Mountains** (p608) or **Ténéré Desert** (p609) of northern Niger by camel or in the relative comfort of a 4WD.
- Losing yourself in the deepest Sahara as you range north to **Araouane** (p528) or the salt mines of **Taoudenni** (p525) by camel or 4WD.
- Kicking back on a long, slow boat trip up the **Niger River** (see p510) from Mopti to Timbuktu.
- Cycling through the otherworldly **Sindou Peaks** (p158) in southwestern Burkina Faso.

trails and gear rental outlets) are usually non-existent. Guides are aplenty, but few have expertise (eg climbing) to do more than point you in the right direction. For this reason, you'll generally have to be pretty self-sufficient, or expect to pay high prices (eg to rent a 4WD for desert expeditions) to get your expedition underway.

## Cycling

In several parts of West Africa (in particular, tourist areas such as the Gambian coast), bicycles can be hired by the hour, day or week, and can be a good way to tour a town or area. Your choice may range from a new, imported mountain bike (*vélo tout terrain* in French or VTT) to ancient, single gear, steel roadsters. Choice of bicycles is more limited but generally available in Banfora (p155) in Burkina Faso's southwest for off-road expeditions into the surrounding areas.

Away from tourist areas, it's almost always possible to find locals willing to rent their bicycles for the day; good places to inquire include the market or your hotel. Costs range from US$1 to US$10 per day, depending on the bicycle and the area. Remember to always check the roadworthiness of your bicycle, especially if you're heading off-road.

For information on cycling in West Africa and on bringing your own bicycle to the region, see p843.

## Desert Expeditions

The Sahara offers a vast desert world to explore. You'll obviously cover far more territory if you rent a 4WD, but remember that costs are expensive and more than a few days are probably beyond the means of most solo travellers. This is especially true when you factor in high fuel costs and the requirement for most expeditions that you take a minimum of two 4WDs (in case one breaks down). Seeking out other travellers to share costs for longer expeditions is a good idea.

Another option is to travel by camel, which is more economical, environmentally friendly and allows you to experience the desert (and get to know your desert companions) at a more leisurely pace. One such trip involves joining one of the epic salt caravans, which travel between Timbuktu (Tombouctou) and the salt mines of Taoudenni in Mali; for more information, see p525.

The most rewarding former Saharan caravan towns, which serve as gateways to the Sahara's incomparable sand dune, oasis and desert-massif scenery, include Atâr (p562) in Mauritania for 4WD excursions to Chinguetti and beyond; Timbuktu (p521); and Agadez (p604), for camel and 4WD tours of the Aïr Mountains and Ténéré Desert. Each of these towns is well set up with vehicles and guides just dying to take you out into another world.

## Fishing

There is reportedly some excellent deep-sea sport fishing off the West African coast, including off Côte d'Ivoire, The Gambia, Mauritania, Senegal and Sierra Leone. Expect costs to start at well over US$100 a day per person. Good places to start your inquiries are top-end hotels and local boat clubs. See the Activities sections of the Directories in each individual country chapter.

## Football (Soccer)

Football is Africa's most popular sport. If you want to play, the universities and municipal stadiums are by far the best places to find a good-quality game, but in most towns are patches of ground where matches are played most evenings (in coastal areas, the beach is used). The ball may be just a bundle of rags, and each goal a couple of sticks, not necessarily opposite each other. You may have to deal with puddles, ditches and the odd goat or donkey wandering across the pitch, but the game itself will be taken seriously and can be exhilaratingly fun, fast and furious. Foreigners are usually warmly welcomed and joining in a game is one of the best ways to meet people. If you bring along your own ball (deflated for travelling) you'll be a big hit.

For more information on football in West Africa, see p43.

## Hiking

West Africa has many interesting possibilities for hiking, but the set-up in this region is very different from that in East or Southern Africa. There are few wilderness areas with good walking infrastructure, such as detailed maps, marked trails or trail accommodation. Much of the hiking is also through populated areas, where paths pass through fields and villages.

All of which means that as long as you don't mind roughing it, hiking can be a great way to interact with the locals; on foot you can meet on more equal terms rather than staring at each other through the windows of a bush taxi. As there's very little formal organisation, expect to arrange everything yourself. Plan on being self-sufficient (bring a good water filter/purifier) and be prepared to adapt your plans. Hiring a local guide (either for the entire expedition or to lead you from village to village) is usually a good idea. In some places, because of the distances involved (or just to take a break from walking), it may also be necessary to use donkeys, hitching or public transport to get around.

Among the better hiking destinations are northern and northwestern Cameroon (p220), Cape Verde (p250), the Fouta Djalon area of Guinea (p432), along the famous Bandiagara Escarpment in Mali (p539) and in the fascinating hill country around Kpalimé in Togo (see p790). For some of the best of these hiking areas, see p809, as well as the individual country chapters.

## River Journeys

There's something special about passing your days floating down one of Africa's great rivers. When the destination is Timbuktu, the trip could take on the stuff of legend. Indeed, the most memorable of river journeys is between Mopti and Timbuktu in Mali (p510), although a host of other pirogue, *pinasse* (larger motorised boats, carrying cargo and anything from 10 to 100 passengers) and public ferry journeys are possible between Bamako and Gao. One thing to remember, however, is that water levels are usually only high enough to make major river trips between July or August and December.

Elsewhere, shorter trips are possible in Niger in Niamey (p588), Boubon (p593) and most of the Niger River towns between Niamey and the Malian border. Boat journeys are possible on Lake Volta, Ghana (p372), and in Gambia (p327) and Senegal (p744). Travelling by boat is a wonderful way to island hop and is especially enjoyable in Cape Verde (p253) and Guinea-Bissau (p461).

## Rock Climbing

West Africa has little climbing. While expats living in, say, Guinea or Ghana may find some outcrops suitable for one-pitch routes or bouldering, as a visitor it's not really worth lugging rock-climbing equipment around West Africa. Other well-known 'climbing' destinations such as Mt Cameroon (p192) and Mt Fogo (p246) are actually strenuous hikes that involve no technical climbing.

The main exception is the area of Hombori in Mali, where some spectacular rock formations stand high above the desert and attract a small but growing number of serious rock climbers from Europe; see p533. Another area with some rock-climbing potential is the Falaise de Bandiagara (p513), in

## WEST AFRICA'S TOP BEACHES

- The beaches around Freetown (p760), Sierra Leone.
- Kokrobite (p354) and Gomoa Fetteh (p356), Ghana.
- Sassandra (p275), Côte d'Ivoire.
- Kribi (p217), Cameroon.
- Cap Skiring (p732), Senegal's Casamance region.
- Nearly anywhere in Cape Verde (p250).
- Guinea-Bissau's Arquipélago dos Bijagós (p450).

Mali. The famous French climber Catherine Destiville established some routes here (and featured prominently in a TV film, *Solo in Mali*, about climbing in Dogon Country) some years ago, and groups from Europe occasionally follow her footsteps (and handholds). The Mandara Mountains (p211) of northern Cameroon are another possibility.

### Swimming & Water Sports

All along the coast of West Africa, you have a choice of beaches where swimming is an attraction. Some beaches are very touristy, whereas others may be inhabited by local fishing communities or be completely deserted. For the potential dangers of swimming at many West African beaches, see p817.

A safer, if less adventurous, option may be to use a *piscine* (swimming pool) – major hotels often have pools that nonguests can use for a small fee.

There are sailing clubs in cities along the coast, but they rarely have boats for hire. Your other option is to hire a small boat at a tourist area such as The Gambia's Atlantic Coast (p303) or Senegal's Petite Côte (p701). Day trips on large crewed yachts are available in Dakar, where you'll also find sailboards, scuba diving and kayaking. Sailboarding is possible elsewhere in Senegal (p738), The Gambia, Freetown, Sierra Leone (p768), Abidjan and Sassandra in Côte d'Ivoire (p284), and Lomé and Lake Togo in Togo (p802).

## BOOKS

Our selection of the best books about West Africa are found on p19, while other suggestions are littered throughout the chapters on the region's history (p30), culture (p39), arts and craftwork (p67), music (p58) and people (p73). Some other good books about the region are listed here.

*Travels in West Africa*, by Mary Kingsley, was written in the late 19th century and, despite the title, is mostly confined to Cameroon and Gabon. It captures the spirit of the age, as the author describes encounters with wild places and wild people, all the while gathering fish specimens and facing every calamity with flamboyance, good humour and typically Victorian fortitude.

*Impossible Journey: Two Against the Sahara*, by Michael Asher, is an enthralling account of a west-to-east camel crossing of the Sahara, starting in Mauritania and passing through Mali and Niger before ending at the Nile.

*Anatomy of Restlessness*, by Bruce Chatwin, is a collection of writings which includes discussion of Chatwin's most recurring theme, the clash between nomads and settled civilisations, as well as a section on his 1970 visit to Timbuktu. This theme is also explored in his famous book *The Songlines*, which includes brief descriptions of Mauritania's nomadic Namadi people. Chatwin's bewitching *Photographs & Notebooks* contains an intriguingly eclectic collection of pictures and observations from his travels, mainly in Mauritania, Mali and Benin.

For a more unusual kind of travel book, try *The Ends of the Earth* by Robert Kaplan. The author visits areas frequently seen as cultural, political and ecological devastation zones, including West Africa, analysing what he sees (Liberian refugee camps, the breakdown of society in Sierra Leone, the massive growth of urban poverty along the coastal strip from Lomé to Abidjan) and about which he cannot help but be darkly pessimistic.

*Designing West Africa: Prelude to 21st Century Calamity*, by Peter Schwab, is a trenchant critique of the mistakes made in the postcolonial period; it has extensive sections on Senegal, Côte d'Ivoire, Nigeria, Liberia, Guinea, and Ghana

Lonely Planet also publishes a guide to *The Gambia & Senegal*.

## CHILDREN

Your children have a big advantage over the rest of us – having yet to acquire the stereotypes about Africa to which the rest

**TEN WEST AFRICA BOOKS FOR KIDS**

Start searching for children's books on West Africa and you'll quickly discover a whole library of everything from folk tales to simply told histories that you never knew existed. Aimed at children learning about the diverse peoples of region, the *Heritage Library of African Peoples: West Africa* is an excellent series. Otherwise, here are some of our favourites:

- *Why Mosquitoes Buzz in People's Ears: A West African Tale* by Verna Aardema (suitable 4 to 8 years)
- *Anansi Does the Impossible!* by Verna Aardema (suitable 4 to 8 years)
- *The Adventures of Spider: West African Folktales* by Joyce Cooper Arkhurst (suitable 4 to 10 years)
- *The Cow-Tail Switch and Other West African Stories* by Harold Courlander (suitable 9 to 12 years)
- *The Singing Man* by Angela Shelf Medearis (suitable 3 to 8 years)
- *The Hunterman and the Crocodile* by Baba Wague Diakite (suitable 4 to 7 years)
- *The Three Birds from Olongo* by Agbo Folarin (suitable 4 to 8 years)
- *Ancient West African Kingdoms: Ghana, Mali and Songhai* by Mary Quigley (suitable 9 to 12 years)
- *Mansa Musa: The Lion of Mali* by Khephra Burns (suitable 8 to 12 years)
- *Sundiata: The Lion King of Mali* by David Wisniewski (suitable 4 to 8 years)

of us are exposed, their first impression of the continent is likely to be the warmth and friendliness of the people. Indeed, many West Africans have grown up in large families and children help break the ice and open doors to closer contact with local people who are generally very friendly, helpful and protective towards children. The result is that travelling with children in West Africa adds a whole new dimension to your journey. Apart from anything else, because foreign children are an unusual sight, they're a great conversation starter.

## Practicalities

In West African countries with a mainstream tourism industry (eg Senegal and The Gambia), some package-tour hotels cater for families with children, and in large cities, top-end hotels usually have rooms with three or four beds for only slightly more than a double. Alternatively, arranging an extra bed or mattress so that children can share a standard adult double is generally easy and inexpensive.

As for hotels, you'll almost certainly want something with a private bathroom and hot water, thereby precluding most budget accommodation.

That said, there are very few child-oriented facilities in the region. In nontourist hotels there are generally no discounts for children. Likewise, on public transport, if you want a seat it has to be paid for. Most young local

children travel for free on buses, but spend the whole journey on their parent's lap.

In addition to the length and discomfort involved in road journeys, possible concerns include the scarcity of medical facilities, especially outside major cities, and the difficulty of finding clean, decent bathrooms outside of midrange and top-end hotels. Canned baby foods, disposable nappies, wipes and other items are available in some capitals, but not everywhere, and they are expensive. It's best to avoid feeding your children street food. Powdered milk and sometimes also baby cereal (usually with sugar in it) are relatively widely available, even in smaller towns.

There are other factors to bear in mind when travelling with kids. The rainy season may mean that temperatures are lower, but the risks of malaria and other mosquito-borne diseases are higher. At all times, bring mosquito nets along for your children and ensure that they sleep under them. Bring child-friendly mosquito repellent and long-sleeved shirts and trousers.

We received the following letter from a Canadian family who travelled for six weeks in Senegal, Guinea and Guinea-Bissau with a one-year-old:

'In West Africa, travelling with a baby was not too difficult, even though life is different. People constantly wanted to touch him, and even though this bothered us on occasion, it was not serious. Most of the time we enjoyed the contact. We learned to travel light, and went with one 50L backpack and a baby carrier which also carried another 10L of luggage. Clothes could be washed every day, and dried while wearing them.

We used small chlorine pills to clean water that was not bottled – apparently iodine may be harmful to children.

In every capital we found nappies at grocery stores selling imported items. Sometimes the quality was poor so we secured them with strong sticky tape.

Baby cereal and powdered milk were available in most towns, even small villages, and prices were similar to those at home.

In Senegal our baby got a rash caused by the heat and humidity. This was not dangerous, and with soothing powder it was gone in two days.'

*Gino Bergeron, Julie Morin*
*& 'little Thomas'*

For more information and hints on travelling with children, Lonely Planet's *Travel with Children* is highly recommended.

### Sights & Activities
Regional highlights that appeal to adults (markets, mosques, mud-brick architecture, endless desert wilderness) often don't have such an attraction for children. Additionally, distances (and waiting times) can be long, especially on public transport. It's a good idea to have a supply of distractions, as well as some food, as what's available en route is often not suitable.

The specific highlights kids are sure to enjoy include the otherworldly villages and festivals of the Dogon Country (Mali; p513) and the Tamberma Valley (Togo; p799), the chance to tell their friends that they've been to Timbuktu (p521), the stilt villages of Ganvié (p102), a trip down the Niger River (p510) and the beaches, castles and markets all along the West African coast

### CLIMATE CHARTS
For more information on the climate in the region, see p18 and the charts on p814.

## COURSES
For a region so diverse in languages, music and arts, West Africa has few courses where you can learn more. In Benin, there are Fon language courses in Cotonou (p98), while you can improve either your French- or Hausa-language skills in Niamey (p588). Lomé has a Prannic healing school (p781), while musicians should head for Klouto (p791) where there are classes in singing, drumming and traditional medicine. For all of Mali's rich musical heritage, only Motel Savanne (p502) in Ségou promises occasional drumming instruction.

In Boké (p432) in Guinea and Latrikunda in The Gambia, the highly recommended **Batafon Arts** (www.batafonarts.co.uk) run dance and percussion courses and can also arrange accommodation. For more information see p840.

## CUSTOMS
Except in CFA-zone countries, the import and export of local currency is either prohibited or severely restricted – typically limited to about US$10 – although enforcement of this regulation is fairly lax. As part of their fiscal control, some countries use currency declaration forms. More commonly, control consists simply of asking how much currency you have. Or, you may occasionally be asked to open your wallet or show the contents of your pockets – wallets bulging with cash is likely to prompt underpaid and ever-hopeful airport agents (ie police and customs officials) to suddenly discover (ie invent) fictitious currency regulations which you've just violated by a sum roughly equivalent to the amount you have in your wallet.

To avoid a scenario like this, it's worth doing a bit of advance planning before getting to the airport. Divide your money and store it in several places so it's not all in one lump, and try to look as savvy as possible when going through customs checks. Responding creatively to questions is also helpful, for example explaining that you relied on a credit card for the majority of your expenses (be prepared to show a card), or (if it's true) explaining that you're just in transit and thus don't have much money with you.

For specific customs regulations of West African countries, see the Customs section of the Directory in each individual country chapter.

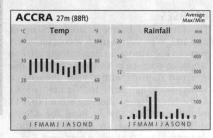

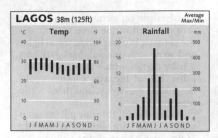

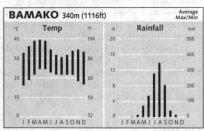

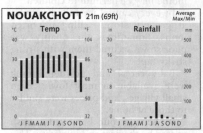

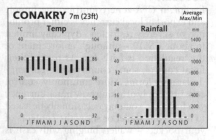

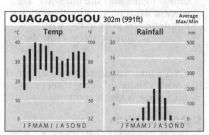

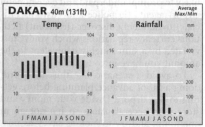

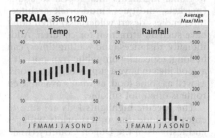

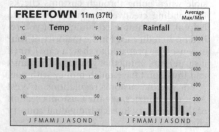

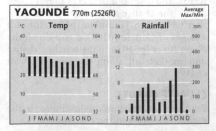

## PRESERVING WEST AFRICA'S HERITAGE

After the plundering of African artefacts by colonial officials and, later, by private collectors, most West African countries prohibit the export of antiquities (from tribal masks to archaeological finds). In Mali, Nigeria and Ghana in particular – countries with a rich tradition of highly prized and beautiful artworks and handicrafts – you must obtain an export permit from the Department of Antiquities or from the national museum in Bamako, Lagos or Accra if you want to take anything older than 100 years old out of the country. Even then, expect to explain why you're taking Africa's heritage off the continent and to pay very high export duties.

Very little art purchased by nonexperts fits this description. Most art that is 'very old' in the words of many a trader is actually recently made, but traders realise that tourists prefer dusty, more authentic-looking pieces than shiny, new mass-produced 'art'. In such cases, it's more a matter of being hassled by customs than doing something illegal. To avoid difficulties later, if the piece looks old, it might be worth having it checked before you purchase.

# DANGERS & ANNOYANCES

It's difficult to make generalisations about the personal-safety situation in West Africa. While there may be considerable risk in some areas, other places are completely safe. The danger of robbery with violence is much more prevalent in cities and towns than in rural or wilderness areas, where it's relatively rare. Most cities have their dangerous streets and beaches, but towns can differ; there's more of a danger in places frequented by wealthy foreigners than in those off the usual tourist track.

The Sahel countries are among the safer places in the world, but Dakar has become much worse in recently and many travellers have had bags snatched and pockets picked, sometimes violently (see p687). In cities such as Banjul (The Gambia), Ouagadougou (Burkina Faso), Niamey (Niger) and Bamako (Mali), attacks are not unknown, but violence is rarer. Travellers have, on occasion, been pushed to the ground and had daypacks or cameras stolen, but they haven't been knifed

or otherwise injured. (In these cities, it's very rare to hear of thieves carrying guns.)

In some of the southern cities, the picture is different. The places with the worst safety records are Lagos (Nigeria) and Abidjan (Côte d'Ivoire). In countries recovering from civil war (eg Sierra Leone and Liberia) another danger is that of harassment and violence by rebel groups or former combatants, especially in rural areas. More specific details are given in the individual country chapters.

## Safety Tips

The warnings in the previous section are not designed to put you off travelling in West Africa, but they should make you more aware of the dangers. Some simple precautions will hopefully ensure that you have a trouble-free trip. Remember, many thousands of travellers enjoy travel throughout this region and have no problems. The recommendations listed here are particularly relevant to cities, although some may apply to other places (especially those which get lots of tourists) as well.

- Carry as little as possible. Thieves will be less interested if you're not carrying a daypack, camera and personal stereo. Consider leaving them in your room. Even passports, travellers cheques and credit cards can be left behind if the hotel has a reliable safe or security box. Never take valuables to beaches, which are often hotspots for thieves. If your hotel isn't too secure, though, then you will have to carry your valuables with you. Work out which is the safest option on a case-by-case basis. (Note that in many countries you're required to carry your passport at all times – although you're very unlikely to be stopped in the street by police and asked for it.)
- Be discreet. Don't wear jewellery or watches. Use a separate wallet for day-to-day purchases, and keep the bulk of your cash out of sight, hidden in a pouch under loose-fitting clothing.
- Try not to look lost. Walk purposefully and confidently, and don't obviously refer to this guidebook or a map. Photocopy or tear out the pages you need, or duck into a shop or café to have a look at the map and get your bearings.
- Avoid back streets and risky areas at night. Take a taxi. A dollar or two for the fare might save you a lot of pain and trouble.

- Avoid getting in taxis with two or more men inside – especially at night and especially if you're female – even (or especially) if the driver says they are his 'friends'.
- Consider hiring somebody locally to accompany you when walking around a risky area. It's usually not too difficult to find someone who wouldn't mind earning a few dollars for warding off potential molesters – ask at your hotel for a reliable recommendation.
- If possible, keep your backpack or suitcase locked whenever you leave it anywhere, whether it be the roof of a bush taxi or your hotel room.

## Scams

The main annoyance you'll come across in West Africa are the various hustlers, touts and con men who prey on tourists. Most tourists succumb at some stage (these guys are either good or numbingly persistent). If this sounds daunting, remember that scams are only likely to be tried in tourist areas and that on most occasions, you're more likely to come across genuine hospitality.

### A NICE WELCOME

You may be invited to stay in someone's house in exchange for a meal and drinks, but your new friend's appetite for food and beer may make this an expensive deal. More seriously, while you are dining, someone else will be back at the house going through your bag. This scam is only likely to be tried in tourist areas and would-be dance and drumming teachers are among the decoys.

### DUD CASSETTES

Street sellers walk around with boxes of cassettes by local musicians. You browse, you choose, you pay. And then when you get back to your hotel and open the box, it's got a cheap blank tape inside. Or the tape itself is missing, or the music is by a completely different artist. Tapes sealed in cellophane are normally fine, but look at, or try to listen to, tapes before buying them.

### POLICE & THIEVES

If you're unwise enough to sample local narcotics, don't be surprised if dealers are in cahoots with the local police, who then come to your hotel or stop you in the street and find

you 'in possession'. We've received reports of travellers being stung by con men claiming to know somebody living in Bamako/Dakar/ Conakry (or wherever you are) from Sydney/ Washington/Manchester/Berlin (or wherever you're from). They're having a party tonight and there'll be music, beer and good times. By the time you arrive, other local guests are already there, and you're assured the Aussie/ American/Brit/German you've come to meet will be here soon. In the meantime how about smoking some grass? You decline, but some of the other guests light up, at which point, enter the police stage left.

### REMEMBER ME?

A popular trick in the tourist areas is for local lads to approach you in the street pretending to be a hotel employee or 'son of the owner'. There's been a mix-up at the shop. Can you lend him some money? You can take it off the hotel bill later. He'll know your name and room number, and even give you a receipt. But, surprise, surprise, back at the hotel they've never heard of him.

### SMOKESCREENS

Some travellers warn of hustlers who begin talking to you, meeting any resistance with a loud and obscene argument and an apparent potential for violence. Don't rise to it. If necessary, go into a shop or restaurant and ask for help. Your 'assailant' will soon be chased off.

### SOCK SELLERS

A youth approaches you in the street with socks for sale. You say no, but he follows, whereupon his buddy approaches from the other side and also tries to persuade you to buy the socks. He bends down to show you how well the socks would go with your outfit. Irritated and distracted, you bend down to fend him off and, whoosh, the other guy relieves you of your wallet. The solution? Be firm, walk purposefully, and never buy socks in the street.

### SPIKED DRINKS

It doesn't happen frequently, but often enough that you need to watch out: don't accept drinks from newly found acquaintances on buses or trains, or you may soon find yourself asleep, while your 'acquaintance' runs off with your wallet.

---

**LATEST TRAVEL ADVICE**

Lonely Planet's website (www.lonelyplanet.com) contains information on what's new, the latest safety reports, and reports from other travellers recounting their experiences while on the road. Most governments have travel advisory services detailing terrorism updates, potential pitfalls and areas to avoid. Some of these include the following:

**Australian Department of Foreign Affairs & Trade** ( ☎ 02-6261 1111; www.dfat.gov.au)
**Canadian Department of Foreign Affairs & International Trade** ( ☎ 1-800-267-6788; www.voyage
.gc.ca/dest/consular_home-en.asp)
**New Zealand Ministry of Foreign Affairs & Trade** ( ☎ 04-439 8000; www.mft.govt.nz/travel/)
**UK Foreign & Commonwealth Office** ( ☎ 0870-6060290; www.fco.gov.uk)
**US Department of State** ( ☎ 202-647-4000; www.travel.state.gov/travel_warnings.html)

---

## Security

To keep your money, passport and tickets safe from pickpockets, secure a pouch under your clothes. Your money should be divided into several stashes and stored in various places on your body. If your hotel seems trustworthy, you can leave some in the hotel safe, preferably in some sort of lockable pouch or at least in a signature-sealed envelope so that any tampering will be clear. When walking about town, keep a small amount of cash, including ready change and small bills, separate from your other money, so that you don't need to pull out large wads of bills for paying taxi fares or making purchases. This may be useful as a decoy to give to any assailant if you happen to be robbed, while the remainder of your valuables remain hidden.

## Swimming Safety

Although West Africa's beaches can seem inviting, remember that you know nothing about local swimming conditions. In many places along the West African Coast, the beaches can slope steeply and the waves can create a vicious undertow. Never plunge into the ocean without first seeking reliable local advice.

## DISABLED TRAVELLERS

West Africa has few facilities for the disabled. This, combined with weak infrastructure in the region, can make travel difficult, although it's not impossible. Few hotels have lifts (and those that do are generally expensive), streets may be either badly potholed or else unpaved, footpaths are few and far between, and ramps and other things to ease access are often nonexistent. While accommodation at many budget hotels is on the ground floor, bathroom access can be difficult, and doors are not always wide enough for wheelchairs. Fortunately, these facts are counterbalanced by the fact that West Africans are usually very accommodating and willing to offer whatever assistance they can, as long as they understand what you need.

As for transport, most taxis in the region are small sedans, and buses are not wheelchair equipped. Minibuses and larger 4WD vehicles can usually be arranged through car-rental agencies in major towns and cities, although this will be pricey.

In general, travel and access will probably be easiest in places with relatively good tourism infrastructure, such as some of the coastal areas of Senegal and The Gambia or, to a lesser extent, Mali. As far as we are aware, there are no facilities in the region specifically aimed at blind travellers.

Organisations that disseminate information, advice and assistance on world travel for the mobility impaired include the following:

**Access-able Travel Source** ( ☎ 303-232 2979; www
.access-able.com; PO Box 1796, Wheat Ridge, CO 80034, USA)
**Accessible Travel & Leisure** ( ☎ 01452-729 739; www
.accessibletravel.co.uk; Avionics House, Naas Lane, Gloucester GL2 2SN, UK) Claims to be the biggest UK holiday company dealing with travel for the disabled and encourages people with a disability to travel independently.
**Holiday Care** ( ☎ 0845-124 9971; www.holidaycare.org
.uk; 2nd fl, Imperial Buildings, Victoria Rd, Horley, Surrey RH6 7PZ, UK)
**Mobility International USA** ( ☎ 541-343 1284; www
.miusa.org; PO Box 10767, Eugene, OR 97440, USA)
**National Information Communication Awareness Network** ( ☎ 02-6285 3713; www.nican.com.au; PO Box 407, Curtin ACT 2605, Australia)

**Royal Association for Disability & Rehabilitation**
(RADAR; ☎ 020-7250 3222; www.radar.org.uk; Unit 12,
250 City Rd, London EC1V 8AF, UK) Publishes a useful guide
called *Holidays & Travel Abroad: A Guide for Disabled People*.

## EMBASSIES & CONSULATES

It's important to realise what your own embassy can and can't do to help if you get into trouble.

Generally speaking, embassy staff have mastered the sympathetic look but remain representatives of governments who aren't in the least sympathetic in emergencies if the trouble is remotely your own fault. Remember that you are bound by the laws of the country you are in and this is very much the approach your embassy will take. Your embassy will not be sympathetic if you end up in jail after committing a crime locally, even if such actions are legal in your own country.

In genuine emergencies you might get some assistance, but only if other channels have been exhausted. For example, if you need to get home urgently, a free ticket home is unlikely as the embassy would expect you to have insurance. If you have all your money and documents stolen, it might assist with getting a new passport, but a loan for onward travel will be out of the question.

Some embassies used to keep letters for travellers or have a small reading room with newspapers and magazines from home, but few provide these services any more.

See the individual country chapters for addresses and contact details of embassies and consulates. Note that in some parts of Africa, countries are represented by an 'honorary consul' who is not a full-time diplomat but usually an expatriate with limited (and rarely visa- or passport-issuing) duties. If your country does not have an embassy in a particular country, another embassy will likely be designated to look after your interests (eg Canadian embassies often have an 'Australian interests' section).

## GAY & LESBIAN TRAVELLERS

Homosexuality is illegal in 13 out of the 17 countries covered in this book; the exceptions are Burkina Faso, Côte d'Ivoire and Niger, while Guinea-Bissau has no laws that explicitly ban homosexuality.

Regardless of the legality, however, all countries covered in this book are conservative in their attitudes towards gays and les-bians, and gay sexual relationships are taboo and rare to the point of nonexistence (homosexual activity does occur, especially among younger men). In most places, discretion is key and public displays of affection should be avoided, advice which applies to homosexual and heterosexual couples as a means of showing sensitivity to local feelings.

In the hotels of some countries (eg Guinea and Sierra Leone), same-sex couples, regardless of whether they are indeed a 'couple', will most likely be refused permission to share a room.

An excellent website to get the low-down on local laws and attitudes to homosexuality is the South African-based **Behind the Mask** (www.mask.org.za) which has detailed information on each country. **Global Gayz** (www.globalgayz.com) is another good resource with some information for (mainly Anglophone) West African countries.

A US-based tour company offering specialist tours for gay men and women, including to West Africa, is **David Tours** (☎ 949-723 0699; www.davidtours.com; 310 Dahlia Pl, Suite A, Corona del Mar, CA 92625-2821, USA).

## HOLIDAYS

A highlight of any trip to West Africa is witnessing one of the many ceremonies that are an integral part of traditional culture in the region. Events such as naming ceremonies, weddings and circumcisions take place everywhere, and if you're lucky, you may be invited to take part. You'll also see village festivals, where people celebrate the end of a harvest, give thanks to a deity or honour their ancestors. While some of the larger ones attract people from across the region, all these ceremonies usually involve singing, dancing (often masked), music and other festivities, and are fascinating to watch.

For specific information on holidays celebrated in each country, see the Holidays section of the Directory in each country chapter.

### Islamic Holidays

Important Islamic holidays, when much of West Africa's commercial life grinds to a halt, include the following:

**Tabaski** Also called Eid al-Kebir; commemorates Abraham's readiness to sacrifice his son on God's command, and the last-minute substitution of a ram. It also coincides with the end of the pilgrimage to Mecca, and is the most important Muslim event, marked in most countries by great feasts with roasted sheep and a two-day public holiday.

**Eid al-Fitr** The second major Islamic holiday, it marks the end of Ramadan, the annual fasting month when Muslims do not eat or drink during daylight hours, but break their fast after sundown. Throughout Ramadan, offices usually grind to a halt in the afternoon.

**Eid al-Moulid** Celebrates the birthday of the Prophet Mohammed. It occurs about three months after Tabaski.

Since the Islamic calendar is based on 12 lunar months totalling 354 or 355 days, these holidays are always about 11 days earlier than the previous year. The exact dates depend on the moon and are announced for certain only about a day in advance. Estimated dates for these events are:

| Event | 2006 | 2007 | 2008 | 2009 | 2010 |
|---|---|---|---|---|---|
| Ramadan begins | 24 Sep | 13 Sep | 2 Sep | 22 Aug | 11 Aug |
| Eid al-Fitr | 23 Oct | 12 Oct | 1 Oct | 20 Sep | 9 Sep |
| Tabaski | 30 Dec | 19 Dec | 8 Dec | 28 Nov | 17 Nov |
| Eid al-Moulid | 10 Apr | 31 Mar | 20 Mar | 9 Mar | 27 Feb |

## Public Holidays

In addition to the Islamic ceremonies, there are many public holidays – either government or religious – when businesses are

---

**TABASKI**

Two weeks before Tabaski, sheep prices steeply rise, as every family is expected to provide one during the celebrations. Those who cannot afford a sheep are socially embarrassed and most will do anything to scrape up the money. One-third of the slaughtered animal is supposed to be given to the poor, one-third to friends, and one-third is left for the family. If you can manage to get an invitation to a Tabaski meal (it usually takes place after prayers at the mosque), you'll be participating in Muslim West Africa's most important and festive day of the year. It's celebrated with particular colour (and cavalry processions) in Kano, Nigeria (p659), but is also a festive time in Senegal and Mali. Here and elsewhere during Tabaski (and during Eid al-Fitr and the other Islamic holidays), you'll see entire families dressed in their finest clothes, strolling in the streets or visiting the mosque.

---

closed. Public holidays vary from country to country, but some – including Christmas and New Year's Day – are observed throughout the region. Government holidays are often marked with parades, dancing and other events, while the Christian religious holidays invariably centre around beautiful church services and singing.

See the Directory in individual country chapters for country-specific listings.

## INSURANCE

A travel insurance policy to cover theft and loss is recommended, and some sort of medical insurance is essential. Always check the small print when shopping around. Some policies specifically exclude 'dangerous activities', which can include scuba diving, motorcycling and even trekking, and a locally acquired motorcycle licence may not be valid under some policies. Also, some policies offer lower and higher medical-expense options, with the higher ones chiefly for countries such as the USA, which have extremely high medical costs.

Hospitals in Africa are not free, and the good ones are not cheap. If your policy requires you to pay on the spot and claim later, make sure you keep all documentation. Some policies ask you to call collect (reverse charges) to a centre in your home country where an immediate assessment of your problem is made.

Check in particular that the policy covers an emergency flight home, as emergency air evacuations can be extremely expensive. Worldwide cover to travellers from over 44 countries is available online at www.lonely planet.com/travel_services.

For further information on health insurance see p852, and for car insurance, see p837.

## INTERNET ACCESS

You'll find Internet cafés in all capital cities, although the situation elsewhere varies enormously from country to country. Costs are usually inexpensive, but the general rule is that you pay more for less – hi-tech places with the latest computers and fast connections generally cost around US$2 an hour while cheap places in out-of-the-way towns, with painfully slow connections, sometimes charge by the minute and have been known to charge six times that price.

---

**FRENCH KEYBOARDS**   *Amy Karafin*

Many Internet cafés in Francophone West Africa have 'French' keyboards, which can slow you down when typing if you're not used to them. Happily, though, some are loaded with English-language settings. To 'Anglicise' a keyboard, look for a 'Fr' icon on the bottom right of the screen, and scroll up to click on 'En'.

---

For things like burning photo CDs, you're unlikely to find much beyond the capital cities. For more information on travelling with a portable computer, see www.teleadapt.com.

Unless you're using a free, web-based email address, such as **Yahoo** (www.yahoo.com), **Hotmail** (www.hotmail.com) or **Google** (www.gmail .com), you'll need to plan in order to be able to access your Internet mail account. You'll need: your incoming (POP or IMAP) mail server name, your account name and password. Your ISP or network supervisor will be able to give you these. Armed with this information, you can access your Internet mail account from any web-connected machine in the world, provided it runs some kind of software (remember that Netscape and Internet Explorer both have mail modules). It pays to become familiar with the process for doing this before you leave home.

For everything else, such as wireless or connecting your own laptop to a local server, West Africa is still at the early stages of its Internet revolution. Expect that to change, but in the meantime, such services are few and far between and only in upper midrange and top-end hotels in some capital cities.

## LAUNDRY

Outside of top-end hotels, laundry is washed by hand, often with brushes or on cement or rocks, which will cause your clothes to wear quickly if you spend much time in the region. Everything is always impeccably pressed (included in the price). Places charge per piece. At budget hotels, it may be as low as US$0.10 or US$0.20 per piece, and rates are sometimes negotiable. Rates are higher at top-end and midrange hotels, sometimes several dollars per piece. In the rainy season it may take longer to get your clothes back, as drying time depends on the sun.

Dry-cleaning services are limited to major cities. In most West African countries, it's a good idea to wash your own 'smalls' (socks and underwear) as it's considered impolite in many places if you ask someone else to do this.

## MAPS

The Michelin map *Africa: North and West* (sheet No 953, formerly No 153, scale 1:4,000,000) is one of the best and most detailed, and something of a classic. It's lent its name to the **153 Club** (www.the153club.org) whose members have driven across the Sahara and West Africa. Whether you join the club or not, the map – together with this guide – is something no overland driver should be without. Even so, expect a few discrepancies between the map and reality, especially regarding road information, as old tracks get upgraded and once-smooth highways become potholed disasters. The map excludes the southernmost portion of Cameroon.

Other maps include the Bartholemew *Africa West* (1:3,500,000), which lacks the route accuracy of the Michelin but has the advantage of contour shading. Another option is the similar map put out by RV Reise- und Verkehrsverlag in Germany (which also excludes southern Cameroon).

Maps of individual countries are described in detail in the relevant chapters, but worth noting are the maps produced by the Institut Géographique National (IGN). The *Pays et Villes du Monde* series (1:1,000,000) and the more recent IGN *Carte Touristique* (1:2,000,000) have country maps, which are excellent and available for most countries in West Africa. For good topographical detail, IGN also produces the *Carte Internationale du Monde* sheets (1:1,000,000), which are devoted to West Africa; the only problem is that they were surveyed in the 1960s and don't seem to have been updated since.

## MONEY

For travel in West Africa, it's best to come with a combination of cash (euros in Francophone countries, while US dollars and, to a lesser extent, UK pounds are often preferred elsewhere), travellers cheques and credit/debit card (Visa only in almost all countries).

Throughout the regional chapters and in countries where inflation is high, prices are quoted in US dollars. For a full list of exchange rates, see the table inside the front cover of this book.

## ATMs

ATMs exist in a few capitals and, occasionally, other large cities in West Africa. In theory, they accept credit and debit cards from banks with reciprocal agreements. In almost all cases, Visa is the only credit/debit card accepted with MasterCard rarely possible. And then, there are the machines themselves. While in a few countries you'll meet with success, there are enough problems – including finding a machine inoperable, or losing your card – that it's best to regard them only as an emergency standby. The main exceptions to this are Côte d'Ivoire, where you may need to rely on ATMs (see p287 for details) and Burkina Faso (p167), where ATMs abound.

Whenever you do use an ATM, expect to be slugged with prohibitive bank fees from your bank back home (€15 is not unusual for a CFA200,000 transaction). For this reason, always take out the maximum the ATM allows.

## Black Market

In some countries, artificially low fixed exchange rates create a demand for unofficial hard currency, so you can get more local money by changing on the so-called 'black market'. In CFA-zone countries, this is not a consideration because local currency is easily converted and the rate is pegged to the euro. In some other countries, banks and forex bureaus offer floating rates, so any black market has also disappeared, although you may be offered from 5% to 10% more than bank rates by shady characters on the street, who often hang out around markets or outside banks and post offices. Unofficial moneychangers are also tolerated by the authorities in many border areas, where there are rarely banks.

Although you may have no choice at a border crossing, the general rule throughout West Africa is to only change money on the street when absolutely necessary. The chances of getting ripped off are high, and even if the moneychanger is honest, you don't know who's watching from the other side of the street. Even at borders, be alert, as changers are notorious for pulling all sorts of stunts with bad rates and folded notes.

Try to anticipate your needs and change enough in advance to cover yourself on

weekends and during non-banking hours. If you do get stuck outside banking hours, you can try changing money at top-end hotels or tour companies, although rates are likely to be poor. Airport exchange bureaus are often open longer hours and on weekends. Another option, and much better than changing on the street, is to ask discreetly at a shop selling imported items. 'The banks are closed, do you know anyone who can help me…?' is a better approach than 'Do you want to change money?'

In countries with a real black market (eg Guinea and Nigeria), where you can get considerably more for your money, don't forget that this is morally questionable and against the law. What's more, dealers often work with corrupt policemen and can trap you in a set-up where you may be 'arrested', shaken down and eventually lose all your money.

## Cash & Travellers Cheques

The best strategy is to take a mixture of cash and travellers cheques, although both have their downsides. Cash is king in terms of convenience and always easiest to change, but cannot be replaced if lost or stolen. Travellers cheques are refundable if lost or stolen, but in some countries (ie Cameroon, Côte d'Ivoire and Guinea-Bissau), they're either difficult to exchange, attract high exchange commissions, or both. Throughout the region, most banks outside of the capital city simply won't accept travellers cheques.

Well-known brands of travellers cheques are better as they're more likely to be recognised by bank staff. Amex, followed by Visa and Thomas Cook/MasterCard, are the most widely accepted, and some banks will take only one of these three. Wherever you are in the region, most banks require you to show your original purchase receipts in order to change travellers cheques, so it's essential to bring these. Carry them with you (separately from your cheques), but also leave a copy at home, as well as elsewhere in your luggage in case the original receipts or the cheques themselves are stolen.

For both cash and travellers cheques, take a mixture of high and low denominations. Rates are better for high denominations but you may need some small amounts if you're about to leave the region, or a certain country, and only need to change a small amount. Also, a supply of small denomination cash

## 17 COUNTRIES, 10 CURRENCIES

The difficulties of juggling the currencies of the 17 countries in this book is ameliorated by the fact that eight countries (Benin, Burkina Faso, Côte d'Ivoire, Guinea-Bissau, Mali, Niger, Senegal and Togo) use the West African CFA (Communauté Financière Africaine) franc which can be used (or exchanged for local currency) in some other countries, such as The Gambia, Guinea and Ghana.

The CFA is fixed against (and supported by) the euro at a rate of 655.967:1, making it a 'hard' currency. One result of this arrangement is that most banks change euros into CFA without charging a fee or commission. At hotels and forex bureaus, expect rates of 650 or lower, and plan on paying commissions when changing euro (or any other currency) travellers cheques into CFA.

In recent years, the political leaders of The Gambia, Ghana, Guinea, Nigeria and Sierra Leone – the majority of West Africa's non-CFA block – have spoken of moving towards their own common currency, to be known as the 'eco', which would later merge with the CFA and thereby create a single currency throughout most of West Africa. Progress towards that goal remains slow, however. In the meantime, countries outside the CFA zone each have their own individual currencies.

Cameroon, as well as neighbouring Central African countries, uses the Central African CFA franc, which is linked to the euro at almost the same rate as the West African CFA franc, and with the West African CFA at a rate of one to one. However, you can't make payments with Central African CFA in the West African CFA zone or vice versa.

notes (eg US$1 and US$5 and the euro equivalent) can come in handy for cases when change is unavailable.

In addition to your main travel funds, carry an additional stash of cash – perhaps about US$300 or the euro equivalent – with you, preferably kept separate from the rest of your cash and travellers cheques. This will serve as a contingency fund for emergencies.

Note that the USA changed the design of the US$100 bill in the mid-1990s and old-style US$100 notes are not accepted at places that don't have a light machine for checking watermarks.

### Changing Money

In CFA-zone countries, the best currency to travel with is definitely the euro. Other major international currencies such as the US dollar and the UK pound can be changed in capital cities and tourist areas, but at less-favourable rates. In the non-CFA countries, the best currency to travel with is US dollars, with euros, UK pounds and other major currencies accepted in larger cities.

The main places to change money are banks and forex bureaus. Where they exist, forex bureaus are often more efficient than banks, usually offer slightly higher rates and are open longer hours, though many don't accept travellers cheques. Charges and commissions vary, with some banks and forex bureaus charging a flat fee, and others a percentage commission; some charge both

a fee and a commission. The bank or forex bureau with the higher commission may also offer a higher exchange rate though, so you could still be better off.

Towards the end of your trip, ensure that you're not left with large amounts of local currency. Apart from export restrictions, exchanging CFA francs in countries outside the region is nearly impossible, except for France. In most countries in the CFA zone, it's relatively easy to change remaining CFA into euros, but difficult to change CFA to dollars. On leaving non-CFA countries, it's usually not possible to reconvert local currency into foreign currency, except in The Gambia, where it's relatively straight-forward, although rates are low. Try and come to an arrangement with other travellers if you think you're going to be caught with a surfeit of local cash.

Also, note that if you're travelling between the West African and Central African CFA zones (eg from Niger to Cameroon), it's easy to change CFA notes of one zone for those of the other at banks, but more difficult to change coins.

### Credit Cards

You can rarely use a credit card to pay for items, and such occasions are limited to top-end hotels and restaurants, car-rental companies and occasionally air tickets; an extra commission is often attached, usually ranging from 3% to 15%. You can use your

Visa card (rarely MasterCard) to withdraw cash at some banks, especially in countries that use CFA. However, as with ATMs and except as noted in the country chapters, it's best not to count on this as computer breakdowns and other problems can leave you stranded. Where credit-card advances are possible, the process is sometimes straightforward with minimal hassle, but usually it's time consuming – sometimes taking up to a day or more. It can also be expensive if extra commissions are charged, and the maximum withdrawal amount is often restricted.

Watching a person put your card through the electronic credit card machine (as opposed to letting them do it out of sight) is a good idea to ensure you don't receive unwanted bills back home.

An advantage of debit cards is that there's no bill to pay (assuming you have the money in your account), so they're more suited for longer travels. However, unless the card carries the Visa logo it's unlikely to be accepted by many car-rental agencies and by some banks and ATMs. As well as the risk being higher if the card is stolen, debit cards are not very practical in much of West Africa.

### International Transfers

International money transfers may have the attraction of saving you from carrying large amounts of money and can be useful for topping up your funds, but these advantages may be outweighed by the fact that the process is generally expensive and time consuming – it's generally best used only as a last resort. Transfers usually take at least three to four days, and sometimes several weeks to clear, and occasionally there are hassles such as the local agent (banks or, in some countries, post offices) denying receiving your money. If you do need to transfer money, ask your forwarding bank to send you separate confirmation with full details, including the routing or transfer number, account and branch numbers, and address and telephone contacts. With this, you can then go to the recipient bank with proof that your money has been sent.

Most countries will only give you cash in local currency. Check the regulations in advance to avoid winding up with large sums of unconvertible currency.

Western Union Money Transfer has representatives in many West African countries, and is a good starting point, although its local partners are not always particularly efficient.

### Tipping

There are few clear rules on tipping in West Africa. In general, only the wealthy (ie well-to-do locals and nearly all foreign visitors) are expected to tip. Anyone staying in a fancy hotel would be expected to tip porters and other staff, but there would not be the same expectation from a backpacker in a cheap hotel.

Everyone – locals and foreigners – is expected to tip 10% at the better restaurants, although service is sometimes included in the bill. At more basic restaurants and eating houses no tips are expected. There's a grey area between these two classes of restaurants, where tipping is rarely expected from locals, but may be expected of foreigners. Even wealthier West Africans will sometimes tip at smaller restaurants – not so much because it's expected, but as a show of status.

Locals seldom tip in privately hired taxis, but some drivers expect well-heeled travellers to tip about 10%, especially if you have hired the vehicle for a lengthy trip. On most short trips, however, loose change is normally appreciated. In shared taxis around cities tipping is almost unheard of. If you rent a car with driver, a tip is always expected, usually about 10% of the total rental cost, and more if it is a multiday rental or if your driver has been exceptionally good.

## PHOTOGRAPHY & VIDEO

You'll find plenty of subjects in West Africa for photography (with a video or camera), but if this is a primary reason for your visit try to avoid the harmattan season, which is at its height in many areas of the region from late December to February (see p18 for more details).

### Film & Equipment

Film in West Africa is imported and expensive (at least US$6/14 for 24/36 exposures). Outside capital cities, only standard print film (not slide or large format) is available. Also, even if the expiry date is still good, film may have been damaged by the heat. It's best to bring all you need with you.

The sunlight in West Africa is frequently very intense, so most people find 100 ISO perfectly adequate, with possibly 200 ISO or 400 ISO for long-lens shots or visits to coastal areas in the rainy season.

Useful photographic accessories might include a small flash, a cable or remote shutter release, filters and a cleaning kit (essential if you're going to be in the desert or in the Sahel during the harmattan). Also, remember to take spare batteries.

Finally, some airports have X-ray machines for checking baggage that may not be safe for film. Even so-called film-safe models affect high-speed film (1000 ISO and higher), especially if the film goes through several checks, so you may want to use a protective lead bag – they're fairly inexpensive. Alternatively, carry your film in your pocket or small plastic container, and have it checked manually by customs officials.

For video cameras, you may find tapes in capitals and other large towns, but qualities and formats vary. While travelling, you can recharge batteries in hotels as you go along, so take the necessary charger, plugs (see the Practicalities box in the Directory section of each country chapter) and transformer for the country you are visiting.

For digital camera equipment and accessories, you may find batteries etc in the better photo shops in major capital cities in the region, but you're better off being self-sufficient and bringing everything you need with you from home.

## Hints

### CAMERA CARE
Factors that can spoil your camera or film include heat, humidity, very fine sand, saltwater and sunlight. Take appropriate precautions.

### EXPOSURE
When photographing animals or people, take light readings on the subject and not the brilliant African background or your shots will turn out underexposed.

### PHOTOGRAPHING PEOPLE
Ask permission before photographing people, and respect their wishes. While some West Africans may like being photographed, others don't. They may be superstitious about your camera, suspicious of your motives, or simply interested in whatever economic advantage they can gain from your desire to

photograph them and demand a fee. Other locals maintain their pride and never want to be photographed, money or not.

Given that cameras are a relative luxury in most of the region, some people may agree to be photographed in exchange for receiving a copy. If you don't carry a Polaroid camera, take their address and make it clear that you'll post the photo. Your promise will be taken seriously. Never say you'll send a photo and then not do it. If you know you won't be able to come through on a promise, just say that so many people ask you for photos that it's impossible to send one to everyone. A digital camera has the advantage of being able to show the subject his or her image.

Video photographers should follow the same rules, as most locals find them even more annoying and offensive than still cameras. The bottom line is always ask permission first, whether you have a still camera or a video camera.

### PHOTOGRAPHY BOOKS
For more advice, Lonely Planet's *Travel Photography: A Guide to Taking Better Pictures* by Richard I'Anson is an excellent resource, full of helpful tips for photography while on the road. For more specific advice, Lonely Planet also publishes *Landscape Photography* by Peter Eastway and *People Photography* by Michael Coyne.

### RESTRICTIONS
Avoid taking pictures of bridges, dams, airports, military equipment, government buildings and anything else that could be considered strategic. You may be arrested or have your film and camera confiscated. Some countries – usually those with precarious military governments – are particularly sensitive. If in doubt, ask first.

### SACRED SITES
Some local people may be offended if you take pictures of their place of worship or a natural feature with religious significance. In some instances, dress may be important. In mosques, for instance, wearing long trousers and removing your shoes may make it more likely that your hosts won't object.

### TIMING
The best times to take photographs on sunny days are the first two hours after

sunrise and the last two before sunset. This takes advantage of the colour-enhancing rays cast by a low sun. Filters (eg ultraviolet, polarising or 'skylight') can also help produce good results; ask for advice in a good camera shop.

### WILDLIFE PHOTOGRAPHY

For wildlife shots, a good lightweight 35mm SLR camera with a lens between 210mm and 300mm should do the trick. Videos with zoom facility may be able to get closer. If your subject is nothing but a speck in the distance, try to resist wasting film, but keep the camera ready.

## POST

Postal services are moderately reliable in most West African capitals and cities. In rural areas, though, service can range from slow to nonexistent. For details on rates and prices, see the Directory in individual country chapters.

Letters sent from a major capital take about a week to 10 days to reach most of Europe, and at least two weeks to reach North America or Australasia – although it's sometimes much longer. For more speed and certainty, a few countries have 'express' services, but the main alternative (though expensive) is a courier service. DHL, for example, has offices in most West African capitals.

If you're only going to be in West Africa for a few weeks, it's unlikely it'll be worth arranging for mail to be sent to you, if only because in such a short time frame the margin of error is small. However, if you're planning on spending months travelling through the region, there are a couple of ways that you can receive mail.

The most common way to receive mail is the poste restante service offered by post offices, where letters are held for your collection. Although some smaller post offices may offer this service, using the main post office in a capital or large city is strongly advised. Letters should be addressed clearly to you, with your family name in capitals and underlined, at Poste Restante, General Post Office (English-speaking countries) or PTT (Francophone countries), then the town and country where you want to collect the mail.

To collect your mail, you generally need to show your passport or other identification. Letters sometimes take a few weeks to work their way through the system, so have them sent to a place where you're going to be for a while, or will be passing through more than once. Some poste restante services levy a nominal charge when you collect mail, and many limit the length of time they will hold letters (usually one month).

Some hotels and tour companies operate mail-holding services, and Amex customers can have mail sent to company branches.

## SHOPPING

A major feature of travel in West Africa is the range of art and craftwork found in the region. This includes masks, statues and other woodcarvings, textiles with a fantastic variety of colours and patterns, glass beads and jewellery made from gold and silver, as well as a fascinating assortment of pots, urns, stools, weapons, musical instruments and more.

Whether you're a serious collector or looking for a souvenir from your trip, you'll find plenty to choose from, and prices are more reasonable than they are at home. Of course, many of the items you'll see in shops and markets are made expressly for the tourist trade, although they are often copies of traditional items. Even contemporary pieces of art are usually based on traditional designs.

Making items for sale is not new to West Africa: among the oldest 'tourist' art in sub-Saharan Africa was that produced by the Sapi people of Sierra Leone in the 15th century – they sold ivory salt pots and trumpets to the Portuguese traders.

See p67 for more details of the types of art and craftwork available. As well as these, other items commonly seen in West Africa are baskets and pottery with intricate designs, which are almost always produced by women. Leatherwork, with colourful incised patterns, mostly made from goat hide, are created in the Sahel and Sahara region.

Cassettes of local music are also a good buy. However, remember that the trade in pirated music is devastating for often struggling musicians who receive no royalties from the tape you buy for a pittance. For more details see p58, as well as the Shopping sections of individual town entries.

### Bargaining

In many West African countries, bargaining over prices is a way of life. Visitors often have difficulty with this idea, as they're used to things having a fixed value, whereas in West Africa, commodities are considered to be worth whatever their seller can get for them. It really is no different to the concept of an auction and should be treated as one more intriguing aspect of travel in the region.

### BASICS

In markets selling items such as fruit and vegetables, traders will sometimes put their price higher when they see you, a wealthy foreigner. If you pay this – whether out of ignorance or guilt about how much you have compared with most locals – you may be considered foolish, but you'll be doing fellow travellers a disservice by creating the impression that all foreigners are willing to pay any price. You may also harm the local economy: by paying these high prices you put some items out of the locals' reach. And who can blame the traders – why sell something to a local when foreigners will pay twice as much? So, in cases such as this, you may need to bargain over the price.

Having said that, many traders will quote you the same price that locals pay, particularly away from cities or tourist areas, so it's important not to go around expecting everybody to charge high prices. It's also wise to keep things in perspective and not haggle over a few cents. After the first few days in a country (when you'll inevitably pay over the odds a few times) you'll soon get to learn the standard prices for basic items. Remember though that prices can change depending on where you buy. For example, a soft drink in a city may be one-third the price you'll pay in a remote rural area, where transport costs have to be paid. Conversely, fruit and vegetables are cheaper in the areas where they're actually grown.

### SOUVENIRS

At craft stalls, where items are specifically for tourists, it's a completely different story, and bargaining is very much expected. The trader's aim is to identify the highest price you're willing to pay. Your aim is to find the price below which the vendor will not sell. People have all sorts of formulae for working out what this should be, but there are no hard-and-fast rules. Some traders may initially ask a price four (or more) times higher than what they're prepared to accept, although it's usually lower than this. Decide what you want to pay or what others have told you they've

paid; your first offer should be about half this. At this stage, the vendor may laugh or feign outrage, while you plead abject poverty. The trader's price then starts to drop from the original quote to a more realistic level. When it does, you begin making better offers until you arrive at a mutually agreeable price.

And that's the crux – mutually agreeable. Travellers often moan about how they were 'overcharged' by souvenir traders. But, when things have no fixed price, nobody really gets overcharged. If you don't like the price, then don't pay it.

The best results when bargaining come from a friendly and spirited exchange. Better still, take the time to sit with the trader, drink tea with him, ask about his family or get him to explain the history of the piece you're wanting to buy. Bargaining is so much more fun for both sides if you take the time to get to know who you're dealing with. It won't necessarily mean that you make a purchase but you could just make a new friend and, at the very least, you'll counter the impression that all tourists arrive loaded up with cash and little time to engage with locals.

There's never any point in losing your temper. If the effort seems a waste of time, politely take your leave. Sometimes traders will call you back if they think their stubbornness may be counterproductive. Very few will pass up the chance of making a sale, however thin the profit.

If traders won't come down to a price you feel is fair (or if you can't afford the asking price), it either means they really aren't making a profit, or that if you don't pay their prices, they know somebody else will.

## Bringing Items Home

When you buy a new woodcarving you may find it has cracked by the time you get home. New wood must be dried slowly. Wrapping the carvings in plastic bags with a small water tray enclosed is one technique. If you see tiny bore marks with white powder, it means the powder-post beetle (often confused with termites) is having a fiesta. There are three remedies – zap the beasts in a microwave, stick the piece in the freezer for a week, or drench it with lighter fluid. You could try fumigating items. Be warned that if you have wooden objects with insect damage, the items may be seized by customs on your return home

(Australia is very strict on this) and you will have to pay to have them fumigated.

If you buy textiles, note that some dyes, including indigo, may not be colour-fast. Soaking cloth in vinegar or very salty water may stop the dye running, but this method should only be used on cloth of one colour. Adinkra cloth is not meant to be washed.

For advice on preserving West Africa's heritage by not purchasing antiquities, and thereby avoiding the ire of customs officials, see p815.

## SOLO TRAVELLERS

Travelling on your own is a great way to make new friends – the opportunity to meet locals is greatly enhanced if you're not part of a large group – and to ensure that you have the freedom to follow your own itinerary. The downside is that hotel rooms cost more for individual travellers (a single room is rarely half the price of a double room). If you don't speak the local language, you may also find yourself frustrated in having little more than broken conversations with locals, and in countries where few tourists are found (eg Guinea), you may end up feeling pretty isolated. If you want to travel in Francophone countries and think you may end up pining for a new travel buddy, head for those countries with more well-worn travellers paths (eg Mali, Senegal or Burkina Faso).

## TELEPHONE & FAX

Telephone and fax connections to places outside West Africa are reasonably good, as the transmission is via satellite, though it's generally much easier and less expensive to call in the other direction – from the USA, Europe or Australasia to West Africa. Calls between African countries, however, are often relayed on land lines or through Europe, which means the reception is frequently bad – assuming you can get a call through in the first place. Things are improving, but slowly.

Costs for international calls and faxes to Europe, the USA or Australasia start at about US$3 to US$4 per minute, with a few countries offering slightly reduced rates at night and on weekends.

Dial-direct or 'home-direct' numbers are available from a few countries. With these, you dial an operator in your home country, who can reverse the charges, or to charge the call to a phone-company charge card or your home number. These home-direct numbers are toll free, but if you are using a phone booth you may need a coin or phonecard to be connect. Check with your phone company for access numbers and a listing of countries where they have home-direct numbers.

Country codes for dialling West African countries are given inside the front cover of this book.

### Fax

Most cities and large towns have public telephone offices at the post office where you can make international calls and send faxes. There are also private telecommunications centres in major towns and cities throughout the region. Sending a fax from a hotel is much more expensive.

### Mobile Phones

People in West Africa love their mobile (cell) phones and they are becoming common in larger cities, where they can be easily and inexpensively rented or purchased. In capitals and larger towns, street vendors sell mobile phone top-up cards for a mobile phone you've rented or bought locally, although these are only valid once you've purchased a SIM card from a local carrier. Mobiles are also becoming increasingly popular with hotels and businesses since land lines are often unreliable. Although coverage is being constantly extended, you're unlikely to get a signal outside larger towns. See the Directory in individual country chapters for details on the situation in the country you'll be visiting.

In some countries (eg Mali), usage has reached a point where companies offer night-time deals for calling internationally from your mobile, which can work out cheaper than using fixed lines.

A European or North American mobile phone will probably have reception in most West African countries, whereby your carrier's local partner will allow you to receive and send text messages, as well as phone calls, although the latter can be extremely expensive. Remember that if someone calls your mobile phone while you're in West Africa, you may pay the bulk of the charge.

### Phonecards

In many West African countries you can buy phonecards at post offices or phone offices, or at shops near cardphones. These usually make international calls slightly cheaper, but the cards are generally only sold during regular business hours so you may need to plan ahead. At some airports and top-end hotels in the major capitals, telephones may accept credit cards, but at high rates.

## TIME

Burkina Faso, Côte d'Ivoire, The Gambia, Ghana, Guinea, Guinea-Bissau, Liberia, Mali, Mauritania, Senegal, Sierra Leone and Togo are on GMT/UTC. Cape Verde is one hour behind. Benin, Cameroon, Niger and Nigeria are one hour ahead. None of the West African countries in this book observe daylight saving.

For a comprehensive guide to time zones in the region, see pp902–3.

## TOILETS

There are two main types of toilet: Western sit-down, with a bowl and seat; and African squat, with a hole in the ground. Standards vary tremendously, from pristine to those that leave little to the imagination as to the health or otherwise of the previous occupant.

In rural areas, squat toilets are built over a deep hole in the ground. These are called 'long drops', and the waste matter just fades away naturally, as long as the hole isn't filled with too much other rubbish (such as paper or synthetic materials, including tampons).

Some Western toilets aren't plumbed in, but just balanced over a long drop, although the lack of running water makes such mechanisms one of the least successful forms of cross-cultural exchange. In our experience, a non-contact hole in the ground is better than a filthy bowl to hover over any day.

## TOURIST INFORMATION

With just a handful of exceptions, West Africa's tourism authorities are not geared up for tourism, and there are few tourist offices abroad. Some countries run small tourist offices at their embassies, which may be helpful for getting moderately useful brochures or general travel information.

Once in West Africa, some countries have Ministry of Tourism information offices, but apart from offering a few old brochures they're unlikely to be of much assistance. Notable exceptions, where a town or city may have a genuinely useful tourist office, are listed in individual country chapters.

You'll usually have more success inquiring with staff at tour companies or hotels.

## VISAS

This section contains general information about visas – for country-specific visa information, see the Directory sections of individual country chapters.

The general rule for West Africa is to get your visas before leaving home. They are rarely issued at land borders and only occasionally at airports. Also, if you're flying from outside Africa, many airlines won't let you on board without a visa anyway.

Visa agencies are worth considering if you need visas to several countries before you leave, or if there's no relevant embassy in your country. For longer trips or more flexibility, it's possible to get most of your visas in the region as you go, although this requires some advance planning and careful checking of the location of embassies for the countries in question – most West African countries have insufficient resources to maintain expensive embassies in many countries.

Visa fees average between US$20 and US$50, with prices depending on where you apply and your nationality. Multi-entry visas cost more than single-entry visas. Check the visa's validity length and its start date when deciding where to make your application. When applying for a visa, you may have to show proof that you intend to leave the country (eg an air ticket) or that you have enough funds to support yourself during your visit.

Most visa applications require between two and four identical passport photos, either black and white or colour. Inexpensive photo shops are found throughout the region, and rural areas often have a village photographer who can do the job for you.

## WOMEN TRAVELLERS

When travelling in West Africa – solo or with other women – you're unlikely to encounter any more difficulties than you would elsewhere in the world. The female authors of this book have travelled for extended periods (including solo travel) and/or lived in West Africa without incident and most did their research for this book travelling alone.

For more information on the situation for women travellers in specific countries, see the Women Travellers section in the Directory of the relevant country chapter.

## Hints

Although women will undoubtedly attract more attention than men, more often than not you'll meet only warmth and hospitality, and find that you receive kindness and special treatment that you wouldn't be shown if you were a man. While you're likely to hear some horror stories (often of dubious accuracy) from expats who may be appalled at the idea of solo female travel, it's worth remembering that the incidence of rape or other real harm is extremely rare.

With that in mind, it's important to not let these concerns ruin your trip. Remember that some sections of the region, such as parts of the Sahel, are wonderfully hassle free. You'll also have the opportunity to meet local women, something which few male travellers have the chance to do on the same terms. Good places to try include tourist offices, government departments or even your hotel, where at least some of the staff are likely to be formally educated young to middle-aged women. In rural areas, starting points include female teachers at a local school, or staff at a health centre where language barriers are less likely to be a problem.

That said, it's inevitable that you'll attract some attention. Here are a few tips:

- Dress modestly. This is the most successful strategy for minimising unwanted attention. Wear trousers or a long skirt, and a conservative top with a sleeve. Tucking your hair under a cap or tying it back, especially if it's blonde, sometimes helps.
- Use common sense, trust your instincts and take the usual precautions when out. For example, if possible, avoid going out alone in the evenings, particularly on foot. Avoid isolated areas, roadways and beaches during both day and evening hours, and be cautious on beaches, many of which can become isolated very quickly. Throughout the region, hitching alone is not recommended.
- Don't worry about being rude, and don't feel the need to explain yourself. If you try to start explaining why you don't want to meet for a drink/go to a nightclub/get married on the spot, it may be interpreted as flirting. The more you try to explain, the more you'll see your hopeful suitor's eyes light up with that pleased, knowing look – 'ah, she's just playing hard to get, but really, she wants me…'

> **'C'EST MADAME? OU BIEN, MADEMOISELLE?'**
>
> Women travelling on their own through Francophone West Africa will undoubtedly hear these words: ad nauseam (translated, the phrase means 'are you married or not?'). Sometimes, for example, when you're filling out forms or registering at a hotel, it's not ill-intentioned. But all too often, it's a leering soldier or border official who's a little too eager for company. Although there's not much you can do to prevent the question, having at least a fictitious husband – ideally one who will be arriving imminently at that very place – can help in avoiding further advances. If you're travelling with a male companion, a good way to avoid unwanted interest is to introduce him as your husband. If you're questioned as to why your husband/children aren't with you, just explain that you'll be meeting them later.

- Ignore hissing, calls of '*chérie*', or whatever – if you respond, it may be interpreted as a lead on.
- Wear a wedding ring or carry photos of 'your' children, which will make you appear less 'available'.
- Avoid direct eye contact with local men; dark sunglasses help. There are, however, times when a cold glare is an effective riposte to an unwanted suitor.
- On public transport, sit next to a woman if possible.
- If you need help (eg directions), ask a woman first. That said, local women are less likely than men to have had an education that included learning in English. You'll find this to be a major drawback in getting to meet and talk with them.
- Going to the nearest public place, such as the lobby of a hotel, usually works in getting rid of any hangers-on. If they still persist however, asking the receptionist to call the police usually frightens them off.

## Tampons & Sanitary Pads

Tampons (imported from Europe) are available from pharmacies or large supermarkets in capitals throughout West Africa, and occasionally in other large towns. Elsewhere, the only choice is likely to be sanitary pads so you may want to bring an emergency supply.

# Transport in West Africa

## CONTENTS

# GETTING THERE & AWAY

This chapter tells you how to reach West Africa by air, land and sea from other parts of the world, and outlines the routes for onward travel from the region. For details of travel once you are in the region between one country and its neighbours see the Getting There & Away section in the relevant country chapter. Flights, tours and rail tickets can be booked online at www.lonelyplanet.com/travel_services.

## ENTRY REQUIREMENTS
### Entering West Africa
Entering West Africa is generally hassle-free, provided you have all your documents in order. For details of the visa requirements for each country covered in this guide, see the Directory section of each individual country chapter.

## AIR
Many major European airlines fly to West Africa, with Air France undoubtedly the airline with the greatest coverage. Of the

> **THINGS CHANGE**
>
> The information in this chapter is particularly vulnerable to change. International air fares are volatile, schedules change, special deals come and go, and rules are amended. Airlines and governments seem to take a perverse pleasure in making fare structures and regulations as complicated as possible. In addition, the travel industry is highly competitive and agents' prices vary considerably.
>
> Fares quoted in this book are approximate and based on the rates advertised by travel agents at the time of going to press. Airlines and travel agents mentioned in this chapter do not necessarily constitute a recommendation.
>
> Ensure that you get quotes and advice from as many airlines and travel agents as possible – and make sure you understand how fares and tickets work – before you part with your hard-earned cash. The details given in this chapter should be regarded as pointers and are not a substitute for your own careful, up-to-date research.

African airlines, Royal Air Maroc and Air Sénégal International in particular have good connections throughout the region while Point Afrique has revolutionised travel to West Africa with its extensive network connecting Paris, Marseilles and Mulhouse with cities and towns across the region.

### Airports & Airlines
International airports with the greatest number of incoming flights (and the best onward connections) include Dakar (Senegal), Abidjan (Côte d'Ivoire), Accra (Ghana), Bamako (Mali), Lagos (Nigeria) and Douala (Cameroon). There are also international airports at: Cotonou (Benin); Ouagadougou and Bobo-Dioulasso (Burkina Faso); Yaoundé and Garoua (Cameroon); Conakry (Guinea); Monrovia (Liberia); Mopti and Gao (Mali); Nouakchott, Nouâdhibou and Atâr (Mauritania); Niamey and Agadez

(Niger); Kano and Port Harcourt (Nigeria); Praia and Sal (Cape Verde); Banjul (Gambia); and Bissau (Guinea-Bissau).

Airlines flying to and from West Africa:
**Afriqiyah** (8U; www.afriqiyah.aero) Hub: Tripoli.
**Air Algérie** (AH; www.airalgerie.dz) Hub: Algiers.
**Air Burkina** (2J; www.air-burkina.com) Hub: Ouagadougou.
**Air France** (AF; www.airfrance.com) Hub: Paris Charles De Gaulle.
**Air Gabon** Hub: Libreville.
**Air Guinée** (2U; www.mirinet.com/airguinee) Hub: Conakry.
**Air Ivoire** (VU; www.airivoire.com) Hub: Abidjan.
**Air Luxor** (LK; www.airluxor.com) Hub: Lisbon.
**Air Mali** (XG) Hub: Bamako.
**Air Mauritanie** (MR; www.airmauritanie.mr) Hub: Nouakchott.
**Air Sénégal International** (V7; www.air-senegal-international.com) Hub: Dakar.
**Alitalia** (AZ; www.alitalia.com) Hub: Rome.
**American Airlines** (AA; www.aa.com) Hub: New York.

**British Airways** (BA; www.britishairways.com) Hub: London Heathrow.
**Cameroon Airlines** (UY; www.cameroon-airlines.com) Hub: Douala.
**EgyptAir** (MS; www.egyptair.com.eg) Hub: Cairo.
**Emirates** (EK; www.emirates.com) Hub: Dubai.
**Ethiopian Airlines** (ET; www.flyethiopian.com/et/) Hub: Addis Ababa.
**Ghana Airways** (GH; www.ghana-airways.com) Hub: Accra.
**Ghana International Airlines** (GO; www.fly-ghana.com) Hub: Accra.
**Go-Voyages** (www.govoyages.com) Hub: Paris.
**Iberia** (IB; www.iberia.com) Hub: Madrid.
**Interair** (D6; www.interair.co.za) Hub: Johannesburg.
**Kenya Airways** (KQ; www.kenya-airways.com) Hub: Nairobi.
**KLM-Royal Dutch Airlines** (KL; www.klm.com) Hub: Amsterdam.
**Lufthansa Airlines** (LH; www.lufthansa.com) Hub: Frankfurt.
**Middle East Airlines** (ME; www.mea.com.lb) Hub: Rafic Hariri International Airport, Beirut.
**Point Afrique** (www.point-afrique.coms) Hub: Paris.
**Royal Air Maroc** (AT; www.royalairmaroc.com) Hub: Casablanca.
**Slok Air** (SO; www.slokairinternational.com) Hub: Banjul.
**SN Brussels** (SN; www.flysn.com) Hub: Brussels.
**South African Airways** (SA; www.flysaa.com) Hub: Johannesburg.
**Swiss International Airlines** (LX; www.swiss.com) Hub: Zurich.
**TACV** (VR; www.tacv.cv)
**TAP Air Portugal** (TP; www.flytap.com) Hub: Lisbon.
**Toumaï Air Tchad** Hub: N'Djaména.
**Tunis Air** (TU; www.tunisair.com.tr) Hub: Tunis.
**Virgin Nigeria** (VK; www.virginnigeria.com) Hub: Lagos.
**West Coast Airways** (WCG) Hub: Accra.

## Tickets

Buying cheap air tickets in West Africa isn't easy. Usually the best deal you can get is an airline's official excursion fare and there is no discount on single tickets unless you qualify for a 'youth' or 'student' rate, with sometimes significant discounts for people under 26 (sometimes 23) or in full-time education. Cheaper tickets are easier to come by from travel agents in cities which handle plenty of international traffic (eg Dakar or Abidjan). If you're stuck in Bissau or Monrovia, however, you won't have much choice about fares or airlines.

Charter flights (eg Point Afrique or Go-Voyages) are generally direct and cheaper

### DON'T FORGET...

There are a few essential things that you must have when you arrive at your first West African border:

- valid entry visa, unless you are entering a country where the visa is available on arrival;
- your up-to-date international vaccination booklet (*livre jeune*) which contains proof of yellow fever vaccination;
- enough empty pages in your passport as African officials love stamps (for visas, entry and exit stamps, and registration with police within some countries) – so make sure you have at least two pages per country;
- a passport that expires at least six months after your trip ends – it's not mandatory in all cases but some officials will cause problems if your passport is about to run out;
- the patience of a saint as African bureaucracy can be epic in its obsession with minutiae;
- an awareness that some African officials will assure you that your perfectly valid visa has expired – unless it has, they're just asking for a bribe.

### A FEW THINGS ABOUT POINT AFRIQUE

Point Afrique is one of the best things to happen to West African tourism in ages. Their flights are generally cheaper than the established carriers, they can take you places that no other airlines can (from Gao to Agadez and plenty of other desert oases or West African capitals) and they don't penalise you for entering West Africa at one place and leaving from another. Their low prices have also prompted other airlines to lower their fares.

There are some things to remember if you're travelling with Point Afrique. For a start, they're a charter company that leases planes from other airlines (at the time of writing, these included Air Mediterranée and Axis Airways). Because they have neither the government backing nor profit margins of national carriers, they operate their flights only if there are enough passengers to make it viable. While flights are rarely cancelled, they may be combined with other routes – for example, one of our Agadez–Paris flights flew via Tamanrasset, Marseilles and required a change of plane.

Point Afrique is way down the pecking order when it comes to airport berths, which means they may be unable to confirm your details (departure airport or time) until 15 days before your departure, a factor which needs to be taken into consideration if you're booking onward flights.

Prices are also something to watch out for as the prices quoted on their website do not include airport taxes. The taxes for each airport are listed on Point Afrique's website and must be added to the quoted price (which still usually falls far below the fares of other carriers).

than scheduled flights, so they're well worth considering. Some charter flights come as part of a package that includes accommodation and other services, but most charter companies sell 'flight only' tickets, which can be good deals.

Once you have your ticket, keep a note of the number, flight numbers, dates, times and other details, and keep the information somewhere separate from your money and valuables. The easiest thing to do is to take a few photocopies – carry one with you and leave another at home. If the ticket is lost or stolen, this will help you get a replacement.

It's sensible to buy travel insurance early. If you get it the week before you fly, you may find, for example, that you're not covered for delays to your flight caused by industrial action. For more details see p819.

A few hours surfing the Web can help give you an idea of what you can expect in the way of good fares as well as be a useful source of information on routes and timetables. Remember that most online flight reservation services need credit-card details and, as many are US-based, they may only deliver to North American addresses.

Following are a few online booking services that may be useful.

**American Express Travel** (www.itn.net)
**Atrapalo** (www.atrapalo.com)
**Cheap Tickets** (www.cheaptickets.com)
**Despegar** (www.despegar.es)
**ebookers** (www.ebookers.com)

**Expedia.com** (www.expedia.com)
**Lowestfare.com** (www.lowestfare.com)
**Orbitz** (www.orbitz.com)
**STA Travel** (www.sta.com)
**Travelocity** (www.travelocity.com)
**Travel.com.au** (www.travel.com.au)

For airline websites, see p830. There's also a full list of recommended travel agencies in the sections which follow. See p840 for more information on tours.

## Travellers with Special Needs

If you have special needs of any sort – you've broken a leg, you're vegetarian, travelling in a wheelchair, taking the baby, terrified of flying – you should let the airline know as soon as possible so that they can make arrangements.

Airports in West Africa can be pretty basic and services such as escorts, ramps, lifts, accessible toilets and reachable phones are generally scarce and basic. Deaf travellers can ask for airport and in-flight announcements to be written down for them.

Children under two travel for 10% of the standard fare (or free, on some airlines), as long as they don't occupy a seat. They don't get a baggage allowance either. 'Skycots' should be provided by the airline if requested in advance; these will take a child weighing up to about 10kg. Children between two and 12 can usually occupy a seat for half to two-thirds of the full fare, and do get a baggage allowance. Pushchairs can usually be taken as hand luggage.

## Africa

### EAST OR SOUTH AFRICA

For travellers going to/from East or Southern Africa, the hubs are Nairobi (Kenya), Addis Ababa (Ethiopia), and Johannesburg (South Africa), all of which have direct connections to West Africa – generally Accra or Abidjan, and sometimes to Lagos and Bamako.

Airlines to try include South African Airways (which has connections from Johannesburg to Abidjan, Accra and Lagos), Ethiopian Airlines, Ghana Airways, Cameroon Airlines, Kenya Airways (with flights from Nairobi to Abidjan, Lagos and Douala), Virgin Nigeria Airways (between Lagos and Johannesburg) and Interair (which flies between Johannesburg and Bamako).

Expect to pay anywhere from US$700 upwards between Nairobi and Abidjan (Douala to Nairobi is US$950), about US$600 for a return excursion fare between Johannesburg and Accra, and US$550 one way between Johannesburg and Lagos. Depending on which airline you use, you may fly a somewhat circuitous route (eg, Johannesburg to Abidjan via Addis Ababa on Ethiopian Airlines). Also keep in mind that flying across Africa – and particularly between East and West Africa – can be slow and subject to delays and cancellations. If you have connecting flights, allow yourself plenty of time.

**STA** ( ☎ 0861 781 781; www.statravel.co.za) has several branches in South Africa, and is a good place to start for arranging discounted fairs. In Nairobi, try **Let's Go Travel** ( ☎ 20-4447151; www.lets-go-travel.net).

### CENTRAL AFRICA

Toumaï Air Tchad offers a weekly flight between Niamey and N'Djaména (Chad, US$685) and one between Douala and Brazzaville (Congo). Air Gabon has five weekly flights between Douala and Libreville (Gabon). Flights with Afriqiyah go via N'Djaména, while Cameroon Air has weekly flights to Bangui (Central African Republic).

### NORTH AFRICA

The best connections from North Africa are on Royal Air Maroc, which has flights from Casablanca (Morocco) to Abidjan, Bamako,

Conakry, Dakar, Douala and Nouakchott. The best deals are into Dakar, with return fares from Casablanca for around US$525. Tunis Air also flies from Tunis to Dakar via Nouakchott. Air Algérie flies between Algiers and Nouakchott, Ouagadougou, Niamey and Agadez among other West African cities. Egypt Air flies into Kano from Cairo. An interesting alternative is Afriqiyah, which flies to West African airports from Europe with a stop in Tripoli (Libya).

## Australasia & the Middle East

There are flights on Qantas and South African Airways from Perth and Sydney to Johannesburg, from where you can connect to several West African destinations, including Accra, Abidjan, Douala and Lagos. Plan on paying around A$2350/NZ$3500 for the full routing. It's also possible to fly via Europe.

More exotic alternatives include flying with Emirates to Dubai from where there are onward connections to Lagos and Accra (around A$2300) or with Egypt Air via Cairo to Accra, Abidjan or Lagos (from A$2350).

Both **STA Travel** ( ☎ 1300 733 035; www.statravel.com.au) and **Flight Centre** ( ☎ 133 133; www.flightcentre.com.au) have offices throughout Australia. For online bookings, try www.travel.com.au.

In New Zealand, both **Flight Centre** ( ☎ 0800 243 544; www.flightcentre.co.nz) and **STA Travel** ( ☎ 0508 782 872; www.statravel.co.nz) have branches throughout the country. The site www.travel.co.nz is recommended for online bookings.

For more options check the ads in travel magazines and weekend newspapers, including the Saturday issues of the *Sydney Morning Herald* or the *Age* in Australia, and the *New Zealand Herald* in New Zealand.

## Continental Europe

You can fly from any European capital to any capital city in West Africa, but some routes are more popular and frequent (and usually cheaper) than others.

Charter airlines such as Point Afrique offer the best deals with flights from Paris, Marseilles and Mulhouse to West African capitals (Cotonou, Ouagadougou, Niamey and Bamako) and a host of smaller towns, such as Mopti and Gao (Mali), Atâr (Mauritania) and Agadez (Niger). One-way fares start from around €175, although most are closer to €220 plus tax. Go-Voyages also flies to Agadez from Paris.

European travel agencies offer an abundance of charter flights to The Gambia, Senegal and, to a lesser extent, Cape Verde. These start at around €500 but are all-inclusive deals that include accommodation and only work for short, specific periods unless you can get a flight-only package. As such, they're not the best if you're planning to remain in West Africa for a while or visiting a number of countries not covered by the package.

For more established carriers, Paris is a good hub (see opposite). Return fares on scheduled flights from France to several West African capitals start from €675. Air France has four weekly flights between Paris and Port Harcourt (Nigeria).

It's also worth looking at flights from other cities. From Madrid, for example, you can get a return flight on Iberia (or Air Sénégal International) to Dakar for about €640 or a return Madrid–Casablanca–Bamako flight with Iberia or Royal Air Maroc for around €660.

From Brussels, SN Brussels Airlines flies to Dakar, Conakry, Banjul, Freetown and Monrovia from €750, while TAP Air Portugal connects Lisbon with Sal (Cape Verde) and Bissau (Guinea-Bissau). From Frankfurt, Lufthansa operates three weekly flights to Lagos, while KLM offers twice weekly flights between Amsterdam and Kano (Nigeria).

Another interesting option is to fly to Las Palmas in the Canary Islands, from where you can get flights on Air Mauritanie to Nouakchott and Nouâdhibou.

If you don't mind travelling via Tripoli, Afriqiyah Airways flies from Brussels, Paris and Geneva to Kano, Niamey, Bamako, Ouagadougou, Abidjan, Accra, Lomé, Cotonou, Lagos and Douala. There are also plans to fly to Dakar. Fares vary, but start from around €650 return.

Recommended agencies in continental Europe include the following:

**Airfair** ( ☎ 020 620 5121; www.airfair.nl; The Netherlands)

**Barcelo Viajes** ( ☎ 902 116 226; www.barceloviajes.com; Spain)

**Connections** ( ☎ 02-550 01 00; www.connections.be; Belgium) Offices throughout the country.

**CTS Viaggi** ( ☎ 06 462 0431; www.cts.it; Italy)

**Expedia** (www.expedia.de; Germany)

**Nouvelles Frontières** ( ☎ 0825 000 747; www.nouvelles-frontieres.fr; France) Also in Belgium, Switzerland.

**STA Travel** ( ☎ 01805 456 422; www.statravel.de; Germany) Also has offices in other countries.

**Voyageurs du Monde** ( ☎ 0892 688 363; www.vdm.com; France)

If you didn't come to West Africa on a return ticket, you can buy flights to any major European airport from most West African capital cities. The best places to try are Dakar and Abidjan, followed by Accra and possibly Bamako. Fares average from about US$750 but can be higher. For good places to buy tickets, see the individual country chapters.

## North America

The most reliable flights are those with Royal Air Maroc, which flies from New York to Abidjan, Bamako, Conakry, Dakar and Nouakchott, via Casablanca. Return prices range from US$1200 to US$1450. Air Sénégal International also has direct flights between New York and Dakar for a similar price. You may also find some flights between New York and Accra (Ghana Airways or American Airlines), while Continental Airlines have had a Newark–Lagos service planned since late 2004, but it has been repeatedly delayed by US air traffic authority restrictions.

From Canada, there are no direct flights to West Africa. You'll need to go via New York, or via London or another European capital.

Most travellers go via Europe – usually London or Paris. Fares on these tickets (from the east coast) start at about US$1000, with most closer to US$1300. If you can find a good deal on the transatlantic leg of the trip, it can be cheaper to buy one ticket to London, and then a separate, discounted ticket onwards from there.

**Council Travel** ( ☎ 800-226 8624; www.ciee.org; 205 E 42 St, New York, NY 10017), America's largest student travel organisation, has around 60 offices in the USA. Call the head office for the office nearest you or visit its website. **STA Travel** ( ☎ 800-777 0112; www.statravel.com) has offices in many major US cities; call the tollfree 800 number for office locations or visit its website. **Pan Express Travel** (www.panexpresstravel.com) is also worth trying.

**Travel CUTS** ( ☎ 800-667 2887; www.travelcuts.com) is Canada's national student travel agency and has offices in all major cities.

Some of the companies listed on p840 also sell flights.

---

**STARTING YOUR JOURNEY IN PARIS**

To an extent far greater than other colonial powers in Africa, France retains strong links with its former colonies. One of the benefits of this is that Paris has the best transport links (both in terms of coverage and price) to West Africa and is, therefore, the best starting point for your West African journey. Starting your journey in Paris can also have the advantage of allowing you to pick up hard-to-get visas as most Francophone West African countries who have few embassies around the world, certainly have one in Paris. And besides, there are worse places to wait for your passport to be returned or for your flight to leave.

---

In addition to the Internet, good places to start your search include the weekend editions of major newspapers such as the *New York Times* on the east coast, the *Los Angeles Times* or *San Francisco Examiner-Chronicle* on the west coast, the *Globe & Mail*, *Toronto Star* and *Vancouver Sun* in Canada, or in travel magazines for travel agents' advertisements.

## UK

Numerous airlines fly between Britain and West Africa, with the majority of flights connecting Anglophone countries, especially Ghana and Nigeria with British Airways, Ghana Airways, Ghana International Airways and KLM-Royal Dutch Airlines. If you want to avoid Lagos, British Airways flies into Abuja five times a week.

For connections to Francophone countries, Afriqiyah (via Tripoli), Cameroon Airlines, Ethiopian Airlines (via Addis Ababa) and Royal Air Maroc (via Casablanca) are often better, while TAP Air Portugal (via Lisbon) is good for Cape Verde and Guinea-Bissau.

Scheduled return flights from London to Dakar start at about UK£475, while London to Accra costs from UK£450 to UK£600 and London to Lagos about UK£500. With luck, you may occasionally find specials to any of these places from around UK£400. Low-season return fares between London and Abidjan or Bamako are around UK£450 to UK£575. During popular periods (such as peak tourist seasons or at busy holiday

times such as Christmas or the end of Ramadan), prices may rise by another UK£75 to UK£100.

Cheaper fares are available to Banjul on charter flights catering for package tourists. Flights go mostly from London, but there are also departures from regional airports. The leading charter flight and tour operator is the **Gambia Experience** ( ☎ 0845-3334567; www .gambia.co.uk). You can buy flight tickets directly from the operators or from many high street travel agents. Flight-only fares start at around UK£325 to UK£375, but some agents offer special deals that include accommodation – often in reasonable hotels – for only a little extra. Even if you don't stay in the hotel all the time, it can still be worth taking this offer; the airport transfers and first- or last-night bed can be very useful. You may also find charter flights heading to Ghana.

There are many travel agents competing for your business. London is usually the best place to buy a ticket, although there are specialist travel agents outside the capital. It's worth checking the ads in weekend newspapers or travel magazines, or in *Time Out*, but the following places are a starting point for discounted tickets. (Some of the agencies listed on p840 also sell tickets.)

**Africa Travel Centre** ( ☎ 0845 450 1520; www .africatravel.co.uk; 21 Leigh St, London WC1H 9EW)

**STA Travel** ( ☎ 020-7361 6142, 7581 4132; www .statravel.co.uk) Has offices throughout the country.

**Trailfinders** ( ☎ 020-7938 3939; www.trailfinders.co.uk) Has offices across the UK.

## LAND
### Border Crossings

If you're travelling independently overland to West Africa – whether cycling, driving your own car or taking public transport – you can approach the region from three main directions: from the north, across the Sahara; from the south and southeast, through the countries bordering southern and eastern Cameroon; or from the east, through Chad.

If you're coming from the north, the main border-crossing point into West Africa is just north of Nouâdhibou, via Morocco and the Western Sahara. There are also crossings at Bordj-Mokhtar and at Assamakka, where the trans-Saharan routes through Algeria enter Mali and Niger, respectively. For more information, see p838.

If you come into West Africa from the south or southeast, the main border-crossing points are at Garoua-Boulaï or Kenzou (for the Central African Republic); at Kousséri, Bongor or Léré (for Chad); Moloundou, in Cameroon's far southeastern corner (for Congo); Kye Ossi (for Gabon); and Ebebi-yin or Campo (for Equatorial Guinea). For more information, see p839.

Your final option is to come into West Africa from the east. In addition to the route from N'djaména (Chad) to Kousséri (Cameroon), from where you can then continue to Nigeria, or else head south into Cameroon, it's also possible to take the 'long way around', crossing the border on the northern side of Lake Chad, on the route to Nguigmi (Niger). For more information, see p838.

More details on the various border crossings are given in the Getting There & Away sections of the relevant country chapters.

## Car & Motorcycle

Driving your own car or motorbike to West Africa (and then around the region and possibly onwards to East or Southern Africa) is a vast subject beyond the scope of this book. Some recommended manuals covering this subject are listed following. These cover matters such as equipment, carnets, insurance, recommended routes, driving techniques, maintenance, repairs, navigation and survival. However, they are usually thin on practical information about places to eat and sleep (mainly because most overlanders use their vehicle as a mobile hotel) and on general background information about the country, including history, economy etc.

- *Adventure Motorcycling Handbook,* by Chris Scott, covers all parts of the world where tar roads end. It contains stacks of good information on the Sahara and West Africa, all combined with humour and personal insights.
- *Africa by Road,* by Bob Swain & Paula Snyder, is recommended once you're across the desert although it's many years out of date for the more practical information and on road conditions. Much of the no-nonsense detail on everything from paperwork and supplies to driving techniques still holds.
- *Sahara Overland,* by Chris Scott, is the finest, most recent and most comprehen-

sive book on all aspects of Saharan travel by two or four wheels, with information on established and newer routes (including those in Mauritania, Mali and Niger), and more than 100 maps. Chris Scott's highly recommended website, www .sahara-overland.com, has updates of the book, as well as letters from travellers and extensive related information.

- *The Sahara Handbook,* by Simon Glen, is an outdated but useful manual if you're coming to West Africa overland in your own vehicle. It concentrates on the Algerian routes (rather than the generally used Western Sahara route), it also includes coverage of the northern Sahel.

Anyone who is planning to take their own vehicle with them needs to check in advance what spare parts and petrol are likely to be available (see opposite). A number of documents are also required:

**Carnet** See opposite.

**Green card** Issued by insurers. Insurance for some countries is only obtainable at the border. Check with your insurance company or automobile association before leaving home. See opposite for further advice.

**International Driving Permit (IDP)** Although most foreign licences are acceptable in West African countries, an IDP issued by your local automobile association is highly recommended. For more information, see below.

**Vehicle registration documents** In addition to carrying all ownership papers, check with your insurer whether you're covered for the countries you intend to visit and whether third-party cover is included.

The documentation required when bringing your own vehicle to West Africa is covered in considerable detail in the specialist manuals listed on left. For some more tips on driving in the region in general, see p847.

### DRIVING LICENCE

To drive a car or motorbike in West Africa you will need a driving licence and, ideally, an International Driving Permit (IDP). If you intend to hire a car, you will need your driving licence and an IDP. IDPs are easy and cheap to get in your home country – they're usually issued by major motoring associations, such as the AA in Britain – and are useful if you're driving in countries where your own licence may not be recognised (officially or unofficially). They have the added advantage

---

## CARNETS

A *carnet de passage* is like a passport for your car, a booklet that is stamped on arrival and departure from a country to ensure that you export the vehicle again after you've imported it. It's usually issued by an automobile association in the country where the vehicle is registered. Most countries of West Africa require a carnet although rules change frequently.

The sting in the tail with a carnet is that you usually have to lodge a deposit to secure it. If you default on the carnet – that is, you don't have an export stamp to match the import one – then the country in question can claim your deposit, which can be up to 300% of the new value of the vehicle. You can get around this problem with bank guarantees or carnet insurance, but you still have to fork out in the end if you default.

Should the worst occur and your vehicle is irretrievably damaged in an accident or catastrophic breakdown, you'll have to argue it out with customs officials. Having a vehicle stolen can be even worse, as you may be suspected of having sold it.

The carnet may need to specify any pricey spare parts that you're planning to carry, such as a gearbox, which is designed to prevent any spare part importation rackets. Contact your local automobile association for details about necessary documentation at least three months in advance.

---

of being written in several languages, with a photo and many stamps, and so look more impressive when presented to car-rental clerks or policemen at road blocks.

### FUEL & SPARE PARTS

The quality, availability and price of fuel (petrol and diesel – called *essence* and *gasoil*, respectively, in the Francophone countries, *gasolina* and *diesel*, or sometimes *gasóleo*, in Lusophone countries) varies depending on where you are, and between rural and urban areas. Where taxation, subsidies or currency rates make petrol cheaper in one country than its neighbour, you'll inevitably find traders who've carried large drums across the border and sell 'black market' fuel at the roadside. However, watch out for fuel sold in plastic bags or small containers along the roadside. While sometimes it's fine, it's often diluted with water or kerosene.

African mechanics are masters of ingenuity, using endlessly recycled parts to coax life out of ageing machines that would have long ago been consigned to the scrap heap in the West. That said, they're often unable to help with newer-model vehicles – for these, either bring your own spare parts, or check with your manufacturer for a list of accredited parts suppliers in West Africa. Be warned, however, there may be very few of the latter and in some cases none at all.

### INSURANCE

Insurance is compulsory in most West African countries, and is highly advisable.

Given the large number of minor accidents, not to mention major ones, fully comprehensive insurance (as opposed to third party) is strongly advised, both for your own and any rental vehicle. Car-hire companies customarily supply insurance, but check carefully the cover and conditions.

Make certain that you're covered for off-piste travel, as well as travel between countries (if you're planning cross-border excursions). A locally acquired motorcycle licence is not valid under some policies.

In the event of an accident, make sure you submit the accident report as soon as possible to the insurance company or, if hiring, the car-hire company.

### SHIPPING A VEHICLE

If you want to travel in West Africa using your own car or motorbike, but don't fancy the Sahara crossing, another option is to ship it. The usual way of doing this is to load the car onto a ship in Europe and take it off again at either Dakar or Banjul (although Abidjan and Tema, in Ghana, are other options).

Costs start from US$500, but US$1000 is generally closer to the mark depending on the size of the vehicle and the final destination. Apart from cost, your biggest problem is likely to be security – many drivers report theft of items from the inside and outside (such as lights and mirrors) of their car. Vehicles are usually left unlocked for the crossing and when in storage at the destination port, so chain or lock all equipment into fixed boxes inside the vehicle. Getting a vehicle out of port is frequently a nightmare, requiring visits to several different offices where stamps must be obtained and mysterious fees paid at every turn. You could consider using an official handling agent or an unofficial 'fixer' to take your vehicle through all this.

## From Chad

If you're entering West Africa from Chad, the most arduous, if adventurous, route goes via Nguigmi in Niger. Unless you have your own vehicle, finding public transport on the Chadian side of the border can require extreme patience. From Nguigmi, weekly Landcruisers make the dusty day-long journey from Nguigmi to Mao in Chad. From Mao you may have to wait several days before you find something to get you to N'Djaména. For more information, see p617.

Between Cameroon and Chad, the main border crossing is between Maroua (Cameroon) and Kousséri, although the actual border is at Nguelé. Corrupt officials abound here. For more adventure, try the crossings further south to the towns of Bongor or Léré; the former requires a pirogue (dugout canoe) across the Logone River. For details see p225.

There are no official border crossings between Nigeria and Chad although the countries do share a short border. For transiting through Cameroon without the need for a visa, see p671).

## From the North – Crossing the Sahara

Three main routes cross the Sahara to West Africa: the Route du Hoggar (through Algeria and Niger); Route du Tanezrouft (through Algeria and Mali); and the Western Sahara Route (through Morocco and Western Sahara into Mauritania). A fourth option crosses between Libya and Niger via Bilma. For most of the past decade, the Tanezrouft and Hoggar routes have been unused by travellers due to the security situation in the region. The Hoggar route has begun to open up again, although the Western Sahara route remains the most popular overland way to travel to West Africa. With any of these routes, you'll need to get a thorough update on the security situation before setting off. Anybody planning to travel in the Sahara should check out the excellent website put together by Chris Scott, www.sahara-overland.com, as well as get some of the books recommended. Be

sure to bring sufficient food, water and warm clothes for the journey.

### ROUTE DU HOGGAR

The Route du Hoggar through Algeria and Niger is sealed, except for the 600km section between Tamanrasset ('Tam') and Arlit, although the road is in poor condition on many sections. The fabulous Hoggar Mountains and Aïr Mountains are worthy diversions, and the route passes several magnificent outcrops of wind-eroded rocks, while Agadez, at the end of the route, is one of the most interesting desert towns in West Africa.

The Route du Hoggar was passable as this book went to print, with access via Tunisia or from northern Algeria. The crossing is quite trouble-free, although if you don't have your own vehicle it involves hitching a ride in trucks or with travellers in their vehicles between Tamanrasset and Arlit, from where there are buses to Agadez. Few travellers make the journey in reverse, due in large part to the difficulty of getting an Algerian visa in Niger – Algerian visas and arrangements with an Algerian travel agency must have been made prior to reaching the border.

Travel in southern Algeria is increasingly popular, and northern Niger has stabilised somewhat. That said, a group of more than 30 Western tourists were kidnapped in the Algerian Sahara in 2003 and not released until months later in Mali; one woman died while held hostage. The situation remains fragile, and you should check out security issues and the route's current status before proceeding, especially if you plan on heading away from the main road into more remote areas. Banditry still occurs – a French tourist was killed near Agadez in November 2005 – but the stories are usually widely publicised in Agadez and, to a lesser extent, Tamanrasset, so keep your ear to the ground. Also, check in with the police before setting out, and where possible, avoid travelling at night.

### ROUTE DU TANEZROUFT

The Route du Tanezrouft runs through Algeria and Mali, via Adrar and the border at Bordj-Mokhtar, ending in Gao. It's technically easier than the Route du Hoggar. The dirt section is more than 1300km long and has a reputation for being a trail of unrelenting monotony, although some travellers find that the sheer size and remoteness of the desert is better appreciated here. Much of this is, however, theoretical because although the situation has stabilised somewhat in the region, the route is still considered dangerous and cannot be recommended. Help, should you need it, is likely to be a long time coming.

### WESTERN SAHARA ROUTE

Travel through Morocco is straightforward (see Lonely Planet's *Morocco* guide). About 500km south of Agadir you enter the disputed territory of Western Sahara, where the main road continues along the coast to Dakhla, from where it's another 460km to Nouâdhibou in Mauritania. In Dakhla, there are a few cheap hotels and a camp site (which also has some rooms) where all the overlanders stay. This is also the best place to find other travellers to team up with, or to look for a lift. If you're hitching, there's a thriving trade in second-hand cars being driven from Europe (especially France) to sell in West Africa, and these drivers are sometimes happy to pick up travellers, although sharing costs is expected. Use some care when finding a lift; hitchers are not always allowed in Mauritanian vehicles, and there have been occasional scams where hitchers with local drivers have been abandoned in the desert unless they pay a large 'fee'. Apart from hitching, there's no public transport along this route.

Until recently, all travel south of Dakhla needed to be done in a military convoy. Now, the convoy has been disbanded and it's possible to continue independently, though it's still advisable for vehicles (especially 2WDs) to go in a group. It's also now legal for travellers to go south to north, although most traffic continues to be in the other direction.

The road is now entirely sealed to Nouakchott, except for the 3km no-man's-land that separates the two border posts. In the border areas in particular, the area is littered with landmines, so stay on the main track. Coming from Morocco, you can buy the Mauritanian visa at the border (€20). Expect to pay about €20 for 'taxes'. Crossing the border is straightforward, although the currency declaration forms (which are officially no longer necessary) are sometimes asked for by officials, and, of course, if you can't present it, they will expect a small bribe. There are searches for alcohol at the Mauritanian bor-

der, and heavy fines if you are caught with it. After Mauritanian border formalities it's approximately 100km further to Nouâdhibou.

For more details on this route, see p575.

### From the South & Southeast

There are two main crossing points between Cameroon and the Central African Republic (CAR), but roads which are dire at the best of times are catastrophic in the rainy season. The standard route is via Garoua-Boulaï, which straddles the border. Buses and trucks go to Bangui, taking two days with an overnight in Bouar. An equally rough alternative is to go to Batouri further south and cross via Kenzou to Berbérati. For information on routes into CAR, see (p225)

The overland route to Congo is an epic journey traversing long, rutted tracks (which are almost impassable in the rainy season) through dense rainforest. The route goes via Yokadouma, Moloundou and on to the border crossing at Sokambo on the Ngoko River. After crossing the river, there's onward transport to Pokola, where you must register with the Congolese police, and Brazzaville. For more details, see p225.

The main border crossings into Equatorial Guinea and Gabon are a few kilometres from each other, accessible from the Cameroonian town of Amban. In Ambam the road splits, the easterly route heading for Bitam and Libreville (Gabon) and the westerly route heading for Ebebiyin and Bata (Equatorial Guinea). There's also a border crossing into Equatorial Guinea on the coast near Campo, but it's frequently closed and should not be relied on. See p225 for more detailed information.

## SEA

For most people, reaching West Africa by sea is not a viable consideration. The days of working your passage on commercial boats are long gone, although a few lucky travellers do manage to hitch rides on private yachts sailing from Spain, Morocco or the Canary Islands to Senegal, The Gambia and beyond.

Alternatively, several cargo shipping companies run from Europe to West Africa, with comfortable officer-style cabins available to the public. The main operator is **Grimaldi Freighter Cruises** ( ☎ 081-496 203; www .grimaldi-freightercruises.com; Via Marchese Campodisola

13, 80133 Naples, Italy), which has boats from Tilbury (London), Antwerp and elsewhere in Europe to Abidjan, Dakar, Douala, Cotonou, Tema (Ghana) and Lagos (though not all stops on all sailings), and one route from Antwerp to Brazil via Dakar.

Prices vary depending on the quality of the ship and on the cabin (inside cabins are cheaper), but expect to pay from US$1250 per person one way between Europe and Dakar in a double cabin. A typical voyage from London takes about eight days to Dakar and 13 days to Abidjan. There's a full list of Europe-wide ticket agents on the Grimaldi website, while in the UK you could also contact **Strand Voyages** ( ☎ 020-7766 8220; www.strandtravel.co.uk; 1 Adam St, London WC2N 6AB).

Also worth checking out in the USA is **Freighter Travel** (www.freightertravel.info) which has routes operated by other lines.

For further information, *Travel by Cargo Ship*, a handy book by Hugo Verlomme, and *Cargo Ship Cruising*, by Robert Kane, are both worth seeking out, although they're almost a decade old.

There are no organised passenger services by boat between Cameroon and Equatorial Guinea or Gabon, although ad hoc transport can sometimes be arranged to Malabo from Limbe; for further details see p226.

## TOURS

Two main sorts of tour are available. On an overland tour, you go from Europe to West Africa by land, visiting several countries along the way. Most are anywhere between two and six months long. On an inclusive tour you fly to your destination and spend two to three weeks in a single country. Between these two types is the option of joining an overland tour for a short section (usually three to five weeks), flying out and back at either end. In addition to the tours listed here, some of the specialist travel agents listed on p833 can be of assistance.

### Inclusive Tours

This type of tour includes your international flight, transport around the country, food, accommodation, excursions, local guide and so on. They are usually around two to three weeks long, and ideal if you want to visit West Africa, but lack the time or inclination for long-distance overland trucks or to organise things yourself.

The number of inclusive tour companies operating in West Africa is much smaller than in East or Southern Africa, but there's still a fair selection. As with flights and overland tours, a good place to look is the advertisements in the weekend newspapers and travel magazines. Several companies are listed following, but this list is not exhaustive.

### AUSTRALASIA & CANADA

**Fresh Tracks** ( ☎ 800-690 4859; www.freshtracks.com) Canadian company.

**Peregrine Adventures** ( ☎ 03-9662 2700; www.peregrineadventures.com) Australian company offering tours to Mali.

### FRANCE & SPAIN

**Explorator** ( ☎ 01 53 45 85 85; www.explorator.fr) Destinations include the Sahara region, Senegal, The Gambia and Mali.

**Montañas del Mundo** ( ☎ 96 373 0067; www.montanasdelmundo.es) Valencia-based company.

**Nouvelles Frontières** ( ☎ 0825 000 744; www.nouvelles-frontieres.fr) Branches in France and French-speaking countries offering a wide range of mainstream holidays and adventurous tours to Senegal, Mali and Burkina Faso.

**Point Afrique** ( ☎ 01 44 88 58 39; www.point-afrique.com) Excellent tours across the region where no-one else goes and cheap charter flights.

**Terres d'Aventure** ( ☎ 0825 847 800; www.terdav.com) Adventurous trips in West Africa and the Sahara region, including Senegal and Mauritania.

**Voyageurs en Afrique** ( ☎ 0892 239 494; www.vdm.com) Worldwide tour company with tours across West Africa, including Mali, Guinea, Senegal and Mauritania.

### UK

**Batafon Arts** ( ☎ 01273-605791; www.batafonarts.co.uk) Dance and percussion courses/tours in Guinea and The Gambia.

**Explore Worldwide** ( ☎ 0870-333 4001; www.explore.co.uk; 1 Frederick St, Aldershot GU11 1LQ) Well-established company offering a wide range of adventurous and active tours and treks.

**Gambia Experience** ( ☎ 0845-3334567; www.gambia.co.uk) Leading operator of package holidays to The Gambia, with some options in Senegal, plus a selection of specialist birding, fishing and cultural tours; sells excellent-value charter flights.

**Guerba** ( ☎ 01373-826611; www.guerba.com) Offers tours to Mali and Niger.

**Karamba Experience** ( ☎ 01263-735097; www.karamba.co.uk) Holidays in Senegal, The Gambia and Ghana concentrating on learning to play drums and other African instruments.

**Limosa Holidays** ( ☎ 01263-578143; www.limosaholi days.co.uk) Specialist birding trips, including The Gambia, Cape Verde and Senegal.

**Naturetrek** ( ☎ 01962-733051; www.naturetrek.co.uk) Bird and wildlife specialists offering tours in Mali and The Gambia.

**Tim Best Travel** ( ☎ 020-7591 0300; www.timbest travel.co.uk) Recommended and experienced company that can take you to Niger and Mali (including the Festival in the Desert in January).

**Wildwings** ( ☎ 0117-965 8333; www.wildwings.co.uk; 577-579 Fishponds Rd, Bristol BS16 3AF) Birding and wild-life specialists; expeditions and tours worldwide, including Cameroon and The Gambia.

### USA

**Access Africa** ( ☎ 212-368 6561; www.accessafrica .com) Tours to most countries in the region, including Mali, Cameroon, Nigeria, Ghana and Senegal.

**Adventure Center** ( ☎ 510-654 1879; www.adventure center.com) Multicountry tours, as well as those tailored to Mali, Mauritania, The Gambia, Senegal and Ghana.

**Africa Desk** ( ☎ 301-591 0923; www.africadesk.com) Tours to many countries in the region.

**Born Free Safaris** ( ☎ 800-372 3274; www.bornfree safaris.com) Tours to Ghana, Senegal, The Gambia, Mali and Benin.

**Mountain Travel-Sobek** ( ☎ 510-549 6000; www .mtsobek.com) Two- to three-week tours in Mali, Burkina Faso, Ghana, Togo and Benin.

**Museum for African Art** ( ☎ 718-784 7700; www .africanart.org) Cultural tours.

**Spector Travel** ( ☎ 617-351 0111; www.spectortravel .com) An Africa specialist, with tours to Mali, The Gambia, Senegal, Cameroon and elsewhere in the region.

**Turtle Tours** ( ☎ 888-299 1439; www.turtletours.com) Tours for individuals and small groups in Mauritania, Mali and Niger and other countries in the region.

**Wilderness Travel** ( ☎ 800-368 2794; www.wilder nesstravel.com) Trips to Niger, Mali, Burkina Faso and Ghana.

## Overland Tours

For these trips, you travel in an 'overland truck' with about 15 to 28 other people, a couple of drivers/leaders, plus tents and other equipment. Food is bought along the way and the group cooks and eats together. Most of the hassles (such as border crossings) are taken care of by the leader. Disadvantages include a fixed itinerary and the possibility of spending a long time with other people in relatively close confines. Having said that, overland truck tours are extremely popular.

The overland-tour market is dominated by British companies, although passengers come from many parts of the world. Most tours start in London and travel to West Africa via Europe and Morocco. Tours can be 'slow' or 'fast', depending on the number of places visited along the way. For those with limited time, most overland companies arrange shorter trips – for example London to Banjul or Dakar. For those with more time, there's also the option to do the West Africa trip as part of a longer trans-Africa trip to or from Nairobi or Harare. Most overland companies can arrange your flights to join and leave the tour.

Among the UK-based overland tour companies offering trips in West Africa are the following:

**Dragoman** ( ☎ 0870-4994475; www.dragoman.co.uk)
**Oasis Overland** ( ☎ 01963-363400; www.oasisover land.com)

# GETTING AROUND

This chapter outlines the various ways of travelling around West Africa. For more details see the Getting There & Away and Getting Around sections of the Directory in each individual country chapter.

## AIR

West Africa is an enormous area, and if your time is limited, a few flights around the region can considerably widen your options. For those who are on tight schedules, flying can save hours or days, even within a country.

Although the airports in capital cities are large and cavernous (and occasionally even modern), some smaller West African airports are little more than single-shed terminals. At all of them, don't be surprised if you spend half a day at check-in (bring a good book).

### Airlines in West Africa

There's not always a lot of choice for getting around West Africa by air, with only two or three airlines operating between most major cities. Regional airlines that enjoy the most extensive networks are Air Sénégal International and, to a lesser extent, Air Burkina. Air Mauritanie and Cameroon Airlines also fly to a number of airports but their safety record is not what it could be. Ghana Airways is notorious for cancellations and delays.

Reputable travel agents throughout the region (see the individual country chapters) can sometimes also find tickets for international airlines (especially Afriqiyah and Air France) as they hop between West African cities as part of their intercontinental routes. Point Afrique is also talking of starting a cut-price Bamako–Dakar route, although this was yet to begin at the time of writing.

For a full list of airlines that fly to West Africa, see p830. Of these, Afriqiyah, Air Burkina, Air Ivoire, Cameroon Airlines, Ghana Airways, Air Sénégal International and Virgin Nigeria all operate flights within West Africa, whether within individual countries or between the countries of the region.

Other airlines that also operate 'domestic' West African services (again, either within or between West African countries) include the following:

**Aero** (AJ; ☎ 496 1340 in Nigeria; www.acn.aero) Hub: Lagos. Domestic Nigerian airline.

**Air CM** ( ☎ 01 53 41 00 50 in France; www.aircm.com) Has a twice weekly connection between Paris and the Cap and plenty of good package deals.

**Air Niamey** Hub: Niamey.

**Air Saint Louis** ( ☎ 644 8629; www.airsaintlouis.com) Hub: Dakar. Flights from Dakar to Saint-Louis.

**Antrak** ( ☎ 769458 in Ghana; www.antrak-gh.net) Hub: Accra. Domestic Ghanaian airline that also flies to Ouagadougou and Lagos.

**Bellview** (B3; www.flybellviewair.com) Hub: Lagos. Domestic Nigerian airline that also flies to Cotonou, Accra, Freetown, Banjul, Abidjan and Dakar.

**Benin Golf Air** (A8; www.beningolfair.com) Hub: Cotonou.

**Chanchangi Airlines** (3U; www.chanchangi-airlines .com) Hub: Lagos. Domestic Nigerian Airline.

**Hôtel Kalissai** ( ☎ 994 8600; www.kalissai.com) Arranges flights from the aerodrome in Abéné to Dakar

---

## CHECKING IN

In many West African cities, check-in procedures are as much of an adventure as the flight itself. Conakry wins our vote as the airport with the most disorganised and chaotic check-in procedures, but every traveller probably has their own 'favourites'. Lagos is another notorious one. The fun starts from the moment you enter the airport. Underpaid security personnel, in an effort to subsidise their meagre incomes, often view the baggage check procedures as a chance to elicit bribes from tourists. After searching your bag, they will ask what you might have for them or, alternatively, try to convince you that you've violated some regulation. Be compliant with requests to open your baggage, be friendly and respectful, smile a lot, and you should soon be on your way. Also remember that, in some cases, officials may search your bag out of genuine curiosity so put your dirty underwear on top and watch their interest evaporate.

After getting past the initial baggage check, you'll need to join the fray by the check-in counter. While some places have lines, many don't – just a sweaty mass of people, all waving their tickets and talking loudly to a rather beleaguered-looking check-in clerk. Although everyone with a confirmed ticket usually gets on the flight, confirmed passengers are 'bumped' just frequently enough to cause many people, locals and foreigners alike, to panic and lose all sense and civility when it seems there may not be enough seats to go around. The West African answer to this situation is the 'fixer' – enterprising locals who make their living by getting people smoothly checked in and through other formalities such as customs and airport tax. Sometimes they practically see you into your seat – all for fees ranging from a dollar or two up to about US$10. If you don't have a confirmed booking, the fee may be more, as some money has to go to the boarding pass clerk.

Without the services of a fixer, the best strategy for avoiding the chaotic scene is to arrive early at the airport – ideally at the start of the official reporting time or earlier. This way, you also have a better chance of getting a confirmed seat if too many 'confirmed' tickets have been sold.

Once you have your boarding pass in hand, there's usually a second luggage inspection as you pass from the check-in terminal to the waiting area. Then it's just a matter of waiting. Have a good book with you, or a pen and paper for catching up on correspondence, and perhaps a few pieces of fruit. Don't schedule any other critical plans for the day (especially connecting flights), and try to calm any frustration you may feel by remembering that by West African standards you're one of a privileged few who have the financial resources to even contemplate flying – and that your journey would be several days to several weeks longer via bush taxi, and much more uncomfortable.

**Senegalair Avion Taxis** ( ☎ 821 3425) Flies mainly to Simenti in Parc National du Niokolo-Koba, though they can also arrange flights elsewhere.

**Slok Air** (SO; www.slokairinternational.com) Hub: Banjul. Gambian airline that connects Banjul with Dakar, Freetown, Monrovia, Accra, Conakry, Abidjan & Cotonou.

**Sophia Airlines** ( ☎ 34-713434 in Côte d'Ivoire) Hub: Abidjan. Domestic Ivorian airline.

**Sosoliso** (SO; www.sosoliso.airline.com) Hub: Lagos. Domestic Nigerian Airline.

Air safety is a major concern in West Africa and a spate of accidents (especially in Nigeria) means that you should always be wary of the region's local airlines, particularly the smaller operators. For more details on the air safety record of individual airlines, see www.airsafe.com/index.html.

### Tickets

Because of the long distances, fares within West Africa are not cheap. Flying from Dakar (Senegal) to Abidjan (Côte d'Ivoire), for example, is equivalent to flying halfway across the USA. Some sample one-way fares are: Dakar to Bamako in Mali (about 500km) US$157; Banjul (The Gambia) to Accra in Ghana (about 1000km) US$355; and Abidjan to Douala (about 1500km) US$415. Return fares are usually double the one-way fares, though less expensive excursion fares are occasionally available, as are youth or student fares. For comprehensive information on flying from specific West African cities, see the Transport sections in the individual country chapters.

Once you've bought your ticket, reconfirm your reservation several times at least, especially if the airline you're flying with has a less-than-stellar reputation for reliability. After the flight, if you checked luggage, hold on to your baggage claim ticket until you've exited the baggage claim area at your destination, as you'll often be required to show it.

### BICYCLE

While cycling isn't exactly common in West Africa, there is a small but steady number of travellers who visit the region on bicycle. As long as you have sufficient time, and a willingness to rough things, cycling is an excellent way to get to know West Africa, as you'll often stay in small towns and villages, interact more with the local people without vehicle windows and other barriers

between you, and eat West African food more frequently.

Because of the distances involved, you'll need to plan your food and water needs in advance, and pay careful attention to choosing a route in order to avoid long stretches of semidesert, areas with no villages or heavily travelled roads. In general, cycling is best well away from urban areas, and in the early morning and late afternoon hours. When calculating your daily distances, plan on taking a break during the hottest midday period, and don't count on covering as much territory each day as you might in a northern European climate. Countries that are particularly good for cycling include southern Senegal, The Gambia, southern Ghana, Togo and Benin; in all, distances between major points of interest are fairly manageable.

Mountain bikes are most suitable for cycling in West Africa, and will give you the greatest flexibility in setting your route. While heavy, single-speed bicycles can be rented in many towns (and occasionally mountain bikes), they're not good for anything other than short local rides, so you should plan on bringing your own bicycle into the country if you will be riding extended distances. To rent a bike locally, ask staff at hotels, or inquire at bicycle repair stands (every town market has one).

Apart from water, your main concern is likely to be motorists. Cyclists are regarded as 2nd-class citizens in West Africa, even more than they are in Western countries, so make sure you know what's coming up behind you and be prepared to take evasive action onto the verge, as local cyclists are often forced to do. A small rear-view mirror will well worth considering, especially if you'll be cycling in urban areas or along heavily travelled roads.

In the region, the best time to cycle is in the cooler, dry period from mid-October to February. Even so, you'll need to work out a way to carry at least 4L of water, and you'll also need to carry a water filter and purifier. If you get tired, or simply want to cut out the boring bits, bikes can easily be carried on bush taxis, though you'll likely want to carry some rags to wrap around the gearing for protection. You'll need to pay a luggage fee for this, but it shouldn't be more than one-third to one-half the price of the journey.

Wherever you go, be prepared to be met with great local curiosity (as well as much goodwill). As in most places in the world, don't leave your bike unattended for any lengthy period of time unless it's locked, and try to secure the main removable pieces. Taking your bike into your hotel room, should you decide to take a break from camping, is generally no problem (and is a good idea). If you're camping near settlements in rural areas, ask the village headman each night where you can stay. Even if you don't have a tent, he'll find you somewhere to sleep.

You'll need to carry sufficient spares, and be proficient at repairs. In particular, punctures will be frequent. Take at least four spare inner tubes, some tyre repair material and a spare tyre. Consider the number of tube patches you might need, square it, and pack those too. Some people don't like them, but we've found inner-tube protectors indispensable for minimising punctures.

A highly recommended contact is **Bicycle Africa** ( ☎ /fax 1-206-767-0848; www.ibike.org/bikeafrica; 4887 Columbia Drive South, Seattle, WA98108-1919, USA), which is part of the International Bicycle Fund, a low-budget, socially conscious organisation that arranges tours in some West African countries, provides fact sheets and posts letters from travellers who've travelled by bike in the area. Another useful resource is the **Cyclists' Touring Club** (CTC; ☎ 01483-417 217; www.ctc.org.uk), a UK-based organisation which offers good tips and information sheets on cycling in different parts of the world.

## Transporting your Bicycle

If you're planning to bring your bike with you on the plane to West Africa, some airlines ask that you partially dismantle it and put the pieces in a large bag or box. Bike boxes are available at some airports. Otherwise, you can arrange one in advance with your local bicycle shop. To fit it in the box, you'll usually need to take off (or turn) the handlebars, pedals and seat, and will need to deflate the tyres. Some airlines don't charge, while others (including many charter airlines) may levy an extra fee – usually about US$50 – because bike boxes are not standard size. Some airlines are willing to take your bike 'as is' – you can just wheel it to the check-in desk – although here, too, you'll still need to partially deflate the tyres, and usually also tie the handlebars into the frame. Check with the airline in advance about what their regulations are. If you don't want to be bothered

with transport, and have plenty of time, you can also cycle to West Africa from Europe, coming down through Morocco and Mauritania, but this is a major undertaking.

## BOAT

At several points along the West African coast you can travel by boat, either on a large passenger vessel or by local canoe. Some of the local canoe trips are definitely of the informal variety, and many are dangerous. Countries where ferries provide an important means of coastal transport include Sierra Leone (p771), Liberia (p481) and Guinea-Bissau (p461).

There are two ferries a week between Limbe (Cameroon) and Calabar (Nigeria). Decidedly dodgy speed boats also make the trip, see p671). Other places where you can cross international borders by boat are by barge from Guinea to Mali (p437), from Kamsar (Guinea) to Bissau (p437) and, once it resumes services, by ferry between Conakry (Guinea) and Freetown (Sierra Leone; p771).

On most major rivers in the region, pirogues, *pinasses* (larger motorised boats, carrying cargo and anything from 10 to 100 passengers) and/or public ferries serve towns and villages along the way, and can be an excellent way to see the country. Some involve a simple river crossing, others can be a longer expedition where you sleep by the riverbank. One of the most popular boat trips for travellers is along the Niger River in Mali, especially between Mopti and Timbuktu. For more information on Niger River trips, see p510 and p545. Other riverboat options exist, for example along the Gambia and Senegal rivers. Remember that many such journeys are only possible at certain times of the year (usually August to December) when water levels are still high enough after the rains.

Whether you're renting a pirogue or *pinasse*, or taking a public ferry, make sure what food and water is included in the price you pay and it's always worth taking more just in case. On some journeys, you'll often be able to buy snacks and fruit along the way. Also bring something to protect yourself from the sun, as few boats have any shade, and something to waterproof your gear. Avoid getting on boats that are overloaded, or setting off when the weather is bad, especially on sea routes in coastal areas.

## BUS

Long-distance buses (sometimes called a 'big bus' or *grand car*, to distinguish it from a minibus) vary in size – from 35 to 70 seats – and services vary between countries and areas. On the main routes buses are good quality, with a reliable service and fixed departure times (although arrival times may be more fluid depending on anything from checkpoints and breakdowns to the number of towns they stop in along the way).

On quiet roads in rural areas, buses may be decrepit, and may frequently breakdown and regularly stop. These buses have no timetable, and usually go when full or when the driver feels like it. They are usually very overcrowded. In contrast, with some of the better lines on major routes, where the one-person-per-seat rule is usually respected. Generally, bus fares are cheaper than bush taxi fares for a comparable route and are usually quicker.

You may arrange a long ride by bus (or bush taxi), and find yourself transferring to another vehicle somewhere along the way. There's no need to pay more – your driver pays your fare directly to the driver of the next vehicle – but unfortunately it can mean long waits while the arrangements are made.

### Reservations

On some main-route buses, you can reserve in advance, which is advisable. In some countries you book a place but not a specific seat. Just before the bus leaves, names get called out in the order that tickets were bought, and you get on and choose the seat you want. Seats to the front tend to be better ventilated and more comfortable. If you suffer from motion sickness, try to get a seat towards the front or in the middle. Whichever end of the bus you sit in, it's worth trying to get a seat on the side that will be away from direct sunlight for most of the journey.

## CAR & MOTORCYCLE

For advice on the necessary documentation and insurance that you'll need if you're bringing your own vehicle to West Africa, general information on shipping your vehicle to West Africa and the availability of fuel and spare parts in the region, see p836.

### Hire

There are car rental agencies in most capital cities and tourist areas. Most international companies (Hertz, Avis, etc) are represented, plus smaller independent operators, but renting is invariably expensive – you can easily spend in one day what you'd pay for a week's rental in Europe or the USA. If the small operators charge less, it's usually because the vehicles are older and sometimes not well maintained. But it can simply be because their costs are lower and they can do a better deal, so if you have the time, check around for bargains. You will need to put down a large deposit (credit cards are usually, but not always good for this).

It's very unlikely you'll be allowed to take a rental car across a border, but if you are (for example from The Gambia into Senegal), make sure the paperwork is valid. If you're uncertain about driving, most companies provide a chauffeur at very little extra cost, and with many, a chauffeur is mandatory. In many cases it's cheaper to go with a chauffeur as you will pay less for insurance. It's also prudent, as getting stuck on your own is no fun and chauffeurs generally know the intricacies of checkpoint etiquette.

In tourist areas, such as The Gambia and Senegal, and in some parts of Mali and Burkina Faso, it's possible to hire mopeds and motorbikes. In most other countries there is no formal rental available, but if you want to hire a motorbike (and know how to ride one) you can arrange something by asking at an auto parts shop or repair yard, or by asking at the reception of your hotel. You can often be put in touch with someone who doesn't mind earning some extra cash by renting out their wheels for a day or two. Remember, though, that matters such as insurance will be easily overlooked, which is fine until you have an accident and find yourself liable for all bills. Also, if you do this, be sure to check out the motorbike in advance to see that it's in acceptable mechanical condition.

### Road Rules

The most important thing to be aware of is that throughout West Africa traffic drives on the right – as in continental Europe and the USA – even in countries that have a British colonial heritage (such as The Gambia).

## HITCHING

In many countries, as you venture further into rural areas, the frequency of buses or bush taxis drops – sometimes to nothing. Then the

**TRANSPORT IN WEST AFRICA**

## ROAD DISTANCES (KM)

| | Abidjan (Côte d'Ivoire) | Accra (Ghana) | Bamako (Mali) | Banjul (The Gambia) | Bissau (Guinea-Bissau) | Conakry (Guinea) | Cotonou (Benin) | Dakar (Senegal) | Freetown (Sierra Leone) | Lagos (Nigeria) | Lomé (Togo) | Monrovia (Liberia) | Niamey (Niger) | Nouakchott (Mauritania) | Ouagadougou (Burkina Faso) | Praia (Cape Verde) |
|---|---|---|---|---|---|---|---|---|---|---|---|---|---|---|---|---|
| Accra (Ghana) | 560 | | | | | | | | | | | | | | | |
| Bamako (Mali) | 1160 | 1710 | | | | | | | | | | | | | | |
| Banjul (The Gambia) | 2490 | 3210 | 1340 | | | | | | | | | | | | | |
| Bissau (Guinea-Bissau) | 2180 | 2900 | 1460 | 310 | | | | | | | | | | | | |
| Conakry (Guinea) | 1700 | 2260 | 920 | 1230 | 980 | | | | | | | | | | | |
| Cotonou (Benin) | 910 | 360 | 2020 | 3360 | 3110 | 2610 | | | | | | | | | | |
| Dakar (Senegal) | 2790 | 3350 | 1420 | 300 | 585 | 1530 | 3360 | | | | | | | | | |
| Freetown (Sierra Leone) | 1590 | 2090 | 1210 | 1440 | 1190 | 320 | 2440 | 1740 | | | | | | | | |
| Lagos (Nigeria) | 1030 | 480 | 2140 | 3480 | 3230 | 2730 | 120 | 3560 | 2560 | | | | | | | |
| Lomé (Togo) | 760 | 200 | 1870 | 3220 | 2970 | 2460 | 160 | 3290 | 2290 | 280 | | | | | | |
| Monrovia (Liberia) | 1020 | 1520 | 1040 | 1860 | 1610 | 740 | 1870 | 2160 | 570 | 1990 | 1720 | | | | | |
| Niamey (Niger) | 1570 | 1390 | 1410 | 2750 | 2880 | 2320 | 1040 | 2740 | 2900 | 1160 | 1190 | 2330 | | | | |
| Nouakchott (Mauritania) | 2800 | 3360 | 1650 | 870 | 1180 | 2100 | 3670 | 570 | 2320 | 3790 | 3560 | 2730 | 3050 | | | |
| Ouagadougou (Burkina Faso) | 1070 | 970 | 900 | 2240 | 2360 | 1820 | 1120 | 2240 | 2400 | 1240 | 1240 | 1830 | 500 | 3830 | | |
| Praia (Cape Verde) | 3140 | 3860 | 2420 | 1270 | 960 | 1880 | 4070 | 680 | 2150 | 4190 | 4190 | 2570 | 3830 | 1250 | 2860 | |
| Yaoundé (Cameroon) | 2650 | 2100 | 3760 | 4410 | 4160 | 4350 | 1740 | 4670 | 4120 | 1620 | 1620 | 3610 | 2090 | 5240 | 2860 | 5120 |

### CAR HIRE, CHICKENS & OTHER HAZARDS OF THE ROAD

If you've never driven in a developing country before, hiring a self-drive car is not something to be undertaken lightly. Road conditions outside the capital are bad and, apart from potholes and the inevitable chickens, dangers include people and cows and other animals moving into your path. Keep in mind that many locals have not driven themselves, and are thus not aware of braking distances and similar concepts. Smaller roads are not sealed, so you need to be able to drive on dirt (and sometimes on sand). One of the biggest hazards is overtaking blind or on curves. Moderate your speed accordingly, and when going around curves or blind spots, be prepared to react to oncoming vehicles in your lane. If you see some branches in the road, it's usually a sign that there is a problem or a stopped vehicle in the road ahead, so you'll need to go slow.

There are very few signposts, so you should take a map and be able to read it. Remember, however, that roads get washed away in the rainy seasons and what looks like a fine piece of tarmac on paper may not correspond with reality. Also, outside capital cities, phones are few and far between, should you need to contact your rental company in case of a breakdown, and cellular telephone networks often don't reach rural areas.

Throughout the region, driving at night is unsafe; try to avoid doing so. If you do need to drive in the dark, be particularly alert for vehicles stopped in the roadway with no lights or hazard warnings. Basic mechanical knowledge – at the very least being able to change a wheel – is very useful. It's almost always best to take a local chauffeur along. In addition to having mechanical knowledge, and (usually) knowledge of the route, they can often be helpful as translators.

---

only way around is to ride on local trucks, as the locals do. A 'fare' is payable to the driver, so in cases like this the line between hitching and public transport is blurred – but if it's the only way to get around, you don't have a choice anyway. Usually you'll be riding on top of the cargo – it may be cotton or rice in sacks, which are quite comfy, but it might be logs or oil drums, which aren't.

If you want to hitch because there's no public transport leaving imminently from the *gare routière*, you'll normally have to go well beyond the town limits, as bush taxi drivers may take umbrage at other vehicles 'stealing' their customers. Even so, you'll probably still have to pay for your lift – but at least you'll get moving more quickly.

Hitching in the Western sense (ie because you don't want to get the bus, or more specifically because you don't want to pay) is also possible, but may take a long time. The only people giving free lifts are likely to be foreign expatriates, volunteer aid workers, or the occasional well-off local (very few West Africans own a car).

Most people with space in their car want payment – usually on a par with what a bus would have cost. The most common vehicles for lifts of this sort are driven by locals working for international agencies, government bodies or aid and relief organisations; all over West Africa you'll see smart Land Cruisers with words and badges on the doors (eg Unesco, Ministry of Energy or MSF), never more than a few years old, always going too fast, and always full of people. But if you've been waiting all day and one of these stops for you, you'll probably get in, however uncomfortable you may feel about it.

That said, as in any other part of the world, hitching or accepting lifts is never entirely safe, and we don't recommend it. Travellers who decide to hitch should understand that they are taking a small but potentially serious risk. If you're planning to travel this way, take advice from other hitchers (locals or travellers) first. Hitching in pairs is obviously safer, and hitching through less salubrious suburbs, especially at night, is asking for trouble. Throughout most of the region, women should avoid hitching alone.

## LOCAL TRANSPORT

The most common forms of public transport in West Africa are bus (*car* in some Francophone countries) and bush taxi *(taxi brousse)*. Buses may be run by state-owned or private companies, but bush taxis are always private, although the driver is rarely the owner of the vehicle. Vehicles are usually located at bus and bush taxi parks, called *gare routière* or sometimes *autogare* in Francophone countries, 'garage', 'lorry park' or 'motor park'

## ROAD SAFETY

Road safety (together with malaria) is probably your biggest safety risk in West Africa. Bush taxi drivers, in particular, race along at hair-raising speeds and overtake blind to reach their destination before another car can get in front of them in the queue for the return journey. Drivers can be sleepy from a long day, and drink-driving is a problem. Travelling early in the morning is one step you can take to cut the risk, as drivers are fresher and roads less travelled. Avoid night travel at all costs. If you are in a vehicle and feel unsafe, if it's a heavily travelled route, you can take your chances and get out at a major station to switch to another car (though don't expect a refund, and the second vehicle may not be much better). You can complain about dangerous driving, but this usually doesn't have any effect and, unless things are really out of control, you'll seldom get support from the others. Saying that you're feeling sick seems to get better results. Drivers are often quite considerate to ill or infirm passengers and, in any case, seem to care more about keeping vomit off their seats than about dying under the wheels of an oncoming lorry. You might be able to rally other passengers to your side this way as well. Most locals take a stoic approach to the situation, with many viewing accidents as a matter of the will of God or Allah. (This explains slogans such as 'Allahu Akhbar' painted on vehicles – probably in the belief that a bit of extra help from above might see the vehicle through the day's runs.) Drivers seem to discredit the idea that accidents are in any way related to vehicle speed or condition, or to wild driving practices.

in English-speaking countries and *paragem* in Portuguese-speaking countries. The *gare routière* or motor park is usually (though not always) in the centre of town, near the market. Most large cities have several *gares routières*, one for each main direction or destination and may be located on the road out of town headed in that direction.

In some countries, buses are common for intercity routes and bush taxis are hard to find; in other countries it's the reverse. Either way, travel generally costs between US$1 and US$2 per 100km, although fares depend on the quality of the vehicle and the route. On routes between countries (eg between Ouagadougou in Burkina Faso and Bamako in Mali), costs can be more because drivers have to pay additional fees (official and unofficial) to cross the border. You can save a bit of money by taking one vehicle to the border and then another on the other side, but this can considerably prolong the trip.

In many countries, transport fares are fixed by the government, so the only way the bush taxi drivers can earn a bit more is to charge for luggage. Local people accept this, so travellers should too, unless of course it is unreasonable. The fee for a medium-sized rucksack is around 10% of the fare. Small bags will be less, and are often not charged at all. If you think you're being overcharged, ask other passengers, out of earshot of the driver. Once you know the proper rate, bargaining will be easy and the price should soon fall.

## Bus

Within some capital cities, you may find well-developed city bus and minibus networks connecting the city centre and suburbs. In most other cities, it's minibuses only.

## Bush Taxi

A bush taxi is effectively a small bus. Almost without exception, bush taxis leave when full of passengers, not according to any timetable that a non-African would recognise. As soon as one car leaves, the next one starts to fill. Depending on the popularity of the route, the car may take half an hour or several days to fill. Either way, drivers jealously guard their car's place in the queue.

Early customers can choose where to sit. Latecomers get no choice and are assigned to the least comfortable seats – usually at the back, where the seating is cramped and stuffy, seat springs work their way into any orifice and window-winders jam into knees. If you have a choice, the best seats are those in the front, near the window. Some travellers prefer the very front, though you're first in line if there's a collision. Better is the row behind the driver, near a window (ideally one that works), and preferably on the side with more shade during the journey.

If a bush taxi looks like it's going to get uncomfortably full you can always buy two seats for yourself – it's simply double the price. Likewise, if you want to charter the whole car, take the price of one seat and multiply it by the number available. Occasionally you may also need to add a bit more for luggage, although in our experience this is rarely requested for charters.

If a group of passengers has been waiting a long time, and there are only two or three seats to fill, they may club together and pay extra so as to get moving. If you do this, don't expect a discount because you're saving the driver the hassle of looking for other passengers – time ain't money in Africa. If you pick up someone along the way, however, the fare they pay goes to the passengers who bought the seats, not to the driver.

The best time by far to catch bush taxis is early morning; after that, you may have difficulty finding vehicles on many routes. Sometimes, however, departures are determined by market days, in which case afternoon may be best.

There are three main types of bush taxi in West Africa, as follows.

### MINIBUS

Some routes are served by minibuses (minicars) – usually seating about 12 to 20 passengers. In some countries these are just large bush taxis, while in others they fill a category between bus and bush taxi. They're typically about 25% cheaper than Peugeot 504s, and sometimes more comfortable, depending on how full they are. They're also slower and tend to stop more, and police checks at roadblocks take longer to negotiate because there are more passengers to search.

### PEUGEOT TAXI

Peugeot 504s, assembled in Nigeria or imported from Europe, are used all over West Africa and are also called cinq-cent-quatre, Peugeot taxi, sept place and brake. With three rows of seats, they're built to take the driver plus seven passengers. In some countries this limit is observed. In others it's flagrantly flaunted. All 504s in Mali, for example, take the driver plus nine passengers. In Guinea you might be jammed in with at least a dozen adults, plus children and bags, with more luggage and a couple of extra passengers riding on the roof. That these cars do hundreds of thousands of kilometres on some of the worst roads in the world is a credit to the manufacturer and the ingenuity of local mechanics.

While some drivers are safe and considerate, others verge on insanity. Some cars are

relatively new (there are quite a few Peugeot 505s, the later model, around these days) and well maintained, with comfortable seats. Others are very old, reduced to nothing more than chassis, body and engine: there's more weld than original metal, tyres are bald, most upholstery is missing, and little extras like windows, door handles and even exhaust pipes fell by the roadside long ago.

### PICK-UP

With wooden seats down the sides, covered pick-ups (bâchés) are definitely 2nd class, but are sometimes the only kind of bush taxi available. They take around 16 passengers but are invariably stuffed with people and baggage, plus a few chickens, and your feet may be higher than your waist from resting on a sack of millet. Up on the roof go more bags, bunches of bananas, extra passengers and goats (also live). Bâché rides are often very slow, and police checks at roadblocks are interminable as drivers or passengers frequently lack vital papers. The ride is guaranteed to be unpleasant unless you adopt an African attitude, which means each time your head hits the roof as the vehicle descends into yet another big pothole, you roar with laughter. There's nothing like local humour to change an otherwise miserable trip into a tolerable, even enjoyable, experience.

---

### TOUTS AT THE GARE ROUTIÈRE

At most gares routières (motor parks), bush taxis leave on a fill-up-and-go basis, but problems arise when you get more than one vehicle covering the same route. This is when a tout (sometimes called a cotiman) can earn money by persuading you to take 'his' car. Most will tell you anything to get you on board: 'this one is very fast', 'this minibus is leaving now', 'this bus is a good cheap price' etc. Another trick involves putting your bags on the roof rack as a 'deposit' against you taking another car (which means you shouldn't give up your bags until you're sure you'll go with them).

Don't think that you're being targeted because you're a wealthy foreigner – the touts hassle everybody. In the end, it's always somewhat of a gamble, but the vehicle that has the most passengers will usually be the one to depart first.

## Taxi

### MOTORCYCLE TAXI

In some countries, motorcycle taxis (*moto-taxis* or *motos*) are used. While they're often cheaper than shared taxis and handy for zipping around, safety can be an issue. If you have a choice, it's usually better to pay slightly more and go with a regular shared taxi.

### PRIVATE TAXI

Only in the bigger cities, such as Dakar, Abidjan and Ouagadougou, do taxis have meters (*compteurs*). Otherwise, bargaining is required or you'll be given the legally fixed rate. In any case, determine the fare before getting into the taxi. The fare from most airports into town is fixed, but some drivers (in Dakar, for example) will try to charge at least double these. In places like Bamako, it costs up to 50% more to go into town from the airport than it takes to go the other way. The price always includes luggage unless you have a particularly bulky item. Also, fares invariably go up at night, and sometimes even in rainy weather.

As an alternative to hiring a car, consider using a taxi by the day. It will probably cost you less (anywhere from about US$20 to US$50 per day), and if the car breaks down it will be the driver's problem. You can either hire a city taxi or a bush taxi (although in most places, you'll find that city taxis won't have the necessary paperwork for long-distance routes), or alternatively, ask around at your hotel and arrange something privately. Whatever vehicle you go with, make sure it's mechanically sound before agreeing to anything. Even if you know nothing about cars, just looking at the bodywork or listening to the engine will give you an idea. Also, don't forget to check the tyres. If they're completely bald, or badly out of alignment, it's probably better to look for another vehicle. If you're going on a longer trip, it's also worth checking that there's a spare (and the tools to change it). Hiring a car for a short test run in town is a good way to check out both vehicle and driver before finalising arrangements for a longer trip.

The price you pay will have to be worth the driver taking it out of public service for the day. If you want a deal including petrol, he'll reduce the speed to a slow trot and complain every time you take a detour. A fixed daily rate for the car, while you pay extra for

fuel, is easier to arrange. Finding a car with a working petrol gauge may be tricky, but you can work on the theory that the tank will be empty when you start, and if you allow for 10km per litre on reasonable roads (more on bad roads) you should be OK.

### SHARED TAXI

Many cities have shared taxis, which will stop and pick up more passengers even if they already have somebody inside. Some run on fixed routes, and are effectively a bus, only quicker and more comfortable. Others go wherever the first passenger wants to go, and other people will only be picked up if they're going in the same direction. They normally shout the name of the suburb or a landmark they're heading for as the taxi goes past. In some places, it's common for the waiting passengers to call out the name of their destination or point in the desired direction as the taxi passes by. Once you've got the hang of the shared taxi system, it's quick, safe and inexpensive, and an excellent way to get around cities – and also a good way to experience local life. It's also one of West Africa's great bargains, as fares seldom exceed US$0.30. It's always worth checking the fare before you get in the car, though, as they're not always fixed, and meters don't apply to shared trips. If you're the first person in the taxi, make it clear that you're expecting the driver to pick up others and that you don't want a private hire (*déplacement, depo*, 'charter' or 'town trip') all to yourself.

## TOURS

Compared with most areas of the world, West Africa has few tour operators. There are exceptions – such as heavily touristed areas like Mali, Senegal and Agadez in Niger – but not many. Tour companies are usually based in the capital cities, and typically offer excursions for groups (rather than individuals) from one-day to one-week trips, or longer. Good West African companies who organise tours beyond the borders of their own country include the following:

### BENIN

**CPN Les Papillons** ( ☎ 22 54 07 13; cpnlespapillons@yahoo.com)

**La Train d'Ebene** ( ☎ 21 31 38 62) Two- and seven-day tours are available in restored colonial railroad cars.

**BURKINA FASO**
**L'Agence Tourisme** ( ☎ 50 31 84 43; www.agence
-tourisme.com)
**Meycom Voyages** ( ☎ 50 33 09 83; meycom@fasonet.bf )

**CAMEROON**
**Safar Tours** ( ☎ 222 8703; www.safartours.com)

**CÔTE D'IVOIRE**
**Net Voyages Côte d'Ivoire** ( ☎ 20-336121,
info@voyager-en-afrique.com; Immeuble Borija, Ave
Nogués, Le Plateau)
**Osmosis Akan** ( ☎ 07-801518, osmosisak@yahoo.fr;
Immeuble Singer Porte S 11, Le Plateau)
**Prestige Voyages** ( ☎ 22-417673, prestigevoyages@
yahoo.fr; Rue Des Jardins, Centre Commercial Louis Panis,
Les Deux Plateaux)

**MALI**
**TAM Voyages** ( ☎ 221 9210; www.tamvoyage.com)
**Toguna Adventure Tours** ( ☎ /fax 2297853;
togunaadventure@afribone.net.ml)

**MAURITANIA**
**Allal Amatlich** ( ☎ 546 47 18; 647 88 68)
**Bab Sahara** ( ☎ 647 39 66)
**Bivouac Tours** ( ☎ 546 45 95)
**Ouadane Tours** ( ☎ 646 93 82, 634 72 73)
**Salima Voyages** ( ☎ 546 46 11).
**Tivoujar** ( ☎ 678 13 42, 625 51 82; www.vuedenhaut.com)

**SIERRA LEONE**
**Facts Finding Tours** ( ☎ 076-903675,
factsfinding@yahoo.com; Lumley Beach Rd, Freetown) The
knowledgeable Kenneth Gbengba leads personalized bird-
and wildlife-watching tours across the country.
**IPC Travel** ( ☎ 221481; ipc@sierratel.sl, 22 Siaka Stevens
St) IPC offers several excellent city, peninsula and island
tours and will be heading out to the provinces soon.

**TOGO**
**Henry Loïc** ( ☎ 927 52 03; africatoy@hotmail.com) This
enthusiastic French biologist and off-roader offers 4WD
'raids' of the surrounding countryside and countries (€45
per person per day, or €150 for four people per day).

There are also plenty of hotels or guides
who offer less professional tours that may
be little more than a man with an underutilised car. On most tours, the larger the
group, the lower the cost per person. Information on local tour operators is given
in the individual country chapters. Companies offering tours to West Africa are
listed on p840.

---

**WEST AFRICA'S TOP THREE
TRAIN RIDES**

Taking the train in Africa is like the ultimate
road movie with the colours, smells and im-
probabilities of life writ large. More than a
form of transport, West African trains are
like moving cities, a stage for street performers, marketplaces, and prayer halls.
And like most forms of transport in West
Africa, you'll have plenty of time to contemplate the experience, whether waiting on a
platform for your train to appear a mere 12
hours after its scheduled arrival or stopped
on remote rails in the middle of nowhere for
no apparent reason. But for all their faults
(and there are many) the trains work and
are an essential part of the West African
experience. Our three favourites:

- Zouérat to Nouâdhibou, Mauritania (see
  p576) – one of the great train experiences of the world on the longest train
  in the world.

- Dakar to Bamako (p743 and p546) –
  another of Africa's great epics, at once
  endlessly fascinating and interminable
  (up to 40 hours).

- Yaoundé to N'Gaoundéré, Cameroon
  (p228) – like crossing a continent, from
  the arid north to the steamy south, with
  glorious rainforests en route.

---

# TRAIN

There are railways in Mauritania (p576),
Senegal, Mali, Côte d'Ivoire, Ghana, Burkina
Faso, Togo, Benin, Nigeria and Cameroon.
Most services run only within the country of
operation, but there are international services, notably between Dakar and Bamako.
At the time of writing, passenger services between Ouagadougou and Abidjan were suspended due to the conflict in Côte d'Ivoire.

Some trains are relatively comfortable,
with 1st-class coaches, which may be air-
conditioned. Some also have sleeping
compartments, with two or four bunks.
Other services are 2nd or 3rd class only,
and conditions can be uncomfortable, with
no lights, no toilets and no glass in the
windows (no fun on long night journeys).
Some trains have a restaurant on board, but
you can usually buy things to eat and drink
at every station along the way.

# Health

## CONTENTS

As long as you stay up-to-date with your vaccinations and take basic preventive measures, you'd have to be pretty unlucky to succumb to most of the health hazards covered in this chapter. Africa certainly has an impressive selection of tropical diseases on offer, but you're more likely to get a bout of diarrhoea (in fact, you should bank on it), a cold or an infected mosquito bite than an exotic disease such as sleeping sickness. When it comes to injuries (as opposed to illness), the most likely reason for needing medical help in Africa is as a result of road accidents – vehicles are rarely well-maintained, the roads are potholed and poorly lit, and drink driving is common.

# BEFORE YOU GO

A little planning before departure, particularly for pre-existing illnesses, will save you a lot of trouble later. Before a long trip get a check-up from your dentist and from your doctor if you have any regular medication or chronic illness, eg high blood pressure and asthma. You should also organise spare contact lenses and glasses (and take your optical prescription with you), get a first aid and medical kit together, and arrange necessary vaccinations.

It's tempting to leave it all to the last minute – don't! Many vaccines don't take effect until two weeks after you've been immunised, so visit a doctor four to eight weeks before departure. Ask your doctor for an International Certificate of Vaccination (otherwise known as the yellow booklet), which will list all the vaccinations you've received. This is mandatory for the African countries that require proof of yellow fever vaccination upon entry, but it's a good idea to carry it anyway wherever you travel.

Travellers can register with the **International Association for Medical Advice to Travellers** (IMAT; www.iamat.org). Its website can help travellers find a doctor who has recognised training. Those heading off to very remote areas might like to do a first-aid course (contact the Red Cross or St John's Ambulance) or attend a remote medicine first aid course, such as that offered by the **Royal Geographical Society** (www.wildernessmedicaltraining.co.uk).

If you are bringing medications with you, carry them in their original containers, clearly labelled. A signed and dated letter from your physician describing all medical conditions and medications, including generic names, is also a good idea. If carrying syringes or needles be sure to have a physician's letter documenting their medical necessity.

How do you go about getting the best possible medical help? It's difficult to say – it really depends on the severity of your illness or injury and the availability of local help. If malaria is suspected, seek medical help as soon as possible or begin self-medicating if you are off the beaten track (see p856).

## INSURANCE

Find out in advance whether your insurance plan will make payments to providers or will reimburse you later for overseas health expenditures (in many countries doctors expect payment in cash). It's vital to ensure that your travel insurance will cover the emergency transport required to get you to a hospital in a major city, to better facilities elsewhere in Africa, or all the way home by air and with a medical attendant if necessary. Not all insurance covers this, so check the contract carefully. If you need medical help, your insurance company might be able to help locate the nearest hospital or clinic, or you can ask at your hotel. In an emergency, contact your embassy or consulate.

The **African Medical and Research Foundation** (Amref; www.amref.org) provides an air evacuation service in medical emergencies in some African countries, as well as air ambulance transfers between medical facilities. Money paid by members for this service goes into providing grass-roots medical assistance for local people.

## RECOMMENDED VACCINATIONS

The **World Health Organization** (www.who.int/en/) recommends that all travellers be covered for diphtheria, tetanus, measles, mumps, rubella and polio, as well as for hepatitis B, regardless of their destination. Planning to travel is a great time to ensure that all routine vaccination cover is complete. The consequences of these diseases can be severe, and outbreaks of them do occur.

According to the **Centers for Disease Control and Prevention** (www.cdc.gov), the following vaccinations are recommended for all parts of Africa: hepatitis A, hepatitis B, meningococcal meningitis, rabies and typhoid, and boosters for tetanus, diphtheria and measles. Yellow fever is not necessarily recommended for all parts of Africa, although the certificate is an entry requirement for many countries (see p858).

## MEDICAL CHECKLIST

It is a very good idea to carry a medical and first aid kit with you, to help yourself in the case of minor illness or injury. Following is a list of items you should consider packing.

- Acetaminophen (paracetamol) or aspirin
- Acetazolamide (Diamox) for altitude sickness (prescription only)
- Adhesive or paper tape
- Antibacterial ointment (prescription only) for cuts and abrasions (eg Bactroban)
- Antibiotics (prescription only), eg ciprofloxacin (Ciproxin) or norfloxacin (Utinor)
- Antidiarrhoeal drugs (eg loperamide)
- Antihistamines (for hayfever and allergic reactions)
- Antiinflammatory drugs (eg ibuprofen)
- Antimalaria pills
- Bandages, gauze, gauze rolls

- DEET-containing insect repellent for the skin
- Iodine tablets (for water purification)
- Oral rehydration salts
- Permethrin-containing insect spray for clothing, tents, and bed nets
- Pocket knife
- Scissors, safety pins, tweezers
- Sterile needles, syringes and fluids if travelling to remote areas
- Steroid cream or hydrocortisone cream (for allergic rashes)
- Sun block
- Syringes and sterile needles
- Thermometer

If you are travelling through a malarial area – particularly an area where falciparum malaria predominates – consider taking a self-diagnostic kit that can identify malaria in the blood from a finger prick.

## INTERNET RESOURCES

There is a wealth of travel health advice on the Internet. For further information, the **Lonely Planet website** (www.lonelyplanet.com) is a good place to start. The **World Health Organization** (www.who.int/en/) publishes a superb book called *International Travel and Health,* which is revised annually and is available online at no cost. Other websites of general interest are **MD Travel Health** (www.mdtravelhealth.com) which provides complete travel health recommendations for every country, updated daily, also at no cost; the **Centers for Disease Control and Prevention** (www.cdc.gov) and **Fit for Travel** (www.fitfortravel.scot.nhs.uk), which has up-to-date information about outbreaks and is very user-friendly.

It's also a good idea to consult your government's travel health website before departure, if one is available:
**Australia** (www.dfat.gov.au/travel/)
**Canada** (www.hc-sc.gc.ca/english/index.html)
**UK** (www.doh.gov.uk/traveladvice/index.htm)
**USA** (www.cdc.gov/travel/)

## FURTHER READING

*A Comprehensive Guide to Wilderness and Travel Medicine* by Eric A Weiss (1998)
*Healthy Travel* by Jane Wilson-Howarth (1999)
*Healthy Travel Africa* by Isabelle Young (2000)
*How to Stay Healthy Abroad* by Richard Dawood (2002)
*Travel in Health* by Graham Fry (1994)
*Travel with Children* by Cathy Lanigan (2004)

# IN TRANSIT

## DEEP VEIN THROMBOSIS (DVT)

Blood clots can form in the legs during flights, chiefly because of prolonged immobility. This formation of clots is known as deep vein thrombosis (DVT), and the longer the flight, the greater the risk. Although most blood clots are reabsorbed uneventfully, some might break off and travel through the blood vessels to the lungs, where they could cause life-threatening complications.

The chief symptom of DVT is swelling or pain of the foot, ankle or calf, usually but not always on just one side. When a blood clot travels to the lungs, it could cause chest pain and breathing difficulty. Travellers with any of these symptoms should immediately seek medical attention.

To prevent the development of DVT on flights you should walk about the cabin, perform isometric compressions of the leg muscles (ie contract the leg muscles while sitting), drink plenty of fluids, and avoid alcohol.

## JET LAG & MOTION SICKNESS

If you're crossing more than five time zones you could suffer jet lag, resulting in insomnia, fatigue, malaise or nausea. To avoid jet lag drink plenty of fluids (nonalcoholic) and eat light meals. Upon arrival, get exposure to natural sunlight and readjust your schedule (for meals, sleep, etc) as soon as possible.

Antihistamines such as dimenhydrinate (Dramamine) and meclizine (Antivert, Bonine) are usually the first choice for treating motion sickness. The main side effect of these drugs is drowsiness. A herbal alternative is ginger (in the form of ginger tea, biscuits or crystallized ginger), which works like a charm for some people.

# IN WEST AFRICA

## AVAILABILITY & COST OF HEALTH CARE

Health care in Africa is varied: it can be excellent in the major cities, which generally have well-trained doctors and nurses, but it is often patchy off the beaten track. Medicine and even sterile dressings and intravenous fluids might need to be purchased from a local pharmacy by patients or their rela-

tives. The standard of dental care is equally variable, and there is an increased risk of hepatitis B and HIV transmission via poorly sterilised equipment. By and large, public hospitals in Africa offer the cheapest service, but will have the least up-to-date equipment and medications; mission hospitals (where donations are the usual form of payment) often have more reasonable facilities; and private hospitals and clinics are more expensive but tend to have more advanced drugs and equipment and better trained medical staff.

Most drugs can be purchased over the counter in Africa, without a prescription. Many drugs for sale in Africa might be ineffective: they might be counterfeit or might not have been stored under the right conditions. The most common examples of counterfeit drugs are malaria tablets and expensive antibiotics, such as ciprofloxacin. Most drugs are available in capitals, but remote villages will be lucky to have a couple of paracetamol tablets. It is recommended that all drugs for chronic diseases be brought from home. Also, the availability and efficacy of condoms cannot be relied on – bring contraception. Condoms bought in Africa might not be of the same quality as in Europe or Australia, and they might not have been correctly stored.

There is a high risk of contracting HIV from infected blood if you receive a blood transfusion in Africa. The **BloodCare Foundation** (www.bloodcare.org.uk) is a useful source of safe, screened blood, which can be transported to any part of the world within 24 hours.

The cost of health care might seem cheap compared to first world countries, but good care and drugs might be not be available. Evacuation to good medical care (within Africa or to your own country) can be very expensive. Unfortunately, adequate health care is available only to very few Africans.

## INFECTIOUS DISEASES

It's a formidable list but, as we say, a few precautions go a long way…

### Cholera

Although small outbreaks can occur, cholera is usually only a problem during natural or artificial disasters. Travellers are rarely affected. It is caused by a bacteria and spread via contaminated drinking water. The main symptom is profuse watery diarrhoea, which causes debilitation if fluids are not replaced quickly. An oral cholera vaccine is available in the USA, but it is not particularly effective. Most cases of cholera could be avoided by making sure you drink clean water and by avoiding potentially contaminated food. Treatment is by fluid replacement (orally or via a drip), but sometimes antibiotics are needed. Self-treatment is not advised.

### Dengue Fever

Found in Senegal, Burkina Faso, Guinea, and some parts of East and Southern Africa, dengue fever (also called 'breakbone fever') is spread through the bite of the mosquito. It causes a feverish illness with headache and muscle pains similar to those experienced with a bad, prolonged attack of influenza. There might be a rash. Self-treatment: paracetamol and rest.

### Diphtheria

Spread through close respiratory contact, diphtheria is found in all of Africa. It usually causes a temperature and a severe sore throat. Sometimes a membrane forms across the throat, and a tracheostomy is needed to prevent suffocation. Vaccination is recommended for those likely to be in close contact with the local population in infected areas. More important for long stays than for short-term trips, the vaccine is given as an injection alone or with tetanus, and lasts 10 years.

### Filariasis

Tiny worms migrating in the lymphatic system cause filariasis. It is found in most of West, Central, East and Southern Africa, and in Sudan in North Africa. A bite from an infected mosquito spreads the infection. Symptoms include itching and swelling of the legs and/or genitalia. Treatment is available.

### Hepatitis A

Found in all of Africa, Hepatitis A is spread through contaminated food (particularly shellfish) and water. It causes jaundice and is rarely fatal, but can cause prolonged lethargy and delayed recovery. If you've had hepatitis A, you shouldn't drink alcohol for up to six months after, but once you've recovered, there won't be any long-term problems. The first symptoms include dark urine and a yellow colour to the whites of the eyes. Sometimes a fever and abdominal pain might occur. Hepatitis A vaccine (Avaxim, VAQTA, Havrix) is

given as an injection: a single dose will give protection for a year, and a booster after a year gives 10-year protection. Hepatitis A and typhoid vaccines can also be given as a single dose vaccine (Hepatyrix or Viatim).

### Hepatitis B

Spread through infected blood, contaminated needles and sexual intercourse, Hepatitis B is found in Africa. It can be spread from an infected mother to the baby in childbirth. It affects the liver, causing jaundice and occasionally liver failure. Most people recover completely, but some might be chronic carriers of the virus, which can lead eventually to cirrhosis or liver cancer. Those visiting high-risk areas for long periods or with increased social or occupational risk should be immunised. Many countries now give Hepatitis B as part of the routine childhood vaccination. It is given singly or can be given at the same time as Hepatitis A (Hepatyrix).

A course of vaccinations will give protection for at least five years. It can be given over four weeks or six months.

### HIV

Human immunodeficiency virus (HIV), the virus that causes acquired immune deficiency syndrome (AIDS), is a huge problem in Africa, but is most acutely felt in sub-Saharan Africa. The virus is spread through infected blood and blood products, by sexual intercourse with an infected partner and from an infected mother to her baby during childbirth and breastfeeding. It can be spread through 'blood to blood' contacts, such as with contaminated instruments during medical, dental, acupuncture and other body-piercing procedures, and through sharing used intravenous needles. At present there is no cure; medication that might keep the disease under control is available, but these drugs are too expensive for the overwhelming majority of Africans, and are not readily available for travellers either. If you think you might have been infected with HIV, a blood test is necessary; a three-month gap after exposure and before testing is required to allow antibodies to appear in the blood.

### Leptospirosis

This is found in West and Southern Africa; in Chad, Congo and Democratic Republic of the Congo in Central Africa; in Algeria,

Morocco and Sudan in North Africa; and in Ethiopia and Somalia in East Africa. It is spread through the excreta of infected rodents, especially rats. It can cause hepatitis and renal failure, which might be fatal. It is unusual for travellers to be affected unless living in poor sanitary conditions. It causes a fever and sometimes jaundice.

## Malaria

One million children die annually from malaria in Africa. The risk of malarial transmission at altitudes higher than 2000m is rare. The disease is caused by a parasite in the bloodstream spread via the bite of the female Anopheles mosquito. There are several types of malaria; falciparum malaria being the most dangerous type and the predominant form in Africa. Infection rates vary with season and climate, so check out the situation before departure. Unlike most other diseases regularly encountered by travellers, there is no vaccination against malaria (yet). However, several different drugs are used to prevent malaria, and new ones are in the pipeline. Up-to-date advice from a travel health clinic is essential as some medication is more suitable for some travellers than others. The pattern of drug-resistant malaria is changing rapidly, so what was advised several years ago might no longer be the case.

Malaria can present in several ways. The early stages include headache, fever, general aches and pains, and malaise, which could be mistaken for flu. Other symptoms include

abdominal pain, diarrhoea and a cough. Anyone who gets a fever in a malarial area should assume infection until a blood test proves negative, even if you have been taking antimalarial medication. If not treated, the next stage could develop within 24 hours, particularly if falciparum malaria is the parasite: jaundice, then reduced consciousness and coma (known as cerebral malaria) followed by death. Treatment in hospital is essential, and the death rate can still be as high as 10% even in the best intensive-care facilities.

Many travellers are under the impression that malaria is a mild illness, treatment is always easy and successful, and taking antimalarial drugs causes more illness through side effects than actually getting malaria. In Africa, this is unfortunately not true. Side effects of the medication depend on the drug being taken. Doxycycline can cause heartburn and indigestion; mefloquine (Larium) can cause anxiety attacks, insomnia, nightmares and (rarely) severe psychiatric disorders; chloroquine can cause nausea and hair loss; and proguanil can cause mouth ulcers. These side effects are not universal, and can be minimized by taking medication correctly, eg with food. Also, some people should not take a particular antimalarial drug, eg people with epilepsy should avoid mefloquine, and doxycycline should not be taken by pregnant women or children younger than 12.

If you decide that you really do not wish to take antimalarial drugs, you must understand the risks, and be obsessive about avoiding mosquito bites. Use nets and insect repellent, and report any fever or flulike symptoms to a doctor as soon as possible. Some people advocate homeopathic preparations against malaria, such as Demal200, but as yet there is no conclusive evidence that this is effective, and many homeopaths do not recommend their use.

People of all ages can contract malaria, and falciparum causes the most severe illness. Repeated infections might result eventually in less serious illness. Malaria in pregnancy frequently results in miscarriage or premature labour. Adults who have survived childhood malaria have developed immunity and usually only develop mild cases of malaria; most Western travellers have no immunity at all. Immunity wanes after 18 months of nonexposure, so even if you have had malaria in the past and used

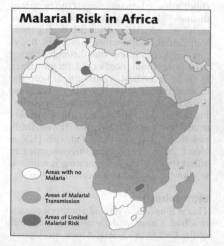

**Malarial Risk in Africa**

Areas with no Malaria

Areas of Malarial Transmission

Areas of Limited Malarial Risk

**THE ANTIMALARIAL A TO D**

**A** – Awareness of the risk. No medication is totally effective, but protection of up to 95% is achievable with most drugs, as long as other measures have been taken.

**B** – Bites – avoid at all costs. Sleep in a screened room, use a mosquito spray or coils, sleep under a permethrin-impregnated net. Cover up at night with long trousers and long sleeves, preferably with permethrin-treated clothing. Apply appropriate re-pellent to all areas of exposed skin in the evenings.

**C** – Chemical prevention (ie antimalarial drugs) is usually needed in malarial areas. Expert advice is needed as resistance patterns can change, and new drugs are in development. Not all antimalarial drugs are suitable for everyone. Most antimalarial drugs need to be started at least a week in advance and continued for four weeks after the last possible exposure to malaria.

**D** – Diagnosis. If you have a fever or flulike illness within a year of travel to a malarial area, malaria is a possibility, and immediate medical attention is necessary.

to live in a malaria-prone area, you might no longer be immune.

If you are planning a journey in a malarial area, particularly where falciparum malaria predominates, consider taking standby treatment. Standby treatment should be seen as emergency treatment aimed at saving the patient's life and not as routine self-medication. It should be used only if you will be far from medical facilities and have been advised about the symptoms of malaria and how to use the medication. Medical advice should be sought as soon as possible to confirm whether the treatment has been successful. The type of standby treatment used will depend on local conditions, such as drug resistance, and on what antimalarial drugs were being used before standby treatment. This is worthwhile because you want to avoid contracting a particularly serious form such as cerebral malaria, which affects the brain and central nervous system and can be fatal in 24 hours. Self-diagnostic kits, which can identify malaria in the blood from a finger prick, are also available in the West (see p853).

The risks from malaria to both mother and foetus during pregnancy are considerable. Unless good medical care can be guaranteed, travel throughout Africa when pregnant – particularly to malarial areas – should be discouraged unless essential.

## Meningococcal Meningitis

Meningococcal infection is spread through close respiratory contact and is more likely in crowded situations, such as dormitories, buses and clubs. Infection is uncommon in travellers. Vaccination is recommended for long stays and is especially important towards the end of the dry season, which varies across the continent (see p18). Symptoms include a fever, severe headache, neck stiffness and a red rash. Immediate medical treatment is necessary.

The ACWY vaccine is recommended for all travellers in sub-Saharan Africa. This vaccine is different from the meningococcal meningitis C vaccine given to children and adolescents in some countries; it is safe to be given both types of vaccine.

## Onchocerciasis

Also known as 'river blindness', this is caused by the larvae of a tiny worm, which is spread by the bite of a small fly. The earliest sign of infection is intensely itchy, red, sore eyes. Travellers are rarely severely affected. Treatment in a specialised clinic is curative.

## Poliomyelitis

Generally spread through contaminated food and water. It is one of the vaccines given in childhood and should be boosted every 10 years, either orally (a drop on the tongue) or as an injection. Polio can be carried asymptomatically (ie showing no symptoms) and could cause a transient fever. In rare cases it causes weakness or paralysis of one or more muscles, which might be permanent. The World Health Organization (WHO) state that Nigeria and Niger are polio hotspots following recent outbreaks.

## Rabies

Rabies is spread by receiving the bites or licks of an infected animal on broken skin. It's fatal once the clinical symptoms start (which might be up to several months after the injury), so postbite vaccination should be given as soon as possible. Postbite vaccination (whether or not you've been vaccinated before the bite) prevents the virus from spreading to the central nervous system. Animal handlers should be vaccinated, as should those travelling to remote areas where a source of postbite vaccine is not available within 24 hours. Three preventive injections are needed in a month. If you have not been vaccinated you will need a course of five injections starting 24 hours or as soon as possible after the injury. If you have been vaccinated, you will need fewer postbite injections, and have more time to seek medical aid.

### Schistosomiasis

Also called bilharzia, this disease is spread by flukes that are carried by a species of freshwater snail. The flukes are carried inside the snail, which then sheds them into slow-moving or still water. The parasites penetrate human skin during paddling or swimming and then migrate to the bladder or bowel. They are passed out via stool or urine and can contaminate fresh water, where the cycle starts again. Avoid paddling or swimming in suspect freshwater lakes or slow-running rivers. There may be no symptoms or there may be a transient fever and rash, and advanced cases can have blood in the stool or in the urine. A blood test can detect antibodies if you have been exposed, and treatment is then possible in travel or infectious disease clinics. If not treated the infection can cause kidney failure or permanent bowel damage. It isn't possible for you to infect others.

### Tuberculosis (TB)

TB is spread through close respiratory contact and occasionally through infected milk or milk products. BCG (Bacille Calmette-Guérin) vaccination is recommended for those likely to be mixing closely with the local population, although it gives only moderate protection against TB. It is more important for long stays than for short-term stays. Inoculation with the BCG vaccine is not available in all countries. It is given routinely to many children in developing countries. The vaccination causes a small permanent scar at the site of injection, and is usually given in a specialised chest clinic. It is a live vaccine and should not be given to pregnant women or immunocompromised individuals.

TB can be asymptomatic, only being picked up on a routine chest X-ray. Alternatively, it can cause a cough, weight loss or fever, sometimes months or even years after exposure.

### Typhoid

This is spread through food or water contaminated by infected human faeces. The first symptom is usually a fever or a pink rash on the abdomen. Sometimes septicaemia (blood poisoning) can occur. A typhoid vaccine (typhim Vi, typherix) will give protection for three years. In some countries, the oral vaccine Vivotif is also available. Antibiotics are usually given as treatment, and death is rare unless septicaemia occurs.

### Trypanosomiasis

Spread via the bite of the tsetse fly, trypanosomiasis, also called 'sleeping sickness', causes a headache, fever and eventually coma. There is an effective treatment.

### Yellow Fever

Travellers should carry a certificate as evidence of vaccination if they have recently been in an infected country, to avoid any possible difficulties with immigration. For a full list of these countries visit the **World Health Organization website** (www.who.int/en/) or the **Centers for Disease Control and Prevention website** (www.cdc.gov/travel). There is always the possibility that a traveller without a legally required, up-to-date certificate will be vaccinated and detained in isolation at the port of arrival for up to 10 days or possibly repatriated.

Yellow fever is spread by infected mosquitoes. Symptoms range from a flulike illness to severe hepatitis (liver inflammation) jaundice and death. The yellow fever vaccin-

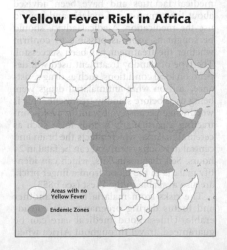

**Yellow Fever Risk in Africa**

Areas with no Yellow Fever

Endemic Zones

## MANDATORY YELLOW FEVER VACCINATION

■ North Africa – Not mandatory for any of North Africa, but Algeria, Libya and Tunisia require evidence of yellow fever vaccination if entering from an infected country. It is recommended for travellers to Sudan, and might be given to unvaccinated travellers leaving the country.

■ Central Africa – Mandatory in Central African Republic (CAR), Congo, Democratic Republic of the Congo, Equatorial Guinea and Gabon, and recommended in Chad.

■ West Africa – Mandatory in Benin, Burkina Faso, Cameroon, Côte d'Ivoire, Ghana, Liberia, Mali, Niger, Sao Tome & Principe and Togo, and recommended for The Gambia, Guinea, Guinea-Bissau, Mauritania, Nigeria, Senegal and Sierra Leone.

■ East Africa – Mandatory in Rwanda; it is advised for Burundi, Ethiopia, Kenya, Somalia, Tanzania and Uganda.

■ Southern Africa – Not mandatory for entry into any countries of Southern Africa, although it is necessary if entering from an infected country.

ation must be given at a designated clinic and is valid for 10 years. It is a live vaccine and must not be given to immunocompromised or pregnant travellers.

## TRAVELLER'S DIARRHOEA

It's not inevitable that you will get diarrhoea while travelling in Africa, but it's certainly likely. Diarrhoea is the most common travel-related illness – figures suggest that at least half of all travellers to Africa will get diarrhoea at some stage. Sometimes dietary changes, such as increased spices or oils, are the cause. To help prevent diarrhoea, avoid tap water unless you're sure it's safe to drink (see p860). You should only eat cooked or peeled fresh fruits or vegetables, and be wary of dairy products that might contain unpasteurised milk. Although freshly cooked food can often be a safe option, plates or serving utensils might be dirty, so you should be very selective when eating food from street vendors (make sure that cooked food is piping hot all the way through). If you develop

diarrhoea, be sure to drink plenty of fluids, preferably an oral rehydration solution containing water, and some salt and sugar. A few loose stools don't require treatment but, if you start having more than four or five a day, you should start taking an antibiotic (often a quinoline drug, such as ciprofloxacin or norfloxacin) and an antidiarrhoeal agent (such as loperamide) if you are not within easy reach of a toilet. If diarrhoea is bloody, persists for over 72 hours or is accompanied by fever, shaking chills or severe abdominal pain, you should seek medical attention.

## Amoebic Dysentery

Contracted by eating contaminated food and water, amoebic dysentery causes blood and mucus in the faeces. It can be relatively mild and tends to come on gradually, but seek medical advice if you think you have the illness as it won't clear up without treatment (which is with specific antibiotics).

## Giardiasis

Like amoebic dysentery, this caused by ingesting contaminated food or water. The illness appears a week or more after you have been exposed to the parasite. Giardiasis might cause only a short-lived bout of traveller's diarrhoea, but it can cause persistent diarrhoea. Seek medical advice if you suspect you have giardiasis, but if you are in a remote area you could start a course of antibiotics.

## ENVIRONMENTAL HAZARDS
### Heat Exhaustion

This condition occurs following heavy sweating and excessive fluid loss with inadequate replacement of fluids and salt, and is common in hot climates when taking exercise before full acclimatisation. Symptoms include headache, dizziness and tiredness. Dehydration is happening by the time you feel thirsty – aim to drink sufficient water to produce pale, diluted urine. Treatment: fluid replacement with water and/or fruit juice, and cooling by cold water and fans. The treatment of the salt-loss component consists of consuming salty fluids as in soup, and adding a bit more salt to food than usual.

## Heatstroke

Heat exhaustion is a precursor to the much more serious heatstroke. In this case there is damage to the sweating mechanism, with an excessive rise in body temperature; irrational and hyperactive behaviour; and eventually loss of consciousness and death. Rapid cooling by spraying the body with water and fanning is best. Emergency fluid and electrolyte replacement is required by intravenous drip.

## Insect Bites & Stings

Mosquitoes might not always carry malaria or dengue fever, but they (and other insects) can cause irritation and infected bites. To avoid these, take the same precautions as you would for avoiding malaria (see p856). Use DEET-based insect repellents. Excellent clothing treatments are also available; mosquitos that land on treated clothing will die.

Bee and wasp stings cause real problems only to those who have a severe allergy to the stings (anaphylaxis.) If you are one of these people, carry an 'epipen' – an adrenaline (epinephrine) injection, which you can give yourself. This could save your life.

Sandflies are found around the beaches. They usually only cause a nasty itchy bite but can carry a rare skin disorder called cutaneous leishmaniasis. Prevention of bites with DEET-based repellents is sensible.

Scorpions are frequently found in arid or dry climates. They can cause a painful bite that is sometimes life-threatening. If bitten by a scorpion, take a painkiller. Medical treatment should be sought if collapse occurs.

Bed bugs are found in hostels and cheap hotels and lead to itchy, lumpy bites. Spraying the mattress with crawling insect killer after changing bedding will get rid of them.

Scabies are also found in cheap accommodation. These tiny mites live in the skin, often between the fingers and they cause an intensely itchy rash. The itch is easily treated with malathion and permethrin lotion from a pharmacy; other members of the household also need treating to avoid spreading scabies, even if they do not show any symptoms.

## Snake Bites

Avoid getting bitten! Don't walk barefoot, or stick your hand into holes or cracks. However, 50% of those bitten by venomous snakes are not actually injected with poison. If bitten by a snake, do not panic. Immobilise the bitten limb with a splint (such as a stick) and apply a bandage over the site, with firm pressure (similar to bandaging a sprain). Do not apply a tourniquet, or cut or suck the bite. Get medical help as soon as possible so antivenom can be given if needed.

## Water

Never drink tap water unless it has been boiled, filtered or chemically disinfected (eg, with iodine tablets). Never drink from streams, rivers and lakes. It's best to avoid drinking from pumps and wells – some do bring pure water to the surface, but the presence of animals can contaminate supplies.

## TRADITIONAL MEDICINE

At least 80% of the African population relies on traditional medicine, often because conventional Western-style medicine is too expensive, because of prevailing cultural attitudes and beliefs, or simply because in some cases it works. It might also be because there's no other choice: a World Health Organization survey found that although there was only one medical doctor for every 50,000 people in Mozambique, there was a traditional healer for every 200 people.

Although some African remedies seem to work on malaria, sickle cell anaemia, high blood pressure and some AIDS symptoms, most African healers learn their art by apprenticeship, so education (and consequently application of knowledge) is inconsistent and unregulated. Conventionally trained physicians in South Africa, for example, angrily describe how their AIDS patients die of kidney failure because a *sangoma* (traditional healer) has given them an enema containing an essence made from powerful roots. Likewise, when traditional healers administer 'injections' with porcupine quills, knives or dirty razor blades, diseases are often spread or created rather than cured.

Rather than attempting to stamp out traditional practices, or pretend they aren't happening, a positive step taken by some African countries is the regulation of traditional medicine by creating healers' associations and offering courses on such topics as sanitary practices. It remains unlikely in the short term that even a basic level of conventional Western-style medicine will be made available to all the people of Africa (even though the cost of doing so is less than the annual military budget of some Western countries). Traditional medicine, on the other hand, will almost certainly continue to be practised widely throughout the continent.

# Language

## CONTENTS

West Africa's myriad ethnic groups speak several hundred local languages, many subdivided into numerous distinct dialects. The people of Nigeria – West Africa's most populous country – speak at least 350 languages and dialects, while even tiny Guinea-Bissau (population just over one million) has around 20 languages.

Consequently, common languages are absolutely essential, and several are used. These may be the language of the largest group in a particular area or country. For example, Hausa has spread out from its northern Nigerian heartland to become widely understood as a trading language in the eastern parts of West Africa. Similarly, Dioula has become a common tongue in markets over much of the western part of the region. Also widespread are the former colonial languages of French, English and Portuguese. In some areas, the common tongue is a creole – a combination of native African and imported European languages.

# COLONIAL LANGUAGES

## FRENCH

Though we've generally only included the polite form of address with the following phrases – *vous* (you) – the informal mode *tu* is used much more commonly in West Africa; you'll hear less *s'il vous plaît* and more *s'il te plaît* (which may be considered impolite in France unless spoken between good friends). If in doubt in Africa (when dealing with border officials or any older people) it's always safer to use the polite *vous* form. The pronunciation guides included with each French phrase should help you in getting your message across.

If you fancy getting stuck into your *français* to a greater extent than is possible with what we include here, Lonely Planet's compact *French Phrasebook* offers a handy, pocket-sized guide to the language that will cover all your travel needs and more.

### Accommodation

| I'm looking for a ... | Je cherche ... | zher shersh ... |
|---|---|---|
| campground | un camping | un kom·peeng |
| hotel | un hôtel | un o·tel |

**Where is a cheap hotel?**
*Où est-ce qu'on peut trouver un hôtel pas cher?*
oo es·kon per troo·vay un o·tel pa shair

**Could you write the address, please?**
*Est-ce que vous pourriez écrire l'adresse, s'il vous plaît?*
e·sker voo poo·ryay ay·kreer la·dres seel voo play

**Do you have any rooms available?**
*Est-ce que vous avez des chambres libres?*
e·sker voo·za·vay day shom·brer lee·brer

## How much is it per night/person?

*Quel est le prix par nuit/personne?*
kel e ler pree par nwee/par per·son

## May I see it?

*Est-ce que je peux voir la chambre?*
es·ker zher per vwa la shom·brer

## I'd like (a) ...

*Je voudrais ...*     zher voo·dray ...

**single room**
*une chambre à un lit*    ewn shom·brer a un lee

**double-bed room**
*une chambre avec un*    ewn shom·brer a·vek
  *grand lit*            un gron lee

**room with two beds**
*une chambre avec des*   ewn shom·brer a·vek day
  *lits jumeaux*         lee zhew·mo

## Where is the bathroom?

*Où est la salle de bains?*   oo e la sal der bun

**air-conditioning**
*climatisation*     klee·ma·tee·za·syon

**hot water**
*eau chaude*      leeo shod

**key**
*clef/clé*        klef/klay

**sheet**
*drap*          drap

**shower**
*douche*       doosh

**toilet**
*les toilettes*     lay twa·let

## Conversation & Essentials

| | | |
|---|---|---|
| **Hello.** | *Bonjour.* | bon·zhoor |
| **Hi.** | *Salut.* (inf) | sa·loo |
| **Goodbye.** | *Au revoir.* | o·rer·vwa |
| **Yes.** | *Oui.* | wee |
| **No.** | *Non.* | no |
| **Please.** | *S'il vous plaît.* | seel voo play |
| | *S'il te plaît.* (inf) | seel ter play |
| **Thank you.** | *Merci.* | mair·see |
| **You're welcome.** | *Je vous en prie.* | zher voo·zon pree |
| | *De rien.* (inf) | der ree·en |
| **Excuse me.** | *Excusez-moi.* | ek·skew·zay·mwa |
| **Sorry.** (forgive me) | *Pardon.* | par·don |

**(Have a) good evening.**
*Bonne soirée.*     bon swa·ray

**What's your name?**
*Comment vous*     ko·mon voo·za·pay·lay voo
  *appelez-vous?*
*Comment tu*      ko·mon tew ta·pel
  *t'appelles?* (inf)

**My name is ...**
*Je m'appelle ...*    zher ma·pel ...

**Where are you from?**
*De quel pays êtes-vous?*   der kel pay·ee et·voo
*De quel pays es-tu?* (inf) der kel pay·ee e·tew

**I'm from ...**
*Je viens de ...*     zher vyen der ...

**I like ...**
*J'aime ...*       zhem ...

**I don't like ...**
*Je n'aime pas ...*    zher nem pa ...

---

### DON'T BE LOST FOR WORDS IN ... !

| Country | Official Language | Principal African Languages (in this guide) |
|---|---|---|
| Benin | French | Fon, Hausa, Yoruba |
| Burkina Faso | French | Dioula, Fon, Hausa, Moré, Senoufo |
| Cape Verde | Portuguese | Crioulo |
| Côte d'Ivoire | French | Dan (Yacouba), Dioula, Hausa, Senoufo |
| Gambia | English | Diola (Jola), Mandinka, Wolof |
| Ghana | English | Ewe, Ga, Hausa, Twi |
| Guinea | French | Fula (Futa Djalon), Malinké, Susu |
| Guinea-Bissau | Portuguese | Crioulo |
| Liberia | English | Dan (Yacouba) |
| Mali | French | Bambara, Malinké, Sangha dialect, Senoufo, Tamashek |
| Mauritania | Arabic (French also still in common use) | Dioula, Fula (Fulfulde), Hassaniya, Wolof |
| Niger | French | Djerma, Fon, Hausa, Tamashek |
| Nigeria | English | Hausa, Igbo, Yoruba |
| Senegal | French | Crioulo, Diola, Fula (Fulfulde), Malinké, Mandinka, Wolof |
| Sierra Leone | English | Krio |
| Togo | French | Ewe, Fon, Kabyé, Mina |

LANGUAGE

## Directions

**Where is ...?**
*Où est ...?*                  oo e ...
**Go straight ahead.**
*Continuez tout droit.*        kon·teen·way too drwa
**Turn left.**
*Tournez à gauche.*            toor·nay a gosh
**Turn right.**
*Tournez à droite.*            toor·nay a drwat
**How many kilometres is ...?**
*À combien de kilomètres*      a kom·byun der kee·lo·me·trer
*est ...?*                     e ...

---

### EMERGENCIES

**Help!**
*Au secours!*                  o skoor
**There's been an accident!**
*Il y a eu un accident!*       eel ya ew un ak·see·don
**I'm lost.**
*Je me suis égaré/e. (m/f)*    zhe me swee·zay·ga·ray
**Leave me alone!**
*Fichez-moi la paix!*          fee·shay·mwa la pay

**Call ...!**          *Appelez ...!*        a·play ...
 **a doctor**         *un médecin*         un mayd·sun
 **the police**       *la police*          la po·lees

---

## Health

**I'm ill.**           *Je suis malade.*       zher swee ma·lad
**antiseptic**         *l'antiseptique*       lon·tee·sep·teek
**condoms**            *des préservatifs*     day pray·zair·va·teef
**contraceptive**      *le contraceptif*      ler kon·tra·sep·teef
**diarrhoea**          *la diarrhée*          la dya·ray
**medicine**           *le médicament*        ler may·dee·ka·mon
**nausea**             *la nausée*            la no·zay
**sunblock cream**     *la crème solaire*     la krem so·lair
**tampons**            *des tampons*          day tom·pon
                       *hygiéniques*          ee·zhen·eek

**I'm ...**            *Je suis ...*          zher swee ...
 **asthmatic**         *asthmatique*          (z)as·ma·teek
 **diabetic**          *diabétique*           dee·a·bay·teek
 **epileptic**         *épileptique*          (z)ay·pee·lep·teek

**I'm allergic**       *Je suis*              zher swee
**to ...**             *allergique ...*       za·lair·zheek ...
 **antibiotics**       *aux antibiotiques*    o zon·tee·byo·teek
 **nuts**              *aux noix*             o nwa
 **peanuts**           *aux cacahuètes*       o ka·ka·wet

## Language Difficulties

**Do you speak English?**
*Parlez-vous anglais?*
par·lay·voo zong·lay

**Does anyone here speak English?**
*Y a-t-il quelqu'un qui parle anglais?*
ya·teel kel·kung kee par long·glay
**I don't understand.**
*Je ne comprends pas.*
zher ner kom·pron pa
**Could you write it down, please?**
*Est-ce que vous pourriez l'écrire, s'il vous plaît?*
es·ker voo poo·ryay lay·kreer seel voo play
**Can you show me (on the map)?**
*Pouvez-vous m'indiquer (sur la carte)?*
poo·vay·voo mun·dee·kay (sewr la kart)

## Numbers

| 0 | *zero* | zay·ro |
|---|---|---|
| 1 | *un* | un |
| 2 | *deux* | der |
| 3 | *trois* | trwa |
| 4 | *quatre* | ka·trer |
| 5 | *cinq* | sungk |
| 6 | *six* | sees |
| 7 | *sept* | set |
| 8 | *huit* | weet |
| 9 | *neuf* | nerf |
| 10 | *dix* | dees |
| 11 | *onze* | onz |
| 12 | *douze* | dooz |
| 13 | *treize* | trez |
| 14 | *quatorze* | ka·torz |
| 15 | *quinze* | kunz |
| 16 | *seize* | sez |
| 17 | *dix-sept* | dee·set |
| 18 | *dix-huit* | dee·zweet |
| 19 | *dix-neuf* | deez·nerf |
| 20 | *vingt* | vung |
| 21 | *vingt et un* | vung tay un |
| 22 | *vingt-deux* | vung·der |
| 30 | *trente* | tront |
| 40 | *quarante* | ka·ront |
| 50 | *cinquante* | sung·kont |
| 60 | *soixante* | swa·sont |
| 70 | *soixante-dix* | swa·son·dees |
| 80 | *quatre-vingts* | ka·trer·vung |
| 90 | *quatre-vingt-dix* | ka·trer·vung·dees |
| 100 | *cent* | son |
| 1000 | *mille* | meel |

## Shopping & Services

**I'd like to buy ...**
*Je voudrais acheter ...*       zher voo·dray ash·tay ...
**How much is it?**
*C'est combien?*                say kom·byun
**May I look at it?**
*Est-ce que je peux le voir?*   es·ker zher per ler vwar

**I'm just looking.**
*Je regarde.*    zher rer·gard
**It's cheap.**
*Ce n'est pas cher.*    ser nay pa shair
**It's too expensive.**
*C'est trop cher.*    say tro shair

| | | |
|---|---|---|
| **Can I pay by ...?** | *Est-ce que je peux* | es·ker zher per |
| | *payer avec ...?* | pay·yay a·vek ... |
| **credit card** | *ma carte de* | ma kart der |
| | *crédit* | kray·dee |
| **travellers** | *des chèques* | day shek |
| **cheques** | *de voyage* | der vwa·yazh |

| | | |
|---|---|---|
| **I want to** | *Je voudrais* | zher voo·dray |
| **change ...** | *changer ...* | shon·zhay ... |
| **(cash) money** | *de l'argent* | der lar·zhon |
| **travellers** | *des chèques* | day shek |
| **cheques** | *de voyage* | der vwa·yazh |

| | | |
|---|---|---|
| **more** | *plus* | plew |
| **less** | *moins* | mwa |
| **smaller** | *plus petit* | plew per·tee |
| **bigger** | *plus grand* | plew gron |

| | | |
|---|---|---|
| **I'm looking** | *Je cherche ...* | zhe shersh ... |
| **for ...** | | |
| **a bank** | *une banque* | ewn bonk |
| **the ... embassy** | *l'ambassade* | lam·ba·sahd |
| | *de ...* | der ... |
| **the hospital** | *l'hôpital* | lo·pee·tal |
| **the market** | *le marché* | ler mar·shay |
| **the police** | *la police* | la po·lees |
| **the post office** | *le bureau de* | ler bew·ro der |
| | *poste* | post |
| **a public phone** | *une cabine* | ewn ka·been |
| | *téléphonique* | tay·lay·fo·neek |
| **a public toilet** | *les toilettes* | lay twa·let |
| **the telephone** | *la centrale* | la san·tral |
| **centre** | *téléphonique* | tay·lay·fo·neek |
| **the tourist** | *l'office de* | lo·fees der |
| **office** | *tourisme* | too·rees·mer |

**What time does it open/close?**
*Quelle est l'heure d'ouverture/de fermeture?*
kel ay lur doo·ver·tewr/der fair·mer·tewr

## Time & Dates
**What time is it?**
*Quelle heure est-il?*    kel er e til
**It's (8) o'clock.**
*Il est (huit) heures.*    il e (weet) er
**It's half past ...**
*Il est (...) heures et*    il e (...) er e
*demie.*    day·mee

| | | |
|---|---|---|
| **When?** | *Quand?* | kon |
| **in the morning** | *du matin* | dew ma·tun |
| **in the afternoon** | *de l'après-midi* | der la·pray·mee·dee |
| **in the evening** | *du soir* | dew swar |
| **today** | *aujourd'hui* | o·zhoor·dwee |
| **tomorrow** | *demain* | der·mun |
| **yesterday** | *hier* | yair |

| | | |
|---|---|---|
| **Monday** | *lundi* | lun·dee |
| **Tuesday** | *mardi* | mar·dee |
| **Wednesday** | *mercredi* | mair·krer·dee |
| **Thursday** | *jeudi* | zher·dee |
| **Friday** | *vendredi* | von·drer·dee |
| **Saturday** | *samedi* | sam·dee |
| **Sunday** | *dimanche* | dee·monsh |

| | | |
|---|---|---|
| **January** | *janvier* | zhon·vyay |
| **February** | *février* | fayv·ryay |
| **March** | *mars* | mars |
| **April** | *avril* | a·vreel |
| **May** | *mai* | may |
| **June** | *juin* | zhwun |
| **July** | *juillet* | zhwee·yay |
| **August** | *août* | oot |
| **September** | *septembre* | sep·tom·brer |
| **October** | *octobre* | ok·to·brer |
| **November** | *novembre* | no·vom·brer |
| **December** | *décembre* | day·som·brer |

## Transport
**What time does ... leave/arrive?**
*À quelle heure part/arrive ...?*
a kel er par/a·reev ...

| | | |
|---|---|---|
| **boat** | | |
| *le bateau* | | ler ba·to |
| **bus** | | |
| *le bus* | | ler bews |
| **train** | | |
| *le train* | | ler trun |

**I want to go to ...**
*Je voudrais aller à ...*
zher voo·dray a·lay a ...
**Which bus goes to ...?**
*Quel autobus/car part pour ...?*
kel o·to·boos/ka par poor ...
**Does this bus go to ...?**
*Ce car·là va·t·il à ...?*
ser ka·la va·til a ...
**Please tell me when we arrive in ...**
*Dîtes-moi quand on arrive à ... s'il vous plaît.*
deet·mwa kon·don a·reev a ... seel voo play
**Stop here, please.**
*Arrêtez ici, s'il vous plaît.*
a·ray·tay ee·see seel voo play

| the first | *le premier* (m) | ler prer·myay |
| | *la première* (f) | la prer·myair |
| the last | *le dernier* (m) | ler dair·nyay |
| | *la dernière* (f) | la dair·nyair |
| ticket | *billet* | bee·yay |
| ticket office | *le guichet* | ler gee·shay |
| timetable | *l'horaire* | lo·rair |
| train station | *la gare* | la gar |
| daily | *chaque jour* | shak zhoor |
| early | *tôt* | to |
| late | *tard* | tar |

| I'd like to hire | *Je voudrais* | zher voo·dray |
| a/an ... | *louer ...* | loo·way ... |
|   car | *une voiture* | ewn vwa·tewr |
|   4WD | *un quatre-quatre* | un kat·kat |
|   motorbike | *une moto* | ewn mo·to |
|   bicycle | *un vélo* | un vay·lo |

| petrol/gas | *essence* | ay·sons |
| diesel | *diesel* | dyay·zel |

**Is this the road to ...?**
| *C'est la route pour ...?* | say la root poor ... |

**Where's a service station?**
| *Où est-ce qu'il y a* | oo es·keel ya |
| *une station-service?* | ewn sta·syon·ser·vees |

**Please fill it up.**
| *Le plein, s'il vous plaît.* | ler plun seel voo play |

**I need a mechanic.**
| *J'ai besoin d'un* | zhay ber·zwun dun |
| *mécanicien.* | may·ka·nee·syun |

## PORTUGUESE

Like French, Portuguese is a Romance language (ie one closely derived from Latin). In West Africa it's the official language in Cape Verde and Guinea-Bissau.

Note that Portuguese uses masculine and feminine word endings, usually '-o' and '-a' respectively – to say 'thank you', a man will therefore say *obrigado*, a woman, *obrigada*.

## Accommodation
**I'm looking for a ...**
| *Procuro ...* | proo·*koo*·roo·... |
|   **campground** | |
|   *um parque de campismo* | oong park·de kang·*peezh*·moo |
|   **hotel** | |
|   *um hotel* | oong oo·*tel* |

**I'd like a ... room.**
| *Queria um quarto de ...* | kree·a oong *kwarr*·too de ... |
|   **double** | |
|   *casal* | ka·*zal* |

|   **single** | |
|   *individual* | ing·dee·vee·*dwal* |
|   **twin** | |
|   *duplo* | doo·ploo |

**How much is it per ...?**
| *Quanto custa por ...?* | kwang·too koos·ta porr ... |
|   **night** | |
|   *uma noite* | oo·ma noyt |
|   **person** | |
|   *pessoa* | pso·a |

## Conversation & Essentials
| Hello. | *Bom dia.* | bong *dee*·a |
| Hi. | *Olá/Chao.* | o·*la*/chow |
| Good day. | *Bom dia.* | bong *dee*·a |
| Goodbye. | *Adeus/Chao.* | a·*dyoos*/chow |
| See you later. | *Até logo.* | a·*te* lo·goo |
| How are you? | *Como está?* | ko·moo shta |
| Fine, and you? | *Tudo bem, e tu?* | too·doo beng e too |
| Yes. | *Sim.* | seeng |
| No. | *Não.* | nowng |
| Please. | *Faz favor.* | fash fa·*vorr* |
| Thank you (very | *(Muito)* | *(mweeng*·too) |
| much). | *Obrigado/a.* (m/f) | o·bree·*ga*·doo/da |
| You're welcome. | *De nada.* | de na·da |
| Excuse me. | *Desculpe.* | des·*koolp* |
| (before asking a question/making a request) | | |
| What's your | *Como se chama?* | ko·moo se sha·ma |
| name? | | |
| My name is ... | *Chamo-me ...* | sha·moo·me ... |
| Where are you | *De onde é?* | de ong·de e |
| from? | | |
| I'm from ... | *Sou (da/do/de) ...* | so (da/do/de) ... |

## Directions
**Where is ...?**
| *Onde fica ...?* | ongd *fee*·ka ... |

**Can you show me (on the map)?**
| *Pode mostrar-me* | pod moos·*trarrm* |
| *(no mapa)?* | (noo *ma*·pa) |

**How far is it?**
| *Qual a distância daqui?* | kwal a dees·*tan*·see·a da·*kee* |

| Turn ... | *Vire ...* | veer ... |
|   left | *à esquerda* | a *skerr*·da |
|   right | *à direita* | a dee·*ray*·ta |

| straight ahead | *em frente* | eng frengt |
| north | *norte* | nort |
| south | *sul* | sool |
| east | *este* | esht |
| west | *oeste* | oo·*esht* |

**LANGUAGE**

### EMERGENCIES

**Help!**
*Socorro!* — soo-*ko*-rroo

**I'm lost.**
*Estou perdido/a.* (m/f) — shto perr-*dee*-doo/da

**Where are the toilets?**
*Onde ficam* — *ong*-de fee-kam
*os lavabos?* — oos la-*va*-boos

**Go away!**
*Vai-te embora!* — vai-te eng-*bo*-ra

**Call ...!**
*Chame ...!* — sham ...
  **a doctor**
  *um médico* — oong me-dee-koo
  **the police**
  *a polícia* — a poo-lee-*see*-a

## Health

**I'm ill.**
*Estou doente.* — shto doo-*engt*

**I need a doctor (who speaks English).**
*Preciso de um médico* — pre-*see*-zoo de oong me-dee-koo
*(que fale inglês).* — (ke fal eeng-*glesh*)

| antiseptic | *antiséptico* | an-tee-*sep*-tee-koo |
| asthma | *asma* | *azh*-ma |
| condoms | *preservativo* | pre-zer-va-*tee*-voo |
| diarrhea | *diarréia* | dee-a-*ray*-a |
| fever | *febre* | febr |
| painkillers | *analgésicos* | a-nal-*zhe*-zee-koos |
| sanitary napkins | *pensos higiénicos* | peng-*soosh* ee-zhee-e-nee-koosh |
| tampons | *tampões* | tang-*poyngsh* |

**I'm allergic to ...**
*Sou alérgico/a à ...* — so a-lerr-*zhee*-koo/ka a ...
  **antibiotics**
  *antibióticos* — ang-tee-*byo*-tee-koos
  **peanuts**
  *amendoins* — a-meng-*doyngs*
  **penicillin**
  *penicilina* — pnee-see-*lee*-na

## Language Difficulties

**Do you speak English?**
*Fala inglês?* — *fa*-la eeng-*glesh*

**Does anyone here speak English?**
*Alguém aqui fala inglês?* — al-*geng* a-*kee* fa-la eeng-*glesh*

**I (don't) understand.**
*(Não) Entendo.* — (nowng) eng-*teng*-doo

**Could you please write it down?**
*Pode por favor escrever* — po-de-porr fa-*vorr* es-kre-*verr*
*num papel?* — noom pa-*pel*

## Numbers

| 0 | *zero* | ze-roo |
| 1 | *um/uma* (m/f) | oong/oo-ma |
| 2 | *dois/duas* (m/f) | doys/dwash |
| 3 | *três* | tresh |
| 4 | *quatro* | kwa-troo |
| 5 | *cinco* | seeng-koo |
| 6 | *seis* | saysh |
| 7 | *sete* | set |
| 8 | *oito* | oy-too |
| 9 | *nove* | nov |
| 10 | *dez* | desh |
| 11 | *onze* | ongz |
| 12 | *doze* | doz |
| 13 | *treze* | trez |
| 14 | *quatorze* | ka-torrz |
| 15 | *quinze* | keengz |
| 16 | *dezesseis* | dze-saysh |
| 17 | *dezesete* | dze-set |
| 18 | *dezoito* | dzoy-too |
| 19 | *dezenove* | dze-nov |
| 20 | *vinte* | veengt |
| 21 | *vinte e um* | veengt e oong |
| 22 | *vinte e dois* | veengt e doysh |
| 30 | *trinta* | treeng-ta |
| 40 | *quarenta* | kwa-reng-ta |
| 50 | *cinquenta* | seeng-kweng-ta |
| 60 | *sessenta* | se-seng-ta |
| 70 | *setenta* | steng-ta |
| 80 | *oitenta* | oy-teng-ta |
| 90 | *noventa* | noo-veng-ta |
| 100 | *cem* | sang |
| 200 | *duzentos* | doo-zeng-toosh |
| 1000 | *mil* | meel |

## Shopping & Services

**What time does ... open?**
*A que horas abre ...?* — a ke o-ras abr ...

**I'd like to buy ...**
*Queria comprar ...* — kree-rya kom-prarr ...

**How much is it?**
*Quanto é?* — kwang-too e

**That's too expensive.**
*É muito caro.* — e mweeng-too ka-roo

**Where is ...?**
*Onde fica ...?* — ong-de fee-ka ...
  **a bank**
  *o banco* — oo ban-koo
  **the ... embassy**
  *a embaixada do/da ...* — a eng-bai-sha-da doo/da ...
  **a market**
  *o mercado* — oo merr-ka-doo
  **a pharmacy/chemist**
  *uma farmácia* — oo-ma far-ma-sya

**the police station**
*o posto de polícia*    oo pos·too·de poo·*lee*·see·a
**the post office**
*o correio*    oo coo·*ray*·oo

**Can I pay ...?**
*Posso pagar com ...?*    po·soo pa·*garr* kom ...
  **by credit card**
  *cartão de crédito*    karr·*towng* de kre·dee·too
  **by travellers cheque**
  *traveler cheque*    tra·ve·ler *she*·kee

**less**    *menos*    me·noos
**more**    *mais*    maizh
**big**    *grande*    grangd
**small**    *pequeno/a* (m/f)    pke·noo/na

**Where can I ...?**
*Onde posso ...?*    on·de po·soo ...
  **change a travellers cheque**
  *trocar traveler cheques*    troo·karr tra·ve·*ler* she·kes
  **change money**
  *trocar dinheiro*    troo·kar dee·*nyay*·roo

## Time & Dates
**What time is it?**
*Que horas são?*    ke o·ras sowng
**It's (ten) o'clock.**
*São (dez) horas.*    sowng (desh) o·ras
**When?**
*Quando?*    kwang·doo

**now**    *agora*    a·go·ra
**today**    *hoje*    ozh
**tomorrow**    *amanhã*    a·ma·nyang

**Monday**    *segunda-feira*    sgoon·da·fay·ra
**Tuesday**    *terça-feira*    terr·sa·fay·ra
**Wednesday**    *quarta-feira*    kwarr·ta·fay·ra
**Thursday**    *quinta-feira*    keeng·ta·fay·ra
**Friday**    *sexta-feira*    saysh·ta·fay·ra
**Saturday**    *sábado*    sa·ba·doo
**Sunday**    *domingo*    doo·meeng·goo

## Transport
**Which ... goes**    *Qual o ... que*    kwal oo ... ke
**to ...?**    *vai para ...?*    vai pa·ra ...
  **boat**    *barco*    barr·koo
  **local bus**    *autocarro*    ow·too·ka·rroo
  **train**    *comboio*    kom·boy·oo

**Is this the (bus) to ...?**
*Este (autocarro)*    esht (ow·to·ka·rroo)
*vai para ...?*    vai pa·ra ...?

**What time does it leave?**
*Que horas sai?*    ke o·ras sai
**What time does it get to ...?**
*Que horas chega a ...?*    ke o·ras she·ga a ...
**A ticket to ...**
*Um bilhete para ...*    oong bee·*lyet* pa·ra ...

**I'd like to hire a/an ...**
*Queria alugar ...*
ke·rya a·loo·garr ...
  **4WD**
  *um quatro por quatro*    oom kwa·troo por kwa·troo
  **bicycle**
  *uma bicicleta*    oo·ma bee·see·*kle*·ta
  **car**
  *um carro*    oong ka·rroo
  **motorbike**
  *uma motocicleta*    oo·ma mo·too·see·*kle*·ta

**Is this the road to ...?**
*Esta é a estrada para ...?*
esh·ta e a es·tra·da pa·ra ...
**Where's a gas/petrol station?**
*Onde fica um posto de gasolina?*
on·de fee·ka oong pos·too de ga·zoo·lee·na
**Please fill it up.**
*Enche o depósito, por favor.*
en·she oo de·po·see·too porr fa·vorr
**I need a mechanic.**
*Preciso de um mecânico.*
pre·see·soo de oong me·ka·nee·koo

**diesel**    *diesel*    dee·sel
**petrol/gas**    *gasolina*    ga·zoo·lee·na

# AFRICAN LANGUAGES

Representing many African languages in the Roman alphabet is a difficult task, as many of Africa's languages don't have an official wrtten form. In our written representations, italics indicates which syllable takes the stress within a word. Syllables themselves are separated by dots.

## BAMBARA & DIOULA
Differences between Bambara and Dioula (also known as Jula) are relatively minor and the two languages share much of their vocabulary, eg 'Goodbye' in Bambara is *kan·bay*, in Dioula it is *an·bay*.

Bambara (called *bamanakan* in Bambara) is the predominant indigenous language of Mali, while Dioula is widely spoken as a first language in Côte d'Ivoire and Burkina Faso. Dioula is one of West Africa's major lingua francas (a common language used for communication between groups with different mother tongues) so the words and phrases included following can be used not only in Burkina Faso, Côte d'Ivoire and Mali but also in southeastern Mauritania (Néma and south), eastern Senegal, and parts of Gambia. In addition there are distinct similarities between Bambara/Dioula and the Mandinka of northern Gambia and parts of southern Senegal, and most Senoufo speakers in southern Mali (Sikasso region), southwestern Burkina Faso, and northern Côte d'Ivoire (Korhogo region) can speak Bambara/Dioula. It's not hard to see that some knowledge of it will prove very useful in this part of West Africa!

Bambara and Dioula are normally written using a phonetic alphabet; in this guide we've mostly used letters common to English. Some specific pronunciations you'll need to be aware of are:

| | |
|---|---|
| a | as in 'far' |
| e | as in 'bet' |
| i | as in 'marine' |
| o | as in 'hot' |
| u | between the 'u' in 'pull' and the 'oo' in 'boot' |
| g | always hard, as in 'get' |
| j | as in 'jet' |
| ñ | as in the 'ni' in 'onion' |
| ng | as the 'ng' in 'sing' – indicates that the preceding vowel is nasal |
| r | almost a 'd' sound |

In the following phrase lists variation in vocabulary is indicated by (B) for Bambara and (D) for Dioula.

## Greetings

The response to any of the following greetings (beginning with i-ni- ... ) is n-ba (for men) and n-seh (for women).

| | |
|---|---|
| **Hello.** | i-ni-che |
| **Hello.** (to someone working) | i-ni-baa-ra (literally, to you and your work) |
| **Good morning.** | i-ni-so-go-ma (sunrise to midday) |
| **Good afternoon.** | i-ni-ti-le (12 noon to 3 pm) |
| **Good evening.** | i-ni-wu-la (3 pm to sunset) |
| **Good night.** | i-ni-su (sunset to sunrise) |

> ### ARABIC ISLAMIC GREETINGS
> Traditional Arabic Islamic greetings are very common in Muslim West Africa – they're easy to learn and will be very much appreciated.
>
> **Greetings.**
> salaam aleikum (peace be with you)
> **Greetings to you too.**
> aleikum asalaam (and peace be with you)

| | |
|---|---|
| **Goodbye.** | kan-beng (B) |
| | an-beng (D) |
| **Please.** | S'il vous plaît. (French) |
| **Thank you.** | i-ni-che/ba-si-tay (lit: no problem) |
| **Sorry/Pardon.** | ha-ke-to |
| **Yes.** | a-wo |
| **No.** | a-yee (B)/uh-uh (D) |
| **How are you?** | i-ka-kéné |
| **I'm fine.** | tu-ro-te |
| **And you?** | e-dung? |
| **Can you help me please?** | ha-ke-to, i-bay-say-ka nn de-me wa? |
| **Do you speak English?** | i-be-say-ka aang-gi-li-kaang meng wa? |
| **Do you speak French?** | i-be-se-ka tu-ba-bu-kan meng wa? |
| **I only speak English.** | nn-be-se-ka aang-gi-li-kaang meng do-ron |
| **I speak a little French.** | nn-be-se-ka tu-ba-bu-kan meng do-nee |
| **I understand.** | nn-y'a-fa-mu |
| **I don't understand.** | nn-m'a-fa-mu |
| **What's your (first) name?** | i-to-go? |
| **My name is ...** | nn-to-go ... |
| **Where are you from?** | i-be-bo-ming? |
| **I'm from ...** | nn-be-bo ... |
| **Where is ...?** | ... be-ming? |
| **Is it far?** | a-ka-jang-wa? |
| **straight ahead** | a-be-ti-leng |
| **left** | nu-man-bo-lo-fe (lit: nose-picking hand) |
| **right** | ki-ni-bo-lo-fe (lit: rice-eating hand) |
| **How much is this?** | ni-ñe-jo-li-ye? |
| **That's too much.** | a-ka-ge-leng—ba-ri-ka! (lit: lower the price) |
| **Leave me alone!** | bo'i-sa! |
| **1** | ke-leng |
| **2** | fi-la (or fla) |
| **3** | saab-ba |
| **4** | na-ni |
| **5** | du-ru |

| | | | | |
|---|---|---|---|---|
| 6 | *wo*·ro | 4 | *kwa*·tu |
| 7 | *wo*·lon·fla | 5 | *sin*·ku |
| 8 | *shay*·ging | 6 | *say*·es |
| 9 | *ko*·nong·taang | 7 | *se*·tee |
| 10 | taang | 8 | *oy*·tu |
| 11 | *taang*·ni·kay·len | 9 | *no*·vee |
| 12 | *taang*·ni·*fla* | 10 | des |
| 13 | *taang*·ni·*sa*·ba | 11 | *oan*·zee |
| 14 | *taang*·ni·*na*·ni | 12 | *do*·zee |
| 15 | *taang*·ni·*doo*·ru | 13 | *tre*·zee |
| 16 | *taang*·ni·*wo*·ro | 14 | ka·*to*·zee |
| 17 | *taang*·ni·*wo*·lon·fla | 15 | *kin*·zee |
| 18 | *taang*·ni·*shay*·ging | 16 | dee·za·*say*·es |
| 19 | *taang*·ni ko·non·*taang* | 17 | dee·za·*se*·tee |
| 20 | mu·*gang* | 18 | dee·*zoy*·tu |
| 30 | *bi*·saab·ba | 19 | dee·za·*no*·vee |
| 31 | *bi*·saab·ba·ni·*ke*·leng | 20 | *vin*·tee |
| 40 | *bi*·na·ni | 30 | *trin*·ta |
| 50 | *bi*·du·ru | 100 | sen |
| 60 | *bi*·wo·ro | 1000 | meel |
| 70 | *bi*·wo·lon·*fla* | | |
| 80 | *bi*·shay·ging | | |
| 90 | *bie*·ko·non·taang | | |
| 100 | *ke*·me | | |
| 1000 | wa | | |
| 5000 | *wa*·du·ru | | |

# CRIOULO

Crioulo is a Portuguese-based creole spoken (with more or less mutual intelligibility) in the Cape Verde islands, Guinea-Bissau (where it's the lingua franca and 'market language') and parts of Senegal and Gambia. Nearly half the Crioulo speakers of Cape Verde are literate in Portuguese but since independence in 1975 Crioulo has become increasingly dominant; upwards of 70% of the country's population speak Crioulo. Even allowing for regional differences the phrases listed below should be understood in both Cape Verde and Guinea-Bissau.

| | |
|---|---|
| Good morning. | bom·*dee*·a |
| Good evening. | bow·a *no*·tay |
| Goodbye. | na·buy |
| How are you? | ou·*kor*·po ees·ta·*bon?* |
| I'm fine. | ta·*bon* |
| Please. | pur·fa·*bor* |
| Thank you. | ob·ree·*ga*·do |
| How much is it? | kal e *pre*·su |

| | |
|---|---|
| 1 | aan |
| 2 | dos |
| 3 | tres |

# DAN (YACOUBA)

Dan (also known as Yacouba) is one of the principal African languages spoken in Côte d'Ivoire (in and around Man). There are also a significant number of Dan speakers in Liberia (where it's referred to as 'Gio'). There are a couple of major dialects and more than 20 sub-dialects; as a result most communication between different language groups in the region is carried out in Dioula (see the Bambara/Dioula section on p867 for a comprehensive list of Dioula words and phrases).

| | |
|---|---|
| Good morning. | un-*zhoo*·ba·bo (to a man) |
| Good morning. | *na*·ba·bo (to a woman) |
| Good evening. | un-*zhoo*·attoir (to a man) |
| Good evening. | *na*·attoir (to a woman) |
| How are you? | bwee·*aar*·way |
| Thank you. | ba·lee·ka |

# DIOLA (JOLA)

The Diola people inhabit the Casamance region of Senegal, and also the south-western parts of Gambia, where their name is spelt Jola. Their language is Diola, also known as Jola, which should not be confused with the Dioula/Jula spoken widely in other parts of West Africa.

Diola society is segmented and very flexible, so several dialects have developed which may not be mutually intelligible between different groups even though the area inhabited by the Diola is relatively small.

| Hello/Welcome. | ka·sou·mai·kep |
| (response) | ka·sou·mai·kep |
| Goodbye. | ou·ka·to·rra |

## DIOULA (JULA)

See Bambara/Dioula (p867).

## DJERMA (ZARMA)

After Hausa, Djerma (pronounced 'jer-ma', also known as Zarma) is Niger's most common African language (people with Djerma as their first language make up around a quarter of the country's population). It's spoken mostly in the western regions including around Niamey, and it is one of the official national languages used for radio broadcasts.

| Good morning. | ma·teen·ke·nee |
| Good evening. | ma·teen·hee·ree |
| How are you? | bar·ka? |
| Thank you. | fo·fo |
| Goodbye. | ka·la ton·ton |

## EWE

Ewe (pronounced 'ev-vay') is the major indigenous language of southern Togo. It is also an official language of instruction in primary and secondary schools in Ghana where it's spoken mainly in the east of the country; you'll find that Twi (the language of the Ashanti and the Fanti, see p876) is the more universally spoken language of Ghana. There are also several closely related languages and dialects of Ewe spoken in Benin.

| Good morning/ | nee·lye·nee·aa |
| Good evening. | |
| (response) | mee·lay |
| What's your name? | n·ko·wo·day? |
| My name is ... | nk·nee·n·yay ... |
| How are you? | nee·fo·a? |
| I'm fine. | mee·fo |
| Thank you. | mou·do, ack·pay·now |
| Goodbye. | mee·a do·go |

## FON (FONGBE)

Fon (called *Fongbe* in the language itself) belongs to the Kwa group of the Gbe language family, *gbe* being the Fon word for 'language'. It is another of the major lingua francas of West Africa, spoken for the most part in Nigeria and Benin, but also used widely in Côte d'Ivoire, Burkina Faso, Niger and Togo. While Fon is subject to clear dialectal variation depending on region, you should find that the list of words and phrases below will be universally understood.

The Fon language is written using the IPA (International Phonetic Alphabet); for the sake of simplicity we've used a pronunciation system that uses letters common to English. Fon is a tone language (ie intended meaning is dependent upon changes in pitch within the normal range of a speaker's voice) with a standard system of five tones; in this guide we have simplified things by using only two written accents for tones: an acute accent (eg **á**) for a high tone; a grave accent (eg **à**) for a low tone; an unmarked vowel has a mid-tone.

Pronounce letters as you would in English, keeping the following points in mind:

| a | as in 'far' |
| e | as in 'met' |
| i | as in 'marine' |
| o | either as in 'hot' or as in 'for' |
| u | as in 'put' |
| g | as in 'go' |
| h | silent |
| ng | indicates that the preceding vowel is nasalised, eg the 'ing' sound in 'sing' |
| ñ | as the 'ni' in 'onion' |

| Hello. | ò·kú |
| Goodbye. | é·dà·bò |
| Please. | kèng·kéng·lèng |
| Thank you. | à·wà·nu |
| You're welcome. | é·sù·kpé·a |
| Sorry/Pardon. | kèng·kéng·lèng |
| Yes. | eng |
| No. | é·wo |
| How are you? | ne·à·dè·gbòng? |
| I'm fine. | ùn·dò·gàng·jí |
| And you? | hwe·lo? |
| Can you help me please? | kèng·kéng·lèng· dá·lò·mì? |

| Do you speak ...? | à·sè ... à? |
| English | glèng·síng·gbè |
| French | flàng·sé·gbè |

| I only speak English. | glèng·síng·gbè ké·dé·wè·ùn·sè |
| I speak a little French. | ùn·sè flàng·sé·gbè kpè·dè |
| I understand. | ùn·mò·nu·jé·mè |

| I don't understand. | ùn·mò·nu·jé·mè·a |
| What's your name? | ne·à·nò·ñí? |
| My name is ... | ùn·nò·ñí ... |
| Where are you from? | tò·té·mè·nù·wé·ñí·wè? |
| I'm from ... | ... nù·wé·ñí·mì |
| Where is ...? | fi·té·wé ...? |
| Is it far? | e·ling·wé·a? |
| straight ahead | tre·le·le |
| left | à·myò |
| right | à·ɗi·sí |
| How much is this? | nà·bí·wè·ñí·é·lò? |
| That's too much. | é·vá·khì·díng |
| Leave me alone! | jo·mí·dó! |

| 1 | ò·de |
| 2 | ò·wè |
| 3 | à·tòng |
| 4 | e·nè |
| 5 | à·tóng |
| 6 | à·yì·zéng |
| 7 | te·we |
| 8 | ta·to |
| 9 | téng·nè |
| 10 | wo |
| 11 | wo·dò·kpó |
| 12 | we·wè |
| 13 | wa·tòng |
| 14 | we·nè |
| 15 | à·fò·tòn |
| 16 | à·fò·tòng·nù·kúng·dò·pó |
| 17 | à·fò·tóng·nu·kúng·wè |
| 18 | à·fò·tóng·nu·kúng·à·tòng |
| 19 | à·fò·tóng·nu·kúng·è·ne |
| 20 | kò |
| 30 | gbàng |
| 40 | kàng·dé |
| 50 | kàng·dé·wo |
| 60 | kàng·dé·ko |
| 70 | kàng·dé·gbàng |
| 80 | kàng·wè |
| 90 | kàng·wè·wo |
| 100 | kàng·wè·kò |
| 1000 | à·fà·tóng |

## FULA (PULAAR)

Fula (which is also known as Pulaar) is one of the languages of the Fula people found across West Africa, from northern Senegal to Sudan in the east, and as far south as Ghana and Nigeria. The Fula are known as Peul in Senegal (they are also called Fulani and Fulbe).

There are two main languages in the Fulani group: Fulfulde, spoken mainly in northern and southern Senegal (includes the dialects known as Tukulor and Fulakunda); Futa Fula (also known as Futa Djalon), the main indigenous language of Guinea, also spoken in eastern Senegal.

It's worth noting that these far-flung languages have many regional dialects which aren't always mutually intelligible between different groups.

## FULFULDE

The following words and phrases should be understood through most parts of Senegal. Note that **ng** should be pronounced as one sound (like the 'ng' in 'sing'); practise isolating this sound and using it at the beginning of a word. The letter **ñ** represents the 'ni' sound in 'onion'.

| Hello. | no ngoolu daa (sg) |
| | no ngoolu dong (pl) |
| Goodbye. | ñalleen e jamm (lit: Have a good day) |
| | mbaaleen e jamm (lit: Have a good night) |
| Please. | njaafodaa |
| Thank you. | a jaaraama (sg) |
| | on jaaraama (pl) |
| You're welcome. | enen ndendidum |
| Sorry/Pardon. | yaafo or achanam hakke |
| Yes. | eey |
| No. | alaa |
| How are you? | no mbaddaa? |
| I'm fine. | mbe de sellee |
| ... and you? | ... an nene? |
| Can you help me please? | ada waawi wallude mi, njaafodaa? |
| Do you speak English/ French? | ada faama engale/faranse? |
| I only speak English. | ko engale tan kaala mi |
| I speak a little French. | mi nani faranse seeda |
| I understand. | mi faami |
| I don't understand. | mi faamaani |
| What's your name? | no mbiyeteedaa? |
| My name is ... | ko ... mbiyetee mi |
| Where are you from? | to njeyedaa? |
| I'm from ... | ko ... njeyaa mi |
| Where is ...? | hoto woni? |
| Is it far? | no woddi? |
| straight ahead | ko yeesu |
| left | nano bang·ge |
| right | nano ñaamo |
| How much is this? | dum no foti jarata? |
| That's too much. | e ne tiidi no feewu |
| Leave me alone! | accam!/oppam mi deeja! |

| 1 | go·o |
|---|---|
| 2 | didi |
| 3 | tati |
| 4 | nayi |
| 5 | joyi |
| 6 | jeego |
| 7 | jeedidi |
| 8 | jeetati |
| 9 | jeenayi |
| 10 | sappo |
| 11 | sappoygoo |
| 12 | sappoydidi |
| 13 | sappoytati |
| 20 | noogaas |
| 30 | chappantati |
| 100 | temedere |
| 1000 | wujenere |

## FUTA FULA (FUTA DJALON)

This variety of Fula known as Futa Fula or Futa Djalon is predominant in the Futa Djalon region of Guinea. It is named after the people who speak it, and is distinct from the variety known as Fulfulde that is spoken in northern and southern Senegal.

| Good morning/Good evening. | on·jaa·ra·ma |
|---|---|
| How are you? | ta·na·la·ton? |
| I'm fine. | ta·na·o·ala |
| Where is ...? | ko·hon·to wo·nee? |
| Thank you. | on·jaa·ra·ma |
| Goodbye. | on·ount·tou·ma |

## GA & ADANGME

Ga (and its very close relative Adangme) is one of the major indigenous languages of Ghana, spoken mostly around Accra.

| Good morning/ Good evening. | meeng·ga·bou |
|---|---|
| How are you? | tey·yo·tain? |
| I'm fine. | ee·o·jo·baan |
| What's your name? | to·cho·bo·tain? |
| My name is ... | a·cho·mee ... |
| Thank you. | o·ye·ra·don |
| Goodbye. | bye·bye |

## HASSANIYA

Hassaniya is a Berber-Arabic dialect which is spoken by Moors of Mauritania. It's also the official language of Mauritania.

| Good morning. | sa·la·ma a·lay·koum |
|---|---|
| Good evening. | ma·sa el·hair |

| How are you? | ish·ta·ree? |
|---|---|
| Thank you. | shu·kraan |
| Goodbye. | ma·sa·laam |

## HAUSA

Hausa is spoken and understood in a vast area of West Africa and beyond. Dialectal variation is not extreme in Hausa so the phrases included in this language guide will be universally understood, and will prove useful in Benin, Burkina Faso, Côte d'Ivoire, Niger, Nigeria and northern Ghana (where it is the principal language of trade).

Hausa is a tone language (where variations in the pitch of a speaker's voice has a direct influence on intended meaning) with three basic tones assigned to vowels: low, high and rising-falling. Standard written Hausa isn't marked for tones and the pronunciation guide for the words and phrases included below doesn't show them either. Your best bet is to learn with your ears by noting the inflection of African speakers.

The consonants **b**, **d** and **k** have 'glottalised' equivalents where air is exhaled forcefully from the larynx (the voice box); these glottal consonants are represented in this guide by **B**, **D** and **K** respectively.

Distinctions in vowel length are also overlooked in standard written Hausa. In this guide long vowels are represented by double vowels, eg *aa'aa* (no).

| Hello. | sannu |
|---|---|
| (response) | yauwaa sannu |
| Good morning. | eenaa kwanaa |
| Good morning. | lapeeyaloh (response) |
| Good evening. | eenaa eenee |
| Good evening. | lapeeyalo (response) |
| Goodbye. | sai wani lookachi |
| Please. | don allaa |
| Thank you. | naa goodee |
| Don't mention it/ It's nothing. | baa koomi |
| Sorry/Pardon. | yi haKurii, ban ji ba |
| Yes. | ii |
| No. | aa'aa |
| How are you? | inaa gajiyaa? |
| I'm fine. | baa gajiyaa |
| And you? | kai fa? |
| What's your name? | yaayaa suunanka? |
| My name is ... | suunaanaa ... |
| Where are you from? | daga inaa ka fitoo? |
| I'm from ... | naa fitoo daga ... |

| | |
|---|---|
| **Can you help me please?** | don allaah, koo zaa ka taimakee ni? |
| **Do you speak English/ French?** | kanaa jin ingiliishii/ faransancii? |
| **I speak only English.** | inaa jin ingiliishii kawai |
| **I speak a little French.** | inaa jin faransancii kaDan |
| **I understand.** | naa gaanee |
| **I don't understand.** | ban gaanee ba |
| **Where is ...?** | inaa ...? |
| **Is it far ...?** | da niisaa ...? |
| **straight ahead** | miiKee sambal |
| **left** | hagu |
| **right** | daama |
| **How much is this?** | nawa nee wannan? |
| **That's too much.** | akwai tsaadaa ga wannan |
| **Leave me alone!** | tafi can! |

| | |
|---|---|
| **1** | d'aya |
| **2** | biyu |
| **3** | uku |
| **4** | hud'u |
| **5** | biyar |
| **6** | shida |
| **7** | bakwai |
| **8** | takwas |
| **9** | tara |
| **10** | gooma |
| **11** | gooma shaa d'aya |
| **12** | gooma shaa biyu |
| **13** | gooma shaa uku |
| **14** | goma shaa hud'u |
| **15** | goma shaa biyar |
| **16** | gooma shaa shida |
| **17** | gooma shaa bakwai |
| **18** | gooma shaa takwas |
| **19** | gooma shaa tara |
| **20** | ashirin |
| **30** | talaatin |
| **40** | arba'in |
| **50** | hamsin |
| **60** | sittin |
| **70** | saba'in |
| **80** | tamaanin |
| **90** | casa'in |
| **100** | d'arii |
| **1000** | dubuu |

## IGBO (IBO)

Igbo, also known as Ibo, is the predominant indigenous language of Nigeria's southeast, where it is afforded the status of official language; it's used in the media and in government, and is the main lingua franca of the region. There are over 30 dialects of Igbo, each with varying degrees of mutual intelligibility.

| | |
|---|---|
| **Good morning.** | ee-*bow*-la-chee |
| **Good evening.** | na-*no*-na |
| **How are you?** | ee-*may*-na aan-*ghan*? |
| **Thank you.** | ee-*may*-na |
| **Goodbye.** | *kay*-may-see-a |

## KABYÉ

After Ewé, Kabyé is Togo's most common African language, predominant in the Kara region. One Kabyé word you'll always hear is *yovo* (white person).

| | |
|---|---|
| **Good morning** | un-la-*wa*-lay |
| **How are you?** | be-ja-un-sema |
| **I'm fine.** | a-*la*-fia |
| **Thank you.** | un-la-*ba*-lay |
| **Goodbye.** | be-*la*-bee-ta-si |

## KRIO

Krio is Sierra Leone's most common non-colonial language. Its major ingredient is English, but its sound system and grammar have been enriched by various West African languages. Because Krio was imported by different slave groups, there are strong differences between the Krio spoken in various regions, so strong in fact that some people find it easier to understand the Krio of Nigeria than the Krio spoken in other parts of Sierra Leone.

| | |
|---|---|
| **Hello.** | kou-shay |
| **Hi, mate!** | e bo! |
| **How are you?** | how-dee bo-dee? |
| **I'm fine.** | bo-dee fine/ no bad (more common) |
| **Thank God.** | a tel god tenk-kee |
| **Thank you.** | tenk-kee |
| **Please.** | dou-ya (a-beg) (added for emphasis) |
| **Goodbye.** | we go see back |
| **How much?** | ow mus? |
| **food** | chop |
| **Sierra Leone** | salone |

## MALINKÉ

Malinké is spoken in the region around the borders between Senegal, Mali and Guinea. It's one of Senegal's six national languages. While it's very similar in some respects to the Mandinka spoken in Gambia and Senegal (they share much of their vocabulary), the two are classed as separate languages.

| Good morning. | nee·so·ma |
| Good evening. | nee·woo·la |
| How are you? | tan·aas·te? |
| Thank you. | nee·kay |
| Goodbye. | m·ba·ra·wa |

## MANDINKA

Mandinka is the language of the Mandinka people found largely in central and northern Gambia, and in parts of southern Senegal. The people and their language are also called Mandingo and they're closely related to other Mande-speaking groups such as the Bambara of Mali, where they originate. Mandinka is classed as one of Senegal's national languages.

In this guide, **ng** should be pronounced as the 'ng' in 'sing' and **ñ** represents the 'ni' sound in 'onion'.

| Hello. | i/al be ñaading (sg/pl) |
| Good bye. | fo tuma doo |
| Please. | dukare |
| Thank you. | i/al ning bara (sg/pl) |
| You're welcome. | mbee le dentaala/wo teng fengti (lit: It's nothing) |
| Sorry/Pardon. | hakko tuñe |
| Yes. | haa |
| No. | hani |
| How are you? | i/al be kayrato? (sg/pl) |
| I'm fine. | tana tenna (lit: I'm out of trouble) |
| | kayra dorong (lit: peace only) |
| And you? | ite fanang? |
| What's your name? | i too dung? |
| My name is ... | ntoo mu ... leti |
| Where are you from? | i/al bota munto? (sg/pl) |
| I'm from ... | mbota ... |
| Can you help me please? | i/al seng maakoy noo, dukare? (sg/pl) |
| Do you speak English/ French? | ye angkale/faranse kango moyle? |
| I speak only English. | nga angkale kango damma le moy |
| I speak a little French. | nga faranse kango domonding le moy |
| I understand. | ngaa kalamuta le/ngaa fahaam le |
| I don't understand. | mmaa kalamuta/mmaa fahaam |
| Where is ...? | ... be munto? |
| Is it far? | faa jamfata? |

| Go straight ahead. | sila tiling jan kilingo |
| left | maraa |
| right | bulu baa |
| How much is this? | ñing mu jelu leti? |
| That's too much. | a daa koleyaata baake |
| Leave me alone! | mbula! |

| 1 | kiling |
| 2 | fula |
| 3 | saba |
| 4 | naani |
| 5 | luulu |
| 6 | wooro |
| 7 | woorowula |
| 8 | sey |
| 9 | kononto |
| 10 | tang |
| 11 | tang ning kiling |
| 12 | tang ning fula |
| 13 | tang ning saba |
| 20 | muwaa |
| 30 | tang saba |
| 100 | keme |
| 1000 | wili kiling |

## MINA (GENGBE)

Mina, also known as Gengbe, is the language of trade in southern Togo, especially along the coast. It belongs to the Gbe (gbe meaning 'language') subgroup of the vast Kwa language family. Other Gbe languages of Togo include Ajagbe, Fongbe, Maxigbe and Wacigbe.

| Good morning. | so·bay·do |
| (response) | dosso |
| How are you? | o·foin? |
| I'm fine. | aaaa ('a' as in 'bat') |
| Thank you. | ack·pay |
| Goodbye. | so·day·lo |

## MORÉ

Moré (the language of the Mossi) is spoken by more than half the population of Burkina Faso – with over 4½ million speakers it's the country's principal indigenous language.

| Good morning. | yee·bay·ro |
| Good evening. | nay·za·bree |
| How are you? | la·fee·bay·may? |
| I'm fine. | la·fee·bay·la |
| Thank you. | un·pus·da bar·ka |
| Goodbye. | wen·a·ta·say |

## SANGHA DIALECT

Sangha is one of the main dialects (from around 48 others!) spoken by the Dogon people who inhabit the Falaise de Bandiagara in central Mali. Dialectal variation can be so marked that mutual intelligibility between the many Dogon groups is not always assured.

| Good morning. | a·ga·po |
| Good evening. | dee·ga·po |
| How are you? | ou say·yo? |
| I'm fine. | say·o |
| Thank you. | bee·ray·po |
| Goodbye. | ee·eye·ee way·dang |
| Safe journey! | day·gay·day·ya |

## SENOUFO

The Senoufo words and phrases listed following will prove useful if you're travelling through southern Mali, southwestern Burkina Faso and northern Côte d'Ivoire.

Senoufo pronunciation can be a very difficult prospect for foreigners, and with no official written form the task of matching the sounds of the language with letters on a page presents quite a challenge. The pronunciation system used in this guide provides rough approximations only. Try to pick up the sounds and inflections of the language by listening to fluent Senoufo speakers.

| a | as in 'far' |
| e | as in 'bet' |
| é | as the 'ay' in 'bay' |
| i | as in 'marine' |
| o | as in 'hot' |
| u | between the 'u' in 'pull' and the 'oo' in 'boot' |
| g | always hard, as in 'get' |
| ñ | as in the 'ni' in 'onion' |
| ng | as the 'ng' in 'sing' – indicates that the preceding vowel is nasal |

| Hello. | kéné |
| Goodbye. | wu·ñe·té·re |
| Thank you. | fa·na |
| Sorry/Pardon. | ya·hé·ya |
| Yes. | huu or mi·lo·go |
| No. | mé·tye |
| How are you? | ma·cho·lo·go·la? |
| I'm fine. | min·bé·gé·ba·mén |
| And you? | mohn·dohn? |

| What's your name? | men·ma·mi·in·ye? |
| My name is ... | men·min·ye ... |

| Do you speak ...? | mun·na ... chi·yé·ré·lu·gu·la? |
| English | aan·gi·li·kan |
| French | tu·ba·bu·kan |

| I only speak English. | min·na aan·gi·li·kan chi·yé·re·ye·ké·né |
| I speak a little French. | min·na tu·ba·bu·kan chi·yé·re tye·ri·ye |
| Can you help me please? | na·pu·gu? |
| I don't understand. | min·nay·chi·men |
| Where are you from? | shi·mo·na yi·ri·ré? |
| I'm from ... | min·na·yi·ri ... |
| Where is ...? | shi·ong·ye ...? |
| Is it far? | ka·lé·li·la? |
| left | ka·mohn |
| right | kin·yi·ka·ni·gi·he·ye·ré |
| How much is this? | jur·gi·na·de·le? |
| That's too much! | ka·la·ra·wa·a, de! |
| Leave me alone! | yi·ri·wa! or me·ya·ba! |

### Numbers

Numbers in Senoufo can be a very complicated affair. For example, the number 'one hundred' translates literally as 'two-times-five-times-two-times-four-plus-two-times-ten' – use the numbers in the Bambara/Dioula section (p867) and you'll have no trouble being understood.

## SUSU

Susu is Guinea's third–most common indigenous language. It's spoken mainly in the south around Conakry.

| Good morning. | tay·na ma·ree |
| Good evening. | tay·na ma·fay·yen |
| How are you? | o·ree to·na·mo? |
| Thank you. | ee·no·wa·lee |
| Goodbye. | oo·ne·gay·say·gay |

## TAMASHEK

Tamashek (spelt variously 'Tamasheq', 'Tamachek', 'Tamajeq' and more!) is the language of the Tuareg. There are two main dialects: Eastern, spoken in western Niger and eastern Mali; Western, spoken in western Niger, the Gao region of Mali, and northern Nigeria.

| How do you do? | met·al·ee·kha? (pol)/o·yeek? (inf) |
| I'm fine. | eel·kha·rass |

| How's the heat? | min·ee·twi·xe? (a traditional greeting) |
| Good/Fine. | ee·zott |
| How much? | min·ee·kit? |
| Thank you. | tan·oo·mert |
| Goodbye. | harr·sad |

## TWI

Twi (pronounced 'chwee'), the language of the Ashanti, is the most widely spoken African language in Ghana, where it's the official language of education and literature. Along with Fanti it belongs to the large Akan language family. Most of the dialects within this group are mutually intelligible.

| Hello. | a·kwa·ba |
| (response) | yaa |
| Good morning. | ma·cheeng |
| Good evening. | ma·jo |
| Are you going to ... | ya·co ...? |
| Goodbye. | ma·krow |
| Safe journey. | nan·tee yee·yay |
| Let's go. | yen·co |
| How are you? | ay·ta·sein? |
| I'm fine. | ay·ya |
| Please. | me·pa·wo·che·o |
| Thank you. | may·da·say |
| Yes. | aan |
| No. | da·be |
| Do you speak English? | wo·te bro·fo aan·na |
| I don't understand. | um·ta se |
| I'd like ... | me·pay ... |

| 1 | bee·a·ko |
| 2 | a·bee·eng |
| 3 | a·bee·e·sa |
| 4 | a·nang |
| 5 | a·nuhm |
| 6 | a·see·ya |
| 7 | a·song |
| 8 | a·wo·twe |
| 9 | a·kruhng |
| 10 | du |
| 11 | du·bee·a·ko |
| 20 | a·dwo·nu |
| 100 | o·ha |
| 1000 | a·pem |

## WOLOF

Wolof (spelt Ouolof in French) is the language of the Wolof people, who are found in Senegal, particularly in the central area north and east of Dakar, along the coast, and in the western regions of Gambia. The Wolof spoken in Gambia is slightly different to the Wolof spoken in Senegal; the Gambian Wolof people living on the north bank of the Gambia River speak the Senegalese variety. Wolof is used as a common language in many parts of Senegal and Gambia, often instead of either French or English, and some smaller groups complain about the increasing 'Wolofisation' of their culture.

For some traditional Arabic Islamic greetings which are used in Muslim West Africa, see p868.

Most consonants are pronounced as they are in English; when they are doubled they are pronounced with greater emphasis. Some vowels have accented variants.

| a | as in 'at' |
| à | as in 'far' |
| e | as in 'bet' |
| é | as in 'whey' |
| ë | as the 'u' in 'but' |
| i | as in 'it' |
| o | as in 'hot' |
| ó | as in 'so' |
| u | as in 'put' |
| g | as in 'go' |
| ñ | as the 'ni' in 'onion' |
| ng | as in 'sing'; practise making this sound at the beginning of a word |
| r | always rolled |
| s | as in 'so', not as in 'as' |
| w | as in 'we' |
| x | as the 'ch' in Scottish loch |

| Hello. | Na nga def. (sg) |
| | Na ngeen def. (pl) |
| Good morning. | Jàmm nga fanaane. |
| Good afternoon. | Jàmm nga yendoo. |
| Goodnight. | Fanaanal jàmm. |
| Goodbye. | Ba beneen. |
| Please. | Su la nexee. |
| Thank you. | Jërëjëf. |
| You're welcome. | Agsil/agsileen ak jàmm . (sg/pl) |
| Sorry/Pardon. | Baal ma. |
| Yes. | Waaw. |
| No. | Déedéet. |
| How are you? | Jàmm nga/ngeen am? (sg/pl) |
| | (lit: Have you peace?) |
| I'm fine. | Jàmm rekk. |
| And you? | Yow nag? |
| How is your family? | Naka waa kër ga? |

**LANGUAGE**

| | |
|---|---|
| What's your first name? | Naka nga/ngeen tudd? (sg/pl) |
| What's your last name? | Naka nga sant? |
| My name is ... | Maa ngi tudd ... |
| Where do you live? | Fan nga dëkk? |
| Where are you from? | Fan nga/ngeen jòge? (sg/pl) |
| I'm from ... | Maa ngi jòge ... |
| Do you speak English/ French? | Dégg nga.Angale/ Faranse? (sg/pl) |
| I speak only English. | Angale rekk laa dégg. |
| I speak a little French. | Dégg naa tuuti Faranse. |
| I don't speak Wolof/French. | Màn dégguma Wolof/ Faranse. |
| I understand. | Dégg naa. |
| I don't undestand. | Dégguma. |
| I'd like ... | Dama bëggoon ... |
| Where is ...? | Fan la ...? |
| Is it far? | Sore na? |
| straight ahead | cha kanam |
| left | cammooñ |
| right | ndeyjoor |
| Get in! | Dugghal waay! |
| How much is this? | Lii ñaata? |
| It's too much. | Seer na torob. |
| Leave me alone! | May ma jàmm! |

| | |
|---|---|
| Monday | altine |
| Tuesday | talaata |
| Wednesday | àllarba |
| Thursday | alxames |
| Friday | àjjuma |
| Saturday | gaawu |
| Sunday | dibéer |

| | |
|---|---|
| 0 | tus |
| 1 | benn |
| 2 | ñaar |
| 3 | ñett |
| 4 | ñeent |
| 5 | juróom |
| 6 | juróom-benn |
| 7 | juróom- ñaar |
| 8 | juróom- ñett |
| 9 | juróom- ñeent |
| 10 | fukk |
| 11 | fukk-ak-benn |
| 12 | fukk-ak-ñaar |
| 13 | fukk-ak-ñett |
| 14 | fukk-ak-ñeent |
| 15 | fukk-ak-juróom |
| 16 | fukk-ak-juróom benn (lit: ten-and-five one) |
| 17 | fukk-ak-juróom ñaar |
| 18 | fukk-ak-juróom ñett |
| 19 | fukk-ak-juróom ñeent |
| 20 | ñaar-fukk (lit: two-ten) |
| 30 | fanweer |
| 40 | ñeent-fukk (lit: four-ten) |
| 50 | juróom-fukk (lit: five-ten) |
| 60 | juróom-benn-fukk (lit: five-one-ten) |
| 70 | juróom-ñaar-fukk (lit: five two-ten) |
| 80 | juróom-ñett-fukk |
| 90 | juróom-ñeent-fukk |
| 100 | téeméer |
| 1000 | junne |

## YORUBA

Yoruba belongs to the Kwa group of the Ede language family (ede is the Yoruba word for 'language'). Along with Fon it is one of the main lingua francas in much of the eastern part of West Africa but it is principally spoken as a first language in Benin and Nigeria. As with the majority of indigenous West African languages, Yoruba is subject to a degree of dialectal variation, not surprising given the broad geographical area its speakers are found in; fortunately, the majority of these variants are mutually intelligible.

Yoruba is normally written using the IPA (International Phonetic Alphabet). It is a tone language, ie changes in voice-pitch are important in giving words their intended meaning. To give a comprehensive description of the five tone Yoruba vowel system would require more space than we have available here. For simplicity we've used an acute accent (eg á) to represent a high tone, a grave accent (eg à) to represent a low tone; unmarked vowels take a mid-tone.

The pronunciations we give for the words and phrases below are approximations only. Pronounce letters as you would in English, keeping the following points in mind:

| | |
|---|---|
| a | as in 'far' |
| e | as in 'met' |
| i | as in 'marine' |
| o | as in 'hot'; as in 'or' |
| u | as in 'put' |
| g | as in 'go' |
| h | not pronounced |
| ng | indicates that the preceding vowel is nasalised, eg the 'ing' in 'sing' |

| | |
|---|---|
| Hello. | bá·o |
| Goodbye. | ó·dà·bò |

| | | | |
|---|---|---|---|
| Please. | e·dá·kuhn | 1 | e·ní |
| Thank you. | e·she·wu | 2 | è·jì |
| You're welcome. | e·wo·lè | 3 | e·ta |
| Sorry/Pardon. | e·dá·kuhn | 4 | e·ring |
| Yes. | e | 5 | à·rúng |
| No. | è·ré·wo | 6 | è·fà |
| How are you? | shé·wà·dá·da? | 7 | è·je |
| I'm fine. (And you?) | à·dú·kpé (è·nyi·na·nkó?) | 8 | è·jo |
| What's your name? | bá·wo·le·má·jé? | 9 | e·saang |
| My name is ... | mo·má·jé ... | 10 | e·wa |
| Where are you from? | à·rá·ibo·lo·jé? | 11 | mó·kàang·la |
| I'm from ... | à·rá ... ni mi | 12 | mé·ji·la |
| Can you help me | e·dá·kuhn e·ràang· | 13 | mé·tà·la |
| please? | mí·ló·wó? | 14 | mé·ri·la |
| Do you speak English? | she·gbó ge·sì? | 15 | má·rùhng·la |
| Do you speak French? | she·gbó fraang·sé? | 16 | mé·ring·dó·gúhng |
| I only speak English. | ge·sì ni·kaang nì·mo·gbó | 17 | mé·tá·dó·gúhng |
| I speak a little | mo·gbó fraang·sé dí·è | 18 | mé·jì·dó·gúhng |
| French. | | 19 | ò·kaang·dó·gúhng |
| I don't understand. | kò·yé·mi·sí | 20 | ò·gúhng |
| Where is ...? | ibo ni ...? | 30 | mé·wa·lé·ló·gbòng |
| Is it far? | o jin·ni? | 40 | ò·gbòng |
| straight ahead | tro·lo·lo | 50 | mé·wà·lé·ló·gbòng |
| left | ò·túhng | 60 | ò·gòng·lé·ló·gbòng |
| right | ò·sìng | 70 | ò·gúhng·mé·wa·lé·ló·gbòng |
| How much is this? | é·lo·lè·yi? | 80 | ò·gbòng·mé·jì |
| That's too much. | ó·wáang·jù | 90 | mé·wa·lé·ló·gbong·mé·jì |
| Leave me alone! | fi·mí·nlè! | 100 | ò·gúhng·lé·ló·gbong·mé·jì |

Also available from Lonely Planet:
*French Phrasebook*

LANGUAGE

# Glossary

The following is a list of words and acronyms used in this book that you are likely to come across in West Africa. For a detailed food & drink glossary, see p55.

**abusua** – clan or organisation of the Akan
**adinkra** – hand-made printed cloth from Ghana worn primarily by the Ashanti on solemn occasions
**Afrique Occidentale Française** – see *French West Africa*
**Afro-beat** – a fusion of African music, jazz and soul originated and popularised by Fela Kuti of Nigeria; along with juju it's the most popular music in Nigeria
**Akan** – a major group of peoples along the south coast of West Africa; includes the Ashanti and Fanti peoples
**akuaba** – Ashanti carved figure
**aluguer** – for hire (sign in minibus)
**animism** – the base of virtually all traditional religions in Africa; the belief that there is a spirit in all natural things and the worship of those spirits, particularly human spirits (those of ancestors) which are thought to continue after death and have the power to bestow protection
**asantehene** – the king or supreme ruler of the Ashanti people
**Ashanti** – the largest tribal group in Ghana, concentrated around Kumasi
**aso adire** – a broad term for dyed cloth, a common handicraft found in many markets in Nigeria
**auberge** – in France it's a hostel, but in West Africa it's used to mean any small hotel
**autogare** – see *gare routière*
**autoroute** – major road or highway

**bâché** – covered pick-up ('ute') used as a basic bush taxi (from the French word for tarpaulin)
**banco** – bank
**barco** – large boat
**balafon** – xylophone
**Bambara** – Mali's major ethnic group found in the centre and south and famous for its art, especially wooden carvings
**banco** – clay or mud used for building
**bar-dancing** – term widely used throughout the region for a bar which also has music (sometimes live) and dancing in the evening
**barrage** – dam across river, or roadblock
**bidon** – large bottle, container or jerry can
**bidonville** – shantytown
**blai** – coiled baskets
**bogolan cloth** – often simply called mud cloth, this is cotton cloth with designs painted on using various types of mud for colour; made by the *Bambara* people of Mali but is found throughout the region
**boîte** – small nightclub (literally 'box')
**bolong** – literally 'river' in Mandinka, but when used in English context it means creek or small river
**bombax tree** – see *fromager tree*
**boubou** – the common name for the elaborate robe-like outfit worn by men and women; also called 'grand boubou'
**boukarous** – open-sided, circular mud huts
**BP** – Boîte Postale (PO Box)
**brake** – see *Peugeot taxi*
**Bundu** – Krio word for 'secret society'; used in Liberia and in certain parts of Sierra Leone and Côte d'Ivoire; includes the Poro society for men and the Sande for women
**Burkinabé** – adjective for Burkina Faso
**bush taxi** – along with buses, this is the most common form of public transport in West Africa; there are three main types of bush taxi in West Africa: Peugeot taxi, minibus and pick-up (bâché)
**buvette** – refreshment stall

**cadeau** – gift, tip, bribe or a handout
**campement** – loosely translated as 'hostel', 'inn' or 'lodge', or even 'motel', but it is not a camping ground (ie, a place for tents); traditionally, campements offered simple accommodation but many today have quality and prices on a par with mid-range hotels
**canoa** – motor-canoe
**car** – large bus, see also *petit car*
**carnet** – document required if you are bringing a car into most of the countries of the region
**car rapide** – minibus, usually used in cities; often decrepit, may be fast or very slow
**carrefour** – literally 'crossroads', but also used to mean meeting place
**carrefour des jeunes** – youth centre
**carte jaune** – vaccination certificate
**cascata** – waterfall
**case** – hut
**case à étage** – two-storey mud house
**case à impluvium** – huge round hut with a hole in the roof to collect rainwater
**case de passage** – very basic place to sleep (often near bus stations) with a bed or mat on the floor and little else, and nearly always doubling as a brothel; also called 'chambre de passage' or 'maison de passage'
**CFA** – the principal currency of the region; used in Benin, Burkina Faso, Côte d'Ivoire, Guinea-Bissau, Mali, Niger, Senegal and Togo

**chambre de passage** – see *case de passage*

**chasée submersible** – see *pont submersible*

**chèche** – light cotton cloth in white or indigo blue that Tuareg men wear to cover their head and face

**chiwara** – a headpiece carved in the form of an antelope and used in ritualistic dances by the Bambara

**cidade** – city

**cinq-cent-quatre** – 504; see *Peugeot taxi*

**climatisée** – air-conditioned; often shortened to 'clim'

**coladeiras** – old-style music; romantic, typically sentimental upbeat love songs

**commissariat** – police station

**compteur** – meter in taxi

**correios** – post office

**couchette** – sleeping berth on a train

**courrier postale** – postal van; sometimes the only means of public transport between towns in rural areas

**cotton tree** – see *fromager tree*

**CRI** – Campements Rurals Integrés; system of village-run campements in the Casamance region of Senegal

**croix d'Agadez** – Tuareg talisman that protects its wearer from the 'evil eye'

**Dahomey** – pre-independence name of Benin

**dash** – bribe or tip (noun); also used as a verb, 'You dash me something...'

**demi-pension** – half board (dinner, bed and breakfast)

**déplacement** – a taxi or boat that you 'charter' for yourself

**djembe** – type of drum

**Dogon** – people found in Mali, east of Mopti; famous for their cliff dwellings, cosmology and arts

**durbar** – ceremony or celebration, usually involving a cavalry parade, found, for example, in the Muslim northern Nigerian states

**dournis** – minibus

**Ecomog** – Ecowas Monitoring Group; a military force made up of soldiers from the member armies of Ecowas

**Ecowas** – Economic Community of West African States

**Eid al-Fitr** – feast to celebrate the end of Ramadan

**Eid al-Kabir** – see *Tabaski*

**Empire of Ghana** – no geographic connection with the present-day country of Ghana; one of the great *Sahel* empires that flourished in the 8th to 11th centuries AD and covered much of present-day Mali and parts of Senegal

**Empire of Mali** – Islamic Sahel empire that was at its peak in the 14th century, covering the region between present-day Senegal and Niger; its capital was at Koumbi Saleh in southern Mauritania

**essence** – petrol (gas) for car

**fado** – haunting melancholy blues-style Portuguese music

**fanals** – large lanterns; also the processions during which the lanterns are carried through the streets

**fanicos** – laundry men

**Fanti** – part of the Akan group of people based along the coast in southwest Ghana and Côte d'Ivoire; traditionally fishing people and farmers

**fête** – festival

**fêtes des masques** – ceremony with masks

**fetish** – sacred objects or talismans in traditional religions, sometimes called 'charms'

**fiche** – form (to complete)

**Foulbé** – see *Fula*

**French West Africa** – area of West and Central Africa acquired by France at the Berlin Conference in 1884-85 which divided Africa up between the European powers; 'Afrique Occidentale Française' in French

**fromager tree** – found throughout West Africa and also known as the 'bombax tree', 'kapok tree' or 'cotton tree', it is recognisable by its yellowish bark, large pod-like fruit and exposed roots

**Fula** – a people spread widely through West Africa, mostly nomadic cattle herders; also known as 'Fulani', 'Peul' or 'Foulbé'

**fula-fula** – converted truck or pick-up; rural public transport

**funaná** – distinctive fast-paced music with a Latin rhythm that's great for dancing; usually features players on the accordion and tapping with metal

**gara** – thin cotton material

**garage** – bush taxi and bus park

**gare lagunaire** – lagoon ferry terminal

**gare maritime** – ferry terminal

**gare routière** – bus and bush-taxi station, also called 'gare voiture' or 'autogare'

**gare voiture** – see *gare routière*

**gargotte** – small, local eatery

**gasoil** – diesel fuel

**gendarmerie** – police station/post

**girba** – water bag

**gîte** – in France, this mean a small hotel or holiday cottage with self-catering facilities; in West Africa it is occasionally used interchangeably with auberge and campement

**Gold Coast** – pre-independence name for modern state of Ghana

**goudron** – tar (road)

**Grain Coast** – old name for Liberia

**grand boubou** – see *boubou*

**gué** – ford or low causeway across river

**Hausa** – people originally from northern Nigeria and southern Niger, mostly farmers and traders

**highlife** – a style of music, originating in Ghana, combining West African and Western influences

**hôtel de ville** – town hall

**ibeji** – Yoruba carved twin figures

**IDP** – International Driving Permit

**Igbo** – one of the three major people groups in Nigeria, concentrated predominantly in the southeast

**IGN** – Institute Géographique National; the French IGN produces maps of most West African countries; several West African countries have their own IGN institution, although maps are not always available

**IMF** – International Monetary Fund

**immeuble** – large building, for example, office block

**impluvium** – large round traditional house with roof constructed to collect rain water in central tank or bowl

**insha'allah** – God willing, ie hopefully (Arabic, but used by Muslims in Africa)

**jali** – see *griot*

**jardim** – garden

**juju** – the music style characterised by tight vocal harmonies and sophisticated guitar work, backed by traditional drums and percussion; it is very popular in southern Nigeria, most notably with the Yoruba; see also voodoo

**kandab** – a large belt used to climb trees to collect palm wine

**kandonga** – truck or pick-up

**kapok tree** – see *fromager tree*

**kente cloth** – probably the most expensive material in West Africa; made with finely woven cotton, and sometimes silk, by Ghana's Ashanti people

**Kingdom of Benin** – no relation to the present-day country, this was one of the great West African kingdoms (13th to 19th centuries); based in Nigeria around Benin City and famous for its bronzes

**kola nuts** – extremely bitter nuts sold everywhere on the streets and known for their mildly hallucinogenic and caffeine-like effects; they are offered as gifts at weddings and other ceremonies

**kora** – harp-like musical instrument with over 20 strings

**kwotenai kanye** – earrings

**line** – fixed-route shared taxi

**Lobi** – people based in southwest Burkina Faso and northern Côte d'Ivoire, famous for their figurative sculpture and compounds known as soukala

**lorry park** – see *motor park*

**lumo** – weekly market, usually in border areas

**luttes** – traditional wrestling matches

**lycée** – secondary school

**macaco** – monkey; a popular meat dish in upcountry Guinea-Bissau

**mairie** – town hall; mayor's office

**maison de passage** – see *case de passage*

**malafa** – crinkly voile material worn as a veil by women in Mauritania

**Malinké** – Guinea's major ethnic group, the people are also found in southern Mali, northwestern Côte d'Ivoire

and eastern Senegal; closely related to the Bambara and famous for having one of the great West African empires; also related to the Mandinka

**Mandinka** – people group based in central and northern Gambia and Senegal; also the name of their language, which is closely related to Malinké; both Malinké and Mandinka are part of the wider Manding group.

**maquis** – rustic open-air restaurant; traditionally open only at night

**marché** – market

**marigot** – creek

**mbalax** – percussion-driven, Senegalese dance music

**mercado** – market

**mestizos** – people of mixed European and African descent

**mobylette** – moped

**Moors** – also called 'Maurs'; the predominant nomadic people of Mauritania, now also well known as merchants and found scattered over French-speaking West Africa

**mornas** – old-style music; mournful and sad, similar to the Portuguese fado style from whence they may have originated

**Moro-Naba** – the king of the Mossi people

**Mossi** – the people who occupy the central area of Burkina Faso and comprise about half the population of Burkina Faso as well as the bulk of Côte d'Ivoire's migrant labour force

**motor park** – bus and bush-taxi park (English-speaking countries); also called 'lorry park'

**moto–taxi** – motorcycle taxi

**Mourides** – the most powerful of the Islamic brotherhoods in Senegal

**mud-cloth** – see *bogolan cloth*

**NEPA** – National Electric Power Authority in Nigeria; supplier of the highly erratic electricity

**nomalies** – sandstone ancestor figures

**OAU** – Organisation of African Unity

**oba** – a Yoruba chief or ruler

**occasion** – a lift or place in a car or bus (often shortened to 'occas')

**orchestra** – in West Africa, this means a group playing popular music

**pagne** – a length of colourful cloth worn around the waist as a skirt

**paillote** – a thatched sun shelter (usually on a beach or around an open-air bar-restaurant)

**palava** – meeting place

**paletuviers** – mangroves

**papelaria** – newsagency

**paragem** – bus and bush-taxi park

**pastel com diablo dentro** – literally 'pastry with the devil inside'; a mix of fresh tuna, onions and tomatoes wrapped in a pastry made from boiled potatoes and corn flour, deep fried and served hot

**patron** – owner, boss
**péage** – toll
**peintures rupestres** – rock paintings
**pensão** – hotel or guesthouse
**pension** – simple hotel or hostel, or 'board'; see also *demi-pension*
**pension complet** – full board (lunch, dinner, bed and breakfast)
**pension simple** – bed and breakfast
**petit car** – minibus
**pétrole** – kerosene
**Peugeot taxi** – one of the main types of bush taxi; also called 'brake', 'cinq-cent-quatre', 'Peugeot 504' or sept-place
**Peul** – see *Fula*
**pinasse** – large pirogue, usually used on rivers, for hauling people and cargo
**pirogue** – traditional canoe, either a small dugout or large, narrow sea-going wooden fishing boat
pharmacie de garde (all-night pharmacy)
**piste** – track or dirt road
**poda-poda** – minibus
**pont submersible** – a bridge or causeway across a river which is covered when the water is high
**posuban** – ensemble of statues representing a proverb or event in Fanti culture
**pousada** – guesthouse
**pousada municipal** – town guesthouse
**praça** – park or square
**praia** – beach
**préfecture** – police headquarters
**PTT** – post (and often telephone) office in Francophone countries

**quatre-quatre** – 4WD or 4x4, a four-wheel drive vehicle

**Ramadan** – Muslim month of fasting
**residencial** – guesthouse
**rond-point** – roundabout
**rua** – street

**Sahel** – dry savanna area south of the Sahara desert; most of Senegal, Gambia, Mali, Burkina Faso and Niger
**Samory Touré** – Guinean hero who led the fight against the French colonialists in the late 19th century
**Scramble for Africa** – term used for the land-grabbing frenzy in the 1880s by the European powers in which France, Britain and Germany laid claim to various parts of the continent
**sept-place** – Peugeot taxi seven-seater (usually carrying up to 12 people)
**serviette** – towel (in bathroom)
**serviette de table** – table napkin, serviette

**serviette hygiénique** – sanitary pad (feminine pad, feminine towel)
**sharia** – Muslim law
**shukublai** – distinctive baskets that are traditionally made by Temne women in Sierra Leone
**Songhaï** – ethnic group located primarily in northeastern Mali and western Niger along the Niger River
**soukala** – a castle-like housing compound of the Lobi tribe found in the Bouna area of southern Burkina Faso
**spirale antimostique** – mosquito coil
**sûreté** – police station
**syndicat d'initiative** – tourist information office

**Tabaski** – Eid al-Kabir; also known as the Great Feast, this is the most important celebration throughout West Africa
**taguelmoust** – shawl or scarf worn as headgear by *Tuareg* men
**tama** – hand-held drum
**tampon** – stamp (eg, in passport)
**tampon hygiénique** – tampon; see also *serviette hygiénique*
**tampon periodique** – see *tampon hygiénique*
**tata somba** – a castle-like house of the Betamaribé tribe who live in northwestern Benin
**taxi brousse** – bush taxi
**taxi-course** – shared taxi (in cities)
**taxi-moto** – see *moto-taxi*
**télécentre** – privately run telecommunications centres
**toca-toca** – small minibus in Bissau
**togu-na** – traditional Dogon shelter where men sit and socialise
**totem** – used in traditional religions, similar to a fetish
**toubab** – white person; term used primarily in Gambia, Senegal, Mali and some other Sahel countries
**town trip** – private hire (taxi)
**tro-tro** – a minibus or pick-up
**Tuareg** – nomadic descendants of the North African Berbers; found all over the Sahara, especially in Mali, Niger and southern Algeria

**voodoo** – the worship of spirits with supernatural powers widely practised in southern Benin and Togo; also called 'juju'

**wassoulou** – singing style made famous by Mali's Oumou Sangaré
**WHO** – World Health Organization
**Wolof** – Senegal's major ethnic group; also found in Gambia
**woro-woro** – minibus

**Yoruba** – a major ethnic group concentrated in southwestern Nigeria

**zemi-john** – motorcycle-taxi

# Behind the Scenes

## THIS BOOK

The first two editions of West Africa were written and researched by Alex Newton. Alex was joined by David Else for the 3rd edition while the 4th edition was updated by David Else, Alex Newton, Jeff Williams, Mary Fitzpatrick and Miles Roddis. For the 5th edition Mary Fitzpatrick was the coordinating author; she was ably assisted by Andrew Burke, Greg Campbell, Bethune Carmichael, Matthew Fletcher, Anthony Ham, Amy Karafin, Frances Linzee Gordon, Kim Wildman and Isabelle Young. Anthony Ham assumed the mantle as coordinating author and also researched Burkina Faso and Mali for this, the 6th edition. His intrepid cohorts included James Bainbridge, who covered Benin and Togo; Tim Bewer, who took on Guinea, Sierra Leone and Côte d'Ivoire; Jean-Bernard Carillet, who roughed it in Mauritania; Paul Clammer, who ventured into Nigeria and Cameroon; Mary Fitzpatrick, who updated Liberia; Michael Grosberg, who worked up a sweat in Ghana; Katharina Kane, who did the hard yards in the Gambia and Senegal; Robert Landon, who swept through Cape Verde and Guinea-Bissau; and Matt Phillips who swept through Mali. Jane Cornwell wrote the Music chapter and Michael Benanav contributed to the 'Timbuktu Salt Trade' boxed text. This guidebook was commissioned in Lonely Planet's Melbourne office, and produced by the following:

**Commissioning Editors** Will Gourlay, Stefanie di Trocchio, Marg Toohey
**Coordinating Editor** Kate McLeod
**Coordinating Cartographer** Diana Duggan

**Coordinating Layout Designer** Carol Jackson
**Managing Cartographer** Shahara Ahmed
**Assisting Editors** Elizabeth Anglin, Yvonne Byron, Monique Choy, Gennifer Ciavarra, Kate James, Pat Kinsella, Kim Noble, Sally O'Brien
**Assisting Cartographers** Clare Capell, Julie Dodkins, Tony Fankhauser, Josh Geoghegan, Valentina Kremenchutskaya
**Assisting Layout Designers** Jim Hsu, Wibowo Rusli, Cara Smith
**Colour Designer** Margie Jung
**Cover Designer** Aleksandra Djuric
**Project Manager** Nancy Ianni
**Managing Editor** Brigitte Ellemor
**Language Content Coordinator** Quentin Frayne

**Thanks to** Sally Darmody, Mark Germanchis, Kate McDonald, Raphael Richards, Celia Wood

## THANKS
### ANTHONY HAM

Special thanks to Hamadou Ouologuem (Chine) for being such a wonderful companion in Mali. Karen Crabb also went beyond the call of duty. Thanks also to Amadou Maiga (Bamako), Azima Ag Mohamed Ali (Timbuktu), Franz Olthof (Bamako), Mac (Sévaré), Jutta (Sévaré), Sidibe (Bamako), Olivier (Mopti), Elaine Belleza (Bamako) and everyone at the Hôtel Tamana. Michael Benanav and Justin Bakule were exceptionally helpful. In Burkina Faso, a huge thank you to Eugène Compaoré and also to Vincent Cougou Cyr, Laurent Santou, Jala Amadou, Camille, Alain and

---

**THE LONELY PLANET STORY**

The story begins with a classic travel adventure: Tony and Maureen Wheeler's 1972 journey across Europe and Asia to Australia. There was no useful information about the overland trail then, so Tony and Maureen published the first Lonely Planet guidebook to meet a growing need.

From a kitchen table, Lonely Planet has grown to become the largest independent travel publisher in the world, with offices in Melbourne (Australia), Oakland (USA) and London (UK). Today Lonely Planet guidebooks cover the globe. There is an ever-growing list of books and information in a variety of media. Some things haven't changed. The main aim is still to make it possible for adventurous travellers to get out there – to explore and better understand the world.

At Lonely Planet we believe travellers can make a positive contribution to the countries they visit – if they respect their host communities and spend their money wisely. Every year 5% of company profit is donated to charities around the world.

Mamadou. Thanks also to David Andrew for his information on bird-watching in the region.

In the LP offices, the wise and witty Will Gourlay is an editor without peer. Thanks also to all my co-authors. Special thanks especially to my mother and friend, Jan, who taught me to love Africa; Ron, the most faithful follower of my journeys; Greta who was born during my first trip to Ouagadougou and who had her 4th birthday while I was in Timbuktu; and my special Alex. Back home in Spain, overdue thanks to Javier Gomez Aranda and to Marina and Alberto. And a special dedication to Rodrigo – may you one day know the magic of Africa.

And to Marina – thank you for bringing Africa alive with the sound of children laughing and for being the perfect companion wherever we find ourselves in the world.

## JAMES BAINBRIDGE

I was helped considerably in Togo and Benin by the Peace Corps folks I met in *gare routierés* (minibus stations), bars and via email. In Togo, they included Charlotte, Erin and Ricardo in Kara, and Laura and Lee in Dapaong; in Benin, Brian in Natitingou, David in Djougo, Katherine in Parakou, the two Erins in Abomey, Felcie in Camaté-Shakaloké, and Brendan in Challa-Ogoi. The same applies to the legion of African hoteliers, taxi drivers and dudes in the street who went to great pains to help. In Lomé, thanks to Albert from IFDC, and a huge shout out to Guillaume and Lena, Daniel and Awaussi. In Cotonou, special thanks go to Daniel from the US embassy, John at the American Cultural Centre, the two Ronalds at Novotel Orisha, and to the Beninese immigration officials who helped me learn the names of the kings of Dahomey.

## TIM BEWER

The number of people that a guidebook researcher relies upon during the course of a project is astounding. I literally owe thanks to thousands. The following were especially helpful. In Sierra Leone, Bimbola Carrol, Sanira Deen, Toufic Haroun, Alhaji Siaka, Umaru Woody and Tony Yazbeck helped make getting to know Sierra Leone an immense pleasure. I'm especially grateful to Edleen Elba, who had no idea what she was getting in to. In Guinea, the biggest thanks of all goes to 'The Mighty' Kanfos, truly a friend of everyone. I also can't thank Millimouno ('Mr Robert') Saa enough for everything he did for me. Ahmedou Barry, John Chen, Mamadou Daïmou Diallo, Jen Jalovec, Karen Smid, Christy Sommers and Faya Tengbe Tonguino offered

good advice and good company. Thanks also to Louise Bedichek, Amy Karafin, Stephen Peterson, Reimer Priester, Olive Sawyerr and Erik Vickstrom. For helping get Côte d'Ivoire in good shape, I owe immense gratitude to Pauline Bax, Béatrice Grandcolas and Daniel Kouaho who helped far beyond my expectations. Special thanks also to Bob Barad, Sidibe Boubakar, Kale Gbegbe, Thomas Hofnung, Tanya Kerssen and those who asked to remain anonymous. In Lonely Planet world, it was a genuine pleasure to work with Will Gourlay, Anthony Ham and Kate McLeod.

## JEAN-BERNARD CARILLET

I'd like to express my deepest gratitude to Will Gourlay for having placed once again his trust in a damn Frenchman – thanks again! Anthony Ham deserves plaudits for its support and constant *bonne humeur* – a true pleasure to work with. A big thanks also to the carto team for their accomplishments. At home, I'd like to thank my little Eva, who gives a meaning and a direction to my otherwise gypsy life. And I won't forget my Mum for her generous care and attention. In Mauritania and in Paris, big thanks to Michel, Sylvie, Frederique, Veronique, Leila, Isselmou, Idoumou, Sidi Ould Amine, Boubacar, Philippe, Herrmann, Patrice and Gerard who did their best to open doors. Lastly, to the Mauritanians I met while on the road – thanks for your friendliness and courteousness.

## PAUL CLAMMER

At Lonely Planet, thanks to Will Gourlay for sending me to some crazy, dusty corners. In Cameroon, Becks and Justin Marshall turned their Landcruiser into a fine research vehicle for a week in the highlands, while Jane and Jerry Flood were excellent company in Yaoundé, as was Sam Bishop in Maroua. Jenny Hislop and Julie Bryant enlivened N'Gaoundéré no end. Kris Gorham and his iPod provided The Boss and *Born to Run* at a crucial moment. Thanks also to Marta Sabbadini in Douala. In Calabar, thanks to Peter Jenkins and Liza Gadsby of Pandrillus. In Lagos, thanks to the hospitality to Mal and Awoba Wallace, and Mark and Mandy Cruise.

## MARY FITZPATRICK

I owe a debt of thanks to Lou Mazel at the US embassy in Monrovia (world traveller and cultural connoisseur par excellence) without whose very generous assistance the Liberia chapter would be only a shadow of what it now is. Many, many thanks, and here's wishing you safe and happy travels wherever in the world you may find yourself. A big thank you also to Reg Hoyt, who offered invaluable help this time around, as well as on several previous occasions, with information on Sapo National Park. Finally, I'm grateful to co-author Tim Bewer for help filling in various missing bits and pieces. At home, my thanks go to Rick and to Christopher for so tolerantly abiding my long hours at the computer, and to Rick for the infusion of adventure and energy during our first unanticipated forays into Liberia almost a decade ago.

## MICHAEL GROSBERG

An enormous *grazie* goes out to Emmanuele and Francesca Santi for providing companionship, conversation and help during my travels and a pad to crash in Accra. Thanks to Mohammed Ali for sharing his insight and knowledge about Ghana and his brother Ahmad Tijani Ali for showing me around Kumasi. To Tanya Accone for her advice and enthusiasm about travel in Ghana; Reverend Emmanuel K Mustafa whose conversation made a long delay and flight to Tamale go quicker; Mahesh V Daswani for his hospitality in Kumasi; J Otanka Obetsebi-Lamptey, the Minister of Tourism, and everyone from the Ghana Tourism Board who provided assistance; Rachel Pringle for sharing her experiences travelling in the country; Robert Apinling from Tamale for his thoughts about northern Ghana; Alex Solomon for her UN-related facts on the country; Marc Gidal for sharing his knowledge of the country's music. And Rebecca Tessler for keeping me going with her emails and text messages in times of need. And last but not least to my niece Sashi, for just being the Sashers.

## KATHARINA KANE

Big thanks to Souleymane Kane for being patient enough to see his fiancée bent over manuscripts until the day before the wedding. Thanks also to his entire family, particularly to Yeya Sy for taking up endless babysitting duties. My parents, brothers and sisters – you've been amazingly patient. In Dakar, thanks to Romuauld Taylor, Mady Kane and Cherif Bojang at the 221. Jean at l'Océanium – your enthusiasm is infectious! Héle'ne, thanks for introducing me to Angelique Dhiedhiou. Still in Dakar, thanks to Stephanie and Baba, Sandrine and Marcus for friendship and advice, as well as Nounou and his entire, wonderful team for far too many things that can be listed. For accompanying me on my many travels, I'd like to thank Djiby Pene, Modou the taxi driver, and particularly Daby Ba, for staying cool during the car accident. Thanks to the hospital staff in Dakar, and particularly Idy Faye for late hour consultations. In Thiès, thanks to Beuz, you're doing a great job! In Saint-Louis, I'm grateful to Jean-Jacques Bancal, Bamba and Amadou Cissé. Thanks to Anthony in Palmarin, Bouba with the mobilette in Toubakouta and Ousmane with the mobilette in Foundiougne. In Eastern Senegal, I could only complete my work thanks to Pape Samba and his mum, Pape Moussa, Modou Senn and his driver, and Numu Diallo, for his insights into the region. Jean-Baptiste, Augustin Diatta, Veronique Chiche and Dr Teneng – greatest respect for all your amazing work in the Casamance! Sandy Haessner – you're an amazing photographer, let's build projects! And Maurice Phillips, Peter Borshik, Astrid Bojang, Nina, EJ and the Egalitarian – you've been incredibly helpful in The Gambia.

All my close ones that are far, thanks for everything and apologies should I have forgotten anyone in writing – I haven't in thought.

## ROBERT LANDON

I want to thank Paulo Bellot for his excellent company; Veronica and Mario for introducing me to the Bijagos people; Manuel for his generous leads; Will Gourlay et al for their patience; Carlos for crash pad and cat patrol; my parents for many things; and the 7am coffee klatch, including HP, for long-distance support.

## MATT PHILLIPS

I'd like to thank my fiancée George for her devotion, support, understanding, humour, enthusiasm and love. I wouldn't be thanking anyone if not for Will Gourlay sending my butt back to Africa – thanks Will! Anthony Ham deserves huge thanks for his hard work, as does Shahara Ahmed and everyone at Lonely Planet, Melbourne. Where would I be without my Mum – thanks for your and Bernie's support, smiles and laughter. Equally loving and supportive, my Dad and Vikki have always taught me to dream big. Thanks to my sister Pam and Dr Dave for being my biggest London fans and support. While far from me in miles, but close to my heart are my sisters Margaret and Eunice, and their children Alex, Bonnie, Lizzy and Rose – thanks for keeping me in your thoughts. I owe mighty thanks to my wonderful friends in Vancouver, London and Spain for getting me this far and for their constant support. To Niger – thanks for opening your arms and always trying to show me your best side. Lastly, to the Nigeriens I met along the way – thanks for your kindness, generosity and putting up with my pathetic abuse of the French language.

## OUR READERS

**Many thanks to the travellers who used the last edition and wrote to us with helpful hints, useful advice and interesting anecdotes:**

**A** Leslie Abramson, Ife Adedeji, Albert Afolabi, Leila Akahloun, Katherine Aldrich, Olivia Almeida-Duque, Ghislaine Annez, Daniel Atsu, Jeffrey Austin **B** Aaron & Karen Barnett, Penny Barten, John Barthelme, Marlon Basel, Frederick Basset, Mike Beck, Gisa Becker, Agnes Beckers, Helen Beecher Bryant, Joachim Behrmann, Mar Belke, Michael Benanav, Kenneth Bengtsson, James Bird, Stephanie Biron, Kendra Bischoff, Haralampos Bizas, Margaret Blanchard, Martinette Boonekamp, Ellen Bork, Carol Bouchard, Ellen Boucherie, Eithne Bradley, Jeroen Bremmer, Kate Bretherton, Claudio Brigati, David Briston, Ron Broadfoot, Lisa Brooks, Christiane Bruno, Jill Buckler, Christof Buehler **C** Sergio Cacopardo, Alicia Caldwell, Genevieve Campbell, Nigel Canavan, Adrian Carr, Pierpaolo Cautela, Manuela Cedarmas, Mia Chabot, Lottie Chambers, Catherine Chapdelaine, Janet Cherry, Na Choo, Ian Clements, Brad Clinehens, Sarah Coleman, Kenny Collyer, Rich Cookson, Melissa Cortale, Julia & Peter Craig, Delbert Crane, Pierre-Antoine Cristofini, Dave "Backflipper" Croft, Brian Cruickshank, Sam Culpin **D** Liesbeth Daffe, Kristin Daley, Sarah Davies, Kim de Kort, Kees & Petra de Leeuw, Dietrich de Roeck, Richard Desomme, Karin Detloff, Peter Devries, Filiep Dewitte, Mark Dixon, Adeola Dokunx, Dennis Dolmans, John Donegan, Anneke Donker, Sandrine Dossou-Yovo, Naomi Doumbia, Crystal Dreisbach, Rudy du Chau **E** Heinz Effertz, Sandra Egger, Emmanuel Ekong, Wouter Endert, Andrew Esiebo **F** Jane Federman, Travis Ferland, Dagmar Fiala, Hanne Finholt, Sarah Florenz, Frances Foster, J A Fraser, Rich Freedman, Alex Friedman, Dottie Fugiel **G** Alexander Garcia, Maike Gardner, Jean Pierre Gatien, Michael Gillich, Bart Goossens, Michael Gran, William Greenberg, Sarah Greenfield, Ben Guerard **H** Hugh Hadley, Edward Hambarchian, Gunner Hamlyn, Mark Hanis, Sue Hardy, Anne Harkin-Camara, Sabine Hazbrouck, Manu Herbstein, Michael Hicks, Laura Higgins, Michiel Hillenius, Gunther Hofer, Martin Holland, Karl Holm, Micki Honkanen, Rhoda Houge, Monika Hoyer, Adam Hughes, Sierra Hutchinson **I** Iain Ilich **J** Gert Jan, Tansy Jefferies, Marianne Jonker **K** Daniel Kayser, Peter Kell, Ralph & Ute Kettritz, David Kitson, Carol Klein, Catherine Koch, Foong Swee Kong, Georges Korb, Karen Kort, Raghav Kotval, Nancy Kramer, Barbara Kreijtz, Jennifer Krischer, Marjan Kroone, Chichi Kwame Mensah **L** Henry Landman, Erik Laridon, Jesse Larson, Linda Layfield, Simon Lee, Veronique Lefebvre, Sophie Lefever, Eve Levin, Jan Lewis, Maarten Licht, Debbie Ling, David Lloyd, Metka Locicnik, Gustaf Lorentz, Gerd Lotze, Rolf-Dieter Luck, Patrizio Luntini **M** Brian MacDomhnaill, Jenny MacDougall, Jim Mackie, John Maclachlan, Sean Maher, Julie Markham, Roy Marokus, Andreas Martin, Carmen Martin, Kent Maxwell, Fidel Mbhele, Matt McClure, Ewan McCowen, Gareth McFeely, Dana McNairn, Katia Medeot, Marielle Meeuwissen, François Meignant, Joke & Frans Meijer, Evelyn Menke, Christiane Moeller Hadi, Claudia Montulet, Mike Moore, Stuart Moore, Thomas Morgan, Anita Moss, Nelly Moudime, Sonja Munnix, Kiruba Murugaiah **N** Imene Nater, Seen Yee Neo, Paul Neumann, Kwame Nkrumah-Boateng, Ute Norman **O** Derik Olson, Chuck Onyiliogwu, Camilla Opoku, Kevin Ormond, Tania Ortiz de Zuniga, Wanda Ot, Peter Ottis **P** Bjvrn Parmentier, Cochard Patrick, Robert Patterson, Urbana Pleme, Marisca Postma, Blake Evans Pritchard, G P Pullen **Q** Patrick Quanston **R** Maggie Racklyeft, Elizabeth Raitt, Samantha Reid, Claire & Kodjikeka Reindorp, Sebastian Reinelt, Bas Renes, Sabine Richard, Steven Riley, Michael Rimmer, Judith Ripoll, Flavia Robin, Dusseaux Rodolphe, Justiniano Rodrigues, Kathryn Roe, Hans Rossel, Emanuele Rossi, Dominik Röttgers, Christopher Ruane, Shawn Rubin **S** Maja Sajovic, Anna Salter, Stefan Samuelsson, Renate Schaefer, Clement Schenk, Heiner H Schmitt, Annekatrin Scholze, Chris Scott, Owen Shahadah, Eyal Shemen, Daniel Siebers, Aric Sigman, John Simister, David K Smith, Jonathan Smith, Martin Smith, Elisa Snel, Heleen Snoep, Jo Somers, Eric Spanjaard, Hartley Springman, Pauline Stannard, Nancy Steedle, Marc Steegen, Laura Stevens, Raffaella Stucchi, Mohar Subbiah, Lars Suess, Robin Syred **T** Nathan Taku, Jay E Taylor, Ingrid Teige, Asif Tejani, April Thompson, Dirk Thys van den Audenaerde, Nigel Tickner, Ehiaghe Timothy, Chiara Trapani, Konrad Tuchscherer **V** Clive Vacher, Patrick van der Hijden, Marc van der Kuil, Ronald van Engers, Saskia van Grinsven, Marieke van Meerten, Marielle van Stiphout, Robin Vandenberg, Anthony Vandyk, Marie-Jeanne Vantuykom, Bart & Linda Verhaak, Ingram Verina, Rob Verweijen, Peter Vibede **W** John Waddell, Karin Wandschura, Natasha Weiner, Saga Wendén, Jane Wenman, Laura Westberg, David & Rayna Wigglesworth, Rachel Willetts, Errol Williams, Martin Willoughby-Thomas, Klaus Winterling, Manfred Wolfensberger, Hayley Wood, A Wootton, **Y** Najim Yassine **Z** David Zeitlyn, Henk Zilverberg, Rene Zorn

## ACKNOWLEDGEMENTS

Many thanks to the following for the use of their content:

Globe on back cover 'Mountain High Maps®' Copyright ©1993 Digital Wisdom, Inc.'

### SEND US YOUR FEEDBACK

We love to hear from travellers – your comments keep us on our toes and help make our books better. Our well-travelled team reads every word on what you loved or loathed about this book. Although we cannot reply individually to postal submissions, we always guarantee that your feedback goes straight to the appropriate authors, in time for the next edition. Each person who sends us information is thanked in the next edition – and the most useful submissions are rewarded with a free book.

To send us your updates – and find out about Lonely Planet events, newsletters and travel news – visit our award-winning website: **www.lonelyplanet.com/feedback**.

Note: We may edit, reproduce and incorporate your comments in Lonely Planet products such as guidebooks, websites and digital products, so let us know if you don't want your comments reproduced or your name acknowledged. For a copy of our privacy policy visit www.lonelyplanet.com/privacy.

# Index

INDEX

**INDEX**

INDEX

000 Map pages
000 Photograph pages

**INDEX**

**INDEX**

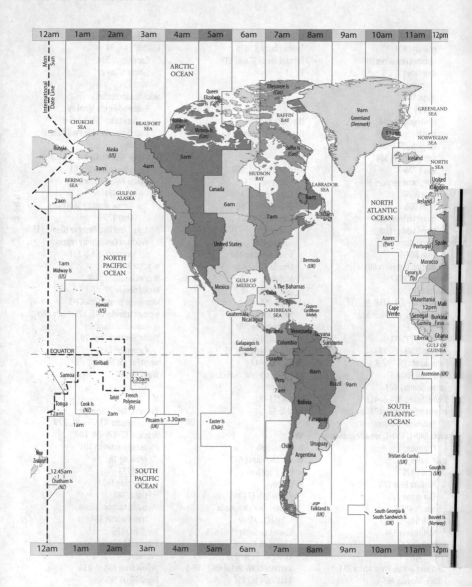